# Conference of the North American Chapter of the Association for Computational Linguistics: Human Language Technologies

# (NAACL HLT 2015)

AA005014

**Denver, Colorado, USA**
**31 May – 5 June 2015**

**Volume 1 of 2**

ISBN: 978-1-5108-0445-6

**Printed from e-media with permission by:**

Curran Associates, Inc.
57 Morehouse Lane
Red Hook, NY 12571

**Some format issues inherent in the e-media version may also appear in this print version.**



Printed by Curran Associates, Inc. (2015)

For permission requests, please contact the Association for Computational Linguistics at the address below.

Association for Computational Linguistics
209 N. Eighth Street
Stroudsburg, Pennsylvania 18360

Phone: 1-570-476-8006
Fax: 1-570-476-0860

acl@aclweb.org

**Additional copies of this publication are available from:**

Curran Associates, Inc.
57 Morehouse Lane
Red Hook, NY 12571 USA
Phone: 845-758-0400
Fax: 845-758-2634
Email: curran@proceedings.com
Web: www.proceedings.com

NAACL HLT 2015

# The 2015 Conference of the North American Chapter of the Association for Computational Linguistics: Human Language Technologies

## Proceedings of the Conference

May 31 – June 5, 2015
Denver, Colorado, USA

**Platinum**

Bloomberg

**Gold**

Google™

Goldman Sachs

A9™

IBM Watson

**Silver**

NUANCE

SDL Research

**Bronze**

YAHOO! LABS

**Supporters**

digital roots

W UNIVERSITY of WASHINGTON Computational Linguistics

**Overseas student fellowship sponsors**

BAOBAB

# Message from the General Chair

Welcome to NAACL-HLT 2015 – at its $14^{th}$ edition! Computational Linguistics has grown into one of the most exciting and diverse research communities, with an ever increasing number of researchers, many big and small companies, and a vibrant community of learners eager to get prepared to take on some of the fun and exciting challenges in the field. This year's NAACL-HLT conference is a testimony to the vibrancy and vitality of this community.

Some of the highlights of this year's program include two excellent invited speakers – Lillian Lee from Cornell and Fei-fei Li from Stanford – who will talk about the exciting research going on at the intersection of our field with social sciences and computer vision; many interesting paper presentations on cutting-edge research in computational linguistics, culminating with three best paper awards that will be presented in a plenary session during the last day of the conference; several excellent student-authored papers and dissertation proposals as part of the student research workshop; many exciting demos showing the latest in terms of developed systems available in our field; six tutorials on some of the most up-and-coming research topics in computational linguistics; several workshops on diverse topics ranging from multiword expressions and metaphors to clinical psychology and educational applications, including thirteen (!) one-day workshops and SEMEVAL as a two-day workshop; the fourth joint conference on lexical and computational semantics *SEM as a collocated conference; and, last but not least: a country line dance lesson!

As with any event of this scale, it would have not been possible without the hard work of a wonderful group of people. I would like to thank Priscilla Rasmussen for the zillions of bits and pieces that she has been doing on an everyday basis, to make sure that every single logistical detail of the forthcoming NAACL-HLT was ironed out. It is no overstatement to say that the success (and fun!) of this year's conference is in large part due to Priscilla.

I am also grateful to Hal Daumé III for getting us started on this "NAACL-HLT 2015" journey, and being always willing to help with advice and information from his experience from previous years. Lucy Vanderwende and Daniel Marcu have also graciously agreed to "pass the baton" conversations that were very helpful and informative.

I was extremely fortunate to have the chance to work with the best committee ever: Joyce Chai and Anoop Sarkar (program chairs); Cornelia Caragea and Bing Liu (workshop co-chairs); Yang Liu and Thamar Solorio (tutorial co-chairs); Shibamouli Lahiri, Karen Mazidi and Alisa Zhila (student co-chairs) and Diana Inkpen and Smaranda Muresan (faculty advisors) for the student research workshop; Matt Gerber, Catherine Havasi, and Finley Lacatusu (demo co-chairs); Annie Louise (student volunteer coordinator); Kevin Cohen (local sponsorship chair); Saif Mohammad (publicity chair); Matt Post and Adam Lopez (publication co-chairs); Peter Ljunglöf (website chair); Aurelia Bunescu (handbook cover designer); Graeme Hirst and Joel Tetreault (treasurers); Asli Celikyilmaz and Julia Hockenmaier (sponsorship co-chairs).

I am also grateful to our sponsors for their generous contributions, which made the conference possible: A9, Baobab, Bloomberg, Digital Roots, Goldman Sachs, Google, IBM, Information Sciences Institute, National Science Foundation, Nuance, SDL, University of Washington Computational Linguistics, Yahoo Labs.

Finally, my gratitude goes to everyone else who contributed to the success of the conference: area chairs, workshop organizers, tutorial presenters, student mentors, and reviewers. And of course my deepest thanks to you, the attendees: you are the life and spirit of this entire conference.

Here is to an enjoyable NAACL-HLT 2015, and many more exciting conferences to come!

Rada Mihalcea, University of Michigan
NAACL 2015 General Chair

# Message from the Program Chairs

Welcome to the 2015 Conference of the North American Chapter of the Association for Computational Linguistics – Human Language Technologies or NAACL HLT 2015 for short.

This year, we received the largest number of submissions in the history of NAACL: a total of 714 submissions with 402 long paper submissions and 312 short papers submissions. From these, 117 long papers (62 oral presentations and 55 poster presentations) and 69 short papers (24 oral presentations and 45 poster presentations) were accepted to appear at the conference.

The submissions to NAACL HLT 2015 were assigned to 18 technical areas including a new topic area called *Language and Vision*. This track was introduced with an intent to broaden research on natural language processing that is situated in a rich visual and perceptual context. We received 16 submissions for this area and seven of them will be presented at the conference.

For NAACL HLT 2015 we initiated a meta review process, where each paper received an analysis of the merits of the paper from the area chair's perspective that was based on the reviewer comments, the reviewer discussion and the author rebuttal. We found the meta reviews very helpful in consolidating the reviews and providing justifications for final decisions. As this was an experiment this year, the meta reviews were not sent to the authors.

Based on comments from reviewers, nominations from area chairs, and rankings from the best paper committee, three papers were selected to receive the best paper awards at the conference.

Continuing the tradition, NAACL HLT 2015 will feature 19 papers which were accepted for publication in the Transactions of the Association for Computational Linguistics (TACL). The TACL papers were split into 10 oral presentations and 9 poster presentatons.

We are very pleased to have two exciting keynote talks: one by Professor Lillian Lee (Cornell University) and the other by Professor Fei-fei Li (Stanford University).

There are many people to thank for who have worked diligently to make NAACL HLT 2015 possible. Thanks to the 32 area chairs for their hard work on recruiting reviewers, managing reviews, leading discussions, and making recommendations. All the area chairs are listed in the Program Committee section of the Front Matter. Thanks to Chris Callison-Burch, David Mimno, Sameer Pradhan, and Philip Resnik for stepping in to serve as area co-chairs at the last minute when we were faced with an unexpectedly large number of submissions in some tracks.

Following what was done in the last NAACL conference, we used the paper assignment tool developed by Mark Dredze to assign papers to reviewers. Thanks to Mark Dredze and Jiang Guo for their hard work on assigning papers to reviewers based on their preferences. We had to especially rely on this tool this year because the distribution of submissions across areas was very different from past trends.

This program certainly would not be possible without the help of the 460 reviewers. Their names are listed in the Program Committee section. In particular, 116 reviewers from this list were recognized by the area chairs as best reviewers who have turned in exceptionally well-written and constructive reviews and who have actively engaged in the post-rebuttal discussions. The names of the best reviewers are marked with * in the list of reviewers.

We are also indebted to the best paper award committee which consists of Claire Cardie, Daniel Gildea, Daniel Marcu, and Fernando Pereira. Their time and effort in recommending the best paper awards is much appreciated.

We also would like to thank Hal Daumé III, Kristina Toutanova, and Lucy Vanderwende for generously sharing their experience in organizing prior NAACL/ACL conferences and for their advice. We are grateful for the guidance and the support of the NAACL president Hal Daumé III, and the NAACL board. We also would like to thank the publication co-chairs Matt Post and Adam Lopez for putting together the proceedings and the conference handbook; and Paolo Gai and Rich Gerber from Softconf for always being responsive to our requests.

We would like to thank the ACL Business Manager Priscilla Rasmussen. She was our *go to* person who knew all details of the conference in and out. We are very grateful for her help.

Finally, this conference could not have happened without the efforts of the general chair, Rada Mihalcea. She made sure the various sections of NAACL organization worked well together. Her monthly newsletters informed all the organizers about what was being done by everyone else. We are very thankful for her leadership in the organization of NAACL HLT 2015.

We hope you will enjoy NAACL HLT 2015!

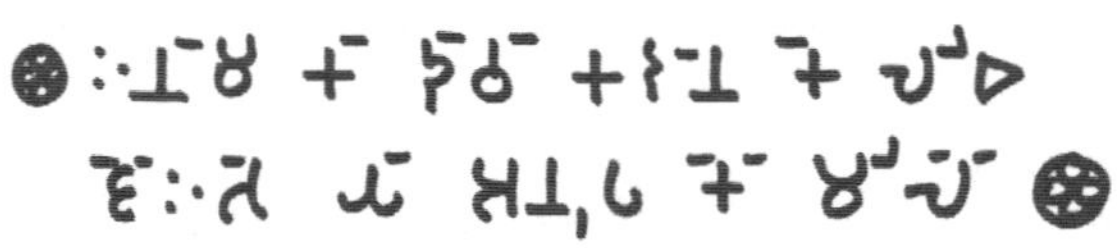

NAACL HLT 2015 Program Co-Chairs
Joyce Chai, Michigan State University
Anoop Sarkar, Simon Fraser University

# Organizing Committee

**General Chair**
Rada Mihalcea, University of Michigan, USA

**Local Arrangements Chair**
Priscilla Rasmussen, ACL Business Manager

**Program Committee Co-chairs**
Joyce Chai, Michigan State University, USA
Anoop Sarkar, Simon Fraser University, Canada

**Workshop Co-chairs**
Cornelia Caragea, University of North Texas, USA
Bing Liu, University of Illinois at Chicago, USA

**Tutorial Co-chairs**
Yang Liu, University of Texas at Dallas, USA
Thamar Solorio, University of Alabama at Birmingham, USA

**Student Research Workshop Co-chairs**
*Student Co-chairs*
Shibamouli Lahiri, University of Michigan, USA
Karen Mazidi, University of North Texas, USA
Alisa Zhila, Instituto Politécnico Nacional (National Polytechnic Institute), Mexico
*Faculty Advisors*
Diana Inkpen, University of Ottawa, Canada
Smaranda Muresan, Columbia University, USA

**Demo Co-chairs**
Matt Gerber, University of Virginia, USA
Catherine Havasi, Massachusetts Institute of Technology, USA
Finley Lacatusu, Language Computer Corporation, USA

**Student Volunteer Coordinator**
Annie Louis, University of Edinburgh, UK

**Reviewing Coordinators**
Mark Dredze, Johns Hopkins University
Jiang Guo, Harbin Institute of Technology

**Local Sponsorship Chair**
Kevin B. Cohen, University of Colorado, USA

**Publicity Chair**
Saif M. Mohammad, National Research Council Canada

**Publication Co-chairs**
Matt Post, John Hopkins University, USA
Adam Lopez, University of Edinburgh, UK

**Conference Handbook Editor**
Matt Post, Johns Hopkins University

**Website Chair**
Peter Ljunglöf, University of Gothenburg and Chalmers University of Technology, Sweden

**Business Manager**
Priscilla Rasmussen

# Program Committee

**Program Committee Co-chairs**
Joyce Chai, Michigan State University, USA
Anoop Sarkar, Simon Fraser University, Canada

**Area Chairs**

*Dialogue and Interactive Systems*
Jason D. Williams, Microsoft Research

*Discourse and Pragmatics*
Ani Nenkova, University of Pennsylvania
Vincent Ng, University of Texas at Dallas

*Generation and Summarization*
Chris Callison-Burch, University of Pennsylvania
Fei Liu, Carnegie Mellon University

*Information Extraction and Question Answering*
Alan Ritter, The Ohio State University
Bowen Zhou, IBM Research

*Information Retrieval*
David Smith, Northeastern University

*Language and Vision*
Julia Hockenmaier, University of Illinois at Urbana-Champaign

*Language Resources and Evaluation*
Will Lewis, Microsoft Research
Sameer Pradhan, Harvard University

*Linguistic and Psycholinguistic Aspects of CL*
William Schuler, The Ohio State University

*Machine Learning for NLP*
Amarnag Subramanya, Google Research
Tong Zhang, Baidu Inc. and Rutgers University

*Machine Translation*
Bill Byrne, Cambridge University
Hany Hassan, Microsoft Research
Kevin Knight, Information Sciences Institute, University of Southern California
Haitao Mi, IBM Research

*NLP for Web, Social Media and Social Sciences*
Brendan O'Connor, University of Massachusetts
Philip Resnik, University of Maryland

*NLP-enabled Technology*
Richard Socher, Stanford University

*Phonology, Morphology, and Word Segmentation*
Sami Virpioja, Lingsoft and Aalto University

*Semantics*
Dipanjan Das, Google
William Dolan, Microsoft Research
Luke Zettlemoyer, University of Washington

*Sentiment Analysis and Opinion Mining*
Saif M. Mohammad, National Research Council Canada
Jerry Zhu, University of Wisconsin-Madison

*Spoken Language Processing*
Xiaodong He, Microsoft Research

*Tagging, Chunking, Syntax, and Parsing*
Noah Smith, Carnegie Mellon University
Yue Zhang, Singapore University of Technology and Design

*Text Categorization and Topic Models*
Jordan Boyd-Graber, University of Colorado at Boulder
David Mimno, Cornell University

**Primary Reviewers**

The list of all reviewers for NAACL HLT 2015. The area chairs also picked the best reviewers in their track. These best reviewers are marked with an asterisk in the list which is alphabetical on the last name. Multiple asterisks mean that multiple area chairs chose that reviewer to be the best in their track.

Amjad Abu-Jbara, Mikhail Ageev, Eneko Agirre, *Gregory Aist, Jan Alexandersson, *James Allan, Jesse Anderton, Jacob Andreas, Nicholas Andrews, Gabor Angeli, *Yoav Artzi, Nicholas Asher, Javed Aslam, Michael Auli, amittai axelrod.

Anton Bakalov, Kirk Baker, *Timothy Baldwin, Miguel Ballesteros, David Bamman, *Srinivas Bangalore, *Mohit Bansal, *Marco Baroni, Roberto Basili, Daniel Bauer, Beata Beigman Klebanov, *Emily M. Bender, Michael Bendersky, Jonathan Berant, Taylor Berg-Kirkpatrick, Sabine Bergler, Delphine Bernhard, Pushpak Bhattacharyya, *Klinton Bicknell, Dan Bikel, Steven Bird, Anders Björkelund, *Graeme Blackwood, Eduardo Blanco, John Blitzer, Nathan Bodenstab, Bernd Bohnet, Johan Bos, Alexandre Bouchard, Kristy Boyer, Chris Brew, *Chris Brockett, Paul Buitelaar, Wray Buntine, *David Burkett, *Benjamin Börschinger.

Aoife Cahill, Nicoletta Calzolari, Marine Carpuat, Xavier Carreras, Marc-Allen Cartright, Damir Cavar, Asli Celikyilmaz, *Daniel Cer, Nathanael Chambers, Ming-Wei Chang, Wanxiang Che, Boxing Chen, Hsin-Hsi Chen, Chen Chen, Wenliang Chen, *Colin Cherry, *Jackie Chi Kit Cheung, *David Chiang, Christian Chiarcos, Jinho D. Choi, *Yejin Choi, Jennifer Chu-Carroll, Christopher Cieri, Philipp Cimiano, *Stephen Clark, *Jonathan Clark, Martin Cmejrek, Shay B. Cohen, Trevor Cohn, *John Conroy, Paul Cook, Dan Cristea, Peter Culicover, Aron Culotta.

Robert Daland, Jeff Dalton, Pradipto Das, *Hal Daumé III, Adrià de Gispert, Vera Demberg, *Steve DeNeefe, Pascal Denis, Leon Derczynski, David DeVault, *Jacob Devlin, *Barbara Di Eugenio, Mona Diab, *Laura Dietz, *Doug Downey, Gabriel Doyle, Eduard Dragut, Mark Dredze, Markus Dreyer, Lan Du, *Kevin Duh, Ewan Dunbar, *Greg Durrett, Chris Dyer.

Sauleh Eetemadi, Markus Egg, Koji Eguchi, Patrick Ehlen, Andreas Eisele, Jacob Eisenstein, Jason Eisner, Desmond Elliott, Tamer Elsayed, *Micha Elsner, Ahmad Emami, *Katrin Erk.

Anthony Fader, James Fan, *Manaal Faruqui, Afsaneh Fazly, Marcello Federico, *Christian Federmann, Yang Feng, Vanessa Wei Feng, Minwei Feng, *Katja Filippova, Nicholas FitzGerald, Jeffrey Flanigan, Radu Florian, Sandiway Fong, *George Foster, Jennifer Foster, Diego Frassinelli.

**Michel Galley, Michael Gamon, Sudeep Gandhe, Juri Ganitkevitch, *Qin Gao, *Claire Gardent, Milica Gasic, Niyu Ge, George Giannakopoulos, Daniel Gildea, *Kevin Gimpel, Filip Ginter, *Roxana Girju, Peter B. Golbus, Yoav Goldberg, Dan Goldwasser, Sharon Goldwater, Jeff Good, Kyle Gorman, Cyril Goutte, Joao Graca, Stephan Greene, Edward Grefenstette, Stig-Arne Grönroos, Weiwei Guo, Iryna Gurevych, *Carlos Gómez-Rodríguez.

Nizar Habash, Eva Hajicova, John Hale, Keith Hall, *David Hall, Michael Hammond, *Sanda Harabagiu, *Eva Hasler, Claudia Hauff, Kenneth Heafield, John Henderson, Aurélie Herbelot, Jack Hessel, Derrick Higgins, Julia Hirschberg, *Graeme Hirst, Anna Hjalmarsson, Micah Hodosh, *Dirk Hovy, Eduard Hovy, *Yuening Hu, Zhongqiang Huang, Minlie Huang, Liang Huang, Ruihong Huang, *Mans Hulden, Rebecca Hwa.

Gonzalo Iglesias, Ryu Iida, Diana Inkpen, Amy Isard, Abe Ittycheriah.

Jagadeesh Jagarlamudi, *Jing Jiang, Richard Johansson, Mark Johnson, *Michael Johnston, Shafiq Joty, Dan Jurafsky, *David Jurgens.

*Min-Yen Kan, Pallika Kanani, *Saurabh Kataria, Daisuke Kawahara, *Andrew Kehler, *Frank Keller, Svetlana Kiritchenko, Alexandre Klementiev, Alistair Knott, Philipp Koehn, Oskar Kohonen, Kazunori Komatani, Terry Koo, Anna Korhonen, Alexander Kotov, Zornitsa Kozareva, Jayant Krishnamurthy, Kriste Krstovski, Canasai Kruengkrai, Lun-Wei Ku, *Marco Kuhlmann, *Roland Kuhn, Shankar Kumar, Jonathan K. Kummerfeld, *Tom Kwiatkowski.

Igor Labutov, D Terence Langendoen, *Guy Lapalme, **Mirella Lapata, Jey Han Lau, *Alon Lavie, *Hung-yi Lee, Sungjin Lee, Yoong Keok Lee, Moontae Lee, Maider Lehr, Tao Lei, Alessandro Lenci, *Omer Levy, Shoushan Li, Fangtao Li, Jiwei Li, Junyi Jessy Li, Jinyu Li, Percy Liang, Mark Liberman, *Shou-de Lin, *Chin-Yew Lin, Xiao Ling, *Yang Liu, Lemao Liu, Jingjing Liu, Qun Liu, *Yang Liu, Adam Lopez, *Annie Louis, Bin Lu, Xiaoqiang Luo, Thang Luong.

Wei-Yun Ma, *Andrew Maas, Wolfgang Macherey, Nitin Madnani, Suresh Manandhar, Gideon Mann, *Christopher D. Manning, *Daniel Marcu, Katja Markert, André F. T. Martins, Yuval Marton, Sameer Maskey, *Michael Maxwell, Diana Maynard, Diana McCarthy, David McClosky, Ryan McDonald, *Bridget McInnes, Louise McNally, *Arul Menezes, Florian Metze, Timothy Miller, Eleni Miltsakaki, *Margaret Mitchell, Yusuke Miyao, Samaneh Moghaddam, Karo Moilanen, Christof Monz, *Taesun Moon, *Robert Moore, Roser Morante, Alessandro Moschitti, *Robert Munro, Brian Murphy.

Mikio Nakano, Preslav Nakov, Roberto Navigli, *Graham Neubig, Guenter Neumann, Hwee Tou Ng, Viet-An Nguyen, Malvina Nissim, Joakim Nivre.

Alice Oh, *Manabu Okumura, Miles Osborne, Myle Ott, Karolina Owczarzak.

Ulrike Pado, *Alexis Palmer, *Martha Palmer, Sinno J. Pan, Siddharth Patwardhan, Michael J. Paul, Virgil Pavlu, *Ted Pedersen, Gerald Penn, Jose Manuel Perea-Ortega, Slav Petrov, Olivier Pietquin, Tommi Pirinen, Emily Pitler, Massimo Poesio, Hoifung Poon, *Andrei Popescu-Belis, Matt Post, Emily Prud'hommeaux, Stephen Pulman, Matthew Purver.

Xian Qian, *Chris Quirk.

Altaf Rahman, Owen Rambow, Antoine Raux, Sujith Ravi, Kyle Rawlins, Siva Reddy, Roi Reichart, David Reitter, Sebastian Riedel, Jason Riesa, Stefan Riezler, German Rigau, *Ellen Riloff, *Laura Rimell, *Eric Ringger, *Brian Roark, Kirk Roberts, Hannah Rohde, Carolyn Rose, Andrew Rosenberg, Sara Rosenthal, Paolo Rosso, *Michael Roth, Teemu Ruokolainen, Irene Russo.

*Kenji Sagae, Alicia Sagae, Saurav Sahay, Rajhans Samdani, *Murat Saraclar, *Giorgio Satta, Asad Sayeed, David Schlangen, Nathan Schneider, Alexandra Schofield, *Lane Schwartz, H. Andrew Schwartz, Holger Schwenk, Hendra Setiawan, Izhak Shafran, Ekaterina Shutova, Khalil Sima'an, Sameer Singh, *Kairit Sirts, Gabriel Skantze, Linfeng Song, Caroline Sporleder, Vivek Srikumar, Manfred Stede, Mark Steedman, Amanda Stent, Brandon Stewart, Veselin Stoyanov, Weiwei Sun, *Mihai Surdeanu, Anders Søgaard.

Partha P. Talukdar, *Joel Tetreault, *Kapil Thadani, Jörg Tiedemann, Christoph Tillmann, Ivan Titov,

*Kristina Toutanova, David Traum, Reut Tsarfaty, Oren Tsur, Yoshimasa Tsuruoka, *Peter Turney, *Oscar Täckström.

Jakob Uszkoreit.

Tim Van de Cruys, *Benjamin Van Durme, **Lucy Vanderwende, Yannick Versley, Aline Villavicencio.

*Xiaojun Wan, *Stephen Wan, Haifeng Wang, Lidan Wang, Lu Wang, Zhiguo Wang, *William Yang Wang, *Taro Watanabe, Andy Way, *Bonnie Webber, David Weir, David Weiss, *Michael White, Janyce Wiebe, Michael Wiegand, Shuly Wintner, Andreas Witt, *Kam-Fai Wong, Kristian Woodsend.

*Fei Xia, Yunqing Xia, Bing Xiang, Tong Xiao, Peng Xu, Wei Xu, Jia Xu, Nianwen Xue.

Hui Yang, Bishan Yang, Muyun Yang, Yi Yang, *Xuchen Yao, Mahsa Yarmohammadi, *Wen-tau Yih, Dani Yogatama, Jianxing Yu, *François Yvon.

Fabio Massimo Zanzotto, Alessandra Zarcone, *Rabih Zbib, Richard Zens, Ke Zhai, Min Zhang, Lei Zhang, Hao Zhang, Hai Zhao, Guodong Zhou, Xiaodan Zhu, Chengqing Zong, *Geoffrey Zweig.

# Invited Talk: “Big data pragmatics!”, or, “Putting the ACL in computational social science”, or, if you think these title alternatives could turn people on, turn people off, or otherwise have an effect, this talk might be for you.

**Lillian Lee**

Cornell University

## Abstract

What effect does language have on people?

You might say in response, "Who are you to discuss this problem?" and you would be right to do so; this is a Major Question that science has been tackling for many years. But as a field, I think natural language processing and computational linguistics have much to contribute to the conversation, and I hope to encourage the community to further address these issues.

This talk will focus on the effect of phrasing, emphasizing aspects that go beyond just the selection of one particular word over another. The issues we'll consider include: Does the way in which something is worded in and of itself have an effect on whether it is remembered or attracts attention, beyond its content or context? Can we characterize how different sides in a debate frame their arguments, in a way that goes beyond specific lexical choice (e.g., "pro-choice" vs. "pro-life")? The settings we'll explore range from movie quotes that achieve cultural prominence; to posts on Facebook, Wikipedia, Twitter, and the arXiv; to framing in public discourse on the inclusion of genetically-modified organisms in food.

Joint work with Lars Backstrom, Justin Cheng, Eunsol Choi, Cristian Danescu-Niculescu-Mizil, Jon Kleinberg, Bo Pang, Jennifer Spindel, and Chenhao Tan.

## Biography

Lillian Lee is a professor of computer science and of information science at Cornell University, and the co-Editor-in-Chief, together with Michael Collins, of Transactions of the ACL. Her research interests include natural language processing and computational social science. She is the recipient of the inaugural Best Paper Award at HLT-NAACL 2004 (joint with Regina Barzilay), a citation in “Top Picks: Technology Research Advances of 2004” by Technology Research News (also joint with Regina Barzilay), and an Alfred P. Sloan Research Fellowship; and in 2013, she was named a Fellow of the Association for the Advancement of Artificial Intelligence (AAAI). Her group's work has received several mentions in the popular press, including The New York Times, NPR's All Things Considered, and NBC's The Today Show, and one of her co-authored papers was publicly called “boring” by Youtubers Rhett and Link, in a video viewed over 1.8 million times.

# Invited Talk: A Quest for Visual Intelligence in Computers

**Fei-Fei Li**

Stanford University

## Abstract

More than half of the human brain is involved in visual processing. While it took mother nature billions of years to evolve and deliver us a remarkable human visual system, computer vision is one of the youngest disciplines of AI, born with the goal of achieving one of the loftiest dreams of AI. The central problem of computer vision is to turn millions of pixels of a single image into interpretable and actionable concepts so that computers can understand pictures just as well as humans do, from objects, to scenes, activities, events and beyond. Such technology will have a fundamental impact in almost every aspect of our daily life and the society as a whole, ranging from e-commerce, image search and indexing, assistive technology, autonomous driving, digital health and medicine, surveillance, national security, robotics and beyond. In this talk, I will give an overview of what computer vision technology is about and its brief history. I will then discuss some of the recent work from my lab towards large scale object recognition and visual scene story telling. I will particularly emphasize on what we call the "three pillars" of AI in our quest for visual intelligence: data, learning and knowledge. Each of them is critical towards the final solution, yet dependent on the other. This talk draws upon a number of projects ongoing at the Stanford Vision Lab.

## Biography

Dr. Fei-Fei Li is an Associate Professor in the Computer Science Department at Stanford, and the Director of the Stanford Artificial Intelligence Lab and the Stanford Vision Lab. Her research areas are in machine learning, computer vision and cognitive and computational neuroscience, with an emphasis on Big Data analysis. Dr. Fei-Fei Li has published more than 100 scientific articles in top-tier journals and conferences, including Nature, PNAS, Journal of Neuroscience, CVPR, ICCV, NIPS, ECCV, IJCV, IEEE-PAMI, etc. Dr. Fei-Fei Li obtained her B.A. degree in physics from Princeton in 1999 with High Honors, and her PhD degree in electrical engineering from California Institute of Technology (Caltech) in 2005. She joined Stanford in 2009 as an assistant professor, and was promoted to associate professor with tenure in 2012. Prior to that, she was on faculty at Princeton University (2007-2009) and University of Illinois Urbana-Champaign (2005-2006). Dr. Fei-Fei Li is a speaker at TED2015 main conference, a recipient of the 2014 IBM Faculty Fellow Award, 2011 Alfred Sloan Faculty Award, 2012 Yahoo Labs FREP award, 2009 NSF CAREER award, the 2006 Microsoft Research New Faculty Fellowship and a number of Google Research awards. Work from Fei-Fei's lab have been featured in a number of popular press magazines and newspapers including New York Times, Wired Magazine, and New Scientists.

# Table of Contents

# Conference Program

**Monday, June 1, 2015**

**07:30–08:45** ***Registration and Breakfast***

08:45–09:00 *Welcome to NAACL HLT 2015*
Rada Mihalcea

09:00–10:10 *Invited Talk: "Big data pragmatics!", or, "Putting the ACL in computational social science", or, if you think these title alternatives could turn people on, turn people off, or otherwise have an effect, this talk might be for you*
Lillian Lee

**10:10–10:40** ***Break***

**10:40–12:20 Session 1A: Semantics (Long Papers)**

**Monday, June 1, 2015 (continued)**

**10:40–12:20 Session 1B: Tagging, Chunking, Syntax and Parsing (Long + TACL Papers)**

10:40–11:05 *Randomized Greedy Inference for Joint Segmentation, POS Tagging and Dependency Parsing*
Yuan Zhang, Chengtao Li, Regina Barzilay and Kareem Darwish

11:05–11:30 *An Incremental Algorithm for Transition-based CCG Parsing*
Bharat Ram Ambati, Tejaswini Deoskar, Mark Johnson and Mark Steedman

11:30–11:55 *Because Syntax Does Matter: Improving Predicate-Argument Structures Parsing with Syntactic Features*
Corentin Ribeyre, Eric Villemonte de la Clergerie and Djamé Seddah

11:55–12:20 *[TACL] Exploring Compositional Architectures and Word Vector Representations for Prepositional Phrase Attachment*
Yonatan Belinkov, Tao Lei, Regina Barzilay, Amir Globerson

**10:40–12:20 Session 1C: Information Retrieval, Text Categorization, Topic Modeling (Long Papers)**

10:40–11:05 *A Hybrid Generative/Discriminative Approach To Citation Prediction*
Chris Tanner and Eugene Charniak

11:05–11:30 *Weakly Supervised Slot Tagging with Partially Labeled Sequences from Web Search Click Logs*
Young-Bum Kim, Minwoo Jeong, Karl Stratos and Ruhi Sarikaya

11:30–11:55 *Not All Character N-grams Are Created Equal: A Study in Authorship Attribution*
Upendra Sapkota, Steven Bethard, Manuel Montes and Thamar Solorio

11:55–12:20 *Effective Use of Word Order for Text Categorization with Convolutional Neural Networks*
Rie Johnson and Tong Zhang

**12:20–14:00** ***Lunch***

**Monday, June 1, 2015 (continued)**

**14:00–15:15 Session 2A: Generation and Summarization (Long Papers)**

14:00–14:25 *Transition-Based Syntactic Linearization*
Yijia Liu, Yue Zhang, Wanxiang Che and Bing Qin

14:25–14:50 *Extractive Summarisation Based on Keyword Profile and Language Model*
Han Xu, Eric Martin and Ashesh Mahidadia

14:50–15:15 *HEADS: Headline Generation as Sequence Prediction Using an Abstract Feature-Rich Space*
Carlos A. Colmenares, Marina Litvak, Amin Mantrach and Fabrizio Silvestri

**14:00–15:15 Session 2B: Language and Vision (Long Papers)**

14:00–14:25 *What's Cookin'? Interpreting Cooking Videos using Text, Speech and Vision*
Jonathan Malmaud, Jonathan Huang, Vivek Rathod, Nicholas Johnston, Andrew Rabinovich and Kevin Murphy

14:25–14:50 *Combining Language and Vision with a Multimodal Skip-gram Model*
Angeliki Lazaridou, Nghia The Pham and Marco Baroni

14:50–15:15 *Discriminative Unsupervised Alignment of Natural Language Instructions with Corresponding Video Segments*
Iftekhar Naim, Young C. Song, Qiguang Liu, Liang Huang, Henry Kautz, Jiebo Luo and Daniel Gildea

**14:00–15:15 Session 2C: NLP for Web, Social Media and Social Sciences (Long Papers)**

14:00–14:25 *TopicCheck: Interactive Alignment for Assessing Topic Model Stability*
Jason Chuang, Margaret E. Roberts, Brandon M. Stewart, Rebecca Weiss, Dustin Tingley, Justin Grimmer and Jeffrey Heer

14:25–14:50 *Inferring latent attributes of Twitter users with label regularization*
Ehsan Mohammady Ardehaly and Aron Culotta

14:50–15:15 *A Neural Network Approach to Context-Sensitive Generation of Conversational Responses*
Alessandro Sordoni, Michel Galley, Michael Auli, Chris Brockett, Yangfeng Ji, Margaret Mitchell, Jian-Yun Nie, Jianfeng Gao and Bill Dolan

**Monday, June 1, 2015 (continued)**

**15:15–16:00 Session 3A: Generation and Summarization (Short Papers)**

15:15–15:30 *How to Make a Frenemy: Multitape FSTs for Portmanteau Generation*
Aliya Deri and Kevin Knight

15:30–15:45 *Aligning Sentences from Standard Wikipedia to Simple Wikipedia*
William Hwang, Hannaneh Hajishirzi, Mari Ostendorf and Wei Wu

15:45–16:00 *Inducing Lexical Style Properties for Paraphrase and Genre Differentiation*
Ellie Pavlick and Ani Nenkova

**15:15–16:00 Session 3B: Information Extraction and Question Answering (Short Papers)**

15:15–15:30 *Entity Linking for Spoken Language*
Adrian Benton and Mark Dredze

15:30–15:45 *Spinning Straw into Gold: Using Free Text to Train Monolingual Alignment Models for Non-factoid Question Answering*
Rebecca Sharp, Peter Jansen, Mihai Surdeanu and Peter Clark

15:45–16:00 *Personalized Page Rank for Named Entity Disambiguation*
Maria Pershina, Yifan He and Ralph Grishman

**15:15–16:00 Session 3C: Machine Learning for NLP (Short Papers)**

15:15–15:30 *When and why are log-linear models self-normalizing?*
Jacob Andreas and Dan Klein

15:30–15:45 *Deep Multilingual Correlation for Improved Word Embeddings*
Ang Lu, Weiran Wang, Mohit Bansal, Kevin Gimpel and Karen Livescu

15:45–16:00 *Disfluency Detection with a Semi-Markov Model and Prosodic Features*
James Ferguson, Greg Durrett and Dan Klein

**16:00–16:30** ***Break***

**Monday, June 1, 2015 (continued)**

**16:30–18:00 One minute madness (Long + TACL papers)**

**Session P1A: 18:00–19:30 Poster session 1A: Long + TACL papers**

*Empty Category Detection With Joint Context-Label Embeddings*
Xun Wang, Katsuhito Sudoh and Masaaki Nagata

*Incrementally Tracking Reference in Human/Human Dialogue Using Linguistic and Extra-Linguistic Information*
Casey Kennington, Ryu Iida, Takenobu Tokunaga and David Schlangen

*Digital Leafleting: Extracting Structured Data from Multimedia Online Flyers*
Emilia Apostolova, Payam Pourashraf and Jeffrey Sack

*Multi-Target Machine Translation with Multi-Synchronous Context-free Grammars*
Graham Neubig, Philip Arthur and Kevin Duh

*Sign constraints on feature weights improve a joint model of word segmentation and phonology*
Mark Johnson, Joe Pater, Robert Staubs and Emmanuel Dupoux

*Semi-Supervised Word Sense Disambiguation Using Word Embeddings in General and Specific Domains*
Kaveh Taghipour and Hwee Tou Ng

*Continuous Space Representations of Linguistic Typology and their Application to Phylogenetic Inference*
Yugo Murawaki

*Interpreting Compound Noun Phrases Using Web Search Queries*
Marius Pasca

*Lexicon-Free Conversational Speech Recognition with Neural Networks*
Andrew Maas, Ziang Xie, Dan Jurafsky and Andrew Ng

*I Can Has Cheezburger? A Nonparanormal Approach to Combining Textual and Visual Information for Predicting and Generating Popular Meme Descriptions*
William Yang Wang and Miaomiao Wen

*A Transition-based Algorithm for AMR Parsing*
Chuan Wang, Nianwen Xue and Sameer Pradhan

**Monday, June 1, 2015 (continued)**

*The Geometry of Statistical Machine Translation*
Aurelien Waite and Bill Byrne

*Data-driven sentence generation with non-isomorphic trees*
Miguel Ballesteros, Bernd Bohnet, Simon Mille and Leo Wanner

*Latent Domain Word Alignment for Heterogeneous Corpora*
Hoang Cuong and Khalil Sima'an

*Extracting Human Temporal Orientation from Facebook Language*
H. Andrew Schwartz, Gregory Park, Maarten Sap, Evan Weingarten, Johannes Eichstaedt, Margaret Kern, David Stillwell, Michal Kosinski, Jonah Berger, Martin Seligman and Lyle Ungar

*An In-depth Analysis of the Effect of Text Normalization in Social Media*
Tyler Baldwin and Yunyao Li

*Using Summarization to Discover Argument Facets in Online Idealogical Dialog*
Amita Misra, Pranav Anand, Jean E. Fox Tree and Marilyn Walker

*Active Learning with Rationales for Text Classification*
Manali Sharma, Di Zhuang and Mustafa Bilgic

*Inferring Temporally-Anchored Spatial Knowledge from Semantic Roles*
Eduardo Blanco and Alakananda Vempala

*A Dynamic Programming Algorithm for Tree Trimming-based Text Summarization*
Masaaki Nishino, Norihito Yasuda, Tsutomu Hirao, Shin-ichi Minato and Masaaki Nagata

*Modeling Word Meaning in Context with Substitute Vectors*
Oren Melamud, Ido Dagan and Jacob Goldberger

*Corpus-based discovery of semantic intensity scales*
Chaitanya Shivade, Marie-Catherine de Marneffe, Eric Fosler-Lussier and Albert M. Lai

*Dialogue focus tracking for zero pronoun resolution*
Sudha Rao, Allyson Ettinger, Hal Daumé III and Philip Resnik

*Déjà Image-Captions: A Corpus of Expressive Descriptions in Repetition*
Jianfu Chen, Polina Kuznetsova, David Warren and Yejin Choi

**Session P1B: 19:30–21:00 Poster session 1B: Long + TACL papers**

**Monday, June 1, 2015 (continued)**

*The Unreasonable Effectiveness of Word Representations for Twitter Named Entity Recognition*
Colin Cherry and Hongyu Guo

*Is Your Anchor Going Up or Down? Fast and Accurate Supervised Topic Models*
Thang Nguyen, Jordan Boyd-Graber, Jeffrey Lund, Kevin Seppi and Eric Ringger

*Grounded Semantic Parsing for Complex Knowledge Extraction*
Ankur P. Parikh, Hoifung Poon and Kristina Toutanova

*Sentiment after Translation: A Case-Study on Arabic Social Media Posts*
Mohammad Salameh, Saif Mohammad and Svetlana Kiritchenko

*Using External Resources and Joint Learning for Bigram Weighting in ILP-Based Multi-Document Summarization*
Chen Li, Yang Liu and Lin Zhao

*Transforming Dependencies into Phrase Structures*
Lingpeng Kong, Alexander M. Rush and Noah A. Smith

*Improving the Inference of Implicit Discourse Relations via Classifying Explicit Discourse Connectives*
Attapol Rutherford and Nianwen Xue

*Solving Hard Coreference Problems*
Haoruo Peng, Daniel Khashabi and Dan Roth

*Pragmatic Neural Language Modelling in Machine Translation*
Paul Baltescu and Phil Blunsom

*Key Female Characters in Film Have More to Talk About Besides Men: Automating the Bechdel Test*
Apoorv Agarwal, Jiehan Zheng, Shruti Kamath, Sriramkumar Balasubramanian and Shirin Ann Dey

*[TACL] Dense Event Ordering with a Multi-Pass Architecture*
Nathanael Chambers, Taylor Cassidy, Bill McDowell, and Steven Bethard

*[TACL] Locally Non-Linear Learning for Statistical Machine Translation via Discretization and Structured Regularization*
Jonathan H. Clark, Chris Dyer, and Alon Lavie

*[TACL] SPRITE: Generalizing Topic Models with Structured Priors*
Michael J. Paul and Mark Dredze

**Monday, June 1, 2015 (continued)**

*[TACL] Reasoning about Quantities in Natural Language*
Subhro Roy, Tim Vieira, and Dan Roth

*[TACL] A sense-topic model for WSI with unsupervised data enrichment*
Jing Wang, Mohit Bansal, Kevin Gimpel, Brian D. Ziebart, and Clement T. Yu

**Tuesday, June 2, 2015**

**07:30–09:00** ***Registration and Breakfast***

**09:00–10:40** **Session 4A: Dialogue and Spoken Language Processing (Long Papers)**

09:00–09:25 *Semantic Grounding in Dialogue for Complex Problem Solving*
Xiaolong Li and Kristy Boyer

09:25–09:50 *Learning Knowledge Graphs for Question Answering through Conversational Dialog*
Ben Hixon, Peter Clark and Hannaneh Hajishirzi

09:50–10:15 *Sentence segmentation of aphasic speech*
Kathleen C. Fraser, Naama Ben-David, Graeme Hirst, Naida Graham and Elizabeth Rochon

10:15–10:40 *Semantic parsing of speech using grammars learned with weak supervision*
Judith Gaspers, Philipp Cimiano and Britta Wrede

**09:00–10:40 Session 4B: Machine Learning for NLP (Long Papers)**

09:00–09:25 *Early Gains Matter: A Case for Preferring Generative over Discriminative Crowdsourcing Models*
Paul Felt, Kevin Black, Eric Ringger, Kevin Seppi and Robbie Haertel

09:25–09:50 *Optimizing Multivariate Performance Measures for Learning Relation Extraction Models*
Gholamreza Haffari, Ajay Nagesh and Ganesh Ramakrishnan

09:50–10:15 *Convolutional Neural Network for Paraphrase Identification*
Wenpeng Yin and Hinrich Schütze

10:15–10:40 *Representation Learning Using Multi-Task Deep Neural Networks for Semantic Classification and Information Retrieval*
Xiaodong Liu, Jianfeng Gao, Xiaodong He, Li Deng, Kevin Duh and Ye-Yi Wang

**09:00–10:40 Session 4C: Phonology, Morphology and Word Segmentation (Long Papers)**

09:00–09:25 *Inflection Generation as Discriminative String Transduction*
Garrett Nicolai, Colin Cherry and Grzegorz Kondrak

09:25–09:50 *Penalized Expectation Propagation for Graphical Models over Strings*
Ryan Cotterell and Jason Eisner

09:50–10:15 *Joint Generation of Transliterations from Multiple Representations*
Lei Yao and Grzegorz Kondrak

10:15–10:40 *Prosodic boundary information helps unsupervised word segmentation*
Bogdan Ludusan, Gabriel Synnaeve and Emmanuel Dupoux

**10:40–11:15 *Break***

**11:15–12:30 Session 5C: Morphology, Syntax, Multilinguality, and Applications (Short Papers)**

11:15–11:30 *Paradigm classification in supervised learning of morphology*
Malin Ahlberg, Markus Forsberg and Mans Hulden

11:30–11:45 *Shift-Reduce Constituency Parsing with Dynamic Programming and POS Tag Lattice*
Haitao Mi and Liang Huang

11:45–12:00 *Unsupervised Code-Switching for Multilingual Historical Document Transcription*
Dan Garrette, Hannah Alpert-Abrams, Taylor Berg-Kirkpatrick and Dan Klein

12:00–12:15 *Matching Citation Text and Cited Spans in Biomedical Literature: a Search-Oriented Approach*
Arman Cohan, Luca Soldaini and Nazli Goharian

12:15–12:30 *Effective Feature Integration for Automated Short Answer Scoring*
Keisuke Sakaguchi, Michael Heilman and Nitin Madnani

**12:30–14:00 *Lunch***

**14:00–15:15 Session 6A: Generation and Summarization (Long Papers)**

14:00–14:25 *Socially-Informed Timeline Generation for Complex Events*
Lu Wang, Claire Cardie and Galen Marchetti

14:25–14:50 *Movie Script Summarization as Graph-based Scene Extraction*
Philip John Gorinski and Mirella Lapata

14:50–15:15 *Toward Abstractive Summarization Using Semantic Representations*
Fei Liu, Jeffrey Flanigan, Sam Thomson, Norman Sadeh and Noah A. Smith

**14:00–15:15 Session 6B: Discourse and Coreference (Long Papers)**



**14:00–15:15 Session 6C: Information Extraction and Question Answering (Long Papers)**



**15:15–15:45 *Break***

**15:45–17:00 Session 7A: Semantics (Long + TACL Papers)**

15:45–16:10 *High-Order Low-Rank Tensors for Semantic Role Labeling*
Tao Lei, Yuan Zhang, Lluís Màrquez, Alessandro Moschitti and Regina Barzilay

16:10–16:35 *[TACL] Large-scale Semantic Parsing without Question-Answer Pairs*
Siva Reddy, Mirella Lapata, and Mark Steedman

16:35–17:00 *[TACL] A Large Scale Evaluation of Distributional Semantic Models: Parameters, Interactions and Model Selection*
Gabriella Lapesa and Stefan Evert

**15:45–17:00 Session 7B: Information Extraction and Question Answering (Long + TACL Papers)**

15:45–16:10 *Lexical Event Ordering with an Edge-Factored Model*
Omri Abend, Shay B. Cohen and Mark Steedman

16:10–16:35 *[TACL] Entity disambiguation with web links*
Andrew Chisholm and Ben Hachey

16:35–17:00 *[TACL] A Joint Model for Entity Analysis: Coreference, Typing, and Linking*
Greg Durrett and Dan Klein

**15:45–17:00 Session 7C: Machine Translation (Long Papers)**

15:45–16:10 *Bag-of-Words Forced Decoding for Cross-Lingual Information Retrieval*
Felix Hieber and Stefan Riezler

16:10–16:35 *Accurate Evaluation of Segment-level Machine Translation Metrics*
Yvette Graham, Timothy Baldwin and Nitika Mathur

16:35–17:00 *Leveraging Small Multilingual Corpora for SMT Using Many Pivot Languages*
Raj Dabre, Fabien Cromieres, Sadao Kurohashi and Pushpak Bhattacharyya

**Session P2A: 17:00–18:30 Poster session 2A: Short papers**

**Session P2B: 18:30–20:00 Poster session 2B: Short papers**

**Tuesday, June 2, 2015 (continued)**

*Unediting: Detecting Disfluencies Without Careful Transcripts*
Victoria Zayats, Mari Ostendorf and Hannaneh Hajishirzi

*Type-Driven Incremental Semantic Parsing with Polymorphism*
Kai Zhao and Liang Huang

*Template Kernels for Dependency Parsing*
Hillel Taub-Tabib, Yoav Goldberg and Amir Globerson

*Embedding a Semantic Network in a Word Space*
Richard Johansson and Luis Nieto Piña

*Random Walks and Neural Network Language Models on Knowledge Bases*
Josu Goikoetxea, Aitor Soroa and Eneko Agirre

*Identification and Characterization of Newsworthy Verbs in World News*
Benjamin Nye and Ani Nenkova

*Enhancing Sumerian Lemmatization by Unsupervised Named-Entity Recognition*
Yudong Liu, Clinton Burkhart, James Hearne and Liang Luo

*Extracting Information about Medication Use from Veterinary Discussions*
Haibo Ding and Ellen Riloff

*Reserating the awesometastic: An automatic extension of the WordNet taxonomy for novel terms*
David Jurgens and Mohammad Taher Pilehvar

*Cross-lingual Text Classification Using Topic-Dependent Word Probabilities*
Daniel Andrade, Kunihiko Sadamasa, Akihiro Tamura and Masaaki Tsuchida

**Wednesday, June 3, 2015**

**07:30–09:00** ***Registration and Breakfast***

09:00–10:10 *Invited Talk: A Quest for Visual Intelligence in Computers*
Fei-fei Li

**10:10–10:40** ***Break***

**10:40–11:55** **Session 8A: NLP for Web, Social Media and Social Sciences (Long + TACL Papers)**

10:40–11:05 *Testing and Comparing Computational Approaches for Identifying the Language of Framing in Political News*
Eric Baumer, Elisha Elovic, Ying Qin, Francesca Polletta and Geri Gay

11:05–11:30 *[TACL] Extracting Lexically Divergent Paraphrases from Twitter*
Wei Xu, Alan Ritter, Chris Callison-Burch, William B. Dolan, and Yangfeng Ji

11:30–11:55 *Echoes of Persuasion: The Effect of Euphony in Persuasive Communication*
Marco Guerini, Gözde Özbal and Carlo Strapparava

**10:40–11:55** **Session 8B: Language and Vision (Long + TACL Papers)**

10:40–11:05 *Translating Videos to Natural Language Using Deep Recurrent Neural Networks*
Subhashini Venugopalan, Huijuan Xu, Jeff Donahue, Marcus Rohrbach, Raymond Mooney and Kate Saenko

11:05–11:30 *[TACL] A Bayesian Model of Grounded Color Semantics*
Brian McMahan and Matthew Stone

11:30–11:55 *Learning to Interpret and Describe Abstract Scenes*
Luis Gilberto Mateos Ortiz, Clemens Wolff and Mirella Lapata

**10:40–11:55 Session 8C: Machine Translation (Long + TACL Papers)**

10:40–11:05 *A Comparison of Update Strategies for Large-Scale Maximum Expected BLEU Training*
Joern Wuebker, Sebastian Muehr, Patrick Lehnen, Stephan Peitz and Hermann Ney

11:05–11:30 *[TACL] Gappy Pattern Matching on GPUs for On-Demand Extraction of Hierarchical Translation Grammars*
Hua He, Jimmy Lin, and Adam Lopez

11:30–11:55 *Learning Translation Models from Monolingual Continuous Representations*
Kai Zhao, Hany Hassan and Michael Auli

**11:55–13:00** ***Lunch***

**13:00–14:00 NAACL Business Meeting**

**14:00–15:15 Session 9A: Lexical Semantics and Sentiment Analysis (Long Papers)**

14:00–14:25 *A Corpus and Model Integrating Multiword Expressions and Supersenses*
Nathan Schneider and Noah A. Smith

14:25–14:50 *Good News or Bad News: Using Affect Control Theory to Analyze Readers' Reaction Towards News Articles*
Areej Alhothali and Jesse Hoey

14:50–15:15 *Do We Really Need Lexical Information? Towards a Top-down Approach to Sentiment Analysis of Product Reviews*
Yulia Otmakhova and Hyopil Shin

**Wednesday, June 3, 2015 (continued)**

**14:00–15:15 Session 9B: NLP-enabled Technology (Long + TACL Papers)**

14:00–14:25 *How to Memorize a Random 60-Bit String*
Marjan Ghazvininejad and Kevin Knight

14:25–14:50 *[TACL] Building a State-of-the-Art Grammatical Error Correction System*
Alla Rozovskaya and Dan Roth

14:50–15:15 *[TACL] Predicting the Difficulty of Language Proficiency Tests*
Lisa Beinborn, Torsten Zesch, and Iryna Gurevych

**14:00–15:15 Session 9C: Linguistic and Psycholinguistic Aspects of CL (Long Papers)**

14:00–14:25 *A Bayesian Model for Joint Learning of Categories and their Features*
Lea Frermann and Mirella Lapata

14:25–14:50 *Shared common ground influences information density in microblog texts*
Gabriel Doyle and Michael Frank

14:50–15:15 *Hierarchic syntax improves reading time prediction*
Marten van Schijndel and William Schuler

**15:15–15:45** ***Break***

**15:45–17:15 Best Paper Plenary Session**

15:45–16:15 *Retrofitting Word Vectors to Semantic Lexicons*
Manaal Faruqui, Jesse Dodge, Sujay Kumar Jauhar, Chris Dyer, Eduard Hovy and Noah A. Smith

16:15–16:45 *"You're Mr. Lebowski, I'm the Dude": Inducing Address Term Formality in Signed Social Networks*
Vinodh Krishnan and Jacob Eisenstein

16:45–17:15 *Unsupervised Morphology Induction Using Word Embeddings*
Radu Soricut and Franz Och

**17:15–17:30** ***Best paper awards and Closing Remarks***

# Unsupervised Induction of Semantic Roles within a Reconstruction-Error Minimization Framework

**Ivan Titov** **Ehsan Khoddam**
University of Amsterdam
{titov|e.khoddammohammadi}@uva.nl

## Abstract

We introduce a new approach to unsupervised estimation of feature-rich semantic role labeling models. Our model consists of two components: (1) an encoding component: a semantic role labeling model which predicts roles given a rich set of syntactic and lexical features; (2) a reconstruction component: a tensor factorization model which relies on roles to predict argument fillers. When the components are estimated jointly to minimize errors in argument reconstruction, the induced roles largely correspond to roles defined in annotated resources. Our method performs on par with most accurate role induction methods on English and German, even though, unlike these previous approaches, we do not incorporate any prior linguistic knowledge about the languages.

## 1 Introduction

Shallow semantic representations, and semantic role labels in particular, have a long history in linguistics (Fillmore, 1968). More recently, with an emergence of large annotated resources such as PropBank (Palmer et al., 2005) and FrameNet (Baker et al., 1998), automatic semantic role labeling (SRL) has attracted a lot of attention (Gildea and Jurafsky, 2002; Carreras and Màrquez, 2005; Surdeanu et al., 2008; Hajič et al., 2009; Das et al., 2010).

Semantic role representations encode the underlying predicate-argument structure of sentences, or, more specifically, for every predicate in a sentence they identify a set of arguments and associate each argument with an underlying *semantic role*, such as an agent (an initiator or doer of the action) or a patient (an affected entity). Semantic roles have many potential applications in NLP and have been shown to benefit question answering (Shen and Lapata, 2007; Kaisser and Webber, 2007), textual entailment (Sammons et al., 2009), machine translation (Wu and Fung, 2009; Liu and Gildea, 2010; Wu et al., 2011; Gao and Vogel, 2011), and dialogue systems (Basili et al., 2009; van der Plas et al., 2009), among others.

Most current statistical approaches to SRL are supervised, requiring large quantities of human annotated data to estimate model parameters. However, such resources are expensive to create and only available for a small number of languages. Moreover, when moved to a new domain (e.g., from news corpora to blogs or biomedical texts), the performance of these models tends to degrade substantially (Pradhan et al., 2008). The scarcity of annotated data has motivated the research into unsupervised learning of semantic representations (Swier and Stevenson, 2004; Grenager and Manning, 2006; Lang and Lapata, 2010; Lang and Lapata, 2011a; Lang and Lapata, 2011b; Titov and Klementiev, 2012a; Fürstenau and Rambow, 2012; Garg and Henderson, 2012). The existing methods have a number of serious shortcomings. First, they make very strong assumptions, for example, assuming that arguments are conditionally independent of each other given the predicate. Second, unlike state-of-the-art supervised parsers, they rely on a very simplistic set of features of a sentence. These factors lead to models being insufficiently expressive to capture the syntax-semantics interface, inadequate



*Human Language Technologies: The 2015 Annual Conference of the North American Chapter of the ACL*, pages 1–10,
Denver, Colorado, May 31 – June 5, 2015. 

handling of language ambiguity and, overall, introduces a restrictive upper bound on their performance. Moreover, these approaches are especially problematic for languages with freer word order than English, where richer features are necessary to account for interactions between surface realizations, syntax and semantics. For example, the two most accurate previous models (Titov and Klementiev, 2012a; Lang and Lapata, 2011a) both treat the role induction task as clustering of argument signatures: an argument signature encodes key syntactic properties of an argument realization and consists of a syntactic function of an argument along with additional information such as an argument position with respect to the predicate. Though it is possible to design signatures which mostly map to a single role, this set-up limits oracle performance even for English, and can be quite restrictive for languages with freer word order. These shortcomings are inherent limitations of the modeling frameworks used in previous work (primarily generative modeling or agglomerative clustering), and cannot be addressed by simply incorporating more features or relaxing some of the modeling assumptions.

In this work, we propose a method for effective unsupervised estimation of feature-rich models of semantic roles. We demonstrate that reconstruction-error objectives, which have been shown to be effective primarily for training neural networks, are well suited for inducing feature-rich log-linear models of semantics. Our model consists of two components: a log-linear feature-rich semantic role labeler and a tensor-factorization model which captures interaction between semantic roles and argument fillers. When estimated jointly on unlabeled data, roles induced by the model mostly corresponds to roles defined in existing resources by annotators.

Our method rivals the most accurate semantic role induction methods on English and German (Titov and Klementiev, 2012a; Lang and Lapata, 2011a). Importantly, no prior knowledge about the languages was incorporated in our feature-rich model, whereas the clustering counterparts relied on language-specific argument signatures. These languages-specific priors were crucial for their success. For example, using English-specific argument signatures for German with the Bayesian model of Titov and Klementiev (2012a) results in a drop of performance from clustering F1 of 80.9% to considerably lower 78.3% (our model yields 81.4%). This confirms the intuition that using richer features helps to capture the syntax-semantics interface in multilingual settings, reducing the need for language-specific model engineering, as is highly desirable in unsupervised learning.

The rest of the paper is structured as follows. Section 2 begins with a definition of the semantic role labeling task and discusses some specifics of the unsupervised setting. In Section 3, we describe our approach, starting with a general motivation and proceeding to technical details of the model (Section 3.3) and the learning procedure (Section 3.4). Section 4 provides both evaluation and analysis. Finally, additional related work is presented in Section 5.

## 2 Task Definition

The SRL task involves prediction of predicate argument structure, i.e. both identification of arguments and assignment of labels according to their underlying semantic role. For example, in the following sentences:

**(a)** $[_{Agent}$ Mary$]$ opened $[_{Patient}$ the door$]$.

**(b)** $[_{Patient}$ The door$]$ opened.

**(c)** $[_{Patient}$ The door$]$ was opened $[_{Agent}$ by Mary$]$.

*Mary* always takes an agent role for the predicate *open*, and *door* is always a patient.

In this work we focus on the labeling stage of semantic role labeling. Identification, though an important problem, can be tackled with heuristics (Lang and Lapata, 2011a; Grenager and Manning, 2006; de Marneffe et al., 2006), with unsupervised techniques (Abend et al., 2009) or potentially by using a supervised classifier trained on a small amount of data.

## 3 Approach

At the core of our approach is a statistical model encoding an interdependence between a semantic role structure and its realization in a sentence. In the unsupervised learning setting, sentences, their syntactic representations and argument positions (denoted by $x$) are observable whereas the associated semantic roles $\boldsymbol{r}$ are latent and need to be induced by the model. The idea which underlines much of latent variable modeling is that a good latent representation is the one which helps us to reconstruct $x$. In practice, we are not interested in predicting $x$, as $x$ is observable, but rather interested in inducing appropriate latent representations (i.e. $\boldsymbol{r}$). Thus, it is crucial to design the model in such a way that the good $\boldsymbol{r}$ (the one predictive of $x$) indeed encodes roles, rather than some other form of abstraction.

In what follows, we will refer to roles using their names, though, in the unsupervised setting, our method, as any other latent variable model, will not yield human-interpretable labels for them. We will use the following sentence as a motivating example in our discussion of the model:

$[_{Agent}$ The police$]$ charged $[_{Patient}$ the demonstrators$]$ $[_{Instrument}$ with batons$]$.

The model consists of two components. The first component is responsible for prediction of argument tuples based on roles and the predicate. In our experiments, in this component, we represent arguments as lemmas of their lexical heads (e.g., *baton* instead of *with batons*). We also restrict ourselves to only verbal predicates. Intuitively, we can think of predicting one argument at a time (see Figure 1(b)): an argument (e.g., *demonstrator* in our example) is predicted based on the predicate lemma (*charge*), the role assigned to this argument (i.e. `Patient`) and other role-argument pairs ((`Agent`, *police*) and (`Instrument`, *baton*)). While learning to predict arguments, the inference algorithm will search for role assignments which simplify this prediction task as much as possible. Our hypothesis is that these assignments will correspond to roles accepted in linguistic theories (or, more importantly, useful in practical applications). Why is this hypothesis plausible? Primarily because these semantic representations were introduced as an abstraction capturing the essence of a situation (or a event). And the underlying situation and participant roles in this situation (rather than surface linguistic details like argument order or syntactic functions) are precisely what impose constraints on admissible argument tuples.

The reconstruction component is not the only part of the model. Crucially, what we referred to above as 'searching for role assignments to simplify argument prediction' would actually correspond to learning another component: a semantic role labeler which predicts roles relying on a rich set of sentence features. These two components will be estimated jointly in such a way as to minimize errors in recovering arguments. The role labeler will be the end-product of learning: it will be used to process new sentences, and it will be compared to existing methods in our evaluation.

### 3.1 Shortcomings of generative modeling

The above paragraph can be regarded as our desiderata; now we discuss how to achieve them. The standard way to approach latent variable modeling is to use the generative framework: that is to define a family of joint models $p(x, y|\theta)$ and estimate the parameters $\theta$ by, for example, maximizing the likelihood. Generative models of semantics (Titov and Klementiev, 2012a; Titov and Klementiev, 2011; Modi et al., 2012; O'Connor, 2013; Kawahara et al., 2014) necessarily make very strong independence assumptions (e.g., arguments are conditionally independent of each other given the predicate) and use simplistic features of $x$ and $y$. Thus, they cannot meet the desiderata stated above. Importantly, they are also much more simplistic in their assumptions than state-of-the-art supervised role labelers (Erk and Pado, 2006; Johansson and Nugues, 2008; Das et al., 2010).

### 3.2 Reconstruction error minimization

Generative modeling is not the only way to learn latent representations. One alternative, popular in the neural network community, is to instead use autoencoders and optimize the reconstruction error (Hinton, 1989; Vincent et al., 2008). In autoencoders, a latent representation $y$ (their hidden layer) is predicted from $x$ by an encoding model and then this $y$ is used to recover $\tilde{x}$ with a reconstruction model (see Figure 1(a)). Parameters of the encoding and reconstruction components are chosen so as to minimize some form of the reconstruction error, for example, the Euclidean distance $\Delta(x, \tilde{x}) = ||x - \tilde{x}||_2$. Though currently popular only within the deep learning community, latent variable models other than neural networks can also be trained this way, moreover:

- the encoding and reconstruction models can belong to different model families;

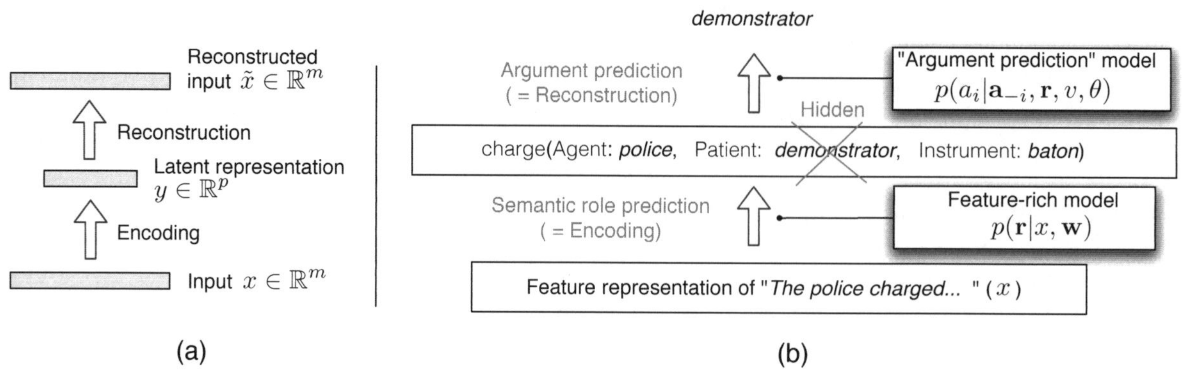


Figure 1: (a) An autoencoder from $\mathbb{R}^m$ to $\mathbb{R}^p$ (typically $p < m$). (b) Modeling roles within the reconstruction-error minimization framework.

- the reconstruction component may be focused on recovering a part of $x$ rather than the entire $x$, and, in doing so, can rely not only on $y$ but on the remaining part of $x$.

These observations are crucial as they allow us to implement our desiderata. More specifically, the encoding model will be a feature-rich classifier which predicts semantic roles for a sentence, and the reconstruction model is the model which predicts an argument given its role, and given the rest of the arguments and their roles. The idea of training linear models by minimizing the reconstruction error was previously explored by Daumé (2009) and very recently by Ammar et al. (2014).

### 3.3 Modeling semantics within the reconstruction-error framework

There are several possible ways to translate the ideas above into a specific method, and we consider one of the simplest instantiations. For simplicity, in the discussion (but not in our experiments), we assume that exactly one predicate is realized in each sentence $x$. As we mentioned above, we focus only on argument labeling: we assume that arguments $\boldsymbol{a} = (a_1, \dots, a_N)$, $a_i \in \mathcal{A}$, are known, and only their roles $\boldsymbol{r} = (r_1, \dots, r_N)$, $r_i \in \mathcal{R}$ need to be induced. For the encoder (i.e. the semantic role labeler), we use a log-linear model:

$$p(\boldsymbol{r}|x, \boldsymbol{w}) \propto \exp(\boldsymbol{w}^T \boldsymbol{g}(x, \boldsymbol{r})),$$

where $\boldsymbol{g}(x, \boldsymbol{r})$ is a feature vector encoding interactions between sentence $x$ and the semantic role representation $\boldsymbol{r}$. Any model can be used here as long as the posterior distributions of roles $r_i$ can be efficiently computed or approximated (we will see why in Section 3.4). In our experiments, we used a model which factorizes over individual arguments (i.e. a set of independent logistic regression classifiers).

The reconstruction component predicts an argument (e.g., the $i$th argument $a_i$) given the semantic roles $\boldsymbol{r}$, the predicate $v$ and other arguments $\boldsymbol{a}_{-i} = (a_1, \dots, a_{i-1}, a_{i+1}, \dots, a_N)$ with a bilinear softmax model:

$$p(a_i|\boldsymbol{a}_{-i}, \boldsymbol{r}, v, C, \boldsymbol{u}) = \frac{\exp(\boldsymbol{u}_{a_i}^T C_{v,r_i}^T \sum_{j \neq i} C_{v,r_j} \boldsymbol{u}_{a_j})}{Z(\boldsymbol{r}, v, i)}, \quad (1)$$

$\boldsymbol{u}_a \in \mathbb{R}^d$ (for every $a \in \mathcal{A}$) and $C_{v,r} \in \mathbb{R}^{k \times d}$ (for every verb $v$ and every role $r \in \mathcal{R}$) are model parameters, $Z(\boldsymbol{r}, v, i)$ is the partition function ensuring that the probabilities sum to one. Intuitively, embeddings $\boldsymbol{u}_a$, when learned from data, will encode semantic properties of an argument: for example, embeddings for the words *demonstrator* and *protestor* should be somewhere near each other in $\mathbb{R}^d$ space, and further away from that for the word *cat*. The product $C_{v,r}\boldsymbol{u}_a$ is a $k$-dimensional vector encoding beliefs about other arguments based on the argument-role pair $(a, r)$. For example, seeing the argument *demonstrator* in the `Patient` position for the predicate *charge*, one would predict that the `Agent` is perhaps the word *police*, and the role `Instrument` is filled by the word *baton* or perhaps (a water) *cannon*. On the contrary, if the `Patient` is *cat* then the `Agent` is more likely to be *dog* than *police*. In turn, the dot product $(C_{v,r_i}\boldsymbol{u}_{a_i})^T C_{v,r_j}\boldsymbol{u}_{a_j}$ is large if these expectations are met for the argument pair $(a_i, a_j)$, and small otherwise. Intuitively, this objective corresponds to scoring argument tuples according to

$$h(\boldsymbol{a}, \boldsymbol{r}, v, C, \boldsymbol{u}) = \sum_{i \neq j} \boldsymbol{u}_{a_i}^T C_{v,r_i}^T C_{v,r_j} \boldsymbol{u}_{a_j}, \quad (2)$$

hinting at connections to (coupled) tensor and matrix factorization methods (Nickel et al., 2011; Yılmaz et al., 2011; Bordes et al., 2011; Riedel et al., 2013) and distributional semantics (Mikolov et al., 2013; Pennington et al., 2014). Note also that the reconstruction model does not have access to any features of the sentence (e.g., argument order or syntax), forcing the roles to convey all the necessary information.

This factorization can be thought of as a generalization of the notion of selection preferences. Selectional preferences characterize the set of arguments licensed for a given role of a given predicate: for example, `Agent` for the predicate *charge* can be *police* or *dog* but not *table* or *idea*. In our generalization, we model soft restrictions imposed not only by the role itself but also by other arguments and their assignment to roles.

In practice, we extend the model slightly: (1) we introduce a word-specific bias (a scalar $b_a$ for every $a \in \mathcal{A}$) in the argument prediction model (equation (1)); (2) we smooth the model by using a sum of predicate-specific and cross-predicate projection matrices $(C_{v,r} + C_r)$ instead of just $C_{v,r}$.

### 3.4 Learning

Parameters of both model components ($\boldsymbol{w}$, $\boldsymbol{u}$ and $C$) are learned jointly: the natural objective associated with every sentence would be the following:

$$\sum_{i=1}^{N} \log \sum_{\boldsymbol{r}} p(a_i|\boldsymbol{a}_{-i}, \boldsymbol{r}, v, C, \boldsymbol{u}) p(\boldsymbol{r}|x, \boldsymbol{w}). \quad (3)$$

However optimizing this objective is not practical in its exact form for two reasons: (1) marginalization over $\boldsymbol{r}$ is exponential in the number of arguments; (2) the partition function $Z(\boldsymbol{r}, v, i)$ requires summation over the entire set of potential argument lemmas. We use existing techniques to address both challenges.

In order to deal with the first challenge, we use a basic mean-field approximation. Namely, instead of computing an expectation of $p(a_i|\boldsymbol{a}_{-i}, \boldsymbol{r}, v, C, \boldsymbol{u})$ under $p(\boldsymbol{r}|x, \boldsymbol{w})$, as in (3), we use the posterior distributions $\mu_{is} = p(\boldsymbol{r_i} = s|x, \boldsymbol{w})$ and score the argument predictions as

$$p(a_i|\boldsymbol{a}_{-i}, \boldsymbol{\mu}, v, C, \boldsymbol{u}) = \frac{\exp(\phi_i(a_i, \boldsymbol{a}_{-i}))}{Z(\boldsymbol{\mu}, v, i)} \quad (4)$$

$$\phi_i(a_i, \boldsymbol{a}_{-i}) = \boldsymbol{u}_{a_i}^T (\sum_s \mu_{is} C_{v,s})^T \times \sum_{j \neq i} (\sum_s \mu_{js} C_{v,s}) \boldsymbol{u}_{a_j},$$

where $\boldsymbol{\mu}$ are the posteriors for all the arguments, and $\phi_i(a, \boldsymbol{a}_{-i})$ is the score associated with predicting lemma $a$ for the argument $i$.

In order to address the second problem, the computation of $Z(\boldsymbol{\mu}, v, i)$, we use a negative sampling technique (see, e.g., Mikolov et al. (2013)). More specfically, we get rid of the softmax in equation (4) and optimize the following sentence-level objective:

$$\sum_{i=1}^{N} [\log \sigma(\phi_i(a_i, \boldsymbol{a}_{-i})) - \sum_{a' \in S} \log \sigma(\phi_i(a', \boldsymbol{a}_{-i}))], \quad (5)$$

where $S$ is a random sample of $n$ elements from the unigram distribution of lemmas, and $\sigma$ is the logistic sigmoid function.

Assuming that the posteriors $\boldsymbol{\mu}$ can be derived in a closed form, the gradients of the objective (5) with respect to parameters of both the encoding component ($\boldsymbol{w}$) and the reconstruction component ($C$, $\boldsymbol{u}$ and $\boldsymbol{b}$) can be computed using back propagation. In our experiments, we used the AdaGrad algorithm (Duchi et al., 2011) to perform the optimization.

The learning algorithm is quite efficient, as the reconstruction computation is bilinear, whereas the computation of the posteriors $\boldsymbol{\mu}$ (and the computation of their gradients) from the semantic roler labeling component (encoder) is not much more expensive than discriminative supervised learning of the role labeler. Moreover, the computations can be sped up substantially by observing that the sum $\sum_s \mu_{is} C_{v,s}$ in expression (4) can be precomputed for all $i$, and reused across predictions of different arguments of the same predicate. At test time, only the linear semantic role labeler is used, so the inference is straightforward.

## 4 Experiments

### 4.1 Data and evaluation metrics

We considered English and German in our experiments. For each language, we replicated experimental set-ups used in previous work.

For English, we followed Lang and Lapata (2010) and used the dependency version of PropBank (Palmer et al., 2005) released for the CoNLL 2008 shared task (Surdeanu et al., 2008). The dataset is divided into three segments. As in the previous work on unsupervised role labeling, we used the largest segment (the original CoNLL training set, sections 2-21) both for evaluation and learning. This is permissible as unsupervised models do not use gold labels in training. The two small segments (sections 22 and 23) were used for model development. In our experiments, we relied on gold standard syntax and gold standard argument identification, as this set-up allows us to evaluate against much of the previous work. We refer the reader to Lang and Lapata (2010) for details of the experimental set-up.

There has not been much work on unsupervised induction of roles for languages other than English, perhaps primarily because of the above-mentioned model limitations. For German, we replicate the set-up considered in Titov and Klementiev (2012b). They used the CoNLL 2009 version (Hajič et al., 2009) of the SALSA corpus (Burchardt et al., 2006). Instead of using syntactic parses provided in the CoNLL dataset, they re-parsed it with the MALT dependency parser (Nivre et al., 2004). Similarly, rather than relying on gold standard annotations for argument identification, they used a supervised classifier to predict argument positions. Details of the preprocessing can be found in Titov and Klementiev (2012b).

As in most previous work on unsupervised SRL, we evaluate our model using purity, collocation and their harmonic mean F1. *Purity* (PU) measures the average number of arguments with the same gold role label in each cluster, *collocation* (CO) measures to what extent a specific gold role is represented by a single cluster. More formally:

$$PU = \frac{1}{N} \sum_i \max_j |G_j \cap C_i|$$

where if $C_i$ is the set of arguments in the $i$-th induced cluster, $G_j$ is the set of arguments in the $j$th gold cluster, and $N$ is the total number of arguments. Similarly, for collocation:

$$CO = \frac{1}{N} \sum_j \max_i |G_j \cap C_i|$$

We compute the aggregate PU, CO, and F1 scores over all predicates in the same way as Lang and Lapata (2010): we weight the scores for each predicate by the number of times its arguments occur and compute the weighted average.

### 4.2 Parameters and features

For the semantic role labeling (encoding) component, we relied on 14 feature patterns used for argument labeling in a popular supervised role labeler (Johansson and Nugues, 2008). These patterns include non-trivial syntactic features, such as a dependency path between the target predicate and the considered argument. The resulting feature space is quite large (49,474 feature instantiations for our English dataset) and arguably sufficient to accurately capture syntax-semantics interface for most languages. We refer the reader to the original publication for details (Johansson and Nugues, 2008: Table 2). Importantly, the dimensionality of the feature space is very different from the one used typically in unsupervised SRL. In principle, any features could be used here but we chose these 14 feature patterns, as they all are fairly simple and generic. They can also be easily extracted from any treebank. We used the same feature patterns both for English and German. However, there is little doubt that some language-specific feature engineering and the use of language-specific priors or constraints (e.g., posterior regularization (Ganchev et al., 2010)) would benefit the performance. Faithful to our goal of constructing the simplest possible feature-rich model, we use logistic classifiers independently predicting role distribution for every argument.

For the reconstruction component, both for English and German, we set the embedding dimensionality $d$, the projection dimensionality $k$ and the number of negative samples $n$ to 30, 15 and 20, respectively. The model was not sensitive to the parameter $|\mathcal{R}|$, defining the number of roles as long it was large enough (see Section 4.3 for more discussion). For training, we used uniform random initialization and AdaGrad (Duchi et al., 2011). Any model selections (e.g., choosing the number of epochs) was done on the basis of the respective held-out set.

### 4.3 Results

#### 4.3.1 English

Table 1 summarizes the results of our method, as well as those of alternative approaches and baselines.

Following (Lang and Lapata, 2010), we use a baseline (*SyntF*) which simply clusters predicate arguments according to the dependency relation to their head. A separate cluster is allocated for each of 20 most frequent relations in the dataset and an additional cluster is used for all other relations. As observed in the previous work (Lang and Lapata, 2011a), this is a hard baseline to beat.

We also compare with previous approaches: the latent logistic classification model (Lang and Lapata, 2010) (labeled *LLogistic*), the agglomerative clustering method (Lang and Lapata, 2011a) (*Agglom*), the graph partitioning approach (Lang and Lapata, 2011b) (*GraphPart*), the global role ordering model (Garg and Henderson, 2012) (*RoleOrdering*). We also report results of an improved version of *Agglom*, recently reported by Lang and Lapata (2014) (*Agglom+*). The strongest previous model is *Bayes*: *Bayes* is the most accurate ('coupled') version of the Bayesian model of Titov and Klementiev (2012a), estimated from the CoNLL dataset without relying on any external data. Titov and Klementiev (2012a) also showed that using Brown clusters induced from a large external corpus resulted in an 0.5% improvement in F1 but that version is not entirely comparable to other systems induced solely from the CoNLL text.

Our model outperforms or performs on par with best previous models in terms of F1. Interestingly, the purity and collocation balance is very different for our model and for the rest of the systems. In fact, our model induces at most 4-6 roles (even if $|\mathcal{R}|$ is much larger). On the contrary, *Bayes* predicts more than 30 roles for the majority of frequent predicates (e.g., 43 roles for the predicate *include* or 35 for *say*). Though this tendency reduces the purity scores for our model, this also means that our roles are more human interpretable. For example, agents and patients are clearly identifiable in the model predictions. Our model has similar purity to the syntactic baseline but outperforms it vastly according to the collocation metric, suggesting that we go substantially beyond recovering syntactic relations.

| | PU | CO | F1 |
|---|---|---|---|
| Our Model | 79.7 | 86.2 | **82.8** |
| Bayes | 89.3 | 76.6 | 82.5 |
| Agglom+ | 87.9 | 75.6 | 81.3 |
| RoleOrdering | 83.5 | 78.5 | 80.9 |
| Agglom | 88.7 | 73.0 | 80.1 |
| GraphPart | 88.6 | 70.7 | 78.6 |
| LLogistic | 79.5 | 76.5 | 78.0 |
| SyntF | 81.6 | 77.5 | 79.5 |

Table 1: Results on English (PropBank / CoNLL 2008).

In additional experiments, we observed that our model, in some regimes, starts to induce roles specific to individual verb senses or specific to groups of semantically similar predicates. This suggests that adding a latent variable capturing predicate senses and conditioning the reconstruction component on this variable may not only result in a more informative semantic representation (i.e. include verb senses) but also improve the role induction performance. We leave this exploration for future work.

#### 4.3.2 German

For German, we replicate the experimental set-up previously used by Titov and Klementiev (2012b). As for English, we report results of the syntactic baseline (*SyntF*). The results for all approaches are presented in Table 2. We compare against *Bayes (De)* – the *Bayes* model with argument signatures specialized for German (as reported in Titov and Klementiev (2012b)). We also consider the original

| | PU | CO | F1 |
|---|---|---|---|
| Our Model | 76.4 | 87.0 | **81.4** |
| Bayes (De) | 86.8 | 75.7 | 80.9 |
| Bayes (En) | 80.6 | 76.0 | 78.3 |
| SyntF | 83.1 | 79.3 | 81.2 |

Table 2: Results on German (SALSA / CoNLL 2009).

version of the *Bayes* model (denoted as *Bayes (En)*).

Recently, Lang and Lapata (2014) evaluated their *Agglom+* on a version of the same German SALSA dataset. Their best result is F1 of 79.2%, however, this score and our results are not directly comparable. Instead of using the CoNLL dataset, they processed the corpus themselves. They also relied on syntactic features from a constituent parser whereas we used dependency representations.

The overall picture for German closely resembles the one for English. Our method achieves results comparable to the best method evaluated in this setting. Importantly, parameters and features of our model for German and English are identical. On the contrary, one can see that specialization of argument signatures was crucial for the Bayesian model. Also, similarly to English, our method induces less fine-grain sets of semantic roles but achieves much higher collocation scores.

## 5 Additional Related Work

In recent years, unsupervised approaches to semantic role induction have attracted considerable attention. However, there exist other ways to address lack of coverage provided by existing semantically-annotated resources.

One natural direction is semi-supervised role labeling, where both annotated and unannotated data is used to estimate a model. Previous semi-supervised approaches to SRL can be mostly regarded as extensions to supervised learning by either incorporating word features induced from unnannoted texts (Collobert and Weston, 2008; Deschacht and Moens, 2009) or creating some form of 'surrogate' supervision (He and Gildea, 2006; Fürstenau and Lapata, 2009). Benefits from using unlabeled data were moderate, and more significant for the harder SRL version, frame-semantic parsing (Das and Smith, 2011).

Another important direction includes cross-lingual approaches (Pado and Lapata, 2009; van der Plas et al., 2011; Kozhevnikov and Titov, 2013) which leverage resources from resource-rich languages, as well as parallel data, to produce annotation or models for resource-poor languages. However, both translation shifts and noise in word alignments harm the performance of cross-lingual methods. Nevertheless, even joint unsupervised induction across languages appears to be beneficial (Titov and Klementiev, 2012b).

Unsupervised learning has also been one of the central paradigms for the closely-related area of relation extraction (RE), where several techniques have been proposed to cluster semantically similar verbalizations of relations (Lin and Pantel, 2001; Banko et al., 2007; Yao et al., 2011). Similarly to SRL, unsupervised methods for RE mostly rely on generative modeling and agglomerative clustering.

From the learning perspective, methods which use the reconstruction-error objective to estimate linear models (Ammar et al., 2014; Daumé III, 2009) are certainly related. However, they do not consider learning factorization models, and they also do not deal with semantics. Tensor factorization methods used in the context of modeling knoweldge bases (e.g., (Bordes et al., 2011)) are also close in spirit. However, they do not deal with inducing semantics but rather factorize existing relations (i.e. rely on semantics).

## 6 Conclusions and Discussion

This work introduces a method for inducing feature-rich semantic role labelers from unannoated text. In our approach, we view a semantic role representation as an encoding of a latent relation between a predicate and a tuple of its arguments. We capture this relation with a probabilistic tensor factorization model. The factorization model (relying on semantic roles) and a feature-rich model (predicting the roles) are jointly estimated by optimizing an objective which favours accurate reconstruction of arguments given the latent semantic representation (and other arguments). Our estimation method yields a semantic role labeler which achieves state-of-the-art results both on English and German.

Unlike previous work on role induction, in our

approach, virtually any computationally tractable structured model can be used as a role labeler, including almost any semantic role labeler introduced in the context of supervised SRL (see, e.g., CoNLL shared tasks (Carreras and Màrquez, 2005; Surdeanu et al., 2008; Hajič et al., 2009)). This opens interesting possibilities to extend our approach to the semi-supervised setting. Previous unsupervised SRL models make too strong assumption and use too limited features to effectively exploit labeled data. For our model, the reconstruction objective can be easily combined with the likelihood objective, yielding a potentially powerful semi-supervised method. We leave this direction for future work.


### Acknowledgements

This work is partially supported by a Google focused award on natural language understanding. The authors thank Dipanjan Das, Ashutosh Modi, Alexis Palmer and the anonymous reviewers for their suggestions.


## References


O. Abend, R. Reichart, and A. Rappoport. 2009. Unsupervised argument identification for semantic role labeling. In *ACL-IJCNLP*.

W. Ammar, C. Dyer, and N. Smith. 2014. Conditional random field autoencoders for unsupervised structured prediction. In *NIPS*.

Collin F. Baker, Charles J. Fillmore, and John B. Lowe. 1998. The Berkeley FrameNet project. In *ACL-COLING*.

M. Banko, M. J. Cafarella, S. Soderland, M. Broadhead, and O. Etzioni. 2007. Open information extraction from the web. In *IJCAI*.

R. Basili, D. De Cao, D. Croce, B. Coppola, and A. Moschitti. 2009. Cross-language frame semantics transfer in bilingual corpora. In *CICLING*.

A. Bordes, J. Weston, R. Collobert, and Y. Bengio. 2011. Learning structured embeddings of knowledge bases. In *AAAI*.

A. Burchardt, K. Erk, A. Frank, A. Kowalski, S. Pado, and M. Pinkal. 2006. The SALSA corpus: a german corpus resource for lexical semantics. In *LREC*.

X. Carreras and L. Màrquez. 2005. Introduction to the CoNLL-2005 Shared Task: Semantic Role Labeling. In *CoNLL*.

R. Collobert and J. Weston. 2008. A unified architecture for natural language processing: Deep neural networks with multitask learning. In *ICML*.

D. Das and N. A. Smith. 2011. Semi-supervised frame-semantic parsing for unknown predicates. In *ACL*.

D. Das, N. Schneider, D. Chen, and N. A. Smith. 2010. Probabilistic frame-semantic parsing. In *NAACL*.

H. Daumé III. 2009. Unsupervised search-based structured prediction. In *ICML*.

M.-C. de Marneffe, B. MacCartney, and C.r D. Manning. 2006. Generating typed dependency parses from phrase structure parses. In *LREC*.

K. Deschacht and M.-F. Moens. 2009. Semi-supervised semantic role labeling using the latent words language model. In *Proceedings of EMNLP*.

J. Duchi, E. Hazan, and Y. Singer. 2011. Adaptive subgradient methods for online learning and stochastic optimization. *The Journal of Machine Learning Research*, 12:2121–2159.

K. Erk and S. Pado. 2006. Shalmaneser–a toolchain for shallow semantic parsing. In *LREC*.

C. J. Fillmore. 1968. The case for case. In Bach E. and Harms R.T., editors, *Universals in Linguistic Theory*, pages 1–88. Holt, Rinehart, and Winston, New York.

H. Fürstenau and M. Lapata. 2009. Graph alignment for semi-supervised semantic role labeling. In *EMNLP*.

H. Fürstenau and O. Rambow. 2012. Unsupervised induction of a syntax-semantics lexicon using iterative refinement. In *Proceedings of the First Joint Conference on Lexical and Computational Semantics*.

K. Ganchev, J. Graca, J. Gillenwater, and B. Taskar. 2010. Posterior regularization for structured latent variable models. *Journal of Machine Learning Research (JMLR)*, 11:2001–2049.

Q. Gao and S. Vogel. 2011. Corpus expansion for statistical machine translation with semantic role label substitution rules. In *ACL:HLT*.

N. Garg and J. Henderson. 2012. Unsupervised semantic role induction with global role ordering. In *ACL*.

D. Gildea and D. Jurafsky. 2002. Automatic labelling of semantic roles. *Computational Linguistics*, 28(3):245–288.

T. Grenager and C. Manning. 2006. Unsupervised discovery of a statistical verb lexicon. In *EMNLP*.

J. Hajič, M. Ciaramita, R. Johansson, D. Kawahara, M.A. Martí, L. Màrquez, A. Meyers, J. Nivre, S. Padó, J. Štěpánek, P. Straňák, M. Surdeanu, N. Xue, and Y. Zhang. 2009. The CoNLL-2009 shared task: Syntactic and semantic dependencies in multiple languages. In *Proceedings of the 13th Conference on Computational Natural Language Learning (CoNLL-2009), June 4-5*.

S. He and D. Gildea. 2006. Self-training and co-training for semantic role labeling: Primary report. Technical report, Technical Report 891, University of Rochester.

G. E. Hinton. 1989. Connectionist learning procedures. *Artificial intelligence*, 40(1):185–234.

R. Johansson and P. Nugues. 2008. Dependency-based syntactic-semantic analysis with PropBank and NomBank. In *CoNLL*.

M. Kaisser and B. Webber. 2007. Question answering based on semantic roles. In *ACL Workshop on Deep Linguistic Processing*.

D. Kawahara, D. Peterson, O. Popescu, and M. Palmer. 2014. Inducing example-based semantic frames from a massive amount of verb uses. In *EACL*.

M. Kozhevnikov and I. Titov. 2013. Crosslingual transfer of semantic role models. In *ACL*.

J. Lang and M. Lapata. 2010. Unsupervised induction of semantic roles. In *ACL*.

J. Lang and M. Lapata. 2011a. Unsupervised semantic role induction via split-merge clustering. In *ACL*.

J. Lang and M. Lapata. 2011b. Unsupervised semantic role induction with graph partitioning. In *EMNLP*.

J. Lang and M. Lapata. 2014. Similarity-driven semantic role induction via graph partitioning. *Computational Linguistics*, 40(3):633–669.

D. Lin and P. Pantel. 2001. DIRT – discovery of inference rules from text. In *KDD*.

D. Liu and D. Gildea. 2010. Semantic role features for machine translation. In *Coling*.

T. Mikolov, K. Chen, G. Corrado, and J. Dean. 2013. Efficient estimation of word representations in vector space. *arXiv preprint arXiv:1301.3781*.

A. Modi, I. Titov, and A. Klementiev. 2012. Unsupervised induction of frame-semantic representations. In *NAACL Workshop on Inducing Linguistic Structure*.

M. Nickel, V. Tresp, and H.-P. Kriegel. 2011. A three-way model for collective learning on multi-relational data. In *ICML*.

J. Nivre, J. Hall, and J. Nilsson. 2004. Memory-based dependency parsing. In *Proc. of the Eighth Conference on Computational Natural Language Learning*, pages 49–56, Boston, USA.

B. O'Connor. 2013. Learning frames from text with an unsupervised latent variable model. Technical report, CMU.

S. Pado and M. Lapata. 2009. Cross-lingual annotation projection for semantic roles. *Journal of Artificial Intelligence Research*, 36:307–340.

M. Palmer, D. Gildea, and P. Kingsbury. 2005. The proposition bank: An annotated corpus of semantic roles. *Computational Linguistics*, 31(1):71–106.

J. Pennington, R. Socher, and C. D. Manning. 2014. Glove: Global vectors for word representation. In *EMNLP*.

S. Pradhan, W. Ward, and J. H. Martin. 2008. Towards robust semantic role labeling. *Computational Linguistics*, 34:289–310.

S. Riedel, L. Yao, A. McCallum, and B. M. Marlin. 2013. Relation extraction with matrix factorization and universal schemas. In *NAACL*.

M. Sammons, V. Vydiswaran, T. Vieira, N. Johri, M. Chang, D. Goldwasser, V. Srikumar, G. Kundu, Y. Tu, K. Small, J. Rule, Q. Do, and D. Roth. 2009. Relation alignment for textual entailment recognition. In *Text Analysis Conference (TAC)*.

D. Shen and M. Lapata. 2007. Using semantic roles to improve question answering. In *EMNLP*.

M. Surdeanu, A. Meyers, R. Johansson, L. Màrquez, and J. Nivre. 2008. The CoNLL-2008 shared task on joint parsing of syntactic and semantic dependencies. In *CoNLL 2008: Shared Task*.

R. Swier and S. Stevenson. 2004. Unsupervised semantic role labelling. In *EMNLP*.

I. Titov and A. Klementiev. 2011. A Bayesian model for unsupervised semantic parsing. In *ACL*.

I. Titov and A. Klementiev. 2012a. A Bayesian approach to semantic role induction. In *EACL*.

I. Titov and A. Klementiev. 2012b. Crosslingual induction of semantic roles. In *ACL*.

L. van der Plas, J. Henderson, and P. Merlo. 2009. Domain adaptation with artificial data for semantic parsing of speech. In *NAACL*.

L. van der Plas, P. Merlo, and J. Henderson. 2011. Scaling up automatic cross-lingual semantic role annotation. In *ACL*.

P. Vincent, H. Larochelle, Y. Bengio, and P.-A. Manzagol. 2008. Extracting and composing robust features with denoising autoencoders. In *ICML*.

D. Wu and P. Fung. 2009. Semantic roles for SMT: A hybrid two-pass model. In *NAACL*.

D. Wu, M. Apidianaki, M. Carpuat, and L. Specia, editors. 2011. *Proc. of Fifth Workshop on Syntax, Semantics and Structure in Statistical Translation*. ACL.

L. Yao, A. Haghighi, S. Riedel, and A. McCallum. 2011. Structured relation discovery using generative models. In *EMNLP*.

K. Y. Yılmaz, A. T. Cemgil, and U. Simsekli. 2011. Generalised coupled tensor factorisation. In *NIPS*.

# Predicate Argument Alignment using a Global Coherence Model

**Travis Wolfe, Mark Dredze, and Benjamin Van Durme**
Johns Hopkins University
Baltimore, MD, USA

## Abstract

We present a joint model for predicate argument alignment. We leverage multiple sources of semantic information, including temporal ordering constraints between events. These are combined in a max-margin framework to find a globally consistent view of entities and events across multiple documents, which leads to improvements over a very strong local baseline.

## 1 Introduction

Natural language understanding (NLU) requires analysis beyond the sentence-level. For example, an *entity* may be mentioned multiple times in a discourse, participating in various events, where each event may itself be referenced elsewhere in the text. Traditionally the task of *coreference resolution* has been defined as finding those entity mentions within a single document that co-refer, while *cross-document coreference resolution* considers a wider discourse context across many documents, yet still pertains strictly to entities.

Predicate argument alignment, or entity-event cross-document coreference resolution, enlarges the set of possible co-referent elements to include the mentions of situations in which entities participate. This expanded definition drives practitioners towards a more complete model of NLU, where systems must not only consider who is mentioned, but also what happened. However, despite the drive towards an expanded notion of discourse, models typically are formulated with strong notions of local-independence: viewing a multi-document task as one limited to individual pairs of sentences. This creates a mis-match between the goals of such work – considering entire documents – with the systems – consider individual sentences.

In this work, we consider a system that takes a document level view in considering coreference for entities and predictions: the task of predicate argument linking. We treat this task as a global inference problem, leveraging multiple sources of semantic information identified at the document level. Global inference for this problem is mostly unexplored, with the exception of Lee et al. (2012) (discussed in § 8). Especially novel here is the use of document-level temporal constraints on events, representing a next step forward on the path to full understanding.

Our approach avoids the pitfalls of local inference while still remaining fast and exact. We use the pairwise features of a very strong predicate argument aligner (Wolfe et al., 2013) (competitive with the state-of-the-art (Roth, 2014)), and add quadratic factors that constrain local decisions based on global document information. These global factors lead to superior performance compared to the previous state-of-the-art. We release both our code and data.[1]

## 2 Model

Consider the two sentences from the document pair shown in Figure 1. These sentences describe the same event, although with different details. The source sentence has four predicates and four arguments, while the target has three predicates and three arguments. In this case, one of the predicates from each sentence aligns, as do three of the arguments. We also show additional information potentially helpful to determining alignments: temporal relations between the predicates. The goal of predicate argument alignment is to assign these links indicating coreferent predicates and arguments across a document pair (Roth and Frank, 2012).

Previous work by Wolfe et al. (2013) formulated

[1] `https://github.com/hltcoe/parma2`



*Human Language Technologies: The 2015 Annual Conference of the North American Chapter of the ACL*, pages 11–20,
Denver, Colorado, May 31 – June 5, 2015. 

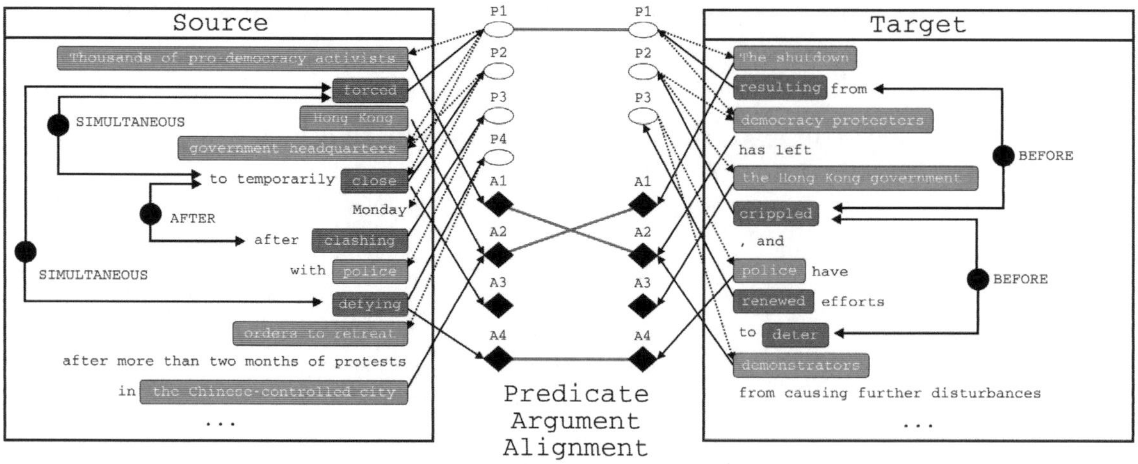


Figure 1: An example analysis and predicate argument alignment task between a source and target document. Predicates appear as hollow ovals, have blue mentions, and are aligned considering their arguments (dashed lines). Arguments, in black diamonds with green mentions, represent a document-level entity (coreference chain), and are aligned using their predicate structure and mention-level features. The alignment choices appear in the middle in red. Temporal relation information is lifted into the global inference over alignments.

this as a binary classification problem: given a pair of arguments or predicates, construct features and score the pair, where scores above threshold indicate links. A binary classification framework has advantages: it's fast since individual decisions can be made quickly, but it comes at the cost of global information across links. The result may be links that conflict in their interpretation of the document. Figure 1 makes clear that jointly considering all links at once can aid individual decisions, for example, by including temporal ordering of predicates.

The global nature of this task is similar to word alignment for machine translation (MT). Many systems consider alignment links between words individually, selecting the best link for each word independently of the other words in the sentence. Just as with an independent linking strategy in predicate argument alignment, this can lead to inconsistencies in the output. Lacoste-Julien et al. (2006) introduced a model that jointly resolved word alignments based on the introduction of quadratic variables, factors that depend on two alignment decisions which characterize patterns that span word-word links. Their approach achieved improved results even in the presence of little training data.

We present a global predicate argument alignment model based on considering quadratic interactions between alignment variables to captures patterns we expect in coherent discourse. We introduce factors which are comprised of a binary variable, multiple quadratic constraints on that variable, and features that determine the cost associated with that variable in order to characterize the dependence between alignment decisions.

While the mathematical framework we use is similar to Lacoste-Julien et al. (2006), predicate argument alignment greatly differs from word alignment; thus our joint factors are based on different sources of regularity. Word alignment favors monotonicity in word order, but this effect is very weak in predicate argument alignment: aligned items can be spread throughout a document, and are often nested, gapped, or shuffled. Instead, we encode assumptions about consistency of temporal relations between coreferent events, coherence between predicates and arguments that appear in both documents, and fertility (to prevent over-alignment). We also note that our setting has much less data than typical word alignment tasks, as well as richer features that utilize semantic resources.

**Notation** An alignment between an item indexed by $i$ in the source document and $j$ in the target document is represented by variable $z_{ij} \in \{0, 1\}$, where $z_{ij} = 1$ indicates that items $i$ and $j$ are aligned. In some cases, we will explicitly indicate when the two items are predicates as $z^p_{ij}$; an argument alignment will be $z^a_{ij}$. We represent all alignments for a document pair as matrix $\mathbf{z}$.

For clarity, we omit any variable representing observed data when discussing feature functions; alignment variables are endowed with this information. For each pair of items we use "local" feature functions $\mathbf{f}(\cdot)$ and corresponding parameters $w$, which capture the similarity between two items without the context of other alignments.

$$s_{ij} = w \cdot \mathbf{f}(z_{ij}) \quad (1)$$

where $s_{ij}$ is the score of linking items $i$ and $j$.

Using only local features, our system would greedily select alignments. To capture global aspects we add joint factors that capture effects between alignment variables. Each joint factor $\phi$ is comprised of a constrained binary variable $z_\phi$ associated with features $\mathbf{f}(\phi)$ that indicates when the factor is active. Together with parameters $w$ these form additional scores $s_\phi$ for the objective:

$$s_\phi = w \cdot \mathbf{f}(\phi) \quad (2)$$

The full linear scoring function on alignments sums over both local similarity and joint factors:

$$\sum_{ij} s_{ij} z_{ij} + \sum_{\phi \in \Phi} s_\phi z_\phi . \quad (3)$$

Lastly, it is convenient to describe the local feature functions and their corresponding alignment variable as factors with no constraints, and we will do so when describing the full score function.

## 3 Local Factors

Local factors encode features based on the mention pair, which include a wide variety of similarity measures, e.g. whether two headwords appear as synonyms in WordNet, gender agreement based on possessive pronouns. We adopt the features of Wolfe et al. (2013), a strong baseline system which doesn't use global inference.[2] These features are built on top of a variety of semantic resources (PPDB (Ganitkevitch et al., 2013), WordNet (Miller, 1995), FrameNet (Baker et al., 1998)) and methods for comparing mentions (tree edit distance (Yao et al., 2013), string transducer (Andrews et al., 2012)).

## 4 Joint Factors

Our goal is to develop joint factors that improve over the feature rich local factors baseline by considering global information.

**Fertility** A common mistake when making independent classification decisions is to align many source items to a single target item. While each link looks promising on its own, they clearly cannot all be right. Empirically, the training set reveals that many to one alignments are uncommon; thus many to one predictions are likely errors. We add a fertility factor for predicates and arguments, where fertility is defined as the number of links to an item. Higher fertilities are undesired and are thus penalized. Formally, for matrix $\mathbf{z}$, the fertility of a row $i$ or column $j$ is the sum of that row or column. We discuss fertility in terms of rows below.

We include two types of fertility factors. First, factor $\phi_{\text{fert1}}$ distinguishes between rows with at least one link from those with none. For row $i$, we add one instance of the linear factor $\phi_{\text{fert1}}$ with constraints

$$z_{\phi_{\text{fert1}}} \geq z_{ij} \; \forall j \quad (4)$$

The cost associated with $z_{\phi_{\text{fert1}}}$, which we will refer to as $s_{\text{fert1}}$, will be incurred any time an item is mentioned in both documents. For data sets with many singletons, $s_{\text{fert1}}$ more strongly penalizes non-singleton rows, reflecting this pattern in the training data. We make $s_{\text{fert1}}$ parametric, where the features of the $\phi_{\text{fert1}}$ factor allow us to learn different weights for predicates and arguments, as well as the size of the row, i.e. number of items in the pairing.

The second fertility factory $\phi_{\text{fert2}}$ considers items with a fertility greater than one, penalizing items for having too many links. Its binary variable has the

[2] Some features inspect the apparent predicate argument structure, based on things like dependency parses, but the model may not inspect more than one of its own decisions (joint factors) while scoring an alignment.

quadratic constraints:

$$z_{\phi_{\text{fert2}}} \geq z_{ij} z_{ik} \; \forall j < k \tag{5}$$

This factor penalizes rows that have fertility of at least two, but does not distinguish beyond that. An alternative would be to introduce a factor for every pair of variables in a row, each with one constraint. This would heavily penalize fertilities greater than two. We found that the resulting quadratic program took longer to solve and gave worse results.

Since documents have been processed to identify in-document coreference chains, we do not expect multiple arguments from a source document to align to a single target item. For this reason, we expect $\phi_{\text{fert2}}$ for arguments to have a large negative weight. In contrast, since predicates do not form chains, we may have multiple source predicates for one target.

We note an important difference between our fertility factor compared with Lacoste-Julien et al. (2006). We parameterize fertility for only two cases (1 and 2) whereas they consider fertility factors from 2 to $D$. We do not parameterize fertilities higher than two because they are not common in our dataset and come at a high computational cost.

The features $\mathbf{f}(\phi)$ for both $\phi_{\text{fert1}}$ and $\phi_{\text{fert2}}$ are an intercept feature (which always fires), indicator features for whether this row corresponds to an argument or a predicate, and a discretized feature for how many alignments are in this row.

**Predicate Argument Structure** We expect structure among links that involve a predicate and its associated arguments. Therefore, we add joint factors that consider a predicate and its associated alignments: the predicate argument structure. We determine this structure from a dependency parse, though the idea is general to any semantic binding, e.g. FrameNet or Propbank style parses. Given a coherent discourse, there are several expected types of patterns in the PAS; we add factors for these.

**Predicate-centric** We begin with a predicate-centric factor, which views scores an alignment between predicates based on their arguments, i.e. the two predicates share the same arguments. Ideally, two predicates can only align when their arguments are coreferent. However, in practice we may incorrectly resolve argument links, or there may be implicit arguments that do not appear as syntactic dependencies of the predicate trigger. Therefore, we settle for a weaker condition, that there should be *some* overlap in the arguments of two coreferent predicates.

For every predicate alignment $z^p_{ij}$, we add a factor $\phi_{\text{psa}}$ whose score $s_{\text{psa}}$ is a penalty for having no argument overlap; predicates share arguments (`psa`). To constrain the variable of $\phi_{\text{psa}}$, we add a quadratic constraint that considers every possible pair of argument alignments that might overlap:

$$z_{\phi_{\text{psa}}} \geq z^p_{ij}\big(1 - \max_{\substack{k \in \text{args}(p_i) \\ l \in \text{args}(p_j)}} z^a_{kl}\big) \tag{6}$$

where $\text{args}(p_i)$ finds the indices of all arguments governed by the predicate $p_i$.

**Entity-centric** We expect similar behavior from arguments (entities). If an entity appears in two documents, it is likely that this entity will be mentioned in the context of a common predicate, i.e. arguments share predicates (`asp`). For a given argument alignment $z^a_{ij}$ we add quadratic constraints so that $z_{\phi_{\text{asp}}}$ represents a penalty for two arguments not sharing a single predicate:

$$z_{\phi_{\text{asp}}} \geq z^a_{ij}\big(1 - \max_{\substack{k \in \text{preds}(a_i) \\ l \in \text{preds}(a_j)}} z^p_{kl}\big) \tag{7}$$

where $\text{preds}(a_i)$ finds the indices of all predicates that govern any mention of argument $a_i$.

The features $\mathbf{f}(\phi)$ for both `psa` and `asp` are an intercept feature and a bucketed count of the size of $\text{args}(p_i) \times \text{args}(p_j)$ or $\text{preds}(a_i) \times \text{preds}(a_j)$ respectively.

**Temporal Information** Temporal ordering, in contrast to textual ordering, can indicate when predicates cannot align: we expect aligned predicates in both documents to share the same temporal relations. SemEval 2013 included a task on predicting temporal relations between events (UzZaman et al., 2013). Many systems produced partial relations of events in a document based on lexical aspect and tense, as well as discourse connectives like "during" or "after". We obtain temporal relations with CAEVO, a state-of-the-art sieve-based system (Chambers et al., 2014).

TimeML (Pustejovsky et al., 2003), the format for specifying temporal relations, defines relations between predicates (e.g. *immediately before* and *simultaneous*), each with an inverse (e.g. *immediately after* and *simultaneous* respectively). We will refer to a relation as $R$ and its inverse as $R^{-1}$. Suppose we had $p_a$ and $p_b$ in the source document, $p_x$ and $p_y$ in the target document, and $p_a R_1 p_b$, $p_x R_2 p_y$. Given this configuration the following alignments conflict with the in-doc relations:

| $z_{ax}$ | $z_{by}$ | $z_{ay}$ | $z_{bx}$ | In-Doc Relations |
|---|---|---|---|---|
| * | * | 1 | 1 | $R_1 = R_2$ |
| 1 | 1 | * | * | $R_1 = R_2^{-1}$ |

where 1 means there is a link and * means there is a link or no link (wildcard). The simplest example that fits this pattern is: 'a before b', 'x before y', 'a corefers with y', and 'b corefers with x' implies a conflict.

We introduce a factor that penalizes these conflicting configurations. In every instance where the predicted temporal relation for a pair of predicate alignments matches one of the conflict patterns above, we add a factor using $z_{\phi_{\text{temp}}}$:

$$\begin{aligned} z_{\phi_{\text{temp}}} &\geq z_{ay} z_{bx} \\ &\text{if } p_a R_1 p_b, p_x R_2 p_y, R_1 = R_2 \\ z_{\phi_{\text{temp}}} &\geq z_{ax} z_{by} \\ &\text{if } p_a R_1 p_b, p_x R_2 p_y, R_1 = R_2^{-1} \end{aligned} \tag{8}$$

Thus $s_{\phi_{\text{temp}}}$ is the cost of disagreeing with the in-doc temporal relations. This is a general technique for incorporating relational information into coreference decisions. It only requires specifying when two relations are incompatible, e.g. `spouseOf` and `siblingOf` are incompatible relations (in most states). We leave this for future work.

Since CAEVO gives each relation prediction a probability, we incorporate this into the feature by indicating the probability of a conflict *not* arising:

$$\mathbf{f}(\phi_{\text{temp}}) = \log\left(1 - p(R_1)p(R_2) + \epsilon\right) \tag{9}$$

$\epsilon$ avoids large negative values since CAEVO probabilities are not perfectly calibrated. We use $\epsilon = 0.1$, allowing feature values of at most $-2.3$.

**Summary** The objective is a linear function over binary variables. There is a local similarity score coefficient on every alignment variable, and a joint factor similarity score on every quadratic variable. These quadratic variables are constrained by products of the original alignment variables. Decoding an alignment requires solving this quadratically constrained integer program; in practice is can be solved quickly without relations.

```
def train(alignments):
  w = init_weights()
  working_set = set()
  while True:
    xi = solve_ILP(w, working_set)
    c = most_violated_constraint(w, alignments)
    working_set.add(c)
    if hinge(c, w) < xi:
      break

def most_violated_constraint(w, alignments):
  delta_features = vector()
  loss = 0
  for z in alignments:
    z_mv = make_ILP(z)
    for phi in factors:
      costs = dot(w, phi.features)
      z_mv.add_terms(costs, phi.vars)
      z_mv.add_constraints(phi.constraints)
    solve_ILP(z_mv)
    mu = (z.size + k) / (avg_z_size + k)
    delta_features += mu * (f(z) - f(z_mv))
    loss += mu * Delta(z, z_mv)
  return Constraint(delta_features, loss)

def hinge(c, w):
  return max(0, c.loss - dot(w, c.delta_features))
```

Figure 2: Learning algorithm (caching and ILP solver not shown). The sum in each constraint is performed once when finding the constraint, and implicitly thereafter.

## 5 Inference

**Learning** We use the supervised structured SVM formulation of Joachims et al. (2009). As is common in structure prediction we use margin rescaling and 1 slack variable, with the structural SVM objective:

$$\begin{gathered} \min_{w} ||w||_2^2 + C\xi \\ \text{s.t. } \xi \geq 0 \\ \xi + \sum_{i=1}^{N} w \cdot f(z_i) \geq \sum_{i=1}^{N} w \cdot f(\hat{z}_i) + \Delta(z_i, \hat{z}_i) \\ \forall \hat{z}_i \in \mathcal{Z}_i \end{gathered} \tag{10}$$

where $\mathcal{Z}_i$ is the set of all possible alignments that have the same shape as $z_i$.

The score function for an alignment uses three types of terms: weights, features, and alignment variables. When we decode, we take the product of the weights and the features to get the costs for the ILP (e.g. $s_\phi = w \cdot \mathbf{f}(\phi)$). When we optimize our SVM objective, we take the product of the alignment variables and the features to get modified features for the SVM:

$$f(z) = \sum_{ij} z_{ij}\mathbf{f}(z_{ij}) + \sum_{\phi \in \Phi} z_\phi \mathbf{f}(\phi) \tag{11}$$

Since we cannot iterate over the exponentially many margin constraints, we solve for this optimization using the cutting-plane learning algorithm. This algorithm repeatedly asks the "separation oracle" for the most violated SVM constraint, which finds this constraint by solving:

$$\arg\max_{\hat{z}_1 \ldots \hat{z}_N} \sum_i w \cdot f(\hat{z}_i) + \Delta(z_i, \hat{z}_i) \tag{12}$$

subject to the constraints defined by the joint factors. When the separation oracle returns a constraint that is not violated or is already in the working set, then we have a guarantee that we solved the original SVM problem with exponentially many constraints. This is the most time-consuming aspect of learning, but since the problem decomposes over document alignments, we cache solutions on a per document alignment basis. With caching, we only call the separation oracle around 100-300 times.

We implement the separation oracle using an ILP solver, CPLEX,[3] due to complexity of the discrete optimization problem: there are $2^{m^n}$ possible alignments for and $m \times n$ alignment grid. In practice this is solved very efficiently, taking less than a third of a second per document alignment on average. We would like $\Delta$ to be F1, but we need a decomposable loss to include it in a linear objective (Taskar et al., 2003). Instead, we use Hamming loss as a surrogate, as in Lacoste-Julien et al. (2006).

Our training data is heavily biased towards negative examples, performing poorly on F1 since precision and recall are unbalanced. We use an asymmetric version of Hamming loss that incurs $c_{FP}$ cost for predicting an alignment for two unaligned items and $c_{FN}$ for predicting no alignment for two aligned items. We fixed $c_{FP} = 1$ and tuned $c_{FN} \in \{1, 2, 3, 4\}$ on dev data. Additionally we found it useful to tune the scale of the loss function across $\{\frac{1}{2}, 1, 2, 4\}$. Previous work, such as Joachims et al. (2009), use a hand-chosen constant for the scale of the Hamming loss, but we observe some sensitivity in this parameter and choose to optimize it.

[3] `http://www-01.ibm.com/software/commerce/optimization/cplex-optimizer/`

**Decoding** Following Wolfe et al. (2013), we tune the threshold for classification $\tau$ on dev data to maximize F1 (via linesearch). For SVMs $\tau$ is typically fixed at 0: this is not necessarily good practice when your training loss differs from test loss (Hamming vs F1). In our case this extra parameter is worth allocating a portion of training data to enable tuning. Tuning $\tau$ addresses the same problem as using an asymmetric Hamming loss, but we found that doing both led to better results.[4] Since we are using a global scoring function rather than a set of classifications, $\tau$ is implemented as a test-time unary factor on every alignment.

## 6 Experiments

**Data** We consider two datasets for evaluation. The first is a cross-document entity and event coreference resolution dataset called the Extended Event Coref Bank (EECB) created by Lee et al. (2012) and based on a corpus from Bejan and Harabagiu (2010). The dataset contains clusters of news articles taken from Google News with annotations about coreference over entities and events. Following the procedure of Wolfe et al. (2013), we select the first document in every cluster and pair it with every other document in the cluster.

The second dataset (RF) comes from Roth and Frank (2012). The dataset contains pairs of news articles that describe the same news story, and are annotated for predicate links between the document pairs. Due to the lack of annotated arguments, we can only report predicate linking performance and the `psa` and `asp` factors do not apply. Lastly, the size of the RF data should be noted as it is much smaller than EECB: the test set has 60 document pairs and the dev set has 10 document pairs.

[4] Only tuning $\tau$ performed almost as well as tuning $\tau$ and the Hamming loss, but not tuning $\tau$ performed much worse than only tuning the Hamming loss at train time.

Both datasets are annotated with parses and in-document coreference labels provided by the toolset of Napoles et al. (2012)[5] and are available with our code release. Due to the small data size, we use $k$-fold cross validation for both datasets. We choose $k = 10$ for RF due to its very small size (more folds give more training examples) and $k = 5$ on EECB to save computation time (amount of training data in EECB is less of a concern). Hyperparameters were chosen by hand using using cross validation on the EECB dataset using F1 as the criteria (rather than Hamming). Figures report averages across these folds.

**Systems** Following Roth and Frank (2012) and Wolfe et al. (2013) we include a *Lemma* baseline for identifying alignments which will align any two predicates or arguments that have the same lemmatized head word.[6] The *Local* baseline uses the same features as Wolfe et al., but none of our joint factors. In addition to running our joint model with all factors, we measure the efficacy of each individual factor by evaluating each with the local features.

For evaluation we use a generous version of F1 that is defined for alignment labels composed of sure, $G_s$, and possible links, $G_p$ and the system's proposed links $H$ (following Cohn et al. (2008), Roth and Frank (2012) and Wolfe et al. (2013)).

$$P = \frac{|H \cap G_p|}{|H|} \quad R = \frac{|H \cap G_s|}{|G_s|} F = \frac{2PR}{P + R}$$

Note that the EECB data does not have a sure and possible distinction, so $G_s = G_p$, resulting in standard F1. In addition to F1, we separately measure predicate and argument F1 to demonstrate where our model makes the largest improvements.

We performed a one-sided paired-bootstrap test where the null hypothesis was that the joint model was no better than the *Local* baseline (described in Koehn (2004)). Cases where $p < 0.05$ are bolded.

[5]`https://github.com/cnap/anno-pipeline`

[6]The lemma baseline is obviously sensitive to the lemmatizer used. We used the Stanford CoreNLP lemmatizer (Manning et al., 2014) and found it yielded slightly better results than previously reported as the lemma baseline (Roth and Frank, 2012), so we used it for all systems to ensure fairness and that the baseline is as strong as it could be.

## 7 Results

Results for EECB and RF are reported in Table 7. As previously reported, using just local factors (features on pairs) improves over lemma baselines (Wolfe et al., 2013). The joint factors make statistically significant gains over local factors in almost all experiments. Fertility factors provide the largest improvements from any single constraint. A fertility penalty actually allows the pairwise weights to be more optimistic in that they can predict more alignments for reasonable pairs, allowing the fertility penalty to ensure only the best is chosen. This penalty also prevents the "garbage collecting" effect that arises for instances that have rare features (Brown et al., 1993).

Temporal constraints are relatively sparse, appearing just 2.8 times on average. Nevertheless, it was very helpful across all experiments, though only statistically significantly on the RF dataset. This is one of the first results to demonstrate benefits of temporal relations affecting an downstream task. Perhaps surprisingly, these improvements result from a a temporal relation system that has relatively poor absolute performance. Despite this, improvements are possibly due to the orthogonal nature of temporal information; no other feature captures this signal. This suggests that future work on temporal relation prediction may yield further improvements and deserves more attention as a useful feature for semantic tasks in NLP.

The predicate-centric factors improved performance significantly on both datasets. For the predicate-centric factor, when a predicate was aligned there is a 72.3% chance that there was at least one argument aligned as well, compared to only 14.1% of case of non-aligned predicates. As mentioned before, the reason the former number isn't 100% is primarily due to implicit arguments and errors in argument identification. The argument-centric features helped almost as much as the predicate-centric version, but the improvements were not significant on the EECB dataset. Running the same diagnostic as the predicate-centric feature reveals similar support: in 57.1% of the cases where an argument was aligned, at least one predicate it partook in was aligned too, compared to 7.6% of cases for non-aligned arguments. Both the

| | EECB | | | | | | | | |
|---|---|---|---|---|---|---|---|---|---|
| | F1 | P | R | Arg F1 | Arg P | Arg R | Pred F1 | Pred P | Pred R |
| Lemma | 68.1 | 79.3 * | 59.6 | 61.7 | 79.1 * | 50.6 | 75.0 | 87.3 * | 65.7 |
| Local | 73.0 | 75.8 | **70.5** | 67.7 | 76.3 | **60.8** | 78.7 | 81.4 | 76.2 |
| +Fertility | 77.1 * | 83.9 * | 71.3 | 66.6 | 80.9 * | 56.6 | 82.8 * | 87.4 * | **78.7** * |
| +Predicate-centric | 74.1 * | 80.7 * | 68.6 | 67.4 | 81.6 * | 57.3 | 79.7 * | 85.0 * | 75.1 |
| +Argument-centric | 73.7 | 81.2 * | 67.5 | 66.8 | **83.0** * | 55.9 | 79.3 | 85.1 * | 74.3 |
| +Temporal | 73.7 | 78.2 * | 69.7 | **67.9** | 80.6 * | 58.7 | 79.0 | 82.1 | 76.1 |
| +All Factors | **77.5** * | **86.3** * | 70.3 | 65.8 | 83.1 * | 54.5 | **83.7** * | **89.7** * | 78.4 * |

| | RF | | |
|---|---|---|---|
| | Pred F1 | Pred P | Pred R |
| Lemma | 52.4 | 47.6 | 58.2 * |
| Local | 58.1 | **63.5** | 53.6 |
| +Fertility | **60.0** | 57.4 | **62.4** * |
| +Predicate-centric | NA | NA | NA |
| +Argument-centric | NA | NA | NA |
| +Temporal | 59.0 | 57.4 | 60.6 * |
| +All factors | 59.4 | 56.9 | 62.2 * |

Figure 3: Cross validation results for EECB (above) (Lee et al., 2012) and RF (left) (Roth and Frank, 2012). Statistically significant improvements from Local marked * ($p < 0.05$ using a one-sided paired-bootstrap test) and best results are bolded.

predicate- and argument-centric improve similarly across both predicates and arguments on EECB.

While each of the joint factors all improve over the baselines on RF, the full model with all the joint factors does not perform as well as with some factors excluded. Specifically, the fertility model performs the best. We attribute this small gap to lack of training data (RF only contains 64 training document pairs in our experiments), as this is not a problem on the larger EECB dataset.

Additionally, the joint models seem to trade precision for recall on the RF dataset compared to the *Local* baseline. Note that both models are tuned to maximize F1, so this tells you more about the shape of the ROC curve as opposed to either models' ability to achieve either high precision or recall. Since we don't see this behavior on the EECB corpus, it is more likely that this is a property of the data than the model.

## 8 Related Work

The task of predicate argument linking was introduced by Roth and Frank (2012), who used a graph parameterized by a small number of semantic features to express similarities between predicates and used min-cuts to produce an alignment. This was followed by Wolfe et al. (2013), who gave a locally-independent, feature-rich log-linear model that utilized many lexical semantic resources, similar to the sort employed in RTE challenges.

Lee et al. (2012) considered a similar problem but sought to produce *clusters* of entities and events rather than an alignment between two documents with the goal of improving coreference resolution. They used features which consider previous event and entity coreference decisions to make future coreference decisions in a greedy manner. This differs from our model which is built on non-greedy joint inference, but much of the signal indicating when two mentions corefer or are aligned is similar.

In the context of in-document coreference resolution, Recasens et al. (2013) sought to overcome the problem of opaque mentions[7] by finding high-precision paraphrases of entities by pivoting off verbs mentioned in similar documents. We address the issue of opaque mentions not by building a paraphrase table, but by jointly reasoning about entities that participate in coreferent events (c.f. §4); the approaches are complementary.

In this work we incorporate ordering information of events. Though we consider it an upstream task, there is a line of work trying to predict temporal relations between events (Pustejovsky et al., 2003; Mani et al., 2006; Chambers et al., 2014). Our results indicate this is a useful source of information, one of the first results to show an improvement from this

[7]A lexically disparate description of an entity.

type of system (Glavaš and Šnajder, 2013).

We utilize an ILP to improve upon a pipelined system, similar to Roth and Yih (2004), but our work differs in that we do not use piecewise-trained classifiers. Our local similarity scores are calibrated according to a global objective by propagating the gradient back from the loss to every parameter in the model. When using piecewise training, local classifiers must focus more on recall (in the spirit of Weiss and Taskar (2010)) than they would for an ordinary classification task with no global objective. Our method trains classifiers jointly with a global convex objective. While our training procedure requires decoding an integer program, the parameters we learn are globally optimal.

## 9 Conclusion

We presented a max-margin quadratic cost model for predicate argument alignment, seeking to exploit discourse level semantic features to improve on previous, locally independent approaches. Our model includes factors that consider fertility of predicates and arguments, the predicate argument structure present in coherent discourses, and soft constraints on predicate coreference determined by a temporal relation classifier. We have shown that this model significantly improves upon prior work which uses extensive lexical resources but without the benefit of joint inference. Additionally, this is one of the first demonstrations of the benefits of temporal relation identification. Overall, this work demonstrates the benefits of considering global document information as part of natural language understanding.

Future work should extend the problem formulation of predicate argument alignment to consider *incremental* linking: starting with a pair of documents, perform linking, and then continue to add in documents over time. This problem formulation would capture the evolution of a breaking news story, which closely matches the type of data (news articles) considered in this work (EECB and RF datasets). This formulation ties into existing work on news summarization, topic detection and tracking, an multi-document NLU. This goes hand with work on better intra-document relation prediction methods, such as the temporal relation model used in this work, to lead to better joint linking decisions.

## References


Nicholas Andrews, Jason Eisner, and Mark Dredze. 2012. Name phylogeny: A generative model of string variation. In *EMNLP-CoNLL*, pages 344–355. ACL.

Collin F. Baker, Charles J. Fillmore, and John B. Lowe. 1998. The berkeley framenet project. In *Proceedings of the 36th Annual Meeting of the Association for Computational Linguistics and 17th International Conference on Computational Linguistics - Volume 1*, ACL '98, pages 86–90, Stroudsburg, PA, USA. Association for Computational Linguistics.

Cosmin Adrian Bejan and Sanda Harabagiu. 2010. Unsupervised event coreference resolution with rich linguistic features. In *Proceedings of the 48th Annual Meeting of the Association for Computational Linguistics*, ACL '10, pages 1412–1422, Stroudsburg, PA, USA. Association for Computational Linguistics.

Peter F. Brown, Stephen A. Della Pietra, Vincent J. Della Pietra, Meredith J. Goldsmith, Jan Hajic, Robert L. Mercer, and Surya Mohanty. 1993. But dictionaries are data too. In *Proceedings of the Workshop on Human Language Technology*, HLT '93, pages 202–205, Stroudsburg, PA, USA. Association for Computational Linguistics.

Nathanael Chambers, Taylor Cassidy, Bill McDowell, and Steven Bethard. 2014. Dense event ordering with a multi-pass architecture. *Transactions of the Association for Computational Linguistics*, 2.

Trevor Cohn, Chris Callison-Burch, and Mirella Lapata. 2008. Constructing corpora for the development and evaluation of paraphrase systems. *Comput. Linguist.*, 34(4):597–614, December.

Juri Ganitkevitch, Benjamin Van Durme, and Chris Callison-Burch. 2013. PPDB: The paraphrase database. In *Proceedings of NAACL-HLT*, pages 758–764, Atlanta, Georgia, June. Association for Computational Linguistics.

Goran Glavaš and Jan Šnajder. 2013. Recognizing identical events with graph kernels. In *Proceedings of the 51st Annual Meeting of the Association for Computational Linguistics (Volume 2: Short Papers)*, pages 797–803, Sofia, Bulgaria, August. Association for Computational Linguistics.

Thorsten Joachims, Thomas Finley, and Chun-Nam John Yu. 2009. Cutting-plane training of structural svms. *Mach. Learn.*, 77(1):27–59, October.

Philipp Koehn. 2004. Statistical significance tests for machine translation evaluation. In Dekang Lin and Dekai Wu, editors, *Proceedings of EMNLP 2004*, pages 388–395, Barcelona, Spain, July. Association for Computational Linguistics.

Simon Lacoste-Julien, Benjamin Taskar, Dan Klein, and Michael I. Jordan. 2006. Word alignment via quadratic assignment. In Robert C. Moore, Jeff A. Bilmes, Jennifer Chu-Carroll, and Mark Sanderson, editors, *HLT-NAACL*. The Association for Computational Linguistics.

Heeyoung Lee, Marta Recasens, Angel Chang, Mihai Surdeanu, and Dan Jurafsky. 2012. Joint entity and event coreference resolution across documents. In *Proceedings of the 2012 Joint Conference on Empirical Methods in Natural Language Processing and Computational Natural Language Learning*, EMNLP-CoNLL '12, pages 489–500, Stroudsburg, PA, USA. Association for Computational Linguistics.

Inderjeet Mani, Marc Verhagen, Ben Wellner, Chong Min Lee, and James Pustejovsky. 2006. Machine learning of temporal relations. In *Proceedings of the 21st International Conference on Computational Linguistics and the 44th annual meeting of the Association for Computational Linguistics*, pages 753–760. Association for Computational Linguistics.

Christopher D. Manning, Mihai Surdeanu, John Bauer, Jenny Finkel, Steven J. Bethard, and David McClosky. 2014. The Stanford CoreNLP natural language processing toolkit. In *Proceedings of 52nd Annual Meeting of the Association for Computational Linguistics: System Demonstrations*, pages 55–60.

George A. Miller. 1995. Wordnet: A lexical database for english. *Communications of the ACM*, 38:39–41.

Courtney Napoles, Matthew Gormley, and Benjamin Van Durme. 2012. Annotated gigaword. In *AKBC-WEKEX Workshop at NAACL 2012*, June.

James Pustejovsky, Jos Castao, Robert Ingria, Roser Saur, Robert Gaizauskas, Andrea Setzer, and Graham Katz. 2003. Timeml: Robust specification of event and temporal expressions in text. In *in Fifth International Workshop on Computational Semantics (IWCS-5)*.

Marta Recasens, Matthew Can, and Daniel Jurafsky. 2013. Same referent, different words: Unsupervised mining of opaque coreferent mentions. In *Proceedings of the 2013 Conference of the North American Chapter of the Association for Computational Linguistics: Human Language Technologies*, pages 897–906, Atlanta, Georgia, June. Association for Computational Linguistics.

Michael Roth and Anette Frank. 2012. Aligning predicate argument structures in monolingual comparable texts: a new corpus for a new task. In *Proceedings of the First Joint Conference on Lexical and Computational Semantics - Volume 1: Proceedings of the main conference and the shared task, and Volume 2: Proceedings of the Sixth International Workshop on Semantic Evaluation*, SemEval '12, pages 218–227, Stroudsburg, PA, USA. Association for Computational Linguistics.

Dan Roth and Wen-tau Yih. 2004. A linear programming formulation for global inference in natural language tasks. In *In Proceedings of CoNLL-2004*, pages 1–8.

Michael Roth. 2014. *Inducing Implicit Arguments via Cross-document Alignment: A Framework and its Applications*. Ph.D. thesis, Heidelberg University, June.

Ben Taskar, Carlos Guestrin, and Daphne Koller. 2003. Max-margin markov networks. MIT Press.

Naushad UzZaman, Hector Llorens, Leon Derczynski, James Allen, Marc Verhagen, and James Pustejovsky. 2013. Semeval-2013 task 1: Tempeval-3: Evaluating time expressions, events, and temporal relations. In *Second Joint Conference on Lexical and Computational Semantics (*SEM), Volume 2: Proceedings of the Seventh International Workshop on Semantic Evaluation (SemEval 2013)*, pages 1–9, Atlanta, Georgia, USA, June. Association for Computational Linguistics.

David Weiss and Benjamin Taskar. 2010. Structured prediction cascades. *Journal of Machine Learning Research - Proceedings Track*, 9:916–923.

Travis Wolfe, Benjamin Van Durme, Mark Dredze, Nicholas Andrews, Charley Bellar, Chris Callison-Burch, Jay DeYoung, Justin Snyder, Jonathann Weese, Tan Xu, and Xuchen Yao. 2013. Parma: A predicate argument aligner. In *Proceedings of the 51th Annual Meeting of the Association for Computational Linguistics (Volume 2: Short Papers)*. Association for Computational Linguistics, July.

Xuchen Yao, Benjamin Van Durme, Chris Callison-burch, and Peter Clark. 2013. Answer extraction as sequence tagging with tree edit distance. In *In North American Chapter of the Association for Computational Linguistics (NAACL*.

# Improving unsupervised vector-space thematic fit evaluation via role-filler prototype clustering

**Clayton Greenberg, Asad Sayeed and Vera Demberg**
Computational Linguistics and Phonetics / M[2]CI Cluster of Excellence
Saarland University
66123 Saarbrücken, Germany
{claytong,asayeed,vera}@coli.uni-saarland.de

## Abstract

Most recent unsupervised methods in vector space semantics for assessing thematic fit (e.g. Erk, 2007; Baroni and Lenci, 2010; Sayeed and Demberg, 2014) create prototypical role-fillers without performing word sense disambiguation. This leads to a kind of sparsity problem: candidate role-fillers for different senses of the verb end up being measured by the same "yardstick", the single prototypical role-filler.

In this work, we use three different feature spaces to construct robust unsupervised models of distributional semantics. We show that correlation with human judgements on thematic fit estimates can be improved consistently by clustering typical role-fillers and then calculating similarities of candidate role-fillers with these cluster centroids. The suggested methods can be used in any vector space model that constructs a prototype vector from a non-trivial set of typical vectors.

## 1 Introduction

Thematic fit estimations can be quite useful for many NLP applications and also for cognitive models of human language processing difficulty, since human processing difficulty is highly sensitive to semantic plausibilities (Ehrlich and Rayner, 1981). For example, we expect that after the word *mash*, *banana* would be easier to process because it fits well as the patient, or direct object, of *mash*, but *milk* would be harder to process because it does not fit well.

A common method for estimating the thematic fit between a verb and a proposed role filler involves computing a centroid, or vector average, over the most typical role fillers for that verb, and then calculating the cosine similarity between this centroid and the proposed role filler (Baroni and Lenci, 2010; Blacoe and Lapata, 2012; Erk, 2012). For instance, we use the cosine of the angle between the *banana* vector and a vector average of the 20 nouns that, according to training data, are most likely to be mashed as a score for how well *banana* fits as the patient of *mash*. Hopefully, the *banana* vector will be closer to the centroid than *milk*, so *banana* will have a higher cosine similarity to the centroid, and thus a higher thematic fit score, than *milk*.

This conceptualization assumes that the most typical fillers for a verb-role will all be variants of a single prototype, i.e. distributionally similar to each other. However, such an assumption may not be true for ambiguous verbs. A verb with many different senses may have typical fillers for each sense, which fit relatively equally well, but are distributionally very different from one another. This means that the calculated prototypical filler will be a mixture of the arguments that are typical role fillers for the main senses of the verb. For example, consider the verb *serve*, for which the 24 most typical prepositional arguments related via the preposition *with* fall into three different senses, as illustrated in Figure 1.

Supposing that the centroid occupies a part of the vector space between two typical role fillers, but is relatively far from any one of the typical role fillers from which it was composed, as in Figure 1, none of the original typical role fillers will achieve high the-



*Human Language Technologies: The 2015 Annual Conference of the North American Chapter of the ACL*, pages 21–31,
Denver, Colorado, May 31 – June 5, 2015. 

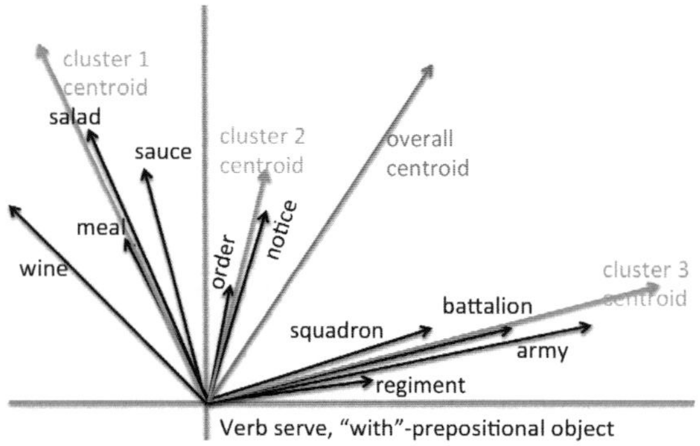


Figure 1: Illustration of *TypeDM* centroid for with-PP arguments of the verb *serve*.

matic fit scores. Also, verbs will be "penalized" for having many senses in that it will seem as though no role filler fits as well as they do with unambiguous verbs. This may produce inconsistent judgements when comparing one verb that is highly polysemous with a second, more restrictive verb whose meaning overlaps with the most dominant meanings of the first verb. For example, *cut* can be used in the sense of "cutting costs," which carries with it restrictions on instruments, locations, and so on that somewhat overlap with *eliminate* as in "eliminating costs." Things that are plausible to be eliminated are also plausible to be cut. But *cut* is also used in the sense of "cutting a cake" or "cutting (editing) a film." Without taking word sense into account, *costs* would be judged by the model as being less appropriate as a patient of *cut* than it should, and also its score for filling the patient role of *eliminate* would be infelicitously higher than its score for filling the patient role of *cut*.

One possible solution to this problem would be to do full word sense disambiguation on the resources from which these vector spaces are constructed. Then, there would be separate entries in the space for each meaning. This would however increase the overall size of the vector space by a significant factor and also cause an additional burden on corpus construction and annotation, even if automatic.

In this paper, we will approach the verb-role sense problem by clustering the most typical role-filler vectors and calculating the maximal cosine similarity for a candidate role filler with respect to each cluster prototype vector. So, to estimate the thematic fit of *salad* as an item with which something is served, in the vector space represented by Figure 1, we would use the cosine similarity with the nearest cluster centroid, the cluster 1 centroid. For a thematic fit task, the correlation between calculated estimates and human judgements can be expected to improve. In particular, good role fillers that are very different from one another and belong to different senses of a verb can all be assigned thematic fit scores as high as those of good role fillers of monosemous verbs.

We will evaluate our system using three distributional spaces: $TypeDM$ (Baroni and Lenci, 2010), which is based on a syntactic dependency parser, $SDDM$ (Sayeed and Demberg, 2014), which uses features obtained from the semantic role labeller SENNA (Collobert et al., 2011), and $SDDMX$, a novel extension of $SDDM$. This way, we can draw conclusions about feature space-specific and feature space-general trends.

The effects of clustering and choice of distributional space will be evaluated against the Padó (2007) and McRae et al. (1998) datasets of human judgements on thematic fit of agent and patient roles, and the Ferretti et al. (2001) datasets of human judgements on thematic fit of instrument and location roles. These different roles are conceptually interesting to compare, as instruments tend to be more strongly constrained by verbs than locations.

## 2 Background and related work

### 2.1 Thematic fit

The fit of a filler of a thematic role can be characterized as a semantic constraint on what can fill potentially available syntactic slots for a given predicate. For example, not every noun can satisfy the agent or patient roles of the typically transitive verb *eat*. There must be a valid "eater" for the agent and a valid "eatee" for the patient. Some nouns are simply more plausible than others in these positions: *lunch* is eaten, but rarely ever eats. But there can also be optional role assignments: there are certain utensils with which one is more or less likely to eat (i.e., appropriate instrument role-fillers) and even places where one is more or less likely to eat (i.e., location roles).

| Verb | Noun | Semantic role | Score |
|---|---|---|---|
| advise | doctor | agent | 6.8 |
| advise | doctor | patient | 4.0 |
| confuse | baby | agent | 3.7 |
| confuse | baby | patient | 6.0 |
| eat | lunch | agent | 1.1 |
| eat | lunch | patient | 6.9 |
| kill | lion | agent | 2.7 |
| kill | lion | patient | 4.9 |
| kill | man | agent | 3.4 |
| kill | man | patient | 5.4 |

Table 1: Sample of judgements from Padó (2007).

In order to model thematic roles, we use the insight that thematic fit correlates with human plausibility judgements (Padó et al., 2009; Vandekerckhove et al., 2009). Therefore, we can use datasets of human plausibility judgements to evaluate computational thematic fit estimates. One such dataset by Padó (2007) includes 18 verbs with up to 12 candidate nominal arguments and totals 414 verb-noun-role triples. The words were chosen based on their frequencies in the Penn Treebank and FrameNet. Human participants were asked to rate the appropriateness of given nouns as agents and as patients for given verbs on a scale from 1 to 7. The judgements were then averaged. We provide a small sample of these judgements in Table 1.

We use three other datasets as well. Ferretti et al. (2001) provide two datasets, one with 248 verb-instrument pairs and one with 274 verb-location pairs. Additionally, McRae et al. (1998) give a dataset of 1444 more agent/patient judgements. We write agent/patient as such because like Padó (2007), the agent plausibility and patient plausibility are given in the same dataset, albeit separately. Once again, human participants were asked to rate the appropriateness of given nouns as locations, instruments, and agents/patients, respectively, of the verbs in each dataset on a scale from 1 to 7. We will make use of these in our evaluation in order to see how well the models and algorithms we propose apply to various thematic roles, not just the most commonly tested and to-date most accurately estimated roles of agent and patient.

## 2.2 Distributional Semantics

### 2.2.1 Distributional Memory

Our semantic modeling technique comes from Baroni and Lenci (2010), who developed an explicitly multifunctional, i.e. not tightly bound to a particular task, framework for recording distributional information about linguistic co-occurrence. Distributional Memory (DM) records frequency information about links between words in a sentence as a third order tensor, in which words or lemmata are represented as two of the tensor axes and the syntactic or semantic link between them is the third axis.

The following corpora were used to construct the Baroni and Lenci (2010) version of DM:

- ukWaC, a corpus of about two billion words collected by crawling the `.uk` web domain (Ferraresi et al., 2008).
- WackyPedia, a snapshot selection of Wikipedia articles.
- The British National Corpus (BNC), a 100-million word corpus including documents such as books and periodicals.

The sentences from these sources were first run through MaltParser (Nivre et al., 2007). The dependency links (e.g. `SBJ`, `NMOD`) were run through a set of hand-crafted patterns to identify higher-level lexicalized links (e.g. `as-long-as`, `in-a-kind-of`). They then counted link type frequencies, so that links that involve the same lexical item (e.g. `long`, `kind`, as in the lexicalized links just mentioned) were collapsed into a single link, and the number of surface form realizations was used as the frequency count. All words were lemmatized and stored with basic part of speech information.

All these counts were then adjusted by Local Mutual Information (Baroni and Lenci, 2010), which is given by

$$LMI(i, j, k) = O_{ijk} \log \frac{O_{ijk}}{E_{ijk}} \quad (1)$$

where $i, j$ are words, $k$ is the link between them, $O$ is the observed frequency, and $E$ is the expected frequency under independence. Tuples with nonpositive LMI values were removed. They called this tensor $TypeDM$.

### 2.2.2 DM Based on Semantic Role Labels

In order to create a competitor to the much less manually pruned cousin of *TypeDM* named DepDM, Sayeed and Demberg (2014) based *SDDM* (short for SENNA-DepDM) on similar corpora but used alternative features. Namely, this tensor was built from ukWaC and BNC, but the features came from a semantic role labelling (SRL) system called SENNA (Collobert and Weston, 2007; Collobert et al., 2011). SENNA uses a multi-layer neural network architecture that learns in a sliding window over token sequences working on raw text instead of syntactic parses, as other semantic role labellers do (Bohnet, 2010). SENNA extracts word features related to identity, capitalization, and suffix/tense (approximated by the last two characters of the word). From these features, in a process similar to decoding a conditional random field, the network derives features related to verb position, part of speech, and chunk membership.

SENNA was trained on PropBank and large amounts of unlabelled data. It achieves a role labelling F-score of 75.49% (in this case, tested on CoNNL 2005 data), which is slightly lower than state of the art SRL systems which use parse trees as input.

*SDDM* was built by running the sentences from the input corpora through SENNA and using the role labels as links between predicates and role-fillers. Unlike *TypeDM*, *SDDM* required almost no further processing; the raw frequency counts of triples were used in the LMI calculation.

In this paper, we present *SDDMX*, an extended version of the *SDDM* model[1]. *SDDMX* contains the same links as *SDDM* and also contains links between nouns that belong to the same predicate instance, using the predicate as a link label. For example, supposing that during training the system encountered *the man eats a donut* with a role link between *man* and *eat* and another role link between *donut* and *eat*, then in *SDDMX*, a link was created between *man* and *donut*. This link was labelled with the verb lemma for the 400 most frequent verbs (`eat` in our example), and `vb` otherwise.

Sayeed and Demberg (2014) found that although

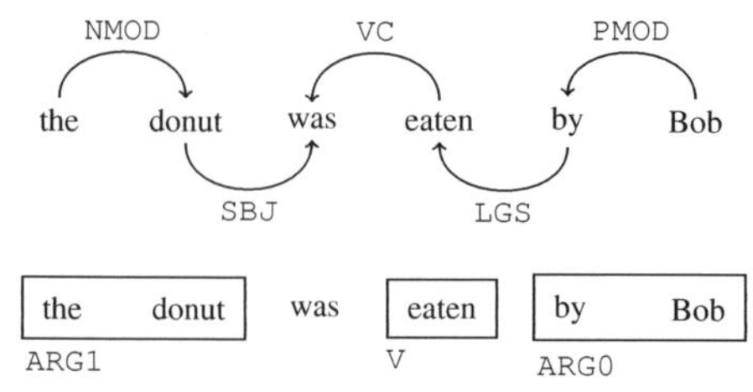


Figure 2: The same sentence with MaltParser (above) and SENNA (below) labels. Sayeed and Demberg (2014) used a simplified approach similar to the head percolation table of Magerman (1994) to find head nouns from SENNA annotation.

*SDDM* is an arguably simpler DM model than *TypeDM*, it performs nearly as well as *TypeDM* on a thematic fit estimation task using the Padó (2007) and McRae et al. (1998) agent/patient datasets. They also found that averaging the thematic fit scores of *SDDM* with those of *TypeDM* outperforms *TypeDM* alone and nearly reaches the performance of a supervised model (Herdağdelen and Baroni, 2009). This suggests that *TypeDM* and *SDDM* cover different aspects of the corpora on which they were trained. Links generated by SENNA may directly access semantic role features that the MaltParser-based *TypeDM* must infer through hand-crafted rules, such as tagging the subject as a patient instead of an agent in passive-voice contexts. Figure 2 illustrates the differences between the labelling approaches.

We make use of the *SDDM*, *SDDMX*, and *TypeDM* tensors in our experiments to demonstrate how our techniques improve performance in thematic fit modelling across different feature spaces.

### 2.2.3 Centroid-based thematic fit calculation in DM

Investigating alternative ways to calculate thematic fit over the DM framework is a major goal of this work, so we now describe the baseline process.

Baroni and Lenci (2010) used the following approach to estimate thematic fit on the Padó (2007) agent/patient dataset: To assess the fit of a noun $w_1$ in a role $r$ for a verb $w_2$, they construct a centroid from the 20 highest-ranked fillers for $r$ with $w_2$ selected by LMI, using the relevant syntactic dependency links, such as subject and object, instead of

[1]We provide *SDDM* and *SDDMX* at `http://rollen.mmci.uni-saarland.de/`.

thematic roles. To illustrate, in order to determine how well *workshop* fits as a location for *eat*, they would construct a centroid of other locations for *eat* that appear in the DM, e.g. *kitchen, restaurant, cafeteria* up to 20.

Each of these top 20 represent a "slice" of the tensor along one of the word axes. One such slice, corresponding to $w_1$, is a matrix of links and words to which $w_1$ is connected. This tensor slice is collapsed into a vector whose components are word-link pairs. This is the vector of $w_1$.

All 20 such vectors are added up and the sum is the centroid that represents, e.g., the typical locations of *eat*. Then a vector is constructed from the slice of the tensor corresponding to *workshop*. The thematic fit score is the cosine of the location centroid of *eat* and the vector of *workshop*.

Accessing thematic roles in *SDDM* and *SDDMX* is straightforward, as the links in these models are PropBank roles. Agent is `ARG0`, patient is `ARG1`, location is `ARGM-LOC`, and we use a combination of `ARGM-MNR`, `ARG2`, and `ARG3` to represent instruments, based on a translation of the roles used by Ferretti et al. (2001). The role mapping for *TypeDM* involves a combination of `sbj_tr` and `subj_intr` (transitive and intransitive subjects) for agents, `obj` for patients, the prepositional links `in`, `at`, and `on` for locations, and `with` for instruments.

### 2.3 Word Sense Disambiguation in Distributional Models

While distributional models carry important information about the relative frequencies of word usages, and perhaps even phrase usages, they often must collapse such usages into one representation. For example, suppose within the domain of cooking recipes, *serve* occurs in its food sense (see cluster 1 in Figure 1) 97% of the time. The other senses will have negligible effect on the representation of *serve* because their frequencies are so much lower. But in a web crawl, the distribution is quite likely to be more uniform, which means the senses will "split the difference" in the representation and end up not being that similar to any instance of *serve*.

Many systems work to alleviate this problem by performing manipulations on words as they occur in training corpora (e.g., Thater et al., 2011). Namely, the base vector for the potentially ambiguous word is contextualized, as in scaled element-wise, by the vectors of the neighboring words for that instance. This is quite intuitive because if *serve* and *cake* occur next to each other, the chance that a non-food sense of the word *serve* was intended would be extremely small, in fact much smaller than a corpus-wide distribution would predict. These systems have been effective at improving correlation with human judgements for a verb-object composition model, i.e. approximating a vector for *serve cake* given a vector for *serve* and a vector for *cake* (Kartsaklis et al., 2014), and also reducing noise in similarity scores for a nearest neighbor-based prepositional phrase attachment disambiguator (Greenberg, 2014).

It remains a choice of the system whether to store explicit senses separately, and relatedly, whether to consult a knowledge base for the number of senses for each word, or even for meaning representations of those senses. Using a task-general knowledge base, in addition to the inherent cost of building one, is not particularly suited for our task because the items to be disambiguated are verb-role pairs, as opposed to just verbs, and usually such knowledge bases do not handle individual thematic roles separately. For instance, it may be optimal to analyze *serve* as having three senses with respect to instruments, two senses with respect to patients, and one sense with respect to agents.

Assigning semantic categories to the slots of a verb subcategorization frame harks back to work by Resnik (1996) and Rooth et al. (1999). Resnik's work presupposes predefined noun classes obtained from WordNet. Rooth et al. induced latent role-filler classes via expectation maximization. Erk et al. (2010) found that neither are good models of thematic fit. Padó et al. (2009) provided thematic fit scores that take into account verb class using a supervised model. In the vector space context, inducing different vectors for multiple verb senses has been investigated recently by Reisinger and Mooney (2010), Huang et al. (2012), and Neelakantan et al. (2014), although these were not focused on role-fillers for verbs. Our contribution is to make use of a large-scale, unsupervised vector space model to provide thematic fit scores after inducing implicit verb sense classes relative to thematic role.

## 3 Methods

We begin our discussion of sense disambiguation for thematic fit with the following insight: the baseline ($Centroid$) method takes as input a set of typical role-fillers, the highest-ranked ones according to the DM, and returns a single prototype vector. However, if we allow the system to return a *set* of prototype vectors, then the framework gains the capacity to handle multiple senses of the verb-role pair.

The first choice is how to handle the output. Now instead of one cosine similarity, we would have a set of cosines corresponding to the similarities between the test role-filler and each prototype vector in the set. But if we make the theoretical assumption that each prototype corresponds to a sense, then roughly only one should apply at a time. So, we choose to use the one that is most relevant, i.e. similar, to the test role-filler. Therefore, we use the maximum of the cosine similarities as the thematic fit score.

### 3.1 One best or nearest

In the extreme case, we can just use the unaltered set of highly-ranked role-fillers as our set of prototypes. For example, if we query $TypeDM$ for the top four instrument-fillers of *eat*, we would retrieve *spoon, hand, bread,* and *sauce*. Then, to assign a thematic fit score for *fork* as an instrument-filler, we compute the cosine similarities of (*fork, spoon*), (*fork, hand*), (*fork, bread*), and (*fork, sauce*). The cosine similarity of (*fork, spoon*) is the highest, so this cosine determines the score. We refer to this method as $OneBest$. Note that $OneBest$ requires the calculation of a large number of cosines, which is a relatively expensive operation given the sparse representations of words in DM spaces.

The number of retrieved top role-fillers ($n$) appears to be the only parameter for $OneBest$. Yet, this method poses a few theoretical questions. First, there most likely should be an upper bound on the number of role-fillers that the system can retrieve at once. Mathematically, allowing the system to retrieve the entire relevant cross-section of the tensor would be equivalent to reducing the thematic fit evaluation task to a binary decision, i.e. whether the verb-role has occurred with the test role-filler in the training data. So, we would not be able to model any graded effect on the fit of two seen role-fillers, even if one of them fits with the verb-role better than the other. Also, psycholinguistically, it seems implausible that one must remember all of the times that one has encountered a word in order to use it. Therefore, we impose 50 as an arbitrary upper bound on $n$. We also set a lower bound of 10 on $n$ because values smaller than this generated quite erratic sets of top role-fillers.

Second, $OneBest$ might return a cosine of 1.0 if the DM retrieves the test role-filler itself as one of the top role-fillers. This could unfairly help the correlation between the cosines returned by the system and human judgements because the good role-fillers would all have the same cosine value, thus reducing the effect of the cosine ratings produced for the more distant (interesting) role-fillers. Therefore, we prohibit our system from returning any cosines of 1.0. The test role-filler thus achieves a high score by having a closely related role-filler in the prototype set, not by being present itself.

### 3.2 Clustering

In order to reduce noise from $OneBest$, we cluster similar top role-fillers together, calculate centroids for each cluster, and use these cluster centroids as the prototype set. This way, the presence of an anomalous vector in the centroid set has less effect. We use the group average agglomerative clustering package within NLTK (Bird et al., 2009). This algorithm works by initializing each top role-filler in its own cluster and iteratively combining the two most similar clusters.

For the stopping criterion, which determines the final number of clusters for the verb-role, we use the Variance Ratio Criterion ($VRC$) method (Caliński and Harabasz, 1974). Let $c$ be the baseline centroid of all top role-fillers retrieved, $f$ be a top role-filler, and $c_f$ be the cluster centroid of the cluster to which $f$ is assigned. Then, this method works by (a) calculating the $VRC$ metric for each number of clusters ($k$), given by

$$VRC(k) = \frac{SS_B}{k-1} / \frac{SS_W}{n-k} \quad (2)$$

where we define

$$SS_B = \sum_f (1 - \cos^2(c_f, c)) \quad (3)$$

and

$$SS_W = \sum_f (1 - \cos^2(f, c_f)) \quad (4)$$

and then (2) choosing the final number of clusters such that

$$\omega_k = (VRC_{k+1} - VRC_k) - (VRC_k - VRC_{k-1}) \quad (5)$$

is minimized. Intuitively, this procedure is meant to find the number of clusters for which adding another cluster does not explain significantly more variance in the data. Also, note that the $VRC$ metric is equivalent to the F-score in a one way ANOVA.

The main drawback of the $VRC$ method is that it cannot evaluate fewer than three clusters, due to having both a $VRC_{k+1}$ and a $VRC_{k-1}$ term in Equation (5). However, as long as enough top role-fillers are retrieved, it should not hurt the system. Equivalently, we set $VRC_0$ and $VRC_1$ equal to $VRC_2$. To examine the effect of this choice, we evaluate two clustering methods: *2Clusters*, which chooses two clusters for every verb-role, and *kClusters*, which dynamically chooses a number of clusters between 3 and 10 based on the above criterion.

Once again, the system is prohibited from returning a cosine of 1.0. This means that if the DM retrieves the test role-filler itself as one of the top role-fillers, the system would skip comparing the test role-filler against itself if it were in a singleton cluster, but would not skip it if it were a member of a cluster of size two or greater. The alternative to this would have been removing the test role-filler before clustering, but we saw these role-filler-specific partitions as a form of supervision.

### 3.3 Evaluation procedure

The *Centroid*, *OneBest*, *2Clusters*, and *kClusters* methods each determine their own prototype vector set for a verb-role, and then return the maximum cosine similarity value for each test role-filler. Prototype sets are stored in a dictionary so they can be reused. It is necessary to expand the sparse data structure of each vector in order to efficiently compute all of the necessary cosine similarities. Finally, we calculate Spearman's $\rho$ values to measure the correlations between these sets of thematic fit scores and the four datasets of human judgements.

| Dataset | *SDDM(X)* | *TypeDM* |
|---|---|---|
| Padó (2007) | 98.6 | 100.0 |
| McRae et al. (1998) | 96.0 | 95.2 |
| Ferretti et al. (2001) inst. | 94.0 | 93.1 |
| Ferretti et al. (2001) loc. | 99.6 | 98.9 |

Table 2: Coverage (%) by dataset for each DM model.

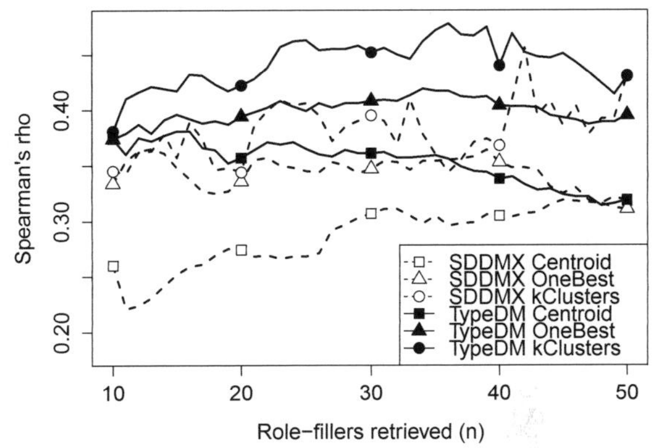


Figure 3: Spearman's $\rho$ values for Ferretti et al. (2001) instruments vs. the number of vectors retrieved.

For our main experiment, we always retrieve the top 20 highest-ranked role-fillers for the verb-role pair to compute the prototype set. This allows our work to be more directly comparable with other implementations. Also, choosing a value of $n$ that maximizes $\rho$ would make this unsupervised system more supervised. However, it is useful to know how the number of top role-fillers retrieved affects the correlation with human judgements, so as a follow-up experiment, we evaluate versions of the *Centroid*, *OneBest*, and *kClusters* methods, with the *SDDMX* and *TypeDM* models, retrieving from 10 to 50 top role-fillers, against the Ferretti et al. (2001) instruments dataset.

## 4 Results

In Table 2, we report the coverage percentages for the DM models on each of the thematic fit datasets. Note that since *SDDM* and *SDDMX* differ only in the additional links added between existing pairs of words, their coverages are the same.

Figure 3 shows the relationship between the number of vectors retrieved from the DM model and the correlation of the system with human judgements.

| | Padó (2007) agents | | | McRae et al. (1998) agents | | | Ferretti et al. (2001) instruments | | |
|---|---|---|---|---|---|---|---|---|---|
| | *SDDM* | *SDDMX* | *TypeDM* | *SDDM* | *SDDMX* | *TypeDM* | *SDDM* | *SDDMX* | *TypeDM* |
| *Centroid* | 0.515 | 0.528 | **0.535** | 0.371 | 0.394 | 0.359 | 0.193 | 0.274 | 0.357 |
| *OneBest* | 0.321 | 0.324 | 0.464 | 0.375 | 0.376 | **0.431** | 0.274 | 0.336 | 0.394 |
| *2Clusters* | 0.489 | 0.412 | 0.522 | 0.367 | 0.373 | 0.370 | 0.252 | 0.331 | 0.388 |
| *kClusters* | 0.281 | 0.322 | 0.460 | 0.396 | 0.394 | 0.416 | 0.335 | 0.344 | **0.422** |
| | **Padó (2007) patients** | | | **McRae et al. (1998) patients** | | | **Ferretti et al. (2001) locations** | | |
| | *SDDM* | *SDDMX* | *TypeDM* | *SDDM* | *SDDMX* | *TypeDM* | *SDDM* | *SDDMX* | *TypeDM* |
| *Centroid* | 0.511 | 0.505 | 0.525 | 0.133 | 0.131 | 0.343 | 0.187 | 0.248 | 0.230 |
| *OneBest* | 0.447 | 0.467 | 0.509 | 0.214 | 0.233 | 0.307 | 0.234 | 0.276 | 0.244 |
| *2Clusters* | 0.526 | 0.498 | 0.551 | 0.175 | 0.166 | **0.353** | 0.294 | 0.249 | 0.235 |
| *kClusters* | 0.401 | 0.428 | **0.555** | 0.212 | 0.227 | 0.350 | 0.293 | **0.326** | 0.289 |
| | **All from Padó (2007)** | | | **All from McRae et al. (1998)** | | | **All datasets** | | |
| | *SDDM* | *SDDMX* | *TypeDM* | *SDDM* | *SDDMX* | *TypeDM* | *SDDM* | *SDDMX* | *TypeDM* |
| *Centroid* | 0.512 | 0.521 | 0.530 | 0.237 | 0.251 | 0.325 | 0.258 | 0.296 | 0.354 |
| *OneBest* | 0.385 | 0.395 | 0.482 | 0.273 | 0.287 | 0.345 | 0.275 | 0.304 | 0.359 |
| *2Clusters* | 0.508 | 0.458 | **0.532** | 0.252 | 0.256 | 0.336 | 0.287 | 0.289 | 0.366 |
| *kClusters* | 0.343 | 0.375 | 0.503 | 0.287 | 0.294 | **0.359** | 0.294 | 0.317 | **0.385** |

Table 3: Spearman's $\rho$ for each method on each dataset and on all datasets together, using the 20 highest ranked words per verb-role.

The first six sections of Table 3 give the Spearman's $\rho$ values for our four centroid set construction methods evaluated against the four datasets of human judgements, organized by thematic role, all using the 20 highest-ranked words per verb-role. We note that the $\rho$ value for the Padó (2007) dataset using *TypeDM* and the *Centroid* method is slightly higher than the value reported in Baroni and Lenci (2010) due to correcting some transpositions in the original file. Finally, the last three sections of Table 3 give the performance of each method on the two whole agent/patient datasets (for comparison with previous work), as well as on all datasets merged together.

## 5 Discussion

While *SDDM* and *SDDMX* have marginally better coverage than *TypeDM*, we do not expect that this had an effect on our results. Figure 3 shows that for the various numbers of vectors retrieved from the DM models, *kClusters* consistently outperforms *OneBest*, which consistently outperforms *Centroid* on the Ferretti et al. (2001) instruments dataset. So, using just a single centroid that is a mixture of all possible good role-fillers for a verb leads to problems due to conflating different word meanings. But at the other extreme, we see how the $\rho$ values for the *OneBest* method peak (at $n = 13$ for *SDDMX* and $n = 34$ for *TypeDM*) and then decrease instead of increasing monotonically. This is because we disallowed cosines of 1.0 and because as we increase the number of vectors retrieved, the easier it becomes to be close to one of the prototype vectors, regardless of thematic fit distinctions within the prototype set.

For the model comparison, we see that while *TypeDM* generally performs better than *SDDMX* on instruments, clustering reduces the gap considerably. Also *SDDMX* outperforms *TypeDM* for all methods on locations as shown in Table 3. This difference suggests that locations appear in sufficiently diverse syntactic configurations such that the handcrafted rules from *TypeDM* do not work well.

From the All datasets section of Table 3, we see that both *OneBest* and *kClusters* improve the $\rho$ values over the *Centroid* baseline for all three DM models. This holds, too, for the individual instruments and locations datasets. Also, the two clustering methods perform better than *Centroid* on Padó (2007) patients with all DM models and on McRae et al. (1998) patients with *TypeDM*. The fact that *Centroid* performs best on Padó (2007) agents confirms previous analyses that have shown that the distribution of objects is more sensitive to verb sense than subjects. *kClusters* outperforming *OneBest* in a majority of cases suggests that clustering has successfully smoothed the top role-fillers, thus capturing sense-like patterns in the verb-roles.

As an example of the effect of the *kClusters* method, we obtained the following top 20 instrument-fillers for the verb "eat" in 4 clusters using *TypeDM*:

- *gusto, relish*
- *family, friend*
- *chopstick, finger, fork, hand, knife, spoon*
- *appetite, bread, butter, cheese, food, meal, meat, mouth, rice, sauce*

The *VRC* method selected 7 to 9 clusters a little more often than 3 to 6, which is perhaps more clusters than the number of senses we could expect from a task general knowledge base. We can see from this example that the four clusters do not all correspond to separate senses, but instead, they rather nicely separate out noise from true instruments. Note that since these role-fillers came from *TypeDM*, they appeared as the object of "with," as a proxy for finding instruments. The true instruments ended up all in the third cluster, which created a cluster centroid that is less affected by noise and errors from the syntactic or semantic parse. So, the higher number of senses seems appropriate for this task and data.

We attribute the differences in results between the Padó (2007) and McRae et al. (1998) datasets to the differences in how these datasets were constructed. First, the Padó (2007) dataset contains only frequent verbs and most, but not all, of the verb-role pairs contain well-fitting and poorly-fitting role-fillers. The latter point is especially important because if the range of human judgements is small for a certain verb, then it is much more difficult to achieve a large $\rho$ value regardless of the general performance level of the system. McRae et al. (1998), however, selected role-fillers much more automatically for their psycholinguistic study, so the data points do not necessarily reflect a typical sample of thematic role fitness decisions that occur in naturalistic language samples. So, it makes sense that the McRae et al. (1998) $\rho$ values are systematically lower than those of Padó (2007). In fact, the Padó (2007) $\rho$ values approach the ceiling of 0.6 as approximated by the supervised system.

Lastly, the effect of clustering was larger on instruments and locations than on agents and patients. A possible explanation is that instruments and locations are less-precisely defined thematic roles and better explained by several subclasses, i.e. clusters. In addition it could be that clustering helps to combat SRL inconsistencies.

## 6 Conclusions and future work

We show that clustering verb-roles into "senses" within a vector space framework achieves a higher correlation with human judgements on thematic fit over pure *Centroid* and *OneBest* methods. While we demonstrated this using the Distributional Memory technique by Baroni and Lenci (2010), the method will also be applicable to other vector space models.

This task has also been useful for comparing among DM models and the different thematic fit datasets. In particular, we can qualitatively evaluate how reliable syntax can be for determining the semantic notion of thematic fit, and the relative strength of human intuitions on verb-imposed restrictions on the various roles (agent, patient, instrument, and location).

In future work, we can investigate more sophisticated methods of vector clustering (such as expectation maximization and non-negative matrix factorization), interactions with verb and noun frequency, and interactions with number of word senses from a task-general knowledge-base such as WordNet. It would be especially useful to evaluate this system of a dataset of human judgements with verbs that systematically vary in polysemy, as this would more clearly expose the general trends we wish to model computationally.

## Acknowledgments

This research was funded by the German Research Foundation (DFG) as part of SFB 1102: "Information Density and Linguistic Encoding." Also, the authors wish to thank the three anonymous reviewers whose valuable ideas contributed to this paper.

## References


Baroni, M. and Lenci, A. (2010). Distributional memory: A general framework for corpus-based semantics. *Computational Linguistics*, 36(4):673–721.

Bird, S., Klein, E., and Loper, E. (2009). *Natural Language Processing with Python*. O'Reilly Media.

Blacoe, W. and Lapata, M. (2012). A comparison of vector-based representations for semantic composition. In *Proceedings of the 2012 Joint Conference on Empirical Methods in Natural Language Processing and Computational Natural Language Learning*, pages 546–556, Jeju Island, Korea. Association for Computational Linguistics.

Bohnet, B. (2010). Very high accuracy and fast dependency parsing is not a contradiction. In *Proceedings of the 23rd International Conference on Computational Linguistics*, COLING '10, pages 89–97, Stroudsburg, PA, USA. Association for Computational Linguistics.

Caliński, T. and Harabasz, J. (1974). A dendrite method for cluster analysis. *Communications in Statistics-Simulation and Computation*, 3(1):1–27.

Collobert, R. and Weston, J. (2007). Fast semantic extraction using a novel neural network architecture. In *Proceedings of the 45th Annual Meeting of the Association of Computational Linguistics*, pages 560–567, Prague, Czech Republic. Association for Computational Linguistics.

Collobert, R., Weston, J., Bottou, L., Karlen, M., Kavukcuoglu, K., and Kuksa, P. (2011). Natural language processing (almost) from scratch. *The Journal of Machine Learning Research*, 12:2493–2537.

Ehrlich, S. F. and Rayner, K. (1981). Contextual effects on word perception and eye movements during reading. *Journal of verbal learning and verbal behavior*, 20(6):641–655.

Erk, K. (2007). A simple, similarity-based model for selectional preferences. In *Proceedings of the 45th Annual Meeting of the Association of Computational Linguistics*, pages 216–223, Prague, Czech Republic. Association for Computational Linguistics.

Erk, K. (2012). Vector space models of word meaning and phrase meaning: A survey. *Language and Linguistics Compass*, 6(10):635–653.

Erk, K., Padó, S., and Padó, U. (2010). A flexible, corpus-driven model of regular and inverse selectional preferences. *Computational Linguistics*, 36(4):723–763.

Ferraresi, A., Zanchetta, E., Baroni, M., and Bernardini, S. (2008). Introducing and evaluating ukwac, a very large web-derived corpus of english. *Proceedings of the 4th Web as Corpus Workshop (WAC-4) Can we beat Google*, pages 47–54.

Ferretti, T. R., McRae, K., and Hatherell, A. (2001). Integrating verbs, situation schemas, and thematic role concepts. *Journal of Memory and Language*, 44(4):516–547.

Greenberg, C. (2014). Disambiguating prepositional phrase attachment sites with sense information captured in contextualized distributional data. In *Proceedings of the ACL 2014 Student Research Workshop*, pages 71–77, Baltimore, Maryland, USA. Association for Computational Linguistics.

Herdağdelen, A. and Baroni, M. (2009). BagPack: A general framework to represent semantic relations. In *Proceedings of the Workshop on Geometrical Models of Natural Language Semantics*, pages 33–40, Athens, Greece. Association for Computational Linguistics.

Huang, E. H., Socher, R., Manning, C. D., and Ng, A. Y. (2012). Improving word representations via global context and multiple word prototypes. In *Proceedings of the 50th Annual Meeting of the Association for Computational Linguistics: Long Papers - Volume 1*, ACL '12, pages 873–882, Stroudsburg, PA, USA. Association for Computational Linguistics.

Kartsaklis, D., Kalchbrenner, N., and Sadrzadeh, M. (2014). Resolving lexical ambiguity in tensor regression models of meaning. In *Proceedings of the 52nd Annual Meeting of the Association for Computational Linguistics (Vol. 2: Short Papers)*, pages 212–217, Baltimore, USA. Association for Computational Linguistics.

Magerman, D. M. (1994). *Natural Lagnuage Parsing as Statistical Pattern Recognition*. PhD thesis, Stanford University.

McRae, K., Spivey-Knowlton, M. J., and Tanenhaus, M. K. (1998). Modeling the influence of thematic fit (and other constraints) in on-line sentence comprehension. *Journal of Memory and Language*, 38(3):283–312.

Neelakantan, A., Shankar, J., Passos, A., and McCallum, A. (2014). Efficient non-parametric estimation of multiple embeddings per word in vector space. In *Proceedings of the 2014 Conference on Empirical Methods in Natural Language Processing (EMNLP)*, pages 1059–1069. Association for Computational Linguistics.

Nivre, J., Hall, J., Nilsson, J., Chanev, A., Eryigit, G., Kübler, S., Marinov, S., and Marsi, E. (2007). Maltparser: A language-independent system for data-driven dependency parsing. *Natural Language Engineering*, 13(2):95–135.

Padó, U. (2007). *The integration of syntax and semantic plausibility in a wide-coverage model of human sentence processing*. PhD thesis, Saarland University.

Padó, U., Crocker, M. W., and Keller, F. (2009). A probabilistic model of semantic plausibility in sentence processing. *Cognitive Science*, 33(5):794–838.

Reisinger, J. and Mooney, R. J. (2010). Multi-prototype vector-space models of word meaning. In *Human Language Technologies: The 2010 Annual Conference of the North American Chapter of the Association for Computational Linguistics*, HLT '10, pages 109–117, Stroudsburg, PA, USA. Association for Computational Linguistics.

Resnik, P. (1996). Selectional constraints: An information-theoretic model and its computational realization. *Cognition*, 61(1):127–159.

Rooth, M., Riezler, S., Prescher, D., Carroll, G., and Beil, F. (1999). Inducing a semantically annotated lexicon via em-based clustering. In *Proceedings of the 37th Annual Meeting of the Association for Computational Linguistics on Computational Linguistics*, ACL '99, pages 104–111, Stroudsburg, PA, USA. Association for Computational Linguistics.

Sayeed, A. and Demberg, V. (2014). Combining unsupervised syntactic and semantic models of thematic fit. In *Proceedings of the first Italian Conference on Computational Linguistics (CLiC-it 2014)*.

Thater, S., Fürstenau, H., and Pinkal, M. (2011). Word meaning in context: A simple and effective vector model. In *Proceedings of 5th International Joint Conference on Natural Language Processing*, pages 1134–1143, Chiang Mai, Thailand. Asian Federation of Natural Language Processing.

Vandekerckhove, B., Sandra, D., and Daelemans, W. (2009). A robust and extensible exemplar-based model of thematic fit. In *EACL 2009, 12th Conference of the European Chapter of the Association for Computational Linguistics, Proceedings of the Conference, Athens, Greece, March 30 - April 3, 2009*, pages 826–834.

# A Compositional and Interpretable Semantic Space

**Alona Fyshe,[1] Leila Wehbe,[1] Partha Talukdar,[2] Brian Murphy,[3] and Tom Mitchell[1]**
[1] Machine Learning Department, Carnegie Mellon University, Pittsburgh, USA
[2] Indian Institute of Science, Bangalore, India
[3] Queen's University Belfast, Belfast, Northern Ireland
afyshe@cs.cmu.edu, lwehbe@cs.cmu.edu, ppt@serc.iisc.in,
brian.murphy@qub.ac.uk, tom.mitchell@cs.cmu.edu

## Abstract

Vector Space Models (VSMs) of Semantics are useful tools for exploring the semantics of single words, and the composition of words to make phrasal meaning. While many methods can estimate the meaning (i.e. vector) of a phrase, few do so in an interpretable way. We introduce a new method (CNNSE) that allows word and phrase vectors to adapt to the notion of composition. Our method learns a VSM that is both tailored to support a chosen semantic composition operation, and whose resulting features have an intuitive interpretation. Interpretability allows for the exploration of phrasal semantics, which we leverage to analyze performance on a behavioral task.

## 1 Introduction

Vector Space Models (VSMs) are models of word semantics typically built with word usage statistics derived from corpora. VSMs have been shown to closely match human judgements of semantics (for an overview see Sahlgren (2006), Chapter 5), and can be used to study semantic composition (Mitchell and Lapata, 2010; Baroni and Zamparelli, 2010; Socher et al., 2012; Turney, 2012).

Composition has been explored with different types of composition functions (Mitchell and Lapata, 2010; Mikolov et al., 2013; Dinu et al., 2013) including higher order functions (such as matrices) (Baroni and Zamparelli, 2010), and some have considered which corpus-derived information is most useful for semantic composition (Turney, 2012; Fyshe et al., 2013). Still, many VSMs act like a black box - it is unclear what VSM dimensions represent (save for broad classes of corpus statistic types) and what the application of a composition function to those dimensions entails. Neural network (NN) models are becoming increasingly popular (Socher et al., 2012; Hashimoto et al., 2014; Mikolov et al., 2013; Pennington et al., 2014), and some model introspection has been attempted: Levy and Goldberg (2014) examined connections between layers, Mikolov et al. (2013) and Pennington et al. (2014) explored how shifts in VSM space encodes semantic relationships. Still, interpreting NN VSM dimensions, or factors, remains elusive.

This paper introduces a new method, Compositional Non-negative Sparse Embedding (CNNSE). In contrast to many other VSMs, our method learns an *interpretable* VSM that is tailored to suit the semantic composition function. Such interpretability allows for deeper exploration of semantic composition than previously possible. We will begin with an overview of the CNNSE algorithm, and follow with empirical results which show that CNNSE produces:

1. more interpretable dimensions than the typical VSM,
2. composed representations that outperform previous methods on a phrase similarity task.

Compared to methods that do not consider composition when learning embeddings, CNNSE produces:

1. better approximations of phrasal semantics,
2. phrasal representations with dimensions that more closely match phrase meaning.



*Human Language Technologies: The 2015 Annual Conference of the North American Chapter of the ACL*, pages 32–41,
Denver, Colorado, May 31 – June 5, 2015. 

## 2 Method

Typically, word usage statistics used to create a VSM form a sparse matrix with many columns, too unwieldy to be practical. Thus, most models use some form of dimensionality reduction to compress the full matrix. For example, Latent Semantic Analysis (LSA) (Deerwester et al., 1990) uses Singular Value Decomposition (SVD) to create a compact VSM. SVD often produces matrices where, for the vast majority of the dimensions, it is difficult to interpret what a high or low score entails for the semantics of a given word. In addition, the SVD factorization does not take into account the phrasal relationships between the input words.

### 2.1 Non-negative Sparse Embeddings

Our method is inspired by Non-negative Sparse Embeddings (NNSEs) (Murphy et al., 2012). NNSE promotes interpretability by including sparsity and non-negativity constraints into a matrix factorization algorithm. The result is a VSM with extremely coherent dimensions, as quantified by a behavioral task (Murphy et al., 2012). The output of NNSE is a matrix with rows corresponding to words and columns corresponding to latent dimensions.

To interpret a particular latent dimension, we can examine the words with the highest numerical values in that dimension (i.e. identify rows with the highest values for a particular column). Though the representations in Table 1 were created with our new method, CNNSE, we will use them to illustrate the interpretability of both NNSE and CNNSE, as the form of the learned representations is similar. One of the dimensions in Table 1 has top scoring words *guidance, advice* and *assistance* - words related to help and support. We will refer to these word list summaries as the dimension's **interpretable summarization**. To interpret the meaning of a particular word, we can select its highest scoring dimensions (i.e. choose columns with maximum values for a particular row). For example, the interpretable summarizations for the top scoring dimensions of the word *military* include both positions in the military (e.g. commandos), and military groups (e.g. paramilitary). More examples in Supplementary Material (http://www.cs.cmu.edu/~fmri/papers/naacl2015/).

NNSE is an algorithm which seeks a lower dimensional representation for $w$ words using the $c$-dimensional corpus statistics in a matrix $X \in \mathbb{R}^{w \times c}$. The solution is two matrices: $A \in \mathbb{R}^{w \times \ell}$ that is sparse, non-negative, and represents word semantics in an $\ell$-dimensional latent space, and $D \in \mathbb{R}^{\ell \times c}$: the encoding of corpus statistics in the latent space. NNSE minimizes the following objective:

$$\underset{A,D}{\operatorname{argmin}} \frac{1}{2} \sum_{i=1}^{w} \left\| X_{i,:} - A_{i,:} \times D \right\|^2 + \lambda_1 \left\| A_{i,:} \right\|_1 \quad (1)$$

$$\text{st: } D_{i,:} D_{i,:}^T \leq 1, \forall\, 1 \leq i \leq \ell \quad (2)$$

$$A_{i,j} \geq 0,\ 1 \leq i \leq w,\ 1 \leq j \leq \ell \quad (3)$$

where $A_{i,j}$ indicates the entry at the $i$th row and $j$th column of matrix $A$, and $A_{i,:}$ indicates the $i$th row of the matrix. The $L_1$ constraint encourages sparsity in $A$; $\lambda_1$ is a hyperparameter. Equation 2 constrains $D$ to eliminate solutions where the elements of $A$ are made arbitrarily small by making the norm of $D$ arbitrarily large. Equation 3 ensures that $A$ is non-negative. Together, $A$ and $D$ factor the original corpus statistics matrix $X$ to minimize reconstruction error. One may tune $\ell$ and $\lambda_1$ to vary the sparsity of the final solution.

Murphy et al. (2012) solved this system of constraints using the Online Dictionary Learning algorithm described in Mairal et al. (2010). Though Equations 1-3 represent a non-convex system, when solving for $A$ with $D$ fixed (and vice versa) the loss function is convex. Mairal et al. break the problem into two alternating optimization steps (solving for $A$ and $D$) and find the system converges to a stationary solution. The solution for $A$ is found with a LARS implementation for lasso regression (Efron et al., 2004); $D$ is found via gradient descent. Though the final solution may not be globally optimal, this method is capable of handling large amounts of data and has been shown to produce useful solutions in practice (Mairal et al., 2010; Murphy et al., 2012).

### 2.2 Compositional NNSE

We add an additional constraint to the NNSE loss function that allows us to learn a latent representation that respects the notion of semantic composition. As we will see, this change to the loss function has a huge effect on the learned latent space. Just as

Table 1: CNNSE interpretable summarizations for the top 3 dimensions of an adjective, noun and adjective-noun phrase.

| military | aid | military aid (observed) |
|---|---|---|
| servicemen, commandos, military intelligence | guidance, advice, assistance | servicemen, commandos, military intelligence |
| guerrilla, paramilitary, anti-terrorist | mentoring, tutoring, internships | guidance, advice, assistance |
| conglomerate, giants, conglomerates | award, awards, honors | compliments, congratulations, replies |

the $L_1$ regularizer can have a large impact on sparsity, our composition constraint represents a considerable change in composition compatibility.

Consider a phrase $p$ made up of words $i$ and $j$. In the most general setting, the following composition constraint could be applied to the rows of matrix A corresponding to $p$, $i$ and $j$:

$$A_{(p,:)} = f(A_{(i,:)}, A_{(j,:)}) \tag{4}$$

where $f$ is some composition function. The composition function constrains the space of learned latent representations $A \in \mathbb{R}^{w \times \ell}$ to be those solutions that are compatible with the composition function defined by $f$. Incorporating $f$ into Equation 1 we have:

$$\underset{A,D,\Omega}{\operatorname{argmin}} \sum_{i=1}^{w} \frac{1}{2}\|X_{i,:} - A_{i,:} \times D\|^2 + \lambda_1 \|A_{i,:}\|_1 + \frac{\lambda_c}{2} \sum_{\substack{\text{phrase } p, \\ p=(i,j)}} \left(A_{(p,:)} - f(A_{(i,:)}, A_{(j,:)})\right)^2 \tag{5}$$

Where each phrase $p$ is comprised of words $(i, j)$ and $\Omega$ represents all parameters of $f$ to be optimized. We have added a squared loss term for composition, and a new regularization parameter $\lambda_c$ to weight the importance of respecting composition. We call this new formulation Compositional Non-Negative Sparse Embeddings (CNNSE). Some examples of the interpretable representations learned by CNNSE for adjectives, nouns and phrases appear in Table 1.

There are many choices for $f$: addition, multiplication, dilation, etc. (Mitchell and Lapata, 2010). Here we choose $f$ to be weighted addition because it has has been shown to work well for adjective noun composition (Mitchell and Lapata, 2010; Dinu et al., 2013; Hashimoto et al., 2014), and because it lends itself well to optimization. Weighted addition is:

$$f(A_{(i,:)}, A_{(j,:)}) = \alpha A_{(i,:)} + \beta A_{(j,:)} \tag{6}$$

This choice of $f$ requires that we simultaneously optimize for $A$, $D$, $\alpha$ and $\beta$. However, $\alpha$ and $\beta$ are simply constant scaling factors for the vectors in $A$ corresponding to adjectives and nouns. For adjective-noun composition, the optimization of $\alpha$ and $\beta$ can be absorbed by the optimization of $A$. For models that include noun-noun composition, if $\alpha$ and $\beta$ are assumed to be absorbed by the optimization of $A$, this is equivalent to setting $\alpha = \beta$.

We can further simplify the loss function by constructing a matrix $B$ that imposes the composition by addition constraint. $B$ is constructed so that for each phrase $p = (i, j)$: $B_{(p,p)} = 1$, $B_{(p,i)} = -\alpha$, and $B_{(p,j)} = -\beta$. For our models, we use $\alpha = \beta = 0.5$, which serves to average the single word representations. The matrix $B$ allows us to reformulate the loss function from Eq 5:

$$\underset{A,D}{\operatorname{argmin}} \frac{1}{2}\|X - AD\|_F^2 + \lambda_1 \|A\|_1 + \frac{\lambda_c}{2}\|BA\|_F^2 \tag{7}$$

where $F$ indicates the Frobenius norm. $B$ acts as a selector matrix, subtracting from the latent representation of the phrase the average latent representation of the phrase's constituent words.

We now have a loss function that is the sum of several convex functions of $A$: squared reconstruction loss for $A$, $L_1$ regularization and the composition constraint. This sum of sub-functions is the format required for the alternating direction method of multipliers (ADMM) (Boyd, 2010). ADMM substitutes a dummy variable $z$ for $A$ in the sub-functions:

$$\underset{A,D}{\operatorname{argmin}} \frac{1}{2}\|X - AD\|_F^2 + \lambda_1 \|z_1\|_1 + \frac{\lambda_c}{2}\|Bz_c\|_F^2 \tag{8}$$

and, in addition to constraints in Eq 2 and 3, incorporates constraints $A = z_1$ and $A = z_c$ to ensure dummy variables match $A$. ADMM uses an augmented Lagrangian to incorporate and relax these new constraints. We optimize for $A, z_1$ and $z_c$ separately, update the dual variables and repeat until convergence (see Supplementary material for Lagrangian form, solutions and updates). We modified code for ADMM, which is available online[1]. ADMM is used when solving for $A$ in the Online Dictionary Learning algorithm, solving for $D$ remains unchanged from the NNSE implementation (see Algorithms 1 and 2 in Supplementary Material).

We use the weighted addition composition function because it performed well for adjective-noun composition in previous work (Mitchell and Lapata, 2010; Dinu et al., 2013; Hashimoto et al., 2014), maintains the convexity of the loss function, and is easy to optimize. In contrast, an element-wise multiplication, dilation or higher-order matrix composition function will lead to a non-convex optimization problem which cannot be solved using ADMM. Though not explored here, we hypothesize that $A$ could be molded to respect many different composition functions. However, if the chosen composition function does not maintain convexity, finding a suitable solution for $A$ may prove challenging. We also hypothesize that even if the chosen composition function is not the "true" composition function (whatever that may be), the fact that $A$ can change to suit the composition function may compensate for this mismatch. This has the flavor of variational inference for Bayesian methods: an approximation in place of an intractable problem often yields better results with limited data, in less time.

## 3 Data and Experiments

We use the semantic vectors made available by Fyshe et al. (2013), which were compiled from a 16 billion word subset of ClueWeb09 (Callan and Hoy, 2009). We used the 1000 dependency SVD dimensions, which were shown to perform well for composition tasks. Dependency features are tuples consisting of two POS tagged words and their dependency relationship in a sentence; the feature value is the pointwise positive mutual information (PPMI) for the tuple. The dataset is comprised of 54,454 words and phrases. We randomly split the approximately 14,000 adjective noun phrases into a train (2/3) and test (1/3) set. From the test set we removed 200 randomly selected phrases as a development set for parameter tuning. We did not lexically split the train and test sets, so many words appearing in training phrases also appear in test phrases. For this reason we cannot make specific claims about the generalizability of our methods to unseen words.

[1] http://www.stanford.edu/~boyd/papers/admm/

Table 2: Median rank, mean reciprocal rank (MRR) and percentage of test phrases ranked perfectly (i.e. first in a sorted list of approx. 4,600 test phrases) for four methods of estimating the test phrase vectors. $\text{w.add}_{\text{SVD}}$ is weighted addition of SVD vectors, $\text{w.add}_{\text{NNSE}}$ is weighted addition of NNSE vectors.

| Model | Med. Rank | MRR | Perfect |
|---|---|---|---|
| $\text{w.add}_{\text{SVD}}$ | 99.89 | 35.26 | 20% |
| $\text{w.add}_{\text{NNSE}}$ | 99.80 | 28.17 | 16% |
| Lexfunc | 99.65 | 28.96 | 20% |
| CNNSE | **99.91** | **40.65** | **26%** |

NNSE has one parameter to tune ($\lambda_1$); CNNSE has two: $\lambda_1$ and $\lambda_c$. In general, these methods are not overly sensitive to parameter tuning, and searching over orders of magnitude will suffice. We found the optimal settings for NNSE were $\lambda_1 = 0.05$, and for CNNSE $\lambda_1 = 0.05, \lambda_c = 0.5$. Too large $\lambda_1$ leads to overly sparse solutions, too small reduces interpretability. We set $\ell = 1000$ for both NNSE and CNNSE and altered sparsity by tuning only $\lambda_1$.

### 3.1 Phrase Vector Estimation

To test the ability of each model to estimate phrase semantics we trained models on the training set, and used the learned model and the composition function to estimate vectors of held out phrases. We sort the vectors for the test phrases, $X_{test}$, by their cosine distance to the predicted phrase vector $\hat{X}_{(p,:)}$.

We report two measures of accuracy. The first is median rank accuracy. Rank accuracy is: $100 \times (1 - \frac{r}{P})$, where $r$ is the position of the correct phrase in the sorted list of test phrases, and $P = |X_{test}|$ (the number of test phrases). The second measure is mean reciprocal rank (MRR), which is often used to evaluate information retrieval tasks (Kantor and Voorhees, 2000). MRR is

$$100 \times (\frac{1}{P}\sum_{i=1}^{P}(\frac{1}{r})). \quad (9)$$

For both rank accuracy and MRR, a perfect score is 100. However, MRR places more emphasis on ranking items close to the top of the list, and less on differences in ranking lower in the list. For example, if the correct phrase is always ranked 2, 50 or 100 out of list of 4600, median rank accuracy would be 99.95, 98.91 or 97.83. In contrast, MRR would be 50, 2 or 1. Note that rank accuracy and reciprocal rank produce identical orderings of methods. That is, whatever method performs best in terms of rank accuracy will also perform best in terms of reciprocal rank. MRR simply allows us to discriminate between very accurate models. As we will see, the rank accuracy of all models is very high ($> 99\%$), approaching the rank accuracy ceiling.

### 3.1.1 Estimation Methods

We will compare to two other previously studied composition methods: weighted addition (**w.add$_{\mathbf{SVD}}$**), and **lexfunc** (Baroni and Zamparelli, 2010). Weighted addition finds $\alpha, \beta$ to optimize

$$(X_{(p,:)} - (\alpha X_{(i,:)} + \beta X_{(j,:)}))^2$$

Note that this optimization is performed over the SVD matrix $X$, rather than on $A$. To estimate $X$ for a new phrase $p = (i, j)$ we compute

$$\hat{X}_{(p,:)} = \alpha X_{(i,:)} + \beta X_{(j,:)}$$

Lexfunc finds an adjective-specific matrix $M_i$ that solves

$$X_{(p,:)} = M_i X_{(j,:)}$$

for all phrases $p = (i, j)$ for adjective $i$. We solved each adjective-specific problem with Matlab's partial least squares implementation, which uses the SIMPLS algorithm (Dejong, 1993). To estimate $X$ for a new phrase $p = (i, j)$ we compute

$$\hat{X}_{(p,:)} = M_i X_{(j,:)}$$

We also optimized the weighted addition composition function over NNSE vectors, which we call **w.add$_{\mathbf{NNSE}}$**. After optimizing $\alpha$ and $\beta$ using the training set, we compose the latent word vectors to estimate the held out phrase:

$$\hat{A}_{(p,:)} = \alpha A_{(i,:)} + \beta A_{(j,:)}$$

For CNNSE, as in the loss function, $\alpha = \beta = 0.5$ so that the average of the word vectors approximates the phrase.

$$\hat{A}_{(p,:)} = 0.5 \times (A_{(i,:)} + A_{(j,:)})$$

Crucially, w.add$_{\text{NNSE}}$ estimates $\alpha, \beta$ *after* learning the latent space $A$, whereas CNNSE *simultaneously* learns the latent space $A$, while taking the composition function into account. Once we have an estimate $\hat{A}_{(p,:)}$ we can use the NNSE and CNNSE solutions for $D$ to estimate the corpus statistics X.

$$\hat{X}_{(p,:)} = \hat{A}_{(p,:)} D$$

Results for the four methods appear in Table 2. Median rank accuracies were all within half a percentage point of each other. However, MRR shows a striking difference in performance. CNNSE has MRR of 40.64, more than 5 points higher than the second highest MRR score belonging to w.add$_{\text{SVD}}$ (35.26). CNNSE ranks the correct phrase in the first position for 26% of phrases, compared to 20% for w.add$_{\text{SVD}}$. Lexfunc ranks the correct phrase first for 20% of the test phrases, w.add$_{\text{NNSE}}$ 16%. So, while all models perform quite well in terms of rank accuracy, when we use the more discriminative MRR, CNNSE is the clear winner. Note that the performance of w.add$_{\text{NNSE}}$ is much lower than CNNSE. Incorporating a composition constraint into the learning algorithm has produced a latent space that surpasses all methods tested for this task.

We were surprised to find that lexfunc performed relatively poorly in our experiments. Dinu et al. (2013) used simple unregularized regression to estimate $M$. We also replicated that formulation, and found phrase ranking to be worse when compared to the Partial Least Squares method described in Baroni and Zamparelli (2010). In addition, Baroni and Zamparelli use 300 SVD dimensions to estimate $M$. We found that, for our dataset, using all 1000 dimensions performed slightly better.

We hypothesize that our difference in performance could be due to the difference in input corpus statistics (in particular the thresholding of infrequent words and phrases), or due to the fact that we did not specifically create the training and tests sets to evenly distribute the phrases for each adjective. If an adjective $i$ appears only in phrases in the test set, lexfunc cannot estimate $M_i$ using training data (a hindrance not present for other methods, which require only that the adjective appear in the training data). To compensate for this possibly unfair train/test split, the results in Table 2 are calculated over only those adjectives which could be estimated using the training set.

Though the results reported here are not as high as previously reported, lexfunc was found to be only slightly better than w.add$_{SVD}$ for adjective noun composition (Dinu et al., 2013). CNNSE outperforms w.add$_{SVD}$ by a large margin, so even if Lexfunc could be tuned to perform at previous levels on this dataset, CNNSE would likely still dominate.

### 3.1.2 Phrase Estimation Errors

None of the models explored here are perfect. Even the top scoring model, CNNSE, only identifies the correct phrase for 26% of the test phrases. When a model makes a "mistake", it is possible that the top-ranked phrase is a synonym of, or closely related to, the actual phrase. To evaluate mistakes, we chose test phrases for which all 4 models are incorrect and produce a different top ranked phrase (likely these are the most difficult phrases to estimate). We then asked Mechanical Turk (Mturk `http://mturk.com`) users to evaluate the mistakes. We presented the 4 mistakenly top-ranked phrases to Mturk users, who were asked to choose the one phrase most related to the actual test phrase.

We randomly selected 200 such phrases and asked 5 Mturk users to evaluate each, paying $0.01 per answer. We report here the results for questions where a majority (3) of users chose the same answer (82% of questions). For all Mturk experiments described in this paper, a screen shot of the question appears in the Supplementary Material.

Table 3 shows the Mturk evaluation of model mistakes. CNNSE and lexfunc make the most reasonable mistakes, having their top-ranked phrase chosen as the most related phrase 35.4% and 31.7% of the time, respectively. This makes us slightly more comfortable with our phrase estimation results (Table 2); though lexfunc does not reliably predict the correct phrase, it often chooses a close approximation. The mistakes from CNNSE are chosen slightly more often than lexfunc, indicating that CNNSE also has the ability to reliably predict the correct phrase, or a phrase deemed more related than those chosen by other methods.

Table 3: A comparison of mistakes in phrase ranking across 4 composition methods. To evaluate mistakes, we chose phrases for which all 4 models rank a different (incorrect) phrase first. Mturk users were asked to identify the phrase that was semantically closest to the target phrase.

| Model | Predicted phrase deemed closest match to actual phrase |
|---|---|
| w.add$_{SVD}$ | 21.3% |
| w.add$_{NNSE}$ | 11.6% |
| Lexfunc | 31.7% |
| **CNNSE** | **35.4%** |

## 3.2 Interpretability

Though our improvement in MRR for phrase vector estimation is compelling, we seek to explore the meaning encoded in the word space features. We turn now to the *interpretation* of phrasal semantics and semantic composition.

### 3.2.1 Interpretability of Latent Dimensions

Due to the sparsity and non-negativity constraints, NNSE produces dimensions with very coherent semantic groupings (Murphy et al., 2012). Murphy et al. used an intruder task to quantify the interpretability of semantic dimensions. The intruder task presents a human user with a list of words, and they are to choose the one word that does not belong in the list (Chang et al., 2009). For example, from the list (red, green, desk, pink, purple, blue), it is clear to see that the word "desk" does not belong in the list of colors.

To create questions for the intruder task, we selected the top 5 scoring words in a particular dimension, as well as a low scoring word from that same dimension such that the low scoring word is also in the top 10th percentile of another dimension. Like the word "desk" in the example above, this low scoring word is called the *intruder*, and the human subject's task is to select the intruder from a shuffled list of 6 words. Five Mturk users answered each question, each paid $0.01 per answer. If Mturk users identify a high percentage of intruders, this indicates that the latent representation groups words in a human-interpretable way. We chose 100 questions for each of the NNSE, CNNSE and SVD representations. Because the output of lexfunc is the SVD

Table 4: Quantifying the interpretability of learned semantic representations via the intruder task. Intruders detected: % of questions for which the majority response was the intruder. Mturk agreement: the % of questions for which a majority of users chose the same response.

| Method | Intruders Detected | Mturk Agreement |
|---|---|---|
| SVD | 17.6% | 74% |
| NNSE | 86.2% | 94% |
| CNNSE | 88.9% | 90% |

representation $X$, SVD interpretability is a proxy for lexfunc interpretability.

Results for the intruder task appear in Table 4. Consistent with previous studies, NNSE provides a much more interpretable latent representation than SVD. We find that the additional composition constraint used in CNNSE has maintained the interpretability of the learned latent space. Because intruders detected is higher for CNNSE, but agreement amongst Mturk users is higher for NNSE, we consider the interpretability results for the two methods to be equivalent. Note that SVD interpretability is close to chance ($1/6 = 16.7\%$).

#### 3.2.2 Coherence of Phrase Representations

The dimensions of NNSE and CNNSE are comparably interpretable. But, has the composition constraint in CNNSE resulted in better phrasal representations? To test this, we randomly selected 200 phrases, and then identified the top scoring dimension for each phrase in both the NNSE and CNNSE models. We presented Mturk users with the interpretable summarizations for these top scoring dimensions. Users were asked to select the list of words (interpretable summarization) most closely related to the target phrase. Mturk users could also select that neither list was related, or that the lists were equally related to the target phrase. We paid $0.01 per answer and had 5 users answer each question. In Table 5 we report results for phrases where the majority of users selected the same answer (78% questions). CNNSE phrasal representations are found to be much more consistent, receiving a positive evaluation almost twice as often as NNSE.

Together, these results show that CNNSE representations maintain the interpretability of NNSE dimensions, while improving the coherence of phrase representations.

Table 5: Comparing the coherence of phrase representations from CNNSE and NNSE. Mturk users were shown the interpretable summarization for the top scoring dimension of target phrases. Representations from CNNSE and NNSE were shown side by side and users were asked to choose the list (summarization) most related to the phrase, or that the lists were equally good or bad.

| Model | Model representation deemed most consistent with phrase |
|---|---|
| **CNNSE** | **54.5%** |
| NNSE | 29.5% |
| Both | 4.5% |
| Neither | 11.5% |

### 3.3 Evaluation on Behavioral Data

We now compare the performance of various composition methods on an adjective-noun phrase similarity dataset (Mitchell and Lapata, 2010). This dataset is comprised of 108 adjective-noun phrase pairs split into high, medium and low similarity groups. Similarity scores from 18 human subjects are averaged to create one similarity score per phrase pair. We then compute the cosine similarity between the composed phrasal representations of each phrase pair under each compositional model. As in Mitchell and Lapata (2010), we report the correlation of the cosine similarity measures to the behavioral scores. We withheld 12 of the 108 questions for parameter tuning, four randomly selected from each of the high, medium and low similarity groups.

Table 6 shows the correlation of each model's similarity scores to behavioral similarity scores. Again, Lexfunc performs poorly. This is probably attributable to the fact that there are, on average, only 39 phrases available for training each adjective in the dataset, whereas the original Lexfunc study had at least 50 per adjective (Baroni and Zamparelli, 2010). CNNSE is the top performer, followed closely by weighted addition. Interestingly, weighted NNSE correlation is lower than CNNSE by nearly 0.15, which shows the value of allowing the learned latent space to conform to the desired composition function.

### 3.3.1 Interpretability and Phrase Similarity

CNNSE has the additional advantage of interpretability. To illustrate, we created a web page to explore the dataset under the CNNSE model. The page `http://www.cs.cmu.edu/~fmri/papers/naacl2015/cnnse_mitchell_lapata_all.html` displays phrase pairs sorted by average similarity score. For each phrase in the pair we show a summary of the CNNSE composed phrase meaning. The scores of the 10 top dimensions are displayed in descending order. Each dimension is described by its interpretable summarization. As one scrolls down the page, the similarity scores increase, and the number of dimensions shared between the phrase pairs (highlighted in red) increases. Some phrase pairs with high similarity scores share no top scoring dimensions. Because we can interpret the dimensions, we can begin to understand how the CNNSE model is failing, and how it might be improved.

For example, the phrase pair judged most similar by the human subjects, but that shares none of the top 10 dimensions in common, is "large number" and "great majority" (behavioral similarity score 5.61/7). Upon exploration of CNNSE phrasal representations, we see that the representation for "great majority" suffers from the multiple word senses of majority. Majority is often used in political settings to describe the party or group with larger membership. We see that the top scoring dimension for "great majority" has top scoring words "candidacy, candidate, caucus", a politically-themed dimension. Though the CNNSE representation is not incorrect for the word, the common theme between the two test phrases is not political.

The second highest scoring dimension for "large number" is "First name, address, complete address". Here we see another case of the collision of multiple word senses, as this dimension is related to identifying numbers, rather than the quantity-related sense of number. While it is satisfying that the word senses for majority and number have been separated out into different dimensions for each word, it is clear that both the composition and similarity functions used for this task are not gracefully handling multiple word senses. To address this issue, we could partition the dimensions of $A$ into sense-related groups and use the maximally correlated groups to score phrase pairs. CNNSE interpretability allows us to perform these analyses, and will also allow us to iterate and improve future compositional models.

Table 6: Correlation of phrase similarity judgements (Mitchell and Lapata, 2010) to pairwise distances in several adjective-noun composition models.

| Model | Correlation to behavioral data |
|---|---|
| w.add$_{\text{SVD}}$ | 0.5377 |
| w.add$_{\text{NNSE}}$ | 0.4469 |
| Lexfunc | 0.1347 |
| **CNNSE** | **0.5923** |

## 4 Conclusion

We explored a new method to create an interpretable VSMs that respects the notion of semantic composition. We found that our technique for incorporating phrasal relationship constraints produced a VSM that is more consistent with observed phrasal representations and with behavioral data.

We found that, compared to NNSE, human evaluators judged CNNSE phrasal representations to be a better match to phrase meaning. We leveraged this improved interpretability to explore composition in the context of a previously published compositional task. We note that the collision of word senses often hinders performance on the behavioral data from Mitchell and Lapata (2010).

More generally, we have shown that incorporating constraints to represent the task of interest can improve a model's performance on that task. Additionally, incorporating such constraints into an *interpretable* model allows for a deeper exploration of performance in the context of evaluation tasks.

**Acknowledgments**

This work was supported in part by a gift from Google, NIH award 5R01HD075328, IARPA award FA865013C7360, DARPA award FA8750-13-2-0005, and by a fellowship to Alona Fyshe from the Multimodal Neuroimaging Training Program (NIH awards T90DA022761 and R90DA023420).

## References

Marco Baroni and Roberto Zamparelli. Nouns are vectors, adjectives are matrices: Representing adjective-noun constructions in semantic space. In *Proceedings of the 2010 Conference on Empirical Methods in Natural Language Processing*, pages 1183–1193. Association for Computational Linguistics, 2010.

Stephen Boyd. Distributed Optimization and Statistical Learning via the Alternating Direction Method of Multipliers. *Foundations and Trends in Machine Learning*, 3(1):1–122, 2010. ISSN 1935-8237. doi: 10.1561/2200000016.

Jamie Callan and Mark Hoy. The ClueWeb09 Dataset, 2009. URL `http://boston.lti.cs.cmu.edu/Data/clueweb09/`.

Jonathan Chang, Jordan Boyd-Graber, Sean Gerrish, Chong Wang, and David M Blei. Reading Tea Leaves : How Humans Interpret Topic Models. In *Advances in Neural Information Processing Systems*, pages 1–9, 2009.

Scott Deerwester, Susan T. Dumais, George W. Furnas, Thomas K. Landauer, and Richard Harshman. Indexing by Latent Semantic Analysis. *Journal of the American Society for Information Science*, 41(6):391–407, 1990.

S Dejong. SIMPLS - An alternative approach to partial least squares regression. *Chemometrics and Intelligent Laboratory Systems*, 18(3):251–263, 1993. ISSN 01697439. doi: 10.1016/0169-7439(93)85002-x.

Georgiana Dinu, Nghia The Pham, and Marco Baroni. General estimation and evaluation of compositional distributional semantic models. In *Workshop on Continuous Vector Space Models and their Compositionality*, Sofia, Bulgaria, 2013.

Bradley Efron, Trevor Hastie, Iain Johnstone, and Robert Tibshirani. Least angle regression. *Annals of Statistics*, 32(2):407–499, 2004.

Alona Fyshe, Partha Talukdar, Brian Murphy, and Tom Mitchell. Documents and Dependencies : an Exploration of Vector Space Models for Semantic Composition. In *Computational Natural Language Learning*, Sofia, Bulgaria, 2013.

Kazuma Hashimoto, Pontus Stenetorp, Makoto Miwa, and Yoshimasa Tsuruoka. Jointly learning word representations and composition functions using predicate-argument structures. *Proceedings of the Conference on Empirical Methods on Natural Language Processing*, pages 1544–1555, 2014.

Paul B. Kantor and Ellen M. Voorhees. The TREC-5 Confusion Track: Comparing Retrieval Methods for Scanned Text. *Information Retrieval*, 2:165–176, 2000. ISSN 1386-4564, 1573-7659. doi: 10.1023/A:1009902609570.

Omer Levy and Yoav Goldberg. Neural Word Embedding as Implicit Matrix Factorization. In *Advances in Neural Information Processing Systems*, pages 1–9, 2014.

Julien Mairal, Francis Bach, J Ponce, and Guillermo Sapiro. Online learning for matrix factorization and sparse coding. *The Journal of Machine Learning Research*, 11:19–60, 2010.

Tomas Mikolov, Ilya Sutskever, Kai Chen, Greg Corrado, and Jeff Dean. Distributed representations of words and phrases and their compositionality. In *Proceedings of Neural Information Processing Systems*, pages 1–9, 2013.

Jeff Mitchell and Mirella Lapata. Composition in distributional models of semantics. *Cognitive science*, 34(8):1388–429, November 2010. ISSN 1551-6709. doi: 10.1111/j.1551-6709.2010.01106.x.

Brian Murphy, Partha Talukdar, and Tom Mitchell. Learning Effective and Interpretable Semantic Models using Non-Negative Sparse Embedding. In *Proceedings of Conference on Computational Linguistics (COLING)*, 2012.

Jeffrey Pennington, Richard Socher, and Christopher D Manning. GloVe : Global Vectors for Word Representation. In *Conference on Empirical Methods in Natural Language Processing*, Doha, Qatar, 2014.

Magnus Sahlgren. *The Word-Space Model Using distributional analysis to represent syntagmatic and paradigmatic relations between words.* Doctor of philosophy, Stockholm University, 2006.

Richard Socher, Brody Huval, Christopher D. Manning, and Andrew Y. Ng. Semantic Compositionality through Recursive Matrix-Vector Spaces. In *Conference on Empirical Methods in Natural Language Processing and Computational Natural Language Learning*, 2012.

Peter D Turney. Domain and Function : A Dual-Space Model of Semantic Relations and Compositions. *Journal of Artificial Intelligence Research*, 44:533–585, 2012.

# Randomized Greedy Inference for Joint Segmentation, POS Tagging and Dependency Parsing

**Yuan Zhang, Chengtao Li, Regina Barzilay**
Computer Science and Artificial Intelligence Laboratory
Massachusetts Institute of Technology
{yuanzh, ctli, regina}@csail.mit.edu

**Kareem Darwish**
ALT Research Group
Qatar Computing Research Institute
kdarwish@qf.org.qa

## Abstract

In this paper, we introduce a new approach for joint segmentation, POS tagging and dependency parsing. While joint modeling of these tasks addresses the issue of error propagation inherent in traditional pipeline architectures, it also complicates the inference task. Past research has addressed this challenge by placing constraints on the scoring function. In contrast, we propose an approach that can handle arbitrarily complex scoring functions. Specifically, we employ a randomized greedy algorithm that jointly predicts segmentations, POS tags and dependency trees. Moreover, this architecture readily handles different segmentation tasks, such as morphological segmentation for Arabic and word segmentation for Chinese. The joint model outperforms the state-of-the-art systems on three datasets, obtaining 2.1% TedEval absolute gain against the best published results in the 2013 SPMRL shared task.[1]

## 1 Introduction

Parsing accuracy is greatly impacted by the quality of preprocessing steps such as tagging and word segmentation. Li et al. (2011) report that the difference between using the gold POS tags and using the automatic counterparts reaches about 6% in dependency accuracy. Prior research has demonstrated that joint prediction alleviates error propagation inherent in pipeline architectures, where mistakes cascade from one task to the next (Bohnet et al., 2013; Tratz, 2013; Hatori et al., 2012; Zhang et al., 2014a). However, jointly modeling all the processing tasks inevitably increases inference complexity. Prior work addressed this challenge by introducing constraints on scoring functions to keep inference tractable (Qian and Liu, 2012).

In this paper, we propose a method for joint prediction that imposes no constraints on the scoring function. The method is able to handle high-order and global features for each individual task (e.g., parsing), as well as features that capture interactions between tasks. The algorithm achieves this flexibility by operating over full assignments that specify segmentation, POS tags and dependency tree, moving from one complete configuration to another.

Our approach is based on the randomized greedy algorithm from our earlier dependency parsing system (Zhang et al., 2014b). We extend this algorithm to jointly predict the segmentation and the POS tags in addition to the dependency parse. The search space for the algorithm is a combination of parse trees and lattices that encode alternative morphological and POS analyses. The inference algorithm greedily searches over this space, iteratively making local modifications to POS tags and dependency trees. To overcome local optima, we employ multiple restarts.

This simple, yet powerful approach can be easily applied to a range of joint prediction tasks. In prior work, joint models have been designed for a specific language. For instance, joint models for Chinese are designed with word segmentation in mind (Hatori et al., 2012), while algorithms for processing Semitic languages are tailored for morpho-

[1] The source code is available at https://github.com/yuanzh/SegParser.



*Human Language Technologies: The 2015 Annual Conference of the North American Chapter of the ACL*, pages 42–52,
Denver, Colorado, May 31 – June 5, 2015. 

logical analysis (Tratz, 2013; Goldberg and Elhadad, 2011). In contrast, we show that our algorithm can be effortlessly applied to all these distinct languages. Language-specific characteristics drive the lattice construction and the feature selection, while the learning and inference methods are language-agnostic.

We evaluate our model on three datasets: SPMRL (Modern Standard Arabic), classical Arabic and CTB5 (Chinese). Our model consistently outperforms state-of-the-art systems designed for these languages. We obtain a 2.1% TedEval gain against the best published results in the 2013 SPMRL shared task (Seddah et al., 2013). The joint model results in significant gains against its pipeline counterpart, yielding 2.4% absolute F-score increase in dependency parsing on the same dataset. Our analysis reveals that most of this gain comes from the improved prediction on OOV words.

## 2 Related Work

**Joint Segmentation, POS tagging and Syntactic Parsing** It has been widely recognized that joint prediction is an appealing alternative for pipeline architectures (Goldberg and Tsarfaty, 2008; Hatori et al., 2012; Habash and Rambow, 2005; Gahbiche-Braham et al., 2012; Zhang and Clark, 2008; Bohnet and Nivre, 2012). These approaches have been particularly prominent for languages with difficult preprocessing, such as morphologically rich languages (e.g., Arabic and Hebrew) and languages that require word segmentation (e.g., Chinese). For the former, joint prediction models typically rely on a lattice structure to represent alternative morphological analyses (Goldberg and Tsarfaty, 2008; Tratz, 2013; Cohen and Smith, 2007). For instance, transition-based models intertwine operations on the lattice with operations on a dependency tree. Other joint architectures are more decoupled: in Goldberg and Tsarfaty (2008), a lattice is used to derive the best morphological analysis for each part-of-speech alternative, which is in turn provided to the parsing algorithm. In both cases, tractable inference is achieved by limiting the representation power of the scoring function. Our model also uses a lattice to encode alternative analyses. However, we employ this structure in a different way. The model samples the full path from the lattice, which corresponds to a valid segmentation and POS tagging assignment. Then the model improves the path and the corresponding tree via a hill-climbing strategy. This architecture allows us to incorporate arbitrary features for segmentation, POS tagging and parsing.

In joint prediction models for Chinese, lattice structures are not typically used. Commonly these models are formulated in a transition-based framework at the character level (Zhang and Clark, 2008; Zhang et al., 2014a; Wang and Xue, 2014). While this formulation can handle a large space of possible word segmentations, it can only capture features that are instantiated based on the stack and queue status. Our approach offers two advantages over prior work: (1) we can incorporate arbitrary features for word segmentation and parsing; (2) we demonstrate that a lattice-based approach commonly used for other languages can be effectively utilized for Chinese.

**Randomized Greedy Inference** Our prior work has demonstrated that a simple randomized greedy approach delivers near optimal dependency parsing (Zhang et al., 2014b). Our analysis explains this performance with the particular properties of the search space in dependency parsing. We show how to apply this strategy to a more challenging inference task and demonstrate that a randomized greedy algorithm achieves excellent performance in a significantly larger search space.

## 3 Randomized Greedy System for Joint Prediction

In this section, we introduce our model for joint morphological segmentation, tagging and parsing. Our description will first assume that word boundaries are provided (e.g., the case of Arabic). Later, we will describe how this model can be applied to a joint prediction task that involves word segmentation (e.g., Chinese).

### 3.1 Notation

Let $x = \{x_i\}_{i=1}^{|x|}$ be a sentence of length $|x|$ that consists of tokens $x_i$. We use $s = \{s_i\}_{i=1}^{|x|}$ to denote a segmentation of all the tokens in sentence $x$, and $s_i = \{s_{i,j}\}_{j=1}^{|s_i|}$ to denote a segmentation of the token $x_i$, where $s_{i,j}$ is the $j$th morpheme of the token $x_i$. Similarly, we use $t$, $t_i$ and $t_{i,j}$ for the POS

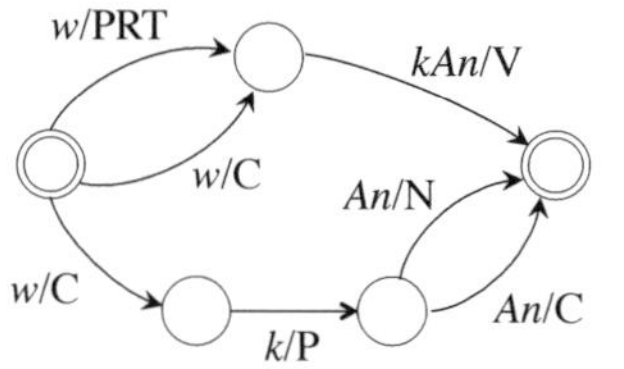


Figure 1: Example lattice structures for the Arabic token "*wkAn*". It has two candidate segmentations: *w*+*kAn* or *w*+*k*+*An*. The first segmentation consists of two morphemes. The first morpheme *w* has two candidate POS.

tags for each sentence, token and morpheme. We use $y$ to denote a dependency tree over morphemes, and $y_{i,j}$ to denote the head of morpheme $s_{i,j}$. During training, the algorithm is provided with tuples that specify ground truth values for all the variables $\mathcal{D} = \{(x, \hat{s}, \hat{t}, \hat{y})\}$.

We also assume access to a morphological analyzer and a POS tagger that provide candidate analyses. Specifically, for each token $x_i$, the algorithm is provided with candidate segmentations $\mathcal{S}_i$, and candidate POS tags $\mathcal{T}_i$ and $\mathcal{T}_{i,j}$. These alternative analyses are captured in the **lattice structure** (see Figure 1 for an example). Finally, we use $\mathcal{Y}$ to denote the set of all valid dependency trees defined over morphemes.

### 3.2 Decoding

We parameterize the scoring function as

$$score(x, s, t, y) = \theta \cdot f(x, s, t, y) \quad (1)$$

where $\theta$ is the parameter vector and $f(x, s, t, y)$ is the feature vector associated with the sentence and all variables.

The goal of decoding is to find a set of valid values for $(s, t, y) \in \mathcal{S} \times \mathcal{T} \times \mathcal{Y}$ that maximizes the score defined in Eq. 1. Our randomized greedy algorithm finds a high scoring assignment for $(s, t, y)$ via a hill-climbing process with multiple random restarts. (Section 3.3 describes how the parameters $\theta$ are learned.)

Figure 2 shows the framework of our randomized greedy algorithm. First, we draw a full path from the lattice structure in two steps: (1) sampling a morphological segmentation $s$ from $\mathcal{S}$; (2) sampling POS tags $t$ for each morpheme. Next, we sample a dependency tree $y$ from the parse space. Based on this random starting point, we iteratively hill-climb $t$ and $y$ in a bottom-up order.[2] In our earlier work (Zhang et al., 2014b), we showed this strategy guarantees that we can climb to any target tree in a finite number of steps. We repeat the sampling and the hill-climbing processes above until we do not find a better solution for $K$ iterations. We introduce the details of this process below.

**SampleSeg and SamplePOS:** Given a sentence $x$, we first draw segmentations $s$ and POS tags $t^{(0)}$ from the first-order distribution using the current learned parameter values. For segmentation, first-order features only depend on each token $x_i$ and its morphemes $s_{i,j}$. Similarly, for POS, first-order features are defined based on $s_{i,j}$ and $t_{i,j}$. The sampling process is straightforward due to the fact that the candidate sets $|\mathcal{S}_i|$ and $|\mathcal{T}_{i,j}|$ are both small. We can enumerate and compute the probabilities proportional to the exponential of the first-order scores as follows.[3]

$$\begin{aligned} p(s_i) &\propto \exp\{\theta \cdot f(x, s_i)\} \\ p(t_{i,j}) &\propto \exp\{\theta \cdot f(x, s_i, t_{i,j})\} \end{aligned} \quad (2)$$

**SampleTree:** Given a random sample of the segmentations $s$ and the POS tags $t^{(0)}$, we draw a random tree $y^{(0)}$ from the first-order distribution using Wilson's algorithm (Wilson, 1996).[4]

**HillClimbPOS:** After sampling the initial values $s$, $t^{(0)}$ and $y^{(0)}$, the hill-climbing algorithm improves the solution via locally greedy changes. The hill-climbing algorithm iterates between improving the POS tags and the dependency tree. For POS tagging, it updates each $t_{i,j}$ in a bottom-up order as follows

$$t_{i,j} \leftarrow \underset{t_{i,j} \in \mathcal{T}_{i,j}}{\arg\max}\, score(x, s, t_{i,j}, t_{-(i,j)}, y) \quad (3)$$

where $t_{-(i,j)}$ are the rest of the POS tags when we update $t_{i,j}$.

[2]We do not hill-climb segmentation, or else we have to jointly find the optimal $t$ and $y$, and the resulting computational cost is too high.

[3]We notice that the distribution becomes significantly sharper after training for several epochs. Therefore, we also smooth the distribution by multiplying the score with a scaling factor.

[4]We also smooth the distribution in the same way as in segmentation and POS tagging.

**Input:** parameter $\theta$, sentence $x$
**Output:** segmentations $s$, POS tags $t$ and dependency tree $y$

1: $s \leftarrow SampleSeg(x)$
2: $t^{(0)} \leftarrow SamplePos(x, s)$
3: $y^{(0)} \leftarrow SampleTree(x, s, t^{(0)})$
4: $k = 0$
5: **repeat**
6: $\quad t^{(k+1)} \leftarrow HillClimbPOS(x, s, t^{(k)}, y^{(k)})$
7: $\quad y^{(k+1)} \leftarrow HillClimbTree(x, s, t^{(k+1)}, y^{(k)})$
8: $\quad k \leftarrow k + 1$
9: **until** no change in this iteration
10: **return** $(s, t^{(k)}, y^{(k)})$

Figure 2: The hill-climbing algorithm with random initializations. Details of the sampling and hill-climbing functions in Line 1-3 and 6-7 are provided in Section 3.2.

**HillClimbTree:** We improve the dependency tree $y$ via a similar hill-climbing process. Specifically, we greedily update the head $y_{i,j}$ of each morpheme in a bottom-up order as follows

$$y_{i,j} \leftarrow \arg\max_{y_{i,j} \in \mathcal{Y}_{i,j}} score(x, s, t, y_{i,j}, y_{-(i,j)}) \quad (4)$$

where $\mathcal{Y}_{i,j}$ is the set of candidate heads such that changing $y_{i,j}$ to any candidate does not violate the tree constraint.

### 3.3 Training

We learn the parameters $\theta$ in a max-margin framework, using on-line updates. For each update, we need to compute the segmentations, POS tags and the tree that maximize the cost-augmented score:

$$(\tilde{s}, \tilde{t}, \tilde{y}) = \arg\max_{s \in \mathcal{S}, t \in \mathcal{T}, y \in \mathcal{Y}} \{\theta \cdot f(x, s, t, y) + Err(s, t, y)\} \quad (5)$$

where $Err(s, t, y)$ is the number of errors of $(s, t, y)$ against the ground truth $(\hat{s}, \hat{t}, \hat{y})$. The parameters are then updated to guide the selection against the violation. This is done via standard passive-aggressive updates (Crammer et al., 2006).

### 3.4 Adapting to Chinese Joint Prediction

In this section we describe how the proposed model can be adapted to languages that do not delineate words with spaces, and thus require word segmentation. The main difference lies in the construction of the lattice structure. We employ a state-of-the-art word segmenter to produce candidate word boundaries. We consider boundaries common across all the top-$k$ candidates as true word boundaries. The remaining tokens (i.e., strings between these boundaries) are treated as words to be further segmented and labeled with POS tags. Figure 3 shows an example of the Chinese word lattice structure we construct. Once the lattice is constructed, the joint prediction model is applied as described above.

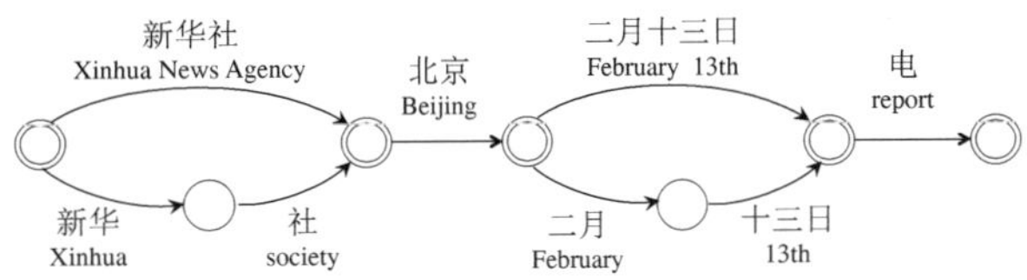


Figure 3: Example lattice structures for the Chinese sentence “新华社北京二月十三日电” (Xinhua Press at Beijing reports on February 13th). The token 新华社 has two candidate segmentations: 新华社 or 新华 + 社.

## 4 Features

**Segmentation Features** For both Arabic and Chinese, each segmentation is represented by its score from the preprocessing system, and by the corresponding morphemes (or words in Chinese). Following previous work (Zhang and Clark, 2010), we also add character-based features for Chinese word segmentation, including the first and the last characters in the word, and the length of the word.

**POS Tag Features** Table 1 summarizes the POS tag features employed by the model. First, we use the feature templates proposed in our previous work on Arabic joint parsing and POS correction (Zhang et al., 2014c). In addition, we incorporate character-based features specifically designed for Chinese. These features are mainly inspired by previous transition-based models on Chinese joint POS tagging and word segmentation (Zhang and Clark, 2010).

**Dependency Parsing Features** The feature templates for dependency parsing are mainly drawn from our previous work (Zhang et al., 2014b). Fig-

| | |
|---|---|
| 1-gram | $\langle t_0, w_{-2}\rangle, \langle t_0, w_{-1}\rangle, \langle t_0, w_0\rangle, \langle t_0, w_1\rangle, \langle t_0, w_2\rangle,$ $\langle t_0, w_{-1}, w_0\rangle, \langle t_0, w_0, w_1\rangle, \langle s(t_0)\rangle, \langle t_0, s(t_0)\rangle$ |
| 2-gram | $\langle t_{-1}, t_0\rangle, \langle t_{-2}, t_0\rangle, \langle t_{-1}, t_0, w_{-1}\rangle, \langle t_{-1}, t_0, w_0\rangle$ |
| 3-gram | $\langle t_{-1}, t_0, t_1\rangle, \langle t_{-2}, t_0, t_1, \rangle, \langle t_{-1}, t_0, t_2\rangle,$ $\langle t_{-2}, t_0, t_2\rangle$ |
| 4-gram | $\langle t_{-2}, t_{-1}, t_0, t_{+1}\rangle, \langle t_{-2}, t_{-1}, t_0, t_2\rangle,$ $\langle t_{-2}, t_0, t_1, t_2\rangle$ |
| 5-gram | $\langle t_{-2}, t_{-1}, t_0, t_1, t_2\rangle$ |
| Character | $\langle t_0, pre_1(w_0)\rangle, \langle t_0, pre_2(w_0)\rangle, \langle t_0, suf_1(w_0)\rangle,$ $\langle t_0, suf_2(w_0)\rangle, \langle t_0, c_n(w_0)\rangle, \langle t_0, len(w_0)\rangle$ |

Table 1: POS tag feature templates. $t_0$ and $w_0$ denotes the POS tag and the word at the current position. $t_{-x}$ and $t_x$ denote left and right context tags, and similarly for words. $s(\cdot)$ denotes the score of the POS tag produced by the preprocessing tagger. The last row shows the "Character"-based features for Chinese. $pre_1(\cdot)$ and $pre_2(\cdot)$ denote the word prefixes with one and two characters respectively. $suf_1(\cdot)$ and $suf_2(\cdot)$ denote the word suffixes similarly. $c_n(\cdot)$ denotes the $n$-th character in the word. $len(\cdot)$ denotes the length of the word, capped at 5 if longer.

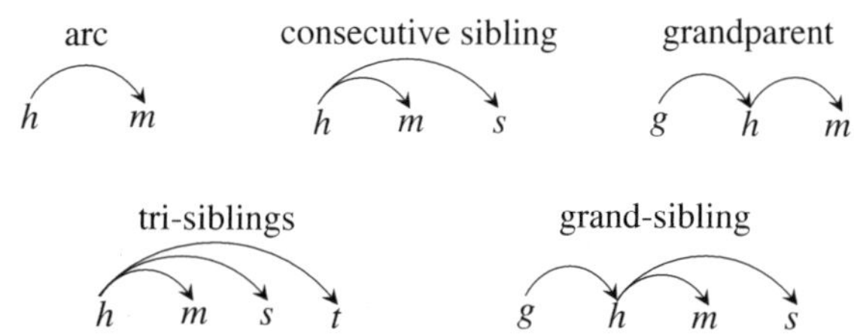


Figure 4: First- to third-order dependency parsing features.

ure 4 shows the first- to third-order feature templates that we use in our model. We also use global features to capture the adjacent conjuncts agreement in a coordination structure, and the valency patterns for each POS category. Note that most dependency features are implicitly cross-task in that they include POS tag and segmentation information. For example, the standard feature involves the POS tags of the words on both ends of the arc.

## 5 Experimental Setup

### 5.1 Datasets

We evaluate our model on two Arabic datasets and one Chinese dataset. For the first Arabic dataset, we use the dataset used in the Statistical Parsing of Morphologically Rich Languages (SPMRL) Shared Task 2013 (Seddah et al., 2013).[5] We follow the official split for training, development and testing set. We use the core set of 12 POS categories provided by Marton et al. (2013). In the second Arabic dataset, the training set is a dependency conversion of the Arabic Treebank, which primarily includes Modern Standard Arabic (MSA) text. However, we test on a new corpus, which consists of classical Arabic text obtained from the Comprehensive Islamic Library (CIS).[6] A native Arabic speaker with background in computational linguistics annotated the morphological segmentation and POS tags. This corpus is an excellent testbed for a joint model because classical Arabic may use rather different vocabulary from MSA, while their syntactic grammars are very similar to each other. Therefore incorporating syntactic information should be particularly beneficial to morphological segmentation and POS tagging. For Chinese, we use the Chinese Penn Treebank 5.0 (CTB5) and follow the split in previous work (Zhang and Clark, 2010).

| Dataset | | SPMRL | Classical | CTB5 |
|---|---|---|---|---|
| Language | | Arabic | Arabic | Chinese |
| Train | #sent | 14.4k | 15.4k | 17.5k |
| | #token | 451k | 573k | 442k |
| Dev. | #sent | 1.8k | – | 348 |
| | #token | 56.9k | – | 6.6k |
| Test. | #sent | 1.8k | 163 | 348 |
| | #token | 55.6k | 7.9k | 8.0k |

Table 2: Statistics of datasets.

Table 2 summarizes the statistics of the datasets. For the SPMRL test set, we follow the common practice which limits the sentence lengths up to 70 (Seddah et al., 2013). For classical Arabic and Chinese, we evaluate on all the test sentences.

### 5.2 Generating Lattice Structures

In this section we introduce the methodology for constructing candidate sets for segmentation and

[5] This dataset is originally provided by the LDC (Maamouri et al., 2004), specifically its SPMRL 2013 dependency instance, derived from the Columbia Catib Treebank (Habash and Roth, 2009; Habash et al., 2009) and extended according to the SPMRL 2013 extension scheme (Seddah et al., 2013).

[6] This classical Arabic dataset is publicly available at `http://farasa.qcri.org/`

MADA analysis

| Word *Emlyp* |
|---|
| *Emly*/NOUN+*p*/NSUFF, gen:f/num:s/per:na |
| *Emly*/ADJ+*p*/NSUFF, gen:f/num:s/per:na |
| *Eml*/NOUN+*y*/NSUFF+*p*/PRON, gen:m/num:d/per:na |

Lattice structure

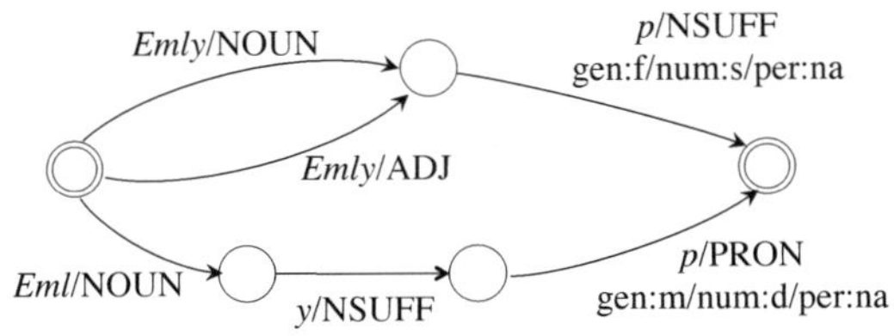


Figure 5: Example MADA analysis for the word *Emlyp* and the corresponding lattice structure.

POS tagging. Table 3 provides statistics on the generated candidate sets.

**SPMRL 2013** Following Marton et al. (2013), we use the MADA system to generate candidate morphological analyses and POS tags. For each token in the sentence, MADA provides a list of possible morphological analyses and POS tags, each associated with a score. The score of each segmentation or POS tag equals the highest score of the MADA analysis in which it appears. In addition, we associate each segmentation with MADA analyses on gender, number and person. Figure 5 shows an example of MADA output for the token *Emlyp* and the corresponding lattice structure.

**Classical Arabic** We construct the lattice for this corpus in a similar fashion to the SPMRL dataset with two main departures. First, we use the Arabic morphological analyzer developed by Darwish et al. (2014) because MADA is primarily trained for MSA and performs poorly on classical Arabic. Second, we implement a CRF-based morpheme-level POS tagger and generate the POS tag candidates for each morpheme based on their marginal probabilities, truncated by a probability threshold.

**CTB5** We first re-train the Stanford Chinese word segmenter on CTB5 and generate a top-10 list for each sentence.[7] We treat the word boundaries shared across all the 10 candidates as the confident ones, and construct the lattice as described in Section 3.4. Our model then focuses on disambiguating the rest of the word boundaries in the candidates. To generate POS candidates, we apply a CRF-based tagger with Chinese-specific features used in previous work (Hatori et al., 2011).

[7]We use 10-fold cross validation to avoid overfitting on the training set.

| Dataset | Seg | | | POS | |
|---|---|---|---|---|---|
| | F1 | Oracle | Avg. $\|\mathcal{S}_i\|$ | F1 | Avg. $\|\mathcal{T}_{i,j}\|$ |
| SPMRL | 99.4 | 99.8 | 1.23 | 96.9 | 1.71 |
| Classical | 92.4 | 97.0 | 1.16 | 82.4 | 3.01 |
| CTB5 | 95.3 | 99.0 | 1.22 | 91.4 | 2.02 |

Table 3: Quality of the lattice structures on each dataset. For SPMRL and CTB5, we show the statistics on the development sets. For classical Arabic, we directly show the statistics on the testing set because the development set is not available.

### 5.3 Evaluation Measures

Following standard practice in previous work (Hatori et al., 2012; Zhang et al., 2014a), we use F-score as the evaluation metric for segmentation, POS tagging and dependency parsing. We report the morpheme-level F-score for Arabic and the word-level F-score for Chinese. In addition, we use TedEval (Tsarfaty et al., 2012) to evaluate the joint prediction on the SPMRL dataset, because TedEval score is the only evaluation metric used in the official report. We directly use the evaluation tools provided on the SPMRL official website.[8]

### 5.4 Baselines

**State-of-the-Art Systems** For the SPMRL dataset, we directly compare with Björkelund et al. (2013). This system achieves the best TedEval score in the track of dependency parsing with predicted information and we directly republish the official result. We also compute the F-score of this system on each task using our own evaluation script.[9] For the CTB5 dataset, we directly compare to the arc-eager system by Zhang et al. (2014a), which slightly outperforms the arc-standard system by Hatori et al. (2012).

[8]http://www.spmrl.org/spmrl2013-sharedtask.html

[9]F-score evaluation for Arabic is not straightforward due to the stem changes in the morphological analysis. Therefore, the comparison of F-scores is only approximate.

| Model | SPMRL | | | | Classical Arabic | | CTB5 | | |
|---|---|---|---|---|---|---|---|---|---|
| | Seg | POS | Dep | TedEval | Seg | POS | Seg | POS | Dep |
| Pipeline | 99.18 | 95.76 | 84.79 | 92.86 | 92.37 | 82.40 | 97.45 | 93.42 | 79.46 |
| Joint | **99.52** | **97.43** | **87.23** | **93.87** | **94.35** | **84.44** | **98.04** | **94.47** | **82.01** |
| Best Published | 96.42 | 91.66 | 82.41 | 91.74 | – | – | 97.76 | 94.36 | 81.70 |

Table 4: Segmentation, POS tagging and unlabeled attachment dependency F-scores (%) and TedEval score (%) on different datasets. The first line denotes the performance by the pipeline variation of our model. The second row shows the results by our joint model. "Best Published" includes the best reported results: Björkelund et al. (2013) for the SPMRL 2013 shared task and Zhang et al. (2014a) for the CTB5 dataset. Note that the POS F-scores are not directly comparable because Björkelund et al. (2013) use a different POS tagset from us.

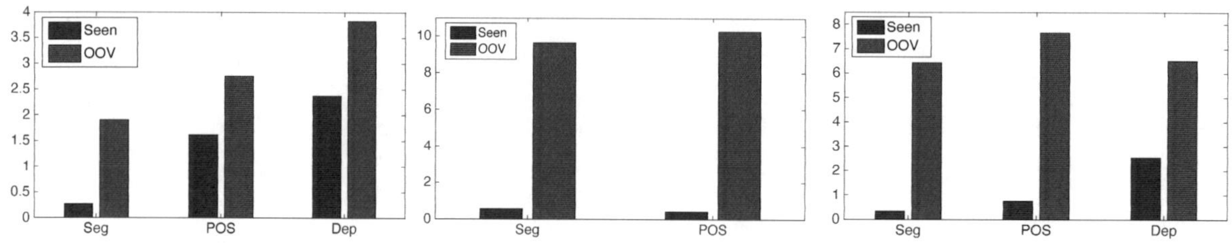


(a) SPMRL (b) Classical Arabic (c) CTB5

Figure 6: Absolute F-score (%) improvement of the joint model over the pipeline counterpart on seen and out-of-vocabulary (OOV) words.

**System Variants** We also compare against a pipeline variation of our model. In our pipeline model, we predict segmentations and POS tags by the same system that we use to generate candidates. The subsequent standard parsing model then operates on the predicted segmentations and POS tags.

### 5.5 Experimental Details

Following our earlier work (Zhang et al., 2014b), we train a first-order classifier to prune the dependency tree space.[10] Following common practice, we average parameters over all iterations after training with passive-aggressive online learning algorithm (Crammer et al., 2006; Collins, 2002). We use the same adaptive random restart strategy as in our earlier work (Zhang et al., 2014b) and set $K = 300$. In addition, we also apply an aggressive early-stop strategy during training for efficiency. If we have found a violation against the ground truth during the first 50 iterations, we immediately stop and update the parameters based on the current violation. The reasoning behind this early-stop strategy is that weaker violations for some training sentences are already sufficient for separable training sets (Huang et al., 2012).

## 6 Results

**Comparison to State-of-the-art Systems** Table 4 summarizes the performance of our model and the best published results for the SPMRL and the CTB5 datasets.[11] On both datasets, our system outperforms the baselines. On the SPMRL 2013 shared task, our approach yields a 2.1% TedEval score gain over the top performing system (Björkelund et al., 2013). We also improve the segmentation and dependency F-scores by 3.1% and 4.8% respectively. Note that the POS F-scores are not directly comparable because Björkelund et al. (2013) use a different POS tagset from us. On the CTB5 dataset, we outperform the state-of-the-art with respect to all

[10]We set the probability threshold to 0.05 and limit the number of candidate heads up to 20, which gives a 99.5% pruning recall on both the SPMRL and the CTB5 development sets.

[11]We are not aware of any published results on the Classical Arabic Dataset.

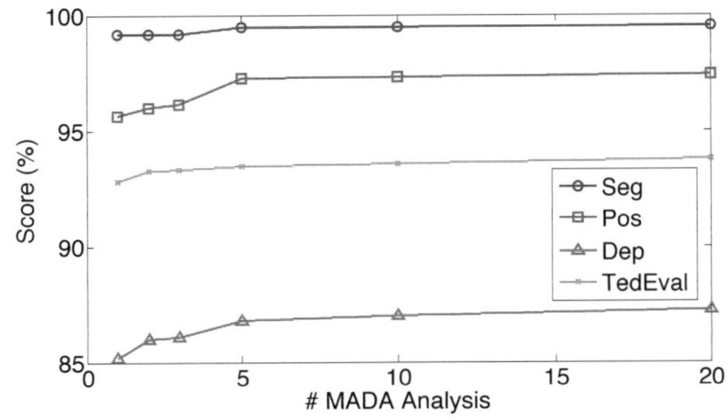


Figure 7: Performance with different sizes of the candidate sets on the SPMRL dataset. The graph shows the TedEval and F-scores when considering the best $k$ analyses by MADA, and the variation is achieved by changing $k$.

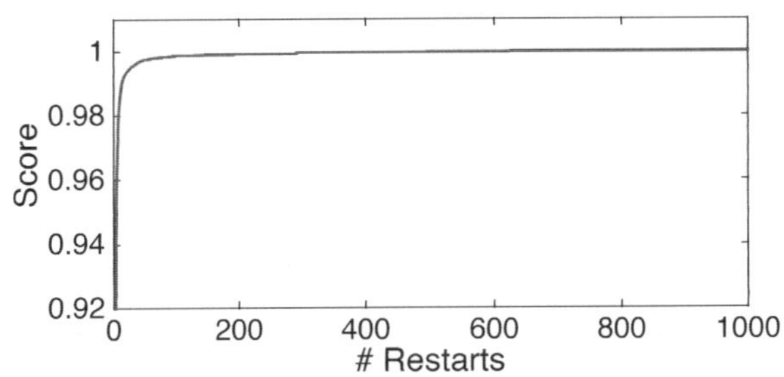


Figure 8: The normalized score of the output tree as the function of the number of restarts. We normalize scores of each sentence by the highest score among 3,000 restarts for this sentence. We show the curve up to 1,000 restarts because it reaches convergence after 500 restarts.

tasks: segmentation (0.3%), tagging (0.1%), and dependency parsing (0.3%).[12]

**Impact of the Joint Prediction** As Table 4 shows, our joint prediction model consistently outperforms the corresponding pipeline model in all three tasks. This observation is consistent with findings in previous work (Hatori et al., 2012; Tratz, 2013). We also observe that gains are higher (2%) on the classical Arabic dataset, which demonstrates that joint prediction is particularly helpful in bridging the gap between MSA and classical Arabic.

[12]Zhang et al. (2014a) improve the dependency F-score to 82.14% by adding manually annotated intra-word dependency information. Even without such gold word structure annotations, our model still achieves a comparable result.

| Dataset | Seg | | POS | | Dep | |
|---|---|---|---|---|---|---|
| | Seen | OOV | Seen | OOV | Seen | OOV |
| SPMRL | 48.4 | 27.8 | 44.7 | 15.0 | 15.9 | 17.5 |
| Classical | 13.8 | 34.8 | 4.2 | 17.2 | – | – |
| CTB5 | 20.3 | 25.7 | 14.2 | 19.9 | 13.0 | 15.6 |

Table 5: F-score error reductions (%) of the joint model over the pipeline counterpart on seen and OOV words.

Figure 6 shows the break of the improvement based on seen and out-of-vocabulary (OOV) words. As expected, across all languages OOV words benefit more from the joint prediction, as they constitute a common source of error propagation in a pipeline model. The extent of improvement depends on the underlying accuracy of the preprocessing for segmentation and POS tagging on OOV words. For instance, we observe a higher gain (7%) on Chinese OOV words which have a 61.5% accuracy when processed by the original stand-along POS tagger. On the SPMRL dataset, the gain on OOV words is lower (3%), while preprocessing accuracy is higher (82%). Their error reductions on OOV words are nevertheless close to each other. Table 5 summarizes the results on F-score error reduction.

We also observe that the error reductions of OOV words/morphemes on the Chinese and the Classical Arabic dataset are larger than that of the in-vocabulary counterparts (e.g. 26% vs. 20% on Chinese word segmentation). However, we have the opposite observation on the segmentation and POS tagging on the SPMRL dataset (28% vs. 48%). This can be explained by analyzing the oracle performance in which we select the best solution from possible candidates. The oracle error reduction of OOV morphemes in the SPMRL dataset is relatively low (44%), compared to the 61% oracle error reduction of OOV morphemes in the Classical Arabic dataset.

**Impact of the Number of Alternative Analyses** In Figure 7, we plot the performance on the SPMRL dataset as a function of the number $k$ of MADA analyses that we use to construct the candidate sets. For low $k$, increasing the number of analyses improves performance across all evaluation metrics. However, the performance converges at around $k = 15$.

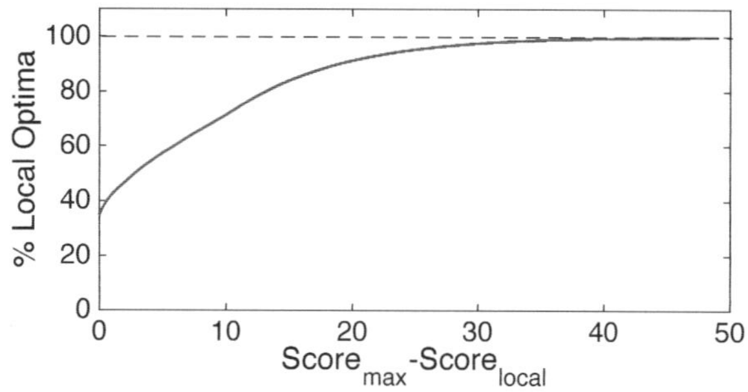


Figure 9: Cumulative distribution function (CDF) for the number of local optima versus the score of these local optima obtained from each restart, on the SPMRL dataset. The score captures the difference between a local optimum and the best one among 3,000 restarts.

**Convergence Properties** To assess the quality of the approximation obtained by the randomized greedy inference, we would like to compare it against the optimal solution. Following our earlier work (Zhang et al., 2014b), we use the highest score among 3,000 restarts for each sentence as a proxy for the optimal solution. Figure 8 shows the normalized score of the retrieved solution as a function of the number of restarts. We observe that most sentences converge quickly.[13] Specifically, more than 97% of the sentences converge within first 300 restarts. Since for the vast majority of cases our system converges fast, we achieve a comparable speed to that of other state-of-the-art joint systems. For example, our model achieves high performance on Chinese at about 0.5 sentences per second. The speed is about the same as that of the transition-based system (Hatori et al., 2012) with beam size 64, the setting that achieved best accuracy in their work.

**Quality of Local Optima** Figure 9 shows the cumulative distribution function (CDF) for the number of local optima versus the score of these local optima obtained from each restart. More specifically, the score captures the difference between a local optimum and the maximal score among 3,000 restarts. We can see that most of the local optima reached by hill-climbing have scores close to the maximum. For instance, about 30% of the local optima are identical to the best solution, namely $score_{max} - score_{local} = 0$.

[13]As expected, we also observe that convergence is slower when comparing to standard dependency parsing with a similar randomized greedy algorithm (Zhang et al., 2014b), because joint prediction results in a harder inference problem.

## 7 Conclusions

In this paper, we propose a general randomized greedy algorithm for joint segmentation, POS tagging and dependency parsing. On both Arabic and Chinese, our model achieves improvement on the three tasks over state-of-the-art systems and pipeline variants of our system. In particular, we demonstrate that OOV words benefits more from the power of joint prediction. Finally, our experimental results show that increasing candidate sizes improves performance across all evaluation metrics.

## Acknowledgments

This research is developed in a collaboration of MIT with the Arabic Language Technologies (ALT) group at Qatar Computing Research Institute (QCRI) within the Interactive sYstems for Answer Search (IYAS) project. The authors acknowledge the support of the U.S. Army Research Office under grant number W911NF-10-1-0533, and of the DARPA BOLT program. We thank Meishan Zhang and Anders Björkelund for answering questions and sharing the outputs of their systems. We also thank the MIT NLP group and the ACL reviewers for their comments. Any opinions, findings, conclusions, or recommendations expressed in this paper are those of the authors, and do not necessarily reflect the views of the funding organizations.

## References

Anders Björkelund, Ozlem Cetinoglu, Richárd Farkas, Thomas Mueller, and Wolfgang Seeker. 2013. (re)ranking meets morphosyntax: State-of-the-art results from the SPMRL 2013 shared task. In *Proceedings of the Fourth Workshop on Statistical Parsing of Morphologically-Rich Languages*, pages 135–145, Seattle, Washington, USA, October. Association for Computational Linguistics.

Bernd Bohnet and Joakim Nivre. 2012. A transition-based system for joint part-of-speech tagging and labeled non-projective dependency parsing. In *Proceedings of the 2012 Joint Conference on Empirical Methods in Natural Language Processing and Computa-*

*tional Natural Language Learning*, pages 1455–1465. Association for Computational Linguistics.

Bernd Bohnet, Joakim Nivre, Igor Boguslavsky, Richárd Farkas, Filip Ginter, and Jan Hajic. 2013. Joint morphological and syntactic analysis for richly inflected languages. *TACL*, 1:415–428.

Shay B Cohen and Noah A Smith. 2007. Joint morphological and syntactic disambiguation. In *Proceedings of EMNLP*.

Michael Collins. 2002. Discriminative training methods for hidden markov models: Theory and experiments with perceptron algorithms. In *Proceedings of the Conference on Empirical Methods in Natural Language Processing - Volume 10*, EMNLP '02. Association for Computational Linguistics.

Koby Crammer, Ofer Dekel, Joseph Keshet, Shai Shalev-Shwartz, and Yoram Singer. 2006. Online passive-aggressive algorithms. *The Journal of Machine Learning Research*.

Kareem Darwish, Ahmed Abdelali, and Hamdy Mubarak. 2014. Using stem-templates to improve arabic pos and gender/number tagging. In *International Conference on Language Resources and Evaluation (LREC-2014)*.

Souhir Gahbiche-Braham, Hélene Bonneau-Maynard, Thomas Lavergne, and François Yvon. 2012. Joint segmentation and pos tagging for arabic using a crf-based classifier. In *LREC*, pages 2107–2113.

Yoav Goldberg and Michael Elhadad. 2011. Joint hebrew segmentation and parsing using a pcfg-la lattice parser. In *Proceedings of the 49th Annual Meeting of the Association for Computational Linguistics: Human Language Technologies: short papers-Volume 2*, pages 704–709. Association for Computational Linguistics.

Yoav Goldberg and Reut Tsarfaty. 2008. A single generative model for joint morphological segmentation and syntactic parsing. In *ACL*, pages 371–379. Citeseer.

Nizar Habash and Owen Rambow. 2005. Arabic tokenization, part-of-speech tagging and morphological disambiguation in one fell swoop. In *Proceedings of the 43rd Annual Meeting on Association for Computational Linguistics*, pages 573–580. Association for Computational Linguistics.

Nizar Habash and Ryan Roth. 2009. Catib: The columbia arabic treebank. In *Proceedings of the ACL-IJCNLP 2009 Conference Short Papers*, pages 221–224, Suntec, Singapore, August. Association for Computational Linguistics.

Nizar Habash, Reem Faraj, and Ryan Roth. 2009. Syntactic Annotation in the Columbia Arabic Treebank. In *Proceedings of MEDAR International Conference on Arabic Language Resources and Tools*, Cairo, Egypt.

Jun Hatori, Takuya Matsuzaki, Yusuke Miyao, and Jun'ichi Tsujii. 2011. Incremental joint pos tagging and dependency parsing in chinese. In *IJCNLP*, pages 1216–1224. Citeseer.

Jun Hatori, Takuya Matsuzaki, Yusuke Miyao, and Jun'ichi Tsujii. 2012. Incremental joint approach to word segmentation, pos tagging, and dependency parsing in chinese. In *Proceedings of the 50th Annual Meeting of the Association for Computational Linguistics: Long Papers-Volume 1*, pages 1045–1053. Association for Computational Linguistics.

Liang Huang, Suphan Fayong, and Yang Guo. 2012. Structured perceptron with inexact search. In *Proceedings of the 2012 Conference of the North American Chapter of the Association for Computational Linguistics: Human Language Technologies*, pages 142–151. Association for Computational Linguistics.

Zhenghua Li, Min Zhang, Wanxiang Che, Ting Liu, Wenliang Chen, and Haizhou Li. 2011. Joint models for chinese pos tagging and dependency parsing. In *Proceedings of the 2011 Conference on Empirical Methods in Natural Language Processing*, pages 1180–1191. Association for Computational Linguistics, July.

Mohamed Maamouri, Ann Bies, Tim Buckwalter, and Wigdan Mekki. 2004. The Penn Arabic Treebank: Building a Large-Scale Annotated Arabic Corpus. In *NEMLAR Conference on Arabic Language Resources and Tools*.

Yuval Marton, Nizar Habash, Owen Rambow, and Sarah Alkhulani. 2013. Spmrl'13 shared task system: The cadim arabic dependency parser. In *Proceedings of the Fourth Workshop on Statistical Parsing of Morphologically-Rich Languages*, pages 76–80.

Xian Qian and Yang Liu. 2012. Joint chinese word segmentation, pos tagging and parsing. In *Proceedings of the 2012 Joint Conference on Empirical Methods in Natural Language Processing and Computational Natural Language Learning*, pages 501–511. Association for Computational Linguistics.

Djamé Seddah, Reut Tsarfaty, Sandra Kübler, Marie Candito, Jinho D. Choi, Richárd Farkas, Jennifer Foster, Iakes Goenaga, Koldo Gojenola Galletebeitia, Yoav Goldberg, Spence Green, Nizar Habash, Marco Kuhlmann, Wolfgang Maier, Joakim Nivre, Adam Przepiórkowski, Ryan Roth, Wolfgang Seeker, Yannick Versley, Veronika Vincze, Marcin Woliński, Alina Wróblewska, and Eric Villemonte de la Clergerie. 2013. Overview of the SPMRL 2013 shared task: A cross-framework evaluation of parsing morphologically rich languages. In *Proceedings of the Fourth Workshop on Statistical Parsing of Morphologically-Rich Languages*, pages 146–182, Seattle, Washington, USA, October. Association for Computational Linguistics.

Stephen Tratz. 2013. A cross-task flexible transition model for arabic tokenization, affix detection, affix labeling, pos tagging, and dependency parsing. In *Fourth Workshop on Statistical Parsing of Morphologically Rich Languages*, page 34. Citeseer.

Reut Tsarfaty, Joakim Nivre, and Evelina Andersson. 2012. Joint evaluation of morphological segmentation and syntactic parsing. In *Proceedings of the 50th Annual Meeting of the Association for Computational Linguistics: Short Papers-Volume 2*, pages 6–10. Association for Computational Linguistics.

Zhiguo Wang and Nianwen Xue. 2014. Joint pos tagging and transition-based constituent parsing in chinese with non-local features. In *Proceedings of the 52nd Annual Meeting of the Association for Computational Linguistics (Volume 1: Long Papers)*, pages 733–742, Baltimore, Maryland, June. Association for Computational Linguistics.

David Wilson. 1996. Generating random spanning trees more quickly than the cover time. In *Proceedings of the twenty-eighth annual ACM symposium on Theory of computing*, pages 296–303. ACM.

Yue Zhang and Stephen Clark. 2008. Joint word segmentation and pos tagging using a single perceptron. In *ACL*, pages 888–896.

Yue Zhang and Stephen Clark. 2010. A fast decoder for joint word segmentation and pos-tagging using a single discriminative model. In *Proceedings of the 2010 Conference on Empirical Methods in Natural Language Processing*, pages 843–852. Association for Computational Linguistics.

Meishan Zhang, Yue Zhang, Wanxiang Che, and Ting Liu. 2014a. Character-level chinese dependency parsing. In *ACL*.

Yuan Zhang, Tao Lei, Regina Barzilay, and Tommi Jaakkola. 2014b. Greed is good if randomized: New inference for dependency parsing. In *EMNLP*.

Yuan Zhang, Tao Lei, Regina Barzilay, Tommi Jaakkola, and Amir Globerson. 2014c. Steps to excellence: Simple inference with refined scoring of dependency trees. In *ACL*.

# An Incremental Algorithm for Transition-based CCG Parsing

**Bharat Ram Ambati[1] , Tejaswini Deoskar[1] , Mark Johnson[2] , Mark Steedman[1]**
[1] ILCC, School of Informatics, University of Edinburgh
[2] Department of Computing, Macquarie University
bharat.ambati@ed.ac.uk, mark.johnson@mq.edu.au, {tdeoskar,steedman}@inf.ed.ac.uk

## Abstract

Incremental parsers have potential advantages for applications like language modeling for machine translation and speech recognition. We describe a new algorithm for incremental transition-based Combinatory Categorial Grammar parsing. As English CCGbank derivations are mostly right branching and non-incremental, we design our algorithm based on the dependencies resolved rather than the derivation. We introduce two new actions in the shift-reduce paradigm based on the idea of 'revealing' (Pareschi and Steedman, 1987) the required information during parsing. On the standard CCGbank test data, our algorithm achieved improvements of 0.88% in labeled and 2.0% in unlabeled F-score over a greedy non-incremental shift-reduce parser.

## 1 Introduction

Combinatory Categorial Grammar (CCG) (Steedman, 2000) is an efficiently parseable, yet linguistically expressive grammar formalism. In addition to predicate-argument structure, CCG elegantly captures the unbounded dependencies found in grammatical constructions like relativization, coordination etc. Availability of the English CCGbank (Hockenmaier and Steedman, 2007) has enabled the creation of several robust and accurate wide-coverage CCG parsers (Hockenmaier and Steedman, 2002; Clark and Curran, 2007; Zhang and Clark, 2011). While the majority of CCG parsers use chart-based approaches (Hockenmaier and Steedman, 2002; Clark and Curran, 2007), there has been some work on developing shift-reduce parsers for CCG (Zhang and Clark, 2011; Xu et al., 2014). Most of these parsers model normal-form CCG derivations (Eisner, 1996), which are mostly right-branching trees : hence are not incremental in nature. The dependency models of Clark and Curran (2007) and Xu et al. (2014) model dependencies rather than derivations, but do not guarantee incremental analyses.

Besides being cognitively plausible (Marslen-Wilson, 1973), incremental parsing is more useful than non-incremental parsing for some applications. For example, an incremental analysis is required for integrating syntactic and semantic information into language modeling for statistical machine translation (SMT) and automatic speech recognition (ASR) (Roark, 2001; Wang and Harper, 2003).

This paper develops a new incremental shift-reduce algorithm for parsing CCG by building a dependency graph in addition to the CCG derivation as a representation. The dependencies in the graph are extracted from the CCG derivation. A node can have multiple parents, and hence we construct a dependency graph rather than a tree. Two new actions are introduced in the shift-reduce paradigm for "revealing" (Pareschi and Steedman, 1987) unbuilt structure during parsing. We build the dependency graph in parallel to the incremental CCG derivation and use this graph for revealing, via these two new actions. On the standard CCGbank test data, our algorithm achieves improvements of 0.88% in labeled F-score and 2.0% in unlabeled F-score over a greedy non-incremental shift-reduce algorithm. As our algorithm does not model derivations, but rather models transitions, we do not need a treebank



*Human Language Technologies: The 2015 Annual Conference of the North American Chapter of the ACL*, pages 53–63,
Denver, Colorado, May 31 – June 5, 2015. 

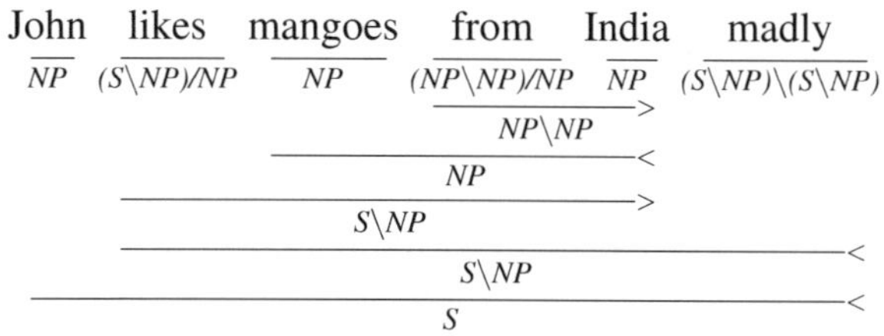


Figure 1: Normal form CCG derivation.

of incremental CCG derivations and can train on the dependencies in the existing treebank. Our approach can therefore be adapted to other languages with dependency treebanks, since CCG lexical categories can be easily extracted from dependency treebanks (Cakici, 2005; Ambati et al., 2013).

The rest of the paper is arranged as follows. Section 2 gives a brief introduction to related work in the areas of CCG parsing and incremental parsing. In section 3, we describe our incremental shift-reduce parsing algorithm. Details about the experiments, evaluation metrices and analysis of the results are in section 4. We conclude with possible future directions in section 5.

## 2 Related Work

In this section, we first give a brief introduction to various available CCG parsers. Then we describe approaches towards incremental and greedy parsing.

### 2.1 CCG Parsers

There has been a significant amount of work on developing chart-based parsers for CCG. Both generative (Hockenmaier and Steedman, 2002) and discriminative (Clark et al., 2002; Clark and Curran, 2007; Auli and Lopez, 2011; Lewis and Steedman, 2014) models have been developed. As these parsers employ a bottom-up chart-parsing strategy and use normal-form CCGbank derivations which are right-branching, they are not incremental in nature. In an SVO (Subject-Verb-Object) language, these parsers first attach the object to the verb and then the subject.

Two major works in shift-reduce CCG parsing with accuracies competitive with the widely used Clark and Curran (2007) parser (C&C) are Zhang and Clark (2011) and Xu et al. (2014). Zhang and Clark (2011) used a global linear model trained discriminatively with the averaged perceptron (Collins, 2002) and beam search for their shift-reduce CCG parser. Xu et al. (2014) developed a dependency model for shift-reduce CCG parsing using a dynamic oracle technique. Unlike the chart parsers, both these parsers can produce fragmentary analyses when a complete spanning analysis is not found. Both these shift-reduce parsers are more incremental than standard chart based parsers. But, as they employ an arc-standard (Yamada and Matsumoto, 2003) shift-reduce strategy on CCG-bank, given an SVO language, these parsers are not guaranteed to attach the subject before the object.

### 2.2 Incremental Parsers

A strictly incremental parser is one which computes the relationship between words as soon as they are encountered in the input. Shift-reduce CCG parsers rely either on CCGbank derivations (Zhang and Clark, 2011) which are non-incremental, or on dependencies (Xu et al., 2014) which could be incremental in simple cases, but do not guarantee incrementality. Hassan et al. (2009) developed a semi-incremental CCG parser by transforming the English CCGbank into left branching derivation trees. The strictly incremental version performed with very low accuracy but a semi-incremental version gave a balance between incrementality and accuracy. There is also some work on incremental parsing using grammar formalisms other than CCG like phrase structure grammar (Collins and Roark, 2004) and tree substitution grammar (Sangati and Keller, 2013).

### 2.3 Greedy Parsers

There has been a significant amount of work on greedy shift-reduce dependency parsing. The Malt parser (Nivre et al., 2007) is one of the earliest parsers based on this paradigm. Goldberg and Nivre (2012) improved learning for greedy parsers by using dynamic oracles rather than a single static transition sequence as the oracle. In all the standard shift-reduce parsers, when two trees combine, only the top node (root) of each tree participates in the action. Sartorio et al. (2013) introduced a technique where in addition to the root node, nodes on the right and left periphery respectively are also available for attachment in the parsing process. A non-monotonic parsing strategy was introduced by Honnibal et al. (2013), where an action taken during the parsing process is revised based on future context.

| | | | | | | | |
|---|---|---|---|---|---|---|---|
| (1) | S | [ | $NP_{John}$ | | | | |
| (2) | S | [ | $NP_{John}$ | $(S\backslash NP)/NP_{likes}$ | | | |
| (3) | S | [ | $NP_{John}$ | $(S\backslash NP)/NP_{likes}$ | $NP_{mangoes}$ | | |
| (4) | S | [ | $NP_{John}$ | $(S\backslash NP)/NP_{likes}$ | $NP_{mangoes}$ | $(NP\backslash NP)/NP_{from}$ | |
| (5) | S | [ | $NP_{John}$ | $(S\backslash NP)/NP_{likes}$ | $NP_{mangoes}$ | $(NP\backslash NP)/NP_{from}$ | $NP_{India}$ |
| (6) | RR | [ | $NP_{John}$ | $(S\backslash NP)/NP_{likes}$ | $NP_{mangoes}$ | $NP\backslash NP_{from}$ | |
| (7) | RR | [ | $NP_{John}$ | $(S\backslash NP)/NP_{likes}$ | $NP_{mangoes}$ | | |
| (8) | RR | [ | $NP_{John}$ | $S\backslash NP_{likes}$ | | | |
| (9) | S | [ | $NP_{John}$ | $S\backslash NP_{likes}$ | $(S\backslash NP)\backslash(S\backslash NP)_{madly}$ | | |
| (10) | RR | [ | $NP_{John}$ | $S\backslash NP_{likes}$ | | | |
| (11) | RL | [ | $S_{likes}$ | | | | |

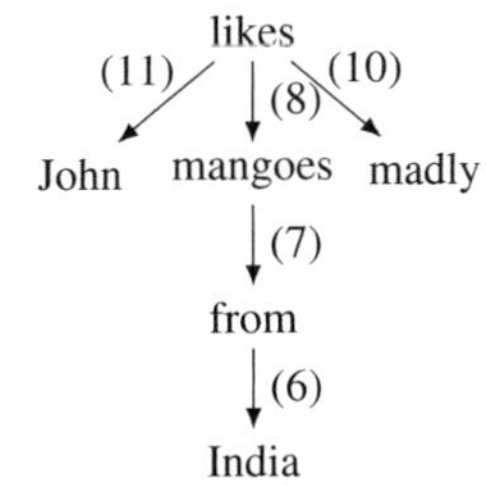


Figure 2: NonInc - Sequence of actions with parser configuration and the corresponding dependency graph.

Though the performance of these greedy parsers is less accurate than related parsers using a beam (Zhang and Nivre, 2011), greedy parsers are interesting as they are very fast and are practically useful in large-scale applications such as parsing the web and online machine translation or speech recognition. In this work, we develop a new greedy transition-based algorithm for incremental CCG parsing, which is more incremental than Zhang and Clark (2011) and Xu et al. (2014) and more accurate than Hassan et al. (2009). Our algorithm is not strictly incremental as we only produce derivations which are compatible with the Strict Competence Hypothesis (Steedman, 2000) (details in §3.2.3).

## 3 Algorithms

We first describe the Zhang and Clark (2011) style shift-reduce algorithm for CCG parsing. Then we explain our incremental algorithm based on the "revealing" technique for shift-reduce CCG parsing.

### 3.1 Non Incremental Algorithm (NonInc)

This is our baseline algorithm and is similar to Zhang and Clark (2011)'s algorithm (henceforth NonInc). It consists of an input buffer and a stack and has four major parsing actions.

- Shift - X `(S)` : Pushes a word from the input buffer to the stack and assigns a CCG category X. This action performs category disambiguation as well, as X can be any of the categories assigned by a supertagger.
- Reduce Left - X `(RL)` : Pops the top two nodes from the stack, combines them into a new node and pushes it back onto the stack with a category X. This corresponds to binary rules in the CCGbank (e.g. CCG combinators like function application, composition etc., and punctuation rules). In this action the right node is the head and hence the left node is reduced.
- Reduce Right - X `(RR)` : This action is similar to the RL (Reduce Left -X) action, except that in this action the right node is reduced since the left node is the head.
- Unary - X `(U)` : Pops the top node from the stack, converts it into a new node with category X and pushes it back on the stack. The head remains the same in this action. This action corresponds to unary rules in the CCGbank (unary type-changing and type-raising rules).

Figure 1 shows a normal-form CCG derivation for an example sentence 'John likes mangoes from India madly'. Figure 2 shows the sequence of steps using the NonInc algorithm for parsing the sentence. For simplicity and space reasons, unary productions leading to `NP` are not described. From step 1 through step 5, the first five words in the sentence (John, likes, mangoes, from, India) are shifted with corresponding categories using shift actions (S). In step 6, `(NP\NP)/NP:from` and `NP:India` are combined using the Reduce-Right (RR) action to form `NP\NP:from` which is combined with `NP:mangoes` in step 7 to form `NP:mangoes`. Step 8 combines `(S\NP)/NP:likes` with `NP:mangoes` to form `S\NP:likes` using RR action. Then the next word 'madly' is shifted in step 9, which is then combined with `S\NP:likes` in step 10. In step 11, `NP:John` and `S\NP:likes` are combined using Reduce-Left (RL) action leading to `S:likes`. The parsing process terminates at this step as there are no more tokens in the input buffer and as there is only a single node left in the stack.

| | | | | | |
|---|---|---|---|---|---|
| (1) | S | [ | $NP_{John}$ | | |
| (2) | S | [ | $NP_{John}$ | $(S\backslash NP)/NP_{likes}$ | |
| (3) | RL | [ | $S/NP_{likes}$ | | |
| (4) | S | [ | $S/NP_{likes}$ | $NP_{mangoes}$ | |
| (5) | RR | [ | $S_{likes}$ | | |
| (6) | S | [ | $S_{likes}$ | $(NP\backslash NP)/NP_{from}$ | |
| (7) | S | [ | $S_{likes}$ | $(NP\backslash NP)/NP_{from}$ | $NP_{India}$ |
| (8) | RR | [ | $S_{likes}$ | $NP\backslash NP_{from}$ | |
| (9) | RRev | [ | $S_{likes}$ | | |
| (10) | S | [ | $S_{likes}$ | $(S\backslash NP)\backslash(S\backslash NP)_{madly}$ | |
| (11) | LRev | [ | $S_{likes}$ | | |

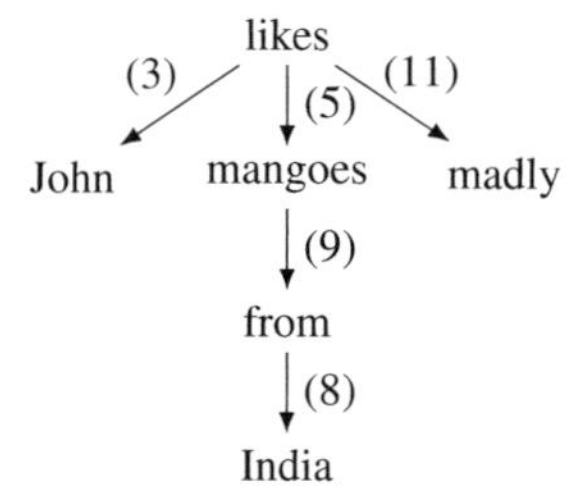


Figure 3: RevInc - Sequence of actions with parser configuration and the corresponding dependency graph.

We use indexed CCG categories (Clark et al., 2002) and obtain the CCG dependencies after every action to build the dependency graph in parallel to the CCG derivation. This is similar to Xu et al. (2014) but differs from Zhang and Clark (2011), who extract the dependencies at the end after obtaining a derivation for the entire sentence. Figure 2 also shows the dependency graph generated and the arc labels give the step ID after which the dependency is generated.

### 3.2 Revealing based Incremental Algorithm (RevInc)

The NonInc algorithm described above is not incremental because it relies purely on the mostly right-branching CCG derivation. In our example sentence, the verb (likes) combines with the subject (John) only at the end (step ID = 11) after all the remaining words in the sentence are processed, making the parse non-incremental. In this section we describe a new incremental algorithm based on a 'revealing' technique (Pareschi and Steedman, 1987) which tries to build the most incremental derivation.

#### 3.2.1 Revealing

Pareschi and Steedman (1987)'s original version of revealing was defined in terms of (implicitly higher-order) unification. It was based on the following observation. If we think of categories as terms in a logic programming language, then while we usually think of CCG combinatory rules like the following as applying with the two categories on the left $X/Y$ and $Y$ as inputs, say instantiated as $S/NP$ and $NP$, to define the category $X$ on the right as $S$, in fact instantiating *any* two of those categories defines the third.

$$X/Y \quad Y \Longrightarrow X$$

For example, if we define $X$ and $X/Y$ as $S$ and $S/NP$, we clearly define $Y$ as $NP$. They proposed to use unification-based revealing to recover unbuilt constituents in from the result of overly-greedy incremental parsing. A related second-order matching-based mechanism was used by (Kwiatkowski et al., 2010) to decompose logical forms for semantic parser induction.

The present incremental parser uses a related revealing technique confined to the right periphery. Using CCG combinators and rules like type-raising followed by forward composition, we combine nodes in the stack if there is a dependency between them. However, this can create problems for the newly shifted node as its dependent might already have been reduced. For instance, if the object 'mangoes' is reduced after it is shifted to the stack, then it won't be available for the preposition phrase (PP) 'from India' (of course, this goes for more complex NPs as well). We have to extract 'mangoes', which is hidden in the derivation, so as to make the correct attachment to the PP. This is where revealing comes into play. Mangoes is 'revealed' so that it is available to attach to the PP following it, although it has already been reduced. To handle this, in addition to the four actions of the NonInc algorithm, we introduce two new actions: Left Reveal (`LRev`) and Right Reveal (`RRev`). For this, after every action, in addition to updating the stack we also keep track of the dependencies resolved and update the dependency graph accordingly[1]. In other words, we build the dependency graph for the

[1]Xu et al. (2014) also obtain CCG dependencies after every action. But they don't have a dependency graph which is updated based on the CCG derivation and used in the CCG parsing (in our case for LRev and RRev actions).

(a) RRev (b) LRev

Figure 4: RRev and LRev actions.

sentence in parallel to the CCG derivation. As these dependencies are extracted from the CCG derivation, a node can have multiple parents and hence we construct a dependency graph rather than a tree.

- Left Reveal (LRev) : Pop the top two nodes in the stack (left, right). Identify the left node's child with a subject dependency. Abstract over this child node and split the category of left node into two categories. Combine the nodes using CCG combinators accordingly. VP modifiers like VP coordination require this action.
- Right Reveal (RRev) : Pop the top two nodes in the stack (left, right). Check the right periphery of the left node in the dependency graph, extract all the nodes with compatible CCG categories and identify all the possible nodes that the right node can combine with. Abstract over this node (e.g. object), split the category into two categories accordingly and combine the nodes using CCG combinators. Constructions like NP coordination, and PP attachment require this action.

### 3.2.2 Worked Example

Figure 3 shows the sequence of steps for the example sentence described above. In steps 1 and 2, the first two words in the sentence: 'John' and 'likes', are shifted from the input buffer to the stack. In addition to standard CCG combinators of application and composition, we also use type-raising followed by forward composition[2]. In step 3, the category of the left node 'John', NP, is type-raised to S/(S\NP) which is then combined with the category of right node 'likes', (S\NP)/NP, using forward composition operator to yield the category S/NP. This step also updates the dependency graph with an edge between 'John' and 'likes', where 'likes' is the parent and 'John' is the child. The next word 'mangoes' is shifted in step 4 and combined with S/NP:likes in step 5 using RR action yielding S:likes. After this step, the dependency graph will have 'likes' as the root, with 'John' and 'mangoes' as its children. In this way, as our algorithm tries to be more incremental, both subject and object arguments are resolved as soon as the corresponding tokens are shifted to the stack.

In steps 6 and 7, the next two words 'from' and 'India' are shifted to the stack. Step 8 combines (NP\NP)/NP:from and NP:India using RR action to form NP\NP:from. Now, we apply the RRev action in step 9 to correctly attach 'from' to 'mangoes'. In RRev we first check the right periphery and identify a possible node to be attached, 'mangoes', which is the object argument of the verb 'likes'. We abstract over this object and split the category in the following manner: If X is the category of the left node and Y\Y is the category of the right node, then X is split into X/Y and Y with corresponding heads. The head of the left node will be the head of X/Y, and the dependency graph helps in identifying the correct head for Y. Now, Y and Y\Y can be combined using the backward application rule to form Y, which can be combined with X/Y to form X back. In our example sentence, S:likes is split into S/NP:likes and NP:mangoes. NP:mangoes is combined with NP\NP:from to form NP:mangoes, which in return combines with S/NP:likes and forms back S:likes. Figure 4(a) sketches this process. This action also updates the dependency graph with a dependency between 'mangoes' and 'from'.

The next word 'madly' is shifted in step 10, after which the stack has two nodes S:likes and (S\NP)\(S\NP):madly. We apply the LRev action to combine these two nodes. We abstract over the subject of the left node, 'likes', and split the category. Here, S:likes is split into NP:John and S\NP:likes. S\NP:likes is combined with (S\NP)\(S\NP):madly to form S\NP:likes,

[2]Type-raising followed by forward composition is treated as a single step. Without this, after type-raising, the parser has to check all possible actions before applying forward composition, making it slower.

which in return combines with NP:John and forms back S:likes. The dependency graph is updated with a dependency between 'likes' and 'madly'. Note that the final output is a standard CCG tree. Figure 4(b) shows this LRev action.

#### 3.2.3 Analysis

Our incremental algorithm uses a combination of the CCG derivation and a dependency graph that helps to 'reveal' unbuilt structure in the CCG derivation by identifying heads of the revealed categories. For example in Figure-4a, in RRev action, S:likes is split into S/NP:likes and NP:mangoes. The splitting of categories is deterministic but the right periphery of the dependency graph helps in identifying the head, which is 'mangoes'. The theoretical idea of 'revealing' is from Pareschi and Steedman (1987), but they used only a toy grammar without a model or empirical results. Checking the right periphery is similar to Sartorio et al. (2013) and abstracting over the left or right argument is similar to Dalrymple et al. (1991). Currently, we abstract only over arguments. Adding a new action to abstract over the verb as well will make our algorithm handle ellipses in the sentences like 'John likes mangoes and Mary too' similar to Dalrymple et al. (1991) but we leave that for future work.

Our system is monotonic in the sense that the set of dependency relationships grows monotonically during the parsing process. Our algorithm gives derivations almost as incremental as Hassan et al. (2009) but without changing the lexical categories and without backtracking. The only change we made to the CCGbank is making the main verb the head of the auxiliary rather than the reverse as in CCGbank derivations. In the right derivational trees of CCGbank, the main verb is the head for its right side arguments and the auxiliary verb is the head for the left side arguments in the derivation. Not changing the head rule would make our algorithm use the costly reveal actions significantly more, which we avoid by changing the head direction. 3% of the total dependencies are affected by this modification.

Though our algorithm can be completely incremental, we currently compromise incrementality in the following cases:

(a) no dependency between the nodes in the stack
(b) unary type-changing and non-standard binary rules
(c) adjuncts like VP modifiers and coordinate constructions like VP, sentential coordination.

We find empirically that extending incrementality to cover these cases actually reduces parsing performance significantly. It also violates the Strict Competence Hypothesis (SCH) (Steedman, 2000), which argues on evolutionary and developmental grounds that the parser can only build constituents that are typable by the competence grammar. We explored the adjunct case of attaching only the preposition first rather than creating a complete prepositional phrase and then attaching it to correct parent. In our example sentence, this would be the case of attaching the preposition 'from' to its parent using RRev and then combining the NP 'India' accordingly as opposed to creating the preposition phrase 'from India' first and then using RRev action to attach it to the correct parent. Though the former is more incremental, it is inconsistent with the SCH. The latter analysis is consistent with strict competence and also gave better parsing performance while compromising incrementality only slightly. The empirical impact of these differing degrees of incrementality on extrinsic evaluation of our algorithm in terms of language modeling for SMT or ASR is left for future work.

Using our incremental algorithm, we converted the CCGbank derivations into a sequence of shift-reduce actions. We could convert around 98% of the derivations, which is the coverage of our algorithm, recovering around 99% dependencies. Problematic cases are mainly the ones which involve non-standard binary rules, and punctuations with lexical CCG categories other than 'conj', used as a conjunction, or ',' which is treated as a punctuation mark.

## 4 Experiments and Results

We re-implemented Zhang and Clark (2011)'s model for our experiments. We used their global linear model trained with the averaged perceptron (Collins, 2002). We applied the early-update strategy of Collins and Roark (2004) while training. In this strategy, when we don't use a beam, decoding is stopped when the predicted action is different from the gold action and weights are updated accordingly. We use the feature set of Zhang and Clark (2011) (Z&C) for the NonInc algorithm. This feature set comprises of features over the top four nodes in the stack and the next four words in the input buffer. Complete details of the feature set can be found in their paper. For our own model, RevInc, in addition to these features used for NonInc, we also provide features based on the right periphery of top node in the stack. For nodes in the right periphery, we provide uni-gram and bi-gram features based on the node's CCG category. For example, if S0 is the node on the top of the stack, B1 is the bottom most node in the right periphery, and c represent the node's CCG category, then B1c, and B1cS0c are the uni-gram and bi-gram features respectively.

Unlike Z&C, we do not use a beam for our experiments, although we use a beam of 16 for comparison of our results with their parser. The latter gives competitive results with the state-of-the-art CCG parsers. Z&C and Xu et al. (2014), use C&C's `generate` script and unification mechanism respectively to extract dependencies for evaluation. C&C's grammar doesn't cover all the lexical categories and binary rules in the CCGbank. To avoid this, we adapted Hockenmaier's scripts used for extracting dependencies from the CCGbank derivations. These are the two major divergences in our re-implementation from Z&C.

### 4.1 Data and Settings

We use standard CCGbank training (sections 02 – 21), development (section 00) and testing (section 23) splits for our experiments. All sentences in the training set are used to train NonInc. But for RevInc, we used 98% of the training set (the coverage of our algorithm). We use automatic POS-tags and lexical CCG categories assigned using the C&C POS tagger and supertagger respectively for development and test data. For training data, these tags are assigned using ten-way jackknifing. Also, for lexical CCG categories, we use a multitagger which assigns k-best supertags to a word rather than 1-best supertagging (Clark and Curran, 2004). The number of supertags assigned to a word depends on a $\beta$ parameter. Unlike Z&C, the default value of $\beta$ gave us better results rather than decreasing the value. Not using a beam could be the reason for this.

Following Z&C and Xu et al. (2014), during training, we also provide the gold CCG lexical category to the list of CCG lexical categories for a word if it is not assigned by the supertagger.

### 4.2 Connectedness and Waiting Time

Before evaluating the performance of our algorithm, we introduce two measures of incrementality: connectedness and waiting time. In a shift-reduce parser, a derivation is fully connected when all the nodes in the stack are connected leading to only one node in the stack at any point of time. We measure the average number of nodes in the stack before shifting a new token from input buffer to the stack, which we call as connectedness. For a fully connected incremental parser like Hassan et al. (2009), connectedness would be one. As our RevInc algorithm is not fully connected, this number will be greater than one. For example, in a noun phrase 'the big book', when 'the' and 'big' are in the stack, as there is no dependency between these two words, our algorithm doesn't combine these two nodes resulting in having two nodes in the stack[3]. Second column in Table 1 gives this number for both NonInc and RevInc algorithms. Though our algorithm is not fully connected, connectedness of our algorithm is significantly lower than the NonInc algorithm as our algorithm is more incremental.

| *Algorithm* | *Connectedness* | *Waiting Time* |
|---|---|---|
| NonInc | 4.62 | 2.98 |
| RevInc | **2.15** | **0.69** |

Table 1: Connectedness and waiting time.

We define waiting time as the number of nodes that need to be shifted to the stack before a dependency between any two nodes in the stack is resolved. In our example sentence, there is a dependency between 'John' and 'likes'. For NonInc, this dependency is resolved only after all the four remaining words in the sentence are shifted. In other words, it has to wait for four more words before this dependency is resolved and hence the waiting time is four. Whereas, in our RevInc algorithm, this dependency is resolved immediately, without waiting for more words to be shifted, and hence the waiting time is zero. The third column in Table 1 gives the waiting time for both the algorithms. Since we compromised incrementality in cases like coordination, waiting time for our RevInc algorithm is not zero but it is significantly lower than the

[3]This is a case where the dependencies are not true to the CCG grammar, and make our algorithm less incremental than SCH would allow.

| *Algorithm* | *UP* | *UR* | *UF* | *LP* | *LR* | *LF* | *Cat Acc.* |
|---|---|---|---|---|---|---|---|
| NonInc (beam=1) | **92.57** | 82.60 | 87.30 | **85.12** | 75.96 | 80.28 | 91.10 |
| RevInc (beam=1) | 91.62 | **85.94** | **88.69** | 83.42 | **78.25** | **80.75** | 90.87 |
| NonInc (beam=16) | 92.71 | 89.66 | 91.16 | 85.78 | 82.96 | 84.35 | 92.51 |
| Z&C (beam=16)* | - | - | - | 87.15 | 82.95 | 85.00 | 92.77 |

Table 2: Performance on the development data. *: These results are from the Z&C paper.

NonInc algorithm and hence more incremental. This property is likely to be crucial for future applications in ASR and SMT language modeling.

### 4.3 Results and Analysis

We trained the perceptron for both NonInc and RevInc algorithms using the CCGbank training data for 30 iterations, and the models which gave best results on development data are directly used for test data. Table 2 gives the unlabeled precision (UP), recall (UR), F-score (UF) and labeled precision (LP), recall (LR), F-score (LF) results of both NonInc and RevInc approaches on the development data. Last column in the table gives the category accuracy. We used the modified CCGbank for all experiments, including NonInc, for consistent comparisons. For NonInc, the modification decreased unlabeled F-score by 0.45%, without a major difference in labeled F-score.

Our incremental algorithm gives 1.39% and 0.47% improvements over the NonInc algorithm in unlabeled and labeled F-scores respectively. For both unlabeled and labeled scores, precision of RevInc is slightly lower than NonInc but the recall of RevInc is much higher than NonInc resulting in a better F-score for RevInc. As NonInc is not incremental and as it uses more context to the right while making a decision, it makes more precise actions. But, on the other hand, if a node is reduced, it is not available for future actions. This is not a problem for our RevInc algorithm which is the reason for higher recall. For example, in the example sentence, 'John likes mangoes from India madly', if the object 'mangoes' is reduced after it got shifted to the stack, then in case of NonInc, the preposition phrase 'from India' can never be attached to 'mangoes'. But, RevInc makes the correct attachment using `RRev` action. Category accuracy of NonInc is better than RevInc, since NonInc can use more context before taking a complex action and is less prone to error propagation compared to RevInc.

To compare these results in the perspective of Z&C's parser we also trained our NonInc parser with a beam size of 16 similar to Z&C. The second last row in Table 2 (NonInc (beam=16)) shows these results and the last row presents the results from their paper. Results with our implementation of Z&C are 0.65% lower than the published results, possibly due to the modification made in the head rule, and other minor differences like the supertagger beta value. Unlabeled and labeled F-scores of our RevInc parser are lower than these numbers. But, given that our RevInc parser doesn't use any beam, these margins are reasonable.

We also analyzed the label-wise scores of both NonInc and RevInc. In general, NonInc is better in precision and RevInc is better in recall. In the case of verbal arguments `((S\NP)/NP)` and verbal modifiers `((S\NP)\(S\NP))`, the F-score of RevInc is better than that of NonInc. But NonInc performed better than RevInc in the case of preposition phrase (PP) attachments `((NP\NP)/NP, (((S\NP)\(S\NP))/NP)`. More context is required for better PP attachment which is provided by the fact that NonInc has a context of several unreduced types for the model to work with, whereas RevInc has fewer. Whereas actions like `LRev` are required to correctly attach the verbal modifiers ('madly') if the subject argument ('John') of the verb ('likes') is reduced early. Table 3 gives the results of these CCG lexical categories.

| *Category* | *RevInc* | *NonInc* |
|---|---|---|
| (NP\NP)/**NP** | 81.36 | **83.21** |
| (NP**NP**)/NP | 78.66 | **82.94** |
| ((S\NP)\(S\NP))/**NP** | 65.09 | **66.98** |
| ((S\NP)\(**S\NP**))/NP | 62.69 | **65.89** |
| ((S[dcl]\NP)/**NP** | **78.96** | 78.29 |
| ((S[dcl]**NP**)/NP | **76.71** | 75.22 |
| (S\NP)\(**S\NP**) | **80.49** | 76.90 |

Table 3: Label-wise F-score of RevInc and NonInc parsers (both with beam=1). Argument slots in the relation are in bold.

| *Algorithm* | *UP* | *UR* | *UF* | *LP* | *LR* | *LF* | *Cat Acc.* |
|---|---|---|---|---|---|---|---|
| NonInc (beam=1) | **92.45** | 82.16 | 87.00 | **85.59** | 76.06 | 80.55 | 91.39 |
| RevInc (beam=1) | 91.83 | **86.35** | **89.00** | 84.02 | **79.00** | **81.43** | 91.17 |
| NonInc (beam=16) | 92.68 | 89.57 | 91.10 | 86.20 | 83.32 | 84.74 | 92.70 |
| Z&C (beam=16)* | - | - | - | 87.43 | 83.61 | 85.48 | 93.12 |
| Hassan et al. 09* | - | - | 86.31 | - | - | - | - |

Table 4: Performance on the test data. *: These results are from their paper.

We also analyzed the performance of the greedy (beam=1) NonInc and RevInc parsers in terms of parsing speed (excluding pos tagger and supertagger time). NonInc and RevInc parse 110 and 125 sentences/second respectively. Despite the complexity of the revealing actions, RevInc is faster than the NonInc. Significant amount of parsing time is spent on the feature extraction step. Features from top four nodes in the stack and their children are extracted for both the algorithms. Since the average connectedness of RevInc and NonInc are 4.62 and 2.15 respectively, on average, all four nodes in the stack are processed for NonInc and only two nodes are processed for RevInc. Because of this there is significant reduction in the feature extraction step for RevInc compared to NonInc. Also, the complex LRev and RRev actions only constituted 5% of the total actions in the parsing process.

Table 4 presents the results of our approaches on test data. Our incremental algorithm, RevInc, gives 2.0% and 0.88% improvements over NonInc in unlabeled and labeled F-scores respectively on the test data. Results of RevInc without a beam are reasonably close to the results of Z&C which uses a beam of 16. We compare our results with Incremental+Lookahead model of Hassan et al. (2009). They reported 86.31% unlabeled F-score on test data which is 2.69% lower. Note that these F-scores are not directly comparable since Hassan et al. (2009) use simplified lexicalized CCG categories. Our evaluation is based on CCG dependencies which are different from dependencies in the dependency grammar. Hence, we can't directly compare our results with dependency parsers like Zhang and Nivre (2011) and Honnibal et al. (2013).

## 5 Conclusion and Future Plan

We have designed and implemented a new incremental shift-reduce algorithm based on a version of revealing for parsing CCG (Pareschi and Steedman, 1987). On the standard CCGbank test data, our algorithm achieved improvements of 0.88% and 2.0% in labeled and unlabeled F-scores respectively over the baseline non-incremental shift-reduce algorithm. We achieved this without changing any CCG lexical categories and only changing a single head rule of making the main verb rather than the auxiliary verb the head. Our algorithm models transitions rather than incremental derivations, and hence we don't need an incremental CCGbank. Our approach can therefore be adapted to languages with dependency treebanks, since CCG lexical categories can be easily extracted from dependency treebanks (Cakici, 2005; Ambati et al., 2013). We also designed new measures of incrementality and showed that our algorithm is more incremental than the standard shift-reduce CCG parsing algorithm.

We expect to improve our current model in a number of ways. Providing information about lexical category probabilities (Auli and Lopez, 2011) assigned by the supertagger can be useful during parsing. We would like to explore the limited use of a beam to handle lexical ambiguity by only keeping analyses derived from distinct lexical categories in the beam. Following Xu et al. (2014), we also plan to explore a dynamic oracle strategy. Ultimately, we intend to evaluate the impact of our incremental parser extrinsically in terms of language modeling for SMT or ASR.

## Acknowledgments

We thank Mike Lewis, Greg Coppola, Francesco Sartorio and Siva Reddy for helpful discussions. We also thank the three anonymous reviewers for their useful suggestions. This work was supported by ERC Advanced Fellowship 249520 GRAMPLUS, EU IST Cognitive Systems IP Xperience and ARC Discovery grant DP 110102506.

## References


Bharat Ram Ambati, Tejaswini Deoskar, and Mark Steedman. 2013. Using CCG categories to improve Hindi dependency parsing. In *Proceedings of the 51st Annual Meeting of the Association for Computational Linguistics (Volume 2: Short Papers)*, pages 604–609, Sofia, Bulgaria.

Michael Auli and Adam Lopez. 2011. A Comparison of Loopy Belief Propagation and Dual Decomposition for Integrated CCG Supertagging and Parsing. In *Proceedings of the 49th Annual Meeting of the Association for Computational Linguistics: Human Language Technologies*, pages 470–480, Portland, Oregon, USA, June.

Ruken Cakici. 2005. Automatic induction of a CCG grammar for Turkish. In *Proceedings of the ACL Student Research Workshop*, pages 73–78, Ann Arbor, Michigan.

Stephen Clark and James R. Curran. 2004. The importance of supertagging for wide-coverage CCG parsing. In *Proceedings of COLING-04*, pages 282–288.

Stephen Clark and James R. Curran. 2007. Wide-coverage efficient statistical parsing with CCG and log-linear models. *Computational Linguistics*, 33.

Stephen Clark, Julia Hockenmaier, and Mark Steedman. 2002. Building Deep Dependency Structures using a Wide-Coverage CCG Parser. In *ACL*, pages 327–334.

Michael Collins and Brian Roark. 2004. Incremental Parsing with the Perceptron Algorithm. In *Proceedings of the 42nd Meeting of the Association for Computational Linguistics (ACL'04), Main Volume*, pages 111–118, Barcelona, Spain, July.

Michael Collins. 2002. Discriminative training methods for hidden Markov models: theory and experiments with perceptron algorithms. In *Proceedings of the conference on Empirical methods in natural language processing*, EMNLP '02, pages 1–8.

Mary Dalrymple, Stuart M Shieber, and Fernando CN Pereira. 1991. Ellipsis and higher-order unification. *Linguistics and philosophy*, 14(4):399–452.

Jason Eisner. 1996. Efficient Normal-Form Parsing for Combinatory Categorial Grammar. In *Proceedings of the 34th Annual Meeting of the Association for Computational Linguistics*, pages 79–86, Santa Cruz, California, USA, June.

Yoav Goldberg and Joakim Nivre. 2012. A Dynamic Oracle for Arc-Eager Dependency Parsing. In *Proceedings of COLING 2012*, pages 959–976, Mumbai, India, December.

Hany Hassan, Khalil Sima'an, and Andy Way. 2009. Lexicalized Semi-Incremental Dependency Parsing. In *Proceedings of the Recent Advances in NLP (RANLP'09)*, Borovets, Bulgaria.

Julia Hockenmaier and Mark Steedman. 2002. Generative models for statistical parsing with Combinatory Categorial Grammar. In *Proceedings of the 40th Annual Meeting on Association for Computational Linguistics*, ACL '02, pages 335–342, Philadelphia, Pennsylvania.

Julia Hockenmaier and Mark Steedman. 2007. CCGbank: A Corpus of CCG Derivations and Dependency Structures Extracted from the Penn Treebank. *Computational Linguistics*, 33(3):355–396.

Matthew Honnibal, Yoav Goldberg, and Mark Johnson. 2013. A Non-Monotonic Arc-Eager Transition System for Dependency Parsing. In *Proceedings of the Seventeenth Conference on Computational Natural Language Learning*, pages 163–172, Sofia, Bulgaria, August.

Tom Kwiatkowski, Luke Zettlemoyer, Sharon Goldwater, and Mark Steedman. 2010. Inducing probabilistic CCG grammars from logical form with higher-order unification. In *Proceedings of the 2010 Conference on Empirical Methods in Natural Language Processing*, pages 1223–1233, Cambridge, MA, October.

Mike Lewis and Mark Steedman. 2014. A* CCG Parsing with a Supertag-factored Model. In *Proceedings of the 2014 Conference on Empirical Methods in Natural Language Processing*, Doha, Qatar, October.

W. Marslen-Wilson. 1973. Linguistic structure and speech shadowing at very short latencies. *Nature.*, 244:522–533.

Joakim Nivre, Johan Hall, Jens Nilsson, Atanas Chanev, Gülsen Eryigit, Sandra Kübler, Svetoslav Marinov, and Erwin Marsi. 2007. Maltparser: A language-independent system for data-driven dependency parsing. *Natural Language Engineering*, 13(2):95–135.

Remo Pareschi and Mark Steedman. 1987. A lazy way to chart-parse with categorial grammars. In *Proceedings of the 25th Annual Meeting of the Association for Computational Linguistics*, pages 81–88, Stanford, California, USA, July.

Brian Roark. 2001. Probabilistic top-down parsing and language modeling. *Computational Linguistics*, 27:249–276.

Federico Sangati and Frank Keller. 2013. Incremental Tree Substitution Grammar for Parsing and Sentence Prediction. In *Transactions of the Association for Computational Linguistics (TACL)*.

Francesco Sartorio, Giorgio Satta, and Joakim Nivre. 2013. A Transition-Based Dependency Parser Using a Dynamic Parsing Strategy. In *Proceedings of the 51st Annual Meeting of the Association for Computational Linguistics (Volume 1: Long Papers)*, pages 135–144, Sofia, Bulgaria, August.

Mark Steedman. 2000. *The Syntactic Process*. MIT Press, Cambridge, MA, USA.

Wen Wang and Mary Harper. 2003. Language modeling using a statistical dependency grammar parser. In *Proceedings of the International Workshop on Automatic Speech Recognition and Understanding*, US Virgin Islands.

Wenduan Xu, Stephen Clark, and Yue Zhang. 2014. Shift-Reduce CCG Parsing with a Dependency Model. In *Proceedings of the 52nd Annual Meeting of the Association for Computational Linguistics (Volume 1: Long Papers)*, pages 218–227, Baltimore, Maryland, June.

Hiroyasu Yamada and Yuji Matsumoto. 2003. Statistical Dependency Analysis with Support Vector Machines. In *In Proceedings of IWPT*, pages 195–206.

Yue Zhang and Stephen Clark. 2011. Shift-Reduce CCG Parsing. In *Proceedings of the 49th Annual Meeting of the Association for Computational Linguistics: Human Language Technologies*, pages 683–692, Portland, Oregon, USA, June.

Yue Zhang and Joakim Nivre. 2011. Transition-based Dependency Parsing with Rich Non-local Features. In *Proceedings of the 49th Annual Meeting of the Association for Computational Linguistics: Human Language Technologies*, pages 188–193, Portland, Oregon, USA.

# Because Syntax Does Matter: Improving Predicate-Argument Structures Parsing with Syntactic Features

**Corentin Ribeyre**[⋆ °] **Eric Villemonte de la Clergerie**[⋆] **Djamé Seddah**[⋆ ◇]
[⋆]Alpage, INRIA
[°]Univ Paris Diderot, Sorbonne Paris Cité
[◇] Université Paris Sorbonne
firstname.lastname@inria.fr

## Abstract

Parsing full-fledged predicate-argument structures in a deep syntax framework requires graphs to be predicted. Using the DeepBank (Flickinger et al., 2012) and the Predicate-Argument Structure treebank (Miyao and Tsujii, 2005) as a test field, we show how transition-based parsers, extended to handle connected graphs, benefit from the use of topologically different syntactic features such as dependencies, tree fragments, spines or syntactic paths, bringing a much needed context to the parsing models, improving notably over long distance dependencies and elided coordinate structures. By confirming this positive impact on an accurate 2nd-order graph-based parser (Martins and Almeida, 2014), we establish a new state-of-the-art on these data sets.

## 1 Introduction

For the majority of the state-of-the-art parsers that routinely reach ninety percent performance plateau in capturing tree structures, the question of *what next* crucially arises. Indeed, it has long been thought that the bottleneck preventing the advent of accurate syntax-to-semantic interfaces lies in the quality of the preceding phase of analysis: the better the parse, the better the output. The truth is that most of the structures used to train current parsing models are degraded versions of a more informative data set: the Wall Street journal section of the Penn treebank (PTB, (Marcus et al., 1993)) which is often stripped of its richer set of annotations (*i.e.* traces and functional labels are removed), while, for reasons of efficiency and availability, projective dependency trees are often given preference over richer graph structures (Nivre and Nilsson, 2005; Sagae and Tsujii, 2008). This led to the emergence of *surface* syntax-based parsers (Charniak, 2000; Nivre, 2003; Petrov et al., 2006) whose output cannot by themselves be used to extract full-fledged predicate-argument structures. For example, control verb constructions, it-cleft structures, argument sharing in ellipsis coordination, etc. are among the phenomena requiring a graph to be properly accounted for. The dichotomy between what can usually be parsed with high accuracy and what lies in the deeper syntactic description has initiated a line of research devoted to closing the gap between surface syntax and richer structures. For most of the previous decade, the term *deep syntax* was used for rich parsing models built upon enriched versions of a constituency treebank, either with added HPSG or LFG annotation or CCG (almost) full rewrites (Miyao and Tsujii, 2005; Cahill et al., 2004; Hockenmaier, 2003). Its use now spreads by misnomer to models that provide more abstract structures, capable of generalizing classical functional labels to more semantic (in a logical view) arguments, potentially capable of neutralizing diathesis distinctions and of providing accurate predicate-argument structures. Although the building of syntax-to-semantic interface seems inextricably linked to an efficient parsing stage, inspirational works on semantic role labelling (Toutanova et al., 2005) and more recently on broad coverage semantic parsing (Du et al., 2014) that provide state-of-the-art results without relying on surface syntax, lead us to question the usefulness of syntactic parses for predicate-argument structure parsing.

In this study, we investigate the impact of syntactic features on a transition-based graph parser by testing on two treebanks. We take advantage of the recent release for the *SemEval 2014 shared task* on semantic dependency parsing, by Oepen et



*Human Language Technologies: The 2015 Annual Conference of the North American Chapter of the ACL*, pages 64–74,
Denver, Colorado, May 31 – June 5, 2015. 

al. (2014) of two semantic-based treebanks, derived from two HPSG resources, the DeepBank (DM, (Flickinger et al., 2012)) and the Enju's predicate argument structure (PAS, (Miyao and Tsujii, 2005)), to investigate the impact of syntactic features on a transition-based graph parser. Our results show that surface syntactic features significantly improve the parsing of predicate-argument structures. More specifically, we show that adding syntactic context improves the recognition of long distance dependencies and elliptical constructions. We finally discuss the usefulness of our approach, when applied on a second-order model based on dual decomposition (Martins and Almeida, 2014), showing that our use of syntactic features enhances this model accuracy and provides state-of-the-art performance.

## 2 Deep Syntax and Underspecified Semantic Corpora

**DeepBank Corpus** Semantic dependency graphs in the DM Corpus are the result of a two-step simplification of the underspecified logical-form meaning representations, based on Minimal Recursion Semantic (MRS, (Copestake et al., 1995; Copestake et al., 2005)), derived from the manually annotated DeepBank treebank (Flickinger et al., 2012). First, Oepen and Lønning (2006) define a conversion from original MRS formulae to variable-free Elementary Dependency Structures (EDS), which (a) maps each predication in the MRS logical-form meaning representation to a node in a dependency graph and (b) transforms argument relations represented by shared logical variables into directed dependency links between graph nodes. Then, in a second conversion step, the EDS graphs are further reduced into strict bi-lexical form, *i.e.* a set of directed, binary dependency relations holding exclusively between lexical units (Ivanova et al., 2012). Even though both conversion steps are, by design, lossy, DM semantic dependency graphs present a true subset of the information encoded in the full, original MRS data set.

**Predicate-Argument Structure Corpus** Enju Predicate-Argument Structures (PAS Corpus) are derived from the automatic HPSG-style annotation of the Penn Treebank (Miyao and Tsujii, 2004) that was primarily used for the development of the Enju parsing system (Miyao and Tsujii, 2005). The PAS data set is an extraction of predicate-argument structures from the Enju HPSG treebank and contains word-to-word semantic dependencies. Each dependency type is made of two elements: a coarse part-of-speech of the head predicate dependent (e.g. verb and adjective), and the argument (e.g. ARG1 and ARG2).

Although both are derived from HSPG resources (a hand-crafted grammar for DM, a treebank-based one for PAS), they differ in their core linguistic choices (functional heads vs lexical heads, coordination scheme, *etc.*) leading to different views of the predicate argument structure for the same sentence (Ivanova et al., 2012). Thus, even though both corpora may appear to contain a similar number of dependency labels, as shown in Table 1, their annotation schemes depict a deeply divergent linguistic reality exposed by two very different distributions. In DM, 9 labels account for almost 95% of all dependencies whereas a label set twice as large covers the same percentage for PAS, as shown in Table 2. Furthermore, semantically empty elements are widespread in the DeepBank (around 21.5%), compared to a low rate of 4.3% in PAS. In other words, the latter is somewhat more *dense* and consequently more syntactic. This is due to the fact that PAS integrates markers for infinitives, auxiliaries, and most punctuation marks into its graphs, whereas DM considers them as semantically void. DM corpus is clearly heading toward more semantic analysis while the PAS corpus aims at providing a more abstract deep syntax analysis than regular surface syntax trees. Both treebanks are used in their bilexical dependency formats.

| | DM Corpus | | PAS Corpus | |
|---|---|---|---|---|
| | Train | Dev | Train | Dev |
| # Sentences | 32,389 | 1,614 | 32,389 | 1,614 |
| # Tokens | 742,736 | 36,810 | 742,736 | 36,810 |
| % Void tokens | 21.63 | 21.58 | 4.30 | 4.25 |
| # Planar graphs | 18,855 | 972 | 17,477 | 953 |
| # Non planar | 13,534 | 642 | 14,912 | 661 |
| # Edges | 559,975 | 27,779 | 723,445 | 35,573 |
| % Crossing edges | 4.24 | 4.05 | 5.69 | 4.46 |
| Label set | 52 | 36 | 43 | 40 |

Table 1: DM and PAS treebank properties

| DM LABELS | % | PAS LABELS | % |
|---|---|---|---|
| ARG1 | 37.89 | adj_ARG1 | 13.46 |
| ARG2 | 23.08 | noun_ARG1 | 9.54 |
| compound | 11.01 | prep_ARG2 | 9.51 |
| BV | 10.39 | prep_ARG1 | 9.37 |
| root | 5.77 | verb_ARG2 | 9.34 |
| poss | 2.23 | verb_ARG1 | 9.23 |
| -and-c | 2.02 | det_ARG1 | 9.13 |
| loc | 1.38 | punct_ARG1 | 5.23 |
| ARG3 | 1.21 | root | 4.48 |
| *times* | *0.87* | aux-ARG2 | 3.06 |
| *mwe* | *0.85* | aux-ARG1 | 3.05 |
| *appos* | *0.72* | coord-ARG2 | 2.35 |
| *conj* | *0.57* | coord-ARG1 | 2.35 |
| *neg* | *0.47* | comp-ARG1 | 1.85 |
| *subord* | *0.43* | conj-ARG1 | 1.20 |
| *-or-c* | *0.31* | poss-ARG2 | 0.89 |
| *-but-c* | *0.20* | poss-ARG1 | 0.85 |
| **total** | **94.98** | **total** | **94.89** |

Table 2: Breakdown of Label Statistics.
*Cell values in italics not counted in the* DM *total.*

## 3 Transition-based Graphs Parsing

$$
\begin{array}{lll}
(\sigma, w_i|\beta, A) & \vdash (\sigma|w_i, \beta, A) & \text{(shift)}\\
(\sigma|w_j|w_i, \beta, A) & \vdash (\sigma|w_i, \beta, A \cup (w_i, r, w_j)) & \text{(lR)}\\
(\sigma|w_j|w_i, \beta, A) & \vdash (\sigma|w_j, \beta, A \cup (w_j, r, w_i)) & \text{(rR)}\\
(\sigma|w_j|w_i, \beta, A) & \vdash (\sigma|w_j|w_i, \beta, A \cup (w_i, r, w_j)) & \text{(lA)}\\
(\sigma|w_j|w_i, \beta, A) & \vdash (\sigma|w_j, w_i|\beta, A \cup (w_j, r, w_i)) & \text{(rA)}\\
(\sigma|w_i, \beta, A) & \vdash (\sigma, \beta, A) & \text{(pop0)}
\end{array}
$$

Figure 1: Set of transitions for dependency graphs.

Shift-reduce transition-based parsers essentially rely on *configurations* formed of a stack and a buffer, with stack transitions used to move from a configuration to the next one, until reaching a final configuration. Following Kübler et al. (2009), we define a configuration by $c = (\sigma, \beta, \mathcal{A})$ where $\sigma$ denotes a stack of words $w_i$, $\beta$ a buffer of words, and $\mathcal{A}$ a set of dependency arcs of the form $(w_i, r, w_j)$, with $w_i$ the head, $w_j$ the dependent, and $r$ a label in some set $R$. As shown in Figure 1, besides the usual *shift* and *reduce* transitions (lR & rR) of the *arc-standard* strategy, we introduced the new left and right *attach* (lA & rA) transitions for adding new dependencies (while keeping the dependent on the stack) and a *pop0* transition to remove a word from the stack after attachment of its dependents. All the transitions that add an edge must also satisfy the condition that the newly created edge does not introduce a cycle or multiple edges between the same pair of nodes. It is to be noted that the *pop0* action may also be used to remove words with no heads.

| | | |
|---|---|---|
| $\text{Word}_{\sigma_1,\sigma_2,\sigma_3}$ | $\text{Lemma}_{\sigma_1,\sigma_2,\sigma_3}$ | $\text{POS}_{\sigma_1,\sigma_2,\sigma_3}$ |
| $\text{Word}_{\beta_1,\beta_2}$ | $\text{Lemma}_{\beta_1,\beta_2}$ | $\text{POS}_{\beta_1,\beta_2,\beta_3}$ |
| $\text{leftPOS}_{\sigma_1,\sigma_2}$ | $\text{rightPOS}_{\sigma_1,\sigma_2}$ | $\text{leftLabel}_{\sigma_1,\sigma_2}$ |
| $\text{rightLabel}_{\sigma_1,\sigma_2}$ | $a$ | $d_{12}\ d'_{11}$ |

Table 3: Baseline features for the parser.
$X\sigma_i, \ldots, \sigma_j$ stands for $X\sigma_i, \ldots, X\sigma_j$.

We base our work on the the DAG parser of Sagae and Tsujii (2008) (henceforth S&T) which we extended with the set of actions displayed above (Figure 1) to cope with partially connected planar graphs, and we gave it the ability to take advantage of an extended set of features. Finally, for efficiency reasons (memory consumption and speed), we replaced the original Maxent model with an averaged structured perceptron (Freund and Schapire, 1999; Collins, 2002).

## 4 Feature Design

### 4.1 Baseline Features

We define $\text{Word}_{\beta_i}$ (resp. $\text{Lemma}_{\beta_i}$ and $\text{POS}_{\beta_i}$) as the word (resp. lemma and part-of-speech) at position $i$ in the queue. The same goes for $\sigma_i$, which is the position $i$ in the stack. Let $d_{i,j}$ be the distance between $\text{Word}_{\sigma_i}$ and $\text{Word}_{\sigma_j}$. We also define $d'_{i,j}$, the distance between $\text{Word}_{\beta_i}$ and $\text{Word}_{\sigma_j}$. In addition, we define $\text{leftPOS}_{\sigma_i}$ (resp. $\text{leftLabel}_{\sigma_i}$) the part-of-speech (resp. the label if any) of the word immediately to the left of $\sigma_i$, and the same goes for $\text{rightPOS}_{\sigma_i}$ (resp. $\text{rightLabel}_{\sigma_i}$). Finally, $a$ is the previous action predicted by the parser. Table 3 lists our baseline features. $X\sigma_i, \sigma_j, \sigma_k$ means that we use $X\sigma_i$, $X\sigma_j$, $X\sigma_k$ as unigram features as well as bigram and trigram features.

### 4.2 Syntactic Features

We combined the previous features with different types of syntactic features (constituents and dependencies), our intuition being that syntax and semantic are interdependent, and that syntactic features should therefore help predicate-argument parsing. In fact, we considered that the low density of syntactic information (compared to regular dependency treebanks) would be counterbalanced by adding more context. We considered the following pieces of information in particular.

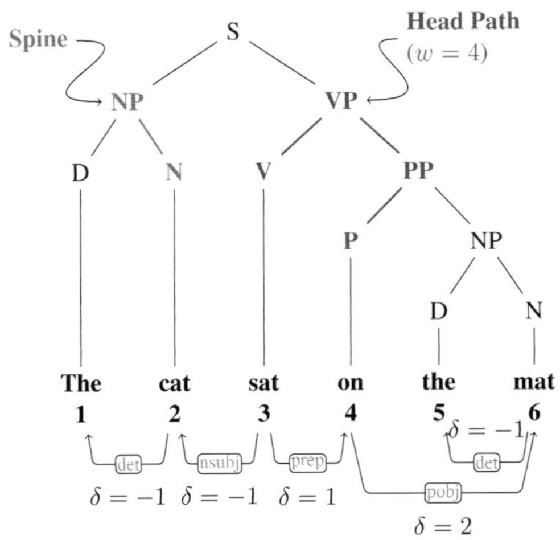


Figure 2: Schema of Syntactic Features

**Constituent Tree Fragments** These consist of fragments of syntactic trees predicted by the Petrov et al. (2006) parser in a 10-way jackknife setting. They can be used as enhanced POS or as features.

**Spinal Elementary Trees** A full set of parses was reconstructed from the tree fragments using a slightly tweaked version of the CoNLL 2009 shared task processing tools (Hajič et al., 2009). We then extracted a *spine grammar* (Seddah, 2010) using the head percolation table of the Bikel (2002) parser, slightly modified to avoid certain determiners being marked as heads in certain configurations. The resulting spines were assigned in a deterministic way (red part in Figure 2).

**Predicted MATE Dependency Labels** These consist of the dependency labels predicted by the MATE parser (Bohnet, 2010), trained on a Stanford surface dependency version of the Penn Treebank. We combined the labels with a distance $\delta = t - h$ where $t$ is the token position and $h$ the head position (brown labels and $\delta$ in Figure 2). In addition, we expanded these features with the part-of-speech of the head of a given token (HPOS). The idea is to evaluate the informativeness of more abstract syntactic features since a <LABEL,HPOS> pair can be seen as generalizing many constituent subtrees.

**Constituent Head Paths.** Inspired by Björkelund et al. (2013), we used MATE dependencies to extract the shortest path between a token and its lexical head and included the path length $w$ (in terms of traversed nodes) as a feature (blue part in Figure 2). The global idea is to use the phrase-based features to provide different kinds of syntactic context and the dependency-based features to provide generalisations over the functional label governing a token. The spines are seen as deterministic supertags, bringing a vertical context.

We report, in Table 4, the counts for each syntactic feature on each set.

| | TREE FRAG. | MATE LABELS+$\delta$ | SPINES TREES | HEAD PATHS |
|---|---|---|---|---|
| TRAIN | 648 | 1305 | 637 | 27,670 |
| DEV | 272 | 742 | 265 | 3,320 |
| TEST | 273 | 731 | 268 | 2,389 |

Table 4: Syntactic features statistics (Counts).

## 5 Experiments

**Experimental Setup** Both DM and PAS treebanks consist of texts from the PTB and which were either automatically derived from the original annotations or annotated with a hand-crafted grammar (see above). We use them in their bi-lexical dependency format, aligned at the token level as provided by Oepen et al. (2014)[1]. The following split is used: sections 00-19 for training, 20 for the dev. set and 21 for test[2]. All predicted parses are evaluated against the gold standard with *labeled precision, recall and f-measure* metrics.

**Results** Our experiments are based on the evaluation of the combinations of the 4 main types of syntactic features described in section 4: tree fragments (BKY), predicted mate dependencies (BN) and their extension with POS heads (BN(HPOS)), spinal elementary trees (SPINES) and head paths (PATHS).

The results are shown in Tables 5 and 6. All improvements from the baseline are significant with a p-value $p < 0.05$. There was no significant difference of the same p value between our two best mod-

[1]This alignment entailed the removal of all unparsed sentences.

[2]We used the same unusual split as in (Oepen et al., 2014) to be able to conduct meaningful comparisons with others.

els for each of the treebanks. [3]

As expected from the rapid overview of our datasets exposed earlier in section 2, the use of each single feature alone increases the performance over the baseline by 0.5 points for the BN feature in DM to 1.44 for PATHS, and by 1.10 for the SPINES to 1.85 for the PATHS features in PAS. Looking at the conjunction of two classes in the DM table, it seems that dependency-based features benefit from the extra context brought by constituents features, reaching an increase of 2.21 points for BKY+BN(HPOS). Interestingly, the maximum gain is brought by the addition of topologically different phrase-based features such as SPINES (+2.80, inherently vertical) or BKY (+2.76, often wider) to the previous best. Regarding PAS, similar trends can be observed, although the gains are more distributed. As opposed to DM where the conjunction of more features led to inferior results, here using a four-features class provides the second best improvement (ALL(HPOS) = BKY+BN(HPOS)+SPINES+PATHS), +2.82) while removing the SPINES slightly increases the score (+2.92). In fact, adding too many features to the model slightly degrades our scores, at least with regard to DM which has a larger label set than PAS.

Results show that syntactic information improves our parser performances. As each feature represents one unique piece of information, they benefit from being combined in order to provide more structural information.

## 6 Results Analysis

Following Mcdonald and Nivre (2007), we conducted an error analysis based on the two best models and the baseline for each corpus. As shown in section 5, syntactic features greatly improve semantic parsing. However, it is interesting to explore more precisely what kind of syntactic information boosts or penalizes our predictions. We consider, among other factors, the impact in terms of distance between the head and the dependent (edge length) and the labels. We also explore several linguistic phenomena well known to be difficult to recover.

[3]We tested the statistical significance between our best models and the baseline with the paired bootstrap test (Berg-Kirkpatrick et al., 2012).

| DM Corpus (dev. set) | LP | LR | LF | |
|---|---|---|---|---|
| BASELINE | 83.66 | 80.33 | 81.97 | |
| BN | 84.12 | 80.91 | 82.48 | +0.51 |
| BKY | 85.10 | 81.70 | 83.36 | +1.39 |
| SPINES | 84.72 | 81.31 | 82.98 | +1.01 |
| PATHS | 85.15 | 81.74 | 83.41 | +1.44 |
| BN(HPOS) | **85.63** | **82.19** | **83.88** | **+1.91** |
| BKY+SPINES | 85.41 | 81.88 | 83.61 | +1.64 |
| SPINES+PATHS | 85.49 | 82.01 | 83.71 | +1.74 |
| BKY+BN | 85.47 | 82.08 | 83.74 | +1.77 |
| BKY+PATHS | 85.70 | 82.22 | 83.92 | +1.95 |
| BN(HPOS)+SPINES | 85.94 | 82.48 | 84.17 | +2.20 |
| BKY+BN(HPOS) | 85.96 | 82.46 | 84.18 | +2.21 |
| BN(HPOS)+PATHS | 85.97 | 82.59 | 84.25 | +2.28 |
| BN+SPINES | 86.05 | 82.55 | 84.26 | +2.29 |
| BN+PATHS | **86.05** | **82.64** | **84.31** | **+2.34** |
| BKY+SPINES+PATHS | 85.64 | 82.23 | 83.90 | +1.93 |
| BKY+BN+SPINES | 85.88 | 82.50 | 84.16 | +2.19 |
| BKY+BN(HPOS)+SPINES | 86.38 | 82.81 | 84.56 | +2.59 |
| BN(HPOS)+SPINES+PATHS | 86.28 | 82.91 | 84.56 | +2.59 |
| BKY+BN(HPOS)+PATHS | 86.49 | 82.94 | 84.68 | +2.71 |
| BKY+BN+PATHS | **86.55** | **82.98** | **84.73** | +2.76 |
| BN+SPINES+PATHS | **86.59** | **83.02** | **84.77** | +2.80 |
| ALL | 85.73 | 82.27 | 83.96 | +1.99 |
| ALL(HPOS) | **86.13** | **82.64** | **84.35** | **+2.38** |

Table 5: Best results and gains on DM corpus.

| PAS Corpus (dev. set) | LP | LR | LF | |
|---|---|---|---|---|
| BASELINE | 86.95 | 83.45 | 85.17 | |
| SPINES | 88.15 | 84.47 | 86.27 | +1.10 |
| BN | 88.21 | 84.77 | 86.46 | +1.29 |
| BN(HPOS) | 88.55 | 85.00 | 86.74 | +1.57 |
| BKY | 88.63 | 84.97 | 86.76 | +1.59 |
| PATHS | **88.85** | **85.24** | **87.01** | **+1.84** |
| BKY+SPINES | 88.84 | 85.20 | 86.98 | +1.81 |
| SPINES+PATHS | 89.04 | 85.45 | 87.21 | +2.04 |
| BN(HPOS)+SPINES | 89.18 | 85.49 | 87.30 | +2.13 |
| BN(HPOS)+PATHS | 89.17 | 85.62 | 87.36 | +2.19 |
| BN+PATHS | 89.32 | 85.74 | 87.49 | +2.32 |
| BKY+PATHS | 89.44 | 85.72 | 87.54 | +2.37 |
| BKY+BN | 89.30 | 85.87 | 87.55 | +2.38 |
| BN+SPINES | 89.48 | 85.81 | 87.60 | +2.43 |
| BKY+BN(HPOS) | **89.49** | **85.80** | **87.61** | **+2.44** |
| BKY+SPINES+PATHS | 89.35 | 85.54 | 87.40 | +2.23 |
| BKY+BN+SPINES | 89.56 | 86.02 | 87.75 | +2.58 |
| BN(HPOS)+SPINES+PATHS | 89.76 | 86.15 | 87.92 | +2.75 |
| BN+SPINES+PATHS | 89.88 | 86.13 | 87.96 | +2.79 |
| BKY+BN+PATHS | 89.82 | 86.20 | 87.97 | +2.80 |
| BKY+BN(HPOS)+PATHS | **89.93** | **86.32** | **88.09** | +2.92 |
| ALL | 89.70 | 86.11 | 87.87 | +2.70 |
| ALL(HPOS) | **89.91** | **86.14** | **87.99** | +2.82 |

Table 6: Best results and gains on PAS.

### 6.1 Breakdown by Labels

In Figures 3(a) and 4(a), we detail the scores for the five most frequent labels.

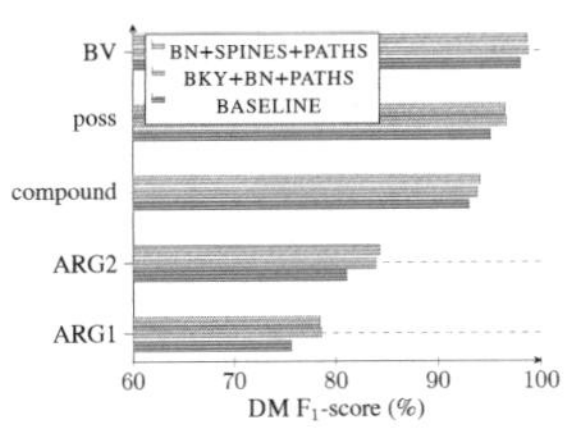


(a) Most frequent labels.

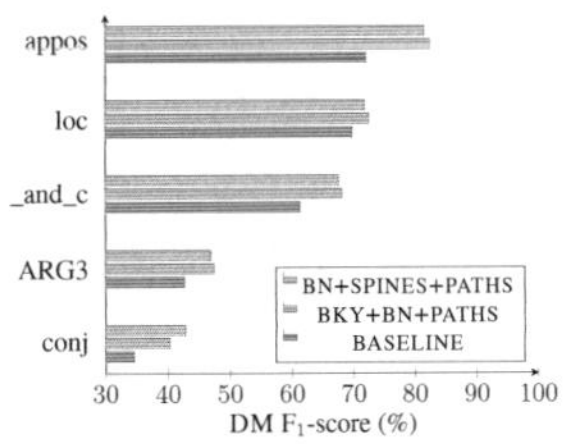


(b) Best improved labels.

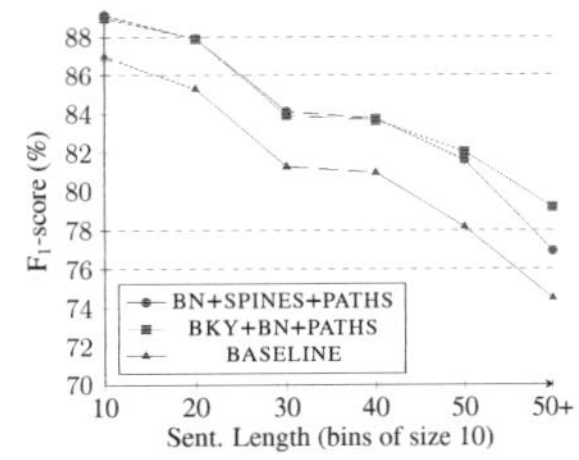


(c) Sentence length.

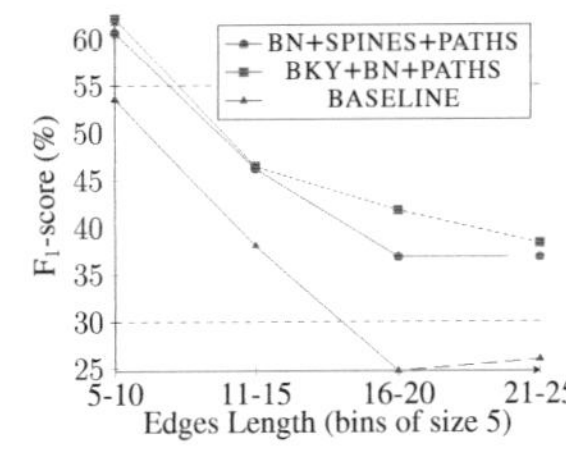


(d) Long-distance dependencies.

Figure 3: Error analysis on DM (dev. set).

As observed in the charts, the scores are higher for the most frequent labels on both corpora, especially when dealing with verbal arguments. There are also two interesting cases for DM: the predictions of *_and_c* and *ARG3* edges show an improvement by at least 5 points (Figures 3(b) & 4(b)), showing that the recovery of coordination structures and the disambiguation of less frequent or more distant arguments is achieved by adding non-local features.

### 6.2 Length Factor

Longer sentences are notoriously difficult to parse for most parsing models. Figures 3(c) and 4(c) show the $F_1$-measure of our models with respect to sentence length (in bins of size 10: 1-10, 11-20, etc.) for the DM and PAS corpora.

It is worth noting that we greatly improve the scores for longer sentences. The use of paths and of the output of a graph-based parser (Bohnet, 2010) favors the capture of complex dependencies and enhances the learning of these constructions for our local transition-based parser. However, we also observe that the features are not able to completely stop the loss of $F_1$-score for longer sentences. The slopes of the curves in the different charts show the same trend: the longer the sentence, the lower the score.

### 6.3 Linguistic Factors

We now center our analysis on long-distance dependencies (LDDs), by focusing our attention on edges length, *i.e.* the distance between two words linked by an edge. We will then concentrate on subject ellipsis, in a treatment of LDDs more similar to the linguistic definition of Cahill et al. (2004).

**Long-distance Dependencies (LDDs)** For many systems, LDDs are difficult to recover because they are generally under-represented in the training corpus and the constructions involved in LDDs often require deep linguistic knowledge to be recovered. In Figure 7, we report the distribution of long-distance dependencies by bins of size 5 up to 40. They only account for 15% of all the dependencies in both corpora. The longest dependencies consist of the first and second arguments of the verb as well as coordination links. In the case of elided coordination structures, we have long-distance dependencies when two coordinated verbs share the same first or second argument, which explains the distribution of lengths.

| BINS | 5-10 | 11-15 | 16-20 | 21-25 | 26-40 |
|---|---|---|---|---|---|
| DM | 2907 | 734 | 329 | 141 | 92 |
| PAS | 3705 | 1007 | 408 | 175 | 127 |

Table 7: Number of LDDs edges (dev. set).

As outlined in Figures 3(d) and 4(d), we can see that without structural information such as spines, surfacic dependencies or paths, the longest dependencies have low $F_1$-scores. When using these features, our models tend to perform better, with a gain of up to 25 points for high-dependency lengths (bins between 16-20 and 21-25).

In Table 8, we show the global improvement when considering edge lengths between 5 and 40. For both corpora, the improvement is the same (around 9 points), showing that structural information is the key to better predictions. Looking into this improvement more closely, we found that PATHS combined with BN tend to be crucial, whereas SPINES

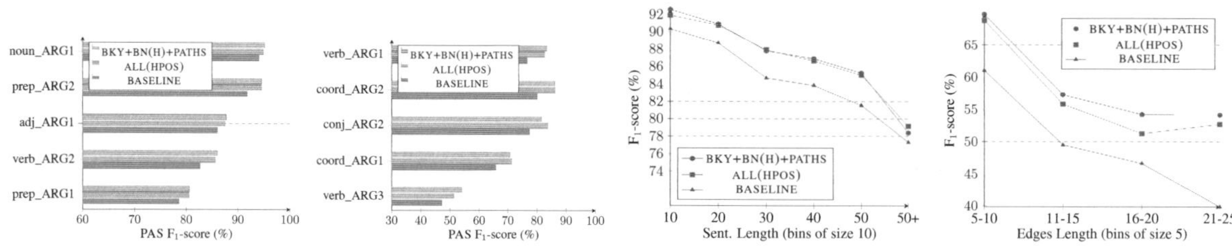


(a) Most frequent labels. (b) Best improved labels. (c) Sentence length. (d) Long-distance dependencies.

Figure 4: Error analysis on PAS (dev. set).
BKY+BN(H)+PATHS stands for BKY+BN(HPOS)+PATHS.

may sometimes penalize the models. Even though, BN+SPINES+PATHS is the best model for DM, a spine is only a *partial projection* which lacks attachment information. Spines alone only therefore provide a local context and are unable to cope well with LDDs.

**Coordination Structures** We now focus on structures with subject ellipsis. We extracted them by using a simple graph pattern, *i.e.* two verbs with a shared *ARG1* and a coordination dependency.

Our best models' scores are displayed in Tables 9. Once again, our models improve the $F_1$ score, but not in the same proportion. DM considers the conjunction as a semantically empty word and attaches an edge *_and_c* between the two verbs to mark the coordination. Consequently this edge is more difficult to predict, because it is less informative, our baseline model relying on tokens, lemmas and POS.

We note that the difference in the number of evaluated dependencies in both corpora comes from an annotation scheme divergence between PAS and DM regarding subject ellipsis. DM opts for coordinate structures with a chain of dependencies rooted at the first conjunct, the coordinating conjunctions being therefore semantically empty. In PAS, the final coordinating conjunction and each coordinating conjunction is a two-place predicate, taking left and right conjuncts as its arguments.

The gain of 6.30 points for DM (Table 9(a), resp. +3 for PAS) indicates that, when an annotation scheme is designed to have many semantically empty words, using syntactic information tends to enhance the parser accuracy. This gives a clear insight into what type of information is required to parse semantic graphs: the greater the distance between the head and the dependent, the larger the context needed to disambiguate the attachments.

### 6.4 Ruling out the Structural Factor Bias

It may argued that the improvement we noticed could stem from a potentially strong overlap between surface trees and predicate-argument structures, both in terms of edges and labels. In fact, the conversion from surfacic parses into predicate-argument structures requires a large amount of edges relabeling (for instance, when *nsubj* is relabeled to *ARG1*).

| | PAS | DM |
|---|---|---|
| Overlap | +2.87 | +2.67 |
| Rest | +2.70 | +2.74 |

We tested this hypothesis by computing the number of common edges between MATE predictions and DM and PAS. The overlap corresponds to about 22% of all edges in PAS and 27% in DM. Although important, it does not represent the majority of dependencies in our corpora, because most of edges are not present in surface predictions. We evaluated the improvement of the overlap as well as for the rest. Results show that our best models perform roughly the same on both sets. Interestingly, as opposed to PAS's model, DM's model performs better on the non-overlap part. This suggests that the use of PTB-based features is somehow not optimal when applied on a none PTB-based treebank, such as DM which comes from a handcrafted grammar.

## 7 Discussion

Our point was to prove that providing more syntactic context, in the form of phrased-based tree fragments and surface dependencies, helps transition-

| | LP | LR | LF | |
|---|---|---|---|---|
| BASELINE | 54.95 | 42.53 | 47.95 | |
| BN+SPINES+PATHS | 64.23 | 50.55 | 56.57 | +8.62 |
| BKY+BN+PATHS | 64.88 | 50.90 | 57.05 | **+9.10** |

(a) DM Corpus (dev. set).

| | LP | LR | LF | |
|---|---|---|---|---|
| BASELINE | 66.62 | 50.17 | 57.23 | |
| ALL(HPOS) | 74.03 | 57.58 | 64.78 | +7.55 |
| BKY+BN(HPOS)+PATHS | 74.62 | 58.95 | 65.86 | **+8.73** |

(b) PAS Corpus (dev. set).

Table 8: Long-distance dependencies eval. (dev sets).

| | LP | LR | LF | |
|---|---|---|---|---|
| BASELINE | 90.00 | 48.57 | 63.09 | |
| BN+SPINES+PATHS | 96.02 | 53.65 | 68.84 | +5.85 |
| BKY+BN+PATHS | 96.07 | 54.29 | 69.37 | **+6.28** |

(a) on DM (dev. set, 315 dependencies).

| | LP | LR | LF | |
|---|---|---|---|---|
| BASELINE | 97.51 | 61.48 | 75.41 | |
| ALL(HPOS) | 97.86 | 64.78 | 77.96 | +2.55 |
| BKY+BN(HPOS)+PATHS | 98.57 | 65.09 | 78.41 | **+3.00** |

(b) on PAS (dev. set, 636 dependencies).

Table 9: Shared subjects coordinations eval. (dev sets).

based parsers to predict predicate-argument structures, especially for LDDs. Yet, compared to state-of-the-art systems, our results built on the S&T parser score lower than the top performers (Table 10).
However, we are currently extending a more advanced lattice-aware transition-based parser (DSR) with beams (Villemonte De La Clergerie, 2013) that takes advantage of cutting-edge techniques (dynamic programming, averaged perceptron with early updates, *etc.* following (Goldberg et al., 2013; Huang et al., 2012)) [4], which proves effective by reaching the state-of-the-art on PAS, outperforming Thomson et al. (2014) and second to the model of Martins and Almeida (2014). [5]

The point here is that using the same syntactic features as our base system exhibits the same improvement over a now much stronger baseline. We can conjecture that the ambiguities added by the relative scarcity of the deep annotations is efficiently handled by a more complete exploration of the search space, made possible by beam optimization.

We can also wonder whether the lower improvement brought to DM parsing by the PTB-based syntactic features does not come from the fact that the DM corpus and the PTB have divergent annotation schemes. In that aspect, PTB syntactic features may add some noise to the learning process, because they give more weight to conflicting decisions that led to correct structures in one but not in the other scheme.

By using features which, to a certain extent, (i) extend the domain of locality available at a given node and (ii) generalize some structural and functional contexts otherwise unavailable, we tried to overcome the main issue of transition-based parsers: they remain local in the sense that they lack a global view of the whole sentence.

**Impact Beyond Transition-based Parser** Of course, it can be argued that improving over a somewhat weak baseline is of limited interest. Our point was to investigate how the direct parsing of relatively sparse graph structures would benefit from the inclusion of more context via the use of topologically different syntactic pieces of information. However in that work, we mostly focused on transition based-parsing, which raises the question of the impact of our feature-set on a much more powerful and state-of-the-art model such as the TURBOSEMANTICPARSER developed by Martins and Almeida (2014).

To this end, we extended the T.PARSER so that it could cope with our syntactic features and studied the interaction of our best feature set with second order features (*i.e.* grand-parents and co-parents). Results in Table 11 show that the gain brought by adding syntactic features (+2.14 on DM over the baseline) is higher than the sole use of second order ones (+1.09). Furthermore, the gain brought by

[4] It uses a different set of transitions, notably *pop* actions instead of *left* and *right reduce*, and a *swap* that allow limited amount of non-planarity. Such a set raises issues with beams (several paths leading to a same item, final items reached with paths of various lengths, ...), overcome by adding a 'noop' action only applied on final items to balance path lengths.

[5] Leaving aside the multiple (19) ensemble models of Du et al. (2014), because of the impracticability of the approach.

| | PAS | DM |
|---|---|---|
| (T.PARSER+features, this paper) | 92.11 | 89.70 |
| (Du et al., 2014) | 92.04 | 89.40 |
| (Martins and Almeida, 2014) | 91.76 | 89.16 |
| (DSR, this paper) | 90.13 | 85.66 |
| (Thomson et al., 2014) | 89.63 | 83.97 |
| (S&T, this paper) | 87.5 | 83.84 |
| (DSR, this paper, no feat) | 87.02 | 83.91 |
| (S&T, this paper, no feat) | 84.18 | 81.17 |

Table 10: Comparison with the State-of-the-Art.

the second-order features is reduced by half when used jointly with our feature set (+1.09 vs +0.57 with them). However, although we could assess that the need of second order models is thus alleviated, the conjunction of both types of features still improves the parser performance by an overall gain of 1.62 points on DM (1.18 on PAS), suggesting that both feature sets contribute to different types of "structures". In short, the use of syntactic features is also relevant with a strong baseline, as they provide a global view to graph-based models, establishing a new state-of-the-art on these corpora.

| | -SYNT. FEAT. | +SYNT. FEAT. | $\delta$ |
|---|---|---|---|
| DM, baseline | 86.99 | 89.13 | *+2.14* |
| +grandparent | 87.66 | 89.43 | *+1.77* |
| +co-parents | 88.08 | 89.7 | **+1.62** |
| PAS, baseline | 89.73 | 91.68 | *+1.95* |
| +grandparent | 90.15 | 91.92 | *+1.77* |
| +co-parents | 90.93 | 92.11 | **+1.18** |

Table 11: LF Results for T.PARSER (test set).
*Baseline = arc-factored + siblings*

**Related Work** A growing interest for semantic parsing has emerged over the past few years, with the availability of resources such as PropBank and NomBank (Palmer et al., 2005; Meyers et al., 2004) built on top of the Penn Treebank. The shallow semantic annotations they provide were among the targets of successful shared tasks on semantic role labeling (Surdeanu et al., 2008; Carreras and Màrquez, 2005). Actually, the conjoint use of such annotations with surface syntax dependencies bears some resemblance with predicate-argument structure parsing like we presented here. However, they diverge in that Propbank/Nombank annotations do not form connected graphs by themselves, as they only cover argument identification and nominal predicates. The range of phenomena they describe is also limited, compared to a full predicate-argument analysis as provided by DM and PAS (Oepen et al., 2014). More importantly, as pointed out by Yi et al. (2007), being verb-specific, Propbank's roles do not generalize well beyond the ARG0 argument (i.e. the subject/agent role) leading to inconsistencies.
However, the advent of such semantic-based resources have ignited a fruitful line of research, of which the use of heterogeneous sources of information to boost parsing performance has been investigated over the past decade (Chen and Rambow, 2003; Tsuruoka et al., 2004) with a strong regain of interest raised by the work of Moschitti et al. (2008), Henderson et al. (2008), Sagae (2009).

## 8 Conclusion

We described the use and combination of several kinds of syntactic features to improve predicate-argument parsing. To do so, we tested our approach of injecting surface-syntax features by thoroughly evaluating their impact on one transition-based graph parser, then validating on two more efficient parsers, over two deep syntax and semantic treebanks. Results of the syntax-enhanced *semantic* parsers exhibit a constant improvement, regardless of the annotation scheme and the parser used.
The question is now to establish whether will this be verified in other semantic data sets? From the parsing of deep syntax treebanks *a la* Meaning Text Theory (Ballesteros et al., 2014), to Framenet semantic parsing (Das et al., 2014) or data-driven approaches closer to ours (Flanigan et al., 2014), it is difficult to know which models will predominate from this bubbling field and what kind of semantic data sets will benefit the most from syntax.

## Acknowledgements

We would like to thank Kenji Sagae and André F. T. Martins for making their parsers available and for kindly answering our questions. We also thank our anonymous reviewers for their comments. This work was partly funded by the Program "Investissements d'avenir" managed by Agence Nationale de la Recherche ANR-10-LABX-0083 (Labex EFL).

## References


Miguel Ballesteros, Bernd Bohnet, Simon Mille, and Leo Wanner. 2014. Deep-syntactic parsing. In *In Proc. of COLING*, Dublin, Ireland.

Taylor Berg-Kirkpatrick, David Burkett, and Dan Klein. 2012. An Empirical Investigation of Statistical Significance in NLP. In *Proc. of the 2012 Joint Conference on Empirical Methods in Natural Language Processing and Computational Natural Language Learning*, pages 995–1005.

Daniel M. Bikel. 2002. Design of a multi-lingual, parallel-processing statistical parsing engine. In *Proc. of the second international conference on Human Language Technology Research*, pages 178–182. Morgan Kaufmann Publishers Inc. San Francisco, CA, USA.

Anders Björkelund, Ozlem Cetinoglu, Richárd Farkas, Thomas Mueller, and Wolfgang Seeker. 2013. (re)ranking meets morphosyntax: State-of-the-art results from the SPMRL 2013 shared task. In *Proc. of the Fourth Workshop on Statistical Parsing of Morphologically-Rich Languages*, pages 135–145, October.

Bernd Bohnet. 2010. Very high accuracy and fast dependency parsing is not a contradiction. In *Proc. of the 23rd International Conference on Computational Linguistics*, pages 89–97.

Aoife Cahill, Michael Burke, Ruth O'Donovan, Josef van Genabith, and Andy Way. 2004. Long-Distance Dependency Resolution in Automatically Acquired Wide-Coverage PCFG-Based LFG Approximations. In *Proc. of ACL*, pages 320–327.

Xavier Carreras and Lluís Màrquez. 2005. Introduction to the conll-2005 shared task: Semantic role labeling. In *Proc. of the Ninth Conference on Computational Natural Language Learning*, pages 152–164.

Eugene Charniak. 2000. A maximum-entropy-inspired parser. In *Proc. of the 1st Annual Meeting of the North American Chapter of the ACL (NAACL)*, Seattle.

John Chen and Owen Rambow. 2003. Use of deep linguistic features for the recognition and labeling of semantic arguments. In *Proc. of the 2003 conference on Empirical methods in natural language processing*, pages 41–48. Association for Computational Linguistics.

Michael Collins. 2002. Discriminative training methods for hidden markov models: Theory and experiments with perceptron algorithms. In *Proc. of the ACL-02 Conference on Empirical Methods in Natural Language Processing - Volume 10*, pages 1–8.

Ann Copestake, Dan Flickinger, Rob Malouf, Susanne Riehemann, and Ivan Sag. 1995. Translation using minimal recursion semantics. In *Proc. of the Sixth International Conference on Theoretical and Methodological Issues in Machine Translation*, pages 15–32. Citeseer.

Ann Copestake, Dan Flickinger, Carl Pollard, and Ivan A Sag. 2005. Minimal recursion semantics: An introduction. *Research on Language and Computation*, 3(2-3):281–332.

Dipanjan Das, Desai Chen, André FT Martins, Nathan Schneider, and Noah A Smith. 2014. Frame-semantic parsing. *Computational Linguistics*, 40(1):9–56.

Yantao Du, Fan Zhang, Weiwei Sun, and Xiaojun Wan. 2014. Peking: Profiling syntactic tree parsing techniques for semantic graph parsing. In *Proc. of the 8th International Workshop on Semantic Evaluation*, pages 459–464.

Jeffrey Flanigan, Sam Thomson, Jaime Carbonell, Chris Dyer, and Noah A. Smith. 2014. A discriminative graph-based parser for the abstract meaning representation. In *in Proc. of ACL*, Baltimore, US.

Daniel Flickinger, Yi Zhang, and Valia Kordoni. 2012. DeepBank: a dynamically annotated treebank of the wall street journal. In *Proc. of the Eleventh International Workshop on Treebanks and Linguistic Theories*, pages 85–96.

Yoav Freund and Robert E. Schapire. 1999. Large margin classification using the perceptron algorithm. *Machine learning*, 37(3):277–296.

Yoav Goldberg, Kai Zhao, and Liang Huang. 2013. Efficient implementation of beam-search incremental parsers. In *Proc. of the 51st Annual Meeting of the Association for Computational Linguistics (ACL)*, Sophia, Bulgaria.

Jan Hajič, Massimiliano Ciaramita, Richard Johansson, Daisuke Kawahara, Maria Antònia Martí, Lluís Màrquez, Adam Meyers, Joakim Nivre, Sebastian Padó, Jan Štěpánek, et al. 2009. The conll-2009 shared task: Syntactic and semantic dependencies in multiple languages. In *Proc. of the Thirteenth Conference on Computational Natural Language Learning: Shared Task*, pages 1–18.

James Henderson, Paola Merlo, Gabriele Musillo, and Ivan Titov. 2008. A latent variable model of synchronous parsing for syntactic and semantic dependencies. In *Proc. of the Twelfth Conference on Computational Natural Language Learning*, pages 178–182.

Julia Hockenmaier. 2003. *Data and models for statistical parsing with Combinatory Categorial Grammar*. Ph.D. thesis.

Liang Huang, Suphan Fayong, and Yang Guo. 2012. Structured perceptron with inexact search. In *Proc. of HLT-NAACL 2012*, pages 142–151.

Angelina Ivanova, Stephan Oepen, Lilja Øvrelid, and Dan Flickinger. 2012. Who did what to whom?: A contrastive study of syntacto-semantic dependencies. In *Proc. of the sixth linguistic annotation workshop*, pages 2–11.

Sandra Kübler, Ryan McDonald, and Joakim Nivre. 2009. *Dependency Parsing*. Morgan and Claypool Publishers.

Mitchell Marcus, Beatrice Santorini, and Mary Ann Marcinkiewicz. 1993. Building a large annotated corpus of English: The Penn Treebank. *Computational Linguistics*, 19(2):313–330.

T. André F. Martins and C. Mariana S. Almeida. 2014. Priberam: A turbo semantic parser with second order features. In *Proc. of the 8th International Workshop on Semantic Evaluation*, pages 471–476.

Ryan Mcdonald and Joakim Nivre. 2007. Characterizing the errors of data-driven dependency parsing models. In *Proc. of the Conference on Empirical Methods in Natural Language Processing and Natural Language Learning*.

Adam Meyers, Ruth Reeves, Catherine Macleod, Rachel Szekely, Veronika Zielinska, Brian Young, and Ralph Grishman. 2004. Annotating noun argument structure for nombank. In *LREC*, volume 4, pages 803–806.

Yusuke Miyao and Jun'ichi Tsujii. 2004. Deep Linguistic Analysis for the Accurate Identification of Predicate-Argument Relations. In *Proc. of the 18th International Conference on Computational Linguistics*, pages 1392–1397, Geneva, Switzerland.

Yusuke Miyao and Jun'ichi Tsujii. 2005. Probabilistic disambiguation models for wide-coverage HPSG parsing. In *Proc. of ACL 2005*, pages 83–90.

Alessandro Moschitti, Daniele Pighin, and Roberto Basili. 2008. Tree kernels for semantic role labeling. *Computational Linguistics*, 34(2):193–224.

Joakim Nivre and Jens Nilsson. 2005. Pseudo-projective dependency parsing. In *Proc. of the 43rd Annual Meeting on Association for Computational Linguistics*, pages 99–106. Association for Computational Linguistics.

Joakim Nivre. 2003. An efficient algorithm for projective dependency parsing. In *Proc. of the 8th International Workshop on Parsing Technologies (IWPT*. Citeseer.

Stephan Oepen and Jan Tore Lønning. 2006. Discriminant-based mrs banking. In *Proc. of the 5th international conference on language resources and evaluation (lrec 2006)*.

Stephan Oepen, Marco Kuhlmann, Yusuke Miyao, Daniel Zeman, Dan Flickinger, Jan Hajic, Angelina Ivanova, and Yi Zhang. 2014. Semeval 2014 task 8: Broad-coverage semantic dependency parsing. In *Proc. of the 8th International Workshop on Semantic Evaluation*, pages 63–72.

Martha Palmer, Daniel Gildea, and Paul Kingsbury. 2005. The proposition bank: An annotated corpus of semantic roles. *Computational Linguistics*, 31(1):71–106.

Slav Petrov, Leon Barrett, Romain Thibaux, and Dan Klein. 2006. Learning accurate, compact, and interpretable tree annotation. In *Proc. of the 21st International Conference on Computational Linguistics and 44th Annual Meeting of the Association for Computational Linguistics*.

Kenji Sagae and Jun'ichi Tsujii. 2008. Shift-reduce dependency DAG parsing. In *Proc. of the 22nd International Conference on Computational Linguistics (Coling 2008)*, pages 753–760.

Kenji Sagae. 2009. Analysis of discourse structure with syntactic dependencies and data-driven shift-reduce parsing. In *Proc. of the 11th International Conference on Parsing Technologies*, pages 81–84. Association for Computational Linguistics.

Djamé Seddah. 2010. Exploring the spinal-stig model for parsing french. In *Proc. of the Seventh conference on International Language Resources and Evaluation (LREC'10)*.

Mihai Surdeanu, Richard Johansson, Adam Meyers, Lluís Màrquez, and Joakim Nivre. 2008. The conll-2008 shared task on joint parsing of syntactic and semantic dependencies. In *Proc. of the Twelfth Conference on Computational Natural Language Learning*, pages 159–177. Association for Computational Linguistics.

Sam Thomson, Brendan O'Connor, Jeffrey Flanigan, David Bamman, Jesse Dodge, Swabha Swayamdipta, Nathan Schneider, Chris Dyer, and A. Noah Smith. 2014. CMU: Arc-Factored, Discriminative Semantic Dependency Parsing. In *Proc. of the 8th International Workshop on Semantic Evaluation*, pages 176–180.

Kristina Toutanova, Aria Haghighi, and Christopher D Manning. 2005. Joint learning improves semantic role labeling. In *Proc. of the 43rd Annual Meeting on Association for Computational Linguistics*, pages 589–596.

Yoshimasa Tsuruoka, Yusuke Miyao, and Jun'ichi Tsujii. 2004. Towards efficient probabilistic hpsg parsing: integrating semantic and syntactic preference to guide the parsing. In *Proc. of the IJCNLP-04 Workshop on Beyond Shallow Analyses*. Citeseer.

Éric Villemonte De La Clergerie. 2013. Exploring beam-based shift-reduce dependency parsing with DyALog: Results from the SPMRL 2013 shared task. In *4th Workshop on Statistical Parsing of Morphologically Rich Languages (SPMRL'2013)*.

Szu-Ting Yi, Edward Loper, and Martha Palmer. 2007. Can semantic roles generalize across genres? In *HLT-NAACL*, pages 548–555.

# A Hybrid Generative/Discriminative Approach To Citation Prediction

**Chris Tanner**
Brown University
Providence, RI
christanner@cs.brown.edu

**Eugene Charniak**
Brown University
Providence, RI
ec@cs.brown.edu

## Abstract

Text documents of varying nature (e.g., summary documents written by analysts or published, scientific papers) often cite others as a means of providing evidence to support a claim, attributing credit, or referring the reader to related work. We address the problem of predicting a document's cited sources by introducing a novel, discriminative approach which combines a content-based generative model (LDA) with author-based features. Further, our classifier is able to learn the importance and quality of each topic within our corpus – which can be useful beyond this task – and preliminary results suggest its metric is competitive with other standard metrics (Topic Coherence). Our flagship system, *Logit-Expanded,* provides state-of-the-art performance on the largest corpus ever used for this task.

## 1 Introduction

The amount of digital documents (both online and offline) continues to grow greatly for several reasons, including the eagerness of users to generate content (e.g., social media, Web 2.0) and the decrease in digital storage costs. Many different types of documents link to or cite other documents (e.g., websites, analyst summary reports, academic research papers), and they do so for various reasons: to provide evidence, attribute credit, refer the reader to related work, etc. Given the plethora of documents, it can be highly useful to have a system which can automatically predict relevant citations, for this could (1) aid authors in citing relevant, useful sources which they may otherwise not know about; and (2) aid readers in finding useful documents which otherwise might not have been discovered, due to the documents' being unpopular or poorly cited by many authors. Specifically, we are interested in *citation prediction* – that is, we aim to predict which *sources* each report document cites. We define a *report* as any document that cites another document in our corpus, and a *source* as a document that is cited by at least one report. Naturally, many documents within a corpus can be both a report and a source. Note, we occasionally refer to *linking* a report and source, which is synonymous with saying the report cites the source.

*Citation prediction* can be viewed as a special case of the more general, heavily-researched area of *link prediction.* In fact, past research mentioned in Section 2 refers to this exact task as both *citation prediction* and *link prediction*. However, *link prediction* is a commonly used phrase which may be used to describe other problems not concerning documents and citation prediction. In these general cases, a link may be relatively abstract and represent any particular relationship between other objects (such as users' interests or interactions). Traditionally, popular techniques for link prediction and recommendation systems have included feature-based classification, matrix factorization, and other collaborative filtering approaches – all of which typically use meta-data features (e.g., names and interests) as opposed to modelling complete content such as full text documents (Sarwar et al., 2001; Al Hasan and Zaki, 2011). However, starting with Hofmann and Cohn's (2001) seminal work on ci-



*Human Language Technologies: The 2015 Annual Conference of the North American Chapter of the ACL*, pages 75–83,
Denver, Colorado, May 31 – June 5, 2015. 

tation prediction (PHITS), along with Erosheva et. al.'s (2004) work (LinkLDA), content-based modelling approaches have extensively used generative models – while largely ignoring meta-data features which collaborative filtering approaches often use – thus creating somewhat of a dichotomy between two approaches towards the same problem. We demonstrate that combining (1) a simple, yet effective, generative approach to modelling content with (2) author-based features into a discriminative classifier can improve performance. We show state-of-the-art performance on the largest corpus for this task. Finally, our classifier learns the importance of each topic within our corpus, which can be useful beyond this task.

In the next section, we describe related research. In Section 3 we describe our models and motivations for them. In Section 4 we detail our experiments, including data and results, and compare our work to the current state-of-the-art system. We finally conclude in Section 5.

## 2 Related Work

Hofmann and Cohn's (2001) *PHITS* seminal work on citation prediction included a system that was based on probabilistic latent semantic analysis (PLSA) (Hofmann, 1999). Specifically, they extended PLSA by representing each distinct link to a document as a separate word token – as shown in Equation 1 and represented by $s_l$. (Note: Table 1 displays common notation that is used consistently throughout this paper.) PHITS assumes both the links and words are generated from the same global topic distributions, and like PLSA, a topic distribution is inferred for each document in the corpus.

$$P(w_i|d_j) = \sum_{k=1}^{K} P(w_i|z_k)P(z_k|d_j),$$
$$P(s_l|d_j) = \sum_{k=1}^{K} P(s_l|z_k)P(z_k|d_j) \quad (1)$$

Later, Erosheva et. al.'s (2004) system replaced PLSA with LDA as the fundamental generative process; thus, the topic distributions were assumed to be sampled from a Dirichlet prior, as depicted in the plate notation of Figure 1. We will refer to this model as it is commonly referred, *LinkLDA*, and it

| | |
|---|---|
| M | total # documents in the corpus (both reports and sources) |
| N | # of words in the particular document |
| r | a report document |
| s | a source document |
| d | a document (report and/or source) |
| w | a word in a document |
| K | total # of topics |
| $z$ | a particular topic |
| V | corpus' vocabulary size |
| $\alpha, \beta$ | concentration parameters to corpus-wide Dirichlet priors |
| $\triangle(p)$ | a simplex of dimension (p-1) |
| $L$ | number of citations in a particular document |
| $\Omega_{kd'}$ | probability of a link to document $d'$ w.r.t. topic $k$ |
| $s_l$ | a token representing a link to source $s$ |

Table 1: Notation Guide

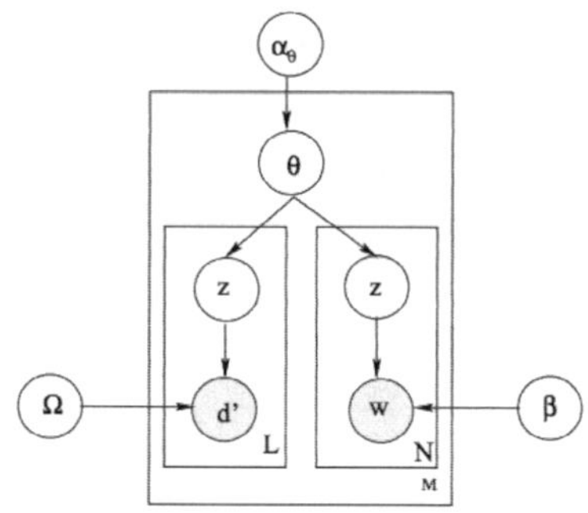


Figure 1: Plate notation of LinkLDA

is the closest model to our baseline approach (later introduced as *LDA-Bayes*).

Others have researched several variants of this LDA-inspired approach, paving the field with promising, generative models. For example, Link-PLSA-LDA is the same as LinkLDA but it treats the generation of the source documents as a separate process inferred by PLSA (Nallapati et al., 2008). Related, Cite-LDA and Cite-PLSA-LDA (Kataria et al., 2010) extend LinkLDA and Link-PLSA-LDA, respectively, by asserting that the existence of a link between a report and source is influenced by the context of where the citation link occurs within the report document. Note, the authors supplemented corpora to include context that surrounds each citation; however, there is currently no freely-available, widely-used corpus which allows one to discern *where* citations appear within each report. Therefore, few systems rely on citation context.

*TopicBlock* (Ho et al., 2012) models citation prediction with a hierarchical topic model but only uses the first 200 words of each document's abstract. To our knowledge, *Topic-Link-LDA* (Liu et al., 2009) is the only research which includes both author information and document content into a generative model in order to predict citations. *Topic-Link-LDA* estimates the probability of linking a report-source pair according to the similarity between the documents' (1) author communities and (2) topic distributions – these two latent groups are linearly combined and weighted, and like the aforementioned systems, are inferred by a generative process. PMTLM (Zhu et al., 2013) is reported as the current state-of-the-art system. In short, it is equivalent to PLSA but extended by having a variable associated with each document, which represents that document's propensity to form a link.

As mentioned, although Collaborative Filtering has been used towards citation prediction (McNee et al., 2002), there is little research which includes features based on the entire content (i.e., documents). Very recently, (Wilson et al., 2014) used topic modelling to help predict movie recommendations. Specifically, one feature into their system was the KL-divergence between candidate items' topic distributions, but applying this towards citation prediction has yet to be done. Most similar to our work, (Bethard and Jurafsky, 2010) used a classifier to predict citations, based on meta-data features and compressed topic information (e.g., one feature is the cosine similarity between a report-source pair's topic distribution). As explained in Section 4, we expand the topic information into a vector of length $K$, which not only improves performance but yields an estimate of the most important, "quality" topics. Further, our system also uses our *LDA-Bayes* baseline as a feature, which by itself yields excellent results compared to other systems on our large corpus. Notably, Bethard and Jurafsky's system (2010) also differs from ours in that (1) their system has an iterative process that alternates between retrieving candidate source documents and learning model weights by training a supervised classifier; and (2) they only assume access to the content of the abstract, not the entire documents. Nonetheless, we use their system's most useful features to construct a comparable system (which we name **WSIC** – "Who Should I Cite"), which we describe in more detail in Section 3.3 and show results for in Section 4.3.

# 3 New Models

## 3.1 LDA-Bayes

For a baseline system, we first implemented LDA (Blei et al., 2003) topic modelling and ran it on our entire corpus. However, unlike past systems, after our model was trained, we performed citation prediction (i.e., $P(s|r)$) according to Equation 2. Notice, although LDA does not explicitly estimate $P(s|z)$, we can approximate it via Bayes Rule, and we consequently call our baseline *LDA-Bayes*. Doing so allows us to include the prior probability of the given source being cited (i.e., $P(s)$), according to the maximum-likelihood estimate seen during training.

$$P(s|r) = \sum_{k}^{K} P(s|z_k)P(z_k|r),$$
$$\text{where } P(s|z_j) = \frac{P(z_j|s)P(s)}{\sum_{s'} P(z_j|s')P(s')} \quad (2)$$

Of the past research which uses generative models for citation prediction, we believe LinkLDA is the only other system in which a source's prior citation probability plays any role in training the model. Specifically, in LinkLDA, the prediction metric is identical to ours in that the topics are marginalized over topics (Equation 3). It differs, however, in that their model directly infers $P(s|z_k)$, for it treats each citation link as a word token. Although this does not explicitly factor in each source's prior probability of being cited, it is implicitly influenced by such, for the sources which are more heavily cited during training will tend to have a higher probability of being generated from topics.

$$P(s|r) = \sum_{k}^{K} P(s|z_k)P(z_k|r), \quad (3)$$

Note: the other generative models mentioned in Section 2, after inference, predict citations by sampling from a random variable (typically a Bernoulli or Poisson distribution) which has been conditioned on the topic distributions.

## 3.2 Logit-Expanded

In attempt to combine the effectiveness of LDA in generating useful topics with the ability of dis-

Table 2: A randomly chosen report and its predicted sources, per LDA-Bayes, illustrating that a report and predicted source may be contextually similar but that their titles may have few words in common.

**Report:** Japanese Dependency Structure Analysis Based On Support Vector Machines (2000)

| Position | Cited Source? | Year | Source Name |
|---|---|---|---|
| 1 | | 1996 | A Maximum Entropy Approach To Natural Language Processing Natural Language Processing |
| 2 | | 1993 | Building A Large Annotated Corpus Of English: The Penn Treebank |
| 3 | | 1996 | A Maximum Entropy Model For Part-Of-Speech Tagging |
| 4 | | 1994 | A Syntactic Analysis Method Of Long Japanese Sentences Based On The Detection Of Conjunctive Structures |
| 5 | | 1992 | Class-Based N-Gram Models Of Natural Language |
| ... | | ... | ... |
| 11 | | 1996 | Three New Probabilistic Models For Dependency Parsing: An Exploration |
| 12 | | 2000 | Introduction To The CoNLL-2000 Shared Task: Chunking |
| 13 | | 1995 | A Model-Theoretic Coreference Scoring Scheme |
| 14 | | 1988 | A Stochastic Parts Program And Noun Phrase Parser For Unrestricted Text |
| 15 | ✓ | 1999 | Japanese Dependency Structure Analysis Based On Maximum Entropy Models |

criminative classifiers to learn important features for classification, we use logistic regression with a linear kernel. Specifically, we train using L2-regularization, which during test time allows us to get a probability estimate for each queried vector (i.e., a report-source pair).

The details of the training and testing data are provided in Section 4.2. However, it is important to understand that each training and testing instance corresponds to a distinct report-source document pair and is represented as a single fixed-length vector. The vector is comprised of the following features, which our experiments illustrate are useful for determining if there exists a link between the associated report and source:

#### 3.2.1 Topic/Content-Based Features

- **LDA-Bayes:** Our baseline system showed strong results by itself, so we include its predictions as a feature (that is, $P(s|r)$).

- **Topics:** LDA-Bayes ranks report-source pairs by marginalizing over all topics (see Equation 2); however, we assert that not all topics are equally important. Allowing each topic to be represented as its own feature, while keeping the value based on the report-source's relationship for that topic (i.e., the absolute value of the difference), can potentially allow the logistic regression to learn both (1) the importance for report-source pairs to be generally similar across most topics and (2) the relative importance of each topic. For all of our experiments (including LDA-Bayes) we used 125 topics to model the corpus; thus, this feature becomes expanded to 125 individual indices within our vector, which is why we name this system Logit-Expanded. Namely, $\forall i \in K$, let feature $f_i = |\theta_{r_i} - \theta_{s_i}|$.

#### 3.2.2 Meta-data Features

- **Report Author Previously Cited Source?:** We believe authors have a tendency to cite documents they have cited in the past

- **Report Author Previously Cited a Source Author?:** Authors also have a tendency to "subscribe" to certain authors and are more familiar with particular people's works, and thus cite those papers more often.

- **Prior Citation Probability:** A distinguishing feature of our LDA-Bayes model is that it factors in the prior probability of a source being cited, based on the maximum likelihood estimate from the training data. So, we explicitly include this as a feature.

- **Number of Overlapping Authors:** Authors have a tendency to cite their co-authors, in part because their co-authors' past work has an increased chance of being relevant.

- **Number of Years between Report and Source:** Authors tend to cite more recent papers.

- **Title Similarity between Report and Source:** As shown in Table 2, some sources erroneously returned by our baseline system could have been discarded had we judged them by how dissimilar their titles are from the report's title. In Table 2's example, the one correct source to find (within $\sim$12,000) was returned at position 15 and has many words in common with the report (namely, "Japanese Dependency Structure Analysis Based On" appears in the titles of both the report and correctly predicted source).

### 3.3 WSIC (Who Should I Cite?)

In attempt to compare our systems against Bethard and Jurafsky's system (2010), we implemented the features they concluded to be most useful for retrieval, and like our Logit-Expanded system, used logistic regression as the mechanism for learning citation prediction. Instead of using only the text from the abstracts, like in their research, to make the comparison more fair we used text from the entire documents – just like we did for the rest of our systems. Specifically, adhering to their naming convention, the features from their system that we used are: *citation-count, venue-citation-count, author-citation-count, author-h-index, age (# years between report and source), terms-citing, topics, authors, authors-cited-article, and authors-cited-author.*

## 4 Experiments

### 4.1 Corpora

The past research mentioned in Section 2 primarily makes use of three corpora: Cora, CiteSeer, and WebKB. As shown in Table 3, these corpora are relatively small with ~3,000 documents, an average of less than three links per document, and a modest number of unique word types.

We wanted to use a corpus which was larger, provided the complete text of the original documents, and included meta-data such as author information. Thus, we used the ACL Anthology (Radev et al., 2013) (the December 2013 release), which provides author and year information for each paper, and the corpus details are listed in Table 3. For the task of citation prediction, we are the first to use full content information from a corpus this large.

### 4.2 Training/Testing Data

The research listed in Section 2 commonly uses 90% of all positive links (i.e., a distinct report-to-source instance) for training purposes and 10% for testing. LDA-based topic modelling approaches, which are standard for this task, require that at testing time each report and candidate source has already been observed during training. This is because at test time the topic distribution for each document must have already been inferred. Additionally, it is common to make the assumption that the corpus is split into a bipartite graph: a priori we know which documents are reports and which are sources, with most being both. At testing time, one then predicts sources from the large set of candidate sources, all of which were seen at some point during training (as either a report or a source document).

We follow suit with the past research and randomly split the ACL Anthology's report-to-source links (citations) into 90% for training and 10% for testing, with the requirement that every candidate source document during testing was seen during training as either a report or a source – ensuring we have a topic distribution for each document. On average, each report has 6.8 sources, meaning typically at test time each report has just a few (e.g., 1-5) sources which we hope to predict from our 12,265 candidate sources. For all of our experiments, the systems (e.g., LDA-Bayes, LinkLDA, Logit-Expanded, etc) were evaluated on the exact same randomly chosen split of training/testing data.

As for training Logit-Expanded, naturally there are vastly more negative examples (i.e., no link between the given report-source pair) than positive examples; most sources are not cited for a given report. This represents a large class-imbalance problem, which could make it difficult for the classifier to learn our task. Consequently, we downsampled the negative examples. Specifically, for each report, we included all positive examples (the cited sources), and for each positive example, we included 5 randomly selected negative examples (sources). Note, for testing our system, we still need to evaluate every possible candidate report-source pair – that is ~12,265 candidate sources per tested report.

Table 3: Report-to-Source Citation Prediction Corpora

| | Cora | CiteSeer | WebKB | ACL |
|---|---|---|---|---|
| # docs | 2,708 | 3,312 | 3,453 | 17,298 |
| # links | 5,429 | 4,608 | 1,733 | 106,992 |
| vocab size | 1,433 | 3,703 | 24,182 | 137,885 |
| # authors | - | - | - | 14,407 |

### 4.3 Results

#### 4.3.1 Report-To-Source Citation Prediction

First, we tested our LDA-Bayes baseline system and compared it to LinkLDA and PMTLM (Zhu et

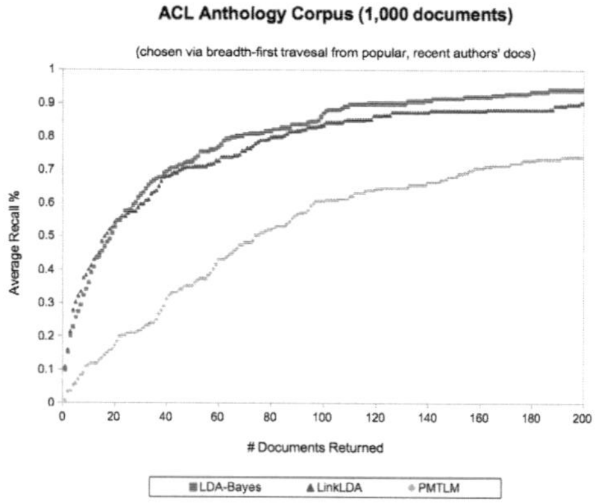


Figure 2: Average Recall Performance across all Reports from a 1,000 document subset of the ACL Anthology

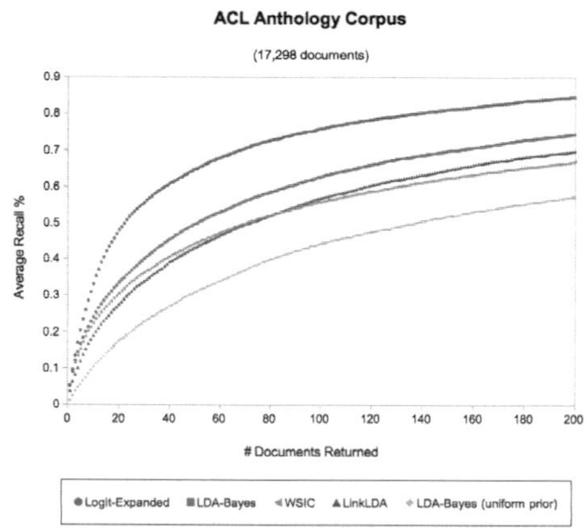


Figure 3: Average Recall Performance across all reports from the full ACL Anthology

al., 2013) – the current state-of-the-art system. Due to the slow running time of PMTLM, we restricted our preliminary experiment to just 1,000 documents of the ACL Anthology, and Figure 2 shows the average recall performance across all reports. Surprisingly, PMTLM performed worst. Note: the authors of PMTLM compared their system to LinkLDA for a different task (predicting research area) but did not compare to LinkLDA during their analysis of citation prediction performance. Thus, it was not previously asserted that PMTLM would outperform LinkLDA.

As we can see, LDA-Bayes, despite being simple, performs well. As mentioned, LDA-Bayes explicitly captures the prior probability of each source being cited (via maximum-likelihood estimate), whereas LinkLDA and PMTLM approximates this during inference. We believe this contributes towards the performance differences.

It was expected that when run on the entire ACL corpus, WSIC and our Logic-Expanded systems would have sufficient data to learn authors' citing preferences and would outperform the other generative models. As shown in Figure 3 and 4, our flagship Logit-Expanded system greatly outperformed all other systems, while our baseline LDA-Bayes continued to offer strong results. Note, the full recall performance results include returning 12,265 sources, but we only show the performance for returning the first 200 returned sources. Further, Table 4 shows the same experimental results but for the performance when returning just the first 50 predicted sources per report.

Table 4: Performance of each system, averaged across all reports while returning the top 50 predicted sources for each. 125 topics were used for every system.

| | recall | precision | fscore |
|---|---|---|---|
| Logit-Expanded | .647 | .016 | .031 |
| LDA-Bayes | .496 | .012 | .024 |
| WSIC | .442 | .011 | .021 |
| LinkLDA | .431 | .011 | .021 |
| LDA-Bayes (uniform prior) | .309 | .007 | .014 |

Again, we further see how effective it is to have a model influenced by a source's prior probability, for when we change LDA-Bayes such that $P(SourceCited)$ is uniform for all sources, performance falls greatly – represented as *LDA (uniform prior)*.

We analyzed the benefits of each feature of Logit-Expanded in 2 ways: (1) starting with the full-feature set experiment (whose results we showed), we evaluate each feature by running an experiment whereby the said feature is removed; and (2) starting with our LDA-Bayes baseline as the only feature for our Logit-Expanded system, we evaluate each feature by running an experiment whereby the said feature is paired with LDA-Bayes as the only two features used. For both of these approaches, we measure performance by looking at recall, precision, and f-score when returning the first 50 predicted sources. The results are shown in Table 5; technique (1) is shown in column *removal*, and (2)

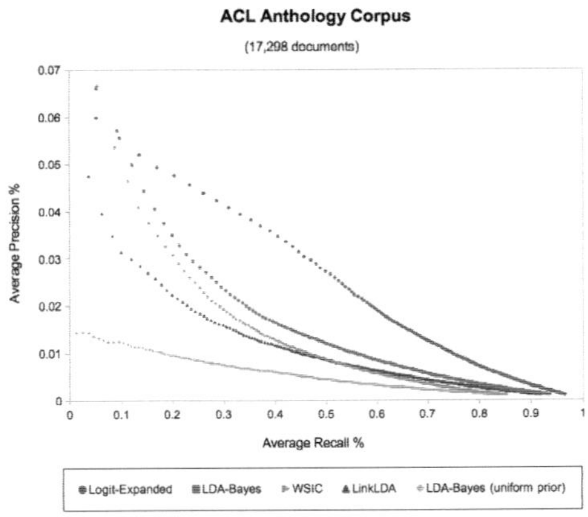


Figure 4: Recall vs Precision Performance across all Reports from the full ACL Anthology. Logit-Expanded's slight blips at recall = 0.25, 0.33, and 0.5 is due to the truth set having many reports with only 4, 3, or 2 golden sources, respectively.

is in column *addage*.

Table 5 reveals insightful results: it is clear that LDA-Bayes is a strong baseline and useful feature to include in our system, for removing it from our feature list causes performance to decrease more than removing any other feature. *PrevCitedSource* and *Topics Expanded* are the second and third strongest features, respectively. We suspect that *PrevCitedSource* was a good feature because our corpus was sufficiently large; had our corpus been much smaller, there might not have been enough data for this feature to provide any benefit. Next, *Title Similarity* and *# Shared Authors* were comparably good features. *PrevCitedAuthor* and *# Years Between* were the worst features, as we see negligible performance difference when we (1) pair either with LDA-Bayes, or (2) remove either from our full feature list. An explanation for the former feature's poor performance could be that authors vary in (1) how often they repeatedly cite authors, and most likely (2) many authors have small publication histories within training, so it might be unwise to base prediction on this limited information. Last, it is worth noting that when we pair Topics Expanded with LDA-Bayes, that alone is not enough to give the best performance from a pair. An explanation is that it dominates the system with too much content-based (i.e., topic) information, overshadowing the prior-citation-probability that plays a role in LDA-Bayes. Supporting this idea, we see the biggest performance increase when we pair LDA-Bayes with the PrevCitedSource feature – a non-topic-based feature, which provides the system with a different *type* of data to leverage.

Table 5: Analysis of each feature used in Logit-Expanded. Results based on the first 50 sources returned, averaged over all reports. Our *Starting Point** system listed within the "Addage" columns used LDA-Bayes as the only feature. Our *Starting Point** system within the "Removal" columns used every feature.

| | Addage | | | Removal | | |
|---|---|---|---|---|---|---|
| | recall | precision | fscore | recall | precision | fscore |
| Starting Point* | .496 | .012 | .024 | .647 | .016 | .031 |
| LDA-Bayes | - | - | - | **.583** | **.014** | **.028** |
| Topics Expanded | **.564** | **.014** | **.027** | **.606** | **.015** | **.028** |
| PrevCitedSource | **.581** | **.014** | **.028** | **.599** | **.014** | **.028** |
| PrevCitedAuthor | .484 | .012 | .023 | .641 | .016 | .030 |
| # Shared Authors | .543 | .013 | .026 | .636 | .015 | .029 |
| Prior Prob. Cited | .501 | .012 | .023 | .639 | .015 | .030 |
| Title Similarity | .513 | .012 | .023 | .623 | .015 | .029 |
| # Years Between | .498 | .012 | .023 | .645 | .016 | .030 |

Additionally, when using only the metadata features (i.e., not LDA-Bayes or Topics-Expanded), performance for returning 50 sources averaged 0.403, 0.010, and 0.019 for recall, precision, and fscore, respectively – demonstrating that the metadata features alone do not yield strong results but that they complement the LDA-Bayes and Topics-Expanded features.

### 4.3.2 Topic Importance

Although Report-to-Source citation prediction was our primary objective, our feature representation of topics allows logistic regression to appropriately learn which *topics* are most useful for predicting citations. In turn, these topics are arguably the most cohesive; thus, our system, as a byproduct, provides a metric for measuring the "quality" of each topic. Namely, the weight associated with each topic feature indicates the topic's importance – the lower the weight the better.

Table 6 shows our system's ranking of the most important topics, signified by "Logit-weight." We did not prompt humans to evaluate the quality of the topics, so in attempt to offer a comparison, we also rank each topic according to two popular metrics: Pointwise Mutual Information (PMI) and Topic Coherence (TC) (Mimno et al., 2011). For a topic $k$, let $V^{(k)}$ represent the top M words for $K$; where $V^{(k)} = (v_i^{(k)}, ..., v_M^{(k)})$ and $D(v)$ represents the document frequency of word type $v$. Then, $PMI(k)$ is defined by Equation 4 and $TC(k)$ is defined by Equation 5.

In Table 6, we see that our most useful topic (Topic 49) concerns vision research, and since our corpus is heavily filled with research concerning (non-vision-related) natural language processing, it makes sense for this topic to be highly important for predicting citations. Similarly, we see the other top-ranking topics all represent a well-defined, subfield of natural language processing research, including parsing, text generation, and Japanese-English machine translation.

$$PMI(k; V^{(k)}) = \sum_{m=2}^{M} \sum_{l=1}^{m-1} \log \frac{p(V_m^{(k)}, V_l^{(k)})}{p(V_m^{(k)})p(V_l^{(k)})} \quad (4)$$

$$TC(k; V^{(k)}) = \sum_{m=2}^{M} \sum_{l=1}^{m-1} \log \frac{D(V_m^{(k)}, V_l^{(k)})}{D(V_m^{(k)})} \quad (5)$$

Table 7 shows the worst 5 topics according to Logit-Expanded. Topic 96 concerns Wikipedia as a corpus, which naturally encompasses many areas of research, and as we would expect, the mention of such is probably a poor indicator for predicting citations. Topic 77 concerns artifacts from the OCR-rendering of our corpus, which offers no meaningful information. In general, the worst-ranking topics concern words that span many documents and do not represent cohesive, well-defined areas of research. Additionally, in both Table 6 and 7 we see that Pointwise Mutual Information (PMI) disagrees quite a bit with our Logit-Expanded's ranking, and from this initial result, it appears Logit-Expanded's ranking might be a better metric than PMI – at least in terms of quantifying relevance towards documents being related and linked via a citation.

This cursory, qualitative critique of the metrics warrants more research, ideally with human-evaluation. However, one can see how these metrics differ: TC and PMI are both entirely concerned with just the co-occurrence of terms, normalized by the general popularity of the said terms. Therefore, words could highly co-occur together but otherwise represent nothing special about the corpus at large. On the other hand, Logit-Expanded's ranking is mainly concerned with quantifying how well each topic represents discriminatively useful content within a document.

Table 6: The highest quality topics (out of 125), sorted according to Logit-Expanded's estimate. Topics are also ranked according to Pointwise Mutual Information (PMI) and Topic Coherence (TC).

| Logit's Rank | PMI Rank | TC Rank | Logit Weight | Topic # | Top Words |
|---|---|---|---|---|---|
| 1 | 116 | 103 | -5.50 | 49 | image, visual, multimodal, images, spatial, gesture, objects, object, video, scene, instructions, pointing |
| 2 | 33 | 44 | -4.76 | 25 | grammar, parsing, grammars, left, derivation, terminal, nonterminal, items, free, string, item, derivations, cfg |
| 3 | 68 | 37 | -4.71 | 65 | generation, generator, generated, realization, content, planning, choice, nlg, surface, generate |
| 4 | 49 | 27 | -4.28 | 32 | noun, nouns, phrases, adjectives, adjective, compound, verb, head, compounds, preposition |
| 5 | 107 | 61 | -4.24 | 0 | japanese, ga, expressions, wo, accuracy, bunsetsu, ni, dictionary, wa, kanji, noun, expression |

Table 7: The lowest quality topics (out of 125), sorted by Logit-Expanded's estimate. Topics are also ranked according to Pointwise Mutual Information (PMI) and Topic Coherence (TC).

| Logit's Rank | PMI Rank | TC Rank | Logit Weight | Topic # | Top Words |
|---|---|---|---|---|---|
| 121 | 13 | 110 | -1.45 | 96 | wikipedia, links, link, articles, article, title, page, anchor, pages, wiki, category, attributes |
| 122 | 83 | 122 | -1.20 | 77 | x1, x2, c1, c2, p2, a1, p1, a2, r1, l1, xf, fi |
| 123 | 42 | 36 | -1.09 | 91 | annotation, agreement, annotated, annotators, annotator, scheme, inter, annotate, gold, kappa |
| 124 | 10 | 34 | -0.75 | 43 | selection, learning, active, selected, random, confidence, sample, sampling, cost, size, select |
| 125 | 65 | 115 | -0.33 | 30 | region, location, texts, city, regions, weather, locations, map, place, geographic, country |

## 5 Conclusions

We have provided a strong baseline, LDA-Bayes, which when run on the largest corpus for this task, offers compelling performance. We have demonstrated that modelling the prior probability of each candidate source being cited is simple yet important, for it allows all of our systems to outperform the previous state-of-the-art – our large corpus helps towards making this a useful feature, too.

Our biggest contribution is our new system, Logit-Expanded, which combines both the effectiveness of the generative model LDA with the power of logistic regression to discriminately learn important features for classification. By representing each topic as its own feature, while still modelling the relationship between the candidate report-source pair, we allow our system to learn (1) that having similar topic distributions between reports and sources is indicative of a link, and (2) which topics are most important for predicting a link. Because we used a linear kernel, we are able to discern exactly how important it ranks each topic. A cursory, qualitative assessment of its metric shows promising and competitive performance with that of Pointwise Mutual Information and Topic Coherence.

## References


Mohammad Al Hasan and Mohammed J Zaki. 2011. A survey of link prediction in social networks. In *Social network data analytics*, pages 243–275. Springer.

Steven Bethard and Dan Jurafsky. 2010. Who should i cite: learning literature search models from citation behavior. In *Proceedings of the 19th ACM international conference on Information and knowledge management*, pages 609–618. ACM.

David M Blei, Andrew Y Ng, and Michael I Jordan. 2003. Latent dirichlet allocation. *the Journal of machine Learning research*, 3:993–1022.

Elena Erosheva, Stephen Fienberg, and John Lafferty. 2004. Mixed-membership models of scientific publications. *Proceedings of the National Academy of Sciences of the United States of America*, 101(Suppl 1):5220–5227.

Qirong Ho, Jacob Eisenstein, and Eric P Xing. 2012. Document hierarchies from text and links. In *Proceedings of the 21st international conference on World Wide Web*, pages 739–748. ACM.

David Hofmann and Thomas Cohn. 2001. The missing link-a probabilistic model of document content and hypertext connectivity. In *Proceedings of the 2000 Conference on Advances in Neural Information Processing Systems. The MIT Press*, pages 430–436.

Thomas Hofmann. 1999. Probabilistic latent semantic indexing. In *Proceedings of the 22nd annual international ACM SIGIR conference on Research and development in information retrieval*, pages 50–57. ACM.

Saurabh Kataria, Prasenjit Mitra, and Sumit Bhatia. 2010. Utilizing context in generative bayesian models for linked corpus. In *AAAI*, volume 10, page 1.

Yan Liu, Alexandru Niculescu-Mizil, and Wojciech Gryc. 2009. Topic-link lda: joint models of topic and author community. In *proceedings of the 26th annual international conference on machine learning*, pages 665–672. ACM.

Sean M McNee, Istvan Albert, Dan Cosley, Prateep Gopalkrishnan, Shyong K Lam, Al Mamunur Rashid, Joseph A Konstan, and John Riedl. 2002. On the recommending of citations for research papers. In *Proceedings of the 2002 ACM conference on Computer supported cooperative work*, pages 116–125. ACM.

David Mimno, Hanna M Wallach, Edmund Talley, Miriam Leenders, and Andrew McCallum. 2011. Optimizing semantic coherence in topic models. In *Proceedings of the Conference on Empirical Methods in Natural Language Processing*, pages 262–272. Association for Computational Linguistics.

Ramesh M Nallapati, Amr Ahmed, Eric P Xing, and William W Cohen. 2008. Joint latent topic models for text and citations. In *Proceedings of the 14th ACM SIGKDD international conference on Knowledge discovery and data mining*, pages 542–550. ACM.

DragomirR. Radev, Pradeep Muthukrishnan, Vahed Qazvinian, and Amjad Abu-Jbara. 2013. The acl anthology network corpus. *Language Resources and Evaluation*, pages 1–26.

Badrul Sarwar, George Karypis, Joseph Konstan, and John Riedl. 2001. Item-based collaborative filtering recommendation algorithms. In *Proceedings of the 10th international conference on World Wide Web*, pages 285–295. ACM.

Jobin Wilson, Santanu Chaudhury, Brejesh Lall, and Prateek Kapadia. 2014. Improving collaborative filtering based recommenders using topic modelling. *arXiv preprint arXiv:1402.6238*.

Yaojia Zhu, Xiaoran Yan, Lise Getoor, and Cristopher Moore. 2013. Scalable text and link analysis with mixed-topic link models. In *Proceedings of the 19th ACM SIGKDD international conference on Knowledge discovery and data mining*, pages 473–481. ACM.

# Weakly Supervised Slot Tagging with Partially Labeled Sequences from Web Search Click Logs

**Young-Bum Kim**[†] **Minwoo Jeong**[†] **Karl Stratos**[‡] **Ruhi Sarikaya**[†]

[†]Microsoft Corporation, Redmond, WA
[‡]Columbia University, New York, NY
{ybkim, minwoo.jeong, ruhi.sarikaya}@microsoft.com
stratos@cs.columbia.edu

## Abstract

In this paper, we apply a weakly-supervised learning approach for slot tagging using conditional random fields by exploiting web search click logs. We extend the constrained lattice training of Täckström et al. (2013) to non-linear conditional random fields in which latent variables mediate between observations and labels. When combined with a novel initialization scheme that leverages unlabeled data, we show that our method gives significant improvement over strong supervised and weakly-supervised baselines.

## 1 Introduction

A key problem in natural language processing (NLP) is to effectively utilize large amounts of unlabeled and partially labeled data in situations where little or no annotations are available for a task of interest. Many recent work tackled this problem mostly in the context of part-of-speech (POS) tagging by transferring POS tags from a supervised language via automatic alignment and/or constructing tag dictionaries from the web (Das and Petrov, 2011; Li et al., 2012; Täckström et al., 2013).

In this work, we attack this problem in the context of slot tagging, where the goal is to find correct semantic segmentation of a given query, which is an important task for information extraction and natural language understanding. For instance, answering the question "when is the new bill murray movie release date?" requires recognizing and labeling key phrases: e.g., "bill murray" as `actor` and "movie" as `media type`.

The standard approach to slot tagging involves training a sequence model such as a conditional random field (CRF) on manually annotated data. An obvious limitation of this approach is that it relies on fully labeled data, which is both difficult to adapt and changing tasks and schemas. Certain films, songs, and books become more or less popular over time, and the performance of models trained on outdated data will degrade. If not updated, models trained on live data feeds such as movies, songs and books become obsolete over time and their accuracy will degrade. In order to achieve high accuracy continuously data and even model schemas have to be refreshed on a regular basis.

To remedy this limitation, we propose a weakly supervised framework that utilizes the information available in web click logs. A web click log is a mapping from a user query to URL link. For example, users issuing queries about movies tend to click on links from the IMDB.com or rottentomatoes.com, which provide rich structured data for entities such as title of the movie ("The Matrix"), the director ("The Wachowski Brothers"), and the release date ("1999"). Web click logs present an opportunity to learn semantic tagging models from large-scale and naturally occurring user interaction data (Volkova et al., 2013).

While some previous works (Li et al., 2009) have applied a similar strategy to incorporate click logs in slot tagging, they do not employ recent advances in machine learning to effectively leverage the incomplete annotations. In this paper, we pursue and extend learning from partially labeled sequences, in particular the approach of Täckström et al. (2013).



*Human Language Technologies: The 2015 Annual Conference of the North American Chapter of the ACL*, pages 84–92,
Denver, Colorado, May 31 – June 5, 2015. ©2015 Association for Computational Linguistics

Instead of projecting labels from a high-resource to a low-resource languages via parallel text and word alignment, we project annotations from structured data found in click logs. This can be seen as a benefit since typically a much larger volume of click log data is available than parallel text for low-resource languages.

We also extend the constrained lattice training method of Täckström et al. (2013) from linear CRFs to non-linear CRFs. We propose a perceptron training method for hidden unit CRFs (Maaten et al., 2011) that allows us to train with partially labeled sequences. We show that combined with a novel pre-training methodology that leverages large quantities of unlabeled data, this training method achieves significant improvements over several strong baselines.

## 2 Model definitions and training methods

In this section, we describe the two sequence models in our experiments: a conditional random field (CRF) of Lafferty et al. (2001) and a hidden unit CRF (HUCRF) of Maaten et al. (2011). Note that since we only have partially labeled sequences, we need a technique to learn from incomplete data. For a CRF, we follow a variant of the training method of Täckström et al. (2013). In addition, we make a novel extension of their method to train a HUCRF from partially labeled sequences. The resulting perceptron-style algorithm (Figure 2) is simple but effective. Furthermore, we propose an initialization scheme that naturally leverages unlabeled data for training a HUCRF.

### 2.1 Partially Observed CRF

A first-order CRF parametrized by $\theta \in \mathbb{R}^d$ defines a conditional probability of a label sequence $y = y_1 \dots y_n$ given an observation sequence $x = x_1 \dots x_n$ as follows:

$$p_\theta(y|x) = \frac{\exp(\theta^\top \Phi(x, y))}{\sum_{y' \in \mathcal{Y}(x)} \exp(\theta^\top \Phi(x, y'))}$$

where $\mathcal{Y}(x)$ is the set of all possible label sequences for $x$ and $\Phi(x, y) \in \mathbb{R}^d$ is a global feature function that decomposes into local feature functions $\Phi(x, y) = \sum_{j=1}^n \phi(x, j, y_{j-1}, y_j)$ by the first-order Markovian assumption. Given fully labeled sequences $\{(x^{(i)}, y^{(i)})\}_{i=1}^N$, the standard training method is to find $\theta$ that maximizes the log likelihood of the label sequences under the model with $l_2$-regularization:

$$\theta^* = \arg\max_{\theta \in \mathbb{R}^d} \sum_{i=1}^N \log p_\theta(y^{(i)}|x^{(i)}) - \frac{\lambda}{2} ||\theta||^2$$

Unfortunately, in our problem we do not have fully labeled sequences. Instead, for each token $x_j$ in sequence $x_1 \dots x_n$ we have the following two sources of label information:

- A set of allowed label types $\mathcal{Y}(x_j)$. (Label dictionary)
- A label $\tilde{y}_j$ transferred from a source data. (Optional: transferred label)

Täckström et al. (2013) propose a different objective that allows training a CRF in this scenario. To this end, they define a constrained *lattice* $\mathcal{Y}(x, \tilde{y}) = \mathcal{Y}(x_1, \tilde{y}_1) \times \dots \times \mathcal{Y}(x_n, \tilde{y}_n)$ where at each position $j$ a set of allowed label types is given as:

$$\mathcal{Y}(x_j, \tilde{y}_j) = \begin{cases} \{\tilde{y}_j\} & \text{if } \tilde{y}_j \text{ is given} \\ \mathcal{Y}(x_j) & \text{otherwise} \end{cases}$$

In addition to these existing constraints, we introduce constraints on the *label structure*. In our segmentation problem, labels are structured (e.g., some label types cannot follow certain others). We can easily incorporate this restriction by disallowing invalid label types as a post-processing step of the form:

$$\mathcal{Y}(x_j, \tilde{y}_j) \leftarrow \mathcal{Y}(x_j, \tilde{y}_j) \cap \overline{\mathcal{Y}}(x_{j-1}, \tilde{y}_{j-1})$$

where $\overline{\mathcal{Y}}(x_{j-1}, \tilde{y}_{j-1})$ is the set of valid label types that can follow $\mathcal{Y}(x_{j-1}, \tilde{y}_{j-1})$.

Täckström et al. (2013) define a conditional probability over label lattices for a given observation sequence $x$:

$$p_\theta(\mathcal{Y}(x, \tilde{y})|x) = \sum_{y \in \mathcal{Y}(x, \tilde{y})} p_\theta(y|x)$$

Given a label dictionary $\mathcal{Y}(x_j)$ for every token type $x_j$ and training sequences $\{(x^{(i)}, \tilde{y}^{(i)})\}_{i=1}^N$ where $\tilde{y}^{(i)}$ is (possibly non-existent) transferred labels for

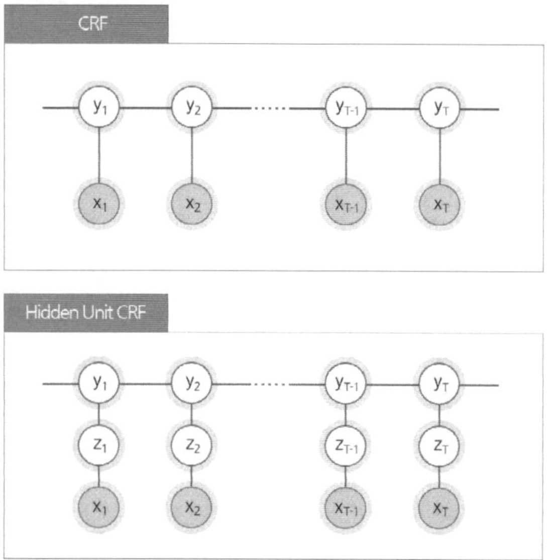


Figure 1: Illustration of CRFs and hidden unit CRFs

$x^{(i)}$ and, the new training method is to find $\theta$ that maximizes the log likelihood of the label lattices:

$$\theta^* = \arg\max_{\theta \in \mathbb{R}^d} \sum_{i=1}^{N} \log p_\theta(\mathcal{Y}(x^{(i)}, \tilde{y}^{(i)})|x^{(i)}) - \frac{\lambda}{2}||\theta||^2$$

Since this objective is non-convex, we find a local optimum with a gradient-based algorithm. The gradient of this objective at each example $(x^{(i)}, \tilde{y}^{(i)})$ takes an intuitive form:

$$\begin{aligned} &\frac{\partial}{\partial \theta} \log p_\theta(\mathcal{Y}(x^{(i)}, \tilde{y}^{(i)})|x^{(i)}) - \frac{\lambda}{2}||\theta||^2 \\ &= \sum_{y \in \mathcal{Y}(x^{(i)}, \tilde{y})} p_\theta(y|x^{(i)}) \Phi(x^{(i)}, y) \\ &\quad - \sum_{y \in \mathcal{Y}(x^{(i)})} p_\theta(y|x^{(i)}) \Phi(x^{(i)}, y) - \lambda\theta \end{aligned}$$

This is the same as the standard CRF training except the first term where the gold features $\Phi(x^{(i)}, y^{(i)})$ are replaced by the expected value of features in the constrained lattice $\mathcal{Y}(x^{(i)}, \tilde{y})$.

### 2.2 Partially Observed HUCRF

While effective, a CRF is still a linear model. To see if we can benefit from nonlinearity, we use a HUCRF (Maaten et al., 2011): a CRF that introduces a layer of binary-valued hidden units $z = z_1 \dots z_n \in \{0,1\}$ for each pair of label sequence $y = y_1 \dots y_n$ and observation sequence $x = x_1 \dots x_n$. A HUCRF parametrized by $\theta \in \mathbb{R}^d$ and $\gamma \in \mathbb{R}^{d'}$ defines a joint probability of $y$ and $z$ conditioned on $x$ as follows:

$$p_{\theta,\gamma}(y, z|x) = \frac{\exp(\theta^\top \Phi(x, z) + \gamma^\top \Psi(z, y))}{\sum_{\substack{z' \in \{0,1\}^n \\ y' \in \mathcal{Y}(x, z')}} \exp(\theta^\top \Phi(x, z') + \gamma^\top \Psi(z', y'))}$$

where $\mathcal{Y}(x, z)$ is the set of all possible label sequences for $x$ and $z$, and $\Phi(x, z) \in \mathbb{R}^d$ and $\Psi(z, y) \in \mathbb{R}^{d'}$ are global feature functions that decompose into local feature functions:

$$\Phi(x, z) = \sum_{j=1}^{n} \phi(x, j, z_j)$$

$$\Psi(z, y) = \sum_{j=1}^{n} \psi(z_j, y_{j-1}, y_j)$$

In other words, it forces the interaction between the observations and the labels at each position $j$ to go through a latent variable $z_j$: see Figure 1 for illustration. Then the probability of labels $y$ is given by marginalizing over the hidden units,

$$p_{\theta,\gamma}(y|x) = \sum_{z \in \{0,1\}^n} p_{\theta,\gamma}(y, z|x)$$

As in restricted Boltzmann machines (Larochelle and Bengio, 2008), hidden units are conditionally independent given observations and labels. This allows for efficient inference with HUCRFs despite their richness (see Maaten et al. (2011) for details).

#### 2.2.1 Training with partially labeled sequences

We extend the perceptron training method of Maaten et al. (2011) to train a HUCRF from partially labeled sequences. This can be viewed as a modification of the constrained lattice training method of Täckström et al. (2013) for HUCRFs.

A sketch of our training algorithm is shown in Figure 2. At each example, we predict the most likely label sequence with the current parameters. If this sequence does not violate the given constrained lattice, we make no updates. If it does, we predict the most likely label sequence within the con-

**Input**: constrained lattices $\{(x^{(i)}, \tilde{y}^{(i)})\}_{i=1}^{N}$, step size $\eta$
**Output**: HUCRF parameters $\Theta := \{\theta, \gamma\}$

1. Initialize $\Theta$ randomly.
2. Repeatedly select $i \in \{1 \dots N\}$ at random:
   (a) $y^* \leftarrow \arg\max_{y \in \mathcal{Y}(x^{(i)})} p_\Theta(y|x^{(i)})$
   (b) If $y^* \notin \mathcal{Y}(x^{(i)}, \tilde{y}^{(i)})$:
      i. $y^+ \leftarrow \arg\max_{y \in \mathcal{Y}(x^{(i)}, \tilde{y}^{(i)})} p_\Theta(y|x^{(i)})$
      ii. Make parameter updates:

$$\Theta \leftarrow \Theta + \eta \times \frac{\partial}{\partial \Theta}\Big(p_\Theta(y^+, z^+|x^{(i)}) - p_\Theta(y^*, z^*|x^{(i)})\Big)$$

where the following hidden units are computed in closed-form (see Gelfand et al. (2010)):

$$z^+ := \arg\max_z p_\Theta(z|x^{(i)}, y^+)$$
$$z^* := \arg\max_z p_\Theta(z|x^{(i)}, y^*)$$

Figure 2: A sketch of the perceptron training algorithm for a partially observed hidden unit CRF.

strained lattice. We treat this as the gold label sequence, and perform the perceptron updates accordingly (Gelfand et al., 2010). Even though this training algorithm is quite simple, we demonstrate its effectiveness in our experiments.

#### 2.2.2 Initialization from unlabeled data

Rather than initializing the model parameters randomly, we propose an effective initialization scheme (in a similar spirit to the pre-training methods in neural networks) that naturally leverages unlabeled data.

First, we cluster observation types in unlabeled data and treat the clusters as labels. Then we train a fully supervised HUCRF on this clustered data to learn parameters $\theta$ for the interaction between observations and hidden units $\Phi(x, z)$ and $\gamma$ for the interaction between hidden units and labels $\Phi(z, y)$. Finally, for task/domain specific training, we discard $\gamma$ and use the learned $\theta$ to initialize the algorithm in Figure 2. We hypothesize that if the clusters are non-trivially correlated to the actual labels, we can capture the interaction between observations and hidden units in a meaningful way.

## 3 Mining Click Log Data

We propose using search click logs which consist of queries and their corresponding web documents. Clicks are an implicit signal for related entities and information in the searched document. In this work, we will assume that the web document is *structured* and generated from an underlying database. Due to the structured nature of the web, this is not an unrealistic assumption (see Adamic and Huberman (2002) for discussion). Such structural regularities make obtaining annotated queries for learning a semantic slot tagger almost cost-free.

As an illustration of how to project annotation, consider Figure 3, where we present an example taken from queries about video games. In the figure, the user queries are connected to a structured document via a click log, and then the document is parsed and stored in a structured format. Then annotation types are projected to linked queries through structural alignment. In the following subsections we describe each step in our log mining approach in detail.

### 3.1 Click Logs

Web search engines keep a record of search queries, clicked document and URLs which reveal the user behavior. Such records are proven to be useful in improving the quality of web search. We focus on utilizing query-to-URL click logs that are essentially a mapping from queries to structured web documents. In this work, we use a year's worth of query logs (from July 2013 to June 2014) at a commercial search engine. We applied a simple URL normalization procedure to our log data including trimming and removal of prefixes, e.g. "www".

### 3.2 Parsing Structured Web Document

A simple wrapper induction algorithm described in Kushmerick (1997) is applied for parsing web documents. Although it involves manually engineering a rule-based parser and is therefore website-specific, a single wrapper often generates large amounts of data for large structured websites, for example IMDB. Furthermore, it is very scalable to large quantities of data, and the cost of writing such a rule-based sys-

Figure 3: An example illustrating annotation projection via click-log and wrapper induction.

tem is typically much lower than the annotation cost of queries.

Figure 4 shows the statistics of parsed web documents on 24 domains with approximately 500 template rules. One of the chosen domains in our experiment, Music, has over 130 million documents parsed by our approach.

### 3.3 Annotation Projection via Structural Alignment

We now turn to the annotation projection step where structural alignment is used to transfer type annotation from structured data to queries. Note that this is different from the word-based or phrase-based alignment scenario in machine translation since we need to align a word sequence to a type-value pair.

Let us assume that we are given the user query as a word sequence, $w = w_1, w_2, \ldots, w_n$ and a set of structured data, $s = \{s_1, s_2, \ldots, s_m\}$, where $s_i$ is a pair of slot-type and value. We define a measurement of dissimilarity between word tokens and slots, $dist(w_i, s_j) = 1 - sim(w_i, s_j)$ where $sim(\cdot, \cdot)$ is cosine similarity over character trigrams of $w_i$ and $s_j$. Next we construct a $n$-by-$n$ score matrix $S$ of which element is $\max_j dist(w_{t' \ldots t}, s_j)$ meaning that a score of the most similar type-value $s_j$ and a segment $\{t' \ldots t\}$ where $1 \leq t' < t \leq n$. Finally, given this approximate score matrix $S$, we use a dynamic programming algorithm to find the optimal segments to minimize the objective function:

$$T(t) = \min_{t' < t} T(t')S(t', t).$$

Our approach results in a large amount of high-quality partially-labeled data: 314K, 1.2M, and 1.1M queries for the Game, Movie and Music domain, respectively.

## 4 Experiments

To test the effectiveness of our approach, we perform experiments on a suite of three entertainment domains for slot tagging: queries about movies, music, and games. For each domain, we have two types of data: engineered data and log data. *Engineered data* is a set of synthetic queries to mimic the behavior of users. This data is created during development at which time no log data is available. *Log data* is a set of queries created by actual users using deployed spoken dialogue systems: thus it is directly transcribed from users' voice commands with automatic speech recognition (ASR). In general we found log data to be fairly noisy, containing many ASR and grammatical errors, whereas engineered data consisted of clean, well-formed text.

Not surprisingly, synthetic queries in engineered data are not necessarily representative of real queries in log data since it is difficult to accurately simulate what users' queries will be before a fully functioning system is available and real user data can be gathered. Hence this setting can greatly benefit from weakly-supervised learning methods such as ours since it is critical to learn from new incoming log data. We use search engine log data to project lattice constraints for weakly supervised learning.

In this setup, a user issues a natural language query to retrieve movies, music titles, games and/or information there of. For instance, a user could say

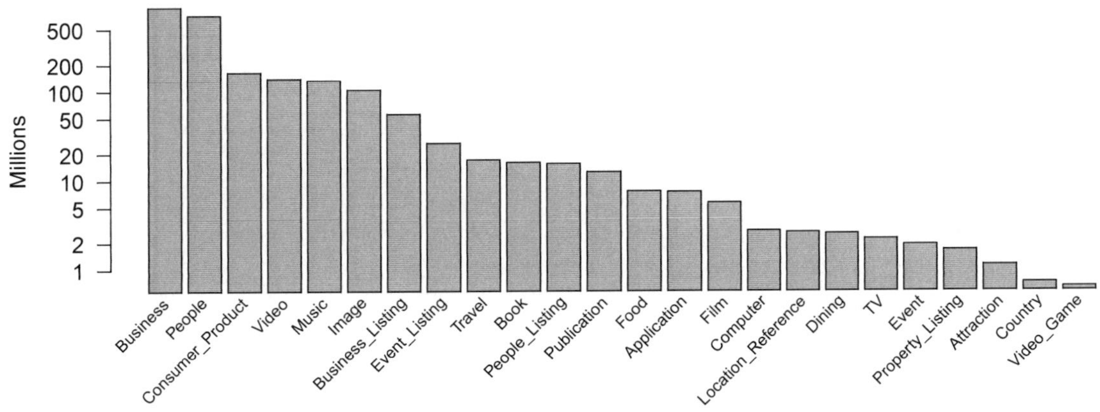


Figure 4: Statistics of structured web documents. The vertical axis shows the number of documents (in millions); the horizontal axis shows the web domain types.

"play the latest batman movie" or "find beyonce's music". Our slot sequence tagger is trained with variants of CRF using lexical features, gazetteers, Brown clusters and context words. The domains consist of 35 slot types for movies, 25 for music and 24 for games. Slot types correspond to both named entities (e.g., game name, music title, movie name) as well as more general categories (genre, media type, description). Table 1 shows the size of the datasets used in our experiments.

| Domains | Training | Test |
|---|---|---|
| games | 32017 | 5508 |
| movies | 48173 | 7074 |
| music | 46377 | 8890 |

Table 1: Labeled data set size for games, movies and music domains partitioned into training and test set.

| Domains | Engineered | Log | Diff. |
|---|---|---|---|
| games | 89.63 | 68.58 | 21.05 |
| movies | 88.67 | 74.21 | 14.45 |
| music | 88.77 | 37.13 | 51.64 |
| AVG. | 89.02 | 59.97 | 29.05 |

Table 2: The difference in F1 performance of CRF models trained only on engineered data but tested on both engineered and log data.

### 4.1 Discrepancy between Engineered Data and Log Data

To empirically highlight the need for learning from real user queries, we first train a standard CRF on the (fully labeled) engineered data and test it on the log data. We have manually annotated some log data for evaluation purposes. For features in the CRF, we use n-grams, gazetteer, and clusters. The clusters were induced from a large body of unlabeled data which consist of log data and click log data. Table 2 shows the F1 scores in this experiment. They indicate that a model fully supervised with engineered data performs very poorly on log data. The difference between the scores within engineered data and the scores in log data is very large (29.05 absolute F1).

### 4.2 Experiments with CRF Variants

Our main contribution is to leverage search log data to improve slot tagging in spoken dialogue systems. In this section, we assume that we have no log data in training slot taggers.[1]

For parameter estimation, both CRFs and POCRFs employ L-BFGS, while POHUCRF uses

[1]In practice, this assumption is not necessarily true because a deployed system can benefit from actual user logs. However, this controlled setting allows us to show the benefits of employing web search click log data.

| Domains | games | music | movies | AVG. |
|---|---|---|---|---|
| CRF | 74.21 | 37.13 | 68.58 | 59.97 |
| POCRF | 77.23 | 44.55 | 76.89 | 66.22 |
| POHCRF | 78.93 | 46.81 | 76.46 | 67.40 |
| POHCRF+ | **79.28** | **47.35** | **78.33** | **68.32** |

Table 3: The F1 performance of variants of CRF across three domains, test on log data

average perceptron. We did not see a significant difference between perceptron and LBFGS in accuracy, but perceptron is faster and thus favorable for training complex HUCRF models. We used 100 as the maximum iteration count and 1.0 for the L2 regularization parameter. The number of hidden variables per token is set to 300. The same features described in the previous section are used here.

We perform experiments with the following CRF variants (see Section 2):

- CRF: A fully supervised linear-chain CRF trained with manually labeled engineered samples.
- POCRF: A partially observed CRF of Täckström et al. (2013) trained with both manually labeled engineered samples and click logs.
- POHUCRF: A partially observed hidden unit CRF (Figure 2) trained with both manually labeled engineered samples and click logs.
- POHUCRF+: POHUCRF with pre-training.

Table 3 summarizes the performance of these CRF variants. All results were tested on log data only. A standard CRF without click log data yields 59.97% of F1 on average. By using click log data, POCRF consistently improves F1 scores across domains, resulting into 66.22% F1 measure. Our model POHUCRF achieves extra gains on games and music, achieving 67.4% F1 measure on average. Finally, the pre-training approach yields significant additional gains across all domains, achieving 68.32% average performance. Overall we achieve a relative error reduction of about 21% over vanilla CRFs.

| Domain | CRF | HUCRF | HUCRF+ |
|---|---|---|---|
| alarm | 91.79 | 91.79 | **91.96** |
| calendar | 87.60 | 87.65 | **88.21** |
| communication | 91.84 | 92.49 | **92.80** |
| note | 87.72 | 88.48 | **88.72** |
| ondevice | 89.37 | 90.14 | **90.64** |
| places | 88.02 | 88.64 | **88.99** |
| reminder | 87.72 | 89.21 | **89.72** |
| weather | 96.93 | 97.38 | **97.63** |
| AVG. | 90.12 | 90.75 | **91.08** |

Table 4: Performance comparison between HUCRF and HUCRF with pre-training.

### 4.3 Weakly-Supervised Learning without Projected Annotations via Pre-Training

We also present experiments within Cortana personal assistant domain where the click log data is not available. The amount of training data we used was from 50K to 100K across different domains and the test data was from 5k to 10k. In addition, the unlabeled log data were used and their amount was from 100k to 200k.

In this scenario, we have access to both engineered and log data to train a model. However, we do not have access to web search click log data. The goal of these experiments is to show the effectiveness of the HUCRF and pre-training method in the absence of weakly supervised labels projected via click logs. Table 4 shows a series of experiments on eight domains.

For all domains other than alarm, using non-linear CRF (HUCRF) improve performance from 90.12% to 90.75% on average. Initializing HUCRF with pretraining (HUCRF+) boosts the performance up to 91.08%, corresponding to a 10% decrease in error relative to a original CRF. Notably in the weather and reminder domains, we have relative error reduction of 23 and 16%, respectively. We speculate that pretraining is helpful because it provides better initialization for training HUCRF: initialization is important since the training objective of HUCRF is non-convex.

In general, we find that HUCRF delivers better performance than standard CRF: when the training procedure is initialized with pretraining (HUCRF+), it improves further.

## 5 Related Work

Previous works have explored weakly supervised slot tagging using aligned labels from a database as constraints. Wu and Weld (2007) train a CRF on heuristically annotated Wikipedia articles with relations mentioned in their structured infobox data. Li et al. (2009) applied a similar strategy incorporating structured data projected through click-log data as both heuristic labels and additional features. Knowledge graphs and search logs have been also considered as extra resources (Liu et al., 2013; El-Kahky et al., 2014; Anastasakos et al., 2014; Sarikaya et al., 2014; Marin et al., 2014).

Distant supervision methods (Mintz et al., 2009; Riedel et al., 2010; Surdeanu et al., 2012; Agichtein and Gravano, 2000) learn to extract relations from text using weak supervision from related structured data sources such as Freebase or Wikipedia. These approaches rely on named entity recognition as a pre-processing step to identify text spans corresponding to candidate slot values. In contrast, our approach jointly segments and predicts slots.

Works on weakly supervised POS tagging are also closely related to ours (Toutanova and Johnson, 2007; Haghighi and Klein, 2006). Täckström et al. (2013) investigate weakly supervised POS tagging in low-resource languages, combining dictionary constraints and labels projected across languages via parallel corpora and automatic alignment. Our work can be seen as an extension of their approach to the structured-data projection setup presented by Li et al. (2009). A notable component of our extension is that we introduce a training algorithm for learning a hidden unit CRF of Maaten et al. (2011) from partially labeled sequences. This model has a set of binary latent variables that introduce non-linearity by mediating between observations and labels.

## 6 Conclusions

In this paper, we applied weakly-supervised learning approach for slot tagging, projecting annotations from structured data to user queries by leveraging click log data. We extended the Täckström et al. (2013) model to nonlinear CRFs by introducing latent variables and applying a novel pre-training methodology. The proposed techniques provide an effective way to leverage incomplete and ambiguous annotations from large amounts of naturally occurring click log data. All of our improvements taken together result in a 21% error reduction over vanilla CRFs trained on engineered data used during system development.

## References


Lada A Adamic and Bernardo A Huberman. 2002. Zipfs law and the internet. *Glottometrics*, 3(1):143–150.

Eugene Agichtein and Luis Gravano. 2000. Snowball: Extracting relations from large plain-text collections. In *Proceedings of the fifth ACM conference on Digital libraries*.

Tasos Anastasakos, Young-Bum Kim, and Anoop Deoras. 2014. Task specific continuous word representations for mono and multi-lingual spoken language understanding. In *Acoustics, Speech and Signal Processing (ICASSP), 2014 IEEE International Conference on*, pages 3246–3250. IEEE.

Dipanjan Das and Slav Petrov. 2011. Unsupervised part-of-speech tagging with bilingual graph-based projections. In *Proceedings of the 49th Annual Meeting of the Association for Computational Linguistics: Human Language Technologies-Volume 1*, pages 600–609. Association for Computational Linguistics.

Ali El-Kahky, Xiaohu Liu, Ruhi Sarikaya, Gokhan Tur, Dilek Hakkani-Tur, and Larry Heck. 2014. Extending domain coverage of language understanding systems via intent transfer between domains using knowledge graphs and search query click logs. In *Acoustics, Speech and Signal Processing (ICASSP), 2014 IEEE International Conference on*, pages 4067–4071. IEEE.

Andrew Gelfand, Yutian Chen, Laurens Maaten, and Max Welling. 2010. On herding and the perceptron cycling theorem. In *Advances in Neural Information Processing Systems*, pages 694–702.

Aria Haghighi and Dan Klein. 2006. Prototype-driven learning for sequence models. In *Proceedings of the main conference on Human Language Technology Conference of the North American Chapter of the Association of Computational Linguistics*.

Nicholas Kushmerick. 1997. *Wrapper induction for information extraction*. Ph.D. thesis, University of Washington.

John Lafferty, Andrew McCallum, and Fernando CN Pereira. 2001. Conditional random fields: Probabilistic models for segmenting and labeling sequence data. In *Proceedings of the 18th International Conference on Machine Learning*, pages 282–289.

Hugo Larochelle and Yoshua Bengio. 2008. Classification using discriminative restricted boltzmann machines. In *Proceedings of the 25th international conference on Machine learning*.

Xiao Li, Ye-Yi Wang, and Alex Acero. 2009. Extracting structured information from user queries with semi-supervised conditional random fields. In *Proceedings of the 32nd international ACM SIGIR conference on Research and development in information retrieval*.

Shen Li, Joao V Graça, and Ben Taskar. 2012. Wiki-ly supervised part-of-speech tagging. In *Proceedings of the 2012 Joint Conference on Empirical Methods in Natural Language Processing and Computational Natural Language Learning*, pages 1389–1398. Association for Computational Linguistics.

Xiaohu Liu, Ruhi Sarikaya, Chris Brockett, Chris Quirk, William B Dolan, and Bill Dolan. 2013. Paraphrase features to improve natural language understanding. In *INTERSPEECH*, pages 3776–3779.

Laurens Maaten, Max Welling, and Lawrence K Saul. 2011. Hidden-unit conditional random fields. In *International Conference on Artificial Intelligence and Statistics*.

Alex Marin, Roman Holenstein, Ruhi Sarikaya, and Mari Ostendorf. 2014. Learning phrase patterns for text classification using a knowledge graph and unlabeled data. In *Fifteenth Annual Conference of the International Speech Communication Association*.

Mike Mintz, Steven Bills, Rion Snow, and Dan Jurafsky. 2009. Distant supervision for relation extraction without labeled data. In *Proceedings of the Joint Conference of the 47th Annual Meeting of the ACL and the 4th International Joint Conference on Natural Language Processing of the AFNLP: Volume 2-Volume 2*.

Sebastian Riedel, Limin Yao, and Andrew McCallum. 2010. Modeling relations and their mentions without labeled text. In *Machine Learning and Knowledge Discovery in Databases*.

Ruhi Sarikaya, Asli Celikyilmaz, Anoop Deoras, and Minwoo Jeong. 2014. Shrinkage based features for slot tagging with conditional random fields. In *Proc. of Interspeech*.

Mihai Surdeanu, Julie Tibshirani, Ramesh Nallapati, and Christopher D Manning. 2012. Multi-instance multi-label learning for relation extraction. In *Proceedings of the 2012 Joint Conference on Empirical Methods in Natural Language Processing and Computational Natural Language Learning*.

Oscar Täckström, Dipanjan Das, Slav Petrov, Ryan McDonald, and Joakim Nivre. 2013. Token and type constraints for cross-lingual part-of-speech tagging.

Kristina Toutanova and Mark Johnson. 2007. A bayesian lda-based model for semi-supervised part-of-speech tagging. In *Advances in Neural Information Processing Systems*, pages 1521–1528.

Svitlana Volkova, Pallavi Choudhury, Chris Quirk, Bill Dolan, and Luke S Zettlemoyer. 2013. Lightly supervised learning of procedural dialog systems. In *ACL*.

Fei Wu and Daniel S Weld. 2007. Autonomously semantifying wikipedia. In *Proceedings of the sixteenth ACM conference on Conference on information and knowledge management*.

# Not All Character $N$-grams Are Created Equal: A Study in Authorship Attribution

**Upendra Sapkota** and **Steven Bethard**
The University of Alabama at Birmingham
1300 University Boulevard
Birmingham, AL 35294, USA
{upendra,bethard}@cis.uab.edu

**Manuel Montes-y-Gómez**
Instituto Nacional de Astrofísica
Optica y Electrónica
Puebla, Mexico
mmontesg@ccc.inaoep.mx

**Thamar Solorio**
University of Houston
4800 Calhoun Rd
Houston, TX, 77004, USA
solorio@cs.uh.edu

## Abstract

Character $n$-grams have been identified as the most successful feature in both single-domain and cross-domain Authorship Attribution (AA), but the reasons for their discriminative value were not fully understood. We identify subgroups of character $n$-grams that correspond to linguistic aspects commonly claimed to be covered by these features: morpho-syntax, thematic content and style. We evaluate the predictiveness of each of these groups in two AA settings: a single domain setting and a cross-domain setting where multiple topics are present. We demonstrate that character $n$-grams that capture information about affixes and punctuation account for almost all of the power of character $n$-grams as features. Our study contributes new insights into the use of $n$-grams for future AA work and other classification tasks.

## 1 Introduction

Authorship Attribution (AA) tackles the problem of determining who, among a set of authors, wrote the document at hand. AA has relevant applications ranging from plagiarism detection (Stamatatos, 2011) to Forensic Linguistics, such as identifying authorship of threatening emails or malicious code. Applied areas such as law and journalism can also benefit from authorship attribution, where identifying the true author of a piece of text (such as a ransom note) may help save lives or catch the offenders.

We know from state of the art research in AA that the length of the documents and the number of potential candidate authors have an important effect on the accuracy of AA approaches (Moore, 2001; Luyckx and Daelemans, 2008; Luyckx and Daelemans, 2010). We can also point out the most common features that have been used successfully in AA work, including: bag-of-words (Madigan et al., 2005; Stamatatos, 2006), stylistic features (Zheng et al., 2006; Stamatatos et al., 2000), and word and character level $n$-grams (Kjell et al., 1994; Keselj et al., 2003; Peng et al., 2003; Juola, 2006).

The utility of bag-of-words features is well understood: they effectively capture correlations between authors and topics (Madigan et al., 2005; Kaster et al., 2005). The discriminative value of these features is thus directly related to the level of content divergence among authors and among train and test sets.

The utility of stylistic features is also well understood: they model author preferences for the use of punctuation marks, emoticons, white spaces, and other traces of writing style. Such preferences are less influenced by topic, and directly reflect some of the unique writing patterns of an author.

Character $n$-grams are the single most successful feature in authorship attribution (Koppel et al., 2009; Frantzeskou et al., 2007; Koppel et al., 2011), but the reason for their success is not well understood. One hypothesis is that character $n$-grams carry a little bit of everything: lexical content, syntactic content, and even style by means of punctuation and white spaces (Koppel et al., 2011). While this argument seems plausible, it falls short of a rigorous explanation.

In this paper, we investigate what in the make-up



*Human Language Technologies: The 2015 Annual Conference of the North American Chapter of the ACL*, pages 93–102,
Denver, Colorado, May 31 – June 5, 2015. 

of these small units of text makes them so powerful. Our goal is two-fold: on the one hand we want to have a principled understanding of character $n$-grams that will inform their use as features for AA and other tasks; on the other hand we want to make AA approaches more accessible to non-experts so that, for example, they could be acceptable pieces of evidence in criminal cases.

The research questions we aim to answer are:

- *Are all character $n$-grams equally important?* For example, are the prefix of '**the**re', the suffix of 'brea**the**' and the whole word '**the**' all equivalent? More generally, are character $n$-grams that capture morpho-syntactic information, thematic information and style information equally important?

- *Are the character $n$-grams that are most important for single-domain settings also the most important for cross-domain settings?* Which character $n$-grams are more like bag-of-words features (which tend to track topics), and which are more like stylistic features (which tend to track authors)?

- *Do different classifiers agree on the importance of the different types of character $n$-grams?* Are some character $n$-grams consistently the best regardless of the learning algorithm?

- *Are some types of character $n$-grams irrelevant in AA tasks?* Are there categories of character $n$-grams that we can exclude and get similar (or better) performance than using all $n$-grams? If there are, are they the same for both single-domain and cross-domain AA settings?

Our study shows that using the default bag-of-words representation of char $n$-grams results in collapsing sequences of characters that correspond to different linguistic aspects, and that this yields suboptimal prediction performance. We further show that we can boost accuracy by loosing some categories of $n$-grams. Char $n$-grams closely related to thematic content can be completely removed without loss of accuracy, even in cases where the train and test sets have the same topics represented, a counter-intuitive argument. Given the wide spread use of char $n$-grams in text classification tasks, our findings have significant implications for future work in related areas.

## 2 Categories of Character $N$-grams

To answer our research questions and explore the value of character $n$-grams in authorship attribution, we propose to separate character $n$-grams into ten distinct categories. Unlike previous AA work where all character $n$-grams were combined into a single bag-of-$n$-grams, we evaluate each category separately to understand its behavior and effectiveness in AA tasks. These categories are related to the three linguistic aspects hypothesized to be represented by character $n$-grams: morpho-syntax (as represented by affix-like $n$-grams), thematic content (as represented by word-like $n$-grams) and style (as represented by punctuation-based $n$-grams). We refer to these three aspects as super categories (SC).

The following sections describe the different types of $n$-grams. We use the sentence in Table 1 as a running example for the classes and in Table 2 we show the resulting $n$-grams in that sentence. For ease of understanding, we replace spaces in $n$-grams with underscores (_).

| |
|---|
| The actors wanted to see if the pact seemed like an old-fashioned one. |

Table 1: Example sentence to demonstrate the selection of different $n$-gram categories.

### 2.1 Affix $n$-grams

Character $n$-grams are generally too short to represent any deep syntax, but some of them can reflect morphology to some degree. In particular, we consider the following affix-like features by looking at $n$-grams that begin or end a word:

**prefix** A character $n$-gram that covers the first $n$ characters of a word that is at least $n + 1$ characters long.

**suffix** A character $n$-gram that covers the last $n$ characters of a word that is at least $n + 1$ characters long.

**space-prefix** A character $n$-gram that begins with a space.

| SC | Category | Character $n$-grams |
|---|---|---|
| affix | *prefix* | **act** wan pac **see** lik fas |
| | *suffix* | ors ted **act** med ike ned |
| | *space-prefix* | _ac _wa _to _se _if _th _pa _li _an _ol _on |
| | *space-suffix* | he_ rs_ ed_ to_ ee_ if_ ct_ ke_ an_ |
| word | *whole-word* | The **see** the old **one** |
| | *mid-word* | cto tor ant nte eem eme ash shi hio ion **one** |
| | *multi-word* | e_a s_w d_t o_s e_i f_t e_p t_s d_l n_o d_o |
| punct | *beg-punct* | -fa |
| | *mid-punct* | d-f |
| | *end-punct* | ld- ne. |

Table 2: Example of the $n$-gram categories ($n$ = 3) for the sentence in Table 1. The first column represents the super category (SC). The $n$-grams that appear in more than one category are in bold.

**space-suffix** A character $n$-gram that ends with a space.

### 2.2 Word $n$-grams

While character $n$-grams are often too short to capture entire words, some types can capture partial words and other word-relevant tokens. We consider the following such features:

**whole-word** A character $n$-gram that covers all characters of a word that is exactly $n$ characters long.

**mid-word** A character $n$-gram that covers $n$ characters of a word that is at least $n + 2$ characters long, and that covers neither the first nor the last character of the word.

**multi-word** $N$-grams that span multiple words, identified by the presence of a space in the middle of the $n$-gram.

### 2.3 Punctuation $n$-grams

The main stylistic choices that character $n$-grams can capture are the author's preferences for particular patterns of punctuation. The following features characterize punctuation by its location in the $n$-gram.

**beg-punct** A character $n$-gram whose first character is punctuation, but middle characters are not.

**mid-punct** A character $n$-gram with at least one punctuation character that is neither the first nor the last character.

**end-punct** A character $n$-gram whose last character is punctuation, but middle characters are not.

The above ten categories are intended to be disjoint, so that a character $n$-gram belongs to exactly one of the categories. For $n$-grams that contain both spaces and punctuation, we first categorize by punctuation and then by spaces. For example, 'e,_' is assigned to the *mid-punct* category, not the *space-suffix* category.

We have observed that in our data almost 80% of the $n$-grams in the *punct-beg* and *punct-mid* categories contain a space. This tight coupling of punctuation and spaces is due to the rules of English orthography: most punctuation marks require a space following them. The 20% of $n$-grams that have punctuation but no spaces correspond mostly to the exceptions to this rule: quotation marks, mid-word hyphens, etc. An interesting experiment for future work would be to split out these two types of punctuation into separate feature categories.

## 3 Datasets

We consider two corpora, a single-domain corpus, where there is only one topic that all authors are writing about, and a multi-domain corpus, where there are multiple different topics. The latter allows us to test the generalization of AA models, by testing them on a different topic from that used for training.

The first collection is the CCAT topic class, a subset of the Reuters Corpus Volume 1 (Lewis et al., 2004). Although this collection was not gathered for the goal of doing authorship attribution studies, previous work has reported results for AA with 10 and 50 authors (Stamatatos, 2008; Plakias and Stamatatos, 2008; Escalante et al., 2011). We refer to these as CCAT_10 and CCAT_50, respectively. Both CCAT_10 and CCAT_50 belong to CCAT category (about corporate/industrial news) and are balanced across authors, with 100 documents sampled for each author. Manual inspection of the dataset revealed that some of the authors in this collection consistently used signatures at the end of documents. Also, we noticed some writers use quotations a lot. Con-

| Corpus | #authors | #docs /author/topic | #sentences /doc | #words /doc |
|---|---|---|---|---|
| CCAT_10 | 10 | 100 | 19 | 425 |
| CCAT_50 | 50 | 100 | 19 | 415 |
| Guardian1 | 13 | 13 | 53 | 1034 |
| Guardian2 | 13 | 65 | 10 | 207 |

Table 3: Some statistics about the datasets.

sidering these parts of text for measuring the frequencies of character $n$-grams is not a good idea because signatures provide direct clues about the authorship of document and quotations do not reflect the author's writing style. Therefore, to clean up the CCAT collection, we preprocessed it to remove signatures and quotations from each document. Since the CCAT collection contains documents belonging to only corporate/industrial topic category, this will be our single-domain collection.

The other collection consists of texts published in The Guardian daily newspaper written by 13 authors in four different topics (Stamatatos, 2013). This dataset contains opinion articles on the topics: World, U.K., Society, and Politics. Following prior work, to make the collection balanced across authors, we choose at most ten documents per author for each of the four topics. We refer to this corpus as Guardian1. We also consider a variation of this corpus that makes it more challenging but that more closely matches realistic scenarios of forensic investigation that deal with short texts such as tweets, SMS, and emails. We chunk each of the documents by sentence boundaries into five new short documents. We refer to this corpus as Guardian2.

Table 3 shows some of the statistics of the CCAT and Guardian corpora and Table 4 presents some of the top character $n$-grams for each category (taken from an author in the Guardian data, but the top $n$-grams look qualitatively similar for other authors).

| SC | Category | $N$-grams | | | | |
|---|---|---|---|---|---|---|
| **affix** | *prefix* | tha | the | wit | con | hav |
| | *suffix* | ing | hat | ion | ent | ers |
| | *space-prefix* | _th | _of | _to | _an | _in |
| | *space-suffix* | he_ | of_ | to_ | ed_ | ng_ |
| **word** | *whole-word* | the | and | for | was | not |
| | *mid-word* | tio | ati | iti | men | ent |
| | *multi-word* | e_t | s_a | t_t | s_t | n_t |
| **punct** | *beg-punct* | ._T | 's_ | ,_t | ,_a | ._I |
| | *mid-punct* | s,_ | e,_ | s._ | e's | y's |
| | *end-punct* | es, | on. | on, | es. | er, |

Table 4: Top character 3-grams in each category for author 'Catherine Bennet' in the cross-domain training data.

## 4 Experimental Settings

We performed various experiments using different categories of character $n$-grams. We chose $n$=3 since our preliminary experiments found character 3-grams to be more effective than other higher level character $n$-grams. For each category, we considered only those 3-grams that occur at least five times in the training documents.

The performance of different authorship attribution models was measured in terms of accuracy. In the single-domain CCAT experiments, accuracy was measured using the train/test partition of prior work. In the cross-domain Guardian experiments, accuracy was measured by considering all 12 possible pairings of the 4 topics, treating one topic as training data and the other as testing data, and averaging accuracy over these 12 scenarios. This ensured that in the cross-domain experiments, the topics of the training data were always different from that of the test data.

We trained support vector machine (SVM) classifiers using the Weka implementation (Witten and Frank, 2005) with default parameters. We also ran some comparative experiments with the Weka implementation of naive Bayes classifiers and the LibSVM implementation of SVMs. In the results below, when performance of a single classifier is presented, it is the result of Weka's SVM, which generally gave the best performance. When performance of other classifiers are presented, the classifiers are explicitly indicated.

## 5 Experimental Results and Evaluation

In this section, we present various results on authorship attribution tasks using both single as well as cross-domain datasets. We will explore character $n$-grams in depth and try to understand why they are so effective in discriminating authors.

### 5.1 Which $n$-gram Categories are Most Author-Discriminative?

After breaking character $n$-grams into ten disjoint categories, we empirically illustrate what categories are

| | affix | | | | word | | | punct | | |
|---|---|---|---|---|---|---|---|---|---|---|
| **Dataset** | *prefix* | *suffix* | *space-prefix* | *space-suffix* | *multi-word* | *whole-word* | *mid-word* | *beg-punct* | *mid-punct* | *end-punct* |
| **CCAT_10** | **74.6** | **71.0** | **71.2** | 66.0 | 65.8 | 48.0 | **70.0** | 60.2 | 35.4 | 56.2 |
| **CCAT_50** | **61.9** | **59.6** | **57.0** | 51.0 | 51.2 | 35.4 | **61.0** | 39.7 | 12.4 | 36.5 |

(a) Single Domain

| | affix | | | | word | | | punct | | |
|---|---|---|---|---|---|---|---|---|---|---|
| **Dataset** | *prefix* | *suffix* | *space-prefix* | *space-suffix* | *multi-word* | *whole-word* | *mid-word* | *beg-punct* | *mid-punct* | *end-punct* |
| **Guardian1** | **41.6** | 36.7 | **41.9** | 38.1 | 32.2 | 38.1 | 37.8 | **43.5** | **46.1** | 37.3 |
| **Guardian2** | **31.0** | 26.9 | **29.7** | 27.0 | 23.2 | 26.8 | 27.2 | **33.6** | **33.5** | 24.5 |

(b) Cross-Domain

Table 5: Accuracy of AA classifiers trained on each of the character $n$-gram categories. The top four accuracies for each dataset are in bold.

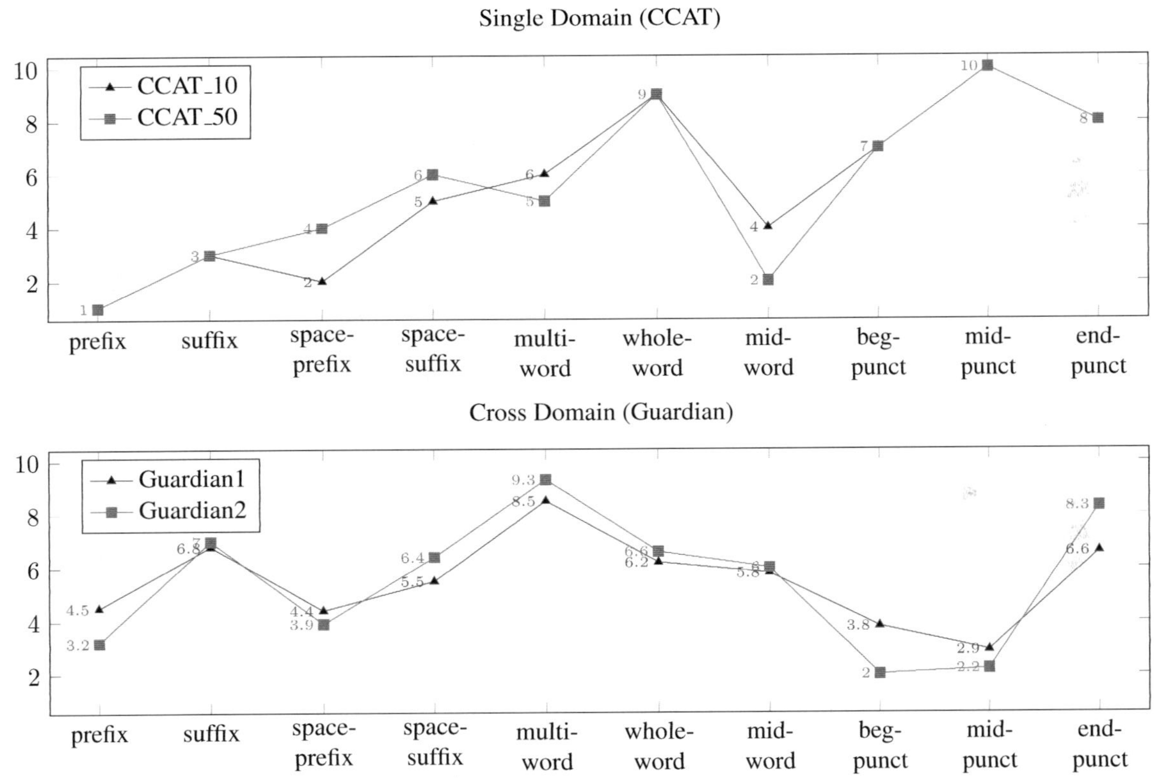


Figure 1: Average rank of the performance of each $n$-gram category on the single-domain CCAT tasks (top) and the cross-domain Guardian tasks (bottom).

most discriminative. Table 5 shows the accuracy of each type of $n$-gram for each of the different corpora.

Table 5(a) shows that the top four categories for single-domain AA are: *prefix*, *suffix*, *space-prefix*, and *mid-word*. These four categories have the best performance on both CCAT_10 and CCAT_50. In contrast, Table 5(b) shows that the top four categories for cross-domain AA are: *prefix*, *space-prefix*, *beg-punct*, and *mid-punct*.

For both single-domain and cross-domain AA, *prefix* and *space-prefix* are strong features, and are generally better than the suffix features, perhaps because authors have more control over prefixes in English, while suffixes are often obligatory for grammatical reasons. For cross-domain AA, *beg-punct* and *mid-punct* are the top features, likely because an author's use of punctuation is consistent even when the topic changes. For single-domain AA, *mid-word* was also a good feature, probably because it captured lexical information that correlates with authors' preferences towards writing about specific topics.

Figure 1 shows an alternate view of these results, graphing the rank of each $n$-gram type. For computing the rank, the accuracies of the ten different $n$-gram type classifiers are sorted in decreasing order and ranked from 1 to 10 respectively with ties getting the same rank. For the Guardian corpora, the average rank of each $n$-gram category was computed by averaging its rank across the 12 possible test/train cross-domain combinations. In both of the single-domain CCAT corpora, the classifier based on *prefix* $n$-grams had the top accuracy (rank 1), and the classifier based on *mid-punct* had the worst accuracy (rank 10). In both of the cross-domain Guardian corpora, on the other hand, *mid-punct* was among the top-ranked $n$-gram categories. This suggests that punctuation features generalize the best across topic, but if AA is more of a topic classification task (as in the single-domain CCAT corpora), then punctuation adds little over other features that more directly capture the topic.

Since our cross-domain datasets are small, we performed a small number of planned comparisons using a two-tailed t-test over the accuracies on the Guardian1 and Guardian2 corpora. We found that in both corpora, the best punctuation category (*punct-mid*) is better than the best word category (*whole-word*) with $p < 0.001$. In the Guardian2 corpus, the best affix category (*space-prefix*) is also better than the best word category (*whole-word*) with $p < 0.05$, but this does not hold in the Guardian1 corpus ($p = 0.14$). Also, we observed that in both Guardian1 and Guardian2 datasets, both *punct-mid* and *space-prefix* are better than *multi-word* ($p < 0.01$).

Overall, we see that **affix** $n$-grams are generally effective in both single-domain and cross-domain settings, **punctuation** $n$-grams are effective in cross-domain settings, and *mid-word* is the only effective **word** $n$-gram, and only in the single-domain setting.

## 5.2 Do Different Classifiers Agree on the Importance of Different $n$-gram Types?

The previous experiments have shown, for example, that *prefix* $n$-grams are universally predictive in AA tasks, that *mid-word* $n$-grams are good predictors in single-domain settings, and that *beg-punct* $n$-grams are good predictors in cross-domain settings. But are these facts about the $n$-gram types themselves, or are these results only true for the specific SVM classifiers we trained?

| Comparison | CCAT | Guardian |
|---|---|---|
| **Weka SVM vs LibSVM** | 0.93 | 0.81 |
| **Weka SVM vs Naive Bayes** | 0.73 | 0.57 |
| **LibSVM vs Naive Bayes** | 0.77 | 0.44 |

Table 6: Spearman's rank correlation coefficient ($\rho$) for each pair of classifiers on the single-domain (CCAT) and cross-domain (Guardian) settings.

To see whether certain types of $n$-grams are fundamentally good or bad, regardless of the classifier, we compare performance of the different $n$-gram types for three classifiers: Weka SVM classifiers (as used in our other experiments), LibSVM classifiers and Weka's naive Bayes classifiers[1]. Figure 2 shows the $n$-gram category rankings for all these classifiers[2] for both the single-domain CCAT and the cross-domain Guardian settings.

Across the different classifiers, the pattern of feature rankings are similar. Table 6 shows the Spearman's rank correlation coefficient ($\rho$) for the per-$n$-gram-type accuracies of each pair of classifiers. We observe fairly high correlations, with $\rho$ above 0.70 for all single-domain pairings, and between 0.44 and 0.81 for cross-domain pairings.

As in Section 5.1, *prefix* and *space-prefix* are among the most predictive $n$-gram types. In the single-domain settings, we again see that *suffix* and *mid-word* are also highly predictive, while in the cross-domain settings, we again see that *beg-punct* and *mid-punct* are highly predictive. These results all confirm that some types of $n$-grams are fundamentally more predictive than others, and our results are not specific to the particular type of classifier used.

[1]Weka SVM and LibSVM are both support vector machine classifiers, but Weka uses Platt's sequential minimal optimization algorithm while LibSVM uses working set selection with second order information. The result is that they achieve different performance on our AA tasks.

[2]We also tried a decision tree classifier, C4.5 (J48) from WEKA, and it produced similar patterns (not shown).

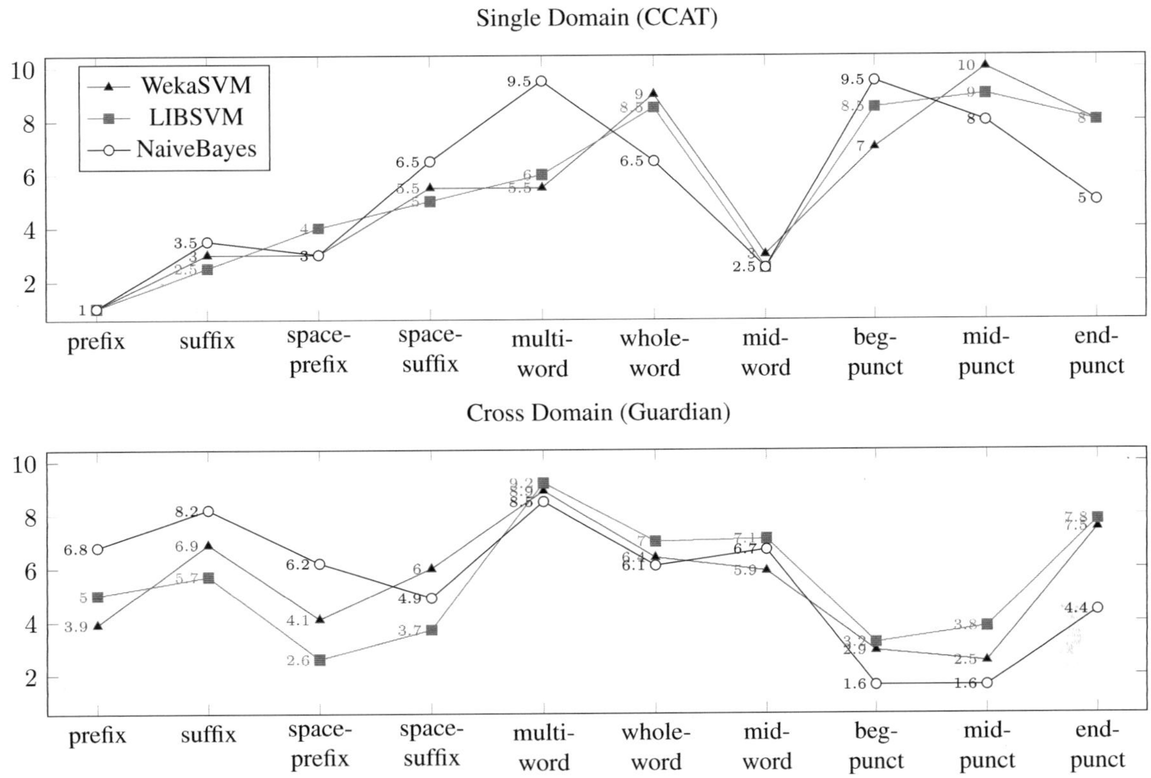


Figure 2: Average rank of the performance of each $n$-gram category across different types of classifiers on the single-domain CCAT task (top) and the cross-domain Guardian task (bottom).

### 5.3 Are Some Character $N$-grams Irrelevant?

In the previous sections, we have seen that some types of character $n$-grams are more predictive than others - **affix** $n$-grams performed well in both single domain and cross-domain settings and **punctuation** $n$-grams performed well in cross-domain settings. In general, **word** $n$-grams were not as predictive as other types of $n$-grams (with the one exception being *mid-word* $n$-grams in the single domain setting). Given this poor performance of **word** $n$-grams, a natural question is: could we exclude these features entirely and achieve similar performance?

Our goal then is to compare a model trained on **affix** $n$-grams and **punct** $n$-grams against a model trained on "all" $n$-grams. We consider two definitions of "all":

**all-untyped** The traditional approach to extracting $n$-grams where $n$-gram types are ignored (e.g., 'the' as a whole word is no different from 'the' in the middle of a word)

**all-typed** The approach discussed in this paper, where $n$-grams of different types are distinguished (equivalent to the set of all **affix+punct+word** $n$-grams).

We compare these models trained on all the $n$-grams to our **affix+punct** model.

Table 7 shows this analysis. For either definition of "all", the model that discards all **word** features achieves performance as high or higher than the model with all of the features, and does so with only about two thirds of the features. This is not too surprising in the cross-domain Guardian tasks, where the **word** $n$-grams were among the worst features. On the single-domain CCAT tasks this result is more surprising, since we have discarded the *mid-word* $n$-grams, which was one of the best single-domain $n$-gram types. This indicates that whatever information *mid-word* is capturing it is also being captured in other ways via **affix** and **punct** $n$-grams. Of all 1024 possible combinations of features, we tried a

| Dataset | all-untyped | | all-typed | | affix+punct | |
|---|---|---|---|---|---|---|
| | Acc | *N* | Acc | *N* | Acc | *N* |
| **CCAT_10** | 77.8 | *8245* | 77.2 | *9715* | **78.8** | *5474* |
| **CCAT_50** | 69.2 | *14461* | 69.1 | *17062* | **69.3** | *9966* |
| **Guardian1** | 55.6 | *5689* | 53.6 | *6966* | **57.0** | *3822* |
| **Guardian2** | 45.9 | *5687* | 45.6 | *6965* | **48.0** | *3820* |

Table 7: Results of excluding **word** $n$-grams, compared to using all $n$-grams, either in the traditional approach (untyped $n$-grams) or in the approach of this paper (typed $n$-grams). Accuracy (Acc) and the number of features (*N* in italics) are reported for each classifier. The best accuracy for each dataset is in bold.

| |
|---|
| To use old-fashioned language, she is motherly - a plump, rosy-cheeked woman of Kent, whom nature seemed to have created to raise children. |
| To use old-fas ned lan age, she is mot rly - a plump, rosy-che ked woman of Kent, whom nature seemed to have cre ted to raise chi ren. |

Table 8: Example sentence showing the opacity of each character. Darkness of character is determined by the number of categories it belongs to (lowest=lighter, highest=darkest color). Categories in **word** are discarded.

number of different combinations and were unable to identify one that outperformed **affix+punct**. Overall, this experiment gives compelling evidence that **affix** and **punct** $n$-grams are more important than **word** $n$-grams.

## 6 Analysis

We did a manual exploration of our datasets. In our cross-domain dataset, the character 3-gram 'sti' shows up as both *prefix* and *mid-word*. All 13 authors use 'sti' frequently as a *mid-word* $n$-gram in words such as in**sti**tution, exi**sti**ng, ju**sti**ce, and di**sti**nction. For example:

- The government's story is that the exi**sti**ng warheads might be deteriorating.
- For all the ju**sti**ce of many of his accusations, the result is occasionally as dreadful as his title suggests.

But only six authors use 'sti' as a *prefix*, in examples like:

- Their mission was to convince tourists that Britain was **sti**ll open for business.
- There aren't even any dead people on it, since by the very act of being dead and **sti**ll famous, they assert their long-term impact.

Thus 'sti' as a *prefix* is predictive of authorship even though 'sti' as a *mid-word* $n$-gram is not. Notably, under the traditional untyped bag-of-$n$-grams approach, both versions of 'sti' would have been treated the same, and this discriminative power would have been lost.

As already demonstrated in Section 5 that **affix+punct** features perform better than using all the features, we would like to use an example from our dataset to visualize the text when features in SC **word** are discarded. Out of seven categories in **affix** and **punct**, we computed in how many of them each character belongs to, three being the maximum possible value. Therefore, we show each character with different opacity level depending on number of categories it belongs to: zero will get white color (word related $n$-grams), one will get 33% black, two will get 67% black, and three will get 100% black. In Table 8, we show an example sentence before (first row of Table 8) and after (second row of Table 8) showing the opacity level of each character. It is clear that the darkest characters are those around the punctuation characters and those around spaces are second darkest, while the lightest (with 0% darkness) are the ones in the middle of long words. This gives us an idea about the characters in a text that are important for AA tasks.

## 7 Discussion

Various hypotheses have been put forth to explain the "black magic" (Kestemont, 2014) behind the success of character $n$-gram features in authorship attribution. Kestemont (2014) conjectured that their utility was in capturing function words and morphology. Koppel et al. (2009) suggested that they were capturing topic information in single domain settings, and style and syntactic information in cross-domain settings. Our study provides empirical evidence for testing these claims. We did indeed find that the ability of character $n$-grams to capture morphology is useful, as reflected in the high prediction performance of **af-**

**fix** $n$-grams in both single-domain and cross-domain settings. And we found that **word** $n$-grams (capturing topic information) were useful in single domain settings, while **puct** $n$-grams (capturing style information) were useful in cross-domain settings. We further found that **word** $n$-grams are unnecessary, even in single-domain settings. Models based only on **affix** and **punct** $n$-grams performed as well as models with all $n$-grams regardless of whether it was a single-domain or cross-domain authorship attribution task.

Our findings on the value of selecting $n$-grams according to the linguistic aspect they represent may also be beneficial in other classification tasks where character $n$-grams are commonly used. Promising tasks are those related to the stylistic analysis of texts, such as native language identification, document similarity and plagiarism detection.

Morphologically speaking, English is a poor language. The fact that we identified significant differences in performance by selecting $n$-gram categories that are related to affixation in this poorly inflected language suggests that we may find even larger differences in performance in morphologically richer languages. We leave this research question for future work.

## Acknowledgements

This research was partially supported by NSF awards 1462141 and 1254108. It was also supported in part by the CONACYT grant 134186 and the WIQ-EI IRSES project (grant no. 269180) within the FP 7 Marie Curie.

## References

H. J. Escalante, T. Solorio, and M. Montes-y Gomez. 2011. Local histograms of character n-grams for authorship attribution. In *Proceedings of the 49th Annual Meeting of the Association for Computational Linguistics: Human Language Technologies*, pages 288–298, Portland, Oregon, USA, June. Association for Computational Linguistics.

G. Frantzeskou, E. Stamatatos, S. Gritzalis, and C. E. Chaski. 2007. Identifying authorship by byte-level n-grams: The source code author profile (SCAP) method. *Journal of Digital Evidence*, 6(1).

P. Juola. 2006. Authorship attribution. *Foundations and Trends in Information Retrieval*, 1(3):233–334, December.

A. Kaster, S. Siersdorfer, and G. Weikum. 2005. Combining text and linguistic document representations for authorship attribution. In *SIGIR Workshop: Stylistic Analysis of Text for Information Access (STYLE*, pages 27–35.

V. Keselj, F. Peng, N. Cercone, and C. Thomas. 2003. N-gram based author profiles for authorship attribution. In *Proceedings of the Pacific Association for Computational Linguistics*, pages 255–264.

M. Kestemont. 2014. Function words in authorship attribution. From black magic to theory? In *CLFL*, pages 59–66, Gothenburg, Sweden, April.

Bradley Kjell, W.Addison Woods, and Ophir Frieder. 1994. Discrimination of authorship using visualization. *Information Processing & Management*, 30(1):141 – 150.

M. Koppel, J. Schler, and S. Argamon. 2009. Computational methods in authorship attribution. *Journal of the American Society for Information Science and Technology*, 60(1):9–26.

M. Koppel, J. Schler, and S. Argamon. 2011. Authorship attribution in the wild. *Language Resources and Evaluation*, 45:83–94.

D. D. Lewis, Y. Yang, T. G. Rose, and F. Li. 2004. RCV1: A new benchmark collection for text categorization research. *Journal of Machine Learning Research*, 5:361–397.

K. Luyckx and W. Daelemans. 2008. Authorship attribution and verification with many authors and limited data. In *Proceedings of the 22nd International Conference on Computational Linguistics (COLING 2008)*, pages 513–520, Manchester, UK, August.

K. Luyckx and W. Daelemans. 2010. The effect of author set size and data size in authorship attribution. *Literary and Linguistic Computing*, pages 1–21, August.

D. Madigan, A. Genkin, S. Argamon, D. Fradkin, and L. Ye. 2005. Author identification on the large scale. In *Proceedings of CSNA/Interface 05*.

R. Moore. 2001. There's no data like more data (but when will enough be enough?). In *Proceedings of the IEEE International Workshop on Intelligent Signal Processing*, Budapest, Hungary.

F. Peng, D. Schuurmans, V. Keselj, and S. Wang. 2003. Language independent authorship attribution using character level language models. In *10th Conference of the European Chapter of the Association for Computational Linguistics, EACL*, pages 267–274.

S. Plakias and E. Stamatatos. 2008. Tensor space models for authorship attribution. In *Proceedings of the 5th Hellenic Conference on Artificial Intelligence: Theories, Models and Applications*, volume 5138 of *LNCS*, pages 239–249, Syros, Greece.

E. Stamatatos, G. Kokkinakis, and N. Fakotakis. 2000. Automatic text categorization in terms of genre and author. *Computational Linguistics*, 26(4):471–495, December.

E. Stamatatos. 2006. Authorship attribution based on feature set subspacing ensembles. *International Journal on Artificial Intelligence tools*, 15(5):823–838.

E. Stamatatos. 2008. Author identification: Using text sampling to handle the class imbalance problem. *Information Processing and Managemement*, 44:790–799.

E. Stamatatos. 2011. Plagiarism detection using stopword n-grams. *Journal of the American Society for Information Science and Technology*, 62(12):2512–2527.

E. Stamatatos. 2013. On the robustness of authorship attribution based on character n-gram features. *Journal of Law & Policy*, 21(2):421 – 439.

I. H. Witten and E. Frank. 2005. *Data Mining: Practical Machine Learning Tools and Techniques*. Morgan Kauffmann, 2nd edition.

R. Zheng, Jiexun Li, Hsinchun Chen, and Zan Huang. 2006. A framework for authorship identification of online messages: Writing-style features and classification techniques. *J. Am. Soc. Inf. Sci. Technol.*, 57(3):378–393, February.

# Effective Use of Word Order for Text Categorization with Convolutional Neural Networks

**Rie Johnson**
RJ Research Consulting
Tarrytown, NY, USA
riejohnson@gmail.com

**Tong Zhang**
Baidu Inc., Beijing, China
Rutgers University, Piscataway, NJ, USA
tzhang@stat.rutgers.edu

## Abstract

Convolutional neural network (CNN) is a neural network that can make use of the internal structure of data such as the 2D structure of image data. This paper studies CNN on text categorization to exploit the 1D structure (namely, word order) of text data for accurate prediction. Instead of using low-dimensional word vectors as input as is often done, we directly apply CNN to high-dimensional text data, which leads to directly learning embedding of small text regions for use in classification. In addition to a straightforward adaptation of CNN from image to text, a simple but new variation which employs bag-of-word conversion in the convolution layer is proposed. An extension to combine multiple convolution layers is also explored for higher accuracy. The experiments demonstrate the effectiveness of our approach in comparison with state-of-the-art methods.

## 1 Introduction

Text categorization is the task of automatically assigning pre-defined categories to documents written in natural languages. Several types of text categorization have been studied, each of which deals with different types of documents and categories, such as topic categorization to detect discussed topics (e.g., sports, politics), spam detection (Sahami et al., 1998), and sentiment classification (Pang et al., 2002; Pang and Lee, 2008; Maas et al., 2011) to determine the sentiment typically in product or movie reviews. A standard approach to text categorization is to represent documents by *bag-of-word vectors*, namely, vectors that indicate which words appear in the documents but do not preserve word order, and use classification models such as SVM.

It has been noted that loss of word order caused by bag-of-word vectors (*bow vectors*) is particularly problematic on sentiment classification. A simple remedy is to use word bi-grams in addition to unigrams (Blitzer et al., 2007; Glorot et al., 2011; Wang and Manning, 2012). However, use of word $n$-grams with $n > 1$ on text categorization in general is not always effective; e.g., on topic categorization, simply adding phrases or $n$-grams is not effective (see, e.g., references in (Tan et al., 2002)).

To benefit from word order on text categorization, we take a different approach, which employs *convolutional neural networks (CNN)* (LeCun et al., 1986). CNN is a neural network that can make use of the internal structure of data such as the *2D structure* of image data through convolution layers, where each computation unit responds to a small region of input data (e.g., a small square of a large image). We apply CNN to text categorization to make use of the *1D structure* (word order) of document data so that each unit in the convolution layer responds to a small region of a document (a sequence of words).

CNN has been very successful on image classification; see e.g., the winning solutions of ImageNet Large Scale Visual Recognition Challenge (Krizhevsky et al., 2012; Szegedy et al., 2014; Russakovsky et al., 2014).

On text, since the work on token-level applications (e.g., POS tagging) by Collobert et al. (2011), CNN has been used in systems for entity search, sentence modeling, word embedding learning, product feature mining, and so on (Xu and Sarikaya, 2013; Gao et al., 2014; Shen et al., 2014; Kalchbrenner et al., 2014; Xu et al., 2014; Tang et al., 2014; Weston



*Human Language Technologies: The 2015 Annual Conference of the North American Chapter of the ACL*, pages 103–112,
Denver, Colorado, May 31 – June 5, 2015. 

et al., 2014; Kim, 2014). Notably, in many of these CNN studies on text, the first layer of the network converts words in sentences to *word vectors* by table lookup. The word vectors are either trained as part of CNN training, or fixed to those learned by some other method (e.g., word2vec (Mikolov et al., 2013)) from an additional large corpus. The latter is a form of semi-supervised learning, which we study elsewhere. We are interested in the effectiveness of CNN itself *without aid of additional resources*; therefore, word vectors should be trained as part of network training if word vector lookup is to be done.

A question arises, however, whether word vector lookup in a purely supervised setting is really useful for text categorization. The essence of convolution layers is to *convert text regions of a fixed size (e.g., "am so happy" with size 3) to feature vectors*, as described later. In that sense, a word vector learning layer is a special (and unusual) case of convolution layer with region size one. Why is size one appropriate if bi-grams are more discriminating than unigrams? Hence, we take a different approach. We *directly apply CNN to high-dimensional one-hot vectors*; i.e., we *directly* learn *embedding*[1] of text regions without going through word embedding learning. This approach is made possible by solving the computational issue[2] through efficient handling of high-dimensional sparse data on GPU, and it turned out to have the merits of improving accuracy with fast training/prediction and simplifying the system (fewer hyper-parameters to tune). Our CNN code for text is publicly available on the internet[3].

We study the effectiveness of CNN on text categorization and explain why CNN is suitable for the task. Two types of CNN are tested: *seq-CNN* is a straightforward adaptation of CNN from image to text, and *bow-CNN* is a simple but new variation of CNN that employs bag-of-word conversion in the convolution layer. The experiments show that seq-CNN outperforms bow-CNN on sentiment classification, vice versa on topic classification, and the winner generally outperforms the conventional bag-of-$n$-gram vector-based methods, as well as previous CNN models for text which are more complex. In particular, to our knowledge, this is the first work that has successfully used word order to improve topic classification performance. A simple extension that combines multiple convolution layers (thus combining multiple types of text region embedding) leads to further improvement. Through empirical analysis, we will show that CNN can make effective use of high-order $n$-grams when conventional methods fail.

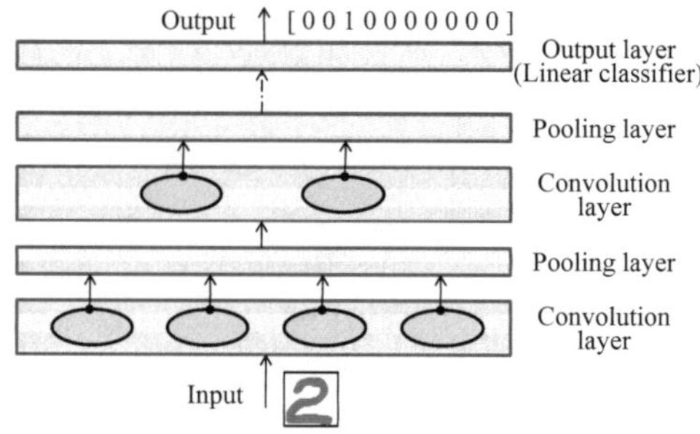


Figure 1: Convolutional neural network.

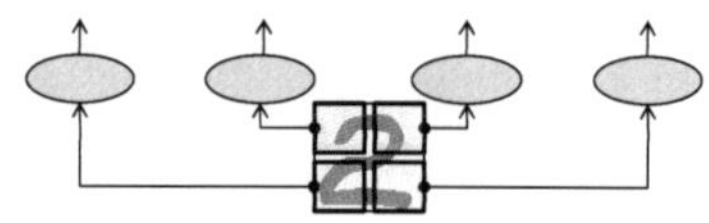

Figure 2: Convolution layer for image. Each computation unit (oval) computes a non-linear function $\boldsymbol{\sigma}(\mathbf{W} \cdot \mathbf{r}_\ell(\mathbf{x}) + \mathbf{b})$ of a small region $\mathbf{r}_\ell(\mathbf{x})$ of input image $\mathbf{x}$, where weight matrix $\mathbf{W}$ and bias vector $\mathbf{b}$ are shared by all the units in the same layer.

## 2 CNN for document classification

We first review CNN applied to image data and then discuss the application of CNN to document classification tasks to introduce seq-CNN and bow-CNN.

### 2.1 Preliminary: CNN for image

CNN is a feed-forward neural network with convolution layers interleaved with pooling layers, as illustrated in Figure 1, where the top layer performs classification using the features generated by the layers below. A convolution layer consists of several computation units, each of which takes as input a *region vector* that represents a small region of the input image and applies a non-linear function to it. Typically, the region vector is a concatenation of pixels in the region, which would be, for example,

[1]We use the term 'embedding' loosely to mean a structure-preserving function, in particular, a function that generates low-dimensional features that preserve the predictive structure.

[2]CNN implemented for image would not handle sparse data efficiently, and without efficient handling of sparse data, convolution over high-dimensional one-hot vectors would be computationally infeasible.

[3]`riejohnson.com/cnn_download.html`

75-dimensional if the region is $5 \times 5$ and the number of *channels* is three (red, green, and blue). Conceptually, computation units are placed over the input image so that the entire image is collectively covered, as illustrated in Figure 2. The region stride (distance between the region centers) is often set to a small value such as 1 so that regions overlap with each other, though the stride in Figure 2 is set larger than the region size for illustration.

A distinguishing feature of convolution layers is *weight sharing*. Given input $\mathbf{x}$, a unit associated with the $\ell$-th region computes $\boldsymbol{\sigma}(\mathbf{W} \cdot \mathbf{r}_\ell(\mathbf{x}) + \mathbf{b})$, where $\mathbf{r}_\ell(\mathbf{x})$ is a region vector representing the region of $\mathbf{x}$ at location $\ell$, and $\boldsymbol{\sigma}$ is a predefined component-wise non-linear activation function, (e.g., applying $\sigma(x) = \max(x, 0)$ to each vector component). The matrix of *weights* $\mathbf{W}$ and the vector of *biases* $\mathbf{b}$ are learned through training, and they are *shared* by the computation units in the same layer. This weight sharing enables learning useful features irrespective of their location, while preserving the location where the useful features appeared.

We regard the output of a convolution layer as an 'image' so that the output of each computation unit is considered to be a 'pixel' of $m$ channels where $m$ is the number of weight vectors (i.e., the number of rows of $\mathbf{W}$) or the number of *neurons*. In other words, *a convolution layer converts image regions to $m$-dim vectors*, and the locations of the regions are inherited through this conversion.

The output image of the convolution layer is passed to a pooling layer, which essentially shrinks the image by merging neighboring pixels, so that higher layers can deal with more abstract/global information. A pooling layer consists of pooling units, each of which is associated with a small region of the image. Commonly-used merging methods are average-pooling and max-pooling, which respectively compute the channel-wise average/maximum of each region.

## 2.2 CNN for text

Now we consider application of CNN to text data. Suppose that we are given a document $D = (w_1, w_2, \ldots)$ with vocabulary $V$. CNN requires vector representation of data that preserves internal locations (word order in this case) as input. A straightforward representation would be to treat each word as a pixel, treat $D$ as if it were an image of $|D| \times 1$ pixels with $|V|$ channels, and to represent each pixel (i.e., each word) as a $|V|$-dimensional one-hot vector[4]. As a running toy example, suppose that vocabulary $V = \{$ "don't", "hate", "I", "it", "love" $\}$ and we associate the words with dimensions of vector in alphabetical order (as shown), and that document $D$="I love it". Then, we have a document vector:

$$\mathbf{x} = [\,0\,0\,1\,0\,0\,|\,0\,0\,0\,0\,1\,|\,0\,0\,0\,1\,0\,]^\top .$$

### 2.2.1 seq-CNN for text

As in the convolution layer for image, we represent each region (which each computation unit responds to) by a concatenation of the pixels, which makes $p|V|$-dimensional region vectors where $p$ is the region size fixed in advance. For example, on the example document vector $\mathbf{x}$ above, with $p = 2$ and stride 1, we would have two regions "I love" and "love it" represented by the following vectors:

$$\mathbf{r}_0(\mathbf{x}) = \left[\begin{array}{c|c} 0 & \text{don't} \\ 0 & \text{hate} \\ \mathbf{1} & \mathbf{I} \\ 0 & \text{it} \\ 0 & \text{love} \\ \text{—} & \\ 0 & \text{don't} \\ 0 & \text{hate} \\ 0 & \text{I} \\ 0 & \text{it} \\ \mathbf{1} & \mathbf{love} \end{array}\right] \qquad \mathbf{r}_1(\mathbf{x}) = \left[\begin{array}{c|c} 0 & \text{don't} \\ 0 & \text{hate} \\ 0 & \text{I} \\ 0 & \text{it} \\ \mathbf{1} & \mathbf{love} \\ \text{—} & \\ 0 & \text{don't} \\ 0 & \text{hate} \\ 0 & \text{I} \\ \mathbf{1} & \mathbf{it} \\ 0 & \text{love} \end{array}\right]$$

The rest is the same as image; *the text region vectors are converted to feature vectors*, i.e., the convolution layer learns to *embed text regions* into low-dimensional vector space. We call a neural net with a convolution layer with this region representation *seq-CNN* ('seq' for keeping sequences of words) to distinguish it from *bow-CNN*, described next.

### 2.2.2 bow-CNN for text

A potential problem of seq-CNN however, is that unlike image data with 3 RGB channels, the number of 'channels' $|V|$ (size of vocabulary) may be very large (e.g., 100K), which could make each region vector $\mathbf{r}_\ell(\mathbf{x})$ very high-dimensional if the region size

[4]Alternatively, one could use *bag-of-letter-n-gram vectors* as in (Shen et al., 2014; Gao et al., 2014) to cope with out-of-vocabulary words and typos.

$p$ is large. Since the dimensionality of region vectors determines the dimensionality of weight vectors, having high-dimensional region vectors means more parameters to learn. If $p|V|$ is too large, the model becomes too complex (w.r.t. the amount of training data available) and/or training becomes unaffordably expensive even with efficient handling of sparse data; therefore, one has to lower the dimensionality by lowering the vocabulary size $|V|$ and/or the region size $p$, which may or may not be desirable, depending on the nature of the task.

An alternative we provide is to perform bag-of-word conversion to make region vectors $|V|$-dimensional instead of $p|V|$-dimensional; e.g., the example region vectors above would be converted to:

$$\mathbf{r}_0(\mathbf{x}) = \begin{bmatrix} 0 \\ 0 \\ \mathbf{1} \\ 0 \\ \mathbf{1} \end{bmatrix} \begin{matrix} \text{don't} \\ \text{hate} \\ \mathbf{I} \\ \text{it} \\ \mathbf{love} \end{matrix} \qquad \mathbf{r}_1(\mathbf{x}) = \begin{bmatrix} 0 \\ 0 \\ 0 \\ \mathbf{1} \\ \mathbf{1} \end{bmatrix} \begin{matrix} \text{don't} \\ \text{hate} \\ \text{I} \\ \mathbf{it} \\ \mathbf{love} \end{matrix}$$

With this representation, we have fewer parameters to learn. Essentially, the expressiveness of bow-convolution (which loses word order only within small regions) is somewhere between seq-convolution and bow vectors.

#### 2.2.3 Pooling for text

Whereas the size of images is fixed in image applications, documents are naturally variable-sized, and therefore, with a fixed stride, the output of a convolution layer is also variable-sized as shown in Figure 3. Given the variable-sized output of the convolution layer, standard pooling for image (which uses a fixed pooling region size and a fixed stride) would produce variable-sized output, which can be passed to another convolution layer. To produce fixed-sized output, which is required by the fully-connected top layer[5], we fix the number of pooling units and dynamically determine the pooling region size on each data point so that the entire data is covered without overlapping.

In the previous CNN work on text, pooling is typically max-pooling over the entire data (i.e., one

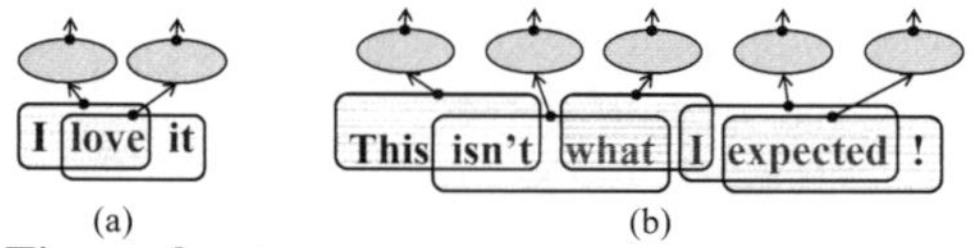

Figure 3: Convolution layer for variable-sized text.

pooling unit associated with the whole text). The *dynamic k-max pooling* of (Kalchbrenner et al., 2014) for sentence modeling extends it to take the $k$ largest values where $k$ is a function of the sentence length, but it is again over the entire data, and the operation is limited to max-pooling. Our pooling differs in that it is a natural extension of standard pooling for image, in which not only max-pooling but other types can be applied. With multiple pooling units associated with different regions, the top layer can receive locational information (e.g., if there are two pooling units, the features from the first half and last half of a document are distinguished). This turned out to be useful (along with average-pooling) on topic classification, as shown later.

### 2.3 CNN vs. bag-of-$n$-grams

Traditional methods represent each document *entirely* with one bag-of-$n$-gram vector and then apply a classifier model such as SVM. However, since high-order $n$-grams are susceptible to data sparsity, use of a large $n$ such as 20 is not only infeasible but also ineffective. Also note that a bag-of-$n$-gram represents each $n$-gram by a one-hot vector and ignores the fact that some $n$-grams share constituent words. By contrast, CNN internally learns *embedding of text regions* (given the consituent words as input) *useful for the intended task*. Consequently, a large $n$ such as 20 can be used especially with the bow-convolution layer, which turned out to be useful on topic classification. A neuron trained to assign a large value to, e.g., "I love" (and a small value to "I hate") is likely to assign a large value to "we love" (and a small value to "we hate") as well, *even though "we love" was never seen during training*. We will confirm these points empirically later.

### 2.4 Extension: parallel CNN

We have described CNN with the simplest network architecture that has one pair of convolution and pooling layers. While this can be extended in several ways (e.g., with deeper layers), in our experiments, we explored *parallel CNN*, which has two or

[5]In this work, the top layer is fully-connected (i.e., each neuron responds to the entire data) as in CNN for image. Alternatively, the top layer could be convolutional so that it can receive variable-sized input, but such CNN would be more complex.

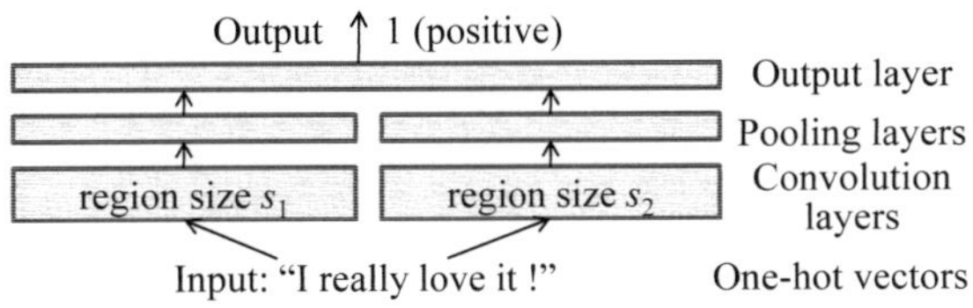


Figure 4: CNN with two convolution layers in parallel.

more convolution layers in parallel[6], as illustrated in Figure 4. The idea is to learn multiple types of embedding of small text regions so that they can complement each other to improve model accuracy. In this architecture, multiple convolution-pooling pairs with different region sizes (and possibly different region vector representations) are given one-hot vectors as input and produce feature vectors for each region; the top layer takes the concatenation of the produced feature vectors as input.

## 3 Experiments

We experimented with CNN on two tasks, topic classification and sentiment classification. Detailed information for reproducing the results is available on the internet along with our code.

### 3.1 CNN

We fixed the activation function to rectifier $\sigma(x) = \max(x, 0)$ and minimized square loss with $L_2$ regularization by *stochastic gradient descent* (SGD). We only used the 30K words that appeared most frequently in the training set; thus, for example, in seq-CNN with region size 3, a region vector is 90K dimensional. Out-of-vocabulary words were represented by a zero vector. On bow-CNN, to speed up computation, we used *variable region stride* so that a larger stride was taken where repetition[7] of the same region vectors can be avoided by doing so. Padding[8] size was fixed to $p - 1$ where $p$ is the region size.

[6]Similar architectures have been used for image. Kim (2014) used it for text, but it was on top of a word vector conversion layer.

[7]For example, if we slide a window of size 3 over "* * foo * *" where "*" is out of vocabulary, a bag of "foo" will be repeated three times with stride fixed to 1.

[8]As is commonly done, to the beginning and the end of each document, special words that are treated as unknown words (and converted to zero vectors instead of one-hot vectors) were added as 'padding'. The purpose is to equally treat the words at the edge and words in the middle.

We used two techniques commonly used with CNN on image, which typically led to small performance improvements. One is *dropout* (Hinton et al., 2012) optionally applied to the input to the top layer. The other is *response normalization* as in (Krizhevsky et al., 2012), which in our case scales the output of the pooling layer $\mathbf{z}$ at each location by multiplying $(1 + |\mathbf{z}|^2)^{-1/2}$.

### 3.2 Baseline methods

For comparison, we tested SVM with the linear kernel and fully-connected neural networks (see e.g., Bishop (1995)) with bag-of-$n$-gram vectors as input. To experiment with fully-connected neural nets, as in CNN, we minimized square loss with $L_2$ regularization and optional dropout by SGD, and activation was fixed to rectifier. To generate bag-of-$n$-gram vectors, on topic classification, we first set each component to $\log(x + 1)$ where $x$ is the word frequency in the document and then scaled them to unit vectors, which we found always improved performance over raw frequency. On sentiment classification, as is often done, we generated binary vectors and scaled them to unit vectors. We tested three types of bag-of-$n$-gram: bow1 with $n \in \{1\}$, bow2 with $n \in \{1, 2\}$, and bow3 with $n \in \{1, 2, 3\}$; that is, bow1 is the traditional bow vectors, and with bow3, each component of the vectors corresponds to either uni-gram, bi-gram, or tri-gram of words.

We used SVMlight[9] for the SVM experiments.

**NB-LM** We also tested NB-LM, which first appeared (but without performance report[10] ) as NB-SVM in WM12 (Wang and Manning, 2012) and later with a small modification produced performance that exceeds state-of-the-art supervised methods on IMDB (which we experimented with) in MMRB14 (Mesnil et al., 2014). We experimented with the MMRB14 version, which generates binary bag-of-$n$-gram vectors, multiplies the component for each $n$-gram $f_i$ with $\log(P(f_i|Y = 1)/P(f_i|Y = -1))$ (*NB-weight*) where the probabilities are estimated using the training data, and does logistic regression training. We used MMRB14's software[11] with a modification so that

[9]`http://svmlight.joachims.org/`

[10]WM12 instead reported the performance of an ensemble of NB and SVM as it performed better.

[11]`https://github.com/mesnilgr/nbsvm`

the regularization parameter can be tuned on development data.

### 3.3 Model selection

For all the methods, the hyper-parameters such as net configurations and regularization parameters were chosen based on the performance on the development data (held-out portion of the training data), and using the chosen hyper-parameters, the models were re-trained using all the training data.

### 3.4 Data, tasks, and data preprocessing

**IMDB: movie reviews** The IMDB dataset (Maas et al., 2011) is a benchmark dataset for sentiment classification. The task is to determine if the movie reviews are positive or negative. Both the training and test sets consist of 25K reviews. For preprocessing, we tokenized the text so that emoticons such as ":-)" are treated as tokens and converted all the characters to lower case.

**Elec: electronics product reviews** Elec consists of electronic product reviews. It is part of a large Amazon review dataset (McAuley and Leskovec, 2013). We chose electronics as it seemed to be very different from movies. Following the generation of IMDB (Maas et al., 2011), we chose the training set and the test set so that one half of each set consists of positive reviews and the other half is negative, regarding rating 1 and 2 as negative and 4 and 5 as positive, and that the reviewed products are disjoint between the training set and test set. Note that to extract text from the original data, we *only* used the *text section*, and we did *not* use the *summary section*. This way, we obtained a test set of 25K reviews (same as IMDB) and training sets of various sizes. The training and test sets are available on the internet[12]. Data preprocessing was the same as IMDB.

**RCV1: topic categorization** RCV1 is a corpus of Reuters news articles as described in LYRL04 (Lewis et al., 2004). RCV1 has 103 topic categories in a hierarchy, and one document may be associated with more than one topic. Performance on this task (multi-label categorization) is known to be sensitive to thresholding strategies, which are algorithms additional to the models we would like to test. Therefore, we also experimented with single-label categorization to assign one of 55 second-level topics to each document to directly evaluate models. For this task, we used the documents from a one-month period as the test set and generated various sizes of training sets from the documents with *earlier* dates. Data sizes are shown in Table 1. As in LYRL04, we used the concatenation of the headline and text elements. Data preprocessing was the same as IMDB except that we used the stopword list provided by LYRL04 and regarded numbers as stopwords.

| | label | #train | #test | #class |
|---|---|---|---|---|
| Table 2 | single | 15,564 | 49,838 | 55 |
| Fig. 6 | single | varies | 49,838 | 55 |
| Table 4 | multi | 23,149 | 781,265 | 103 |

Table 1: RCV1 data summary.

### 3.5 Performance results

Table 2 shows the error rates of CNN in comparison with the baseline methods. The first thing to note is that on all the datasets, the best-performing CNN outperforms the baseline methods, which demonstrates the effectiveness of our approach.

To look into the details, let us first focus on CNN with one convolution layer (seq- and bow-CNN in the table). On sentiment classification (IMDB and Elec), the configuration chosen by model selection was: region size 3, stride 1, 1000 weight vectors, and max-pooling with one pooling unit, for both types of CNN; seq-CNN outperforms bow-CNN, as well as all the baseline methods except for one. Note that with a small region size and max-pooling, if a review contains a short phrase that conveys strong sentiment (e.g., "A great movie!"), the review could receive a high score irrespective of the rest of the review. It is sensible that this type of configuration is effective on sentiment classification.

By contrast, on topic categorization (RCV1), the configuration chosen for bow-CNN by model selection was: region size 20, variable-stride$\geq$2, average-pooling with 10 pooling units, and 1000 weight vectors, which is very different from sentiment classification. This is presumably because on topic classification, a larger context would be more predictive than short fragments ($\rightarrow$ larger region size), the entire document matters ($\rightarrow$ the effectiveness of average-pooling), and the location of predictive text also matters ($\rightarrow$ multiple pooling units). The last

[12] `riejohnson.com/cnn_data.html`

point may be because news documents tend to have crucial sentences (as well as the headline) at the beginning. On this task, while both seq and bow-CNN outperform the baseline methods, bow-CNN outperforms seq-CNN, which indicates that in this setting the merit of having fewer parameters is larger than the benefit of keeping word order in each region.

Now we turn to parallel CNN. On IMDB, seq2-CNN, which has two seq-convolution layers (region size 2 and 3; 1000 neurons each; followed by one unit of max-pooling each), outperforms seq-CNN. With more neurons (3000 neurons each; Table 3) it further exceeds the best-performing baseline, which is also the best previous supervised result. We presume the effectiveness of seq2-CNN indicates that the length of predictive text regions is variable.

The best performance 7.67 on IMDB was obtained by 'seq2-bow$n$-CNN', equipped with three layers in parallel: two seq-convolution layers (1000 neurons each) as in seq2-CNN above and one layer (20 neurons) that *regards the entire document as one region* and represents the region (document) by a bag-of-$n$-gram vector (bow3) as input to the computation unit; in particular, we generated bow3 vectors by multiplying the NB-weights with binary vectors, motivated by the good performance of NB-LM. This third layer is a bow-convolution layer[13] with one region of variable size that takes one-hot vectors with $n$-gram vocabulary as input to learn document embedding. The seq2-bow$n$-CNN for Elec in the table is the same except that the regions sizes of seq-convolution layers are 3 and 4. On both datasets, performance is improved over seq2-CNN. The results suggest that what can be learned through these three layers are distinct enough to complement each other. The effectiveness of the third layer indicates that not only short word sequences but also global context in a large window may be useful on this task; thus, inclusion of a bow-convolution layer with $n$-gram vocabulary with a large fixed region size might be even more effective, providing more focused context, but we did not pursue it in this work.

**Baseline methods** Comparing the baseline methods with each other, on sentiment classification, reducing the vocabulary to the most frequent $n$-grams

[13]It can also be regarded as a fully-connected layer that takes bow3 vectors as input.

| methods | IMDB | Elec | RCV1 |
|---|---|---|---|
| SVM bow3 (30K) | 10.14 | 9.16 | 10.68 |
| SVM bow1 (all) | 11.36 | 11.71 | 10.76 |
| SVM bow2 (all) | 9.74 | 9.05 | 10.59 |
| SVM bow3 (all) | 9.42 | 8.71 | 10.69 |
| NN bow3 (all) | 9.17 | 8.48 | 10.67 |
| NB-LM bow3 (all) | 8.13 | 8.11 | 13.97 |
| bow-CNN | 8.66 | 8.39 | **9.33** |
| seq-CNN | 8.39 | 7.64 | 9.96 |
| seq2-CNN | 8.04 | 7.48 | – |
| seq2-bow$n$-CNN | **7.67** | **7.14** | – |

Table 2: Error rate (%) comparison with bag-of-$n$-gram-based methods. Sentiment classification on IMDB and Elec (25K training documents) and 55-way topic categorization on RCV1 (16K training documents). '(30K)' indicates that the 30K most frequent $n$-grams were used, and '(all)' indicates that all the $n$-grams (up to 5M) were used. CNN used the 30K most frequent words.

| | | |
|---|---|---|
| SVM bow2 [WM12] | 10.84 | – |
| WRRBM+bow [DAL12] | 10.77 | – |
| NB+SVM bow2 [WM12] | 8.78 | ensemble |
| NB-LM bow3 [MMRB14] | 8.13 | – |
| Paragraph vectors [LM14] | 7.46 | unlabeled data |
| seq2-CNN (3K×2) [Ours] | 7.94 | – |
| seq2-bow$n$-CNN [Ours] | **7.67** | – |

Table 3: Error rate (%) comparison with previous best methods on IMDB.

notably hurt performance (also observed on NB-LM and NN) even though some reduction is a common practice. Error rates were clearly improved by addition of bi- and tri-grams. By contrast, on topic categorization, bi-grams only slightly improved accuracy, and reduction of vocabulary did not hurt performance. NB-LM is very strong on IMDB and poor on RCV1; its effectiveness appears to be data-dependent, as also observed by WM12.

**Comparison with state-of-the-art results** As shown in Table 3, the previous best supervised result on IMDB is 8.13 by NB-LM with bow3 (MMRB14), and our best error rate 7.67 is better by nearly 0.5%. (Le and Mikolov, 2014) reports 7.46 with the semi-supervised method that learns low-dimensional vector representations of documents from unlabeled data. Their result is not directly comparable with our supervised results due to use of additional resource. Nevertheless, our best result rivals their result.

We tested bow-CNN on the multi-label topic categorization task on RCV1 to compare with

| models | micro-F | macro-F |
|---|---|---|
| LYRL04's best SVM | 81.6 | 60.7 |
| bow-CNN | **84.0** | **64.8** |

Table 4: RCV1 micro-averaged and macro-averaged F-measure results on multi-label task with LYRL04 split.

LYRL04. We used the same thresholding strategy as LYRL04. As shown in Table 4, bow-CNN outperforms LYRL04's best results even though our data preprocessing is much simpler (no stemming and no tf-idf weighting).

**Previous CNN** We focus on the sentence classification studies due to its relation to text categorization. Kim (2014) studied fine-tuning of pre-trained word vectors to produce input to parallel CNN. He reported that performance was poor when word vectors were trained as part of CNN training (i.e., no additional method/corpus). On our tasks, we were also unable to outperform the baselines with this type of model. Also, with our approach, a system is simpler with one fewer layer – no need to tune the dimensionality of word vectors or meta-parameters for word vector learning.

Kalchbrenner et al. (2014) proposed complex modifications of CNN for sentence modeling. Notably, given word vectors $\in \mathbb{R}^d$, their convolution with $m$ feature maps produces for each region a matrix $\in \mathbb{R}^{d \times m}$ (instead of a vector $\in \mathbb{R}^m$ as in standard CNN). Using the provided code, we found that their model is too resource-demanding for our tasks. On IMDB and Elec[14] the best error rates we obtained by training with various configurations that fit in memory for 24 hours each on GPU (cf. Fig 5) were 10.13 and 9.37, respectively, which is no better than SVM bow2. Since excellent performances were reported on short sentence classification, we presume that their model is optimized for short sentences, but not for text categorization in general.

**Performance dependency** CNN training is known to be expensive, compared with, e.g., linear models – linear SVM with bow3 on IMDB only takes 9 minutes using SVMlight (single-core) on a high-end Intel CPU. Nevertheless, with our code on GPU, CNN training only takes minutes (to a few hours) on these datasets shown in Figure 5.

[14]We could not train adequate models on RCV1 on either Tesla K20 or M2070 due to memory shortage.

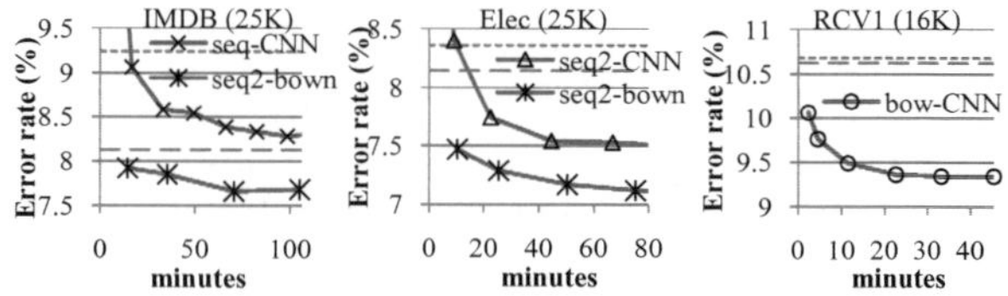


Figure 5: Training time (minutes) on Tesla K20. The horizontal lines are the best-performing baselines.

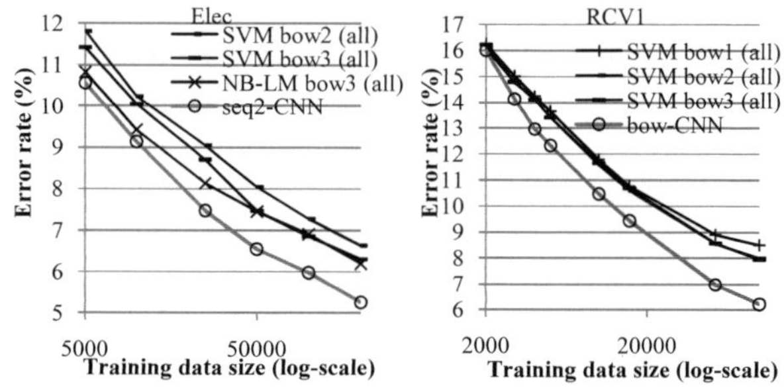


Figure 6: Error rate in relation to training data size. For readability, only representative methods are shown.

Finally, the results with training sets of various sizes on Elec and RCV1 are shown in Figure 6.

### 3.6 Why is CNN effective?

In this section we explain the effectiveness of CNN through looking into what it learns from training.

First, for comparison, we show the $n$-grams that SVM with bow3 found to be the most predictive; i.e., the following $n$-grams were assigned the 10 largest weights by SVM with binary features on Elec for the negative and positive class, respectively:

- poor, useless, returned, not worth, return, worse, disappointed, terrible, worst, horrible
- great, excellent, perfect, love, easy, amazing, awesome, no problems, perfectly, beat

Note that, even though SVM was also given bi- and tri-grams, the top 10 features chosen by SVM with binary features are mostly uni-grams; furthermore, the top 100 features (50 for each class) include 28 bi-grams but only four tri-grams. This means that, with the given size of training data, SVM still heavily counts on uni-grams, which could be ambiguous, and cannot fully take advantage of higher-order $n$-grams. By contrast, NB-weights tend to promote $n$-grams with a larger $n$; the 100 features that were assigned the largest NB-weights are 7 uni-, 33 bi-, and 60 tri-grams. However, as seen above, NB-weights do not always lead to the best performance.

| | |
|---|---|
| N1 | completely useless ., return policy . |
| N2 | it won't even, but doesn't work |
| N3 | product is defective, very disappointing ! |
| N4 | is totally unacceptable, is so bad |
| N5 | was very poor, it has failed |
| P1 | works perfectly !, love this product |
| P2 | very pleased !, super easy to, i am pleased |
| P3 | 'm so happy, it works perfect, is awesome ! |
| P4 | highly recommend it, highly recommended ! |
| P5 | am extremely satisfied, is super fast |

Table 5: Examples of predictive text regions in the training set.

| |
|---|
| were unacceptably bad, is abysmally bad, were universally poor, was hugely disappointed, was enormously disappointed, is monumentally frustrating, are endlessly frustrating |
| best concept ever, best ideas ever, best hub ever, am wholly satisfied, am entirely satisfied, am incredicbly satisfied, 'm overall impressed, am awfully pleased, am exceptionally pleased, 'm entirely happy, are acoustically good, is blindingly fast, |

Table 6: Examples of text regions that contribute to prediction. They are from the *test set*, and they did *not* appear in the training set, either entirely or partially as bi-grams.

In Table 5, we show some of text regions learned by seq-CNN to be predictive on Elec. This net has one convolution layer with region size 3 and 1000 neurons; thus, embedding by the convolution layer produces a 1000-dim vector for each region, which (after pooling) serves as features in the top layer where weights are assigned to the 1000 vector components. In the table, N$i$/P$i$ indicates the component that received the $i$-th highest weight in the top layer for the negative/positive class, respectively. The table shows the text regions (in the training set) whose embedded vectors have a large value in the corresponding component, i.e., predictive text regions.

Note that the embedded vectors for the text regions listed in the same row are close to each other as they have a large value in the same component. That is, Table 5 also shows that the *proximity of the embedded vectors* tends to reflect the *proximity in terms of the relations to the target classes* (positive/negative sentiment). This is the effect of embedding, which helps classification by the top layer.

With the bag-of-$n$-gram representation, only the $n$-grams that appear in the training data can participate in prediction. By contrast, one strength of CNN is that $n$-grams (or text regions of size $n$) *can contribute to accurate prediction even if they did not appear in the training data*, as long as (some of) their constituent words did, because input of embedding is the constituent words of the region. To see this point, in Table 6 we show the text regions from the *test set*, which *did not appear in the training data*, either entirely or partially as bi-grams, and yet whose embedded features have large values in the heavily-weighted (predictive) component thus contributing to the prediction. There are many more of these, and we only show a small part of them that fit certain patterns. One noticeable pattern is (be-verb, adverb, sentiment adjective) such as "am entirely satisfied" and "'m overall impressed". These adjectives alone could be ambiguous as they may be negated. To know that the writer is indeed "satisfied", we need to see the sequence "am satisfied", but the insertion of adverb such as "entirely" is very common. "best X ever' is another pattern that a discriminating pair of words are not adjacent to each other. These patterns require tri-grams for disambiguation, and seq-CNN successfully makes use of them even though the exact tri-grams were not seen during training, as a result of learning, e.g., "am X satisfied" with non-negative X (e.g., "am very satisfied", "am so satisfied") to be predictive of the positive class through training. That is, CNN can effectively use word order when bag-of-$n$-gram-based approaches fail.

## 4 Conclusion

This paper showed that CNN provides an alternative mechanism for effective use of word order for text categorization through direct embedding of small text regions, different from the traditional bag-of-$n$-gram approach or word-vector CNN. With the parallel CNN framework, several types of embedding can be learned and combined so that they can complement each other for higher accuracy. State-of-the-art performances on sentiment classification and topic classification were achieved using this approach.

## Acknowledgements

We thank the anonymous reviewers for useful suggestions. The second author was supported by NSF IIS-1250985 and NSF IIS-1407939.

## References


Christopher Bishop. 1995. *Neural networks for pattern recognition*. Oxford University Press.

John Blitzer, Mark Dredze, and Fernando Pereira. 2007. Biographies, bollywood, boom-boxes, and blenders: Domain adaptation for sentiment classification. In *Proceedings of ACL*.

Ronan Collobert, Jason Weston, Léon Bottou, Michael Karlen, Koray Kavukcuoglu, and Pavel Kuksa. 2011. Natural language processing (almost) from scratch. *Journal of Machine Learning Research*, 12:2493–2537.

Jianfeng Gao, Patric Pantel, Michael Gamon, Xiaodong He, and Li dent. 2014. Modeling interestingness with deep neural networks. In *Proceedings of EMNLP*.

Xavier Glorot, Antoine Bordes, and Yoshua Bengio. 2011. Domain adaptation for large-scale sentiment classification: A deep learning approach. In *Proceedings of ICML*.

Geoffrey E. Hinton, Nitish Srivastava, Alex Krizhevsky, Ilya Sutskever, and Ruslan R. Salakhutdinov. 2012. Improving neural networks by preventing co-adaptation of feature detectors. *arXiv:1207.0580*.

Nal Kalchbrenner, Edward Grefenstette, and Phil Blunsom. 2014. A convolutional neural network for modeling sentences. In *Proceedings of ACL*.

Yoon Kim. 2014. Convolutional neural networks for sentence classification. In *Proceedings of EMNLP*, pages 1746–1751.

Alex Krizhevsky, Ilya Sutskever, and Geoffrey E. Hinton. 2012. ImageNet classification with deep convolutional neural networks. In *Proceedings of NIPS*.

Quoc Le and Tomas Mikolov. 2014. Distributed representations of sentences and documents. In *Proceedings of ICML*.

Yann LeCun, León Bottou, Yoshua Bengio, and Patrick Haffner. 1986. Gradient-based learning applied to document recognition. In *Proceedings of the IEEE*, pages 2278–2324.

David D. Lewis, Yiming Yang, Tony G. Rose, and Fan Li. 2004. RCV1: A new benchmark collection for text categorization research. *Journal of Marchine Learning Research*, 5:361–397.

Andrew L. Maas, Raymond E. Daly, Peter T. Pham, Dan Huang, Andrew Y. Ng, and Christopher Potts. 2011. Learning word vectors for sentiment analysis. In *Proceedings of ACL*.

Julian McAuley and Jure Leskovec. 2013. Hidden factors and hidden topics: Understanding rating dimensions with review text. In *RecSys*.

Grégoire Mesnil, Tomas Mikolov, Marc'Aurelio Ranzato, and Yoshua Bengio. 2014. Ensemble of generative and discriminative techniques for sentiment analysis of movie reviews. *arXiv:1412.5335v5 (4 Feb 2015 version)*.

Tomas Mikolov, Ilya Sutskever, Kai Chen, Greg Corrado, and Jeffrey Dean. 2013. Distributed representations of words and phrases and their compositionality. In *Proceedings of NIPS*.

Bo Pang and Lillian Lee. 2008. Opinion mining and sentiment analysis. *Foundations and Trends in Information Retrieval*, 2(1–2):1–135.

Bo Pang, Lillian Lee, and Shivakumar Vaithyanathan. 2002. Thumbs up? sentiment classification using machine learning techniques. In *Proceedings of Conference on Empirical Methods in Natural Language Processing (EMNLP)*, pages 79–86.

Olga Russakovsky, Jia Deng, Hao Su, Jonathan Krause, Sanjeev Satheesh, Sean Ma, Zhiheng Huang, Andrej Karpathy, Aditya Khosla, Michael Bernstein, Alexander C. Berg, and Li Fei-Fei. 2014. ImageNet Large Scale Visual Recognition Challenge. *arXiv:1409.0575*.

Mehran Sahami, Susan Dumais, David Heckerman, and Eric Horvitz. 1998. A bayesian approach to filtering junk e-mail. In *Proceedings of AAAI'98 Workshop on Learning for Text Categorization*.

Yelong Shen, Xiaodong He, Jianfeng Gao, Li Deng, and Grégoire Mensnil. 2014. A latent semantic model with convolutional-pooling structure for information retrieval. In *Proceedings of CIKM*.

Christian Szegedy, Wei Liu, Yangqing Jia, Pierre Sermanet, Scott Reed, Dragomir Anguelov, Dumitru Erhan, Vincent Vanhoucke, and Andrew Rabinovich. 2014. Going deeper with convolutions. *arXiv:1409.4842*.

Chade-Meng Tan, Yuan-Fang Wang, and Chan-Do Lee. 2002. The use of bigrams to enhance text categorization. *Information Processing and Management*, 38:529–546.

Duyu Tang, Furu Wei, Nan Yang, Ming Zhou, Ting Liu, and Bing Qin. 2014. Learning sentiment-specific word embedding for twitter sentiment classification. In *Proceedings of ACL*, pages 1555–1565.

Sida Wang and Christopher D. Manning. 2012. Baselines and bigrams: Simple, good sentiment and topic classification. In *Proceedings of ACL (short paper)*.

Jason Weston, Sumit Chopra, and Keith Adams. 2014. #tagspace: Semantic embeddings from hashtags. In *Proceedings of EMNLP*, pages 1822–1827.

Puyang Xu and Ruhi Sarikaya. 2013. Convolutional neural network based triangular crf for joint intent detection and slot filling. In *ASRU*.

Liheng Xu, Kang Liu, Siwei Lai, and Jun Zhao. 2014. Product feature mining: Semantic clues versus syntactic constituents. In *Proceedings of ACL*.

# Transition-Based Syntactic Linearization

**Yijia Liu †‡, Yue Zhang †, Wanxiang Che ‡, Bing Qin ‡**
†Singapore University of Technology and Design
‡Research Center for Social Computing and Information Retrieval
Harbin Institute of Technology, China
{yjliu,car,bqin}@ir.hit.edu.cn yue_zhang@sutd.edu.sg

## Abstract

Syntactic linearization algorithms take a bag of input words and a set of optional constraints, and construct an output sentence and its syntactic derivation simultaneously. The search problem is NP-hard, and the current best results are achieved by bottom-up best-first search. One drawback of the method is low efficiency; and there is no theoretical guarantee that a full sentence can be found within bounded time. We propose an alternative algorithm that constructs output structures from left to right using beam-search. The algorithm is based on incremental parsing algorithms. We extend the transition system so that word ordering is performed in addition to syntactic parsing, resulting in a linearization system that runs in guaranteed quadratic time. In standard evaluations, our system runs an order of magnitude faster than a state-of-the-art baseline using best-first search, with improved accuracies.

## 1 Introduction

*Linearization* is the task of ordering a bag of words into a grammatical and fluent sentence. Syntax-based linearization algorithms generate a sentence along with its syntactic structure. Depending on how much syntactic information is available as inputs, recent work on syntactic linearization can be classified into *free word ordering* (Wan et al., 2009; Zhang et al., 2012; de Gispert et al., 2014), which orders a bag of words without syntactic constraints, *full tree linearization* (He et al., 2009; Bohnet et al., 2010; Song et al., 2014), which orders a bag of words given a full-spanning syntactic tree, and *partial tree linearization* (Zhang, 2013), which orders a bag of words given some syntactic relations between them as partial constraints.

| | |
|---|---|
| Initial State | $([\,], [1...n], \emptyset)$ |
| Final State | $([\,], [\,], A)$ |
| Induction Rules: | |
| SHIFT | $\dfrac{(\sigma, [i\|\beta], A)}{([\sigma\|\ i], \beta, A)}$ |
| LEFTARC | $\dfrac{([\sigma\|j\ i], \beta, A)}{([\sigma\|i], \beta, A \cup \{j \leftarrow i\})}$ |
| RIGHTARC | $\dfrac{([\sigma\|j\ i], \beta, A)}{([\sigma\|j], \beta, A \cup \{j \rightarrow i\})}$ |

Figure 1: The *arc-standard* parsing algorithm.

The search space for syntactic linearization is huge. Even with a full syntax tree being available as constraints, permutation of nodes on each level is an NP-hard problem. As a result, heuristic search has been adopted by most previous work, and the best results have been achieved by a time-constrained best-first search framework (White, 2004a; White and Rajkumar, 2009; Zhang and Clark, 2011b; Song et al., 2014). Though empirically highly accurate, one drawback of this approach is that there is no asymptotic upper bound on the time complexity of finding the first full sentence. As a result, it can take 5–10 seconds to process a sentence, and sometimes fail to yield a full sentence at timeout. This issue is more severe for larger bags of words, and makes the algorithms practically less useful.

We study the effect of an alternative learning and search framework for the linearization prob-



*Human Language Technologies: The 2015 Annual Conference of the North American Chapter of the ACL*, pages 113–122,
Denver, Colorado, May 31 – June 5, 2015. 

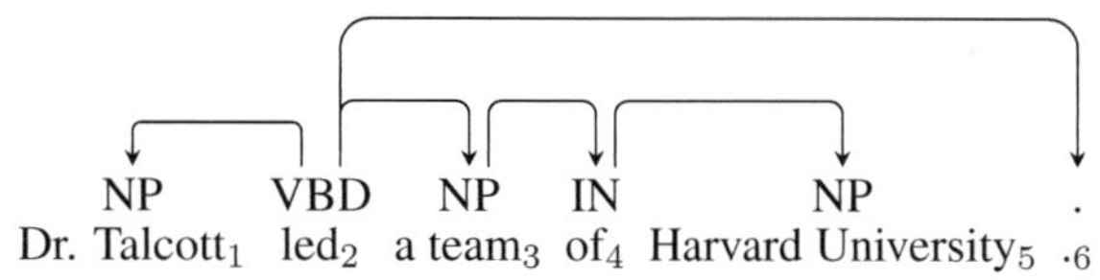


Figure 2: Example dependency tree.

lem, which has a theoretical upper bound on the time complexity, and always yields a full sentence in quadratic time. Our method is inspired by the connection between syntactic linearization and syntactic parsing: both build a syntactic tree over a sentence, with the former performing word ordering in addition to derivation construction. As a result, syntactic linearization can be treated as a generalized form of parsing, for which there is no input word order, and therefore extensions to parsing algorithms can be used to perform linearization.

For syntactic parsing, the algorithm of Zhang and Nivre (2011) gives competitive accuracies under linear complexity. Compared with parsers that use dynamic programming (McDonald and Pereira, 2006; Koo and Collins, 2010), the efficient beam-search system is more suitable for the NP-hard linearization task. We extend the parser of Zhang and Nivre (2011), so that word ordering is performed in addition to syntactic tree construction. Experimental results show that the transition-based linearization system runs an order of magnitude faster than a state-of-the-art best-first baseline, with improved accuracies in standard evaluation. Our linearizer is publicly available under GPL at `http://sourceforge.net/projects/zgen/`.

## 2 Transition-Based Parsing

The task of *dependency parsing* is to find a *dependency tree* given an input sentence. Figure 2 shows an example dependency tree, which consists of *dependency arcs* that represent syntactic relations between pairs of words. A transition-based dependency parsing algorithm (Nivre, 2008) can be formalized as a *transition system*, $S = (C, T, c_s, C_t)$, where $C$ is the set of states, $T$ is a set of transition actions, $c_s$ is the initial state and $C_t$ is a set of terminal states. The parsing process is modeled as an application of a sequence of actions, transducing the initial state into a final state, while constructing dependency arcs. Each state in the transition system can be formalized as a tuple $(\sigma, \beta, A)$, where $\sigma$ is a stack that maintains a partial derivation, $\beta$ is a buffer of incoming input words and $A$ is the set of dependency relations that have been built.

| | Transition | $\sigma$ | $\beta$ | A |
|---|---|---|---|---|
| 0 | | [] | [1...6] | $\emptyset$ |
| 1 | SHIFT | [1] | [2...6] | |
| 2 | SHIFT | [1 2] | [3...6] | |
| 3 | SHIFT | [1 2 3] | [4...6] | |
| 4 | SHIFT | [1 2 3 4] | [5,6] | |
| 5 | SHIFT | [1 2 3 4 5] | [6] | |
| 6 | RIGHTARC | [1 2 3 4] | [6] | $A \cup \{4 \rightarrow 5\}$ |
| 7 | RIGHTARC | [1 2 3] | [6] | $A \cup \{3 \rightarrow 4\}$ |
| 8 | RIGHTARC | [1 2] | [6] | $A \cup \{2 \rightarrow 3\}$ |
| 9 | SHIFT | [1 2 6] | [] | |
| 10 | RIGHTARC | [1 2] | [] | $A \cup \{2 \rightarrow 6\}$ |
| 11 | LEFTARC | [2] | [] | $A \cup \{1 \leftarrow 2\}$ |

Table 1: *arc-standard* transition action sequence for parsing the sentence in Figure 2.

Our work is based on the *arc-standard* algorithm (Nivre, 2008). The deduction system of the *arc-standard* algorithm is shown in Figure 1. In this system, three transition actions are used: LEFTARC, RIGHTARC and SHIFT. Given a state $s = ([\sigma|\, j\ i], [k|\beta], A)$,

- LEFTARC builds an arc $\{j \leftarrow i\}$ and pops $j$ off the stack.
- RIGHTARC builds an arc $\{j \rightarrow i\}$ and pops $i$ off the stack.
- SHIFT removes the front word $k$ from the buffer $\beta$, and shifts it onto the stack.

In the notations above, $i$, $j$ and $k$ are word indices of an input sentence. The *arc-standard* system assumes that each input word has been assigned a part-of-speech (POS) tag.

The sentence in Figure 2 can be parsed by the transition sequence shown in Table 1. Given an input sentence of $n$ words, the algorithm takes $2n$ transitions to construct an output, because each word needs to be shifted onto the stack once and popped off once before parsing finishes, and all the transition actions are either shifting or popping actions.

| | |
|---|---|
| Initial State | $([\,], set(1..n), \emptyset)$ |
| Final State | $([\,], \emptyset, A)$ |

Induction Rules:

| | |
|---|---|
| SHIFT-*i*-POS | $\dfrac{(\sigma, \rho, A)}{([\sigma \vert i], \rho - \{i\}, A)}$ |
| LEFTARC | $\dfrac{([\sigma \vert j\ i], \rho, A)}{([\sigma \vert i], \rho, A \cup \{j \leftarrow i\})}$ |
| RIGHTARC | $\dfrac{([\sigma \vert j\ i], \rho, A)}{([\sigma \vert j], \rho, A \cup \{j \rightarrow i\})}$ |

Figure 3: Deduction system for transition-based linearization. Indices $i$, $j$ do not reflect word order.

## 3 Transition-Based Linearization

The main difference between linearization and dependency parsing is that the input words are unordered for linearization, which results in an unordered buffer $\rho$. At a certain state $s = (\sigma, \rho, A)$, any word in the buffer $\rho$ can be shifted onto the stack. In addition, unlike a parser, the vanilla linearization task does not assume that input words are assigned POS. To extend the *arc-standard* algorithm for linearization, we incorporate word and POS into the SHIFT operation, transforming the *arc-standard* SHIFT operation to SHIFT-*Word-POS*, which selects the word *Word* from the buffer $\rho$, tags it with *POS* and shifts it onto the stack. Since the order of words in an output sentence equals to the order in which they are shifted onto the stack, word ordering is performed along with the parsing process.

Under such extension, the sentence in Figure 2 can be generated by the transition sequence (SHIFT-*Dr. Talcott*-NP, SHIFT-*led*-VBD, SHIFT-*of*-NP, SHIFT-*a team*-NP, SHIFT-*of*-IN, SHIFT-*Harvard University*-NP, RIGHTARC, RIGHTARC, RIGHTARC, RIGHTARC, SHIFT-.-., RIGHTARC, LEFTARC), given the unordered bag of words (*Dr. Talcott*, *led*, *a team*, *of*, *Harvard University*, .).

The deduction system for the linearization algorithm is shown in Figure 3. Given an input bag of $n$ words, this algorithm also takes $2n$ transition actions to construct an output, by the same reason as the *arc-standard* parser.

### 3.1 Search and Learning

We apply the learning and search framework of Zhang and Clark (2011a), which gives state-of-the-art transition-based parsing accuracies and runs in linear time (Zhang and Nivre, 2011). Pseudocode of the search algorithm is shown in Algorithm 1. It performs beam-search by using an agenda to keep the $k$-best states at each incremental step. When decoding starts, the agenda contains only the initial state. At each step, each state in the agenda is advanced by applying all possible transition actions (GETPOSSIBLEACTIONS), leading to a set of new states. The $k$ best are selected for the new states, and used to replace the current states in the agenda, before the next decoding step starts. Given an input bag of $n$ words, the process repeats for $2n$ steps, after which all the states in the agenda are terminal states, and the highest-scored state in the agenda is taken for the final output. The complexity of this algorithm is $n^2$, because it takes a fixed $2n$ steps to construct an output, and in each step the number of possible SHIFT action is proportional to the size of $\rho$.

**Algorithm 1:** transition-based linearization

```
Input: C, a set of input syntactic constraints
Output: The highest-scored final state
candidates ← ([ ], set(1..n), ∅)
agenda ← ∅
for i ← 1..2n do
    for s in candidates do
        for action in GETPOSSIBLEACTIONS(s, C) do
            agenda ← APPLY(s, action)
    candidates ← TOP-K(agenda)
    agenda ← ∅
best ← BEST(candidates)
return best
```

The search algorithm ranks search hypotheses, which are sequences of state transitions, by their scores. A global linear model is used to score search hypotheses. Given a hypothesis $h$, its score is calculated by:

$$Score(h) = \Phi(h) \cdot \vec{\theta},$$

where $\vec{\theta}$ is the parameter vector of the model and $\Phi(h)$ is the global feature vector of $h$, extracted by instantiating the feature templates in Table 2 according to each state in the transition sequence.

In the table, $S_0$ represents the first word on the top of the stack, $S_1$ represents the second word on the top of the stack, $w$ represents a word and $p$ rep-

| Unigrams |
|---|
| $S_0w$; $S_0p$; $S_{0,l}w$; $S_{0,l}p$; $S_{0,r}w$; $S_{0,r}p$; |
| $S_{0,l2}w$; $S_{0,l2}p$; $S_{0,r2}w$; $S_{0,r2}p$; |
| $S_1w$; $S_1p$; $S_{1,l}w$; $S_{1,l}p$; $S_{1,r}w$; $S_{1,r}p$; |
| $S_{1,l2}w$; $S_{1,l2}p$; $S_{1,r2}w$; $S_{1,r2}p$; |
| **Bigram** |
| $S_0wS_{0,l}w$; $S_0wS_{0,l}p$; $S_0pS_{0,l}w$; $S_0pS_{0,l}p$; |
| $S_0wS_{0,r}w$; $S_0wS_{0,r}p$; $S_0pS_{0,r}w$; $S_0pS_{0,r}p$; |
| $S_1wS_{1,l}w$; $S_1wS_{1,l}p$; $S_1pS_{1,l}w$; $S_1pS_{1,l}p$; |
| $S_1wS_{1,r}w$; $S_1wS_{1,r}p$; $S_1pS_{1,r}w$; $S_1pS_{1,r}p$; |
| $S_0wS_1w$; $S_0wS_1p$; $S_0pS_1w$; $S_0pS_1p$ |
| **Trigram** |
| $S_0wS_0pS_{0,l}w$; $S_0wS_{0,l}wS_{0,l}p$; $S_0wS_0pS_{0,l}p$; |
| $S_0pS_{0,l}wS_{0,l}p$; $S_0wS_0pS_{0,r}w$; $S_0wS_{0,l}wS_{0,r}p$; |
| $S_0wS_0pS_{0,r}p$; $S_0pS_{0,r}wS_{0,r}p$; |
| $S_1wS_1pS_{1,l}w$; $S_1wS_{1,l}wS_{1,l}p$; $S_1wS_1pS_{1,l}p$; |
| $S_1pS_{1,l}wS_{1,l}p$; $S_1wS_1pS_{1,r}w$; $S_1wS_{1,l}wS_{1,r}p$; |
| $S_1wS_1pS_{1,r}p$; $S_1pS_{1,r}wS_{1,r}p$; |
| **Linearizion** |
| $w_0$; $p_0$; $w_{-1}w_0$; $p_{-1}p_0$; $w_{-2}w_{-1}w_0$; $p_{-2}p_{-1}p_0$; |
| $S_{0,l}wS_{0,l2}w$; $S_{0,l}pS_{0,l2}p$; $S_{0,r2}wS_{0,r}w$; $S_{0,r2}pS_{0,r}p$; |
| $S_{1,l}wS_{1,l2}w$; $S_{1,l}pS_{1,l2}p$; $S_{1,r2}wS_{1,r}w$; $S_{1,r2}pS_{1,r}p$; |

Table 2: Feature templates.

resent a POS-tag. The feature templates can be classified into four types: *unigram*, *bigram*, *trigram* and *linearization*. The first three types are taken from the dependency parser of Zhang and Nivre (2011), which capture context information for $S_0$, $S_1$ and their modifiers. The original feature templates of Zhang and Nivre (2011) also contain information of the front words on the buffer. However, since the buffer is unordered for linearization, we do not include these features.

The *linearization* feature templates are specific for linearization, and captures surface ngram information. Each search state represents a partially linearized sentence. We represents the last word in the partially linearized sentence as $w_0$ and the second last as $w_{-1}$.

Given a set of labeled training examples, the averaged perceptron (Collins, 2002) with early update (Collins and Roark, 2004; Zhang and Nivre, 2011) is used to train the parameters $\vec{\theta}$ of the model.

## 3.2 Input Syntactic Constraints

The use of syntactic constraints to achieve better linearization performance has been studied in previous work. Wan et al. (2009) employ POS constraints

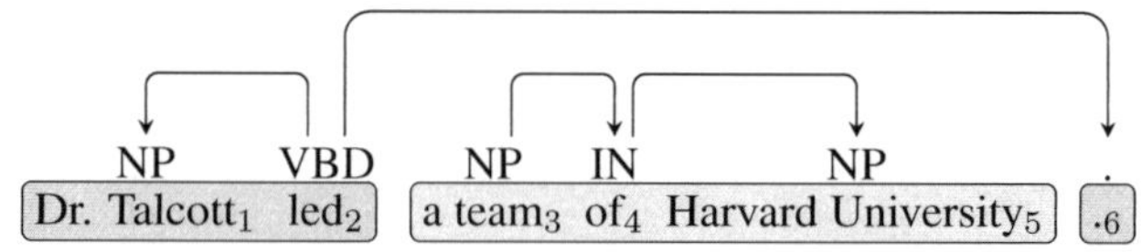


Figure 4: Example partial tree. Words in the same sub dependency trees are grouped by rounded boxes. Word indices do not specify their orders. Base phrases (e.g. *Dr. Talcott*) are treated as single words.

in learning a dependency language model. Zhang and Clark (2011b) take supertags as constraints to a CCG linearizer. Zhang (2013) demonstrates the possibility of *partial-tree linearization*, which allows a whole spectrum of input syntactic constraints. In practice, input syntactic constraints, including POS and dependency relations, can be obtained from earlier stage of a generation pipeline, such as lexical transfer results in machine translation.

It is relatively straightforward to apply input constraints to a best-first system (Zhang, 2013), but less so for beam-search. In this section, we utilize the input syntactic constraints by letting the information decide the possible actions for each state, namely the return value of GETPOSSIBLEACTIONS in Algorithm 1, thus, when input POS-tags and dependencies are given, the generation system can achieve more specified outputs.

### 3.2.1 POS Constraints

POS is the simplest form of constraints to the transition-based linearization system. When the POS of an input word is given, the POS-tag component in SHIFT-*Word-POS* operation is fixed, and the number of SHIFT actions for the word is reduced from the number of all POS to 1.

### 3.2.2 Partial Tree Constraints

In partial tree linearization, a set of dependency arcs that form a partial dependency tree is given to the linearization system as input constraints. Figure 4 illustrate an example. The search space can be reduced by ignoring the transition sequences that do not result in a dependency tree that is consistent with the input constraints. Take the partial tree in Figure 4 for example. At the state $s =$ ([*Harvard University*$_5$], set(1..n)-$\{5\}$, $\emptyset$), it is illegal to shift the base phrase *a team*$_3$ onto the stack, be-

**Algorithm 2:** GETPOSSIBLEACTIONS for partial tree linearization, where $C$ is a partial tree

```
Input: A state s = ([σ|j i], ρ, A) and partial tree C
Output: A set of possible transition actions T
1  if s.σ is empty then
2      for k ∈ s.ρ do
3          T ← T ∪ (SHIFT, POS, k)
4  else
5      if REDUCABLE(s, i, j, C) then
6          T ← T ∪ (LEFTARC)
7      if REDUCABLE(s, j, i, C) then
8          T ← T ∪ (RIGHTARC)
9      for k ∈ s.β do
10         if SHIFTLEGAL(s, k, C) then
11             T ← T ∪ (SHIFT, POS, k)
12 return T
```

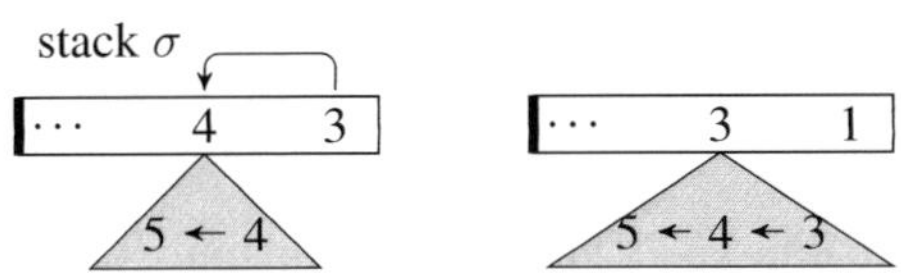


(a) (b)

Figure 5: Two conditions for a valid LEFTARC action in partial-tree linearization. The indices correspond to those in Figure 4. A shaded triangle represents the readily built arcs under a root word.

cause this action will result in a sub-sequence (*Harvard University*$_5$, *a team*$_3$, *of*$_4$), which cannot have the dependency arcs $\{3 \rightarrow 4\}, \{4 \rightarrow 5\}$ by using *arc-standard* actions.

Algorithm 3 shows pseudocode of GETPOSSIBLEACTIONS when $C$ is a partial tree. Given a state $s = ([\sigma|j\ i], \rho, A)$ the LEFTARC action builds an arc $\{j \leftarrow i\}$ and pops the word $j$ off the stack. Since the popped word $j$ cannot be linked to any words in future transitions, all the descendants of $j$ should have been processed and removed from the stack. In addition, constrained by the given partial tree, the arc $\{j \leftarrow i\}$ should be an arc in $C$ (Figure 5a), or $j$ should be the root of a sub dependency tree in $C$ (Figure 5b). We denote the conditions as REDUCABLE($s$, $i$, $j$, $C$) (lines 5-6). The case for RIGHTARC is similar to LEFTARC (lines 7-8).

For the SHIFT action, the conditions are more complex. Due to space limitation, we briefly sketch

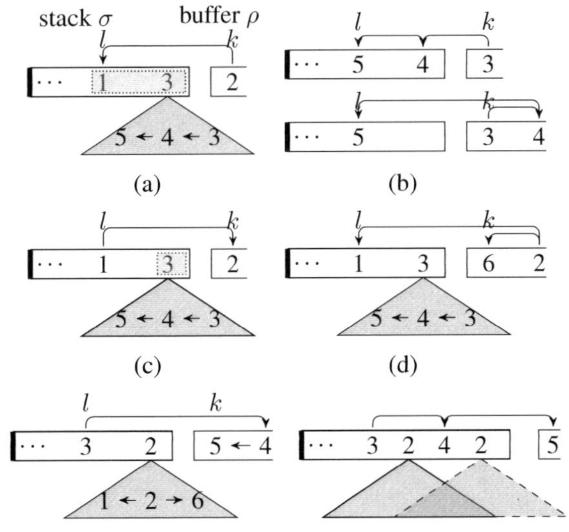


(a) (b) (c) (d) (e)

Figure 6: 5 relations between $k$ and $l$. The indices correspond to those in Figure 4. The words in green boxes must have arcs with $k$ in future transitions.

the SHIFTLEGAL function below. Detailed algorithm pseudocode for SHIFTLEGAL is given in the supplementing material. For a word $k$ in $\rho$ to be shifted onto the stack, all the words on the stack must satisfy certain constraints. There are 5 possible relations between $k$ and a word $l$ on the stack. (1) If $l$ is a child of $k$ in $C$ (Figure 6a), all the words on the stack from $l$ to the top of the stack should be *reducable to* $k$, because only LEFTARC can be applied between $k$ and these words in future actions. (2) If $l$ is a grand child of $k$ (Figure 6b), no legal sentence can be constructed if $k$ is shifted onto the stack. (3) If $l$ is the parent of $k$ (Figure 6c), legal SHIFTs require all the words on the stack from $l$ to the top to be *reducable* to $k$. (4) If $l$ is a grand parent of $k$, all the words on the stack from $l$ to the top will become descendants of $l$ in the output (Figure 6e). Thus these words must be descendants of $l$ in $C$, or the root of different subdependency trees. (5) If $l$ is a siblings of $k$, we denote $a$ as the least common ancestor of $k$ and $l$. $a$ will become in the buffer and $l$ should be a direct child of $a$. All the words from $l$ to the top of the stack should be the descendants of $a$ in the output (Figure 6d), and thus $a$ should have the same conditions as in (4). Finally, if no word on the stack is in the same subdependency tree as $k$ in $C$, then $k$ can be safely shifted.

**Algorithm 3:** GETPOSSIBLEACTIONS for full tree linearization, where $C$ is a full tree

**Input**: A state $s = ([\sigma|j\ i], \rho, A)$ and gold tree $C$
**Output**: A set of possible transition actions $T$

1 $T \leftarrow \emptyset$
2 **if** $s.\sigma$ *is empty* **then**
3     **for** $k \in s.\rho$ **do**
4         $T \leftarrow T \cup (\text{SHIFT}, POS, k)$
5 **else**
6     **if** $\exists j, j \in (\text{DESCENDANTS}(i) \cap s.\rho)$ **then**
7         **for** $j \in (\text{DESCENDANTS}(i) \cap s.\rho)$ **do**
8             $T \leftarrow T \cup (\text{SHIFT}, POS, j)$
9     **else**
10         **if** $\{j \rightarrow i\} \in C$ **then**
11             $T \leftarrow T \cup (\text{RIGHTARC})$
12         **else if** $\{j \leftarrow i\} \in C$ **then**
13             $T \leftarrow T \cup (\text{LEFTARC})$
14         **else**
15             **for** $k \in (\text{SIBLINGS}(i) \cup \text{HEAD}(i)) \cap s.\rho$ **do**
16                 $T \leftarrow T \cup (\text{SHIFT}, POS, k)$
17 **return** $T$

#### 3.2.3 Full Tree Constraints

Algorithm 2 can also be used with full-tree constraints, which are a special case of partial-tree constraints. However, there is a conceptually simpler algorithm that leverages full-tree constraints. Because tree linearization is frequently studied in the literature, we describe this algorithm in Algorithm 3. When the stack is empty, we can freely move any word in the buffer $\rho$ onto the stack (line 2-4). If not all the descendants of the stack top $i$ have been processed, the next transition actions should move them onto the stack, so that arcs can be constructed between $i$ and these words (line 6-8). If all the descendants of $i$ have been processed, the next action should eagerly build arcs between top two words $i$ and $j$ on the stack (line 10-13). If no arc exists between $i$ and $j$, the next action should shift the parent word of $i$ or a word in $i$'s sibling tree (line 14-16).

## 4 Experiments

We follow previous work and conduct experiments on the Penn Treebank (PTB), using Wall Street Journal sections 2–21 for training, 22 for development testing and 23 for final testing. Gold-standard dependency trees are derived from bracketed sentences in the treebank using Penn2Malt[1], and base noun phrases are treated as a single word (Wan et al., 2009; Zhang, 2013). The BLEU score (Papineni et al., 2002) is used to evaluate the performance of linearization, which has been adopted in former literals (Wan et al., 2009; White and Rajkumar, 2009; Zhang and Clark, 2011b) and recent shared-tasks (Belz et al., 2011). We use our implementation of the best-first system of Zhang (2013), which gives the state-of-the-art results, as the baseline.

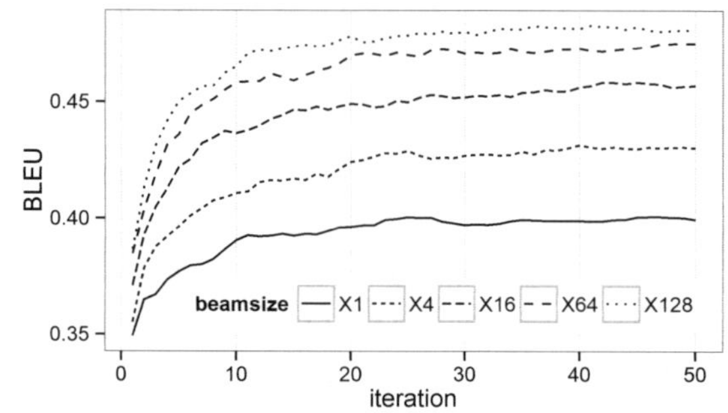


Figure 7: Dev. results with different beam sizes.

### 4.1 Influence of Beam size

We first study the influence of beam size by performing free word ordering on the development test data. BLEU score curves with different beam sizes are shown in Figure 7. From this figure, we can see that the systems with beam 64 and 128 achieve the best results. However, the 128-beam system does not improve the performance significantly (48.2 vs 47.5), but runs twice slower. As a result, we set the beam size to 64 in the remaining experiments.

### 4.2 Input Syntactic Constraints

To test the effectiveness of GETPOSSIBLEACTIONS under different input constraints, we follow Zhang (2013) and feed different amounts of POS-tags and dependencies to our transition-based linearization system. Input syntactic constraints are obtained by randomly sampling POS and dependencies from the gold dependency tree. Nine development experiments under different inputs are performed, and the

[1] http://stp.lingfil.uu.se/~nivre/research/Penn2Malt.html

| | no pos no dep | | 50% pos no dep | | all pos no dep | | no pos 50% dep | | 50% pos 50% dep | | all pos 50% dep | | no pos all dep | | 50% pos all dep | | all pos all dep | |
|---|---|---|---|---|---|---|---|---|---|---|---|---|---|---|---|---|---|---|
| | BL | SP | BL | SP | BL | SP | BL | SP | BL | SP | BL | SP | BL | SP | BL | SP | BL | SP |
| Z13 | 42.9 | 4872 | 43.4 | 4856 | 44.7 | 4826 | 50.5 | 4790 | 51.4 | 4737 | 52.2 | 4720 | 73.3 | 4600 | 74.7 | 4431 | 76.3 | 4218 |
| Ours | 47.5 | 155 | 47.9 | 119 | 48.8 | 74 | 54.8 | 132 | 55.2 | 91 | 56.2 | 41 | 77.8 | 40 | 79.1 | 28 | 81.1 | 22 |

Table 3: Partial-tree linearizion results on the development test set. *BL* – the BLEU score, *SP* – number of milliseconds to order one sentence. Z13 refers to the best-first system of Zhang (2013).

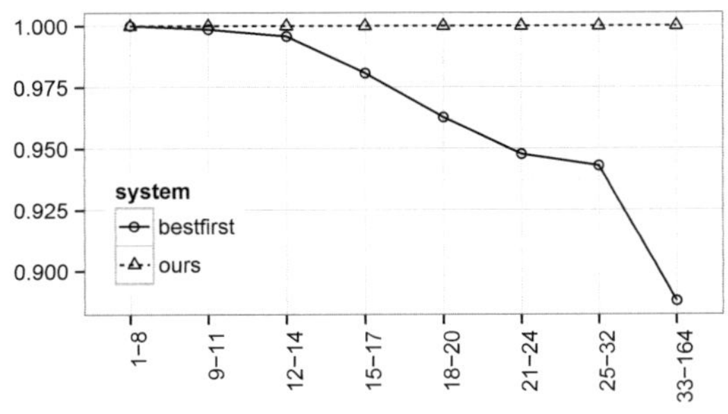


Figure 8: Comparison between transition-based and best-first systems on surface string brevity.

| | Precision | | Recall | | F | |
|---|---|---|---|---|---|---|
| len | Z13 | ours | Z13 | ours | Z13 | ours |
| $< 5$ | 24.63 | 20.45 | 14.56 | 21.82 | 18.3 | 21.11 |
| $< 10$ | 15.20 | 16.33 | 10.59 | 15.88 | 12.48 | 16.1 |
| $< 15$ | 10.82 | 14.73 | 9.38 | 14.08 | 10.05 | 14.4 |
| $< 30$ | 8.18 | 12.54 | 8.26 | 12.43 | 8.22 | 12.49 |

Table 4: Precision, recall and F-score comparison on different spans lengths.

BLEU scores along with the average time to order one sentence are shown in Table 3.

With more syntactic information in the input, our linearization system achieves better performance, showing that GETPOSSIBLEACTIONS can take advantage of the input constraints and yield more specified output. In addition, because input constraints reduce the search space, the systems with more syntactic information achieve faster decoding speeds. In comparison with Zhang (2013), the transition-based system achieves improved accuracies under the settings, and the decoding speed can be over two orders of magnitude faster (22ms vs. 4218ms). We give more detailed analysis next.

### 4.3 Comparison with Best-First

The beam-search linearizer takes a very different search strategy compared with best-first search, which affects the error distribution. As mentioned earlier, one problem of best-first is the lack of theoretical guarantee on time complexity. As a result, a time constraint is used and default output can be constructed when no full output is found (White, 2004b; Zhang and Clark, 2011b). This may result in incomplete output sentences and intuitively, this problem is more severe for larger bag of words. In contrast, the transition-based linearization algorithm takes $|2n|$ steps to generate a sentence and thus guarantees to order all the input words. Figure 8 shows the results by comparing the brevity scores (i.e. the number of words in the output divided by the number of words in reference sentence) on different sizes of inputs. Best-search can fail to order all the input words even on bags of 9 – 11 words, and the case is more severe for larger bag of words. On the other hand, the transition-based method uses all the input words to generate output and the brevity score is constant 1. Since the BLEU score consists two parts: the n-gram precision and brevity, this comparison partly explains why the transition-based linearization algorithm achieves higher BLEU scores.

To further compare the difference between the two systems, we evaluate the qualities of projective spans, which are dependency treelets. Both systems build outputs bottom-up by constructing projective spans, and a break-down of span accuracies against span sizes shows the effects of the different search algorithms. The results are shown in Table 4. According to this table, the best-first system tends to construct smaller spans more precisely, but the recall is relatively lower. Overall, higher F-scores are achieved by the transition-based system.

During the decoding process, the best-first system compares spans of different sizes and expands

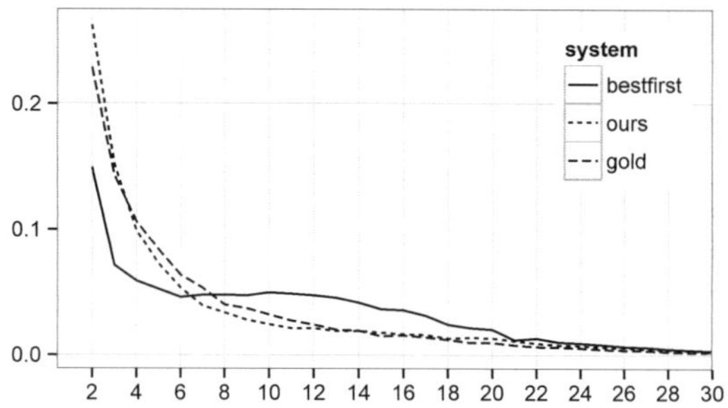


Figure 9: Distributions of spans outputted by the best-first, transition-based systems and the gold trees.

| | no pos no dep | all pos no dep | all pos all dep |
|---|---|---|---|
| Wan et al. (2009) | - | 33.7 | - |
| Zhang and Clark (2011b) | - | 40.1 | - |
| Zhang et al. (2012) | - | 43.8 | - |
| Zhang (2013) | 44.7 | 46.8 | 76.2 |
| This paper | **49.4** | **50.8** | **82.3** |

Table 5: Final results.

those that have higher scores. As a result, the number of expanded spans do not have a fixed correlation with the size, and there can be fewer but better small spans expanded. In contrast, the transition-based system models transition sequences rather than individual spans, and therefore the distribution of spans of different sizes in each hypothesis resembles that of the training data. Figure 9 verifies the analysis by counting the distributions of spans with respect to the length, in the search algorithms of the two systems and the gold dependency trees. The distribution of the transition-based system is closer to that of gold dependency trees, while the best-first system outputs less smaller spans and more longer ones. This explains the higher precision for the best-first system on smaller spans.

### 4.4 Final Results

The final results on the test set of Penn Treebank are shown in Table 5. Compared with previous studies, our transition-based linearization system achieves the best results on all the tests. Table 6 shows some example output sentences, when there are no input constraints. For longer sentences, the transition-based method gives noticeably better results.

| | output | BL |
|---|---|---|
| ref. | There is no asbestos in our products now . | |
| Z13 | There is no asbestos now in our products . | 43.5 |
| ours | There is now our products in no asbestos . | 17.8 |
| ref. | Previously , watch imports were denied such duty-free treatment . | |
| Z13 | such duty-free treatment Previously , watch imports were denied . | 67.6 |
| ours | Previously , watch imports were denied such duty-free treatment . | 100 |
| ref. | Despite recent declines in yields , investors continue to pour cash into money funds . | |
| Z13 | continue yields investors pour to recent declines in cash , into money funds | 20.1 |
| ours | Despite recent declines in yields into money funds , investors continue to pour cash . | 67.0 |

Table 6: Example outputs.

## 5 Related Work

The input to practical natural language generation (NLG) system (Reiter and Dale, 1997) can range from a bag of words and phrases to a bag of lemmas without punctuation (Belz et al., 2011). The linearization module of this paper can serve as the final stage in a pipeline when the bag of words and their optional syntactic information are given. There has also been work to jointly perform linearization and morphological generation (Song et al., 2014).

There has been work on linearization with unlabeled and labeled dependency trees (He et al., 2009; Zhang, 2013). These methods mostly use greedy or best-first algorithms to order each tree node. Our work is different by performing word ordering using a transition process.

Besides dependency grammar, linearization with other syntactic grammars, such as CFG and CCG (White and Rajkumar, 2009; Zhang and Clark, 2011b), has also been studied. In this paper, we adopt the dependency grammar for transition-based linearization. However, since transition-based parsing algorithms has been successfully applied to different grammars, including CFG (Sagae et al., 2005) and CCG (Xu et al., 2014), our linearization method can be applied to these grammars.

## 6 Conclusion

We studied transition-based syntactic linearization as an extension to transition-based parsing. Compared with best-first systems, the advantage of our transition-based algorithm includes bounded time complexity, and the guarantee to yield full sentences when given a bag of words. Experimental results show that our algorithm achieves improved accuracies, with significantly faster decoding speed compared with a state-of-the-art best-first baseline. We publicly release our code at `http://sourceforge.net/projects/zgen/`.

For future work, we will study the incorporation of large-scale language models, and the integration of morphology generation and linearization.

## Acknowledgments

We thank the anonymous reviewers for their constructive comments. This work was supported by the National Key Basic Research Program of China via grant 2014CB340503 and the Singapore Ministry of Education (MOE) AcRF Tier 2 grant T2MOE201301 and SRG ISTD 2012 038 from Singapore University of Technology and Design.

## References

Anja Belz, Mike White, Dominic Espinosa, Eric Kow, Deirdre Hogan, and Amanda Stent. 2011. The first surface realisation shared task: Overview and evaluation results. In *Proceedings of the Generation Challenges Session at the 13th European Workshop on Natural Language Generation*, pages 217–226, Nancy, France, September. Association for Computational Linguistics.

Bernd Bohnet, Leo Wanner, Simon Mill, and Alicia Burga. 2010. Broad coverage multilingual deep sentence generation with a stochastic multi-level realizer. In *Proceedings of the 23rd International Conference on Computational Linguistics (Coling 2010)*, pages 98–106, Beijing, China, August. Coling 2010 Organizing Committee.

Michael Collins and Brian Roark. 2004. Incremental parsing with the perceptron algorithm. In *Proceedings of the 42nd Meeting of the Association for Computational Linguistics (ACL'04), Main Volume*, pages 111–118, Barcelona, Spain, July.

Michael Collins. 2002. Discriminative training methods for hidden markov models: Theory and experiments with perceptron algorithms. In *Proceedings of the 2002 Conference on Empirical Methods in Natural Language Processing*, pages 1–8. Association for Computational Linguistics, July.

Adrià de Gispert, Marcus Tomalin, and Bill Byrne. 2014. Word ordering with phrase-based grammars. In *Proceedings of the 14th Conference of the European Chapter of the Association for Computational Linguistics*, pages 259–268, Gothenburg, Sweden, April. Association for Computational Linguistics.

Wei He, Haifeng Wang, Yuqing Guo, and Ting Liu. 2009. Dependency based chinese sentence realization. In *Proceedings of the Joint Conference of the 47th Annual Meeting of the ACL and the 4th International Joint Conference on Natural Language Processing of the AFNLP*, pages 809–816, Suntec, Singapore, August. Association for Computational Linguistics.

Terry Koo and Michael Collins. 2010. Efficient third-order dependency parsers. In *Proceedings of the 48th Annual Meeting of the Association for Computational Linguistics*, pages 1–11, Uppsala, Sweden, July. Association for Computational Linguistics.

Ryan T McDonald and Fernando CN Pereira. 2006. Online learning of approximate dependency parsing algorithms. In *EACL*.

Joakim Nivre. 2008. Algorithms for deterministic incremental dependency parsing. *Computational Linguistics*, 34(4):513–553.

Kishore Papineni, Salim Roukos, Todd Ward, and Wei-Jing Zhu. 2002. Bleu: a method for automatic evaluation of machine translation. In *Proceedings of 40th Annual Meeting of the Association for Computational Linguistics*, pages 311–318, Philadelphia, Pennsylvania, USA, July. Association for Computational Linguistics.

Ehud Reiter and Robert Dale. 1997. Building applied natural language generation systems. *Nat. Lang. Eng.*, 3(1):57–87, March.

Kenji Sagae, Alon Lavie, and Brian MacWhinney. 2005. Automatic measurement of syntactic development in child language. In *Proceedings of the 43rd Annual Meeting of the Association for Computational Linguistics (ACL'05)*, pages 197–204, Ann Arbor, Michigan, June. Association for Computational Linguistics.

Linfeng Song, Yue Zhang, Kai Song, and Qun Liu. 2014. Joint morphological generation and syntactic linearization. In *AAAI*, pages 1522–1528.

Stephen Wan, Mark Dras, Robert Dale, and Cécile Paris. 2009. Improving grammaticality in statistical sentence generation: Introducing a dependency spanning tree algorithm with an argument satisfaction model. In *Proceedings of the 12th Conference of the European Chapter of the ACL (EACL 2009)*, pages 852–860, Athens, Greece, March. Association for Computational Linguistics.

Michael White and Rajakrishnan Rajkumar. 2009. Perceptron reranking for CCG realization. In *Proceedings of the 2009 Conference on Empirical Methods in Natural Language Processing*, pages 410–419, Singapore, August. Association for Computational Linguistics.

Michael White. 2004a. Reining in CCG chart realization. In *In Proc. INLG-04*, pages 182–191.

Michael White. 2004b. Reining in ccg chart realization. In *Natural Language Generation*, pages 182–191. Springer.

Wenduan Xu, Stephen Clark, and Yue Zhang. 2014. Shift-reduce ccg parsing with a dependency model. In *Proceedings of the 52nd Annual Meeting of the Association for Computational Linguistics (Volume 1: Long Papers)*, pages 218–227, Baltimore, Maryland, June. Association for Computational Linguistics.

Yue Zhang and Stephen Clark. 2011a. Syntactic processing using the generalized perceptron and beam search. *Computational Linguistics*, 37(1):105–151.

Yue Zhang and Stephen Clark. 2011b. Syntax-based grammaticality improvement using CCG and guided search. In *Proceedings of the 2011 Conference on Empirical Methods in Natural Language Processing*, pages 1147–1157, Edinburgh, Scotland, UK., July. Association for Computational Linguistics.

Yue Zhang and Joakim Nivre. 2011. Transition-based dependency parsing with rich non-local features. In *Proceedings of the 49th Annual Meeting of the Association for Computational Linguistics: Human Language Technologies*, pages 188–193, Portland, Oregon, USA, June. Association for Computational Linguistics.

Yue Zhang, Graeme Blackwood, and Stephen Clark. 2012. Syntax-based word ordering incorporating a large-scale language model. In *Proceedings of the 13th Conference of the European Chapter of the Association for Computational Linguistics*, pages 736–746, Avignon, France, April. Association for Computational Linguistics.

Yue Zhang. 2013. Partial-tree linearization: Generalized word ordering for text synthesis. In *IJCAI*.

# Extractive Summarisation Based on Keyword Profile and Language Model

**Han Xu** **Eric Martin** **Ashesh Mahidadia**

School of Computer Science and Engineering
UNSW, Sydney, NSW, Australia, 2052
hanx,emartin,ashesh@cse.unsw.edu.au

## Abstract

We present a statistical framework to extract information-rich citation sentences that summarise the main contributions of a scientific paper. In a first stage, we automatically discover salient keywords from a paper's citation summary, keywords that characterise its main contributions. In a second stage, exploiting the results of the first stage, we identify citation sentences that best capture the paper's main contributions. Experimental results show that our approach using methods rooted in quantitative statistics and information theory outperforms the current state-of-the-art systems in scientific paper summarisation.

## 1 Introduction and Motivation

Science is not an isolated endeavour, but benefits from and expands on the work of others, with more or less cross fertilisation between disciplines. The interdependent nature of research has naturally resulted in a network of scientific areas with dense interconnections between related fields. Though research is a highly specialised activity, researchers find themselves constantly in need to explore the network further from the core of their research. Tools that can facilitate understanding the key contributions of papers in those parts of the network being explored can only prove highly valuable.

As an example of such tools, we focus on an application that automatically extracts information-rich sentences describing the main contributions of a given paper. From which corpus the extraction could take place? A natural answer is the abstract of the paper. However, the contributions as perceived by the authors can significantly deviate from those judged extrospectively by the community over time (Mei and Zhai, 2008). Instead, we take as corpus the set of citing sentences to the paper (from other papers). Indeed, those sentences can arguably be deemed as a form of crowd-sourced review of the paper's main contributions. The set of citing sentences is referred to as the *citation summary* of the target paper. Elkiss et al. (2008) carried out a large-scale study and confirmed that citation summaries contain extra information that does not appear in paper abstracts. In addition, they found that the "self-cohesion", measured as the average cosine similarity between sentences, is consistently higher in a paper's citation summary than in its abstract: the former is more focused than the latter in describing papers' main contributions. This work presents our efforts in advancing research along this direction.

Section 2 formally defines the problem we aim to solve: summarise scientific papers using the most informative and diversified part of their citation summaries. It surveys several prominent related studies, and introduces the data used in our experiments and evaluations. In Section 3, we present our statistical framework built upon quantitative statistics and information theory. In Section 4, we evaluate and compare the performance of our method with state-of-the-art systems. We conclude and point to future directions in Section 5.

## 2 Problem Statement

The problem we tackle in this paper is to generate an *extractive summary* (usually, we will simply say *summary*) from its citation summary. More specifically, we opt for a two stage approach. In the first stage, we automatically discover salient keywords from a paper's citation summary, keywords that are essential in characterising the paper's main contributions. The second stage, exploiting the results of the first stage, identifies citation sentences (to the paper) that best capture the paper's main contributions.

A word of caution: by utilising only citation summaries, one should not expect to obtain well formulated, readily consumable summaries of papers. Indeed, a citation sentence may be not all about the cited paper, but also talk about the citing paper and other co-cited papers, which disqualify citation sum-



*Human Language Technologies: The 2015 Annual Conference of the North American Chapter of the ACL*, pages 123–132,
Denver, Colorado, May 31 – June 5, 2015. ©2015 Association for Computational Linguistics

maries as a premium source of sentences for building highly readable summaries (Siddharthan and Teufel, 2007). Moreover, a summary built from citing sentences that come for a pool of multiple citing papers is bound to lack coherence. Therefore, it is more appropriate to consider that the output of such a system is to extrinsically gauge a system's effectiveness in indexing information-rich citing sentences containing keywords that facilitate rapidly grasping a paper's important contributions, rather than be treated as a polished, readable summary for human consumption (Qazvinian et al., 2013).

### 2.1 Related Work

Qazvinian and Radev (2008) first experimented with citation summary based paper summarisations. They proposed a graph-based method, C-LexRank, that first generates a citation summary network for a paper by mapping citing sentences to vertices and creating edges from their lexical similarities. Clusters of sentences capturing the same contribution of the paper are then identified through link-based community detection. Finally, the most central sentence of each cluster is found using a weighted random walk and selected to form a paper summary meant to comprehensively cover the paper's main contributions. Mohammad et al. (2009) further adapted the C-LexRank to multi-document summarisation in an attempt to generate surveys for scientific paradigms.

In a later paper, Qazvinian et al. (2010) proposed a more computationally efficient summariser that does not require clustering citing sentences. As a first step, key phrases are automatically identified as significant n-grams with positive point-wise divergence (Tomokiyo, 2003) from a foreground language model estimated using the citation summary of a paper w.r.t. a background language model built from a large set of paper abstracts. A greedy algorithm is subsequently applied to select citing sentences and form a summary that maximises key phrase coverage.

Mei and Zhai (2008) presented a sophisticated generative approach that frames summarisation under an Information Retrieval (IR) context. Specifically, an impact language model for a paper is first built as a mixture of a language model estimated from the paper's own text, and a weighted citation language model based on its collective citation contexts, using a compound coefficient reflecting both a sentence's proximity to the citation label (anchor) in the citing paper and the citing paper's authority calculated from the citation network using PageRank (Brin and Page, 1998). Finally, documents (sentences in the target paper) that are closest to the query (the impact language model of the target paper) are extracted to form a summary using ad-hoc document retrieval. Note that Mei and Zhai (2008) utilised extra information (i.e., paper full texts and citation networks) to produce summaries that consist of sentences from papers' own texts rather than their citation summaries, making their task related to but different to ours.

### 2.2 Data

The experiments and evaluations presented here have been based on Qazvinian's single paper summarisation corpus[1]. The dataset consists of 25 highly cited papers in the ACL Anthology Network (AAN) (Radev et al., 2009) from 5 different domains: Dependency Parsing (DP), Phrase Based Machine Translation (PBMT), Text Summarisation (SUM), Question Answering (QA) and Textual Entailment (TE). There are two files provided for each paper: a citation summary file containing all citing sentences to it, and a manually constructed key fact file containing its main contributions hand picked by human annotators after reading the citation summary. The manual annotation has been performed independently by annotators, and a phrase needed to be marked by at least 2 annotators to be qualified as capturing a paper's key fact (Qazvinian and Radev, 2008). This corpus represents a gold standard in research paper summarisation and it has been widely used in system evaluations (Qazvinian and Radev, 2008; Qazvinian et al., 2010).

## 3 Our Approach

In this section, we first introduce our quantitative statistical method to automatically construct a *keyword profile* of a paper and statistically capture a paper's main contributions in terms of words from its citation summary. We then discuss how we construct a *keyword profile language model*. Finally, we elaborate on how we cast the task of sentence selection from the citation summary as language model divergence based IR in a probabilistic framework.

### 3.1 Paper Keyword Profile

As indicated in Section 1, the citation summary of a paper can be deemed a collective review of its contributions. Therefore, the main contributions of a

[1] http://www-personal.umich.edu/~vahed/data.html

paper are salient keywords, those keywords which are commonly used by its citers to refer to it and are statistically over-represented in the paper's citation summary w.r.t. the overall distribution of such words across other papers' citation summaries. Put another way, the salience of a word in characterising a paper's main contributions is qualified along *over-representedness* and *exclusiveness* dimensions. Clearly, a proper statistical model of words distribution is required in order to measure words' salience in a paper's citation summary. Consider five papers, $D_1, \ldots, D_5$ with citation summaries $CS_1, \ldots, CS_5$. We aim at identifying salient keywords from $D_1$'s citation summary $CS_1$, that map to $D_1$'s main contributions. To decide whether a word $W$ is a characterising keyword of $D_1$, we first collect all $n$ citing sentences containing $W$ from $CS_1, \ldots, CS_5$; suppose there are $n = 20$ of them. Then for each citing sentence $S$ amongst those 20, we perform the binary test: success iff $S$ belongs to $CS_1$. Suppose that there are $k = 18$ successes and 2 failures. This represents a surprising observation: one would expect a word of no characterising power to appear in roughly the same number of sentences in $CS_1, \ldots, CS_5$, assuming all citation summaries have the same number of sentences[2]. So one would heuristically conclude that $W$ is a good candidate keyword for $D_1$, a keyword that is likely to represent a main contribution.

The previous process can be abstracted as sampling without replacement from a finite set whose elements can be classified into mutually exclusive binary categories, which itself follows a Hypergeometric distribution. Let $N$ be the total number of citing sentences in citation summaries for papers belonging to collection $C$, $K$ be the number of sentences in paper $D$'s citation summary, $n$ be the total number of citing sentences containing a certain word $W$, and $X$ be the number of citing sentences containing $W$ in $D$'s citation summary. The probability of observing exactly $k$ citing sentences in $D$'s citation summary containing $W$ is:

$$H(X{=}k|N,K,n) = \frac{\binom{K}{k}\binom{N-K}{n-k}}{\binom{N}{n}} \quad (1)$$

We can then calculate a p-value to the observed number of $x$ citing sentences in $D$'s citation summary that contain word $W$ using the Hypergeometric test, which in turn is used to measure word $W$'s salience in characterising $D$'s main contributions:

$$S(W) \stackrel{def}{=} P(X{\geq}x) = 1 - \sum_{i=0}^{x-1} H(X{=}i|N,K,n) \quad (2)$$

[2]This assumption is only made to simplify the discussion.

The smaller the value of $S(W)$, the more salient $W$ is. Also, words not appearing in $D$'s citation summary have a maximum p-value of 1.0, and common words appearing in many papers' citation summaries are expected to have larger p-values than words that are more exclusively used when citing paper $D$.

It is worth pointing out that the above formulation can be equivalently expressed as applying the one-tailed Fisher's exact test to measure strengths of statistical associations between words and paper's citation summaries at the sentence level. Our choice of this statistical procedure has been informed by (Moore, 2004). Prior to this work, Dunning (1993) was pointing out that some commonly used methods such as the Pearson's $\chi^2$ test are inappropriate for measuring textual associations due to the fact that the underlying normality assumption is usually violated in textual data. He was subsequently introducing the log-likelihood ratio test (LLR) and showing that it can yield more reliable results. The LLR was then and has since been widely adopted in statistical NLP as a measure of strength of association (Moore, 2004). For instance, Lin and Hovy (2000) successfully applied LLR in mining "topic signatures" of pre-classified document collections. But to further verify LLR's validity applied to rare events, Moore (2004) performed an empirical study comparing results obtained using LLR and Fisher's exact test on bilingual word association and found that albeit being a good approximation to Fisher's exact test, LLR can still introduce a substantial amount of error and the author went on to advocate the use of Fisher's exact test where computationally feasible. Recall that we measured associational strengths at the sentence level. This resulted in marginal frequencies in the order of only hundreds for Qazvinian's small corpus. We therefore followed this empirical advice and used the one-tailed Fisher's exact test (i.e., Hypergeometric test) as our measure of textual association to perform keyword profiling of a scientific paper.

To obtain a set of keywords likely to map to a paper's main contributions, one can simply sort all words according to their statistical significance and pick the top few (e.g., 10 words with the smallest p-values). A more statistically tenable scheme would be to identify the keywords of a paper as all words appearing in its citation summary with p-values below some significance level. A technicality here is that in the identification of keywords, multiple Hypergeometric tests have been performed. For example, all unique words that appeared in the collection of citation summaries have been individually tested for their salience in a target paper's citation summary in succession. The significance level used to qualify a word as a keyword thus requires correction for multiple tests to reduce type I errors. However, we shall show that the rigid statistical significance is not crucial in our subsequent building of a keyword language model for a paper, and so we did not perform multiple tests corrections, but simply used the raw p-values in subsequent analysis.

Another technicality is special handling of citation anchors. Cited authors' names, almost systematically appearing in citing sentences, are bound to be identified as salient keywords. We thus substituted all citation anchors appearing in a paper's citation summary with the pseudo token "targetanchor" if they refer to the target paper, and "otheranchor" if they refer to other co-cited papers.

Furthermore, our keyword profiling approach allows for a flexible control of the level of selectiveness in its statistical procedure through the choice of the benchmarking collection $C$. For example, we can choose to use a heterogeneous collection of papers covering multiple domains. Words that are salient in characterising a domain may then evaluate to a high salience for a paper in $C$ on that domain (e.g., word "parsing" for domain Dependency Parsing (DP)). We can also choose $C$ to be a homogeneous collection of papers from the same domain. Only words that are salient in characterising a single paper will then be evaluated to a high salience for that paper (e.g., if $C$ is on DP, "parsing" will not show up as a salient word for any paper in $C$). Recall from Section 2.2 that we use as data papers from five domains. We exploited the homogeneity of this data and performed keyword profiling intra-domain. This effectively made the keyword profiling all the more selective that the keywords identified for a paper only characterise its *unique* contributions w.r.t. its domain, using five highly cited papers. We shall show in the next section that it is this high selectiveness in keyword profiling that bestows our approach its high discriminative power.

For paper P05-1013, Table 2 lists the top 10 keywords identified from its citation summary using our method, while Table 1 lists the humanly selected gold standard key facts (Qazvinian and Radev, 2008). It can be seen that our method is highly effective in identifying the paper's main contributions which closely mirror those picked by human experts. We term our word list ranked by p-values the *keyword profile* of the paper; it statistically and objectively captures words' salience (measured along the dimensions of over-representedness and exclusiveness) in characterising the paper's main contributions using the statistical surprise given by Hypergeometric tests. While only unigram keywords were considered here, our method can be easily extended to cope with higher order n-gram "key phrases". This is left for future work.

| Fact id | Fact | Occurence | Pyramid tier |
|---|---|---|---|
| 1 | non-projective<br>pseudo-projective<br>projectivizing<br>projective graphs<br>projectivization transformation | 15<br>6<br>1<br>1<br>1 | 19 |
| 4 | czech<br>swedish | 6<br>5 | 8 |
| 2 | data-driven<br>training data | 4<br>2 | 6 |
| 5 | maltparser | 4 | 4 |
| 3 | nonterminal categories in constituency | 1 | 1 |

Table 1: Gold standard key facts of P05-1013 (Qazvinian and Radev, 2008) ordered by importance. The pyramid tier might not be the sum of the occurrences of facts, as multiple facts can appear in the same sentence.

| Salience rank | Word | P-value |
|---|---|---|
| 1 | non-projective | 1.54e-08 |
| 2 | pseudo-projective | 5.61e-06 |
| 3 | transformation | 4.47e-05 |
| 4 | transformations | 1.26e-04 |
| 5 | maltparser | 3.48e-04 |
| 6 | swedish | 7.53e-04 |
| 7 | danish | 1.56e-03 |
| 8 | following | 2.64e-03 |
| 9 | arcs | 2.64e-03 |
| 10 | dependencies | 4.43e-03 |

Table 2: Extracted keywords for P05-1013, ranked by decreasing Hypergeometric test significance.

### 3.2 Keyword Profile Language Model

Each sentence in a paper's citation summary covers keywords (possibly none) that map to the paper's main contributions. Intuitively, a good summarisation should be short, and consist of citing sentences that maximise keywords coverage w.r.t. an arbitrarily imposed summary length limit (Qazvinian and Radev, 2008). A good summariser should thus pick citing sentences that contain as many non-redundant keywords as possible. We have shown in the last section that not all keywords are of equal importance, so a good summariser should favour sentences covering the most important ones. Intuitively, the keyword profile of a paper containing valuable information on words' salience in characterising the paper's main contributions should be utilised to drive such a discriminative sentence selection process.

Based on the previous considerations, we use a paper's keyword profile to build a discriminative unigram language model that directly encodes words' salience as pseudo generative probabilities to facilitate the seamless incorporation of such information into a generic probabilistic framework. More specifically, we directly translate words' salience (in the form of p-values) into a discriminative unigram language model of a paper that assigns high probabilities to its characterising keywords. The pseudo generative probability of word $W$ according to a paper $D$'s keyword profile language model $M_{kp}$ is:

$$P(W|M_{kp}) = -\frac{1}{Z}\log(S(W)) \quad (3)$$

where $S(W)$ denotes the salience of word $W$ in characterising paper $D$ calculated using (2), and $Z$ is a normalisation factor. An intuitive interpretation of (3) is to deem $-\log(S(W))$ a pseudo word count of $W$, where more salient words have higher pseudo counts; this makes $Z$ the total length of the pseudo document generated from the paper's keyword profile. We disregard actual word counts to make the keyword profile language model directly encode words' salience. Also, in the previous step, keyword profiling had already implicitly taken such information into account, providing another justification for this design decision. Table 3 shows a miniature example to illustrate how a keyword profile language model is built. In this example, $W_5$ is automatically eliminated from the resulting language model because it has lowest salience in characterising the imaginary document. Any word $S$ with salience value $S(W)$ close to but strictly less than 1.0 would still have a tiny pseudo probability in the resulting keyword profile language model (e.g., $W_4$). Words with low salience are not necessarily stop words (*e.g.*, $W_4$ and $W_5$), and neither is the reverse true: a content word can possibly be used across the document collection and thus evaluate to a very low salience (and so have a nul or low pseudo generative probability in the resulting keyword profile language model) for the document under consideration. For example, "parsing" would have a low salience for any paper in a collection on Dependency Parsing. It can be seen that our method amounts to a highly adaptive data driven term weighting framework. For brevity, from now on, we use KPLM to refer to keyword profile language model.

| **Word** | **Salience** $S(W)$ | **Pseudo count** $-\log(S(W))$ | $P(W\|M_{kp})$ |
|---|---|---|---|
| $W_1$ | 0.01 | 4.61 | 0.605 |
| $W_2$ | 0.10 | 2.30 | 0.303 |
| $W_3$ | 0.50 | 0.69 | 0.091 |
| $W_4$ | 0.99 | 0.01 | 0.001 |
| $W_5$ | 1.00 | 0.00 | 0.000 |

Table 3: Keyword profile language model built for an imaginary document consists of only 5 distinct words.

Although implicitly conveyed in the formulation of KPLM above, it should be made clear that the KPLM is a pseudo language model that encodes words' salience in the form of pseudo generative probabilities, which functions as a language model, yet should not be interpreted as a true language model under the traditional definition. A traditional unigram language model is constructed using the actual term frequencies in the document, the resulting model capturing generative probabilities. In contrast, the KPLM of a document is built using pseudo term frequencies that directly encode words' salience in characterising a document's contents, measured using a sophisticated quantitative statistical procedure. It can thus be interpreted as a probabilistic description of the document's keywords with significantly boosted discriminative power. Having clarified the nature of KPLM, we treat it as a language model in the rest of the paper.

## 3.3 KPLM Based Summarisation

### 3.3.1 Sentence Selection

The KPLM of a paper is a discriminative generative model that incorporates words' salience in characterising a paper's main contributions. It thus represents an effective language model from which a model citing sentence covering the paper's main contributions could be sampled from[3]. So by measuring the statistical surprise between the realistic language model estimated from each citing sentence with the KPLM of a paper, we can select the set of citing sentences that conform best to the optimal model given by the the KPLM and build a summary that well captures keywords. More specifically, we adopt the negative cross entropy retrieval model (Zhai, 2008), use the KPLM of a paper as the

[3]A pseudo citing sentence sampled from KPLM in this manner would simply be a bag of words, not a grammatical sentence. So here "model" has the favour of keywords coverage.

sole document model, and measure the cross entropy of multiple query models from it (one for each citing sentence in that paper's citation summary). Citing sentences whose Maximum Likelihood Estimation (MLE) language models are closest to the paper's KPLM are taken as building blocks of the summary.

Formally, let $S$ be a citing sentence and let $c(W, S)$ denote the number of occurrences of word $W$ in $S$. The MLE language model $M_{mle}$ of $S$ is the relative frequency of word $W$ in $S$:

$$P(W|M_{mle})=\frac{c(W,S)}{|S|} \tag{4}$$

Subsequently, the score for a citing sentence $S$ is given by its negative cross entropy with the $M_{kp}$:

$$\begin{aligned} Score(S) &= -H(M_{mle}||M_{kp}) \\ &= \sum_{W \in V} P(W|M_{mle}) \log(P(W|M_{kp})) \end{aligned} \tag{5}$$

The larger a citing sentence's score, the closer it is to the cited paper's KPLM, thus the higher the citing sentence would be ranked. To summarise a paper, one can just pick the top $k$ ranked citing sentences where $k$ is the imposed summary length limit.

We are not the first to cast the task of summarisation as document retrieval. Mei and Zhai (2008) pioneered in utilising language models and divergence based IR to select sentences to build summaries. While similar in the fundamental methodology, our approach should be distinguished from this work. First, Mei and Zhai cast the task as ad-hoc retrieval, using the "impact language model" of a paper as sole query, while the paper's sentences are treated as documents whose Kullback-Leibler divergence (Kullback and Leibler, 1951) with the query model is measured in turn. Estimating reliable language models for short documents is challenging due to data sparseness and thus requires prudent smoothing. We purposefully reversed the roles of sentence model and document model, using the shorter sentences as queries and measuring their cross entropy with a sole document model (the KPLM)[4]. This represents a more natural formulation resulting in simpler language models that require fewer parameter estimations. Second, while the impact language model in (Mei and Zhai, 2008) is partially weighted using citing paper authority and sentence proximity to the citation anchor in the citing paper, it is still largely based on actual word occurrences. In contrast, KPLM directly models words' salience in characterising a paper's main contributions using its keyword profile, with expectedly more discriminative power. Last, Mei and Zhai's estimation of an impact language model for a paper assumes the reliable estimation of its citing papers' authority, which cannot always be guaranteed, for example when a paper receives citations from new papers that themselves have not been cited enough. Furthermore, while a citation network can be unavailable, the estimation of KPLM requires only the citation summaries of papers, which is arguably more robust.

### 3.3.2 Top Sentence Re-ranking

As discussed in Section 3.2, a good summary should capture the most salient keywords of a paper, but also cover as many non-redundant keywords as possible. A summary built using our method is likely to contain citing sentences that concentrate on and repetitively cover salient keywords of the target paper, which may fall short in keywords diversity. Indeed, we can see in the top part of Table 4 that the summary of paper P05-1012 repetitively covers a single keyword, "Minimum Spanning Tree", while it fails to capture other key concepts.

To leverage the diversity in keywords captured in a summary, a simple heuristic is to select the next sentence from a pool of top ranked sentences least similar to the existing summary. From an information theoretic point of view, this amounts to choosing the next sentence that carries the most *extra* information (i.e., statistical surprise), w.r.t. the current contents of the summary. This formulation intuitively suggests that cross entropy, as a natural measure of statistical surprise, could again be employed.

We first need to abstract a citing sentence and the citation summary into probabilistic distributions before their cross entropy can be measured. Again we use unigram language modelling. Since both texts are small in size, data sparseness becomes a major issue, as nul dimensions in the MLE language models would make cross entropy not measurable. Smoothing as a way to alleviate data sparseness is thus required. Another issue that also arises from the texts' small size is the non-negligible amount of cross entropy contributed from non-content words in both texts (English stop words plus the two pseudo tokens: "targetanchor" and "otheranchor"). We therefore remove those non-content words prior to

[4] Kullback-Leibler divergence, used in (Mei and Zhai, 2008), is unsuitable to our task, as it is not formalised as ad-hoc retrieval (i.e., single query, multiple documents). Instead we compare multiple query models (MLE's of citing sentences) to a single document model (KPLM of the cited paper), making KL-divergence scores not comparable due to query specific entropy terms. See (Zhai, 2008) for a detailed analysis.

language model construction to eliminate their noise in the cross entropy calculation. Experiments did support this design decision, and better results have been achieved with non-content words removed.

We perform Dirichlet Prior Smoothing (Zhai and Lafferty, 2001) to both the citing sentence MLE and the summary MLE using the KPLM of the paper as a background model using a Dirichlet Prior (DP) of 20. The choice of 20 has been based on the observation that citing sentences are short (32 words on average) and a large DP is prone to generate overly smoothed language models that are dominated by the KPLM, thus lack discriminative power. Here we choose to use this empirically selected DP parameter without attempting to fine-tune it for best results.

In summary, we implement a top sentence re-ranking heuristic that iteratively selects the next sentence to be appended to the existing summary whose smoothed language model is with the largest cross entropy (so it contains most extra information) with a smoothed language mode built for the summary at its current stage. We shall demonstrate how our top sentence re-ranking method introduces a major performance boost in the next section. For a quick inspection of the effectiveness of this method, compare the summaries constructed for paper P05-1012 with and without sentence re-reranking in Table 4. It shows that the summary constructed with sentence re-ranking covers key facts more comprehensively. The pseudo code for our re-ranking strategy is shown in Algorithm 1. It adopts a straightforward re-ranking approach that simply uses the top $k$+5 retrieved citing sentences in the previous step as the candidate pool; at each iteration, it selects the best sentence based on its cross entropy with the summary at the current stage. A more sophisticated re-ranking method is to combine the two cross entropy scores in some way (e.g., Maximal Marginal Relevance (Carbonell and Goldstein, 1998)) so that the final score for a citing sentence reflects its value in capturing salient keywords that have not yet been included in the summary. We leave the study of a more sophisticated re-ranking scheme for future work.

**Algorithm 1** Top Sentence Re-ranking

```
function TOPSENTENCERERANKER
    k ← summary length limit
    top_sent ← top_k_plus_5_sents[0]
    es ← top_sent
    cp ← top_k_plus_5_sents - top_sent
    for s in cp do
        cp_lms[s] ← DPSmoothed(s)
    for i = 2 to k do
        es_lm ← DPSmoothed(es)
        s ← argmax_{s∈cp}(CE(cp_lms||es_lm))
        es ← es + s
        cp ← cp − s
        cp_lms ← cp_lms − cp_lms[s]
    return es
```

## 4 Experimental Setup

### 4.1 Evaluation Method

Following Qazvinian et al. (2008; 2010), we use the pyramid method (Nenkova and Passonneau, 2004) at sentence level to evaluate our system's performance. The pyramid score is a fact-based evaluation method that has been especially popular in evaluating extractive summarisation systems. It has been widely adopted because it incorporates both fact coverage and fact importance into the scoring process, which resonates well with the goals of summarisation (Qazvinian et al., 2010). More specifically, the pyramid method scores a summary using the ratio between the total facts weights of the facts it covers and that of an optimal summary. First a fact weights pyramid is built using some facts weighting method and each fact is subsequently put into its perspective pyramid tier. Qazvinian et al. (2008; 2010) built a weights pyramid for each paper and assigned each humanly discovered fact into a tier according to the number of citing sentences the fact occurs in that paper's citation summary. For example, fact $f_i$ appearing in $|f_i|$ citing sentences in the citation summary of paper $D$ is assigned to the tier $T_{|f_i|}$ in $D$'s fact weights pyramid $P_D$. Let $F_i$ denotes the number of facts in the summary $ES$ in tier $T_i$ of $P_D$. The total facts weights $ES$ covers is calculated as:

$$W(ES)=\sum_{i=1}^{n} i \cdot F_i \quad (6)$$

where $n$ is the highest tier of $P_D$. Let $ES_{optimal}$ be the optimal summary for $D$ w.r.t. the summary length limit ($ES_{optimal}$ can be found using heuristic-driven exhaustive search). The pyramid score for $ES$ is finally calculated as:

$$Score(ES)=W(ES)/W(ES_{optimal}) \quad (7)$$

Note again that we used exactly the same corpus and evaluation method as in (Qazvinian and Radev, 2008; Qazvinian et al., 2010), which makes our results directly comparable to those described in those papers. Furthermore, both papers report on performance of various baseline methods which are also directly comparable to ours (see next section). We compare our results with the current state-of-the-art; readers are encouraged to refer to (Qazvinian

| Rank | Summary |
|---|---|
| **KPLM without sentence re-ranking (Pyramid score: 0.23)** | |
| 1 | 3.1 decoding mcdonald et al (2005b) use the chu-liuedmonds (cle) algorithm to solve the maximum **spanning tree** problem. |
| 2 | thus far, the formulation follows mcdonald et al (2005b) and corresponds to the maximum **spanning tree** (mst) problem. |
| 3 | while we have presented signi cant improvements using additional constraints, one may won5even when caching feature extraction during training mcdonald et al (2005a) still takes approximately 10 minutes to train. |
| 4 | we have successfully replicated the state-of-the-art results for dependency parsing (mcdonald et al, 2005a) for both czech and english, using bayes point machines. |
| 5 | the search for the best parse can then be formalized as the search for the maximum **spanning tree** (mst) (mcdonald et al, 2005b). |
| **KPLM with sentence re-ranking (Pyramid score: 0.73)** | |
| 1 | 3.1 decoding mcdonald et al (2005b) use the chu-liuedmonds (cle) algorithm to solve the maximum **spanning tree** problem. |
| 2 | to learn these structures we used online **large-margin** learning (mcdonald et al, 2005) that empirically provides state-of-the-art performance for czech. |
| 3 | while we have presented signi cant improvements using additional constraints, one may won5even when caching feature extraction during training mcdonald et al (2005a) still takes approximately 10 minutes to train. |
| 4 | mcdonald et al (2005a) introduce a dependency parsing framework which treats the task as searching for the **projective tree** that **maximises the sum of local dependency scores**. |
| 5 | we take as our starting point a re-implementation of mcdonald's state-of-the-art dependency parser (mcdonald et al, 2005a). |

Table 4: Summaries of paper P05-1012 produced using KPLM. Key facts in citing sentences are highlighted and OCR and sentence segmentation errors have been retained as they originally appeared in the corpus.

and Radev, 2008; Qazvinian et al., 2010) for cross-referencing results from a broader set of systems.

## 4.2 Results and Discussion

Table 5 shows the pyramid score evaluation results for the 25 papers. To facilitate comparison and cross-referencing, the table has been formatted as close as possible to Table 7 in (Qazvinian and Radev, 2008) with figures in the Gold and C-LexRank columns directly copied over. Note that a Gold pyramid score less than 1 suggests that there are more facts than can be covered using $k$ sentences for that paper's citation summary. It can be seen that KPLM based summarisation achieves quite comparable results (especially in terms of the median score) with C-LexRank, even without top sentence re-ranking. When the re-ranking is introduced, our system outperforms the current state-of-the-art C-LexRank by a measurable margin. Albeit the perceived differences in the results, a one-tailed Wilcoxon signed-rank test indicated that our results are not statistically superior at significance level 0.05 (Z=-1.22, P=0.11). A power analysis reveals that in order to achieve a statistically significant result on this small sample of 25 papers, a system would need to score a medium to large effect size (Cohen's d $>$ 0.53), which is a challenging task considering C-LexRank's strong baseline performance. We hope this analysis can inform future studies using Qazvinian's 25 papers corpus. Nevertheless, it should be pointed out that our approach is not only substantially simpler than C-LexRank, it also yields more interpretable results.

We know of a more recent set of results reported in (Qazvinian et al., 2013), which again confirmed C-LexRank's state-of-the-art status with a mean pyramid score of 0.799 (cf. Table 6 in (Qazvinian et al., 2013)). However those results are not comparable with ours for the following reasons. First, Qazvinian et al. (2013) used a slightly different corpus with 30 papers (5 extra papers from the Conditional Random Field domain). Second, results were based on a summary length limit of 200 words, so roughly equivalent to 6.3 sentences per paper, giving evaluations an extra edge. Both changes boosted system performance in those evaluations, as evidenced by comparing Table 7 in (Qazvinian and Radev, 2008) and Table 6 in (Qazvinian et al., 2013).

Qazvinian et al. (2010) used the same corpus and evaluation method as our work; however the results have been presented as box plots (cf. Figure 1 in (Qazvinian et al., 2010)) from which only the five-number summary (i.e., minimum, lower quartile, median, upper quartile and maximum) of the pyramid scores can be reconstructed and consequently no significance test can be performed. Compared with the best performing variants of the system devised in (Qazvinian et al., 2010) based on unigrams, bigrams and trigrams, our system (KPLM+TSR) achieves a higher median score (0.86 vs. 0.80), as well as a lower score variation across the 25 papers.

An arbitrarily imposed constraint in the evaluations is the summary length limit, which may be changed to suit a specific application context. The summarisation task becomes increasingly more challenging when summary length limit is further tightened as this would require a summariser to pinpoint the best sentences from a potentially large cita-

| Domain | Paper | Gold | C-LexRank | KPLM | KPLM+TSR |
|---|---|---|---|---|---|
| DP | C96-1058 | 1.00 | 0.73 | 0.33 | 0.56 |
| | P97-1003 | 1.00 | 0.40 | 0.79 | 0.79 |
| | P99-1065 | 0.94 | 0.67 | 0.62 | 0.76 |
| | P05-1013 | 1.00 | 0.67 | 0.66 | 0.66 |
| | P05-1012 | 0.95 | 0.62 | 0.23 | 0.73 |
| PBMT | N03-1017 | 0.96 | 0.64 | 0.60 | 0.60 |
| | W03-0301 | 1.00 | 1.00 | 0.80 | 0.80 |
| | J04-4002 | 1.00 | 0.48 | 0.86 | 0.89 |
| | N04-1033 | 1.00 | 0.85 | 0.57 | 0.86 |
| | P05-1033 | 1.00 | 0.85 | 0.97 | 0.97 |
| SUMM | A00-1043 | 1.00 | 0.95 | 0.50 | 0.50 |
| | A00-2024 | 1.00 | 0.60 | 0.60 | 0.60 |
| | C00-1072 | 1.00 | 0.93 | 0.87 | 0.93 |
| | W00-0403 | 1.00 | 0.70 | 0.81 | 0.54 |
| | W03-0510 | 1.00 | 0.83 | 1.00 | 1.00 |
| QA | A00-1023 | 1.00 | 0.86 | 0.88 | 1.00 |
| | W00-0603 | 1.00 | 0.60 | 0.44 | 0.94 |
| | P02-1006 | 1.00 | 0.87 | 0.93 | 0.93 |
| | D03-1017 | 1.00 | 0.85 | 0.70 | 0.90 |
| | P03-1001 | 1.00 | 0.59 | 0.94 | 0.44 |
| TE | D04-9907 | 1.00 | 0.94 | 0.77 | 0.91 |
| | H05-1047 | 1.00 | 1.00 | 0.83 | 0.83 |
| | H05-1079 | 1.00 | 0.56 | 0.78 | 0.89 |
| | W05-1203 | 1.00 | 0.71 | 1.00 | 1.00 |
| | P05-1014 | 1.00 | 0.78 | 0.89 | 1.00 |
| | **Mean** | **0.99** | **0.75** | **0.73** | **0.80** |
| | **Median** | **1.00** | **0.73** | **0.79** | **0.86** |

Table 5: Summary pyramid score evaluation results with summary length limit $k = 5$.

tion summary. A desirable property of a good summariser is thus the ability in maintaining its performance while the task becomes increasingly demanding. To further evaluate KPLM's performance under increasingly more stringent summary length limits, we gathered the pyramid scores with summary length limit $k$ decreasing from 5 to 1 and visualised the results in Figure 1. We can see that KPLM's performance decays quite gracefully as more stringent limits are imposed. Even under the harshest constraint with the summary length limit sets to 1, our system still managed a mean pyramid score of close to 0.6 across the 25 papers. Indeed, it can be seen that the variance in pyramid scores gradually spreads wider (the dark band in the figure marks out 95% confidence interval of the mean scores), but this phenomenon is expected as the error margin also shrinks along with the summary length limit.

## 5 Conclusion and Future Work

We designed a statistical framework to summarise scientific papers, using methods rooted in quantitative statistics and information theory. We first built a keyword profile for a paper using a quantitative statistical method that captures its charac-

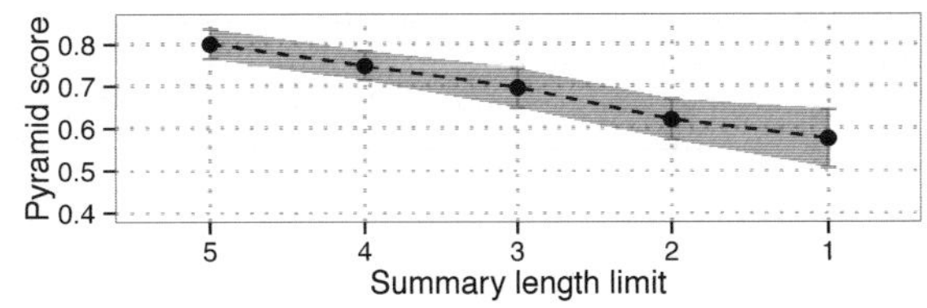


Figure 1: Pyramid scores of KPLM+TSR under different summary length limits.

terising keywords that are both overly represented and relatively exclusively used in the paper's citation summary. We then used the keyword profile of a paper to build a discriminative pseudo unigram language model that directly incorporates words' salience in characterising a paper's main contributions into pseudo generative probabilities. Based on the fact that a paper's KPLM represents an effective language model from which pseudo citing sentences with good coverage of important keywords could be sampled, we cast the task of summarisation as language model divergence based IR. Finally, we implemented an information-driven sentence reranking algorithm that can effectively leverage diversity in keyword coverage in summaries produced. Experimental results show that our approach outperforms the current state-of-the-art systems in scientific paper summarisation, which is also with good resilience to more stringent summary length limits.

In the future, we plan to extend our approach to higher order n-grams and see whether larger information units (phrases) would help boost summarisation performance. We also plan to apply our method to the problem of multi-document summarisation. In particular, we are very interested to test our system's performance on automatically generating a technical survey of a scientific paradigm, which thanks to the authors of (Mohammad et al., 2009; Qazvinian et al., 2013), has been established as a well-defined task with high-quality open data. Finally, while we have shown that our approach is effective in summarising a scientific paper's major contributions using its citation summary text, further experiments are required to test our method's effectiveness on more generic summarisation tasks and texts genres.

## Acknowledgement

We thank Vahed Qazvinian for making the 25 paper summarisation corpus publicly available; without it, our formal evaluations would have been impossible. We also thank the anonymous reviewers for their highly constructive comments.

## References


Brin, Sergey and Page, Larry. 1998 The anatomy of a large-scale hypertextual web search engine. In *Proceedings of the 7th International Conference on World Wide Web*, pp. 107–117.

Carbonell, Jaime and Goldstein, Jade. 1998 The use of MMR, diversity-based reranking for reordering documents and producing summaries. In *Proceedings of the SIGIR*, pp. 335–336.

Elkiss, Aaron and Shen, Siwei and Fader, Anthony and Erkan, Güneş and States, David and Radev, Dragomir. 2008 Blind men and elephants: What do citation summaries tell us about a research article?. *Journal of the American Society for Information Science and Technology*, vol. 59, no. 1, pp. 51–62.

Kullback, S. and Leibler, R. A. 1951 On information and sufficiency. *The Annals of Mathematical Statistics*, vol. 22, no. 1, pp. 79–86.

Mei, Qiaozhu and Zhai, Chengxiang. 2008 Generating impact-based summaries for scientific literature. In *Proceedings of the ACL*, pp. 816–824.

Mohammad, Saif and Dorr, Bonnie and Egan, Melissa and Hassan, Ahmed and Muthukrishan, Pradeep and Qazvinian, Vahed and Radev, Dragomir and Zajic, David. 2009 Using citations to generate surveys of scientific paradigms. In *Proceedings of the HLT-NAACL*, pp. 584–592.

Nenkova, Ani and Passonneau, Rebecca. 2004 Evaluating content selection in summarization: The pyramid method. In *Proceedings of the HLT-NAACL*, pp. 145–152.

Qazvinian, Vahed and Radev, Dragomir. 2008 Scientific paper summarization using citation summary networks. In *Proceedings of the 22nd International Conference on Computational Linguistics*, pp. 689–696.

Qazvinian, Vahed and Radev, Dragomir and Özgür, Arzucan. 2010 Citation summarization through keyphrase extraction. In *Proceedings of the 23rd International Conference on Computational Linguistics*, pp. 895–903.

Dunning Ted. 1993 Accurate methods for the statistics of surprise and coincidence. *Computational Linguistics*, vol. 19, no. 1, pp. 61–74.

Lin, Chin-Yew and Hovy, Eduard. 2000 The automated acquisition of topic signatures for text summarization. In *Proceedings of the 18th conference on Computational Linguistics*, pp. 495–501.

Moore. Robert C. 2004 On log-likelihood-ratios and the significance of rare events. In *Proceedings of EMNLP*, pp. 333–340.

Qazvinian, Vahed and Radev, Dragomir and Mohammad, Saif and Dorr, Bonnie and Zajic, David and Whidby, Michael and Moon, Taesun. 2013 Generating extractive summaries of scientific paradigms. *Journal of Artificial Intelligence Research (JAIR)*, vol. 46, pp.165–201.

Radev, Dragomir and Pradeep, Muthukrishnan and Qazvinian, Vahed. 2009 The ACL anthology network corpus. In *Proceedings of the ACL workshop on Natural Language Processing and Information Retrieval for Digital Libraries*, pp. 54–61.

Siddharthan, Advaith. and Teufel, Simone. 2007 Whose idea was this, and why does it matter? In *Proceedings of the NAACL/HLT*, pp. 316–323.

Tomokiyo, Takashi and Hurst, Matthew. 2003 A language model approach to keyphrase extraction. In *Proceedings of the ACL'03 workshop on Multiword expressions*, pp. 33–40.

Zhai, Chengxiang. 2008 Statistical language models for information retrieval a critical review. *Foundations and Trends in Information Retrieval*, vol. 2, no. 3, pp. 137–213.

Zhai, Chengxiang and Lafferty, John. 2001 A study of smoothing methods for language models applied to ad hoc information retrieval. In *Proceedings of the 24th Annual International ACM SIGIR Conference on Research and Development in Information Retrieval*, pp. 334–342.

# HEADS: Headline Generation as Sequence Prediction Using an Abstract Feature-Rich Space

**Carlos A. Colmenares***
Google Inc.
Brandschenkestrasse 110
8002 Zurich, Switzerland
crcarlos@google.com

**Marina Litvak**
Shamoon College
of Engineering
Beer Sheva, Israel
marinal@sce.ac.il

**Amin Mantrach** **Fabrizio Silvestri**
Yahoo Labs.
Avinguda Diagonal 177
08018 Barcelona, Spain
{amantrach,silvestr}@yahoo-inc.com

## Abstract

Automatic headline generation is a sub-task of document summarization with many reported applications. In this study we present a sequence-prediction technique for learning how editors title their news stories. The introduced technique models the problem as a discrete optimization task in a feature-rich space. In this space the global optimum can be found in polynomial time by means of dynamic programming. We train and test our model on an extensive corpus of financial news, and compare it against a number of baselines by using standard metrics from the document summarization domain, as well as some new ones proposed in this work. We also assess the readability and informativeness of the generated titles through human evaluation. The obtained results are very appealing and substantiate the soundness of the approach.

## 1 Introduction

Document summarization, also known as text summarization, is the process of automatically abridging text documents. Although traditionally the final objective of text summarization is to produce a paragraph or abstract that summarizes a rather large collection of texts (Mani and Maybury, 1999; Das and Martins, 2007; Nenkova and McKeown, 2012), the task of producing a very short summary comprised of 10–15 words has also been broadly studied. There have been many reported practical applications for this endeavor, most notably, efficient web browsing on hand-held devices (Buyukkokten et al., 2001), generation of TV captions (Linke-Ellis, 1999), digitization of newspaper articles that have uninformative headlines (De Kok, 2008), and headline generation in one language based on news stories written in another (Banko et al., 2000; Zajic et al., 2002).

In general terms, a headline of a news article can be defined as a short statement that gives a reader a general idea about the main contents of the story it entitles (Borko and Bernier, 1987; Gattani, 2007). The objective of our study is to develop a novel technique for generating informative headlines for news articles, albeit to conduct experiments we focused on finance articles written in English. In this work we make a number of contributions concerning statistical models for headline generation, training of the models, and their evaluation, specifically:

- We propose a model that learns how an editor generates headlines for news articles, where a headline is regarded as a compression of its article's text. Our model significantly differs from others in the way it represents possible headlines in a feature-rich space. The model tries to learn how humans discern between good and bad compressions. Furthermore, our model can be trained with any monolingual corpus consisting of titled articles, because it does not request special conditions on the headlines' structure or provenance.
- We suggest a slight change of the Margin Infused Relaxed Algorithm (Crammer and Singer, 2003) to fit our model, which yields better empirical results.

* Work done during an internship at Yahoo Labs.



*Human Language Technologies: The 2015 Annual Conference of the North American Chapter of the ACL*, pages 133–142,
Denver, Colorado, May 31 – June 5, 2015. 

- We present a simple and elegant algorithm that runs in polynomial time and finds the global optimum of our objective function. This represents an important advantage of our proposal because many former techniques resort to heuristic-driven search algorithms that are not guaranteed to find the global optimum.

- With the intention of overcoming several problems suffered by traditional metrics for automatically evaluating the quality of proposed headlines, we propose two new evaluation metrics that correlate with ratings given by human annotators.

## 2 Related work

There has been a significant amount of research about headline generation. As noted by Gattani (2007), it is possible to identify three main trends of techniques broadly employed through different studies:

**Rule-based approaches.** These methods make use of handcrafted linguistically-based rules for detecting or compressing important parts in a document. They are simple and lightweight, but fail at exploring complex relationships in the text. The most representative model for this group is the Hedge Trimmer (Dorr et al., 2003).

**Statistics-based approaches.** These methods make use of statistical models for learning correlations between words in headlines and in the articles. The models are fit under supervised learning environments and therefore need large amounts of labelled data. One of the most influential works in this category is the Naïve Bayes approach presented by Banko et al. (2000), and augmented in works such as Jin and Hauptmann (2001; Zajic et al. (2002). The use of statistical models for learning pruning-rules for parse trees has also been studied, the most notable work on this area is presented in Knight and Marcu (2001) and extended by Unno et al. (2006).

**Summarization-based approaches.** Headlines can be regarded as very short summaries, therefore traditional summarization methods could be adapted for generating one-line compressions; the common trend consists in performing multiple or combined steps of sentence selection and compression (Hajime et al., 2013; Martins and Smith, 2009). The main problem with these approaches is that they make use of techniques that were not initially devised for generating compressions of less than 10% of the original content, which directly affects the quality of the resulting summary (Banko et al., 2000). It is noteworthy to highlight that most of the modern summarization-based techniques opt for generating headlines just by recycling and reordering words present in the article, which also raises the risk of losing or changing the contextual meaning of the reused words (Berger and Mittal, 2000).

An area that deals with a target similar to headline generation is multi-sentence compression, where its objective is to produce a single short phrase that abridges a set of sentences that conform a document. The main difference between both practices is that headline generation is more strict about the length of the generated output, which should consist of about eight tokens (Banko et al., 2000), whereas the latter accepts longer results. One of the most recent and competitive approaches for multi-sentence compression is described by Filippova (2010).

## 3 Background on sequence prediction

Sequence models have been broadly used for many Natural Language Processing tasks, such as identification of sentence boundaries (Reynar and Ratnaparkhi, 1997), named entity recognition (McCallum and Li, 2003), part of speech tagging (Kupiec, 1992), dependency tree parsing (McDonald et al., 2005), document summarization (Shen et al., 2007), and single-sentence compression (McDonald, 2006; Nomoto, 2007). These models are formalizations of relationships between observed sequences of variables and predicted categories for each one. Mathematically, let $\mathcal{X} = \{x_1, x_2, ..., x_N\}$ be a finite set of possible atomic observations, and let $\mathcal{Y} = \{y_1, y_2, ..., y_M\}$ be a finite set of possible categories that each atomic observation could belong to.

Statistical sequence models try to approximate a probability distribution $P$ with parameters $\phi$ capable of predicting for any sequence of $n$ observations $\boldsymbol{x} \in \mathcal{X}^n$, and any sequence of assigned categories per observation $\boldsymbol{y} \in \mathcal{Y}^n$, the probability $P(\boldsymbol{y}|\boldsymbol{x}; \phi)$. The final objective of these models is to predict the most likely sequence of categories $\hat{\boldsymbol{y}} \in \mathcal{Y}^n$ for any arbitrary observation sequence, which can be expressed as:

$$\hat{\boldsymbol{y}} = \arg\max_{\boldsymbol{y} \in \mathcal{Y}^n} P(\boldsymbol{y}|\boldsymbol{x}; \phi)$$

There have been many proposals for modelling the probability distribution $P$. Some of the most popular proposals are Hidden Markov Models (Rabiner and Juang, 1986), local log-linear classifiers, Maximum Entropy Markov Models (McCallum et al., 2000), and Conditional Random Fields (Lafferty et al., 2001). The following two sections will briefly introduce the latter, together with a widely used improvement of the model.

### 3.1 Conditional Random Fields (CRF)

As presented by Lafferty et al. (2001), CRF are sequence prediction models where no Markov assumption is made on the sequence of assigned categories $\boldsymbol{y}$, but a factorizable global feature function is used so as to transform the problem into a log-linear model in feature space. Formally, CRF model the probability of a sequence in the following way:

$$P(\boldsymbol{y}|\boldsymbol{x}; \phi) = \frac{exp\{\boldsymbol{w} \cdot \boldsymbol{F}(\boldsymbol{x}, \boldsymbol{y})\}}{Z(\boldsymbol{x})}$$

Where $\phi = \{\boldsymbol{w}\}$ and $\boldsymbol{w} \in \mathbb{R}^m$ is a weight vector, $\boldsymbol{F} : \mathcal{X}^n \times \mathcal{Y}^n \rightarrow \mathbb{R}^m$ is a global feature function of $m$ dimensions, and $Z(\boldsymbol{x})$ is a normalization function. Moreover, the global feature function is defined in the following factored way:

$$\boldsymbol{F}(\boldsymbol{x}, \boldsymbol{y}) = \sum_{i=1}^{n} \boldsymbol{f}(\boldsymbol{x}, i, y_{i\text{-}1}, y_i)$$

where $\boldsymbol{f} : \mathcal{X}^* \times \mathbb{N}^+ \times \mathcal{Y} \times \mathcal{Y} \rightarrow \mathbb{R}^m$ is a local feature function. Due to this definition, it can be shown that the decoding of CRF is equivalent to:

$$\hat{\boldsymbol{y}} = \arg\max_{\boldsymbol{y} \in \mathcal{Y}^n} \boldsymbol{w} \cdot \boldsymbol{F}(\boldsymbol{x}, \boldsymbol{y})$$

Which is a linear classification in a feature space. The fact that the local feature function $\boldsymbol{f}$ only depends on the last two assigned categories allows the global optimum of the model to be found by means of a tractable algorithm, whereas otherwise it would be necessary to explore all the $|\mathcal{Y}|^n$ possible solutions.

### 3.2 CRF with state sequences

Since CRF do not assume independence between assigned categories, it is possible to extend the local feature function for enabling it to keep more information about previous assigned categories and not just the last category. These models are derived from the work on weighted automata and transducers presented in studies such as Mohri et al. (2002). Let $\mathcal{S}$ be a state space, $s_0$ be a fixed initial empty state, and let function $g : \mathcal{S} \times \mathcal{X}^* \times \mathbb{N}^+ \times \mathcal{Y} \rightarrow \mathcal{S}$ model state transitions. Then the global feature function can be redefined as:

$$\boldsymbol{F}(\boldsymbol{x}, \boldsymbol{y}) = \sum_{i=1}^{n} \boldsymbol{f}(\boldsymbol{x}, i, s_{i\text{-}1}, y_i), \quad s_i = g(s_{i\text{-}1}, \boldsymbol{x}, i, y_i)$$

This slight change adds a lot of power to CRF because it provides the model with much more information that it can use for learning complex relations. Finally, the best candidate can be found by solving:

$$\hat{\boldsymbol{y}} = \arg\max_{\boldsymbol{y} \in \mathcal{Y}^n} \boldsymbol{w} \cdot \left[ \sum_{i=1}^{n} \boldsymbol{f}(\boldsymbol{x}, i, s_{i\text{-}1}, y_i) \right] \qquad (1)$$

## 4 Model description: headlines as bitmaps

We model headline generation as a sequence prediction task. In this manner a news article is seen as a series of observations, where each is a possible token in the document. Furthermore, each observation can be assigned to one of two categories: in-headline, or not in-headline. Note that this approach allows a generated headline to be interpreted as a bitmap over the article's tokens.

If this set-up was used for a CRF model, the standard local feature function $\boldsymbol{f}(\boldsymbol{x}, i, y_{i\text{-}1}, y_i)$ would only be able to know whether the previous token was taken or not, which would not be very informative. For solving the problem we integrate a state sequence into the model, where a state $s \in \mathcal{S}$ holds the following information:

- The last token that was chosen as part of the headline.
- The part-of-speech tag[1] of the second-to-last word that was selected as part of the headline.

[1] We used the set of 45 tags from the Penn Treebank Tag-Set.

- The number of words already chosen to be part of the headline, which could be zero.

Therefore, the local feature function $\boldsymbol{f}(\boldsymbol{x}, i, s_{i\text{-}1}, y_i)$ will not only know about the whole text and the current token $x_i$, whose category $y_i$ is to be assigned, but it will also hold information about the headline constructed so far. In our model, the objective of the local feature function is to return a vector that describes in an abstract euclidean space the outcome of placing, or not placing, token $x_i$ in the headline, provided that the words previously chosen form the state $s_{i\text{-}1}$. We decide to make this feature vector consist of 23 signals, which only fire if the token $x_i$ is placed in the headline (i.e., $y_i = 1$). The signals can be grouped into the following five sets:

**Language-model features:** they assess the grammaticality of the headline being built. The first feature is the bigram probability of the current token, given the last one placed on the headline. The second feature is the trigram probability of the PoS tag of the current token, given the tags of the two last tokens on the headline.

**Keyword features:** binary features that help the model detect whether the token under analysis is a salient word. The document's keywords are calculated as a preprocessing step via TF-IDF weighting, and the features fire depending on how good or bad the current token $x_i$ is ranked with respect to the others on the text.

**Dependency features:** in charge of informing the model about syntactical dependencies among the tokens placed on the headline. For this end the dependency tree of all the sentences in the news article are computed as a pre-processing step[2].

**Named-entity features:** help the system identify named entities[3] in the text, including those that are composed of contiguous tokens.

**Headline-length features:** responsible for enabling the model to decide whether a headline is too short or too long. As many previous studies report, an ideal headline must have from 8 to 10 tokens (Banko et al., 2000). Thus, we include three binary features that correspond to the following conditions: (1) if the headline length so far is less than or equal to seven; (2) if the headline length so far is greater than or equal to 11; (3) if the token under analysis is assigned to the headline, which is a bias feature.

## 5 Decoding the model

Decoding the model involves solving equation (1) being given a weight vector $\boldsymbol{w}$, whose value stays unchanged during the process. A naive way of solving the optimization problem would be to try all possible $|\mathcal{Y}|^n$ sequence combinations, which would lead to an intractable procedure. In order to design a polynomial algorithm that finds the global optimum of the aforementioned formula, the following four observations must be made:

**(1)** Our model is designed so that the local feature function only fires when a token is selected for being part of a headline. Then, when evaluating an arbitrary solution $\boldsymbol{y}$, only the tokens placed on the headline must be taken into account.

**(2)** When applying the local feature function to a particular token $x_i$ (assuming $y_i = 1$), the result of the function will vary only depending on the provided previous state $s_{i\text{-}1}$; all the other parameters are fixed. Moreover, a new state $s_i$ will be generated, which in turn will include token $x_i$. This implies that the entire evaluation of a solution can be completely modeled as a sequence of state transitions; i.e., it becomes possible to recover a solution's bitmap from a sequence of state transitions and vice-versa.

**(3)** When analyzing the local feature function at any token $x_i$, the amount of different states $s_{i\text{-}1}$ that can be fed to the function depend solely on the tokens taken before, for which there are $2^{i\text{-}1}$ different combinations. Nevertheless, because a state only holds three pieces of information, a better upper-bound to the number of possible reachable states is equal to $i^2 \times |PoS|$, which accounts to: all possible candidates for the last token chosen before $x_i$, times all possible combinations of total number of tokens taken before $x_i$, times all possible PoS tags of the one-before-last token taken before $x_i$.

**(4)** The total amount of producible states in the whole text is equal to $\sum_{i=1}^{n} i^2 \times |PoS| = O(n^3 \times |PoS|)$. If the model is also constrained to produce headlines containing no more than $H$ tokens, the asymptotic bound drops to $O(H \times n^2 \times |PoS|)$.

[2] We use the Stanford toolkit for computing parse trees.

[3] We only use PER, LOC, and ORG as entity annotations.

The final conclusion of these observations is as follows: since any solution can be modelled as a chain of state sequences, the global optimum can be found by generating all possible states and fetching the one that, when reached from the initial state, yields the maximum score. This task is achievable with a number of operations linearly proportional to the number of possible states, which at the same time is polynomial with respect to the number of tokens in the document. In conclusion, the model can be decoded in quadratic time. The pseudo-code in algorithm 1 gives a sketch of a $O(H \times n^2 \times |PoS|)$ bottom-up implementation.

## 6 Training the model: learning what human-generated headlines look like

The global feature function $\boldsymbol{F}$ is responsible for taking a document and a bitmap, and producing a vector that describes the candidate headline in an abstract feature space. We defined the feature function so it only focuses on evaluating how a series of tokens that comprise a headline relate to each other and to the document as a whole. This implies that if $\boldsymbol{h} = \{h_1, h_2, ..., h_k\}$ is the tokenized form of any arbitrary headline consisting of $k$ tokens, and we define vectors $\boldsymbol{a} \in \mathcal{X}^{k+n}$ and $\boldsymbol{b} \in \mathcal{Y}^{k+n}$ as:

$$\boldsymbol{a} = \{h_1, h_2, ..., h_k, x_1, x_2, ..., x_n\}$$

$$\boldsymbol{b} = \{1_1, 1_2, ..., 1_k, 0_1, 0_2, ..., 0_n\}$$

where $\boldsymbol{a}$ is the concatenation of $\boldsymbol{h}$ and $\boldsymbol{x}$, and $\boldsymbol{b}$ is a bitmap for only selecting the actual headline tokens, it follows that the feature vector that results from calling the global feature function, which we define as

$$\boldsymbol{u} = \boldsymbol{F}(\boldsymbol{a}, \boldsymbol{b}) \qquad (2)$$

is equivalent to a description of how headline $\boldsymbol{h}$ relates to document $\boldsymbol{x}$. This observation is the core of our learning algorithm, because it implies that it is possible to "insert" a human-generated headline in the text and get its description in the abstract feature space induced by $\boldsymbol{F}$. The objective of the learning process will consist in molding a weight vector $\boldsymbol{w}$, such that it makes the decoding algorithm favor headlines whose descriptions in feature space resemble the characteristics of human-generated titles.

For training the model we follow the on-line learning schemes presented by Collins (2002) and applied in studies that deal with CRF models with state sequences, such as the dependency parsing model of McDonald et al. (2005). The learning framework consists of an averaged perceptron that iteratively sifts through the training data and performs the following error-correction update at each step:

$$\boldsymbol{w}^* \leftarrow \boldsymbol{w} + \tau \times (\boldsymbol{u} - \hat{\boldsymbol{v}}), \quad \hat{\boldsymbol{v}} = \boldsymbol{F}(\boldsymbol{x}, \hat{\boldsymbol{y}})$$

where $\boldsymbol{u}$ is the vector defined in equation (2), $\hat{\boldsymbol{y}}$ is the result of solving equation (1) with the current weight

**Algorithm 1** Sketch of a bottom-up algorithm for finding the top-scoring state $s^*$ that leads to the global optimum of our model's objective function. It iteratively computes two functions: $\pi(i, l)$, which returns the set of all reachable states that correspond to headlines having token-length $l$ and finishing with token $x_i$, and $\alpha(s)$, which returns the maximum score that can be obtained by following a chain of state sequences that ends in the provided state, and starts on $s_0$.

```
//Constants.
H ← Max. number of allowed tokens in headlines.
n ← Number of tokens in the document.
x ← List of n tokens (document).
w ← Weight vector.
g ← State transition function.
f ← Local feature function.
s0 ← Init state.
//Variables.
π ← new Set<State>[n + 1][H + 1]({})
α ← new Float[|State|](−∞)
s* ← s0
//Base cases.
α(s0) ← 0
for i in {0, ..., n} do
    π(i, 0) ← {s0}
//Bottom-up fill of π and α.
for l in {1, ..., H} do
    for i in {l, ..., n} do
        for j in {l − 1, ..., i − 1} do
            for z in π(j, l − 1) do
                s ← g(z, x, i, 1)
                s_score ← α(z) + w · f(x, i, z, 1)
                π(i, l) ← π(i, l) ∪ {s}
                α(s) ← max(α(s), s_score)
                if α(s) > α(s*) then
                    s* ← s
```

vector, and $\tau \in \mathbb{R}$ is a learning factor. We try three different values for $\tau$, which lead to the following learning algorithms:

- **Perceptron:** $\tau = 1$
- **MIRA:** $\tau = max\left(0, \frac{1-\boldsymbol{w}\cdot(\boldsymbol{u}-\hat{\boldsymbol{v}})}{||\boldsymbol{u}-\hat{\boldsymbol{v}}||^2}\right)$
- **Forced-MIRA:** $\tau = \frac{1-\boldsymbol{w}\cdot(\boldsymbol{u}-\hat{\boldsymbol{v}})}{||\boldsymbol{u}-\hat{\boldsymbol{v}}||^2}$

The first value is a simple averaged perceptron as presented by Collins (2002), the second value is a Margin Infused Relaxed Algorithm (MIRA) as presented by Crammer and Singer (2003), and the third value is a slight variation to the MIRA update. We propose it for making the algorithm acknowledge that the objective feature vector $\boldsymbol{u}$ cannot be produced from document $\boldsymbol{x}$, and thus force an update at every step. The reason for this is that if $\boldsymbol{w}\cdot\boldsymbol{u} > \boldsymbol{w}\cdot\hat{\boldsymbol{v}}$, then MIRA sets $\tau = 0$, because an error was not made (i.e. the human-generated headline got a higher score than all of the others). Nevertheless, we observed in our experiments that this behaviour biases the process towards learning weights that exploit patterns that can occur in human-generated titles, but are almost never observed in the titles that can be generated by our model, which hinders the quality of the final headlines.

# 7 Automatic evaluation set-up

## 7.1 Evaluation metrics

For performing an automatic evaluation of the headlines generated by our system we follow the path taken by related work such as Zajic et al. (2004) and use a subset of the ROUGE metrics for comparing candidate headlines with reference ones, which have been proven to strongly correlate with human evaluations (Lin, 2003; Lin, 2004).

We decide to use as metrics ROUGE-1, ROUGE-2, and ROUGE-SU. We also propose as an experimental new metric a weighted version of ROUGE-SU, which we name ROUGE-WSU. The rationale of our proposal is that ROUGE-SU gives the same importance to all skip-bigrams extracted from a phrase no matter how far apart they are. We address the problem by weighting each shared skip-gram between phrases by the inverse of the token's average gap distance. Formally:

$$Sim(R,C) = \frac{\sum\limits_{(a,b)\in su(R)\cap su(C)} \frac{2}{dist_R(a,b)+dist_C(a,b)}}{\sum\limits_{(a,b)\in su(R)} \frac{1}{dist_R(a,b)}}$$

Where function $dist_H(a,b)$ returns the skip distance between tokens "$a$" and "$b$" in headline $H$, and $su(H)$ returns all skip-bigrams in headline $H$.

With the objective of having a metric capable of detecting abstract concepts in phrases and comparing headlines at a semantic level, we resort to Latent Semantic Indexing (LSI) (Deerwester et al., 1990). We use the method for extracting latent concepts from our training corpus so as to be able to represent text in an abstract latent space. We then compute the similarity of a headline with respect to a news article by calculating the cosine similarity of their vector representations in latent space.

## 7.2 Baselines

In order to have a point of reference for interpreting the performance of our model, we implement four baseline models. We arbitrarily decide to make all the baselines generate, if possible, nine-token-long headlines, where the last token must always be a period. This follows from the observation that good headlines must contain about eight tokens (Banko et al., 2000). The implemented baselines are the following:

**Chunked first sentence:** the first eight tokens from the article, plus a period at the end.

**Hidden Markov Model:** as proposed by Zajic et al. (2002), but adapted for producing eight-token sentences, plus an ending period.

**Word Graphs:** as proposed by Filippova (2010). This is a state-of-the-art multi-sentence compression algorithm. To ensure it produces headlines as output, we keep the shortest path in the graph with length equal to or greater than eight tokens. An ending period is appended if not already present. Note that the original algorithm would produce the top-k shortest paths and keep the one with best average edge weight, not caring about its length.

**Keywords:** the top eight keywords in the article, as ranked by TF-IDF weighting, sorted in descending order of relevance. This is not a real baseline because it does not produce proper headlines, but it is used for naively trying to maximize the achievable value of the evaluation metrics. This is based on the assumption that keywords are the most likely tokens to occur in human-generated headlines.

### 7.3 Experiments and Results

We trained our model with a corpus consisting of roughly 1.3 million financial news articles fetched from the web, written in English, and published on the second half of 2012. We decided to add three important constraints to the learning algorithm which proved to yield positive empirical results:

**(1)** Large news articles are simplified by eliminating their most redundant or least informative sentences. For this end, the text ranking algorithm proposed by Mihalcea and Tarau (2004) is used for discriminating salient sentences in the article. Furthermore, a news article is considered large if it has more than 300 tokens, which corresponds to the average number of words per article in our training set.

**(2)** Because we observed that less than 2% of the headlines in the training set contained more than 15 tokens, we constraint the decoding algorithm to only generate headlines consisting of 15 or fewer tokens.

**(3)** We restrain the decoding algorithm from placing symbols such as commas, quotation marks, and question marks on headlines. Nonetheless, only headlines that end with a period are considered as solutions; otherwise the model tends to generate non-conclusive phrases as titles.

For automated testing purposes we use a training set consisting of roughly 12,000 previously unseen articles, which were randomly extracted from the initial dataset before training. The evaluation consisted in producing seven candidate headlines per article: one for each of the four baselines, plus one for each of the three variations of our model (each differing solely on the scheme used to learn the weight vector). Then each candidate is compared against the article's reference headline by means of the five proposed metrics.

Table 1 summarizes the obtained results of the models with respect to the ROUGE metrics. The results show that our model, when trained with our proposed forced-MIRA update, outperforms all the other baselines on all metrics, except for ROUGE-2, where all differences are statistically significant when assessed via a paired t-test ($p < 0.001$). Also, as initially intended, the keywords baseline does produce better scores than all the other methods, therefore it is considered as a naive upper-bound. It must be highlighted that all the numbers on the table are rather low, this occurs because, as noted by Zajic et al. (2002), humans tend to use a very different vocabulary and writing-style on headlines than on articles. The effect of this is that our methods and baselines are not capable of producing headlines with wordings strongly similar to human-written ones, which as a consequence makes it almost impossible to obtain high ROUGE scores.

| | R-1 | R-2 | R-SU | R-WSU |
|---|---|---|---|---|
| **Perceptron** | 0.157 | 0.056 | 0.053 | 0.082 |
| **MIRA** | 0.172 | 0.042 | 0.057 | 0.084 |
| **f-MIRA** | **0.187** | 0.054 | **0.065** | **0.095** |
| 1$^{st}$sent. | 0.076 | 0.021 | 0.025 | 0.038 |
| HMM | 0.090 | 0.009 | 0.023 | 0.038 |
| Word graphs | 0.174 | **0.060** | 0.060 | 0.084 |
| Keywords | **0.313** | 0.021 | **0.112** | **0.148** |

Table 1: Result of the evaluation of our models and baselines with respect to ROUGE metrics.

For having a more objective assessment of our proposal, we carried out a human evaluation of the headlines generated by our model when trained with the f-MIRA scheme and the word graphs approach by Filippova (2010). For this purpose, 100 articles were randomly extracted from the test set and their respective candidate headlines were generated. Then different human raters were asked to evaluate on a Likert scale, from 1 to 5, both the grammaticality and informativeness of the titles. Each article-headline pair was annotated by three different raters. The median of their ratings was chosen as a final mark. As a reference, the raters were also asked to annotate the actual human-generated headlines from the articles, although they were not informed about the provenance of the titles. We measured inter-judge agreement by means of their Intra-Class Correlation (ICC) (Cicchetti, 1994). The ICC for grammaticality was $0.51 \pm 0.07$, which represents fair agreement, and the ICC for informativeness was $0.63 \pm 0.05$, which represents substantial agreement.

Table 2 contains the results of the models with

| | H. Len. | LSI | Gram. | Inf. |
|---|---|---|---|---|
| **Perceptron** | 10.096 | 0.446 | – | – |
| **MIRA** | 13.045 | 0.463 | – | – |
| **f-MIRA** | 11.737 | **0.491** | 3.45 | **2.94** |
| 1[st]sent. | 8.932 | 0.224 | – | – |
| HMM | 9.000 | 0.172 | – | – |
| Word graphs | 10.973 | 0.480 | **3.69** | 2.32 |
| Keywords | 9.000 | **0.701** | – | – |
| Reference | 11.898 | **0.555** | **4.49** | **4.14** |

Table 2: Result of the evaluation of our models and baselines with LSI document similarity, grammaticality and informativeness as assessed by human raters, and average headline length.

respect to the LSI document similarity metric, and the human evaluations for grammaticality and informativeness. For exploratory purposes the table also contains the average length for the generated headlines of each of the models (which also counts the imposed final period). The results in this table are satisfying: with respect to LSI document similarity, our model outperforms all of the baselines and its value is close to the one achieved by human-generated headlines. On the other hand, the human evaluations are middling: the word-graphs method produces more readable headlines, but our model proves to be more informative because it does better work at detecting abstract word relationships in the text. All differences in this table are statistically significant when computed as paired t-tests ($p < 0.001$).

It is worth noting that the informativeness of human-generated headlines did not get a high score. The reason for this is the fact that editors tend to produce rather sensationalist or partially informative titles so as to attract the attention of readers and engage them to read the whole article; human raters penalized the relevance of such headlines, which was reflected on this final score.

Finally, table 3 contains the mutual correlation between automated and manual metrics. The first thing to note is that none of the used metrics proved to be good for assessing grammaticality of headlines. It is also worth noting that our proposed metric ROUGE-WSU performs as well as the other ROUGE metrics, and that the proposed LSI document similarity does not prove to be as strong a metric as the others.

| | R-1 | R-2 | R-SU | R-WSU | LSI-DS |
|---|---|---|---|---|---|
| **Gram.** | -0.130 | -0.084 | -0.131 | -0.132 | -0.015 |
| **Inf.** | 0.561 | 0.535 | 0.557 | 0.542 | 0.370 |

Table 3: Spearman correlation between human-assessed metrics and automatic ones.

## 8 Conclusions and Discussion

In this study we proposed a CRF model with state transitions. The model tries to learn how humans title their articles. The learning is performed by means of a mapping function that, given a document, translates headlines to an abstract feature-rich space, where the characteristics that distinguish human-generated titles can be discriminated. This abstraction allows our model to be trained with any monolingual corpus of news articles because it does not impose conditions on the provenance of stories' headlines –i.e, our model maps reference headlines to a feature space and only learns what abstract properties characterize them. Furthermore, our model allows defining the task of finding the best possible producible headline as a discrete optimization problem. By doing this each candidate headline is modelled as a path in a graph of state sequences, thus allowing the best-scoring path to be found in polynomial time by means of dynamic programming. Our results, obtained through reliable automatic and human-assessed evaluations, provide a proof of concept for the soundness of our model and its capabilities. Additionally, we propose a new evaluation metric, ROUGE-WSU, which, as shown in table 3, correlates as good as traditional ROUGE metrics with human evaluations for informativeness of headlines.

The further work we envisage for augmenting our research can be grouped in the following areas:

- Exploring more advanced features that manage to detect abstract semantic relationships or discourse flows in the compressed article.
- Complementing our system with a separate translation model capable of transforming to "Headlinese" the titles generated with the language used in the bodies of articles.
- Attempting to achieve a more objective evaluation of our generated headlines, through the use of semantic-level measures.

## Acknowledgments

We thank Jordi Atserias, Horacio Saggion, Horacio Rodríguez, and Xavier Carreras, who helped and supported us during the development of this study.

## References

[Banko et al.2000] Michele Banko, Vibhu O. Mittal, and Michael J. Witbrock. 2000. Headline generation based on statistical translation. *Proceedings of the 38th Annual Meeting on Association for Computational Linguistics.*

[Berger and Mittal2000] B. Berger and N. Mittal. 2000. Discourse segmentation in aid of document summarization. *Proceedings of the Hawaii International Conference on System Sciences, Minitrack on Digital Documents Understanding.*

[Borko and Bernier1987] H. Borko and C. Bernier. 1987. Abstracting concepts and methods. *New York: Academic Press.*

[Buyukkokten et al.2001] Orkut Buyukkokten, Hector Garcia-Molina, and Andreas Paepcke. 2001. Seeing the whole in parts: text summarization for web browsing on handheld devices. *Proceedings of the 10th international conference on World Wide Web. ACM.*

[Cicchetti1994] Domenic V. Cicchetti. 1994. Guidelines, criteria, and rules of thumb for evaluating normed and standardized assessment instruments in psychology. *Psychological assessment 6.4.*

[Collins2002] Michael Collins. 2002. Discriminative training methods for hidden markov models: Theory and experiments with perceptron algorithms. *Proceedings of the ACL-02 conference on Empirical methods in natural language processing-Volume 10.*

[Crammer and Singer2003] Koby Crammer and Yoram Singer. 2003. Ultraconservative online algorithms for multiclass problems. *The Journal of Machine Learning Research 3.*

[Das and Martins2007] Dipanjan Das and André FT Martins. 2007. A survey on automatic text summarization. *Literature Survey for the Language and Statistics II course at CMU 4*, pages 192–195.

[De Kok2008] D. De Kok. 2008. Headline generation for dutch newspaper articles through transformation-based learning. *Master Thesis.*

[Deerwester et al.1990] Scott C. Deerwester et al. 1990. Indexing by latent semantic analysis. *JASIS 41.6.*

[Dorr et al.2003] Bonnie Dorr, David Zajic, and Richard Schwartz. 2003. Hedge trimmer: a parse-and-trim approach to headline generation. *Proceedings of the HLT-NAACL 03 on Text summarization workshop*, pages 1–8.

[Filippova2010] Katja Filippova. 2010. Multi-sentence compression: Finding shortest paths in word graphs. *Proceedings of the 23rd International Conference on Computational Linguistics.*

[Gattani2007] Akshay Kishore Gattani. 2007. Automated natural language headline generation using discriminative machine learning models. *Diss. Simon Fraser University.*

[Hajime et al.2013] Morita Hajime et al. 2013. Subtree extractive summarization via submodular maximization. *Proceedings of 51st Annual Meeting of the Association for Computational Linguistics.*

[Jin and Hauptmann2001] Rong Jin and Alexander G. Hauptmann. 2001. Title generation using a training corpus. *CICLing '01: Proceedings of the Second International Conference on Computational Linguistics and Intelligent Text Processing*, pages 208–215.

[Knight and Marcu2001] Kevin Knight and Daniel Marcu. 2001. Summarization beyond sentence extraction: A probabilistic approach to sentence compression. *Artificial Intelligence 139.1*, pages 91–107.

[Kupiec1992] Julian Kupiec. 1992. Robust part-of-speech tagging using a hidden markov model. *Computer Speech and Language 6.3.*

[Lafferty et al.2001] John Lafferty, Andrew McCallum, and Fernando CN Pereira. 2001. Conditional random fields: Probabilistic models for segmenting and labeling sequence data.

[Lin2003] C.Y. Lin. 2003. Cross-domain study of n-gram co-occurrence metrics. *Proceedings of the Workshop on Machine Translation Evaluation, New Orleans, USA.*

[Lin2004] Chin-Yew Lin. 2004. Rouge: A package for automatic evaluation of summaries. *Text Summarization Branches Out: Proceedings of the ACL-04 Workshop.*

[Linke-Ellis1999] N. Linke-Ellis. 1999. Closed captioning in america: Looking beyond compliance. *Proceedings of the TAO Workshop on TV Closed Captions for the Hearing Impaired People, Tokyo, Japan*, pages 43–59.

[Mani and Maybury1999] Inderjeet Mani and Mark T. Maybury Maybury. 1999. *Advances in automatic text summarization*, volume 293. Cambridge: MIT press.

[Martins and Smith2009] André F.T. Martins and Noah A. Smith. 2009. Summarization with a joint model for sentence extraction and compression. *NAACL-HLT Workshop on Integer Linear Programming for NLP, Boulder, USA.*

[McCallum and Li2003] Andrew McCallum and Wei Li. 2003. Early results for named entity recognition with conditional random fields, feature induction and web-enhanced lexicons. *Proceedings of the seventh conference on Natural language learning at HLT-NAACL 2003-Volume 4.*

[McCallum et al.2000] Andrew McCallum, Dayne Freitag, and Fernando CN Pereira. 2000. Maximum entropy markov models for information extraction and segmentation. *ICML.*

[McDonald et al.2005] Ryan McDonald, Koby Crammer, and Fernando Pereira. 2005. Online large-margin training of dependency parsers. *Proceedings of the 43rd Annual Meeting on Association for Computational Linguistics.*

[McDonald2006] Ryan T. McDonald. 2006. Discriminative sentence compression with soft syntactic evidence. *EACL.*

[Mihalcea and Tarau2004] Rada Mihalcea and Paul Tarau. 2004. Textrank: Bringing order into texts. *Association for Computational Linguistics.*

[Mohri et al.2002] Mehryar Mohri, Fernando Pereira, and Michael Richard. 2002. Weighted finite-state transducers in speech recognition. *Computer Speech and Language 16.1.*

[Nenkova and McKeown2012] Ani Nenkova and Kathleen McKeown. 2012. A survey of text summarization techniques. *Mining Text Data. Springer US*, pages 43–76.

[Nomoto2007] Tadashi Nomoto. 2007. Discriminative sentence compression with conditional random fields. *Information processing and management 43.6.*

[Rabiner and Juang1986] Lawrence Rabiner and Biing-Hwang Juang. 1986. An introduction to hidden markov models. *ASSP Magazine, IEEE 3.1*, pages 4–16.

[Reynar and Ratnaparkhi1997] Jeffrey C. Reynar and Adwait Ratnaparkhi. 1997. A maximum entropy approach to identifying sentence boundaries. *Proceedings of the fifth conference on Applied natural language processing.*

[Shen et al.2007] Dou Shen et al. 2007. Document summarization using conditional random fields. *IJCAI. Vol. 7.*

[Unno et al.2006] Yuya Unno et al. 2006. Trimming cfg parse trees for sentence compression using machine learning approaches. *Proceedings of the COLING/ACL on Main conference poster sessions.*

[Zajic et al.2002] David Zajic, Bonnie Dorr, and Richard Schwartz. 2002. Automatic headline generation for newspaper stories. *Workshop on Automatic Summarization.*

[Zajic et al.2004] David Zajic, Bonnie Dorr, and Richard Schwartz. 2004. Bbn/umd at duc-2004: Topiary. *Proceedings of the HLT-NAACL 2004 Document Understanding Workshop, Boston.*

# What's Cookin'? Interpreting Cooking Videos using Text, Speech and Vision

**Jonathan Malmaud, Jonathan Huang, Vivek Rathod, Nick Johnston, Andrew Rabinovich, and Kevin Murphy**
Google
1600 Amphitheatre Parkway
Mountain View, CA 94043
malmaud@mit.edu
{jonathanhuang, rathodv, nickj, amrabino, kpmurphy}@google.com

## Abstract

We present a novel method for aligning a sequence of instructions to a video of someone carrying out a task. In particular, we focus on the cooking domain, where the instructions correspond to the recipe. Our technique relies on an HMM to align the recipe steps to the (automatically generated) speech transcript. We then refine this alignment using a state-of-the-art visual food detector, based on a deep convolutional neural network. We show that our technique outperforms simpler techniques based on keyword spotting. It also enables interesting applications, such as automatically illustrating recipes with keyframes, and searching within a video for events of interest.

## 1 Introduction

In recent years, there have been many successful attempts to build large "knowledge bases" (KBs), such as NELL (Carlson et al., 2010), KnowItAll (Etzioni et al., 2011), YAGO (Suchanek et al., 2007), and Google's Knowledge Graph/ Vault (Dong et al., 2014). These KBs mostly focus on declarative facts, such as "Barack Obama was born in Hawaii". But human knowledge also encompasses procedural information not yet within the scope of such declarative KBs – instructions and demonstrations of how to dance the tango, for example, or how to change a tire on your car. A KB for organizing and retrieving such procedural knowledge could be a valuable resource for helping people (and potentially even robots – e.g., (Saxena et al., 2014; Yang et al., 2015)) learn to perform various tasks.

In contrast to declarative information, procedural knowledge tends to be inherently multimodal. In particular, both language and perceptual information are typically used to parsimoniously describe procedures, as evidenced by the large number of "how-to" videos and illustrated guides on the open web. To automatically construct a multimodal database of procedural knowledge, we thus need tools for extracting information from both textual and visual sources. Crucially, we also need to figure out how these various kinds of information, which often complement and overlap each other, fit together to a form a structured knowledge base of procedures.

As a small step toward the broader goal of aligning language and perception, we focus in this paper on the problem of aligning video depictions of procedures to steps in an accompanying text that corresponds to the procedure. We focus on the cooking domain due to the prevalence of cooking videos on the web and the relative ease of interpreting their recipes as linear sequences of canonical actions. In this domain, the textual source is a user-uploaded recipe attached to the video showing the recipe's execution. The individual steps of procedures are cooking actions like "peel an onion", "slice an onion", etc. However, our techniques can be applied to any domain that has textual instructions and corresponding videos, including videos at sites such as youtube.com, howcast.com, howdini.com or videojug.com.

The approach we take in this paper leverages the fact that the speech signal in instructional videos is often closely related to the actions that the person is performing (which is not true in more general



*Human Language Technologies: The 2015 Annual Conference of the North American Chapter of the ACL*, pages 143–152,
Denver, Colorado, May 31 – June 5, 2015. 

videos). Thus we first align the instructional steps to the speech signal using an HMM, and then refine this alignment by using a state of the art computer vision system.

In summary, our contributions are as follows. First, we propose a novel system that combines text, speech and vision to perform an alignment between textual instructions and instructional videos. Second, we use our system to create a large corpus of 180k aligned recipe-video pairs, and an even larger corpus of 1.4M short video clips, each labeled with a cooking action and a noun phrase. We evaluate the quality of our corpus using human raters. Third, we show how we can use our methods to support applications such as within-video search and recipe auto-illustration.

## 2 Data and pre-processing

We first describe how we collected our corpus of recipes and videos, and the pre-processing steps that we run before applying our alignment model. The corpus of recipes, as well as the results of the alignment model, will be made available for download at `github.com/malmaud/whats_cookin`.

### 2.1 Collecting a large corpus of cooking videos with recipes

We first searched Youtube for videos which have been automatically tagged with the Freebase mids /m/01mtb (Cooking) and /m/0p57p (recipe), and which have (automatically produced) English-language speech transcripts, which yielded a collection of 7.4M videos. Of these videos, we kept the videos that also had accompanying descriptive text, leaving 6.2M videos.

Sometimes the recipe for a video is included in this text description, but sometimes it is stored on an external site. For example, a video's text description might say "Click here for the recipe". To find the recipe in such cases, we look for sentences in the video description with any of the following keywords: "recipe", "steps", "cook", "procedure", "preparation", "method". If we find any such tokens, we find any URLs that are mentioned in the same sentence, and extract the corresponding document, giving us an additional 206k documents. We then combine the original descriptive text with any additional text that we retrieve in this way.

| Class | Precision | Recall | F1 |
|---|---|---|---|
| Background | 0.97 | 0.95 | 0.96 |
| Ingredient | 0.93 | 0.95 | 0.94 |
| Recipe step | 0.94 | 0.95 | 0.94 |

Table 1: Test set performance of text-based recipe classifier.

Finally, in order to extract the recipe from the text description of a video, we trained a classifier that classifies each sentence into 1 of 3 classes: *recipe step*, *recipe ingredient*, or *background*. We keep only the videos which have at least one ingredient sentence and at least one recipe sentence. This last step leaves us with 180,000 videos.

To train the recipe classifier, we need labeled examples, which we obtain by exploiting the fact that many text webpages containing recipes use the machine-readable markup defined at `http://schema.org/Recipe`. From this we extract 500k examples of recipe sentences, and 500k examples of ingredient sentences. We also sample 500k sentences at random from webpages to represent the non-recipe class. Finally, we train a 3-class naïve Bayes model on this data using simple bag-of-words feature vectors. The performance of this model on a separate test set is shown in Table 1.

### 2.2 Parsing the recipe text

For each recipe, we apply a suite of in-house NLP tools, similar to the Stanford Core NLP pipeline. In particular, we perform POS tagging, entity chunking, and constituency parsing (based on a re-implementation of (Petrov et al., 2006)).[1] Following (Druck and Pang, 2012), we use the parse tree structure to partition each sentence into "micro steps". In particular, we split at any token categorized by the parser as a conjunction only if that token's parent in the sentence's constituency parse is a verb phrase. Any recipe step that is missing a verb is considered noise and discarded.

We then label each recipe step with an optional action and a list of 0 or more noun chunks. The ac-

[1]Sometimes the parser performs poorly, because the language used in recipes is often full of imperative sentences, such as "Mix the flour", whereas the parser is trained on newswire text. As a simple heuristic for overcoming this, we classify any token at the beginning of a sentence as a verb if it lexically matches a manually-defined list of cooking-related verbs.

tion label is the lemmatized version of the head verb of the recipe step. We look at all chunked noun entities in the step which are the direct object of the action (either directly or via the preposition "of", as in "Add a cup of flour").

We canonicalize these entities by computing their similarity to the list of ingredients associated with this recipe. If an ingredient is sufficiently similar, that ingredient is added to this step's entity list. Otherwise, the stemmed entity is used. For example, consider the step "Mix tomato sauce and pasta"; if the recipe has a known ingredient called "spaghetti", we would label the action as "mix" and the entities as "tomato sauce" and "spaghetti", because of its high semantic similarity to "pasta". (Semantic similarity is estimated based on Euclidean distance between word embedding vectors computed using the method of (Mikolov et al., 2013) trained on general web text.)

In many cases, the direct object of a transitive verb is elided (not explicitly stated); this is known as the "zero anaphora" problem. For example, the text may say "Add eggs and flour to the bowl. Mix well.". The object of the verb "mix" is clearly the stuff that was just added to the bowl (namely the eggs and flour), although this is not explicitly stated. To handle this, we use a simple recency heuristic, and insert the entities from the previous step to the current step.

### 2.3 Processing the speech transcript

The output of Youtube's ASR system is a sequence of time-stamped tokens, produced by a standard Viterbi decoding system. We concatenate these tokens into a single long document, and then apply our NLP pipeline to it. Note that, in addition to errors introduced by the ASR system[2], the NLP system can introduce additional errors, because it does not work well on text that may be ungrammatical and which is entirely devoid of punctuation and sentence boundary markers.

To assess the impact of these combined sources of error, we also collected a much smaller set of 480 cooking videos (with corresponding recipe text) for which the video creator had uploaded a manually curated speech transcript; this has no transcription errors, it contains sentence boundary markers, and it also aligns whole phrases with the video (instead of just single tokens). We applied the same NLP pipeline to these manual transcripts. In the results section, we will see that the accuracy of our end-to-end system is indeed higher when the speech transcript is error-free and well-formed. However, we can still get good results using noisier, automatically produced transcripts.

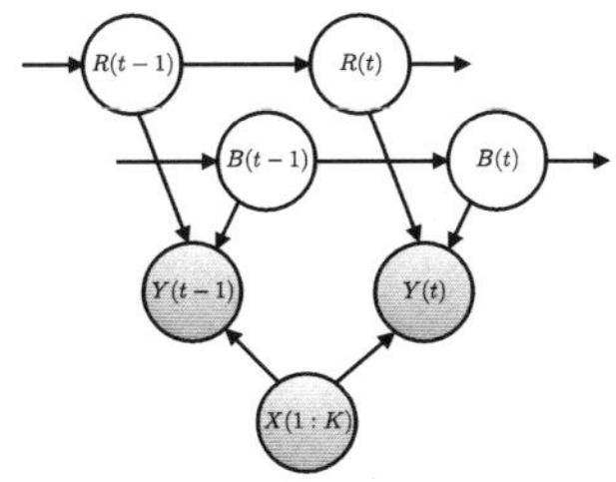


Figure 1: Graphical model representation of the factored HMM. See text for details.

## 3 Methods

In this section, we describe our system for aligning instructional text and video.

### 3.1 HMM to align recipe with ASR transcript

We align each step of the recipe to a corresponding sequence of words in the ASR transcript by using the input-output HMM shown in Figure 1. Here $X(1:K)$ represents the textual recipe steps (obtained using the process described in Section 2.2); $Y(1:T)$ represent the ASR tokens (spoken words); $R(t) \in \{1, \ldots, K\}$ is the recipe step number for frame $t$; and $B(t) \in \{0, 1\}$ represents whether timestep $t$ is generated by the background ($B = 1$) or foreground model ($B = 0$). This background variable is needed since sometimes sequences of spoken words are unrelated to the content of the recipe, especially at the beginning and end of a video.

The conditional probability distributions (CPDs) for the Markov chain is as follows:

$$p(R(t) = r | R(t-1) = r') = \begin{cases} \alpha & \text{if } r = r'+1 \\ 1-\alpha & \text{if } r = r' \\ 0.0 & \text{otherwise} \end{cases}$$

$$p(B(t) = b | B(t-1) = b) = \gamma.$$

[2]According to (Liao et al., 2013), the Youtube ASR system we used, based on using Gaussian mixture models for the acoustic model, has a word error rate of about 52% (averaged over all English-language videos; some genres, such as news, had lower error rates). The newer system, which uses deep neural nets for the acoustic model, has an average WER of 44%; however, this was not available to us at the time we did our experiments.

This encodes our assumption that the video follows the same ordering as the recipe and that background/foreground tokens tend to cluster together. Obviously these assumptions do not always hold, but they are a reasonable approximation.

For each recipe, we set $\alpha = K/T$, the ratio of recipe steps to transcript tokens. This setting corresponds to an *a priori* belief that each recipe step is aligned with the same number of transcript tokens. The parameter $\gamma$ in our experiments is set by cross-validation to $0.7$ based on a small set of manually-labeled recipes.

For the foreground observation model, we generate the observed word from the corresponding recipe step via:

$$\log p(Y(t) = y|R(t) = k, X(1:K), B(t) = 0) \propto \max(\{\text{WordSimilarity}(y, x) : x \in X(k)\}),$$

where $X(k)$ is the set of words in the $k$'th recipe step, and WordSimilarity$(s, t)$ is a measure of similarity between words $s$ and $t$, based on word vector distance.

If this frame is aligned to the background, we generate it from the empirical distribution of words, which is estimated based on pooling all the data:

$$p(Y(t) = y|R(t) = k, B(t) = 1) = \hat{p}(y).$$

Finally, the prior for $p(B(t))$ is uniform, and $p(R(1))$ is set to a delta function on $R(1) = 1$ (i.e., we assume videos start at step 1 of the recipe).

Having defined the model, we "flatten" it to a standard HMM (by taking the cross product of $R_t$ and $B_t$), then estimate the MAP sequence using the Viterbi algorithm. See Figure 2 for an example.

Finally, we label each segment of the video as follows: use the segmentation induced by the alignment, and extract the action and object from the corresponding recipe step as described in Section 2.2. If the segment was labeled as background by the HMM, we do not apply any label to it.

### 3.2 Keyword spotting

A simpler approach to labeling video segments is to just search for verbs in the ASR transcript, and then to extract a fixed-sized window around the timestamp where the keyword occurred. We call this approach "keyword spotting". A similar method from (Yu et al., 2014) filters ASR transcripts by part-of-speech tag and finds tokens that match a small vocabulary to create a corpus of video clips (extracted from instructional videos), each labeled with an action/object pair.

In more detail, we manually define a whitelist of ~200 actions (all transitive verbs) of interest, such as "add", "chop", "fry", etc. We then identify when these words are spoken (relying on the POS tags to filter out non-verbs), and extract an 8 second video clip around this timestamp. (Using 2 seconds prior to the action being mentioned, and 6 seconds following.) To extract the object, we take all tokens tagged as "noun" within 5 tokens after the action.

### 3.3 Hybrid HMM + keyword spotting

We cannot use keyword spotting if the goal is to align instructional text to videos. However, if our goal is just to create a labeled corpus of video clips, keyword spotting is a reasonable approach. Unfortunately, we noticed that the quality of the labels (especially the object labels) generated by keyword spotting was not very high, due to errors in the ASR. On the other hand, we also noticed that the recall of the HMM approach was about 5 times lower than using keyword spotting, and furthermore, that the temporal localization accuracy was sometimes worse.

To get the best of both worlds, we employ the following hybrid technique. We perform keyword spotting for the action in the ASR transcript as before, but use the HMM alignment to infer the corresponding object. To avoid false positives, we only use the output of the HMM for this video if at least half of the recipe steps are aligned by it to the speech transcript; otherwise we back off to the baseline approach of extracting the noun phrase from the ASR transcript in the window after the verb.

### 3.4 Temporal refinement using vision

In our experiments, we noticed that sometimes the narrator describes an action before actually performing it (this was also noted in (Yu et al., 2014)). To partially combat this problem, we used computer vision to refine candidate video segments as follows. We first trained visual detectors for a large collection of food items (described below). Then, given a candidate video segment annotated with an action/object pair (coming from any of the previous

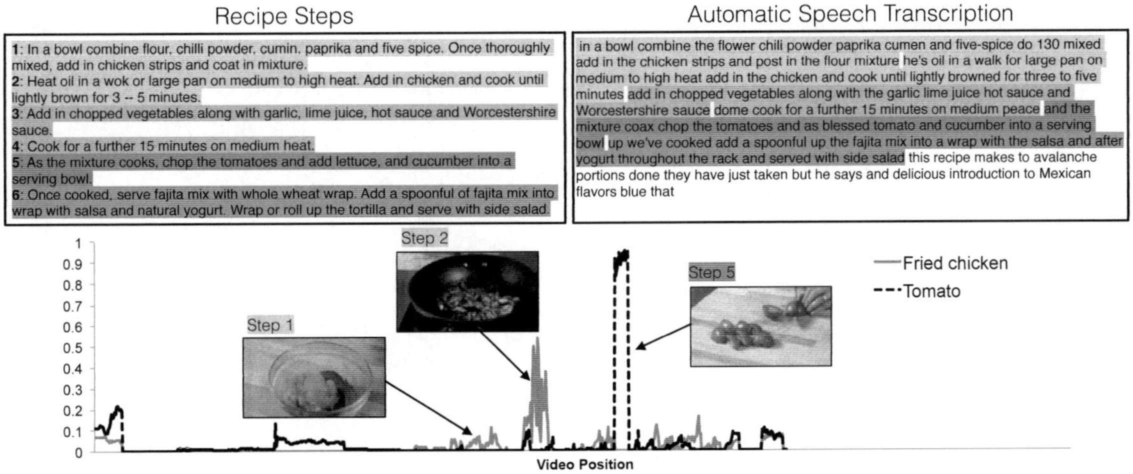


Figure 2: Examples from a Chicken Fajitas recipe at https://www.youtube.com/watch?v=mGpvZE3udQ4 (figure best viewed in color). Top: Alignment between (left) recipe steps to (right) automatic speech transcript. Tokens from the ASR are allowed to be classified as background steps (see e.g., the uncolored text at the end). Bottom: Detector scores for two ingredients as a function of position in the video.

three methods), we find a translation of the window (of up to 3 seconds in either direction) for which the average detector score corresponding to the object is maximized. The intuition is that by detecting when the object in question is visually present in the scene, it is more likely that the corresponding action is actually being performed.

**Training visual food detectors.** We trained a deep convolutional neural network (CNN) classifier (specifically, the 16 layer VGG model from (Simonyan and Zisserman, 2014)) on the FoodFood-101 dataset of (Bossard et al., 2014), using the Caffe open source software (Jia et al., 2014). The Food-101 dataset contains 1000 images for 101 different kinds of food. To compensate for the small training set, we pretrained the CNN on the ImageNet dataset (Russakovsky et al., 2014), which has 1.2M images, and then fine-tuned on Food-101. After a few hours of fine tuning (using a single GPU), we obtained 79% classification accuracy (assuming all 101 labels are mutually exclusive) on the test set, which is consistent with the state of the art results.[3]

[3]In particular, the website https://www.metamind.io/vision/food (accessed on 2/25/15) claims they also got 79% on this dataset. This is much better than the 56.4% for a CNN reported in (Bossard et al., 2014). We believe the main reason for the improved performance is the use of pre-training on ImageNet.

We then trained our model on an internal, proprietary dataset of 220 million images harvested from Google Images and Flickr. About 20% of these images contain food, the rest are used to train the background class. In this set, there are 2809 classes of food, including 1005 raw ingredients, such as avocado or beef, and 1804 dishes, such as ratatouille or cheeseburger with bacon. We use the model trained on this much larger dataset in the current paper, due to its increased coverage. (Unfortunately, we cannot report quantitative results, since the dataset is very noisy (sometimes half of the labels are wrong), so we have no ground truth. Nevertheless, qualitative behavior is reasonable, and the model does well on Food-101, as we discussed above.)

**Visual refinement pipeline.** For storage and time efficiency, we downsample each video temporally to 5 frames per second and each frame to $224 \times 224$ before applying the CNN. Running the food detector on each video then produces a vector of scores (one entry for each of 2809 classes) per timeframe.

There is not a perfect map from the names of ingredients to the names of the detector outputs. For example, an omelette recipe may say "egg", but there are two kinds of visual detectors, one for "scrambled egg" and one for "raw egg". We therefore decided to define the match score between an ingredient and a frame by taking the maximum score for that frame over all detectors whose names matched any of the ingredient tokens (after lemmatization and stopword filtering).

Finally, the match score of a video segment to an object is computed by taking the average score of all frames within that segment. By then scoring and maximizing over all translations of the candidate segment (of up to three seconds away), we produce a final "refined" segment.

### 3.5 Quantifying confidence via vision and affordances

The output of the keyword spotting and/or HMM systems is an (action, object) label assigned to certain video clips. In order to estimate how much confidence we have in that label (so that we can trade off precision and recall), we use a linear combination of two quantities: (1) the final match score produced by the visual refinement pipeline, which measures the visibility of the object in the given video segment, and (2) an *affordance probability*, measuring the probability that $o$ appears as a direct object of $a$.

The affordance model allows us to, for example, prioritize a segment labeled as (peel, garlic) over a segment labeled as (peel, sugar). The probabilities $P(\text{object} = o|\text{action} = a)$ are estimated by first forming an inverse document frequency matrix capturing action/object co-occurrences (treating actions as documents). To generalize across actions and objects we form a low-rank approximation to this IDF matrix using a singular value decomposition and set affordance probabilities to be proportional to exponentiated entries of the resulting matrix. Figure 3 visualizes these affordance probabilities for a selected subset of frequently used action/object pairs.

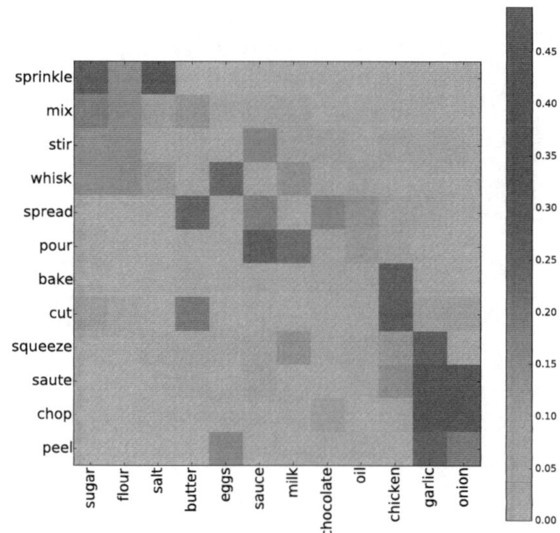


Figure 3: Visualization of affordance model. Entries $(a, o)$ are colored according to $P(\text{object} = o \mid \text{action} = a)$.

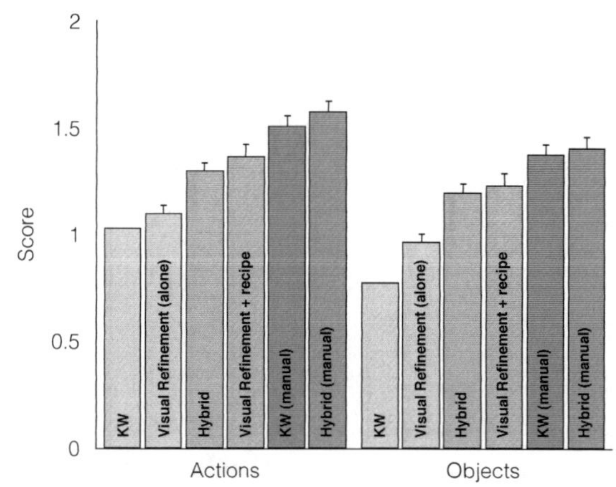


Figure 4: Clip quality, as assessed by Mechanical Turk experiments on 900 trials. Figure best viewed in color; see text for details.

## 4 Evaluation and applications

In this section, we experimentally evaluate how well our methods work. We then briefly demonstrate some prototype applications.

### 4.1 Evaluating the clip database

One of the main outcomes of our process is a set of video clips, each of which is labeled with a verb (action) and a noun (object). We generated 3 such labeled corpora, using 3 different methods: keyword spotting ("KW"), the hybrid HMM + keyword spotting ("Hybrid"), and the hybrid system with visual food detector ("visual refinement"). The total number of clips produced by each method is very similar, approximately 1.4 million. The coverage of the clips is approximately 260k unique (action, noun phrase) pairs.

To evaluate the quality of these methods, we created a random subset of 900 clips from each corpus using stratified sampling. That is, we picked an action uniformly at random, and then picked a corresponding object for that action from its support set uniformly at random, and finally picked a clip with that (action, object) label uniformly at random from the clip corpuses produced in Section 3; this ensures

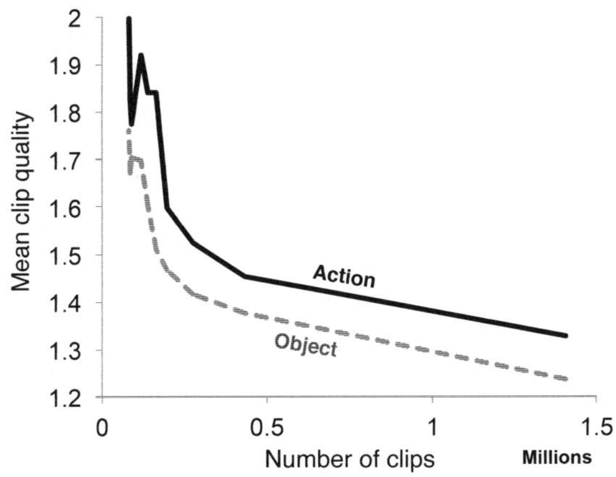


Figure 5: Average clip quality (precision) after filtering out low confidence clips versus # clips retained (recall).

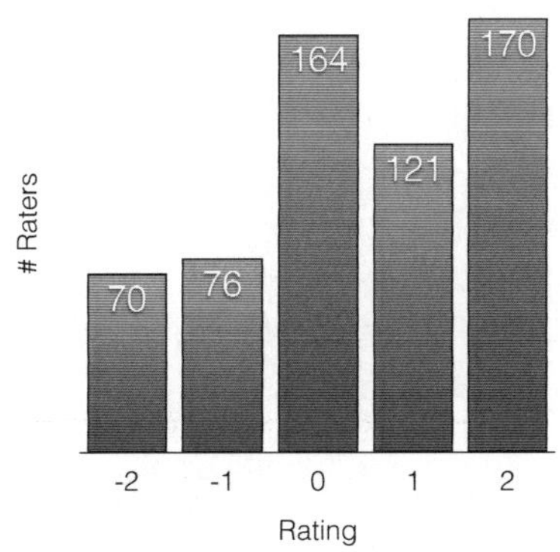


Figure 6: Histogram of human ratings comparing recipe steps against ASR descriptions of a video clip. "2" indicate a strong preference for the recipe step; "-2" a strong preference for the transcript. See text for details.

the test set is not dominated by frequent actions or objects.

We then performed a Mechanical Turk experiment on each test set. Each clip was shown to 3 raters, and each rater was asked the question "How well does this clip show the given action/object?". Raters then had to answer on a 3-point scale: 0 means "not at all", 1 means "somewhat", and 2 means "very well".

The results are shown in Figure 4. We see that the quality of the hybrid method is significantly better than the baseline keyword spotting method, for both actions and objects.[4] While a manually curated speech transcript indeed yields better results (see the bars labeled 'manual'), we observe that automatically generated transcripts allow us to perform almost as well, especially using our alignment model with visual refinement.

Comparing accuracy on actions against that on objects in the same figure, we see that keyword spotting is far more accurate for actions than it is for objects (by over 30%). This disparity is not surprising since keyword spotting searches only for action keywords and relies on a rough heuristic to recover objects. We also see that using alignment (which extracts the object from the "clean" recipe text) and visual refinement (which is trained explicitly to detect ingredients) both help to increase the relative accuracy of objects — under the hybrid method, for example, the accuracy for actions is only 8% better than that of objects.

Note that clips from the HMM and hybrid methods varied in length between 2 and 10 seconds (mean 4.2 seconds), while clips from the keyword spotting method were always exactly 8 seconds. Thus clip length is potentially a confounding factor in the evaluation when comparing the hybrid method to the keyword-spotting method; however, if there is a bias to assign higher ratings to longer clips (which are *a priori* more likely to contain a depiction of a given action than shorter clips), it would benefit the keyword spoting method.

Segment confidence scores (from Section 3.5) can be used to filter out low confidence segments, thus improving the precision of clip retrieval at the cost of recall. Figure 5 visualizes this trade-off as we vary our confidence threshold, showing that indeed, segments with higher confidences tend to have the highest quality as judged by our human raters. Moreover, the top 167,000 segments as ranked by our confidence measure have an average rating exceeding 1.75.

We additionally sought to evaluate how well recipe steps from the recipe body could serve as captions for video clips in comparison to the often noisy ASR transript, which serves as a rough proxy for evaluating the quality of the alignment model as well as demonstration a potential application of our method for "cleaning up" noisy ASR captions into complete grammatical sentences. To that end, we randomly selected 200 clips from our corpus that

[4]Inter-rater agreement, measured via Fleiss's kappa by aggregating across all judgment tasks, is .41, which is statistically significant at a $p < .05$ level.

both have an associated action keyword from the transcript as well as an aligned recipe step selected by the HMM alignment model. For each clip, three raters on Mechanical Turk were shown the clip, the text from the recipe step, and a fragment of the ASR transcript (the keyword, plus 5 tokens to the left and right of the keyword). Raters then indicated which description they preferred: 2 indicates a strong preference for the recipe step, 1 a weak preference, 0 indifference, -1 a weak preference for the transcript fragment, and -2 a strong preference. Results are shown in Figure 6. Excluding raters who indicated indiffierence, 67% of raters preferred the recipe step as the clip's description.

A potential confound for using this analysis as a proxy for the quality of the alignment model is that the ASR transcript is generally an ungrammatical sentence fragment as opposed to the grammatical recipe steps, which is likely to reduce the raters' approval of ASR captions in the case when both accurately describe the scene. However, if users still on average prefer an ASR sentence fragment which describes the clip correctly versus a full recipe step which is unrelated to the scene, then this experiment still provides evidence of the quality of the alignment model.

### 4.2 Automatically illustrating a recipe

One useful byproduct of our alignment method is that each recipe step is associated with a segment of the corresponding video.[5] We use a standard keyframe selection algorithm to pick the best frame from each segment. We can then associate this frame with the corresponding recipe step, thus automatically illustrating the recipe steps. An illustration of this process is shown in Figure 7.

### 4.3 Search within a video

Another application which our methods enable is search within a video. For example, if a user would like to find a clip illustrating how to knead dough, we can simply search our corpus of labeled clips,

Figure 8: Searching for "knead dough". Note that the videos have automatically been advanced to the relevant frame.

and return a list of matches (ranked by confidence). Since each clip has a corresponding "provenance", we can return the results to the user as a set of videos in which we have automatically "fast forwarded" to the relevant section of the video (see Figure 8 for an example). This stands in contrast to standard video search on Youtube, which returns the whole video, but does not (in general) indicate where within the video the user's search query occurs.

## 5 Related work

There are several pieces of related work. (Yu et al., 2014) performs keyword spotting in the speech transcript in order to label clips extracted from instructional videos. However, our hybrid approach performs better; the gain is especially significant on automatically generated speech transcripts, as shown in Figure 4.

The idea of using an HMM to align instructional steps to a video was also explored in (Naim et al., 2014). However, their conditional model has to generate images, whereas ours just has to generate ASR words, which is an easier task. Furthermore, they only consider 6 videos collected in a controlled lab setting, whereas we consider over 180k videos collected "in the wild".

Another paper that uses HMMs to process recipe text is (Druck and Pang, 2012). They use the HMM to align the steps of a recipe to the comments made by users in an online forum, whereas we align the steps of a recipe to the speech transcript. Also, we use video information, which was not considered in this earlier work.

(Joshi et al., 2006) describes a system to automatically illustrate a text document, however they only generate one image, not a sequence, and their techniques are very different.

There is also a large body of other work on connecting language and vision; we only have space

[5]The HMM may assign multiple non-consecutive regions of the video to the same recipe step (since the background state can turn on and off). In such cases, we just take the "convex hull" of the regions as the interval which corresponds to that step. It is also possible for the HMM not to assign a given step to any interval of the video.

Figure 7: Automatically illustrating a Guacamole recipe from `https://www.youtube.com/watch?v=H7Ne3s202lU`.

to briefly mention a few key papers. (Rohrbach et al., 2012b) describes the MPII Cooking Composite Activities dataset, which consists of 212 videos collected in the lab of people performing various cooking activities. (This extends the dataset described in their earlier work, (Rohrbach et al., 2012a).) They also describe a method to recognize objects and actions using standard vision features. However, they do not leverage the speech signal, and their dataset is significantly smaller than ours.

(Guadarrama et al., 2013) describes a method for generating subject-verb-object triples given a short video clip, using standard object and action detectors. The technique was extended in (Thomason et al., 2014) to also predict the location/ place. Furthermore, they use a linear-chain CRF to combine the visual scores with a simple (s,v,o,p) language model (similar to our affordance model). They applied their technique to the dataset in (Chen and Dolan, 2011), which consists of 2000 short video clips, each described with 1-3 sentences. By contrast, we focus on aligning instructional text to the video, and our corpus is significantly larger.

(Yu and Siskind, 2013) describes a technique for estimating the compatibility between a video clip and a sentence, based on relative motion of the objects (which are tracked using HMMs). Their method is tested on 159 video clips, created under carefully controlled conditions. By contrast, we focus on aligning instructional text to the video, and our corpus is significantly larger.

## 6 Discussion and future work

In this paper, we have presented a novel method for aligning instructional text to videos, leveraging both speech recognition and visual object detection. We have used this to align 180k recipe-video pairs, from which we have extracted a corpus of 1.4M labeled video clips – a small but crucial step toward building a multimodal procedural knowlege base. In the future, we hope to use this labeled corpus to train visual action detectors, which can then be combined with the existing visual object detectors to interpret novel videos. Additionally, we believe that combining visual and linguistic cues may help overcome longstanding challenges to language understanding, such as anaphora resolution and word sense disambiguation.

**Acknowledgments.** We would like to thank Alex Gorban and Anoop Korattikara for helping with some of the experiments, and Nancy Chang for feedback on the paper.

## References

Lukas Bossard, Matthieu Guillaumin, and Luc Van Gool. 2014. Food-101 – mining discriminative components with random forests. In *Proc. European Conf. on Computer Vision*.

A. Carlson, J. Betteridge, B. Kisiel, B. Settles, E. Hruschka Jr., and T. Mitchell. 2010. Toward an architecture for never-ending language learning. In *Procs. AAAI*.

David L Chen and William B Dolan. 2011. Collecting highly parallel data for paraphrase evaluation. In *Proc. ACL*, HLT '11, pages 190–200, Stroudsburg, PA, USA. Association for Computational Linguistics.

X. Dong, E. Gabrilovich, G. Heitz, W. Horn, N. Lao, K. Murphy, T. Strohmann, S. Sun, and W. Zhang. 2014. Knowledge vault: A web-scale approach to probabilistic knowledge fusion. In *Proc. of the Int'l Conf. on Knowledge Discovery and Data Mining*.

Gregory Druck and Bo Pang. 2012. Spice it up?: Mining

refinements to online instructions from user generated content. In *Proc. ACL*, pages 545–553.

O. Etzioni, A. Fader, J. Christensen, S. Soderland, and Mausam. 2011. Open Information Extraction: the Second Generation. In *Intl. Joint Conf. on AI*.

S. Guadarrama, N. Krishnamoorthy, G. Malkarnenkar, S. Venugopalan, R. Mooney, T. Darrell, and K. Saenko. 2013. YouTube2Text: Recognizing and describing arbitrary activities using semantic hierarchies and Zero-Shot recognition. In *Intl. Conf. on Computer Vision*, pages 2712–2719.

Yangqing Jia, Evan Shelhamer, Jeff Donahue, Sergey Karayev, Jonathan Long, Ross Girshick, Sergio Guadarrama, and Trevor Darrell. 2014. Caffe: Convolutional architecture for fast feature embedding, 20 June.

Dhiraj Joshi, James Z Wang, and Jia Li. 2006. The story picturing Engine-A system for automatic text illustration. *ACM Trans. Multimedia Comp., Comm. and Appl.*, 2(1):1–22.

Hank Liao, Erik McDermott, and Andrew Senior. 2013. Large scale deep neural network acoustic modeling with semi-supervised training data for YouTube video transcription. In *ASRU (IEEE Automatic Speech Recognition and Understanding Workshop)*.

Tomas Mikolov, Kai Chen, Greg Corrado, and Jeffrey Dean. 2013. Efficient estimation of word representations in vector space. http://arxiv.org/abs/1301.3781.

I Naim, Y C Song, Q Liu, H Kautz, J Luo, and D Gildea. 2014. Unsupervised alignment of natural language instructions with video segments. In *Procs. of AAAI*.

Slav Petrov, Leon Barrett, Romain Thibaux, and Dan Klein. 2006. Learning accurate, compact, and interpretable tree annotation. In *Proceedings of the 21st International Conference on Computational Linguistics and 44th Annual Meeting of the Association for Computational Linguistics*, pages 433–440, Sydney, Australia, July. Association for Computational Linguistics.

M Rohrbach, S Amin, M Andriluka, and B Schiele. 2012a. A database for fine grained activity detection of cooking activities. In *CVPR*, pages 1194–1201.

Marcus Rohrbach, Michaela Regneri, Mykhaylo Andriluka, Sikandar Amin, Manfred Pinkal, and Bernt Schiele. 2012b. Script data for Attribute-Based recognition of composite activities. In *Proc. European Conf. on Computer Vision*, pages 144–157.

Olga Russakovsky, Jia Deng, Hao Su, Jonathan Krause, Sanjeev Satheesh, Sean Ma, Zhiheng Huang, Andrej Karpathy, Aditya Khosla, Michael Bernstein, Alexander C. Berg, and Li Fei-Fei. 2014. ImageNet Large Scale Visual Recognition Challenge. http://arxiv.org/abs/1409.0575.

Ashutosh Saxena, Ashesh Jain, Ozan Sener, Aditya Jami, Dipendra K Misra, and Hema S Koppula. 2014. RoboBrain: Large-Scale knowledge engine for robots. http://arxiv.org/pdf/1412.0691.pdf.

Karen Simonyan and Andrew Zisserman. 2014. Very deep convolutional networks for Large-Scale image recognition, 4 September. http://arxiv.org/abs/1409.1556.

F. M. Suchanek, G. Kasneci, and G. Weikum. 2007. YAGO: A Large Ontology from Wikipedia and WordNet. *J. Web Semantics*, 6:203217.

J Thomason, S Venugopalan, S Guadarrama, K Saenko, and R Mooney. 2014. Integrating language and vision to generate natural language descriptions of videos in the wild. In *Intl. Conf. on Comp. Linguistics*.

Yezhou Yang, Yi Li, Cornelia Fermüller, and Yiannis Aloimonos. 2015. Robot learning manipulation action plans by watching unconstrained videos from the world wide web. In *The Twenty-Ninth AAAI Conference on Artificial Intelligence (AAAI-15)*.

Haonan Yu and JM Siskind. 2013. Grounded language learning from video described with sentences. In *Proc. ACL*.

Shoou-I Yu, Lu Jiang, and Alexander Hauptmann. 2014. Instructional videos for unsupervised harvesting and learning of action examples. In *Intl. Conf. Multimedia*, pages 825–828. ACM.

# Combining Language and Vision with a Multimodal Skip-gram Model

**Angeliki Lazaridou   Nghia The Pham   Marco Baroni**
Center for Mind/Brain Sciences
University of Trento
{angeliki.lazaridou|thenghia.pham|marco.baroni}@unitn.it

## Abstract

We extend the SKIP-GRAM model of Mikolov et al. (2013a) by taking visual information into account. Like SKIP-GRAM, our *multimodal* models (MMSKIP-GRAM) build vector-based word representations by learning to predict linguistic contexts in text corpora. However, for a restricted set of words, the models are also exposed to visual representations of the objects they denote (extracted from natural images), and must predict linguistic and visual features jointly. The MMSKIP-GRAM models achieve good performance on a variety of semantic benchmarks. Moreover, since they propagate visual information to all words, we use them to improve image labeling and retrieval in the zero-shot setup, where the test concepts are never seen during model training. Finally, the MMSKIP-GRAM models discover intriguing visual properties of abstract words, paving the way to realistic implementations of embodied theories of meaning.

## 1 Introduction

Distributional semantic models (DSMs) derive vector-based representations of meaning from patterns of word co-occurrence in corpora. DSMs have been very effectively applied to a variety of semantic tasks (Clark, 2015; Mikolov et al., 2013b; Turney and Pantel, 2010). However, compared to human semantic knowledge, these purely textual models, just like traditional symbolic AI systems (Harnad, 1990; Searle, 1984), are severely impoverished, suffering of *lack of grounding* in extra-linguistic modalities (Glenberg and Robertson, 2000). This observation has led to the development of *multimodal distributional semantic models* (MDSMs) (Bruni et al., 2014; Feng and Lapata, 2010; Silberer and Lapata, 2014), that enrich linguistic vectors with perceptual information, most often in the form of visual features automatically induced from image collections.

MDSMs outperform state-of-the-art text-based approaches, not only in tasks that directly require access to visual knowledge (Bruni et al., 2012), but also on general semantic benchmarks (Bruni et al., 2014; Silberer and Lapata, 2014). However, current MDSMs still have a number of drawbacks. First, they are generally constructed by first separately building linguistic and visual representations of the same concepts, and then merging them. This is obviously very different from how humans learn about concepts, by hearing words in a situated perceptual context. Second, MDSMs assume that both linguistic and visual information is available for all words, with no generalization of knowledge across modalities. Third, because of this latter assumption of full linguistic and visual coverage, current MDSMs, paradoxically, cannot be applied to computer vision tasks such as image labeling or retrieval, since they do not generalize to images or words beyond their training set.

We introduce the *multimodal skip-gram* models, two new MDSMs that address all the issues above. The models build upon the very effective skip-gram approach of Mikolov et al. (2013a), that constructs vector representations by learning, incrementally, to predict the linguistic contexts in which target words occur in a corpus. In our extension, for a subset of the target words, relevant visual evidence from



*Human Language Technologies: The 2015 Annual Conference of the North American Chapter of the ACL*, pages 153–163,
Denver, Colorado, May 31 – June 5, 2015. 

natural images is presented together with the corpus contexts (just like humans hear words accompanied by concurrent perceptual stimuli). The model must learn to predict these visual representations jointly with the linguistic features. The joint objective encourages the propagation of visual information to representations of words for which no direct visual evidence was available in training. The resulting multimodally-enhanced vectors achieve remarkably good performance both on traditional semantic benchmarks, and in their new application to the "zero-shot" image labeling and retrieval scenario. Very interestingly, indirect visual evidence also affects the representation of abstract words, paving the way to ground-breaking cognitive studies and novel applications in computer vision.

## 2 Related Work

There is by now a large literature on multimodal distributional semantic models. We focus here on a few representative systems. Bruni et al. (2014) propose a straightforward approach to MDSM induction, where text- and image-based vectors for the same words are constructed independently, and then "mixed" by applying the Singular Value Decomposition to their concatenation. An empirically superior model has been proposed by Silberer and Lapata (2014), who use more advanced visual representations relying on images annotated with high-level "visual attributes", and a multimodal fusion strategy based on stacked autoencoders. Kiela and Bottou (2014) adopt instead a simple concatenation strategy, but obtain empirical improvements by using state-of-the-art convolutional neural networks to extract visual features, and the skip-gram model for text. These and related systems take a two-stage approach to derive multimodal spaces (unimodal induction followed by fusion), and they are only tested on concepts for which both textual and visual labeled training data are available (the pioneering model of Feng and Lapata (2010) did learn from text and images jointly using Topic Models, but was shown to be empirically weak by Bruni et al. (2014)).

Howell et al. (2005) propose an incremental multimodal model based on simple recurrent networks (Elman, 1990), focusing on *grounding propagation* from early-acquired concrete words to a larger vocabulary. However, they use subject-generated features as surrogate for realistic perceptual information, and only test the model in small-scale simulations of word learning. Hill and Korhonen (2014), whose evaluation focuses on how perceptual information affects different word classes more or less effectively, similarly to Howell et al., integrate perceptual information in the form of subject-generated features and text from image annotations into a skip-gram model. They inject perceptual information by merging words expressing perceptual features with corpus contexts, which amounts to linguistic-context re-weighting, thus making it impossible to separate linguistic and perceptual aspects of the induced representation, and to extend the model with non-linguistic features. We use instead authentic image analysis as proxy to perceptual information, and we design a robust way to incorporate it, easily extendible to other signals, such as feature norm or brain signal vectors (Fyshe et al., 2014).

The recent work on so-called *zero-shot learning* to address the annotation bottleneck in image labeling (Frome et al., 2013; Lazaridou et al., 2014; Socher et al., 2013) looks at image- and text-based vectors from a different perspective. Instead of combining visual and linguistic information in a common space, it aims at learning a mapping from image- to text-based vectors. The mapping, induced from annotated data, is then used to project images of objects that were not seen during training onto linguistic space, in order to retrieve the nearest word vectors as labels. Multimodal word vectors should be better-suited than purely text-based vectors for the task, as their similarity structure should be closer to that of images. However, traditional MDSMs cannot be used in this setting, because they do not cover words for which no manually annotated training images are available, thus defeating the generalizing purpose of zero-shot learning. We will show below that our multimodal vectors, that are not hampered by this restriction, do indeed bring a significant improvement over purely text-based linguistic representations in the zero-shot setup.

Multimodal language-vision spaces have also been developed with the goal of improving caption generation/retrieval and caption-based image retrieval (Karpathy et al., 2014; Kiros et al., 2014;

Mao et al., 2014; Socher et al., 2014). These methods rely on necessarily limited collections of captioned images as sources of multimodal evidence, whereas we automatically enrich a very large corpus with images to induce general-purpose multimodal word representations, that could be used as input embeddings in systems specifically tuned to caption processing. Thus, our work is complementary to this line of research.

## 3 Multimodal Skip-gram Architecture

### 3.1 Skip-gram Model

We start by reviewing the standard SKIP-GRAM model of Mikolov et al. (2013a), in the version we use. Given a text corpus, SKIP-GRAM aims at inducing word representations that are good at predicting the *context* words surrounding a *target* word. Mathematically, it maximizes the objective function:

$$\frac{1}{T}\sum_{t=1}^{T}\left(\sum_{-c\leq j\leq c, j\neq 0}\log p(w_{t+j}|w_t)\right) \tag{1}$$

where $w_1, w_2, ..., w_T$ are words in the training corpus and $c$ is the size of the window around target $w_t$, determining the set of context words to be predicted by the induced representation of $w_t$. Following Mikolov et al., we implement a subsampling option randomly discarding context words as an inverse function of their frequency, controlled by hyperparameter $t$. The probability $p(w_{t+j}|w_t)$, the core part of the objective in Equation 1, is given by softmax:

$$p(w_{t+j}|w_t) = \frac{e^{u'^{T}_{w_{t+j}} u_{w_t}}}{\sum_{w'=1}^{W} e^{u'^{T}_{w'} u_{w_t}}} \tag{2}$$

where $u_w$ and $u'_w$ are the context and target vector representations of word $w$ respectively, and $W$ is the size of the vocabulary. Due to the normalization term, Equation 2 requires $O(|W|)$ time complexity. A considerable speedup to $O(\log |W|)$, is achieved by using the hierarchical version of Equation 2 (Morin and Bengio, 2005), adopted here.

### 3.2 Injecting visual knowledge

We now assume that word learning takes place in a *situated* context, in which, for a subset of the target words, the corpus contexts are accompanied by a

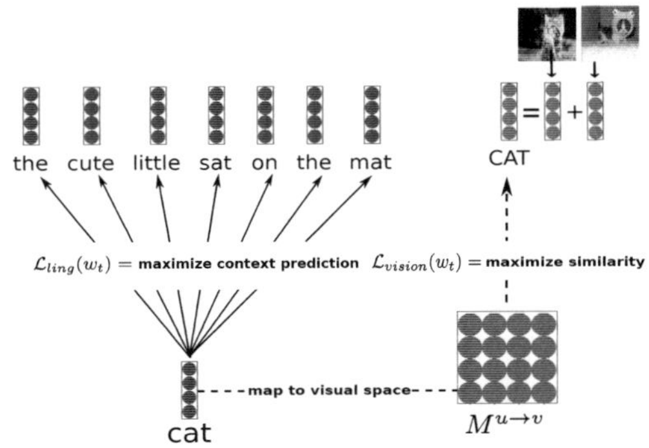


Figure 1: "Cartoon" of MMSKIP-GRAM-B. Linguistic context vectors are actually associated to classes of words in a tree, not single words. SKIP-GRAM is obtained by ignoring the visual objective, MMSKIP-GRAM-A by fixing $M^{u\to v}$ to the identity matrix.

visual representation of the concepts they denote (just like in a conversation, where a linguistic utterance will often be produced in a visual scene including some of the word referents). The visual representation is also encoded in a vector (we describe in Section 4 below how we construct it). We thus make the skip-gram "multimodal" by adding a second, *visual* term to the original *linguistic* objective, that is, we extend Equation 1 as follow:

$$\frac{1}{T}\sum_{t=1}^{T}(\mathcal{L}_{ling}(w_t) + \mathcal{L}_{vision}(w_t)) \tag{3}$$

where $\mathcal{L}_{ling}(w_t)$ is the text-based skip-gram objective $\sum_{-c\leq j\leq c, j\neq 0}\log p(w_{t+j}|w_t)$, whereas the $\mathcal{L}_{vision}(w_t)$ term forces word representations to take visual information into account. Note that if a word $w_t$ is not associated to visual information, as is systematically the case, e.g., for determiners and non-imageable nouns, but also more generally for any word for which no visual data are available, $\mathcal{L}_{vision}(w_t)$ is set to 0.

We now propose two variants of the visual objective, resulting in two distinguished multi-modal versions of the skip-gram model.

### 3.3 Multi-modal Skip-gram Model A

One way to force word embeddings to take visual representations into account is to try to directly increase the similarity (expressed, for example, by the *cosine*) between linguistic and visual representations, thus aligning the dimensions of the linguistic vector with those of the visual one (recall that we are inducing the first, while the second is fixed), and making the linguistic representation of a concept "move" closer to its visual representation. We maximize similarity through a max-margin framework commonly used in models connecting language and vision (Weston et al., 2010; Frome et al., 2013). More precisely, we formulate the visual objective $\mathcal{L}_{vision}(w_t)$ as:

$$-\sum_{w' \sim P_n(w)} \max(0, \gamma - cos(u_{w_t}, v_{w_t}) + cos(u_{w_t}, v_{w'})) \quad (4)$$

where the minus sign turns a loss into a cost, $\gamma$ is the margin, $u_{w_t}$ is the target multimodally-enhanced word representation we aim to learn, $v_{w_t}$ is the corresponding visual vector (fixed in advance) and $v_{w'}$ ranges over visual representations of words (featured in our image dictionary) randomly sampled from distribution $P_n(w_t)$. These random visual representations act as "negative" samples, encouraging $u_{w_t}$ to be more similar to its own visual representation than to that of other words. The sampling distribution is currently set to uniform, and the number of negative samples controlled by hyperparameter $k$.

### 3.4 Multi-modal Skip-gram Model B

The visual objective in MMSKIP-GRAM-A has the drawback of assuming a direct comparison of linguistic and visual representations, constraining them to be of equal size. MMSKIP-GRAM-B lifts this constraint by including an extra layer mediating between linguistic and visual representations (see Figure 1 for a sketch of MMSKIP-GRAM-B). Learning this layer is equivalent to estimating a cross-modal mapping matrix from linguistic onto visual representations, jointly induced with linguistic word embeddings. The extension is straightforwardly implemented by substituting, into Equation 4, the word representation $u_{w_t}$ with $z_{w_t} = M^{u \rightarrow v} u_{w_t}$, where $M^{u \rightarrow v}$ is the cross-modal mapping matrix to be induced. To avoid overfitting, we also add an L2 regularization term for $M^{u \rightarrow v}$ to the overall objective (Equation 3), with its relative importance controlled by hyperparamer $\lambda$.

## 4 Experimental Setup

The parameters of all models are estimated by backpropagation of error via stochastic gradient descent. Our text corpus is a Wikipedia 2009 dump comprising approximately 800M tokens.[1] To train the multimodal models, we add visual information for 5,100 words that have an entry in ImageNet (Deng et al., 2009), occur at least 500 times in the corpus and have concreteness score $\geq 0.5$ according to Turney et al. (2011). On average, about 5% tokens in the text corpus are associated to a visual representation. To construct the visual representation of a word, we sample 100 pictures from its ImageNet entry, and extract a 4096-dimensional vector from each picture using the Caffe toolkit (Jia et al., 2014), together with the pre-trained convolutional neural network of Krizhevsky et al. (2012). The vector corresponds to activation in the top (FC7) layer of the network. Finally, we average the vectors of the 100 pictures associated to each word, deriving 5,100 aggregated visual representations.

**Hyperparameters** For both SKIP-GRAM and the MMSKIP-GRAM models, we fix hidden layer size to 300. To facilitate comparison between MMSKIP-GRAM-A and MMSKIP-GRAM-B, and since the former requires equal linguistic and visual dimensionality, we keep the first 300 dimensions of the visual vectors. For the linguistic objective, we use hierarchical softmax with a Huffman frequency-based encoding tree, setting frequency subsampling option $t = 0.001$ and window size $c = 5$, without tuning. The following hyperparameters were tuned on the text9 corpus:[2] MMSKIP-GRAM-A: $k$=20, $\gamma$=0.5; MMSKIP-GRAM-B: $k$=5, $\gamma$=0.5, $\lambda$=0.0001.

## 5 Experiments

### 5.1 Approximating human judgments

**Benchmarks** A widely adopted way to test DSMs and their multimodal extensions is to measure how well model-generated scores approximate human similarity judgments about pairs of words. We put together various benchmarks covering diverse aspects of meaning, to gain insights on the effect of perceptual information on different similarity facets. Specifically, we test on general relatedness (*MEN*, Bruni et al. (2014), 3K pairs), e.g., pickles are related to hamburgers, semantic ($\approx$ taxonomic) simi-

[1] http://wacky.sslmit.unibo.it

[2] http://mattmahoney.net/dc/textdata.html

larity (*Simlex-999*, Hill et al. (2014), 1K pairs; *SemSim*, Silberer and Lapata (2014), 7.5K pairs), e.g., pickles are similar to onions, as well as visual similarity (*VisSim*, Silberer and Lapata (2014), same pairs as SemSim with different human ratings), e.g., pickles look like zucchinis.

**Alternative Multimodal Models** We compare our models against several recent alternatives. We test the vectors made available by Kiela and Bottou (2014). Similarly to us, they derive textual features with the skip-gram model (from a portion of the Wikipedia and the British National Corpus) and use visual representations extracted from the ESP data-set (von Ahn and Dabbish, 2004) through a convolutional neural network (Oquab et al., 2014). They concatenate textual and visual features after normalizing to unit length and centering to zero mean. We also test the vectors that performed best in the evaluation of Bruni et al. (2014), based on textual features extracted from a 3B-token corpus and SIFT-based Bag-of-Visual-Words visual features (Sivic and Zisserman, 2003) extracted from the ESP collection. Bruni and colleagues fuse a weighted concatenation of the two components through SVD. We further re-implement both methods with our own textual and visual embeddings as CONCATENATION and SVD (with target dimensionality 300, picked without tuning). Finally, we present for comparison the results on *SemSim* and *VisSim* reported by Silberer and Lapata (2014), obtained with a stacked-autoencoders architecture run on textual features extracted from Wikipedia with the Strudel algorithm (Baroni et al., 2010) and attribute-based visual features (Farhadi et al., 2009) extracted from ImageNet.

All benchmarks contain a fair amount of words for which we did not use direct visual evidence. We are interested in assessing the models both in terms of how they fuse linguistic and visual evidence when they are both available, and for their robustness in lack of full visual coverage. We thus evaluate them in two settings. The visual-coverage columns of Table 1 (those on the right) report results on the subsets for which all compared models have access to direct visual information for both words. We further report results on the full sets ("100%" columns of Table 1) for models that can propagate visual information and that, consequently, can meaningfully be tested on words without direct visual representations.

**Results** The state-of-the-art visual CNN FEATURES alone perform remarkably well, outperforming the purely textual model (SKIP-GRAM) in two tasks, and achieving the best absolute performance on the visual-coverage subset of Simlex-999. Regarding multimodal *fusion* (that is, focusing on the visual-coverage subsets), both MMSKIP-GRAM models perform very well, at the top or just below it on all tasks, with comparable results for the two variants. Their performance is also good on the full data sets, where they consistently outperform SKIP-GRAM and SVD (that is much more strongly affected by lack of complete visual information). They're just a few points below the state-of-the-art MEN correlation (0.8), achieved by Baroni et al. (2014) with a corpus 3 larger than ours and extensive tuning. MMSKIP-GRAM-B is close to the state of the art for Simlex-999, reported by the resource creators to be at 0.41 (Hill et al., 2014). Most impressively, MMSKIP-GRAM-A reaches the performance level of the Silberer and Lapata (2014) model on their SemSim and VisSim data sets, despite the fact that the latter has full visual-data coverage and uses attribute-based image representations, requiring supervised learning of attribute classifiers, that achieve performance in the semantic tasks comparable or higher than that of our CNN features (see Table 3 in Silberer and Lapata (2014)). Finally, if the multimodal models (unsurprisingly) bring about a large performance gain over the purely linguistic model on visual similarity, the improvement is consistently large also for the other benchmarks, confirming that multimodality leads to better semantic models in general, that can help in capturing different types of similarity (general relatedness, strictly taxonomic, perceptual).

While we defer to further work a better understanding of the relation between multimodal grounding and different similarity relations, Table 2 provides qualitative insights on how injecting visual information changes the structure of semantic space. The top SKIP-GRAM neighbours of *donuts* are places where you might encounter them, whereas the multimodal models relate them to other take-away food, ranking visually-similar pizzas at the top. The *owl* example shows how multimodal

| Model | *MEN* | | *Simlex-999* | | *SemSim* | | *VisSim* | |
|---|---|---|---|---|---|---|---|---|
| | 100% | 42% | 100% | 29% | 100% | 85% | 100% | 85% |
| KIELA AND BOTTOU | - | 0.74 | - | 0.33 | - | 0.60 | - | 0.50 |
| BRUNI ET AL. | - | 0.77 | - | 0.44 | - | 0.69 | - | 0.56 |
| SILBERER AND LAPATA | - | - | - | - | 0.70 | - | 0.64 | - |
| CNN FEATURES | - | 0.62 | - | 0.54 | - | 0.55 | - | 0.56 |
| SKIP-GRAM | 0.70 | 0.68 | 0.33 | 0.29 | 0.62 | 0.62 | 0.48 | 0.48 |
| CONCATENATION | - | 0.74 | - | 0.46 | - | 0.68 | - | 0.60 |
| SVD | 0.61 | 0.74 | 0.28 | 0.46 | 0.65 | 0.68 | 0.58 | 0.60 |
| MMSKIP-GRAM-A | 0.75 | 0.74 | 0.37 | 0.50 | 0.72 | 0.72 | 0.63 | 0.63 |
| MMSKIP-GRAM-B | 0.74 | 0.76 | 0.40 | 0.53 | 0.66 | 0.68 | 0.60 | 0.60 |

Table 1: Spearman correlation between model-generated similarities and human judgments. Right columns report correlation on visual-coverage subsets (percentage of original benchmark covered by subsets on first row of respective columns). First block reports results for out-of-the-box models; second block for visual and textual representations alone; third block for our implementation of multimodal models.

| *Target* | SKIP-GRAM | MMSKIP-GRAM-A | MMSKIP-GRAM-B |
|---|---|---|---|
| donut | fridge, diner, candy | pizza, sushi, sandwich | pizza, sushi, sandwich |
| owl | pheasant, woodpecker, squirrel | eagle, woodpecker, falcon | eagle, falcon, hawk |
| mural | sculpture, painting, portrait | painting, portrait, sculpture | painting, portrait, sculpture |
| tobacco | coffee, cigarette, corn | cigarette, cigar, corn | cigarette, cigar, smoking |
| depth | size, bottom, meter | sea, underwater, level | sea, size, underwater |
| chaos | anarchy, despair, demon | demon, anarchy, destruction | demon, anarchy, shadow |

Table 2: Ordered top 3 neighbours of example words in purely textual and multimodal spaces. Only *donut* and *owl* were trained with direct visual information.

models pick taxonomically closer neighbours of concrete objects, since often closely related things also look similar (Bruni et al., 2014). In particular, both multimodal models get rid of squirrels and offer other birds of prey as nearest neighbours. No direct visual evidence was used to induce the embeddings of the remaining words in the table, that are thus influenced by vision only by propagation. The subtler but systematic changes we observe in such cases suggest that this indirect propagation is not only non-damaging with respect to purely linguistic representations, but actually beneficial. For the concrete *mural* concept, both multimodal models rank paintings and portraits above less closely related sculptures (they are not a form of painting). For *tobacco*, both models rank cigarettes and cigar over coffee, and MMSKIP-GRAM-B avoids the arguably less common "crop" sense cued by corn. The last two examples show how the multimodal models turn up the embodiment level in their representation of abstract words. For *depth*, their neighbours suggest a concrete marine setup over the more abstract measurement sense picked by the MMSKIP-GRAM neighbours. For *chaos*, they rank a demon, that is, a concrete agent of chaos at the top, and replace the more abstract notion of despair with equally gloomy but more imageable shadows and destruction (more on abstract words below).

### 5.2 Zero-shot image labeling and retrieval

The multimodal representations induced by our models should be better suited than purely text-based vectors to label or retrieve images. In particular, given that the quantitative and qualitative results collected so far suggest that the models propagate visual information across words, we apply them to image labeling and retrieval in the challenging zero-shot setup (see Section 2 above).[3]

[3] We will refer here, for conciseness' sake, to *image* labeling/retrieval, but, as our visual vectors are aggregated representations of images, the tasks we're modeling consist, more precisely, in labeling a set of pictures denoting the same object and retrieving the corresponding set given the name of the object.

**Setup** We take out as test set 25% of the 5.1K words we have visual vectors for. The multimodal models are re-trained without visual vectors for these words, using the same hyperparameters as above. For both tasks, the search for the correct word label/image is conducted on the whole set of 5.1K word/visual vectors.

In the image labeling task, given a visual vector representing an image, we map it onto word space, and label the image with the word corresponding to the nearest vector. To perform the vision-to-language mapping, we train a Ridge regression by 5-fold cross-validation on the test set (for SKIP-GRAM only, we also add the remaining 75% of word-image vector pairs used in estimating the multimodal models to the Ridge training data).[4]

In the image retrieval task, given a linguistic/multimodal vector, we map it onto visual space, and retrieve the nearest image. For SKIP-GRAM, we use Ridge regression with the same training regime as for the labeling task. For the multimodal models, since maximizing similarity to visual representations is already part of their training objective, we do not fit an extra mapping function. For MMSKIP-GRAM-A, we directly look for nearest neighbours of the learned embeddings in visual space. For MMSKIP-GRAM-B, we use the $M^{u \to v}$ mapping function induced while learning word embeddings.

**Results** In image labeling (Table 3) SKIP-GRAM is outperformed by both multimodal models, confirming that these models produce vectors that are directly applicable to vision tasks thanks to visual propagation. The most interesting results however are achieved in image retrieval (Table 4), which is essentially the task the multimodal models have been implicitly optimized for, so that they could be applied to it without any specific training. The strategy of directly querying for the nearest visual vectors of the MMSKIP-GRAM-A word embeddings works remarkably well, outperforming on the higher ranks SKIP-GRAM, which requires an ad-hoc mapping function. This suggests that the multimodal embeddings we are inducing, while general enough to achieve good performance in the semantic tasks discussed above, encode sufficient visual information for direct application to image analysis tasks. This is especially remarkable because the word vectors we are testing were not matched with visual representations at model training time, and are thus multimodal only by propagation. The best performance is achieved by MMSKIP-GRAM-B, confirming our claim that its $M^{u \to v}$ matrix acts as a multimodal mapping function.

| | P@1 | P@2 | P@10 | P@20 | P@50 |
|---|---|---|---|---|---|
| SKIP-GRAM | 1.5 | 2.6 | 14.2 | 23.5 | 36.1 |
| MMSKIP-GRAM-A | 2.1 | 3.7 | 16.7 | 24.6 | 37.6 |
| MMSKIP-GRAM-B | 2.2 | 5.1 | 20.2 | 28.5 | 43.5 |

Table 3: Percentage precision@$k$ results in the zero-shot image labeling task.

| | P@1 | P@2 | P@10 | P@20 | P@50 |
|---|---|---|---|---|---|
| SKIP-GRAM | 1.9 | 3.3 | 11.5 | 18.5 | 30.4 |
| MMSKIP-GRAM-A | 1.9 | 3.2 | 13.9 | 20.2 | 33.6 |
| MMSKIP-GRAM-B | 1.9 | 3.8 | 13.2 | 22.5 | 38.3 |

Table 4: Percentage precision@$k$ results in the zero-shot image retrieval task.

### 5.3 Abstract words

We have already seen, through the *depth* and *chaos* examples of Table 2, that the indirect influence of visual information has interesting effects on the representation of abstract terms. The latter have received little attention in multimodal semantics, with Hill and Korhonen (2014) concluding that abstract nouns, in particular, do not benefit from propagated perceptual information, and their representation is even harmed when such information is forced on them (see Figure 4 of their paper). Still, embodied theories of cognition have provided considerable evidence that abstract concepts are also grounded in the senses (Barsalou, 2008; Lakoff and Johnson, 1999). Since the word representations produced by MMSKIP-GRAM-A, including those pertaining to abstract concepts, can be directly used to search for near images in visual space, we decided to verify, experimentally, if these near images (of concrete things) are relevant not only for concrete words, as

[4] We use one fold to tune Ridge $\lambda$, three to estimate the mapping matrix and test in the last fold. To enforce strict zero-shot conditions, we exclude from the test fold labels occurring in the LSVRC2012 set that was employed to train the CNN of Krizhevsky et al. (2012), that we use to extract visual features.

expected, but also for abstract ones, as predicted by embodied views of meaning.

More precisely, we focused on the set of 200 words that were sampled across the USF norms concreteness spectrum by Kiela et al. (2014) (2 words had to be excluded for technical reasons). This set includes not only concrete (*meat*) and abstract (*thought*) nouns, but also adjectives (*boring*), verbs (*teach*), and even grammatical terms (*how*). Some words in the set have relatively high concreteness ratings, but are not particularly imageable, e.g.: *hot, smell, pain, sweet.* For each word in the set, we extracted the nearest neighbour picture of its MMSKIP-GRAM-A representation, and matched it with a random picture. The pictures were selected from a set of 5,100, all labeled with distinct words (the picture set includes, for each of the words associated to visual information as described in Section 4, the nearest picture to its aggregated visual representation). Since it is much more common for concrete than abstract words to be directly represented by an image in the picture set, when searching for the nearest neighbour we excluded the picture labeled with the word of interest, if present (e.g., we excluded the picture labeled *tree* when picking the nearest neighbour of the word *tree*). We ran a CrowdFlower[5] survey in which we presented each test word with the two associated images (randomizing presentation order of nearest and random picture), and asked subjects which of the two pictures they found more closely related to the word. We collected minimally 20 judgments per word. Subjects showed large agreement (median proportion of majority choice at 90%), confirming that they understood the task and behaved consistently.

We quantify performance in terms of proportion of words for which the number of votes for the nearest neighbour picture is significantly above chance according to a two-tailed binomial test. We set significance at $p<0.05$ after adjusting all p-values with the Holm correction for running 198 statistical tests. The results in Table 5 indicate that, in about half the cases, the nearest picture to a word MMSKIP-GRAM-A representation is meaningfully related to the word. As expected, this is more often the case for concrete than abstract words. Still, we also observe a significant preference for the model-predicted nearest picture for about one fourth of the abstract terms. Whether a word was exposed to direct visual evidence during training is of course making a big difference, and this factor interacts with concreteness, as only two abstract words were matched with images during training.[6] When we limit evaluation to word representations that were not exposed to pictures during training, the difference between concrete and abstract terms, while still large, becomes less dramatic than if all words are considered.

| | *global* | $\|words\|$ | *unseen* | $\|words\|$ |
|---|---|---|---|---|
| all | 48% | 198 | 30% | 127 |
| concrete | 73% | 99 | 53% | 30 |
| abstract | 23% | 99 | 23% | 97 |

Table 5: Subjects' preference for nearest visual neighbour of words in Kiela et al. (2014) vs. random pictures. Figure of merit is percentage proportion of significant results in favor of nearest neighbour across words. Results are reported for the whole set, as well as for words above (*concrete*) and below (*abstract*) the concreteness rating median. The *unseen* column reports results when words exposed to direct visual evidence during training are discarded. The *words* columns report set cardinality.

Figure 2: Examples of nearest visual neighbours of some abstract words: on the left, cases where subjects preferred the neighbour to the random foil; on the right, cases where they did not.

Figure 2 shows four cases in which subjects expressed a strong preference for the nearest visual neighbour of a word. *Freedom, god* and *theory* are strikingly in agreement with the view, from embodied theories, that abstract words are grounded in rel-

[5]http://www.crowdflower.com

[6]In both cases, the images actually depict concrete senses of the words: a memory board for *memory* and a stop sign for *stop*.

evant concrete scenes and situations. The *together* example illustrates how visual data might ground abstract notions in surprising ways. For all these cases, we can borrow what Howell et al. (2005) say about visual propagation to abstract words (p. 260):

> Intuitively, this is something like trying to explain an abstract concept like *love* to a child by using concrete examples of scenes or situations that are associated with love. The abstract concept is never fully grounded in external reality, but it does inherit some meaning from the more concrete concepts to which it is related.

Of course, not all examples are good: the last column of Figure 2 shows cases with no obvious relation between words and visual neighbours (subjects preferred the random images by a large margin).

The multimodal vectors we induce also display an interesting intrinsic property related to the hypothesis that grounded representations of abstract words are more complex than for concrete ones, since abstract concepts relate to varied and composite situations (Barsalou and Wiemer-Hastings, 2005). A natural corollary of this idea is that visually-grounded representations of abstract concepts should be more diverse: If you think of dogs, very similar images of specific dogs will come to mind. You can also imagine the abstract notion of freedom, but the nature of the related imagery will be much more varied. Recently, Kiela et al. (2014) have proposed to measure abstractness by exploiting this very same intuition. However, they rely on manual annotation of pictures via Google Images and define an *ad-hoc* measure of *image dispersion*. We conjecture that the representations naturally induced by our models display a similar property. In particular, the *entropy* of our multimodal vectors, being an expression of how varied the information they encode is, should correlate with the degree of abstractness of the corresponding words. As Figure 3(a) shows, there is indeed a difference in entropy between the most concrete (*meat*) and most abstract (*hope*) words in the Kiela et al. set.

To test the hypothesis quantitatively, we measure the correlation of entropy and concreteness on the 200 words in the Kiela et al. (2014) set.[7] Figure 3(b) shows that the entropies of both the

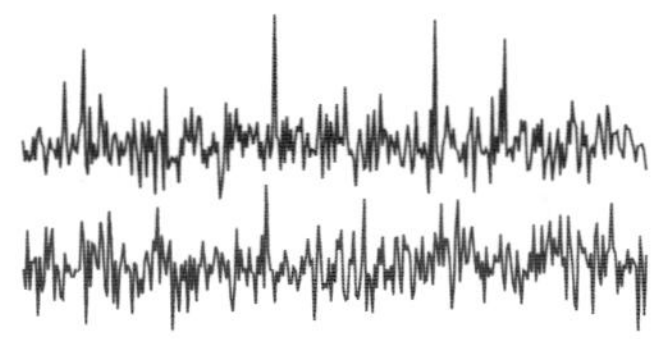

(a)

| Model | $\rho$ |
|---|---|
| WORD FREQUENCY | 0.22 |
| KIELA ET AL. | -0.65 |
| SKIP-GRAM | 0.05 |
| MMSKIP-GRAM-B | 0.04 |
| MMSKIP-GRAM-A | **-0.75** |
| MMSKIP-GRAM-B* | -0.71 |

(b)

Figure 3: (a) Distribution of MMSKIP-GRAM-A vector activation for *meat* (blue) and *hope* (red). (b) Spearman $\rho$ between concreteness and various measures on the Kiela et al. (2014) set.

MMSKIP-GRAM-A representations and those generated by mapping MMSKIP-GRAM-B vectors onto visual space (MMSKIP-GRAM-B*) achieve very high correlation (but, interestingly, not MMSKIP-GRAM-B). This is further evidence that multimodal learning is grounding the representations of both concrete and abstract words in meaningful ways.

## 6 Conclusion

We introduced two multimodal extensions of SKIP-GRAM. MMSKIP-GRAM-A is trained by directly optimizing the similarity of words with their visual representations, thus forcing maximum interaction between the two modalities. MMSKIP-GRAM-B includes an extra mediating layer, acting as a cross-modal mapping component. The ability of the models to *integrate* and *propagate* visual information resulted in word representations that performed well in both semantic and vision tasks, and could be used as input in systems benefiting from prior visual knowledge (e.g., caption generation). Our results with abstract words suggest the models might also help in tasks such as metaphor detection, or even retrieving/generating pictures of abstract concepts. Their incremental nature makes them well-suited for cognitive simulations of grounded language acquisition, an avenue of research we plan to explore further.


## Acknowledgments

We thank Adam Liska, Tomas Mikolov, the reviewers and the NIPS 2014 Learning Semantics audience. We were supported by ERC 2011 Starting Independent Research Grant n. 283554 (COMPOSES).


[7] Since the vector dimensions range over the real number line, we calculate entropy on vectors that are unit-normed after adding a small constant insuring all values are positive.

## References


Marco Baroni, Eduard Barbu, Brian Murphy, and Massimo Poesio. 2010. Strudel: A distributional semantic model based on properties and types. *Cognitive Science*, 34(2):222–254.

Marco Baroni, Georgiana Dinu, and Germán Kruszewski. 2014. Don't count, predict! a systematic comparison of context-counting vs. context-predicting semantic vectors. In *Proceedings of ACL*, pages 238–247, Baltimore, MD.

Lawrence Barsalou and Katja Wiemer-Hastings. 2005. Situating abstract concepts. In D. Pecher and R. Zwaan, editors, *Grounding Cognition: The Role of Perception and Action in Memory, Language, and Thought*, pages 129–163. Cambridge University Press, Cambridge, UK.

Lawrence Barsalou. 2008. Grounded cognition. *Annual Review of Psychology*, 59:617–645.

Elia Bruni, Gemma Boleda, Marco Baroni, and Nam Khanh Tran. 2012. Distributional semantics in Technicolor. In *Proceedings of ACL*, pages 136–145, Jeju Island, Korea.

Elia Bruni, Nam Khanh Tran, and Marco Baroni. 2014. Multimodal distributional semantics. *Journal of Artificial Intelligence Research*, 49:1–47.

Stephen Clark. 2015. Vector space models of lexical meaning. In Shalom Lappin and Chris Fox, editors, *Handbook of Contemporary Semantics, 2nd ed.* Blackwell, Malden, MA. In press; `http://www.cl.cam.ac.uk/~sc609/pubs/sem_handbook.pdf`.

Jia Deng, Wei Dong, Richard Socher, Lia-Ji Li, and Li Fei-Fei. 2009. Imagenet: A large-scale hierarchical image database. In *Proceedings of CVPR*, pages 248–255, Miami Beach, FL.

Jeffrey L Elman. 1990. Finding structure in time. *Cognitive science*, 14(2):179–211.

Ali Farhadi, Ian Endres, Derek Hoiem, and David Forsyth. 2009. Describing objects by their attributes. In *Proceedings of CVPR*, pages 1778–1785, Miami Beach, FL.

Yansong Feng and Mirella Lapata. 2010. Visual information in semantic representation. In *Proceedings of HLT-NAACL*, pages 91–99, Los Angeles, CA.

Andrea Frome, Greg Corrado, Jon Shlens, Samy Bengio, Jeff Dean, Marc'Aurelio Ranzato, and Tomas Mikolov. 2013. DeViSE: A deep visual-semantic embedding model. In *Proceedings of NIPS*, pages 2121–2129, Lake Tahoe, NV.

Alona Fyshe, Partha P Talukdar, Brian Murphy, and Tom M Mitchell. 2014. Interpretable semantic vectors from a joint model of brain-and text-based meaning. In *In Proceedings of ACL*, pages 489–499.

Arthur Glenberg and David Robertson. 2000. Symbol grounding and meaning: A comparison of high-dimensional and embodied theories of meaning. *Journal of Memory and Language*, 3(43):379–401.

Stevan Harnad. 1990. The symbol grounding problem. *Physica D: Nonlinear Phenomena*, 42(1-3):335–346.

Felix Hill and Anna Korhonen. 2014. Learning abstract concept embeddings from multi-modal data: Since you probably can't see what I mean. In *Proceedings of EMNLP*, pages 255–265, Doha, Qatar.

Felix Hill, Roi Reichart, and Anna Korhonen. 2014. SimLex-999: Evaluating semantic models with (genuine) similarity estimation. http://arxiv.org/abs/arXiv:1408.3456.

Steve Howell, Damian Jankowicz, and Suzanna Becker. 2005. A model of grounded language acquisition: Sensorimotor features improve lexical and grammatical learning. *Journal of Memory and Language*, 53:258–276.

Yangqing Jia, Evan Shelhamer, Jeff Donahue, Sergey Karayev, Jonathan Long, Ross Girshick, Sergio Guadarrama, and Trevor Darrell. 2014. Caffe: Convolutional architecture for fast feature embedding. *arXiv preprint arXiv:1408.5093*.

Andrej Karpathy, Armand Joulin, and Li Fei-Fei. 2014. Deep fragment embeddings for bidirectional image sentence mapping. In *Proceedings of NIPS*, pages 1097–1105, Montreal, Canada.

Douwe Kiela and Léon Bottou. 2014. Learning image embeddings using convolutional neural networks for improved multi-modal semantics. In *Proceedings of EMNLP*, pages 36–45, Doha, Qatar.

Douwe Kiela, Felix Hill, Anna Korhonen, and Stephen Clark. 2014. Improving multi-modal representations using image dispersion: Why less is sometimes more. In *Proceedings of ACL*, pages 835–841, Baltimore, MD.

Ryan Kiros, Ruslan Salakhutdinov, and Richard Zemel. 2014. Unifying visual-semantic embeddings with multimodal neural language models. In *Proceedings of the NIPS Deep Learning and Representation Learning Workshop*, Montreal, Canada. Published online: `http://www.dlworkshop.org/accepted-papers`.

Alex Krizhevsky, Ilya Sutskever, and Geoffrey Hinton. 2012. ImageNet classification with deep convolutional neural networks. In *Proceedings of NIPS*, pages 1097–1105, Lake Tahoe, Nevada.

George Lakoff and Mark Johnson. 1999. *Philosophy in the Flesh: The Embodied Mind and Its Challenge to Western Thought.* Basic Books, New York.

Angeliki Lazaridou, Elia Bruni, and Marco Baroni. 2014. Is this a wampimuk? cross-modal mapping between distributional semantics and the visual world. In *Proceedings of ACL*, pages 1403–1414, Baltimore, MD.

Junhua Mao, Wei Xu, Yi Yang, Jiang Wang, and Alan Yuille. 2014. Explain images with multimodal recurrent neural networks. In *Proceedings of the NIPS Deep Learning and Representation Learning Workshop*, Montreal, Canada. Published online: `http://www.dlworkshop.org/accepted-papers`.

Tomas Mikolov, Ilya Sutskever, Kai Chen, Greg Corrado, and Jeff Dean. 2013a. Distributed representations of words and phrases and their compositionality. In *Proceedings of NIPS*, pages 3111–3119, Lake Tahoe, NV.

Tomas Mikolov, Wen-tau Yih, and Geoffrey Zweig. 2013b. Linguistic regularities in continuous space word representations. In *Proceedings of NAACL*, pages 746–751, Atlanta, Georgia.

Frederic Morin and Yoshua Bengio. 2005. Hierarchical probabilistic neural network language model. In *Proceedings of AISTATS*, pages 246–252, Barbados.

Maxime Oquab, Leon Bottou, Ivan Laptev, and Josef Sivic. 2014. Learning and transferring mid-level image representations using convolutional neural networks. In *Proceedings of CVPR*.

John Searle. 1984. *Minds, Brains and Science*. Harvard University Press, Cambridge, MA.

Carina Silberer and Mirella Lapata. 2014. Learning grounded meaning representations with autoencoders. In *Proceedings of ACL*, pages 721–732, Baltimore, Maryland.

Josef Sivic and Andrew Zisserman. 2003. Video Google: A text retrieval approach to object matching in videos. In *Proceedings of ICCV*, pages 1470–1477, Nice, France.

Richard Socher, Milind Ganjoo, Christopher Manning, and Andrew Ng. 2013. Zero-shot learning through cross-modal transfer. In *Proceedings of NIPS*, pages 935–943, Lake Tahoe, NV.

Richard Socher, Quoc Le, Christopher Manning, and Andrew Ng. 2014. Grounded compositional semantics for finding and describing images with sentences. *Transactions of the Association for Computational Linguistics*, 2:207–218.

Peter Turney and Patrick Pantel. 2010. From frequency to meaning: Vector space models of semantics. *Journal of Artificial Intelligence Research*, 37:141–188.

Peter Turney, Yair Neuman, Dan Assaf, and Yohai Cohen. 2011. Literal and metaphorical sense identification through concrete and abstract context. In *Proceedings of EMNLP*, pages 680–690, Edinburgh, UK.

Luis von Ahn and Laura Dabbish. 2004. Labeling images with a computer game. In *Proceedings of CHI*, pages 319–326, Vienna, Austria.

Jason Weston, Samy Bengio, and Nicolas Usunier. 2010. Large scale image annotation: learning to rank with joint word-image embeddings. *Machine learning*, 81(1):21–35.

# Discriminative Unsupervised Alignment of Natural Language Instructions with Corresponding Video Segments

**Iftekhar Naim**[1], **Young Chol Song**[1], **Qiguang Liu**[1], **Liang Huang**[2], **Henry Kautz**[1], **Jiebo Luo**[1] and **Daniel Gildea**[1]
[1]Department of Computer Science, University of Rochester, Rochester, NY 14627
[2]Queens College & Graduate Center, City University of New York, Flushing, NY 11367

## Abstract

We address the problem of automatically aligning natural language sentences with corresponding video segments without any direct supervision. Most existing algorithms for integrating language with videos rely on hand-aligned parallel data, where each natural language sentence is manually aligned with its corresponding image or video segment. Recently, fully unsupervised alignment of text with video has been shown to be feasible using hierarchical generative models. In contrast to the previous generative models, we propose three latent-variable discriminative models for the unsupervised alignment task. The proposed discriminative models are capable of incorporating domain knowledge, by adding diverse and overlapping features. The results show that discriminative models outperform the generative models in terms of alignment accuracy.

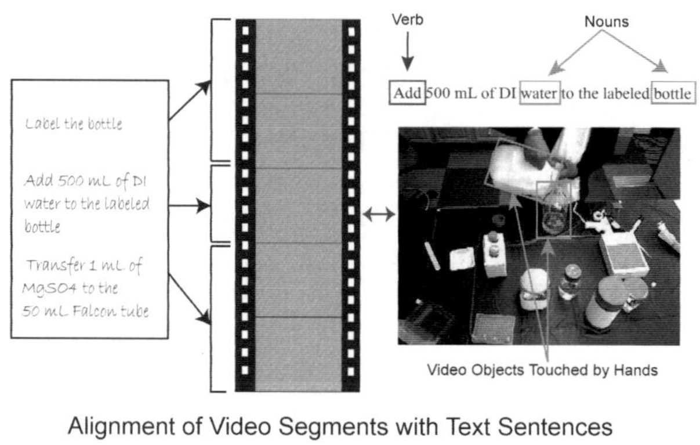


Figure 1: The proposed discriminative learning algorithm aligns protocol sentences to corresponding video frames. We incorporate features that can learn the co-occurrences of nouns and verbs in the sentences with the objects in the video.

## 1 Introduction

Learning to integrate natural language descriptions with video events is attracting increasing attention in the natural language processing and computer vision communities. The Grounded Language Learning task aims to map the meaning of natural language expressions to their corresponding referents in videos (e.g., objects, actions, and events) without any dictionary. Most existing grounded language learning algorithms are either supervised or weakly-supervised. During the training stage, they assume each video is pre-segmented to chunks of short duration, and each video segment is manually aligned with a natural language sentence that describes that segment. Manually aligning each video segment with a sentence is tedious, especially for long videos. Therefore, it is desirable to automatically align video segments with their corresponding natural language sentences without direct supervision.

Recently, Naim et al. (2014) proposed an unsupervised learning algorithm for automatically aligning sentences in a document with corresponding video segments. Given a sequence of natural language instructions and an unaligned video recording of a person following these instructions, a hierarchical generative model was applied to align each instruc-



*Human Language Technologies: The 2015 Annual Conference of the North American Chapter of the ACL*, pages 164–174,
Denver, Colorado, May 31 – June 5, 2015. 

tion to its corresponding video segment, and to align nouns in each instruction to their corresponding objects in the video. We extend this generative alignment framework by applying several discriminative models with latent variables. Discriminative models are attractive as they can easily incorporate domain knowledge by adding many diverse, overlapping, and complex features. By incorporating a large number of features and regularizing their weights properly, discriminative models have been shown to outperform generative models in many natural language processing tasks (Collins, 2002; Dyer et al., 2011; Yu et al., 2013).

Similar to Naim et al. (2014), we applied our algorithm to align the natural language instructions for biological experiments in "wet laboratories" with recorded videos of people performing these experiments. Typically, each wetlab experiment has a protocol written in natural language, describing the sequence of steps necessary for that experiment. However, these instructions are often incomplete, and do not spell out implicit assumptions and knowledge, causing the results to be difficult to reproduce (Begley and Ellis, 2012). Given a set of such wetlab experiment protocols and associated videos, our initial goal is to infer the correct alignment between the steps mentioned in the protocol and corresponding video segments in which a person performs these steps (Figure 1). The aligned and segmented output of the system described in this paper can eventually be used to learn detailed visual models of correctly performed activities and to identify experimental anomalies.

In this paper, we apply three latent discriminative learning algorithms: latent conditional random field (LCRF), latent structured perceptron (LSP), and latent structured support vector machine (LSSVM) for unsupervised alignment of video with text. We show that discriminative models outperform the existing generative models by incorporating diverse features. While the previous models only considered the mappings of nouns to blobs, and ignored verbs, we incorporated the co-occurrences of verbs with blobs as features in our model. Finally, we propose a constrained variant of the standard LSP and LSSVM update rule, which provided better alignment accuracy and more stable convergence on our datasets.

## 2 Background Research

### 2.1 Unsupervised Grounded Language Learning

Most existing grounded language learning algorithms for integrating language with vision rely on either a fully supervised (Kollar et al., 2010; Matuszek et al., 2012) or a weakly supervised training stage (Yu and Ballard, 2004; Kate and Mooney, 2007; Krishnamurthy and Kollar, 2013; Yu and Siskind, 2013; Krishnamoorthy et al., 2013; Rohrbach et al., 2013; Tellex et al., 2013). The fully supervised methods assume that each sentence in the training data is manually paired with the corresponding image or video segment, and furthermore, each word or phrase in a sentence is already mapped to its corresponding blob or action in the image or video segment. Given the detailed annotations, these methods train a set of classifiers to recognize perceptual representations for commonly used words or phrases. After the initial fully supervised training stage, these methods can learn the meaning of new words as they are encountered. Such detailed supervision is difficult to obtain, and as a result most of the recent grounded language learning algorithms rely on weaker supervision (Krishnamurthy and Kollar, 2013; Yu and Siskind, 2013; Krishnamoorthy et al., 2013; Rohrbach et al., 2013; Tellex et al., 2013), where each image or video frame is manually paired with corresponding sentence, but the mapping between objects and words is not provided, and instead learned and inferred automatically as latent variables. Manually pairing each video segment or image frame with the corresponding sentence can be tedious, especially for long videos. Furthermore, these methods can be relatively difficult to extend to new domains, as this may require collecting new annotated data.

Recently, Naim et al. (2014) proposed a fully unsupervised approach for aligning wetlab experiment videos with associated text protocols, without any direct supervision. They proposed a hierarchical generative model to infer the alignment between each video segment with corresponding protocol sentence, and also the mapping of each blob with corresponding noun in that sentence. First, it models the generation of each video segment from one of the sentences in the protocol using a Hidden

Markov Model (HMM) (Rabiner, 1989; Vogel et al., 1996). Next, each tracked object or blob in a video segment is generated from one of the nouns in the corresponding sentence using IBM Model 1 (Brown et al., 1993), a generative model frequently used in machine translation. The IBM Model 1 probabilities are incorporated as emission probabilities in HMM. The transition probabilities are parameterized using the jump size, i.e., the difference between the alignments of two consecutive video segments. They also extended IBM Model 1 by introducing latent variables for each noun, allowing some of the non-object nouns to be unobserved in the video. While the alignment results are encouraging, and show that unsupervised alignment is feasible, they considered the mappings between nouns and blobs only, and ignored the verbs and other relations in the sentences. Moreover, incorporating domain knowledge is not straightforward in these generative models.

### 2.2 Discriminative Word Alignment

In machine translation, alignment of the words in source language with the words in target language has traditionally been done using the IBM word alignment models (Brown et al., 1993), which are generative models, and typically trained using Expectation Maximization (Dempster et al., 1977). Early attempts (Blunsom and Cohn, 2006; Taskar et al., 2005) towards discriminative word alignment relied on supervised hand-aligned parallel corpora. Dyer et al. (2011) first applied a latent variable conditional random field (LCRF) to perform unsupervised discriminative word alignment. They treated the words' alignments as latent variables, and formulated the task as predicting the target sentence, given the source sentence. We apply similar latent variable discriminative models for unsupervised alignment of sentences with video segments.

## 3 Problem Formulation and Notations

The input to our system is a dataset containing $N$ pairs of observations $\{(\mathbf{x}_i, \mathbf{y}_i)\}_{i=1}^N$, where $\mathbf{x}_i$ represents the $i^{th}$ experiment protocol, and $\mathbf{y}_i$ represents a video of a person carrying out the instructions in that protocol. The protocols are not necessarily unique, as we have multiple videos of different people carrying out the same protocol.

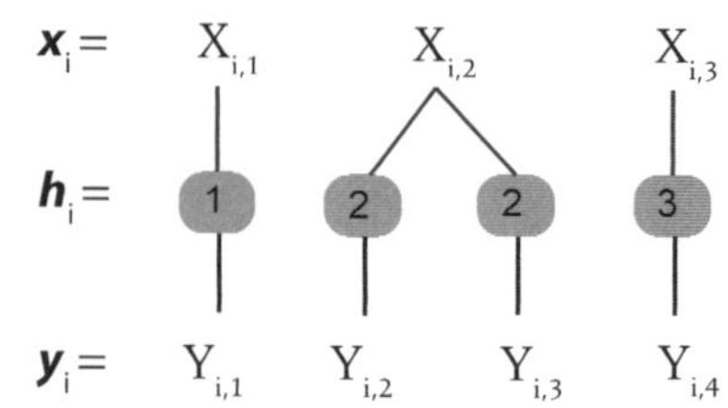


Figure 2: Each $X_{i,m}$ is a sentence in the protocol, consisting of the nouns and verbs in the sentence, and each $Y_{i,n}$ is a video chunk represented by the set of blobs touched by hands in that chunk. The alignment $\mathbf{h}_i = [1, 2, 2, 3]$ maps each video chunk to the corresponding sentence.

We apply similar data preprocessing as Naim et al. (2014). First, we parse each protocol sentence using the two-stage Charniak-Johnson parser (Charniak and Johnson, 2005), and extract the head nouns and verbs from each sentence. Let $m_i$ be the number of sentences in the protocol $\mathbf{x}_i$. We represent $\mathbf{x}_i$ as a sequence of sets $\mathbf{x}_i = [X_{i,1}, \ldots, X_{i,m_i}]$, where $X_{i,m}$ is the set of nouns and verbs in the $m^{th}$ sentence of $\mathbf{x}_i$. Each video $\mathbf{y}_i$ is segmented into a sequence of chunks, each one second long. For each video chunk, we determine the set of objects touched by the participant's hands using automated image segmentation and tracking. We ignore the chunks over which no object is touched by a hand. Let $n_i$ be the number of chunks in $\mathbf{y}_i$. We represent the video $\mathbf{y}_i$ as a sequence of sets: $\mathbf{y}_i = [Y_{i,1}, \ldots, Y_{i,n_i}]$, one for each video chunk, where $Y_{i,n}$ is the set of objects or blobs touched by hands in the $n^{th}$ chunk of $\mathbf{y}_i$. If $V_Y$ is the set of all blobs in the videos, then $Y_{i,n} \subseteq V_Y$.

Our goal is to learn the alignment $\mathbf{h}_i$ between the sentences in $\mathbf{x}_i$ with their corresponding video chunks in $\mathbf{y}_i$ (Figure 2). Formally, $\mathbf{h}_i[n] \in \{1, \ldots, m_i\}$, for $1 \leq n \leq n_i$, where $\mathbf{h}_i[n] = m$ indicates that the video segment $Y_{i,n}$ is aligned to the protocol sentence $X_{i,m}$.

## 4 Discriminative Alignment

To formulate the alignment problem as a discriminative learning task, we assume the text sequence $\mathbf{x}_i$ as the observed input, and the video sequence $\mathbf{y}_i$ as the output sequence that we aim to predict. Since the alignments are unknown, we treat them as latent variables. Let $\mathbf{h}_i$ be the hidden alignment vector for an observation pair $(\mathbf{x}_i, \mathbf{y}_i)$. The feature function $\mathbf{\Phi}(\mathbf{x}_i, \mathbf{y}_i, \mathbf{h}_i)$ maps the input observation $(\mathbf{x}_i, \mathbf{y}_i)$, and their latent alignment vector $\mathbf{h}_i$ to a $d$-dimensional feature vector. Our goal is to learn the weights $\mathbf{w} \in \mathbb{R}^d$ for these features.

### 4.1 Latent Variable Conditional Random Field

Given a text sequence $\mathbf{x}_i$ and a video sequence $\mathbf{y}_i$ with lengths $|\mathbf{x}_i| = m_i$ and $|\mathbf{y}_i| = n_i$, the conditional probability of the video sequence is:

$$\begin{aligned} p(\mathbf{y}_i|\mathbf{x}_i) &= p(\mathbf{y}_i, n_i|\mathbf{x}_i) \\ &= p(\mathbf{y}_i|\mathbf{x}_i, n_i)\, p(n_i|\mathbf{x}_i) \end{aligned} \quad (1)$$

Since we only aim to learn the alignments given $(\mathbf{x}_i, \mathbf{y}_i)$, we ignore the length probability $p(n_i|\mathbf{x}_i)$, and consider only the first term:

$$p(\mathbf{y}_i|\mathbf{x}_i, n_i) = \sum_{\mathbf{h}_i} p(\mathbf{y}_i, \mathbf{h}_i|\mathbf{x}_i, n_i) \quad (2)$$

We model the conditional probability $p(\mathbf{y}_i, \mathbf{h}_i|\mathbf{x}_i, n_i)$ using a log-linear model:

$$p(\mathbf{y}_i, \mathbf{h}_i|\mathbf{x}_i, n_i) = \frac{\exp \mathbf{w}^T \mathbf{\Phi}(\mathbf{x}_i, \mathbf{y}_i, \mathbf{h}_i)}{Z(\mathbf{x}_i, n_i)}, \quad (3)$$

where $Z(\mathbf{x}_i, n_i) = \sum_{\mathbf{y}} \sum_{\mathbf{h}} \exp \mathbf{w}^T \mathbf{\Phi}(\mathbf{x}_i, \mathbf{y}, \mathbf{h})$. To keep our models tractable, we assume our feature function $\mathbf{\Phi}$ decomposes linearly, similar to a linear-chain graphical model:

$$\mathbf{\Phi}(\mathbf{x}_i, \mathbf{y}_i, \mathbf{h}_i) = \sum_{n=1}^{n_i} \phi(X_{i,m}, Y_{i,n}, m, n, m'),$$

where $\mathbf{h}_i[n] = m$ and $\mathbf{h}_i[n-1] = m'$. Therefore, each factor in our linear chain graph structure depends on the alignment state for the current and the previous video chunk. For any two consecutive alignment states $\mathbf{h}_i[n] = m$ and $\mathbf{h}_i[n-1] = m'$, we represent the factor potential as:

$$\Psi(X_{i,m}, Y_{i,n}, m, n, m') = \exp\left[\mathbf{w}^T \phi(X_{i,m}, Y_{i,n}, m, n, m')\right]$$

Our goal is to maximize the following log-likelihood function:

$$L(\mathbf{w}) = \sum_{i=1}^{N} \log \sum_{\mathbf{h}_i} p(\mathbf{y}_i, \mathbf{h}_i|\mathbf{x}_i, n_i). \quad (4)$$

The gradient of the log-likelihood function with respect to the weight parameters is:

$$\frac{\partial L}{\partial \mathbf{w}} = \sum_{i=1}^{N} \Big[\mathbb{E}_{p(\mathbf{h}|\mathbf{x}_i, n_i, \mathbf{y}_i)} [\mathbf{\Phi}(\mathbf{x}_i, \mathbf{y}_i, \mathbf{h})] - \mathbb{E}_{p(\mathbf{y}, \mathbf{h}|\mathbf{x}_i, n_i)} [\mathbf{\Phi}(\mathbf{x}_i, \mathbf{y}, \mathbf{h})]\Big] \quad (5)$$

We apply the stochastic gradient descent algorithm (Vishwanathan et al., 2006) to maximize the conditional log-likelihood. For each observation $(\mathbf{x}_i, \mathbf{y}_i)$, we perform forward-backward dynamic programming to estimate the two expectation terms in equation 5, as discussed next.

#### 4.1.1 Estimation of $\mathbb{E}_{p(\mathbf{h}|\mathbf{x}_i, n_i, \mathbf{y}_i)} [\mathbf{\Phi}(\mathbf{x}_i, \mathbf{y}_i, \mathbf{h})]$

To estimate the first expectation term in equation 5, we need to sum over all the possible alignment states $h[n] = m$, where $n \in \{1, \ldots, n_i\}$ and $m \in \{1, \ldots, m_i\}$. Since the output sequence $\mathbf{y}_i$ is given, we refer to this stage as "forced" forward-backward stage. The forward messages $\alpha_n^F[m] \propto p(Y_{i,1}, \ldots, Y_{i,n}, \mathbf{h}[n] = m \mid \mathbf{x}_i)$ are estimated using the following recursion:

$$\alpha_n^F(m) = \sum_{m'} \alpha_{n-1}^F(m')\, \Psi(X_{i,m}, Y_{i,n}, m, n, m')$$

where $m'$ is one of the predecessors of the alignment state $h[n] = m$. Assuming no restrictions on the possible alignments, the computational complexity of each iteration on a single observation pair $(\mathbf{x}_i, \mathbf{y}_i)$ is $O(m_i^2 n_i d)$ for $m_i$ sentences, $n_i$ video chunks, and $d$ dimensional features. However, we allow only a constant number of predecessor and successor states for each alignment state, and hence the computational complexity becomes $O(m_i n_i d)$. Similarly, we apply backward recursions, with the same computational complexity.

#### 4.1.2 Estimation of $\mathbb{E}_{p(\mathbf{y}, \mathbf{h}|\mathbf{x}_i, n_i)} [\mathbf{\Phi}(\mathbf{x}_i, \mathbf{y}, \mathbf{h})]$

While computing the second expectation term, we assume only $\mathbf{x}_i$ and the number of video chunks $n_i$ are observed, and we need to sum probabilities over all possible alignments $h[n] = m$ and all possible video sequences $\mathbf{y}$. Again we apply forward-backward. The computational complexity, however, grows significantly, as we need to sum over all possible set of blobs that may be touched by hands in each video segment. The forward message $\alpha_n(m)$ is computed as:

$$\alpha_n(m) = \sum_{m'} \alpha_{n-1}(m') \sum_{Y \subseteq V_Y} \Psi(X_{im}, Y, m, n, m')$$

There can be $2^{|V_Y|} - 1$ possible subset of blobs at each of the alignment position, and the overall computational complexity becomes $O(2^{|V_Y|} m_i n_i d)$, which is prohibitively expensive, even for a small number of blobs. In our videos, the hands never touch more than 3 objects at a time. So we considered only the non-empty subsets with 3 or less elements: $P = \{S : S \subseteq V_Y, |S| \leq 3, S \neq \emptyset\}$. The pruning of larger subsets reduces the complexity to $O(|V_Y|^3 m_i n_i d)$. We can further reduce computation by decomposing the forward-backward recursions to the co-occurrence features and alignment path features:

$$\Psi(X_{im}, Y, m, n, m') = \Psi_{co}(X_{im}, Y) \Psi_{ap}(m, n, m')$$

The potential due to alignment path features ($\Psi_{ap}$) does not depend on the subset of blobs, and only depends on the current and previous alignment states $h[n] = m$ and $h[n-1] = m'$. On the other hand, the co-occurrence potential $\Psi_{co}$ for a given set of blobs $Y$ depends only on the sentence that it is being aligned to, and does not depend on the video chunk index $n$. Therefore we can decompose the forward recursion as:

$$\alpha_n(m) = \sum_{m'} \alpha_{n-1}(m') \, \Psi_{ap}(m, n, m') \, \delta(m)$$

where $\delta(m) = \sum_{Y \in P} \Psi_{co}(X_{im}, Y)$. We can precompute the values of $\delta(m)$ for each of the $m_i$ sentences, which takes $O(m_i d |V_Y|^3)$ operations. Finally, we run forward recursions over all the alignment states using the precomputed values, and the complexity becomes $O(m_i d |V_Y|^3 + m_i n_i d)$ Similarly the backward recursion becomes:

$$\beta_n(m) = \sum_{m'} \beta_{n+1}(m') \, \Psi_{ap}(m', n{+}1, m) \, \delta(m')$$

The alignment state transition probabilities $\xi_n(m', m)$ represents the probability $p(\mathbf{h}_{n-1} = m', \mathbf{h}_n = m \mid \mathbf{x}_i)$, which can be estimated by marginalizing over all possible sets of blobs:

$$\xi_n(m', m) \propto \alpha_{n-1}(m') \Psi_{ap}(m, n, m') \delta(m) \beta_n(m)$$

### 4.2 Latent Variable Structured Perceptron

Structured Perceptron (Collins, 2002) has become a popular method for discriminative structured learning due to its relatively fast convergence rate and theoretical convergence guarantee. Since true alignments are unknown, we apply the latent variable structured perceptron algorithm (Liang et al., 2006; Sun et al., 2009; Yu et al., 2013) for our discriminative alignment task.

We iteratively scan through our dataset, one protocol and video pair $(\mathbf{x}_i, \mathbf{y}_i)$ at a time. First, we infer the best alignment $\mathbf{h}_i^{Forced}$ for the given observation pair $(\mathbf{x}_i, \mathbf{y}_i)$ and the current weight vector $\mathbf{w}$:

$$\mathbf{h}_i^{Forced} = \arg\max_{\mathbf{h}} \mathbf{w}^T \mathbf{\Phi}(\mathbf{x}_i, \mathbf{y}_i, \mathbf{h}). \quad (6)$$

This step is known as Forced Decoding, as we are given both the protocol sentences and the associated video chunks. Forced decoding is performed using Viterbi-like dynamic programming (Algorithm 1), where the dynamic programming states are the alignment states $(m, n)$ such that $h[n] = m$.

**Algorithm 1** Perceptron Forced-Decoding

**Input:** Observation pair $(\mathbf{x}_i, \mathbf{y}_i)$ and a weight vector $\mathbf{w}$.
$m_i \leftarrow$ length$(\mathbf{x}_i)$, and $n_i \leftarrow$ length$(\mathbf{y}_i)$,
$D[m, n] \leftarrow -\infty$ for $0 \leq m \leq m_i$ and $0 \leq n \leq n_i$
$D[0, 0] \leftarrow 0$
**for** $m = 1$ to $m_i$ **do**
  **for** $n = 1$ to $n_i$ **do**
    **for each** $(m', n-1) \in$ Predecessors$(m, n)$ **do**
      $\mathbf{\Phi} \leftarrow$ create-features$(X_{i,m}, Y_{i,n}, m, n, m')$
      **if** $D[m', n-1] + \mathbf{w}^T \mathbf{\Phi} > D[m, n]$ **then**
        $D[m, n] \leftarrow D[m', n-1] + \mathbf{w}^T \mathbf{\Phi}$
        Backpointers$[m, n] \leftarrow m'$
$\mathbf{h}_i^{Forced} \leftarrow$ Backtrack($D$, Backpointers)
Return $\mathbf{h}_i^{Forced}$

Next, we decode both the highest scoring alignment $\hat{\mathbf{h}}_i$ and video sequence $\hat{\mathbf{y}}_i$, given the protocol $\mathbf{x}_i$ and the number of video chunks $n_i$.

$$\hat{\mathbf{h}}_i, \hat{\mathbf{y}}_i = \arg\max_{\mathbf{h}, \mathbf{y}} \mathbf{w}^T \mathbf{\Phi}(\mathbf{x}_i, \mathbf{y}, \mathbf{h}) \quad (7)$$

We refer to this step as Full Decoding (Algorithm 2). The dynamic programming is similar to that for forced decoding, except that we need to find the best set of blobs given a set of nouns, for every protocol sentence $X_{i,m}$:

$$B[m] = \arg\max_{S \in P} \mathbf{w}_{co}^T \mathbf{\Phi}_{\mathbf{co}}(X_{i,m}, S) \quad (8)$$

where $P$ is the pruned set of blobs and $\mathbf{\Phi_{co}}(X_{i,m}, S)$ is a vector containing only the co-occurrence features, and $\mathbf{w}_{co}$ contains their corresponding weights. The detailed algorithm is described in Algorithm 2. Finally, we update the weight vector $\mathbf{w}$:

$$\mathbf{w}^{(new)} = \mathbf{w}^{(old)} + \mathbf{\Phi}(\mathbf{x}_i, \mathbf{y}_i, \mathbf{h}_i^{Forced}) - \mathbf{\Phi}(\mathbf{x}_i, \hat{\mathbf{y}}_i, \hat{\mathbf{h}}_i)$$

**Algorithm 2** Perceptron Full Decoding

```
Input: Input protocol x_i, set of all blobs V_Y, number of video
    chunks n_i, weight vector w.
m_i ← length(x_i)
D[m, n] ← −∞ for 0 ≤ m ≤ m_i and 0 ≤ n ≤ n_i
B[m] ← ∅ for 0 ≤ m ≤ m_i
D[0, 0] ← 0
P ← {S : S ⊂ V_Y, |S| ≤ 3, S ≠ ∅}    // precompute the
    pruned list of subsets of blobs
for m = 1 to m_i do
    B[m] ← arg max_{S∈P} w_co^T Φ_co(X_{i,m}, S)
    for n = 1 to n_i do
        for each (m', n − 1) ∈ Predecessors(m, n) do
            Φ ← create-features(X_{i,m}, B[m], m, n, m')
            if D[m', n − 1] + w^T Φ > D[m, n] then
                D[m, n] ← D[m', n − 1] + w^T Φ
                Backpointer[m, n] ← m'
ĥ_i ← Backtrack(D, Backpointers)
ŷ_i ← [B[ĥ_{i,1}], . . . , B[ĥ_{i,n_i}]]
Return ĥ_i, ŷ_i
```

### 4.3 Constrained Decoding

During the full decoding of $(\hat{\mathbf{h}}_i, \hat{\mathbf{y}}_i)$, we have no information regarding how many video chunks to assign to each sentence. As a result, the full decoding is unlikely to predict the correct video sequence, no matter how many training iterations performed. In practice, the unconstrained full decoding often ends up aligning too many video chunks to one of the protocol sentences.

To address this problem, we modified the perceptron update rule. Instead of performing unconstrained full decoding, we constrain the alignment $\hat{\mathbf{h}}_i$ to be same as the forced alignment $\mathbf{h}_i^{Forced}$, and infer the best sequence of video chunks $\hat{\mathbf{y}}_i^{Constr}$ under this constraint:

$$\hat{\mathbf{y}}_i^{Constr} = \arg\max_{\mathbf{y}} \mathbf{w}^T \mathbf{\Phi}(\mathbf{x}_i, \mathbf{y}, \mathbf{h}_i^{Forced})$$

We refer to this decoding step as "constrained decoding" (Algorithm 3), and refer to this constrained LSP variant as LSP-C. The modified weight update rule is:

$$\mathbf{w}^{(new)} = \mathbf{w}^{(old)} + \mathbf{\Phi}(\mathbf{x}_i, \mathbf{y}_i, \mathbf{h}_i^{Forced}) - \mathbf{\Phi}(\mathbf{x}_i, \hat{\mathbf{y}}_i^{Constr}, \mathbf{h}_i^{Forced})$$

**Algorithm 3** Perceptron Constrained-Decoding

```
Input: Input protocol x_i, set of all blobs V_Y, number of video
    chunks n_i, forced alignment h_i^Forced, weight vector w.
P ← {S : S ⊂ V_Y, |S| ≤ 3, S ≠ ∅}
for n = 1 to n_i do
    m ← h_i^Forced[n]
    Ŷ_{i,n}^Constr ← arg max_{S∈P} w_co^T Φ_co(X_{i,m}, S)
Return ŷ_i^Constr = [Ŷ_{i,1}^Constr, . . . , Ŷ_{i,n_i}^Constr]
```

### 4.4 Latent Structured SVM

Structured SVM can be formulated by extending structured perceptron with two simple modifications: (1) incorporating a large-margin regularization term, and (2) incorporating a general loss function, instead of the zero-one loss of perceptron. The regularization reduces overfitting by keeping feature weights relatively small. Let the loss-augmented full decoding be:

$$(\hat{\mathbf{y}}_i, \hat{\mathbf{h}}_i) = \arg\max_{\mathbf{y},\mathbf{h}} \mathbf{w}^T \mathbf{\Phi}(\mathbf{x}_i, \mathbf{y}, \mathbf{h}) + \mathcal{L}_i(\mathbf{y}, \mathbf{h}),$$

where $\mathcal{L}_i(\mathbf{y}, \mathbf{h})$ is the loss function for the $i^{th}$ observation. LSSVM minimizes the following objective function:

$$C(w) = \frac{1}{N} \sum_{i=1}^{N} \Big( \mathbf{w}^T \mathbf{\Phi}(\mathbf{x}_i, \hat{\mathbf{y}}_i, \hat{\mathbf{h}}_i) + \mathcal{L}_i(\hat{\mathbf{y}}_i, \hat{\mathbf{h}}_i) - \mathbf{w}^T \mathbf{\Phi}(\mathbf{x}_i, \mathbf{y}_i, \mathbf{h}_i^{Forced}) \Big) + \frac{\lambda}{2} \|w\|^2,$$

which is non-convex and non-differentiable, and optimized utilizing the subgradient method (Ratliff et al., 2007). We perform online learning, and the subgradient in each iteration is:

$$g_i(\mathbf{w}) = \mathbf{\Phi}(\mathbf{x}_i, \hat{\mathbf{y}}_i, \hat{\mathbf{h}}_i) - \mathbf{\Phi}(\mathbf{x}_i, \mathbf{y}_i, \mathbf{h}_i^{Forced}) + \lambda \mathbf{w}.$$

Similar to LSP-C, we can obtain a constrained variant LSSVM-C, by replacing loss-augmented decoding with a constrained variant, where we fix $\hat{\mathbf{h}}_i$ to forced alignment $\mathbf{h}_i^{Forced}$.

### 4.5 Latent Variables to Map Blobs to Nouns

Given a sentence $X_{i,n}$ and a video segment $Y_{i,m}$, we further introduce additional latent variables to map each blob in $Y_{i,m}$ to one of the nouns in $X_{i,n}$. These latent variables are similar to the IBM Model 1 latent variables of Naim et al. (2014). Instead of turning on the (noun, blob) co-occurrence feature for every noun and blob in $X_{i,n}$ and $Y_{i,m}$, the latent variables map each blob to one of the nouns only. For LCRF, we sum over all the latent variables for estimating the expectations. For LSP and LSSVM, the (noun,blob) feature with maximum feature weight triggers for each blob.

## 5 Feature Design

The features used in our discriminative models can be grouped in two categories: (1) co-occurrence features, and (2) alignment path features. The co-occurrence features depend only on a protocol sentence and the video segment it aligns to. The alignment path features, on the other hand, do not depend on the co-occurrence of sentence and video segment, and instead capture general alignment properties, e.g., jump size and the distance of an alignment state from the diagonal.

### 5.1 Co-occurrence Features

The co-occurrence features included in our experiments are:

- *Co-occurrence of Nouns and Blobs:* For each noun in the input protocols and each blob in the videos, we add a boolean feature (noun, blob), which is turned on if we align a sentence containing that noun with a video segment containing that blob.

- *Co-occurrence of Verbs and Blobs:* For each verb in the input protocols and each blob in the videos, we add a boolean feature. This feature captures the observation that certain verbs are more likely to occur with certain objects (e.g., 'write' co-occurs with 'pen', 'aspirate' co-occurs with 'pipette').

We experimented with co-occurrence features of the form: (noun, verb, blob) triplets. However, including these features did not provide any noticeable gain, while significantly increasing the computation time, as the number of features increased drastically. Therefore, we did not include these features in our final experiments.

### 5.2 Alignment Path Features

Alignment path features depend on the current alignment state $\mathbf{h}[n] = m$, and the previous alignment states $\mathbf{h}[n-1] = m'$. These features do not depend on the nouns and verbs in the sentences and the blobs in the video segments. We used the following alignment path features:

- *Jump Size:* Since we allow monotonic jumps only, the jump sizes can be either zero or one. Therefore, we added two features for these two jump sizes.

- *Positional Features:* we added positional features (Dyer et al., 2011) to discourage alignment states that are too far from the diagonal. For each alignment state $(m, n)$, we estimate normalized distance from the diagonal as $|\frac{m}{m_i} - \frac{n}{n_i}|$. Again we used boolean features by assigning this normalized distance to five equally spaced bins.

The alignment features are not updated by the LSP-C and LSSVM-C methods, as they assume $\mathbf{h}_i^{Forced}$ and $\hat{\mathbf{h}}_i$ to be identical.

## 6 Results

Our dataset contains 12 wetlab experiment videos, for 3 different protocols (4 videos per protocol). Each protocol contains natural language instructions for an actual biological experiment. On average, each protocol has 9 steps, and 24 sentences. The videos are recorded using an RGB-D Kinect camera, in a mock wetlab setup. The average video length is $\sim$ 5 minutes. There are 34 unique nouns and 25 unique verbs in the protocols, and 22 distinct blobs in the videos.

We follow the same data pre-processing technique as described by Naim et al. (2014). The number of blobs is assumed to be known apriori. We oversegment each frame into many superpixels using the SLIC Superpixels algorithm (Achanta et al., 2012). We combine multiple adjacent superpixels into a blob, based on a pre-trained Gaussian mixture

| Dataset | Average Alignment Accuracy (%) | | | | | | | |
|---|---|---|---|---|---|---|---|---|
| | LHMM | LCRF | LSP | LSP-C | LSP-H | LSSVM | LSSVM-C | LSSVM-H |
| Manual-Tracking | 75.58 | **85.09** | 79.64 | 80.68 | 80.41 | 79.64 | 80.68 | 80.41 |
| Auto-Tracking | 64.04 | **65.59** | 61.99 | 63.95 | 65.27 | 61.99 | 63.95 | 65.27 |

Table 1: Alignment accuracy (% of video chunks aligned to the correct protocol step) for both manual and automatic tracking data. LHMM is the existing state-of-the-art generative model. For the variants of latent perceptron (LSP) and latent structured SVM (LSSVM), "C" indicates constrained decoding, and "H" indicates hybrid update.

color model and their boundary maps (Luo and Guo, 2003), and track each blob using a 3D Kalman filter. In order to isolate alignment error from computer vision tracking and segmentation error, we manually tracked and annotated each of the video segments with the set of blobs touched by hands using the video annotation tool Anvil (Kipp, 2012). The alignment accuracies are reported both for the manual and automated tracking datasets. Parsing error is relatively small. The Charniak-Johnson parser correctly identified the nouns and verbs for most sentences, except for several single-word imperative sentences (e.g., Mix.), for which the verbs were mistakenly parsed as nouns.

We experimented with the latent CRF (LCRF), latent perceptron (LSP) and its constrained variant (LSP-C), and latent SVM (LSSVM) and its constrained variant (LSSVM-C). Furthermore, we tried two hybrid variants LSP-H and LSSVM-H, where we started with constrained decoding, and later switched to full decoding. We experimented by incorporating additional latent variables for Blob-to-Noun mapping (Section 4.5), which significantly improved alignment accuracy for LCRF, but decreased accuracy for LSP and LSSVM and their variants. We report the best result for each model. The discriminative algorithms are compared with the state-of-the-art LHMM model (Naim et al., 2014), which is a generative HMM with latent variables for blob-to-noun mapping and the observation states of each noun.

We initialized the weights for co-occurrence and jump size features to the log-probabilities learned by the generative HMM model. All the other features are initialized to zero. For both LHMM and the discriminative models, we used monotonic jumps as they performed better than the non-monotonic jumps. We used the same learning rate $\eta = \frac{0.001}{\sqrt{t}}$ (where $t$ is the iteration number) for all the discriminative models, and the LSSVM regularization constant $\lambda = 0.001$. All the Perceprton and SVM variants performed "weight averaging" (Collins, 2002). The number of iterations are set to 100 for all the algorithms.

Table 1 shows that the discriminative models, especially LCRF and LSP-H/LSSVM-H, outperform the generative model LHMM both on the manual-tracking and auto-tracking datasets. For the manual-tracking dataset, the difference between LHMM and each of the discriminative models is statistically significant (p-value $< 0.0001$). On the auto-tracking dataset, however, the differences are not significant (p-value $> 0.1$). Table 2 shows an example of an alignment obtained by LCRF for a short segment of a manually tracked video.

The average running time for each iteration per video is 0.8 seconds for LHMM, 1.1 seconds for LSP and LSSVM, and 2.5 seconds for LCRF on a 2.9 GHz Intel Core-i7 processor and 8GB RAM.

## 7 Discussions and Future Work

The results show that discriminative methods outperform the generative LHMM model on both the manual and auto-tracking datasets. We achieved the best overall accuracy using the LCRF model. LCRF takes expectations over all possible alignment states and video sequences. On the other hand, LSP and LSSVM consider the highest scoring prediction only, which is similar to the hard-decision decoding. With no information regarding how many video segments to align to each sentence, LSP and LSSVM could not correctly predict the output video sequences during full decoding, and the weight vectors did not converge. By constraining the alignment to the forced alignment, we avoid aggressive updates, which may have helped LSP-C and LSSVM-C to learn better alignments. However, constrained decoding has a limitation that it can not update align-

| Start (s) | End (s) | Blobs in Hands | Detected Nouns | Detected Verbs | Protocol Sentence |
|---|---|---|---|---|---|
| 40.58 | 42.58 | boat | boat, scale | place | place the plastic boat on the scale . |
| 42.58 | 42.90 | boat | scale | | zero the scale . |
| 42.90 | 48.48 | base | spatula, base, boat | measure | using the spatula , measure 20 g of lb broth base into the plastic boat . |
| 48.48 | 58.95 | base, spatula | spatula, base, boat | measure | using the spatula , measure 20 g of lb broth base into the plastic boat . |
| 58.95 | 65.93 | base | spatula, base, boat | measure | using the spatula , measure 20 g of lb broth base into the plastic boat . |
| 65.93 | 80.90 | boat, bottle | base, bottle | pour | pour the lb broth base into the 1000 ml bottle . |
| 83.80 | 84.80 | water | water | add | add 800 ml of di water . |
| 84.80 | 88.95 | water | water, sink | use | use the di water near the sink . |
| 88.95 | 96.68 | water, bottle | water, sink | use | use the di water near the sink . |
| 96.68 | 104.67 | water | mix | | mix . |
| 108.15 | 118.12 | bottle | cap, bottle, water | put, shake, mix | put a cap on the bottle and shake to mix the dry ingredients with the water . |

Table 2: An example of an alignment, obtained for a part of a manually tracked video. We notice several incorrect parses, e.g., the verbs "mix" and "zero" were not detected correctly.

ment path features. LCRF sums over all possible output and latent variables, which includes the correct solution, and hence constrained decoding is not necessary. While the latent variables for blob-to-noun mappings improved the alignment accuracy for LCRF, it did not improve alignment accuracy for LSP and LSSVM and their variants, presumably because of their hard-decision decoding approach.

Among the different variants of LSP and LSSVM, we obtained the best accuracy with the hybrid variants (LSP-H and LSSVM-H), where we started with constrained decoding, and then switched to standard updates. While these hybird approaches provided better accuracy, they still suffer from the issue of not converging. The feature weights learned by LSSVM and its variants were smaller than that for LSP (due to regularization). However, they always resulted in the same forced decoding alignments in our experiments, and obtained same alignment accuracy.

Unlike the previous models, we considered the co-occurrences of verbs with blobs in the video. The highest weighted features include: *(write, pen)*, *(aspirate, pipette)*, which agree with our intuition. Our immediate next step will be to automatically learn a dictionary of hand motion patterns, and consider the co-occurrence of these patterns with verbs in the sentences. Some of the objects in our video are small and thin (e.g., pen, pipette, spatula, plastic boat), and were not reliably detected by the computer vision segmentation and tracking system. This may be the reason why we achieved relatively smaller improvements on the auto-tracking dataset.

Our alignment models are different from the traditional discriminative approaches in that our cost function is not same as our evaluation criteria. Although our goal is to improve alignment accuracy, the objective function that we minimize is either the negative conditional log-likelihood (LCRF) or the number of mis-predicted video segments (LSSVM). Since the ground truth alignments are unknown, we could not integrate alignment error in our objective function. The proposed discriminative models outperform LHMM despite the fact that the discriminative models are simpler – lacking latent variables for the observation states of nouns. The alignment accuracy of the discriminative models is expected to improve even further once these latent variables are incorporated.

## 8 Conclusion

We proposed three discriminative unsupervised alignment algorithms and their novel variants using constrained decoding. The proposed algorithms incorporate overlapping features to capture the co-occurrences of nouns and verbs with video blobs, and outperform the state-of-the-art latent HMM model via discriminative training.

**Acknowledgments** Funded by NSF IIS-1446996, ONR N00014-11-10417, Intel ISTCPC, DoD SBIR N00014-12-C-0263, DARPA FA8750-13-2-0041 (DEFT), NSF IIS-1449278, and a Google Faculty Research Award.

## References


R. Achanta, A. Shaji, K. Smith, A. Lucchi, P. Fua, and Sabine Susstrunk. 2012. SLIC superpixels compared to state-of-the-art superpixel methods. *IEEE Transactions on Pattern Analysis and Machine Intelligence*, 34(11):2274–2282.

C. Glenn Begley and Lee M. Ellis. 2012. Drug development: Raise standards for preclinical cancer research. *Nature*, 483(7391):531–533.

Phil Blunsom and Trevor Cohn. 2006. Discriminative word alignment with conditional random fields. In *Proceedings of the 21st International Conference on Computational Linguistics and the 44th Annual Meeting of the Association for Computational Linguistics*, ACL-44, pages 65–72, Stroudsburg, PA, USA. Association for Computational Linguistics.

Peter F. Brown, Stephen A. Della Pietra, Vincent J. Della Pietra, and Robert L. Mercer. 1993. The mathematics of statistical machine translation: Parameter estimation. *Computational Linguistics*, 19(2):263–311.

Eugene Charniak and Mark Johnson. 2005. Coarse-to-fine n-best parsing and maxent discriminative reranking. In *ACL*.

Michael Collins. 2002. Discriminative training methods for Hidden Markov Models: Theory and experiments with perceptron algorithms. In *Proceedings of the 2002 Conference on Empirical Methods in Natural Language Processing*.

A. P. Dempster, N. M. Laird, and D. B. Rubin. 1977. Maximum likelihood from incomplete data via the *EM* algorithm. *Journal of the Royal Statistical Society*, 39(1):1–21.

Chris Dyer, Jonathan Clark, Alon Lavie, and Noah A Smith. 2011. Unsupervised word alignment with arbitrary features. In *Proceedings of the 49th Annual Meeting of the Association for Computational Linguistics: Human Language Technologies-Volume 1*, pages 409–419. Association for Computational Linguistics.

Rohit J Kate and Raymond J Mooney. 2007. Learning language semantics from ambiguous supervision. In *AAAI*, volume 7, pages 895–900.

M Kipp. 2012. Anvil: A universal video research tool. *Handbook of Corpus Phonology. Oxford University Press*.

Thomas Kollar, Stefanie Tellex, Deb Roy, and Nicholas Roy. 2010. Toward understanding natural language directions. In *Human-Robot Interaction (HRI), 2010 5th ACM/IEEE International Conference on*, pages 259–266. IEEE.

Niveda Krishnamoorthy, Girish Malkarnenkar, Raymond Mooney, Kate Saenko, and Sergio Guadarrama. 2013. Generating natural-language video descriptions using text-mined knowledge. In *Proceedings of the National Conference on Artificial Intelligence (AAAI-13)*, volume 2013, page 3.

Jayant Krishnamurthy and Thomas Kollar. 2013. Jointly learning to parse and perceive: Connecting natural language to the physical world. *Transactions of the Assoc. for Comp. Ling.*, 10:193–206.

Percy Liang, Alexandre Bouchard-Côté, Dan Klein, and Ben Taskar. 2006. An end-to-end discriminative approach to machine translation. In *Proceedings of the 21st International Conference on Computational Linguistics and 44th Annual Meeting of the Association for Computational Linguistics*, pages 761–768, Sydney, Australia, July.

Jiebo Luo and Cheng-en Guo. 2003. Perceptual grouping of segmented regions in color images. *Pattern Recognition*, 36(12):2781 – 2792.

Cynthia Matuszek, Nicholas Fitzgerald, Luke Zettlemoyer, Liefeng Bo, and Dieter Fox. 2012. A joint model of language and perception for grounded attribute learning. In *Proceedings of the 29th International Conference on Machine Learning (ICML-2012)*, pages 1671–1678.

Iftekhar Naim, Young Song, Qiguang Liu, Henry Kautz, Jiebo Luo, and Daniel Gildea. 2014. Unsupervised alignment of natural language instructions with video segments. In *Proceedings of Twenty-Eighth AAAI Conference on Artificial Intelligence*.

Lawrence R. Rabiner. 1989. A tutorial on Hidden Markov Models and selected applications in speech recognition. *Proceedings of the IEEE*, 77(2):257–286.

Nathan Ratliff, J. Andrew (Drew) Bagnell, and Martin Zinkevich. 2007. (Online) subgradient methods for structured prediction. In *Eleventh International Conference on Artificial Intelligence and Statistics (AIStats)*, March.

M. Rohrbach, Wei Qiu, I. Titov, S. Thater, M. Pinkal, and B. Schiele. 2013. Translating video content to natural language descriptions. In *14th IEEE International Conference on Computer Vision (ICCV)*, pages 433–440, Dec.

X. Sun, T. Matsuzaki, D. Okanohara, and J. Tsujii. 2009. Latent variable perceptron algorithm for structured classification. In *Proceedings of the 21st International Joint Conference on Artificial Intelligence (IJCAI 2009)*, pages 1236–1242.

Ben Taskar, Simon Lacoste-Julien, and Dan Klein. 2005. A discriminative matching approach to word alignment. In *Proceedings of the Conference on Human Language Technology and Empirical Methods in Natural Language Processing*, HLT '05, pages 73–80, Stroudsburg, PA, USA. Association for Computational Linguistics.

Stefanie Tellex, Pratiksha Thaker, Joshua Joseph, and Nicholas Roy. 2013. Learning perceptually grounded word meanings from unaligned parallel data. *Machine Learning*, pages 1–17.

SVN Vishwanathan, Nicol N Schraudolph, Mark W Schmidt, and Kevin P Murphy. 2006. Accelerated training of conditional random fields with stochastic gradient methods. In *Proceedings of the 23rd international conference on Machine learning*, pages 969–976. ACM.

Stephan Vogel, Hermann Ney, and Christoph Tillmann. 1996. HMM-based word alignment in statistical translation. In *COLING-96*, pages 836–841, Copenhagen, Denmark.

Chen Yu and Dana H Ballard. 2004. On the integration of grounding language and learning objects. In *AAAI*, volume 4, pages 488–493.

Haonan Yu and Jeffrey Mark Siskind. 2013. Grounded language learning from video described with sentences. In *Proceedings of the 51st Annual Meeting of the Association for Computational Linguistics (ACL-13)*, volume 1, pages 53–63.

Heng Yu, Liang Huang, Haitao Mi, and Kai Zhao. 2013. Max-violation perceptron and forced decoding for scalable MT training. In *Conference on Empirical Methods in Natural Language Processing (EMNLP-13)*.

# TopicCheck: Interactive Alignment for Assessing Topic Model Stability

**Jason Chuang*** jason@chuang.ca

**Margaret E. Roberts†** Political Science, U. California, San Diego, meroberts@ucsd.edu

**Brandon M. Stewart†** Government, Harvard University, bstewart@fas.harvard.edu

**Rebecca Weiss†** Communication, Stanford University, rjweiss@stanford.edu

**Dustin Tingley** Government, Harvard University, dtingley@gov.harvard.edu

**Justin Grimmer** Political Science, Stanford University, jgrimmer@stanford.edu

**Jeffrey Heer** Computer Science & Eng., University of Washington, jheer@uw.edu

## Abstract

Content analysis, a widely-applied social science research method, is increasingly being supplemented by topic modeling. However, while the discourse on content analysis centers heavily on reproducibility, computer scientists often focus more on scalability and less on coding reliability, leading to growing skepticism on the usefulness of topic models for automated content analysis. In response, we introduce TopicCheck, an interactive tool for assessing topic model stability. Our contributions are threefold. First, from established guidelines on reproducible content analysis, we distill a set of design requirements on how to computationally assess the stability of an automated coding process. Second, we devise an interactive alignment algorithm for matching latent topics from multiple models, and enable sensitivity evaluation across a large number of models. Finally, we demonstrate that our tool enables social scientists to gain novel insights into three active research questions.

## 1 Introduction

Content analysis — the examination and systematic categorization of written texts (Berelson, 1952) — is a fundamental and widely-applied research method in the social sciences and humanities (Krippendorff, 2004a), found in one third of all articles published in major communication journals (Wimmer and Dominick, 2010). Initial reading and coding, two labor-intensive steps in the analysis process, are increasingly replaced by computational approaches such as statistical topic modeling (Grimmer, 2013; McFarland et al., 2013; Roberts et al., 2014a).

However, while the discourse on content analysis overwhelmingly centers around the reproducibility and generalizability of a coding scheme (Krippendorff, 2004b; Lombard et al., 2002), computer scientists tend to focus more on increasing the scale of analysis and less on establishing coding reliability. Machine-generated latent topics are often taken on faith to be a truthful and consistent representation of the underlying corpus, but in practice exhibit significant variations among models or modeling runs. These unquantified uncertainties fuel growing skepticism (Schmidt, 2012) and hamper the continued adoption (Grimmer and Stewart, 2011) of topic models for automated content analysis.

In response, we introduce TopicCheck, an interactive tool for assessing the stability of topic models. Our threefold contributions are as follows.

First, from established guidelines on reproducible content analysis, we distill a set of design requirements on how to computationally assess the stability of an automated coding process. We advocate for the use of multiple models for analysis, a user-driven approach to identify acceptable levels of coding uncertainty, and providing users with the capability to inspect model output at all levels of detail.

Second, we devise an interactive *up-to-one* alignment algorithm for assessing topic model stability. Through repeated applications of a topic model to generate multiple outputs, our tool allows users to inspect whether the model consistently uncover the

*Work completed while at Stanford University and the University of Washington, and submitted while at the Allen Institute for Artificial Intelligence.

†These authors contributed equally to this paper.



*Human Language Technologies: The 2015 Annual Conference of the North American Chapter of the ACL*, pages 175–184,
Denver, Colorado, May 31 – June 5, 2015. 

same set of concepts. We allow users to interactively define groupings of matching topics, and present the aligned topics using an informative tabular layout, so that users can quickly identify stable topical groupings as well as any inconsistencies.

Finally, in three case studies, we demonstrate that our tool allows social scientists to gain novel insights into active and ongoing research questions. We provide an in-depth look at the multi-modality of topic models. We document how text pre-processing alters topical compositions, causing shifts in definitions and the removal of select topics. We report on how TopicCheck supports the validity of newly-proposed communication research methods.

## 2 Background

Manual approaches to extract information from textual data — reading the source documents and codifying notable concepts — do not scale. For example, Pew Research Center produces the News Coverage Index (2014) to measure the quality of news reporting in the United States. Intended to track 1,450 newspapers nationwide, their purely manual efforts only cover 20 stories per day. Researchers stand to lose rich details in their data when their attention is limited to a minuscule fraction of the available texts.

Critical of approaches that "*[make] restrictive assumptions or [are] prohibitively costly*," Quinn et al. (2010) discuss the use of topic models (Blei et al., 2003) to enable large-scale text analysis by using machine-generated latent topics to approximate previously manually-crafted codes. Automated content analysis has enabled groundbreaking massive studies (Grimmer, 2013; McFarland et al., 2013; Roberts et al., 2014a). While this initial uptake of topic models is encouraging, an over-emphasis on scalability and the use of a single model for analysis invites skepticism and threatens continued adoption.

### 2.1 Coding Reliability & Growing Skepticism

Coding reliability is critical to content analysis. When social scientists devise a coding scheme, they must clearly articulate the definition of their codes in such a way that any person can consistently apply the given codes to all documents in a corpus.

Despite high labor cost, content analysis is typically conducted with multiple coders in order to establish coding reliability; the proper application of reliability measures is heavily discussed and debated in the literature (Krippendorff, 2004b; Lombard et al., 2002). In contrast, software packages (McCallum, 2013; Řehůřek and Sojka, 2010) and graphical tools (Chaney and Blei, 2014; Chuang et al., 2012b) have made topic models accessible, cheap to compute, easy to deploy, but they almost always present users with a single model without any measure of uncertainty; we find few studies on topic model sensitivity and no existing tool to support such analyses.

Schmidt (2012) summarizes the view among digital humanists, a group of early adopters of topic models, on the experience of working with uncertain modeling results: "*A poorly supervised machine learning algorithm is like a bad research assistant. It might produce some unexpected constellations that show flickers of deeper truths; but it will also produce tedious, inexplicable, or misleading results. ... [Excitement] about the use of topic models for discovery needs to be tempered with skepticism about how often the unexpected juxtapositions... will be helpful, and how often merely surprising.*"

Researchers increasingly voice skepticism about the validity of using single models for analysis. In a comprehensive survey of automatic content analysis methods, Grimmer et al. (2011) highlight the need to validate models through close reading and model comparison, and advise against the use of software that "*simply provide the researcher with output*" with no capability to ensure the output is conceptually valid and useful. Chuang et al. (2012a) report that findings from one-off modeling efforts may not sustain under scrutiny. Schmidt (2012) argues that computer-aided text analysis should incorporate competing models or "*humanists are better off applying zero computer programs.*"

### 2.2 Uncertainties in Topic Models

While topic models remove some issues associated with human coding, they also introduce new sources of uncertainties. We review three factors related to our case studies: multi-modality, text preprocessing, and human judgment of topical quality.

Roberts et al. (2014b) examine the multi-modal distributions of topic models that arise due to the non-convex nature of the underlying optimization. They characterize the various local solutions, and demonstrate that the spread of topics can lead to contradictory analysis outcomes. The authors note that optimal coding may not necessarily correspond to models that yield the highest value of the objective function, but there is currently a paucity of computational tools to inspect how the various modes differ, help researchers justify why one local mode might be preferred over another on the basis of their domain knowledge, or for an independent researcher to validate another's modeling choices.

Fokkens et al. (2013) report widespread reproducibility failures in natural language processing when they replicate — and fail to reproduce — the results reported on two standard experiments. The authors find that minor decisions in the modeling process can impact evaluation results, including two factors highly relevant to topic modeling: differences in text pre-processing and corpus vocabulary.

The word intrusion test (Chang et al., 2009; Lau et al., 2014) is considered the current state-of-the-art approach to assess topical quality, and captures human judgment more accurately than other topical coherence measures (Stevens et al., 2012; Wallach et al., 2009). However, in this approach, users inspect only a single latent topic at a time without access to the overall set of topics. As a part of this paper, we investigate whether exposure to multiple competing models affects human judgment, and whether model consistency impacts topical coherence.

### 2.3 Reproducibility of a Coding Process

While no single definition exists for the process of content analysis, a frequently-cited and wide-applied template is provided by Krippendorff (1989; 2004b) who recommends four steps to safeguard the reproducibility of a coding process. Practitioners must demonstrate *coder reliability*, *a decisive agreement coefficient*, *an acceptable level of agreement*, and test *individual variables*.

To the best of our knowledge, our paper is the first to convert guidelines on reproducible human coding into software design requirements on validating automated content analysis. Our interactive alignment algorithm is the first implementation of these guidelines. Our case studies represent the first reports on the impact of computationally quantifying topic model uncertainties, situated within the context of real-world ongoing social science research.

Much of the research on topic modeling focuses on model designs (Blei et al., 2004; Blei and Lafferty, 2006; Rosen-Zvi et al., 2004) or inference algorithms (Anandkumar et al., 2012). Our tool is complementary to this large body of work, and supports real-world deployment of these techniques. Interactive topic modeling (Hu et al., 2014) can play a key role to help users not only verify model consistency but actively curate high-quality codes; its inclusion is beyond the scope of a single conference paper. While supervised learning (Settles, 2011) has been applied to content analysis, it represents the application of a pre-defined coding scheme to a text corpus, which is different from the task of devising a coding scheme and assessing its reliability.

## 3 Validation Tool Design Requirements

A measure of coding reproducibility is whether a topic model can consistently uncover the same set of latent topics. We assume that users have a large number of topic model outputs, presumed to be identical, and that the users wish to examine unexpected variations among the outputs. To guide tool development, we first identify software design requirements, to meet the standards social scientists need to demonstrate producible coding.

### 3.1 Topical Mapping & Up-to-One Alignment

A key difference exists between measuring inter-coder agreement and assessing topic model variations. In a manual coding process, human coders are provided code identifiers; responses from different coders can be unambiguously mapped onto a common scheme. No such mapping exists among the output from repeated runs of a topic model. Validation tools must provide users with **effective means to generate topical mapping**.

However, the general alignment problem of optimally mapping *multiple* topics from one model to *multiple* topics in another model is both ill-defined and computationally intractable. Since our tool is to support the comparison of similar — and supposedly identical — model output, we impose the following constraint. A latent topic belonging to a model may align with *up to one* latent topic in another model. We avoid the more restrictive constraint of *one-to-one* alignment. Forcing a topic to always map onto another topic may cause highly dissimilar topics to be grouped together, obscuring critical mismatches. Instead, up-to-one mapping allows for two potential outcomes, both of which correspond directly to the intended user task: recognize consistent patterns across the models (when alignment occurs) and identify any deviations (when alignment fails).

### 3.2 Guidelines Adapted for Topic Models

We synthesize the following four requirements from Krippendorff's guidelines (2004b).

To calculate the equivalent of *coder reliability*, we advocate the **use of multiple models to determine modeling consistency**, which may be determined from the repeated applications of the same topic model, a search through the parameter space of a model, or the use of multiple models.

Selecting an appropriate *agreement coefficient* depends on the underlying data type, such as binary, multivariate, ordered, or continuous codes (Cohen, 1960; Holsti, 1969; Krippendorff, 1970; Osgood, 1959; Scott, 1995). No widely-accepted similarity measure exists for aligning latent topics, which are probability distributions over a large vocabulary. We argue that validation tools must be sufficiently modular, in order to **accept any user-defined topical similarity measure** for aligning latent topics.

*Acceptable level of agreement* depends on the purpose of the analysis, and should account for the costs of drawing incorrect conclusions from a coding scheme. For example, do "*human lives hang on the results of a content analysis?*" (Krippendorff, 2004b). Validation tools must **allow users to set the appropriate acceptable level of agreement**, and help users determine — rather than dictate — when topic models match and what constitutes reasonable variations in the model output.

Finally, Krippendorff points out that aggregated statistics can obscure critical reliability failures, and practitioners must test *individual variables*. We interpret this recommendation as the need to **present users with not a single overall alignment score but details at all levels**: models, topics, and constituent words within each latent topic.

## 4 Interactive Topical Alignment

We introduce TopicCheck, an implementation of our design specifications. At the core of this tool is an interactive topical alignment algorithm.

### 4.1 Hierarchical Clustering with Constraints

Our algorithm can be considered as hierarchical agglomerative clustering with up-to-one mapping constraints. As input, it takes in three arguments: a list of topic models, a topical similarity measure, and a matching criterion. As output, it generates a list of topical groups, where each group contains a list of topics with at most one topic from each model.

At initialization, we create a topical group for every topic in every model. We then iteratively merge the two most similar groups based on the user-supplied topical similarity measure, provided that the groups satisfy the user-specified matching criterion and the mapping constraints. When no new groups can be formed, the algorithm terminates and returns a sorted list of final topical groups.

During the alignment process, the following two invariants are guaranteed: Every topic is always assigned to exactly one group; every group contains at most one topic from each model. A topic model $m$ consists of a list of latent topics. A latent topic $t$ is represented by a probability distribution over words. A topical group $g$ also consists of a list of latent topics. Let $|m|$, $|t|$, and $|g|$ denote the number of models, topics, and groups respectively. We create a total of $|g| = |m| \times |t|$ initial topical groups. Although $|g|$ decreases by 1 after each merge, $|g| \geq |t|$ at all times. At the end of alignment, $|g| = |t|$ if and only if perfect alignment occurs and every group contains exactly one topic from each model.

Users may supply any topical similarity measure that best suits their analysis needs. We select cosine similarity for our three case studies, though our software is modular and accepts any input. As a first implementation, we apply single-linkage clustering criteria when comparing the similarity of two topical groups. Single-linkage clustering is computationally efficient (Sibson, 1973), so that users may interact with the algorithm and receive feedback in real-time; our procedure generalizes to other linkage criteria such as complete-linkage or average-linkage.

At each merge step, the most similar pair of topical groups are identified. If they meet the matching criteria and the mapping constraints, the pair is combined into a new group. Otherwise, the algorithm iteratively examines the next most similar pair until either a merge occurs or when all pairs are ex-

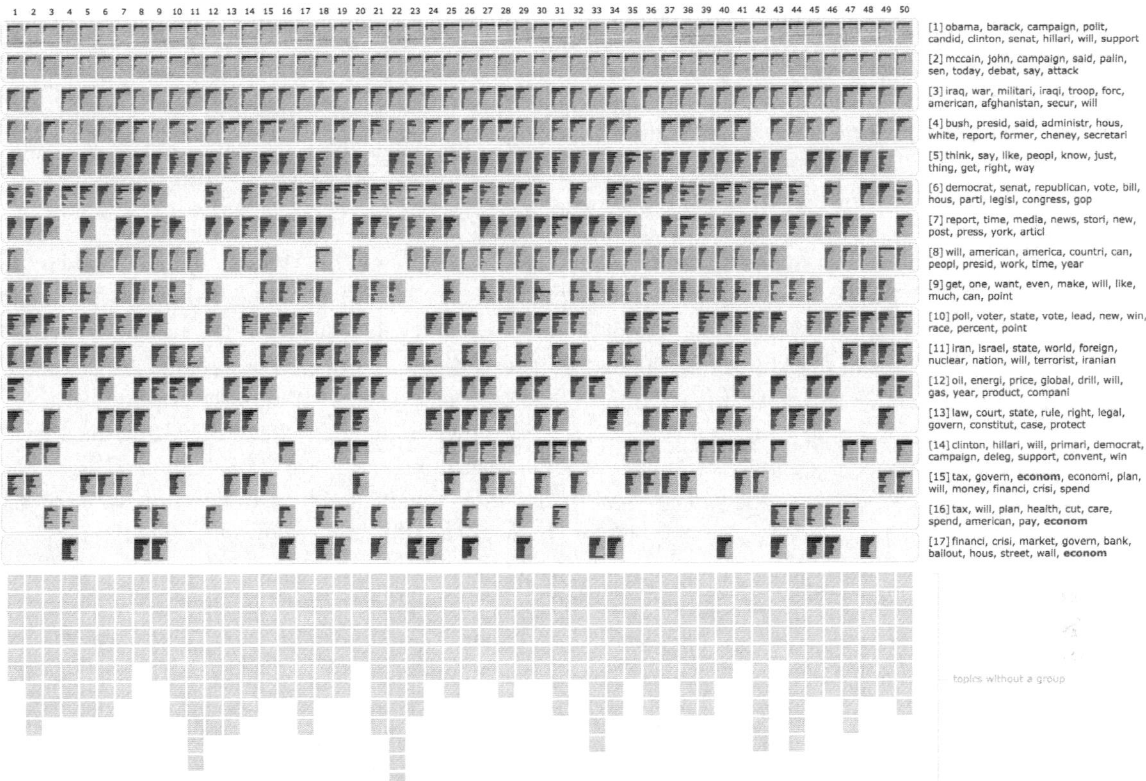


Figure 1: This chart shows topics uncovered from 13,250 political blogs (Eisenstein and Xing, 2010) by 50 structural topic models (Roberts et al., 2013). Latent topics are represented as rectangles; bar charts within the rectangles represent top terms in a topic. Topics belonging to the same model are arranged in a column; topics assigned to the same group are arranged in a row. This chart is completely filled with topics only if perfect alignment occurs. When topics in a model fail to align with topics in other models, empty cells appear in its column. Similarly, when topics in a group are not consistently uncovered by all models, empty cells appear in its row. Hovering over a term highlights all other occurrences of the same term. Top terms belonging to each topical group are shown on the right; they represent the most frequent words over all topics in the group, by summing their probability distributions.

Figure 2: Continued from Figure 1, users may decrease the similarity threshold to generate additional groupings of topics that are less consistent, uncovered by as few as 3 of the 50 modeling runs.

hausted, at which point the procedure terminates.

Users can specify a similarity threshold, below which topical groups are considered to differ too much to be matched. Two groups are allowed to merge only if both of the following conditions are met: their similarity is above the user-defined similarity threshold *and* every topic in the combined group belongs to a different model.

### 4.2 Tabular Layout and User Interactions

We devise a tabular layout to present the alignment output at all levels of detail: groups, models, topics, and words. Users can interact with the algorithm, redefine matching criteria, and inspect the aligned models interactively in real-time.

We arrange topical groups as rows and topic models as columns as shown in Figure 1. A topic assigned to group $g_i$ and belonging to model $m_j$ is placed at the intersection of row $i$ and column $j$. Our up-to-one mapping ensures at most one topic per each cell. A table of size $|g| \times |m|$ will only be completely filled with topics if perfect alignment occurs. When topics in model $m_j$ fail to align with topics in other models, empty cells appear in column $j$. Similarly, when topics in group $g_i$ are not consistently uncovered by all models, empty cells appear in row $i$. Within each topic, we show the probability distribution of its constituent words as a bar chart.

Users define three parameters in our tool. First, they may set the matching criteria, and define how aggressively the topics are merged into groups. Second, users may alter the number of topical groups to reveal. Rather than displaying numerous sparse groups, the tool shows only the top groups as determined by their topical weight. Topics in all remaining groups are placed at the bottom of the table and marked as *ungrouped*. Third, users may adjust the number of top terms to show, as a trade-off between details vs. overview. Increasing the number of terms allows users to inspect the topics more carefully, but the cells take up more screen space, reducing the number of visible groups. Decreasing the number of terms reduces the size of each cell, allowing users to see more groups and observe high-level patterns.

The tabular layout enables rapid visual assessment of consistency within a model or a group. We further facilitate comparisons via brushing and linking (Becker and Cleveland, 1987). When users hover over a word on the right hand side or over a bar within the bar charts, we highlight all other occurrences of the same word. For example, in Figure 1, hovering over the term *econom* reveals that the word is common in three topical groups.

## 5 Deployment and Initial Findings

We implemented our alignment algorithm and user interface in JavaScript, so they are easily accessible within a web browser; topical similarity is computed on a Python-backed web server. We report user responses and initial findings from deploying the tool on three social science research projects. Interactive versions of the projects are available at `http://content-analysis.info/naacl`.

### 5.1 A Look at Multi-Modal Solutions

We deployed TopicCheck on topic models generated by Roberts et al. (2014b) to examine how model output clusters into local modes. As the models are produced by 50 runs of an identical algorithm with all pre-processing, parameters, and hyper-parameters held constant, we expect minimal variations.

As shown in Figure 1, we observe that the top two topical groups, about Barack Obama and John McCain respectively, are consistently uncovered across all runs. The third topical group, about the Iraqi and Afghani wars (defined by a broader set of terms) is also consistently generated by 49 of the 50 runs.

Toward the bottom of the chart, we observe signs of multi-modality. Topical groups #15 to #17 represent variations of topics about the economy. Whereas group #15 is about the broader economy, groups #16 and #17 focus on taxes and the financial crisis, respectively. Half of the runs produced the broader economy topic; the other runs generated only one or two of the specialized subtopics. No single model uncovered all three, suggesting that the inference algorithm converged to one of two distinct local optimal solutions. In Figure 2, by lowering the matching criteria and revealing additional groups, we find that the model continues to produce interesting topics such as those related to global warming (group #24) or women's rights (group #25), but these topics are not stable across the multiple modes.

### 5.2 Text Pre-Processing & Replication Issues

We conducted an experiment to investigate the effects of rare word removal using TopicCheck. As a part of our research, we had collected 12,000 news reports from five different international news sources over a period of ten years, to study systematic differences in news coverage on the rise of China, between western and Chinese media.

While many modeling decisions are involved in our analysis, we choose rare word removal for two reasons. First, though the practice is standard, to the best of our knowledge, we find no systematic studies on how aggressively one should cull the vocabulary.

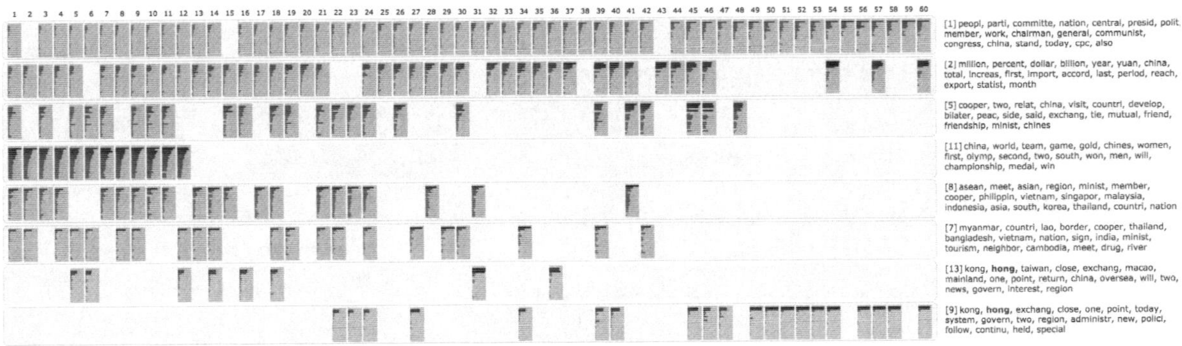


Figure 3: While rare word removal is generally considered to have limited impact on topic model output, we find evidence to the contrary. By varying the removal threshold, for this corpus of international news reports on the rise of China, we observe that topics such as group #11 on the Beijing Olympics begin to disappear. Topics about Hong Kong appear sporadically. On top of the inconsistency issues, different pre-processing settings lead to drifts in topic definitions. For milder removal thresholds (toward the left), group #13 discusses Hong Kong within the context of Taiwan and Macau. With more aggressive filtering (toward the right), group #14 shifts into discussions about Hong Kong itself such as *one country two systems* and the *special administrative region*. Unchecked, these seemingly minor text pre-processing decisions may eventually lead researchers down different paths of analysis.

Second, as latent topics are typically defined through their top words, filtering words that occur only in a small fraction of the documents is generally considered to have limited impact on model output.

We trained structural topic models (Roberts et al., 2013) based on a subset of the corpus with 2,398 documents containing approximately 20,000 unique words. We applied 10 different settings where we progressively removed a greater number of rare terms beyond those already filtered by the default settings while holding all other parameters constant. The number of unique words retained by the models were 1,481 (default), 904, 634, 474, 365, . . ., down to 124 for the 10 settings. We generated 6 runs of the model at each setting, for a total of 60 runs. Removed words are assigned a value of 0 in the topic vector when computing cosine similarity.

We observe significant changes to the model output across the pre-processing settings, as shown in Figure 3. The six models on the far left (columns 1 to 6) represent standard processing; rare word removal ranges from the mildest (columns 7 to 12) to the most aggressive (columns 55 to 60) as the columns move from left to right across the chart.

While some topical groups (e.g., #1 on the communist party) are stable across all settings, many others fade in and out. Group #11 on the Beijing Olympics is consistent under standard processing and the mildest removal, but disappears completely afterward. We find two topical groups about Hong Kong that appear sporadically. On top of the instability issues, we observe that their content drifts across the settings. With milder thresholds, topical group #13 discusses Hong Kong within the context of Taiwan and Macau. With more aggressive filtering, topical group #14 shifts into discussions about Hong Kong itself such as *one country two systems* and the *special administrative region*. Unchecked, these minor text pre-processing decisions may lead researchers down different paths of analysis.

### 5.3 News Coverage & Topical Coherence

Agenda-setting refers to observations by McCombs et al. (1972) that the media play an important role in dictating issues of importance for voters, and by Iyengar et al. (1993) that news selection bias can determine how the public votes. Studying agenda-setting requires assessing the amount of coverage paid to specific issues. Previous manual coding efforts are typically limited to either a single event or subsampled so thinly that they lose the ability to consistently track events over time. Large-scale analysis (e.g., for an entire federal election) remains beyond the reach of most communication scholars.

As part of our research, we apply topic modeling to closed-captioning data from over 200,000 hours of broadcasts on all mainstream news networks, to track the full spectrum of topics across all media out-

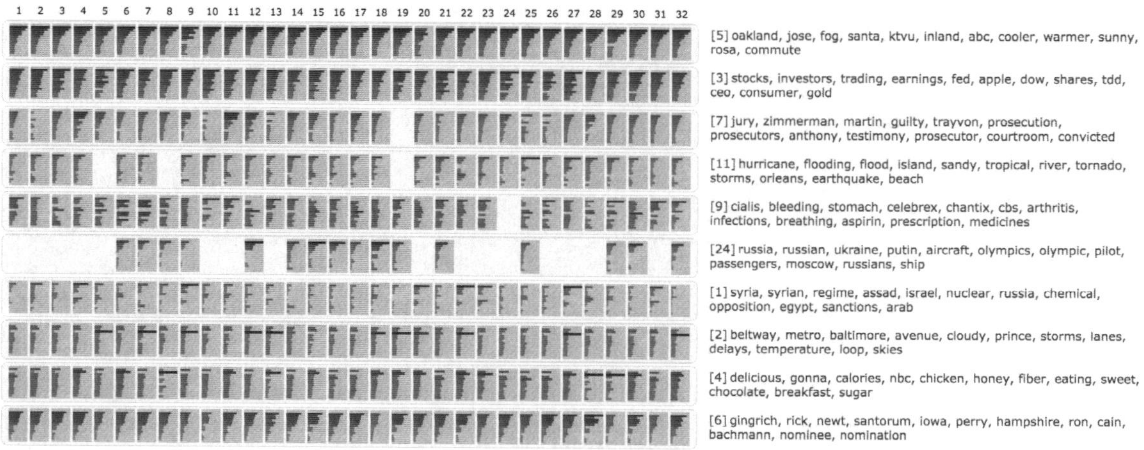


Figure 4: To enable large-scale studies of agenda-setting, we applied topic modeling to closed-captioning of over 200,000 hours of broadcasts, to estimate coverage in mainstream news networks. Through TopicCheck, the researchers find consistent topical groups that correspond to known major news categories. Group #9 represents topics about advertisements and valuable data to study the relationships between broadcasters and advertisers.

lets. We conduct word intrusion tests (Chang et al., 2009) on Amazon Mechanical Turk, and obtain over 50,000 user ratings to identify high quality topics. However, to establish topic modeling as a valid research method, we must demonstrate the reliability of how we include or exclude topics in our analyses.

By applying TopicCheck to 32 runs of the same topic model, as shown in Figure 4, we confirm that the consistent topical groupings capture at least four major known news categories: weather (such as group #5), finance (group #3), major events (group #7 on the Trayvon Martin shooting), and natural disasters (group #11 on Hurricane Katrina). We find additional evidence supporting the use of topic models, including the consistent appearance of advertising topics (group #9 on the sales of prescription medicine to senior citizens, a major demographic of the broadcast news audience). These topics may enable studies on the relationship between broadcasters and advertisers, an important but difficult question to address because few previous studies have the resources to codify advertisement content.

However, event-specific topics tend to appear less consistently (such as group #24 on Russia, its conflict with Ukraine, and the Sochi Olympics). We note the lack of consistent topics on supreme court cases, an expected but missing news category, which warrants more in-depth investigations.

We compare human judgment of topical quality when examining multiple models and those based on word intrusion tests. We calculate the aggregated topical coherence scores for each topical grouping. We find that consistent topical groups tend to receive higher coherence scores. However, topics about natural disasters receive low scores with a high variance (avg 0.5371; stdev 0.2497); many of them would have previously been excluded from analysis.

## 6 Discussions

To many social scientists, statistical models are measurement tools for inspecting social phenomena, such as probing recurring language use in a text corpus with topic models. In this light, instruments with known performance characteristics — including well-quantified uncertainties and proper coverage — are more valuable than potentially powerful but inconsistent modeling approaches.

Our initial findings suggest that a single topic model may not capture all perspectives on a dataset, as evident in the multiple local solutions about the economy, Hong Kong, and natural disasters in the three case studies respectively. By exposing model stability, our tool can help researchers validate modeling decisions, and caution against making too general a claim about any single modeling result.

We hypothesize that the low coherence scores for topics about natural disasters might derive from two causes. First, news media might cover an event differently (e.g., focusing on economic vs. humanitarian issues during Hurricane Katrina). Second, unfolding events may naturally have less stable vocabularies. In both cases, detecting and pinpointing reporting bias is central to the study of agenda-setting. These observations suggest that for certain applications, identifying consistent topics across multiple models may be equally critical as, if not more than, enforcing topical coherence within a single model.

Increasingly, text analysis relies on data-dependent modeling decisions. Rare word removal can substantively alter analysis outcomes, but selecting an appropriate threshold requires inspecting the content of a text corpus. TopicCheck can help archive the exact context of analysis, allowing researchers to justify — and readers to verify and challenge — modeling decisions through access to data.

Finally, topic modeling has dramatically lowered the costs associated with content analysis, allowing hundreds of models to be built in parallel. The current intended user task for TopicCheck is to validate the stability of presumably identical models. We plan to develop additional tools to help social scientists design better models, and actively explore the effects of alternative coding schemes.

## 7 Conclusion

We present TopicCheck for assessing topic model stability. Through its development, we demonstrate that existing research on reproducible manual codification can be transferred and applied to computational approaches such as automated content analysis via topic modeling. We hope this work will help computer scientists and social scientists engage in deeper conversations about research reproducibility for large-scale computer-assisted text analysis.

## Acknowledgments

This research was supported in part by a grant from the Brown Institute for Media Innovation.

## References

Anima Anandkumar, Yi kai Liu, Daniel J. Hsu, Dean P Foster, and Sham M Kakade. 2012. A spectral algorithm for latent dirichlet allocation. In *Neural Information Processing Systems (NIPS)*, pages 917–925.

Richard A. Becker and William S. Cleveland. 1987. Brushing scatterplots. *Technometrics*, 29(2):127–142.

Bernard Berelson. 1952. *Content analysis in communication research*. Free Press.

David M. Blei and John D. Lafferty. 2006. Dynamic topic models. In *International Conference on Machine Learning (ICML)*, pages 113–120.

David M. Blei, Andrew Y. Ng, and Michael I. Jordan. 2003. Latent Dirichlet allocation. *Journal of Machine Learning Research*, 3(1):993–1022.

David M. Blei, Thomas L. Griffiths, Michael I. Jordan, and Joshua B. Tenenbaum. 2004. Hierarchical topic models and the nested chinese restaurant process. In *Neural Information Processing Systems (NIPS)*.

Allison June-Barlow Chaney and David M. Blei. 2014. Visualizing topic models. In *International Conference on Weblogs and Social Media (ICWSM)*, pages 419–422.

Jonathan Chang, Jordan Boyd-Graber, Chong Wang, Sean Gerrish, and David M. Blei. 2009. Reading tea leaves: How humans interpret topic models. In *Neural Information Processing Systems (NIPS)*, pages 288–296.

Jason Chuang, Christopher D. Manning, and Jeffrey Heer. 2012a. Interpretation and trust: Designing model-driven visualizations for text analysis. In *Conference on Human Factors in Computing Systems (CHI)*, pages 443–452.

Jason Chuang, Christopher D. Manning, and Jeffrey Heer. 2012b. Termite: Visualization techniques for assessing textual topic models. In *Advanced Visual Interfaces (AVI)*.

Jacob Cohen. 1960. A coefficient of agreement for nominal scales. *Educational and Psychological Measurement*, 20:37–46.

Jacob Eisenstein and Eric Xing. 2010. *The CMU 2008 Political Blog Corpus*. Carnegie Mellon University.

Antske Fokkens, Marieke van Erp, Marten Postma, Ted Pedersen, Piek Vossen, and Nuno Freire. 2013. Offspring from reproduction problems: What replication failure teaches us. In *Annual Meeting of the Association for Computational Linguistics (ACL)*, pages 1691–1701.

Justin Grimmer and Brandon M. Stewart. 2011. Text as data: The promise and pitfalls of automatic content analysis methods for political texts. *Political Analysis*, 21(3):267–297.

Justin Grimmer. 2013. Appropriators not position takers: The distorting effects of electoral incentives on congressional representation. *American Journal of Political Science*, 57(3):624–642.

Ole R. Holsti. 1969. *Content analysis for the social sciences and humanities*. Addison-Wesley Publishing Company.

Yuening Hu, Jordan Boyd-Graber, Brianna Satinoff, and Alison Smith. 2014. Interactive topic modeling. *Machine Learning*, 95(3):423–469.

Shanto Iyengar and Adam Simon. 1993. News coverage of the gulf crisis and public opinion: A study of agenda-setting, priming, and framing. *Communication Research*, 20(3):365–383.

Klaus Krippendorff. 1970. Bivariate agreement coefficients for reliability of data. In E. R. Borgatta and G. W. Bohrnstedt, editors, *Sociological methodology*, pages 139–150. John Wiley & Sons.

Klaus Krippendorff. 1989. Content analysis. In E. Barnouw, G. Gerbner, W. Schramm, T. L. Worth, and L. Gross, editors, *International encyclopedia of communication*. Oxford University Press.

Klaus Krippendorff. 2004a. *Content analysis: An introduction to its methodology*. Sage, 2nd edition.

Klaus Krippendorff. 2004b. Reliability in content analysis: Some common misconceptions and recommendations. *Human Communication Research*, 30(3):411–433.

Jey Han Lau, David Newman, and Timothy Baldwin. 2014. Machine reading tea leaves: Automatically evaluating topic coherence and topic model quality. In *Conference of the European Chapter of the Association for Computational Linguistics (EACL)*, pages 530–539.

Matthew Lombard, Jennifer Snyder-Duch, and Cheryl Campanella Bracken. 2002. Content analysis in mass communication: Assessment and reporting of intercoder reliability. *Human Communication Research*, 28(4):587–604.

Andrew McCallum. 2013. MALLET: A machine learning for language toolkit. `http://mallet.cs.umass.edu`.

Maxwell E. McCombs and Donald L. Shaw. 1972. The agenda-setting function of mass media. *Public Opinion Quarterly*, 36(5):176–187.

Daniel A. McFarland, Daniel Ramage, Jason Chuang, Jeffrey Heer, and Christopher D. Manning. 2013. Differentiating language usage through topic models. *Poetics: Special Issue on Topic Models and the Cultural Sciences*, 41(6):607–625.

C. E. Osgood. 1959. The representational model and relevant research. In I. de Sola Pool, editor, *Trends in content analysis*, pages 33–88. University of Illinois Press.

Ted Pedersen. 2008. Empiricism is not a matter of faith. *Computational Linguistics*, 34(3):465–470.

Pew Research Journalism Project. 2014. News coverage index methodology. `http://www.journalism.org/news_index_methodology/99/`.

Kevin M. Quinn, Burt L. Monroe, Michael Colaresi, Michael H. Crespin, and Dragomir R. Radev. 2010. How to analyze political attention with minimal assumptions and costs. *American Journal of Political Science*, 54(1):209–228.

Radim Řehůřek and Petr Sojka. 2010. Software framework for topic modelling with large corpora. In *LREC Workshop on New Challenges for NLP Frameworks*, pages 45–50.

Margaret E. Roberts, Brandon M. Stewart, Dustin Tingley, and Edoardo M. Airoldi. 2013. The structural topic model and applied social science. In *NIPS Workshop on Topic Models*.

Margaret E. Roberts, Brandon Stewart, Dustin Tingley, Chris Lucas, Jetson Leder-Luis, Bethany Albertson, Shana Gadarian, and David Rand. 2014a. Topic models for open-ended survey responses with applications to experiments. *American Journal of Political Science*. Forthcoming.

Margaret E. Roberts, Brandon M. Stewart, and Dustin Tingley. 2014b. Navigating the local modes of big data: The case of topic models. In R. Michael Alvarez, editor, *Data Science for Politics, Policy and Government*. In Press.

Michal Rosen-Zvi, Thomas Griffiths, Mark Steyvers, and Padhraic Smyth. 2004. The author-topic model for authors and documents. In *Conference on Uncertainty in Artificial Intelligence (UAI)*, pages 487–494.

Benjamin M. Schmidt. 2012. Words alone: Dismantling topic models in the humanities. *Journal of Digital Humanities*, 2(1).

William A. Scott. 1995. Reliability of content analysis:: The case of nominal scale coding. *Public Opinion Quarterly*, 19(3):321–325.

Burr Settles. 2011. Closing the loop: Fast, interactive semi-supervised annotation with queries on features and instances. In *Empirical Methods in Natural Language Processing (EMNLP)*, pages 1467–1478.

Robin Sibson. 1973. SLINK: an optimally efficient algorithm for the single-link cluster method. *The Computer Journal*, 16:30–34.

Keith Stevens, Philip Kegelmeyer, David Andrzejewski, and David Buttler. 2012. Exploring topic coherence over many models and many topics. In *Conference on Empirical Methods on Natural Language Processing and Computational Natural Language Learning (EMNLP-CoNLL)*, pages 952–961.

Hanna M. Wallach, Iain Murray, Ruslan Salakhutdinov, and David Mimno. 2009. Evaluation methods for topic models. In *International Conference on Machine Learning (ICML)*, pages 1105–1112.

Roger Wimmer and Joseph Dominick. 2010. *Mass Media Research: An Introduction*. Cengage Learning.

# Inferring latent attributes of Twitter users with label regularization

**Ehsan Mohammady Ardehaly** and **Aron Culotta**
Department of Computer Science
Illinois Institute of Technology
Chicago, IL 60616
emohamm1@hawk.iit.edu, aculotta@iit.edu

## Abstract

Inferring latent attributes of online users has many applications in public health, politics, and marketing. Most existing approaches rely on supervised learning algorithms, which require manual data annotation and therefore are costly to develop and adapt over time. In this paper, we propose a lightly supervised approach based on label regularization to infer the age, ethnicity, and political orientation of Twitter users. Our approach learns from a heterogeneous collection of soft constraints derived from Census demographics, trends in baby names, and Twitter accounts that are emblematic of class labels. To counteract the imprecision of such constraints, we compare several constraint selection algorithms that optimize classification accuracy on a tuning set. We find that using no user-annotated data, our approach is within 2% of a fully supervised baseline for three of four tasks. Using a small set of labeled data for tuning further improves accuracy on all tasks.

## 1 Introduction

Data annotation is a key bottleneck in applying supervised machine learning to language processing problems. This is especially problematic in streaming settings such as social media, where models quickly become dated as new linguistic patterns emerge. An attractive alternative is *lightly supervised learning* (Schapire et al., 2002; Jin and Liu, 2005; Chang et al., 2007; Graça et al., 2007; Quadrianto et al., 2009; Mann and McCallum, 2010; Ganchev et al., 2010). In this approach, classifiers are trained from a set of domain-specific *soft* constraints, rather than individually labeled instances. For example, *label regularization* (Mann and McCallum, 2007; Graça et al., 2007) uses prior knowledge of the expected label distribution to fit a model from large pools of unlabeled instances. Similarly, annotating features with their expected class frequency has proven to be an efficient way of bootstrapping from domain knowledge (Druck et al., 2009; Melville et al., 2009; Settles, 2011).

In this paper we use lightly supervised learning to infer the age, ethnicity, and political orientation of Twitter users. Lightly supervised learning provides a natural method for incorporating the rich, declarative constraints available in social media. Our approach pairs unlabeled Twitter data with constraints from county demographics, trends in first names, and exemplar Twitter accounts strongly associated with a class label.

Prior applications of label regularization use a small number of highly-accurate constraints; for example, Mann and McCallum (2007) use a single constraint that is the true label proportions of an unlabeled dataset, and Ganchev and Das (2013) use cross-lingual constraints from aligned text. In contrast, we use hundreds of constraints that are heterogeneous, overlapping, and noisy. For example, we constrain the predicted attributes of users from a county to match those collected by the Census, despite the known non-representativeness of Twitter users (Mislove et al., 2011). Furthermore, users from that county who list first names in their profile have additional constraints imposed upon them, which may conflict with the county constraints.



*Human Language Technologies: The 2015 Annual Conference of the North American Chapter of the ACL*, pages 185–195,
Denver, Colorado, May 31 – June 5, 2015. 

To deal with such noisy constraints, we explore forward selection algorithms that choose from hundreds of soft constraints to optimize accuracy on a tuning set. We find that this approach is competitive with a fully supervised approach, with the added advantage of being less reliant on labeled data and therefore easier to update over time. Our primary research questions and answers are as follows:

**RQ1. What effect do noisy constraints have on label regularization?** We find that simply using all constraints, ignoring noise and overlap, results in surprisingly high accuracy, within 2% of a fully-supervised approach on three of four tasks. For age classification, the constraint noise appears to substantially degrade accuracy.

**RQ2. How can we select the most useful constraints?** Using a small tuning set, we find that our forward selection algorithms improve label regularization accuracy while using fewer than 10% of the available constraints. Constraint selection improves age classification accuracy by nearly 18% (absolute).

**RQ3. Which constraints are most informative?** We find that follower constraints result in the highest accuracy in isolation, yet the constraint types appear to be complementary. For three of four tasks, combining all constraint types leads to the highest accuracy.

In the following, we first review related work in lightly supervised learning and latent attribute inference, then describe the Twitter data and constraints. Next, we formalize the label regularization problem and our constraint selection algorithms. Finally, we present empirical results on four classification tasks and conclude with a discussion of future work.

## 2 Related Work

Inferring demographic attributes of users in social media with supervised learning is a growing area of interest, with applications in public health (Dredze, 2012), politics (O'Connor et al., 2010) and marketing (Gopinath et al., 2014). Attributes considered include age (Nguyen et al., 2011; Al Zamal et al., 2012), ethnicity (Pennacchiotti and Popescu, 2011; Rao et al., 2011), and political orientation (Conover et al., 2011; Barberá, 2013).

The main of drawback supervised learning in social media is that human annotation is expensive and error-prone, and collecting pseudo-labeled data by self-identifying keywords is noisy and biased (e.g., searching for profiles that mention political orientation). For these reasons we investigate lightly-supervised learning, which takes advantage of the plentiful unlabeled data.

Previous work in lightly-supervised learning has developed methods to train classifiers from prior knowledge of label proportions (Jin and Liu, 2005; Chang et al., 2007; Musicant et al., 2007; Mann and McCallum, 2007; Quadrianto et al., 2009; Liang et al., 2009; Ganchev et al., 2010; Mann and McCallum, 2010; Chang et al., 2012; Wang et al., 2012; Zhu et al., 2014) or prior knowledge of features-label associations (Schapire et al., 2002; Haghighi and Klein, 2006; Druck et al., 2008; Melville et al., 2009). In addition to standard document categorization tasks, lightly supervised approaches have been applied to named-entity recognition (Mann and McCallum, 2010; Ganchev and Das, 2013; Wang and Manning, 2014), dependency parsing (Druck et al., 2009; Ganchev et al., 2009), language identification (King and Abney, 2013), and sentiment analysis (Melville et al., 2009).

One similarly-motivated work is that of Chang et al. (2010), who infer race/ethnicity of online users using name and ethnicity distributions provided by the U.S. Census Bureau. This external data is incorporated into the model as a prior; however, no linguistic content is used in the model, limiting the coverage of the resulting approach. Oktay et al. (2014) extend the work of Chang et al. (2010) to also include statistics over first names.

Other work has inferred population-level statistics from social media; e.g., Eisenstein et al. (2011) use geolocated tweets to predict zip-code statistics of demographic attributes of users, and Schwartz et al. (2013) predict county health statistics from Twitter. However, no user-level attributes are predicted.

Patrini et al. (2014) build a Learning with Label Proportions (LLP) model with the objective to learn a supervised classifier when, instead of labels, only label proportions for bags of observations are known. Their empirical results demonstrate that their algorithms compete with or are just percents of AUC away from the supervised learning approach.

In preliminary work (Mohammady and Culotta, 2014), we fit a regression model to predict the ethnicity distribution of a county based on its Twitter usage, then applied the regression model to classify individual users. In contrast, here we use label regularization, which can more naturally be applied to user-level classification and can incorporate a wider range of constraint types.

## 3 Data

In this section we describe all data and constraints collected for our experiments.

### 3.1 Labeled Twitter Data

For validation (and for tuning some of the methods) we annotate Twitter users according to age, ethnicity, and political orientation. We collects four disjoint datasets for this purpose:

**Race/ethnicity**: This data set comes from the research of Mohammady and Culotta (2014). They categorized 770 Twitter profiles into one of four categories (Asian, Black, Latino, White). They used the Twitter Streaming API to obtain a random sample of 1,000 users, filtered to the United States. These were manually categorized by analyzing the profile, tweets, and profile image for each user, discarding those for which race could not be determined (230/1,000; 23%). The category frequency is Asian (22), Black (263), Latino (158), White (327). For each user, they collected the 200 most recent tweets using the Twitter API. We refer to this dataset as the **race** dataset.

**Age**: Annotating Twitter users by age can be difficult, since it is rarely explicitly mentioned. Similar to prior work (Rao et al., 2010; Al Zamal et al., 2012), we divide users into those below 25 and those above above 25 years old. Using the idea from Al Zamal et al. (2012), we use the Twitter search API to find tweets with phrases like "happy 30th birthday to me," and then we collect those users and download their 200 most recent tweets using the Twitter API. We collect 1,436 users (771 below 25 and 665 above 25). While this sampling procedure introduces some selection bias, it provides a useful form of validation in the absence of expedient alternatives. We refer to this dataset as the **age** dataset.

**Politician**: Inspired by works of (Cohen and Ruths, 2013), we select the official Twitter accounts of members of the U.S. Congress. We select 189 Democratic accounts and and 188 Republican accounts and download their most recent 200 tweets. We refer to this dataset as the **politician** dataset.

**Politician-follower**: As the **politician** dataset is not representative of typical users, we collect a separate political datasets. We first collect a list of followers of the official Twitter accounts for both parties ("thedemocrats" and "gop"). We randomly select 598 likely Democrats and 632 likely Republicans, and download the most recent 200 tweets for each user. While the labels for these data may contain moderate noise (since not everyone who follows "gop" is Republican), a manual inspection did not reveal any mis-annotations. We refer to this as the **politician-follower** dataset.[1]

We split each of the datasets above into 40% tuning/training and 60% testing (though not all methods will use the training set, as we describe below).

### 3.2 Unlabeled Twitter Data

Label regularization depends on a pool of unlabeled data, along with soft constraints over the label proportions in that data. Since many of our constraints involve location, we use the Twitter streaming API to collect 1% of geolocated tweets, using a bounding box of the United States (48 contiguous states plus Hawaii and Alaska). In order to assign each tweet to a county, we use the U.S. Census' center of population data.[2] We use this data to map each geolocated Twitter user to a corresponding county. We use the k-d tree algorithm (Maneewongvatana and Mount, 2002) to find the nearest center of population for each tweet and use a threshold to discard tweets that are not within a specified distance of any county center. In total, we collect 18 million geolocated tweets from 2.7 million unique users.

[1] We were unfortunately unable to obtain the annotated political data of Cohen and Ruths (2013) for direct comparison.

[2] https://www.census.gov/geo/reference/centersofpop.html

### 3.3 Constraints

Finally, we describe the soft constraints used by label regularization. Each constraint will apply to a (possibly overlapping) subset of users from the unlabeled Twitter data. For all constraints below, we only include the constraint for consideration if at least 1,000 unlabeled Twitter users are matched. For example, if we only have 500 users from a county, we will not use that county's demographics as a constraint. This is to ensure that there is sufficient unlabeled data for learning. We consider three classes of constraints:

**County constraints (cnt)**: The U.S. Census produces annual estimates of the ethnicity and age demographics for each county. We use the most recent decennial census (2010) to compute the proportion of each county that is below and above 25 years old (to match the labels of the annotated data). We additionally use the 2012 updated estimates of ethnicity by county, restricting to Asian, Black, Latino, and White. Each constraint, then, is applied to the users assigned to that county in the unlabeled data. For example, there are 46K unlabeled users from Cook County, which the Census estimates as 45% White. We consider 3,000 total counties as constraints, of which roughly 500 are retained for consideration after filtering those that match fewer than 1,000 users.

**Name constraints (nam)**: Silver and McCanc (2014) recently demonstrated how a person's first name can often indicate their age. The Social Security Administration reports the frequencies of names given to children born in a given year,[3] and its actuarial tables[4] estimate how many people born in a given year are still alive. From these data, one can estimate the age distribution of people with a given name. For example, the median age of someone named "Brittany" is 23. With this approach, we can assign constraints indicating the fraction of people with a given name that are above and below 25 years old.

For each user in the unlabeled Twitter data, we parse the "name" field of the profile, assuming that the first token represents the first name. Constraints are assigned to users with matching names. We consider more than 50K total name constraints, of which we retain 175 that match a sufficient number of users. For example, there are roughly 1,600 unlabeled users with the first name Katherine; the constraint specifies that 86% of them are under 25.

**Follower constraints (fol)**: Our final type of constraint uses Twitter accounts and hashtags strongly associated with a class label. The constraint applies to users that follow such exemplar accounts or use such hashtags. We consider two sources of such constraints. For age and race, we download demographic data for 1K websites from Quantcast.com, an audience measurement company that tracks the demographics of visitors to millions of websites (Kamerer, 2013). We then identify the Twitter accounts for each website. For example, one constraint indicates that 12% of Twitter users who follow "oprah" are Latino. For political constraints, we manually identify 18 Twitter accounts or hashtags that are strongly associated with either Democrats or Republicans.[5] The constraint specifies that 90% of users that follow one of these accounts (or use one of these hashtags) are affiliated with the corresponding party. (We omit constraints use to construct the labeled data for the **politician-follower** data.)

## 4 Label Regularization

Our goal is to learn a classification model using the unlabeled Twitter data and the constraints described above. The idea of label regularization is to define an objective function that enforces that the predicted label distribution for a set of unlabeled data closely matches the expected distribution according to a constraint.

We select multinomial logistic regression as our classification model. Given a feature vector $x$, a class label $y$, and set of parameter vectors $\theta = \{\theta_{y_1} \ldots \theta_{y_k}\}$ (one vector per class), the conditional distribution of $y$ given $x$ is defined as follows:

$$p_\theta(y|x) = \frac{\exp(\theta_y \cdot x)}{\sum_{y'} \exp(\theta_{y'} \cdot x)}$$

[3] `http://www.ssa.gov/oact/babynames/`

[4] `http://www.ssa.gov/oact/NOTES/as120/LifeTables_Tbl_7.html`

[5] For Democrats: thedemocrats, wegoted, dccc, collegedems, dennis_kucinich, sensanders, repjohnlewis, keithellison, #p2. For Republicans: gop, nrsc, the_rga, repronpaul, senrandpaul, senmikelee, repjustinamash, gopleader, #tcot

Typically, $\theta$ is set to maximize the likelihood of a labeled training set. Instead, we will optimize the objective defined in Mann and McCallum (2007), using only unlabeled data and constraints.

Let $U = \{U_1 \dots U_k\}$ be a set of sets, where $U_j$ consists of unlabeled feature vectors $x$. The elements of $U$ may be overlapping. Let $\tilde{p}_j$ be the expected label distribution of $U_j$. E.g., $\tilde{p}_j = \{.9, .1\}$ would indicate that 90% of examples in $U_j$ are expected to have class label 0. The combination of $(U_j, \tilde{p}_j)$ is called a **constraint**.

Our goal, then, is to set $\theta$ so that the predicted label distribution matches $\tilde{p}_j$, for all $j$. Since using the predicted class counts results in an objective that is non-differentiable, Mann and McCallum (2007) instead use the model's posterior distribution:

$$\hat{q}_j(y) = \sum_{x \in U_j} p_\theta(y|x)$$

$$\hat{p}_j(y) = \frac{\hat{q}_j(y)}{\sum_{y'} \hat{q}_j(y')}$$

where $\hat{p}_j$ is the normalized form of $\hat{q}_j$. Then, we want to set $\theta$ such that $\hat{p}_j$ and $\tilde{p}_j$ are close. Mann and McCallum (2007) use KL-divergence, which is equivalent to augmenting the likelihood with a Dirichlet prior over expectations where values for the priors are proportional to $\tilde{p}_j$. KL-divergence can be factored into two parts:

$$= -\sum_y \tilde{p}_j(y) \log \hat{p}_j(y) + \sum_y \tilde{p}_j(y) \log \tilde{p}_j(y)$$
$$= H(\tilde{p}_j, \hat{p}_j) - H(\tilde{p}_j)$$

where $H(\tilde{p}_j)$ is constant for each j, and so we need to minimize $H(\tilde{p}_j, \hat{p}_j)$ in order to minimize KL-divergence, where $H(\tilde{p}_j, \hat{p}_j)$ is the cross-entropy of the hypothesized distribution and the expected distribution for $U_j$.

We additionally use L2 regularization, resulting in our final objective function:

$$J(\theta) = \sum_j H(\tilde{p}_j, \hat{p}_j) + \frac{1}{\lambda} \sum_y ||\theta_y||_2^2$$

In practice we find that $\lambda$ does not need tuning for each data set. We set it simply to:

$$\lambda = \frac{C}{\sum_j |U_j|}$$

We set C to 1.3e10 in our experiments. Mann and McCallum (2007) compute the gradient of cross-entropy as follows:

$$\frac{\partial}{\partial \theta_k} H(\tilde{p}_j, \hat{p}_j) = -\sum_{x \in U_j} \sum_y p_\theta(y|x) x_k$$
$$\times \left( \frac{\tilde{p}_j(y)}{\hat{p}_j(y)} - \sum_{y'} \frac{\tilde{p}_j(y) \times p_\theta(y'|x)}{\hat{p}_j(y)} \right)$$

The gradient for $\theta_k$ is then a sum of the gradients for each constraint $j$. In order to minimize the objective function, we use gradient descent with L-BFGS (Byrd et al., 1995). (While the objective is not guaranteed to be convex, this approximation has worked well in prior work.) To help reduce overfitting, we use early-stopping (10 iterations).

**Temperature**: Mann and McCallum (2007) find that sometimes label regularization returns a degenerate solution. For example, for a three class problem with constraint $\tilde{p}_j(y) = \{.5, .35, .15\}$, it may find a solution such that $p_\theta(y) = \{.5, .35, .15\}$ for every instance and as a result all of the instances are assigned the same label. To avoid this behavior Mann and McCallum (2007) introduce a temperature parameter $T$ into the classification function as follows:

$$p_\theta(y|x) = \frac{\exp(\theta_y \cdot x/T)}{\sum_y \exp(\theta_y \cdot x/T)}$$

In practice we find that we can set $T$ to two for binary classification and ten for multi-class problems.

While the approach described above closely follows Mann and McCallum (2007), we note two important distinctions: we use no labeled data in our objective, and we consider a set of hundreds of noisy, overlapping constraints (as opposed to only a handful of precise constraints).

### 4.1 Constraint Selection

As described above, our proposed constraints are undoubtedly inexact. For example, it is generally accepted that social media users are not a representative sample of the population. E.g., younger, urban and minority populations tend to be overrepresented on Twitter (Mislove et al., 2011; Lenhart and Fox, 2009), and Latino users tend to be underrepresented on Facebook (Watkins, 2009). Thus, it is incorrect to assume that the demographics of Twitter users from a county match those of all people from a county. While it may be possible to directly adjust for these mismatches using techniques from survey reweighting (Gelman, 2007), it is difficult to precisely quantify the proper weights in this context.

Instead, we propose a search-based approach inspired by feature selection algorithms commonly used in machine learning (Guyon and Elisseeff, 2003). The idea is to select the subset of constraints that result in the most accurate model. We first assume the presence of a small set of labeled data $L = \{(x_1, y_1) \ldots (x_n, y_n)\}$. Given a set of constraints $C = \{(U_1, \tilde{p}_1) \ldots (U_k, \tilde{p}_k)\}$, the search objective is to select a subset of constraints $C^* \subseteq C$ to minimize error on $L$:

$$C^* \leftarrow \operatorname*{argmin}_{C' \subseteq C} E(p_{C'}(y|x), L)$$

where $E(\cdot)$ is a classification error function, and $p_{C'}(y|x)$ is the model fit by label regularization using constraint set $C'$.

In our experiments, $|C|$ is in the hundreds, so exhaustive, exponential search is impractical. Instead, we consider the following greedy and pseudo-greedy forward-selection algorithms:

- **Greedy (grdy):** Standard greedy search. At each iteration, we select the constraint that leads to the greatest accuracy improvement on $L$.
- **Semi-greedy (semi):** Rather than selecting the constraint that improves accuracy the most, we randomly select from the top three constraints (Hart and Shogan, 1987).
- **Improved-greedy (imp):** The same as **grdy**, but after each iteration, optionally remove a single constraint. We consider each currently selected constraint, and compute the accuracy attained by removing this constraint from the set. We remove the constraint that improves accuracy the most (if any exists). This constraint is removed from consideration in future iterations.
- **Grasp (grsp):** Greedy Randomized Adaptive Search Procedures (Feo and Resende, 1995) combines **semi** and **imp**.

We run each selection algorithm for 140 iterations (as we discuss below, accuracy plateaus well before then). Then, we select the constraint set that results in the highest accuracy. While this search procedure is computationally expensive, it is fortunately easily parallelizable (by partitioning by constraint), which we take advantage of in our implementation. All constraint selection algorithms use the 40% of the labeled data reserved for training/tuning. After we finalized all models using the tuning data, we then used them to classify the 60% of labeled data reserved for testing.

## 5 Baselines

We compare label regularization with standard logistic regression (**logistic**) trained using the 40% of labeled data reserved for training/tuning. We also consider several heuristic baselines:

- **Name heuristic, race classification**: We implement the method proposed by (Mohammady and Culotta, 2014), using the top 1000 most popular last names with their race distribution from the U.S. Census Bureau to infer race/ethnicity of users based of most probable race according last name. If the last name is not among the top 1000 most popular for a given race, we simply predict White (the most frequent class).
- **Name heuristic, age classification**: We use the heuristic described in Section 3.3 that estimates a person's age by their first name. Given the age distribution of a first name, we classify the user according to the more probable class.
- **Follower heuristic, political classification**: We reuse the exemplar accounts used in the follower constraint in Section 3.3. That is, rather than using the fact that a user follows "dennis_kucinich" as a soft constraint, we classify such a user as a Democrat. If a user follows more than one of the exemplar accounts, we select the more frequent party.[6] In case of ties (or if the user does not follow any of the accounts), we classify at random.

[6]For the **politician-follower** data the heuristic does not use "thedemocrats" and "gop," because these were used for the original annotation.

| | race | age | pol | pol-f | avg |
|---|---|---|---|---|---|
| **heuristic** | 43.7 | 56.0 | 89.4 | 65.4 | 63.6 |
| **logistic** | 81.0 | **83.3** | **93.8** | 68.7 | **81.7** |
| **all-const** | | | | | |
| **cnt** | 61.9 | 45.5 | 58.1 | 60.6 | 56.5 |
| **fol** | 67.3 | 61.4 | **93.8** | 60.7 | 70.8 |
| **nam** | | 55.6 | | | |
| **cnt fol** | 79.4 | 45.5 | 79.3 | 67.9 | 68.0 |
| **cnt nam** | | 44.1 | | | |
| **fol nam** | | 55.9 | | | |
| **cnt fol nam** | | 44.0 | | | |
| **imp-greedy** | | | | | |
| **cnt** | 80.1 | 76.6 | 65.6 | 58.9 | 70.3 |
| **fol** | 76.6 | 66.1 | 86.8 | 69.1 | 74.7 |
| **nam** | | 68.3 | | | |
| **cnt fol** | **82.3** | 75.2 | 88.1 | **74.3** | 80.0 |
| **cnt nam** | | 79.2 | | | |
| **fol nam** | | 68.1 | | | |
| **cnt fol nam** | | 75.2 | | | |

Table 1: Accuracy on the *testing* set. **all-const** does no constraint selection; **imp-greedy** selects constraints to maximize accuracy on the tuning set using the Improved-greedy algorithm.

**Features:** For all models, we use a standard bag-of-words representation consisting of a binary term vector for the 200 tweets of each user, their description field, and their name field. We differentiate between terms used in the description, tweet text, and name field, and also indicate hashtags. Finally, we include additional features indicating the accounts followed by each user.

## 6 Results

Table 1 shows the classification accuracy on the test set for each of the four tasks (F1 results are similar). We begin by comparing **heuristic** and **logistic** to the **all-const** results, which is our proposed label regularization approach using no constraint selection (i.e., no user-labeled data). We can see that for three of the four tasks (**race**, **pol**, **pol-f**), label regularization accuracy is either the same as **logistic** or within 2%. That is, using no user-annotated data, we can obtain accuracy competitive with logistic regression.

For **age**, however, label regularization does quite poorly; only using the **fol** constraints surpasses the heuristic baseline. We suspect that this is in part due to the greater noise in age constraints — Twitter users are particularly non-representative of the overall population according to age. To summarize our answer to **RQ1**, label regularization appears to perform quite well under a moderate amount of constraint noise, but can still fail under excessive noise.

| | all | grdy | semi | imp | grsp |
|---|---|---|---|---|---|
| **Race** | 77.9 | 82.5 | 82.5 | **82.8** | **82.8** |
| **Age** | 48.4 | 82.8 | **84.3** | 82.6 | **84.3** |
| **Politician** | 84.0 | 98.7 | 96.0 | **99.3** | 96.7 |
| **Politic-fol** | 61.8 | 79.1 | 77.0 | **79.5** | 77.0 |
| **Average** | 68.0 | 85.7 | 85.0 | **86.0** | 85.2 |

Table 2: Comparison of the accuracy of constraint selection algorithms on the *tuning* set. **all** uses all possible constraints.

We next consider the effect of the constraint selection algorithms. Table 2 compares the four different constraint selection algorithms, along with the model that selects all constraints. We report the accuracy for each approach considering all constraint types (county, follow, and name, where applicable). Importantly, this accuracy is computed on the *tuning* set, not the test set. The goal here is to determine which search algorithm is able to find the best approximate solution. By comparing with **all**, we can see that constraint selection can significantly improve accuracy on the tuning set (by 18% absolute on average). The differences among the selection algorithms do not appear to be significant.

Figure 1 plots the accuracy at each iteration of constraint select for three of the datasets. The main conclusion we draw from these figures is that high accuracy can be achieved with only a small number of constraints, provided they are carefully chosen. Each method is very close to convergence after using only 20 constraints (selected from hundreds). When examining which constraints are selected, we find that those that apply to many users are often preferred, presumably because there is more data to inform the final model.

Returning to Table 1, we have also listed the accuracy of the **imp-greedy** selection method (which performed best on the tuning set), further strati-

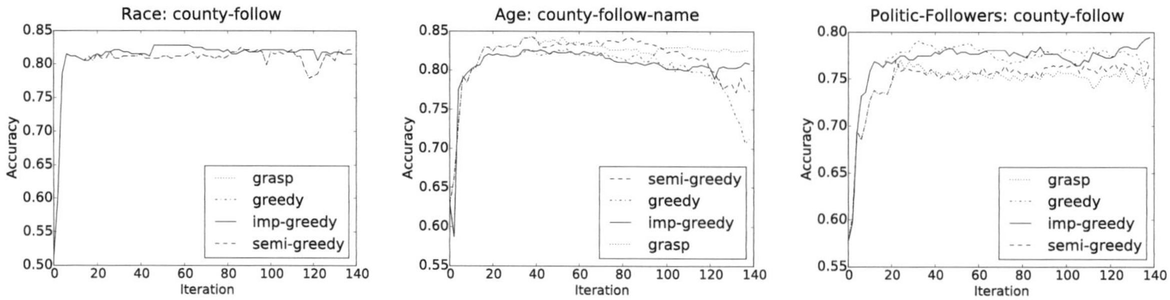


(a) (b) (c)

Figure 1: Accuracy per iteration of constraint selection for three classification tasks.

fied by constraint type. Note that **imp-greedy** selects the constraints that perform best on the tuning set, fits the classification model, and then classifies the testing set. We can see that for three of the four tasks (**race**, **age**, **pol-f**), **imp-greedy** results in higher accuracy than using all the constraints. This is particularly pronounced for **age**: the best result without constraint selection is 61.4, compared with 79.2 for **imp-greedy**. Furthermore, **imp-greedy** outperforms **logistic** on two of four tasks, suggesting that using unlabeled data can improve accuracy. Note that both **imp-greedy** and **logistic** use the same amount of labeled data, though in different ways: **logistic** performs standard supervised classification; **imp-greedy** uses the labeled data to perform constraint selection for label regularization. Thus, to summarize our answer to **RQ2**, we find that **imp-greedy** provides a robust method to select constraints in the presence of noise. While it comes at the cost of a small amount of labeled data, it is less reliant on this data than a traditional supervised approach, and so may be more applicable in streaming settings.

To answer **RQ3**, we can compare the accuracies provided by each of the constraint types in Table 1. For **all-const**, the follower constraints (**fol**) outperform the county constraints (**cnt**) for all tasks, while the name constraint (which only applies to **age**), falls between the two. Including both **cnt** and **fol** improves accuracy on two of the four tasks. These trends change somewhat for **imp-greedy**. The **cnt** constraints are superior for two tasks, while **fol** are superior for the other two. The **nam** constraints again fall between the two. Unlike for **all-const**, using more constraint types improves accuracy on three of four tasks. These differences suggest that the constraint selection algorithms allow label regularization to be more robust to noisy and conflicting constraints. That is, using constraint selection, we can view constraint engineering akin to feature engineering in discriminative, supervised learning methods — developers can add many types of constraints to the model without (much) fear of reducing accuracy. The usual caveat of overfitting applies here as well; indeed, comparing the accuracies on the tuning set (Table 2) with those on the testing set (Table 1) suggests that some over-tuning has occurred, most notably on **age** and **pol**.

We further examined the coefficients of the models trained using each constraint type. We find, for example, that county constraints result in models with large coefficients for location-specific terms (e.g., college names for younger users, southern cities for Republican users), while follower constraints tend to learn models dominated by follower features ("thenation" for Democrats, "glennbeck" for Republicans). Similarly, name constraints result in models dominated by name features. This analysis helps explain how combining constraint types can improve overall accuracy, since each type emphasizes different subsets of features.

This difference between constraint types is further shown in Table 3, which lists the top features for the semi-greedy constraint selection algorithm, fit using different subsets of constraints. In this table, the italicized words are the words from the description field of the user's profile, the underlined words are followed accounts, and the bold words are the words

| *age* | **under 25** | **above 25** |
|---|---|---|
| **County** | athens *tech uga virginia georgia* | airport nashvillescene at theonion *and* |
| **Follow** | altpress colourlovers hotnewhiphop planetminecraft me | newsobserver baseballamerica peopleenespanol breakingnews hogshaven |
| **Name** | **katherine diana** me my this | **debra lori sandra janet** *No Desc* |
| *politician* | **Democratic** | **Republican** |
| **County** | *oregon* eugene oregon nesn *university* | colts beach tahoe *indiana* jgfortwayne |
| **Follow** | keithellison repjohnlewis sensanders thinkprogres thenation | gopleader senmikelee senrandpaul gop glennbeck |

Table 3: Top features learned by label regularization for the age and politician datasets using semi-greedy constraint selection. Models were fit separately for each constraint type (county, follow, name). Italicized words are from the description field, bold words are from the name field, and underlined words are followed accounts.

from the name field of the user profile. In the first row, we display the top features for a model fit using only county constraints. College names appear as top features for younger users, and "airport" and @NashvilleScene (a newspaper) are for older users. The second row of Table 3 shows the top features for following constraints; some news channels are appear for younger (Alternative Press) and older (The News & Observer) users. The third row shows the top features for name constraints, and some names are in the top features for younger (Katherine and Diana) and older (Debra, Lori, Sandra, and Janet). In addition, the absence of a profile description is indicative of older users.

The bottom of Table 3 shows top features for the politician dataset. The first row shows that some colleges, a sports network in New England, and locations in the Pacific Northwest are indicative of Democrats. Indiana-related terms are strong indicators of Republicans: *indiana*, the Indianapolis Colts (an American football team), and 'jgfortwayne' (The Journal Gazette, a newspaper in Fort Wayne, Indiana). This aligns with the strong support of the Republican party in Indiana.[7] The second row shows top-ranked following features. Accounts 'keithellison' and 'repjohnlewis' are top features for Democratic Party; these belong to Keith Ellison and John Robert Lewis, members of the Democratic leadership of the House of Representatives. On other hand, the 'gopleader' (the official account for the Republican's majority leader in the House) and 'senmikelee' (Republican Senator Mike Lee from Utah) are the top features for Republicans.

## 7 Conclusions and Future work

While label regularization has been used on a number of NLP tasks, we have presented evidence that it is applicable to latent attribute inference even using many noisy, heterogeneous constraints. We have compared a number of constraint selection algorithms and found they can make label regularization more robust to noisy constraints, allowing developers to combine many rich constraint types without reducing accuracy.

There are many avenues for future work. Most pressing is the need to directly address the sampling bias created when constraints derived from the overall population are applied to online users. We plan to explore alternative optimization strategies to explicitly address this issue. Finally, additional research should quantify how responsive label regularization approaches are to the changing linguistic patterns common in online data.

## References


F Al Zamal, W Liu, and D Ruths. 2012. Homophily and latent attribute inference: Inferring latent attributes of twitter users from neighbors. In *ICWSM*.

Pablo Barberá. 2013. Birds of the same feather tweet together. bayesian ideal point estimation using twitter data. *Proceedings of the Social Media and Political Participation, Florence, Italy*, pages 10–11.


[7] `http://en.wikipedia.org/wiki/Politics_of_Indiana`

Richard H Byrd, Peihuang Lu, Jorge Nocedal, and Ciyou Zhu. 1995. A limited memory algorithm for bound constrained optimization. *SIAM Journal on Scientific Computing*, 16(5):1190–1208.

M. Chang, L. Ratinov, and D. Roth. 2007. Guiding semi-supervision with constraint-driven learning. In *ACL*, pages 280–287, Prague, Czech Republic, 6. Association for Computational Linguistics.

Jonathan Chang, Itamar Rosenn, Lars Backstrom, and Cameron Marlow. 2010. epluribus: Ethnicity on social networks. In *ICWSM*.

Ming-Wei Chang, Lev Ratinov, and Dan Roth. 2012. Structured learning with constrained conditional models. *Machine learning*, 88(3):399–431.

Raviv Cohen and Derek Ruths. 2013. Classifying political orientation on twitter: It's not easy! In *ICWSM*.

Michael D Conover, Bruno Gonçalves, Jacob Ratkiewicz, Alessandro Flammini, and Filippo Menczer. 2011. Predicting the political alignment of twitter users. In *Privacy, security, risk and trust (passat), 2011 ieee third international conference on and 2011 ieee third international conference on social computing (socialcom)*, pages 192–199. IEEE.

M. Dredze. 2012. How social media will change public health. *IEEE Intelligent Systems*, 27(4):81–84.

Gregory Druck, Gideon Mann, and Andrew McCallum. 2008. Learning from labeled features using generalized expectation criteria. In *Proceedings of the 31st Annual International ACM SIGIR Conference on Research and Development in Information Retrieval*, pages 595–602.

Gregory Druck, Gideon Mann, and Andrew McCallum. 2009. Semi-supervised learning of dependency parsers using generalized expectation criteria. In *ACL*.

Jacob Eisenstein, Noah A. Smith, and Eric P. Xing. 2011. Discovering sociolinguistic associations with structured sparsity. In *Proceedings of the 49th Annual Meeting of the Association for Computational Linguistics: Human Language Technologies - Volume 1*, HLT '11, page 13651374, Stroudsburg, PA, USA. Association for Computational Linguistics.

Thomas A Feo and Mauricio GC Resende. 1995. Greedy randomized adaptive search procedures. *Journal of global optimization*, 6(2):109–133.

Kuzman Ganchev and Dipanjan Das. 2013. Cross-lingual discriminative learning of sequence models with posterior regularization. In *EMNLP*, pages 1996–2006.

Kuzman Ganchev, Jennifer Gillenwater, and Ben Taskar. 2009. Dependency grammar induction via bitext projection constraints. In *Proceedings of the Joint Conference of the 47th Annual Meeting of the ACL and the 4th International Joint Conference on Natural Language Processing of the AFNLP: Volume 1-Volume 1*, pages 369–377. Association for Computational Linguistics.

Kuzman Ganchev, Joo Graca, Jennifer Gillenwater, and Ben Taskar. 2010. Posterior regularization for structured latent variable models. *J. Mach. Learn. Res.*, 11:20012049, August.

Andrew Gelman. 2007. Struggles with survey weighting and regression modeling. *Statistical Science*, 22(2):153–164.

Shyam Gopinath, Jacquelyn S Thomas, and Lakshman Krishnamurthi. 2014. Investigating the relationship between the content of online word of mouth, advertising, and brand performance. *Marketing Science*, 33(2):241–258.

Joao Graça, Kuzman Ganchev, and Ben Taskar. 2007. Expectation maximization and posterior constraints. In *NIPS*, volume 20, pages 569–576.

Isabelle Guyon and André Elisseeff. 2003. An introduction to variable and feature selection. *The Journal of Machine Learning Research*, 3:1157–1182.

Aria Haghighi and Dan Klein. 2006. Prototype-driven learning for sequence models. In *Proceedings of the main conference on Human Language Technology Conference of the North American Chapter of the Association of Computational Linguistics*, pages 320–327. Association for Computational Linguistics.

J Pirie Hart and Andrew W Shogan. 1987. Semi-greedy heuristics: An empirical study. *Operations Research Letters*, 6(3):107–114.

Rong Jin and Yi Liu. 2005. A framework for incorporating class priors into discriminative classification. In *In PAKDD*.

David Kamerer. 2013. Estimating online audiences: Understanding the limitations of competitive intelligence services. *First Monday*, 18(5).

Ben King and Steven Abney. 2013. Labeling the languages of words in mixed-language documents using weakly supervised methods. In *Proceedings of NAACL-HLT*, pages 1110–1119.

Amanda Lenhart and Susannah Fox. 2009. Twitter and status updating. pew internet & american life project.

Percy Liang, Michael I. Jordan, and Dan Klein. 2009. Learning from measurements in exponential families. In *Proceedings of the 26th Annual International Conference on Machine Learning*, ICML '09, page 641648, New York, NY, USA. ACM.

Songrit Maneewongvatana and David M Mount. 2002. Analysis of approximate nearest neighbor searching with clustered point sets. *Data Structures, Near Neighbor Searches, and Methodology*, 59:105–123.

Gideon S. Mann and Andrew McCallum. 2007. Simple, robust, scalable semi-supervised learning via expectation regularization. In *Proceedings of the 24th Inter-*

*national Conference on Machine Learning*, ICML '07, page 593600, New York, NY, USA. ACM.

Gideon S. Mann and Andrew McCallum. 2010. Generalized expectation criteria for semi-supervised learning with weakly labeled data. *J. Mach. Learn. Res.*, 11:955984, March.

Prem Melville, Wojciech Gryc, and Richard D. Lawrence. 2009. Sentiment analysis of blogs by combining lexical knowledge with text classification. In *Proceedings of the 15th ACM SIGKDD International Conference on Knowledge Discovery and Data Mining*, KDD '09, page 12751284, New York, NY, USA. ACM.

Alan Mislove, Sune Lehmann, Yong-Yeol Ahn, Jukka-Pekka Onnela, and J. Niels Rosenquist. 2011. Understanding the demographics of twitter users. In *Proceedings of the Fifth International AAAI Conference on Weblogs and Social Media (ICWSM'11)*, Barcelona, Spain.

Ehsan Mohammady and Aron Culotta. 2014. Using county demographics to infer attributes of twitter users. In *ACL Joint Workshop on Social Dynamics and Personal Attributes in Social Media*.

D.R. Musicant, J.M. Christensen, and J.F. Olson. 2007. Supervised learning by training on aggregate outputs. In *Seventh IEEE International Conference on Data Mining, 2007. ICDM 2007*, pages 252–261.

Dong Nguyen, Noah A. Smith, and Carolyn P. Ros. 2011. Author age prediction from text using linear regression. In *Proceedings of the 5th ACL-HLT Workshop on Language Technology for Cultural Heritage, Social Sciences, and Humanities*, LaTeCH '11, page 115123, Stroudsburg, PA, USA. Association for Computational Linguistics.

Brendan O'Connor, Ramnath Balasubramanyan, Bryan R. Routledge, and Noah A. Smith. 2010. From Tweets to polls: Linking text sentiment to public opinion time series. In *International AAAI Conference on Weblogs and Social Media*, Washington, D.C.

Huseyin Oktay, Aykut Firat, and Zeynep Ertem. 2014. Demographic breakdown of twitter users: An analysis based on names. In *Academy of Science and Engineering (ASE)*.

Giorgio Patrini, Richard Nock, Tiberio Caetano, and Paul Rivera. 2014. (almost) no label no cry. In Z. Ghahramani, M. Welling, C. Cortes, N.D. Lawrence, and K.Q. Weinberger, editors, *Advances in Neural Information Processing Systems 27*, pages 190–198. Curran Associates, Inc.

Marco Pennacchiotti and Ana-Maria Popescu. 2011. A machine learning approach to twitter user classification. In Lada A. Adamic, Ricardo A. Baeza-Yates, and Scott Counts, editors, *ICWSM*. The AAAI Press.

Novi Quadrianto, Alex J. Smola, Tiberio S. Caetano, and Quoc V. Le. 2009. Estimating labels from label proportions. *J. Mach. Learn. Res.*, 10:23492374, December.

Delip Rao, David Yarowsky, Abhishek Shreevats, and Manaswi Gupta. 2010. Classifying latent user attributes in twitter. In *Proceedings of the 2Nd International Workshop on Search and Mining User-generated Contents*, SMUC '10, page 3744, New York, NY, USA. ACM.

Delip Rao, Michael J. Paul, Clayton Fink, David Yarowsky, Timothy Oates, and Glen Coppersmith. 2011. Hierarchical bayesian models for latent attribute detection in social media. In Lada A. Adamic, Ricardo A. Baeza-Yates, and Scott Counts, editors, *ICWSM*. The AAAI Press.

Robert E. Schapire, Marie Rochery, Mazin G. Rahim, and Narendra K. Gupta. 2002. Incorporating prior knowledge into boosting. In *Proceedings of the Nineteenth International Conference*, pages 538–545.

H Andrew Schwartz, Johannes C Eichstaedt, Margaret L Kern, Lukasz Dziurzynski, Stephanie M Ramones, Megha Agrawal, Achal Shah, Michal Kosinski, David Stillwell, Martin E P Seligman, and Lyle H Ungar. 2013. Personality, gender, and age in the language of social media: the open-vocabulary approach. *PloS one*, 8(9):e73791. PMID: 24086296.

Burr Settles. 2011. Closing the loop: Fast, interactive semi-supervised annotation with queries on features and instances. In *Proceedings of the Conference on Empirical Methods in Natural Language Processing*, pages 1467–1478. Association for Computational Linguistics.

Nate Silver and Allison McCanc. 2014. How to tell someone's age when all you know is her name. Retrieved from http://fivethirtyeight.com/features/how-to-tell-someones-age-when-all-you-know-is-her-name/.

Mengqiu Wang and Christopher D. Manning. 2014. Cross-lingual projected expectation regularization for weakly supervised learning. *TACL*, 2:55–66.

Zuoguan Wang, Siwei Lyu, Gerwin Schalk, and Qiang Ji. 2012. Learning with target prior. In F. Pereira, C.J.C. Burges, L. Bottou, and K.Q. Weinberger, editors, *Advances in Neural Information Processing Systems 25*, pages 2231–2239. Curran Associates, Inc.

Samuel Craig Watkins. 2009. *The young and the digital: what the migration to social-network sites, games, and anytime, anywhere media means for our future*. Beacon Press.

Jun Zhu, Ning Chen, and Eric P Xing. 2014. Bayesian inference with posterior regularization and applications to infinite latent svms. *Journal of Machine Learning Research*, 15:1799–1847.

# A Neural Network Approach to Context-Sensitive Generation of Conversational Responses

Alessandro Sordoni[1*†] Michel Galley[2†] Michael Auli[3*] Chris Brockett[2]
Yangfeng Ji[4*] Margaret Mitchell[2] Jian-Yun Nie[1*] Jianfeng Gao[2] Bill Dolan[2]

[1]DIRO, Université de Montréal, Montréal, QC, Canada
[2]Microsoft Research, Redmond, WA, USA
[3]Facebook AI Research, Menlo Park, CA, USA
[4]Georgia Institute of Technology, Atlanta, GA, USA

## Abstract

We present a novel response generation system that can be trained end to end on large quantities of unstructured Twitter conversations. A neural network architecture is used to address sparsity issues that arise when integrating contextual information into classic statistical models, allowing the system to take into account previous dialog utterances. Our dynamic-context generative models show consistent gains over both context-sensitive and non-context-sensitive Machine Translation and Information Retrieval baselines.

Figure 1: Example of three consecutive utterances occurring between two Twitter users $A$ and $B$.

## 1 Introduction

Until recently, the goal of training open-domain conversational systems that emulate human conversation has seemed elusive. However, the vast quantities of conversational exchanges now available on social media websites such as Twitter and Reddit raise the prospect of building data-driven models that can begin to communicate conversationally. The work of Ritter et al. (2011), for example, demonstrates that a response generation system can be constructed from Twitter conversations using statistical machine translation techniques, where a status post by a Twitter user is "translated" into a plausible looking response.

However, an approach such as that presented in Ritter et al. (2011) does not address the challenge of generating responses that are sensitive to the context of the conversation. Broadly speaking, context may be linguistic or involve grounding in the physical or virtual world, but we here focus on linguistic context. The ability to take into account previous utterances is key to building dialog systems that can keep conversations active and engaging. Figure 1 illustrates a typical Twitter dialog where the contextual information is crucial: the phrase "good luck" is plainly motivated by the reference to "your game" in the first utterance. In the MT model, such contextual sensitivity is difficult to capture; moreover, naive injection of context information would entail unmanageable growth of the phrase table at the cost of increased sparsity, and skew towards rarely-seen context pairs. In most statistical approaches to machine translation, phrase pairs do not share statistical weights regardless of their intrinsic semantic commonality.

We propose to address the challenge of context-sensitive response generation by using continuous representations or *embeddings* of words and phrases to compactly encode semantic and syntactic similarity. We argue that embedding-based models af-

*The entirety of this work was conducted while at Microsoft Research.

†Corresponding authors: Alessandro Sordoni (sordonia@iro.umontreal.ca) and Michel Galley (mgalley@microsoft.com).



*Human Language Technologies: The 2015 Annual Conference of the North American Chapter of the ACL*, pages 196–205,
Denver, Colorado, May 31 – June 5, 2015. 

ford flexibility to model the transitions between consecutive utterances and to capture long-span dependencies in a domain where traditional word and phrase alignment is difficult (Ritter et al., 2011). To this end, we present two simple, context-sensitive response-generation models utilizing the Recurrent Neural Network Language Model (RLM) architecture of (Mikolov et al., 2010). These models first encode past information in a hidden continuous representation, which is then decoded by the RLM to promote plausible responses that are simultaneously fluent and contextually relevant. Unlike typical complex task-oriented multi-modular dialog systems (Young, 2002; Stent and Bangalore, 2014), our architecture is *completely data-driven* and can easily be trained end-to-end using unstructured data without requiring human annotation, scripting, or automatic parsing.

This paper makes the following contributions. We present a neural network architecture for response generation that is both context-sensitive and data-driven. As such, it can be trained from end to end on massive amounts of social media data. To our knowledge, this is the first application of a neural-network model to open-domain response generation, and we believe that the present work will lay groundwork for more complex models to come. We additionally introduce a novel multi-reference extraction technique that shows promise for automated evaluation.

## 2 Related Work

Our work naturally lies in the path opened by Ritter et al. (2011), but we generalize their approach by exploiting information from a larger context. Ritter et al. and our work represent a radical paradigm shift from other work in dialog. More traditional dialog systems typically tease apart dialog management (Young, 2002) from response generation (Stent and Bangalore, 2014), while our holistic approach can be considered a first attempt to accomplish both tasks jointly. While there are previous uses of machine learning for response generation (Walker et al., 2003), dialog state tracking (Young et al., 2010), and user modeling (Georgila et al., 2006), many components of typical dialog systems remain hand-coded: in particular, the labels and attributes defining dialog states. In contrast, the dialog state in our neural network model is completely latent and directly optimized towards end-to-end performance. In this sense, we believe the framework of this paper is a significant milestone towards more data-driven and less hand-coded dialog processing.

Continuous representations of words and phrases estimated by neural network models have been applied on a variety of tasks ranging from Information Retrieval (IR) (Huang et al., 2013; Shen et al., 2014), Online Recommendation (Gao et al., 2014b), Machine Translation (MT) (Auli et al., 2013; Cho et al., 2014; Kalchbrenner and Blunsom, 2013; Sutskever et al., 2014), and Language Modeling (LM) (Bengio et al., 2003; Collobert and Weston, 2008). Gao et al. (2014a) successfully use an embedding model to refine the estimation of rare phrase-translation probabilities, which is traditionally affected by sparsity problems. Robustness to sparsity is a crucial property of our method, as it allows us to capture context information while avoiding unmanageable growth of model parameters.

Our work extends the Recurrent Neural Network Language Model (RLM) of (Mikolov et al., 2010), which uses continuous representations to estimate a probability function over natural language sentences. We propose a set of conditional RLMs where contextual information (i.e., past utterances) is encoded in a continuous context vector to help generate the response. Our models differ from most previous work in the way the context vector is constructed. For example, Mikolov and Zweig (2012) and Auli et al. (2013) use a pre-trained topic model. In our models, the context vector is learned along with the conditional RLM that generates the response. Additionally, the learned context encodings do not exclusively capture contentful words. Indeed, even "stop words" can carry discriminative power in this task; for example, all words in the utterance "how are you?" are commonly characterized as stop words, yet this is a contentful dialog utterance.

## 3 Recurrent Language Model

We give a brief overview of the Recurrent Language Model (RLM) (Mikolov et al., 2010) architecture that our models extend. A RLM is a generative model of sentences, i.e., given sentence $s = s_1, \ldots, s_T$, it estimates:

$$p(s) = \prod_{t=1}^{T} p(s_t | s_1, \ldots, s_{t-1}). \quad (1)$$

The model architecture is parameterized by three weight matrices, $\Theta_{\text{RNN}} = \langle W_{in}, W_{out}, W_{hh} \rangle$: an input matrix $W_{in}$, a recurrent matrix $W_{hh}$ and an output matrix $W_{out}$, which are usually initialized randomly. The rows of the input matrix $W_{in} \in \mathbb{R}^{V \times K}$ contain the $K$-dimensional embeddings for each word in the language vocabulary of size $V$. Let us denote by $s_t$ both the vocabulary token and its one-hot representation, i.e., a zero vector of dimensionality $V$ with a 1 corresponding to the index of the $s_t$ token. The embedding for $s_t$ is then obtained by $s_t^\top W_{in}$. The recurrent matrix $W_{hh} \in \mathbb{R}^{K \times K}$ keeps a history of the subsequence that has already been processed. The output matrix $W_{out} \in \mathbb{R}^{K \times V}$ projects the hidden state $h_t$ into the output layer $o_t$, which has an entry for each word in the vocabulary $V$. This value is used to generate a probability distribution for the next word in the sequence. Specifically, the forward pass proceeds with the following recurrence, for $t = 1, \ldots, T$:

$$h_t = \sigma(s_t^\top W_{in} + h_{t-1}^\top W_{hh}), \quad o_t = h_t^\top W_{out} \quad (2)$$

where $\sigma$ is a non-linear function applied element-wise, in our case the logistic sigmoid. The recurrence is seeded by setting $h_0 = 0$, the zero vector. The probability distribution over the next word given the previous history is obtained by applying the softmax activation function:

$$P(s_t = w | s_1, \ldots, s_{t-1}) = \frac{\exp(o_{tw})}{\sum_{v=1}^{V} \exp(o_{tv})}. \quad (3)$$

The RLM is trained to minimize the negative log-likelihood of the training sentence $s$:

$$L(s) = -\sum_{t=1}^{T} \log P(s_t | s_1, \ldots, s_{t-1}). \quad (4)$$

The recurrence is unrolled backwards in time using the back-propagation through time (BPTT) algorithm (Rumelhart et al., 1988), and gradients are accumulated over multiple time-steps.

## 4 Context-Sensitive Models

We distinguish three linguistic entities in a conversation between two users $A$ and $B$: the context[1] $c$, the message $m$ and response $r$. The context $c$ represents a sequence of past dialog exchanges of any length; then $B$ emits a message $m$ to which $A$ reacts by formulating its response $r$ (see Figure 1).

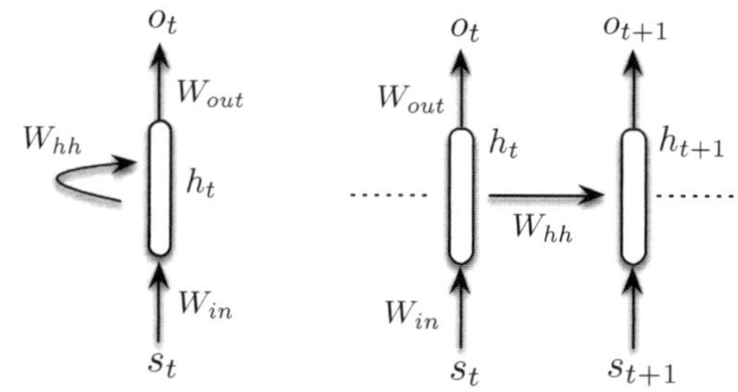


Figure 2: Compact representation of an RLM (left) and unrolled representation for two time steps (right).

We use three context-based generation models to estimate a generation model of the response $r$, $r = r_1, \ldots, r_T$, conditioned on past information $c$ and $m$:

$$p(r|c, m) = \prod_{t=1}^{T} p(r_t | r_1, \ldots, r_{t-1}, c, m). \quad (5)$$

These three models differ in the manner in which they compose the context-message pair $(c, m)$.

### 4.1 Tripled Language Model

In our first model, dubbed RLMT, we straightforwardly concatenate each utterance $c$, $m$, $r$ into a single sentence $s$ and train the RLM to minimize $L(s)$. Given $c$ and $m$, we compute the probability of the response as follows: we perform the forward propagation over the known utterances $c$ and $m$ to obtain a hidden state encoding useful information about previous utterances. Subsequently, we compute the likelihood of the response from that hidden state.

An issue with this simple approach is that the concatenated sentence $s$ will be very long on average, especially if the context comprises multiple utterances. Modelling such long-range dependencies with an RLM is difficult and is still considered an open problem (Pascanu et al., 2013). We will consider RLMT as an additional context-sensitive baseline for the models we present next.

### 4.2 Dynamic-Context Generative Model I

The above limitation of RLMT can be addressed by strengthening the context bias. In our second model (DCGM-I), the context and the message are encoded

[1]In this work, the context is purely linguistic, but future work might integrate further contextual information, e.g., geographical location, time information, or other forms of grounding.

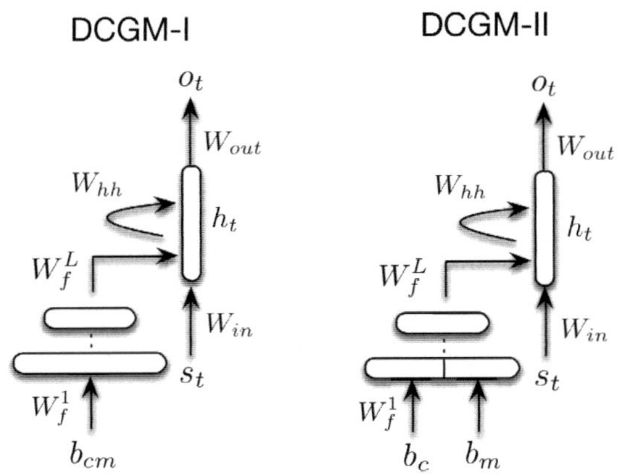


Figure 3: Compact representations of DCGM-I (left) and DCGM-II (right). The decoder RLM receives a bias from the context encoder. In DCGM-I, we encode the bag-of-words representation of both $c$ and $m$ in a single vector $b_{cm}$. In DCGM-II, we concatenate the representations $b_c$ and $b_m$ on the first layer to preserve order information.

into a fixed-length vector representation the is used by the RLM to decode the response. This is illustrated in Figure 3 (left). First, we consider $c$ and $m$ as a single sentence and compute a single bag-of-words representation $b_{cm} \in \mathbb{R}^V$. Then, $b_{cm}$ is provided as input to a multilayered non-linear forward architecture that produces a fixed-length representation that is used to bias the recurrent state of the decoder RLM. At training time, both the context encoder and the RLM decoder are learned so as to minimize the negative log-probability of the generated response.

The parameters of the model are $\Theta_{\text{DCGM-I}} = \langle W_{in}, W_{hh}, W_{out}, \{W_f^\ell\}_{\ell=1}^L \rangle$, where $\{W_f^\ell\}_{\ell=1}^L$ are the weights for the $L$ layers of the feed-forward context networks. The fixed-length context vector $k_L$ is obtained by forward propagation of the network:

$$\begin{aligned} k_1 &= b_{cm}^\top W_f^1 \\ k_\ell &= \sigma(k_{\ell-1}^\top W_f^\ell) \quad \text{for } \ell = 2, \cdots, L \end{aligned} \tag{6}$$

The rows of $W_f^1$ contain the embeddings of the vocabulary.[2] These are different from those employed in the RLM and play a crucial role in promoting the specialization of the context encoder to a distinct task. The hidden layer of the decoder RLM takes the following form:

$$h_t = \sigma(h_{t-1}^\top W_{hh} + k_L + s_t^\top W_{in}) \tag{7a}$$

$$o_t = h_t^\top W_{out} \tag{7b}$$

$$p(s_{t+1}|s_1, \ldots, s_{t-1}, c, m) = \text{softmax}(o_t) \tag{7c}$$

This model conditions on the previous utterances via biasing the hidden layer state on the context representation $k_L$. Note that the context representation does not change through time. This is useful because: (a) it forces the context encoder to produce a representation general enough to be useful for generating all words in the response and (b) it helps the RLM decoder to remember context information when generating long responses.

### 4.3 Dynamic-Context Generative Model II

Because DCGM-I does not distinguish between $c$ and $m$, that model has the propensity to underestimate the strong dependency that holds between $m$ and $r$. Our third model (DCGM-II) addresses this issue by concatenating the two linear mappings of the bag-of-words representations $b_c$ and $b_m$ in the input layer of the feed-forward network representing $c$ and $m$ (see Figure 3 right). Concatenating continuous representations prior to deep architectures is a common strategy to obtain order-sensitive representations (Bengio et al., 2003; Devlin et al., 2014).

The forward equations for the context encoder are:

$$\begin{aligned} k_1 &= [b_c^\top W_f^1, b_m^\top W_f^1], \\ k_\ell &= \sigma(k_{\ell-1}^\top W_f^\ell) \quad \text{for } \ell = 2, \cdots, L \end{aligned} \tag{8}$$

where $[x, y]$ denotes the concatenation of $x$ and $y$ vectors. In DCGM-II, the bias on the recurrent hidden state and the probability distribution over the next token are computed as described in Eq. 7.

## 5 Experimental Setting

### 5.1 Dataset Construction

For computational efficiency and to alleviate the burden of human evaluators, we restrict the context sequence $c$ to a single sentence. Hence, our dataset is composed of "triples" $\tau \equiv (c_\tau, m_\tau, r_\tau)$ consisting of three sentences. We mined 127M context-message-response triples from the Twitter FireHose, covering the 3-month period June 2012 through August 2012.

[2]Notice that the first layer of the encoder network is linear. We found that this helps learning the embedding matrix as it reduces the vanishing gradient effect partially due to stacking of squashing non-linearities (Pascanu et al., 2013).

| Corpus | # Triples | Avg # Ref | [Min,Max] # Ref |
|---|---|---|---|
| Tuning | 2118 | 3.22 | [1, 10] |
| Test | 2114 | 3.58 | [1, 10] |

Table 1: Number of triples, average, minimum and maximum number of references for tuning and test corpora.

Only those triples where context and response were generated by the same user were extracted. To minimize noise, we selected triples that contained at least one frequent bigram that appeared more than 3 times in the corpus. This produced a corpus of 29M Twitter triples. Additionally, we hired crowdsourced raters to evaluate approximately 33K candidate triples. Judgments on a 5-point scale were obtained from 3 raters apiece. This yielded a set of 4232 triples with a mean score of 4 or better that was then randomly binned into a tuning set of 2118 triples and a test set of 2114 triples[3]. The mean length of responses in these sets was approximately 11.5 tokens, after cleanup (e.g., stripping of emoticons), including punctuation.

### 5.2 Automatic Evaluation

We evaluate all systems using BLEU (Papineni et al., 2002) and METEOR (Banerjee and Lavie, 2005), and supplement these results with more targeted human pairwise comparisons in Section 6.3. A major challenge in using these automated metrics for response generation is that the set of reasonable responses in our task is potentially vast and extremely diverse. The dataset construction method just described yields only a single reference for each status. Accordingly, we extend the set of references using an IR approach to mine potential responses, after which we have human judges rate their appropriateness. As we see in Section 6.3, it turns out that by optimizing systems towards BLEU using mined multi-references, BLEU rankings align well with human judgments. This lays groundwork for interesting future correlation studies.

**Multi-reference extraction** We use the following algorithm to better cover the space of reasonable responses. Given a test triple $\tau \equiv (c_\tau, m_\tau, r_\tau)$, our goal is to mine other responses $\{r_{\tilde{\tau}}\}$ that fit the context and message pair $(c_\tau, m_\tau)$. To this end, we first select a set of 15 candidate triples $\{\tilde{\tau}\}$ using an IR system. The IR system is calibrated in order to select candidate triples $\tilde{\tau}$ for which both the message $m_{\tilde{\tau}}$ and the response $r_{\tilde{\tau}}$ are similar to the original message $m_\tau$ and response $r_\tau$. Formally, the score of a candidate triple is:

$$s(\tilde{\tau}, \tau) = d(m_{\tilde{\tau}}, m_\tau)\,(\alpha\, d(r_{\tilde{\tau}}, r_\tau) + (1-\alpha)\epsilon), \quad (9)$$

where $d$ is the bag-of-words BM25 similarity function (Robertson et al., 1995), $\alpha$ controls the impact of the similarity between the responses and $\epsilon$ is a smoothing factor that avoids zero scores for candidate responses that do not share any words with the reference response. We found that this simple formula provided references that were both diverse and plausible. Given a set of candidate triples $\{\tilde{\tau}\}$, human evaluators are asked to rate the quality of the response within the new triples $\{(c_\tau, m_\tau, r_{\tilde{\tau}})\}$. After human evaluation, we retain the references for which the score is 4 or better on a 5 point scale, resulting in 3.58 references per example on average (Table 1). The average lengths for the responses in the multi-reference tuning and test sets are 8.75 and 8.13 tokens respectively.

### 5.3 Feature Sets

The response generation systems evaluated in this paper are parameterized as log-linear models in a framework typical of statistical machine translation (Och and Ney, 2004). These log-linear models comprise the following feature sets:

**MT** MT features are derived from a large response generation system built along the lines of Ritter et al. (2011), which is based on a phrase-based MT decoder similar to Moses (Koehn et al., 2007). Our MT feature set includes the following features that are common in Moses: forward and backward maximum likelihood "translation" probabilities, word and phrase penalties, linear distortion, and a modified Kneser-Ney language model (Kneser and Ney, 1995) trained on Twitter responses. For the translation probabilities, we built a very large phrase table of 160.7 million entries by first filtering out Twitterisms (e.g., long sequences of vowels, hashtags), and then selecting candidate phrase pairs using Fisher's exact test (Ritter et al., 2011). We also included MT decoder features specifically motivated by the response generation task: Jaccard distance between source and

[3]The Twitter ids of the tuning and test sets along with the code for the neural network models may be obtained from http://research.microsoft.com/convo/

| System | BLEU |
|---|---|
| RANDOM | 0.33 |
| MT | 3.21 |
| HUMAN | 6.08 |

Table 2: Multi-reference corpus-level BLEU obtained by leaving one reference out at random.

target phrase, Fisher's exact probability, and a score relating the lengths of source and target phrases.

**IR** We also use an IR feature built from an index of triples, whose implementation roughly matches the $\mathrm{IR}_{\mathrm{status}}$ approach described in Ritter et al. (2011): For a test triple $\tau$, we choose $r_{\tilde{\tau}}$ as the candidate response iff $\tilde{\tau} = \arg\max_{\tilde{\tau}} d(m_\tau, m_{\tilde{\tau}})$.

**CMM** Neither MT nor IR traditionally take into account contextual information. Therefore, we take into consideration context and message matches (CMM), i.e., exact matches between $c$, $m$ and $r$. We define 8 features as the [1-4]-gram matches between $c$ and the candidate reply $r$ and the [1-4]-gram matches between $m$ and the candidate reply $r$. These exact matches help capture and promote contextual information in the replies.

**RLMT, DCGM-I, DCGM-II** We consider the RLM trained on the concatenated triples, denoted as RLMT (Section 4.1), to be a context-sensitive RLM baseline. Each neural network model contributes an additional feature corresponding to the likelihood of the candidate response given context and message.

### 5.4 Model Training

The proposed models are trained on a 4M subset of the triple data. The vocabulary consists of the most frequent $V = 50K$ words. In order to speed up training, we use the Noise-Contrastive Estimation (NCE) loss, which avoids repeated summations over $V$ by approximating the probability of the target word (Gutmann and Hyvärinen, 2010). Parameter optimization is done using Adagrad (Duchi et al., 2011) with a mini-batch size of 100 and a learning rate $\alpha = 0.1$, which we found to work well on held-out data. In order to stabilize learning, we clip the gradients to a fixed range $[-10, 10]$, as suggested in Mikolov et al. (2010). All the parameters of the neural models are sampled from a normal distribution $\mathcal{N}(0, 0.01)$ while the recurrent weight $W_{hh}$ is initialized as a random orthogonal matrix and scaled by 0.01. To prevent over-fitting, we evaluate performance on a held-out set during training and stop when the objective increases. The size of the RLM hidden layer is set to $K = 512$, where the context encoder is a 512, 256, 512 multilayer network. The bottleneck in the middle compresses context information that leads to similar responses and thus achieves better generalization. The last layer embeds the context vector into the hidden space of the decoder RLM.

### 5.5 Rescoring Setup

We evaluate the proposed models by rescoring the $n$-best candidate responses obtained using the MT phrase-based decoder and the IR system. In contrast to MT, the candidate responses provided by IR have been created by humans and are less affected by fluency issues. The different $n$-best lists will provide a comprehensive testbed for our experiments. First, we augment the $n$-best list of the tuning set with the scores of the model of interest. Then, we run an iteration of MERT (Och, 2003) to estimate the log-linear weights of the new features. At test time, we rescore the test $n$-best list with the new weights.

## 6 Results

### 6.1 Lower and Upper Bounds

Table 2 shows the expected upper and lower bounds for this task as suggested by BLEU scores for human responses and a random response baseline. The RANDOM system comprises responses randomly extracted from the triples corpus. HUMAN is computed by choosing one reference amongst the multi-reference set for each context-status pair.[4] Although the scores are lower than those usually reported in SMT tasks, the ranking of the three systems is unambiguous.

### 6.2 BLEU and METEOR

The results of automatic evaluation using BLEU and METEOR are presented in Table 3, where some broad patterns emerge. First, both metrics indicate that a phrase-based MT decoder outperforms a purely IR approach. Second, adding CMM features

[4] For the human score, we compute corpus-level BLEU with a sampling scheme that randomly leaves out one reference - the human sentence to score - for each reference set. This sampling scheme (repeated with 100 trials) is also applied for the MT and RANDOM system so as to make BLEU scores comparable.

| MT $n$-best | BLEU (%) | METEOR (%) |
|---|---|---|
| MT $_{9\text{ feat.}}$ | 3.60 (-9.5%) | 9.19 (-0.9%) |
| CMM $_{9\text{ feat.}}$ | 3.33 (-16%) | 9.34 (+0.7%) |
| ▷ MT + CMM $_{17\text{ feat.}}$ | 3.98 (-) | 9.28 (-) |
| RLMT $_{2\text{ feat.}}$ | 4.13 (+3.7%) | 9.54 (+2.7%) |
| DCGM-I $_{2\text{ feat.}}$ | 4.26 (+7.0%) | 9.55 (+2.9%) |
| DCGM-II $_{2\text{ feat.}}$ | 4.11 (+3.3%) | 9.45 (+1.8%) |
| DCGM-I + CMM $_{10\text{ feat.}}$ | 4.44 (+11%) | 9.60 (+3.5%) |
| DCGM-II + CMM $_{10\text{ feat.}}$ | 4.38 (+10%) | 9.62 (+3.5%) |

| IR $n$-best | BLEU (%) | METEOR (%) |
|---|---|---|
| IR $_{2\text{ feat.}}$ | 1.51 (-55%) | 6.25 (-22%) |
| CMM $_{9\text{ feat.}}$ | 3.39 (-0.6%) | 8.20 (+0.6%) |
| ▷ IR + CMM $_{10\text{ feat.}}$ | 3.41 (-) | 8.04 (-) |
| RLMT $_{2\text{ feat.}}$ | 2.85 (-16%) | 7.38 (-8.2%) |
| DCGM-I $_{2\text{ feat.}}$ | 3.36 (-1.5%) | 7.84 (-2.5%) |
| DCGM-II $_{2\text{ feat.}}$ | 3.37 (-1.1%) | 8.22 (+2.3%) |
| DCGM-I + CMM $_{10\text{ feat.}}$ | 4.07 (+19%) | 8.67 (+7.8%) |
| DCGM-II + CMM $_{10\text{ feat.}}$ | 4.24 (+24%) | 8.61 (+7.1%) |

Table 3: Context-sensitive ranking results on both MT (left) and IR (right) $n$-best lists, $n = 1000$. The subscript $_{\text{feat.}}$ indicates the number of features of the models. The log-linear weights are estimated by running one iteration of MERT. We mark by ($\pm$%) the relative improvements with respect to the reference system (▷).

to the baseline systems helps. Third, the neural network models contribute measurably to improvement: RLMT and DCGM models outperform baselines, and DCGM models provide more consistent gains than RLMT.

**MT vs. IR** BLEU and METEOR scores indicate that the phrase-based MT decoder outperforms a purely IR approach, despite the fact that IR proposes fluent human generated responses. This may be because the IR model only loosely captures important patterns between message and response: It ranks candidate responses solely by the similarity of their message with the message of the test triple (§5.3). As a result, the top ranked response is likely to drift from the purpose of the original conversation. The MT approach, by contrast, more directly models statistical patterns between message and response.

**CMM** MT+CMM, totaling 17 features (9 from MT + 8 CMM), improves 0.38 BLEU points, a 9.5% relative improvement, over the baseline MT model. IR+CMM, with 10 features (IR + word penalty + 8 CMM), benefits even more, attaining 1.8 BLEU points and 1.5 METEOR points over the IR baseline. Figure 4 (a) and (b) plots the magnitude of the learned CMM feature weights for MT+CMM and IR+CMM. CMM features help in both these hypothesis spaces and especially on the IR $n$-best list. Figure 4 (b) supports the hypothesis formulated in the previous paragraph: Since IR solely captures inter-message similarities, the matches between message and response are important, while context matches help in providing additional gains. The phrase-based statistical patterns captured by the MT system do a good job in explaining away 1-gram and 2-gram message matches (Figure 4 (a)) and the performance gain mainly comes from context matches. On the other hand, we observe that 4-gram matches may be important in selecting appropriate responses. Inspection of the tuning set reveals instances where responses contain long subsequences of their corresponding messages, e.g., $m$ = "good night best friend, I love you", $r$ = "I love you too, good night best friend". Although infrequent, such higher-order n-gram matches, when they occur, may provide a more robust signal of the quality of the response than 1- and 2-gram matches, given the highly conversational nature of our dataset.

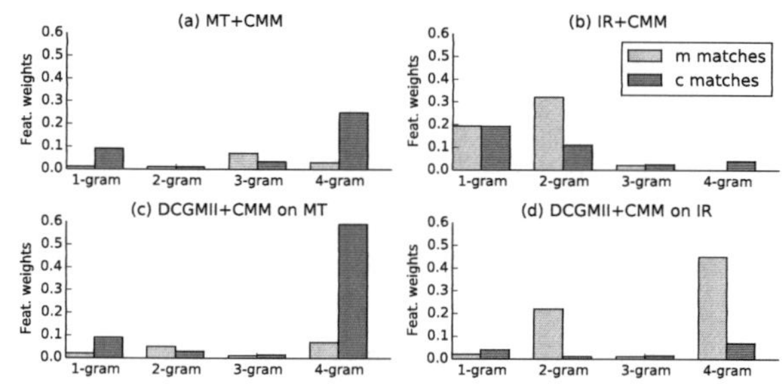


Figure 4: Comparison of the weights of learned CMM features for MT+CMM and IR+CMM systems (a) et (b) and DCGM-II+CMM on MT and IR (c) and (d).

**RLMT and DCGM** Both RLMT and DCGM models outperform their respective MT and IR baselines. Both models also exhibit similar performance and show improvements over the MT+CMM models, albeit using a lower dimensional feature space. We believe that their similar performance is due to the limited diversity of MT $n$-best list together with gains in fluency stemming from the strong language

| System A | System B | Gain (%) | CI |
|---|---|---|---|
| HUMAN | MT+CMM | 13.6* | [12.4,14.8] |
| DCGM-II | MT | 1.9* | [0.8, 2.9] |
| DCGM-II+CMM | MT | 3.1* | [2.0, 4.3] |
| DCGM-II+CMM | MT+CMM | 1.5* | [0.5, 2.5] |
| DCGM-II | IR | 5.2* | [4.0, 6.4] |
| DCGM-II+CMM | IR | 5.3* | [4.1, 6.6] |
| DCGM-II+CMM | IR+CMM | 2.3* | [1.2, 3.4] |

Table 4: Pairwise human evaluation scores between System A and B. The first (second) set of results refer to the MT (IR) hypothesis list. The asterisk means agreement between human preference and BLEU rankings.

model provided by the RLM. In the case of IR models, on the other hand, there is more headroom for improvement and fluency is already guaranteed. Any gains must come from context and message matches. Hence, RLMT underperforms with respect to both DCGM and IR+CMM. The DCGM models appear to have better capacity to retain contextual information and thus achieve similar performance to IR+CMM despite their lack of exact n-gram match information.

In the present experimental setting, no striking performance difference can be observed between the two versions of the DCGM architecture. If multiple sequences were used as context, we expect that the DCGM-II model would likely benefit more owing to the separate encoding of message and context.

**DCGM+CMM** We also investigated whether mixing exact CMM n-gram overlap with semantic information encoded by the DCGM models can bring additional gains. DCGM-{I-II}+CMM systems each totaling 10 features show increases of up to 0.48 BLEU points over MT+CMM and up to 0.88 BLEU over the model based on Ritter et al. (2011). METEOR improvements similarly align with BLEU improvements both for MT and IR lists. We take this as evidence that CMM exact matches and DCGM semantic matches interact positively, a finding that comports with Gao et al. (2014a), who show that semantic relationships mined through phrase embeddings correlate positively with classic co-occurrence-based estimations. Analysis of CMM feature weights in Figure 4 (c) and (d) suggests that 1-gram matches are explained away by the DCGM model, but that higher order matches are important. It appears that DCGM models might be improved by preserving word-order information in context and message encodings.

### 6.3 Human Evaluation

Human evaluation was conducted using crowd-sourced annotators. Annotators were asked to compare the quality of system output responses pairwise ("Which is better?") in relation to the context and message strings in the 2114 item test set. Identical strings were held out, so that the annotators only saw those outputs that differed. Paired responses were presented in random order to the annotators, and each pair of responses was judged by 5 annotators.

Table 4 summarizes the results of human evaluation, giving the difference in mean scores (pairwise preference margin) between systems and 95% confidence intervals generated using Welch's t-test. Identical strings not shown to raters are incorporated with an automatically assigned score of 0.5. The pattern in these results is clear and consistent: context-sensitive systems (+CMM) outperform non-context-sensitive systems, with preference gains as high as approximately 5.3% in the case of DCGM-II+CMM versus IR, and about 3.1% in the case of DCGM-II+CMM versus MT. Similarly, context-sensitive DCGM systems outperform non-DCGM context-sensitive systems by 1.5% (MT) and 2.3% (IR). These results are consistent with the automated BLEU rankings and confirm that our best performing DCGM models outperform both raw baseline and the context-sensitive baseline using CMM features.

### 6.4 Discussion

Table 5 provides examples of responses generated on the tuning corpus by the MT-based DCGM-II+CMM system, our best system in terms of both BLEU and human evaluation. Responses from this system are on average shorter (8.95 tokens) than the original human responses in the tuning set (11.5 tokens). Overall, the outputs tend to be generic or commonplace, but are often reasonably plausible in the context as in examples 1-3, especially where context and message contain common conversational elements. Example 2 illustrates the impact of context-sensitivity: the word "book" in the response is not found in the message. Nonetheless, longer generated responses are apt to degrade both syntactically and in terms of content. We notice that longer responses are likely to present

| # | Context $c$ | Message $m$ | Generated Response $r$ |
|---|---|---|---|
| 1 | noone can help this time its just i need a support system | well im here to support you. whenever you need me. | thank you, i appreciate it thank you |
| 2 | nothin much, and how's the book?! | its good but i'm only like halfway through cuz i don't feel like reading. i'm so bored ... | that's good! i have the book but i'm bored too. |
| 3 | i know! what have you been up to? | nothing really. just enjoying summer and working. what about you? | that's good! nothing much just listening to music and you? |
| 4 | thanks, your way better though | i'm just good at expressing it that's but trust me you are freakin amazing and waay better | i know, i don't trust you, i love you too! thank you |
| 5 | thanks. yeah i am good thanks! good, but angry! | sorry you're angry, been there, i hope it dies down. | i hope so too, i'm not angry!! |
| 6 | figures. bass. never ate bass. | bass is extremely mild with very few bones. my favorite after catfish | that's one of the bones, chuck bass is mine too. |
| 7 | today i will walk for miles. clear sky clear mind. | love walking. it's too hot to walk this month. i haven't moved. frozen. heat freeze. | it's too hot for you to get up to honey if you have frozen yogurt to you. |
| 8 | arresting people over "nasty tweets"? please. i'm not condoning what the lad did but arresting him is a tad silly. | it appears he may have sent death threats to others while all this was kicking off too. | i did! he was armed with nuclear threats? that's what's happening to you. |

Table 5: Sample responses produced by the MT-based DCGM-II+CMM system.

information that conflicts either internally within the response itself, or is at odds with the context, as in examples 4-5. This is not unsurprising, since our model lacks mechanisms both for reflecting agent intent in the response and for maintaining consistency with respect to sentiment polarity. Longer context and message components may also result in responses that wander off-topic or lapse into incoherence as in 6-8, especially when relatively low frequency unigrams ("bass", "threat") are echoed in the response. In general, we expect that larger datasets and incorporation of more extensive contexts into the model will help yield more coherent results in these cases. Consistent representation of agent intent is outside the scope of this work, but will likely remain a significant challenge.

## 7 Conclusion

We have formulated a neural network architecture for data-driven response generation trained from social media conversations, in which generation of responses is conditioned on past dialog utterances that provide contextual information. We have proposed a novel multi-reference extraction technique allowing for robust automated evaluation using standard SMT metrics such as BLEU and METEOR. Our context-sensitive models consistently outperform both context-independent and context-sensitive baselines by up to 11% relative improvement in BLEU in the MT setting and 24% in the IR setting, albeit using a minimal number of features. As our models are completely data-driven and self-contained, they hold the potential to improve fluency and contextual relevance in other types of dialog systems.

Our work suggests several directions for future research. We anticipate that there is much room for improvement if we employ more complex neural network models that take into account word order within the message and context utterances. Direct generation from neural network models is an interesting and potentially promising next step. Future progress in this area will also greatly benefit from thorough study of automated evaluation metrics.

## Acknowledgments

We thank Alan Ritter, Ray Mooney, Chris Quirk, Lucy Vanderwende, Susan Hendrich and Mouni Reddy for helpful discussions, as well as the three anonymous reviewers for their comments.

## References

Michael Auli, Michel Galley, Chris Quirk, and Geoffrey Zweig. 2013. Joint language and translation modeling with recurrent neural networks. In *Proc. of EMNLP*, pages 1044–1054.

Satanjeev Banerjee and Alon Lavie. 2005. METEOR: An automatic metric for MT evaluation with improved correlation with human judgments. In *Proc. of ACL Workshop on Intrinsic and Extrinsic Evaluation Measures for Machine Translation and/or Summarization*, pages 65–72, Ann Arbor, Jun.

Yoshua Bengio, Rejean Ducharme, and Pascal Vincent. 2003. A neural probabilistic language model. *Journ. Mach. Learn. Res.*, 3:1137–1155.

Kyunghyun Cho, Bart van Merrienboer, Çaglar Gülçehre, Fethi Bougares, Holger Schwenk, and Yoshua Bengio. 2014. Learning phrase representations using RNN encoder-decoder for statistical machine translation. *Proc. of EMNLP*.

Ronan Collobert and Jason Weston. 2008. A unified architecture for natural language processing: Deep neural networks with multitask learning. In *Proc. of ICML*, pages 160–167. ACM.

Jacob Devlin, Rabih Zbib, Zhongqiang Huang, Thomas Lamar, Richard Schwartz, and John Makhoul. 2014. Fast and robust neural network joint models for statistical machine translation. In *Proc. of ACL*.

John Duchi, Elad Hazan, and Yoram Singer. 2011. Adaptive subgradient methods for online learning and stochastic optimization. *Journ. Mach. Learn. Res.*, 12:2121–2159.

Jianfeng Gao, Xiaodong He, Wen tau Yih, and Li Deng. 2014a. Learning continuous phrase representations for translation modeling. In *Proc. of ACL*, pages 699–709.

Jianfeng Gao, Patrick Pantel, Michael Gamon, Xiaodong He, and Li Deng. 2014b. Modeling interestingness with deep neural networks. In *Proc. of EMNLP*, pages 2–13.

Kallirroi Georgila, James Henderson, and Oliver Lemon. 2006. User simulation for spoken dialogue systems: Learning and evaluation. In *Proc. of Interspeech/ICSLP*.

Michael Gutmann and Aapo Hyvärinen. 2010. Noise-contrastive estimation: A new estimation principle for unnormalized statistical models. In *Proc. of AISTATS*, pages 297–304.

Po-Sen Huang, Xiaodong He, Jianfeng Gao, Li Deng, Alex Acero, and Larry Heck. 2013. Learning deep structured semantic models for web search using clickthrough data. In *Proc. of CIKM*, pages 2333–2338.

Nal Kalchbrenner and Phil Blunsom. 2013. Recurrent continuous translation models. *Proc. of EMNLP*, pages 1700–1709.

Reinhard Kneser and Hermann Ney. 1995. Improved backing-off for M-gram language modeling. In *Proc. of ICASSP*, pages 181–184, May.

Philipp Koehn, Hieu Hoang, Alexandra Birch, Chris Callison-Burch, Marcello Federico, Nicola Bertoldi, Brooke Cowan, Wade Shen, Christine Moran, Richard Zens, Chris Dyer, Ondrej Bojar, Alexandra Constantin, and Evan Herbst. 2007. Moses: Open Source Toolkit for Statistical Machine Translation. In *Proc. of ACL Demo and Poster Sessions*, pages 177–180.

Tomas Mikolov and Geoffrey Zweig. 2012. Context Dependent Recurrent Neural Network Language Model.

Tomas Mikolov, Martin Karafiát, Lukas Burget, Jan Cernocký, and Sanjeev Khudanpur. 2010. Recurrent neural network based language model. In *Proc. of INTERSPEECH*, pages 1045–1048.

Franz Josef Och and Hermann Ney. 2004. The alignment template approach to machine translation. *Comput. Linguist.*, 30(4):417–449.

Franz Josef Och. 2003. Minimum error rate training in statistical machine translation. In *Proc. of ACL*, pages 160–167.

Kishore Papineni, Salim Roukos, Todd Ward, and Wei-Jing Zhu. 2002. BLEU: a method for automatic evaluation of machine translation. In *Proc. of ACL*, pages 311–318.

Razvan Pascanu, Tomas Mikolov, and Yoshua Bengio. 2013. On the difficulty of training recurrent neural networks. *Proc. of ICML*, pages 1310–1318.

Alan Ritter, Colin Cherry, and William B. Dolan. 2011. Data-driven response generation in social media. In *Proc. of EMNLP*, pages 583–593.

Stephen E Robertson, Steve Walker, Susan Jones, et al. 1995. Okapi at TREC-3.

David E. Rumelhart, Geoffrey E. Hinton, and Ronald J. Williams. 1988. Learning representations by back-propagating errors. In James A. Anderson and Edward Rosenfeld, editors, *Neurocomputing: Foundations of Research*, pages 696–699. MIT Press, Cambridge, MA, USA.

Yelong Shen, Xiaodong He, Jianfeng Gao, Li Deng, and Grégoire Mesnil. 2014. A latent semantic model with convolutional-pooling structure for information retrieval. In *Proc. of CIKM*, pages 101–110.

Amanda Stent and Srinivas Bangalore. 2014. *Natural Language Generation in Interactive Systems*. Cambridge University Press.

Ilya Sutskever, Oriol Vinyals, and Quoc V. V Le. 2014. Sequence to sequence learning with neural networks. *Proc. of NIPS*.

Marilyn A. Walker, Rashmi Prasad, and Amanda Stent. 2003. A trainable generator for recommendations in multimodal dialog. In *Proc. of EUROSPEECH*.

Steve Young, Milica Gašić, Simon Keizer, François Mairesse, Jost Schatzmann, Blaise Thomson, and Kai Yu. 2010. The hidden information state model: A practical framework for pomdp-based spoken dialogue management. *Comput. Speech Lang.*, 24(2):150–174.

Steve Young. 2002. Talking to machines (statistically speaking). In *Proc. of INTERSPEECH*.

# How to Make a Frenemy: Multitape FSTs for Portmanteau Generation

**Aliya Deri and Kevin Knight**
Information Sciences Institute
Department of Computer Science
University of Southern California
{aderi, knight}@isi.edu

## Abstract

A portmanteau is a type of compound word that fuses the sounds and meanings of two component words; for example, "frenemy" (friend + enemy) or "smog" (smoke + fog). We develop a system, including a novel multitape FST, that takes an input of two words and outputs possible portmanteaux. Our system is trained on a list of known portmanteaux and their component words, and achieves 45% exact matches in cross-validated experiments.

| $W^1$ | $W^2$ | PM |
|---|---|---|
| affluence | influenza | affluenza |
| anecdote | data | anecdata |
| chill | relax | chillax |
| flavor | favorite | flavorite |
| guess | estimate | guesstimate |
| jogging | juggling | joggling |
| sheep | people | sheeple |
| spanish | english | spanglish |
| zeitgeist | ghost | zeitghost |

Table 1: Valid component words and portmanteaux.

## 1 Introduction

Portmanteaux are new words that fuse both the sounds and meanings of their component words. Innovative and entertaining, they are ubiquitous in advertising, social media, and newspapers (Figure 1). Some, like "frenemy" (friend + enemy), "brunch" (breakfast + lunch), and "smog" (smoke + fog), express such unique concepts that they permanently enter the English lexicon.

Portmanteau generation, while seemingly trivial for humans, is actually a combination of two complex natural language processing tasks: (1) choosing component words that are both semantically and phonetically compatible, and (2) blending those words into the final portmanteau. An end-to-end system that is able to generate novel portmanteaux with minimal human intervention would be not only a useful tool in areas like advertising and journalism, but also a notable achievement in creative NLP.

Figure 1: A *New Yorker* headline portmanteau.

Due to the complexity of both component word selection and blending, previous portmanteau generation systems have several limitations. The Nehovah system (Smith et al., 2014) combines words only at exact grapheme matches, making the generation of more complex phonetic blends like "frenemy" or "brunch" impossible. Özbal and Strappavara (2012) blend words phonetically and allow inexact matches but rely on encoded human knowledge, such as sets of similar phonemes and semantically related words. Both systems are rule-based, rather than data-driven, and do not train or test their systems with real-world portmanteaux.

In contrast to these approaches, this paper presents a data-driven model that accomplishes (2) by blending two given words into a portmanteau. That is, with an input of "friend" and "enemy," we want to generate "frenemy."



*Human Language Technologies: The 2015 Annual Conference of the North American Chapter of the ACL*, pages 206–210,
Denver, Colorado, May 31 – June 5, 2015. 

$F_1$ $R_1$ $EH_3$ $N_3$ $D_4$ $T_1$ $OW_1$ $F_1$ $UW_3$

$EH_3$ $N_3$ $AH_5$ $M_5$ $IY_5$ $T_2$ $ER_3$ $K_5$ $IY_5$

Figure 2: Derivations for friend + enemy → "frenemy" and tofu + turkey → "tofurkey." Subscripts indicate the step applied to each phoneme.

We take a statistical modeling approach to portmanteau generation, using training examples (Table 1) to learn weights for a cascade of finite state machines. To handle the 2-input, 1-output problem inherent in the task, we implement a multitape FST.

This work's contributions can be summarized as:

- a portmanteau generation model, trained in an unsupervised manner on unaligned portmanteaux and component words,
- the novel use of a multitape FST for a 2-input, 1-output problem, and
- the release of our training data.[1]

## 2 Definition of a portmanteau

In this work, a portmanteau PM and its pronunciation $PM_{pron}$ have the following constraints:

- PM has exactly 2 component words $W^1$ and $W^2$, with pronunciations $W^1_{pron}$ and $W^2_{pron}$.
- All of PM's letters are in $W^1$ and $W^2$, and all phonemes in $PM_{pron}$ are in $W^1_{pron}$ and $W^2_{pron}$.
- All pronunciations use the Arpabet symbol set.
- Portmanteau building occurs at the phoneme level. $PM_{pron}$ is built through the following steps (further illustrated in Figure 2):

1. 0+ phonemes from $W^1_{pron}$ are output.
2. 0+ phonemes from $W^2_{pron}$ are deleted.
3. 1+ phonemes from $W^1_{pron}$ are aligned with an equal number of phonemes from $W^2_{pron}$. For each aligned pair of phonemes $(x, y)$, either $x$ or $y$ is output.
4. 0+ phonemes from $W^1_{pron}$ are deleted, until the end of $W^1_{pron}$.
5. 0+ phonemes from $W^2_{pron}$ are output, until the end of $W^2_{pron}$.

[1]Available at both authors' websites.

## 3 Multitape FST model

Finite state machines (FSMs) are powerful tools in NLP and are frequently used in tasks like machine transliteration and pronunciation. Toolkits like Carmel and OpenFST allow rapid implementations of complex FSM cascades, machine learning algorithms, and $n$-best lists.

Both toolkits implement two types of FSMs: finite state acceptors (FSAs) and finite state transducers (FSTs), and their weighted counterparts (wFSAs and wFSTs). An FSA has one input tape; an FST has one input and one output tape.

What if we want a one input and two output tapes for an FST? Three input tapes for an FSA? Although infrequently explored in NLP research, these "multitape" machines are valid FSMs.

In the case of converting $\{W^1_{pron}, W^2_{pron}\}$ to $PM_{pron}$, an interleaved reading of two tapes would be impossible with a traditional FST. Instead, we model the problem with a 2-input, 1-output FST (Figure 3). Edges are labeled $x : y : z$ to indicate input tapes $W^1_{pron}$ and $W^2_{pron}$ and output tape $PM_{pron}$, respectively.

## 4 FSM Cascade

We include the multitape model as part of an FSM cascade that converts $W^1$ and $W^2$ to PM (Figure 4).

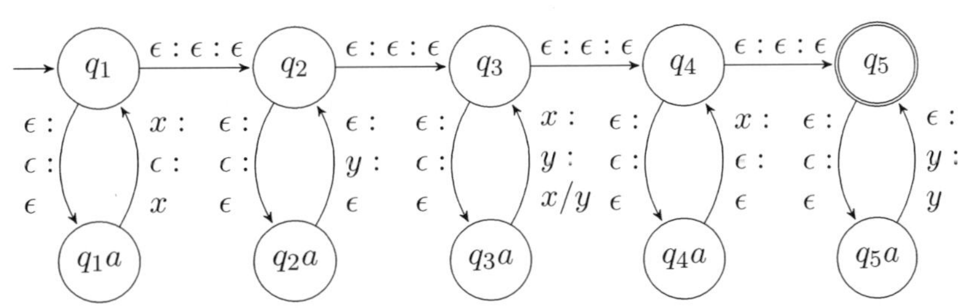


Figure 3: A 2- input, 1-output wFST for portmanteau pronunciation generation.

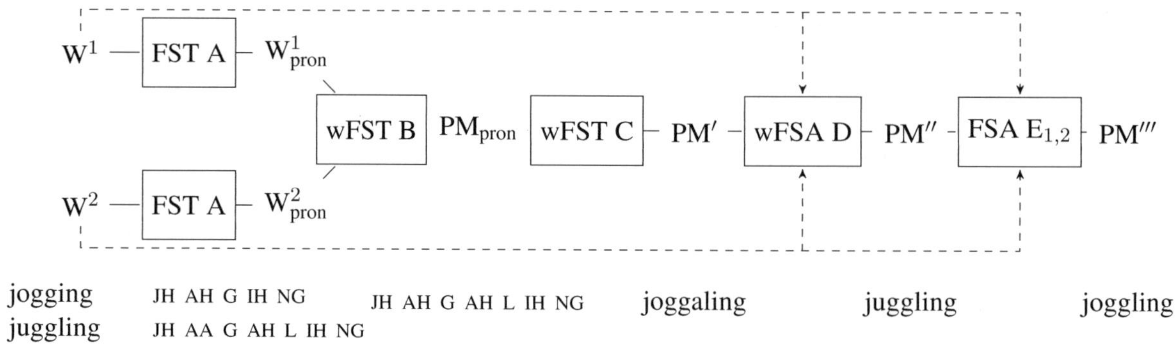


Figure 4: The FSM cascade for converting $W^1$ and $W^2$ into a PM, and an illustrative example.

| phonemes | | | $P(x, y \to z)$ | | |
|---|---|---|---|---|---|
| $x$ | $y$ | $z$ | cond. | joint | mixed |
| AA | AA | AA | 1.000 | 0.017 | 1.000 |
| AH | ER | AH | 0.424 | 0.007 | 0.445 |
| AH | ER | ER | 0.576 | 0.009 | 0.555 |
| P | B | P | 0.972 | 0.002 | 1.000 |
| P | B | B | 0.028 | N/A | N/A |
| Z | SH | SH | 1.000 | N/A | N/A |
| JH | AO | JH | 1.000 | N/A | N/A |

Table 2: Sample learned phoneme alignment probabilities for each method.

| step $k$ | description | $P(k)$ |
|---|---|---|
| 1 | $W^1_{\text{pron}}$ keep | 0.68 |
| 2 | $W^2_{\text{pron}}$ delete | 0.55 |
| 3 | align | 0.74 |
| 4 | $W^1_{\text{pron}}$ delete | 0.64 |
| 5 | $W^2_{\text{pron}}$ keep | 0.76 |

Table 3: Learned step probabilities. The probabilities of keeping and aligning are higher than those of deleting, showing a tendency to preserve the component words.

We first generate the pronunciations of $W^1$ and $W^2$ with FST A, which functions as a simple look-up from the CMU Pronouncing Dictionary (Weide, 1998).

Next, wFST B, the multitape wFST from Figure 3, translates $W^1_{\text{pron}}$ and $W^2_{\text{pron}}$ into $PM_{\text{pron}}$. wFST C, built from aligned graphemes and phonemes from the CMU Pronunciation Dictionary (Galescu and Allen, 2001), spells $PM_{\text{pron}}$ as $PM'$.

To improve $PM'$, we now use three FSAs built from $W^1$ and $W^2$. The first, wFSA D, is a smoothed "mini language model" which strongly prefers letter trigrams from $W^1$ and $W^2$. The second and third, FSA $E_1$ and FSA $E_2$, accept all inputs except $W^1$ and $W^2$.

## 5 Data

We obtained examples of portmanteaux and component words from Wikipedia and Wiktionary lists (Wikipedia, 2013; Wiktionary, 2013). We reject any that do not satisfy our constraints–for example, portmanteaux with three component words ("turkey" + "duck" + "chicken" $\to$ "turducken") or without any overlap ("arpa" + "net" $\to$ "arpanet"). From 571 examples, this yields 401 $\{W^1, W^2, PM\}$ triples.

We also use manual annotations of $PM_{\text{pron}}$ for learning the multitape wFST B weights and for mid-cascade evaluation.

We randomly split the data for 10-fold cross-validation. For each iteration, 8 folds are used for training data, 1 for dev, and 1 for test. Training data is used to learn wFST B weights (Section 6) and dev data is used to learn reranking weights (Section 7).

## 6 Training

FST A is unweighted and wFST C is pretrained. wFSA D and FSA $E_{1,2}$ are built at runtime.

We only need to learn wFST B weights, which we can reduce to weights on transitions $q_k \to q_k a$ and $q_3 a \to q_3$ from Figure 3. The weights $q_k \to q_k a$ represent the probability of each step, or $P(k)$. The weights $q_3 a \to q_3$ represent the probability of generating phoneme $z$ from input phonemes $x$ and $y$, or $P(x, y \to z)$.

| model | % exact | | avg. dist. | | % 1k-best | |
|---|---|---|---|---|---|---|
| | dev | test | dev | test | dev | test |
| cond | 28.9 | 29.9 | 1.6 | 1.6 | 92.0 | **91.2** |
| joint | **44.6** | **44.6** | **1.5** | **1.5** | 91.0 | 89.7 |
| mixed | 31.9 | 33.4 | 1.6 | 1.5 | **92.8** | 91.0 |
| rerank | **51.4** | **50.6** | **1.2** | **1.3** | **93.1** | **91.5** |

Table 4: $\text{PM}_{\text{pron}}$ results pre- and post-reranking.

| PM | % exact | avg. dist. | % 1k-best |
|---|---|---|---|
| PM′ | 12.03 | 5.31 | 42.35 |
| PM″ | 42.14 | 1.80 | 58.10 |
| PM‴ | **45.39** | **1.59** | **61.35** |

Table 5: PM results on cross-validated test data.

We use expectation maximization (EM) to learn these weights from our unaligned input and output, $\{\text{W}^1_{\text{pron}}, \text{W}^2_{\text{pron}}\}$ and $\text{PM}_{\text{pron}}$. We use three different methods of normalizing fractional counts. The learned phoneme alignment probabilities $P(x, y \rightarrow z)$ (Table 2) vary across these methods, but the learned step probabilities $P(k)$ (Table 3) do not.

### 6.1 Conditional Alignment

Our first learning method models phoneme alignment $P(x, y \rightarrow z)$ conditionally, as $P(z|x, y)$. Since $P(z|x, y)$ tends to be larger than step probabilities $P(k)$, the model prefers to align phonemes when possible, rather than keep or delete them separately. This creates longer alignment regions.

Additionally, during training a potential alignment $P(x|x, y)$ can compete only with its pair $P(y|x, y)$, making it more difficult to zero out an alignment's probability. The conditional method therefore also learns more potential alignments between phonemes.

### 6.2 Joint Alignment

Our second learning method models $P(x, y \rightarrow z)$ jointly, as $P(z, x, y)$. Since $P(z, x, y)$ is relatively low compared to the step probabilities, this method prefers very short alignments–the reverse of the effect seen in the conditional method.

However, the model can also zero out the probabilities of unlikely aligments, so overall it learns fewer possible alignments between phonemes.

| $\text{W}^1$ | $\text{W}^2$ | gold PM | hyp. PM |
|---|---|---|---|
| affluence | influenza | affluenza | affluenza |
| architecture | ecology | arcology | architecology |
| chill | relax | chillax | chilax |
| friend | enemy | frenemy | frienemy |
| japan | english | japlish | japanglish |
| jeans | shorts | jorts | js |
| jogging | juggling | joggling | joggling |
| man | purse | murse | mman |
| tofu | turkey | tofurkey | tofurkey |
| zeitgeist | ghost | zeitghost | zeitghost |

Table 6: Component words and gold and hypothesis PMs.

### 6.3 Mixed Alignment

Our third learning method initializes alignment probabilities with the joint method, then normalizes them so that $P(x|x, y)$ and $P(y|x, y)$ sum to 1. This "mixed" method, like the joint method, is more conservative in learning phoneme alignments. However, like the conditional method, it has high alignment probabilities and prefers longer alignments.

## 7 Model Combination and Reranking

Using the methods from sections 6.1, 6.2, and 6.3, we train three models and produce three different 1000-best lists of $\text{PM}_{\text{pron}}$ candidates for dev data. We combine these three lists into a single one, and compute the following features for each candidate: model scores, $\text{PM}_{\text{pron}}$ length, percentage of $\text{W}^1_{\text{pron}}$ or $\text{W}^2_{\text{pron}}$ in $\text{PM}_{\text{pron}}$, and percentage of $\text{PM}_{\text{pron}}$ in $\text{W}^1_{\text{pron}}$ or $\text{W}^2_{\text{pron}}$. We also include a binary feature for whether $\text{PM}_{\text{pron}}$ matches $\text{W}^1_{\text{pron}}$ or $\text{W}^2_{\text{pron}}$.

We then compute feature weights using the averaged perceptron algorithm (Zhou et al., 2006), and use them to rerank the candidate list, for both dev and test data. We combine the reranked $\text{PM}_{\text{pron}}$ lists to generate wFST C's input.

## 8 Evaluation

We evaluate our model's generation of $\text{PM}_{\text{pron}}$ pre- and post-reranking against our manually annotated $\text{PM}_{\text{pron}}$. We also compare PM′, PM″, and PM‴. For both $\text{PM}_{\text{pron}}$ and PM, we use three metrics:

- percent of 1-best results that are exact matches,
- average Levenshtein edit distance of 1-bests, and
- percent of 1000-best lists with an exact match.

## 9 Results and Discussion

We first evaluate the model at $PM_{pron}$. Table 4 shows that, despite less than 50% exact matches, over 90% of the 1000-best lists contain the correct pronunciation. This motivates our model combination and reranking, which increase exact matches to over 50%.

Next, we evaluate PM (Table 5). A component word mini-LM dramatically improves $PM''$ compared to $PM'$. Filtering out component words provides additional gain, to 45% exact matches.

In comparison, a baseline that merges $W^1_{pron}$ and $W^2_{pron}$ at the first shared phoneme achieves 33% exact matches for $PM_{pron}$ and 25% for PM.

Table 6 provides examples of system output. Perfect outputs include "affluenza," "joggling," "tofurkey," and "zeitghost." For others, like "chilax" and "frienemy," the discrepancy is negligible and the hypothesis PM could be considered a correct alternate output. Some hypotheses, like "architecology" and "japanglish," might even be considered superior to their gold counterparts. However, some errors, like "js" and "mman," are clearly unacceptable system outputs.

## 10 Conclusion

We implement a data-driven system that generates portmanteaux from component words. To accomplish this, we use an FSM cascade, including a novel 2-input, 1-output multitape FST, and train it on existing portmanteaux. In cross-validated experiments, we achieve 45% exact matches and an average Levenshtein edit distance of 1.59.

In addition to improving this model, we are interested in developing systems that can select component words for portmanteaux and reconstruct component words from portmanteaux. We also plan to research other applications for multi-input/output models.

## 11 Acknowledgements

We would like to thank the anonymous reviewers for their helpful comments, as well as our colleagues Qing Dou, Tomer Levinboim, Jonathan May, and Ashish Vaswani for their advice. This work was supported in part by DARPA contract FA-8750-13-2-0045.

## References

Lucian Galescu and James F Allen. 2001. Bi-directional conversion between graphemes and phonemes using a joint n-gram model. In *4th ISCA Tutorial and Research Workshop (ITRW) on Speech Synthesis*.

Gözde Özbal and Carlo Strapparava. 2012. A computational approach to the automation of creative naming. In *Proceedings of the 50th Annual Meeting of the Association for Computational Linguistics: Long Papers - Volume 1*, ACL '12, pages 703–711. Association for Computational Linguistics.

Michael R Smith, Ryan S Hintze, and Dan Ventura. 2014. Nehovah: A neologism creator nomen ipsum. In *Proceedings of the International Conference on Computational Creativity*, pages 173–181. ICCC.

Robert Weide. 1998. The CMU pronunciation dictionary, release 0.6.

Wikipedia. 2013. List of portmanteaus. `http://en.wikipedia.org/w/index.php?title=List_of_portmanteaus&oldid=578952494`. [Online; accessed 01-November-2013].

Wiktionary. 2013. Appendix:list of portmanteaux. `http://en.wiktionary.org/w/index.php?title=Appendix:List_of_portmanteaux&oldid=23685729`. [Online; accessed 02-November-2013].

Zhengyu Zhou, Jianfeng Gao, Frank K. Soong, and Helen Meng. 2006. A comparative study of discriminative methods for reranking LVCSR n-best hypotheses in domain adaptation and generalization. In *2006 IEEE International Conference on Acoustics Speech and Signal Processing, ICASSP 2006, Toulouse, France*, pages 141–144.

# Aligning Sentences from Standard Wikipedia to Simple Wikipedia

**William Hwang, Hannaneh Hajishirzi, Mari Ostendorf, and Wei Wu**
{wshwang, hannaneh, ostendor, weiwu}@u.washington.edu
University of Washington

## Abstract

This work improves monolingual sentence alignment for text simplification, specifically for text in standard and simple Wikipedia. We introduce a method that improves over past efforts by using a greedy (vs. ordered) search over the document and a word-level semantic similarity score based on Wiktionary (vs. WordNet) that also accounts for structural similarity through syntactic dependencies. Experiments show improved performance on a hand-aligned set, with the largest gain coming from structural similarity. Resulting datasets of manually and automatically aligned sentence pairs are made available.

## 1 Introduction

Text simplification can improve accessibility of texts for both human readers and automatic text processing. Although simplification (Wubben et al., 2012) could benefit from data-driven machine translation, paraphrasing, or grounded language acquisition techniques, e.g. (Callison Burch and Osborne, 2003; Fung and Cheung, 2004; Munteanu and Marcu, 2005; Smith et al., 2010; Ganitkevitch et al., 2013; Hajishirzi et al., 2012; Kedziorski et al., 2014), work has been limited because available parallel corpora are small (Petersen and Ostendorf, 2007) or automatically generated are noisy (Kauchak, 2013).

Wikipedia is potentially a good resource for text simplification (Napoles and Dredze, 2010; Medero and Ostendorf, 2009), since it includes *standard* articles and their corresponding *simple* articles in English. A challenge with automatic alignment is that standard and simple articles can be written independently so they are not strictly parallel, and have very different presentation ordering. A few studies use editor comments attached to Wikipedia edit logs to extract pairs of simple and difficult words (Yatskar et al., 2010; Woodsend and Lapata, 2011). Other methods use text-based similarity techniques (Zhu et al., 2010; Coster and Kauchak, 2011; Kauchak, 2013), but assume sentences in standard and simple articles are ordered relatively.

In this paper, we align sentences in standard and simple Wikipedia using a greedy method that, for every simple sentence, finds the corresponding sentence (or sentence fragment) in standard Wikipedia. Unlike other methods, we do not make any assumptions about the relative order of sentences in standard and simple Wikipedia articles. We also constrain the many-to-one matches to cover sentence fragments. In addition, our method takes advantage of a novel word-level semantic similarity measure that is built on top of Wiktionary (vs. WordNet) which incorporates structural similarity represented in syntactic dependencies. The Wiktionary-based similarity measure has the advantage of greater word coverage than WordNet, while the use of syntactic dependencies provides a simple mechanism for approximating semantic roles.

Here, we report the first manually annotated dataset for evaluating alignments for text simplification, develop and assess a series of alignment methods, and automatically generate a dataset of sentence pairs for standard and simple Wikipedia. Experiments show that our alignment method significantly outperforms previous methods on the hand-aligned



*Human Language Technologies: The 2015 Annual Conference of the North American Chapter of the ACL*, pages 211–217,
Denver, Colorado, May 31 – June 5, 2015. 

| | | |
|---|---|---|
| Good | Apple sauce or applesauce is a puree made of apples. | Applesauce (or applesauce) is a sauce that is made from stewed or mashed apples. |
| Good Partial | Commercial versions of applesauce are really available in supermarkets | It is easy to make at home, and *it is also sold already made in supermarkets as a common food.* |
| Partial | *Applesauce* is a sauce that is *made from* stewed and mashed apples. | *Applesauce is made by* cooking down apples with water or apple cider to the desired level. |

Table 1: Annotated examples: the matching regions for partial and good partial are italicized.

set of standard and simple Wikipedia article pairs. The datasets are publicly available to facilitate further research on text simplification.

## 2 Background

Given comparable articles, sentence alignment is achieved by leveraging the sentence-level similarity score and the sequence-level search strategy.

**Sentence-Level Scoring:** There are two main approaches for sentence-level scoring. One approach, used in Wikipedia alignment (Kauchak, 2013), computes sentence similarities as the cosine distance between vector representations of tf.idf scores of the words in each sentence. Other approaches rely on word-level $\sigma(w, w')$ semantic similarity scores $s(W, W') = \frac{1}{Z}\sum_{w \in W} \max_{w' \in W'} \sigma(w, w') idf(w)$. Previous work use WordNet-based similarity (Wu and Palmer, 1994; Mohler and Mihalcea, 2009; Hosseini et al., 2014), distributional similarity (Guo and Diab., 2012), or discriminative similarity (Hajishirzi et al., 2010; Rastegari et al., 2015).

In this paper, we leverage pairwise word similarities, and introduce two novel word-level semantic similarity metrics and show that they outperform the previous metrics.

**Sequence-Level Search:** There are several sequence-level alignment strategies (Shieber and Nelken, 2006). In (Zhu et al., 2010), sentence alignment between simple and standard articles is computed without constraints, so every sentence can be matched to multiple sentences in the other document. Two sentences are aligned if their similarity score is greater than a threshold. An alternative approach is to compute sentence alignment with a sequential constraint, i.e. using dynamic programming (Coster and Kauchak, 2011; Barzilay and Elhadad, 2003). Specifically, the alignment is computed by a recursive function that optimizes alignment of one or two consecutive sentences in one article to sentences in the other article. This method relies on consistent ordering between two articles, which does not always hold for Wikipedia articles.

## 3 Simplification Datasets

We develop datasets of aligned sentences in standard and simple Wikipedia. Here, we describe the *manually annotated* dataset and leave the details of the *automatically generated* dataset to Section 5.2.

**Manually Annotated:** For every sentence in a standard Wikipedia article, we create an HTML survey that lists sentences in the corresponding simple article and allow the annotator to judge each sentence pair as a good, good partial, partial, or bad match (examples in Table 1): *Good:* The semantics of the simple and standard sentence completely match, possibly with small omissions (e.g., pronouns, dates, or numbers). *Good Partial:* A sentence completely covers the other sentence, but contains an additional clause or phrase that has information which is not contained within the other sentence. *Partial:* The sentences discuss unrelated concepts, but share a short related phrase that does not match considerably. *Bad:* The sentences discuss unrelated concepts.

The annotators were native speaker, hourly paid, undergraduate students. We randomly selected 46 article pairs from Wikipedia (downloaded in June 2012) that started with the character 'a'. In total, 67,853 sentence pairs were annotated (277 good, 281 good partial, 117 partial, and 67,178 bad). The kappa value for interannotator agreement is 0.68 (13% of articles were dual annotated). Most disagreements between annotators are confusions between 'partial' and 'good partial' matches. The manually annotated dataset is used as a test set for evaluating alignment methods as well as tuning parameters for generating automatically aligned pairs across standard and simple Wikipedia.

## 4 Sentence Alignment Method

We use a sentence-level similarity score that builds on a new word-level semantic similarity, described below, together with a greedy search over the article.

### 4.1 Word-Level Similarity

Word-level similarity functions return a similarity score $\sigma(w_1, w_2)$ between words $w_1$ and $w_2$. We introduce two novel similarity metrics: Wiktionary-based similarity and structural semantic similarity.

**WikNet Similarity:** The Wiktionary-based semantic similarity measure leverages synonym information in Wiktionary as well as word-definition cooccurrence, which is represented in a graph and referred to as WikNet. In our work, each lexical content word (noun, verb, adjective and adverb) in the English Wiktionary is represented by one node in WikNet. If word $w_2$ appears in any of the sense definitions of word $w_1$, one edge between $w_1$ and $w_2$ is added, as illustrated in Figure 1. We prune the WikNet using the following steps: i) morphological variations are mapped to their baseforms; ii) atypical word senses (e.g. "obsolete," "Jamaican English") are removed; and iii) stopwords (determined based on high definition frequency) are removed. After pruning, there are roughly 177k nodes and 1.15M undirected edges. As expected, our Wiktionary based similarity metric has a higher coverage of 71.8% than WordNet, which has a word coverage of 58.7% in our annotated dataset.

Motivated by the fact that the WikNet graph structure is similar to that of many social networks (Watts and Strogatz, 1998; Wu, 2012), we characterize semantic similarity with a variation on a link-based node similarity algorithm that is commonly applied for person relatedness evaluations in social network studies, the Jaccard coefficient (Salton and McGill, 1983), by quantifying the number of shared neighbors for two words. More specifically, we use the extended Jaccard coefficient, which looks at neighbors within an n-step reach (Fogaras and Racz, 2005) with an added term to indicate whether the words are direct neighbors. In addition, if the words or their neighbors have synonym sets in Wiktionary, then the shared synonyms are used in the extended Jaccard measure. If the two words are in each other's synonym lists, then the similarity is set to

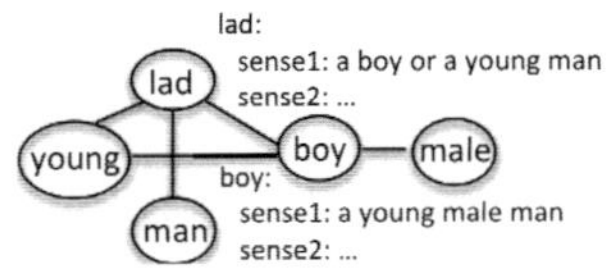


Figure 1: Part of WikNet with words "boy" and "lad".

1 otherwise, $\sigma_{wk}(w_1, w_2) = \sum_{l=0}^{n} J_l^s(w_1, w_2)$, for $J_l^s(w_1, w_2) = \frac{\Gamma_l(w_1) \cap_{syn} \Gamma_l(w_2)}{\Gamma_l(w_1) \cup \Gamma_l(w_2)}$ where $\Gamma_l(w_i)$ is the $l$-step neighbor set of $w_i$, and $\cap_{syn}$ accounts for synonyms if any. We precomputed similarities between pairs of words in WikNet to make the alignment algorithm more efficient. The WikNet is available at `http://ssli.ee.washington.edu/tial/projects/simplification/`.

**Structural Semantic Similarity:** We extend the word-level similarity metric to account for both semantic similarity between words, as well as the dependency structure between the words in a sentence. We create a triplet for each word using Stanford's dependency parser (de Marneffe et al., 2006). Each triplet $t_w = (w, h, r)$ consists of the given word $w$, its head word $h$ (governor), and the dependency relationship (e.g., modifier, subject, etc) between $w$ and $h$. The similarity between words $w_1$ and $w_2$ combines the similarity between these three features in order to boost the similarity score of words whose head words are similar and appear in the same dependency structure: $\sigma_{ss_{wk}}(w_1, w_2) = \sigma_{wk}(w_1, w_2) + \sigma_{wk}(h_1, h_2)\sigma_r(r_1, r_2)$ where $\sigma_{wk}$ is the WikNet similarity and $\sigma_r(r_1, r_2)$ represents dependency similarity between relations $r_1$ and $r_2$ such that $\sigma_r = 0.5$ if both relations fall into the same category, otherwise $\sigma_r = 0$.

### 4.2 Greedy Sequence-level Alignment

To avoid aligning multiple sentences to the same content, we require one-to-one matches between sentences in standard and simple Wikipedia articles using a greedy algorithm. We first compute similarities between all sentences $S_j$ in the simple article and $A_i$ in standard article using a sentence-level similarity score. Then, our method iteratively selects the most similar sentence pair $S^*, A^* = \arg\max s(S_j, A_i)$ and removes all other pairs associated with the respective sentences, repeating until all sentences in the shorter document are aligned. The cost of aligning sentences in two articles $S, A$ is $O(mn)$ where $m, n$ are the number of sentences in

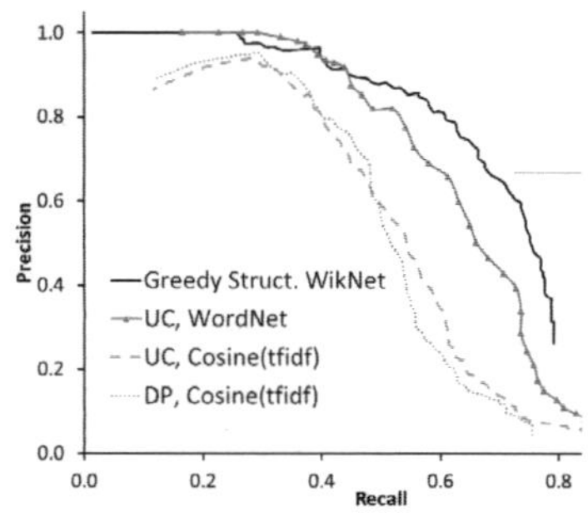


Figure 2: Precision-recall curve for our method vs. baselines.

articles $S$ and $A$, respectively. The run time of our method using WikNet is less than a minute for the sentence pairs in our test set.

Many simple sentences only match with a fragment of a standard sentence. Therefore, we extend the greedy algorithm to discover good partial matches as well. The intuition is that two sentences are good partial matches if a simple sentence has higher similarity with a fragment of a standard sentence than the complete sentence. We extract fragments for every sentence from the Stanford syntactic parse tree (Klein and Manning, 2003). The fragments are generated based on the second level of the syntactic parse tree. Specifically, each fragment is a S, SBAR, or SINV node at this level. We then calculate the similarity between every simple sentence $S_j$ with every standard sentence $A_i$ as well as fragments of the standard sentence $A_i^k$. The same greedy algorithm is then used to align simple sentences with standard sentences or their fragments.

## 5 Experiments

We test our method on all pairs of standard and simple sentences for each article in the hand-annotated data (no training data is used). For our experiments, we preprocess the data by removing topic names, list markers, and non-English words. In addition, the data was tokenized, lemmatized, and parsed using Stanford CoreNLP (Manning et al., 2014).

### 5.1 Results

**Comparison to Baselines:** The baselines are our implementations of previous work: *Unconstrained WordNet* (Mohler and Mihalcea, 2009), which uses an unconstrained search for aligning sentences and WordNet semantic similarity (in particular Wu-Palmer (1994)); *Unconstrained Vector Space* (Zhu et al., 2010), which uses a vector space representation and an unconstrained search for aligning sentences; and *Ordered Vector Space* (Coster and Kauchak, 2011), which uses dynamic programming for sentence alignment and vector space scoring.

| Good vs. Others | Max F1 | AUC |
|---|---|---|
| Greedy Struc. WikNet ($sim_G, \sigma_{ss_{wk}}$) | **0.712** | **0.694** |
| Unconst. WordNet ($sim_{UC}, \sigma_{wd}$) | 0.636 | 0.651 |
| Ordered Vec. Space ($sim_{DP}, s_{cos}$) | 0.564 | 0.495 |
| Unconst. Vec. Space ($sim_{UC}, s_{cos}$) | 0.550 | 0.509 |
| Good & Good Partial vs. Others | | |
| Greedy Struc. WikNet ($sim_G, \sigma_{ss_{wk}}$) | **0.607** | **0.529** |
| Unconst. WordNet ($sim_{UC}, \sigma_{wd}$) | 0.515 | 0.499 |
| Ordered Vec. Space ($sim_{DP}, s_{cos}$) | 0.415 | 0.387 |
| Unconst. Vec. Space ($sim_{UC}, s_{cos}$) | 0.431 | 0.391 |

Table 2: Max F1, AUC for identifying good matches and identifying good & good partial matches.

We compare our method (*Greedy Structural WikNet*) that combines the novel Wiktionary-based structural semantic similarity score with a greedy search to the baselines. Figure 2 and Table 2 show that our method achieves higher precision-recall, max F1, and AUC compared to the baselines. The precision-recall score is computed for good pairs vs. other pairs (good partial, partial, and bad).

From error analysis, we found that most mistakes are caused by missing good matches (lower recall). As shown by the graph, we obtain high precision (about .9) at recall 0.5. Thus, applying our method on a large dataset yields high quality sentence alignments that would benefit data-driven learning in text simplification.

Table 2 also shows that our method outperforms the baselines in identifying good and good partial matches. Error analysis shows that our fragment generation technique does not generate all possible or meaningful fragments, which suggests a direction for future work. We list a few qualitative examples in Table 3.

**Ablation Study:** Table 4 shows the results of ablating each component of our method, sequence-level alignments and word-level similarity.

*Sequence-level Alignment:* We study the contribution of the greedy approach in our method by using word-level structural semantic WikNet similarity $\sigma_{ss(wk)}$ and replacing the sequence-level greedy search strategy with dynamic programming and un-

| | | |
|---|---|---|
| Good | The castle was later incorporated into the construction of Ashtown Lodge which was to serve as the official residence of the Under Secretary from 1782. | After the building was made bigger and improved, it was used as the house for the Under Secretary of Ireland from 1782. |
| Good Partial | Mozart's Clarinet Concerto and Clarinet Quintet are both in A major, and generally Mozart was more likely to use clarinets in A major than in any other key besides E-flat major | Mozart used clarinets in A major often. |

Table 3: Qualitative examples of the good and good partial matches identified by our method.

| Sequence-level | Max F1 | AUC |
|---|---|---|
| Greedy ($sim_G, \sigma_{ss_{wk}}$) | **0.712**$^+$ | **0.694**$^+$ |
| Ordered ($sim_{DP}, \sigma_{ss_{wk}}$) | 0.656$^+$ | 0.610$^+$ |
| Unconstrained ($sim_{UC}, \sigma_{ss_{wk}}$) | 0.689 | 0.689 |
| **Word-level** | **Max F1** | **AUC** |
| Structural WikNet ($sim_G, \sigma_{ss_{wk}}$) | **0.712**$^+$ | **0.694**$^+$ |
| WordNet ($sim_G, \sigma_{wd}$) | 0.665$^+$ | 0.663$^+$ |
| Structural WordNet ($sim_G, \sigma_{ss_{wd}}$) | 0.685 | 0.679 |
| WikNet ($sim_G, \sigma_{wk}$) | 0.697 | 0.669 |

Table 4: Max F1, AUC for ablation study on word-level and sequence-level similarity scores. Values with the $^+$ superscript are significant with p<0.05.

constrained approaches. As expected, the dynamic programming approach used in previous work does not perform as well as our method, even with the structural semantic WikNet similarity, because the simple Wikipedia articles are not explicit simplifications of standard articles.

*Word-level Alignment:* Table 4 also shows the contribution of the structural semantic WikNet similarity measure $\sigma_{ss_{wk}}$ vs. other word-level similarities (WordNet similarity $\sigma_{wd}$, structural semantic WordNet similarity $\sigma_{ss_{wd}}$, and WikNet similarity $\sigma_{wk}$). In all the experiments, we use the sequence-level greedy alignment method. The structural semantic similarity measures improve over the corresponding similarity measures for both WordNet and WikNet. Moreover, WikNet similarity outperforms WordNet, and the structural semantic WikNet similarity measure achieves the best performance.

### 5.2 Automatically Aligned Data

We develop a parallel corpus of aligned sentence pairs between standard and simple Wikipedia, together with their similarity scores. In particular, we use our best case method to align sentences from 22k standard and simple articles, which were download in April 2014. To speed up our method, we index the similarity scores of frequent words and distribute computations over multiple CPUs.

We release a dataset of aligned sentence pairs, with a scaled threshold greater than 0.45.[1] Based on the precision-recall data, we choose a scaled threshold of 0.67 (P = 0.798, R = 0.599, F1 = 0.685) for good matches, and 0.53 (P = 0.687, R = 0.495, F1 = 0.575) for good partial matches. The selected thresholds yield around 150k good matches, 130k good partial matches, and 110k uncategorized matches. In addition, around 51.5 million potential matches, with a scaled score below 0.45, are pruned from the dataset.

## 6 Conclusion and Future Work

This work introduces a sentence alignment method for text simplification using a new word-level similarity measure (using Wiktionary and dependency structure) and a greedy search over sentences and sentence fragments. Experiments on comparable standard and simple Wikipedia articles outperform current baselines. The resulting hand-aligned and automatically aligned datasets are publicly available.

Future work involves developing text simplification techniques using the introduced datasets. In addition, we plan to improve our current alignment technique with better text preprocessing (e.g., coreference resolution (Hajishirzi et al., 2013)), learning similarities, as well as phrase alignment techniques to obtain better partial matches.

**Acknowledgments** This research was supported in part by grants from the NSF (IIS-0916951) and (IIS-1352249). The authors also wish to thank Alex Tan and Hayley Garment for annotations, and the anonymous reviewers for their valuable feedback.

[1] http://ssli.ee.washington.edu/tial/projects/simplification/

## References


[Barzilay and Elhadad2003] Regina Barzilay and Noemie Elhadad. 2003. Sentence alignment for monolingual comparable corpora. In *Proceedings of the Conference on Empirical Methods in Natural Language Processing (EMNLP)*.

[Callison Burch and Osborne2003] Chris Callison Burch and Miles Osborne. 2003. Bootstrapping parallel corpora. In *Proceedings of the Human Language Technologies - North American Chapter of the Association for Computational Linguistics Workshop on Building and Using Parallel Texts: Data Driven Machine Translation and Beyond - Volume 3 (HLT NAACL PARALLEL)*.

[Coster and Kauchak2011] William Coster and David Kauchak. 2011. Simple english Wikipedia: A new text simplification task. In *Proceedings of the Conference of the North American Chapter of the Association for Computational Linguistics: Human Language Technologies (NAACL HLT)*.

[de Marneffe et al.2006] Marie-Catherine de Marneffe, Bill MacCartney, and Christopher D. Manning. 2006. Generating typed dependency parses from phrase structure parses. In *Proceedings of the International Conference on Language Resources and Evaluation (LREC)*.

[Fogaras and Racz2005] Daniel Fogaras and Balazs Racz. 2005. Scaling link-based similarity search. In *Proceedings of the International Conference on World Wide Web (WWW)*, pages 641–650.

[Fung and Cheung2004] Pascale Fung and Percy Cheung. 2004. Mining Very-Non-Parallel Corpora: Parallel Sentence and Lexicon Extraction via Bootstrapping and EM. In *Proceedings of the Conference on Empirical Methods in Natural Language Processing (EMNLP)*.

[Ganitkevitch et al.2013] Juri Ganitkevitch, Benjamin Van Durme, and Chris Callison-Burch. 2013. PPDB: The paraphrase database. In *Proceedings of the Conference of the North American Chapter of the Association for Computational Linguistics: Human Language Technologies (NAACL HLT)*, pages 758–764, Atlanta, Georgia, June. Association for Computational Linguistics.

[Guo and Diab.2012] Weiwei Guo and Mona Diab. 2012. Modeling semantic textual similarity in the latent space. In *Proceedings of the Conference of the Association for Computational Linguistics (ACL)*.

[Hajishirzi et al.2010] Hannaneh Hajishirzi, Wen-tau Yih, and Aleksander Kolcz. 2010. Adaptive near-duplicate detection via similarity learning. In *Proceedings of the Association for Computing Machinery Special Interest Group in Information Retrieval(ACM SIGIR)*, pages 419–426.

[Hajishirzi et al.2012] Hannaneh Hajishirzi, Mohammad Rastegari, Ali Farhadi, and Jessica Hodgins. 2012. Semantic understanding of professional soccer commentaries. In *Proceedings of the Conference on Uncertainty in Artificial Intelligence (UAI)*.

[Hajishirzi et al.2013] Hannaneh Hajishirzi, Leila Zilles, Daniel S Weld, and Luke S Zettlemoyer. 2013. Joint coreference resolution and named-entity linking with multi-pass sieves. In *Proceedings of the Conference on Empirical Methods in Natural Language Processing (EMNLP)*.

[Hosseini et al.2014] Mohammad Javad Hosseini, Hannaneh Hajishirzi, Oren Etzioni, and Nate Kushman. 2014. Learning to solve arithmetic word problems with verb categorization. In *Proceedings of the Conference on Empirical Methods in Natural Language Processing (EMNLP)*.

[Kauchak2013] David Kauchak. 2013. Improving text simplification language modeling using unsimplified text data. In *Proceedings of the Conference of the Association for Computational Linguistics (ACL)*.

[Kedziorski et al.2014] Rik Koncel Kedziorski, Hannaneh Hajishirzi, and Ali Farhadi. 2014. Multi-resolution language grounding with weak supervision. In *Proceedings of the Conference on Empirical Methods in Natural Language Processing (EMNLP)*, pages 386–396.

[Klein and Manning2003] Dan Klein and Christopher D. Manning. 2003. Accurate unlexicalized parsing. In *Proceedings of the Conference of the Association for Computational Linguistics (ACL)*, pages 423–430.

[Manning et al.2014] Christopher D. Manning, Mihai Surdeanu, John Bauer, Jenny Finkel, Steven J. Bethard, and David McClosky. 2014. The Stanford CoreNLP natural language processing toolkit. In *Proceedings of the Conference of the Association for Computational Linguistics: System Demonstrations (ACL)*, pages 55–60.

[Medero and Ostendorf2009] Julie Medero and Mari Ostendorf. 2009. Analysis of vocabulary difficulty using wiktionary. In *Proceedings of the Speech and Language Technology in Education Workshop (SLaTE)*.

[Mohler and Mihalcea2009] Michael Mohler and Rada Mihalcea. 2009. Text-to-text semantic similarity for automatic short answer grading. In *Proceedings of the Conference of the European Chapter of the Association for Computational Linguistics (EACL)*.

[Munteanu and Marcu2005] Dragos Stefan Munteanu and Daniel Marcu. 2005. Improving machine translation performance by exploiting non-parallel corpora. *Computational Linguistics*.

[Napoles and Dredze2010] Courtney Napoles and Mark Dredze. 2010. Learning simple wikipedia: a cogitation in ascertaining abecedarian language. In *Proceedings of the North American Chapter of the Association for Computational Linguistics: Human Language Technologies Workshop on Computation Linguistics and Writing: Writing Processes and Authoring Aids (NAACL HLT)*.

[Petersen and Ostendorf2007] Sarah Petersen and Mari Ostendorf. 2007. Text simplification for langauge learners: A corpus analysis. In *Proceedings of the Speech and Language Technology in Education Workshop (SLaTE)*.

[Rastegari et al.2015] Mohammad Rastegari, Hannaneh Hajishirzi, and Ali Farhadi. 2015. Discriminative and consistent similarities in instance-level multiple instance learning. In *Proceedings of Computer Vision and Pattern Recognition (CVPR)*.

[Salton and McGill1983] Gerard Salton and Michael McGill. 1983. *Introduction to Modern Information Retrieval*. McGraw-Hill.

[Shieber and Nelken2006] Stuart Shieber and Rani Nelken. 2006. Towards robust context-sensitive sentence alignment for monolingual corpora. In *Proceedings of the Conference of the Association for Computational Linguistics (ACL)*.

[Smith et al.2010] Jason R. Smith, Chris Quirk, and Kristina Toutanova. 2010. Extracting parallel sentences from comparable corpora using document level alignment. In *Proceedings of the Conference of the North American Chapter of the Association for Computational Linguistics: Human Language Technologies (NAACL HLT)*.

[Watts and Strogatz1998] Duncan J. Watts and Steven H. Strogatz. 1998. Collective dynamics of small-world networks. *Nature*, pages 440–442.

[Woodsend and Lapata2011] Kristian Woodsend and Mirella Lapata. 2011. Wikisimple: Automatic simplification of wikipedia articles. In *Proceedings of the Association for Advancement of Artificial Intelligence Conference on Artificial Intelligence (AAAI)*, pages 927–932, San Francisco, CA.

[Wu and Palmer1994] Zhibiao Wu and Martha Palmer. 1994. Verbs semantics and lexical selection. In *Proceedings of the Conference of the Association for Computational Linguistics (ACL)*.

[Wu2012] Wei Wu. 2012. *Graph-based Algorithms for Lexical Semantics and its Applications*. Ph.D. thesis, University of Washington.

[Wubben et al.2012] Sander Wubben, Antal Van Den Bosch, and Emiel Krahmer. 2012. Sentence simplification by monolingual machine translation. In *Proceedings of the Conference of the Association for Computational Linguistics (ACL)*, pages 1015–1024.

[Yatskar et al.2010] Mark Yatskar, Bo Pang, Cristian Danescu-Niculescu-Mizil, and Lillian Lee. 2010. For the sake of simplicity: Unsupervised extraction of lexical simplifications from wikipedia. In *Proceedings of the Conference of the North American Chapter of the Association for Computational Linguistics: Human Language Technologies (NAACL HLT)*.

[Zhu et al.2010] Zhemin Zhu, Delphine Bernhard, and Iryna Gurevych. 2010. A monolingual tree-based translation model for sentence simplification. In *Proceedings of the International Conference on Computational Linguistics (COLING)*.

# Inducing Lexical Style Properties for Paraphrase and Genre Differentiation

**Ellie Pavlick**
University of Pennsylvania
epavlick@seas.upenn.edu

**Ani Nenkova**
University of Pennsylvania
nenkova@seas.upenn.edu

## Abstract

We present an intuitive and effective method for inducing style scores on words and phrases. We exploit signal in a phrase's rate of occurrence across stylistically contrasting corpora, making our method simple to implement and efficient to scale. We show strong results both intrinsically, by correlation with human judgements, and extrinsically, in applications to genre analysis and paraphrasing.

## 1 Introduction

True language understanding requires comprehending not just what is said, but how it is said, yet only recently have computational approaches been applied to the subtleties of tone and style. As the expectations on language technologies grow to include tailored search, context-aware inference, and analysis of author belief, an understanding of style becomes crucial.

Lexical features have proven indispensable for the good performance of most applications dealing with language. Particularly, more generalized characterizations of the lexicon (Brown et al., 1992; Wilson et al., 2005; Feng et al., 2013; Ji and Lin, 2009; Resnik, 1995) have become key in overcoming issues with lexical sparseness and in providing practical semantic information for natural language processing systems (Miller et al., 2004; Rutherford and Xue, 2014; Velikovich et al., 2010; Dodge et al., 2012). Most work on stylistic variation, however, has focused on larger units of text (Louis and Nenkova, 2013; Danescu-Niculescu-Mizil et al., 2012; Greene and Resnik, 2009; Xu et al., 2012) and studies of style at the lexical level have been scant. The few recent efforts (Brooke et al., 2010; Brooke and Hirst, 2013b; Brooke and Hirst, 2013a) have been motivated by the need to categorize genre in multiple continuous dimensions and focused on applying standard methods for lexical characterization via graph propagation or crowdsourcing.

| Formal/Casual | Complex/Simple |
|---|---|
| jesus/my gosh | great/a lot |
| 18 years/eighteen | cinema/a movie |
| respiratory/breathing | a large/a big |
| yes/yeah | music/the band |
| decade/ten years | much/many things |
| 1970s/the seventies | exposure/the show |
| foremost/first of all | relative/his family |
| megan/you there | matters/the things |
| somewhere/some place | april/apr |
| this film/that movie | journal/diary |
| full/a whole bunch | the world/everybody |
| otherwise/another thing | burial/funeral |
| father/my dad | rail/the train |
| recreation/hobby | physicians/a doctor |

Table 1: Paraphrases with large style differences. Our method learns these distinctions automatically.

We propose a simple and flexible method for placing phrases along a style spectrum. We focus on two dimensions: formality and complexity. We evaluate the resulting scores in terms of their correlation with human judgements as well as their utility in two tasks. First, we use the induced dimensions to identify stylistic shifts in paraphrase, allowing us to differentiate stylistic properties in the Paraphrase Database (PPDB) with high accuracy. Second, we test how well the induced scores capture differences between genres, and explore the extent to which these differences are due to topic versus lexical choice between stylistically different expressions for the same content. We show that style alone



*Human Language Technologies: The 2015 Annual Conference of the North American Chapter of the ACL*, pages 218–224,
Denver, Colorado, May 31 – June 5, 2015. ©2015 Association for Computational Linguistics

does differentiate between genres, and that the combined indicators of style and topic are highly effective in describing genre in a way consistent with human judgements.

## 2 Method

We focus on two style dimensions: formality and complexity. We define formal language as the way one talks to a superior, whereas casual language is used with friends. We define simple language to be that used to talk to children or non-native English speakers, whereas more complex language is used by academics or domain experts.

We use the Europarl corpus of parliamentary proceedings as an example of formal text and the Switchboard corpus of informal telephone conversations as casual text. We use articles from Wikipedia and simplified Wikipedia (Coster and Kauchak, 2011) as examples of complex and simple language respectively. For each style dimension, we subsample sentences from the larger corpus so that the two ends of the spectrum are roughly balanced. We end up with roughly 300K sentences each for formal/casual text and about 500K sentences each for simple/complex text.[1]

Given examples of language at each end of a style dimension, we score a phrase by the log ratio of the probability of observing the word in the reference corpus (REF) to observing it in the combined corpora (ALL). For formality the reference corpus is Europarl and the combined data is Europarl and Switchboard together. For complexity, the reference corpus is normal Wikipedia and the combined data is normal and simplified Wikipedia together. Specifically, we map a phrase $w$ onto a style dimension via:

$$\text{FORMALITY}(w) = \log\left(\frac{P(w \mid REF)}{P(w \mid ALL)}\right).$$

We assign formality scores to phrases up to three words in length that occur at least three times total in ALL, regardless of whether they occur in both corpora. Phrases which do not occur at all in REF are treated as though they occurred once.

[1]Number of words: casual (2MM), formal (7MM), simple (9MM), complex (12MM).

## 3 Evaluation

We first assess the intrinsic quality of the scores returned by our method by comparing against subjective human judgements of stylistic properties.

**Phrase-level human judgements** For each of our style dimensions, we take a random sample of 1,000 phrases from our corpora. We show each phrase to 7 workers on Amazon Mechanical Turk (MTurk) and ask the worker to indicate using a sliding bar (corresponding to a 0 to 100 scale) where they feel each word falls on the given style spectrum (e.g. casual to formal). Workers were given a high-level description of each style (like those given at the beginning of Section 2) and examples to guide their annotation.

| | Formal | Casual | Complex | Simple |
|---|---|---|---|---|
| Low $\sigma$ | exchange<br>proceedings<br>scrutiny | , uh<br>all that stuff<br>pretty much | per capita<br>referendum<br>proportional | is not<br>the night<br>up |
| High $\sigma$ | his speech<br>in return for<br>of the series | radio<br>are really<br>to move into | mid<br>japan<br>os | possible<br>center of<br>sets |

Table 2: Phrases with high and low levels of annotator agreement, measured by the variance of the human raters' scores (Low $\sigma$ = high agreement).

We estimate inter-annotator agreement by computing each rater's correlation with the average of the others. The inter-annotator correlation was reasonably strong on average ($\rho = 0.65$). However, not all phrases had equally strong levels of human agreement. Table 2 shows some examples of phrases which fell "obviously" on one end of a style spectrum (i.e. the variance between humans' ratings was low) and some other examples which were less clear.

**Quality of automatic scores** We compute the correlation of our method's score with the average human rating for each phrase. The results are summarized in Table 4. The log-ratio score correlates with the human score significantly above chance, even matching inter-human levels of correlation on the formality dimension.

## 4 Applications

We evaluate the acquired style mappings in two tasks: finding paraphrase pairs with differences in style and characterizing genre variation.

| | | | | | | |
|---|---|---|---|---|---|---|
| agreed | → | great | → | sure | → | yeah |
| assumes | → | implies | → | imagine | → | guess |
| currently | → | today | → | now | → | nowadays |
| most beautiful | → | very nice | → | really nice | → | really pretty |
| following a | → | in the aftermath | → | in the wake | → | right after |
| the man who | → | one who | → | the one that | → | the guy that |

Table 3: Groups of paraphrases ordered from most formal (left) to least formal (right), as described in Section 4.1.

| | Spearman $\rho$ | |
|---|---|---|
| | Formality | Complexity |
| Inter-annotator | 0.654 | 0.657 |
| Log-ratio score | 0.655 | 0.443 |

Table 4: First row: mean correlation of each rater's scores with the average of the others. Second row: correlation of our automatic style score with the average human score.

### 4.1 Differentiating style in paraphrases

Paraphrases are usually defined as "meaning equivalent" words or phrases. However, many paraphrases, even while capturing the same meaning overall, display subtle differences which effect their substitutability (Gardiner and Dras, 2007).

For example, paraphrasing "I believe that we have..." as "I think we got..." preserves the meaning but causes a clear change in style, from a more formal register to a casual one. It has been proposed that paraphrases are rarely if ever perfectly equivalent, but instead represent *near synonyms* (Edmonds and Hirst, 2002), which contain subtle differences in meaning and connotation.

We test whether our method can tease apart stylistic variation given a set of "equivalent" phrases. We use phrase pairs from the Paraphrase Database (PPDB) (Ganitkevitch et al., 2013). Using the scoring method described in Section 2, we identify paraphrase pairs which display stylistic variation along a particular dimension. We can find pairs $\langle w1, w2 \rangle$ in PPDB for which $\text{FORMALITY}(w1) - \text{FORMALITY}(w2)$ is large; Table 1 gives some examples of pairs identified using this method. We can also view paraphrases along a continuum; Table 3 shows groups of paraphrases ordered from most formal to most casual and Figure 1 shows how paraphrases of the phrase *money* rank along the formality and complexity dimensions. For example, we capture the fact that *money* is more formal but simpler than the idiomatic expression *a fortune*.

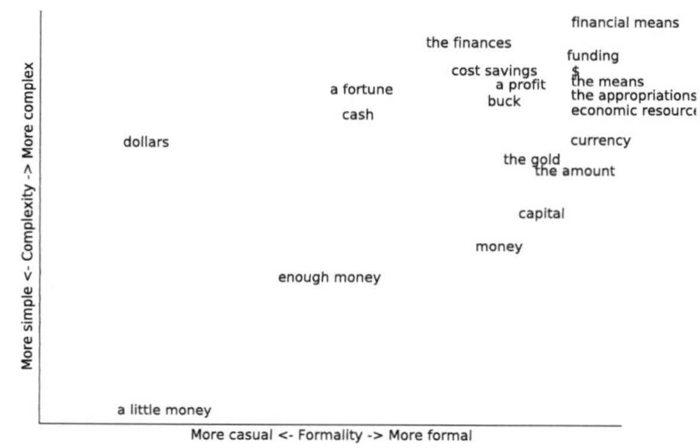


Figure 1: Several paraphrases for *money* ranked according to automatically learned style dimensions.

**Pairwise human judgements** To evaluate the goodness of our style-adapted paraphrases, we take a random sample of 3,000 paraphrase pairs from PPDB and solicit MTurk judgements. We show workers each paraphrase pair and ask them to choose which of the words is more casual, or to indicate "no difference." We also carry out the analogous task for the complexity distinction. We take the majority of 7 judgements as the true label for each pair.

In only 9% of the 3,000 paraphrase pairs, turkers decided there was no stylistic difference in the pair, indicating that indeed formality and complexity differences are truly characteristic of paraphrases. In further analysis we ignore the pairs for which the consensus was no difference but note that in further work we need to automate the identification of stylistically equivalent paraphrases.

**Automatically differentiating paraphrases** Using the human judgements, we compute the accuracy of our method for choosing which word in a pair is more formal (complex). We use the magnitude of the difference in formality (complexity) score as a measure of our method's confidence in its prediction. E.g. the smaller the gap in FORMALITY, the less confident our method is that there is a true style difference. Table 5 shows pairwise accuracy as a function of confidence: it is well above the 50% random baseline, reaching 90% for the high-confidence predictions in the complexity dimension.

| | Pairwise accuracy | | |
|---|---|---|---|
| | Top 10% | Top 25% | Overall |
| Complexity | 0.90 | 0.88 | 0.74 |
| Formality | 0.72 | 0.73 | 0.68 |

Table 5: Pairwise accuracy for paraphrase pairs at varying levels confidence. Top 10% refers to the 10% of pairs with largest difference in log-ratio style score. Random guessing achieves an accuracy of 0.5.

### 4.2 Genre characterization

Now we explore if the dimensions we learned at the sub-sentential level can be used to capture stylistic variation at the sentence and genre level.

**Sentence-level human judgements** We gather human ratings of formality and complexity for 900 sentences from the MASC corpus (Ide et al., 2010): 20 sentences from each of 18 genres.[2] Recently data from this corpus has been used to study genre difference in terms of pronoun, named entity, punctuation and part of speech usage (Passonneau et al., 2014). We use the data to test a specific hypothesis that automatically induced scores for lexical style are predictive of perceptions of sentence- and genre-level style.

We average 7 independent human scores to get sentence-level style scores. To get genre-level style scores, we use the the average of the 20 sentence-level scores for the sentences belonging to that genre.

In human perception, the formality and complexity dimensions are highly correlated (Spearman $\rho = 0.7$). However, we see many interesting examples of sentences which break this trend (Table 6). Overall, inter-annotator correlations are reasonably strong ($\rho \approx 0.5$), but as in the phrase-level annotations, we see some sentences for which the judgement seems unanimous among annotators and some sentences for which there is very little consensus (Table 7). We discuss this variation further in Section 5.

| | |
|---|---|
| Formal/Simple | has dr. miller left the courtroom? |
| Formal/Simple | i want to thank you for listening tonight. |
| Casual/Complex | right. cuz if we have a fixed number of neurons-? |
| Casual/Complex | i was actually thinking we could use the warping factors that we compute for the mfcc's |

Table 6: Some examples of sentences for which the generally high correlation between formality and complexity does not hold.

**Automatically characterizing genre** The extent to which genre is defined by topic versus style is an open question. We therefore look at two methods for genre-level style characterization, which we apply at the sentence-level as well as at the genre-level.

First, we take the average formality (complexity) score of all words in the text, which we refer to as the "all words" method. Using the style score alone in this way will likely to conflate aspects of topic with aspects of style. For example, the word *birthday* receives a very low formality score whereas the phrase *united nations* receives a very high formality score, reflecting the tendency of certain topics to be discussed more formally than others.

Figure 2: Authors reveal style by choosing casual terms or formal terms for the same concept. Shown is a casual sentence (left) and a formal sentence (right) on the same topic. Alternative paraphrases are ordered casual (top) to formal (bottom).

We therefore use a second method, which we refer to as "PP only", in which we look only at the words in the text which belong to one of our paraphrase sets (as in Figure 3), allowing us to control for topic and focus only on stylistic word choice. In "PP only", we consider a word to be formal if it appears on the formal side of the set (i.e. there are

[2]Court transcripts, debate transcripts, face-to-face conversations, blogs, essays, fiction, jokes, letters, technical writing, newspaper, twitter, email, ficlets (short fan fiction), government documents, journal entries, movie scripts, non-fiction, and travel guides. We omit the "telephone" genre, since it is too similar to the Switchboard corpus and may inflate results.

| | | |
|---|---|---|
| Formal | Low $\sigma$ | whereupon, the proceedings were adjourned at 4:20 p.m. |
| Formal | High $\sigma$ | mr. president , you have 90 seconds |
| Casual | Low $\sigma$ | is she, what grade is she in? |
| Casual | High $\sigma$ | they bring to you and your loved ones. |
| Complex | Low $\sigma$ | let me abuse the playwright and dismiss the penultimate scene |
| Complex | High $\sigma$ | revealing to you my family 's secret because my late dad 's burial is over. |
| Simple | Low $\sigma$ | you 're not the only one |
| Simple | High $\sigma$ | facebook can get you fired , dumped , and yes , evicted |

Table 7: Style ratings of sentences with high and low levels of human agreement, measured by the variance of the human raters' scores (Low $\sigma$ = high agreement).

more phrases to its left than to its right). We then score the overall formality of the text as the proportion of times a formal phrase was chosen when a more casual paraphrase could have been chosen instead. The intuition is captured in Figure 2: when an author is writing about a given topic, she encounters words for which there exist a range of paraphrases. Her lexical choice in these cases signals the style independent of the topic.

Table 8 shows how well our two scoring methods correlate with the human judgements of sentences' styles. The "all words" method performs very well, correlating with humans nearly as well as humans correlate with each other. Interestingly, when using paraphrases only we maintain significant correlations. This ability to differentiate stylistic variation without relying on cues from topic words could be especially important for tasks such as bias detection (Recasens et al., 2013) and readability (Callan, 2004; Kanungo and Orr, 2009).

| | Formality | | Complexity | |
|---|---|---|---|---|
| | Sent. | Genre | Sent. | Genre |
| Inter-anno. | 0.47 | – | 0.48 | – |
| All words | 0.44 | 0.77 | 0.43 | 0.80 |
| PP only | 0.18 | 0.63 | 0.23 | 0.45 |

Table 8: Spearman $\rho$ of automatic rankings with human rankings. Genres are the concatenation of sentences from that genre. In "all words," a text's score is the average log-ratio style score of its words. In "PP only," a text's score is the proportion of times a formal term was chosen when more casual paraphrases existed, effectively capturing style independent of topic.

## 5 Discussion

Characterization of style at the lexical level is an important first step in complex natural language tasks, capturing style information in a way that is portable across topics and applications. An interesting open question is the extent to which style is defined at the lexical level versus at the sentential level: how strongly are human perceptions of style influenced by topic and context as opposed to by lexical choice? One interesting phenomenon we observe is that inter-annotator correlations are lower at the sentence level ($\rho \approx 0.5$) than at the word- and phrase-level ($\rho \approx 0.65$). Tables 7 offers some insight: for many of the sentences for which human agreement is low, there seems to be some mismatch between the topic and the typical style of that topic (e.g. talking formally about family life, or talking in relatively complex terms about Facebook). When humans are making judgements at the lexical level, such contextual mismatches don't arise, which might lead to higher overall agreements. Interesting future work will need to explore how well humans are able to separate style from topic at the sentence- and document-level, and how the lexical choice of the author/speaker affects this distinction.

## 6 Conclusion

We present a simple and scalable method for learning fine-grained stylistic variation of phrases. We demonstrate good preliminary results on two relevant applications: identifying stylistic differences in paraphrase, and characterizing variations between genres. Our method offers a simple and flexible way of acquiring stylistic annotations at web-scale, making it a promising approach for incorporating nuanced linguistic information into increasingly complex language applications.[3]

[3]All human and log-ratio scores discussed are available at http://www.seas.upenn.edu/~nlp/resources/style-scores.tar.gz

## References


Julian Brooke and Graeme Hirst. 2013a. Hybrid models for lexical acquisition of correlated styles. In *Proceedings of the Sixth International Joint Conference on Natural Language Processing*, pages 82–90.

Julian Brooke and Graeme Hirst. 2013b. A multi-dimensional bayesian approach to lexical style. In *Proceedings of the 2013 Conference of the North American Chapter of the Association for Computational Linguistics: Human Language Technologies*, pages 673–679.

Julian Brooke, Tong Wang, and Graeme Hirst. 2010. Automatic acquisition of lexical formality. In *Proceedings of the 23rd International Conference on Computational Linguistics: Posters*, pages 90–98.

Peter F. Brown, Peter V. deSouza, Robert L. Mercer, Vincent J. Della Pietra, and Jenifer C. Lai. 1992. Class-based n-gram models of natural language. *Comput. Linguist.*, 18(4):467–479, December.

Kevyn Collins-Thompson Jamie Callan. 2004. A language modeling approach to predicting reading difficulty.

William Coster and David Kauchak. 2011. Simple english wikipedia: a new text simplification task. In *Proceedings of the 49th Annual Meeting of the Association for Computational Linguistics: Human Language Technologies: short papers-Volume 2*, pages 665–669. Association for Computational Linguistics.

Cristian Danescu-Niculescu-Mizil, Justin Cheng, Jon Kleinberg, and Lillian Lee. 2012. You had me at hello: How phrasing affects memorability. In *Proceedings of the 50th Annual Meeting of the Association for Computational Linguistics: Long Papers-Volume 1*, pages 892–901. Association for Computational Linguistics.

Jesse Dodge, Amit Goyal, Xufeng Han, Alyssa Mensch, Margaret Mitchell, Karl Stratos, Kota Yamaguchi, Yejin Choi, Hal Daumé III, Alexander C. Berg, and Tamara L. Berg. 2012. Detecting visual text. In *Human Language Technologies: Conference of the North American Chapter of the Association of Computational Linguistics, Proceedings,*, pages 762–772.

Philip Edmonds and Graeme Hirst. 2002. Near-synonymy and lexical choice. *Computational linguistics*, 28(2):105–144.

Song Feng, Jun Seok Kang, Polina Kuznetsova, and Yejin Choi. 2013. Connotation lexicon: A dash of sentiment beneath the surface meaning. In *Proceedings of the 51st Annual Meeting of the Association for Computational Linguistics, ACL*, pages 1774–1784.

Juri Ganitkevitch, Benjamin Van Durme, and Chris Callison-Burch. 2013. PPDB: The paraphrase database. In *Proceedings of NAACL-HLT*, pages 758–764, Atlanta, Georgia, June. Association for Computational Linguistics.

Mary Gardiner and Mark Dras. 2007. Corpus statistics approaches to discriminating among near-synonyms.

Stephan Greene and Philip Resnik. 2009. More than words: Syntactic packaging and implicit sentiment. In *Proceedings of human language technologies: The 2009 annual conference of the north american chapter of the association for computational linguistics*, pages 503–511. Association for Computational Linguistics.

Nancy Ide, Christiane Fellbaum, Collin Baker, and Rebecca Passonneau. 2010. The manually annotated sub-corpus: A community resource for and by the people. In *Proceedings of the ACL 2010 conference short papers*, pages 68–73. Association for Computational Linguistics.

Heng Ji and Dekang Lin. 2009. Gender and animacy knowledge discovery from web-scale n-grams for unsupervised person mention detection. In *Proceedings of the 23rd Pacific Asia Conference on Language, Information and Computation, PACLIC*, pages 220–229.

Tapas Kanungo and David Orr. 2009. Predicting the readability of short web summaries. In *Proceedings of the Second ACM International Conference on Web Search and Data Mining*, pages 202–211. ACM.

Annie Louis and Ani Nenkova. 2013. What makes writing great? first experiments on article quality prediction in the science journalism domain. *TACL*, 1:341–352.

Scott Miller, Jethran Guinness, and Alex Zamanian. 2004. Name tagging with word clusters and discriminative training. In *HLT-NAACL 2004: Main Proceedings*, pages 337–342.

Rebecca J. Passonneau, Nancy Ide, Songqiao Su, and Jesse Stuart. 2014. Biber redux: Reconsidering dimensions of variation in american english. In *Proceedings of COLING 2014, the 25th International Conference on Computational Linguistics: Technical Papers*, pages 565–576, Dublin, Ireland, August. Dublin City University and Association for Computational Linguistics.

Marta Recasens, Cristian Danescu-Niculescu-Mizil, and Dan Jurafsky. 2013. Linguistic models for analyzing and detecting biased language. In *ACL (1)*, pages 1650–1659.

Philip Resnik. 1995. Using information content to evaluate semantic similarity in a taxonomy. In *Proceedings of the Fourteenth International Joint Conference on Artificial Intelligence, IJCAI*, pages 448–453.

Attapol Rutherford and Nianwen Xue. 2014. Discovering implicit discourse relations through brown cluster pair representation and coreference patterns. In

*Proceedings of the 14th Conference of the European Chapter of the Association for Computational Linguistics, EACL*, pages 645–654.

Leonid Velikovich, Sasha Blair-Goldensohn, Kerry Hannan, and Ryan T. McDonald. 2010. The viability of web-derived polarity lexicons. In *Human Language Technologies: Conference of the North American Chapter of the Association of Computational Linguistics, Proceedings,*, pages 777–785.

Theresa Wilson, Janyce Wiebe, and Paul Hoffmann. 2005. Recognizing contextual polarity in phrase-level sentiment analysis. In *Proceedings of the Conference on Human Language Technology and Empirical Methods in Natural Language Processing*, HLT '05, pages 347–354.

Wei Xu, Alan Ritter, Bill Dolan, Ralph Grishman, and Colin Cherry. 2012. Paraphrasing for style. In *COLING*, pages 2899–2914.

# Entity Linking for Spoken Language

**Adrian Benton**
Human Language Technology
Center of Excellence
Johns Hopkins University
Baltimore, MD, USA
adrian@jhu.edu

**Mark Dredze**
Human Language Technology
Center of Excellence
Johns Hopkins University
Baltimore, MD, USA
mdredze@jhu.edu

## Abstract

Research on entity linking has considered a broad range of text, including newswire, blogs and web documents in multiple languages. However, the problem of entity linking for spoken language remains unexplored. Spoken language obtained from automatic speech recognition systems poses different types of challenges for entity linking; transcription errors can distort the context, and named entities tend to have high error rates. We propose features to mitigate these errors and evaluate the impact of ASR errors on entity linking using a new corpus of entity linked broadcast news transcripts.

## 1 Introduction

Entity linking identifies for each textual mention of an entity a corresponding entry contained in a knowledge base, or indicates when no such entry exits (NIL). Numerous studies have explored entity linking in a wide range of domains, including newswire (Milne and Witten, 2008; Mcnamee et al., 2009; McNamee and Dang, 2009; Dredze et al., 2010), blog posts (Ji et al., 2010), web pages (Demartini et al., 2012; Lin et al., 2012), social media (Cassidy et al., 2012; Guo et al., 2013a; Shen et al., 2013; Liu et al., 2013), email (Gao et al., 2014) and multi-lingual documents (Mayfield et al., 2011; McNamee et al., 2011; Wang et al., 2012). A common theme across all these settings requires addressing two difficulties in linking decisions: matching the textual name mention to the form contained in the knowledge base, and using contextual clues to disambiguate similar entities. However, all of these studies have focused on written language, while linking of spoken language remains untested. Yet many intended applications of entity linking, such as supporting search (Hachey et al., 2013) and identifying relevant sources for reports (He et al., 2010; He et al., 2011), linking of spoken language is critical. Search results regularly include audio content (e.g. YouTube) and numerous information sources are audio recordings (e.g. media reports.) An evaluation of entity linking for spoken language can help clarify issues and challenges in this domain.

In addition to the two main challenges discussed above, audio entity linking presents two parallel difficulties that arise from automatic transcription (ASR) of speech. First, the context can be both shorter (than newswire formats) and contain ASR errors, which can make the context of the mention less like supporting material in the knowledge base. Second, named entities are often more difficult to recognize (Huang, 2005; Horlock and King, 2003); they are often out-of-vocabulary and less common overall in training data. This can mislead the name matching techniques on which most entity linking systems depend.

In this paper we consider the task of entity linking for spoken language by evaluating linking on transcripts of broadcast news. We select broadcast news as a comparable domain of spoken language to newswire documents, which have been the focus of considerable research for entity linking (Mcnamee et al., 2009; Ji et al., 2010). We chose this comparable domain to focus on issues introduced because of a transition to spoken language from written, as opposed to issues that arise from a general domain shift associated with conversational speech, an issue that has been previously studied in the shift from written news to written conversations (weblogs, social



*Human Language Technologies: The 2015 Annual Conference of the North American Chapter of the ACL*, pages 225–230,
Denver, Colorado, May 31 – June 5, 2015. 

media, etc.) (Baldwin et al., 2013; Han et al., 2013).

We proceed as follows. We first introduce a new broadcast news dataset annotated for entity linking. We then propose new features based on ASR output to address the two sources of error specific to spoken language: 1) context errors and shortening, 2) name mention transcription errors. We then test our features on the automated output of an ASR system to validate our findings.

## 2 Entity Linked Spoken Language Data

We created entity linking annotations for HUB4 (Fiscus et al., 1997), a manually-transcribed broadcast news corpus. We used gold named entity annotations from Parada et al. (2011), who manually annotated 9971 utterances with CONLL style (Tjong Kim Sang and De Meulder, 2003) named entities. We selected 2140 person entities and obtained entity linking decisions with regards to the TAC KBP knowledge base (Mcnamee et al., 2009; Ji et al., 2010), which contains 818,741 entries derived from Wikipedia.

Annotations were initially obtained using Amazon Mechanical Turk (Callison-Burch and Dredze, 2010) using the same entity linking annotation scheme as Mayfield et al. (2011). Turkers were asked which of five provided Wikipedia articles matched a person mention highlighted in a displayed utterance. The provided Wikipedia articles were selected based on token overlap between the mention and article title, weighted by TFIDF. In addition to selecting one of the five articles, turkers could select "None of the above", "Not enough information" or "Not a person". We collected one Turker annotation per query and manually verified and corrected each provided label. For mentions that were not matched to an article, we verified that the article was not in the KB, or manually assigned a KB entry otherwise. Because we manually corrected each annotation, mistakes and biases resulting from crowdsourced annotations are not present in this corpus. Of the 2140 annotated mentions, 41% ($n$=887) were NIL, compared to 54.6% in TAC-KBP 2010 (Ji et al., 2010) and 57.1% in TAC-KBP 2009 (Mcnamee et al., 2009). The named entity and linking annotations can be found at https://github.com/mdredze/speech_ner_entity_linking_data/releases/tag/1.0.

We divided the 2140 mentions into 60% train ($n = 1283$) and 40% test ($n = 857$.) We ensured that the 1218 unique mention strings were disjoint between the two sets, i.e. no mention in the test data was observed during training.

Each instance is represented by the query (mention string) and document context. Unlike written articles, broadcast news does not indicate where one topic starts and another ends. Therefore, we experimented with different size contexts by including the utterance containing the name mention and up to eight utterances before and after so long as they occurred within 150 seconds of the start of the utterance containing the name mention. We found that five utterances before and after gave the highest average accuracy when using a standard set of features on the reference transcript to perform entity linking; we use this setting in the experiments below.

## 3 Entity Linking System

For entity linking, we use Slinky (Benton et al., 2014), an entity linking system that uses parallel processing of queries and candidates in a learned cascade to achieve fast and accurate entity linking performance. We use standard features from McNamee et al. (2012) as described in Benton et al. (2014). For a query $q$ composed of a context (multiple utterances) and a named entity string, Slinky first triages (Dredze et al., 2010; McNamee et al., 2012; Guo et al., 2013b) the query to identify a set of candidates $C_q$ in the knowledge base that may correspond to the mention string. Up to 1000 candidates are considered, though its usually much fewer. The system then extracts features based on query and candidate pairs and ranks them using a series of classifiers. The candidates are then ordered by their final scores; the highest ranking candidate is selected as the system's prediction. NIL is included as a candidate for every query and is then ranked by the system. For all training settings, we sweep over hyper-parameters using 5-fold cross validation on the training data to find the most accurate system. Reported results are based on the test data.

### 3.1 Spoken Language Features

ASR transcription errors pose a challenge for standard text processing features, which rely on textual similarity to measure relatedness of both context and entity mention strings. However, ASR errors are not random; incorrectly decoded words may be phonetically similar to the original spoken words. This suggests that similarity can still be captured by considering phonetic similarity.

We experiment with four feature types.

- **Text**: Our baseline system uses features based on the text of the mention string and document. We used the feature set presented by McNamee et al. (2012) and used in Benton et al. (2014), which was the best performing submission in the TAC-KBP 2009 entity linking task. These features include, among others, features that compare the candidate entity name to the mention string as well as the document's terms to those stored in the candidate's description in the KB. These include the dice coefficient, cosine similarity (boolean and weighted), and proportion of candidate tokens in the query document.
- **Phone**: Words in the document, mention string as well as the knowledge base are represented as phone sequences instead of text. We convert all words to phones using a grapheme string to phone (G2P) system.
- **Metaphones**: Two distinct phones can sound similar, yet still appear different when matching phones. Metaphones (Philips, 1990), a more recent version of Soundex, map similar sounding phones to the same representation. We convert the phones used in the previous paragraph to metaphones.
- **Lattice**: Expected word counts of the query document from the ASR lattice. Extracted unigrams are treated as a weighted bag-of-words for the query document. We compute all the features that use the query document's content and weigh them by the term's expectation.

The features in each of the above sets depend on their representation of the text (e.g. text, phone, metaphone, lattice). Additionally, we include the following features in all experiments: *Bias* features that fire for all candidates, only non-`NIL` candidates, and only `NIL` candidates; `NIL` features indicative of being linked to no article in the knowledge base such as the mention string is only 1 or 2 characters/tokens, the number of candidates emitted by the triager; and the *Popularity* (number of Wikipedia in-links) of the candidate.

**Triage** The above feature sets change the ranking of candidates. We also modified the triage methods that produce $C_q$ based on these new features. For **Text** we used the triage methods of Mcnamee et al. (2009): string similarity based on character/token n-gram overlap, same acronym, exact match, etc. **Phone** triage used the same heuristics but based on phone representations of the mention strings and candidate names. **Metaphone** triage worked as in phone, but used metaphones. When two representations are used we take the union of their candidates.

**G2P System** For phone features we use a G2P system based on the Sequitur G2P grapheme-phone-converter (Bisani and Ney, 2008). We trained the system on version 0.7a of CMUdict[1] (stress omitted from phone sequences, case-insensitive for graphemes), by predicting the phoneme sequence of an English token given its string (G2P). The language model was a 9-gram model with modified Kneser-Ney smoothing applied. For **Phone** features we converted each token to its best phone representation, where each phone, as well as diphthong, is represented by a single character for similarity matching.

## 4 Experiments

We evaluate reference transcripts and output from two ASR systems run on our dataset (HUB4). We use Kaldi (Povey et al., 2011) trained on the spoken version of the Wall Street Journal corpus (Paul and Baker, 1992).[2] The first system (*mono*) relies on an HMM whose hidden states are context-independent phones. The second system (*tri4b*) uses an HMM that outputs phones dependent on their immediate left and right contexts. These systems respectively achieve 70.6% and 50.7% WER over our training set, where high error rates are likely due to a shift in domain from primarily financial news to the wider

[1] http://www.speech.cs.cmu.edu/cgi-bin/cmudict

[2] Linguistic Data Consortium number LDC94S13A.

| | Reference | mono | tri4b |
|---|---|---|---|
| WER | - | 71% | 51% |
| Mention WER | - | 90% | 63% |
| Mention Exact | - | 5% | 22% |
| Text | 0.77/0.77 | 0.44/0.48 | 0.56/0.55 |
| Phone | 0.77/0.79 | 0.42/0.45 | 0.47/0.46 |
| Text+Phn | 0.81/0.81 | 0.45/0.49 | 0.58/0.61* |
| Text+Phn+Latt | - | 0.45/0.49 | 0.59/0.60* |
| Metaphone | 0.52/0.61 | 0.43/48 | 0.52/0.56 |
| Text+Metaphn | 0.78/0.78 | 0.45/0.50 | 0.59/0.61* |
| Text+Metaphn+Latt | - | **0.45/0.51** | **0.59/0.63**** |

Table 1: Performance of different feature sets for reference transcripts and ASR output (mono, tri4b). Results are cross-fold validation/test accuracy. Significance of system test accuracy compared to the Text baseline computed with two-sample proportion test. (* $p < 0.05$, ** $p < 0.01$).

| | Text | Phone | Text+Phn |
|---|---|---|---|
| Reference | 0.92/0.87 | 0.95/0.91 | 0.98/0.97 |
| mono | 0.48/0.13 | 0.50/0.17 | 0.51/0.19 |
| tri4b | 0.68/0.47 | 0.71/0.52 | 0.73/0.56 |

Table 2: Overall/non-NIL triager recall.

| | Text | Phone | Text+Phn | T+P+Latt |
|---|---|---|---|---|
| Reference | 0.82 | 0.82 | 0.85 | 0.85 |
| tri4b | 0.76 | 0.62 | 0.77 | 0.78 |

Table 3: Cross validation accuracy evaluated over only those queries whose correct candidate was output by the triager for both tri4b and reference.

| tri4b | Reference |
|---|---|
| on joseph | Don Joseph |
| ira magazine | Ira Magaziner |
| bob defiance | Bob Mathias |
| gave deforest | Dave Deforest |
| georgia the books | George W. Bush's |
| george w. porsche | George W. Bush |
| louis freer | Louis Freeh |
| norman monetta | Norman Mineta |
| edward and | Edward Egan |
| keith clarke | Nikki Clark |

Table 4: Examples of improved linking accuracy.

news variety in HUB4. These higher error settings test the limits of entity linking in noisy ASR.

To find the ASR-corrupted mention string used for the query $q$ we align the ASR transcript by token-level edit distance – additions and deletions cost 1, while substitutions cost the Jaccard distance between two tokens. This is done at both training and test time, and allows us to evaluate performance of entity linking features without worrying about errors introduced by a named entity recognizer on the transcripts.

**Entity Linking System Training** The entity linking system relies on a linear Ranking SVM objective (Joachims, 2006), and the optimal slack parameter $C$ was chosen using 5-fold cross validation over the training set ($C$ varied from 1 and $5 \times 10^{-5 \ldots 3}$). During cross-validation, mention string types were kept disjoint between the train and development folds. Ranking was performed over the (up to) 1000 candidates produced by triage selected from the TAC-KBP 2009/10 KB (Mcnamee et al., 2009; Ji et al., 2010). Using the selected $C$ we trained over the entire training set and evaluated on the test set.

## 5 Results

Table 1 reports both the average accuracy for 5-fold cross validation (CV) on train and for the best tuned system from CV on test data. The reference test accuracy is relatively high, but lags behind person entity linking for written language. When accurate transcripts are available, entity linking for spoken language, while harder, achieves just a little behind written language. However, on ASR transcripts, accuracy drops considerably: 0.77 reference to 0.48 (mono, 71% WER) or 0.55 (tri4b, 51% WER). Our features improve accuracy for both ASR systems. Metaphone features do better than Phone features. Lattice do not show significant improvements, likely because they help with context but not mentions (see below.) When combined with text, both metaphone and phone features do similarly.

The majority of our improvement comes from improvements to recall. Table 3 shows the accuracy of queries for which the triager found the correct candidate in *both* the reference transcript and tri4b, providing a consistent set for comparison. For these queries, tri4b is much closer to the results obtained on reference and much higher than the best results in Table 1. This is encouraging, especially given the 50% WER of tri4b; entity linking accuracy is not seriously impacted by noisy transcripts, provided that the correct candidate is recalled for ranking.

Table 2 shows the recall of the triager on the reference, tri4b and mono transcripts. Reference recall is quite high, while recall for the ASR systems is much lower. Here, our features dramatically improve the recall, giving the ranker an opportunity to correctly score these queries. The challenge of recall is that many of the mention strings are incorrectly recognized. Table 1 shows the WER of the mention string and the number of mention strings for which the recognition is completely correct. Unsurprisingly, error rates for mentions are higher than the overall WER. In short, success on ASR transcripts is primarily dictated by the effectiveness of finding candidates in triage, which is much harder given the low recognition rate. Our features most benefit overall accuracy by improving recall.

Finally, Table 4 provides example of improved recall: mention strings that are incorrectly recognized by the tri4b ASR system leading to linking failures, but are then correctly linked by our improved features. These examples demonstrate the effectiveness of phonetic matching, retrieving the correct "George W. Bush" when the recognizer output "Georgia the Books."

## 6 Conclusion

We have conducted the first analysis of entity linking for spoken language. Our new features, which rely on phonetic representations of words and expected counts of the lattice for context, improve the accuracy of an entity linker on ASR output. Our analysis reveals that while the linker is not sensitive to large drops in error rates in the context, it is highly sensitive to error rates in mention strings, due to a drop in triage recall. Our features improve the overall accuracy by improving the recall of the triager. Future work should focus on additional methods for identifying relevant KB candidates given inaccurate transcriptions of mention strings.

## References


Timothy Baldwin, Paul Cook, Marco Lui, Andrew MacKinlay, and Li Wang. 2013. How noisy social media text, how diffrnt social media sources. In *Proceedings of the 6th International Joint Conference on Natural Language Processing (IJCNLP 2013)*, pages 356–364.

Adrian Benton, Jay Deyoung, Adam Teichert, Mark Dredze, Benjamin Van Durme, Stephen Mayhew, and Max Thomas. 2014. Faster (and better) entity linking with cascades. In *NIPS Workshop on Automated Knowledge Base Construction*.

Maximilian Bisani and Hermann Ney. 2008. Joint-sequence models for grapheme-to-phoneme conversion. In *Speech Communication*, volume 50, pages 434–451.

Chris Callison-Burch and Mark Dredze. 2010. Creating speech and language data with amazon's mechanical turk. In *Workshop on Creating Speech and Language Data With Mechanical Turk at NAACL-HLT*.

Taylor Cassidy, Heng Ji, Lev-Arie Ratinov, Arkaitz Zubiaga, and Hongzhao Huang. 2012. Analysis and enhancement of wikification for microblogs with context expansion. In *COLING*, pages 441–456.

Gianluca Demartini, Djellel Eddine Difallah, and Philippe Cudré-Mauroux. 2012. Zencrowd: Leveraging probabilistic reasoning and crowdsourcing techniques for large-scale entity linking. In *Proceedings of the 21st International Conference on World Wide Web*, WWW '12, pages 469–478, New York, NY, USA. ACM.

Mark Dredze, Paul McNamee, Delip Rao, Adam Gerber, and Tim Finin. 2010. Entity disambiguation for knowledge base population. In *COLING*.

Jonathan Fiscus, John Garofolo, Mark Przybocki, William Fisher, and David Pallett. 1997. 1997 english broadcast news speech (hub4). In *LDC98S71*.

Ning Gao, Douglas Oard, and Mark Dredze. 2014. A test collection for email entity linking. In *NIPS Workshop on Automated Knowledge Base Construction*.

Stephen Guo, Ming-Wei Chang, and Emre Kiciman. 2013a. To link or not to link? a study on end-to-end tweet entity linking. In *NAACL*.

Yuhang Guo, Bing Qin, Yuqin Li, Ting Liu, and Sheng Li. 2013b. Improving candidate generation for entity linking. In *Natural Language Processing and Information Systems*, pages 225–236. Springer.

Ben Hachey, Will Radford, Joel Nothman, Matthew Honnibal, and James R. Curran. 2013. Evaluating entity linking with wikipedia. *Artificial Intelligence*, 194(0):130 – 150. Artificial Intelligence, Wikipedia and Semi-Structured Resources.

Bo Han, Paul Cook, and Timothy Baldwin. 2013. Lexical normalization for social media text. *ACM Trans. Intell. Syst. Technol.*, 4(1):5:1–5:27, February.

Qi He, Jian Pei, Daniel Kifer, Prasenjit Mitra, and Lee Giles. 2010. Context-aware citation recommendation. In *Proceedings of the 19th International Conference* on World Wide Web, WWW '10, pages 421–430, New York, NY, USA. ACM.

Qi He, Daniel Kifer, Jian Pei, Prasenjit Mitra, and C. Lee Giles. 2011. Citation recommendation without author supervision. In *Proceedings of the Fourth ACM International Conference on Web Search and Data Mining*, WSDM '11, pages 755–764, New York, NY, USA. ACM.

James Horlock and Simon King. 2003. Named entity extraction from word lattices. *Eurospeech*.

Fei Huang. 2005. *Multilingual Named Entity Extraction and Translation from Text and Speech*. Ph.D. thesis, Carnegie Mellon University.

Heng Ji, Ralph Grishman, Hoa Trang Dang, Kira Griffitt, and Joe Ellis. 2010. Overview of the tac 2010 knowledge base population track. *Third Text Analysis Conference (TAC 2010)*.

Thorsten Joachims. 2006. Training linear svms in linear time. In *Proceedings of the ACM Conference on Knowledge Discovery and Data Mining (KDD)*.

Thomas Lin, Oren Etzioni, et al. 2012. Entity linking at web scale. In *Proceedings of the Joint Workshop on Automatic Knowledge Base Construction and Web-scale Knowledge Extraction*, pages 84–88. Association for Computational Linguistics.

Xiaohua Liu, Yitong Li, Haocheng Wu, Ming Zhou, Furu Wei, and Yi Lu. 2013. Entity linking for tweets. In *ACL*.

James Mayfield, Dawn Lawrie, Paul McNamee, and DouglasW. Oard. 2011. Building a cross-language entity linking collection in twenty-one languages. In Pamela Forner, Julio Gonzalo, Jaana Kekäläinen, Mounia Lalmas, and Marteen de Rijke, editors, *Multilingual and Multimodal Information Access Evaluation*, volume 6941 of *Lecture Notes in Computer Science*, pages 3–13. Springer Berlin Heidelberg.

Paul McNamee and Hoa Trang Dang. 2009. Overview of the TAC 2009 knowledge base population track. In *TAC*.

Paul Mcnamee, Mark Dredze, Adam Gerber, Nikesh Garera, Tim Finin, James Mayfield, Christine Piatko, Delip Rao, David Yarowsky, and Markus Dreyer. 2009. Hltcoe approaches to knowledge base population at tac 2009. In *Text Analysis Conference (TAC*.

Paul McNamee, James Mayfield, Douglas W. Oard, Tan Xu, Ke Wu, Veselin Stoyanov, and David Doerman. 2011. Cross-language entity linking in maryland during a hurricane. In *TAC*.

Paul McNamee, Veselin Stoyanov, James Mayfield, Tim Finin, Tim Oates, Tan Xu, Douglas Oard, and Dawn Lawrie. 2012. HLTCOE participation at TAC 2012: Entity linking and cold start knowledge base construction. In *TAC*.

David N. Milne and Ian H. Witten. 2008. Learning to link with wikipedia. In *CIKM*, pages 509–518.

Carolina Parada, Mark Dredze, and Frederick Jelinek. 2011. Oov sensitive named-entity recognition in speech. In *International Speech Communication Association (INTERSPEECH)*.

Douglas Paul and Janet Baker. 1992. The design for the wall street journal-based csr corpus. In *DARPA Speech and Language Workshop*. Morgan Kaufmann Publishers.

Lawrence Philips. 1990. Hanging on the metaphone. *Computer Language*, 7(12 (December)).

Daniel Povey, Arnab Ghoshal, Gilles Boulianne, Lukas Burget, Ondrej Glembek, Nagendra Goel, Mirko Hannemann, Petr Motlicek, Yanmin Qian, Petr Schwarz, Jan Silovsky, Georg Stemmer, and Karel Vesely. 2011. The kaldi speech recognition toolkit. In *IEEE 2011 Workshop on Automatic Speech Recognition and Understanding*. IEEE Signal Processing Society, December. IEEE Catalog No.: CFP11SRW-USB.

Wei Shen, Jianyong Wang, Ping Luo, and Min Wang. 2013. Linking named entities in tweets with knowledge base via user interest modeling. In *KDD*.

Erik F Tjong Kim Sang and Fien De Meulder. 2003. Introduction to the conll-2003 shared task: Language-independent named entity recognition. In *Proceedings of the seventh conference on Natural language learning at HLT-NAACL 2003-Volume 4*, pages 142–147. Association for Computational Linguistics.

Zhichun Wang, Juanzi Li, Zhigang Wang, and Jie Tang. 2012. Cross-lingual knowledge linking across wiki knowledge bases. In *Proceedings of the 21st International Conference on World Wide Web*, WWW '12, pages 459–468, New York, NY, USA. ACM.

# Spinning Straw into Gold: Using Free Text to Train Monolingual Alignment Models for Non-factoid Question Answering

**Rebecca Sharp[1], Peter Jansen[1], Mihai Surdeanu[1], and Peter Clark[2]**
[1] University of Arizona, Tucson, AZ, USA
[2] Allen Institute for Artificial Intelligence, Seattle, WA, USA
{bsharp,pajansen,msurdeanu}@email.arizona.edu
peterc@allenai.org

## Abstract

Monolingual alignment models have been shown to boost the performance of question answering systems by "bridging the lexical chasm" between questions and answers. The main limitation of these approaches is that they require semistructured training data in the form of question-answer pairs, which is difficult to obtain in specialized domains or low-resource languages. We propose two inexpensive methods for training alignment models solely using free text, by generating artificial question-answer pairs from discourse structures. Our approach is driven by two representations of discourse: a shallow sequential representation, and a deep one based on Rhetorical Structure Theory. We evaluate the proposed model on two corpora from different genres and domains: one from Yahoo! Answers and one from the biology domain, and two types of non-factoid questions: manner and reason. We show that these alignment models trained directly from discourse structures imposed on free text improve performance considerably over an information retrieval baseline and a neural network language model trained on the same data.

## 1 Introduction

Question Answering (QA) is a challenging task that draws upon many aspects of NLP. Unlike search or information retrieval, answers infrequently contain lexical overlap with the question (e.g. *What should we eat for breakfast? – Zoe's Diner has good pancakes*), and require QA models to draw upon more complex methods to bridge this "lexical chasm" (Berger et al., 2000). These methods range from robust shallow models based on lexical semantics, to deeper, explainably-correct, but much more brittle inference methods based on first order logic.

Berger et al. (2000) proposed that this "lexical chasm" might be partially bridged by repurposing statistical machine translation (SMT) models for QA. Instead of translating text from one language to another, these monolingual alignment models learn to translate from question to answer[1], learning common associations from question terms such as *eat* or *breakfast* to answer terms like *kitchen, pancakes, or cereal*.

While monolingual alignment models have enjoyed a good deal of recent success in QA (see related work), they have expensive training data requirements, requiring a large set of aligned in-domain question-answer pairs for training. For low-resource languages or specialized domains like science or biology, often the only option is to enlist a domain expert to generate gold QA pairs – a process that is both expensive and time consuming. All of this means that only in rare cases are we accorded the luxury of having enough high-quality QA pairs to properly train an alignment model, and so these models are often underutilized or left struggling for resources.

Making use of recent advancements in discourse parsing (Feng and Hirst, 2012), here we address this issue, and investigate whether alignment models for QA can be trained from artificial question-answer pairs generated from discourse structures imposed on free text. We evaluate our methods on two corpora, generating alignment models for an open-domain community QA task using Gigaword[2], and for a biology-domain QA task using a biology textbook.

[1] In practice, alignment for QA is often done from answer to question, as answers tend to be longer and provide more opportunity for association (Surdeanu et al., 2011).

[2] LDC catalog number LDC2012T21



*Human Language Technologies: The 2015 Annual Conference of the North American Chapter of the ACL*, pages 231–237,
Denver, Colorado, May 31 – June 5, 2015. 

The contributions of this work are:

1. We demonstrate that by exploiting the discourse structure of free text, monolingual alignment models can be trained to surpass the performance of models built from expensive in-domain question-answer pairs.
2. We compare two methods of discourse parsing: a simple sequential model, and a deep model based on Rhetorical Structure Theory (RST) (Mann and Thompson, 1988). We show that the RST-based method captures within and across-sentence alignments and performs better than the sequential model, but the sequential model is an acceptable approximation when a discourse parser is not available.
3. We evaluate the proposed methods on two corpora, including a low-resource domain where training data is expensive (biology).
4. We experimentally demonstrate that monolingual alignment models trained using our method considerably outperform state-of-the-art neural network language models in low resource domains.

## 2 Related Work

Lexical semantic models have shown promise in bridging Berger et al.'s (2000) "lexical chasm." In general, these models can be classified into alignment models (Echihabi and Marcu, 2003; Soricut and Brill, 2006; Riezler et al., 2007; Surdeanu et al., 2011; Yao et al., 2013) which require structured training data, and language models (Jansen et al., 2014; Sultan et al., 2014; Yih et al., 2013), which operate over free text. Here, we close this gap in resource availability by developing a method to train an alignment model over free text by making use of discourse structures.

Discourse has been previously applied to QA to help identify answer candidates that contain explanatory text (e.g. Verberne et al. (2007)). Jansen et al. (2014) proposed a reranking model that used both shallow and deep discourse features to identify answer structures in large answer collections across different tasks and genres. Here we use discourse to impose structure on free text to create inexpensive knowledge resources for monolingual alignment. Our work is conceptually complementary to that of Jansen et al. – where they explored largely unlexicalized discourse structures to identify explanatory text, we use discourse to learn lexicalized models for semantic similarity.

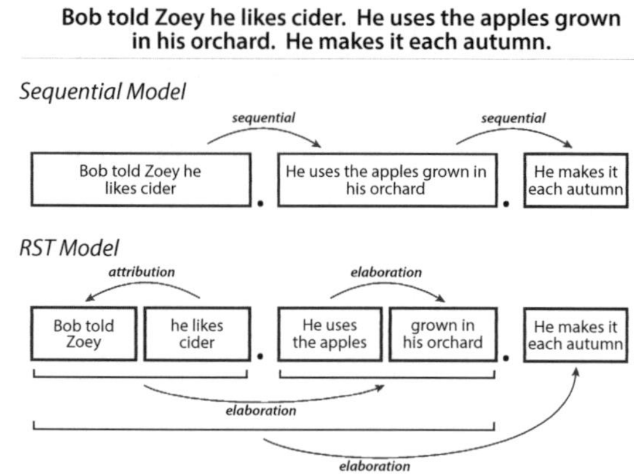


Figure 1: An example of the alignments produced by the two discourse models. The sequential model aligns pairs of consecutive sentences, capturing intersentence associations such as *cider–apples*, and *orchard–autumn*. The RST model generates alignment pairs from participants in all (binary) discourse relations, capturing both intrasentence and intersentence alignments, including *apples–orchard, cider–apples*, and *cider–autumn*.

Our work is conceptually closest to that of Hickl et al. (2006), who created artificially aligned pairs for textual entailment. Taking advantage of the structure of news articles, wherein the first sentence tends to provide a broad summary of the article's contents, Hickl et al. aligned the first sentence of each article with its headline. By making use of automated discourse parsing, here we go further and impose alignment structure over an entire text.

## 3 Approach

A written text is not simply a collection of sentences, but rather a flowing narrative where sentences and sentence elements depend on each other for meaning – a concept known as cohesion (Halliday and Hasan, 2014). Here we examine two methods for generating alignment training data from free text that make use of cohesion: a shallow method that uses only intersentence structures, and a deep method that uses both intrasentence and intersentence structures. We additionally attempt to separate the contribution of discourse from that of alignment in general by comparing these models against a baseline alignment model which aligns sentences at random.

The first model, the sequential discourse model (SEQ), considers that each sentence continues the narrative of the previous one, and creates artificial question-answer pairs from all pairs of consecutive sentences. Thus, this model takes advantage of intersentence cohesion by aligning the content words[3] in each sentence with the content words in the following sentence. For example, in the passage in Figure 1, this model would associate *cider* in the first sentence with *apples* and *orchard* in the second sentence.

The second model uses RST to capture discourse cohesion both within and across sentence boundaries. We extracted RST discourse structures using an in-house parser (Surdeanu et al., 2015), which follows the architecture introduced by Hernault et al. (2010) and Feng and Hirst (2012). The parser first segments text into elementary discourse units (EDUs), which may be at sub-sentence granularity, then recursively connects neighboring units with binary discourse relations, such as *Elaboration* or *Contrast*.[4] Our parser differs from previous work with respect to feature generation in that we implement all features that rely on syntax using solely dependency syntax. For example, a crucial feature used by the parser is the dominance relations of Soricut and Marcu (2003), which capture syntactic dominance between discourse units located in the same sentence. While originally these dominance relations were implemented using constituent syntax, we provide an equivalent implementation that relies on dependency syntax. The main advantage to this approach is speed: the resulting parser performs at least an order of magnitude faster than the parser of Feng and Hirst (2012).

Importantly, we generate artificial alignment pairs from this imposed structure by aligning the governing text (nucleus) with its dependent text (satellite).[5] Turning again to the example in Figure 1, this RST-based model captures additional alignments that are both intrasentence, e.g., *apples–orchard*, and intersentence, e.g., *cider–autumn*.

[3]In pilot experiments, we found that aligning only nouns, verbs, adjectives, and adverbs yielded higher performance.

[4]The RST parser performs better on relations which occur more frequently. We use only relations that occurred at least 1% of the time. This amounted to six relations: *elaboration*, *attribution*, *background*, *contrast*, *same-unit*, and *joint*. Using all relations slightly improves performance by 0.3% P@1.

[5]Pilot experiments showed that this direction of alignment performed better than aligning from satellite to nucleus.

## 4 Models and Features

We evaluate the contribution of these alignment models using a standard reranking architecture (Jansen et al., 2014). The initial ranking of candidate answers is done using a shallow candidate retrieval (CR) component.[6] Then, these answers are reranked using a more expressive model that incorporates alignment features alongside the CR score. As a learning framework we use SVM$^{rank}$, a Support Vector Machine tailored for ranking.[7] We compare this alignment-based reranking model against one that uses a state-of-the-art recurrent neural network language model (RNNLM) (Mikolov et al., 2010; Mikolov et al., 2013), which has been successfully applied to QA previously (Yih et al., 2013).

**Alignment Model:** The alignment matrices were generated with IBM Model 1 (Brown et al., 1993) using GIZA++ (Och and Ney, 2003), and the corresponding models were implemented as per Surdeanu et al. (2011) with a global alignment probability. We extend this alignment model with features from Fried et al. (In press) that treat each (source) word's probability distribution (over destination words) in the alignment matrix as a distributed semantic representation, and make use the Jensen-Shannon distance (JSD)[8] between these conditional distributions. A summary of all these features is shown in Table 1.

**RNNLM:** We learned word embeddings using the `word2vec` RNNLM of Mikolov et al. (2013), and include the cosine similarity-based features described in Table 1.

## 5 Experiments

We tested our approach in two different domains, open-domain and cellular biology. For consistency we use the same corpora as Jansen et al. (2014), which are described briefly here.

**Yahoo! Answers (YA):** Ten thousand open-domain *how* questions were randomly chosen from the Ya-

[6]We use the same cosine similarity between question and answer lemmas as Jansen et al. (2014), weighted using *tf.idf*.

[7]`http://www.cs.cornell.edu/people/tj/svm_light/svm_rank.html`

[8]Jensen-Shannon distance is based on Kullback-Liebler divergence but is a distance metric (finite and symmetric).

| | Feature Group | Feature Descriptions |
|---|---|---|
| Alignment Models | Global Alignment Probability | p(Q\|A) according to IBM Model 1 (Brown et al., 1993) |
| | Jenson-Shannon Distance (JSD) | Pairwise JSDs were found between the probability distribution of each content word in the question and those in the answer. The **mean, minimum, and maximum JSD values** were used as features. Additionally, composite vectors were formed which represented the entire question and the entire answer and the **overall JSD** between these two vectors was also included as a feature. See Fried et. al (In press) for additional details. |
| RNNLM | Cosine Similarity | Similar to Jansen et al. (2014), we include as features the **maximum and average pairwise cosine similarity** between question and answer words, as well as the **overall similarity** between the composite question and answer vectors. |

Table 1: Feature descriptions for alignment models and RNNLM baseline.

hoo! Answers[9] community question answering corpus and divided: 50% for training, 25% for development, and 25% for test. Candidate answers for a given question are selected from the corresponding answers proposed by the community (each question has an average of 9 answers).

**Biology QA (Bio):** 183 *how* and 193 *why* questions in the cellular biology domain were hand-crafted by a domain expert, and paired with gold answers in the Campbell's Biology textbook (Reece et al., 2011). Each paragraph in the textbook was considered as a candidate answer. As there were few questions, five fold cross-validation was used with three folds for training, one for development, and one for test.

**Alignment Corpora**: To train the alignment models we generated alignment pairs from two different resources: Annotated Gigaword (Napoles et al., 2012) for YA, and the textbook for Bio. Each was discourse parsed with the RST discourse parser described in Section 3, which is implemented in the FastNLPProcessor toolkit[10], using the MaltParser[11] for syntactic analysis.

### 5.1 Results and Discussion

Figure 2 shows the performance of the discourse models against the number of documents used to train the alignment model.[12] We used the standard implementation for P@1 (Manning et al., 2008) with the adaptations for Bio described in Jansen et al. (2014). We address the following questions.

[9]http://answers.yahoo.com

[10]http://github.com/sistanlp/processors

[11]http://www.maltparser.org/

[12]For space reasons the graph for Bio *how* is not shown, but the pattern is essentially identical to Bio *why*.

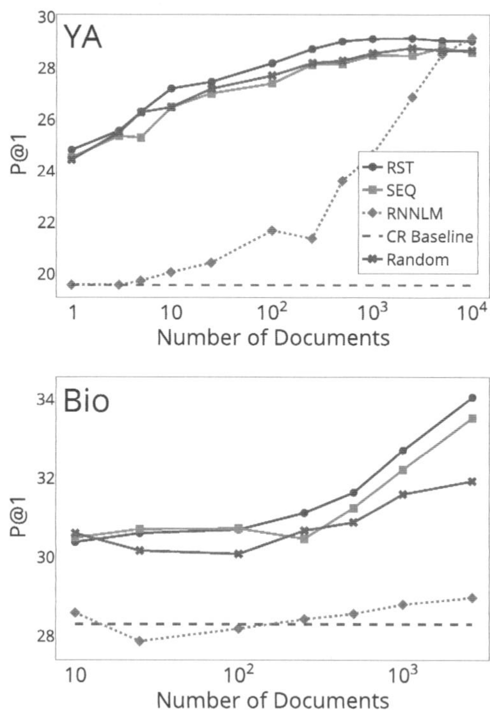


Figure 2: Overall performance for the two discourse-based alignment models, compared against the CR baseline, random baselines, and a RNNLM-based reranker. The $x$ axis indicates the number of training documents used to construct all models. Each point represents the average of 10 samples of training documents.

**How does the performance of the RST and SEQ models compare?** Comparing the two principal alignment models, the RST-based model significantly outperforms the SEQ model by about 0.5% P@1 in both domains ($p < 0.001$ for Bio and $p < 0.01$ for YA)[13]. This shows that deep discourse anal-

[13]All reported statistics were performed at the endpoints, i.e., when all training data is used, using bootstrap resampling with

ysis (as imperfect as it is today) is beneficial.

**How does the performance of the RST model compare to a model trained on in-domain pairs?** Both the RST and SEQ results for YA are *higher* than that of an alignment model trained on explicit in-domain question-answer pairs. Fried et. al (In press) trained an identical alignment model using approximately 65k QA pairs from the YA corpus, and report a performance of 27.24% P@1, or nearly 2 points lower than our model trained using 10,000 Gigaword documents. This is an encouraging result, which further demonstrates that: (a) discourse analysis can be exploited to generate artificial semi-structured data for alignment, and (b) the sequential model, which also outperforms Fried et. al, can be used as a reasonable proxy for discourse when a parser is not available.

**How does the performance of the RST model compare to previous work?** Comparing our work to Jansen et al. (2014), the most relevant prior work, we notice two trends. First, our discourse-based alignment models outperform their CR + RNNLM model, which peaks at 26.6% P@1 for YA and 31.7% for Bio *why*. While some of this difference can be assigned to implementation differences (e.g., we consider only content words for both alignment and RNNLM, where they used all words), this result again emphasizes the value of our approach. Second, the partially lexicalized discourse structures used by Jansen et. al to identify explanatory text in candidate answers perform better than our approach, which relies solely on lexicalized alignment. However, we expect that our two approaches are complementary, because they address different aspects of the QA task (structure vs. similarity).

**How do the RST and SEQ models compare to the non-alignment baselines?** In Bio, both the RST and SEQ alignment models significantly outperform the RNNLM and CR baselines ($p < 0.001$). In YA, the RST and SEQ models significantly outperform the CR baseline ($p < 0.001$), and though they considerably outperform the the RNNLM baseline for most training document sizes, when all 10,000 documents are used for training, they do not perform better. This shows that alignment models are more robust to little training data, but RNNLMs catch up when considerable data is available.

10,000 iterations.

**How does the SEQ model compare to the RND baseline?** In Bio, the SEQ model significantly outperforms the RND baseline ($p < 0.001$) but in YA it does not. This is likely due to differences in the size of the document which was randomized. In YA, the sentences were randomized within Gigaword articles, which are relatively short (averaging 19 sentences), whereas in Bio the randomization was done at the textbook level. In practice, as document size decreases, the RND model approaches the SEQ model.

**Why does performance plateau in YA and not in Bio?** With Bio, we exploit all of the limited in-domain training data, and continue to see performance improvements. With YA, however, performance asymptotes for the alignment models when trained beyond 10,000 documents, or less than 1% of the Gigaword corpus. Similarly, when trained over the entirety of Gigaword (two orders of magnitude more data), our RNNLM improves only slightly, peaking at approximately 30.5% P@1 (or, a little over 1% P@1 higher). We hypothesize that this limitation comes from failing to take context into account. In open domains, alignments such as *apple – orchard* may interfere with those from different contexts, e.g., *apple – computer*, and add noise to the answer selection process.

## 6 Conclusion

We propose two inexpensive methods for training alignment models using solely free text, by generating artificial question-answer pairs from discourse structures. Our experiments indicate that these methods are a viable solution for constructing state-of-the-art QA systems for low-resource domains, or languages where training data is expensive and/or limited. Since alignment models have shown utility in other tasks (e.g. textual entailment), we hypothesize that these methods for creating inexpensive and highly specialized training data could be useful for tasks other than QA.

## Acknowledgments

We thank the Allen Institute for AI for funding this work.

## References


Adam Berger, Rich Caruana, David Cohn, Dayne Freytag, and Vibhu Mittal. 2000. Bridging the lexical chasm: Statistical approaches to answer finding. In *Proceedings of the 23rd Annual International ACM SIGIR Conference on Research & Development on Information Retrieval*, Athens, Greece.

Peter F. Brown, Stephen A. Della Pietra, Vincent J. Della Pietra, and Robert L. Mercer. 1993. The mathematics of statistical machine translation: Parameter estimation. *Computational Linguistics*, 19(2):263–311.

Abdessamad Echihabi and Daniel Marcu. 2003. A noisy-channel approach to question answering. In *Proceedings of the 41st Annual Meeting on Association for Computational Linguistics-Volume 1*, pages 16–23. Association for Computational Linguistics.

Vanessa Wei Feng and Graeme Hirst. 2012. Text-level discourse parsing with rich linguistic features. In *Proceedings of the Association for Computational Linguistics*.

Daniel Fried, Peter Jansen, Gustave Hahn-Powell, Mihai Surdeanu, and Peter Clark. In press. Higher-order lexical semantic models for non-factoid answer reranking. *Transactions of the Association for Computational Linguistics*.

Michael Alexander Kirkwood Halliday and Ruqaiya Hasan. 2014. *Cohesion in english*. Routledge.

H. Hernault, H. Prendinger, D. duVerle, and M. Ishizuka. 2010. HILDA: A discourse parser using support vector machine classification. *Dialogue and Discourse*, 1(3):1–33.

Andrew Hickl, John Williams, Jeremy Bensley, Kirk Roberts, Bryan Rink, and Ying Shi. 2006. Recognizing textual entailment with lccs groundhog system. In *Proceedings of the Second PASCAL Challenges Workshop*.

Peter Jansen, Mihai Surdeanu, and Peter Clark. 2014. Discourse complements lexical semantics for non-factoid answer reranking. In *Proceedings of the 52nd Annual Meeting of the Association for Computational Linguistics (ACL)*.

William C. Mann and Sandra A. Thompson. 1988. Rhetorical structure theory: Toward a functional theory of text organization. *Text*, 8(3):243–281.

Christopher D. Manning, Prabhakar Raghavan, and Hinrich Schütze. 2008. *Introduction to Information Retrieval*. Cambridge University Press.

Tomas Mikolov, Martin Karafiat, Lukas Burget, Jan Cernocky, and Sanjeev Khudanpur. 2010. Recurrent neural network based language model. In *Proceedings of the 11th Annual Conference of the International Speech Communication Association (INTERSPEECH 2010)*.

Tomas Mikolov, Kai Chen, Greg Corrado, and Jeffrey Dean. 2013. Efficient estimation of word representations in vector space. In *Proceedings of the International Conference on Learning Representations (ICLR)*.

Courtney Napoles, Matthew Gormley, and Benjamin Van Durme. 2012. Annotated gigaword. In *Proceedings of the Joint Workshop on Automatic Knowledge Base Construction and Web-scale Knowledge Extraction*, AKBC-WEKEX '12, pages 95–100, Stroudsburg, PA, USA. Association for Computational Linguistics.

Franz Josef Och and Hermann Ney. 2003. A systematic comparison of various statistical alignment models. *Computational Linguistics*, 29(1):19–51.

J.B. Reece, L.A. Urry, M.L. Cain, S.A. Wasserman, and P.V. Minorsky. 2011. *Campbell Biology*. Pearson Benjamin Cummings.

Stefan Riezler, Alexander Vasserman, Ioannis Tsochantaridis, Vibhu Mittal, and Yi Liu. 2007. Statistical machine translation for query expansion in answer retrieval. In *Proceedings of the 45th Annual Meeting of the Association for Computational Linguistics (ACL)*, pages 464–471, Prague, Czech Republic.

Radu Soricut and Eric Brill. 2006. Automatic question answering using the web: Beyond the factoid. *Journal of Information Retrieval - Special Issue on Web Information Retrieval*, 9(2):191–206.

R. Soricut and D. Marcu. 2003. Sentence level discourse parsing using syntactic and lexical information. In *Proceedings of the Human Language Technology and North American Association for Computational Linguistics Conference*.

Md. Arafat Sultan, Steven Bethard, and Tamara Sumner. 2014. Back to basics for monolingual alignment: Exploiting word similarity and contextual evidence. *Transactions of the Association for Computational Linguistics*, 2:219–230.

Mihai Surdeanu, Massimiliano Ciaramita, and Hugo Zaragoza. 2011. Learning to rank answers to non-factoid questions from web collections. *Computational Linguistics*, 37(2):351–383.

Mihai Surdeanu, Thomas Hicks, and Marco A. Valenzuela-Escárcega. 2015. Two practical rhetorical structure theory parsers. In *Proceedings of the North American Chapter of the Association for Computational Linguistics (NAACL): Software Demonstrations*.

Susan Verberne, Lou Boves, Nelleke Oostdijk, Peter-Arno Coppen, et al. 2007. Discourse-based answering of why-questions. *Traitement Automatique des Langues, Discours et document: traitements automatiques*, 47(2):21–41.

Xuchen Yao, Benjamin Van Durme, Chris Callison-Burch, and Peter Clark. 2013. Semi-markov phrase-based monolingual alignment. In *Proceedings of EMNLP*.

Wen-tau Yih, Ming-Wei Chang, Christopher Meek, and Andrzej Pastusiak. 2013. Question answering using enhanced lexical semantic models. In *Proceedings of the 51st Annual Meeting of the Association for Computational Linguistics (ACL)*.

# Personalized Page Rank for Named Entity Disambiguation

**Maria Pershina** **Yifan He** **Ralph Grishman**
Computer Science Department
New York University
New York, NY 10003, USA
{pershina,yhe,grishman}@cs.nyu.edu

## Abstract

The task of Named Entity Disambiguation is to map entity mentions in the document to their correct entries in some knowledge base. We present a novel graph-based disambiguation approach based on Personalized PageRank (PPR) that combines local and global evidence for disambiguation and effectively filters out noise introduced by incorrect candidates. Experiments show that our method outperforms state-of-the-art approaches by achieving 91.7% in micro- and 89.9% in macroaccuracy on a dataset of 27.8K named entity mentions.

## 1 Introduction

Name entity disambiguation (NED) is the task in which entity mentions in a document are mapped to real world entities. NED is both useful on its own, and serves as a valuable component in larger Knowledge Base Construction systems (Mayfield, 2014).

Since the surge of large, publicly available knowledge bases (KB) such as Wikipedia, the most popular approach has been linking text mentions to KB nodes (Bunescu and Paşca, 2006). In this paradigm, the NED system links text mentions to the KB, and quite naturally utilizes information in the KB to support the linking process. Recent NED systems (Cucerzan, 2007; Ratinov et al., 2011; Alhelbawy and Gaizauskas, 2014) usually exploit two types of KB information: *local* information, which measures the similarity between the text mention and the a candidate KB node; and *global* information, which measures how well the candidate entities in a document are connected to each other, with the assumption that entities appearing in the same document should be coherent. Both types of features have their strengths and drawbacks: local features better encode similarity between a candidate and a KB node, but overlook the coherence between entities; global features are able to exploit interlinking information between entities, but can be noisy if they are used by their own, without considering information from the text and the KB (cf. Section 4).

In this paper, we propose to disambiguate NEs using a Personalized PageRank (PPR)-based random walk algorithm. Given a document and a list of entity mentions within the document, we first construct a graph whose vertices are linking candidates and whose edges reflects links in Wikipedia. We run the PPR algorithm on this graph, with the constraint that we only allow the highest scored candidate for each entity to become the start point of a hop. As all candidates but the correct one are erronous and probably misleading, limiting the random walk to start from the most promising candidates effectively filters out potential noise in the Personalized PageRank process.

Our method has the following properties: 1) as our system is based on a random walk algorithm, it does not require training model parameters ; 2) unlike previous PageRank based approaches in NED (Alhelbawy and Gaizauskas, 2014) which mainly rely on global coherence, our method is able to better utilize the local similarity between a candidate and a KB node (Section 3); and 3) we tailor the Personalized PageRank algorithm to only focus on one high-confidence entity at a time to reduce noise (Section 4).

## 2 Related Work

Early attempts at the NED tasks use local and surface level information. Bunescu and Paşca



*Human Language Technologies: The 2015 Annual Conference of the North American Chapter of the ACL*, pages 238–243,
Denver, Colorado, May 31 – June 5, 2015. 

(2006) first utilize information in a knowledge base (Wikipedia) to disambiguate names, by calculating similarity between the context of a name mention and the taxonomy of a KB node.

Later research, such as Cucerzan (2007) and Milne and Witten (2008) extends this line by exploring richer feature sets, such as coherence features between entities. Global coherence features have therefore been widely used in NED research (see e.g. (Ratinov et al., 2011), (Hoffart et al., 2011), and (Cheng and Roth, 2013)) and have been applied successfully in TAC shared tasks (Cucerzan, 2011). These methods often involve optimizing an objective function that contains both local and global terms, and thus requires training on an annotated or distantly annotated dataset.

Our system performs collective NED using a random walk algorithm that does not require supervision. Random walk algorithms such as PageRank (Page et al., 1999) and Personalized PageRank (Jeh and Widom, 2003) have been successfully applied to NLP tasks, such as Word Sense Disambiguation (WSD: (Sinha and Mihalcea, 2007; Agirre and Soroa, 2009)).

Alhelbawy and Gaizauskas (2014) successfully apply the PageRank algorithm to the NED task. Their work is the closest in spirit to ours and performs well without supervision. We try to further improve their model by using a PPR model to better utilize local features, and by adding constraints to the random walk to reduce noise.

## 3 The Graph Model

We construct a graph representation $G(V, E)$ from the document $D$ with pre-tagged named entity textual mentions $M = \{m_1, ..., m_k\}$. For each entity mention $m_i \in M$ there is a list of candidates in KB $C_i = \{c_1^i, ..., c_{n_i}^i\}$. Vertices $V$ are defined as pairs

$$V = \{\ (m_i, c_j^i) \mid m_i \in M, c_j^i \in C_i\ \},$$

corresponding to the set of all possible KB candidates for different mentions in $M$. Edges are undirected and exist between two vertices if the two candidates are directly linked in the knowledge base, but no edge is allowed between candidates for the same named entity. Every vertex $(m, c)$ is associated with an initial similarity score between entity mention $m$ and candidate $c$ (Figure 1).

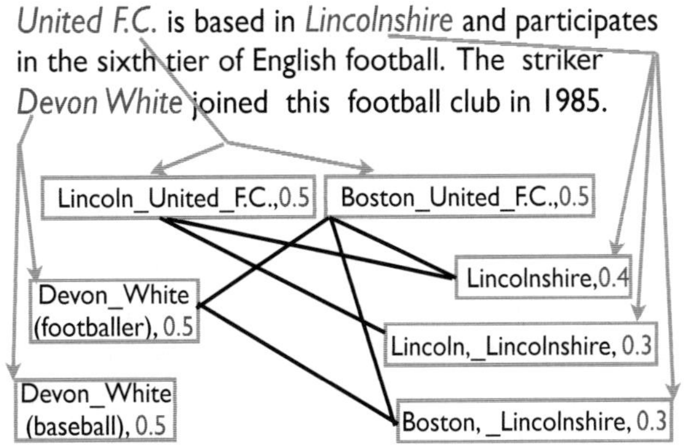


Figure 1: A toy document graph for three entity mentions: *United F.C., Lincolnshire, Devon White*. Candidates and their initial similarity scores are generated for each entity mention.

### 3.1 Vertices

**Candidates.** Given named entity mentions $M$ in the document, we need to generate all possible candidates for every mention $m \in M$. We first perform coreference resolution on the whole document and expand $m$ to the longest mention in the coreference chain. We then add a Wikipedia entry $c$ to the candidate set $C_i$ for mention $m_i$ if 1) the title of $c$ is the same as the expanded form of $m_i$, or 2) string $m_i$ redirects to page $c$, or 3) $c$ appears in a disambiguation page with title $m_i$.

**Initial Similarity.** Initial similarity $iSim$ for vertex $(m, c)$ describes how similar entity mention $m$ to candidate $c$ is. It is independent from other candidates in the graph $G$. We experiment with the local measure (localSim), based on the local information about the entity in the text, and the global measure (popSim), based on the global importance of the entity. Initial similarity scores of all candidates for a single named entity mention are normalized to sum to 1.

- **localSim**: The local similarity score is produced by a MaxEnt model trained on the TAC2014 EDL training data (LDC2014E15). MaxEnt features include string similarity between the title of the Wikipedia entry and the entity mention, such as edit distance, whether the text mention starts or ends with the Wikipedia title, etc; and whether they have the same type (e.g. person, organization, location, etc).

- **popSim**: We use the Freebase popularity as an alternative similarity measure. The Freebase popularity is a function of entity's incoming and outgoing link counts in Wikipedia and Freebase.[1]

### 3.2 Edges

Edges in our graph model represent relations between candidates. We insert an edge between two candidates if the Wikipedia entry corresponding to either of the two candidates contains a link to the other candidate. We assume that this relation is bidirectional and thus this edge is undirected.

There is a toy document graph in Figure 1 with three entity mentions and seven candidates: three candidates generated for *Lincolnshire*, and two candidates generated for *United F.C.* and *Devon White* each. Each graph node $e(m, c)$ is a pair of an entity mention $m$ and a candidate $c$; every node is assigned an initial score, normalized across all candidates for the same entity. An edge is drawn between two candidates for different entities whenever there is a link from the Wikipedia page for one candidate to the Wikipedia page for another. There is no edge between candidates competing for the same entity.

## 4 The Challenge

A successful entity disambiguation algorithm would benefit from both the initial similarity between candidate and entity, as well as the coherence among entities in the same document. We assume that every entity can refer to at most one in the list of possible candidates, so all candidates except for the correct one for each entity are erroneous and will introduce noise into the document graph. Based on this observation, we contend that the typical random walk approach, which computes coherence of one candidate to the whole graph, is not suitable for our scenario. To address this problem, we propose to consider pairwise relations between every two nodes, given by PPR scores, compute the contribution of every node to the coherence of the other, and impose *aggregation constraints* to avoid redundant contributions.

### 4.1 Personalized PageRank

The PageRank algorithm considers random walk on a graph, where at each step with probability $\epsilon$ (teleport probability) we jump to a randomly selected node on a graph, and with probability $1 - \epsilon$ we follow a random outgoing edge of the current node. Stationary distribution of this walk gives PageRank weights associated with each node. Personalized PageRank is the same as PageRank, except that all teleports are made to the same source node, for which we are personalizing the PageRank.

### 4.2 Coherence and Constraints

The *coherence* of the node $e$ to the graph $G$ quantifies how well node $e$ "fits" into this graph. Intuitively, pairwise weights $PPR(s \to e)$ represent relationships between nodes in the graph: the higher the weight is, the more relevant endpoint $e$ is for the source $s$. Candidate nodes in the graph have different quality, measured by their initial similarity $iSim$. Thus, coherence of the node $e$ to the graph $G$ due to the presence of node $s$ is given by

$$coh_s(e) = PPR(s \to e) \cdot iSim(s), \qquad (1)$$

where relevance *e* for $s$ is weighted by the $iSim(s)$, which is the similarity between entity $e$ and candidate $s$. We experiment with a MaxEnt-trained local score and the Freebase popularity as the $iSim$ in Section 5.

We observe that summing the contributions $coh_s(e)$ for all nodes $s \in V$ would accumulate noise, and therefore impose two *aggregation constraints* to take into account this nature of document graph $G$. Namely, to compute coherence $coh(e)$ of the node $e(m, c)$, corresponding to the entity mention $m$ and the candidate $c$, to the graph $G$ we enforce:

**(c1)** ignore contributions from candidate nodes competing for an entity $m$;
**(c2)** take only one, highest contribution from candidate nodes, competing for an entity $m' \neq m$;

The first constraint **(c1)** means that alternative candidates $\bar{e}(m, \bar{c})$, generated for the same entity mention $m$, should not contribute to the coherence of $e(m, c)$, as only one candidate per entity can be correct. For the same reason the second constraint **(c2)** picks the single candidate node $s(m', c')$ for entity $m' \neq m$ with the highest contribution $coh_s(e)$ towards $e$. So these constraints guarantee that exactly *one* and the *most relevant* candidate per entity will contribute

[1] https://developers.google.com/freebase/v1/search

to the coherence of the node $e$. Thus, the set of contributors towards $coh(e)$ is defined as

$$CONTR_{e(m,c)} = \{ (m', \underset{c}{\text{argmax}}\, coh_{(m',c)}(e) ) \in V,\ m' \neq m \} \quad (2)$$

Then coherence of the node $e$ to graph $G$ is given by

$$coh(e) = \sum_{s \in CONTR_{e(m,c)}} coh_s(e) \quad (3)$$

Consider the example in Figure 1, which has two connected components. Candidate Devon_White_(baseball) is disconnected from the rest of the graph and can neither contribute towards any other candidate nor get contributions from other nodes. So its coherence is zero. All other candidates are connected, i.e. belong to the same connected component. Thus, the random walker, started from any node in this component, will land at any other node in this component with some positive likelihood.

Let us consider the $CONTR_{e(m,c)}$ for entity mention *m* = *Lincolnshire* and candidate $c$ = Lincolnshire, 0.4,. Without our constraints, nodes Devon_White_(footballer), 0.5, Lincoln_United_F.C., 0.5, Boston_United_F.C., 0.5, Lincoln_Lincolnshire, 0.3, Boston_Lincolnshire, 0.3 can all potentially contribute towards coherence of Lincolnshire, 0.4.

However, **(c1)** and **(c2)** will eliminate contribution from some of the candidates: Constraint **(c1)** does not allow Lincoln_Lincolnshire, 0.3 and Boston_Lincolnshire, 0.3 to contribute, because they compete for the same entity mention as candidate Lincolnshire, 0.4; constraint **(c2)** will allow only one contribution from either Lincoln_United_F.C., 0.5 or Boston_United_F.C., 0.5 whichever is bigger, since they compete for the same entity mention *United F.C.*. Therefore, set $CONTR_{e(m,c)}$ for entity mention *m* = *Lincolnshire* and candidate $c$ = Lincolnshire, 0.4, will contain only two contributors: candidate Devon_White_(footballer), 0.5, for entity mention *Devon_White,* and exactly one of the candi dates for entity mention *United F.C.*

### 4.3 PPRSim

Our goal is to find the best candidate for every entity given a candidate's coherence and its initial similarity to the entity. To combine the coherence score $coh(e)$ with $iSim(e)$, we weight the latter with an average value of $PPR$ weights used in coherence computation (3) across all nodes in the document graph $G(V, E)$:

$$PPR_{avg} = \frac{\sum_{e \in V} \sum_{s \in CONTR_e} PPR(s \rightarrow e)}{|V|} \quad (4)$$

Thus, the final score for node $e$ is a linear combination

$$score(e) = coh(e) + PPR_{avg} \cdot iSim(e) \quad (5)$$

If the document graph has no edges then $PPR_{avg}$ is zero and for any node $e$ its coherence $coh(e)$ is zero as well. In this case we set $score(e)$ to its initial similarity $iSim(e)$ for all nodes $e$ in the graph $G$. Finally, PPRSim disambiguates entity mention $m$ with the highest scored candidate $c \in C_m$ :

$$disambiguate(m) = \underset{c \in C_m}{\text{argmax}}\ score(m, c) \quad (6)$$

To resolve ties in (6) we pick a candidate with the most incoming wikipedia links.

Thus, candidate Devon_White_(footballer), 0.5 in Figure 1 will get higher overall score than its competitor, Devon_White_(baseball), 0.5. Their initial scores are the same, 0.5, but the latter one is disconnected from other nodes in the graph and thus has a zero coherence. So, entity mention *Devon White* will be correctly disambiguated with the candidate Devon_White_(footballer), 0.5. This candidate is directly connected to Boston_United_F.C., 0.5 and has a shortest path of length 3 to Lincolnshire_United_F.C., 0.5, and therefore contributes more towards Boston_United_F.C., 0.5, and boosts its coherence to make it the correct disambiguation for *United F.C.* Similarly, *Lincolnshire* is correctly disambiguated with Boston_Lincolnshire_F.C., 0.3.

## 5 Experiments and Results.

**Data.** For our experiments we use dataset AIDA[2]. All textual entity mentions are manually disambiguated against Wikipedia links (Hoffart et al.,

[2]http://www.mpi-inf.mpg.de/yago-naga/aida/

| Models | Cucerzan | Kulkarni | Hoffart | Shirakawa | Alhelbawy | iSim | PPR | PPRSim |
|---|---|---|---|---|---|---|---|---|
| Micro | 51.03 | 72.87 | 81.82 | 82.29 | 87.59 | 62.61 | 85.56 | 91.77 |
| Macro | 43.74 | 76.74 | 81.91 | 83.02 | 84.19 | 72.21 | 85.86 | 89.89 |

Table 1: Performance of PPRSim compared to baselines and state-of-the-art models on AIDA dataset. Baselines iSim and PPR choose a candidate with the highest initial similarity or coherence correspondingly.

2011). There are 34,965 annotated mentions in 1393 documents. Only mentions with a valid entry in the Wikipedia KB are considered (Hoffart et al., 2011), resulting in a total of 27,816 mentions. We use a Wikipedia dump from June 14, 2014, as the reference KB. Our set of candidates is publicly available for experiments[3].

**Evaluation.** We use two evaluation metrics: (1) Microaccuracy is the fraction of correctly disambiguated entities; (2) Macroaccuracy is the proportion of textual mentions, correctly disambiguated per entity, averaged over all entities.

**PPR.** We adopt the Monte Carlo approach (Fogaras and Racz, 2004) for computing Personalized PageRank. It performs a number of independent random walks for every source node and takes an empirical distribution of ending nodes to obtain PPR weights with respect to the source. We initialized 2,000 random walks for every source node, performed 5 steps of PPR, and computed PPR weights from all iterations dropping walks from the first one. The teleport probability is set to 0.2.

**Baselines.** We performed a set of experiments using initial similarity and Personalized PageRank weights. Model iSim uses only Freebase scores and achieves microaccuracy of $62.61\%$ (Table 1). PPR model picks a candidate with highest coherence, computed in (3), where no initial similarity is used ($iSim \equiv 1.0$) and no constraints are applied. It has microaccuracy of $85.56\%$. This is a strong baseline, proving that coherence (3), solely based on PPR weights, is very accurate. We also reimplemented the most recent state-of-the-art approach by Alhelbawy (2014) based on the PageRank. We ran it on our set of candidates with freebase scores and got $82.2\%$ and $80.2\%$ in micro- and macroaccuracy correspondingy.

[3]https://github.com/masha-p/PPRforNED

| PPRSim | Micro | Macro |
|---|---|---|
| $iSim \equiv 1.0$ | 85.56 | 85.86 |
| $iSim =$ localSim | 87.01 | 86.65 |
| $iSim =$ popSim | 90.26 | 88.98 |
| +(c1) | 90.52 | 89.21 |
| +(c2) | 91.68 | 89.78 |
| +(c1),(c2) | 91.77 | 89.89 |

Table 2: Performance of PPRSim with different initial similarities and constraints.

**Results.** We observe that PPR combined with global similarity popSim achieves a microaccuracy of $90.2\%$ (Table 2). Adding constraints into the coherence computation further improves the performance to $91.7\%$. Interestingly, (c2) is more accurate than (c1). When put together, (c1)+(c2) performs better than each individual constraint (Table 2). Thus, combining coherence and initial similarity via (5) improves both micro- and macroaccuracy, outperforming state-of-the-art models (Table 1).

## 6 Conclusion and Future Work

In this paper we devise a new algorithm for collective named entity disambiguation based on Personalized PageRank. We show how to incorporate pairwise constraints between candidate entities by using PPR scores and propose a new robust scheme to compute coherence of a candidate entity to a document. Our approach outperforms state-of-the-art models and opens up many opportunities to employ pairwise information in NED. For future work, we plan to explore other strategies and constraints for noise reduction in the document graph.

## References


Eneko Agirre and Aitor Soroa. 2009. Personalizing PageRank for word sense disambiguation. In *Proceedings of the 12th Conference of the European Chapter of the ACL*, pages 33–41, Athens, Greece.

Ayman Alhelbawy and Robert Gaizauskas. 2014. Graph Ranking for Collective Named Entity Disambiguation. In *Proceedings of the 52nd Annual Meeting of the Association for Computational Linguistics (Volume 2: Short Papers)*, pages 75–80.

Razvan Bunescu and Marius Paşca. 2006. Using encyclopedic knowledge for named entity disambiguation. In *Proceedings of the 11th Conference of the European Chapter of the Association for Computational Linguistics*.

Xiao Cheng and Dan Roth. 2013. Relational inference for wikification. In *Proceedings of the 2013 Conference on Empirical Methods in Natural Language Processing*, pages 1787–1796, Seattle, WA.

Silviu Cucerzan. 2007. Large-scale named entity disambiguation based on Wikipedia data. In *Proceedings of the 2007 Joint Conference on Empirical Methods in Natural Language Processing and Computational Natural Language Learning*, pages 708–716.

Silviu Cucerzan. 2011. Tac entity linking by performing full-document entity extraction and disambiguation. In *Proceedings of the 2011 TAC Workshop*, pages 708–716.

Fogaras and Racz. 2004. Towards scaling fully personalized page rank. In *Proceedings of the 3rd Workshop on Algorithms and Models for the Web-Graph (WAW)*, pages 105–117.

Johannes Hoffart, Mohamed Amir Yosef, Ilaria Bordino, Hagen Fürstenau, Manfred Pinkal, Marc Spaniol, Bilyana Taneva, Stefan Thater, and Gerhard Weikum. 2011. Robust disambiguation of named entities in text. In *Proceedings of the Conference on Empirical Methods in Natural Language Processing*, pages 782–792.

Glen Jeh and Jennifer Widom. 2003. Scaling personalized web search. In *Proceedings of the 12th International Conference on World Wide Web*, pages 271–279.

James Mayfield. 2014. Cold start knowledge base population at tac 2014. In *Proceedings of the 2014 TAC Workshop*.

David Milne and Ian H. Witten. 2008. Learning to link with wikipedia. In *Proceedings of the 17th ACM Conference on Information and Knowledge Management*, pages 509–518.

Lawrence Page, Sergey Brin, Rajeev Motwani, and Terry Winograd. 1999. The pagerank citation ranking: Bringing order to the web. Technical Report 1999-66, Stanford InfoLab.

Lev Ratinov, Dan Roth, Doug Downey, and Mike Anderson. 2011. Local and global algorithms for disambiguation to wikipedia. In *Proceedings of the 49th Annual Meeting of the Association for Computational Linguistics: Human Language Technologies*, pages 1375–1384, Portland, OR.

Ravi Sinha and Rada Mihalcea. 2007. Unsupervised graph-basedword sense disambiguation using measures of word semantic similarity. In *Proceedings of the International Conference on Semantic Computing*, pages 363–369.

# When and why are log-linear models self-normalizing?

**Jacob Andreas** and **Dan Klein**
Computer Science Division
University of California, Berkeley
{jda,klein}@cs.berkeley.edu

## Abstract

Several techniques have recently been proposed for training "self-normalized" discriminative models. These attempt to find parameter settings for which unnormalized model scores approximate the true label probability. However, the theoretical properties of such techniques (and of self-normalization generally) have not been investigated. This paper examines the conditions under which we can expect self-normalization to work. We characterize a general class of distributions that admit self-normalization, and prove generalization bounds for procedures that minimize empirical normalizer variance. Motivated by these results, we describe a novel variant of an established procedure for training self-normalized models. The new procedure avoids computing normalizers for most training examples, and decreases training time by as much as factor of ten while preserving model quality.

## 1 Introduction

This paper investigates the theoretical properties of log-linear models trained to make their unnormalized scores approximately sum to one.

Recent years have seen a resurgence of interest in log-linear approaches to language modeling. This includes both conventional log-linear models (Rosenfeld, 1994; Biadsy et al., 2014) and neural networks with a log-linear output layer (Bengio et al., 2006). On a variety of tasks, these LMs have produced substantial gains over conventional generative models based on counting $n$-grams. Successes include machine translation (Devlin et al., 2014) and speech recognition (Graves et al., 2013). However, log-linear LMs come at a significant cost for computational efficiency. In order to output a well-formed probability distribution over words, such models must typically calculate a normalizing constant whose computational cost grows linearly in the size of the vocabulary.

Fortunately, many applications of LMs remain well-behaved even if LM scores do not actually correspond to probability distributions. For example, if a machine translation decoder uses output from a pre-trained LM as a feature inside a larger model, it suffices to have all output scores on approximately the same scale, even if these do not sum to one for every LM context. There has thus been considerable research interest around training procedures capable of ensuring that unnormalized outputs for every context are "close" to a probability distribution. We are aware of at least two such techniques: noise-contrastive estimation (NCE) (Vaswani et al., 2013; Gutmann and Hyvärinen, 2010) and explicit penalization of the log-normalizer (Devlin et al., 2014). Both approaches have advantages and disadvantages. NCE allows fast training by dispensing with the need to ever compute a normalizer. Explicit penalization requires full normalizers to be computed during training but parameterizes the relative importance of the likelihood and the "sum-to-one" constraint, allowing system designers to tune the objective for optimal performance.

While both NCE and explicit penalization are observed to work in practice, their theoretical properties have not been investigated. It is a classical result that empirical minimization of *classification error* yields models whose predictions generalize well. This paper instead investigates a notion of *normalization error*, and attempts to understand the conditions under which unnormalized model scores are a reliable surrogate for probabilities. While language modeling serves as a motivation and running example, our results apply to any log-linear model, and may be of general use for efficient classification and decoding.

Our goals are twofold: primarily, to provide intuition about how self-normalization works, and why it behaves as observed; secondarily, to back these intuitions with formal guarantees, both about classes of normalizable distributions and parameter estimation procedures. The paper is built around two questions:



*Human Language Technologies: The 2015 Annual Conference of the North American Chapter of the ACL*, pages 244–249,
Denver, Colorado, May 31 – June 5, 2015. 

*When* can self-normalization work—for which distributions do good parameter settings exist? And *why* should self-normalization work—how does variance of the normalizer on held-out data relate to variance of the normalizer during training? Analysis of these questions suggests an improvement to the training procedure described by Devlin et al., and we conclude with empirical results demonstrating that our new procedure can reduce training time for self-normalized models by an order of magnitude.

## 2 Preliminaries

Consider a log-linear model of the form

$$p(y|x;\boldsymbol{\theta}) = \frac{\exp\{\theta_y^\top x\}}{\sum_{y'} \exp\{\theta_{y'}^\top x\}} \tag{1}$$

We can think of this as a function from a *context* $x$ to a probability distribution over *decisions* $y_i$, where each decision is parameterized by a weight vector $\theta_y$.[1] For concreteness, consider a language modeling problem in which we are trying to predict the next word after the context *the ostrich*. Here $x$ is a vector of features on the context (e.g. $x = \{$`1-2=the_ostrich, 1=the, 2=ostrich,` $\ldots\}$), and $y$ ranges over the full vocabulary (e.g. $y_1 =$ `the`, $y_2 =$ `runs`, $\ldots$).

Our analysis will focus on the standard log-linear case, though later in the paper we will also relate these results to neural networks. We are specifically concerned with the behavior of the normalizer or *partition function*

$$Z(x;\boldsymbol{\theta}) \stackrel{\text{def}}{=} \sum_y \exp\{\theta_y^\top x\} \tag{2}$$

and in particular with choices of $\boldsymbol{\theta}$ for which $Z(x;\boldsymbol{\theta}) \approx 1$ *for most* $x$.

To formalize the questions in the title of this paper, we introduce the following definitions:

**Definition 1.** A log-linear model $p(y|x,\boldsymbol{\theta})$ is *normalized* with respect to a set $\mathcal{X}$ if for every $x \in \mathcal{X}$, $Z(x;\boldsymbol{\theta}) = 1$. In this case we call $\mathcal{X}$ *normalizable* and $\boldsymbol{\theta}$ *normalizing*.

Now we can state our questions precisely: What distributions are normalizable? Given data points

[1] An alternative, equivalent formulation has a single weight vector and a feature function from contexts and decisions onto feature vectors.

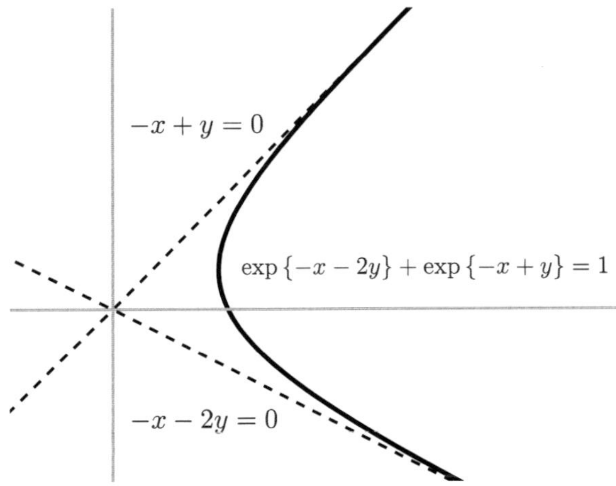


Figure 1: A normalizable set, the solutions $[x, y]$ to $Z([x,y];\{[-1,1],[-1,-2]\}) = 1$. The set forms a smooth one-dimensional manifold bounded on either side by the hyperplanes normal to $[-1,1]$ and $[-1,-2]$.

from a normalizable $\mathcal{X}$, how do we find a normalizing $\boldsymbol{\theta}$?

In sections 3 and 4, we do not analyze whether the setting of $\boldsymbol{\theta}$ corresponds to a good classifier—only a good normalizer. In practice we require both good normalization *and* good classification; in section 5 we provide empirical evidence that both are achievable.

Some notation: Weight vectors $\theta$ (and feature vectors $x$) are $d$-dimensional. There are $k$ output classes, so the total number of parameters in $\boldsymbol{\theta}$ is $kd$. $||\cdot||_p$ is the $\ell_p$ vector norm, and $||\cdot||_\infty$ specifically is the max norm.

## 3 When should self-normalization work?

In this section, we characterize a large class of datasets (i.e. distributions $p(y|x)$) that are normalizable either exactly, or approximately in terms of their marginal distribution over *contexts* $p(x)$. We begin by noting simple features of Equation 2: it is convex in $x$, so in particular its level sets enclose convex regions, and are manifolds of lower dimension than the embedding space.

As our definition of normalizability requires the existence of a normalizing $\boldsymbol{\theta}$, it makes sense to begin by fixing $\boldsymbol{\theta}$ and considering contexts $x$ for which it is normalizing.

**Observation.** *Solutions* $x$ *to* $Z(x;\boldsymbol{\theta}) = 1$, *if any exist, lie on the* boundary *of a convex region in* $\mathbb{R}^d$.

This follows immediately from the definition of a convex function, but provides a concrete example of a set for which $\boldsymbol{\theta}$ is normalizing: the solution set of $Z(x;\boldsymbol{\theta}) = 1$ has a simple geometric interpretation as a particular kind of smooth surface. An example is depicted in Figure 1.

We cannot expect real datasets to be this well behaved, so seems reasonable to ask whether "good-enough" self-normalization is possible for datasets (i.e. distributions $p(x)$) which are only close to some exactly normalizable distribution.

**Definition 2.** A context distribution $p(x)$ is *D-close* to a set $\mathcal{X}$ if

$$\mathbb{E}_p\left[\inf_{x^*\in\mathcal{X}} ||X - x^*||_\infty\right] = D \tag{3}$$

**Definition 3.** A context distribution $p(x)$ is *$\varepsilon$-approximately normalizable* if $\mathbb{E}_p|\log Z(X;\boldsymbol{\theta})| \leq \varepsilon$.

**Theorem 1.** *Suppose $p(x)$ is $D$-close to $\{x : Z(x;\boldsymbol{\theta}) = 1\}$, and each $||\theta_i||_\infty \leq B$. Then $p(x)$ is $dBD$-approximately normalizable.*

*Proof sketch.*[2] Represent each $X$ as $X^* + X^-$, where $X^*$ solves the optimization problem in Equation 3. Then it is possible to bound the normalizer by $\log\exp\{\tilde{\theta}^\top X^-\}$, where $\tilde{\theta}$ maximizes the magnitude of the inner product with $X^-$ over $\boldsymbol{\theta}$.

In keeping with intuition, data distributions that are close to normalizable sets are themselves approximately normalizable on the same scale.[3]

## 4 Why should self-normalization work?

So far we have given a picture of what approximately normalizable distributions look like, but nothing about how to find normalizing $\boldsymbol{\theta}$ from training data in practice. In this section we prove that any procedure that causes training contexts to approximately normalize will also have log-normalizers close to zero in unseen contexts. As noted in the introduction, this does not follow immediately from corresponding results for *classification* with log-linear models. While the two problems are related (it would be quite surprising to have uniform convergence for classification but not normalization), we nonetheless have a different function class and a different loss, and need new analysis.

**Theorem 2.** *Consider a sample $(X_1, X_2, \ldots)$, with all $||X||_\infty \leq R$, and $\boldsymbol{\theta}$ with each $||\theta_i||_\infty \leq B$. Additionally define $\hat{\mathcal{L}} = \frac{1}{n}\sum_i |\log Z(X_i)|$ and $\mathcal{L} = \mathbb{E}|\log Z(X)|$. Then with probability $1-\delta$,*

$$|\hat{\mathcal{L}} - \mathcal{L}| \leq 2\sqrt{\frac{dk(\log dBR + \log n) + \log\frac{1}{\delta}}{2n}} + \frac{2}{n} \tag{4}$$

*Proof sketch.* Empirical process theory provides standard bounds of the form of Equation 4 (Kakade, 2011) in terms of the size of a *cover* of the function class under consideration (here $Z(\cdot;\boldsymbol{\theta})$). In particular, given some $\alpha$, we must construct a finite set of $\hat{Z}(\cdot;\theta)$ such that some $\hat{Z}$ is everywhere a distance of at most $\alpha$ from every $Z$. To provide this cover, it suffices to provide a cover $\hat{\boldsymbol{\theta}}$ for $\boldsymbol{\theta}$. If the $\hat{\boldsymbol{\theta}}$ are spaced at intervals of length $D$, the size of the cover is $(B/D)^{kd}$, from which the given bound follows.

This result applies uniformly across choices of $\boldsymbol{\theta}$ regardless of the training procedure used—in particular, $\boldsymbol{\theta}$ can be found with NCE, explicit penalization, or the variant described in the next section.

As hoped, sample complexity grows as the number of features, and not the number of contexts. In particular, skip-gram models that treat context words independently will have sample efficiency multiplicative, rather than exponential, in the size of the conditioning context. Moreover, if some features are correlated (so that data points lie in a subspace smaller than $d$ dimensions), similar techniques can be used to prove that sample requirements depend only on this effective dimension, and not the true feature vector size.

We emphasize again that this result says nothing about the *quality* of the self-normalized model (e.g. the likelihood it assigns to held-out data). We defer a theoretical treatment of that question to future work. In the following section, however, we provide experimental evidence that self-normalization does not significantly degrade model quality.

## 5 Applications

As noted in the introduction, previous approaches to learning approximately self-normalizing distributions have either relied on explicitly computing the

[2]Full proofs of all results may be found in the Appendix.

[3]Here (and throughout) it is straightforward to replace quantities of the form $dB$ with $B$ by working in $\ell_2$ instead of $\ell_\infty$.

normalizer for each training example, or at least keeping track of an estimate of the normalizer for each training example.

Our results here suggest that it should be possible to obtain approximate self-normalizing behavior without *any* representation of the normalizer on some training examples—as long as a sufficiently large fraction of training examples are normalized, then we have some guarantee that with high probability the normalizer will be close to one on the remaining training examples as well. Thus an unnormalized likelihood objective, coupled with a penalty term that looks at only a small number of normalizers, might nonetheless produce a good model. This suggests the following:

$$l(\boldsymbol{\theta}) = \sum_i \theta_{y_i}^\top x_i + \frac{\alpha}{\gamma} \sum_{h \in H} (\log Z(x_h; \boldsymbol{\theta}))^2 \quad (5)$$

where the parameter $\alpha$ controls the relative importance of the self-normalizing constraint, $H$ is the set of indices to which the constraint should be applied, and $\gamma$ controls the size of $H$, with $|H| = \lceil n\gamma \rceil$. Unlike the objective used by Devlin et al. (2014) most examples are *never* normalized during training. Our approach combines the best properties of the two techniques for self-normalization previously discussed: like NCE, it does not require computation of the normalizer on all training examples, but like explicit penalization it allows fine-grained control over the tradeoff between the likelihood and the quality of the approximation to the normalizer.

We evaluate the usefulness of this objective with a set of small language modeling experiments. We train a log-linear LM with features similar to Biadsy et al. (2014) on a small prefix of the Europarl corpus of approximately 10M words.[4] We optimize the objective in Equation 5 using Adagrad (Duchi et al., 2011). The normalized set $H$ is chosen randomly for each new minibatch. We evaluate using two metrics: BLEU on a downstream machine translation task, and *normalization risk* $R$, the average magnitude of the log-normalizer on held-out data. We measure the response of our training to changes in $\gamma$ and $\alpha$. Results are shown in Table 1 and Table 2.

[4]This prefix was chosen to give the fully-normalized model time to finish training, allowing a complete comparison. Due to the limited LM training data, these translation results are far from state-of-the-art.

| | Normalized fraction ($\gamma$) | | | | |
|---|---|---|---|---|---|
| | 0 | 0.001 | 0.01 | 0.1 | 1 |
| $R_{\text{train}}$ | 22.0 | 1.7 | 1.5 | 1.5 | 1.5 |
| $R_{\text{test}}$ | 21.6 | 1.7 | 1.5 | 1.5 | 1.5 |
| BLEU | 1.5 | 19.1 | 19.2 | 20.0 | 20.0 |

Table 1: Result of varying normalized fraction $\gamma$, with $\alpha = 1$. When no normalization is applied, the model's behavior is pathological, but when normalizing only a small fraction of the training set, performance on the downstream translation task remains good.

| | Normalization strength ($\alpha$) | | | |
|---|---|---|---|---|
| $\alpha$ | 0.01 | 0.1 | 1 | 10 |
| $R_{\text{train}}$ | 20.4 | 9.7 | 1.5 | 0.5 |
| $R_{\text{test}}$ | 20.1 | 9.7 | 1.5 | 0.5 |
| BLEU | 1.5 | 2.6 | 20.0 | 16.9 |

Table 2: Result of varying normalization parameter $\alpha$, with $\gamma = 0.1$. Normalization either too weak or too strong results in poor performance on the translation task, emphasizing the importance of training procedures with a tunable normalization parameter.

Table 1 shows that with small enough $\alpha$, normalization risk grows quite large. Table 2 shows that forcing the risk closer to zero is not necessarily desirable for a downstream machine translation task. As can be seen, no noticeable performance penalty is incurred when normalizing only a tenth of the training set. Performance gains are considerable: setting $\gamma = 0.1$, we observe a roughly tenfold speedup over $\gamma = 1$.

On this corpus, the original training procedure of Devlin et al. with $\alpha = 0.1$ gives a BLEU score of 20.1 and $R_{\text{test}}$ of 2.7. Training time is equivalent to choosing $\gamma = 1$, and larger values of $\alpha$ result in decreased BLEU, while smaller values result in significantly increased normalizer risk. Thus we see that we can achieve smaller normalizer variance and an order-of-magnitude decrease in training time with a loss of only 0.1 BLEU.

## 6 Relation to neural networks

Our discussion has focused on log-linear models. While these can be thought of as a class of single-layer neural networks, in practice much of the demand for fast training and querying of log-linear LMs comes from deeper networks. All of the proof techniques used in this paper can be combined straightforwardly with existing tools for covering the output spaces of neural networks (Anthony and Bartlett, 2009). If optimization of the self-normalizing portion of the objective is deferred to a post-processing step after standard (likelihood) training, and restricted to parameters in the output layers, then Theorem 2 applies exactly.

## 7 Conclusion

We have provided both qualitative and formal characterizations of "self-normalizing" log-linear models, including what we believe to be the first theoretical guarantees for self-normalizing training procedures. Motivated by these results, we have described a novel objective for training self-normalized log-linear models, and demonstrated that this objective achieves significant performance improvements without a decrease in the quality of the models learned.

## A Quality of the approximation

*Proof of Theorem 1.* Using the definitions of $X^*$, $X^-$ and $\tilde{\theta}$ given in the proof sketch for Theorem 1,

$$\begin{aligned}
&\mathbb{E}|\log(\sum \exp\{\theta_i^\top X\})| \\
&\quad = \mathbb{E}|\log(\sum \exp\{\theta_i^\top (X^* + X^-)\})| \\
&\quad \le \mathbb{E}|\log(\exp\{\tilde{\theta}^\top X^-\} \sum \exp\{\theta_i^\top X^*\})| \\
&\quad \le \mathbb{E}|\log(\exp\{\tilde{\theta}^\top X^-\})| \\
&\quad \le dDB \qquad \square
\end{aligned}$$

## B Generalization error

**Lemma 3.** *For any $\boldsymbol{\theta}_1$, $\boldsymbol{\theta}_2$ with $||\theta_{1,i} - \theta_{2,i}||_\infty \le D \stackrel{\text{def}}{=} \alpha/dR$ for all $i$,*

$$||\log Z(x;\boldsymbol{\theta}_1)| - |\log Z(x;\boldsymbol{\theta}_2)|| \le \alpha \tag{6}$$

*Proof.*

$$\begin{aligned}
&||\log Z(x;\boldsymbol{\theta}_1)| - |\log Z(x;\boldsymbol{\theta}_2)|| \\
&\quad \le |\log Z(x;\boldsymbol{\theta}_1) - \log Z(x;\boldsymbol{\theta}_2)| \\
&\quad \le \log \frac{Z(x;\boldsymbol{\theta}_1)}{Z(x;\boldsymbol{\theta}_2)} \qquad \text{(w.l.o.g.)} \\
&\quad = \log \frac{\sum_i \exp\left\{(\theta_{1i} - \theta_{2i})^\top x\right\} \exp\left\{\theta_{2i}^\top x\right\}}{\sum_i \exp\left\{\theta_{2i}^\top x\right\}} \\
&\quad \le dDR + \log \frac{Z(x;\boldsymbol{\theta}_2)}{Z(x;\boldsymbol{\theta}_2)} = \alpha \qquad \square
\end{aligned}$$

**Corollary 4.** *The set of partition functions $\mathcal{Z} = \{Z(\cdot;\boldsymbol{\theta}) : ||\theta||_\infty \le B \ \forall\theta \in \boldsymbol{\theta}\}$ can be covered on on the $\ell_\infty$ ball of radius $R$ by a grid of $\hat{\boldsymbol{\theta}}$ with distance $D$. The size of this cover is*

$$|\hat{\mathcal{Z}}| = \left(\frac{B}{D}\right)^{dk} = \left(\frac{dBR}{\alpha}\right)^{dk} \tag{7}$$

*Proof of Theorem 2.* From a standard discretization lemma (Kakade, 2011) and Corollary 4, we immediately have that with probabilty $1 - \delta$,

$$\begin{aligned}
&\sup_{Z\in\mathcal{Z}} |\hat{\mathcal{L}} - \mathcal{L}| \le \\
&\quad \le \inf_\alpha 2\sqrt{\frac{dk(\log dBR - \log\alpha) + \log\frac{1}{\delta}}{2n}} + 2\alpha
\end{aligned}$$

Taking $\alpha = 1/n$,

$$\le 2\sqrt{\frac{dk(\log dBR + \log n) + \log\frac{1}{\delta}}{2n}} + \frac{2}{n} \qquad \square$$


## Acknowledgements

The authors would like to thank Peter Bartlett, Robert Nishihara and Maxim Rabinovich for useful discussions. This work was partially supported by BBN under DARPA contract HR0011-12-C-0014. The first author is supported by a National Science Foundation Graduate Fellowship.


## References


Martin Anthony and Peter Bartlett. 2009. *Neural network learning: theoretical foundations*. Cambridge University Press.

Yoshua Bengio, Holger Schwenk, Jean-Sébastien Senécal, Fréderic Morin, and Jean-Luc Gauvain. 2006. Neural probabilistic language models. In *Innovations in Machine Learning*, pages 137–186. Springer.

Fadi Biadsy, Keith Hall, Pedro Moreno, and Brian Roark. 2014. Backoff inspired features for maximum entropy language models. In *Proceedings of the Conference of the International Speech Communication Association*.

Jacob Devlin, Rabih Zbib, Zhongqiang Huang, Thomas Lamar, Richard Schwartz, and John Makhoul. 2014. Fast and robust neural network joint models for statistical machine translation. In *Proceedings of the Annual Meeting of the Association for Computational Linguistics*.

John Duchi, Elad Hazan, and Yoram Singer. 2011. Adaptive subgradient methods for online learning and stochastic optimization. *Journal of Machine Learning Research*, 12:2121–2159.

Alex Graves, Navdeep Jaitly, and Abdel-rahman Mohamed. 2013. Hybrid speech recognition with deep bidirectional LSTM. In *IEEE Workshop on Automatic Speech Recognition and Understanding*, pages 273–278.

Michael Gutmann and Aapo Hyvärinen. 2010. Noise-contrastive estimation: A new estimation principle for unnormalized statistical models. In *Proceedings of the International Conference on Artificial Intelligence and Statistics*, pages 297–304.

Sham Kakade. 2011. Uniform and empirical covering numbers. `http://stat.wharton.upenn.edu/~skakade/courses/stat928/lectures/lecture16.pdf`.

Ronald Rosenfeld. 1994. *Adaptive statistical language modeling: a maximum entropy approach*. Ph.D. thesis.

Ashish Vaswani, Yinggong Zhao, Victoria Fossum, and David Chiang. 2013. Decoding with large-scale neural language models improves translation. In *Proceedings of the Conference on Empirical Methods in Natural Language Processing*.

# Deep Multilingual Correlation for Improved Word Embeddings

**Ang Lu**[1], **Weiran Wang**[2], **Mohit Bansal**[2], **Kevin Gimpel**[2], **and Karen Livescu**[2]
[1]Department of Automation, Tsinghua University, Beijing, 100084, China
lva11@mails.tsinghua.edu.cn
[2]Toyota Technological Institute at Chicago, Chicago, IL, 60637, USA
{weiranwang, mbansal, kgimpel, klivescu}@ttic.edu

## Abstract

Word embeddings have been found useful for many NLP tasks, including part-of-speech tagging, named entity recognition, and parsing. Adding multilingual context when learning embeddings can improve their quality, for example via canonical correlation analysis (CCA) on embeddings from two languages. In this paper, we extend this idea to learn *deep non-linear transformations* of word embeddings of the two languages, using the recently proposed deep canonical correlation analysis. The resulting embeddings, when evaluated on multiple word and bigram similarity tasks, consistently improve over monolingual embeddings and over embeddings transformed with linear CCA.

## 1 Introduction

Learned word representations are widely used in NLP tasks such as tagging, named entity recognition, and parsing (Miller et al., 2004; Koo et al., 2008; Turian et al., 2010; Täckström et al., 2012; Huang et al., 2014; Bansal et al., 2014). The idea in such representations is that words with similar context have similar meaning, and hence should be nearby in a clustering or vector space. Continuous representations are learned with neural language models (Bengio et al., 2003; Mnih and Hinton, 2007; Mikolov et al., 2013) or spectral methods (Deerwester et al., 1990; Dhillon et al., 2011).

The context used to learn these representations is typically the set of nearby words of each word occurrence. Prior work has found that adding **translational context** results in better representations (Diab and Resnik, 2002; Täckström et al., 2012; Bansal et al., 2012; Zou et al., 2013). Recently, Faruqui and Dyer (2014) applied canonical correlation analysis (CCA) to word embeddings of two languages, and found that the resulting embeddings represent word similarities better than the original monolingual embeddings.

In this paper, we follow the same intuition as Faruqui and Dyer (2014) but rather than learning linear transformations with CCA, we permit the correlated information to lie in nonlinear subspaces of the original embeddings. We use the recently proposed deep canonical correlation analysis (DCCA) technique of Andrew et al. (2013) to learn nonlinear transformations of two languages' embeddings that are highly correlated. We evaluate our DCCA-transformed embeddings on word similarity tasks like WordSim-353 (Finkelstein et al., 2001) and SimLex-999 (Hill et al., 2014), and also on the bigram similarity task of Mitchell and Lapata (2010) (using additive composition), obtaining consistent improvements over the original embeddings and over linear CCA. We also compare tuning criteria and ensemble methods for these architectures.

## 2 Method

We assume that we have initial word embeddings for two languages, denoted by random vectors $\mathbf{x} \in \mathbb{R}^{D_x}$ and $\mathbf{y} \in \mathbb{R}^{D_y}$, and a set of bilingual word pairs. Our goal is to obtain a representation for each language that incorporates useful information from both $\mathbf{x}$ and $\mathbf{y}$. We consider the two input monolingual word embeddings as different views of the same latent semantic signal. There are multiple ways to incorporate multilingual information into word embeddings. Here we follow Faruqui and Dyer (2014) in taking a CCA-based approach, in which we project the original embeddings onto their maximally correlated subspaces. However, instead of relying on linear correlation, we learn more powerful non-linear transformations of each view via deep networks.

**Canonical Correlation Analysis** A popular method for multi-view representation learning is canonical correlation analysis (CCA; Hotelling, 1936). Its objective is to find two vectors $\mathbf{u} \in \mathbb{R}^{D_x}$



*Human Language Technologies: The 2015 Annual Conference of the North American Chapter of the ACL*, pages 250–256,
Denver, Colorado, May 31 – June 5, 2015. 

and $\mathbf{v} \in \mathbb{R}^{D_y}$ such that projections of the two views onto these vectors are maximally (linearly) correlated:

$$\max_{\mathbf{u}\in\mathbb{R}^{D_x},\mathbf{v}\in\mathbb{R}^{D_y}} \frac{\mathbb{E}\left[(\mathbf{u}^\top\mathbf{x})(\mathbf{v}^\top\mathbf{y})\right]}{\sqrt{\mathbb{E}\left[(\mathbf{u}^\top\mathbf{x})^2\right]}\sqrt{\mathbb{E}\left[(\mathbf{v}^\top\mathbf{y})^2\right]}} = \frac{\mathbf{u}^\top\boldsymbol{\Sigma}_{xy}\mathbf{v}}{\sqrt{\mathbf{u}^\top\boldsymbol{\Sigma}_{xx}\mathbf{u}}\sqrt{\mathbf{v}^\top\boldsymbol{\Sigma}_{yy}\mathbf{v}}} \quad (1)$$

where $\boldsymbol{\Sigma}_{xy}$ and $\boldsymbol{\Sigma}_{xx}$ are the cross-view and within-view covariance matrices. (1) is extended to learn multi-dimensional projections by optimizing the sum of correlations in all dimensions, subject to different projected dimensions being uncorrelated. Given sample pairs $\{(\mathbf{x}_i, \mathbf{y}_i)\}_{i=1}^N$, the empirical estimates of the covariance matrices are $\hat{\boldsymbol{\Sigma}}_{xx} = \frac{1}{N}\sum_{i=1}^N \mathbf{x}_i\mathbf{x}_i^\top + r_x\mathbf{I}$, $\hat{\boldsymbol{\Sigma}}_{yy} = \frac{1}{N}\sum_{i=1}^N \mathbf{y}_i\mathbf{y}_i^\top + r_y\mathbf{I}$ and $\hat{\boldsymbol{\Sigma}}_{xy} = \frac{1}{N}\sum_{i=1}^N \mathbf{x}_i\mathbf{y}_i^\top$ where $(r_x, r_y) > 0$ are **regularization** parameters (Hardoon et al., 2004; De Bie and De Moor, 2003). Then the optimal $k$-dimensional projection mappings are given in closed form via the rank-$k$ singular value decomposition (SVD) of the $D_x \times D_y$ matrix $\hat{\boldsymbol{\Sigma}}_{xx}^{-1/2}\hat{\boldsymbol{\Sigma}}_{xy}\hat{\boldsymbol{\Sigma}}_{yy}^{-1/2}$.

## 2.1 Deep Canonical Correlation Analysis

A linear feature mapping is often not sufficiently powerful to faithfully capture the hidden, non-linear relationships within the data. Recently, Andrew et al. (2013) proposed a nonlinear extension of CCA using deep neural networks, dubbed deep canonical correlation analysis (DCCA) and illustrated in Figure 1. In this model, two (possibly deep) neural networks $\mathbf{f}$ and $\mathbf{g}$ are used to extract features from each view, and trained to maximize the correlations between outputs in the two views, measured by a linear CCA step with projection mappings $(\mathbf{u}, \mathbf{v})$. The neural network weights and the linear projections are optimized together using the objective

$$\max_{\mathbf{W_f},\mathbf{W_g},\mathbf{u},\mathbf{v}} \frac{\mathbf{u}^\top\boldsymbol{\Sigma}_{fg}\mathbf{v}}{\sqrt{\mathbf{u}^\top\boldsymbol{\Sigma}_{ff}\mathbf{u}}\sqrt{\mathbf{v}^\top\boldsymbol{\Sigma}_{gg}\mathbf{v}}}, \quad (2)$$

where $\mathbf{W_f}$ and $\mathbf{W_g}$ are the weights of the two networks and $\boldsymbol{\Sigma}_{fg}$, $\boldsymbol{\Sigma}_{ff}$ and $\boldsymbol{\Sigma}_{gg}$ are covariance matrices computed for $\{\mathbf{f}(\mathbf{x}_i), \mathbf{g}(\mathbf{y}_i)\}_{i=1}^N$ in the same way as CCA. The final transformation is the composition of the neural network and CCA projection, e.g., $\mathbf{u}^\top\mathbf{f}(\mathbf{x})$ for the first view. Unlike CCA, DCCA does not have a closed-form solution, but the parameters can be learned via gradient-based optimization, with either batch algorithms like L-BFGS as in (Andrew et al., 2013) or a mini-batch stochastic gradient descent-like approach as in (Wang et al., 2015). We choose the latter in this paper.

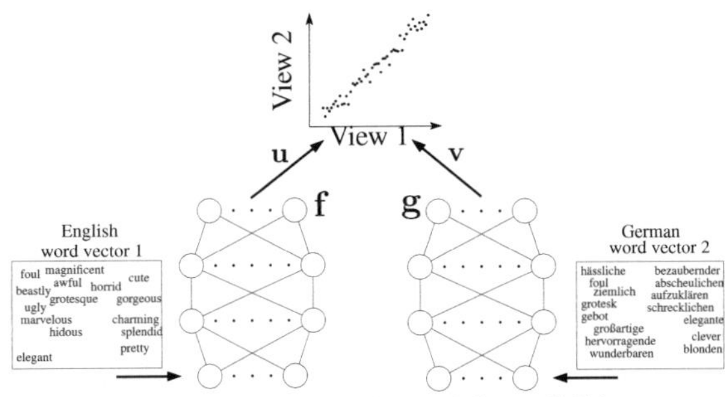

Figure 1: Illustration of deep CCA.

An alternative nonlinear extension of CCA is kernel CCA (KCCA) (Lai and Fyfe, 2000; Vinokourov et al., 2003), which introduces nonlinearity through kernels. DCCA scales better with data size, as KCCA involves the SVD of an $N \times N$ matrix. Andrew et al. (2013) showed that DCCA achieves better correlation on held-out data than CCA/KCCA, and Wang et al. (2015) found that DCCA outperforms CCA and KCCA on a speech recognition task.

# 3 Experiments

We use English and German as our two languages. Our original monolingual word vectors are the same as those used by Faruqui and Dyer (2014). They are 640-dimensional and are estimated via latent semantic analysis on the WMT 2011 monolingual news corpora.[1] We use German-English translation pairs as the input to CCA and DCCA, using the same set of 36K pairs as used by Faruqui and Dyer. These pairs contain, for each of 36K English word types, the single most frequently aligned German word. They were obtained using the word aligner in `cdec` (Dyer et al., 2010) run on the WMT06-10 news commentary corpora and Europarl. After training, we apply the learned CCA/DCCA projection mappings to the original English word embeddings (180K words) and use these transformed embeddings for our evaluation tasks.

## 3.1 Evaluation Tasks

We compare our DCCA-based embeddings to the original word vectors and to CCA-based em-

[1] www.statmt.org/wmt11/

beddings on several tasks. We use WordSim-353 (Finkelstein et al., 2001), which contains 353 English word pairs with human similarity ratings. It is divided into WS-SIM and WS-REL by Agirre et al. (2009) to measure similarity and relatedness. We also use SimLex-999 (Hill et al., 2014), a new similarity-focused dataset consisting of 666 noun pairs, 222 verb pairs, and 111 adjective pairs. Finally, we use the bigram similarity dataset from Mitchell and Lapata (2010) which has 3 subsets, adjective-noun (AN), noun-noun (NN), and verb-object (VN), and dev and test sets for each. For the bigram task, we simply add the word vectors output by CCA or DCCA to get bigram vectors.[2]

All task datasets contain pairs with human similarity ratings. To evaluate embeddings, we compute cosine similarity between the two vectors in each pair, order the pairs by similarity, and compute Spearman's correlation ($\rho$) between the model's ranking and human ranking.

### 3.2 Training

We normalize the 36K training pair vectors to unit norm (as also done by Faruqui and Dyer). We then remove the per-dimension mean and standard deviation of this set of training pairs, as is typically done in neural network training (LeCun et al., 1998). We do the same to the original 180K English word vectors (normalize to unit norm, remove the mean/standard deviation of the size-36K training set), then apply our CCA/DCCA mappings to these 180K vectors. The resulting 180K vectors are further normalized to zero mean before cosine similarities between test pairs are computed, as also done by Faruqui and Dyer.

For both CCA and DCCA, we tune the output dimensionality among factors in $\{0.2, 0.4, 0.6, 0.8, 1.0\}$ of the original embedding dimension (640), and regularization $(r_x, r_y)$ from $\{10^{-6}, 10^{-5}, 10^{-4}, 10^{-3}\}$, based on the 7 tuning tasks discussed below.

For DCCA, we use standard deep neural networks with rectified linear units and tune the depth (1 to 4 hidden layers) and layer widths (in $\{128, 256, 512, 1024, 2048, 4096\}$) separately for each language. For optimization, we use stochastic gradient descent (SGD) as described by Wang et al. (2015). We tune SGD hyperparameters on a small grid, choosing a mini-batch size of 3000, learning rate of $0.0001$, and momentum of $0.99$.

### 3.3 Tuning

Our main results are based on tuning hyperparameters (of CCA/DCCA) on 7 word similarity tasks.[3] We perform additional experiments in which we tune on the development sets for the bigram tasks. We set aside WS-353, SimLex-999, and the test sets of the bigram tasks as held-out test sets. We consider two tuning criteria:

**BestAvg**: Choose the hyperparameters with the best average performance across the 7 tuning tasks. This is the only tuning criterion used for CCA.

**MostBeat**: For DCCA, choose the hyperparameters that beat the best CCA embeddings on a maximum number of the 7 tasks; to break ties here, choose the hyperparameters with the best average performance. The idea is that we want to find a setting that generalizes to many tasks.

We also consider simple ensembles by averaging the cosine similarities from the three best settings under each of these two criteria.

### 3.4 Results

Table 1 shows our main results on the word and bigram similarity tasks. All values are Spearman's correlation ($\rho$). We show the original word vector results, the best-tuned CCA setting (CCA-1), the ensemble of the top-3 CCA settings (CCA-Ens), and the same for DCCA (with both tuning criteria). The DCCA results show an overall improvement on most tasks over linear CCA (all of the shaded DCCA results are better than all corresponding CCA results).

Each of our tuning criteria for DCCA performs well, and almost always better than CCA. BestAvg is better on some tasks while MostBeat is better on others; we report both here to bring attention to and promote discussion about the effects of tuning methods when learning representations in the absence of supervision or in-domain tuning data.

In Table 2, we report additional bigram similarity results obtained by tuning on the dev sets of the bi-

[2] We also tried multiplication but it performed worse. In future work, we will directly train on bigram translation pairs.

[3] RG-65 (Rubenstein and Goodenough, 1965), MC-30 (Miller and Charles, 1991), MTurk-287 (Radinsky et al., 2011), MTurk-771, MEN (Bruni et al., 2014), Rare Word (Luong et al., 2013), and YP-130 (Yang and Powers, 2006).

| Embeddings | WS-353 | WS-SIM | WS-REL | SL-999 | AN | NN | VN | Avg | Dim |
|---|---|---|---|---|---|---|---|---|---|
| Original | 46.7 | 56.3 | 36.6 | 26.5 | 26.5 | 38.1 | 34.1 | 32.9 | 640 |
| CCA-1 | 67.2 | 73.0 | 63.4 | 40.7 | 42.4 | 48.1 | 37.4 | 42.6 | 384 |
| CCA-Ens | 67.5 | 73.1 | 63.7 | 40.4 | 42.0 | **48.2** | 37.8 | 42.7 | 384 |
| DCCA-1 (BestAvg) | 69.6 | 73.9 | 65.6 | 38.9 | 35.0 | 40.9 | **41.3** | 39.1 | 128 |
| DCCA-Ens (BestAvg) | **70.8** | **75.2** | **67.3** | 41.7 | 42.4 | 45.7 | 40.1 | 42.7 | 128 |
| DCCA-1 (MostBeat) | 68.6 | 73.5 | 65.7 | **42.3** | **44.4** | 44.7 | 36.7 | 41.9 | 384 |
| DCCA-Ens (MostBeat) | 69.9 | 74.4 | 66.7 | **42.3** | 43.7 | 47.4 | 38.8 | **43.3** | 384 |

Table 1: Main results on word and bigram similarity tasks, tuned on 7 development tasks (see text for details). Shading indicates a result that matches or improves the best linear CCA result; boldface indicates the best result in a given column. See Section 3.4 for discussion on NN results.

| Embeddings | AN | NN | VN | Avg |
|---|---|---|---|---|
| CCA | 42.4 | **48.1** | 37.4 | 42.6 |
| Deep CCA | **45.5** | 47.1 | **45.1** | **45.9** |

Table 2: Bigram results, tuned on bigram dev sets.

gram tasks themselves (as provided by Mitchell and Lapata), since the 7 tuning tasks are not particularly related to the bigram test sets. We see that DCCA can achieve even stronger improvements over CCA and overall using these related dev sets.

We note that the performance on the NN task does not improve. The typical variance of annotator scores for each bigram pair was larger for the NN dataset than for the other bigram datasets, suggesting noisier annotations. Also, we found that the NN annotations often reflected topical relatedness rather than functional similarity, e.g., *television set* and *television programme* are among the most similar noun-noun bigrams. We expect that multilingual information would help embeddings to more closely reflect functional similarity.

For DCCA, we found that the best-performing networks were typically asymmetric, with 1 to 2 layers on the English side and 2 to 4 on the German side. The best network structure on the bigram VN development set is 640-128-128 for the English view and 640-128-512-128 for the German view, with a final CCA projection layer with dimensionality 128 for each language.

## 4 Discussion

**Normalization and Evaluation** We note that the cosine similarity (and thus Spearman's $\rho$) between a pair of words is not invariant to the series of simple (affine) transformations done by the normalizations in our procedure. For their baseline, Faruqui and Dyer (2014) did not remove the standard deviation

| better with DCCA | | worse with DCCA | |
|---|---|---|---|
| arrive | come | author | creator |
| locate | find | leader | manager |
| way | manner | buddy | companion |
| recent | new | crowd | bunch |
| take | obtain | achieve | succeed |
| boundary | border | attention | interest |
| win | accomplish | join | add |
| contemplate | think | mood | emotion |

Table 3: Highly-similar pairs in SimLex-999 that improved/degraded the most under DCCA. Pairs are sorted in decreasing order according to the amount of improvement/degradation.

of the 36K training set for the 180K English vocabulary during testing. We have accidentally found that this normalization step alone greatly improves the performance of the original vectors.

For example, the WS-353 correlation improves from 46.7 to 67.1, essentially matching the linear CCA correlations, though DCCA still outperforms them both. This indicates that the cosine similarity is not stable, and it is likely better to learn a distance/similarity function (using labeled tuning data) atop the learned features such that similarities between selected pairs will match the human similarities, or such that the rankings will match.

**Error Analysis** We analyze high-similarity word pairs that change the most with DCCA, as compared to both linear CCA and the original vectors.

For a word pair $w$, we use $r(w)$ to refer to its similarity rank, subscripting it whether it is computed according to human ratings ($r_h$) or if based on cosine similarity via the original vectors ($r_o$), CCA-1 ($r_c$), or DCCA-1 MostBeat ($r_d$). We define $\delta_a(w) = |r_a(w) - r_h(w)|$ and compute $\Delta(w) =$

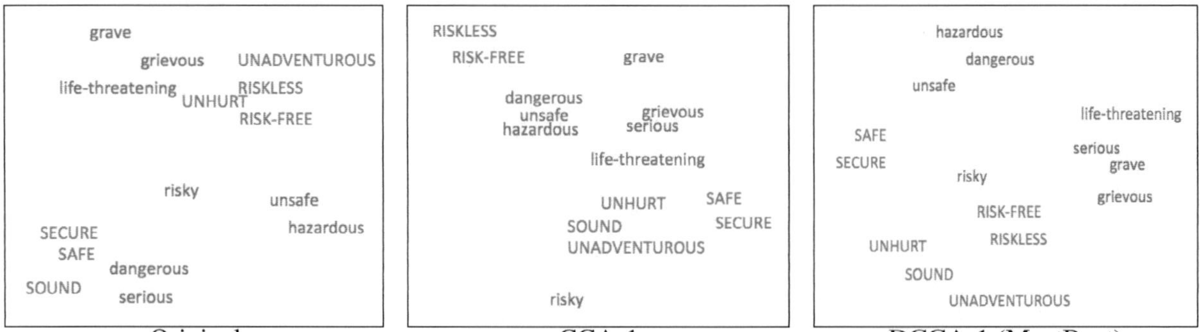


Original CCA-1 DCCA-1 (MostBeat)

Figure 2: t-SNE visualization of synonyms (green) and antonyms (red, capitalized) of *dangerous*.

$\delta_d(w) - (\delta_c(w) + \delta_o(w))$. If $\Delta(w) < 0$, then word pair $w$ was closer to the human ranking using DCCA. Table 3 shows word pairs from SimLex-999 with high human similarity ratings ($\geq$ 7 out of 10); column 1 shows pairs with smallest $\Delta$ values, and column 2 shows pairs with largest $\Delta$ values.

Among pairs in column 1, many contain words with several senses. Using bilingual information is likely to focus on the most frequent sense in the bitext, due to our use of the most frequently-aligned German word in each training pair. By contrast, using only monolingual context is expected to find an embedding that blends the contextual information across all word senses.

Several pairs from column 2 show hypernym rather than paraphrase relationships, e.g., *author-creator* and *leader-manager*. Though these pairs are rated as highly similar by annotators, linear CCA made them less similar than the original vectors, and DCCA made them less similar still. This matches our intuition that bilingual information should encourage paraphrase-like similarity and thereby discourage the similarity of hypernym-hyponym pairs.

**Visualizations** We visualized several synonym-antonym word lists and often found that DCCA more cleanly separated synonyms from antonyms than CCA or the original vectors. An example of the clearest improvement is shown in Fig. 2.

## 5 Related work

Previous work has successfully used translational context for word representations (Diab and Resnik, 2002; Zhao et al., 2005; Täckström et al., 2012; Bansal et al., 2012; Faruqui and Dyer, 2014), including via hand-designed vector space models (Peirsman and Padó, 2010; Sumita, 2000) or via unsupervised LDA and LSA (Boyd-Graber and Blei, 2009; Zhao and Xing, 2006).

There have been other recent deep learning approaches to bilingual representations, e.g., based on a joint monolingual and bilingual objective (Zou et al., 2013). There has also been recent interest in learning bilingual representations without using word alignments (Chandar et al., 2014; Gouws et al., 2014; Kočiský et al., 2014; Vulic and Moens, 2013).

This research is also related to early examples of learning bilingual lexicons using monolingual corpora (Koehn and Knight, 2002; Haghighi et al., 2008); the latter used CCA to find matched word pairs. Irvine and Callison-Burch (2013) used a supervised learning method with multiple monolingual signals. Finally, other work on CCA and spectral methods has been used in the context of other types of views (Collobert and Weston, 2008; Dhillon et al., 2011; Klementiev et al., 2012; Chang et al., 2013).

## 6 Conclusion

We have demonstrated how bilingual information can be incorporated into word embeddings via deep canonical correlation analysis (DCCA). The DCCA embeddings consistently outperform linear CCA embeddings on word and bigram similarity tasks. Future work could compare DCCA to other non-linear approaches discussed in §5, compare different languages as multiview context, and extend to aligned phrase pairs, and to unaligned data.

## Acknowledgments

We are grateful to Manaal Faruqui for sharing resources, and to Chris Dyer, David Sontag, Lyle Ungar, and anonymous reviewers for helpful input.

## References


Eneko Agirre, Enrique Alfonseca, Keith Hall, Jana Kravalova, Marius Pacsca, and Aitor Soroa. 2009. A study on similarity and relatedness using distributional and wordnet-based approaches. In *Proceedings of HLT-NAACL*.

Galen Andrew, Raman Arora, Jeff Bilmes, and Karen Livescu. 2013. Deep canonical correlation analysis. In *Proceedings of ICML*.

Mohit Bansal, John DeNero, and Dekang Lin. 2012. Unsupervised translation sense clustering. In *Proceedings of NAACL-HLT*.

M. Bansal, K. Gimpel, and K. Livescu. 2014. Tailoring continuous word representations for dependency parsing. In *Proceedings of ACL*.

Yoshua Bengio, Réjean Ducharme, Pascal Vincent, and Christian Janvin. 2003. A neural probabilistic language model. *JMLR*, 3:1137–1155, March.

Jordan Boyd-Graber and David M Blei. 2009. Multilingual topic models for unaligned text. In *Proceedings of UAI*.

Elia Bruni, Nam-Khanh Tran, and Marco Baroni. 2014. Multimodal distributional semantics. *J. Artif. Intell. Res.(JAIR)*, 49:1–47.

Sarath Chandar, Stanislas Lauly, Hugo Larochelle, Mitesh Khapra, Balaraman Ravindran, Vikas Raykar, and Amrita Saha. 2014. An autoencoder approach to learning bilingual word representations. In *Proceedings of NIPS*.

Kai-Wei Chang, Wen-tau Yih, and Christopher Meek. 2013. Multi-relational latent semantic analysis. In *Proceedings of EMNLP*.

Ronan Collobert and Jason Weston. 2008. A unified architecture for natural language processing: Deep neural networks with multitask learning. In *Proceedings of ICML*.

Tijl De Bie and Bart De Moor. 2003. On the regularization of canonical correlation analysis. *Int. Sympos. ICA and BSS*, pages 785–790.

Scott C. Deerwester, Susan T. Dumais, Thomas K. Landauer, George W. Furnas, and Richard A. Harshman. 1990. Indexing by latent semantic analysis. *JASIS*, 41(6):391–407.

Paramveer Dhillon, Dean P. Foster, and Lyle H. Ungar. 2011. Multi-view learning of word embeddings via CCA. In *Proceedings of NIPS*.

Mona Diab and Philip Resnik. 2002. An unsupervised method for word sense tagging using parallel corpora. In *Proceedings of ACL*.

C. Dyer, A. Lopez, J. Ganitkevitch, J. Weese, F. Ture, P. Blunsom, H. Setiawan, V. Eidelman, and P. Resnik. 2010. cdec: A decoder, alignment, and learning framework for finite-state and context-free translation models. In *Proceedings of ACL*.

Manaal Faruqui and Chris Dyer. 2014. Improving vector space word representations using multilingual correlation. In *Proceedings of EACL*.

Lev Finkelstein, Evgeniy Gabrilovich, Yossi Matias, Ehud Rivlin, Zach Solan, Gadi Wolfman, and Eytan Ruppin. 2001. Placing search in context: The concept revisited. In *Proceedings of WWW*.

Stephan Gouws, Yoshua Bengio, and Greg Corrado. 2014. Bilbowa: Fast bilingual distributed representations without word alignments. *arXiv preprint arXiv:1410.2455*.

Aria Haghighi, Percy Liang, Taylor Berg-Kirkpatrick, and Dan Klein. 2008. Learning bilingual lexicons from monolingual corpora. In *Proceedings of ACL*.

David R. Hardoon, Sandor Szedmak, and John Shawe-Taylor. 2004. Canonical correlation analysis: An overview with application to learning methods. *Neural Computation*, 16(12):2639–2664, December.

Felix Hill, Roi Reichart, and Anna Korhonen. 2014. Simlex-999: Evaluating semantic models with (genuine) similarity estimation. *arXiv preprint arXiv:1408.3456*.

Harold Hotelling. 1936. Relations between two sets of variates. *Biometrika*, 28(3/4):321–377, December.

Fei Huang, Arun Ahuja, Doug Downey, Yi Yang, Yuhong Guo, and Alexander Yates. 2014. Learning representations for weakly supervised natural language processing tasks. *Computational Linguistics*, 40(1).

Ann Irvine and Chris Callison-Burch. 2013. Supervised bilingual lexicon induction with multiple monolingual signals. In *Proceedings of HLT-NAACL*, pages 518–523.

Alexandre Klementiev, Ivan Titov, and Binod Bhattarai. 2012. Inducing crosslingual distributed representations of words.

Tomáš Kočiský, Karl Moritz Hermann, and Phil Blunsom. 2014. Learning bilingual word representations by marginalizing alignments. *arXiv preprint arXiv:1405.0947*.

Philipp Koehn and Kevin Knight. 2002. Learning a translation lexicon from monolingual corpora. In *Proceedings of the ACL Workshop on Unsupervised Lexical Acquisition*.

Terry Koo, Xavier Carreras, and Michael Collins. 2008. Simple semi-supervised dependency parsing. In *Proceedings of ACL*.

P. L. Lai and C. Fyfe. 2000. Kernel and nonlinear canonical correlation analysis. *Int. J. Neural Syst.*, 10(5):365–377, October.

Yann LeCun, Leon Bottou, Genevieve B. Orr, and Klaus-Robert Müller. 1998. Efficient backprop. volume

1524 of *Lecture Notes in Computer Science*, pages 9–50, Berlin. Springer-Verlag.

Minh-Thang Luong, Richard Socher, and Christopher D. Manning. 2013. Better word representations with recursive neural networks for morphology. In *Proceedings of CoNLL.*

Tomas Mikolov, Ilya Sutskever, Kai Chen, Greg Corrado, and Jeffrey Dean. 2013. Distributed representations of words and phrases and their compositionality. In *Proceedings of NIPS*.

George A Miller and Walter G Charles. 1991. Contextual correlates of semantic similarity. *Language and cognitive processes*, 6(1):1–28.

Scott Miller, Jethran Guinness, and Alex Zamanian. 2004. Name tagging with word clusters and discriminative training. In *Proceedings of HLT-NAACL.*

Jeff Mitchell and Mirella Lapata. 2010. Composition in distributional models of semantics. *Cognitive Science*, 34(8):1388–1439.

Andriy Mnih and Geoffrey Hinton. 2007. Three new graphical models for statistical language modelling. In *Proceedings of ICML.*

Yves Peirsman and Sebastian Padó. 2010. Cross-lingual induction of selectional preferences with bilingual vector spaces. In *Proceedings of HLT-NAACL.*

Kira Radinsky, Eugene Agichtein, Evgeniy Gabrilovich, and Shaul Markovitch. 2011. A word at a time: computing word relatedness using temporal semantic analysis. In *Proceedings of WWW.*

Herbert Rubenstein and John B Goodenough. 1965. Contextual correlates of synonymy. *Communications of the ACM*, 8(10):627–633.

Eiichiro Sumita. 2000. Lexical transfer using a vector-space model. In *Proceedings of ACL.*

Oscar Täckström, Ryan McDonald, and Jakob Uszkoreit. 2012. Cross-lingual word clusters for direct transfer of linguistic structure. In *Proceedings of HLT-NAACL.*

Joseph Turian, Lev-Arie Ratinov, and Yoshua Bengio. 2010. Word representations: A simple and general method for semi-supervised learning. In *Proceedings of ACL.*

Alexei Vinokourov, Nello Cristianini, and John Shawe-Taylor. 2003. Inferring a semantic representation of text via cross-language correlation analysis. In *Proceedings of NIPS*.

Ivan Vulic and Marie-Francine Moens. 2013. A study on bootstrapping bilingual vector spaces from non-parallel data (and nothing else). In *Proceedings of EMNLP*.

Weiran Wang, Raman Arora, Karen Livescu, and Jeff Bilmes. 2015. Unsupervised learning of acoustic features via deep canonical correlation analysis. In *Proceedings of ICASSP*.

Dongqiang Yang and David MW Powers. 2006. Verb similarity on the taxonomy of wordnet. *Proceedings of GWC-06*, pages 121–128.

Bing Zhao and Eric P Xing. 2006. Bitam: Bilingual topic admixture models for word alignment. In *Proceedings of the COLING/ACL on Main conference poster sessions*, pages 969–976. ACL.

Bing Zhao, Eric P Xing, and Alex Waibel. 2005. Bilingual word spectral clustering for statistical machine translation. In *Proceedings of the ACL Workshop on Building and Using Parallel Texts.*

Will Y Zou, Richard Socher, Daniel M Cer, and Christopher D Manning. 2013. Bilingual word embeddings for phrase-based machine translation. In *Proceedings of EMNLP*.

# Disfluency Detection with a Semi-Markov Model and Prosodic Features

**James Ferguson, Greg Durrett** and **Dan Klein**
Computer Science Division
University of California, Berkeley
{jferguson,gdurrett,klein}@berkeley.edu

## Abstract

We present a discriminative model for detecting disfluencies in spoken language transcripts. Structurally, our model is a semi-Markov conditional random field with features targeting characteristics unique to speech repairs. This gives a significant performance improvement over standard chain-structured CRFs that have been employed in past work. We then incorporate prosodic features over silences and relative word duration into our semi-CRF model, resulting in further performance gains; moreover, these features are not easily replaced by discrete prosodic indicators such as ToBI breaks. Our final system, the semi-CRF with prosodic information, achieves an F-score of 85.4, which is 1.3 $F_1$ better than the best prior reported F-score on this dataset.

## 1 Introduction

Spoken language is fundamentally different from written language in that it contains frequent disfluencies, or parts of an utterance that are corrected by the speaker. Removing these disfluencies is desirable in order to clean the input for use in downstream NLP tasks. However, automatically identifying disfluencies is challenging for a number of reasons. First, disfluencies are a syntactic phenomenon, but defy standard context-free parsing models due to their parallel substructures (Johnson and Charniak, 2004), causing researchers to employ other approaches such as pipelines of sequence models (Qian and Liu, 2013) or incremental syntactic systems (Honnibal and Johnson, 2014). Second, human processing of spoken language is complex and mixes acoustic and syntactic indicators (Cutler et al., 1997), so an automatic system must employ features targeting all levels of the perceptual stack to

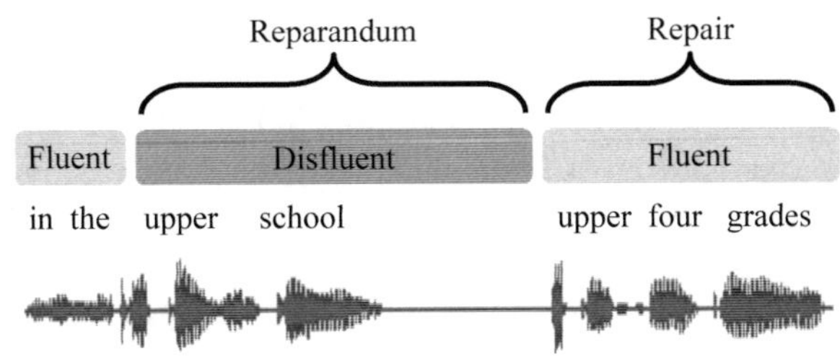


Figure 1: Example of a disfluency where the speaker corrected *upper school*. Our model considers both transcribed text and the acoustic signal and predicts disfluencies as complete chunks using a semi-Markov conditional random field.

achieve high performance. In spite of this, the primary thread of work in the NLP community has focused on identifying disfluencies based only on lexicosyntactic cues (Heeman and Allen, 1994; Charniak and Johnson, 2001; Snover et al., 2004; Rasooli and Tetreault, 2013). A separate line of work has therefore attempted to build systems that leverage prosody as well as lexical information (Shriberg et al., 1997; Liu et al., 2003; Kim et al., 2004; Liu et al., 2006), though often with mixed success.

In this work, we present a model for disfluency detection that improves upon model structures used in past work and leverages additional prosodic information. Our model is a semi-Markov conditional random field that distinguishes disfluent chunks (to be deleted) from fluent chunks (everything else), as shown in Figure 1. By making chunk-level predictions, we can incorporate not only standard token-level features but also features that can consider the entire reparandum and the start of the repair, enabling our model to easily capture parallelism between these two parts of the utterance.[1] This frame-

[1]The reparandum and repair are important concepts that we will refer to in this paper, but the model does not distinguish the repair from other fluent text which follows.



*Human Language Technologies: The 2015 Annual Conference of the North American Chapter of the ACL*, pages 257–262,
Denver, Colorado, May 31 – June 5, 2015. ©2015 Association for Computational Linguistics

work also enables novel prosodic features that compute pauses and word duration based on alignments to the speech signal itself, allowing the model to capture acoustic cues like pauses and hesitations that have proven useful for disfluency detection in earlier work (Shriberg et al., 1997). Such information has been exploited by NLP systems in the past via ToBI break indices (Silverman et al., 1992), a mid-level prosodic abstraction that might be indicative of disfluencies. These have been incorporated into syntactic parsers with some success (Kahn et al., 2005; Dreyer and Shafran, 2007; Huang and Harper, 2010), but we find that using features on predicted breaks is ineffective compared to directly using acoustic indicators.

Our implementation of a baseline CRF model already achieves results comparable to those of a high-performance system based on pipelined inference (Qian and Liu, 2013). Our semi-CRF with span features improves on this, and adding prosodic indicators gives additional gains. Our final system gets an F-score of 85.4, which is 1.3 $F_1$ better than the best prior reported F-score on this dataset (Honnibal and Johnson, 2014).

## 2 Experimental Setup

Throughout this work, we make use of the Switchboard corpus using the train/test splits specified by Johnson and Charniak (2004) and used in other work. We use the provided transcripts and gold alignments between the text and the speech signal. We follow the same preprocessing regimen as past work: we remove partial words, punctuation, and capitalization to make the input more realistic.[2] Finally, we use predicted POS tags from the Berkeley parser (Petrov et al., 2006) trained on Switchboard.

## 3 Model

Past work on disfluency detection has employed CRFs to predict disfluencies using a IOBES tag set (Qian and Liu, 2013). An example of this is shown in Figure 2. One major shortcoming of this model is that beginning and ending of a disfluency are not decided jointly: because features in the CRF are local to emissions and transitions, features in this model cannot recognize that a proposed disfluency begins with *upper* and ends before another occurrence of *upper* (see Figure 1). Identifying instances of this parallelism is key to accurately predicting disfluencies. Past work has captured information about repeats using token-level features (Qian and Liu, 2013), but these still apply to either the beginning or ending of a disfluency in isolation. Such features are naturally less effective on longer disfluencies as well, and roughly 15% of tokens occurring in disfluencies are in disfluencies of length 5 or greater. The presence of these longer disfluencies suggests using a more powerful semi-CRF model as we describe in the next section.

### 3.1 Semi-CRF Model

The model that we propose in this work is a semi-Markov conditional random field (Sarawagi and Cohen, 2004). Given a sentence $x = (x_1, \ldots, x_n)$ the model considers sequences of labeled spans $\bar{s} = ((\ell_1, b_1, e_1), (\ell_2, b_2, e_2), \ldots, (\ell_k, b_k, e_k))$, where $\ell_i \in \{\text{Fluent}, \text{Disfluent}\}$ is a label for each span and $b_i, e_i \in \{0, 1 \ldots n\}$ are fenceposts for each span such that $b_i < e_i$ and $e_i = b_{i+1}$. The model places distributions over these sequences given the sentence as follows:

$$p_\theta(\bar{s}|x) \propto \exp\left(\theta^\top \sum_{i=1}^{k} f(x, (\ell_i, b_i, e_i))\right) \quad (1)$$

where $f$ is a feature function that computes features for a span given the input sentence. In our model we constrain the transitions so that fluent spans can only be followed by disfluent spans. For this task, the spans we are predicting correspond directly to the reparanda of disfluencies, since these are the parts of the input sentences that should be removed. Note that our feature function can jointly inspect both the beginning and ending of the disfluency; we will describe the features of this form more specifically in Section 3.2.2.

To train our model, we maximize conditional log likelihood of the training data augmented with a loss function via softmax-margin (Gimpel and Smith, 2010). Specifically, during training, we maximize $\mathcal{L}(\theta) = \sum_{i=1}^{d} \log p'_\theta(\bar{s}|x)$, where $p'_\theta(\bar{s}|x) = p_\theta(\bar{s}|x) \exp(\ell(\bar{s}, \bar{s}^*))$. We take the loss function

[2] As described in Honnibal and Johnson (2014), we computed features over sentences with filler words (*um* and *uh*) and the phrases *I mean* and *you know* removed.

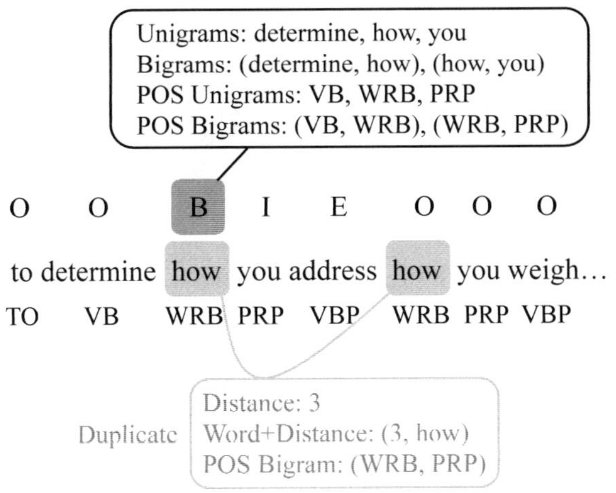


Figure 2: Token features for CRF and semi-CRF models.

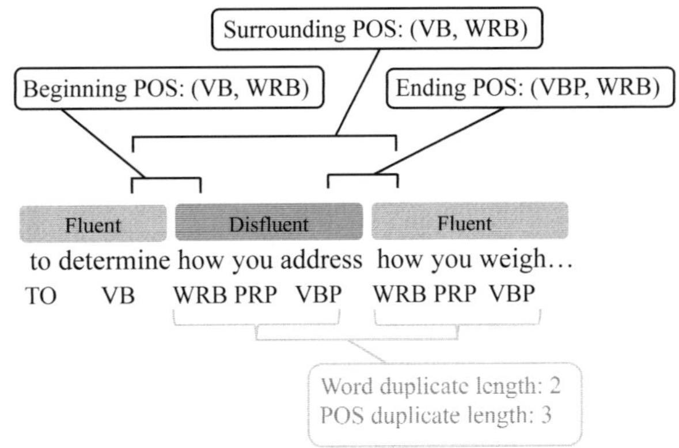


Figure 3: Span features for semi-CRF model.

$\ell$ to be token-level asymmetric Hamming distance (where the output is viewed as binary edited/non-edited). We optimize with the AdaGrad algorithm of Duchi et al. (2011) with $L_2$ regularization.

### 3.2 Features

Features in our semi-CRF factor over spans, which cover the reparandum of a proposed disfluency, and thus generally end at the beginning of the repair. This means that they can look at information throughout the reparandum as well as the repair by looking at content following the span. Many of our features are inspired by those in Qian and Liu (2013) and Honnibal and Johnson (2014). We use a combination of features that are fired for each token within a span, and features that consider properties of the span as a whole.

#### 3.2.1 Token Features

Figure 2 depicts the token-level word features we employ in both our basic CRF and our semi-CRF models. Similar to standard sequence modeling tasks, we fire word and predicted part-of-speech unigrams and bigrams in a window around the current token. In addition, we fire features on repeated words and part-of-speech tags in order to capture the fact that the repair is typically a partial copy of the reparandum, with possibly a word or two switched out. Specifically, we fire features on the distance to any duplicate words or parts-of-speech in a window around the current token, conjoined with the word identity itself or its POS tag (see the *Duplicate* box in Figure 2). We also fire similar features for POS tags since substituted words in the repair frequently have the same tag (compare *address* and *weigh*). Finally, we include a duplicate bigram feature that fires if the bigram formed from the current and next words is repeated later on. When this happens, we fire an indicator for the POS tags of the bigram. In Figure 2, this feature is fired for the word *how* because *how you* is repeated later on, and contains the POS tag bigram (*WRB, PRP*).

Table 1 shows the results for using these features in a CRF model run on the development set.[3]

#### 3.2.2 Span Features

In addition to features that fire for each individual token, the semi-CRF model allows for the inclusion of features that look at characteristics of the proposed span as a whole, allowing us to consider the repair directly by firing features targeting the words following the span. These are shown in Figure 3. Critically, repeated sequences of words and parts-of-speech are now featurized in a coordinated way, making it less likely that spurious repeated content will cause the model to falsely posit a disfluency.

We first fire an indicator of whether or not the entire proposed span is later repeated, conjoined with the length of the span. Because many disfluencies

[3] We created our development set by randomly sampling documents from the training set. Compared to the development set of Johnson and Charniak (2004), this more closely matches the disfluency distribution of the corpus: their development set has 0.53 disfluent tokens per sentence, while our set has 0.38 per sentence, and the training set has 0.37 per sentence.

| | Prec. | Rec. | $F_1$ |
|---|---|---|---|
| CRF | 84.0 | 82.1 | 83.0 |
| Semi-CRF | 88.6 | 81.7 | 85.0 |
| Semi-CRF + Prosody | 89.5 | 82.7 | 86.0 |

Table 1: Disfluency results on the development set. Adding span features on top of a CRF baseline improves performance, and including raw acoustic information gives further performance gains.

are just repeated phrases, and longer phrases are generally not repeated verbatim in fluent language, this feature is a strong indicator of disfluencies when it fires on longer spans. For similar reasons, we fire features for the length of the longest repeated sequences of words and POS tags (the bottom box in Figure 3). In addition to general repeated words, we fire a separate feature for the number of uncommon words (appearing less than 50 times in the training data) contained in the span that are repeated later in the sentence; consider *upper* from Figure 1, which would be unlikely to be repeated on its own as compared to stopwords. Lastly, we include features on the POS tag bigrams surrounding each span boundary (top of Figure 3), as well as the bigram formed from the POS tags immediately before and after the span. These features aim to capture the idea that a disfluency is a mistake with a disjuncture before the repair, so the ending bigram will generally not be a commonly seen fluent pair, and the POS tags surrounding the reparandum should be fluent if the reparandum were removed.

Table 1 shows that the additional features enabled by the CRF significantly improve performance on top of the basic CRF model.

## 4 Exploiting Acoustic Information

Section 3 discussed a primarily structural improvement to disfluency detection. Henceforth, we will use the semi-CRF model exclusively and discuss two methods of incorporating acoustic duration information that might be predictive of disfluencies. Our results will show that features targeting raw acoustic properties of the signal (Section 4.1) are quite effective, while using ToBI breaks as a discrete indicator to import the same information does not give benefits (Section 4.2)

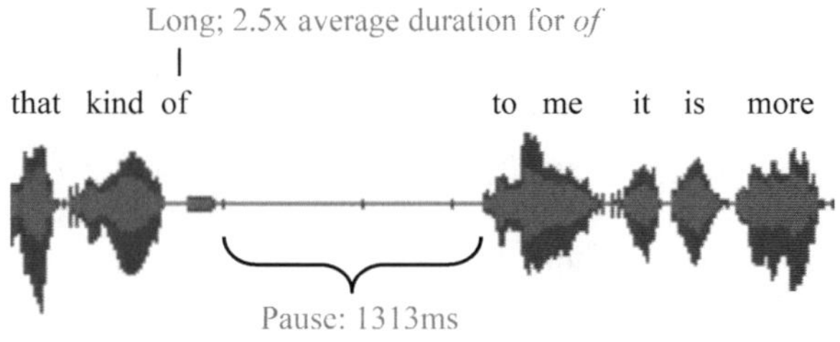


Figure 4: Raw acoustic features. The combination of a long pause and considerably longer than average duration for *of* is a strong indicator of a disfluency.

### 4.1 Raw Acoustic Features

The first way we implemented this information was in the form of raw prosodic features related to pauses between words and word duration. To compute these features, we make use of the alignment between the speech signal and the raw text. Pauses are then simply identified by looking for pairs of words whose alignments are not flush. The specific features used are indicators of the existence of a pause immediately before or after a span, and the total number of pauses contained within a span. Word duration is computed based on the deviation of a word's length from its average length averaged over all occurrences in the corpus.[4] We fire duration features similar to the pause features, namely indicators of whether the duration of the first and last words in a span deviate beyond some threshold from the average, and the total number of such deviations within a span. As displayed in Table 1, adding these raw features results in improved performance on top of the gains from the semi-CRF model.

### 4.2 ToBI Features

In addition to the raw acoustic features, we also tried utilizing discrete indicators of acoustic information, specifically ToBI break indices (Silverman et al., 1992). Previous work has shown performance improvements resulting from the use of such discrete information in other tasks, such as parsing (Kahn et al., 2005; Dreyer and Shafran, 2007; Huang and Harper, 2010). We chose to focus specifically on ToBI breaks rather than on ToBI tones because tonal information has appeared relatively less

[4]Note that this averages over multiple speakers as well.

| | Disfluency | | |
|---|---|---|---|
| | Prec. | Rec. | $F_1$ |
| Baseline | 88.61 | 81.69 | 85.01 |
| AuToBI *3, 4* | 88.46 | 81.92 | 85.06 |
| CRF ToBI | 88.42 | 81.96 | 85.07 |
| Raw acoustic | 89.53 | 82.74 | **86.00** |

Table 2: Disfluency results with predicted ToBI features on the development set. We compare our baseline semi-CRF system (Baseline) with systems that incorporate prosody via predictions from the AuToBI system of Rosenberg (2010) and from our CRF ToBI predictor, as well as the full system using raw acoustic features.

| | Prec. | Rec. | $F_1$ |
|---|---|---|---|
| Johnson and Charniak (2004) | – | – | 79.7 |
| Qian and Liu (2013) | – | – | 83.7 |
| Honnibal and Johnson (2014) | – | – | 84.1 |
| CRF | 88.7 | 78.8 | 83.4 |
| Semi-CRF | 90.1 | 80.0 | 84.8 |
| Semi-CRF + Prosody | 90.0 | 81.2 | 85.4 |

Table 3: Disfluency prediction results on the test set; our base system outperforms that of Honnibal and Johnson (2014), a state-of-the-art system on this dataset, and incorporating prosody further improves performance.

useful for this task (Shriberg et al., 1997). Moreover, the ToBI break specification (Hirschberg and Beckman, 1992) stipulates a category for strong disjuncture with a pause (*2*) as well as a pause marker (*p*), both of which correlate well with disfluencies on gold-annotated ToBI data.

To investigate whether this correlation translates into a performance improvement for a disfluency detection system like ours, we add features targeting ToBI annotations as follows: for each word in a proposed disfluent span, we fire a feature indicating the break index on the fencepost following that word, conjoined with where that word is in the span (beginning, middle, or end).

We try two different ways of generating the break indices used by these features. The first is using the AuToBI system of Rosenberg (2010), a state-of-the-art automatic ToBI prediction systems based on acoustic information which focuses particularly on detecting occurrences of *3* and *4*. Second, we use the subset of Switchboard labeled with ToBI breaks (Taylor et al., 2003) to train a CRF-based ToBI predictor. This model employs both acoustic and lexical features, which are both useful for ToBI prediction despite breaks being a seemingly more acoustic phenomenon (Rosenberg, 2010). The acoustic indicators that we use are similar to the ones described in Section 4 and our lexical features consist of a set of standard surface features similar to those used in Section 3.2.1.

In Table 2 we see that neither source of predicted ToBI breaks does much to improve performance. In particular, the gains from using raw acoustic features are substantially greater despite the fact that the predictions were made in part using similar raw acoustic features. This is somewhat surprising, since intuitively, ToBI should be capturing information very similar to what pauses and word durations capture, particularly when it is predicted based partially on these phenomena. However, our learned ToBI predictor only gets roughly 50 $F_1$ on break prediction, so ToBI prediction is clearly a hard task even with sophisticated features. The fact that ToBI cannot be derived from acoustic features also indicates that it may draw on information posterior to signal processing, such as syntactic and semantic cues. Finally, pauses are also simply more prevalent in the data than ToBI markers of interest: there are roughly 40,000 pauses on the ToBI-annotated subset of the dataset, yet there are fewer than 10,000 *2* or *p* break indices. The ToBI predictor is therefore trained to ignore information that may be relevant for disfluency detection.

## 5 Results and Conclusion

Table 3 shows results on the Switchboard test set. Our final system substantially outperforms the results of prior work, and we see that this is a result of both incorporating span features via a semi-CRF as well as incorporating prosodic indicators.

## Acknowledgments

This work was partially supported by BBN under DARPA contract HR0011-12-C-0014 and by a Facebook Fellowship for the second author. Thanks to the anonymous reviewers for their helpful comments.

## References


Eugene Charniak and Mark Johnson. 2001. Edit Detection and Parsing for Transcribed Speech. In *Proceedings of the North American Chapter of the Association for Computational Linguistics*.

Anne Cutler, Delphine Dahan, and Wilma van Donselaar. 1997. Prosody in the Comprehension of Spoken Language: A Literature Review. *Language and Speech*, 40(2):141–201.

Markus Dreyer and Izhak Shafran. 2007. Exploiting Prosody for PCFGs with Latent Annotations. In *Proceedings of Interspeech*.

John Duchi, Elad Hazan, and Yoram Singer. 2011. Adaptive Subgradient Methods for Online Learning and Stochastic Optimization. *Journal of Machine Learning Research*, 12:2121–2159, July.

Kevin Gimpel and Noah A. Smith. 2010. Softmax-Margin CRFs: Training Log-Linear Models with Cost Functions. In *Proceedings of the North American Chapter for the Association for Computational Linguistics*.

Peter Heeman and James Allen. 1994. Detecting and Correcting Speech Repairs. In *Proceedings of the Association for Computational Linguistics*.

Julia Hirschberg and Mary E. Beckman. 1992. The tobi annotation conventions. Online at http://www.cs.columbia.edu/ julia/files/conv.pdf.

Matthew Honnibal and Mark Johnson. 2014. Joint Incremental Disfluency Detection and Dependency Parsing. *Transactions of the Association of Computational Linguistics – Volume 2, Issue 1*, pages 131–142.

Zhongqiang Huang and Mary Harper. 2010. Appropriately Handled Prosodic Breaks Help PCFG Parsing. In *Proceedings of the North American Chapter of the Association for Computational Linguistics*.

Mark Johnson and Eugene Charniak. 2004. A TAG-based Noisy-channel Model of Speech Repairs. In *Proceedings of the Association for Computational Linguistics*.

Jeremy G. Kahn, Matthew Lease, Eugene Charniak, Mark Johnson, and Mari Ostendorf. 2005. Effective Use of Prosody in Parsing Conversational Speech. In *Proceedings of the Conference on Empirical Methods in Natural Language Processing*.

Joungbum Kim, Sarah E Schwarm, and Mari Ostendorf. 2004. Detecting Structural Metadata with Decision Trees and Transformation-Based Learning. In *Proceedings of the North American Chapter of the Association for Computational Linguistics*.

Yang Liu, Elizabeth Shriberg, and Andreas Stolcke. 2003. Automatic Disfluency Identification in Conversational Speech Using Multiple Knowledge Sources. In *Proceedings of Eurospeech*.

Yang Liu, E. Shriberg, A. Stolcke, D. Hillard, M. Ostendorf, and M. Harper. 2006. Enriching Speech Recognition with Automatic Detection of Sentence Boundaries and Disfluencies. *Transactions of Audio, Speech and Language Processing*, 14(5):1526–1540, September.

Slav Petrov, Leon Barrett, Romain Thibaux, and Dan Klein. 2006. Learning Accurate, Compact, and Interpretable Tree Annotation. In *Proceedings of the Conference on Computational Linguistics and the Association for Computational Linguistics*.

Xian Qian and Yang Liu. 2013. Disfluency Detection Using Multi-step Stacked Learning. In *Proceedings of the North American Chapter of the Association for Computational Linguistics*.

Mohammad Sadegh Rasooli and Joel Tetreault. 2013. Joint Parsing and Disfluency Detection in Linear Time. In *Proceedings of the Conference on Empirical Methods in Natural Language Processing*.

Andrew Rosenberg. 2010. AuToBI - A Tool for Automatic ToBI Annotation. In *Proceedings of Interspeech*.

Sunita Sarawagi and William W. Cohen. 2004. Semi-Markov Conditional Random Fields for Information Extraction. In *Proceedings of Advances in Neural Information Processing Systems*.

Elizabeth Shriberg, Rebecca Bates, and Andreas Stolcke. 1997. A Prosody-only Decision-tree Model for Disfluency Detection. In *Proceedings of Eurospeech*.

Kim Silverman, Mary Beckman, John Pitrelli, Mari Ostendorf, Colin Wightman, Patti Price, Janet Pierrehumbert, and Julia Hirschberg. 1992. ToBI: A Standard for Labeling English Prosody. In *Proceedings of the International Conference on Spoken Language Processing*.

Matthew Snover, Bonnie Dorr, and Richard Schwartz. 2004. A Lexically-Driven Algorithm for Disfluency Detection. In *Proceedings of the North American Chapter of the Association for Computational Linguistics*.

Ann Taylor, Mitchell Marcus, and Beatrice Santorini. 2003. The penn treebank: An overview.

# Empty Category Detection With Joint Context-Label Embeddings

**Xun Wang, Katsuhito Sudoh** and **Masaaki Nagata**
NTT Communication Science Laboratories
Kyoto 619-0237, Japan
wang.xun,sudoh.katsuhito,nagata.masaaki@lab.ntt.co.jp

## Abstract

This paper presents a novel technique for empty category (EC) detection using distributed word representations. A joint model is learned from the labeled data to map both the distributed representations of the contexts of ECs and EC types to a low dimensional space. In the testing phase, the context of possible EC positions will be projected into the same space for empty category detection. Experiments on Chinese Treebank prove the effectiveness of the proposed method. We improve the precision by about 6 points on a subset of Chinese Treebank, which is a new state-of-the-art performance on CTB.

## 1 Introduction

The empty category (EC) is an important concept in linguistic theories. It is used to describe nominal words that do not have explicit phonological forms (they are also called "covert nouns"). This kind of grammatical phenomenons is usually caused by the omission or dislocation of nouns or pronouns. Empty categories are the "hidden" parts of text and are essential for syntactic parsing (Gabbard et al., 2006; Yang and Xue, 2010). As a basic problem in NLP, the resolution of ECs also has a huge impact on lots of downstream tasks, such as co-reference resolution (Ponzetto and Strube, 2006; Kong and Ng, 2013), long distance dependency relation analysis (Marcus et al., 1993; Xue et al., 2005). Research also uncovers the important role of ECs in machine translation. Some recent work (Chung and Gildea, 2010; Xiang et al., 2013) demonstrates the improvements they manage to obtain through EC detection in Chinese-English translation.

To resolve ECs, we need to decide 1) the position and type of the EC and 2) the content of the EC (to which element the EC is linked to if plausible). Existing research mainly focuses on the first problem which is referred to as EC detection (Cai et al., 2011; Yang and Xue, 2010), and so is this paper. As ECs are words or phrases inferable from their context, previous work mainly designs features mining the contexts of ECs and then trains classification models or parsers using these features (Xue and Yang, 2013; Johnson, 2002; Gabbard et al., 2006; Kong and Zhou, 2010). One problem with these human-developed features are that they are not fully capable of representing the semantics and syntax of contexts. Besides, the feature engineering is also time consuming and labor intensive.

Recently neural network models have proven their superiority in capturing features using low dense vector compared with traditional manually designed features in dozens of NLP tasks (Bengio et al., 2006; Collobert and Weston, 2008; Socher et al., 2010; Collobert et al., 2011; Li and Hovy, 2014; Li et al., 2014).

This paper demonstrates the advantages of distributed representations and neural networks in predicting the locations and types of ECs. We formulate the EC detection as an annotation



*Human Language Technologies: The 2015 Annual Conference of the North American Chapter of the ACL*, pages 263–271,
Denver, Colorado, May 31 – June 5, 2015. 

task, to assign predefined labels (EC types) to given contexts. Recently, Weston et al. (2011) proposed a system taking advantages of the hidden representations of neural networks for image annotation which is to annotate images with a set of textual words. Following the work, we design a novel method for EC detection. We represent possible EC positions using the word embeddings of their contexts and then map them to a low dimension space for EC detection.

Experiments on Chinese Treebank show that the proposed model obtains significant improvements over the previous state-of-the-art methods based on strict evaluation metrics. We also identify the dependency relations between ECs and their heads, which is not reported in previous work. The dependency relations can help us with the resolution of ECs and benefit other tasks, such as full parsing and machine translation in practice.

## 2 Proposed Method

We represent each EC as a vector by concatenating the word embeddings of its contexts. As is shown in Fig. 1, we learn a map $MAP_A$ from the annotated data, to project the ECs' feature vectors to a low dimension space $K$. Meanwhile, we also obtain the distributed representations of EC types in the same low dimension space $K$. In the testing phase, for each possible EC position, we use $MAP_A$ to project its context feature to the same space and further compare it with the representations of EC types for EC detection.

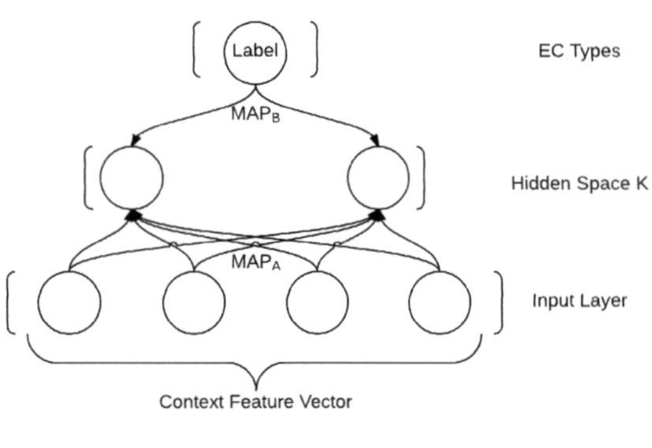


Figure 1: System Architecture

Distributed representations are good at capturing the semantics and syntax of contexts. For example, with word embeddings we are able to tell that "吃/eat" and "喝/drink" have a closer relationship than "吃/eat" and "走/walk" or "喝/drink" and "走/walk". Thus the knowledge we learn from: "EC(你/You)-吃/have-EC(晚饭/supper)-了/past tense marker-么/question marker" could help us to detect ECs in sentences such as "EC(你/You)-饮料/beverage-喝/drink-了/past tense marker-么/question marker", which are similar, though different from the original sentence.

Below is a list of EC types contained in the Chinese Treebank, which are also the types of EC we are to identity in this work.

- pro: small pro, refer to dropped pronouns.
- PRO: big PRO, refer to shared elements in control structures or elements that have generic references.
- OP: null operator, refer to empty relative pronouns.
- T: trace left by A'-movement, e.g., topicalization, relativization.
- RNR: used in right nodes rising.
- *: trace left by passivization, raising.
- Others: other ECs.

According to the reason that one EC is caused, we are able to assign it one of the above categories.

We can formulate EC detection as a combination of a two-class classification problem (is there an EC or not) and a seven-class classification problem (what type the EC is if there is one) following the two-pass method. For one-pass method, EC detection can be formulated as an eight-class (seven EC types listed above plus a dummy "No" type) classification problem. Previous research shows there is no significant differences between their performances (Xue and Yang, 2013). Here we adopt the one-pass method for simplicity.

## 2.1 System Overview

The proposed system consists of two maps.

$MAP_A$ is from the feature vector of an EC position to a low dimensional space.

$$MAP_A : R^n \rightarrow R^k, k \ll n \\ f_A(X) \rightarrow W_A X \tag{1}$$

$MAP_A$ is a linear transformation, and $W_A$ is a $k * n$ matrix.

The other one is from labels to the same low dimensional space.

$$MAP_B : \{Label_1, Label_2, ...\} \in R \rightarrow R^k \\ f_B(Label_i) \rightarrow W_B^i \tag{2}$$

$MAP_B$ is also a linear transformation. $W_B^i$ is a $k$ dimensional vector and it is also the distributed representation of $Label_i$ in the low dimensional space.

The two maps are learned from the training data simultaneously. In the testing phase, for any possible EC position to be classified, we extract the corresponding feature vector $X$, and then map it to the low dimensional space using $f_A(X) = W_A X$. Then we have $g_i(X)$ for each $Label_i$ as follows:

$$g_i(X) = (f_A(X))^T W_B^i \tag{3}$$

For each possible label $Label_i$, $g_i(X)$ is the score that the example having a $Label_i$ and the label predicted for the example is the $i$ that maximizes $g_i(X)$.

Following the method of Weston et al. (2011), we try to minimize a weighted pairwise loss, learned using stochastic gradient descent:

$$\sum_X \sum_{i \neq c} L(rank_c(X)) \max(0, (g_i(X) - g_c(X))) \tag{4}$$

Here $c$ is the correct label for example $X$, and $rank_c(X)$ is the rank of $Label$ $c$ among all possible labels for $X$. $L$ is a function which reflects our attitude towards errors. A constant function $L = C$ implies we aim to optimize the full ranking list. Here we adopt $L(\alpha) = \sum_{i=1}^{\alpha} 1/i$, which aims to optimize the top 1 in the ranking list, as stated in (Usunier et al., 2009). The learning rate and some other parameters of the stochastic gradient descent algorithm are to be optimized using the development set.

An alternative method is to train a neural network model for multi-class classification directly. It is plausible when the number of classes is not large. One of the advantages of representing ECs and labels in a hidden space is that EC detection usually serves as an intermediate task. Usually we want to know more about the ECs such as their roles and explicit content. Representing labels and ECs as dense vectors will greatly benefit other work such as EC resolution or full parsing. Besides, such a joint embedding framework can scale up to the large set of labels as is shown in the image annotation task (Weston et al., 2011), which makes the identification of dependency types of ECs (which is a large set) possible.

## 2.2 Context Features Construction

### 2.2.1 Defining Locations

In a piece of text, possible EC positions can be described with references to tokens, e.g., before the $n^{th}$ token (Yang and Xue, 2010). One problem with such methods is that if there are more than one ECs preceding the $n^{th}$ token, they will occupy the same position and can not be distinguished. One solution is to decide the number of ECs for each position, which complicates the problem. But if we do nothing, some ECs will be ignored.

A compromised solution is to describe positions using parse trees (Xue and Yang, 2013). Adjacent ECs before a certain token usually have different head words, which means they are attached to different nodes (head words) in a parse tree. Therefore it is possible to define positions using "head word, following word" pairs. Thus the problem of EC detection can be formulated as a classification problem: for each "head word, following word" pair, what is the type of the EC? An example is shown in figure 2, in which there are 2 possible EC positions, (吃, 了) and (吃, 。)[1].

[1]Note that there are still problems with the tree based method. As is shown in Fig. 3, the pro and T are attached to the same head word (告别) and share the same

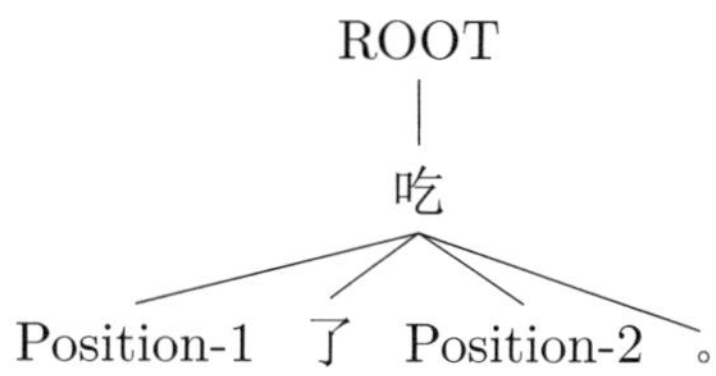


Figure 2: Possible EC Positions in a Dependency Tree

Besides, we keep punctuations in the parse tree so that we can describe all the possible positions using the "head node, following word" pairs, as no elements will appear after a full stop in a sentence.

### 2.2.2 Feature Extraction

The feature vector is constructed by concatenating the word embeddings of context words that are expected to contribute to the detection of ECs.

1. The head word (except the dummy root node). Suppose words are represented using $d$ dimension vectors, we need $d$ elements to represent this feature. The distributed representations of the head word would be placed at the corresponding positions.

2. The following word in the text. This feature is extracted using the same method with head words.

3. "Nephews", the sons of the following word. We choose the leftmost two.

4. Words in dependency paths. ECs usually have long distance dependencies with words which cannot be fully captured by the above categories. We need a new feature to describe such long distance semantic relations: Dependency Paths. From the training data, we collect all the paths from root nodes to ECs (ECs excluded) together with dependency types. Below we give an example to illustrate the extraction of this kind of features using a complex sentence with a multi-layer hierarchical dependency tree as in Fig. 3. If we have $m$ kinds of such paths with different path types or dependency types, we need $md$ elements to represent this kind of features. The distributed representations of the words would be placed at the corresponding positions in the feature vector and the remaining are set to 0.

Previous work usually involves lots of syntactic and semantic features. In the work of (Xue and Yang, 2013), 6 kinds of features are used, including those derived from constituency parse trees, dependency parse trees, semantic roles and others. Here we use only the dependency parse trees for the feature extraction. The words in dependency paths we use have proven their potential in representing the meanings of text in frame identification (Hermann et al., 2014).

Take the OP in the sentence shown in Fig. 3 for example. For the OP, its head word is "的", its following word is "告别" and its nephews are "NULL" and "NULL" (ECs are invisible).

The dependency path from root to OP is: $Root \xrightarrow{ROOT}$ 举行/hold $\xrightarrow{COMP}$ 仪式/ceremony $\xrightarrow{RELC}$ 的/DE $\xrightarrow{COMP}$ OP

For such a path, we have the following subpaths:

$$Root \xrightarrow{ROOT} . \xrightarrow{COMP} . \xrightarrow{RELC} X$$
$$Root \xrightarrow{ROOT} . \xrightarrow{COMP} X$$
$$Root \xrightarrow{ROOT} X$$

For the position of the OP in the given example, the words with corresponding dependency paths are "的", "仪式" and "举行". Similarly, we collects all the paths from other ECs in the training examples to build the feature template.

In the testing phase, for each possible EC position, we place the distributed representations of the right words at the corresponding positions of its feature vector.

following word (德国). But such phenomenas are rare, so here we still adopt the tree based method.

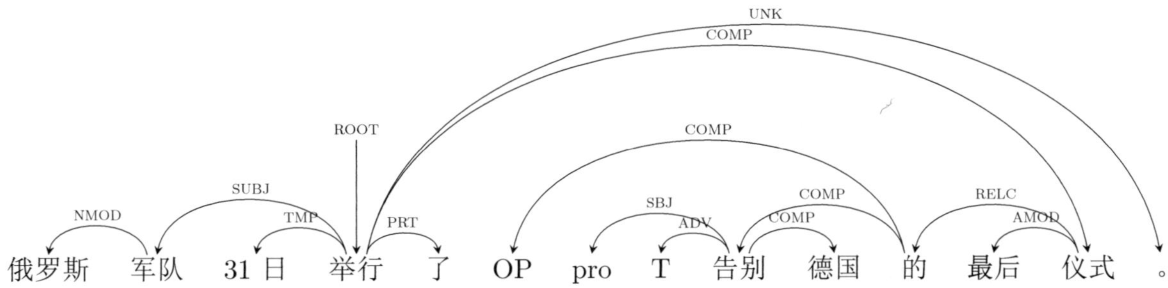


俄罗斯/Russian 军队/troops 31 日/31rd 举行/hold 了/past-tense-marker 告别/farewell 德国/Germany 的/DE 最后/final 仪式/ceremony 。

Figure 3: ECs in a Dependency Tree

| | Train | Dev | Test |
|---|---|---|---|
| File | 81-325, 400-454<br>500-554, 590-596<br>600-885, 900 | 41-80 | 1-40<br>901-931 |
| #pro | 1023 | 166 | 297 |
| #PRO | 1089 | 210 | 298 |
| #OP | 2099 | 301 | 575 |
| #T | 1981 | 287 | 527 |
| #RNR | 91 | 15 | 32 |
| #* | 22 | 0 | 19 |
| #Others | 0 | 0 | 0 |
| Total | 6305 | 979 | 1748 |

Table 1: Data Division and EC Distribution

# 3 Experiments on CTB

## 3.1 Data

The proposed method can be applied to various kinds of languages as long as annotated corpus are available. In our experiments, we use a subset of Chinese Treebank V7.0.

We split the data set into three parts, training, development and test data. Following the previous research, we use File 1-40 and 901-931 as the test data, File 41-80 as the development data. The training data includes File {81-325, 400-454, 500-554, 590-596, 6000-885, 900}. The development data is used to tune parameters and the final results are reported on the test data. CTB trees are transferred to dependency trees for feature extraction with ECs preserved (Xue, 2007).

The distributed word representation we use is learned using the word2vec toolkit (Mikolov et al., 2013). We train the model on a large Chinese news copora provided by Sogou[2], which contains about 1 billion words after necessary preprocessing. The text is segmented into words using ICTCLAS(Zhang et al., 2003)[3].

## 3.2 Experiment Settings

**Initialization** $W_A$ is initialized according to $uniform[-\frac{24}{d_{in}+d_{hidden}}, \frac{24}{d_{in}+d_{hidden}}]$.
And $W_B$ is initialized using
$uniform[-\frac{24}{d_{hidden}+d_{out}}, \frac{24}{d_{hidden}+d_{out}}]$.
Here $d_{in}, d_{hidden}$ and $d_{out}$ are the dimensions of the input layer, the hidden space and the label space.

**Parameter Tuning** To optimize the parameters, firstly, we set the dimension of word vectors to be 80, the dimension of hidden space to be 50. We search for the suitable learning rate in $\{\underline{10^{-1}}, 10^{-2}, 10^{-4}\}$. Then we deal with the dimension of word vectors $\{\underline{80}, 100, 200\}$. Finally we tune the dimension of hidden space in $\{50, 200, \underline{500}\}$ against the F-1 scores. . Those underlined figures are the value of the parameters after optimization. We use the stochastic gradient descent algorithm to optimize the model. The details can be checked here (Weston et al., 2011). The maximum iteration number we used is 10K. In the following experiments,

[2]http://www.sogou.com/labs/dl/cs.html

[3]The word segment standards used by CTB and ICTCLAS are roughly the same with minor differences.

we set the parameters to be learning rate=$10^{-1}$, word vector dimension=80 and hidden layer dimension=500.

From the experiments for parameter tuning, we find that for the word embeddings in the proposed model, low dimension vectors are better than high dimensions one for low dimension vectors are better in sharing meanings. For the hidden space which represents inputs as uninterpreted vectors, high dimensional vectors are better than low dimensional vectors. The learning rates also have an impact on the performance. If the learning rate is too small, we need more iterations to achieve convergence. If we stop iterations too early, we will suffer under-fitting.

### 3.3 Results

#### 3.3.1 Metrics and Evaluation

Previous work reports results based on different evaluation metrics. Some work uses linear positions to describe ECs. ECs are judged on a "whether there is an EC of type A before a certain token in the text" basis (Cai et al., 2011). Collapsing ECs before the same token to one, Cai et al. (2011) has 1352 ECs in the test data. Xue and Yang (2013) has stated that some ECs that share adjacent positions have different heads in the parse tree. They judge ECs on a "whether there is an EC of type A with a certain head word and a certain following token in the text" basis. Using this kind of metric, they gets 1765 ECs.

Here we use the same evaluation metric with Xue and Yang (2013). Note that we still cannot describe all the 1838 ECs in the corpora, for on some occasions ECs preceding the same token share the same head word. We also omit some ECs which cause cycles in dependency trees as described in the previous sections. We have 1748 ECs, 95% of all the ECs in the test data, very close to 1765 used by Xue and Yang (2013). The total number of ECs has an impact on the recall. In Table 3, we include results based on each method's own EC count (1748, 1765, 1352 for Ours, Xue's and Cai's respectively) and the real total EC count 1838 (figures in brackets).

Yang and Xue (2010) report an experiment result based on a classification model in a unified

| Type | PRO | pro | T | OP | RNR | * | Others | Total |
|---|---|---|---|---|---|---|---|---|
| | 297 | 298 | 575 | 527 | 32 | 19 | 0 | 1748 |
| Xue | 305 | 298 | 584 | 527 | 32 | 19 | 0 | 1765 |
| Cai | 299 | 290 | 578 | 134 | 32 | 19 | 0 | 1352 |

Table 2: EC Distribution in the Test Data

| class | correct | p | r | F1 |
|---|---|---|---|---|
| PRO | 162 | .479 | .545 | .510 |
| pro | 161 | .564 | .540 | .552 |
| OP | 409 | .707 | .776 | .740 |
| T | 506 | .939 | .88 | .908 |
| RNR | 23 | .767 | .719 | .742 |
| * | 0 | 0 | 0 | 0 |
| Overall | 1261 | .712 | .721 (.686) | .717 (.699) |
| (Xue) | 903 | .653 | .512 (.491) | .574 (.561) |
| (Cai) | 737 | .660 | .545 (.401) | .586 (.499) |

Table 3: Performance on the CTB Test Data

parsing frame. We do not include it for it uses different and relativelyThe distributions of ECs in the test data are shown in Table 2.

The results are shown in Table 3. We present the results for each kind of EC and compare our results with two previous state-of-the-art methods(Cai et al., 2011; Xue and Yang, 2013).

The proposed method yields the newest state-of-the-art performances on CTB as far as we know. We also identify the dependency types between ECs and their heads. Some ECs, such as pro and PRO, are latent subjects of sentences. They usually serve as $SBJ$ with very few exceptions. While the others may play various roles. There are 31 possible $(EC, Dep)$ pairs. Using the same model, the overall result is $p = 0.701, r = 0.703, f = 0.702$.

#### 3.3.2 Analysis

We compare the effectiveness of different features by eliminating each kind of features described in the previous section. As Table 4 shows, the most important kind is the dependency paths, which cause a huge drop in performance if eliminated. Dependency paths encode words and path pattern information which is proved essential for the detection of ECs. Besides, headwords are also useful. While for the

| | -dep | -head | -following | -nephews |
|---|---|---|---|---|
| F1 | .501 | .604 | .703 | .716 |
| | (-.216) | (-.103) | (-.014) | (-.001) |

Table 4: Effectiveness of Features

others, we cannot easily make the conclusion that they are of little usage in the identification of ECs. They are not fully explored in the proposed model, but may be vital for EC detection in reality.

Worth to mention is that of the several kinds of ECs, the proposed method shows the best performance on ECs of type T, which represents ECs that are the trace of "A'"-movement, which moves a word to a position where no fixed grammatical function is assigned. Here we give an example:

"[ ] 看起来/seem A 喜欢/like B."
"A 看起来/seem (EC) 喜欢/like B."

A is moved to the head of the sentence as the topic (topicalization) and left a trace which is the EC. To detect this EC, we need information about the action "喜欢/like", the link verb "看起来/seem" and the arguments "A" and "B". ECs of type *T* are very common in Chinese, since Chinese is a topic-prominent language. Using distributed representations, it is easy to encode the context information in our feature vectors for EC detection.

We also have satisfying results and significant improvements for the other types except * (trace of A-movement), which make up about 1% of all the ECs in the test data. Partly because there are too few * examples in the training data. We need to further improve our models to detect such ECs.

## 4 Discussion

The proposed method is capable of handling large set of labels. Hence it is possible to detect EC types and dependency types simultaneously. Besides, some other NLP tasks can also be formulated as annotation tasks, and therefore can be resolved using the same scheme, such as the frame identification for verbs (Hermann et al., 2014).

This work together with some previous work that uses classification methods (Cai et al., 2011; Xue and Yang, 2013; Xue, 2007), regards ECs in a sentence as independent to each other and even independent to words that do not appear in the feature vectors. Such an assumption makes it easier to design models and features but does not reflect the grammatic constraints of languages. For example, simple sentences in Chinese contain one and only one subject, whether it is an EC or not. If it is decided there is an EC as a subject in a certain place, there should be no more ECs as subjects in the same sentence. But such an important property is not reflected in these classification models. Methods that adopt parsing techniques take the whole parse tree as input and output a parse tree with EC anchored. So we can view the sentence as a whole and deal with ECs with regarding to all the words in the sentence. Iida and Poesio (2011) also take the grammar constraints into consideration by formulating EC detection as an ILP problem. But they usually yield poor performances compared with classification methods partly because the methods they use can not fully explore the syntactic and semantic features.

## 5 Related Work

Empty category is a complex problem (Li and Hovy, 2015). Existing methods for EC detection mainly explores syntactic and semantic features using classification models or parsing techniques.

Johnson (2002) proposes a simple pattern based algorithm to recover ECs, both the positions and their antecedents in phrase structure trees. Gabbard et al. (2006) presents a two stage parser that uses syntactical features to recover Penn Treebank style syntactic analyses, including the ECs. The first stage, sentences are parse as usual without ECs, and in the second stage, ECs are detected using a learned model with rich text features in the tree structures. Kong and Zhou (2010) reports a tree kernel-based model which takes as input parse trees for EC detection. They also deal with EC resolution, to link ECs to text pieces if possible. They reports their results on Chinese Treebank. Yang and Xue (2010) try to restore ECs from parse trees using a Maximum Entropy model. Iida and Poesio (2011) propose an cross-lingual ILP-based model for zero anaphora detection. Cai et al. (2011) reports a classification model for EC detection. Their method is based on "is there an EC *before* a certain token".

Recently Xue and Yang (2013) further develop the method of Yang and Xue (2010) and explore rich syntactical and semantical features, including paths in parse trees and semantic roles, to train an ME classification model for EC detection and yield the best performance reported using a strict evaluation metric on Chinese Treebank as far as we know.

As we have stated, the traditional features used by above methods are not good at capturing the meanings of contexts. Currently the distributed representations together with deep neural networks have proven their ability not only in representing meaning of words, inferring words from the context, but also in representing structures of text (Socher et al., 2010; Li et al., 2015). Deep neural networks are capable of learning features from corpus, therefore saves the labor of feature engineering and have proven their ability in lots of NLP task (Collobert et al., 2011; Bengio et al., 2006).

The most relevant work to this paper are that of Weston et al. (2011) and that of Hermann et al. (2014). Weston et al. (2011) propose a deep neural network scheme exploring the hidden space for image annotation. They map both the images and labels to the same hidden space and annotate new images according to their representations in the hidden space. Hermann et al. (2014) extend the scheme to frame identification, for which they obtain satisfying results. This paper further uses it for empty category detection with features designed for EC detection.

Compared with previous research, the proposed model simplifies the feature engineering greatly and produces distributed representations for both ECs and EC types which will benefit other tasks.

## 6 Conclusion

In this paper, we propose a new empty category detection method using distributed word representations. Using the word embeddings of the contexts of ECs as features enables us to employ rich information in the context without much feature engineering. Experiments on CTB have verified the advantages of the proposed method. We successfully beat the existing state-of-the-art methods based on a strict evaluation metric. The proposed method can be further applied to other languages such as Japanese. We will further explore the feasibility of using neural networks to resolve empty categories: to link ECs to their antecedents.

## References


Yoshua Bengio, Holger Schwenk, Jean-Sébastien Senécal, Fréderic Morin, and Jean-Luc Gauvain. 2006. Neural probabilistic language models. In *Innovations in Machine Learning*, pages 137–186. Springer.

Shu Cai, David Chiang, and Yoav Goldberg. 2011. Language-independent parsing with empty elements. In *Proceedings of the 49th Annual Meeting of the Association for Computational Linguistics: Human Language Technologies: short papers-Volume 2*, pages 212–216. Association for Computational Linguistics.

Tagyoung Chung and Daniel Gildea. 2010. Effects of empty categories on machine translation. In *Proceedings of EMNLP*, pages 636–645. ACL.

Ronan Collobert and Jason Weston. 2008. A unified architecture for natural language processing: Deep neural networks with multitask learning. In *Proceedings of the 25th international conference on Machine learning*, pages 160–167. ACM.

Ronan Collobert, Jason Weston, Léon Bottou, Michael Karlen, Koray Kavukcuoglu, and Pavel Kuksa. 2011. Natural language processing (almost) from scratch. *The Journal of Machine Learning Research*, 12:2493–2537.

Ryan Gabbard, Mitchell Marcus, and Seth Kulick. 2006. Fully parsing the penn treebank. In *Proceedings of the main conference on human language technology conference of the North American chapter of the association of computational linguistics*, pages 184–191. Association for Computational Linguistics.

Karl Moritz Hermann, Dipanjan Das, Jason Weston, and Kuzman Ganchev. 2014. Semantic frame identification with distributed word representations. In *Proceedings of ACL*.

Ryu Iida and Massimo Poesio. 2011. A cross-lingual ilp solution to zero anaphora resolution. In *Proceedings of the 49th Annual Meeting of the Association for Computational Linguistics: Human Language Technologies-Volume 1*, pages 804–813. Association for Computational Linguistics.

Mark Johnson. 2002. A simple pattern-matching algorithm for recovering empty nodes and their antecedents. In *Proceedings of the 40th Annual Meeting on Association for Computational Linguistics*, pages 136–143. ACL.

Fang Kong and Hwee Tou Ng. 2013. Exploiting zero pronouns to improve chinese coreference resolution. In *EMNLP*, pages 278–288.

Fang Kong and Guodong Zhou. 2010. A tree kernel-based unified framework for chinese zero anaphora resolution. In *Proceedings of the 2010 Conference on Empirical Methods in Natural Language Processing*, pages 882–891. Association for Computational Linguistics.

Jiwei Li and Eduard Hovy. 2014. A model of coherence based on distributed sentence representation. In *Proceedings of the 2014 Conference on Empirical Methods in Natural Language Processing*, pages 2061–2069.

Jiwei Li and Eduard Hovy. 2015. The nlp engine: A universal turing machine for nlp. *arXiv preprint arXiv:1503.00168*.

Jiwei Li, Rumeng Li, and Eduard Hovy. 2014. Recursive deep models for discourse parsing. In *Proceedings of the 2014 Conference on Empirical Methods in Natural Language Processing*, pages 2061–2069.

Jiwei Li, Dan Jurafsky, and Eudard Hovy. 2015. When are tree structures necessary for deep learning of representations? *arXiv preprint arXiv:1503.00185*.

Mitchell P Marcus, Mary Ann Marcinkiewicz, and Beatrice Santorini. 1993. Building a large annotated corpus of english: The penn treebank. *Computational linguistics*, 19(2):313–330.

Tomas Mikolov, Ilya Sutskever, Kai Chen, Greg S Corrado, and Jeff Dean. 2013. Distributed representations of words and phrases and their compositionality. In *Proceedings of NIPS2013*, pages 3111–3119.

Simone Paolo Ponzetto and Michael Strube. 2006. Exploiting semantic role labeling, wordnet and wikipedia for coreference resolution. In *Proceedings of the main conference on Human Language Technology Conference of the North American Chapter of the Association of Computational Linguistics*, pages 192–199. Association for Computational Linguistics.

Richard Socher, Christopher D Manning, and Andrew Y Ng. 2010. Learning continuous phrase representations and syntactic parsing with recursive neural networks. In *Proceedings of the NIPS-2010 Deep Learning and Unsupervised Feature Learning Workshop*, pages 1–9.

Nicolas Usunier, David Buffoni, and Patrick Gallinari. 2009. Ranking with ordered weighted pairwise classification. In *Proceedings of ICML2009*, pages 1057–1064. ACM.

Jason Weston, Samy Bengio, and Nicolas Usunier. 2011. Wsabie: Scaling up to large vocabulary image annotation. In *Proceedings of IJCAI2011*, volume 11, pages 2764–2770.

Bing Xiang, Xiaoqiang Luo, and Bowen Zhou. 2013. Enlisting the ghost: Modeling empty categories for machine translation. In *ACL (1)*, pages 822–831. Citeseer.

Nianwen Xue and Yaqin Yang. 2013. Dependency-based empty category detection via phrase structure trees. In *HLT-NAACL*, pages 1051–1060.

Naiwen Xue, Fei Xia, Fu-Dong Chiou, and Marta Palmer. 2005. The penn chinese treebank: Phrase structure annotation of a large corpus. *Natural language engineering*, 11(02):207–238.

Nianwen Xue. 2007. Tapping the implicit information for the ps to ds conversion of the chinese treebank. In *Proceedings of the Sixth International Workshop on Treebanks and Linguistics Theories*.

Yaqin Yang and Nianwen Xue. 2010. Chasing the ghost: recovering empty categories in the chinese treebank. In *Proceedings of the 23rd International Conference on Computational Linguistics: Posters*, pages 1382–1390. ACL.

Hua-Ping Zhang, Hong-Kui Yu, De-Yi Xiong, and Qun Liu. 2003. Hhmm-based chinese lexical analyzer ictclas. In *Proceedings of the second SIGHAN workshop on Chinese language processing-Volume 17*, pages 184–187. Association for Computational Linguistics.

# Incrementally Tracking Reference in Human/Human Dialogue Using Linguistic and Extra-Linguistic Information

**Casey Kennington**
CITEC, Bielefeld University
Universitätsstraße 25
Bielefeld Germany
ckennington@cit-ec.uni-bielefeld.de

**Ryu Iida**
NICT UCRI
Seika-cho, Soraku-gun
Kyoto, Japan
ryu.iida@nict.go.jp

**Takenobu Tokunaga**
Tokyo Institute of Technology
Ôokayama, Meguro
Tokyo, Japan
take@cs.titech.ac.jp

**David Schlangen**
Bielefeld University
Universitätsstraße 25
Bielefeld Germany
david.schlangen@uni-bielefeld.de

## Abstract

A large part of human communication involves referring to entities in the world and often these entities are objects that are visually present for the interlocutors. A system that aims to resolve such references needs to tackle a complex task: objects and their visual features need to be determined, the referring expressions must be recognised, and extra-linguistic information such as eye gaze or pointing gestures need to be incorporated. Systems that can make use of such information sources exist, but have so far only been tested under very constrained settings, such as WOz interactions. In this paper, we apply to a more complex domain a reference resolution model that works incrementally (i.e., word by word), grounds words with visually present properties of objects (such as shape and size), and can incorporate extra-linguistic information. We find that the model works well compared to previous work on the same data, despite using fewer features. We conclude that the model shows potential for use in a real-time interactive dialogue system.

## 1 Introduction

Referring to entities in the world via definite descriptions makes up a large part of human communication (Poesio and Vieira, 1997). In task-oriented situations, these references are often to entities that are visible in the shared environment. This kind of reference has attracted attention in recent computational research, but the kinds of interactions studied are often fairly restricted in controlled lab situations (Tanenhaus and Spivey-Knowlton, 1995) or simulated human/computer interactions, (Schlangen et al., 2009; Kousidis et al., 2013; Chai et al., 2014). In such task-oriented, co-located settings, interlocutors can make use of extra-linguistic cues such as gaze or pointing gestures. Furthermore, listeners resolve references as they unfold, often identifying the referred entity before the end of the reference (Tanenhaus and Spivey-Knowlton, 1995; Spivey et al., 2002), however research in reference resolution has mostly focused on full, completed referring expressions.

In this paper we make a first move towards addressing somewhat more complex domains. We apply a model of reference resolution, which has been tested in a simpler setup, on more natural data coming from a corpus of human/human interactions. The model is *incremental* in that it does not wait until the end of an utterance to process, rather it updates its interpretation at each word increment. The model can also incorporate other modalities, such as gaze or pointing cues (deixis) incrementally. We also model the saliency of the context, and show that the model can easily take such contextual information into account. The model improves over previous work on reference resolution applied to the same data (Iida et al., 2010; Iida et al., 2011).

The paper is structured as follows: in the following section we discuss related work on incremental resolution of referring expressions. We explain the model that we use in Section 3 and the data we apply it to in Section 4. We then describe the experiments and the results and provide a discussion.

## 2 Related Work

*Reference resolution* (RR), which is the task of resolving referring expressions (REs) to what they are



*Human Language Technologies: The 2015 Annual Conference of the North American Chapter of the ACL*, pages 272–282,
Denver, Colorado, May 31 – June 5, 2015. 

intended to refer to, has been well-studied in various fields such as psychology (Isaacs and Clark, 1987; Tanenhaus and Spivey-Knowlton, 1995), linguistics (Pineda and Garza, 2000), as well as human/human (Iida et al., 2010) and human/machine interaction (Prasov and Chai, 2010; Siebert and Schlangen, 2008; Schlangen et al., 2009). In recent years, multi-modal corpora have emerged which provide RR with important contextual information: collecting dialogue between two humans (Tokunaga et al., 2012; Spanger et al., 2012), between a human and a (simulated) dialogue system (Kousidis et al., 2013; Liu et al., 2013), with gaze, information about the shared environment, and in some cases deixis.

It has been shown that incorporating gaze improves RR in a situated setting because speakers need to look at and distinguish from distractors the objects they are describing: this has been shown in a static scene on a computer screen (Prasov and Chai, 2008), in human-human interactive puzzle tasks (Iida et al., 2010; Iida et al., 2011), in web browsing (Hakkani-tür et al., 2014), and in a moving car where speakers look at objects in their vicinity (Misu et al., 2014). Incorporating pointing (deictic) gestures is also potentially useful in situated RR; as for example Matuszek et al. (2014) have shown in work on resolving objects processed by computer vision techniques. Chen and Eugenio (2012) looked into reference in multi-modal settings, with focus on co-referential pronouns and pointing gestures. However, these approaches were applied in settings in which communication between the two interlocutors was constrained, or the developed systems did not process incrementally. Kehler (2000) presented approach that focused more on interaction in a map task, though the model was not incremental, nor did grounding occur between language and world, as we do here.

Incremental RR has also been studied in a number of papers, including a framework for fast incremental interpretation (Schuler et al., 2009), a Bayesian filtering model approach that was sensitive to disfluencies (Schlangen et al., 2009), a model that used Markov Logic Networks to resolve objects on a screen (Kennington and Schlangen, 2013), a model of RR and incremental feedback (Traum et al., 2012), and an approach that used a semantic representation to refer to objects (Peldszus et al., 2012; Kennington et al., 2014). However, the approaches reported there did not incorporate multi-modal information, were too slow to work in real-time, were evaluated on constrained data, or only focused on a specific type of RR, ignoring pronouns or deixis.

In this paper, we opted to use the model presented in Kennington et al. (2013), the *simple incremental update model* (SIUM). It has been tested extensively against data from a puzzle-playing human/computer interaction domain (the PENTO data, (Kousidis et al., 2013)); it can incorporate multi-modal information, works in real-time, and can resolve definite, exophoric, and deictic references in a single framework, all of which makes it a potential candidate for working in an interactive, multi-modal dialogue system. The model is similar to the one proposed in Funakoshi et al. (2012), which could resolve descriptions, anaphora, and deixis in a unified manner, but that model does not work incrementally.[1]

The main contributions of this paper are the more thorough exposition of the model (in Section 3) and its application and evaluation on much less constrained, more interactive (and hence realistic) data than what it has previously been tested on (Section 4). Moreover, the data set used here is also from a typologically very different language (Japanese) than what the model has been previously tested on (German), and so the robustness of the model against these differences is also investigated.

We will now describe the model, and that will be followed by a description of the corpus we used.

## 3 The Simple Incremental Update Model

Following Kennington et al. (2013) and Kennington et al. (2014), we model the task at hand as one of recovering $I$, the intention of the speaker making the RE, where $I$ ranges over the possible alternatives (the objects in the domain). This recovery proceeds incrementally (word by word), for RE of arbitrary length. That is, if $U$ denotes the current word, we are interested in $P(I|U)$, the current hypothesis about

[1]It can be argued that any non-incremental model could be made into an incremental one by applying that model at each word (Khouzaimi et al., 2014), but we would argue that more modeling effort is required in order for the model to work in an interactive dialogue system, see (Schlangen and Skantze, 2009; Aist et al., 2007; Skantze and Schlangen, 2009; Skantze and Hjalmarsson, 1991).

the intended referent, given the observed word. We assume the presence of an unobserved, latent variable $R$, which models properties of the candidate objects such as colour or shape; explained further below), and so the computation formally is:

$$P(I|U) = \sum_{r \in R} \frac{P(I, U, R)}{P(U)} \quad (1)$$

Which, after making some independence assumptions, can be factored into:

$$P(I|U) = \frac{1}{P(U)} P(I) \sum_{r \in R} P(U|R)P(R|I) \quad (2)$$

This is an update model in the usual sense that the posterior $P(I|U)$ at one step becomes the prior $P(I)$ at the next. $P(R|I)$ provides the link between the intentions (that is, objects) and the properties (e.g., the colour and shape of each object), and $P(U|R)$ the link between properties and (observed) words. Being incremental, this model is computed at each word. As properties play an important role in this model, they will now be explained.

**Properties** The variable $R$ models visual or abstract properties of entities (such as real-world objects or linguistic entities) and their selection for verbalisation in the referring expression. The simple assumption made by the model is that only such properties can be selected for verbalisation which the candidate object actually has. Hence, the starting point for the model is a representation of the world and the current dialogue context in terms of the properties of the objects. For this paper, this means properties belonging to objects in the shared work space.

We will explain the properties we used in our implementation of this model (henceforth SIUM, i.e., *simple incremental update model*), the motivation for using them, and give an example of applying the model in Section 5.

## 4 The REX Data

The corpora presented in Iida et al. (2011) and Spanger et al. (2012) are a collection of human/human interaction data where the participants collaboratively solved Tangram puzzles. In this setting, anaphoric references (i.e., pronoun references to entities in an earlier utterance, e.g., "move *it* to the left") and exophoric references via definite descriptions (i.e., references to real-world objects, e.g., "*that* one" or "the big triangle") are common (note that both refer in different ways to objects that are physically present). The corpus also records an added modality: the gaze of the puzzle *solver* (SV) who gives the instructions and that of the *operator* (OP), who moves the tangram pieces. The mouse pointer controlled by the OP could also be considered a modality, used as a kind of pointing gesture that both participants can observe. The goal of the task was to arrange puzzle pieces on a board into a specified shape (example in Figure 1), which was only known to SV and hidden from OP. The language of the dialogues was Japanese.

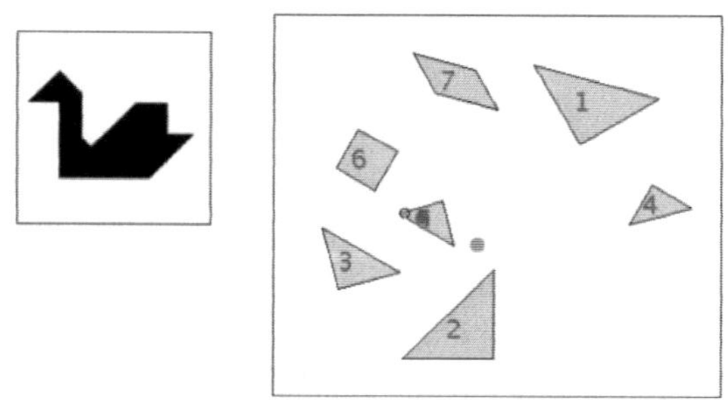


Figure 1: Example Tangram Board; the goal shape is the swan in the top left, the shared work area is the large board on the right, the mouse cursor and OP gaze (blue dot) are on object 5, the SV gaze is the red dot (gaze points were not seen by the participants).

This environment provided frequent use of REs that aimed to distinguish puzzle pieces (and piece groups) from each other. The following are some example REs from the REX corpus:

(1) a. *chicchai sankakkei*
 b. small triangle

(2) a. *sono ichiban migi ni shippo ni natte iru sankakkei*
 b. that most right tail becoming triangle
 'that right-most triangle that is the tail'

Example (1) is a typical example of an RE as found in the corpus. Note that this at the same time constitutes the whole utterance, which hence can be classified as a non-sentential utterance (Schlangen, 2004). Its transliteration consists of 8 Japanese characters, which could be tokenized into two words. The more difficult RE shown in Example (2) requires the model to learn how spatial placements map to certain descriptions. Moreover, Japanese is a head-final language where comparative landmark pieces are uttered before the referent. Also, because this was a highly interactive setting, many exophoric pronouns were used, e.g., *sore* and *sono*, both meaning *that*.[2] Pronoun references like this made up around 32% of the utterances.

Corpus annotations included (for both participants) transcriptions of utterances, the object being looked at any given time, the object being pointed at or manipulated by the mouse, segmentation of the REs and the corresponding referred object or objects. The spatial layout of the board was recorded each time an object was manipulated. Further details of the corpus can be found in (Iida et al., 2011). In order to directly compare our work with previous work, in our evaluations below we consider the same annotated REs. Iida et al. (2011) applied a support vector machine-based ranking algorithm (Joachims, 2002) to the task of resolving REs in this corpus. They used a total of 36 binary features in the SVM classifier, which predicted the referred object. They further used a separate model for pronoun utterances and non-pronoun utterances, allowing the classifier to learn patterns without confusing utterance types. More details on the results of these models are given below.

The SIU-model has previously been applied to two datasets from the Pentomino domain (Kennington et al., 2013), where the speaker's goal was to identify one out of a set of tetris-like (but consisting of five instead of four blocks) puzzle pieces. However, in these datasets, the references were "one-shot" and not embedded in longer dialogues, as is the case in the REX corpus. A summary of differences between the two tasks is summarised in Table 1. Applying SIUM to data like that found in the REX corpus is a natural next step to test the abilities of the model as a RR component in a dialogue system.

[2]To be precise, *sono* is a demonstrative adjective.

| | PENTO | REX |
|---|---|---|
| language | **German** | **Japanese** |
| language type | SVO | SOV |
| phrase type | head-initial | head-final |
| avg utt length | 7-8 | 4-5 |
| number of objects | 15 | 7 |
| interactivity | human-wizard | human-human |
| recorded gaze | SV (speaker) | SV, OP |
| % of pronoun utts | 0% | 32% |

Table 1: Summary of differences between PENTO and REX tasks.

## 5 Experiment

**Procedure** The procedure for this experiment is as follows. In order to compare our results directly with those of Iida et al. (2011), we provide our model with the same training and evaluation data, in a 10-fold cross-validation of the 1192 REs from 27 dialogues (the T2009-11 corpus in Tokunaga et al. (2012)). For development, we used a separate part of the REX corpus (N2009-11) that was structured similarly to the one used in our evaluation.

**Task** The task is RR. At each increment, SIUM returns a distribution over all objects; the probability for each object represents the strength of the belief that it is the referred one. The argmax of the distribution is chosen as the hypothesised referred object.

**P(R|I)** $P(R|I)$ models the likelihood of selecting a property of a candidate object for verbalisation; this likelihood is assumed to be uniform for all the properties that the candidate object has.[3] We derive these properties from a representation of the scene; similar to how Iida et al. (2011) computed features to present to their classifier: namely **Ling** (linguistic features), **TaskSp** (task specific features), and **Gaze** (from SV only). Some features were binary, others such as shape and size had more values. Table 2 shows all the properties that were used here. Each will now be explained.

**Ling** Each object had a shape, size, and relative position to the other pieces. We determined by hand

[3]Uniformity in the likelihood of the properties isn't an ideal approach as certain properties could be more likely to be selected than others; we leave a more principled approach to using saliency to help determine the likelihood of the properties to future work.

| Ling | TaskSp |
|---|---|
| tri/squ/pgram | most_recent_move |
| small/med/big | mouse_pointed |
| left/mid/right | |
| prev_referred | **Gaze** |
| top/cen/bottom | most_gazed_at |
| referred_5 | gazed_at_in_utt |
| referred_10 | longest_gazed_at |
| referred_20 | recent_fixation |

Table 2: List of properties used for each source of information.

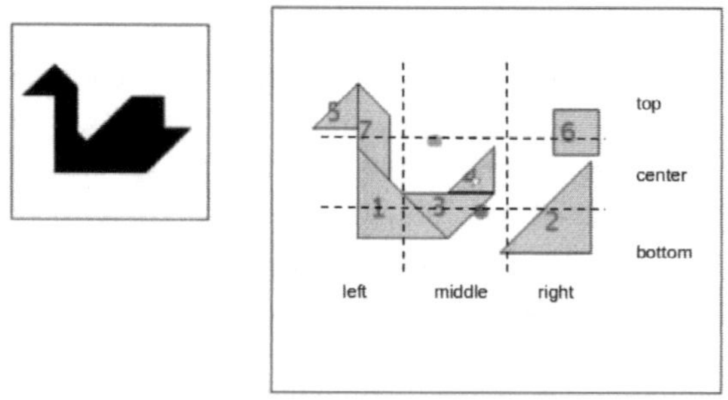


Figure 2: Tangram later in the dialogue; the notion of *right-ness* and other spatial concepts changes throughout the dialogue (compare to Figure 1), the grids are added to show which objects receive which horizontal and which vertical properties.

the shape and size properties which remained static through each dialogue. The position properties were derived from the corpus logs. For each object, the centroid of each object was computed. Then, the vertical and horizontal range for all of the objects was calculated and then split into three even sections in each dimension (see Figure 2). An object with a centroid in the left-most section of the horizontal range received a `left` property, similarly `middle` and `right` properties were calculated for corresponding objects. For vertical placement, `top`, `center` and `bottom` properties were given to objects in the respective vertical segments. Figure 2 shows an example segmentation. Each object had a vertical and a horizontal property at all times, however, moving an object could result in a change of one of these spatial properties as the dialogue progressed. As an example, compare Figure 1, which is a snapshot of the interaction towards the beginning, and Figure 2, which shows a later stage of the game board; spatial layout changes throughout the dialogue.

These properties differ somewhat from the features for the Ling model presented in Iida et al. (2011). Three features that we did use as properties had to do with reference recency: the most recently referred object received the `referred_X` properties, if an object was referred to in the past 5, 10, or 20 seconds.

**TaskSp** Iida et al. (2011) used 14 task-specific features, three of which they found to be the most informative in their model. Here, we will only use the two most informative features as properties (the third one, whether or not an object was being manipulated at the beginning of the RE, did not improve results in a held-out test): the object that was most recently moved received the `most_recent_move` property and objects that have the mouse cursor over them received the `mouse_pointed` property (see Figure 2; object 4 would receive both of these properties, but only for the duration that the mouse was actually over it). Each of these properties can be extracted directly from the corpus annotations.

**Gaze** Similar to Iida et al. (2011), we consider gaze during a window of 1500ms before the onset of the RE. The object that was gazed at the longest during that time received a `longest_gazed_at` property, the object which was fixated upon most recently during that interval before the RE onset received a `recent_fixation` property, and the object which had the most fixations received the `most_gazed_at` property. During a RE, an object received the `gazed_at_in_utt` property if it is gazed at during the RE up until that point. These properties can be extracted directly from the corpus annotations. Other gaze features are not really accessible to an incremental model such as this, as gaze features extracted from gaze activity over the RE can only be computed when it is complete. Our Gaze properties are made up of these 4 properties, as opposed to the 14 features in Iida et al. (2011).

**P(U|R)** $P(U|R)$ is the model that connects the property selected for verbalisation with a way of verbalising it (a value for $U$). Instead of directly learning this model from data, which would suffer from data sparseness, we trained a naive Bayes model for $P(R|U)$ (as, according to Bayes' rule, $P(U|R)$ is equal to $P(R|U)P(U)\frac{1}{P(R)}$, which, plugged in into formula (2), cancels out $\frac{1}{P(U)}$; further assuming the $P(R)$ is uniform, we can directly replace $P(U|R)$ with $P(R|U)$ here). On the language side (the variable $U$ in the model), we used n-grams over Japanese characters (we attempted tokenisation of the REs into words, but found that using characters worked just as well in the held-out set).

**P(I)** The prior $P(I)$ is the posterior of the previously computed increment. In the first increment, it can simply be set to a uniform distribution. Here, we apply a more informative prior based on saliency. We learn a *context model* which is queried when the first word begins, taking information about the context immediately before the beginning of the RE into account, producing a distribution over objects, which becomes $P(I)$ of the first increment in the RE. The context model itself is a simple application of the SIUM, where instead of being a word, $U$ is a token that represents saliency. The context model thus learns what properties are important to the pre-RE context and provides an up-to-date distribution over the objects as a RE begins.

### 5.1 Example

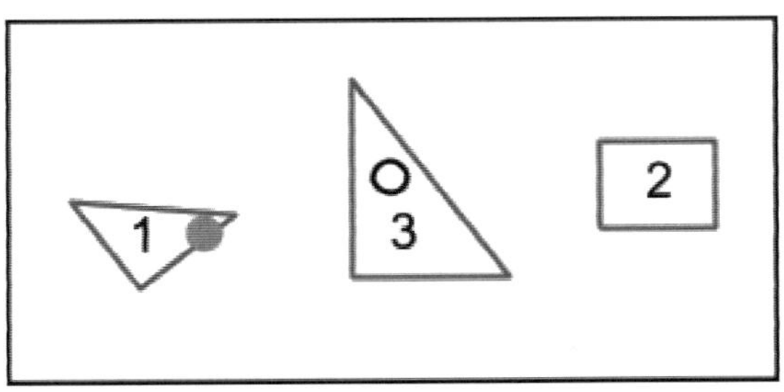


Figure 3: Example scene with two triangles and one square, 1 is being looked at by the SV, 3 was recently moved and the mouse pointer is still over it.

We will now give a simple example of how the model is applied to the REX data using a subset of the above properties for the RE *small triangle*. Table 3 shows a simple normalised co-occurrence count of how many times properties were observed as belonging to a referred object (the basis for $P(U|R)$). Figure 3 shows the current toy scene, and Table 4 shows the properties that each object in the scene has during the utterance. Table 5 shows the full application of the model by summing over the properties for the product $P(U|R)P(R|I)$ and multiplying by the prior $P(I)$, the posterior of the previous step. Included in this example is how the initial prior is computed from the context model.

| property | *small* | *triangle* | *square* | ⟨*context*⟩ |
|---|---|---|---|---|
| **small** | .87 | .02 | .4 | .04 |
| **big** | .01 | .08 | .02 | .05 |
| **triangle** | .04 | .88 | .01 | .09 |
| **square** | .04 | .01 | .9 | .09 |
| **left** | .06 | .07 | .06 | .09 |
| **center** | .04 | .03 | .04 | .07 |
| **right** | .04 | .06 | .05 | .03 |
| **most_gazed** | .07 | .09 | .07 | .6 |
| **recent_move** | .03 | .1 | .04 | .56 |
| **mouse_pointed** | .08 | .05 | .06 | .71 |

Table 3: Applications of $P(U|R)$, for some values of $U$ and $R$; we assume that this model is learned from data (rows are excerpted from a larger distribution over all the words in the vocabulary)

| property | 1 | 2 | 3 |
|---|---|---|---|
| **small** | 0.25 | 0.33 | 0 |
| **big** | 0 | 0 | 0.2 |
| **triangle** | 0.25 | 0 | 0.2 |
| **square** | 0 | 0.33 | 0 |
| **left** | 0.25 | 0 | 0 |
| **center** | 0 | 0 | 0.2 |
| **right** | 0 | 0.33 | 0 |
| **most_gazed** | 0.25 | 0 | 0 |
| **recent_move** | 0 | 0 | 0.2 |
| **mouse_pointed** | 0 | 0 | 0.2 |

Table 4: $P(R|I)$, for our example domain. The probability mass is distributed over the number of properties that a candidate object actually has.

Before the RE even begins, the prior saliency yields that 3 is the most likely object to be referred; it was the most salient in that it was the most recently moved object and the mouse pointer was still over it. However, initial prior information alone is not enough to resolve the intended object; for that the RE is needed. After the word *small* is uttered, 1 is the most likely referred object. After *triangle*, 1 remains the highest in the distribution. With the RE alone, in this case there would have been enough information to infer that 1 was the referred object, but adding the prior information provided additional evidence.

| $I$ | $U$ | $\Sigma\, P(U\|R) * P(R\|I)$ | $P(I\|U)$ |
|---|---|---|---|
| 1 | $\langle$*context*$\rangle$ | $.25(.04+.09+.09+.6)$ | .37 |
| 2 | | $.33(.04+.09+.03)$ | .095 |
| 3 | | $.2(.05+.09+.07+.56+.71)$ | .535 |
| 1 | *small* | $.25(.87+.04+.06+.07)$ | .65 |
| 2 | | $.33(.87+.04+.04)$ | .2 |
| 3 | | $.2(.01+.04+.04+.03+.08)$ | .15 |
| 1 | *triangle* | $.25(.02+.88+.07+.09)$ | .81 |
| 2 | | $.33(.02+.01+.06)$ | .028 |
| 3 | | $.2(.08+.88+.03+.1+.05)$ | .162 |

Table 5: Application of RE *small triangle*, where 1 is the referred object

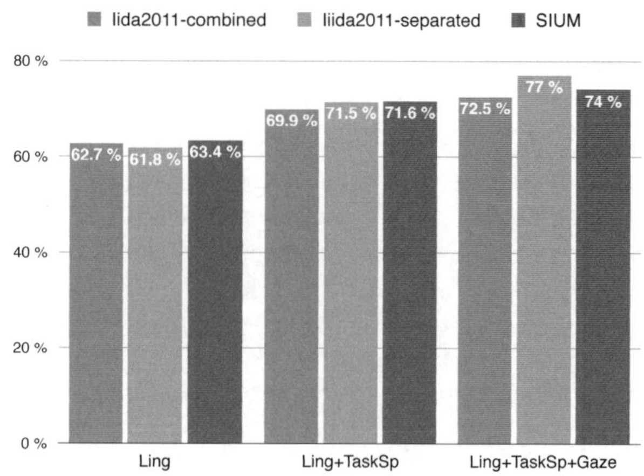


Figure 4: Comparison of model accuracies; our SIUM approach generally performs better over the combined model presented in Iida et al., (2011)

**Evaluation Metrics** We report results of our evaluation in referential accuracy on utterances that were annotated as referring to a single object (references to group objects is left for future work). Going beyond Iida et al. (2011), our model computes a resolution hypothesis incrementally; for the performance of this aspect of the system we followed previously used metrics for evaluation (Schlangen et al., 2009; Kennington et al., 2013):

**first correct**: how deep into the RE does the model predict the referent for the first time?

**first final**: how deep into the RE does the model predict the correct referent and keep that decision until the end?

**edit overhead**: how often did the model unnecessarily change its prediction (the only *necessary* prediction happens when it first makes a correct prediction)?

We compare non-incremental results to three evaluations performed in Iida et al. (2011), namely when Ling is used alone, Ling+TaskSP used together, and Ling+TaskSp+Gaze. Furthermore, they show results of models where a separate part handled REs that used pronouns, as well as a part that handled the non-pronoun REs, and a combined model that handled both types of expressions.

# 6 Results

## 6.1 Reference Resolution

Results of our evaluation are shown in Figure 4. The SIUM model performs better than the combined approach of Iida et al. (2011), and performs better than their separated model—when not including gaze (there is a significant difference between SIUM and the separated models for Ling+TaskSp, though SIUM only got one more correct than the separated model). This is a welcome result, as it shows that our very simple incremental model that uses a basic classifier is comparable to a non-incremental approach that uses a more complicated classifier. It further shows that the SIUM model is robust to using TaskSp and Gaze features as properties, as long as those features are available immediately before the RE begins, or during the RE.

The best-performing approach is the Iida2011-separated model with gaze. This is the case for several reasons: first, their models use features that are not available to our incremental model (e.g., their model uses 14 gaze features, some of which were based on the entire RE, ours only uses 4 properties). Second, and more importantly, separated models means less feature confusion: in Iida et al. (2011) (Section 5.2), the authors give a comparison of the most informative features for each model; task and gaze features were prominent for the pronoun model, whereas gaze and language features were prominent for the non-pronoun model. We also tested SIUM under separated conditions to better compare with the approaches presented here. The separated models, however, did not improve. This, we assume, is because the model grounds *language* with properties (see Discussion below). An interactive dialogue system might not have the luxury of choosing between two models at runtime. We assume that a model that can sufficiently handle both

|  | 1-5 | 6-8 | 9-14 |
|---|---|---|---|
| first correct (% into RE) | 35.47 | 22.34 | 14.8 |
| first final (% into RE) | 69.0 | 49.85 | 48.0 |
| edit overhead (all lengths) | 0.88% |  |  |
| never correct (all lengths) | 5.5% |  |  |

Table 6: Incremental results for SIUM, numbers represent % into RE.

types of utterances is to be preferred to one that doesn't.

### 6.2 Incremental Behaviour

Table 6 shows how our model fares using the incremental metrics described earlier. (As this has not been done in Iida et al. (2011), direct comparison is not possible.) For the evaluation, REs are binned into short, normal, and long (1-5, 6-8, 9-14 characters, respectively, based on what the average numbers of words in REs in this corpus is), to make relative statements ("% into the utterance") comparable.

Ideally, a system would make the first correct decision as early as possible without changing that decision. The results in the table show a respectable incremental model; on average it picks the right object early, with some edit overhead (making unnecessary changes in its prediction), finally fixing on a final decision before the end of the RE with low edit overhead, meaning it rarely changes its mind once it has made a decision. In some cases, SIUM never guessed the correct object, labeled *never correct* in the table. These incremental results are consistent with previous work for the SIUM; overall, the model is stable across the RE.

### 6.3 Discussion

Despite being very simple, there is an important difference that allows SIUM to improve over previous work. It learns to connect object properties selected for verbalisation to ways of verbalising them, and forms a stochastic expectation about which properties might be selected for verbalisation (namely, those that are present). This represents a type of *grounding* (Harnad, 1990; Roy, 2005).[4] In terms of the SIUM formalism, the link between object and words is mediated by the properties the object has

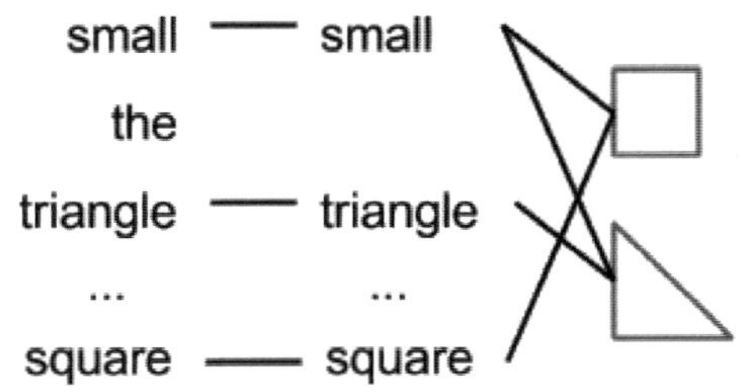


Figure 5: Words that describe objects are linked via a hand-coded `compatibility` function; links from words to multiple properties can exist, provided it is coded.

and by a stochastic process of associating words with properties. Figure 6 visualises this: each word has a stochastic connection between each property and objects have a set of properties. The property names are arbitrary as long as they are consistent. In contrast, previous work in RR (Iida et al., 2011; Chai et al., 2014) used a hand-coded concept-labeled semantic representation and checked if aspects of the RE match that of a particular object. If so, a binary *compatibility* feature was set. Figure 5 shows this; words can only link to objects via hand-crafted rules (e.g., the word or FOL predicate and property string must match). By the way SIUM uses properties, it can also perform (exophoric) pronoun resolution, deixis (the mouse pointer) and definite descriptions, in a single framework. This is a nice feature of the model: adding additional modalities does not require model reformulation.

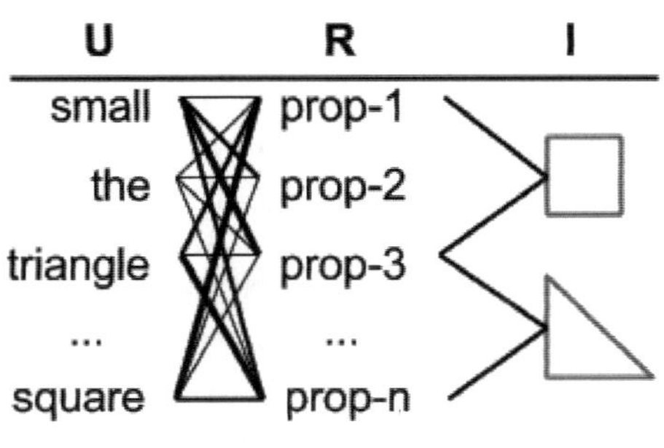


Figure 6: Words that describe objects are linked via properties stochastically: thicker lines between $U$ and $R$ represent higher probabilities. The lines between $R$ and $I$ denote a property belonging to an object. The cardinality of $U$ does not equal $R$.

[4]Not to be confused with *building common ground* (Clark, 1996) which is also referred to as *grounding*.

Incorporating saliency information via a context model is also a nice feature of the model. In this paper, we computed the initial $P(I)$ using a context model instantiated by SIUM. By considering only this saliency information, the context model can predict the referred object in 41% of the cases. It also learned which properties were important for saliency (that is, these are the properties that the model would most likely select): `recently_fixated`, `most_gaze_at`, `longest_gazed_at`, `prev_ref`, as might be expected. In less than 2% of the cases, the context model referred to the correct object, but was wrongly "overruled" when processing the corresponding RE.

There were shortcomings, however. In previous work, it was shown that SIUM performed well when REs contained pronouns (see Kennington et al. (2013), experiment 2). However, in the current work we observed that REs with pronouns were more difficult for the model to resolve than the model presented in Iida et al. (2011). We surmise that SIUM had a difficult time grounding certain properties, as the Japanese pronoun *sore* can be used anaphorically or demonstratively in this kind of context (i.e., sometimes *sore* refers to previously-manipulated objects, or objects that are newly identified with a mouse pointer over them); the model presented in Iida et al. (2011) made more use of contextual information when pronouns were used, particularly in the combined model which incorporated gaze information, as shown above.

## 7 Conclusion

The SIUM is a model of RR that grounds language with the world, works incrementally, can incorporate modalities such as gaze and deixis, and can resolve multiple kinds of RRs in a single framework. This paper represents the natural next step in evaluating SIUM in a setting that was less constrained and more interactive, with added knowledge that it can work in more than one language.

There is more to be tested for SIUM. A common form of RR happens collaboratively over multiple utterances (Clark and Wilkes-Gibbs, 1986; Heeman and Hirst, 1995), SIUM has only been tested on isolated REs. Though SIUM required fewer features (realised as properties) than previous work, those properties still need to be computed. We leave for future work investigation of a version of the model that can ground language with raw(er) information from the world (e.g., vision information), eliminating the need to determine properties.

**Acknowledgements** Thanks to the anonymous reviewers for their excellent comments and suggestions.

## References

Gregory Aist, James Allen, Ellen Campana, Carlos Gomez Gallo, Scott Stoness, and Mary Swift. 2007. Incremental understanding in human-computer dialogue and experimental evidence for advantages over nonincremental methods. In *Pragmatics*, volume 1, pages 149–154, Trento, Italy.

Joyce Y Chai, Lanbo She, Rui Fang, Spencer Ottarson, Cody Littley, Changsong Liu, and Kenneth Hanson. 2014. Collaborative effort towards common ground in situated human-robot dialogue. In *Proceedings of the 2014 ACM/IEEE international conference on Human-robot interaction*, pages 33–40, Bielefeld, Germany.

Lin Chen and Barbara Di Eugenio. 2012. Co-reference via Pointing and Haptics in Multi-Modal Dialogues. In *Proceedings of the 2012 Conference of the North American Chapter of the Association for Computational Linguistics: Human Language Technologies*, pages 523–527. Association for Computational Linguistics.

Herbert H Clark and Deanna Wilkes-Gibbs. 1986. Referring as a collaborative process. *Cognition*, 22:1–39.

Herbert H Clark. 1996. *Using Language*. Cambridge University Press.

Kotaro Funakoshi, Mikio Nakano, Takenobu Tokunaga, and Ryu Iida. 2012. A Unified Probabilistic Approach to Referring Expressions. In *Proceedings of the 13th Annual Meeting of the Special Interest Group on Discourse and Dialogue*, pages 237–246, Seoul, South Korea, July. Association for Computational Linguistics.

Dilek Hakkani-tür, Malcolm Slaney, Asli Celikyilmaz, and Larry Heck. 2014. Eye Gaze for Spoken Language Understanding in Multi-Modal Conversational Interactions. In *ICMI*.

Stevan Harnad. 1990. The Symbol Grounding Problem. *Physica D*, 42:335–346.

Peter a. Heeman and Graeme Hirst. 1995. Collaborating on Referring Expressions. *Computational Linguistics*, 21(3):32.

Ryu Iida, Shumpei Kobayashi, and Takenobu Tokunaga. 2010. Incorporating Extra-linguistic Information into Reference Resolution in Collaborative Task Dialogue. In *Proceedings of the 48th Annual Meeting of the Association for Computational Linguistic*, pages 1259—-1267, Uppsala, Sweden.

Ryu Iida, Masaaki Yasuhara, and Takenobu Tokunaga. 2011. Multi-modal Reference Resolution in Situated Dialogue by Integrating Linguistic and Extra-Linguistic Clues. In *Proceedings of the 5th International Joint Conference on Natural Language Processing (IJCNLP 2011)*, pages 84–92.

Ellen a. Isaacs and Herbert H. Clark. 1987. References in conversation between experts and novices. *Journal of Experimental Psychology: General*, 116(1):26–37.

Thorsten Joachims. 2002. Optimizing search engines using clickthrough data. In *Proceedings of the eighth ACM SIGKDD international conference on Knowledge discovery and data mining - KDD '02*, pages 133–142.

Andrew Kehler. 2000. Cognitive Status and Form of Reference in Multimodal Human-Computer Interaction. In *AAAI 00, The 15th Annual Conference of the American Association for Artificial Intelligence*, pages 685–689.

Casey Kennington and David Schlangen. 2013. Situated incremental natural language understanding using Markov Logic Networks. *Computer Speech & Language*, pages –.

Casey Kennington, Spyros Kousidis, and David Schlangen. 2013. Interpreting Situated Dialogue Utterances: an Update Model that Uses Speech, Gaze, and Gesture Information. In *SIGdial 2013*.

Casey Kennington, Spyros Kousidis, and David Schlangen. 2014. Situated Incremental Natural Language Understanding using a Multimodal, Linguistically-driven Update Model. In *CoLing 2014*.

Hatim Khouzaimi, Romain Laroche, and Fabrice Lefevre. 2014. An easy method to make dialogue systems incremental. In *Proceedings of the 15th Annual Meeting of the Special Interest Group on Discourse and Dialogue (SIGDIAL)*, pages 98–107, Philadelphia, PA, U.S.A. Association for Computational Linguistics.

Spyros Kousidis, Casey Kennington, and David Schlangen. 2013. Investigating speaker gaze and pointing behaviour in human-computer interaction with the mint.tools collection. In *SIGdial 2013*.

Changsong Liu, Rui Fang, Lanbo She, and Joyce Chai. 2013. Modeling Collaborative Referring for Situated Referential Grounding. In *Proceedings of the SIGDIAL 2013 Conference*, pages 78–86, Metz, France, August. Association for Computational Linguistics.

Cynthia Matuszek, Liefeng Bo, Luke Zettlemoyer, and Dieter Fox. 2014. Learning from Unscripted Deictic Gesture and Language for Human-Robot Interactions. In *Aaai*. AAAI Press.

Teruhisa Misu, Antoine Raux, Ian Lane, and Moffett Field. 2014. Situated Language Understanding at 25 Miles per Hour. In *SIGdial 2014*, pages 22–31, Philadelphia, PA, U.S.A. Association for Computational Linguistics.

Andreas Peldszus, Okko Buß, Timo Baumann, and David Schlangen. 2012. Joint Satisfaction of Syntactic and Pragmatic Constraints Improves Incremental Spoken Language Understanding. In *Proceedings of the 13th EACL*, pages 514–523, Avignon, France, April. Association for Computational Linguistics.

Luis Pineda and Gabriela Garza. 2000. A Model for Multimodal Reference Resolution. *Computational Linguistics*, 26:139–193.

Massimo Poesio and Renata Vieira. 1997. A Corpus-Based Investigation of Definite Description Use. *Computational Linguistics*, 24(2):47, June.

Zahar Prasov and Joyce Y. Chai. 2008. What's in a gaze? In *Proceedings of the 13th international conference on Intelligent user interfaces - IUI '08*, page 20.

Zahar Prasov and Joyce Y Chai. 2010. Fusing Eye Gaze with Speech Recognition Hypotheses to Resolve Exophoric References in Situated Dialogue. In *Emnlp 2010*, number October, pages 471–481.

Deb Roy. 2005. Grounding words in perception and action: Computational insights. *Trends in Cognitive Sciences*, 9(8):389–396, August.

David Schlangen and Gabriel Skantze. 2009. A general, abstract model of incremental dialogue processing. *Proceedings of the 12th Conference of the European Chapter of the Association for Computational Linguistics on EACL 09*, 2(1):710–718.

David Schlangen, Timo Baumann, and Michaela Atterer. 2009. Incremental Reference Resolution: The Task, Metrics for Evaluation, and a Bayesian Filtering Model that is Sensitive to Disfluencies. In *Proceedings of the 10th SIGdial*, number September, pages 30–37, London, UK. Association for Computational Linguistics.

David Schlangen. 2004. *A Coherence-Based Approach to the Interpretation of Non-Sentential Utterances in Dialogue*. Ph.D. thesis, University of Edinburgh.

William Schuler, Stephen Wu, and Lane Schwartz. 2009. A Framework for Fast Incremental Interpretation during Speech Decoding. *Computational Linguistics*, 35(3):313–343.

Alexander Siebert and David Schlangen. 2008. A Simple Method for Resolution of Definite Reference in a Shared Visual Context. In *Proceedings of the 9th SIGdial*, number June, pages 84–87, Columbus, Ohio. Association for Computational Linguistics.

Gabriel Skantze and Anna Hjalmarsson. 1991. Towards Incremental Speech Production in Dialogue Systems. In *Word Journal Of The International Linguistic Association*, pages 1–8, Tokyo, Japan, September.

Gabriel Skantze and David Schlangen. 2009. Incremental dialogue processing in a micro-domain. *Proceedings of the 12th Conference of the European Chapter of the Association for Computational Linguistics on EACL 09*, (April):745–753.

Philipp Spanger, Masaaki Yasuhara, Ryu Iida, Takenobu Tokunaga, Asuka Terai, and Naoko Kuriyama. 2012. REX-J: Japanese referring expression corpus of situated dialogs. *Language Resources and Evaluation*, 46(3):461–491, December.

Michael J Spivey, Michael K Tanenhaus, Kathleen M Eberhard, and Julie C Sedivy. 2002. Eye movements and spoken language comprehension: Effects of visual context on syntactic ambiguity resolution. *Cognitive Psychology*, 45(4):447–481.

Michael K Tanenhaus and Michael J Spivey-Knowlton. 1995. Integration of visual and linguistic information in spoken language comprehension. *Science*, 268:1632.

Takenobu Tokunaga, Ryu Iida, Asuka Terai, and Naoko Kuriyama. 2012. The REX corpora : A collection of multimodal corpora of referring expressions in collaborative problem solving dialogues. In *Proceedings of the Eigth International Conference on Language Resources and Evaluation (LREC 2012)*, pages 422–429.

David Traum, David Devault, Jina Lee, Zhiyang Wang, and Stacy Marsella. 2012. Incremental dialogue understanding and feedback for multiparty, multimodal conversation. In *Lecture Notes in Computer Science (including subseries Lecture Notes in Artificial Intelligence and Lecture Notes in Bioinformatics)*, volume 7502 LNAI, pages 275–288. Springer.

# Digital Leafleting: Extracting Structured Data from Multimedia Online Flyers

**Emilia Apostolova**
BrokerSavant Inc.
2506 N. Clark St, 415
Chicago, IL 60614, USA
emilia@brokersavant.com

**Payam Pourashraf**
DePaul University
243 S Wabash Ave
Chicago, IL 60604, USA
ppourash@cdm.depaul.edu

**Jeffrey Sack**
BrokerSavant Inc.
2506 N. Clark St, 415
Chicago, IL 60614, USA
jeff@brokersavant.com

## Abstract

Marketing materials such as flyers and other infographics are a vast online resource. In a number of industries, such as the commercial real estate industry, they are in fact the only authoritative source of information. Companies attempting to organize commercial real estate inventories spend a significant amount of resources on manual data entry of this information. In this work, we propose a method for extracting structured data from free-form commercial real estate flyers in PDF and HTML formats. We modeled the problem as text categorization and Named Entity Recognition (NER) tasks and applied a supervised machine learning approach (Support Vector Machines). Our dataset consists of more than 2,200 commercial real estate flyers and associated manually entered structured data, which was used to automatically create training datasets. Traditionally, text categorization and NER approaches are based on textual information only. However, information in visually rich formats such as PDF and HTML is often conveyed by a combination of textual and visual features. Large fonts, visually salient colors, and positioning often indicate the most relevant pieces of information. We applied novel features based on visual characteristics in addition to traditional text features and show that performance improved significantly for both the text categorization and NER tasks.

## 1 Introduction

Digital flyers are the preferred and sometimes only method of conveying offerings information in a number of broker-based industries. Such industries typically lack a centralized database or an established source of information. Organizing such content typically involves manual data entry, an expensive and labour intensive effort. Further challenge is that available offerings constantly change and manually entered data often results in out-dated inventories.

In particular, the commercial real estate industry in the US (unlike residential real estate[1]) does not have a centralized database or an established source of information. A number of commercial real estate inventories collect commercial real estate data using information from flyers, contacting brokers, or visiting physical sites[2]. The data is manually entered in structured form. At the same time, inventories change on a daily basis. As a result, the collected information is typically sparse and often outdated. In fact, commercial real estate brokers often need to rely on networking and chance in preference to consulting third party listing databases.

While brokers do not often update third party inventory databases, they do create marketing materials (usually PDF flyers and/or HTML emails/web pages) that contain all relevant listing information. Virtually all commercial real estate offerings come with a publicly available marketing material that contains all relevant listing information. Figures 1 and 2 show two typical commercial real estate flyers.

[1]The US Multiple Listing Services (MLS), governed by the National Association of Realtors, represents the US residential real estate.

[2]LoopNet, subsidiary of CoStar Group Inc., is the most heavily trafficked online commercial real estate inventory.



*Human Language Technologies: The 2015 Annual Conference of the North American Chapter of the ACL*, pages 283–292,
Denver, Colorado, May 31 – June 5, 2015. ©2015 Association for Computational Linguistics

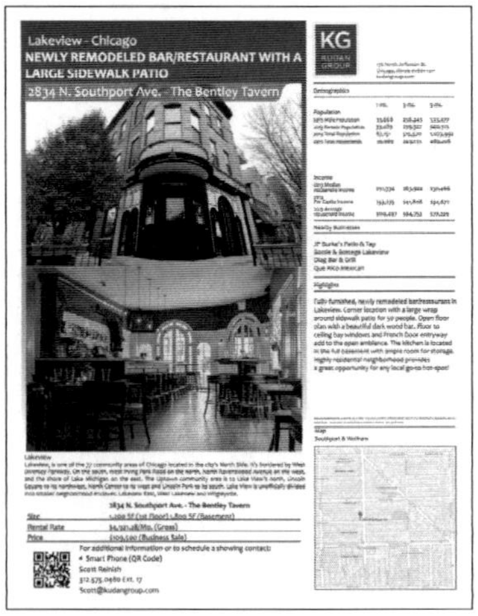


Figure 1: An example of a commercial real estate flyer © Kudan Group Real Estate.

Our goal is to utilize this publicly available information and extract structured data that can be continuously updated for a reliable centralized database of offerings.

Commercial listing information is typically summarized in a structured form suitable for targeted property searches. The most important information consists of the various categories of the offering. For example, the transaction type (*sale*, *lease*, and/or *investment*), the property type (*industrial, retail, office*, etc.), the location of the property (its full geocoded address), the size of the property, the contact information of the brokers representing the property, etc.

This information is typically present in text form within the flyer. However, flyers and similar marketing materials are essentially multi-media documents. In addition to text, information is also conveyed by attributes such as font size, color, positioning, and images. For example, the listing address of the flyer on Figure 1 can be easily identified by its prominent color, size, and positioning (*2834 N. Southport Ave*, upper left corner). While the address of the broker firm shown in the same flyer is considered non-essential information and lacks such visual prominence (*156 North Jefferson St.*, upper right corner). In fact, it is very difficult and sometimes impossible to distinguish between the two address types when considering a text-only version of the flyer. Similarly, the transaction type (*For Sale*) of the property on Figure 2 is prominently shown in a large font and distinctive color. To account for the multi-media nature of the dataset, we attempt to combine textual and visual features for the task of automatic extraction of structured information from free-form commercial real estate flyers.

The problem of extracting structured data from flyers was modeled as text categorization and Named Entity Recognition (NER) tasks as described in Section *Problem Definition* below. Typically, both text categorization and NER approaches are applied to genres with exclusively text-based content (newswires, scientific publications, blogs and other social media texts). As a result, the feature space of NER and text categorization involves purely textual features: word attributes and characteristics, their contexts and frequencies. However, textual information in visually rich formats, such as PDF and HTML, is interlaced with typographic and other visually salient characteristics. In this study, we propose several novel features that take visual characteristics into account and show that performance improves significantly on both the text categorization and NER tasks.

## 2 Problem Definition

Given a commercial real estate flyer, our task is to extract structured information that can be used as input to a commercial real estate listing service. This information includes categories associated with the property (property type and transaction type) and a list of property attributes (address, space information, and broker information).

The task of identifying a list of categories was modeled as a text categorization task. The categories and associated types are summarized in Table 1. Both text categorization tasks (identifying the Transaction and Property Types) are multi-label classification tasks, i.e. multiple category labels can be assigned to each listing. For example, properties are often offered for both *sale* and *lease* and belong to both transaction types. Similarly, a retail building could offer an associated office unit and belongs to property types *retail* and *office*.

The task of identifying values of specific listing attributes was modeled as a Named Entity Recognition (NER) task. The various NER types and de-

| | |
|---|---|
| Transaction Type | A listing can have one or more of the following transaction types: *sale, lease, investment*. |
| Property Type | A listing can have one or more of the following property types: *retail, office, industrial, land, multi-family*. |

Table 1: Types and descriptions of flyer categories.

scriptions are summarized in Table 2. The named entities represent a typical set of attributes collected by commercial real estate listing services. They are 1) one or more brokers representing the property and their contact information; 2) the full address of the property broken down into individual address fields; 3) one or more spaces including their sizes and types (e.g. sizes of available units in a shopping mall, the sizes of a warehouse building and associated office building, etc.).

| | |
|---|---|
| Broker Name<br>Broker Email<br>Broker Phone | The contact information of all listing brokers, including full name, email address, phone number. |
| Company Name | The brokerage company name. |
| Street<br>City<br>Neighborhood<br>State<br>Zip | The address information of the listing address including street or intersection, city, state, and, zip code. |
| Space Size and Type | Size and attributes of relevant spaces (e.g. *27,042 SF building, 4.44 acres site*, etc.); Includes the numeric value, unit of measure, whether the value is a part of a range (min or max) or exact value, as well as the space type *(unit, building,lot)*; Excludes size information of non-essential listing attributes (e.g. basement size or parking lot size). |

Table 2: Types and descriptions of named entities relevant to extracting listing information from commercial real estate flyers.

The problem of automatically extracting structured information from real estate flyers was then implemented as a combination of the text categorization and NER tasks.

# 3 Method

## 3.1 Dataset

The dataset consists of 2,269 commercial real estate flyers submitted to a listing service[3] over a period of one year. It represents over 450 US locations, over 90 commercial real estate companies and over 800 commercial real estate brokers. The flyers were generated using different tools and formats and represent a wide variety of styles. Typically, the same broker can represent properties of various categories and transaction types. The text categorization was evaluated using the full dataset of 2,269 flyers with 5-fold cross validation. For the NER task, we used 60 percent of the flyers for training (a total of 1,361 flyers), and the remaining 40 percent for testing (a total of 908 flyers).

All flyers (PDF and HTML) were converted to a common format (HTML)[4]. The flyers were converted to text using an HTML parser and extracting DOM[5] text elements while preserving some of the white space formatting. In some cases, text was presented inside embedded images within the flyer. Since the majority of flyers, however, were mostly in text format, OCR[6] was not used and text within images was discarded. The median number of characters, tokens, and sentences for flyers are 2106, 424, and 72 respectively.

## 3.2 Training Data Transformation

In previous work, we have created a tool used to annotate HTML flyers and evaluated the NER task on a subset of 800 manually annotated flyers. However, the manual annotation proved a laborious task (the same listing attribute typically appears multiple times in the document) and resulted in moderate inter-annotator agreement. In this work, instead of manually annotating the full set of 2,269 flyers, we used listing data entered by professional data en-

[3]© BrokerSavant Inc.

[4]PDFs were converted to HTML using the PDFTOHTML conversion program `http://pdftohtml.sourceforge.net/`. While the open-source tool occasionally misaligned text, performance was satisfactory and the use of more accurate commercial PDF-to-HTML5 conversion tool was deemed unnecessary.

[5]Document Object Model.

[6]Optical Character Recognition.

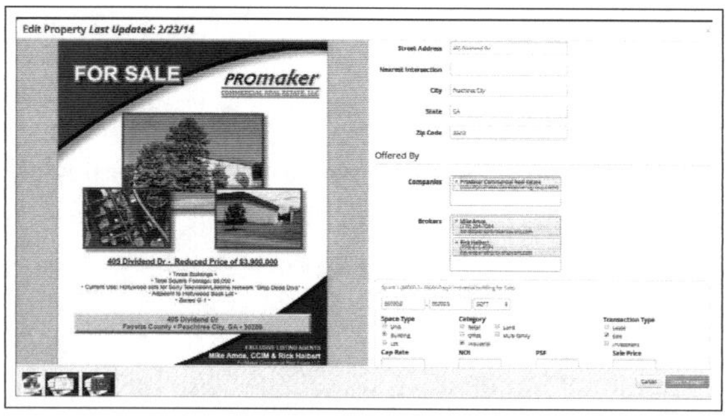

Figure 2: An example of a commercial real estate flyer and manually entered listing information © ProMaker Commercial Real Estate LLC, © BrokerSavant Inc.

try staff employed by the listing service[7]. Figure 2 shows an example of a real estate flyer and the corresponding manually entered listing data.

To generate a dataset for the text categorization tasks we assigned the list of manually entered labels for transaction and property types to each flyer. For example, the flyer from Figure 2 was assigned to transaction type *sale* and property type *industrial*.

To generate annotated data for the NER task, we had to convert the stand-alone listing information to annotated text in which each occurrence of the field values was marked with the corresponding entity type via string matching. The manually entered listing data, however, introduced some text variations and did not always match the text in the corresponding flyer. For example, the same street and intersection address could be expressed in a variety of ways (e.g. *'Westpark Drive and Main Street' vs 'Westpark Dr & Main St'; '123 North Main Road' vs '123 N Main'*, etc.). Similarly, broker names, phones, and company names could have a variety of alternative representations (e.g. *'Michael R. Smith' vs 'Mike Smith CCIM'; 'Lee and Associates' vs 'Lee & Associates of IL LLC'; '773-777-0000 ext 102' vs '773.777.0000x102'*, etc.). Lastly, space size information was always entered in square feet, while at the same time it could be expressed as both square feet and acres (with various precision points) in the corresponding flyer (e.g. *53796 sf, 1.235 acres, 1.23 acres*, etc.).

To account for the various ways in which an attribute value can be expressed in the text we hand-crafted a small set of rules and regular expressions that allowed us to find most of its alternative representations. In some cases, however, the listing value was not found in the corresponding flyer text. In the case of such a discrepancy, the flyer was simply discarded from the training set used for the corresponding named entity type. Such discrepancies could occur for several reasons. In some cases, the manually hand-crafted rules and regular expressions did not cover all possible variants in which the value could be expressed. On occasion, the text containing the attribute value was in image format (inside embedded images). We also noted a few instances of incorrectly entered manual data. As a result, only a portion of the training data (a total of 1,361 flyers) was used for the training of individual named entity types. We were able to automatically annotate 878 flyers used for training the address named entity recognizer (street or intersection, city, state, zip), 1145 flyers used for training the broker information named entity recognizer (broker name, phone, email, company) and 1242 flyers for training the space named entity recognizer (size and space type).

### 3.3 Data Pre-processing

As mentioned earlier, all flyers (PDF and HTML) were converted to a common format (HTML). An HTML parser was then used to create a text representation of the flyer. The text was tokenized and tokens were normalized (all tokens were converted to lower case and digits were converted to a common format).

As noted previously, data entry staff were able to quickly spot listing attributes of interest solely because of their visual characteristics. To account for such visual characteristics we included typographic and other visual features associated with tokens or text chunks for both the text categorization and NER tasks. Typographic and visual features were based on the computed HTML style attributes for each DOM element containing text.

Computing the HTML style attributes is a complex task since they are typically defined by a combination of CSS[8] files, in-lined HTML style attributes, and browser defaults. The complexities of style definition, inheritance, and overwriting are handled by

[7] © BrokerSavant Inc.

[8] Cascading Style Sheets.

browsers[9]. We used the Chrome browser to dynamically compute the style of each DOM element and output it as inline style attributes. To achieve this we programmatically inserted a javascript snippet that inlines the computed style and saves the new version of the HTML on the local file system utilizing the HTML5 *saveAs* interface[10]. We then normalized the style attribute values for font size, RGB color, and Y coordinate as described in the following sections.

### 3.4 Text Categorization

The text categorization task involves labeling all flyers with appropriate transaction types and property types as shown in Table 1. This is a multi-label classification task as in all cases a flyer can have more than one label (e.g. Transaction Type: *sale, lease*; Property Type: *retail, office*).

We applied a supervised Machine Learning approach to the task utilizing Support Vector Machines (SVM) (Vapnik, 2000) using the LibSVM library (Chang and Lin, 2011). SVM was a sensible choice as it has been shown to be one of the top performers on a number of text categorization tasks (Joachims, 1998; Yang and Liu, 1999; Sebastiani, 2002).

Category information such as the transaction type and property type are one of the key pieces of information in a flyer. However, they are not always explicitly mentioned in the flyer and in some cases the data entry person needs to read the full content of the flyer to infer the property type. For example, an *industrial* property might be inferred by a mention of a particular zoning category and description of loading docks; a *retail* property type might be inferred by mentions of retail neighbors (e.g. *Staples, Bed Bath and Beyond*, etc) and traffic counts; an *investment* property type can be inferred by description of NOI (net operating income) and Cap Rates (the ratio between the NOI and capital cost of a property), etc. At the same time, when present, terms indicating the transaction and property types typically appear prominently in large fonts. For example, the property type of the flyer shown on Figure 1 is prominently shown in large font (*Restaurant* indicates *retail* property type). Similarly, the transaction type of the flyer shown on Figure 2 is again prominently displayed in a large font (*For Sale*). The classifiers could then benefit from both the full text of the flyers, combined with some information of the visual prominence of individual words.

We used 'bag-of-words' representation (token unigrams) and modeled the task as a binary classification for each category label. As a term weighting scheme, we first used TF-IDF as one of the most common weighting schemes used for term categorization (Lan et al., 2005; Soucy and Mineau, 2005). This served as a performance baseline. To account for visually prominent characteristics of important document terms we also introduced a term weight that takes into account the relative font size of the term. As a measure of the relative font size, we used the percentile rank of the term font size, compared to all term font sizes in the document. For example, a weight of 0.9 is assigned to terms whose font size is greater than 90% of all tokens within the current document. The font size percentile was then used as a term weighting scheme (instead of TF-IDF). Table 3 summarizes the results of 5-fold cross validation using the full dataset of 2,269 flyers. We used a linear kernel model with the default parameters.

| | | TF-IDF | Font Size Pctl |
|---|---|---|---|
| Property type | P | 79.57 | 85.04 |
| | R | 85.27 | 84.16 |
| | F | 82.32 | **84.6** |
| Transaction type | P | 87.56 | 89.64 |
| | R | 92.87 | 94.60 |
| | F | 90.14 | **92.05** |

Table 3: Results from applying SVM on the task of identifying flyer Property Types (*retail, office, industrial, land, multi-family*) and Transaction Types (*sale, lease, investment*). We used 'bag-of-words' representation (unigrams) applying two different term weight schemes: TF-IDF and the relative percentile rank of the term font size. P=precision, R=recall, F=f1 score.

In both text categorization tasks the Font Size Percentile term weight significantly outperformed the TF-IDF term weight scheme[11].

[9]We attempted to use an HTML renderer from the Cobra java toolkit `http://lobobrowser.org/cobra.jsp` to compute HTML style attributes. However, this renderer produced poor results on our dataset and failed to accurately compute the pixel location of text elements.

[10]`https://github.com/eligrey/FileSaver.js`

[11]The difference is statistically significant with p value $<$ 0.05% using Z-test on two proportions.

### 3.5 Named Entity Recognition

A supervised machine learning approach was then applied to the task of identifying the named entities shown in Table 2. The task was modeled as a **BIO** classification task, classifiers identify the **B**eginning, the **I**nside, and **O**utside of the text segments. We first used a traditional set of text-based features for the classification task. Table 4 lists the various text-based features used. In all cases, a sliding window including the 6 preceding and 6 following tokens was used as features.

| Feature Name | Description |
|---|---|
| Token | A normalized string representation of the token. All tokens were converted to lower case and all digits were converted to a common format. |
| Token Orth | The token orthography. Possible values are lowercase (all token characters are lower case), all capitals (all token characters are upper case), upper initial (the first token character is upper case, the rest are lower case), mixed (any mixture of upper and lower case letters not included in the previous categories). |
| Token Kind | Possible values are word, number, symbol, punctuation. |
| Regex type | Regex-based rules were used to mark chunks as one of 3 regex types: email, phone number, zip code. |
| Gazetteer | Text chunks were marked as possible US cities or states based on US Census Bureau city and state data. www.census.gov/geo/maps-data/data/gazetteer2013.html. |

Table 4: List of text-based features used for the NER task. A sliding window of the 6 preceding and 6 following tokens was used for all features.

As noted previously, data entry staff were able to quickly spot named entities of interest solely because of their visual characteristics. To account for such visual characteristics, we also included visual features associated with text chunks. We used the computed HTML style attributes for each DOM element containing text. Table 5 lists the computed visual features and shows details on how we normalized the style attribute values for font size, RGB color, and Y coordinate.

We then applied SVM on the NER task using the LibSVM library. We again chose SVMs as they have been shown to perform well on a variety of

| Feature Name | Description |
|---|---|
| Font Size | The computed *font-size* attribute of the surrounding HTML DOM element, normalized to 7 basic sizes (*xx-small, x-small, small, medium, large, x-large, xx-large*). |
| Color | The computed *color* attribute of the surrounding HTML DOM element. The RGB values were normalized to a set of 100 basic colors. We converted the RGB values to the YUV color space, and then used Euclidian distance to find the most similar basic color approximating human perception. |
| Y Coordinate | The computed *top* attribute of the surrounding HTML DOM element, i.e. the y-coordinate in pixels. The pixel locations was normalized to 150 pixel increments (roughly 1/5th of the visible screen for the most common screen resolution.) |

Table 5: List of visual features used for the NER task. A sliding window of 6 preceding and 6 following DOM elements were used for all features.

NER tasks, for example (Isozaki and Kazawa, 2002; Takeuchi and Collier, 2002; Mayfield et al., 2003; Ekbal and Bandyopadhyay, 2008). We used a linear kernel model with the default parameters. The multi-class problem was converted to binary problems using the one-vs-others scheme.

As described earlier, we used a portion of the total training data (a total of 1,361 flyers) for the NER tasks. We were able to automatically annotate and use as training data 878 flyers used for address named entities, 1,145 flyers used for broker information named entities, and 1,242 flyers for space named entities. Results were evaluated against the manually entered data for the full test set of 908 flyers. We first used the trained classifiers to find named entities, including their boundaries and types. The predicted named entities were then used to generate listing data as follows. For attributes that have a single value per flyer, we used the predicted named entity of the corresponding type with the highest probability estimate[12]. Single value listing attributes are the fields of the listing address (street or intersection, city, state, zip). Flyers contain a single list-

[12]We used the LibSVM probability estimates for each predicted named entity.

ing, which in turn has a single address. In contrast, broker information and space information are multi-value attributes. A listing is typically represented by multiple brokers and can contain multiple spaces. To construct listing information in the case of multi-value attributes, we used all predicted named entities of the corresponding types. The predicted listing information was then compared to the gold standard of manually entered listing data.

The construction of listing data (for comparison with manually entered data) resulted in a strict performance measure. We consider an answer to be correct only if both the entity boundaries and entity type are accurately predicted. In addition, in the case of single value attributes, only the highest ranking named entity (based on estimated probabilities) was retained.

Results are shown in Table 6. We compared performance of classifiers using only textual features (first 3 columns), versus performance using both textual and visual features (next 3 columns).

| Named Entity | Pt | Rt | Ft | Pv+t | Rv+t | Fv+t |
|---|---|---|---|---|---|---|
| Broker Name | 93.3 | 81.2 | 86.9 | 95.9 | 85.5 | 90.4 |
| Broker Email | 95.6 | 83.6 | 89.2 | 95.8 | 86.5 | 90.9 |
| Broker Phone | 95.4 | 82.6 | 88.6 | 95.7 | 83.3 | 89.1 |
| Company Name | 97.6 | 93.9 | 95.7 | 98.2 | 94.9 | 96.5 |
| Street | 77.0 | 83.4 | 80.1 | 81.4 | 88.6 | 84.9 |
| City | 88.1 | 96.1 | 91.9 | 92.0 | 98.3 | 95.0 |
| State | 93.1 | 98.6 | 95.8 | 95.4 | 99.4 | 97.3 |
| Zip | 92.0 | 86.7 | 89.3 | 96.3 | 86.4 | 91.1 |
| Space Size | 76.8 | 57.9 | 66.0 | 80.1 | 65.7 | 72.2 |
| Space Type | 66.7 | 62.6 | 64.6 | 68.8 | 66.7 | 67.8 |
| OVERALL | 87.7 | 80.3 | 83.8 | 89.7 | 83.5 | 86.5 |

Table 6: Results from applying SVM using the textual features described in Table 4, as well as both the textual and visual features described in Tables 4 and 5. t=textual features only, v+t=visual + textual features, P=Precision, R=Recall, F=F1-score

The addition of visual features significantly[13] increased the overall F1-score from 83.8 to 86.5%. Performance gains are more significant for named entities that are typically visually salient and are otherwise difficult (or impossible) to identify in a text-only version of the flyers. In particular, improvements were most significant for named entities referring to space information. A flyer typically describes multiple spaces, however, only a few of these are considered relevant for the purposes of listing services. For example, the size of an office space is typically entered, while the size of an office associated with a retail or industrial space is typically omitted. Similarly, lot size is included in building and land listings, but excluded when the listing refers to a unit (or multiple units) within a building. Essential space information is usually prominently displayed and as a result easy to identify. Similarly, named entities referring to address information also showed overall significant improvement. As noted earlier, the property address (vs other addresses in the flyer) is typically visually prominent. In both cases, visual features proved useful predictors.

[13]The difference is statistically significant with p value $<$ 0.05% using Z-test on two proportions.

## 4 Discussion

In both the text categorization and NER tasks performance improved significantly over the baseline with the addition of typographic and visual features. However, in both cases, improvements were somewhat moderate (around 3% on average). Further improvement could be achieved by including features that account for additional visual characteristics, such as a measure of how eye-catching or striking the relative font color differences are, the perceived contrast between foreground and background colors, etc.

In future work, we could also add to the overall system an image classification component. It has been noted that occasionally the only indicator of the property type of a flyer is present in embedded flyer images and not present in the flyer text. For example, a number of flyers display images of the inside and outside of restaurants, gas stations, shopping malls and thus specify the property type as *retail* without giving additional textual clues. Similarly, an image of a warehouse, a land parcel, or an areal photo of a shopping center explicitly identify the listing property type.

Lastly, it should be noted that an overall system performance baseline is one that measures the average performance of data entry staff in commercial real estate listing services. However, the terms and conditions of most listing services prohibit gathering and using data for such purposes. We were able to collect a very small set of listings (100 listings) from several listing services[14] and evaluate the precision of a limited set of listing fields. We compared the values of manually entered listing fields against the associated flyer (considered to be the gold standard). The precision of property type, transaction type, space type, and space size was measured as 97%, 79%, 72%, and 73% respectively. While results are not conclusive, this preliminary evaluation suggests that machine learning could achieve performance on par with the performance of manual data entry.

## 5 Related Work

A number of studies survey and compare term weighting schemes and feature selection methods for text categorization, for example (Salton and Buckley, 1988; Yang and Pedersen, 1997; Debole and Sebastiani, 2004; Soucy and Mineau, 2005; Lan et al., 2005; Lan et al., 2009). They describe supervised and traditional term weighting schemes. All, however, are only considering the textual information in documents such as the term frequency, the collection frequency, combined with normalization factors, various information theory functions and statistics metrics.

A number of term weighting schemes have been suggested for web retrieval and classification that rely on the HTML DOM structure. (Cutler et al., 1997; Cutler et al., 1999; Riboni, 2002; Kwon and Lee, 2000). The idea is that terms appearing in different HTML elements of a document may have different significance in identifying the document (e.g. terms in HTML titles and headings vs HTML body). In our dataset, however, visually salient information does not fall into any distinctive HTML element type. Instead all text is typically presented in *div* elements whose style characteristics are defined by a number of css descriptors complicated by external css files, css inlining, style inheritance, and browser defaults.

Nadeau and Satoshi (2007) present a survey of NER and describe the feature space of NER research. While they mention multi-media NER in the context of video/text processing, all described features/approaches focus only on textual representation.

The literature on Information Extraction from HTML resources is dominated by various approaches based on wrapper induction (Kushmerick, 1997; Kushmerick, 2000). Wrapper inductions rely on common HTML structure (based on the HTML DOM) and formatting features to extract structured information from similarly formatted HTML pages. This approach, however, is not applicable to the genres of marketing materials (PDF and HTML) since they typically do not share any common structure that can be used to identify relevant named entities. Laender et al. (2002) present a survey of data extraction techniques and tools from structured or semi-structured web resources.

Cai et al. (2003) present a vision-based segmentation algorithm of web pages that uses HTML layout features and attempts to partition the page at the semantic level. In (Burget and Rudolfova, 2009) authors propose web-page block classification based on visual features. Yang and Zhang (2001) build a content tree of HTML documents based on *visual consistency* inferred semantics. Burget (2007) proposes a layout based information extraction from HTML documents and states that this visual approach is more robust than traditional DOM-based methods.

Changuel et al.(2009a) describe a system for automatically extracting author information from web-pages. They use spatial information based on the depth of the text node in the HTML DOM tree. In (Changuel et al., 2009b) and (Hu et al., 2006), the authors proposed a machine learning method for title extraction and utilize format information such as font size, position, and font weight. In (Zhu et al., 2007) authors use layout information based on font size and weight for NER for automated expense reimbursement.

None of the above studies, however, include computed HTML style attributes (as seen in browsers), and as a result are not applicable to the vast majority of web pages which do not rely on HTML layout tags or DOM-structure to describe style.

## 6 Conclusion

In this study, we generated dataset and features from available commercial real estate flyers and associ-

[14]Due to data usage restrictions we were unable to collect a larger dataset or reveal the identity of the source listing services.

ated manually entered listing data. This approach precludes the need for manual linguistic annotation and instead relies on existing data available from commercial real estate listing services. We modeled the structured data extraction task as text categorization and NER tasks and applied machine learning (SVM) on the automatically generated training datasets. The learned models were then applied on our test set and the predicted values were used to reconstruct listing data matching the manually entered fields. Results suggest that this completely automated approach could substitute or enhance the existing manual data entry workflows.

In addition, we have shown that ubiquitous online formats such as PDF and HTML often exploit the interaction of textual and visual elements. Specifically, in the marketing domain, information is often augmented or conveyed by non-textual features such as positioning, font size, color, and images. We explored the use of novel features capturing the visual characteristics of marketing flyers. Results show that the addition of visual features improved overall performance significantly in the context of text categorization and NER.

## References


Radek Burget and Ivana Rudolfova. 2009. Web page element classification based on visual features. In *Intelligent Information and Database Systems, 2009. ACIIDS 2009. First Asian Conference on*, pages 67–72. IEEE.

Radek Burget. 2007. Layout based information extraction from html documents. In *Document Analysis and Recognition, 2007. ICDAR 2007. Ninth International Conference on*, volume 2, pages 624–628. IEEE.

Deng Cai, Shipeng Yu, Ji-Rong Wen, and Wei-Ying Ma. 2003. Extracting content structure for web pages based on visual representation. In *Web Technologies and Applications*, pages 406–417. Springer.

Chih-Chung Chang and Chih-Jen Lin. 2011. LIBSVM: A library for support vector machines. *ACM Transactions on Intelligent Systems and Technology*, 2:27:1–27:27. Software available at `http://www.csie.ntu.edu.tw/~cjlin/libsvm`.

Sahar Changuel, Nicolas Labroche, and Bernadette Bouchon-Meunier. 2009a. Automatic web pages author extraction. In *Flexible Query Answering Systems*, pages 300–311. Springer.

Sahar Changuel, Nicolas Labroche, and Bernadette Bouchon-Meunier. 2009b. A general learning method for automatic title extraction from html pages. In *Machine Learning and Data Mining in Pattern Recognition*, pages 704–718. Springer.

Michal Cutler, Yungming Shih, and Weiyi Meng. 1997. Using the structure of html documents to improve retrieval. In *USENIX Symposium on Internet Technologies and Systems*, pages 241–252.

Michal Cutler, Hongou Deng, SS Maniccam, and Weiyi Meng. 1999. A new study on using html structures to improve retrieval. In *Tools with Artificial Intelligence, 1999. Proceedings. 11th IEEE International Conference on*, pages 406–409. IEEE.

Franca Debole and Fabrizio Sebastiani. 2004. Supervised term weighting for automated text categorization. In *Text mining and its applications*, pages 81–97. Springer.

Asif Ekbal and Sivaji Bandyopadhyay. 2008. Named entity recognition using support vector machine: A language independent approach. *International Journal of Computer Systems Science & Engineering*, 4(2).

Yunhua Hu, Hang Li, Yunbo Cao, Li Teng, Dmitriy Meyerzon, and Qinghua Zheng. 2006. Automatic extraction of titles from general documents using machine learning. *Information processing & management*, 42(5):1276–1293.

Hideki Isozaki and Hideto Kazawa. 2002. Efficient support vector classifiers for named entity recognition. In *Proceedings of the 19th international conference on Computational linguistics-Volume 1*, pages 1–7. Association for Computational Linguistics.

Thorsten Joachims. 1998. *Text categorization with support vector machines: Learning with many relevant features*. Springer.

Nicholas Kushmerick. 1997. *Wrapper induction for information extraction*. Ph.D. thesis, University of Washington.

Nicholas Kushmerick. 2000. Wrapper induction: Efficiency and expressiveness. *Artificial Intelligence*, 118(1):15–68.

Oh-Woog Kwon and Jong-Hyeok Lee. 2000. Web page classification based on k-nearest neighbor approach. In *Proceedings of the fifth international workshop on on Information retrieval with Asian languages*, pages 9–15. ACM.

Alberto HF Laender, Berthier A Ribeiro-Neto, Altigran S da Silva, and Juliana S Teixeira. 2002. A brief survey of web data extraction tools. *ACM Sigmod Record*, 31(2):84–93.

Man Lan, Chew-Lim Tan, Hwee-Boon Low, and Sam-Yuan Sung. 2005. A comprehensive comparative study on term weighting schemes for text categorization with support vector machines. In *Special interest tracks and posters of the 14th international conference on World Wide Web*, pages 1032–1033. ACM.

Man Lan, Chew Lim Tan, Jian Su, and Yue Lu. 2009. Supervised and traditional term weighting methods for automatic text categorization. *Pattern Analysis and Machine Intelligence, IEEE Transactions on*, 31(4):721–735.

James Mayfield, Paul McNamee, and Christine Piatko. 2003. Named entity recognition using hundreds of thousands of features. In *Proceedings of the seventh conference on Natural language learning at HLT-NAACL 2003-Volume 4*, pages 184–187. Association for Computational Linguistics.

David Nadeau and Satoshi Sekine. 2007. A survey of named entity recognition and classification. *Lingvisticae Investigationes*, 30(1):3–26.

Daniele Riboni. 2002. *Feature selection for web page classification*. na.

Gerard Salton and Christopher Buckley. 1988. Term-weighting approaches in automatic text retrieval. *Information processing & management*, 24(5):513–523.

Fabrizio Sebastiani. 2002. Machine learning in automated text categorization. *ACM computing surveys (CSUR)*, 34(1):1–47.

Pascal Soucy and Guy W Mineau. 2005. Beyond tfidf weighting for text categorization in the vector space model. In *IJCAI*, volume 5, pages 1130–1135.

Koichi Takeuchi and Nigel Collier. 2002. Use of support vector machines in extended named entity recognition. In *proceedings of the 6th conference on Natural language learning-Volume 20*, pages 1–7. Association for Computational Linguistics.

Vladimir Vapnik. 2000. *The nature of statistical learning theory*. springer.

Yiming Yang and Xin Liu. 1999. A re-examination of text categorization methods. In *Proceedings of the 22nd annual international ACM SIGIR conference on Research and development in information retrieval*, pages 42–49. ACM.

Yiming Yang and Jan O Pedersen. 1997. A comparative study on feature selection in text categorization. In *ICML*, volume 97, pages 412–420.

Yudong Yang and HongJiang Zhang. 2001. Html page analysis based on visual cues. In *Document Analysis and Recognition, 2001. Proceedings. Sixth International Conference on*, pages 859–864. IEEE.

Guangyu Zhu, Timothy J Bethea, and Vikas Krishna. 2007. Extracting relevant named entities for automated expense reimbursement. In *Proceedings of the 13th ACM SIGKDD international conference on Knowledge discovery and data mining*, pages 1004–1012. ACM.

# Multi-Target Machine Translation with Multi-Synchronous Context-free Grammars

**Graham Neubig, Philip Arthur, Kevin Duh**
Graduate School of Information Science
Nara Institute of Science and Technology
8916-5 Takayama-cho, Ikoma-shi, Nara, Japan
{neubig,philip.arthur.om0,kevinduh}@is.naist.jp

## Abstract

We propose a method for simultaneously translating from a single source language to multiple target languages T1, T2, etc. The motivation behind this method is that if we only have a weak language model for T1 and translations in T1 and T2 are associated, we can use the information from a strong language model over T2 to disambiguate the translations in T1, providing better translation results. As a specific framework to realize multi-target translation, we expand the formalism of synchronous context-free grammars to handle multiple targets, and describe methods for rule extraction, scoring, pruning, and search with these models. Experiments find that multi-target translation with a strong language model in a similar second target language can provide gains of up to 0.8-1.5 BLEU points.[1]

## 1 Introduction

In statistical machine translation (SMT), the great majority of work focuses on translation of a single language pair, from the source $F$ to the target $E$. However, in many actual translation situations, identical documents are translated not from one language to another, but between a large number of different languages. Examples of this abound in commercial translation, and prominent open data sets used widely by the MT community include UN documents in 6 languages (Eisele and Chen, 2010), European Parliament Proceedings in 21 languages (Koehn, 2005), and video subtitles on TED in as many as 50 languages (Cettolo et al., 2012).

[1]Code and data to replicate the experiments can be found at http://phontron.com/project/naacl2015

Figure 1: An example of multi-target translation, where a second target language is used to assess the quality of the first target language.

However, despite this abundance of multilingual data, there have been few attempts to take advantage of it. One exception is the *multi-source* SMT method of Och and Ney (2001), which assumes a situation where we have multiple source sentences, and would like to combine the translations from these sentences to create a better, single target translation.

In this paper, we propose a framework of *multi-target* SMT. In multi-target translation, we translate $F$ to not a single target $E$, but to a set of sentences $\mathcal{E} = \langle E_1, E_2, \ldots, E_{|\mathcal{E}|} \rangle$ in multiple target languages (which we will abbreviate T1, T2, etc.). This, in a way, can be viewed as the automated version of the multi-lingual dissemination of content performed by human translators when creating data for the UN, EuroParl, or TED corpora mentioned above.

But what, one might ask, do we expect to gain by generating multiple target sentences at the same time? An illustrative example in Figure 1 shows three potential Chinese T1 translations for an Arabic input sentence. If an English speaker was asked to simply choose one of the Chinese translations, they



*Human Language Technologies: The 2015 Annual Conference of the North American Chapter of the ACL*, pages 293–302,
Denver, Colorado, May 31 – June 5, 2015. 

likely could not decide which is correct. However, if they were additionally given English T2 translations corresponding to each of the Chinese translations, they could easily choose the third as the most natural, even without knowing a word of Chinese.

Translating this into MT terminology, this is equivalent to generating two corresponding target sentences $E_1$ and $E_2$, and using the naturalness of $E_2$ to help decide which $E_1$ to generate. Language models (LMs) are the traditional tool for assessing the naturalness of sentences, and it is widely known that larger and stronger LMs greatly help translation (Brants et al., 2007). It is easy to think of a situation where we can only create a weak LM for T1, but much more easily create a strong LM for T2. For example, T1 could be an under-resourced language, or a new entrant to the EU or UN.

As a concrete method to realize multi-target translation, we build upon Chiang (2007)'s framework of synchronous context free grammars (SCFGs), which we first overview in Section 2.[2] SCFGs are an extension of context-free grammars that define rules that synchronously generate source and target strings $F$ and $E$. We expand this to a new formalism of multi-synchronous CFGs (MSCFGs, Section 3) that simultaneously generate not just two, but an arbitrary number of strings $\langle F, E_1, E_2, \ldots, E_N\rangle$. We describe how to acquire these from data (Section 4), and how to perform search, including calculation of LM probabilities over multiple target language strings (Section 5).

To evaluate the effectiveness of multi-target translation in the context of having a strong T2 LM to help with T1 translation, we perform experiments on translation of United Nations documents (Section 6). These experiments, and our subsequent analysis, show that the framework of multi-target translation can, indeed, provide significant gains in accuracy (of up to 1.5 BLEU points), particularly when the two target languages in question are similar.

## 2 Synchronous Context-Free Grammars

We first briefly cover SCFGs, which are widely used in MT, most notably in the framework of hierarchical phrase-based translation (Hiero; Chiang (2007)). SCFGs are based on synchronous rules defined as tuples of $X$, $\gamma$, and $\alpha$

$$X \rightarrow \langle \gamma, \alpha \rangle, \tag{1}$$

where $X$ is the head of the rule, and $\gamma$ and $\alpha$ are strings of terminals and indexed non-terminals on the source and target side of the grammar. Each non-terminal on the right side is indexed, with non-terminals with identical indices corresponding to each-other. For example, a synchronous rule could take the form of[3]

$$X \rightarrow \langle X_0 \text{ of the } X_1,\ X_0 \text{ des } X_1 \rangle. \tag{2}$$

By simply generating from this grammar, it is possible to generate a string in two languages synchronously, as shown in Figure 2 (a). When we are already given a source side sentence and would like to using an SCFG to generate the translation, we find all rules that match the source side and perform search using the CKY+ algorithm (Chappelier et al., 1998). When we would additionally like to consider

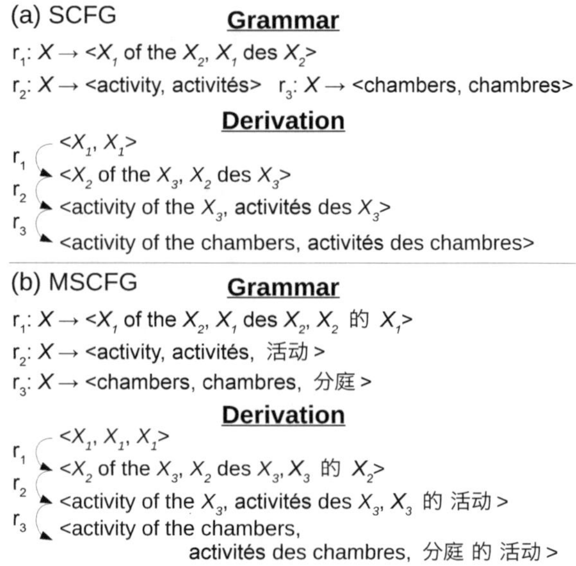


Figure 2: Synchronous grammars and derivations using (a) standard SCFGs and (b) the proposed MSCFGs.

[2]One could also consider a multi-target formulation of phrase-based translation (Koehn et al., 2003), but generating multiple targets while considering reordering in phrase-based search is not trivial. We leave this to future work.

[3]It is possible to use symbols other than $X$ (e.g.: $NP$, $VP$) to restrict rule application to follow grammatical structure, but we focus on the case with a single non-terminal.

an LM, as is standard in SMT, we perform a modified version of CKY+ that approximately explores the search space using a method such as cube pruning (Chiang, 2007).

## 3 Multi-Synchronous CFGs

In this section, we present the basic formalism that will drive our attempts at multi-target translation. Specifically, we propose a generalization of SCFGs, which we will call multi-synchronous context free grammars (MSCFGs). In an MSCFG, the elementary structures are rewrite rules containing not a source and target, but an arbitrary number $M$ of strings

$$X \rightarrow \langle \eta_1, ..., \eta_M \rangle, \quad (3)$$

where $X$ is the head of the rule and $\eta_m$ is a string of terminal and non-terminal symbols.[4] In this paper, for notational convenience, we will use a specialized version of Equation 3 in which we define a single $\gamma$ as the source side string, and $\alpha_1, ...\alpha_N$ as an arbitrary number $N$ of target side strings:

$$X \rightarrow \langle \gamma, \alpha_1, ..., \alpha_N \rangle. \quad (4)$$

Therefore, at each derivation step, one non-terminal in $\gamma$ is chosen and all the nonterminals with same indices in $\alpha_1, ..., \alpha_N$ will be rewritten using a single rule. Figure 2 (b) gives an example of generating sentences in three languages using MSCFGs. Translation can also be performed by using the CKY+ algorithm to parse the source side, and then generate targets in not one, but multiple languages.

It can be noted that this formalism is a relatively simple expansion of standard SCFGs. However, the additional targets require non-trivial modifications to the standard training and search processes, which we discuss in the following sections.

## 4 Training Multi-Synchronous Grammars

This section describes how, given a set of parallel sentences in $N$ languages, we can create translation models (TMs) using MSCFGs.

[4]We will also make the restriction that indices are linear and non-deleting, indicating that each non-terminal index present in any of the strings will appear exactly once in all of the strings. Thus, MSCFGs can also be thought of as a subset of the "generalized multi-text grammars" of Melamed et al. (2004).

### 4.1 SCFG Rule Extraction

First, we briefly outline rule extraction for SCFGs in the standard two-language case, as proposed by Chiang (2007). We first start by preparing two corpora in the source and target language, $\mathcal{F}$ and $\mathcal{E}$, and obtaining word alignments for each sentence automatically, using a technique such as the IBM models implemented by GIZA++ (Och and Ney, 2003).

We then extract initial phrases for each sentence. Given a source $f_1^J$, target $e_1^I$, and alignment $A = \{\langle i_1, i'_1 \rangle, \ldots, \langle i_{|A|}, i'_{|A|} \rangle\}$ where $i$ and $i'$ represent indices of aligned words in $F$ and $E$ respectively. First, based on this alignment, we extract all pairs of phrases $BP = \{\langle f_{i_1}^{j_1}, e_{i'_1}^{j'_1} \rangle, \ldots, \langle f_{i_{|BP|}}^{j_{|BP|}}, e_{i'_{|BP|}}^{j'_{|BP|}} \rangle\}$, where $f_{i_1}^{j_1}$ is a substring of $f_1^J$ spanning from $i_1$ to $j_1$, and $e_{i'_1}^{j'_1}$ is analogous for the target side. The criterion for whether a phrase $\langle f_i^j, e_{i'}^{j'} \rangle$ can be extracted or not is whether there exists at least one alignment in $A$ that falls within the bounds of both $f_i^j$ and $e_{i'}^{j'}$, and no alignments that fall within the bounds of one, but not the other. It is also common to limit the maximum length of phrases to be less than a constant $S$ (in our experiments, 10). The `phrase-extract` algorithm of Och (2002) can be used to extract phrases that meet these criteria.

Next, to create synchronous grammar rules, we cycle through the phrases in $BP$, and extract all potential rules encompassed by this phrase. This is done by finding all sets of 0 or more non-overlapping sub-phrases of initial phrase $\langle f_i^j, e_{i'}^{j'} \rangle$, and replacing them by non-terminals to form rules. In addition, it is common to limit the number of non-terminals to two and not allow consecutive non-terminals on the source side to ensure search efficiency, and limit the number of terminals to limit model size (in our experiments, we set this limit to five).

### 4.2 MSCFG Rule Extraction

In this section, we generalize the rule extraction process in the previous section to accommodate multiple targets. We do so by first independently creating alignments between the source corpus $\mathcal{F}$, and each of $N$ target corpora $\{\mathcal{E}_1, \ldots, \mathcal{E}_N\}$.

Given a particular sentence we now have source $F$, $N$ target strings $\{E_1, \ldots, E_N\}$, and $N$ alignments $\{A_1, \ldots, A_N\}$. We next independently extract initial phrases for each of the $N$ languages using the standard bilingual `phrase-extract` algorithm, yielding initial phrase sets $\{BP_1, \ldots, BP_N\}$. Finally, we convert these bilingual sets of phrases into a single set of multilingual phrases. This can be done by noting that all source phrases $f_i^j$ will be associated with a set of 0 or more phrases in each target language. We define the set of multilingual phrases associated with $f_i^j$ as the cross product of these sets. In other words, if $f_i^j$ is associated with 2 phrases in T1, and 3 phrases in T2, then there will be a total of $2*3 = 6$ phrase triples extracted as associated with $f_i^j$.[5]

Once we have extracted multilingual phrases, the remaining creation of rules is essentially the same as the bilingual case, with sub-phrases being turned into non-terminals for the source and all targets.

### 4.3 Rule Scoring

After we have extracted rules, we assign them feature functions. In traditional SCFGs, given a source and target $\gamma$ and $\alpha_1$, it is standard to calculate the log forward and backward translation probabilities $P(\gamma|\alpha_1)$ and $P(\alpha_1|\gamma)$, log forward and backward lexical translation probabilities $P_{lex}(\gamma|\alpha_1)$ and $P_{lex}(\alpha_1|\gamma)$, a word penalty counting the non-terminals in $\alpha_1$, and a constant phrase penalty of 1.

In our MSCFG formalism, we also add new features regarding the additional targets. Specifically in the case where we have one additional target $\alpha_2$, we add the log translation probabilities $P(\gamma|\alpha_2)$ and $P(\alpha_2|\gamma)$, log lexical probabilities $P_{lex}(\gamma|\alpha_2)$ and $P_{lex}(\alpha_2|\gamma)$, and word penalty for $\alpha_2$. In addition, we add log translation probabilities that consider both targets at the same time $P(\gamma|\alpha_1, \alpha_2)$ and $P(\alpha_1, \alpha_2|\gamma)$. As a result, compared to the 6-feature set in standard SCFGs, an MSCFG rule with two targets will have 13 features.

### 4.4 Rule Table Pruning

In MT, it is standard practice to limit the number of rules used for any particular source $\gamma$ to ensure realistic search times and memory usage. This limit is generally imposed by ordering rules by the phrase probability $P(\alpha_1|\gamma)$ and only using the top few (in our case, 10) for each source $\gamma$. However, in the MSCFG case, this is not so simple. As the previous section mentioned, in the two-target MSCFG, we have a total of three probabilities conditioned on $\gamma$: $P(\alpha_1, \alpha_2|\gamma)$, $P(\alpha_1|\gamma)$, $P(\alpha_2|\gamma)$. As our main motivation for multi-target translation is to use T2 to help translation of T1, we can assume that the final of these three probabilities, which only concerns T2, is of less use. Thus, we propose two ways for pruning the rule table based on the former two.

The first method, which we will call *T1+T2*, is based on $P(\alpha_1, \alpha_2|\gamma)$. The use of this probability is straightforward, as it is possible to simply list the top rules based on this probability. However, this method also has a significant drawback. If we are mainly interested in accurate generation of the T1 sentence, there is a possibility that the addition of the T2 phrase $\alpha_2$ will fragment the probabilities for $\alpha_1$. This is particularly true when the source and T1 are similar, while T2 is a very different language. For example, in the case of a source of English, T1 of French, and T2 of Chinese, translations of English to French will have much less variation than translastions of English to Chinese, due to less freedom of translation and higher alignment accuracy between English and French. In this situation, the pruned model will have a variety of translations in T2, but almost no variety in T1, which is not conducive to translating T1 accurately.

As a potential solution to this problem, we also test a *T1* method, which is designed to maintain variety of T1 translations for each rule. In order to do so, we first list the top $\alpha_1$ candidates based only on the $P(\alpha_1|\gamma)$ probability. Each $\alpha_1$ will be associated with one or more $\alpha_2$ rule, and thus we choose the $\alpha_2$ resulting in the highest joint probability of the two targets $P(\alpha_1, \alpha_2|\gamma)$ as the representative rule for $\alpha_1$. This pruning method has the potential advantage of increasing the variety in the T1 translations, but also has the potential disadvantage of artificially reducing genuine variety in T2. We examine which method is more effective in the experiments section.

## 5 Search with Multiple LMs

LMs computes the probability $P(E)$ of observing a particular target sentence, and are a fundamental

[5]Taking the cross-product here has the potential for combinatorial explosion as more languages are added, but in our current experiments with two target languages this did not cause significant problems, and we took no preventative measures.

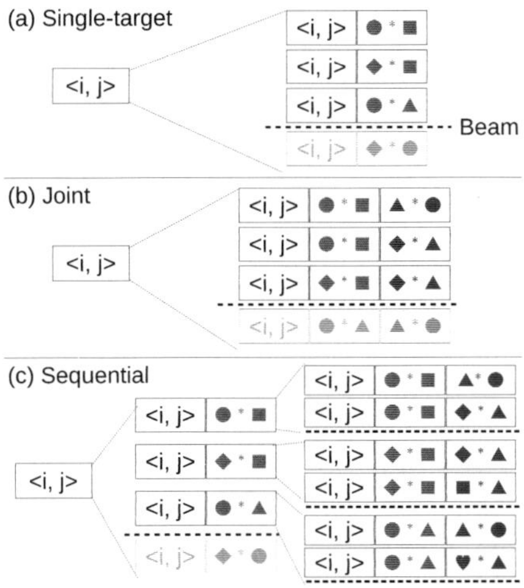


Figure 3: State splitting with (a) one LM, (b) two LMs with joint search, and (c) two LMs with sequential search, where T1 and T2 are the first (red) and second (blue) columns respectively.

part of both standard SMT systems and the proposed method. Unlike the other features assigned to rules in Section 4.3, LM probabilities are non-local features, and cannot be decomposed over rules. In case of $n$-gram LMs, this probability is defined as:

$$P_{LM}(E) = \prod_{i=1}^{|E|+1} p(e_i|e_{i-n+1}, \dots, e_{i-2}, e_{i-1}) \quad (5)$$

where the probabilities of the next word $e_i$ depend on the previous $n-1$ words.

When not considering an LM, it is possible to efficiently find the best translation for an input sentence $f_1^J$ using the CKY+ algorithm, which performs dynamic programming remembering the most probable translation rule for each state corresponding to source span $f_i^j$. When using an LM, it is further necessary split each state corresponding to $f_i^j$ to distinguish between not only the span, but also the strings of $n-1$ boundary words on the left and right side of the translation hypothesis, as illustrated in Figure 3 (a). As this expands the search space to an intractable size, this space is further reduced based on a limit on expanded edges (the pop limit), or total states per span (the stack limit), through a procedure such as cube pruning (Chiang, 2007).

In a multi-target translation situation with one LM for each target, managing the LM state becomes more involved, as we need to keep track of the $n-1$ boundary words for both targets. We propose two methods for handling this problem.

The first method, which we will dub the *joint* search method, is based on consecutively expanding the LM states of both T1 and T2. As shown in the illustration in Figure 3 (b), this means that each post-split search state will be annotated with boundary words from both targets. This is a natural and simple expansion of the standard search algorithm, simply using a more complicated representation of the LM state. On the other hand, because the new state space is the cross-product of all sets of boundary words in the two languages, the search space becomes significantly larger, with the side-effect of reducing the diversity of T1 translations for the same beam size. For example, in the figure, it can be seen that despite the fact that 3 hypotheses have been expanded, we only have 2 unique T1 LM states.

Our second method, which we will dub the *sequential* search method, first expands the state space of T1, then later expands the search space of T2. This procedure can be found in Figure 3 (c). It can be seen that by first expanding the T1 space we ensure diversity in the T1 search space, then additionally expand the states necessary for scoring with the T2 LM. On the other hand, if the T2 LM is important for creating high-quality translations, it is possible that the first pass of search will be less accurate and prune important hypotheses.

## 6 Experiments

### 6.1 Experimental Setup

We evaluate the proposed multi-target translation method through translation experiments on the MultiUN corpus (Eisele and Chen, 2010). We choose this corpus as it contains a large number of parallel documents in Arabic (ar), English (en), Spanish (es), French (fr), Russian (ru), and Chinese (zh), languages with varying degrees of similarity. We use English as our source sentence in all cases, as it is the most common actual source language for UN documents. To prepare the data, we first deduplicate the sentences in the corpus, then hold out 1,500 sentences each for tuning and test. In our basic training setup, we use 100k sentences for training both the TM and the T1 LM. This somewhat small number is to simulate a T1 language that has relatively few resources. For the T2 language, we assume we have a large language model trained on all of the UN data, amounting to 3.5M sentences total.

As a decoder, we use the Travatar (Neubig, 2013) toolkit, and implement all necessary extensions to the decoder and rule extraction code to allow for multiple targets. Unless otherwise specified, we use joint search with a pop limit of 2,000, and T1 rule pruning with a limit of 10 rules per source rule. BLEU is used for both tuning and evaluating all models. In particular, we tune and evaluate all models based on T1 BLEU, simulating a situation similar to that in the introduction, where we want to use a large LM in T2 to help translation in T1. In order to control for optimizer instability, we follow Clark et al. (2011)'s recommendation of performing tuning 3 times, and reporting the average of the runs along with statistical significance obtained by pairwise bootstrap resampling (Koehn, 2004).

### 6.2 Main Experimental Results

In this section we first perform experiments to investigate the effectiveness of the overall framework of multi-target translation.

We assess four models, starting with standard single-target SCFGs and moving gradually towards our full MSCFG model:

**SCFG:** A standard SCFG grammar with only the source and T1.

**SCFG+T2Al:** SCFG constrained during rule extraction to only extract rules that also match the T2 alignments. This will help measure the effect, if any, of being limited by T2 alignments in rule extraction.

**MSCFG-T2LM:** The MSCFG, without using the T2 LM. Compared to SCFG+T2Al, this will examine the effect caused by adding T2 rules in scoring (Section 4.3) and pruning (Section 4.4) the rule table.

**MSCFG:** The full MSCFG model with the T2 LM.

The result of experiments using all five languages as T1, and the remaining four languages as T2 for all of these methods is shown in Table 1.

| T1 | T2 | SCFG | SCFG +T2Al | MSCFG -T2LM | MSCFG |
|---|---|---|---|---|---|
| ar | es | 24.97 | 25.11 | 24.79 | †**25.19** |
| | fr | | 24.70 | 24.73 | 24.89 |
| | ru | | 24.54 | 24.62 | 24.48 |
| | zh | | 24.21 | 24.16 | 23.95 |
| es | ar | 42.15 | 41.73 | 41.21 | 41.22 |
| | fr | | 42.20 | 41.84 | ‡**42.91** |
| | ru | | 41.62 | 41.90 | 41.98 |
| | zh | | 41.80 | 41.61 | 41.65 |
| fr | ar | 37.21 | 37.26 | 37.03 | 37.41 |
| | es | | 37.25 | 37.22 | ‡**38.67** |
| | ru | | 37.11 | 37.31 | ‡37.79 |
| | zh | | 37.14 | 37.29 | 36.99 |
| ru | ar | 26.20 | 25.91 | 25.67 | 25.86 |
| | es | | 26.17 | 26.01 | †**26.45** |
| | fr | | 26.07 | 25.77 | 26.29 |
| | zh | | 25.53 | 25.57 | 25.52 |
| zh | ar | 21.16 | 21.06 | 20.85 | 20.84 |
| | es | | 21.39 | 21.31 | 21.33 |
| | fr | | †**21.60** | 21.28 | 21.16 |
| | ru | | 20.50 | 21.15 | 21.14 |

Table 1: Results for standard Hiero (SCFG), SCFG with T2 extraction constraints (SCFG+T2Al), a multi-SCFG minus the T2 LM (MSCFG-T2LM), and full multi-target translation (MSCFG). Bold indicates the highest BLEU score, and daggers indicate statistically significant gains over SCFG (†: $p < 0.05$, ‡: $p < 0.01$)

First, looking at the overall results, we can see that MSCFGs with one of the choices of T2 tends to outperform SCFG for all instances of T1. In particular, the gain for the full MSCFG model is large for the cases where the two target languages are French and Spanish, with en-fr/es achieving a gain of 1.46 BLEU points, and en-es/fr achieving a gain of 0.76 BLEU points over the baseline SCFG. This is followed by Arabic, Russian and Chinese, which all saw small gains of less than 0.3 when using Spanish as T2, with no significant difference for Chinese. This result indicates that multi-target MT has the potential to provide gains in T1 accuracy, particularly in cases where the languages involved are similar to each other.

It should be noted however, that positive results are sensitive to the languages chosen for T1 and T2,

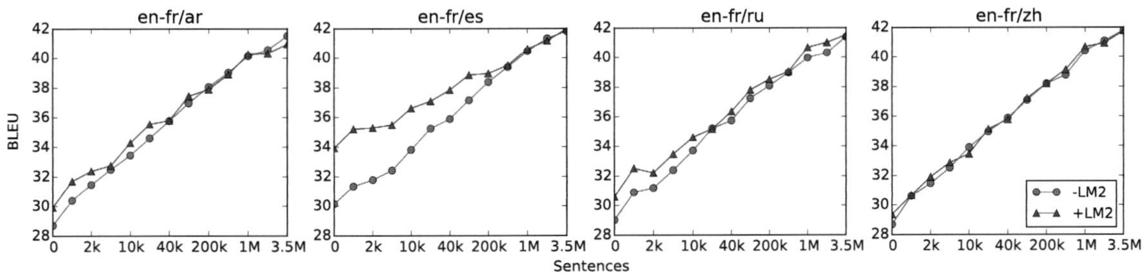


Figure 4: BLEU scores for different T1 LM sizes without (-LM2) or with (+LM2) an LM for the second target.

| T2 | SCFG | +T2Al |
|---|---|---|
| ar | 223M | 46.5M |
| es | | 134M |
| ru | | 70.8M |
| zh | | 26.0M |

Table 2: Differences in rule table sizes for a T1 of French.

and in the cases involving Russian or Chinese, there is often even a drop in accuracy compared to the baseline SCFG. The reason for this can be seen by examining the results for SCFG+T2Al and MSCFG-T2LM. It can be seen that in the cases where there is an overall decrease in accuracy, this decrease can generally be attributed to a decrease when going from SCFG to SCFG+T2Al (indicating that rule extraction suffers from the additional constraints imposed by T2), or a decrease from SCFG+T2Al to MSCFG-LM2 (indicating that rule extraction suffers from fragmentation of the T1 translations by adding the T2 translation). On the other hand, we can see that in the majority of cases, going from MSCFG-LM2 to MSCFG results in at least a small gain in accuracy, indicating that a T2 LM is generally useful, after discounting any negative effects caused by a change in the rule table.

In Table 2 we show additional statistics illustrating the effect of adding a second language on the number of rules that can be extracted. From these results, we can see that all languages reduce the number of rules extracted, with the reduction being greater for languages with a larger difference from English and French, providing a convincing explanation for the drop in accuracy observed between these two settings.

### 6.3 Effect of T1 Language Model Strength

The motivation for multi-target translation stated in the introduction was that information about T2 may give us hints about the appropriate translation in T1. It is also a reasonable assumption that the less information we have about T1, the more valuable the information about T2 may be. To test this hypothesis, we next show results of experiments in which we vary the size of the training data for the T1 LM in intervals from 0 to 3.5M sentences. For T2, we either use no LM (MSCFG-T2LM) or an LM trained on 3.5M sentences (MSCFG). The results for when French is used as T1 are shown in Figure 4.

From these results, we can see that this hypothesis is correct. When no T1 LM is used, we generally see some gain in translation accuracy by introducing a strong T2 LM, with the exception of Chinese, which never provides a benefit. When using Spanish as T2, this benefit continues even with a relatively strong T1 LM, with the gap closing after we have 400k sentences of data. For Arabic and Russian, on the other hand, the gap closes rather quickly, with consistent gains only being found up to about 20-40k sentences. In general this indicates that the more informative the T2 LM is in general, the more T1 data will be required before the T2 LM is no longer able to provide additional gains.

### 6.4 Effect of Rule Pruning

Next we examine the effect of the rule pruning methods explained in Section 4.4. We set T1 to either French or Chinese, and use either the naive pruning criterion using T1+T2, or the criterion that picks the top translations in T1 along with their most probable T2 translation. Like previous experiments, we

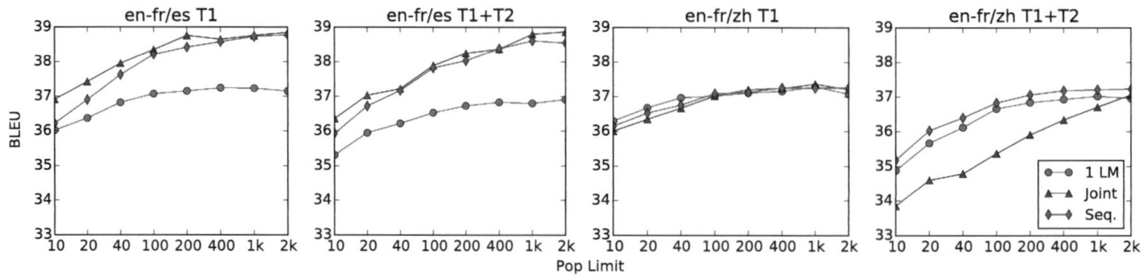


Figure 5: The impact of search on accuracy. Lines indicate a single LM (1 LM), two LMs with joint search (Joint) or two LMs with sequential search (Seq.) for various pop limits and pruning criteria.

| | T1=fr | | T1=zh | |
|---|---|---|---|---|
| T2 | T1+T2 | T1 | T1+T2 | T1 |
| ar | 36.21 | **37.41** | 20.35 | **20.84** |
| es | **38.68** | 38.67 | 20.73 | **21.33** |
| fr | - | | 20.49 | **21.16** |
| ru | 37.14 | **37.79** | 19.87 | **21.14** |
| zh | 36.41 | **36.99** | - | |

Table 3: BLEU scores by pruning criterion. Columns indicate T1 (fr or zh) and the pruning criterion (T1+T2 joint probability, or T1 probability plus max T2). Rows indicate T2.

use the top 10 rules for any particular $F$.

Results are shown in Table 3. From these results we can see that in almost all cases, pruning using T1 achieves better results. This indicates the veracity of the observation in Section 4.4 that considering multiple T2 for a particular T1 causes fragmentation of TM probabilities, and that this has a significant effect on translation results. Interestingly, the one exception to this trend is T1 of French and T2 of Spanish, indicating that with sufficiently similar languages, the fragmentation due to the introduction of T2 translations may not be as much of a problem.

It should be noted that in this section, we are using the joint search algorithm, and the interaction between search and pruning will be examined more completely in the following section.

### 6.5 Effect of Search

Next we examine the effect of the search algorithms suggested in Section 5. To do so, we perform experiments where we vary the search algorithm (joint or sequential), the TM pruning criterion (T1 or T1+T2), and the pop limit. For sequential search, we set the pop limit of T2 to be 10, as this value did not have a large effect on results. For reference, we also show results when using no T2 LM.

From the BLEU results shown in Figure 5, we can see that the best search algorithm depends on the pruning criterion and language pair.[6] In general, when trimming using T1, we achieve better results using joint search, indicating that maintaining T1 variety in the TM is enough to maintain search accuracy. On the other hand, when using the T1+T2 pruned model when T2 is Chinese, sequential search is better. This shows that in cases where there are large amounts of ambiguity introduced by T2, sequential search effectively maintains necessary T1 variety before expanding the T2 search space. As there is no general conclusion, an interesting direction for future work is search algorithms that can combine the advantages of these two approaches.

## 7 Related Work

While there is very little previous work on multi-target translation, there is one line of work by González and Casacuberta (2006) and Pérez et al. (2007), which adapts a WFST-based model to output multiple targets. However, this purely monotonic method is unable to perform non-local reordering, and thus is not applicable most language pairs. It is also motivated by efficiency concerns, as opposed to this work's objective of learning from a T2 language.

Factored machine translation (Koehn and Hoang, 2007) is also an example where an LM over a second

[6]Results for model score, a more direct measure of search errors, were largely similar.

stream of factors (for example POS tags, classes, or lemmas) has been shown to increase accuracy. These factors are limited, however, by the strong constraint of being associated with a single word and not allowing reordering, and thus are not applicable to our setting of using multiple languages.

There has also been work on using multiple languages to improve the quality of extracted translation lexicons or topic models (Mausam et al., 2009; Baldwin et al., 2010; Mimno et al., 2009). These are not concerned with multi-target translation, but may provide us with useful hints about how to generate more effective multi-target translation models.

## 8 Conclusion

In this paper, we have proposed a method for multi-target translation using a generalization of SCFGs, and proposed methods to learn and perform search over the models. In experiments, we found that these models are effective in the case when a strong LM exists in a second target that is highly related to the first target of interest.

As the overall framework of multi-target translation is broad-reaching, there are a still many challenges left for future work, a few of which we outline here. First, the current framework relies on data that is entirely parallel in all languages of interest. Can we relax this constraint and use comparable data, or apply MSCFGs to pivot translation? Second, we are currently performing alignment independently for each target. Can we improve results by considering all languages available (Lardilleux and Lepage, 2009)? Finally, in this paper we considered the case where we are only interested in T1 accuracy, but optimizing translation accuracy for two or more targets, possibly through the use of multi-metric optimization techniques (Duh et al., 2012) is also an interesting future direction.

## Acknowledgments

The authors thank Taro Watanabe and anonymous reviewers for helpful suggestions. This work was supported in part by JSPS KAKENHI Grant Number 25730136 and the Microsoft CORE project.

## References

Timothy Baldwin, Jonathan Pool, and Susan Colowick. 2010. PanLex and LEXTRACT: Translating all words of all languages of the world. In *Proc. COLING*, pages 37–40.

Thorsten Brants, Ashok C. Popat, Peng Xu, Franz J. Och, and Jeffrey Dean. 2007. Large language models in machine translation. In *Proc. EMNLP*, pages 858–867.

Mauro Cettolo, Christian Girardi, and Marcello Federico. 2012. WIT3: web inventory of transcribed and translated talks. In *Proc. EAMT*, pages 261–268.

Jean-Cédric Chappelier, Martin Rajman, et al. 1998. A generalized CYK algorithm for parsing stochastic CFG. In *TAPD*, pages 133–137.

David Chiang. 2007. Hierarchical phrase-based translation. *Computational Linguistics*, 33(2):201–228.

Jonathan H. Clark, Chris Dyer, Alon Lavie, and Noah A. Smith. 2011. Better hypothesis testing for statistical machine translation: Controlling for optimizer instability. In *Proc. ACL*, pages 176–181.

Kevin Duh, Katsuhito Sudoh, Xianchao Wu, Hajime Tsukada, and Masaaki Nagata. 2012. Learning to translate with multiple objectives. In *Proc. ACL*.

Andreas Eisele and Yu Chen. 2010. MultiUN: A multilingual corpus from United Nation documents. In *Proc. LREC*.

M. Teresa González and Francisco Casacuberta. 2006. Multi-target machine translation using finite-state transducers. In *Proc. of TC-Star Speech to Speech Translation Workshop*, pages 105–110.

Philipp Koehn and Hieu Hoang. 2007. Factored translation models. In *Proc. EMNLP*.

Phillip Koehn, Franz Josef Och, and Daniel Marcu. 2003. Statistical phrase-based translation. In *Proc. HLT*, pages 48–54.

Philipp Koehn. 2004. Statistical significance tests for machine translation evaluation. In *Proc. EMNLP*.

Philipp Koehn. 2005. Europarl: A parallel corpus for statistical machine translation. In *Proc. MT Summit*, pages 79–86.

Adrien Lardilleux and Yves Lepage. 2009. Sampling-based multilingual alignment. In *Proc. RANLP*, pages 214–218.

Mausam, Stephen Soderland, Oren Etzioni, Daniel Weld, Michael Skinner, and Jeff Bilmes. 2009. Compiling a massive, multilingual dictionary via probabilistic inference. In *Proc. ACL*, pages 262–270.

I. Dan Melamed, Giorgio Satta, and Benjamin Wellington. 2004. Generalized multitext grammars. In *Proc. ACL*, pages 661–668.

David Mimno, Hanna M. Wallach, Jason Naradowsky, David A. Smith, and Andrew McCallum. 2009. Polylingual topic models. In *Proc. EMNLP*, pages 880–889.

Graham Neubig. 2013. Travatar: A forest-to-string machine translation engine based on tree transducers. In *Proc. ACL Demo Track*, pages 91–96.

Franz Josef Och and Hermann Ney. 2001. Statistical multi-source translation. In *Proc. MT Summit*, pages 253–258.

Franz Josef Och and Hermann Ney. 2003. A systematic comparison of various statistical alignment models. *Computational Linguistics*, 29(1):19–51.

Franz Josef Och. 2002. *Statistical machine translation: from single-word models to alignment templates*. Ph.D. thesis, RWTH Aachen.

Alicia Pérez, M. Teresa González, M. Inés Torres, and Francisco Casacuberta. 2007. Speech-input multi-target machine translation. In *Proc. WMT*, pages 56–63.

# Sign constraints on feature weights improve a joint model of word segmentation and phonology

**Mark Johnson**
Macquarie University
Sydney, Australia
Mark Johnson@MQ.edu.au

**Joe Pater**
University of Massachusetts, Amherst
Amherst, MA, USA
pater@linguist.umass.edu

**Robert Staubs**
University of Massachusetts, Amherst
Amherst, MA, USA
rstaubs@linguist.umass.edu

**Emmanuel Dupoux**
École des Hautes Etudes
en Sciences Sociales, ENS, CNRS,
Paris, France
emmanuel.dupoux@gmail.com

## Abstract

This paper describes a joint model of word segmentation and phonological alternations, which takes unsegmented utterances as input and infers word segmentations and underlying phonological representations. The model is a Maximum Entropy or log-linear model, which can express a probabilistic version of Optimality Theory (OT; Prince and Smolensky (2004)), a standard phonological framework. The features in our model are inspired by OT's Markedness and Faithfulness constraints. Following the OT principle that such features indicate "violations", we require their weights to be non-positive. We apply our model to a modified version of the Buckeye corpus (Pitt et al., 2007) in which the only phonological alternations are deletions of word-final /d/ and /t/ segments. The model sets a new state-of-the-art for this corpus for word segmentation, identification of underlying forms, and identification of /d/ and /t/ deletions. We also show that the OT-inspired sign constraints on feature weights are crucial for accurate identification of deleted /d/s; without them our model posits approximately 10 times more deleted underlying /d/s than appear in the manually annotated data.

## 1 Introduction

This paper unifies two different strands of research on word segmentation and phonological rule induction. The *word segmentation task* is the task of segmenting utterances represented as sequences of phones into sequences of words. This is an idealisation of the lexicon induction problem, since the resulting words are phonological forms for lexical entries.

In its simplest form, the data for a word segmentation task is obtained by looking up the words of an orthographic transcript (of, say, child-directed speech) in a pronouncing dictionary and concatenating the results. However, this formulation significantly oversimplifies the problem because it assumes that each token of a word type is pronounced identically in the form specified by the pronouncing dictionary (usually its citation form). In reality there is usually a significant amount of pronunciation variation from token to token.

The Buckeye corpus, on which we base our experiments here, contains manually-annotated surface phonetic representations of each word as well as the corresponding underlying form (Pitt et al., 2007). For example, a token of the word "lived" has the underlying form /l.ih.v.d/ and could have the surface form [l.ah.v] (we follow standard phonological convention by writing underlying forms with slashes and surface forms with square brackets, and use the Buckeye transcription format).

There is a large body of work in the phonological literature on inferring phonological rules mapping underlying forms to their surface realisations. While most of this work assumes that the underlying forms are available to the inference procedure, there is work that induces underlying forms as well as the phonological processes that map them to sur-



*Human Language Technologies: The 2015 Annual Conference of the North American Chapter of the ACL*, pages 303–313,
Denver, Colorado, May 31 – June 5, 2015. 

face forms (Eisenstat, 2009; Pater et al., 2012).

We present a model that takes a corpus of unsegmented surface representations of sentences and infers a word segmentation and underlying forms for each hypothesised word. We test this model on data derived from the Buckeye corpus where the only phonological variation consists of word-final /d/ and /t/ deletions, and show that it outperforms a state-of-the-art model that only handles word-final /t/ deletions.

Our model is a MaxEnt or log-linear model, which means that it is formally equivalent to a Harmonic Grammar, which is a continuous version of Optimality Theory (OT) (Smolensky and Legendre, 2005). We use features inspired by OT, and show that sign constraints on feature weights result in models that recover underlying /d/s significantly more accurately than models that don't include such contraints. We present results suggesting that these constraints simplify the search problem that the learner faces.

The rest of this paper is structured as follows. The next section describes related work, including previous work that this paper builds on. Section 3 describes our model, while section 4 explains how we prepared the data, presents our experimental results and investigates the effects of design choices on model performance. Section 5 concludes the paper and discusses possible future directions.

## 2 Background and related work

The *word segmentation task* is the task of segmenting utterances represented as sequences of phones into sequences of words. Elman (1990) introduced the word segmentation task as a simplified form of lexical acquisition, and Brent and Cartwright (1996) and Brent (1999) introduced the *unigram model of word segmentation*, which forms the basis of the model used here. Goldwater et al. (2009) described a non-parametric Bayesian model of word segmentation, and highlighted the importance of contextual dependencies. Johnson (2008) and Johnson and Goldwater (2009) showed that word segmentation accuracy improves when phonotactic constraints on word shapes are incorporated into the model. That model has been extended to also exploit stress cues (Börschinger and Johnson, 2014), the "topics" present in the non-linguistic context (Johnson et al., 2010) and the special properties of function words (Johnson et al., 2014).

Liang and Klein (2009) proposed a simple unigram model of word segmentation much like the original Brent unigram model, and introduced a "word length penalty" to avoid under-segmentation that we also use here. (As Liang et al note, without this the maximum likelihood solution is not to segment utterances at all, but to analyse each utterance as a single word). Berg-Kirkpatrick et al. (2010) extended this model by defining the unigram distribution with a MaxEnt model. The MaxEnt features can capture phonotactic generalisations about possible word shapes, and their model achieves a state-of-the-art word segmentation f-score.

The *phonological learning* task is to learn the phonological mapping from underlying forms to surface forms. Johnson (1984) and Johnson (1992) describe a search procedure for identifying underlying forms and the phonological rules that map them to surface forms given surface forms organised into inflectional paradigms. Goldwater and Johnson (2003) and Goldwater and Johnson (2004) showed how Harmonic Grammar phonological constraint weights (Smolensky and Legendre, 2005) can be learnt using a Maximum Entropy parameter estimation procedure given data consisting of underlying and surface word form pairs. There is now a significant body of work using Maximum Entropy techniques to learn phonological constraint weights (see esp. Hayes and Wilson (2008), as well as the review in Coetzee and Pater (2011)).

Recently there has been work attempting to integrate these two approaches. The word segmentation work generally ignores pronunciation variation by assuming that the input to the learner consists of sequences of citation forms of words, which is highly unrealistic. The phonology learning work has generally assumed that the learner has access to the underlying forms of words, which is also unrealistic.

In the word segmentation area, Elsner et al. (2012) and Elsner et al. (2013) generalise the Goldwater bigram model by assuming that the bigram model generates underlying forms, which a finite state transducer maps to surface forms. While this is an extremely general model, inference in such a model is very challenging, and they restrict attention to transducers where the underlying to surface mapping consists of simple substitutions, so their model cannot handle the deletion phenomena studied here. Börschinger et al. (2013) also generalise the Goldwater bigram model by including an underlying-to-surface mapping, but their mapping only allows word-final underlying /t/ to be deleted, which enables them to use a straight-forward generalisation of Goldwater's Gibbs sampling inference procedure.

In phonology, Eisenstat (2009) and Pater et al. (2012) showed how to generalise a MaxEnt model so it also learns underlying forms as well as MaxEnt phonological constraint weights given surface forms in paradigm format. The vast sociolinguistic literature on /t/-/d/-deletion is surveyed in Coetzee and Pater (2011), together with prior OT and MaxEnt analyses of the phenomena.

## 2.1 The Berg-Kirkpatrick et al. model

This section contains a more technical description of the Berg-Kirkpatrick et al. (2010) MaxEnt unigram model of word segmentation, which our model directly builds on. Our model integrates the MaxEnt unigram word segmentation model of Berg-Kirkpatrick et al. with the MaxEnt phonology models developed by Goldwater and Johnson (2003) and Goldwater and Johnson (2004). Because both kinds of models are MaxEnt models, this integration is fairly easy, and the inference procedure requires optimisation of a fairly straight-forward objective function. We use a customised version of the OWLQN-LBFGS procedure (Andrew and Gao, 2007) that allows us to impose sign constraints on individual feature weights.

As is standard in the word-segmentation literature, the model's input is a sequence of utterances $D = (w_1, \ldots, w_n)$, where each utterance $w_i = (w_{i,1}, \ldots, w_{i,m_i})$ is a sequence of (surface) phones. The Berg-Kirkpatrick et al model is a unigram model, so it defines a probability distribution over possible words $s$, where $s$ is also a sequence of phones. The probability of an utterance $w$ is the sum of the probability of all word sequences that generate it:

$$\mathrm{P}(w \mid \theta) = \sum_{\substack{s_1 \ldots s_\ell \\ \text{s.t.} s_1 \ldots s_\ell = w}} \prod_{j=1}^{\ell} \mathrm{P}(s_j \mid \theta)$$

Berg-Kirkpatrick et al's model of word probabilities $\mathrm{P}(s \mid \theta)$ is a MaxEnt model with parameters $\theta$, where the features $f(s)$ of surface form $s$ are chosen to encourage the model to generalise appropriately over word shapes. While they don't describe their features in complete detail, they include features for each word $s$, features for the prefix and suffix of $s$ and features for the CV skeleton of the prefix and suffix of $s$.

In more detail, $\mathrm{P}(s \mid \theta)$ is a MaxEnt model as follows:

$$\mathrm{P}(s \mid \theta) = \frac{1}{Z} \exp(\theta \cdot f(s)), \text{ where:}$$
$$Z = \sum_{s' \in \mathcal{S}} \exp(\theta \cdot f(s'))$$

The set of possible surface word forms $\mathcal{S}$ is the set of substrings (i.e., sequences of phones) occuring in the training data $D$ that are shorter than a user-specified length bound. We follow Berg-Kirkpatrick in imposing a length bound on possible words; for the Brent corpus the maximum word length is 10 phones, while for the Buckeye corpus the maximum word length is 15 phones (reflecting the fact that words are longer in this adult-directed corpus).

While restricting the set of possible word forms $\mathcal{S}$ to the substrings appearing in $D$ is reasonable for a simple multinomial model like the one in Liang and Klein (2009), it's interesting that this produces good results with a MaxEnt model like Berg-Kirkpatrick et al's, since one might expect such a model would have to learn generalisations about *impossible word shapes* in order to perform well. Because $\mathcal{S}$ only contains a small fraction of the possible phone strings, one might worry that the model would not see enough "impossible words" to learn to distinguish possible words from impossible ones, but the model's good performance suggests this is not the case.[1]

[1]The non-parametric Bayesian approach of Goldwater et al. (2009) and Johnson (2008) can be viewed as setting $\mathcal{S}$ to the set of all possible phone strings (i.e., a possible word can be any string of phones, whether or not it appears in $D$). The success of Berg-Kirkpatrick et al's approach suggests that these non-parametric methods might not be necessary here, i.e., the set of substrings actually occuring in $D$ is "large enough" to enable the model to learn "implicit negative evidence" generalisations about impossible word shapes.

Berg-Kirkpatrick et al follow Liang et al in using maximum likelihood estimation to estimate their model's parameters (Berg-Kirkpatrick et al actually use $L_2$-regularised maximum likelihood estimates). As Liang et al note, it's easy to show that the maximum likelihood segmentation leaves each utterance unsegmented, i.e., each utterance is analysed as a single word. To avoid this, Berg-Kirkpatrick et al follow Liang et al by multiplying the word probabilities by a *word length penalty* term. Thus the likelihood $L_D$ they actually maximise is as shown below:

$$L_D(\theta) = \prod_{i=1}^{n} \mathrm{P}(w_i \mid \theta)$$

$$\mathrm{P}(w \mid \theta) = \sum_{\substack{s_1 \ldots s_\ell \\ \text{s.t.} s_1 \ldots s_\ell = w}} \prod_{j=1}^{\ell} \mathrm{P}(s_j \mid \theta) \exp(-|s_i|^d)$$

where $d$ is a constant chosen to optimise segmentation performance. This means that the model is deficient, i.e., $\sum_{s \in \mathcal{S}} \mathrm{P}(s \mid \theta) < 1$. (Because our model uses a word length penalty in the same way, it too is deficient).

As Figure 1 shows, performance is very sensitive to the word length penalty parameter $d$: the best word segmentation on the Brent corpus is obtained when $d \approx 1.6$, while the best segmentation on the Buckeye corpus is obtained when $d \approx 1.5$. As far as we know there is no principled way to set $d$ in an unsupervised fashion, so this sensitivity to $d$ is perhaps the greatest weakness of this kind of model.

Even so, it's interesting that a unigram model without the kind of inter-word dependencies that Goldwater et al. (2009) argues for can do so well. It's possible that the improvement that Goldwater et al found with the bigram model is because modelling individual bigram dependencies splits the data in a way that reduces overlearning (Börschinger et al., 2012).

## 3 A MaxEnt unigram model of word segmentation and word-final /d/ and /t/ deletion

This section explains how we extend the Berg-Kirkpatrick et al. (2010) model to handle a set $\mathcal{P}$ of phonological processes, where a phonological process $p \in \mathcal{P}$ is a partial, non-deterministic function

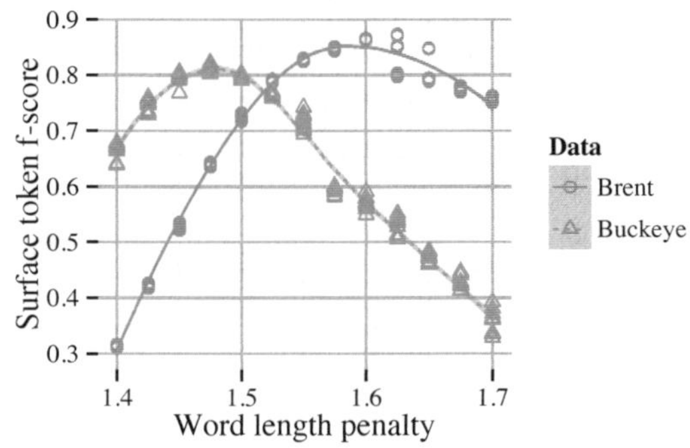


Figure 1: Sensitivity of surface token f-score to word length penalty factor $d$ for the Brent and Buckeye corpora on data with no /d/ or /t/ deletions. Performance is sensitive to the value of the word length penalty $d$, and the optimal value of $d$ depends on the corpus.

mapping underlying forms to surface forms. For example, word-final /t/ deletion is the function mapping underlying underlying forms ending in /t/ to surface forms lacking that final segment.

Our model is also a unigram model, but it defines a distribution over pairs $(s, u)$ of surface/underlying form pairs, where $s$ is a surface form and $u$ is an underlying form. Below we allow this distribution to condition on phonological properties of the neighbouring surface forms.

The set $\mathcal{X}$ of possible $(s, u)$ surface/underlying form pairs is defined as follows. For each surface form $s \in \mathcal{S}$ (the set of length-bounded phone substrings of the data $D$), $(s, s) \in \mathcal{X}$. In addition, if $u \in \mathcal{S}$ and some phonological alternation $p \in \mathcal{P}$ maps $u$ to a surface form $s \in p(u) \in \mathcal{S}$, then $(s, u) \in \mathcal{X}$. That is, we require that potential underlying forms appear as surface substrings somewhere in the data $D$ (which means this model cannot handle e.g., absolute neutralisation).

In the experiments below, we let $\mathcal{P}$ be phonological processes that delete word-final /d/ and /t/ phonemes. Given the Buckeye data, ([l.ih.v], /l.ih.v/), ([l.ih.v], /l.ih.v.d/) and ([l.ih.v], /l.ih.v.t/) are all members of $\mathcal{X}$ (i.e., candidate $(s, u)$ pairs), corresponding to "live", "lived" and the non-word "livet" respectively, where the latter two surface forms are generated by final /d/ and /t/ deletion respectively.

Word-final /d/ and /t/ deletion depends on various aspects of the phonological context, such as whether the following word begins with a consonant or a vowel. Our model handles this dependency by learning a conditional model over surface/underlying form pairs $(s, u) \in \mathcal{X}$ that depends on the phonological context $c$:

$$\begin{aligned} \mathrm{P}(s, u \mid c, \theta) &= \frac{1}{Z_c} \exp(\theta \cdot f(s, u, c)), \text{ where:} \\ Z_c &= \sum_{(s,u) \in \mathcal{X}} \exp(\theta \cdot f(s, u, c)) \end{aligned}$$

In our experiments below, the set of possible contexts is $\mathcal{C} = \{\mathrm{C}, \mathrm{V}, \#\}$, encoding whether the following word begins with a consonant, a vowel or is the end of the utterance respectively. We leave for future research the exploration of other sorts of contextual conditioning. Note that the set $\mathcal{X}$ is the same for all contexts $c$; we show below that restricting attention to just those surface/underlying pairs appearing in the context $c$ degrades the model's performance. In other words, the model benefits from the implicit negative evidence provided by underlying/surface pairs that do not occur in a given context.

We define the probability of a surface form $s \in \mathcal{S}$ in a context $c \in \mathcal{C}$ by marginalising out the underlying form:

$$\mathrm{P}(s \mid c, \theta) = \sum_{u:(s,u) \in \mathcal{X}} \mathrm{P}(s, u \mid c, \theta)$$

We optimise a penalised log likelihood $Q_D(\theta)$, with the word length penalty term $d$ applied to the underlying form $u$.

$$\begin{aligned} Q(s \mid c, \theta) &= \sum_{u:(s,u) \in \mathcal{X}} \mathrm{P}(s, u \mid c, \theta) \exp(-|u|^d) \\ Q(w \mid \theta) &= \sum_{\substack{s_1 \ldots s_\ell \\ \text{s.t.} s_1 \ldots s_\ell = w}} \prod_{j=1}^{\ell} Q(s_j \mid c, \theta) \\ Q_D(\theta) &= \sum_{i=1}^{n} \log Q(w_i \mid \theta) - \lambda \|\theta\|_1 \end{aligned}$$

We are somewhat cavalier about the conditional contexts $c$ here: in our model below the context $c$ for a word is determined by the following word, so one can view our model as a generative model that generates the words in an utterance from right to left.

Because our model is a MaxEnt model, we have considerable freedom in the choice of features, and as Berg-Kirkpatrick et al. (2010) emphasise, the choice of features directly determines the kinds of generalisations the model can learn. The features $f(s, u, c)$ of a surface form $s$, underlying form $u$ and context $c$ we use here are inspired by OT. We describe our features using an example where $s =$ [l.ih.v], $u =$ /l.ih.v.t/ and $c =$ C (i.e., the word is followed by a consonant).

**Underlying form lexical features:** A feature for each underlying form $u$. In our example, the feature is `<U l ih v t>`. These features enable the model to learn language-specific lexical entries. There are 4,803,734 underlying form lexical features (one for each possible substring in the training data).

**Surface markedness features:** The length of the surface string (`<#L 3>`), the number of vowels (`<#V 1>`) (this is a rough indication of the number of syllables), the surface suffix (`<Suffix v>`), the surface prefix and suffix CV shape (`<CVPrefix CV>` and `<CVSuffix VC>`), and suffix+context CV shape (`<CVContext _C>` and `<CVContext C _C>`). There are 108 surface markedness features.

**Faithfulness features:** A feature for each divergence between underlying and surface forms (in this case, `<*F t>`). There are two faithfulness features.

We used $L_1$ regularisation here, rather than the $L_2$ regularisation used by Berg-Kirkpatrick et al. (2010), in the hope that its sparsity-inducing "feature selection" capabilities would enable it to "learn" lexical entries for the language, as well as precisely which markedness features are required to account for the data. However, we found that the choice of $L_1$ versus $L_2$ regression makes little difference, and the model is insensitive to the value of the regulariser constant $\lambda$ (we set to $\lambda = 1$ in the experiments below).

We developed a specially modified version of the LBFGS-OWLQN optimisation procedure for optimising $L_1$-regularised loss functions (Andrew and

Gao, 2007) that allows us to constrain certain feature weights $\theta_k$ to have a particular sign. This is a natural extension of the LBFGS-OWLQN procedure since it performs orthant-constrained line searches in any case. We describe experiments below where we require the feature weights for the markedness and faithfulness features to be non-positive, and where the underlying lexical form features are required to be non-negative. The requirement that the lexical form features are positive, combined with the sparsity induced by the $L_1$ regulariser, was intended to force the model to learn an explicit lexicon encoded by the underlying form features with positive weights (although our results below suggest that it did not in fact do this).

The inspiration for the requirement that markedness and faithfulness features are non-positive comes from OT, which claims that the presence of such features can only reduce the "harmony", i.e., the well-formedness, of an $(s, u)$ pair. Versions of Harmonic Grammar that aim to produce OT-like behavior with weighted constraints often bound weights at zero (see e.g. Pater (2009)). The results below are the first to show that these constraints matter for word segmentation.

## 4 Experimental results

This section describes the experiments we performed to evaluate the model just described. We first describe how we prepared the data on which the model is trained and evaluated, and then we describe the performance of that model. Finally we perform an analysis of how the model's performance varies as parameters of the model are changed.

We ran this model on data extracted from the Buckeye corpus of conversational speech (Pitt et al., 2007) which was modified so the only alternations it contained are final /d/ and /t/ deletions. The Buckeye corpus gives a surface realisation and an underlying form for each word token, and following Börschinger et al. (2013), we prepared the data as follows. We used the Buckeye underlying forms as our underlying forms. Our surface forms were also identical to the Buckeye underlying forms, except when the underlying form ends in either a /d/ or a /t/. In this case, if the Buckeye surface form does not end in an allophonic variant of that segment, then our surface form consists of the Buckeye underlying form with that final segment deleted. Thus the only phonological variation in our data are deletions of word-final /d/ and /t/ appearing in the Buckeye corpus, otherwise our surface forms are identical to Buckeye underlying forms.

For example, consider a token whose Buckeye underlying form is /l.ih.v.d/ "lived". If the Buckeye surface form is [l.ah.v] then our surface form would be [l.ih.v], while if the Buckeye surface form is [l.ah.v.d] then our surface form would be [l.ih.v.d].

We now present some descriptive statistics on our data. The data contains 48,796 sentences and 890,597 segments. The longest sentence has 187 segments. The "gold" data has the following properties. There are 236,996 word boundaries, 285,792 word tokens, and 9,353 underlying word types. The longest word has 17 segments. Of the 41,186 /d/s and 73,392 /t/s in the underlying forms, 24,524 /d/s and 40,720 /t/s are word final, and of these 13,457 /d/s and 11,727 /t/s are deleted (i.e., do not appear on the surface).

Our model considers all possible substrings of length 15 or less as a possible surface form of a word, yielding 4,803,734 possible word types and 5,292,040 possible surface/underlying word type pairs. Taking the 3 contexts derived from the following word into account, there are 4,969,718 possible word+context types. When all possible surface/underlying pairs are considered in all possible contexts there are 15,876,120 possible surface/underlying/context triples.

Table 1 summarises the major experimental results for this model, and compares them to the results of Börschinger et al. (2013). Note that their model only recovers word-final /t/ deletions and was run on data without word-final /d/ deletions, so it is solving a simpler problem than the one studied here. Even so, our model achieves higher overall accuracies.

We also conducted experiments on several of the design choices in our model. Figure 2 shows the effect of the sign constraints on feature weights discussed above. This plot shows that the contraints on the weights of markedness and faithfulness features seems essential for good word segmentation performance. Interestingly, we found that the weight constraints make very little difference if the data does

| | Börschinger et al. 2013 | Our model |
|---|---|---|
| Surface token f-score | 0.72 | **0.76** (0.01) |
| Underlying type f-score | — | 0.37 (0.02) |
| Deleted /t/ f-score | 0.56 | **0.58** (0.03) |
| Deleted /d/ f-score | — | 0.62 (0.19) |

Table 1: Results summary for our model compared to that of the Börschinger et al. (2013) model. Surface token f-score is the standard token f-score, while underlying type or "lexicon" f-score measures the accuracy with which the underlying word types are recovered. Deleted /t/ and /d/ f-scores measure the accuracy with which the model recovers segments that don't appear in the surface. These results are averaged over 40 runs (standard deviations in parentheses) with the word length penalty $d = 1.525$ applied to underlying forms; standard deviations are given in parentheses.

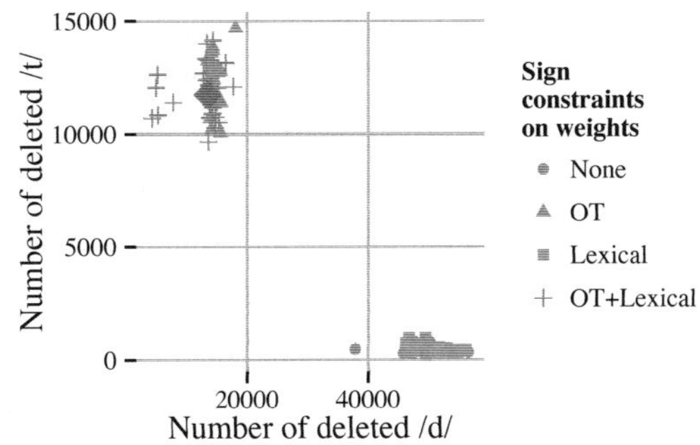


Figure 3: The effect of constraints feature weights on the number of deleted underlying /d/ and /t/ segments posited by the model ($d$ = 1.525). The red diamond indicates the 13,457 deleted underlying /d/ and 11,727 deleted underlying /t/ in the "gold" data.

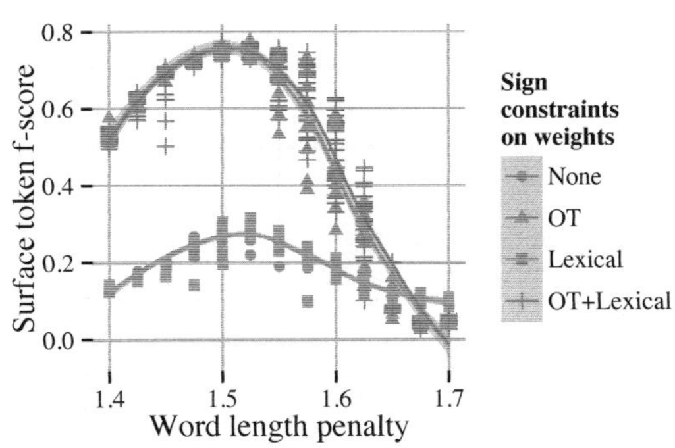


Figure 2: The effect of constraints on feature weights on surface token f-score. "OT" indicates that the markedness and faithfulness features are required to be non-positive, while "Lexical" indicates that the underlying lexical features are required to be non-negative.

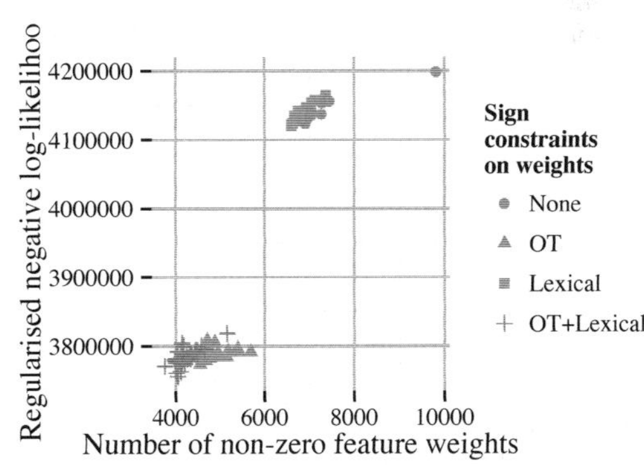


Figure 4: The regularised log-likelihood as a function of the number of non-zero weights for different constraints on feature weights ($d = 1.525$).

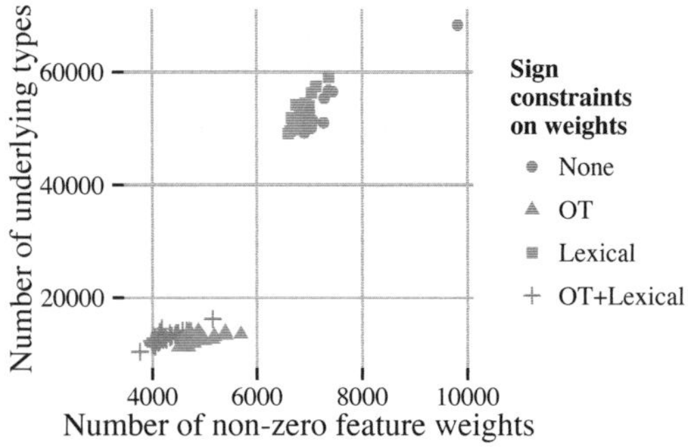


Figure 5: The number of underlying types proposed by the model as a function of the number of non-zero weights, for different constraints on feature weights ($d = 1.525$). There are 9,353 underlying types in the "gold" data.

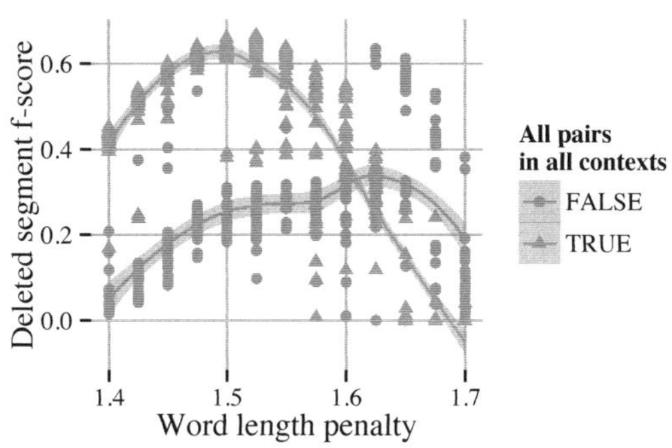


Figure 6: F-score for deleted /d/ and /t/ recovery as a function of word length penalty $d$ and whether all surface/underlying pairs $\mathcal{X}$ are included in all contexts $\mathcal{C}$ ($d = 1.525$).

not any /t/ or /d/ deletions (i.e., the case that Berg-Kirkpatrick et al. (2010) studied).

Investigating this further, we found that the weight constraints on the markedness and faithfulness features has a dramatic effect on the recovery of underlying segments, particularly underlying /d/s. Figure 3 shows that with these constraints the model recovers approximately the correct number of deleted underlying segments, while without this constraint the model posits far too many underlying /d/s. Figure 4 shows that these constraints help the model find higher regularised likelihood sets of feature weights with fewer non-zero feature weights.

We examined how the number of non-zero feature weights (most of which are for underlying type features) relate to the number of underlying types posited by the model. Figure 5 shows that the weight constraints on markedness and faithfulness constraints have great impact on the number of non-zero feature weights and on the number of underlying forms the model posits. In all cases, the model recovers far more underlying forms than it finds non-zero weights.

The lexicon weight constraints have much less impact than the OT weight constraints. As Figure 3 shows, without the OT weight constraints the models posit too many deleted /d/ and essentially no deleted /t/. Figure 4 shows that OT weight constraints enable the model to find higher likelihood solutions, i.e., the OT weight constraints help search. Inspired by a reviewer's comments, we studied type-token ratios and the number of boundaries our models posit. We found that the models without OT weight constraints posit far too few word boundaries compared to the gold data, so the number of surface tokens is too low, so the words are too long, and the number of underlying types is too high. This is consistent with Figures 4–5.

We also examined whether it is necessary to consider all surface/underlying pairs $\mathcal{X}$ in each context $\mathcal{C}$, or whether it is possible to restrict attention to the much smaller sets $\mathcal{X}_c$ that occur in each $c \in \mathcal{C}$ (this dramatically reduces the amount of memory required and speeds the computation). Figure 6 shows that working with the smaller, context-specific sets dramatically decreases the model's ability to recover deleted segments.

## 5 Conclusions and future work

The MaxEnt unigram model of word segmentation developed by Berg-Kirkpatrick et al. (2010) integrates straight-forwardly with the MaxEnt phonology models of Goldwater and Johnson (2003) to produce a MaxEnt model that jointly models word segmentation and the mapping from underlying to surface forms.

We tested our model on data derived from the manually-annotated Buckeye corpus of conversational speech (Pitt et al., 2007) in which the only phonological alternations are deletions of word-final /d/ and /t/ segments. We demonstrated that our model improves on the state-of-the-art for word segmentation, recovery of underlying forms and recovery of deleted segments for this corpus.

Our model is a MaxEnt or log-linear unigram model over the set of possible surface/underlying form pairs. Inspired by the work of Berg-Kirkpatrick et al. (2010), the set of surface/underlying form pairs our model calculates the partition function over is restricted to those actually appearing in the training data, and doesn't include all logically possible pairs. We found that even with this restriction, the model produces good results.

Because our model is a Maximum Entropy or log-linear model, it is formally an instance of a Harmonic Grammar (Smolensky and Legendre, 2005), so we investigated features inspired by OT, which is a discretised version of Harmonic Grammar that has been extensively developed in the linguistics literature. The features our model uses consist of underlying form features (one for each possible underlying form), together with markedness and faithfulness phonological features inspired by OT phonological analyses. According to OT, these markedness and faithfulness features should always have negative weights (i.e., when such a feature "fires", it should always make the analysis less probable). We found that constraining feature weights in this way dramatically improves the model's accuracy, apparently helping to find higher likelihood solutions.

Looking forwards, a major drawback of the MaxEnt approaches to word segmentation are their sensitivity to the *word length penalty* parameter, which this model shares with the models of Berg-Kirkpatrick et al. (2010) and (Liang and Klein, 2009) on which it is based. It would be very desirable to have a principled way to set this parameter in an unsupervised manner.

Because our goal was to explore the MaxEnt approach to joint segmenation and alternation, we deliberately used a minimal feature set here. As the reviewers pointed out, we did not include any morphological features, which could have a major impact on the model. Investigating the impact of richer feature sets, including a combination of phonotactic and morphological features, would be an excellent topic for future work.

It would be interesting to extend this approach to a wider range of phonological processes in addition to the word-final /t/ and /d/ deletion studied here. Because this model enumerates the possible surface/underlying/context triples before beginning to search for potential surface and underlying words, its memory requirements would grow dramatically if the set of possible surface/underlying alternations were increased. (The fact that we only considered word final /d/ and /t/ deletions means that there are only three possible underlying word forms for each surface word forms). Perhaps there is a way of identifying potential underlying forms that avoids enumerating them. For example, it might be possible to sample possible underlying word forms during the learning process rather than enumerating them ahead of time, perhaps by adapting non-parametric Bayesian approaches (Goldwater et al., 2009; Johnson and Goldwater, 2009; Börschinger et al., 2013).

## Acknowledgments

This research was supported under the Australian Research Council's *Discovery Projects* funding scheme (project numbers DP110102506 and DP110102593), by the Mairie de Paris, the fondation Pierre Gilles de Gennes, the École des Hautes Etudes en Sciences Sociales, the École Normale Supérieure, the Region Ile de France, by the US National Science Foundation under Grant No. S121000000211 to the third author and Grant BCS-424077 to the University of Massachusetts, and by grants from the European Research Council (ERC-2011-AdG-295810 BOOTPHON) and the Agence Nationale pour la Recherche (ANR-10-LABX-0087 IEC, ANR-10-IDEX-0001-02 PSL*). We'd also like to thank the three anonymous reviewers for helpful comments and suggestions.

## References

Galen Andrew and Jianfeng Gao. 2007. Scalable training of l1-regularized log-linear models. In *Proceedings of the 24th International Conference on Machine Learning*, ICML '07, pages 33–40, New York, New York. ACM.

Taylor Berg-Kirkpatrick, Alexandre Bouchard-Côté, John DeNero, and Dan Klein. 2010. Painless unsupervised learning with features. In *Human Language Technologies: The 2010 Annual Conference of the North American Chapter of the Association for Computational Linguistics*, pages 582–590. Association for Computational Linguistics.

Benjamin Börschinger and Mark Johnson. 2014. Exploring the role of stress in Bayesian word segmentation using adaptor grammars. *Transactions of the Association for Computational Linguistics*, 2(1):93–104.

Benjamin Börschinger, Katherine Demuth, and Mark Johnson. 2012. Studying the effect of input size for Bayesian word segmentation on the Providence corpus. In *Proceedings of the 24th International Conference on Computational Linguistics (Coling 2012)*, pages 325–340, Mumbai, India. Coling 2012 Organizing Committee.

Benjamin Börschinger, Mark Johnson, and Katherine Demuth. 2013. A joint model of word segmentation and phonological variation for English word-final /t/-deletion. In *Proceedings of the 51st Annual Meeting of the Association for Computational Linguistics (Volume 1: Long Papers)*, pages 1508–1516, Sofia, Bulgaria. Association for Computational Linguistics.

M. Brent and T. Cartwright. 1996. Distributional regularity and phonotactic constraints are useful for segmentation. *Cognition*, 61:93–125.

M. Brent. 1999. An efficient, probabilistically sound algorithm for segmentation and word discovery. *Machine Learning*, 34:71–105.

Andries Coetzee and Joe Pater. 2011. The place of variation in phonological theory. In John Goldsmith, Jason Riggle, and Alan Yu, editors, *The Handbook of Phonological Theory*, pages 401–431. Blackwell, 2nd edition.

Sarah Eisenstat. 2009. Learning underlying forms with MaxEnt. Master's thesis, Brown University.

Jeffrey Elman. 1990. Finding structure in time. *Cognitive Science*, 14:197–211.

Micha Elsner, Sharon Goldwater, and Jacob Eisenstein. 2012. Bootstrapping a unified model of lexical and phonetic acquisition. In *Proceedings of the 50th Annual Meeting of the Association for Computational Linguistics*, pages 184–193, Jeju Island, Korea. Association for Computational Linguistics.

Micha Elsner, Sharon Goldwater, Naomi Feldman, and Frank Wood. 2013. A joint learning model of word segmentation, lexical acquisition, and phonetic variability. In *Proceedings of the 2013 Conference on Empirical Methods in Natural Language Processing*, pages 42–54, Seattle, Washington, USA, October. Association for Computational Linguistics.

Sharon Goldwater and Mark Johnson. 2003. Learning OT constraint rankings using a Maximum Entropy model. In J. Spenader, A. Eriksson, and Osten Dahl, editors, *Proceedings of the Stockholm Workshop on Variation within Optimality Theory*, pages 111–120, Stockholm. Stockholm University.

Sharon Goldwater and Mark Johnson. 2004. Priors in Bayesian learning of phonological rules. In *Proceedings of the Seventh Meeting Meeting of the ACL Special Interest Group on Computational Phonology: SIGPHON 2004*.

Sharon Goldwater, Thomas L. Griffiths, and Mark Johnson. 2009. A Bayesian framework for word segmentation: Exploring the effects of context. *Cognition*, 112(1):21–54.

Bruce Hayes and Colin Wilson. 2008. A Maximum Entropy model of phonotactics and phonotactic learning. *Linguistic Inquiry*, 39(3):379–440.

Mark Johnson and Sharon Goldwater. 2009. Improving nonparameteric Bayesian inference: experiments on unsupervised word segmentation with adaptor grammars. In *Proceedings of Human Language Technologies: The 2009 Annual Conference of the North American Chapter of the Association for Computational Linguistics*, pages 317–325, Boulder, Colorado, June. Association for Computational Linguistics.

Mark Johnson, Katherine Demuth, Michael Frank, and Bevan Jones. 2010. Synergies in learning words and their referents. In J. Lafferty, C. K. I. Williams, J. Shawe-Taylor, R.S. Zemel, and A. Culotta, editors, *Advances in Neural Information Processing Systems 23*, pages 1018–1026.

Mark Johnson, Anne Christophe, Emmanuel Dupoux, and Katherine Demuth. 2014. Modelling function words improves unsupervised word segmentation. In *Proceedings of the 52nd Annual Meeting of the Association for Computational Linguistics*, pages 282–292. Association for Computational Linguistics, June.

Mark Johnson. 1984. A discovery procedure for certain phonological rules. In *10th International Conference on Computational Linguistics and 22nd Annual Meeting of the Association for Computational Linguistics*.

Mark Johnson. 1992. Identifying a rule's context from data. In *The Proceedings of the 11th West Coast Conference on Formal Linguistics*, pages 289–297, Stanford, CA. Stanford Linguistics Association.

Mark Johnson. 2008. Using Adaptor Grammars to identify synergies in the unsupervised acquisition of linguistic structure. In *Proceedings of the 46th Annual Meeting of the Association of Computational Linguistics*, pages 398–406, Columbus, Ohio. Association for Computational Linguistics.

Percy Liang and Dan Klein. 2009. Online EM for unsupervised models. In *Proceedings of Human Language Technologies: The 2009 Annual Conference of the North American Chapter of the Association for Computational Linguistics*, pages 611–619, Boulder, Colorado, June. Association for Computational Linguistics.

Joe Pater, Robert Staubs, Karen Jesney, and Brian Smith. 2012. Learning probabilities over underlying representations. In *Proceedings of the Twelfth Meeting of the ACL-SIGMORPHON: Computational Research in Phonetics, Phonology, and Morphology*, pages 62–71.

Joe Pater. 2009. Weighted constraints in generative linguistics. *Cognitive Science*, 33:999–1035.

Mark A. Pitt, Laura Dilley, Keith Johnson, Scott Kiesling, William Raymond, Elizabeth Hume, and Eric Fosler-Lussier. 2007. Buckeye corpus of conversational speech.

Alan Prince and Paul Smolensky. 2004. *Optimality Theory: Constraint Interaction in Generative Grammar*. Blackwell.

Paul Smolensky and Géraldine Legendre. 2005. *The Harmonic Mind: From Neural Computation To Optimality-Theoretic Grammar*. The MIT Press.

# Semi-Supervised Word Sense Disambiguation Using Word Embeddings in General and Specific Domains

**Kaveh Taghipour**
Department of Computer Science
National University of Singapore
13 Computing Drive
Singapore 117417
kaveh@comp.nus.edu.sg

**Hwee Tou Ng**
Department of Computer Science
National University of Singapore
13 Computing Drive
Singapore 117417
nght@comp.nus.edu.sg

## Abstract

One of the weaknesses of current supervised word sense disambiguation (WSD) systems is that they only treat a word as a discrete entity. However, a continuous-space representation of words (word embeddings) can provide valuable information and thus improve generalization accuracy. Since word embeddings are typically obtained from unlabeled data using unsupervised methods, this method can be seen as a semi-supervised word sense disambiguation approach. This paper investigates two ways of incorporating word embeddings in a word sense disambiguation setting and evaluates these two methods on some SensEval/SemEval lexical sample and all-words tasks and also a domain-specific lexical sample task. The obtained results show that such representations consistently improve the accuracy of the selected supervised WSD system. Moreover, our experiments on a domain-specific dataset show that our supervised baseline system beats the best knowledge-based systems by a large margin.

## 1 Introduction

Because of the ambiguity of natural language, many words can have different meanings in different contexts. For example, the word "bank" has two different meanings in "the bank of a river" and "a bank loan". While it seems simple for humans to identify the meaning of a word according to the context, word sense disambiguation (WSD) (Ng and Lee, 1996; Lee and Ng, 2002) is a difficult task for computers and thus requires sophisticated means to achieve its goal. Part of this ambiguity may be resolved by considering part-of-speech (POS) tags but the word senses are still highly ambiguous even for the same part-of-speech. Machine translation is probably the most important application of word sense disambiguation. In machine translation, different senses of a word cause a great amount of ambiguity for automated translation and it negatively affects the results. Hence, an accurate WSD system can benefit machine translation significantly and improve the results (Chan et al., 2007; Carpuat and Wu, 2007; Vickrey et al., 2005). Moreover, Zhong and Ng (2012) have shown that word sense disambiguation improves information retrieval by proposing a method to use word senses in a language modeling approach to information retrieval.

The rest of this paper is organized as follows. Section 2 gives a literature review of related work, including a review of semi-supervised word sense disambiguation and distributed word representation called word embeddings. The method and framework used in this paper are explained in Section 3. Finally, we evaluate the system in Section 4 and conclude the paper in Section 5.

## 2 Related Work

The method that we use in this paper is a semi-supervised learning method which incorporates knowledge from unlabeled datasets by using word embeddings. This section is a literature review of previous work on semi-supervised word sense disambiguation and various methods of obtaining word embeddings.



*Human Language Technologies: The 2015 Annual Conference of the North American Chapter of the ACL*, pages 314–323,
Denver, Colorado, May 31 – June 5, 2015. 

### 2.1 Semi-Supervised Word Sense Disambiguation

Among various types of semi-supervised learning approaches, *co-training* and *self-training* are probably the most common. These methods randomly select a subset of a large unlabeled dataset and classify these samples using one (self-training) or two (co-training) classifiers, trained on a smaller set of labeled samples. After assigning labels to the new samples, these methods select the samples that were classified with a high confidence (according to a selection criterion) and add them to the set of labeled data. These methods have been used in the context of word sense disambiguation. Mihalcea (2004) used both co-training and self-training to make use of unlabeled datasets for word sense disambiguation. Mihalcea also introduced a technique for combining co-training and majority voting, called *smoothed co-training*, and reported improved results. Another related study was done by (Pham et al., 2005). In (Pham et al., 2005), some semi-supervised learning techniques were used for word sense disambiguation. Pham et al. employed co-training and spectral graph transduction methods in their experiments and obtained significant improvements over a supervised method.

Another semi-supervised learning method used for word sense disambiguation is Alternating Structure Optimization (ASO), first introduced by (Ando and Zhang, 2005) and later applied to word sense disambiguation tasks by (Ando, 2006). This algorithm learns a predictive structure shared between different problems (disambiguation of a target word). Semi-supervised application of the ASO algorithm was shown to be useful for word sense disambiguation and improvements can be achieved over a supervised predictor (Ando, 2006).

This paper uses a different method proposed by (Turian et al., 2010) that can be applied to a wide variety of supervised tasks in natural language processing. This method uses distributed word representations (word embeddings) as additional feature functions in supervised tasks and is shown to improve the accuracy of named-entity recognition (NER) and chunking. In this paper, we also follow the same approach for word sense disambiguation. The key idea is that a system without a continuous-space representation of words ignores the similarity of words completely and relies only on their discrete form. However, when a distributed representation for words is added to the system, the classifier can make use of the notion of *similarity* of words and learn the relationships between class labels and words.

In addition to using *raw* word embeddings, we also propose a method to *adapt* embeddings for each classification task. Since word embeddings do not include much task-specific discriminative information, we use a neural network to modify word vectors to tune them for our WSD tasks. We show that this process results in improved accuracy compared to raw word embeddings.

Recently, obtaining word embeddings in an unsupervised manner from large text corpora has attracted the attention of many researchers (Collobert and Weston, 2008; Mnih and Hinton, 2009; Mikolov et al., 2013a; Mikolov et al., 2013b). Subsequently, there have been some published word embeddings and some software for training word embeddings.

For word sense disambiguation, there are very few open source programs. Since we are interested in a fully supervised WSD tool, IMS (It Makes Sense) (Zhong and Ng, 2010) is selected in our work. This system allows addition of extra features in a simple way and hence is a good choice for testing the effect of word embeddings as additional features. Moreover, the scores reported for IMS are competitive with or better than state-of-the-art systems (Zhong and Ng, 2010).

### 2.2 Word Embeddings

There are several types of word representations. A *one-hot* representation is a vector where all components except one are set to zero and the component at the index associated with a word is set to one. This type of representation is the sparsest word representation and does not carry any information about word similarity. Another popular approach is to use the methods mainly applied in information retrieval. Latent Semantic Analysis (LSA) and Latent Dirichlet Allocation (LDA) are such examples, and word representations produced by these methods can also be used in other applications. However, a dense distributed representation for words (word embeddings) can learn more complex relationships between words and hence, it can be useful in a wide range of applications. We only focus on word embeddings in this paper and apply them to word sense disambiguation.

Word embeddings are distributed representations of words and contain some semantic and syntactic information (Mikolov et al., 2013c). Such representations are usually produced by neural networks. Examples of such neural networks are (log-)linear networks (Mikolov et al., 2013a), deeper feed-forward neural networks (Bengio et al., 2003; Collobert and Weston, 2008), or recurrent neural networks (Mikolov et al., 2010). Moreover, it has been shown that deep structures may not be needed for word embeddings estimation (Lebret et al., 2013) and shallow structures can obtain relatively high quality representations for words (Mikolov et al., 2013b).

In this paper, we have used the word embeddings created and published by (Collobert and Weston, 2008). Throughout this paper, we refer to these word embeddings as 'CW'. This method is proposed in (Collobert and Weston, 2008) and explained further in (Collobert et al., 2011). The authors use a feed-forward neural network to produce word representations. In order to train the neural network, a large text corpus is needed. Collobert and Weston (2008) use Wikipedia (Nov. 2007 version containing 631 million words) and Reuters RCV1 (containing 221 million words) (Lewis et al., 2004) as their text corpora and Stochastic Gradient Descent (SGD) as the training algorithm. The training algorithm selects a window of text randomly and then replaces the middle word with a random word from the dictionary. Then the original window of text and the corrupted one is given to the neural network. The neural network computes $f(x)$ and $f(x^{(w)})$, where $x$ is the original window of text, $x^{(w)}$ is the same window of text with the middle word replaced by word $w$, and $f(.)$ is the function that the neural network represents. After computing $f(x)$ and $f(x^{(w)})$, the training algorithm uses a *pairwise ranking* cost function to train the network. The training algorithm minimizes the cost function by updating the parameters (including word embeddings) and as a consequence of using the pairwise ranking cost function, this neural network tends to assign higher scores to *valid* windows of texts and lower scores to *incorrect* ones. After training the neural network, the word vectors

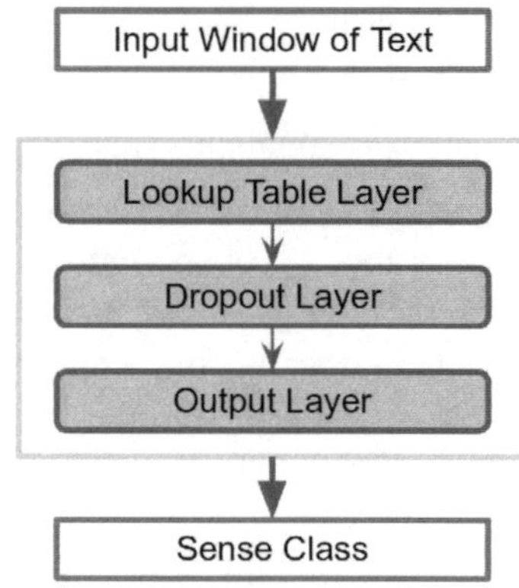


Figure 1: The neural network architecture for adaptation of word embeddings.

in the lookup table layer form the word embeddings matrix. Collobert et al. (2011) have made this matrix available for public use and it can be accessed online[1].

## 3 Method

In this section, we first explain our novel task-specific method of *adapting* word embeddings and then describe our framework in which raw or adapted word embeddings are included in our word sense disambiguation system. To the best of our knowledge, the use of word embeddings for semi-supervised word sense disambiguation is novel.

### 3.1 Adaptation of Word Embeddings

Word embeddings capture some semantic and syntactic information and usually similar words have similar word vectors in terms of distance measures. However, in a classification task, it is better for word embeddings to also include some task specific discriminative information. In order to add such information to word embeddings, we modify word vectors using a neural network (Figure 1) to obtain *adapted* word embeddings. This section explains this process in detail.

The neural network that we used to adapt word embeddings is similar to the *window approach* network introduced by (Collobert and Weston, 2008). This neural network includes the following layers:

[1] http://ml.nec-labs.com/senna

- Lookup table layer: This layer includes three lookup tables. The first lookup table assigns a vector to each input word, as described earlier. The second lookup table maps each word to a vector with respect to the capitalization feature. Finally, the third lookup table maps each word to its corresponding vector based on the word's POS tag.

- Dropout layer: In order to avoid overfitting, we added a dropout layer (Hinton et al., 2012) to the network to make use of its regularization effect. During training, the dropout layer copies the input to the output but randomly sets some of the entries to zero with a probability $p$, which is usually set to 0.5. During testing, this layer produces the output by multiplying the input vector by $1 - p$ (see (Hinton et al., 2012) for more information).

- Output layer: This layer linearly maps the input vector $X$ to a $C$-dimensional vector $Y$ (equation 1) and then applies a SoftMax operation (Bridle, 1990) over all elements of $Y$ (equation 2):

$$Y = WX + b \tag{1}$$

$$p(t|I) = \frac{\exp(Y_t)}{\sum_{j=1}^{C} \exp(Y_j)} \quad 1 \leq t \leq C \tag{2}$$

  where $I$ is the input window of text and $t$ is a class label (sense tag in WSD). The output of the output layer can be interpreted as a conditional probability $p(t|I)$ over tags given the input text.

This architecture is similar to the network used by (Collobert and Weston, 2008) but it does not include a hidden layer. Since the number of training samples for each word type in WSD is relatively small, we did not use a hidden layer to decrease the model size and consequently overfitting, as much as possible. Moreover, we added the dropout layer and observed increased generalization accuracy subsequently.

In order to train the neural network, we used Stochastic Gradient Descent (SGD) and error backpropagation to minimize negative log-likelihood cost function for each training example $(I, t)$ (equation 3).

$$-\log p(t|I) = \log(\sum_{j=1}^{C} exp(Y_j)) - Y_t \tag{3}$$

During the training process, the inputs are the windows of text surrounding the target word with their assigned POS tags. We used fixed learning rate (0.01) during training, with no momentum.

Since the objective is to adapt word embeddings using the neural network, we initialized the lookup table layer parameters using pre-trained word embeddings and trained a model for each target word type. After the training process completes, the modified word vectors form our adapted word embeddings, which will be used in exactly the same way as the original embeddings. Section 3.2 explains the way we use word embeddings to improve a supervised word sense disambiguation system.

### 3.2 Framework

The supervised system that we used for word sense disambiguation is an open source tool named IMS (Zhong and Ng, 2010). This software extracts three types of features and then uses Support Vector Machines (SVM) as the classifier. The three types of features implemented in IMS are explained below.

- POS tags of surrounding words: IMS uses the POS tags of all words in a window size of 7, surrounding the target ambiguous word. POS tag features are limited to the current sentence and neighboring sentences are not considered.

- Surrounding words: Additionally, the surrounding words of a target word (after removing stop words) are also used as features in IMS. However, unlike POS tags, the words occurring in the immediately adjacent sentences are also included.

- Local collocations: Finally, 11 local collocations around the target word are considered as features. These collocations also cover a window size of 7, where the target word is in the middle.

All mentioned features are binary features and will be used by the classifier in the next phase. After extracting these features, the classifier (SVM) is used to train a model for each target word. In the test phase, the model is used to classify test samples and assign a sense tag to each sample.

This supervised framework with separate feature extraction and classification phases makes it easy to add any number of features and in our case, word embeddings. In order to make use of word embeddings trained by a neural network, we follow the approach of (Turian et al., 2010) and include word embeddings for all words in the surrounding window of text, given a target ambiguous word. We use the words from immediately adjacent sentences if the window falls beyond the current sentence boundaries. Since each word type has its own classification model, we do not add the word embeddings for the target word because the same vector will be used in all training and test samples and will be useless.

After extraction of the three mentioned types of features, $d.(w-1)$ features will be added to each sample, where $d$ is the word embeddings dimension and $w$ is the number of words in the window of text surrounding the target word (window size). $w$ is one of the hyper-parameters of our system that can be tuned for each word type separately. However, since the training sets for some of the benchmark tasks are small, tuning the window size will not be consistent over different tuning sets. Thus, we decided to select the same window size for all words in a task and tune this parameter on the whole tuning set instead. After augmenting the features, a model is trained for the target word and then the classifier can be used to assign the correct sense to each test sample.

However, since the original three types of features are binary, newly added real-valued word embeddings do not fit well into the model and they tend to decrease performance. This problem is addressed in (Turian et al., 2010) and a simple solution is to scale word embeddings. The following conversion is suggested by (Turian et al., 2010):

$$E \leftarrow \sigma \cdot E/stddev(E) \qquad (4)$$

where $\sigma$ is a scalar hyper-parameter denoting the desired standard deviation, $E$ is the word embeddings matrix and $stddev(.)$ is the standard deviation function, which returns a scalar for matrix $E$. However, different dimensions of word embedding vectors may have different standard deviations and Equation 4 may not work well. In this case, per-dimension scaling will make more sense. In order to scale the word embeddings matrix, we use Equation 5 in our experiments:

$$E_i \leftarrow \sigma \cdot E_i/stddev(E_i), \quad i: 1, 2, ..., d \qquad (5)$$

where $E_i$ denotes the $i^{th}$ dimension of word embeddings. Like (Turian et al., 2010), we also found that $\sigma = 0.1$ is a good choice for the target standard deviation and works well.

## 4 Results and Discussion

We evaluate our word sense disambiguation system experimentally by using standard benchmarks. The two major tasks in word sense disambiguation are *lexical sample task* and *all-words task*. For each task, we explain our experimental setup first and then present the results of our experiments for the two mentioned tasks. Although most benchmarks are general domain test sets, a few domain-specific test sets also exist (Koeling et al., 2005; Agirre et al., 2010).

### 4.1 Lexical Sample Tasks

We have evaluated our system on SensEval-2 (SE2) and SensEval-3 (SE3) lexical sample tasks and also the domain-specific test set (we call it DS05) published by (Koeling et al., 2005). This subsection describes our experiments and presents the results of these tasks.

#### 4.1.1 Experimental Setup

Most lexical sample tasks provide separate training and test sets. Some statistics about these tasks are given in Table 1.

| | SE2 | SE3 | DS05 |
|---|---|---|---|
| #Word types | 73 | 57 | 41 |
| #Training samples | 8,611 | 8,022 | - |
| #Test samples | 4,328 | 3,944 | 10,272 |

Table 1: Statistics of lexical sample tasks

The DS05 dataset does not provide any training instances. In order to train models for DS05 (and later for the SE3 all-words task), we generated training samples for the top 60% most frequently occurring polysemous content words in Brown Corpus, using the approach described in (Ng et al., 2003; Chan and Ng, 2005). This dataset is automatically created by processing parallel corpora without any manual sense annotation effort. We used the following six English-Chinese parallel corpora: Hong Kong Hansards, Hong Kong News, Hong Kong Laws, Sinorama, Xinhua News, and the English translations of Chinese Treebank. Similar to (Zhong and Ng, 2010), we obtained word alignments using GIZA++ (Och and Ney, 2000). Then, for each English word, the aligned Chinese word is used to find the corresponding sense tag for the English word. Finally, we made use of examples from the DSO corpus (Ng and Lee, 1996) and SEMCOR (Miller et al., 1994) as part of our training data. Table 2 shows some statistics of our training data.

| POS | #word types |
|---|---|
| Adj. | 5,129 |
| Adv. | 28 |
| Noun | 11,445 |
| Verb | 4,705 |
| Total | 21,307 |

Table 2: Number of word types in each part-of-speech (POS) in our training set

Since the dataset used by (Zhong and Ng, 2010) does not cover the specific domains of DS05 (Sports and Finance), we added a few samples from these domains to improve our baseline system. For each target word, we *randomly* selected 5 instances (a sentence including the target word) for Sports domain and 5 instances for Finance domain from the Reuters (Rose et al., 2002) dataset's Sports and Finance sections and manually sense annotated them. Annotating 5 instances per word and domain takes about 5 minutes. To make sure that these instances are not the same samples in the test set, we filtered out all documents containing at least one of the test instances and selected our training samples from the rest of the collection. After removing samples with *unclear* tags, we added the remaining instances (187 instances for Sports domain and 179 instances for Finance domain) to our original training data (Zhong and Ng, 2010). We highlight this setting in our experiments by 'CC' (concatenation).

We used the published CW word embeddings and set the word embeddings dimension to 50 in all our experiments. Finally, in order to tune the window size hyper-parameter, we randomly split our training sets into two parts. We used 80% for training models and the remaining 20% for evaluation. After tuning the window size, we used the original complete training set for training our models.

#### 4.1.2 Results

In order to select a value for the window size parameter, we performed two types of tuning. The first method, which (theoretically) can achieve higher accuracies, is per-word tuning. Since each word type has its own model, we can select different window sizes for different words. The second method, on the other hand, selects the same value for the window size for all word types in a task, and we call it per-task tuning.

Although, per-word tuning achieved very high accuracies on the held-out development set, we observed that it performed poorly on the test set. Moreover, the results of per-word tuning are not stable and different development sets lead to different window sizes and also fluctuating accuracies. This is because the available training sets are small and using 20% of these samples as the development set means that the development set only contains a small number of samples. Thus the selected development sets are not proper representatives of the test sets and the tuning process results in overfitting the parameters (window sizes) to the development sets, with low generalization accuracy. However, per-task tuning is relatively stable and performs better on the test sets. Thus we have selected this method of tuning in all our experiments. Mihalcea (2004) also reports that per-word tuning of parameters is not helpful and does not result in improved performance.

We also evaluated our system separately on the word types in each part-of-speech (POS) for SE2 and SE3 lexical sample tasks. The results are included in Table 3 and Table 4. According to these tables, word embeddings do not affect all POS types uniformly. For example, on SE2, the improvement achieved on verbs is much larger than the other two POS types and on SE3, adjectives benefited from word embeddings more than nouns and verbs. However, this table also shows that improvements from word embeddings are consistent over POS types and both lexical sample tasks.

| | SE2 | | |
|---|---|---|---|
| **POS** | **#word types** | **baseline** | **CW (17)** |
| Adj. | 15 | 67.45% | 67.72% |
| Noun | 29 | 69.39% | 69.38% |
| Verb | 29 | 60.45% | 61.89% |

Table 3: The scores for each part-of-speech (POS) on SE2 lexical sample tasks. The window size is shown inside brackets.

| | SE3 | | |
|---|---|---|---|
| **POS** | **#word types** | **baseline** | **CW (9)** |
| Adj. | 5 | 45.93% | 47.81% |
| Noun | 32 | 73.44% | 73.83% |
| Verb | 20 | 74.12% | 74.17% |

Table 4: The scores for each part-of-speech (POS) on SE3 lexical sample tasks. The window size is shown inside brackets.

Finally, we evaluated the effect of word embeddings and the adaptation process. Table 5 summarizes our findings on SE2 and SE3 lexical sample tasks. According to this table, both types of word embeddings lead to improvements on lexical sample tasks. We also performed a one-tailed paired t-test to see whether the improvements are statistically significant over the baseline (IMS). The improvements obtained using CW word embeddings over the baseline are significant ($p < 0.05$) in both lexical sample tasks. Furthermore, the results show that adapted word embeddings achieve higher scores than raw word embeddings. We have included the scores obtained by the first and the second best participating systems in these lexical sample tasks and also the Most Frequent Sense (MFS) score. The results also show that the Dropout layer increases performance significantly. The reason behind this observation is that without Dropout, word embeddings are overfitted to the training data and when they are used as extra features in IMS, the classifier does not generalize well to the test set. Since adaptation without Dropout leads to worse performance, we include Dropout in all other experiments and only report results obtained using Dropout.

Similarly, Table 6 presents the results obtained

| | **SE2** | **SE3** |
|---|---|---|
| IMS (baseline) | 65.3% | 72.7% |
| IMS + CW | 66.1%$^*$ (17) | 73.0%$^*$ (9) |
| IMS + adapted CW | **66.2%$^*$ (5)** | **73.4%$^*$ (7)** |
| – Dropout | 65.4% (7) | 72.7% (7) |
| Rank 1 system | 64.2% | 72.9% |
| Rank 2 system | 63.8% | 72.6% |
| MFS | 47.6% | 55.2% |

Table 5: Lexical sample task results. The values inside brackets are the selected window sizes and statistically significant ($p < 0.05$) improvements are marked with '*'.

from our experiments on the DS05 dataset. In this table, as explained earlier, 'CC' denotes the additional manually tagged instances. For comparison purposes, we included the results reported by two state-of-the-art knowledge-based systems, namely $\text{PPR}_{\text{w2w}}$ (Agirre et al., 2014) and Degree (Ponzetto and Navigli, 2010).

Table 6 shows that IMS performs worse than $\text{PPR}_{\text{w2w}}$ on Sports and Finance domains but IMS + CC outperforms $\text{PPR}_{\text{w2w}}$. One of the reasons behind this observation is *unseen* sense tags. For example, in the sentence "the winning goal came with less than a minute left to play[2]", the sense tag for word 'goal' is 'goal%1:04:00::'. However, the training data for IMS does not contain any sample with this sense tag and so it is impossible for IMS to assign this tag to any test instances. On the other hand, the manually annotated instances (CC) include samples with this tag and therefore IMS + CC is able to associate a target word with this sense tag.

According to Table 6, adding word embeddings results in improved performance over the baseline (IMS + CC). Moreover, adapting word embeddings is found to increase accuracy in most cases.

### 4.2 All-Words Task

We also evaluated the performance of our system on the SensEval-3 (SE3) all-words task. Next, we explain our setup and then present the results of our evaluation.

[2]This example is taken from WordNet v3.1.

| | BNC | Sports | Finance | Total |
|---|---|---|---|---|
| IMS | 48.7% | 41.4% | 53.4% | 47.8% |
| IMS + CC (baseline) | 51.7% | 55.7% | 62.1% | 56.4% |
| IMS + CC + CW (3) | 51.9% | 56.1%$^*$ | **62.3%** | 56.7%$^*$ |
| IMS + CC + adapted CW (3) | **52.3%**$^*$ | **57.1%**$^*$ | 62.0% | **57.1%**$^*$ |
| $PPR_{w2w}$ | 37.7% | 51.5% | 59.3% | 49.3% |
| Degree | - | 42.0% | 47.8% | - |

Table 6: DS05 task results. The values inside brackets are the selected window sizes and statistically significant ($p < 0.05$) improvements over 'IMS + CC' are marked with '*'.

### 4.2.1 Experimental Setup

All-words tasks do not provide any training samples and only include a test set (see Table 7). In order to train our system for SE3 all-words task, we used the automatically labeled training samples used earlier for training models for DS05 (see section 4.1.1). Table 2 shows some statistics about our training set.

| | SE3 |
|---|---|
| #Word types | 963 |
| #Test samples | 2,041 |

Table 7: Statistics of SE3 all-words task

Similar to the lexical sample tasks, we tune our system on 20% of the original training set. After obtaining window size parameter via tuning, we train on the whole training set and test on the given standard test set.

### 4.2.2 Results

The results of the evaluation on SE3 all-words task are given in Table 8. This table shows that CW word embeddings improve the accuracy. Similar to the results obtained for the lexical sample tasks, we observe some improvement by adapting word embeddings for SE3 all-words task as well. For comparison purposes, we have included the official scores of rank 1 and rank 2 participating systems in SE3 all-words task and the WordNet first sense (WNs1) score.

| | SE3 |
|---|---|
| IMS (baseline) | 67.6% |
| IMS + CW | 68.0%$^*$ (9) |
| IMS + adapted CW | **68.2%$^*$ (9)** |
| Rank 1 system | 65.2% |
| Rank 2 system | 64.6% |
| WNs1 | 62.4% |

Table 8: SE3 all-words task results. The values inside brackets are the selected window sizes and statistically significant ($p < 0.05$) improvements over the IMS baseline are marked with '*'.

## 5 Conclusion

Supervised word sense disambiguation systems usually treat words as discrete entities and consequently ignore the concept of *similarity* between words. However, by adding word embeddings, some of the samples that cannot be discriminated based on the original features (surrounding words, collocations, POS tags) have more chances to be classified correctly. Moreover, word embeddings are likely to contain valuable linguistic information too. Hence, adding continuous-space representations of words can provide valuable information to the classifier and the classifier can learn better discriminative criteria based on such information.

In this paper, we exploited a type of word embeddings obtained by feed-forward neural networks. We also proposed a novel method (i.e., adaptation) to add discriminative information to such embeddings. These word embeddings were then added to a supervised WSD system by augmenting the original binary feature space with real-valued representations for all words occurring in a window of text. We evaluated our system on two general-domain lexical sample tasks, an all-words task, and also a domain-specific dataset and showed that word embeddings consistently improve the accuracy of a supervised word sense disambiguation system, across different datasets. Moreover, we observed that adding discriminative information by adapting word embeddings further improves the accuracy of our word sense disambiguation system.

## Acknowledgments

This research is supported by the Singapore National Research Foundation under its International Research Centre @ Singapore Funding Initiative and administered by the IDM Programme Office.

## References

Eneko Agirre, Oier Lopez de Lacalle, Christiane Fellbaum, Shu-Kai Hsieh, Maurizio Tesconi, Monica Monachini, Piek Vossen, and Roxanne Segers. 2010. SemEval-2010 task 17: All-words word sense disambiguation on a specific domain. In *Proceedings of the 5th International Workshop on Semantic Evaluation*, pages 75–80.

Eneko Agirre, Oier López de Lacalle, and Aitor Soroa. 2014. Random walks for knowledge-based word sense disambiguation. *Computational Linguistics*, 40(1):57–84.

Rie Kubota Ando and Tong Zhang. 2005. A framework for learning predictive structures from multiple tasks and unlabeled data. *Journal of Machine Learning Research*, 6:1817–1853.

Rie Kubota Ando. 2006. Applying alternating structure optimization to word sense disambiguation. In *Proceedings of the Tenth Conference on Computational Natural Language Learning*, pages 77–84.

Yoshua Bengio, Réjean Ducharme, Pascal Vincent, and Christian Janvin. 2003. A neural probabilistic language model. *Journal of Machine Learning Research*, 3:1137–1155.

John S Bridle. 1990. Probabilistic interpretation of feedforward classification network outputs, with relationships to statistical pattern recognition. *Neurocomputing*, pages 227–236.

Marine Carpuat and Dekai Wu. 2007. Improving statistical machine translation using word sense disambiguation. In *Proceedings of the 2007 Joint Conference on Empirical Methods in Natural Language Processing and Computational Natural Language Learning*, pages 61–72.

Yee Seng Chan and Hwee Tou Ng. 2005. Scaling up word sense disambiguation via parallel texts. In *Proceedings of the 20th National Conference on Artificial Intelligence*, pages 1037–1042.

Yee Seng Chan, Hwee Tou Ng, and David Chiang. 2007. Word sense disambiguation improves statistical machine translation. In *Proceedings of the 45th Annual Meeting of the Association for Computational Linguistics*, pages 33–40.

Ronan Collobert and Jason Weston. 2008. A unified architecture for natural language processing: Deep neural networks with multitask learning. In *Proceedings of the 25th International Conference on Machine Learning*, pages 160–167.

Ronan Collobert, Jason Weston, Léon Bottou, Michael Karlen, Koray Kavukcuoglu, and Pavel Kuksa. 2011. Natural language processing (almost) from scratch. *Journal of Machine Learning Research*, 12:2493–2537.

Geoffrey E. Hinton, Nitish Srivastava, Alex Krizhevsky, Ilya Sutskever, and Ruslan Salakhutdinov. 2012. Improving neural networks by preventing co-adaptation of feature detectors. *Computing Research Repository*, abs/1207.0580.

Rob Koeling, Diana McCarthy, and John Carroll. 2005. Domain-specific sense distributions and predominant sense acquisition. In *Proceedings of the Conference on Human Language Technology and Empirical Methods in Natural Language Processing*, pages 419–426.

Rémi Lebret, Joël Legrand, and Ronan Collobert. 2013. Is deep learning really necessary for word embeddings? In *Neural Information Processing Systems: Deep Learning Workshop*.

Yoong Keok Lee and Hwee Tou Ng. 2002. An empirical evaluation of knowledge sources and learning algorithms for word sense disambiguation. In *Proceedings of the 2002 Conference on Empirical Methods in Natural Language Processing*, pages 41–48.

David D. Lewis, Yiming Yang, Tony G. Rose, and Fan Li. 2004. RCV1: A new benchmark collection for text categorization research. *Journal of Machine Learning Research*, 5:361–397.

Rada Mihalcea. 2004. Co-training and self-training for word sense disambiguation. In *Proceedings of the 8th Conference on Computational Natural Language Learning*, pages 33–40.

Tomas Mikolov, Martin Karafiát, Lukáš Burget, Jan Černockỳ, and Sanjeev Khudanpur. 2010. Recurrent neural network based language model. In *Proceedings of the Eleventh Annual Conference of the International Speech Communication Association*.

Tomas Mikolov, Kai Chen, Greg Corrado, and Jeffrey Dean. 2013a. Efficient estimation of word representations in vector space. *In Proceedings of Workshop at International Conference on Learning Representations*.

Tomas Mikolov, Ilya Sutskever, Kai Chen, Greg Corrado, and Jeffrey Dean. 2013b. Distributed representations of words and phrases and their compositionality. In *Advances in Neural Information Processing Systems 26*, pages 3111–3119.

Tomas Mikolov, Wen-tau Yih, and Geoffrey Zweig. 2013c. Linguistic regularities in continuous space word representations. In *Proceedings of the 2013 Conference of the North American Chapter of the Association for Computational Linguistics: Human Language Technologies*, pages 746–751.

George A. Miller, Martin Chodorow, Shari Landes, Claudia Leacock, and Robert G. Thomas. 1994. Using a semantic concordance for sense identification. In *Proceedings of the Workshop on Human Language Technology*, pages 240–243.

Andriy Mnih and Geoffrey E. Hinton. 2009. A scalable hierarchical distributed language model. In *Advances in Neural Information Processing Systems 21*, pages 1081–1088.

Hwee Tou Ng and Hian Beng Lee. 1996. Integrating multiple knowledge sources to disambiguate word sense: An exemplar-based approach. In *Proceedings of the 34th Annual Meeting of the Association for Computational Linguistics*, pages 40–47.

Hwee Tou Ng, Bin Wang, and Yee Seng Chan. 2003. Exploiting parallel texts for word sense disambiguation: An empirical study. In *Proceedings of the 41st Annual Meeting of the Association for Computational Linguistics*, pages 455–462.

Franz Josef Och and Hermann Ney. 2000. Improved statistical alignment models. In *Proceedings of the 38th Annual Meeting of the Association for Computational Linguistics*, pages 440–447.

Thanh Phong Pham, Hwee Tou Ng, and Wee Sun Lee. 2005. Word sense disambiguation with semi-supervised learning. In *Proceedings of the 20th National Conference on Artificial Intelligence*, pages 1093–1098.

Simone Paolo Ponzetto and Roberto Navigli. 2010. Knowledge-rich word sense disambiguation rivaling supervised systems. In *Proceedings of the 48th Annual Meeting of the Association for Computational Linguistics*, pages 1522–1531.

Tony Rose, Mark Stevenson, and Miles Whitehead. 2002. The Reuters Corpus Volume 1 – from yesterday's news to tomorrow's language resources. In *Proceedings of the Third International Conference on Language Resources and Evaluation*, pages 827–832.

Joseph Turian, Lev-Arie Ratinov, and Yoshua Bengio. 2010. Word representations: A simple and general method for semi-supervised learning. In *Proceedings of the 48th Annual Meeting of the Association for Computational Linguistics*, pages 384–394.

David Vickrey, Luke Biewald, Marc Teyssier, and Daphne Koller. 2005. Word-sense disambiguation for machine translation. In *Proceedings of the Conference on Human Language Technology and Empirical Methods in Natural Language Processing*, pages 771–778.

Zhi Zhong and Hwee Tou Ng. 2010. It Makes Sense: a wide-coverage word sense disambiguation system for free text. In *Proceedings of the 48th Annual Meeting of the Association for Computational Linguistics System Demonstrations*, pages 78–83.

Zhi Zhong and Hwee Tou Ng. 2012. Word sense disambiguation improves information retrieval. In *Proceedings of the 50th Annual Meeting of the Association for Computational Linguistics*, pages 273–282.

# Continuous Space Representations of Linguistic Typology and their Application to Phylogenetic Inference

**Yugo Murawaki**
Graduate School of Information Science and Electrical Engineering
Kyushu University
Fukuoka, Japan
murawaki@ait.kyushu-u.ac.jp

## Abstract

For phylogenetic inference, linguistic typology is a promising alternative to lexical evidence because it allows us to compare an arbitrary pair of languages. A challenging problem with typology-based phylogenetic inference is that the changes of typological features over time are less intuitive than those of lexical features. In this paper, we work on reconstructing typologically natural ancestors To do this, we leverage dependencies among typological features. We first represent each language by continuous latent components that capture feature dependencies. We then combine them with a typology evaluator that distinguishes typologically natural languages from other possible combinations of features. We perform phylogenetic inference in the continuous space and use the evaluator to ensure the typological naturalness of inferred ancestors. We show that the proposed method reconstructs known language families more accurately than baseline methods. Lastly, assuming the monogenesis hypothesis, we attempt to reconstruct a common ancestor of the world's languages.

## 1 Introduction

Linguistic typology is a cross-linguistic study that classifies the world's languages according to structural properties such as complexity of syllable structure and object-verb ordering. The availability of a large typology database (Haspelmath et al., 2005) makes it possible to take computational approaches to this area of study (Daumé III and Campbell, 2007; Georgi et al., 2010; Rama and Kolachina, 2012). In this paper, we consider its application to phylogenetic inference. We aim at reconstructing evolutionary trees that illustrate how modern languages have descended from common ancestors.

Typological features have two advantages over other linguistic traits. First, they allow us to compare an arbitrary pair of languages. By contrast, historical linguistics has worked on regular sound changes (see (Bouchard-Côté et al., 2013) for computational models). Glottochronology and computational phylogenetics make use of the presence and absence of lexical items (Swadesh, 1952; Gray and Atkinson, 2003). All these approaches require that certain sets of cognates, or words with common etymological origins, are shared by the languages in question. For this reason, it is hardly possible to use lexical evidence to search for external relations involving language isolates and tiny language families such as Ainu, Basque, and Japanese. For these languages, typology can be seen as the last hope.

The second advantage is that typological features are potentially capable of tracing evolutionary history on the order of 10,000 years because they change far more slowly than lexical traits. A glottochronological study indicates that even if Japanese is genetically related to Korean, they diverged from a common ancestor no earlier than 6,700 years ago (Hattori, 1999). Even the basic vocabulary vanishes so rapidly that after some 6,000 years, the retention rate becomes comparable to chance similarity. By contrast, the word order of Japanese, for example is astonishingly stable. It remains intact from the earliest attested data. Thus we argue that if we manage to develop a statistical model of typological



*Human Language Technologies: The 2015 Annual Conference of the North American Chapter of the ACL*, pages 324–334,
Denver, Colorado, May 31 – June 5, 2015. 

| | Munda | Mon-Khmer |
|---|---|---|
| **grammar** | synthetic | analytic |
| **word order** | head-last, OV, postpositional | head-first, VO, prepositional |
| **affixation** | pre/infixing, suffixing | pre/infixing or isolating |
| **fusion** | agglutinative | fusional |
| **consonants** | stable/assimilative | shifting/dissimilative |
| **vowels** | harmonizing/stable | reducing/diphthongizing |

Table 1: Typological comparison of the Munda and Mon-Khmer branches of the Austroasiatic languages. An abridged version of Table 1 of (Donegan and Stampe, 2004).

changes with predictive power, we can understand a much deeper past.

A challenging problem with typology-based inference is that the changes of typological features over time are less intuitive than those of lexical features. Regular sound changes have been well known since the time of the Neogrammarians. The binary representations of lexical items commonly used in computational phylogenetics correspond to their their presence and absence. The alternations of each feature value can be straightforwardly interpreted as the birth and death (Le Quesne, 1974) of a lexical item. By contrast, it is difficult to understand how a language switches from SOV to SVO.

Practically speaking, since each language is represented by a vector of categorical features, we can easily perform distance-based hierarchical clustering. Still, the extent to which the resultant tree reflects evolutionary history is unclear. Teh et al. (2008) proposed a generative model for hierarchical clustering, which straightforwardly explains evolutionary history. However, features used in their experiments were binarized in a one-versus-rest manner (i.e., expanding a feature with $K$ possible values into $K$ binary features) (Daumé III and Campbell, 2007) although the model itself had an ability to handle categorical values. With the independence assumption of binary features, the model was likely to reconstruct ancestors with logically impossible states.

Typological studies have shown that dependencies among typological features are not limited to the categorical constraints. For example, object-verb ordering is said to imply adjective-noun ordering (Greenberg, 1963). A natural question arises as to what would happen to adjective-noun ordering if object-verb ordering were altered. While dependencies among feature *pairs* were discussed in previous studies (Greenberg, 1978; Dunn et al., 2011), dependencies among more than two features are yet to be exploited.

To gain a better insight into typological changes, we take Austroasiatic languages as an example. Table 1 compares some typological features of the Munda and Mon-Khmer branches. Although their genetic relationship was firmly established, they are almost opposite in structure. Their common ancestor is considered to have been Mon-Khmer-like. This indicates that the holistic changes have happened in the Munda branch (Donegan and Stampe, 2004). To generalize from this example, we suggest the following hypotheses:

1. The holistic polarization can be explained by latent components that control dependencies among observable features.
2. Typological changes can occur in a way such that typologically unnatural intermediate states are avoided.

To incorporate these hypotheses, we propose continuous space representations of linguistic typology. Specifically, we use an autoencoder (see (Bengio, 2009) for a review) to map each language into the latent space. In analogy with principal component analysis (PCA), each element of the encoded vector is referred to as a component. We combine the autoencoder with a typology evaluator that distinguishes typologically natural languages from other possible combinations of features.

Armed with the typology evaluator, we perform phylogenetic inference in the continuous space. The evaluator ensures that inferred ancestors are also typologically natural. The inference procedure is guided by known language families so that each component's stability with respect to evolutionary history can be learned. To evaluate the proposed method, we hide some trees to see how well they are reconstructed.

Lastly, we build a binary tree on top of known language families. This experiment is based on a controversial assumption that the world's languages descend from one common ancestor. Our goal here is not to address the validity of the monogenesis hypothesis. Rather, we address the questions of how the common ancestor looked like if it existed and how modern languages have evolved from it.

## 2 Related Work

In linguistic typology, much attention has been given to non-tree-like evolution (Trubetzkoy, 1928). Daumé III (2009) incorporated linguistic areas into a phylogenetic model and reported that the extended model outperformed a simple tree model. This result motivates us to use known language families for supervision rather than to perform phylogenetic inference in purely unsupervised settings.

Dunn et al. (2011) applied a state-process model to reference phylogenetic trees to test if a pair of features is independent. The model they adopted can hardly be extended to handle multiple features. They separately applied the model to each language family and claimed that most dependencies were lineage-specific rather than universal tendencies. However, each known language family is so shallow in time depth that few feature changes can be observed in it (Croft et al., 2011). We mitigate data sparsity by letting our model share parameters among language families all over the world.

## 3 Data and Preprocessing

### 3.1 Typology Database and Phylogenetic Trees

The typology database we used is the *World Atlas of Language Structures* (WALS) (Haspelmath et al., 2005). As of 2014, it contains 2,679 languages and 192 typological features. It covers less than 15% of the possible language/feature pairs, however.

WALS provides phylogenetic trees but they only have two layers above individual languages: family and genus. Language families include Indo-European, Austronesian and Niger-Congo, and genera within Indo-European include Germanic, Indic and Slavic. For more detailed trees, we used hierarchical classifications provided by Ethnologue (Lewis et al., 2014). The mapping between WALS and Ethnologue was done using ISO 639-3 language codes. We manually corrected some obsolete language codes used by WALS and dropped languages without language codes. We also excluded languages labeled by Ethnologue as Deaf sign language, Mixed language, Creole or Unclassified. For both WALS and Ethnologue trees, we removed intermediate nodes that had only one child. Language isolates were treated as family trees of their own. We obtained 193 family trees for WALS and 189 for Ethnologue.

We made no further modifications to the trees although we were aware that some language families and their subgroups were highly controversial. In the future work, the Altaic language family, for example, should be disassembled into Turkic, Mongolic and Tungusic to test if the Altaic hypothesis is valid (Vovin, 2005).

Next, we removed features with low coverage. Some features such as "Inclusive/Exclusive Forms in Pama-Nyungan" (39B) and "Irregular Negatives in Sign Languages" (139A) were not supposed to cover the world. We selected 98 features that covered at least 10% of languages.[1]

We used the original, categorical feature values. The mergers of some fine-grained feature values seem desirable (Daumé III and Campbell, 2007; Greenhill et al., 2010; Dunn et al., 2011). Some features like "Consonant Inventories" might be better represented as real-valued features. We leave them for future work.

In the end, we created two sets of data. The first set PARTIAL was used to train the typology evaluator. We selected 887 languages that covered at least 30% of features. The second set FULL was for phylogenetic inference. We chose language families in each of which at least 30% of features were covered by one or more languages in the family. The numbers of language families (including language isolates) were reduced to 103 for WALS and 110 for Ethnologue.

### 3.2 Missing Data Imputation

We imputed missing data using the R package *missMDA* (Josse et al., 2012). It handled missing values using multiple correspondence analysis (MCA). Specifically, we used the imputeMCA function to

[1] Additional cleanup is needed. For example, the high-coverage feature "The Position of Negative Morphemes in SOV Languages" (144L) is not defined for non-SOV languages. A natural solution is to add another feature value (*Undefined*).

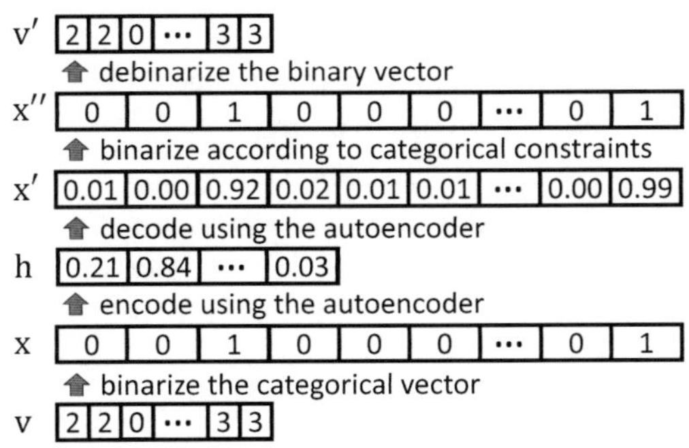


Figure 1: Representations of a language.

predict missing feature values. The substituted data are used (1) to train the typology evaluator and (2) to initialize phylogenetic inference.

To evaluate the performance of missing data imputation, we hid some known features to see how well they were predicted. A 10-fold cross-validation test using the PARTIAL dataset showed that 64.6% of feature values were predicted correctly. It considerably outperformed (1) the random baseline of 22.4% and (2) the most-frequent-value baseline of 28.1%. Thus our assumption of dependencies among features was confirmed.

## 4 Typology Evaluator

We use a combination of an autoencoder to transform typological features into continuous latent components, and an energy-based model to evaluate how a given feature vector is typologically natural.

We begin with the autoencoder. Figure 1 shows various representations of a language. The original feature representation $\mathrm{v}$ is a vector of categorical features. $\mathrm{v}$ is binarized into $\mathrm{x} \in \{0,1\}^{d_0}$ in a one-versus-rest manner. $\mathrm{x}$ is mapped by an encoder to a latent representation $\mathrm{h} \in [0,1]^{d_1}$, in which $d_1$ is the dimension of the latent space:

$$\mathrm{h} = s(\mathrm{W_e x} + \mathrm{b_e}),$$

where $s$ is the sigmoid function, and matrix $\mathrm{W_e}$ and vector $\mathrm{b_e}$ are weight parameters to be estimated. A decoder then maps $\mathrm{h}$ back to $\mathrm{x}'$ through a similar transformation:

$$\mathrm{x}' = s(\mathrm{W_d h} + \mathrm{b_d}).$$

We use tied weights: $\mathrm{W_d} = \mathrm{W_e}^T$. Note that $x'$ is a real vector. To recover a categorical vector, we need to first binarize $\mathrm{x}'$ according to categorical constraints and then to debinarize the resultant vector.

The training objective of the autoencoder alone is to minimize cross-entropy of reconstruction:

$$L_{\mathrm{AE}}(\mathrm{x}, \mathrm{x}') = -\sum_{k=1}^{d} x_k \log x'_k + (1 - x_k)\log(1 - x'_k),$$

where $x_k$ is the $k$-th element of $\mathrm{x}$.

Next, we plug an energy-based model into the autoencoder. It gives a probability to $\mathrm{x}$.

$$p(\mathrm{x}) = \frac{\exp(\mathrm{W_s}^T \mathrm{g})}{\sum_{\mathrm{x}'} \exp(\mathrm{W_s}^T \mathrm{g}')},$$
$$\mathrm{g} = s(\mathrm{W_l h} + \mathrm{b_l}),$$

where vector $\mathrm{W_s}$, matrix $\mathrm{W_l}$ and bias term $\mathrm{b_l}$ are the weights to be estimated. $\mathrm{h}$ is mapped to $\mathrm{g} \in [0,1]^{d_2}$ before evaluation. This transformation is motivated by our speculation that typologically natural languages may not be linearly separable from unnatural ones in the latent space since biplots of principal components of PCA often show sinusoidal waves (Novembre and Stephens, 2008). The denominator sums over all possible states of $\mathrm{x}'$, including those which violate categorical constraints. By maximizing the average log probability of training data, we can distinguish typologically natural languages from other possible combinations of features.

Given a set of $N$ languages with missing data imputed,[2] our training objective is to maximize the following:

$$\sum_{i=1}^{N} (-L_{\mathrm{AE}}(\mathrm{x}_i, \mathrm{x}'_i) + C \log p(\mathrm{x}_i))),$$

where $C$ is some constant. Weights are optimized by the gradient-based AdaGrad algorithm (Duchi et al., 2011) with a mini-batch. A problem with this optimization is that the derivative of the second term contains an expectation that involves a summation over all possible states of $\mathrm{x}'$, which is computationally intractable. Inspired by contrastive divergence (Hinton, 2002), we do not compute the expectation exactly but approximate it by few negative samples collected from Gibbs samplers.

### 4.1 Mixing Languages: An Experiment

To analyze the continuous space representations, we generated mixtures of two languages, which were

[2] We tried a joint inference of weight optimization and missing data imputation but dropped it for its instability. A cross-validation test revealed that the joint inference caused a big accuracy drop in missing data imputation.

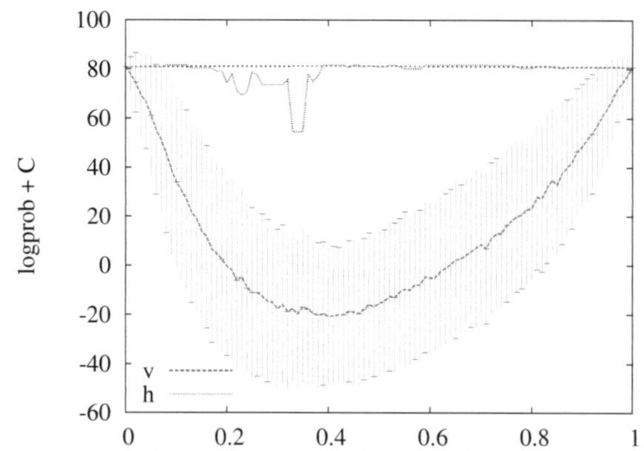

Figure 2: Mixtures of Mundari (a Munda language) and Khmer (a Mon-Khmer language). The transitions from Mundari (leftmost) to Khmer (rightmost). The vertical axis denotes typological naturalness $\log p(\mathrm{x}) + C$.

potential candidates for their common ancestor. The pair of languages $A$ and $B$ was mixed in two ways. First, we replaced elements of $A$'s categorical vector $\mathrm{v}_A$ with $\mathrm{v}_B$, with the specified probability. We repeated this procedure 1,000 times to obtain a mean and a standard deviation. Second, we applied linear interpolation of two vectors $\mathrm{h}_A$ and $\mathrm{h}_B$ and mapped the resultant vector to $\mathrm{v}'$. In this experiment, $d_0 = 539$ and we set $d_1 = 100$ and $d_2 = 10$.

Figure 2 shows the case of the Austroasiatic languages. In the original, categorical representations, the mixtures of two languages form a deep valley (i.e., typologically unnatural intermediate states). By contrast, the continuous space representations allow a language to change into another without harming typological naturalness. This indicates that in the continuous space, we can easily reconstruct typologically natural ancestors. The major feature changes include "postpositional" to "prepositional" (0.46–0.47), "strongly suffixing" to "little affixation" (0.53–0.54) and "SOV" to "SVO" (0.60–0.61).

## 5 Phylogenetic Inference

### 5.1 Tree Model

We use continuous space representations and the typology evaluator for phylogenetic inference. Our strategy is to find a tree in which (1) nodes are typologically natural and (2) edges are shorter by the principle of Occam's razor. The first point is realized by applying the typology evaluator. To implement the second point, we define a probability distribution over a parent-to-child move in the continuous space.

We assume that latent components are independent. For the $k$-th component, the node's value $h_k$ is drawn from a Normal distribution with mean $h_k^{\mathrm{P}}$ (its parent's value) and precision $\lambda_k$ (inverse variance). The further the node moves, the smaller probability it receives. Precision controls each component's stability with respect to evolutionary history.

We set a gamma prior over $\lambda_k$, with hyperparameters $\alpha$ and $\beta$.[3] Taking advantage of the conjugacy property, we marginalize out $\lambda_k$. Suppose that we have drawn $n$ samples and let $m_i$ be the difference between the $i$-th node and its parent, $h_k - h_k^{\mathrm{P}}$. Then the posterior hyperparameters are $\alpha_n = \alpha + n/2$ and $\beta_n = \beta + \frac{1}{2}\sum_{i=1}^{n} m_i^2$. The posterior predictive distribution is Student's $t$-distribution (Murphy, 2007):

$$p_k(h_k | h_k^{\mathrm{P}}, M_{\mathrm{hist}}, \alpha, \beta) = t_{2\alpha_n}(h_k | h_k^{\mathrm{P}}, \sigma^2 = \beta_n/\alpha_n),$$

where $M_{\mathrm{hist}}$ is a collection of $\alpha$, $\beta$ and a history of previously observed differences. The probability of a parent-to-child move is a product of the probabilities of its component moves:

$$p_{\mathrm{MOVE}}(\mathrm{h}|\mathrm{h}^{\mathrm{P}}, M_{\mathrm{hist}}) = \prod_{k=1}^{d} p_k(h_k | h_k^{\mathrm{P}}, M_{\mathrm{hist}}).$$

The root node is drawn from a uniform distribution.

To sum up, the probability of a phylogenetic tree $\tau$ is given by $p_{\mathrm{EVAL}}(\mathrm{tree}) \times p_{\mathrm{CONT}}(\mathrm{tree})$, where

$$\begin{aligned} p_{\mathrm{EVAL}}(\mathrm{tree}) &= \mathrm{Uniform}(\mathrm{tree}) \prod_{\mathrm{x} \in \mathrm{nodes}(\tau)} p(\mathrm{x}), \\ p_{\mathrm{CONT}}(\mathrm{tree}) &= \mathrm{Uniform}(\mathrm{root}) \\ &\quad \times \prod_{(\mathrm{h},\mathrm{h}^{\mathrm{P}}) \in \mathrm{edges}(\tau)} p_{\mathrm{MOVE}}(\mathrm{h}|\mathrm{h}^{\mathrm{P}}, M_{\mathrm{hist}}). \end{aligned}$$

$\mathrm{nodes}(\tau)$ is the set of nodes in $\tau$, and $\mathrm{edges}(\tau)$ is the set of edges in $\tau$, We abuse notation as $M_{\mathrm{hist}}$ is updated each time a node is observed.

### 5.2 Inference

Given observed data, we aim at reconstructing the best phylogenetic tree. The data observed are (1) leaves (with some missing feature values) and (2) some tree topologies. We need to infer (1) the missing feature values of leaves, (2) the latent components of internal nodes including the root and (3) the remaining portion of tree topologies. Since leaves

[3] In the experiments, we set $\alpha = \beta = 0.1$.

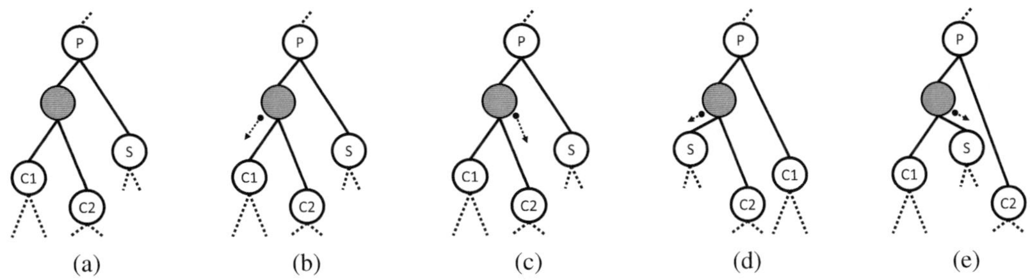


Figure 3: SWAP operator. The gray circle is the target node. Its parent P, sibling S and two children C1 and C2 are shown. (a) The current state. (b–e) The proposed states. (b–c) The topology remains the same but the target is moved toward C1 and C2, respectively. (d) C1 is swapped for S. (e) C2 is swapped for S.

are tied to observed categorical vectors, our inference procedures also work on them. We map categorical vectors into the latent space every time we attempt to change a feature value. By contrast, we adopt latent vectors as the primary representations of internal nodes.

Take the Indo-European language family for example. Its tree topology is given but the states of its internal nodes such as Indo-European, Germanic and Indic need to be inferred. Dutch has some missing feature values. Although they have been imputed with multiple correspondence analysis, its close relatives such as Danish and German might be helpful for better estimation.

We need to infer portions of tree topologies even though a set of trees (language families) is given. To evaluate the performance of phylogenetic inference, we hide some trees to see how well they are reconstructed. To reconstruct a common ancestor of the world's languages, we build a binary tree on top of the set of trees. Note that while we only infer binary trees, a node may have more than two children in the fixed portions of tree topologies.

We use Gibbs sampling for inference. We define four operators, CAT, COMP, SWAP and MOVE. The first tree operators correspond to missing feature values, latent components and tree topologies, respectively.

CAT – For the target categorical feature of a leaf node, we sample from $K$ possible values. Let $\mathrm{x}'$ be a binary feature representation with the target feature value altered, let $\mathrm{h}^{\mathrm{P}}$ be the state of the node's parent, and let $\mathrm{h}' = s(\mathrm{W_e x}' + \mathrm{b_e})$. The probability of choosing $\mathrm{x}'$ is proportional to $p(\mathrm{x}')\, p_{\mathrm{MOVE}}(\mathrm{h}'|\mathrm{h}^{\mathrm{P}}, M_{\mathrm{hist}})$, where $\mathrm{h}$ is removed from the history. The second term is omitted if the target node has no parent.[4]

COMP – For the target $k$-th component of an internal node, we choose its new value using the Metropolis algorithm. It stochastically proposes a new state and accepts it with some probability. If the proposal is rejected, the current state is reused as the next state. The proposal distribution $Q(h'_k|h_k)$ is a Gaussian distribution centered at $h_k$. The acceptance probability is $a(h_k, h'_k) = \min(1, P(h'_k)/P(h_k))$, where $P(h'_k)$ is defined as

$$P(h'_k) = p(\mathrm{x}')\, p_{\mathrm{MOVE}}(\mathrm{h}'|\mathrm{h}^{\mathrm{P}}, M_{\mathrm{hist}}) \prod_{\mathrm{h}^{\mathrm{C}} \in \mathrm{children}(\mathrm{h}')} p_{\mathrm{MOVE}}(\mathrm{h}^{\mathrm{C}}|\mathrm{h}', M_{\mathrm{hist}})$$

where $\mathrm{children}(\mathrm{h}')$ is the set of the target node's children.

SWAP – For the target internal node (which cannot be the root), we use the Metropolis-Hastings algorithm to locally rearrange its neighborhood in a way similar to Li et al. (2000). We first propose a new state as illustrated in Figure 3. The target node has a parent P, a sibling S and two children C1 and C2. From among S, C1 and C2, we choose two nodes. If C1 and C2 are chosen, the topology remains the same; otherwise S is swapped for one of the node's children. It is shown that one topology can be transformed into any other topology in a finite number of steps (Li et al., 2000).

To improve mobility, we also move the target node toward C1, C2 or S, depending on the proposed topology. Here the selected node is denoted by $*$. We first draw $r'$ from a log-normal distribution whose underlying Gaussian distribution has

[4]It is easy to extend the operator to handle internal nodes supplied with some categorical features.

mean $-1$ and variance 1. The target's proposed state is $\mathrm{h}' = (1 - r')\mathrm{h} + r'\mathrm{h}^*$. $r'$ can be greater than 1, and in that case, the proposed state $\mathrm{h}'$ is more distant from $\mathrm{h}^*$ than the current state h. This ensures that the transition is reversible because $r = 1/r'$. The acceptance probability can be calculated in a similar manner to that described for COMP.

MOVE – Propose to move the target internal node, without swapping its neighbors.

For initialization, missing feature values are imputed by *missMDA*. The initial tree is constructed by distance-based agglomerative clustering. The state of an internal node is set to the average of those of its children.

## 6 Experiments

### 6.1 Reconstruction of Known Family Trees

#### 6.1.1 Data and Method

We first conducted a quantitative evaluation of phylogenetic inference, using known family trees. We ran 5-fold cross-validations. For each of WALS and Ethnologue, we subdivided a set of language families into 5 subsets with roughly the same number of leaves. Because of some huge language families, the number of language families per subset was uneven. We disassembled family trees in the target subset and to let the model reconstruct a binary tree for each language family. Unlike ordinary held-out evaluation, this experiment used all data for inference at once.

#### 6.1.2 Model Settings

We used the parameter settings described in Section 4.1. For phylogenetic inference, we ran 9,000 burn-in iterations after which we collected 100 samples at an interval of 10 iterations.

For comparison, we performed average-link agglomerative clustering (ALC). It has two variants, ALC-CAT and ALC-CONT. ALC-CAT worked on categorical features and used the ratio of disagreement as a distance metric. ALC-CONT performed clustering in the continuous space, using cosine distance. In other words, we can examine the effects of the typology evaluator and precision parameters. For these models, missing feature values are imputed by *missMDA*.

#### 6.1.3 Evaluation Measures

We present purity (Heller and Ghahramani, 2005), subtree (Teh et al., 2008) and outlier fraction

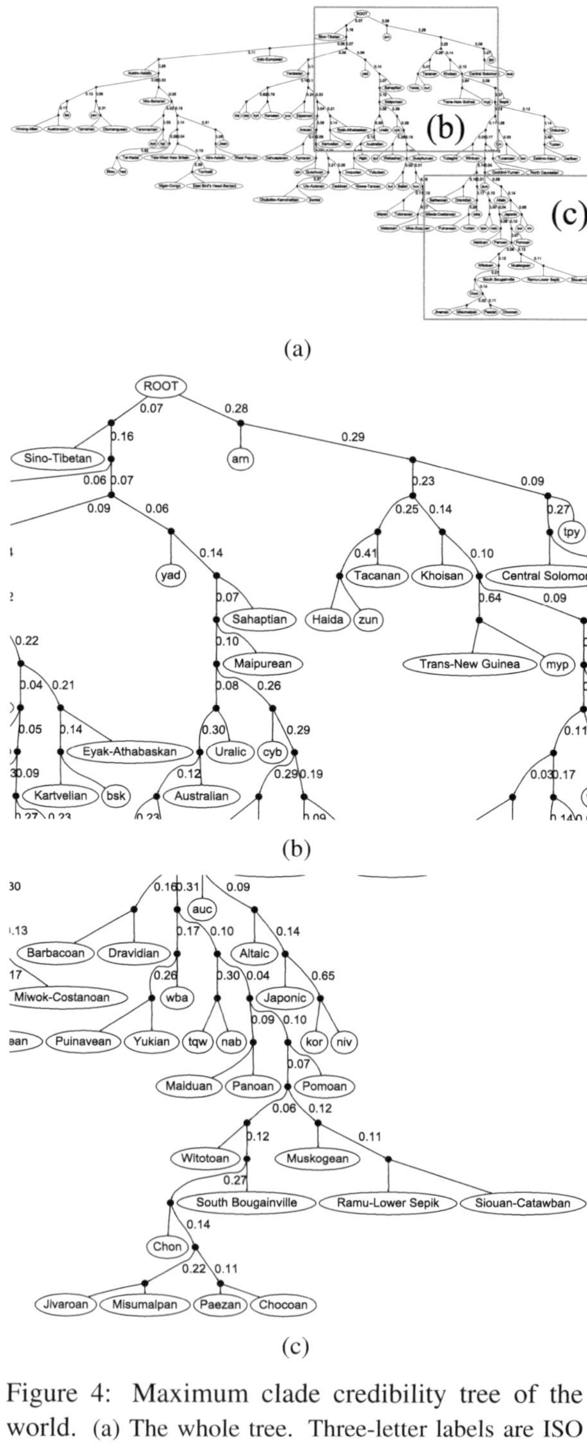


Figure 4: Maximum clade credibility tree of the world. (a) The whole tree. Three-letter labels are ISO 639-3 codes. Nodes below language families are omitted. (b–c) Portions of the tree are enlarged.

scores (Krishnamurthy et al., 2012). All scores are between 0 and 1 and higher scores are better. We calculated these scores for each language family and

| | WALS | | | | | | Ethnologue | |
|---|---|---|---|---|---|---|---|---|
| | purity | | subtree | | outlier | | outlier | |
| ALC-CAT | .500 | .557 | .608 | .626 | .343 | .330 | **.358** | **.398** |
| ALC-CONT | .503 | .557 | **.630** | .630 | .343 | .330 | .353 | .395 |
| Proposed | **.522** | **.572** | .603 | **.651** | **.351** | **.346** | .356 | .394 |

Table 2: Results of the reconstruction of known family trees. Macro-averages are followed by micro-averages.

report macro- and micro-averages. Only non-trivial family trees (trees with more than two children) were considered.

Purity and subtree scores compare inferred trees with gold-standard class labels. In WALS, genera were treated as class labels because they were the only intermediate layer between families and leaves. By contrast, Ethnologue provided more complex trees and we were unable to assign one class label to each language. For this reason, only outlier fraction scores are reported for Ethnologue.

#### 6.1.4 Results

Table 2 shows the scores for reconstructed family trees. The proposed method outperformed the baselines in 5 out of 8 metrics. Three methods performed almost equally for Ethnologue. We suspect that typological features reflect long term trends in comparison to Ethnologue's fine-grained classification. For WALS, the proposed method was beaten by average-link agglomerative clustering only in the macro-average of subtree scores. One possible explanation is randomness of the proposed method. Apparently, random sampling distributed errors more evenly than deterministic clustering. It was penalized more often by subtree scores because they required that all leaves of an internal node belonged to the same class.

### 6.2 Reconstruction of a Common Ancestor of the World's Languages

We reconstructed a single tree that covers the world. To do this, we build a binary tree on top of known language families, a product of historical linguistics. It is generally said that historical linguistics cannot go far beyond 6,000–7,000 years (Nichols, 2011). Here we attempt to break the brick wall.

It is no surprise that this experiment is full of problems and difficulties. No quantitative evaluation is possible. Underlying assumptions are questionable. No one knows for sure if there was such a thing as one common ancestor of all modern languages. Moreover, *language capacity* of humans, in addition to languages themselves, is likely to have evolved over time (Nichols, 2011). This casts doubt on the applicability of the typology evaluator, which is trained on modern languages, to languages of far distant past. Nevertheless, it is fascinating to make inference on the world's ancestral languages.

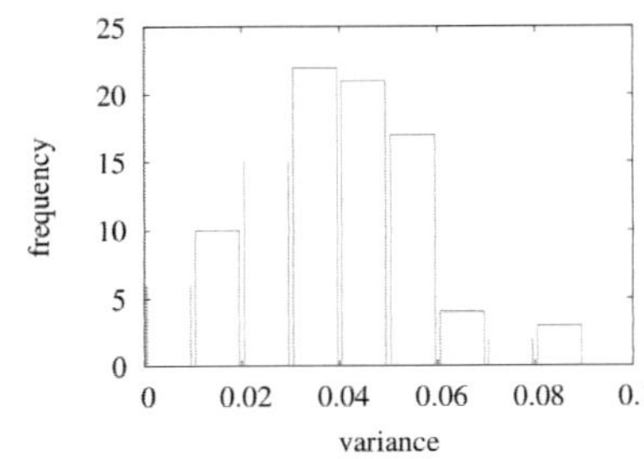

Figure 5: Histogram of posterior variances $\sigma^2 = \beta_n/\alpha_n$ of the 4,000th sample.

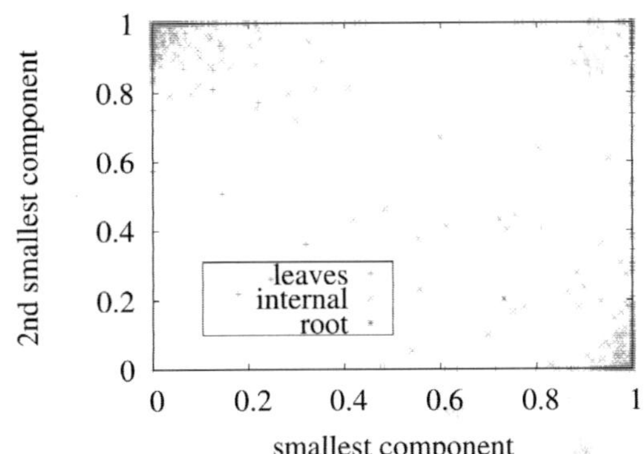

Figure 6: Scatter plot of languages using the components with the two smallest variances.

We used Ethnologue as the known tree topologies. For Gibbs sampling, we ran 3,000 burn-in iterations after which we collected 100 samples at an interval of 10 iterations.

Figure 4 shows a reconstructed tree. To summarize multiple sample trees, we constructed a maximum clade credibility tree. For each clade (a set of all leaves that share a common ancestor), we calculated the fraction of times it appears in the collected samples, which we call a *support* in this pa-

| Features | Frequencies/Values |
|---|---|
| Consonant Inventories | 95 Average |
| | 5 Moderately small |
| Vowel Quality Inventories | 85 Average (5-6) |
| | 15 Small (2-4) |
| Syllable Structure | 100 Moderately complex |
| | 0 Complex |
| Coding of Nominal Plurality | 97 Plural suffix |
| | 2 Plural word |
| | 1 No plural |
| | 0 Plural clitic |
| Order of Numeral and Noun | 61 Noun-Numeral |
| | 39 Numeral-Noun |
| Position of Case Affixes | 61 No case affixes or adp. clitics |
| | 39 Case suffixes |
| Ord. of SOV | 61 SOV |
| | 38 SVO |
| | 1 No dominant order |
| Ord. of Adposition and NP | 91 Postpositions |
| | 9 Prepositions |
| Ord. of Adjective and Noun | 87 Noun-Adjective |
| | 13 Adjective-Noun |

Table 3: Some features of the world's ancestor with sample frequencies.

per. A tree was scored by the product of supports of all clades within it, and we created a tree that maximized the score. Each edge label shows the support of the corresponding clade. As indicated by generally low supports, the sample trees were very unstable. Some geographically distant groups of languages were clustered near the bottom. We partially attribute this to the *underspecificity* of linguistic typology: even if a pair of languages shares the same feature vector, they are not necessarily the same language. This problem might be eased by incorporating geospatial information into phylogenetic inference (Bouckaert et al., 2012).

Table 3 shows some features of the root. The reconstructed ancestor is moderate in phonological typology, uses suffixing in morphology and prefers the SOV word order. The inferred word order agrees with speculations given by previous studies (Maurits and Griffiths, 2014).

Figure 5 shows the histogram of variance parameters. Some latent components had smaller variances and thus were more stable with respect to evolutionary history. Figure 6 displays languages using the components with the two smallest variances. Unlike PCA plots, data concentrated at the edges.

We used a geometric mean of $p_{\text{MOVE}}$ of multiple samples to calculate how a modern language is similar to another. The case of Japanese is shown in Table 4. This ranked list is considerably different from that of disagreement rates of categorical vectors (Spearman's $\rho = 0.76$). When features' stability with respect to evolutionary history is considered, Japanese is less closer to Korean and Ainu than to some Tibeto-Burman languages south of the Himalayas. As the importance of these minor languages of Northeast India is recognized, the Sino-Tibetan tree might be drastically revised in the future (Blench and Post, 2013). The least similar languages include the Malayo-Polynesian and Nilo-Saharan languages.

| Rank | Language | Classificatoin | Logprob. |
|---|---|---|---|
| 1 | (Japanese) | Japonic | 76.8 |
| 2 | Shuri | Japonic | -37.7 |
| 3 | Khalkha | Altaic>Mongolic | -200.0 |
| 4 | Lepcha | Sino-Tibetan>Tibeto-Burman | -201.9 |
| 5 | Chuvash | Altaic>Turkic | -205.5 |
| 6 | Deuri | Sino-Tibetan>Tibeto-Burman | -218.3 |
| 7 | Urum | Altaic>Turkic | -218.6 |
| 8 | Ordos | Altaic>Mongolic | -219.0 |
| 9 | Uzbek | Altaic>Turkic | -219.6 |
| 10 | Archi | N. Caucasian>E. Caucasian | -221.5 |
| 131 | Korean | (isolate) | -265.7 |
| 493 | Ainu | (isolate) | -409.9 |

Table 4: Modern languages ranked by the similarity to Japanese.

## 7 Conclusion

In this paper, we proposed continuous space representations of linguistic typology and used them for phylogenetic inference. Feature dependencies are a major focus of linguistic typology, and typology data have occasionally been used for computational phylogenetics. To our knowledge, however, we are the first to integrate the two lines of research. In addition, the continuous space representations underlying interdependent discrete features are applicable to other data including phonological inventories (Moran et al., 2014).

We believe that typology provides important clues for long-term language change. The currently available database only contains modern languages, but we expect that data of some ancestral languages could greatly facilitate computational approaches to diachronic linguistics.

## Acknowledgment

This work was partly supported by JSPS KAKENHI Grant Number 26730122.

## References


Yoshua Bengio. 2009. Learning deep architectures for AI. *Foundations and Trends in Machine Learning*, 2(1):1–127.

Roger Blench and Mark W. Post. 2013. Rethinking Sino-Tibetan phylogeny from the perspective of North East Indian languages. In Nathan Hill and Tom Owen-Smith, editors, *Trans-Himalayan Linguistics*, pages 71–104. De Gruyter.

Alexandre Bouchard-Côté, David Hall, Thomas L. Griffiths, and Dan Klein. 2013. Automated reconstruction of ancient languages using probabilistic models of sound change. *PNAS*, 110(11):4224–4229.

Remco Bouckaert, Philippe Lemey, Michael Dunn, Simon J. Greenhill, Alexander V. Alekseyenko, Alexei J. Drummond, Russell D. Gray, Marc A. Suchard, and Quentin D. Atkinson. 2012. Mapping the origins and expansion of the Indo-European language family. *Science*, 337(6097):957–960.

William Croft, Tanmoy Bhattacharya, Dave Kleinschmidt, D. Eric Smith, and T. Florian Jaeger. 2011. Greenbergian universals, diachrony, and statistical analyses. *Linguistic Typology*, 15(2):433–453.

Hal Daumé III and Lyle Campbell. 2007. A Bayesian model for discovering typological implications. In *ACL*, pages 65–72.

Hal Daumé III. 2009. Non-parametric Bayesian areal linguistics. In *HLT-NAACL*, pages 593–601.

Patricia Donegan and David Stampe. 2004. Rhythm and the synthetic drift of Munda. In Rajendra Singh, editor, *The Yearbook of South Asian Languages and Linguistics*, pages 3–36. Mouton de Gruyter.

John Duchi, Elad Hazan, and Yoram Singer. 2011. Adaptive subgradient methods for online learning and stochastic optimization. *The Journal of Machine Learning Research*, 12:2121–2159.

Michael Dunn, Simon J. Greenhill, Stephen C. Levinson, and Russell D. Gray. 2011. Evolved structure of language shows lineage-specific trends in word-order universals. *Nature*, 473(7345):79–82.

Ryan Georgi, Fei Xia, and William Lewis. 2010. Comparing language similarity across genetic and typologically-based groupings. In *COLING*, pages 385–393.

Russell D. Gray and Quentin D. Atkinson. 2003. Language-tree divergence times support the Anatolian theory of Indo-European origin. *Nature*, 426(6965):435–439.

Joseph H. Greenberg, editor. 1963. *Universals of language*. MIT Press.

Joseph H. Greenberg. 1978. Diachrony, synchrony and language universals. In Joseph H. Greenberg, Charles A. Ferguson, and Edith A. Moravesik, editors, *Universals of human language*, volume 1. Stanford University Press.

Simon J. Greenhill, Quentin D. Atkinson, Andrew Meade, and Russel D. Gray. 2010. The shape and tempo of language evolution. *Proc. of the Royal Society B*, 277(1693):2443–2450.

Martin Haspelmath, Matthew Dryer, David Gil, and Bernard Comrie, editors. 2005. *The World Atlas of Language Structures*. Oxford University Press.

Shiro Hattori. 1999. *Nihongo no keito (The Genealogy of Japanese)*. Iwanami Shoten.

Katherine A. Heller and Zoubin Ghahramani. 2005. Bayesian hierarchical clustering. In *ICML*, pages 297–304.

Geoffrey E. Hinton. 2002. Training products of experts by minimizing contrastive divergence. *Neural Computation*, 14(8):1771–1800.

Julie Josse, Marie Chavent, Benot Liquet, and François Husson. 2012. Handling missing values with regularized iterative multiple correspondence analysis. *Journal of Classification*, 29(1):91–116.

Akshay Krishnamurthy, Sivaraman Balakrishnan, Min Xu, and Aarti Singh. 2012. Efficient active algorithms for hierarchical clustering. In *ICML*, pages 887–894.

Walter J. Le Quesne. 1974. The uniquely evolved character concept and its cladistic application. *Systematic Biology*, 23(4):513–517.

M. Paul Lewis, Gary F. Simons, and Charles D. Fennig, editors. 2014. *Ethnologue: Languages of the World, 17th Edition*. SIL International. Online version: http://www.ethnologue.com.

Shuying Li, Dennis K. Pearl, and Hani Doss. 2000. Phylogenetic tree construction using Markov chain Monte Carlo. *Journal of the American Statistical Association*, 95(450):493–508.

Luke Maurits and Thomas L. Griffiths. 2014. Tracing the roots of syntax with Bayesian phylogenetics. *PNAS*, 111(37):13576–13581.

Steven Moran, Daniel McCloy, and Richard Wright, editors. 2014. *PHOIBLE Online*. Max Planck Institute for Evolutionary Anthropology, Leipzig.

Kevin P. Murphy. 2007. Conjugate Bayesian analysis of the Gaussian distribution. Technical report, University of British Columbia.

Johanna Nichols. 2011. Monogenesis or polygenesis: A single ancestral language for all humanity? In Maggie Tallerman and Kathleen R. Gibson, editors, *The Oxford Handbook of Language Evolution*, pages 558–572. Oxford Univ Press.

John Novembre and Matthew Stephens. 2008. Interpreting principal component analyses of spatial population genetic variation. *Nature Genetics*, 40(5):646–649.

Taraka Rama and Prasanth Kolachina. 2012. How good are typological distances for determining genealogical relationships among languages? In *COLING Posters*, pages 975–984.

Morris Swadesh. 1952. Lexicostatistic dating of prehistoric ethnic contacts. *Proc. of American Philosophical Society*, 96:452–463.

Yee Whye Teh, Hal Daumé III, and Daniel Roy. 2008. Bayesian agglomerative clustering with coalescents. In *NIPS*, pages 1473–1480.

Nikolai Sergeevich Trubetzkoy. 1928. Proposition 16. In *Acts of the First International Congress of Linguists*, pages 17–18.

Alexander Vovin. 2005. The end of the Altaic controversy. *Central Asiatic Journal*, 49(1):71–132.

# Interpreting Compound Noun Phrases Using Web Search Queries

**Marius Paşca**
Google Inc.
1600 Amphitheatre Parkway
Mountain View, California 94043
mars@google.com

## Abstract

A weakly-supervised method is applied to anonymized queries to extract lexical interpretations of compound noun phrases (e.g., *"fortune 500 companies"*). The interpretations explain the subsuming role (*"listed in"*) that modifiers (*fortune 500*) play relative to heads (*companies*) within the noun phrases. Experimental results over evaluation sets of noun phrases from multiple sources demonstrate that interpretations extracted from queries have encouraging coverage and precision. The top interpretation extracted is deemed relevant for more than 70% of the noun phrases.

## 1 Introduction

**Motivation**: Semantic classes of interest to Web users are often expressed as lexical class labels (e.g., *"fortune 500 companies"*, *"italian composers"*, *"victorinox knives"*). Each class label hints at the implicit properties shared among its instances (e.g., *general electric*, *gaetano donizetti*, *swiss army jetsetter* respectively). Class labels allow for the organization of instances into hierarchies, which in turn allows for the systematic development of knowledge repositories. This motivates research efforts to acquire as many relevant class labels of instances as possible, which have received particular emphasis (Wang and Cohen, 2009; Dalvi et al., 2012; Flati et al., 2014). The efforts are part of the larger area of extracting open-domain facts and relations (Banko et al., 2007; Hoffart et al., 2013; Yao and Van Durme, 2014), ultimately delivering richer results in Web search.

Different methods can associate instances (*general electric*) with both class labels (*"fortune 500 companies"*) and facts (<*general electric*, *founded in*, *1892*>) extracted from text. But the class labels tend to be extracted, maintained and used separately from facts. Beyond organizing the class labels hierarchically (Kozareva and Hovy, 2010), the meaning of a class label is rarely explored (Nastase and Strube, 2008), nor is it made available downstream to applications using the extracted data.

**Contributions**: The method introduced in this paper is the first to exploit Web search queries to uncover the semantics of open-domain class labels in particular; and of compound noun phrases in general. The method extracts candidate, lexical interpretations of compound noun phrases from queries. The interpretations turn implicit properties or subsuming roles (*"listed in"*, *"from"*, *"made by"*) that modifiers (*fortune 500*, *italian*, *victorinox*) play within longer noun phrases (*"fortune 500 companies"*, *"italian composers"*, *"victorinox knives"*) into explicit strings. The roles of modifiers relative to heads of noun phrase compounds cannot be characterized in terms of a finite list of possible compounding relationships (Downing, 1977). Hence, the interpretations are not restricted to a closed, pre-defined set. Experimental results over evaluation sets of noun phrases from multiple sources demonstrate that interpretations can be extracted from queries for a significant fraction of the input noun phrases. Without relying on syntactic analysis, extracted interpretations induce implicit bracketings over the interpreted noun phrases. The bracketings reveal the multiple senses, some of which are more rare but still plausible, in which the same noun phrase can be sometimes explained. The quality of interpretations is encouraging, with at least one interpretation deemed relevant among the top 3 retrieved for 77% of the



*Human Language Technologies: The 2015 Annual Conference of the North American Chapter of the ACL*, pages 335–344,
Denver, Colorado, May 31 – June 5, 2015. 

noun phrases with extracted interpretations. The top interpretation is deemed relevant for more than 70% of the noun phrases.

**Applications**: The extracted interpretations can serve as a bridge connecting class labels and facts. Relevant interpretations allow one to potentially derive missing facts (<*general electric*, *listed in*, *fortune 500*>) from existing class labels (<*general electric*, *fortune 500 companies*>) and vice versa. In addition, relevant interpretations of class labels are themselves class labels inferred for the same instances. Examples are <*general electric*, *companies listed in fortune 500*>, or <*general electric*, *companies in fortune 500*>, based on <*general electric*, *fortune 500 companies*>. If the input class labels are organized hierarchically (<*fortune 500 companies*, *companies*>), interpretations explain why more specific class labels (*"fortune 500 companies"*, *"german companies"*, *"dow jones industrial average companies"*, *"french companies"*) do not merely belong under more general ones (*"companies"*), but do so along shared interpretations (*companies*→*listed in*→{*fortune 500*, *dow jones industrial average companies*}; vs. {*companies*→*from*→{*germany*, *france*}); and, more generally, aid in the better understanding of noun phrases.

## 2 Interpreting Noun Phrases

**Hypothesis**: Let $N$ be a compound noun phrase, containing a head $H$ preceded by modifiers $M$. Each of $H$ and $M$ may contain one or multiple tokens. Being a compound, the sequence of modifiers and head in $N$ act as a single noun (Downing, 1977; Hendrickx et al., 2013). If $N$ is relevant and of interest to Web users, then in a sufficiently large corpus it will eventually be referred to in relatively more verbose search queries, which explain the implicit role that modifiers $M$ play relative to the head $H$.

**Acquisition from Queries**: To illustrate the intuition above, consider the noun phrases *"water animals"* and *"zone 7 plants"*. If enough Web users are interested in the concepts represented by these noun phrases, then the phrases are likely to be submitted as search queries. In addition, some Web users seeking similar information are likely to submit queries that make the role of the modifiers *water* and *zone 7* explicit, such as *"animals living in water"* or *"plants that grow in zone 7"*.

As illustrated in Figure 1, the extraction method

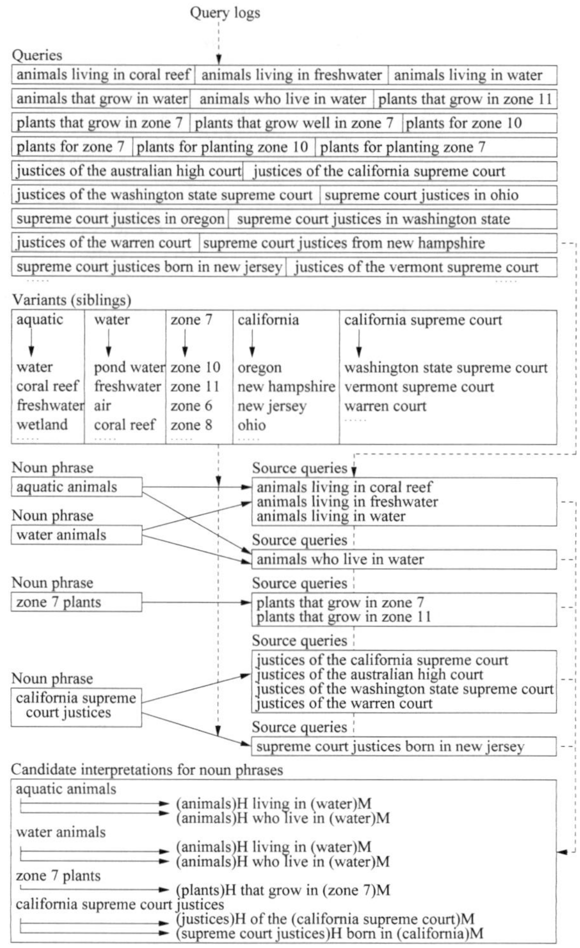


Figure 1: Overview of extraction of interpretations of noun phrases from Web search queries

proposed in this paper takes as input a vocabulary of noun phrases, as well as a set of anonymized queries from which possible interpretations for the noun phrases must be extracted. The extraction consists of several steps: (1) the selection of a subset of queries that may be candidate interpretations of some yet-to-be-specified noun phrases; (2) the matching of the selected queries to the noun phrases to interpret; and (3) the aggregation of matched queries into candidate interpretations extracted for a noun phrase.

**Queries as Candidate Interpretations**: The input queries are matched against the extraction patterns from Table 1. The use of targeted patterns in information extraction has been suggested before (Hearst, 1992; Fader et al., 2011). In our case, the patterns match queries that start with an arbitrary ngram $H$, followed by what is likely a

| Extraction Pattern<br>→ Examples of Matched Queries |
|---|
| Passive constructs: |
| $H$ [VBN\|VBD\|VBG] [<anything>] $M$ [<anything>] |
| → (plants)$_H$ grown in (zone 7)$_M$ |
| → (supreme court justices)$_H$ born in (new jersey)$_M$ |
| → (medicinal plants)$_H$ used as (ayurvedic)$_M$ drugs |
| → (manipulatives)$_H$ used in (elementary math)$_M$ |
| Prepositional constructs: |
| $H$ [IN\|TO] [<anything>] $M$ [<anything>] |
| → (plants)$_H$ for (zone 7)$_M$ |
| → (justices)$_H$ of the (california supreme court)$_M$ |
| → (medicinal plants)$_H$ in (ayurvedic)$_M$ products |
| → (math manipulatives)$_H$ for (elementary)$_M$ level |
| Relative pronoun constructs: |
| $H$ [that\|who\|which] [<anything>] $M$ [<anything>] |
| → (plants)$_H$ that grow in (zone 7)$_M$ |
| → (animals)$_H$ who live in (water)$_M$ |
| → (medicinal plants)$_H$ that are used in (ayurveda)$_M$ |
| → (math manipulatives)$_H$ that are taught in the (elementary)$_M$ classroom |

Table 1: Extraction patterns matched against queries to identify candidate interpretations ($H$, $M$=head and modifier of a hypothetical noun phrase)

passive, prepositional or relative-pronoun construct, followed by another ngram $M$, and optionally followed by other tokens. The ngrams $H$ and $M$ contain one or more tokens. The patterns effectively split matching queries into four consecutive sequences of tokens $Q$=[$Q_1$ $Q_2$ $Q_3$ $Q_4$], where $H$ and $M$ correspond to $Q_1$ and $Q_3$, and $Q_4$ may be empty. For example, the pattern in the lower portion of Table 1 matches the query *"(plants)$_H$ that grow in (zone 7)$_M$"*, which is one of the queries shown in the upper portion of Figure 1.

**Mapping Noun Phrases to Interpretations**: Each noun phrase to interpret is split into all possible decompositions of two consecutive sequences of tokens $N$=[$N_1$ $N_2$], where the two sequences correspond to a hypothetical modifier and a hypothetical head of the noun phrase. For example, the noun phrase *"zone 7 plants"* is split into [*"zone"*, *"7 plants"*] and separately into [*"zone 7"*, *"plants"*]. If $N_1$ and $Q_3$, and $N_2$ and $Q_1$ respectively, match, then the matching query $Q$ (e.g., *"(plants)$_H$ that grow in (zone 7)$_M$"*) is retained as a candidate interpretation of the noun phrase $N$ (*"(zone 7)$_M$ (plants)$_H$"*), as shown in the middle portion of Figure 1.

**Mapping via Modifier Variants**: At its simplest, the matching of the hypothetical modifier relies on strict string matching. Alternatively, original modifiers in the noun phrases to interpret may be matched to queries via expansion variants. Variants are phrases that likely play the same role, and therefore share interpretations, as modifiers relative to the head in a noun phrase. Variants allow for the extraction of candidate interpretations that may otherwise not be available in the input data. For example, in Figure 1, the variant *new jersey* available for *california* allows for the matching of *california* in the noun phrase *"(california)$_M$ (supreme court justices)$_H$"*, with *new jersey* in the query *"(supreme court justices)$_H$ born in (new jersey)$_M$"*. The candidate interpretation *"(supreme court justices)$_H$ born in (california)$_M$"* is extracted for the noun phrase *"(california)$_M$ (supreme court justices)$_H$"*, even though the query *"supreme court justices born in california"* is not present among the input queries.

Possible sources of variants include distributionally similar phrases (Lin and Wu, 2009), where the phrases most similar to a modifier would act as its variants. Mappings from adjectival modifiers in noun phrases (e.g., *aquatic* in *"aquatic animals"* in Figure 1) into the nominal counterparts (e.g., *water*) that are likely to occur in interpretations (e.g., *"(animals)$_H$ who live in (water)$_M$"*) are also useful. Concretely, as described later in Section 3, variants are generated using WordNet (Fellbaum, 1998), distributional similarities and Wikipedia.

**Aggregation of Candidate Interpretations**: Candidate interpretations of a noun phrase are aggregated from source queries that matched the noun phrase. The frequency score of a candidate interpretation is the weighted sum of the frequencies of source queries from which the candidate interpretation is collected, possibly via variants of modifiers. In the weighted sum, the weights are similarity scores between the original modifier from the noun phrase, on one hand, and the variant from the source query into which the modifier was mapped, on the other hand. For example, in Figure 1, the frequency score of the candidate interpretation *"(plants)$_H$ that grow in (zone 7)$_M$"* for the noun phrase *"(zone 7)$_M$ (plants)$_H$"* is the weighted sum of the frequencies of the source queries *"plants that grow in zone 7"* and *"plants that grow in zone 11"*. The weights for the variants *zone 7* and *zone 11* relative to the original modifier *zone 7* may be 1.0 (identity) and 0.8 (distributional similarity), whereas the weights of adjectival modifiers such as *water* for *aquatic* may be 1.0. Separately from the frequency score, a penalty score is computed that penalizes interpretations containing extraneous tokens. Specifically, the penalty counts the number of nouns or adjectives located outside the modifier and head. Candidate interpretations extracted for a noun phrase are ranked in increasing order of their penalty scores or, in case of ties, in decreasing order of their frequency scores.

## 3 Experimental Setting

**Sources of Textual Data**: The experiments rely on a random sample of around 1 billion fully-anonymized Web search queries in English. The sample is drawn from queries submitted to a general-purpose Web search engine. Each query is available independently from other queries, and is accompanied by its frequency of occurrence in the query logs.
**Sources of Variants**: The original form of the modifiers is denoted as **orig-phrase**. Three types of variant phrases are collected for the purpose of matching modifiers within noun phrases to interpret, with phrases from queries. Relations encoded as Value-Of, Related-Noun and Derivationally-Related relations in WordNet (Fellbaum, 1998) are the source of **adj-noun** variants. They map around 6,000 adjectives into one or more nouns (e.g., (*french→france*), (*electric→electricity*), (*aquatic→water*)). A repository of distributionally similar phrases, collected in advance (Lin and Wu, 2009) from a sample of around 200 million Web documents in English, is the source of **dist-sim** variants. For each of around 1 million phrases, the variants consist of their 50 most similar phrases (e.g., *art garfunkel→{carly simon, melissa manchester, aaron neville, ..}*).

A snapshot of all Wikipedia articles in English, as available in June 2014, is the source of **wiki-templ** variants. For each of around 50,000 phrases, their wiki-templ variants are collected from Wikipedia categories sharing a common parent Wikipedia category (e.g., *"albums by artist"*) and having a common head (*"art garfunkel albums"*, *"black sabbath albums"*, *"metallica albums"*). The different modifiers (*art garfunkel*, *black sabbath*, *metallica*) that accompany the shared head are collected as variants of one another. Among the four types of variants, wiki-templ variants are applied only when the noun phrase to interpret, and the source Wikipedia category names from which the variants were collected, have the same head. For example, *X=art garfunkel→{black sabbath, metallica, 50 cent, ..}* is applied only in the context of the noun phrase *"X albums"*.
**Vocabularies of Noun Phrases**: The extraction method acquires interpretations from queries, for noun phrases from three vocabularies. **ListQ** is a set of phrases *X* (e.g., *"aramaic words"*) from queries in the form [*list of X*], where the frequency of the query [*X*] is at most 100 times higher than the frequency of the query [*list of X*], and the frequency of the latter is at least 5. **IsA** is a set of class labels (e.g., *"academy award nominees"*), originally extracted from Web documents via Hearst patterns (Hearst, 1992), and associated with at least 25 instances each (e.g., *zero dark thirty*). **WikiC** is a set of Wikipedia categories that contain some tokens in lowercase beyond prepositions and determiners, and whose heads are plural-form nouns (e.g., *"french fiction writers"*). Only phrases that are one of the full-length queries from the input set of Web search queries are retained in the respective sets, as vocabularies of noun phrases to interpret; other phrases are discarded.

| Vocabulary | Relative Coverage | | | |
|---|---|---|---|---|
| | R | Q | I | I / Q |
| ListQ | 406,249 | 406,249 | 277,193 | 0.682 |
| IsA | 613,148 | 405,262 | 282,927 | 0.698 |
| WikiC | 248,615 | 87,878 | 63,518 | 0.723 |

Table 2: Relative coverage of noun phrase interpretation, over noun phrases from various vocabularies (R=number of raw noun phrases; Q=subset of noun phrases from R that are queries; I=subset of noun phrases from Q with some extracted interpretation(s); I/Q=fraction of noun phrases from Q that are present in I)

**Parameter Settings**: The noun phrases to interpret and queries are both part-of-speech tagged (Brants, 2000). From among candidate interpretations extracted for a noun phrase, interpretations whose penalty score is higher than 1 are discarded. When computing the frequency score of a candidate interpretation as the weighted sum of the frequencies of source queries, the weights assigned to various variants are 1.0, for orig-phrase, adj-noun and wiki-templ variants; and the available distributional similarity scores within [0.0, 1.0], for dist-sim variants.

## 4 Evaluation Results

**Relative Coverage**: Because it is not feasible to manually compile the exhaustive sets of all string forms of valid interpretations of all (or many) noun phrases, we compute relative instead of absolute coverage. As illustrated in Table 2, some interpretations are extracted from queries for more than 500,000 of the noun phrases from all input vocabu-

| Gold Set: Sample of Noun Phrases |
|---|
| ListQ: 1911 pistols, 2009 movies, alabama sororities, alaskan towns, american holidays, aramaic words, argumentative essays, arm loans, army ranks, .., yugioh movies |
| IsA: academy award nominees, addicting games, advanced weapons systems, android tablet, application layer protocols, astrological signs, automotive parts, .., zip code |
| WikiC: 2k sports games, aaliyah songs, advertising slogans, airline tickets, alan jackson songs, ancient romans, andrea bocelli albums, athletic shoes, .., wii accessories |

Table 3: Gold sets of 100 noun phrases per vocabulary

laries, or around 70% of all input noun phrases.

**Precision of Interpretations**: From an input vocabulary, an initial weighted sample of 150 noun phrases with some extracted interpretations is manually inspected. The sampling weight is the frequency of the noun phrases as queries. A noun phrase from the selected sample is either retained, or discarded if deemed to be a non-interpretable phrase. A noun phrase is not interpretable if it is in fact an instance (*"new york"*, *"alicia keys"*) rather than a class; or it is not a properly formed noun phrase (*"watch movies"*); or does not refer to a meaningful class (*"3 significant figures"*). The manual inspection ends, once a sample of 100 noun phrases has been retained. The procedure gives weighted random samples of 100 noun phrases, drawn from each of the ListQ, IsA and WikiC vocabularies. The samples, shown in Table 3, constitute the gold sets of phrases ListQ, IsA and WikiC, over which precision of interpretations is computed. Note that, since the samples are random, Wikipedia categories that contribute to the automatic construction of wiki-templ variants may be selected as gold phrases in WikiC. This is the case for three of the gold phrases in WikiC.

The top 20 interpretations extracted for each gold phrase are manually annotated with correctness labels. As shown in Table 4, an interpretation is annotated as: correct and generic, or correct and specific, if relevant; okay, if useful but containing non-essential information; or wrong. To compute the precision score over a gold set of phrases, the correctness labels are converted to numeric values. Precision of a ranked list of extracted interpretations is the average of the correctness values of the interpretations in the list.

Table 5 provides a comparison of precision scores at various ranks in the extracted lists of interpretations, as an average over all phrases from a gold set.

| Label (Score) → Examples of (Noun Phrase: Interpretation) |
|---|
| cg (1.0) → (good short stories: short stories that are good), (bay area counties: counties in the bay area), (fourth grade sight words: sight words in fourth grade), (army ranks: ranks from the army), (who wants to be a millionaire winners: winners of who wants to be a millionaire), (us visa: visa for us) |
| cs (1.0) → (brazilian dances: dances of the brazilian culture), (tsunami charities: charities that gave to the tsunami), (stephen king books: books published by stephen king), (florida insurance companies: insurance companies headquartered in florida), (florida insurance companies: insurance companies operating in florida), (us visa: visa required to enter us) |
| qq (0.5) → (super smash bros brawl characters: characters meant to be in super smash bros brawl), (carribean islands: islands by the carribean), (pain assessment tool: tool for recording pain assessment) |
| xw (0.0) → (periodic functions: functions of periodic distributions), (simpsons episodes: episodes left of simpsons), (atm card: card left in wachovia atm) |

Table 4: Examples of interpretations manually annotated with each correctness label (cg=correct generic; cs=correct specific; qq=okay; xw=incorrect)

| Gold Set | Precision@N | | | | |
|---|---|---|---|---|---|
| | @1 | @3 | @5 | @10 | @20 |
| ListQ | 0.770 | 0.708 | 0.655 | 0.568 | 0.465 |
| IsA | 0.730 | 0.598 | 0.530 | 0.423 | 0.329 |
| WikiC | 0.780 | 0.647 | 0.561 | 0.455 | 0.357 |

Table 5: Average precision, at various ranks in the ranked lists of interpretations extracted for noun phrases from various sets of gold phrases

At ranks 1, 5 and 20, precision scores vary between 0.770, 0.655 and 0.465 respectively, for the ListQ gold set; and between 0.730, 0.530 and 0.329 respectively, for the IsA gold set.

**Presence of Relevant Interpretations**: Sometimes it is difficult to even manually enumerate as many as 20 distinct, relevant string forms of interpretations for a given noun phrase. Measuring precision at a particular rank (e.g., 20) in a ranked list of interpretations may be too conservative. Table 6 summarizes a different type of scoring metric, namely the presence of any relevant interpretation, among the interpretations extracted up to a particular rank. Relevance is flexibly defined, by requiring the interpretations to have been assigned a certain correctness label, then computing the average number of gold phrases for which such interpretations are present up to a particular rank. When considering only interpretations annotated as correct and generic or correct and specific, in the second row of each vertical

| Gold Set | Selected Correctness Labels | | | Average presence of any interpretations with any of the selected correctness labels | | | | |
|---|---|---|---|---|---|---|---|---|
| | cg | cs | qq | @1 | @3 | @5 | @10 | @20 |
| ListQ | √ | √ | √ | 0.790 | 0.860 | 0.870 | 0.880 | 0.880 |
| | √ | √ | | 0.750 | 0.810 | 0.830 | 0.840 | 0.840 |
| | √ | | | 0.720 | 0.780 | 0.790 | 0.800 | 0.800 |
| | | √ | | 0.030 | 0.160 | 0.360 | 0.450 | 0.460 |
| IsA | √ | √ | √ | 0.750 | 0.800 | 0.810 | 0.830 | 0.830 |
| | √ | √ | | 0.710 | 0.770 | 0.790 | 0.800 | 0.800 |
| | √ | | | 0.650 | 0.690 | 0.710 | 0.710 | 0.720 |
| | | √ | | 0.060 | 0.220 | 0.350 | 0.480 | 0.520 |
| WikiC | √ | √ | √ | 0.810 | 0.900 | 0.920 | 0.930 | 0.930 |
| | √ | √ | | 0.750 | 0.830 | 0.860 | 0.860 | 0.870 |
| | √ | | | 0.640 | 0.730 | 0.750 | 0.750 | 0.760 |
| | | √ | | 0.110 | 0.210 | 0.370 | 0.520 | 0.560 |

Table 6: Average of scores indicating the presence or absence of any interpretations annotated with a correctness label from a particular subset of correctness labels. Computed over interpretations extracted up to various ranks in the ranked lists of extracted interpretations (cg=correct generic; cs=correct specific; qq=okay)

| Noun Phrase → Multiple-Bracketing Interpretations |
|---|
| african american women writers → (writers)$_H$ who wrote about (african american)$_M$ women, (women writers)$_H$ who are (african american)$_M$, (writers)$_H$ who cover (african american)$_M$ women struggles |
| chinese traditional instruments → (traditional instruments)$_H$ of (china)$_M$, (instruments)$_H$ used in (chinese traditional)$_M$ music |
| elementary math manipulatives → (manipulatives)$_H$ for (elementary math)$_M$, (math manipulatives)$_H$ in the (elementary)$_M$ classroom, (manipulatives)$_H$ used in (elementary math)$_M$, (math manipulatives)$_H$ for (elementary)$_M$ level |
| global corporate tax rates → (corporate tax rates)$_H$ around the (world)$_M$, (tax rates)$_H$ on (global corporate)$_M$ profits |

Table 7: Sample of noun phrases from the ListQ gold set, whose top 10 extracted interpretations induce multiple pairs of a head and a modifier of the noun phrases (H=head; M=modifier)

portion in Table 6, the scores at rank 5 are 0.830 for ListQ, 0.790 for IsA and 0.860 for WikiC. Alternatively, in the fourth rows of each vertical portion, the scores at rank 5 are 0.360, 0.350 and 0.370 respectively. The scores indicate that at least one of the top 5 interpretations is correct and specific for about a third of the noun phrases in the gold sets.

**Induced Modifiers, Heads and Interpretations**: When a candidate interpretation is extracted for a noun phrase, the interpretation effectively induces a particular bracketing over the noun phrase, as it splits it into a modifier and a head. For an ambiguous

| Presence of Multiple Bracketings | | | |
|---|---|---|---|
| Vocabulary | ListQ | IsA | WikiC |
| Fraction of Noun Phrases | 0.110 | 0.124 | 0.051 |

Table 8: Fraction of noun phrases that have some extracted interpretation(s) and contain at least 3 tokens, whose interpretations induce multiple (rather than single) bracketings over interpreted noun phrases. The presence of multiple bracketings for a noun phrase is equivalent to the presence of multiple pairs of a head and a modifier, as induced by the top 10 interpretations extracted for the noun phrase

| Noun Phrase → Extracted Interpretations |
|---|
| beatles songs → (songs)$_H$ sung by the (beatles)$_M$, (songs)$_H$ about the (beatles)$_M$ |
| company accounts → (accounts)$_H$ maintained by the (company)$_M$, (accounts)$_H$ owed to a (company)$_M$ |
| florida insurance companies → (insurance companies)$_H$ headquartered in (florida)$_M$, (insurance companies)$_H$ insuring in (florida)$_M$ |
| german food → (food)$_H$ eaten in (germany)$_M$, (food)$_H$ produced in (germany)$_M$, (food)$_H$ that originated in (germany)$_M$ |
| math skills → (skills)$_H$ needed for (math)$_M$, (skills)$_H$ learned in (math)$_M$, (skills)$_H$ gained from studying (math)$_M$ |
| michael jackson song → (song)$_H$ written by (michael jackson)$_M$, (song)$_H$ sung by (michael jackson)$_M$, (song)$_H$ about (michael jackson)$_M$ |

Table 9: Sample of alternative relevant interpretations extracted among the top 20 interpretations for noun phrases from the ListQ gold set (H=head; M=modifier)

noun phrase, multiple bracketings may be possible, each corresponding to a different interpretation. Interpretations extracted from queries do capture such multiple bracketings, even for phrases from the gold sets, as illustrated in Table 7. Over all noun phrases from the input vocabularies that have some extracted interpretations and contain at least 3 tokens, about 10% (ListQ and IsA) and 5% (WikiC) of the noun phrases have multiple bracketings induced by their top 10 interpretations, as shown in Table 8.

Table 9 shows examples of noun phrases with multiple extracted interpretations that induce identical bracketings, but capture distinct interpretations.

**Impact of Variants**: Variants of modifiers provide alternatives in extracting candidate interpretations, even when the modifiers from the noun phrases are not present in their original form in the interpretations. For example, the adj-noun variant *ethiopia* of the modifier *ethiopian* leads to the extraction of the interpretation *"runners from ethiopia"* for the noun phrase *"ethiopian runners"*. Similarly, wiki-

| Vocab | Variant Type | | | |
|---|---|---|---|---|
| | orig-phrase | adj-noun | dist-sim | wiki-templ |
| Interpretations produced by variant type (not exclusive): | | | | |
| ListQ | 0.453 | 0.089 | 0.642 | 0.017 |
| IsA | 0.389 | 0.121 | 0.597 | 0.003 |
| WikiC | 0.191 | 0.097 | 0.603 | 0.425 |
| Interpretations produced only by variant type (exclusive): | | | | |
| ListQ | 0.281 | 0.069 | 0.450 | 0.005 |
| IsA | 0.299 | 0.099 | 0.491 | 0.001 |
| WikiC | 0.086 | 0.076 | 0.351 | 0.225 |

Table 10: Impact of various types of variants of modifiers, on the coverage of noun phrase interpretations. Computed as the fraction of the top 10 extracted interpretations produced by a particular variant type, and possibly by other variant types (upper portion); or produced only by a particular variant type, and by no other variant types (lower portion) (Vocab=vocabulary of noun phrases)

| Variant Types | | | | Impact on Precision | | |
|---|---|---|---|---|---|---|
| O | A | D | W | Cvg | P@5 | C@5 |
| √ | - | - | - | 74 | 0.433 | 0.581 |
| - | √ | - | - | 16 | 0.474 | 0.562 |
| - | - | √ | - | 66 | 0.478 | 0.651 |
| - | - | - | √ | 2 | 0.166 | 0.500 |
| - | √ | √ | √ | 73 | 0.484 | 0.657 |
| √ | - | √ | √ | 97 | 0.641 | 0.835 |
| √ | √ | - | √ | 83 | 0.448 | 0.590 |
| √ | √ | √ | - | 99 | 0.649 | 0.828 |
| √ | - | - | - | 74 | 0.433 | 0.581 |
| √ | √ | - | - | 81 | 0.453 | 0.592 |
| √ | - | √ | - | 96 | 0.635 | 0.833 |
| √ | - | - | √ | 76 | 0.429 | 0.578 |
| √ | √ | √ | √ | 100 | 0.655 | 0.830 |

Table 11: Impact of various types of variants of modifiers, on the precision of noun phrase interpretations. Computed over the ListQ gold set, at rank 5 in the ranked lists of extracted interpretations, when various variant types are allowed (√) or temporarily not allowed (-) to produce interpretations (O=orig-phrase variant type; A=adj-noun variant type; D=dist-sim variant type; W=wiki-templ variant type; Cvg=number of noun phrases from the gold set with some interpretation(s) produced by the allowed variant types; P@5=precision at rank 5; C@5=average presence of any interpretations annotated as correct and generic (cg) or correct and specific (cs), among interpretations up to rank 5)

templ variants *metallica* and *50 cent* of the modifier *art garfunkel*, in the context *"X albums"*, allow for the extraction of the interpretation *"albums sold by art garfunkel"* for the noun phrase *"art garfunkel albums"*, via the interpretations *"albums sold by metallica"* and *"albums sold by 50 cent"*.

Table 10 quantifies the impact of various types of variants, on the coverage of noun phrase interpretations. The scores provided for each variant type correspond to either non-exclusive (upper portion of the table) or exclusive (lower portion) contribution of that variant type towards some extracted interpretations. In other words, in the lower portion, the scores capture the fraction of the top 10 interpretations that are produced only by that particular variant type. Three conclusions can be drawn from the results. First, all variant types contribute to increasing coverage, relative to using only orig-phrase variants. Second, dist-sim variants have a particularly strong impact. Third, wiki-templ variants have a strong impact, but only when the contexts from which they were collected match the context of the noun phrase being interpreted. On the WikiC vocabulary in the lower portion of Table 10, the scores for wiki-templ illustrate the potential that contextual variants have in extracting additional interpretations.

Table 11 again quantifies the impact of variant types, but this time on the coverage and, more importantly, accuracy of interpretations extracted for phrases from the gold sets. The scores are computed over the ranked lists of interpretations from the ListQ gold set, as certain types of variants are temporarily disabled in ablation experiments. The upper portion of the table shows results when only one of the variant types is enabled. It shows that none of the variant types, taken in isolation, can match what they achieve when combined together, in terms of both coverage and accuracy. The middle portion of the table shows results when all but one of the variant types are enabled. Each of the variant types incrementally contributes to higher coverage and accuracy over the combination of the other variant types. The incremental contribution of wiki-templ variants is the smallest. The lower portion of Table 11 gives the incremental contribution of the variant types, relative to using only the orig-phrase variant type. The last row of Table 11 corresponds to all variant types being enabled.

**Discussion**: Independently of the choice of the textual data source (e.g., documents, queries) from which interpretations are extracted, a noun phrase is intuitively more difficult to interpret if it is relatively more rare or more complex (i.e., longer). Additional experiments quantify the effect, by measuring the correlation between the presence of some extracted interpretations for an input noun phrase, on one hand; and the frequency of the noun phrase as a query (in Table 12), on the other hand. In Table 12,

| Vocabulary | Noun Phrases With : Without Interpretation(s) | | |
|---|---|---|---|
| | I : ¬I | $A_I$ : $A_{\neg I}$ | $M_I$ : $M_{\neg I}$ |
| ListQ | 2.14 : 1 | 2.93 : 1 | 2.65 : 1 |
| IsA | 2.31 : 1 | 5.76 : 1 | 3.26 : 1 |
| WikiC | 2.60 : 1 | 3.72 : 1 | 3.63 : 1 |

Table 12: Correlation between coverage, measured as the presence of some extracted interpretation(s) for a noun phrase, on one hand; and frequency of the noun phrase as a query, on the other hand (I=number of noun phrases that are queries and have some extracted interpretation(s); ¬I=number of noun phrases that are queries and do not have any extracted interpretation(s); A=average query frequency of noun phrases as queries; M=median query frequency of noun phrases as queries)

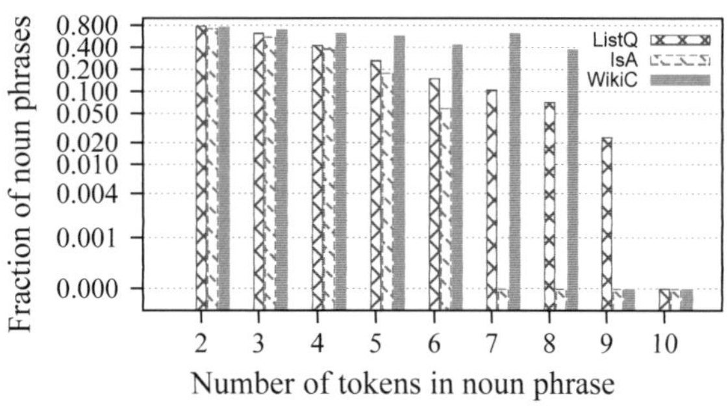


Figure 2: Ability to extract interpretations for noun phrases, as a function of the length of noun phrases. Computed as the fraction of noun phrases from an input vocabulary with a particular number of tokens, for which there are some extracted interpretation(s)

the effect is visible in that query frequency is higher for noun phrases with some extracted interpretations vs. noun phrases with none. For example, the average query frequency is almost three times higher for the former than for the latter, for the ListQ vocabulary. Similarly, in Figure 2, a larger fraction of the input noun phrases with a particular number of tokens have some extracted interpretations, when the number of tokens is lower rather than higher. The effect is somewhat less pronounced for, but still applicable to, the WikiC vocabulary, with some extracted interpretations being present for 75%, 71%, 63%, and 37% of the noun phrases containing 2, 3, 4 and 8 tokens respectively. That a larger fraction of the longer noun phrases can be interpreted in the WikiC vocabulary is attributed to the role of wiki-templ variants in extracting interpretations that would otherwise not be available.

**Interpretations from Queries vs. Documents**: For completeness, additional experiments evaluate the interpretations extracted from queries, relative to a gold standard introduced in (Hendrickx et al., 2013). The gold standard consists of a gold set of 181 compound noun phrases (e.g., *"accounting principle"* and *"application software"*), their manually-assembled gold paraphrases (e.g., *"principle of accounting"*, *"software to make applications"*), and associated scoring metrics referred to as non-isomorphic and isomorphic. Note that, in comparison to the ListQ, IsA and WikiC evaluation sets, the gold standard in (Hendrickx et al., 2013) may contain relatively less popular gold phrases. As many as 45 gold paraphrases are available per gold phrase on average. They illustrate the difficulty of any attempt to manually assemble exhaustive sets of all strings that are valid interpretations of a noun phrase. For example, the gold paraphrases of the gold phrase *blood cell* include *"cell that is found in the blood"*, but not the arguably equally-relevant *"cell found in the blood"*. In addition, more than one human annotators independently provide the same gold paraphrase for only a tenth of all gold paraphrases. See (Hendrickx et al., 2013) for details on the gold standard and scoring metrics. The gold set is added as another input vocabulary to the method proposed here. After inspection of a training set of compound noun phrases also introduced in (Hendrickx et al., 2013), the parameter settings are modified to only retain interpretations whose penalty score is 0.

The isomorphic and non-isomorphic scores reward coverage and accuracy respectively. For the ranked candidate interpretations extracted from queries for the gold set, they are 0.037 and 0.556 respectively. In comparison to previous methods that operate over documents instead of queries, the isomorphic score is much lower for our method (e.g., 0.037 vs. 0.130 (Van de Cruys et al., 2013)). It suggests that queries cannot reliably provide an exhaustive list of all possible strings available in the gold standard for each gold phrase. However, the non-isomorphic score is higher for our method than for the best method operating over documents (i.e., 0.556 vs. 0.548 (Hendrickx et al., 2013)). In fact, the non-isomorphic score using queries would be 0.745 instead of 0.556, if it were computed over only the 135 gold noun phrases with some extracted interpretations. The results suggests that the method proposed here extracts more accurate interpretations from queries, than previous methods extract from documents. Higher accuracy is preferable in scenarios like Web search, where it is important to accurately trigger structured results.

**Error Analysis**: The relative looseness of the extraction patterns applied to queries causes interpretations containing undesirable tokens to be extracted. In addition, part-of-speech tagging errors lead to interpretations receiving artificially low penalty scores, and therefore being considered to be of higher quality than they should be. For example, *phd* in the interpretation *"job for phd in chemistry"* is incorrectly tagged as a past participle verb. As a result, the computed penalty score is too low.

Occasionally, the presence of additional tokens within an interpretation is harmless (e.g., *"issues of controversy in society"* for *"controversial issues"*, *"foods allowed on a high protein low carb diet"* for *"high protein low carb foods"*), if not necessary (e.g., *"dances with brazilian origin"* for *"brazilian dances"*, *"artists of the surrealist movement"* for *"surrealist artists"*, *"options with weekly expirations"* for *"weekly options"*). But often it leads to incorrect interpretations (e.g., *"towns of alaska map"* for *"alaska towns"*, *"processes in chemical vision"* for *"chemical processes"*).

Variants of modifiers occasionally lead to incorrect interpretations for a noun phrase, even if the interpretations may be correct for the individual variants. The phenomenon is an instance of semantic drift, wherein variants do share many properties but still diverge in others. Examples are *"words that are bleeped similarly"* extracted for *"bleeped words"* via the variant *bleeped→spelled*. Separately, linguistic constructs that negate or at least alter the desired meaning affect the understanding of text in general and also affect the extraction of interpretations in particular. Examples are *"heaters with no electricity"* for *"electric heaters"*, and *"animal that used to be endangered"* for *"endangered animal"*.

## 5 Related Work

Relevant interpretations extracted from queries act as a potential bridge between facts, on one hand, and class labels, on the other hand, available for instances. The former might be inferred from the latter and vice versa. There are two previous studies that are relevant to the task of extracting facts from existing noun phrases. First, (Yahya et al., 2014) extract facts for attributes of instances, without requiring the presence of the verbal predicates usually employed (Fader et al., 2011) in open-domain information extraction. Second, in (Nastase and Strube, 2008), relations encoded implicitly within Wikipedia categories are converted into explicit relations. As an example, the relation *<deconstructing harry, directed, woody allen>* is obtained from the fact that *deconstructing harry* is listed under *"movies directed by woody allen"* in Wikipedia. The method in (Nastase and Strube, 2008) relies on manually-compiled knowledge, and does not attempt to interpret compound noun phrases.

Since relevant interpretations paraphrase the noun phrases which they interpret, a related area of research is paraphrase acquisition (Madnani and Dorr, 2010; Ganitkevitch et al., 2013). Previous methods for the acquisition of paraphrases of compound noun phrases (Kim and Nakov, 2011; Van de Cruys et al., 2013) operate over documents, and may rely on text analysis tools including syntactic parsing (Nakov and Hearst, 2013). In contrast, the method proposed here extracts interpretations from queries, and applies part of speech tagging. Queries were used as a textual data source in other tasks in open-domain information extraction (Jain and Pennacchiotti, 2010; Pantel et al., 2012).

## 6 Conclusion

Interpretations extracted from queries explain the roles that modifiers play within longer noun phrases. Current work explores the interpretation of noun phrases containing multiple modifiers (e.g., *"$(french)_{M1}$ $(healthcare)_{M2}$ $(companies)_{H}$"* by separately interpreting *"$(french)_{M1}$ $(companies)_{H}$"* and *"$(healthcare)_{M2}$ $(companies)_{H}$"*); the grouping of lexically different but semantically equivalent interpretations (e.g., *"dances of brazilian origin"*, *"dances from brazil"*); the collection of more variants from Wikipedia and other resources; the incorporation of variants of heads (*physicists→scientists* for interpreting the phrase *"belgian physicists"*), which likely need to be more conservatively applied than for modifiers; and the use of query sessions, as an alternative to sets of disjoint queries.

## Acknowledgments

The paper benefits from comments from Jutta Degener, Mihai Surdeanu and Susanne Riehemann. Data extracted by Haixun Wang and Jian Li is the source of the IsA vocabulary of noun phrases used in the evaluation.

## References


M. Banko, Michael J Cafarella, S. Soderland, M. Broadhead, and O. Etzioni. 2007. Open information extraction from the Web. In *Proceedings of the 20th International Joint Conference on Artificial Intelligence (IJCAI-07)*, pages 2670–2676, Hyderabad, India.

T. Brants. 2000. TnT - a statistical part of speech tagger. In *Proceedings of the 6th Conference on Applied Natural Language Processing (ANLP-00)*, pages 224–231, Seattle, Washington.

B. Dalvi, W. Cohen, and J. Callan. 2012. Websets: Extracting sets of entities from the Web using unsupervised information extraction. In *Proceedings of the 5th ACM Conference on Web Search and Data Mining (WSDM-12)*, pages 243–252, Seattle, Washington.

P. Downing. 1977. On the creation and use of English compound nouns. *Language*, 53:810–842.

A. Fader, S. Soderland, and O. Etzioni. 2011. Identifying relations for open information extraction. In *Proceedings of the 2011 Conference on Empirical Methods in Natural Language Processing (EMNLP-11)*, pages 1535–1545, Edinburgh, Scotland.

C. Fellbaum, editor. 1998. *WordNet: An Electronic Lexical Database and Some of its Applications*. MIT Press.

T. Flati, D. Vannella, T. Pasini, and R. Navigli. 2014. Two is bigger (and better) than one: the Wikipedia Bitaxonomy project. In *Proceedings of the 52nd Annual Meeting of the Association for Computational Linguistics (ACL-14)*, pages 945–955, Baltimore, Maryland.

J. Ganitkevitch, B. Van Durme, and C. Callison-Burch. 2013. PPDB: The paraphrase database. In *Proceedings of the 2013 Conference of the North American Association for Computational Linguistics (NAACL-HLT-13)*, pages 758–764, Atlanta, Georgia.

M. Hearst. 1992. Automatic acquisition of hyponyms from large text corpora. In *Proceedings of the 14th International Conference on Computational Linguistics (COLING-92)*, pages 539–545, Nantes, France.

I. Hendrickx, Z. Kozareva, P. Nakov, D. Ó Séaghdha, S. Szpakowicz, and T. Veale. 2013. SemEval-2013 task 4: Free paraphrases of noun compounds. In *Proceedings of the 7th International Workshop on Semantic Evaluation (SemEval-14)*, pages 138–143, Atlanta, Georgia.

J. Hoffart, F. Suchanek, K. Berberich, and G. Weikum. 2013. YAGO2: a spatially and temporally enhanced knowledge base from Wikipedia. *Artificial Intelligence Journal. Special Issue on Artificial Intelligence, Wikipedia and Semi-Structured Resources*, 194:28–61.

A. Jain and M. Pennacchiotti. 2010. Open entity extraction from Web search query logs. In *Proceedings of the 23rd International Conference on Computational Linguistics (COLING-10)*, pages 510–518, Beijing, China.

N. Kim and P. Nakov. 2011. Large-scale noun compound interpretation using bootstrapping and the Web as a corpus. In *Proceedings of the 2011 Conference on Empirical Methods in Natural Language Processing (EMNLP-11)*, pages 648–658, Edinburgh, Scotland.

Z. Kozareva and E. Hovy. 2010. A semi-supervised method to learn and construct taxonomies using the web. In *Proceedings of the 2010 Conference on Empirical Methods in Natural Language Processing (EMNLP-10)*, pages 1110–1118, Cambridge, Massachusetts.

D. Lin and X. Wu. 2009. Phrase clustering for discriminative learning. In *Proceedings of the 47th Annual Meeting of the Association for Computational Linguistics (ACL-IJCNLP-09)*, pages 1030–1038, Singapore.

N. Madnani and B. Dorr. 2010. Generating phrasal and sentential paraphrases: a survey of data-driven methods. *Computational Linguistics*, 36(3):341–387.

P. Nakov and M. Hearst. 2013. Semantic interpretation of noun compounds using verbal and other paraphrases. *ACM Transactions on Speech and Language Processing*, 10(3):1–51.

V. Nastase and M. Strube. 2008. Decoding Wikipedia categories for knowledge acquisition. In *Proceedings of the 23rd National Conference on Artificial Intelligence (AAAI-08)*, pages 1219–1224, Chicago, Illinois.

P. Pantel, T. Lin, and M. Gamon. 2012. Mining entity types from query logs via user intent modeling. In *Proceedings of the 50th Annual Meeting of the Association for Computational Linguistics (ACL-12)*, pages 563–571, Jeju Island, Korea.

T. Van de Cruys, S. Afantenos, and P. Muller. 2013. MELODI: A supervised distributional approach for free paraphrasing of noun compounds. In *Proceedings of the 7th International Workshop on Semantic Evaluation (SemEval-14)*, pages 144–147, Atlanta, Georgia.

R. Wang and W. Cohen. 2009. Automatic set instance extraction using the Web. In *Proceedings of the 47th Annual Meeting of the Association for Computational Linguistics (ACL-IJCNLP-09)*, pages 441–449, Singapore.

M. Yahya, S. Whang, R. Gupta, and A. Halevy. 2014. ReNoun: Fact extraction for nominal attributes. In *Proceedings of the 2014 Conference on Empirical Methods in Natural Language Processing (EMNLP-14)*, pages 325–335, Doha, Qatar.

X. Yao and B. Van Durme. 2014. Information extraction over structured data: Question Answering with Freebase. In *Proceedings of the 52nd Annual Meeting of the Association for Computational Linguistics (ACL-14)*, pages 956–966, Baltimore, Maryland.

# Lexicon-Free Conversational Speech Recognition with Neural Networks


**Andrew L. Maas,* Ziang Xie,* Dan Jurafsky, Andrew Y. Ng**
Stanford University
Stanford, CA 94305, USA
{amaas, zxie, ang}@cs.stanford.edu, jurafsky@stanford.edu



## Abstract

We present an approach to speech recognition that uses only a neural network to map acoustic input to characters, a character-level language model, and a beam search decoding procedure. This approach eliminates much of the complex infrastructure of modern speech recognition systems, making it possible to directly train a speech recognizer using errors generated by spoken language understanding tasks. The system naturally handles out of vocabulary words and spoken word fragments. We demonstrate our approach using the challenging Switchboard telephone conversation transcription task, achieving a word error rate competitive with existing baseline systems. To our knowledge, this is the first entirely neural-network-based system to achieve strong speech transcription results on a conversational speech task. We analyze qualitative differences between transcriptions produced by our lexicon-free approach and transcriptions produced by a standard speech recognition system. Finally, we evaluate the impact of large context neural network character language models as compared to standard $n$-gram models within our framework.


## 1 Introduction

Users increasingly interact with natural language understanding systems via conversational speech interfaces. Google Now, Microsoft Cortana, and Apple Siri are all systems which rely on *spoken language understanding* (SLU), where transcribing speech is a single step within a larger system. Building such systems is difficult because spontaneous, conversational speech naturally contains repetitions, disfluencies, partial words, and out of vocabulary (OOV) words (De Mori et al., 2008; Huang et al., 2001). Moreover, SLU systems must be robust to transcription errors, which can be quite high depending on the task and domain.

Modern systems for large vocabulary continuous speech recognition (LVCSR) use hidden Markov models (HMMs) to handle sequence processing, word-level language models, and a pronunciation lexicon to map words into phonetic pronunciations (Saon and Chien, 2012). Traditional systems use Gaussian mixture models (GMMs) to build a mapping from sub-phonetic states to audio input features. The resulting speech recognition system contains many sub-components, linguistic assumptions, and typically over ten thousand lines of source code. Within the past few years LVCSR systems improved by replacing GMMs with deep neural networks (DNNs) (Dahl et al., 2011; Hinton et al., 2012), drawing on early work on with hybrid GMM-NN architectures (Bourlard and Morgan, 1993). Both HMM-GMM and HMM-DNN systems remain difficult to build, and nearly impossible to efficiently optimize for downstream SLU tasks. As a result, SLU researchers typically operate on an $n$-best list of possible transcriptions and treat the LVCSR system as a black box.

Recently Graves and Jaitly (2014) demonstrated an approach to LVCSR using a neural network trained with the connectionist temporal classification (CTC) loss function (Graves et al., 2006). Us-

*Authors contributed equally.



*Human Language Technologies: The 2015 Annual Conference of the North American Chapter of the ACL*, pages 345–354,
Denver, Colorado, May 31 – June 5, 2015. 

ing the CTC loss function the authors built a neural network which directly maps audio input features to a sequence of characters. By re-ranking word-level $n$-best lists generated from an HMM-DNN system the authors obtained competitive results on the Wall Street Journal corpus.

Our work builds upon the foundation introduced by Graves and Jaitly (2014). Rather than reasoning at the word level, we train and decode our system by reasoning entirely at the character-level. By reasoning over characters we eliminate the need for a lexicon, and enable transcribing new words, fragments, and disfluencies. We train a deep bi-directional recurrent neural network (DBRNN) to directly map acoustic input to characters using the CTC loss function introduced by Graves and Jaitly (2014). We are able to efficiently and accurately perform transcription using only our DBRNN and a character-level language model (CLM), whereas previous work relied on $n$-best lists from a baseline HMM-DNN system. On the challenging Switchboard telephone conversation transcription task, our approach achieves a word error rate competitive with existing baseline HMM-GMM systems. To our knowledge, this is the first entirely neural-network-based system to achieve strong speech transcription results on a conversational speech task.

Section 2 reviews the CTC loss function and describes the neural network architecture we use. Section 3 presents our approach to efficiently perform first-pass decoding using a neural network for character probabilities and a character language model. Section 4 presents experiments on the Switchboard corpus to compare our approach to existing LVCSR systems, and evaluates the impact of different language models. In Section 5, we offer insight on how the CTC-trained system performs speech recognition as compared to a standard HMM-GMM model, and finally conclude in Section 6.

## 2 Model

We address the complete LVCSR problem. Our system trains on utterances which are labeled by word-level transcriptions and contain no indication of when words occur within an utterance. Our approach consists of two neural networks which we integrate during a beam search decoding procedure. Our first neural network, a DBRNN, maps acoustic input features to a probability distribution over characters at each time step. Our second system component is a neural network character language model. Neural network CLMs enable us to leverage high order $n$-gram contexts without dramatically increasing the number of free parameters in our language model. To facilitate further work with our approach we make our source code publicly available. [1]

### 2.1 Connectionist Temporal Classification

We train neural networks using the CTC loss function to do maximum likelihood training of letter sequences given acoustic features as input. This is a direct, discriminative approach to building a speech recognition system in contrast to the generative, noisy-channel approach which motivates HMM-based speech recognition systems. Our application of the CTC loss function follows the approach introduced by Graves and Jaitly (2014), but we restate the approach here for completeness.

CTC is a generic loss function to train systems on sequence problems where the alignment between the input and output sequence are unknown. CTC accounts for time warping of the output sequence relative to the input sequence, but does not model possible re-orderings. Re-ordering is a problem in machine translation, but is not an issue when working with speech recognition – our transcripts provide the exact ordering in which words occur in the input audio.

Given an input sequence $X$ of length $T$, CTC assumes the probability of a length $T$ character sequence $C$ is given by,

$$p(C|X) = \prod_{t=1}^{T} p(c_t|X). \tag{1}$$

This assumes that character outputs at each timestep are conditionally independent given the input. The distribution $p(c_t|X)$ is the output of some predictive model.

CTC assumes our ground truth transcript is a character sequence $W$ with length $\tau$ where $\tau \leq T$. As a result, we need a way to construct possibly shorter output sequences from our length $T$ sequence of

[1] Available at: `deeplearning.stanford.edu/lexfree`

character probabilities. The CTC *collapsing function* achieves this by introducing a special *blank* symbol, which we denote using "_", and collapsing any repeating characters in the original length $T$ output. This output symbol contains the notion of *junk* or *other* so as to not produce a character in the final output hypothesis. Our transcripts $W$ come from some set of symbols $\zeta'$ but we reason over $\zeta = \zeta' \cup \_$.

We denote the collapsing function by $\kappa(\cdot)$ which takes an input string and produces the unique collapsed version of that string. As an example, here are the set of strings $Z$ of length $T = 3$ such that $\kappa(z) = \texttt{hi}, \forall z \in Z$:

$$Z = \{\texttt{hhi}, \texttt{hii}, \texttt{\_hi}, \texttt{h\_i}, \texttt{hi\_}\}.$$

There are a large number of possible length $T$ sequences corresponding to a final length $\tau$ transcript hypothesis. The CTC objective function $\mathcal{L}_{\text{CTC}}(X, W)$ is a likelihood of the correct final transcript $W$ which requires integrating over the probabilities of all length $T$ character sequences $C_W = \{C : \kappa(C) = W\}$ consistent with $W$ after applying the collapsing function,

$$\begin{aligned} \mathcal{L}_{\text{CTC}}(X, W) &= \sum_{C_W} p(C|X) \\ &= \sum_{C_W} \prod_{t=1}^{T} p(c_t|X). \end{aligned} \quad (2)$$

Using a dynamic programming approach we can exactly compute this loss function efficiently as well as its gradient with respect to our probabilities $p(c_t|X)$.

### 2.2 Deep Bi-Directional Recurrent Neural Networks

Our loss function requires at each time $t$ a probability distribution $p(c|x_t)$ over characters $c$ given input features $x_t$. We model this distribution using a DBRNN because it provides an expressive model which explicitly accounts for the sequential relationships that should exist in our task. Moreover, the DBRNN is a relatively straightforward neural network architecture to specify, and allows us to learn parameters from data rather than more explicitly specifying how to convert audio features into characters. Figure 1 shows a DBRNN with two hidden layers.

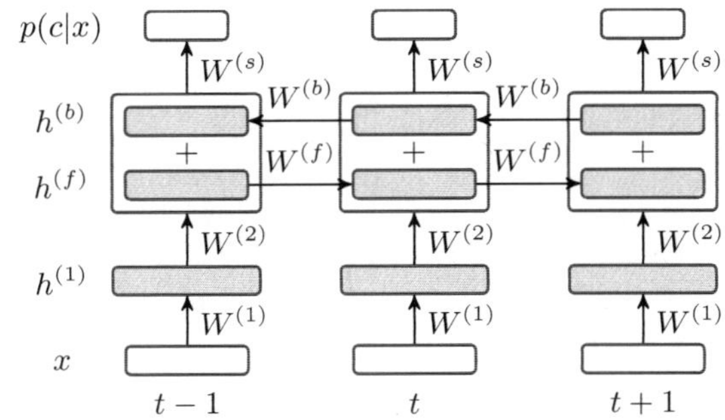


Figure 1: Deep bi-directional recurrent neural network to map input audio features $X$ to a distribution $p(c|x_t)$ over output characters at each timestep $t$. The network contains two hidden layers with the second layer having bi-directional temporal recurrence.

A DBRNN computes the distribution $p(c|x_t)$ using a series of hidden layers followed by an output layer. Given an input vector $x_t$ the first hidden layer activations are a vector computed as,

$$h^{(1)} = \sigma(W^{(1)T} x_t + b^{(1)}), \quad (3)$$

where the matrix $W^{(1)}$ and vector $b^{(1)}$ are the weight matrix and bias vector. The function $\sigma(\cdot)$ is a point-wise nonlinearity. We use $\sigma(z) = \min(\max(z, 0), \mu)$. This is a rectified linear activation function clipped to a maximum possible activation of $\mu$ to prevent overflow. Rectified linear hidden units have been show to work well in general for deep neural networks, as well as for acoustic modeling of speech data (Glorot et al., 2011; Zeiler et al., 2013; Dahl et al., 2013; Maas et al., 2013)

We select a single hidden layer $j$ of the network to have temporal connections. Our temporal hidden layer representation $h^{(j)}$ is the sum of two partial hidden layer representations,

$$h_t^{(j)} = h_t^{(f)} + h_t^{(b)}. \quad (4)$$

The representation $h^{(f)}$ uses a weight matrix $W^{(f)}$ to propagate information forwards in time. Similarly, the representation $h^{(b)}$ propagates information backwards in time using a weight matrix $W^{(b)}$. These partial hidden representations both take input from the previous hidden layer $h^{(j-1)}$ using a weight matrix $W^{(j)}$,

$$h_t^{(f)} = \sigma(W^{(j)T} h_t^{(j-1)} + W^{(f)T} h_{t-1}^{(f)} + b^{(j)}),$$
$$h_t^{(b)} = \sigma(W^{(j)T} h_t^{(j-1)} + W^{(b)T} h_{t+1}^{(b)} + b^{(j)}). \quad (5)$$

Note that the recurrent forward and backward hidden representations are computed entirely independently from each other. As with the other hidden layers of the network we use $\sigma(z) = \min(\max(z, 0), \mu)$.

All hidden layers aside from the first hidden layer and temporal hidden layer use a standard dense weight matrix and bias vector,

$$h^{(i)} = \sigma(W^{(i)T} h^{(i-1)} + b^{(i)}). \quad (6)$$

DBRNNs can have an arbitrary number of hidden layers, but we assume that only one hidden layer contains temporally recurrent connections.

The model outputs a distribution $p(c|x_t)$ over a set of possible characters $\zeta$ using a *softmax* output layer. We compute the softmax layer as,

$$p(c = c_k|x_t) = \frac{\exp(-(W_k^{(s)T} h^{(:)} + b_k^{(s)}))}{\sum_{j=1}^{|\zeta|} \exp(-(W_j^{(s)T} h^{(:)} + b_j^{(s)}))}, \quad (7)$$

where $W_k^{(s)}$ is the $k$'th column of the output weight matrix $W^{(s)}$ and $b_k^{(s)}$ is a scalar bias term. The vector $h^{(:)}$ is the hidden layer representation of the final hidden layer in our DBRNN.

We can directly compute a gradient for all weights and biases in the DBRNN with respect to the CTC loss function and apply batch gradient descent.

## 3 Decoding

Our decoding procedure integrates information from the DBRNN and language model to form a single cohesive estimate of the character sequence in a given utterance. For an input sequence $X$ of length $T$ our DBRNN produces a set of probabilities $p(c|x_t)$, $t = 1, \ldots, T$. Again, the character probabilities are a categorical distribution over the symbol set $\zeta$.

### 3.1 Decoding Without a Language Model

As a baseline, we use a simple, greedy approach to decoding the DBRNN outputs (Graves and Jaitly, 2014). The simplest form of decoding does not employ the language model and instead finds the highest probability character transcription given only the DBRNN outputs. This process selects a transcript hypothesis $W^*$ by making a greedy approximation,

$$\begin{aligned} W^* &= \arg\max_W p(W|X) \approx \kappa(\arg\max_C p(C|X)) \\ &= \kappa(\arg\max_C \prod_{t=1}^{T} p(c_t|X)). \end{aligned} \quad (8)$$

This decoding procedure ignores the issue of many time-level character sequences mapping to the same final hypothesis, and instead considers only the most probable character at each point in time. Because our model assumes the character labels for each timestep are conditionally independent, $C^*$ is simply the most probable character at each timestep in our DBRNN output. As a result, this decoding procedure is very fast to compute, requiring only time $O(T|\zeta|)$.

### 3.2 Beam Search Decoding

To decode while taking language model probabilities into account, we use a beam search to combine a character language model and the outputs of our DBRNN. This search-based decoding method does not make a greedy approximation and instead assigns probability to a final hypothesis by integrating over all character sequences consistent with the hypothesis under our collapsing function $\kappa(\cdot)$. Algorithm 1 outlines our decoding procedure.

We note that our decoding procedure is significantly simpler, and in practice faster, than previous decoding procedures applied to CTC models. This is due to reasoning at the character level without a lexicon so as to not introduce difficult multi-level constraints to obey during the decoding search procedure. While a softmax over words is typically the bottleneck in neural network language models, a softmax over possible characters is comparatively cheap to compute. Our character language model is applied at every time step, while word models can only be applied when we consider adding a space or by computing the likelihood of a sequence being the prefix of a word in the lexicon (Graves and Jaitly, 2014). Additionally, our lexicon-free approach re-

**Algorithm 1** Beam Search Decoding: Given the likelihoods from our DBRNN and our character language model, for each time step $t$ and for each string $s$ in our current previous hypothesis set $Z_{t-1}$, we consider extending $s$ with a new character. Blanks and repeat characters with no separating blank are handled separately. For all other character extensions, we apply our character language model when computing the probability of $s$. We initialize $Z_0$ with the empty string $\varnothing$. Notation: $\zeta'$: character set excluding "_", $s+c$: concatenation of character $c$ to string $s$, $|s|$: length of $s$, $p_b(c|x_{1:t})$ and $p_{nb}(c|x_{1:t})$: probability of $s$ ending and not ending in blank conditioned on input up to time $t$, $p_{tot}(c|x_{1:t})$: $p_b(c|x_{1:t}) + p_{nb}(c|x_{1:t})$

**Inputs** CTC likelihoods $p_{ctc}(c|x_t)$, character language model $p_{clm}(c|s)$
**Parameters** language model weight $\alpha$, insertion bonus $\beta$, beam width $k$
**Initialize** $Z_0 \leftarrow \{\varnothing\}$, $p_b(\varnothing|x_{1:0}) \leftarrow 1$, $p_{nb}(\varnothing|x_{1:0}) \leftarrow 0$
**for** $t = 1, \ldots, T$ **do**
  $Z_t \leftarrow \{\}$
  **for** $s$ **in** $Z_{t-1}$ **do**
    $p_b(s|x_{1:t}) \leftarrow p_{ctc}(\_|x_t) p_{tot}(s|x_{1:t-1})$ ▷ Handle blanks
    $p_{nb}(s|x_{1:t}) \leftarrow p_{ctc}(c|x_t) p_{nb}(s|x_{1:t-1})$ ▷ Handle repeat character collapsing
    Add $s$ to $Z_t$
    **for** $c$ **in** $\zeta'$ **do**
      $s^+ \leftarrow s + c$
      **if** $c \neq s_{t-1}$ **then**
        $p_{nb}(s^+|x_{1:t}) \leftarrow p_{ctc}(c|x_t) p_{clm}(c|s)^\alpha p_{tot}(c|x_{1:t-1})$
      **else**
        $p_{nb}(s^+|x_{1:t}) \leftarrow p_{ctc}(c|x_t) p_{clm}(c|s)^\alpha p_b(c|x_{1:t-1})$ ▷ Repeat characters have "_" between
      **end if**
      Add $s^+$ to $Z_t$
    **end for**
  **end for**
  $Z_t \leftarrow k$ most probable $s$ by $p_{tot}(s|x_{1:t})|s|^\beta$ in $Z_t$ ▷ Apply beam
**end for**
**Return** $\arg\max_{s \in Z_t} p_{tot}(s|x_{1:T})|s|^\beta$

moves the difficulties of handling OOV words during decoding, which is typically a troublesome issue in speech recognition systems.

## 4 Experiments

We perform LVCSR experiments on the 300 hour Switchboard conversational telephone speech corpus (LDC97S62). Switchboard utterances are taken from approximately 2,400 conversations among 543 speakers. Each pair of speakers had never met, and converse no more than once about a given topic chosen randomly from a set of 50 possible topics. Utterances exhibit many rich, complex phenomena that make spoken language understanding difficult. Table 2 shows example transcripts from the corpus.

For evaluation, we report word error rate (WER) and character error rate (CER) on the HUB5 Eval2000 dataset (LDC2002S09). This test set consists of two subsets, Switchboard and CallHome. The CallHome subset represents a mismatched test condition as it was collected from phone conversations among family and friends rather than strangers directed to discuss a particular topic. The mismatch makes the CallHome subset quite difficult overall. The Switchboard evaluation subset is substantially easier, and represents a better match of test data to our training corpus. We report WER and CER on the test set as a whole, and additionally report WER for each subset individually.

### 4.1 Baseline Systems

We build two baseline LVCSR systems to compare our approach to standard HMM-based approaches.

| Method | CER | EV | CH | SWBD |
|---|---|---|---|---|
| HMM-GMM | 23.0 | 29.0 | 36.1 | 21.7 |
| HMM-DNN | 17.6 | 21.2 | 27.1 | 15.1 |
| HMM-SHF | NR | NR | NR | 12.4 |
| CTC no LM | 27.7 | 47.1 | 56.1 | 38.0 |
| CTC+5-gram | 25.7 | 39.0 | 47.0 | 30.8 |
| CTC+7-gram | 24.7 | 35.9 | 43.8 | 27.8 |
| CTC+NN-1 | 24.5 | 32.3 | 41.1 | 23.4 |
| CTC+NN-3 | 24.0 | 30.9 | 39.9 | 21.8 |
| CTC+RNN | 24.9 | 33.0 | 41.7 | 24.2 |
| CTC+RNN-3 | 24.7 | 30.8 | 40.2 | 21.4 |

Table 1: Character error rate (CER) and word error rate results on the Eval2000 test set. We report word error rates on the full test set (EV) which consists of the Switchboard (SWBD) and CallHome (CH) subsets. As baseline systems we use an HMM-GMM system and HMM-DNN system. We evaluate our DBRNN trained using CTC by decoding with several character-level language models: 5-gram, 7-gram, densely connected neural networks with 1 and 3 hidden layers (NN-1, and NN-3), as well as recurrent neural networks s with 1 and 3 hidden layers. We additionally include results from a state-of-the-art HMM-based system (HMM-DNN-SHF) which does not report performance on all metrics we evaluate (NR).

First, we build an HMM-GMM system using the Kaldi open-source toolkit[2] (Povey et al., 2011). The baseline recognizer has 8,986 sub-phone states and 200K Gaussians trained using maximum likelihood. Input features are speaker-adapted MFCCs. Overall, the baseline GMM system setup largely follows the existing `s5b` Kaldi recipe, and we defer to previous work for details (Vesely et al., 2013).

We additionally built an HMM-DNN system by training a DNN acoustic model using maximum likelihood on the alignments produced by our HMM-GMM system. The DNN consists of five hidden layers, each with 2,048 hidden units, for a total of approximately 36 million (M) free parameters in the acoustic model.

Both baseline systems use a bigram language model built from the 3M words in the Switchboard transcripts interpolated with a second bigram language model built from 11M words on the Fisher English Part 1 transcripts (LDC2004T19). Both LMs are trained using interpolated Kneser-Ney smoothing. For context we also include WER results from a state-of-the-art HMM-DNN system built with quinphone phonetic context and Hessian-free sequence-discriminative training (Sainath et al., 2014).

### 4.2 DBRNN Training

We train a DBRNN using the CTC loss function on the entire 300hr training corpus. The input features to the DBRNN at each timestep are MFCCs with context window of $\pm 10$ frames. The DBRNN has 5 hidden layers with the third containing recurrent connections. All layers have 1824 hidden units, giving about 20M trainable parameters. In preliminary experiments we found that choosing the middle hidden layer to have recurrent connections led to the best results.

The output symbol set $\zeta$ consists of 33 characters including the special blank character. Note that because speech recognition transcriptions do not contain proper casing or punctuation, we exclude capital letters and punctuation marks with the exception of "`-`", which denotes a partial word fragment, and "`'`", as used in contractions such as "`can't`."

We train the DBRNN from random initial parameters using the gradient-based Nesterov's accelerated gradient (NAG) algorithm as this technique is sometimes beneficial as compared with standard stochastic gradient descent for deep recurrent neural network training (Sutskever et al., 2013). The NAG algorithm uses a step size of $10^{-5}$ and a momentum of 0.95. After each epoch we divide the learning rate by 1.3. Training for 10 epochs on a single GTX 570 GPU takes approximately one week.

### 4.3 Character Language Model Training

The Switchboard corpus transcripts alone are too small to build CLMs which accurately model general orthography in English. To learn how to spell words more generally we train our CLMs using a corpus of 31 billion words gathered from the web (Heafield et al., 2013). Our language models use sentence start and end tokens, `<s>` and `</s>`, as

[2] `http://kaldi.sf.net`

well as a <null> token for cases when our context window extends past the start of a sentence.

We build 5-gram and 7-gram CLMs with modified Kneser-Ney smoothing using the KenLM toolkit (Heafield et al., 2013). Building traditional $n$-gram CLMs is for $n > 7$ becomes increasingly difficult as the model free parameters and memory footprint become unwieldy. Our 7-gram CLM is already 21GB; we were not able to build higher order $n$-gram models to compare against our neural network CLMs.

Following work illustrating the effectiveness of neural network CLMs (Sutskever et al., 2011) and word-level LMs for speech recognition (Mikolov et al., 2010), we train and evaluate two variants of neural network CLMs: standard feedfoward deep neural networks (DNNs) and a recurrent neural network (RNN). The RNN CLM takes one character at a time as input, while the non-recurrent CLM networks use a context window of 19 characters. All neural network CLMs use the rectified linear activation function, and the layer sizes are selected such that each has about 5M parameters (20MB).

The DNN models are trained using standard backpropagation using Nesterov's accelerated gradient with a learning rate of 0.01 and momentum of 0.95 and a batch size of 512. The RNN is trained using backpropagation through time with a learning rate of 0.001 and batches of 128 utterances. For both model types we halve the learning rate after each epoch. The DNN models were trained for 10 epochs, and the RNN models for 5 epochs.

All neural network CLMs were trained using a combination of the Switchboard and Fisher training transcripts which in total contain approximately 23M words. We also performed experiments with CLMs trained from a large corpus of web text, but found these CLMs to perform no better than transcript-derived CLMs for our task.

### 4.4 Results

After training the DBRNN and CLMs we run decoding on the Eval2000 test set to obtain CER and WER results. For all experiments using a CLM we use our beam search decoding algorithm with $\alpha = 1.25$, $\beta = 1.5$ and a beam width of 100. We found that larger beam widths did not significantly improve performance. Table 1 shows results for the DBRNN as well as baseline systems.

The DBRNN performs best with the 3 hidden layer DNN CLM. This DBRNN+NN-3 attains both CER and WER performance comparable to the HMM-GMM baseline system, albeit substantially below the HMM-DNN system. Neural networks provide a clear gain as compared to standard $n$-gram models when used for DBRNN decoding, although the RNN CLM does not produce any gain over the best DNN CLM.

Without a language model the greedy DBRNN decoding procedure loses relatively little in terms of CER as compared with the DBRNN+NN-3 model. However, this 3% difference in CER translates to a 16% gap in WER on the full Eval2000 test set. Generally, we observe that small CER differences translate to large WER differences. In terms of character-level performance it appears as if the DBRNN alone performs well using only acoustic input data. Adding a CLM yields only a small CER improvement, but guides proper spelling of words to produce a large reduction in WER.

## 5 Analysis

To better see how the DBRNN performs transcription we show the output probabilities $p(c|x)$ for an example utterance in Figure 2. The model tends to output mostly blank characters and only spike long enough for a character to be the most likely symbol for a few frames at a time. The dominance of the blank class is not forced, but rather learned by the DBRNN during training. We hypothesize that this spiking behavior results in more stable results as the DBRNN only produces a character when its confidence of seeing that character rises above a certain threshold. Note that this a dramatic contrast to HMM-based LVCSR systems, which, due to the nature of generative models, attempt to explain almost all timesteps as belonging to a phonetic substate.

Next, we qualitatively compare the DBRNN and HMM-GMM system outputs to better understand how the DBRNN approach might interact with SLU systems. This comparison is especially interesting because our best DBRNN system and the HMM-GMM system have comparable WERs, removing the confound of overall quality when comparing hypotheses. Table 2 shows example test set utterances along with transcription hypotheses from the HMM-

| # | Method | Transcription |
|---|---|---|
| | Truth | yeah i went into the i do not know what you think of *fidelity* but |
| (1) | HMM-GMM | yeah when the i don't know what you think of fidel it even them |
| | CTC+CLM | yeah i went to i don't know what you think of fidelity but um |
| | Truth | no no speaking of weather do you carry a altimeter slash *barometer* |
| (2) | HMM-GMM | no i'm not all being the weather do you uh carry a uh helped emitters last brahms her |
| | CTC+CLM | no no beating of whether do you uh carry a uh a time or less barometer |
| | Truth | i would ima- well yeah it is i know you are able to stay home with them |
| (3) | HMM-GMM | i would amount well yeah it is i know um you're able to stay home with them |
| | CTC+CLM | i would ima- well yeah it is i know uh you're able to stay home with them |

Table 2: Example test set utterances with a ground truth transcription and hypotheses from our method (CTC+CLM) and a baseline HMM-GMM system of comparable overall WER. The words *fidelity* and *barometer* are not in the lexicon of the HMM-GMM system.

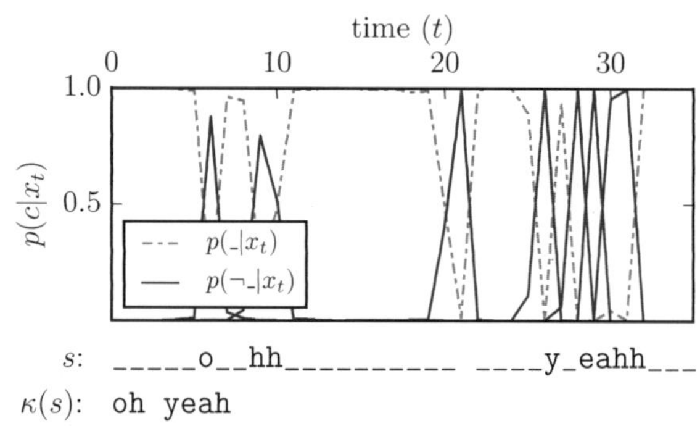


Figure 2: DBRNN character probabilities over time for a single utterance along with the per-frame most likely character string $s$ and the collapsed output $\kappa(s)$. Due to space constraints we only show a distinction in line type between the blank symbol _ and non-blank symbols.

GMM and DBRNN+NN-3 systems.

The DBRNN sometimes correctly transcribes OOV words with respect to our audio training corpus. We find that OOVs tend to trigger clusters of errors in the HMM-GMM system, an observation that has been systematically explored in previous work (Goldwater et al., 2010). As shown in example utterance (3), HMM-GMM errors can introduce word substitution errors which may alter meaning whereas the DBRNN system outputs word fragments or non-words which are phonetically similar and may be useful input features for SLU systems. Unfortunately the Eval2000 test set does not offer a rich set of utterances containing OOVs or fragments to perform a deeper analysis. The HMM-GMM and best DBRNN system achieve identical WERs on the subset of test utterances containing OOVs and the subset of test utterances containing fragments.

Finally, we quantitatively compare how character probabilities from the DBRNN align with phonetic segments from the HMM-GMM system. We generate HMM-GMM forced alignments on a large sample of the training set, and separate utterances into monophone segments. For each monophone, we compute the average character probabilities from the DBRNN by aligning the beginning of each monophone segment, treating it as time 0. We measure time using feature frames rather than seconds. Figure 3 shows character probabilities over time for the phones *k*, *sh*, *w*, and *uw*.

Although the CTC model does not explicitly compute a forced alignment as part of training, we see significant rises in character probabilities corresponding to particular phones during HMM-GMM-aligned monophone segments. This indicates that the CTC model automatically learns a reasonable alignment of characters to the audio. Generally, the CTC model tends to produce character spikes towards the beginning of monophone segments. This is especially evident in plosive consonants such as *k* and *t*. For liquids and glides (*r*, *l*, *w*, *y*), the CTC model does not produce characters until later in the monophone segment. For vowels the CTC character

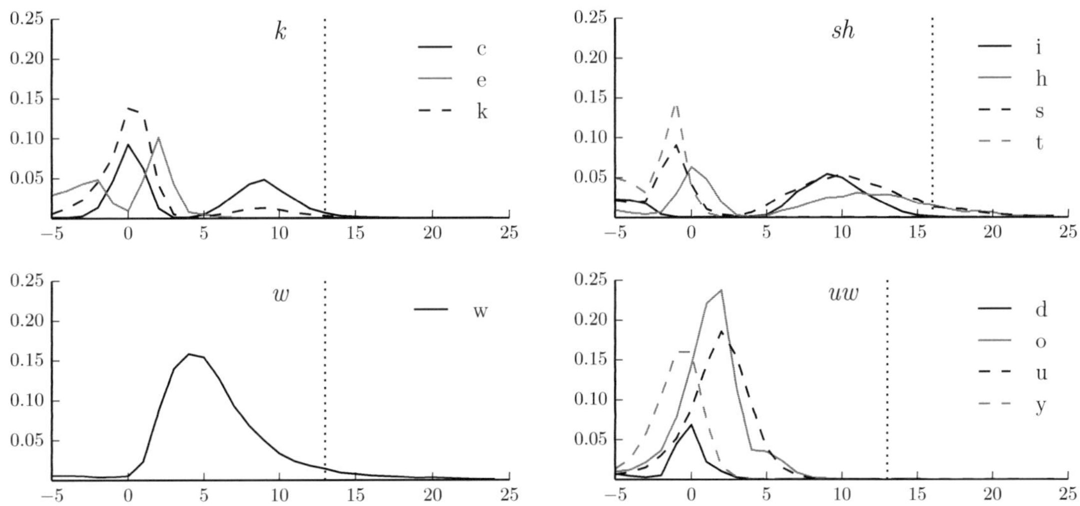


Figure 3: Character probabilities from the CTC-trained neural network averaged over monophone segments created by a forced alignment of the HMM-GMM system. Time is measured in frames, with 0 indicating the start of the monophone segment. The vertical dotted line indicates the average duration of the monophone segment. We show only characters with non-trivial probability for each phone while excluding the blank and space symbols.

probabilities generally rise slightly later in the phone segment as compared to consonants. This may occur to avoid the large contextual variations in vowel pronunciations at phone boundaries. For certain consonants we observe CTC probability spikes before the monophone segment begins, as is the case for *sh*. The probabilities for *sh* additionally exhibit multiple modes, suggesting that CTC may learn different behaviors for the two common spellings of the sibilant *sh*: the letter sequence "sh" and the letter sequence "ti".

## 6 Conclusion

We presented an LVCSR system consisting of two neural networks integrated via beam search decoding that matches the performance of an HMM-GMM system on the challenging Switchboard corpus. We built on the foundation of Graves and Jaitly (2014) to vastly reduce the overall complexity required for LVCSR systems. Our method yields a complete first-pass LVCSR system with about 1,000 lines of code — roughly an order of magnitude less than high performance HMM-GMM systems. Operating entirely at the character level yields a system which does not require assumptions about a lexicon or pronunciation dictionary, instead learning orthography and phonics directly from data. We hope the simplicity of our approach will facilitate future research in improving LVCSR with CTC-based systems and jointly training LVCSR systems for SLU tasks. DNNs have already shown great results as acoustic models in HMM-DNN systems. We free the neural network from its complex HMM infrastructure, which we view as the first step towards the next wave of advances in speech recognition and language understanding.

## Acknowledgments

We thank Awni Hannun for his contributions to the software used for experiments in this work. We also thank Peng Qi and Thang Luong for insightful discussions, and Kenneth Heafield for help with the KenLM toolkit. Our work with HMM-GMM systems was possible thanks to the Kaldi toolkit and its contributors. Some of the GPUs used in this work were donated by the NVIDIA Corporation. AM was supported as an NSF IGERT Traineeship Recipient under Award 0801700. ZX was supported by an NDSEG Graduate Fellowship.

## References


H. Bourlard and N. Morgan. 1993. *Connectionist Speech Recognition: A Hybrid Approach*. Kluwer Academic Publishers, Norwell, MA.

G. E. Dahl, D. Yu, and L. Deng. 2011. Large vocabulary continuous speech recognition with context-dependent DBN-HMMs. In *Proc. ICASSP*.

G. E. Dahl, T. N. Sainath, and G. E. Hinton. 2013. Improving Deep Neural Networks for LVCSR using Rectified Linear Units and Dropout. In *ICASSP*.

R. De Mori, F. Bechet, D. Hakkani-Tur, M. McTear, G. Riccardi, and G. Tur. 2008. Spoken language understanding. *Signal Processing Magazine, IEEE*, 25(3):50–58.

X. Glorot, A. Bordes, and Y Bengio. 2011. Deep Sparse Rectifier Networks. In *AISTATS*, pages 315–323.

S. Goldwater, D. Jurafsky, and C. Manning. 2010. Which Words are Hard to Recognize? Prosodic, Lexical, and Disfluency Factors That Increase Speech Recognition Error Rates. *Speech Communications*, 52:181–200.

A. Graves and N. Jaitly. 2014. Towards End-to-End Speech Recognition with Recurrent Neural Networks. In *ICML*.

A. Graves, S. Fernández, F. Gomez, and J. Schmidhuber. 2006. Connectionist temporal classification: Labelling unsegmented sequence data with recurrent neural networks. In *ICML*, pages 369–376. ACM.

K. Heafield, I. Pouzyrevsky, J. H. Clark, and P. Koehn. 2013. Scalable modified Kneser-Ney language model estimation. In *ACL-HLT*, pages 690–696, Sofia, Bulgaria.

G. E. Hinton, L. Deng, D. Yu, G. E. Dahl, A. Mohamed, N. Jaitly, A. Senior, V. Vanhoucke, P. Nguyen, T. Sainath, and B. Kingsbury. 2012. Deep neural networks for acoustic modeling in speech recognition. *IEEE Signal Processing Magazine*, 29(November):82–97.

X. Huang, A. Acero, H.-W. Hon, et al. 2001. *Spoken language processing*, volume 18. Prentice Hall Englewood Cliffs.

A. Maas, A. Hannun, and A. Ng. 2013. Rectifier Nonlinearities Improve Neural Network Acoustic Models. In *ICML Workshop on Deep Learning for Audio, Speech, and Language Processing*.

T. Mikolov, M. Karafiát, L. Burget, J. Cernockỳ, and S. Khudanpur. 2010. Recurrent neural network based language model. In *INTERSPEECH*, pages 1045–1048.

D. Povey, A. Ghoshal, G. Boulianne, L. Burget, O. Glembek, K. Veselý, N. Goel, M. Hannemann, P. Motlicek, Y. Qian, P. Schwarz, J. Silovsky, and G. Stemmer. 2011. The kaldi speech recognition toolkit. In *ASRU*.

T. N. Sainath, I. Chung, B. Ramabhadran, M. Picheny, J. Gunnels, B. Kingsbury, G. Saon, V. Austel, and U. Chaudhari. 2014. Parallel deep neural network training for lvcsr tasks using blue gene/q. In *INTERSPEECH*.

G. Saon and J. Chien. 2012. Large-vocabulary continuous speech recognition systems: A look at some recent advances. *IEEE Signal Processing Magazine*, 29(6):18–33.

I. Sutskever, J. Martens, and G. E. Hinton. 2011. Generating text with recurrent neural networks. In *ICML*, pages 1017–1024.

I. Sutskever, J. Martens, G. Dahl, and G. Hinton. 2013. On the Importance of Momentum and Initialization in Deep Learning. In *ICML*.

K. Vesely, A. Ghoshal, L. Burget, and D. Povey. 2013. Sequence-discriminative training of deep neural networks. In *Interspeech*.

M. D. Zeiler, M. Ranzato, R. Monga, M. Mao, K. Yang, Q.V. Le, P. Nguyen, A. Senior, V. Vanhoucke, J. Dean, and G. E. Hinton. 2013. On Rectified Linear Units for Speech Processing. In *ICASSP*.

# I Can Has Cheezburger?
# A Nonparanormal Approach to Combining Textual and Visual Information for Predicting and Generating Popular Meme Descriptions

**William Yang Wang** and **Miaomiao Wen**
School of Computer Science
Carnegie Mellon University
Pittsburgh, PA 15213

## Abstract

The advent of social media has brought Internet memes, a unique social phenomenon, to the front stage of the Web. Embodied in the form of images with text descriptions, little do we know about the "language of memes". In this paper, we statistically study the correlations among popular memes and their wordings, and generate meme descriptions from raw images. To do this, we take a multimodal approach—we propose a robust nonparanormal model to learn the stochastic dependencies among the image, the candidate descriptions, and the popular votes. In experiments, we show that combining text and vision helps identifying popular meme descriptions; that our nonparanormal model is able to learn dense and continuous vision features jointly with sparse and discrete text features in a principled manner, outperforming various competitive baselines; that our system can generate meme descriptions using a simple pipeline.

## 1 Introduction

In the past few years, Internet memes become a new, contagious social phenomenon: it all starts with an image with a witty, catchy, or sarcastic sentence, and people circulate it from friends to friends, colleagues to colleagues, and families to families. Eventually, some of them go viral on the Internet.

Meme is not only about the funny picture, the Internet culture, or the emotion that passes along, but also about the richness and uniqueness of its language: it is often highly structured with special written style, and forms interesting and subtle connotations that resonate among the readers. For example, the LOL cat memes (e.g., Figure 1) often include superimposed text with broken grammars and/or spellings.

Figure 1: An example of the LOL cat memes.

Even though the memes are popular over the Internet, the "language of memes" is still not well-understood: there are no systematic studies on predicting and generating popular Internet memes from the Natural Language Processing (NLP) and Computer Vision (CV) perspectives.

In this paper, we take a multimodal approach to predict and generate popular meme descriptions. To do this, we collect a set of original meme images, a list of candidate descriptions, and the corresponding votes. We propose a robust nonparanormal approach (Liu et al., 2009) to model the multimodal stochastic dependencies among images, text, and votes. We then introduce a simple pipeline for generating meme descriptions combining reverse image search and traditional information retrieval approaches. In empirical experiments, we show that our model outperforms strong discriminative baselines by very large margins in the regression/ranking experiments, and that in the generation experiment, the nonparanormal outperforms the second-best supervised baseline by 4.35 BLEU points, and obtains a BLEU score improvement of 4.48 over an unsupervised recurrent neural network language model



*Human Language Technologies: The 2015 Annual Conference of the North American Chapter of the ACL*, pages 355–365,
Denver, Colorado, May 31 – June 5, 2015. 

trained on a large meme corpus that is almost 90 times larger. Our contributions are three-fold:

- We are the first to study the "language of memes" combining NLP, CV, and machine learning techniques, and show that combining the visual and textual signals helps identifying popular meme descriptions;
- Our approach empowers Internet users to select better wordings and generate new memes automatically;
- Our proposed robust nonparanormal model outperforms competitive baselines for predicting and generating popular meme descriptions.

In the next section, we outline related work. In Section 3, we introduce the theory of copula, and our nonparanormal approach. In Section 4, we describe the datasets. We show the prediction and generation results in Section 5 and Section 6. Finally, we conclude in Section 7.

## 2 Related Work

Although the language of Internet memes is a relatively new research topic, our work is broadly related to studies on predicting popular social media messages (Hong et al., 2011; Bakshy et al., 2011; Artzi et al., 2012). Most recently, Tan et al. (2014) study the effect on wordings for Tweets. However, none of the above studies have investigated multimodal approaches that combine text and vision.

Recently, there has been growing interests in inter-disciplinary research on generating image descriptions. Gupta el al. (2009) have studied the problem of constructing plots from video understanding. The work by Farhadi et al. (2010) is among the first to generate sentences from images. Kulkarni et al. (2011) use linguistic constraints and a conditional random field model for the task, whereas Mitchell et al. (2012) leverage syntactic information and co-occurrence statistics and Dodge et al. (2012) use a large text corpus and CV algorithms for detecting visual text. With the surge of interests in deep learning techniques in NLP (Socher et al., 2013; Devlin et al., 2014) and CV (Krizhevsky et al., 2012; Oquab et al., 2013), there have been several unrefereed manuscripts on parsing images and generating text descriptions lately (Vinyals et al., 2014; Chen and Zitnick, 2014; Donahue et al., 2014; Fang et al., 2014; Karpathy and Fei-Fei, 2014) using neural network models. Although the above studies have shown interesting results, our task is arguably more complex than generating text descriptions: in addition to the visual and textual signals, we have to model the popular votes as a third dimension for learning. For example, we cannot simply train a convolutional neural network image parser on billions of images, and use recurrent neural networks to generate texts such as *"There is a white cat sitting next to a laptop."* for Figure 1. Additionally, since not all images are suitable as meme images, collecting training images is also more challenging in our task.

In contrast to prior work, we take a very different approach: we investigate copula methods (Schweizer and Sklar, 1983; Nelsen, 1999), in particular, the nonparanormals (Liu et al., 2009), for joint modeling of raw images, text descriptions, and popular votes. Copula is a statistical framework for analyzing random variables from Statistics (Liu et al., 2012), and often used in Economics (Chen and Fan, 2006). Only until very recently, researchers from the machine learning and information retrieval communities (Ghahramani et al., 2012; Han et al., 2012; Eickhoff et al., 2013). start to understand the theory and the predictive power of copula models. Wang and Hua (2014) are the first to introduce semiparametric Gaussian copula (a.k.a. nonparanormals) for text prediction. However, their approach may be prone to overfitting. In this work, we generalize Wang and Hua's method to jointly model text and vision features with popular votes, while scaling up the model using effective dropout regularization.

## 3 Our Approach

A key challenge for joint modeling of text and vision is that, because textual features are often relatively sparse and discrete, while visual features are typically dense and continuous, it is difficult to model them jointly in a principled way.

To avoid comparing "apple and oranges" in the same probabilistic space, we propose the nonparanormal approach, which extends the Gaussian graphical model by transforming its variables by smooth functions. More specifically, for each dimension of textual and visual features, instead of

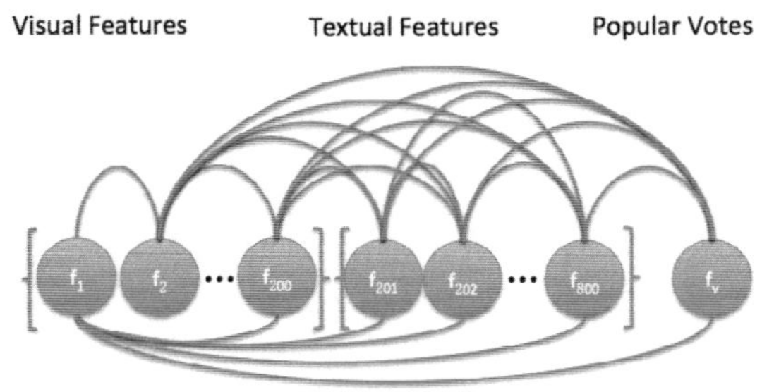


Figure 2: Our nonparanormal method extends Gaussian by transforming each dimension with a smooth function, and jointly models the stochastic dependencies among textual and visual features, as well as the popular votes by the crowd.

using raw counts or histograms, we first use *probability integral transform* to generate empirical cumulative density functions (ECDF): now instead of the probability density function (PDF) space, we are working in the ECDF space where the value of each feature is based on the rank, and is strictly restricted between 0 and 1. Then, we use kernel density estimation to smooth out the zeroing features[1]. Finally, now textual and visual features are compatible, and we then build a parametric Gaussian copula model to estimate the pair-wise correlations among the covariate and the dependent variable.

In this section, we first explain the visual and textual features used in this study. Then, we introduce the theory of copula, and describe the robust nonparanormal. Finally, we show a simple pipeline for generating meme descriptions.

### 3.1 Features

**Textual Features** To model the meme descriptions, we take a broad range of textual features into considerations:

- **Lexical Features**: we extract unigrams and bigrams from meme descriptions as surface-level lexical features.
- **Part-of-Speech Features**: to model shallow syntactic cues, we extract lexicalized part-of-speech features using the Stanford part-of-speech tagger (Toutanova et al., 2003).
- **Dependency Triples**: to better understand the deeper syntactic dependencies of keywords in memes, we have also extracted typed dependency triples (e.g., *subj(I,are)*) using the MaltParser (Nivre et al., 2007).
- **Named Entity Features**: after browsing the dataset, we notice that certain names are often mentioned in memes (e.g. "Drake", "Kenye West", and "Justin Bieber"), so we utilize the Stanford named entity recognizer (Finkel et al., 2005) to extract lexicalized named entities.
- **Frame-Semantics Features**: SEMAFOR (Das et al., 2010) is a state-of-the-art frame-semantics parser that produces FrameNet-style semantic annotation. We use SEMAFOR to extract frame-level semantic features.

[1]This is necessary for the normal inversion of the ECDFs, which we will describe in Section 3.2.

Figure 3: An example of the standard SIFT keypoints detected on the "doge" meme.

**Visual Features** A key insight on viral memes is that the images producing a shared social signal are typically inter-related in style. For example, LOLcats are an early series of memes involving funny cat photos. Similarly, "Bieber memes" involve modified pictures of Bieber.

Therefore, we hypothesize that, by extracting visual features, it is of crucial importance to capture the entities, objects, and styles as visual words in these inter-related meme images. The popular visual bag-of-words representation (Sivic and Zisserman, 2003) is used to describe images:

1. **PHOW Features Extraction**: unlike text features, SIFT first detects the Harris keypoints from an image, and then describes each keypoint with a vector. An example of the SIFT frames are shown in Figure 3. PHOW (Bosch et al., 2007) is a dense and multi-scale variant of the Scale Invariant Feature Transform (SIFT) descriptors. Using PHOW, we obtain about 20K keypoints for each image.

2. **Elkan K-means Clustering** is the clustering method (Elkan, 2003) that we use to obtain the vocabulary for visual words. Comparing to other variants of K-means, this method quickly constructs the codebook from PHOW keypoints.
3. **Bag-of-Words Histograms** are used to represent each image. We match the PHOW keypoints of each image with the vocabulary that we extract from the previous step, and generate a $1 \times 200$ sized visual bag-of-words vector.

### 3.2 The Theory of Copula

In the Statistics literature, copula is widely known as a family of distribution function. The idea behind copula theory is that the cumulative distribution function (CDF) of a random vector can be represented in the form of uniform marginal cumulative distribution functions, and a copula that connects these marginal CDFs, which describes the correlations among the input random variables. However, in order to have a valid multivariate distribution function regardless of $n$-dimensional covariates, not every function can be used as a copula function. The central idea behind copula, therefore, can be summarize by the Sklar's theorem and the corollary.

**Theorem 1 (Sklar's Theorem (1959))** *Let $F$ be the joint cumulative distribution function of $n$ random variables $X_1, X_2, ..., X_n$. Let the corresponding marginal cumulative distribution functions of the random variable be $F_1(x_1), F_2(x_2), ..., F_n(x_n)$. Then, if the marginal functions are continuous, there exists a unique copula $C$, such that*

$$F(x_1, ..., x_n) = C[F_1(x_1), ..., F_n(x_n)]. \quad (1)$$

Furthermore, if the distributions are continuous, the multivariate dependency structure and the marginals might be separated, and the copula can be considered independent of the marginals (Joe, 1997; Parsa and Klugman, 2011). Therefore, the copula does not have requirements on the marginal distributions, and any arbitrary marginals can be combined and their dependency structure can be modeled using the copula. The inverse of Sklar's Theorem is also true in the following:

**Corollary 1** *If there exists a copula $C : (0,1)^n$ and marginal cumulative distribution functions $F_1(x_1), F_2(x_2), ..., F_n(x_n)$, then $C[F_1(x_1), ..., F_n(x_n)]$ defines a multivariate cumulative distribution function.*

### 3.3 The Nonparanormal

To model multivariate text and vision variables, we choose the nonparanormal (NPN) as the copula function in this study, which can be explained in the following two parts.

#### The Nonparametric Estimation

Assume we have $n$ random variables of vision and text features $X_1, X_2, ..., X_n$. The problem is that text features are sparse, so we need to perform nonparametric kernel density estimation to smooth out the distribution of each variable. Let $f_1, f_2, ..., f_n$ be the unknown density, we are interested in deriving the shape of these functions. Assume we have $m$ samples, the kernel density estimator can be defined as:

$$\hat{f}_h(x) = \frac{1}{m}\sum_{i=1}^{m} K_h(x - x_i) \quad (2)$$

$$= \frac{1}{mh}\sum_{i=1}^{m} K\left(\frac{x - x_i}{h}\right) \quad (3)$$

Here, $K(\cdot)$ is the kernel function, where in our case, we use the Box kernel[2] $K(z)$:

$$K(z) = \frac{1}{2}, |z| \leq 1, \quad (4)$$

$$= 0, |z| > 1. \quad (5)$$

Comparing to the Gaussian kernel and other kernels, the Box kernel is simple, and computationally inexpensive. The parameter $h$ is the bandwidth for smoothing[3].

Now, we can derive the empirical cumulative distribution functions

$$\hat{F}_{X_1}(\hat{f}_1(X_1)), \hat{F}_{X_2}(\hat{f}_2(X_2)), ..., \hat{F}_{X_n}(\hat{f}_n(X_n))$$

of the smoothed covariates, as well as the dependent variable $y$ (which is the reciprocal rank of the popular votes of a meme) and its CDF $\hat{F}_y(\hat{f}(y))$. The

[2]It is also known as the original Parzen windows (Parzen, 1962).

[3]In our implementation, we use the default $h$ of the Box kernel in the *ksdensity* function in Matlab.

empirical cumulative distribution functions are defined as:

$$\hat{F}(\nu) = \frac{1}{m}\sum_{i=1}^{m} \mathbf{I}\{x_i \leq \nu\} \quad (6)$$

where $\mathbf{I}\{\cdot\}$ is the indicator function, and $\nu$ indicates the current value that we are evaluating. Note that the above step is also known as *probability integral transform* (Diebold et al., 1997), which allows us to convert any given continuous distribution to random variables having a uniform distribution. This is crucial for text: instead of using the raw counts, we are now working with uniform marginal CDFs, which helps coping with the overfitting issue due to noise and data sparsity. We also use the same procedure to transform the vision features into CDF space to be compatible with text features.

### The Robust Estimation of Copula

Now that we have obtained the marginals, and then the joint distribution can be constructed by applying the copula function that models the stochastic dependencies among marginal CDFs:

$$\begin{aligned}&\hat{F}(\hat{f}_1(X_1), ..., \hat{f}_1(X_n), \hat{f}(y))\\ &= C[\hat{F}_{X_1}(\hat{f}_1(X_1)), ..., \hat{F}_{X_n}(\hat{f}_n(X_n)), \hat{F}_y(\hat{f}_y(y))]\end{aligned} \quad (7)$$

In this work, we apply the parametric Gaussian copula to model the correlations among the text features and the label. Assume $x_i$ is the smoothed version of random variable $X_i$, and $y$ is the smoothed label, we have:

$$\begin{aligned}&F(x_1, ..., x_n, y)\\ &= \Phi_\Sigma\Big(\Phi^{-1}[F_{x_1}(x_1)], ..., \Phi^{-1}[F_{x_n}(x_n)], \Phi^{-1}[F_y(y)]\Big)\end{aligned} \quad (8)$$

where $\Phi_\Sigma$ is the joint cumulative distribution function of a multivariate Gaussian with zero mean and $\Sigma$ variance. $\Phi^{-1}$ is the inverse CDF of a standard Gaussian. In this parametric part of the model, the parameter estimation boils down to the problem of learning the covariance matrix $\Sigma$ of this Gaussian copula. In this work, we perform standard maximum likelihood estimation (MLE) for the $\Sigma$ matrix, where we follow the details from prior work (Wang and Hua, 2014).

To avoid overfitting, traditionally, one resorts to classic regularization techniques such as Lasso (Tibshirani, 1996). While Lasso is widely used, the non-differentiable nature of the $L_1$ norm often make the objective function difficult to optimize. In this work, we propose dropout training (Hinton et al., 2012) as copula regularization. Dropout was proposed by Hinton et al. as a method to prevent feature co-adaptation in the deep learning framework, but recently studies (Wager et al., 2013) also show that its behaviour is similar to $L_2$ regularization, and can be approximated efficiently (Wang and Manning, 2013) in many other machine learning tasks. Another advantage of dropout training is that, unlike Lasso, it does not require all the features for training, and training is "embarrassingly" parallelizable.

In Gaussian copula estimation context, we can introduce another dimension $\ell$: the number of dropout learners, to extend the $\Sigma$ into a dropout tensor. Essentially, the task becomes the estimation of

$$\Sigma_1, \Sigma_2, ..., \Sigma_\ell$$

where the input feature space for each dropout component is randomly corrupted by $(1 - \delta)$ percent of the original dimension. In the inference time, we use geometric mean to average the predictions from each dropout learner, and generate the final prediction. Note that the final $\Sigma$ matrix has to be symmetric and positive definite, so we apply tiny random Gaussian noise $\epsilon$ to maintain the property.

### Computational Complexity

One important question regarding the proposed nonparanormal model is the corresponding computational complexity. This boils down to the estimation of the $\hat{\Sigma}$ matrix (Liu et al., 2012): one only needs to calculate the correlation coefficients of $n(n-1)/2$ pairs of random variables. Christensen (2005) shows that sorting and balanced binary trees can be used to calculate the correlation coefficients with complexity of $O(n \log n)$. Therefore, the computational complexity of MLE for the proposed model is $O(n \log n)$.

### Efficient Approximate Inference

In this prediction task, in order to perform the exact inference of the conditional probability distribution $p(F_y(y)|F_{x_1}(x_1), ..., F_{x_n}(x_n))$, one needs to solve the mean response $\hat{\mathbf{E}}(F_y(y)|F_{x_1}(x_1), ..., F_{x_1}(x_1))$ from a joint distribution of high-dimensional Gaussian copula. Unfortunately, the exact inference can be

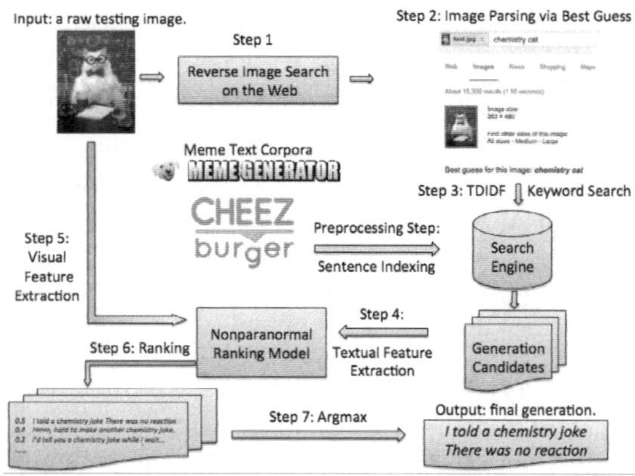


Figure 4: Our pipeline for generating memes from raw images.

intractable in the multivariate case, and approximate inference, such as Markov Chain Monte Carlo sampling (Gelfand and Smith, 1990; Pitt et al., 2006) is often used for posterior inference. In this work, we propose an efficient sampling method to derive $y$ given the text features — we sample $\hat{F_y(y)}$ s.t. it maximizes the joint high-dimensional Gaussian copula density:

$$\arg\max_{\hat{F_y(y)} \in (0,1)} \frac{1}{\sqrt{\det \Sigma}} \exp\left(-\frac{1}{2}\Delta^T \cdot (\Sigma^{-1} - \mathbf{I}) \cdot \Delta\right) \tag{9}$$

where

$$\Delta = \begin{pmatrix} \Phi^{-1}(F_{x_1}(x_1)) \\ \vdots \\ \Phi^{-1}(F_{x_n}(x_n)) \\ \Phi^{-1}(F_y(y)) \end{pmatrix}$$

This approximate inference scheme using maximum density sampling from the Gaussian copula significantly relaxes the complexity of inference. Finally, to derive $\hat{y}$, the last step is to compute the inverse CDF of $\hat{F_y(y)}$. A detailed description of the inference algorithm can be found in our prior work (Wang and Hua, 2014).

### 3.4 A Simple Meme Generation Pipeline

Now after we train a nonparanormal model for ranking meme descriptions, we show the simple meme generation pipeline in Figure 4.

Given a test image, we disguise as the Internet Explorer, and query Google's "Search By Image" inverse image search service[4]. By comparing the query image with all possible images with their captions in Google's database, a "Best Guess" of the keywords in the image is then revealed.

Using the extracted image keywords, we further query a TF-IDF based Lucene[5] meme search engine, which we indexed with a large number of Web-crawled meme descriptions. After we obtain the candidate generations, we then extract all the text and vision features that we described in Section 3.1. Finally, our nonparanormal model ranks all possible candidates, and selects the final generation with the highest posterior.

## 4 Datasets

We collected meme images and text descriptions[6] from two popular meme websites[7]. In the prediction experiment, we use 3,008 image-description pairs for training, and 526 image-description pairs for testing. In the generation experiment, we use 269,473 meme descriptions to index the meme search engine, and 50 randomly selected images for testing. During training, we convert the raw counts of popular votes into reciprocal ranks (e.g., the most popular text descriptions will all have a reciprocal rank of 1, and $n$-th popular one will have a score of $1/n$).

## 5 Prediction Experiments

In the first experiment, we compare the proposed NPN with various baselines in a prediction task, since prior literature (Hodosh et al., 2013) also suggests using ranking based evaluation for associating images with text descriptions. Throughout the experiment sections, we set $\ell = 10$, and $\delta = 80$ as the dropout hyperparameters.

**Baselines:**

The baselines are standard squared-loss linear regression, linear kernel SVM, and non-linear (Gaussian) kernel SVM. In a recent empirical study (Fernández-Delgado et al., 2014) that evaluates 179 classifiers from 17 families on 121 UCI datasets, the authors find that Gaussian SVM is one of the top performing classifiers. We use the Statistical Toolbox's linear regression implementation in Matlab, and LibSVM (Chang and Lin, 2011) for

[4] http://www.google.com/imghp/

[5] http://lucene.apache.org/

[6] http://www.cs.cmu.edu/~yww/data/meme_dataset.zip.

[7] memegenerator.net and cheezburger.com

training and testing the SVM models. The hyperparameter $C$ in linear SVM, and the $\gamma$ and $C$ hyperparameters in Gaussian SVM are tuned on the training set using 10-fold cross-validation.

**Evaluation Metrics:**

Spearman's correlation (Hogg and Craig, 1994) and Kendall's tau (Kendall, 1938) have been widely used in many real-valued prediction (regression) problems in NLP (Albrecht and Hwa, 2007; Yogatama et al., 2011), and here we use them to measure the quality of predicted values $\hat{\mathbf{y}}$ by comparing to the vector of ground truth $\mathbf{y}$. Kendall's tau is a nonparametric statistical metric that have shown to be inexpensive, robust, and representation independent (Lapata, 2006). We use paired two-tailed t-test to measure the statistical significance.

## 5.1 Comparison with Various Baselines

The first two figures in Figure 5 show the learning curve of our system, comparing other baselines. We see that when increasing the amount of training data, our approach clearly dominates all other methods by a large margin. Linear and Gaussian SVMs perform similarly, and have good performances with only 25% of the training data, but the improvements are not large when increasing the amount of training data.

In the last two figures in Figure 5, we increase the amount of features, and compare various models. We see that the linear regression model overfits with 600 features, and Gaussian SVM outperforms the linear SVM. We see that our NPN model clearly outperforms all baselines by a big gap, and does not overfit.

## 5.2 Combination of Text and Vision

In Table 1, we systematically compare the contributions of each feature set. First, we see that bigram features clearly improve the performance on top of unigram features. Second, named entities are crucial for further boosting the performance. Third, adding the shallow part-of-speech features does not benefit all models, but the dependency triples are shown to be useful for all methods. Finally, we see that using semantic features helps increasing the performances for most of the cases, and combining text and vision features in our NPN framework doubles the performance for associating popular votes, meme images, and text descriptions.

| Feature Sets | LR | LSVM | GSVM | NPN |
|---|---|---|---|---|
| Unigrams | 0.152 | 0.158 | 0.176 | **0.241*** |
| + Bigrams | 0.163 | 0.248 | 0.279 | **0.318*** |
| + Named Entities | 0.188 | 0.296 | 0.312 | **0.339*** |
| + Part-of-Speech | 0.184 | 0.318 | 0.337 | **0.343** |
| + Dependency | 0.191 | 0.322 | 0.348 | **0.350** |
| + Semantics | 0.183 | 0.368 | **0.388** | 0.367 |
| All Text + Vision | 0.413 | 0.415 | 0.451 | **0.754*** |

| | | | | |
|---|---|---|---|---|
| Unigrams | 0.102 | 0.105 | 0.118 | **0.181*** |
| + Bigrams | 0.115 | 0.164 | 0.187 | **0.237*** |
| + Named Entities | 0.127 | 0.202 | 0.213 | **0.248*** |
| + Part-of-Speech | 0.125 | 0.218 | 0.232 | **0.239** |
| + Dependency | 0.130 | 0.223 | 0.242 | **0.255** |
| + Semantics | 0.124 | 0.257 | **0.270** | **0.270** |
| All Text + Vision | 0.284 | 0.288 | 0.314 | **0.580*** |

Table 1: The Spearman correlation (top table) and Kendall's $\tau$ (bottom table) for comparing various text features and combining with vision features. The best results of each row are highlighted in **bold**. * indicates $p < .001$ comparing to the second best result.

## 5.3 The Effects of Dropout Training for Nonparanormals

As we mentioned before, because NPNs model the complex network of random variables, a key issue for training NPN is to prevent the model from overfitting to the training data. So far, none of the prior work have investigated dropout training for regularizing the nonparanormals or even copula in general. To empirical test the effects of dropout training for nonparanormals, in addition to our datasets, we also compare with the unregularized copula from Wang and Hua (2014) on predicting financial risks from earnings calls. Table 2 clearly suggests that dropout training for NPNs significant improves the performances on various datasets.

## 5.4 Qualitative Analysis

Table 3 shows the top ranked text features that are highly correlated with popular votes. We see that the named entity features are useful: Paul Walker, UPS, Bruce Willis, Pencil Guy, Amy Winehouse are recognized as entities in the meme dataset. Dependency triples, as a less-understood feature set, also perform well in this task. For example, *xcomp(tell,mean)*

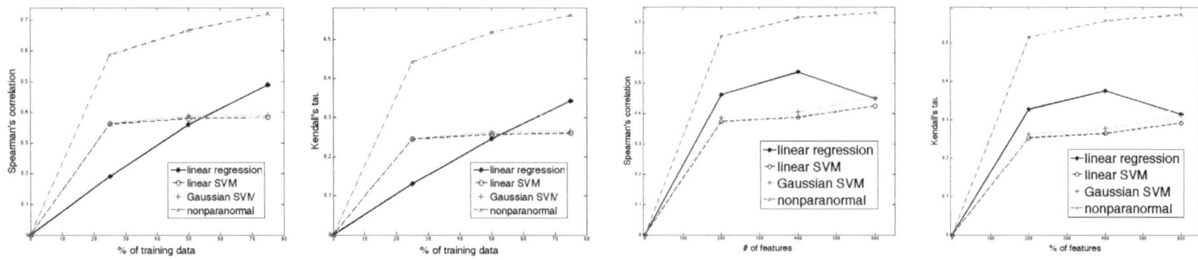


Figure 5: Two figures on the left: varying the amount of training data. L(1): Spearman. L(2): Kendall. Two figures on the right: varying the amount of features. R(1): Spearman. R(2): Kendall.

| Datasets | No Dropout | With Dropout |
|---|---|---|
| Meme | 0.625 | **0.754*** |
| Finance (pre2009) | 0.416 | **0.482*** |
| Finance (2009) | 0.412 | **0.445*** |
| Finance (post2009) | 0.377 | **0.409*** |
| Meme | 0.491 | **0.580*** |
| Finance (pre2009) | 0.307 | **0.349*** |
| Finance (2009) | 0.302 | **0.318*** |
| Finance (post2009) | 0.282 | **0.297*** |

Table 2: The effects of dropout training for NPNs on meme and other datasets. The best results of each row are highlighted in **bold**. * indicates $p < .001$ comparing to the no dropout setting.

| Top 1-10 | Top 11-20 | Top 21-30 |
|---|---|---|
| paul/PER | FE_party_you | new |
| xcomp(tell,mean) | dep(when,but) | FE_Entity_it |
| possessive('s,it) | ..._: | bruce/PER |
| yo_daw | FE_Theme_i | FE_party_we |
| pobj(vegas,in) | on_a | FE_Food_fat |
| ups/ORG | FE_Exp._they | <start>_make |
| into | FE_Entity_you | so_you |
| so_you're | <start>_how | penci/PER |
| FE_Cognizer_i | of_the | y |
| yo_. | pobj(life,of) | winehouse/PER |

Table 3: Top-30 linguistic features that are highly correlated with the popular votes.

captures the dependency relation of the popular meme series "You mean to tell me...". Interestingly, the transitional dependency feature *dep(when,but)* plays an important role in the language of memes. The object of a preposition, such as *pobj(vegas,in)* and *pobj(life,of)*, also made the list.

Bigrams are shown to be important features as usual. For example, "Yo daw" is a popular meme based on rapper Xzibit's famous reality car show "Pimp My Ride", where the rapper customizes people's car according to personal preferences. This viral meme follows the pattern[8] of "Yo daw(g), I herd you like $X$ (noun), so I put an $X$ in your $Y$ (noun) so you can $W$ (verb) while you $Z$ (verb)."

The use of pronouns, captured by frame semantics features, is associated with popular memes. We hypothesize that by using pronouns such as "i", "you", "we", and "they", the meme recalls personal experiences and emotions, thus connects better with the audience. Finally, we see that the punctuation bigram "..._:" is an important feature in the language of memes, and Web dialect such as "y" (why) also exhibits high correlation with the popular votes.

## 6 Generation Experiments

In this section, we investigate the performance of our meme generation system using 50 test meme images. To quantitatively evaluate our system, we compare with both unsupervised and supervised baselines. For the unsupervised baselines, we compare with a compact recurrent neural network language model (RNNLM) (Mikolov, 2012) trained on the 3,008 text descriptions of our meme training set, as well as a full model of RNNLM trained on a large meme corpus of 269K sentences[9]. For the supervised baselines, all models are trained on the 3,008 training image-description pairs with labels. All these models can be viewed as different re-ranking methods for the retrieved candidate descriptions. We use BLEU score (Papineni et al., 2002) as the evaluation metric, since the generation task can be viewed as translating raw images into sentences, and it is

[8] http://knowyourmeme.com/memes/xzibit-yo-dawg

[9] Note that there are no image features feeding to the unsupervised RNN models.

Figure 6: Examples from the meme generation experiment. First row: the chemistry cat meme. Second row: the forever alone meme. Third row: the Batman slaps Robin meme. Left column: human generated top-voted meme descriptions on memegenerator.net at the time of writing. Middle column: generated output from RNNLM. Right column: generated output from NPNs.

used in many caption generation studies (Vinyals et al., 2014; Chen and Zitnick, 2014; Donahue et al., 2014; Fang et al., 2014; Karpathy and Fei-Fei, 2014).

The generation result is shown in Table 4. Note that when combining B-1 to B-4 scores, BLEU includes a brevity penalty as described in the original BLEU paper. We see that our NPN model outperforms the best supervised baseline by 4.35 BLEU points, while also obtaining an advantage of 4.48 BLEU points over the full RNNLM, which is trained on a corpus that is $\sim$90 times larger, in an unsupervised fashion. When breaking down the results, we see that our NPN's advantage is on generating longer phrases, typically trigrams and four-grams, comparing to the other models. This is very interesting, because generating high-quality long phrases is difficult, since the memes are often short.

| Systems | BLEU | B-1 | B-2 | B-3 | B-4 |
|---|---|---|---|---|---|
| RNN-C | 19.52 | 62.2 | 21.2 | 12.1 | 9.0 |
| RNN-F | 23.76 | 72.2 | **31.4*** | 16.2 | 8.7 |
| LR | 23.89 | **72.3** | 28.3 | 15.0 | 10.6 |
| LSVM | 21.06 | 65.0 | 24.8 | 13.1 | 9.3 |
| GSVM | 20.63 | 66.2 | 22.8 | 12.8 | 9.3 |
| NPN | **28.24*** | 66.9 | 29.0 | **19.7*** | **16.6*** |

Table 4: The BLEU scores for generating memes from images. B-1 to B-4: BLEU unigram to four-grams. The best BLEU results are highlighted in **bold**. * indicates $p < .001$ comparing to the second best system.

We show some generation examples in Figure 6. We see that on the left column, the reference memes are the ones with top votes by the crowd. The first *chemistry cat* meme includes puns, the second *forever alone* meme includes reference to the life simulation video game, while the last *Batman* meme has interesting conversations. In the second column, we see that the memes generated by the full RNNLM model are short, which corresponds to the quantitative results in Table 4. In the third column, our NPN meme generator was able to generate longer descriptions. Interestingly, it also creates a pun for the *chemistry cat* meme. Our generation on the *forever alone* meme is also accurate. In the Batman example, we show that the NPN model makes a sentence-image-mismatch type of error: although the generated sentence includes the entities Batman and Robin, as well as their slapping activity, it was originally created for the "overly attached girlfriend" meme[10].

## 7 Conclusions

In this paper, we study the language of memes by jointly learning the image, the description, and the popular votes. In particular, we propose a robust nonparanormal approach to transform all vision and text features into the cumulative density function space. By learning the stochastic dependencies, we show that our model significantly outperforms various competitive baselines in the prediction experiments. In addition, we also propose a simple pipeline for generating memes from raw images, drawing the wisdom from reverse image search and traditional information retrieval perspectives. Finally, we show that our model obtains significant BLEU point improvements over an unsupervised RNNLM baseline trained on a larger corpus, as well as other strong supervised baselines.

[10]http://www.overlyattachedgirlfriend.com

## References


Joshua Albrecht and Rebecca Hwa. 2007. Regression for sentence-level mt evaluation with pseudo references. In *Proceedings of ACL*.

Yoav Artzi, Patrick Pantel, and Michael Gamon. 2012. Predicting responses to microblog posts. In *Proceedings of NAACL-HLT*.

Eytan Bakshy, Jake M Hofman, Winter A Mason, and Duncan J Watts. 2011. Everyone's an influencer: quantifying influence on twitter. In *Proceedings of WSDM*, pages 65–74. ACM.

Anna Bosch, Andrew Zisserman, and Xavier Munoz. 2007. Image classification using random forests and ferns.

Chih-Chung Chang and Chih-Jen Lin. 2011. Libsvm: a library for support vector machines. *ACM TIST*.

Xiaohong Chen and Yanqin Fan. 2006. Estimation of copula-based semiparametric time series models. *Journal of Econometrics*.

Xinlei Chen and C Lawrence Zitnick. 2014. Learning a recurrent visual representation for image caption generation. *arXiv preprint arXiv:1411.5654*.

David Christensen. 2005. Fast algorithms for the calculation of kendalls $\tau$. *Computational Statistics*.

Dipanjan Das, Nathan Schneider, Desai Chen, and Noah A Smith. 2010. Probabilistic frame-semantic parsing. In *Proceedings of NAACL-HLT*.

Jacob Devlin, Rabih Zbib, Zhongqiang Huang, Thomas Lamar, Richard Schwartz, and John Makhoul. 2014. Fast and robust neural network joint models for statistical machine translation. In *Proceedings of ACL*.

Francis X Diebold, Todd A Gunther, and Anthony S Tay. 1997. Evaluating density forecasts.

Jesse Dodge, Amit Goyal, Xufeng Han, Alyssa Mensch, Margaret Mitchell, Karl Stratos, Kota Yamaguchi, Yejin Choi, Hal Daumé III, Alexander C Berg, et al. 2012. Detecting visual text. In *Proceedings of the NAACL-HLT*.

Jeff Donahue, Lisa Anne Hendricks, Sergio Guadarrama, Marcus Rohrbach, Subhashini Venugopalan, Kate Saenko, and Trevor Darrell. 2014. Long-term recurrent convolutional networks for visual recognition and description. *arXiv preprint arXiv:1411.4389*.

Carsten Eickhoff, Arjen P. de Vries, and Kevyn Collins-Thompson. 2013. Copulas for information retrieval. In *Proceedings of the 36th International ACM SIGIR Conference on Research and Development in Information Retrieval*.

Charles Elkan. 2003. Using the triangle inequality to accelerate k-means. In *ICML*, volume 3, pages 147–153.

Hao Fang, Saurabh Gupta, Forrest Iandola, Rupesh Srivastava, Li Deng, Piotr Dollár, Jianfeng Gao, Xiaodong He, Margaret Mitchell, John Platt, et al. 2014. From captions to visual concepts and back. *arXiv preprint arXiv:1411.4952*.

Ali Farhadi, Mohsen Hejrati, Mohammad Amin Sadeghi, Peter Young, Cyrus Rashtchian, Julia Hockenmaier, and David Forsyth. 2010. Every picture tells a story: Generating sentences from images. In *Computer Vision–ECCV 2010*, pages 15–29. Springer.

Manuel Fernández-Delgado, Eva Cernadas, Senén Barro, and Dinani Amorim. 2014. Do we need hundreds of classifiers to solve real world classification problems? *Journal of Machine Learning Research*, 15:3133–3181.

Jenny Rose Finkel, Trond Grenager, and Christopher Manning. 2005. Incorporating non-local information into information extraction systems by gibbs sampling. In *Proceedings of the 43rd Annual Meeting on Association for Computational Linguistics*, pages 363–370. Association for Computational Linguistics.

Alan Gelfand and Adrian Smith. 1990. Sampling-based approaches to calculating marginal densities. *Journal of the American statistical association*.

Zoubin Ghahramani, Barnabás Póczos, and Jeff Schneider. 2012. Copula-based kernel dependency measures. In *Proceedings of the 29th International Conference on Machine Learning*.

Abhinav Gupta, Praveen Srinivasan, Jianbo Shi, and Larry S Davis. 2009. Understanding videos, constructing plots learning a visually grounded storyline model from annotated videos. In *Computer Vision and Pattern Recognition, 2009. CVPR 2009. IEEE Conference on*, pages 2012–2019. IEEE.

Fang Han, Tuo Zhao, and Han Liu. 2012. Coda: High dimensional copula discriminant analysis. *Journal of Machine Learning Research*.

Geoffrey E Hinton, Nitish Srivastava, Alex Krizhevsky, Ilya Sutskever, and Ruslan R Salakhutdinov. 2012. Improving neural networks by preventing co-adaptation of feature detectors. *arXiv preprint arXiv:1207.0580*.

Micah Hodosh, Peter Young, and Julia Hockenmaier. 2013. Framing image description as a ranking task: Data, models and evaluation metrics. *J. Artif. Intell. Res.(JAIR)*, 47:853–899.

Robert V Hogg and Allen Craig. 1994. Introduction to mathematical statistics.

Liangjie Hong, Ovidiu Dan, and Brian D Davison. 2011. Predicting popular messages in twitter. In *Proceedings of WWW*.

Harry Joe. 1997. *Multivariate models and dependence concepts*.

Andrej Karpathy and Li Fei-Fei. 2014. Deep visual-semantic alignments for generating image descriptions. *Stanford University Technical Report.*

Maurice Kendall. 1938. A new measure of rank correlation. *Biometrika.*

Alex Krizhevsky, Ilya Sutskever, and Geoffrey E Hinton. 2012. Imagenet classification with deep convolutional neural networks. In *Advances in neural information processing systems*, pages 1097–1105.

Girish Kulkarni, Visruth Premraj, Sagnik Dhar, Siming Li, Yejin Choi, Alexander C Berg, and Tamara L Berg. 2011. Baby talk: Understanding and generating image descriptions. In *Proceedings of the 24th CVPR.* Citeseer.

Mirella Lapata. 2006. Automatic evaluation of information ordering: Kendall's tau. *Computational Linguistics.*

Han Liu, John Lafferty, and Larry Wasserman. 2009. The nonparanormal: Semiparametric estimation of high dimensional undirected graphs. *The Journal of Machine Learning Research*, 10:2295–2328.

Han Liu, Fang Han, Ming Yuan, John Lafferty, and Larry Wasserman. 2012. High-dimensional semiparametric gaussian copula graphical models. *The Annals of Statistics.*

Tomáš Mikolov. 2012. *Statistical language models based on neural networks.* Ph.D. thesis, Ph. D. thesis, Brno University of Technology.

Margaret Mitchell, Xufeng Han, Jesse Dodge, Alyssa Mensch, Amit Goyal, Alex Berg, Kota Yamaguchi, Tamara Berg, Karl Stratos, and Hal Daumé III. 2012. Midge: Generating image descriptions from computer vision detections. In *Proceedings of EACL.*

Roger B Nelsen. 1999. *An introduction to copulas.* Springer Verlag.

Joakim Nivre, Johan Hall, Jens Nilsson, Atanas Chanev, Gülsen Eryigit, Sandra Kübler, Svetoslav Marinov, and Erwin Marsi. 2007. Maltparser: A language-independent system for data-driven dependency parsing. *Natural Language Engineering*, 13(02):95–135.

Maxime Oquab, Leon Bottou, Ivan Laptev, Josef Sivic, et al. 2013. Learning and transferring mid-level image representations using convolutional neural networks.

Kishore Papineni, Salim Roukos, Todd Ward, and Wei-Jing Zhu. 2002. Bleu: a method for automatic evaluation of machine translation. In *Proceedings of ACL*, pages 311–318. Association for Computational Linguistics.

Rahul A Parsa and Stuart A Klugman. 2011. Copula regression. *Variance Advancing and Science of Risk.*

Emanuel Parzen. 1962. On estimation of a probability density function and mode. *The annals of mathematical statistics.*

Michael Pitt, David Chan, and Robert Kohn. 2006. Efficient bayesian inference for gaussian copula regression models. *Biometrika.*

Berthold Schweizer and Abe Sklar. 1983. *Probabilistic metric spaces.*

Josef Sivic and Andrew Zisserman. 2003. Video google: A text retrieval approach to object matching in videos. In *Proceedings of ICCV*, pages 1470–1477. IEEE.

Abe Sklar. 1959. *Fonctions de répartition à n dimensions et leurs marges.* Université Paris 8.

Richard Socher, Alex Perelygin, Jean Y Wu, Jason Chuang, Christopher D Manning, Andrew Y Ng, and Christopher Potts. 2013. Recursive deep models for semantic compositionality over a sentiment treebank. In *Proceedings of EMNLP*, pages 1631–1642. Citeseer.

Chenhao Tan, Lillian Lee, and Bo Pang. 2014. The effect of wording on message propagation: Topic- and author-controlled natural experiments on twitter. In *Proceedings of ACL.*

Robert Tibshirani. 1996. Regression shrinkage and selection via the lasso. *Journal of the Royal Statistical Society. Series B (Methodological)*, pages 267–288.

Kristina Toutanova, Dan Klein, Christopher D Manning, and Yoram Singer. 2003. Feature-rich part-of-speech tagging with a cyclic dependency network. In *Proceedings of NAACL-HLT.*

Oriol Vinyals, Alexander Toshev, Samy Bengio, and Dumitru Erhan. 2014. Show and tell: A neural image caption generator. *arXiv preprint arXiv:1411.4555.*

Stefan Wager, Sida Wang, and Percy Liang. 2013. Dropout training as adaptive regularization. In *Advances in Neural Information Processing Systems*, pages 351–359.

William Yang Wang and Zhenhao Hua. 2014. A semiparametric gaussian copula regression model for predicting financial risks from earnings calls. In *Proceedings of ACL.*

Sida Wang and Christopher Manning. 2013. Fast dropout training. In *Proceedings of ICML.*

Dani Yogatama, Michael Heilman, Brendan O'Connor, Chris Dyer, Bryan R Routledge, and Noah A Smith. 2011. Predicting a scientific community's response to an article. In *Proceedings of EMNLP.*

# A Transition-based Algorithm for AMR Parsing

**Chuan Wang**
Brandeis University
cwang24@brandeis.edu

**Nianwen Xue**
Brandeis University
xuen@brandeis.edu

**Sameer Pradhan**
Harvard Medical School
Sameer.Pradhan@childrens.harvard.edu

## Abstract

We present a two-stage framework to parse a sentence into its Abstract Meaning Representation (AMR). We first use a dependency parser to generate a dependency tree for the sentence. In the second stage, we design a novel transition-based algorithm that transforms the dependency tree to an AMR graph. There are several advantages with this approach. First, the dependency parser can be trained on a training set much larger than the training set for the tree-to-graph algorithm, resulting in a more accurate AMR parser overall. Our parser yields an improvement of 5% absolute in F-measure over the best previous result. Second, the actions that we design are linguistically intuitive and capture the regularities in the mapping between the dependency structure and the AMR of a sentence. Third, our parser runs in nearly linear time in practice in spite of a worst-case complexity of $O(n^2)$.

## 1 Introduction

Abstract Meaning Representation (AMR) is a rooted, directed, edge-labeled and leaf-labeled graph that is used to represent the meaning of a sentence. The AMR formalism has been used to annotate the AMR Annotation Corpus (Banarescu et al., 2013), a corpus of over 10 thousand sentences that is still undergoing expansion. The building blocks for an AMR representation are concepts and relations between them. Understanding these concepts and their relations is crucial to understanding the meaning of a sentence and could potentially benefit a number of natural language applications such as Information Extraction, Question Answering and Machine Translation.

The property that makes AMR a graph instead of a tree is that AMR allows reentrancy, meaning that the same concept can participate in multiple relations. Parsing a sentence into an AMR would seem to require graph-based algorithms, but moving to graph-based algorithms from the typical tree-based algorithms that we are familiar with is a big step in terms of computational complexity. Indeed, quite a bit of effort has gone into developing grammars and efficient graph-based algorithms that can be used to parse AMRs (Chiang et al., 2013).

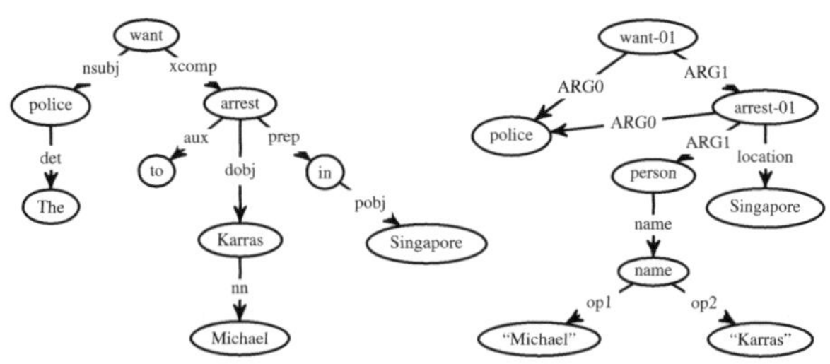


(a) Dependency tree (b) AMR graph

Figure 1: Dependency tree and AMR graph for the sentence, "The police want to arrest Micheal Karras in Singapore."

Linguistically, however, there are many similarities between an AMR and the dependency structure of a sentence. Both describe relations as holding between a head and its dependent, or between a parent and its child. AMR concepts and relations abstract away from actual word tokens, but there are regularities in their mappings. Content words generally be-



*Human Language Technologies: The 2015 Annual Conference of the North American Chapter of the ACL*, pages 366–375,
Denver, Colorado, May 31 – June 5, 2015. ©2015 Association for Computational Linguistics

come concepts while function words either become relations or get omitted if they do not contribute to the meaning of a sentence. This is illustrated in Figure 1, where 'the' and 'to' in the dependency tree are omitted from the AMR and the preposition 'in' becomes a relation of type *location*. In AMR, reentrancy is also used to represent co-reference, but this only happens in some limited contexts. In Figure 1, 'police' is both an argument of 'arrest' and 'want' as the result of a control structure. This suggests that it is possible to transform a dependency tree into an AMR with a limited number of actions and learn a model to determine which action to take given pairs of aligned dependency trees and AMRs as training data.

This is the approach we adopt in the present work, and we present a transition-based framework in which we parse a sentence into an AMR by taking the dependency tree of that sentence as input and transforming it to an AMR representation via a series of actions. This means that a sentence is parsed into an AMR in two steps. In the first step the sentence is parsed into a dependency tree with a dependency parser, and in the second step the dependency tree is transformed into an AMR graph. One advantage of this approach is that the dependency parser does not have to be trained on the same data set as the dependency to AMR transducer. This allows us to use more accurate dependency parsers trained on data sets much larger than the AMR Annotation Corpus and have a more advantageous starting point. Our experiments show that this approach is very effective and yields an improvement of 5% absolute over the previously reported best result (Flanigan et al., 2014) in F-score, as measure by the Smatch metric (Cai and Knight, 2013).

The rest of the paper is as follows. In §2, we describe how we align the word tokens in a sentence with its AMR to create a span graph based on which we extract contextual information as features and perform actions. In §3, we present our transition-based parsing algorithm and describe the actions used to transform the dependency tree of a sentence into an AMR. In §4, we present the learning algorithm and the features we extract to train the transition model. In §5, we present experimental results. §6 describes related work, and we conclude in §7.

## 2 Graph Representation

Unlike the dependency structure of a sentence where each word token is a node in the dependency tree and there is an inherent alignment between the word tokens in the sentence and the nodes in the dependency tree, AMR is an abstract representation where the word order of the corresponding sentence is not maintained. In addition, some words become abstract concepts or relations while other words are simply deleted because they do not contribute to meaning. The alignment between the word tokens and the concepts is non-trivial, but in order to learn the transition from a dependency tree to an AMR graph, we have to first establish the alignment between the word tokens in the sentence and the concepts in the AMR. We use the aligner that comes with JAMR (Flanigan et al., 2014) to produce this alignment. The JAMR aligner attempts to greedily align every concept or graph fragment in the AMR graph with a contiguous word token sequence in the sentence.

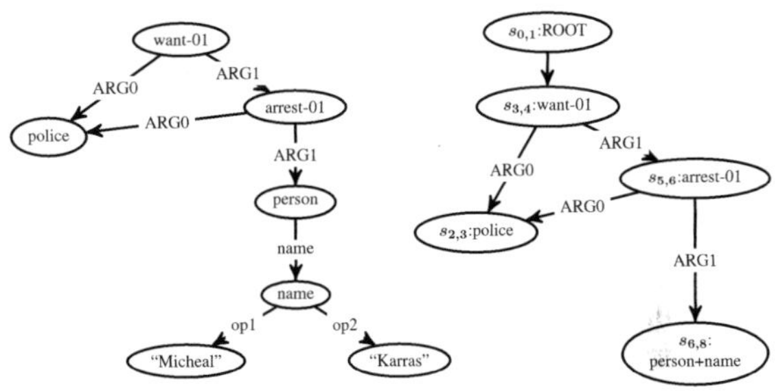


(a) AMR graph (b) Span graph

Figure 2: AMR graph and its span graph for the sentence, "The police want to arrest Micheal Karras."

We use a data structure called **span graph** to represent an AMR graph that is aligned with the word tokens in a sentence. For each sentence $w = w_0, w_1, \ldots, w_n$, where token $w_0$ is a special root symbol, a **span graph** is a directed, labeled graph $G = (V, A)$, where $V = \{s_{i,j} | i, j \in (0, n) \text{ and } j > i\}$ is a set of nodes, and $A \subseteq V \times V$ is a set of arcs. Each node $s_{i,j}$ of $G$ corresponds to a continuous span $(w_i, \ldots, w_{j-1})$ in sentence $w$ and is indexed by the starting position $i$. Each node is assigned a **concept** label from a set $L_V$ of concept labels and each arc is assigned a **relation** label from a set $L_A$

of relation labels, respectively.

For example, given an AMR graph $G_{AMR}$ in Figure 2a, its span graph $G$ can be represented as Figure 2b. In span graph $G$, node $s_{3,4}$'s sentence span is *(want)* and its concept label is *want-01*, which represents a single node *want-01* in AMR. To simplify the alignment, when creating a span graph out of an AMR, we also collapse some AMR subgraphs in such a way that they can be deterministically restored to their original state for evaluation. For example, the four nodes in the AMR subgraph that correspond to span *(Micheal, Karras)* is collapsed into a single node $s_{6,8}$ in the span graph and assigned the concept label *person+name*, as shown in Figure 3. So the concept label set that our model predicts consists of both those from the concepts in the original AMR graph and those as a result of collapsing the AMR subgraphs.

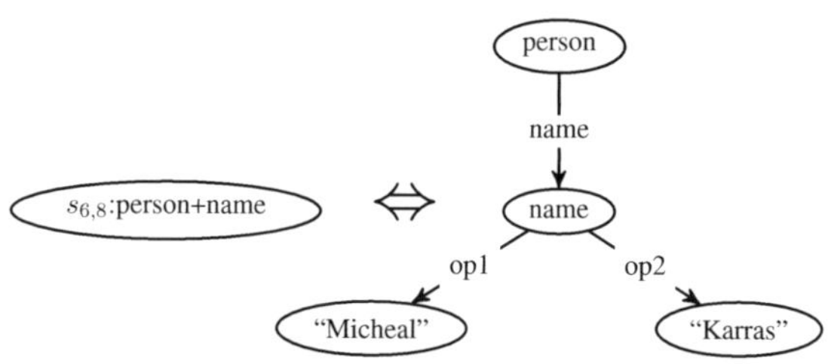


Figure 3: Collapsed nodes

Representing AMR graph this way allows us to formulate the AMR parsing problem as a joint learning problem where we can design a set of actions to simultaneously predict the concepts (nodes) and relations (arcs) in the AMR graph as well as the labels on them.

## 3 Transition-based AMR Parsing

### 3.1 Transition System

Similar to transition-based dependency parsing (Nivre, 2008), we define a *transition system* for AMR parsing as a quadruple $S = (S, T, s_0, S_t)$, where

- $S$ is a set of parsing *states* (configurations).
- $T$ is a set of parsing *actions* (transitions), each of which is a function $t : S \to S$.
- $s_0$ is an *initialization function*, mapping each input sentence $w$ and its dependency tree $D$ to an *initial state*.
- $S_t \subseteq S$ is a set of *terminal states*.

Each state (configuration) of our transition-based parser is a triple $(\sigma, \beta, G)$. $\sigma$ is a buffer that stores indices of the nodes which have not been processed and we write $\sigma = \sigma_0|\sigma'$ to indicate that $\sigma_0$ is the topmost element of $\sigma$. $\beta$ is also a buffer $[\beta_0, \beta_1, \ldots, \beta_j]$ and each element $\beta_i$ of $\beta$ indicates the edge $(\sigma_0, \beta_i)$ which has not been processed in the partial graph. We also write $\beta = \beta_0|\beta'$ to indicate the topmost element of $\beta$ is $\beta_0$. We use span graph $G$ to store the partial parses for the input sentence $w$. Note that unlike traditional transition-based syntactic parsers which store partial parses in the stack structure and build a tree or graph incrementally, here we use $\sigma$ and $\beta$ buffers only to guide the parsing process (which node or edge to be processed next) and the actual tree-to-graph transformations are applied to $G$.

When the parsing procedure starts, $\sigma$ is initialized with a post-order traversal of the input dependency tree $D$ with topmost element $\sigma_0$, $\beta$ is initialized with node $\sigma_0$'s children or set to null if $\sigma_0$ is a leaf node. $G$ is initialized with all the nodes and edges of $D$. Initially, all the nodes of $G$ have a span length of one and all the labels for nodes and edges are set to null. As the parsing procedure goes on, the parser will process all the nodes and their outgoing edges in dependency tree $D$ in a bottom-up left-right manner, and at each state certain action will be applied to the current node or edge. The parsing process will terminate when both $\sigma$ and $\beta$ are empty.

The most important part of the transition-based parser is the set of actions (transitions). As stated in (Sartorio et al., 2013), the design space of possible actions is actually infinite since the set of parsing states is infinite. However, if the problem is amenable to transition-based parsing, we can design a finite set of actions by categorizing all the possible situations we run into in the parsing process. In §5.2 we show this is the case here and our action set can account for almost all the transformations from dependency trees to AMR graphs.

We define 8 types of actions for the actions set $T$, which is summarized in Table 1. The action set could be divided into two categories based on conditions of buffer $\beta$. When $\beta$ is not empty, parsing decisions are made based on the edge $(\sigma_0, \beta_0)$; oth-

| Action | Current state ⇒ Result state | Assign labels | Precondition |
|---|---|---|---|
| NEXT EDGE-$l_r$ | $(\sigma_0\|\sigma', \beta_0\|\beta', G) \Rightarrow (\sigma_0\|\sigma', \beta', G')$ | $\delta[(\sigma_0, \beta_0) \rightarrow l_r]$ | $\beta$ is not empty |
| SWAP-$l_r$ | $(\sigma_0\|\sigma', \beta_0\|\beta', G) \Rightarrow (\sigma_0\|\beta_0\|\sigma', \beta', G')$ | $\delta[(\beta_0, \sigma_0) \rightarrow l_r]$ | |
| REATTACH$_k$-$l_r$ | $(\sigma_0\|\sigma', \beta_0\|\beta', G) \Rightarrow (\sigma_0\|\sigma', \beta', G')$ | $\delta[(k, \beta_0) \rightarrow l_r]$ | |
| REPLACE HEAD | $(\sigma_0\|\sigma', \beta_0\|\beta', G) \Rightarrow (\beta_0\|\sigma', \beta = CH(\beta_0, G'), G')$ | NONE | |
| REENTRANCE$_k$-$l_r$ | $(\sigma_0\|\sigma', \beta_0\|\beta', G) \Rightarrow (\sigma_0\|\sigma', \beta_0\|\beta', G')$ | $\delta[(k, \beta_0) \rightarrow l_r]$ | |
| MERGE | $(\sigma_0\|\sigma', \beta_0\|\beta', G) \Rightarrow (\tilde{\sigma}\|\sigma', \beta', G')$ | NONE | |
| NEXT NODE-$l_c$ | $(\sigma_0\|\sigma_1\|\sigma', [], G) \Rightarrow (\sigma_1\|\sigma', \beta = CH(\sigma_1, G'), G')$ | $\gamma[\sigma_0 \rightarrow l_c]$ | $\beta$ is empty |
| DELETE NODE | $(\sigma_0\|\sigma_1\|\sigma', [], G) \Rightarrow (\sigma_1\|\sigma', \beta = CH(\sigma_1, G'), G')$ | NONE | |

Table 1: Transitions designed in our parser. $CH(x, y)$ means getting all node $x$'s children in graph $y$.

erwise, only the current node $\sigma_0$ is examined. Also, to simultaneously make decisions on the assignment of concept/relation label, we augment some of the actions with an extra parameter $l_r$ or $l_c$. We define $\gamma : V \rightarrow L_V$ as the concept labeling function for nodes and $\delta : A \rightarrow L_A$ as the relation labeling function for arcs. So $\delta[(\sigma_0, \beta_0) \rightarrow l_r]$ means assigning relation label $l_r$ to arc $(\sigma_0, \beta_0)$. All the actions update buffer $\sigma$, $\beta$ and apply some transformation $G \Rightarrow G'$ to the partial graph. The 8 actions are described below.

- NEXT-EDGE-$l_r$ (ned). This action assigns a relation label $l_r$ to the current edge $(\sigma_0, \beta_0)$ and makes no further modification to the partial graph. Then it pops out the top element of buffer $\beta$ so that the parser moves one step forward to examine the next edge if it exists.

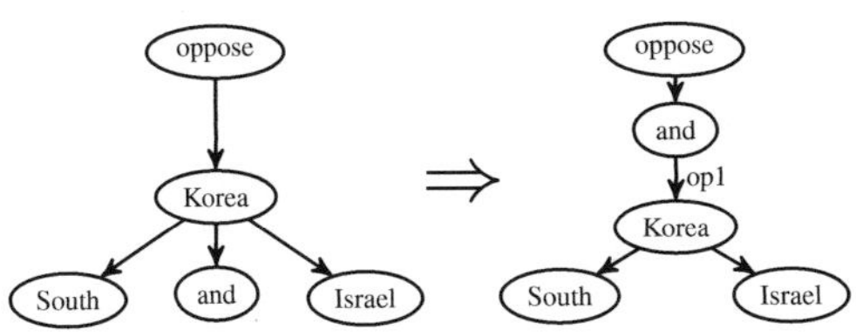


Figure 4: SWAP action

- SWAP-$l_r$ (sw). This action reverses the dependency relation between node $\sigma_0$ and $\beta_0$ and then makes node $\beta_0$ as new head of the subgraph. Also it assigns relation label $l_r$ to the arc $(\beta_0, \sigma_0)$. Then it pops out $\beta_0$ and inserts it into $\sigma$ right after $\sigma_0$ for future revisiting. This action is to resolve the difference in the choice of head between the dependency tree and the AMR graph. Figure 4 gives an example of applying SWAP-op1 action for arc (*Korea*, *and*) in the dependency tree of sentence "South Korea and Israel oppose ...".

- REATTACH$_k$-$l_r$ (reat). This action removes the current arc $(\sigma_0, \beta_0)$ and reattaches node $\beta_0$ to some node $k$ in the partial graph. It also assigns a relation label $l_r$ to the newly created arc $(k, \beta_0)$ and advances one step by popping out $\beta_0$. Theoretically, the choice of node $k$ could be any node in the partial graph under the constraint that arc $(k, \beta_0)$ doesn't produce a self-looping cycle. The intuition behind this action is that after swapping a head and its dependent, some of the dependents of the old head should be reattached to the new head. Figure 5 shows an example where node *Israel* needs to be reattached to node *and* after a head-dependent swap.

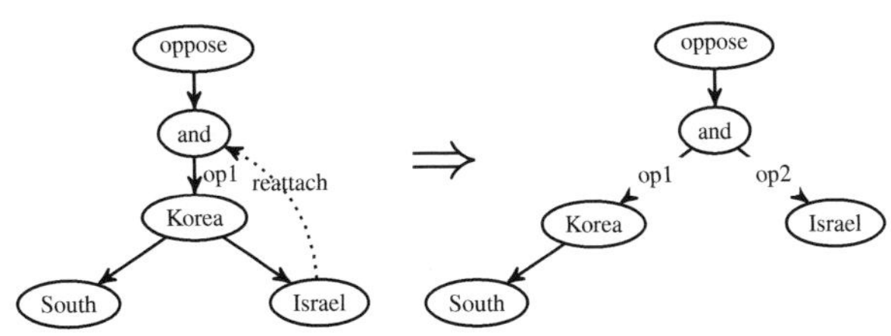


Figure 5: REATTACH action

- REPLACE-HEAD (rph). This action removes node $\sigma_0$, replaces it with node $\beta_0$. Node $\beta_0$ also inherits all the incoming and outgoing arcs of $\sigma_0$. Then it pops out $\beta_0$ and inserts it into the top position of buffer $\sigma$. $\beta$ is re-initialized with all the children of $\beta_0$ in the transformed graph $G'$. This action targets nodes in the dependency tree that do not correspond to concepts in AMR graph and become a relation instead. An example is provided in Figure 6, where node *in*, a preposition, is replaced with node *Singapore*, and in a subsequent NEXT-EDGE action that examines arc (*live*, *Singapore*), the arc is labeled *location*.

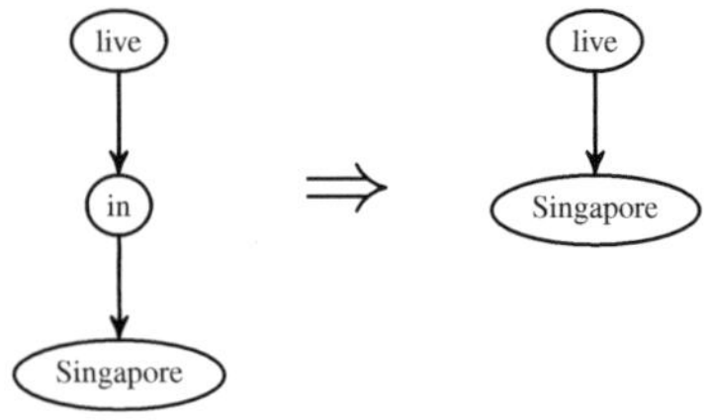


Figure 6: REPLACE-HEAD action

- REENTRANCE$_k$-$l_r$ (reen). This is the action that transforms a tree into a graph. It keeps the current arc unchanged, and links node $\beta_0$ to every possible node $k$ in the partial graph that can also be its parent. Similar to the REATTACH action, the newly created arc $(k, \beta_0)$ should not produce a self-looping cycle and parameter $k$ is bounded by the sentence length. In practice, we seek to constrain this action as we will explain in §3.2. Intuitively, this action can be used to model co-reference and an example is given in Figure 7.

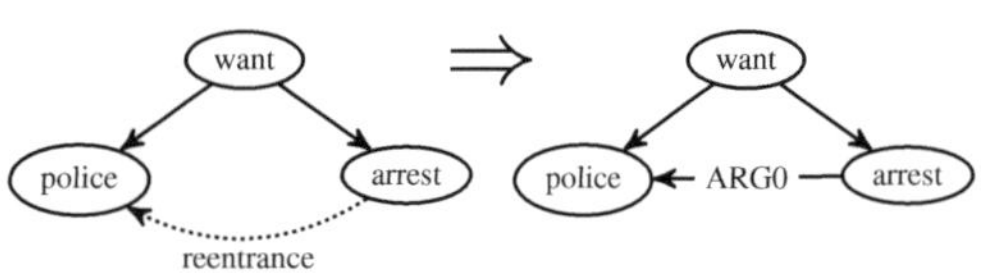


Figure 7: REENTRANCE action

- MERGE (mrg). This action merges nodes $\sigma_0$ and $\beta_0$ into one node $\tilde{\sigma}$ which covers multiple words in the sentence. The new node inherits all the incoming and outgoing arcs of both nodes $\sigma_0$ and $\beta_0$. The MERGE action is intended to produce nodes that cover a continuous span in the sentence that corresponds to a single name entity in AMR graph. see Figure 8 for an example.

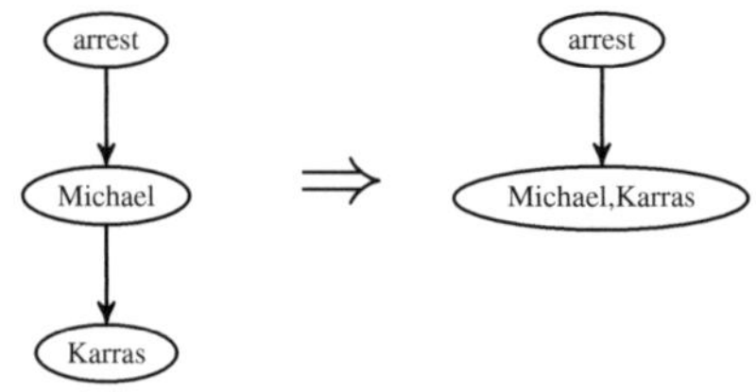


Figure 8: MERGE action

When $\beta$ is empty, which means all the outgoing arcs of node $\sigma_0$ have been processed or $\sigma_0$ has no outgoing arcs, the following two actions can be applied:

- NEXT-NODE-$l_c$ (nnd). This action first assigns a concept label $l_c$ to node $\sigma_0$. Then it advances the parsing procedure by popping out the top element $\sigma_0$ of buffer $\sigma$ and re-initializes buffer $\beta$ with all the children of node $\sigma_1$ which is the current top element of $\sigma$. Since this action will be applied to every node which is kept in the final parsed graph, concept labeling could be done simultaneously through this action.
- DELETE-NODE (dnd). This action simply deletes the node $\sigma_0$ and removes all the arcs associated with it. This action models the fact that most function words are stripped off in the AMR of a sentence. Note that this action only targets function words that are leaves in the dependency tree, and we constrain this action by only deleting nodes which do not have outgoing arcs.

When parsing a sentence of length $n$ (excluding the special root symbol $w_0$), its corresponding dependency tree will have $n$ nodes and $n - 1$ arcs. For projective transition-based dependency parsing, the parser needs to take exactly $2n - 1$ steps or actions. So the complexity is $O(n)$. However, for our tree-to-graph parser defined above, the actions needed are no longer linearly bounded by the sentence length. Suppose there are no REATTACH, REENTRANCE and SWAP actions during the parsing process, the algorithm will traverse every node and edge in the dependency tree, which results in $2n$ actions. However, REATTACH and REENTRANCE actions would add extra edges that need to be re-processed and the SWAP action adds both nodes and edges that need to be re-visited. Since the space of all possible extra edges is $(n-2)^2$ and revisiting them only adds more actions linearly, the total asymptotic runtime complexity of our algorithm is $O(n^2)$.

In practice, however, the number of applications of the REATTACH action is much less than the worst case scenario due to the similarities between the dependency tree and the AMR graph of a sentence. Also, nodes with reentrancies in AMR only account for a small fraction of all the nodes, thus making the REENTRANCE action occur at constant times. These allow the tree-to-graph parser to parse a sentence in nearly linear time in practice.

### 3.2 Greedy Parsing Algorithm

**Algorithm 1** Parsing algorithm

**Input:** sentence $w = w_0 \dots w_n$ and its dependency tree $D_w$
**Output:** parsed graph $G_p$
1: $s \leftarrow s_0(D_w, w)$
2: **while** $s \notin S_t$ **do**
3: $\quad \mathcal{T} \leftarrow$ all possible actions according to $s$
4: $\quad bestT \leftarrow \arg\max_{t \in \mathcal{T}} score(t, c)$
5: $\quad s \leftarrow$ apply $bestT$ to $s$
6: **end while**
7: **return** $G_p$

Our parsing algorithm is similar to the parser in (Sartorio et al., 2013). At each parsing state $s \in S$, the algorithm greedily chooses the parsing action $t \in T$ that maximizes the score function $score()$. The score function is a linear model defined over parsing action $t$ and parsing state $s$.

$$score(t, s) = \vec{\omega} \cdot \phi(t, s) \tag{1}$$

where $\vec{\omega}$ is the weight vector and $\phi$ is a function that extracts the feature vector representation for one possible state-action pair $\langle t, s \rangle$.

First, the algorithm initializes the state $s$ with the sentence $w$ and its dependency tree $D_w$. At each iteration, it gets all the possible actions for current state $s$ (line 3). Then, it chooses the action with the highest score given by function $score()$ and applies it to $s$ (line 4-5). When the current state reaches a terminal state, the parser stops and returns the parsed graph.

As pointed out in (Bohnet and Nivre, 2012), constraints can be added to limit the number of possible actions to be evaluated at line 3. There could be formal constraints on states such as the constraint that the SWAP action should not be applied twice to the same pair of nodes. We could also apply soft constraints to filter out unlikely concept labels, relation labels and candidate nodes $k$ for REATTACH and REENTRANCE. In our parser, we enforce the constraint that NEXT-NODE-$l_c$ can only choose from concept labels that co-occur with the current node's lemma in the training data. We also empirically set the constraint that REATTACH$_k$ could only choose $k$ among $\sigma_0$'s grandparents and great grandparents. Additionally, REENTRANCE$_k$ could only choose $k$ among its siblings. These constraints greatly reduce the search space, thus speeding up the parser.

## 4 Learning

### 4.1 Learning Algorithm

As stated in section 3.2, the parameter of our model is weight vector $\vec{\omega}$ in the score function. To train the weight vector, we employ the averaged perceptron learning algorithm (Collins, 2002).

**Algorithm 2** Learning algorithm

**Input:** sentence $w = w_0 \dots w_n, D_w, G_w$
**Output:** $\vec{\omega}$
1: $s \leftarrow s_0(D_w, w)$
2: **while** $s \notin S_t$ **do**
3: $\quad \mathcal{T} \leftarrow$ all possible actions according to $s$
4: $\quad bestT \leftarrow \arg\max_{t \in \mathcal{T}} score(t, s)$
5: $\quad goldT \leftarrow oracle(s, G_w)$
6: $\quad$ **if** $bestT \neq goldT$ **then**
7: $\quad\quad \vec{\omega} \leftarrow \vec{\omega} - \phi(bestT, s) + \phi(goldT, s)$
8: $\quad$ **end if**
9: $\quad s \leftarrow$ apply $goldT$ to $s$
10: **end while**

For each sentence $w$ and its corresponding AMR annotation $G_{AMR}$ in the training corpus, we could get the dependency tree $D_w$ of $w$ with a dependency parser. Then we represent $G_{AMR}$ as span graph $G_w$, which serves as our learning target. The learning algorithm takes the training instances ($w$, $D_w$, $G_w$), parses $D_w$ according to Algorithm 1, and get the best action using current weight vector $\vec{\omega}$. The gold action for current state $s$ is given by consulting span graph $G_w$, which we formulate as a function $oracle()$ (line 5). If the gold action is equal to the best action we get from the parser, then the best action is applied to current state; otherwise, we update the weight vector (line 6-7) and continue the parsing procedure by applying the gold action.

### 4.2 Feature Extraction

| Single node features |
|---|
| $\bar{\sigma}_0.w, \bar{\sigma}_0.lem, \bar{\sigma}_0.ne, \bar{\sigma}_0.t, \bar{\sigma}_0.dl, \bar{\sigma}_0.len$ |
| $\bar{\beta}_0.w, \bar{\beta}_0.lem, \bar{\beta}_0.ne, \bar{\beta}_0.t, \bar{\beta}_0.dl, \bar{\beta}_0.len$ |
| $\bar{k}.w, \bar{k}.lem, \bar{k}.ne, \bar{k}.t, \bar{k}.dl, \bar{k}.len$ |
| $\bar{\sigma}_{0p}.w, \bar{\sigma}_{0p}.lem, \bar{\sigma}_{0p}.ne, \bar{\sigma}_{0p}.t, \bar{\sigma}_{0p}.dl$ |
| Node pair features |
| $\bar{\sigma}_0.lem + \bar{\beta}_0.t, \bar{\sigma}_0.lem + \bar{\beta}_0.dl$ |
| $\bar{\sigma}_0.t + \bar{\beta}_0.lem, \bar{\sigma}_0.dl + \bar{\beta}_0.lem$ |
| $\bar{\sigma}_0.ne + \bar{\beta}_0.ne, \bar{k}.ne + \bar{\beta}_0.ne$ |
| $\bar{k}.t + \bar{\beta}_0.lem, \bar{k}.dl + \bar{\beta}_0.lem$ |
| Path features |
| $\bar{\sigma}_0.lem + \bar{\beta}_0.lem + path_{\sigma_0,\beta_0}$ |
| $\bar{k}.lem + \bar{\beta}_0.lem + path_{k,\beta_0}$ |
| Distance features |
| $dist_{\sigma_0,\beta_0}$ |
| $dist_{k,\beta_0}$ |
| $dist_{\sigma_0,\beta_0} + path_{\sigma_0,\beta_0}$ |
| $dist_{\sigma_0,\beta_0} + path_{k,\beta_0}$ |
| Action specific features |
| $\bar{\beta}_0.lem + \bar{\beta}_0.nswp$ |
| $\bar{\beta}_0.reph$ |

Table 2: Features used in our parser. $\bar{\sigma}_0, \bar{\beta}_0, \bar{k}, \bar{\sigma}_{0p}$ represents elements in feature context of nodes $\sigma_0, \beta_0, k, \sigma_{0p}$, separately. Each atomic feature is represented as follows: $w$ - word; $lem$ - lemma; $ne$ - name entity; $t$ - POS-tag; $dl$ - dependency label; $len$ - length of the node's span.

For transition-based dependency parsers, the feature context for a parsing state is represented by the neighboring elements of a word token in the stack containing the partial parse or the buffer containing unprocessed word tokens. In contrast, in our tree-to graph parser, as already stated, buffers $\sigma$ and $\beta$ only specify which arc or node is to be examined next. The feature context associated with current arc or node is mainly extracted from the partial graph $G$. As a result, the feature context is different for the different types of actions, a property that makes our parser very different from a standard transition-based dependency parser. For example, when evaluating action SWAP we may be interested in features about individual nodes $\sigma_0$ and $\beta_0$ as well as features involving the arc $(\sigma_0, \beta_0)$. In contrast, when evaluating action REATTACH$_k$, we want to extract not only features involving $\sigma_0$ and $\beta_0$, but also information about the reattached node $k$. To address this problem, we define the feature context as $\langle\bar{\sigma}_0, \bar{\beta}_0, \bar{k}, \bar{\sigma}_{0p}\rangle$, where each element $\bar{x}$ consists of its atomic features of node $x$ and $\sigma_{0p}$ denotes the immediate parent of node $\sigma_0$. For elements in feature context that are not applicable to the candidate action, we just set the element to NONE and only extract features which are valid for the candidate action. The list of features we use is shown in Table 2.

Single node features are atomic features concerning all the possible nodes involved in each candidate state-action pair. We also include path features and distance features as described in (Flanigan et al., 2014). A path feature $path_{x,y}$ is represented as the dependency labels and parts of speech on the path between nodes $x$ and $y$ in the partial graph. Here we combine it with the lemma of the starting and ending nodes. Distance feature $dist_{x,y}$ is the number of tokens between two node $x, y$'s spans in the sentence. Action-specific features record the history of actions applied to a given node. For example, $\bar{\beta}_0.nswp$ records how many times node $\beta_0$ has been swapped up. We combine this feature with the lemma of node $\beta_0$ to prevent the parser from swapping a node too many times. $\bar{\beta}_0.reph$ records the word feature of nodes that have been replaced with node $\beta_0$. This feature is helpful in predicting relation labels. As we have discussed above, in an AMR graph, some function words are deleted as nodes but they are crucial in determining the relation label between its child and parent.

## 5 Experiments

### 5.1 Experiment Setting

Our experiments are conducted on the newswire section of AMR Annotation Corpus (LDC2013E117) (Banarescu et al., 2013).

We follow Flanigan et al. (2014) in setting up the train/development/test splits[1] for easy comparison: 4.0k sentences with document years 1995-2006 as the training set; 2.1k sentences with document year 2007 as the development set; 2.1k sentences with document year 2008 as the test set, and only using AMRs that are tagged `::preferred`. Each sentence $w$ is preprocessed with the Stanford CoreNLP toolkit (Manning et al., 2014) to get part-of-speech tags, name entity information, and basic dependencies. We have verified that there is no overlap between the training data for the Stanford CoreNLP toolkit[2] and the AMR Annotation Corpus. We evaluate our parser with the Smatch tool (Cai and Knight, 2013), which seeks to maximize the semantic overlap between two AMR annotations.

### 5.2 Action Set Validation

One question about the transition system we presented above is whether the action set defined here can cover all the situations involving a dependency-to-AMR transformation. Although a formal theoretical proof is beyond the scope of this paper, we can empirically verify that the action set works well in practice. To validate the actions, we first run the $oracle()$ function for each sentence $w$ and its dependency tree $D_w$ to get the "pseudo-gold" $G'_w$. Then we compare $G'_w$ with the gold-standard AMR graph represented as span graph $G_w$ to see how similar they are. On the training data we got an overall 99% F-score for all $\langle G'_w, G_w \rangle$ pairs, which indicates that our action set is capable of transforming each sentence $w$ and its dependency tree $D_w$ into its gold-standard AMR graph through a sequence of actions.

### 5.3 Results

Table 3 gives the precision, recall and F-score of our parser given by Smatch on the test set. Our parser achieves an F-score of 63% (Row 3) and the result is 5% better than the first published result reported in (Flanigan et al., 2014) with the same training and test set (Row 2). We also conducted experiments on the test set by replacing the parsed graph with gold relation labels or/and gold concept labels. We can see in Table 3 that when provided with gold concept and relation labels as input, the parsing accuracy improves around 8% F-score (Row 6). Rows 4 and 5 present results when the parser is provided with just the gold relation labels (Row 4) or gold concept labels (Row 5), and the results are expectedly lower than if both gold concept and relation labels are provided as input.

| | Precision | Recall | F-score |
|---|---|---|---|
| JAMR | .52 | .66 | .58 |
| Our parser | **.64** | .62 | **.63** |
| Our parser $+l_{gr}$ | .68 | .65 | .67 |
| Our parser $+l_{gc}$ | .69 | .67 | .68 |
| Our parser $+l_{grc}$ | .72 | .70 | .71 |

Table 3: Results on the test set. Here, $l_{gc}$ - gold concept label; $l_{gr}$ - gold relation label; $l_{grc}$ - gold concept label and gold relation label.

### 5.4 Error Analysis

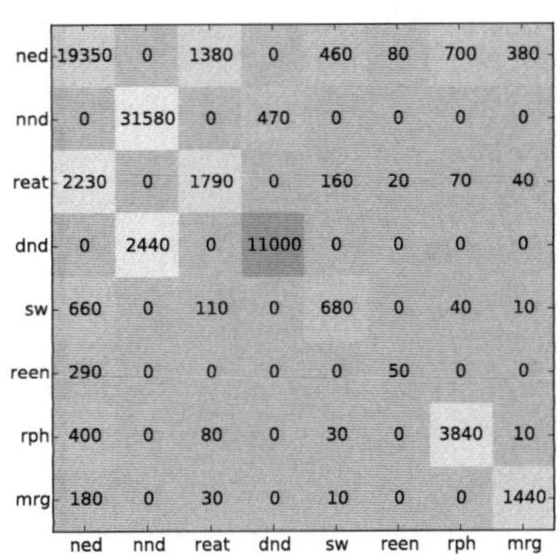


Figure 9: Confusion Matrix for actions $\langle t_g, t \rangle$. Vertical direction goes over the correct action type, and horizontal direction goes over the parsed action type.

Wrong alignments between the word tokens in the sentence and the concepts in the AMR graph account for a significant proportion of our AMR parsing errors, but here we focus on errors in the transition from the dependency tree to the AMR graph. Since in our parsing model, the parsing process has been decomposed into a sequence of actions applied to the input dependency tree, we can use the $oracle()$ function during parsing to give us the cor-

[1]A script to create the train/dev/test partitions is available at the following URL: `http://goo.gl/vA32iI`

[2]Specifically we used CoreNLP toolkit v3.3.1 and parser model wsjPCFG.ser.gz trained on the WSJ treebank sections 02-21.

rect action $t_g$ to take for a given state $s$. A comparison between $t_g$ and the best action $t$ actually taken by our parser will give us a sense about how accurately each type of action is applied. When we compare the actions, we focus on the structural aspect of AMR parsing and only take into account the eight action types, ignoring the concept and edge labels attached to them. For example, NEXT-EDGE-$ARG0$ and NEXT-EDGE-$ARG1$ would be considered to be the same action and counted as a match when we compute the errors even though the labels attached to them are different.

Figure 9 shows the confusion matrix that presents a comparison between the parser-predicted actions and the correct actions given by $oracle()$ function. It shows that the NEXT-EDGE (ned), NEXT-NODE (nnd), and DELETENODE (dnd) actions account for a large proportion of the actions. These actions are also more accurately applied. As expected, the parser makes more mistakes involving the REATTACH (reat), REENTRANCE (reen) and SWAP (sw) actions. The REATTACH action is often used to correct PP-attachment errors made by the dependency parser or readjust the structure resulting from the SWAP action, and it is hard to learn given the relatively small AMR training set. The SWAP action is often tied to coordination structures in which the head in the dependency structure and the AMR graph diverges. In the Stanford dependency representation which is the input to our parser, the head of a coordination structure is one of the conjuncts. For AMR, the head is an abstract concept signaled by one of the coordinating conjunctions. This also turns out to be one of the more difficult actions to learn. We expect, however, as the AMR Annotation Corpus grows bigger, the parsing model trained on a larger training set will learn these actions better.

## 6 Related Work

Our work is directly comparable to JAMR (Flanigan et al., 2014), the first published AMR parser. JAMR performs AMR parsing in two stages: concept identification and relation identification. They treat concept identification as a sequence labeling task and utilize a semi-Markov model to map spans of words in a sentence to concept graph fragments. For relation identification, they adopt the graph-based techniques for non-projective dependency parsing. Instead of finding maximum-scoring trees over words, they propose an algorithm to find the maximum spanning connected subgraph (MSCG) over concept fragments obtained from the first stage. In contrast, we adopt a transition-based approach that finds its root in transition-based dependency parsing (Yamada and Matsumoto, 2003; Nivre, 2003; Sagae and Tsujii, 2008), where a series of actions are performed to transform a sentence to a dependency tree. As should be clear from our description, however, the actions in our parser are very different in nature from the actions used in transition-based dependency parsing.

There is also another line of research that attempts to design graph grammars such as hyperedge replacement grammar (HRG) (Chiang et al., 2013) and efficient graph-based algorithms for AMR parsing. Existing work along this line is still theoretical in nature and no empirical results have been reported yet.

## 7 Conclusion and Future Work

We presented a novel transition-based parsing algorithm that takes the dependency tree of a sentence as input and transforms it into an Abstract Meaning Representation graph through a sequence of actions. We show that our approach is linguistically intuitive and our experimental results also show that our parser outperformed the previous best reported results by a significant margin. In future work we plan to continue to perfect our parser via improved learning and decoding techniques.

## Acknowledgments

We want to thank the anonymous reviewers for their suggestions. We also want to thank Jeffrey Flanigan, Xiaochang Peng, Adam Lopez and Giorgio Satta for discussion about ideas related to this work during the Fred Jelinek Memorial Workshop in Prague in 2014. This work was partially supported by the National Science Foundation via Grant No.0910532 entitled Richer Representations for Machine Translation. All views expressed in this paper are those of the authors and do not necessarily represent the view of the National Science Foundation.

## References


Laura Banarescu, Claire Bonial, Shu Cai, Madalina Georgescu, Kira Griffitt, Ulf Hermjakob, Kevin Knight, Philipp Koehn, Martha Palmer, and Nathan Schneider, 2013. Abstract Meaning Representation for Sembanking. In *Proceedings of the 7th Linguistic Annotation Workshop and Interoperability with Discourse*, pages 178–186. Association for Computational Linguistics.

Bernd Bohnet and Joakim Nivre. 2012. A transition-based system for joint part-of-speech tagging and labeled non-projective dependency parsing. In *Proceedings of the 2012 Joint Conference on Empirical Methods in Natural Language Processing and Computational Natural Language Learning*, pages 1455–1465. Association for Computational Linguistics.

Shu Cai and Kevin Knight. 2013. Smatch: an evaluation metric for semantic feature structures. In *Proceedings of the 51st Annual Meeting of the Association for Computational Linguistics (Volume 2: Short Papers)*, pages 748–752. Association for Computational Linguistics.

David Chiang, Jacob Andreas, Daniel Bauer, Karl Moritz Hermann, Bevan Jones, and Kevin Knight. 2013. Parsing graphs with hyperedge replacement grammars. In *Proceedings of the 51st Annual Meeting of the Association for Computational Linguistics (Volume 1: Long Papers)*, pages 924–932, Sofia, Bulgaria, August. Association for Computational Linguistics.

Michael Collins and Brian Roark. 2004. Incremental parsing with the perceptron algorithm. In *Proceedings of the 42nd Annual Meeting on Association for Computational Linguistics*, page 111. Association for Computational Linguistics.

Michael Collins. 2002. Discriminative training methods for hidden markov models: Theory and experiments with perceptron algorithms. In *Proceedings of the ACL-02 conference on Empirical methods in natural language processing-Volume 10*, pages 1–8. Association for Computational Linguistics.

Jeffrey Flanigan, Sam Thomson, Jaime Carbonell, Chris Dyer, and Noah A. Smith. 2014. A discriminative graph-based parser for the abstract meaning representation. In *Proceedings of the 52nd Annual Meeting of the Association for Computational Linguistics (Volume 1: Long Papers)*, pages 1426–1436, Baltimore, Maryland, June. Association for Computational Linguistics.

Dan Klein and Christopher D Manning. 2003. Accurate unlexicalized parsing. In *Proceedings of the 41st Annual Meeting on Association for Computational Linguistics-Volume 1*, pages 423–430. Association for Computational Linguistics.

Christopher D. Manning, Mihai Surdeanu, John Bauer, Jenny Finkel, Steven J. Bethard, and David McClosky. 2014. The Stanford CoreNLP natural language processing toolkit. In *Proceedings of 52nd Annual Meeting of the Association for Computational Linguistics: System Demonstrations*, pages 55–60.

Joakim Nivre. 2003. An efficient algorithm for projective dependency parsing. In *Proceedings of the 8th International Workshop on Parsing Technologies (IWPT)*. Citeseer.

Joakim Nivre. 2007. Incremental non-projective dependency parsing. In *Human Language Technologies 2007: The Conference of the North American Chapter of the Association for Computational Linguistics; Proceedings of the Main Conference*, pages 396–403. Association for Computational Linguistics.

Joakim Nivre. 2008. Algorithms for deterministic incremental dependency parsing. *Computational Linguistics*, 34(4):513–553.

Joakim Nivre. 2009. Non-projective dependency parsing in expected linear time. In *Proceedings of the Joint Conference of the 47th Annual Meeting of the ACL and the 4th International Joint Conference on Natural Language Processing of the AFNLP: Volume 1-Volume 1*, pages 351–359. Association for Computational Linguistics.

Kenji Sagae and Jun'ichi Tsujii. 2008. Shift-reduce dependency dag parsing. In *Proceedings of the 22nd International Conference on Computational Linguistics-Volume 1*, pages 753–760. Association for Computational Linguistics.

Francesco Sartorio, Giorgio Satta, and Joakim Nivre. 2013. A transition-based dependency parser using a dynamic parsing strategy. In *Proceedings of the 51st Annual Meeting of the Association for Computational Linguistics (Volume 1: Long Papers)*, pages 135–144. Association for Computational Linguistics.

Hiroyasu Yamada and Yuji Matsumoto. 2003. Statistical dependency analysis with support vector machines. In *Proceedings of IWPT*, volume 3.

# The Geometry of Statistical Machine Translation

**Aurelien Waite, William Byrne**
Department of Engineering, University of Cambridge, UK
aaw35@cam.ac.uk, wjb31@cam.ac.uk

## Abstract

Most modern statistical machine translation systems are based on linear statistical models. One extremely effective method for estimating the model parameters is minimum error rate training (MERT), which is an efficient form of line optimisation adapted to the highly non-linear objective functions used in machine translation. We describe a polynomial-time generalisation of line optimisation that computes the error surface over a plane embedded in parameter space. The description of this algorithm relies on convex geometry, which is the mathematics of polytopes and their faces.

Using this geometric representation of MERT we investigate whether the optimisation of linear models is tractable in general. Previous work on finding optimal solutions in MERT (Galley and Quirk, 2011) established a worst-case complexity that was exponential in the number of sentences, in contrast we show that exponential dependence in the worst-case complexity is mainly in the number of features.

Although our work is framed with respect to MERT, the convex geometric description is also applicable to other error-based training methods for linear models. We believe our analysis has important ramifications because it suggests that the current trend in building statistical machine translation systems by introducing a very large number of sparse features is inherently not robust.

## 1 Introduction

The linear model of Statistical Machine Translation (SMT) (Och and Ney, 2002) casts translation as a search for translation hypotheses under a linear combination of weighted features: a source language sentence $\mathbf{f}$ is translated as

$$\hat{\mathbf{e}}(\mathbf{f};\mathbf{w}) = \underset{\mathbf{e}}{\operatorname{argmax}}\{\mathbf{w}\mathbf{h}(\mathbf{e},\mathbf{f})\} \tag{1}$$

where translation scores are a linear combination of the $D \times 1$ feature vector $\mathbf{h}(\mathbf{e},\mathbf{f}) \in \mathbb{R}^D$ under the $1 \times D$ model parameter vector $\mathbf{w}$.

Convex geometry (Ziegler, 1995) is the mathematics of such linear equations presented as the study of convex polytopes. We use convex geometry to show that the behaviour of training methods such as MERT (Och, 2003; Macherey et al., 2008), MIRA (Crammer et al., 2006), PRO (Hopkins and May, 2011), and others converge with a high feature dimension. In particular we analyse how robustness decreases in linear models as feature dimension increases. We believe that severe overtraining is a problem in many current linear model formulations due to this lack of robustness.

In the process of building this geometric representation of linear models we discuss algorithms such as the Minkowski sum algorithm (Fukuda, 2004) and projected MERT (Section 4.2) that could be useful for designing new and more robust training algorithms for SMT and other natural language processing problems.

## 2 Training Linear Models

Let $\mathbf{f}_1 \ldots \mathbf{f}_S$ be a set of $S$ source language sentences with reference translations $\mathbf{r}_1 \ldots \mathbf{r}_S$. The goal is to estimate the model parameter vector $\mathbf{w}$ so as to minimize an error count based on an automated metric, such as BLEU (Papineni et al., 2002), assumed to be



*Human Language Technologies: The 2015 Annual Conference of the North American Chapter of the ACL*, pages 376–386,
Denver, Colorado, May 31 – June 5, 2015. 

additive over sentences:

$$\hat{\mathbf{w}} = \underset{\mathbf{w}}{\text{argmin}} \sum_{s=1}^{S} E(\hat{\mathbf{e}}(\mathbf{f}_s; \mathbf{w}), \mathbf{r}_s) \quad (2)$$

Optimisation can be made tractable by restricting the search to rescoring of K-best lists of translation hypotheses, $\{\mathbf{e}_{s,i}, 1 \leq i \leq K\}_{s=1}^{S}$ . For $\mathbf{f}_s$, let $\mathbf{h}_{s,i} = \mathbf{h}(\mathbf{e}_{s,i}, \mathbf{f}_s)$ be the feature vector associated with hypothesis $\mathbf{e}_{s,i}$. Restricted to these lists, the general decoder of Eqn. 1 becomes

$$\hat{\mathbf{e}}(\mathbf{f_s}; \mathbf{w}) = \underset{\mathbf{e}_{s,i}}{\text{argmax}}\{\mathbf{w}\mathbf{h}(\mathbf{e}_{s,i}, \mathbf{f}_s)\} \quad (3)$$

Although the objective function in Eqn. (2) cannot be solved analytically, MERT as described by Och (2003) can be performed over the K-best lists. The line optimisation procedure considers a subset of parameters defined by the line $\mathbf{w}^{(0)} + \gamma\mathbf{d}$, where $\mathbf{w}^{(0)}$ corresponds to an initial point in parameter space and $\mathbf{d}$ is the direction along which to optimise. Eqn. (3) can be rewritten as:

$$\hat{\mathbf{e}}(\mathbf{f_s}; \gamma) = \underset{\mathbf{e_{s,i}}}{\text{argmax}}\{\mathbf{w}^{(0)}\mathbf{h}_{s,i} + \gamma\mathbf{d}\mathbf{h}_{s,i})\} \quad (4)$$

Line optimisation reduces the $D$-dimensional procedure in Eqn. (2) to a 1-Dimensional problem that can be easily solved using a geometric algorithm for many source sentences (Macherey et al., 2008).

More recently, Galley and Quirk (2011) have introduced linear programming MERT (LP-MERT) as an exact search algorithm that reaches the global optimum of the training criterion. A hypothesis $\mathbf{e}_{s,i}$ from the $s$th K-best list can be selected by the decoder only if

$$\mathbf{w}(\mathbf{h}_{s,j} - \mathbf{h}_{s,i}) \leq 0 \text{ for } 1 \leq j \leq K \quad (5)$$

for some parameter vector $\mathbf{w} \neq \mathbf{0}$. If such a solution exists then the system of inequalities is *feasible*, and defines a convex region in parameter space within which any parameter $\mathbf{w}$ will yield $\mathbf{e}_{s,i}$. Testing the system of inequalities in (5) and finding a parameter vector can be cast as a linear programming feasibility problem (Galley and Quirk, 2011), and this can be extended to find a parameter vector that optimizes Eqn. 2 over a collection of K-best lists. We discuss the complexity of this operation in Section 4.1.

Hopkins and May (2011) note that for the $s$th source sentence, the parameter $\mathbf{w}$ that correctly ranks its $K$-best list must satisfy the following set of constraints for $1 \leq i, j \leq K$:

$$\mathbf{w}(\mathbf{h}_{s,j} - \mathbf{h}_{s,i}) \leq 0 \text{ if } \Delta(\mathbf{e}_{s,i}, \mathbf{e}_{s,j}) \geq 0 \quad (6)$$

where $\Delta$ computes the difference in error between two hypotheses. The difference vectors $(\mathbf{h}_{s,j} - \mathbf{h}_{s,i})$ associated with each constraint can be used as input vectors for a binary classification problem in which the aim is to predict whether the the difference in error $\Delta(\mathbf{e}_{s,i}, \mathbf{e}_{s,j})$ is positive or negative. Hopkins and May (2011) call this algorithm Pairwise Ranking Optimisation (PRO). Because there are $SK^2$ difference vectors across all source sentences, a subset of constraints is sampled in the original formulation; with effcient calculation of rankings, sampling can be avoided (Dreyer and Dong, 2015).

The online error based training algorithm MIRA (Crammer et al., 2006) is also used for SMT (Watanabe et al., 2007; Chiang et al., 2008; Chiang, 2012). Using a sentence-level error function, a set of $S$ oracle hypotheses are indexed with the vector $\hat{\mathbf{i}}$:

$$\hat{i}_s = \underset{i}{\text{argmin}}\, E(\mathbf{e}_{s,i}, \mathbf{r}_s) \text{ for } 1 \leq s \leq S$$

For a given $s$ the objective at iteration $n+1$ is :

$$\underset{\mathbf{w}^{(n+1)}}{\text{minimise}} \ \frac{1}{2}\|\mathbf{w}^{(n+1)} - \mathbf{w}^{(n)}\|^2 + C\sum_{j=1}^{K}\xi_j \quad (7)$$

$$\text{subject to } \xi_j \geq 0 \text{ and for } 1 \leq j \leq K, \hat{i}_s \neq j :$$
$$\mathbf{w}^{(n+1)}(\mathbf{h}_{s,j} - \mathbf{h}_{s,\hat{i}_s}) + \Delta(\mathbf{e}_{s,\hat{i}_s}, \mathbf{e}_{s,j}) - \xi_j \leq 0$$

where $\{\xi\}$ are slack variables added to allow infeasible solutions, and $C$ controls the trade-off between error minimisation and margin maximisation. The online nature of the optimiser results in complex implementations, therefore batch versions of MIRA have been proposed (Cherry and Foster, 2012; Gimpel and Smith, 2012).

Although MERT, LP-MERT, PRO, and MIRA carry out their search in very different ways, we can compare them in terms of the constraints they are attempting to satisfy. A feasible solution for LP-MERT is also an optimal solution for MERT, and vice versa. The constraints (Eqn. (5)) that define LP-MERT are a subset of the constraints (Eqn. (6))

that define PRO and so a feasible solution for PRO will also be feasible for LP-MERT; however the converse is not necessarily true. The constraints that define MIRA (Eqn. (7)) are similar to the LP-MERT constraints (5), although with the addition of slack variables and the $\Delta$ function to handle infeasible solutions. However, if a feasible solution is available for MIRA, then these extra quantities are unnecessary. With these quantities removed, then we recover a 'hard-margin' optimiser, which utilises the same constraint set as in LP-MERT. In the feasible case, the solution found by MIRA is also a solution for LP-MERT.

### 2.1 Survey of Recent Work

One avenue of SMT research has been to add as many features as possible to the linear model, especially in the form of sparse features (Chiang et al., 2009; Hopkins and May, 2011; Cherry and Foster, 2012; Gimpel and Smith, 2012; Flanigan et al., 2013; Galley et al., 2013; Green et al., 2013). The assumption is that the addition of new features will improve translation performance. It is interesting to read the justification for many of these works as stated in their abstracts. For example Hopkins and May (2011) state that:

> We establish PRO's scalability and effectiveness by comparing it to MERT and MIRA and demonstrate parity on both phrase-based and syntax-based systems

Cherry and Foster (2012) state:

> Among other results, we find that a simple and efficient batch version of MIRA performs at least as well as training online.

Along similar lines Gimpel and Smith (2012) state:

> [We] present a training algorithm that is easy to implement and that performs comparable to others.

In defence of MERT, Galley et al. (2013) state:

> Experiments with up to 3600 features show that these extensions of MERT yield results comparable to PRO, a learner often used with large feature sets.

Green et al. (2013) also note that feature-rich models are rarely used in annual MT evaluations, an observation they use to motivate an investigation into adaptive learning rate algorithms.

Why do such different methods give such remarkably 'comparable' performance in research settings? And why is it so difficult to get general and unambiguous improvements through the use of high dimensional, sparse features? We believe that the explanation is in *feasibility*. If the oracle index vector $\hat{\mathbf{i}}$ is feasible then all training methods will find very similar solutions. Our belief is that as the feature dimension increases, the chance of an oracle index vector being feasible also increases.

## 3 Convex Geometry

We now build on the description of LP-MERT to give a geometric interpretation to training linear models. We first give a concise summary of the fundamentals of convex geometry as presented by (Ziegler, 1995) after which we work through the example in Cer et al. (2008) to provide an intuition behind these concepts.

### 3.1 Convex Geometry Fundamentals

In this section we reference definitions from convex geometry (Ziegler, 1995) in a form that allows us to describe SMT model parameter optimisation.

**Vector Space** The real valued vector space $\mathbb{R}^D$ represents the space of all finite $D$-dimensional feature vectors.

**Dual Vector Space** The dual vector space $(\mathbb{R}^D)^*$ are the real linear functions $\mathbb{R}^D \to \mathbb{R}$.

**Polytope** The polytope $H_s \subseteq \mathbb{R}^D$ is the convex hull of the finite set of feature vectors associated with the $K$ hypotheses for the $s$th sentence, i.e. $H_s = \mathrm{conv}(\mathbf{h}_{s,1}, \ldots, \mathbf{h}_{s,K})$.

**Faces in $\mathbb{R}^D$** Suppose for $\mathbf{w} \in (\mathbb{R}^D)^*$ that $\mathbf{wh} \leq \max_{\mathbf{h}' \in H_s} \mathbf{wh}'$, $\forall\, \mathbf{h} \in H_s$. A *face* is defined as

$$F = \{\mathbf{h} \in H_s : \mathbf{wh} = \max_{\mathbf{h}' \in H_s} \mathbf{wh}'\} \qquad (8)$$

**Vertex** A face consisting of a single point is called a *vertex*. The set of vertices of a polytope is denoted $\mathrm{vert}(H_s)$.

**Edge** An *edge* is a face in the form of a line segment between two vertices $\mathbf{h}_{s,i}$ and $\mathbf{h}_{s,j}$ in the polytope $H_s$. The edge can be written as $[\mathbf{h}_{s,i}, \mathbf{h}_{s,j}] = \mathrm{conv}(\mathbf{h}_{s,i}, \mathbf{h}_{s,j})$. If an edge exists then the following

| | $h_{LM}$ : $\log(P_{LM}(\mathbf{e}))$ | $h_{TM}$ : $\log(P_{TM}(\mathbf{f}|\mathbf{e}))$ |
|---|---|---|
| $\mathbf{e}_1$ | -0.1 | -1.2 |
| $\mathbf{e}_2$ | -1.2 | -0.2 |
| $\mathbf{e}_3$ | -0.9 | -1.6 |
| $\mathbf{e}_4$ | -0.9 | -0.1 |
| $\mathbf{e}_5$ | -0.8 | -0.9 |

Table 1: An example set of two dimensional feature vectors (after Cer et al. (2008), Table 1) with language model ($h_{LM}$) and translation model ($h_{TM}$) components. A fifth feature vector has been added to illustrate redundancy.

modified system from (5) is feasible

$$\begin{aligned} &\mathbf{w}(\mathbf{h}_j - \mathbf{h}_i) = 0 \quad (9)\\ &\mathbf{w}(\mathbf{h}_k - \mathbf{h}_i) < 0,\ 1 \le k \le K, k \ne i, k \ne j\\ &\mathbf{w}(\mathbf{h}_l - \mathbf{h}_j) < 0,\ 1 \le l \le K, l \ne i, l \ne j \end{aligned}$$

which implies that $[\mathbf{h}_{s,i}, \mathbf{h}_{s,j}]$ defines a decision boundary in $(\mathbb{R}^D)^*$ between the parameters that maximise $\mathbf{h}_{s,i}$ and those that maximise $\mathbf{h}_{s,j}$.

**Normal Cone** For the face $F$ in polytope $H_s$ the normal cone $N_F$ takes the form.

$$\begin{aligned} N_F = \{\mathbf{w} : \mathbf{w}(\mathbf{h}_{s,j} - \mathbf{h}_{s,i}) \le 0, \forall \mathbf{h}_{s,i} \in \text{vert}(F),\\ \forall \mathbf{h}_{s,j} \in \text{vert}(H_s)\} \quad (10) \end{aligned}$$

If the face is a vertex $F = \{\mathbf{h}_{s,i}\}$ then its normal cone $N_{\{\mathbf{h}_{s,i}\}}$ is the set of feasible parameters that satisfy the system in (5).

**Normal Fan** The set of all normal cones associated with the faces of $H_s$ is called the *normal fan* $\mathcal{N}(H_s)$.

### 3.2 Drawing a Normal Fan

Following the example in Cer et al. (2008) we analyze a system based on two features: the translation $P_{TM}(\mathbf{f}|\mathbf{e})$ and language $P_{LM}(\mathbf{e})$ models. For brevity we omit the common sentence index, so that $\mathbf{h}_i = \mathbf{h}_{s,i}$. The system produces a set of four hypotheses which yield four feature vectors $\{\mathbf{h}_1, \mathbf{h}_2, \mathbf{h}_3, \mathbf{h}_4\}$ (Table 1). To this set of four hypotheses, we add a fifth hypothesis and feature vector $\mathbf{h}_5$ to illustrate an infeasible solution. These feature vectors are plotted in Figure 1.

The feature vectors form a polytope $H$ shaded in light blue. From Figure 1 we see that $\mathbf{h}_4$ satisfies the conditions for a vertex in Eqn. (8), because we can draw a decision boundary that interests the vertex and no other $\mathbf{h} \in H$. We also note $\mathbf{h}_5$ is not a vertex, and is *redundant* to the description of H.

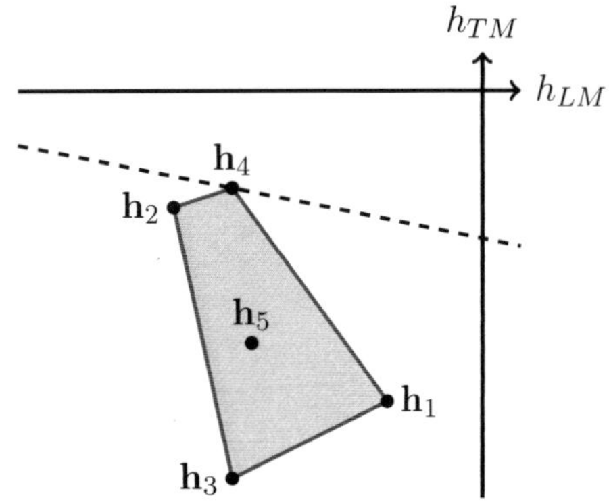


Figure 1: A geometric interpretation of LP-MERT (after Cer et al. (2008) and Galley and Quirk (2011)). The decision boundary represented by the dashed line intersects the polytope at only $\mathbf{h}_4$, making it a vertex. No decision boundary intersects $\mathbf{h}_5$ without intersecting other points in the polytope, making $\mathbf{h}_5$ redundant.

Figure 1 of Cer et al. (2008) actually shows a normal fan, although it is not described as such. We now describe how this geometric object is constructed step by step in Figure 2. In Part (a) we identify the edge $[\mathbf{h}_4, \mathbf{h}_1]$ in $\mathbb{R}^2$ with a decision boundary represented by a dashed line. We have also drawn a vector $\mathbf{w}$ normal to the decision boundary that satisfies Eqn. (8). This parameter would result in a tied model score such that $\mathbf{w}\mathbf{h}_4 = \mathbf{w}\mathbf{h}_1$. When moving to $(\mathbb{R}^2)^*$ we see that the normal cone $N_{[\mathbf{h}_4,\mathbf{h}_1]}$ is a ray parallel to $\mathbf{w}$. This ray can be considered as the set of parameter vectors that yield the edge $[\mathbf{h}_4, \mathbf{h}_1]$. The ray is also a decision boundary in $(\mathbb{R}^2)^*$, with parameters on either side of the decision boundary maximising either $\mathbf{h}_4$ or $\mathbf{h}_1$. Any vector parallel to the edge $[\mathbf{h}_4, \mathbf{h}_1]$, such as $(\mathbf{h}_1 - \mathbf{h}_4)$, can be used to define this decision boundary in $(\mathbb{R}^2)^*$.

Next in Part (b), with the same procedure we define the normal cone for the edge $[\mathbf{h}_3, \mathbf{h}_1]$. Now both the edges from parts (a) and (b) share the the vertex $\mathbf{h}_1$. This implies that any parameter vector that lies between the two decision boundaries (i.e. between the two rays $N_{[\mathbf{h}_3,\mathbf{h}_1]}$ and $N_{[\mathbf{h}_4,\mathbf{h}_1]}$) would maximise the vertex $\mathbf{h}_1$: this is the set of vectors that comprise

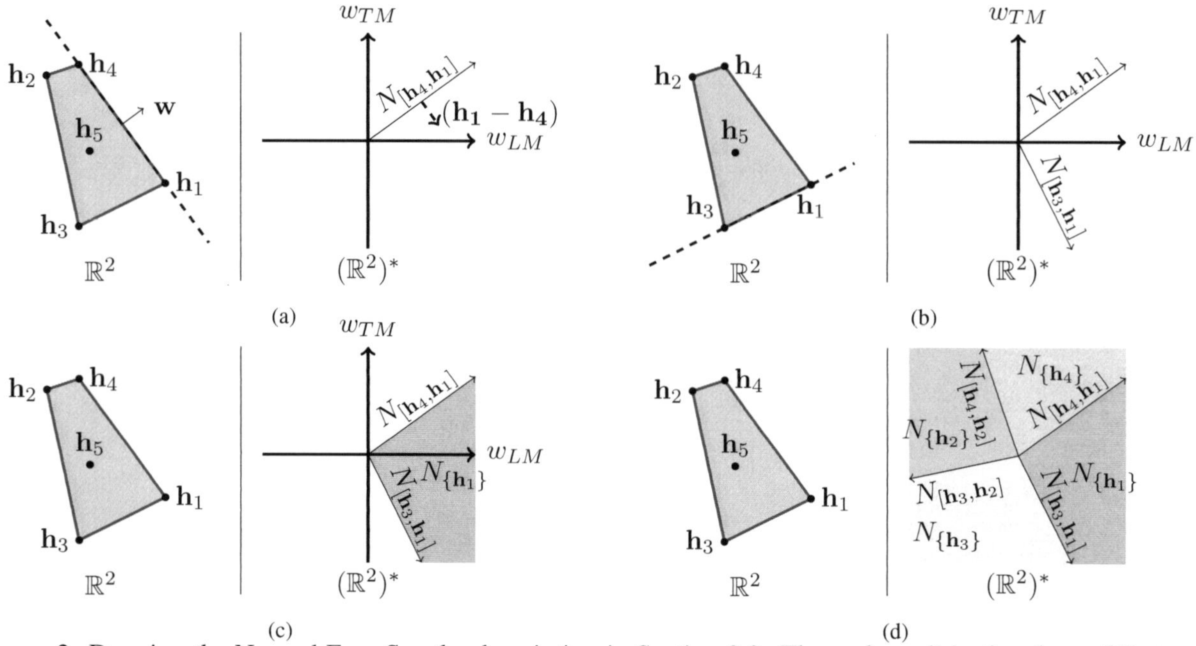


Figure 2: Drawing the Normal Fan. See the description in Section 3.2. The end result in the r.h.s. of Part (d) reproduces Figure 1 from Cer et al. (2008), identifying the normal cones for all vertices.

normal cone of the vertex $N_{\{\mathbf{h}_1\}}$.

In Part (c) we have shaded and labelled $N_{\{\mathbf{h}_1\}}$. Note that no other edges are needed to define this normal cone; these other edges are redundant to the normal cone's description.

Finally in Part (d) we draw the full fan. We have omitted the axes in $(\mathbb{R}^2)^*$ for clarity. The normal cones for all 4 vertices have been identified.

## 4 Training Set Geometry

The previous discussion treated only a single sentence. For a training set of $S$ input sentences, let $\mathbf{i}$ be an index vector that contains $S$ elements. Each element is an index $i_s$ to a hypothesis and a feature vector for the $s$th sentence. A particular $\mathbf{i}$ specifies a set of hypotheses drawn from each of the K-best lists. LP-MERT builds a set of $K^S$ feature vectors associated with $S$ dimensional index vectors $\mathbf{i}$ of the form $\mathbf{h}_\mathbf{i} = \mathbf{h}_{1,i_1} + \ldots + \mathbf{h}_{S,i_S}$. The polytope of these feature vectors is then constructed.

In convex geometry this operation is called the *Minkowski sum* and for the polytopes $H_s$ and $H_t$, is defined as (Ziegler, 1995)

$$H_s + H_t := \{\mathbf{h} + \mathbf{h}' : \mathbf{h} \in H_s, \mathbf{h}' \in H_t\} \quad (11)$$

We illustrate this operation in the top part of Figure 3. The Minkowski sum is commutative and associative and generalises to more than two polytopes (Gritzmann and Sturmfels, 1992).

For the polytopes $H_s$ and $H_t$ the *common refinement* (Ziegler, 1995) is

$$\mathcal{N}(H_s) \wedge \mathcal{N}(H_t) := \{N \cap N' : N \in \mathcal{N}(H_s), N' \in \mathcal{N}(H_t)\} \quad (12)$$

Each cone in the common refinement is the set of parameter vectors that maximise two faces in $H_s$ and $H_t$. This operation is shown in the bottom part of Figure 3.

As suggested by Figure 3 the Minkowski sum and common refinement are linked by the following

**Proposition 1.** $\mathcal{N}(H_s + H_t) = \mathcal{N}(H_s) \wedge \mathcal{N}(H_t)$

*Proof.* See Gritzmann and Sturmfels (1992) □

This implies that, with $\mathbf{h}_\mathbf{i}$ defined for the index vector $\mathbf{i}$, the Minkowski sum defines the parameter vectors that satisfy the following (Tsochantaridis et al., 2005, Eqn. 3)

$$\mathbf{w}(\mathbf{h}_{s,j} - \mathbf{h}_{s,i_s}) \leq 0,\ 1 \leq s \leq S, 1 \leq j \leq K \quad (13)$$

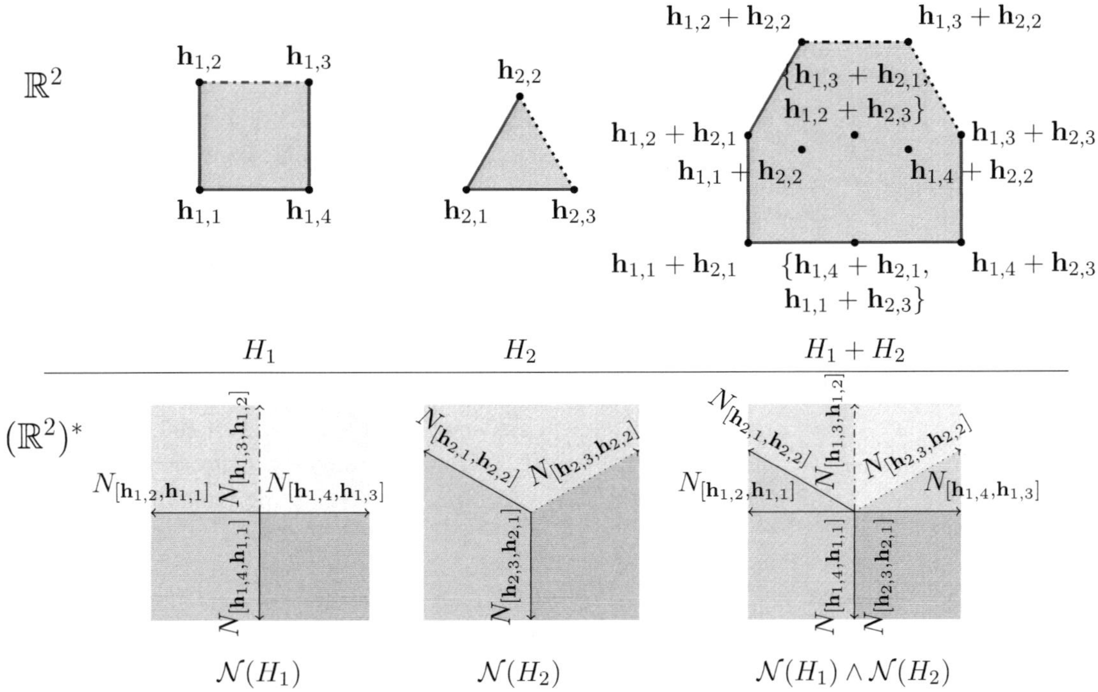


Figure 3: An example of the equivalence between the Minkowski sum and the common refinement.

### 4.1 Computing the Minkowski Sum

In the top part of the Figure 3 we see that computing the Minkowski sum directly gives 12 feature vectors, 10 of which are unique. Each feature vector would have to be tested under LP-MERT. In general there are $K^S$ such feature vectors and exhaustive testing is impractical. LP-MERT performs a lazy enumeration of feature vectors as managed through a divide and conquer algorithm. We believe that in the worst case the complexity of this algorithm could be $O(K^S)$.

The lower part of Figure 3 shows the computation of the common refinement. The common refinement appears as if one normal fan was superimposed on the other. We can see there are six decision boundaries associated with the six edges of the Minkowski sum. Even in this simple example, we can see that the common refinement is an easier quantity to compute than the Minkowski sum.

We now briefly describe the algorithm of Fukuda (2004) that computes the common refinement. Consider the example in Figure 3. For $H_1$ and $H_2$ we have drawn an edge in each polytope with a dashed line. The corresponding decision boundaries in their normal fans have also been drawn with dashed lines.

Now consider the vertex $\mathbf{h}_{1,3} + \mathbf{h}_{2,2}$ in $H = H_1 + H_2$ and note it has two incident edges. These edges are parallel to edges in the summand polytopes and correspond to decision boundaries in the normal cone $N_{\{\mathbf{h}_{1,3}+\mathbf{h}_{2,2}\}}$.

We can find the redundant edges in the Minkowski sum by testing the edges suggested by the summand polytopes. If a decision boundary in $(\mathbb{R}^D)^*$ is redundant, then we can ignore the feature vector that shares the decision boundary. For example $\mathbf{h}_{1,4} + \mathbf{h}_{2,2}$ is redundant and the decision boundary $N_{[\mathbf{h}_{1,3},\mathbf{h}_{1,4}]}$ is also redundant to the description of the normal cone $N_{\{\mathbf{h}_{1,3}+\mathbf{h}_{2,2}\}}$. The test for redundant edges can be performed by a linear program.

Given a Minkowski sum $H$ we can define an undirected cyclic graph $G(H) = (\text{vert}(H), E)$ where $E$ is the set of edges. The degree of a vertex in $G(H)$ is the number of edges incident to a vertex; $\delta$ is denoted as the maximum degree of the vertices.

The linear program for testing redundancy of decision boundaries has a runtime of $O(D^{3.5}\delta)$ (Fukuda, 2004). Enumerating the vertices of graph $G(H)$ is not trivial due to it being an undirected and cyclic graph. The solution is to use a *reverse search* algorithm (Avis and Fukuda, 1993). Essen-

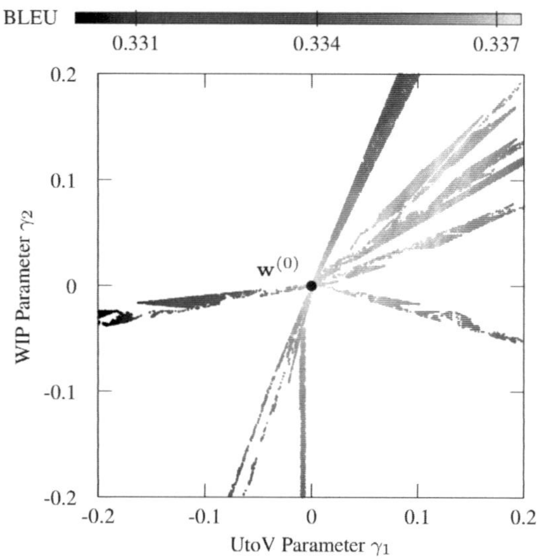


Figure 4: The BLEU score over a 1502 sentence tune set for the CUED Russian-to-English (Pino et al., 2013) system over two parameters. Enumerated vertices of the Minkowski sum are shown in the shaded regions.

tially reverse search transforms the graph into a tree. The vertex associated with $\mathbf{w}^{(0)}$ is denoted as the root of the tree, and from this root vertices are enumerated in reverse order of model score under $\mathbf{w}^{(0)}$. Each branch of the tree can be enumerated independently, which means that the enumeration can be parallelised.

The complexity of the full algorithm is $O(\delta(D^{3.5}\delta)|\operatorname{vert}(H)|)$ (Fukuda, 2004). In comparison with the $O(K^S)$ for LP-MERT the worst case complexity of the reverse search algorithm is linear with respect to the size of $\operatorname{vert}(H)$.

### 4.2 Two Dimensional Projected MERT

We now explore whether the reverse search algorithm is a practical method for performing MERT using an open source implementation of the algorithm (Weibel, 2010). For reasons discussed in the next section, we wish to reduce the feature dimension. For $M < D$, we can define a projection matrix $A_{M+1,D}$ that maps $\mathbf{h}_i \in \mathbb{R}^D$ into $\mathbb{R}^{M+1}$ as $A_{M+1,D}\mathbf{h}_i = \tilde{\mathbf{h}}_i$, $\tilde{\mathbf{h}}_i \in \mathbb{R}^{M+1}$. There are technical constraints to be observed, discussed in Waite (2014). We note that when $M = 1$ we obtain Eqn. (4).

For our demonstration, we plot the error count over a plane in $(\mathbb{R}^D)^*$. Using the CUED Russian-to-English (Pino et al., 2013) entry to WMT'13 (Bojar et al., 2013) we build a tune set of 1502 sentences. The system uses 12 features which we initially tune with lattice MERT (Macherey et al., 2008) to get a parameter $\mathbf{w}^{(0)}$. Using this parameter we generate 1000-best lists. We then project the feature functions in the 1000-best lists to a 3-dimensional representation that includes the source-to-target phrase probability (UtoV), the word insertion penalty (WIP), and the model score due to $\mathbf{w}^{(0)}$. We use the Minkowski sum algorithm to compute BLEU as $\gamma \in (\mathbb{R}^2)^*$ is applied to the parameters from $\mathbf{w}^{(0)}$.

Figure 4 displays some of the characteristics of the algorithm[1]. This plot can be interpreted as a 3-dimensional version of Figure 3 in Macherey et al. (2008) where we represent the BLEU score as a heatmap instead of a third axis. Execution was on 12 CPU cores, leading to the distinct search regions, demonstrating the parallel nature of the algorithm. Weibel (2010) uses a depth-first enumeration order of $G(H)$, hence the narrow and deep exploration of $(\mathbb{R}^D)^*$. A breadth-first ordering would focus on cones closer to $\mathbf{w}^{(0)}$. To our knowledge, this is the first description of a generalised line optimisation algorithm that can search all the parameters in a plane in polynomial time. Extensions to higher dimensional search are straightforward.

## 5 Robustness of Linear Models

In the previous section we described the Minkowski sum polytope. Let us consider the following upper bound theorem

**Theorem 1.** *Let $H_1, \ldots, H_S$ be polytopes in $\mathbb{R}^D$ with at most $N$ vertices each. Then for $D > 2$ the upper bound on number of vertices of $H_1 + \ldots + H_S$ is $O(S^{D-1}K^{2(D-1)})$.*

*Proof.* See Gritzmann and Sturmfels (1992) □

Each vertex $\mathbf{h_i}$ corresponds to a single index vector $\mathbf{i}$, which itself corresponds to a single set of selected hypotheses. Therefore the number of distinct sets of hypotheses that can be drawn

[1] A replication of this experiment forms part of the UCAM-SMT tutorial at `http://ucam-smt.github.io`

from the $S$ $K$-best lists in bounded above by $O(\min(K^S, S^{D-1}K^{2(D-1)}))$.

For low dimension features, i.e. for $D$ : $S^{D-1}K^{2(D-1)} \ll K^S$, the optimiser is therefore tightly constrained. It cannot pick arbitrarily from the individual $K$-best lists to optimise the overall BLEU score. We believe this acts as an *inherent form of regularisation*.

For example, in the system of Section 4.2 (D=12, S=1502, K=1000), only $10^{-4403}$ percent of the $K^S$ possible index vectors are feasible. However, if the feature dimension $D$ is increased to $D = 493$, then $S^{D-1}K^{2(D-1)} \gg K^S$ and this inherent regularisation is no longer at work: any index vector is feasible, and sentence hypotheses can chosen arbitrarily to optimise the overall BLEU score.

This exponential relationship of feasible solutions with respect to feature dimension can be seen in Figure 6 of Galley and Quirk (2011). At low feature dimension, they find that the LP-MERT algorithm can run to completion for a training set size of hundreds of sentences. As feature dimension increases, the runtime increases exponentially.

PRO and other ranking methods are similarly constrained for low dimensional feature vectors.

**Theorem 2.** *If H is a D-dimensional polytope, then for* $D \geq 3$ *the following is an upper bound on the number of edges* $|E|$

$$|E| \leq \binom{|\operatorname{vert}(H)|}{2} \tag{14}$$

*Proof.* This is a special case of the upper bound theorem. See Ziegler (1995, Theorem 8.23). □

Each feasible pairwise ranking of pairs of hypotheses corresponds to an edge in the Minkowski sum polytope. Therefore in low dimension ranking methods also benefit from this inherent regularisation.

For higher dimensional feature vectors, these upper bounds no longer guarantee that this inherent regularisation is at work. The analysis suggests - but does not imply - that index vectors, and their corresponding solutions, can be picked arbitrarily from the $K$-best lists. For MERT overtraining is clearly a risk.

MIRA and related methods have a regularisation mechanism due to the margin maximisation term in

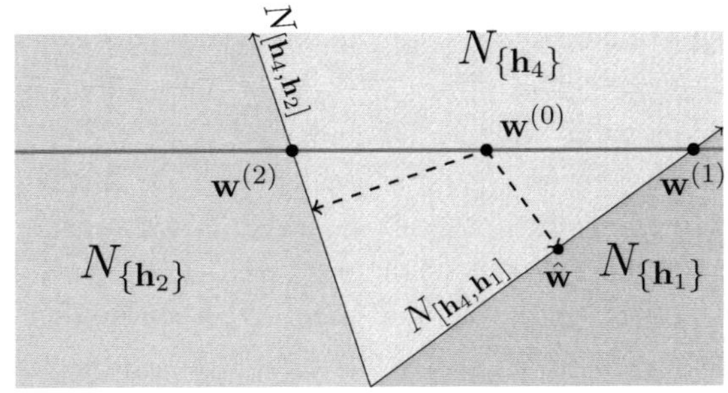


Figure 5: We redraw the normal fan from Figure 2 with potential optimal parameters under the $\ell_2$ regularisation scheme of Galley et al. (2013) marked. The thick red line is the subspace of $(\mathbb{R}^2)^*$ optimised. The dashed lines mark the distances between the decision boundaries and $\mathbf{w}^{(0)}$.

their objective functions. Although this form of regularisation may be helpful in practice, there is no guarantee that it will prevent overtraining due to the exponential increase in feasible solutions. For example the adaptive learning rate method of Green et al. (2013) finds gains of over 13 BLEU points in the training set with the addition of 390,000 features, yet only 2 to 3 BLEU points are found in the test set.

### 5.1 A Note on Regularisation

The above analysis suggest a need for regularisation in training with high dimensional feature vectors. Galley et al. (2013) note that regularisation is hard to apply to linear models due to the magnitude invariance of $\mathbf{w}$ in Eqn. (1). Figure 2 makes the difficulty clear: the normal cones are determined entirely by the feature vectors of the training samples, and within any particular normal cone a parameter vector can be chosen with arbitrary magnitude. This renders schemes such as L1 or L2 normalisation ineffective. To avoid this, Galley et al. (2013) describe a regularisation scheme for line optimisation that encourages the optimal parameter to be found close to $\mathbf{w}^{(0)}$. The motivation is that $\mathbf{w}^{(0)}$ should be a trusted initial point, perhaps taken from a lower-dimensional model. We briefly discuss the challenges of doing this sort of regularisation in MERT.

In Figure 5 we reproduce the normal fan from Figure 2. In this diagram we represent the set of parameters considered by a line optimisation as a thick red line. Let us assume that both $\mathbf{e}_1$ and $\mathbf{e}_2$ have a similarly low error count. Under the regularisation scheme of Galley et al. (2013) we have a choice of $\mathbf{w}^{(1)}$ or $\mathbf{w}^{(2)}$, which are equidistant from $\mathbf{w}^{(0)}$. In this affine projection of parameter space it is unclear which one is the optimum. However, if we consider the normal fan as a whole we can clearly see that $\hat{\mathbf{w}} \in N_{\{\mathbf{h}_i\}}$ is the optimal point under the regularisation. However, it is not obvious in the projected parameter space that $\hat{\mathbf{w}}$ is the better choice. This analysis suggests that direct intervention, e.g. monitoring BLEU on a held-out set, may be more effective in avoiding overtraining.

## 6 Discussion

The main contribution of this work is to present a novel geometric description of MERT. We show that it is possible to enumerate all the feasible solutions of a linear model in polynomial time using this description. The immediate conclusion from this work is that the current methods for estimating linear models as done in SMT works best for low dimensional feature vectors.

We can consider the SMT linear model as a member of a family of linear models where the output values are highly structured, and where each input yields a candidate space of possible output values. We have already noted that the constraints in (13) are shared with the structured-SVM (Tsochantaridis et al., 2005), and we can also see the same constraints in Eqn. 3 of Collins (2002). It is our belief that our analysis is applicable to all models in this family and extends far beyond the discussion of SMT here.

We note that the upper bound on feasible solutions increases polynomially in training set size $S$, whereas the number of possible solutions increases exponentially in $S$. The result is that the ratio of feasible to possible solutions decreases with $S$. Our analysis suggests that inherent regularisation should be improved by increasing training set size. This confirms most researchers intuition, with perhaps even larger training sets needed than previously believed.

Another avenue to prevent overtraining would be to project high-dimensional feature sets to low dimensional feature sets using the technique described in Section 4.1. We could then use existing training methods to optimise over the projected feature vectors.

We also note that non-linear models methods, such as neural networks (Schwenk et al., 2006; Kalchbrenner and Blunsom, 2013; Devlin et al., 2014; Cho et al., 2014) and decision forests (Criminisi et al., 2011) are not bound by these analyses. In particular neural networks are non-linear functions of the features, and decision forests actively reduce the number of features for individual trees in the forrest. From the perspective of this paper, the recent improvements in SMT due to neural networks are well motivated.

## Acknowledgments

This research was supported by a doctoral training account from the Engineering and Physical Sciences Research Council.

## References

David Avis and Komei Fukuda. 1993. Reverse search for enumeration. *Discrete Applied Mathematics*, 65:21–46.

Ondřej Bojar, Christian Buck, Chris Callison-Burch, Christian Federmann, Barry Haddow, Philipp Koehn, Christof Monz, Matt Post, Radu Soricut, and Lucia Specia. 2013. Findings of the 2013 Workshop on Statistical Machine Translation. In *Proceedings of the Eighth Workshop on Statistical Machine Translation*, pages 1–44, Sofia, Bulgaria, August. Association for Computational Linguistics.

Daniel Cer, Dan Jurafsky, and Christopher D. Manning. 2008. Regularization and search for minimum error rate training. In *Proceedings of the Third Workshop on Statistical Machine Translation*, pages 26–34, Columbus, Ohio, June. Association for Computational Linguistics.

Colin Cherry and George Foster. 2012. Batch tuning strategies for statistical machine translation. In *Proceedings of the 2012 Conference of the North American Chapter of the Association for Computational Linguistics: Human Language Technologies*, pages 427–436, Montréal, Canada, June. Association for Computational Linguistics.

David Chiang, Yuval Marton, and Philip Resnik. 2008. Online large-margin training of syntactic and structural translation features. In *Proceedings of the 2008 Conference on Empirical Methods in Natural Language Processing*, pages 224–233, Honolulu, Hawaii, October. Association for Computational Linguistics.

David Chiang, Kevin Knight, and Wei Wang. 2009. 11,001 new features for statistical machine translation. In *Proceedings of Human Language Technologies: The 2009 Annual Conference of the North American Chapter of the Association for Computational Linguistics*, pages 218–226, Boulder, Colorado, June. Association for Computational Linguistics.

David Chiang. 2012. Hope and fear for discriminative training of statistical translation models. *The Journal of Machine Learning Research*, 13(1):1159–1187.

Kyunghyun Cho, Bart van Merrienboer, Caglar Gulcehre, Dzmitry Bahdanau, Fethi Bougares, Holger Schwenk, and Yoshua Bengio. 2014. Learning phrase representations using RNN encoder–decoder for statistical machine translation. In *Proceedings of the 2014 Conference on Empirical Methods in Natural Language Processing (EMNLP)*, pages 1724–1734, Doha, Qatar, October. Association for Computational Linguistics.

Michael Collins. 2002. Discriminative training methods for hidden Markov models: Theory and experiments with perceptron algorithms. In *Proceedings of the 2002 Conference on Empirical Methods in Natural Language Processing*, pages 1–8. Association for Computational Linguistics, July.

Koby Crammer, Ofer Dekel, Joseph Keshet, Shai Shalev-Shwartz, and Yoram Singer. 2006. Online passive-aggressive algorithms. *The Journal of Machine Learning Research*, 7:551–585.

A. Criminisi, J. Shotton, and E. Konukoglu. 2011. Decision forests for classification, regression, density estimation, manifold learning and semi-supervised learning. Technical report, Microsoft Research.

Jacob Devlin, Rabih Zbib, Zhongqiang Huang, Thomas Lamar, Richard Schwartz, and John Makhoul. 2014. Fast and robust neural network joint models for statistical machine translation. In *Proceedings of the 52nd Annual Meeting of the Association for Computational Linguistics (Volume 1: Long Papers)*, pages 1370–1380, Baltimore, Maryland, June. Association for Computational Linguistics.

Markus Dreyer and Yuanzhe Dong. 2015. APRO: All-pairs ranking optimization for MT tuning. In *Proceedings of the 2015 Conference of the North American Chapter of the Association for Computational Linguistics: Human Language Technologies*.

Jeffrey Flanigan, Chris Dyer, and Jaime Carbonell. 2013. Large-scale discriminative training for statistical machine translation using held-out line search. In *Proceedings of the 2013 Conference of the North American Chapter of the Association for Computational Linguistics: Human Language Technologies*, pages 248–258, Atlanta, Georgia, June. Association for Computational Linguistics.

Komei Fukuda. 2004. From the zonotope construction to the Minkowski addition of convex polytopes. *Journal of Symbolic Computation*, 38(4):1261–1272.

Michel Galley and Chris Quirk. 2011. Optimal search for minimum error rate training. In *Proceedings of the 2011 Conference on Empirical Methods in Natural Language Processing*, pages 38–49, Edinburgh, Scotland, UK., July. Association for Computational Linguistics.

Michel Galley, Chris Quirk, Colin Cherry, and Kristina Toutanova. 2013. Regularized minimum error rate training. In *Proceedings of the 2013 Conference on Empirical Methods in Natural Language Processing*, pages 1948–1959, Seattle, Washington, USA, October. Association for Computational Linguistics.

Kevin Gimpel and Noah A. Smith. 2012. Structured ramp loss minimization for machine translation. In *Proceedings of the 2012 Conference of the North American Chapter of the Association for Computational Linguistics: Human Language Technologies*, pages 221–231, Montréal, Canada, June. Association for Computational Linguistics.

Spence Green, Sida Wang, Daniel Cer, and Christopher D. Manning. 2013. Fast and adaptive online training of feature-rich translation models. In *Proceedings of the 51st Annual Meeting of the Association for Computational Linguistics (Volume 1: Long Papers)*, pages 311–321, Sofia, Bulgaria, August. Association for Computational Linguistics.

Peter Gritzmann and Bernd Sturmfels. 1992. Minkowski addition of polytopes: Computational complexity and applications to Gröbner bases. *SIAM Journal on Discrete Mathematics*, 6(2).

Mark Hopkins and Jonathan May. 2011. Tuning as ranking. In *Proceedings of the 2011 Conference on Empirical Methods in Natural Language Processing*, pages 1352–1362, Edinburgh, Scotland, UK., July. Association for Computational Linguistics.

Nal Kalchbrenner and Phil Blunsom. 2013. Recurrent continuous translation models. In *Proceedings of the 2013 Conference on Empirical Methods in Natural Language Processing*, pages 1700–1709, Seattle, Washington, USA, October. Association for Computational Linguistics.

Wolfgang Macherey, Franz Och, Ignacio Thayer, and Jakob Uszkoreit. 2008. Lattice-based minimum error rate training for statistical machine translation. In *Proceedings of the 2008 Conference on Empirical Methods in Natural Language Processing*, pages 725–734, Honolulu, Hawaii, October. Association for Computational Linguistics.

Franz Josef Och and Hermann Ney. 2002. Discriminative training and maximum entropy models for statistical machine translation. In *Proceedings of 40th*

*Annual Meeting of the Association for Computational Linguistics*, pages 295–302, Philadelphia, Pennsylvania, USA, July. Association for Computational Linguistics.

Franz Josef Och. 2003. Minimum error rate training in statistical machine translation. In *Proceedings of the 41st Annual Meeting of the Association for Computational Linguistics*, pages 160–167, Sapporo, Japan, July. Association for Computational Linguistics.

Kishore Papineni, Salim Roukos, Todd Ward, and Wei-Jing Zhu. 2002. Bleu: a method for automatic evaluation of machine translation. In *Proceedings of 40th Annual Meeting of the Association for Computational Linguistics*, pages 311–318, Philadelphia, Pennsylvania, USA, July. Association for Computational Linguistics.

Juan Pino, Aurelien Waite, Tong Xiao, Adrià de Gispert, Federico Flego, and William Byrne. 2013. The University of Cambridge Russian-English system at WMT13. In *Proceedings of the Eighth Workshop on Statistical Machine Translation*, pages 200–205, Sofia, Bulgaria, August. Association for Computational Linguistics.

Holger Schwenk, Daniel Dechelotte, and Jean-Luc Gauvain. 2006. Continuous space language models for statistical machine translation. In *Proceedings of the COLING/ACL 2006 Main Conference Poster Sessions*, pages 723–730, Sydney, Australia, July. Association for Computational Linguistics.

Ioannis Tsochantaridis, Thorsten Joachims, Thomas Hofmann, and Yasemin Altun. 2005. Large margin methods for structured and interdependent output variables. In *Journal of Machine Learning Research*, pages 1453–1484.

Aurelien Waite. 2014. *The Geometry of Statistical Machine Translation*. Ph.D. thesis, University of Cambridge, Cambridge, United Kingdom.

Taro Watanabe, Jun Suzuki, Hajime Tsukada, and Hideki Isozaki. 2007. Online large-margin training for statistical machine translation. In *Proceedings of the 2007 Joint Conference on Empirical Methods in Natural Language Processing and Computational Natural Language Learning*, pages 764–773.

Christophe Weibel. 2010. Implementation and parallelization of a reverse-search algorithm for minkowski sums. In *Proceedings of the 12th Workshop on Algorithm Engineering and Experiments (ALENEX 2010)*, pages 34–42. SIAM.

G Ziegler. 1995. *Lectures on Polytopes*. Springer-Verlag.

# Data-driven sentence generation with non-isomorphic trees

**Miguel Ballesteros**[1] **Bernd Bohnet**[2] **Simon Mille**[1] **Leo Wanner**[1,3]
[1]Natural Language Processing Group, Pompeu Fabra University, Barcelona, Spain
[2]Google Inc.
[3]Catalan Institute for Research and Advanced Studies (ICREA)
[1,3]{name.lastname}@upf.edu [2]bohnetbd@google.com

## Abstract

Abstract structures from which the generation naturally starts often do not contain any functional nodes, while surface-syntactic structures or a chain of tokens in a linearized tree contain all of them. Therefore, data-driven linguistic generation needs to be able to cope with the projection between non-isomorphic structures that differ in their topology and number of nodes. So far, such a projection has been a challenge in data-driven generation and was largely avoided. We present a fully stochastic generator that is able to cope with projection between non-isomorphic structures. The generator, which starts from PropBank-like structures, consists of a cascade of SVM-classifier based submodules that map in a series of transitions the input structures onto sentences. The generator has been evaluated for English on the Penn-Treebank and for Spanish on the multi-layered Ancora-UPF corpus.

## 1 Introduction

Applications such as machine translation that inherently draw upon sentence generation increasingly deal with deep meaning representations; see, e.g., (Aue et al., 2004; Jones et al., 2012; Andreas et al., 2013). Deep representations tend to differ in their topology and number of nodes from the corresponding surface structures since they do not contain, e.g., any functional nodes, while syntactic structures or chains of tokens in linearized trees do. This means that sentence generation needs to be able to cope with the projection between non-isomorphic structures. However, most of the recent work in data-driven sentence generation still avoids this challenge. Some systems focus on syntactic generation (Bangalore and Rambow, 2000; Langkilde-Geary, 2002; Filippova and Strube, 2008) or linearization and inflection (Filippova and Strube, 2007; He et al., 2009; Wan et al., 2009; Guo et al., 2011a), and avoid thus the need to cope with this projection all together; some use a rule-based module to handle the projection between non-isomorphic structures (Knight and Hatzivassiloglou, 1995; Langkilde and Knight, 1998; Bohnet et al., 2011); and some adapt the meaning structures to be isomorphic with syntactic structures (Bohnet et al., 2010). However, it is obvious that a "syntacticization" of meaning structures can be only a temporary workaround and that a rule-based module raises the usual questions of coverage, maintenance and portability.

In this paper, we present a fully stochastic generator that is able to cope with the projection between non-isomorphic structures.[1] Such a generator can be used as a stand-alone application and also, e.g., in text simplification (Klebanov et al., 2004) or deep machine translation (Jones et al., 2012) (where the transfer is done at a deep level). In abstractive summarization, it facilitates the generation of the summaries, and in extractive summarization a better sentence fusion.[2]

[1]The data-driven sentence generator is available for public downloading at https://github.com/talnsoftware/deepgenerator/wiki.

[2]For all of these applications, the deep representation can be obtained by a deep parser, such as, e.g., (Ballesteros et al., 2014a).



*Human Language Technologies: The 2015 Annual Conference of the North American Chapter of the ACL*, pages 387–397,
Denver, Colorado, May 31 – June 5, 2015. 

The generator, which starts from elementary predicate-argument lexico-structural structures as used in sentence planning by Stent et al. (2004), consists of a cascade of Support Vector Machines (SVM)-classifier based submodules that map the input structures onto sentences in a series of transitions. Following the idea presented in (Ballesteros et al., 2014b), a separate SVM-classifier is defined for the mapping of each linguistic category. The generator has been tested on Spanish with the multi-layered Ancora-UPF corpus (Mille et al., 2013) and on English with an extended version of the dependency Penn TreeBank (Johansson and Nugues, 2007).

The remainder of the paper is structured as follows. In the next section, we briefly outline the fundamentals of sentence generation as we view it in our work, focusing in particular on the most challenging part of it: the transition between the non-isomorphic predicate-argument lexico-structural structures and surface-syntactic structures. Section 3 outlines the setup of our system. Section 4 discusses the experiments we carried out and the results we obtained. In Section 5, we briefly summarize related work, before in Section 6 some conclusions are drawn and future work is outlined.

## 2 The Fundamentals

Sentence generation realized in this paper is part of the sentence synthesis pipeline argued for by Mel'čuk (1988). It consists of a sequence of two mappings:

1. Predicate-argument lexico-structural structure $\rightarrow$ Syntactic structure
2. Syntactic Structure $\rightarrow$ Linearized structure

Following the terminology in (Mel'čuk, 1988), we refer to the predicate-argument lexico-structural structures as "deep-syntactic structures" (DSyntSs) and to the syntactic structures as "surface-syntactic structures" (SSyntSs).

While SSyntSs and linearized structures are isomorphic, the difference in the linguistic abstraction of the DSyntSs and SSyntSs leads to divergences that impede the isomorphy between the two and make the first mapping a challenge for statistical generation. Therefore, we focus in this section on the presentation of the DSyntSs and SSyntSs and the mapping between them.

### 2.1 DSyntSs and SSyntSs

#### 2.1.1 Input DSyntSs

DSyntSs are very similar to the PropBank (Babko-Malaya, 2005) structures and the structures as used for the deep track of the First Surface Realization Shared Task (SRST, (Belz et al., 2011)) annotations. DSyntSs are connected trees that contain only meaning-bearing lexical items and both predicate-argument (indicated by Roman numbers: *I, II, III, IV, ...*) and lexico-structural, or deep-syntactic, (*ATTR(ibutive)*, *APPEND(itive)* and *COORD(inative)*) relations. In other words, they do not contain any punctuation and functional nodes, i.e., governed elements, auxiliaries and determiners. Governed elements such governed prepositions and subordinating conjunctions are dropped because they are imposed by sub-categorization restrictions of the predicative head and void of own meaning—as, for instance, *to* in *give TO your friend* or *that* in *I know that you will come.*[3] Auxiliaries do not appear as nodes in DSyntSs. Rather, the information they encode is captured in terms of tense, aspect and voice attributes of the corresponding full verbal nodes. Equally, determiners are substituted by attribute–value pairs of givenness they encode, assigned to their governors. See Figure 1 (a) for a sample DSyntS.[4]

#### 2.1.2 SSyntSs

SSyntSs are connected dependency trees in which the nodes are labeled by open or closed class lexical items and the edges by grammatical function relations of the type 'subject', 'oblique_object', 'adverbial', 'modifier', etc. A SSyntS is thus a typical dependency tree as used in data-driven syntactic parsing (Hajič et al., 2009) and generation (Belz et al., 2011). See Figure 1 (b) for illustration of a SSyntS.

[3] In contrast, *on* in *the bottle is on the table* is not dropped because it is semantic.

[4] "That" is considered a kind of determiner (to be derived from the Information Structure). This is the reason to omit it in the deep structure.

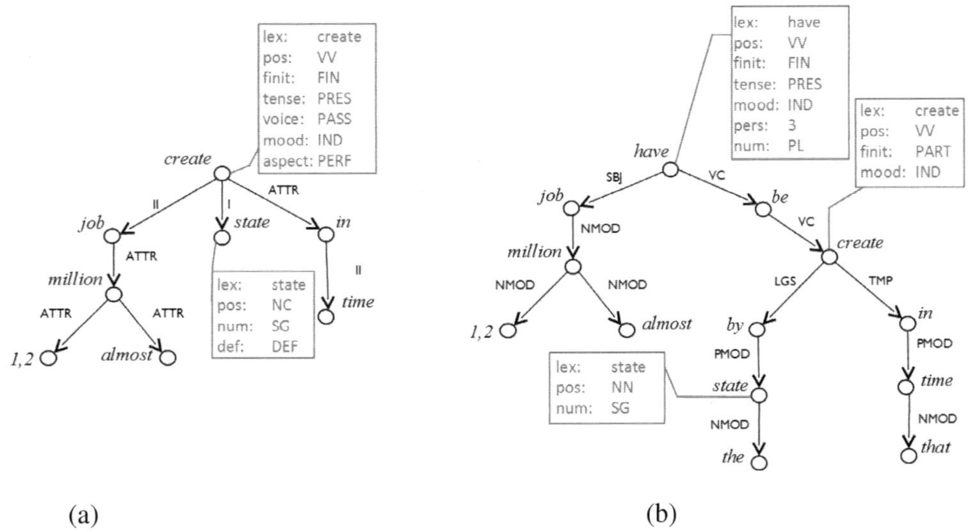


Figure 1: A DSyntS (a) and its corresponding SSyntS (b) for the sentence *Almost 1.2 million jobs have been created by the state in that time*

### 2.2 Projection of DSyntS to SSyntS

In order to project a DSyntS onto its corresponding SSyntS in the course of generation (where both DSyntSs and their corresponding SSyntSs are stored in the 14-column CoNLL'09 format), the following types of actions need to be performed:[5]

**1.** Project each node in the DSyntS onto its SSynS-correspondence. This correspondence can be a single node, as, e.g., *job* $\rightarrow$ [*NN*] (where *NN* is a noun), or a subtree (*hypernode*, known as *syntagm* in linguistics), as, e.g., *time* $\rightarrow$ [*DT NN*] (where *DT* is a determiner and *NN* a noun) or *create* $\rightarrow$ [$V_{\text{AUX}}$ $V_{\text{AUX}}$ *VB IN*] (where $V_{\text{AUX}}$ is an auxiliary, *VB* a full verb and *IN* a preposition). In formal terms, we assume any SSyntS-correspondence to be a hypernode with a cardinality $\geq 1$.
**2.** Generate the correct lemma for the nodes in SSyntS that do not have a 1:1 correspondence with an origin DSyntS node (as *DT* and $V_{\text{AUX}}$ above).[6]
**3.** Establish the dependencies within the individual SSyntS-hypernodes.
**4.** Establish the dependencies between the SSyntS-hypernodes (more precisely, between the nodes of different SSyntS-hypernodes) to obtain a connected SSyntS-tree.

[5]For Spanish, we apply after the DSyntS–SSyntS transition in a postprocessing stage rules for the generation of relative pronouns that are implied by the the SSyntS. Since we cannot count on the annotation of coreference in the training data, we do not treat other types of referring expressions.

[6]The lemmas of nodes with 1:1 correspondence are the same in both structures.

### 2.3 Treebanks used in the experiments

#### 2.3.1 Spanish Treebank

For the validation of the performance of our generator on Spanish, we use the AnCora-UPF treebank, which contains only about 100,000 tokens, but which has been manually annotated and validated on the SSyntS- and DSyntS-layers, such that its quality is rather high. The deep annotation does not contain any functional prepositions since they have been removed for all predicates of the corpus, and the DSyntS-relations have been edited following annotation guidelines. AnCora-UPF SSyntSs are annotated with fine-grained dependencies organized in a hierarchical scheme (Mille et al., 2012), in a similar fashion as the dependencies of the Stanford Scheme (de Marneffe et al., 2006).[7] Thus, it is possible to use the full set of labels or to reduce it according to our needs. We performed preliminary experiments in order to assess which tag granularity is better suited for generation and came up with the 31-label tagset.

[7]The main difference with the Stanford scheme is that in AnCora-UPF no distinction is explicitly made between argumental and non-argumental dependencies.

### 2.3.2 English Treebank

For the validation of the generator on English, we use the dependency Penn TreeBank (about 1,000,000 tokens), which we extend by a DSynt layer defined by the same deep dependency relations, features and node correspondences as the Spanish DSynt layer. The Penn TreeBank DSynt layer is obtained by a rule-based graph transducer. The transducer removes definite and indefinite determiners, auxiliaries, THAT complementizers, TO infinitive markers, and a finite list of functional prepositions. The functional prepositions have been manually compiled from the description and examples of the roles in the PropBank and NomBank annotations of the 150 most frequent predicates of the corpus. A dictionary has been built, which contains for each of the 150 predicates the argument slots (roles) and the prepositions associated to it, such that given a predicate and a preposition, we know to which role it corresponds. Consider, for illustration, Figure 2, which indicates that for the nominal predicate *plan_01*, a dependent introduced by the preposition *to* corresponds to the second argument of *plan_01*, while a dependent introduced by *for* is its third argument.

```
plan_01 : predicate_ {
 NN = {
  to = {DeepRel = II}
  for = {DeepRel = III}
}}
```

Figure 2: A sample (partial) mapping dictionary entry

For each possible surface dependency relation between a governor and a dependent, a default mapping is provided, which is applied if

(i) The syntactic structure fulfills the conditions of the default mapping (e.g., '*subject*' is by default mapped onto '*I*' unless it is the subject of a passive verb, in which case it is mapped to the second argument '*II*'), and

(ii) The pair governor–dependent is not found in the dictionary; that is, if the dependent of the SSyntS dependency relation is a preposition found in the governor's entry in the dictionary, the information provided in the dictionary is used instead of the default mapping.[8]

For instance, in the sentence *Sony announced its plans to hire Mr. Guber*, *to* is a dependent of *plan* with the SSyntS dependency *NMOD*. *NMOD* is by default mapped onto the deep relation *ATTR*, but since in the dictionary entry of *plan* it is stated that a dependent introduced by *to* is mapped to 'II' (cf. Figure 2), *II* is the relation that appears in the DSyntS-annotation.

The features *definiteness*, *voice*, *tense*, *aspect* in the *FEATS* column of the CoNLL format capture the information conveyed by determiners and auxiliaries. The conversion procedure maps surface dependency relations as found in the Penn TreeBank onto the restricted set of deep dependency relations as described in Section 2.1.1.

The nodes in the original (surface-oriented) and deep annotations are connected through their IDs. In the *FEATS* column of the output CoNLL file, *id0* indicates the deep identifier of a word, while *id1* indicates the ID of the surface node it corresponds to. There are less nodes in DSyntSs than in SSyntSs since SSyntSs contain all the words of a sentence. Hence, a DSynt-node can correspond to several SSyntS nodes. Multiple correspondences are indicated by the presence of the *id2* (*id3*, *id4*, etc) feature in the *FEATS* column.

## 3 Deep Generation

### 3.1 Baselines

Since no available data-driven generator uses as input DSyntSs, we developed as baselines two rule-based graph transducer generators which produce for English respectively Spanish the best possible SSyntSs, using only the information contained in the starting DSyntS.

The two baseline generators are structured similarly: both contain around 50 graph transducer rules, separated into two clusters. The first cluster maps DSyntS-nodes onto SSyntS-nodes, while the second one handles the introduction of SSyntS dependency relations between the generated SSyntS-nodes. For instance, in English, one rule maps DSyntS-nodes that have a one-to-one correspondence in the SSyntS

[8] In the PropBank annotation, a distinction is made between external and internal arguments, such that for some predicates the arguments are numbered starting from '0', and for other starting from '1'. This has been normalized in order to make all arguments start from '1' for all predicates.

**if** $N_1$ is a $V_{fin}$ **and** (($R_{1,2}$ == I **and** $N_1$ is in active voice **and** $N_2$ is **not** *by*)
**or** ($R_{1,2}$ == II **and** $N_1$ is in passive voice))
  **if** ∃ one-to-one correspondence between $N_{D_i}$ **and** $N_{S_i}$
    **then** introduce *SBJ* between $N_{S_1}$ **and** $N_{S_2}$
  **else**
    **if** $N_{S_2}$ is top node of the SSyntS hypernode **and** (($N_{S_1}$ is top node of the SSynt hypernode **and** is AUX)
     **or** ($N_{S_1}$ is the bottom node of the SSynt hypernode **and** is $V_{fin}$)
     **or** ($N_{S_1}$ is **not** top node **or** bottom node of the SSynt-hypernode **and** is AUX))
    **then** introduce *SBJ* between $N_{S_1}$ **and** $N_{S_2}$
    **endif**
**endif**

Figure 3: Sample graph transducer rule

(simple nouns, verbs, adverbs, adjectives, etc.), 22 rules map DSyntS-nodes that have a one-to-many correspondence in the SSyntS (N → DET+NN, N → DET+NN+governed PREP, V → AUX+VV, V → *that* COMPL+AUX+VV+governed PREP, etc.), and 25 rules generate the dependency relations.[9] The transduction rules apply in two phases, see Figure 3. During the first phase, all nodes and intra-hypernode dependencies are created in the output structure. During the second phase, all inter-hypernode dependencies are established. Since there are one-to-many DSyntS-SSyntS correspondences, the rules of the second phase have to ensure that the correct output nodes are targeted, i.e., that *jobs* in Figure 1(b) is made a dependent of *have*, and not of *been* or *created*, which all correspond to *create* in the input. Consider, for illustration of the complexity of the rule-based generator, the transduction rule in Figure 3. The rule creates the SSynt dependency relation *SBJ* (*subject*) in a target SSyntS (with a governor node $N_{D_1}$ and a dependent node $N_{D_2}$ linked by a deep dependency relation $R_{1,2}$ in the input DSyntS and two nodes $N_{S_1}$ and $N_{S_2}$ which correspond to $N_{D_1}$ and $N_{D_2}$ respectively in the target SSyntS).

The evaluation shows that all straightforward mappings are performed correctly; English auxiliaries, *that* complementizers, infinitive markers and determiners are introduced, and so are Spanish auxiliaries, reflexive pronouns, and determiners. That is, the rules produce well-formed SSyntSs of all possible combinations of auxiliaries, conjunctions and/or prepositions for verbs, determiners and/or prepositions for nouns, adjectives and adverbs.

When there are several possible mappings, the baseline takes decisions by default. For example, when a governed preposition must be introduced, we always introduce the most common one (*of* in English, *de* 'of' in Spanish).

### 3.2 Data-Driven Generator

The data-driven generator is defined as a tree transducer framework that consists of a cascade of 6 data-driven small tasks; cf. Figure 4. The first four tasks capture the actions 1.–4. from Section 2.2; the 5th linearizes the obtained SSyntS. Figure 4 provides a sample input and output of each submodule. The system outputs a 14 column CoNLL'09 linearized format without morphological inflections or punctuation marks.

In the next sections, we discuss how these actions are realized and how they are embedded into the overall generation process.

The intra- and inter-hypernode dependency determination works as an informed dependency parser that uses the DSyntS as input. The search space is thus completely pruned. Note also that for each step, the space of classes for the SVMs is based on linguistic facts extracted from the training corpus (for instance, for the preposition generation SVM, the classes are the possible prepositions; for the auxiliary generation SVM, the possible auxiliaries, etc.).

#### 3.2.1 Hypernode Identification

Given a node $n_d$ from the DSyntS, the system must find the shape of the surface hypernode that corresponds to $n_d$ in the SSyntS. The hypernode identification SVMs use the following features:

> PoS of $n_d$, PoS of $n_d$'s head, verbal voice (*active*, *passive*) and aspect (*perfective*, *progressive*) of the current node, lemma of $n_d$, and $n_d$'s dependencies.

In order to simplify the task, we define the shape of a surface hypernode as a list of surface PoS tags. This unordered list contains the PoS of each of the lemmas contained within the hypernode and a tag that encodes the original deep node; for instance:

[9]'N' stands for "noun", 'NN' for "common noun", 'DET' for "determiner", 'PREP' for "preposition", 'V' for "verb", 'AUX' for "auxiliary verb", 'VV' for "main verb", and 'COMPL' for "complementizer".

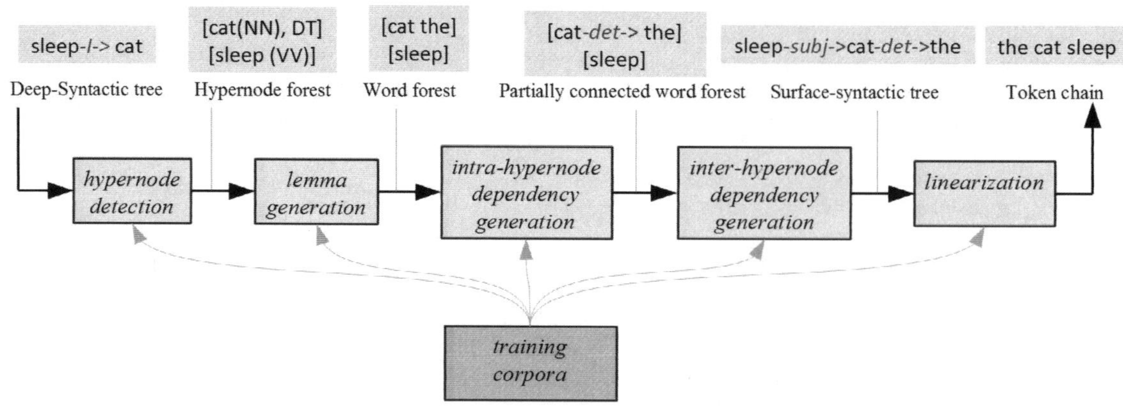


Figure 4: Workflow of the Data-Driven Generator.

[ NN(deep), DT]

For each deep, i.e., DSyntS, PoS tag (which can be one of the following four: *N* (noun), *V* (verb), *Adv* (adverb), *A* (adjective)), a separate multi-class classifier is defined.[10] For instance, in the case of *N*, the N-classifier will use the above features to assign to the a DSynt-node with PoS *N* the most appropriate (most likely) hypernode—in this case, [*NN*(deep), *DT*].

### 3.2.2 Lemma Generation

Once the hypernodes of the SSyntS under construction have been produced, the functional nodes that have been newly introduced in the hypernodes must be assigned a lemma label. The lemma generation SVMs use the following features of the deep nodes $n_d$ in the hypernodes to select the most likely lemma:

> verbal finiteness (*finite, infinitive, gerund, participle*) and aspect (*perfective, progressive*), degree of definiteness of nouns, PoS of $n_d$, lemma of $n_d$, PoS of the head of $n_d$

Again, for each surface PoS tag, a separate classifier is defined. Thus, the DT-classifier would pick for the hypernode [*NN*(deep), *DT*] the most likely lemma for the *DT*-node (optimally, a determiner).

[10]As will be seen in the discussion of the results, the strategy proposed by Ballesteros et al. (2014b) to define a separate classifier for each linguistic category here and in the other stages largely pays off because it reduces the classification search space enormously and thus leads to a higher accuracy.

### 3.2.3 Intra-hypernode Dependency Generation

Given a hypernode and its lemmas provided by the two previous stages, the dependencies (i.e., the dependency attachments and dependency labels) between the elements of the created SSyntS hypernodes must be determined (and thus also the governors of the hypernodes). For this task, the intra-hypernode dependency generation SVMs use the following features:

> lemmas included in the hypernode, PoS-tags of the lemmas in the hypernode, *voice* of the head $h$ of the hypernode, deep dependency relation to $h$.

For each kind of hypernode, dynamically a separate classifier is generated.[11] In the case of the hypernode [*NN*(deep), *DT*], the corresponding classifier will create a link between the determiner and the noun, with the noun as head and the determiner as dependent because it is the best link that it can find; cf. Figure 5 for illustration. We ensure that the output of the classifiers is a tree by controlling that every node (except the root) has one and only one governor. The DSynt input is a tree; in the case of hypernodes of cardinality one, the governor/dependent relation is maintained; in the case of hypernodes of higher cardinality, only one node receives an incoming arc and only one can govern another hypernode.

### 3.2.4 Inter-hypernode Dependency Generation

Once the individual hypernodes have been converted into connected dependency subtrees, the hy-

[11]This implies that the number of classifiers varies depending on the training set. For instance, during the intra-hypernode dependency creation for Spanish, 108 SVMs are generated.

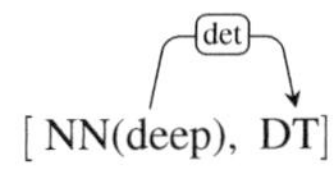


Figure 5: Internal dependency within a hypernode

pernodes must be connected between each other, such that we obtain a complete SSyntS. The inter-hypernode dependency generation SVMs use the following features of a hypernode $s_s$ to determine for each hypernode its governor. For each hypernode with a distinct internal dependency pattern, a separate classifier is dynamically derived (for our treebanks, we obtained 114 different SVM classifiers because they also take into account hypernodes with just one token).:

> the internal dependencies of $s_s$, the head of $s_s$, the lemmas of $s_s$, the PoS of the dependent of the head of $s_s$ in DSyntS

For instance, the classifier for the hypernode [*JJ*(deep)] is most likely to identify as its governor *NN* in the hypernode [*NN*(deep), *DT*]; cf. Figure 6.

The task faced by the inter-hypernode dependency classifiers is the same as that of a dependency parser, only that its search space is very small (which is favorably reflected in the accuracy figures).

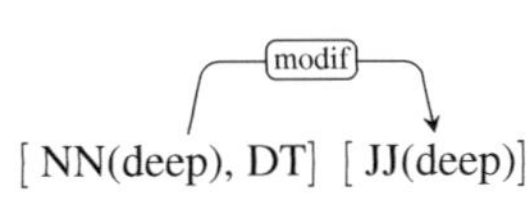


Figure 6: Surface dependencies between two hypernodes.

### 3.3 Linearization

Once we obtained a SSyntS, the linearizer must find the correct order of the words. There is already a body of work available on statistical linearization. Therefore, these tasks were not in the focus of our work. Rather, we adopt the most successful technique of the first SRST (Belz et al., 2011), a bottom-up tree linearizer that orders bottom-up each head and its children (Bohnet et al., 2011; Guo et al., 2011a). This has the advantage that the linear order obtained previously can provide context features for ordering sub-trees higher up in the dependency tree. Each head and its children are ordered with a beam search.

The beam is initialized with entries of single words that are expanded in the next step by the remaining words of the sub-tree, which results in a number of new entries for the next iteration. After the expansion step, the new beam entries are sorted and pruned. We keep the 30 best entries and continue with the expansion and pruning steps until no further nodes of the subtree are left. We take an SVM to obtain the scores for sorting the beam entries, using the same feature templates as in Guo et al. (2011b) and Bohnet et al. (2011).

## 4 Experiments and Results

In our experiments, the Spanish treebank has been divided into: (i) a development set of 219 sentences, with 3,437 tokens in the DSyntS treebank and 4,799 tokens in the SSyntS treebank (with an average of 21.91 words by sentence in SSynt); (ii) a training set of 3,036 sentences, with 57,665 tokens in the DSyntS treebank and 84,668 tokens in the SSyntS treebank (with an average of 27.89 words by sentence in SSynt); and a (iii) a held-out test for evaluation of 258 sentences, with 5,878 tokens in the DSyntS treebank and 8,731 tokens in the SSyntS treebank (with an average of 33.84 words by sentence in SSynt).

For the English treebank, we used a classical split of (i) a training set of 39,279 sentences, with 724,828 tokens in the DSynt treebank and 958,167 tokens in the SSynt treebank (with an average of 24.39 words by sentence in SSynt); and (ii) a test set of 2,399 sentences, with 43,245 tokens in the DSynt treebank and 57,676 tokens in the SSynt treebank (with an average of 24.04 words by sentence in SSynt).

In what follows, we show the system performance on both treebanks. The Spanish treebank was used for development and testing, while the English treebank was only used for testing.

### 4.1 Results

In this section, we present the performance of, first of all, the individual tasks of the data-driven DSyntS–SSyntS projection, since these have been the challenging tasks that we addressed. Table 1 shows similar results for all tasks on the development and test sets with gold-standard input, that is, the results of the classifiers as a stand-alone module, assuming that the previous module provides a perfect output.

| Spanish Dev.set | # | % |
|---|---|---|
| Hypernode identification | 3327/3437 | 96.80 |
| Lemma generation | 724/767 | 94.39 |
| Intra-hypernode dep. generation | 756/756 | 100.00 |
| Inter-hypernode dep. generation | 2628/2931 | 89.66 |
| Spanish Test set | # | % |
| Hyper-node identification | 5640/5878 | 95.95 |
| Lemma generation | 1556/1640 | 94.88 |
| Intra-hypernode dep. generation | 1622/1622 | 100.00 |
| Inter-hypernode dep. generation | 4572/5029 | 90.91 |

Table 1: Results of the evaluation of the SVMs for the non-isomorphic transition for the Spanish DSyntS development and test sets

| English Test set | # | % |
|---|---|---|
| Hyper-node identification | 42103/43245 | 97.36 |
| Lemma generation | 6726/7199 | 93.43 |
| Intra-hypernode dep. generation | 6754/7179 | 94.08 |
| Inter-hypernode dep. generation | 35922/40699 | 88.26 |

Table 2: Results of the evaluation of the SVMs for the non-isomorphic transition for the English DSyntS test set

To have the entire generation pipeline in place, we carried out several linearization experiments, starting from: (i) the SSyntS gold standard, (ii) SSyntSs generated by the rule-based baselines, and (iii) SSyntSs generated by the data-driven deep generator; cf. *surface gen.*, *baseline deep gen*, and *deep gen.* respectively in Tables 3 and 4).[12]

| **Development Set** | BLEU | NIST | Exact |
|---|---|---|---|
| surface gen. | 0.754 | 11.29 | 24.20 % |
| baseline deep gen. | 0.547 | 9.98 | 10.96 % |
| **deep gen.** | **0.582** | 10.78 | 12.33 % |
| **Test Set** | BLEU | NIST | Exact |
| surface gen. | 0.762 | 12.08 | 15.89 % |
| baseline deep gen. | 0.515 | 10.60 | 2.33 % |
| **deep gen.** | **0.542** | 11.24 | 3.49 % |

Table 3: Overview of the results on the Spanish development and test sets excluding punctuation marks after the linearization

[12]Following (Langkilde-Geary, 2002; Belz et al., 2011) and other works on statistical text generation, we access the quality of the linearization module via BLEU score, NIST and exactly matched sentences.

| **Test Set** | BLEU | NIST | Exact |
|---|---|---|---|
| surface gen. | 0.91 | 15.26 | 56.02 % |
| baseline deep gen. | 0.69 | 13.71 | 12.38 % |
| **deep gen.** | **0.77** | 14.42 | 21.05 % |

Table 4: Overview of the results on the English test set excluding punctuation marks after the linearization

### 4.2 Discussion and Error Analysis

In general, Tables 1–4 show that the quality of the presented deep data-driven generator is rather good both during the individual stages of the DSyntS–SSyntS transition and as part of the DSyntS–linearized sentence pipeline.

Two main problems impede an even better performance figures than those reflected in Tables 1 and 2. First, the introduction of prepositions causes most errors in hypernode detection and lemma generation: when a preposition should be introduced or not and which preposition should be introduced depends exclusively on the subcategorization frame of the governor of the DSyntS node. A corpus of a limited size does not capture the subcategorization frames of ALL predicates. This is especially true for our Spanish treebank, which is particularly small. Second, the inter-hypernode dependency suffers from the fact that the SSyntS tagset is quite fine-grained, at least in the case of Spanish, which makes the task of the classifiers harder (e.g., there are nine different types of verbal objects). In spite of these problems, each set of classifiers achieves results above 88% on the test sets.

The results of deep generation in Tables 3 and 4 can be explained by the fact of error propagation: while (only) about 1 out of 10 hypernodes and about 1 out of 10 lemmas are not correct and very little information is lost in the stage of the intra-hypernode dependencies determination, already almost 1.75 out of 10 inter-hypernode dependencies, and finally 1 out 10 linear orderings are incorrect for English and more than 2 out 10 for Spanish.

As already mentioned above, the size of the training corpus strongly affects the results. Thus, for English, for which the size of the training dataset has been 10 times bigger than for Spanish, the data-driven generator provides, without any tuning, more than 0.2 BLEU points more that for Spanish. A bigger corpus also covers more linguistic phenomena (lexical features, subcategorization frames, syntactic sentential constructions, etc.)—which can be also exploited for rule-based generation.

The linearizer also suffers from a small size of the training set. Thus, while the small Spanish training corpus leads to 0.754 BLEU and 0.762 BLEU for the development and test sets respectively, for English, we achieve 0.91 BLEU, which is a very competitive outcome compared to other English linearizers (Song et al., 2014).

We also found that the data-driven generator tends to output slightly shorter sentences, when compared to the rule-based baseline. It is always difficult to find the best evaluation metric for plain text sentences (Smith et al., 2014). In our experiments, we used BLEU, NIST and the exact match metric. BLEU is the average of $n$-gram precisions and includes a brevity penalty, which reduces the score if the length of the output sentence is shorter than the gold. In other words, BLEU favors longer sentences. We believe that this is one of the reasons why the machine-learning based generator shows a bigger difference for the English test set and the Spanish development set than the rule-based baseline. Firstly, there are extremely long sentences in the Spanish test set (31 words per sentence, in the average; the longest being 165 words). Secondly, the English sentences and the Spanish development sentences are much shorter than the Spanish test sentences, such that the ML approach has the potential to perform better.

## 5 Related work

There is an increasing amount of work on statistical sentence generation, although hardly any addresses the problem of deep generation from semantic structures that are not isomorphic with syntactic- structures as a purely data-driven problem (as we do). To the best of our knowledge, the only exception is our earlier work in (Ballesteros et al., 2014b), where we discuss the principles of classifiers for data-driven generators. As already mentioned in Section 1, most of the state-of-the-art work focuses on syntactic generation; see, among others (Bangalore and Rambow, 2000; Langkilde-Geary, 2002; Filippova and Strube, 2008), or only on linearization and inflection (Filippova and Strube, 2007; He et al., 2009; Wan et al., 2009; Guo et al., 2011a). A number of proposals are hybrid in that they combine statistical machine learning-based generation with rule-based generation. Thus, some combine machine learning with pre-generated elements, as, e.g., (Marciniak and Strube, 2004; Wong and Mooney, 2007; Mairesse et al., 2010), or with handcrafted rules, as, e.g., (Ringger et al., 2004; Belz, 2005). Others derive automatically grammars for rule-based generation modules from annotated data, which can be used for surface generation, as, e.g., (Knight and Hatzivassiloglou, 1995; Langkilde and Knight, 1998; Oh and Rudnicky, 2002; Zhong and Stent, 2005; Bohnet et al., 2011; Rajkumar et al., 2011) or for generation from ontology triples, as, e.g., (Gyawali and Gardent, 2013).

## 6 Conclusions

We presented a statistical deep sentence generator that successfully handles the non-isomorphism between meaning representations and syntactic structures in terms of a principled machine learning approach. This generator has been successfully tested on an English and a Spanish corpus, as a stand-alone DSyntS–SSyntS generator and as a part of the generation pipeline. We are currently about to apply it to other languages—including Chinese, French and German. Furthermore, resources are compiled to use it for generation of spoken discourse in Arabic, Polish and Turkish.

We believe that our generator can be used not only in generation *per se*, but also, e.g., in machine translation (MT), since MT could profit from using meaning representations such as DSyntSs, which abstract away from the surface syntactic idiosyncrasies of each language, but are still linguistically motivated, as transfer representations.

## Acknowledgments

Our work on deep stochastic sentence generation is partially supported by the European Commission under the contract numbers FP7-ICT-610411 (project MULTISENSOR) and H2020-RIA-645012 (project KRISTINA).

## References


J. Andreas, A. Vlachos, and S. Clark. 2013. Semantic Parsing as Machine Translation. In *Proceedings of ACL '13*.

A. Aue, A. Menezes, R. Moore, C. Quirk, and E. Ringger. 2004. Statistical Machine Translation Using Labeled Semantic Dependency Graphs. In *Proceedings of TMI '04*.

Olga Babko-Malaya, 2005. *Propbank Annotation Guidelines*.

Miguel Ballesteros, Bernd Bohnet, Simon Mille, and Leo Wanner. 2014a. Deep-syntactic parsing. In *Proceedings of COLING'14*, Dublin, Ireland.

Miguel Ballesteros, Simon Mille, and Leo Wanner. 2014b. Classifiers for Data-Driven Deep Sentence Generation. In *Proceedings of the International Conference of Natural Language Generation (INLG)*.

Srinivas Bangalore and Owen Rambow. 2000. Exploiting a probabilistic hierarchical model for generation. In *Proceedings of the 18th conference on Computational linguistics-Volume 1*, pages 42–48. Association for Computational Linguistics.

Anja Belz, Mike White, Dominic Espinosa, Eric Kow, Deirdre Hogan, and Amanda Stent. 2011. The first surface realisation shared task: Overview and evaluation results. In *Proceedings of the Generation Challenges Session at the 13th European Workshop on Natural Language Generation*, pages 217–226.

Anja Belz. 2005. Statistical generation: Three methods compared and evaluated. In *Proceedings of the 10th European Workshop on Natural Language Generation*, pages 15–23.

Bernd Bohnet, Leo Wanner, Simon Mille, and Alicia Burga. 2010. Broad coverage multilingual deep sentence generation with a stochastic multi-level realizer. In *Proceedings of COLING '10*, pages "98–106".

Bernd Bohnet, Simon Mille, Benoît Favre, and Leo Wanner. 2011. StuMaBa: From deep representation to surface. In *Proceedings of ENLG 2011, Surface-Generation Shared Task*, Nancy, France.

Marie-Catherine de Marneffe, Bill MacCartney, and Christopher D Manning. 2006. Generating typed dependency parses from phrase structure parses. In *Proceedings of the 5th International Conference on Language Resources and Evaluation (LREC)*, volume 6, pages 449–454.

Katja Filippova and Michael Strube. 2007. Generating constituent order in german clauses. In *Proceedings of the Annual Meeting of the Association for Computational Linguistics*, volume 45, page 320.

Katja Filippova and Michael Strube. 2008. Sentence fusion via dependency graph compression. In *Proceedings of the Conference on Empirical Methods in Natural Language Processing*, EMNLP '08, pages 177–185, Stroudsburg, PA, USA. Association for Computational Linguistics.

Yuqing Guo, Deirdre Hogan, and Josef van Genabith. 2011a. Dcu at generation challenges 2011 surface realisation track. In *Proceedings of the Generation Challenges Session at the 13th European Workshop on Natural Language Generation*, pages 227–229, Nancy, France, September. Association for Computational Linguistics.

Yuqing Guo, Haifeng Wang, and Josef Van Genabith. 2011b. Dependency-based n-gram models for general purpose sentence realisation. *Natural Language Engineering*, 17(04):455–483.

B. Gyawali and C. Gardent. 2013. LOR-KBGEN, A Hybrid Approach To Generating from the KBGen Knowledge-Base. In *Proceedings of the KBGen Challenge http://www.kbgen.org/papers/*.

Jan Hajič, Massimiliano Ciaramita, Richard Johansson, Daisuke Kawahara, Maria Antònia Martí, Lluís Màrquez, Adam Meyers, Joakim Nivre, Sebastian Padó, Jan Štěpánek, Pavel Straňák, Mihai Surdeanu, Nianwen Xue, and Yi Zhang. 2009. The CoNLL-2009 shared task: Syntactic and semantic dependencies in multiple languages. In *Proceedings of the 13th Conference on Computational Natural Language Learning (CoNLL-2009), June 4-5*, Boulder, Colorado, USA.

Wei He, Haifeng Wang, Yuqing Guo, and Ting Liu. 2009. Dependency based chinese sentence realization. In *Proceedings of the Joint Conference of the 47th Annual Meeting of the ACL and the 4th International Joint Conference on Natural Language Processing of the AFNLP: Volume 2-Volume 2*, pages 809–816. Association for Computational Linguistics.

Richard Johansson and Pierre Nugues. 2007. Extended constituent-to-dependency conversion for English. In *Proceedings of the 16th Nordic Conference of Computational Linguistics (NODALIDA)*, pages 105–112, Tartu, Estonia, May 25-26.

B. Jones, J. Andreas, D. Bauer, K.M. Hermann, and K. Knight. 2012. Semantics-Based Machine Translation with Hyperedge Replacement Grammars. In *Proceedings of COLING '12*.

Beata Beigman Klebanov, Kevin Knight, and Daniel Marcu. 2004. Text simplification for information-seeking applications. In *On the Move to Meaningful Internet Systems, Lecture Notes in Computer Science*, pages 735–747. Springer Verlag.

Kevin Knight and Vasileios Hatzivassiloglou. 1995. Two-level, many-paths generation. In *Proceedings of the 33rd annual meeting on Association for Computational Linguistics*, pages 252–260. Association for Computational Linguistics.

I. Langkilde and K. Knight. 1998. Generation that exploits corpus-based statistical knowledge. In *Proceedings of the COLING/ACL*, pages 704–710.

Irene Langkilde-Geary. 2002. An empirical verification of coverage and correctness for a general-purpose sentence generator. In *Proceedings of the 12th International Natural Language Generation Workshop*, pages 17–24. Citeseer.

François Mairesse, Milica Gašić, Filip Jurčíček, Simon Keizer, Blaise Thomson, Kai Yu, and Steve Young. 2010. Phrase-based statistical language generation using graphical models and active learning. In *Proceedings of the 48th Annual Meeting of the Association for Computational Linguistics*, pages 1552–1561. Association for Computational Linguistics.

Tomasz Marciniak and Michael Strube. 2004. Classification-based generation using tag. In *Natural Language Generation*, pages 100–109. Springer.

Igor Mel'čuk. 1988. *Dependency Syntax: Theory and Practice*. State University of New York Press, Albany.

Simon Mille, Alicia Burga, Gabriela Ferraro, and Leo Wanner. 2012. How does the granularity of an annotation scheme influence dependency parsing performance? In *Proceedings of COLING 2012*, pages 839–852, Mumbai, India.

Simon Mille, Alicia Burga, and Leo Wanner. 2013. Ancora-upf: A multi-level annotation of spanish. In *Proceedings of the Second International Conference on Dependency Linguistics*, Prague, Czech Republic.

Alice H Oh and Alexander I Rudnicky. 2002. Stochastic natural language generation for spoken dialog systems. *Computer Speech & Language*, 16(3):387–407.

Rajakrishnan Rajkumar, Dominic Espinosa, and Michael White. 2011. The osu system for surface realization at generation challenges 2011. In *Proceedings of the 13th European workshop on natural language generation*, pages 236–238. Association for Computational Linguistics.

Eric Ringger, Michael Gamon, Robert C Moore, David Rojas, Martine Smets, and Simon Corston-Oliver. 2004. Linguistically informed statistical models of constituent structure for ordering in sentence realization. In *Proceedings of the 20th international conference on Computational Linguistics*, page 673. Association for Computational Linguistics.

Aaron Smith, Christian Hardmeier, and Jörg Tiedemann. 2014. Bleu is not the colour: How optimising bleu reduces translation quality.

Linfeng Song, Yue Zhang, Kai Song, and Qun Liu. 2014. Joint morphological generation and syntactic linearization. In *Proceedings of the Twenty-Eighth AAAI Conference on Artificial Intelligence, July 27 - 31, 2014, Québec City, Québec, Canada.*, pages 1522–1528.

A. Stent, R. Prasad, and M. Walker. 2004. Trainable sentence planning for complex information presentation in spoken dialog systems. In *Proceedings of the ACL '04*, pages 79–86.

Stephen Wan, Mark Dras, Robert Dale, and Cécile Paris. 2009. Improving grammaticality in statistical sentence generation: Introducing a dependency spanning tree algorithm with an argument satisfaction model. In *Proceedings of the 12th Conference of the European Chapter of the Association for Computational Linguistics*, pages 852–860. Association for Computational Linguistics.

Yuk Wah Wong and Raymond J Mooney. 2007. Generation by inverting a semantic parser that uses statistical machine translation. In *HLT-NAACL*, pages 172–179.

Huayan Zhong and Amanda Stent. 2005. Building surface realizers automatically from corpora. *Proceedings of UCNLG*, 5:49–54.

# Latent Domain Word Alignment for Heterogeneous Corpora

**Hoang Cuong** and **Khalil Sima'an**
Institute for Logic, Language and Computation
University of Amsterdam
Science Park 107, 1098 XG Amsterdam, The Netherlands
{c.hoang,k.simaan}@uva.nl

## Abstract

This work focuses on the insensitivity of existing word alignment models to domain differences, which often yields suboptimal results on large heterogeneous data. A novel latent domain word alignment model is proposed, which induces domain-conditioned lexical and alignment statistics. We propose to train the model on a heterogeneous corpus under partial supervision, using a small number of seed samples from different domains. The seed samples allow estimating sharper, domain-conditioned word alignment statistics for sentence pairs. Our experiments show that the derived domain-conditioned statistics, once combined together, produce notable improvements both in word alignment accuracy and in translation accuracy of their resulting SMT systems.

## 1 Introduction

Word alignment currently constitutes the basis for phrase extraction and reordering in phrase-based systems, and its statistics provide lexical parameters used for smoothing the phrase pair estimates. For over two decades since IBM models (Brown et al., 1993) and the HMM alignment model (Vogel et al., 1996), word alignment remains an active research line, e.g., see recent work (Simion et al., 2013; Tamura et al., 2014; Chang et al., 2014).

During the past years we witnessed an increasing need to collect and use large *heterogeneous* parallel corpora from different domains and sources, e.g., News, Wikipedia, Parliament Proceedings. It is tacitly assumed that assembling a larger corpus should improve a phrase-based system coverage and performance. Recent work (Sennrich et al., 2013; Carpuat et al., 2014; Cuong and Sima'an, 2014b; Kirchhoff and Bilmes, 2014; Cuong and Sima'an, 2014a) shows that this is not necessarily true as phrase translations as well as (bi- and monolingual) word co-occurrence statistics could differ across domains. This suggests that the word alignment quality obtained from IBM and HMM alignment models might also be affected in heterogeneous corpora.

Intuitively, in heterogeneous data certain words are present across many domains, whereas others are more specific to few domains. This suggests that the translation probabilities for words will be as fractioned as the diversity of its translations across the domains. Furthermore, because the IBM and HMM alignment models use *context-insensitive* conditional probabilities, in heterogeneous corpora the estimates of these probabilities will be aggregated over different domains. Both issues could lead to suboptimal word alignment quality.

Surprisingly, the *insensitivity* of the existing IBM and HMM alignment models to domain differences has not received much attention thus far (see the study of Bach et al. (2008) and Gao et al. (2011) for reference in the literature). We conjecture that this is because it is not fully clear how to define what constitutes a *(sub)-domain*. In this paper we propose to exploit the contrast between the alignment statistics in a handful of *seed samples from different domains* in order to induce domain-conditioned probabilities for each sentence pair in the heterogeneous corpus. Crucially, some sentence pairs will be more similar to a seed domain than others, whereas some sentence



*Human Language Technologies: The 2015 Annual Conference of the North American Chapter of the ACL*, pages 398–408,
Denver, Colorado, May 31 – June 5, 2015. 

pairs might be dissimilar to all seed domains. The number and choice of seed domains depends largely on the available resources but intuitively these seed domains are chosen to be relevant to parts of the heterogeneous corpus. A small number of such seeds can be expected to notably improve word alignment accuracy. In fact, a single seed sample already allows us to exploit the contrast between two parts in the corpus: similar or dissimilar to the seed data.

Considering the small seed samples as *partial supervision*, in this paper we explore the question: *how to obtain better word alignment in a heterogeneous, mix-of-domains corpus?* We present a novel *latent domain HMM alignment model*, which aims to *tighten* the probability estimates of the generative alignment process of a sentence pair, and of the probability estimates of the sentence pair itself for a specific domain. We also present an accompanying training regime *guided* by partial supervision using the seed samples, exploiting the contrast between the domain-conditioned alignment statistics in these samples. This way we aim for an alignment model that is more domain-sensitive than the original HMM alignment model. Once the domain-conditioned statistics are induced, we discuss how to combine them together to express the probability of a sentence pair as a mixture over specific domains.

Finally, we report experimental results over heterogeneous corpora of 1M, 2M and $4M$ sentence pairs, where we are provided domain information for different samples of $10\%$, $5\%$ and $2.5\%$ of the heterogeneous data respectively. A large number of experiments are reported, showing that the latent domain HMM model produces notable improvements in word alignment accuracy over the original HMM alignment model. Furthermore, the translation accuracy of the resulting SMT systems is significantly improved across *four* different translation tasks.

## 2 HMM Alignment Model

In this section, we briefly review the HMM alignment model (Vogel et al., 1996). The generative story of the model is shown in Figure 1. The latent states take values from the target language words and generate source language words.

Formally, we use $\mathbf{e} = (e_1, \ldots, e_I)$ to denote the target sentence with length $I$ and $\mathbf{f} = (f_1, \ldots, f_J)$ to denote the source sentence with length $J$. For an alignment $\mathbf{a} = (a_1, \ldots, a_J)$ of a sentence pair $\langle \mathbf{e}, \mathbf{f} \rangle$, the model factors $P(\mathbf{f}, \mathbf{a}| \mathbf{e})$ into the word translation and transition probabilities:

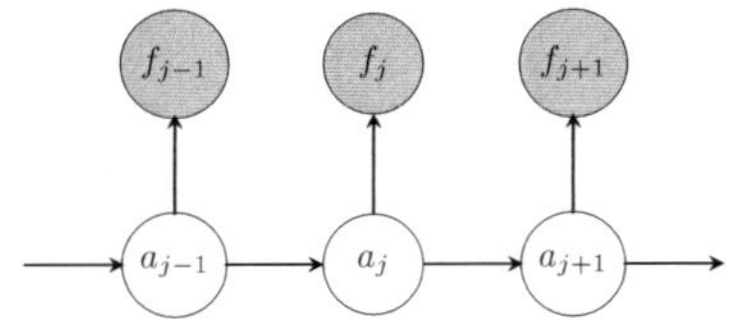


Figure 1: HMM alignment model with observed and latent alignment layers.

$$P(\mathbf{f}, \mathbf{a}| \mathbf{e}) = \prod_{j=1}^{J} P(f_j| e_{a_j}) P(a_j| a_{j-1}). \quad (1)$$

Here, $P(f_j| e_{a_j})$ represents the word translation probabilities and $P(a_j| a_{j-1})$[1] represents the transition probabilities between positions. Note that $P(a_j| a_{j-1})$ depends only on the distance $(a_j - a_{j-1})$. Note also that the first-order dependency model is an extension of the uniform dependency model and zero-order dependency model of IBM models 1 and 2, respectively.

In this work, we model explicitly distances in the range $\pm 5$. Note that *null*-links are also explicitly added in our implementation, following Och and Ney (2003) and Graca et al. (2010).

Once the HMM alignment model is trained, the most probable alignment, $\hat{\mathbf{a}}$ for each sentence pair can be computed by: $\hat{\mathbf{a}} = \text{argmax}_{\mathbf{a}} P(\mathbf{f}, \mathbf{a}| \mathbf{e})$. Here, the search problem can be solved by the Viterbi algorithm.

## 3 Latent Domain HMM Alignment Model

Because the heterogeneous data contains a mix of diverse domains, the induced statistics derived from word alignment models reflect translation preferences aggregated over these domains. In this sense, they can be considered domain-*confused* statistics (Cuong and Sima'an, 2014a). This work thus focuses on more **representative** statistics: the domain-*conditioned* word alignment statistics, i.e., the statistics with respect to each of the diverse domains.

By introducing a latent variable $D$ representing domains of the heterogeneous data, we aim

[1]The "full" formula for transition probabilities would be $P(a_j| a_{j-1}, I)$. For convenience, we ignore $I$ in our presentation.

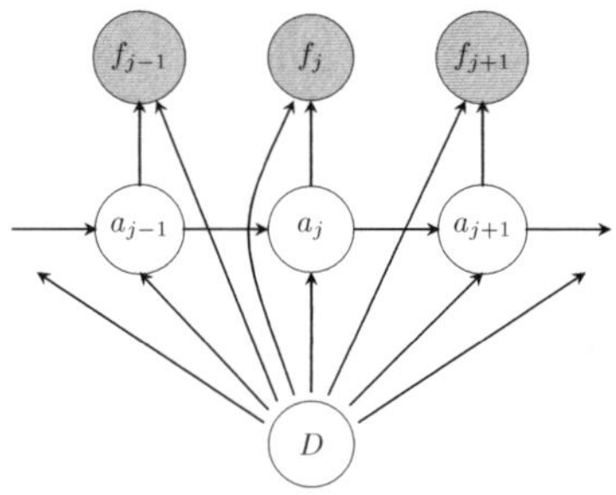


Figure 2: Latent domain HMM alignment model. An additional latent layer representing domains has been conditioned on by both the rest two layers.

to learn the $D$-conditioned word alignment model $P(\mathbf{f},\ \mathbf{a}|\ \mathbf{e},\ D)$.[2] Relying on the HMM alignment model, our latent domain HMM alignment model factors $P(\mathbf{f},\ \mathbf{a}|\ \mathbf{e},\ D)$ into the domain-conditioned word translation and transition probabilities:

$$P(\mathbf{f}, \mathbf{a}|\mathbf{e}, D) = \prod_{j=1}^{J} P(f_j|e_{a_j}, D)P(a_j|a_{j-1}, D). \tag{2}$$

The generative story of the model is shown in Figure 2. Note how domain-conditioned alignment statistics, $P(\cdot|\ \cdot, D)$ contain their former domain-confused alignment statistics, $P(\cdot|\ \cdot)$ as special case

$$P(f_j|e_{a_j}, D) = \frac{P(f_j|e_{a_j})P(D|f_j, e_{a_j})}{\sum_f P(f_j|e_{a_j})P(D|f_j, e_{a_j})}, \tag{3}$$

$$P(a_j|a_{j-1}, D) = \frac{P(a_j|a_{j-1})P(D|a_j, a_{j-1})}{\sum_{a_j} P(a_j|a_{j-1})P(D|a_j, a_{j-1})}. \tag{4}$$

With an additional latent domain layer, it becomes crucial to train the model in an efficient way. As suggested by Eq. 3 and 4, we could simplify training by breaking up the estimation process into two steps. That is, we train alignment parameters, $P(\cdot|\ \cdot)$ or domain parameters, $P(D|\ \cdot,\ \cdot)$ first, hold them fixed before training the other kind of the parameters.[3] Instead, in this work we design an algorithm that trains both of them simultaneously via training domain-conditioned parameters $P(\cdot|\ ,\cdot,\ D)$ directly.

[2] Note that $P(\mathbf{f},\ \mathbf{a}|\ \mathbf{e},\ D)$ contains their former $P(\mathbf{f},\ \mathbf{a}|\ \mathbf{e})$ as special case, i.e., $P(\mathbf{f},\ \mathbf{a}|\ \mathbf{e},\ D) = \frac{P(\mathbf{f},\ \mathbf{a}|\ \mathbf{e})P(D|\ \mathbf{f},\ \mathbf{a},\ \mathbf{e})}{\sum_{\mathbf{f}}\sum_{\mathbf{a}} P(\mathbf{f},\ \mathbf{a}|\ \mathbf{e})P(D|\ \mathbf{f},\ \mathbf{a},\ \mathbf{e})}$.

[3] This training scheme is in fact applied in the work of Cuong and Sima'an (2014a), however, for a different purpose.

### 3.1 Training

Basically, our model can be viewed as having a set, $\Theta$ of $N$ subsets of domain-conditioned parameters, $\Theta_D$ for $N$ different domains, i.e., $\Theta = \{\Theta_{D_1},\ \ldots,\ \Theta_{D_N}\}$. In this work, to simplify the learning problem we assume that the domains are very *different* from each other. If this assumption does not hold, the learning problem would shift from *single-label* learning to *multiple-label* learning. We leave this extension for future work.

Our training procedure seeks the parameters $\Theta$ that maximize the log-likelihood, $\mathcal{L}$ of the data: $\mathcal{L} = \sum_{\langle \mathbf{f},\ \mathbf{e}\rangle} \log \sum_D \sum_{\mathbf{a}} P_{\Theta_D}(\mathbf{f},\ \mathbf{e},\ D,\ \mathbf{a})$. There, however, does not exist a closed-form solution for maximizing $\mathcal{L}$, and EM comes as an alternative solution to fit the model. EM maximizes $\mathcal{L}$ via block-coordinate ascent on a "free energy" lower bound $\mathcal{F}(q,\ \Theta)$ (Neal and Hinton, 1999), using an auxiliary distribution $q$ over both the latent variables: $\mathcal{F}(q,\ \Theta) = \sum_{\langle \mathbf{f},\ \mathbf{e}\rangle} \sum_D \sum_{\mathbf{a}} q \log \frac{P_{\Theta_D}(\mathbf{a},\ D,\ \mathbf{f},\ \mathbf{e})}{q}$.

In the **E**-step of the EM algorithm, we fix $\Theta$ and aim to find the distribution $q^*$ that maximizes $\mathcal{F}(q, \Theta)$ over the heterogeneous data. Simple mathematics lead to $\mathcal{F}(q,\ \Theta) = \sum_{\langle \mathbf{f},\ \mathbf{e}\rangle} \log P_{\Theta}(\mathbf{f},\ \mathbf{e}) - KL[q\ ||\ P_{\Theta_D}(\mathbf{a},\ D|\ \mathbf{f},\ \mathbf{e})]$, where $KL[\cdot\ ||\ \cdot]$ is the Kullback-Leiber divergence between two distributions. The distribution $q^*$ can be thus derived as

$$\begin{aligned} q^* &= \text{argmax}_q\, \mathcal{F}(q,\ \Theta) \\ &= \text{argmin}_q\, KL[q\ ||\ P_{\Theta_D}(\mathbf{a},\ D|\ \mathbf{f},\ \mathbf{e})] \\ &= \frac{P_{\Theta_D}(\mathbf{f},\ \mathbf{a}|\ \mathbf{e},\ D)}{\sum_{\mathbf{a}} P_{\Theta_D}(\mathbf{f},\ \mathbf{a}|\ \mathbf{e},\ D)} P_{\Theta_D}(D|\ \mathbf{f},\ \mathbf{e}). \end{aligned}$$

Here, $P_{\Theta_D}(D|\ \mathbf{f},\ \mathbf{e})$ aims to exploit the contrast between the domain-sensitive alignment statistics. Assigning higher probability to one domain forces lower probability assignment to other domains.

Note that $P_{\Theta_D}(\mathbf{f},\ \mathbf{a}|\ \mathbf{e},\ D)$ is given in Eq. 2 and $\sum_{\mathbf{a}} P_{\Theta_D}(\mathbf{f},\ \mathbf{a}|\ \mathbf{e},\ D)$ can be computed efficiently using dynamic programming.[4] Meanwhile, $P_{\Theta_D}(D|\ \mathbf{f},\ \mathbf{e})$ can be derived by Bayes' rule, i.e.,

$$P_{\Theta_D}(D|\ \mathbf{f},\ \mathbf{e}) \propto P_{\Theta_D}(\mathbf{f},\ \mathbf{e}|\ D)P_{\Theta_D}(D).$$

Here, the estimation of the domain prior parameters is easy, $P_{\Theta_D}(D) \propto \sum_{\langle \mathbf{f},\ \mathbf{e}\rangle} P_{\Theta_D}(D|\ \mathbf{f},\ \mathbf{e})$. The estimation of $P_{\Theta_D}(\mathbf{f},\ \mathbf{e}|\ D)$ raises a task of defining a

[4] Its time complexity is $\mathcal{O}(J \times I^2)$ for each sentence pair $\langle \mathbf{f},\ \mathbf{e}\rangle$ with their length $J$ and $I$ respectively.

**E-step** $\forall D \in \{D_1, \ldots, D_N\}$ do

$$c(D;\, \mathbf{f},\, \mathbf{e}) = P^{(c)}(D|\, \mathbf{f},\, \mathbf{e})$$

$$c(f|\, e;\, \mathbf{f},\, \mathbf{e},\, D) = P^{(c)}(D|\, \mathbf{f},\, \mathbf{e}) \sum_{\mathbf{a}} P^{(c)}(\mathbf{a}|\, \mathbf{f},\, \mathbf{e},\, D) \sum_{j=1}^{J} \delta(f, f_j) \sum_{i=0}^{I} \delta(e,\, e_i)$$

$$c(i|\, i';\, \mathbf{f},\, \mathbf{e},\, D) = P^{(c)}(D|\, \mathbf{f},\, \mathbf{e}) \sum_{\mathbf{a}} P^{(c)}(\mathbf{a}|\, \mathbf{f},\, \mathbf{e},\, D) \sum_{j=1}^{J} \delta(a_j,\, i)\delta(a_{j-1},\, i')$$

**M-step** $\forall D \in \{D_1, \ldots, D_N\}$ do

$$P^{(+)}(f|e, D) = \frac{\sum_{\langle \mathbf{f},\mathbf{e}\rangle} c(f|e; \mathbf{f}, \mathbf{e}, D)}{\sum_f \sum_{\langle \mathbf{f},\mathbf{e}\rangle} c(f|e; \mathbf{f}, \mathbf{e}, D)} \quad P^{(+)}(i|i', D) = \frac{\sum_{\langle \mathbf{f},\mathbf{e}\rangle} c(i|i'; \mathbf{f}, \mathbf{e}, D)}{\sum_i \sum_{\langle \mathbf{f},\mathbf{e}\rangle} c(i|i'; \mathbf{f}, \mathbf{e}, D)} \quad P^{(+)}(D) = \frac{\sum_{\langle \mathbf{f},\mathbf{e}\rangle} c(D; \mathbf{f}, \mathbf{e})}{\sum_D \sum_{\langle \mathbf{f},\mathbf{e}\rangle} c(D; \mathbf{f}, \mathbf{e})}$$

Figure 3: Pseudocode for the training algorithm for the latent domain HMM alignment model. Note that notation $P^{(c)}$ denotes current iteration estimates, and $P^{(+)}$ denotes the re-estimates.

generative process for every sentence pair in the heterogeneous data with respect to a specific domain. Following (Cuong and Sima'an, 2014b), we factor it into two kinds of models in a symmetrized strategy: $P_{\Theta_D}(\mathbf{f},\, \mathbf{e}|\, D) \propto \big(P_{\Theta_D}(\mathbf{e}|\, D)P_{\Theta_D}(\mathbf{f}|\, \mathbf{e},\, D) + P_{\Theta_D}(\mathbf{f}|\, D)P_{\Theta_D}(\mathbf{e}|\, \mathbf{f},\, D)\big)$.

Basically, $P_{\Theta_D}(\cdot|\, \cdot,\, D)$ can be thought of as the domain-conditioned translation models, aiming to model how well a target/source sentence is generated over a source/target sentence with respect to a domain.[5] Meanwhile, $P_{\Theta_D}(\cdot|\, D)$ can be thought of as the domain-conditioned language models (LMs), aiming to model how fluent a source/target sentence with respect to a domain. For simplicity, once the domain-conditioned LMs are trained, they will stay *fixed* during training, i.e., LM probabilities are not parameters in our model.

In the **M**-step of the EM algorithm, we fix the derived $q^*$ and aim to find the parameter set $\Theta^*$ that maximizes $\mathcal{F}(q, \Theta)$ over the data. This can be (easily) done by using $q^*$ to softly fill in the values of $\mathbf{a}$ and $D$ to estimate model parameters.

### Pseudocode

In summary, the model has three kinds of parameters - word translation, word transition, and domain prior parameters. We now summarize the training via presenting the pseudocode.

First, we present expected count notations with respect to domains for the parameters. We use $c(f|\, e;\, \mathbf{f},\, \mathbf{e},\, D)$ to denote the expected counts that word $e$ aligns to word $f$. We use $c(i|\, i';\, \mathbf{f},\, \mathbf{e},\, D)$ to denote the expected counts that two certain consecutive source words $j$ and $j-1$ align to two target words $i$ and $i'$ respectively, i.e., $j$ aligns to $i$ and $j-1$ aligns to $i'$. Finally, we also use $c(D;\, \mathbf{f},\, \mathbf{e})$ to denote the expected count of domain priors. Note that all the expected counts are in the translation $(\mathbf{f}|\, \mathbf{e})$.

Figure 3 represents the pseudocode.

## 4 Learning with Partial Supervision

We now discuss remaining issues on how to guide the learning with partial supervision, i.e., how to use the given domain information of seed samples to guide the learning.

**Number of Domains** The values of $D \in [1..(N+1)]$ depends on the $N$ available seed samples plus the so-called "out-domain," i.e., the part of the heterogeneous data that is dissimilar to all of the $N$ sample domains.

**Parameter Initialization** We first discuss how to initialize the domain prior parameters. If a sentence pair $\langle \mathbf{f},\, \mathbf{e}\rangle$ belongs to a sample with a pre-specified domain $D_i$, we initialize $P(D_i|\, \mathbf{f},\, \mathbf{e})$ close to 1, and, $P(D_{i'}|\, \mathbf{f},\, \mathbf{e})$ close to 0 for other domains $i'$, $i' \neq i$. Furthermore, we uniformly create the domain prior parameters for the rest of sentence pairs.

Uniform initialization for the domain-conditioned alignment parameters is also a reasonable option. Nevertheless, a more effective way is to make use of the domain-specific seed samples and the pool of the rest sentence pairs in the heterogeneous data.[6] That is, we train the model on each of the samples, assign-

[5]Note that $P_{\Theta_D}(\cdot|\, \cdot,\, D) = \sum_{\mathbf{a}} P_{\Theta_D}(\cdot,\, \mathbf{a}|\, \cdot,\, D)$ and it can be thus computed efficiently using dynamic programming.

[6]During the initialization, we assume that the pool of the rest sentence pairs in the heterogeneous data is the exemplifying sample of the out-domain.

ing the derived probabilities as the initialization for their corresponding domain-conditioned alignment parameters. In our implementation, one EM iteration is usually dedicated for this. It should be noted that we ignore the domain prior parameters in the model during the period.

**Parameter Constraints** During training, it would be also necessary to keep the domain prior parameters fixed for all sentence pairs that belong to seed samples. This can be thought of as the constraints derived from the partial knowledge, guiding the learning to a desirable parameter space.

**Domain-conditioned LMs training** We now discuss how to train the domain-conditioned LMs with partial supervision. It would be reasonable to use the domain-specific seed samples to train their exemplifying domain-conditioned LMs, and the pool of the rest sentence pairs to train the out-domain LMs. Nevertheless, the out-domain LMs trained on such a big corpus could dominate the other domain-conditioned LMs. Following Cuong and Sima'an (2014b), we rather create a "pseudo" out-domain sample to train the out-domain LMs, i.e., the creation is via an inspired burn-in period. In brief, an EM iteration is dedicated just to compute $P(D_{OUT}|\ \mathbf{f},\ \mathbf{e})$ for all sentences, ranking them and select a small subset with highest score as the (on the fly) pseudo out-domain sample.

Note that our partial learning framework is very simple. There are various advanced learning framework that are also applicable with the partial supervision, e.g., Posterior Regularization (Ganchev et al., 2010). This leaves much space for future work.

## 5 Domain-conditioned Decoding

At test time, assigning each sentence pair to a single most likely domain (hard decision) is likely to result in sub-optimal performance.[7] Instead we average over domains (soft decision) while predicting the translation. Formally for each sentence pair, $\langle \mathbf{e},\ \mathbf{f} \rangle$, we can find their best Viterbi alignment, $\hat{\mathbf{a}}$ as follows:

$$\begin{aligned}\hat{\mathbf{a}} &= \text{argmax}_{\mathbf{a}} \sum\nolimits_D P(\mathbf{f}, \mathbf{a}, D|\mathbf{e}) \\ &= \text{argmax}_{\mathbf{a}} \sum\nolimits_D P(\mathbf{f}, \mathbf{a}|\mathbf{e}, D)P(D|\mathbf{e}) \\ &= \text{argmax}_{\mathbf{a}} \sum\nolimits_D P(\mathbf{f}, \mathbf{a}|\mathbf{e}, D)P(\mathbf{e}|D)P(D).\end{aligned}$$

Here, we derive the last equation by applying Bayes' rule to $P(D|\ \mathbf{e})$, i.e., $P(D|\ \mathbf{e}) \propto P(\mathbf{e}|\ D)P(D)$. Interestingly, our Viterbi decoding now relies on a mix of domain-conditioned statistics for each sentence pair. The computing of term $\sum_D(\mathbf{a})$ for all possible alignments, $\mathbf{a}$, however, is intractable, making the search problem difficult. Inspired by Liang et al. (2006), we opt instead for a heuristic objective function as follows[8]:

$$\hat{\mathbf{a}} = \underset{\mathbf{a}}{\text{argmax}} \prod\nolimits_D P(\mathbf{f},\ \mathbf{a}|\ \mathbf{e}, D)^{P(\mathbf{e}|\ D)P(D)}. \quad (5)$$

Here, note that $\prod p$ is a lower bound for $\sum p$, when $0 \leq p \leq 1$, according to Jensen's inequality. With Eq. 5, it is straightforward to design a dynamic programming algorithm to decoding, e.g., the Viterbi algorithm. In practice, we observe that the approximation yields good results. Later experiments on word alignment will present this in detail.

## 6 Experimental Setup

In the following experiments, we use three heterogeneous English-Spanish corpora consisting of $1M$, $2M$ and $4M$ sentence pairs respectively. These corpora combine two parts. The first part respectively $0.7M$, $1.7M$ and $3.7M$ is collected from multiple domains and resources including EuroParl (Koehn, 2005), Common Crawl, United Nation, News Commentary. The second part consists of three domain-exemplifying samples consisting of roughly $100K$ sentence pairs for each one (total $300K$). Each of these three samples (manually collected by a commercial partner) exemplifies a specific domain related to **Legal**, **Hardware** and **Pharmacy**.

**Outlook** In Section 7 we examine the word alignment yielded by the HMM alignment model and our latent domain HMM alignment model. In Section 8 we proceed further to examine the translation produced by derived SMT systems.

[7] Later experiments on word alignment will confirm this.

[8] Alternative solutions could be Lagrangian relaxation-based decoder (DeNero and Macherey, 2011; Chang et al., 2014).

| Model | Domain Prior | Prec.↑ | Δ | Rec.↑ | Δ | AER↓ | Δ |
|---|---|---|---|---|---|---|---|
| | | 1 **Million** | | | | | |
| **Model 4** (ref.) | - | 71.56 | - | 64.59 | - | 32.10 | - |
| **Baseline** | - | 66.95 | - | 61.29 | - | 36.00 | - |
| **Latent** | Pharmacy | 67.85 | **+0.90** | 61.72 | **+0.43** | 35.36 | **-0.64** |
| | Legal | 67.57 | **+0.62** | 62.29 | **+1.00** | 35.17 | **-0.83** |
| | Hardware | 69.41 | **+2.46** | 63.58 | **+2.29** | 33.63 | **-2.37** |
| | **Legal + Hardware + Software** | **69.64** | **+2.69** | **63.30** | **+2.01** | **33.68** | **-2.32** |
| | | 2 **Million** | | | | | |
| **Model 4** (ref.) | - | 74.13 | - | 65.30 | - | 30.56 | - |
| **Baseline** | - | 68.34 | - | 61.58 | - | 35.22 | - |
| **Latent** | Pharmacy | 68.85 | **+0.51** | 62.58 | **+1.00** | 34.43 | **-0.79** |
| | Legal | 69.98 | **+1.64** | 64.01 | **+2.43** | 33.13 | **-2.09** |
| | Hardware | 69.45 | **+1.11** | 63.23 | **+1.65** | 33.81 | **-1.41** |
| | **Legal + Hardware + Software** | **71.51** | **+3.17** | **63.87** | **+2.29** | **32.53** | **-2.69** |
| | | 4 **Million** | | | | | |
| **Model 4** (ref.) | - | 75.53 | - | 65.95 | - | 29.58 | - |
| **Baseline** | - | 69.37 | - | 64.30 | - | 33.26 | - |
| **Latent** | Pharmacy | 69.69 | **+0.32** | 62.80 | -1.50 | 33.94 | +0.68 |
| | Legal | 70.51 | **+1.14** | 63.94 | -0.36 | 32.93 | **-0.33** |
| | Hardware | 71.75 | **+2.38** | 64.44 | **+0.14** | 32.10 | **-1.16** |
| | **Legal + Hardware + Software** | **72.16** | **+2.79** | **64.30** | ±0.0 | **31.99** | **-1.27** |

Table 1: Alignment accuracy over heterogeneous corpora.

## 7 Word Alignment Experiment

For alignment accuracy evaluation, we use a data set of 100 sentence pairs with their "golden" alignment from Graca et al. (2008). Here, the golden alignment consists of *sure* links ($S$) and *possible* links ($P$) for each sentence pair. Counting the set of generating *alignment* links ($A$), we report the word alignment accuracy by *precision* ($\frac{|A \cap P|}{|P|}$), *recall* ($\frac{|A \cap S|}{|S|}$), *alignment error rate* (AER) ($1 - \frac{|A \cap P| + |A \cap S|}{|A| + |S|}$) (Och and Ney, 2003).[9]

For all experiments, we use the same training configuration for both the baseline/the latent domain alignment model: 5 iterations for IBM model 1/the latent domain model; 3 iterations for HMM alignment model/the latent domain model. For evaluation, we first align the sentence pairs in both directions and then symmetrize them using the *grow-diag-final* heuristic (Koehn et al., 2003).

For reference we also report the performance of a considerably more expressive Model 4, capable of capturing more structure, but at the expense of intractable inference. Using MGIZA++ (Gao and Vogel, 2008), we run 5 iterations for training Model 1, 3 iterations for training the HMM alignment model, Model 3 and Model 4.

### 7.1 Learning with Single Domain

We first examine the binary case, where we are given domain information in advance for each kind of samples **only**, e.g., Legal, or Pharmacy, or Hardware. For the different sizes of the heterogeneous data ($1M$, $2M$ and $4M$) the seed sample size is thus $10\%$, $5\%$ and $2.5\%$ respectively. Note that in such cases, training the latent domain alignment model induces two domain-conditioned statistics: in-domain vs. out-domain ($D_1$ and $D_2$ respectively). Once the model is trained, we combine the induced domain-conditioned statistics together (Eq. 5) and examine the produced word alignment output.

Table 1 presents the results. Most importantly, it shows that as long as providing domain information for reasonably large enough data, learning the latent domain alignment model notably improves the word alignment accuracy. For instance, given in advance the domain information for a sample of $10\%$, and $5\%$ of the heterogeneous corpora, our model consistently improves the word alignment accuracy in

[9]Note that better results correspond to larger Precision, Recall and to smaller AER.

all cases. Meanwhile, given in advance the domain information for a relatively small sample of 2.5% of the heterogeneous data, the results are mixed. We obtain a good performance/slightly better performance/worse performance with the case of Hardware/Legal/Pharmacy respectively.

**What do domain-conditioned statistics look like?**

To have an idea what the induced statistics look like, we investigate their **conditional entropy**. Here, we present the conditional entropy for the domain-confused/-conditioned word translation statistics induced from the HMM alignment model/its latent domain model. Note that similar results are observed for transition tables.

| Model | Prior | Statistics | $H$(F\| E) |
|---|---|---|---|
| **Baseline** | - | Domain-confused | **1348.53** |
| **Latent** | Hardware | $D_1$-conditioned | **1124.43** |
| | | $D_2$-conditioned | **1354.58** |
| | Legal | $D_1$-conditioned | **1104.58** |
| | | $D_2$-conditioned | **1385.35** |
| | Pharmacy | $D_1$-conditioned | **1115.52** |
| | | $D_2$-conditioned | **1342.54** |

Table 2: Conditional entropy of the statistics.

Formally, for a translation table, $\langle F,\ E\rangle$, its conditional entropy, $H(F|\ E)$ can be estimated from its possible word pairs, $\langle e,\ f\rangle$: $H(F|\ E) = -\sum_e P(e) \sum_f P(f|\ e) \log P(f|\ e)$. Table 2 reveals that the induced $D_1$-conditioned statistics need much less *bits* to represent than the induced domain-confused statistics, e.g., 1124.43, 1104.58, 1115.52 vs. 1348.53. This implies the induced $D_1$-conditioned statistics are much more **predictable** compared to the domain-confused statistics. Meanwhile, the induced $D_2$-conditioned statistics are similar to the domain-confused statistics in terms of the conditional entropy, e.g., 1354.58, 1385.35, 1342.54 vs. 1348.53.

## 7.2 Learning with Multiple Domains

It would be more interesting to learn the latent domain alignment model for multiple domains, rather than learning with each of them separately. In detail, using **all** the seed samples from different domains, we aim to learn four different domain-conditioned statistics simultaneously. Under this setting, we obtain good results, as described in Table 1. For the two cases with the training corpora of 2M and 4M sentence pairs respectively, learning with the combining domain prior knowledge produces the best word alignment accuracy compared to the rest. In the last case with the training corpus of 1M sentence pairs, learning with the combining domain prior knowledge produces compatible with the case of Hardware, i.e., the best binary domain case.

Table 1 also reveals that the performance of our model approaches Model 4, even though Model 4 is much more complex and computationally expensive.

**Domain-conditioned statistics combination**

We also investigate the relation between the number of domain-conditioned statistics "involved" in the Viterbi decoding (Eq. 5) and the word alignment accuracy. Table 3 presents the results in case of using only the induced $D_1$-/, $D_2$-/, $D_3$-/, $D_4$-conditioned statistics separately, and also using their different combinations. Interestingly, we observe that using more domain-conditioned statistics for decoding incrementally improves the word alignment accuracy over the heterogeneous data. While the domain-conditioned statistics are very different in their characteristics from each other, the results reveal how they are *complementary* to the others, conveying a mix of domains for each sentence pair.

| Decoding's Statistics | Prec.↑ | Rec.↑ | AER↓ |
|---|---|---|---|
| Hard Decision (ref.) | 68.49 | 62.80 | 34.48 |
| $D_1$ (Pharmacy) | 64.78 | 59.86 | 37.78 |
| $D_2$ (Legal) | 66.54 | 61.15 | 36.27 |
| $D_3$ (Hardware) | 66.98 | 61.36 | 35.95 |
| $D_4$ (OUT) | 68.46 | 63.01 | 34.38 |
| $D_1 + D_2$ | 66.80 | 61.72 | 35.84 |
| $D_1 + D_2 + D_3$ | 68.54 | 62.80 | 34.46 |
| $D_1 + D_2 + D_3 + D_4$ | **69.64** | **63.30** | **33.68** |

Table 3: Domain-conditioned statistics combination for Viterbi decoding. The reported results are for the heterogeneous corpus of 1M sentence pairs. Similar results are observed for other training data.

Finally, it is also tempting to make a comparison between the *hard* vs. *soft* domain assignment in Viterbi decoding. Here, for hard domain decision we simply do decoding with the following objective function: $\hat{\mathbf{a}} = \mathrm{argmax}_{\mathbf{a}} P(\mathbf{f},\ \mathbf{a}|\ \mathbf{e}, \hat{D})$, where $\hat{D} = \mathrm{argmax}_D P(D|\ \mathbf{e})$. Table 3 presents the results. It reveals that a soft domain assignment on the domain of sentence pairs results in a better alignment accuracy than a hard domain assignment.[10]

## 8 Translation Experiment

In this section, we investigate the contribution of our model in terms of the translation accuracy. Here, we run experiments on the heterogeneous corpora of 1M, 2M, and 4M sentence pairs, testing the translation accuracy over four different domain-specific test sets related to News, Pharmacy, Legal, and Hardware.

We use a standard state-of-the-art phrase-based system as the baseline. Our dense features include MOSES (Koehn et al., 2007) baseline features, plus hierarchical lexicalized reordering model features (Galley and Manning, 2008), and the word-level feature derived from IBM model 1 score, c.f., (Och et al., 2004).[11] The interpolated 5-grams LMs with Kneser-Ney are trained on a very large monolingual corpus of 2B words. We tune the systems using k-best batch MIRA (Cherry and Foster, 2012). Finally, we use MOSES (Koehn et al., 2007) as decoder.

Our system has exactly the same setting with the baseline, except: (1) To learn the translation, we use the alignment result derived from our latent domain HMM alignment model, rather than the HMM alignment model; and (2) We replace the word-level feature with our four domain-conditioned word-level features derived from the latent domain IBM model 1. Here, note that our latent model is learned with the supervision from the combining domain knowledge of all three domain-specific seed samples.

| Data | System | BLEU↑ | METEOR↑ | TER↓ |
|---|---|---|---|---|
| | | **News test** | | |
| 1M | Model 4 (ref.) | 23.6 | 30.8 | 58.3 |
| | Baseline | 23.2 | 30.6 | 58.9 |
| | Our System | 23.5/**+0.3** | 30.8/+0.2 | 58.7/-0.2 |
| 2M | Baseline | 25.9 | 32.4 | 56.1 |
| | Our System | 26.3/**+0.4** | 32.6/**+0.2** | 55.6/**-0.5** |
| 4M | Baseline | 26.8 | 33.0 | 55.0 |
| | Our System | 27.0/**+0.2** | 33.1/+0.1 | 54.7/**-0.3** |
| | | **Pharmacy** | | |
| 1M | Model 4 (ref.) | 54.7 | 43.8 | 33.4 |
| | Baseline | 53.9 | 43.4 | 34.6 |
| | Our System | 54.4/**+0.5** | 43.8/**+0.4** | 34.0/**-0.6** |
| 2M | Baseline | 54.5 | 43.7 | 34.4 |
| | Our System | 55.3/**+0.8** | 44.3/**+0.6** | 33.5/**-0.9** |
| 4M | Baseline | 54.8 | 43.9 | 33.8 |
| | Our System | 55.0/**+0.2** | 44.0/+0.1 | 33.7/-0.1 |
| | | **Legal** | | |
| 1M | Model 4 (ref.) | 56.6 | 44.7 | 34.1 |
| | Baseline | 56.0 | 44.2 | 35.0 |
| | Our System | 57.2/**+1.2** | 44.4/+0.2 | 34.0/**-1.0** |
| 2M | Baseline | 55.8 | 43.9 | 35.4 |
| | Our System | 58.3/**+2.5** | 44.7/**+0.8** | **33.4/-2.0** |
| 4M | Baseline | 55.9 | 43.9 | 34.3 |
| | Our System | 57.3/**+1.4** | 44.4/**+0.5** | 33.4/**-0.9** |
| | | **Hardware** | | |
| 1M | Model 4 (ref.) | 75.4 | 53.6 | 17.7 |
| | Baseline | 74.9 | 53.1 | 19.0 |
| | Our System | 76.8/**+1.9** | 53.9/**+0.8** | 17.3/**-1.7** |
| 2M | Baseline | 75.7 | 53.5 | 18.6 |
| | Our System | 77.4/**+1.7** | 54.3/**+0.8** | 17.0/**-1.6** |
| 4M | Baseline | 77.1 | 54.2 | 17.3 |
| | Our System | 77.9/**+0.8** | 54.5/**+0.3** | 16.7/**-0.6** |

Table 4: Metric scores for the systems, which are averages over multiple runs. Bold results indicate that the comparison is significant over the baseline.

For the News translation task, we tune systems on the News-test 2008 of $2,051$ sentence pairs and test them on the News-test 2013 of $3,000$ sentence pairs from the WMT 2013 shared task (Bojar et al., 2013). For the Pharmacy, Legal, and Hardware translation tasks, we tune systems on three domain-specific dev sets of $1,000$ sentence pairs and test them on three domain-specific test sets of $1,016$, $1,326$ and $1,721$ sentence pairs. We report three metrics - BLEU (Papineni et al., 2002), METEOR (Denkowski and Lavie, 2011) and TER (Snover et al., 2006), with statistical significance at $95\%$ confidence interval

[10] Note that similar results are also observed for training, in which a soft domain assignment using soft EM produces better alignment accuracy than a hard domain assignment using hard EM. (See (Gao et al., 2011) for reference to hard domain assignment to training data.) This is perhaps due to the characteristics of the data we use. For instance, News sentence pairs are useful for translating Legal, Financial or EuroParl to varying degrees.

[11] For every phrase pair $\langle \tilde{f},\ \tilde{e} \rangle$ with their length of $m_{\tilde{f}}$ and $l_{\tilde{e}}$ respectively, the lexical feature estimates a probability in Model 1 style between their word pairs $\langle f_j,\ e_i \rangle$ (i.e. $P(\tilde{f}|\ \tilde{e}) = \frac{\epsilon}{l_{\tilde{e}}} \prod_{j=1}^{m_{\tilde{f}}} \sum_{i=1}^{l_{\tilde{e}}} P(f_j|e_i)$). Note that adding word-level features from both translation sides does not help much, as observed by (Och et al., 2004). We thus add only an one from a translation side.

under paired bootstrap re-sampling.[12] For every system reported, we run the optimizer three times, before running MultEval (Clark et al., 2011) for resampling and significance testing.

| Data | BLEU↑ | METEOR↑ | TER↓ |
|---|---|---|---|
| 1M | +1.0 | +0.4 | -0.9 |
| 2M | +1.4 | +0.6 | -1.3 |
| 4M | +0.7 | +0.3 | -0.5 |

Table 5: Averaged improvements across the tasks.

**Results** are in Table 4, showing significant improvements across four different test sets over different heterogeneous corpora sizes. Table 5 gives a summary of the improvements. On average, over heterogeneous corpora of 1M, 2M and 4M sentence pairs, our system outperforms the baseline by 1.0 BLEU, 1.4 BLEU and 0.7 BLEU, respectively. Finally, we observe that our system produces comparably good performance to the MGIZA++-based system. When 1M data is considered, on *three* of *four* tasks, our system produces at least compatible translation accuracy to the corresponding MGIZA++-based system.

Further analysis reveals that the improvement is due to not only the reduction in alignment error rate, but also the use of the domain-sensitive lexical features. Moreover, the domain-sensitive lexical features is particularly useful when the domain of the test data matches with the domain of seed samplers. This is also widely observed in the literature, e.g., see (Eidelman et al., 2012; Hasler et al., 2014; Hu et al., 2014).

## 9 Related Work and Conclusion

In terms of domain-conditioned statistics for word alignment, a distantly related research line (Tam et al., 2007; Zhao and Xing, 2008) focuses on using document topics to improve the word alignment. In terms of learning word alignment with partial supervision, another distantly related research line focuses on semi-supervised training with partial manual alignments (Fraser and Marcu, 2006; Gao and Vogel, 2010; Gao et al., 2010). Finally, recent work also focuses on data selection (Kirchhoff and Bilmes, 2014; Cuong and Sima'an, 2014b), mixture models (Carpuat et al., 2014), instance weighting (Foster et al., 2010) and latent variable models (Cuong and Sima'an, 2014a) over heterogeneous corpora.

One main contribution of this work is the novelty of exploring the quality of word alignment in heterogeneous corpora. This, surprisingly, has not received much attention thus far (see the study of Bach et al. (2008) and Gao et al. (2011) for reference in the literature). Another major contribution of this work is a learning framework for latent domain word alignment with partial supervision using seed domains. We present its benefits for improving not only the word alignment accuracy, but also the translation accuracy resulting SMT systems produce. We hope this study sparks a new research direction for using domain samples, which is cheap to gather, but has not been exploited before.

One obvious direction for future work might be to integrate the model into fertility-based alignment models (Brown et al., 1993), as well as other recently advanced alignment frameworks, e.g., (Simion et al., 2013; Tamura et al., 2014; Chang et al., 2014). Another interesting direction might be to integrate our model into advanced mixing multiple translation models, improving SMT systems trained on the heterogeneous data (Razmara et al., 2012; Sennrich et al., 2013; Carpuat et al., 2014). Finally, an open question is whether it is possible to learn the latent domain alignment model in a fully unsupervised style. This challenge deserves more attention in future work.

## Acknowledgements

We are indebted to Ivan Titov and three anonymous reviewers for their constructive comments on earlier versions. The first author is supported by the EXPERT (EXPloiting Empirical appRoaches to Translation) Initial Training Network (ITN) of the European Union's Seventh Framework Programme. The second author is supported by VICI grant nr. 277-89-002 from the Netherlands Organization for Scientific Research (NWO).

[12]Note that better results correspond to larger BLEU, METEOR and to smaller TER.

## References


Nguyen Bach, Qin Gao, and Stephan Vogel. 2008. Improving word alignment with language model based confidence scores. In *Proceedings of the Third Workshop on Statistical Machine Translation*.

Ondřej Bojar, Christian Buck, Chris Callison-Burch, Christian Federmann, Barry Haddow, Philipp Koehn, Christof Monz, Matt Post, Radu Soricut, and Lucia Specia. 2013. Findings of the 2013 Workshop on Statistical Machine Translation. In *Proceedings of the Eighth Workshop on Statistical Machine Translation*.

Peter F. Brown, Vincent J. Della Pietra, Stephen A. Della Pietra, and Robert L. Mercer. 1993. The mathematics of statistical machine translation: parameter estimation. *Comput. Linguist.*, 19:263–311, June.

Marine Carpuat, Cyril Goutte, and George Foster. 2014. Linear mixture models for robust machine translation. In *Proceedings of the Ninth Workshop on Statistical Machine Translation*.

Yin-Wen Chang, Alexander M. Rush, John DeNero, and Michael Collins. 2014. A constrained viterbi relaxation for bidirectional word alignment. In *Proceedings of ACL*.

Colin Cherry and George Foster. 2012. Batch tuning strategies for statistical machine translation. In *Proceedings of NAACL HLT*.

Jonathan H. Clark, Chris Dyer, Alon Lavie, and Noah A. Smith. 2011. Better hypothesis testing for statistical machine translation: Controlling for optimizer instability. In *Proceedings of HLT: Short Papers*.

Hoang Cuong and Khalil Sima'an. 2014a. Latent domain phrase-based models for adaptation. In *Proceedings of EMNLP*.

Hoang Cuong and Khalil Sima'an. 2014b. Latent domain translation models in mix-of-domains haystack. In *Proceedings of COLING*.

John DeNero and Klaus Macherey. 2011. Model-based aligner combination using dual decomposition. In *Proceedings of ACL*.

Michael Denkowski and Alon Lavie. 2011. Meteor 1.3: Automatic metric for reliable optimization and evaluation of machine translation systems. In *Proceedings of the Sixth Workshop on Statistical Machine Translation*, WMT '11.

Vladimir Eidelman, Jordan Boyd-Graber, and Philip Resnik. 2012. Topic models for dynamic translation model adaptation. In *Proceedings of ACL: Short Papers*.

George Foster, Cyril Goutte, and Roland Kuhn. 2010. Discriminative instance weighting for domain adaptation in statistical machine translation. In *Proceedings of EMNLP*.

Alexander Fraser and Daniel Marcu. 2006. Semi-supervised training for statistical word alignment. In *Proceedings of ACL*.

Michel Galley and Christopher D. Manning. 2008. A simple and effective hierarchical phrase reordering model. In *Proceedings of EMNLP*.

Kuzman Ganchev, João Graça, Jennifer Gillenwater, and Ben Taskar. 2010. Posterior regularization for structured latent variable models. *J. Mach. Learn. Res.*, 11:2001–2049, August.

Qin Gao and Stephan Vogel. 2008. Parallel implementations of word alignment tool. In *Software Engineering, Testing, and Quality Assurance for Natural Language Processing*, SETQA-NLP '08.

Qin Gao and Stephan Vogel. 2010. Consensus versus expertise: A case study of word alignment with mechanical turk. In *Proceedings of the NAACL HLT 2010 Workshop on Creating Speech and Language Data with Amazon's Mechanical Turk*, CSLDAMT '10.

Qin Gao, Nguyen Bach, and Stephan Vogel. 2010. A semi-supervised word alignment algorithm with partial manual alignments. In *Proceedings of the Joint Fifth Workshop on Statistical Machine Translation and MetricsMATR*, WMT '10.

Qin Gao, Will Lewis, Chris Quirk, and Mei-Yuh Hwang. 2011. Incremental training and intentional over-fitting of word alignment. In *Proceedings of MT Summit XIII*.

Joao Graca, Joana Paulo Pardal, Luisa Coheur, and Diamantino Caseiro. 2008. Building a golden collection of parallel multi-language word alignment. In *Proceedings of the Sixth International Conference on Language Resources and Evaluation (LREC'08)*.

Joao Graca, Kuzman Ganchev, and Ben Taskar. 2010. Learning tractable word alignment models with complex constraints. *Comput. Linguist.*, 36(3):481–504.

Eva Hasler, Phil Blunsom, Philipp Koehn, and Barry Haddow. 2014. Dynamic topic adaptation for phrase-based mt. In *Proceedings of EACL*.

Yuening Hu, Ke Zhai, Vladimir Eidelman, and Jordan Boyd-Graber. 2014. Polylingual tree-based topic models for translation domain adaptation. In *Proceedings of ACL*.

Katrin Kirchhoff and Jeff Bilmes. 2014. Submodularity for data selection in machine translation. In *Proceedings of EMNLP*.

Philipp Koehn, Franz Josef Och, and Daniel Marcu. 2003. Statistical phrase-based translation. In *Proceedings of NAACL*.

Philipp Koehn, Hieu Hoang, Alexandra Birch, Chris Callison-Burch, Marcello Federico, Nicola Bertoldi, Brooke Cowan, Wade Shen, Christine Moran, Richard Zens, Chris Dyer, Ondřej Bojar, Alexandra Constantin, and Evan Herbst. 2007. Moses: Open source toolkit for statistical machine translation. In *Proceedings of the 45th Annual Meeting of the ACL on Interactive Poster and Demonstration Sessions*, ACL '07.

Philipp Koehn. 2005. Europarl: A Parallel Corpus for Statistical Machine Translation. In *Conference Proceedings: the tenth Machine Translation Summit*, pages 79–86, Phuket, Thailand. AAMT, MMichigan0605 AAMT.

Percy Liang, Ben Taskar, and Dan Klein. 2006. Alignment by agreement. In *Proceedings of HLT-NAACL*.

Radford M. Neal and Geoffrey E. Hinton. 1999. Learning in graphical models. chapter A View of the EM Algorithm That Justifies Incremental, Sparse, and Other Variants, pages 355–368. MIT Press.

Franz Josef Och and Hermann Ney. 2003. A systematic comparison of various statistical alignment models. *Comput. Linguist.*, 29(1):19–51, March.

Franz Josef Och, Daniel Gildea, Sanjeev Khudanpur, Anoop Sarkar, Kenji Yamada, Alex Fraser, Shankar Kumar, Libin Shen, David Smith, Katherine Eng, Viren Jain, Zhen Jin, and Dragomir Radev. 2004. A smorgasbord of features for statistical machine translation. In *HLT-NAACL*.

Kishore Papineni, Salim Roukos, Todd Ward, and Wei-Jing Zhu. 2002. Bleu: A method for automatic evaluation of machine translation. In *Proceedings of ACL*.

Majid Razmara, George Foster, Baskaran Sankaran, and Anoop Sarkar. 2012. Mixing multiple translation models in statistical machine translation. In *Proceedings of ACL*.

Rico Sennrich, Holger Schwenk, and Walid Aransa. 2013. A multi-domain translation model framework for statistical machine translation. In *Proceedings of ACL*.

Andrei Simion, Michael Collins, and Cliff Stein. 2013. A convex alternative to ibm model 2. Proceedings of EMNLP.

Matthew Snover, Bonnie Dorr, R. Schwartz, L. Micciulla, and J. Makhoul. 2006. A study of translation edit rate with targeted human annotation. In *Proceedings of AMTA*.

Yik-Cheung Tam, Ian Lane, and Tanja Schultz. 2007. Bilingual lsa-based adaptation for statistical machine translation. *Machine Translation*, 21(4):187–207.

Akihiro Tamura, Taro Watanabe, and Eiichiro Sumita. 2014. Recurrent neural networks for word alignment model. In *Proceedings of ACL*.

Stephan Vogel, Hermann Ney, and Christoph Tillmann. 1996. Hmm-based word alignment in statistical translation. In *Proceedings of COLING*.

Bing Zhao and Eric P. Xing. 2008. Hm-bitam: Bilingual topic exploration, word alignment, and translation. In *Proceedings of NIPS*.

# Extracting Human Temporal Orientation from Facebook Language

**H. Andrew Schwartz,**[1,4] **Gregory J. Park,**[2] **Maarten Sap,**[2] **Evan Weingarten**[3], **Johannes Eichstaedt,**[2]
**Margaret L. Kern,**[5] **David Stillwell,**[6] **Michal Kosinski,**[7] **Jonah Berger,**[3] **Martin Seligman,**[2] **Lyle H. Ungar**[1]
[1]Computer & Information Science, [2]Psychology, [3]Wharton, University of Pennsylvania
[4]Computer Science, Stony Brook University [5]Graduate School of Education, University of Melbourne
[6]Psychometrics Centre, Cambridge University [7]Graduate School of Business, Stanford University
hansens@seas.upenn.edu, gregpark@sas.upenn.edu

## Abstract

People vary widely in their temporal orientation—how often they emphasize the past, present, and future—and this affects their finances, health, and happiness. Traditionally, temporal orientation has been assessed by self-report questionnaires. In this paper, we develop a novel behavior-based assessment using human language on Facebook. We first create a past, present, and future message classifier, engineering features and evaluating a variety of classification techniques. Our message classifier achieves an accuracy of 71.8%, compared with 52.8% from the most frequent class and 58.6% from a model based entirely on time expression features. We quantify a users' overall temporal orientation based on their distribution of messages and validate it against known human correlates: conscientiousness, age, and gender. We then explore social scientific questions, finding novel associations with the factors openness to experience, satisfaction with life, depression, IQ, and one's number of friends. Further, demonstrating how one can track orientation over time, we find differences in future orientation around birthdays.

## 1 Introduction

How much one emphasizes the past, present, or future is predictive of many human factors such as occupational and educational success, engagement in risky behavior, financial stability, depression, and health (Boyd and Zimbardo, 2005; Zimbardo and Boyd, 1999). However, studies on the human experience of time are filled with diverse measurement methods (Strathman and Joireman, 2005), mostly involving questionnaires which are expensive to administer multiple times or at scale and can be subject to confounds when compared to other questionnaire based assessments.

Text mining and language processing techniques can provide a more objective and scalable measurement of *temporal orientation*, one's tendency to emphasize the past, present, or future. Whereas most prior computational linguistics and text mining temporal studies have focused on events, there has been a lack of work looking at the temporal orientation of people. Such measures, which were not practical before the growth of social media, can open many avenues of large-scale psychological discovery into the consequences of temporal orientation and yield applications such as targeted marketing, loan repayment forecasting, understanding economic patterns, or even quantified self-help tools to encourage more future-mindedness.

In this paper, we develop a temporal orientation measure based on language in social media. The measure uses a message-level classifier of past, present, and future, aggregated over users to create user-level assessments. We evaluate the message-level classifier over hand annotated data and the derived user-level model against known human correlates of temporal orientation: *conscientiousness*, age, and gender. To the best of our knowledge, this represents the first paper to study a language-based measure of user-level temporal-orientation.

Our contributions include: (a) the introduction of the task of extracting human temporal orientation from their language use, (b) methodological evaluation and feature engineering for the task, and (c) novel social scientific applications and findings. To-



*Human Language Technologies: The 2015 Annual Conference of the North American Chapter of the ACL*, pages 409–419,
Denver, Colorado, May 31 – June 5, 2015. 

ward (a) and (b), we find that achieving the task is non-trivial as we build on and diverge from related computational linguistics tasks (e.g. time expression recognition) and utilize a classifier capturing non-linear relationships and interactions. Towards (c), we show how our measure usefully informs psychological theory by relating our human assessments to other psychological variables at a scale not easily explored, and by tracking changes in temporal orientation over time.

## 2 Background

Researchers and philosophers have long been interested in the subjective experience of time: how individuals relate to their past, are mindful of their present, and envision their futures (James, 1890; Lewin, 1942). Similarly, computational studies have a rich history on extracting temporal relationships beginning decades ago (Allen, 1983). Here, we provide some background on temporal orientation's broader relevance, on computational techniques used to extract temporal information from text, and on related user-level prediction tasks.

**Temporal orientation and its correlates.** Studies on the human subjective experience of time are filled with diverse measurement methods, varying in their emphasis on cognitive, affective, and/or motivational aspects.[1] Decisions are influenced by the past, present, and mental simulations of possible futures (Seligman et al., 2013).

One widely studied aspect of subjective time is *temporal orientation*, or an individual's tendency to habitually emphasize past, present, or future temporal frames (Boyd and Zimbardo, 2005). Understanding how and why individuals differ in their temporal orientation, can, for example suggest how they can achieve favorable outcomes in areas of life that require substantial long-term planning, including education, higher status occupations, and physical health (Zimbardo and Boyd, 1999; Boyd and Zimbardo, 2005; Steinberg et al., 2009).

Consistent links have been established between temporal orientation and a psychological factor associated with planning, health, and risky behaviors: the personality trait of *conscientiousness*. Conscientious individuals are characterized as self-disciplined, orderly, planful, and reliable (Roberts et al., 2013). Past research has established that highly conscientious people exhibit more future- and less present-oriented (Zimbardo and Boyd, 1999; Webley and Nyhus, 2006; Adams and Nettle, 2009). We use a measure of conscientiousness from the well-established "Big-five" or Five Factor Model of personality (Goldberg, 1990; McCrae and John, 1992). The other four factors, *extraversion* (e.g. active, outgoing, talkative), *agreeableness* (e.g. kind, trusting, generous), *neuroticism* (e.g. touchy, anxious, depressive), and *openness* (e.g. intellectual, artistic, insightful), have been found to have little connection with temporal orientation (Zimbardo and Boyd, 1999).

Other studies have established consistent links between temporal orientation and demographic characteristics. In particular, as one ages they think less about the immediate present and more about the future (Friedman, 2000; Nurmi, 2005; Steinberg et al., 2009), and females tend to think a bit more about the future than males (Keough et al., 1999). However, detailed age trends are not well understood, with studies mostly focusing on adolescents or college-aged students.

For many other important outcomes, such as happiness or well-being, past research leaves us unclear as to the relationship with temporal orientation. Some suggest future-oriented individuals are happier as they engage in more provident behaviors such as saving money and establishing healthier habit (Desmyter and De Raedt, 2012; Diener et al., 2013). This is supported by the connection between future orientation and less depression (Zimbardo and Boyd, 1999). However, others argue that emphasis on the future inhibits ones ability to reflect wisely on the past and savor present experiences (Boniwell et al., 2010). Our study explores this relationship at an unprecedented scale, utilizing the Satisfaction with Life Scale (Diener et al., 1985) and the Center for Epidemiologic Studies Depression Scale, the CES-D (Radloff, 1977). We also look at previously unexplored variables, IQ and number of friends, for which links with temporal orientation seem plausible (e.g. one might suspect it is smart to think about the future, or wonder if one's reflection

[1] For a review, see Strathman et al., 2005.

on the past is related to their popularity as measure by number of friends).

**Related work.** Studying temporal language is by no means new to the field of computational linguistics (or NLP). Most recently, time annotation has gained greater interest with a successive sequence of three SemEval tasks (TempEval-1, -2 and -3).

The SemEval competitions have provided data sets that facilitate the comparison of different methods for evaluating time expressions, events, and temporal relations (Verhagen et al., 2007; Verhagen et al., 2010; UzZaman et al., 2013). Such research on temporal text analysis generally focuses on determining when events start and end or how they relate temporally to each other; specific goals include information extraction of time-dependent facts from news media (Ling and Weld, 2010; Talukdar et al., 2012), or extracting personal histories in social media (Wen et al., 2013). In contrast, our goal is to find the temporal orientation of people.

Of the numerous TempEval tasks, we build upon those which identify time expressions and resolve their expressed time and date relative to the time of writing (e.g. the time expression 'yesterday' in a document written on *January 15, 2014* is resolved as *January 14, 2014*). Many methods have been used, ranging from hand-crafting rules to machine learning models. Unlike other areas of natural language processing where stochastic techniques dominate, rule-based systems have been quite competitive in time expressions recognition, especially in less domain dependent settings or for relaxed matching tasks (UzZaman et al., 2013).

A number of useful toolkits have been produced for temporal text analysis (Verhagen et al., 2005; Ling and Weld, 2010; Chang and Manning, 2012). In this work, we use Stanford University's rule-based temporal tagger, SUTime, which geve accuracy in line with the state-of-the-art systems at identifying time expressions at TempEval (Chang and Manning, 2012).[2] SUTime, built on top of Stanford's part-of-speech and named entity taggers, labels times, durations, intervals, and relative times compared to the time at which the document was written.

Our work fits a growing tradition of computational work to better understand people based on their online behavior. Much of this type of work uses human properties to better perform traditional computational linguistics tasks, while others focus particularly on predicting user attributes. User network information has been used for tweet summarization or filtering (Panigrahy et al., 2012; Chang et al., 2013; Feng and Wang, 2013).

Others utilize psychological knowledge about people, such as exploiting the human tendency to report more positive extreme feelings than negative in order to improve on sentiment analysis (Guerra et al., 2014). Toward attribute prediction, a large proportion of works have focused on demographics (Argamon et al., 2009; Goswami et al., 2009; Burger et al., 2011; Al Zamal et al., 2012; Bergsma et al., 2013; Sap et al., 2014). and personality prediction (Mairesse et al., 2007; Iacobelli et al., 2011; Schwartz et al., 2013; Park et al., 2015).

Human temporal orientation, as we study it here, differs from previous studies of user attribute prediction in that temporal orientation calls for consideration of additional language features (some more sophisticated, such as time expressions), and exploration of classification techniques (e.g. that can capture non-linear relationships or interactions). We also add multidisciplinary applications, showing not just how accurately our models predict, but also studying how temporal orientation relates to other factors, for example, by weighing in on conflicting literature as to whether people who are more future-oriented are more satisfied with their life.

# 3 Method

We develop a methodology for measuring a given social media user's temporal orientation. First, we build a classifier to label whether a message discusses the past, present, or future, and then we quantify users' temporal orientation as the percentage of their messages in each category.

We train a variety of supervised classifiers and explore many features in order to label the temporal

[2] Our goals differ slightly from the TempEval accuracy criteria. For example, when SUTime fails to distinguish "one and a half weeks" from "one week", it does not affect our performance. However, other errors, such as confusing the verb 'march' with the month March will harm our accuracy.

class of a social media message. Because this task is new, it is not clear what classification technique is ideal (for example, it is possible that present orientation is best captured with non-linear relationships), so we explore four techniques:

**logR:** *(logistic regression)*. We use regularized logistic regression (equivalent to maximum entropy) (Fan et al., 2008; Bishop, 2006). From cross-validation over the training data, we chose L1 penalization ($\alpha||\beta||_1$).

**lSVC, rSVC:** *(support vector classification)*. Compared to logR, support vector machines offer non-linear kernel functions (Cortes and Vapnik, 1995), and large-margin optimization for class split. We consider both a linear kernel (lSVC) and a radial basis function kernel (rSVC). From cross-validation over the training data, we chose L1 penalization for lSVC and L2 ($\alpha||\beta||^2$) for rSVC.

**ERTs:** *(forest of extremely randomized trees)*. This technique uses an ensemble of decision trees in which both the feature and cut-point are chosen at each node from a randomly generated set of possible options (Geurts et al., 2006). Such an approach can handle both interactions and non-linear relationships, at the expense of a larger search space. From cross-validation over our training data, we set the following algorithm parameters: we build 1,000 decision trees, using the Gini impurity measure when choosing splits (as opposed to entropy), and selecting each node's feature threshold from among square-root of the total features.

All classifications algorithms were implemented using the scikit-learn toolkit (Pedregosa et al., 2011). Multi-classication over binary classifiers (logR, lSVC, rSVC) was achieved using a series of *one-v-rest* classifiers.

We explore five language-based features:

**ngrams:** *1 to 3 token sequences.* Messages are tokenized using the *happierfuntokenizing* tool[3] which captures common social media tokens such as emoticons, hashtags, and user handles. Features are encoded simply as binary indicators for whether the ngram appears in the message.

**time exs:** *The mean difference between the resolved date-time of all time expressions and the date-time in which the message was posted.* Time expressions are labeled via Stanford's SUTime annotator (Chang and Manning, 2012), discussed previously. Specific features recorded include the temporal difference itself (e.g. -2.5 for "two and half days ago"), its base 2 log ($log(1 + value)$), its absolute value, total number of time expressions, and binary variables indicating if any past, present, or future expressions appear in the text. We also include binary features for each of the named-entity time tags for the time expression provided by SUTime (e.g. "future_ref", "present_ref", "next_immediate").

**POS tags:** *The relative frequency of each part-of-speech tag.* Tagging is done via Stanford's part-of-speech tagger (Toutanova et al., 2003). Stanford's tagger does not have explicit social media tags, but we are most interested in capturing tense which it does well.[4] Also, it is already being used as part of SUTime. Each part-of-speech tag is encoded as the frequency of tag usage ($freq(tag, msg)$) divided by the total number of tokens in the message ($tokens_{msg}$):

$$p(tag|msg) = \frac{freq(tag, msg)}{|tokens_{msg}|}$$

**lexica:** *The relative frequency of categories, based on the Linguistic Inquiry and Word Count (LIWC) dictionary* (Pennebaker et al., 2007). We use the 2007 version of *LIWC* which includes 64 categories of psychologically-relevant language, including past, present, and future verb categories. The features are encoded as the frequency with which a word from a category ($cat$) appeared in the message ($msg$) divided by the total tokens in the message ($tokens_{msg}$):

$$p(cat|msg) = \frac{\sum\limits_{token \in cat} freq(token, msg)}{|tokens_{msg}|}$$

[3]available here:
wwbp.org/public_data/happierfuntokenizing.zip

[4]The Stanford Tagger has well documented errors on microblog text (Derczynski et al., 2013). However, we manually evaluated 49 verbs across 20 randomly selected statuses, and all verb tenses were correctly tagged while 4 non-verbs were incorrectly tagged as base-form verbs.

| Status | R1 | R2 | R3 | Maj |
|---|---|---|---|---|
| *:) today was actually pretty good* | pa | pa | pa | pa |
| *is listening to The Sad Cafe by The Eagles!* | pr | pr | pr | pr |
| *considering checking out base jumping and parkour some time in the future XP* | fu | fu | fu | fu |
| *I just watched Oprah and am posting what it was about.* | pa | pr | pa | pa |
| *really wanted a snow day, but probably not going to get one tomorrow. now homework.* | pr | fu | fu | fu |
| *Another day of great restraint.* | pa | pa | pr | pa |

Table 1: Examples of statuses annotated for temporal classes: past (pa), present/none (pr), and future (fu). R1, R2, R3: judgements from each rater; Maj: choice from majority voting. The bottom three examples illustrate difficult cases.

**lengths:** *mean size of 1grams and number of tokens in the post.*

We found it useful to use a modest variety of feature types and to build on existing work that labels time expressions. While one might expect time expression features to be extremely valuable for this task, we found only 15% of Facebook messages contain them, even though many more communicate a focus on the past or future through other means (e.g. tense or semantic information). All features were limited to those mentioned in at least 0.05% of messages.

At the user-level, we produce three categories of temporal orientation, defined simply as the proportion of a user's total messages ($msgs(user)_{all}$) classified in the given temporal category ($tc \in \{past, present, future\}$):

$$orientation_{tc}(user) = \frac{|msgs_{tc}(user)|}{|msgs_{all}(user)|}$$

We generate three separate variables (summing to one), rather than a single variable temporal index, in order to capture non-linear relationships (i.e., the potential for the present to correlate in the opposite direction of both the past and future). All of our user analyses are based on 100 randomly selected messages from each user.

# 4 Data collection and labeling

We use three social media datasets: the *training set*, *test set*, and *user set*. The *training set* consists of 4,302 Twitter and Facebook annotated messages. The *test set* is a random subset of 500 annotated Facebook messages, representative of messages we will apply our model. Finally, the *user set* contains 531,893 messages from Facebook users with known age, gender, personality, satisfaction with life, depression, IQ and number of Facebook friends. We derived the *test set* from the *user set* in order to establish accuracies of our model over the application domain.

**Training set.** Our training data consists of both Facebook and Twitter messages. For Facebook, 3,000 status updates, sent between March 2009 and October 2011, were randomly sampled from users of the MyPersonality application (Kosinski and Stillwell, 2012; Quercia et al., 2012), who also provided their age and gender. For Twitter, 3,000 messages were sampled from the 1% *random* stream provided by Twitter during September 2012.

Three annotators, undergraduate students at the University of Pennsylvania, independently labeled the temporal orientation of each message. Messages were labeled in units of days past or future (adapted from Liberman et al. (2007)). For example, -7 would be a week ago, $^{-1}/_{24}$ would be an hour ago, 0 would be now (present), and 365 would be a year from now. Inter-annotator agreement, as the intraclass correlation coefficient (Shrout and Fleiss, 1979), was 0.85. Ratings were averaged into a single "time from now" index. For the purposes of this study we then discretized the data into past (mean rating $< 0$), present (mean rating $= 0$), or future (mean rating $> 0$). Annotation of the 6,000 messages took approximately 150 human hours.

When rating, messages were marked 'NA' when they appeared to come from a bot or were composed of song lyrics or quotations. (Removing unoriginal content was desired for the consumer behavior research for which the messages were first labeled.) For our purposes, in order to maximize the training set size, we only removed messages when all three raters chose 'NA', such that there was no average rating available for the message. The resulting final *training set* consisted of 4,302 total messages (2,009 tweets; 2,293 Facebook status updates). Since our application of the data does not include a manual filtering of messages, we created a separate message test set with no filtering in order to accurately evaluate our classifier in the application's setting (below).

**Test set.** Evaluating our classifiers over our annotated training set would not yield an accurate assessment of the performance when applied to the *user set* (described next). Therefore, we randomly selected 500 statuses from the *user set* as our message *test set*.[5] Statuses exclude

[5]While we desired a large training set, the test set only needed to be large enough to evaluate differences in accuracy.

| | mfc | logR | lSVC | rSVC | ERTs | *msgs* |
|---|---|---|---|---|---|---|
| **Accuracy** | .528 | .686 | .708 | .684 | **.718** | *500* |
| past (p, r, f1) | (.00, .00, .00) | (.56, .68, .62) | (.63, .67, .65) | (.63, .56, .59) | (.73, .67, .71) | *131* |
| present (p, r, f1) | (.53, 1.0, .69) | (.80, .74, .77) | (.78, .78, .78) | (.70, .85, .77) | (.74, .84, .79) | *264* |
| future (p, r, f1) | (.00, .00, .00) | (.60, .56, .58) | (.61, .56, .58) | (.69, .43, .53) | (.60, .47, .53) | *105* |

Table 2: Accuracy (percentage classified correct) message classifiers based on different learning algorithms (identified in section 3). Temporal class results are broken down by precision (p), recall (r), and f1 score for each of past (pa), present (pr), and future (fu). Number of messages (*msgs*) are listed on the far right. The most frequent class baseline (mfc) indicates accuracy if only predicting the present class.

reposts of others' statuses and comments on other people's posts, and we found only 2 of the 500 random messages were made by apps (users still choose whether or not to post these to their walls). Three annotators independently classified each status message as predominantly talking about the past, present, or future. The overall rating for each message was determined by a majority vote (when there was a tie: i.e., one of each class, present was used). Agreement among these raters, calculated as the intraclass correlation coefficient, was 0.83. One might suggest some messages do not have a temporal class (e.g. does "I like Selena Gomez" have a predominant temporal class?).[6] Such messages would be marked as 'present' in our annotation scheme. Thus, one might consider our present class to encompass both a present and "non-temporal" class.

**User set.** Human-level data is used to evaluate our model toward understanding the relationship between human temporal orientation and individual characteristics (e.g. demographics, personality). Thus, this data spans both message and user levels, from consenting participants, in the MyPersonality Facebook study (Kosinski and Stillwell, 2012).

We used five subsets of the MyPersonality data in order to capture various psychological and behavioral variables: *user subset 1*: gender, age, and personality; *user subset 2*: satisfaction with life, *user subset 3*: depression, *user subset 4*: IQ, and *user subset 5*: number of friends. For our first subset, gender, age, and personality variables are well represented in the dataset, so we created a stratified sample over 1,520 users. We sampled equal proportions of males and females across 4-year age bins from 13 to 60 (i.e., ages *[13,16], [17,20], . . . ,[57, 60]*), which provides gender- and age-controlled correlations for each personality factor (openness, conscientiousness, extraversion, agreeableness, and neuroticism).

Other variables are more limited. Thus, instead of creating stratified samples, these three subsets include users for whom gender and age information is also available: 1,565 in the case of satisfaction with life, 268 for the CES-D depression scale, 898 for IQ and, 1,000 in the case of number of friends. The gender and age data is then included as covariates in regression analyses to find the relationship between these variables and temporal orientation, controlled for demographics. In all five subsets of the *user set*, we randomly sample 100 messages from each user in order to determine their temporal orientation.

Table 1 shows example status updates along with ratings. As evidenced from the rater agreement, most status updates were fairly easy to determine. Some messages have explicit temporal phrases (e.g. "in the future") while others are more subtle (e.g. relying on verb tense: "is listening ..."). Others, such as the bottom three examples, might reference multiple temporal classes or not include clear verb tense and thus rely on the raters' judgements for what is most dominant.

# 5 Evaluation

We evaluate our past, present, and future message classifier as well as its features. All models were trained over our *training set* and evaluated over the *test set*.

Table 2 compares accuracy of various types of classifiers: logistic regression (logR), linear support vector classifier (lSVC), support vector classifier with rbf kernel (rSVC), and a forest of extremely randomized trees (ERTs). We saw best results from the ERTs classifier, suggesting some of its benefits (capturing non-linear relationships or interactions among features) may help this problem. We also see, from the F1 scores, that all classifiers found the future class most difficult to predict; this was the smallest class and likely subject to the most bias against. All classifiers performed significantly better than the most frequent class baseline with an error reduction of 41% in the case of ERTs ($p < 0.001$ from paired t-test on absolute errors). We selected the ERTs classifier for the remaining experiments.[7]

[6]We attempted to include a non-temporal class and found disagreement. Some argue that every message has a temporal class (e.g. "I like Selena Gomez" is truly signalling present).

[7]This trained classifier is available at: wwbp.org/data.html.

| Past | | Present | | Future | |
|---|---|---|---|---|---|
| type | feature | type | feature | type | feature |
| POS | *verb, past tense* | time exs - | *num of timexs* | lexica | *relativity* |
| ngrams | *was* | POS - | *verb, past tense* | time exs | *num of timexs* |
| lexica - | *common-present verbs* | lexica - | *relativity (in, on, at, ...)* | POS | *verb, base form* |
| lengths | *num of tokens* | lexica | *common-present verbs* | ngrams | *tomorrow* |
| ngrams | *had* | POS | *verbs, 3rd-pers singular* | POS | *to* |

Table 4: Top five most correlated features for each of the temporal classes. '-' indicates negative correlations; positive otherwise. Correlation absolute strengths ranged from Pearson $r = 0.08$ to $0.40$.

| Features | Accuracy | Features | Accuracy |
|---|---|---|---|
| mfc baseline | .528 | all features | **.718** |
| *ngrams* alone | .688 | w/o *ngrams* | .672 |
| *time exs* alone | .586 | w/o *time exs* | .708 |
| *POS tags* alone | .614 | w/o *POS tags* | .712 |
| *lexica* alone | .684 | w/o *lexica* | .702 |
| *lengths* alone | .544 | w/o *lengths* | .718 |

Table 3: Accuracy of our full past, present, future message classifier (top) and an ablation analysis of accuracies when removing each feature type (bottom). The most frequent class baseline (mfc) indicates accuracy if only predicting the present class. The full classifier significantly out-performed using time expressions alone ($p < 0.05$; bolded accuracy).

We did feature ablation analyses as shown in Table 3. Every feature type produced improvement over the baseline and, with the exception of $lengths$, removing any feature resulted in reduced performance (though none strong enough to meet significance at $p < 0.05$). The limited reduction implies that while each feature type may contain temporal information, there is also substantial redundancy across the feature types.

Results when using time-expression alone can be considered another baseline, representing a model based entirely on previous time expression work. A reason for the large advantage of using additional features is that many temporally indicative messages did not contain any time expressions (instead expressing orientation through verb tense or semantics). Indeed, we see from Table 4, which lists the top features for each class, that time expression features were very useful when then occurred. All feature types made it into these top ten lists.

User-level temporal orientation is trivially defined: percentage of a given user's messages that are classified as past, present, or future oriented. Thus, accuracy for each proportion is directly tied to message accuracy. Still, we validate that our approach is in line with psychological theory (discussed in Section 2) by correlating user-level temporal orientations with outcomes whose associations have been previously established: conscientiousness, age, and gender number of users; results controlled for age and gender. In particular, future orientation should be positively correlated with conscientiousness, age, and being female, while present orientation should be negatively correlated. Our results which which are consistent with the literature, can be seen in the top half of Table 5. Among users with personality scores, we found positive correlations between future orientation and seemingly future-oriented questionnaire items: "I make plans and stick to them" ($r = .16$) and "I finish what I start" ($r = .12$). To the best of our knowledge, psychology literature has not established standard correlates of past orientation, so the correlation with age and past orientation, though not surprising, is somewhat novel.

Correlations with questionnaire measures help to establish convergent validity — i.e. our measure is empirically related to other measures in a way that is consistent with theory about the underlying constructs. However, self report questionnaires are often used for convenience, not necessarily because they are most valid (Paulhus and Vazire, 2007). In fact, more objective or behavior-based measures in social science have been called for (Baumeister et al., 2007).

# 6 Exploration

Here we use our language-based user measure to explore behavioral and psychological correlates of temporal orientation. Figure 1 illustrates the user-level distributions of the message classes, broken down by gender, within the stratified sample. All experiments in this section applied our measure over the *user set*. Within users, the mean proportions of past, present, and future messages were 0.24, 0.61, and 0.15 respectively. Among most users, the majority of messages were classified as present, while future-oriented messages were least frequent.

We compare these temporal orientations to user personality, satisfaction with life, IQ, and their number of Facebook friends. We use both Pearson correlation and linear regression (OLS) to estimate relationships between

| Attribute | *N* | Past | Present | Future |
|---|---|---|---|---|
| validation | | | | |
| conscientiousness | *1520* | .02 | **-.08** | **.12** |
| age | *1520* | **.30** | **-.30** | **.15** |
| gender | *1520* | **.10** | **-.15** | **.14** |
| exploration | | | | |
| openness | *1520* | .05 | .04 | **-.12** |
| extraversion | *1520* | -.04 | .03 | .00 |
| agreeableness | *1520* | .00 | -.02 | .04 |
| neuroticism | *1520* | -.01 | -.01 | .04 |
| satisfaction w/ life | *1565* | .00 | -.05 | **.08** |
| depression | *268* | -.14 | **.21** | **-.17** |
| IQ | *898* | **.14** | **-.14** | .05 |
| # of friends | *1000* | **-.15** | **.13** | -.05 |

Table 5: Correlations between user temporal orientation and human attributes. The attributes conscientiousness, age, and gender are well-established in previous literature to be associated with temporal orientation. Gender is coded as 0 = male, 1 = female. **bold**: $p < .01$ after Benjamini-Hochberg multiple comparison correction; *N*: number of users; results controlled for age and gender.

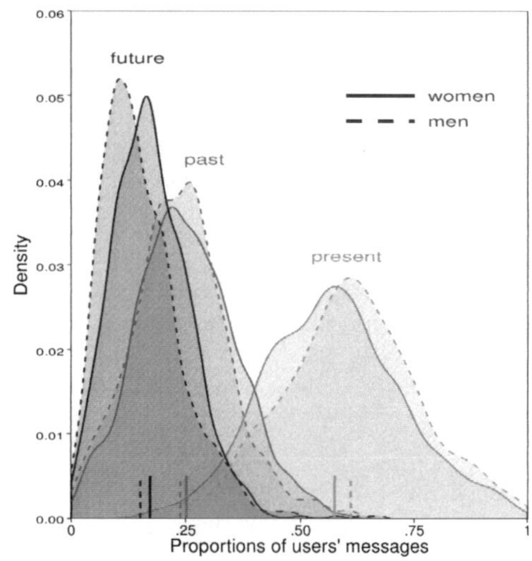


Figure 1: Kernel density estimates of user-level proportions of past, present, and future classified messages, broken down by gender. Vertical bars represent means.

temporal orientation and other variables. In our age and gender stratified sample (1520 users), we calculate Pearson correlations between temporal orientation and age, gender, and measures of openness, conscientiousness, extraversion, agreeableness, and neuroticism. Because fewer users completed measures of satisfaction with life, IQ, and number of friends, we were not able to produce sufficient stratified samples, so we used ordinary least squares linear regression to fit the standardized outcome of interest to standardized temporal orientation also including standardized age and gender as covariates to adjust for their effects. The coefficient, often denoted $\beta$, for temporal orientation then represents the strength of the relationship, controlled for age and gender.

Table 5 lists the correlation coefficients between temporal orientation and user attributes. We found the strongest effects for age, with patterns that are consistent with the psychological literature (Steinberg et al., 2009). Figure 2 illustrates trends from age 13 to 60. Most notably, present orientation decreases steadily across age; past orientation steadily increases, and future orientation increases quickly throughout adolescence, slows in early adulthood, and finally levels off in late adulthood. Female users were significantly more future-oriented, slightly more past-oriented, and significantly less present-oriented than males.

For personality, we found the expected patterns of correlations with conscientiousness, but more interestingly, openness to experience was correlated with lower future orientation (beyond conscientiousness, there was no support in the literature for any of the five personality factors to correlate with temporal orientation). This is surprising when considering openness to experience is characterized by creativity and intellect (McCrae and John, 1992), yet IQ instead correlates with less present and more past orientation, suggesting future orientation characterizes a difference between the two.[8]

We found a modest yet significant positive correlation between future orientation and satisfaction with life, with future orientation associated with higher life satisfaction. On the other hand, we found a stronger negative correlation between future orientation and depression as well as a positive correlation between present orientation and depression. As previously noted, past literature was conflicting on the relationship between these factors, so our study weighs in with a behavior-based assessment in support of a future-oriented people being more satisfied in life and less depressed.

Lastly, we consider whether the use of our language-based measure of temporal orientation can track changes over time. As a proof-of-concept, we focus on patterns around birthdays; excluding messages containing birthday terms and users turning 21, we calculated the standardized proportion of messages which were future-

[8]One interpretation is that our classifier may be more accurate on messages authored by those with higher IQ (i.e. more grammatical sentences); however no significant difference in error was found when spitting messages by the authors' IQ, age, or gender.

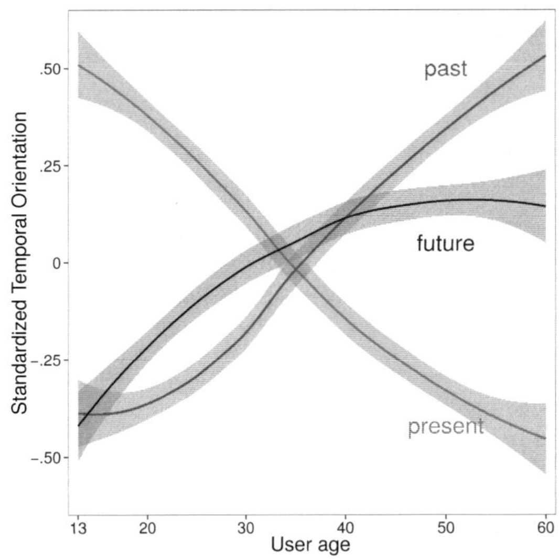


Figure 2: Standardized temporal orientation of users over their age. Shaded area indicates $\pm 1$ standard error around loess smoothed estimates.

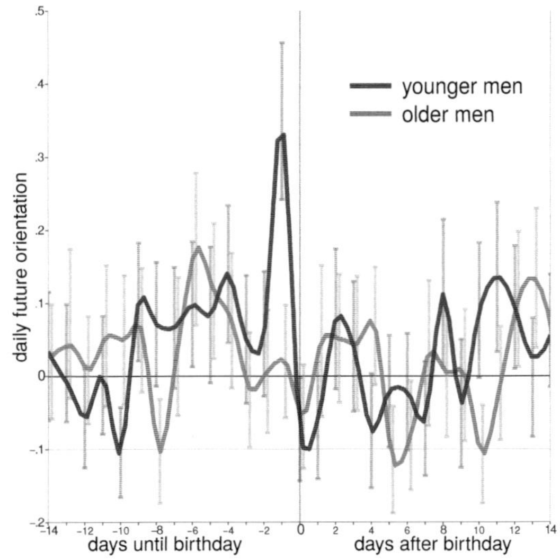


Figure 3: Daily proportion of future-oriented messages leading up to and following birthdays. Younger men: $<$ 23, N = 423; Older men: $\geq$ 23, N = 402.

oriented over two weeks before and after one's birthday. We controlled for individual differences and date effects (e.g. if more people happen to be born near a holiday) by standardizing users' future orientation over all their messages and standardizing daily future orientation scores over all messages from each day. Figure 3 shows the patterns for men $< 23$ and $\geq 23$, suggesting that younger men look forward to their birthdays while older men do not (patterns were less pronounced for women).

# 7 Conclusions

This is, to our knowledge, the first study to automatically assess individual temporal orientation through language, and it constitutes one of the largest (perhaps the largest) studies of temporal orientation. Our message-level past, present, and future classifier achieved an accuracy of 71.8%, well-above most frequent sense, pasts-of-speech only, and time expression only baselines. The associations we found between user-level temporal orientation and conscientiousness, gender, and age validated our novel method against well-established correlates. We then explored novel links with other personality factors, satisfaction with life, depression, IQ, and number of friends.

Our automatic labeling of temporal orientation yielded strong accuracy. There are, however, several ways in which our analysis might be improved or extended. We used a coding scheme that did not allow a "no temporal orientation" class. Separate handling of "non-temporal" messages might provide more nuanced profiles of user orientation. Another simplification was our binning of temporal relations into past, present, and future. One might want to instead use a continuous measure of temporal distance, indicating how far into the past or future a message is oriented, providing a more detailed profile of individual orientations. Among the future-oriented, for example, there may be important differences between those who plan for tomorrow versus those who plan years in advance. Assessing additional characteristics of messages, such as sentiment, may also allow further insight and more nuanced characterizations (e.g. "I will be fine" vs. "I will never be ok").

Whereas prior computational linguistics work with temporal relations has focused on classifying events, we focus on people and open many avenues for social scientific investigations that were previously not very feasible. For instance, temporal orientation was generally treated as a stable trait (with little change through the lifetime); For men, we found age differences in temporal orientation leading up to one's birthday. Learning how, why, and when people become more future-oriented may inform planning and risk assessment interventions, and lead to better understanding of health and economic prosperity.

# 8 Acknowledgments


We thank George Wan for his assistance running prototype classifiers. This work was supported by the Templeton Religion Trust under grant #TRT0048.

# References


Jean Adams and Daniel Nettle. 2009. Time perspective, personality and smoking, body mass, and physical activity: An empirical study. *British Journal of Health Psychology*, 14(1):83–105.

Faiyaz Al Zamal, Wendy Liu, and Derek Ruths. 2012. Homophily and latent attribute inference: Inferring latent attributes of twitter users from neighbors. In *ICWSM*.

James F Allen. 1983. Maintaining knowledge about temporal intervals. *Communications of the ACM*, 26(11):832–843.

Shlomo Argamon, Moshe Koppel, James W. Pennebaker, and Jonathan Schler. 2009. Automatically profiling the author of an anonymous text. *Commun. ACM*, 52(2):119–123, February.

Roy F Baumeister, Kathleen D Vohs, and David C Funder. 2007. Psychology as the science of self-reports and finger movements: Whatever happened to actual behavior? *Perspectives on Psychological Science*, 2(4):396–403.

Shane Bergsma, Mark Dredze, Benjamin Van Durme, Theresa Wilson, and David Yarowsky. 2013. Broadly improving user classification via communication-based name and location clustering on twitter. In *Anuual Meeting of HLT-NAACL*, pages 1010–1019.

Christopher M Bishop. 2006. *Pattern recognition and machine learning*, volume 4. Springer New York.

Ilona Boniwell, Evgeny Osin, P Alex Linley, and Galina V Ivanchenko. 2010. A question of balance: Time perspective and well-being in british and russian samples. *The Journal of Positive Psychology*, 5(1):24–40.

John N Boyd and Philip G Zimbardo. 2005. Time perspective, health, and risk taking. In *Understanding behavior in the context of time*, pages 85–107. Lawrence Erlbaum, Mahwah.

John D Burger, John Henderson, George Kim, and Guido Zarrella. 2011. Discriminating gender on twitter. In *Proceedings of the Conference on Empirical Methods in Natural Language Processing*, pages 1301–1309. Association for Computational Linguistics.

Angel X Chang and Christopher Manning. 2012. Sutime: A library for recognizing and normalizing time expressions. In *LREC*, pages 3735–3740.

Yi Chang, Xuanhui Wang, Qiaozhu Mei, and Yan Liu. 2013. Towards twitter context summarization with user influence models. In *Proceedings of the sixth ACM international conference on Web search and data mining*, pages 527–536. ACM.

Corinna Cortes and Vladimir Vapnik. 1995. Support-vector networks. *Machine learning*, 20(3):273–297.

Leon Derczynski, Diana Maynard, Niraj Aswani, and Kalina Bontcheva. 2013. Microblog-genre noise and impact on semantic annotation accuracy. In *Proceedings of the 24th ACM Conference on Hypertext and Social Media*, pages 21–30. ACM.

Fien Desmyter and Rudi De Raedt. 2012. The relationship between time perspective and subjective well-being of older adults. *Psychologica Belgica*, 52(1):19–38.

ED Diener, Robert A Emmons, Randy J Larsen, and Sharon Griffin. 1985. The satisfaction with life scale. *Journal of personality assessment*, 49(1):71–75.

Ed Diener, Louis Tay, and Shigehiro Oishi. 2013. Rising income and the subjective well-being of nations. *Journal of Personality and Social Psychology*, 104(2):267–276.

Rong-En Fan, Kai-Wei Chang, Cho-Jui Hsieh, Xiang-Rui Wang, and Chih-Jen Lin. 2008. LIBLINEAR: A library for large linear classification. *Journal of Machine Learning Research*, 9:1871–1874.

Wei Feng and Jianyong Wang. 2013. Retweet or not?: personalized tweet re-ranking. In *Proceedings of the sixth ACM international conference on Web search and data mining*, pages 577–586. ACM.

William J Friedman. 2000. The development of children's knowledge of the times of future events. *Child Development*, 71(4):913–932.

Pierre Geurts, Damien Ernst, and Louis Wehenkel. 2006. Extremely randomized trees. *Machine learning*, 63(1):3–42.

Lewis R Goldberg. 1990. An alternative" description of personality": the big-five factor structure. *Journal of Personality and Social Ssychology*, 59(6):1216–1229.

Sumit Goswami, Sudeshna Sarkar, and Mayur Rustagi. 2009. Stylometric analysis of bloggers age and gender. In *Third International AAAI Conference on Weblogs and Social Media*.

Pedro Calais Guerra, Wagner Meira Jr, and Claire Cardie. 2014. Sentiment analysis on evolving social streams: How self-report imbalances can help. In *Proceedings of the 7th ACM international conference on Web search and data mining*, pages 443–452. ACM.

Francisco Iacobelli, Alastair J. Gill, Scott Nowson, and Jon Oberlander. 2011. Large scale personality classification of bloggers. In *Proc of the 4th int conf on Affect comput and intel interaction*, pages 568–577. Springer-Verlag.

William James. 1890. *The principles of psychology*. Henry Holt and Company.

Kelli A Keough, Philip G Zimbardo, and John N Boyd. 1999. Who's smoking, drinking, and using drugs? Time perspective as a predictor of substance use. *Basic and Applied Social Psychology*, 21(2):149–164.

M Kosinski and D Stillwell. 2012. myPersonality research wiki. http://www.mypersonality.org/wiki/.

Kurt Lewin. 1942. Time perspective and morale. In *Resolving social conflicts and Field theory in social science*, pages 80–93. APA, Washington, D. C.

Nira Liberman, Yaacov Trope, Sean M McCrea, and Steven J Sherman. 2007. The effect of level of construal on the temporal distance of activity enactment. *Journal of Experimental Social Psychology*, 43(1):143–149.

Xiao Ling and Daniel S Weld. 2010. Temporal information extraction. In *Proceedings of the 24th AAAI Conference on Artificial Intelligence*.

F. Mairesse, M.A. Walker, M.R. Mehl, and R.K. Moore. 2007. Using linguistic cues for the automatic recognition of personality in conversation and text. *Journal of Artificial Intelligence Research*, 30(1):457–500.

Robert R McCrae and O P John. 1992. An introduction to the five-factor model and its applications. *Journal of Personality*, 60(2):175–215.

Jari-Erik Nurmi. 2005. Thinking about and acting upon the future: Development of future orientation across the life span.

In Alan Strathman and Jeff Joireman, editors, *Understanding behavior in the context of time*, pages 31–57. Lawrence Erlbaum, Mahwah.

Rina Panigrahy, Marc Najork, and Yinglian Xie. 2012. How user behavior is related to social affinity. In *Proceedings of the fifth ACM international conference on Web search and data mining*, pages 713–722. ACM.

Greg Park, H Andrew Schwartz, Johannes C Eichstaedt, Margaret L Kern, David J Stillwell, Michal Kosinski, Lyle H Ungar, and Martin EP Seligman. 2015. Automatic personality assessment through social media language. *Journal of Personality and Social Psychology*.

Delroy L Paulhus and Simine Vazire. 2007. The self-report method. *Handbook of research methods in personality psychology*, pages 224–239.

Fabian Pedregosa, Gaël Varoquaux, Alexandre Gramfort, Vincent Michel, Bertrand Thirion, Olivier Grisel, Mathieu Blondel, Peter Prettenhofer, Ron Weiss, Vincent Dubourg, et al. 2011. Scikit-learn: Machine learning in Python. *The Journal of Machine Learning Research*, 12:2825–2830.

James W. Pennebaker, C.K. Chung, M. Ireland, A. Gonzales, and R.J. Booth. 2007. The development and psychometric properties of liwc2007. *Austin, TX, LIWC. Net*.

Daniele Quercia, Renaud Lambiotte, David Stillwell, Michal Kosinski, and Jon Crowcroft. 2012. The personality of popular facebook users. In *Proceedings of the ACM 2012 conference on Computer Supported Cooperative Work*, pages 955–964. ACM.

Lenore Sawyer Radloff. 1977. The ces-d scale a self-report depression scale for research in the general population. *Applied psychological measurement*, 1(3):385–401.

Brent W Roberts, Carl Lejuez, Robert F Krueger, Jessica M Richards, and Patrick L Hill. 2013. What is conscientiousness and how can it be assessed? *Developmental Psychology*, (online advance publication).

Maarten Sap, Gregory Park, Johannes C. Eichstaedt, Margaret L. Kern, David J. Stillwell, Michal Kosinski, Lyle H. Ungar, and H. Andrew Schwartz. 2014. Developing age and gender predictive lexica over social media. In *EMNLP 2014*, pages 1146–1151. Association for Computational Linguistics.

H Andrew Schwartz, Johannes C Eichstaedt, Margaret L Kern, Lukasz Dziurzynski, Stephanie M Ramones, Megha Agrawal, Achal Shah, Michal Kosinski, David Stillwell, Martin EP Seligman, et al. 2013. Personality, gender, and age in the language of social media: The open-vocabulary approach. *PloS one*, 8(9):e73791.

Martin EP Seligman, Peter Railton, Roy F Baumeister, and Chandra Sripada. 2013. Navigating into the future or driven by the past. *Perspectives on Psychological Science*, 8(2):119–141.

Patrick E Shrout and Joseph L Fleiss. 1979. Intraclass correlations: Uses in assessing rater reliability. *Psychological bulletin*, 86(2):420–428.

Laurence Steinberg, Sandra Graham, Lia OBrien, Jennifer Woolard, Elizabeth Cauffman, and Marie Banich. 2009. Age differences in future orientation and delay discounting. *Child Development*, 80(1):28–44.

Alan Strathman and Jeff Joireman, editors. 2005. *Understanding behavior in the context of time: Theory, research, and application*. Lawrence Erlbaum, Mahwah.

Partha Pratim Talukdar, Derry Wijaya, and Tom Mitchell. 2012. Coupled temporal scoping of relational facts. In *Proceedings of the fifth ACM international conference on Web search and data mining*, pages 73–82. ACM.

Kristina Toutanova, Dan Klein, Christopher D Manning, and Yoram Singer. 2003. Feature-rich part-of-speech tagging with a cyclic dependency network. In *Proceedings of the 2003 Conference of the North American Chapter of the Association for Computational Linguistics on Human Language Technology-Volume 1*, pages 173–180. Association for Computational Linguistics.

Naushad UzZaman, Hector Llorens, Leon Derczynski, Marc Verhagen, James Allen, and James Pustejovsky. 2013. SemEval-2013 task 1: TempEval-3: Evaluating time expressions, events, and temporal relations. In *Proceedings of the 7th International Workshop on Semantic Evaluation*.

Marc Verhagen, Inderjeet Mani, Roser Sauri, Robert Knippen, Seok Bae Jang, Jessica Littman, Anna Rumshisky, John Phillips, and James Pustejovsky. 2005. Automating temporal annotation with TARSQI. In *Proceedings of the ACL 2005 on interactive poster and demonstration sessions*, pages 81–84. Association for Computational Linguistics.

Marc Verhagen, Robert Gaizauskas, Frank Schilder, Mark Hepple, Graham Katz, and James Pustejovsky. 2007. Semeval-2007 task 15: Tempeval temporal relation identification. In *Proceedings of the 4th International Workshop on Semantic Evaluations*, pages 75–80. Association for Computational Linguistics.

Marc Verhagen, Roser Sauri, Tommaso Caselli, and James Pustejovsky. 2010. SemEval-2010 task 13: TempEval-2. In *Proceedings of the 5th International Workshop on Semantic Evaluation*, pages 57–62. Association for Computational Linguistics.

Paul Webley and Ellen K Nyhus. 2006. Parents influence on childrens future orientation and saving. *Journal of Economic Psychology*, 27(1):140–164.

Miaomiao Wen, Zeyu Zheng, Hyeju Jang, Guang Xiang, and Carolyn Penstein Rosé. 2013. Extracting events with informal temporal references in personal histories in online communities. In *Proceedings of 51st annual meeting of the ACL*, pages 836–842.

Philip G Zimbardo and John N Boyd. 1999. Putting time in perspective: A valid, reliable individual-differences metric. *Journal of Personality and Social Psychology*, 77(6):1271–1288.

# An In-depth Analysis of the Effect of Text Normalization in Social Media

**Tyler Baldwin***
baldwin.tyler.s@gmail.com

**Yunyao Li**
IBM Research - Almaden
650 Harry Road
San Jose, CA 95120, USA
yunyaoli@us.ibm.com

## Abstract

Recent years have seen increased interest in text normalization in social media, as the informal writing styles found in Twitter and other social media data often cause problems for NLP applications. Unfortunately, most current approaches narrowly regard the normalization task as a "one size fits all" task of replacing non-standard words with their standard counterparts. In this work we build a taxonomy of normalization edits and present a study of normalization to examine its effect on three different downstream applications (dependency parsing, named entity recognition, and text-to-speech synthesis). The results suggest that how the normalization task should be viewed is highly dependent on the targeted application. The results also show that normalization must be thought of as more than word replacement in order to produce results comparable to those seen on clean text.

## 1 Introduction

The informal writing style employed by authors of social media data is problematic for many natural language processing (NLP) tools, which are generally trained on clean, formal text such as newswire data. One possible solution to this problem is normalization, in which the informal text is converted into a more standard formal form. Because of this, the rise of social media data has coincided with a rise in interest in the normalization problem.

Unfortunately, while many approaches to the problem exist, there are notable limitations to the way in which normalization is examined. First, although social media normalization is universally motivated by pointing to its role in helping downstream applications, most normalization work gives little to no insight into the effect of the normalization process on the downstream application of interest. Further, the normalization process is generally seen to be agnostic of the downstream application, adopting a "one size fits all" view of how normalization should be performed. This view seems intuitively problematic, as different information is likely to be of importance for different tasks. For instance, while capitalization is important for resolving named entities, it is less important for other tasks, such as dependency parsing.

Some recent work has given credence to the idea that application-targeted normalization is appropriate (Wang and Ng, 2013; Zhang et al., 2013). However, how certain normalization actions influence the overall performance of these applications is not well understood. To address this, we design a taxonomy of possible normalization edits based on inspiration from previous work and an examination of annotated data. We then use this taxonomy to examine the importance of individual normalization actions on three different downstream applications: dependency parsing, named entity recognition, and text-to-speech synthesis. The results suggest that the importance of a given normalization edit is highly dependent on the task, making the "one size fits all" approach inappropriate. The results also show that a narrow view of normalization as word replacement is insufficient, as many often-ignored normalization actions prove to be important for certain tasks.

* Work was done while at IBM Research - Almaden.



*Human Language Technologies: The 2015 Annual Conference of the North American Chapter of the ACL*, pages 420–429,
Denver, Colorado, May 31 – June 5, 2015. 

In the next section, we give an overview of previous work on the normalization problem. We then introduce our taxonomy of normalization edits in Section 3. In Section 4, we present our evaluation methodology and present results over the three applications, using Twitter data as a representative domain. Finally, we discuss our results in Section 5 and conclude in Section 6.

## 2 Related Work

Twitter and other social media data is littered with non-standard word forms and other informal usage patterns, making it difficult for many NLP tools to produce results comparable to what is seen on formal datasets. There are two approaches proposed in the literature to handle this problem (Eisenstein, 2013). One approach is to tailor a specific NLP tool towards the data, by using training data from the domain to help the tool learn its specific idiosyncrasies. This approach has been applied with reasonable success on named entity recognition (Liu et al., 2011b; Ritter et al., 2011) as well as on parsing and part-of-speech tagging (Foster et al., 2011).

The other approach is normalization. Rather than tailoring a NLP tool towards the data, normalization seeks to tailor the data towards the tool. This is accomplished by transforming the data into a form more akin to the formal text that NLP tools are generally trained on. While normalization is often more straightforward and more easily applied in instances in which retraining is difficult or impractical, it has potential disadvantages as well, such as the potential loss of pragmatic nuance (Baldwin and Chai, 2011).

Prior to the rise of social media, the normalization process was primarily seen as one of standardizing non-standard tokens found in otherwise clean text, such as numbers, dates, and acronyms (Sproat et al., 2001). However, the current popularity of Twitter and other informal texts has caused the normalization task to take on a broader meaning in these contexts, where the goal is to convert informal text into formal text that downstream applications expect.

Many different approaches to social media normalization have been undertaken. These approaches often draw inspiration from other tasks such as machine translation (Pennell and Liu, 2011; Aw et al., 2006), spell checking (Choudhury et al., 2007) or speech recognition (Kobus et al., 2008). Other approaches include creating automatic abbreviations via a maximum entropy classifier (Pennell and Liu, 2010), creating word association graphs (Sonmez and Ozgur, 2014), and incorporating both rules and statistical models (Beaufort et al., 2010). While most initial approaches used supervised methods, unsupervised methods have recently become popular (Cook and Stevenson, 2009; Liu et al., 2011a; Yang and Eisenstein, 2013; Li and Liu, 2014). Some work has chosen to focus on specific aspects of the normalization process, such as providing good coverage (Liu et al., 2012) or building normalization dictionaries (Han et al., 2012).

In all of the work mentioned above, the normalization task was seen primarily as one of converting non-standard tokens into an equivalent standard form. Similarly, many of these works defined the problem even more narrowly such that punctuation, capitalization, and multi-word replacements were ignored. However, two pieces of recent work have suggested that this understanding of the normalization task is too narrow, as it ignores many other hallmarks of informal writing that are prevalent in social media data. Wang and Ng (2013) present a beam search based approach designed to handle machine translation which incorporates attempts to correct mistaken punctuation and add missing words, such as forms of the verb *to be*. Similarly, Zhang et al. (2013) attempt to perform all actions necessary to create a formal text. In both instances the work was motivated by, and evaluated with respect to, a specific downstream application (machine translation and dependency parsing, respectively). However, not every study that tied the output to an application chose a broad interpretation of the normalization problem (Beaufort et al., 2010; Kaji and Kitsuregawa, 2014).

## 3 Taxonomy of Normalization Edits

In order to understand the impact of individual normalization edits on downstream applications, we first need to define the space of possible normalization edits. While it is not uncommon for normalization work to present some analysis of the data, these analyses are often quite specific to the domain and datasets of interest. Because there is no agreed upon

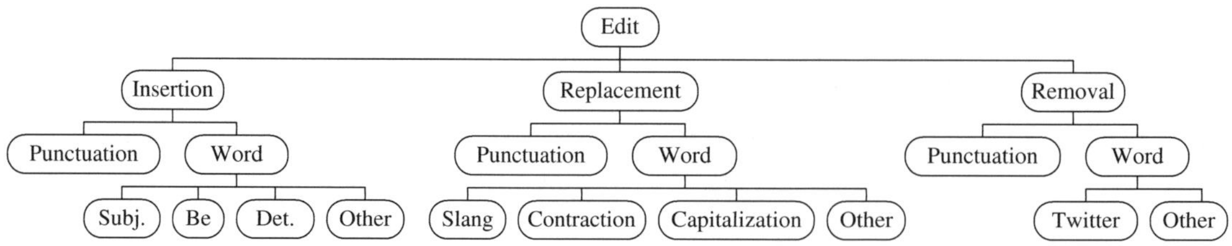


Figure 1: Taxonomy of normalization edits

taxonomy of normalization token or edit types, different analyses often look at different edit types and at different levels of granularity. In an attempt to help future work converge on a common understanding of normalization edits, in this section we present our taxonomy of normalization edits at several different levels of granularity. While it would be difficult for a taxonomy of normalization edits to be universal enough to be appropriate over all datasets and domains, we attempt to provide a taxonomy general enough to give future work a meaningful initial point of reference.

## 3.1 Methodology

Our taxonomy draws inspiration from both previous work and an examination of our own dataset (Section 3.3). In doing so, it attempts to cover normalization edits broadly, including cases that are universally understood to be important, such as slang replacement, as well as cases that are frequently ignored, such as capitalization correction.

One of the guiding principles in the design of our taxonomy was that categories should not be divided so narrowly such that the phenomenon they capture appeared very infrequently in the data. One example of this is our decision not to divide punctuation edits at the lowest level of granularity. While certain clear categories exist (e.g., emoticons), these cases appeared in a small enough percentage of tokens that they would be difficult to examine and likely have a negligible effect on overall performance.

## 3.2 Taxonomy

Our taxonomy of normalization edits is shown in Figure 1. As can be seen, we categorize edits at three levels of granularity.

**Level One.** The primary goal of the level one segmentation is to separate token replacements which are most centrally thought of as part of the normalization task from other instances that may require additional pragmatic inference. Specifically, we separate edits coarsely into three categories:

- **Token Replacements.** Replacing one or more existing tokens with one or more new tokens (e.g., replacing *wanna* with *want to*).
- **Token Additions.** Adding a token that does not replace an existing token (e.g., adding in missing subjects).
- **Token Removals.** Removing a token without replacing it with an equivalent (e.g., removing laughter words such as *lol* and *hahaha*).

**Level Two.** The next level of granularity separates normalization edits over word tokens from those over punctuation:

- **Word.** Replacing, adding, or removing word tokens (depending on parent).
- **Punctuation.** Replacing, adding, or removing punctuation tokens (depending on parent).

**Level Three.** At the final level, we subdivide word edits into groups as appropriate for the edit type. Rather than attempting to keep consistent groups across all leaf nodes, we selected the grouping based on the data distribution. For instance, Twitter-specific tokens (e.g., retweets) are often removed during normalization, so examining the removal of these words as a group is warranted. In contrast, these tokens are never added, so different segmentation is appropriate when examining word addition.

At the lowest level of the taxonomy, word replacements were subdivided as follows:

- **Contraction Replacements.** Unrolling standard contractions (*don't*), common informal cases (*wanna*), and non-standard variations produced via apostrophe omission (*dont*).
- **Slang Replacements.** Replacing slang terms, such as slang shortenings and word elongation.
- **Capitalization Replacements.** Correcting the capitalization of words. The replaced word differs from its replacement by *only* capitalization.
- **Other Replacements.** Correcting unintentional typographic mistakes, such as misspelling and word concatenation.

When segmenting word additions, we note that words that need to be added in a normalization edit were often consciously dropped by the user in the original text. Our categorization reflects this by examining syntactic categories that are often dropped in informal writing:

- **Subject Addition.** Adding in omitted subjects.
- **Determiner Addition.** Adding in omitted determiners (e.g., "[*The*] front row is so close").
- **Be-verb Addition.** Adding in omitted forms of the verb *to be*.
- **Other Addition.** All word additions not covered by the other categories.

Finally, word removals are subdivided into just two categories:

- **Dataset-specific Removals.** Removing tokens that do not appear outside of the dataset in question (e.g., for Twitter: hashtags, @replies, and retweets).
- **Other Removals.** Removing interjections, laughter words, and other expression of emotion (e.g., *ugh*).

Note that we are not suggesting here that dataset-specific words should be removed in all cases. While in many cases they may be removed if they do not have a formal equivalent, they may also be replaced or retained as is, depending on the context.

### 3.3 Dataset

To facilitate our experiments, we collected and annotated a dataset of Twitter posts (tweets) from the TREC Twitter Corpus[1]. The TREC Twitter corpus is a collection of 16 million tweets posted in January and February of 2011. The corpus is designed to be a representative sample of Twitter usage, and as such includes both regular and spam tweets. To build our dataset, we sampled 600 posts at random from the corpus. The tweets were then manually filtered such that tweets that were not in English were replaced with those in English.

To produce our gold standard, two oDesk[2] contractors were asked to manually normalize each tweet in the dataset to its fully grammatical form, as would be found in formal text. Annotation guidelines stipulated that twitter-specific tokens should be retained if important to understanding the sentence, but modified or removed otherwise. As noted, most previous work often stopped short of requiring full grammaticality. However, Zhang et al. (2013) argued that grammaticality should be the ideal end goal of normalization since the models used in downstream applications are typically trained on well-formed sentences. We adopt this methodology here both because we agree with this assertion and because a fully grammatical form is appropriate for all of the downstream applications of interest, allowing for a single unified gold standard that can aid comparison across applications.

During gold standard creation, each normalization edit was labeled with its type, according to the above taxonomy. The distribution of normalization edits in the dataset is given in Table 1. As shown, normalization edits accounted for about 29% of all tokens. Token replacements accounted for just over half of all edits (53%), while token addition (29%) was more common than token removal (18%). One interesting observation is non-capitalization word replacement accounted for only 25% of all normalization edits, intuitively indicating potential drawbacks for the common definition of normalization as one of simple word replacement which ignores capitalization and punctuation.

[1]`http://trec.nist.gov/data/tweets/`
[2]`https://www.odesk.com/`

| Configuration | Count |
|---|---|
| No edit | 8479 |
| All edits | 3411 |
| ADDITION | 993 |
| PUNCT | 437 |
| WORD | 556 |
| BEVERB | 137 |
| DETERMINER | 103 |
| OTHER | 141 |
| SUBJECT | 175 |
| REPLACEMENT | 1797 |
| PUNCT | 312 |
| WORD | 1485 |
| CAPITALIZATION | 634 |
| CONTRACTION | 246 |
| OTHER | 176 |
| SLANG | 429 |
| REMOVAL | 621 |
| PUNCT | 120 |
| WORD | 501 |
| OTHER | 172 |
| TWITTER | 329 |

Table 1: Token counts for each type of normalization edit.

## 4 Evaluation

In this section, we present our examination of the effect of normalization edits on downstream NLP applications. To get a broad understanding of these effects, we examine three very different cases: dependency parsing, named entity recognition (NER), and text-to-speech (TTS) synthesis. We chose these tasks because they each require the extraction of different information from the text. For instance, named entity recognition requires only a shallow syntactic analysis, in contrast to the deeper understanding required for dependency parsing. Similarly, only speech synthesis requires phoneme production, while the other tasks do not. Despite their differences, each of these tasks is relevant to larger applications that would benefit from improved performance on Twitter data, and each has garnered attention in the normalization and Twitter-adaptation literature (Beaufort et al., 2010; Liu et al., 2011b; Zhang et al., 2013).

Although the differences in these tasks also dictates that they be evaluated somewhat differently, we examine them within a common evaluation structure. In all cases, to examine the effects of each normalization edit we model our analyses as ablation studies. That is, for every category in the taxonomy, we examine the effect of performing all normalization edits *except* the relevant case. This allows us to measure the drop in performance solely attributable to each category; the greater the performance drop observed when a given normalization edit is not performed, the greater the importance of performing that edit.

To aid analysis, results are presented in two ways: 1) as raw performance numbers, and 2) as an error rate per-token. These metrics give two different views of the relevance of each edit type. The raw numbers give a sense of the overall impact of a given category, and as such may be impacted by the size of the category, with common edits becoming more important simply by virtue of their frequency. In contrast, the per-token error rate highlights the cost of failing to perform a single instance of a given normalization edit, independent of the frequency of the edit. Both of these measures are likely to be relevant when attempting to improve the performance of a normalization system. Note that since the first measure is one of overall performance, smaller numbers reflect larger performance drops when removing a given type of edit, so that the smaller the number the more critical the need to perform the given type of normalization. In contrast, the latter judgment is one of error rate, and thus interpretation is reversed; the larger the error rate when it is removed, the more critical the normalization edit.

Another commonality among the analyses is that performance is measured relative to the top performance of the *tool*, not the task. That is, following Zhang et al. (2013), we consider the output produced by the tool (e.g., the dependency parser) on the grammatically correct data to be gold standard performance. This means that some output based on our gold standard may in fact be incorrect relative to human judgment, simply because the tool used does not have perfect performance even if the text if fully grammatical. Since the goal is to understand how normalization edits impact the performance, this style of evaluation is appropriate; it considers mistakes attributable to normalization edits as erroneous, but ignores those mistakes attributable to the limitations of the tool.

Finally, to maximize the relevance of the analyses

given here, in each case we employ publicly available and widely used tools.

### 4.1 Parser Evaluation

To examine the effect of normalization on dependency parsing, we employ the Stanford dependency parser[3] (Marneffe et al., 2006). To produce the gold standard dependencies for comparison, the manually grammaticalized tweets (Section 3.3) were run through the parser. To compare the ablation results to the gold standard parses, we adopt a variation of the evaluation method used by Zhang et al. (2013). Given dependency parses from the gold standard and a candidate normalization, we define precision and recall as follows:

$$\text{precision}_{\text{sov}} = \frac{|SOV \cap SOV_{gold}|}{|SOV|} \quad (1)$$

$$\text{recall}_{\text{sov}} = \frac{|SOV \cap SOV_{gold}|}{|SOV_{gold}|} \quad (2)$$

Where $SOV$ and $SOV_{gold}$ are the sets of subject, object, and verb dependencies in the candidate normalization and gold standard, respectively. While Zhang et al. chose to examine subjects and objects separately from verbs, we employ a unified metric to simplify interpretation.

#### 4.1.1 Results

Results of the ablation study are summarized in Table 2. As shown, the performance of a complex task such as dependency parsing is broadly impacted by a variety of normalization edits. Based on the raw F-measure, the more common word replacements proved to be the most critical, although failing to handle token addition and removal edits also resulted in substantial drops in performance. At the lowest level in the taxonomy, slang replacements and subject addition were the most critical edits.

Although many replacement tasks were important in aggregate, on a per-token basis the most important edits were those that required token removal and addition. Perhaps unsurprisingly, failing to add subjects and verbs resulted in the largest issues, as the parser has little chance of identifying these dependencies if the terms simply do not appear in the sentence. However, not all word additions proved critical, as failing to add in a missing determiner generally had little impact on the overall performance. Similarly, failing to correct capitalization did not cause substantial problems for the parser. Some word replacements did prove to be important, with slang and other word replacements showing some of the largest per-token error rates. Removing misleading punctuation or changing non-standard punctuation both proved important, but the per-token effect of punctuation addition was modest.

In general, the results suggest that a complex task such as dependency parsing suffers substantially when the input data differs from formal text in any number of ways. With the exception of capitalization correction, performing almost every normalization edit is necessary to achieve results commensurate with those seen on formal text.

| **Configuration** | **F-measure** | **Per-token Error Rate** |
|---|---|---|
| -ADDITION | 0.790 | 0.00021 |
| -PUNCT | 0.919 | 0.00019 |
| -WORD | 0.842 | 0.00028 |
| -BEVERB | 0.948 | 0.00038 |
| -DETERMINER | 0.980 | 0.00019 |
| -OTHER | 0.959 | 0.00029 |
| -SUBJECT | 0.903 | **0.00055** |
| -REPLACEMENT | **0.710** | 0.00016 |
| -PUNCT | 0.907 | 0.00030 |
| -WORD | **0.754** | 0.00017 |
| -CAPITALIZATION | 0.950 | 0.00008 |
| -CONTRACTION | 0.945 | 0.00023 |
| -OTHER | 0.947 | 0.00030 |
| -SLANG | **0.872** | 0.00030 |
| -REMOVAL | 0.866 | **0.00022** |
| -PUNCT | 0.959 | **0.00034** |
| -WORD | 0.887 | 0.00023 |
| -OTHER | 0.952 | 0.00028 |
| -TWITTER | 0.925 | 0.00023 |

Table 2: Dependency Parser Results.

### 4.2 NER Evaluation

In this section, we examine the effect of each normalization edit on a somewhat more shallow interpretation task, named entity recognition. Unlike dependency parsing which requires an understanding of every token in the text, NER must only determine whether a given token is a named entity, and if so, discover its associated entity type.

[3] Version 2.0.5

The setup for evaluation of normalization edits on named entity recognition closely follows that of dependency parsing. We once again employ a tool from the suite of Stanford NLP tools, the Stanford named entity recognizer[4] (Finkel et al., 2005). We also define precision and recall in a similar manner:

$$\text{precision}_{\text{ner}} = \frac{|ENT \cap ENT_{gold}|}{|ENT|} \quad (3)$$

$$\text{recall}_{\text{ner}} = \frac{|ENT \cap ENT_{gold}|}{|ENT_{gold}|} \quad (4)$$

Where $ENT$ and $ENT_{gold}$ are the sets of entities identified over the candidate normalization and gold standard sentences, respectively. Entities were labeled as one of three classes (`person`, `location`, or `organization`), and two entities were only considered a match if they both selected the same entity and the same entity class.

#### 4.2.1 Results

Table 3 shows the results of the NER ablation study. Unlike dependency parsing, only word replacement edits proved to be critically important for NER tasks, as adding and subtracting words had little impact on the overall performance. Capitalization, which is generally an important feature for the identification of named entities, was unsurprisingly important. Similarly, the replacement of word types other than slang and contraction was important, because many of these instances may come from misspelled named entities. Slang and contractions were less important, as they were generally not used to reference named entities. As the words dropped by Twitter users tend to be function words that are not critical to understanding the sentence they are rarely named entities and have only a small effect on named entity recognition. Similarly, terms that are removed during normalization also tend to not be named entities, and thus has minor overall impact.

A similar phenomenon is observed in the per-token evaluation, where unintentionally produced, non-slang, non-contraction word replacement was seen to be of paramount importance. Punctuation removal was also important on a per-token basis, despite having little impact in aggregate.

Overall, the results given in Table 3 indicate that a focused approach to normalization for named entity recognition is warranted. Unlike dependency parsing that required a broad approach involving token addition and removal, the replacement-centric normalization approach typically employed by previous work is likely to be sufficient when the goal is to improve entity recognition.

[4] Version 1.2.8

| Configuration | F-measure | Per-token Error Rate |
|---|---|---|
| -ADDITION | 0.955 | 0.00005 |
| -PUNCT | 0.973 | 0.00006 |
| -WORD | 0.974 | 0.00005 |
| -BEVERB | 0.998 | 0.00001 |
| -DETERMINER | 0.989 | 0.00011 |
| -OTHER | 0.989 | 0.00008 |
| -SUBJECT | 0.998 | 0.00001 |
| -REPLACEMENT | **0.827** | **0.00010** |
| -PUNCT | 0.962 | 0.00012 |
| -WORD | **0.849** | 0.00010 |
| -CAPITALIZATION | **0.921** | 0.00012 |
| -CONTRACTION | 0.977 | 0.00009 |
| -OTHER | 0.931 | **0.00039** |
| -SLANG | 0.945 | 0.00013 |
| -REMOVAL | 0.956 | 0.00007 |
| -PUNCT | 0.970 | **0.00025** |
| -WORD | 0.960 | 0.00008 |
| -OTHER | 0.973 | 0.00015 |
| -TWITTER | 0.962 | 0.00012 |

Table 3: NER Results.

### 4.3 TTS Evaluation

Unlike the previous two tasks, the TTS problem is complicated by its need for speech production. Similarly, evaluation of speech synthesis is more difficult, as it requires human judgment about the overall quality of the output (Black and Tokuda, 2005). While speech synthesis evaluations often rate performance on a 5 point scale, we adopt a more restricted method, based on the comparison to gold standard methodology used in the previous evaluations. For each tweet and each round of ablation, a synthesized audio file was produced from both the gold standard and ablated version of the tweet. These audio snippets were randomized and presented to human judges who were asked to make a binary judgment as to whether the meaning and understandability of the ablated case was comparable to the gold standard. The accuracy of a given round of ablation is then calculated to be the percentage of tweets judged

| Configuration | F-measure | Per-token Error Rate |
|---|---|---|
| -ADDITION | 0.713 | 0.00029 |
| -PUNCT | 0.920 | 0.00018 |
| -WORD | 0.723 | 0.00050 |
| -BEVERB | 0.903 | 0.00071 |
| -DETERMINER | 0.937 | 0.00061 |
| -OTHER | 0.910 | 0.00064 |
| -SUBJECT | 0.853 | 0.00084 |
| -REPLACEMENT | **0.550** | 0.00025 |
| -PUNCT | 0.877 | 0.00040 |
| -WORD | **0.590** | 0.00028 |
| -CAPITALIZATION | 0.860 | 0.00022 |
| -CONTRACTION | 0.910 | 0.00037 |
| -OTHER | 0.883 | 0.00066 |
| -SLANG | 0.783 | 0.00051 |
| -REMOVAL | 0.580 | **0.00068** |
| -PUNCT | 0.880 | **0.00100** |
| -WORD | 0.600 | 0.00080 |
| -OTHER | 0.837 | **0.00095** |
| -TWITTER | **0.710** | 0.00088 |

Table 4: Text-To-Speech Synthesis Results.

to be similar to the gold standard.

The eSpeak speech synthesizer[5] was used to produce audio files for all tweet variations in the ablation study. As is common for speech synthesizers, eSpeak does perform some amount of TTS-specific normalization natively. While this does influence the normalizations produced, the comparison to gold standard methodology employed in this study helps us to focus on differences that are primarily attributable to the normalization edits we wish to examine, not those produced natively. To obtain the gold standard, two native-English speaking judges were recruited via oDesk. Inter-annotator agreement was moderate, $\kappa = 0.48$.

### 4.3.1 Results

Table 4 shows the results of the speech synthesis study. As shown, the removal of non-standard or out of place tokens was most critical to the production of a normalization that is clearly understandable to human listeners. The aggregate results for token removals were comparable to or better than those of replacements at all levels of the taxonomy, in contrast to the results from the other two tasks, where the larger number of replacements led to the largest performance hits. Meanwhile, word addition proved to be less essential overall.

At the token level, the importance of token removal is even more stark; the per-token error rate of every category of removal is greater than that of all other categories at the same taxonomy level. Although most word additions had a comparatively small effect on performance overall, they were important on a per-token basis. Most notably, subject adding had high per-token importance. In contrast, failing to add missing punctuation was not often marked as erroneous by human judges, nor was failing to normalize capitalization or contractions.

Similar to those on dependency parsing, the results on speech synthesis suggest that a broad approach that considers several different types of normalization edit is necessary to produce results comparable to those seen on clean text. However, at a high level there is a clear divide in importance between normalization types, where the greatest performance gains can be obtained by focusing on the comparatively small number of token removals.

## 5 Discussion

The results presented in Section 4 are consistent with the hypothesis that a "one size fits all" approach to Twitter normalization is problematic, as the importance of a given normalization edit was highly dependent on the intended downstream task. Differences in which edits had the most substantial effect were present at all levels of scrutiny. Adding subjects and other words that a Twitter author dropped can be vitally important if the goal is to improve parsing performance, but can mostly be ignored if the goal is NER. Removing twitter-specific or otherwise non-standard words showed a gradation of importance over the three tasks, with little importance for NER, moderate importance for parsing, and critical importance for speech synthesis. Capitalization correction had negligible impact on the parser or synthesizer, but was helpful for NER.

The importance of different edit types can be seen even at the most coarse level of examination. While normalization for speech synthesis is primarily dependent on removing unknown tokens, normalization that targets name entity recognition would be better served focusing on replacing non-standard to-

[5]Version 1.47.11, `http://espeak.sourceforge.net/`

kens with their standard forms. In contrast, parser-targeted normalization must attend to both of the tasks, as well as the task of restoring dropped tokens.

Despite the differences, there are a few common threads that appear in each evaluation. Most notably, the results suggest that the decision of most recent Twitter normalization work to focus on word replacement was not entirely without merit, as the high frequency of token replacements translated into high overall importance for all tasks. Similarly, the focus on slang was also somewhat reasonable, as failing to handle slang terms had a significant impact on parsing and speech synthesis, though it had little impact on entity recognition. Nonetheless, the results in Section 4 clearly suggest that handling these cases represent only a small fraction of the actions necessary to produce performance comparable to what would be seen on formal text.

Another similarity among all instances was the lack of importance of certain categories. For instance, punctuation addition was not important for any of the three tasks. While Zhang et al. had hypothesized that punctuation addition would be important for dependency parsing, the results given here suggest that the overall impact is minor. Similarly, contraction standardization was not shown to be important in any of the evaluations. Contraction normalization is more representative of how the normalization task was seen prior to the rise of social media normalization, as it represents a fairly minor normalizing action that might still be performed on formal text. Since contractions likely appear in a variety of forms in the data used to train NLP tools, it is unsurprising that these tools are comparatively robust to contraction differences than to cases that are less typically encountered.

## 6 Conclusion

In this work, we presented an in-depth look at the effects of the normalization of Twitter data. To do so, we introduced a taxonomy of normalization edits based on an examination of our Twitter dataset and inspiration from previous work. The taxonomy allowed for normalization edits to be examined systematically at different levels of granularity, and enabled an examination of the effects of not only token replacements, but the token additions and removals that recent work has suggested may have been unjustly ignored.

To understand the effects of each edit, we conducted ablation studies that examined results on three different downstream tasks: dependency parsing, named entity recognition, and text-to-speech synthesis. We found that while some normalization edits were universally important (or unimportant) for the production of accurate results, many differences persist. These results suggest that, for best results, how the normalization task is performed should not be agnostic of the downstream application. Further, our results support the suggestion that in order for downstream applications to produce accurate results, in most cases it is necessary to take a broad view of the normalization task the looks beyond simple word replacements.

## Acknowledgments

The authors would like to thank Benny Kimelfeld for his comments on an early draft of this work. We also thank our anonymous reviewers for their constructive comments and feedback, and Stephanie Mcneish, Lacy Corlis, and Kaila Milos C. Factolerin for their assistance with annotation and evaluation.

## References

AiTi Aw, Min Zhang, Juan Xiao, and Jian Su. 2006. A phrase-based statistical model for sms text normalization. In *ACL*, pages 33–40.

Tyler Baldwin and Joyce Chai. 2011. Beyond normalization: Pragmatics of word form in text messages. In *IJCNLP*, pages 1437–1441, Chiang Mai, Thailand, November. Asian Federation of Natural Language Processing.

Richard Beaufort, Sophie Roekhaut, Louise-Amélie Cougnon, and Cédrick Fairon. 2010. A hybrid rule/model-based finite-state framework for normalizing sms messages. In *ACL*, pages 770–779.

Alan W. Black and Keiichi Tokuda. 2005. The blizzard challenge - 2005: evaluating corpus-based speech synthesis on common datasets. In *INTERSPEECH*, pages 77–80.

Monojit Choudhury, Rahul Saraf, Vijit Jain, Animesh Mukherjee, Sudeshna Sarkar, and Anupam Basu. 2007. Investigation and modeling of the structure of texting language. *IJDAR*, 10(3-4):157–174.

Paul Cook and Suzanne Stevenson. 2009. An unsupervised model for text message normalization. In *CALC*, pages 71–78.

Jacob Eisenstein. 2013. What to do about bad language on the internet. In *NAACL-HLT*, pages 359–369, Atlanta, Georgia, June. Association for Computational Linguistics.

Jenny Rose Finkel, Trond Grenager, and Christopher Manning. 2005. Incorporating non-local information into information extraction systems by gibbs sampling. In *ACL*, pages 363–370, Ann Arbor, Michigan, June. Association for Computational Linguistics.

Jennifer Foster, Özlem Çetinoglu, Joachim Wagner, Joseph Le Roux, Stephen Hogan, Joakim Nivre, Deirdre Hogan, and Josef van Genabith. 2011. hardtoparse: Pos tagging and parsing the twitterverse. volume WS-11-05 of *AAAI Workshops*. AAAI.

Bo Han, Paul Cook, and Timothy Baldwin. 2012. Automatically constructing a normalisation dictionary for microblogs. In *EMNLP-CoNLL*, pages 421–432.

Nobuhiro Kaji and Masaru Kitsuregawa. 2014. Accurate word segmentation and pos tagging for japanese microblogs: Corpus annotation and joint modeling with lexical normalization. In *Proceedings of the 2014 Conference on Empirical Methods in Natural Language Processing (EMNLP)*, pages 99–109, Doha, Qatar, October. Association for Computational Linguistics.

Catherine Kobus, François Yvon, and Géraldine Damnati. 2008. Normalizing SMS: are two metaphors better than one? In *COLING*, pages 441–448.

Chen Li and Yang Liu. 2014. Improving text normalization via unsupervised model and discriminative reranking. In *Proceedings of the ACL 2014 Student Research Workshop*, pages 86–93, Baltimore, Maryland, USA, June. Association for Computational Linguistics.

Fei Liu, Fuliang Weng, Bingqing Wang, and Yang Liu. 2011a. Insertion, deletion, or substitution? normalizing text messages without pre-categorization nor supervision. In *ACL*, pages 71–76.

Xiaohua Liu, Shaodian Zhang, Furu Wei, and Ming Zhou. 2011b. Recognizing named entities in tweets. In *NAACL-HLT*, pages 359–367, Portland, Oregon, USA, June. Association for Computational Linguistics.

Fei Liu, Fuliang Weng, and Xiao Jiang. 2012. A broad-coverage normalization system for social media language. In *ACL*, pages 1035–1044.

Marie-Catherine De Marneffe, Bill MacCartney, and Christopher D. Manning. 2006. Generating typed dependency parses from phrase structure parses. In *LREC*, pages 449–454.

Deana Pennell and Yang Liu. 2010. Normalization of text messages for text-to-speech. In *ICASSP*, pages 4842–4845.

Deana Pennell and Yang Liu. 2011. A character-level machine translation approach for normalization of SMS abbreviations. In *IJCNLP*, pages 974–982.

Alan Ritter, Sam Clark, Mausam, and Oren Etzioni. 2011. Named entity recognition in Tweets: An experimental study. In *EMNLP*, pages 1524–1534.

Cagil Sonmez and Arzucan Ozgur. 2014. A graph-based approach for contextual text normalization. In *Proceedings of the 2014 Conference on Empirical Methods in Natural Language Processing (EMNLP)*, pages 313–324, Doha, Qatar, October. Association for Computational Linguistics.

Richard Sproat, Alan W. Black, Stanley F. Chen, Shankar Kumar, Mari Ostendorf, and Christopher Richards. 2001. Normalization of non-standard words. *Computer Speech & Language*, 15(3):287–333.

Pidong Wang and Hwee Tou Ng. 2013. A beam-search decoder for normalization of social media text with application to machine translation. In *NAACL-HLT*, pages 471–481, Atlanta, Georgia, June. Association for Computational Linguistics.

Yi Yang and Jacob Eisenstein. 2013. A log-linear model for unsupervised text normalization. In *Proceedings of the 2013 Conference on Empirical Methods in Natural Language Processing*, pages 61–72, Seattle, Washington, USA, October. Association for Computational Linguistics.

Congle Zhang, Tyler Baldwin, Howard Ho, Benny Kimelfeld, and Yunyao Li. 2013. Adaptive parser-centric text normalization. In *ACL*, Sofia, Bulgaria, August. Association for Computational Linguistics.

# Using Summarization to Discover Argument Facets in Online Idealogical Dialog

**Amita Misra, Pranav Anand, Jean Fox Tree, and Marilyn Walker**
UC Santa Cruz
Natural Language and Dialogue Systems Lab
1156 N. High. SOE-3
Santa Cruz, California, 95064, USA
amisra2|panand|foxtree|mawalker@ucsc.edu

## Abstract

More and more of the information available on the web is dialogic, and a significant portion of it takes place in online forum conversations about current social and political topics. We aim to develop tools to summarize what these conversations are about. What are the CENTRAL PROPOSITIONS associated with different stances on an issue; what are the abstract objects under discussion that are central to a speaker's argument? How can we recognize that two CENTRAL PROPOSITIONS realize the same FACET of the argument? We hypothesize that the CENTRAL PROPOSITIONS are exactly those arguments that **people** find most salient, and use human summarization as a probe for discovering them. We describe our corpus of human summaries of opinionated dialogs, then show how we can identify similar repeated arguments, and group them into FACETS across many discussions of a topic. We define a new task, ARGUMENT FACET SIMILARITY (AFS), and show that we can predict AFS with a .54 correlation score, versus an ngram system baseline of .39 and a semantic textual similarity system baseline of .45.

| PostID:Turn |
|---|
| **S1:1** Agreed She is ignoring my religious freedom and trying to institute her religion into law. **The law that will bar my family from legal protections. It won't protect her marriage but will bar me and my people from from being full citizens.** She isn't protecting marriage but perserving her heterosexual privledge. |
| **S2:1** How on earth is she impeding on you religious freedom? She isn't trying to take away your right to any religious ceremony. With such a wide-open standard of what constitutes religious freedom that you seem to have, any legislation could be construed as imposing on religious freedom. |
| **S1:2** Because it is her religious belief that marriage is between a man and a woman. **My religious belief is that marriage is between two people that love each other regardless of sex.** She is tying to place her religious belif into law over mine. Who gets hurt here? If my religious belief is put into law she can still marry the person of her choice. If her religious belief gets put into law she can still marry the person of her choice but I do not get to. So I and my people are hurt by codifing her religious belief into law. She is trying to keep gay people out of marriage and thus preserve her heterosexual privledge. |
| **S2:2** But by that definition, either one could be viewed as impeding on religious freedom, including your view impeding on hers ! We don't define imposing on religious freedom on the basis of having different ideals. **It doesn't effect your religion or religious freedom if you don't get benefits under gay marriages.** You can argue in other ways, on other basis, but the idea that not giving gays marriage benefits is imposing on religious freedom is an empty " argument ". |

Figure 1: Gay Marriage Dialog-1.

## 1 Introduction

In the wake of the Penn TreeBank, much progress has been achieved in processing the monologic, informational language characteristic of newswire text. But an increasing share of the text data on the web is unlike newswire in a variety of ways: it is dialogic, opinionated, argumentative. And while some of these dialogs may be a little more than flame wars, a significant portion involve contentful, reasoned disputes on important social and political topics, as exemplified by the forum snippets in Figs. 1 and 3. Studying data like this will undoubtedly help us to understand dialogic and informal argumentative language in general. And, indeed, previous work (Abbott et al., 2011; Somasundaran and Wiebe, 2010) has examined the structure of these discussions – e.g., the argumentative discourse relation a post bears to its parent (agreeing or disagreeing), or the stance that a person takes on an issue.

Our goal here is to develop techniques to recognize the specific arguments and counterarguments people tend to advance, and group them across discussions into the FACETS on which that issue is ar-



*Human Language Technologies: The 2015 Annual Conference of the North American Chapter of the ACL*, pages 430–440,
Denver, Colorado, May 31 – June 5, 2015. 

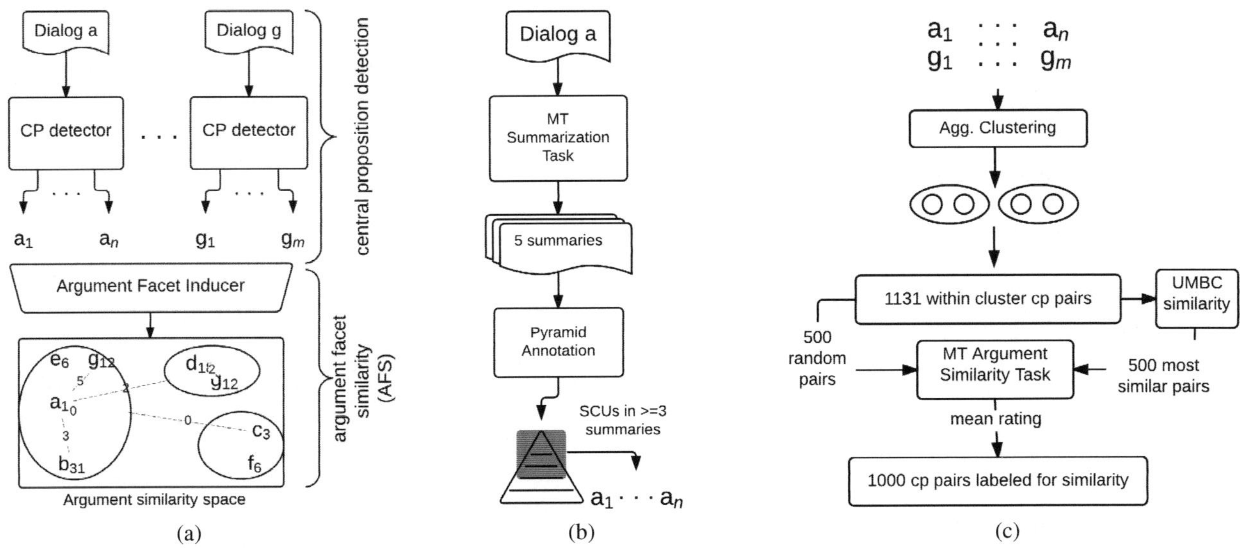


Figure 2: The overall engineering architecture of our approach. (a) Basic engineering approach for extracting CENTRAL PROPOSITIONS and clustering them into argument FACETS across several dialogs; (b) Workflow for 'detecting' central propositions via pyramid evaluation of multiple summaries; (c) Workflow for obtaining gold-standard labels for AFS task.

gued across the population at large. Recognizing the FACETS of an argument automatically entails at least two subtasks, as schematized in Fig. 2a.

| **PostID:Turn** |
| --- |
| **S1:1** Certainly not yours. You should know that I am for no marriage in government. It should be left to a religious institution where it will actually mean something. The states should then go back to doing something that actually makes sense and doesn't reward people like Britney Spears for being white trash. |
| **S2:1** That is all well and good, but it is not the religious ceremony and sanction that gays are looking for. They already have that; there are churches that perform same-sex marriages. **It is the civil benefits that are at issue. Are you saying you would be in favor of foregoing ALL the legal rights and benefits you are afforded by marriage? For example: *Assumption of Spouse's Pension *Automatic Inheritance *Automatic Housing Lease Transfer *Bereavement Leave....** What do you say? |
| **S1:2** yeah I know. I'm saying that there should be a better system. For example, if you had a best friend who you are roommates with... both hetero for the sake of argument... and never wish to get married then **could they get some of the benefits you described**? |

Figure 3: Gay Marriage Dialog-2.

First, there must be a system, the CENTRAL PROPOSITION detector, that can extract the most essential arguments in a particular conversation. Example CENTRAL PROPOSITIONS in Figs. 1 and 3 are provided in bold. Second, there must be another system, the ARGUMENT FACET inducer, that relates these conversation-specific arguments to each other in terms of FACETS, e.g. that identifies the two specific central propositions in Figs. 1 and 3 about "legal protections" and "civil benefits" as the same (abstract) FACET, namely that same-sex marriage is about getting the civil rights benefits of marriage.

We first focus on the question of extracting reliable data for central propositions. See Fig. 2b. We propose that the CENTRAL PROPOSITIONS of a dialog are exactly those arguments that **people** find most salient, which is naturally reflected by their summarization behavior. We then apply the Pyramid method, by which the CENTRAL PROPOSITIONS bubble up to the highest tiers of the pyramid, thereby allowing us to identify them. With the central propositions in hand, we proceed to build the argument facet inducer. We introduce a new task of ARGUMENT FACET SIMILARITY (**AFS**). We discuss how AFS is similar to, but different than SEMANTIC TEXTUAL SIMILARITY (**STS**) (Agirre et al., 2012; Jurgens et al., 2014; Agirre et al., 2013; Beltagy et al., 2014; Han et al., 2013).

Sec. 2 provides a more detailed overview and description of our method, and the data that it produces. Sec. 3 describes our experimental setup for the **AFS** task and then presents our results. We describe a learning approach that achieves correlations of .54 on the **AFS** task, as compared to a baseline correlation of .45 using off-the-shelf modules that are competitive in **STS** tasks. We delay a detailed discussion of related work to Sec. 4 when we can compare it to our own approach. Sec. 5 summarizes the paper and discusses future work.

## 2 Experimental Method

Fig. 2 summarizes our overall method for producing the summary corpus and then extracting arguments and clustering them into FACETS. Our method consists of the following steps:

**S1**: Dialog Selection.

**S2**: MT summarization of dialogs selected in S1.

**S3**: Pyramid annotation of summaries produced by S2 and selection of top-tier pyramid labels as CENTRAL PROPOSITIONS for individual dialogs.

**S4**: Clustering of CENTRAL PROPOSITIONS from S3.

**S5**: MT ARGUMENT FACET SIMILARITY task, using clusters from S4.

**S6**: Train and test a predictor for ARGUMENT FACET SIMILARITY (Sec. 3).

We explain these steps in more detail below.

**S1: Dialog Selection.** We use the publicly available Internet Argument Corpus (IAC) (Walker et al., 2012). We use the links in the meta-data to extract a sequence of turns to build two-party dialog chains like those in Figs. 1 and 3. We extracted 85 dialogs for the topic gay marriage from an original corpus of 1292 discussion threads using these criteria:

- **Number of turns per contributor**: We want dialogs in which substantive issues were discussed, so we extract dialogs with at least 3 turns per conversant that present at least 2 different perspectives on an issue.
- **Author**: Some authors post frequently and would dominate the corpus if we use random selection. To get richer, more diverse dialogs expressing different perspectives, we only select a single dialog between any particular pair of authors from a discussion thread.
- **Word Count in a post**: Some posts are long. To make it practical to collect dialog summaries, we extract dialogs where the number of words per turn is less than 250.

**S2: MT Summarization Task.** The summarization task was run on Mechanical Turk. To get good quality summaries, workers completed a qualification test involving summarizing a sample dialog. Workers were instructed to summarize according to dialog length: dialogs under 750 words in 125 words, and those above 750 in 175 words. We use 45 dialogs in this study and save the other 40 for future work. We collect 5 summaries for each dialog resulting in a dataset of 225 summaries. Fig. 4 provides 2 of the 5 summaries collected for the dialog in Fig. 3.

| |
|---|
| S1 thinks that the government should stay out of marriage and that it should be left to religious institutions. He thinks there needs to be a better system and that single people are the ones that are harmed the most by marriage laws because they are unable to get any of the benefits that married people do even if they want them, or it is important to their situation. S2 says religious ceremonies aren't what gay people want because they already can have them via churches. They want the rights and to keep the government out would be to give up those rights. If single people want those rights they should get married, but he thinks you should be free to marry who you wish. |
| The issue here is whether government or religion should decides the principles of marriage, and who is allowed to get married.<br>Speaker one believes that leaving it up to religions groups does not satisfy what gays are looking for. They are searching for the civil benefits that come with a marriage and would like to be treated equally in that respect. The speaker believes gay should be able to marry a person of their choice and get equal rights.<br>Speaker two opinions that there should indeed be a better system for marriage benefits and that it is all "single" people that get screwed over by marriage's current stature. Speaker two believes that gay people should marry a woman if they want the same rights. |

Figure 4: Two of the 5 Summaries for Dialog-2.

**S3: Pyramid Annotation.** We trained three undergraduates to annotate summaries to produce pyramids. We hypothesize that we can use the Pyramid method to induce the FACETS of a topic across a set of dialogs (Nenkova and Passonneau, 2004). The annotation of Pyramids seeks to uncover the common elements, or summary content units (SCUs), across several summaries (in our case, 5). Each SCU identifies a set of spans that are semantically equivalent. Each SCU also has a unique annotator-generated label that reflects the semantic meaning of the contributions. Because our aim here is to focus on argument propositional content, the annotators were instructed to keep only the main proposition in the SCU as the label, ignoring any attributions or other types of content. See Table 1. Once annotation is complete, the SCUs are ranked based on their frequency across all of the summaries, as shown by the Tier in Fig. 5, which includes data from the two summaries in Fig. 4.

| | |
|---|---|
| Contributor | S1 points to the trend to legalize gay marriage in western countries such as Netherlands, Belgium, and most of Canada |
| Contributor | S1 refutes this assertion, citing a number of countries which recognize same-sex marriage. |
| Contributor | He states the US is more similar to Anglo nations and in many of those gay marriage is legal. |
| Label | A number of countries recognize same-sex marriage. |

Table 1: A sample label after removing the attributions from the SCU contributors.

**S4: SCUs to clusters.** The pyramid structure directly reflects the content that the annotators deem most important in the original dialog. We are interested in the content that bubbles to the top across all the dialogs. We take the Tier 3 and above SCUs as our CENTRAL PROPOSITIONS, and extract the labels of those SCUs. This gives a total of 329 SCU labels. In what follows we treat a cluster of CENTRAL PROPOSITIONS as a FACET label, just as a synset concept in WordNet is labeled by its members.

The purpose of AFS, then, is to provide a similarity metric on these SCU labels. As described below (and sketched in Fig. 2c), we used Mechanical Turk to provide similarity scores between pairs of SCU central propositions. Although, in principle, we could have asked about all possible pairs of the 329 CENTRAL PROPOSITIONS, most pairs are likely to be unrelated, and so we used an initial clustering algorithm to help reduce the work and cost.

To group similar arguments, we performed clustering across our 329 labels. We performed Agglomerative Clustering using Scikit-learn (Agg Clustering in Fig. 2c). (Pedregosa et al., 2011). It recursively merges the pair of clusters that minimally increases a given linkage distance. We used cosine similarity as the distance measure with average linkage criteria. To focus on topic-specific cues, the clustering was performed using only nouns, verbs and adjectives. After generating all pairwise combinations within a cluster, this approach yielded 1131 argument pairs used in the Mechanical Turk AFS task. See Fig. 2c.

**Instructions**
We would like you to classify each of the following sets of pairs based on your perception of how SIMILAR the arguments are, on the following scale, examples follow.
(5) Completely equivalent, mean pretty much exactly the same thing, using different words.
(4) Mostly equivalent, but some unimportant details differ. One argument may be more specific than another or include a relatively unimportant extra fact.
(3) Roughly equivalent, but some important information differs or is missing. This includes cases where the argument is about the same FACET but the authors have different stances on that facet.
(2) Not equivalent, but share some details. For example, talking about the same entities but making different arguments (different facets)
(1) Not equivalent, but are on same topic
(0) On a different topic

**Facet**: A facet is a low level issue that often reoccurs in many arguments in support of the author's stance or in attacking the other author's position. There are many ways to argue for your stance on a topic. For example, in a discussion about the death penalty you may argue in favor of it by claiming that it deters crime. Alternatively, you may argue in favor of the death penalty because it gives victims of the crimes closure. On the other hand you may argue against the death penalty because some innocent people will be wrongfully executed or because it is a cruel and unusual punishment. Each of these specific points is a facet.
For two utterances to be about the same facet, it is not necessary that the authors have the same belief toward the facet. For example, one author may believe that the death penalty is a cruel and unusual punishment while the other one attacks that position. However, in order to attack that position they must be discussing the same facet.

Figure 6: Instructions for AFS MT HIT.

**S5: MT Argument Facet Similarity HIT.** Fig. 6 shows the instructions defining AFS for the MT HIT. Inspired by the scale used for STS, we collected annotations on a 6 point scale. One crucial difference in our formulation was a desire to capture similarity in FACET and argument simultaneously. The use of the value 3 for 'same FACET, contradictory stance' was a well-thought decision in the definition of AFS.

| SCU Label | Used by summarizer? 1 | 2 | 3 | 4 | 5 | Tier |
|---|---|---|---|---|---|---|
| Gay couples are interested in the rights and benefits associated with marriage. | ✓ | ✓ | ✓ | ✓ | ✓ | 5 |
| Gay people should be able to marry a person of their choice and get equal rights. | ✓ | ✓ | ✓ | ✓ | ✓ | 5 |
| Government should not be involved in marriage and marriage should be left to religious institutions. | ✓ | ✓ | ✓ | ✓ | ✓ | 5 |
| Discussion on the civil benefits of marriage and the rights of marriage. | ✓ | | ✓ | ✓ | ✓ | 4 |
| Gay couples are unable to get any benefits that married people do. | ✓ | ✓ | | ✓ | ✓ | 4 |
| There should be a better system for marriage benefits. | | ✓ | ✓ | ✓ | ✓ | 4 |
| Religious ceremonies are not what gay people want. | | ✓ | | ✓ | ✓ | 3 |
| Single people are the ones that are harmed the most by marriage laws. | ✓ | ✓ | ✓ | | | 3 |
| Gay people should marry the opposite sex if they want the same rights. | | | ✓ | ✓ | | 2 |
| Gays have religious ceremonies already can have them via churches | | ✓ | | | | 1 |
| Relation to the issues by consideration of the case of a life-long bachelor uncle | ✓ | | | | | 1 |

Figure 5: Pyramid for Dialog-2. SCU labels in Tiers 3-5 are assumed to be the CENTRAL PROPOSITIONS.

Just as two words can only be antonyms if they are in the same semantic field, two arguments can only be contradictory if they are about the same FACET. Thus, we instruct annotators to give a score of 3 to opposing arguments on the same FACET.

The task was put on Mechanical Turk using two separate batches. For the first batch we randomly selected 500 pairs from our pairs dataset of 1131 pairs. However, our subsequent impression was that the clustering had not filtered out enough of the unrelated pairs (score 0-1). For the second batch we selected the top 500 pairs according to the UMBC similarity score (Han et al., 2013). This gave us a final pair dataset of 1000 pairs. Since AFS is a novel and subjective task, workers took a qualification test. Then each pair was annotated by 5 workers, and one of the authors provided gold standard labels. The HIT allowed 5 AFS judgements per hit, thus the number of pairs annotated by a worker varies from 5 to 1000.

To increase reliability, we removed the annotations from those workers who had attempted less than 4 hits (20 pairs) and had the lowest pairwise correlations with our gold standard annotation. Our final AFS score was the average score across all the annotators. The final AFS score correlated at .7 with our gold standard annotation, showing that the AFS similarity task is well-defined, and understandable by minimally trained annotators on MT. Table 4 provides typical examples of argument pairs and their MT AFS score, along with the predicted scores from some of our models. We discuss the AFS values and interesting cases in Sec. 3 below.

## 3 Machine Learning Experiments and Results

Given the data collected above, we defined a supervised machine learning experiment with AFS as our dependent variable and different collections of features inspired from previous work as our independent variables.

### 3.1 Features

**NGRAM overlap.** This is our primary baseline. For each argument, we extracted all the unigrams, bigrams and trigrams, and then counted how many were in overlap across the two arguments. For unigrams we did not include stop words. Stemmed Ngrams were used to get better overlap.

**UMBC.** This is our secondary baseline. This feature is the Semantic Textual Similarity obtained using UMBC Semantic Similarity tool (Han et al., 2013)

**DISCO Distributionally Similar Category.** We used the distributional similarity tool DISCO with the pre-computed English Wikipedia word space (Kolb, 2008). We extract the top 5 distributionally similar nouns, verbs, and adjectives for each argument. For each argument pair, three vector pairs (over nouns, verbs, and adjectives) are created with this extended vocabulary. Stemming was performed and cosine similarity between these vector pairs was calculated.

**LIWC Category.** This feature set is based on the Linguistics Inquiry Word Count tool (Pennebaker et al., 2001). To tune these features, we first used a set of gay marriage posts from websites such as CreateDebate and ConvinceMe to extract relevant LIWC categories. We supplemented this data with gay marriage posts from 4forums, but excluded the discussion threads in our dialog corpus. From this data, we extracted the LIWC categories most frequent nouns, verbs and adjectives. For the verbs category, we excluded the verbs present in the NLTK stop word list. We retained only semantically rich categories such as Biological Processes, Causation, Cognitive Processes, Humans, Negative Emotion, Positive Emotion, Religion, Sexual, and Social Processes. The score for this set was the LIWC category overlap count across pairs for each category.

**ROUGE Scores.** ROUGE is a family of metrics to determine the quality of a summary by comparing it to other ideal summaries (Lin, 2004). It is based on a number of overlapping units such as n-gram, word sequences, and word pairs. This feature includes all of the rouge f-scores available via the package at https://pypi.python.org/pypi/pyrouge/0.1.0.

### 3.2 Results

Our aim is to predict the similarity among repeated arguments across many discussions in online social and political debate forums, a task we have dubbed ARGUMENT FACET SIMILARITY (**AFS**). Given the CENTRAL PROPOSITIONS from the CP detector (see Fig. 2a), we need to train an argument FACET inducer. We define AFS as a regression problem and evaluate support vector regression and linear regression for 10-fold cross validation using the Weka machine learning toolkit (Hall et al., 2005).

| Classifier | RMS | MAE | R |
|---|---|---|---|
| **SMO** | 1.0208 | 0.8019 | 0.532 |
| **Linear Regression** | 0.9996 | 0.8003 | 0.540 |

Table 2: Support Vector and Linear Regression. RMS: Root Mean Squared Error, MAE: Mean Absolute Error, R: Correlation Coefficient.

Table 2 shows that the results for support vector regression are worse than the linear regression model using our proposed features combined with UMBC, hence we focus hereon on linear regression. Table 3 provides the correlations, MAE, and RMS values for models produced using various sets of features. We considered two baselines, simple Ngram overlap and the off-the-shelf UMBC STS metric (Han et al., 2013). In general, we found that Ngram overlap (Row 1) performed best alone of our features, but falls short of the UMBC baseline (Row 2). It is interesting that Ngram alone outperforms distributional measures (which Conrad & Wiebe found most helpful) as well as Rouge (which contains metrics insensitive to linear adjacency).

| Row | Feature Set | R | MAE | RMS |
|---|---|---|---|---|
| 1 | **NGRAM (N)** | 0.39 | 0.90 | 1.09 |
| 2 | **UMBC (U)** | 0.46 | 0.86 | 1.06 |
| 3 | **LIWC (L)** | 0.32 | 0.92 | 1.13 |
| 4 | **DISCO (D)** | 0.33 | 0.93 | 1.12 |
| 5 | **ROUGE (R)** | 0.34 | 0.91 | 1.12 |
| 6 | **N-U** | 0.47 | 0.85 | 1.05 |
| 7 | **N-L** | 0.45 | 0.86 | 1.06 |
| 8 | **N-R** | 0.42 | 0.88 | 1.08 |
| 9 | **N-D** | 0.41 | 0.89 | 1.08 |
| 10 | **U-R** | 0.48 | 0.84 | 1.04 |
| 11 | **U-L** | 0.51 | 0.83 | 1.02 |
| 12 | **U-D** | 0.45 | 0.86 | 1.06 |
| 13 | **N-L-R** | 0.48 | 0.84 | 1.04 |
| 14 | **U-L-R** | 0.53 | 0.81 | 1.00 |
| 15 | **N-L-R-D** | 0.50 | 0.83 | 1.03 |
| 16 | **N-L-R-U** | 0.54 | 0.80 | 1.00 |
| 17 | **N-L-R-D-U** | 0.54 | 0.80 | 1.00 |

Table 3: Results for Different Individual Features and Feature Combinations.

Table 3, Row 15, shows that the best correlation that is achievable without UMBC is the combination of Ngram, LIWC, ROUGE and DISCO (NLRD). This combination significantly improves over the UMBC baseline of 0.46 to 0.50 (paired $t$-test, $p <$ .05).

We then tested combinations of of features to determine which feature sets are complementary. LIWC + NGRAM is significantly different than NGRAM alone ($p < 0.01$), and ROUGE + NGRAM is significantly different than NGRAM alone ($p = 0.03$), but DISCO does not add anything ($p = 0.2$). This shows that LIWC and ROUGE features complement Ngram features. Other combinations of interest are NGRAM + LIWC (Row 7) which amazingly performs as well as UMBC while UMBC includes sentence alignment, a model of negation, and distributional measures (Han et al., 2013). This suggests that AFS is clearly a different task that STS. Additionally we also combined our proposed set of features with UMBC. A comparison of Row 15 (our feature set) with Rows 16 and 17 of Table 3 where we combine our features with UMBC shows that this improves the correlation further, from the UMBC baseline of 0.46 to 0.54 ($p < 0.01$.)

| Row | N | L | U | NLRD | NLRDU | MT AFS | Arg1 | Arg2 |
|---|---|---|---|---|---|---|---|---|
| 1 | 1.38 | 1.50 | **0.37** | 1.31 | 0.40 | 0.00 | **everyone has the freedom of speech** | **service in the military** |
| 2 | 2.00 | 2.02 | **1.55** | 2.33 | 1.86 | 1.14 | **gay people should be able to marry a person of their choice and get equal rights** | **referring to namecalling and violence from the original post that was opposing gay rights** |
| 3 | 2.00 | 1.29 | 2.52 | **1.37** | 1.54 | 1.33 | Constitutional right to be opposed to gay marriage as well as gay people themselves | arguing about marriage benefits between single people and married |
| 4 | 2.00 | 1.70 | 2.74 | **1.77** | 1.98 | 1.80 | people should not pick and choose what they want equal rights on. | people did not want gay marriage |
| 5 | 1.38 | 1.92 | 0.88 | **1.94** | 1.64 | 2.50 | the Republicans creating another Holocaust | No republican in leadership would call for the extermination of gays |
| 6 | 1.69 | 2.02 | **2.58** | 1.89 | 2.49 | 2.60 | **homosexuals have all the same rights as heterosexuals** | **Opposition to equal rights for gay couples.** |
| 7 | 1.83 | 2.40 | 1.46 | **2.81** | 2.51 | 3.00 | There was prejudice against gays in 1909 just as there is now | it is prejudice as opposed to religious or moral beliefs which fuel the anti-gay agenda; |
| 8 | 2.00 | 1.70 | **3.16** | 1.73 | 2.41 | 3.40 | **homosexual relationships should not compare to heterosexual marriages because only heterosexuals are legally allowed to marry** | **marriage should be between a heterosexual couple** |
| 9 | 2.00 | 2.70 | 2.09 | 2.83 | **3.03** | 3.50 | it is prejudice as opposed to religious or moral beliefs which fuel the anti-gay agenda; | when people claim religion in doing prejudice they are actually abandoning their morals |
| 10 | **2.94** | 2.02 | 2.93 | 2.18 | 2.70 | 3.50 | **gay people should be able to marry a person of their choice and get equal rights.** | **Gay couples are unable to get any benefits that married people do.** |
| 11 | 2.14 | 1.50 | **2.91** | 2.08 | 2.62 | 3.60 | **Paul Cameron is the voice of the Republicans** | **Conversation about Paul Cameron** |
| 12 | 2.63 | 3.63 | 2.60 | **3.75** | 3.57 | 4.17 | in opening this opportunity for gay marriage, the definition of marriage will change | opponents of homosexual marriage tend to argue that a change to marriage law would make it too open ended |
| 13 | **4.23** | 2.72 | 2.26 | 4.82 | 4.12 | 4.50 | AIDs was initially spread in the United States primarily by homosexuals. | No one argues the point that AIDs was spread in the United States by homosexuals. |

Table 4: Predicted Scores for each model and the Mechanical Turk AFS gold standard for selected argument pairs from the pairs dataset. Best performing model for each pair is shown in **bold**. The table is sorted by the AFS score (gold standard). The argument pairs shown in **bold** are cases where UMBC by itself beats our proposed model. KEY: Feature sets model. N = NGRAM, U = UMBC STS tool, L = Linguistic Inquiry and Word Count; R = Rouge, D = DISCO, AFS= Mean of Mechanical Turker AFS scores, our gold standard. For example, NLRD means a combination of NGRAM, LIWC, ROUGE and DISCO.

It is also interesting to examine the differences in model scores for particular argument pairs as shown in Table 4. The best performing model for each row is in **bold** in Table 4. As described in the HIT instructions in Fig. 6, values of AFS near 0 (Row 1) indicate different topics and no similarity. Values near 1 indicate same topic but different arguments (Rows 2,3). Values of 3 and above indicate same FACET (Rows 7,8), and values near 5 are same facet and very similar argument (Rows 12 and 13). Both Arg1 and Arg2 in Row 10 makes the same argument but Arg1 includes additional argumentation. In Row 12, there is very low Ngram overlap, but strong AFS and NLRD performs better than the other models, and LIWC performs well by itself.

In Row 1, UMBC performs the best with a predicted score of 0.37 as opposed to an AFS score of 0.00. Other rows where UMBC on its own provides the best performance are highlighted in the table with Arg1 and Arg2 in **bold**. The top performance of NLRD in Row 5 without UMBC perhaps arises from the semantic information that extermination and holocau are somehow related. NGRAM overlap does the best in Row 13 despite the fact that the phrase *No one argues the point that* does not participate in the NGRAM overlap.

## 4 Related Work

Our approach draws on three different strands of related work: (1) argument mining; (2) semantic textual similarity; and (3) dialog summarization, which we discuss and compare with our work below.

**Argument Mining.** The study of the structure of arguments has a long tradition in logic, rhetoric and psychology (Walton et al., 2008; Reed and Rowe, 2004; Walton, 2009; Gilbert, 1997; Jackson and Jacobs, 1980; Madnani et al., 2012). Much of this work has been on formal (legal or political) argumentation, and the small computational literature that has applied the rhetorical categories of this research has likewise focused on formal, monologic text (Feng and Hirst, 2011; Palau and Moens, 2009; Goudas et al., 2014). More recent work (Ghosh et al., 2014) has attempted to apply these theories to dialogic text in online forums. Ghosh et al. label spans in conversations with attacking moves (CALL-OUTS) and their corresponding argumentative TARGETS in another speaker's utterance, and they attempt to learn these callout-target pairs in a supervised framework. Other work attempts to identify general categories of speech-acts such as disagreements or justifications (Misra and Walker, 2015; Biran and Rambow, 2011).

What unites all of the above approaches is an interest in understanding the detailed rheotrical structure of a particular linguistic interaction (monologic or dialogic). Our present work is focused instead on inducing the recurring FACETS in a particular topic domain via weakly supervised learning over several dialogic interactions. Several different threads of recent research on argument mining have strong parallels with this goal (Conrad et al., 2012; Boltuzic and Šnajder, 2014; Hasan and Ng, 2014).

Conrad & Wiebe construct an argument mining system on monologic weblog and news data about universal healthcare. One component of their system identifies ARGUING SEGMENTS and the second component labels the segments with the relevant stance-specific ARGUMENT TAGS. They show that distributional similarity features help identify arguments that belong to the same tag set (notably, we did not find distributional similarity helpful for **AFS**.) Boltuzic & Snajder pursue argument mining on comment streams. Instead of hand-generating argument tags like Conrad & Wiebe, they select short sentential summaries of the key arguments for a given topic from a debate website, and then label comments on the same topic from a different website with the most closely matching summary. The same problem on debate posts is tackled as a "reason classification" problem (Hasan and Ng, 2014), with a probabilistic framework for argument recognition (reason classification) that operates jointly with the related task of stance classification.

All of these approaches differ from ours in three respects. First, they all assume a finite set of topic-specific labels that are determined in some form by the researchers themselves. In contrast, we seek to uncover popular facets via clustering the central propositions across the dialogs. After our own initial categorical efforts, we feel that the argument "topics" have such nuance that they resist clear labels or category membership. Instead, we feel that a scale such as AFS is a better fit, both for the diversity of the data itself and for the idea of inducing FACETS bottom up. Second, these approaches assume the labels are dependent on a particular *stance* towards an issue, whereas our facets are deliberately designed to unify across stance disagreement. Finally, all other approaches in argument mining work from the source text itself. We instead (to our knowledge, for the first time) work from human summaries of dialogs because it is an open question whether the CENTRAL PROPOSITIONS for a dialog are really identifiable as continuous spans of text in the dialog itself. (Indeed, our corpus will allow us to determine how true that assumption is.)

**Semantic Textual Similarity.** There appears to be similarity between FACET induction and aspect learning in sentiment analysis (Brody and Elhadad, 2010), but FACETS are propositional abstract objects, while aspects can usually be described as nouns or properties. Facet induction is more similar to work on **STS** (Mihalcea et al., 2006; Yeh et al., 2009; Agirre et al., 2012; Han et al., 2013; Jurgens et al., 2014). Calculating similarity is a central aspect of AFS. Our scale and MT task for AFS was inspired by the STS task and definition. In addition, as a baseline we apply an off-the-shelf system that calculates STS (UMBC) and compare it with our own system (Han et al., 2013). In order to avoid asking for judgements for many unrelated arguments (CENTRAL PROPOSITIONS), and to make the AFS task more doable for Turkers, we also use UMBC as a filter on pairs of CENTRAL PROPOSITIONS as part of making our HIT. This biases the distribution of the training set to having a much larger set of more similar pairs, which has been a problem for previous work (Boltuzic and Šnajder, 2014), where the vast majority of pairs that were labelled were unrelated. However the AFS task is clearly different than STS, partly because the data is dialogic and partly because it is argumentative. Our results show that we can improve on STS systems for the AFS task.

**Dialog Summarization.** Much previous work on dialog summarization focused on extracting phenomena specific to meetings, such as action items or decisions (Murray et al., 2006; Hsueh and Moore, 2008; Whittaker et al., 2012; Janin et al., 2004; Carletta, 2007). Other approaches, like our work, use semantic similarity metrics to identify the most central or important utterances of a spoken dialog (Gurevych and Strube, 2004), but do not attempt to find the FACETS of a set of arguments across multiple dialogs. Another parallel may exist between work on nuclearity in RST and its use in summarization (Marcu, 1999). However our notion of a CENTRAL PROPOSITION is different than nuclearity in RST, since FACETS are derived from CENTRAL PROPOSITIONS that rise to the top of the pyramid across summarizers, and then (via AFS) across many dialogs on a topic, while RST nuclearity is only defined for a span of text by a single speaker.

Other work examines how social phenomena affect summarization, such as a study of how the politeness level in computer-generated dialogs impacted summaries (Roman et al., 2006). Emotion naturally occurs in the IAC, and summarizers' orientation to emotion is intriguing. Emotional information has been observed even in summaries of professional chats discussing technology (Zhou and Hovy, 2005). However the instructions to our Pyramid annotators were to not include information of this type in the pyramids. We are currently collecting an additional summary corpus using a method that we expect to result in more evaluative and emotional assessments in summaries.

## 5 Conclusion

This paper presents a method and results for extracting FACETS of a topic, across multiple informal arguments on the same topic. We first use human summarization of dialogs as a probe to determine the CENTRAL PROPOSITIONS of each dialog. Then we use clustering in combination with measures of SEMANTIC SIMILARITY to group the CENTRAL PROPOSITIONS into the important FACETS of an argument across many different dialogs. Importantly, we **do not** attempt to enumerate the possible FACETS for an argument in advance, believing that bottom-up discovery of FACETS is a better fit to the problem.

This paper contributes to the current state of knowledge in three ways: (1) we collected summaries of spontaneously-produced written dialog of high social and political importance (available from `http://nlds.soe.ucsc.edu/summarycorpus`). (2) we proposed a novel application of the pyramid summarization scheme to the task of FACET induction; and (3) we introduce a new task of ARGUMENT FACET SIMILARITY (**AFS**) aimed at identifying FACETS across opinionated dialogs and show that we can identify AFS with a correlation of .54 as opposed to a baseline of .46 provided by a system designed for a similar task. We suspect that the summarize-and-collate approach used here could be promisingly applied to produce annotations on a range of subjective, holistic properties of dialog.

In future work, we aim to expand on this work in several ways. First, we hope to expand summaries, similarity judgments, and systems to several topics beyond gay marriage. We believe, for example, that the features and the system we have trained for AFS will apply to other domains without retraining, since none of the features are topic specific, but we have not shown that. In addition, we aim to develop additional features and improve on the results reported here. For example, we believe that it is possible that other off-the-shelf systems, such as for example one for sentence specificity (Louis and Nenkova, 2011; Louis and Nenkova, 2012), might possibly help with aspects of this task. In addition, in future, we aim to automatically identify CENTRAL PROPOSITIONS without the mediation of human summarizers and evaluators. Given the summaries that we have collected for each dialog, we plan to examine the relationship between the contributors to the related pyramid and the original source text, to determine whether indeed there are surface features of the source that would allow us to treat CENTRAL PROPOSITION detection as an extractive task.

**Acknowledgments** This work was funded by NSF GRANT IIS-1302668, Grant NPS-BAA-03, and an IARPA Grant on Persuasion in Dialogue to UCSC by subcontract from the University of Maryland.

## References


Rob Abbott, Marilyn Walker, Jean E. Fox Tree, Pranav Anand, Robeson Bowmani, and Joseph King. 2011. How can you say such things?!?: Recognizing Disagreement in Informal Political Argument. In *Proceedings of the ACL Workshop on Language and Social Media*.

Eneko Agirre, Mona Diab, Daniel Cer, and Aitor Gonzalez-Agirre. 2012. Semeval-2012 task 6: A pilot on semantic textual similarity. In *Proceedings of the First Joint Conference on Lexical and Computational Semantics-Volume 1: Proceedings of the main conference and the shared task, and Volume 2: Proceedings of the Sixth International Workshop on Semantic Evaluation*, pages 385–393. Association for Computational Linguistics.

Eneko Agirre, Daniel Cer, Mona Diab, Aitor Gonzalez-Agirre, and Weiwei Guo. 2013. Sem 2013 shared task: Semantic textual similarity, including a pilot on typed-similarity. In *In* SEM 2013: The Second Joint Conference on Lexical and Computational Semantics. Association for Computational Linguistics*. Citeseer.

Islam Beltagy, Katrin Erk, and Raymond Mooney. 2014. Probabilistic soft logic for semantic textual similarity. *Proceedings of Association for Computational Linguistics (ACL-14)*.

O. Biran and O. Rambow. 2011. Identifying justifications in written dialogs. In *2011 Fifth IEEE International Conference on Semantic Computing (ICSC)*, pages 162–168. IEEE.

Filip Boltuzic and Jan Šnajder. 2014. Back up your stance: Recognizing arguments in online discussions. In *Proceedings of the First Workshop on Argumentation Mining*, pages 49–58.

Samuel Brody and Noemie Elhadad. 2010. An unsupervised aspect-sentiment model for online reviews. In *Human Language Technologies: The 2010 Annual Conference of the North American Chapter of the Association for Computational Linguistics*, pages 804–812. Association for Computational Linguistics.

Jean Carletta. 2007. Unleashing the killer corpus: experiences in creating the multi-everything ami meeting corpus. *Language Resources and Evaluation*, 41(2):181–190.

Alexander Conrad, Janyce Wiebe, et al. 2012. Recognizing arguing subjectivity and argument tags. In *Proceedings of the Workshop on Extra-Propositional Aspects of Meaning in Computational Linguistics*, pages 80–88. Association for Computational Linguistics.

Vanessa Wei Feng and Graeme Hirst. 2011. Classifying arguments by scheme. In *Proceedings of the 49th Annual Meeting of the Association for Computational Linguistics: Human Language Technologies-Volume 1*, pages 987–996. Association for Computational Linguistics.

Debanjan Ghosh, Smaranda Muresan, Nina Wacholder, Mark Aakhus, and Matthew Mitsui. 2014. Analyzing argumentative discourse units in online interactions. *ACL 2014*, page 39.

Michael A. Gilbert. 1997. Coalescent argumentation.

Theodosis Goudas, Christos Louizos, Georgios Petasis, and Vangelis Karkaletsis. 2014. Argument extraction from news, blogs, and social media. In *Artificial Intelligence: Methods and Applications*, pages 287–299. Springer.

I. Gurevych and M. Strube. 2004. Semantic similarity applied to spoken dialogue summarization. In *Proceedings of the 20th international conference on Computational Linguistics*, pages 764–771. ACL.

M. Hall, F. Eibe, G. Holms, B. Pfahringer, P. Reutemann, and I. Witten. 2005. The weka data mining software: An update. *SIGKDD Explorations*, 11(1).

Lushan Han, Abhay Kashyap, Tim Finin, James Mayfield, and Jonathan Weese. 2013. Umbc ebiquity-core: Semantic textual similarity systems. *Atlanta, Georgia, USA*, page 44.

Kazi Saidul Hasan and Vincent Ng. 2014. Why are you taking this stance? identifying and classifying reasons in ideological debates. In *Proceedings of the Conference on Empirical Methods in Natural Language Processing*.

P.Y. Hsueh and J. Moore. 2008. Automatic decision detection in meeting speech. *Machine Learning for Multimodal Interaction*, pages 168–179.

Sally Jackson and Scott Jacobs. 1980. Structure of conversational argument: Pragmatic bases for the enthymeme. *Quarterly Journal of Speech*, 66(3):251–265.

A. Janin, J. Ang, S. Bhagat, R. Dhillon, J. Edwards, J. Macias-Guarasa, N. Morgan, B. Peskin, E. Shriberg, A. Stolcke, et al. 2004. The icsi meeting project: Resources and research. In *Proceedings of the 2004 ICASSP NIST Meeting Recognition Workshop*.

David Jurgens, Mohammad Taher Pilehvar, and Roberto Navigli. 2014. Semeval-2014 task 3: Cross-level semantic similarity. *SemEval 2014*, page 17.

P. Kolb. 2008. Disco: A multilingual database of distributionally similar words. In *Proceedings of KONVENS-2008*.

C.-Y. Lin. 2004. Rouge: A package for automatic evaluation of summaries rouge: A package for automatic evaluation of summaries. In *Proceedings of the Workshop on Text Summarization Branches Out (WAS 2004)*.

Annie Louis and Ani Nenkova. 2011. Automatic identification of general and specific sentences by leveraging discourse annotations. In *IJCNLP*, pages 605–613.

Annie Louis and Ani Nenkova. 2012. A corpus of general and specific sentences from news. In *LREC*, pages 1818–1821.

Nitin Madnani, Michael Heilman, Joel Tetreault, and Martin Chodorow. 2012. Identifying high-level organizational elements in argumentative discourse. In *Proceedings of the 2012 Conference of the North American Chapter of the Association for Computational Linguistics: Human Language Technologies*, NAACL HLT '12, pages 20–28, Stroudsburg, PA, USA. Association for Computational Linguistics.

Daniel Marcu. 1999. Discourse trees are good indicators of importance in text. *Advances in automatic text summarization*, pages 123–136.

Rada Mihalcea, Courtney Corley, and Carlo Strapparava. 2006. Corpus-based and knowledge-based measures of text semantic similarity. In *AAAI*, volume 6, pages 775–780.

Amita Misra and Marilyn A Walker. 2015. Topic independent identification of agreement and disagreement in social media dialogue. In *Proceedings of the SIGDIAL 2013 Conference: The 15th Annual Meeting of the Special Interest Group on Discourse and Dialogue*.

G. Murray, S. Renals, J. Carletta, and J. Moore. 2006. Incorporating speaker and discourse features into speech summarization. In *Proceedings of the main conference on Human Language Technology Conference of the North American Chapter of the Association of Computational Linguistics*, pages 367–374. Association for Computational Linguistics.

A. Nenkova and R. Passonneau. 2004. Evaluating content selection in summarization: The pyramid method. In *Proceedings of HLT-NAACL*, volume 2004.

Raquel Mochales Palau and Marie-Francine Moens. 2009. Argumentation mining: the detection, classification and structure of a rguments in text. In *Proceedings of the 12th international conference on artificial int elligence and law*, pages 98–107. ACM.

F. Pedregosa, G. Varoquaux, A. Gramfort, V. Michel, B. Thirion, O. Grisel, M. Blondel, P. Prettenhofer, R. Weiss, V. Dubourg, J. Vanderplas, A. Passos, D. Cournapeau, M. Brucher, M. Perrot, and E. Duchesnay. 2011. Scikit-learn: Machine learning in Python. *Journal of Machine Learning Research*, 12:2825–2830.

J. W. Pennebaker, L. E. Francis, and R. J. Booth, 2001. *LIWC: Linguistic Inquiry and Word Count.*

Chris Reed and Glenn Rowe. 2004. Araucaria: Software for argument analysis, diagramming and representation. *International Journal on Artificial Intelligence Tools*, 13(04):961–979.

N. Roman, P. Piwek, P. Carvalho, and M. B. R. Ariadne. 2006. Politeness and bias in dialogue summarization: two exploratory studies. In J. Shanahan, Y. Qu, and J. Wiebe, editors, *Computing attitude and affect in text: theory and applications*, volume 20 of *The Information Retrieval Series*. Springer.

S. Somasundaran and J. Wiebe. 2010. Recognizing stances in ideological on-line debates. In *Proceedings of the NAACL HLT 2010 Workshop on Computational Approaches to Analysis and Generation of Emotion in Text*, pages 116–124. Association for Computational Linguistics.

Marilyn Walker, Pranav Anand, Rob Abbott, Jean E. Fox Tree, Craig Martell, and Joseph King. 2012. That's your evidence?: Classifying stance in online political debate. *Decision Support Sciences*.

Douglas Walton, Chris Reed, and Fabrizio Macagno. 2008. *Argumentation Schemes*. Cambridge University Press.

Douglas Walton. 2009. Argumentation theory: A very short introduction. In Guillermo Simari and Iyad Rahwan, editors, *Argumentation in Artificial Intelligence*, pages 1–22. Springer US.

S. Whittaker, V. Kalnikaité, and P. Ehlen. 2012. Markup as you talk: establishing effective memory cues while still contributing to a meeting. In *Proceedings of the ACM 2012 conference on Computer Supported Cooperative Work*, pages 349–358. ACM.

Eric Yeh, Daniel Ramage, Christopher D Manning, Eneko Agirre, and Aitor Soroa. 2009. Wikiwalk: random walks on wikipedia for semantic relatedness. In *Proceedings of the 2009 Workshop on Graph-based Methods for Natural Language Processing*, pages 41–49. Association for Computational Linguistics.

L. Zhou and E. Hovy. 2005. Digesting virtual geek culture: The summarization of technical internet relay chats. In *Proceedings of the 43rd Annual Meeting on Association for Computational Linguistics*, pages 298–305. ACL.

# Active Learning with Rationales for Text Classification

**Manali Sharma, Di Zhuang** and **Mustafa Bilgic**
Department of Computer Science
Illinois Institute of Technology
Chicago, IL USA
{msharm11, dzhuang3}@hawk.iit.edu and mbilgic@iit.edu

## Abstract

We present a simple and yet effective approach that can incorporate rationales elicited from annotators into the training of any off-the-shelf classifier. We show that our simple approach is effective for multinomial naïve Bayes, logistic regression, and support vector machines. We additionally present an active learning method tailored specifically for the learning with rationales framework.

## 1 Introduction

Annotating documents for supervised learning is a tedious, laborious, and time consuming task for humans. Given huge amounts of unlabeled documents, it is impractical for annotators to go over each document and provide a label. To reduce the annotation time and effort, various approaches such as semi-supervised learning (Chapelle et al., 2006) that utilizes both labeled and unlabeled data, and active learning (Settles, 2012) that carefully chooses instances for annotation have been developed. To further minimize the human effort, recent work looked at eliciting domain knowledge, such as rationales and feature annotations, from the annotators instead of just the labels of documents.

One of the bottlenecks in eliciting domain knowledge from annotators is that the traditional supervised learning approaches cannot readily handle the elicited rich feedback. To address this issue, many methods have been developed that are classifier-specific. Examples include knowledge-based neural networks (e.g., (Towell and Shavlik, 1994), (Girosi and Chan, 1995), (Towell et al., 1990)), knowledge-based support vector machines (Fung et al., 2002), pooling multinomial naïve Bayes (Melville and Sindhwani, 2009), incorporating constraints into the training of naïve Bayes (Stumpf et al., 2007), and converting rationales and feature annotations into constraints for support vector machines (e.g., (Small et al., 2011) and (Zaidan et al., 2007)). Being classifier-specific limits their applicability when one wants to test a different classifier for his/her domain, necessitating an approach that can be utilized by several off-the-shelf classifiers.

In this paper we present a simple and yet effective approach that can incorporate the elicited rationales in the form of feature annotations into the training of any off-the-shelf classifier. We empirically show that it is effective at incorporating rationales into the learning of naïve Bayes, logistic regression, and support vector machines using four text categorization datasets. We further discuss a novel active learning strategy specifically geared towards the learning with rationales framework and empirically show that it improves over traditional active learning.

The rest of the paper is organized as follows. In Section 2, we provide a brief background on eliciting rationales in the context of active learning. In Section 3, we describe our approach for incorporating rationales into the training of classifiers and compare learning without rationales and learning with rationales. In Section 4, we present an active learning method using the learning with rationales framework and present relevant results. Finally, we discuss limitations and future work in Section 5, related work in Section 6, and conclude in Section 7.



*Human Language Technologies: The 2015 Annual Conference of the North American Chapter of the ACL*, pages 441–451,
Denver, Colorado, May 31 – June 5, 2015. 

## 2 Background

In this section, we provide a brief background on data annotation with rationales in the context of active learning and introduce the notation to be used throughout the paper.

Let $\mathcal{D}$ be a set of document-label pairs $\langle x, y \rangle$, where the label (value of $y$) is known only for a small subset $\mathcal{L} \subset \mathcal{D}$ of the documents: $\mathcal{L} = \{\langle x, y \rangle\}$ and the rest $\mathcal{U} = \mathcal{D} \setminus \mathcal{L}$ consists of the unlabeled documents: $\mathcal{U} = \{\langle x, ? \rangle\}$. We assume that each document $x^i$ is represented as a vector of features (most commonly as a bag-of-words model with a dictionary of predefined set of phrases, which can be unigrams, bigrams, etc.): $x^i \triangleq \{f_1^i, f_2^i, \cdots, f_n^i\}$. Each feature $f_j^i$ represents the binary presence (or absence), frequency, or tf-idf representation of the word/phrase $j$ in document $x^i$. Each label $y \in \mathcal{Y}$ is discrete-valued variable $\mathcal{Y} \triangleq \{y_1, y_2, \cdots, y_l\}$.

Typical greedy active learning algorithms iteratively select a document $\langle x, ? \rangle \in \mathcal{U}$, query a labeler for its label $y$, and incorporate the new document $\langle x, y \rangle$ into its training set $\mathcal{L}$. This process continues until a stopping criterion is met, usually until a given budget, $B$, is exhausted.

In the learning with rationales framework, in addition to querying for label $y^i$ of a document $x^i$, the active learner asks the labeler to provide a rationale, $R(x^i)$ for the chosen label. The rationale in its most general form consists of a subset of the terms that are present in $x^i$: $R(x^i) = \{f_k^i : j \in x^i\}$. Note that there might be cases where the labeler cannot pinpoint any phrase as a rationale, in which case $R(x^i)$ is allowed to be $\phi$. Algorithm 1 formally describes the active learning process that elicits rationales from the labeler.

The goal of eliciting rationales is to improve the learning efficiency by incorporating domain knowledge. However, it is not trivial to integrate domain knowledge into state-of-the-art classifiers, such as logistic regression and support vector machines.

Next, we describe our approach for incorporating rationales into the learning process.

**Algorithm 1** Active Learning with Rationales

**Input:** $\mathcal{U}$ - unlabeled documents, $\mathcal{L}$ - labeled documents, $\theta$ - underlying classification model, $B$ - budget
**repeat**
  $x^* = \underset{x \in \mathcal{U}}{\operatorname{argmax}}\, utility(x|\theta)$
  request label and rationale for this label
  $\mathcal{L} \leftarrow \mathcal{L} \cup \{\langle x^*, y^*, R(x^*) \rangle\}$
  $\mathcal{U} \leftarrow \mathcal{U} \setminus \{\langle x^* \rangle\}$
  Train $\theta$ on $\mathcal{L}$
**until** Budget $B$ is exhausted; e.g., $|\mathcal{L}| = B$

## 3 Learning with Rationales

In this section we first provide the formulation of our approach to incorporate rationales into learning and then present the results to compare *learning without rationales* (Lw/oR) and *learning with rationales* (LwR) on four datasets. We evaluate our approach using multinomial naïve Bayes, logistic regression, and support vector machines classifiers.

### 3.1 Training a Classifier Using Labels and Rationales

Like most previous work, we assume that the rationales, i.e. the phrases, returned by the labeler already exist in the dictionary of the vectorizer. Hence, rationales correspond to features in our vector representation. It is possible that the labeler returns a phrase that is currently not in the dictionary; for example, the labeler might return a phrase that consists of three words whereas the representation has single words and bi-grams only. In that case, the representation can be enriched by creating and adding a new feature that represents the phrase returned by the labeler.

Our simple approach works as follows: we modify the features of the annotated document $\langle x^*, y^*, R(x^*) \rangle$ to emphasize the rationale(s) and de-emphasize the remaining phrases in that document. We simply multiply the features corresponding to phrase(s) that are returned as rationale(s) by weight $r$ and we multiply the remaining features in the document by weight $o$, where $r > o$, and $r$ and $o$ are hyper-parameters. The modified document becomes:

$$x_{\prime}^{i} = \langle r \times f_j^i, \forall f_j^i \in R(x^i); o \times f_j^i, \forall f_j^i \notin R(x^i), \rangle \tag{1}$$

Note that the rationales are tied to their documents for which they were provided as rationales. One phrase might be a rationale for the label of one document and yet it might not be the rationale for the label of another document. Hence, the feature weightings are done at the document level, rather than globally. To illustrate this concept, we provide an example dataset below with three documents. In these documents, the words that are returned as rationales are underlined.

*Document 1: This is a great movie.*

*Document 2: The plot was great, but the performance of the actors was terrible. Avoid it.*

*Document 3: I've seen this at an outdoor cinema; great atmosphere. The movie was terrific.*

As these examples illustrate, the word "great" appears in all three documents, but it is marked as a rationale only for Document 1. Hence, we do not weight the rationales globally; rather, we modify only the labeled document using its particular rationale. Table 1 illustrates both the Lw/oR and LwR representations for these documents.

Table 1: The Lw/oR binary representation (top) and its LwR transformation (bottom) for Documents 1, 2, and 3. Stop words are removed. LwR multiplies the rationales with $r$ and other features with $o$.

| | great | movie | plot | performance | actor | terrible | avoid | outdoor | cinema | atmosphere | terrific |
|---|---|---|---|---|---|---|---|---|---|---|---|
| **Lw/oR Representation (binary)** | | | | | | | | | | | |
| D1 | 1 | 1 | | | | | | | | | |
| D2 | 1 | | 1 | 1 | 1 | 1 | 1 | | | | |
| D3 | 1 | 1 | | | | | | 1 | 1 | 1 | 1 |
| **LwR Transformation of the binary Lw/oR repr.** | | | | | | | | | | | |
| D1 | $r$ | $o$ | | | | | | | | | |
| D2 | $o$ | | $o$ | $o$ | $o$ | $r$ | $r$ | | | | |
| D3 | $o$ | $o$ | | | | | | $o$ | $o$ | $o$ | $r$ |

This approach is simple, intuitive, and classifier-agnostic. As we will show later, it is quite effective empirically as well. To gain a theoretical understanding of this approach, consider the work on regularization: the aim is to build a sparse/simple model that can capture the most important features of the training data and thus have large weights for important features and small/zero weights for irrelevant features. For example, consider the gradient for $w_j$ of feature $f_j$ for logistic regression with $l_2$ regularization (assuming $y$ is binary with 0/1):

$$\nabla w_j = C \times \sum_{x^l \in \mathcal{L}} f_j^l \times (y^l - P(y = 1|x^l)) - w_j \quad (2)$$

where $C$ is the complexity parameter that balances between fit to the data and the model complexity.

With our rationales framework, the gradient for $w_j$ will be:

$$\begin{aligned} \nabla w_j = \\ C \times \Bigg( & \sum_{x^l \in \mathcal{L}: f_j^l \in R(x^l)} r \times f_j^l \times (y^l - P(y^l = 1|x^l)) \\ + & \sum_{x^l \in \mathcal{L}: f_j^l \notin R(x^l)} o \times f_j^l \times (y^l - P(y^l = 1|x^l)) \Bigg) \\ - w_j & \qquad (3) \end{aligned}$$

In the above equation, a feature $f_j$ contributes more to the gradient of its weight $w_j$ when a document in which it is marked as a rationale is misclassified. When $f_j$ appears in another document $x^k$ but is not a rationale, it's contribution to the gradient is muted by $o$. And hence, when $r > o$, this framework implicitly provides more granular (per instance-feature combination) regularization by placing a higher importance on the contribution of the rationales versus non-rationales in each document.[1]

Note that in our framework the rationales are tied to their own documents; that is, we do not weight rationales and non-rationales globally. In addition to providing more granular regularization, this approach has the benefit of allowing different rationales to contribute differently to the objective function of the trained classifier. For example, consider the case where the number of documents in which one word $f_j$ (e.g., "excellent") is marked as a rationale is much more than the number of documents where another word $f_k$ (e.g., "good") is marked as

[1]The justification for our approach is similar for support vector machines. The idea is also similar for multinomial naïve Bayes with Dirichlet priors $\alpha_j$. For a fixed Dirichlet prior with $\langle \alpha_1, \alpha_2, \cdots, \alpha_n \rangle$ setting, when $o < 1$ for a feature $f_j$, its counts are smoothed more.

a rationale. Then, the first sum in equation 3 will range over more documents for the gradient of $w_j$ compared to the gradient of $w_k$, giving more importance to $w_j$ than to $w_k$. In the traditional feature annotation work, this can be achieved only if the labeler can rank the features; even then, it is often very difficult, if not impossible, for the labelers to determine how much more important one feature is compared to another.

## 3.2 Experiments Comparing Lw/oR to LwR

In this section we first describe the settings, datasets, and classifiers used for our experiments and how we simulated a human labeler to provide rationales. Then, we present the results comparing the learning curves achieved with *learning without rationales* (Lw/oR) and *learning with rationales* (LwR).

### 3.2.1 Methodology

For this study, we used four text classification datasets. The IMDB dataset consists of 25K movie reviews (Maas et al., 2011). The SRAA[2] dataset consists of 48K documents that discuss either auto or aviation. Nova is a text classification dataset used in active learning challenge (Guyon, 2011) and contains 12K documents. WvsH is a 20 Newsgroups[3] dataset in which we use the Windows vs. hardware categories, and it contains 1176 documents.

To make sure our approach works across representations, we experimented with both binary and tf-idf representations for these text datasets. We evaluated our strategy using multinomial naïve Bayes, logistic regression, and support vector machines, as these are strong classifiers for text classification. We used the scikit-learn (Pedregosa et al., 2011) implementation of these classifiers with their default parameter settings for our experiments.

To compare various strategies, we used learning curves. The initially labeled dataset was bootstrapped using 10 documents by picking 5 random documents from each class. A budget ($B$) of 200 documents was used in our experiments, because most of the learning curves flatten out after about 200 documents. We evaluated all the strategies using AUC (Area Under an ROC Curve) measure. The code to repeat our experiments is available at Github `http://www.cs.iit.edu/~ml/code/`.

While incorporating the rationales into learning, we set the weights for rationales and the remaining features of a document as 1 and 0.01 respectively (i.e. $r = 1$ and $o = 0.01$). That is, we did not overemphasize the features corresponding to rationales but rather de-emphasized the remaining features in the document. These weights worked reasonably well for all four datasets, across all three classifiers, and for both binary and tf-idf data representations.

Obviously, these are not necessarily the best weight settings one can achieve; the optimal settings for $r$ and $o$ depend on many factors, such as the extent of the knowledge of the labeler (i.e., how many words a labeler can recognize), how noisy the labeler is, and how much labeled data we have in our training set. Ideally, one should have $r >> o$ when the labeled data is small and $r$ should be closer to $o$ when the labeled data is large; a more practical approach would be to tune for these parameters (e.g., cross-validation) at each step of the learning curve. However, in our experiments, we fixed $r$ and $o$ and we found that most settings where $r > o$ worked quite well.

### 3.2.2 Simulating the Human Expert

Like most literature on feature labeling, we constructed an artificial labeler to simulate a human labeler. Every time a document is annotated, we asked the artificial labeler to mark a word as a rationale for that document's label. We allowed the labeler to return any one (and not necessarily the top one) of the positive words as a rationale for a positive document and any one of the negative words as a rationale for a negative document. If the labeler did not recognize any of the words as positive (negative) in a positive (negative) document, we let the labeler return nothing as the rationale. To make this as practical as possible in a real-world setting, we constructed the artificial labeler to recognize only the most apparent words in the documents. For generating rationales, we chose only the positive (negative) features that had the highest $\chi^2$ (chi-squared) statistic in at least 5% of the positive (negative) documents. This resulted in an overly-conservative labeler that recognized only a tiny subset of the words. For example,

[2] http://people.cs.umass.edu/ mccallum/data.html
[3] http://qwone.com/ jason/20Newsgroups/

the artificial labeler knew about only 49 words (23 for one class and 26 for the other class) for IMDB, 67 words (32 for one class and 35 for the other class) for SRAA, 95 words (42 for one class and 53 for the other class) for WvsH, and 111 words (31 for one class and 80 for the other class) for the Nova dataset.

To determine whether the rationales selected by this artificial labeler are meaningful, we printed out the actual words used as rationales, and we ourselves verified that these words are human-recognizable words that could be naturally provided as rationales for classification. For example, the positive terms for the IMDB dataset included "great", "excellent", and "wonderful" and the negative terms included "worst", "bad", and "waste."

### 3.2.3 Results

Next, we compare Lw/oR to LwR. Figure 1 presents the learning curves for random sampling on four text classification datasets with binary and tf-idf representations and using multinomial naïve Bayes, logistic regression, and support vector machines. Figure 1 shows that even though the artificial labeler knew only about a tiny subset of the vocabulary, and returned any *one* word, rather than the top word or all the words, as rationale, LwR still drastically outperformed Lw/oR across all datasets, classifiers, and representations. This shows that our method for incorporating rationales into the learning process is empirically effective.

We used the default complexity parameters for logistic regression and support vector machines and used Laplace smoothing for multinomial naïve Bayes. In our rationale framework, most features were non-rationales, and hence in Equation 3, most features appeared in the second summation term, with $o = 0.01$. We tested whether the improvements that LwR provide over Lw/oR are simply due to implicit higher regularization for most of the features with $o = 0.01$, and hence experimented with equation 2 (which is Lw/oR) using $C = 0.01$. We observed that setting $C = 0.01$ and indiscriminately regularizing all the terms did not improve Lw/oR, further providing experimental evidence that the improvements provided by LwR are not due to just higher regularization, but they are due to a more fine-grained regularization, as explained in Section 3.1.

Even though LwR provides huge benefits, providing both a label and a rationale is expected to take more time of the labeler than simply providing a label. However, the improvements of LwR over Lw/oR is so huge that it might be worth spending the extra time in providing rationales. For example, in order to achieve a target AUC of 0.95 for SRAA dataset (using tf-idf representation with MNB classifier), Lw/oR required labeling 656 documents, whereas LwR required annotating a mere 29 documents, which is 22.6 times reduction in the number of documents. As another example, in order to achieve a target AUC of 0.8 for WvsH dataset (using binary representation with SVM classifier), Lw/oR required labeling 113 documents, whereas LwR achieved this target with only 13 documents.

(Zaidan et al., 2007) conducted user studies and showed that providing 5 to 11 rationales and a class label per document takes roughly twice the time of providing only the label for the document. (Raghavan et al., 2006) also conducted user studies and showed that labeling instances takes five times more time than labeling features. We worked with simulated user and showed that a document that is annotated with a label and a single rationale can be worth as many as 22 documents that are annotated with only a label and thus these results suggest that LwR, compared to Lw/oR, can lead to significant time savings for the annotator.

## 4 Active Learning with Rationales

So far we have seen that LwR provides drastic improvements over Lw/oR. Both these strategies selected documents randomly for labeling. Active learning (Settles, 2012) aims to carefully choose instances for labeling to improve over random sampling. Many successful active learning approaches have been developed for instance labeling (e.g. (Lewis and Gale, 1994), (Seung et al., 1992), (Roy and McCallum, 2001)), feature labeling (e.g. (Druck et al., 2009)), and rotating between instance and feature labeling (e.g. (Raghavan and Allan, 2007), (Druck et al., 2009), (Attenberg et al., 2010), (Melville and Sindhwani, 2009)). In this section, we introduce an active learning strategy that can utilize the learning with rationales framework.

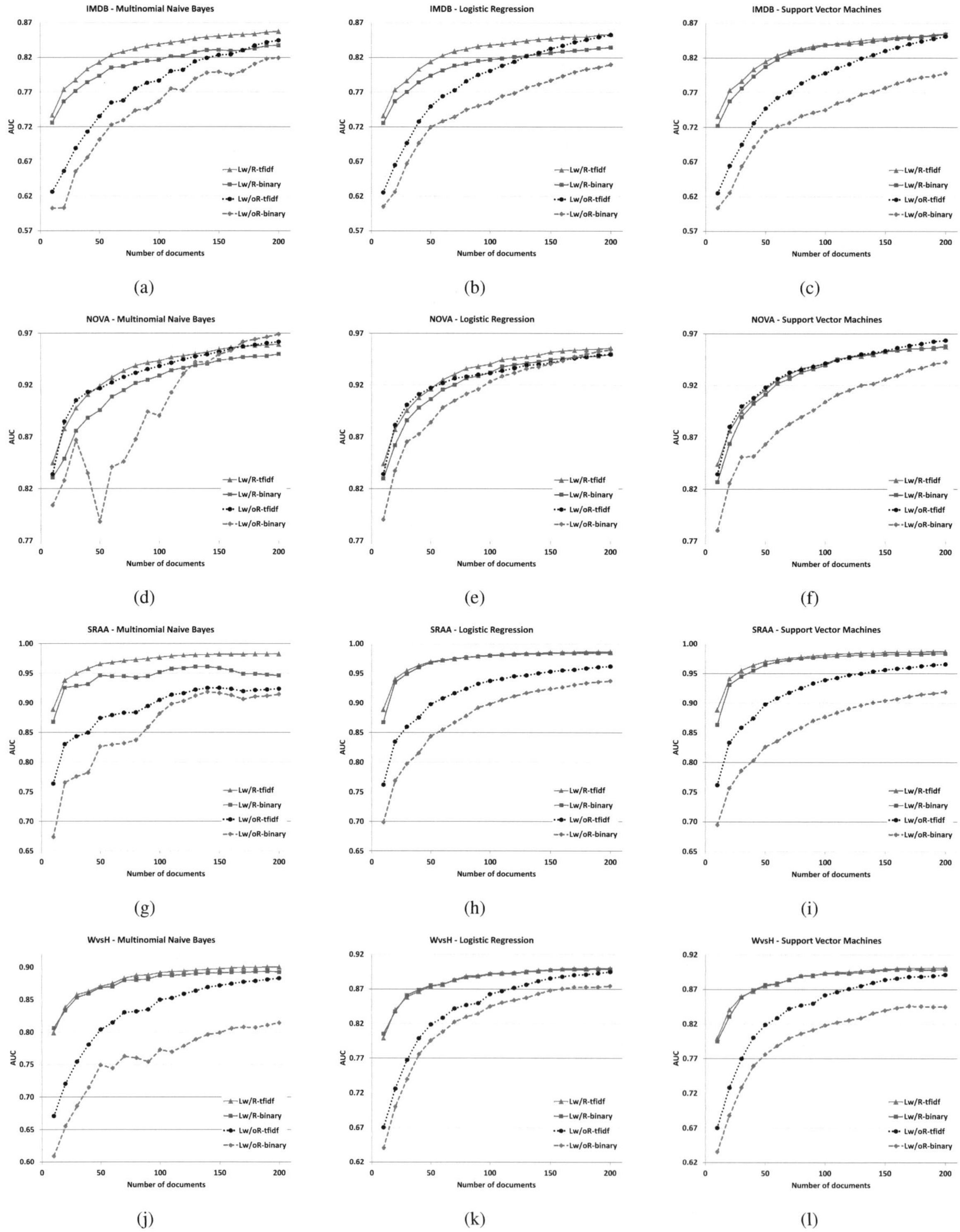


Figure 1: Comparison of Lw/oR with LwR. LwR provides drastic improvements over Lw/oR for all datasets with binary and tf-idf representations and using all three classifiers.

### 4.1 Active Learning to Select Documents based on Rationales

Arguably, one of the most successful active learning strategies for text categorization is uncertainty sampling, which was first introduced by (Lewis and Catlett, 1994) for probabilistic classifiers and later formalized for support vector machines (Tong and Koller, 2001). The idea is to label instances for which the underlying classifier is uncertain, i.e., the instances that are close to the decision boundary of the model. It has been successfully applied to text classification tasks in numerous publications, including (Zhu and Hovy, 2007), (Sindhwani et al., 2009), and (Segal et al., 2006).

We adapt uncertainty sampling for the learning with rationales framework. To put simply, when the underlying model is uncertain about an unlabeled document, we look whether the unlabeled document contains words/phrases that were returned as rationales for any of the existing labeled documents. More formally, let $R^+$ denote the union of all the rationales returned for the positive documents so far. Similarly, let $R^-$ denote the union of all the rationales returned for the negative documents so far. An unlabeled document can be of these three types:

1. Type1: has no words in common with $R^+$ and $R^-$.
2. Type2: has word(s) in common with either $R^+$ or $R^-$ but not both.
3. Type3: has at least one word in common with $R^+$ and at least one word in common with $R^-$.

One would imagine that labeling each of the type1, type2, and type3 documents has its own advantage. Labeling type1 documents has the potential to elicit new domain knowledge, i.e., terms that were not provided as a rationale for any of the existing labeled documents. It also carries the risk of containing little to no useful information for the classifier (e.g., a neutral review). For type2 documents, even though the document shares a word that was returned as a rationale for another document, the classifier is still uncertain about the document either because that word is not weighted high enough by the classifier and/or there are other words that pull the classification decision in the other direction, making the classifier uncertain. Type3 documents contain conflicting words/phrases and are potentially harder cases, however, they also have the potential to resolve the conflicts for the classifier.

Building on our previous work (Sharma and Bilgic, 2013) we devised an active learning approach, where given uncertain documents, the active learner prefers instances of type3 over type1 and type2. We call this strategy as *uncertain-prefer-conflict* (UNC-PC) because type3 documents carry conflicting words (with respect to rationales) whereas type1 and type2 do not. The difference between this approach and our previous work (Sharma and Bilgic, 2013) is that in (Sharma and Bilgic, 2013), we selected uncertain instances based on model's perceived conflict whereas in this work, we are selecting documents based on conflict caused by the domain knowledge provided by the labeler. Next, we compare the vanilla uncertainty sampling (UNC) and UNC-PC strategies using LwR to see if using uncertain documents of type3 could improve active learning.

### 4.2 Active Learning with Rationales Experiments

We used the same four text datasets and evaluated our method UNC-PC using multinomial naïve Bayes, logistic regression, and support vector machines. For the active learning strategies, we used a bootstrap of 10 random documents, and labeled five documents at each round of active learning. We used a budget of 200 documents for all methods. UNC simply picks the top five uncertain documents, whereas UNC-PC looks at top 20 uncertain documents and picks five uncertain documents giving preference to the conflicting cases (type 3) over the non-conflicting cases (type1 and type2). We repeated each experiment 10 times starting with a different bootstrap at each trial and report the average results.

In Figure 2 we show the learning curves comparing UNC-PC with UNC for multinomial naïve Bayes. (Logistic regression and SVM curves are omitted due to space.) Since the results for LwR using tf-idf representation are better than the results using the binary representation, we compared UNC-PC to UNC for LwR using only the tf-idf representation. We see that for multinomial naïve

Bayes, UNC-PC improves over traditional uncertainty, UNC, on two datasets, and hurts performance on one dataset. Next, we discuss the significance results for all classifiers.

Table 2 shows the paired t-test results comparing the learning curves of UNC-PC with the learning curves of UNC at each step of the active learning (i.e, if the average of one learning curve is significantly better or worse than the average of the learning curve of the other). If UNC-PC has a higher average AUC than UNC with a t-test significance level of 0.05 or better, it is a Win (W), if it has significantly lower performance, it is a Loss (L), and if the difference is not statistically significant, the result is a Tie (T).

Using multinomial naïve Bayes, UNC-PC wins over UNC for two of the datasets (IMDB and WvsH), does not cause any significant changes for Nova (ties all the time), and loses for SRAA. Using logistic regression, UNC-PC wins for two datasets (Nova and SRAA), ties for WvsH and loses for IMDB. Using support vector machines, UNC-PC wins for three datasets (Nova, SRAA, and WvsH) and loses for IMDB. The t-test results show that UNC-PC often improves learning over UNC.

Table 2: Significant W/T/L counts for UNC-PC versus UNC. UNC-PC improves over UNC significantly for all three classifiers and most of the datasets.

| UNC baseline | MNB | LR | SVM |
|---|---|---|---|
| UNC-PC | 2/1/1 | 2/1/1 | 3/0/1 |

## 5 Limitations and Future Work

A limitation of our work is that we simulated the labeler in our experiments. Even though we simulated the labeler in a very conservative way (that is, our simulated labeler knows only a few most apparent words) and asked the simulated labeler to provide any one (rather than the top) rationale, a user study is needed to i) experiment with potentially noisy labelers, and ii) measure how much actual time saving LwR provides over Lw/oR.

Another line of future work is to allow the labeler to provide richer feedback. This is especially useful for resolving conflicts that stem from seemingly conflicting words and phrases. For example, for the movie review "The plot was great, but the performance of the actors was terrible. Avoid it." the word "great" is at odds with the words "terrible" and "avoid". If the labeler is allowed to provide richer feedback, saying that the word "great" refers to the plot, "terrible" refers to the performance, and "avoid" refers to the movie, then the learner might be able to learn to resolve similar conflicts in other documents. However, this requires a conflict resolution mechanism in which the labeler can provide rich feedback, and a learner that can utilize such rich feedback. This is an exciting future research direction that we would like to pursue.

We showed that our strategy to incorporate rationales works well for text classification. The proposed framework can potentially be used for non-text domains where the domain experts can provide rationales for their decisions, such as medical domain where the doctor can provide a rationale for his/her diagnosis and treatment decisions. Each domain is expected to have its own unique research challenges and working with other domains is another interesting future research direction.

## 6 Related Work

The closest related work deals with eliciting rationales from users and incorporating them into the learning (e.g., (Zaidan et al., 2007), (Donahue and Grauman, 2011), (Zaidan et al., 2008), and (Parkash and Parikh, 2012)). However, much of this work is specific to a particular classifier, such as support vector machines. The framework we present is classifier-agnostic and we have shown that it works across classifiers and feature representations. Additionally, we provide a novel active learning approach tailored for the learning with rationales framework.

Another line of related work is the recent work on active learning with instance and feature annotations (e.g., (Melville and Sindhwani, 2009), (Druck et al., 2009), (Small et al., 2011), (Stumpf et al., 2008), (Raghavan and Allan, 2007), and (Attenberg et al., 2010)). The main difference between the feature annotation work and the learning with rationales framework is that the feature annotations are not tied to particular instances, whereas in the learning with rationales framework, the documents and their rationales are coupled together. Even though

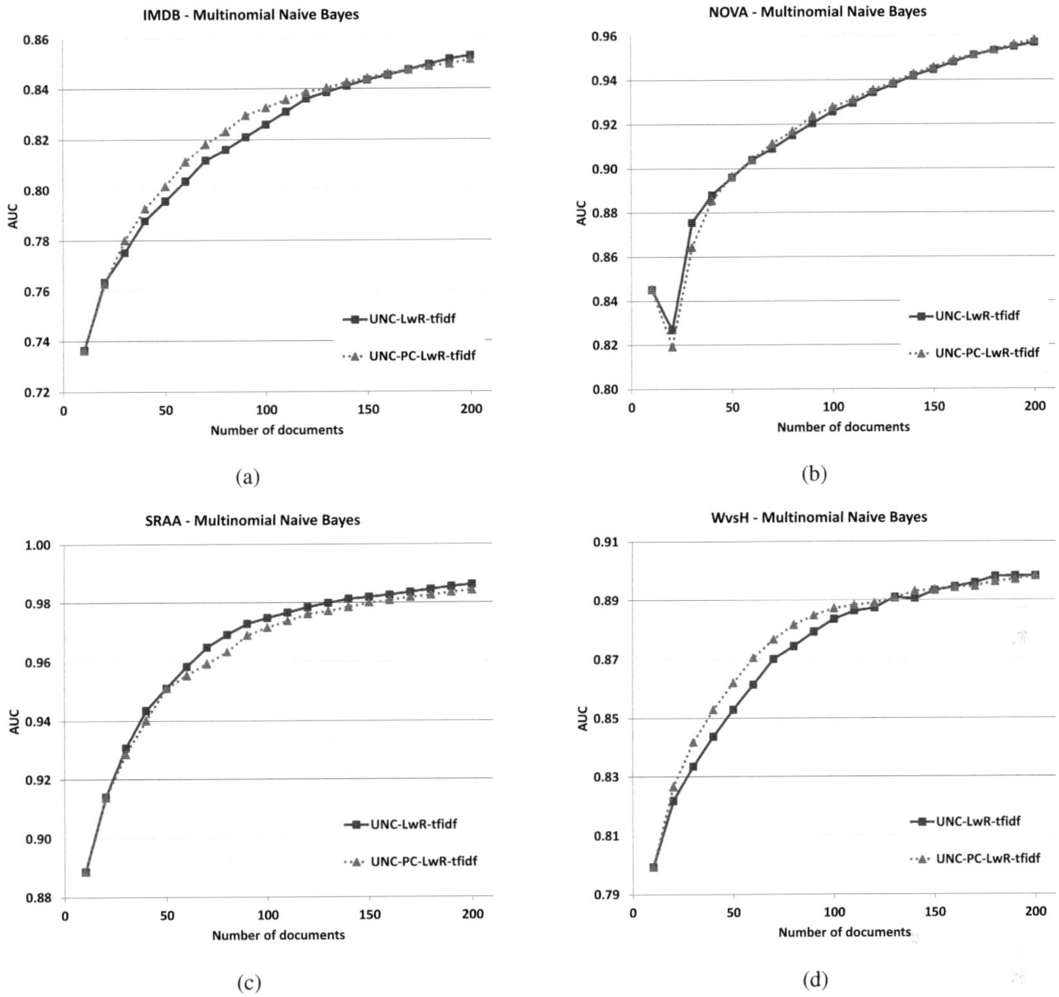


Figure 2: Comparison of LwR using UNC and UNC-PC for all datasets with tf-idf representation and using multinomial naïve Bayes classifier.

feature annotation work can be utilized for the learning with rationales framework by decoupling rationales from their documents, this is expected to result in information loss (such as weighting features globally rather than locally). The precise effect of decoupling rationales and documents on the classifier performance still needs to be tested empirically.

## 7 Conclusion

We introduced a novel framework to incorporate rationales into active learning for text classification. Our simple strategy to incorporate rationales can utilize any off-the-shelf classifier. The empirical evaluations on four text datasets with binary and tf-idf representations and three classifiers showed that our proposed method utilizes rationales effectively. Additionally, we presented an active learning strategy that is tailored specifically for the learning with rationales framework and empirically showed that it improved active learning.

## Acknowledgment

This material is based upon work supported by the National Science Foundation CAREER award no. 1350337.

## References


Josh Attenberg, Prem Melville, and Foster Provost. 2010. A unified approach to active dual supervision for labeling features and examples. In *European conference on Machine learning and knowledge discovery in databases*, pages 40–55.

Olivier Chapelle, Bernhard Schölkopf, and Alexander Zien, editors. 2006. *Semi-Supervised Learning*. MIT Press, Cambridge, MA.

Jeff Donahue and Kristen Grauman. 2011. Annotator rationales for visual recognition. In *Computer Vision (ICCV), 2011 IEEE International Conference on*, pages 1395–1402.

G. Druck, B. Settles, and A. McCallum. 2009. Active learning by labeling features. In *Proceedings of the 2009 Conference on Empirical Methods in Natural Language Processing: Volume 1-Volume 1*, pages 81–90.

Glenn M Fung, Olvi L Mangasarian, and Jude W Shavlik. 2002. Knowledge-based support vector machine classifiers. In *Advances in neural information processing systems*, pages 521–528.

Federico Girosi and Nicholas Tung Chan. 1995. Prior knowledge and the creation of virtual examples for rbf networks. In *Neural Networks for Signal Processing [1995] V. Proceedings of the 1995 IEEE Workshop*, pages 201–210.

Isabell Guyon. 2011. Results of active learning challenge.

D.D. Lewis and J. Catlett. 1994. Heterogeneous uncertainty sampling for supervised learning. In *Proceedings of the eleventh international conference on machine learning*, pages 148–156.

David D. Lewis and William A. Gale. 1994. A sequential algorithm for training text classifiers. In *ACM SIGIR Conference on Research and Development in Information Retrieval*, pages 3–12.

Andrew L Maas, Raymond E Daly, Peter T Pham, Dan Huang, Andrew Y Ng, and Christopher Potts. 2011. Learning word vectors for sentiment analysis. In *Proceedings of the 49th Annual Meeting of the Association for Computational Linguistics: Human Language Technologies-Volume 1*, pages 142–150.

Prem Melville and Vikas Sindhwani. 2009. Active dual supervision: Reducing the cost of annotating examples and features. In *Proceedings of the NAACL HLT 2009 Workshop on Active Learning for Natural Language Processing*, pages 49–57.

Amar Parkash and Devi Parikh. 2012. Attributes for classifier feedback. In *Computer Vision–ECCV 2012*, pages 354–368. Springer.

F. Pedregosa, G. Varoquaux, A. Gramfort, V. Michel, B. Thirion, O. Grisel, M. Blondel, P. Prettenhofer, R. Weiss, V. Dubourg, J. Vanderplas, A. Passos, D. Cournapeau, M. Brucher, M. Perrot, and E. Duchesnay. 2011. Scikit-learn: Machine learning in Python. *Journal of Machine Learning Research*, 12:2825–2830.

Hema Raghavan and James Allan. 2007. An interactive algorithm for asking and incorporating feature feedback into support vector machines. In *Proceedings of the 30th annual international ACM SIGIR conference on Research and development in information retrieval*, pages 79–86.

Hema Raghavan, Omid Madani, and Rosie Jones. 2006. Active learning with feedback on features and instances. *Journal of Machine Learning Research*, 7:1655–1686.

Nicholas Roy and Andrew McCallum. 2001. Toward optimal active learning through sampling estimation of error reduction. In *International Conference on Machine Learning*, pages 441–448.

Richard Segal, Ted Markowitz, and William Arnold. 2006. Fast uncertainty sampling for labeling large e-mail corpora. In *Conference on Email and Anti-Spam*.

Burr Settles. 2012. *Active Learning*. Synthesis Lectures on Artificial Intelligence and Machine Learning. Morgan & Claypool Publishers.

H. S. Seung, M. Opper, and H. Sompolinsky. 1992. Query by committee. In *ACM Annual Workshop on Computational Learning Theory*, pages 287–294.

Manali Sharma and Mustafa Bilgic. 2013. Most-surely vs. least-surely uncertain. In *IEEE 13th International Conference on Data Mining*, pages 667–676.

Vikas Sindhwani, Prem Melville, and Richard D Lawrence. 2009. Uncertainty sampling and transductive experimental design for active dual supervision. In *Proceedings of the International Conference on Machine Learning*, pages 953–960.

Kevin Small, Byron Wallace, Thomas Trikalinos, and Carla E Brodley. 2011. The constrained weight space svm: learning with ranked features. In *Proceedings of the 28th International Conference on Machine Learning (ICML-11)*, pages 865–872.

Simone Stumpf, Vidya Rajaram, Lida Li, Margaret Burnett, Thomas Dietterich, Erin Sullivan, Russell Drummond, and Jonathan Herlocker. 2007. Toward harnessing user feedback for machine learning. In *Proceedings of the 12th international conference on Intelligent user interfaces*, pages 82–91.

S. Stumpf, E. Sullivan, E. Fitzhenry, I. Oberst, W.K. Wong, and M. Burnett. 2008. Integrating rich user feedback into intelligent user interfaces. In *Proceedings of the 13th international conference on Intelligent user interfaces*, pages 50–59.

Simon Tong and Daphne Koller. 2001. Support vector machine active learning with applications to text classification. *Journal of Machine Learning Research*, 2:45–66.

Geoffrey G Towell and Jude W Shavlik. 1994. Knowledge-based artificial neural networks. *Artificial intelligence*, 70(1):119–165.

Geofrey G Towell, Jude W Shavlik, and Michiel Noordewier. 1990. Refinement of approximate domain theories by knowledge-based neural networks. In *Proceedings of the eighth National conference on Artificial intelligence*, pages 861–866.

Omar Zaidan, Jason Eisner, and Christine D Piatko. 2007. Using" annotator rationales" to improve machine learning for text categorization. In *HLT-NAACL*, pages 260–267.

Omar F Zaidan, Jason Eisner, and Christine Piatko. 2008. Machine learning with annotator rationales to reduce annotation cost. In *Proceedings of the NIPS* 2008 Workshop on Cost Sensitive Learning*.

J. Zhu and E. Hovy. 2007. Active learning for word sense disambiguation with methods for addressing the class imbalance problem. In *Proceedings of the 2007 Joint Conference on Empirical Methods in Natural Language Processing and Computational Natural Language Learning*, pages 783–790.

# Inferring Temporally-Anchored Spatial Knowledge from Semantic Roles

**Eduardo Blanco** and **Alakananda Vempala**
Human Intelligence and Language Technologies Lab
University of North Texas
Denton, TX, 76203
eduardo.blanco@unt.edu, AlakanandaVempala@my.unt.edu

## Abstract

This paper presents a framework to infer spatial knowledge from verbal semantic role representations. First, we generate potential spatial knowledge deterministically. Second, we determine whether it can be inferred and a degree of certainty. Inferences capture that something is located or is not located somewhere, and temporally anchor this information. An annotation effort shows that inferences are ubiquitous and intuitive to humans.

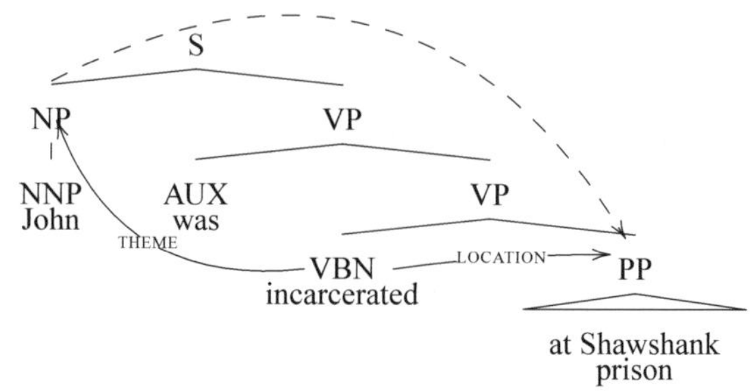


Figure 1: Semantic roles (solid arrows) and additional spatial knowledge (discontinuous arrow).

## 1 Introduction

Extracting semantic relations from text is at the core of text understanding. Semantic relations encode semantic connections between words. For example, from (1) *Bill couldn't handle the pressure and quit yesterday*, one could extract that the CAUSE of *quit* was *the pressure*. Doing so would help answering question *Why did Bill quit?* and determining that *the pressure* started before Bill *quit*.

In the past years, computational semantics has received a significant boost. But extracting all semantic relations in text—even in single sentences—is still an elusive goal. Most existing approaches target either a single relation, e.g., PART-WHOLE (Girju et al., 2006), or relations that hold between arguments following some syntactic construction, e.g., possessives (Tratz and Hovy, 2013). Among the latter kind, the task of verbal semantic role labeling focuses on extracting semantic links exclusively between verbs and their arguments. PropBank (Palmer et al., 2005) is a popular corpus for this task, and tools to extract verbal semantic roles have been proposed for years (Carreras and Màrquez, 2005).

Some semantic relations hold forever, e.g., the CAUSE of event *quit* in example (1) above is *pressure*. Discussing when this CAUSE holds is somewhat artificial: at some point Bill *quit*, and he did so because of *the pressure*. But LOCATION and other semantic relations often do not hold forever. For example, while buildings typically have one location during their existence, people and objects such as cars and books do not: they participate in events and as a result their locations change.

This paper presents a framework to infer temporally-anchored spatial knowledge from verbal semantic roles. Specifically, our goal is to infer whether something is located somewhere or not located somewhere, and temporally anchor this spatial information. Consider sentence (2) *John was incarcerated at Shawshank prison* and its semantic roles (Figure 1, solid arrows). Given these roles, we aim at inferring that *John* had LOCATION *Shawshank prison* during event *incarcerated*, and that he (probably) did not have this LOCATION before and after (discontinuous arrow). Our intuition is that knowing that *incarcerated* has THEME *John* and LOCATION *Shawshank prison* will help making these inferences. As we shall discuss, sometimes we have evidence that something is (or is not) located somewhere, but cannot completely commit.

We target temporally-anchored spatial knowledge between intra-sentential arguments of verbs, not only between arguments of the same verb as exemplified in Figure 1. The main contributions are:



*Human Language Technologies: The 2015 Annual Conference of the North American Chapter of the ACL*, pages 452–461,
Denton, Colorado, May 31 – June 5, 2015. 

(1) analysis of spatial knowledge inferable from PropBank-style semantic roles; (2) annotations of temporally-anchored LOCATION relations on top of OntoNotes;[1] (3) supervised models to infer the additional spatial knowledge; and (4) experiments detailing results using lexical, syntactic and semantic features. The framework presented here infers over 44% spatial knowledge on top of the PropBank-style semantic roles annotated in OntoNotes (certYES and certNO labels, Section 3.3).

## 2 Semantic Roles and Additional Spatial Knowledge

We denote a semantic relation R between $x$ and $y$ as R($x$, $y$). R($x$, $y$) could be read "$x$ has R $y$", e.g., AGENT(*moved*, *John*) could be read "moved has AGENT John". Semantic roles[2] are semantic relations R($x$, $y$) such that $x$ is a verb and $y$ is an argument of $x$. We refer to any spatial relation LOCATION($x$, $y$) where (1) $x$ is not a verb, or (2) $x$ is a verb but $y$ is not a argument of $x$, as additional spatial knowledge. As we shall see, we target additional spatial knowledge beyond plain LOCATION($x$, $y$) relations, which only specify the location $y$ of $x$. Namely, we consider polarity, i.e., whether something is or is not located somewhere, and temporally anchor this information.

This paper complements semantic role representations with additional spatial knowledge. We follow a practical approach by inferring spatial knowledge from PropBank-style semantic roles. We believe this is an advantage since PropBank is well-known in the field and several tools to predict PropBank roles are documented and publicly available.[3] The work presented here could be incorporated into any NLP pipeline after role labeling without modifications to other components.

### 2.1 PropBank and OntoNotes

PropBank (Palmer et al., 2005) adds semantic role annotations on top of the parse trees of the Penn Treebank. It uses a set of numbered arguments[4] ($\text{ARG}_0$, $\text{ARG}_1$, etc.) and modifiers (ARGM-TMP, ARGM-MNR, etc.). Numbered arguments do not share a common meaning across verbs, they are defined on verb-specific framesets. For example, $\text{ARG}_2$ is used to indicate "*employer*" with verb *work.01* and "*expected terminus of sleep*" with verb *sleep.01* (Table 1). Unlike numbered arguments, modifiers have the same meaning across verbs (Table 2).

| |
|---|
| [Mr. Cray]$_{\text{ARG}_0}$ [will]$_{\text{ARGM-MOD}}$ [work]$_{verb}$ [for the Colorado Springs CO company]$_{\text{ARG}_2}$ [as an independent contractor]$_{\text{ARG}_1}$. |
| [I]$_{\text{ARG}_0}$'d [slept]$_{verb}$ [through my only previous brush with natural disaster]$_{\text{ARG}_2}$, [...] |

Table 1: Examples of PropBank annotations.

| | |
|---|---|
| ARGM-LOC: location | ARGM-CAU: cause |
| ARGM-EXT: extent | ARGM-TMP: time |
| ARGM-DIS: discourse connective | ARGM-PNC: purpose |
| ARGM-ADV: general-purpose | ARGM-MNR: manner |
| ARGM-NEG: negation marker | ARGM-DIR: direction |
| ARGM-MOD: modal verb | |

Table 2: Argument modifiers in PropBank.

The original PropBank corpus consists of (1) 3,327 framesets, each frameset defines the numbered roles for a verb, and (2) actual semantic role annotations (numbered arguments and modifiers) for 112,917 verbs. On average, each verb has 1.93 numbered arguments and 0.66 modifiers annotated. Only 7,198 verbs have an ARGM-LOC annotated, i.e., location information is present in 6.37% of verbs. For more information about PropBank and examples, refer to the annotation guidelines.[5]

OntoNotes (Hovy et al., 2006) is a more recent corpus that includes POS tags, word senses, parse trees, speaker information, named entities, PropBank-style semantic roles and coreference. While the original PropBank annotations were done exclusively in the news domain, OntoNotes includes other genres as well: broadcast and telephone conversations, weblogs, etc. Because of the additional annotation layers and genres, we work with OntoNotes instead of PropBank.

[1] Available at http://hilt.cse.unt.edu/

[2] We use *semantic role* to refer to PropBank-style (verbal) semantic roles. NomBank (Meyers et al., 2004) and FrameNet (Baker et al., 1998) also annotate semantic roles.

[3] E.g., http://cogcomp.cs.illinois.edu/page/software, http://ml.nec-labs.com/senna/;

[4] Numbered arguments are also referred to as *core*.

[5] http://verbs.colorado.edu/~mpalmer/projects/ace/PBguidelines.pdf

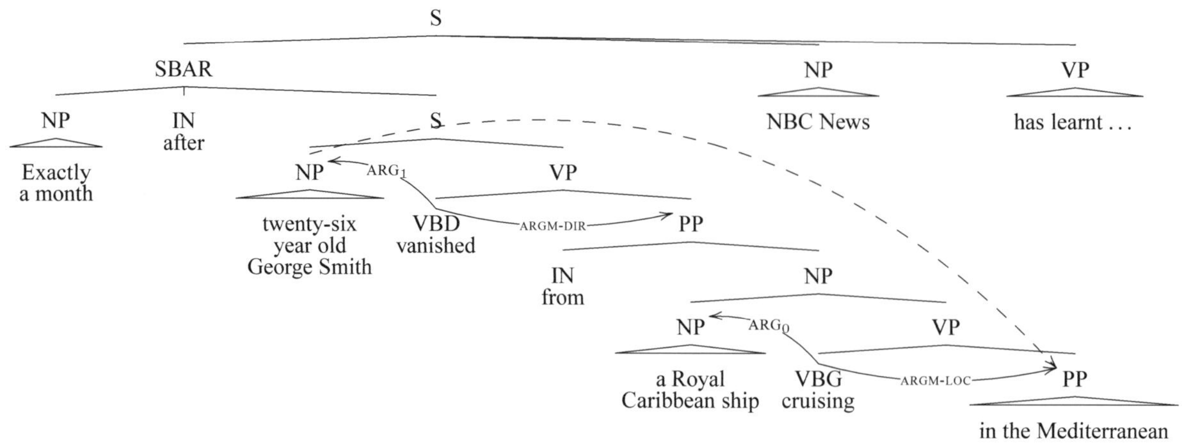


Figure 2: Semantic roles (solid arrows) and additional spatial knowledge (discontinuous arrow) of type (1b). The additional LOCATION(*a Royal Caribbean ship*, *in the Mediterranean*) of type (1a) is not shown.

### 2.2 Additional Spatial Knowledge

Sentences contain spatial information beyond ARGM-LOC semantic role, i.e., beyond links between verbs and their arguments. There are two main types of additional LOCATION($x$, $y$) relations:[6] (1) those whose arguments $x$ and $y$ are semantic roles of a verb, and (2) those whose arguments $x$ and $y$ are not semantic roles of a verb.

The first kind can be further divided into (1a) those whose arguments are semantic roles of the same verb (Figure 1), and (1b) those whose arguments are semantic roles of different verbs. Figure 2 illustrates type (1b). Semantic roles indicate $\text{ARG}_1$ and ARGM-DIR of *vanished*, and $\text{ARG}_0$ and ARGM-LOC of *cruising*. In this example, one can infer that *twenty-six year old George Smith* ($\text{ARG}_1$ of vanished) has LOCATION *in the Mediterranean* (ARGM-LOC of *cruising*) during the *cruising* event.

The second kind of additional LOCATION($x$, $y$) is exemplified in the following sentence: *[Residents of Biddeford apartments]*$_{\text{ARG}_0}$ *can [enjoy]*$_{\text{verb}}$ *[the recreational center]*$_{\text{ARG}_1}$ *[free of charge]*$_{\text{MANNER}}$. LOCATION(*recreational center*, *Biddeford apartments*) could be inferred yet *Biddeford apartments* is not a semantic role of a verb.[7] Inferring this kind of relations would require splitting semantic roles; one could also extract that the *residents* have LOCATION *Biddeford apartments*.

In this paper, we focus on extracting additional spatial knowledge of type (1), and reserve type (2) for future work. More specifically, we infer spatial knowledge between $x$ and $y$, where the following semantic roles exist: $\text{ARG}_i(x_{pred}, x)$ and ARGM-LOC($y_{pred}$, $y$). $\text{ARG}_i$ indicates any numbered argument ($\text{ARG}_0$, $\text{ARG}_1$, $\text{ARG}_2$, etc.) and $x_{pred}$ ($y_{pred}$) indicates the verbal predicate to which $x$ ($y$) attaches. Targeting additional spatial knowledge exclusively for numbered arguments is not a significant limitation: most semantic roles annotated in OntoNotes (75%) are numbered arguments, and it is pointless to infer spatial knowledge for most modifiers, e.g., ARGM-EXT, ARGM-DIS, ARGM-ADV, ARGM-MOD, ARGM-NEG, ARGM-DIR.

## 3 Annotating Spatial Knowledge

Annotating all additional spatial knowledge in OntoNotes inferable from semantic roles is a daunting task. OntoNotes is a large corpus with 63,918 sentences and 9,924 ARGM-LOC semantic roles annotated. Our goal is not to present an extensive annotation effort, but rather show that additional temporally-anchored spatial knowledge can be (1) annotated reliably by non-experts following simple guidelines, and (2) inferred automatically using supervised machine learning. Thus, we focus on 200 sentences from OntoNotes that have at least one ARGM-LOC role annotated.

[6] Both ARGM-LOC($x$, $y$) and LOCATION($x$, $y$) encode the same meaning, but we use ARGM-LOC for the PropBank semantic role and LOCATION for additional spatial knowledge.

[7] Note that the head of $\text{ARG}_0$ is *residents*, not the apartments.

**foreach** *sentence s* **do**
  **foreach** *sem. role* ARGM-LOC($y_{pred}$, $y$) $\in s$ **do**
    **foreach** *sem. role* ARG$_i$($x_{pred}$, $x$) $\in s$ **do**
      **if** *is_valid(x, y)* **then**
        Is $x$ located at $y$ before $y_{pred}$?
        Is $x$ located at $y$ during $y_{pred}$?
        Is $x$ located at $y$ after $y_{pred}$?

Algorithm 1: Procedure to generate potential additional spatial knowledge of type (1) (Section 2.2).

Obviously, [the pilot]$_{\text{ARG0}, v_1}$ did[n't]$_{\text{ARGM-NEG}, v_1}$ [think]$_{v_1}$ [too much]$_{\text{ARGM-EXT}, v_1}$ [about [what]$_{\text{ARG1}, v_2}$ was [happening]$_{v_2}$ [on the ground]$_{\text{ARGM-LOC}, v_2}$, or ... ]$_{\text{ARG1}, v_1}$

Figure 3: Sample sentence and semantic roles. Pair (x: *about what was happening on the ground*, y: *on the ground*) is invalid because x contains y.

All potential additional spatial knowledge is generated with Algorithm 1, and a manual annotation effort determines whether spatial knowledge should be inferred. Algorithm 1 loops over all ARGM-LOC roles, and generates questions regarding whether spatial knowledge can be inferred for any numbered argument within the same sentence. $is\_valid(x, y)$ returns True if (1) $x$ is not contained in $y$ and (2) $y$ is not contained in $x$. Considering invalid pairs would be trivial or nonsensical, e.g., pair (x: *about what was happening on the ground*, y: *on the ground*) is invalid in the sentence depicted in Figure 3.

### 3.1 Annotation Process and Guidelines

In a first batch of annotations, two annotators were asked questions generated by Algorithm 1 and required to answer YES or NO. The only information they had available was the source sentence without semantic role information. Feedback from this first attempt revealed that (1) because of the nature of $x$ or $y$, sometimes questions are pointless, and (2) because of uncertainty, sometimes it is not correct to answer YES or NO, even tough there is some evidence that makes either answer likely.

Based on this feedback, and inspired by previous annotation guidelines (Saurí and Pustejovsky, 2012), in a second batch we allowed five answers:

- `certYES`: I am certain that the answer is yes.
- `probYES`: It is probable that the answer is yes, but it is not guaranteed.
- `certNO`: I am certain that the answer is no.
- `probNO`: It is probable that the answer is no, but it is not guaranteed.
- UNK: There is not enough information to answer, I can't tell the location of $x$.

The goal is to infer spatial knowledge as gathered by humans when reading text. Thus, annotators were encouraged to use commonsense and world knowledge. While simple and somewhat open to interpretation, these guidelines allowed as to gather annotations with "good reliability" (Section 3.3.1).

### 3.2 Annotation Examples

In this section, we present annotation examples after resolving conflicts (Figure 4). These examples show that ambiguity is common and sentences must be fully interpreted before annotating.

Sentence 4(a) has four semantic roles for verb *collecting* (solid arrows), and annotators are asked to decide whether ARG$_0$ and ARG$_1$ of *collecting* are located at the ARGM-LOC before, during or after *collecting* (discontinuous arrows). Annotators interpreted that the *FBI agents and divers* (ARG$_0$) and *evidence* (ARG$_1$) were located *at Lake Logan* (ARGM-LOC) during *collecting* (`certYES`). They also annotated that the *FBI agents and divers* were likely to be located at *Lake Logan* before and after (`probYES`). Finally, they determined that the *evidence* was located *at Lake Logan* before the *collecting* (`certYES`), but probably not after (`probNO`). These annotations reflect the natural reading of sentence 4(a): (1) people and whatever they collect are located where the collecting takes place during the event, (2) people collecting are likely to be at that location before and after (i.e., presumably they do not arrive immediately before and leave immediately after), and (3) the objects being collected are located at that location before collecting, but probably not after.

Sentence 4(b) is more complex. First, potential relation LOCATION(*in sight*, *at the intersection*) is annotated UNK: it is nonsensical to ask for the location of *sight*. Second, the *Disney symbols* are never located *at the intersection* (`certNO`). Third, both *the car* and *security guard* were located *at the intersection* during the stop for sure (`certYES`). Fourth, annotators interpreted that *the car* was not *at the intersection* before (`certNO`), but they were not sure about after (`probNO`). Fifth, they considered that the *security guard* was probably located *at the intersec-*

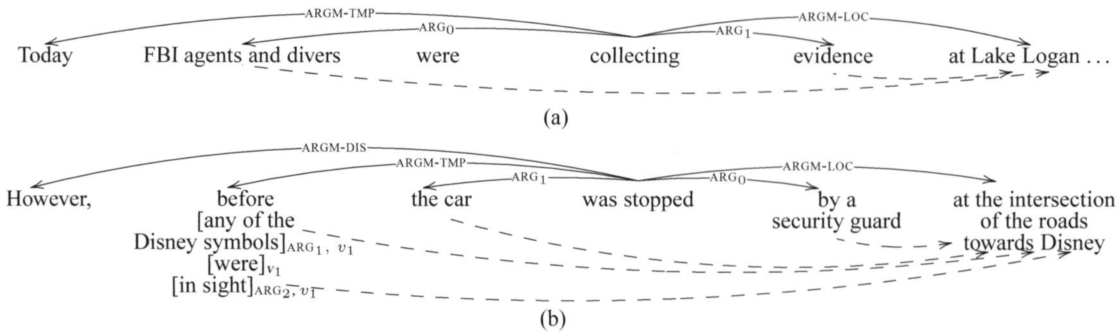


| $x$ | $y$ | $y_{pred}$ | Before | During | After |
|---|---|---|---|---|---|
| FBI agents and divers | at Lake Logan | collecting | probYES | certYES | probYES |
| evidence | at Lake Logan | collecting | certYES | certYES | probNO |
| any of the Disney symbols | at the intersection of the roads ... | stopped | certNO | certNO | certNO |
| in sight | at the intersection of the roads ... | stopped | UNK | UNK | UNK |
| the car | at the intersection of the roads ... | stopped | certNO | certYES | probNO |
| by a security guard | at the intersection of the roads ... | stopped | probYES | certYES | probYES |

Figure 4: Examples of semantic role representations (solid arrows), potential additional spatial knowledge (discontinuous arrows) and annotations with respect to the verb to which $y$ attaches (*collecting* or *stopped*).

| | Label | | | | | | | | | |
|---|---|---|---|---|---|---|---|---|---|---|
| | certYES | | probYES | | certNO | | probNO | | UNK | |
| | # | % | # | % | # | % | # | % | # | % |
| Before | 100 | 15.04 | 225 | 33.83 | 57 | 8.57 | 248 | 37.29 | 35 | 5.26 |
| During | 477 | 71.51 | 36 | 5.40 | 60 | 9.00 | 59 | 8.85 | 35 | 5.25 |
| After | 140 | 21.12 | 344 | 51.89 | 57 | 8.60 | 87 | 13.12 | 35 | 5.28 |
| All | 717 | **35.94** | 605 | 30.33 | 174 | **8.72** | 394 | 19.75 | 105 | 5.26 |

Table 3: Annotation counts. Over 44% of potential spatial knowledge can be inferred (certYES and certNO).

*tion* before and after. In other words, annotators understood that (1) the car was moving down a road and arrived at the intersection; (2) then, it was pulled over by a security guard who is probably stationed at the intersection; and (3) after the stop, the car probably continued with its route but the guard probably stayed at the intersection.

### 3.3 Annotation Analysis

Each annotator answered 1,995 questions generated with Algorithm 1. Basic label counts after resolving conflicts are shown in Table 3. First, it is worth noting that annotators used UNK to answer only 5.26% of questions. Thus, over 94% of times ARGM-LOC semantic role is found, additional spatial knowledge can be inferred with some degree of certainty. Second, annotators were certain about the additional spatial knowledge, i.e., labels certYES and certNO, 35.94% and 8.72% of times respectively. Thus, 44% of times one encounters ARGM-LOC semantic role, additional spatial knowledge can be inferred with certainty. Finally, annotators answered around 50% of questions with probYES or probNO. In other words, they found it likely that spatial information can be inferred, but were not completely certain.

| | Observed | Cohen Kappa |
|---|---|---|
| Before | 89.0% | 0.845 |
| During | 91.2% | 0.848 |
| After | 87.8% | 0.814 |
| All | 89.8% | 0.862 |

Table 4: Inter-annotation agreements. Kappa scores indicate "good reliability".

#### 3.3.1 Inter-Annotator Agreements

Table 4 presents observed agreements, i.e., raw percentage of equal annotations, and Cohen Kappa scores (Cohen, 1960) per temporal anchor and for all questions. Kappa scores are above 0.80, indicating "good reliability" (Artstein and Poesio, 2008).

| | No. | Name | Description |
|---|---|---|---|
| | 0 | temporal anchor | are we predicting LOCATION($x$, $y$) before, during or after $y_{pred}$? |
| lexical | 1–4 | first word, POS tag | first word and POS tag in $x$ and $y$ |
| | 5–8 | last word, POS tag | last word and POS tag in $x$ and $y$ |
| | 9,10 | num tokens | number of tokens in $x$ and $y$ |
| | 11,12 | subcategory | concatenation of (1) $x$'s children and (2) $y$'s children |
| | 13 | direction | whether $x$ occurs before or after $y$ |
| syntactic | 14,15 | syntactic node | syntactic node of $x$ and $y$ |
| | 16–19 | head word, POS tag | head word and POS tag of $x$ and $y$ |
| | 20–23 | left and right sibling | syntactic nodes of the left and right siblings of $x$ and $y$ |
| | 24–27 | parent node and index | syntactic nodes and child indices of parents of $x$ and $y$ |
| | 28 | common subsumer | syntactic node subsuming $x$ and $y$ |
| | 29 | syntactic path | syntactic path between $x$ and $y$ |
| semantic | 30–33 | word, POS tag | predicate and POS tag of $x_{pred}$ and $y_{pred}$ |
| | 34 | isRole | semantic role label between $x_{pred}$ and $x$ |
| | 35 | same predicate | whether $x_{pred}$ and $y_{pred}$ are the same token |
| | 36–39 | firstRole, lastRole | the first and last semantic roles of $x_{pred}$ and $y_{pred}$ |
| | 40–59 | hasRole | flags indicating whether $x_{pred}$ and $y_{pred}$ have each semantic role |
| | 60–99 | role index and node | for each semantic role, the order of appearance and syntactic node |
| | 100 | x_containedIn_y_role | semantic role of $y_{pred}$ that fully contains $x$ |
| | 101 | y_containedIn_x_role | semantic role of $x_{pred}$ that fully contains $y$ |

Table 5: Feature set to infer temporally-anchored spatial knowledge from semantic role representations.

We believe the high Kappa scores are due to the fact that we start from PropBank-style roles instead of plain text, and questions asked are intuitive. Note that not all disagreements are equal, e.g., the difference between `certYES` and `certNO` is much larger than the difference between `certYES` and `probYES`.

## 4 Inferring Spatial Knowledge

We follow a standard supervised machine learning approach. The 200 sentences were divided into train (80%) and test (20%), and the corresponding instances assigned to the train and test sets.[8] We trained an SVM with RBF kernel using scikit-learn (Pedregosa et al., 2011). Parameters $C$ and $\gamma$ were tuned using 10-fold cross-validation with the training set, and results are calculated with test instances.

### 4.1 Feature selection

Selected features (Table 5) are a mix of lexical, syntactic and semantic features, and are extracted from tokens (words and POS tags), full parse trees and semantic roles. Lexical and syntactic features are standard in semantic role labeling (Gildea and Jurafsky, 2002) and we do not elaborate on them. Hereafter we describe semantic features, which include any feature derived from semantic role representations.

[8]Splitting instances randomly would be unfair, as instances from the same sentence would be assigned to the train and test sets. Thank you to an anonymous reviewer for pointing this out.

| |
|---|
| Sentence: [In this laboratory]$_{\text{ARGM-LOC}, v_1}$ [I]$_{\text{ARG}_0, v_1}$'m [surrounded]$_{v_1}$ [by the remains of [20 service members who]$_{\text{ARG}_1, v_2}$ are in the process of being [identified]$_{v_2}$]$_{\text{ARG}_1, v_1}$ |
| Potential additional spatial knowledge: x: *20 service members who*, y: *In this laboratory*; x_containedIn_y_role = ARG$_1$ |
| Sentence: [Children]$_{\text{ARG}_0, v_1}$ can get to [know]$_{v_1}$ [different animals and plants, and [even some crops that]$_{\text{ARG}_1, v_2}$ are [rarely]$_{\text{ARGM-ADV}, v_2}$ [seen]$_{v_2}$ [in our daily life]$_{\text{ARGM-LOC}, v_2}$]$_{\text{ARG}_1, v_1}$. |
| Potential additional spatial knowledge: x: *Children*, y: *in our daily life*; y_containedIn_x_role = ARG$_1$ |

Figure 5: Pairs (x, y) for which *x_containedIn_y_role* and *y_containedIn_x_role* features have a value.

Features 30–33 correspond to the surface form and POS tag of the verbs to which $x$ and $y$ attach to. Feature 34 indicates the semantic role between $x_{pred}$ and $x$; note that the semantic role between $y_{pred}$ and $y$ is always ARGM-LOC (Algorithm 1). Feature 35 distinguishes inferences of type (1a) from (1b) (Section 2.2): it indicates whether both $x$ and $y$ attach to the same verb, as in Figure 1, or not, as in Figure 2. Features 36–39 encode the first and last semantic role of $x_{pred}$ and $y_{pred}$ by order of appearance. Features 40–59 are binary flags signalling which se-

| | | Before | | | During | | | After | | | All | | |
|---|---|---|---|---|---|---|---|---|---|---|---|---|---|
| | | P | R | F | P | R | F | P | R | F | P | R | F |
| most frequent baseline | certYES | 0.11 | 1.00 | 0.20 | 0.74 | 1.00 | 0.85 | 0.26 | 1.00 | 0.42 | 0.37 | 1.00 | 0.54 |
| | other labels | 0.00 | 0.00 | 0.00 | 0.00 | 0.00 | 0.00 | 0.00 | 0.00 | 0.00 | 0.00 | 0.00 | 0.00 |
| | weighted avg. | 0.01 | 0.11 | 0.02 | 0.54 | 0.74 | 0.63 | 0.07 | 0.26 | 0.11 | 0.14 | 0.37 | **0.20** |
| most frequent per temporal anchor baseline | certYES | 0.00 | 0.00 | 0.00 | 0.75 | 1.00 | 0.86 | 0.00 | 0.00 | 0.00 | 0.75 | 0.62 | 0.68 |
| | probYES | 0.00 | 0.00 | 0.00 | 0.00 | 0.00 | 0.00 | 0.45 | 1.00 | 0.62 | 0.45 | 0.56 | 0.50 |
| | probNO | 0.38 | 1.00 | 0.55 | 0.00 | 0.00 | 0.00 | 0.00 | 0.00 | 0.00 | 0.38 | 0.62 | 0.47 |
| | other labels | 0.00 | 0.00 | 0.00 | 0.00 | 0.00 | 0.00 | 0.00 | 0.00 | 0.00 | 0.00 | 0.00 | 0.00 |
| | weighted avg. | 0.14 | 0.38 | 0.21 | 0.57 | 0.75 | **0.65** | 0.20 | 0.45 | 0.28 | 0.50 | 0.53 | **0.50** |
| lexical features | certYES | 0.13 | 0.20 | 0.16 | 0.74 | 1.00 | 0.85 | 0.53 | 0.29 | 0.37 | 0.63 | 0.75 | 0.69 |
| | probYES | 0.39 | 0.34 | 0.36 | 0.00 | 0.00 | 0.00 | 0.56 | 0.90 | 0.69 | 0.51 | 0.63 | 0.56 |
| | certNO | 0.00 | 0.00 | 0.00 | 0.00 | 0.00 | 0.00 | 0.00 | 0.00 | 0.00 | 0.00 | 0.00 | 0.00 |
| | probNO | 0.39 | 0.53 | 0.45 | 0.00 | 0.00 | 0.00 | 0.00 | 0.00 | 0.00 | 0.39 | 0.37 | 0.38 |
| | UNK | 0.00 | 0.00 | 0.00 | 0.00 | 0.00 | 0.00 | 0.00 | 0.00 | 0.00 | 0.00 | 0.00 | 0.00 |
| | weighted avg. | 0.31 | 0.35 | 0.32 | 0.54 | 0.74 | 0.63 | 0.44 | 0.56 | 0.47 | 0.47 | 0.55 | **0.50** |
| lexical + syntactic features | certYES | 0.41 | 0.47 | 0.44 | 0.74 | 0.99 | 0.85 | 0.27 | 0.09 | 0.13 | 0.67 | 0.72 | 0.70 |
| | probYES | 0.53 | 0.34 | 0.41 | 0.00 | 0.00 | 0.00 | 0.54 | 0.90 | 0.67 | 0.54 | 0.63 | 0.58 |
| | certNO | 0.33 | 0.10 | 0.15 | 0.00 | 0.00 | 0.00 | 0.00 | 0.00 | 0.00 | 0.25 | 0.04 | 0.06 |
| | probNO | 0.38 | 0.64 | 0.48 | 0.00 | 0.00 | 0.00 | 0.00 | 0.00 | 0.00 | 0.38 | 0.44 | 0.41 |
| | UNK | 1.00 | 0.12 | 0.22 | 1.00 | 0.12 | 0.22 | 1.00 | 0.12 | 0.22 | 1.00 | 0.12 | 0.22 |
| | weighted avg. | 0.48 | 0.43 | **0.41** | 0.61 | 0.74 | 0.64 | 0.42 | 0.51 | 0.41 | 0.57 | 0.56 | **0.53** |
| lexical + semantic features | certYES | 0.18 | 0.20 | 0.19 | 0.74 | 1.00 | 0.85 | 0.65 | 0.31 | 0.42 | 0.67 | 0.76 | 0.71 |
| | probYES | 0.48 | 0.42 | 0.44 | 0.00 | 0.00 | 0.00 | 0.57 | 0.92 | 0.70 | 0.54 | 0.66 | 0.60 |
| | certNO | 0.00 | 0.00 | 0.00 | 0.00 | 0.00 | 0.00 | 0.00 | 0.00 | 0.00 | 0.00 | 0.00 | 0.00 |
| | probNO | 0.35 | 0.51 | 0.41 | 0.00 | 0.00 | 0.00 | 0.00 | 0.00 | 0.00 | 0.35 | 0.35 | 0.35 |
| | UNK | 0.00 | 0.00 | 0.00 | 0.00 | 0.00 | 0.00 | 0.00 | 0.00 | 0.00 | 0.00 | 0.00 | 0.00 |
| | weighted avg. | 0.33 | 0.37 | 0.34 | 0.54 | 0.74 | 0.63 | 0.47 | 0.57 | **0.49** | 0.49 | 0.56 | **0.52** |
| all features | certYES | 0.50 | 0.20 | 0.29 | 0.76 | 0.97 | 0.85 | 0.50 | 0.14 | 0.22 | 0.73 | 0.70 | 0.71 |
| | probYES | 0.51 | 0.36 | 0.42 | 0.50 | 0.14 | 0.22 | 0.56 | 0.93 | 0.70 | 0.55 | 0.66 | 0.60 |
| | certNO | 0.33 | 0.10 | 0.15 | 0.00 | 0.00 | 0.00 | 0.00 | 0.00 | 0.00 | 0.11 | 0.04 | 0.05 |
| | probNO | 0.40 | 0.72 | 0.51 | 0.00 | 0.00 | 0.00 | 0.00 | 0.00 | 0.00 | 0.39 | 0.50 | 0.44 |
| | UNK | 1.00 | 0.12 | 0.22 | 0.33 | 0.12 | 0.18 | 0.50 | 0.12 | 0.20 | 0.50 | 0.12 | 0.20 |
| | weighted avg. | 0.49 | 0.44 | **0.41** | 0.61 | 0.73 | **0.65** | 0.46 | 0.54 | 0.45 | 0.56 | 0.57 | **0.55** |

Table 6: Results obtained with two baselines, and training with several feature combinations. Models are trained with all instances (before, during and after).

mantic roles $x_{pred}$ and $y_{pred}$ have, and features 60–99 capture the index of each role (first, second, third, etc.) and its syntactic node (NP, PP, SBAR, etc.).

Finally, features 100 and 101 capture the semantic role of $x_{pred}$ and $y_{pred}$ which fully contain $y$ and $x$ respectively, if such roles exists. These features are especially designed for our inference task and are exemplified in Figure 5.

## 5 Experiments and Results

Results obtained with the test set using two baselines and models trained with several feature combinations are presented in Table 6. The *most frequent* baseline always predicts `certYES`, and the *most frequent per temporal anchor* baseline predicts `probNO`, `certYES` and `probYES` for instances with temporal anchor *before*, *during* and *after* respectively. The *most frequent* baseline obtains a weighted F-measure of 0.20, and *most frequent per temporal anchor* baseline 0.50. Results with supervised models are better, but we note that always predicting `certYES` for *during* instances obtains the same F-measure than using all features (0.65).

The bottom block of Table 6 presents results using all features. The weighted F-measure is 0.55, and the highest F-measures are obtained with labels `certYES` (0.71) and `probYES` (0.60). Results with `certNO` and `probNO` are lower (0.05 and 0.44), we believe this is due to the fact that few instances are annotated with this labels (8.72% and 19.75%, Table 3). Results are higher (0.65) with *during* instances than with *before* and *after* instances (0.41 and 0.45). These results are intuitive: certain events such as *press* and *write* require participants to be located where the event occurs only during the event.

### 5.1 Feature Ablation and Detailed Results

The weighted F-measure using lexical features is the same than with the *most frequent per temporal anchor* baseline (0.50). F-measures go up with *before* (0.21 vs. 0.32, 52.38%) and *after* (0.28 vs. 0.47, 67.85%) instances, but slightly down with *during* instances (0.65 vs. 0.63, −3.08%).

Complementing lexical features with syntactic and semantic features brings the overall weighted F-measure slightly up: 0.53 with syntactic and 0.52 with semantic features (+0.03 and +0.02, 6% and 4%). *Before* instances benefit the most from syntactic features (0.32 vs. 0.41, 28.13%), and *after* instances benefit from semantic features (0.47 vs. 0.49, 4.26%). *During* instances do not benefit from semantic features, and only gain 0.01 F-measure (1.59%) with syntactic features.

Finally, combining lexical, syntactic and semantic features obtains the best overall results (weighted F-measure: 0.55 vs. 0.53 and 0.52, 3.77% and 5.77%). We note, however, that *before* instances do not benefit from including semantic features (same F-measure, 0.41), and the best results for *after* instances are obtained with lexical and semantic features (0.49 vs. 0.45, 8.16%),

## 6 Related Work

Tools to extract the PropBank semantic roles we infer from have been studied for years (Carreras and Màrquez, 2005; Hajič et al., 2009; Lang and Lapata, 2010). These systems only extract semantic links between predicates and their arguments, not between arguments of predicates. In contrast, this paper complements semantic role representations with spatial knowledge for numbered arguments.

There have been several proposals to extract semantic links not annotated in well-known corpora such as PropBank (Palmer et al., 2005), FrameNet (Baker et al., 1998) or NomBank (Meyers et al., 2004). Gerber and Chai (2010) augment NomBank annotations with additional numbered arguments appearing in the same or previous sentences; posterior work obtained better results for the same task (Gerber and Chai, 2012; Laparra and Rigau, 2013). The SemEval-2010 Task 10: Linking Events and their Participants in Discourse (Ruppenhofer et al., 2009) targeted cross-sentence missing numbered arguments in PropBank and FrameNet. We have previously proposed an unsupervised framework to compose semantic relations out of previously extracted relations (Blanco and Moldovan, 2011; Blanco and Moldovan, 2014a), and a supervised approach to infer additional argument modifiers (ARGM) for verbs in PropBank (Blanco and Moldovan, 2014b). Unlike the current work, these previous efforts (1) improve the semantic representation of verbal and nominal predicates, or (2) infer relations between arguments of the same predicate. None of them target temporally-anchored spatial knowledge or account for uncertainty.

Attaching temporal information to semantic relations is uncommon. In the context of the TAC KBP temporal slot filling track (Garrido et al., 2012; Surdeanu, 2013), relations common in information extraction (e.g., SPOUSE, COUNTRY_OF_RESIDENCY) are assigned a temporal interval indicating when they hold. The task proved very difficult, and the best system achieved 48% of human performance. Unlike this line of work, the approach presented in this paper starts from semantic role representations, targets temporally-anchored LOCATION relations, and accounts for degrees of uncertainty (`certYES` / `certNO` vs. `probYES` / `probNO`).

The task of spatial role labeling (Hajič et al., 2009; Kolomiyets et al., 2013) aims at thoroughly representing spatial information with so-called spatial roles, i.e., trajector, landmark, spatial and motion indicators, path, direction, distance, and spatial relations. Unlike us, the task does not consider temporal spans nor certainty. But as the examples throughout this paper show, doing so is useful because (1) spatial information for most objects changes over time, and (2) humans sometimes can only state that an object is *probably* located somewhere. In contrast to this task, we infer temporally-anchored spatial knowledge as humans intuitively understand it, and purposely avoid following any formalism.

## 7 Conclusions

Semantic roles encode semantic links between a verb and its arguments. Among other role labels, PropBank uses numbered arguments ($\text{ARG}_0$, $\text{ARG}_1$, etc.) to encode the core arguments of a verb, and ARGM-LOC to encode the location. This paper exploits these numbered arguments and ARGM-LOC in order to infer temporally-anchored spatial knowledge. This knowledge encodes whether a numbered argument $x$ is or is not located in a location $y$, and temporally anchors this information with respect to the verb to which $y$ attaches.

An annotation effort with 200 sentences from OntoNotes has been presented. First, potential additional spatial knowledge is generated automatically (Algorithm 1). Then, annotators following straightforward guidelines answer questions asking for intuitive spatial information, including uncertainty. The result is annotations with high inter-annotator agreements that encode spatial knowledge as understood by humans when reading text.

Experimental results show that inferring additional spatial knowledge can be done with a modest weighted F-measure of 0.55. Results are higher for `certYES` and `probYES` (0.71 and 0.60), the labels that indicate that something is certainly or probably located somewhere. Simple majority baselines provide strong results, but combining lexical, syntactic and semantic features yields the best results (0.50 vs. 0.55). Inferring spatial knowledge for numeric arguments before and after an event occurs is harder than during the event (0.41 and 0.45 vs. 0.65).

The most important conclusion of this work is the fact that given an ARGM-LOC semantic role, temporally-anchored spatial knowledge can be inferred for numbered arguments in the same sentence. Indeed, annotators answered 44% of questions with `certYES` or `certNO`, and 50% of questions with `probYES` or `probNO`. Another important observation is that spatial knowledge can be inferred from most verbs, not only motion verbs. While it is fairly obvious to infer from *John went to Paris* that he had LOCATION *Paris* after *went* but not before or during, we have shown that verbs such as *incarcerated* (Figure 1) also grant spatial inferences.

## References


Ron Artstein and Massimo Poesio. 2008. Inter-coder agreement for computational linguistics. *Computational Linguistics*, 34(4):555–596, December.

Collin F. Baker, Charles J. Fillmore, and John B. Lowe. 1998. The Berkeley FrameNet Project. In *Proceedings of the 17th international conference on Computational Linguistics*, Montreal, Canada.

Eduardo Blanco and Dan Moldovan. 2011. Unsupervised learning of semantic relation composition. In *Proceedings of the 49th Annual Meeting of the Association for Computational Linguistics (ACL 2011)*, pages 1456–1465, Portland, Oregon.

Eduardo Blanco and Dan Moldovan. 2014a. Composition of semantic relations: Theoretical framework and case study. *ACM Trans. Speech Lang. Process.*, 10(4):17:1–17:36, January.

Eduardo Blanco and Dan Moldovan. 2014b. Leveraging verb-argument structures to infer semantic relations. In *Proceedings of the 14th Conference of the European Chapter of the Association for Computational Linguistics (EACL 2014)*, pages 145–154, Gothenburg, Sweden.

Xavier Carreras and Lluís Màrquez. 2005. Introduction to the CoNLL-2005 shared task: semantic role labeling. In *CONLL '05: Proceedings of the Ninth Conference on Computational Natural Language Learning*, pages 152–164.

J. Cohen. 1960. A Coefficient of Agreement for Nominal Scales. *Educational and Psychological Measurement*, 20(1):37.

Guillermo Garrido, Anselmo Peñas, Bernardo Cabaleiro, and Álvaro Rodrigo. 2012. Temporally anchored relation extraction. In *Proceedings of the 50th Annual Meeting of the Association for Computational Linguistics: Long Papers - Volume 1*, ACL '12, pages 107–116.

Matthew Gerber and Joyce Chai. 2010. Beyond NomBank: A Study of Implicit Arguments for Nominal Predicates. In *Proceedings of the 48th Annual Meeting of the Association for Computational Linguistics*, pages 1583–1592, Uppsala, Sweden, July.

Matthew Gerber and Joyce Chai. 2012. Semantic role labeling of implicit arguments for nominal predicates. *Computational Linguistics*, 38:755–798, 2012.

Daniel Gildea and Daniel Jurafsky. 2002. Automatic labeling of semantic roles. *Computational Linguistics*, 28(3):245–288, September.

Roxana Girju, Adriana Badulescu, and Dan Moldovan. 2006. Automatic discovery of part-whole relations. *Computational Linguistics*, 32(1):83–135, March.

Jan Hajič, Massimiliano Ciaramita, Richard Johansson, Daisuke Kawahara, Maria Antònia Martí, Lluís

Màrquez, Adam Meyers, Joakim Nivre, Sebastian Padó, Jan Štěpánek, Pavel Straňák, Mihai Surdeanu, Nianwen Xue, and Yi Zhang. 2009. The conll-2009 shared task: Syntactic and semantic dependencies in multiple languages. In *Proceedings of the Thirteenth Conference on Computational Natural Language Learning: Shared Task*, CoNLL '09, pages 1–18.

Eduard Hovy, Mitchell Marcus, Martha Palmer, Lance Ramshaw, and Ralph Weischedel. 2006. OntoNotes: the 90% Solution. In *NAACL'06: Proceedings of the Human Language Technology Conference of the NAACL*, pages 57–60, Morristown, NJ, USA.

Oleksandr Kolomiyets, Parisa Kordjamshidi, Marie-Francine Moens, and Steven Bethard. 2013. Semeval-2013 task 3: Spatial role labeling. In *Second Joint Conference on Lexical and Computational Semantics (*SEM), Volume 2: Proceedings of the Seventh International Workshop on Semantic Evaluation (SemEval 2013)*, pages 255–262.

Joel Lang and Mirella Lapata. 2010. Unsupervised induction of semantic roles. In *Human Language Technologies: The 2010 Annual Conference of the North American Chapter of the Association for Computational Linguistics*, HLT '10, pages 939–947.

Egoitz Laparra and German Rigau. 2013. Impar: A deterministic algorithm for implicit semantic role labelling. In *Proceedings of the 51st Annual Meeting of the Association for Computational Linguistics (Volume 1: Long Papers)*, pages 1180–1189, Sofia, Bulgaria, August.

A. Meyers, R. Reeves, C. Macleod, R. Szekely, V. Zielinska, B. Young, and R. Grishman. 2004. The NomBank Project: An Interim Report. In A. Meyers, editor, *HLT-NAACL 2004 Workshop: Frontiers in Corpus Annotation*, pages 24–31, Boston, Massachusetts, USA, May.

Martha Palmer, Daniel Gildea, and Paul Kingsbury. 2005. The Proposition Bank: An Annotated Corpus of Semantic Roles. *Computational Linguistics*, 31(1):71–106.

F. Pedregosa, G. Varoquaux, A. Gramfort, V. Michel, B. Thirion, O. Grisel, M. Blondel, P. Prettenhofer, R. Weiss, V. Dubourg, J. Vanderplas, A. Passos, D. Cournapeau, M. Brucher, M. Perrot, and E. Duchesnay. 2011. Scikit-learn: Machine learning in Python. *Journal of Machine Learning Research*, 12:2825–2830.

Josef Ruppenhofer, Caroline Sporleder, Roser Morante, Collin Baker, and Martha Palmer. 2009. SemEval-2010 Task 10: Linking Events and Their Participants in Discourse. In *Proceedings of the Workshop on Semantic Evaluations: Recent Achievements and Future Directions (SEW-2009)*, pages 106–111, Boulder, Colorado, June.

Roser Saurí and James Pustejovsky. 2012. Are you sure that this happened? assessing the factuality degree of events in text. *Computational Linguistics*, 38(2):261–299, June.

Mihai Surdeanu. 2013. Overview of the tac2013 knowledge base population evaluation: English slot filling and temporal slot filling. In *Proceedings of the TAC-KBP 2013 Workshop*.

Stephen Tratz and Eduard Hovy. 2013. Automatic interpretation of the english possessive. In *Proceedings of the 51st Annual Meeting of the Association for Computational Linguistics (Volume 1: Long Papers)*, pages 372–381. Association for Computational Linguistics.

# A Dynamic Programming Algorithm for Tree Trimming-based Text Summarization

**Masaaki Nishino[1], Norihito Yasuda[2], Tsutomu Hirao[1], Shin-ichi Minato[2,3], Masaaki Nagata[1]**
[1]NTT Communication Science Laboratories, NTT Corporation
[2]ERATO Minato Discrete Structure Manipulation System Project, JST
[3]Graduate School of Information Science and Technology, Hokkaido University
nishino.masaaki@lab.ntt.co.jp

## Abstract

Tree trimming is the problem of extracting an optimal subtree from an input tree, and sentence extraction and sentence compression methods can be formulated and solved as tree trimming problems. Previous approaches require integer linear programming (ILP) solvers to obtain exact solutions. The problem of this approach is that ILP solvers are black-boxes and have no theoretical guarantee as to their computation complexity. We propose a dynamic programming (DP) algorithm for tree trimming problems whose running time is $O(NL \log N)$, where $N$ is the number of tree nodes and $L$ is the length limit. Our algorithm exploits the zero-suppressed binary decision diagram (ZDD), a data structure that represents a family of sets as a directed acyclic graph, to represent the set of subtrees in a compact form; the structure of ZDD permits the application of DP to obtain exact solutions, and our algorithm is applicable to different tree trimming problems. Moreover, experiments show that our algorithm is faster than state-of-the-art ILP solvers, and that it scales well to handle large summarization problems.

## 1 Introduction

Extractive text summarization and sentence compression are tasks that basically select a subset of the input set of textual units that is appropriate as a summary or a compressed sentence. Current text summarization and sentence compression methods regard the problem of extracting such a subset as a combinatorial optimization problem (e.g., (Filatova and Hatzivassiloglou, 2004; McDonald, 2007; Lin and Bilmes, 2010)). Tree trimming, the problem of finding an optimal subtree of an input tree, is one kind of these combinatorial optimization problems, and it is used in three classes of text summarizations: sentence compression (Filippova and Strube, 2008; Filippova and Altun, 2013), single-document summarization (Hirao et al., 2013), and the combination of sentence compression and single-document summarization (Kikuchi et al., 2014). In these tasks, the set of input textual units is represented as a rooted tree whose nodes correspond to the minimum textual units such as sentences and words. Next, a subset is made by forming a subtree by trimming the input tree. Since the optimal trimmed subtree preserves the relationships between textual units, it is a concise representation of the original set that preserves linguistic quality.

A shortcoming of tree trimming-based methods is that they are formulated as integer linear programming (ILP) problems and so an ILP solver is needed to solve them. Although modern ILP solvers can solve many instances of tree trimming problems in a short time, there is no theoretical guarantee that they obtain an optimal solution. Furthermore, even if an optimal solution can be obtained, we cannot estimate the running time. Estimating the running time is critical for practical applications.

In this paper, we propose a dynamic programming (DP) algorithm for tree trimming problems that focus on text summarization. The algorithm can solve all three different classes of tree trimming problems proposed so far in a unified way, and it can always find an optimal solution in $O(NL \log N)$ time for these problems, where $N$ is the number of nodes of the input tree and $L$ is the length limit. The running time of our algorithm only depends on $N$ and $L$ and



*Human Language Technologies: The 2015 Annual Conference of the North American Chapter of the ACL*, pages 462–471,
Denver, Colorado, May 31 – June 5, 2015. 

so is independent of the input trees structure. Finding an exact solution is important since we can use it to evaluate the performance of heuristic algorithms.

The key idea of our algorithm is to use the zero-suppressed binary decision diagram (ZDD) (Minato, 1993) to represent the set of all subtrees of the input tree. ZDD is a data structure that represents a family of sets as a directed acyclic graph (DAG). It can represent a family of sets in compressed form. We use ZDD to represent the set of subtrees of the input tree, and then run a DP algorithm on the ZDD to obtain the optimal solution that satisfies the length limit. The algorithm runs in time $O(|Z|L)$, where $|Z|$ is the number of nodes of ZDD, and $L$ is the length limit. Although the number of ZDD nodes depends on the set we want to represent, we can give theoretical upper bounds when we represent the set of all subtrees of an input tree. ZDD uses $O(N \log N)$ nodes to represent the set of all subtrees of an $N$ node input tree. Hence the DP algorithm runs in $O(NL \log N)$ time. The main virtues of the proposed algorithm are that (1) it can always find an exact solution, (2) its running time is theoretically guaranteed, and (3) it can solve the three known tree trimming problems. Furthermore, our algorithm is fast enough to be practical and scalable. Since text summarization methods are often applied to large scale inputs (e.g., (Christensen et al., 2014; Nakao, 2000)), scalability is important. We compare it to state-of-the-art ILP solvers and confirm that the proposed algorithm can be hundreds of times faster.

Since our method assumes known formuations for text summarization, the summary created by our algorithm is exactly the same as that obtained by applying previous methods. However, we believe that algorithmic improvements in computational cost is as important as improvements in accuracy in order to make better practical systems.

## 2 Tree Trimming Problems

We briefly review the three tree trimming formulations used in text summarization and sentence compression. They all try to find the subtree that maximizes the sum of item weights while satisfying the length limit. Let $D = \{e_1, \ldots, e_N\}$ be the input set of textual units, where $e_i$ represents the $i$-th unit. We use $w_i$ and $l_i$ to represent the weight and length of $e_i$, respectively. Given length limit $L$, these methods solve the following optimization problem:

$$\begin{aligned} &\underset{T \subseteq D}{\text{Maximize}} \sum_{e_i \in T} w_i \\ &\text{Subject to } T \in \mathcal{T} \text{ and } \sum_{e_i \in T} l_i \leq L \,, \end{aligned} \tag{1}$$

where $T \subseteq D$ and $\mathcal{T} \subseteq 2^D$. We use $\mathcal{T}$ to represent the set of subtrees that can be feasible solutions if we ignore the length limit. The following problems employ different $\mathcal{T}$ to match each problem setting. If $\mathcal{T} = 2^D$, i.e., $\mathcal{T}$ equals the set of all possible subsets of $D$, it is equivalent to the 0-1 knapsack problem, and is solved with the standard DP algorithm.

**Sentence Extraction** Hirao et al. (2013) proposed a single-document summarization algorithm to solve a tree trimming problem. They represent a document as a set of elementary discourse units (EDUs) and then select an optimal subset to make a summary. Each EDU is a minimal unit that composes the discourse structure of the document; it usually corresponds to a clause. Their summarization method first represents a document as a dependency discourse tree (DEP-DT) that represents the dependency structure between EDUs. DEP-DT is a rooted tree in which each node corresponds to an EDU. They then select the rooted subtree that maximizes the sum of weights and satisfies the length limit to make a summary, where we say a subtree is rooted if it contains the root node of the input tree. This problem can be formulated as the combinatorial optimization problem of Eq.(1), where $\mathcal{T}$ is the set of all rooted subtrees of the input DEP-DT.

**Sentence Compression** Filippova and Strube (2008) proposed a sentence compression method based on the trimming of a word dependency tree. Its recently proposed variant shows state-of-the-art performance (Filippova and Altun, 2013). They trim a syntactical dependency tree to compress a sentence. Their formulation is similar to the previous sentence extraction method except that it allows the root node of a subtree to be other than the root node of the input tree. In other words, their formulation allows multiple candidate root nodes for a subtree. We represent such a set of candidate root nodes as $R$, and the set of possible solutions $\mathcal{T}$ for this formulation

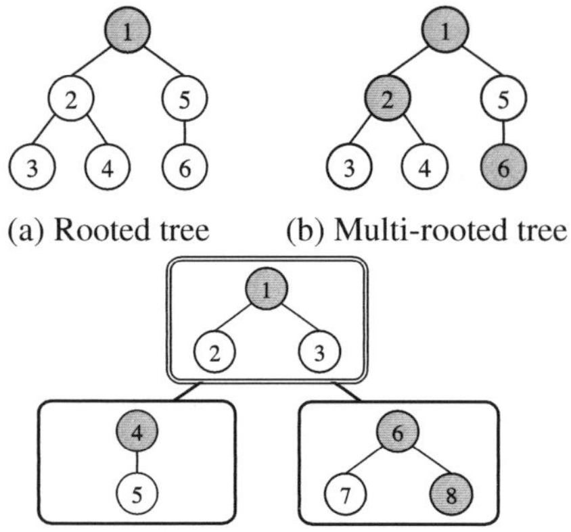

(a) Rooted tree (b) Multi-rooted tree

(c) Nested tree

Figure 1: Example trees.

is the set of all subtrees of the input tree whose root node is contained in $R$.

**Sentence Extraction & Compression** Kikuchi et al. (2014) proposed a single-document summarization method that can select compressed sentences. It is an extension of the sentence extraction method proposed in (Hirao et al., 2013). They represent a document as a sentence dependency tree that is obtained from DEP-DT, and then represent each sentence in the sentence dependency tree as a word dependency tree. In the following, inner trees refer to the word dependency trees that correspond to sentences, while the outer tree represents the sentence dependency tree that represents a document. Hence a document is represented as a nested tree where each node of the outer tree corresponds to an inner tree. They then make a summary by first selecting a rooted subtree of the outer tree, and then selecting a subtree for each inner tree that corresponds to a node of the selected subtree of the outer tree. Each inner tree has multiple root candidate nodes, and the root node of a subtree of an inner tree is a root candidate node of the tree. The set of feasible solutions, $\mathcal{T}$, corresponds to all possible nested trees constructed in this way[1].

Fig. 1 shows example input trees used in the above three tasks: (a) a rooted tree used in sentence extraction, (b) a multi-rooted tree used in sentence compression, and (c) a nested tree used in sentence extraction & compression. Gray nodes are root candidate nodes. Each tree yields a different set of valid subtrees. Tab. 1 shows examples of valid and invalid subtrees of each input tree, where we assume that each subtree in $\mathcal{T}$ is represented by a set of nodes that is contained in the subtree.

Table 1: Examples of valid and invalid subtrees of the input trees in Fig. 1

| | Valid | Invalid |
|---|---|---|
| Rooted tree | $e_1e_2e_3$, $e_1e_2e_5$ | $e_2e_3e_4$, $e_6$ |
| Multi-rooted tree | $e_1e_2e_5$, $e_2e_3e_4$ | $e_3$, $e_5e_6$ |
| Nested tree | $e_1e_2e_4$, $e_1e_4e_5e_8$ | $e_4e_5e_6$, $e_1e_2e_7$ |

## 3 Zero-suppressed Binary Decision Diagram (ZDD)

The key idea of the proposed algorithm is to represent the set of candidate subtrees $\mathcal{T}$ as a zero-suppressed binary decision diagram (ZDD) (Minato, 1993). ZDD is a variant of binary decision diagram (BDD) (Bryant, 1986; Akers, 1978), and is a data structure that can succinctly represent a family of sets as a DAG. ZDD has two types of nodes, namely branch nodes and terminal nodes. Branch nodes are non-terminal nodes. Each branch node has exactly two out edges, called low-edge and high-edge, and a label that represents the item that the node corresponds to. We use $\mathrm{hi}(i)$, $\mathrm{lo}(i)$, and $\mathrm{v}(i)$ to represent the node pointed to by the high-edge, low-edge, and the label of the $i$-th node of the ZDD, respectively. The branch node that has no parent node is the root node. Terminal nodes have no outgoing edges, and a ZDD has exactly two terminal nodes whose labels are $\top$ and $\bot$. A path from the root node to terminal node $\top$ represents a set of items contained in the family of sets represented by the ZDD. We can recover the set of items that corresponds to a path by selecting the labels of the branch nodes whose high-edges lie on the path.

Fig. 2(a) is a ZDD that represents the family of sets $\{e_1e_2, e_2e_3, e_1e_3\}$. We use circles to represent branch nodes and rectangles to represent the terminal nodes. A dashed edge represents a low-edge and full edge represents a high-edge. The number on each circle node represents the label of the node. For example, the label of the root node of the ZDD

[1] Kikuchi et al. (2014) set further constraints on possible subtrees of a syntactical tree. Our method can also cope with these additional constraints (see Sect. 7).

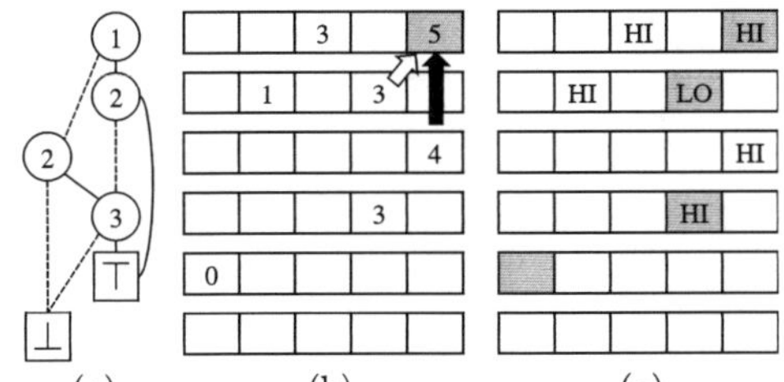


Figure 2: An example ZDD and how the dynamic programming algorithm works with the ZDD. (a) An example ZDD that represents the family of sets $\{e_1e_2, e_1e_3, e_2e_3\}$, (b) table $S$ and (c) table $B$ after completion of the table filling phase.

in Fig. 2(a) is 1. The ZDD has three different paths that start at the root node and end at $\top$. Each path corresponds to an item contained in the family of sets.

In the following, let $z_1, \ldots, z_{|Z|}$ be the nodes of a ZDD. We use $Z$ to represent a ZDD, and $|Z|$ to represent the number of nodes in $Z$. We assume $i < \text{hi}(i), \text{lo}(i)$ for every $i = 1, \ldots, |Z| - 2$. $z_1$ corresponds to the root node, and $z_{|Z|-1}, z_{|Z|}$ corresponds to $\top$ and $\bot$ terminal nodes, respectively. We also assume that the ZDD is ordered, i.e., there is a total order on the labels, and the label of a parent node comes before that of a child node for every parent-child node pair. The ZDD in Fig. 2(a) is an ordered ZDD whose order is $e_1, e_2, e_3$.

## 4 Dynamic Programming Algorithm for Tree Trimming Problems

Our algorithm takes the following three-step procedure. First, we represent the set of subtrees $\mathcal{T}$ for each tree trimming problem as a ZDD. Then we apply a bottom-up and table-filling style DP algorithm to the ZDD. Finally, we backtrack the filled table to obtain an optimal solution.

Our algorithm is similar to the standard DP algorithm for the 0-1 knapsack problem, which solves the problem in $O(NL)$ time with $N$ items and length limit $L$. The DP algorithm solves a knapsack problem by filling an $N \times (L+1)$ table by recursively exploiting previously computed partial solutions. Our algorithm also fills a table for problem solving, but the table's size is $|Z| \times (L + 1)$. That is, the size of the table equals the number of nodes of the ZDD

**Algorithm 1** Dynamic Programming Algorithm

**Input:** ZDD $Z$ that represent $\mathcal{T}$, length limit $L$, and $w_i$, $l_i$ for $1 \leq i \leq N$
**Output:** Optimal subtree **r**
1: Initialize $S[i][j] \leftarrow -\infty$ **for all** $i, j$.
2: $S[|Z| - 1][0] \leftarrow 0$.
3: **for** $i = |Z| - 2, \ldots, 1$ **do**
4:   **for** $j = 0, \ldots, L$ **do**
5:     **if** $j \geq l_{\text{v}(i)}$ **and** $S[\text{hi}(i)][j - l_{\text{v}(i)}] + w_{\text{v}(i)} > S[\text{lo}(i)][j]$ **then**
6:       $S[i][j] \leftarrow S[\text{hi}(i)][j - l_{\text{v}(i)}] + w_{\text{v}(i)}$
7:       $B[i][j] \leftarrow HI$
8:     **else**
9:       $S[i][j] \leftarrow S[\text{lo}(i)][j]$, $B[i][j] \leftarrow LO$
10: $k^* \leftarrow \text{argmax}_{0 \leq k \leq L} S[1][k]$
11: $i \leftarrow 1$, $j \leftarrow k^*$, $\mathbf{r} \leftarrow \emptyset$
12: **while** $(i, j) \neq (|Z| - 1, 0)$ **do**
13:   **if** $B[i][j] = HI$ **then**
14:     $\mathbf{r} \leftarrow \mathbf{r} \cup \{\text{v}(i)\}$, $i \leftarrow \text{hi}(i)$, $j \leftarrow j - l_{\text{v}(i)}$
15:   **else**
16:     $i \leftarrow \text{lo}(i)$
17: **return r**

that represents a set of subtrees $\mathcal{T}$. The tables can be seen as the set of $|Z|$ arrays with $(L+1)$ entries, and each array is associated with each ZDD node. We fill these tables by referring to previously computed results by using the ZDD's structure.

Alg. 1 is the DP algorithm that can solve the problem of Eq.(1), given the ZDD that represents the family of sets $\mathcal{T}$. We first prepare two tables, $S$ and $B$; both have $|Z| \times (L + 1)$ entries. Table $S$ is used for storing intermediate weights, and $B$ is used for storing information used in recovering the optimal solution. We first fill the elements in $S$ and $B$ while traversing the ZDD in order from the terminal nodes to the root node. We then use $B$ to recover the solution that maximizes the weight. In the table filling phase (lines 1 to 9), we update $S[i][j]$ and $B[i][j]$, recursively. Weight $S[i][j]$ represents the maximum weight of the ZDD path from the $i$-th node to the $\top$ terminal node, whose total length is $j$. We compare $S[\text{hi}(i)][j - l_{\text{v}(i)}] + w_{\text{v}(i)}$ and $S[\text{lo}(i)][j]$, and select the maximum weight to set $S[i][j]$. The value of $B[i][j]$ stores which candidate we set to $S[i][j]$. If we use the former one, we set label $HI$ to $B[i][j]$, otherwise $LO$. After filling the table, we run a backtracking procedure to obtain an optimal solution. In the backtracking phase (lines 10 to 16), we start from $B[i][k^*]$ and repeat backtracking using the entries of $B$.

We give here a proof of the correctness of the algorithm. We use the fact that the ZDD is constructed recursively; given the $i$-th branch node $z_i$ of a ZDD, the subgraph induced by the set of nodes that are descendants of $z_i$ is also a ZDD. Let the ZDD whose root node is $z_i$ be $Z_i$, and the family of sets represented by $Z_i$ be $\mathcal{T}_i$. Family of sets $\mathcal{T}_i$, $\mathcal{T}_{\text{lo}(i)}$ and $\mathcal{T}_{\text{hi}(i)}$ satisfy the following relationship.

$$\mathcal{T}_i = \mathcal{T}_{\text{lo}(i)} \cup \{e_{\text{v}(i)} \cup T | T \in \mathcal{T}_{\text{hi}(i)}\}$$

**Proposition 1.** *Alg. 1 can find the optimal solution of the problem of Eq.(1), where we assume $\mathcal{T}$ is represented as an ordered ZDD.*

*Proof.* We use induction to give a proof that $S[i][j] = \max_T \sum_{e_i \in T} w_i$ after running our algorithm, where $T$ is a set of tree nodes that satisfies $T \in \mathcal{T}_i$ and $\sum_{e_i \in T} l_i = j$. If $i = |Z| - 1$, then $\mathcal{T}_i = \{\emptyset\}$ and $S[i][0] = 0$ and $S[i][j] = -\infty$ for $j \neq 0$, which satisfies the condition. Suppose that $S[\text{lo}(i)][j]$ and $S[\text{hi}(i)][j]$ both satisfy the condition for $j = 0, \ldots, L$. If the set that maximizes $S[i][j]$ does not have $e_{\text{v}(i)}$, then the set is contained in $\mathcal{T}_{\text{lo}(i)}$, and its size is $j$. Therefore, the maximum weight equals $S[\text{lo}(i)][j]$ (Alg.1 line 9). Otherwise, the set that maximizes $S[i][j]$ has $e_{\text{v}(i)}$, so the item is contained in $\{e_{\text{v}(i)} \cup T | T \in \mathcal{T}_{\text{hi}(i)}\}$, and its weight is $S[\text{hi}(i)][j - l_{\text{v}(i)}] + w_{\text{v}(i)}$ (Alg.1 line 6). Since $Z_1$ corresponds to the root node and it represents all possible solutions, $\max_j S[1][j]$ is the maximum weight of the subset that satisfies the length limit and is contained in $\mathcal{T}$. □

**Proposition 2.** *The time and space complexity of Alg. 1 are both $O(|Z|L)$.*

*Proof.* We have to store tables $S, B$ and solution $\mathbf{r}$. The tables have $|Z| \times (L+1)$ entries and $|Z| \geq |\mathbf{r}|$, the space complexity is $O(|Z|L)$. For the time complexity, filling entries in $S$ and $B$ requires $O(|Z|L)$ time since to fill an entry requires constant time. Backtracking requires at most $N$ updates, hence the time complexity is $O(|Z|L)$. □

We show an example of our algorithm in Fig. 2. Suppose that $D = \{e_1e_2, e_1e_3, e_2e_3\}$, $(l_1, l_2, l_3) = (1, 1, 3)$ and $(w_1, w_2, w_3) = (2, 1, 3)$. Set $D$ is represented as the ZDD in Fig. 2(a). Let $L = 4$ and run the DP algorithm yielding tables $S$ and $B$ shown in

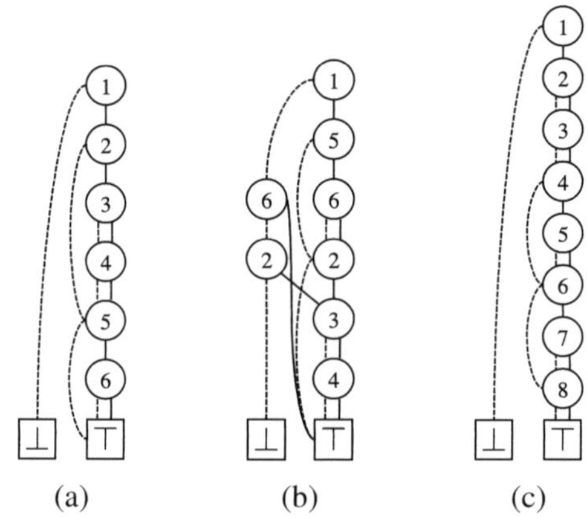


Figure 3: Example ZDDs representing the set of trimmed subtrees of the trees in Fig. 1. (a) Rooted-tree, (b) multi-rooted tree, and (c) nested-tree

Fig. 2(b,c). Suppose that we want to fill entry $S[1][4]$ (the upper right cell). There are two possible paths to reach the entry; the first path takes the high-edge from $S[2][3]$, and the second path takes the low-edge from $S[3][4]$. We use hollow and black arrows to represent these paths in Fig. 2(b). Since the former path results in weight 5, which is higher than that of the later path, hence we set $S[1][4] = 5$ and $B[1][4] =$ HI. After filling all the entries in tables, we can see $S[1][4]$ has the maximum weight, and the backtracking from $B[1][4] \to B[2][3] \to B[4][3] \to B[5][0]$. $B[5][0]$ corresponds to the $\top$ terminal node, and the backtracking yields the optimal solution $e_1e_3$.

## 5 ZDD Sizes

We give upper bounds on the size of the ZDD representing the family of sets $\mathcal{T}$ of Eq.(1) for the three problems. The number of subtrees contained in $\mathcal{T}$ may grow exponentially with the size of the original tree, however, we can represent them as a ZDD with very few nodes. Since the running time of our algorithm is $O(|Z|L)$, these theoretical upper bounds determine the running time of the proposed tree trimming algorithms.

We first give a proof of the size of the ZDD that represents all rooted subtrees of a given tree.

**Proposition 3.** *Given a tree with $N$ nodes, we can construct a ZDD that represents all rooted subtrees of the tree whose number of nodes is $N+2$, if we use a depth first pre-order of tree nodes as the order* *of ZDD labels.*

This result can be derived from the result of (Knuth, 2011), Chap.7.1.4, exercise 266. Fig. 3(a) is a ZDD that represents the set of all rooted subtrees of the tree in Fig. 1(a), where we employ pre-ordering $e_1, e_2, e_3, e_4, e_5, e_6$.

We next show the size of the ZDDs that represent the set of all subtrees of a multi-rooted tree.

**Proposition 4.** *Given an $N$ node tree and the set of candidate root nodes $R$, the set of all possible subtrees can be represented by a ZDD whose number of nodes is $O(N \log |R|)$.*

*Proof.* (Sketch) The set of all possible subtrees can be represented as the union of the sets of rooted subtrees for different root $r \in R$. The set of rooted subtrees for a root node $r$ can be represented as a ZDD that has $O(N)$ nodes, hence the set of ZDDs for different root nodes has $O(N|R|)$ nodes in total. We can further reduce this upper bound by employing appropriate depth first pre-ordering so as to share as many ZDD substructures as possible, and this ordering results in a union ZDD whose number of nodes is $O(N \log |R|)$. □

This proposition is related to a recently proved result that the set of all subtrees of an $N$-node tree can be represented as a ZDD whose number of nodes is $O(N \log N)$ (Yasuda et al., 2014). This is a special case of the above theorem that $R$ equals the set of all nodes of the tree, i.e., $|R| = N$. The key point is to use the *heaviest-last depth first pre-order* as the ZDD label order. In this order, a node with the heaviest weight always comes after other siblings, where we define the weight of a node as the size of the maximum rooted subtree $T \in \mathcal{T}$ that is contained in its descendant tree. Fig. 3(b) is an example of the ZDD that represents the set of all possible rooted subtrees of the multi-rooted tree in Fig. 1(b), where the heaviest-last depth first pre-order is $e_1, e_5, e_6, e_2, e_3, e_4$.

The upper bound size of a ZDD for nested subtrees can be estimated by combining the above two theoretical results on rooted subtrees and multi-rooted subtrees.

**Proposition 5.** *For a nested tree whose sum of the number of nodes of inner trees is $N$, and the sets of candidate root nodes for inner trees are $R_1, \ldots, R_M$, where $M$ is the number of inner trees, we can represent the set of possible nested subtrees by $O(N \log |R^*|)$, where $|R^*| = \max_i |R_i|$.*

*Proof.* (Sketch) The ZDD corresponding to the set of nested subtrees can be constructed as follows: first we make ZDDs that represent the set of rooted subtrees of the outer tree and inner trees. The outer tree is represented as a ZDD with $O(N)$ nodes, and the $i$-th inner tree is represented as a ZDD with $O(N_i \log |R_i|)$ nodes, where $N_i$ is the number of nodes of the $i$-th inner tree. Then we can construct the ZDD for the nested tree by replacing each ZDD node of the outer-tree ZDD with the inner-tree ZDD corresponding to that node. □

Fig. 3(c) is a ZDD that represents the set of nested subtrees of the tree in Fig. 1(c), where we employ the order $e_1, e_2, e_3, e_4, e_5, e_6, e_7, e_8$.

We can directly prove the running time of the DP algorithm by exploiting the above three results to show the DP algorithm for the three problems takes $O(NL)$, $O(NL \log |R|)$, and $O(NL \log |R^*|)$ time, respectively. Here we assume that a ZDD that represents the set $\mathcal{T}$ is given. We need additional time for constructing a ZDD that represents $\mathcal{T}$ i.e. the input tree. However, ZDD construction also can be done in $O(|Z|)$ for the three tree trimming problems. We show details of ZDD construction in the next section.

## 6 Efficient ZDD Construction

We introduce here an efficient algorithm for constructing a ZDD that is used in the tree trimming problems. A ZDD can be constructed by repeatedly applying set operations between intermediate ZDDs, however, this process may be too slow since the running time of the set operations depends on the size of input and output ZDDs.

We first show the flow of an efficient ZDD construction algorithm for multi-rooted trees. This algorithm also can be used for constructing a ZDD for all rooted subtrees of a tree since a single-root tree is also a multi-rooted tree. The algorithm consists of two steps: first, we determine the appropriate order of ZDD nodes. We then use the top-down ZDD construction algorithm shown in (Knuth, 2011) (Chap.7.1.4, Exercise 55) to construct a ZDD. The top-down algorithm can efficiently construct a ZDD that represents the set of all connected components of a graph, and we can use it for constructing the set of all rooted subtrees with small modification. The running time of top-down construction algorithms may not be $O(|Z|)$, but our modified algorithm can obtain the ZDD in $O(|Z|)$ time by exploiting the structure of the input tree to avoid to make unnecessary ZDD nodes.

We can extend this ZDD construction algorithm to create ZDDs that represent the set of nested subtrees. We first compute the orders of outer tree and each inner tree, and then construct ZDDs for them using the top-down construction algorithm. Finally, we obtain the required ZDD by replacing ZDD nodes of the outer tree with the corresponding inner ZDDs. These procedure also can be done in $O(|Z|)$ time, since constructing the ZDDs for each tree takes time proportional to its size, and the ZDD substitution phase also takes time proportional to ZDD size.

## 7 Discussion

When solving a tree trimming problem, we sometimes want to add constraints to the problem so as to obtain better results. For example, Kikuchi et al. (2014) use additional constraints to set the minimum number of words (say $\theta$ words) extracted from a sentence if the sentence is contained in a summary, and require each selected inner tree to contain at least one verb and noun if the inner tree has them. Since our tree trimming approach can work once the ZDD that represents the set of feasible solutions is constructed, adding new constraints to the set of solutions can be easily performed by applying ZDD operations. These operations can be performed efficiently for many cases and the proposed approach will still work well. Moreover, we can extend the algorithm to construct ZDDs that represent the extended set of feasible solutions. We can also give theoretical upper bounds for the new constraint-added problem. In this nested tree case, we can prove that the number of ZDD nodes is $O(N\theta \log |R^*|)$.

## 8 Experiments

We conduct experiments on the three tree trimming tasks of text summarization, sentence compression, and the combination of summarization and text compression. For the text summarization experiments, we use the test collection for summarization evaluation contained in the RST Discourse Treebank (RST-DTB) (Carlson et al., 2001), which is used in the previous work. The test collection consists of 30 documents with the reference summaries whose length is about 10% of the original document. We used the same parameters used in the previous papers. For sentence compression, we use the English compression corpus used in (Filippova and Strube, 2008), which consists of 82 news stories selected from the British National Corpus and American News Text Corpus, and consists of more than 1,300 sentences. We set the sizes of compressed sentences to be 70% of the original length, which is used in the original paper. We compare the proposed algorithm to Gurobi 5.5.0, a widely used commercial ILP solver[2]. It was run in the default settings and we used single-thread mode. We run Gurobi until it finds an optimal solution. Our algorithm was implemented in C++, and all experiments were conducted on a Linux machine with a Xeon E5-2670 2.60 GHz CPU and 192 GB RAM.

Fig. 4 compares the running time of our algorithm (includes ZDD construction time) and Gurobi. Each plotted marker in the figures represents a test instance, and if the position of a marker is below the dashed line, it means that our method is faster than Gurobi. We can see that our method is always faster than Gurobi; it was, at most, 300, 10, and 50 times faster in sentence extraction, sentence compression, and extraction & compression, respectively. Fig. 5,6 shows the relation between the input tree size and the ZDD construction times, and the relation between the input tree size and converted ZDD size respectively. These results show that both ZDD sizes and construction time were linear to the number of input tree nodes. The number of ZDD nodes looks like smaller than the $O(N \log N)$ bounds for multi-rooted trees and nested trees. This result is caused since the set of root candidate nodes $R$ is small comparing with $N$ for a typical input document.

Next we conduct experiments to assess the scalability of the proposed method by solving problems with different input sizes. We choose the nested tree

[2]We also used CPLEX 12.5.1.0, but Gurobi shows better performance in most cases.

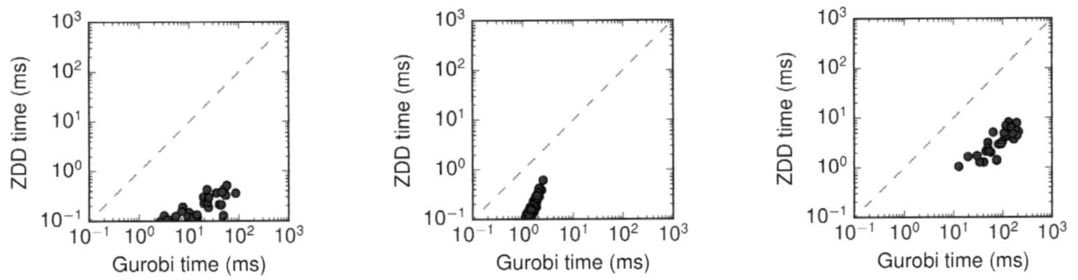


(a) Sentence extraction (b) Sentence compression (c) Extraction & compression

Figure 4: Performance comparison between the proposed method and Gurobi

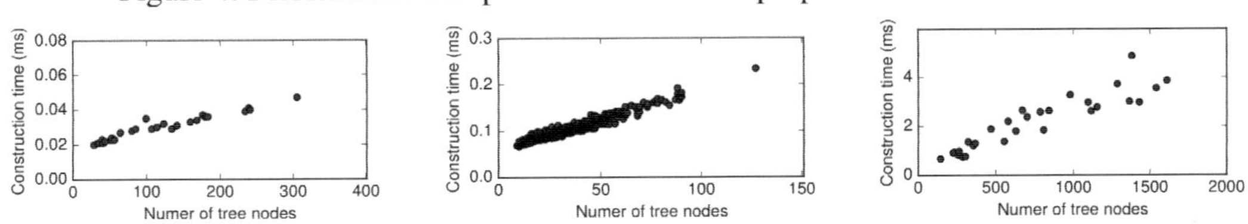


(a) Sentence extraction (b) Sentence compression (c) Extraction & compression

Figure 5: ZDD construction time with number of input tree nodes

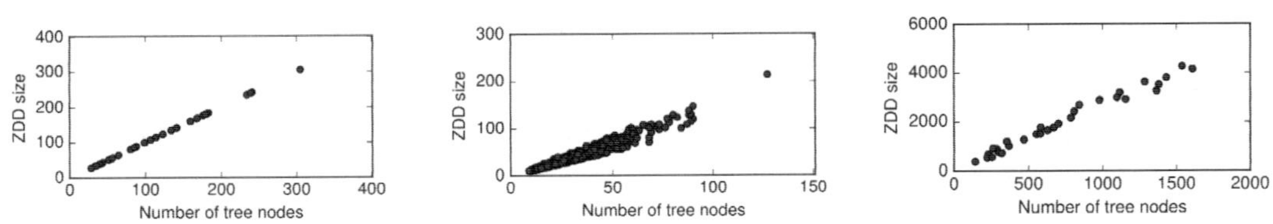


(a) Sentence extraction (b) Sentence compression (c) Extraction & compression

Figure 6: ZDD sizes with number of input tree nodes

trimming problem since it is the most complex problem. We make a large artificial nested tree by concatenating outer-trees of the nested trees of 30 RST-DT datasets. The results are shown in Fig. 7, and it shows that out method scales well with large inputs comparing with Gurobi.

## 9 Related Work

Recently proposed text summarization and sentence compression methods solve a task by formulating it as a combinatorial optimization problem (McDonald, 2007; Woodsend and Lapata, 2010; Martins and Smith, 2009; Clarke and Lapata, 2008). These combinatorial optimization-based formulations enable flexible models that can reflect the properties required. However, their complexity makes it difficult to solve optimization problems efficiently. These problems can be solved by using ILP solvers, however, they may fail to find optimal solutions and they have no guarantee on the running time. Since the proposed method is a DP algorithm and it has a theoretical guarantee, it always find an optimal solution in time proportional to the size of the input tree.

Our method also can be seen as a kind of fast text summarization algorithm. Previous fast algorithms are approximate algorithms (Qian and Liu, 2013; Lin and Bilmes, 2010; Lin and Bilmes, 2011; Davis et al., 2012), while our algorithm is an exact algorithm. Of course, there is a difference in task hardness since previous methods were designed for multi-document summarization and ours for single document summarization. Those works suggest

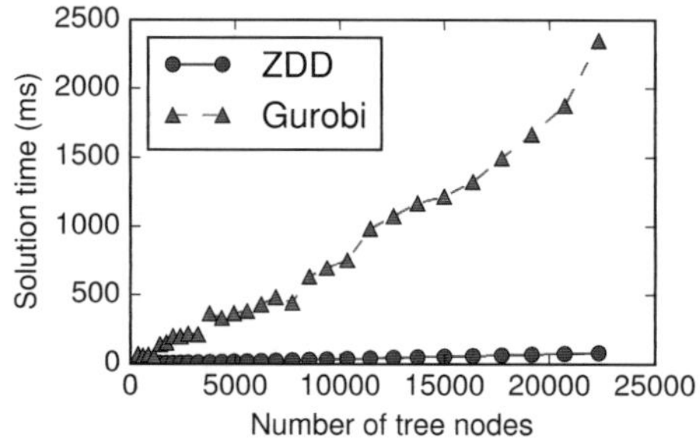


Figure 7: Solution time of our algorithm and Gurobi with different input tree sizes.

that algorithms that have guarantees on both running time and quality of solutions are highly demanding, and the proposed pseudo-polynomial time exact algorithm is valuable.

The Zero-suppressed Binary Decision Diagram (ZDD) (Minato, 1993) is a variant of the Binary Decision Diagram (BDD) (Akers, 1978; Bryant, 1986). BDD is a data structure that represents a Boolean function as a DAG, and ZDD can represent a family of sets in a compact form. Recently, ZDD and BDD have been used for solving optimization problems (Bergman et al., 2014a; Bergman et al., 2014b); they find the optimal solution by representing the set of feasible solutions in a BDD or its variants. Compared to these optimization methods, the proposed method differs in two main points. First, the proposed algorithm extends the ZDD-based optimization algorithm to solve knapsack problems. Second, it offers proofs of the size of ZDDs representing trimmed subtrees.

The ZDD-based method presented in this paper is related to our previous work of a BDD-constrained search (BCS) method (Nishino et al., 2015). In BCS, a BDD is used to solve constraints-added variants of shortest path problems on a DAG, and a 0-1 knapsack problem with additional constraints also can be solved by BCS. The main advantage of the DP-algorithm shown in this paper is that it has a theoretical guarantee on its running time which depends on only the size of the input tree. This advantage comes from using ZDD instead of BDD, and designing an algorithm specialized for variants of the knapsack problem. Though not obvious, it is possible to extend BCS to use ZDD instead of BDD and employ the label order used in this paper to give a theoretical bound that only depends on the size of an input tree. Nevertheless, the bound attained with this extension is worse than that shown in this paper.

## 10 Conclusion

We have proposed a DP algorithm for the tree trimming problems that appear in text summarization. Our approach always finds an optimal solution, and it runs in $O(NL \log N)$ time, where $N$ is the number of tree nodes and $L$ is the length limit. The key to our approach is to represent a set of subtrees of an input tree as a ZDD. By using ZDD, we can give a theoretical guarantee of the running time of the algorithm. Experiments show that the proposal allows three different tree trimming problems to be solved in the same way.

## References

Sheldon B. Akers. 1978. Binary decision diagrams. *Computers, IEEE Transactions on*, C-27(6):509–516.

David Bergman, Andre A. Cire, and Willem-Jan van Hoeve. 2014a. MDD propagation for sequence constraints. *Journal of Artificial Intelligence Research*, 50:697–722.

David Bergman, Andre A Cire, Willem-Jan van Hoeve, and Tallys Yunes. 2014b. BDD-based heuristics for binary optimization. *Journal of Heuristics*, 20(2):211–234.

Randal E Bryant. 1986. Graph-based algorithms for boolean function manipulation. *Computers, IEEE Transactions on*, C-35(8):677–691.

Lynn Carlson, Daniel Marcu, and Mary Ellen Okurowski. 2001. Building a discourse-tagged corpus in the framework of rhetorical structure theory. In *Proceedings of the Second SIGdial Workshop on Discourse and Dialogue - Volume 16*, SIGDIAL'01, pages 1–10.

Janara Christensen, Stephen Soderland, Gagan Bansal, and Mausam. 2014. Hierarchical summarization: Scaling up multi-document summarization. In *Proceedings of the 52nd Annual Meeting of the Association for Computational Linguistics*, ACL'14, pages 902–912.

James Clarke and Mirella Lapata. 2008. Global inference for sentence compression an integer linear programming approach. *Journal of Artificial Intelligence Research*, 31(1):399–429.

Sashka T. Davis, John M. Conroy, and Judith .D. Schlesinger. 2012. Occams – an optimal combinatorial covering algorithm for multi-document summarization. In *IEEE 12th International Conference on Data Mining Workshops*, ICDMW, pages 454–463.

Elena Filatova and Vasileios Hatzivassiloglou. 2004. A formal model for information selection in multi-sentence text extraction. In *Proceedings of the 20th International Conference on Computational Linguistics*, COLING'04.

Katja Filippova and Yasemin Altun. 2013. Overcoming the lack of parallel data in sentence compression. In *Proceedings of the 2013 Conference on Empirical Methods in Natural Language Processing*, EMNLP'13, pages 1481–1491.

Katja Filippova and Michael Strube. 2008. Dependency tree based sentence compression. In *Proceedings of the Fifth International Natural Language Generation Conference*, INLG'08, pages 25–32.

Tsutomu Hirao, Yasuhisa Yoshida, Masaaki Nishino, Norihito Yasuda, and Masaaki Nagata. 2013. Single-document summarization as a tree knapsack problem. In *Proceedings of the 2013 Conference on Empirical Methods in Natural Language Processing*, EMNLP'13, pages 1515–1520.

Yuta Kikuchi, Tsutomu Hirao, Hiroya Takamura, Manabu Okumura, and Masaaki Nagata. 2014. Single document summarization based on nested tree structure. In *Proceedings of the 52nd Annual Meeting of the Association for Computational Linguistics*, ACL'14, pages 315–320.

Donald E Knuth. 2011. *The Art of Computer Programming, Volume 4A: Combinatorial Algorithms, Part 1*. Addison-Wesley.

Hui Lin and Jeff Bilmes. 2010. Multi-document summarization via budgeted maximization of submodular functions. In *Human Language Technologies: The 2010 Annual Conference of the North American Chapter of the Association for Computational Linguistics*, NAACL/HLT'10, pages 912–920.

Hui Lin and Jeff Bilmes. 2011. A class of submodular functions for document summarization. In *Proceedings of the 49th Annual Meeting of the Association for Computational Linguistics: Human Language Technologies*, ACL/HLT'11, pages 510–520.

André FT Martins and Noah A Smith. 2009. Summarization with a joint model for sentence extraction and compression. In *Proceedings of the Workshop on Integer Linear Programming for Natural Langauge Processing*, pages 1–9.

Ryan McDonald. 2007. A study of global inference algorithms in multi-document summarization. In *Proceedings of the 9th European Conference on Information Retrieval*, ECIR'07, pages 557–564.

Shin-ichi Minato. 1993. Zero-suppressed BDDs for set manipulation in combinatorial problems. In *Design Automation, 1993. 30th Conference on*, DAC'93, pages 272–277.

Yoshio Nakao. 2000. An algorithm for one-page summarization of a long text based on thematic hierarchy detection. In *Proceedings of the 38th Annual Meeting of the Association for Computational Linguistics*, ACL'00, pages 302–309.

Masaaki Nishino, Norihito Yasuda, Shin-ichi Minato, and Masaaki Nagata. 2015. BDD-constrained search: A unified approach to constrained shortest path problems. In *Proceedings of the 29th AAAI Conference on Artificial Intelligence*, AAAI'15, pages 1219–1225.

Xian Qian and Yang Liu. 2013. Fast joint compression and summarization via graph cuts. In *Proceedings of the 2013 Conference on Empirical Methods in Natural Language Processing*, EMNLP'13, pages 1492–1502.

Kristian Woodsend and Mirella Lapata. 2010. Automatic generation of story highlights. In *Proceedings of the 48th Annual Meeting of the Association for Computational Linguistics*, ACL'10, pages 565–574.

Norihito Yasuda, Masaaki Nishino, and Shin-ichi Minato. 2014. On the size of the zero-suppressed binary decision diagram that represents all the subtrees in a tree. In *Trends and Applications in Knowledge Discovery and Data Mining*, Lecture Notes in Computer Science, pages 504–510.

# Modeling Word Meaning in Context with Substitute Vectors

**Oren Melamud**
Computer Science Dept.
Bar-Ilan University
melamuo@cs.biu.ac.il

**Ido Dagan**
Computer Science Dept.
Bar-Ilan University
dagan@cs.biu.ac.il

**Jacob Goldberger**
Faculty of Engineering
Bar-Ilan University
goldbej@eng.biu.ac.il

## Abstract

Context representations are a key element in distributional models of word meaning. In contrast to typical representations based on neighboring words, a recently proposed approach suggests to represent a context of a target word by a *substitute vector*, comprising the potential fillers for the target word slot in that context. In this work we first propose a variant of substitute vectors, which we find particularly suitable for measuring context similarity. Then, we propose a novel model for representing word meaning in context based on this context representation. Our model outperforms state-of-the-art results on lexical substitution tasks in an unsupervised setting.

## 1 Introduction

Following the distributional hypothesis (Firth, 1957), distributional models represent the meaning of a word type as an aggregation of its contexts. A recent line of work addresses polysemy of word types by representing the meaning (or sense) of each word instance individually as induced by its particular context. The context-sensitive meaning of a word instance is commonly called the word meaning *in context*, as opposed to the word meaning *out-of-context* of a word type.

A key element of distributional models is the choice of context representation. A context of a word instance is typically represented by an unordered collection of its first-order neighboring words, called *bag-of-words* (BOW). In contrast, Yatbaz et al. (2012) proposed to represent this context as a second-order *substitute vector*. Instead of the neighboring words themselves, a substitute vector

| | |
|---|---|
| our proposals will unlock _new_ ways of raising the finance needed to develop businesses. | |
| representations of context | |
| BOW | proposals, raising, unlock, ways |
| substitutes | alternate, proposing, infinite, various |
| representation of word meaning in context | |
| paraphrases | new, innovative, different, alternative, novel |

Table 1: Example for BOW and substitute vector representations for a context of the target word *new*. The paraphrase vector is the representation learned by our model for the meaning of *new* in this context. Only the first few entries for each vector are shown.

includes the potential filler words for the target word slot, weighted according to how 'fit' they are to fill the target slot given the neighboring words. For example, the substitute vector representing the context "I __ my smartphone." (target slot underlined), would typically include potential slot fillers such as *love*, *lost*, *upgraded*, etc.

Melamud et al. (2014) argued that substitute vectors are potentially more informative than traditional context representations since the fitness of the fillers is estimated using an $n$-gram language model, thereby capturing information embedded in the neighboring word order. They showed promising results on measuring word similarity out-of-context with a distributional model based on this approach.

In this paper we first propose a variant of substitute vectors as a context representation, which we find particularly suitable for measuring context similarity. Then, we extend the work in Melamud et al. (2014) by proposing a novel distributional model for representing word meaning in context, based on this context representation. Like sub-



*Human Language Technologies: The 2015 Annual Conference of the North American Chapter of the ACL*, pages 472–482,
Denver, Colorado, May 31 – June 5, 2015. ©2015 Association for Computational Linguistics

stitute vectors, the word representations learned by our model are second-order vectors, which we call *paraphrase vectors*. Table 1 illustrates the difference between BOW and substitute vector context representations, as well as our representation for a word in context. Our model outperforms state-of-the-art results on lexical substitution tasks while learning from plain text in an unsupervised setting. [1]

## 2 Background

A key element in distributional models of word meaning is the choice of context representation. Traditional out-of-context distributional models aggregate the observed contexts of a target word type to derive its representation. More recent models of word meaning in context typically bias such a word type representation towards the context of each particular word instance using context similarity measures. The typical choice for context representation is a *bag-of-words* (BOW) context vector. In this vector each neighboring word type is assigned with a weight, such as its count (Erk and Padó, 2010) or *tf-idf* (Reisinger and Mooney, 2010). A more recent variant of this approach is the *continuous bag-of-words* (CBOW) vector, where context is represented as an average, or *tf-idf* weighted average, of dense low dimensional vector representations of the neighboring words (Huang et al., 2012). Context similarity is typically computed using vector Cosine.

Several types of models of word meaning in context were recently proposed in the literature, mostly based on variants of BOW context representations. Thater et al. (2011) aggregate the contexts of a target word type into a sparse syntax-based context feature vector. Then, they generate a biased vector representation by reducing the weight of each context feature the less similar it is to the context of the given word instance. Reisinger and Mooney (2010) and Huang et al. (2012) use context clustering to induce multiple word senses for a target word type, where each sense is represented by a different context feature vector. Then, they choose for each word instance the sense vector most similar to its given context. Ó Séaghdha and Korhonen (2014) use LDA (Blei et al., 2003) to aggregate word collocations to distributions over topics. Then, word meaning is represented by distributions that can be conditioned on (and hence biased towards) the given context.

## 3 Substitute Vectors

In this work we propose to use a little-known context modeling paradigm, representing a context word window as a *substitute vector* (Yatbaz et al., 2012). Unlike traditional context representations, a substitute vector does not comprise the first-order neighboring words of the target word. Instead it includes the second-order potential fillers for the target word slot, weighted according to how 'fit' they are to fill the target slot given the neighboring words. More formally, we denote a word window context around a target word slot as $c$, and the substitute vector representing $c$ as $\vec{s}_c$. $\vec{s}_c[v]$ is the fitness weight of word $v$ to fill the target slot in context $c$, for every word $v$ in the target word vocabulary. For example, the substitute vector $\vec{s}_c$ = [big 0.35, good 0.28, bold 0.05, ...] may represent the context $c$ = "It's a __ move.".

Yatbaz et al. (2012) used a Kneser-Ney smoothed $n$-gram language model (Kneser and Ney, 1995) to estimate conditional probability as the fitness weight $\vec{s}_c[v] = p(v|c)$. Using a smoothed language model is essential since context-word collocation counts are too sparse when the context considered is an entire word window. We note that given the nature of $n$-gram language models this representation is sensitive to word order. This property makes it appealing as it is potentially more informative than the traditional unordered BOW context representations.

## 4 A Model for Word Meaning in Context

The main contribution of this paper is in proposing a model for word meaning in context, which is based on substitute vector context representations instead of the traditional bag-of-words representations. To achieve this we first propose a variant of substitute vectors as our context representation. Then, we consider an out-of-context representation for a word type as the average of the substitute vector representations of its observed contexts. Finally, the in-context representation for a given word instance is a weighted average of its observed contexts. In this weighted average, contexts are weighted higher the more similar they are to the given context, using

[1]Our source code is publicly available at: www.cs.biu.ac.il/nlp/resources/downloads/word2parvec/

| ... the very essence or heart of being a _*coach*_. | |
|---|---|
| $c$ | ... the very essence or heart of being a ____. |
| $\vec{s}_c$ | christian, non-smoker, traitor, grandparent |
| $\vec{p}_u$ | coach, bus, train, boat |
| $\vec{p}_{u,c}$ | coach, teacher, writer, manager |

Table 2: The substitute vector $\vec{s}_c$ for context $c$, the out-of-context paraphrase vector $\vec{p}_u$ for the word type $u$ = *coach*, and the in-context paraphrase vector $\vec{p}_{u,c}$ for $u$ in context $c$, as learned by our model. Only the first few vector entries (weights omitted) are shown. $\vec{s}_c$, $\vec{p}_u$ and $\vec{p}_{u,c}$ are defined formally in sections 4.1 and 4.2.

a substitute vector similarity measure. Intuitively, with this weighting scheme, we wish to consider mostly the word type contexts that induce a sense similar to that of the given word instance, under the premise that similar contexts induce similar word senses. The resulting word representation is biased towards the given context on one hand due to the context weighting scheme, and is bounded to the target word type spectrum of meanings on the other hand as only contexts of that word type are taken into consideration.

Table 2 exemplifies a context substitute vector and both out-of-context and in-context word representations learned by our model for a word instance. It is evident in this case that our in-context representation comprises suitable paraphrases in contrast to the out-of-context representation. We evaluate these word representations quantitatively in Section 6. We next describe our model in more detail.

### 4.1 Context representation

We wish the context representation in our model to be optimized for measuring context similarity, which is typically used to bias in-context word representations towards a given context.

For the purpose of measuring similarity between contexts, we consider in this section the contexts as 'targets'. Accordingly, we observe that the substitute vector of a word window context $c$ can be considered as a vector of first-order co-occurrence features of $c$, as it consists of slot filler words that are likely to co-occur with this context. Hence, we follow prior work and propose to use *Positive PMI* (PPMI) as our substitute vector feature weights, instead of the conditional probabilities used by Yatbaz et al. (2012), and vector Cosine as our context similarity function (Bullinaria and Levy, 2007):

| Q: the transcendental meditation people advertised this: meditation can _fix_ many sicknesses. | |
|---|---|
| substitutes | relieve, circumvent, alleviate |
| $R_{sub}$: use the results of your analysis to suggest design changes that would _fix_ these problems. | |
| substitutes | overcome, solve, alleviate |
| $R_{cbow}$: _fix_ in your mind a picture of heavenly worship that is real and eternal. | |
| substitutes | echoing, send, stick |

Table 3: Example for a context of the word *fix*, Q, and the two contexts of *fix*, $R_{sub}$ and $R_{cbow}$, most similar to it, based on substitute vector and CBOW similarity, respectively. The substitute vectors are illustrated below each context (selected substitutes in the top-10 entries shown).

$$\vec{s}_c[v] = PPMI(c, v) = \max(0, PMI(c, v)) \quad (1)$$

$$sim(c, c') = cos(\vec{s}_c, \vec{s}_{c'}) \quad (2)$$

where $\vec{s}_c[v]$ is the fitness weight for word $v$ in the substitute vector of context $c$, PMI is point-wise mutual information (Church and Hanks, 1990), and $sim(c, c')$ is our context similarity measure. We note that a context $c$ in our setting stands for an entire word window rather than a single context word. We therefore follow Yatbaz et al. (2012) using an $n$-gram language model to estimate $PMI(c, v)$, as detailed in Section 5.

Table 3 illustrates an example of a given context and the contexts most similar to it, as retrieved by our substitute vector and continuous bag-of-words context similarity measures. It is evident in this case that our measure correlates with the induced senses better than the bag-of-words measure. We suggest this context similarity measure as a standalone contribution, which may be useful in other settings as well. We evaluate it quantitatively in Section 5.

### 4.2 Modeling word meaning

**Word meaning out-of-context** We first define our *out-of-context* representation for target word type $u$, as an average of the substitute vectors of its contexts:

$$\vec{p}_u = \frac{1}{|C_u|} \sum_{i \in C_u} \vec{s}_i \quad (3)$$

where $C_u$ is a collection of the contexts observed for target word type $u$ in a learning corpus, and $\vec{s}_i$ are their substitute vectors.

**Word meaning in context** Next, following Erk and Padó (2010), to represent the meaning of word $u$ in context $c$, we would like to alter the out-of-context representation by theoretically averaging only over contexts that induce a word sense similar to that of the given context. To approximate this objective we use a weighted average of all contexts of $u$, where contexts are weighted according to their similarity to the given context:

$$\vec{p}_{u,c} = \frac{1}{Z} \sum_{i \in C_{cu}} sim(c, i) \cdot \vec{s}_i \quad (4)$$

where $C_{cu} = C_u \cup c$ ($u$'s corpus contexts plus the given context) and $Z$ is a normalization factor.

$\vec{p}_{u,c}[v] = \frac{1}{Z} \sum_{i \in C_{cu}} sim(c, i) \cdot \vec{s}_i[v]$ is the average fitness of $v$ within the contexts of $u$, biased to those similar to $c$. We consider this a context-sensitive similarity score, indicative of the likelihood of $v$ to be a paraphrase of $u$ in context $c$.[2] Thus, we name our in-context representation for a word instance as its *paraphrase vector*.

Finally, $\vec{p}^{\,m}_{u,c}$ denotes a word representation as defined in Equation (4), where only the top-$m$ percent of the contexts in $C_{cu}$ most similar to $c$ are averaged. Using low values for $m$ means injecting a stronger bias in our model towards the given context.

## 5 Evaluating Context Representations

As described in Section 4, our model for word meaning in context utilizes a context similarity measure under the premise that similar contexts induce similar target word senses. In this section we describe a focused evaluation of our proposed similarity measure and prior methods with respect to this objective. This evaluation suggests that our measures may be useful as a component in other models as well.

### 5.1 Task description

Given a word window context $c$ of a target word $u$, we wish to evaluate context similarity measures on their ability to retrieve other contexts of $u$ from $C_u$ that induce a similar sense. To perform such an evaluation we want a dataset of target words with thousands of sense tagged contexts in $C_u$ for each target word $u$. Since available manually sense-tagged datasets, such as SemCor (Mihalcea, 1998), are not large enough for this purpose, we adopted a pseudo-word approach, with which we can automatically generate as many tagged contexts as we wish.

Pseudo-word methods consider a set of real words as pseudo-senses of an artificial pseudo-word (Pilehvar and Navigli, 2014). Specifically, we adopted a simple approach following Otrusina and Smrz (2010) to generate our pseduo-words. First, we sampled 100 words randomly from our learning corpus, ukWaC (Ferraresi et al., 2008). Then we constructed a pseudo-word based on each of these words as follows. We used WordNet (Fellbaum, 2010) to identify all of the word's synsets. Next, for each synset we chose the surface word which is the least polysemous yet occurs in our learning corpus at least 1,000 times, as a *representative* for this synset. Then, we created a pseudo-word whose pseudo-senses are the set of the representative words. For example, the pseudo-word that was generated based on the word *promote* is *elevate_encourage_advertise*. Finally, we sampled from our learning corpus 1,000 contexts for each pseudo-sense word, and for each pseudo-word we mixed together all contexts of its pseudo-sense words. The original pseudo-sense word for each context was recorded as its sense tag.

Next, for each pseudo-word, we sampled a single *query context* from all of its mixed contexts and then ranked the remaining contexts according to each of the compared context similarity measures. We computed precision at top-1, top-1% and average precision for the ranked lists, where a true-positive is a context with an identical sense tag as the query context. We repeated this procedure, sampling 100 different query contexts and computed the mean precision values. Finally, we report for each compared method, the average of the mean precision values for all 100 pseudo-words. Our pseudo-word dataset consists on average around 4.5 senses and 4,500 tagged contexts per pseudo-word. [3]

### 5.2 Compared methods

All compared methods are unsupervised and use the plain text of ukWaC (Ferraresi et al., 2008), a two

[2]This can be considered an in-context extension of the out-of-context similarity score proposed by Melamud et al. (2014).

[3]Our pseudo-word dataset is available at: www.cs.biu.ac.il/nlp/resources/downloads/word2parvec/

billion word web corpus, as their learning corpus. We converted every word that occurs less than 100 times in the corpus to a special rare-word token, and all numbers to a special number token, obtaining a vocabulary of a little under 200K word types.

#### 5.2.1 Substitute vector similarity

We learned a 5-gram Kneser-Ney language model from our learning corpus using KenLM (Heafield et al., 2013). Following Yatbaz et al. (2012), we used FASTSUBS (Yuret, 2012) with this language model to efficiently generate substitute vectors pruned to their top-$n$ substitutes, $v_1..v_n$, and normalized such that $\sum_{i=1..n} p(v_i|c) = 1$. In order to make our substitute vectors compatible with the pseudo-word setting, for each substitute vector we replaced the entries of all of the pseudo-sense words with a single pseudo-word entry, and assigned it with the sum of the conditional probabilities of the pseudo-sense words. Next, we computed the Positive PMI weights for the substitutes, $\vec{s}_c[v_i] = PPMI(v_i, c) = \max(0, \log(\frac{p(v_i|c)}{p(v_i)}))$, where $p(v_i)$ is the unigram probability of the word $v_i$ in our learning corpus. The unigram probability of a pseudo-word is the sum of the probabilities of its pseudo-sense words. Finally, we computed context similarity as substitute vector Cosine.

$SUB_{weight,n}$ denotes our similarity measure, where $n$ is the pruning factor and $weight \in \{cond, ppmi\}$ denotes conditional probabilities and PPMI fitness weights, respectively. We note that by using a 5-gram language model we consider a context word window of 4 words on each side of the target word.

#### 5.2.2 Bag-of-words similarity

Bag-of-words similarity between two context word windows is computed as vector Cosine between their bag-of-words vector representations. We use $BOW_{weight,l}$ to denote these context similarity measures, where $l$ is the size of the context word window on each side of the target word (we use *sent* to denote the entire sentence), and *weight* $\in$ {*tf*, *tfidf*} stands for term frequency and *tf-idf* weights, respectively. $CBOW_{weight,l}$ is used to denote the same for the continuous bag-of-words method, which is based on averaging the dense vector word representations. We used *word2vec* (Mikolov et al., 2013) to learn these dense vectors.[4]

| Method | P@1 | P@1% | AvgPrec |
|---|---|---|---|
| $SUB \cdot CBOW$ | **80.6** | **67.1** | **44.5** |
| $SUB_{ppmi,1000}$ | 73.1 | 60.0 | **44.0** |
| $SUB_{ppmi,100}$ | **74.5** | **61.0** | 42.8 |
| $CBOW_{tfidf,8w}$ | 68.4 | 58.0 | 43.5 |
| $SUB_{cond,1000}$ | 63.6 | 53.0 | 38.6 |
| $SUB_{cond,100}$ | 63.1 | 52.7 | 38.5 |
| $BOW_{tfidf,sent}$ | 62.8 | 51.3 | 34.6 |
| *Random* | 30.4 | 30.4 | 30.4 |

Table 4: Precision values for compared context similarity measures. Only the best performing configurations for BOW and CBOW are shown.

### 5.3 Results

The results presented in Table 4 support our hypothesis that our proposed substitute vector similarity measure is particularly suitable for measuring context similarity, at least in our setting. Our similarity measures outperform both CBOW and BOW baselines on P@1 and P@1%, with statistical significance at $p < 0.01$ for $SUB_{ppmi,100}$, and $p < 0.05$ for $SUB_{ppmi,1000}$, on a paired t-test. On average precision they perform similarly to CBOW. Within the substitute vector measures, our proposed PPMI weights significantly outperform the previously used conditional probabilities, and the choice of pruning factor has a small impact. Within the bag-of-words measures, the CBOW measure significantly outperforms the BOW measure, with an optimal window size of 8 (on each side). This suggests that CBOW's ability to capture context word similarities via its dense word representations is beneficial.

Finally, *SUB·CBOW* denotes a combined similarity measure, which is the geometrical mean between the scores of the best configurations of the respective methods. We see that this combination yields substantial improvement, outperforming all other baselines across all precision categories, with $p < 0.0001$ for P@1 and P@1%. We hypothesize that this is due to the synergy between the word order sensitivity of *SUB* and the word similarities and larger window size captured by *CBOW*.

[4]We experimented with various parameters of word2vec, observing small differences in performance. We report here the results with the best configuration (cbow 1, negative sampling 15, window size 8).

## 6 Evaluating Word Representations

Models of word meaning in context are commonly evaluated in lexical substitution tasks on predicting paraphrases of a target word that preserve its meaning in a given context. Conveniently, our paraphrase vector representations for words include exactly these predictions. We evaluated our model on two lexical substitution datasets under two types of tasks and compared it to the state-of-the-art as described next.

### 6.1 Lexical substitution datasets

The dataset introduced in the lexical substitution task of SemEval 2007 (McCarthy and Navigli, 2007), denoted here LS07, is the most widely used for the evaluation of lexical substitution. It consists of 10 sentences extracted from a web corpus for each of 201 target words (nouns, verbs, adjectives and adverbs), or altogether 2,010 word instances in sentential context, split into 300 trial sentences and 1,710 test sentences. The gold standard provided with this dataset is a weighted lemmatized paraphrase list for each word instance, based on manual annotations.

A more recent dataset (Kremer et al., 2014), denoted LS14, provides the same kind of data as LS07, but instead of target words that were specifically selected to be ambiguous as in LS07, the target words here are simply all the content words in text documents extracted from news and fiction corpora. LS14 is also much larger than LS07 with over 15K target word instances.

### 6.2 Predicting lexical substitutions

#### 6.2.1 Task description

In SemEval 2007 the lexical substitution task organizers evaluated participant systems on their ability to predict the paraphrases in the gold standard of the LS07 test-set in a few subtasks (1) *best* and *best-mode* - evaluate the quality of the best predictions (2) *oot* and *oot-mode* (out of ten) - evaluate the coverage of the gold paraphrase list by the top ten best predictions.[5] We performed this evaluation on both the LS07 and LS14 datasets.

[5]For brevity we do not describe the details of these subtasks. We report only *recall* scores as in this task *recall=precision* for all methods that predict paraphrases to all of the instances in the dataset, as we did.

#### 6.2.2 Compared methods

We used the same learning corpus and substitute vector generation procedure as described in Section 5. For every target word type $u$ (not lemmatized) in the LS07 and LS14 datasets, we sampled a collection of 20K sentence contexts from our learning corpus (or less for word types with lower frequency), denoted $C_u$.[6] Next, we generated substitute vectors, pruned to top-100 entries, for these contexts. For every target word type $u$, we discarded the contexts in $C_u$ where $u$ itself is not in the top-100 predicted substitutes, assuming that either these contexts are not typical to $u$, or that the quality of the predicted substitutes is low. This omits approximately 25% of all contexts. Finally, we generated top-100 and top-1000 substitute vectors for all of the instances in the LS07 and LS14 datasets.

We used a generalization of PPMI, called *Shifted PPMI* (Levy and Goldberg, 2014), as our substitute vector fitness weights: $SPPMI(v, c; s) = \max(0, PPMI(v, c) - s)$, where $s$ is a global shift constant. Levy and Goldberg (2014) showed that SPPMI outperformed PPMI on various semantic tasks. We tuned the value of $s \in \{0.0, 1.0, 2.0, 3.0\}$ on the trial portion of the LS07 dataset and used the best value, 2.0, on the LS07 test set and on LS14. We omit results based on conditional probability weights for brevity as they were substantially worse. Next, for every LS07/LS14 instance of word $u$ in context $c$ we generated a paraphrase vector according to Equation (4). We used the paraphrase vectors sorted by entry scores as our paraphrase predictions. $P_n^{in}$ (in-context) denotes this method, where $n$ is the pruning factor used for generating the substitute vectors of the lexical substitution datasets.[7]

As baseline, we generated our meaning out-of-context paraphrase vectors according to Equation (3), denoted $P^{out}$. We also used *word2vec* (Mikolov et al., 2013) to generate dense word vectors for all word types in our learning corpus.[8] Para-

[6]In general, we observed that the results improve the more contexts are sampled up to $\sim 10K$ contexts per word type.

[7]For the learning corpus contexts we always used top-100 substitute vectors to reduce computational complexity.

[8]We experimented with 600-dimension vectors, negative sampling value 15, both skip and cbow options, and various window sizes, and tuned these parameters on the trial portion of the LS07 dataset.

phrase predictions for this baseline, denoted $w2v^{out}$, were computed as the words most similar to the target word based on dense vector Cosine similarities, ignoring the context (out-of-context).

In the *best* subtasks we used only the top ranked lemmatized paraphrase (best prediction) suggested by each of the compared methods. In the *oot* subtasks we used the top-10 lemmatized paraphrases.

To the best of our knowledge, Biemann and Riedl (2013) is the only prior work that attempted to perform the original SemEval 2007 task on the LS07 dataset, learning only from corpus data like we do. They merged Gigaword (Parker et al., 2011) and LLC (Richter et al., 2006) as their learning corpus, which is similar in size to ours. We denote by *Biemann*$^{in}$ and *Biemann*$^{out}$ the reported results for their in-context and out-of-context methods, respectively. There is no previously reported result for this task on LS14.

### 6.2.3 Results

The results are shown in Table 5. First, we note that our out-of-context method significantly outperforms the out-of-context word2vec baseline on all subtasks in both LS07 and LS14, showing that our model performs well on predicting paraphrases even out-of-context. Furthermore, our meaning in-context methods show significant additional gains in performance on LS07, with top-1000 pruning performing a little better than top-100. On LS14 we see smaller gains, which may be due to the fact that its target words are less ambiguous by construction. This behavior is consistent with similar findings in Kremer et al. (2014). Finally, both *Biemann*$^{out}$ and *Biemann*$^{in}$ exhibit substantially lower performance on LS07 than our methods, achieving scores that are close to the word2vec baseline.

We note that all ten systems that participated in the original SemEval 2007 task on the LS07 dataset followed a two-step scheme (1) generating paraphrase candidates using a manually constructed thesaurus, such as WordNet; (2) ranking the candidates according to the given context based on data from various learning corpora. We stress that in contrast to all these systems, our model does not utilize manually constructed thesauri, and therefore addresses a much harder problem of predicting paraphrase substitutes out of the entire vocabulary, rather

| Method | best | best-m | oot | oot-m |
|---|---|---|---|---|
| LS07 test-set | | | | |
| $P^{in}_{1000}$ | **12.72** | **21.71** | **36.37** | **52.03** |
| $P^{in}_{100}$ | 12.25 | 20.73 | 35.54 | 50.98 |
| $P^{out}$ | 10.68 | 18.29 | 32.58 | 46.34 |
| $w2v^{out}_{skip,4w}$ | 8.25 | 13.41 | 29.27 | 39.92 |
| *Biemann*$^{in}$ | n/a | n/a | 27.48 | 37.19 |
| *Biemann*$^{out}$ | n/a | n/a | 27.02 | 37.35 |
| LS14 all | | | | |
| $P^{in}_{1000}$ | **8.07** | **17.37** | **26.67** | **46.23** |
| $P^{in}_{100}$ | 7.93 | 16.97 | 26.24 | 45.58 |
| $P^{out}$ | 7.80 | 16.90 | 25.57 | 44.66 |
| $w2v^{out}_{skip,4w}$ | 5.99 | 12.21 | 22.66 | 36.98 |

Table 5: *best* and *oot* subtasks scores for all compared methods. best-m and oot-m stand for the *mode* scores.

than merely ranking a small given set of candidates. Even so, in the *best* subtasks we achieve top results with respect to the reported score range of these systems, 2.98-12.90 for *best*, and 4.72-20.73 for *best-mode*. In comparison to the reported *oot* score range, our results are lower than average.

## 6.3 Ranking lexical substitutions

### 6.3.1 Task description

Most works that used the LS07 dataset after SemEval 2007, as well as the results reported for LS14, focused only on candidate ranking. Instead of using a thesaurus, they obtained the set of paraphrase candidates for each target type by pooling the annotated gold-standard paraphrases from all of its instances.[9] The quality of the rankings with respect to the gold standard was measured using Generalized Average Precision (GAP) (Kishida, 2005). Furthermore, all of the works compared in this section discarded multi-word expression substitutes from the original gold standard, and omitted instances who thus remained with no gold paraphrases. We follow the same evaluation settings for this task.

### 6.3.2 Compared methods

We observe that in this task, the objective is to rank candidates that are known to be semantically similar to the target word in some context. Therefore, we hypothesize that possibly more focus should be given in this case to assessing the

[9] A target type is defined as the pair (word lemma, pos), where pos $\in$ {noun, verb, adjective, adverb}.

compatibility between the candidates and the given context versus their semantic similarity to the target word. To this end, we explore strategies with different points of balance between these two factors. On one hand we evaluate the scores assigned to the candidates by our out-of-context paraphrase vector representation, which is based only on semantic similarity. Similarly, we also evaluate rankings based on word2vec similarity scores, with a range of learning parameters (same range as used in Section 6.2) and report the best results that we were able to obtain. On the other hand, we ignore the target word identity and consider only context compatibility by ranking candidates based on their conditional probabilities to fill the target word slot, as reflected in the respective context substitute vector representation, denoted $S_{cond,1000}$.

Finally, we rank the candidates using the scores in our in-context paraphrase vectors from Section 6.2. However, this time we check the effect of injecting a stronger bias towards the given context $c$, by averaging only the top-$m$ percent contexts most similar to $c$, for $m \in \{1\%, 5\%, 10\%, 100\%\}$, as described in Section 4.2. We denote this as $P_n^{in,m}$. We do not report results based on conditional probability weights, as they perform substantially worse than our SPPMI weights. We also report the most recent state-of-the-art results on both LS07 and LS14. On LS07, we report our results both on the test-set and on the entire dataset (trial+test).

#### 6.3.3 Results

The results are shown in Table 6. Looking first at the results on the LS07 dataset, we see that not surprisingly both our out-of-context method, $P^{out}$, and the word2vec baseline, $w2v^{out}_{skip,2w}$, which ignore the given context, achieve relatively low results. $S_{cond,1000}$ that considers only the context compatibility performs a little better. Next, we see that our in-context method, $P_{1000}^{in,100\%}$ outperforms all of the above, but $P_{1000}^{in,5\%}$, which is more strongly biased to context compatibility performs even better. For brevity, we report only the results for $m = 5\%$, which performed best on the trial portion of LS07, but the results are almost as good for $m = 1\%$ and $m = 10\%$. This supports our hypothesis that in the ranking task more focus is to be given to context compatibility. As in the prediction task in Section 6.2, the pruning factor of 100 performed slightly (up to half a point) worse than 1000.

| Method | Resources | LS07 test | LS07 all | LS14 all |
|---|---|---|---|---|
| $P_{1000}^{in,5\%}$ | UW | **55.2** | **55.1** | **50.2** |
| $P_{1000}^{in,100\%}$ | UW | 52.0 | 51.7 | 50.0 |
| $S_{cond,1000}$ | UW | 48.6 | 48.4 | 46.4 |
| $P^{out}$ | UW | 46.6 | 45.9 | 47.9 |
| $w2v^{out}_{skip,2w}$ | UW | 45.2 | 45.2 | 46.5 |
| Random | UW | 29.7 | 30.0 | 33.8 |
| Kremer, 2014† | GW | n/a | 52.5 | 47.8 |
| Thater, 2011 | GW | n/a | 51.7 | n/a |
| Séaghdha, 2014 | WP,BN | n/a | 49.5 | n/a |
| Moon, 2013 | UW,BN,WN<br>GW,WN | n/a<br>n/a | 47.1<br>46.7 | n/a<br>n/a |
| Szarvas, 2013b | LLC,WN | n/a | 55.0* | n/a |
| Szarvas, 2013a | LLC,WN | n/a | 52.4* | n/a |

Table 6: GAP scores for compared methods. UW = ukWaC; GW = Gigaword; WP = Wikipedia; WN = WordNet; BN = British National Corpus (Aston and Burnard, 1998).
† A re-implementation of the model in Thater, 2011.
* Obtained by a supervised method.

In comparison to previous results, our method achieves the best reported GAP score to date, on par with Szarvas et al. (2013b). However, we note that both Szarvas et al. (2013b) and Szarvas et al. (2013a) follow a supervised approach, training on the LS07 gold standard with 10-fold cross validation, as well as incorporate features from WordNet. Therefore, they cannot be directly compared with unsupervised models, such as our own. Our model and previous works used different learning corpora that are similar in size. Moon and Erk (2013) reported results for both Gigaword and ukWaC, showing minor differences in performance.

The results on LS14 exhibit a similar behavior with our method outperforming the state-of-the-art. However, as also reported in Kremer et al. (2014), the performance gain achieved by taking the given context into consideration is smaller than in LS07. Again, this seems to be due to the nature of LS14, which is not biased to ambiguous target words.

| Benchmark | Orig | 1000 | 100 |
|---|---|---|---|
| best | 12.7 | 12.1 | 11.2 |
| best-m | 21.7 | 20.9 | 19.7 |
| oot | 36.3 | 34.8 | 32.5 |
| oot-m | 52.0 | 50.4 | 46.4 |
| GAP test | 55.2 | 52.0 | 50.9 |
| GAP all | 55.1 | 51.8 | 50.7 |

Table 7: The effect of context clustering on our model's performance on LS07. *Orig* stands for best configuration of our model with no clustering, and 1000/100 stand for the same configuration with that number of clusters.

### 6.4 Computational efficiency and clustering

To generate our in-context paraphrase predictions for an instance of a target word $u$, our model performs a weighted average over all of its context substitute vectors in $C_u$. The run-time complexity of this procedure is reasonably efficient at $O(|C_u| \cdot n)$, where $n$ is the vector pruning factor. This is comparable to the complexity of the state-of-the-art algorithm before this work (Thater et al., 2011) and even to word2vec's dense vector computations. As a point of reference, in our experiments it took ~300 msec to generate an in-context paraphrase vector for a given word instance on a modest single core, which was only about 3 times slower than the word2vec computation.

Memory consumption of our model is not an issue when operating in an 'offline' mode. In this mode all the target word instances in a test set (such as LS07 or LS14), can first be sorted according to their word type. Then, while processing all instances of the same word type $u$ one after the other, only the substitute vectors in $C_u$ need to be loaded into memory. In contrast, in an 'online' mode, to be ready for any arbitrary word instance input, our model would need to keep in memory substitute vectors for all the word types in the vocabulary $V$. The space complexity in this case is $O(|C_u| \cdot n \cdot |V|)$, which can easily reach memory consumptions in the order of ~100 GB or more, requiring a large-scale server.

To address this challenge, we present a more coarse-grained variant of our model, where for each word type $u$ we keep only $k$ substitute vectors instead of all individual context vectors, thereby bounding the memory consumption to $O(k \cdot n \cdot |V|)$. To this end, for each word type $u$ we used spherical $k$-means to cluster the ~20,000 substitute vectors in $C_u$ into either 100 or 1000 clusters. Then, instead of $C_u$, we used the collection of its cluster centroids, pruned to their top-100 entries. Table 7 shows the results when applying this to our best performing configurations on the LS07 dataset. The results show relative performance degradation when fewer clusters are used, indicating that some relevant information may be lost in this process. However, absolute performance remains competitive, suggesting that this is a viable option when memory consumption is a concern. The results on the LS14 dataset show similar trends.

## 7 Discussion and Future Work

We proposed a model for word meaning in context whose main novelty is in representing contexts as substitute vectors. Our model outperformed state-of-the-art baselines in both predicting and ranking paraphrases of words in context in two different lexical substitution tasks. As another potential contribution, the context similarity measures used in our model performed well on a targeted evaluation, suggesting that they may be useful as a component in other applications as well.

Substitute vectors were successfully used earlier for performing part-of-speech and word sense induction tasks (Baskaya et al., 2013; Yatbaz et al., 2014), not addressed in this work. These works took a different approach, embedding words in a low dimensional space, based on target-substitute pairs sampled from substitute vectors. It would be interesting to explore how our approach applies to these tasks.

Finally, a preliminary qualitative analysis showed that low quality substitute vectors may be a factor limiting our model's performance. This suggests that generating substitute vectors with better language models, such as neural language models, is a potential path to further improvements.

## Acknowledgments

We thank our reviewers for their helpful remarks. This work was partially supported by the Israel Science Foundation grant 880/12, the German Research Foundation through the German-Israeli Project Cooperation (DIP, grant DA 1600/1-1), and the European Community's Seventh Framework Programme (FP7/2007-2013) grant 287923 (EXCITEMENT).

## References


Guy Aston and Lou Burnard. 1998. *The BNC handbook: exploring the British National Corpus with SARA*. Capstone.

Osman Baskaya, Enis Sert, Volkan Cirik, and Deniz Yuret. 2013. Ai-ku: Using substitute vectors and co-occurrence modeling for word sense induction and disambiguation. In *Proceedings of the SemEval*.

Chris Biemann and Martin Riedl. 2013. Text: Now in 2d! a framework for lexical expansion with contextual similarity. *Journal of Language Modelling*, 1(1):55–95.

David M. Blei, Andrew Y. Ng, and Michael I. Jordan. 2003. Latent Dirichlet allocation. *Journal of Machine Learning Research*, 3:993–1022.

John A. Bullinaria and Joseph P. Levy. 2007. Extracting semantic representations from word co-occurrence statistics: A computational study. *Behavior Research Methods*, 39(3):510–526.

Kenneth W. Church and Patrick Hanks. 1990. Word association norms, mutual information, and lexicography. *Computational Linguistics*, 16(1):22–29.

Katrin Erk and Sebastian Padó. 2010. Exemplar-based models for word meaning in context. In *Proceedings of ACL (short papers)*.

Christiane Fellbaum. 2010. *WordNet*. Springer.

Adriano Ferraresi, Eros Zanchetta, Marco Baroni, and Silvia Bernardini. 2008. Introducing and evaluating ukwac, a very large web-derived corpus of English. In *Proceedings of the 4th Web as Corpus Workshop (WAC-4)*.

John R. Firth. 1957. A synopsis of linguistic theory 1930-1955. *Studies in linguistic analysis*, pages 1–32.

Kenneth Heafield, Ivan Pouzyrevsky, Jonathan H. Clark, and Philipp Koehn. 2013. Scalable modified Kneser-Ney language model estimation. In *Proceedings of ACL*.

Eric H. Huang, Richard Socher, Christopher D. Manning, and Andrew Y. Ng. 2012. Improving word representations via global context and multiple word prototypes. In *Proceedings of ACL*.

Kazuaki Kishida. 2005. *Property of average precision and its generalization: An examination of evaluation indicator for information retrieval experiments*. National Institute of Informatics Tokyo, Japan.

Reinhard Kneser and Hermann Ney. 1995. Improved backing-off for $m$-gram language modeling. In *Proceedings of ICASSP*.

Gerhard Kremer, Katrin Erk, Sebastian Padó, and Stefan Thater. 2014. What substitutes tell us-analysis of an all-words lexical substitution corpus. In *Proceedings of EACL*.

Omer Levy and Yoav Goldberg. 2014. Neural word embeddings as implicit matrix factorization. In *Proceedings of NIPS*.

Diana McCarthy and Roberto Navigli. 2007. Semeval-2007 task 10: English lexical substitution task. In *Proceedings of SemEval*.

Oren Melamud, Ido Dagan, Jacob Goldberger, Idan Szpektor, and Deniz Yuret. 2014. Probabilistic modeling of joint-context in distributional similarity. In *Proceedings of CoNLL*.

Rada Mihalcea. 1998. Semcor semantically tagged corpus. *Unpublished manuscript*.

Tomas Mikolov, Kai Chen, Greg Corrado, and Jeffrey Dean. 2013. Efficient estimation of word representations in vector space. *arXiv preprint arXiv:1301.3781*.

Taesun Moon and Katrin Erk. 2013. An inference-based model of word meaning in context as a paraphrase distribution. *ACM Trans. Intell. Syst. Technol.*, 4(3):42:1–42:28.

Diarmuid Ó Séaghdha and Anna Korhonen. 2014. Probabilistic distributional semantics with latent variable models. *Computational Linguistics*, 40(3):587–631.

Lubomir Otrusina and Pavel Smrz. 2010. A new approach to pseudoword generation. In *Proceedings of LREC*.

Robert Parker, David Graff, Junbo Kong, Ke Chen, and Kazuaki Maeda. 2011. English gigaword fifth edition, june. *Linguistic Data Consortium, LDC2011T07*.

Mohammad Taher Pilehvar and Roberto Navigli. 2014. A large-scale pseudoword-based evaluation framework for state-of-the-art word sense disambiguation. *Computational Linguistics*, 40(4):837–881.

Joseph Reisinger and Raymond J. Mooney. 2010. Multi-prototype vector-space models of word meaning. In *Human Language Technologies: The 2010 Annual Conference of the North American Chapter of the Association for Computational Linguistics*.

Matthias Richter, Uwe Quasthoff, Erla Hallsteinsdóttir, and Chris Biemann. 2006. Exploiting the Leipzig corpora collection. *Proceesings of the IS-LTC*.

György Szarvas, Chris Biemann, Iryna Gurevych, et al. 2013a. Supervised all-words lexical substitution using delexicalized features. In *Proceedings of HLT-NAACL*.

György Szarvas, Róbert Busa-Fekete, and Eyke Hüllermeier. 2013b. Learning to rank lexical substitutions. In *Proceedings of EMNLP*.

Stefan Thater, Hagen Fürstenau, and Manfred Pinkal. 2011. Word meaning in context: A simple and effective vector model. In *Proceedings of IJCNLP*.

Mehmet Ali Yatbaz, Enis Sert, and Deniz Yuret. 2012. Learning syntactic categories using paradigmatic representations of word context. In *Proceedings of EMNLP*.

Mehmet Ali Yatbaz, Enis Rıfat Sert, and Deniz Yuret. 2014. Unsupervised instance-based part of speech induction using probable substitutes. In *Proceedings of COLING*.

Deniz Yuret. 2012. FASTSUBS: An efficient and exact procedure for finding the most likely lexical substitutes based on an $n$-gram language model. *Signal Processing Letters, IEEE*, 19(11):725–728.

# Corpus-based discovery of semantic intensity scales

**Chaitanya Shivade[†], Marie-Catherine de Marneffe[§], Eric Fosler-Lussier[†], Albert M. Lai[*]**
[†]Department of Computer Science and Engineering,
[§]Department of Linguistics,
[*]Department of Biomedical Informatics,
The Ohio State University, Columbus OH 43210, USA.
shivade@cse.ohio-state.edu, mcdm@ling.ohio-state.edu
fosler@cse.ohio-state.edu, albert.lai@osumc.edu

## Abstract

Gradable terms such as *brief*, *lengthy* and *extended* illustrate varying degrees of a scale and can therefore participate in comparative constructs. Knowing the set of words that can be compared on the same scale and the associated ordering between them (*brief* < *lengthy* < *extended*) is very useful for a variety of lexical semantic tasks. Current techniques to derive such an ordering rely on WordNet to determine which words belong on the same scale and are limited to adjectives. Here we describe an extension to recent work: we investigate a fully automated pipeline to extract gradable terms from a corpus, group them into clusters reflecting the same scale and establish an ordering among them. This methodology reduces the amount of required handcrafted knowledge, and can infer gradability of words independent of their part of speech. Our approach infers an ordering for adjectives with comparable performance to previous work, but also for adverbs with an accuracy of 71%. We find that the technique is useful for inferring such rankings among words across different domains, and present an example using biomedical text.

## 1 Introduction

Gradability (Sapir, 1944) is a property of words that identifies different degrees of the quality the word denotes. For example, adjectives such as *large*, *huge* and *gigantic* present different degrees of size or volume. Similarly, adverbs such as *approximately*, *almost* and *roughly* present different degrees of how accurate a measurement is. Thus, one of the characteristics of gradable terms is that they participate in a scale and can be ordered along that scale: for example, *good* < *great* < *excellent* (Kennedy, 2007). Another characteristic is that gradable terms can appear in comparative constructions, e.g., "A is larger than B". Such comparative judgments are a psychological process that precedes judgments of counting, e.g., "A is twice as large as B" (Sapir, 1944).

Modern NLP systems face the challenge of interpreting language as close to human perception as possible. Modeling gradable terms as well as their associated meaning and ordering is an important aspect of this challenge. Such information can be very useful for a variety of inference tasks, such as sentiment analysis (Pang and Lee, 2008) and textual inference (Dagan et al., 2006). However, current lexical resources, like WordNet (Fellbaum, 1998), lack annotations capturing the gradability of words. This weakens the notion of similarity: although words such as *small* and *minuscule* illustrate varying degrees of size, they are listed as synonyms in WordNet.

Recently, there has been a lot of interest in exploring different approaches to derive an ordering among gradable adjectives based on their semantics (Ruppenhofer et al., 2014; Sheinman et al., 2013; Schulam and Fellbaum, 2010). de Melo and Bansal (2013) propose a novel Mixed Integer Linear Programming (MILP) based approach, publish a gold standard dataset and report the best performance on ordering scalar adjectives on this dataset. However, these approaches are limited in two ways. First, they depend on a manually created resource, such



*Human Language Technologies: The 2015 Annual Conference of the North American Chapter of the ACL*, pages 483–493,
Denver, Colorado, May 31 – June 5, 2015. 

as WordNet or FrameNet (Baker et al., 1998). Lexical patterns (e.g., 'not just $x$ but $y$') are used both to extract words that belong to the same scale and to determine the direction of the ordering (e.g., in the above pattern, $x$ is weaker than $y$). However, this extraction process gives noisy results that require filtering using an electronic thesaurus. The domain of application is thus restricted to words that exist in an electronic thesaurus. Second, previous work is limited to the study of adjectives.

In this paper, we propose a fully automated pipeline that uses structural patterns to extract gradable terms from a corpus, cluster them into groups that reflect the same semantic scale of comparison, and finally rank them using de Melo and Bansal's MILP technique to establish an ordering among them. We also explore how the technique fares on domain-specific (biomedical) text, deriving scales for domain-specific terms that might not exist in thesauri. Our approach achieves a comparable performance to previous studies on scalar adjectives, and can be reliably extended to adverbs.

## 2 Related work

Hatzivassiloglou and McKeown (1993) present the first work on automatically clustering adjectives that belong to the same scale, identifying scalar adjectives based on the intuition that similar nouns are modified by similar adjectives. They use a hierarchical clustering algorithm on a newswire corpus for grouping similar adjectives, but do not provide ranking among a given cluster of related adjectives.

Assuming a pair of related adjectives, de Marneffe et al. (2010) use reviews from the Internet Movie Database and their associated ratings to infer an ordering in the adjective pair. Kim and de Marneffe (2013) also obtain an ordering given a pair of adjectives, using distributional word vectors derived from a recursive neural network.

Sheinman et al. (2013) and de Melo and Bansal (2013) present similar approaches, which make use of WordNet *dumbbells* to determine words that belong to the same scale as proposed in Sheinman et al. (2012). A WordNet *dumbbell* is a representation involving an antonym pair (e.g., *small* and *large*) as two ends of a semantic scale with semantically similar adjectives arranged in a radial fashion around each adjective. The antonym acting as a centroid and its synonyms as members of a cluster represent words that most likely participate in the same scale. For example, the antonym pair (*small, large*) results in the dumbbell with clusters (*small, tiny, pocket-size, smallish*) and (*large, gigantic, monstrous, huge*) at the two ends. It should be noted that even with such a representation, there can be words that fall into the same WordNet synset but do not participate in the scalar relationship (e.g., *violent* with respect to *supernatural* and *affected*). This is primarily because of polysemy and semantic drift (de Melo and Bansal, 2013).

Sheinman et al. (2013) present a two-step approach for establishing an ordering among scalar adjectives. They extract adjectives from the Web using lexical patterns indicative of the direction of the scalar relationship between a pair of adjectives. Two sets of patterns are defined: *mild* patterns in which participating words are such that the first word has a weaker semantic intensity than the second word (e.g., '$*$ but not $*$' – *good but not great*); and *intense* patterns, in which the first word has a stronger semantic intensity than the second word (e.g., 'not $*$ but still $*$' – *not freezing but still cold*). In the first step, they assign a positive score to an adjective if it is seen as a part of the intense pattern and a negative score if seen as part of the mild pattern. In the second step, they use these scores to partition the adjectives into two subsets one representing *mild* and the other representing *intense* adjectives. They perform this partitioning recursively to obtain a complete ordering for a given cluster of adjectives from a WordNet dumbbell.

de Melo and Bansal (2013) improve upon Sheinman et al. (2013) by refining their lexical patterns, and refer to them as "strong-weak" and "weak-strong" patterns. Using frequencies of occurrence for a pair of adjectives across the strong-weak and weak-strong patterns in a corpus, they define an overall weak-strong score. They optimize for this score using MILP. The constraints of the MILP model two types of strength relationships: the strength relationships between two adjectives in a pair with a possible third adjective, and synonymy relationship between two adjectives based on information from an external resource. Given a cluster of terms, the MILP produces an ordering of the cluster members using frequency counts of instances where these members are found in strong-weak and weak-strong patterns. To evaluate their approach, de Melo and Bansal construct a manually curated gold standard of 88 clusters, each with a cardinality of three or more adjectives. These 88 clusters are randomly drawn from all possible clusters that are either half of a WordNet dumbbell. Two annotators manually examined these clusters to remove words that did not belong to the same scale. Further, all pairs within these clusters were annotated for scalar relationship: is the adjective in a pair weaker than the other, stronger than the other, or of equivalent intensity. The output of the MILP was tested on these 88 clusters (569 word pairs). They achieve a pairwise accuracy of 78.2%.

# 3 Our approach

## 3.1 Extraction using structural patterns

As observed by Ruppenhofer et al. (2014), lexical pattern-based approaches suffer from a coverage issue. This is because these patterns consist of longer n-grams, which are sparsely found in a small dataset. Therefore, Sheinman et al. (2013) use the Web as their corpus, and de Melo & Bansal use Google N-grams (Brants and Franz, 2006). However, this results in a large number of instances where satisfied lexical patterns do not correspond to adjectives (e.g., *sometimes but not always*). Moreover, since the Google N-grams corpus is limited to 5-grams, adjective pairs of interest beyond a five-word window are lost.

To deal with these shortcomings, we use *Tregex* (Levy and Andrew, 2006), which enables pattern matching on parse trees based on syntactic relationships and regular expression matches on nodes. Using Tregex, we transform de Melo and Bansal's weak-strong and strong-weak lexical patterns into structural patterns. For example, one way of expanding the lexical pattern '$*$ but not $*$' into a structural Tregex pattern for adjectives is 'ADJP< ((ADJP<JJ) $ (CC<but)$(RB<not)$ (ADJP<JJ)).' Similarly, a structural pattern for adverbs can be written as 'ADVP< ((ADVP<RB) $ (CC<but)$(RB<not)$ (ADVP<RB)).' These patterns are available for download[1].

[1]http://web.cse.ohio-state.edu/~shivade/naacl2015

Introducing tree patterns requires parsing a corpus: while this additional step in the pipeline might lead to error propagation, the advantages of the structural patterns are that (i) they are more robust than the lexical ones and (ii) restricting results to a desired part-of-speech comes for free. In the experiments reported here, we use the Stanford parser v3.3.1 (Klein and Manning, 2003).

## 3.2 Automatic clustering

In order to determine a ranking of words based on their semantic intensity, the first step is to determine words that belong to the same scale of meaning. As pointed out earlier, previous work (de Melo and Bansal, 2013; Sheinman et al., 2013) use WordNet *dumbbells*, and this restricts the utility of these approaches to the scope of a manually created lexical resource. We overcome this limitation by automatically clustering words that belong to the same scale. As the clustering algorithm, we use the Matlab (2014) implementation of K-means++ (Arthur and Vassilvitskii, 2007), a hard clustering algorithm[2] with cosine similarity as a distance metric. Following Hatzivassiloglou and McKeown (1993), we use context vectors to represent the words to cluster. They make use of standard context vectors for clustering adjectives, where context for every adjective comprises of nouns it modifies across all sentences in a corpus.

However, recent work shows promise for context vectors embedded in a compressed semantic space that are derived using neural networks: Baroni et al. (2014) compare standard context vectors with embedded vectors for a wide range of lexical semantic tasks and found embedded vectors to yield better results. We therefore generate context vectors and compare the utility of both skip-gram and continuous bag of words (CBOW) representations using the `word2vec` tool (Mikolov et al., 2013) for our task. These two representations have demonstrated varying degrees of success in different NLP tasks (Baroni et al., 2014; Bansal et al., 2014). Given a

[2]The choice of a hard-clustering algorithm was mostly for implementational convenience, but carries with it the issue that polysemous words can only appear in one semantic cluster. We leave the issue of deriving a soft clustering approach that works with context vectors, a separate research problem in its own right, to future work.

window size $w$, the CBOW model predicts the current word given the neighboring words as context. In contrast, the skip-gram model predicts the neighboring words given the current word. We used $w = 5$ and found CBOW to yield better results for our task. Thus the terms extracted from a corpus by the structural patterns are automatically clustered, and these clusters are used as an input to the ranking algorithm.

### 3.3 Ranking based on semantic intensity

Once the terms have been clustered, the second step is to provide a ranking between the cluster members. To do so, we use the MILP implementation provided by de Melo and Bansal (2013). This method computes an overall weak-strong score for a pair of adjectives based on the frequency of that pair in the matches for weak-strong and strong-weak patterns. The MILP then uses these scores among all relevant pairs of adjectives belonging to the same scale, capturing complex interactions to infer an ordering among them.

### 3.4 Data: PubMed corpus

In this work, we want to provide an approach that can infer scalar orderings for any domain-specific terms. Such terms might be absent from existing thesauri. Our approach is thus corpus-based as outlined above. We chose to test the robustness of our technique on PubMed, a large domain-specific corpus of biomedical texts. It is a free resource developed and maintained by the National Center for Biotechnology Information at the National Library of Medicine. It provides access to scientific abstracts, full text articles and associated resources. We used $10,875,982$ freely available abstracts (not full text articles) from PubMed as our corpus. This corresponds to $88,303,272$ sentences in total, where the average length of a sentence is 28 words (including punctuations). We used this corpus to find instances of the structural strong-weak and weak-strong patterns, both for adjectives and adverbs.

## 4 Comparison with the gold standard of de Melo & Bansal

To evaluate our approach, we need to establish how good the clustering step is, as well as how good the ranking step is. Each step is evaluated separately using annotations obtained from Amazon Mechanical Turk.

### 4.1 Clustering

In order to evaluate the automatic clustering procedure that uses K-means++ and word vectors, we start with the gold standard provided by de Melo and Bansal (2013): as mentioned above, their data set has 88 gold standard clusters, corresponding to 346 adjectives, annotated by humans for scale ordering. One problem with evaluating a hard clustering algorithm is that the same word may appear in multiple WordNet synsets, corresponding to multiple clusters (soft clustering). We therefore made a "hard cluster version" of the de Melo & Bansal dataset by removing any adjectives that occur in multiple clusters, and then eliminating any singleton clusters. This resulted in a gold standard set of 256 adjectives belonging to 84 clusters.

We clustered the 256 adjectives from the gold standard data subset into 84 clusters: the representation for each adjective was a neural embedding derived using the `word2vec` tool trained on our PubMed data. We experimented with both the skip-gram and continuous bag of words (CBOW) models to derive vectors of dimension sizes varying from 200 to 800 in increments of 100. To choose the right dimensionality and the best model, we evaluated the quality of the automatically derived 84 clusters against the gold standard. As a metric of evaluation for cluster quality, we follow Hatzivassiloglou and McKeown (1993) and use F1 calculated by comparing equivalence relations generated by the clusters (as implemented in LingPipe (2008)). We found that the CBOW model gave clusters closer to the gold standard than the skip-gram model. We found that a dimension size of 600 for the vectors yielded clusters with a maximum F1 score of 57%. Thus, we were able to fix the parameters for our clustering task. Figure 1 summarizes the results of this experiment.

In their study, Hatzivassiloglou and McKeown (1993) evaluate the results of their clustering on a small set of 21 adjectives. They presented the 21 adjectives to 9 annotators and asked them to partition these adjectives such that each partition contain adjectives that belong to the same scale. They re-

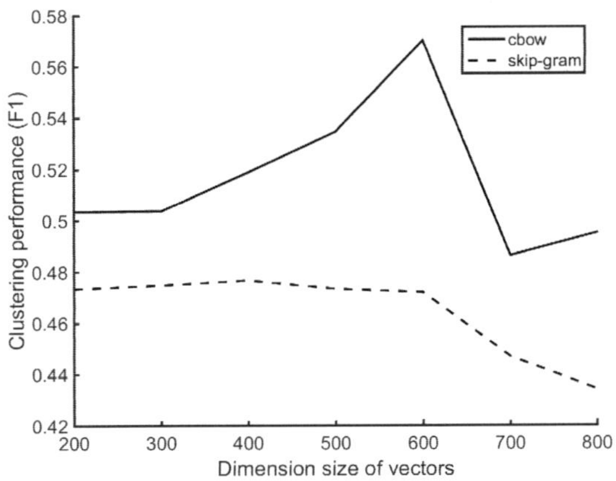


Figure 1: Comparison of CBOW and skip-gram for clustering of adjectives.

port a best F1 score of 48% but note that such score does not seem to reflect the quality of the clustering. We observe the same problem: our automatically derived clusters have a different organization for words that belong to the same cluster than the gold standard clusters, but in a way that seems intuitive. Some differences between our automatically derived clusters and the gold standard clusters are illustrated in Table 1. For example, the adjectives *false* and *misleading* belong to the same cluster in both the gold standard as well as the automatic clustering output. However, the automatic clustering groups the adjectives *false* and *misleading* together with *unreliable* and *wrong*, whereas the gold standard groups *false* and *misleading* with *deceptive* and *fraudulent*. Both clusterings are plausible, though. The adjectives *fraudulent* and *deceptive* become part of new clusters in our automatic clustering. It could be argued that the gold standard cluster "deceptive, false, fraudulent, misleading" represents different degrees of "trickery," whereas the automatic cluster "false, misleading, unreliable, wrong" represent different degrees of "wrongness." Thus, although both clusters contain different adjectives, they group adjectives that are on the same scale of a different meaning.

Therefore, to evaluate the quality of the automatic clustering, we sampled 50 clusters containing three or more adjectives (corresponding to a total of 190 adjectives) from all the generated clusters and obtained annotations using Amazon Mechanical Turk (AMT), a crowdsourcing platform that has been shown useful for a number of NLP tasks (Snow et al., 2008). Annotators (workers, in AMT parlance) were presented with 15 clusters in each worker session, whose members were each associated with a checkbox. For each cluster, workers had to uncheck the adjectives that did not belong to the same scale. The nature of the annotation task does involve inherent subjectivity which cannot be avoided. We tried to minimize this by giving detailed instructions with accompanying examples to achieve coherent annotations. To make sure workers were paying attention to the task, 2 clusters among the 15 clusters they saw were clusters for which we a priori knew which adjectives should be removed (e.g., *beautiful, pretty,* and *rainy* where *rainy* had to be unchecked). Most workers did the task well: we only had to discard annotations from 4 worker sessions (out of 140). We ended up with annotations from 8 to 10 workers per cluster. To create a gold standard, we retained in each cluster only those words that were ascertained to be in the same cluster by 6 or more annotators.

For each cluster, we calculated an accuracy score equivalent to the number of correct adjectives (determined to be on the same scale by the annotators) divided by the total number of adjectives in the generated cluster. This accuracy was averaged across all 50 clusters, and yielded a final micro-averaged accuracy of 74.36% as seen in Table 2.

### 4.2 Ranking

Since our end goal is to establish an ordering among scalar adjectives, we use the automatically derived clusters (rather than the WordNet dumbbells) as input to the MILP algorithm. To determine the performance of the ranking produced by the MILP algorithm, we use AMT to obtain pairwise ranking annotations for all unique adjective pairs within a cluster. Workers were presented with 15 word pairs in each worker session. For each pair $(a1, a2)$, the worker had to pick one of four options: (1) $a1$ is stronger than $a2$, (2) $a2$ is stronger than $a1$, (3) both are equally strong, and (4) $a1$ and $a2$ are not comparable. Option (4) was present because our clusters possibly contained adjectives that are not on the same scale. As in the previous task for getting annotations for clusters, we inserted two items with a clear ranking (e.g., *hot, hotter*) for every set of 15

| Gold standard clusters | Automatic clusters |
|---|---|
| deceptive, false, fraudulent, misleading | false, misleading, unreliable, wrong |
| evil, immoral, sinful, wrong | desperate, humiliated, immoral, insane, sinful |
| dangerous, risky, suicidal, unreliable | dangerous, harmful, toxic |

Table 1: Example comparison of automatically derived clusters against gold standard clusters from WordNet.

| Data | Corpus for strength counts in MILP ranking | Clustering Accuracy | Ranking Pairwise Accuracy |
|---|---|---|---|
| Clusters automatically derived from non-polysemous WordNet adjectives | Google N-grams | 74.36 | 84.74 |
| | PubMed | 74.36 | 69.23 |
| PubMed-derived clustering: | | | |
| Regular adjectives | PubMed | 86.26 | 70.37 |
| Domain-specific adjectives | PubMed | 64.30 | – |
| PubMed-derived clustering: | | | |
| Regular adverbs | PubMed | 89.36 | 71.00 |
| Domain-specific adverbs | PubMed | 53.80 | – |

Table 2: AMT-based evaluations of cluster accuracy and pairwise ranking accuracy of systems that vary in the source of clustering data, source of strength counts, and part of speech. For comparison, the approach used by de Melo and Bansal (2013) achieves a pairwise ranking accuracy of 76.1% on the non-polysemous WordNet clusters.

pairs to avoid random annotations. Each set was annotated by 10 workers. All workers passed all the checks and we did not discard any annotations for this task. To create a gold standard we assigned each pair one of four labels, *weaker, stronger, equal,* or *not comparable*. A value was assigned based on a majority vote. In case of a tie, the pair was assigned a label of being *equal*.

In order to compute a ranking, the MILP needs two inputs: 1) the cluster of terms that are on the same scale, and 2) the counts for how many times all pairs of adjectives in that cluster satisfied the weak-strong and strong-weak patterns (henceforth referred to as "strength counts"). In the first experiment of ranking adjectives, we ran the full pipeline used by (de Melo and Bansal, 2013) on the 256 adjective (84 hard cluster) subset of their gold standard (see Section 4.1). Thus, this experiment uses hand-corrected WordNet dumbbells to determine adjectives on the same scale of semantic intensity, followed by the MILP using strength counts from the Google N-gram corpus, to determine the ranking. Their pipeline resulted in a pairwise accuracy of 76.1% which serves as a baseline for comparison. In the second experiment of ranking adjectives, we used the 50 automatically derived adjective clusters described in Section 4.1 as an input for the MILP. Since these adjectives originate from WordNet dumbbells, we refer to them as "WordNet adjective clusters." We determined the ranking for adjectives within these clusters using strength counts obtained from our PubMed corpus. We obtained an accuracy of 69.23% across 105 pairs. The strength counts for all adjectives in these clusters, from Google N-grams corpus, used in the experiments of (de Melo and Bansal, 2013) were also available to us by the authors. We repeated the previous experiment by substituting strength counts from PubMed corpus with these strength counts from the Google N-grams corpus and obtained an accuracy of 84.74% across 119 pairs.[3] It appears from our experiment that pattern counts from a general corpus

[3]The MILP does not produce a strength relationship between a pair of adjectives if there are no strength counts for this pair. Hence, we observe a difference in the number of pairs for which accuracy is determined in the two ranking experiments.

is a better match for determining the adjective ordering than a more-limited domain corpus, despite the limitation of Google N-grams being restricted to 5-word sequences. We think this is because of two reasons: First, Google N-grams is a very large corpus compared to the one we use. Second, our corpus consists of abstracts and not full text of scientific articles from PubMed. Hence there is less variety in the language used; capturing fewer comparative constructs than Google N-grams. However, it is interesting that we can still extract patterns from domain-specific corpora to act as constraints for the MILP process.

## 5 Rankings for adjectives extracted from PubMed

We also desired to see how well our approach does on terms that are not specifically in WordNet, but present in a domain-specific corpus such as PubMed. We therefore also evaluate the clustering and ranking steps on a set of adjectives extracted from the PubMed data using structural patterns.

### 5.1 Clustering

Since there was no gold standard reflecting ideal clustering of data, we explored heuristic measures to choose parameters for our clustering step. We used CBOW vectors over skip-gram vectors since these were more effective in the previous experiment. Since the true value for number of clusters $k$ was unknown, we chose $k$ such that the average cardinality of a cluster was three. The value of $k$ was found to be the same ($k = 375$) for all clustering experiments conducted using vector dimension sizes varying from 200 to 800 in increments of 100. To choose the right dimension size $d$ of the CBOW vectors for this fixed value of $k$, we obtained clusters for incremental values of $d$ from 200 to 800 in increments of 100. We determined the number of identical clusters obtained using a particular value of $d$ with its next increment. The lowest value of $d$ which resulted in a maximum number of identical clusters with its next increment was chosen: $d = 400$.

Using vectors of 400 dimensions, we obtained 375 adjective clusters with cardinality varying from 1 to 9. Since these clusters were derived from our biomedical dataset, they comprised of domain-specific adjectives, which are quite unfamiliar even to native English speakers. We manually partitioned the clusters into two sets: (i) containing domain-specific words, and (ii) containing words used in day-to-day English (henceforth referred to as "regular" terms). Examples of clusters from both sets are summarized in Table 3. The clusters we obtain look reasonable, grouping together adjectives that pertain to the same scale. The first cluster of domain-specific adjectives qualifies the nouns corresponding to different types of protein with varying degree of specificity, the second cluster contains different qualifications of a tumor, and adjectives in the third cluster qualify different parts of a living cell. For the regular adjective clusters, the clusters look intuitive too, except for the first cluster. The adjectives *male* and *female* are not scalar, but match the structural patterns, and are grouped together with adjectives describing age qualifications, due to a strong context overlap in which these words are used.

| |
|---|
| **Clusters of domain-specific adjectives** |
| cytokine, gm-csf, ifn-gamma, il-10, il-12, il-2 |
| benign, malignant, metastatic, neoplastic, squamous |
| mitochondrial, nuclear, ribosomal |
| **Clusters of regular adjectives** |
| female, male, middle-aged, older, young, younger |
| accurate, precise, reliable, reproducible, robust |
| additive, insignificant, negligible |

Table 3: Examples of automatically derived adjective clusters from PubMed abstracts.

We randomly sampled 25 clusters from each set, "regular adjectives" and "domain-specific adjectives", for our evaluation. We evaluated the clustering quality of the regular adjectives using the exact same approach as described in Section 4.1. We obtained a clustering accuracy of 86.26% for 25 clusters across 101 regular adjectives. This is substantially better than the performance of clustering in the previous experiment. We believe that this is due to the fact that the adjectives in the dataset used in the previous experiment originate from WordNet and contain many words (e.g., *handsome*, *crazy*, *spicy*), which are less likely to be found in scientific abstracts. Therefore, the context vectors learnt for these words are possibly less accurate compromising the clustering quality.

For the domain-specific adjectives, the annotations require specialized skills. PubMed hosts scientific articles from different disciplines of biological sciences. We obtained annotations from three annotators specializing in disciplines of Biomedical Informatics, Biochemistry, and Nursing. To create the gold standard, a word was retained or discarded from a cluster if two or more annotators agreed on it. We obtained a clustering accuracy of 64.3% for 25 clusters across 101 domain-specific adjectives.

### 5.2 Ranking

We obtained gold standard annotations for ranking using AMT for these 25 "regular adjective" clusters derived from the PubMed corpus using the exact same methodology as described in Section 4.2. The strength counts for these adjectives were also derived from the PubMed corpus. We obtained an accuracy of 70.37% across 109 pairs, indicating a similar level of performance to WordNet-based clusters.

Our expert annotators for the domain-specific adjectives faced problems in assessing an ordering between adjectives in a cluster. They report that for majority of the clusters, the ordering of the words would vary given the context. For example, consider the following modifications of the domain specific adjectives of the third cluster in Table 3: ribosomal particles, mitochondiral compartments and nuclear compartments, representing different parts of a living cell. If we consider "number of" as the relation in context, we get (*ribosomal* > *mitochondrial* > *nuclear*) as an ordering since number of ribosomal particles is greater than number of mitochondrial compartments, and number of mitochondrial compartments is greater than number of nuclear compartments. However, if we consider "size of" as the context, the ordering is reversed.

## 6 Extension to adverbs

A novelty of our approach is that we can also apply the technique to other parts of speech (e.g., adverbs). The structural patterns we describe in Section 3.1 also enable us to extract candidate scalar adverbs. We follow a similar approach to adjectives: extract adverbs, derive strength counts and rank them using the MILP.

| **Clusters of domain-specific adverbs** |
| --- |
| anteriorly, caudally, distally, proximally |
| chromosomally, clonally, genetically, phenotypically |
| neonatally, prenatally, postnatally |
| **Clusters of regular adverbs** |
| always, certainly, inevitably, invariably, universally |
| marginally, modestly, slightly, somewhat |
| excessively, inappropriately, overly |

Table 4: Examples of automatically derived adverb clusters from PubMed abstracts.

### 6.1 Clustering

We used CBOW vectors to perform clustering and derived $k = 300$ and $d = 250$ using the approach described in Section 5. As with the adjective clusters, we found that there were also domain-specific adverbs, illustrated in Table 4. Again, the clusters obtained look reasonable. The first cluster of domain-specific adverbs describes relative position of a body part, the second cluster corresponds to adverbs describing identity of a gene that may have an observable effect, the third cluster represents temporal descriptions that relate an event to child birth. The clustering of regular adverbs is accurate, except for the third cluster where *inappropriately* was found to be an outlier based on our annotations. We followed a similar approach to the adjective experiment, creating two partitions for domain-specific and regular adverbs and sampling 25 clusters from each. Annotations for regular adverbs were obtained from AMT while annotations for domain-specific adverbs were obtained from 3 domain experts. The annotation process for both clusters of adverbs was identical to that of adjectives. We obtained a micro-averaged accuracy of 89.36% for 25 clusters across 104 regular adverbs and a 53.8% for 25 clusters across 89 domain-specific adverbs.

| Accuracy | POS | Examples |
|---|---|---|
| Good | Adj | serious<br>$<$ life-threatening<br>$<$ fatal |
| Good | Adv | considerably<br>$<$ significantly<br>$<$ dramatically |
| Average | Adj | common<br>$<$ frequent<br>$=$ prevalent |
| Average | Adv | slightly<br>$<$ modestly<br>$<$ marginally |
| Bad | Adj | useful $<$ helpful |
| Bad | Adv | continuously $=$ regularly |

Table 5: Example rankings for adjectives and adverbs from PubMed data.

### 6.2 Ranking

As in the case of adjectives, our annotators for domain-specific adverbs faced a challenge in ranking adverbs due to lack of context. Therefor we do not report results on ranking of adverbs. We obtained gold standard annotations for ranking using AMT for 25 clusters of regular adverbs derived from the PubMed corpus, using the exact same methodology as described in Section 4.2. The strength counts for these adverbs were also derived from the PubMed corpus. We obtained an accuracy of 71.00% across 38 pairs – a performance similar to the adjectives. However, we observe that there are a large number of pairs for which there are no strength counts, and the MILP does not generate a ranking. Table 5 shows sample results for ranking adjectives and adverbs from the PubMed data.

## 7 Limitations and future work

We present an approach to gradable modifier ordering that replaces WordNet-based clusters with automatically derived word clusters, replaces lexical patterns with structural patterns, and show that the approach has utility for not only discovering adjective patterns but also adverb patterns in biomedical text. We observe that while automatic ranking based on semantic intensity can be successful established between regular terms, doing so for domain-specific terms requires knowledge of context.

We plan to expand the structure patterns derived from the lexical patterns of de Melo and Bansal (2013), looking for new patterns that could be more suited for adverbs. We also plan to investigate soft clustering algorithms such as (Pereira et al., 1993) that may allow us to model polysemous words better. Furthermore, recent studies have compared traditional vectors against embedded vectors (such as the CBOW vectors used in this study) for different lexical semantic tasks (Levy and Goldberg, 2014; Baroni et al., 2014), which suggests that such a comparison for our clustering task could be insightful.

Our experimental results show that automatic clustering of gradable words produces promising results. However, we also observe that with domain-specific words, context is important for establishing a ranking between words that is based on semantic intensity. Thus, rather than clustering adjectives or adverbs in isolation, a joint with the clustering of nouns or verbs with which they occur is a possible direction of research. Finally, studies deriving a ranking based on semantic intensities are limited to unigrams belonging to different parts of speech. Our future work would focus on performing a similar task on bigrams consisting of adverb-adjective pairs (e.g., *somewhat unclear* $<$ *quite hard* $<$ *very difficult*) that exhibit properties of gradability.

## Acknowledgements

We would like to thank Mohit Bansal and Gerard de Melo for providing the implementation and results of the experiments from their previous work. Research reported in this publication was supported by the National Library of Medicine of the National Institutes of Health under award number R01LM011116. The content is solely the responsibility of the authors and does not necessarily represent the official views of the National Institutes of Health.

## References

David Arthur and Sergei Vassilvitskii. 2007. K-means++: The advantages of careful seeding. In *Proceedings of the Eighteenth Annual ACM-SIAM Sympo-*

*sium on Discrete Algorithms*, SODA '07, pages 1027–1035, Philadelphia, PA, USA. Society for Industrial and Applied Mathematics.

Collin F. Baker, Charles J. Fillmore, and John B. Lowe. 1998. The Berkeley FrameNet project. In *Proceedings of the 36th Annual Meeting of the Association for Computational Linguistics and 17th International Conference on Computational Linguistics - Volume 1*, ACL '98, pages 86–90, Stroudsburg, PA, USA.

Mohit Bansal, Kevin Gimpel, and Karen Livescu. 2014. Tailoring continuous word representations for dependency parsing. In *Proceedings of the Annual Meeting of the Association for Computational Linguistics*.

Marco Baroni, Georgiana Dinu, and Germán Kruszewski. 2014. Don't count, predict! A systematic comparison of context-counting vs. context-predicting semantic vectors. In *Proceedings of the 52nd Annual Meeting of the Association for Computational Linguistics (Volume 1: Long Papers)*, pages 238–247. Association for Computational Linguistics.

Thorsten Brants and Alex Franz. 2006. The Google Web 1T 5-gram Version 1.1.

Ido Dagan, Oren Glickman, and Bernardo Magnini. 2006. The PASCAL recognising textual entailment challenge. In Joaquin Quiñonero Candela, Ido Dagan, Bernardo Magnini, and Florence DAlché-Buc, editors, *Proceedings of the First International Conference on Machine Learning Challenges: Evaluating Predictive Uncertainty Visual Object Classification, and Recognizing Textual Entailment*, volume 3944 of *Lecture Notes in Computer Science*, pages 177–190, Berlin, Heidelberg, April.

Marie-Catherine de Marneffe, Christopher D. Manning, and Christopher Potts. 2010. "Was it good? It was provocative". Learning the meaning of scalar adjectives. In *Proceedings of the 48th Annual Meeting of the Association for Computational Linguistics*, pages 167–176, July.

Gerard de Melo and Mohit Bansal. 2013. Good, Great, Excellent: Global Inferences of Semantic Intensities. *Transactions of the Association of Computational Linguistics*, 1(July):279–290.

Christiane Fellbaum. 1998. *WordNet: An Electronic Lexical Database*. Bradford Books.

Vasileios Hatzivassiloglou and Kathleen R. McKeown. 1993. Towards the automatic identification of adjectival scales. In *Proceedings of the 31st Annual meeting on Association for Computational Linguistics*, pages 172–182, Morristown, NJ, USA, June.

Christopher Kennedy. 2007. Vagueness and grammar: the semantics of relative and absolute gradable adjectives. *Linguistics and Philosophy*, 30(1):1–45, March.

Joo-Kyung Kim and Marie-Catherine de Marneffe. 2013. Deriving Adjectival Scales from Continuous Space Word Representations. *Proceedings of the 2013 Conference on Empirical Methods in Natural Language Processing*, pages 1625–1630.

Dan Klein and Christopher D. Manning. 2003. Accurate Unlexicalized Parsing. In *Proceedings of the 41st Annual Meeting on Association for Computational Linguistics - Volume 1*, ACL '03, pages 423–430, Stroudsburg, PA, USA.

Roger Levy and Galen Andrew. 2006. Tregex and Tsurgeon: tools for querying and manipulating tree data structures. In *Proceedings of the Fifth International Conference on Language Resources and Evaluation*, pages 2231–2234. Citeseer.

Omer Levy and Yoav Goldberg. 2014. Linguistic Regularities in Sparse and Explicit Word Representations. In *Proceedings of the Eighteenth Conference on Computational Language Learning*, Batimore, Maryland USA. Association for Computational Linguistics.

2008. LingPipe 4.1.0.

Tomas Mikolov, Ilya Sutskever, Kai Chen, Greg S. Corrado, and Jeff Dean. 2013. Distributed Representations of Words and Phrases and their Compositionality. In *Advances in Neural Information Processing Systems*, pages 3111–3119.

Bo Pang and Lillian Lee. 2008. Opinion mining and sentiment analysis. *Found. Trends Inf. Retr.*, 2(1-2):1–135, January.

Fernando Pereira, Naftali Tishby, and Lillian Lee. 1993. Distributional clustering of English words. In *Proceedings of the 31st Annual Meeting on Association for Computational Linguistics*, ACL '93, pages 183–190, Stroudsburg, PA, USA.

Josef Ruppenhofer, Michael Wiegand, and Jasper Brandes. 2014. Comparing methods for deriving intensity scores for adjectives. In *14th Conference of the European Chapter of the Association for Computational Linguistics*, pages 117–122, Gothenburg, Sweden.

Edward Sapir. 1944. Grading, A Study in Semantics. *Philosophy of Science*, 11(2):93–116.

Peter F Schulam and Christiane Fellbaum. 2010. Automatically determining the semantic gradation of German adjectives. *Semantic Approaches to Natural Language Proceedings, Saarbruecken, Germany*, page 163.

Vera Sheinman, Takenobu Tokunaga, Isaac Julien, Peter Schulam, and Christiane Fellbaum. 2012. Refining WordNet adjective dumbbells using intensity relations. In *Sixth International Global Wordnet Conference*, pages 330–337, Matsue, Japan.

Vera Sheinman, Christiane Fellbaum, Isaac Julien, Peter Schulam, and Takenobu Tokunaga. 2013. Large, huge or gigantic? Identifying and encoding intensity relations among adjectives in WordNet. *Language Resources and Evaluation*, 47(3):797–816, January.

Rion Snow, Brendan O'Connor, Daniel Jurafsky, and Andrew Y. Ng. 2008. Cheap and fast—but is it good?: evaluating non-expert annotations for natural language tasks. In *Proceedings of the 2008 Conference on Empirical Methods in Natural Language Processing*, pages 254–263, Honolulu, USA, October.

# Dialogue focus tracking for zero pronoun resolution

**Sudha Rao**[1,3], **Allyson Ettinger**[2], **Hal Daumé III**[1,3], **Philip Resnik**[2,3]
[1]Computer Science, [2]Linguistics, [3]UMIACS
University of Maryland
raosudha@cs.umd.edu, aetting@umd.edu, hal@cs.umd.edu, resnik@umd.edu

## Abstract

We take a novel approach to zero pronoun resolution in Chinese: our model explicitly tracks the flow of focus in a discourse. Our approach, which generalizes to *deictic* references, is not reliant on the presence of overt noun phrase antecedents to resolve to, and allows us to address the large percentage of "non-anaphoric" pronouns filtered out in other approaches. We furthermore train our model using readily available parallel Chinese/English corpora, allowing for training without hand-annotated data. Our results demonstrate improvements on two test sets, as well as the usefulness of linguistically motivated features.

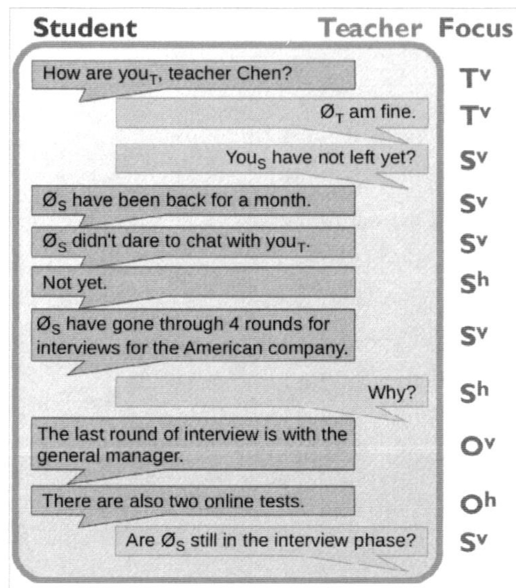


Figure 1: A conversation between a student and a teacher. The text has been translated from Mandarin, but zero pronouns are retained and indexed with their referent: (T)eacher or (S)tudent.

## 1 Introduction

"Pro-drop" languages like Chinese, Japanese and Turkish allow for dropping of pronouns when the referents of those pronouns can be inferred. English is typically *not* pro-drop, but is unusual in that regard: two thirds of languages documented in WALS (Haspelmath et al., 2005) can be categorized as pro-drop. In such languages, sentences are frequently characterized by "zero pronouns": gaps in the sentence which in English would hold an overt pronoun. In some languages, verbal morphology or clitics elsewhere in the sentence are sufficient to resolve the ambiguity of dropped pronouns; in other languages, there is *no* overt marking at all in the sentence and the referent of the dropped pronoun must be resolved using pragmatic information.

Our work departs from mainstream work on zero pronoun resolution in that we focus primarily on the resolution of *deictic* zero pronouns. Unlike an *anaphoric* zero pronoun (Section 2), whose reference must be specified by a noun phrase occurring previously in the text, a *non-anaphoric* zero pronoun refers to an entity that is salient from larger units of discourse (such as full sentences or passages) or from the extralinguistic environment (outside of the text altogether). Although anaphoric zero pronoun resolution has been the focus of most past work (Yeh and Chen, 2007; Chen and Ng, 2014), 50% or fewer of zero pronouns in natural Chinese text are anaphoric (Zhao and Ng, 2007; Kong and Zhou, 2010). Our approach allows for generalization to non-anaphoric pronouns, focusing in particular on *deictic* non-anaphoric zero pronouns, which



*Human Language Technologies: The 2015 Annual Conference of the North American Chapter of the ACL*, pages 494–503,
Denver, Colorado, May 31 – June 5, 2015. 

refer to salient entities in the environment (such as the speaker, hearer or pragmatically accessible referent) without requiring any introduction in the preceding text. Figure 1 shows an example conversation in which zero pronouns are frequently used to refer to speaker or listener, and would be translated to English as "I" or "you."

We propose a model for resolving deictic zero pronouns that draws inspiration from ideas in Centering Theory (Grosz et al., 1995): discourses tend to settle on a particular *focus* for a time, before switching. Furthermore, we presume that *when* a switch happens, there is likely to be an overt cue of this. For example, in Figure 1, the initial focus on **T** is signaled with the overt second person pronoun in the first utterance; the switch of focus to **S** in the third utterance is also signaled by an overt "you." However, at that point, the focus remains on **S** for several utterances until "The last round..." at which point it switches away from the speakers. It is brought back to **S** in the last utterance, which can be inferred from the fact that **S** is the most recent focus that fits the required semantic constraints.

To account for these phenomena, **we develop a novel sequential model for zero pronoun resolution that explicitly tracks the conversation focus in a dialogue** (Section 3). We test, using data from Chinese SMS ("texting") dialogues, the hypothesis that our model can predict the identity of pronouns (at a granularity of the person attribute: first, second, or third person—with particular focus on first and second person) based on a variety of features of the utterance context, without reference to a particular antecedent (Section 4.3). In this way, we address a much higher percentage of the zero pronouns found in Chinese texts, and particularly in dialogue.

Our second contribution is to show that **one can train a zero pronoun resolution system using supervision coming from English translations of the Chinese text** (Section 2.2). This obviates the need for expensive linguistic annotation of Chinese and allows us to use plentiful parallel data to train our model. Our results confirm that even though this "translation as annotation" process is noisy, it is still possible to learn on large amounts of "bronze standard" data.

## 2 Linguistic motivation

Handling zero pronouns in Chinese (or other pro-drop language) involves two separate tasks: (1) Zero pronoun identification: locating and marking the gaps corresponding to zero pronouns; and (2) Zero pronoun resolution: determining the entity referred to by the zero pronoun. Our focus is the latter task.

Zero pronoun resolution, like general pronoun resolution, is almost universally approached as a problem of linking a pronoun to an overt noun phrase antecedent in the text. However, while some zero pronouns do have overt noun phrase antecedents, many other zero pronouns do not. In fact, (Zhao and Ng, 2007) report that just 52% of zero pronouns in their training set (and 46% of zero pronouns in their test set) are "anaphoric." Kong and Zhou (Kong and Zhou, 2010) report just 41%. Some zero pronouns fail to link to an antecedent because they refer to facts or events described by larger phrases or full sentences earlier in the text, preventing coreference with a single noun phrase. Other zero pronouns, particularly in dialogue settings, are *deictic*, pointing to salient entities in the environment without requiring introduction by an overt mention in the text.

### 2.1 Dialogue focus

A central principle of document cohesion that underlies frameworks such as Centering Theory (Grosz et al., 1995) states that discourses tend to settle on a particular focus for a time, before eventually switching to a new one. The status of a particular focus within this flow of discourse is typically signaled by the form of the expression chosen to point to it. When a focus is introduced (or returned to), a full (overt) noun phrase is generally used to indicate it. While that entity remains in focus, subsequent mentions can be realized with less explicit forms. In English, these less explicit forms are overt pronouns. In Chinese (and pro-drop languages more generally), these focus continuations are generally realized as zero pronouns.

We see in this example an illustration of these discourse principles:

1. In pro-drop languages (Chinese), overt pronouns introduce switches in focus, while zero

pronouns are used while an established focus continues.
2. In non-pro-drop languages (English), overt pronouns serve the focus-continuation function.
3. There are "deictic" exceptions to these rules, licensed by environmental salience of the referent and inferable from the meaning of the utterance (final question of the example).

Importantly, these continuations and switches of foci occur for the most part at the level of the syntactic clause. This is thus the level at which we model, assigning labels to individual clauses, which will in turn indicate the identity of any dropped subject pronoun in that clause.[1] In identifying focus, we remain at the granularity of the "person" attribute (first, second, or third person). This is the most relevant granularity for deictic pronoun resolution, as the intent is to capture the alternation between speakers within that dialogue (first and second person), along with switches of focus to any referents external to the dialogue (third person).

### 2.2 Translation as annotation

Currently, most state-of-the-art machine learning systems for Chinese zero pronoun resolution are supervised, requiring manually resolved pronouns for training. We hypothesize comparable distribution between zero pronouns in a pro-drop language, and overt pronouns in a *non*-pro-drop language. More specifically, because non-pro-drop languages lack zero pronouns, the discourse functions that are served by zero pronouns in pro-drop languages *must* in non-pro-drop languages be served by overt pronouns.

To be more concrete, the original Mandarin SMS conversation from Figure 1 is reproduced in Table 1, together with a human translation into English. Indeed, we see in the example in Figure 1 that the zero pronouns on the Chinese side correspond to overt pronouns on the English side. For this reason we make use of a parallel (Chinese/English) corpus for training of our sequence labeling model, deriving the identities of missing pronouns from the English translation of the Chinese text rather than from coreference relations with antecedents in the Chinese text. Our model thus does not rely on the availability of hand-annotated data for training.

[1]Although Mandarin does license dropped object pronouns, we focus in this paper only on subject pronouns, as the syntactic subject is (a) more consistently dropped in Mandarin, and (b) more tightly tied to the notion of focus of conversation that motivates our model; see also a discussion of the centering hierarchy in Chinese (Wang, 2011). Relatedly, we filter out possessive pronouns in subject position, as they do not point to the topical entity represented by the full noun phrase.

## 3 Our focus tracking model

Given a Chinese dialogue, our goal is to identify zero pronouns and resolve them either as deictic (first or second person) or non-deictic (third person). We use off-the-shelf tools for the identification of the zero pronouns (described in Section 4.1) and focus on the *resolution* task.

In our implementation, we *jointly* predict the *focus* and identify the number of the pronoun that would be used. For instance, when **S** is speaking about herself, we consider this a "**1**" label; when **S** is speaking about her conversation partner, we consider this a "**2**" label. This numbering corresponds to which pronominal form would be required in English.[2]

### 3.1 Supervision via bronze standard data

We obtain "bronze" standard (as opposed to "gold" standard) data by looking at human-produced English translations of Chinese utterances, such as those seen in Table 1. Our label set consists of two properties: the *person* being referred to (first person, second person or third person), and whether the reference is overt or not (visible or hidden). The "visible" three labels correspond to clauses in which an overt subject pronoun appears *on the English side.* Chinese clauses bearing this label may have an overt or a zero pronoun subject—if the Chinese side contains a zero pronoun subject, then this label will be used to determine the correct person attribute (first, second, or third) of the unseen pronoun.

**1v:** Overt English first person pronoun: "I" or "we"
**2v:** Overt English second person pronoun: "you"
**3v:** Overt English third person pronoun: "he", "she", "it", "they"

[2]We ignore morphological issues in English dealing with possession and grammatical role, since these are exogenous to the resolution task.

| | Original Mandarin | English Translation | Label |
|---|---|---|---|
| 1) **Student** | 陈老师你还好吗 | How are you, Teacher Chen? | 2v |
| 2) **Teacher** | ∅ 好啊，你还没走？ | I am fine. You have not left yet? | 1v, 2v |
| 3) **Student** | ∅ 回来有一个月 ∅ 不敢给你说话 | I have been back for a month.<br>I didn't dare to chat with you. | 1v, 1v |
| 4) **Student** | 没呢 | Not yet. | 1h |
| 5) **Student** | 美国的面试 ∅ 进行了 4 轮了 | I have gone through 4 rounds of interviews for the American (company). | 1v |
| 6) **Teacher** | 为什么 | Why? | 2h |
| 7) **Student** | 最后一轮是跟总经理 | The last round of interview is with the general manager. | 3v |
| 8) **Student** | 还有两次网上测验 | There are also two online tests. | 3h |
| 9) **Teacher** | ∅ 还在面试阶段吗 | Are you still in the interview phase? | 2v |

Table 1: Sample Chinese SMS conversation with English translation and derived labels.

However, there are plenty of utterances (e.g., Table 1 lines 4 and 6) in which the English translation does not contain an overt subject. This can happen in English in imperative constructions, (some) questions, and general informal communication.[3] In these cases, we introduce "hidden" person labels whose role is to carry forward the focus from the previous utterance. For instance, in utterance 4, even though there is no subject on the English side, we carry forward the fact that the most-recent referent was "first person" and denote this with "1h."

Because we are jointly modeling the focus shift and the pronoun realization aspects, when the speaker shifts, the "hidden" person must flip. For example, in utterance (5) the **Student** overtly refers to herself, yielding a label of "1v." The next utterance is by the **Teacher** but lacks an English subject. The focus remains on the **Student** and therefore this utterance is labeled "2h" meaning that the focus is on the *other* speaker, and it is non-overt in English.

**1h:** subject being continued is first person
**2h:** subject being continued is second person
**3h:** subject being continued is anything else

Finally, we introduced a seventh label for instances in which no overt subject pronoun appears on the English side, and no focus has yet been established from prior clauses (this applies only at the beginning of a discourse).

**None:** no subject and no focus yet established

[3]This can also happen due to imperfect zero pronoun identification (Section 4.1).

In Table 1, the rightmost column shows the label assignment for the sample SMS exchange. (The utterances on lines 2 and 3 contain two clauses each, and thus two labels each.)

### 3.2 Features

We included in our model the following features. Note that these features are based solely on the *Chinese side*. Linguistic motivations for each feature category are described.

**Subject continuation:** a value indicating the *person* (1, 2, 3) of the most recent overt NP that was a direct descendent of an IP node (the most recent overt NP in structural subject position—including, if overt, the subject of the current clause). *The most recent overt NP subject is a strong candidate for coreference with a zero pronoun. This feature comes closest to attempting antecedent selection.*

**Verb:** the first verb in the VP that is sister to the subject NP (the VP of which that NP is the subject). *The nature of the verb can provide information relevant to inferring the identity of deictic forms.* For example: the Chinese verb *guji* ("reckon") is intuitively biased toward first-person subject; our training data accordingly show 68% of clauses with *guji* as verb feature were assigned first-person subject labels.

**Participant index:** a value indicating the index of the conversational participant. *To capture regularities, if any exist, in the pronoun use of a speaker.*

**Participant switch:** a binary value indicating whether the current utterance represents a change of speaker relative to the previous clause. *Switches in* *speaker may, particularly in tandem with other features, be informative about topic.*

**Object (downstream):** the direct object of the VP sister to the subject (if any). *This feature exploits the fact that pronouns occurring as direct objects within a clause cannot be the same as the (zero) pronoun in subject position of that clause.*

**Has question particle:** a binary value indicating whether the clause contains a) a question particle or *wh*-word, or b) a question mark. *This feature is likely to be a strong indicator of that the subject pronoun is* not *first person (also used by (Chen and Ng, 2013)).* For example, in our training data we found that only 16% of the clauses with question particle were marked with first person label i.e. 1v or 1h.

**Bag of words:** all words occurring in the clause. *Apart from the verb, other words can also be highly informative about the nature of the subject.*

**Bag of parts of speech:** all parts of speech occurring in the clause. *The structural make-up of clause may be informative about focus, for instance in the case of passive or possessive constructions.*

**Hidden subject particles:** a feature indicating whether the clause consists of a list of phrases consistently tagged with empty categories on the Chinese side, but consistently translated without subject pronouns on the English side (thus likely to correspond to labels 1h-3h). *This feature is intended to help the model in recognizing clauses consistently corresponding to "hidden" labels.*

In addition, for the features that consist of sequence (bag of words, bag of part of speech, object, etc.) we additionally compute bigrams and trigrams.

### 3.3 Structured prediction

We cast the above model as a sequence labeling problem over visible and hidden labels. We consider each conversation segment in the SMS as an input data sequence $\boldsymbol{x} = \langle x_1, x_2, \ldots, x_n \rangle$ where each $x_i$ corresponds to a clause in Chinese. Each clause in Chinese is assigned a label from the label space $Y$ = {1v, 2v, 3v, 1h, 2h, 3h, none}. The task then is to assign labels $\boldsymbol{y} = \langle y_1, y_2, \ldots, y_n \rangle$ to the input data sequence from the label space $Y$ based on the features described in Section 3.2. At training time we assign labels to the input sequence using the "bronze standard" method described in Section 3.1.

To train the sequence labeling model, we use an online variant of the DAgger imitation learning algorithm (Ross et al., 2011) as implemented in the Vowpal Wabbit machine learning library (Langford et al., 2007; Daumé III et al., 2014). DAgger, like its predecessor SEARN (Daumé III et al., 2009), solves structured prediction problems by transforming them into sequential decision making problems. In the case of sequence labeling, the natural order for sequence decision making is left-to-right. At test time, inference is performed greedily. At training time, the learning algorithm attempts to balance between training on "oracle" states (prefixes of decisions made optimally according to the true labels) and training on "system" states (prefixes of decisions made sub-optimally according to the learned model). The online variant of DAgger balances this trade-off by slowly transitioning from making past decisions optimally to making them using the currently learned predictor.

## 4 Experiments

Our goal in our experiments is to answer the following questions:

1. How well does the bronze-standard annotation capture the underlying truth? (Section 4.2).
2. Is our model able to leverage both dialogue structure and semantic content to accurately resolve pronouns? (Section 4.3)
3. How important are the different components in our model in making effective predictions? (Section 4.4)

In the following sections, we describe the experiments we perform aimed at answering these questions. First, we describe the data we use for experimentation.

### 4.1 Experimental setup

For training our focus-tracking model, we use Chinese-English parallel data from the SMS/chat domain available as part of training data used in the Machine Translation task under the DARPA BOLT project. The training data consisted of $117k$ sentences. We test our model on heldout SMS/Chat data consisting of 1152 sentences (hand-annotated,

|  | Bronze Training | SMS Test | OntoNotes Test |
|---|---|---|---|
| **# tokens** | $1,007,722$ | $8104$ | $108,531$ |
| **# sents** | $129,190$ | $1152$ | $9607$ |
| **# dialog** | $3309$ | $34$ | $257$ |
| **# types** | $26,519$ | $1747$ | $4753$ |

Table 2: Dataset statistics; numbers are for the Chinese side of the data. English has 25% more tokens and roughly as many types.

as described in Section 4.2), and on telephone conversation data from the OntoNotes corpus (Hovy et al., 2006), consisting of 5000 sentences. Full data statistics are provided in Table 2.

We perform zero pronoun identification using the method of (Cai et al., 2011), which automatically recovers empty categories corresponding to dropped pronouns, integrating these empty categories into syntactic parses. Syntactic parses were obtained with the Berkeley parser (Petrov and Klein, 2007). These parses were then used to split the Chinese utterances into single-clause units, based on IP and CP clausal nodes. These clauses were aligned with clauses in the English translation, which were used to determine the identity of the clausal subject, for extracting the 1v, 2v, ... label for each utterance.[4]

For our machine learning systems, we use Vowpal Wabbit (Langford et al., 2007) with default hyperparameter settings. We train on 75% of the training data and retain 25% as development data on which to perform early stopping. We run 20 iterations by default and take the parameters with best development performance based on sequence labeling accuracy.

### 4.2 Gold standard test set

Although we can use "bronze standard" annotations for learning, evaluating against a bronze standard is not directly useful. Therefore, we annotated our test set (1152 utterances) by hand. In particular, for the SMS/chat test set, we recruited three linguistically-informed native Mandarin speakers to annotate Chinese clauses containing empty categories. The clauses were labeled with a person number (1,2,3) when the empty category corresponded to such a pronoun; or "none" in spurious cases.[5]

[4]Sometimes English syntactic parses were not well-aligned with the Chinese IP/CP nodes; in practice, we split the English utterances based on end-of-clause punctuation and aligned Chinese and English clauses based on a simple order heuristic.

| Pronoun | Precision | Recall | F-measure |
|---|---|---|---|
| **1p** | 0.75 | 0.43 | 0.55 |
| **2p** | 0.61 | 0.32 | 0.42 |
| **3p** | 0.52 | 0.45 | 0.49 |
| **Micro-avg** | 0.62 | 0.41 | 0.50 |

Table 3: Bronze vs Gold labels

In our annotated data,[6] 32% of identified zero pronouns were first person, 17% were second person, 25% were third person and 26% do not have a referent (were spurious). Of the correctly identified zero pronouns, a majority of pronouns (about 2/3) are deictic: referring either to the speaker or listener. The remainder are third person and mostly anaphoric.[7] Since the annotators labeled the empty categories obtained from an automatic zero pronoun identification method (Cai et al., 2011), 26% spurious cases suggest that the accuracy of this method is only 74% on the SMS test data set.

We then used these annotations to evaluate our bronze standard label assignment method against the gold standard judgments. Table 3 shows the precision, recall and F-measure of the bronze annotations when evaluated against the gold annotations. We use micro-averaging to average the precision, recall and F-measure values against different sets. In this method we sum up the individual true positives (TP), false positives (FP), and false negatives (FN) of the system for different sets and then apply them to get the statistics. For example, precision across two sets 1 and 2 is given by (TP1 + TP2)/(TP1 + TP2 + FP1 + FP2). We can see a fairly significant discrepancy between our bronze labels and the gold labels. One major—and unfortunately inevitable—reason for this discrepancy is a high proportion of utterances in the English translation data which have

[5]Note that under this annotation scheme, our evaluations will be partially constrained by (Cai et al., 2011) performance, in including no zero pronouns that were missed by that method—however, use of the "none" label allows filtering out of any spuriously-identified zero pronouns.

[6]Annotations are available at www.umiacs.umd.edu/~raosudha/LDC2013E83-BOLT-P2R2-cmn-SMS-CHT-dev.annotated.

[7]In an in-person dialogue, a third person pronoun might be used in a deictic manner, as in "*She* is really smart" while pointing at someone. This rarely occurs in SMS/chat because there is no shared environment beyond the two dialogue participants.

been translated with the subject pronouns still absent. This is partially due to the casual nature of the text, and partially because the quality (fluency) of English translations in this data is at times dubious.

While there may be a systematicity to this kind of subject omission on the English side, this was not a factor taken into account by our human annotators. So while our own model may stand a chance at predicting "hidden" labels (no overt pronoun on English side) in such instances, the annotators will never assign a label of "none" to a location at which a pronoun could reasonably have been inserted.

### 4.3 Overall system efficacy

In this section we discuss the overall efficacy of our proposed method in comparison to a few alternatives. These alternatives are:

**Random guessing baseline.** A naïve system that makes predictions uniformly at random.

**Subject continuation baseline.** This is a rule-based approach that mimics the intuitions described in Section 2. In particular, for a Chinese utterance, we check whether the current utterance has an overt pronominal subject. If so, we assign a label of 1v, 2v or 3v depending on the person of this subject. If the current utterance has a non-pronominal subject, we assign 3h. Otherwise we "carry forward" the subject from the previous utterance, flipping the 1p/2p as necessary when the speaker changes; these are labeled as 1h, 2h or 3h.

**Minimal model baseline.** In the minimal model, we restrict our model to use just three features: participant index, participant switch and subject continuation feature. This is a machine learning variant of the rule-based subject continuation baseline.

**Oracle upper bound.** None of the proposed models can hope to achieve 100% accuracy on this task because the gold annotation data consists of 26% "no pronoun" cases. Since all of our approaches *must* predict a pronoun when a zero pronoun has been identified, their performance (namely, their precision) is upper-bounded away from 100%.

The summary of results (micro-averaged across 1p, 2p and 3p) are shown in Table 5. These results show that on both the SMS data (on which the model was developed) and the OntoNotes data (on which the model was applied blindly), our full model is able to substantially outperform the baselines. In fact, on OntoNotes, despite a potential domain mismatch (from SMS/chat to telephone conversations), our full model was the only baseline to beat random guessing! Across both data sets, the minimal model tends to have high precision and low recall; the behavior of the other approaches varies across the tasks. On the SMS/chat data, our model achieves a 14% relative improvement over the best baseline; on an OntoNotes data, a 50% relative improvement.

| | **SMS/chat Micro-average** | | | **OntoNotes Micro-average** | | |
|---|---|---|---|---|---|---|
| **System** | **Pre** | **Rec** | **F** | **Pre** | **Rec** | **F** |
| Random | 0.24 | 0.25 | 0.24 | 0.18 | 0.26 | 0.22 |
| Minimal | 0.42 | 0.23 | 0.30 | 0.30 | 0.07 | 0.11 |
| SubjCont | 0.32 | **0.42** | 0.36 | **0.31** | 0.15 | 0.20 |
| **Full Model** | **0.59** | 0.31 | **0.41** | 0.30 | **0.36** | **0.33** |
| Upper Bound | 0.74 | 1.00 | 0.85 | 0.55 | 1.00 | 0.71 |

Table 5: Summary of results for different comparator models against the gold standard labels from SMS data (left) and OntoNotes (right).

More specific breakdowns of performance by different pronouns (1p, 2p and 3p) are shown for the subject continuation baseline and the full model in Table 4. In these tables, we also report results when evaluated on the OntoNotes test set in these Tables. As we can see, the subject continuation baseline massively overpredicts third person pronouns in the SMS data, leading to an overall low score. In comparison, our model tends to have much higher precision (at the expense of recall) across the board on the SMS data, leading to a 14% relative improvement over the subject continuation baseline.

Since, to our knowledge, no prior work (see Section 5) has focused on deictic pronoun restoration, it is not possible to directly compare our results to previously published results. Although it is an apples-to-oranges comparison, a state-of-the-art *anaphoric* zero pronoun resolution system (Chen and Ng, 2014) achieves a precision of 13.3, a recall of 32.2 and an F-measure of 18.8 on the *telephone conversation* part of the OntoNotes data, but does so addressing the complementary problem of correctly choosing antecedents from previous overt noun phrases.

Another reasonable comparison would be with a

| Subject Continuation Baseline | | | | | | |
|---|---|---|---|---|---|---|
| | SMS Test set | | | OntoNotes Test set | | |
| **Pronoun** | **Precision** | **Recall** | **F-measure** | **Precision** | **Recall** | **F-measure** |
| **1p** | 0.43 | 0.28 | 0.34 | 0.29 | 0.08 | 0.13 |
| **2p** | 0.27 | 0.19 | 0.22 | 0.28 | 0.11 | 0.16 |
| **3p** | 0.29 | 0.75 | 0.42 | 0.32 | 0.21 | 0.25 |
| **Micro-avg** | 0.32 | 0.42 | 0.36 | 0.31 | 0.15 | 0.20 |

| Our Full Model | | | | | | |
|---|---|---|---|---|---|---|
| | SMS Test set | | | OntoNotes Test set | | |
| **Pronoun** | **Precision** | **Recall** | **F-measure** | **Precision** | **Recall** | **F-measure** |
| **1p** | 0.64 | 0.47 | 0.54 | 0.27 | 0.58 | 0.37 |
| **2p** | 0.55 | 0.21 | 0.31 | 0.25 | 0.23 | 0.24 |
| **3p** | 0.50 | 0.18 | 0.27 | 0.40 | 0.28 | 0.33 |
| **Micro-avg** | 0.59 | 0.31 | 0.41 | 0.30 | 0.36 | 0.33 |

Table 4: Results across different pronoun categories for (top) subject continuation and (bottom) our full model.

| | SMS/chat Micro-average | | | OntoNotes Micro-average | | |
|---|---|---|---|---|---|---|
| **System** | **Pre** | **Rec** | **F** | **Pre** | **Rec** | **F** |
| Minimal (M) | 0.42 | 0.23 | 0.30 | 0.30 | 0.07 | 0.11 |
| M + question | 0.44 | 0.23 | 0.30 | 0.31 | 0.07 | 0.12 |
| M + object | 0.43 | 0.23 | 0.30 | 0.30 | 0.07 | 0.12 |
| M + verb | 0.58 | 0.29 | 0.39 | 0.32 | 0.13 | 0.18 |
| M + pos | 0.52 | 0.30 | 0.38 | 0.23 | 0.27 | 0.25 |
| M + bow | 0.59 | 0.28 | 0.38 | 0.30 | 0.35 | 0.32 |
| **Full Model** | 0.59 | 0.31 | 0.41 | 0.30 | 0.36 | 0.33 |

Table 6: Summary of results for feature ablation against the gold standard labels from SMS data (left) and OntoNotes (right).

model trained on gold annotated data (instead of bronze data). Owing to cost, we could not obtain gold annotations for the full training set; however, a leave-one-out cross validation on the gold annotated test set (of SMS data) gave an F-measure of 0.47, versus 0.41 for our model trained on bronze labels. This suggests the noisy bronze labels are indeed useful for this task.

### 4.4 Feature ablations

In order to investigate the individual contributions of each of our features, we performed feature ablation experiments, pairing our Minimal Model with a single feature at a time and retraining the model with this pairing. The results of these experiments can be seen in Table 6. We see in this table that for the SMS data, the Verb feature creates the greatest improvement over the Minimal Model, followed by Bag of Words and Bag of POS. This supports the hypothesis that the verb is informative with respect to the nature of its subject, as are the other words of the clause, and their parts of speech. For the OntoNotes corpus, however, the Bag of Words feature performs best by a large margin. Interesting, although the Bag of Words features are clearly the most useful, the linguistically motivated features (verb/question) performing well supports our linguistic intuitions.

## 5 Discussion and related work

Past approaches to zero pronoun resolution focus exclusively on anaphoric zero pronouns approached as a task of antecedent identification. Almost all work makes use of syntactic structure, with differences primarily in how that structure is used. (Yeh and Chen, 2007) take a rule-based, Centering Theory-inspired approach based on a system of constraints to guide selection of zero pronoun antecedents. In the same year, (Zhao and Ng, 2007) introduced a supervised learning approach for both zero pronoun identification and antecedent selection based on engineered features; these engineered features were replaced with a tree-kernel by (Kong and Zhou, 2010), who jointly perform zero pronoun identification, anaphoricity determination, and antecedent selection. Recently, (Chen and Ng, 2013) built upon the model introduced by Zhao and Ng, introducing additional features and allowing coreference links between multiple zero pronouns. Chen and Ng (2013) also test their model on automatically identified zero pronouns and automatically generated parse trees, thus presenting the first end-to-end Chinese zero pronoun resolver.

These approaches are mostly complementary to our task, since they focus on resolving anaphoric zero pronouns (the minority!) while we focus on resolving deictic non-anaphoric zero pronouns. In particular, for an end-to-end system that resolves both deictic and anaphoric zero pronouns, one could first take our approach and whenever our model predicts "third person," which is often an anaphoric reference, one could apply one of these prior approaches for further reference resolution.

The only work we are aware of that does not require linguistically annotated data for zero pronoun resolution is that of (Chen and Ng, 2014). They hypothesize that zero pronouns and overt pronouns have *similar* distributions, and train an unsupervised model on *overt* pronouns and then apply this model to *zero* pronouns. This model performs on par with their previous (2013) supervised model. Despite this, their unsupervised model only agrees with their supervised model on 55% of zero pronoun antecedents, suggesting that this hypothesis is weak.

In particular, the complementarity of zero versus overt pronoun usage has been studied within various domains of linguistics. The Position of Antecedent Hypothesis (Carminati, 2002) states that null and overt pronouns have different antecedent selection preferences: null pronouns prefer antecedents in subject positions, while overt pronouns prefer antecedents in non-subject positions. This hypothesis has been supported by studies in a variety of pro-drop languages (e.g., (Alonso-Ovalle et al., 2002) (Kweon, 2011)). Switching of reference has been identified as one of the main constraints regulating use of zero versus overt pronouns in the variationist literature (see (Cameron, 1992) for sociolinguistic studies of the phenomenon in Spanish). The importance of topically-coherent discourse sequences—and the role of linguistic and extralinguistic indicators of such sequences—has also been examined in child language acquisition, e.g., (Rohde and Frank, 2014).

Our main result shows that although our bronze standard labels are noisy (Section 4.3), they are nonetheless useful for learning to resolve deictic pronouns. Moreover, one oft-heralded advantage of the translation-as-annotation scheme (Carpuat and Wu, 2007) is that it naturally integrates into a machine translation framework, since one is learning to predict precisely what is necessary for successful translation; evaluating whether this hypothesis is true is currently an open question. One limitation of our approach is the coarseness of the labeling granularity (1p, 2p, 3p). Our ultimate plan is to provide all possibilities (e.g., both singular and plural for 1p, weighted) to a machine translation system, and let other components (e.g., language model) determine selection. For now, we believe that there is significant value in intrinsic evaluation of our approach for a problem that has not previously received significant attention.

## Acknowledgments

This research was supported in part by the BOLT program of the Defense Advanced Research Projects Agency, Contract No. HR0012-12-C-0015. Any opinions, findings, conclusions or recommendations expressed in this paper are those of the authors and do not necessarily reflect the view of DARPA. The authors would like to thank three anonymous reviewers for providing helpful comments and also acknowledge people from Computational Linguistics and Information Processing (CLIP) lab at University of Maryland for helpful discussions.

## References

[Alonso-Ovalle et al.2002] Luis Alonso-Ovalle, Susana Fernández-Solera, Lyn Frazier, and Charles Clifton. 2002. Null vs. overt pronouns and the topic-focus articulation in Spanish. *Journal of Italian Linguistics*, 14:151–170.

[Cai et al.2011] Shu Cai, David Chiang, and Yoav Goldberg. 2011. Language-independent parsing with empty elements. In *Proceedings of the 49th Annual Meeting of the Association for Computational Linguistics: Human Language Technologies: short papers-Volume 2*, pages 212–216. Association for Computational Linguistics.

[Cameron1992] Richard Cameron. 1992. *Pronominal and null subject variation in Spanish: Constraints, dialects, and functional compensation*. Ph.D. thesis, University of Pennsylvania.

[Carminati2002] Maria Nella Carminati. 2002. *The processing of Italian subject pronouns*. Ph.D. thesis, University of Massachusetts at Amherst.

[Carpuat and Wu2007] Marine Carpuat and Dekai Wu.

2007. Improving statistical machine translation using word sense disambiguation. In *In EMNLP*.

[Chen and Ng2013] Chen Chen and Vincent Ng. 2013. Chinese zero pronoun resolution: Some recent advances. In *Proceedings of the 2013 Conference on Empirical Methods in Natural Language Processing*, pages 1360–1365.

[Chen and Ng2014] Chen Chen and Vincent Ng. 2014. Chinese zero pronoun resolution: An unsupervised probabilistic model rivaling supervised resolvers. In *Proceedings of the 2014 Conference on Empirical Methods in Natural Language Processing*. Association for Computational Linguistics.

[Daumé III et al.2009] Hal Daumé III, John Langford, and Daniel Marcu. 2009. Search-based structured prediction. *Machine learning*, 75(3):297–325.

[Daumé III et al.2014] Hal Daumé III, John Langford, and Stephane Ross. 2014. Efficient programmable learning to search. *arXiv preprint arXiv:1406.1837*.

[Grosz et al.1995] Barbara J Grosz, Scott Weinstein, and Aravind K Joshi. 1995. Centering: A framework for modeling the local coherence of discourse. *Computational linguistics*, 21(2):203–225.

[Haspelmath et al.2005] Martin Haspelmath, Matthew Dryer, David Gil, and Bernard Comrie, editors. 2005. *The World Atlas of Language Structures*. Oxford University Press.

[Hovy et al.2006] Eduard Hovy, Mitchell Marcus, Martha Palmer, Lance Ramshaw, and Ralph Weischedel. 2006. Ontonotes: the 90% solution. In *NAACL*.

[Kong and Zhou2010] Fang Kong and Guodong Zhou. 2010. A tree kernel-based unified framework for Chinese zero anaphora resolution. In *Proceedings of the 2010 Conference on Empirical Methods in Natural Language Processing*, pages 882–891. Association for Computational Linguistics.

[Kweon2011] Soo-Ok Kweon. 2011. Processing null and overt pronoun subject in ambiguous sentences in Korean. *International Journal of Linguistics*, 3(1).

[Langford et al.2007] John Langford, Lihong Li, and Alexander Strehl. 2007. Vowpal wabbit online learning project. http://hunch.net/?p=309.

[Petrov and Klein2007] S. Petrov and D. Klein. 2007. Improved inference for unlexicalized parsing. In *Proceedings of NAACL HLT 2007*, pages 404–411.

[Rohde and Frank2014] Hannah Rohde and Michael C Frank. 2014. Markers of topical discourse in child-directed speech. *Cognitive science*, 38(8):1634–1661.

[Ross et al.2011] Stéphane Ross, Geoff J. Gordon, and J. Andrew Bagnell. 2011. A reduction of imitation learning and structured prediction to no-regret online learning. In *Proceedings of the Workshop on Artificial Intelligence and Statistics (AIStats)*.

[Wang2011] Deliang Wang. 2011. *Anaphora Resolution in Chinese from the Centering Perspective*. Foreign Language Teaching and Research Press.

[Yeh and Chen2007] Ching-Long Yeh and Yi-Chun Chen. 2007. Zero anaphora resolution in Chinese with shallow parsing. *Journal of Chinese Language and Computing*, 17(1):41–56.

[Zhao and Ng2007] Shanheng Zhao and Hwee Tou Ng. 2007. Identification and resolution of Chinese zero pronouns: A machine learning approach. In *Proceedings of the 2007 Joint Conference on Empirical Methods on Natural Language Processing and Computational Natural Language Learning*, pages 541–550.

# Déjà Image-Captions: A Corpus of Expressive Descriptions in Repetition

**Jianfu Chen**[†] and **Polina Kuznetsova**[†] and **David S. Warren**[†] and **Yejin Choi**[‡]
Stony Brook University[†] University of Washington[‡]
{jianchen,pkuznetsova,warren}@cs.stonybrook.edu[†], yejin@cs.washington.edu[‡]

## Abstract

We present a new approach to harvesting a large-scale, high quality image-caption corpus that makes a better use of already existing web data with no additional human efforts. The key idea is to focus on *Déjà Image-Captions*: *naturally* existing image descriptions that are *repeated almost verbatim* – by more than one individual for different images. The resulting corpus provides association structure between 4 million images with 180K unique captions, capturing a rich spectrum of everyday narratives including figurative and pragmatic language. Exploring the use of the new corpus, we also present new conceptual tasks of visually situated paraphrasing, creative image captioning, and creative visual paraphrasing.

## 1 Introduction

The use of multimodal web data has been a recurring theme in many recent studies integrating language and vision, e.g., image captioning (Ordonez et al., 2011; Hodosh et al., 2013; Mason and Charniak, 2014; Kuznetsova et al., 2014), text-based image retrieval (Rasiwasia et al., 2010; Rasiwasia et al., 2007), and entry-level categorization (Ordonez et al., 2013; Feng et al., 2015).

However, much research integrating complex textual descriptions to date has been based on datasets that rely on substantial human curation or annotation (Hodosh et al., 2013; Rashtchian et al., 2010; Lin et al., 2014), rather than using the web data in the wild as is (Ordonez et al., 2011; Kuznetsova et al., 2014). The need for human curation limits the potential scale of the multimodal dataset. Without human curation, however, the web data introduces significant noise. In particular, everyday captions often contain extraneous information that is not directly relevant to what the image shows (Kuznetsova et al., 2013b; Hodosh et al., 2013).

In this paper, we present a new approach to harvesting a large-scale, high quality image-caption corpus that makes a better use of already existing web data with no additional human efforts. Figure 1 shows sample captions in the resulting corpus, e.g., *"butterfly resting on a flower"* and *"evening walk along the beach"*. Notably, some of these are figurative, e.g., *"rippled sky"* and *"sun is going to bed."*

The key idea is to focus on *Déjà Image-Captions*, i.e., naturally existing image captions that are *repeated almost verbatim* by more than one individual for different images. The hypothesis is that such captions represent common visual content across multiple images, hence are more likely to be free of unwanted extraneous information (e.g., specific names, time, or any other personal information) and better represent visual concepts. A surprising aspect of our study is that such a strict data filtration scheme can still result in a large-scale corpus; sifting through 760 million image-caption pairs, we harvest as many as 4 million image-caption pairs with 180K unique captions.

The resulting corpus, *Déjà Image Captions*, provides several unique properties that complement human-curated or crowd-sourced datasets. First, as our approach is fully automated, it can be readily applied to harvesting a new dataset from the ever changing multimodal web data. Indeed, a recent internet report estimates that billions of new photographs are being uploaded daily (Meeker, 2014). In contrast, human-annotated datasets are costly to scale to different domains.

Second, datasets that are harvested from the web



*Human Language Technologies: The 2015 Annual Conference of the North American Chapter of the ACL*, pages 504–514,
Denver, Colorado, May 31 – June 5, 2015. 

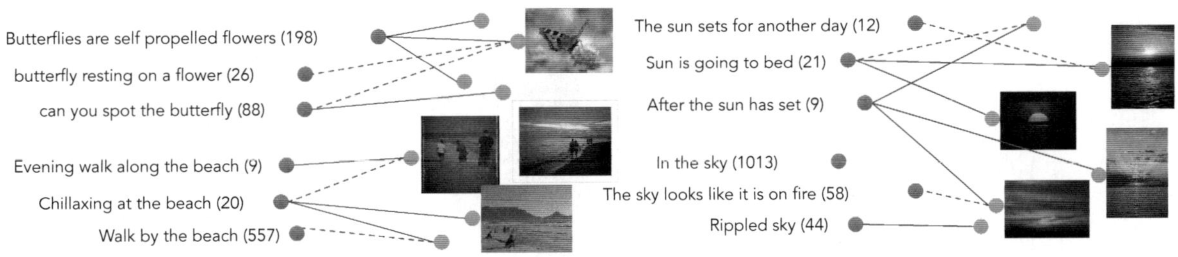


Figure 1: The image-caption association graph of *Déjà Image-Captions.* Solid lines represent original captions and dotted lines represent paraphrase captions. This corpus reflects a rich spectrum of everyday narratives people use in online activities including figurative language (e.g., *"Sun is going to bed"*), casual language (e.g., *Chillaxing at the beach"*), and conversational language (e.g., *"Can you spot the butterfly"*). The numbers in the parenthesis show the cardinality of images associated with each caption. Surprisingly, some of these descriptions are highly expressive, almost *creative*, and yet not unique — as all these captions are repeated almost verbatim by different individuals describing different images.

can complement those based on prompted human annotations. The latter in general are literal and mechanical readings of the visual scenes, while the former reflect a rich spectrum of natural language utterances in everyday narratives, including figurative, pragmatic, and conversational language, e.g., *"can you spot the butterfly"* (Figure 1). Therefore, this dataset offers unique opportunities for grounding figurative and metaphoric expressions using visual context.

In conjunction with the new corpus, publicly shared at `http://www.cs.stonybrook.edu/~jianchen/deja.html`, we also present three new tasks: *visually situated paraphrases* (§5); *creative image captioning* (§7), and *creative visual paraphrasing* (§7). The central algorithm component in addressing all these tasks is a simple and yet effective approach to image caption transfer that exploits the unique association structure of the resulting corpus (§3).

Our empirical results collectively demonstrate that when the web data is available at such scale, it is possible to obtain a large-scale, high-quality dataset with significantly less noise. We hope that our approach would be only one of the first attempts, and inspire future research to develop better ways of making use of ever-growing multimodal web data. Although it is unlikely that the automatically gathered datasets can completely replace the curated descriptions written in a controlled setting, our hope is to find ways to complement human annotated datasets in terms of both the scale and also the diversity of the domain and language.

The remainder of this paper is organized as follows. First we describe the dataset collection procedure and insights (§2). We then present a new approach to image caption transfer based on the association structure of the corpus (§3) followed by experimental results (§4). After then we present new conceptual tasks: *visual paraphrasing* (§5), *creative image captioning*, and *creative visual paraphrasing* (§7), interleaved with corresponding experimental results (§6, §8).

## 2 Dataset - Captions in Repetition

Our corpus consists of three components (Table 1):

**MAIN SET** The first step is to crawl as many image-caption pairs as possible. We use flickr.com search API to crawl 760 million pairs in total. The API allows searching images within a given time window, which enables exhaustive search over any time span. To ensure visual correspondence between images and captions, we set query terms using 693 most frequent nouns from the dataset of Ordonez et al. (2011), and systematically slide time windows over the year 2013.[1] For each image, we segment its title and the first line of its description into sentences.

The crawled dataset at this point includes a lot of noise in the captions. Hence we apply initial filtering rules to reduce the noise. We retain only those image-sentence pairs in which the sentence contains the query noun, and does not contain personal information indicators such as first-person pronouns. We

[1]To ensure enough number of images are associated with each caption, we further search captions with no more than 10 associated images across *all* years.

| set | # captions | # images |
|---|---|---|
| MAIN | 176,780 | 3,967,524 |
| PARAPHRASE | 7,570 human-annotated triples<br>353,560 auto-generated triples | |
| FIGURATIVE | 6,088 quotations | 180,185 |
| | 18,179 quotations + predicted figurative captions | 413,698 |

Table 1: Corpus Statistics

| | mean | std | 25% | 50% | 75% | max |
|---|---|---|---|---|---|---|
| #imgs. | 22.4 | 47.6 | 4 | 10 | 25 | 4617 |
| #tokens | 4.9 | 3.3 | 3 | 4 | 5 | 178 |

Table 2: Percentiles of the image count associated with each caption and the number of tokens in each caption.

want captions that are more than simple keywords, thus we discard trivial captions that do not include at least one verb, preposition, or adjective.

The next step is to find captions in repetition. For this purpose, we transform captions into *canonical forms*. We lemmatize all words, convert prepositions to a special token "IN"[2], and discard function words, numbers, and punctuations. For instance, "*The bird flies in blue sky*" and "*A bird flying into the blue sky*" have the same canonical form, "*bird fly IN blue sky*". We then retain only those captions that are repeated with respect to their canonical forms by more than one user, and for distinctly different images to ensure the generality of the captions.

Retaining only captions that are repeated verbatim may seem overly restrictive. Nonetheless, because we start with as many as 760 million pairs, this procedure yields nearly 180K unique captions associated with nearly 4M images.[3] What is more surprising, as will be shown later, is that many of these captions are highly expressive. Table 2 shows the distribution of the number of images associated with each caption.[4] The median and mean are 10 and 22.4 respectively, showing a high degree of connectivities between captions and images.

**PARAPHRASE SET** Our dataset collection procedure finds *one-to-many* relations between captions and images. To extend these relations to *many-to-many*, we introduce *visually-situated paraphrases* (or *visual paraphrases* for shorthand) (§5). A visual paraphrase relation is a triple $(i, c, p)$, where image $i$ has an original caption $c$, caption $p$ is the visual paraphrase for $c$ situated in image $i$. We collect visual paraphrases for sample images in our dataset, using both crowd sourcing (7,570 triples) and an automatic algorithm (353,560 triples) (see §5 for details). Figure 2 shows example visual paraphrases.

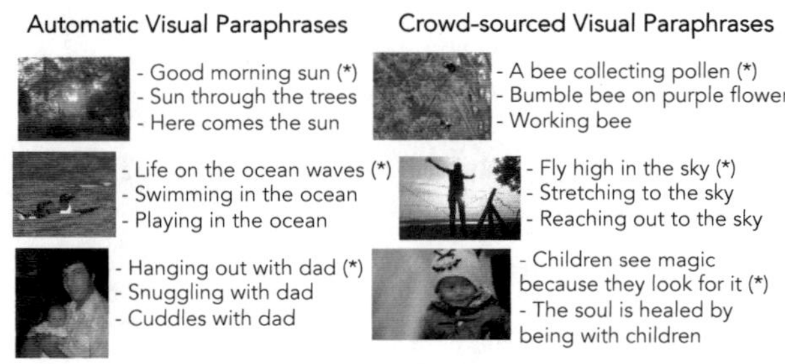


Figure 2: Example visual paraphrases: automatic (left) and crowd-sourced (right). The first caption marked with * indicates the original caption of the corresponding image. Some paraphrases are not strictly equivalent to the original caption if considered out of context, while they are pragmatically adequate paraphrases given the image.

| figure of speech | #caps. | example (#imgs.) |
|---|---|---|
| quotation&idiom | 70 | The early bird gets the worm (77) |
| personification | 43 | Meditating cat (38) |
| metaphor | 24 | Wine is the answer (7) |
| question | 18 | Do you see the moon (82) |
| dialog | 11 | Hello little flower (37) |
| anaphora | 6 | Beads, beads and more beads (62) |
| simile | 5 | The lake is like glass (23) |
| hyperbole | 1 | In the land of a billion lights (3) |

Table 3: Distribution of figurative language out of 1000 random captions (171 figurative captions in total)

Formally, our corpus represents a bipartite graph $G = (T, V, E)$, in which the set of captions $T$ and the set of images $V$ are connected by typed edges $e(c, i, t)$, where caption $c \in T$, image $i \in V$, and edge type $t \in \{original, paraphrase\}$, which denotes whether the image-caption association is given by the original caption or by a visual paraphrase.

**FIGURATIVE SET** We find that many repeating captions are surprisingly lengthy and expressive, most of which turn out to be idiomatic expressions and quotations, e.g., *"faith is the bird that feels the light when the dawn is still dark"* from Tagore's poem. We look up `goodreads.com`

[2] We do this transformation so as not to over-count unique captions with trivial variations, but merging prepositions can sometimes combine prepositions that are not semantically compatible. We therefore also keep original captions with original prepositions.

[3] We also keep user annotated image tags if available.

[4] Without counting additional edges created by visual paraphrasing (§5).

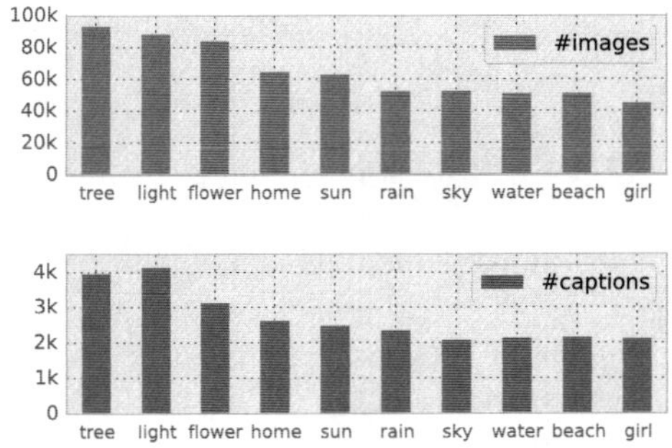


Figure 3: Top 10 queries with the largest number of images and unique captions

| polarity | % in all caps. | mean/median #imgs. per cap. | example (#imgs) |
|---|---|---|---|
| pos. | 8% | 20 / 8 | Happy bride and groom (282)<br>The rock and pool,<br>is nice and cool (4) |
| neg. | 2% | 19.5 / 7 | Bad day at the office (269)<br>Crying lightning (147) |

Table 4: Distribution of caption sentiment. The polarity is determined by comparing number of positive words and negative words (>: positive; <: negative) according to a sentiment lexicon (Wilson et al., 2005) (counting only words of *strong* polarity).

and brainyquotes.com to identify 6K quotation captions illustrated by 180K images. We also present a manual labeling on a small subset of the data (Table 3) to provide better insights into the degree and types of figurative speech used in natural captions. Using these labels we build a classifier (§7) to further detect 18K figurative captions associated with 410K images.

**INSIGHTS** As additional insights into the dataset, Figure 3 shows statistics of the visual content, Table 5 shows syntactic types of the captions, and Table 4 shows positive and negative sentiment in captions.

## 3 Image Captioning using Association Structure

We demonstrate the usefulness of the association between images and captions via retrieval-based image captioning. Given a query image $q$ and the corpus $G = (T, V, E)$, the task is to find a caption $c \in T$ that maximizes an affinity function $\mathcal{A}(q, c)$, which measures how well the caption $c$ fits the query image $q$,

$$c^* = \arg\max_{c \in T}\{\mathcal{A}(q, c)\} \quad (1)$$

**Visual Neighborhood:** Each textual description, e.g., *"reading a book"*, can associate with many different visual instantiations (Figure 4a). Our dataset $G = (T, V, E)$ serves as a database to navigate the possible visual instantiations of descriptive captions as observed in online photo sharing communities. Let $\mathcal{N}_c = \{i | e(c, i, original) \in E\}$ denote the set of adjacent nodes (i.e., visual instantiations) of a caption $c$. To quantify how well a caption $c$ describe a query image $q$, we propose to examine caption $c$'s visual neighborhood $\mathcal{N}_c$ as provided in our dataset. Concretely, the affinity $\mathcal{A}(q, c)$ of a query image $q$ to a caption $c$ is a function $\phi(q, \mathcal{N}_c)$ of $q$ and the visual neighborhood $\mathcal{N}_c$ defined as:

$$\mathcal{A}(q, c) = \phi(q, \mathcal{N}_c) = \frac{1}{\sigma}\sum_{i=1}^{\sigma} sim(q, \mathcal{N}_c^i) \quad (2)$$

where $\sigma$ is a parameter; $sim(\cdot, \cdot)$ is a similarity function of two images; and $\mathcal{N}_c = [\mathcal{N}_c^1, \mathcal{N}_c^2, ..., \mathcal{N}_c^{|\mathcal{N}_c|}]$ is sorted by $sim(q, \mathcal{N}_c^i)$ in *descending* order.

Figure 4a illustrates the key insight: instead of directly transferring the caption of the single image with the closest visual similarity to the query image (Ordonez et al., 2011), we propose to retrieve a caption based on the aggregated visual similarity between its visual neighborhood and the query image. The idea is to prefer a caption for which the query image is likely to be a *prototypical* visual rendering (Ordonez et al., 2013; Deselaers and Ferrari, 2011), hence avoid an unusual association between the text

| type | %caps. | %imgs. | mean #imgs. | std #imgs. |
|---|---|---|---|---|
| verb | 45% | 44% | 22 | 9 |
| | be, have, do, look,<br>go, make, come, get,<br>wait, take, love, play,<br>walk, fly, see, watch,<br>find, live, sleep, fall | | Sky is the limit (3057)<br>Home is where the heart is (2480)<br>Lunch is served (2443)<br>Let them eat cake (2193)<br>Follow the yellow brick road (2077) | |
| prep | 44% | 41% | 21 | 9 |
| | in, of, on,<br>at, with, for,<br>from, by,<br>over, through | | On the road (4617)<br>After the rains (4450)<br>Under the bridge (3443)<br>At the beach (3203) | |
| adj | 11% | 15% | 30 | 15 |
| | old, little, new,<br>red, blue, more,<br>white, big, beautiful,<br>black | | Home sweet home (2398)<br>Good morning sun (1122)<br>Cabbage white butterfly (976)<br>Next door neighbors (838) | |

Table 5: Statistics on the syntactic composition of captions. *verb*: captions with at least one verb. *prep*: prepositional phrases (without any verbs). *adj*: adjective phrases (without any verbs and prepositions). For each caption type, we also show the *top words* that appear in the most number of captions (left), and the *top captions* that are associated with largest number of images (right).

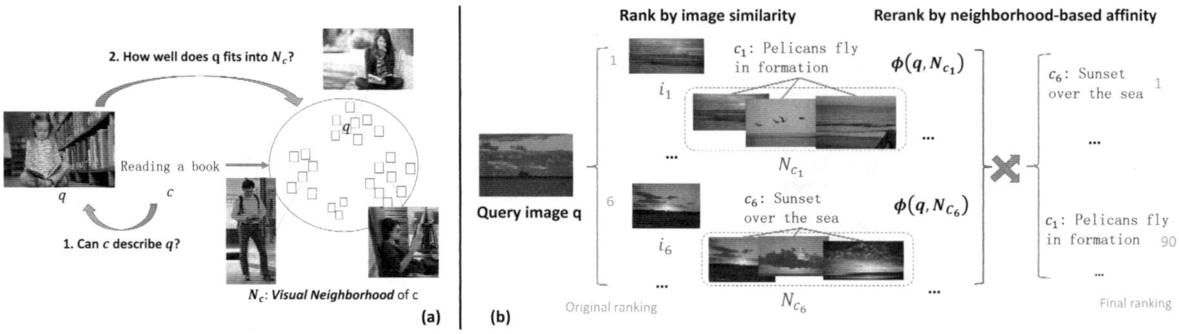


Figure 4: (a) Using the association structure, we retrieve a caption for which the query image is likely to be a *prototypical* visual rendering. We hypothesize that there can be multiple visual prototypes of a caption. (b) Reranking by visual neighborhood proximity.

and the visual information. Also, we hypothesize that there could be several diverse visual prototypes of any given textual description $c$, so we focus on only the top $\sigma$ nearest members of $\mathcal{N}_c$.

We apply the neighborhood-based affinity for image captioning via reranking (Figure 4b): first we retrieve a pool of $K$ candidate captions by finding top $K$ closest images based on their direct visual similarity to the query image, then compute the neighborhood-based affinity to rerank the captions.[5] The proposed approach is similar in spirit to the non-parametric K nearest neighbor approach of (Boiman et al., 2008) in modeling image-to-concept similarity rather than image-to-image similarity, but differs in that our work is in the context of image description generation rather than classification.

## 4 Experiments: Association Structure Improves Image Captioning

**Baselines:** The proposed approach (to be referred as ASSOC) requires one-to-many mappings between captions and images *at scale* — a unique property of our dataset. We compare against two baselines: instance-based retrieval of (Ordonez et al., 2011) (INSTANCE) and Kernel Canonical Correlation Analysis (KCCA) (Hardoon et al., 2004; Hodosh et al., 2013). We implement KCCA with Hardoon's code[6]. We use a linear kernel since non-linear kernels like RBF showed worse performance.

[5]We set $K = 100$ and choose parameter $\sigma$ using a held-out development set of 300 images. If there are less than $\sigma$ available images, we use them all.

[6]http://www.davidroihardoon.com/Professional/Code_files/kcca_package.tar.gz

| method | BLEU | METEOR |
|---|---|---|
| INSTANCE | *0.125* | *0.029* |
| KCCA | 0.118 | $0.024^{**}$ |
| ASSOC$^{gi}$ w/ all | 0.130 | 0.031 |
| ASSOC$^{g+t}$ w/ all | 0.133 | 0.030 |
| ASSOC$^{ti}$ w/ all | 0.126 | 0.029 |
| ASSOC$^{gi}$ w/ $\sigma$ | $0.172^{**}$ | $0.033^{*}$ |
| ASSOC$^{g+t}$ w/ $\sigma$ | $0.159^{**}$ | $0.033^{*}$ |
| ASSOC$^{ti}$ w/ $\sigma$ | **0.184**$^{**}$ | **0.034**$^{**}$ |

Table 6: Automatic evaluation for image captioning: The superscripts denote the image feature for reranking; gi: GIST; ti: Tinyimage; g+t:= gi + ti. We report the best setting (gt) for INSTANCE and KCCA. Results statistically significant compared to INSTANCE with two-tailed $t$-test are indicated with * ($p < 0.05$) and ** ($p < 0.005$).

**Configurations:** For image features, we follow (Ordonez et al., 2011) to experiment with two global image descriptors and their combination: a) the GIST feature that represents the dominant spatial structure of a scene (Oliva and Torralba, 2001); b) the Tinyimage feature that represents the overall color of an image (Torralba et al., 2008); c) a combination of the two. We compute the similarity as $sim(Q, I) = -\|Q - I\|^2$. The INSTANCE and the KCCA approaches use the feature combination. The ASSOC approach also use the combination for preparing candidate captions, but can use different features for reranking.

**Dataset:** We randomly sample 1000 images with unique captions as test set. The rest of the corpus is the pool of caption retrieval after *discarding*: (1) the original caption $c$ and all of its associated images, to avoid potential unfair advantage toward ASSOC and (2) the 10K captions used for training KCCA and all

| reranking feature | INSTANCE | ASSOC |
|---|---|---|
| gi | 42% | 58% |
| g+t | 50% | 50% |
| ti | 46% | 54% |

Table 7: Human evaluation for image captioning: the % of cases judged as visually more *relevant*, in pairwise comparisons. gi: GIST; ti: Tinyimage; g+t:= gi+ti.

of their associated images (about 280K).

**Evaluation.** Automatic evaluation remains to be a challenge (Elliott and Keller, 2014). We report both BLEU (Papineni et al., 2002) at 1 without brevity penalty, and METEOR (Banerjee and Lavie, 2005) with balanced precision and recall. Table 6 shows the results: the ASSOC approach (w/ $\sigma$) significantly outperforms the two baselines. The largest improvement over INSTANCE is 60% higher in BLEU, and 44% higher in METEOR, demonstrating the benefit of the innate association structure of our corpus. Using *all* visual neighborhood (ASSOC w/ all) does not yield as strong results as selective neighborhood (ASSOC w/ $\sigma$), confirming our hypothesis that each visual concept can have diverse visual renderings.

We also compute crowd-sourced evaluation on a subset (200 images) randomly sampled out of the test set. For each query image, we present two captions generated by two competing methods in a random order. Turkers choose the caption that is more relevant to the visual content of the given image. We aggregate the choices of three turkers by majority voting. As shown in Table 7, ASSOC shows overall improvement over baselines, where the difference is more pronounced when reranking is based on feature sets that differ from the one used during the candidate retrieval.

# 5 Image Captioning using Visual Paraphrases

We present an exploration of *visually situated paraphrase* (or *visual paraphrase* in short hand), and demonstrate their utility for image captioning. Formally, given our corpus $G = (T, V, E)$, a visual paraphrase relation is a triple $(i, c, p)$, where given an image $i \in V$ and its original caption $c \in T$ (i.e., $e(c, i, original) \in E$), $p \in T$ is a visual paraphrase for $c$ situated in a visual context given by the image $i$ (i.e, $e(p, i, paraphrase) \in E$). We collect visual paraphrases using both human annotation and an automatic algorithm.

**(1) Visual Paraphrasing using Crowd-sourcing:** We use Amazon Mechanical Turk to annotate visual paraphrases for a subset of images in our corpus. Given each image with its original caption, we showed 10 randomly sampled candidate captions from our dataset that share at least one physical-object noun[7] with the original caption. Turkers choose all candidate captions that could also describe the given image. We collect 7,570 $(i, c, p)$ paraphrase triples in total.

**(2) Visual Paraphrasing using Associative Structure:** We also propose an algorithm for automatic visual paraphrasing by adapting the ASSOC algorithm for image captioning (§3) as follows: given an image-caption pair $(i, c)$, it first prepares a set of candidate captions that share the largest number of physical-object nouns with $c$, which are likely to be semantically close to $c$; then we rerank the candidate captions using the same neighborhood-based affinity as described in §3.

We apply this algorithm to generate a large set of visual paraphrases. For each caption in our corpus, we randomly sample two of its associated images, and generate one visual paraphrase for each image-caption pair, which yields 353,560 $(i, c, p)$ triples. See Figure 2 for example paraphrases.

## 5.1 Image Captioning using Visual Paraphrasing

We propose to utilize automatically-generated visual paraphrases to improve the ASSOC approach (§3) for image captioning. One potential limitation of the ASSOC approach is that for some captions, the number of associated images might be too small for reliable estimations of the neighborhood based affinity. We hypothesize that for a caption with a small visual neighborhood, merging its neighborhood with those associated with its *visual paraphrases* will give a more reliable estimation of the affinity between a query image and that caption. Thus we modify the ASSOC approach as follows.

After preparing a pool of $K$ candidate captions $\{c_1, c_2, \ldots, c_K\}$, automatically generate a visual paraphrase $(i_i, c_i, p_i)$ for each $(i_i, c_i)$; then rerank the candidate captions by the following affinity function that merges the visual neighborhood from the

[7]under the WordNet "physical_entity.n.01" synset

| method | BLEU | METEOR | AMT |
|---|---|---|---|
| INSTANCE | 0.125 | 0.029 | N/A |
| $\text{ASSOC}^{\text{gi}}$ | 0.172 | 0.033 | 45% |
| $\text{ASSOC}^{\text{gi}}_{\text{para}}$ | **0.187** | **0.036** | 55% |
| $\text{ASSOC}^{\text{ti}}$ | 0.184 | 0.034 | 45% |
| $\text{ASSOC}^{\text{ti}}_{\text{para}}$ | **0.197** | **0.036** | 55% |

Table 8: Automatic and human evaluation of exploiting visual paraphrases for image captioning. The superscripts represent the image feature used in the reranking step; gi: GIST; ti: Tinyimage. The AMT column shows the percentages of captions preferred by human as of better visual relevance, in pairwise comparisons. The improvement of $\text{ASSOC}_{\text{para}}$ over ASSOC is significant at $p < 0.002$ for BLEU, and $p < 0.03$ for METEOR with two tailed $t$-test.

paraphrase,

$$\mathcal{A}(q, C_i) = \phi(q, \mathcal{N}_{c_i} \cup \mathcal{N}_{p_i}) \tag{3}$$

## 6 Experiments: Visual Paraphrasing Improves Image Captioning

The experimental configuration basically follows §4. We compare $\text{ASSOC}_{\text{para}}$, the visual-paraphrase augmented approach, to the vanilla ASSOC approach. The image feature setting is the one with which the ASSOC approach performs best. Both approaches use the GIST+Tinyimage feature to prepare candidate captions, then use either the GIST or Tinyimage feature for reranking.

Table 8 shows that the $\text{ASSOC}_{\text{para}}$ approach significantly improves the vanilla ASSOC method under both automatic and human evaluation. As a reference, the first row shows the performance of the INSTANCE method (§4). The ASSOC method significantly improves over the INSTANCE method. On a similar vein, the $\text{ASSOC}_{\text{para}}$ method further improves over the ASSOC method, as automatic paraphrases provide a better visual neighborhood. This improvement is remarkable since the paraphrasing association is added automatically without any supervised training. This demonstrates the usefulness of the bipartite association structure of our corpus.

## 7 Image Captioning with Creativity

Naturally existing captions reflect everyday narratives, which in turn reflect figurative language use such as metaphor, simile, and personification. To gain better insights, one of the authors manually categorized a set of 1000 random captions. About 17% are identified as figurative. Table 3 shows the distribution over different types of figurative captions.

**Creative Language Classifier:** Using the small set of labels described above, we train a simple binary classifier to identify captions with creative language.[8] Using this classifier, we can control the degree of literalness or creativity in generated captions. Based on 5-fold cross-validation, the classifier performs with 77% precision and 43% recall.

Importantly, a high-precision and low-recall classifier suffices our purpose. It is because in the context of creative captioning and creative paraphrasing presented below, we only need to detect *some* figurative captions, not *all*.

### 7.1 Creative Image Captioning

Given a query image $q$, we describe it with the most appropriate figurative caption. We propose the $\text{ASSOC}_{\text{creative}}$ approach that alters the ASSOC approach (§3) to return a *figurative* caption from the candidate pool, excluding *literal* captions.

### 7.2 Creative Visual Paraphrasing

Given a query image $q$ and its *original* caption $c$, we rephrase $c$ to a more creative and inspirational caption that still describes $q$. We use the $\text{PARA}_{\text{creative}}$ approach that changes our automatic visual paraphrasing algorithm (§5), by retrieving only figurative captions.

## 8 Experiments: Creative Image Captioning and Paraphrasing

### 8.1 Creative Captioning

We compare the $\text{ASSOC}_{\text{creative}}$ approach to the vanilla ASSOC approach. With the ASSOC approach, the top-rank caption is usually literal. Both approaches use the GIST+Tinyimage feature for preparing candidate captions, and the Tinyimage feature for reranking, which is the best setting for the ASSOC approach (§4).

Similarly to §4, we sample 200 test images from our corpus, and use AMT to compare two algorithms in terms of *visual relevance* and *creativity* separately. For creativity, we ask turkers to choose one

[8] We use a random forest classifier with features including words indicating reasoning (but, could, that), generality (never, always), caption length, abstract nouns (life, and hope), and whether the caption is a known idiom or quotation.

| method | creativity | relevance |
|---|---|---|
| ASSOC | 33% | 41% |
| ASSOC$_{creative}$ | 67% | 59% |

Table 9: Human evaluation for creative captioning: % of captions preferred by judges in pairwise comparisons

of the two captions that is more creative and inspirational than the other to describe each given test image. Results are shown in Table 9.

(1) *Creativity.* For 2/3 of the query images, captions produced by the ASSOC$_{creative}$ method are judged as more creative than those produced by the ASSOC method. This result indirectly validates that the figurativeness classifier has a reasonable precision to control the literalness of the system caption.

(2) *Visual relevance.* Interestingly, not only the captions from the ASSOC$_{creative}$ method are favored as creative, they are also judged as visually more relevant than those from the ASSOC method, despite that each figurative caption has lower neighborhood-based affinity than the literal counterpart. We conjecture that it is easier for human judges to be imaginative and draw visual relevance between the query image and figurative captions than the literal counterparts. This result also suggests that figurative language may be of practical use in image caption applications as a means to smooth the potentially brittle system output. Figure 5 shows example system output.

### 8.2 Creative Visual Paraphrasing

We test 200 images that are associated with *literal* captions as predicted by the figurativeness classifier. The PARA$_{creative}$ approach competes against two baselines: 1) the ORIGINAL captions , and 2) a text-only variant of the PARA$_{caption}$ approach sans visual processing: it randomly chooses a figurative caption that shares the largest number of physical-object nouns with the original caption, without looking at the query image. This is for evaluating the effect of visual context.

In addition to the evaluations as in §8.1, we also use a *multiple-choice* setting that allows a turker to choose zero to two captions that are visually relevant to the query image. See Table 10 for results, and Figure 5 for example outputs.

| method | creativity | relevance | |
|---|---|---|---|
| | | *single* | *multiple* |
| ORIGINAL | 32% | 80% | 87% |
| PARA$_{creative}$ | 68% | 20% | 60% |
| PARA$_{caption}$ | 56% | 47% | 63% |
| PARA$_{creative}$ | 44% | 53% | 74% |

Table 10: Human eval for creative visual paraphrasing

**I. Comparing original captions with creative paraphrases (ORIGINAL vs. PARA$_{creative}$):** The paraphrases are preferred over the original literal captions as more creative most of the time. As for the visual relevance, the original captions are favored over the paraphrases most of the time in the single-choice competition. However, when we use a multiple-choice setting, paraphrases has a reasonable relevance rate (60%), despite the simplicity of the algorithm. The fact that the original captions has a high relevance rate (87%) shows that in our corpus the captions have high visual relevance to their associated images most of the time.

**II. Creative paraphrasing with and without the visual context (PARA$_{caption}$ vs. PARA$_{creative}$):** In terms of creativity, the PARA$_{caption}$ method is preferred over the PARA$_{creative}$ method. We conjecture that without conditioning on the visual content, PARA$_{caption}$ method tends to retrieve more unexpected captions that make turkers think they are more fun and creative. As for the visual relevance, by conditioning on the visual context given by query images, the PARA$_{creative}$ method significantly improves the visual relevance over the text-only counterpart, PARA$_{caption}$ method. This result highlights the pragmatic differences between visually-situated paraphrasing and text-based paraphrasing.

## 9 Related work

**Image-caption corpus:** Our work contributes to the line of research that makes use of internet web imagery and text (Ordonez et al., 2011; Berg et al., 2010) by detecting the visually relevant text (Dodge et al., 2012) and reducing the noise (Kuznetsova et al., 2013b; Kuznetsova et al., 2014). Compared to datasets with crowd-sourced captions (Hodosh et al., 2013; Lin et al., 2014), in which each image is annotated with several captions, our dataset presents several images for each caption, a subset of which also includes visually situated paraphrases. The as-

Figure 5: Examples of creative captioning and creative visual paraphrasing. The left column shows good examples in blue, and the right column shows bad examples in red. The captions marked with * are the original captions of the corresponding query images.

sociation structure of our dataset is analogous to that of ImageNet (Deng et al., 2009). Unlike ImageNet that is built for nouns (physical objects) listed under WordNet (Miller, 1995), our corpus is built for expressive phrases and full sentences and constructed without human curation. Our corpus has several unique properties to complement existing corpora. As explored in a very recent work of (Gong et al., 2014), we expect that it is possible to combine crowd-sourced and web-harvested datasets and achieve the best of both worlds.

**Image captioning:** Our work contributes to the increasing body of research on retrieval-based image captioning (Ordonez et al., 2011; Hodosh et al., 2013; Hodosh and Hockenmaier, 2013; Socher et al., 2014), by providing a new large-scale corpus with unique association structure between images and captions, by proposing an algorithm that exploits the structure, and by exploring two new dimensions: (i) visually situated paraphrasing (and its utility for retrieval-based image captioning), and (ii) creative image captioning.

**Paraphrasing:** Most previous studies in paraphrasing have focused exclusively on text, and the primary goal has been learning *semantic* equivalence of phrases that would be true out of context (e.g., (Barzilay and McKeown, 2001; Pang et al., 2003; Dolan et al., 2004; Ganitkevitch et al., 2013)), rather than targeting *situated* or *pragmatic* equivalence given a context. Emerging efforts began exploring paraphrases that are situated in video content (Chen and Dolan, 2011), news events (Zhang and Weld, 2013), and knowledge base (Berant and Liang, 2014). Our work is the first to introduce *visually situated paraphrasing* in which the task is to find paraphrases that are conditioned on both the input text as well as the visual context. (Chen and Dolan, 2011) collected situated paraphrases only through crowd sourcing, while we also explore automatic collection, and further test the quality of automatic paraphrases by using the learned paraphrases in an extrinsic evaluation setting.

**Figurative language:** There has been substantial work for detecting and interpreting figurative language (Shutova, 2010; Li et al., 2013; Kuznetsova et al., 2013a; Tsvetkov et al., 2014), while relatively less work on *generating* creative or figurative language (Veale, 2011; Ozbal and Strapparava, 2012). We probe data-driven approaches to creative language generation in the context of image captioning.

## 10 Conclusion

To conclude, we have provided insights into making a better use of multimodal web data in the wild, resulting in a large-scale corpus, *Deja Image-Captions*, with several unique properties to complement datasets with crowdsourced captions. To validate the usefulness of the corpus, we proposed new image captioning algorithms using the associative structure, which we extended to several related tasks ranging from visually situated paraphrasing to enhanced image captioning. In the process we have also explored several new tasks: visually situated paraphrasing, creative image captioning, and creative caption paraphrasing.

**Acknowledgement** The research is supported in part by NSF Award IIS 1447549 and IIS 1408287.

## References


Satanjeev Banerjee and Alon Lavie. 2005. METEOR: An automatic metric for MT evaluation with improved correlation with human judgments. In *Proceedings of the ACL Workshop on Intrinsic and Extrinsic Evaluation Measures for Machine Translation and/or Summarization*, pages 65–72.

Regina Barzilay and Kathleen R. McKeown. 2001. Extracting paraphrases from a parallel corpus. In *Proceedings of the 39th Annual Meeting on Association for Computational Linguistics*, pages 50–57. Association for Computational Linguistics.

Jonathan Berant and Percy Liang. 2014. Semantic Parsing via Paraphrasing. In *Association for Computational Linguistics (ACL)*.

Tamara L. Berg, Alexander C. Berg, and Jonathan Shih. 2010. Automatic attribute discovery and characterization from noisy web data. In *ECCV 2010*, pages 663–676. Springer.

Oren Boiman, Eli Shechtman, and Michal Irani. 2008. In defense of Nearest-Neighbor based image classification. In *IEEE Conference on Computer Vision and Pattern Recognition, 2008. CVPR 2008*, pages 1–8, June.

David L. Chen and William B. Dolan. 2011. Collecting highly parallel data for paraphrase evaluation. In *Proceedings of the 49th Annual Meeting of the Association for Computational Linguistics: Human Language Technologies-Volume 1*, pages 190–200. Association for Computational Linguistics.

Jia Deng, Wei Dong, Richard Socher, Li-Jia Li, Kai Li, and Li Fei-Fei. 2009. Imagenet: A large-scale hierarchical image database. In *Computer Vision and Pattern Recognition, 2009. CVPR 2009. IEEE Conference on*, pages 248–255. IEEE.

Thomas Deselaers and Vittorio Ferrari. 2011. Visual and semantic similarity in imagenet. In *Computer Vision and Pattern Recognition (CVPR), 2011 IEEE Conference on*, pages 1777–1784. IEEE.

Jesse Dodge, Amit Goyal, Xufeng Han, Alyssa Mensch, Margaret Mitchell, Karl Stratos, Kota Yamaguchi, Yejin Choi, Hal Daumé III, Alexander C. Berg, and others. 2012. Detecting visual text. In *Proceedings of the 2012 Conference of the North American Chapter of the Association for Computational Linguistics: Human Language Technologies*, pages 762–772. Association for Computational Linguistics.

Bill Dolan, Chris Quirk, and Chris Brockett. 2004. Unsupervised construction of large paraphrase corpora: Exploiting massively parallel news sources. In *Proceedings of the 20th international conference on Computational Linguistics*, page 350. Association for Computational Linguistics.

Desmond Elliott and Frank Keller. 2014. Comparing automatic evaluation measures for image description. In *Proceedings of the 52nd Annual Meeting of the Association for Computational Linguistics*, volume 2, pages 452–457.

Song Feng, Sujith Ravi, Ravi Kumar, Polina Kuznetsova, Wei Liu, Alexander C. Berg, Tamara L. Berg, and Yejin Choi. 2015. Refer-to-as Relations as Semantic Knowledge. In *AAAI Conference on Artificial Intelligence*.

Juri Ganitkevitch, Benjamin Van Durme, and Chris Callison-Burch. 2013. PPDB: The Paraphrase Database. In *Proceedings of NAACL-HLT*, pages 758–764, Atlanta, Georgia, June. Association for Computational Linguistics.

Yunchao Gong, Liwei Wang, Micah Hodosh, Julia Hockenmaier, and Svetlana Lazebnik. 2014. Improving Image-Sentence Embeddings Using Large Weakly Annotated Photo Collections. In *ECCV 2014*, pages 529–545. Springer.

David Hardoon, Sandor Szedmak, and John Shawe-Taylor. 2004. Canonical correlation analysis: An overview with application to learning methods. *Neural computation*, 16(12):2639–2664.

Micah Hodosh and Julia Hockenmaier. 2013. Sentence-based image description with scalable, explicit models. In *Proceedings of the IEEE Conference on Computer Vision and Pattern Recognition Workshops*, pages 294–300.

Micah Hodosh, Peter Young, and Julia Hockenmaier. 2013. Framing image description as a ranking task: data, models and evaluation metrics. *Journal of Artificial Intelligence Research*, 47(1):853–899.

Polina Kuznetsova, Jianfu Chen, and Yejin Choi. 2013a. Understanding and Quantifying Creativity in Lexical Composition. In *EMNLP*, pages 1246–1258.

Polina Kuznetsova, Vicente Ordonez, Alexander C. Berg, Tamara L. Berg, and Yejin Choi. 2013b. Generalizing Image Captions for Image-Text Parallel Corpus. In *ACL (2)*, pages 790–796.

Polina Kuznetsova, Vicente Ordonez, Tamara Berg, and Yejin Choi. 2014. TreeTalk: Composition and Compression of Trees for Image Descriptions. *Transactions of the Association for Computational Linguistics*.

Hongsong Li, Kenny Q. Zhu, and Haixun Wang. 2013. Data-Driven Metaphor Recognition and Explanation. *TACL*, 1:379–390.

Tsung-Yi Lin, Michael Maire, Serge Belongie, James Hays, Pietro Perona, Deva Ramanan, Piotr Dollár, and C. Lawrence Zitnick. 2014. Microsoft COCO: Common Objects in Context. In *ECCV*, Zürich.

Rebecca Mason and Eugene Charniak. 2014. Nonparametric Method for Data-driven Image Captioning. In *NAACL*.

Mary Meeker. 2014. *Internet Trends 2014*.

George A. Miller. 1995. WordNet: a lexical database for English. *Communications of the ACM*, 38(11):39–41.

Aude Oliva and Antonio Torralba. 2001. Modeling the shape of the scene: A holistic representation of the spatial envelope. *International journal of computer vision*, 42(3):145–175.

Vicente Ordonez, Girish Kulkarni, and Tamara L. Berg. 2011. Im2text: Describing Images Using 1 Million Captioned Photographs. In *NIPS*, volume 1, page 4.

Vicente Ordonez, Jia Deng, Yejin Choi, Alexander C. Berg, and Tamara L. Berg. 2013. From large scale image categorization to entry-level categories. In *Computer Vision (ICCV), 2013 IEEE International Conference on*, pages 2768–2775. IEEE.

Gozde Ozbal and Carlo Strapparava. 2012. A Computational Approach to the Automation of Creative Naming. In *Proceedings of the 50th Annual Meeting of the Association for Computational Linguistics (Volume 1: Long Papers)*, pages 703–711, Jeju Island, Korea, July. Association for Computational Linguistics.

Bo Pang, Kevin Knight, and Daniel Marcu. 2003. Syntax-based alignment of multiple translations: Extracting paraphrases and generating new sentences. In *Proceedings of the 2003 Conference of the North American Chapter of the Association for Computational Linguistics on Human Language Technology-Volume 1*, pages 102–109. Association for Computational Linguistics.

Kishore Papineni, Salim Roukos, Todd Ward, and Wei-Jing Zhu. 2002. BLEU: a method for automatic evaluation of machine translation. In *Proceedings of the 40th annual meeting on association for computational linguistics*, pages 311–318. Association for Computational Linguistics.

Cyrus Rashtchian, Peter Young, Micah Hodosh, and Julia Hockenmaier. 2010. Collecting Image Annotations Using Amazon's Mechanical Turk. In *Proceedings of the NAACL HLT 2010 Workshop on Creating Speech and Language Data with Amazon's Mechanical Turk*, CSLDAMT '10, pages 139–147, Stroudsburg, PA, USA. Association for Computational Linguistics.

Nikhil Rasiwasia, Pedro J. Moreno, and Nuno Vasconcelos. 2007. Bridging the gap: Query by semantic example. *Multimedia, IEEE Transactions on*, 9(5):923–938.

Nikhil Rasiwasia, Jose Costa Pereira, Emanuele Coviello, Gabriel Doyle, Gert R.G. Lanckriet, Roger Levy, and Nuno Vasconcelos. 2010. A New Approach to Cross-modal Multimedia Retrieval. In *Proceedings of the International Conference on Multimedia*, MM '10, pages 251–260, New York, NY, USA. ACM.

Ekaterina Shutova. 2010. Models of metaphor in NLP. In *Proceedings of the 48th Annual Meeting of the Association for Computational Linguistics*, ACL '10, pages 688–697, Stroudsburg, PA, USA. Association for Computational Linguistics.

Richard Socher, Andrej Karpathy, Quoc V. Le, Christopher D. Manning, and Andrew Y. Ng. 2014. Grounded compositional semantics for finding and describing images with sentences. *Transactions of the Association for Computational Linguistics*, 2:207–218.

Antonio Torralba, Robert Fergus, and William T. Freeman. 2008. 80 million tiny images: A large data set for nonparametric object and scene recognition. *Pattern Analysis and Machine Intelligence, IEEE Transactions on*, 30(11):1958–1970.

Yulia Tsvetkov, Leonid Boytsov, Anatole Gershman, Eric Nyberg, and Chris Dyer. 2014. Metaphor detection with cross-lingual model transfer. In *Proceedings of ACL*.

Tony Veale. 2011. Creative Language Retrieval: A Robust Hybrid of Information Retrieval and Linguistic Creativity. In *Proceedings of the 49th Annual Meeting of the Association for Computational Linguistics: Human Language Technologies*, pages 278–287, Portland, Oregon, USA, June. Association for Computational Linguistics.

Theresa Wilson, Janyce Wiebe, and Paul Hoffmann. 2005. Recognizing contextual polarity in phrase-level sentiment analysis. In *Proceedings of the conference on human language technology and empirical methods in natural language processing*, pages 347–354. Association for Computational Linguistics.

Congle Zhang and Daniel S Weld. 2013. Harvesting Parallel News Streams to Generate Paraphrases of Event Relations. In *EMNLP*, pages 1776–1786.

# Inferring Missing Entity Type Instances for Knowledge Base Completion: New Dataset and Methods

**Arvind Neelakantan***
Department of Computer Science
University of Massachusetts, Amherst
Amherst, MA, 01003
arvind@cs.umass.edu

**Ming-Wei Chang**
Microsoft Research
1 Microsoft Way
Redmond, WA 98052, USA
minchang@microsoft.com

## Abstract

Most of previous work in knowledge base (KB) completion has focused on the problem of relation extraction. In this work, we focus on the task of inferring missing entity type instances in a KB, a fundamental task for KB competition yet receives little attention.

Due to the novelty of this task, we construct a large-scale dataset and design an automatic evaluation methodology. Our knowledge base completion method uses information within the existing KB and external information from Wikipedia. We show that individual methods trained with a *global* objective that considers unobserved cells from both the entity and the type side gives consistently higher quality predictions compared to baseline methods. We also perform manual evaluation on a small subset of the data to verify the effectiveness of our knowledge base completion methods and the correctness of our proposed automatic evaluation method.

## 1 Introduction

There is now increasing interest in the construction of knowledge bases like *Freebase* (Bollacker et al., 2008) and *NELL* (Carlson et al., 2010) in the natural language processing community. KBs contain facts such as *Tiger Woods* is an *athlete*, and *Barack Obama* is the *president of USA*. However, one of the main drawbacks in existing KBs is that they are incomplete and are missing important facts (West et al., 2014), jeopardizing their usefulness in downstream tasks such as question answering. This has led to the task of completing the knowledge base entries, or Knowledge Base Completion (KBC) extremely important.

In this paper, we address an important subproblem of knowledge base completion— inferring missing entity type instances. Most of previous work in KB completion has only focused on the problem of relation extraction (Mintz et al., 2009; Nickel et al., 2011; Bordes et al., 2013; Riedel et al., 2013). Entity type information is crucial in KBs and is widely used in many NLP tasks such as relation extraction (Chang et al., 2014), coreference resolution (Ratinov and Roth, 2012; Hajishirzi et al., 2013), entity linking (Fang and Chang, 2014), semantic parsing (Kwiatkowski et al., 2013; Berant et al., 2013) and question answering (Bordes et al., 2014; Yao and Durme, 2014). For example, adding entity type information improves relation extraction by 3% (Chang et al., 2014) and entity linking by 4.2 F1 points (Guo et al., 2013). Despite their importance, there is surprisingly little previous work on this problem and, there are no datasets publicly available for evaluation.

We construct a large-scale dataset for the task of inferring missing entity type instances in a KB. Most of previous KBC datasets (Mintz et al., 2009; Riedel et al., 2013) are constructed using a single snapshot of the KB and methods are evaluated on a subset of facts that are hidden during training. Hence, the methods could be potentially evaluated by their ability to predict *easy* facts that the KB already contains. Moreover, the methods are not directly evaluated

* Most of the research conducted during summer internship at Microsoft.



*Human Language Technologies: The 2015 Annual Conference of the North American Chapter of the ACL*, pages 515–525,
Denver, Colorado, May 31 – June 5, 2015. 

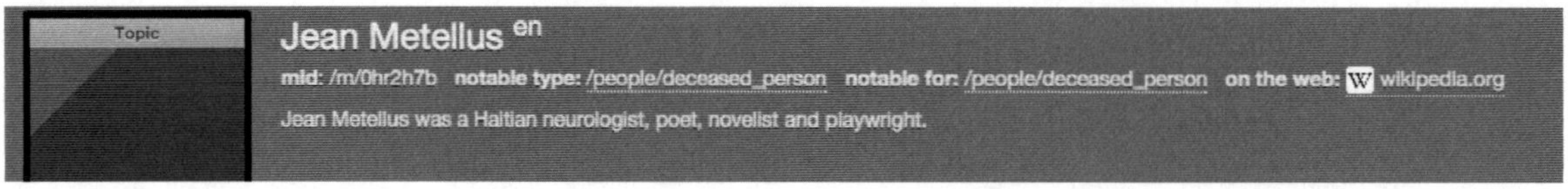


Figure 1: Freebase description of *Jean Metellus* can be used to infer that the entity has the type */book/author*. This missing fact is found by our algorithm and is still missing in the latest version of Freebase when the paper is written.

on their ability to predict missing facts. To overcome these drawbacks we construct the train and test data using two snapshots of the KB and evaluate the methods on predicting facts that are added to the more recent snapshot, enabling a more realistic and challenging evaluation.

Standard evaluation metrics for KBC methods are generally *type-based* (Mintz et al., 2009; Riedel et al., 2013), measuring the quality of the predictions by aggregating scores computed within a type. This is not ideal because: (1) it treats every entity type equally not considering the distribution of types, (2) it does not measure the ability of the methods to rank predictions across types. Therefore, we additionally use a global evaluation metric, where the quality of predictions is measured within and across types, and also accounts for the high variance in type distribution. In our experiments, we show that models trained with negative examples from the entity side perform better on type-based metrics, while when trained with negative examples from the type side perform better on the global metric.

In order to design methods that can rank predictions *both* within and across entity (or relation) types, we propose a *global objective* to train the models. Our proposed method combines the advantages of previous approaches by using negative examples from both the entity and the type side. When considering the same number of negative examples, we find that the linear classifiers and the low-dimensional embedding models trained with the global objective produce better quality ranking within and across entity types when compared to training with negatives examples only from entity or type side. Additionally compared to prior methods, the model trained on the proposed global objective can more reliably suggest confident entity-type pair candidates that could be added into the given knowledge base.

Our contributions are summarized as follows:

- We develop an evaluation framework comprising of methods for dataset construction and evaluation metrics to evaluate KBC approaches for missing entity type instances. The dataset and evaluation scripts are publicly available at `http://research.microsoft.com/en-US/downloads/df481862-65cc-4b05-886c-acc181ad07bb/default.aspx`.
- We propose a global training objective for KBC methods. The experimental results show that both linear classifiers and low-dimensional embedding models achieve best overall performance when trained with the global objective function.
- We conduct extensive studies on models for inferring missing type instances studying the impact of using various features and models.

## 2 Inferring Entity Types

We consider a KB $\Lambda$ containing entity type information of the form $(e, t)$, where $e \in E$ ($E$ is the set of all entities) is an entity in the KB with type $t \in T$ ($T$ is the set of all types). For example, $e$ could be *Tiger Woods* and $t$ could be *sports athlete*. As a single entity can have multiple types, entities in Freebase often miss some of their types. The aim of this work is to infer missing entity type instances in the KB. Given an unobserved fact (an entity-type pair) in the training data $(e, t) \notin \Lambda$ where entity $e \in E$ and type $t \in T$, the task is to infer whether the KB currently misses the fact, i.e., infer whether $(e, t) \in \Lambda$. We consider entities in the intersection of Freebase and Wikipedia in our experiments.

### 2.1 Information Resources

Now, we describe the information sources used to construct the feature representation of an entity to infer its types. We use information in Freebase and external information from Wikipedia to complete the KB.

- **Entity Type Features**: The entity types observed in the training data can be a useful signal to infer missing entity type instances. For example, in our snapshot of *Freebase*, it is not uncommon to find an entity with the type */people/deceased_person* but missing the type */people/person*.

- **Freebase Description**: Almost all entities in *Freebase* have a short one paragraph description of the entity. Figure 1 shows the *Freebase* description of *Jean Metellus* that can be used to infer the type */book/author* which *Freebase* does not contain as the date of writing this article.

- **Wikipedia**: As external information, we include the *Wikipedia* full text article of an entity in its feature representation. We consider entities in Freebase that have a link to their Wikipedia article. The *Wikipedia* full text of an entity gives several clues to predict it's entity types. For example, Figure 2 shows a section of the *Wikipedia* article of *Claire Martin* which gives clues to infer the type */award/award_winner* that *Freebase* misses.

## 3 Evaluation Framework

In this section, we propose an evaluation methodology for the task of inferring missing entity type instances in a KB. While we focus on recovering entity types, the proposed framework can be easily adapted to relation extraction as well.

First, we discuss our two-snapshot dataset construction strategy. Then we motivate the importance of evaluating KBC algorithms globally and describe the evaluation metrics we employ.

### 3.1 Two Snapshots Construction

In most previous work on KB completion to predict missing relation facts (Mintz et al., 2009; Riedel et al., 2013), the methods are evaluated on a subset of facts from a *single* KB snapshot, that are hidden while training. However, given that the missing entries are usually selected randomly, the distribution of the selected unknown entries could be very different from the actual missing facts distribution. Also, since any fact could be potentially used for evaluation, the methods could be evaluated on their ability to predict easy facts that are already present in the KB.

To overcome this drawback, we construct our train and test set by considering *two* snapshots of the knowledge base. The *train* snapshot is taken from an earlier time without special treatment. The *test* snapshot is taken from a later period, and a KBC algorithm is evaluated by its ability of recovering newly added knowledge in the test snapshot. This enables the methods to be directly evaluated on facts that are missing in a KB snapshot. Note that the facts that are added to the test snapshot, in general, are more subtle than the facts that they already contain and predicting the newly added facts could be harder. Hence, our approach enables a more realistic and challenging evaluation setting than previous work.

We use manually constructed *Freebase* as the KB in our experiments. Notably, Chang et al. (2014) use a two-snapshot strategy for constructing a dataset for relation extraction using automatically constructed *NELL* as their KB. The new facts that are added to a KB by an automatic method may not have all the characteristics that make the two snapshot strategy more advantageous.

We construct our train snapshot $\Lambda_0$ by taking the *Freebase* snapshot on $3^{rd}$ September, 2013 and consider entities that have a link to their Wikipedia page. KBC algorithms are evaluated by their ability to predict facts that were added to the $1^{st}$ June, 2014 snapshot of *Freebase* $\Lambda$. To get negative data, we make a closed world assumption treating any unobserved instance in *Freebase* as a negative example. Unobserved instances in the *Freebase* snapshot on $3^{rd}$ September, 2013 and $1^{st}$ June, 2014 are used as negative examples in training and testing respectively.[1]

The positive instances in the test data $(\Lambda - \Lambda_0)$ are facts that are newly added to the test snapshot $\Lambda$. Using the entire set of negative examples in the test data is impractical due to the large number of negative examples. To avoid this we only add the negative types

[1]Note that some of the negative instances used in training could be positive instances in test but we do not remove them during training.

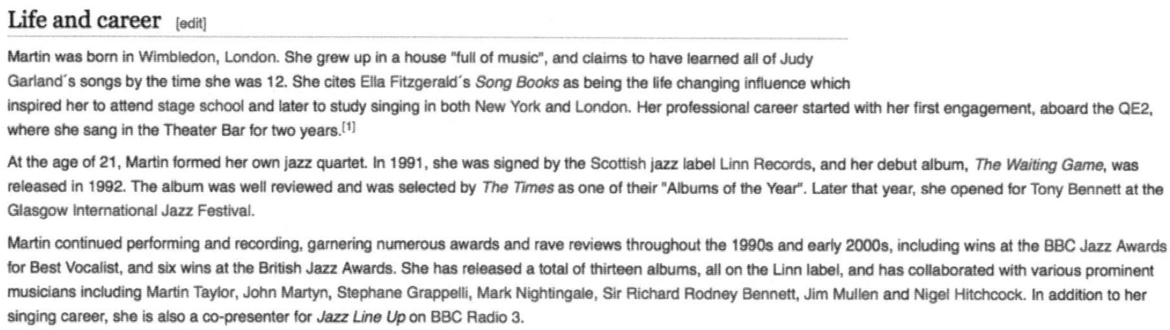
Life and career [edit]

Martin was born in Wimbledon, London. She grew up in a house "full of music", and claims to have learned all of Judy Garland's songs by the time she was 12. She cites Ella Fitzgerald's *Song Books* as being the life changing influence which inspired her to attend stage school and later to study singing in both New York and London. Her professional career started with her first engagement, aboard the QE2, where she sang in the Theater Bar for two years.[1]

At the age of 21, Martin formed her own jazz quartet. In 1991, she was signed by the Scottish jazz label Linn Records, and her debut album, *The Waiting Game*, was released in 1992. The album was well reviewed and was selected by *The Times* as one of their "Albums of the Year". Later that year, she opened for Tony Bennett at the Glasgow International Jazz Festival.

Martin continued performing and recording, garnering numerous awards and rave reviews throughout the 1990s and early 2000s, including wins at the BBC Jazz Awards for Best Vocalist, and six wins at the British Jazz Awards. She has released a total of thirteen albums, all on the Linn label, and has collaborated with various prominent musicians including Martin Taylor, John Martyn, Stephane Grappelli, Mark Nightingale, Sir Richard Rodney Bennett, Jim Mullen and Nigel Hitchcock. In addition to her singing career, she is also a co-presenter for *Jazz Line Up* on BBC Radio 3.

Figure 2: A section of the *Wikipedia* article of *Claire Martin* which gives clues that entity has the type */award/award_winner*. This currently missing fact is also found by our algorithm.

of entities that have at least one new fact in the test data. Additionally, we add a portion of the negative examples for entities which do not have new fact in the test data and that were unused during training. This makes our dataset quite challenging since the number of negative instances is much larger than the number of positive instances in the test data.

It is important to note that the goal of this work is not to predict facts that emerged between the time period of the train and test snapshot[2]. For example, we do not aim to predict the type */award/award_winner* for an entity that won an award after $3^{rd}$ September, 2013. Hence, we use the *Freebase* description in the training data snapshot and *Wikipedia* snapshot on $3^{rd}$ September, 2013 to get the features for entities.

One might worry that the new snapshot might contain a significant amount of emerging facts so it could not be an effective way to evaluate the KBC algorithms. Therefore, we examine the difference between the training snapshot and test snapshot manually and found that this is likely not the case. For example, we randomly selected 25 */award/award_winner* instances that were added to the test snapshot and found that all of them had won at least one award before $3^{rd}$ September, 2013.

Note that while this automatic evaluation is closer to the real-world scenario, it is still not perfect as the new KB snapshot is still incomplete. Therefore, we also perform human evaluation on a small dataset to verify the effectiveness of our approach.

[2]In this work, we also do not aim to correct existing false positive errors in *Freebase*

### 3.2 Global Evaluation Metric

*Mean average precision* (MAP) (Manning et al., 2008) is now commonly used to evaluate KB completion methods (Mintz et al., 2009; Riedel et al., 2013). MAP is defined as the mean of *average precision* over all entity (or relation) types. MAP treats each entity type equally (not explicitly accounting for their distribution). However, some types occur much more frequently than others. For example, in our large-scale experiment with 500 entity types, there are many entity types with only 5 instances in the test set while the most frequent entity type has tens of thousands of missing instances. Moreover, MAP only measures the ability of the methods to correctly rank predictions within a type.

To account for the high variance in the distribution of entity types and measure the ability of the methods to correctly rank predictions across types we use global average precision (GAP) (similarly to micro-F1) as an additional evaluation metric for KB completion. We convert the multi-label classification problem to a binary classification problem where the label of an entity and type pair is true if the entity has that type in *Freebase* and false otherwise. GAP is the average precision of this transformed problem which can measure the ability of the methods to rank predictions both within and across entity types.

Prior to us, Bordes et al. (2013) use mean reciprocal rank as a global evaluation metric for a KBC task. We use average precision instead of mean reciprocal rank since MRR could be biased to the top predictions of the method (West et al., 2014)

While GAP captures global ordering, it would be

beneficial to measure the quality of the top $k$ predictions of the model for bootstrapping and active learning scenarios (Lewis and Gale, 1994; Cucerzan and Yarowsky, 1999). We report G@k, GAP measured on the top $k$ predictions (similarly to *Precision@k* and *Hits@k*). This metric can be reliably used to measure the overall quality of the top $k$ predictions.

## 4 Global Objective for Knowledge Base Completion

We describe our approach for predicting missing entity types in a KB in this section. While we focus on recovering entity types in this paper, the methods we develop can be easily extended to other KB completion tasks.

### 4.1 Global Objective Framework

During training, only positive examples are observed in KB completion tasks. Similar to previous work (Mintz et al., 2009; Bordes et al., 2013; Riedel et al., 2013), we get negative training examples by treating the unobserved data in the KB as negative examples. Because the number of unobserved examples is much larger than the number of facts in the KB, we follow previous methods and sample few unobserved negative examples for every positive example.

Previous methods largely neglect the sampling methods on unobserved negative examples. The proposed global object framework allows us to systematically study the effect of the different sampling methods to get negative data, as the performance of the model for different evaluation metrics does depend on the sampling method.

We consider a training snapshot of the KB $\Lambda_0$, containing facts of the form $(e, t)$ where $e$ is an entity in the KB with type $t$. Given a fact $(e, t)$ in the KB, we consider two types of negative examples constructed from the following two sets: $\mathcal{N}_E(e, t)$ is the "negative entity set", and $\mathcal{N}_T(e, t)$ is the "negative type set". More precisely,

$$\mathcal{N}_E(e,t) \subset \{e' | e' \in E, e' \neq e, (e', t) \notin \Lambda_0\},$$

and

$$\mathcal{N}_T(e,t) \subset \{t' | t' \in T, t' \neq t, (e, t') \notin \Lambda_0\}.$$

Let $\theta$ be the model parameters, $m = |\mathcal{N}_E(e,t)|$ and $n = |\mathcal{N}_T(e,t)|$ be the number of negative examples and types considered for training respectively. For each entity-type pair $(e, t)$, we define the scoring function of our model as $s(e, t|\theta)$.[3] We define two loss functions one using negative entities and the other using negative types:

$$L_E(\Lambda_0, \theta) = \sum_{(e,t)\in\Lambda_0, e'\in\mathcal{N}_E(e,t)} [s(e', t) - s(e,t) + 1]_+^k,$$

and

$$L_T(\Lambda_0, \theta) = \sum_{(e,t)\in\Lambda_0, t'\in\mathcal{N}_T(e,t)} [s(e, t') - s(e,t) + 1]_+^k,$$

where $k$ is the power of the loss function ($k$ can be 1 or 2), and the function $[\cdot]_+$ is the hinge function.

The global objective function is defined as

$$\min_\theta Reg(\theta) + CL_T(\Lambda_0, \theta) + CL_E(\Lambda_0, \theta), \quad (1)$$

where $Reg(\theta)$ is the regularization term of the model, and $C$ is the regularization parameter. Intuitively, the parameters $\theta$ are estimated to rank the observed facts above the negative examples with a margin. The total number of negative examples is controlled by the size of the sets $\mathcal{N}_E$ and $\mathcal{N}_T$. We experiment by sampling only entities or only types or both by fixing the total number of negative examples in Section 5.

The rest of section is organized as follows: we propose three algorithms based on the global objective in Section 4.2. In Section 4.3, we discuss the relationship between the proposed algorithms and existing approaches. Let $\Phi(e) \rightarrow R^{d_e}$ be the feature function that maps an entity to its feature representation, and $\Psi(t) \rightarrow R^{d_t}$ be the feature function that maps an entity type to its feature representation.[4] $d_e$ and $d_t$ represent the feature dimensionality of the entity features and the type features respectively. Feature representations of the entity types ($\Psi$) is only used in the embedding model.

[3]We often use $s(e, t)$ as an abbreviation of $s(e, t|\theta)$ in order to save space.

[4]This gives the possibility of defining features for the labels in the output space but we use a simple one-hot representation for types right now since richer features did not give performance gains in our initial experiments.

**Algorithm 1** The training algorithm for Linear.Adagrad.

Initialize $\mathbf{w}_t = 0, \forall t = 1 \ldots |T|$
**for** $(e, t) \in \Lambda_0$ **do**
  **for** $e' \in \mathcal{N}_E(e, t)$ **do**
    **if** $\mathbf{w}_t^T \Phi(e) - \mathbf{w}_t^T \Phi(e') - 1 < 0$ **then**
      AdaGradUpdate$(w_t, \Phi(e') - \Phi(e))$
    **end if**
  **end for**
  **for** $t' \in \mathcal{N}_T(e, t)$ **do**
    **if** $\mathbf{w}_t^T \Phi(e) - \mathbf{w}_{t'}^T \Phi(e) - 1 < 0$ **then**
      AdaGradUpdate$(w_t, -\Phi(e))$
      AdaGradUpdate$(w_{t'}, \Phi(e))$.
    **end if**
  **end for**
**end for**

### 4.2 Algorithms

We propose three different algorithms based on the global objective framework for predicting missing entity types. Two algorithms use the linear model and the other one uses the embedding model.

**Linear Model** The scoring function in this model is given by $s(e, t|\theta = \{\mathbf{w}_t\}) = \mathbf{w}_t^T \Phi(e)$, where $\mathbf{w}_t \in R^{d_e}$ is the parameter vector for target type $t$. The regularization term in Eq. (1) is defined as follows: $R(\theta) = 1/2 \sum_{t=1} \mathbf{w}_t^T \mathbf{w}_t$. We use $k = 2$ in our experiments. Our first algorithm is obtained by using the dual coordinate descent algorithm (Hsieh et al., 2008) to optimize Eq. (1), where we modified the original algorithm to handle multiple weight vectors. We refer to this algorithm as **Linear.DCD**.

While DCD algorithm ensures convergence to the global optimum solution, its convergence can be slow in certain cases. Therefore, we adopt an online algorithm, Adagrad (Duchi et al., 2011). We use the hinge loss function ($k = 1$) with no regularization ($Reg(\theta) = \emptyset$) since it gave best results in our initial experiments. We refer to this algorithm as **Linear.Adagrad**, which is described in Algorithm 1. Note that AdaGradUpdate$(x, g)$ is a procedure which updates the vector $x$ with the respect to the gradient $g$.

**Embedding Model** In this model, vector representations are constructed for entities and types using linear projection matrices. Recall $\Psi(t) \rightarrow R^{d_t}$ is the feature function that maps a type to its feature representation. The scoring function is given by

**Algorithm 2** The training algorithm for the embedding model.

Initialize $\mathbf{V}, \mathbf{U}$ randomly.
**for** $(e, t) \in \Lambda_0$ **do**
  **for** $e' \in \mathcal{N}_E(e, t)$ **do**
    **if** $s(e, t) - s(e', t) - 1 < 0$ **then**
      $\mu \leftarrow \mathbf{V}^T \Psi(t)$
      $\eta \leftarrow \mathbf{U}^T (\Phi(e') - \Phi(e))$
      **for** $i \in 1 \ldots d$ **do**
        AdaGradUpdate$(\mathbf{U}_i, \mu[i](\Phi(e') - \Phi(e)))$
        AdaGradUpdate$(\mathbf{V}_i, \eta[i]\Psi(t))$
      **end for**
    **end if**
  **end for**
  **for** $t' \in \mathcal{N}_T(e, t)$ **do**
    **if** $s(e, t) - s(e, t') - 1 < 0$ **then**
      $\mu \leftarrow \mathbf{V}^T (\Psi(t') - \Psi(t))$
      $\eta \leftarrow \mathbf{U}^T \Phi(e)$
      **for** $i \in 1 \ldots d$ **do**
        AdaGradUpdate$(\mathbf{U}_i, \mu[i]\Phi(e))$
        AdaGradUpdate$(\mathbf{V}_i, \eta[i](\Psi(t') - \Psi(t)))$
      **end for**
    **end if**
  **end for**
**end for**

$$s(e, t|\theta = (\mathbf{U}, \mathbf{V})) = \Psi(t)^T \mathbf{V} \mathbf{U}^T \Phi(e),$$

where $\mathbf{U} \in R^{d_e \times d}$ and $\mathbf{V} \in R^{d_t \times d}$ are projection matrices that embed the entities and types in a $d$-dimensional space. Similarly to the linear classifier model, we use the l1-hinge loss function ($k = 1$) with no regularization ($Reg(\theta) = \emptyset$). $\mathbf{U}_i$ and $\mathbf{V}_i$ denote the $i$-th column vector of the matrix $\mathbf{U}$ and $\mathbf{V}$, respectively. The algorithm is described in detail in Algorithm 2.

The embedding model has more expressive power than the linear model, but the training unlike in the linear model, converges only to a local optimum solution since the objective function is non-convex.

### 4.3 Relationship to Existing Methods

Many existing methods for relation extraction and entity type prediction can be cast as a special case under the global objective framework. For example, we can consider the work in relation extraction (Mintz et al., 2009; Bordes et al., 2013; Riedel et al., 2013) as models trained with $\mathcal{N}_T(e, t) = \emptyset$. These models are trained only using negative entities which we refer to as Negative Entity (NE) objective. The entity type prediction model in Ling and Weld (2012) is a linear model with $\mathcal{N}_E(e, t) = \emptyset$ which

| | 70 types | 500 types |
|---|---|---|
| Entities | 2.2M | 2.2M |
| Training Data Statistics ($\Lambda_0$) | | |
| positive example | 4.5M | 6.2M |
| max #ent for a type | 1.1M | 1.1M |
| min #ent for a type | 6732 | 32 |
| Test Data Statistics ($\Lambda - \Lambda_0$) | | |
| positive examples | 163K | 240K |
| negative examples | 17.1M | 132M |
| negative/positive ratio | 105.22 | 554.44 |

Table 1: Statistics of our dataset. $\Lambda_0$ is our training snapshot and $\Lambda$ is our test snapshot. An example is an entity-type pair.

we refer to as the Negative Type (NT) objective. The embedding model described in Weston et al. (2011) developed for image retrieval is also a special case of our model trained with the NT objective.

While the $NE$ or $NT$ objective functions could be suitable for some classification tasks (Weston et al., 2011), the choice of objective functions for the KBC tasks has not been well motivated. Often the choice is made neither with theoretical foundation nor with empirical support. To the best of our knowledge, the global objective function, which includes both $\mathcal{N}_E(e,t)$ and $\mathcal{N}_T(e,t)$, has not been considered previously by KBC methods.

## 5 Experiments

In this section, we give details about our dataset and discuss our experimental results. Finally, we perform manual evaluation on a small subset of the data.

### 5.1 Data

First, we evaluate our methods on 70 entity types with the most observed facts in the training data.[5] We also perform large-scale evaluation by testing the methods on 500 types with the most observed facts in the training data.

Table 1 shows statistics of our dataset. The number of positive examples is much larger in the training data compared to that in the test data since the test set contains only facts that were added to the more recent snapshot. An additional effect of this is that most of the facts in the test data are about entities that are not very well-known or famous. The high negative to positive examples ratio in the test data makes this dataset very challenging.

[5] We removed few entity types that were trivial to predict in the test data.

### 5.2 Automatic Evaluation Results

Table 2 shows automatic evaluation results where we give results on 70 types and 500 types. We compare different aspects of the system on 70 types empirically.

**Adagrad Vs DCD** We first study the linear models by comparing Linear.DCD and Linear.AdaGrad. Table 2a shows that Linear.AdaGrad consistently performs better for our task.

**Impact of Features** We compare the effect of different features on the final performance using Linear.AdaGrad in Table 2b. Types are represented by boolean features while Freebase description and Wikipedia full text are represented using *tf-idf* weighting. The best MAP results are obtained by using all the information (T+D+W) while best GAP results are obtained by using the Freebase description and Wikipedia article of the entity. Note that the features are simply concatenated when multiple resources are used. We tried to use *idf* weighting on type features and on all features, but they did not yield improvements.

**The Importance of Global Objective** Table 2c and 2d compares global training objective with NE and NT training objective. Note that all the three methods use the same number of negative examples. More precisely, for each $(e,t) \in \Lambda_0$, $|\mathcal{N}_E(e,t)| + |\mathcal{N}_T(e,t)| = m + n = 2$. The results show that the global training objective achieves best scores on both MAP and GAP for classifiers and low-dimensional embedding models. Among NE and NT, NE performs better on the type-based metric while NT performs better on the global metric.

**Linear Model Vs Embedding Model** Finally, we compare the linear classifier model with the embedding model in Table 2e. The linear classifier model performs better than the embedding model in both MAP and GAP.

We perform large-scale evaluation on 500 types with the description features (as experiments are expensive) and the results are shown in Table 2f.

| Features | Algorithm | MAP | GAP |
|---|---|---|---|
| Description | Linear.Adagrad | 29.17 | 28.17 |
| | Linear.DCD | 28.40 | 27.76 |
| Description + Wikipedia | Linear.Adagrad | **33.28** | **31.97** |
| | Linear.DCD | 31.92 | 31.36 |

(a) Adagrad vs. Dual coordinate descent (DCD). Results are obtained using linear models trained with global training objective (m=1, n=1) on 70 types.

| Features | MAP | GAP |
|---|---|---|
| Type (T) | 12.33 | 13.58 |
| Description (D) | 29.17 | 28.17 |
| Wikipedia (W) | 30.81 | 30.56 |
| D + W | 33.28 | **31.97** |
| T + D + W | **36.13** | 31.13 |

(b) Feature Comparison. Results are obtained from using Linear.Adagrad with global training objective (m=1, n=1) on 70 types.

| Features | Objective | MAP | GAP |
|---|---|---|---|
| D + W | NE (m = 2) | 33.01 | 23.97 |
| | NT (n = 2) | 31.61 | 29.09 |
| | Global (m = 1, n = 1) | 33.28 | **31.97** |
| T + D + W | NE (m = 2) | 34.56 | 21.79 |
| | NT (n = 2) | 34.45 | 31.42 |
| | Global (m = 1, n = 1) | **36.13** | 31.13 |

(c) Global Objective vs NE and NT. Results are obtained using Linear.Adagrad on 70 types.

| Features | Objective | MAP | GAP |
|---|---|---|---|
| D + W | NE (m = 2) | 30.92 | 22.38 |
| | NT (n = 2) | 25.77 | 23.40 |
| | Global (m = 1, n = 1) | **31.60** | **30.13** |
| T + D + W | NE (m = 2) | 28.70 | 19.34 |
| | NT (n = 2) | 28.06 | 25.42 |
| | Global (m = 1, n = 1) | 30.35 | 28.71 |

(d) Global Objective vs NE and NT. Results are obtained using the embedding model on 70 types.

| Features | Model | MAP | GAP | G@1000 | G@10000 |
|---|---|---|---|---|---|
| D + W | Linear.Adagrad | 33.28 | **31.97** | **79.63** | **68.08** |
| | Embedding | 31.60 | 30.13 | 73.40 | 64.69 |
| T + D + W | Linear.Adagrad | **36.13** | 31.13 | 70.02 | 65.09 |
| | Embedding | 30.35 | 28.71 | 62.61 | 64.30 |

(e) Model Comparison. The models were trained with the global training objective (m=1, n=1) on 70 types.

| Model | MAP | GAP | G@1000 | G@10000 |
|---|---|---|---|---|
| Linear.Adagrad | **13.28** | **20.49** | **69.23** | **60.14** |
| Embedding | 9.82 | 17.67 | 55.31 | 51.29 |

(f) Results on 500 types using Freebase description features. We train the models with the global training objective (m=1, n=1).

Table 2: Automatic Evaluation Results. Note that $m = |\mathcal{N}_E(e,t)|$ and $n = |\mathcal{N}_T(e,t)|$.

One might expect that with the increased number of types, the embedding model would perform better than the classifier since they share parameters across types. However, despite the recent popularity of embedding models in NLP, linear model still performs better in our task.

### 5.3 Human Evaluation

To verify the effectiveness of our KBC algorithms, and the correctness of our automatic evaluation method, we perform manual evaluation on the top 100 predictions of the output obtained from two different experimental setting and the results are shown in Table 3. Even though the automatic evaluation gives pessimistic results since the test KB is also incomplete[6], the results indicate that the automatic evaluation is correlated with manual evaluation. More excitingly, among the 179 unique instances we manually evaluated, 17 of them are still[7] missing in Freebase which emphasizes the effectiveness of our approach.

[6]This is true even with existing automatic evaluation methods.

[7]at submission time.

| Features | G@100 | G@100-M | Accuracy-M |
|---|---|---|---|
| D + W | **87.68** | **97.31** | **97** |
| T + D + W | 84.91 | 91.47 | 88 |

Table 3: Manual vs. Automatic evaluation of top 100 predictions on 70 types. Predictions are obtained by training a linear classifier using Adagrad with global training objective (m=1, n=1). G@100-M and Accuracy-M are computed by manual evaluation.

### 5.4 Error Analysis

- **Effect of training data**: We find the performance of the models on a type is highly dependent on the number of training instances for that type. For example, the linear classifier model when evaluated on 70 types performs 24.86 % better on the most frequent 35 types compared to the least frequent 35 types. This indicates bootstrapping or active learning techniques can be profitably used to provide more supervision for the methods. In this case, G@k would be an useful metric to compare the effectiveness of the different methods.

- **Shallow Linguistic features**: We found some of the false positive predictions are caused by the use of shallow linguistic features. For example, an entity who has acted in a movie and composes music only for television shows is wrongly tagged with the type /film/composer since words like "movie", "composer" and "music" occur frequently in the Wikipedia article of the entity (`http://en.wikipedia.org/wiki/J._J._Abrams`).

## 6 Related Work

**Entity Type Prediction and Wikipedia Features** Much of previous work (Pantel et al., 2012; Ling and Weld, 2012) in entity type prediction has focused on the task of predicting entity types at the sentence level. Yao et al. (2013) develop a method based on matrix factorization for entity type prediction in a KB using information within the KB and New York Times articles. However, the method was still evaluated only at the sentence level. Toral and Munoz (2006), Kazama and Torisawa (2007) use the first line of an entity's Wikipedia article to perform named entity recognition on three entity types.

**Knowledge Base Completion** Much of precious work in KB completion has focused on the problem of relation extraction. Majority of the methods infer missing relation facts using information within the KB (Nickel et al., 2011; Lao et al., 2011; Socher et al., 2013; Bordes et al., 2013) while methods such as Mintz et al. (2009) use information in text documents. Riedel et al. (2013) use both information within and outside the KB to complete the KB.

**Linear Embedding Model** Weston et al. (2011) is one of first work that developed a supervised linear embedding model and applied it to image retrieval. We apply this model to entity type prediction but we train using a different objective function which is more suited for our task.

## 7 Conclusion and Future Work

We propose an evaluation framework comprising of methods for dataset construction and evaluation metrics to evaluate KBC approaches for inferring missing entity type instances. We verified that our automatic evaluation is correlated with human evaluation, and our dataset and evaluation scripts are publicly available.[8] Experimental results show that models trained with our proposed global training objective produces higher quality ranking within and across types when compared to baseline methods.

In future work, we plan to use information from entity linked documents to improve performance and also explore active leaning, and other human-in-the-loop methods to get more training data.

## References

Jonathan Berant, Vivek Srikumar, Pei-Chun Chen, Abby Vander Linden, Brittany Harding, Brad Huang, and Christopher D. Manning. 2013. Semantic parsing on freebase from question-answer pairs. In *Empirical Methods in Natural Language Processing.*

Kurt Bollacker, Colin Evans, Praveen Paritosh, Tim Sturge, and Jamie Taylor. 2008. Freebase: a collaboratively created graph database for structuring human knowledge. In *Proceedings of the ACM SIGMOD International Conference on Management of Data.*

[8] `http://research.microsoft.com/en-US/downloads/df481862-65cc-4b05-886c-acc181ad07bb/default.aspx`

Antoine Bordes, Nicolas Usunier, Alberto Garcia-Duran, Jason Weston, and Oksana Yakhnenko. 2013. Translating embeddings for modeling multi-relational data. In *Advances in Neural Information Processing Systems.*

Antoine Bordes, Sumit Chopra, and Jason Weston. 2014. Question answering with subgraph embeddings. In *Empirical Methods in Natural Language Processing.*

Andrew Carlson, Justin Betteridge, Bryan Kisiel, Burr Settles, Estevam R. Hruschka, and A. 2010. Toward an architecture for never-ending language learning. In *In AAAI.*

Kai-Wei Chang, Wen tau Yih, Bishan Yang, and Christopher Meek. 2014. Typed tensor decomposition of knowledge bases for relation extraction. In *Proceedings of the 2014 Conference on Empirical Methods in Natural Language Processing.*

Silviu Cucerzan and David Yarowsky. 1999. Language indep endent named entity recognition combining morphological and contextual evidence. In *oint SIGDAT Conference on Empirical Methods in Natural Language Processing and Very Large Corpora.*

John Duchi, Elad Hazan, and Yoram Singer. 2011. Adaptive subgradient methods for online learning and stochastic optimization. In *Journal of Machine Learning Research.*

Yuan Fang and Ming-Wei Chang. 2014. Entity linking on microblogs with spatial and temporal signals. In *Transactions of the Association for Computational Linguistics.*

Stephen Guo, Ming-Wei Chang, and Emre Kiciman. 2013. To link or not to link? a study on end-to-end tweet entity linking. In *The North American Chapter of the Association for Computational Linguistics.*, June.

Hannaneh Hajishirzi, Leila Zilles, Daniel S. Weld, and Luke Zettlemoyer. 2013. Joint coreference resolution and named-entity linking with multi-pass sieves. In *Empirical Methods in Natural Language Processing.*

Cho-Jui Hsieh, Kai-Wei Chang, Chih-Jen Lin, S. Sathiya Keerthi, and S. Sundararajan. 2008. A dual coordinate descent method for large-scale linear svm. In *International Conference on Machine Learning.*

Jun'ichi Kazama and Kentaro Torisawa. 2007. Exploiting wikipedia as external knowledge for named entity recognition. In *Joint Conference on Empirical Methods in Natural Language Processing and Computational Natural Language Learning.*

Tom Kwiatkowski, Eunsol Choi, Yoav Artzi, and Luke. Zettlemoyer. 2013. Scaling semantic parsers with on-the-fly ontology matching. In *Empirical Methods in Natural Language Processing.*

Ni Lao, Tom Mitchell, and William W. Cohen. 2011. Random walk inference and learning in a large scale knowledge base. In *Conference on Empirical Methods in Natural Language Processing.*

David D. Lewis and William A. Gale. 1994. A sequential algorithm for training text classifiers. In *ACM SIGIR Conference on Research and Development in Information Retrieval.*

Xiao Ling and Daniel S. Weld. 2012. Fine-grained entity recognition. In *Association for the Advancement of Artificial Intelligence.*

Christopher D. Manning, Prabhakar Raghavan, and Hinrich Schütze. 2008. Introduction to information retrieval. In *Cambridge University Press, Cambridge, UK.*

Mike Mintz, Steven Bills, Rion Snow, and Dan Jurafsky. 2009. Distant supervision for relation extraction without labeled data. In *Association for Computational Linguistics and International Joint Conference on Natural Language Processing.*

Maximilian Nickel, Volker Tresp, and Hans-Peter Kriegel. 2011. A three-way model for collective learning on multi-relational data. In *International Conference on Machine Learning.*

Patrick Pantel, Thomas Lin, and Michael Gamon. 2012. Mining entity types from query logs via user intent modeling. In *Association for Computational Linguistics.*

Lev Ratinov and Dan Roth. 2012. Learning-based multi-sieve co-reference resolution with knowledge. In *Joint Conference on Empirical Methods in Natural Language Processing and Computational Natural Language Learning.*

Sebastian Riedel, Limin Yao, Andrew McCallum, and Benjamin M. Marlin. 2013. Relation extraction with matrix factorization and universal schemas. In *The North American Chapter of the Association for Computational Linguistics.*

Richard Socher, Danqi Chen, Christopher Manning, and Andrew Y. Ng. 2013. Reasoning with neural tensor networks for knowledge base completion. In *Advances in Neural Information Processing Systems.*

Antonio Toral and Rafael Munoz. 2006. A proposal to automatically build and maintain gazetteers for named entity recognition by using wikipedia. In *European Chapter of the Association for Computational Linguistics.*

Robert West, Evgeniy Gabrilovich, Kevin Murphy, Shaohua Sun, Rahul Gupta, and Dekang Lin. 2014. Knowledge base completion via search-based question answering. In *Proceedings of the 23rd international conference on World wide web*, pages 515–526. International World Wide Web Conferences Steering Committee.

Jason Weston, Samy Bengio, and Nicolas Usunier. 2011. Wsabie: Scaling up to large vocabulary image annotation. In *International Joint Conference on Artificial Intelligence*.

Xuchen Yao and Benjamin Van Durme. 2014. Information extraction over structured data: Question answering with freebase. In *Association for Computational Linguistics*.

Limin Yao, Sebastian Riedel, and Andrew McCallum. 2013. Universal schema for entity type prediction. In *Proceedings of the 2013 Workshop on Automated Knowledge Base Construction*.

# Robust Morphological Tagging with Word Representations

**Thomas Müller** and **Hinrich Schütze**
Center for Information and Language Processing
University of Munich, Germany
muellets@cis.lmu.de

## Abstract

We present a comparative investigation of word representations for part-of-speech (POS) and morphological tagging, focusing on scenarios with considerable differences between training and test data where a *robust* approach is necessary. Instead of adapting the model towards a specific domain we aim to build a robust model across domains. We developed a test suite for robust tagging consisting of six languages and different domains. We find that representations similar to Brown clusters perform best for POS tagging and that word representations based on linguistic morphological analyzers perform best for morphological tagging.

## 1 Introduction

Most natural language processing (NLP) tasks can be better solved if a preprocessor tags each word in the natural language input with a label like "noun, singular" or "verb, past tense" that gives some indication of the syntactic role that the word plays in its context. The most common form of such preprocessing is POS tagging. However, for morphologically rich languages, a large subset of the languages of the world, POS tagging in its original form – where labels are syntactic categories with little or no morphological information – does not make much sense. The reason is that POS and morphological properties are mutually dependent, so solving only one task or solving the tasks sequentially is inadequate. The most important dependence of this type is that POS can be read off morphology in many cases; e.g., the morphological suffix "-iste" is a reliable indicator of the informal second person singular preterite indicative form of a verb in Spanish. In what follows, we use the term "morphological tagging" to refer to "morphological and POS tagging" since morphological tags generally include POS information.

The importance of morphological tagging as part of the computational linguistics processing pipeline motivated us to conduct the research reported in this paper. The specific setting that we address is increasingly recognized as the setting in which most practical NLP takes place: We look at scenarios with considerable differences between the training data and the application data, i.e., between the data that the tagger is trained on and the data that it is applied to. This type of scenario is frequent because of the great diversity and variability of natural language and because of the high cost of annotation – which makes it impossible to create large training sets for each new domain. For this reason, we address morphological tagging in a setting in which training and application data differ.

The most common approach to this setting is domain adaptation. Domain adaptation has been demonstrated to have good performance in scenarios with differently distributed training/test data. However, it has two disadvantages. First, it requires the availability of data from the target domain. Second, we need to do some extra work in domain adaptation – consisting of taking target domain data and using it to adapt our NLP system to the target domain – and we end up with a number of different versions of our NLP system. The extra work required and the pro-



*Human Language Technologies: The 2015 Annual Conference of the North American Chapter of the ACL*, pages 526–536,
Denver, Colorado, May 31 – June 5, 2015. 

liferation of different versions increase the possibility of errors and increase the complexity of deploying NLP technology. Similar to other recent work (Zhang and Wang, 2009), we therefore take an approach that is different from domain adaptation. We build a system that is *robust across domains without any modification*. As a result, no extra work is required when the system is applied to a new domain: there is only one system and we can use it for all domains.

The key to making NLP components robust across domains is *the use of powerful domain-independent representations for words*. One of the main contributions of this paper is that we compare the performance of the most important representations that can be used for this purpose. We find that two of these are best suited for robust tagging. MarLiN (Martin et al., 1998) clusters – a derivative of Brown clusters – perform best for POS tagging. MarLiN clusters are also an order of magnitude more efficient to induce than the original Brown clusters. We provide an open source implementation of MarLiN clustering as part of this publication (Section 8). We compare the word representations to Morphological Analyzers (MAs), which are finite-state transducers that find the stems of a form and use them to derive all its possible morphological readings. MAs produce the best results in our experiments on morphological tagging. Our initial expectation was that domain differences and lack of coverage would put manually created MAs at a disadvantage when compared to learning algorithms that are run on very large text corpora. However, our results clearly show that MA-based representations are the best representations to use for robust morphological tagging.

The motivation for our work is that both morphological tagging and the "robust" application setting are important areas of research in NLP. To support this research, we created an extensive evaluation set for six languages. This involved identifying morphologically rich languages in which usable data sets with different distributional properties were available, designing mappings between different tag sets, organizing a manual annotation effort for one of the six languages and preparing large "general" (not domain-specific) data sets for unsupervised learning of word representations. The preparation and publication (Section 8) of this test suite is in itself a significant contribution.

The remainder of this paper is structured as follows. Section 2 discusses related work. Section 3 presents the representations we tested. Section 4 describes the data sets and the annotation and conversion efforts required to create the in-domain (ID) and out-of-domain (OOD) data sets. In Section 5, we describe the experiments and discuss our findings. In Section 6, we provide an analysis of our results. Section 7 summarizes our findings and contributions.

## 2 Related Work

**Morphological tagging** (Oflazer and Kuruöz, 1994; Hajič and Hladká, 1998) is the task of assigning a morphological reading to a token in context. The morphological reading consists of features such as case, gender, person and tense and is represented as a single tag. This allows for the application of standard sequence labeling algorithms such as Conditional Random Fields (CRFs) (Lafferty et al., 2001), but also puts an upper bound on the accuracy as only readings occurring in the training set can be produced. It is still the standard approach to morphological disambiguation as the number of readings that cannot be produced is usually small.

The related work can be divided in systems that try to exploit certain properties of a language (Habash and Rambow, 2005; Yuret and Türe, 2006) and language-independent systems (Hajič, 2000; Smith et al., 2005). In this paper, we adopt a language-independent approach.

**Semi-supervised learning** attempts to increase the accuracy of a machine learning system by using additional unlabeled data. Word representations, especially Brown clusters, have been extensively used for named entity recognition (NER) (Miller et al., 2004), parsing (Koo et al., 2008) and POS tagging (Collobert and Weston, 2008; Huang et al., 2009). In these papers, word representations were shown to yield consistent improvements and to often outperform traditional semi-supervised methods such as self-training. Prior work on semi-supervised training for morphological tagging includes Spoustová et al. (2009) and Chrupala (2011). In contrast to this earlier work on morphological tagging, we study a number of morphologically more complex and diverse languages. We also compare learned representations to representations obtained from MAs.

**Domain adaptation** (DA) attempts to adapt a model trained on a source domain to a target domain. DA can be broadly divided into supervised and unsupervised approaches depending on whether labeled target domain data is available or not. Among unsupervised approaches to DA, representation learning (Ando and Zhang, 2005; Blitzer et al., 2006) uses the unlabeled target domain data to induce a structure that is suitable for transferring information from the labeled source domain to the target domain. Similar to representation learning for DA, we attempt to include word representations into the model. However, we induce the representation from a *general domain* in an attempt to obtain a model that has robust high accuracy across domains, for the source domain as well as for the target domains, for which neither labeled nor unlabeled training data is available.

## 3 Representations

We survey the following distributional representations: (i) count vectors reduced by a Singular Value Decomposition (SVD), (ii) word clusters induced using the likelihood of a class-based language model, (iii) distributed embeddings trained using a neural network and (iv) accumulated tag counts, a task-specific representation obtained from an automatically tagged corpus.

**Singular value decomposition** of word-feature cooccurrence matrices (Schütze, 1995) has been found to be a fast and efficient way to obtain distributed embeddings. The approach selects a subset of the vocabulary as so-called feature words, usually by including words up to a certain frequency rank. Every word form can then be represented by the accumulated counts of feature words occurring to its left and right. Then an SVD is applied to the cooccurrence matrix as a form of dimension reduction and to reduce sparsity.

We also experimented with unreduced count vectors, but they did not give better results than SVD reduced count vectors. SVD-based representations have been used in English POS induction (Lamar et al., 2010) as well as as features in English POS tagging and syntactic chunking (Huang et al., 2009); they have a similar level of accuracy as unsupervised Hidden Markov Models (HMMs) in these studies.

**Language model-based (LM-based) word clusters** were introduced by Brown et al. (1992) and later found to be helpful in a range of NLP tasks. The basic idea is to find the optimal clustering with respect to the likelihood of a class-based language model:

$$g = \arg\max_{g} \prod_{i=1}^{|D|} p(g(x_i)|g(x_{i-1})) \cdot p(x_i|g(x_i))$$

where $g(x)$ is the cluster assignment function that maps a word form $x$ to a cluster and $|D|$ denotes the length of the training set. Brown et al. (1992) propose a greedy bottom-up algorithm for the optimization that merges the pair of clusters that yields the smallest loss in likelihood; as well as a more efficient approximation of that algorithm that limits the number of clusters under consideration and still works well in practice. It is used by most work in the literature (Liang, 2005; Turian et al., 2010; Koo et al., 2008).

We, however, found the algorithm proposed by Martin et al. (1998) to be faster and to give slightly better results. The algorithm is similar to K-means in that it starts with an initial clustering and greedily improves the objective function by moving single words to their optimal cluster. In contrast to K-means, it updates the objective function immediately. The algorithm has also been shown to work well in unsupervised POS induction (Clark, 2003; Blunsom and Cohn, 2011). Our implementation of this algorithm is called MarLiN and has been made available as open-source software (Section 8). Miller et al. (2004) use tags of different granularity induced from unlabeled text to improve the performance of an averaged perceptron tagger (Collins, 2002) on an English NER task.

The Brown algorithm induces a tree where leaves represent a single word form and the root node the entire vocabulary. Intermediate nodes represent clusters of different sizes and can be addressed by a binary string specifying the path from the root node to the cluster. Brown clusters are also used by Koo et al. (2008) to improve dependency parsing for English and Czech. Chrupala (2011) compare Brown clusters to a Latent Dirichlet Allocation

(LDA) model on Spanish and French morphological tagging and find them to yield similar performance.[1]

**Neural networks** have been used by Collobert and Weston (2008) to train embeddings for POS tagging as well as other NLP tasks. These embeddings – henceforth *CW embeddings* – are trained by building a neural network that given contexts of a word as input is trained to discriminate between the correct center word and a random word. The proposed training algorithm is reported to need several days or even weeks, but has been reimplemented by Al-Rfou et al. (2013), who induced embeddings for the Wikipedias of more than 100 languages. Turian et al. (2010) find that the performance of Brown clusters is competitive with more training intensive embeddings like CW. In our experiments, we find that MarLiN clusters slightly outperform CW. We do not evaluate bag-of-words models such as WORD2VEC (Mikolov et al., 2013), because the ordering of words is essential for finding morphological properties.

**Accumulated tag counts** (ACT) are a form of task-specific sparse representation. The unlabeled corpus is first annotated by a tagger; for each occurring word form, the number of times a specific tag was assigned can then be used as a representation. Goldberg and Elhadad (2013) and (Szántó and Farkas, 2014) show that using such information in the word-preterminal emission probabilities of PCFGs can improve parsing accuracy. Specifically, Szántó and Farkas (2014) show that this approach performs as well as an MA in some cases. We find MAs to be more effective than the accumulated count embeddings; this is not a contradiction as we try to improve the performance of the tagger itself.

## 4 Data Preparation

Our test suite consists of data sets for six different languages: Czech (cs), English (en), German (de), Hungarian (hu), Spanish (es) and Latin (la). Czech, German, Hungarian and Latin are morphologically rich. We chose these languages because they represent different families: Germanic (English, German), Romance (Latin, Spanish), Slavic (Czech) and Finno-Ugric (Hungarian) and different degrees of morphological complexity and syncretism. For example, English and Spanish rarely mark case while the other languages do; and as an agglutinative language, Hungarian features a low number of possible readings for a word form while languages like German can have more than 40 different readings for a word form. An additional criterion was to have a sufficient amount of labeled OOD data. The data sets also feature an interesting selection of domain differences. For example, for Latin we have texts from different epochs while the English data contains canonical and non-canonical text.

**Labeled Data.** This section describes the annotation and conversion we performed to create consistent ID and OOD data sets.[2] No conversion was required for Hungarian, English and Latin as the data is already annotated in a consistent way.

For Hungarian we use the (multi-domain) Szeged Dependency Treebank (Vincze et al., 2010). We use the part that was used in the SPMRL 2013 shared task (Seddah et al., 2013) as ID data (news-wire) and an excerpt from the novel *1984* and a *Windows 2000* manual as OOD data.

For Latin we use the PROIEL treebank (Haug and Jøhndal, 2008). It consists of data from the *Vulgate* (bible text, ≈ 380 AD), *Commentarii de Bello Gallico* (≈ 50 BC), Letters from Cicero to his friend Atticus (≈ 50 BC) and *The Pilgrimage of Aetheria* (≈ 380 AD). We use the biggest text source *(Vulgate)* as ID data and the remainder as OOD data.

For English we use the SANCL shared task data (Petrov and McDonald, 2012), which consists of Ontonotes 4.0 as ID data and five OOD domains from the Google Web treebank: Yahoo! Answers, weblogs, news groups, business reviews and emails. For Czech we use the part of the Prague Dependency Treebank (PDT) (Böhmová et al., 2003) that was used in the CoNLL 2009 shared tasks (Hajič et al., 2009) as ID data. We use the Czech part of the Multext East (MTE) corpus (Erjavec, 2010) as OOD data. MTE consists of translations of the

[1]The authors claim that LDA Gibbs sampling is faster than the induction of Brown clusters because it only depends linearly on the number of clusters. We, however, could not train their models on our bigger data sets as the sampling depends linearly on the number of tokens.

[2]Table 5 of the appendix provides a structured overview over the domains and resources used for each language. The appendix can be found at `http://cistern.cis.lmu.de/marmot/naacl2015/appendix.pdf`.

novel *1984* that have been annotated morphologically. PDT and MTE have been annotated using two different guidelines that without further annotation effort could only be merged by reducing them to a common subset. Specifically, we removed features such as sub POS tags as well as markers for (in)animacy. The PDT features a number of tags that are ambiguous and could not always be resolved. The gender feature Q for example can mean feminine or neuter. If we could not disambiguate such a tag, we removed it; this results in morphological tags that are not present in the MTE corpus and a relatively high number of unseen tags. Instead of describing the conversion process in greater detail we refer to our conversion scripts (Section 8).

For Spanish we use the part of the AnCora corpus (Taulé et al., 2008) of CoNLL 2009 and the IULA treebank (Marimon et al., 2012), which consists of five domains: law, economics, medicine, computer science and environment. We use the AnCora corpus as ID data set and IULA as OOD data set. The two treebanks have been annotated using the same annotation scheme, but slightly different guidelines. Similar to Czech we merged the data sets by deleting features that could not be merged or were not present in one of the treebanks. Again we refer to the conversion script for further details (Section 8).

For German we use the Tiger treebank (Brants et al., 2002) in the same split as Müller et al. (2013) as ID data and the Smultron corpus (Volk et al., 2010) as OOD data. Smultron consists of four parts: a description of Alpine hiking routes, a DVD manual, an excerpt of Sophie's World and economics texts. It has been annotated with POS and syntax, but not with morphological features. We annotated Smultron following the Tiger guidelines. The annotation process was similar to Marimon et al. (2012) in that the data sets were automatically tagged with the MORPH tagger MarMoT (Müller et al., 2013) and then manually corrected by two annotators. This tagger is a strong baseline as we could include features based on gold lemma, POS and syntax (Seeker and Kuhn, 2013). The agreement of the annotators was .9628 and the $\kappa$ agreement .64.[3] As most of the differences between the annotators were cases where only one of the annotators had corrected an obvious error that the other had overlooked, the differences were resolved by the annotators themselves.

We used the provided segmentation if available and otherwise split ID data 8/1/1 into training, development and test sets and OOD data 1/1 into development and test sets if not mentioned otherwise. We thus have a classical setup of in-domain news paper text vs. prose, medical, law, economic or technical texts for Czech, German, Spanish and Hungarian. For English we have canonical vs. non-canonical data and for Latin data of different epochs (ca. 400 AD vs 50 BC). Additionally, for German one of the test domains is written in Swiss German.

Looking at some statistics of the labeled data sets,[4] we find that: Hungarian and Latin are the languages with the highest OOV rates (27% and 37%, which for reasons of consistency we will henceforth write as follows: .27 and .37); Hungarian has a very productive agglutinative morphology while the high number of Latin OOVs can be explained by the small training set (<60,000); Czech features the highest unknown tag rate (.05) as well as the highest unseen word-tag rate (.16). This can be explained by the limits of the conversion procedure we discussed above, e.g., ambiguous features like Q.

**Unlabeled Data.** As unlabeled data we use Wikipedia dumps from 2014 for all languages except for Latin for which we use the Patrologia Latina, a collection of clerical texts from ca. 100 AD to 1200 AD from Corpus Corporum (Roelli, 2014). We do not use the Latin version of Wikipedia because it is written by enthusiasts, not by native speakers, and contains many errors.

We preprocessed the Wikipedia dumps with WIKIPEDIAEXTRACTOR (Attardi and Fuschetto, 2013) and NLTK'S (Bird et al., 2009) implementation of PUNKT (Kiss and Strunk, 2006) to detect sentence boundaries. Tokenization was performed using MAGYARLANC (Hungarian, Zsibrita et al. (2013)), STANFORD TOKENIZER (English, Manning et al. (2014)), FREELING (Spanish, Padró and Stanilovsky (2012)) and CZECHTOK[5] (Czech). For

[3] For calculating $\kappa$, we assume that random agreement occurs when both annotators agree with the reading proposed by the tagger. We then estimate the probability of random agreement by multiplying the individual estimated probabilities of changing the proposed tagging. This yields a random agreement probability of .8965.

[4] Complete tables are in the appendix: Tables 1 and 2.

[5] http://sourceforge.net/projects/

Latin, we removed punctuation because PROIEL does not contain punctuation. We also split off the clitics *ne*, *que* and *ve* if the resulting token was accepted by LatMor (Springmann et al. (2014)). Following common practice, we normalized the text by replacing digits with 0s.[6]

In our experiments, we extract representations for the 250,000 most frequent word types. This vocabulary size is comparable to other work; e.g., Turian et al. (2010) use 269,000 types. This threshold yields low fractions of uncovered tokens[7] for English and Latin (.009 and .02). For the other languages, this fraction rises to .04. We also extract the morphological readings of the words in this vocabulary using MAGYARLANC (Hungarian, Zsibrita et al. (2013)), FreeLing (English and Spanish, Padró and Stanilovsky (2012)), SMOR (German, Schmid et al. (2004)), an MA from Charles University (Czech, Hajič (2001)) and LatMor (Latin, Springmann et al. (2014)). Throughout this paper we extract one feature for each cluster id or MA reading of the current word form. For example, SMOR produces two readings for the German word form *erhielt* 'received': <1><Sg><Past><Ind> and <2><Sg><Past><Ind>, we thus fire two features representing the respective tags whenever *erhielt* is seen in the data. We also experimented with cluster indexes of neighboring uni/bigrams, but obtained no consistent improvement. For the dense embeddings we analogously extract the vector of the current word form.

## 5 Experiments

For all our experiments we use MarMoT (Müller et al., 2013) a joint POS and morphological tagger.[8] The CRF tagger employs a pruning strategy on forward-backward lattices to efficiently handle big tag sets and higher orders. Its feature set is similar to Ratnaparkhi (1996) and Toutanova et al. (2003) and includes prefixes, suffixes, immediate lexical context and shape features based on capitalization, special characters and digits. MarMoT was shown to be a competitive POS and morphological tagger across six languages (Müller et al., 2013). In order to make sure that it is also robust in an OOD setup we compare it to the two popular taggers SVMTool (Giménez and Marquez, 2004) and Morfette (Chrupała et al., 2008). The results are summarized in Table 1.

MarMoT uses stochastic gradient descent and produces different results in each training run. We therefore always report the average of five runs. The OOD numbers are macro-averages over the different OOD data sets of a language. [9] The tables in this paper are based on the development sets; the only exception to this is Table 5, which is based on the test set. MarMoT outperforms SVMTool and Morfette on every language and setup (ID / OOD) except for the Spanish OOD data set. For Czech, German and Latin the improvements over the best baseline are $>1$. Different orders of MarMoT behave as expected: higher-order models (order$>1$) outperform first-order models. The only exception to this is Latin. This suggests a drastic difference of the tag transition probabilities between the Latin ID and OOD data sets. Given the results in Table 1 and for simplicity we use an second-order MarMoT model in all subsequent experiments.

**LM-based clustering.** We first compare different implementations of LM-based clustering. The implementation of Brown clustering by Liang (2005) is most commonly used. Its hierarchical binary structure can be used to extract clusterings of varying granularity by selecting different prefixes of the path from the root to a specific word form. Following other work (Ratinov and Roth, 2009; Turian et al., 2010), we induce 1000 clusters and select path lengths 4, 6, 10 and 20. We call this representation Brown_path. We compare Brown_path to mkcls[10] (Och, 1999) and MarLiN. These implementations just induce flat clusterings of a certain size; we thus run them for cluster sizes 100, 200, 500 and 1000 to also obtain cluster ids of different sizes. The cluster sizes roughly resemble the granularity obtained in Brown$_{\text{path}}$. We call the corresponding mod-

czechtok/

[6]For statistics of the unlabeled data sets cf. Table 3 of the appendix.

[7]Cf. Table 4 in the appendix.

[8]http://cistern.cis.lmu.de/marmot/

[9]Throughout this paper we use the approximate randomization test (Yeh, 2000) to establish significance. To this end, we compare the output of the medians of the five independent models. We regard p-values $<.05$ as significant.

[10]mkcls implements a similar training algorithm as MarLiN, but uses simulated annealing, not greedy maximization.

| | | MarMoT (1) | | MarMoT (2) | | MarMoT (3) | | Morfette | | SVMTool | |
|---|---|---|---|---|---|---|---|---|---|---|---|
| | | ID | OOD | ID | OOD | ID | OOD | ID | OOD | ID | OOD |
| morph | cs | 93.27 | 77.83 | **93.89** | 78.52 | 93.86 | **78.55** | 91.48 | 76.56 | 91.06 | 75.41 |
| | de | 88.90 | 82.74 | 90.26 | 84.19 | **90.54*** | **84.30** | 85.89 | 80.28 | 85.98 | 78.08 |
| | es | 98.21 | 93.24 | **98.22** | 93.62 | 98.16 | 93.42 | 97.95 | **93.97*** | 97.96 | 91.36 |
| | hu | **96.11** | 89.78 | 96.07 | **89.83** | 95.92 | 89.70 | 95.47 | 89.18 | 94.72 | 88.44 |
| | la | 86.09 | **67.90*** | 86.44 | 67.47 | **86.47** | 67.40 | 83.68 | 65.06 | 84.09 | 65.65 |

Table 1: Baseline experiments comparing MarMoT models of different orders with Morfette and SVMTool. Numbers denote average accuracies on ID and OOD development sets on the full morphological tagging task. A result significantly better than the other four ID (resp. OOD) results in its row is marked with $*$.

| | | $\text{Brown}_{\text{flat}}$ | | $\text{Brown}_{\text{path}}$ | | MarLiN | | mkcls | |
|---|---|---|---|---|---|---|---|---|---|
| | | ID | OOD | ID | OOD | ID | OOD | ID | OOD |
| pos | cs | 99.19 | 97.25 | 99.18 | 97.21 | 99.19 | **97.26** | **99.21** | **97.26** |
| | de | 98.08 | 93.42 | 98.07 | 93.47 | 98.10 | 93.44 | **98.11** | **93.64*** |
| | en | 96.99 | 91.67 | 97.02 | 91.71 | 97.01 | 91.71 | **97.03** | **91.86*** |
| | es | 98.84 | 97.91 | 98.84 | **97.97** | **98.87** | **97.97** | 98.84 | 97.90 |
| | hu | 97.95 | 93.40 | 97.89 | 93.39 | 97.98 | 93.36 | **97.99** | **93.42** |
| | la | 96.78 | 86.49 | 96.62 | 86.60 | 96.91 | **87.24** | **96.95** | 87.19 |
| morph | cs | 94.20 | 78.95 | 94.23 | 79.01 | **94.35** | **79.14** | 94.32 | 79.11 |
| | de | 90.71 | 85.39 | 90.75 | 85.44 | **90.78** | **85.58** | 90.68 | 85.47 |
| | es | 98.47 | 95.08 | 98.47 | 95.12 | **98.48** | **95.15** | **98.48** | 95.13 |
| | hu | 96.60 | 90.57 | 96.52 | 90.54 | 96.60 | 90.64 | **96.61** | **90.66** |
| | la | 87.53 | 71.69 | 87.44 | 71.60 | **87.87** | **72.08** | 87.67 | 71.88 |

Table 2: Tagging results for LM-based models

| | | Baseline | | MarLiN | | CW | |
|---|---|---|---|---|---|---|---|
| | | ID | OOD | ID | OOD | ID | OOD |
| pos | cs | 99.00 | 96.80 | **99.16*** | **97.06** | 99.12 | 97.00 |
| | de | 97.87 | 92.21 | **98.03** | **93.35*** | **98.03** | 93.02 |
| | en | 96.92 | 91.12 | **97.05** | 91.72 | 97.00 | **91.86*** |
| | es | 98.62 | 96.70 | 98.79 | **97.82*** | **98.80** | 97.31 |
| | hu | 97.49 | 92.79 | **97.94** | 93.30 | 97.88 | **93.40** |
| | la | 95.80 | 81.92 | **96.35*** | **85.52*** | 95.88 | 84.50 |
| morph | cs | 93.89 | 78.52 | **94.23*** | **78.91** | 94.10 | 78.80 |
| | de | 90.26 | 84.19 | 90.54 | 85.08 | **90.59** | **85.21** |
| | es | 98.22 | 93.62 | **98.44** | **94.97*** | **98.44** | 94.32 |
| | hu | 96.07 | 89.83 | 96.47 | 90.60 | **96.48** | **90.95*** |
| | la | 86.44 | 67.47 | **86.95** | **70.30*** | 86.76 | 69.32 |

Table 3: Tagging results for CW

els $\text{Brown}_{\text{flat}}$, mkcls and MarLiN. The runtime of the Brown algorithm depends quadratically on the number of clusters while mkcls and MarLiN have linear complexity. This is reflected in the training times: For German the Brown algorithm takes $\approx 5000$ min, mkcls $\approx 2000$ min and MarLiN $\approx 500$ min.

Table 2 shows that the absolute differences between systems are small, but overall MarLiN and mkcls are better.[11] We conclude that systems based on the algorithm of Martin et al. (1998) are slightly more accurate for tagging and are several times faster than the more frequently used version of Brown et al. (1992). We thus use MarLiN for the remainder of this paper.

**Neural Network Representations.** We compare MarLiN with the implementation of CW by Al-Rfou et al. (2013). They extracted 64-dimensional representations for only the most frequent 100,000 word forms. To make the comparison fair, we use the intersection of our and their representation vocabularies.[12] The results in Table 3 show that MarLiN is best in 15 out of 22 cases and significantly better in eight. CW is best in 9 out of 22 cases and significantly better in two. We conclude that LM-based representations are more suited for tagging as they can be induced faster, are smaller and give better results.

**SVD and ACT Representations.** For the SVD-based representation we use feature ranks out of {500, 1000} and dimensions out of {50, 100, 200, 500}. We found that l1-normalizing the vectors before and after the SVD improved results slightly. For the accumulated tag counts (ACT) we annotate the data with our baseline model and extract word-tag probabilities. The probabilities are then used as sparse real-valued features. Table 4 shows that all representations outperform the baseline. Improvements are biggest for Latin. Overall, SVD outperforms ACT and is outperformed by MarLiN and MA. MarLiN gives the best representations for POS tagging while MA outperforms MarLiN in MORPH tagging. Table 5 shows that the findings for the baseline, MarLiN and MA also hold for the test set.

[11] $\text{Brown}_{\text{path}}$ reaches the same performance as MarLiN in one case: pos/es/OOD.

[12] We also use representations from Wikipedia (instead of Corpus Corporum) for Latin to increase the similarity of the training data.

| | | Baseline | | ACT | | MarLiN | | MA | | SVD | |
|---|---|---|---|---|---|---|---|---|---|---|---|
| | | ID | OOD | ID | OOD | ID | OOD | ID | OOD | ID | OOD |
| pos | cs | 99.00 | 96.80 | 99.11 | 97.03 | **99.19** | **97.26** | 99.18 | 97.25 | 99.11 | 97.09 |
| | de | 97.87 | 92.21 | 98.00 | 92.92 | **98.10** | **93.44***| 98.00 | 92.87 | 98.09 | 92.88 |
| | en | 96.92 | 91.12 | 96.97 | 91.47 | **97.01** | 91.71 | 96.99 | 91.57 | 97.00 | **91.75** |
| | es | 98.62 | 96.70 | 98.79 | 97.09 | **98.87** | **97.97** | **98.87** | 97.89 | 98.80 | 97.16 |
| | hu | 97.49 | 92.79 | 97.84 | 93.15 | 97.98 | 93.36 | **98.12*** | **93.77*** | 97.86 | 93.30 |
| | la | 95.80 | 81.92 | 96.17 | 83.40 | **96.91** | **87.24*** | 96.81 | 86.31 | 96.36 | 85.01 |
| morph | cs | 93.89 | 78.52 | 94.16 | 78.75 | 94.35 | 79.14 | **94.48*** | **79.41*** | 94.14 | 78.94 |
| | de | 90.26 | 84.19 | 90.56 | 84.78 | **90.78** | 85.58 | 90.75 | **85.75** | 90.69 | 85.15 |
| | es | 98.22 | 93.62 | 98.38 | 93.92 | 98.48 | 95.15 | **98.56*** | **95.43*** | 98.40 | 94.18 |
| | hu | 96.07 | 89.83 | 96.25 | 90.07 | 96.60 | 90.64 | **96.83*** | **91.14*** | 96.46 | 90.50 |
| | la | 86.44 | 67.47 | 86.96 | 68.61 | 87.87 | 72.08 | **88.40*** | **73.23*** | 87.45 | 70.81 |

Table 4: Tagging results for the baseline and four different representations

| | | Baseline | | MarLiN | | MA | |
|---|---|---|---|---|---|---|---|
| | | ID | OOD | ID | OOD | ID | OOD |
| pos | cs | 98.88 | 96.43 | **99.11*** | 96.94 | 99.06 | **96.95** |
| | de | 97.32 | 91.10 | **97.73*** | **92.00*** | 97.60 | 91.49 |
| | en | 97.36 | 89.81 | **97.58*** | **90.65*** | 97.47 | 90.51 |
| | es | 98.66 | 97.94 | **98.94*** | 98.33 | 98.87 | **98.38** |
| | hu | 96.84 | 92.11 | 97.08 | 92.95 | **97.46*** | **93.25*** |
| | la | 93.02 | 81.35 | **95.20** | **87.58*** | 95.11 | 86.45 |
| morph | cs | 93.93 | 77.50 | 94.33 | 78.12 | **94.50*** | **78.37*** |
| | de | 88.41 | 82.78 | 89.18 | 83.91 | **89.32*** | **84.09** |
| | es | 98.30 | 95.65 | 98.53 | 95.92 | **98.54** | **96.33*** |
| | hu | 94.82 | 88.82 | 95.46 | 89.98 | **95.85*** | **90.46*** |
| | la | 82.09 | 65.59 | 84.67 | 71.25 | **85.91*** | **72.42*** |

Table 5: Test set results for: baseline, MarLiN, MA

| | | | $f=0$ | $0<f<10$ | $f>=10$ |
|---|---|---|---|---|---|
| morph | cs | MarLiN | 0.29 | 0.22 | 0.11 |
| | | MA | 0.37 | 0.35 | 0.16 |
| | de | MarLiN | 1.02 | 0.17 | 0.19 |
| | | MA | 0.85 | 0.29 | 0.42 |
| | es | MarLiN | 1.36 | 0.15 | 0.02 |
| | | MA | 1.50 | 0.27 | 0.04 |
| | hu | MarLiN | 0.62 | 0.18 | 0.00 |
| | | MA | 1.07 | 0.20 | 0.03 |
| | la | MarLiN | 3.76 | 0.80 | 0.06 |
| | | MA | 4.98 | 0.69 | 0.09 |

Table 6: Improvement compared to the baseline for different frequency ranges of words on OOD

| | | | | | |
|---|---|---|---|---|---|
| morph | cs | MarLiN | gen 0.70 | cas 0.41 | pos 0.35 |
| | | MA | gen 0.85 | cas 0.51 | pos 0.31 |
| | de | MarLiN | gen 1.23 | pos 1.14 | num 0.62 |
| | | MA | gen 1.37 | pos 0.63 | num 0.59 |
| | es | MarLiN | sub 1.49 | gen 1.21 | pos 1.07 |
| | | MA | sub 1.34 | gen 1.24 | pos 1.10 |
| | hu | MarLiN | cas 0.71 | sub 0.66 | pos 0.52 |
| | | MA | cas 0.88 | sub 0.84 | pos 0.76 |
| | la | MarLiN | pos 5.19 | cas 3.46 | gen 3.25 |
| | | MA | pos 4.68 | gen 3.85 | cas 3.01 |

Table 7: Improvement compared to the baseline for different features

## 6 Analysis

We now analyze why MarLiN and MA perform better than the baseline. First we compare the improvements in absolute error rate over the baseline by grouping word forms by their training set frequency $f$. The number are shown in Table 6. We find that most of the improvement comes from OOV words. Rare words (frequency $<10$) show a smaller, but still important contribution while the contribution of frequent words can be almost neglected for four languages. The exception is German where frequent words contribute more to the error reduction than rare words. This could be caused by syncretisms such as in plural noun phrases where the gender is not marked in determiner and adjective and can only be derived from the head noun; e.g., the adjectives in *schwere Schulfächer* 'difficult school subjects' and *verdächtige Personen* 'suspect persons' are unmarked for gender and the correct genders (neuter vs. feminine) cannot be inferred from distributional information or suffixes for the nouns (although gender is easy to infer distributionally for singular forms of nouns).

Looking at the morphological features with the highest improvement in absolute error rate (Table 7) we find, that the features with the highest improvement are POS, SUB-POS (a finer division of POS, e.g., nouns are split into proper / common nouns), gender, case and number. For all languages POS and – if part of the annotation – SUB-POS are among the three features with the highest improvements. Gender is also always among the three features with the highest improvements for the four languages that have gender (es, de, la, cs). We just discussed an example for German where gender could not be derived from context or inflectional suffixes. Other languages also have word forms that do not mark gender, e.g., Spanish masculine *ave* 'bird' vs. feminine *llave* 'key'. The gender can, however, easily be derived if the word representation encodes whether a word form has been seen with a specific determiner or adjective on its right or left.

Lastly, we use Jaccard similarity[13] to compare the sets of gold and predicted morphological features. Jaccard can be interpreted as a soft variant of accuracy: If the two tags are identical it yields 1 and otherwise it corresponds to the number of correctly predicted features divided by the size of the union of gold and predicted features.

| morph | | cs | de | es | hu | la |
|---|---|---|---|---|---|---|
| | accuracy | 79.41 | 85.72 | 95.43 | 91.14 | 73.23 |
| | Jaccard | 89.89 | 90.71 | 96.77 | 93.52 | 83.68 |

This table demonstrates that the evaluation measure we have used throughout this paper – a tag counts as completely wrong if a single feature was misidentified even though all others are correct – is conservative. On a feature-by-feature basis accuracy would be much higher. The difference is largest for Czech and Latin.

## 7 Conclusion

We have presented a test suite for morphological tagging consisting of in-domain (ID) and out-of-domain (OOD) data sets for six languages: Czech, English, German, Hungarian, Latin and Spanish. We converted some of the data sets to obtain a reasonably consistent annotation and manually annotated the German part of the Smultron treebank. We surveyed four different word representations: SVD-reduced count vectors, LM-based clusters, accumulated tag counts and CW embeddings. We found that the LM-based clusters outperformed the other representations for POS and MORPH tagging, ID and OOD data sets and all languages. We also showed that our implementation of MarLiN (Martin et al., 1998) is an order-of-magnitude more efficient and performs slightly better than the implementation by Liang (2005). We also compared the learned representations to manually created Morphological Analyzers (MAs). We found that MarLiN outperforms MAs in POS tagging, but that it is substantially worse in morphological tagging. In our analysis of the results, we showed that both MarLiN and MAs decrease the error most for out-of-vocabulary words and for the features POS and gender.

[13] $\text{Jaccard}(U,V) = |U \cap V| / |U \cup V|$

## 8 Resources

As part of this publication we also release the following resources at `http://cistern.cis.lmu.de/marmot/`: (i) our implementation of MarLiN as open-source (ii) the morphological layer of the German part of the SMULTRON corpus. For easier reproducibility, we also made (iii) the preprocessed Wikipedia dumps and the induced representation dictionaries available. (iv) Morphological dictionaries were released to the extent this was compatible with the usage agreement. (v) We also published the conversion code for unifying the Spanish and Czech annotations.

## Acknowledgments

We would like to thank the anonymous reviewers for their comments. The first author is a recipient of the Google Europe Fellowship in Natural Language Processing, and this research is supported by this Google Fellowship. The annotation of the SMULTRON data was supported by Deutsche Forschungsgemeinschaft (grant DFG 2246/2, Wordgraph).

## References

Rami Al-Rfou, Bryan Perozzi, and Steven Skiena. 2013. Polyglot: Distributed word representations for multilingual NLP. In *Proceedings of CoNLL*.

Rie Kubota Ando and Tong Zhang. 2005. A high-performance semi-supervised learning method for text chunking. In *Proceedings of ACL*.

Giuseppe Attardi and Antonia Fuschetto. 2013. Wikipedia Extractor. `http://medialab.di.unipi.it/wiki/Wikipedia_Extractor`.

Steven Bird, Ewan Klein, and Edward Loper. 2009. *Natural language processing with Python*. " O'Reilly Media, Inc.".

John Blitzer, Ryan McDonald, and Fernando Pereira. 2006. Domain adaptation with structural correspondence learning. In *Proceedings of EMNLP*.

Phil Blunsom and Trevor Cohn. 2011. A hierarchical Pitman-Yor process HMM for unsupervised part of speech induction. In *Proceedings of ACL-HLT*.

Alena Böhmová, Jan Hajič, Eva Hajičová, and Barbora Hladká. 2003. The Prague dependency treebank. In *Proceedings of Treebanks*. Springer.

Sabine Brants, Stefanie Dipper, Silvia Hansen, Wolfgang Lezius, and George Smith. 2002. The TIGER treebank. In *Proceedings of the workshop on treebanks and linguistic theories*.

Peter F. Brown, Peter V. Desouza, Robert L. Mercer, Vincent J. Della Pietra, and Jenifer C. Lai. 1992. Class-based n-gram models of natural language. *Computational linguistics*.

Grzegorz Chrupała, Georgiana Dinu, and Josef Van Genabith. 2008. Learning morphology with Morfette. In *Proceedings of LREC*.

Grzegorz Chrupala. 2011. Efficient induction of probabilistic word classes with LDA. In *Proceedings of IJCNLP*.

Alexander Clark. 2003. Combining distributional and morphological information for part of speech induction. In *Proceedings of EACL*.

Michael Collins. 2002. Discriminative training methods for hidden Markov models: Theory and experiments with perceptron algorithms. In *Proceedings of EMNLP*.

Ronan Collobert and Jason Weston. 2008. A unified architecture for natural language processing: Deep neural networks with multitask learning. In *Proceedings of ICML*.

Tomaž Erjavec. 2010. MULTEXT-East version 4: Multilingual morphosyntactic specifications, lexicons and corpora. In *Proceedings of LREC*.

Jesús Giménez and Lluis Marquez. 2004. SVMTool: A general POS tagger generator based on support vector machines. In *Proceedings of LREC*.

Yoav Goldberg and Michael Elhadad. 2013. Word segmentation, unknown-word resolution, and morphological agreement in a Hebrew parsing system. *Computational Linguistics*.

Nizar Habash and Owen Rambow. 2005. Arabic tokenization, part-of-speech tagging and morphological disambiguation in one fell swoop. In *Proceedings of ACL*.

Jan Hajič and Barbora Hladká. 1998. Tagging inflective languages: Prediction of morphological categories for a rich, structured tagset. In *Proceedings of Coling*.

Jan Hajič, Massimiliano Ciaramita, Richard Johansson, Daisuke Kawahara, Maria Antònia Martí, Lluís Màrquez, Adam Meyers, Joakim Nivre, Sebastian Padó, Jan Štěpánek, et al. 2009. The CoNLL-2009 shared task: Syntactic and semantic dependencies in multiple languages. In *Proceedings of CoNLL*.

Jan Hajič. 2000. Morphological tagging: Data vs. dictionaries. In *Proceedings of NAACL*.

Jan Hajič. 2001. Czech Free Morphology.

Dag TT Haug and Marius Jøhndal. 2008. Creating a parallel treebank of the old Indo-European bible translations. In *Proceedings of LaTeCH*.

Zhongqiang Huang, Vladimir Eidelman, and Mary Harper. 2009. Improving a simple bigram hmm part-of-speech tagger by latent annotation and self-training. In *Proceedings of NAACL*.

Tibor Kiss and Jan Strunk. 2006. Unsupervised multilingual sentence boundary detection. *Computational Linguistics*.

Terry Koo, Xavier Carreras, and Michael Collins. 2008. Simple semi-supervised dependency parsing. In *Proceedings of ACL*.

John Lafferty, Andrew McCallum, and Fernando Pereira. 2001. Conditional random fields: Probabilistic models for segmenting and labeling sequence data. In *Proceedings of ICML*.

Michael Lamar, Yariv Maron, Mark Johnson, and Elie Bienenstock. 2010. SVD and clustering for unsupervised POS tagging. In *Proceedings of ACL*.

Percy Liang. 2005. *Semi-supervised learning for natural language*. Ph.D. thesis, Massachusetts Institute of Technology.

Christopher D. Manning, Mihai Surdeanu, John Bauer, Jenny Finkel, Steven Bethard, and David McClosky. 2014. The Stanford CoreNLP natural language processing toolkit. In *Proceedings of ACL: System Demonstrations*.

Montserrat Marimon, Beatriz Fisas, Núria Bel, Marta Villegas, Jorge Vivaldi, Sergi Torner, Mercè Lorente, Silvia Vázquez, and Marta Villegas. 2012. The IULA treebank. In *Proceedings of LREC*.

Sven Martin, Jorg Liermann, and Hermann Ney. 1998. Algorithms for bigram and trigram word clustering. *Speech communication*.

Tomas Mikolov, Kai Chen, Greg Corrado, and Jeffrey Dean. 2013. Efficient estimation of word representations in vector space. In *Proceedings of ICLR: Workshop*.

Scott Miller, Jethran Guinness, and Alex Zamanian. 2004. Name tagging with word clusters and discriminative training. In *Proceedings of NAACL-HLT*.

Thomas Müller, Helmut Schmid, and Hinrich Schütze. 2013. Efficient higher-order CRFs for morphological tagging. In *Proceedings of EMNLP*.

Franz J. Och. 1999. An efficient method for determining bilingual word classes. In *Proceedings of EACL*.

Kemal Oflazer and İlker Kuruöz. 1994. Tagging and morphological disambiguation of turkish text. In *Proceedings of the Applied natural language processing*.

Lluís Padró and Evgeny Stanilovsky. 2012. Freeling 3.0: Towards wider multilinguality. In *Proceedings of LREC*.

Slav Petrov and Ryan McDonald. 2012. Overview of the 2012 shared task on parsing the web. In *Proceedings of SANCL*.

Lev Ratinov and Dan Roth. 2009. Design challenges and misconceptions in named entity recognition. In *Proceedings of CoNLL*.

Adwait Ratnaparkhi. 1996. A maximum entropy model for part-of-speech tagging. In *Proceedings of EMNLP*.

Phillip Roelli. 2014. Corpus Corporum. `http://www.mlat.uzh.ch/MLS/`.

Helmut Schmid, Arne Fitschen, and Ulrich Heid. 2004. SMOR: A German computational morphology covering derivation, composition and inflection. In *Proceedings of LREC*.

Hinrich Schütze. 1995. Distributional part-of-speech tagging. In *Proceedings of EACL*.

Djamé Seddah, Reut Tsarfaty, Sandra Kübler, Marie Candito, Jinho Choi, Richárd Farkas, Jennifer Foster, Iakes Goenaga, Koldo Gojenola, Yoav Goldberg, et al. 2013. Overview of the SPMRL 2013 shared task: Cross-framework evaluation of parsing morphologically rich languages. In *SPMRL*. Association for Computational Linguistics.

Wolfgang Seeker and Jonas Kuhn. 2013. The effects of syntactic features in automatic prediction of morphology. In *Proceedings of EMNLP*.

Noah A. Smith, David A. Smith, and Roy W. Tromble. 2005. Context-based morphological disambiguation with random fields. In *Proceedings of EMNLP*.

Drahomíra "johanka" Spoustová, Jan Hajič, Jan Raab, and Miroslav Spousta. 2009. Semi-supervised training for the averaged perceptron pos tagger. In *Proceedings of EACL*.

Uwe Springmann, Dietmar Najock, Hermann Morgenroth, Helmut Schmid, Annette Gotscharek, and Florian Fink. 2014. OCR of historical printings of Latin texts: problems, prospects, progress. In *Proceedings of DATeCH*.

Zsolt Szántó and Richárd Farkas. 2014. Special techniques for constituent parsing of morphologically rich languages. In *Proceedings of EACL*.

Mariona Taulé, Maria Antònia Martí, and Marta Recasens. 2008. Ancora: Multilevel annotated corpora for Catalan and Spanish. In *Proceedings of LREC*.

Kristina Toutanova, Dan Klein, Christopher D. Manning, and Yoram Singer. 2003. Feature-rich part-of-speech tagging with a cyclic dependency network. In *Proceedings of NAACL*.

Joseph Turian, Lev Ratinov, and Yoshua Bengio. 2010. Word representations: A simple and general method for semi-supervised learning. In *Proceedings of ACL*.

Veronika Vincze, Dóra Szauter, Attila Almási, György Móra, Zoltán Alexin, and János Csirik. 2010. Hungarian dependency treebank. In *Proceedings of LREC*.

Martin Volk, Anne Göhring, Torsten Marek, and Yvonne Samuelsson. 2010. SMULTRON (version 3.0) — The Stockholm MULtilingual parallel TReebank.

Alexander Yeh. 2000. More accurate tests for the statistical significance of result differences. In *Proceedings of COLING*.

Deniz Yuret and Ferhan Türe. 2006. Learning morphological disambiguation rules for Turkish. In *Proceedings of NAACL*.

Yi Zhang and Rui Wang. 2009. Cross-domain dependency parsing using a deep linguistic grammar. In *Proceedings of ACL-AFNLP*.

János Zsibrita, Veronika Vincze, and Richárd Farkas. 2013. magyarlanc: A toolkit for morphological and dependency parsing of Hungarian. In *Proceedings of RANLP*.

# English orthography is not "close to optimal"

**Garrett Nicolai** and **Grzegorz Kondrak**
Department of Computing Science
University of Alberta
{nicolai,gkondrak}@ualberta.ca

## Abstract

In spite of the apparent irregularity of the English spelling system, Chomsky and Halle (1968) characterize it as "near optimal". We investigate this assertion using computational techniques and resources. We design an algorithm to generate word spellings that maximize both phonemic transparency and morphological consistency. Experimental results demonstrate that the constructed system is much closer to optimality than the traditional English orthography.

## 1 Introduction

English spelling is notorious for its irregularity. Kominek and Black (2006) estimate that it is about 3 times more complex than German, and 40 times more complex than Spanish. This is confirmed by lower accuracy of letter-to-phoneme systems on English (Bisani and Ney, 2008). A survey of English spelling (Carney, 1994) devotes 120 pages to describe phoneme-to-letter correspondences, and lists 226 letter-to-phoneme rules, almost all of which admit exceptions. Numerous proposals have been put forward for spelling reforms over the years, ranging from small changes affecting a limited set of words to complete overhauls based on novel writing scripts (Venezky, 1970).

In spite of the perceived irregularity of English spellings, Chomsky and Halle (1968) assert that they remarkably well reflect abstract underlying forms, from which the surface pronunciations are generated with "rules of great generality and wide applicability". They postulate two principles of an optimal orthographic system: (1) it should have "one representation for each lexical entry" (*consistency*); and, (2) "phonetic variation is not indicated where it is predictable by a general rule" (*predictability*). They conclude that "conventional orthography is [...] a near optimal system for the lexical representation of English words" (page 49), which we refer to as the *optimality claim*.

Chomsky and Halle's account of English orthography is not without its detractors. Steinberg (1973) argues against the idea that speakers store abstract underlying forms of separate morphemes and apply sequences of phonological rules during composition. Sampson (1985) cites the work of Yule (1978) in asserting that many common English word-forms provide counter-evidence to their vowel alternation observations. Derwing (1992) maintains that the observations only hold for five vowel alternations that can be predicted with simple spelling rules. According to Nunn (2006), the idea that spelling represents an abstract phonological level has been abandoned by most linguists. Sproat (2000) notes that few scholars of writing systems would agree with Chomsky and Halle, concluding that the evidence for a consistent morphological representation in English orthography is equivocal.

It is not our goal to formulate yet another proposal for reforming English orthography, nor even to argue that there is a need for such a reform. Furthermore, we refrain from taking into account other potential advantages of the traditional orthography, such as reflecting archaic pronunciation of native words, preserving the original spelling of loanwords, or maintaining orthographic similarity to cognates in other languages. Although these may be valid concerns, they are not considered as such by Chomsky and Halle. Instead, our primary objective is a deeper understanding of how the phono-



*Human Language Technologies: The 2015 Annual Conference of the North American Chapter of the ACL*, pages 537–545,
Denver, Colorado, May 31 – June 5, 2015. 

logical and morphological characteristics of English are reflected in its traditional orthography, which is currently the dominant medium of information exchange in the world.

In this paper, we investigate the issue of orthographic optimality from the computational perspective. We define metrics to quantify the degree of optimality of a spelling system in terms of phonemic transparency and morphological consistency. We design an algorithm to generate an orthography that maximizes both types of optimality, and implement it using computational tools and resources. We show experimentally that the traditional orthography is much further from optimality than our constructed system, which contradicts the claim of Chomsky and Halle.

## 2 Optimality

In this section, we define the notions of phonemic and morphemic optimality, and our general approach to quantifying them. We propose two theoretical orthographies that are phonemically and morphologically optimal, respectively. We argue that no orthographic system for English can be simultaneously optimal according to both criteria.

### 2.1 Phonemic optimality

A purely phonemic system would have a perfect one-to-one relationship between graphemes and phonemes. Rogers (2005) states that no standard writing system completely satisfies this property, although Finnish orthography comes remarkably close. For our purposes, we assume the International Phonetic Alphabet (IPA) transcription to be such an ideal system. For example, the IPA transcription of the word *viscosity* is [vɪskɑsəti]. We obtain the transcriptions from a digital dictionary that represents the General American pronunciation of English.

Phonemic transparency can be considered in two directions: from letters to phonemes, and vice versa. The pronunciation of Spanish words is recoverable from the spelling by applying a limited set of rules (Kominek and Black, 2006). However, there is some ambiguity in the opposite direction; for example, the phoneme [b] can be expressed with either 'b' or 'v'. As a result, it is not unusual for native Spanish speakers to make spelling mistakes. On the other hand, the orthography of Serbo-Croatian was originally created according to the rule "write as you speak", so that the spelling can be unambiguously produced from pronunciation. This does not mean that the pronunciation is completely predictable from spelling; for example, lexical stress is not marked (Sproat, 2000).

In this paper, we measure phonemic transparency by computing average perplexity between graphemes and phonemes. Roughly speaking, phonemic perplexity indicates how many different graphemes on average correspond to a single phoneme, while graphemic perplexity reflects the corresponding ambiguity of graphemes. We provide a formal definition in Section 5.

### 2.2 Morphological optimality

A purely morphemic writing system would have a unique graphemic representation for each morpheme. Chinese is usually given as an example of a near-morphemic writing system. In this paper, we construct an abstract morphemic spelling system for English by selecting a single alphabetic form for each morpheme, and simply concatenating them to make up words. For example, the morphemic spelling of *viscosity* could be 'viscous·ity'.[1]

We define morphemic optimality to correspond to the consistency principle of Chomsky and Halle. The rationale is that a unique spelling for each morpheme should allow related words to be readily identified in the mental lexicon. Sproat (2000) distinguishes between morpheme-oriented "deep" orthographies, like Russian, and phoneme-oriented "shallow" orthographies, like Serbo-Croatian.

We propose to measure morphemic consistency by computing the average edit distance between morpheme representations in different word-forms. The less variation morpheme spellings exhibit in a writing system, the higher the corresponding value of the morphemic transparency will be. We define the measure in Section 5.

It is impossible to achieve complete phonemic and morphemic optimality within one system designed for English spelling. For example, the stem morpheme of verb forms *hearing* and *heard* is

[1]Non-traditional spellings are written within single quotes. Morphemes may be explicitly separated by the centered dot character.

spelled identically but pronounced differently. If we changed the spellings to indicate the difference in pronunciation, we would move towards phonemic optimality, but away from morphemic optimality. Apart from purely phonographic or logographic variants, any English spelling system must be a compromise between phonemic and morphemic transparency. In this paper, we attempt to algorithmically create an orthography that simultaneously approaches the optimality along both dimensions.

## 3 Algorithm

In this section, we describe our algorithm for generating English spellings (Figure 1), which serves as a constructive proof that the traditional orthography is not optimal. Our objective is to find the best compromise between phonemic transparency and morphemic consistency. Section 3.1 explains how we derive a unique representation for each morpheme. Section 3.2 shows how the morpheme representations are combined into word spellings. Without a loss of generality, the generated spellings are composed of IPA symbols.

// Create word sets<br>
1: **for each** word $w$ in lexicon $L$ **do**<br>
2:     **for each** morpheme $m$ in $w$ **do**<br>
3:         add $w$ to word set $S_m$<br>
// Generate morpheme representations<br>
4: **for each** word set $S_m$ **do**<br>
5:     $m_0 :=$ longest representation of $m$<br>
6:     **for each** word $w$ in $S_m$ **do**<br>
7:         $a_w :=$ alignment of $m_0$ and $w$<br>
8:         add $a_w$ to multi-alignment $A$<br>
9:     **for each** position i in $A$ **do**<br>
10:         select representative phoneme $r[i]$<br>
11:     $r_m := r[1..|m_0|]$<br>
// Adopt a surface phoneme predictor<br>
12: *Pronounce* := *Predictor (L)*<br>
// Generate word representations<br>
13: **for each** word $w = m_1 \ldots m_k$ **do**<br>
14:     $r := r_{m_1} \cdot \ldots \cdot r_{m_k}$<br>
15:     **for each** phoneme $r[i]$ in $r$ **do**<br>
16:         **if** *Pronounce*$(r[i]) \neq w[i]$ **then**<br>
17:             $r[i] := w[i]$<br>
18:     $r_w := r[1..|w|]$

Figure 1: Spelling generation algorithm. All representations consists of phonemes.

### 3.1 Morpheme representations

We start by identifying all morphemes in the lexicon, and associating each morpheme with sets of words that contain it (lines 1–3 in Figure 1). An example word set that corresponds to the morpheme *atom* is shown in Table 1. Words may belong to more than one set. For example, the word *atomic* will also be included in the word set that corresponds to the morpheme *-ic*. We make no distinction between bound and free morphemes.

As can be seen in Table 1, English morphemes often have multiple phonemic realizations. The objective of the second step (lines 4–11) is to follow the consistency principle by establishing a single representation of each morpheme. They suggest that orthographic representations should reflect the underlying forms of morphemes as much as possible. Unfortunately, underlying forms are not attested, and there is no commonly accepted algorithm to construct them. Instead, our algorithm attempts to establish a sequence of phonemes that is maximally similar to the attested surface allomorphs.

Table 1 shows an example of generating the common representation for a morpheme. We extract the phonemic representation of each allomorph in the word set, and perform a multi-alignment of the representations by pivoting on the longest representation of the morpheme (lines 5–8). For each position in the multi-alignment, we identify the set of phonemes corresponding to that position. If there is no variation within a position, we simply adopt the common phoneme. Otherwise, we choose the phoneme that is most preferred in a fixed hierarchy of phonemes. In this case, since [æ] and [ɑ] are preferred to [ə], the resulting morpheme representation is ‘ætɑm’.

For selecting between variant phonemes, we follow a manually-constructed hierarchy of phonemes (Table 2), which roughly follows the principle of least effort. The assumption is that the phonemes requiring more articulatory effort to produce are more likely to represent the underlying phoneme. Within a single row, phonemes are listed in the order of preference. For example, alveolar fricatives like [s]

| | | | | | | | | | | | |
|---|---|---|---|---|---|---|---|---|---|---|---|
| | | | æ | t | ə | m | | | | | *atom* |
| | | | æ | t | ə | m | z | | | | *atoms* |
| | | | ə | t | ɑ | m | ɪ | k | | | *atomic* |
| | | | ə | t | ɑ | m | ɪ | k | l | i | *atomically* |
| s | ʌ | b | ə | t | ɑ | m | ɪ | k | | | *subatomic* |
| | | | æ | t | ɑ | m | | | | | |

Table 1: Extracting the common morphemic representation .

are preferred to post-alveolar ones like [ʃ], in order to account for palatalization. Since our representations are not intended to represent actual underlying forms, the choice of a particular phoneme hierarchy affects only the shape of the generated word spellings.

### 3.2 Word representations

Ideally, polymorphemic words should be represented by a simple concatenation of the corresponding morpheme representations. However, for languages that are not purely concatenative, this approach may produce forms that are far from the phonemic realizations. For example, assuming that the words *deceive* and *deception* share a morpheme, a spelling 'deceive·ion' would fail to convey the actual pronunciation [dəsɛpʃən]. The predictability principle of Chomsky and Halle implies that phonetic variation should only be indicated where it is not predictable by general rules. Unfortunately, the task of establishing such a set of general rules, which we discuss in Section 7, is not at all straightforward. Instead, we assume the existence of an oracle (line 12 in Figure 1) which predicts the surface pronunciation of each phoneme found in the concatenation of the morphemic forms.

In our algorithm (lines 13–18), the default spelling of the word is composed of the representations of its constituent morphemes conjoined with a separator character. If the predicted pronunciation matches the actual surface phoneme, the "underlying" phoneme is preserved; otherwise, it is substituted by the surface phoneme. This modification helps to maintain the resulting word spellings reasonably close to the surface pronunciation.

For example, consider the word *sincerity*. Suppose that our algorithm derives the representations of the two underlying morphemes as 'sɪnsir' and 'ɪti'. If, given the input 'sɪnsir·ɪti', the predictor correctly generates the surface pronunciation [sɪnsɛrəti], we adopt the input as our final spelling. However, if the prediction is [sɪnsirəti] instead, our final spelling becomes 'sɪnsɛr·ɪti', in order to avoid a potentially misleading spelling. Since the second vowel was incorrectly predicted, we determine it to be unpredictable, and thus represent it with the surface phoneme, rather than the underlying one. The choice of the predictor affects only the details of the generated spellings.

| | |
|---|---|
| Stops | b d g p t k |
| Affricates | dʒ tʃ |
| Fricatives | ð v z ʒ θ f s ʃ h |
| Nasals | m n ŋ |
| Liquids | l r |
| Glides | j w |
| Diphthongs | aɪ ɔɪ aʊ |
| Tense vowels | i e o u ɑ |
| Lax vowels | æ ɛ ɔ ʊ ʌ |
| Reduced vowels | ɪ ə |
| deletion | _ |

Table 2: Hierarchy of phonemes.

## 4 Implementation

In this section, we describe the specific data and tools that we use in our implementation of the algorithm described in the previous section.

### 4.1 Data

For the implementation of our spelling generation algorithm, we require a lexicon that contains morphological segmentation of phonemic representations of words. Since we have been been unsuccessful in finding such a lexicon, we extract the necessary information from two different resources: the CELEX lexical database (Baayen et al., 1995), which includes morphological analysis of words, and the Combilex speech lexicon (Richmond et al., 2009), which contains high-quality phonemic transcriptions. After intersecting the lexicons, and pruning it of proper nouns, function words, duplicate forms, and multi-word entries, we are left with approximately 51,000 word-forms that are annotated both morphologically and phonemically.

In order to segment phonemic representations into constituent morphemes, we apply a high-precision phonetic aligner (Kondrak, 2000) to link letters and phonemes using the procedure described in (Dwyer and Kondrak, 2009). In rare cases where the phonetic aligner fails to produce an alignment, we back-off to alignment generated with *m2m-aligner* (Jiampojamarn et al., 2007), an unsupervised EM-based algorithm. We found that this approach worked better for our purposes than relying on the alignments provided in Combilex. We use the same approach to align variant phonemic representations of morphemes as described in Section 3.1.

The morphological information contained in CELEX is incomplete for our purposes, and requires further processing. For example, the word *amputate* is listed as monomorphemic, but in fact contains the suffix *-ate*. However, *amputee* is analyzed as

$$amputee = amputate - ate + ee.$$

This allows us to identify the stem as *amput*, which in turn implies the segmentations *amput·ee*, *amput·ate*, and *amput·at·ion*.

Another issue that requires special handling in CELEX involves recovering reduced geminate consonants. For example, the word *interrelate* is pronounced with a single [r] phoneme at the morpheme boundary. However, when segmenting the phoneme sequence, we need to include [r] both at the end of *inter-* and at the beginning of *relate*.

### 4.2 Predictor

The role of the predictor mentioned in Section 3.2 is performed by DIRECTL+ (Jiampojamarn et al., 2010), a publicly available discriminative string transducer. It takes as input a sequence of common morpheme representations, determined using the method described above, and produces the predicted word pronunciation. Since DIRECTL+ tends to make mistakes related to the unstressed vowel reduction phenomenon in English, we refrain from replacing the "underlying" phonemes with either [ə] or [ɪ].

An example derivation is shown in Table 3, where the *Underlying* string represents the input to DIRECTL+, *Predicted* is its output, *Surface* is the actual pronunciation, and *Respelling* is the spelling generated according to the algorithm in Figure 1.

| | | | | | | | |
|---|---|---|---|---|---|---|---|
| Underlying: | foto | + | græf | + | ər | + | z |
| Predicted: | fotə | | græf | | ər | | z |
| Surface: | fətɑ | | grəf | | ər | | z |
| Respelling: | fotɑ | · | græf | · | ər | · | z |

Table 3: Deriving the spelling of the word *photographers*.

Since DIRECTL+ requires a training set, we split the lexicon into two equal-size parts with no morpheme overlap, and induce two separate models on each set. Then we apply each model as the predictor on the other half of the lexicon. This approach simulates the human ability to guess pronunciation from the spelling. Jiampojamarn et al. (2010) report that DIRECTL+ achieves approximately 90% word accuracy on the letter-to-phoneme conversion task on the CELEX data.

## 5 Evaluation measures

In this section, we define our measures of phonemic transparency and morphemic consistency.

### 5.1 Phonemic transparency

Kominek and Black (2006) measure the complexity of spelling systems by calculating the average perplexity of phoneme emissions for each letter. The total perplexity is the sum of each letter's perplexity weighted by its unigram probability. Since their focus is on the task of inducing text-to-speech rules, they also incorporate letter context into this definition. Thus, a system that is completely explained by a set of rules has a perplexity of 1.

The way we compute perplexity differs in several aspects. Whereas Kominek and Black (2006) calculate the perplexity of single letters, we take as units substrings derived from many-to-many alignment, with the length limited to two characters. Some letter bigrams, such as $ph$, $th$, and $ch$, are typically pronounced as a single phoneme, while the letter $x$ often corresponds to the phoneme bigram [ks]. By considering substrings we obtain a more realistic estimate of spelling perplexity.

We calculate the average orthographic perplexity using the standard formulation:

$$P_{ave} = \sum_{c} P_c e^{-\sum_{i} P_i log P_i} \quad (1)$$

| System | *viscous* | *viscosity* |
|---|---|---|
| T.O. | viscous | viscosity |
| IPA | vɪskəs | vɪskɑsəti |
| M-CAT | viscous | viscous·ity |
| ALG | vɪskɑs | vɪskɑs·ɪti |
| SR | viscous | viscosity |
| SS | viscus | viscosity |

Table 4: Example spellings according to various systems.

| System | Orth | Phon | Morph |
|---|---|---|---|
| T.O. | 2.32 | 2.10 | 96.11 |
| IPA | 1.00 | 1.00 | 93.94 |
| M-CAT | 2.51 | 2.36 | 100.00 |
| ALG | 1.33 | 1.72 | 98.90 |
| SR | 2.27 | 2.15 | 96.57 |
| SS | 1.60 | 1.72 | 94.72 |

Table 5: Orthographic, phonemic and morphemic optimality of spelling systems.

where $P_c$ is the probability of a grapheme substring in the dictionary, and $P_i$ is the probability that the grapheme substring is pronounced as the phoneme substring $i$. Note that this formulation is not contingent on any set of rules.

In a similar way, we compute the phonemic perplexity in the opposite direction, from phonemes to letters. The orthographic and the phonemic perplexity values quantify the transparency of a spelling system with respect to reading and writing, respectively.

### 5.2 Morphemic consistency

Little (2001) proposes to calculate the morphemic optimality of English spellings by computing the average percentage of "undisturbed letters" in the polymorphemic words with respect to the base form. For example, four of five letters of the base form *voice* are present in *voicing*, which translates into 80% optimal. The examples given in the paper allow us to interpret this measure as a function of edit distance normalized by the length of the base form.

We make three modifications to the original method. First, we compute the average over all words in the lexicon rather than over word sets, which would give disproportionate weight to words in smaller word sets. Second, we normalize edit distance by the number of phonemes in a word, rather than by the number of letters in a spelling, in order to avoid penalizing systems that use shorter spellings. Finally, we consider edit operations to apply to substrings aligned to substrings of phonemes, rather than to individual symbols. In this way, the maximum number of edit operations is equal to the number of phonemes. The modified measure yields a score between 0 and 100%, with the latter value representing morphemic optimality.

As an example, consider the word set consisting of six word-forms: *snip*, *snips*, *snipped*, *snipping*, *snippet*, and *snippets*. The first two words, which represent the base morpheme as *snip*, receive a perfect score of 1 for morphemic consistency. The remaining four words, which have the morpheme as *snipp*, obtain the score of 75% because one of the four phonemes is spelled differently from the base form. For free morphemes, the base form is simply the spelling of the morpheme, but for bound morphemes, we take the majority spelling of the morpheme.

## 6 Quantitative comparison

We compare the traditional English orthography (T.O.) to three hypothetical systems: phonemic transcription (IPA), morpheme concatenation (M-CAT), and the orthography generated by the algorithm described in Section 3 (ALG). In addition, we consider two proposals submitted to the English Spelling Society: a minimalist spelling reform (SR) of Gibbs (1984), and the more comprehensive SoundSpel (SS) of Rondthaler and Edward (1986). Table 4 lists the spellings of the words *viscous* and *viscosity* in various orthographies.

Table 5 shows the values of orthographic and phonemic transparency, as well as morphemic consistency for the evaluated spelling systems. By definition, phonemic transcription obtains the optimal transparency scores of 1, while simple morphological concatenation receives a perfect 100% in terms of morphemic consistency.

The results in Table 5 indicate that traditional orthography scores poorly according to all three measures. Its low orthographic and phonemic transparency is to be expected, but its low morphemic

| Rule | Input | Output |
|---|---|---|
| e-deletion | voice·ing | voicing |
| y-replacement | industry·al | industrial |
| k-insertion | panic·ing | panicking |
| e-insertion | church·s | churches |
| consonant doubling | get·ing | getting |
| f-voicing | knife·s | knives |

Table 6: Common English spelling rules with examples.

| Rule | Writing | Reading |
|---|---|---|
| e-deletion | 98.8 | 67.1 |
| y-replacement | 93.5 | 95.8 |
| k-insertion | 100.0 | 1.0 |
| e-insertion | 100.0 | 98.7 |
| consonant doubling | 96.3 | 36.3 |
| f-voicing | 33.3 | 14.7 |

Table 7: Applicability of common spelling rules.

consistency is striking. Traditional orthography is not only far from optimality, but overall seems no more optimal than any other of the evaluated systems.

Searching for the explanation of this surprising result, we find that much of the morphemic score deduction can be attributed to small changes like dropping of the silent *e*, as in 'make' + 'ing' = 'making'. These types of inconsistencies counter-weigh the high marks that traditional orthography gets for maintaining consistent spelling in spite of unstressed vowel reductions.

The prevalence of silent $e$'s in traditional orthography undeniably diminishes its morphemic consistency. Nor is the device necessary to represent the pronunciation of the preceding vowel; for example, SoundSpel has those words as 'maek' and 'maeking'. However, one can argue that such minor alterations should not be penalized because English speakers subconsciously take them into account while reading. In the next section, we describe an experiment in which we pre-process words with such orthographic rules, in order to determine how much they influence the optimality picture.

## 7 Spelling rules

Table 6 lists six common English spelling rules that affect letters at morpheme boundaries, of which the first five are included in the textbook account of Jurafsky and Martin (2009, page 63). We conducted an experiment to determine the applicability of these rules by computing how often they fired when triggered by the correct environment.[2] We tested the rules in both directions, with respect to both writing and reading applicability. Writing rules are applied to morphemes when they are in the correct environment. For example, the *k-insertion* rule fires if the morpheme ends in a $c$ and the next morpheme begins with $e$ or $i$, as in *panic·ing*. On the other hand, reading may involve recovering the morphemes from the surface forms. For example, if the stem ends in a $tt$ and the affix begins with an $i$, the *consonant doubling* rule implies that the free form of the morpheme ends in a single $t$, as in *getting*.

The results in Table 7 show that the rules, with the exception of the *f-voicing* rule, have high applicability in writing. Most rules, however, cannot be trusted to recover the morpheme spellings from the surface form. For example, following the consonant doubling rule would cause the reader to incorrectly infer from the word *butted* that the spelling of the verb is *but*. This is significant considering that Chomsky and Halle define orthography as a system for *readers* (page 49).

Notwithstanding the unreliability of the spelling rules, we incorporate them into the computation of the morphemic consistency of the traditional orthography. We apply the rules from a reading perspective, but assume some morphemic knowledge of a reader. Whereas we consider a rule to misfire if it does not apply in the correct environment when calculating applicability, as in Table 7, when calculating morphemic consistency, we allow the rules to be more flexible. We consider a morpheme to match the prototype if either the observed form or the form modified by the spelling rule matches the prototype.

## 8 Discussion

Figure 2 shows a two-dimensional plot of orthographic perplexity vs. morphemic consistency. The (unattainable) optimality is represented by the lower

[2]The conditioning environments of the rules were implemented according to the guidelines provided at *http://www.phonicslessons.co.uk/englishspellingrules.html*.

left corner of the plot. The effect of accommodating the spelling rules within the traditional orthography is illustrated by an arrow, which indicates an increase in morphemic consistency from 96.11 to 98.90.

The ALG(L) system represents a version of the ALG system in which the IPA symbols are respelled using combinations of the 26 letters of the Roman alphabet, with the morpheme boundary symbol removed. This change, which is intended to make the comparison with the traditional orthography more interpretable, increases the orthographic perplexity from 1.33 to 1.58. Furthermore, we ensure that ALG(L) contains no homographs (which consitute 2.6% of the lexicon in ALG) by reverting to a traditional spelling of a morpheme if necessary. Since the respelling applies to all instances of that morpheme, it has no effect on the morphemic consistency, but results in a small increase of the orthographic perplexity to 1.61.

The plot in Figure 2 shows that, even after accounting for the orthographic rules, traditional orthography does not surpass the level of morphemic consistency of ALG. With the same writing script and no homographs, ALG(L) is less than half the distance from the orthographic optimality. On the other hand, neither of the spelling reform proposals is substantially better overall than the traditional orthography.

Inspection of the spellings generated by our algorithm reveals that it generally maintains consistent spellings of morphemes. In fact, it only makes a change from the underlying form in 3660 cases, or 7.2% of the words in the dictionary. Consider the morpheme *transcribe*, which is traditionally spelled as 'transcrip' in *transcription*. Even if we disregard the final 'e' by invoking the *e-deletion* spelling rule, the morphemic consistency in the traditional orthography is still violated by the 'b'/'p' alternation. Our predictor, however, considers this a predictable devoicing assimilation change, which occurs in a number of words, including *subscription* and *absorption*. Consequently, the spellings generated by the algorithm preserve the morpheme's 'b' ending in all words that contain it. In addition, the algorithm avoids spurious idiosyncrasies such as *four*/*forty*, which abound in traditional orthography.

The spellings generated by the algorithm are also

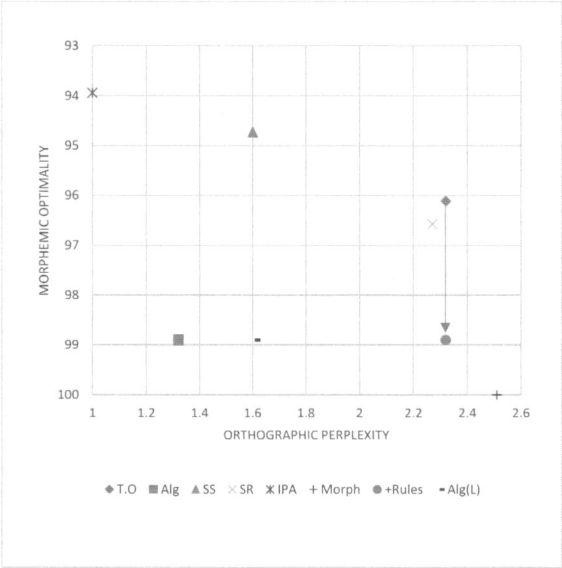


Figure 2: Morphemic and orthographic optimality of various spelling systems.

much more phonemically transparent, particularly for vowels. Phonemically, ALG(L) improves on the traditional orthography mostly by making the spelling more predictable, For example, 'a' represents the phoneme [æ] in 91.7% of the cases in the generated spellings, as opposed to only 36.5% in traditional orthography.

## 9 Conclusion

We have analyzed English orthography in terms of morphemic consistency and phonemic transparency. According to the strict interpretation of morphemic consistency, traditional orthography is closer to the level of a phonemic transcription than to that of a morphemic concatenation. Even if orthographic rules are assumed to operate cost-free as a preprocessing step, the orthographic perplexity of traditional orthography remains high.

While phonemic transparency and morphemic consistency are at odds with each other, we have provided a constructive proof that it is possible to create a spelling system for English that it is substantially closer to theoretical optimality than the traditional orthography, even when it is constrained by the traditional character set. This contradicts the claim that English orthography is near optimal.

## Acknowledgments

This research was supported by the Natural Sciences and Engineering Research Council of Canada, and the Alberta Innovates – Technology Futures.

## References

Harald R. Baayen, Richard Piepenbrock, and Leon Gulikers. 1995. *The CELEX Lexical Database. Release 2 (CD-ROM)*. Linguistic Data Consortium, University of Pennsylvania, Philadelphia, Pennsylvania.

Maximilian Bisani and Hermann Ney. 2008. Joint-sequence models for grapheme-to-phoneme conversion. *Speech Communication*, 50(5):434–451.

Edward Carney. 1994. *A Survey of English Spelling*. Routledge.

Noam Chomsky and Morris Halle. 1968. The sound pattern of English.

Bruce L Derwing. 1992. Orthographic aspects of linguistic competence. *The linguistics of literacy*, pages 193–210.

Kenneth Dwyer and Grzegorz Kondrak. 2009. Reducing the annotation effort for letter-to-phoneme conversion. In *Proceedings of ACL-IJCNLP*, pages 127–135.

Stanley Gibbs. 1984. The Simplified Spelling Society's 1984 proposals. *Journal of the Simplified Spelling Society*, 2:32.

Sittichai Jiampojamarn, Grzegorz Kondrak, and Tarek Sherif. 2007. Applying many-to-many alignments and hidden markov models to letter-to-phoneme conversion. In *Human Language Technologies 2007: The Conference of the North American Chapter of the Association for Computational Linguistics; Proceedings of the Main Conference*, pages 372–379, Rochester, New York, April. Association for Computational Linguistics.

Sitichai Jiampojamarn, Colin Cherry, and Grzegorz Kondrak. 2010. Integrating Joint n-gram Features into a Discriminative Training Framework. In *Proceedings of NAACL-2010*, Los Angeles, CA, June. Association for Computational Linguistics.

Dan Jurafsky and James H Martin. 2009. *Speech & language processing*. Pearson Education India, 2nd edition.

John Kominek and Alan W. Black. 2006. Learning pronunciation dictionaries: Language complexity and word selection strategies. In *HLT-NAACL*, pages 232–239.

Grzegorz Kondrak. 2000. A new algorithm for the alignment of phonetic sequences. In *Proceedings of NAACL 2000: 1st Meeting of the North American Chapter of the Association for Computational Linguistics*, pages 288–295.

Joseph R Little. 2001. The optimality of English spelling.

Anneke Marijke Nunn. 2006. *Dutch orthography: A systematic investigation of the spelling of Dutch words*. The Hague: Holland Academic Graphics.

Korin Richmond, Robert AJ Clark, and Susan Fitt. 2009. Robust LTS rules with the Combilex speech technology lexicon. pages 1295–1298, September.

Henry Rogers. 2005. *Writing Systems*. Blackwell.

Edward Rondthaler and J LIAS Edward. 1986. Dictionary of simplified American Spelling.

Geoffrey Sampson. 1985. *Writing systems: A linguistic introduction*. Stanford University Press.

Richard Sproat. 2000. *A computational Theory of Writing Systems*. Cambridge.

Danny D Steinberg. 1973. Phonology, reading, and Chomsky and Halle's optimal orthography. *Journal of Psycholinguistic Research*, 2(3):239–258.

Richard L Venezky. 1970. *The structure of English orthography*, volume 82. Walter de Gruyter.

Valerie Yule. 1978. Is there evidence for Chomsky's interpretation of English spelling? *Spelling Progress Bulletin*, 18(4):10–12.

# LCCT: A Semi-supervised Model for Sentiment Classification

**Min Yang**[1] **Wenting Tu**[1] **Ziyu Lu**[1] **Wenpeng Yin**[2] **Kam-Pui Chow**[1]
[1]Department of Computer Science, The University of Hong Kong, Hong Kong
{myang,wttu,zylu,chow}@cs.hku.hk
[2]Center for Information and Language Processing, University of Munich, Germany
wenpeng@cis.lmu.de

## Abstract

Analyzing public opinions towards products, services and social events is an important but challenging task. An accurate sentiment analyzer should take both lexicon-level information and corpus-level information into account. It also needs to exploit the domain-specific knowledge and utilize the common knowledge shared across domains. In addition, we want the algorithm being able to deal with missing labels and learning from incomplete sentiment lexicons. This paper presents a LCCT (**L**exicon-based and **C**orpus-based, **C**o-**T**raining) model for semi-supervised sentiment classification. The proposed method combines the idea of lexicon-based learning and corpus-based learning in a unified co-training framework. It is capable of incorporating both domain-specific and domain-independent knowledge. Extensive experiments show that it achieves very competitive classification accuracy, even with a small portion of labeled data. Comparing to state-of-the-art sentiment classification methods, the LCCT approach exhibits significantly better performances on a variety of datasets in both English and Chinese.

## 1 Introduction

Due to the popularity of opinion-rich resources (e.g., online review sites, forums, blogs and the microblogging websites), people express their opinions all over the Internet. Motivated by the demand of gleaning insights from such valuable data, a flurry of research devotes to the task of extracting people's opinions from online reviews. Such opinions could be expressed on products, services or policies, etc (Pang and Lee, 2008). Existing sentiment analysis approaches can be divided into two categories based on the source of information they use: the lexicon-based approach (Turney, 2002; Dave et al., 2003) and the corpus-based approach (Pang et al., 2002; Blitzer et al., 2007; Wan, 2009). The lexicon-based approach counts positive and negative terms in a review based on the sentiment dictionary and classifies the document as positive if it contains more positive terms than negative ones. On the contrary, the corpus-based approach uses supervised learning algorithms to train a sentiment classifier.

Further study (Kennedy and Inkpen, 2006; Andreevskaia and Bergler, 2008; Qiu et al., 2009) shows that corpus-based and lexicon-based approaches have complementary performances. Specifically, the corpus-based approach has high precision but low recall on positive instances, while the lexicon-based approach has high recall but low precision on positive instances. In fact, corpus-based approaches are over conservative in classifying instances as positive, because positive reviews usually contain many neutral statements. In contrast, the lexicon-based approaches tend to classify negative or neutral instances as positive when there are a few positive words appear in the document. It motivates us to develop a new approach that achieves good performance on both precision and recall evaluations.

Besides reviews on products and services, another rich source of opinion data are social reviews in forums, blogs and microblogging websites. Different from product reviews, the social reviews are not associated with numerical ratings, making it difficult to perform supervised classification. Since manual labeling is time consuming and expensive, it is



*Human Language Technologies: The 2015 Annual Conference of the North American Chapter of the ACL*, pages 546–555,
Denver, Colorado, May 31 – June 5, 2015. 

preferable to label a small portion of social reviews to perform semi-supervised learning, leveraging information from both labeled and unlabeled data.

In this paper, we propose a novel approach to handle the above two challenges. We presents the LCCT Model (**L**exicon-based and **C**orpus-based, **C**o-**T**raining Model), which treats the lexicon-based information and the corpus-based information as two views, and combine them via co-training (Blum and Mitchell, 1998). The algorithm naturally incorporates the framework of semi-supervised learning, as missing labels in each view can be estimated by the classifier trained from the other view. The proposed LCCT model exploits the complementary performance associated with the lexicon-based and the corpus-based approaches, taking the best of each side to improve the overall performance. We present a novel semi-supervised sentiment-aware LDA approach to build the lexicon-based classifier, which uses a minimal set of seed words (e.g., "good","happy" as positive seeds) as well as document sentiment labels to construct a domain-specific sentiment lexicon. This model reflects the domain-specific knowledge. We employ the stacked denoising auto-encoder (Vincent et al., 2008; Glorot et al., 2011) to build the corpus-based classifier. As Glorot et al. (Glorot et al., 2011) point out, the intermediate abstractions extracted in this way tend to reflect the domain-independent knowledge, unifying information across all domains. Finally, we use a co-training algorithm to combine the corpus-based and lexicon-based classifiers and to combine the domain-specific knowledge and the domain-independent knowledge.

The main contributions of our approach are three-folded. First, we propose a method that exploits both general domain-independent knowledge and specific domain-dependent knowledge, behaving like a human being when she analyzes the text. Second, we complement the lexicon-based approach and the corpus-based approach to overcome their respective classification biases. Third, our approach is capable of levering labeled and unlabeled data, unifying them into a semi-supervised learning framework. We conduct extensive experiments to verify the effectiveness of the proposed approach on real-world social reviews. The experiment results show that our model substantially outperforms the state-of-the-art methods in analyzing sentiments in online reviews.

## 2 Related Works

Sentiment analysis of natural language texts is an active research field. The papers by Pang and Lee (Pang and Lee, 2008) and Liu (Liu, 2012) describe most of the existing techniques for sentiment analysis and opinion mining. Sentiment analysis approaches can be categorized into lexicon-based approaches (Turney, 2002; Kennedy and Inkpen, 2006; Andreevskaia and Bergler, 2008) and corpus-based approaches (Pang et al., 2002; Blitzer et al., 2007; Wan, 2009). The lexicon-based approach uses a dictionary of opinion words (e.g., "good" and "bad") to identify the sentiment of a text. In contrast, the corpus-based approach can be seen as a statistical learning approach (Pang et al., 2002; Whitelaw et al., 2005; Wiebe and Riloff, 2005; Ye et al., 2009). The performance of corpus-based methods often degenerates when the labeled training data is insufficient.

As we have discussed earlier, corpus-based algorithms are overly conservative on positive reviews, while lexicon-based approaches are overly aggressive on positive reviews. There are several literature integrating both methods (Kennedy and Inkpen, 2006; Andreevskaia and Bergler, 2008; Qiu et al., 2009; Zhang et al., 2011). These methods require either a complete lexicon or a fully labeled corpus being available, which might not be true in practice. The method in this paper, in contrast, uses incomplete lexicon and partially labeled corpus as training examples.

On the other hand, there are semi-supervised methods in sentiment analysis which handle incomplete data (Wan, 2009; Dasgupta and Ng, 2009; Li et al., 2010; Zhou et al., 2010; Biyani et al., 2013). Nevertheless, none of them combines the lexicon-based and corpus-based approaches and thus they do not solve the bias problem in sentiment classification.

## 3 LCCT Model

In the LCCT model, we use a novel semi-supervised sentiment-aware LDA model to build the lexicon-based model. We use stacked denoising auto-encoder (Vincent et al., 2008; Glorot et al., 2011) to build the corpus-based model. Finally, a co-training algorithm is employed for semi-supervised sentiment classification, and the two classifiers from corpus-based method and lexicon-based method are combined. The overall structure of the model is illustrated by Figure 1.

### 3.1 Lexicon-based Approach

For building the lexicon-based model, the key challenge is that a single word can carry multiple sentiment meanings in different domains, so that a general-purpose sentiment lexicon is less accurate than domain-specific lexicons. To solve this problem, we build a domain-specific sentiment lexicon by semi-supervised sentiment-aware LDA (ssLDA). The ssLDA method takes semi-supervised data as input.

#### 3.1.1 Semi-supervised Sentiment-aware LDA

In this section, we describe how each word of the corpus is generated by the ssLDA model, then illustrate its inference method. Each document has three classes of topics: $K^{(p)}$ positive sentiment topics, $K^{(n)}$ negative sentiment topics, and $K^{(u)}$ neutral sentiment topics. Each document is a mixture of the three classes of topics. Each topic is associated with a multinomial distribution over words. To prevent conceptual confusion, we use a superscript "$(p)$" and "$(n)$" to indicate variables relating to positive and negative sentiment topics, and a superscript "$(u)$" to indicate variables relating to neutral sentiment topics. In addition, we assume that the vocabulary consists of $V$ distinct words indexed by $\{1, \ldots, V\}$.

For each word $w$, there is a multinomial distribution determining which class of topics that $w$ belongs to. This prior distribution is sampled from a Dirichlet distribution $\text{Dir}(\lambda)$, where $\lambda = (\lambda^{(p)}, \lambda^{(n)}, \lambda^{(u)})$ is a vector of three scalars. For documents with different sentiment labels, we choose different values of $\lambda$, so that words in the document with a positive label has a higher probability belonging to positive topics, and vice versa. In the semi-supervised setting, a document usually doesn't have a sentiment label. In that case, the value of $\lambda$ is equal to $(\frac{1}{3}, \frac{1}{3}, \frac{1}{3})$.

Given the class of topics, there is another multinomial distribution indicating the particular topic that the word belongs to. If it turns out that the word belongs to a positive sentiment class, then its topic distribution is drawn from a biased Dirichlet prior $\phi_w^{(p)} \sim \text{Dir}(\beta_w^{(p)})$. The vector $\beta_w^{(p)} \in \mathbb{R}^V$ is constructed by

$$\beta_{w,k}^{(p)} := \gamma_0(1 - \omega_w) + \gamma_1 \omega_w \quad \text{for } k \in \{1, \ldots, K\} \tag{1}$$

We set $\omega_w = 1$ if the word $w$ is a positive seed word, otherwise, we set $\omega_w = 0$. The scalars $\gamma_0$ and $\gamma_1$ are hyperparameters. Intuitively, the biased prior enforces a positive seed word more probably drawn from a positive sentiment topic. The distributions $\phi_{\text{w}}^{(\text{n})} \sim \text{Dir}(\beta_w^{(n)})$ and $\phi_w^{(u)} \sim \text{Dir}(\beta_w^{(u)})$ for negative and neutral sentiment topics are similarly constructed. Once the topic is determined, the word is generated from a multinomial distribution that associates with the topic. We summarize the generative process of the ssLDA model as below:

1. For each word $w$ in the vocabulary, draw the distributions of topics for three sentiment classes: $\phi_w^{(p)} \sim \text{Dir}(\beta_w^{(p)})$, $\phi_w^{(n)} \sim \text{Dir}(\beta_w^{(n)})$ and $\phi_w^{(u)} \sim \text{Dir}(\beta_w^{(u)})$.

2. For each topic $k$, draw the distribution over words: $\theta_k^{(p)} \sim \text{Dir}(\alpha)$, $\theta_k^{(n)} \sim \text{Dir}(\alpha)$ and $\theta_k^{(u)} \sim \text{Dir}(\alpha)$.

3. For each document in the corpus
   (a) Draw sentiment class distribution $p$ from either $\text{Dir}(\lambda^{(p)})$, $\text{Dir}(\lambda^{(n)})$ or $\text{Dir}(\lambda^{(u)})$ based on the document's sentiment label.
   (b) For each word in document, Draw sentiment class indicator $c \sim \text{Mult}(p)$, then generate the word's topic $z$ from $\text{Mult}(\phi_w^{(c)})$, and generate the word $w$ from $\text{Mult}(\theta_z^{(c)})$.

Given hyper-parameters $\alpha$, $\lambda$, and $\{\beta^{(s)}, \beta^{(n)}, \beta^{(u)}\}$, our goal is to estimate the latent variables in the ssLDA model. We present a collapsed Gibbs-sampling algorithm, which iteratively takes a word $w$ from the corpus and samples the topic that the word belongs to. The reader may refer to (Yang et al., 2014) for a detailed derivation of the sampling procedure. Let the whole corpus excluding the current word be denoted by $D$. Let $n_{i,w}^{(p)}$ (or $n_{j,w}^{(n)}$, or $n_{k,w}^{(u)}$) indicate the number of occurrences of positive sentiment topic $i^{(p)}$ (or negative sentiment topic $j^{(n)}$, or neutral sentiment topic $k^{(u)}$) with word $w$ in

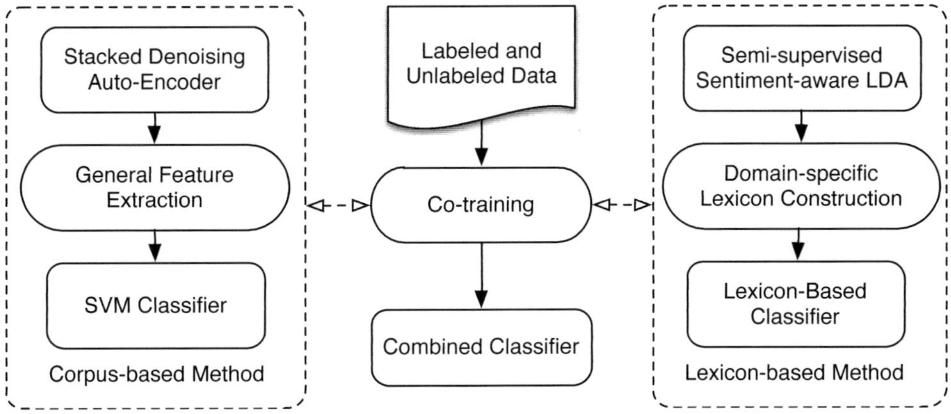


Figure 1: Algorithm Overview

the whole corpus. Let $m_i^{(p)}$ (or $m_j^{(n)}$, or $m_k^{(u)}$) indicate the number of occurrence of positive sentiment topic $i^{(p)}$ (or negative sentiment topic $j^{(n)}$, or neutral sentiment topic $k^{(u)}$) in the current document. Then, the posterior probability that the current word $w$ belongs to a specific topic is presented as follow

$$\Pr\left(z = i^{(p)}|D\right) \propto (\lambda^{(p)} + \sum_{i=1}^{K^{(p)}} m_i^{(p)}) \cdot \frac{\alpha + m_i^{(p)}}{K^{(p)}\alpha + \sum_{i'=1}^{K^{(p)}} m_{i'}^{(p)}} \cdot \frac{\beta_{i,w}^{(p)} + n_{i,w}^{(p)}}{\sum_{w'=1}^{V}\left(\beta_{i,w'}^{(p)} + n_{i,w'}^{(p)}\right)} \quad (2)$$

$$\Pr\left(z = j^{(n)}|D\right) \propto (\lambda^{(p)} + \sum_{i=1}^{K^{(p)}} m_i^{(p)}) \cdot \frac{\alpha + m_j^{(n)}}{K^{(n)}\alpha + \sum_{j'=1}^{K^{(n)}} m_{j'}^{(n)}} \cdot \frac{\beta_{j,w}^{(n)} + n_{i,w}^{(n)}}{\sum_{w'=1}^{V}\left(\beta_{j,w'}^{(n)} + n_{j,w'}^{(n)}\right)} \quad (3)$$

$$\Pr\left(z = k^{(u)}|D\right) \propto (\lambda^{(p)} + \sum_{i=1}^{K^{(p)}} m_i^{(p)}) \cdot \frac{\alpha + m_k^{(u)}}{K^{(u)}\alpha + \sum_{k'=1}^{K^{(u)}} m_{u'}^{(n)}} \cdot \frac{\beta_{k,w}^{(u)} + n_{k,w}^{(u)}}{\sum_{w'=1}^{V}\left(\beta_{k,w'}^{(u)} + n_{k,w'}^{(u)}\right)} \quad (4)$$

By equations (2), (3), and (4), we can sample the topic $z$ for each word. In the Gibbs sampling procedure, we only need to maintain the counters $n^{(p)}$, $n^{(n)}$, $n^{(u)}$, $m^{(p)}$, $m^{(n)}$ and $m^{(u)}$, which takes $O(1)$ time to update for each iteration.

#### 3.1.2 Lexicon Construction and Sentiment Classification

Once we obtain the topic of each word, we obtain the value of hidden variables $p^{(c)}, \theta^{(c)}, \phi^{(c)}$, where $c \in \{p, n, u\}$. The goal is to use these values to construct a sentiment lexicon, which assigns sentiment scores to each word. In particular, we need the probability that each word $w$ appears in a certain sentiment class, i.e. we want to calculate $\Pr\left(c \in \{p, n, u\}|w\right)$ for the sentiment indicator $c$. We use $\gamma_w^{(p)}$, $\gamma_w^{(n)}$, $\gamma_w^{(u)}$ to represent these probabilities. By the ssLDA's model specification, we define

$$\gamma_w^{(p)} := \Pr\left(c = p|w\right) \propto p^{(p)} \cdot \sum_{i=1}^{K^{(p)}} \theta_{i,w}^{(p)} \phi_{w,i}^{(p)} \quad (5)$$

$$\gamma_w^{(n)} := \Pr\left(c = n|w\right) \propto p^{(n)} \cdot \sum_{j=1}^{K^{(n)}} \theta_{i,w}^{(n)} \phi_{w,j}^{(n)} \quad (6)$$

$$\gamma_w^{(u)} := \Pr\left(c = u|w\right) \propto p^{(u)} \cdot \sum_{k=1}^{K^{(u)}} \theta_{i,w}^{(u)} \phi_{w,k}^{(u)} \quad (7)$$

We construct the sentiment lexicon for each word $w$ by comparing $\gamma_w^{(p)}$, $\gamma_w^{(n)}$ and $\gamma_w^{(u)}$. If $\gamma_w^{(p)}$ is the greatest value, then the word $w$ is considered to convey positive sentiment, and is added to the positive sentiment lexicon with weight $\gamma_w^{(p)}$. If $\phi_{1,w}^{(s)}$ is the greatest, then the word $w$ is added to the negative sentiment lexicon with weight $-\gamma_w^{(n)}$. Otherwise, the word $w$ is considered neutral and not included in the sentiment lexicon.

It remains to classify the sentiment for each document. We aggregate the weights for each word, so that the document is classified as "positive" if the accumulated weight is larger than zero; Otherwise, it is classified as "negative". The proposed model is a semi-supervised method since it is capable of processing documents without the sentiment label. This property makes the proposed method suitable for co-training.

### 3.2 Corpus-based Method

The deep learning approach, especially Stacked Denoising Auto-encoders (SDA), has been shown highly beneficial for extracting domain-independent knowledge (Glorot et al., 2011). Thus, we use SDA to construct the corpus-based sentiment classifier. The stacked autoencoder method was introduced by Rumelhart, Hinton and Williams (Rumelhart et al., 1985) and its denoising variant was proposed by Vincent et al. (Vincent et al., 2010). Recently, it has become an essential building block in deep learning architectures. A basic denoising autoencoder consists of an input layer, a hidden layer and an output layer. The procedure can be interpreted into two phases, i.e., encode and decode. In the encoding phrase, an encoder function is employed to map input data into a feature vector $h$. For each sample $x$ from input dataset $\{x^{(1)}, \ldots, x^{(N)}\}$, we have

$$h = f(U^T(x + \epsilon) + b) \tag{8}$$

where $f(x)$ is sigmoid activation function, $U$ is the weight matrix between input layer and hidden layer, $b_h$ is the bias of each input layer neuron and $\epsilon$ is a random Gaussian noise. In the decoding phrase, a decoder function is deployed to remap the feature vector in the feature space back to the input space, producing a reconstruction $\hat{x}$. The decoder function takes the following form

$$\hat{x} = f(V^T h + b') \tag{9}$$

where $f(x)$ is also a sigmoid function, $V$ is the weight matrix between the hidden layer and the output layer, and $b$' is the bias. The parameters of the SDA models, namely $\theta = \{U, V, b, b'\}$, are learned by minimizing the reconstruction error $L(x, \hat{x})$ over all training instances:

$$J(\theta) = \sum_{x^{(t)}} L(x^{(t)}, \hat{x}^{(t)}) \tag{10}$$

where $L(\cdot, \cdot)$ is measure of discrepancy. Popular choices of $L$ include squared error and Kullback-Liebler divergence. By iteratively adding autoencoders on top of a trained denoising autoencoder, we obtain the stacked denoising autoencoder (SDA). Once trained, their parameters can be used to initialize a supervised learning algorithm. In this paper, SDA is learnt in a greedy layer-wise fashion using stochastic gradient descent. For the first layer, the decoder is activated by a sigmoid function, and the Kullback-Liebler divergence is used as the reconstruction error. For the remaining layers, we use the softplus function for activation. After the SDA parameters are trained (on both labeled and unlabeled data) and the high-level representation of each data instance is obtained, a SVM classifier is employed using the resulting representation (of labeled data) to train a sentiment classifier.

### 3.3 Combining two Methods with Co-training

**Algorithm 1** Co-training with corpus-based and lexicon-based methods

- Inputs: labeled training data $\boldsymbol{L}$, unlabeled training data $\boldsymbol{U}$
- Create a pool $\boldsymbol{U}'$ of examples by choosing $u$ unlabeled examples at random, then loop for $k$ iterations
  - use $\boldsymbol{L}$ and $\boldsymbol{U}$ to train a corpus-based classifier $f_1$, then use $f_1$ to label samples from $\boldsymbol{U}'$. Let $\boldsymbol{A}_1$ be the set of $p$ positive and $n$ negative most confidently labeled examples.
  - use $\boldsymbol{L}$ and $\boldsymbol{U}$ to train a lexicon-based classifier $f_2$, then use $f_2$ to label samples from $\boldsymbol{U}'$. Let $\boldsymbol{A}_2$ be the set of $p$ positive and $n$ negative most confidently labeled examples.
  - Add $f_1$ and $f_2$ to the set $\boldsymbol{C}$ of classifiers and add the self-labeled examples $\boldsymbol{A}_1 \cup \boldsymbol{A}_2$ to the labeled dataset $\boldsymbol{L}$. Randomly choose $2p + 2n$ examples from $\boldsymbol{U}$ to replenish $\boldsymbol{U}'$
- For testing, run all classifiers in $\boldsymbol{C}$ and output the majority vote.

We employ a variant of co-training algorithm to train the classifier with a small number of labeled data and a large number of unlabeled data. The co-training approach is well known for semi-supervised approach (Blum and Mitchell, 1998). For our problem, the two views of co-training are lexicon-based method (domain-specific knowledge) and corpus-based method (domain-independent knowledge). Initially, both classifiers are trained with the partially available labels, as described by the above two subsections. Then, we use one of the two classifiers to label the unlabeled documents, adding its labels to the pool of labeled data, re-training the other classifier using the new labeled data. The procedure is performed iteratively. After a sufficient number of iterations, we obtain a set of classifiers and we combine them using a majority-voting scheme to predict the sentiment label for test data. The details of the algorithm are summarized in Algorithm 1.

## 4 Experiments

In this section, we compare the proposed LCCT model with state-of-the-art methods in sentiment classification. The experiment demonstrates the superior performance of our approach.

### 4.1 Datasets

We conduct experiments on English and Chinese reviews from three datasets. In this subsection, we describe the datasets.

**Movie Review (MR) dataset in English** The movie reviews are selected if the rating was stars or a numerical score. In this paper, we use the Movie Review dataset containing 1000 positive examples and 1000 negative examples (Pang and Lee, 2004). Positive labels were assigned to reviews that had a rating above 3.5 stars and negative labels were assigned to the rest (Pang and Lee, 2004).

**SemEval-2013 (SemEval) dataset in English** This dataset is constructed for the Twitter sentiment analysis task (Task 2) in the Semantic Evaluation of Systems challenge (SemEval-2013). All the tweets were manually annotated by 5 Amazon Mechanical Turk workers with negative, positive and neutral labels. SemEval contains 13,975 tweets with 2,186 negative, 6,440 neutrals and 5,349 positives tweets. We collect the 2,186 negative tweets and 5,349 positive tweets as the training data.

**COAE-2009 (COAE) dataset in Chinese** This dataset is provided by COAE 2009 [1] (Task 4). The corpus consists of 39,976 documents and 50 topics. The topics cover education, entertainment, finance, computer, etc. In this paper, we select the 2202 negative and 1248 positive documents as our dataset.

In all experiments, data preprocessing is performed. For English dataset, the texts are first tokenized using the natural language toolkit NLTK[2].

[1] http://ir-china.org.cn/coae2009.html

[2] http://www.nltk.org

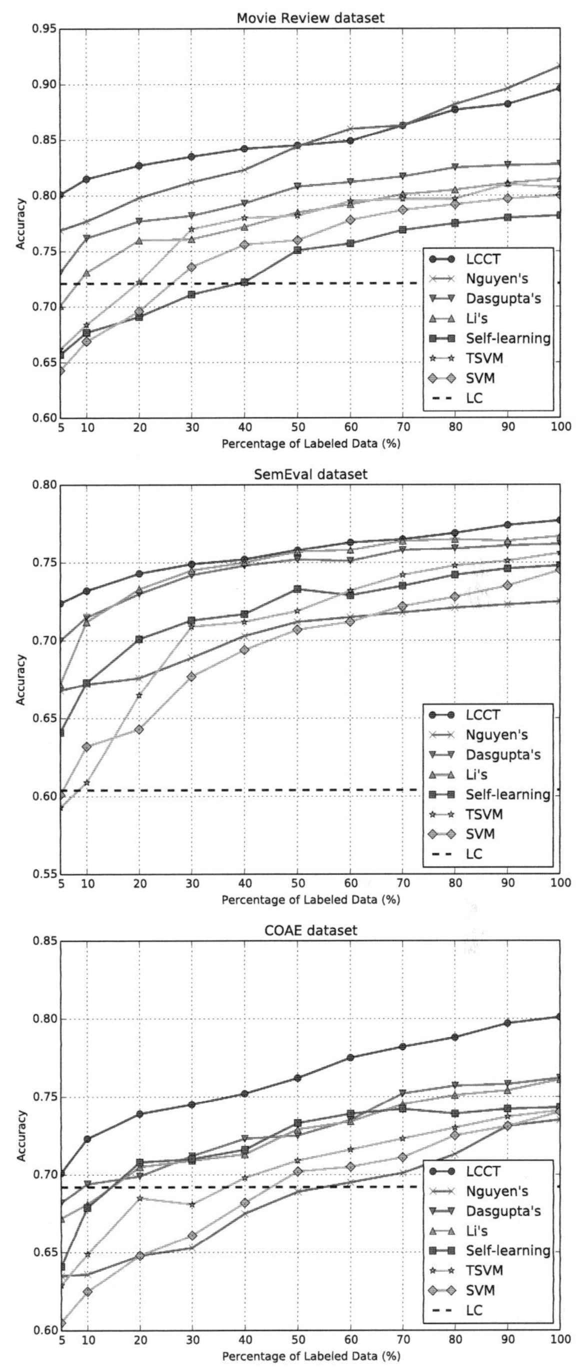


Figure 2: Comparing classification accuracy by varying the percentage of labeled data from 5% to 100%. The LCCT model is robust to incomplete data.

Then, we remove non-alphabet characters, numbers, pronoun, punctuation and stop words from the text. Finally, the WordNet stemmer[3] is applied to reduce the vocabulary size and settle the issue of data sparseness. For Chinese dataset, we first perform Chinese word segmentation with a popular Chinese auto-segmentation system ICTCLAS[4]. Then, the words about time, numeral words, pronoun and punctuation are removed as they are unrelated to the sentiment analysis task.

### 4.2 Implementation Details

We specify the hyper-parameters we use for the experiments. For all datasets, we choose $\alpha = 0.5$, $\lambda^{(p)} = (0.95, 0.25, 0.4)$, $\lambda^{(n)} = (0.25, 0.95, 0.4)$, $\lambda^{(u)} = (0.6, 0.6, 0.4)$ and $(\gamma_0, \gamma_1) = (0.25, 0.75)$. We use cross-validation to set the number of topics on datasets MR, SemEval and COAE as 20, 10 and 20, respectively. The seed words used to construct English and Chinese lexicons are the same as in previous literatures (Xie and Li, 2012) and (Yang et al., 2014). For the corpus-based method, each document is transformed into binary vectors which encodes the presence/absence of the terms. The autoencoder is constructed with 500 input neurons and 200 hidden neurons. Each autoencoder is trained by back propagation with 400 iterations.

For all datasets, we set the iteration number of co-training to be $k = 50$. Other parameters of co-training are chosen by cross-validation: $u$ is set to be $10\%$ of all unlabeled data, the sum of $p$ and $n$ are $0.8\%$ of all unlabeled data, while their ratio are determined by the ratio of positive and negative samples in labeled training data.

### 4.3 Baseline Methods

In this paper, we evaluate and compare our approach with an unsupervised method, two supervised methods and a variety of semi-supervised methods:

SVM: 5000 words with greatest information gain are chosen as features. In our experiment, we use the LibLinear[5] implementation of SVM.

Lexical Classifier (LC): This method calculates the number of positive words and negative words contained in the Opinion Lexicon (Hu and Liu, 2004) for English texts or the HowNet[6] lexicon for Chinese texts. If the positive sentiment words are more than negative words, then the document is classified as positive, and vice versa.

Self-learning: Following the idea of (Zhu, 2006), this method uses the unlabeled data in a bootstrapping way. The SVM classifier is used to select most confident unlabeled samples in each iteration.

Transductive SVM (TSVM) : Following the idea of (Joachims, 1999), this method seeks the largest separation between labeled and unlabeled data through regularization. We implement it with the SVM-light toolkit [7].

Dasgupta's method: This is a popular semi-supervised approach to automatic sentiment classification proposed by Dasgupta and Ng (Dasgupta and Ng, 2009). The unambiguous reviews are first mined using spectral techniques, then classified by a combination of active learning, transductive learning, and ensemble learning.

Li's method: This method is proposed in (Li et al., 2010). An unsupervised bootstrapping method is adopted to automatically split documents into personal and impersonal views. Then, two views are combined by an ensemble of individual classifier generated by each view. The co-training algorithm is utilized to incorporate unlabeled data.

Nguyen's method: This method is proposed in (Nguyen et al., 2014), which achieves the state-of-the-art results in supervised sentiment classification. We follow all the settings in (Nguyen et al., 2014). For the document with no associated score, we predict a score for the document as the values of the rating-based features using a regression model learned from SRA14[8] dataset.

### 4.4 Experiment Results

For each dataset, we use $80\%$ instances as the training data and the remaining are used for testing. To test the performance of semi-supervised learning, we randomly select $10\%$ of the training instances as labeled data and treat the remaining as unlabeled. For fair comparison, the fully supervised SVM and Nguyen's method use the $10\%$ labeled data for training.

[3]http://wordnet.princeton.edu/
[4]http://www.ictclas.org
[5]http://www.csie.ntu.edu.tw/~cjlin/liblinear/
[6]http://www.keenage.com/download/sentiment.rar
[7]http://svmlight.joachims.org/
[8]https://sites.google.com/site/nquocdai/resources

| Dataset | SVM | LC | Self-learning | TSVM | Dasgupta's | Li's | Nguyen's | LCCT |
|---|---|---|---|---|---|---|---|---|
| MR | 0.669 | 0.721 | 0.677 | 0.684 | 0.762 | 0.731 | 0.769 | 0.815 |
| SemEval | 0.632 | 0.604 | 0.675 | 0.609 | 0.735 | 0.702 | 0.652 | 0.775 |
| COAE | 0.625 | 0.706 | 0.679 | 0.649 | 0.709 | 0.692 | 0.642 | 0.713 |

Table 1: Comparing classification accuracy with 10% labeled data. The LCCT model performs significantly better

We summarize the experiment results in Table 1. According to Table 1, the proposed LCCT method substantially and consistently outperforms other methods on all the three datasets. This verifies the effectiveness of the proposed approach and demonstrates its advantage in semi-supervised sentiment analysis where reviews are from different domains and different language. For example, the overall accuracy of our algorithm is 5.3% higher than Dasgupta's method and 13.1% higher than TSVM on Movie Reviews dataset. On other datasets, we observe the similar results. To verify that unlabeled data improves the performance, we compare the SVM and Nguyen's classifier trained on 10% of the labeled data with other semi-supervised classifiers. Table 1 shows that the semi-supervised learning methods greatly benefit from using unlabeled data, especially on the Movie Reviews and on the SemEval dataset. Surprisingly, on the COAE dataset, lexicon-based method turns out to outperform SVM, self-learning and TSVM. The reason might be that the topics in the COAE dataset are pretty diverse. Without sufficient labeled data or prior knowledge such as sentiment lexicon, the corpus-based classifiers tend to separate the documents into topical sub-clusters as opposed to sentiment classes.

To understand the performance of our algorithm with respect to different portions of labeled data, we compare our algorithm with baseline methods by varying the percentage of labeled data from 5% to 100%. Figure 2 shows that our approach is robust and achieves excellent performance on different labeling percentages. As expected, having more labeled data improves the performance. The LCCT method achieves a relative high accuracy with 10% of the reviews labeled, better than SVM, TSVM and Self-learning with 100% of the reviews labeled. On the other hand, when all the training data are labeled, LCCT is still significantly more accurate than all the competitors except Nguyen's method. Although, the accuracy of Nguyen's method is slightly better than ours on Movie Reviews dataset, it dosen't perform well on SemEval and COAE datasets since the rating-based features learned from score-associated product reviews cannot significantly benefit the social reviews in forums and blogs, etc. The main advantage of our model comes from its capability of exploiting the complementary information from the lexicon-based approach and the corpus-based approach. Another reason for the effectiveness of our approach is the way that we combine the domain-independent knowledge and the domain-specific knowledge.

It is known that both the corpus-based approach and the lexicon-based approach have classification biases (Kennedy and Inkpen, 2006; Andreevskaia and Bergler, 2008; Qiu et al., 2009). To evaluate the effectiveness of our algorithm in reducing the bias, we compare it with the classifier that only uses one view of the LCCT model: either using the corpus-based view or using the lexicon-based view. The comparison is conducted on the Movie Review dataset. As Table 2 shows, our algorithm achieves good performance on both precision and recall. In contrast, the baseline methods either have high precision but low recall, or have high recall but low precision. The experiment result suggests that combining the two views is essential in eliminating the classification bias.

| Data | Corpus-based | | Lexicon-based | | LCCT | |
|---|---|---|---|---|---|---|
| | Prec. | Rec. | Prec. | Rec. | Prec. | Rec. |
| MR pos | 0.92 | 0.79 | 0.67 | 0.86 | 0.90 | 0.86 |
| MR neg. | 0.78 | 0.90 | 0.80 | 0.58 | 0.88 | 0.89 |

Table 2: Precision and recall on Movie reviews

## 5 Conclusions

We have proposed the LCCT model for semi-supervised sentiment classification, combining the idea of lexicon-based learning and corpus-based learning in a unified co-training framework. It is capable of incorporating both domain-specific and domain-independent knowledge. Comparing to state-of-the-art sentiment classification methods, the LCCT approach exhibits significantly better performances on a variety of datasets in both English and Chinese, even with a small portion of labeled data.

## References


Alina Andreevskaia and Sabine Bergler. 2008. When specialists and generalists work together: Overcoming domain dependence in sentiment tagging. In *ACL*, pages 290–298.

Prakhar Biyani, Cornelia Caragea, Prasenjit Mitra, Chong Zhou, John Yen, Greta E Greer, and Kenneth Portier. 2013. Co-training over domain-independent and domain-dependent features for sentiment analysis of an online cancer support community. In *the 2013 IEEE/ACM International Conference on Advances in Social Networks Analysis and Mining*, pages 413–417. ACM.

John Blitzer, Mark Dredze, and Fernando Pereira. 2007. Biographies, bollywood, boom-boxes and blenders: Domain adaptation for sentiment classification. In *ACL*, volume 7, pages 440–447.

Avrim Blum and Tom Mitchell. 1998. Combining labeled and unlabeled data with co-training. In *COLT*, pages 92–100. ACM.

Sajib Dasgupta and Vincent Ng. 2009. Mine the easy, classify the hard: a semi-supervised approach to automatic sentiment classification. In *ACL-IJCNLP:Volume 2*, pages 701–709. Association for Computational Linguistics.

Kushal Dave, Steve Lawrence, and David M Pennock. 2003. Mining the peanut gallery: Opinion extraction and semantic classification of product reviews. In *WWW*, pages 519–528. ACM.

Xavier Glorot, Antoine Bordes, and Yoshua Bengio. 2011. Domain adaptation for large-scale sentiment classification: A deep learning approach. In *ICML*, pages 513–520.

Minqing Hu and Bing Liu. 2004. Mining and summarizing customer reviews. In *SIGKDD*, pages 168–177. ACM.

Thorsten Joachims. 1999. Transductive inference for text classification using support vector machines. In *ICML*, volume 99, pages 200–209.

Alistair Kennedy and Diana Inkpen. 2006. Sentiment classification of movie reviews using contextual valence shifters. *Computational Intelligence*, 22(2):110–125.

Shoushan Li, Chu-Ren Huang, Guodong Zhou, and Sophia Yat Mei Lee. 2010. Employing personal/impersonal views in supervised and semi-supervised sentiment classification. In *ACL*, pages 414–423. Association for Computational Linguistics.

Bing Liu. 2012. Sentiment analysis and opinion mining. *Synthesis Lectures on Human Language Technologies*, 5(1):1–167.

Dai Quoc Nguyen, Dat Quoc Nguyen, Thanh Vu, and Son Bao Pham. 2014. Sentiment classification on polarity reviews: an empirical study using rating-based features.

Bo Pang and Lillian Lee. 2004. A sentimental education: Sentiment analysis using subjectivity summarization based on minimum cuts. In *ACL*, page 271. Association for Computational Linguistics.

Bo Pang and Lillian Lee. 2008. Opinion mining and sentiment analysis. *Foundations and trends in information retrieval*, 2(1-2):1–135.

Bo Pang, Lillian Lee, and Shivakumar Vaithyanathan. 2002. Thumbs up?: sentiment classification using machine learning techniques. In *EMNLP: Volume 10*, pages 79–86. Association for Computational Linguistics.

Likun Qiu, Weishi Zhang, Changjian Hu, and Kai Zhao. 2009. Selc: a self-supervised model for sentiment classification. In *CIKM*, pages 929–936. ACM.

David E Rumelhart, Geoffrey E Hinton, and Ronald J Williams. 1985. Learning internal representations by error propagation. Technical report, DTIC Document.

Peter D Turney. 2002. Thumbs up or thumbs down?: semantic orientation applied to unsupervised classification of reviews. In *ACL*, pages 417–424. Association for Computational Linguistics.

Pascal Vincent, Hugo Larochelle, Yoshua Bengio, and Pierre-Antoine Manzagol. 2008. Extracting and composing robust features with denoising autoencoders. In *ICML*, pages 1096–1103. ACM.

Pascal Vincent, Hugo Larochelle, Isabelle Lajoie, Yoshua Bengio, and Pierre-Antoine Manzagol. 2010. Stacked denoising autoencoders: Learning useful representations in a deep network with a local denoising criterion. *The Journal of Machine Learning Research*, 9999:3371–3408.

Xiaojun Wan. 2009. Co-training for cross-lingual sentiment classification. In *ACL-IJCNLP: Volume 1-Volume 1*, pages 235–243. Association for Computational Linguistics.

Casey Whitelaw, Navendu Garg, and Shlomo Argamon. 2005. Using appraisal groups for sentiment analysis. In *CIKM*, pages 625–631. ACM.

Janyce Wiebe and Ellen Riloff. 2005. Creating subjective and objective sentence classifiers from unannotated texts. In *Computational Linguistics and Intelligent Text Processing*, pages 486–497. Springer.

Rui Xie and Chunping Li. 2012. Lexicon construction: A topic model approach. In *International Conference on Systems and Informatics (ICSAI)*, pages 2299–2303. IEEE.

Min Yang, Dingju Zhu, Rashed Mustafa, and Kam-Pui Chow. 2014. Learning domain-specific sentiment lexicon with supervised sentiment-aware lda. *ECAI 2014*, pages 927–932.

Qiang Ye, Ziqiong Zhang, and Rob Law. 2009. Sentiment classification of online reviews to travel destinations by supervised machine learning approaches. *Expert Systems with Applications*, 36(3):6527–6535.

Ley Zhang, Riddhiman Ghosh, Mohamed Dekhil, Meichun Hsu, and Bing Liu. 2011. Combining lexiconbased and learning-based methods for twitter sentiment analysis. *HP Laboratories, Technical Report HPL-2011*, 89.

Shusen Zhou, Qingcai Chen, and Xiaolong Wang. 2010. Active deep networks for semi-supervised sentiment classification. In *Coling: Posters*, pages 1515–1523. Association for Computational Linguistics.

Xiaojin Zhu. 2006. Semi-supervised learning literature survey. *Computer Science, University of Wisconsin-Madison*, 2:3.

# Multiview LSA: Representation Learning via Generalized CCA

**Pushpendre Rastogi**[1] and **Benjamin Van Durme**[1,2] and **Raman Arora**[1]
[1]Center for Language and Speech Processing
[2]Human Language Technology Center of Excellence
Johns Hopkins University

## Abstract

*Multiview LSA (MVLSA)* is a generalization of Latent Semantic Analysis (LSA) that supports the fusion of arbitrary views of data and relies on Generalized Canonical Correlation Analysis (GCCA). We present an algorithm for fast approximate computation of GCCA, which when coupled with methods for handling missing values, is general enough to approximate some recent algorithms for inducing vector representations of words. Experiments across a comprehensive collection of test-sets show our approach to be competitive with the state of the art.

## 1 Introduction

Winograd (1972) wrote that: *"Two sentences are paraphrases if they produce the same representation in the internal formalism for meaning"*. This intuition is made soft in vector-space models (Turney and Pantel, 2010), where we say that expressions in language are paraphrases if their representations are *close* under some distance measure.

One of the earliest linguistic vector space models was Latent Semantic Analysis (LSA). LSA has been successfully used for Information Retrieval but it is limited in its reliance on a single matrix, or *view*, of term co-occurrences. Here we address the single-view limitation of LSA by demonstrating that the framework of Generalized Canonical Correlation Analysis (GCCA) can be used to perform Multiview LSA (MVLSA). This approach allows for the use of an arbitrary number of views in the induction process, including embeddings induced using other algorithms. We also present a fast approximate method for performing GCCA and approximately recover the objective of (Pennington et al., 2014) while accounting for missing values.

Our experiments show that MVLSA is competitive with state of the art approached for inducing vector representations of words and phrases. As a methodological aside, we discuss the (in-)significance of conclusions being drawn from comparisons done on small sized datasets.

## 2 Motivation

LSA is an application of Principal Component Analysis (PCA) to a term-document cooccurrence matrix. The principal directions found by PCA form the basis of the vector-space in which to represent the input terms (Landauer and Dumais, 1997). A drawback of PCA is that it can leverage only a single source of data and it is sensitive to scaling.

An arguably better approach to representation learning is Canonical Correlation Analysis (CCA) that induces representations that are maximally *correlated* across two views, allowing the utilization of two distinct sources of data. While an improvement over PCA, being limited to only two views is unfortunate in light of the fact that many sources of data (perspectives) are frequently available in practice. In such cases it is natural to extend CCA's original objective of maximizing correlation between two views by maximizing some measure of the matrix $\Phi$ that contains all the pairwise correlations between linear projections of the *covariates*. This is how Generalized Canonical Correlation Analysis (GCCA) was first derived by Horst (1961). Recently these intuitive ideas about benefits of leveraging multiple sources of data have received strong theoretical backing due to the work by Sridharan and



*Human Language Technologies: The 2015 Annual Conference of the North American Chapter of the ACL*, pages 556–566,
Denver, Colorado, May 31 – June 5, 2015. 

Kakade (2008) who showed that learning with multiple views is beneficial since it reduces the complexity of the learning problem by restricting the search space. Recent work by Anandkumar et al. (2014) showed that at least three views are necessary for recovering hidden variable models.

Note that there exist different variants of GCCA depending on the measure of $\Phi$ that we choose to maximize. Kettenring (1971) enumerated a variety of possible measures, such as the spectral-norm of $\Phi$. Kettenring noted that maximizing this spectral-norm is equivalent to finding linear projections of the *covariates* that are most amenable to rank-one PCA, or that can be best explained by a single term factor model. This variant was named *MAX-VAR GCCA* and was shown to be equivalent to a proposal by Carroll (1968), which searched for an auxiliary orthogonal representation $G$ that was maximally correlated to the linear projections of the covariates. Carroll's objective targets the intuition that representations leveraging multiple views should correlate with all provided views as much as possible.

## 3 Proposed Method: MVLSA

Let $X_j \in \mathbb{R}^{N \times d_j}\ \forall j \in [1, \ldots, J]$ be the mean centered matrix containing data from view $j$ such that row $i$ of $X_j$ contains the information for word $w_i$. Let the number of words in the vocabulary be $N$ and number of contexts (columns in $X_j$) be $d_j$. Following standard notation (Hastie et al., 2009) we call $X_j^\top X_j$ the scatter matrix and $X_j(X_j^\top X_j)^{-1}X_j^\top$ the projection matrix.

The objective of *MAX-VAR GCCA* can be written as the following optimization problem: Find $G \in \mathbb{R}^{N \times r}$ and $U_j \in \mathbb{R}^{d_j \times r}$ that solve:

$$\begin{aligned} &\arg\min_{G,U_j} \sum_{j=1}^{J} \left\| G - X_j U_j \right\|_F^2 \\ &\text{subject to } G^\top G = I. \end{aligned} \tag{1}$$

The matrix $G$ that solves problem (1) is our vector representation of the vocabulary. Finding $G$ reduces to spectral decomposition of sum of projection matrices of different views: Define

$$P_j = X_j(X_j^\top X_j)^{-1}X_j^\top, \tag{2}$$

$$M = \sum_{j=1}^{J} P_j. \tag{3}$$

Then, for some positive diagonal matrix $\Lambda$, $G$ and $U_j$ satisfy:

$$MG = G\Lambda, \tag{4}$$

$$U_j = \left(X_j^\top X_j\right)^{-1} X_j^\top G. \tag{5}$$

Computationally storing $P_j \in \mathbb{R}^{N \times N}$ is problematic owing to memory constraints. Further, the scatter matrices may be non-singular leading to an ill-posed procedure. We now describe a novel scalable GCCA with $\ell_2$-regularization to address these issues.

**Approximate Regularized GCCA**: GCCA can be regularized by adding $r_j I$ to scatter matrix $X_j^\top X_j$ before doing the inversion where $r_j$ is a small constant e.g. $10^{-8}$. Projection matrices in (2) and (3) can then be written as

$$\widetilde{P}_j = X_j(X_j^\top X_j + r_j I)^{-1}X_j^\top, \tag{6}$$

$$M = \sum_{j=1}^{J} \widetilde{P}_j. \tag{7}$$

Next, to scale up GCCA to large datasets, we first form a rank-$m$ approximation of projection matrices (Arora and Livescu, 2012) and then extend it to an eigendecomposition for $M$ following ideas by Savostyanov (2014). Consider the rank-$m$ SVD of $X_j$:

$$X_j = A_j S_j B_j^\top,$$

where $S_j \in \mathbb{R}^{m \times m}$ is the diagonal matrix with $m$-largest singular values of $X_j$ and $A_j \in \mathbb{R}^{N \times m}$ and $B_j \in \mathbb{R}^{m \times d_j}$ are the corresponding left and right singular vectors. Given this SVD, write the $j^{th}$ projection matrix as

$$\begin{aligned} \widetilde{P}_j &= A_j S_j^\top (r_j I + S_j S_j^\top)^{-1} S_j A_j^\top, \\ &= A_j T_j T_j^\top A_j^\top, \end{aligned}$$

where $T_j \in \mathbb{R}^{m \times m}$ is a diagonal matrix such that $T_j T_j^\top = S_j^\top (r_j I + S_j S_j^\top)^{-1} S_j$. Finally, we note that the sum of projection matrices can be expressed as $M = \tilde{M}\tilde{M}^\top$ where

$$\tilde{M} = [A_1 T_1 \dots A_J T_J] \in \mathbb{R}^{N \times mJ}.$$

Therefore, eigenvectors of matrix $M$, i.e. the matrix $G$ that we are interested in finding, are the left singular vectors of $\tilde{M}$, i.e. $\tilde{M} = GSV^\top$. These left singular vectors can be computed by using Incremental PCA (Brand, 2002) since $\tilde{M}$ may be too large to fit in memory.

### 3.1 Computing SVD of mean centered $X_j$

Recall that we assumed $X_j$ to be mean centered matrices. Let $Z_j \in \mathbb{R}^{N \times d_j}$ be sparse matrices containing mean-uncentered cooccurrence counts. Let $f_j = n_j \circ t_j$ be the preprocessing function that we apply to $Z_j$:

$$\begin{aligned} Y_j &= f_j(Z_j), &(8)\\ X_j &= Y_j - 1(1^\top Y_j). &(9) \end{aligned}$$

In order to compute the SVD of mean centered matrices $X_j$ we first compute the partial SVD of uncentered matrix $Y_j$ and then update it (Brand (2006) provides details). We experimented with representations created from the uncentered matrices $Y_j$ and found that they performed as well as the mean centered versions but we would not mention them further since it is computationally efficient to follow the principled approach. We note, however, that even the method of mean-centering the SVD produces an approximation.

### 3.2 Handling missing rows across views

With real data it may happen that a term was not observed in a view at all. A large number of missing rows can corrupt the learnt representations since the rows in the left singular matrix become zero. To counter this problem we adopt a variant of the "missing-data passive" algorithm from Van De Velden and Bijmolt (2006) who modified the GCCA objective to counter the problem of missing rows.[1] The objective now becomes:

$$\begin{aligned} &\underset{G,U_j}{\arg\min} \sum_{j=1}^{J} \left\| K_j(G - X_j U_j) \right\|_F^2 \\ &\text{subject to } G^\top G = I, \end{aligned} \quad (10)$$

where $[K_j]_{ii} = 1$ if row $i$ of view $j$ is observed and zero otherwise. Essentially $K_j$ is a diagonal row-selection matrix which ensures that we optimize our representations only on the observed rows. Note that $X_j = K_j X_j$ since the rows that $K_j$ removed were already zero. Let, $K = \sum_j K_j$ then the optima of the objective can be computed by modifying equation (7) as:

$$M = K^{-\frac{1}{2}} (\sum_{j=1}^{J} P_j) K^{-\frac{1}{2}}. \quad (11)$$

Again, if we regularize and approximate the GCCA solution we get $G$ as the left singular vectors of $K^{-\frac{1}{2}}\tilde{M}$. We mean center the matrices using only the observed rows.

Also note that other heuristic weighting schemes could be used here. For example if we modify our objective as follows then we would approximately recover the objective of Pennington et al. (2014):

$$\begin{aligned} &\underset{G,U_j}{\text{minimize:}} \quad \sum_{j=1}^{J} \left\| W_j K_j (G - X_j U_j) \right\|_F^2 \\ &\text{subject to:} \quad G^\top G = I \end{aligned} \quad (12)$$

where

$$\begin{aligned} [W_j]_{ii} &= \left( \frac{w_i}{w_{\max}} \right)^{\frac{3}{4}} \text{ if } w_i < w_{\max} \text{ else } 1, \\ \text{and } w_i &= \sum_k [X_j]_{ik}. \end{aligned}$$

## 4 Data

**Training Data** We used the English portion of the *Polyglot* Wikipedia dataset released by Al-Rfou et

[1] A more recent effort, by van de Velden and Takane (2012), describes newer iterative and non-iterative (Test-Equating Method) approaches for handling missing values. It is possible that using one of those methods could improve performance.

al. (2013) to create 15 *irredundant* views of cooccurrence statistics where element $[z]_{ij}$ of view $Z_k$ represents that number of times word $w_j$ occurred $k$ words behind $w_i$. We selected the top 500K words by occurrence to create our vocabulary for the rest of the paper.

We extracted cooccurrence statistics from a large bitext corpus that was made by combining a number of parallel bilingual corpora as part of the ParaPhrase DataBase (PPDB) project: Table 1 gives a summary, Ganitkevitch et al. (2013) provides further details. Element $[z]_{ij}$ of the *bitext* matrix represents the number of times English word $w_i$ was automatically aligned to the foreign word $w_j$.

We also used the dependency relations in the *Annotated Gigaword Corpus* (Napoles et al., 2012) to create 21 views[2] where element $[z]_{ij}$ of view $Z_d$ represents the number of times word $w_j$ occurred as the governor of word $w_i$ under dependency relation $d$.

We combined the knowledge of paraphrases present in FrameNet and PPDB by using the dataset created by Rastogi and Van Durme (2014) to construct a *FrameNet* view. Element $[z]_{ij}$ of the *FrameNet* view represents whether word $w_i$ was present in frame $f_j$. Similarly we combined the knowledge of morphology present in the *CatVar* database released by Habash and Dorr (2003) and *morpha* released by Minnen et al. (2001) along with *morphy* that is a part of WordNet. The morphological views and the frame semantic views were especially sparse with densities of 0.0003% and 0.03%. While the approach allows for an arbitrary number of distinct sources of semantic information, such as going further to include cooccurrence in WordNet synsets, we considered the described views to be representative, with further improvements possible as future work.

**Test Data** We evaluated the representations on the word similarity datasets listed in Table 2. The first 10 datasets in Table 2 were annotated with different rubrics and rated on different scales. But broadly they all contain human judgements about how similar two words are. The "AN-SYN" and "AN-SEM" datasets contain 4-tuples of analogous words and the

[2]Dependency relations employed: nsubj, amod, advmod, rcmod, dobj, prep_of, prep_in, prep_to, prep_on, prep_for, prep_with, prep_from, prep_at, prep_by, prep_as, prep_between, xsubj, agent, conj_and, conj_but, pobj.

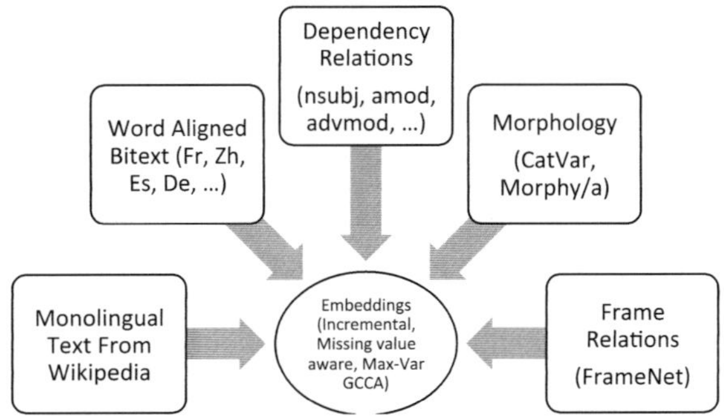


Figure 1: An illustration of datasets used.

| Language | Sentences | English Tokens |
|---|---|---|
| Bitext-Arabic | 8.8M | 190M |
| Bitext-Czech | 7.3M | 17M |
| Bitext-German | 1.8M | 44M |
| Bitext-Spanish | 11.1M | 241M |
| Bitext-French | 30.9M | 671M |
| Bitext-Chinese | 10.3M | 215M |
| Monotext-En-Wiki | 75M | 1700M |

Table 1: Portion of data used to create GCCA representations (in millions).

task is to predict the missing word given the first three. Both of these are open vocabulary tasks while TOEFL is a closed vocabulary task.

### 4.1 Significance of comparison

While surveying the literature we found that performance on word similarity datasets is typically reported in terms of the Spearman correlation between the gold ratings and the cosine distance between normalized embeddings. However researchers do not report measures of significance of the difference between the Spearman Correlations even for comparisons on small evaluation sets.[3] This motivated our defining a method for calculating the *Minimum Required Difference for Significance (MRDS)*.

**Minimum Required Difference for Significance (MRDS)**: Imagine two lists of ratings over the same

[3]For example, the comparative difference by competing algorithms reported by Faruqui et al. (2014) could not be significant for the Word Similarity test set released by Finkelstein et al. (2001), even if we assumed a correlation between competing methods as high as 0.9, with a p value threshold of 0.05. Similar such comparisons on small datasets are performed by Hill et al. (2014a).

| Acronym | Size | $\sigma_{0.01}^{0.5}$ | $\sigma_{0.01}^{0.7}$ | $\sigma_{0.01}^{0.9}$ | $\sigma_{0.05}^{0.5}$ | $\sigma_{0.05}^{0.7}$ | $\sigma_{0.05}^{0.9}$ | Reference |
|---|---|---|---|---|---|---|---|---|
| MEN | 3000 | 4.2 | 3.2 | 1.8 | 3.0 | 2.3 | 1.3 | (Bruni et al., 2012) |
| RW | 2034 | 5.1 | 3.9 | 2.3 | 3.6 | 2.8 | 1.6 | (Luong et al., 2013) |
| SCWS | 2003 | 5.1 | 4.0 | 2.3 | 3.6 | 2.8 | 1.6 | (Huang et al., 2012) |
| SIMLEX | 999 | 7.3 | 5.7 | 3.2 | 5.2 | 4.0 | 2.3 | (Hill et al., 2014b) |
| WS | 353 | 12.3 | 9.5 | 5.5 | 8.7 | 6.7 | 3.9 | (Finkelstein et al., 2001) |
| MTURK | 287 | 13.7 | 10.6 | 6.1 | 9.7 | 7.5 | 4.3 | (Radinsky et al., 2011) |
| WS-REL | 252 | 14.6 | 11.3 | 6.5 | 10.3 | 8.0 | 4.6 | (Agirre et al., 2009) |
| WS-SEM | 203 | 16.2 | 12.6 | 7.3 | 11.5 | 8.9 | 5.1 | -Same-As-Above- |
| RG | 65 | 28.6 | 22.3 | 12.9 | 20.6 | 16.0 | 9.2 | (Rubenstein and Goodenough, 1965) |
| MC | 30 | 41.7 | 32.7 | 19.0 | 30.6 | 23.9 | 13.8 | (Miller and Charles, 1991) |
| AN-SYN | 10675 | - | - | 0.95 | - | - | 0.68 | (Mikolov et al., 2013a) |
| AN-SEM | 8869 | - | - | 1.03 | - | - | 0.74 | -Same-As-Above- |
| TOEFL | 80 | - | - | 8.13 | - | - | 6.63 | (Landauer and Dumais, 1997) |

Table 2: List of test datasets used. The columns headed $\sigma_{p_0}^r$ contain *MRDS* values. The rows for accuracy based test sets contain $\sigma_{p_0}$ which does not depend on $r$. See § 4.1 for details.

items, produced respectively by algorithms $A$ and $B$, and then a list of gold ratings $T$. Let $r_{AT}$, $r_{BT}$ and $r_{AB}$ denote the Spearman correlations between $A:T$, $B:T$ and $A:B$ respectively. Let $\hat{r}_{AT}, \hat{r}_{BT}, \hat{r}_{AB}$ be their empirical estimates and assume that $\hat{r}_{BT} > \hat{r}_{AT}$ without loss of generality.

For word similarity datasets we define $\sigma_{p_0}^r$ as the MRDS, such that it satisfies the following proposition:

$$(r_{AB} < r) \wedge (|\hat{r}_{BT} - \hat{r}_{AT}| < \sigma_{p_0}^r) \implies \textit{pval} > p_0$$

. Here *pval* is the probability of the test statistic under the null hypothesis that $r_{AT} = r_{BT}$ found using the Steiger's test (Steiger, 1980). The above constraint ensures that as long as the correlation between the competing methods is less than $r$ and the difference between the correlations of the scores of the competing methods to the gold ratings is less than $\sigma_{p_0}^r$, then the pvalue of the null hypothesis will be greater than $p_0$. We can then ask what we consider a reasonable upper bound on the agreement of ratings produced by competing algorithms: for instance two algorithms correlating above $0.9$ might not be considered meaningfully different. That leaves us with the second part of the predicate which ensures that as long as the difference between the correlations of the competing algorithms to the gold scores is less than $\sigma_{p_0}^r$ then the null hypothesis is more likely than $p_0$.

We can find $\sigma_{p_0}^r$ as follows: Let *stest* denote Steiger's test predicate which satisfies the following:

$$\textit{stest-p}(\hat{r}_{AT}, \hat{r}_{BT}, r_{AB}, p_0, n) \implies \textit{pval} < p_0$$

Once we define this predicate then we can use it to set up an optimistic problem where our aim is to find $\sigma_{p_0}^r$ by solving the following:

$$\sigma_{p_0}^r = \min\{\sigma | \forall\, 0 < r' < 1\; \textit{stest-p}(r', \min(r' + \sigma, 1), r, p_0, n)\}$$

Note that MRDS is a liberal threshold and it only guarantees that differences in correlations below that threshold can never be statistically significant (under the given parameter settings). MRDS might optimistically consider some differences as significant when they are not, but it is at least useful in reducing some of the noise in the evaluations. The values of $\sigma_{p_0}^r$ are shown in Table 2.

For the accuracy based test-sets we found MRDS$=\sigma_{p_0}$ that satisfied the following:

$$0 < (\hat{\theta}_B - \hat{\theta}_A) < \sigma_{p_0} \implies \mathrm{p}(\theta_B \leq \theta_A) > p_0$$

Specifically, we calculated the posterior probability $\mathrm{p}(\theta_B \leq \theta_A)$ with a flat prior of $\beta(1,1)$ to solve the following:[4] $\sigma_{p_0} = \min\{\sigma | \forall\, 0 < \theta < \min(1-\sigma, 0.9)$ $\mathrm{p}(\theta_B \leq \theta_A | \hat{\theta}_A = \theta, \hat{\theta}_B = \theta + \sigma, n) < p_0\}$ Here $\theta_A$ and $\theta_B$

[4]This instead of using McNemar's test (McNemar, 1947) since the Bayesian approach is tractable and more direct. A calculation with $\beta(0.5, 0.5)$ as the prior changed $\sigma_{0.5}$ from 6.63 to 6.38 for the TOEFL dataset but did not affect MRDS for the AN-SEM and AN-SYN datasets.

are probability of correctness of algorithms $A$, $B$ and $\hat{\theta}_A$, $\hat{\theta}_B$ are observed empirical accuracies.

Unfortunately there are no widely reported train-test splits of the above datasets, leading to potential concerns of *soft supervision* (hyper-parameter tuning) on these evaluations, both in our own work and throughout the existing literature. We report on the resulting impact of various parameterizations, and our final results are based on a single set of parameters used across all evaluation sets.

## 5 Experiments and Results

We wanted to answer the following questions through our experiments: (1) How do hyper-parameters affect performance? (2) What is the contribution of the multiple sources of data to performance? (3) How does the performance of MVLSA compare with other methods? For brevity we show tuning runs only on the larger datasets. We also highlight the top performing configurations in bold using the small threshold values in column $\sigma_{0.05}^{0.09}$ of Table 2.

**Effect of Hyper-parameters** $f_j$: We modeled the preprocessing function $f_j$ as the composition of two functions, $f_j = n_j \circ t_j$. $n_j$ represents nonlinear preprocessing that is usually employed with LSA. We experimented by setting $n_j$ to be: identity; logarithm of count plus one; and the fourth root of the count. $t_j$ represents the truncation of columns and can be interpreted as a type of regularization of the raw counts themselves through which we prune away the noisy contexts. Decrease in $t_j$ also reduces the influence of views that have a large number of context columns and emphasizes the sparser views. Table 3 and Table 4 show the results.

| Test Set | Log | Count | $\text{Count}^{\frac{1}{4}}$ |
|---|---|---|---|
| MEN | 67.5 | 59.7 | **70.7** |
| RW | 31.1 | 25.3 | **37.8** |
| SCWS | 64.2 | 58.2 | **66.6** |
| AN-SYN | 45.7 | 21.1 | **53.6** |
| AN-SEM | 25.4 | 15.9 | **38.7** |

Table 3: Performance versus $n_j$, the non linear processing of cooccurrence counts. $t = 200K$, $m = 500$, $v = 16$, $k = 300$. All the top configurations determined by $\sigma_{0.05}^{0.09}$ are in bold font.

| Test Set | 6.25K | 12.5K | 25K | 50K | 100K | 200K |
|---|---|---|---|---|---|---|
| MEN | 70.2 | **71.2** | **71.5** | **71.6** | **71.2** | **70.7** |
| RW | **41.8** | **41.7** | **41.5** | **40.9** | 39.6 | 37.8 |
| SCWS | **67.1** | **67.3** | **67.1** | **67.0** | **66.9** | **66.6** |
| AN-SYN | 59.2 | **60.0** | **59.5** | 58.4 | 56.1 | 53.6 |
| AN-SEM | 37.7 | **38.6** | **39.4** | **39.2** | 38.4 | **38.7** |

Table 4: Performance versus the truncation threshold, $t$, of raw cooccurrence counts. We used $n_j = \text{Count}^{\frac{1}{4}}$ and other settings were the same as Table 3.

$m$: The number of left singular vectors extracted after SVD of the preprocessed cooccurrence matrices can again be interpreted as a type of regularization, since the result of this truncation is that we find cooccurrence patterns only between the top left singular vectors. We set $m_j = max(d_j, m)$ with $m = [100, 300, 500]$. See table 5.

| Test Set | 100 | 200 | 300 | 500 |
|---|---|---|---|---|
| MEN | 65.6 | 68.5 | **70.1** | **71.1** |
| RW | 34.6 | **36.0** | **37.2** | **37.1** |
| SCWS | 64.2 | **65.4** | **66.4** | **66.5** |
| AN-SYN | 50.5 | **56.2** | **56.4** | **56.4** |
| AN-SEM | 24.3 | 31.4 | 34.3 | **40.6** |

Table 5: Performance versus $m$, the number of left singular vectors extracted from raw cooccurrence counts. We set $n_j = \text{Count}^{\frac{1}{4}}$, $t = 100K$, $v = 25$, $k = 300$.

$k$: Table 6 demonstrates the variation in performance versus the dimensionality of the learnt vector representations of the words. Since the dimensions of the MVLSA representations are orthogonal to each other therefore creating lower dimensional representations is a trivial matrix slicing operation and does not require retraining.

| Test Set | 10 | 50 | 100 | 200 | 300 | 500 |
|---|---|---|---|---|---|---|
| MEN | 49.0 | 67.0 | **69.7** | **70.2** | **70.1** | **69.8** |
| RW | 28.8 | 33.3 | 35.0 | 35.2 | **37.2** | **38.3** |
| SCWS | 57.8 | 64.4 | **65.2** | **66.1** | **66.4** | **65.1** |
| AN-SYN | 9.0 | 41.2 | 52.2 | 55.4 | **56.4** | 54.4 |
| AN-SEM | 2.5 | 21.8 | 34.8 | **35.8** | 34.3 | 33.8 |

Table 6: Performance versus $k$, the final dimensionality of the embeddings. We set $m = 300$ and other settings were same as Table 5.

$v$: Expression 12 describes a method to set $W_j$. We experimented with a different, more global, heuristic to set $[W_j]_{ii} = (K_{ww} \geq v)$, essentially removing all words that did not appear in $v$ views before doing GCCA. Table 7 shows that changes in $v$ are largely inconsequential for performance.

| Test Set | 16 | 17 | 21 | 25 | 29 |
|---|---|---|---|---|---|
| MEN | **70.4** | **70.4** | **70.2** | **70.1** | **70.0** |
| RW | **39.9** | **38.8** | **39.7** | 37.2 | 33.5 |
| SCWS | **67.0** | **66.8** | **66.5** | **66.4** | **65.7** |
| AN-SYN | **56.0** | **55.8** | **55.9** | **56.4** | **56.0** |
| AN-SEM | **34.6** | **34.3** | **34.0** | **34.3** | **34.3** |

Table 7: Performance versus minimum view support threshold $v$, The other hyperparameters were $n_j = \text{Count}^{\frac{1}{4}}$, $m = 300$, $t = 100K$. Though a clear best setting did not emerge, we chose $v = 25$ as the middle ground.

$r_j$: The regularization parameter ensures that all the inverses exist at all points in our method. We found that the performance of our procedure was invariant to $r$ over a large range from 1 to 1e-10. This was because even the 1000th singular value of our data was much higher than 1.

**Contribution of different sources of data** Table 8 shows an ablative analysis of performance where we remove individual views or some combination of them and measure the performance. It is clear by comparing the last column to the second column that adding in more views improves performance. Also we can see that the Dependency based views and the Bitext based views give a larger boost than the morphology and FrameNet based views, probably because the latter are so sparse.

**Comparison to other word representation creation methods** There are a large number of methods of creating representations both multilingual and monolingual. There are many new methods such as by Yu and Dredze (2014), Faruqui et al. (2014), Hill and Korhonen (2014), and Weston et al. (2014) that are performing multiview learning and could be considered here as baselines: however it is not straightforward to use those systems to handle the variety of data that we are using. Therefore, we directly compare our method to the Glove and the SkipGram model of Word2Vec as the performance of those systems is considered state of the art. We trained these two systems on the English portion of the *Polyglot* Wikipedia dataset.[5] We also combined their outputs using MVLSA to create *MV-G-WSG)* embeddings.

We trained our best MVLSA system with data from all views and by using the individual best settings of the hyper-parameters. Specifically the configuration we used was as follows: $n_j = \text{Count}^{\frac{1}{4}}, t = 12.5K, m = 500, k = 300, v = 16$. To make a fair comparison we also provide results where we used only the views derived from the *Polyglot* Wikipedia corpus. See column *MVLSA (All Views)* and *MVLSA (Wiki)* respectively. It is clearly visible that MVLSA on the monolingual data itself is competitive with Glove but worse than Word2Vec on the word similarity datasets and it is substantially worse than both the systems on the AN-SYN and AN-SEM datasets. However with the addition of multiple views MVLSA makes substantial gains, shown in column *MV Gain*, and after consuming the Glove and WSG embeddings it again improves performance by some margins, as shown in column *G-WSG Gain*, and outperforms the original systems. Using GCCA itself for system combination provides closure for the MVLSA algorithm since multiple distinct approaches can now be simply fused using this method. Finally we contrast the Spearman correlations $r_s$ with Glove and Word2Vec before and after including them in the GCCA procedure. The values demonstrate that including Glove and WSG during GCCA actually increased the correlation between them and the learnt embeddings, which supports our motivation for performing GCCA in the first place.

## 6 Previous Work

Vector space representations of words have been created using diverse frameworks including Spectral methods (Dhillon et al., 2011; Dhillon et al., 2012), [6] Neural Networks (Mikolov et al., 2013b; Collobert and Lebret, 2013), and Random Projections (Ravichandran et al., 2005; Bhagat and Ravichan-

[5] We explicitly provided the vocabulary file to Glove and Word2Vec and set the truncation threshold for Word2Vec to 10. Glove was trained for 25 iterations. Glove was provided a window of 15 previous words and Word2Vec used a symmetric window of 10 words.

[6] `cis.upenn.edu/~ungar/eigenwords`

| Test Set | All Views | !Framenet | !Morphology | !Bitext | !Wikipedia | !Dependency | !Morphology !Framenet | !Morphology !Framenet !Bitext |
|---|---|---|---|---|---|---|---|---|
| MEN | **70.1** | **69.8** | **70.1** | **69.9** | 46.4 | 68.4 | **69.5** | 68.4 |
| RW | **37.2** | **36.4** | **36.1** | 32.2 | 11.6 | 34.9 | 34.1 | 27.1 |
| SCWS | **66.4** | **65.8** | **66.3** | 64.2 | 54.5 | **65.5** | **65.2** | 60.8 |
| AN-SYN | **56.4** | **56.3** | **56.2** | 51.2 | 37.6 | 50.5 | 54.4 | 46.0 |
| AN-SEM | 34.3 | 34.3 | 34.3 | **36.2** | 4.1 | 35.3 | 34.5 | 30.6 |

Table 8: Performance versus views removed from the multiview GCCA procedure. !Framenet means that the view containing counts derived from Frame semantic dataset was removed. Other columns are named similarly. The other hyperparameters were $n_j = \text{Count}^{\frac{1}{4}},\ m = 300,\ t = 100K,\ v = 25,\ k = 300$.

| Test Set | Glove | WSG | MV G-WSG | MVLSA Wiki | MVLSA All Views | MVLSA Combined | MV Gain | G-WSG Gain | $r_s$ MVLSA Glove | $r_s$ MVLSA WSG | $r_s$ MV-G-WSG Glove | $r_s$ MV-G-WSG WSG |
|---|---|---|---|---|---|---|---|---|---|---|---|---|
| MEN | 70.4 | 73.9 | **76.0** | 71.4 | 71.2 | **75.8** | −0.2 | 4.6† | 71.9 | 89.1 | 85.8 | 92.3 |
| RW | 28.1 | 32.9 | 37.2 | 29.0 | **41.7** | **40.5** | 12.7† | −1.2 | 72.3 | 74.2 | 80.2 | 75.6 |
| SCWS | 54.1 | 65.6 | 60.7 | 61.8 | **67.3** | **66.4** | 5.5† | −0.9 | 87.1 | 94.5 | 91.3 | 96.3 |
| SIMLEX | 33.7 | 36.7 | 41.1 | 34.5 | **42.4** | **43.9** | 7.9† | 1.5 | 62.4 | 78.2 | 79.3 | 86.0 |
| WS | 58.6 | **70.8** | **67.4** | **68.0** | **70.8** | **70.1** | 2.8† | −0.7 | 72.3 | 88.1 | 81.8 | 91.8 |
| MTURK | **61.7** | **65.1** | 59.8 | 59.1 | 59.7 | **62.9** | 0.6 | 3.2 | 80.0 | 87.7 | 87.3 | 92.5 |
| WS-REL | 53.4 | **63.6** | 59.6 | 60.1 | **65.1** | **63.5** | 5.0† | −1.6 | 58.2 | 81.0 | 69.6 | 85.3 |
| WS-SEM | 69.0 | **78.4** | **76.1** | **76.8** | **78.8** | **79.2** | 2.0 | 0.4 | 74.4 | 90.6 | 83.9 | 94.0 |
| RG | **73.8** | **78.2** | **80.4** | 71.2 | **74.4** | **80.8** | 3.2 | 6.4† | 80.3 | 90.6 | 91.8 | 92.9 |
| MC | **70.5** | **78.5** | **82.7** | **76.6** | **75.9** | **77.7** | −0.7 | 2.8 | 80.1 | 94.1 | 91.4 | 95.8 |
| AN-SYN | 61.8 | 59.8 | 51.0 | 42.7 | 60.0 | **64.3** | 17.3† | 4.3† | | | | |
| AN-SEM | **80.9** | 73.7 | 73.5 | 36.2 | 38.6 | 77.2 | 2.4† | 38.6† | | | | |
| TOEFL | **83.8** | 81.2 | **86.2** | 78.8 | **87.5** | **88.8** | 8.7† | 1.3 | | | | |

Table 9: Comparison of Multiview LSA against Glove and WSG(Word2Vec Skip Gram). Using $\sigma^{0.9}_{0.05}$ as the threshold we highlighted the top performing systems in bold font. † marks significant increments in performance due to use of multiple views in the *Gain* columns. The $r_s$ columns demonstrate that GCCA increased pearson correlation.

dran, 2008; Chan et al., 2011). [7] They have been trained using either one (Pennington et al., 2014) [8] or two sources of cooccurrence statistics (Zou et al., 2013; Faruqui and Dyer, 2014; Bansal et al., 2014; Levy and Goldberg, 2014) [9] or using multi-modal data (Hill and Korhonen, 2014; Bruni et al., 2012).

Dhillon et al. (2011) and Dhillon et al. (2012) were the first to use CCA as the primary method to learn vector representations and Faruqui and Dyer (2014) further demonstrated that incorporating bilingual data through CCA improved performance. More recently this same phenomenon was reported by Hill et al. (2014a) through their experiments over neural representations learnt from MT systems. Various other researchers have tried to improve the performance of their paraphrase systems or vector space models by using diverse sources of information such as bilingual corpora (Bannard and Callison-Burch, 2005; Huang et al., 2012; Zou et al., 2013),[10] structured datasets (Yu and Dredze, 2014; Faruqui et al., 2014) or even tagged images (Bruni

[7] `code.google.com/p/word2vec`, `metaoptimize.com/projects/wordreprs`

[8] `nlp.stanford.edu/projects/glove`

[9] `ttic.uchicago.edu/~mbansal/data/syntacticEmbeddings.zip`, `cs.cmu.edu/~mfaruqui/soft.html`

[10] An example of complementary views: Chan et al. (2011) observed that monolingual distributional statistics are susceptible to conflating antonyms, where bilingual data is not; on the other hand bilingual statistics are susceptible to noisy alignments, where monolingual data is not.

et al., 2012). However, most previous work[11] did not adopt the general, simplifying view that all of these sources of data are just cooccurrence statistics coming from different sources with underlying latent factors.[12]

Bach and Jordan (2005) presented a probabilistic interpretation for CCA. Though they did not generalize it to include GCCA we believe that one could give a probabilistic interpretation of *MAX-VAR GCCA*. Such a probabilistic interpretation would allow for an online-generative model of lexical representations, which unlike methods like Glove or LSA would allows us to naturally perplexity or generate sequences. We also note that Vía et al. (2007) presented a neural network model of GCCA and adaptive/incremental GCCA. To the best of our knowledge both of these approaches have not been used for word representation learning.

CCA is also an algorithm for multi-view learning (Kakade and Foster, 2007; Ganchev et al., 2008) and when we view our work as an application of multi-view learning to NLP, this follows a long chain of effort started by Yarowsky (1995) and continued with *Co-Training* (Blum and Mitchell, 1998), *CoBoosting* (Collins and Singer, 1999) and *2 view perceptrons* (Brefeld et al., 2006).

## 7 Conclusion and Future Work

While previous efforts demonstrated that incorporating two views is beneficial in word-representation learning, we extended that thread of work to a logical extreme and created *MVLSA* to learn distributed representations using data from 46 views![13] Through evaluation of our induced representations, shown in Table 9, we demonstrated that the MVLSA algorithm is able to leverage the information present in multiple data sources to improve performance on a battery of tests against state of the art baselines. In order to perform MVLSA on large vocabularies with up to 500K words we presented a fast scalable algorithm. We also showed that a close variant of the Glove objective proposed by Pennington et al. (2014) could be derived as a heuristic for handling missing data under the MVLSA framework. In order to better understand the benefit of using multiple sources of data we performed MVLSA using views derived only from the monolingual Wikipedia dataset thereby providing a more principled alternative of LSA that removes the need for heuristically combining word-word cooccurrence matrices into a single matrix. Finally, while surveying the literature we noticed that not enough emphasis was being given towards establishing the significance of comparative results and proposed a method, *(MRDS)*, to filter out insignificant comparative gains between competing algorithms.

**Future Work** Column *MVLSA Wiki* of Table 9 shows us that MVLSA applied to monolingual data has mediocre performance compared to the baselines of Glove and Word2Vec on word similarity tasks and performs surprisingly worse on the AN-SEM dataset. We believe that the results could be improved by (1) either using recent methods for handling missing values mentioned in footnote 1 or by using the heuristic count dependent non-linear weighting mentioned by Pennington et al. (2014) and that sits well within our framework as exemplified in Expression 12 (2) by using even more views, which look at the future words as well as views that contain PMI values. Finally, we note that Table 8 shows that certain datasets can actually degrade performance over certain metrics. Therefore we are exploring methods for performing discriminative optimization of weights assigned to views, for purposes of task-based customization of learned representations.


## Acknowledgments

This material is based on research sponsored by the Defense Advanced Research Projects Agency (DARPA) under the Deep Exploration and Filtering of Text (DEFT) Program, agreement number FA8750-13-2-001, as well as the National Science Foundation (NSF), agreement number BCS-1344269. We also thank Juri Ganitkevitch for providing the word aligned bitext corpus.


[11] Ganitkevitch et al. (2013) did employ a rich set of diverse cooccurrence statistics in constructing the initial PPDB, but without a notion of "training" a joint representation beyond random projection to a binary vector subspace (bit-signatures).

[12] Note that while Faruqui et al. (2014) performed belief propagation over a graph representation of their data, such an undirected weighted graph can be viewed as an adjacency matrix, which is then also a cooccurrence matrix.

[13] Code and data available at `www.cs.jhu.edu/~prastog3/mvlsa`

## References


Eneko Agirre, Enrique Alfonseca, Keith Hall, Jana Kravalova, Marius Paşca, and Aitor Soroa. 2009. A study on similarity and relatedness using distributional and wordnet-based approaches. In *Proceedings of NAACL-HLT*. ACL.

Rami Al-Rfou, Bryan Perozzi, and Steven Skiena. 2013. Polyglot: Distributed word representations for multilingual nlp. In *Proceedings of CoNLL*. ACL.

Animashree Anandkumar, Rong Ge, Daniel Hsu, Sham M. Kakade, and Matus Telgarsky. 2014. Tensor decompositions for learning latent variable models. *JMLR*, 15.

Raman Arora and Karen Livescu. 2012. Kernel CCA for multi-view learning of acoustic features using articulatory measurements. *MLSLP*.

Francis R Bach and Michael I Jordan. 2005. A probabilistic interpretation of canonical correlation analysis. *Technical Report 688, Department of Statistics, University of California, Berkeley*.

Colin Bannard and Chris Callison-Burch. 2005. Paraphrasing with bilingual parallel corpora. In *Proceedings of ACL*. ACL.

Mohit Bansal, Kevin Gimpel, and Karen Livescu. 2014. Tailoring continuous word representations for dependency parsing. In *Proceedings of ACL*. ACL.

Rahul Bhagat and Deepak Ravichandran. 2008. Large scale acquisition of paraphrases for learning surface patterns. In *Proceedings of ACL-HLT*.

Avrim Blum and Tom Mitchell. 1998. Combining labeled and unlabeled data with co-training. In *Proceedings of COLT*. ACM.

Matthew Brand. 2002. Incremental singular value decomposition of uncertain data with missing values. In *Computer Vision—ECCV 2002*, pages 707–720. Springer.

Matthew Brand. 2006. Fast low-rank modifications of the thin singular value decomposition. *Linear algebra and its applications*, 415(1).

Ulf Brefeld, Thomas Gärtner, Tobias Scheffer, and Stefan Wrobel. 2006. Efficient co-regularised least squares regression. In *Proceedings of ICML*. ACM.

Elia Bruni, Gemma Boleda, Marco Baroni, and Nam-Khanh Tran. 2012. Distributional semantics in technicolor. In *Proceedings of ACL*. ACL.

J Douglas Carroll. 1968. Generalization of canonical correlation analysis to three or more sets of variables. In *Proceedings of APA*, volume 3.

Tsz Ping Chan, Chris Callison-Burch, and Benjamin Van Durme. 2011. Reranking bilingually extracted paraphrases using monolingual distributional similarity. In *Proceedings of EMNLP Workshop: GEMS*.

Michael Collins and Yoram Singer. 1999. Unsupervised models for named entity classification. In *Proceedings of EMNLP*. ACL.

Ronan Collobert and Rémi Lebret. 2013. Word embeddings through hellinger pca. Technical report, Idiap.

Paramveer Dhillon, Dean Foster, and Lyle Ungar. 2011. Multi-view learning of word embeddings via CCA. In *Procesdings of NIPS*.

Paramveer Dhillon, Jordan Rodu, Dean P Foster, and Lyle H Ungar. 2012. Two step CCA: A new spectral method for estimating vector models of words. In *Proceedings of ICML*. ACM.

Manaal Faruqui and Chris Dyer. 2014. Improving vector space word representations using multilingual correlation. In *Proceedings of EACL*.

Manaal Faruqui, Jesse Dodge, Sujay Jauhar, Chris Dyer, Eduard Hovy, and Noah Smith. 2014. Retrofitting word vectors to semantic lexicons. In *Proceedings of the deep learning and representation learning workshop, NIPS*.

Lev Finkelstein, Evgeniy Gabrilovich, Yossi Matias, Ehud Rivlin, Zach Solan, Gadi Wolfman, and Eytan Ruppin. 2001. Placing search in context: The concept revisited. In *Proceedings of WWW*. ACM.

Kuzman Ganchev, Joao Graca, John Blitzer, and Ben Taskar. 2008. Multi-view learning over structured and non-identical outputs. In *Proceedings of UAI*.

Juri Ganitkevitch, Benjamin Van Durme, and Chris Callison-Burch. 2013. Ppdb: The paraphrase database. In *Proceedings of NAACL-HLT*.

Nizar Habash and Bonnie Dorr. 2003. Catvar: A database of categorial variations for english. In *Proceedings of MT Summit*.

Trevor Hastie, Robert Tibshirani, and Jerome Friedman. 2009. *The Elements Of Statistical Learning*, volume 2. Springer.

Felix Hill and Anna Korhonen. 2014. Learning abstract concept embeddings from multi-modal data: Since you probably can't see what i mean. In *Proceedings of EMNLP*. ACL.

Felix Hill, KyungHyun Cho, Sebastien Jean, Coline Devin, and Yoshua Bengio. 2014a. Not all neural embeddings are born equal. *arXiv preprint arXiv:1410.0718*.

Felix Hill, Roi Reichart, and Anna Korhonen. 2014b. Simlex-999: Evaluating semantic models with (genuine) similarity estimation. *arXiv preprint arXiv:1408.3456*.

Paul Horst. 1961. Generalized canonical correlations and their applications to experimental data. *Journal of Clinical Psychology*, 17(4).

Eric H. Huang, Richard Socher, Christopher D. Manning, and Andrew Y. Ng. 2012. Improving word representations via global context and multiple word prototypes. In *Proceedings of ACL*. ACL.

Sham M Kakade and Dean P Foster. 2007. Multi-view regression via canonical correlation analysis. In *Learning Theory*. Springer.

Jon R Kettenring. 1971. Canonical analysis of several sets of variables. *Biometrika*, 58(3):433–451.

Thomas K Landauer and Susan T Dumais. 1997. A solution to plato's problem: The latent semantic analysis theory of acquisition, induction, and representation of knowledge. *Psychological review*, 104(2):211.

Omer Levy and Yoav Goldberg. 2014. Dependency-based word embeddings. In *Proceedings of ACL*. ACL.

Minh-Thang Luong, Richard Socher, and Christopher D. Manning. 2013. Better word representations with recursive neural networks for morphology. In *Proceedings of CoNLL*. ACL.

Quinn McNemar. 1947. Note on the sampling error of the difference between correlated proportions or percentages. *Psychometrika*, 12(2).

Tomas Mikolov, Ilya Sutskever, Kai Chen, Greg Corrado, and Jeff Dean. 2013a. Distributed representations of words and phrases and their compositionality. In *Proceedings of NIPS*.

Tomas Mikolov, Wen-tau Yih, and Geoffrey Zweig. 2013b. Linguistic regularities in continuous space word representations. In *Proceedings of NAACL-HLT*, pages 746–751.

George A. Miller and Walter G. Charles. 1991. Contextual correlates of semantic similarity. *Language and Cognitive Processes*, 6(1).

Guido Minnen, John Carroll, and Darren Pearce. 2001. Applied morphological processing of english. *Natural Language Engineering*, 7(03).

Courtney Napoles, Matthew Gormley, and Benjamin Van Durme. 2012. Annotated gigaword. In *Proceedings of NAACL Workshop: AKBC-WEKEX*.

Jeffrey Pennington, Richard Socher, and Christopher D. Manning. 2014. Glove: global vectors for word representation. In *Proceedings of EMNLP*. ACL.

Kira Radinsky, Eugene Agichtein, Evgeniy Gabrilovich, and Shaul Markovitch. 2011. A word at a time: Computing word relatedness using temporal semantic analysis. In *Proceedings of WWW*. ACM.

Pushpendre Rastogi and Benjamin Van Durme. 2014. Augmenting framenet via PPDB. In *Proceedings of the Second Workshop on EVENTS: Definition, Detection, Coreference, and Representation*. ACL.

Deepak Ravichandran, Patrick Pantel, and Eduard Hovy. 2005. Randomized algorithms and nlp: Using locality sensitive hash functions for high speed noun clustering. In *Proceedings of ACL*.

Herbert Rubenstein and John B. Goodenough. 1965. Contextual correlates of synonymy. *Communications of the ACM*, 8(10).

Dmitry Savostyanov. 2014. Efficient way to find svd of sum of projection matrices? MathOverflow. URL:http://mathoverflow.net/q/178573 (version: 2014-08-14).

Karthik Sridharan and Sham M Kakade. 2008. An information theoretic framework for multi-view learning. In *Proceedings of COLT*.

James H Steiger. 1980. Tests for comparing elements of a correlation matrix. *Psychological Bulletin*, 87(2).

Peter D Turney and Patrick Pantel. 2010. From frequency to meaning: Vector space models of semantics. *Journal of AI Research*, 37(1).

Michel Van De Velden and Tammo HA Bijmolt. 2006. Generalized canonical correlation analysis of matrices with missing rows: a simulation study. *Psychometrika*, 71(2).

Michel van de Velden and Yoshio Takane. 2012. Generalized canonical correlation analysis with missing values. *Computational Statistics*, 27(3).

Javier Vía, Ignacio Santamaría, and Jesús Pérez. 2007. A learning algorithm for adaptive canonical correlation analysis of several data sets. *Neural Networks*, 20(1).

Jason Weston, Sumit Chopra, and Keith Adams. 2014. #tagspace: Semantic embeddings from hashtags. In *Proceedings of EMNLP*, Doha, Qatar. ACL.

Terry Winograd. 1972. Understanding natural language. *Cognitive psychology*, 3(1):1–191.

David Yarowsky. 1995. Unsupervised WSD rivaling supervised methods. In *Proceedings of ACL*. ACL.

Mo Yu and Mark Dredze. 2014. Improving lexical embeddings with semantic knowledge. In *Proceedings of ACL*. ACL.

Will Zou, Richard Socher, Daniel Cer, and Christopher Manning. 2013. Bilingual word embeddings for phrase-based machine translation. In *Proceedings of EMNLP*. ACL.

# NASARI: a Novel Approach to a Semantically-Aware Representation of Items

**José Camacho-Collados, Mohammad Taher Pilehvar** and **Roberto Navigli**
Department of Computer Science
Sapienza University of Rome
{collados,pilehvar,navigli}@di.uniroma1.it

## Abstract

The semantic representation of individual word senses and concepts is of fundamental importance to several applications in Natural Language Processing. To date, concept modeling techniques have in the main based their representation either on lexicographic resources, such as WordNet, or on encyclopedic resources, such as Wikipedia. We propose a vector representation technique that combines the complementary knowledge of both these types of resource. Thanks to its use of explicit semantics combined with a novel cluster-based dimensionality reduction and an effective weighting scheme, our representation attains state-of-the-art performance on multiple datasets in two standard benchmarks: word similarity and sense clustering. We are releasing our vector representations at http://lcl.uniroma1.it/nasari/.

## 1 Introduction

Obtaining accurate semantic representations of individual word senses or concepts is vital for several applications in Natural Language Processing (NLP) such as, for example, Word Sense Disambiguation (Navigli, 2009; Navigli, 2012), Entity Linking (Bunescu and Paşca, 2006; Rao et al., 2013), semantic similarity (Budanitsky and Hirst, 2006), Information Extraction (Banko et al., 2007), and resource linking and integration (Pilehvar and Navigli, 2014). One prominent semantic representation approach is the distributional semantic model, which represents lexical items as vectors in a semantic space. The weights in these vectors were traditionally computed on the basis of co-occurrence statistics (Salton et al., 1975; Turney and Pantel, 2010; Dinu and Lapata, 2010; Lappin and Fox, 2014), whereas for the more recent generation of distributional models weight computation is viewed as a context prediction problem, often to be solved by using neural networks (Collobert and Weston, 2008; Turian et al., 2010; Mikolov et al., 2013). Unfortunately, unless they are provided with large amounts of sense-annotated data these corpus-based techniques cannot capture polysemy in their representations, as they conflate different meanings of a word into a single vector. Therefore, most sense modeling techniques tend to base their computation on the knowledge obtained from various lexical resources. However, these techniques mainly utilize the knowledge derived from either WordNet (Banerjee and Pedersen, 2002; Budanitsky and Hirst, 2006; Pilehvar et al., 2013) or Wikipedia (Medelyan et al., 2009; Mihalcea, 2007; Dandala et al., 2013; Gabrilovich and Markovitch, 2007; Strube and Ponzetto, 2006), which are, respectively, the most widely-used lexicographic and encyclopedic resources in lexical semantics (Hovy et al., 2013). This restriction to a single resource brings about two main limitations: (1) the sense modeling does not benefit from the complementary knowledge of different resources, and (2) the obtained representations are resource-specific and cannot be used across settings.

In this paper we put forward a novel concept representation technique, called NASARI, which exploits the knowledge available in both types of resource in order to obtain effective representations of arbitrary concepts. The contributions of this paper are threefold. First, we propose a novel technique



*Human Language Technologies: The 2015 Annual Conference of the North American Chapter of the ACL*, pages 567–577,
Denver, Colorado, May 31 – June 5, 2015. 

for rich semantic representation of arbitrary WordNet synsets or Wikipedia pages. Second, we provide improvements over the conventional *tf-idf* weighting scheme by applying lexical specificity (Lafon, 1980), a statistical measure mainly used for term extraction, to the task of computing vector weights in a vector representation. Third, we propose a semantically-aware dimensionality reduction technique that transforms a lexical item's representation from a semantic space of words to one of WordNet synsets, simultaneously providing an implicit disambiguation and a distribution smoothing. We demonstrate that our representation achieves state-of-the-art performance on two different tasks: (1) word similarity on multiple standard datasets: MC-30, RG-65, and WordSim-353 similarity, and (2) Wikipedia sense clustering, in which our unsupervised system surpasses the performance of a state-of-the-art supervised technique that exploits knowledge available in Wikipedia in several languages.

## 2 Semantic Representation of Concepts

**Lexical resources and concepts.** The gist of our approach lies in its combination of knowledge from two different lexical resources: (1) the expert-based lexicographic WordNet, whose basic constituents are synsets, i.e., concepts expressed by sets of synonymous words (Miller et al., 1990), and (2) the collaboratively-constructed encyclopedic Wikipedia, whose articles can be considered as individual concepts. Throughout the paper, by a concept we mean a tuple $b = (p, s)$ where $p$ is a Wikipedia page and $s$ is the corresponding WordNet synset. As a bridge between the two resources we use the synset-to-article mappings provided by BabelNet[1] (Navigli and Ponzetto, 2012), a high coverage multilingual encyclopedic dictionary and semantic network that merges, among other resources, Wikipedia and WordNet. Note that the concept $b$ can also contain a Wikipedia page or a WordNet synset only, if a mapping is not provided by BabelNet.

**Semantic representation: NASARI.** Our concept modeling approach consists of two phases. First, for a given concept, we collect a set of relevant Wikipedia pages by leveraging the structural information in Wikipedia and WordNet (Section 2.1).

[1]http://www.babelnet.org/

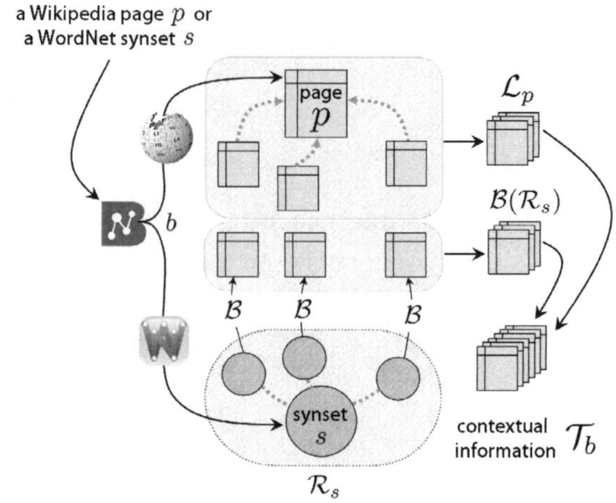


Figure 1: The process of obtaining contextual information for a WordNet synset or a Wikipedia article.

Then, we analyze the obtained contextual information and construct two vector representations of the concept (Section 2.2).

### 2.1 Collecting contextual information

Figure 1 illustrates the process of obtaining a set of relevant Wikipedia pages $\mathcal{T}_b$ as contextual information for a given concept $b = (p, s)$. Let $\mathcal{L}_p$ be the set containing $p$ and all the Wikipedia pages having an outgoing link to $p$, and $\mathcal{R}_s$ be the set consisting of $s$ and all other synsets that are in its direct neighbourhood. We further enrich $\mathcal{R}_s$ by including the coordinate synsets of $s$ and the related synsets from its disambiguated gloss[2]. Let $\mathcal{B}$ be a function mapping each WordNet synset $s'$ to its corresponding Wikipedia page $p$, if such mapping exists in BabelNet, and to the empty set otherwise. Hence, $\mathcal{B}(\mathcal{R}_s) = \cup_{s' \in \mathcal{R}_s} \mathcal{B}(s')$. Then, our contextual information is the set of Wikipedia pages $\mathcal{T}_b = \mathcal{L}_p \cup \mathcal{B}(\mathcal{R}_s)$. In the case either $p$ or $s$ is not present in the concept $b$, we take the contextual information as $\mathcal{T}_b = \mathcal{B}(\mathcal{R}_s)$ or $\mathcal{T}_b = \mathcal{L}_p$, respectively.

### 2.2 Vector construction

By processing the collected contextual information $\mathcal{T}_b$, NASARI represents the concept $b$ as two vectors in two semantic spaces: (1) word-based and (2) synset-based. Let $\mathcal{W}_b$ be the bag of words of all the Wikipedia pages in $\mathcal{T}_b$ after lemmatization and stop-

[2]http://wordnet.princeton.edu/glosstag.shtml

word removal. We use lexical specificity in order to extract the most representative words (Section 2.2.1) and synsets (Section 2.2.2) of $\mathcal{W}_b$.

**Lexical specificity.** Lexical specificity (Lafon, 1980) is a statistical measure that has been used in a wide range of NLP applications, such as textual data analysis (Lebart et al., 1998), term extraction (Drouin, 2003), and domain disambiguation (Camacho Collados et al., 2014). However, to our knowledge, it has never heretofore been used to calculate weights in a vector-based representation (Turney and Pantel, 2010). Lexical specificity is based on the hypergeometric distribution over word frequencies. This statistical measure is particularly suitable for extracting an accurate set of representative terms for a given subcorpus of a reference corpus (Lafon, 1980). Unlike the conventional term frequency-inverse document frequency weighting scheme (Jones, 1972, *tf-idf*), lexical specificity is not especially sensitive to different text lengths.

Assume a reference corpus of $T$ words and a $t$-words subcorpus of that corpus. The goal is to find a set of terms that are peculiar to the subcorpus, but not to the whole reference corpus. Formally, given a word $w$ that occurs $f$ and $k$ times in the corpus and subcorpus, respectively, positive specificity computes the relevance of $w$ to the subcorpus as $P(X \geq k)$ if $k \geq \frac{ft}{T}$, where $X$ is a random variable following a hypergeometric distribution with parameters $f$, $t$ and $T$, and $\frac{ft}{T}$ is the expected value of $X$. In our setting we are only interested in the positive specificity, i.e., the set of most relevant words appearing in the contextual information. We apply the standard procedure of applying $log_{10}$ and then inverting the sign of the specificity probabilities in order to re-scale them to the real line, which is more easily interpretable (Drouin, 2003; Camacho Collados et al., 2014). We only retain words with specificity greater than two, which is equal to $-log_{10}(0.01)$. This threshold leads to a set of representative words that are relevant to the context with a confidence of at least 99%, i.e., $P(X \geq k) \leq 0.01$ (Billami et al., 2014).

### 2.2.1 Word-based representation

This word-based representation models the concept $b$ in a conventional semantic space whose dimensions are individual words. We leverage lexical specificity to compute a weighted set of most representative words for $\mathcal{W}_b$ with respect to the reference corpus, i.e., the whole Wikipedia. As an example, the obtained word-based vector for the *edge of water* sense of *shore* has *water*, *ocean*, *lake*, *beach* and *sea* among its most relevant dimensions.

### 2.2.2 Synset-based representation

Given that the amount of contextual information gathered for a concept can be small, the resulting word-based vector can be sparse and as a consequence prone to noise, especially in the case of less frequent concepts. Therefore, we put forward a method that tackles the issue, providing rich semantically-aware representations. To this end, we group - and thereby generalize - similar dimensions in the obtained word-based vector, to produce a smaller vector in which dimensions are WordNet synsets and weights are computed on the basis of the combined information of the individual words in the group. The generalization procedure can be summarized in two main steps.

First, for each word $w$ in $\mathcal{W}_b$, we obtain from WordNet the set $\mathcal{H}_w$ of all the direct hypernyms of all the synsets containing $w$. For each synset $h \in \mathcal{H}_w$ we check whether there exists another word $w'$ from the contextual information that is a hyponym of $h$, i.e., $h \in \mathcal{H}_w \cap \mathcal{H}_{w'}$. When such is the case, letting $\mathcal{Y}_h$ be the set of all words in the hyponym synsets of $h$, we combine $w$, $w'$ and all the other words in $\mathcal{Y}_h$ into a single dimension represented by their common hypernym $h$. Thus for our earlier example, the three words *ocean*, *lake*, and *sea* are grouped into a single dimension represented by their hypernym, i.e., the synset containing the *body of water* sense of *water* ($water_n^2$ in WordNet 3.0)[3].

Then, we compute the weight associated with the new dimension by calculating the lexical specificity of the word cluster. Formally, we calculate the lexical specificity of $h$ by setting the parameters $k$ and $f$ as the total number of times the words in $\mathcal{Y}_h$ occur in $\mathcal{W}_b$ and the whole Wikipedia, respectively. The values of $t$ and $T$ remain unchanged.

Our generalization procedure is similar to the dimensionality reduction that is performed using singular value decomposition in Latent Semantic Analysis (Landauer and Dumais, 1997, LSA). However,

[3]We denote the $i^{th}$ sense of word $w$ with POS $p$ as $w_p^i$.

LSA is not applicable to our setting because, due to the usage of lexical specificity, our vectors are relatively small in size and different vectors usually have few overlapping dimensions. Moreover, unlike LSA, in which the size-reduced vectors have opaque conflations of multiple words as their dimensions, our new semantic space has human- and machine-readable synsets as its dimensions. Our generalization procedure produces three advantages: (1) it maps the vectors from a word-based semantic space to a lower-dimensional space of synsets, (2) while merging multiple words into a single synset an implicit disambiguation of context words takes place, providing better means for sense distinction, and (3) the dimensionality reduction tackles the potential noise and sparsity, resulting in smoother vectors.

## 3 NASARI for Semantic Similarity

So far we have explained how NASARI constructs two types of representations, i.e., word-based and synset-based, for arbitrary WordNet synsets and Wikipedia pages. In this section we provide a method that leverages NASARI representations for effective measurement of concept and word similarity. Semantic similarity between a pair of lexical items (e.g., words or concepts) lies at the core of many applications in NLP and hence it has received a considerable amount of research interest, leading to a wide range of semantic similarity measures (Mohammad and Hirst, 2012).

### 3.1 Concept similarity

Given a pair of concepts, we first use the procedure described in Section 2 to obtain for each concept the two corresponding vector representations, i.e., word-based and synset-based. For each representation type, we then compute the similarity of the two concepts by comparing their corresponding vectors. This results in two similarity scores, one for each representation type. The final similarity is computed as the average of the two similarity scores. We use Weighted Overlap for comparing vectors.

**Weighted Overlap.** Proposed by Pilehvar et al. (2013), Weighted Overlap (WO) first sorts the elements of each vector $v_i$ and then harmonically weights the overlaps between the two vectors:

$$WO(v_1, v_2) = \frac{\sum_{q \in O} (r_q^1 + r_q^2)^{-1}}{\sum_{i=1}^{|O|} (2i)^{-1}} \quad (1)$$

where $O$ is the set of overlapping dimensions between the two vectors and $r_q^j$ is the rank of dimension $q$ in the vector $v_j$. Given that our vectors are significantly smaller than those in the original setting of WO, the overlaps are also generally smaller in size. Hence, we apply a square root operation to the computed value in order to obtain a more uniformly-distributed range of scores across the similarity scale, i.e., [0, 1]. In our experiments we show the advantage we gain by using WO in comparison to the conventional cosine measure.

**Algorithm 1** NASARI-based word similarity

**Input:** words $w_1$ and $w_2$
**Output:** *Sim*, similarity score

**for each** synonym set $H \in \mathcal{S}$
  **if** $w_1 \in H$ & $w_2 \in H$ **then**
    **return** $Sim = 1$
**for each** word $w_i \in \{w_1, w_2\}$
  $\mathcal{C}_{w_i} \leftarrow \emptyset$, set of concepts associated with $w_i$
  **if** $w_i \in$ *WordNet* & $w_i$ *not* Named Entity **then**
    **for each** sense $s \in$ *WordNet senses* $(w_i)$
      $\mathcal{C}_{w_i} \leftarrow \mathcal{C}_{w_i} \cup \{s\}$
  **else**
    **for each** page $p \in$ *piped links* $(w_i)$
      $\mathcal{C}_{w_i} \leftarrow \mathcal{C}_{w_i} \cup \{p\}$
  $V_i \leftarrow \emptyset$, set of representations for concepts in $\mathcal{C}_{w_i}$
  **for each** concept $c \in \mathcal{C}_{w_i}$
    $v_{wrd} \leftarrow$ NASARI word-based rep. of $c$
    $v_{syn} \leftarrow$ NASARI synset-based rep. of $c$
    $v \leftarrow (v_{wrd}, v_{syn})$
    $V_i \leftarrow V_i \cup \{v\}$
$Sim \leftarrow \max_{v \in V_1, v' \in V_2} \frac{WO(v_{wrd}, v'_{wrd}) + WO(v_{syn}, v'_{syn})}{2}$
**return** *Sim*

### 3.2 Word similarity

Algorithm 1 shows the procedure we devised for measuring semantic similarity between two words. There are three main steps:

1. Given a pair of words $w_1$ and $w_2$ the algorithm first checks whether they are synonymous according to our synonym set collection $\mathcal{S}$. In Section 3.2.1, we explain how we obtain this set. If the words are defined as synonyms in $\mathcal{S}$,

the algorithm returns the maximum similarity score of one (lines 1-3).

2. If the words are not defined as synonyms, we proceed by obtaining, for each word $w_i$, its set of possible senses ($\mathcal{C}_{w_i}$, lines 5-11). We accordingly obtain the set of their respective NASARI vector representations ($V_i$, lines 13-17), two (word-based and synset-based) for each concept in $\mathcal{C}_{w_i}$. Section 3.2.2 describes the concept extraction process.

3. Finally, the algorithm returns the similarity score *Sim* (line 19), calculated as the similarity of the closest senses of $w_1$ and $w_2$. In our default setting, we linearly combine our two vector representations by averaging them (line 18).

#### 3.2.1 Wiktionary synonyms $\mathcal{S}$

Wiktionary is a rich collaboratively-constructed lexical resource that provides a considerable amount of multilingual lexical information for a large number of words. We use this resource in order to obtain sets of synonymous words $\mathcal{S}$. To this end, we first extract all the pre-specified synonymy relations in the English Wiktionary. This results in 17K sets with an average size of 2.8 synonyms.

In order to enrich the set we introduce a method that exploits the multilinguality of Wiktionary to extract synonymous words. Our approach utilizes translations of words in other languages as bridges between synonymous words in English. Specifically, for each sense $s$ of word $w$ in Wiktionary, we first get all the available translations. Assume that the sense $s$ of $w$ translates into the word $t_l$ in language $l$. If there is another word sense $s'$ of another word $w'$ in Wiktionary that is also translated to $t_l$ in language $l$, we hypothesize that $w$ and $w'$ are synonyms. In order to avoid ambiguity, as $t_l$ we only consider words that are monosemous according to language $l$.

This procedure results in around 9K additional synonymous sets with an average size of 2.1. For instance, the Finnish noun *ammatti*, which is monosemous according to Wiktionary, links seven English words into a single set of synonyms: *career*, *business*, *profession*, *occupation*, *trade*, *calling*, and *vocation*. The final synonym set collection $\mathcal{S}$ contains 25K sets, each having, on average, 2.6 words.

#### 3.2.2 Concept extraction

If the two input words $w_1$ and $w_2$ are not found in the same synonym set in $\mathcal{S}$, we proceed by obtaining their sets of senses $\mathcal{C}_{w_1}$ and $\mathcal{C}_{w_2}$, respectively. Depending on the type of $w_i$, we use two different resources for obtaining $\mathcal{C}_{w_i}$: the WordNet sense inventory and Wikipedia.

**WordNet words.** When the word $w_i$ is defined in the WordNet sense inventory and is not a named entity (line 6 in Algorithm 1), we set $\mathcal{C}_{w_i}$ as all the WordNet synsets that contain $w_i$, i.e., $\mathcal{C}_{w_i} = \{\textit{synset } s \in \textit{WordNet} : w_i \in s\}$. We use Stanford Named Entity Recognizer (Finkel et al., 2005) in our experiments.

**WordNet OOV and named entities.** For named entities and words that do not exist in WordNet's vocabulary (OOV) we construct the set $\mathcal{C}_{w_i}$ by exploiting Wikipedia's piped links (line 10 in Algorithm 1). To this end, we take as elements of $\mathcal{C}_{w_i}$ the Wikipedia pages of the hyperlinks which have $w_i$ as their surface form, i.e., *piped-links* $(w_i)$. If $|\mathcal{C}_{w_i}| > 5$, we prune $\mathcal{C}_{w_i}$ to its top-5 pages in terms of their number of ingoing links. Our choice of Wikipedia as a source for named entities is due to its higher coverage in comparison to WordNet.

## 4 Experiments

We evaluated NASARI on two different tasks that require the computation of semantic similarity between words or concepts: word similarity (Section 4.1) and sense clustering (Section 4.2).

### 4.1 Word similarity

#### 4.1.1 Datasets

We took as benchmark for our word similarity experiments three standard datasets that are widely used in the literature: RG-65 (Rubenstein and Goodenough, 1965), MC-30 (Miller and Charles, 1991), and WordSim-353 (Finkelstein et al., 2002; Agirre et al., 2009). WordSim-353 originally conflated similarity and relatedness, leading to high similarity scores for pairs such as *computer-keyboard* despite the dissimilarity in their meanings. To correct the conflation, Agirre et al. (2009) partitioned the dataset into two subsets: relatedness and similarity. Given that our similarity measure is targeted at semantic similarity, we took the similarity subset of

WordSim-353 (WS-Sim) as test bed for our evaluations. The subset comprises 203 word pairs.

### 4.1.2 Experimental setup

In this task, we assess the performance of different systems in terms of Pearson correlation. We compare our system against six similarity measures that have reported best performance on the three datasets. Lin (Lin, 1998) and ADW (Pilehvar et al., 2013) are WordNet-based approaches that leverage the structural information of WordNet for the computation of semantic similarity. Most similar to our work are Explicit Semantic Analysis (Gabrilovich and Markovitch, 2007, ESA), which represents a word in a high-dimensional space of Wikipedia articles, and Salient Semantic Analysis (Hassan and Mihalcea, 2011, SSA), which leverages the linking of concepts within Wikipedia articles for generating *semantic profiles* of words. Word2Vec (Mikolov et al., 2013) and PMI-SVD are the best predictive and co-occurrence models obtained by Baroni et al. (2014) on a 2.8 billion-token corpus that also includes the English Wikipedia.[4] Word2Vec is based on neural network context prediction models (Mikolov et al., 2013), whereas PMI-SVD is a traditional co-occurrence based vector wherein weights are calculated by means of Pointwise Mutual Information (PMI) and the vector's dimension is reduced to 500 by singular value decomposition (SVD). We use the DKProSimilarity (Bär et al., 2013) implementation of Lin and ESA in order to evaluate these measures on the WS-Sim dataset.

### 4.1.3 Results

Table 1 shows the Pearson correlation of the different similarity measures on the three datasets considered. NASARI proves to be highly reliable on the task of word similarity, providing state-of-the-art performance on RG-65 and MC-30, and competitive results on WS-Sim. Importantly, the improvement we attain over measures that utilize as their knowledge base either WordNet (i.e., ADW, Lin) or Wikipedia (i.e., ESA and SSA) shows that our usage of the complementary information of the two types of resource has been helpful. We note that our Wiktionary module detects four additional synonymous pairs (i.e., similarity = 1.0) in MC-30 (13%), eight in RG-65 (12%), and thirteen in WS-Sim (6%) that are not defined as synonyms in WordNet. We also obtain competitive results according to the Spearman correlation (a setting in which the absolute similarity scores do not play a role and it is solely their ranking that matters) on all the three datasets: MC-30 (0.89), RG-65 (0.88), and WS-Sim (0.73).

| Measure | RG-65 | MC-30 | WS-Sim |
|---|---|---|---|
| NASARI | **0.91** | **0.91** | 0.74 |
| SSA | 0.86 | 0.88 | NA |
| Word2Vec | $0.84^{\diamond}$ | $0.83^{\ddagger}$ | $\mathbf{0.76}^{\ddagger}$ |
| Lin | 0.83 | 0.82 | 0.66 |
| ADW | 0.81 | 0.79 | 0.63 |
| PMI-SVD | $0.74^{\diamond}$ | $0.76^{\ddagger}$ | $0.68^{\ddagger}$ |
| ESA | 0.72 | 0.74 | 0.45 |

Table 1: Pearson correlation of different similarity measures on RG-65, MC-30, and WordSim-353 similarity (WS-Sim) datasets. Results for Lin and ESA on RG-65 and MC-30 are taken from (Hassan and Mihalcea, 2011). We show the best performance obtained by Baroni et al. (2014) out of 48 configurations specifically tested on RG-65 (highlighted by $\diamond$) and across different datasets including WS-Sim (highlighted by $\ddagger$).

WS-Sim is the only dataset on which we do not report state-of-the-art performance. An analysis of the outputs of our system on the WS-Sim dataset revealed that there are pairs in this subset of WordSim-353 that are not assigned proper scores according to the similarity scale. Hill et al. (2014) had previously pointed out this deficiency of WS-Sim, mainly due to its original relatedness-based scoring scale. For instance, word pairs that are barely related (e.g., *street-children*) or antonyms (e.g., *profit-loss* and *smart-stupid*) are assigned relatively high similarity values (respectively, 4.9 for the former and 7.3 and 5.8 for the latter case, in the 0-10 scale). In all these cases our system produces more appropriate judgements according to the similarity scale. On the other hand, there are highly similar pairs in the dataset with relatively low gold scores. Examples include *school-center*[5] and *term-life*[6] with the respective gold similarity scores of 3.4 and 4.5, whereas

[4] clic.cimec.unitn.it/composes/semantic-vectors.html

[5] *School* and *center* have a pair of highly similar senses in WordNet 3.0: $center^3_n$: *"a building dedicated to a particular activity"* and $school^2_n$: *"a building where young people receive education."*

[6] *Term* and *life* are in coordinate synsets (with *time period* as their common hypernym) in WordNet 3.0.

| Measure | System type | 500-pair | SemEval |
|---|---|---|---|
| NASARI | unsupervised | **84.6%** | **88.4%** |
| Dan-mono | supervised | 77.4% | 83.5% |
| Dan-multi | supervised | 84.4% | 85.5% |
| *Baseline* | - | 71.4% | 82.5% |

Table 2: Accuracy of different systems on two manually-annotated English datasets for sense clustering in Wikipedia. Dan-mono and Dan-multi are the monolingual and multilingual systems of Dandala et al. (2013).

NASARI computes their similarities as 8.4 and 9.6.

## 4.2 Sense clustering

Our second set of experiments focuses on sense clustering of the Wikipedia sense inventory. Wikipedia can be considered as a sense inventory wherein the different meanings of a word are denoted by the articles listed in its disambiguation page (Mihalcea and Csomai, 2007). Given the high granularity of this inventory, clustering of senses can be highly beneficial to tasks that take this encyclopedic resource as their sense inventory (Hovy et al., 2013), such as Wikipedia-based Word Sense Disambiguation (Mihalcea, 2007; Dandala et al., 2013).

### 4.2.1 Datasets

For the sense clustering task, we take as our benchmark the two datasets created by Dandala et al. (2013). In these datasets, clustering has been viewed as a binary classification problem in which all possible pairings of senses of a word are annotated whether they ought to be clustered or not. The first dataset contains 500 pairs, 357 of which are set to *clustered* and the remaining 143 to *not clustered*. The second dataset, referred to as the SemEval dataset, is based on a set of highly ambiguous words taken from SemEval evaluations (Mihalcea, 2007) and consists of 925 pairs, 162 of which are positively labeled, i.e., clustered.

### 4.2.2 Experimental setup

In this task we use the procedure explained in Section 3.1 for measuring the similarity of concepts. A pair of pages is set to belong to the same cluster if their similarity exceeds the middle point in our similarity scale, i.e., 0.5 in the scale of [0, 1]. We compare our results with the state-of-the-art systems of Dandala et al. (2013) that perform clustering by exploiting the structure and content of an English page (monolingual variant), or several pages in different languages (multilingual variant that uses English, German, Spanish and Italian pages). These systems are essentially multi-feature Support Vector Machine classifiers that use an automatically-labeled dataset for their training.

### 4.2.3 Results

Table 2 lists the results of NASARI as well as the state-of-the-art systems of Dandala et al. (2013). We also report the results for a baseline system that sets all pairs as *not clustered*. As can be seen from the table, our system proves to be highly robust and competitive by outperforming, in an unsupervised setting, the supervised monolingual and multilingual systems of Dandala et al. (2013) on both datasets. As regards the F1, we obtain 72.0% and 64.2% on the 500-pair and SemEval datasets, respectively, a measure that is not reported by Dandala et al. (2013).

## 4.3 Analysis

Recall from Section 2 that our system has two vector representations, for each of which we compute vectors based on lexical specificity. We also mentioned in Section 3 that we opt for Weighted Overlap as our vector comparison method. In order to analyze the impact of each of these elements, we carried out a series of experiments with the conventional logarithmically-scaled *tf-idf* weighting scheme and the cosine vector comparison technique. For a word $w$, we calculate the *tf-idf* by taking *tf* as the frequency of $w$ in the corresponding contextual information, and $idf = log(|D|/|\{p \in D : w \in p\}|)$, where $D$ is the set of all pages in Wikipedia.

Table 3 shows the performance of the NASARI-based similarity system and its individual vector representations for different weight computation schemes, i.e., lexical specificity and *tf-idf*, and for different vector comparison techniques, i.e., cosine and WO, on word similarity and sense clustering datasets. As can be seen from the Table, the performance of the word-based representation consistently improves on both tasks when combined with the additional information from the synset-based vectors, demonstrating that the sense distinctions offered by the generalization process have been beneficial.

Between the two vector comparison methods, WO proves to better suit our specificity-based vec-

| Vector representation | Weighting scheme | Vector comparison | Word similarity | | | Sense clustering | |
|---|---|---|---|---|---|---|---|
| | | | MC-30 | RG-65 | WS-Sim | 500-pair | SemEval |
| Combined | specificity | WO | ⋆**0.91** | ⋆**0.91** | ⋆0.74 | ⋆**84.6%** | ⋆**88.4%** |
| | | cosine | 0.88 | 0.89 | **0.75** | 76.2% | 83.6% |
| | *tf-idf* | WO | 0.85 | 0.87 | 0.73 | 60.4% | 67.8% |
| | | cosine | 0.79 | 0.84 | 0.70 | 81.4% | 86.1% |
| Word-based | specificity | WO | **0.90** | **0.91** | **0.73** | **82.0%** | **85.0%** |
| | | cosine | 0.86 | 0.88 | 0.72 | 73.2% | 83.4% |
| | *tf-idf* | WO | 0.86 | 0.87 | 0.72 | 78.4% | 82.6% |
| | | cosine | 0.83 | 0.87 | 0.71 | 79.2% | 84.4% |
| Synset-based | specificity | WO | **0.91** | **0.90** | **0.75** | 78.8% | 83.8% |
| | | cosine | 0.90 | 0.88 | **0.75** | **79.8%** | **85.0%** |
| | *tf-idf* | WO | 0.86 | 0.85 | 0.73 | 37.2% | 41.1% |
| | | cosine | 0.71 | 0.80 | 0.66 | 79.4% | **85.0%** |
| Word-based | specificity | WO | †0.86 | †0.87 | †0.71 | †80.0% | †85.1% |

Table 3: Performance of NASARI and its individual vector representations for different weight computation schemes, i.e., lexical specificity and *tf-idf*, and for different vector comparison techniques, i.e., cosine and Weighted Overlap (WO), in terms of Pearson correlation (word similarity) and accuracy (sense clustering). The scores highlighted by ⋆ are the ones obtained using our default NASARI setting, and the ones highlighted by † correspond to the setting of our system using Wikipedia as its only knowledge source.

tors by outperforming cosine in most cases. The reason behind the lower performance of WO for the synset-based vectors on the task of sense clustering can be explained by the nature of the corresponding datasets. Since the synset-based vectors and their overlapping dimensions are small, their cosine similarity scores also tend to be relatively low, unlike WO whose range of values is not affected by the number of overlapping dimensions. Given that in the experiments the threshold is fixed to the middle point of the scale (cf. Section 4.2.2), generally low similarity values lead to a high-precision, low-recall system, which is rewarded by higher accuracy performance in datasets in which a large portion of instances are negative. In fact, for the synset-based vector representation weighted using specificity, the F1 performance of the cosine is significantly lower than WO. On the SemEval dataset the F1 performance of WO is 60.1%, whereas cosine attains 37.1%. Similarly, on the 500-pair dataset, WO leads cosine by 16.8%: 68.5% vs. 51.7%.

As far as the weighting scheme is concerned, lexical specificity outperforms *tf-idf* on both tasks, irrespective of the vector comparison technique and representation. We attribute the better performance of lexical specificity to the probabilistic nature of weights in its vectors. The *tf-idf* weighting scheme, in contrast, suffers from insensitivity to the relative size of the contextual information. Thus, subsequently, specificity-based vectors provide the advantage of accurately reducing the vectors' dimension, unlike the *tf-idf* scheme in which the size-insensitive weights are not comparable across vectors. As a result, the specificity-based vectors are substantially smaller in size, bringing about better space utilization and faster running time. In our experiments the vectors obtained by using lexical specificity were, on average, almost nine times (2505 vs. 21825) and four times (335 vs. 1311) smaller than the *tf-idf*-based vectors for the word-based and synset-based vector representations, respectively.

We were also interested in verifying the advantage gained by combining the complementary knowledge of Wikipedia and WordNet. To this end, we carried out an experiment in which NASARI uses Wikipedia as its only knowledge source (i.e., without using WordNet). The last row in the Table (highlighted by †) shows the results for this setting. Note that since WordNet is not used in this setting, we are constrained to the word-based vector representation only. The results show that the combination of the types of resource leads to a consistent performance improvement across tasks and datasets, with the average improvement being 5%.

## 5 Related Work

Given that in this work we focused mainly on similarity for the evaluation of our semantic representation, in addition to concept representation, we also briefly discuss related works for semantic similarity.

**Concept representation.** Distributional semantic models are usually the first choice for representing textual items such as words or sentences (Turney and Pantel, 2010). These models have attracted considerable research interest, resulting in various co-occurrence based representations (Salton et al., 1975; Evert, 2005; Pado and Lapata, 2007; Erk and Padó, 2008) or predictive models (Collobert and Weston, 2008; Turian et al., 2010; Mikolov et al., 2013; Baroni et al., 2014). Although there have been approaches proposed in the literature for learning sense-specific embeddings (Weston et al., 2013; Huang et al., 2012; Neelakantan et al., 2014), their coverage is limited only to those senses that are covered in the underlying corpus. Moreover, the obtained sense representations are usually not linked to any sense inventory, and therefore such linking has to be carried out, either manually, or with the help of sense-annotated data. Hence, unless they are provided with large amounts of sense-annotated data, these techniques cannot furnish an effective representation of word senses in an existing standard sense inventory.

Consequently, most sense modeling techniques have based their representation on the knowledge derived from resources such as WordNet (Mihalcea and Moldovan, 1999; Agirre and Lopez, 2003; Agirre and de Lacalle, 2004; Pilehvar et al., 2013), or Wikipedia (Gabrilovich and Markovitch, 2007; Mihalcea, 2007). None of these techniques, however, combine knowledge from multiple types of resource, making their representations resource-specific and also prone to sparsity. In contrast, our method is based on the complementary knowledge of two different resources and their interlinking, leading to richer semantic representations that are also applicable across resources. Most similar to our combination of complementary knowledge is the work of Franco-Salvador et al. (2014) for cross-lingual document retrieval.

**Concept similarity.** Concept similarity techniques are mainly limited to the knowledge that their underlying lexical resources provide. For instance, methods designed for measuring semantic similarity of WordNet synsets (Banerjee and Pedersen, 2002; Budanitsky and Hirst, 2006; Pilehvar et al., 2013) usually leverage lexicographic or structural information in this lexical resource. Similarly, Wikipedia-based approaches (Hassan and Mihalcea, 2011; Strube and Ponzetto, 2006; Milne and Witten, 2008) do not usually benefit from the expert-based lexico-semantic knowledge provided in WordNet. In contrast, our approach combines knowledge from both resources, providing two advantages: (1) more effective measurement of similarity based on rich semantic representations, and (2) the possibility of measuring cross-resource semantic similarity, i.e., between Wikipedia pages and WordNet synsets.

## 6 Conclusions

In this paper we presented a novel semantic approach, called NASARI, for effective vector representation of arbitrary WordNet synsets and Wikipedia pages. The strength of our approach lies in its combination of complementary knowledge from different types of resource, while at the same time it also benefits from an effective vector representation with two novel features: lexical specificity for the calculation of vector weights and a semantically-aware dimensionality reduction. NASARI attains state-of-the-art performance on multiple standard benchmarks in word similarity as well as Wikipedia sense clustering. We release the representations obtained for all the Wikipedia pages and WordNet synsets in http://lcl.uniroma1.it/nasari/. As future work we plan to integrate NASARI into BabelNet and apply our representation to a multilingual setting, enabling the comparison of pairs of concepts across languages. We also intend to use our approach on the task of multilingual Word Sense Disambiguation.

## Acknowledgments

The authors gratefully acknowledge the support of the ERC Starting Grant MultiJEDI No. 259234.

## References


Eneko Agirre and Oier Lopez de Lacalle. 2004. Publicly available topic signatures for all WordNet nominal senses. In *Proceedings of LREC*, pages 1123–1126, Lisbon, Portugal.

Eneko Agirre and Oier Lopez. 2003. Clustering WordNet word senses. In *Proceedings of RANLP*, pages 121–130, Borovets, Bulgaria.

Eneko Agirre, Enrique Alfonseca, Keith Hall, Jana Kravalova, Marius Paşca, and Aitor Soroa. 2009. A study on similarity and relatedness using distributional and WordNet-based approaches. In *Proceedings of NAACL-HLT*, pages 19–27, Boulder, Colorado.

Satanjeev Banerjee and Ted Pedersen. 2002. An adapted Lesk algorithm for Word Sense Disambiguation using WordNet. In *Proceedings of CICLing*, pages 136–145, Mexico City, Mexico.

Michele Banko, Michael J. Cafarella, Stephen Soderland, Matt Broadhead, and Oren Etzioni. 2007. Open information extraction from the Web. In *Proceedings of IJCAI*, pages 2670–2676, New York, NY, USA.

Daniel Bär, Torsten Zesch, and Iryna Gurevych. 2013. DKPro similarity: An open source framework for text similarity. In *Proceedings of ACL: System Demonstrations*, pages 121–126, Sofia, Bulgaria, August.

Marco Baroni, Georgiana Dinu, and Germán Kruszewski. 2014. Don't count, predict! a systematic comparison of context-counting vs. context-predicting semantic vectors. In *Proceedings of ACL*, pages 238–247, Baltimore, Maryland.

Mokhtar-Boumeyden Billami, José Camacho-Collados, Evelyne Jacquey, and Laurence Kister. 2014. Semantic annotation and terminology validation in full scientific articles in social sciences and humanities (annotation sémantique et validation terminologique en texte intégral en shs) [in french]. In *Proceedings of TALN 2014*, pages 363–376, Marseille, France.

Alexander Budanitsky and Graeme Hirst. 2006. Evaluating WordNet-based measures of Lexical Semantic Relatedness. *Computational Linguistics*, 32(1):13–47.

Razvan Bunescu and Marius Paşca. 2006. Using encyclopedic knowledge for named entity disambiguation. In *Proceedings of EACL*, pages 9–16, Trento, Italy.

Jose Camacho Collados, Mokhtar Billami, Evelyne Jacquey, and Laurence Kister. 2014. Approche statistique pour le filtrage terminologique des occurrences de candidats termes en texte intgral. In *Journées internationales d'Analyse statistique des Données Textuelles*, pages 121–133, Paris, France.

Ronan Collobert and Jason Weston. 2008. A unified architecture for natural language processing: Deep neural networks with multitask learning. In *Proceedings of ICML*, pages 160–167, Helsinki, Finland.

Bharath Dandala, Chris Hokamp, Rada Mihalcea, and Razvan C. Bunescu. 2013. Sense clustering using Wikipedia. In *Proceedings of RANLP*, pages 164–171, Hissar, Bulgaria.

Georgiana Dinu and Mirella Lapata. 2010. Measuring distributional similarity in context. In *Proceedings of EMNLP*, pages 1162–1172, Massachusetts, USA.

Patrick Drouin. 2003. Term extraction using non-technical corpora as a point of leverage. *Terminology*, 9(1):99–115.

Katrin Erk and Sebastian Padó. 2008. A structured vector space model for word meaning in context. In *Proceedings of EMNLP*, pages 897–906, Edinburgh, UK.

Stefan Evert. 2005. *The statistics of word cooccurrences: word pairs and collocations*. Ph.D. thesis, Universitt Stuttgart.

Jenny Rose Finkel, Trond Grenager, and Christopher Manning. 2005. Incorporating non-local information into information extraction systems by gibbs sampling. In *Proceedings of ACL*, pages 363–370, Ann Arbor, Michigan.

Lev Finkelstein, Gabrilovich Evgeniy, Matias Yossi, Rivlin Ehud, Solan Zach, Wolfman Gadi, and Ruppin Eytan. 2002. Placing search in context: The concept revisited. *ACM Transactions on Information Systems*, 20(1):116–131.

Marc Franco-Salvador, Paolo Rosso, and Roberto Navigli. 2014. A knowledge-based representation for cross-language document retrieval and categorization. In *Proceedings of the* $14^{th}$ *Conference on European chapter of the Association for Computational Linguistics (EACL)*, Gothenburg, Sweden.

Evgeniy Gabrilovich and Shaul Markovitch. 2007. Computing semantic relatedness using Wikipedia-based explicit semantic analysis. In *Proceedings of IJCAI*, pages 1606–1611, Hyderabad, India.

Samer Hassan and Rada Mihalcea. 2011. Semantic relatedness using salient semantic analysis. In *Proceedings of AAAI*, pages 884,889, San Francisco, USA.

Felix Hill, Roi Reichart, and Anna Korhonen. 2014. Simlex-999: Evaluating semantic models with (genuine) similarity estimation. arXiv:1408.3456.

Eduard H. Hovy, Roberto Navigli, and Simone Paolo Ponzetto. 2013. Collaboratively built semi-structured content and Artificial Intelligence: The story so far. *Artificial Intelligence*, 194:2–27.

Eric H. Huang, Richard Socher, Christopher D. Manning, and Andrew Y. Ng. 2012. Improving word representations via global context and multiple word prototypes. In *Proceedings of ACL*, pages 873–882, Jeju Island, Korea.

Karen Spärck Jones. 1972. A statistical interpretation of term specificity and its application in retrieval. *Journal of Documentation*, 28:11–21.

Pierre Lafon. 1980. Sur la variabilité de la fréquence des formes dans un corpus. *Mots*, 1:127–165.

Thomas K. Landauer and Susan T. Dumais. 1997. A solution to Plato's problem: The latent semantic analysis theory of acquisition, induction, and representation of knowledge. *Psychological Review*, 104(2):211.

Shalom Lappin and Chris Fox, editors. 2014. *Handbook of Contemporary Semantics – second edition*. Wiley-Blackwell, Malden, MA.

Ludovic Lebart, Andre Salem, and Lisette Berry. 1998. *Exploring textual data*. Kluwer Academic Publishers.

Dekang Lin. 1998. An information-theoretic definition of similarity. In *Proceedings of ICML*, pages 296–304, San Francisco, CA.

Olena Medelyan, David Milne, Catherine Legg, and Ian H. Witten. 2009. Mining meaning from Wikipedia. *International Journal of Human-Computer Studies*, 67(9):716–754.

Rada Mihalcea and Andras Csomai. 2007. Wikify! Linking documents to encyclopedic knowledge. In *Proceedings of ACM on Information and Knowledge management*, pages 233–242, Lisbon, Portugal.

Rada Mihalcea and Dan Moldovan. 1999. An automatic method for generating sense tagged corpora. In *Proceedings of AAAI*, pages 461–466, Orlando, Florida, USA.

Rada Mihalcea. 2007. Using Wikipedia for automatic Word Sense Disambiguation. In *Proceedings of NAACL-HLT-07*, pages 196–203, Rochester, NY.

Tomas Mikolov, Kai Chen, Greg Corrado, and Jeffrey Dean. 2013. Efficient estimation of word representations in vector space. In *Workshop at International Conference on Learning Representations*, Scottsdale, Arizona.

George A. Miller and Walter G. Charles. 1991. Contextual correlates of semantic similarity. *Language and Cognitive Processes*, 6(1):1–28.

George A. Miller, R.T. Beckwith, Christiane D. Fellbaum, D. Gross, and K. Miller. 1990. WordNet: an online lexical database. *International Journal of Lexicography*, 3(4):235–244.

David Milne and Ian H. Witten. 2008. An effective, low-cost measure of semantic relatedness obtained from Wikipedia links. In *Proceedings of the Workshop on Wikipedia and Artificial Intelligence: An Evolving Synergy at AAAI-08*, pages 25–30, Chicago, IL.

Saif Mohammad and Graeme Hirst. 2012. Distributional measures of semantic distance: A survey. *CoRR*, abs/1203.1858.

Roberto Navigli and Simone Paolo Ponzetto. 2012. BabelNet: The automatic construction, evaluation and application of a wide-coverage multilingual semantic network. *Artificial Intelligence*, 193:217–250.

Roberto Navigli. 2009. Word Sense Disambiguation: A survey. *ACM Computing Surveys*, 41(2):1–69.

Roberto Navigli. 2012. A quick tour of Word Sense Disambiguation, induction and related approaches. In *SOFSEM 2012: Theory and practice of computer science*, pages 115–129. Springer.

Arvind Neelakantan, Jeevan Shankar, Alexandre Passos, and Andrew McCallum. 2014. Efficient non-parametric estimation of multiple embeddings per word in vector space. In *Proceedings of EMNLP*, pages 1059–1069, Doha, Qatar.

Sebastian Pado and Mirella Lapata. 2007. Dependency-based construction of semantic space models. *Computational Linguistics*, 33(2):161–199.

Mohammad Taher Pilehvar and Roberto Navigli. 2014. A robust approach to aligning heterogeneous lexical resources. In *Proceedings of ACL*, pages 468–478, Baltimore, USA.

Mohammad Taher Pilehvar, David Jurgens, and Roberto Navigli. 2013. Align, Disambiguate and Walk: a Unified Approach for Measuring Semantic Similarity. In *Proceedings of ACL*, pages 1341–1351, Sofia, Bulgaria.

Delip Rao, Paul McNamee, and Mark Dredze. 2013. Entity linking: Finding extracted entities in a knowledge base. In *Multi-source, Multilingual Information Extraction and Summarization*, pages 93–115.

Herbert Rubenstein and John B. Goodenough. 1965. Contextual correlates of synonymy. *Communications of the ACM*, 8(10):627–633.

Gerard Salton, A. Wong, and C. S. Yang. 1975. A vector space model for automatic indexing. *Communications of the ACM*, 18(11):613–620.

Michael Strube and Simone Paolo Ponzetto. 2006. WikiRelate! computing semantic relatedness using wikipedia. In *Proceedings of the 21st National Conference on Artificial Intelligence*, pages 1419–1424, Boston, Massachusetts.

Joseph Turian, Lev Ratinov, and Yoshua Bengio. 2010. Word representations: A simple and general method for semi-supervised learning. In *Proceedings of ACL*, pages 384–394, Uppsala, Sweden.

Peter D. Turney and Patrick Pantel. 2010. From frequency to meaning: Vector space models of semantics. *Journal of Artificial Intelligence Research*, 37:141–188.

Jason Weston, Antoine Bordes, Oksana Yakhnenko, and Nicolas Usunier. 2013. Connecting language and knowledge bases with embedding models for relation extraction. In *Proceedings of EMNLP*, pages 1366–1371, Seattle, Washington, USA.

# Towards a standard evaluation method for grammatical error detection and correction

**Mariano Felice** and **Ted Briscoe**
ALTA Institute, Computer Laboratory, University of Cambridge
15 JJ Thomson Avenue, Cambridge CB3 0FD, United Kingdom
{mf501,ejb}@cl.cam.ac.uk

## Abstract

We present a novel evaluation method for grammatical error correction that addresses problems with previous approaches and scores systems in terms of improvement on the original text. Our method evaluates corrections at the token level using a globally optimal alignment between the source, a system hypothesis, and a reference. Unlike the M² Scorer, our method provides scores for both detection and correction and is sensitive to different types of edit operations.

## 1 Introduction

A range of methods have been applied to evaluation of grammatical error correction, but no entirely satisfactory method has emerged as yet. Standard metrics (such as accuracy, precision, recall and $F$-score) have been used, but they can lead to different results depending on the criteria used for their computation (Leacock et al., 2014; Chodorow et al., 2012).

Accuracy, for example, can only be computed in cases where we can enumerate all true negatives, which is why it has been mostly used for article and preposition errors (De Felice and Pulman, 2008; Rozovskaya and Roth, 2010). Extending this approach to other error types involves the identification of all *relevant instances* or positions where an error can occur, which is not always easy and renders the evaluation process costly, language-dependent, and possibly inexact. Accuracy has also been criticised as being a poor indicator of predictive power, especially on unbalanced datasets (Manning and Schütze, 1999).

| | |
|---|---|
| **Source**: | You have missed word. |
| **System hypothesis**: | You have missed a word. |
| **System edits**: | ($\epsilon \rightarrow$ a) |
| **Gold edits**: | (word $\rightarrow$ a word) or<br>(word $\rightarrow$ words) |

Figure 1: Mismatch between system and gold standard edits producing the same corrected sentence.

Alternatively, we can compute precision ($P$), recall ($R$) and $F$-score by comparing system edits to gold-standard edits and thus circumvent the problem of counting true negatives. This was the official evaluation scheme adopted for the HOO 2011 (Dale and Kilgarriff, 2011) and HOO 2012 (Dale et al., 2012) shared tasks. However, these metrics can fail when edits are not identical and therefore underestimate system performance (see Figure 1).

This problem was later addressed by the *Max-Match* or *M² Scorer* (Dahlmeier and Ng, 2012), which is able to identify equivalent edits by applying a transitive rule (e.g. ($\epsilon \rightarrow$ a) + (word $\rightarrow$ word) $\Rightarrow$ (word $\rightarrow$ a word)). The scorer also allows for multiple gold standard annotations of each sentence, choosing the ones that maximise overall $F$-score. So far, the M² Scorer has been the most reliable tool for evaluating error correction systems and has been used as the official scorer in the subsequent CoNLL 2013 (Ng et al., 2013), CoNLL 2014 (Ng et al., 2014) and EMNLP 2014 (Mohit et al., 2014) shared tasks. In 2014, system ranking was based on $F_{0.5}$-score, weighting precision twice as highly as recall.

Nevertheless, this method also suffers from a number of limitations:



*Human Language Technologies: The 2015 Annual Conference of the North American Chapter of the ACL*, pages 578–587,
Denver, Colorado, May 31 – June 5, 2015. 

| Source | Annotator 1 | Annotator 2 | | |
|---|---|---|---|---|
| This machines is designed for help people . | (This → These), (is → are), (help → helping) | (machines → machine), (for → to) | | |
| **System hypothesis** | **System edits** | **P** | **R** | **$F_{0.5}$** |
| These machines are designed to help people . | (This → These), (is → are), (for → to) | 0.67 | 0.67 | 0.67 |

Table 1: The M² Scorer is unable to mix and match corrections from different annotators.

| Source | Gold edits | | | |
|---|---|---|---|---|
| Machine is design to help people . | (Machine → Machines), (is design → are designed) | | | |
| **System hypothesis** | **System edits** | **P** | **R** | **$F_{0.5}$** |
| Machine is designed to help people . | (design → designed) | 0.00 | 0.00 | 0.00 |

Table 2: Partial matches are ignored by the M² Scorer.

(a) There is a limit to the number of unchanged words allowed in an edit (2 by default), whose value affects final results.

(b) Given that the computed metrics rely on true positive counts, a baseline system that does not propose any correct edits will not produce informative results ($P = 1$ by definition, $R = 0$ and $F = 0$). The actual error rate and consequent potential for text improvement are not taken into account.

(c) It is not possible to discriminate between a 'do-nothing' baseline system and other systems that only propose wrong corrections, as they will all yield $F = 0$.

(d) System performance is underestimated when using multiple annotations for a sentence, since the scorer will choose the one that maximises $F$-score instead of mixing and matching all the available annotations (see Table 1).

(e) Partial matches are ignored (see Table 2).

(f) Phrase-level edits can produce misleading results, as they may not always reflect effective improvements (see Table 3).

(g) The lack of a true negative count (i.e. the number of non-errors) precludes the computation of accuracy, which is useful for discriminating between systems with $F = 0$.

(h) There is no clear indicator of improvement on the original text after applying the suggested corrections, since an increase in P, R or F does not imply a reduction in the error rate (see Section 2.3.3).

(i) It is not clear how values of $F$ should be interpreted (especially for $F_{0.5}$), as there is no known threshold that would signal improvement. Ranking by $F$-score does not guarantee that the top systems make the source text better.

(j) Detection scores are not computed.

In addition, Leacock et al. (2014) discuss key issues concerning system evaluation, such as the estimation of true negatives and good practices for reporting results, which are currently not addressed by the M² scorer.

## 2 Designing a new evaluation method

A better evaluation method should address the issues described above and use a metric that is meaningful and easy to interpret. We examine these and other related problems, showing how they can be resolved.

The proposed method uses tokens as the unit of evaluation (instead of phrase-level edits), which provides a stable unit of comparison and facilitates the computation of true negatives. In turn, this provides a solution for problems 1.(a), 1.(e), 1.(f) and 1.(g).

| **Source** | **Gold edits** | | | |
|---|---|---|---|---|
| Machine is design to help people . | (Machine → Machines), (is → are), (design → designed) | | | |
| **System hypothesis** | **System edits** | **P** | **R** | **$F_{0.5}$** |
| The machine is designed for helping people . | (Machine is → The machine is), (design → designed), (to help people → for helping people) | 0.33 | 0.33 | 0.33 |
| Machines is a design on the helping of the people . | (Machine → Machines), (is design to help → is a design on the helping of the) | 0.50 | 0.33 | 0.45 |

Table 3: The $M^2$ Scorer evaluates systems based on the number of edits, regardless of their length and their effect on the final corrected sentence. The first hypothesis is better than the second despite having a lower $F_{0.5}$-score.

The following sections describe the three pillars of our method: a new annotation scheme, sentence alignment and metrics.

## 2.1 Annotation

We define a gold standard format where each sentence is annotated with a set of errors and their possible corrections. A sentence can contain zero or more errors, each of which includes information such as type, a flag indicating whether a correction is required, and a list of alternative corrections corresponding to each of the annotators. An error is required to be corrected when all annotators provide a correction for it.

Unlike in other annotation schemes, each error is defined by its locus (regardless of the position of the incorrect tokens in the sentence) and all its alternative corrections must be mutually exclusive. In other words, corrections are grouped whenever they refer to the same underlying error, even if the tokens involved are not contiguous. Listing 1 shows a sample XML annotation for the sentence in Table 1.

Because all the correction alternatives are mutually exclusive, we can directly combine them to generate all possible valid gold standard references. The annotation in Listing 1 would produce the following list of references:

*These* machines *are* designed for *helping* people .

*These* machines *are* designed *to* help people .

This *machine* is designed for *helping* people .

This *machine* is designed *to* help people .

```
<sentence id="1" numann="2">
  <text>
    This machines is designed for help
    people .
  </text>
  <error-list>
    <error id="1" req="yes" type="SVA">
      <alt ann="0">
        <c start="0" end="1">These</c>
        <c start="2" end="3">are</c>
      </alt>
      <alt ann="1">
        <c start="1" end="2">machine</c>
      </alt>
    </error>
    <error id="2" req="yes" type="Vform">
      <alt ann="0">
        <c start="5" end="6">helping</c>
      </alt>
      <alt ann="1">
        <c start="4" end="5">to</c>
      </alt>
    </error>
  </error-list>
</sentence>
```

Listing 1: An example annotated sentence.

By mixing and matching corrections from different annotators, we avoid the performance underestimation described in 1.(d).

## 2.2 Alignment

In order to compute matches for detection and correction, we generate a token-level alignment between a source sentence, a system's hypothesis, and a gold standard reference. Three-way alignments are a special case of *multiple sequence alignment*, a well-known string matching problem in computational biology (Mount, 2004).

We generate an exact (globally optimal) alignment using a dynamic programming implementation of the Sum of Pairs (SP) alignment (Carrillo and Lipman, 1988), shown in Listing 2. Under this model, the score of a multiple alignment is the sum of the scores of each pairwise alignment, so that a globally optimal alignment has minimum SP score. Time and space complexity of the dynamic programming implementation for $k$ strings of length $n$ is $O(n^k)$, which is acceptable for three average-length sentences but can quickly become impractical for a larger number of sequences.

In computational biology, edit costs are defined in terms of mutation probabilities, which are irrelevant to our task. However, we can find new optimal costs by defining a set of constraints that are meaningful for error correction:

(a) Matches have zero cost ($c_{\text{match}} = 0$).

(b) Gaps (insertions or deletions) are more costly than matches ($c_{\text{gap}} > c_{\text{match}}$).

(c) Mismatches (substitutions) are set to be more costly than gaps (insertions or deletions) so as to maximise matches ($c_{\text{mis}} > c_{\text{gap}}$).

Given these constraints, we can set $c_{\text{gap}} = 1$ and $c_{\text{mis}} = 2$; however, they will not necessarily keep gaps aligned (see Table 4). To ensure this, we must place a new constraint on the SP algorithm so that a gap-aligned version (desired alignment) has a lower cost than a gap-unaligned version (initial alignment):

$$\text{cost(A,–)} + \ldots + \text{cost(B,–)} > \text{cost(A,C)} + \ldots + \text{cost(B,–)}$$
$$c_{\text{gap}} + \ldots + c_{\text{gap}} > c_{\text{mis}} + \ldots + c_{\text{gap}}$$
$$4c_{\text{gap}} + c_{\text{mis}} > 2c_{\text{mis}} + 2c_{\text{gap}}$$
$$2c_{\text{gap}} > c_{\text{mis}}$$

Therefore $2c_{\text{gap}} > c_{\text{mis}} > c_{\text{gap}} > c_{\text{match}}$. For our implementation, we adopted $c_{\text{gap}} = 2$ and $c_{\text{mis}} = 3$.

There can be more than one optimal alignment for a given set of strings. Some of these alignments will look more intuitive than others (see Table 5) but they are equally optimal for our evaluation method and will produce the same final results.

| **Initial alignment** | | **Desired alignment** | |
|---|---|---|---|
| A | B | A | B |
| – | C | C | – |
| A | – | A | – |

Table 4: Initial and desired alignments showing differences in the distribution of gaps.

```
/* Initialisation */

cmatch := cost of match
cmis  := cost of mismatch
cgap  := cost of gap

D[0, 0, 0] := 0

D1,2[i, j] := edit_distance(S1[1..i], S2[1..j])
D1,3[i, k] := edit_distance(S1[1..i], S3[1..k])
D2,3[j, k] := edit_distance(S2[1..j], S3[1..k])

/* Recurrences for boundary cells */

D[i, j, 0] := D1,2[i, j] + (i + j) * cgap,
D[i, 0, k] := D1,3[i, k] + (i + k) * cgap,
D[0, j, k] := D2,3[j, k] + (j + k) * cgap,

/* Recurrences for non-boundary cells */

for i := 1 to n1 do
  for j := 1 to n2 do
    for k := 1 to n3 do
      begin
        if (S1[i] = S2[j]) then cij := cmatch
        else cij := cmis;
        if (S1[i] = S3[k]) then cik := cmatch
        else cik := cmis;
        if (S2[j] = S3[k]) then cjk := cmatch
        else cjk := cmis;

        d1 := D[i-1, j-1, k-1] + cij + cik + cjk;
        d2 := D[i-1, j-1, k] + cij + 2 * cgap;
        d3 := D[i-1, j, k-1] + cik + 2 * cgap;
        d4 := D[i, j-1, k-1] + cjk + 2 * cgap;
        d5 := D[i-1, j, k] + 2 * cgap;
        d6 := D[i, j-1, k] + 2 * cgap;
        d7 := D[i, j, k-1] + 2 * cgap;

        D[i, j, k] := Min(d1,d2,d3,d4,d5,d6,d7);
      end;
```

Listing 2: The Sum of Pairs dynamic programming algorithm for the alignment of three sequences, $S_1$, $S_2$ and $S_3$ (adapted from Gusfield (1997)).

## 2.3 Metrics

Once we have an optimal alignment between a source, a hypothesis and a reference, we compute a number of metrics that measure different aspects of performance and can be used for ranking systems.

| | | | | | | | | | | | | | | | | |
|---|---|---|---|---|---|---|---|---|---|---|---|---|---|---|---|---|
| Their | is | wide | spread | usage | of | technology | . | | A | A | A | A | A | A | A | A |
| There | is | widespread | use | | of | technology | . | ⇔ | B | A | B | B | - | A | A | A |
| There | is | widespread | use | | of | technology | . | | B | A | B | B | - | A | A | A |
| Their | is | wide | spread | usage | of | technology | . | | A | A | A | A | A | A | A | A |
| There | is | widespread | | use | of | technology | . | ⇔ | B | A | B | - | B | A | A | A |
| There | is | widespread | | use | of | technology | . | | B | A | B | - | B | A | A | A |

Table 5: Two equally optimal alignments under the SP alignment model.

| Tokens | | | Classification | |
|---|---|---|---|---|
| **Source** | **Hypothesis** | **Reference** | **Detection** | **Correction** |
| a | a | a | TN | TN |
| a | a | b | FN | FN |
| a | a | - | FN | FN |
| a | b | a | FP | FP |
| a | b | b | TP | TP |
| a | b | c | TP | FP, FN, FPN |
| a | b | - | TP | FP, FN, FPN |
| a | - | a | FP | FP |
| a | - | b | TP | FP, FN, FPN |
| a | - | - | TP | TP |
| - | a | a | TP | TP |
| - | a | b | TP | FP, FN, FPN |
| - | a | - | FP | FP |
| - | - | a | FN | FN |

Table 6: Our extended WAS evaluation scheme.

The limitation in 1.(j) is addressed by computing these metrics for both detection and correction.

We adopt an extended version of the Writer-Annotator-System (WAS) evaluation scheme (Chodorow et al., 2012) where each token alignment is classified as a true positive (TP), true negative (TN), false positive (FP) or false negative (FN). As noted by Chodorow et al. (2012), cases where *source* $\neq$ *hypothesis* $\neq$ *reference*[1] are both a FP and a FN for correction,[2] so we introduce a new FPN class to count such cases and adjust our metrics accordingly. Our extended WAS scheme is shown in Table 6.

With these counts, we can compute $P$, $R$ and $F_\beta$ using their standard definitions:

$$P = \frac{\text{TP}}{\text{TP} + \text{FP}} \qquad R = \frac{\text{TP}}{\text{TP} + \text{FN}}$$

$$F_\beta = (1+\beta^2) \cdot \frac{P \cdot R}{(\beta^2 \cdot P) + R}$$

[1]Note that we use different terminology where *source* = *writer*, *hypothesis* = *system* and *reference* = *annotator*.

[2]From a correction perspective, an alignment where $a \neq b \neq c$ generates a FP for the $b$ class and a FN for the $c$ class.

As mentioned in Section 1, the $F$ measure does not shed light on the error rates in the data and is unable to discriminate between a 'do-nothing' baseline and other systems unless TP $> 0$. However, because we now have a TN count, we can address problems 1.(b) and 1.(c) by computing accuracy (*Acc*) as follows:

$$Acc = \frac{\text{TP} + \text{TN}}{\text{TP} + \text{TN} + \text{FP} + \text{FN} - \text{FPN}}$$

Unlike in information retrieval, for example, where the whole document collection is usually unknown to the user so TNs are perhaps less relevant, the sentences fed into an error correction system will be provided by users. In this context, TNs are relevant because they indicate what parts of the text are already correct, allowing users to focus on problematic regions. For this reason, accuracy seems a more appropriate measure of text quality than $F$-score.

#### 2.3.1 Weighted accuracy

Accuracy treats all counts equally, which has two main side effects. A system that introduces the same number of TPs and FPs will have the same accuracy as the 'do-nothing' baseline, in which case we would prefer to keep the original text and rank the system lower, in accord with the choice of $F_{0.5}$ for evaluating the 2014 shared task. Accuracy is also unable to discriminate between systems with different TP and TN counts if their sum is the same.

It is clear that for error correction these counts should be weighted differently. In particular, we would like to:

- Reward correction more than preservation (i.e. $weight_{\text{TP}} > weight_{\text{TN}}$).
- Penalise unnecessary corrections more than uncorrected errors (i.e. $weight_{\text{FP}} > weight_{\text{FN}}$).

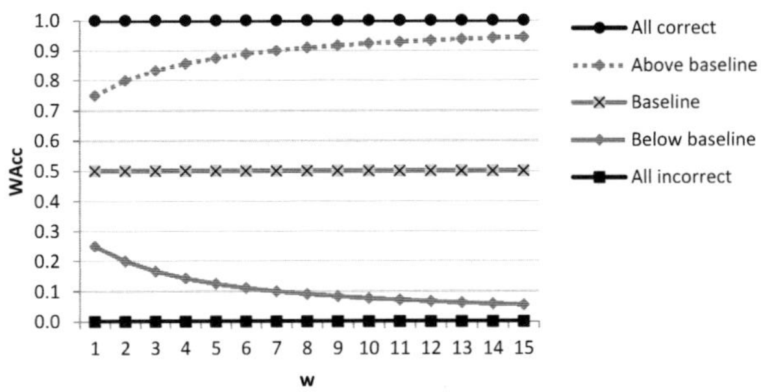


Figure 2: Effect of $w$ on weighted accuracy (WAcc).

We can reformulate accuracy to satisfy these conditions by including a weight factor $w > 1$:

$$
\begin{aligned}
WAcc &= \frac{w \cdot \text{TP} + \text{TN}}{w \cdot \text{TP} + \text{TN} + w \cdot \left(\text{FP} - \frac{\text{FPN}}{2}\right) + \left(\text{FN} - \frac{\text{FPN}}{2}\right)} \\
&= \frac{w \cdot \text{TP} + \text{TN}}{w \cdot \text{TP} + \text{TN} + w \cdot \text{FP} - w \cdot \frac{\text{FPN}}{2} + \text{FN} - \frac{\text{FPN}}{2}} \\
&= \frac{w \cdot \text{TP} + \text{TN}}{w \cdot (\text{TP} + \text{FP}) + \text{TN} + \text{FN} - (w+1) \cdot \frac{\text{FPN}}{2}}
\end{aligned}
$$

Higher values of $w$ will reward and penalise systems more heavily, bringing those below the baseline closer to the lower bound and those above the baseline closer to the upper bound (see Figure 2). As $w$ increases, differences between $WAcc_{\text{sys}}$ and its bounds become less pronounced, which is why we adopt $w = 2$. Regardless of $w$, *WAcc* will always reduce to *Acc* for the 'do-nothing' baseline.

### 2.3.2 Metric behaviour

Before we set out to evaluate and compare systems, we must understand how metrics behave and to what extent they are comparable.

Table 6 indicates that the metrics will always produce the same results for detection and correction unless *source* $\neq$ *hypothesis* $\neq$ *reference* for at least one position in the alignment. A 'do-nothing' baseline will always produce the same results for both aspects, since *source* = *hypothesis* for all positions.

Whenever a gold standard allows for alternative corrections, references that maximise the target metric should be chosen. Nevertheless, we note that the (maximum) score obtained by a system only applies to a given set of chosen references and is therefore only directly comparable to results on the same reference set.

| System | Chosen references | P | R | $F_{0.5}$ |
|---|---|---|---|---|
| **$S_1$** | **1.2, 2.1, 3.1** | **0.60** | **0.20** | **0.43** |
| $S_2$ | 1.2, 2.1, 3.1 | 0.80 | 0.05 | 0.20 |
| $S_1$ | 1.1, 2.1, 3.2 | 0.30 | 0.30 | 0.30 |
| **$S_2$** | **1.1, 2.1, 3.2** | **0.30** | **0.40** | **0.32** |

Table 7: $S_1$ outperforms $S_2$ in terms of overall $F_{0.5}$ but $S_2$ outperforms $S_1$ when evaluated on different references.

To illustrate this, consider two systems ($S_1$ and $S_2$) evaluated on a gold standard containing 3 sentences with 2 correction alternatives each (i.e. six possible references: 1.1, 1.2, 2.1, 2.2, 3.1 and 3.2 respectively). Table 7 shows that, while $S_1$ achieves a higher maximum score than $S_2$, comparing their $F_{0.5}$ scores directly is not possible as they are computed on a different set of references. In fact, $S_2$ could outperform $S_1$ on other reference sets.

### 2.3.3 Measuring improvement

We know that whenever $P > 0.5$, the error rate decreases (and therefore *Acc* increases) so the text is improved.[3] However, an increase in $P$, $R$ or $F$ alone does not necessarily imply an increase in *Acc* or *WAcc*, as illustrated in Table 8.

In order to determine whether a system improves on the source text, we must compare its performance ($WAcc_{\text{sys}}$) with that of the baseline ($WAcc_{\text{base}}$). Because each $WAcc_{\text{sys}}$ is computed from a different set of references, we must compute $WAcc_{\text{base}}$ individually for each system using its chosen references. This is done by using the source sentence as the hypothesis in the existing alignment. Once we have $WAcc_{\text{sys}}$ and $WAcc_{\text{base}}$ for each system, we can compare them to determine if the text has improved. When these two values are equal, there is no benefit to deploying the system.

If we want to compare and rank systems, we need to measure how much the text has been improved or degraded. This can be done using a baseline-normalised metric that measures relative coverage of the area between the baseline and *WAcc* bounds (see Figure 3). This metric, henceforth *Improvement* or

[3] In theory, applying more correct edits than incorrect edits will yield a positive balance. However, in practice, this depends on the edits, especially if they are variable-length phrases. The $P > 0.5$ criterion also only holds for *Acc* and not *WAcc*, as the latter modifies the original proportions by introducing weights.

| System | TP | FP | TN | FN | P | R | $F_{0.5}$ | Acc | WAcc |
|---|---|---|---|---|---|---|---|---|---|
| Baseline | 0 | 0 | 6 | 4 | 1.00 | 0.00 | 0.00 | 0.60 | 0.60 |
| $S_1$ | 4 | 1 | 5 | 0 | 0.80 | 1.00 | 0.83 | 0.90 | 0.87 |
| $S_2$ | 1 | 0 | 6 | 3 | 1.00 | 0.25 | 0.62 | 0.70 | 0.73 |
| $S_3$ | 1 | 1 | 5 | 3 | 0.50 | 0.25 | 0.42 | 0.60 | 0.58 |
| $S_4$ | 4 | 6 | 0 | 0 | 0.40 | 1.00 | 0.45 | 0.40 | 0.40 |

Table 8: An increase in $P$, $R$ or $F$ does not necessarily translate into an increase in *Acc*, assuming all systems are evaluated on the same set of references.

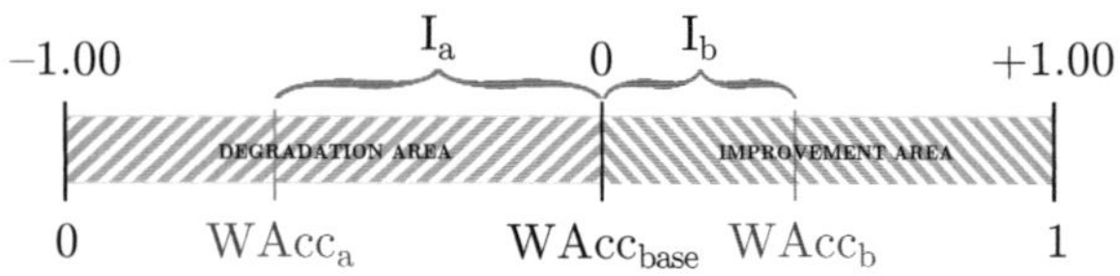


Figure 3: Graphical representation of improvement for two hypothetical systems, a and b. Values of $I$ are shown at the top while values of *WAcc* are shown at the bottom.

| Value | Interpretation |
|---|---|
| 1 | 100% improvement (100% correct text). |
| $>0$ | Relative improvement. |
| 0 | Baseline performance (no change). |
| $<0$ | Relative degradation. |
| -1 | 100% degradation (100% incorrect text). |

Table 9: Interpretation of $I$ values.

$I$, is defined as:

$$I = \begin{cases} \lfloor WAcc_{\text{sys}} \rfloor & \text{if } WAcc_{\text{sys}} = WAcc_{\text{base}} \\ \dfrac{WAcc_{\text{sys}} - WAcc_{\text{base}}}{1 - WAcc_{\text{base}}} & \text{if } WAcc_{\text{sys}} > WAcc_{\text{base}} \\ \dfrac{WAcc_{\text{sys}}}{WAcc_{\text{base}}} - 1 & \text{otherwise} \end{cases}$$

Values of $I$ lie in the $[-1; 1]$ interval and should be interpreted as per Table 9. The use of this metric provides a solution to problems 1.(h) and 1.(i).

The $I$-measure should be computed after maximising system *WAcc* at the sentence level, so as to ensure all the evaluated hypotheses are paired with their highest scoring references.

## 3 Experiments and results

We tested our evaluation method by re-ranking systems in the CoNLL 2014 shared task on grammatical error correction. Re-ranking was limited to the 12 participating teams that made their system's output publicly available.

For the gold standard, we used the shared task test set containing corrections from the two official annotators as well as alternative corrections provided by three participating teams. This version allowed us to generate many more references than the original test set and thus reduce annotator bias.

The corrections extracted from the gold standard were automatically clustered into groups of independent errors based on token overlap. This means that overlapping corrections from different annotators are considered to be mutually exclusive (i.e. alternative) corrections of the same error and are therefore grouped together (the *error* elements in Listing 1). Provided the original annotations are correct, the combination of alternatives will generate all possible valid references. Sentences containing corrections that could not be automatically clustered because they require human knowledge were excluded, leaving a subset of 711 sentences (out of 1,312).

We restrict our analysis to correction, since that is the only aspect reported by the $M^2$ Scorer. Table 10 shows the results of the $M^2$ Scorer using the original annotations as well as a modified version containing mixed-and-matched corrections. Results of our proposed evaluation method are included in Table 11.

As expected, rankings are clearly distinct between the two methods, as they use different units of evaluation (phrase-level edits vs tokens) and maximising metrics ($F_{0.5}$ vs *WAcc*). Results show that only the UFC system is able to beat the baseline (by a small but statistically significant margin), being also the one with consistently highest $P$ (much higher than the rest).

These rankings are affected by the fact that systems were probably optimised for $F_{0.5}$ during development, as it was the official evaluation metric

| System | TP | TN | FP | FN | FPN | P | R | $F_{0.5}$ | Acc | WAcc | $WAcc_{base}$ | I ↓ |
|---|---|---|---|---|---|---|---|---|---|---|---|---|
| UFC | 19 | 13062 | 7 | 665 | 2 | 73.08 | 2.78 | 12.06 | 95.13 | 95.09 | 95.03 | 1.35 |
| BASELINE | 0 | 13078 | 0 | 673 | 0 | 100.00 | 0.00 | 0.00 | 95.11 | 95.11 | 95.11 | 0.00 |
| IITB | 11 | 13057 | 26 | 668 | 4 | 29.73 | 1.62 | 6.65 | 94.98 | 94.82 | 95.06 | -0.25 |
| SJTU | 54 | 12947 | 114 | 649 | 8 | 32.14 | 7.68 | 19.64 | 94.51 | 93.79 | 94.89 | -1.16 |
| CUUI | 290 | 12697 | 337 | 553 | 34 | 46.25 | 34.40 | 43.27 | 93.82 | 91.86 | 93.91 | -2.18 |
| PKU | 128 | 12800 | 283 | 625 | 66 | 31.14 | 17.00 | 26.70 | 93.89 | 92.28 | 94.53 | -2.38 |
| AMU | 219 | 12761 | 322 | 556 | 41 | 40.48 | 28.26 | 37.26 | 93.94 | 92.06 | 94.39 | -2.47 |
| UMC | 179 | 12761 | 314 | 603 | 26 | 36.31 | 22.89 | 32.50 | 93.56 | 91.67 | 94.35 | -2.84 |
| IPN | 25 | 12848 | 251 | 680 | 40 | 9.06 | 3.55 | 6.91 | 93.53 | 92.00 | 94.88 | -3.04 |
| POST | 231 | 12588 | 454 | 574 | 46 | 33.72 | 28.70 | 32.58 | 92.88 | 90.23 | 94.17 | -4.18 |
| RAC | 147 | 12723 | 426 | 623 | 49 | 25.65 | 19.09 | 24.00 | 92.79 | 90.28 | 94.45 | -4.41 |
| CAMB | 386 | 12402 | 641 | 502 | 78 | 37.59 | 43.47 | 38.63 | 92.31 | 88.77 | 93.59 | -5.15 |
| NTHU | 196 | 12620 | 521 | 575 | 54 | 27.34 | 25.42 | 26.93 | 92.48 | 89.44 | 94.44 | -5.29 |

Table 11: Results of our new evaluation method (in percentages). All values of $I$ are statistically significant (two-tailed paired T-test, $p < 0.01$).

| System | Original annotations | | | Mixed annotations | | |
|---|---|---|---|---|---|---|
| | P | R | $F_{0.5}$ ↓ | P | R | $F_{0.5}$ ↓ |
| CUUI | 47.66 | 33.87 | 44.07 | 47.57 | 39.60 | 45.73 |
| AMU | 44.68 | 29.44 | 40.48 | 44.56 | 33.49 | 41.80 |
| CAMB | 39.22 | 41.65 | 39.69 | 39.04 | 48.72 | 40.66 |
| POST | 36.39 | 29.13 | 34.67 | 36.39 | 33.79 | 35.84 |
| NTHU | 33.56 | 28.10 | 32.31 | 33.62 | 31.52 | 33.18 |
| UMC | 34.86 | 20.86 | 30.73 | 34.86 | 23.31 | 31.71 |
| RAC | 33.67 | 19.08 | 29.21 | 33.67 | 21.59 | 30.28 |
| PKU | 32.17 | 19.60 | 28.51 | 32.42 | 21.63 | 29.48 |
| SJTU | 28.00 | 7.08 | 17.60 | 28.00 | 7.46 | 18.06 |
| UFC | 73.08 | 3.26 | 13.83 | 73.08 | 3.39 | 14.31 |
| IPN | 9.16 | 3.87 | 7.20 | 9.16 | 4.09 | 7.34 |
| IITB | 30.30 | 1.74 | 7.07 | 30.30 | 1.81 | 7.31 |
| BASELINE | 100.00 | 0.00 | 0.00 | 100.00 | 0.00 | 0.00 |

Table 10: $M^2$ Scorer results (in percentages).

for the shared task. Rankings by $F_{0.5}$ are almost identical for the two methods (Spearman's rank correlation is 0.9835 with $p < 0.01$), suggesting that there is a statistically significant difference between phrase-level edits and tokens, despite phrases being only 1.12 tokens on average in this dataset.

Spearman's $\rho$ between both scorers ($F_{0.5}$ vs $I$) is $-0.5330$, which suggests they generally produce inverse rankings. Pearson's correlation between token-level $F_{0.5}$ and $I$ is $-0.5942$, confirming the relationship between rankings and our intuition that $F_{0.5}$ is not a good indicator of overall correction quality. While the $I$-measure reflects improvement, $F_{0.5}$ indicates error manipulation. We argue that $I$ is better suited to the needs of end-users (as it indicates whether the output of the system is better than the original text) whereas $F_{0.5}$ is more relevant to system developers (since they need to analyse $P$ and $R$ in order to tune their systems).

Lastly, we verify that mixing and matching corrections from different annotators improves $R$ (see Table 10) and ensures systems are always assigned the maximum possible score.

## 4 Discussion

Automatic evaluation metrics that are based on comparisons with a gold standard are inherently limited by the number of available references. Although this does not pose much problem for tasks such as part-of-speech tagging, it does constrain evaluation for text generation tasks (such as error correction, machine translation or summarisation), where the number of 'correct answers' goes beyond a few collected references.

Sentences can be corrected in many different ways and the fact that a given correction is not matched by any of the references does not necessarily mean that it is not valid. Therefore, we must accept that any metric used in such scenarios will not be perfect. However, it is worth noting that this limitation does not extend to evaluation of error detection *per se* using such metrics.

Finding independent evidence to support one correction over another is also difficult, since the notion of sentence quality is somewhat subjective. Evaluation metrics that rely on a gold standard are es-

| System hypotheses | | Best | |
|---|---|---|---|
| | | $F_{0.5}$ | I |
| a. | The son was died after one year 's treatment and a couple got divorced later after that . | × | |
| b. | The son had died after one year 's and the couple got divorced later after that . | | × |
| a. | Although there might be a lot of challenges along the way in seeking medical attention , such as a financial issues , everyone should be given right of knowing their family 's inherented medical conditions . | × | |
| b. | Although there might be a lot of challenges along the way in seeking medical attention , such as finance , everyone should be given the right of knowing their family 's inherented medical conditions . | | × |
| a. | Taking Angeline Jolie , for example , she is famous but she still reveal the truth about her genetic testing to the development of her breast cancer risk . | × | |
| b. | Taking Angeline Jolie for example , she is famous but she still revealed the truth about her genetic testing on the development of her breast cancer risk . | | × |

Table 12: Example hypotheses produced by two error correction systems (a and b). The last two columns indicate the highest-scoring hypothesis from each pair according to each evaluation metric.

sentially distance metrics, but judging between hypotheses without looking at the source or reference sentences is a distinct task, which is more similar to *sentence quality estimation* for machine translation output.

Our evaluation method overcomes many of the limitations of previous approaches by using a stable unit of evaluation, weighting edit operations in line with the goals of grammatical error correction and making the most of the available annotations. Values of $F$ are always positive, with no clear interpretation or threshold that would indicate improvement of the original text whereas the $I$-measure provides meaningful indicators ($I < 0$ for degradation, $I = 0$ for no change and $I > 0$ for improvement). Table 12 shows a few examples where the $M^2$ Scorer differs from our method, revealing how the $I$-measure is able to pick hypotheses in accord with (at least our) intuitions.

## 5 Conclusion

We have presented a new evaluation method for grammatical error detection and correction that overcomes many of the limitations of previous approaches and provides more meaningful indicators of system performance.

The method is designed to evaluate improvement in correction of the input text by analysing post-system error rate. Improvement is measured using a reformulation of accuracy where TPs and FPs are weighted higher than TNs and FNs, in an attempt to model desirable aspects of correction. We also combine individual corrections from different annotators, as this improves $R$ and ensures systems get the maximum possible score from the available annotations.

Experiments show $I$ and $F_{0.5}$ are inversely correlated and account for different aspects of system performance. Choosing one metric over the other poses a fundamental question about the aims of error correction, whether we prefer a system that tackles few errors but improves the original text or one that handles many more errors but degrades the original. We believe that, from a user perspective, a system that reliably improves text is more desirable.

Future work might usefully explore automated sentence quality estimation, as a component both of grammatical error correction systems and of their evaluation, in order to ameliorate the issue that any set of gold standard references will underspecify the set of possible corrections.

An open-source implementation of our evaluation method is available for download at `https://github.com/mfelice/imeasure`.

## Acknowledgments

We would like to thank Øistein Andersen and Zheng Yuan for their constructive feedback, as well as the anonymous reviewers for their comments and suggestions. We are also grateful to Cambridge English Language Assessment for supporting this research via the ALTA Institute.


## References


Humberto Carrillo and David Lipman. 1988. The multiple sequence alignment problem in biology. *SIAM J. Appl. Math.*, 48(5):1073–1082, October.

Martin Chodorow, Markus Dickinson, Ross Israel, and Joel Tetreault. 2012. Problems in evaluating grammatical error detection systems. In *Proceedings of COLING 2012*, pages 611–628, Mumbai, India, December. The COLING 2012 Organizing Committee.

Daniel Dahlmeier and Hwee Tou Ng. 2012. Better evaluation for grammatical error correction. In *Proceedings of the 2012 Conference of the North American Chapter of the Association for Computational Linguistics: Human Language Technologies*, NAACL 2012, pages 568 – 572, Montreal, Canada.

Robert Dale and Adam Kilgarriff. 2011. Helping Our Own: The HOO 2011 Pilot Shared Task. In *Proceedings of the Generation Challenges Session at the 13th European Workshop on Natural Language Generation*, pages 242–249, Nancy, France, September. Association for Computational Linguistics.

Robert Dale, Ilya Anisimoff, and George Narroway. 2012. HOO 2012: A Report on the Preposition and Determiner Error Correction Shared Task. In *Proceedings of the Seventh Workshop on Building Educational Applications Using NLP*, pages 54–62, Montréal, Canada, June. Association for Computational Linguistics.

Rachele De Felice and Stephen G. Pulman. 2008. A Classifier-Based Approach to Preposition and Determiner Error Correction in L2 English. In *Proceedings of the 22nd International Conference on Computational Linguistics (COLING 2008)*, pages 169–176, Manchester, UK, August. COLING 2008 Organizing Committee.

Dan Gusfield. 1997. *Algorithms on Strings, Trees and Sequences*. Cambridge University Press.

Claudia Leacock, Martin Chodorow, Michael Gamon, and Joel Tetreault. 2014. *Automated Grammatical Error Detection for Language Learners, Second edition*. Synthesis Lectures on Human Language Technologies. Morgan & Claypool Publishers.

Christopher D. Manning and Hinrich Schütze. 1999. *Foundations of Statistical Natural Language Processing*. The MIT Press, Cambridge, Massachusetts.

Behrang Mohit, Alla Rozovskaya, Nizar Habash, Wajdi Zaghouani, and Ossama Obeid. 2014. The First QALB Shared Task on Automatic Text Correction for Arabic. In *Proceedings of the EMNLP 2014 Workshop on Arabic Natural Language Processing (ANLP)*, pages 39–47, Doha, Qatar, October. Association for Computational Linguistics.

David W. Mount. 2004. *Bioinformatics: Sequence and Genome Analysis, Second edition*. Cold Spring Harbor Laboratory Press.

Hwee Tou Ng, Siew Mei Wu, Yuanbin Wu, Christian Hadiwinoto, and Joel Tetreault. 2013. The CoNLL-2013 Shared Task on Grammatical Error Correction. In *Proceedings of the Seventeenth Conference on Computational Natural Language Learning: Shared Task*, pages 1–12, Sofia, Bulgaria, August. Association for Computational Linguistics.

Hwee Tou Ng, Siew Mei Wu, Ted Briscoe, Christian Hadiwinoto, Raymond Hendy Susanto, and Christopher Bryant. 2014. The CoNLL-2014 Shared Task on Grammatical Error Correction. In *Proceedings of the Eighteenth Conference on Computational Natural Language Learning: Shared Task*, pages 1–14, Baltimore, Maryland, June. Association for Computational Linguistics.

Alla Rozovskaya and Dan Roth. 2010. Training paradigms for correcting errors in grammar and usage. In *Human Language Technologies: The 2010 Annual Conference of the North American Chapter of the Association for Computational Linguistics*, HLT '10, pages 154–162, Los Angeles, California. Association for Computational Linguistics.

# Using Zero-Resource Spoken Term Discovery for Ranked Retrieval

**Jerome White**
New York University
Abu Dhabi, UAE
jerome.white@nyu.edu

**Douglas W. Oard**
University of Maryland
College Park, MD USA
oard@umd.edu

**Jiaul Paik**
University of Maryland
College Park, MD USA
jiaul@umd.edu

**Rashmi Sankepally**
University of Maryland
College Park, MD USA
rashmi@umd.edu

**Aren Jansen**
John Hopkins HLTCOE
Baltimore, MD USA
aren@jhu.edu

## Abstract

Research on ranked retrieval of spoken content has assumed the existence of some automated (word or phonetic) transcription. Recently, however, methods have been demonstrated for matching spoken terms to spoken content without the need for language-tuned transcription. This paper describes the first application of such techniques to ranked retrieval, evaluated using a newly created test collection. Both the queries and the collection to be searched are based on Gujarati produced naturally by native speakers; relevance assessment was performed by other native speakers of Gujarati. Ranked retrieval is based on fast acoustic matching that identifies a deeply nested set of matching speech regions, coupled with ways of combining evidence from those matching regions. Results indicate that the resulting ranked lists may be useful for some practical similarity-based ranking tasks.

## 1 Introduction

Despite new methods of interaction, speech continues to be a dominant modality for information exchange, particularly among the half of the world's almost five billion mobile phone users who currently lack text-based Internet access. Recording speech poses no particular problems, but retrieval of spoken content using spoken queries is presently available only for the approximately two dozen languages in which there is an established path to market; English, German, or Chinese, for example. However, many of the mobile-only users who could benefit most from such systems speak only one of the several hundred other languages that each have at least a million speakers;[1] Balochi, Mossi or Quechua, for example. Addressing this challenge in a scalable manner requires an integration of speech processing and information retrieval techniques that can be effectively and affordably extended to a large number of languages.

To this end, the experiments in this paper were conducted in a conventional ranked retrieval framework consisting of spoken queries, spoken "documents" (*responses*, hereafter), graded relevance judgments, and standard evaluation measures. As with other information retrieval tasks, there is an element of uncertainty in our best representations of what was said. Our focus on speech processing techniques that are language-agnostic creates the potential for explosive growth in the uncertainty that our search techniques must accommodate. The design and evaluation of such techniques is therefore the central focus of the work explored in this paper.

Our results are both heartening and disconcerting. On the positive side, useful responses can often be found. As one measure of success, we show that a Mean Reciprocal Rank near 0.5 can be achieved when more than one relevant response exists; this corresponds to a relevant response appearing in the second position of a ranked list, on average (by the harmonic mean). On the negative side, the zero-resource speech processing technique that we rely on to generate indexing terms has quadratic time complexity, making even the hundred-hour scale of

[1]There are 393 languages with at least one million speakers according to Ethnologue.



*Human Language Technologies: The 2015 Annual Conference of the North American Chapter of the ACL*, pages 588–597,
Denver, Colorado, May 31 – June 5, 2015. ©2015 Association for Computational Linguistics

the collection on which we have run our experiments computationally strenuous. We believe, however, that by demonstrating the utility of the techniques introduced in this paper we can help to motivate further work on even more affordable scalable language-agnostic techniques for generating indexable terms from speech.

## 2 Motivation and Related Work

Extending spoken language processing to low-resource languages has been a longstanding goal of the Spoken Web Search task of MediaEval. In this task, research teams are challenged to identify instances of specific spoken terms that are provided as queries in a few hours of speech. Between 2011 and 2013, the task was run three times on a total of 16 different languages (Rajput and Metze, 2011; Metze et al., 2012; Anguera et al., 2013).[2] Two broad classes of techniques over this span proved to be practical: one based on phonetic recognition followed by phonetic matching; the other based on direct matching of acoustic features. Of the two approaches, phonetic recognition was, at the time, slightly more accurate. Directly matching acoustic features, the focus of this paper, potentially offers easier extensibility to additional languages.

From the perspective of information retrieval, the principal limitation of the "spoken term detection" design of the MediaEval task was the restriction to single-term queries. While single-term queries are common in Web search (Spink et al., 2001), the best reported Actual Term Weighted Value (ATWV) from any MediaEval Spoken Web Search participant was 0.4846 (Abad and Astudillo, 2012). This corresponds to a system that correctly detects 48 per cent of all instances of the spoken query terms, while producing at most ten false alarms for every missed detection (Fiscus et al., 2007). Thus, if users are willing to tolerate low precision, moderate levels of recall are possible. Speech search arguably demands higher precision than does Web search, however, since browsing multiple alternatives is easier in text than in speech. One way of potentially improving retrieval performance is to encourage a searcher to speak at length about what they are looking for (Oard, 2012). Such an approach, however, introduces the new challenge of properly leveraging the additional matching potential of verbose multi-term queries (White et al., 2013).

To this end, our work builds on two components: a term matching system, and a test collection. As a term matching system, we used our zero-knowledge speech matching system. In MediaEval 2012, this system achieved an ATWV of 0.321 in the Spoken Web Search task (Jansen et al., 2012). A version of this system has previously been evaluated in an example-based topic classification task using English speech, achieving a classification accuracy of 0.8683 (Drezde et al., 2010). Ranked retrieval using naturally occurring queries is more challenging, however, both because topics in information retrieval are often not easily separable, and because the form of a query may be unlike the form of the responses that are sought. Our goal now, therefore, is to use an information retrieval evaluation framework to drive the development of robust techniques for accommodating representational uncertainty.

Traditional spoken term detection (STD) tries to address uncertainty by learning speech-signal to language-model mappings; using neural networks (Cui et al., 2013; Gales et al., 2014) or Markov models (Chan et al., 2013), for example. From a broad perspective, the method utilized in our work does not use an acoustic model for its analysis. More fundamentally, however, speech signals in our collection map to dozens of smaller terms that are not necessarily the same across utterances of the same word. Thus, it is more accurate to think of the work herein as matching signal features rather than linguistic features.

For this reason, widely used techniques such as stemming, spelling correction, and stopword removal that rely to some extent on linguistic features do not apply in our setting. We therefore rely on term and corpus statistics. Even here there are limitations, since our lexical items are not easily aligned with those found in other collections. For this reason, we can not leverage external corpus statistics from, for example, Google or Wikipedia (Bendersky et al., 2011; Bendersky et al., 2010; Bendersky and Croft, 2008; Lease, 2009), or phrases from search logs (Svore et al., 2010).

Evaluation of ranked retrieval for spoken content

[2]For example, Gujarati, isiNdebele, isiXhosa, Sepedi, Setswana, Telugu, Tshivenda, and Xitsonga.

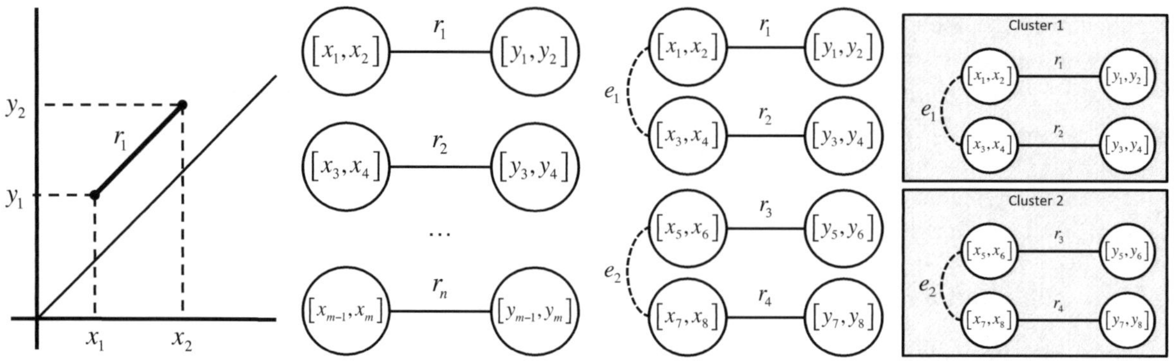


(a) Term discovery. (b) Term extraction. (c) Term overlap. (d) Term clustering.

Figure 1: Overview of the pseudo-term creation process. The term discovery system is run over the audio. A threshold, $\delta$, dictates the acceptable length, $r$, and thus the number of regions extracted. Extracted regions are then made into a graph structure, where vertices are regions of speech, and edges denote a connection between those regions. A second edge set is added based on region overlap. Resulting connected components are then clustered; these clusters are known as *pseudo-terms*.

in low-resource languages has to date been hampered by a lack of suitable test collections. We have therefore made our new test collection freely available for research use in recent shared-task information retrieval evaluations (Oard et al., 2013; Joshi and White, 2014).

## 3 Zero-Resource Term Discovery

In traditional speech retrieval applications, document-level features are derived from the outputs of supervised phonetic or word recognizers. Recent term discovery systems automatically identify repeating words and phrases in large collections of audio (Park and Glass, 2008; Jansen et al., 2010), providing an alternative means of extracting lexical features for retrieval tasks. Critically, this discovery is performed without the assistance of any supervised speech tools by instead resorting to a search for repeated trajectories in a suitable acoustic feature space (for example, Mel Frequency Cepstrum Coefficients (MFCC) and Perceptual Linear Prediction (PLP)) followed by a graph clustering procedure. We refer to the discovered units as *pseudo-terms* (by analogy to the terms built from character sequences that are commonly used in text retrieval), and we can represent each query and response as a set of pseudo-term offsets and durations. We summarize each step in the subsections below. Complete specifications can be found in the literature (Drezde et al., 2010; Jansen and Van Durme, 2011).

### 3.1 Repetition and Clustering

Our test collection consists of nearly 100 hours of speech audio. Term discovery is inherently an $O(n^2)$ search problem, and application to a corpus of this size is unprecedented in the literature. We applied the scalable system described by Jansen and Van Durme (2011), which employs a pure-to-noisy strategy to achieve a very substantial (orders-of-magnitude) speedup over its predecessor state-of-the-art system (Park and Glass, 2008). The system functions by constructing a sparse (thresholded) distance matrix across the frames of the entire corpus and then searching for approximately diagonal line structures in that matrix, as such structures are indicative that a word or phrase has been repeated (Figure 1a).

To cluster the individual acoustic repetitions into pseudo-term categories we apply a simple graph-based procedure. First, we construct an unweighted acoustic similarity graph, where each segment of speech involved in a discovered repetition becomes a vertex, and each match provides an edge (Figure 1b). Since we construct an unweighted graph and employ a simple connected-components clustering, it is es-

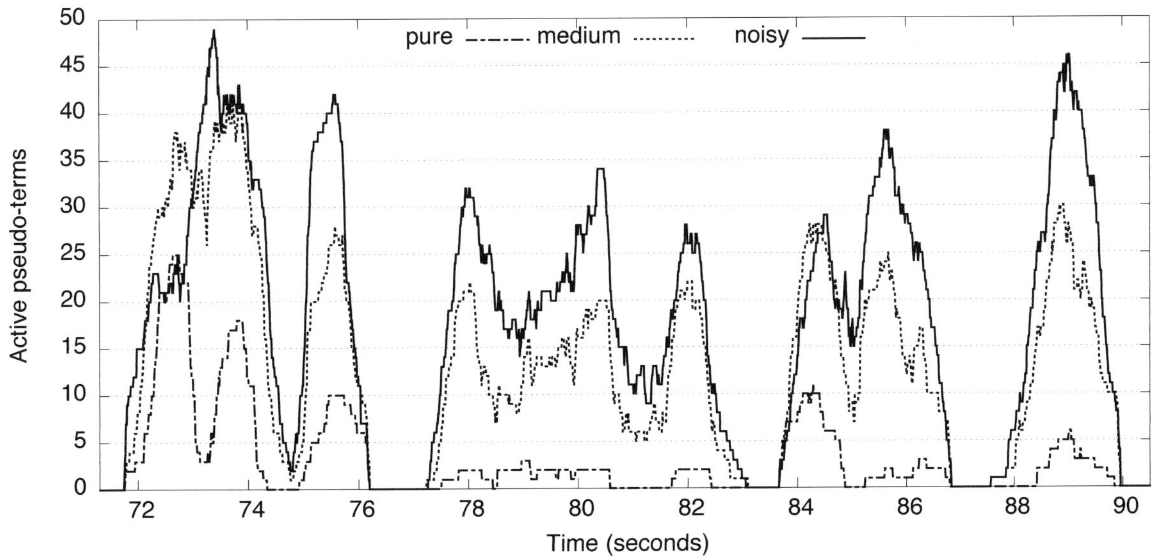


Figure 2: Different pseudo-term nesting structures for various settings of the speech-to-term extraction model. The $y$-axis represents the number of terms extracted at a given period in time. This figure represents an approximately twenty second interval of Query 42.

sential some DTW distance threshold $\delta$ is applied before a repetition is passed along to the clustering procedure. This produces a graph consisting of a set of disconnected "dumbbells."

Finally, the original edge list is augmented with a set of "overlap" edges between corresponding nodes in different dumbbells (Figure 1c); these overlap edges indicate that two nodes correspond to essentially the same segment of speech. For two nodes (two segments of speech) to be considered essentially the same, we require a minimal fractional overlap of 0.97, which is set less than unity to allow some noise in the segment end points. These overlap edges act to effectively merge vertexes across the dumbbells, enabling transitive matches between acoustic segments that did not match directly. The pseudo-terms are defined to be the resulting connected components of the graph, each consisting of a set of corresponding acoustic segments that can occur anywhere in the collection (Figure 1d).

In the experiments described in this paper, three pseudo-term feature variants arising from three settings of the DTW distance threshold are considered. Lower thresholds imply higher fidelity matches that yield fewer and purer pseudo-term clusters. These are referred to as *pure clustering* ($\delta = 0.06$, producing 406,366 unique pseudo-terms), *medium clustering* ($\delta = 0.07$, producing 1,213,223 unique pseudo-terms) and *noisy clustering* ($\delta = 0.075$, producing 1,503,169 unique pseudo-terms).

### 3.2 Nested Pseudo-Terms

Each pseudo-term cluster consists of a list of occurrences. A term is denoted using start and end offsets, in units of 10 milliseconds, from the beginning of the file. It is thus a simple matter of bookkeeping to construct a bag-of-pseudo-terms representation for each query and response. Moreover, because we have start and end offsets for each pseudo-term, we can also construct more sophisticated representations that are based on filtering or grouping the pseudo-terms based on the ways in which they overlap temporally.

One interesting effect of pseudo-term creation is that the pseudo-terms are often "nested," and they are often nested quite deeply. This sort of nesting has previously been explored for phrase indexing, where a longer term contains a shorter term that might also be used independently elsewhere in the collection. As an English text analogy, if we index "White House spokesman" we might well also want to index "White House" and "spokesman"

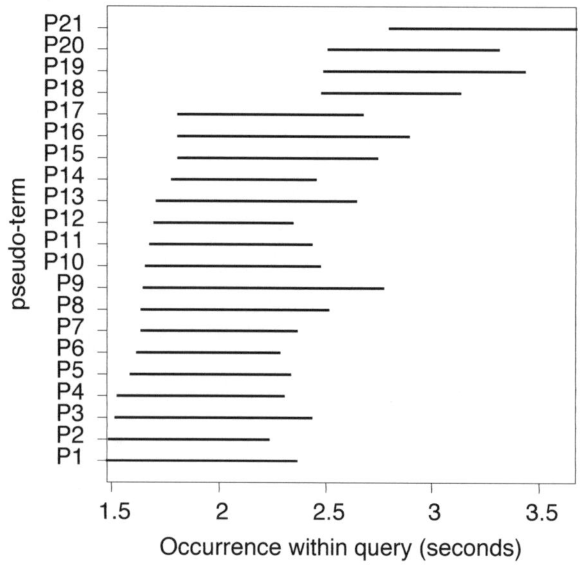


Figure 3: Example of overlapping pseudo-terms within Query 42 under medium clustering. Terms are presented as horizontal bars denoting their start and end time.

separately to support partial matching. Because pseudo-term detection can find any pair of matching regions, we could, continuing the analogy, not only get pseudo-terms for "White House Spokesman" and "White House," but also for parts of those words such as "Whit" and "Whi". Indeed, nesting to depth 50 has been observed in practice for noisy clustering, as displayed in Figure 2. This is a fairly typical pseudo-term nesting graph, in which noisy clustering yields deeper nesting than medium clustering, and much deeper nesting than pure clustering.

Figure 3 shows a collection of pseudo-terms within an overlapping region; in this case a medium clustering representation of the 1.48 second to 3.67 second region of Query 42.[3] As can be seen, calling this "nesting" is somewhat of an oversimplification, the region is actually a set of pseudo-terms that generally overlap to some degree, although not all pseudo-term pairs in one of these "nested" regions actually overlap—pseudo-terms P1 and P21, for example. What gives a nested region its depth is the overlap between pseudo-terms that have adjacent start times. Although in this case, as is typical, there is no one dominating pseudo-term for the entire nested region, there are some cases in which one pseudo-terms is entirely subsumed by another; pseudo-terms P5 and P6, for example. This trait can be leveraged during term matching.

[3]Figure 2 shows the same query between 70 and 90 seconds.

## 4 Retrieval Models

The development of ranking functions, referred to as "retrieval models," proceeded in three stages. To establish a baseline, we first implemented a standard bag-of-words approach. We then looked to techniques from Cross-Language Information Retrieval (CLIR) for inspiration, since CLIR techniques must accommodate some degree of translation ambiguity and for which robust techniques have been established. Our zero-resource pseudo-term discovery techniques result in representations that differ from the CLIR case in two key ways, however: 1) in CLIR the translation relationship is normally represented such that one side (query or document) exhibits no ambiguity, whereas we have ambiguity on both sides; and 2) in CLIR the typical scope of all translation alternatives are aligned, whereas we have complex nested units that contain terms with differing temporal extents. We therefore developed a new class of techniques that leverage the temporal extent of a pseudo-term as a measure of specificity (Figure 2) and the fraction of a nested unit covered by a pseudo-term as a measure of descriptiveness (Figure 3). This section describes each of these three types of retrieval models in turn.

Indri (Strohman et al., 2004) indexes were built using pseudo-terms from pure, medium or noisy clustering; in each case, stemming and stopword removal were disabled. Indri's query language provides operators that make it possible to implement all of our retrieval models using query-time processing from a single index.

### 4.1 Types of Retrieval Models

To explore the balance between specificity and descriptiveness, retrieval models were developed that primarily differed along three dimensions: structured versus unstructured, selective versus inclusive, and weighted versus unweighted. Structured models (*S*) treat nested pseudo-terms with varying levels of synonymy. Unstructured models (*U*) treat nested pseudo-terms as independent. Selective models retain only a subset (1 or n) of the pseudo-terms from each nested region; inclusive models retain them all (*a*). Finally, weighted models (*W*) include a heuristic adjustment to give some pseudo-terms (in our experiments, longer ones) greater influence; unweighted models treat each pseudo-term in the same manner. Table 1 illustrates the weights given to each term by each of the retrieval models defined below. Unweighted models implicitly take a binary approach to term weighting—with unweighted selective models omitting many pseudo-terms—while structured and weighted models yield real values between zero and one. Note that both weighted and unweighted models reward term repetition (term frequency) and term specificity (inverse collection frequency).

### 4.2 Bag-of-Words Baseline (Ua)

Our first set of experiments had three goals: 1) to serve as a dry run for system development, as we had no prior experience with indexing or ranked retrieval based on pseudo-terms; 2) to gain experience with performing relevance judgments using only the audio responses; and 3) to understand the feasibility of speech retrieval based on pseudo-terms. For these initial experiments, each pseudo-term was treated as a "word" in a bag-of-words representation (coded Ua). No consideration was given to term length or nesting. Although this set of runs was largely exploratory, it provided a good baseline for comparison to other methods considered.

### 4.3 Terms as Synonyms (Sa, U1)

Moving beyond the bag of words method of term selection involves various forms of term analysis within an overlapping region. The first family of methods treats terms in each overlapping group as synonymous. Aside from being straightforward, treating terms as unweighted synonyms has been a successful technique in cross-language IR. There are generally two methods that can be used in such cases. The first is to treat all overlapping pseudo-terms as synonyms of a single term. This is accomplished in Indri by placing each pseudo-term in an overlapping region within the `syn` operator. This model is coded Sa.

| | Retrieval Model | | | | | |
|---|---|---|---|---|---|---|
| P. Term | Ua | Sa | U1 | Un | UaW | SaW |
| P21 | 1.00 | 0.05 | | 1.00 | 0.45 | 0.45 |
| P20 | 1.00 | 0.05 | | | 0.43 | 0.22 |
| P19 | 1.00 | 0.05 | | | 0.48 | 0.48 |
| P18 | 1.00 | 0.05 | | | 0.36 | 0.36 |
| P17 | 1.00 | 0.05 | | | 0.45 | 0.06 |
| P16 | 1.00 | 0.05 | | 1.00 | 0.53 | 0.53 |
| P15 | 1.00 | 0.05 | | | 0.48 | 0.11 |
| P14 | 1.00 | 0.05 | | | 0.37 | 0.12 |
| P13 | 1.00 | 0.05 | | | 0.48 | 0.22 |
| P12 | 1.00 | 0.05 | | | 0.36 | 0.02 |
| P11 | 1.00 | 0.05 | | | 0.41 | 0.22 |
| P10 | 1.00 | 0.05 | | | 0.43 | 0.24 |
| P9 | 1.00 | 0.05 | 1.00 | | 0.54 | 0.54 |
| P8 | 1.00 | 0.05 | | | 0.45 | 0.45 |
| P7 | 1.00 | 0.05 | | | 0.39 | 0.04 |
| P6 | 1.00 | 0.05 | | | 0.37 | 0.03 |
| P5 | 1.00 | 0.05 | | | 0.40 | 0.13 |
| P4 | 1.00 | 0.05 | | | 0.41 | 0.08 |
| P3 | 1.00 | 0.05 | | | 0.47 | 0.47 |
| P2 | 1.00 | 0.05 | | | 0.40 | 0.22 |
| P1 | 1.00 | 0.05 | | 1.00 | 0.46 | 0.46 |

Table 1: Weights assigned to pseudo-terms in Figure 3 by each retrieval model (zero values shown as blank).

One risk with the Sa model is that including shorter terms may add more noise than signal. Another method of dealing with alternatives in the cross-language IR literature is to somehow select a single term from the set. For our experiments with this technique, only the longest pseudo-term from an overlapping set is retained; all other ("nested") pseudo-terms are simply deleted from the query. The thinking behind this is that the longest term should contain the greatest amount of information. This method is coded U1.

### 4.4 Length Measure of Specificity (UaW, SaW)

The U1 and Sa models are two extremes on a spectrum of possibilities; thus, models in which some pseudo-terms receive less weight, rather than being ignored entirely, were also explored. Care must be taken, however, to do so in a way that emphasizes coverage rather than nesting depth: more weight should not be given to some region in a query or a response just because it is deeply nested (indicating extreme uncertainty). Both the U1 and Sa models do this, but in a rather unnuanced manner. For a more nuanced approach, inspiration can be found in techniques from cross-language IR that give more weight to some term choices than to others.

Our basic approach is to downweight terms that are dominated temporally by several other terms, where the amount of downweighting is proportional to the number of terms that cover it. This is implemented by adjusting the contribution of each pseudo-term based on the extent of its overlap with other pseudo-terms. This could be done in a way that would give the greatest weight to either the shortest or the longest nested pseudo-term.

Formally, let $T = \{t_1, t_2, \ldots, t_n\}$ be the nested term class, ordered by term length. Let $l(t_i)$ denote the length of term $t_i$, in seconds. Further, let

$$w(t_i) = \frac{\alpha \times l(t_i)}{1 + \alpha \times l(t_i)}$$

be the weight of term $t_i$, where $\alpha$ is a free parameter. For our experiments, $\alpha = 0.5$. The *discounted weight* is

$$d(t_i) = \begin{cases} w(t_i) & i = 1 \\ w(t_i) \times \prod_{j=1}^{i-1} (1 - w(t_j)) & \text{otherwise,} \end{cases}$$

where $t_j$ refers, implicitly, to other members of $T$. The factor $1 - w(t_i)$ is used to discount the weight of $t_i$ due to the contribution made by the previous term(s). We assume $T$ to be in descending order and define two heuristics: *total weight discounted* (UaW) and *longest weight discounted* (SaW). The former uses Indri's `weight` operator to specify term weights at query time; the latter uses `wsyn`.

### 4.5 Coverage Measure of Descriptiveness (Un)

Recall Figure 3, a visual display of pseudo-term overlap within an arbitrary region of speech. Outside of the bounds of that figure there is either silence—no terms to describe a particular segment of time—or a region of terms that describe some other utterance within the overall speech. Of particular note, however, is that within the bounds there are a potentially large number of terms that can be used to *describe* a region of speech. Thus, the larger the number of terms present, the larger the amount of redundancy in the segment of speech each term describes. This observation motivates our final query methodology: removing redundancy within a region by extracting a seemingly descriptive subset of terms from that region. Here we begin to move beyond the ideas inspired by cross-language IR.

Specifically, we posit that an optimal subset contains the beginning and ending terms of the region, along with a series of intra-terms that connect the two. It is with this logic that the *unweighted shortest path* (coded Un) was conceived. Un attempts to find the subset that captures the most information using the smallest number of terms. Formally, consider a directed graph in which the set of vertexes is the set of pseudo-terms within an overlapping region. For an arbitrary pair of vertexes, $u, v \in V$, there is an outgoing edge from $u$ to $v$ if $y(u) \geq x(v)$, where $x(\cdot)$ and $y(\cdot)$ denote the start and end time, respectively, of a given pseudo-term. Further, the weight of such an edge is the difference between these times: $w(u, v) = y(u) - x(v)$. Note that an edge between $u$ and $v$ does not exist if they have the same start time, $x(u) = x(v)$.

Let $\hat{u}$ and $\hat{v}$ be the endpoints of the graph; that is, for all $u, v \in P$, $x(\hat{u}) \leq x(u)$, and $y(\hat{v}) \geq y(v)$. Our objective is to find the shortest path from $\hat{u}$ to $\hat{v}$ that minimizes the standard deviation of the edge weights. Minimizing standard deviation results in a set of terms with more uniform overlaps.

## 5 Building a Test Collection

The test collection was built using actual spoken content from the Avaj Otalo (Patel et al., 2010) "speech forum," an information service that was regularly used by a select group of farmers in Gujarat. These farmers spoke Gujarati, a language native to western parts of India and spoken by more than 65 million people worldwide. Most of the farmers knew no other language, and approximately 30 per cent were unable to read or write. The idea was to provide a resource for the local farming community to exchange ideas and have their questions answered. To this end, farmers would call into an Interactive Voice Response (IVR) system and peruse answers to existing questions, or would pose their own questions for the community. Other farmers would call into the system to leave answers to those questions. On occasion, there were also a small group of system administrators who would periodically call in to leave announcements that they expected would be of interest to the broader farming community. The system was completely automated—no human intervention or call center was involved.

Avaj Otalo's recorded speech was divided into 50 *queries* and 2,999 *responses*. Queries were statements on a particular topic, sometimes phrased as a question, sometimes phrased as an announcement. Responses were sometimes answers to questions, sometimes they were related announcements, and sometimes they were questions on a similar topic. This represented approximately two-thirds of the total audio present in the system. Very short recordings were omitted, as were those in which little speech activity was automatically detected. The average length of a query is approximately 70 seconds ($SD$ = 14.40s), or approximately 61 seconds ($SD$ = 15.76s) after automated silence removal. Raw response lengths averaged 110 seconds ($SD = 88.80$s), and 96.52 seconds ($SD = 82.75$s) after silence was removed.

### 5.1 Relevance Judgments and Evaluation

Pools for judgment were formed by combining the results from every system reported in our results section below, along with several other systems that yielded less interesting results that we omit for space reasons. Three native speakers of Gujarati performed relevance assessment; none of the three had any role in system development. Relevance assessment was performed by listening to the audio and making a graded relevance judgment. Assessors could assign one of the following judgments for each response: 1) unable to assess, 2) not relevant, 3) relevant, and 4) highly relevant.

For evaluation measures that require binary judgments, and for computing inter-annotator agreement, the relevance judgments were subsequently binarized by removing all the unassessable cases. Highly relevant and relevant responses were then collapsed into a single relevant category. To compute NDCG, relevant and highly relevant categories were assigned the scores 1 and 2, respectively, while non-relevant judgments retained a score of 0. Three rounds of relevance assessments were conducted as query models were developed and assessor agreement was characterized.

| | Retrieval Model | | | | | |
|---|---|---|---|---|---|---|
| | U1 | Un | Ua | UaW | Sa | SaW |
| MRR | 0.447 | 0.281 | 0.169 | 0.204 | 0.235 | 0.432 |
| | 0.139 | 0.071 | 0.081 | 0.089 | 0.242 | 0.075 |
| | 0.188 | 0.104 | 0.109 | 0.193 | 0.252 | 0.105 |
| MAP | 0.106* | 0.057 | 0.047 | 0.060* | 0.058 | 0.111 |
| | 0.023 | 0.011 | 0.015 | 0.018 | 0.050 | 0.010 |
| | 0.045 | 0.013 | 0.018 | 0.050 | 0.058 | 0.022 |
| NDCG | 0.237 | 0.216 | 0.206 | 0.219 | 0.214 | 0.284* |
| | 0.122 | 0.098* | 0.187 | 0.195 | 0.243 | 0.194 |
| | 0.142 | 0.089* | 0.219 | 0.191 | 0.285 | 0.230 |

Table 2: Results for pure (top), medium (middle) and noisy (bottom) clustering for the 10 queries for which more than one relevant response is known. Shaded cells are best-performers, per measure; starred values indicate NDCG or MAP is significantly better or worse than same-row Ua (two-sided paired $t$-test, $p < 0.05$).

## 6 Results

Each retrieval model was run for each of the three clustering results. For each method, there were three metrics of interest: normalized discounted cumulative gain (NDCG), mean reciprocal rank (MRR), and mean average precision (MAP). Results are outlined in Table 2. To limit the effect of quantization noise on the evaluation measures, results are reported for queries having three or more relevant documents. There were a total of 10 such queries, having a total of 61 relevant documents and yielding an average of 6.10 documents per query ($SD = 2.13$).

Low baselines for each evaluation were established—as there were none in prior existence by randomly sampling 60 documents from the test collection. For each of the six randomly selected topics, 10 of the 60 randomly selected documents were add to the judgment pool without replacement.

Relevance judgments were performed in an order that obscured, from the assessor, the source of the response being judged. The 10 random selections were then evaluated for each of the six topics as if they had been a system run. None of the 60 randomly selected documents were judged by assessors to be relevant to their respective randomly selected topic; thus the random baseline for each of our measures is zero. Without multiple draws, confidence intervals on this value cannot be established. However, we are confident that random baselines even as high as 0.1 for any of our measures would be surprising.

Pure clustering produced the best results with respect to other clustering domains. SaW was, generally, the best performing retrieval model. Although SaW did not produce the highest pure cluster MRR numbers, it was within 0.015 of U1, the best performing method. This is notable given that the difference between U1 and the third best method was 0.166. Further, given the highly quantized nature of MRR, a difference of 0.015 says little about any overall difference between the rankings. In the case of NDCG, SaW was the best performer with pure clustering, significantly better than BoW with pure clustering and second best overall. Sa with noisy clustering was best numerically with NDCG, but the difference is minuscule (1/1000th).

Under pure clustering, Ua was generally the worst performer. Thus, query refinement using the temporal extent of pseudo-terms is a good idea. Further, the MRR of U1 and SaW both approach one-half. Since MRR is the inverse of the harmonic mean of the rank, we can interpret this as meaning that it is likely that a user will get a relevant document somewhere in the first three positions of the result set. Such a result is encouraging, as it means that, under the correct conditions, a retrieval system built using zero-resource term detection is a potentially useful tool in practice. We should note, however, that this result was obtained for result-rich queries in which three or more relevant responses were known to exist; MRR results on needle-in-a-haystack queries for which only a single relevance response exists would likely be lower. As with all search, precision-biased measures benefit from collection richness.

## 7 Conclusions and Future Work

Recent advances in zero-resource term discovery have facilitated spoken document retrieval without the need for traditional transcription or ASR. There are still open questions, however, as to best practices around building useful IR systems on top of these tools. This work has been a step in filling that void. The results show that these zero-resource methods can be used to find relevant responses, and that in some cases such relevant responses can also be highly ranked. Retrieval results vary depending on how much redundancy exists in the transcribed data, and how that redundancy is handled within the query. One common theme, at least for the techniques that we have explored, is that pure clustering seems to be the best overall choice when ranked retrieval is the goal. A promising next step is to look to techniques from speech retrieval for insights that might be applicable to the zero-resource setting. One possibility in this regard is to explore extending the zero-resource term matching techniques to generate a lattice representation from which expected pseudo-term counts could be computed.

## 8 Acknowledgments

The authors wish to thank Nitendra Rajput for providing the spoken queries and responses, and for early discussions about evaluation design; Komal Kamdar, Dhwani Patel, and Yash Patel for performing relevance assessments; and Nizar Habash for his insightful comments on early drafts. Thanks is also extended to the anonymous reviewers for their comments and suggestions. This work has been supported in part by NSF award 1218159.

## References

Alberto Abad and Ramón Fernandez Astudillo. 2012. The L2F spoken web search system. In *MediaEval*.

Xavier Anguera, Florian Metze, Andi Buzo, Igor Szöke, and Luis Javier Rodríguez-Fuentes. 2013. The spoken web search task. In *MediaEval*.

Michael Bendersky and W. Bruce Croft. 2008. Discovering key concepts in verbose queries. In *Proceedings of the 31st Annual International ACM SIGIR Conference on Research and Development in Rnformation Retrieval*, pages 491–498.

Michael Bendersky, Donald Metzler, and W. Bruce Croft. 2010. Learning concept importance using a weighted dependence model. In *Proceedings of the Third ACM International Conference on Web Search and Data Mining*, pages 31–40.

Michael Bendersky, Donald Metzler, and W. Bruce Croft. 2011. Parameterized concept weighting in verbose queries. In *Proceedings of the 34th International ACM SIGIR Conference on Research and Development in Information Retrieval*, pages 605–614.

Chun-an Chan, Cheng-Tao Chung, Yu-Hsin Kuo, and Lin shan Lee. 2013. Toward unsupervised model-based spoken term detection with spoken queries without annotated data. In *International Conference on Acoustics, Speech and Signal Processing*, pages 8550–8554, May.

Jia Cui, Xiaodong Cui, B. Ramabhadran, J. Kim, B. Kingsbury, J. Mamou, L. Mangu, M. Picheny, T.N. Sainath, and A. Sethy. 2013. Developing speech recognition systems for corpus indexing under the IARPA Babel program. In *International Conference on Acoustics, Speech and Signal Processing*, pages 6753–6757, May.

Mark Drezde, Aren Jansen, Glen Coppersmith, and Ken Church. 2010. NLP on spoken documents without ASR. In *Conference on Empirical Methods on Natural Language Processing*, pages 460–470.

Jonathan Fiscus, Jerome Ajot, John Garofolo, and George Doddington. 2007. Results of the 2006 spoken term detection evaluation. In *SIGIR Workshop on Searching Spontaneous Conversational Speech*, pages 51–57.

Mark Gales, Kate Knill, Anton Ragni, and Shakti Rath. 2014. Speech recognition and keyword spotting for low resource languages: Babel project research at CUED. In *Spoken Language Technologies for Under-Resourced Languages*.

Aren Jansen and Benjamin Van Durme. 2011. Efficient spoken term discovery using randomized algorithms. In *Automatic Speech Recognition and Understanding*.

Aren Jansen, Kenneth Church, and Hynek Hermansky. 2010. Towards spoken term discovery at scale with zero resources. In *Interspeech Conference*, pages 1676–1679.

Aren Jansen, Benjamin Van Durme, and Pascal Clark. 2012. The JHU-HLTCOE spoken web search system for MediaEval. In *MediaEval*.

Hardik Joshi and Jerome White. 2014. Document similarity amid automatically detected terms. Forum for Information Retrieval Evaluation, December.

Matthew Lease. 2009. An improved Markov random field model for supporting verbose queries. In *Proceedings of the 32nd International ACM SIGIR Conference on Research and Development in Information Retrieval*, pages 476–483.

Florian Metze, Nitendra Rajput, Xavier Anguera, Marelie Davel, Guillaume Gravier, Charl van Heerden, Gautam Mantena, Armando Muscariello, Kishore Prahallad, Igor Szoke, and Javier Tejedor. 2012. The spoken web search task at MediaEval 2011. In *International Conference on Acoustics, Speech and Signal Proccessing*, pages 3487–3491.

Douglas Oard, Jerome White, Jiaul Paik, Rashmi Sankepally, and Aren Jansen. 2013. The FIRE 2013 question answering for the spoken web task. Forum for Information Retrieval Evaluation, December.

Douglas W. Oard. 2012. Query by babbling: A research agenda. In *Workshop on Information and Knowledge Management for Developing Regions*, pages 17–22.

Alex Park and James R. Glass. 2008. Unsupervised pattern discovery in speech. *Transactions on Audio, Speech, and Language Processing*, 16(1):186–197.

Neil Patel, Deepti Chittamuru, Anupam Jain, Paresh Dave, and Tapan S. Parikh. 2010. Avaaj Otalo: A field study of an interactive voice forum for small farmers in rural India. In *Human Factors in Computing Systems*, pages 733–742.

Nitendra Rajput and Florian Metze. 2011. Spoken web search. In *MediaEval*.

Amanda Spink, Dietman Wolfram, Bernard Jansen, and Tefko Saracevic. 2001. Searching the Web: The public and their queries. *Journal of the American Society for Information Science and Technology*, 52(3):226–234.

Trevor Strohman, Donald Metzler, Howard Turtle, and W. Bruce Croft. 2004. Indri: A language model-based search engine for complex queries. In *International Conference on Intelligence Analysis*.

Krysta Svore, Pallika Kanani, and Nazan Khan. 2010. How good is a span of terms? exploiting proximity to improve Web retrieval. In *Proceedings of the 33rd International ACM SIGIR Conference on Research and Development in Information Retrieval*, pages 154–161.

Jerome White, Douglas W. Oard, Nitendra Rajput, and Marion Zalk. 2013. Simulating early-termination search for verbose spoken queries. In *Empirical Methods on Natural Language Processing*, pages 1270–1280.

# Constraint-Based Models of Lexical Borrowing

**Yulia Tsvetkov   Waleed Ammar   Chris Dyer**
Language Technologies Institute
Carnegie Mellon University
Pittsburgh, PA, 15213, USA
{ytsvetko, wammar, cdyer}@cs.cmu.edu

## Abstract

Linguistic borrowing is the phenomenon of transferring linguistic constructions (lexical, phonological, morphological, and syntactic) from a "donor" language to a "recipient" language as a result of contacts between communities speaking different languages. Borrowed words are found in all languages, and—in contrast to cognate relationships—borrowing relationships may exist across unrelated languages (for example, about 40% of Swahili's vocabulary is borrowed from Arabic). In this paper, we develop a model of morpho-phonological transformations across languages with features based on universal constraints from Optimality Theory (OT). Compared to several standard—but linguistically naïve—baselines, our OT-inspired model obtains good performance with only a few dozen training examples, making this a cost-effective strategy for sharing lexical information across languages.

## 1 Introduction

We may imagine that globalization is a modern phenomenon, but the lexicons of the world's languages attest to the fact that robust interaction between communities of speakers of different languages is widespread throughout history. Language contact breeds *linguistic borrowing*—a phenomenon as old as language itself—adoption and nativization of phonemes, morphemes, words, and syntactic constructions from another language (Thomason and Kaufman, 2001).

Contact-induced borrowing is a fundamental research topic in linguistics; however, in computational linguistics, very limited work has addressed modeling this phenomenon. The problem we address is the identification of plausible donor words (in the donor language) given a loanword (in the recipient language), and vice versa, identification of loanwords given a donor. For example, given a Swahili loanword *safari* 'journey', our model identifies its Arabic donor سفرية (*sfryh*)[1] 'journey' (§2). Although at a high level, this is an instance of the well-known problem of modeling string transductions, our interest is being able to identify correspondences across languages with minimal supervision, so as to make the technique applicable in low-resource settings. To reduce the supervision burden, we propose a model that includes awareness of the morpho-phonological repair strategies that native speakers of a language subconsciously employ to adapt a loanword to phonological constraints of the recipient language (§3). To this end, we use constraint-based theories of phonology, as exemplified by Optimality Theory (OT) (Prince and Smolensky, 2008; McCarthy, 2009), which non-computational linguistic work has demonstrated to be particularly well suited to account for phonologically complex borrowing processes (Kang, 2011). We operationalize OT constraints as features in our borrowing model (§4).

We conduct a case study on Arabic and Swahili, two unrelated languages with a long history of contact; we then apply the model to additional language pairs (§5). The proposed approach significantly outperforms transliteration and cognate discovery models (§6).

[1] We use Buckwalter notation to write Arabic glosses.



*Human Language Technologies: The 2015 Annual Conference of the North American Chapter of the ACL*, pages 598–608,
Denver, Colorado, May 31 – June 5, 2015. 

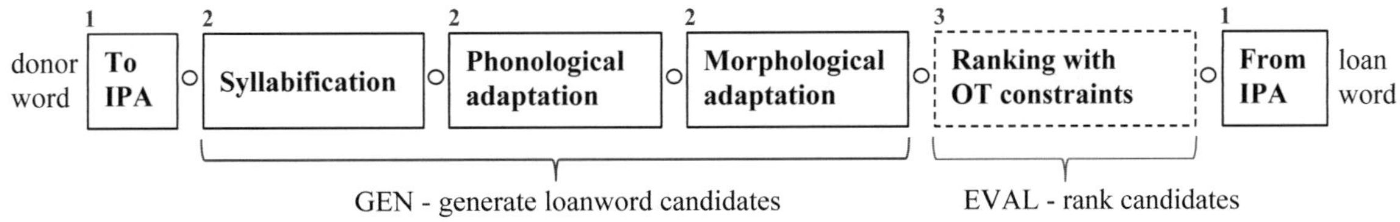


**Figure 1:** Our morpho-phonological borrowing model conceptually has three main parts: (1) conversion of orthographic word forms to pronunciations in IPA format; (2) generation of loanword pronunciation candidates; (3) ranking of generated candidates using Optimality-Theoretic constraints. Part (1) and (2) are rule-based, (1) uses pronunciation dictionaries, (2) is based on prior linguistic studies; part (3) is learned. In (3) we learn OT constraint weights from a few dozen automatically extracted training examples.

## 2 Methodology

Our task is to identify plausible donor–loan word pairs in a language pair. While modeling string transductions is a well-studied problem in NLP, we wish to be able to learn the cross-lingual correspondences from minimal amounts of data, so we propose a linguistically-motivated approach: we formulate a scoring model inspired by Optimality Theory (OT; discussed below), in which borrowing candidates are ranked by universal constraints posited to underly the human faculty of language, and the candidates are determined by transduction processes articulated in prior studies of contact linguistics.

As shown in figure 1, our model is conceptually divided into three main parts: (1) mapping of orthographic word forms in two languages into a common space of their phonetic representation; (2) generation of loanword pronunciation candidates from a donor word; (3) ranking of generated loanword candidates, based on linguistic constraints of the donor and recipient languages. Parts (1) and (2) are rule-based; whereas (3) is learned. Each component of the model is discussed in detail in the following sections.

The model is implemented within a finite-state cascade. Parts (1) and (2) amount to unweighted string transformation operations. In (1), we convert orthographic word forms to their pronunciations in the International Phonetic Alphabet (IPA), these are pronunciation transducers. In (2) we syllabify donor pronunciations, then perform insertion, deletion, and substitution of phonemes and morphemes (affixes), to generate multiple loanword candidates from a donor word. Although string transformation transducers in (2) can generate loanword candidates that are not found in a recipient language vocabulary, such candidates are filtered out due to composition with the recipient language lexicon acceptor.

We perform string transformations from donor to recipient (recapitulating the historical process). However, the resulting relation (i.e., the final composed transducer) is a bidirectional model which can just as well be used to reason about underlying donor forms given recipient forms. To employ the model in a specific direction, one needs to optimize parameters—weights on transitions—to generate a desired set of outputs from a specific input. Our model is trained to discriminate a donor word given a loanword. In part (3), candidates are "evaluated" (i.e., scored) with a weighted sum of universal constraint violations. The non-negative weights, which we call "cost vector", constitute our model parameters and are learned using a small training set of donor–recepient pairs. We use a shortest path algorithm to find the path with the minimal cost.

**OT: constraint-based evaluation** Our decision to evaluate borrowing candidates by weighting counts of "constraint violations" is based on Optimality Theory, which has shown that complex surface phenomena can be well-explained as the interaction of constraints on the form of outputs and the relationships of inputs and outputs (Kager, 1999). Although our linear scoring scheme departs from OT's standard evaluation assumptions (namely, the assumption of an ordinal constraint ranking and strict dominance rather than constraint "weighting"), we are still able to obtain effective models.

Although originally a theory of monolingual phonology, OT has been adapted to account for borrowing by treating the donor language word as the underlying form for the recipient language; that is, the phonological system of the recipient language is encoded as a system of constraints, and these constraints account for how the donor word is adapted when borrowed. There has been substantial prior work in linguistics on borrowing in the OT paradigm (Yip, 1993; Davidson and Noyer, 1997; Jacobs and Gussenhoven, 2000; Kang, 2003; Broselow, 2004; Adler, 2006; Rose and Demuth, 2006; Kenstowicz and Suchato, 2006; Kenstowicz, 2007; Mwita, 2009), but none of it has led to computational realizations.

## 3 Generating loanword candidates

In this section, we use the Arabic–Swahili language-pair to describe the prototypical linguistic adaptation processes that words undergo when borrowed. Then, we describe how we model these processes.[2]

### 3.1 Case study: Arabic–Swahili borrowing

The Swahili lexicon has been influenced by Arabic due to a prolonged period of language contact in the Indian Ocean trading (800 A.D.–1920), as well as the influence of Islam (Rothman, 2002). According to several independent studies, Arabic loanwords constitute from 18% (Hurskainen, 2004) to 40% (Johnson, 1939) of Swahili word types.

Despite a strong susceptibility of Swahili to borrowing and a large fraction of Swahili words originating from Arabic, the two languages are typologically distinct with profoundly dissimilar phonological and morpho-syntactic systems. Therefore, Arabic loanwords have been substantially adapted to conform to Swahili phonotactics, which we survey briefly. First, Arabic has five syllable patterns:[3] CV, CVV, CVC, CVCC, and CVVC (McCarthy, 1985, pp. 23–28), whereas Swahili (like other Bantu languages) is characterized by the syllable ending with a vowel and CV or V syllable structure. At the segment level, Swahili loanword adaptation thus involves extensive vowel epenthesis in consonant clusters and at a syllable final position if the syllable ends with a consonant, e.g., : كتاب (*ktAb*) → *kitabu* 'book' (Polomé, 1967; Schadeberg, 2009; Mwita, 2009). Second, phonological adaptation in Swahili loanwords includes shortening of vowels (unlike Arabic, Swahili does not have phonemic length); substitution of consonants that are found in Arabic but not in Swahili (e.g., emphatic (pharyngealized) /tˤ/→/t/, voiceless velar fricative /x/→/k/, dental fricatives /θ/→/s/, /ð/→/z/, and the voiced velar fricative /ɣ/→/g/); adoption of Arabic phonemes that were not originally present in Swahili /θ/, /ð/, /ɣ/ (e.g., تحذير (*tH*yr*)→ *tahadhari* 'warning'); degemination of Arabic geminate consonants (e.g., شرّ (*$r~*)→ *shari* 'evil'). Finally, adapted loanwords can freely undergo Swahili inflectional and derivational processes, e.g., الوزير (*Alwzyr*) → *waziri* 'minister', *mawaziri* 'ministers', *kiuwaziri* 'ministerial' (Zawawi, 1979; Schadeberg, 2009).

### 3.2 Arabic–Swahili borrowing transducers

We describe unweighted transducers for pronunciation, syllabification, and morphological and phonological adaptation. An example that illustrates some of the possible string transformations by individual components of the model is shown in figure 2. The goal of these transducers is to minimally overgenerate Swahili adapted forms of Arabic words, based on the adaptations described above.

**Pronunciation.** Based on the IPA, we assign shared symbols to sounds that exist in both sound systems of Arabic and Swahili (e.g., nasals /n/, /m/; voiced stops /b/, /d/), and language-specific unique symbols to sounds that are unique to the phonemic inventory of Arabic (e.g., pharyngeal voiced and voiceless fricatives /ħ/, /ʕ/) or Swahili (e.g., velar nasal /ŋ/). For Swahili, we construct a pronunciation dictionary based on the Omniglot grapheme-to-IPA mapping.[4] In Arabic, we use the CMU Arabic vowelized pronunciation dictionary containing about 700K types which has an average of four pronunciations per word (Metze et al., 2010).[5] We then design four transducers—Arabic and Swahili word-to-IPA and IPA-to-word transducers—each as a union of linear chain transducers, as well as one acceptor per pronunciation dictionary listing.

[2] For simplicity, we subsume Omani Arabic and other historical dialects of Arabic under the label "Arabic"; similarly, we subsume Swahili, its dialects and protolanguages under "Swahili".

[3] C stands for consonant, and V for vowel.

[4] www.omniglot.com

[5] Since we are working at the level of word types which have no context, we cannot disambiguate the intended form, so we include all options. For example, for the input word كتابا (*ktAbA*) 'book.sg.indef', we use both pronunciations /kitɑbɑ/ and /kuttɑbɑ/.

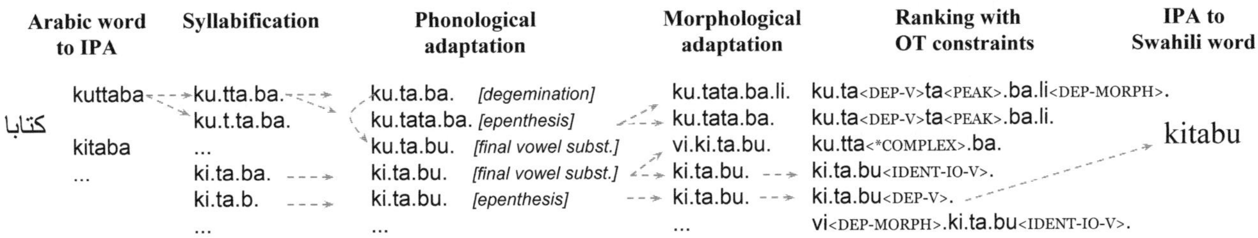


**Figure 2:** An example of an Arabic word كتابا (*ktAbA*) 'book.sg.indef' transformed by our model into a Swahili loanword *kitabu*.

**Syllabification.** Arabic words borrowed into Swahili undergo a repair of violations of the Swahili segmental and phonotactic constraints, for example via vowel epenthesis in a consonant cluster. Importantly, *repair depends upon syllabification.* To simulate plausible phonological repair processes, we generate multiple syllabification variants for input pronunciations. The syllabification transducer optionally inserts syllable separators between phones. For example, for an input phonetic sequence /kuttɑbɑ/, the output strings include /ku.t.tɑ.bɑ/, /kut.tɑ.bɑ/, and /ku.ttɑ.bɑ/ as syllabification variants; each variant violates different constraints and consequently triggers different phonological adaptation.

**Phonological adaptation.** Phonological adaptation of syllabified phone sequences is the crux of the loanword adaptation process. We implement phonological adaptation transducers as a composition of plausible context-dependent insertions, deletions, and substitutions of phone subsets, based on prior studies summarized in §3.1. In what follows, we list phonological adaptation components in the order of transducer composition in the borrowing model. The **vowel deletion** transducer shortens Arabic long vowels and vowel clusters. The **consonant degemination** transducer shortens Arabic geminate consonants, e.g., it degeminates /tt/ in /ku.ttɑ.bɑ/, outputting /ku.tɑ.bɑ/. The **substitution of similar phonemes** transducer substitutes similar phonemes and phonemes that are found in Arabic but not in Swahili (Polomé, 1967, p. 45). For example, the emphatic /tˤ/, /dˤ/, /sˤ/ are replaced by the corresponding non-emphatic segments [t], [d], [s]. The **vowel epenthesis** transducer inserts a vowel between pairs of consonants (/ku.ttɑ.bɑ/ → /ku.tatɑ.bɑ/), and at the end of a syllable, if the syllable ends with a consonant (/ku.t.tɑ.bɑ/ → /ku.ta.tɑ.bɑ/). Sometimes it is possible to predict the final vowel of a word, depending on the word-final coda consonant of its Arabic counterpart: /u/ or /o/ added if an Arabic donor ends with a labial, and /i/ or /e/ added after coronals and dorsals (Mwita, 2009). Following these rules, the **final vowel substitution** transducer complements the inventory of final vowels in loanword candidates.

**Morphological adaptation.** Both Arabic and Swahili have significant morphological processes that alter the appearance of lemmas. To deal with morphological variants, we construct morphological adaptation transducers that optionally strip Arabic concatenative affixes and clitics, and then optionally append Swahili affixes, generating a superset of all possible loanword hypotheses. We obtain the list of Arabic affixes from the Arabic morphological analyzer SAMA (Maamouri et al., 2010); the Swahili affixes are taken from a hand-crafted Swahili morphological analyzer (Littell et al., 2014).

## 4 Learning constraint weights

Due to the computational problems of working with OT (Eisner, 1997; Eisner, 2002), we make simplifying assumptions by (1) bounding the theoretically infinite set of underlying forms with a small linguistically-motivated subset of allowed transformations on donor pronunciations, as described in §3; (2) imposing a priori restrictions on the set of the surface realizations by intersecting the candidate set with the recipient pronunciation lexicon; (3) assuming that the set of constraints is finite and regular (Ellison, 1994); and (4) assigning linear weights to constraints, rather than learning an ordinal constraint ranking (Boersma and Hayes, 2001; Goldwater and

**Faithfulness constraints**

| | |
|---|---|
| MAX-IO-MORPH | no (donor) affix deletion |
| MAX-IO-C | no consonant deletion |
| MAX-IO-V | no vowel deletion |
| DEP-IO-MORPH | no (recipient) affix epenthesis |
| DEP-IO-V | no vowel epenthesis |
| IDENT-IO-C | no consonant substitution |
| IDENT-IO-C-M | no subst. in manner of pronunciation |
| IDENT-IO-C-A | no subst. in place of articulation |
| IDENT-IO-C-S | no subst. in sonority |
| IDENT-IO-C-P | no pharyngeal consonant substitution |
| IDENT-IO-C-G | no glottal consonant substitution |
| IDENT-IO-C-E | no emphatic consonant substitution |
| IDENT-IO-V | no vowel substitution |
| IDENT-IO-V-O | no subst. in vowel openness |
| IDENT-IO-V-R | no subst. in vowel roundness |
| IDENT-IO-V-F | no subst. in vowel frontness |
| IDENT-IO-V-FIN | no final vowel substitution |

**Table 1:** Faithfulness constraints prefer pronounced realizations completely congruent with their underlying forms.

Johnson, 2003).

OT distinguishes "markedness" constraints (McCarthy and Prince, 1995), which detect dispreferred phonetic patterns in the language, and "faithfulness" constraints (Prince and Smolensky, 2008), which ensure correspondences between the underlying form and the surface candidates.[6] The implemented constraints are listed in tables 1 and 2. Faithfulness constraints are integrated in phonological transformation components as transitions following each insertion, deletion, or substitution. Markedness constraints are implemented as standalone identity transducers: inputs are equal outputs, but path weights representing candidate evaluation with respect to violated constraints are different.

The final "loanword transducer" is the composition of all transducers described in §3 and OT constraint transducers. A path in the transducer represents a syllabified phonemic sequence along with (weighted)

[6]To clarify the distinction between faithfulness and markedness constraint groups to the NLP readership, we can draw the following analogy to the components of machine translation or speech recognition: faithfulness constraints are analogical to the translation model or acoustic model (reflecting input), while markedness constraints are analogical to the language model (requiring well-formedness of the output). Without faithfulness constraints, the optimal surface form could differ arbitrarily from the underlying form.

**Markedness constraints**

| | |
|---|---|
| NO-CODA | syllables must not have a coda |
| ONSET | syllables must have onsets |
| PEAK | there is only one syllabic peak |
| SSP | complex onsets rise in sonority, complex codas fall in sonority |
| *COMPLEX-S | no consonant clusters on syllable margins |
| *COMPLEX-C | no consonant clusters within a syllable |
| *COMPLEX-V | no vowel clusters |

**Table 2:** Markedness constraints impose language-specific structural well-formedness of surface realizations.

OT constraints it violates, and shortest path outputs are those, whose cumulative weight of violated constraints is minimal.

OT constraints are realized as features in our linear model, and feature weights are learned in a discriminative training to maximize the accuracy obtained by the loanword transducer on a small development set of donor–recipient pairs. For parameter estimation, we employ the Nelder–Mead algorithm (Nelder and Mead, 1965), a heuristic derivative-free method that iteratively optimizes, based on an objective function evaluation, the convex hull of $n+1$ simplex vertices.[7] The objective function is the "soft accuracy" of the development set, defined as the proportion of correctly identified donor words in the total set of 1-best outputs.

## 5 Adapting the model to a new language

Although we conduct a thorough case study on the Arabic–Swahili language pair, our methodology can easily be generalized to other language pairs. String transformation operations, as well as OT constraints are language-universal. The only adaptation required is a linguistic analysis to identify plausible morpho-phonological repair strategies for the new language pair (i.e., a subset of allowed insertions, deletions and substitutions of phonemes and morphemes). Since we need only to overgenerate candidates (the OT constraints will filter bad outputs), the effort is minimal relative to many other grammar engineering exercises. The second language-specific component is the grapheme-to-IPA converter. While this can be a non-

[7]The decision to use Nelder–Mead rather than more conventional gradient-based optimization algorithms was motivated by practical limitations of the finite-state toolkit we used that made computing derivatives with latent structure impractical.

trivial problem in some cases, the problem is well studied, and many under-resourced languages have "phonographic" systems where orthography corresponds to phonology, rather than organically evolved written forms, which makes the mapping problem trivial.

To illustrate the ease with which a language pair can be engineered, we applied our borrowing model to the French–Romanian language pair. Although French and Romanian are sister languages (both descending from Latin), about 12% of Romanian types are true French borrowings that came into the language in the past few centuries (Schulte, 2009). We employ the GLOBALPHONE pronunciation dictionary for French (Schultz and Schlippe, 2014) (we convert it to IPA), and automatically construct a Romanian pronunciation dictionary using Omniglot grapheme-to-IPA conversion rules.

## 6 Experiments

Our experimental setup is defined as follows. The input to the borrowing model is a loanword candidate in Swahili/Romanian,[8] the outputs are plausible donor words in the Arabic/French monolingual lexicon (i.e., any word in pronunciation dictionary). We train the borrowing model using a small set of training examples, and then evaluate it using a held-out test set. In the rest of this section we describe in detail our datasets, tools, and experimental results.

**Resources** We employ Arabic–English and Swahili–English bitexts to extract a training set (corpora of sizes 5.4M and 14K sentence pairs, respectively), using a cognate discovery technique (Kondrak, 2001). Phonetically and semantically similar strings are classified as cognates; phonetic similarity is the string similarity between phonetic representations, and semantic similarly is approximated by translation.[9] We thereby extract Arabic and Swahili pairs $\langle a, s\rangle$ that are phonetically similar ($\frac{\Delta(a,s)}{\min(|a|,|s|)} < 0.5$) where $\Delta(a, s)$ is the Levenshtein distance between $a$ and $s$ and that are aligned to the same English word $e$. FastAlign (Dyer et al., 2013) is used for word alignments. Given an extracted word pair $\langle a, s\rangle$, we also extract word pairs $\{\langle a', s\rangle\}$ for all proper Arabic words $a'$ which share the same lemma with $a$ producing on average 33 Arabic types per Swahili type. We use MADA (Habash et al., 2009) for Arabic morphological expansion.

From the resulting dataset of 490 extracted Arabic–Swahili borrowing examples,[10] we set aside randomly sampled 73 examples (15%) for evaluation,[11] and use the remaining 417 examples for model parameter optimization. For French–Romanian language pair, we use an existing small annotated set of borrowing examples,[12] with 282 training and 50 (15%) randomly sampled test examples.

We use `pyfst`—a Python interface to OpenFst (Allauzen et al., 2007)—for the borrowing model implementation.[13]

**Baselines** We compare our model to several baselines. In the Levenshtein (L) distance baselines we chose the closest word (either surface or pronunciation-based). In the Levenshtein-weighted (L-W) baselines, we evaluate a variant of the Levenshtein distance tuned to identify cognates (Mann and Yarowsky, 2001; Kondrak and Sherif, 2006); this method was identified by Kondrak and Sherif (2006) among the top three cognate identification methods. In the CRF baselines we generate plausible "transliterations" of the input Swahili (or Romanian) words in the donor lexicon using the model of Ammar et al. (2012), with multiple references in a lattice and without reranking. The CRF transliteration model is a linear-chain CRF where we label each source character with a sequence of target characters. The features are label unigrams, label bigrams, and label

[8]Our model does not provide a mechanism for identifying loanwords in the recipient language; we only model the borrowing process. Classifying loanwords in the recipient language is an interesting but ultimately different problem: the ontological status of words in a lexicon is a difficult problem, even for human experts, however, knowledge of cross-lingual correspondences is a valuable feature, and as such, our work can be understood as enabling this.

[9]This cognate discovery technique is sufficient to extract a small training set, but is not generally applicable, as it requires parallel corpora or manually constructed dictionaries to measure semantic similarity. Large parallel corpora are unavailable for most language pairs, including Swahili–English.

[10]In each training/test example one Swahili word corresponds to all extracted Arabic donor words.

[11]We manually verified that our test set contains clear Arabic–Swahili borrowings. For example, we extract Swahili *kusafiri, safari* and Arabic السفر, يسفر, سفر (*Alsfr, ysAfr, sfr*) all aligned to 'travel'.

[12]`http://wold.clld.org/vocabulary/8`

[13]`https://github.com/vchahun/pyfst`

conjoined with a moving window of source characters. In the OT-uniform baseline, we evaluate the accuracy of the borrowing model with uniform weights, thus shortest paths in the loanwords transducer will be forms violating the fewest constraints.

**Evaluation** In addition to predictive accuracy on all models (if a model produces multiple hypotheses with the same 1-best weight, we count the proportion of correct outputs in this set), we evaluate two particular aspects of our proposed model: (1) appropriateness of the model family, and (2) the quality of the learned OT constraint weights. The first aspect is designed to evaluate whether the morpho-phonological transformations implemented in the model are required *and* sufficient to generate loanwords from the donor inputs. We report two evaluation measures: model *reachability* and *ambiguity*. Reachability is a percentage of test samples that are reachable (i.e., there is a path from the input test example to a correct output) in the loanword transducer. A naïve model which generates all possible strings would score 100% reachability, but it will be hard to set the model parameters such that it discriminates between good and bad candidates. In order to capture this trade-off, we also report the inherent *ambiguity* of our model, which is the average number of outputs potentially generated per input. A generic Arabic–Swahili transducer, for example, has an ambiguity of 786,998—the size of the Arabic pronunciation lexicon.

**Results** The borrowing model reachability and ambiguity are listed in table 3. The model obtains high reachability, while significantly reducing the average number of possible outputs per input: in Arabic from 787K to 857 words, in French from 62K to 12. This result shows that the loanword transducer design, based on the prior linguistic analysis, is a plausible model of word borrowing. Yet, there are on average 33 correct Arabic words out of the possible 857 outputs, thus the second part of the model—OT constraint weights optimization—is crucial.

The accuracy results in table 4 show how challenging the task of modeling lexical borrowing between two distinct languages is, and importantly, that orthographic and phonetic baselines including the state-of-the-art generative model of transliteration are not suitable for this task. Phonetic baselines for Arabic–Swahili perform better than orthographic ones, but substantially worse than OT-based models, even if OT constraints are not weighted. Crucially, the performance of the borrowing model with the learned OT weights corroborates the assumption made in numerous linguistic accounts that OT is an adequate analysis of the lexical borrowing phenomenon.

| | AR–SW | FR–RO |
|---|---|---|
| Reachability | 87.7% | 82.0% |
| Ambiguity | 857 | 12 |

**Table 3:** The evaluation of the borrowing model design. Reachability is a percentage of donor–recipient pairs that are reachable from a donor to a recipient language. Ambiguity is an average number of outputs that the model generates per one input.

| | | Accuracy (%) | |
|---|---|---|---|
| | | AR–SW | FR–RO |
| Orthographic | L | 8.9 | 38.0 |
| | CRF | 16.4 | 36.0 |
| Phonetic | L | 19.8 | 26.3 |
| | L-W | 19.7 | 30.7 |
| OT | OT-U | 29.3 | 58.5 |
| | OT | **48.4** | **75.6** |

**Table 4:** The evaluation of the borrowing model accuracy. The baselines are orthographic (surface) and phonetic (based on pronunciation lexicon) Levenshtein distance (L), heuristic Levenshtein distance with lower penalty on vowel updates and similar letter/phone substitutions (L-W), CRF transliteration, and our model with uniform (OT-U) and learned OT constraint weights assignment.

**Qualitative evaluation** The constraint ranking learned by the borrowing model (constraints are listed in tables 1, 2) is in line with prior linguistic analysis. Space precludes a thorough discussion, but we highlight a few points. In Swahili NO-CODA dominates all other markedness constraints, as expected. Both *COMPLEX-S and *COMPLEX-C, restricting consonant clusters, dominate *COMPLEX-V, confirming that Swahili is more permissive to vowel clusters. SSP—sonority-based constraint—captures a common pattern of consonant clustering, found across languages, and is also learned by our model as undominated by most competitors in Swahili, and as a dominating markedness constraint in Romanian. Finally, vowel epenthesis DEP-IO-V is the most common strategy in Arabic loanword adaptation, and is ranked lower according to the model; however, it is ranked

| EN | AR gloss | AR pronunciation | SW syllabification | Violated OT constraints |
|---|---|---|---|---|
| book | ktAb | kitAb | ki.ta.bu. | IDENT-IO-C-G$\langle A, a\rangle$, DEP-IO-V$\langle \epsilon, u\rangle$ |
| palace | AlqSr | AlqaSr | ka.sri | MAX-IO-MORPH$\langle Al, \epsilon\rangle$, IDENT-IO-C-S$\langle q, k\rangle$, IDENT-IO-C-E$\langle S, s\rangle$, *COMPLEX-C$\langle sr\rangle$, DEP-IO-V$\langle \epsilon, i\rangle$ |
| wage | Ajrh | Aujrah | u.ji.ra. | MAX-IO-V$\langle A, \epsilon\rangle$, ONSET$\langle u\rangle$ , DEP-IO-V$\langle \epsilon, i\rangle$, MAX-IO-C$\langle h, \epsilon\rangle$ |

**Table 5:** Examples of syllabification and OT constraint violations produced by our borrowing model.

highly in the French–Romanian model, where vowel insertion is rare.

A second interesting by-product of our model is an inferred syllabification. While we did not conduct a systematic quantitative evaluation, higher-ranked Swahili outputs tend to contain linguistically plausible syllabifications, although the syllabification transducer inserts optional syllable boundaries between every pair of phones. This result further attests to the plausible constraint ranking learned by the model. Example Swahili syllabifications[14] along with the OT constraint violations produced by the borrowing model are depicted in table 5.

## 7 Discussion

The task of modeling borrowing is unexplored in computational linguistics. In this section we first situate the task with respect to two most closely related research directions: modeling transliteration and cognate forms. We then motivate the new line of research proposed in this work: modeling borrowing.

**Borrowing vs. transliteration** Borrowing is not transliteration. Transliteration refers to writing in a different *orthography*, whereas borrowing refers to *expanding a language* to include words adapted from another language. Unlike borrowing, transliteration is more amenable to orthographic—rather than morpho-phonological—features, although see (Knight and Graehl, 1998). Borrowed words might have begun as transliterations, but a characteristic of borrowed words is that they become assimilated in the linguistic system of the recipient language, and became regular content words, e.g., 'orange' and 'sugar' are English words borrowed from Arabic نارنج (*nArnj*) and السكر (*Alskr*), respectively.

[14]We chose examples from the Arabic–Swahili system because this is a more challenging case due to linguistic discrepancies.

**Borrowing vs. inheritance** Cognates are words in related languages inherited from one word in a common ancestral language (the proto-language). Loanwords, on the other hand, can occur between any languages, either related or not, that historically came into contact. Theoretical analysis of cognates has tended to be concerned with a diachronic point of view, i.e., modeling word changes across time. While of immense scientific interest, language processing applications are arguably better served by models of synchronic processes, peculiar to loanword analysis.

**Why borrowing?** Borrowing is a distinctive and pervasive phenomenon: *all* languages borrowed from other languages at some point in their lifetime, and borrowed words constitute a large fraction of most language lexicons. Another important property of borrowing is that in adaptation of borrowed items, changes in words are systematic, knowledge of morphological and phonological patterns in a language can be used to predict how borrowings will be realized in that language, without having to list them all. Therefore, modeling of borrowing is a task well-suited for computational approaches.

Our suggestion in this work is that we can identify borrowing relations between resource-limited languages and resource-rich donor languages, such as English, French, Spanish, Arabic, Chinese, and Russian. For example, 30–70% of the vocabulary in Vietnamese, Cantonese, and Thai—relatively resource-limited languages spoken by hundreds of millions of people—are borrowed from Chinese and English. Similarly, African languages have been greatly influenced by Arabic, Spanish, English, and French—widely spoken languages such as Swahili, Zulu, Malagasy, Hausa, Tarifit, Yoruba contain up to 40% of loanwords. Indo-Iranian languages—Hindustani, Hindi, Urdu, Bengali, Persian, Pashto—spoken by 860 million, also extensively borrowed from Arabic and English (Haspelmath and Tadmor, 2009). In short, at least a billion people are speaking resource-scarce languages whose lexicons are heavily borrowed from resource-rich languages.

Why is this important? Lexical translations or alignments extracted from large parallel corpora have been widely used to project annotations from high- to low-resource languages (Hwa et al., 2005; Täckström et al., 2013; Ganchev et al., 2009; Tsvetkov et al., 2014, *inter alia*). Unfortunately, parallel resources are unavailable for the majority of resource-limited languages. Loanwords can be used as a source of cross-lingual links complementary to lexical alignments. This holds promise for applying existing cross-lingual methods and bootstrapping linguistic resources in languages where no parallel data is available.

## 8 Related work

With the exception of a study conducted by Blair and Ingram (2003) on generation of borrowed phonemes in English–Japanese language pair (the method does not generalize from borrowed phonemes to borrowed words, and does not rely on linguistic insights), we are not aware of any prior work on computational modeling of lexical borrowing. Few papers only mention or tangentially address borrowing, we briefly list them here. Daumé III (2009) focuses on areal effects on linguistic typology, a broader phenomenon that includes borrowing and genetic relations across languages. This study is aimed at discovering language areas based on typological features of languages. Garley and Hockenmaier (2012) train a maxent classifier with character $n$-gram and morphological features to identify anglicisms (which they compare to loanwords) in an online community of German hip hop fans. List and Moran (2013) have published a toolkit for computational tasks in historical linguistics but remark that "Automatic approaches for borrowing detection are still in their infancy in historical linguistics."

Two related lines of research are transliteration and cognate identification. Knight and Graehl (1998), Al-Onaizan and Knight (2002) developed a finite-state generative model of transliteration, and successfully applied it to Arabic–English named entity translation. Mann and Yarowsky (2001) and Kondrak (2001) identify cognate pairs, based on the learned surface and phonetic similarities, respectively. As our experiments confirm, orthographic and phonetic transliteration and string edit distance methods are not adequate models for the complex borrowing phenomena.

## 9 Conclusion

Given a loanword, our model identifies plausible donor words in a contact language. We show that a discriminative model with Optimality Theoretic features effectively models systematic phonological changes in Arabic–Swahili loanwords. We also found that the model and methodology is generally applicable to other language pairs with minimal engineering effort.

This paper makes two contributions: (1) To the best of our knowledge, this is the first computational model of lexical borrowing. (2) While there are implementations of OT (Hayes et al., 2013), they are used chiefly to facilitate linguistic analysis.

There are numerous research questions that we would like to explore further. Is it possible to monolingually identify borrowed words in a language? Can we automatically identify a donor language (or its phonological properties) for a borrowed word? Since languages may borrow from many sources, can jointly modeling this process lead to better performance? Can we reduce the amount of language-specific engineering required to deploy our model? Can we integrate knowledge of borrowing in downstream NLP applications? We intend to address these questions in future work.

## Acknowledgments

This work was supported by the U.S. Army Research Laboratory and the U.S. Army Research Office under contract/grant number W911NF-10-1-0533. Computational resources were provided by Google in the form of a Google Cloud Computing grant and the NSF through the XSEDE program TG-CCR110017. We are grateful to Nathan Schneider, David Mortensen, Archna Bhatia, Shuly Wintner, Shay Cohen, David Bamman, Noah Smith, and Lori Levin for extensive discussions and constructive feedback.

## References


Allison N Adler. 2006. Faithfulness and perception in loanword adaptation: A case study from Hawaiian. *Lingua*, 116(7):1024–1045.

Yaser Al-Onaizan and Kevin Knight. 2002. Machine transliteration of names in Arabic text. In *Proc. of the ACL workshop on Computational Approaches to Semitic Languages*, pages 1–13.

Cyril Allauzen, Michael Riley, Johan Schalkwyk, Wojciech Skut, and Mehryar Mohri. 2007. OpenFst: A general and efficient weighted finite-state transducer library. In *Implementation and Application of Automata*, pages 11–23. Springer.

Waleed Ammar, Chris Dyer, and Noah A. Smith. 2012. Transliteration by sequence labeling with lattice encodings and reranking. In *Proc. of NEWS workshop at ACL*.

Alan D Blair and John Ingram. 2003. Learning to predict the phonological structure of English loanwords in Japanese. *Applied Intelligence*, 19(1-2):101–108.

Paul Boersma and Bruce Hayes. 2001. Empirical tests of the gradual learning algorithm. *Linguistic inquiry*, 32(1):45–86.

Ellen Broselow. 2004. Language contact phonology: richness of the stimulus, poverty of the base. In *Proc. of NELS*, volume 34, pages 1–22.

Hal Daumé III. 2009. Non-parametric Bayesian areal linguistics. In *Proc. of NAACL*, pages 593–601.

Lisa Davidson and Rolf Noyer. 1997. Loan phonology in Huave: nativization and the ranking of faithfulness constraints. In *Proc. of WCCFL*, volume 15, pages 65–79.

Chris Dyer, Victor Chahuneau, and Noah A. Smith. 2013. A simple, fast, and effective reparameterization of IBM Model 2. In *Proc. of NAACL*.

Jason Eisner. 1997. Efficient generation in primitive Optimality Theory. In *Proc. of EACL*, pages 313–320.

Jason Eisner. 2002. Comprehension and compilation in Optimality Theory. In *Proc. of ACL*, pages 56–63.

T Mark Ellison. 1994. Phonological derivation in Optimality Theory. In *Proc. of CICLing*, pages 1007–1013.

Kuzman Ganchev, Jennifer Gillenwater, and Ben Taskar. 2009. Dependency grammar induction via bitext projection constraints. In *Proc. of ACL*, pages 369–377.

Matt Garley and Julia Hockenmaier. 2012. Beefmoves: dissemination, diversity, and dynamics of English borrowings in a German hip hop forum. In *Proc. of ACL*, pages 135–139.

Sharon Goldwater and Mark Johnson. 2003. Learning OT constraint rankings using a maximum entropy model. In *Proc. of the Stockholm workshop on variation within Optimality Theory*, pages 111–120.

Nizar Habash, Owen Rambow, and Ryan Roth. 2009. MADA+TOKAN: A toolkit for Arabic tokenization, diacritization, morphological disambiguation, POS tagging, stemming and lemmatization. In *Proc. of MEDAR*, pages 102–109.

Martin Haspelmath and Uri Tadmor, editors. 2009. *Loanwords in the World's Languages: A Comparative Handbook*. Max Planck Institute for Evolutionary Anthropology, Leipzig.

Bruce Hayes, Bruce Tesar, and Kie Zuraw. 2013. OTSoft 2.3.2. *software package, http://www.linguistics.ucla.edu/people/hayes/otsoft*.

Arvi Hurskainen. 2004. Loan words in Swahili. In Katrin Bromber and Birgit Smieja, editors, *Globalisation and African Languages*, pages 199–218. Walter de Gruyter.

Rebecca Hwa, Philip Resnik, Amy Weinberg, Clara Cabezas, and Okan Kolak. 2005. Bootstrapping parsers via syntactic projection across parallel texts. *Natural Language Engineering*, 11(3).

Haike Jacobs and Carlos Gussenhoven. 2000. Loan phonology: perception, salience, the lexicon and OT. *Optimality Theory: Phonology, syntax, and acquisition*, pages 193–209.

Frederick Johnson. 1939. *Standard Swahili-English dictionary*. Oxford University Press.

René Kager. 1999. *Optimality Theory*. Cambridge University Press.

Yoonjung Kang. 2003. Perceptual similarity in loanword adaptation: English postvocalic word-final stops in Korean. *Phonology*, 20(2):219–274.

Yoonjung Kang. 2011. Loanword phonology. In Mark van Oostendorp, Colin Ewen, Elizabeth Hume, and Keren Rice, editors, *Companion to Phonology*. Wiley–Blackwell.

Michael Kenstowicz and Atiwong Suchato. 2006. Issues in loanword adaptation: A case study from Thai. *Lingua*, 116(7):921–949.

Michael Kenstowicz. 2007. Salience and similarity in loanword adaptation: a case study from Fijian. *Language Sciences*, 29(2):316–340.

Kevin Knight and Jonathan Graehl. 1998. Machine transliteration. *Computational Linguistics*, 24(4):599–612.

Grzegorz Kondrak and Tarek Sherif. 2006. Evaluation of several phonetic similarity algorithms on the task of cognate identification. In *Proc. of the Workshop on Linguistic Distances*, pages 43–50.

Grzegorz Kondrak. 2001. Identifying cognates by phonetic and semantic similarity. In *Proc. of NAACL*, pages 1–8.

Johann-Mattis List and Steven Moran. 2013. An open source toolkit for quantitative historical linguistics. In *Proc. of ACL (System Demonstrations)*, pages 13–18.

Patrick Littell, Kaitlyn Price, and Lori Levin. 2014. Morphological parsing of Swahili using crowdsourced lexical resources. In *Proc. of LREC*.

Mohamed Maamouri, Dave Graff, Basma Bouziri, Sondos Krouna, and Seth Kulick. 2010. LDC Standard Arabic morphological analyzer (SAMA) v. 3.1. *LDC Catalog No. LDC2010L01. ISBN*, pages 1–58563.

Gideon S Mann and David Yarowsky. 2001. Multipath translation lexicon induction via bridge languages. In *Proc. of HLT-NAACL*, pages 1–8.

John J McCarthy and Alan Prince. 1995. Faithfulness and reduplicative identity. *Beckman et al. (Eds.)*, pages 249–384.

John J McCarthy. 1985. *Formal problems in Semitic phonology and morphology*. Ph.D. thesis, MIT.

John J McCarthy. 2009. *Doing Optimality Theory: Applying theory to data*. John Wiley & Sons.

Florian Metze, Roger Hsiao, Qin Jin, Udhyakumar Nallasamy, and Tanja Schultz. 2010. The 2010 CMU GALE speech-to-text system. In *Proc. of INTERSPEECH*, pages 1501–1504.

Leonard Chacha Mwita. 2009. The adaptation of Swahili loanwords from Arabic: A constraint-based analysis. *Journal of Pan African Studies*.

John A Nelder and Roger Mead. 1965. A simplex method for function minimization. *Computer journal*, 7(4):308–313.

Edgar C Polomé. 1967. *Swahili Language Handbook*. ERIC.

Alan Prince and Paul Smolensky. 2008. *Optimality Theory: Constraint interaction in generative grammar*. John Wiley & Sons.

Yvan Rose and Katherine Demuth. 2006. Vowel epenthesis in loanword adaptation: Representational and phonetic considerations. *Lingua*, 116(7):1112–1139.

Norman C Rothman. 2002. Indian Ocean trading links: The Swahili experience. *Comparative Civilizations Review*, 46:79–90.

Thilo C Schadeberg. 2009. Loanwords in Swahili. In Martin Haspelmath and Uri Tadmor, editors, *Loanwords in the World's Languages: A Comparative Handbook*, pages 76–102. Max Planck Institute for Evolutionary Anthropology.

Kim Schulte. 2009. Loanwords in Romanian. In Martin Haspelmath and Uri Tadmor, editors, *Loanwords in the World's Languages: A Comparative Handbook*, pages 230–259. Max Planck Institute for Evolutionary Anthropology.

Tanja Schultz and Tim Schlippe. 2014. GlobalPhone: Pronunciation dictionaries in 20 languages. In *Proc. of LREC*.

Sarah Grey Thomason and Terrence Kaufman. 2001. *Language contact*. Edinburgh University Press Edinburgh.

Yulia Tsvetkov, Leonid Boytsov, Anatole Gershman, Eric Nyberg, and Chris Dyer. 2014. Metaphor detection with cross-lingual model transfer. In *Proc. of ACL*, pages 248–258.

Oscar Täckström, Dipanjan Das, Slav Petrov, Ryan McDonald, and Joakim Nivre. 2013. Token and type constraints for cross-lingual part-of-speech tagging. *Transactions of the Association for Computational Linguistics*, 1:1–12.

Moira Yip. 1993. Cantonese loanword phonology and Optimality Theory. *Journal of East Asian Linguistics*, 2(3):261–291.

Sharifa Zawawi. 1979. *Loan words and their effect on the classification of Swahili nominals*. Leiden: E.J. Brill.

# Model Invertibility Regularization: Sequence Alignment With or Without Parallel Data

**Tomer Levinboim**[*] levinboim.1@nd.edu

**Ashish Vaswani**[†] avaswani@isi.edu

**David Chiang**[*] dchiang@nd.edu

[*]Dept. of Computer Science and Engineering University of Notre Dame

[†]Information Sciences Institute University of Southern California

## Abstract

We present Model Invertibility Regularization (MIR), a method that jointly trains two directional sequence alignment models, one in each direction, and takes into account the invertibility of the alignment task. By coupling the two models through their parameters (as opposed to through their inferences, as in Liang et al.'s Alignment by Agreement (ABA), and Ganchev et al.'s Posterior Regularization (PostCAT)), our method seamlessly extends to all IBM-style word alignment models as well as to alignment *without* parallel data. Our proposed algorithm is mathematically sound and inherits its convergence guarantees from EM. We evaluate MIR on two tasks: (1) On word alignment, applying MIR on fertility based models we attain higher F-scores than ABA and PostCAT. (2) On Japanese-to-English back-transliteration without parallel data, applied to the decipherment model of Ravi and Knight, MIR learns sparser models that close the gap in whole-name error rate by 33% relative to a model trained on parallel data, and further, beats a previous approach by Mylonakis et al.

## 1 Introduction

The transfer of information between languages is a common natural language phenomenon that is intuitively invertible. For example, in transliteration, a source-language word is mapped to a target language's writing system under a sound preserving mapping (for example, "computer" to Japanese Romaji, "konpyutaa"). The original word should then be recoverable from its transliterated version. Similarly, in translation, the back-translation of the translation of a word is likely to be that same word itself.

In NLP, however, commonly-used generative models describing such phenomena are directional, only concerned with the transfer of source-language symbols to target-language symbols or vice versa, but not both directions. Left unchecked, independently training two such directional models (source-to-target and target-to-source) often yields two models that diverge from this invertibility intuition.

In word alignment, this can lead to disagreements between alignments inferred by a model trained in one direction and those inferred by a model trained in the reverse direction. To remedy this disparity (and other shortcomings), it is common to turn to alignment symmetrization techniques such as grow-diag-final-and (Koehn et al., 2003) which heuristically combines alignments from both directions.

Liang et al. (2006) suggest a more fundamental approach they call Alignment by Agreement (ABA), which jointly trains two word alignment models by maximizing their data-likelihoods along with a regularizer that rewards agreement between their alignment posteriors (computed over each parallel sentence pair). Although their EM-like optimization procedure is heuristic, it proves effective at jointly training bidirectional models. Ganchev et al. (2008) propose another approach for agreement between the directed models by adding constraints on the alignment posteriors. Unlike ABA, their optimization is exact, but it can be computationally expensive, requiring multiple forward-backward inferences in each E-step.

In this paper we develop a different approach for jointly training general bidirectional sequence alignment models called Model Invertibility Regularization, or MIR (Section 3). Our approach has two key benefits over ABA and PostCAT: First, MIR can



*Human Language Technologies: The 2015 Annual Conference of the North American Chapter of the ACL*, pages 609–618, Denver, Colorado, May 31 – June 5, 2015. 

be applied to sequence alignment without parallel data. Second, a single implementation seamlessly extends to all IBM models, including the fertility based models. Furthermore, since `MIR` follows the MAP-EM framework, it inherits its desirable convergence guarantees.

The key idea facilitating the easy extension to complex models and to non-parallel data settings is in our regularizer, which operates on the model parameters as opposed to their inferences. Specifically, `MIR` was designed to reward model pairs whose translation tables respect the invertibility intuition.

We tested `MIR` against competitive baselines on two sequence alignment tasks: word alignment (with parallel data) and back-transliteration decipherment (without parallel data).

On Czech-English and Chinese-English word alignment (Section 5), restricted to the HMM model, `MIR` attains F- and B score improvements that are comparable to those of `ABA` and `PostCAT`. We further apply `MIR` beyond HMM, on the fertility-based IBM Models, showing further gains in F-score compared to the baseline, `ABAandPostCAT`. Interestingly, the HMM alignments obtained by `ABA` and `MIR` are qualitatively different, so that combining the two yields additive gains over each method by itself.

On English-Japanese back-transliteration decipherment (Section 6), we apply `MIR` to the cascade of wFSTs approach proposed by Ravi and Knight (2009). Using `MIR`, we are able to reduce the whole-name error-rate relative to a model trained on parallel data by 33%, as well as significantly outperform the joint model proposed by Mylonakis et al. (2007).

## 2 Background

We are concerned with learning generative models that describe transformations of a source-language sequence $\mathbf{e} = (e_1, \ldots, e_I)$ to a target-language sequence $\mathbf{f} = (f_1, \ldots, f_J)$. We consider two different data scenarios.

In the parallel data setting, each sample in the observed data consists of a pair $(\mathbf{e}, \mathbf{f})$. The generative story assigns the following probability to the event that $\mathbf{f}$ arises from $\mathbf{e}$:

$$p(\mathbf{f} \mid \mathbf{e}; \Theta) = \sum_{\mathbf{a}} p(\mathbf{a}, \mathbf{f} \mid \mathbf{e}; \Theta) \qquad (1)$$

where $\Theta$ denotes the model parameters and $\mathbf{a}$ denotes a hidden variable that corresponds to unknown choices taken in the generative process.

In the non-parallel data setting, only the target sequence $\mathbf{f}$ is observed and the source sequence $\mathbf{e}$ is hidden. The model assigns the following probability to the observed data:

$$p(\mathbf{f}; \Theta) = \sum_{\mathbf{e}} p(\mathbf{e}) \sum_{\mathbf{a}} p(\mathbf{a}, \mathbf{f} \mid \mathbf{e}). \qquad (2)$$

That is, the sequence $\mathbf{f}$ can arise from any sequence $\mathbf{e}$ by first selecting $\mathbf{e} \sim p(\mathbf{e})$ and then proceeding according to the parallel-data generative story (Eq. 1).

Unsupervised training of such models entails maximizing the data log-likelihood $L(\Theta)$:

$$\arg\max_{\Theta} \; L(\Theta) = \arg\max_{\Theta} \; \sum_{x \in X} \log p(\mathbf{x}; \Theta)$$

where $X = \{(\mathbf{e}^n, \mathbf{f}^n)\}_n$ in the parallel data setting and $X = \{(\mathbf{f}^n)\}_n$ in the non-parallel data setting.

Although the structure of $\Theta$ is unspecified, in practice, most models that follow these generative stories contain a word translation table (t-table) denoted $t$, with each parameter $t(f \mid e)$ representing the conditional probability of mapping a given source symbol $e$ to a target symbol $f$.

## 3 Model Invertibility Regularization

In this section we propose a method for jointly training two word alignment models, a source-to-target model $\Theta_1$ and a target-to-source model $\Theta_2$, by regularizing their parameters to respect the invertibility of the alignment task. We therefore name our method *Model Invertibility Regularization* (`MIR`).

### 3.1 Regularizer

Our regularizer operates on the t-table parameters $t_1, t_2$ of the two models, as follows: Let matrices $T_1, T_2$ denote the t-tables $t_1, t_2$ in matrix form and consider their multiplication $T = T_1 T_2$. The resulting matrix $T$ is a stochastic square matrix of dimension $|V_1| \times |V_1|$ where $|V_1|$ denotes the size of the source-language vocabulary. Each entry $T_{ij}$ represents the total probability mass mapped from source word $e_i$ to source word $e_j$ by first applying the source-to-target mapping $T_1$ and then the target-to-source mapping $T_2$.

In particular, each diagonal entry $T_{ii}$ holds the probability of mapping a source symbol back onto itself, a quantity we intuitively believe should be high. We therefore (initially) consider maximizing the trace of $T$:

$$\mathrm{Tr}[T] = \sum_i T_{ii} = \sum_e \sum_f t_1(f \mid e)\, t_2(e \mid f).$$

We further note that $\mathrm{Tr}[T] = \mathrm{Tr}[T_1 T_2] = \mathrm{Tr}[T_2 T_1]$, so that the trace captures equally well how much the target symbols map onto themselves.

Since $T$ is stochastic, setting it to the identity matrix $I$ maximizes its trace. In other words, the more $T_1$ and $T_2$ behave as (pseudo-)inverses of each other, the higher the trace is. This exactly fits with our intuition regarding invertibility.

Unfortunately, the trace is not concave in both $T_1$ and $T_2$, a property which will become desirable in optimization. We therefore modify the trace regularizer by applying the entrywise square root operator on $T_1$, $T_2$ and denote the new term $R$:

$$\begin{aligned} R(t_1, t_2) &= \mathrm{Tr}\left[\sqrt{T_1}\sqrt{T_2}\right] \\ &= \sum_e \sum_f \sqrt{t_1(f \mid e)\, t_2(e \mid f)}. \end{aligned} \qquad (3)$$

Note that $R$ is maximized when $\sqrt{T_1}\sqrt{T_2} = I$.

Concavity of $R$ in both $t_1, t_2$ (or equivalently $T_1, T_2$) follows by observing that it is a sum of concave functions – each term in the summation is a geometric mean, which is concave in its parameters.

## 3.2 Joint Objective Function

We apply MIR in two data scenarios: In the parallel data setting, we observe $N$ sequence pairs $\{\mathbf{x}_1^n\}_n = \{(\mathbf{e}^n, \mathbf{f}^n)\}_n$ or, equivalently, $\{\mathbf{x}_2^n\}_n = \{(\mathbf{f}^n, \mathbf{e}^n)\}_n$.

In the non-parallel setting, two monolingual datasets are observed: $N_1$ source sequences $\{\mathbf{x}_1^n\}_n = \{\mathbf{e}^n\}_n$ and $N_2$ target sequences $\{\mathbf{x}_2^n\}_n = \{\mathbf{f}^n\}_n$.

The probability of the $n$th sample under the $k$th model $\Theta_k$ (for $k \in \{1, 2\}$) is denoted $p_k(\mathbf{x}_k^n; \Theta_k)$. Specifically, in the parallel data setting, the probability of $\mathbf{x}_k^n$ under its model is:[1]

$$\begin{aligned} p_1(\mathbf{x}_1^n; \Theta_1) &= p(\mathbf{f}^n \mid \mathbf{e}^n; \Theta_1) \\ p_2(\mathbf{x}_2^n; \Theta_2) &= p(\mathbf{e}^n \mid \mathbf{f}^n; \Theta_2) \end{aligned}$$

[1] This slight notational abuse helps represent both data scenarios succinctly.

whereas in the non-parallel data setting, the probability is defined as:

$$\begin{aligned} p_1(\mathbf{x}_1^n; \Theta_1) &= p(\mathbf{f}^n; \Theta_1) \\ p_2(\mathbf{x}_2^n; \Theta_2) &= p(\mathbf{e}^n; \Theta_2). \end{aligned}$$

Using the above definitions and the MIR regularizer $R$ (Eq. 3), we formulate an optimization program for maximizing the regularized log-likelihoods of the observed data:

$$\max_{\Theta_1, \Theta_2} \; \lambda R(t_1, t_2) + \sum_{k \in \{1,2\}} \sum_{n=1}^{N_k} \log p_k(\mathbf{x}_k^n; \Theta_k) \qquad (4)$$

where $\lambda \geq 0$ is a tunable hyperparameter (note that, in the parallel case, $N = N_1 = N_2$).

We defer discussion on the relationship and merits of our approach with respect to ABA (Liang et al., 2006) and PostCAT (Ganchev et al., 2008) to Section 4.

## 3.3 Optimization Procedure

Using our concave regularizer, MIR optimization (Eq. 4) neatly falls under the MAP-EM framework (Dempster et al., 1977) and inherits the convergence properties of the underlying algorithms. MAP-EM follows the same structure as standard EM: The E-step remains identical to the standard E-step, while the M-step maximizes the complete-data log-likelihood plus the regularization term. In the case of MIR, the E-step can be carried out independently for each model. The only extra work is in the M-step, which optimizes a single (concave) objective function.

Specifically, let $\mathbf{z}_n$ denote the missing data, where, in the parallel data setting, only the alignment is missing ($\mathbf{z}_k^n = \mathbf{a}_k^n$) and in the non-parallel data setting, both alignment and source symbol are missing ($\mathbf{z}_1^n = (\mathbf{a}_1^n, \mathbf{e}^n)$, $\mathbf{z}_2^n = (\mathbf{a}_2^n, \mathbf{f}^n)$).

In the E-step, each model $\Theta_k$ (for $k \in \{1, 2\}$) is held fixed and its posterior distribution over the missing data $\mathbf{z}_k^n$ is computed per each observation, $\mathbf{x}_k^n$:

$$q_k(\mathbf{z}_k^n, \mathbf{x}_k^n) := p_k(\mathbf{z}_k^n \mid \mathbf{x}_k^n; \Theta_k).$$

In the M-step, the computed posteriors are used to define a convex optimization program that maximizes the regularized sum of expected complete-data log-likelihoods:

$$\max_{\Theta_1,\Theta_2} \lambda R(t_1, t_2) + \sum_{k\in\{1,2\}} \sum_{n=1}^{N_k} q_k(\mathbf{z}_k^n, \mathbf{x}_k^n) \log p_k(\mathbf{x}_k^n, \mathbf{z}_k^n)$$

where $n$ ranges over the appropriate sample set.

Operationally, for models $\Theta_k$ that can be encoded as wFSTs (such as the IBM1, IBM2 and HMM word alignment models), the E-step can be carried out efficiently and exactly using dynamic programming (Eisner, 2002). Other models resort to approximation techniques – for example, the fertility-based word alignment models apply hill-climbing and sampling heuristics in order to efficiently estimate the posteriors (Brown et al., 1993)

From the computed posteriors $q_k$ we collect expected counts for each event, used to construct the M-step optimization objective. Since the MIR regularizer couples only the t-table parameters, the update rule for any remaining parameter is left unchanged (that is, one can use the usual closed-form count-and-divide solution).

Now, let $\mathrm{C}_1^{e,f}$ and $\mathrm{C}_2^{e,f}$ denote the expected counts for the t-table parameters. That is, $\mathrm{C}_k^{e,f}$ denotes the expected number of times a source-symbol type $e$ is seen aligned to a target-symbol type $f$ according to the posterior $q_k$. In the M-step, we maximize the following objective with respect to $t_1$ and $t_2$:

$$\arg\max_{t_1,t_2} \sum_{e,f} \mathrm{C}_1^{e,f} \log t_1(f \mid e) + \sum_{e,f} \mathrm{C}_2^{e,f} \log t_2(e \mid f) + \lambda R(t_1, t_2) \quad (5)$$

which can be efficiently solved using convex programming techniques due to the concavity of $R$ and the complete-data log-likelihoods in both $t_1$ and $t_2$.

In our implementation, we applied Projected Gradient Descent (Bertsekas, 1999; Schoenemann, 2011), where at each step, the parameters are updated in the direction of the M-step objective gradient at $(t_1, t_2)$ and then projected back onto the probability simplex. We used simple stopping conditions based on objective function value convergence and a bounded number of iterations.

## 4 Baselines

### 4.1 Parallel Data Baseline: ABA and PostCAT

Our approach is most similar to Alignment by Agreement (Liang et al., 2006) which uses a single joint objective for two word alignment models. The difference between our objective (Eq. 4) and theirs lies in their proposed regularizer, which rewards the per-sample agreement of the two models' alignment posteriors:

$$\sum_n \log \sum_{\mathbf{z}} p_1(\mathbf{z} \mid \mathbf{x}^n) \cdot p_2(\mathbf{z} \mid \mathbf{x}^n)$$

where $\mathbf{x}^n = (\mathbf{e}^n, \mathbf{f}^n)$ and where $\mathbf{z}$ ranges over the possible alignments between $\mathbf{e}^n$ and $\mathbf{f}^n$ (practically, only over 1-to-1 alignments, since each model is only capable of producing one-to-many alignments).

Liang et al. (2006) note that proper EM optimization of their regularized joint objective leads to an intractable E-step. Unable to exactly and efficiently compute alignment posteriors, they resort to a product-of-marginals heuristic which breaks EM's convergence guarantees, but has a closed-form solution and works well in practice.

MIR regularization has both theoretical and practical advantages compared to ABA, which make our method more convenient and broadly applicable:

1. By regularizing for posterior agreement, ABA is restricted to a parallel data setting, whereas MIR can be applied even without parallel data.

2. The posteriors of more advanced word alignment models (such as fertility-based models) do not correspond to alignments, and furthermore, are already estimated with approximation techniques. Thus, even if we somehow adapt ABA's product-of-marginals heuristic to such models, we run the risk of estimating highly inaccurate posteriors (specifically, zero-valued posteriors). In contrast, MIR extends to all IBM-style word alignment models and does not add heuristics. The M-step computation can be done exactly and efficiently with convex optimization.

3. MIR provides the same theoretical convergence guarantees as the underlying algorithms.

Ganchev et al. (2008) propose PostCAT which uses Posterior Regularization (Ganchev et al., 2010) to enforce posterior agreement between the two models. Specifically, they add a KL-projection step after the E-step of the EM algorithm which returns the posterior $q(z \mid x)$ closest in KL-Divergence to an E-step posterior, but which also upholds certain constraints. The particular constraints they suggest encode alignment agreement *in expectation* between the two models' posteriors. For details, the reader can refer to (Ganchev et al., 2008).

Similarly to ABA, with their suggested alignment agreement constraints PostCAT cannot be applied without parallel data and it is unclear how to extend it to fertility based models (however, it does seems possible to apply other constraints using the general posterior regularization framework).

We compare MIR against ABA and PostCAT in Section 5.

### 4.2 Non-Parallel Data Baseline: bi-EM

Mylonakis et al. (2007) cast the two directional models as a single joint model by reparameterization and normalization. That is, both directional models, consisting of a t-table only, are reparameterized as:

$$t_1(f \mid e) = \frac{\beta_{e,f}}{\sum_f \beta_{e,f}} \qquad t_2(e \mid f) = \frac{\beta_{e,f}}{\sum_e \beta_{e,f}} \tag{6}$$

They then maximize the likelihood of observed *monolingual* sequences from both languages:

$$\max_{\beta} L_1(\{\mathbf{f}^n\};\beta) + L_2(\{\mathbf{e}^n\};\beta) \tag{7}$$

where, for example:

$$\begin{aligned} L_1(\{\mathbf{f}^n\};\beta) &= \log \prod_n p(\mathbf{f}^n) \\ &= \log \prod_n \sum_{\mathbf{e}} p(\mathbf{f}^n \mid \mathbf{e}) p(\mathbf{e}) \\ &= \log \prod_n \sum_{\mathbf{e}} p(\mathbf{e}) \prod_m t_1(f_m^n \mid \mathbf{e}) \end{aligned}$$

Here, $p(\mathbf{e})$ denotes the probability of $\mathbf{e}$ according to a fixed source language model.

Once training of $\beta$ is complete, we can decode an observed target sequence $\mathbf{f}$, by casting $\beta$ back in terms of $t_1$ and apply the Viterbi decoding algorithm.

To solve for $\beta$ in Eq. 7, Mylonakis et al. (2007) propose bi-EM, an iterative EM-style algorithm. The objective function in their M-step is not concave, hinting that a closed-form solution for the maximizer is unlikely. The probability estimate that they use in the M-step appears to maximize an approximation of their M-step objective which omits the normalization factors in Eq. 7.

Nevertheless, bi-EM attains improved results compared to standard EM on both POS-tagging and monotone noun sequence translation without parallel data. We compare MIR against bi-EM in Sec. 6.

## 5 Experiments with Parallel Data

In this section, we compare MIR against standard EM training and ABA on Czech-English and Chinese-English word alignment and translation.

### 5.1 Implementation and Code

For ABA[2] and PostCAT[3] training we used the authors' implementation, which supports the HMM model. Vanilla EM training was done using GIZA++,[4] which supports all IBM models as well as HMM. Our method MIR was implemented on top of GIZA++.[5]

### 5.2 Data

We used the following parallel data to train the word alignment models:

**Chinese-English:** 287K sentence pairs from the NIST 2009 Open MT Evaluation constrained task consisting of 5.3M and 6.6M tokens, respectively.

**Czech-English:** 85K sentence pairs from the News Commentary corpus, consisting of 1.6M and 1.8M tokens, respectively.

Sentence length was restricted to at most 40 tokens.

### 5.3 Word Alignment Experiments

We obtained HMM alignments by running either 5 or 10 iterations (optimized on a held-out validation set) of both IBM Model 1 and HMM. We obtained IBM Model 4 alignments by continuing with 5 iterations of IBM Model 3 and 10 iterations of IBM

[2]http://cs.stanford.edu/~pliang/software/cross-em-aligner-1.3.zip

[3]http://www.seas.upenn.edu/~strctlrn/CAT/CAT.html

[4]http://code.google.com/p/giza-pp/

[5]https://github.com/vaswani/MIR_ALIGNMENT

| Method | Chi-Eng **Align F1** | Cze-Eng **Align F1** |
|---|---|---|
| EM-HMM | 64.6 | 65.0 |
| PostCAT-HMM | 69.8 | 69.6 |
| ABA-HMM | 70.8 | 70.4 |
| MIR-HMM | 70.9 | 69.6 |
| EM-IBM4 | 68.4 | 67.3 |
| MIR-IBM4 | 72.9 | 70.7 |

Table 1: Word alignment F1 scores.

Model 4. We then extracted symmetrized alignments in the following manner: For all HMM models, we used the *posterior decoding* technique described in Liang et al. (2006) as implemented by each package. For IBM Model 4, we used the standard grow-diag-final-and (gdfa) symmetrization heuristic (Koehn et al., 2003).

We tuned MIR's $\lambda$ parameter to maximize alignment F-score on a validation set of 460 hand-aligned Czech-English and 1102 Chinese-English sentences.

Alignment F-scores are reported in Table 1. In particular, the best results were obtained by MIR, when applied to the fertility based IBM4 model - we obtained gains of +2.1% (Chinese-English) and +0.3% (Czech-English) compared to the best competitor.

### 5.4 MT Experiments

We ran MT experiments using the Moses (Koehn et al., 2007) phrase-based translation system.[6] The feature weights were trained discriminatively using MIRA (Chiang et al., 2008), and we used a 5-gram language model trained on the Xinhua portion of English Gigaword (LDC2007T07). All other parameters remained with their default settings. The development data used for discriminative training were: for Chinese-English, data from the NIST 2004 and NIST 2006 test sets; for Czech-English, 2051 sentences from the WMT 2010 shared task. We used case-insensitive IBM B (closest reference length) as our metric.

On both language pairs, ABA, PostCAT and MIR outperform their respective EM baseline with comparable gains overall. However, we noticed that ABA and MIR are not producing the same alignments.

[6] http://www.statmt.org/moses/

| Method | Chi-Eng **NIST08** | Cze-Eng **WMT09** | **WMT10** |
|---|---|---|---|
| EM-HMM | 23.6 | 16.7 | 17.1 |
| PostCAT-HMM | 24.6 | 16.9 | 17.4 |
| MIR-HMM | 24.0 | 17.1 | 17.6 |
| ABA-HMM | 24.4 | 17.1 | 17.7 |
| EM-IBM4 | 24.2 | 16.8 | 17.2 |
| MIR-IBM4 | 24.6 | 17.2 | 17.5 |
| ABA + MIR-HMM | 25.1 | 17.4 | 17.9 |

Table 2: B scores. Combining ABA and MIR HMM alignments improves B score significantly over all other methods.

For example, by combining their HMM alignments (simply concatenating aligned bitexts) the total improvement reaches +1.5 B on the Chinese-to-English task, a statistically significant improvement ($p < 0.05$) according to a bootstrap resampling significance test (Koehn, 2004)). Table 5.4 summarizes our MT results.

## 6 Experiments without Parallel Data

Ravi and Knight (2009) consider the challenging task of learning a Japanese-English back-transliteration model without parallel data. The goal is to correctly decode a list of 100 US senator names written in katakana script, without having access to parallel data. In this section, we reproduce their decipherment experiment and show that applying MIR to their baseline model significantly outperforms both the baseline and the bi-EM method.

### 6.1 Phonetic-Based Japanese Decipherment

Ravi and Knight (2009) construct a English-to-Japanese transliteration model as a cascade of wFSTs (depicted in Figure 1, top). According to their generative story, any word in katakana is generated by re-writing an English word in its English phonetic representation, which is then transformed to a Japanese phonetic representation and finally re-written in katakana script. For example, the word "computer" is mapped to a sequence of 8 English phonemes (k, ah, m, p, y, uw, t, er), which is mapped to a sequence of 9 Japanese phonemes (K, O, N, P, Y, U, T, A, A) and finally to Katakana.

They apply their trained transliteration model to decode a list of 100 US senator names and report a whole-name error-rate (WNER)[7] of 40% with parallel data (trained over 3.3k word pairs), compared to 73% WNER without parallel data (trained over 9.5k Japanese words only), demonstrating the weakness of methods that do not use parallel data.

### 6.2 Forward Pipeline

We reproduced the English-to-Japanese transliteration pipeline of Ravi and Knight (2009) by constructing each of the cascade wFSTs as follows:

1. A unigram language model (LM) of English terms, estimated over the top 40K most frequent capitalized words found in the Gigaword corpus (without smoothing).

2. An English pronunciation wFST from the CMU pronunciation dictionary.[8]

3. An English-to-Japanese phoneme mapping wFST that encodes a phoneme t-table $t_1$ which was designed according to the best setting reported by Ravi and Knight (2009). Specifically, $t_1$ is restricted to either 1-to-1 or 1-to-2 phoneme mappings and maintains consonant parity. See further details in their paper.

4. A hand-built Japanese pronunciation to Katakana wFST (Ravi and Knight, 2009).

### 6.3 Backward Pipeline

`MIR` requires a pipeline in the reverse direction, transliteration of Japanese to English. We constructed a unigram LM of Katakana terms over the top 25K most frequent Katakana words found in the Japanese `2005-2008-news` dictionary from the Leipzig corpora.[9]

The remaining required wFSTs were obtained by inverting the forward model wFSTs (that is, wFSTs 2,3,4 above), and the cascade was composed in the reverse direction. In particular, by inverting $t_1$, we obtained the Japanese-to-English t-table $t_2$ that allows only 2-to-1 or 1-to-1 phoneme mappings.

[7]The percentage of names where any error occurs anywhere in either the first or last name.

[8]`http://www.speech.cs.cmu.edu/cgi-bin/cmudict`

[9]`http://corpora.uni-leipzig.de/`

### 6.4 Training Data

For training data, we used the top 50% most frequent terms from the monolingual data over which we constructed the LM wFSTs. This resulted in a set of 20K English terms (denoted `ENG`) and a set of 13K Japanese terms in Katakana (denoted `KTKN`).

Taking the entire set of monolingual terms led to poor baseline results, probably since uncommon English terms are not transliterated, and uncommon Katakana terms may be borrowed from languages other than English.

In any case, it is important to note that `ENG` and `KTKN` are unrelated, since both were collected over non-parallel corpora.

### 6.5 Training and Tuning

We train and tune 4 models:

`baseline`: the model proposed by Ravi and Knight (2009), which maximizes the likelihood (Eq. 2) of the observed Japanese terms `KTKN`.

`MIR`: Our bidirectional, regularized model, which maximizes the regularized likelihoods (Eq. 4) of both monolingual corpora `ENG`, `KTKN`.

`bi-EM`: The joint model proposed by Mylonakis et al. (2007), which maximizes the likelihoods (Eq. 7) of both monolingual corpora `ENG`, `KTKN`.

`Oracle`: As an upper bound, we train the model of Ravi and Knight (2009) as if it was given the correct English origin for each Japanese term. (over 4.2K *parallel* English-Japanese phoneme sequences).

We train each method for 15 EM iterations, while keeping the LM and pronunciation wFSTs fixed.

Training was done using the Carmel finite-state toolkit.[10] Specifically, `baseline` and `oracle` rely on Carmel exclusively, while for `MIR` and `bi-EM`, we manipulated Carmel to output the E-step posteriors, which we then used to construct and solve the M-step objective using our own implementation.

The different models were tuned over a development set consisting of 50 frequent Japanese terms and their English origin. For each method, we chose the so-called stretch-factor $\alpha \in \{1, 2, 3\}$ used to exponentiate the model parameters before decoding

[10]`http://www.isi.edu/licensed-sw/carmel/`

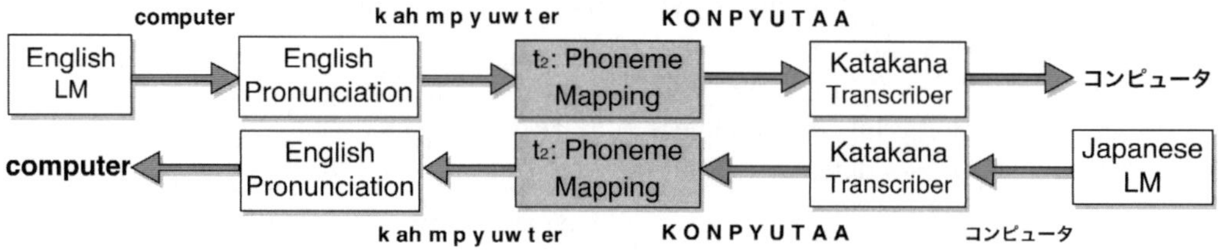


Figure 1: The transliteration generative story as a cascade of wFSTs. Each box represents a transducer. **Top:** transliteration of the word "computer" to Japanese Katakana. **Bottom:** the reverse process. MIR jointly trains the two cascades by maximizing the regularized data log-likelihood with respect to the two (shaded) phoneme mapping models $t_1, t_2$.

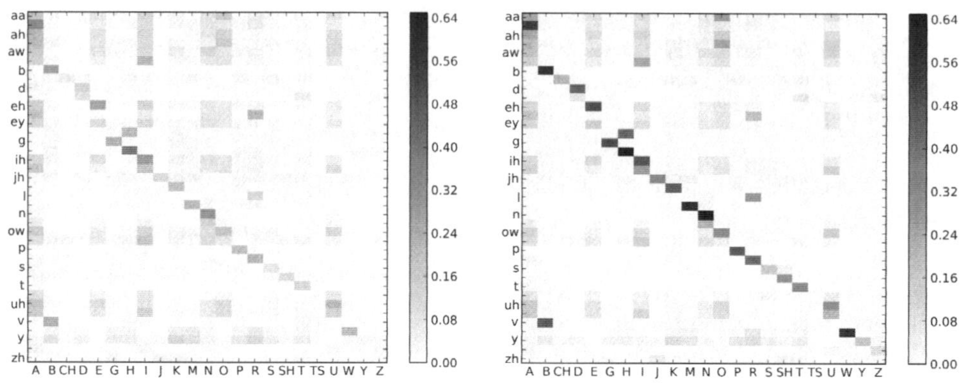

Figure 2: The 1-to-1 mapping submatrix of the $t_1$ transliteration table for independent training (left) and MIR (right). MIR learns sparser, peaked models compared to those learned by independent training.

(see Ravi and Knight (2009)), our model's hyperparameter $\lambda \in \{1, 2, 3, 4\}$, and the number of iterations (up to 15) to minimize WNER on the development set.

We decoded Japanese terms using the Viterbi algorithm, applied on the selected $t_1$ model (using Eq. 6 to convert the bi-EM model $\beta$ back to to $t_1$). Finally, note that ABA training and symmetrization decoding heuristics are inapplicable, since they rely on parallel data.

### 6.6 Senator Name Decoding Results

We compiled our own test set, consisting of 100 US senator names (first and last), and compared the performance of the four algorithms. Table 3 reports WNER, average normalized edit distance (NED) and the number of model parameters ($t_1$) with value greater than 0.01 as an indication of sparsity. Figure 2 further compares the 1-to-1 portions of the best model learned by the baseline method with the best model learned by MIR, showing the difference in parameter sparsity.

| | WNER | NED | $t_1 > 0.01$ |
|---|---|---|---|
| baseline | 67% | 23.2 | 649 |
| bi-EM | 66% | 21.8 | 600 |
| MIR | **59%** | **17.3** | **421** |
| Oracle | 43% | 10.8 | 152 |

Table 3: MIR reduces error rates (WNER, NED) and learns sparser models (number of $t_1$ parameters greater than 0.01) compared to the other models.

Using MIR, we obtained significant reduction in error rates, closing the gap between the baseline method and Oracle, which was trained on parallel data, by 33% in WNER and nearly 50% in NED. This error reduction clearly demonstrates the efficacy of MIR in the non-parallel data setting.

## 7 Conclusion

We presented Model Invertibility Regularization (MIR), an unsupervised method for jointly training bidirectional sequence alignment models with or without parallel data. Our formulation is based on the simple observation that the alignment tasks at hand are inherently invertible and encourages the translation tables in both models to behave like pseudo-inverses of each other.

We derived an efficient MAP-EM algorithm and demonstrated our method's effectiveness on two different alignment tasks. On word alignment, applying MIR on the IBM4 model yielded the highest F scores and the resulting B scores were comparable to that of Alignment by Agreement (Liang et al., 2006) and PostCAT (Ganchev et al., 2008). Our best MT results (up to +1.5 B improvement) were obtained by combining alignments from both MIR and ABA, indicating that the two methods learn complementary alignments. On Japanese-English back-transliteration with no parallel data, we obtained a significant error reduction over two baseline methods (Ravi and Knight, 2009; Mylonakis et al., 2007).

As future work, we plan to apply MIR on large-scale MT decipherment (Ravi and Knight, 2011; Dou and Knight, 2013), where, so far, only a single directional model has been used. Another promising direction is to encourage invertibility not only between words, but between their senses and synonyms.

## Acknowledgements

We would like to thank Markos Mylonakis and Khalil Sima'an for their help in understanding the derivation of their bi-EM method. This work was partially supported by DARPA grants DOI/NBC D12AP00225 and HR0011-12-C-0014 and a Google Faculty Research Award to Chiang.

## References

Dimitri P. Bertsekas. 1999. *Nonlinear Programming*. Athena Scientific.

Peter F. Brown, Stephen A. Della Pietra, Vincent J. Della Pietra, and Robert L. Mercer. 1993. The mathematics of statistical machine translation: Parameter estimation. *Computational Linguistics*, 19:263–311.

David Chiang, Yuval Marton, and Philip Resnik. 2008. Online large-margin training of syntactic and structural translation features. In *Proceedings of EMNLP*.

A. P. Dempster, N. M. Laird, and D. B. Rubin. 1977. Maximum likelihood from incomplete data via the EM algorithm. *Computational Linguistics*, 39(4):1–38.

Qing Dou and Kevin Knight. 2013. Dependency-based decipherment for resource-limited machine translation. In *EMNLP*, pages 1668–1676. ACL.

Jason Eisner. 2002. Parameter estimation for probabilistic finite-state transducers. In *Proceedings of the 40th Annual Meeting on Association for Computational Linguistics*, ACL '02, pages 1–8, Stroudsburg, PA, USA. Association for Computational Linguistics.

Kuzman Ganchev, João V. Graça, and Ben Taskar. 2008. Better alignments = better translations? In *Proceedings of ACL-08: HLT*, pages 986–993, Columbus, Ohio, June. Association for Computational Linguistics.

Kuzman Ganchev, Joao Graça, Jennifer Gillenwater, and Ben Taskar. 2010. Posterior regularization for structured latent variable models. *The Journal of Machine Learning Research*, 11:2001–2049.

Philipp Koehn, Franz Joseph Och, and Daniel Marcu. 2003. Statistical phrase-based translation. In *Proceedings of NAACL*.

Philipp Koehn, Hieu Hoang, Alexandra Birch, Chris Callison-Burch, Marcello Federico, Nicola Bertoldi, Brooke Cowan, Wade Shen, Christine Moran, Richard Zens, et al. 2007. Moses: Open source toolkit for statistical machine translation. In *Proceedings of the 45th Annual Meeting of the ACL on Interactive Poster and Demonstration Sessions*, pages 177–180. Association for Computational Linguistics.

Philipp Koehn. 2004. Statistical significance tests for machine translation evaluation. In *Proceedings of EMNLP*.

Percy Liang, Ben Taskar, and Dan Klein. 2006. Alignment by agreement. In *Proceedings of HLT-NAACL*.

Markos Mylonakis, Khalil Sima'an, and Rebecca Hwa. 2007. Unsupervised estimation for noisy-channel models. In *Proceedings of the 24th International Conference on Machine Learning*, ICML '07, pages 665–672, New York, NY, USA. ACM.

Sujith Ravi and Kevin Knight. 2009. Learning phoneme mappings for transliteration without parallel data. In *Proceedings of Human Language Technologies: The 2009 Annual Conference of the North American Chapter of the Association for Computational Linguistics*, NAACL '09, pages 37–45, Stroudsburg, PA, USA. Association for Computational Linguistics.

Sujith Ravi and Kevin Knight. 2011. Deciphering foreign language. In *Proceedings of the 49th Annual*

*Meeting of the Association for Computational Linguistics: Human Language Technologies - Volume 1*, HLT '11, pages 12–21, Stroudsburg, PA, USA. Association for Computational Linguistics.

Thomas Schoenemann. 2011. Probabilistic word alignment under the $L_0$-norm. In *Proceedings of CoNLL*.

# Jointly Modeling Inter-Slot Relations by Random Walk on Knowledge Graphs for Unsupervised Spoken Language Understanding

**Yun-Nung Chen, William Yang Wang, and Alexander I. Rudnicky**
School of Computer Science, Carnegie Mellon University
5000 Forbes Avenue, Pittsburgh, PA 15213-3891, USA
{yvchen, yww, air}@cs.cmu.edu

## Abstract

A key challenge of designing coherent semantic ontology for spoken language understanding is to consider inter-slot relations. In practice, however, it is difficult for domain experts and professional annotators to define a coherent slot set, while considering various lexical, syntactic, and semantic dependencies. In this paper, we exploit the typed syntactic dependency theory for unsupervised induction and filling of semantics slots in spoken dialogue systems. More specifically, we build two knowledge graphs: a slot-based semantic graph, and a word-based lexical graph. To jointly consider word-to-word, word-to-slot, and slot-to-slot relations, we use a random walk inference algorithm to combine the two knowledge graphs, guided by dependency grammars. The experiments show that considering inter-slot relations is crucial for generating a more coherent and compete slot set, resulting in a better spoken language understanding model, while enhancing the interpretability of semantic slots.

## 1 Introduction

An important requirement for building a successful spoken dialogue system (SDS) is to define a coherent slot set and the corresponding slot-fillers for the spoken language understanding (SLU) component. Unfortunately, since the semantic slots are often mutually-related, it is non-trivial for domain experts and professional annotators to design a such slot set for semantic representation of SLU.

Considering a restaurant domain (Henderson et al., 2012), "*restaurant*" is the target slot, and important adjective modifiers such as "*Asian*" (the restaurant type) and "*cheap*" (the price of the restaurant) should be included in the slot set, so that the semantic representation of SLU can be more coherent and complete. In this case, it is challenging to design such a coherent and complete slot set manually, while considering various lexical, syntactic, and semantic dependencies.

Instead of considering slots independently, this paper takes a data-driven approach to model word-to-word relations via syntactic dependencies and further infer slot-to-slot relations. To do this, we incorporate the typed dependency grammar theory (De Marneffe and Manning, 2008) in a state-of-the-art frame-semantic driven unsupervised slot induction framework (Chen et al., 2013b). In particular, we build two knowledge graphs: a slot-based semantic knowledge graph, and a word-based lexical knowledge graph. Using typed dependency triples, we then study the stochastic relations between slots and words, using a mutually-reinforced random walk inference procedure to combine the two knowledge graphs. In evaluations, we use the jointly learned inter-slot relations to induce a coherent slot set in an unsupervised fashion. Our contributions are three-fold:

- We are among the first to consider unsupervised spoken language understanding combining semantic and lexical knowledge graphs;
- We propose a novel typed syntactic dependency grammar driven random walk model for relation discovery;



*Human Language Technologies: The 2015 Annual Conference of the North American Chapter of the ACL*, pages 619–629,
Denver, Colorado, May 31 – June 5, 2015. ©2015 Association for Computational Linguistics

- Our experimental results suggest that jointly considering inter-slot relations helps obtain a more coherent and complete semantic slot set.

## 2 Related Work

With the recent success of commercial dialogue systems and personal assistants (e.g., Microsoft's Cortana[1], Google Now[2], Apple's Siri[3], and Amazon's Echo[4]), a key focus on developing spoken understanding techniques is the scalability issue.

From the knowledge management perspective, empowering the system with a large knowledge base is of crucial significance to modern spoken dialogue systems. On this end, our work clearly aligns with recent studies on leveraging semantic knowledge graphs for SLU modeling (Heck et al., 2013; Hakkani-Tür et al., 2013; Hakkani-Tür et al., 2014; El-Kahky et al., 2014; Chen et al., 2014a). While leveraging external knowledge is the trend, efficient inference algorithms, such as random walk, are still less-studied for direct inference on knowledge graphs of the spoken contents.

In the natural language processing literature, Lao et al. (2011) used a random walk algorithm to construct inference rules on large entity-based knowledge bases, and leveraged syntactic information for reading the Web (Lao et al., 2012). Even though this work has important contributions, the proposed algorithm cannot learn mutually-recursive relations, and does not to consider lexical items—in fact, more and more studies show that, in addition to semantic knowledge graphs, lexical knowledge graphs (Inkpen and Hirst, 2006; Song et al., 2011; Li et al., 2013b) that model surface-level natural language realization, multiword expressions, and context (Li et al., 2013a), are also critical for short text understanding (Song et al., 2011; Wang et al., 2014).

From the engineering perspective, quick and easy development turnaround time for domain-specific dialogue applications is also critical (Chen and Rudnicky, 2014). Prior work shows that it is possible to use the frame-semantics theory to automatically induce and fill semantic slots (Chen et al., 2013b), and that leveraging distributional semantics helps improving the performance (Chen et al., 2014b). However, prior works treat each slot independently and have not considered the inter-slot relations when inducing the semantic slots. To the best of our knowledge, we are the first to use syntactically-informed random walk algorithms to combine the semantic and lexical knowledge graphs, and not individually but globally inducing the semantic slots for building better unsupervised SLU components.

## 3 The Proposed Framework

We build our approach on top of the recent success of an unsupervised frame-semantic parsing approach (Chen et al., 2013b). The main motivation of prior work is to use a FrameNet-trained statistical probabilistic semantic parser to generate initial frame-semantic parses from automatic speech recognition (ASR) decodings of the raw audio conversation files, and then adapt the FrameNet-style frames to the semantic slots in the target semantic space, so that they can be used practically in the SDSs. Chen et al. formulated the semantic mapping and adaptation problem as a ranking problem to differentiate generic semantic concepts from target semantic space for task-oriented dialogue systems. This paper improves the adaptation process by leveraging distributed word embeddings associated with typed syntactic dependencies between words to infer inter-slot relations (Mikolov et al., 2013b; Mikolov et al., 2013c; Levy and Goldberg, 2014). The proposed framework is shown in Figure 1. In the remainder of the section, we first introduce frame-semantic parsing to obtain slot candidates. With slot candidates, then we train the independent semantic decoders. The adaptation process, which is the main focus of this paper, is performed to decide outputted slots. Finally we can build an SLU model based on the learned semantic decoders and induced slots.

### 3.1 Probabilistic Semantic Parsing

FrameNet is a linguistically-principled semantic resource that offers annotations of predicate-argument semantics, and associated lexical units for English (Baker et al., 1998). FrameNet is developed based on a semantic theory, Frame Semantics (Fill-

[1] http://www.windowsphone.com/en-us/how-to/wp8/cortana

[2] http://www.google.com/landing/now

[3] http://www.apple.com/ios/siri

[4] http://www.amazon.com/oc/echo

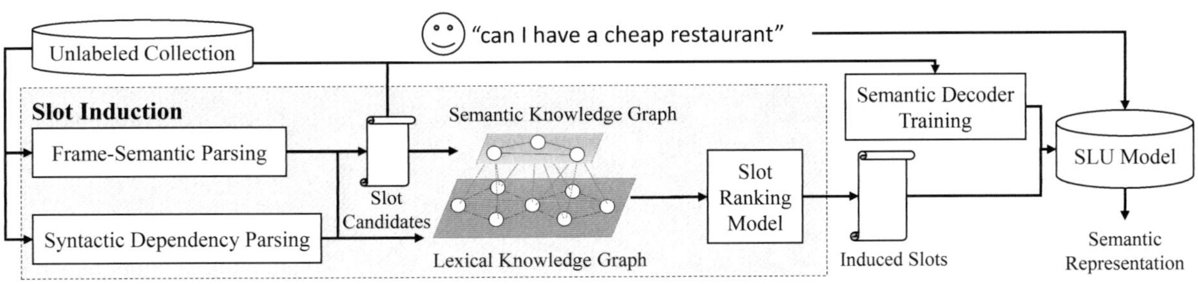


Figure 1: The proposed framework

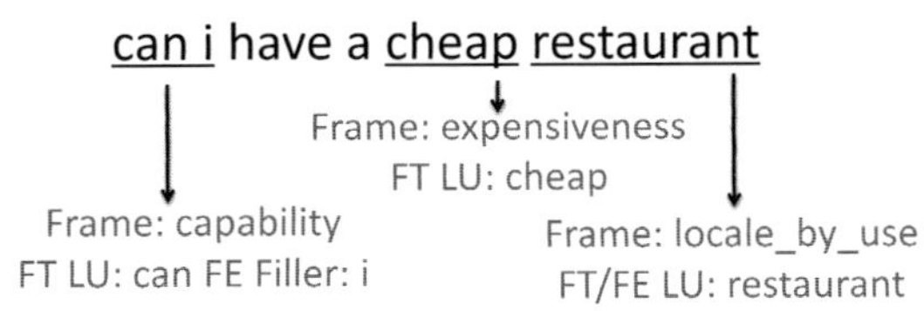


Figure 2: An example of probabilistic frame-semantic parsing on ASR output. FT: frame target. FE: frame element. LU: lexical unit.

more, 1976), which holds that the meaning of most words can be expressed on the basis of semantic frames, which encompass three major components: frame (F), frame elements (FE), and lexical units (LU). For example, the frame "food" contains words referring to items of food. A descriptor frame element within the food frame indicates the characteristic of the food. For example, the phrase "*low fat milk*" should be analyzed with "*milk*" evoking the food frame and "*low fat*" filling the descriptor FE of that frame.

In our approach, we parse all ASR-decoded utterances in our corpus using SEMAFOR[5], a state-of-the-art semantic parser for frame-semantic parsing (Das et al., 2010; Das et al., 2013), and extract all frames from semantic parsing results as slot candidates, where the LUs that correspond to the frames are extracted for slot filling. For example, Figure 2 shows an example of an ASR-decoded text output parsed by SEMAFOR. SEMAFOR generates three frames (capability, expensiveness, and locale_by_use) for the utterance, which we consider as slot candidates for training the SLU model. Note that for each slot candidate, SEMAFOR also includes the corresponding lexical unit (*can i*, *cheap*, and *restaurant*), which we consider as possible slot-fillers.

[5]`http://www.ark.cs.cmu.edu/SEMAFOR/`

### 3.2 Independent Semantic Decoder

With outputted semantic parses, we extract the frames with the top 50 highest frequency as our slot candidates for training SLU. The features for training are generated by word confusion network, where confusion network features are shown to be useful in developing more robust systems for SLU (Hakkani-Tür et al., 2006; Henderson et al., 2012). We build a vector representation of an utterance as $\mathbf{u} = [x_1, ..., x_j, ...]$.

$$x_j = \mathbb{E}[C_u(n\text{-gram}_j)]^{1/|n\text{-gram}_j|}, \tag{1}$$

where $C_u(n\text{-gram}_j)$ counts how many times $n$-gram$_j$ occurs in the utterance $u$, $\mathbb{E}(C_u(n\text{-gram}_j))$ is the expected frequency of $n$-gram$_j$ in $u$, and $|n\text{-gram}_j|$ is the number of words in $n$-gram$_j$.

For each slot candidate $s_i$, we generate a pseudo training data $\mathcal{D}^i$ to train a binary classifier $\mathcal{M}^i$ for predicting the existence of $s_i$ given an utterance, $\mathcal{D}^i = \{(\mathbf{u_k}, l_k^i) \mid \mathbf{u_k} \in \mathbb{R}^+, l_k^i \in \{-1, +1\}\}_{k=1}^K$, where $l_k^i = +1$ when the utterance $u_k$ contains the slot candidate $s_i$ in its semantic parse, $l_k^i = -1$ otherwise, and $K$ is the number of utterances.

### 3.3 Adaptation Process and SLU Model

Since SEMAFOR was trained on FrameNet annotation, which has a more generic frame-semantic context, not all the frames from the parsing results can be used as the actual slots in the domain-specific dialogue systems. For instance, in Figure 2, we see that the frames "expensiveness" and "locale_by_use" are essentially the key slots for the purpose of understanding in the restaurant query domain, whereas

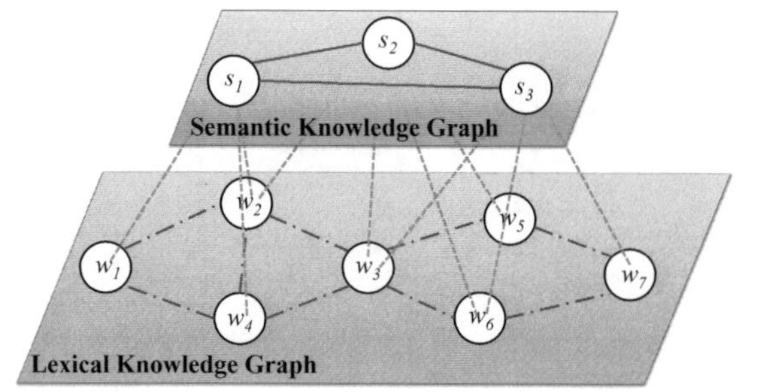


Figure 3: A simplified example of the two knowledge graphs, where a slot candidate $s_i$ is represented as a node in a semantic knowledge graph and a word $w_j$ is represented as a node in a lexical knowledge graph.

the "capability" frame does not convey particular valuable information for SLU. With the trained independent semantic decoders for all slot candidates, adaptation process computes the prominence of slot candidates for ranking and then selects a list of induced slots associated with their corresponding semantic decoders for use in domain-specific dialogue systems, where the detail is described in Section 4.

Then with each induced slot $s_i$ and its corresponding trained semantic decoder $\mathcal{M}^i$, an SLU model can be built to predict whether the semantic slot occurs in the given utterance in a fully unsupervised way. In other words, the SLU model is able to transform the testing utterance into semantic representations without human involvement.

## 4 Slot Ranking Model

The purpose of the ranking model is to distinguish between generic semantic concepts and domain-specific concepts that are relevant to an SDS. To induce meaningful slots for the purpose of SDS, we compute the prominence of the slot candidates using a slot ranking model described below.

With the semantic parses from SEMAFOR, where each frame is viewed independently, so inter-slot relations are not included, the model ranks the slot candidates by integrating two information: (1) the frequency of each slot candidate in the corpus, since slots with higher frequency may be more important. (2) the relations between slot candidates. Assuming that domain-specific concepts are usually related to each other, globally considering inter-slot relations induces a more coherent slot set. Here for baseline scores, we only use the frequency of each slot candidate as its prominence.

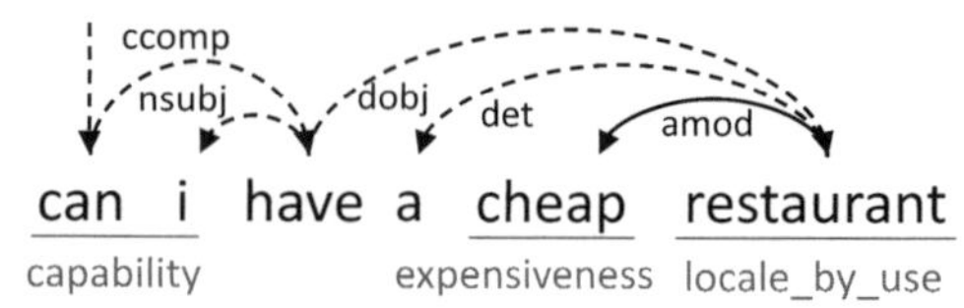


Figure 4: The dependency parsing result on an utterance.

First we construct two knowledge graphs, one is a slot-based semantic knowledge graph and another is a word-based lexical knowledge graph, both of which encode the typed dependency relations in their edge weights. We also connect two graphs to model the relations between slot-filler pairs.

### 4.1 Knowledge Graphs

We construct two undirected graphs, semantic and lexical knowledge graphs. Each node in the semantic knowledge graph is a slot candidate $s_i$ outputted by the frame-semantic parser, and each node in the lexical knowledge graph is a word $w_j$.

- **Slot-based semantic knowledge graph** is built as $G_s = \langle V_s, E_{ss} \rangle$, where $V_s = \{s_i\}$ and $E_{ss} = \{e_{ij} \mid s_i, s_j \in V_s\}$.
- **Word-based lexical knowledge graph** is built as $G_w = \langle V_w, E_{ww} \rangle$, where $V_w = \{w_i\}$ and $E_{ww} = \{e_{ij} \mid w_i, w_j \in V_w\}$.

With two knowledge graphs, we build the edges between slots and slot-fillers to integrate them as shown in Figure 3. Thus the combined graph can be formulated as $G = \langle V_s, V_w, E_{ss}, E_{ww}, E_{ws} \rangle$, where $E_{ws} = \{e_{ij} \mid w_i \in V_w, s_j \in V_s\}$. $E_{ss}$, $E_{ww}$, and $E_{ws}$ correspond to slot-to-slot relations, word-to-word relations, and word-to-slot relations respectively (Chen and Metze, 2012; Chen and Metze, 2013).

### 4.2 Edge Weight Estimation

Considering the relations in the knowledge graphs, the edge weights for $E_{ww}$ and $E_{ss}$ are measured based on the dependency parsing results. The example utterance "*can i have a cheap restaurant*" and its dependency parsing result are illustrated in Figure 4. The arrows denote the de-

| | Typed Dependency Relation | Target Word | Contexts |
|---|---|---|---|
| **Word** | ⟨*restaurant*, AMOD, *cheap*⟩ | *restaurant* | *cheap*/AMOD |
| | | *cheap* | *restaurant*/AMOD$^{-1}$ |
| **Slot** | ⟨locale_by_use, AMOD, expensiveness⟩ | locale_by_use | expensiveness/AMOD |
| | | expansiveness | locale_by_use/AMOD$^{-1}$ |

Table 1: The contexts extracted for training dependency-based word/slot embeddings from the utterance of Fig. 2.

pendency relations from headwords to their dependents, and words on arcs denote types of the dependencies. All typed dependencies between two words are encoded in triples and form a word-based dependency set $\mathcal{T}_w = \{\langle w_i, t, w_j \rangle\}$, where $t$ is the typed dependency between the headword $w_i$ and the dependent $w_j$. For example, Figure 4 generates ⟨*restaurant*, AMOD, *cheap*⟩, ⟨*have*, DOBJ, *restaurant*⟩, etc. for $\mathcal{T}_w$. Similarly, we build a slot-based dependency set $\mathcal{T}_s = \{\langle s_i, t, s_j \rangle\}$ by transforming dependencies between slot-fillers into ones between slots. For example, ⟨*restaurant*, AMOD, *cheap*⟩ from $\mathcal{T}_w$ is transformed into ⟨locale_by_use, AMOD, expensiveness⟩ for building $\mathcal{T}_s$, because both sides of the non-dotted line are parsed as slot-fillers by SEMAFOR.

For the edges within a single knowledge graph, we assign a weight of the edge connecting nodes $x_i$ and $x_j$ as $\hat{r}(x_i, x_j)$, where $x$ is either $s$ or $w$. Since the weights are measured based on the relations between nodes regardless of the directions, we combine the scores of two directional dependencies:

$$\hat{r}(x_i, x_j) = r(x_i \to x_j) + r(x_j \to x_i), \quad (2)$$

where $r(x_i \to x_j)$ is the score estimating the dependency including $x_i$ as a head and $x_j$ as a dependent. In Section 4.2.1 and 4.2.2, we propose two scoring functions for $r(\cdot)$, frequency-based as $r_1(\cdot)$ and embedding-based as $r_2(\cdot)$ respectively.

For the edges in $E_{ws}$, we estimate the edge weights based on the frequency that the slot candidates and the words are parsed as slot-filler pairs. In other words, the edge weight between the slot-filler $w_i$ and the slot candidate $s_j$, $\hat{r}(w_i, s_j)$, is equal to how many times the filler $w_i$ corresponds to the slot candidate $s_j$ in the parsing results.

### 4.2.1 Frequency-Based Measurement

Based on the dependency set $\mathcal{T}_x$, we use $t^*_{x_i \to x_j}$ to denote the most frequent typed dependency with $x_i$ as a head and $x_j$ as a dependent.

$$t^*_{x_i \to x_j} = \arg\max_t C(x_i \xrightarrow[t]{} x_j), \quad (3)$$

where $C(x_i \xrightarrow[t]{} x_j)$ counts how many times the dependency $\langle x_i, t, x_j \rangle$ occurs in the dependency set $\mathcal{T}_x$.

Then the scoring function that estimates the dependency $x_i \to x_j$ is measured as

$$r_1(x_i \to x_j) = C(x_i \xrightarrow[t^*_{x_i \to x_j}]{} x_j), \quad (4)$$

which equals to the highest observed frequency of the dependency $x_i \to x_j$ among all types from $\mathcal{T}_x$.

### 4.2.2 Embedding-Based Measurement

Most neural embeddings use linear bag-of-words contexts, where a window size is defined to produce contexts of the target words (Mikolov et al., 2013c; Mikolov et al., 2013b; Mikolov et al., 2013a). However, some important contexts may be missing due to smaller windows, while larger windows capture broad topical content. A dependency-based embedding approach was proposed to derive contexts based on the syntactic relations the word participates in for training embeddings, where the embeddings are less topical but offer more functional similarity compared to original embeddings (Levy and Goldberg, 2014).

Table 1 shows the extracted dependency-based contexts for each target word from the example in Figure 4, where headwords and their dependents can form the contexts by following the arc on a word in the dependency tree, and $-1$ denotes the directionality of the dependency. After replacing original bag-of-words contexts with dependency-based contexts, we can train dependency-based embeddings for all target words (Yih et al., 2014; Bordes et al., 2011; Bordes et al., 2013).

For training dependency-based word embeddings, each word $w$ is associated with a word vector $\mathbf{v_w} \in$

$\mathbb{R}^d$ and each context $c$ is represented as a context vector $\mathbf{v_c} \in \mathbb{R}^d$, where $d$ is the embedding dimensionality. We learn vector representations for both words and contexts such that the dot product $\mathbf{v_w} \cdot \mathbf{v_c}$ associated with "good" word-context pairs belonging to the training data $\mathcal{D}$ is maximized, leading to the objective function:

$$\arg\max_{\mathbf{v_w},\mathbf{v_c}} \sum_{(w,c)\in\mathcal{D}} \log \frac{1}{1+\exp(-\mathbf{v_c}\cdot\mathbf{v_w})}, \quad (5)$$

which can be trained using stochastic-gradient updates (Levy and Goldberg, 2014). Then we can obtain the dependency-based slot and word embeddings using $\mathcal{T}_s$ and $\mathcal{T}_w$ respectively.

With trained dependency-based embeddings, we estimate the probability that $x_i$ is the headword and $x_j$ is its dependent via the typed dependency $t$ as

$$P(x_i \xrightarrow[t]{} x_j) = \frac{Sim(x_i, x_j/t) + Sim(x_j, x_i/t^{-1})}{2}, \quad (6)$$

where $Sim(x_i, x_j/t)$ is the cosine similarity between the slot/word embeddings $\mathbf{v_{x_i}}$ and the context embeddings $\mathbf{v_{x_j/t}}$ after normalizing to $[0,1]$. Then we can measure the scoring function $r_2(\cdot)$ as

$$r_2(x_i \rightarrow x_j) = C(x_i \xrightarrow[t^*_{x_i\rightarrow x_j}]{} x_j) \cdot P(x_i \xrightarrow[t^*_{x_i\rightarrow x_j}]{} x_j), \quad (7)$$

which is similar to (4) but additionally weighted by the estimated probability. The estimated probability smooths the observed frequency to avoid overfitting due to a smaller dataset.

## 4.3 Random Walk Algorithm

We first compute $L_{ww} = [\hat{r}(w_i, w_j)]_{|V_w|\times|V_w|}$ and $L_{ss} = [\hat{r}(s_i, s_j)]_{|V_s|\times|V_s|}$, where $\hat{r}(w_i, w_j)$ and $\hat{r}(s_i, s_j)$ are either from frequency-based ($r_1(\cdot)$) or embedding-based measurements ($r_2(\cdot)$). Similarly, $L_{ws} = [\hat{r}(w_i, s_j)]_{|V_w|\times|V_s|}$ and $L_{sw} = [\hat{r}(w_i, s_j)]^T_{|V_w|\times|V_s|}$, where $\hat{r}(w_i, s_j)$ is the frequency that $s_j$ and $w_i$ are a slot-filler pair computed in Section 4.2. Then we only keep the top $N$ highest weights for each row in $L_{ww}$ and $L_{ss}$ ($N = 10$), which means that we filter out the edges with smaller weights within the single knowledge graph. Column-normalization are performed for $L_{ww}$, $L_{ss}$, $L_{ws}$, $L_{sw}$ (Shi and Malik, 2000). They can be viewed as word-to-word, slot-to-slot, and word-to-slot relation matrices.

### 4.3.1 Single-Graph Random Walk

Here we run random walk only on the semantic knowledge graph to propagate the scores based on inter-slot relations through the edges $E_{ss}$.

$$R_s^{(t+1)} = (1-\alpha)R_s^{(0)} + \alpha L_{ss} R_s^{(t)}, \quad (8)$$

where $R_s^{(t)}$ denotes the importance scores of the slot candidates $V_s$ in $t$-th iteration. In the algorithm, the score is the interpolation of two scores, the normalized baseline importance of slot candidates ($R_s^{(0)}$), and the scores propagated from the neighboring nodes in the semantic knowledge graph based on slot-to-slot relations via $L_{ss}$. The algorithm will converge when $R_s^{(t+1)} = R_s^{(t)} = R_s^*$ and (9) can be satisfied.

$$R_s^* = \left((1-\alpha)R_s^{(0)}e^T + \alpha L_{ss}\right) R_s^* = M_1 R_s^*, \quad (9)$$

where $e = [1, 1, ..., 1]^T$. It has been shown that the closed-form solution $R_s^*$ of (9) is the dominant eigenvector of $M_1$ (Langville and Meyer, 2005), the eigenvector corresponding to the largest absolute eigenvalue of $M_1$. The solution of $R_s^*$ denotes the updated importance scores for all utterances. Similar to the PageRank algorithm (Brin and Page, 1998), the solution can also be obtained by iteratively updating $R_s^{(t)}$.

### 4.3.2 Double-Graph Random Walk

Here we borrow the idea from two-layer mutually reinforced random walk to propagate the scores based on not only internal importance propagation within the same graph but external mutual reinforcement between different knowledge graphs (Chen and Metze, 2012; Chen and Metze, 2013).

$$\begin{cases} R_s^{(t+1)} = (1-\alpha)R_s^{(0)} + \alpha L_{ss} L_{sw} R_w^{(t)} \\ R_w^{(t+1)} = (1-\alpha)R_w^{(0)} + \alpha L_{ww} L_{ws} R_s^{(t)} \end{cases} \quad (10)$$

In the algorithm, they are the interpolations of two scores, the normalized baseline importance ($R_s^{(0)}$ and $R_w^{(0)}$) and the scores propagated from another graph. For the semantic knowledge graph, $L_{sw} R_w^{(t)}$ is the score from the word set weighted by slot-to-word relations, and then the scores are propagated based on slot-to-slot relations via $L_{ss}$. Similarly, nodes of the lexical knowledge graph also include the scores propagated from the semantic knowledge graph. Then $R_s^{(t+1)}$ and $R_w^{(t+1)}$ can be mutually updated by the latter parts in (10) iteratively. When the algorithm converges, we have $R_s^*$ as follows.

$$\begin{aligned} R_s^* &= (1-\alpha)R_s^{(0)} \quad (11) \\ &+ \alpha L_{ss}L_{sw}\Big((1-\alpha)R_w^{(0)} + \alpha L_{ww}L_{ws}R_s^*\Big) \\ &= \Big((1-\alpha)R_s^{(0)}e^T + \alpha(1-\alpha)L_{ss}L_{sw}R_w^{(0)}e^T \\ &+ \alpha^2 L_{ss}L_{sw}L_{ww}L_{ws}\Big)R_s^* = M_2R_s^*. \end{aligned}$$

The closed-form solution $R_s^*$ of (11) is the dominant eigenvector of $M_2$.

## 5 Experiments

We evaluate our approach in two ways. First, we examine the slot induction accuracy by comparing the ranked list of induced slots with the reference slots created by system developers (Young, 2007). Secondly, with the ranked list of induced slots and their associated semantic decoders, we can evaluate the SLU performance. For the experiments, we evaluate both on ASR transcripts of the raw audio, and on the manual transcripts.

### 5.1 Experimental Setup

In this experiment, we used the Cambridge University SLU corpus, previously used on several other SLU tasks (Henderson et al., 2012; Chen et al., 2013a). The domain of the corpus is about restaurant recommendation in Cambridge; subjects were asked to interact with multiple SDSs in an in-car setting. The corpus contains a total number of 2,166 dialogues, including 15,453 utterances (10,571 for self-training and 4,882 for testing). The data is gender-balanced, with slightly more native than non-native speakers. The vocabulary size is 1868. An ASR system was used to transcribe the speech; the word error rate was reported as 37%. There are 10 slots created by domain experts: addr, area, food, name, phone, postcode, price range, signature, task, and type.

For parameter setting, the damping factor for random walk $\alpha$ is empirically set as 0.9 for all experiments. For training the semantic decoders, we use SVM with a linear kernel to predict each semantic slot. We use Stanford Parser to obtain the collapsed typed syntactic dependencies (Socher et al., 2013) and set the dimensionality of embeddings $d = 300$ in all experiments.

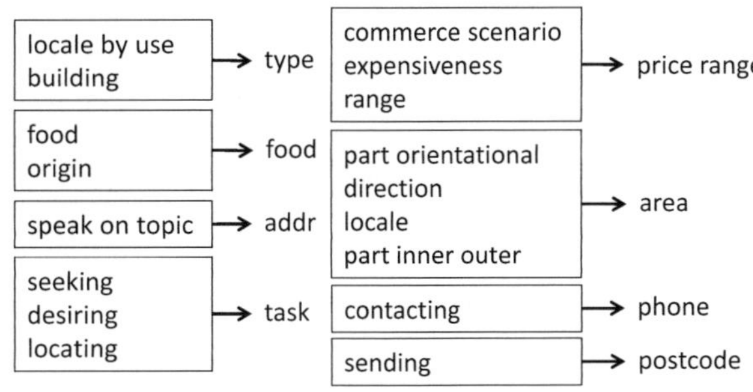


Figure 5: The mappings from induced slots (within blocks) to reference slots (right sides of arrows).

### 5.2 Evaluation Metrics

To eliminate the influence of threshold selection when choosing induced slots, in the following metrics, we take the whole ranking list into account and evaluate the performance by the metrics that are independent of the selected threshold.

#### 5.2.1 Slot Induction

To evaluate the accuracy of the induced slots, we measure their quality as the proximity between induced slots and reference slots. Figure 5 shows the mappings that indicate semantically related induced slots and reference slots (Chen et al., 2013b). For example, "expensiveness $\rightarrow$ price", "food $\rightarrow$ food", and "direction $\rightarrow$ area" show that these induced slots can be mapped into the reference slots defined by experts and carry important semantics in the target domain for developing the task-oriented SDS. Since we define the adaptation task as a ranking problem, with a ranked list of induced slots and associated scores, we can use the standard average precision (AP) and the area under the precision-recall curve (PR-AUC) as our metrics, where the induced slot is counted as correct when it has a mapping to a reference slot.

#### 5.2.2 SLU Model

While semantic slot induction is essential for providing semantic categories and imposing semantic constraints, we are also interested in understanding the performance of our unsupervised SLU models.

| Approach | | | ASR | | | | Manual | | | |
|---|---|---|---|---|---|---|---|---|---|---|
| | | | Slot Induction | | SLU Model | | Slot Induction | | SLU Model | |
| | | | AP | PR-AUC | WAP | AF | AP | PR-AUC | WAP | AF |
| (a) | Baseline (Frequency) | | 56.69 | 54.67 | 35.82 | 43.28 | 53.01 | 50.80 | 36.78 | 44.20 |
| (b) | Single | Frequency | 63.88 | 62.05 | 41.67 | 47.38 | 63.02 | 61.10 | 43.76 | 48.53 |
| (c) | | Embedding | 69.04 | 68.25 | **46.29** | **48.89** | 75.15 | 74.50 | **54.50** | **50.86** |
| (d) | Double | Frequency | 56.83 | 55.31 | 32.64 | 44.91 | 52.12 | 50.54 | 34.01 | 45.05 |
| (e) | | Embedding | **71.48** | **70.84** | 44.06 | 47.91 | **76.42** | **75.94** | 52.89 | 50.40 |

Table 2: The performance of induced slots and corresponding SLU models (%)

For each induced slot with the mapping to a reference slot, we can compute an F-measure of the corresponding semantic decoder, and weight the average precision with corresponding F-measure as weighted average precision (WAP) to evaluate the performance of slot induction and SLU tasks together. The metric scores the ranking result higher if the induced slots corresponding to better semantic decoders are ranked higher. Another metric is the average F-measure (AF), which is the average micro F-measure of SLU models at all cut-off positions in the ranked list. Compared to WAP, AF additionally considers the slot popularity in the dataset.

## 5.3 Evaluation Results

Table 5.1 shows the results on both ASR and manual transcripts. Rows (a) is the baseline only considering the frequency of each slot candidate for ranking (Chen et al., 2013b). Rows (b) and (c) show performance after leveraging a semantic knowledge graph through random walk. Rows (d) and (e) are the results after combining two knowledge graphs. We find almost all results are improved by additionally considering inter-slot relations in terms of single- and double-graph random walk for both ASR and manual transcripts.

### 5.3.1 Slot Induction

For both ASR and manual transcripts, almost all results outperform the baseline, showing that inter-slot relations significantly influence the performance of slot induction. The best performance is from the results of double-graph random walk with the embedding-based measurement, which integrate a semantic knowledge graph and a lexical knowledge graph together and jointly consider slot-to-slot, word-to-word, and word-to-slot relations when scoring the prominence of slot candidates to generate a coherent slot set.

### 5.3.2 SLU Model

For both ASR and manual transcripts, almost all results outperform the baseline, which shows the practical usage for training dialogue systems. The best performance is from the results of single-graph random walk with the embedding-based measurement, which only use the semantic knowledge graph to involve the inter-slot relations. The semantic knowledge graph is not as precise as the lexical one and may be influenced by the performance of the semantic parser more. Although the row (e) does not show better performance than the row (c), double-graph random walk may be more robust because it additionally includes the word relations to avoid only relying on the relations tied with the slot candidates.

## 5.4 Discussion and Analysis

### 5.4.1 Comparing Frequency- and Embedding-Based Measurements

Table 5.1 shows that all results with the embedding-based measurement perform better than those with the frequency-based measurement. The frequency-based measurement also brings large improvement for single-graph approaches, but does not for double-graph ones. The reason is probably that using observed frequencies in the lexical knowledge graph may result in overfitting issues due to the smaller dataset. Additionally including embedding information can smooth the edge weights and deal with data sparsity to improve the performance, especially for the lexical knowledge graph.

#### 5.4.2 Comparing Single- and Double-Graph Approaches

Considering that the embedding-based measurement performs better, we only compare the results of single- and double-graph random walk using this measurement (rows (c) and (e)). It can be seen that the difference between them is not consistent in terms of slot induction and SLU model.

For evaluating slot induction (AP and PR-AUC), the double-graph random walk (row (e)) performs better on both ASR and manual results, which implies that additionally integrating the lexical knowledge graph helps decide a more coherent and complete slot set since we can model the score propagation more precisely (not only slot-level but word-level information). However, for SLU evaluation (WAP and AF), the single-graph random walk (row (c)) performs better, which may imply that the slots carrying the coherent relations from the row (e) may not have good semantic decoder performance so that the performance is decreased a little. For example, double-graph random walk scores the slots local_by_use and expensiveness higher than the slot contacting, while the single-graph method ranks the latter higher. local_by_use and expensiveness are more important on this domain but contacting has very good performance of its semantic decoder, so the double-graph approach does not show the improvement when evaluating SLU models. This allows us to try an improved method of jointly optimizing the slot coherence and SLU performance in the future.

#### 5.4.3 Relation Discovery Analysis

To interpret the inter-slot relations, we output the slot-to-slot relations with highest scores from the best results (row (e) in Table 5.1) in Table 3, and the automatically constructed ontology is shown in Figure 6. It can be shown that the outputted inter-slot relations are reasonable and usually connect two important semantic slots in this restaurant domain. This proves that inter-slot relations help decide a coherent and complete slot set and enhance the interpretability of semantic slots. Therefore, from a practical perspective, developers are able to design the framework of dialogue systems more easily, and the development of SDS can be speeded up with less human effort.

| Rank | Relation |
|---|---|
| 1 | ⟨locale_by_use, NN, food⟩ |
| 2 | ⟨food, AMOD, expensiveness⟩ |
| 3 | ⟨locale_by_use, AMOD, expensiveness⟩ |
| 4 | ⟨seeking, PREP_FOR, food⟩ |
| 5 | ⟨food, AMOD, relational_quantity⟩ |
| 6 | ⟨desiring, DOBJ, food⟩ |
| 7 | ⟨seeking, PREP_FOR, locale_by_use⟩ |
| 8 | ⟨food, DET, quantity⟩ |

Table 3: The top inter-slot relations learned from the training set of ASR outputs.

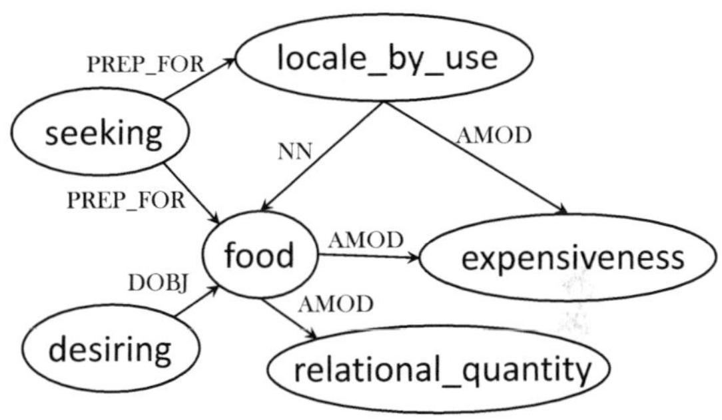


Figure 6: The automatically constructed domain-specific ontology based on Table 3.

## 6 Conclusion

The paper proposes an approach of jointly considering inter-slot relations for slot induction to output a more coherent slot set, where two knowledge graphs, a slot-based semantic knowledge graph and a word-based lexical knowledge graph, are built and combined by a random walk algorithm. The automatically induced slots carry coherent and interpretable relations and can be used for training better SLU models of SDSs in an unsupervised fashion.

## Acknowledgments

We thank Anatole Gershman for helpful discussions and anonymous reviewers for their useful comments. We are also grateful to MetLife's support. Any opinions, findings, and conclusions expressed in this publication are those of the authors and do not necessarily reflect the views of funding agencies.

## References


Collin F Baker, Charles J Fillmore, and John B Lowe. 1998. The Berkeley FrameNet project. In *Proceedings of COLING*, pages 86–90.

Antoine Bordes, Jason Weston, Ronan Collobert, Yoshua Bengio, et al. 2011. Learning structured embeddings of knowledge bases. In *Proceedings of AAAI*.

Antoine Bordes, Nicolas Usunier, Alberto Garcia-Duran, Jason Weston, and Oksana Yakhnenko. 2013. Translating embeddings for modeling multi-relational data. In *Advances in Neural Information Processing Systems*, pages 2787–2795.

Sergey Brin and Lawrence Page. 1998. The anatomy of a large-scale hypertextual web search engine. *Computer networks and ISDN systems*, 30(1):107–117.

Yun-Nung Chen and Florian Metze. 2012. Two-layer mutually reinforced random walk for improved multi-party meeting summarization. In *Proceedings of The 4th IEEE Workshop on Spoken Language Tachnology*, pages 461–466.

Yun-Nung Chen and Florian Metze. 2013. Multi-layer mutually reinforced random walk with hidden parameters for improved multi-party meeting summarization. In *INTERSPEECH*, pages 485–489.

Yun-Nung Chen and Alexander I. Rudnicky. 2014. Dynamically supporting unexplored domains in conversational interactions by enriching semantics with neural word embeddings. In *Proceedings of 2014 IEEE Spoken Language Technology Workshop (SLT)*,.

Yun-Nung Chen, William Yang Wang, and Alexander I. Rudnicky. 2013a. An empirical investigation of sparse log-linear models for improved dialogue act classification. In *Proceedings of ICASSP*, pages 8317–8321.

Yun-Nung Chen, William Yang Wang, and Alexander I Rudnicky. 2013b. Unsupervised induction and filling of semantic slots for spoken dialogue systems using frame-semantic parsing. In *Proceedings of 2013 IEEE Workshop on Automatic Speech Recognition and Understanding (ASRU)*, pages 120–125. IEEE.

Yun-Nung Chen, Dilek Hakkani-Tür, and Gokhan Tur. 2014a. Deriving local relational surface forms from dependency-based entity embeddings for unsupervised spoken language understanding. In *Proceedings of 2014 IEEE Spoken Language Technology Workshop (SLT)*,.

Yun-Nung Chen, William Yang Wang, and Alexander I. Rudnicky. 2014b. Leveraging frame semantics and distributional semantics for unsupervised semantic slot induction in spoken dialogue systems. In *Proceedings of 2014 IEEE Spoken Language Technology Workshop (SLT)*,.

Dipanjan Das, Nathan Schneider, Desai Chen, and Noah A Smith. 2010. Probabilistic frame-semantic parsing. In *Proceedings of The Conference of the North American Chapter of the Association for Computational Linguistics: Human Language Technologies*, pages 948–956.

Dipanjan Das, Desai Chen, André F. T. Martins, Nathan Schneider, and Noah A. Smith. 2013. Frame-semantic parsing. *Computational Linguistics*.

Marie-Catherine De Marneffe and Christopher D Manning. 2008. The Stanford typed dependencies representation. In *Coling 2008: Proceedings of the workshop on Cross-Framework and Cross-Domain Parser Evaluation*, pages 1–8. Association for Computational Linguistics.

Ali El-Kahky, Derek Liu, Ruhi Sarikaya, Gökhan Tür, Dilek Hakkani-Tür, and Larry Heck. 2014. Extending domain coverage of language understanding systems via intent transfer between domains using knowledge graphs and search query click logs. In *Proceedings of ICASSP*.

Charles J Fillmore. 1976. Frame semantics and the nature of language. *Annals of the NYAS*, 280(1):20–32.

Dilek Hakkani-Tür, Frédéric Béchet, Giuseppe Riccardi, and Gokhan Tur. 2006. Beyond ASR 1-best: Using word confusion networks in spoken language understanding. *Computer Speech & Language*, 20(4):495–514.

Dilek Hakkani-Tür, Larry Heck, and Gokhan Tur. 2013. Using a knowledge graph and query click logs for unsupervised learning of relation detection. In *Proceedings of ICASSP*, pages 8327–8331.

Dilek Hakkani-Tür, Asli Celikyilmaz, Larry Heck, Gokhan Tur, and Geoff Zweig. 2014. Probabilistic enrichment of knowledge graph entities for relation detection in conversational understanding. In *Proceedings of INTERSPEECH*.

Larry P Heck, Dilek Hakkani-Tür, and Gokhan Tur. 2013. Leveraging knowledge graphs for web-scale unsupervised semantic parsing. In *Proceedings of INTERSPEECH*.

Matthew Henderson, Milica Gasic, Blaise Thomson, Pirros Tsiakoulis, Kai Yu, and Steve Young. 2012. Discriminative spoken language understanding using word confusion networks. In *Proceedings of SLT*, pages 176–181.

Diana Inkpen and Graeme Hirst. 2006. Building and using a lexical knowledge base of near-synonym differences. *Computational Linguistics*, 32(2):223–262.

Amy N Langville and Carl D Meyer. 2005. A survey of eigenvector methods for web information retrieval. *SIAM review*, 47(1):135–161.

Ni Lao, Tom Mitchell, and William W Cohen. 2011. Random walk inference and learning in a large scale knowledge base. In *Proceedings of the Conference on Empirical Methods in Natural Language Processing*, pages 529–539. Association for Computational Linguistics.

Ni Lao, Amarnag Subramanya, Fernando Pereira, and William W Cohen. 2012. Reading the web with learned syntactic-semantic inference rules. In *Proceedings of the 2012 Joint Conference on Empirical Methods in Natural Language Processing and Computational Natural Language Learning*, pages 1017–1026. Association for Computational Linguistics.

Omer Levy and Yoav Goldberg. 2014. Dependency-based word embeddings. In *Proceedings of ACL*.

Peipei Li, Haixun Wang, Hongsong Li, and Xindong Wu. 2013a. Assessing sparse information extraction using semantic contexts. In *Proceedings of the 22nd ACM international conference on Conference on information & knowledge management*, pages 1709–1714. ACM.

Peipei Li, Haixun Wang, Kenny Q Zhu, Zhongyuan Wang, and Xindong Wu. 2013b. Computing term similarity by large probabilistic isa knowledge. In *Proceedings of the 22nd ACM international conference on Conference on information & knowledge management*, pages 1401–1410. ACM.

Tomas Mikolov, Kai Chen, Greg Corrado, and Jeffrey Dean. 2013a. Efficient estimation of word representations in vector space. In *Proceedings of Workshop at ICLR*.

Tomas Mikolov, Ilya Sutskever, Kai Chen, Greg S Corrado, and Jeff Dean. 2013b. Distributed representations of words and phrases and their compositionality. In *Proceedings of Advances in Neural Information Processing Systems*, pages 3111–3119.

Tomas Mikolov, Wen-tau Yih, and Geoffrey Zweig. 2013c. Linguistic regularities in continuous space word representations. In *HLT-NAACL*, pages 746–751. Citeseer.

Jianbo Shi and Jitendra Malik. 2000. Normalized cuts and image segmentation. *Pattern Analysis and Machine Intelligence, IEEE Transactions on*, 22(8):888–905.

Richard Socher, John Bauer, Christopher D Manning, and Andrew Y Ng. 2013. Parsing with compositional vector grammars. In *Proceedings of the ACL conference*. Citeseer.

Yangqiu Song, Haixun Wang, Zhongyuan Wang, Hongsong Li, and Weizhu Chen. 2011. Short text conceptualization using a probabilistic knowledgebase. In *Proceedings of the Twenty-Second international joint conference on Artificial Intelligence-Volume Volume Three*, pages 2330–2336. AAAI Press.

Fang Wang, Zhongyuan Wang, Zhoujun Li, and Ji-Rong Wen. 2014. Concept-based short text classification and ranking. In *Proceedings of the 23rd ACM International Conference on Conference on Information and Knowledge Management*, pages 1069–1078. ACM.

Wen-tau Yih, Xiaodong He, and Christopher Meek. 2014. Semantic parsing for single-relation question answering. In *Proceedings of ACL*.

Steve Young. 2007. CUED standard dialogue acts. Technical report, Cambridge University Engineering Department.

# Expanding Paraphrase Lexicons by Exploiting Lexical Variants

**Atsushi Fujita**[†] **Pierre Isabelle**[‡]
[†]National Institute of Information and Communications Technology
3-5 Hikaridai, Seika-cho, Souraku-gun, Kyoto, 619-0289, Japan
atsushi.fujita@nict.go.jp
[‡]National Research Council Canada
1200 Montreal Road, Ottawa, Ontario, K1A 0R6, Canada
Pierre.Isabelle@nrc.ca

## Abstract

This study tackles the problem of paraphrase acquisition: achieving high coverage as well as accuracy. Our method first induces paraphrase patterns from given seed paraphrases, exploiting the generality of paraphrases exhibited by pairs of lexical variants, e.g., "amendment" and "amending," in a fully empirical way. It then searches monolingual corpora for new paraphrases that match the patterns. This can extract paraphrases comprising words that are completely different from those of the given seeds. In experiments, our method expanded seed sets by factors of 42 to 206, gaining 84% to 208% more coverage than a previous method that generalizes only identical word forms. Human evaluation through a paraphrase substitution test demonstrated that the newly acquired paraphrases retained reasonable quality, given substantially high-quality seeds.

## 1 Introduction

One of the characteristics of human languages is that the same semantic content can be expressed using several different linguistic expressions, i.e., paraphrases. Dealing with paraphrases is an important issue in a broad range of natural language processing (NLP) tasks (Madnani and Dorr, 2010; Androutsopoulos and Malakasiotis, 2010).

To adequately and robustly deal with paraphrases, a large-scale knowledge base containing words and phrases having approximately the same meaning is indispensable. Thus, the task of automatically creating such large-scale **paraphrase lexicons** has been drawing the attention of many researchers (see Section 2 for details). The challenge is to ensure substantial coverage along with high accuracy despite the natural tension between these factors. Among the different types of language resources, monolingual corpora[1] offer the largest coverage, but the quality of the extracted candidates is generally rather low. The difficulty lies in the manner of distinguishing paraphrases from expressions that stand in different semantic relations, e.g., antonyms and sibling words, using only the statistics estimated from such corpora. In contrast, highly accurate paraphrases can be extracted from parallel or comparable corpora, but their coverage is limited owing to the limited availability of such corpora for most languages.

This study aims to improve coverage while maintaining accuracy. To that end, we propose a method that exploits the generality exhibited by pairs of **lexical variants**. Given a seed set of paraphrase pairs, our method first induces paraphrase patterns by generalizing not only identical word forms (Fujita et al., 2012) but also pairs of lexical variants. For instance, from a seed pair (1a), a pattern (1b) is acquired, where the pair of lexical variants ("amendment", "amending") and the shared word form "regulation" are generalized.

(1) a. amendment of regulation
$\Leftrightarrow$ amending regulation
b. $X$:ment of $Y{:}\phi \Leftrightarrow X$:ing $Y{:}\phi$

With such patterns, new paraphrase pairs that would have been missed using only the surface forms are extracted from a monolingual corpus. Obtainable pairs can include those comprising words that are

[1]The term "monolingual corpora" in this study refers to monolingual non-parallel corpora, unless otherwise explicitly noted. As reviewed in Section 2.1.2, monolingual parallel corpora have also been used as a source of paraphrases.



*Human Language Technologies: The 2015 Annual Conference of the North American Chapter of the ACL*, pages 630–640,
Denver, Colorado, May 31 – June 5, 2015. ©2015 Association for Computational Linguistics

completely different from those of the seed paraphrases, e.g., (2a) and (2b).

(2) a. investment of resources
⇔ investing resources
b. recruitment of engineers
⇔ recruiting engineers

While the generality underlying paraphrases has been exploited either by handcrafted rules (Harris, 1957; Mel'čuk and Polguère, 1987; Jacquemin, 1999; Fujita et al., 2007) or by data-driven techniques (Ganitkevitch et al., 2011; Fujita et al., 2012), we still lack a robust and accurate way of identifying various types of lexical variants. Our method tackles this issue using affix patterns that are also acquired from high-quality seed paraphrases in a fully empirical way. Consequently, our method has the potential to apply to many languages.

## 2 Previous Work

### 2.1 Creating Paraphrase Lexicons

Researchers have been intensively studying methods for automatically creating paraphrase lexicons using various types of corpora. There are two major streams: one that uses monolingual corpora and one that uses parallel or comparable corpora.

#### 2.1.1 Monolingual Corpora

A monolingual corpus is the most promising resource when targeting increased coverage, thanks to the availability of Web-scale monolingual data. Techniques that use such corpora mostly extract pairs of expressions by exploiting the **contextual similarity** associated with the Distributional Hypothesis (Harris, 1954). A given expression is represented with its co-occurring expressions such as adjacent word $n$-grams (Paşca and Dienes, 2005; Bhagat and Ravichandran, 2008; Marton, 2013), nominal elements (Lin and Pantel, 2001; Szpektor et al., 2004; De Saeger et al., 2011), and modifiers and modified words (Hagiwara et al., 2006). The similarity of a pair of expressions is calculated by comparing the distributions of their contexts.

Despite the quantitative advantage, this approach tends to result in low accuracy. This is because contextual information alone often fails to differentiate paraphrases from expressions that have other semantic relations, e.g., antonyms and sibling words.

#### 2.1.2 Parallel and Comparable Corpora

Much effort has gone into compiling monolingual parallel corpora and extracting paraphrases from them by identifying corresponding parts of aligned sentences. Barzilay and McKeown (2001) and Pang et al. (2003) collected multiple human translations of the same source text. Multiple verbalizations of mathematical proofs were also used (Barzilay and Lee, 2002). This triangulating method provides solid anchors that guarantee the semantic equivalence of sentences (or text fragments).

Monolingual comparable corpora are also useful sources of paraphrases. For instance, articles from different newswire services describing the same event can be used in that way (Shinyama et al., 2002; Barzilay and Elhadad, 2003; Dolan et al., 2004; Wubben et al., 2009). Chen and Dolan (2011) created such corpora by collecting multiple descriptions of short movies through crowdsourcing. Web-harvested definition sentences of the same term often contain paraphrases (Hashimoto et al., 2011; Yan et al., 2013).

Bilingual parallel corpora have been recognized as sources of paraphrases since (Bannard and Callison-Burch, 2005). First, a translation table is created using techniques developed for statistical machine translation. Then, pairs of expressions in the same language that share the same translations are extracted. For instance, a pair ("under control", "in check") will be extracted if they are both linked with the German translation "unter controlle." Each paraphrase pair $(e_1, e_2)$ is assigned probabilities, $p(e_2|e_1)$ and $p(e_1|e_2)$, estimated by marginalizing over all the translations $F$ shared by $e_1$ and $e_2$, i.e., $p(e_2|e_1) = \sum_{f \in F} p(e_2|f)p(f|e_1)$.

This **bilingual pivoting** approach inspired further techniques such as the use of syntactic information as the basis of constraints (Callison-Burch, 2008; Zhao et al., 2009), learning patterns using synchronous grammar (Ganitkevitch et al., 2011), uncovering missing links by combining multiple translation tables and other lexical resources (Kok and Brockett, 2010), and re-ranking candidate pairs on the basis of contextual similarity (Chan et al., 2011). Ganitkevitch and Callison-Burch (2014) compiled paraphrase lexicons for various languages on this approach.

Parallel/comparable corpora are useful sources of highly accurate paraphrases. However, for most languages, only small paraphrase lexicons can be created due to the limited availability of such corpora.

#### 2.1.3 Combination of Multiple Corpora

Unlike the above methods, which used only a single type of corpus as sources of paraphrases, Fujita et al. (2012) used both bilingual parallel and monolingual corpora as sources. In that method, paraphrase pairs, e.g., (3a), are first acquired from a bilingual parallel corpus using the bilingual pivoting method and several heuristic filters for drastic noise reduction. Second, each paraphrase pair is generalized into a paraphrase pattern[2], e.g., (3b). Finally, new pairs, e.g., (3c), are extracted from a monolingual corpus using the patterns.

(3) a. amendment of regulation
⇔ amending regulation
b. amendment of $X$ ⇔ amending $X$
c. amendment of documents
⇔ amending documents

Using that method, they were able to expand the seed lexicon by a large multiple (15 to 40 times), and the new paraphrase pairs were of reasonably good quality. However, they introduced variables only for identical word forms shared by both sides of each pair and left corresponding pairs of lexical variants, e.g., ("amendment", "amending") in (3a), untouched.

### 2.2 Dealing with Lexical Variants

In this study, the term **lexical variants** covers, at least, the following three types of word groups.

**Lexical derivations:** different words that share the same stem and a large part of their meaning, e.g., {"develop", "developer", "development", ...}. Words in such a group can have different parts-of-speech.

**Morphological variants:** different surface forms of the same word, e.g., {"amend", "amends", "amending", ...}. These are derived based on processes such as inflection and conjugation.

**Orthographic variants:** different spellings of the same inflectional/conjugation form of the same word, e.g., {"color", "colour"} and {"authorize", "authorise"}.

Several syntactic and semantic theories, such as transformational grammar (Harris, 1957) and Meaning-Text Theory (Mel'čuk and Polguère, 1987), propose a representation of paraphrases that involve alternations of lexical variants. Jacquemin (1999) and Fujita et al. (2007) addressed this type of paraphrase using manually described syntactic transformation patterns in combination with dictionaries of lexical variants.

Catvar (Habash and Dorr, 2003) is a comprehensive lexical derivation database for English. WordNet (Fellbaum, 1998) also contains information of that kind and is currently available for various languages. Despite its high accuracy, manual creation of rich lexical resources requires a large human effort. Gaussier (1999) and Fujita et al. (2007) extracted groups of lexical derivations from a list of headwords of dictionaries through mining affix patterns. This approach significantly reduces human effort, maintaining reasonable accuracy, but the coverage is still limited because of the reliance on manually compiled dictionaries.

## 3 Proposed Method

This study is the first attempt to exploit various types of lexical variants for acquiring paraphrases in a completely empirical way.

Given a seed paraphrase lexicon ($S_{Seed}$) our method (henceforth ***LEXVAR***) expands it in two steps (see also Figure 1).

**Step 1. Learning paraphrase patterns:** From $S_{Seed}$, we learn a set of paraphrase patterns, generalizing various types of lexical variants in addition to identical word forms.

**Step 2. Harvesting new paraphrase pairs:** Using the learned paraphrase patterns, we harvest a set of new paraphrase pairs ($S_{LV}$) from monolingual corpora.

*LEXVAR* subsumes Fujita et al. (2012)'s method explained in Section 2.1.3 (henceforth ***IDENT***), and its output $S_{LV}$ always subsumes *IDENT*'s output ($S_{ID}$). As *LEXVAR* and *IDENT* have the effect of expanding pre-existing paraphrase lexicons, they can be used as a complement to the other methods for acquiring paraphrases, provided they produce a

[2] If a constituency parser is available for the language of interest, one can learn syntax-based patterns during the bilingual pivoting process (Ganitkevitch et al., 2011).

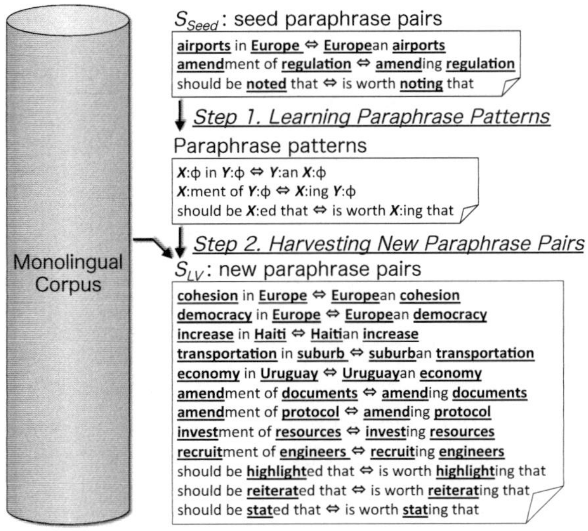


Figure 1: Overview of our proposed method.

sufficient number of high-quality pairs to make lexical generalization possible.

### 3.0 Step 0. Acquiring Seed Paraphrase Pairs

Our method requires as input a seed paraphrase lexicon ($S_{Seed}$) that has high quality and preferably exhibits various lexical correspondences that our method will exploit. For this purpose, paraphrases acquired from bilingual or monolingual parallel corpora are preferable (see Section 2.1.2).

In this study, we take the bilingual pivoting method as an example for the sake of reproducibility. However, the method also outputs a large number of non-paraphrases. To obtain further clean seeds, we apply several filters as described in (Fujita et al., 2012) and discard pairs that have low paraphrase probability, i.e., $p(e_2|e_1) < 0.01$, following the convention in (Du et al., 2010; Max, 2010; Denkowski and Lavie, 2010; Fujita et al., 2012).

Previous work (Chan et al., 2011; Fujita et al., 2012; Ganitkevitch et al., 2013) has proved that the information obtained from monolingual data can be used for assessing bilingually originated paraphrases. Thus, pairs that have low contextual similarity are also filtered out. Among various recipes for computing contextual similarity, we use a simple one: cosine measure of two context vectors comprising adjacent word 1–4 grams of all of the phrase appearances in given monolingual data. For a fair comparison with previous work, we eliminate only pairs that have no shared context, i.e., $Sim(e_1, e_2) = 0$.

### 3.1 Step 1. Learning Paraphrase Patterns

Given a set of seed paraphrases ($S_{Seed}$) we first induce a set of paraphrase patterns. From a seed paraphrase (4a), for instance, while *IDENT* learns (4b), *LEXVAR* generates (4c) by exploiting the generality exhibited by corresponding pairs of lexical variants, i.e., ("amendment", "amending").

(4) a. amendment of regulation
⇔ amending regulation
b. amendment of $X$ ⇔ amending $X$
c. $X$:ment of $Y$:$\phi$ ⇔ $X$:ing $Y$:$\phi$

The central issue at this stage is to robustly and accurately identify various types of lexical variants. We examine a data-driven approach, targeting for increased coverage, but manually created resources such as dictionaries can also be used.

#### 3.1.1 Collecting Affix Patterns

As exemplified by ("$X$:ment", "$X$:ing") in (4c), we represent pairs of lexical variants with **affix patterns**. While Gaussier (1999) considered only suffix patterns, we also deal with prefix patterns such as those exhibited by ("reliable", "unreliable") and ("exist", "coexist") observed in the following paraphrase pairs.

(5) a. is not reliable ⇔ is unreliable
b. exist together with ⇔ coexist with

However, we currently do not consider prefix/suffix combinations, such as ("directly", "indirect") and ("believed", "unbelievable"), and other types of affixes than prefixes and suffixes.

Reliable affix patterns are collected from $S_{Seed}$ (cf., headwords of manually compiled dictionaries (Gaussier, 1999; Fujita et al., 2007)). First, candidates of affix patterns are extracted from $S_{Seed}$ on the following assumption.

> A pair of words will share a definite semantic relation if the words appear on opposite sides of a paraphrase pair and have the same stem.

We do not rely on any language resources to identify the stems of words. Instead, we regard word pairs that share at least one character as candidate

| $\text{Word}_1$ | $\text{Word}_2$ | $\text{Affix}_1$ | $\text{Affix}_2$ | Stem |
|---|---|---|---|---|
| aimed | aims | $X$:ed | $X$:s | aim |
| aimed | achieve | $X$:imed | $X$:chieve | a |
| achieving | aims | $X$:chieving | $X$:ims | a |
| achieving | achieve | $X$:ing | $X$:e | achiev |

Table 1: Candidate pairs of lexical variants and corresponding affix patterns extracted from (6).

| $\text{Affix}_1$ | $\text{Affix}_2$ | # of unique stems length $\geq 5$ | # of unique stems length $<5$ | Result |
|---|---|---|---|---|
| $X$:chieve | $X$:imed | 0 | 1 | Eliminated |
| $X$:chieving | $X$:ims | 0 | 1 | Eliminated |
| $X$:ed | $X$:s | 69 | 22 | Retained |
| $X$:ing | $X$:e | 330 | 70 | Retained |

Table 2: Filtering affix patterns (# of unique stems taken from our experimental result of Europarl setting).

pairs of lexical variants and extract the longest common prefix/suffix as their corresponding affix patterns. From a paraphrase pair (6), for instance, we separately extract four pairs of words and their corresponding affix patterns, as shown in Table 1.

(6) is aimed at achieving ⇔ aims to achieve

Our candidate affix patterns are then filtered using the following criterion (Gaussier, 1999).

> An affix pattern is retained iff it is associated with at least $n$ unique stems that are at least $k$ characters in length.

This criterion relies on two parameters, $n$ and $k$. The parameter $n$ assesses whether a pattern is sufficiently productive. The other ($k$) is more linguistically motivated: a genuine pattern is more likely to be used for long stems, as affixation is a general operation for producing lexical derivations in many languages. In particular, we set $k = 5$ and $n = 2$, as proposed in (Gaussier, 1999). Table 2 presents examples of filtering affix patterns eliminated and retained with this setting.

#### 3.1.2 Generating Paraphrase Patterns

Using the affix patterns acquired in the previous step, paraphrase patterns are generated from the seed paraphrase pairs in $S_{Seed}$. In this step, we exhaustively consider all the combinations of word forms and lexical variants that match one of the affix patterns. From the paraphrase pair (6), the following pattern is generated.

(7) is $X$:ed at $Y$:ing ⇔ $X$:s to $Y$:e

Thanks to the above filtering mechanism, spurious patterns, such as (8), are not generated.

(8) is $X$:imed at $Y$:chieving
⇔ $Y$:ims to $X$:chieve

### 3.2 Step 2. Harvesting New Paraphrase Pairs

Given a set of paraphrase patterns, e.g., (4c) and (7), new paraphrase pairs are harvested from monolingual corpora. In this process, each paraphrase pattern is used as a template such that the expressions that match both sides of the patterns are collected.

Unlike *IDENT*'s patterns, e.g., (4b), *LEXVAR* also collects corresponding pairs of lexical variants designated by each pattern. However, affix pattern alone cannot guarantee the semantic relation between a corresponding pair of words that each paraphrase pattern implicitly requires. For instance, the pattern (9b) is learned from (9a), where a definite relation is assumed between the two elements of ("$X$:$\phi$", "$X$:an").

(9) a. countries of Europe
⇔ European nations
b. countries of $X$:$\phi$ ⇔ $X$:an nations

Word pairs inappropriate for this pattern, e.g., ("uncle", "unclean") and ("beg", "began"), would be extracted alongside appropriate ones, e.g., ("Haiti", "Haitian") and ("suburb", "suburban"). Nonetheless, we suppose that the other surface parts of each paraphrase pair, e.g., "countries of" and "nations" in (9b), can effectively constrain instances, guaranteeing the existence of each entire phrase of the pair.

Pattern matching alone can generate pairs that are not suitable as paraphrases in any context. Thus, we assess the reliability of each pair by calculating contextual similarity between two phrases in the same manner as cleaning $S_{Seed}$: a pair of phrases is eliminated, if the phrases are used in completely dissimilar contexts.

### 3.3 Limitation

While *LEXVAR* exploits a kind of generality of paraphrases exhibited by pairs of lexical variants, it does not exploit paraphrase pairs comprising completely different surface forms such as those pairs in (10).

(10) a. look like ⇔ resemble
b. burst into tears ⇔ cry

To create further large paraphrase lexicons, we need to acquire these idiosyncratic paraphrases by improving existing methods and/or exploring yet another approach.

Another limitation of *LEXVAR* is that it considers only prefixes and suffixes of words as clues of lexical correspondences. We will need extensions to deal with a wider range of lexical correspondences. For instance, depending on the targeted language, other types of affixes, such as infixes and circumfixes, should be taken into account. Gaussier (1999) pointed out that some lexical derivations involve character-level alternations, e.g., "c" and "ç." Fujita et al. (2007) demonstrated that lexical derivations in an ideographic language, i.e., Japanese, can be captured by considering both ideographs and their phonetic transcriptions.

Last but not least, as *LEXVAR* regards only corpus as source, it does not acquire paraphrases that do not appear in a given corpus.

## 4 Expanding Paraphrase Lexicons

To what extent can our *LEXVAR* method expand a given paraphrase lexicon? We examined this, taking English as a target language and the bilingual pivoting method as the means of acquiring $S_{Seed}$.

### 4.1 Seed Paraphrase Pairs

We conducted experiments on the following two corpora configurations.

**Europarl setting:** The English–French version of the Europarl Parallel Corpus[3] comprising 2.0 M sentence pairs (55.7 M words in English and 61.9 M words in French) was used as a bilingual corpus. Its English side and the 2011–2013 editions of News Crawl corpora[4] comprising 52.0 M sentences (1.20 B words) were used as a monolingual corpus.

**NTCIR setting:** The Japanese–English Patent Translation data[5] comprising 3.2 M sentence pairs (107 M words in English and 116 M morphemes in Japanese) was used as a bilingual parallel corpus, while its English side and the 39.9 M sentences (1.36 B words) from the 2006–2007 chapters of NTCIR unaligned patent documents were used as a monolingual corpus.

For learning curve experiments, several sizes of bilingual sub-corpora were created by sub-sampling sentence pairs for both settings.

The other language resources involved in this experiment are as follows.

**Phrase table learner:** SyMGIZA++[6] was used for IBM2 alignment, then grow-diag-final phrase extraction and phrase table pruning were performed using toolkits in Moses[7].

**Tokenizer:** The tokenizer distributed with Moses was used for both English and French texts. For Japanese data, MeCab[8] was used.

**Stoplists:** To perform several types of filtering proposed by Fujita et al. (2012), we used the stoplists available on the Web[9]: 571 English and 463 French words. For Japanese, we manually listed 160 morphemes.

### 4.2 Paraphrase Patterns

Paraphrase patterns were learned from the set of seed paraphrase pairs. Figure 2 shows the numbers of the acquired paraphrase patterns and the percentages of paraphrase pairs in the seed lexicon, $S_{Seed}$, covered by the patterns.

As illustrated by example (4), *LEXVAR* learns more general paraphrase patterns than *IDENT*. Applied to another seed paraphrase pair (11a), *IDENT* will generate another pattern (11b), but *LEXVAR* will not: the corresponding (4c) is already learned.

(11) a. development of tourism
$\Leftrightarrow$ developing tourism
b. development of $X \Leftrightarrow$ developing $X$

On the other hand, *LEXVAR* also learns patterns from seed paraphrase pairs that *IDENT* ignores, e.g., (6) and (9a). Consequently, a wider range of seed paraphrases were involved in learning patterns and more patterns were acquired.

### 4.3 New Paraphrase Pairs

Finally, new paraphrases were acquired from the monolingual data. At this time, only single words

[3] http://statmt.org/europarl/, release 7
[4] http://statmt.org/wmt14/translation-task.html
[5] http://ntcir.nii.ac.jp/PatentMT-2/
[6] http://psi.amu.edu.pl/en/index.php?title=SyMGIZA
[7] http://statmt.org/moses/, RELEASE-2.1.1
[8] https://code.google.com/p/mecab/, version 0.996
[9] http://members.unine.ch/jacques.savoy/clef/

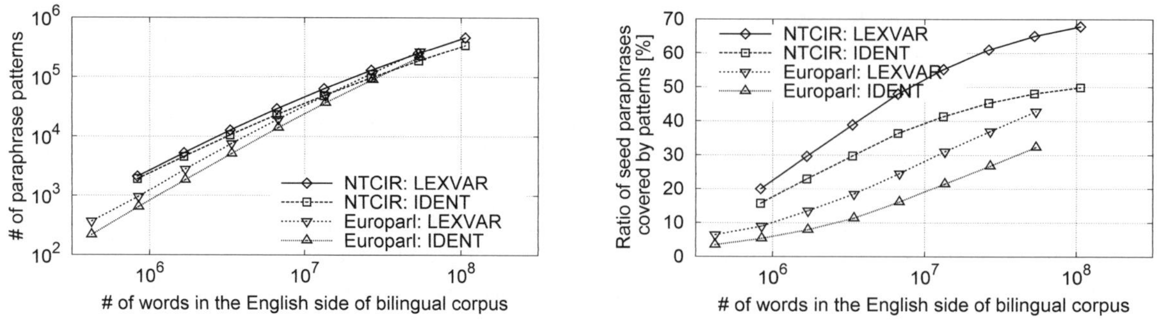


Figure 2: Statistics for the acquired paraphrase patterns: number and coverage against $S_{Seed}$.

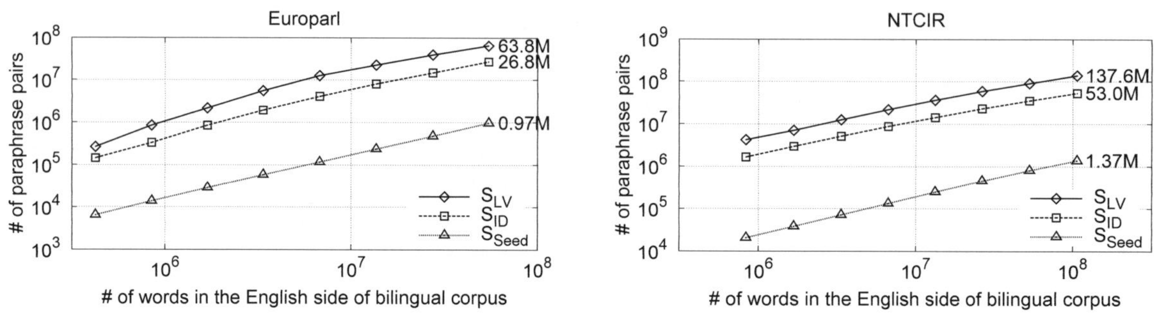


Figure 3: Number of acquired paraphrase pairs (left: Europarl, right: NTCIR).

were regarded as potential slot-fillers for the patterns. Recall that $S_{LV}$ and $S_{ID}$ are the sets of paraphrases generated by *LEXVAR* and *IDENT*, respectively, and $S_{LV} \supseteq S_{ID}$. Pairs that appeared in $S_{Seed}$ and those used in completely dissimilar contexts were excluded from both $S_{ID}$ and $S_{LV}$.

Figure 3 demonstrates that, irrespective of the size of the bilingual corpus, *LEXVAR* yielded far more (relative) coverage of paraphrase pairs $S_{LV}$ than not only $S_{Seed}$ but also $S_{ID}$. When the full bilingual corpora were used, $S_{LV}$ contained 63.8 M and 137.6 M paraphrase pairs in the two respective settings, while $S_{ID}$ contained only 26.8 M and 53.0 M pairs. The seed set $S_{Seed}$ can be pooled with $S_{LV}$; thus, *LEXVAR* expanded $S_{Seed}$ by approximately 67 and 101 times in the two respective settings. Figure 4 illustrates the ratio of the expanded parts of the paraphrase lexicons $S_{LV}$ and $S_{ID}$ against the seed set $S_{Seed}$. The ratio of $S_{LV}$ against $S_{Seed}$ ranged over 41–109 and 100–205 in the two respective settings. This figure also emphasizes the visible advantage of $S_{LV}$ over $S_{ID}$: 84%–208% and 139%–159% more coverage.

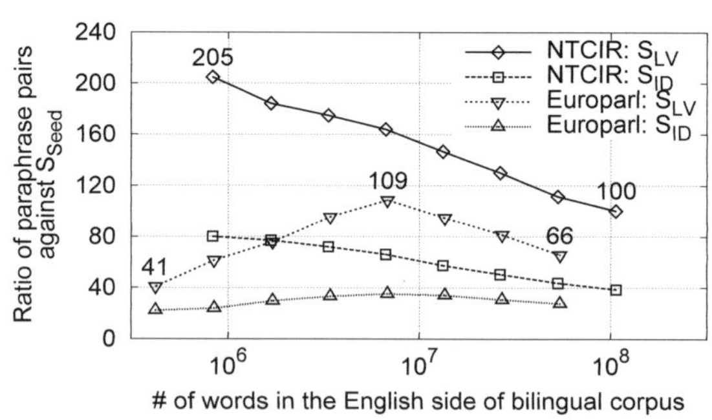


Figure 4: Ratio of $S_{LV}$ and $S_{ID}$ to $S_{Seed}$.

We expected that the more the bilingual data there are, the lower the leverage ratio is, because when a larger bilingual corpus is used, more seed paraphrases can be acquired, and the relative size of the monolingual data compared to the bilingual is lower. While the leverage ratio in the NTCIR setting follows this, the ratio in the Europarl setting does not: it peaks at approximately the middle of the scale. We found that from a very small bilingual corpus, we do not necessarily obtain seed paraphrases that exhibit the generality exploited by *LEXVAR* and *IDENT*. In this case, the leverage ratio cannot be extremely high despite the large difference in the corpora sizes.

*LEXVAR* also largely contributed to discovering paraphrases for phrases that were not paraphrased using only $S_{Seed}$ and $S_{ID}$. The ratio of the numbers of unique left-hand side phrases in $S_{LV}$ to those in $S_{Seed}$ ranged over 65–147 and 92–415 in the two respective settings, gaining 76%–210% and 145%–175% more coverage than $S_{ID}$.

## 5 Quality Assessment

The quality of the created paraphrase lexicons was manually evaluated through a paraphrase substitution test: we generated pairs of paraphrase sentences using the paraphrase lexicons and asked human evaluators to assess their quality.

### 5.1 Criteria and Procedure

Generating paraphrased sentences by substituting words and phrases involves two different tasks: generating new sentences and ensuring that the meaning is preserved. It is therefore straightforward to separately evaluate the **grammaticality** and **meaning equivalence** of each paraphrased sentence (Callison-Burch, 2008).

**Grammaticality:** whether the paraphrased sentence is grammatical

**Meaning equivalence:** whether the meaning of the original sentence is properly preserved by the paraphrased sentence

We adopted the detailed criteria and procedure described in (Fujita, 2013), as they resulted in a reasonably high inter-evaluator agreement ratio. The evaluation protocol is characterized by the following three features introduced for reducing human labor and making results consistent.

**Unit-wise:** Several paraphrase examples for the same source are packaged into an **example unit** and provided at the same time.

**Two-phased:** Evaluators are first asked to assess only the grammaticality of each paraphrased sentence without seeing the original sentence. Then, by comparing each pair of original and paraphrased sentences, they assess to what extent the paraphrased sentence retains the meaning of its counterpart.

**Classification-based:** Evaluators are asked to classify each example into one of the predetermined categories, guided by the decision trees respectively designed for evaluating grammaticality and meaning equivalence.

### 5.2 Data

We used news sentences as in (Callison-Burch, 2008; Fujita et al., 2012): the English sentences from WMT 2011–2013 "newstest" data (9,000 unique sentences). To reduce the human labor for the evaluation, they were restricted to those with moderate length: 10–30 words, which we expected to provide sufficient but succinct context of the substituted phrases. 5,850 sentences were retained.

By substituting phrases in the above sentences using the paraphrase lexicons $S_{Seed}$ and $S_{LV}$ in the Europarl setting, 88,555 example units comprising 1,013,511 paraphrases were generated. For each example unit, 3-best paraphrases were then selected by a 5-gram language model trained on the monolingual data in the Europarl setting with modified Kneser–Ney smoothing using KenLM[10]. Finally, from 31,149 units that contained at least three paraphrases, we randomly sampled 200 example units for 200 unique left-hand side phrases.

### 5.3 Results

We collected evaluations from three native English speakers. Table 3 summarizes the inter-evaluator agreement ratio, Cohen's $\kappa$ (Cohen, 1960). The values for a coarse-grained binary decision[11] were "substantial" for grammaticality and "moderate" for meaning equivalence (Landis and Koch, 1977).

The quality of the examined paraphrase lexicons is measured by the precision of the evaluated examples: an example was regarded as correct if and only if a majority of evaluators (two or three in our case) assigned a label corresponding to the positive class in the binary decision. Table 4 summarizes the results. Despite the low chance of being the 3-best candidates, thanks to various filters,

[10]https://kheafield.com/code/kenlm/

[11]We regarded "Perfect" and "Awkward" for grammaticality, and "Equivalent" and either of three categories of slight differences "Missing Info.," "Additional Info.," and "Ignorable Change" for meaning equivalence as positive. This is consistent with (Callison-Burch, 2008).

| Criterion | Fine-grained | Coarse-grained |
|---|---|---|
| Grammar | 0.51 - 0.56 | 0.64 - 0.79 |
| Meaning | 0.27 - 0.35 | 0.48 - 0.53 |

Table 3: Cohen's $\kappa$ of pairwise agreement.

| Lexicon | $n$ | Grammar | Meaning | Both |
|---|---|---|---|---|
| $S_{Seed}$ | 66 | 0.85 | 0.91 | 0.76 |
| $S_{ID}$ ($\subseteq S_{LV}$) | 339 | 0.84 | 0.78 | 0.66 |
| $S_{LV}$ | 534 | 0.74 | 0.78 | 0.59 |
| Total | 600 | 0.75 | 0.79 | 0.61 |

Table 4: Precision of paraphrase substitution.

paraphrases drawn from $S_{Seed}$ were of substantially high quality. Compared to $S_{Seed}$, paraphrases sampled from $S_{LV}$ have relatively low precision in both grammaticality and meaning equivalence. However, these scores are reasonably high, considering that no use is made of rich language-specific resources[12].

However, more grammatical errors occurred than with $S_{Seed}$ and $S_{ID}$. A manual error analysis revealed that the majority of these errors were caused by the differences of syntactic categories between phrases, e.g., (12).

(12) The safety issue was *considered sufficiently* ( $\Rightarrow$ *sufficient consideration*) serious for all affected parties to be informed.

Differences of grammatical number and determiners were the other major error sources.

(13) Federal Security Service now spread a big network of fake sites and there are tons of *potential buyers* ( $\Rightarrow$ *a potential buyer*) of military weapons.

These types of pairs originally existed in $S_{Seed}$ but were amplified by *LEXVAR*. Ganitkevitch and Callison-Burch (2014) stated that morphological variants of the same word might be desirable depending on the downstream task. For instance, they could be useful for paraphrase recognition tasks including question answering and multi-document summarization. As they are morphological variants rather than genuine paraphrases, substituting them in a given context often degrades grammaticality.

## 6 Conclusion

We proposed a method for expanding given paraphrase lexicons by first inducing paraphrase patterns and then searching monolingual corpora with these patterns for new paraphrase pairs. To the best of our knowledge, this is the first attempt to exploit various types of lexical variants for acquiring paraphrases in a completely empirical way. Our method requires minimal language-dependent resources, i.e., stoplists and tokenizers, other than raw corpora. We demonstrated the quantitative impact of our method and confirmed the potential quality of the expanded paraphrase lexicon.

Our future work is four-fold. (i) Paraphrase lexicons created by different methods and sources have different properties. Designing an overall model to harmonize such heterogeneous lexicons is an important issue. (ii) We aim to investigate an extensive collection of corpora: there are far more corpora than those we used in this experiment. We are also interested in expanding paraphrase lexicons created by a method other than bilingual pivoting; for instance, those extracted from a Web-harvested monolingual comparable corpus (Hashimoto et al., 2011; Yan et al., 2013). (iii) We will apply our method to various languages for demonstrating its applicability, extending it for a wider range of lexical variants depending on the targeted language. (iv) Paraphrases are the fundamental linguistic phenomena that affect a wide range of NLP tasks. We are therefore interested in determining to what extent our paraphrase lexicons can improve the performance of application tasks such as machine translation, text summarization, and text simplification.


## Acknowledgments

We are deeply grateful to Eiichiro Sumita, Masao Utiyama, Taro Watanabe, Kentaro Torisawa, and anonymous reviewers for their valuable comments on the earlier version of this paper. This work was partly supported by JSPS Postdoctoral Fellowship for Research Abroad (FYs 2011–2012) and JSPS KAKENHI Grant-in-Aid for Young Scientists (B) 25730139.


[12]Although we cannot make a direct comparison owing to the differences of data and human evaluators, for reference, Callison-Burch (2008) achieved 0.68, 0.61, and 0.55 precision for grammaticality, meaning equivalence, and both, respectively, by introducing parser-oriented syntactic constraints in bilingual pivoting.

## References


Ion Androutsopoulos and Prodromos Malakasiotis. 2010. A survey of paraphrasing and textual entailment methods. *Journal of Artificial Intelligence Research*, 38:135–187.

Colin Bannard and Chris Callison-Burch. 2005. Paraphrasing with bilingual parallel corpora. In *Proceedings of the 43rd Annual Meeting of the Association for Computational Linguistics (ACL)*, pages 597–604.

Regina Barzilay and Kathleen R. McKeown. 2001. Extracting paraphrases from a parallel corpus. In *Proceedings of the 39th Annual Meeting of the Association for Computational Linguistics (ACL)*, pages 50–57.

Regina Barzilay and Lillian Lee. 2002. Bootstrapping lexical choice via multiple-sequence alignment. In *Proceedings of the 2002 Conference on Empirical Methods in Natural Language Processing (EMNLP)*, pages 164–171.

Regina Barzilay and Noemie Elhadad. 2003. Sentence alignment for monolingual comparable corpora. In *Proceedings of the 2003 Conference on Empirical Methods in Natural Language Processing (EMNLP)*, pages 25–32.

Rahul Bhagat and Deepak Ravichandran. 2008. Large scale acquisition of paraphrases for learning surface patterns. In *Proceedings of the 46th Annual Meeting of the Association for Computational Linguistics (ACL)*, pages 161–170.

Chris Callison-Burch. 2008. Syntactic constraints on paraphrases extracted from parallel corpora. In *Proceedings of the 2008 Conference on Empirical Methods in Natural Language Processing (EMNLP)*, pages 196–205.

Tsz Ping Chan, Chris Callison-Burch, and Benjamin Van Durme. 2011. Reranking bilingually extracted paraphrases using monolingual distributional similarity. In *Proceedings of the Workshop on Geometrical Models of Natual Language Semantics (GEMS)*, pages 33–42.

David L. Chen and William B. Dolan. 2011. Collecting highly parallel data for paraphrase evaluation. In *Proceedings of the 49th Annual Meeting of the Association for Computational Linguistics (ACL)*, pages 190–200.

Jacob Cohen. 1960. A coefficient of agreement for nominal scales. *Educational and Psychological Measurement*, 20(1):37–46.

Stijn De Saeger, Kentaro Torisawa, Masaaki Tsuchida, Jun'ichi Kazama, Chikara Hashimoto, Ichiro Yamada, Jong Hoon Oh, István Varga, and Yulan Yan. 2011. Relation acquisition using word classes and partial patterns. In *Proceedings of the 2011 Conference on Empirical Methods in Natural Language Processing (EMNLP)*, pages 825–835.

Michael Denkowski and Alon Lavie. 2010. METEOR-NEXT and the METEOR paraphrase tables: Improved evaluation support for five target languages. In *Proceedings of the 5th Workshop on Statistical Machine Translation (WMT) and MetricsMATR*, pages 339–342.

Bill Dolan, Chris Quirk, and Chris Brockett. 2004. Unsupervised construction of large paraphrase corpora: Exploiting massively parallel news sources. In *Proceedings of the 20th International Conference on Computational Linguistics (COLING)*, pages 350–356.

Jinhua Du, Jie Jiang, and Andy Way. 2010. Facilitating translation using source language paraphrase lattices. In *Proceedings of the 2010 Conference on Empirical Methods in Natural Language Processing (EMNLP)*, pages 420–429.

Christiane Fellbaum. 1998. *WordNet: An Electronic Lexical Database*. The MIT Press.

Atsushi Fujita, Shuhei Kato, Naoki Kato, and Satoshi Sato. 2007. A compositional approach toward dynamic phrasal thesaurus. In *Proceedings of the ACL-PASCAL Workshop on Textual Entailment and Paraphrasing (WTEP)*, pages 151–158.

Atsushi Fujita, Pierre Isabelle, and Roland Kuhn. 2012. Enlarging paraphrase collections through generalization and instantiation. In *Proceedings of the 2012 Joint Conference on Empirical Methods in Natural Language Processing and Computational Natural Language Learning (EMNLP-CoNLL)*, pages 631–642.

Atsushi Fujita. 2013. A consideration on the methodology for evaluating large-scale paraphrase lexicons. In *Information Processing Society of Japan SIG Notes, NL-214-21*, pages 1–8.

Juri Ganitkevitch, Chris Callison-Burch, Courtney Napoles, and Benjamin Van Durme. 2011. Learning sentential paraphrases from bilingual parallel corpora for text-to-text generation. In *Proceedings of the 2011 Conference on Empirical Methods in Natural Language Processing (EMNLP)*, pages 1168–1179.

Juri Ganitkevitch, Benjamin Van Durme, and Chris Callison-Burch. 2013. PPDB: The paraphrase database. In *Proceedings of Human Language Technologies: The 2013 Annual Conference of the North American Chapter of the Association for Computational Linguistics (NAACL-HLT)*, pages 758–764.

Juri Ganitkevitch and Chris Callison-Burch. 2014. The multilingual paraphrase database. In *Proceedings of the 9th International Conference on Language Resources and Evaluation (LREC)*, pages 4276–4282.

Éric Gaussier. 1999. Unsupervised learning of derivational morphology from inflectional lexicons. In *Proceedings of the Workshop on Unsupervised Learning in Natural Language Processing*, pages 24–30.

Nizar Habash and Bonnie Jean Dorr. 2003. A categorial variation database for English. In *Proceedings of the 2003 Human Language Technology Conference and the North American Chapter of the Association for Computational Linguistics* (*HLT-NAACL*), pages 96–102.

Masato Hagiwara, Yasuhiro Ogawa, and Katsuhiko Toyama. 2006. Selection of effective contextual information for automatic synonym acquisition. In *Proceedings of the 44th Annual Meeting of the Association for Computational Linguistics and the 21st International Conference on Computational Linguistics* (*COLING-ACL*), pages 353–360.

Zellig Harris. 1954. Distributional structure. *Word*, 10(23):146–162.

Zellig Harris. 1957. Co-occurrence and transformation in linguistic structure. *Language*, 33(3):283–340.

Chikara Hashimoto, Kentaro Torisawa, Stijn De Saeger, Jun'ichi Kazama, and Sadao Kurohashi. 2011. Extracting paraphrases from definition sentences on the Web. In *Proceedings of the 49th Annual Meeting of the Association for Computational Linguistics* (*ACL*), pages 1087–1097.

Christian Jacquemin. 1999. Syntagmatic and paradigmatic representations of term variation. In *Proceedings of the 37th Annual Meeting of the Association for Computational Linguistics* (*ACL*), pages 341–348.

Stanley Kok and Chris Brockett. 2010. Hitting the right paraphrases in good time. In *Proceedings of Human Language Technologies: The 2010 Annual Conference of the North American Chapter of the Association for Computational Linguistics* (*NAACL-HLT*), pages 145–153.

J. Richard Landis and Gary G. Koch. 1977. The measurement of observer agreement for categorical data. *Biometrics*, 33(1):159–174.

Dekang Lin and Patrick Pantel. 2001. Discovery of inference rules for question answering. *Natural Language Engineering*, 7(4):343–360.

Nitin Madnani and Bonnie J. Dorr. 2010. Generating phrasal and sentential paraphrases: A survey of data-driven methods. *Computational Linguistics*, 36(3):341–387.

Yuval Marton. 2013. Distributional phrasal paraphrase generation for statistical machine translation. *ACM Transactions on Intelligent Systems and Technology*, 4(3).

Aurélien Max. 2010. Example-based paraphrasing for improved phrase-based statistical machine translation. In *Proceedings of the 2010 Conference on Empirical Methods in Natural Language Processing* (*EMNLP*), pages 656–666.

Igor Mel'čuk and Alain Polguère. 1987. A formal lexicon in Meaning-Text Theory (or how to do lexica with words). *Computational Linguistics*, 13(3-4):261–275.

Marius Paşca and Péter Dienes. 2005. Aligning needles in a haystack: Paraphrase acquisition across the Web. In *Proceedings of the 2nd International Joint Conference on Natural Language Processing* (*IJCNLP*), pages 119–130.

Bo Pang, Kevin Knight, and Daniel Marcu. 2003. Syntax-based alignment of multiple translations: Extracting paraphrases and generating new sentences. In *Proceedings of the 2003 Human Language Technology Conference and the North American Chapter of the Association for Computational Linguistics* (*HLT-NAACL*), pages 102–109.

Yusuke Shinyama, Satoshi Sekine, Kiyoshi Sudo, and Ralph Grishman. 2002. Automatic paraphrase acquisition from news articles. In *Proceedings of the 2002 Human Language Technology Conference* (*HLT*).

Idan Szpektor, Hristo Tanev, Ido Dagan, and Bonaventura Coppola. 2004. Scaling Web-based acquisition of entailment relations. In *Proceedings of the 2004 Conference on Empirical Methods in Natural Language Processing* (*EMNLP*), pages 41–48.

Sander Wubben, Antal van den Bosch, Emiel Krahmer, and Erwin Marsi. 2009. Clustering and matching headlines for automatic paraphrase acquisition. In *Proceedings of the 12th European Workshop on Natural Language Generation* (*EWNLG*), pages 122–125.

Yulan Yan, Chikara Hashimoto, Kentaro Torisawa, Takao Kawai, Jun'ichi Kazama, and Stijn De Saeger. 2013. Minimally supervised method for multilingual paraphrase extraction from definition sentences on the web. In *Proceedings of Human Language Technologies: The 2013 Annual Conference of the North American Chapter of the Association for Computational Linguistics* (*NAACL-HLT*), pages 63–73.

Shiqi Zhao, Haifeng Wang, Ting Liu, and Sheng Li. 2009. Extracting paraphrase patterns from bilingual parallel corpora. *Natural Language Engineering*, 15(4):503–526.

# Diamonds in the Rough: Event Extraction from Imperfect Microblog Data

**Ander Intxaurrondo†, Eneko Agirre†, Oier Lopez de Lacalle†, Mihai Surdeanu‡**
†IXA NLP Group, University of the Basque Country
‡University of Arizona
{ander.intxaurrondo, e.agirre, oier.lopezdelacalle}@ehu.eus
msurdeanu@email.arizona.edu

## Abstract

We introduce a distantly supervised event extraction approach that extracts complex event templates from microblogs. We show that this near real-time data source is more challenging than news because it contains information that is both approximate (e.g., with values that are close but different from the gold truth) and ambiguous (due to the brevity of the texts), impacting both the evaluation and extraction methods. For the former, we propose a novel, "soft", F1 metric that incorporates similarity between extracted fillers and the gold truth, giving partial credit to different but similar values. With respect to extraction methodology, we propose two extensions to the distant supervision paradigm: to address approximate information, we allow positive training examples to be generated from information that is similar but not identical to gold values; to address ambiguity, we aggregate contexts across tweets discussing the same event. We evaluate our contributions on the complex domain of earthquakes, with events with up to 20 arguments. Our results indicate that, despite their simplicity, our contributions yield a statistically-significant improvement of 33% (relative) over a strong distantly-supervised system. The dataset containing the knowledge base, relevant tweets and manual annotations is publicly available.

## 1 Introduction

Twitter is an excellent source of near real-time data on recent events, motivating the need for information extraction (IE) systems that operate on tweets rather than traditional news articles. However, using this data comes with its own challenges: tweets tend to use colloquial speech, noisy syntax and discourse, and, more importantly, the information reported is often inaccurate (e.g., reporting a different but similar magnitude for an earthquake) and ambiguous (e.g., reporting multiple potential earthquake locations, with insufficient context to guess which is the correct one).[1] The top rows in Table 1 show examples of these problems for an actual event in our dataset on earthquakes. This comes in contrast with "traditional" IE work on newswire documents, where information is considerably more accurate than microblog material, and none of the above observations hold (Grishman and Sundheim, 1996; Doddington et al., 2004).

As an example of the benefits of event extraction from a near real-time social-media resource, the last row in Table 1 lists a motivating example, where our system extracts the correct depth of an earthquake from the text tweeted by the U.S. Geological Survey, which is novel information that is missing in our manually-curated knowledge base.

In this work we take a classic event extraction (EE) task, where events are defined by templates containing a predefined set of arguments, and implement it using data from Twitter. We avoid the prohibitive cost of manual annotation through distant supervision (DS): we automatically generate train-

[1] We focus on microblogs here because they commonly contain inaccurate and/or ambiguous information. However, we believe that our contributions extend beyond microblogs because these innacuracies, especially inaccurate information, may appear in news article as well.



*Human Language Technologies: The 2015 Annual Conference of the North American Chapter of the ACL*, pages 641–650,
Denver, Colorado, May 31 – June 5, 2015. 

| | |
|---|---|
| Approximate information | Earthquake in Honduras. So strong it strong it was felt in Guatemala as well. **7.1** offshore atlantic. |
| Ambiguous information | DTN **Indonesia**: *Peru* Earthquake Destroys Homes, Injures 100... |
| | 6.9 magnitude earthquake rocks *Peru*. |
| | U.S.G.S. reports 6.9 Earthquake in *Peru*. NO TSUNAMI threat to Hawaii. |
| Information not in the knowledge base | #Earthquake M 7.0 – Ryukyu Islands, Japan T20:31:27 UTC , 25.95 128.40 depth: **22 km** `<USGS URL>` Local tsunami alert issued |

Table 1: Challenges and opportunities for event extraction from Twitter. The first row shows a tweet with approximate information (in bold); the correct magnitude is 7.3 (cf. Table 2). The second row shows a first tweet with ambiguous information, which leads our baseline model to extract the incorrect country (in bold; correct country is *Peru*). The following two tweets help disambiguate the context. The last row shows a tweet containing information (in bold) that is missing in the knowledge base.

ing data by aligning a knowledge base of known event instances with tweets (Mintz et al., 2009; Hoffmann et al., 2011), which is then used to train a supervised extraction model (sequence tagger in our case). In seminal work on event extraction, (Benson et al., 2011) applied DS to both detect tweets about local events and then extracted values about two arguments (artist and venue). In our work, we work on automatically selected tweets, and scale the task to complex events with a large number of arguments. We focus on the domain of earthquakes, where each event has up to 20 arguments. Table 2 summarizes this task.

The contributions of this work are the following:

**1.** To our knowledge, this is one of the first works that analyzes the problem of distantly supervised extraction of complex events with many arguments from microblogs.

**2.** Our analysis shows (Section 3) that the biggest barrier is that information on Twitter can be *inaccurate* (containing approximately correct event argument values) and *ambiguous* (with insufficient context for accurate extraction). The top two blocks in Table 1 show an example of each. These challenges impact both evaluation and system development.

**3.** The analysis also highlights the need to adapt evaluation metrics to approximately correct information, which may appear both in text and in the knowledge base itself. For example, for a particular earthquake, the USGS reports a depth of 22 km., while NOAA reports 25 km[2]. We propose a new evaluation metric that gives partial credit to extracted argument values based on their similarity to existing values in the knowledge base.

**4.** We introduce two simple strategies that address the above barriers for system development: *approximate matching*, which addresses inaccurate values by allowing the distant supervision process to map values from the knowledge base to text even when they do not match exactly; and *feature aggregation*, which responds to small, ambiguous contexts by aggregating information across multiple tweets for the same event. For example, the first strategy considers the 7.1 magnitude in the first tweet in Table 1 as a training example because it is close to the value in the knowledge base (7.3). The second strategy classifies all instances of *Peru* jointly using a single set of features, extracted from all available tweets for the corresponding earthquake. For example, this feature set contains three values for the feature `previous-word` (*:*, *rocks*, and *in*). Each approach yields 19% relative improvement, 33% in combination.

**5.** We release a public dataset containing a knowledge base of earthquake instances and corresponding tweets for each earthquake[3].

## 2 Experimental framework

In this section we detail the creation of the knowledge base of earthquake events, the collection process for potentially-relevant tweets, and, lastly, our distant supervision framework, which serves as a platform for our contributions (Sections 5 and 6).

### 2.1 Knowledge base and tweet dataset creation

The **knowledge base (KB)** was created from the list of globally significant earthquakes during the 21st century, as reported by Wikipedia.[4] We se-

[2] http://bit.ly/aq9Vxa and http://1.usa.gov/1p1gELB

[3] http://ixa.eus/Ixa/Argitalpenak/Artikuluak/1425465524/publikoak/earthquake-kb-dataset.zip

[4] https://en.wikipedia.org/wiki/List_of_21st-century_earthquakes. Accessed on July 9th,

| Argument Name | Arg. Type | # KB Values | Example Values | # DS Values | # MA Values |
|---|---|---|---|---|---|
| Date | D | 108 | 2009-5-28 | 291 | 706 |
| Time | T | 108 | T08:24:00 | 378 | 589 |
| Country | L | 108 | Honduras | 6294 | 6327 |
| Region | L | 77 | | 2598 | 2663 |
| City | L | 77 | | 1426 | 1723 |
| Latitude | N | 108 | 16.733 | 2 | 28 |
| Longitude | N | 108 | -86.22 | 4 | 28 |
| Dead | N | 71 | 7 | 143 | 984 |
| Injured | N | 39 | | 22 | 192 |
| Missing | N | 8 | | - | 18 |
| Magnitude | N | 108 | 7.3 | 933 | 3403 |
| Depth (km) | N | 99 | 10 | 27 | 313 |
| Countries affected(*) | L | 37 | Guatemala, Belize | 436 | 357 |
| Regions affected(*) | L | 4 | | - | 36 |
| Landslides | B | 8 | | 7 | 9 |
| Tsunami | B | 10 | | 408 | 273 |
| Aftershocks | N | 20 | | 5 | 22 |
| Foreshocks | N | 3 | | 6 | - |
| Duration | T | 7 | | - | 1 |
| Peak accel. | N | 8 | | - | - |
| TOTAL | | 1,116 | | 13,562 | 17,672 |

Table 2: Event arguments and types in the earthquake domain (first and second column), summary statistics for the knowledge base, i.e., the gold truth (third column), and values for one example earthquake (4th column). (*) indicates multi-valued arguments (all other are single-valued). The two rightmost columns give statistics for the number of mentions in the tweets per argument, as obtained through manual annotation (MA) or distant supervision (DS) (cf. Section 2.4). The argument types are the following: *D* date, *T* time, *L* location, *N* numeric, and *B* boolean.

lected earthquakes from the beginning of 2009, with the last reported earthquake happening on July 7th, 2013, and constructed the KB from the above Wikipedia list page and the individual infoboxes. Where necessary, argument values were normalized.[5] See Table 2 for a summary and an example.

We used the Topsy API[6] to search for **tweets** that are potentially relevant for each earthquake. We formed a query using the word "earthquake" plus the location, encoded as a disjunction of city, region, and country arguments. We retrieved tweets from the day before the date and time of the earthquake, up to seven days after. This procedure might also retrieve tweets about aftershocks, which we consider to be different events. We applied an aggressive method to discard aftershock tweets: we only kept tweets up to the first tweet that mentions a time expression more than a minute different from that of the main earthquake (after adjusting for time zone). For example, this heuristic removes all tweets starting with *"A 4.9 earthquake occurred in Ryukyu Islands, Japan on 2010-2-27 T10:33:21 at epicenter."* because the main earthquake occurred on February 26th at 8:31PM UTC. It is important to note that identifying event-relevant tweets is not the focus of this work (hence the simple heuristics used for tweet extraction). We focus instead on the *extraction* of information from such tweets. In a complete system, our approach would follow a component that detects event tweets automatically (Benson et al., 2011). The final dataset contains 108 earthquakes and 7,841 tweets, 72 tweets per earthquake on average, a maximum of 654 and a minimum of 2. 19 earthquakes had less than 10 tweets.

## 2.2 Manual annotation of tweets

In order to analyze the challenges faced by our EE system based on distant supervision, we also manually annotated all tweets.[7] The manual annotation included any mention of an event argument in the tweets. This included information already in the KB, but also information that is missing, caused by: variations of dates and times, similar but not identical latitude/longitude values, different reported numbers for dead/injured/missing etc. The first tweet in Table 1 is an example of this situation: even though the reported magnitude is different from the value in the KB (cf. example in Table 2), it was annotated during this process. In total, we annotated 17,672 mentions (at an average of two event arguments per tweet). Table 2 shows the breakdown per argument (the MA column), compared to the automatic annotations generated through distant supervision (the DS column). Note that some of the arguments have a very different coverage in the tweets compared with the KB. For example, latitude and longitude are rarely present in tweets, but affected countries are commonly mentioned. The quality of the manual annotation was assessed on a 5% sample of the dataset, which was annotated by an additional expert. The agreement was very high: 90% ITA and 85% Fleiss Kappa. Disagreements were generally

2013, at 2PM CET.

[5]Time and date expressions were converted to TimeML. Numerical values in English were converted to numbers, latitude and longitudes were converted to decimal format.

[6]`http://api.topsy.com/doc/`

[7]These manual annotations are used solely for post-hoc analysis, *not* to train our system.

due to missed argument mentions. Note that the cost of annotation was around 75 hours, confirming the cost-saving properties of distant supervision.

### 2.3 Dataset and experiment organization

We sorted the list of earthquakes in the KB chronologically, and chose the earliest 75% of the earthquakes as the training dataset, and the most recent (25%) for testing. The training set contained 81 earthquakes and their corresponding 6078 tweets, while the testing set contained 27 earthquakes and 1763 tweets. All development experiments were performed using 5-fold cross-validation over the training partition, where the folds were organized randomly by earthquake. Each fold contained tweets for around 15 earthquakes, but the number of tweets varied widely, with one fold having 585 tweets and another 2229.

The evaluation compares the argument values induced by our system with those in the gold KB, and computes precision, recall and F1 using the official scorer from the Knowledge Base Population (KBP) Slot Filling (SF) shared task (Surdeanu, 2013). We also incorporated the notion of equivalence classes proposed in the SF task. For instance, if the system predicted *Guerrero State* for the argument `region`, when the KB contains just *Guerrero*, we consider this result correct because the two strings are equivalent in this context. Our equivalence classes also include countries, regions, and cities with hashtags, unnormalized temporal expressions, etc. Where applicable, we checked statistical significance of performance differences using the bootstrap resampling technique proposed in (Berg-Kirkpatrick et al., 2012), in which we draw many simulated test sets by sampling with replacement from the set of earthquakes in the test partition.

### 2.4 Distant supervision for event extraction

For the initial extraction experiment, we followed a traditional distant supervision approach (Mintz et al., 2009), which has four steps: the KB of past events is aligned to the text; a supervised system is trained on the resulting annotated text; the system is run on test data; and the output slot values are inferred from the annotations produced by the system. We thus started by aligning the information in the KB to the training tweets using strict matching[8]. Table 2 compares the number of mentions automatically generated through DS against the number of manually annotated mentions. As expected, the strict matching criterion yields fewer mentions than the manual annotation.

As an example of this process, given the Honduras earthquake in Table 2, this procedure will annotate two argument mentions in the first tweet from Table 1, `country` and `affected-country`, as follows:

> Earthquake in <country>Honduras</country>. So strong it was felt in <affected-country>Guatemala</affected-country> as well. 7.1 offshore atlantic.

Note that the magnitude in the tweet is different from the one reported in the KB and it will thus be left unmarked (we revisit this issue in Section 5).

Using this automatically-generated data, we trained a sequential tagger based on Conditional Random Fields (CRF)[9]. Based on the output of the CRF, we inferred the arguments values using noisy-or (Surdeanu et al., 2012), which selects the value with the largest probability for each single-valued argument by aggregating the individual mention probabilities produced by the CRF.[10] In the case of multi-valued arguments (`affected-country` and `affected-region`) we choose all values that had been annotated by the sequential tagger.

## 3 Initial results and analysis

The left block in Table 3 reports the results on development (5-fold cross-validation) of the initial event

[8]We identified two types of arguments: those that have binary (yes/no) values (`tsunami` and `landslides`) and those having other values. For the first type, we search the tweets corresponding to the target earthquake for a small number of strings (e.g., *tsunami* and *tsunamis*), and annotate all matches (e.g., *<tsunami> tsunami </tsunami>*). For non-binary valued arguments, we searched the tweets for exact occurrences of the corresponding values, and annotated all matching strings. When the same value appears in more than one argument for the same earthquake (e.g., *7* as both magnitude and number of dead people), we choose the most common label (e.g., magnitude cf. Table 2).

[9]We used the linear CRF in Stanford's CoreNLP package, with the default features (word form, PoS, lemma, NERC) for the `macro` configuration: `http://nlp.stanford.edu/software/corenlp.shtml`.

[10]For multi-token mentions (e.g. *New Zealand*) we use the average of the token probabilities.

| | Strict Evaluation | | |
|---|---|---|---|
| System | Prec. | Rec. | F1 |
| DS-CRF | 53.1 | 22.0 | 31.1 |
| MA-CRF | 44.1 | 26.1 | 32.8 |
| | Lenient Evaluation | | |
| DS-CRF | 67.4 | 27.9 | 39.4 |
| MA-CRF | 62.1 | 36.8 | 46.2 |

Table 3: Development: Results for the distant supervision system (DS-CRF). We also include results for the same CRF trained on manual annotations (MA-CRF). The regular evaluation is shown in the left columns and lenient evaluation (cf. Section 4) in the right.

extraction system based on a distantly-supervised CRF (DS-CRF), which notably attains higher precision than recall. These results are fair, e.g., they are comparable to those of (Benson et al., 2011), even though their events had much fewer argument types than ours (two vs. twenty). More importantly, we use this system's output to analyze where the approach could be improved. For the sake of comparison, we trained the same CRF with the manually annotated tweets, cf. Section 2 (MA-CRF). The MA-CRF results in Table 3 indicate that the main loss when doing distant supervision is in recall, but the overall F1 is close. This is remarkable, as the much more expensive MA-CRF (75 hours of human annotation) is taken to be an upperbound for DS-CRF.

Manual inspection showed that that DS-CRF returns fewer argument values than MA-CRF (328 vs. 469), from "easier" (more common) arguments which have a higher chance of appearing both in the text and the KB. Importantly, MA-CRF has lower precision than its distant supervision counterpart because it is trained on manual annotations, which included many mentions not in the KB. The consequence of this strategy is that MA-CRF tends to produce spurious mentions (i.e., mentions not in the KB) at evaluation time, which lowers precision.

In addition, we analyzed the annotations created through distant supervision[11], which produced 13,562 argument mentions in the training tweets (cf. Table 2, which also includes a breakdown by argument). This data contains incorrectly annotated strings (false positives) and also misses relevant argument values (false negatives). A comparison of these DS annotations against the manual annotations on all training tweets (17,672 mentions) yielded that 97.4% were correct, but that 27.4% of the gold manual annotations were missed. This is an important result: it demonstrates that, unlike in the problem of relation extraction (RE) where the major issue is the large percentage (higher than 30%) of false positives in automatically-created annotations (Riedel et al., 2010), here the fundamental roadblock is missing annotations (i.e., false negatives). We explain this difference by the fact that for this event extraction domain, it is trivial to identify domain-relevant tweets, which reduces the number of false positives for event arguments. We believe this generalizes to many other EE domains, e.g., airplane crashes (Reschke et al., 2014) or terrorist attacks, where the event context can be summarized accurately with a small number of keywords (e.g., flight number and date for the airplane crashes domain).

We also did a post-hoc analysis of the quality of the arguments induced by DS-CRF. One of the most significant outcomes of the analysis is that a large portion of numeric values (31.3%) were partially correct, in that the returned values were very similar to those in the KB (see for instance the 7.1 vs. 7.3 example in Section 1). This strongly suggests that the evaluation metric should be more lenient, and give credit to argument values that are similar to the gold ones.

## 4 Lenient evaluation

The previous analysis suggests that traditional evaluation measures unnecessarily penalize arguments containing values that do not match the gold truth exactly. Rather than giving no credit when predicted values are different from gold ones, we devised a simple extension to the KBP evaluation measures that take into account the similarity between the values of system and gold arguments, where the similarity depends on the type of each slot (cf. Table 2). For numeric values, we use the following formula, where $x$ is the predicted value, and $g$ the gold value:

$$sim(x, g) = max\left(1 - \frac{|x - g|}{g}, 0\right) \quad (1)$$

[11] Note that these are the argument mention annotations used to train DS-CRF, not the arguments inferred by the DS-CRF system.

For example, given a gold value of 7.3, a system value of 7.2 would have a similarity of 0.98, and a system value of 14.6 or larger would have a similarity 0. If both values are equal, similarity is 1.

For the other slot types, the similarity function is discrete, with values set to 1 (proposed slot is correct) or 0 (incorrect) as follows. We consider a proposed *temporal* argument as correct if it is within a span of 5 minutes of the corresponding gold temporal value. *Durations* are judged as correct if they are within 10 seconds of the gold values. We considered proposed *dates* as correct if they differ by at most one day from the gold date.[12]

For *location* arguments, we use GeoNames[13] to obtain the coordinates of the locations produced by the system that do not match the information in the KB. Based on the average size of countries, regions, and cities, we consider these additional locations as correct if they are at the following distance (or closer) from the gold locations: 500 kms for countries, 50 kms for regions, and 10 kms for cities.

The original KBP scorer increases the value of True Positives (TP) by 1 every time a predicted argument matches its gold value. In the proposed lenient scorer, TP is increased by the similarity between the predicted and gold values. The precision and recall will be thus calculated as follows (*SYS* for number of predicted argument values, *GOLD* for number of gold argument values):

$$prec = \frac{\sum sim(x, g)}{SYS} \quad (2)$$

$$rec = \frac{\sum sim(x, g)}{GOLD} \quad (3)$$

The right block in Table 3 lists the results under this lenient evaluation for the experiment initially reported in the left block in the same table. As expected, these results are higher than the ones using the strict measure, but maintain the relative order of the systems in each of the evaluation measures. The difference in precision between DS-CRF and MA-CRF decreases, indicating that the new measure assigns partial credit to the larger amount of argument values extracted by MA-CRF. The difference in recall values remains large. We address this in the next section.

[12]These thresholds might change in other domains, but adjusting these values is trivial.

[13]http://www.geonames.org/

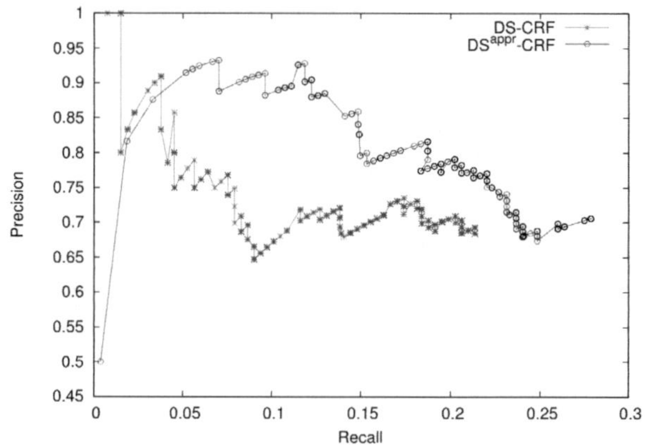


Figure 1: Test: Precision/Recall curves for regular DS and approximate DS on test (lenient evaluation).

| System | Prec. | Rec. | F1 |
|---|---|---|---|
| DS-CRF | 68.4 | 21.3 | 32.5 |
| $DS^{appr}$-CRF | 70.6 | 27.8 | 39.9 † |

Table 4: Test: Regular (DS-CRF) and approximate DS ($DS^{appr}$-CRF) results, with lenient evaluation. † indicates statistically significant improvement over DS-CRF ($p < 0.05$).

## 5 Approximate distant supervision

The previous section demonstrated that many tweets contain argument values which are similar but not identical to the data in the knowledge base. These values would not be annotated during alignment by traditional distant supervision, which expects an exact match between knowledge base values and tweet texts. This means that DS-CRF will be trained with less data than what is available (e.g., without the 7.1 magnitude example in the tweet in Section 2.4). Here we demonstrate that a simple extension to distant supervision that annotates values close to the values in the knowledge base, results in improved performance.

The proposed alignment algorithm scans the training tweets, and labels named and numeric entities as positive argument examples (with the corresponding label from the KB), if they are deemed similar to the gold values according to the similarity formulas introduced in the previous section. This

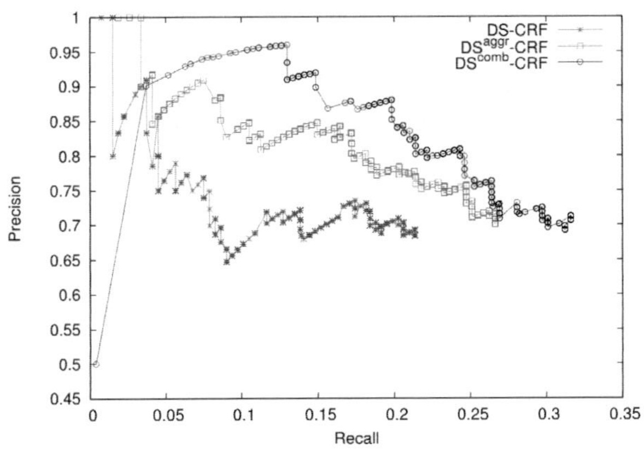


Figure 2: Test: P/R curves for DS-CRF, feature aggregation and combination with approximate DS (lenient evaluation).

is a trivial process for discrete similarities, but requires some care for continuous similarity functions, which are triggered for numeric arguments. In this situation, numeric entities are considered as positive examples only if their similarity function returns a value over a certain threshold with a known argument in the KB. If a numeric mention has more than one matching argument in the KB, the algorithm chooses the argument label with the highest similarity value; if all have the same similarity, the algorithm chooses the most frequent label in training.

We tuned the threshold hyper parameter for numeric values over the training dataset using 5-fold cross validation, which yielded 0.95 as the optimal value. Table 4 shows the results for the test partition using this threshold, and Figure 1 shows the corresponding P/R curves. Both results are generated using the proposed lenient evaluation. The results in the table show that, despite its simplicity, the proposed alignment algorithm yields considerable, statistically-significant improvements. The P/R curves show that the improvement holds for all recall points[14].

## 6 Feature aggregation

The second block in Table 1 illustrates a common scenario on Twitter, where a short, ambiguous tweet derails the extraction. We address this problem of insufficient local context with a method inspired by work in relation extraction, where relation instances between identical entities are classified jointly using the conjunction of features from all instances (Mintz et al., 2009). We adapt this idea to our sequence tagging EE model as follows:

| System | Prec. | Rec. | F1 |
|---|---|---|---|
| DS-CRF | 68.4 | 21.3 | 32.5 |
| DS$^{aggr}$-CRF | 70.1 | 26.6 | 38.6 † |
| DS$^{comb}$-CRF | 69.2 | 31.2 | 43.1 † |
| MA-CRF | 69.1 | 37.9 | 48.9 |

Table 5: Test: Results for regular DS (DS-CRF), DS with feature aggregation (DS$^{aggr}$-CRF), and the DS model that combines feature aggregation and approximate matching (DS$^{comb}$-CRF), with lenient evaluation. † indicates statistically significant improvement over DS-CRF ($p < 0.05$). We include the results of the CRF trained on manual annotations (MA-CRF) as a performance ceiling for this task.

**1:** We focus on location, date and temporal entities (both earthquake time and duration) which are argument candidates that are often ambiguous, i.e., they may be classified as more than one argument type. For example, a location entity may be labeled as `country`, `region`, `country-affected`, etc. We exclude numeric entities due to potential feature collisions between different argument types: we observed that, in training, several earthquakes had different numeric arguments with the same value. For example, the magnitude and depth of the 2012 Zohan earthquake were 5.6. Applying feature aggregation to examples of these arguments would lead to collisions between features from different classes.[15]

**2:** For each token that appears in one of these named entities, we identify all its instances across the relevant tweets, and share features across all these token instances. For example, for the tweets in the second block in Table 1, our approach identifies *Peru* as an argument mention candidate. All three instances of *Peru* are then classified using the same shared features, e.g., using three values for the fea-

[14]The curves for the strict evaluation are similar, and were omitted for brevity.

[15]Initial experiments confirmed this hypothesis: feature aggregation did not improve results for numeric arguments in development. In future work, we will explore multi-instance multi-label algorithms to handle this situation (Surdeanu et al., 2012).

ture `previous-word` (*:*, *rocks*, and *in*). This process is repeated for each earthquake individually, because tokens may be labeled differently in different earthquakes. This approach produced 37% more features than the DS-CRF baseline.[16]

The positive effect of feature aggregation is confirmed by the formal evaluation on the test dataset. Table 5 shows a statistically significant improvement in overall F1, for the lenient evaluation. The P/R curves (Fig. 2) indicate that DS$^{aggr}$-CRF's improvement comes from both better recall and better precision that the DS-CRF baseline.

Table 5 and Fig. 2 also show that the combination of approximate matching and aggregation outperforms the individual models, demonstrating that feature aggregation is complementary to approximate matching. The combined model attains a relative improvement of 33% over the DS-CRF baseline, reaching approximately 88% of the ceiling performance for this task (MA-CRF row, the CRF trained on manual annotations).

## 7 Related work

There has been considerable recent interest in IE from Twitter. However, in general, these works use supervised learning frameworks (Popescu et al., 2011; Ritter et al., 2012), and/or they use either a coarse representation of events, which reduces to topic modeling or classification of entire tweets (Popescu et al., 2011; Becker et al., 2011; Ritter et al., 2012), or a simplified representation of events with few arguments (Sakaki et al., 2010; Popescu et al., 2011; Benson et al., 2011; Ritter et al., 2012). In contrast, our work uses a complex event representation with 20 arguments, and does not require any manual annotation of tweets. Our work is closest, but complementary to the work of (Benson et al., 2011), which also uses distant supervision for event extraction: We provide solutions for two problems they do not address (inaccurate and ambiguous information) and we focus on more complex events (20 arguments vs. two).

This paper is also complementary to systems which detect event-relevant tweets (Sakaki et al., 2010; Petrović et al., 2010). In future work, we plan to replace our simple method of extracting relevant tweets by one of these approaches, producing a system that monitors microblogs in realtime to automatically construct event-specific knowledge bases.

Our work uses the framework of distant supervision, which has also received considerable attention recently. Nevertheless, most of these works focus on the extraction of binary relations from well-formed documents (Mintz et al., 2009; Riedel et al., 2010; Hoffmann et al., 2011; Surdeanu et al., 2012). We use the much noisier Twitter as the underlying text, and extract complex events instead of binary relations. We note, however, that the idea of feature aggregation is inspired by these works (Mintz et al., 2009; Riedel et al., 2010), but, to our knowledge, we are the first to apply it to event extraction and sequence tagging. In the DS space, our work is closest to (Reschke et al., 2014), which use it to extract complex events (airplane crashes) from newswire text. Because they focus on newswire, they do not need to address the potential for inaccurate or ambiguous information, which is the main focus of our work.

| System | Prec. | Rec. | F1 |
|---|---|---|---|
| DS-CRF | 66.21 | 20.66 | 31.49 |
| DS$^{aggr}$-CRF | 68.27 | 25.92 | 37.58 † |
| DS$^{comb}$-CRF | 61.53 | 27.61 | 38.25 † |
| MA-CRF | 68.76 | 27.61 | 39.40 |

Table 6: Test: Replica of the experiments in Table 5 using a threshold of 0.95 for the lenient evaluation measure. All other settings are identical to the experiments in Table 5. † indicates statistically significant improvement over DS-CRF ($p < 0.05$).

## 8 Discussion: An alternate evaluation measure

Designing relevant measures for lenient evaluations, such as the one discussed here, is an open research issue. For example, the method proposed in Section 4 gives partial credit to all reported (positive) numeric values in the interval $[0, 2g]$, where $g$ is the correct value for the corresponding slot (see the equation in Section 4). But other, stricter, measures

[16] We also tried skip-chain CRFs (Getoor and Taskar, 2007), but found that our simpler approach converges considerably faster and produces slightly better results. We do not show those results for brevity.

are certainly possible.[17] For example, one stricter variant of our proposed measure would assign partial credit only for predicted values that have a similarity of 0.95 or higher with the gold truth (inline with our approximate DS training process). For example, for the same gold numeric value $g$, the measure assigns partial credit only for predicted values in the interval $[0.95g, 1.05g]$.

We repeated the experiments in Table 5 using this alternate evaluation measure. The result are summarized in Table 6. The results reported in Table 5 do not alter the findings of the paper. In fact, under this stricter evaluation measure, our results are stronger: DS$^{comb}$-CRF, which combines both our ideas, approaches with nearly 1 F1 point MA-CRF, which trains on manually annotated data.

## 9 Conclusions

To our knowledge, this is one of the first works that analyzes the problem of distantly supervised complex event extraction on microblogs. This near real-time data source is challenging, with inaccurate information and short, ambiguous texts, as shown by our empirical analysis of the dataset. We proposed two simple techniques to address these problems: (a) a novel distant supervision paradigm, which implements an alignment algorithm that allows text snippets that are similar but not identical to argument values in the knowledge base to be annotated (thus producing better training data); and (b) a feature aggregation strategy that provides richer information across tweets to cope with ambiguity. Our results on earthquake-related tweets show that each improvement yields 19% significant improvement when applied on top of a strong system based on sequence tagging (CRFs). We show that these contributions are complementary: a model that combines both performs better than each of the above individual models, with an improvement of 33% over the baseline. All in all, our approach attains approximately 88% of the ceiling performance for this task, which is obtained by a system trained on manually-annotated tweets, validating the hypothesis that distant supervision is useful for a complex event extraction task.

In addition, we devised a lenient evaluation measure which incorporates the similarity between the extracted argument values and the gold truth, rather than considering as correct only the extractions that exactly match the gold values. We show that this evaluation models the event extraction task better, and, furthermore, is more realistic, especially in view of imperfect knowledge bases.

Lastly, we release a dataset containing an event knowledge base constructed from Wikipedia information on earthquakes, which contains 108 earthquakes, 20 different argument types, and 1,116 argument values. The dataset also includes a collection of relevant tweets about these earthquakes, totaling 7,841 tweets. The dataset is publicly available.[18]


## Acknowledgements

This work was partially funded by MINECO (CHIST-ERA READERS project – PCIN-2013-002-C02-01, EXTRECM project – TIN2013-46616-C2-1-R, SKaTeR project – TIN2012-38584-C06-02), and the European Commission (QTLEAP – FP7-ICT-2013.4.1-610516). Ander Intxaurrondo is supported by a PhD grant from the Basque Country Government. The IXA group is funded by the Basque Government (A type Research Group).


[17] We thank the anonymous reviewer for the suggestion.

[18] http://ixa.eus/Ixa/Argitalpenak/Artikuluak/1425465524/publikoak/earthquake-kb-dataset.zip

## References

Hila Becker, Mor Naaman, and Luis Gravano. 2011. Beyond trending topics: Real-world event identication on twitter. In *Proceedings of the Conference of the Association for the Advancement of Articial Intelligence*.

Edward Benson, Aria Haghighi, and Regina Barzilay. 2011. Event discovery in social media feeds. In *Proceedings of the Conference of the Association for Computational Linguistics (ACL)*.

Taylor Berg-Kirkpatrick, David Burkett, and Dan Klein. 2012. An empirical investigation of statistical significance in nlp. In *Proceedings of the 2012 Joint Conference on Empirical Methods in Natural Language Processing and Computational Natural Language Learning*, EMNLP-CoNLL '12, pages 995–1005, Stroudsburg, PA, USA. Association for Computational Linguistics.

G. Doddington, A. Mitchell, M. Przybocki, L. Ramshaw, S. Strassel, and R. Weischedel. 2004. The automatic content extraction (ace) program – tasks, data, and evaluation. In *Proceedings of LREC*.

L. Getoor and B. Taskar, 2007. *Introduction to statistical relational learning*. MIT Press.

R. Grishman and B. Sundheim. 1996. Message understanding conference - 6: A brief history. In *Proceedings of the International Conference on Computational Linguistics*.

Raphael Hoffmann, Congle Zhang, Xiao Ling, Luke Zettlemoyer, and Daniel S. Weld. 2011. Knowledge-based weak supervision for information extraction of overlapping relations. In *Proceedings of the Annual Meeting of the Association for Computational Linguistics (ACL)*.

Mike Mintz, Steven Bills, Rion Snow, and Daniel Jurafsky. 2009. Distant supervision for relation extraction without labeled data. In *Proceedings of the 47th Annual Meeting of the Association for Computational Linguistics*.

Saša Petrović, Miles Osborne, and Victor Lavrenko. 2010. Streaming first story detection with application to twitter. In *Human Language Technologies: The 2010 Annual Conference of the North American Chapter of the Association for Computational Linguistics*, pages 181–189, Los Angeles, California, June. Association for Computational Linguistics.

Ana-Maria Popescu, Marco Pennacchiotti, and Deepa Paranjpe. 2011. Extracting events and event descriptions from twitter. In *Proceedings of the 20th International Conference on World Wide Web*.

Kevin Reschke, Martin Jankowiak, Mihai Surdeanu, Christopher D. Manning, and Daniel Jurafsky. 2014. Event extraction using distant supervision. In *Proceedings of LREC*.

Sebastian Riedel, Limin Yao, and Andrew McCallum. 2010. Modeling relations and their mentions without labeled text. In *Proceedings of the European Conference on Machine Learning and Knowledge Discovery in Databases (ECML PKDD '10)*.

Alan Ritter, Mausam, Oren Etzioni, and Sam Clark. 2012. Open domain event extraction from twitter. In *Proceedings of KDD*.

Takeshi Sakaki, Makoto Okazaki, and Yutaka Matsuo. 2010. Earthquake shakes twitter users: Real-time event detection by social sensors. In *Proceedings of the 19th International Conference on World Wide Web*, WWW '10, pages 851–860, New York, NY, USA. ACM.

Mihai Surdeanu, Julie Tibshirani, Ramesh Nallapati, and Christopher D. Manning. 2012. Multi-instance multi-label learning for relation extraction. In *Proceedings of the 2012 Conference on Empirical Methods in Natural Language Processing and Natural Language Learning (EMNLP-CoNLL)*.

Mihai Surdeanu. 2013. Overview of the tac2013 knowledge base population evaluation: English slot filling and temporal slot filling. In *Proceedings of the TAC-KBP 2013 Workshop*.

# Unsupervised Dependency Parsing: Let's Use Supervised Parsers

**Phong Le** and **Willem Zuidema**
Institute for Logic, Language, and Computation
University of Amsterdam, the Netherlands
{p.le,zuidema}@uva.nl

## Abstract

We present a self-training approach to unsupervised dependency parsing that reuses existing supervised and unsupervised parsing algorithms. Our approach, called 'iterated reranking' (IR), starts with dependency trees generated by an unsupervised parser, and iteratively improves these trees using the richer probability models used in supervised parsing that are in turn trained on these trees. Our system achieves 1.8% accuracy higher than the state-of-the-part parser of Spitkovsky et al. (2013) on the WSJ corpus.

## 1 Introduction

Unsupervised dependency parsing and its supervised counterpart have many characteristics in common: they take as input raw sentences, produce dependency structures as output, and often use the same evaluation metric (DDA, or UAS, the percentage of tokens for which the system predicts the correct head). Unsurprisingly, there has been much more research on supervised parsing – producing a wealth of models, datasets and training techniques – than on unsupervised parsing, which is more difficult, much less accurate and generally uses very simple probability models. Surprisingly, however, there have been no reported attempts to reuse supervised approaches to tackle the unsupervised parsing problem (an idea briefly mentioned in Spitkovsky et al. (2010b)).

There are, nevertheless, two aspects of supervised parsers that we would like to exploit in an unsupervised setting. First, we can increase the model expressiveness in order to capture more linguistic regularities. Many recent supervised parsers use third-order (or higher order) features (Koo and Collins, 2010; Martins et al., 2013; Le and Zuidema, 2014) to reach state-of-the-art (SOTA) performance. In contrast, existing models for unsupervised parsing limit themselves to using simple features (e.g., conditioning on heads and valency variables) in order to reduce the computational cost, to identify consistent patterns in data (Naseem, 2014, page 23), and to avoid overfitting (Blunsom and Cohn, 2010). Although this makes learning easier and more efficient, the disadvantage is that many useful linguistic regularities are missed: an upper bound on the performance of such simple models – estimated by using annotated data – is 76.3% on the WSJ corpus (Spitkovsky et al., 2013), compared to over 93% actual performance of the SOTA supervised parsers.

Second, we would like to make use of information available from lexical semantics, as in Bansal et al. (2014), Le and Zuidema (2014), and Chen and Manning (2014). Lexical semantics is a source for handling rare words and syntactic ambiguities. For instance, if a parser can identify that "he" is a dependent of "walks" in the sentence "He walks", then, even if "she" and "runs" do not appear in the training data, the parser may still be able to recognize that "she" should be a dependent of "runs" in the sentence "she runs". Similarly, a parser can make use of the fact that "sauce" and "John" have very different meanings to decide that they have different heads in the two phrases "ate spaghetti with sauce" and "ate spaghetti with John".

However, applying existing supervised parsing



*Human Language Technologies: The 2015 Annual Conference of the North American Chapter of the ACL*, pages 651–661,
Denver, Colorado, May 31 – June 5, 2015. 

techniques to the task of unsupervised parsing is, unfortunately, not trivial. The reason is that those parsers are optimally designed for being trained on manually annotated data. If we use existing unsupervised training methods (like EM), learning could be easily misled by a large amount of ambiguity naturally embedded in unannotated training data. Moreover, the computational cost could rapidly increase if the training algorithm is not designed properly. To overcome these difficulties we propose a framework, iterated reranking (IR), where existing supervised parsers are trained without the need of manually annotated data, starting with dependency trees provided by an existing unsupervised parser as initialiser. Using this framework, we can employ the work of Le and Zuidema (2014) to build a new system that outperforms the SOTA unsupervised parser of Spitkovsky et al. (2013) on the WSJ corpus.

The contribution of this paper is twofold. First, we show the benefit of using lexical semantics for the unsupervised parsing task. Second, our work is a bridge connecting the two research areas unsupervised parsing and its supervised counterpart. Before going to the next section, in order to avoid confusion introduced by names, it is worth noting that we use *un-trained* existing supervised parsers which will be trained on *automatically annotated* treebanks.

## 2 Related Work

### 2.1 Unsupervised Dependency Parsing

The first breakthrough was set by Klein and Manning (2004) with their dependency model with valence (DMV), the first model to outperform the right-branching baseline on the DDA metric: 43.2% vs 33.6% on sentences up to length 10 in the WSJ corpus. Nine years later, Spitkovsky et al. (2013) achieved much higher DDAs: 72.0% on sentences up to length 10, and 64.4% on all sentences in section 23. During this period, many approaches have been proposed to attempt the challenge.

Naseem and Barzilay (2011), Tu and Honavar (2012), Spitkovsky et al. (2012), Spitkovsky et al. (2013), and Marecek and Straka (2013) employ extensions of the DMV but with different learning strategies. Naseem and Barzilay (2011) use semantic cues, which are event annotations from an out-of-domain annotated corpus, in their model during training. Relying on the fact that natural language grammars must be unambiguous in the sense that a sentence should have very few correct parses, Tu and Honavar (2012) incorporate unambiguity regularisation to posterior probabilities. Spitkovsky et al. (2012) bootstrap the learning by slicing up all input sentences at punctuation. Spitkovsky et al. (2013) propose a complete deterministic learning framework for breaking out of local optima using count transforms and model recombination. Marecek and Straka (2013) make use of a large raw text corpus (e.g., Wikipedia) to estimate stop probabilities, using the reducibility principle.

Differing from those works, Bisk and Hockenmaier (2012) rely on Combinatory Categorial Grammars with a small number of hand-crafted general linguistic principles; whereas Blunsom and Cohn (2010) use Tree Substitution Grammars with a hierarchical non-parametric Pitman-Yor process prior biasing the learning to a small grammar.

### 2.2 Reranking

Our work relies on reranking which is a technique widely used in (semi-)supervised parsing. Reranking requires two components: a $k$-best parser and a reranker. Given a sentence, the parser generates a list of $k$ best candidates, the reranker then rescores those candidates and picks the one that has the highest score. Reranking was first successfully applied to supervised constituent parsing (Collins, 2000; Charniak and Johnson, 2005). It was then employed in the supervised dependency parsing approaches of Sangati et al. (2009), Hayashi et al. (2013), and Le and Zuidema (2014).

Closest to our work is the work series on semi-supervised constituent parsing of McClosky and colleagues, e.g. McClosky et al. (2006), using self-training. They use a $k$-best generative parser and a discriminative reranker to parse unannotated sentences, then add resulting parses to the training treebank and re-train the reranker. Different from their work, our work is for unsupervised dependency parsing, without manually annotated data, and uses iterated reranking instead of single reranking. In addition, both two components, $k$-best parser and reranker, are re-trained after each iteration.

## 3 The IR Framework

Existing training methods for the unsupervised dependency task, such as Blunsom and Cohn (2010), Gillenwater et al. (2011), and Tu and Honavar (2012), are hypothesis-oriented search with the EM algorithm or its variants: training is to move from a point which represents a model hypothesis to another point. This approach is feasible for optimising models using simple features since existing dynamic programming algorithms can compute expectations, which are sums over all possible parses, or to find the best parse in the whole parse space with low complexities. However, the complexity increases rapidly if rich, complex features are used. One way to reduce the computational cost is to use approximation methods like sampling as in Blunsom and Cohn (2010).

### 3.1 Treebank-oriented Greedy Search

Believing that the difficulty of using EM is from the fact that treebanks are 'hidden', leading to the need of computing sum (or max) overall possible treebanks, we propose a greedy local search scheme based on another training philosophy: treebank-oriented search. The key idea is to explicitly search for concrete treebanks which are used to train parsing models. This scheme thus allows supervised parsers to be trained in an unsupervised parsing setting since there is a (automatically annotated) treebank at any time.

Given $\mathcal{S}$ a set of raw sentences, the search space consists of all possible treebanks $\mathcal{D} = \{d(s)|s \in \mathcal{S}\}$ where $d(s)$ is a dependency tree of sentence $s$. The target of search is the optimal treebank $\mathcal{D}^*$ that is as good as human annotations. Greedy search with this philosophy is as follows: starting at an initial point $\mathcal{D}_1$, we pick up a point $\mathcal{D}_2$ among its neighbours $\mathbf{N}(\mathcal{D}_1)$ such that

$$\mathcal{D}_2 = \arg\max_{\mathcal{D} \in \mathbf{N}(\mathcal{D}_1)} f_{\mathcal{D}_1}(\mathcal{D}) \quad (1)$$

where $f_{\mathcal{D}_1}(\mathcal{D})$ is an objective function measuring the goodness of $\mathcal{D}$ (which may or may not be conditioned on $\mathcal{D}_1$). We then continue this search until some stop criterion is satisfied. The crucial factor here is to define $\mathbf{N}(\mathcal{D}_i)$ and $f_{\mathcal{D}_i}(\mathcal{D})$. Below are two special cases of this scheme.

**Semi-supervised parsing using reranking** (McClosky et al., 2006). This reranking is indeed one-step greedy local search. In this scenario, $\mathbf{N}(\mathcal{D}_1)$ is the Cartesian product of $k$-best lists generated by a $k$-best parser, and $f_{\mathcal{D}_i}(\mathcal{D})$ is a reranker.

**Unsupervised parsing with hard-EM** (Spitkovsky et al., 2010b) In hard-EM, the target is to maximise the following objective function with respect to a parameter set $\Theta$

$$L(\mathcal{S}|\Theta) = \sum_{s \in \mathcal{S}} \max_{d \in Dep(s)} \log P_\Theta(d) \quad (2)$$

where $Dep(s)$ is the set of all possible dependency structures of $s$. The two EM steps are thus

- Step 1: $\mathcal{D}_{i+1} = \arg\max_\mathcal{D} P_{\Theta_i}(\mathcal{D})$
- Step 2: $\Theta_{i+1} = \arg\max_\Theta P_\Theta(\mathcal{D}_{i+1})$

In this case, $\mathbf{N}(\mathcal{D}_i)$ is the whole treebank space and $f_{\mathcal{D}_i}(\mathcal{D}) = P_{\Theta_i}(\mathcal{D}) = P_{\arg\max_\Theta P_\Theta(\mathcal{D}_i)}(\mathcal{D})$.

### 3.2 Iterated Reranking

We instantiate the greedy search scheme by iterated reranking which requires two components: a $k$-best parser $P$, and a reranker $R$. Firstly, $\mathcal{D}_1$ is used to train these two components, resulting in $P_1$ and $R_1$. The parser $P_1$ then generates a set of lists of $k$ candidates ${}_k\mathcal{D}_1$ (whose Cartesian product results in $\mathbf{N}(\mathcal{D}_1)$) for the set of training sentences $\mathcal{S}$. The best candidates, according to reranker $R_1$, are collected to form $\mathcal{D}_2$ for the next iteration. This process is halted when a pre-defined stop criterion is met.[1]

It is certain that we can, as in the work of Spitkovsky et al. (2010b) and many bootstrapping approaches, employ only parser $P$. Reranking, however, brings us two benefits. First, it allows us to employ very expressive models like the $\infty$-order generative model proposed by Le and Zuidema (2014). Second, it embodies a similar idea to co-training (Blum and Mitchell, 1998): $P$ and $R$ play roles as two views of the data.

[1]It is worth noting that, although $\mathbf{N}(\mathcal{D}_i)$ has the size $O(k^n)$ where $n$ is the number of sentences, reranking only needs to process $O(k \times n)$ parses if these sentences are assumed to be independent.

### 3.3 Multi-phase Iterated Reranking

Training in machine learning often uses *starting big* which is to use up all training data at the same time. However, Elman (1993) suggests that in some cases, learning should start by training simple models on small data and then gradually increase the model complexity and add more difficult data. This is called *starting small.*

In unsupervised dependency parsing, starting small is intuitive. For instance, given a set of long sentences, learning the fact that the head of a sentence is its main verb is difficult because a long sentence always contains many syntactic categories. It would be much easier if we start with only length-one sentences, e.g "Look!", since there is only one choice which is usually a verb. This training scheme was successfully applied by Spitkovsky et al. (2010a) under the name: Baby Step.

We adopt starting small to construct the multi-phase iterated reranking (MPIR) framework. In phase 0, a parser $M$ with a simple model is trained on a set of short sentences $\mathcal{S}^{(0)}$ as in traditional approaches. This parser is used to parse a larger set of sentences $\mathcal{S}^{(1)} \supseteq \mathcal{S}^{(0)}$, resulting in $\mathcal{D}_1^{(1)}$. $\mathcal{D}_1^{(1)}$ is then used as the starting point for the iterated reranking in phase 1. We continue this process until phase $N$ finishes, with $\mathcal{S}^{(i)} \supseteq \mathcal{S}^{(i-1)}$ $(i = 1..N)$. In general, we use the resulting reranker in the previous phase to generate the starting point for the iterated reranking in the current phase.

## 4 Le and Zuidema (2014)'s Reranker

Le and Zuidema (2014)'s reranker is an exception among supervised parsers because it employs an extremely *expressive* model whose features are $\infty$-order[2]. To overcome the problem of sparsity, they introduced the inside-outside recursive neural network (IORNN) architecture that can estimate tree-generating models including those proposed by Eisner (1996) and Collins (2003a).

### 4.1 The $\infty$-order Generative Model

Le and Zuidema (2014)'s reranker employs the generative model proposed by Eisner (1996). Intuitively, this model is top-down: starting with ROOT, we generate its left dependents and its right dependents. We then generate dependents for each ROOT's dependent. The generative process recursively continues until there is no dependent to generate. Formally, this model is described by the following formula

$$P(d(H)) = \prod_{l=1}^{L} P\left(H_l^L | \mathcal{C}(H_l^L)\right) P\left(d(H_l^L)\right) \times \prod_{r=1}^{R} P\left(H_r^R | \mathcal{C}(H_r^R)\right) P\left(d(H_r^R)\right) \quad (3)$$

where $H$ is the current head, $d(N)$ is the fragment of the dependency parse rooted at $N$, and $\mathcal{C}(N)$ is the context to generate $N$. $H^L, H^R$ are respectively $H$'s left dependents and right dependents, plus $EOC$ (End-Of-Children), a special token to inform that there are no more dependents to generate. Thus, $P(d(ROOT))$ is the probability of generating the entire dependency structure $d$.

Le and Zuidema's $\infty$-order generative model is defined as Eisner's model in which the context $\mathcal{C}^{\infty}(D)$ to generate $D$ contains *all* of $D$'s generated siblings, its ancestors and their siblings. Because of very large fragments that contexts are allowed to hold, traditional count-based methods are impractical (even if we use smart smoothing techniques). They thus introduced the IORNN architecture to estimate the model.

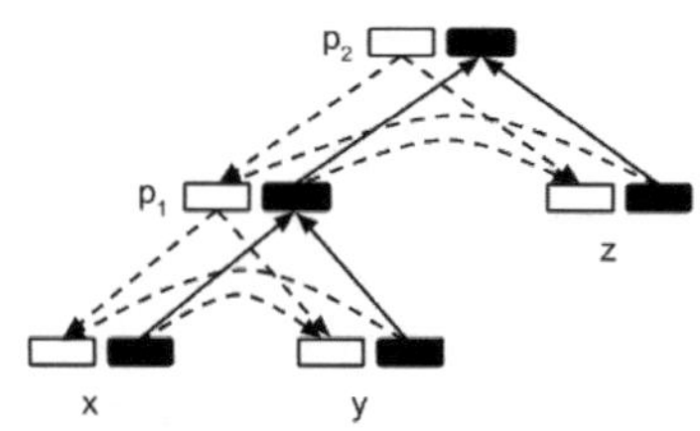


Figure 1: Inside-Outside Recursive Neural Network (IORNN). Black/white rectangles correspond to inner/outer representations.

### 4.2 Estimation with the IORNN

An IORNN (Figure 1) is a recursive neural network whose topology is a tree. What make this network different from traditional RNNs (Socher et al., 2010) is that each tree node $u$ caries two vectors: $\mathbf{i}_u$ - the inner representation, represents the content of the

[2]In fact, the order is finite but unbound.

phrase covered by the node, and $\mathbf{o}_u$ - the outer representation, represents the context around that phrase. In addition, information in an IORNN is allowed to flow not only bottom-up as in RNNs, but also top-down. That makes IORNNs a natural tool for estimating top-down tree-generating models.

Applying the IORNN architecture to dependency parsing is straightforward, along the generative story of the $\infty$-order generative model. First of all, the "inside" part of this IORNN is simpler than what is depicted in Figure 1: the inner representation of a phrase is assumed to be the inner representation of its head. This approximation is plausible since the meaning of a phrase is often dominated by the meaning of its head. The inner representation at each node, in turn, is a function of a vector representation for the word (in our case, the word vectors are initially borrowed from Collobert et al. (2011)), the POS-tag and capitalisation feature.

Without loss of generality and ignoring directions for simplicity, they assume that the model is generating dependent $u$ for node $h$ conditioning on context $\mathcal{C}^\infty(u)$ which contains all of $u$'s ancestors (including $h$) and theirs siblings, and all of previously generated $u$'s sisters. Now there are two types of contexts: *full* contexts of heads (e.g., $h$) whose dependents are being generated, and contexts to generate nodes (e.g., $\mathcal{C}^\infty(u)$). Contexts of the first type are clearly represented by outer representations. Contexts of the other type are represented by *partial outer representations*, denoted by $\bar{\mathbf{o}}_u$. Because the context to generate a node can be constructed recursively by combining the full context of its head and its previously generated sisters, they can compute $\bar{\mathbf{o}}_u$ as a function of $\mathbf{o}_h$ and the inner representations of its previously generated sisters. On the top of $\bar{\mathbf{o}}_u$, they put a softmax layer to estimate the probability $P(x|\mathcal{C}^\infty(u))$.

Training this IORNN is to minimise the cross entropy over all dependents. This objective function is indeed the negative log likelihood $P(\mathcal{D})$ of training treebank $\mathcal{D}$.

### 4.3 The Reranker

Le and Zuidema's (generative) reranker is given by

$$d^* = \arg\max_{d \in {}_k Dep(s)} P(d)$$

where $P$ (Equation 3) is computed by the $\infty$-order generative model which is estimated by an IORNN; and ${}_k Dep(s)$ is a $k$-best list.

## 5 Complete System

Our system is based on the multi-phase IR. In general, any third-party parser for unsupervised dependency parsing can be used in phase 0, and any third-party parser that can generate $k$-best lists can be used in the other phases. In our experiments, for phase 0, we choose the parser using an extension of the DMV model with stop-probability estimates computed on a large corpus proposed by Marecek and Straka (2013). This system has a moderate performance[3] on the WSJ corpus: 57.1% vs the SOTA 64.4% DDA of Spitkovsky et al. (2013). For the other phases, we use the MSTParser[4] (with the second-order feature mode) (McDonald and Pereira, 2006).

Our system uses Le and Zuidema (2014)'s reranker (Section 4.3). It is worth noting that, in this case, each phase with iterated reranking could be seen as an approximation of hard-EM (see Equation 2) where the first step is replaced by

$$\mathcal{D}_{i+1} = \arg\max_{\mathcal{D} \in \mathbf{N}(\mathcal{D}_i)} P_{\Theta_i}(\mathcal{D}) \qquad (4)$$

In other words, instead of searching over the treebank space, the search is limited in a neighbour set $\mathbf{N}(\mathcal{D}_i)$ generated by $k$-best parser $P_i$.

### 5.1 Tuning Parser $P$

Parser $P_i$ trained on $\mathcal{D}_i$ defines neighbour set $\mathbf{N}(\mathcal{D}_i)$ which is the Cartesian product of the $k$-best lists in ${}_k\mathcal{D}_i$. The position and shape of $\mathbf{N}(\mathcal{D}_i)$ is thus determined by two factors: how well $P_i$ can fit $\mathcal{D}_i$, and $k$. Intuitively, the lower the fitness is, the more $\mathbf{N}(\mathcal{D}_i)$ goes far away from $\mathcal{D}_i$; and the larger $k$ is, the larger

[3] Marecek and Straka (2013) did not report any experimental result on the WSJ corpus. We use their source code at `http://ufal.mff.cuni.cz/udp` with the setting presented in Section 6.1. Because the parser does not provide the option to parse unseen sentences, we merge the training sentences (up to length 15) to all the test sentences to evaluate its performance. Note that this result is close to the DDA (55.4%) that the authors reported on CoNLL 2007 English dataset, which is a portion of the WSJ corpus.

[4] `http://sourceforge.net/projects/mstparser/`

$\mathbf{N}(\mathcal{D}_i)$ is. Moreover, the diversity of $\mathbf{N}(\mathcal{D}_i)$ is inversely proportional to the fitness. When the fitness decreases, patterns existing in the training treebank become less certain to the parser, patterns that do not exist in the training treebank thus have more chances to appear in $k$-best candidates. This leads to high diversity of $\mathbf{N}(\mathcal{D}_i)$. We blindly set $k = 10$ in all of our experiments.

With the MSTParser, there are two hyper-parameters: $\texttt{iters}_{\text{MST}}$, the number of epochs, and $\texttt{training-k}_{\text{MST}}$, the $k$-best parse set size to create constraints during training. $\texttt{training-k}_{\text{MST}}$ is always 1 because constraints from $k$-best parses with almost incorrect training parses are useless.

Because $\texttt{iters}_{\text{MST}}$ controls the fitness of the parser to training treebank $\mathcal{D}_i$, it, as pointed out above, determines the distance from $\mathbf{N}(\mathcal{D}_i)$ to $\mathcal{D}_i$ and the diversity of the former. Therefore, if we want to encourage the local search to explore more distant areas, we should set $\texttt{iters}_{\text{MST}}$ low. In our experiments, we test two strategies: (i) MaxEnc, $\texttt{iters}_{\text{MST}} = 1$, maximal encouragement, and (ii) MinEnc, $\texttt{iters}_{\text{MST}} = 10$, minimal encouragement.

### 5.2 Tuning Reranker $R$

Tuning the reranker $R$ is to set values for $\texttt{dim}_{\text{IORNN}}$, the dimensions of inner and outer representations, and $\texttt{iters}_{\text{IORNN}}$, the number of epochs to train the IORNN. Because the $\infty$-order model is very expressive and feed-forward neural networks are universal approximators (Cybenko, 1989), the reranker is capable of perfectly remembering all training parses. In order to avoid this, we set $\texttt{dim}_{\text{IORNN}} = 50$, and set $\texttt{iters}_{\text{IORNN}} = 5$ for *very* early stopping.

### 5.3 Tuning multi-phase IR

Because Marecek and Straka (2013)'s parser does not distinguish training data from test data, we postulate $\mathcal{S}_0 = \mathcal{S}_1$. Our system has $N$ phases such that $\mathcal{S}_0, \mathcal{S}_1$ contain all sentences up to length $l_1 = 15$, $\mathcal{S}_i$ $(i = 2..N)$ contains all sentences up to length $l_i = l_{i-1} + 1$, and $\mathcal{S}_N$ contains all sentences up to length 25. Phase 1 halts after 100 iterations whereas all the following phases run with one iteration. Note that we force the local search in phase 1 to run intensively because we hypothesise that most of the important patterns for dependency parsing can be found within short sentences.

## 6 Experiments

### 6.1 Setting

We use the Penn Treebank WSJ corpus: sections 02-21 for training, and section 23 for testing. We then apply the standard pre-processing[5] for unsupervised dependency parsing task (Klein and Manning, 2004): we strip off all empty sub-trees, punctuation, and terminals (tagged # and $) not pronounced where they appear; we then convert the remaining trees to dependencies using Collins's head rules (Collins, 2003b). Both word forms and gold POS tags are used. The directed dependency accuracy (DDA) metric is used for evaluation.

The vocabulary is taken as a list of words occurring more than two times in the training data. All other words are labelled 'UNKNOWN' and every digit is replaced by '0'. We initialise the IORNN with the 50-dim word embeddings from Collobert et al. (2011) [6] , and train it with the learning rate 0.1,

### 6.2 Results

We compare our system against recent systems (Table 1 and Section 2.1). Our system with the two encouragement levels, MinEnc and MaxEnc, achieves the highest reported DDAs on section 23: 1.8% and 1.2% higher than Spitkovsky et al. (2013) on all sentences and up to length 10, respectively. Our improvements over the system's initialiser (Marecek and Straka, 2013) are 9.1% and 4.4%.

### 6.3 Analysis

In this section, we analyse our system along two aspects. First, we examine three factors which determine the performance of the whole system: encouragement level, lexical semantics, and starting point. We then search for what IR (with the MaxEnc option) contributes to the overall performance by comparing the quality of the treebank resulted in the end of phase 1 against the quality of the treebank given by its initialier, i.e. Marecek and Straka (2013).

**The effect of encouragement level**

Figure 2 shows the differences in DDA between using MaxEnc and MinEnc in each phase: we com-

[5] `http://www.cs.famaf.unc.edu.ar/~francolq/en/proyectos/dmvccm`

[6] `http://ml.nec-labs.com/senna/`. These word embeddings were *unsupervisedly* learnt from Wikipedia.

| System | DDA (@10) |
|---|---|
| Bisk and Hockenmaier (2012) | 53.3 (71.5) |
| Blunsom and Cohn (2010) | 55.7 (67.7) |
| Tu and Honavar (2012) | 57.0 (71.4) |
| Marecek and Straka (2013)[3] | 57.1 (68.8) |
| Naseem and Barzilay (2011) | 59.4 (70.2) |
| Spitkovsky et al. (2012) | 61.2 (71.4) |
| Spitkovsky et al. (2013) | 64.4 (72.0) |
| Our system (MinEnc) | **66.2** (72.7) |
| Our system (MaxEnc) | 65.8 (**73.2**) |

Table 1: Performance on section 23 of the WSJ corpus (all sentences and up to length 10) for recent systems and our system. MinEnc and MaxEnc denote $\texttt{iters}_{\text{MST}} = 10$ and $\texttt{iters}_{\text{MST}} = 1$ respectively.

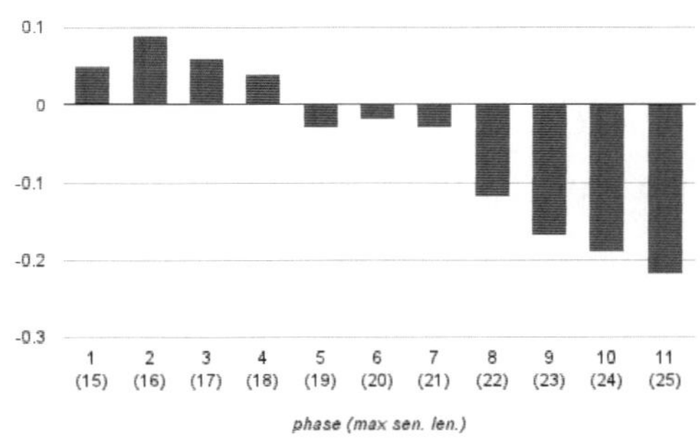


Figure 2: $DDA_{MaxEnc} - DDA_{MinEnc}$ of all phases on the their training sets (e.g., phase 3 with $\mathcal{S}^{(3)}$ containing all training sentences up to length 17).

pute $DDA_{MaxEnc} - DDA_{MinEnc}$ of each phase on its training set (e.g., phase 3 with $\mathcal{S}^{(3)}$ containing all training sentences up to length 17). MinEnc outperforms MaxEnc within phases 1, 2, 3, and 4. However, from phase 5, the latter surpasses the former. It suggests that exploring areas far away from the current point with long sentences is risky. The reason is that long sentences contain more ambiguities than short ones; thus rich diversity, high difference from the current point, but small size (i.e., small $k$) could easily lead the learning to a wrong path.

The performance of the system with the two encouragement levels on section 23 (Table 1) also suggests the same. MaxEnc strategy helps the system achieve the highest accuracy on short sentences (up to length 10). However, it is less helpful than MinEnc when performing on long sentences.

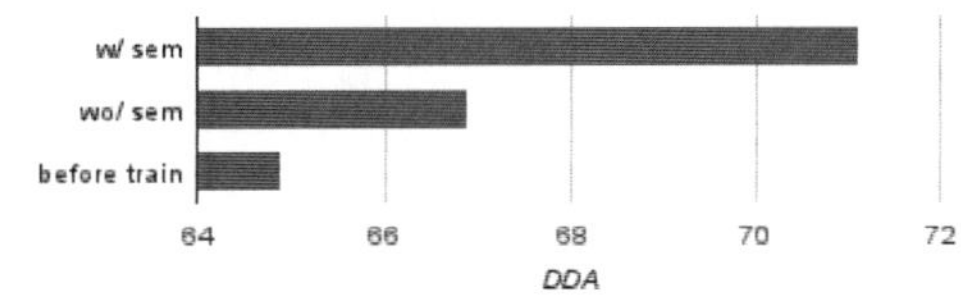


Figure 3: DDA of phase 1 (MaxEnc), with and without the word embeddings (denoted by w/ sem and wo/ sem, respectively), on training sentences up to length 15 (i.e. $\mathcal{S}^{(1)}$).

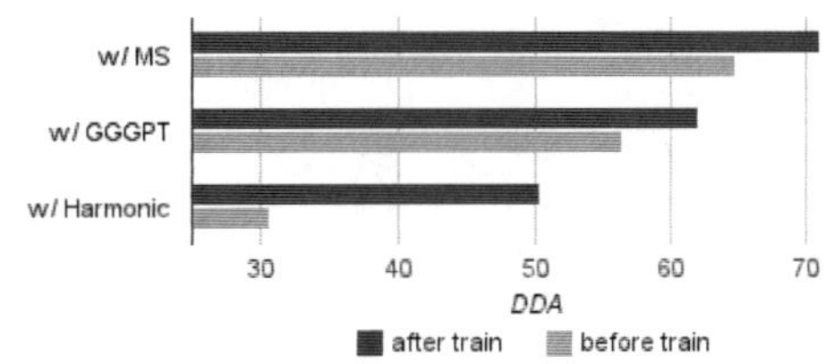


Figure 4: DDA of phase 1 (MaxEnc) before and after training with three different starting points provided by three parsers used in phase 0: MS (Marecek and Straka, 2013), GGGPT (Gillenwater et al., 2011), and Harmonic (Klein and Manning, 2004).

### The role of lexical semantics

We examine the role of the lexical semantics, which is given by the word embeddings. Figure 3 shows DDAs on training sentences up to length 15 (i.e. $\mathcal{S}^{(1)}$) of phase 1 (MaxEnc) with and without the word-embeddings. With the word-embeddings, phase 1 achieves 71.11%. When the word-embeddings are not given, i.e. the IORNN uses randomly generated word vectors, the accuracy drops 4.2%. It shows that lexical semantics plays a decisive role in the performance of the system.

However, it is worth noting that, even without that knowledge (i.e., with the $\infty$-order generative model alone), the DDA of phase 1 is 2% higher than before being trained (66.89% vs 64.9%). It suggests that phase 1 is capable of discovering some useful dependency patterns that are invisible to the parser in phase 0. This, we conjecture, is thanks to high-order features captured by the IORNN.

### The importance of the starting point

Starting point is claimed to be important in local search. We examine this by using three different parsers in phase 0: (i) MS (Marecek and Straka,

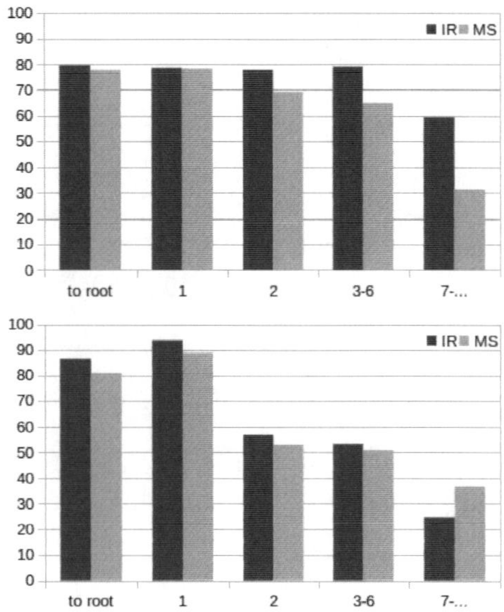


Figure 5: Precision (top) and recall (bottom) over binned HEAD distance of iterated reranking (IR) and its initializer (MS) on the training sentences in phase 1 ($\leq 15$ words).

2013), the parser used in the previous experiments, (ii) GGGPT (Gillenwater et al., 2011)[7] employing an extension of the DMV model and posterior regularization framework for training, and (iii) Harmonic, the harmonic initializer proposed by Klein and Manning (2004).

Figure 4 shows DDAs of phase 1 (MaxEnc) on training sentences up to length 15 with three starting-points given by those parsers. Starting point is clearly very important to the performance of the iterated reranking: the better the starting point is, the higher performance phase 1 has. However, a remarkable point here is that the iterated reranking of phase 1 always finds out more useful patterns for parsing whatever the starting point is in this experiment. It is certainly due to the high order features and lexical semantics, which are not exploited in those parsers.

**The contribution of Iterated Reranking**

We compare the quality of the treebank resulted in the end of phase 1 against the quality of the treebank given by the initialier Marecek and Straka (2013). Figure 5 shows precision (top) and recall (bottom) over binned HEAD distance. IR helps to improve the precision on all distance bins, especially on the bins corresponding to long distances ($\geq 3$). The recall is also improved, except on the bin corresponding to $\geq 7$ (but the F1-score on this bin is increased). We attribute this improvement to the $\infty$-order model which uses very large fragments as contexts thus be able to capture long dependencies.

Figure 6 shows the correct-head accuracies over POS-tags. IR helps to improve the accuracies over almost all POS-tags, particularly nouns (e.g. NN, NNP, NNS), verbs (e.g. VBD, VBZ, VBN, VBG) and adjectives (e.g. JJ, JJR). However, as being affected by the initializer, IR performs poorly on conjunction (CC) and modal auxiliary (MD). For instance, in the treebank given by the initializer, almost all modal auxilaries are dependents of their verbs instead of the other way around.

## 7 Discussion

Our system is different from the other systems shown in Table 1 as it uses an extremely expressive model, the $\infty$-order generative model, in which conditioning contexts are very large fragments. Only the work of Blunsom and Cohn (2010), whose resulting grammar rules can contain large tree fragments, shares this property. The difference is that their work needs a pre-defined prior, namely hierarchical non-parametric Pitman-Yor process prior, to avoid large, rare fragments and for smoothing. The IORNN of our system, in contrast, does that automatically. It learns by itself how to deal with distant conditioning nodes, which are often less informative than close conditioning nodes on computing $P(x|\mathcal{C}^{\infty}(u))$. In addition, smoothing is given free: recursive neural nets are able to map 'similar' fragments onto close points (Socher et al., 2010) thus an unseen fragment tends to be mapped onto a point close to points corresponding to 'similar' seen fragments.

Another difference is that our system exploits lexical semantics via word embeddings, which were learnt unsupervisedly. By initialising the IORNN with these embeddings, the use of this knowledge turns out easy and transparent. Spitkovsky et al. (2013) also exploit lexical semantics but in a limited way, using a context-based polysemous unsuper-

[7] `code.google.com/p/pr-toolkit`

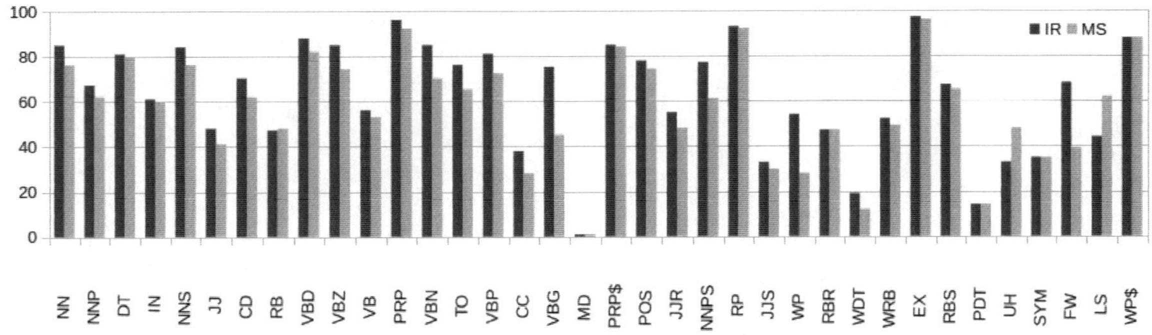


Figure 6: Correct-head accuracies over POS-tags (sorted in the descending order by frequency) of iterated reranking (IR) and its initializer (MS) on the training sentences in phase 1 ($\leq 15$ words).

vised clustering method to tag words. Although their approach can distinguish polysemes (e.g., 'cool' in 'to cool the selling panic' and in 'it is cool'), it is not able to make use of word meaning similarities (e.g., the meaning of 'dog' is closer to 'animal' than to 'table'). Naseem and Barzilay (2011)'s system uses semantic cues from an out-of-domain annotated corpus, thus is not fully unsupervised.

We have showed that IR with a generative reranker is an approximation of hard-EM (see Equation 4). Our system is thus related to the works of Spitkovsky et al. (2013) and Tu and Honavar (2012). However, what we have proposed is more than that: IR is a general framework that we can have more than one option for choosing $k$-best parser and reranker. For instance, we can make use of a generative $k$-best parser and a discriminative reranker that are used for supervised parsing. Our future work is to explore this.

The experimental results reveal that starting point is very important to the iterated reranking with the $\infty$-order generative model. On the one hand, that is a disadvantage compared to the other systems, which use uninformed or harmonic initialisers. But on the other hand, that is an innovation as our approach is capable of making use of existing systems. The results shown in Figure 4 suggest that if phase 0 uses a better parser which uses less expressive model and/or less external knowledge than our model, such as the one proposed by Spitkovsky et al. (2013), we can expect even a higher performance. The other systems, except Blunsom and Cohn (2010), however, might not benefit from using good existing parsers as initializers because their models are not significantly more expressive than others [8].

## 8 Conclusion

We have proposed a new framework, iterated reranking (IR), which trains supervised parsers without the need of manually annotated data by using a unsupervised parser as an initialiser. Our system, employing Marecek and Straka (2013)'s unsupervised parser as the initialiser, the $k$-best MSTParser, and Le and Zuidema (2014)'s reranker, achieved 1.8% DDA higher than the SOTA parser of Spitkovsky et al. (2013) on the WSJ corpus. Moreover, we also showed that unsupervised parsing benefits from lexical semantics through using word-embeddings.

Our future work is to exploit other existing supervised parsers that fit our framework. Besides, taking into account the fast development of the word embedding research (Mikolov et al., 2013; Pennington et al., 2014), we will try different word embeddings.


## Acknowledgments

We thank Remko Scha and three anonymous reviewers for helpful comments. Le thanks Miloš Stanojević for helpful discussion.


[8] In an experiment, we used the Marecek and Straka (2013)'s parser as an initializer for the Gillenwater et al. (2011)'s parser. As we expected, the latter was not able to make use of this.

## References


Mohit Bansal, Kevin Gimpel, and Karen Livescu. 2014. Tailoring continuous word representations for dependency parsing. In *Proceedings of the Annual Meeting of the Association for Computational Linguistics*.

Yonatan Bisk and Julia Hockenmaier. 2012. Simple robust grammar induction with combinatory categorial grammars. In *AAAI*.

Avrim Blum and Tom M. Mitchell. 1998. Combining labeled and unlabeled sata with co-training. In *COLT*, pages 92–100.

Phil Blunsom and Trevor Cohn. 2010. Unsupervised induction of tree substitution grammars for dependency parsing. In *Proceedings of the 2010 Conference on Empirical Methods in Natural Language Processing*, pages 1204–1213. Association for Computational Linguistics.

Eugene Charniak and Mark Johnson. 2005. Coarse-to-fine n-best parsing and maxent discriminative reranking. In *ACL*.

Danqi Chen and Christopher D Manning. 2014. A fast and accurate dependency parser using neural networks. In *Empirical Methods in Natural Language Processing (EMNLP)*.

Michael Collins. 2000. Discriminative reranking for natural language parsing. In *ICML*, pages 175–182.

Michael Collins. 2003a. Head-driven statistical models for natural language parsing. *Computational linguistics*, 29(4):589–637.

Michael Collins. 2003b. Head-driven statistical models for natural language parsing. *Computational Linguistics*, 29(4):589–637.

Ronan Collobert, Jason Weston, Léon Bottou, Michael Karlen, Koray Kavukcuoglu, and Pavel Kuksa. 2011. Natural language processing (almost) from scratch. *The Journal of Machine Learning Research*, 12:2493–2537.

George Cybenko. 1989. Approximation by superpositions of a sigmoidal function. *Mathematics of control, signals and systems*, 2(4):303–314.

Jason M Eisner. 1996. Three new probabilistic models for dependency parsing: An exploration. In *Proceedings of the 16th conference on Computational linguistics-Volume 1*, pages 340–345. Association for Computational Linguistics.

Jeffrey L Elman. 1993. Learning and development in neural networks: The importance of starting small. *Cognition*, 48(1):71–99.

Jennifer Gillenwater, Kuzman Ganchev, João Graça, Fernando Pereira, and Ben Taskar. 2011. Posterior sparsity in unsupervised dependency parsing. *The Journal of Machine Learning Research*, 12:455–490.

Katsuhiko Hayashi, Shuhei Kondo, and Yuji Matsumoto. 2013. Efficient stacked dependency parsing by forest reranking. *Transactions of the Association for Computational Linguistics*, 1(1):139–150.

Dan Klein and Christopher D. Manning. 2004. Corpus-based induction of syntactic structure: Models of dependency and constituency. In *ACL*, pages 478–485.

Terry Koo and Michael Collins. 2010. Efficient third-order dependency parsers. In *Proceedings of the 48th Annual Meeting of the Association for Computational Linguistics*, pages 1–11. Association for Computational Linguistics.

Phong Le and Willem Zuidema. 2014. The inside-outside recursive neural network model for dependency parsing. In *Proceedings of the 2014 Conference on Empirical Methods in Natural Language Processing*. Association for Computational Linguistics.

David Marecek and Milan Straka. 2013. Stop-probability estimates computed on a large corpus improve unsupervised dependency parsing. In *ACL (1)*, pages 281–290.

André FT Martins, Miguel B Almeida, and Noah A Smith. 2013. Turning on the turbo: Fast third-order non-projective turbo parsers. In *Proc. of ACL*.

David McClosky, Eugene Charniak, and Mark Johnson. 2006. Effective self-training for parsing. In *Proceedings of the main conference on human language technology conference of the North American Chapter of the Association of Computational Linguistics*, pages 152–159. Association for Computational Linguistics.

Ryan T. McDonald and Fernando C. N. Pereira. 2006. Online learning of approximate dependency parsing algorithms. In *EACL*.

Tomas Mikolov, Ilya Sutskever, Kai Chen, Greg S Corrado, and Jeff Dean. 2013. Distributed representations of words and phrases and their compositionality. In *Advances in Neural Information Processing Systems*, pages 3111–3119.

Tahira Naseem and Regina Barzilay. 2011. Using semantic cues to learn syntax. In *AAAI*.

Tahira Naseem. 2014. *Linguistically Motivated Models for Lightly-Supervised Dependency Parsing*. Ph.D. thesis, Massachusetts Institute of Technology.

Jeffrey Pennington, Richard Socher, and Christopher D Manning. 2014. Glove: Global vectors for word representation. *Proceedings of the Empiricial Methods in Natural Language Processing (EMNLP 2014)*, 12.

Federico Sangati, Willem Zuidema, and Rens Bod. 2009. A generative re-ranking model for dependency parsing. In *Proceedings of the 11th International Conference on Parsing Technologies*, pages 238–241. Association for Computational Linguistics.

Richard Socher, Christopher D. Manning, and Andrew Y. Ng. 2010. Learning continuous phrase representations and syntactic parsing with recursive neural networks. In *Proceedings of the NIPS-2010 Deep Learning and Unsupervised Feature Learning Workshop*.

Valentin I. Spitkovsky, Hiyan Alshawi, and Daniel Jurafsky. 2010a. From Baby Steps to Leapfrog: How "Less is More" in unsupervised dependency parsing. In *Proc. of NAACL-HLT*.

Valentin I. Spitkovsky, Hiyan Alshawi, Daniel Jurafsky, and Christopher D. Manning. 2010b. Viterbi training improves unsupervised dependency parsing. In *Proceedings of the Fourteenth Conference on Computational Natural Language Learning (CoNLL-2010)*.

Valentin I. Spitkovsky, Hiyan Alshawi, and Daniel Jurafsky. 2012. Bootstrapping dependency grammar inducers from incomplete sentence fragments via austere models. In *Proceedings of the 11th International Conference on Grammatical Inference*.

Valentin I. Spitkovsky, Hiyan Alshawi, and Daniel Jurafsky. 2013. Breaking out of local optima with count transforms and model recombination: A study in grammar induction. In *EMNLP*, pages 1983–1995.

Kewei Tu and Vasant Honavar. 2012. Unambiguity regularization for unsupervised learning of probabilistic grammars. In *Proceedings of the 2012 Joint Conference on Empirical Methods in Natural Language Processing and Computational Natural Language Learning*, pages 1324–1334. Association for Computational Linguistics.

# A Linear-Time Transition System for Crossing Interval Trees

**Emily Pitler** **Ryan McDonald**
Google, Inc.
{epitler,ryanmcd}@google.com

## Abstract

We define a restricted class of non-projective trees that 1) covers many natural language sentences; and 2) can be parsed exactly with a generalization of the popular arc-eager system for projective trees (Nivre, 2003). Crucially, this generalization only adds constant overhead in run-time and space keeping the parser's total run-time linear in the worst case. In empirical experiments, our proposed transition-based parser is more accurate on average than both the arc-eager system or the swap-based system, an unconstrained non-projective transition system with a worst-case quadratic runtime (Nivre, 2009).

## 1 Introduction

Linear-time transition-based parsers that use either greedy inference or beam search are widely used today due to their speed and accuracy (Nivre, 2008; Zhang and Clark, 2008; Zhang and Nivre, 2011). Of the many proposed transition systems (Nivre, 2008), the arc-eager transition system of Nivre (2003) is one of the most popular for a variety of reasons. The arc-eager system has a well-defined output space: it can produce *all* projective trees and *only* projective trees. For an input sentence with $n$ words, the arc-eager system always performs $2n$ operations and each operation takes constant time. Another attractive property of the arc-eager system is the close connection between the parameterization of the parsing problem and the final predicted output structure. In the arc-eager model, each operation has a clear interpretation in terms of constraints on the final output tree (Goldberg and Nivre, 2012), which allows for more robust learning procedures (Goldberg and Nivre, 2012).

The arc-eager system, however, cannot produce trees with crossing arcs. Alternative systems can produce crossing dependencies, but at the cost of taking $O(n^2)$ transitions in the worst case (Nivre, 2008; Nivre, 2009; Choi and McCallum, 2013), requiring more transitions than arc-eager to produce projective trees (Nivre, 2008; Gómez-Rodríguez and Nivre, 2010), or producing trees in an unknown output class[1] (Attardi, 2006).

Graph-based non-projective parsing algorithms, on the other hand, have been able to preserve many of the attractive properties of their corresponding projective parsing algorithms by restricting search to classes of *mildly non-projective trees* (Kuhlmann and Nivre, 2006). Mildly non-projective classes of trees are *characterizable* subsets of directed trees. Classes of particular interest are those that both have high empirical coverage and that can be parsed efficiently. With appropriate definitions of feature functions and output spaces, exact higher-order graph-based non-projective parsers can match the asymptotic time and space of higher-order projective parsers (Pitler, 2014).

In this paper, we propose a class of mildly non-projective trees (§3) and a transition system (§4) that is sound and complete with respect to this class (§5) while preserving desirable properties of arc-eager: it runs in $O(n)$ time in the worst case (§6), and each operation can be interpreted as a prediction about

[1] A characterization independent of the transition system is unknown.



*Human Language Technologies: The 2015 Annual Conference of the North American Chapter of the ACL*, pages 662–671,
Denver, Colorado, May 31 – June 5, 2015. 

the final tree structure. At the same time, it can produce trees with crossing dependencies. Across ten languages, on average 96.7% of sentences have dependency trees in the proposed class (Table 1), compared with 79.4% for projective trees. The implemented mildly non-projective transition-based parser is more accurate than a fully projective parser (arc-eager, (Nivre, 2003)) and a fully non-projective parser (swap-based, (Nivre, 2009)) (§7.1).

## 2 Preliminaries

Given an input sentence $w_1 w_2 \ldots w_n$, a dependency tree for that sentence is a set of vertices $V = \{0, 1, \ldots, n\}$ and arcs $A \subset V \times V$. Each vertex $i$ corresponds to a word in the sentence and vertex 0 corresponds to an artificial *root* word, which is standard in the literature. An arc $(i, j) \in A$ represents a dependency between a modifier $w_j$ and a head $w_i$. Critically, the arc set $A$ is constrained to form a valid *dependency tree*: its root is at the leftmost vertex 0; each vertex $i$ has exactly one incoming arc (except 0, which has no incoming arcs); and there are no cycles. A common extension is to add labels of syntactic relations to each arc. For ease of exposition, we will focus on the unlabeled variant during the discussion but use a labeled variant during experiments.

A dependency tree is *projective* if and only if the nodes in the yield of each subtree form a contiguous interval with respect to the words and their order in the sentence. For instance, the tree in Figure 1a is *non-projective* since the subtrees rooted at *came* and *parade* do not cover a contiguous set of words. Equivalently, a dependency tree is non-projective if and only if the tree cannot be drawn in the plane above the sentence without crossing arcs. As we will see, these *crossing arcs* are a useful measure when defining sub-classes of non-projectivity. We will often reason about the set of vertices *incident* to a particular arc. The incident vertices of an arc are its endpoints: for an arc $(u, v)$, $u$ and $v$ are the two vertices incident to it.

## 3 $k$-Crossing Interval Trees

We begin by defining a class of trees based on restrictions on crossing dependencies. The class definition is independent of any transition system; it is easy to check whether a particular tree is within the class or not. We compare the coverage of this class on various natural language datasets with the coverage of the class of projective trees.

(a) A dependency tree with two disjoint sets (blue and dashed/red and dotted) of crossing arcs (bold).

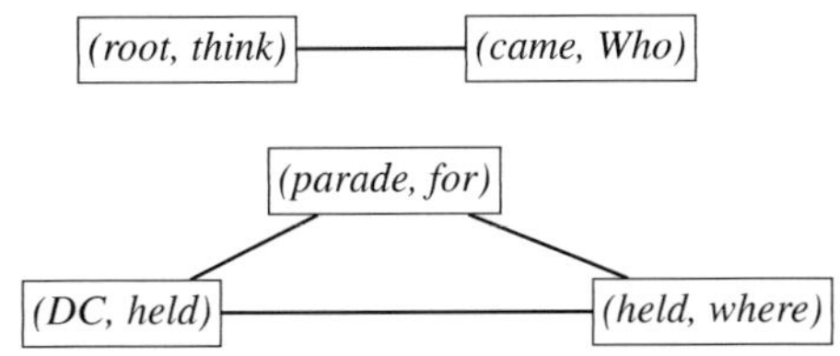


(b) The auxiliary graph for the sentence above. There are two connected components of crossed arcs, one of which corresponds to the crossing interval *[root, came]* and the other *[DC, for]*.

Figure 1: A sentence with two crossing intervals.

**Definition 1.** *Let $A$ be a set of unlabeled arcs. The* Interval *of $A$,* Interval(A)*, is the interval from the leftmost vertex in $A$ to the rightmost vertex in $A$, i.e., Interval(A)* $= [min(V_A), max(V_A)]$*, where* $V_A = \{v : \exists u[(u, v) \in A \vee (v, u) \in A]\}$.

**Definition 2.** *For any dependency tree $T$, the below procedure partitions the crossed arcs in $T$ into disjoint sets $A_1$, $A_2$, $\ldots$, $A_l$ such that Interval($A_1$), Interval($A_2$), $\ldots$, Interval($A_l$) are all vertex-disjoint. These intervals are the* ***crossing intervals*** *of the tree $T$.*

*Procedure:* Construct an auxiliary graph with a vertex for each crossed arc in the original tree. Two such vertices are connected by an arc if the intervals defined by the arcs they correspond to have a non-empty intersection. Figure 1b shows the auxiliary graph for the sentence in Figure 1a. The connected components of this graph form a partition of the graph's vertices, and so also partition the crossed arcs in the original sentence. The intervals defined by these groups cannot overlap, since then the crossed arcs that span the overlapping portion would have been connected by an arc in the auxiliary graph and hence been part of the same connected component. □

**Definition 3.** *A tree is a $k$-*Crossing Interval *tree if for each crossing interval, there exists at most $k$ ver-*

| Language | 2-Crossing Interval | 1-Endpoint-Crossing | Projective |
|---|---|---|---|
| Basque | 93.5 | 94.7 | 74.8 |
| Czech | 97.4 | 98.9 | 77.9 |
| Dutch | 91.4 | 95.8 | 63.6 |
| English | 99.2 | 99.3 | 93.4 |
| German | 94.7 | 96.4 | 72.3 |
| Greek | 99.1 | 99.7 | 84.4 |
| Hungarian | 95.3 | 96.3 | 74.7 |
| Portuguese | 99.0 | 99.6 | 83.3 |
| Slovene | 98.2 | 99.5 | 79.6 |
| Turkish | 99.1 | 99.3 | 89.9 |
| Average | 96.7 | 98.0 | 79.4 |

Table 1: Proportion of trees (excluding punctuation) in each tree class for the CoNLL shared tasks training sets: Dutch, German, Portuguese, and Slovene are from Buchholz and Marsi (2006); Basque, Czech, English, Greek, Hungarian, and Turkish data are from Nivre et al. (2007).

*tices such that a) all crossed arcs within the interval are incident to at least one of these vertices and b) any vertex in the interval that has a child on the far side of its parent is one of these $k$ vertices.*

Figure 1a shows a 2-Crossing Interval tree. For the first crossing interval, *think* and *came* satisfy the conditions; for the second, *parade* and *held* do. The coverage of 2-Crossing Interval trees is shown in Table 1. Across datasets from ten languages with a non-negligible proportion of crossing dependencies, on average 96.7% of dependency trees are 2-Crossing Interval, within 1.3% of the larger 1-Endpoint-Crossing class (Pitler et al., 2013) and substantially larger than the 79.4% coverage of projective trees. Coverage increases as $k$ increases; for 3-Crossing Interval trees, the average coverage reaches 98.6%. Punctuation tokens are excluded when computing coverage to better reflect language specific properties rather than treebank artifacts; for example, the Turkish CoNLL data attaches punctuation tokens to the artificial root, causing a 15% absolute drop in coverage for projective trees when punctuation tokens are included (89.9% vs. 74.7%).

### 3.1 Connections to Other Tree Classes

$k = 0$ or $k = 1$ gives exactly the class of projective trees (even a single crossing implies two vertex-disjoint crossed edges). 2-Crossing Interval trees are a subset of the linguistically motivated 1-Endpoint-Crossing trees (Pitler et al., 2013) (each crossed edge is incident to one of the two vertices for the

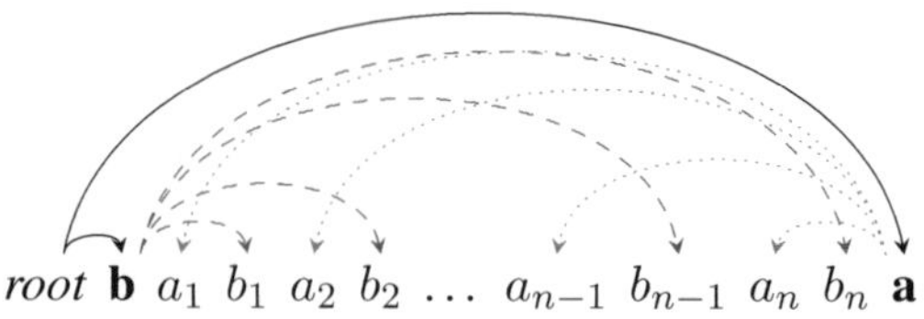


Figure 2: A 2-Crossing Interval tree that is not well-nested and has unbounded block degree.

interval, so all edges that cross it are incident to the *other* vertex for the interval); all of the examples from the linguistics literature provided in Pitler (2013, p.132-136) for 1-Endpoint-Crossing trees are 2-Crossing Interval trees as well. 2-Crossing Interval trees are *not* necessarily *well-nested* and can have unbounded *block degree* (Kuhlmann, 2013). Figure 2 shows an example of a 2-Crossing Interval tree (all crossed edges are incident to either $a$ or $b$; no children are on the far side of their parent) in which the subtrees rooted at $a$ and $b$ are ill-nested and each has a block degree of $n + 1$.

## 4 Two-Registers Transition System

A transition system for dependency parsing comprises: 1) an initial configuration for an input sentence; 2) a set of final configurations after which the parsing derivation terminates; and 3) a set of deterministic *transitions* for transitioning from one configuration to another (Nivre, 2008).

Our transition system builds on one of the most commonly used transition systems for parsing projective trees, the arc-eager system (Nivre, 2003). An arc-eager configuration, $c$, is a tuple, $(\sigma, \beta, A)$, where 1) $\sigma$ is a *stack* consisting of a subset of processed tokens; 2) $\beta$ is a *buffer* consisting of unprocessed tokens; and 3) $A$ is the set of dependency arcs already added to the tree.

We define a new transition system called *two-registers*. Configurations are updated to include two *registers* $R1$ and $R2$, i.e., $c = (\sigma, \beta, R1, R2, A)$. A register contains one vertex or is empty: $R1, R2 \in V \cup \{null\}$. Table 2 defines both the arc-eager and two-registers transition systems. The two-registers system includes the arc-eager transitions (top half of Table 2) and three new transitions that make use of the registers (bottom half of Table 2):

- **Store**: Moves the token at the front of the buffer into the first available register, optionally

Arc-Eager

- Initial configuration: $(\{0\}, \{1, \ldots, n\}, \{\})$
- Terminal configurations $(\sigma, \{\}, A)$

Two-Registers

- Initial configuration: $(\{\}, \{0, \ldots, n\}, null, null, \{\})$
- Terminal configurations: $(\sigma, \{\}, null, null, A)$

| | Transition | $\sigma$ | $\beta$ | $R1$ | $R2$ | $A$ |
|---|---|---|---|---|---|---|
| Arc-Eager | Left-Arc | $\sigma_{m..2}$ | $\beta_{1..n}$ | $R1$ | $R2$ | $A \cup \{(\beta_1, \sigma_1)\}$ |
| Arc-Eager | Right-Arc | $\sigma_{m..1}\|\beta_1$ | $\beta_{2..n}$ | $R1$ | $R2$ | $A \cup \{(\sigma_1, \beta_1)\}$ |
| Arc-Eager | Shift | $\sigma_{m..1}\|\beta_1$ | $\beta_{2..n}$ | $R1$ | $R2$ | $A$ |
| Arc-Eager | Reduce | $\sigma_{m..2}$ | $\beta_{1..n}$ | $R1$ | $R2$ | $A$ |
| + Two-Registers | Store(arc) | $\sigma_{m..1}$ | $\beta_{2..n}$ | $R1'$ | $R2'$ | $A \cup B$ |
| | | Where: | arc $\in$ {left, right, no-arc}<br>$B := \{(\beta_1, R1)\}$ if arc=left, $\{(R1, \beta_1)\}$ if arc=right, and $\emptyset$ otherwise.<br>$R1' := (R1 = null)\ ?\ \beta_1 : R1;\quad R2' := (R1 = null)\ ?\ R2 : \beta_1$. | | | |
| + Two-Registers | Clear | $\sigma_{m..2}\|\psi$ | $\gamma\|\beta_{1..n}$ | $null$ | $null$ | $A$ |
| | | Where: | $\gamma := (\sigma_1 = \beta_1 - 1)\ ?\ \sigma_1 : (R2 = \beta_1 - 1)\ ?\ R2 : null$<br>$\psi := \{\sigma_1\} \cup NotCovered(R1) \cup NotCovered(R2) - \{\gamma\}$ in left-to-right order, where $NotCovered(x) := x$ if no edges in $A$ cover $x$ and $\emptyset$ otherwise. | | | |
| + Two-Registers | Register-Stack(k, dir) | $\sigma_{m..2}\|\psi$ | $\beta_{1..n}$ | $R1$ | $R2$ | $A \cup B$ |
| | | Where: | $k \in \{1, 2\}$ and $dir \in$ {to-register, to-stack}<br>$B := (dir =$ to-register$)\ ?\ \{(\sigma_1, Rk)\} : \{(Rk, \sigma_1)\}$<br>$\psi := (dir =$ to-stack $\wedge\ \sigma_1 < Rk)\ ?\ null : \sigma_1$ | | | |

Table 2: Transitions and the resulting state after each is applied to the configuration $(\sigma_{m..2}|\sigma_1, \beta_1|\beta_{2..n}, R1, R2, A)$.

| Transition | $\sigma$ | $\beta$ | $R1$ | $R2$ | $A$ |
|---|---|---|---|---|---|
| ... | [that we Hans house] | [helped paint] | *null* | *null* | {(*house, the*)} |
| Store(no-arc) | [that we Hans house] | [paint] | helped | *null* | |
| Store(right) | [that we Hans house] | [] | helped | paint | ∪ {(*helped, paint*)} |
| Register-Stack(2, to-stack) | [that we Hans] | [] | helped | paint | ∪ {(*paint, house*)} |
| Register-Stack(1, to-stack) | [that we] | [] | helped | paint | ∪ {(*helped, Hans*)} |
| Register-Stack(1, to-stack) | [that] | [] | helped | paint | ∪ {(*helped, we*)} |
| Register-Stack(1, to-register) | [that] | [] | helped | paint | ∪ {(*that, helped*)} |
| Clear | [that] | [paint] | *null* | *null* | |

Table 3: An excerpt from a gold standard derivation of the sentence in Figure 3. The two words *paint* and *house* are added to the registers and then crossed arcs are added between them and the top of the stack.

| Transition | Precondition | Type |
|---|---|---|
| Left-Arc, Right-Arc | $R1 \notin (\sigma_1, \beta_1) \wedge R2 \notin (\sigma_1, \beta_1)$ | (2) |
| Store(·) | $(R1 = null \vee R2 = null) \wedge (\beta_1 > last)$ | (1) |
| Clear | $(R1 \neq null) \wedge (R2 \neq null \vee \beta_1 = null) \wedge (\sigma_2 < R1) \wedge (\sigma_1 \notin (R1, R2))$ | (1) |
| Register-Stack(k, ·) | $(\sigma_1 > last) \vee (k = 1 \wedge \neg IsCovered(R1))$ | (1) |
| | $\sigma_2 < R_{right}$ | (2) |
| Register-Stack(k, to-register) | $(R_{close}, \sigma_1) \notin A$ | (3) |
| Register-Stack(k, to-stack) | $(\sigma_1, R_{far}) \notin A$ | (3) |

Table 4: Preconditions that ensure the 2-Crossing Interval property for trees output by the two-registers transition system, applied to a configuration $(\sigma_{m..1}, \beta_{1..n}, R1, R2, A)$. If $\sigma_1 < R1$, $R_{close} := R1$ and $R_{far} := R2$; otherwise, $R_{close} := R2$ and $R_{far} := R1$. $R_{right} := (R2 = null)\ ?\ R1 : R2$. Preconditions of type (1) ensure each pair of registers defines a disjoint crossing interval; type (2) that only edges incident to registers are crossed; and type (3) that only registers can have children on the far side of their parent.

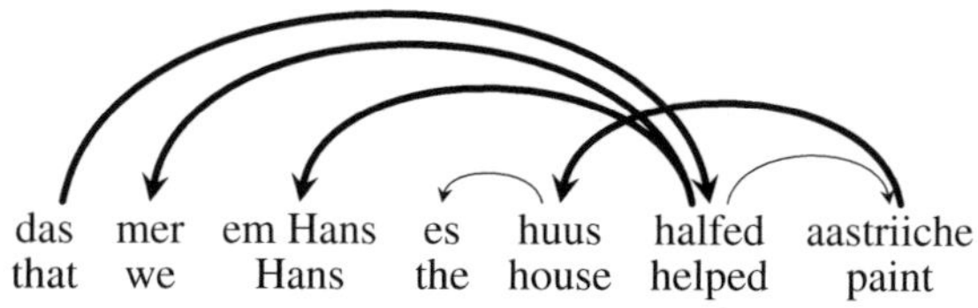


Figure 3: A clause with crossing edges (Shieber, 1985).

adding an arc between this token and the token in the first register.

- **Clear**: Removes tokens from the registers, reducing them completely if they are covered by an edge in $A$ or otherwise placing them back on the stack in order. If either $R2$ or the top of the stack is the token immediately to the left of the front of the buffer, that token is placed back on the buffer instead.
- **Register-Stack**: Adds an arc between the top of the stack and one of the registers.

A derivation excerpt for the clause in Figure 3 is shown in Table 3. The two tokens incident to all crossed arcs *helped* and *paint* are stored in the registers. The crossed arcs are then added through Register-Stack transitions, working outward from the registers through the previous words in the sentence: *(paint, house)*, then *(helped, Hans)*, etc. After all the crossed arcs incident to these two tokens have been added, the registers are cleared.

Preconditions related to rootedness, single-headedness, and acyclicity follow the arc-eager system straightforwardly: each transition that adds an arc $(h, m)$ checks that $m$ is not the root, $m$ does not already have a head, and that $h$ is not a descendant of $m$. Preconditions used to guarantee that trees output by the system are within the desired class are listed in Table 4. In particular, they ensure that all crossed arcs are incident to registers, and that each pair of registers entails an interval corresponding to a self-contained set of crossed edges. To avoid traversing $A$ while checking preconditions, two helper constants are used: *IsCovered($Rk$)*[2] and *last*[3].

[2] $IsCovered(R1)$ is true if there exists an arc in $A$ with endpoints on either side of $R1$. Rather than enumerating arcs, this boolean can be updated in constant time by setting it to true only after a Register-Stack(2, dir) transition with $\sigma_1 < R1$; likewise R2 can only be covered with a Register-Stack(1, dir) transition with $\sigma_1 > R2$.

[3] *last* is used to indicate the rightmost partially processed unreduced vertex after the last pair of registers were cleared (set to the rightmost in $\gamma$, $\psi$ after each Clear transition).

**Lemma 1.** *In the two-registers system, all crossed arcs are added through register-stack operations.*

*Proof.* Suppose for the sake of contradiction that a right arc $(s, b)$ added when $\sigma_1 = s$ and $\beta_1 = b$ is crossed in the final output tree (the argument for left-arcs is identical). Let $(l, r)$ with $l < r$ be an arc that crosses $(s, b)$. One of $\{l, r\}$ must be within the open interval $(s, b)$ and one of $\{l, r\} \notin [s, b]$. When the arc $(s, b)$ is added, no tokens in the open interval $(s, b)$ remain. They cannot be in the stack or buffer since the stack and buffer always remain in order; they cannot be in registers by the precondition $R1 \notin (\sigma_1, \beta_1) \wedge R2 \notin (\sigma_1, \beta_1)$ for Right-Arc transitions. Thus, $(l, r)$ must already have been added. It cannot be that $l \in (s, b)$ and $r > b$, since the rest of the buffer has never been accessible to tokens left of $b$. The ordering must then be $l < s < r < b$. Figure 4 shows that for each way $(l, r)$ could have been added (Right-Arc, 4a; Store(right), 4b; Register-Stack(k, to-stack), 4c; Register-Stack(k, to-register), 4d), it is impossible to keep $s$ unreduced without violating one of the preconditions.

The only other type of arc-adding operation is Store. Similar logic holds: arcs added through Left-Arc and Right-Arc transitions cannot cross these arcs, since they would violate the preconditions $R1 \notin (\sigma_1, \beta_1) \wedge R2 \notin (\sigma_1, \beta_1)$; later arcs involving other registers would imply Clear operations that violate $\sigma_2 < R1 \wedge \sigma_1 \notin (R1, R2)$. □

## 5 Parsing 2-Crossing Interval Trees with the Two-Registers Transition System

In this section we show the correspondence between the two-registers transition system and 2-Crossing Interval trees: each forest output by the transition system is a 2-Crossing Interval tree (*soundness*) and every 2-Crossing Interval tree can be produced by the two-registers system (*completeness*).

### 5.1 Soundness: Two-Registers System → 2-Crossing Interval trees

*Proof.* Every crossed arc is incident to a token that was in a register (Lemma 1). There cannot be any overlap between register arcs where the corresponding tokens were not in the registers simultaneously: the Clear transition updates the book-keeping constant $last$ to be the rightmost vertex associated with

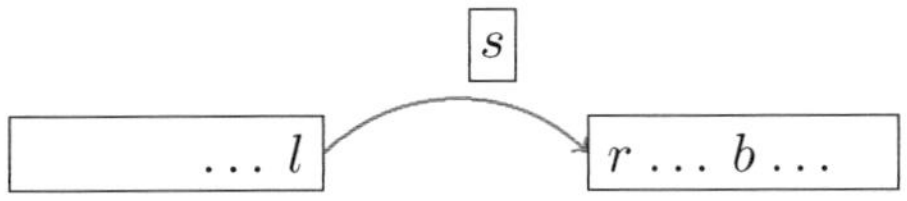


(a) Right-Arc: $s$ would have been in a register, and the Right-Arc would have violated $R1 \notin (\sigma_1, \beta_1) \wedge R2 \notin (\sigma_1, \beta_1)$.

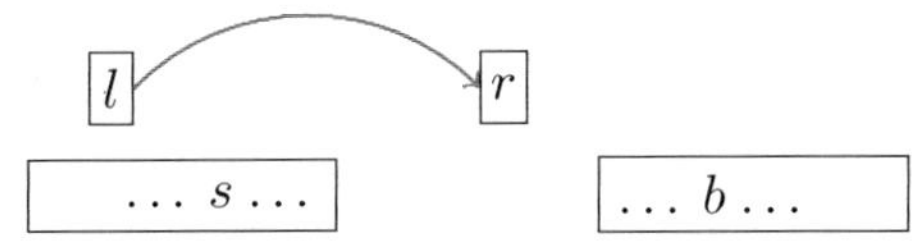


(b) Store(right): $s$ would be on the stack when the registers were cleared, so Clear would have violated $\sigma_2 < R1 \wedge \sigma_1 \notin (R1, R2)$.

(c) Register-Stack(k, to-stack): If $s$ was on the stack, then if $s > R2$, Register-Stack(k, t-stack) would have violated $\sigma_2 < R2$; if $s < R2$, then $s \in (R1, R2)$, and Clear would have violated $\sigma_2 < R1 \wedge \sigma_1 \notin (R1, R2)$. If $s$ instead was in $R2$ (not shown), then it would get covered by $(l, r)$ and reduced by Clear.

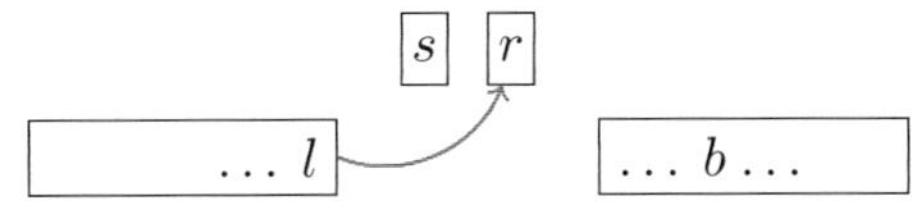


(d) Register-Stack(k, to-register): $s$ must have been in $R2$. $s$ would get covered by $(l, r)$ and reduced by Clear.

Figure 4: If a stack-buffer arc $(s, b)$ is added in the two-registers system, there cannot have been an earlier arc $(l, r)$ with $l < s < r < b$, since it would then be impossible to keep $s$ unreduced without violating the preconditions.

the registers being cleared, and subsequent actions cannot introduce crossed arcs to the $last$ token or to its left (by the $\beta_1 > last$ and $\sigma_1 > last$ preconditions on storing and register-stack arcs, respectively). Thus, each set of tokens that were in registers simultaneously defines a crossing interval. Condition (a) of Definition 3 is satisfied, since all crossed arcs are incident to registers and at most two vertices are in registers at the same time.

Assume that a vertex $h$, $h \notin \{R1, R2\}$, has a child $m$ on the far side of its parent $g$ (i.e., either $h < g < m$ or $m < g < h$). The edge $(h, m)$ is guaranteed to be crossed and so was added through a register-stack arc (Lemma 1). The ordering $h < g < m$ is not possible, since if $(g, h)$ had been added through a left-arc, then $h$ would have been reduced, and if $(g, h)$ and $(h, m)$ were both added through register-stack arcs, then one of them would have violated the $(R_{close}, \sigma_1) \notin A$ or the $(\sigma_1, R_{far}) \notin A$ precondition. Similar reasoning can rule out $m < g < h$. Thus Condition (b) of Definition 3 is also satisfied. □

### 5.2 Completeness: 2-Crossing Interval trees → Two-Registers System

*Proof.* The portions of a 2-Crossing Interval tree in-between the crossing intervals can be constructed using the transitions from arc-eager. For a particular crossing interval $[l, r]$ and a particular choice of two vertices $a$ and $b$ incident to all all crossed arcs in the interval ($l \leq a < b \leq r$), $a$ and $b$ divide the interval into: $L = [l, a)$, $a$, $M = (a, b)$, $b$, $R = (b, r]$. All arcs incident to neither $a$ nor $b$ must lie entirely within $L$, $M$, or $R$.[4]

The parser begins by adding all arcs with both endpoints in $L$, using the standard arc-eager Shift/Reduce/Left-Arc/Right-Arc. It then shifts until $a$ is at the front of the buffer and stores $a$. It then repeats the same process to add the arcs lying entirely in $M$ until $b$ reaches the front of the buffer, adding the parent of $a$ with a Register-Stack(1, to-register) transition if the parent is in $M$ and the arc is uncrossed. $b$ is then stored, adding the arc between $a$ and $b$ if necessary. Throughout this process, the precondition $R1 \notin (\sigma_1, \beta_1) \wedge R2 \notin (\sigma_1, \beta_1)$ for left and right arcs is satisfied.

Next, the parser will repeatedly take Register-Stack transitions, interspersed with Reduce transitions, to add all the arcs with one endpoint in $\{a, b\}$ and the other in $L$ or $M$, working right-to-left from $b$ (i.e., from the top of the stack downwards). No shifts are done at this stage, so the $\sigma_2 < R2$ precondition on Register-Stack arcs is always satisfied. The $\sigma_1 > last$ precondition is also always satisfied since all vertices in the crossing interval will be to the right of the previous crossing interval boundary point. After all these arcs are done, if there are any uncrossed arcs incident to $a$ to the left that go outside of the crossing interval, they are added now with a Register-Stack transition.[5]

[4]E.g., if there were an arc not incident to $a$ or $b$ with one endpoint left of $a$ and one endpoint right of $a$, then this arc must be crossed or lie outside of the crossing interval.

[5]Only possible in the case $l = a$, in which case $\neg$IsCovered$(a)$ and the transition is allowed.

Finally, the arcs with at least one endpoint in $R$ are added, using Register-Stack arcs for those with the other endpoint in $\{a, b\}$ and Left-Arc/Right-Arc for those with both endpoints in $R$. Before any vertex incident to $a$ or $b$ is shifted onto the stack, all tokens on the stack to the right of $b$ are reduced.

After all these arcs are added, the crossing interval is complete. The boundary points of the interval that can still participate in uncrossed arcs with the exterior are left on the stack and buffer after the clear operation, so the rest of the tree is still parsable. □

## 6 Worst-case Runtime

The two-registers system runs in $O(n)$ time: it completes after at most $O(n)$ transitions and each transition takes constant time.

The total number of arc-adding actions (Left-Arc, Right-Arc, Register-Stack, or a Store that includes an arc) is bounded by $n$, as there are at most $n$ arcs in the final output. The net result of {Store, Store, Clear} triples of transitions decreases the number of tokens on the buffer by at least one, so these triples, plus the number of Shifts and Right-Arcs, are bounded by $n$. Finally, each token can be removed completely at most once, so the number of Left-Arcs and Reduces is bounded by $n$. Every transition fell into one of these categories, so the total number of transitions is bounded by $5n = O(n)$.

Each operation can be performed in constant time, as all operations involve moving vertices and/or adding arcs, and at most three vertices are ever moved (Clear) and at most one arc is ever added. Most preconditions can be trivially checked in constant time, such as checking whether a vertex already has a parent or not. The non-trivial precondition to check is acyclicity, and this can also be checked by adding some book-keeping variables that can be updated in constant time (full proof omitted due to space constraints). For example, in the derivation in Table 3, prior to the Register-Stack(2, to-stack) transition, $R1 \rightarrow^A R2$ (*helped* $\rightarrow^A$ *paint*). After the arc $(R2, \sigma_1)$ (*paint*, *house*) is added, $R2 \rightarrow^A \sigma_1$ and by transitivity, $R1 \rightarrow^A \sigma_1$. The top of the stack is then reduced, and since $\sigma_2$ does not have a parent to its right, it is not a descendant of $\sigma_1$, and so after *Hans* becomes the new $\sigma_1$, the system makes the update that $R1$, $R2 \not\rightarrow^A \sigma_1$.

## 7 Experiments

The experiments compare the two-registers transition system for mildly non-projective trees proposed here with two other transition systems: the arc-eager system for projective trees (Nivre, 2003) and the swap-based system for all non-projective trees (Nivre, 2009). We choose the swap-based system as our non-projective baseline as it currently represents the state-of-the-art in transition-based parsing (Bohnet et al., 2013), with higher empirical performance than the Attardi system or pseudo-projective parsing (Kuhlmann and Nivre, 2010).

The arc-eager system is a reimplementation of Zhang and Nivre (2011), using their rich feature set and beam search. The features for the two other transition systems are based on the same set, but with slight modifications to account for the different relevant domains of locality. In particular, for the swap transition system, we updated the features to account for the fact that this transition system is based on the arc-standard model and so the most relevant positions are the top two tokens on the stack. For the two-register system, we added features over properties of the tokens stored in each of the registers. All experiments use beam search with a beam of size 32 and are trained with ten iterations of averaged structured perceptron training. Training set trees that are outside of the reachable class (projective for arc-eager, 2-Crossing Intervals for two-registers) are transformed by lifting arcs (Nivre and Nilsson, 2005) until the tree is within the class. The test sets are left unchanged. We use the standard technique of parameterizing arc creating actions with dependency labels to produce labeled dependency trees.

Experiments use the ten datasets in Table 1 from the CoNLL 2006 and 2007 shared tasks (Buchholz and Marsi, 2006; Nivre et al., 2007). We report numbers using both gold and automatically predicted part-of-speech tags and morphological attribute-values as features. For the latter, the part of speech tagger is a first-order CRF model and the morphological tagger uses a greedy SVM per-attribute classifier. Evaluation uses CoNLL-X scoring conventions (Buchholz and Marsi, 2006) and we report both labeled and unlabeled attachment scores.

| Language | LAS (UAS) eager | swap | two-registers |
|---|---|---|---|
| Basque | 70.50 (78.06) | 69.66 (77.44) | **71.10 (78.57)** |
| Czech | 79.60 (85.55) | **80.74 (86.82)** | 79.75 (85.93) |
| Dutch | 78.69 (81.41) | 79.65 (82.69) | **80.77 (83.91)** |
| English | 90.00 (91.18) | 90.16 (91.29) | **90.36 (91.54)** |
| German | 88.34 (91.01) | 86.76 (89.56) | **89.08 (91.95)** |
| Greek | 77.34 (**84.79**) | 76.90 (84.72) | **77.59** (84.77) |
| Hungarian | 80.00 (84.20) | 79.93 (84.40) | **80.21 (84.91)** |
| Portuguese | **88.30 (91.64)** | 87.92 (91.79) | 87.40 (91.20) |
| Slovene | 75.68 (83.97) | **76.34 (84.47)** | 76.08 (84.33) |
| Turkish | 68.83 (77.34) | 70.71 (79.74) | **70.94 (80.39)** |
| Average | 79.73 (84.92) | 79.88 (85.29) | **80.33 (85.75)** |

Table 5: Labeled and Unlabeled Attachment Scores (LAS and UAS) on the CoNLL 2006/2007 Shared Task datasets (gold part-of-speech tags and morphology).

| Language | Crossed / Uncrossed eager | swap | two-registers |
|---|---|---|---|
| Basque | 33.10 / 83.32 | **39.37** / 82.52 | 34.49 / **83.58** |
| Czech | 43.98 / 87.37 | **68.76 / 87.63** | 55.42 / 87.24 |
| Dutch | 40.08 / **87.66** | **71.08** / 85.70 | 69.19 / 87.08 |
| English | 27.66 / 91.98 | **42.55** / 92.00 | **42.55 / 92.09** |
| German | 55.29 / 91.60 | 72.35 / 89.46 | **75.29 / 91.85** |
| Greek | 29.94 / 84.79 | **33.12** / 84.76 | 30.57 / **84.94** |
| Hungarian | 44.40 / **84.98** | 55.40 / 84.07 | **55.60** / 84.77 |
| Portuguese | 48.17 / **90.98** | **58.64** / 90.79 | 57.07 / 89.96 |
| Slovene | 41.83 / 83.60 | **47.91 / 84.05** | 44.11 / 83.65 |
| Turkish | 45.07 / 86.20 | **70.39** / 86.15 | 56.25 / **87.31** |
| Average | 32.51 / **87.25** | **55.96** / 86.72 | 52.05 / **87.25** |

Table 7: UAS from Table 5 for tokens in which the incoming arc in the gold tree is crossed or uncrossed (recall of both crossed and uncrossed arcs).

| Language | LAS (UAS) eager | swap | two-registers |
|---|---|---|---|
| Basque | **64.36 (73.03)** | 63.23 (72.10) | 64.27 (72.32) |
| Czech | 75.92 (83.79) | **76.92 (84.54)** | 76.37 (83.79) |
| Dutch | 78.59 (81.07) | 79.69 (83.03) | **80.77 (83.71)** |
| English | 88.19 (89.77) | 88.68 (90.32) | **88.93 (90.50)** |
| German | **87.74 (90.62)** | 85.66 (88.40) | 87.60 (90.48) |
| Greek | **77.46 (85.14)** | 76.29 (84.65) | 77.22 (84.82) |
| Hungarian | **75.88** (81.61) | 75.83 (81.89) | 75.71 (**82.43**) |
| Portuguese | **86.07 (90.16)** | 85.65 (89.86) | 85.91 (**90.16**) |
| Slovene | **71.72 (81.69)** | 71.36 (81.63) | 71.58 (81.43) |
| Turkish | 62.18 (74.22) | 63.12 (75.26) | **64.06 (76.82)** |
| Average | 76.81 (83.11) | 76.64 (83.17) | **77.24 (83.65)** |

Table 6: Labeled and Unlabeled Attachment Scores (LAS and UAS) on the CoNLL 2006/2007 Shared Task datasets (predicted part-of-speech tags and morphology).

### 7.1 Results

Table 5 shows the results using gold tags as features, which is the most common set-up in the literature. The two-registers transition system has on average 0.8% absolute higher unlabeled attachment accuracy than arc-eager across the ten datasets investigated. Its UAS is higher than arc-eager for eight out of the ten languages and is up to 2.5% (Dutch) or 3.0% (Turkish) absolute higher, while never more than 0.4% worse (Portuguese). The two-registers transition system is also more accurate than the alternate non-projective swap system on seven out of the ten languages, with more than 1% absolute improvements in UAS for Basque, Dutch, and German. The two-registers transition-system is still on average more accurate than either the arc-eager or swap systems using predicted tags as features (Table 6).

Finally, we analyzed the performance of each of these parsers on both crossed *and uncrossed* arcs. Even on languages with many non-projective sentences, the majority of arcs are not crossed. Table 7 partitions all scoring tokens into those whose incoming arc in the gold tree is crossed and those whose incoming arc is not crossed, and presents the UAS scores from Table 5 for each of these groups. On the crossed arcs, the swap system does the best, followed by the two-registers system, with the arc-eager system about 20% absolute less accurate. On the uncrossed arcs, the arc-eager and two-registers systems are tied, with the swap system less accurate.

## 8 Discussion and Related Work

There has been a significant amount of recent work on non-projective dependency parsing. In the transition-based parsing paradigm, the pseudo-projective parser of Nivre and Nilsson (2005) was an early attempt and modeled the problem by transforming non-projective trees into projective trees via transformations encoded in arc labels. While improving parsing accuracies for many languages, this method was both approximate and inefficient as the increase in the cardinality of the label set affected run time.

Attardi (2006) directly augmented the transition system to permit limited non-projectivity by allowing transitions between words not directly at the top of the stack or buffer. While this transition system had significant coverage, it is unclear how to precisely characterize the set of dependency trees that it covers. Nivre (2009) introduced a transition system that covered all non-projective trees via a new *swap* transition that locally re-ordered words in the sentence. The downside of the swap transition is that it made worst-case run time quadratic. Also, as shown in Table 7, the attachment scores of *uncrossed* arcs decreases compared with arc-eager.

Two other transition systems that can be seen as generalizations of arc-eager are the 2-Planar transition system (Gómez-Rodríguez and Nivre, 2010; Gómez-Rodríguez and Nivre, 2013), which adds a second stack, and the transition system of Choi (Choi and McCallum, 2013), which adds a deque. The arc-eager, 2-registers, 2-planar, and the Choi transition systems can be seen as along a continuum for trading off various properties. In terms of coverage, projective trees (arc-eager) $\subset$ 2-Crossing Interval trees (this paper) $\subset$ 2-planar trees $\subset$ all directed trees (Choi). The Choi system uses a quadratic number of transitions in the worst case, while arc-eager, 2-registers, and 2-planar all use at most $O(n)$ transitions. Checking for cycles does not need to be done at all in the arc-eager system, can be with a few constant operations in the 2-registers system, and can be done in amortized constant time for the other systems (Gómez-Rodríguez and Nivre, 2013).

In the graph-based parsing literature, there has also been a plethora of work on non-projective parsing (McDonald et al., 2005; Martins et al., 2009; Koo et al., 2010). Recent work by Pitler and colleagues is the most relevant to the work described here (Pitler et al., 2012, 2013, 2014). Like this work, Pitler et al. define a restricted class of non-projective trees and then a graph-based parsing algorithm that parses exactly that set.

The register mechanism in two-registers transition parsing bears a resemblance to registers in Augmented Transition Networks (ATNs) (Woods, 1970). In ATNs, global registers are introduced to account for a wide range of natural language phenomena. This includes long-distance dependencies, which is a common source of non-projective trees. While transition-based parsing and ATNs use quite different control and data structures, this observation does raise an interesting question about the relationship between these two parsing paradigms.

There are many additional points of interest to explore based on this study. A first step would be to generalize the two-registers transition system to a $k$-registers system that can parse exactly $k$-Crossing Interval trees. This will necessarily lead to an asymptotic increase in run-time as $k$ approaches $n$. With larger values of $k$, the system would need additional transitions to add arcs between the registers (extending the Store transition to consider all subsets of arcs with the existing registers would become exponential in $k$). If $k$ were to increase all the way to $n$, such a system would probably look very similar to list-based systems that consider all pairs of arcs (Covington, 2001; Nivre, 2008).

Another direction would be to define dynamic oracles around the two-registers transition system (Goldberg and Nivre, 2012; Goldberg and Nivre, 2013). The additional transitions here have interpretations in terms of which trees are still reachable (Register-Stack($\cdot$) adds an arc; Store and Clear indicate that particular vertices should be incident to crossed arcs or are finished with crossed arcs, respectively). The two-registers system is not quite arc-decomposable (Goldberg and Nivre, 2013): if the wrong vertex is stored in a register then a later pair of crossed arcs might both be individually reachable but not jointly reachable. However, there may be a "crossing-sensitive" variant of arc-decomposability that takes into account the vertices crossed arcs are incident to that would apply here.

## 9 Conclusion

In this paper we presented $k$-Crossing Interval trees, a class of mildly non-projective trees with high empirical coverage. For the case of $k = 2$, we also presented a transition system that is sound and complete with respect to this class that is a generalization of the arc-eager transition system and maintains many of its desirable properties, most notably a linear worst-case run-time. Empirically, this transition system outperforms its projective counterpart as well as a quadratic swap-based transition system with larger coverage.

## Acknowledgments

We'd like to thank Mike Collins, Terry Koo, Joakim Nivre, Fernando Pereira, and Slav Petrov for helpful discussions and comments.

## References


G. Attardi. 2006. Experiments with a multilanguage non-projective dependency parser. In *Proceedings of CoNLL*, pages 166–170.

B. Bohnet, J. Nivre, I. Boguslavsky, R. Farkas, F. Ginter, and J. Hajic. 2013. Joint morphological and syntactic analysis for richly inflected languages. *TACL*, 1:415–428.

S. Buchholz and E. Marsi. 2006. CoNLL-X shared task on multilingual dependency parsing. In *Proceedings of CoNLL*, pages 149–164.

J. D. Choi and A. McCallum. 2013. Transition-based dependency parsing with selectional branching. In *ACL*, pages 1052–1062.

M. A. Covington. 2001. A fundamental algorithm for dependency parsing. *Proceedings of the 39th Annual ACM Southeast Conference*, pages 95–102.

Y. Goldberg and J. Nivre. 2012. A dynamic oracle for arc-eager dependency parsing. In *COLING*.

Y. Goldberg and J. Nivre. 2013. Training deterministic parsers with non-deterministic oracles. *TACL*, 1:403–414.

C. Gómez-Rodríguez and J. Nivre. 2010. A transition-based parser for 2-planar dependency structures. In *Proceedings of ACL*, pages 1492–1501.

C. Gómez-Rodríguez and J. Nivre. 2013. Divisible transition systems and multiplanar dependency parsing. *Computational Linguistics*, 39(4):799–845.

T. Koo, A. M. Rush, M. Collins, T. Jaakkola, and D. Sontag. 2010. Dual decomposition for parsing with non-projective head automata. In *Proceedings of EMNLP*, pages 1288–1298.

M. Kuhlmann and J. Nivre. 2006. Mildly non-projective dependency structures. In *Proceedings of COLING/ACL*, pages 507–514.

M. Kuhlmann and J. Nivre. 2010. Transition-based techniques for non-projective dependency parsing. *Northern European Journal of Language Technology*, 2(1):1–19.

M. Kuhlmann. 2013. Mildly non-projective dependency grammar. *Computational Linguistics*, 39(2).

A. F. T. Martins, N. A. Smith, and E. P. Xing. 2009. Concise integer linear programming formulations for dependency parsing. In *Proceedings of ACL*, pages 342–350.

R. McDonald, F. Pereira, K. Ribarov, and J. Hajič. 2005. Non-projective dependency parsing using spanning tree algorithms. In *Proceedings of HLT/EMNLP*, pages 523–530.

J. Nivre and J. Nilsson. 2005. Pseudo-projective dependency parsing. In *Proceedings of ACL*, pages 99–106.

J. Nivre, J. Hall, S. Kübler, R. McDonald, J. Nilsson, S. Riedel, and D. Yuret. 2007. The CoNLL 2007 shared task on dependency parsing. In *Proceedings of the CoNLL Shared Task Session of EMNLP-CoNLL*, pages 915–932.

J. Nivre. 2003. An efficient algorithm for projective dependency parsing. In *Proceedings of the 8th International Workshop on Parsing Technologies*, pages 149–160.

J. Nivre. 2008. Algorithms for deterministic incremental dependency parsing. *Computational Linguistics*, 34(4):513–553.

J. Nivre. 2009. Non-projective dependency parsing in expected linear time. In *Proceedings of ACL*, pages 351–359.

E. Pitler, S. Kannan, and M. Marcus. 2012. Dynamic programming for higher order parsing of gap-minding trees. In *Proceedings of EMNLP*, pages 478–488.

E. Pitler, S. Kannan, and M. Marcus. 2013. Finding optimal 1-Endpoint-Crossing trees. *TACL*, 1(Mar):13–24.

E. Pitler. 2013. Models for improved tractability and accuracy in dependency parsing. *University of Pennsylvania*.

E. Pitler. 2014. A crossing-sensitive third-order factorization for dependency parsing. *TACL*, 2(Feb):41–54.

S. M. Shieber. 1985. Evidence against the context-freeness of natural language. *Linguistics and Philosophy*, 8(3):333–343.

W. A. Woods. 1970. Transition network grammars for natural language analysis. *Communications of the ACM*, 13(10):591–606.

Y. Zhang and S. Clark. 2008. A tale of two parsers: investigating and combining graph-based and transition-based dependency parsing using beam-search. In *Proceedings of EMNLP*, pages 562–571.

Y. Zhang and J. Nivre. 2011. Transition-based dependency parsing with rich non-local features. In *Proceedings of ACL (Short Papers)*, pages 188–193.

# Unsupervised Multi-Domain Adaptation with Feature Embeddings

**Yi Yang** and **Jacob Eisenstein**
School of Interactive Computing
Georgia Institute of Technology
Atlanta, GA 30308
{yiyang+jacobe}@gatech.edu

## Abstract

Representation learning is the dominant technique for unsupervised domain adaptation, but existing approaches have two major weaknesses. First, they often require the specification of "pivot features" that generalize across domains, which are selected by task-specific heuristics. We show that a novel but simple *feature embedding* approach provides better performance, by exploiting the feature template structure common in NLP problems. Second, unsupervised domain adaptation is typically treated as a task of moving from a single source to a single target domain. In reality, test data may be diverse, relating to the training data in some ways but not others. We propose an alternative formulation, in which each instance has a vector of *domain attributes*, can be used to learn distill the domain-invariant properties of each feature.[1]

## 1 Introduction

Domain adaptation is crucial if natural language processing is to be successfully employed in high-impact application areas such as social media, patient medical records, and historical texts. Unsupervised domain adaptation is particularly appealing, since it requires no labeled data in the target domain. Some of the most successful approaches to unsupervised domain adaptation are based on representation learning: transforming sparse high-dimensional surface features into dense vector representations,

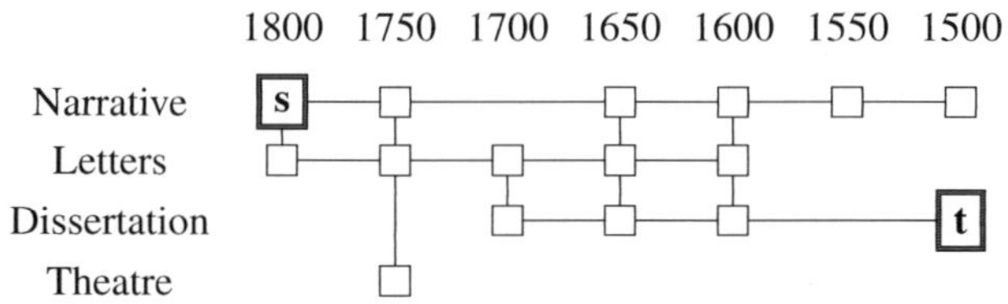


Figure 1: Domain graph for the Tycho Brahe corpus (Galves and Faria, 2010). **Suppose we want to adapt from 19th Century narratives to 16th Century dissertations: can unlabeled data from other domains help?**

which are often more robust to domain shift (Blitzer et al., 2006; Glorot et al., 2011). However, these methods are computationally expensive to train, and often require special task-specific heuristics to select good "pivot features."

A second, more subtle challenge for unsupervised domain adaptation is that it is normally framed as adapting from a single source domain to a single target domain. For example, we may be given part-of-speech labeled text from 19th Century narratives, and we hope to adapt the tagger to work on academic dissertations from the 16th Century. This ignores text from the intervening centuries, as well as text that is related by genre, such as 16th Century narratives and 19th Century dissertations (see Figure 1). We address a new challenge of *unsupervised multi-domain adaptation*, where the goal is to leverage this additional unlabeled data to improve performance in the target domain.[2]

[1] Source code and a demo are available at https://github.com/yiyang-gt/feat2vec

[2] Multiple domains have been considered in **supervised** domain adaptation (e.g., Mansour et al., 2009), but these approaches are not directly applicable when there is no labeled data outside the source domain.



*Human Language Technologies: The 2015 Annual Conference of the North American Chapter of the ACL*, pages 672–682,
Denver, Colorado, May 31 – June 5, 2015. 

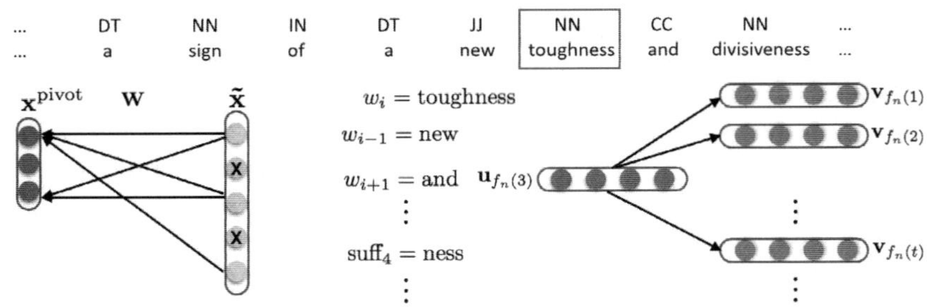


(a) Learning a dense transformation $\mathbf{W}$ by reconstructing pivot features.

(b) Directly learning of feature embeddings by maximizing Skip-Gram objective.

Figure 2: Representation learning techniques in structured feature spaces

We present FEMA (**F**eature **EM**beddings for domain **A**daptation), a novel representation learning approach for domain adaptation in structured feature spaces. Like prior work in representation learning, FEMA learns dense features that are more robust to domain shift. However, rather than performing representation learning by reconstructing pivot features, FEMA uses techniques from neural language models to obtain low-dimensional embeddings directly. FEMA outperforms prior work on adapting POS tagging from the Penn Treebank to web text, and it easily generalizes to unsupervised multi-domain adaptation, further improving performance by learning generalizable models across multiple domains.

## 2 Learning feature embeddings

Feature co-occurrence statistics are the primary source of information driving many unsupervised methods for domain adaptation; they enable the induction of representations that are more similar across the source and target domain, reducing the error introduced by domain shift (Ben-David et al., 2010). For example, both Structural Correspondence Learning (SCL; Blitzer et al., 2006) and Denoising Autoencoders (Chen et al., 2012) learn to reconstruct a subset of "pivot features", as shown in Figure 2(a). The reconstruction function — which is learned from unlabeled data in both domains — is then employed to project each instance into a dense representation, which will hopefully be better suited to cross-domain generalization. The pivot features are chosen to be both predictive of the label and general across domains. Meeting these two criteria requires task-specific heuristics; for example, different pivot selection techniques are employed in SCL for syntactic tagging (Blitzer et al., 2006) and sentiment analysis (Blitzer et al., 2007). Furthermore, the pivot features correspond to a small subspace of the feature co-occurrence matrix. In Denoising Autoencoders, each pivot feature corresponds to a dense feature in the transformed representation, but large dense feature vectors impose substantial computational costs at learning time. In SCL, each pivot feature introduces a new classification problem, which makes computation of the cross-domain representation expensive. In either case, we face a tradeoff between the amount of feature co-occurrence information that we can use, and the computational complexity for representation learning and downstream training.

This tradeoff can be avoided by inducing low dimensional feature embeddings directly. We exploit the tendency of many NLP tasks to divide features into *templates*, with exactly one active feature per template (Smith, 2011); this is shown in the center of Figure 2. Rather than treating each instance as an undifferentiated bag-of-features, we use this template structure to induce *feature embeddings*, which are dense representations of individual features. Each embedding is selected to help predict the features that fill out the other templates: for example, an embedding for the current word feature is selected to help predict the previous word feature and successor word feature, and vice versa; see Figure 2(b). The embeddings for each active feature are then concatenated together across templates, giving a dense representation for the entire instance.

Our approach is motivated by word embeddings,

in which dense representations are learned for individual words based on their neighbors (Turian et al., 2010; Xiao and Guo, 2013), but rather than learning a single embedding for each word, we learn embeddings for each *feature*. This means that the embedding of, say, 'toughness' will differ depending on whether it appears in the current-word template or the previous-word template (see Table 6). This provides additional flexibility for the downstream learning algorithm, and the increase in the dimensionality of the overall dense representation can be offset by learning shorter embeddings for each feature. In Section 4, we show that feature embeddings convincingly outperform word embeddings on two part-of-speech tagging tasks.

Our feature embeddings are based on the skip-gram model, trained with negative sampling (Mikolov et al., 2013a), which is a simple yet efficient method for learning word embeddings. Rather than predicting adjacent words, the training objective in our case is to find feature embeddings that are useful for predicting other active features in the instance. For the instance $n \in \{1 \dots N\}$ and feature template $t \in \{1 \dots T\}$, we denote $f_n(t)$ as the index of the active feature; for example, in the instance shown in Figure 2, $f_n(t) =$ 'new' when $t$ indicates the previous-word template. The skip-gram approach induces distinct "input" and "output" embeddings for each feature, written $\mathbf{u}_{f_n(t)}$ and $\mathbf{v}_{f_n(t)}$, respectively. The role of these embeddings can be seen in the negative sampling objective,

$$\ell_n = \frac{1}{T}\sum_{t=1}^{T}\sum_{t' \neq t}^{T}\Big[\log \sigma(\mathbf{u}_{f_n(t)}^{\top}\mathbf{v}_{f_n(t')}) + k\mathbb{E}_{i\sim P_{t'}^{(n)}} \log \sigma(-\mathbf{u}_{f_n(t)}^{\top}\mathbf{v}_i)\Big], \quad (1)$$

where $t$ and $t'$ are feature templates, $k$ is the number of negative samples, $P_{t'}^{(n)}$ is a *noise distribution* for template $t'$, and $\sigma$ is the sigmoid function. This objective is derived from noise-contrastive estimation (Gutmann and Hyvärinen, 2012), and is chosen to maximize the unnormalized log-likelihood of the observed feature co-occurrence pairs, while minimizing the unnormalized log-likelihood of "negative" samples, drawn from the noise distribution.

Feature embeddings can be applied to domain adaptation by learning embeddings of all features on the union of the source and target data sets; we consider the extension to multiple domains in the next section. The dense feature vector for each instance is obtained by concatenating the feature embeddings for each template. Finally, since it has been shown that nonlinearity is important for generating robust representations (Bengio et al., 2013), we follow Chen et al. (2012) and apply the hyperbolic tangent function to the embeddings. The augmented representation $\mathbf{x}_n^{(\text{aug})}$ of instance $n$ is the concatenation of the original feature vector and the feature embeddings,

$$\mathbf{x}_n^{(\text{aug})} = \mathbf{x}_n \oplus \tanh[\mathbf{u}_{f_n(1)} \oplus \cdots \oplus \mathbf{u}_{f_n(T)}],$$

where $\oplus$ is vector concatenation.

## 3 Feature embeddings across domains

We now describe how to extend the feature embedding idea beyond a single source and target domain, to unsupervised multi-attribute domain adaptation (Joshi et al., 2013). In this setting, each instance is associated with $M$ metadata domain attributes, which could encode temporal epoch, genre, or other aspects of the domain. The challenge of domain adaptation is that the meaning of features can shift across each metadata dimension: for example, the meaning of 'plant' may depend on genre (agriculture versus industry), while the meaning of 'like' may depend on epoch. To account for this, the feature embeddings should smoothly shift over domain graphs, such as the one shown in Figure 1; this would allow us to isolate the domain general aspects of each feature. Related settings have been considered only for supervised domain adaptation, where some labeled data is available in each domain (Joshi et al., 2013), but not in the unsupervised case.

More formally, we assume each instance $n$ is augmented with a vector of $M$ binary domain attributes, $\boldsymbol{z}_n \in \{0,1\}^M$. These attributes may overlap, so that we could have an attribute for the epoch 1800-1849, and another for the epoch 1800-1899. We define $z_{n,0} = 1$ as a shared attribute, which is active for all instances. We capture domain shift by estimating embeddings $\mathbf{h}_i^{(m)}$ for each feature $i$ crossed with each domain attribute $m$. We then compute the embedding for each instance by summing across the relevant domain attributes, as shown

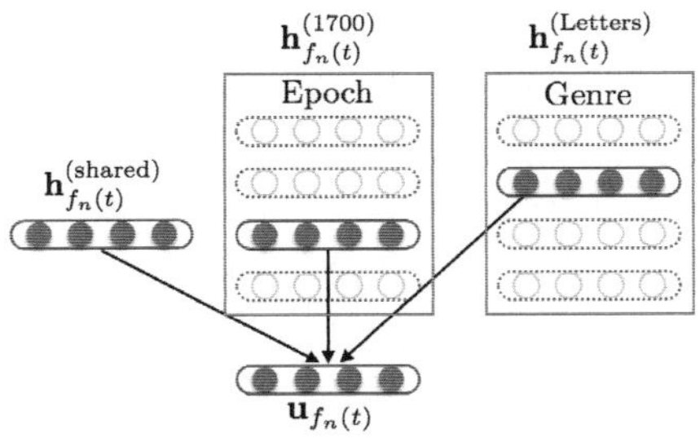


Figure 3: Aggregating multiple embeddings.

in Figure 3. The local "input" feature embedding $\mathbf{u}_{f_n(t)}$ is then defined as the summation, $\mathbf{u}_{f_n(t)} = \sum_{m=0}^{M} z_{n,m}\mathbf{h}^{(m)}_{f_n(t)}$.

The role of the global embedding $\mathbf{h}^{(0)}_i$ is to capture domain-neutral information about the feature $i$, while the other embeddings capture attribute-specific information. The global feature embeddings should therefore be more robust to domain shift, which is "explained away" by the attribute-specific embeddings. We therefore use only these embeddings when constructing the augmented representation, $\boldsymbol{x}_n^{(\text{aug})}$. To ensure that the global embeddings capture all of the domain-general information about each feature, we place an L2 regularizer on the attribute-specific embeddings. Note that we do not learn attribute-specific "output" embeddings $\mathbf{v}$; these are shared across all instances, regardless of domain.

The attribute-based embeddings yield a new training objective for instance $n$,

$$\ell_n = \frac{1}{T}\sum_{t=1}^{T}\sum_{t'\neq t}^{T}\Bigg[\log\sigma\Big(\Big[\sum_{m=0}^{M} z_{n,m}\mathbf{h}^{(m)}_{f_n(t)}\Big]^\top \mathbf{v}_{f_n(t')}\Big) + k\mathbb{E}_{i\sim P^{(n)}_{t'}}\log\sigma\Big(-\Big[\sum_{m=0}^{M} z_{n,m}\mathbf{h}^{(m)}_{f_n(t)}\Big]^\top \mathbf{v}_i\Big)\Bigg]. \quad (2)$$

For brevity, we omit the regularizer from Equation 2. For feature $f_n(t)$, the (unregularized) gradients of $\mathbf{h}^{(m)}_{f_n(t)}$ and $\mathbf{v}_{f_n(t')}$ *w.r.t* $\ell_{n,t}$ are

$$\frac{\partial \ell_{n,t}}{\mathbf{h}^{(m)}_{f_n(t)}} = \frac{1}{T}\sum_{t'\neq t}^{T} z_{n,m}\Big[(1-\sigma(\mathbf{u}^\top_{f_n(t)}\mathbf{v}_{f_n(t')}))\mathbf{v}_{f_n(t')} - k\mathbb{E}_{i\sim P^{(n)}_{t'}}\sigma(\mathbf{u}^\top_{f_n(t)}\mathbf{v}_i)\mathbf{v}_i\Big] \quad (3)$$

$$\frac{\partial \ell_{n,t}}{\mathbf{v}_{f_n(t')}} = \frac{1}{T}\sum_{t'\neq t}^{T}(1-\sigma(\mathbf{u}^\top_{f_n(t)}\mathbf{v}_{f_n(t')}))\mathbf{u}_{f_n(t)}. \quad (4)$$

For each feature $i$ drawn from the noise distribution $P^{(n)}_{t'}$, the gradient of $\mathbf{v}_i$ *w.r.t* $\ell_{n,t}$ is

$$\frac{\partial \ell_{n,t}}{\mathbf{v}_i} = -\frac{1}{T}\sigma(\mathbf{u}^\top_{f_n(t)}\mathbf{v}_i)\mathbf{u}_{f_n(t)}. \quad (5)$$

## 4 Experiments

We evaluate FEMA on part-of-speech (POS) tagging, in two settings: (1) adaptation of English POS tagging from news text to web text, as in the SANCL shared task (Petrov and McDonald, 2012); (2) adaptation of Portuguese POS tagging across a graph of related domains over several centuries and genres, from the Tycho Brahe corpus (Galves and Faria, 2010). These evaluations are complementary: English POS tagging gives us the opportunity to evaluate feature embeddings in a well-studied and high-impact application; Portuguese POS tagging enables evaluation of multi-attribute domain adaptation, and demonstrates the capability of our approach in a morphologically-rich language, with a correspondingly large number of part-of-speech tags (383). As more historical labeled data becomes available for English and other languages, we will be able to evaluate feature embeddings and related techniques there.

### 4.1 Implementation details

While POS tagging is classically treated as a structured prediction problem, we follow Schnabel and Schütze (2014) by taking a classification-based approach. Feature embeddings can easily be used in feature-rich sequence labeling algorithms such as conditional random fields or structured perceptron, but our pilot experiments suggest that with sufficiently rich features, classification-based methods can be extremely competitive on these datasets, at a fraction of the computational cost. Specifically, we apply a support vector machine (SVM) classifier,

| Component | Feature template |
|---|---|
| Lexical (5) | $w_{i-2} = X, w_{i-1} = Y, \ldots$ |
| Affixes (8) | $X$ is prefix of $w_i$, $\lvert X \rvert \leq 4$<br>$X$ is suffix of $w_i$, $\lvert X \rvert \leq 4$ |
| Orthography (3) | $w_i$ contains number, uppercase character, or hyphen |

Table 1: Basic feature templates for token $w_i$.

adding dense features from FEMA (and the alternative representation learning techniques) to a set of basic features.

#### 4.1.1 Basic features

We apply sixteen feature templates, motivated by by Ratnaparkhi (1996). Table 1 provides a summary of the templates; there are four templates each for the prefix and suffix features. Feature embeddings are learned for all lexical and affix features, yielding a total of thirteen embeddings per instance. We do not learn embeddings for the binary orthographic features. Santos and Zadrozny (2014) demonstrate the utility of embeddings for affix features.

#### 4.1.2 Competitive systems

We consider three competitive unsupervised domain adaptation methods. Structural Correspondence Learning (Blitzer et al., 2006, SCL) creates a binary classification problem for each pivot feature, and uses the weights of the resulting classifiers to project the instances into a dense representation. Marginalized Denoising Autoencoders (Chen et al., 2012, mDA) learn robust representation across domains by reconstructing pivot features from artificially corrupted input instances. We use structured dropout noise, which has achieved state-of-art results on domain adaptation for part-of-speech tagging (Yang and Eisenstein, 2014). We also directly compare with WORD2VEC[3] word embeddings, and with a "no-adaptation" baseline in which only surface features are used.

#### 4.1.3 Parameter tuning

All the hyperparameters are tuned on development data. Following Blitzer et al. (2006), we consider pivot features that appear more than 50 times in all the domains for SCL and mDA. In SCL, the parameter $K$ selects the number of singular vectors of the projection matrix to consider; we try values between 10 and 100, and also employ feature normalization and rescaling. For embedding-based methods, we choose embedding sizes and numbers of negative samples from $\{25, 50, 100, 150, 200\}$ and $\{5, 10, 15, 20\}$ respectively. The noise distribution $P_t^{(n)}$ is simply the unigram probability of each feature in the template $t$. Mikolov et al. (2013b) argue for exponentiating the unigram distribution, but we find it makes little difference here. The window size of word embeddings is set as 5. As noted above, the attribute-specific embeddings are regularized, to encourage use of the shared embedding $\mathbf{h}^{(0)}$. The regularization penalty is selected by grid search over $\{0.001, 0.01, 0.1, 1.0, 10.0\}$. In general, we find that the hyperparameters that yield good word embeddings tend to yield good feature embeddings too.

[3]https://code.google.com/p/word2vec/

### 4.2 Evaluation 1: Web text

Recent work in domain adaptation for natural language processing has focused on the data from the shared task on Syntactic Analysis of Non-Canonical Language (SANCL; Petrov and McDonald, 2012), which contains several web-related corpora (newsgroups, reviews, weblogs, answers, emails) as well as the WSJ portion of OntoNotes corpus (Hovy et al., 2006). Following Schnabel and Schütze (2014), we use sections 02-21 of WSJ for training and section 22 for development, and use 100,000 unlabeled WSJ sentences from 1988 for learning representations. On the web text side, each of the five target domains has an unlabeled training set of 100,000 sentences (except the ANSWERS domain, which has 27,274 unlabeled sentences), along with development and test sets of about 1000 labeled sentences each. In the spirit of truly unsupervised domain adaptation, we do not use any target domain data for parameter tuning.

**Settings** For FEMA, we consider only the single-embedding setting, learning a single feature embedding jointly across all domains. We select 6918 pivot features for SCL, according to the method described above; the final dense representation is produced by performing a truncated singular value decomposition on the projection matrix that arises from the

| Target | baseline | MEMM | SCL | mDA | word2vec | FLORS | FEMA |
|---|---|---|---|---|---|---|---|
| NEWSGROUPS | 88.56 | 89.11 | 89.33 | 89.87 | 89.70 | 90.86 | **91.26** |
| REVIEWS | 91.02 | 91.43 | 91.53 | 91.96 | 91.70 | **92.95** | 92.82 |
| WEBLOGS | 93.67 | 94.15 | 94.28 | 94.18 | 94.17 | 94.71 | **94.95** |
| ANSWERS | 89.05 | 88.92 | 89.56 | 90.06 | 89.83 | 90.30 | **90.69** |
| EMAILS | 88.12 | 88.68 | 88.42 | 88.71 | 88.51 | 89.44 | **89.72** |
| AVERAGE | 90.08 | 90.46 | 90.63 | 90.95 | 90.78 | 91.65 | **91.89** |

Table 2: Accuracy results for adaptation from WSJ to Web Text on SANCL dev set.

| Target | baseline | MEMM | SCL | mDA | word2vec | FLORS | FEMA |
|---|---|---|---|---|---|---|---|
| NEWSGROUPS | 91.02 | 91.25 | 91.51 | 91.83 | 91.35 | 92.41 | **92.60** |
| REVIEWS | 89.79 | 90.30 | 90.29 | 90.95 | 90.87 | **92.25** | 92.15 |
| WEBLOGS | 91.85 | 92.32 | 92.32 | 92.39 | 92.42 | 93.14 | **93.43** |
| ANSWERS | 89.52 | 89.74 | 90.04 | 90.61 | 90.48 | 91.17 | **91.35** |
| EMAILS | 87.45 | 87.77 | 88.04 | 88.11 | 88.28 | 88.67 | **89.02** |
| AVERAGE | 89.93 | 90.28 | 90.44 | 90.78 | 90.68 | 91.53 | **91.71** |

Table 3: Accuracy results for adaptation from WSJ to Web Text on SANCL test set.

weights of the pivot feature predictors. The mDA method does not include any such matrix factorization step, and therefore generates a number of dense features equal to the number of pivot features. Memory constraints force us to choose fewer pivots, which we achieve by raising the threshold to 200, yielding 2754 pivot features.

**Additional systems** Aside from SCL and mDA, we compare against published results of FLORS (Schnabel and Schütze, 2014), which uses distributional features for domain adaptation. We also republish the baseline results of Schnabel and Schütze (2014) using the Stanford POS Tagger, a maximum entropy Markov model (MEMM) tagger.

**Results** As shown in Table 2 and 3, FEMA outperforms competitive systems on all target domains except REVIEW, where FLORS performs slightly better. FLORS uses more basic features than FEMA; these features could in principle be combined with feature embeddings for better performance. Compared with the other representation learning approaches, FEMA is roughly 1% better on average, corresponding to an error reduction of 10%. Its training time is approximately 70 minutes on a 24-core machine, using an implementation based on gensim.[4] This is slightly faster than SCL, although slower than mDA with structured dropout noise.

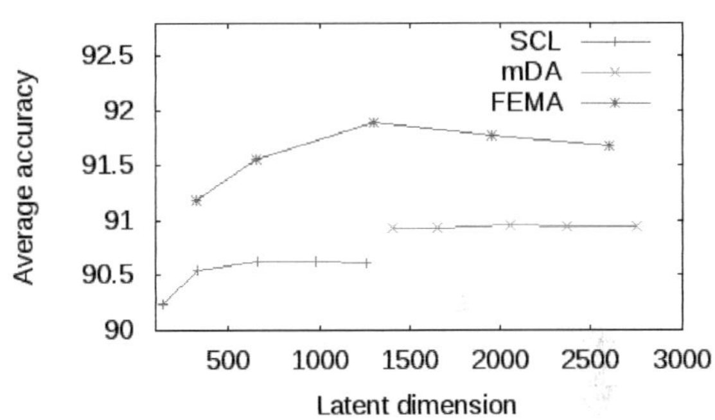


Figure 4: Accuracy results with different latent dimensions on SANCL dev sets.

Figure 4 shows the average accuracy on the SANCL development set, versus the latent dimensions of different methods. The latent dimension of SCL is modulated by the number of singular vectors; we consider sizes 10, 25, 50, 75, and 100. In mDA, we consider pivot feature frequency thresholds 500, 400, 300, 250, and 200. For FEMA, we consider embedding sizes 25, 50, 100, 150, and 200. The resulting latent dimensionality multiplies these sizes by the number of non-binary templates

[4] http://radimrehurek.com/gensim/

| Task | baseline | SCL | mDA | word2vec | FEMA | |
|---|---|---|---|---|---|---|
| | | | | | single embedding | attribute embeddings |
| from 1800-1849 | | | | | | |
| → 1750 | 88.74 | 89.31 | 90.11 | 89.24 | 90.25 | **90.59** |
| → 1700 | 89.97 | 90.41 | 91.39 | 90.51 | 91.61 | **92.03** |
| → 1650 | 85.94 | 86.76 | 87.69 | 86.22 | 87.64 | **88.12** |
| → 1600 | 86.21 | 87.65 | 88.63 | 87.41 | 89.39 | **89.77** |
| → 1550 | 88.92 | 89.92 | 90.79 | 89.85 | 91.47 | **91.78** |
| → 1500 | 85.32 | 86.82 | 87.64 | 86.60 | 89.29 | **89.89** |
| AVERAGE | 87.52 | 88.48 | 89.37 | 88.30 | 89.94 | **90.36** |
| from 1750-1849 | | | | | | |
| → 1700 | 94.37 | 94.60 | 94.86 | 94.60 | 95.14 | **95.22** |
| → 1650 | 91.49 | 91.78 | 92.52 | 91.85 | 92.56 | **93.26** |
| → 1600 | 91.92 | 92.51 | 93.14 | 92.83 | 93.80 | **93.89** |
| → 1550 | 92.75 | 93.21 | 93.53 | 93.21 | **94.23** | 94.20 |
| → 1500 | 89.87 | 90.53 | 91.31 | 91.48 | 92.05 | **92.95** |
| AVERAGE | 92.08 | 92.53 | 93.07 | 92.80 | 93.56 | **93.90** |

Table 4: Accuracy results for adaptation in the Tycho Brahe corpus of historical Portuguese.

13. FEMA dominates the other approaches across the complete range of latent dimensionalities. The best parameters for SCL are dimensionality $K = 50$ and rescale factor $\alpha = 5$. For both FEMA and WORD2VEC, the best embedding size is 100 and the best number of negative samples is 5.

### 4.3 Evaluation 2: Historical Portuguese

Next, we consider the problem of *multi-attribute domain adaptation*, using the Tycho Brahe corpus of historical Portuguese text (Galves and Faria, 2010), which contains syntactic annotations of Portuguese texts in four genres over several centuries (Figure 1). We focus on temporal adaptation: training on the most modern data in the corpus, and testing on increasingly distant historical text.

**Settings** For FEMA, we consider domain attributes for 50-year temporal epochs and genres; we also create an additional attribute merging all instances that are in neither the source nor target domain. In SCL and mDA, 1823 pivot features pass the threshold. Optimizing on a source-domain development set, we find that the best parameters for SCL are dimensionality $K = 25$ and rescale factor $\alpha = 5$. The best embedding size and negative sample number are 50 and 15 for both FEMA and WORD2VEC.

**Results** As shown in Table 4, FEMA outperforms competitive systems on all tasks. The column "single embedding" reports results with a single feature embedding per feature, ignoring domain attributes; the column "attribute embeddings" shows that learning feature embeddings for domain attributes further improves performance, by 0.3-0.4% on average.

## 5 Similarity in the embedding space

The utility of word and feature embeddings for POS tagging task can be evaluated through word similarity in the embedding space, and its relationship to type-level part-of-speech labels. To measure the label consistency between each word and its top $Q$ closest words in the vocabulary we compute,

$$\text{Consistency} = \frac{\sum_{i=1}^{|V|} \sum_{j=1}^{Q} \beta(w_i, c_{ij})}{|V| \times Q} \tag{6}$$

where $|V|$ is the number of words in the vocabulary, $w_i$ is the $i$-th word in the vocabulary, $c_{ij}$ is the $j$-th closest word to $w_i$ in the embedding space (using cosine similarity), $\beta(w_i, c_{ij})$ is an indicator function that is equal to 1 if $w_i$ and $c_{ij}$ have the same most common part-of-speech in labeled data.

We compare feature embeddings of different templates against WORD2VEC embeddings. All embeddings are trained on the SANCL data, which is

| Embedding | $Q = 5$ | $Q = 10$ | $Q = 50$ | $Q = 100$ |
|---|---|---|---|---|
| WORD2VEC | 47.64 | 46.17 | 41.96 | 40.09 |
| FEMA-current | 68.54 | 66.93 | 62.36 | 59.94 |
| FEMA-prev | 55.34 | 54.18 | 50.41 | 48.39 |
| FEMA-next | 57.13 | 55.78 | 52.04 | 49.97 |
| FEMA-all | 70.63 | 69.60 | 65.95 | 63.91 |

Table 5: Label consistency of the $Q$-most similar words in each embedding. FEMA-all is the concatenation of the current, previous, and next-word FEMA embeddings.

also used to obtain the most common tag for each word. Table 5 shows that the FEMA embeddings are more consistent with the type-level POS tags than WORD2VEC embeddings. This is not surprising, since they are based on feature templates that are specifically designed for capturing syntactic regularities. In simultaneously published work, Ling et al. (2015) present "position-specific" word embeddings, which are an alternative method to induce more syntactically-oriented word embeddings.

Table 6 shows the most similar words for three query keywords, in each of four different embeddings. The next-word and previous-word embeddings are most related to syntax, because they help to predict each other and the current-word feature; the current-word embedding brings in aspects of orthography, because it must help to predict the affix features. In morphologically rich languages such as Portuguese, this can help to compute good embeddings for rare inflected words. This advantage holds even in English: the word 'toughness' appears only once in the SANCL data, but the FEMA-current embedding is able to capture its morphological similarity to words such as 'tightness' and 'thickness'. In WORD2VEC, the lists of most similar words tend to combine syntax and topic information, and fail to capture syntactic regularities such as the relationship between 'and' and 'or'.

| | |
|---|---|
| **'new'** | |
| FEMA-current | nephew, news, newlywed, newer, newspaper |
| FEMA-prev | current, local, existing, international, entire |
| FEMA-next | real, big, basic, local, personal |
| WORD2VEC | current, special, existing, newly, own |
| **'toughness'** | |
| FEMA-current | tightness, trespass, topless, thickness, tenderness |
| FEMA-prev | underside, firepower, buzzwords, confiscation, explorers |
| FEMA-next | aspirations, anguish, pointers, organisation, responsibilities |
| WORD2VEC | parenting, empathy, ailment, rote, nerves |
| **'and'** | |
| FEMA-current | amd, announced, afnd, anesthetized, anguished |
| FEMA-prev | or, but, as, when, although |
| FEMA-next | or, but, without, since, when |
| WORD2VEC | but, while, which, because, practically |

Table 6: Most similar words for three queries, in each embedding space.

## 6 Related Work

**Representation learning** Representational differences between source and target domains can be a major source of errors in the target domain (Ben-David et al., 2010). To solve this problem, cross-domain representations were first induced via auxiliary prediction problems (Ando and Zhang, 2005), such as the prediction of *pivot features* (Blitzer et al., 2006). In these approaches, as well as in later work on denoising autoencoders (Chen et al., 2012), the key mechanism is to learn a function to predict a subset of features for each instance, based on other features of the instance. Since no labeled data is required to learn the representation, target-domain instances can be incorporated, revealing connections between features that appear only in the target domain and features that appear in the source domain training data. The design of auxiliary prediction problems and the selection of pivot features both involve heuristic decisions, which may vary depending on the task. FEMA avoids the selection of pivot features by directly learning a low-dimensional representation, through which features in each template predict the other templates.

An alternative is to link unsupervised learning in the source and target domains with the label distribution in the source domain, through the framework of posterior regularization (Ganchev et al., 2010). This idea is applied to domain adaptation by Huang and Yates (2012), and to cross-lingual learning by Ganchev and Das (2013). This approach requires a forward-backward computation for representation learning, while FEMA representations can be learned without dynamic programming, through negative sampling.

**Word embeddings** Word embeddings can be viewed as special case of representation learning, where the goal is to learn representations for each word, and then to supply these representations in place of lexical features. Early work focused on discrete clusters (Brown et al., 1990), while more recent approaches induce dense vector representations; Turian et al. (2010) compare Brown clusters with neural word embeddings from Collobert and Weston (2008) and Mnih and Hinton (2009). Word embeddings can also be computed via neural language models (Mikolov et al., 2013b), or from canonical correlation analysis (Dhillon et al., 2011). Xiao and Guo (2013) induce word embeddings across multiple domains, and concatenate these representations into a single feature vector for labeled instances in each domain, following EasyAdapt (Daumé III, 2007). However, they do not apply this idea to unsupervised domain adaptation, and do not work in the structured feature setting that we consider here. Bamman et al. (2014) learn geographically-specific word embeddings, in an approach that is similar to our multi-domain feature embeddings, but they do not consider the application to domain adaptation. We can also view the distributed representations in FLORS as a sort of word embedding, computed directly from rescaled bigram counts (Schnabel and Schütze, 2014).

Feature embeddings are based on a different philosophy than word embeddings. While many NLP features are lexical in nature, the role of a word towards linguistic structure prediction may differ across feature templates. Applying a single word representation across all templates is therefore suboptimal. Another difference is that feature embeddings can apply to units other than words, such as character strings and shape features. The tradeoff is that feature embeddings must be recomputed for each set of feature templates, unlike word embeddings, which can simply be downloaded and plugged into any NLP problem. However, computing feature embeddings is easy in practice, since it requires only a light modification to existing well-optimized implementations for computing word embeddings.

**Multi-domain adaptation** The question of adaptation across multiple domains has mainly been addressed in the context of supervised multi-domain learning, with labeled data available in all domains (Daumé III, 2007). Finkel and Manning (2009) propagate classification parameters across a tree of domains, so that classifiers for sibling domains are more similar; Daumé III (2009) shows how to induce such trees using a nonparametric Bayesian model. Dredze et al. (2010) combine classifier weights using confidence-weighted learning, which represents the covariance of the weight vectors. Joshi et al. (2013) formulate the problem of multi-attribute multi-domain learning, where all attributes are potential distinctions between domains; Wang et al. (2013) present an approach for automatically partitioning instances into domains according to such metadata features. Our formulation is related to multi-domain learning, particularly in the multi-attribute setting. However, rather than partitioning all instances into domains, the domain attribute formulation allows information to be shared across instances which share metadata attributes. We are unaware of prior research on unsupervised multi-domain adaptation.

## 7 Conclusion

Feature embeddings can be used for domain adaptation in any problem involving feature templates. They offer strong performance, avoid practical drawbacks of alternative representation learning approaches, and are easy to learn using existing word embedding methods. By combining feature embeddings with metadata domain attributes, we can perform domain adaptation across a network of interrelated domains, distilling the domain-invariant essence of each feature to obtain more robust representations.

**Acknowledgments** This research was supported by National Science Foundation award 1349837. We thank the reviewers for their feedback. Thanks also to Hal Daumé III, Chris Dyer, Slav Petrov, and Djamé Seddah.

## References


Rie Kubota Ando and Tong Zhang. 2005. A framework for learning predictive structures from multiple tasks and unlabeled data. *The Journal of Machine Learning Research*, 6:1817–1853.

David Bamman, Chris Dyer, and Noah A. Smith. 2014. Distributed representations of geographically situated language. In *Proceedings of the Association for Computational Linguistics (ACL)*, pages 828–834, Baltimore, MD.

Shai Ben-David, John Blitzer, Koby Crammer, Alex Kulesza, Fernando Pereira, and Jennifer Wortman Vaughan. 2010. A theory of learning from different domains. *Machine learning*, 79(1-2):151–175.

Yoshua Bengio, Aaron Courville, and Pascal Vincent. 2013. Representation learning: A review and new perspectives. *IEEE Transactions on Pattern Analysis and Machine Intelligence*, 35(8):1798–1828.

John Blitzer, Ryan McDonald, and Fernando Pereira. 2006. Domain adaptation with structural correspondence learning. In *Proceedings of Empirical Methods for Natural Language Processing (EMNLP)*, pages 120–128.

John Blitzer, Mark Dredze, and Fernando Pereira. 2007. Biographies, bollywood, boom-boxes and blenders: Domain adaptation for sentiment classification. In *Proceedings of the Association for Computational Linguistics (ACL)*, pages 440–447, Prague.

Peter F. Brown, Vincent J. Della Pietra, Peter V. deSouza, Jenifer C. Lai, and Robert L. Mercer. 1990. Class-Based N-Gram models of natural language. *Computational Linguistics*, 18:18–4.

Minmin Chen, Z. Xu, Killian Weinberger, and Fei Sha. 2012. Marginalized denoising autoencoders for domain adaptation. In *Proceedings of the International Conference on Machine Learning (ICML)*.

Ronan Collobert and Jason Weston. 2008. A unified architecture for natural language processing: Deep neural networks with multitask learning. In *Proceedings of the International Conference on Machine Learning (ICML)*, pages 160–167.

Hal Daumé III. 2007. Frustratingly easy domain adaptation. In *Proceedings of the Association for Computational Linguistics (ACL)*, Prague.

Hal Daumé III. 2009. Bayesian multitask learning with latent hierarchies. In *Proceedings of the Twenty-Fifth Conference on Uncertainty in Artificial Intelligence*, pages 135–142. AUAI Press.

Paramveer Dhillon, Dean P Foster, and Lyle H Ungar. 2011. Multi-view learning of word embeddings via cca. In *Advances in Neural Information Processing Systems*, pages 199–207.

Mark Dredze, Alex Kulesza, and Koby Crammer. 2010. Multi-domain learning by confidence-weighted parameter combination. *Machine Learning*, 79(1-2):123–149.

E. Eaton, M. Desjardins, and T. Lane. 2008. Modeling transfer relationships between learning tasks for improved inductive transfer. *Machine Learning and Knowledge Discovery in Databases*, pages 317–332.

Jenny R. Finkel and Christopher Manning. 2009. Hierarchical bayesian domain adaptation. In *Proceedings of the North American Chapter of the Association for Computational Linguistics (NAACL)*, pages 602–610, Boulder, CO.

Charlotte Galves and Pablo Faria. 2010. Tycho Brahe Parsed Corpus of Historical Portuguese. `http://www.tycho.iel.unicamp.br/~tycho/corpus/en/index.html`.

Kuzman Ganchev and Dipanjan Das. 2013. Cross-lingual discriminative learning of sequence models with posterior regularization. In *Proceedings of Empirical Methods for Natural Language Processing (EMNLP)*, pages 1996–2006.

Kuzman Ganchev, Joao Graça, Jennifer Gillenwater, and Ben Taskar. 2010. Posterior regularization for structured latent variable models. *The Journal of Machine Learning Research*, 11:2001–2049.

Xavier Glorot, Antoine Bordes, and Yoshua Bengio. 2011. Domain adaptation for large-scale sentiment classification: A deep learning approach. In *Proceedings of the International Conference on Machine Learning (ICML)*, Seattle, WA.

Michael U Gutmann and Aapo Hyvärinen. 2012. Noise-contrastive estimation of unnormalized statistical models, with applications to natural image statistics. *The Journal of Machine Learning Research*, 13(1):307–361.

Eduard Hovy, Mitchell Marcus, Martha Palmer, Lance Ramshaw, and Ralph Weischedel. 2006. Ontonotes: the 90% solution. In *Proceedings of the North American Chapter of the Association for Computational Linguistics (NAACL)*, pages 57–60, New York, NY.

Fei Huang and Alexander Yates. 2012. Biased representation learning for domain adaptation. In *Proceedings of Empirical Methods for Natural Language Processing (EMNLP)*, pages 1313–1323.

Mahesh Joshi, Mark Dredze, William W. Cohen, and Carolyn P. Rosé. 2013. What's in a domain? multi-domain learning for multi attribute data. In *Proceedings of the North American Chapter of the Association for Computational Linguistics (NAACL)*, pages 685–690, Atlanta, GA.

Wang Ling, Chris Dyer, Alan Black, and Isabel Trancoso. 2015. Two/too simple adaptations of word2vec for syntax problems. In *Proceedings of the North American Chapter of the Association for Computational Linguistics (NAACL)*, Denver, CO.

Yishay Mansour, Mehryar Mohri, and Afshin Rostamizadeh. 2009. Domain adaptation with multiple sources. In *Neural Information Processing Systems (NIPS)*, pages 1041–1048.

Tomas Mikolov, Kai Chen, Greg Corrado, and Jeffrey Dean. 2013a. Efficient estimation of word representations in vector space. In *Proceedings of International Conference on Learning Representations*.

Tomas Mikolov, Ilya Sutskever, Kai Chen, Greg S Corrado, and Jeff Dean. 2013b. Distributed representations of words and phrases and their compositionality. In *Advances in Neural Information Processing Systems*, pages 3111–3119.

Andriy Mnih and Geoffrey E Hinton. 2009. A scalable hierarchical distributed language model. In *Neural Information Processing Systems (NIPS)*, pages 1081–1088.

Slav Petrov and Ryan McDonald. 2012. Overview of the 2012 shared task on parsing the web. In *Notes of the First Workshop on Syntactic Analysis of Non-Canonical Language (SANCL)*, volume 59.

Adwait Ratnaparkhi. 1996. A maximum entropy model for part-of-speech tagging. In *Proceedings of Empirical Methods for Natural Language Processing (EMNLP)*, pages 133–142.

Cicero D. Santos and Bianca Zadrozny. 2014. Learning character-level representations for part-of-speech tagging. In *Proceedings of the International Conference on Machine Learning (ICML)*, pages 1818–1826.

Tobias Schnabel and Hinrich Schütze. 2014. Flors: Fast and simple domain adaptation for part-of-speech tagging. *Transactions of the Association of Computational Linguistics*, 2:51–62.

Noah A Smith. 2011. Linguistic structure prediction. *Synthesis Lectures on Human Language Technologies*, 4(2):1–274.

Joseph Turian, Lev Ratinov, and Yoshua Bengio. 2010. Word Representation: A Simple and General Method for Semi-Supervised Learning. In *Proceedings of the Association for Computational Linguistics (ACL)*, pages 384–394, Uppsala, Sweden.

Di Wang, Chenyan Xiong, and William Yang Wang. 2013. Automatic domain partitioning for multi-domain learning. In *Proceedings of Empirical Methods for Natural Language Processing (EMNLP)*, pages 869–873.

Min Xiao and Yuhong Guo. 2013. Domain adaptation for sequence labeling tasks with a probabilistic language adaptation model. In *Proceedings of the International Conference on Machine Learning (ICML)*, pages 293–301.

Yi Yang and Jacob Eisenstein. 2014. Fast easy unsupervised domain adaptation with marginalized structured dropout. In *Proceedings of the Association for Computational Linguistics (ACL)*, Baltimore, MD.

# Ontologically Grounded Multi-sense Representation Learning for Semantic Vector Space Models

**Sujay Kumar Jauhar** **Chris Dyer** **Eduard Hovy**
Language Technologies Institute
School of Computer Science
Carnegie Mellon University
Pittsburgh, PA 15213, USA
{sjauhar, cdyer, hovy}@cs.cmu.edu

## Abstract

Words are polysemous. However, most approaches to representation learning for lexical semantics assign a single vector to every surface word type. Meanwhile, lexical ontologies such as WordNet provide a source of complementary knowledge to distributional information, including a word sense inventory. In this paper we propose two novel and general approaches for generating sense-specific word embeddings that are grounded in an ontology. The first applies graph smoothing as a post-processing step to tease the vectors of different senses apart, and is applicable to any vector space model. The second adapts predictive maximum likelihood models that learn word embeddings with latent variables representing senses grounded in an specified ontology. Empirical results on lexical semantic tasks show that our approaches effectively captures information from both the ontology and distributional statistics. Moreover, in most cases our sense-specific models outperform other models we compare against.

## 1 Introduction

Vector space models (VSMs) of word meaning play a central role in computational semantics. These represent meanings of words as contextual feature vectors in a high-dimensional space (Deerwester et al., 1990) or some embedding thereof (Collobert and Weston, 2008) and are learned from unannotated corpora. Word vectors in these continuous space representations can be used for meaningful semantic operations such as computing word similarity (Turney, 2006), performing analogical reasoning (Turney, 2013) and discovering lexical relationships (Mikolov et al., 2013b). They have also proved useful in downstream NLP applications such as information retrieval (Manning et al., 2008) and question answering (Tellex et al., 2003), among others.

However, VSMs remain flawed because they assign a single vector to every word, thus ignoring the possibility that words may have more than one meaning. For example, the word "bank" can either denote a financial institution or the shore of a river. The ability to model multiple meanings is an important component of any NLP system, given how common polysemy is in language. The lack of sense annotated corpora large enough to robustly train VSMs, and the absence of fast, high quality word sense disambiguation (WSD) systems makes handling polysemy difficult.

Meanwhile, lexical ontologies, such as WordNet (Miller, 1995) specifically catalog sense inventories and provide typologies that link these senses to one another. These hand-curated ontologies provide a complementary source of information to distributional statistics. Recent research tries to leverage this information to train better VSMs (Yu and Dredze, 2014; Faruqui et al., 2014), but does not tackle the problem of polysemy. Parallely, work on polysemy for VSMs revolves primarily around techniques that cluster contexts to distinguish between different word senses (Reisinger and Mooney, 2010; Huang et al., 2012), but does not integrate ontologies in any way.

In this paper we present two novel approaches to integrating ontological and distributional sources of information. Our focus is on allowing already existing, proven techniques to be adapted to produce ontologically grounded word sense embeddings. Our first technique is applicable to any sense-agnostic



*Human Language Technologies: The 2015 Annual Conference of the North American Chapter of the ACL*, pages 683–693,
Denver, Colorado, May 31 – June 5, 2015. 

VSM as a post-processing step that performs graph propagation on the structure of the ontology. The second is applicable to the wide range of current techniques that learn word embeddings from predictive models that maximize the likelihood of a corpus (Collobert and Weston, 2008; Mnih and Teh, 2012; Mikolov et al., 2013a). Our technique adds a latent variable representing the word sense to each token in the corpus, and uses EM to find parameters. Using a structured regularizer based on the ontological graph, we learn grounded sense-specific vectors.

There are several reasons to prefer ontologies as distant sources of supervision for learning sense-aware VSMs over previously proposed unsupervised context clustering techniques. Clustering approaches must often parametrize the number of clusters (senses), which is neither known a priori nor constant across words (Kilgarriff, 1997). Also the resulting vectors remain abstract and uninterpretable. With ontologies, interpretable sense vectors can be used in downstream applications such as WSD, or for better human error analysis. Moreover, clustering techniques operate on distributional similarity only whereas ontologies support other kinds of relationships between senses. Finally, the existence of cross-lingual ontologies would permit learning multi-lingual vectors, without compounded errors from word alignment and context clustering.

We evaluate our methods on 3 lexical semantic tasks across 7 datasets and show that our sense-specific VSMs effectively integrate knowledge from the ontology with distributional statistics. Empirically, this results in consistently and significantly better performance over baselines in most cases. In the more marginal cases, analysis reveals that our performance is a result of the deficient structure of the ontology. We discuss and compare the two different approaches from the perspectives of performance, generalizability, flexibility and computational efficiency. Finally, we qualitatively analyze the vectors and show that they indeed capture sense-specific semantics.

## 2 Unified Symbolic and Distributional Semantics

In this section, we present our two techniques for inferring sense-specific vectors grounded in an ontology. We begin with notation. Let $W = \{w_1, ..., w_n\}$ be a set of word types, and $W_s = \{s_{ij} \mid \forall w_i \in W,\ 1 \leq j \leq k_i\}$ a set of senses, with $k_i$ the number of senses of $w_i$. Moreover, let $\Omega = (T_\Omega, E_\Omega)$ be an ontology represented by an undirected graph. The vertices $T_\Omega = \{t_{ij} | \ \forall \ s_{ij} \in W_s\}$ correspond to the word senses in the set $W_s$, while the edges $E_\Omega = \{e^r_{ij-i'j'}\}$ connect some subset of word sense pairs $(s_{ij}, s_{i'j'})$ by semantic relation $r$[1].

### 2.1 Retrofitting Vectors to an Ontology

Our first technique assumes that we already have a vector space embedding of a vocabulary $\hat{U} = \{\hat{u}_i | \ \forall \ w_i \in W\}$. We wish to infer vectors $V = \{v_{ij} | \ \forall \ s_{ij} \in W_s\}$ for word senses that are maximally consistent with both $\hat{U}$ and $\Omega$, by some notion of consistency. We formalize this notion as MAP inference in a Markov network (MN).

The MN we propose contains variables for every vector in $\hat{U}$ and $V$. These variables are connected to one another by dependencies as follows. Variables for vectors $v_{ij}$ and $v_{i'j'}$ are connected iff there exists an edge $e^r_{ij-i'j'} \in E_\Omega$ connecting their respective word senses in the ontology. Furthermore, vectors $\hat{u}_i$ for the word types $w_i$ are each connected to all the vectors $v_{ij}$ of the different senses $s_{ij}$ of $w_i$. If $w_i$ is not contained in the ontology, we assume it has a single unconnected sense and set it's only sense vector $v_{i1}$ to it's empirical estimate $\hat{u}_i$.

The structure of this MN is illustrated in Figure 1, where the neighborhood of the ambiguous word "bank" is presented as a factor graph.

We set each pairwise clique potential to be of the form $\exp(a\|u - v\|^2)$ between neighboring nodes. Here $u$ and $v$ are the vectors corresponding to these nodes, and $a$ is a weight controlling the strength of the relation between them. We use the Euclidean norm instead of a distance based on cosine similarity because it is more convenient from an optimization perspective.

Our inference problem is to find the MAP estimate of the vectors $V$, given $\hat{U}$, which may be stated

[1]For example there might be a "synonym" edge between the word senses "cat(1)" and "feline(1)".

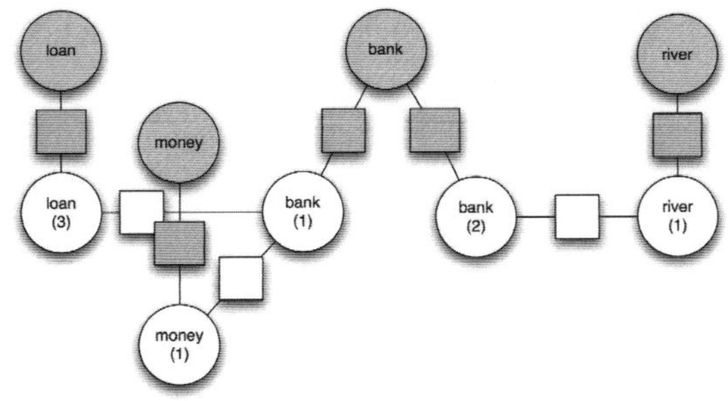


Figure 1: A factor graph depicting the retrofitting model in the neighborhood of the word "bank". Observed variables corresponding to word types are shaded in grey, while latent variables for word senses are in white.

as follows:

$$C(V) = \arg\min_{V} \sum_{i-ij} \alpha \|\hat{u}_i - v_{ij}\|^2 + \sum_{ij-i'j'} \beta_r \|v_{ij} - v_{i'j'}\|^2 \quad (1)$$

Here $\alpha$ is the sense-agnostic weight and $\beta_r$ are relation-specific weights for different semantic relations. This objective encourages vectors of neighboring nodes in the MN to pull closer together, leveraging the tension between sense-agnostic neighbors (the first summation term) and ontological neighbors (the second summation term). This allows the different neighborhoods of each sense-specific vector to tease it apart from its sense-agnostic vector.

Taking the partial derivative of the objective in equation 1 with respect to vector $v_{ij}$ and setting to zero gives the following solution:

$$v_{ij} = \frac{\alpha \hat{u}_i + \sum_{i'j' \in \mathcal{N}_{ij}} \beta_r v_{i'j'}}{\alpha + \sum_{i'j' \in \mathcal{N}_{ij}} \beta_r} \quad (2)$$

where $\mathcal{N}_{ij}$ denotes the set of neighbors of $ij$. Thus, the MAP sense-specific vector is an $\alpha$-weighted combination of its sense-agnostic vector and the $\beta_r$-weighted sense-specific vectors in its ontological neighborhood.

We use coordinate descent to iteratively update the variables $V$ using equation 2. The optimization problem in equation 1 is convex, and we normally converge to a numerically satisfactory stationary point within 10 to 15 iterations. This procedure is summarized in Algorithm 1. The generality of this algorithm allows it to be applicable to any VSM as a computationally attractive post-processing step.

**Algorithm 1** Outputs a sense-specific VSM, given a sense-agnostic VSM and ontology

**function** RETROFIT($\hat{U}, \Omega$)
  $V^{(0)} \leftarrow \{v_{ij}^{(0)} = \hat{u}_i \mid \forall s_{ij} \in W_s\}$
  **while** $\|v_{ij}^{(t)} - v_{ij}^{(t-1)}\| \geq \epsilon \; \forall i, j$ **do**
    **for** $t_{ij} \in T_\Omega$ **do**
      $v_{ij}^{(t+1)} \leftarrow$ update using equation 2
    **end for**
  **end while**
  **return** $V^{(t)}$
**end function**

An implementation of this technique is available at `https://github.com/sjauhar/SenseRetrofit`.

## 2.2 Adapting Predictive Models with Latent Variables and Structured Regularizers

Many successful techniques for semantic representation learning are formulated as models where the desired embeddings are parameters that are learnt to maximize the likelihood of a corpus (Collobert and Weston, 2008; Mnih and Teh, 2012; Mikolov et al., 2013a). In our second approach we extend an existing probability model by adding latent variables representing the senses, and we use a structured prior based on the topology of the ontology to ground the sense embeddings. Formally, we assume a corpus $D = \{(w_1, c_1), \ldots, (w_N, c_N)\}$ of pairs of target and context words, and the ontology $\Omega$, and we wish to infer sense-specific vectors $V = \{v_{ij} \mid \forall\, s_{ij} \in W_s\}$.

Consider a model with parameters $\theta$ ($V \in \theta$) that factorizes the probability over the corpus as $\prod_{(w_i, c_i) \in D} p(w_i, c_i; \theta)$. We propose to extend such a model to learn ontologically grounded sense vectors by presenting a general class of objectives of the following form:

$$C(\theta) = \arg\max_{\theta} \sum_{(w_i, c_i) \in D} \log\Big(\sum_{s_{ij}} p(w_i, c_i, s_{ij}; \theta)\Big) + \log p_\Omega(\theta) \quad (3)$$

This objective introduces latent variables $s_{ij}$ for senses and adds a structured regularizer $p_\Omega(\theta)$

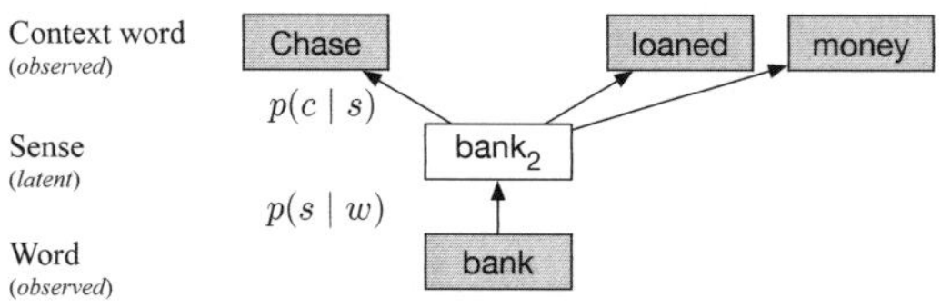


Figure 2: The generative process associated with the skip-gram model, modified to account for latent senses. Here, the context of the ambiguous word "bank" is generated from the selection of a specific latent sense.

that grounds the vectors $V$ in an ontology. This form permits flexibility in the definition of both $p(w_i, c_i, s_{ij}; \theta)$ and $p_\Omega(\theta)$ allowing for a general yet powerful framework for adapting MLE models.

In what follows we show that the popular skip-gram model (Mikolov et al., 2013a) can be adapted to generate ontologically grounded sense vectors. The classic skip-gram model uses a set of parameters $\theta = (U, V)$, with $U = \{u_i \mid \forall c_i \in W\}$ and $V = \{v_i \mid \forall w_i \in W\}$ being sets of vectors for context and target words respectively. The generative story of the skip-gram model involves generating the context word $c_i$ conditioned on an observed word $w_i$. The conditional probability is defined to be $p(c_i \mid w_i; \theta) = \frac{\exp(u_i \cdot v_i)}{\sum_{c_{i'} \in W} \exp(u_{i'} \cdot v_i)}$.

We modify the generative story of the skip-gram model to account for latent sense variables by first selecting a latent word sense $s_{ij}$ conditional on the observed word $w_i$, then generating the context word $c_i$ from the sense distinguished word $s_{ij}$. This process is illustrated in Figure 2. The factorization $p(c_i \mid w_i; \theta) = \sum_{s_{ij}} p(c_i \mid s_{ij}; \theta) \times p(s_{ij} \mid w_i; \theta)$ follows from the chain rule since senses are word-specific. To parameterize this distribution, we define a new set of model parameters $\theta = (U, V, \Pi)$, where $U$ remains identical to the original skip-gram, $V = \{v_{ij} \mid \forall s_{ij} \in W_s\}$ are a set of vectors for word senses, and $\Pi$ are the context-independent sense proportions $\pi_{ij} = p(s_{ij} \mid w_i)$. We use a Dirichlet prior over the multinomial distributions $\pi_i$ for every $w_i$, with a shared concentration parameter $\lambda$.

We define the ontological prior on vectors as $p_\Omega(\theta) \propto \exp(-\gamma \sum_{ij-i'j'} \beta_r \|v_{ij} - v_{i'j'}\|^2)$, where $\gamma$ controls the strength of the prior. We note the similarity to the retrofitting objective in equation 1, except with $\alpha = 0$. This leads to the following realization of the objective in equation 3:

$$C(\theta) = \arg\max_{\theta} \sum_{(w_i,c_i) \in D} \log\Big(\sum_{s_{ij}} p(c_i \mid s_{ij}; \theta) \times p(s_{ij} \mid w_i; \theta)\Big) - \gamma \sum_{ij-i'j'} \beta_r \|v_{ij} - v_{i'j'}\|^2 \quad (4)$$

This objective can be optimized using EM, for the latent variables, and with lazy updates (Carpenter, 2008) every $k$ words to account for the prior regularizer. However, since we are primarily interested in learning good vector representations, and we want to learn efficiently from large datasets, we make the following simplifications. First, we perform "hard" EM, selecting the most likely sense at each position rather than using the full posterior over senses. Also, given that the structured regularizer $p_\Omega(\theta)$ is essentially the retrofitting objective in equation 1, we run retrofitting periodically every $k$ words (with $\alpha = 0$ in equation 2) instead of lazy updates.[2]

The following decision rule is used in the "hard" E-step:

$$s_{ij} = \arg\max_{s_{ij}} p(c_i \mid s_{ij}; \theta^{(t)}) \pi_{ij}^{(t)} \quad (5)$$

In the M-step we use Variational Bayes to update $\Pi$ with:

$$\pi_{ij}^{(t+1)} \propto \frac{\exp\left(\psi\left(\tilde{c}(w_i, s_{ij}) + \lambda \pi_{ij}^{(0)}\right)\right)}{\exp\left(\psi\left(\tilde{c}(w_i) + \lambda\right)\right)} \quad (6)$$

where $\tilde{c}(\cdot)$ is the online expected count and $\psi(\cdot)$ is the digamma function. This approach is motivated by Johnson (2007) who found that naive EM leads to poor results, while Variational Bayes is consistently better and promotes faster convergence of the likelihood function. To update the parameters $U$ and $V$, we use negative sampling (Mikolov et al., 2013a) which is an efficient approximation to the original skip-gram objective. Negative sampling attempts to distinguish between true word pairs in the data, relative to noise. Stochastic gradient descent on the following equation is used to update the model pa-

[2]We find this gives slightly better performance.

rameters $U$ and $V$:

$$\mathcal{L} = \log \sigma(u_i \cdot v_{ij}) + \sum_{\substack{j' \\ j' \neq j}} \log \sigma(-u_i \cdot v_{ij'}) + \sum_{m} \mathbb{E}_{c_{i'} \sim P_n(c)} \left[\log \sigma(-u_{i'} \cdot v_{ij})\right] \tag{7}$$

Here $\sigma(\cdot)$ is the sigmoid function, $P_n(c)$ is a noise distribution computed over unigrams and $m$ is the negative sampling parameter. This is almost exactly the same as negative sampling proposed for the original skip-gram model. The only change is that we additionally take a negative gradient step with respect to all the senses that were not selected in the hard E-step. We summarize the training procedure for the adapted skip-gram model in Algorithm 2.

**Algorithm 2** Outputs a sense-specific VSM, given a corpus and an ontology

```
function SENSEEM(D, Ω)
    θ^(0) ← initialize
    for (w_i, c_i) ∈ D do
        if period > k then
            RETROFIT(θ^(t), Ω)
        end if
        (Hard) E-step:
        s_ij ← find argmax using equation 5
        M-step:
        Π^(t+1) ← update using equation 6
        U^(t+1), V^(t+1) ← update using equation 7
    end for
    return θ^(t)
end function
```

## 3 Evaluation

In this section we detail experimental results on 3 lexical semantics tasks across 8 different datasets. We begin by detailing the training and setup for our experiments.

### 3.1 Resources, Data and Training

We use WordNet (Miller, 1995) as the sense repository and ontology in all our experiments. WordNet is a large, hand-annotated ontology of English composed of 117,000 clusters of senses, or "synsets" that are related to one another through semantic relations such as hypernymy and hyponymy. Each synset additionally comprises a list of sense specific lemmas which we use to form the nodes in our graph. There are 206,949 such sense specific lemmas, which we connect with synonym, hypernym and hyponym[3] relations for a total of 488,432 edges.

To show the applicability of our techniques to different VSMs we experiment with two different kinds of base vectors.

**Global Context Vectors (GC) (Huang et al., 2012):** These word vectors were trained using a neural network which not only uses local context but also defines global features at the document level to further enhance the VSM. We distinguish three variants: the original single-sense vectors (SINGLE), a multi-prototype variant (MULTI), – both are available as pre-trained vectors for download[4] – and a sense-based version obtained by running retrofitting on the original vectors (RETRO).

**Skip-gram Vectors (SG) (Mikolov et al., 2013a):** We use the word vector tool `Word2Vec`[5] to train skip-gram vectors. We define 6 variants: a single-sense version (SINGLE), two multi-sense variants that were trained by first sense disambiguating the entire corpus using WSD tools, – one unsupervised (Pedersen and Kolhatkar, 2009) (WSD) and the other supervised (Zhong and Ng, 2010) (IMS) – a retrofitted version obtained from the single-sense vectors (RETRO), an EM implementation of the skip-gram model with the structured regularizer as described in section 2.2 (EM+RETRO), and the same EM technique but ignoring the ontology (EM). All models were trained on publicly available WMT-2011[6] English monolingual data. This corpus of 355 million words, although adequate in size, is smaller than typically used billion word corpora. We use this corpus because the WSD baseline involves preprocessing the corpus with sense disambiguation, which is slow enough that running it on corpora orders of magnitude larger was infeasible.

Retrofitted variants of vectors (RETRO) are trained using the procedure described in algorithm 1. We set the convergence criteria to $\epsilon = 0.01$ with a maximum number of iterations of 10. The weights

[3]We treat edges as undirected, so hypernymy and hyponymy are collapsed and unified in our representation schema.

[4]`http://nlp.stanford.edu/~socherr/ACL2012_wordVectorsTextFile.zip`

[5]`https://code.google.com/p/word2vec/`

[6]`http://www.statmt.org/wmt11/`

in the update equation 2 are set heuristically: the sense agnostic weight $\alpha$ is 1.0, and relations-specific weights $\beta_r$ are 1.0 for synonyms and 0.5 for hypernyms and hyponyms. EM+RETRO vectors are the exception where we use a weight of $\alpha = 0.0$ instead, as required by the derivation in section 2.2.

For skip-gram vectors (SG) we use the following standard settings, and do not tune any of the values. We filter all words with frequency $< 5$, and pre-normalize the corpus to replace all numeric tokens with a placeholder. We set the dimensionality of the vectors to 80, and the window size to 10 (5 context words to either side of a target). The learning rate is set to an initial value of 0.025 and diminished linearly throughout training. The negative sampling parameter is set to 5. Additionally for the EM variants (section 2.2) we set the Dirichlet concentration parameter $\lambda$ to 1000. We use 5 abstract senses for the EM vectors, and initialize the priors uniformly. For EM+RETRO, WordNet dictates the number of senses; also when available WordNet lemma counts are used to initialize the priors. Finally, we set the retrofitting period $k$ to 50 million words.

### 3.2 Experimental Results

We evaluate our models on 3 kinds of lexical semantic tasks: similarity scoring, synonym selection, and similarity scoring in context.

**Similarity Scoring:** This task involves using a semantic model to assign a score to pairs of words. We use the following 4 standard datasets in this evaluation: WS-353 (Finkelstein et al., 2002), RG-65 (Rubenstein and Goodenough, 1965), MC-30 (Miller and Charles, 1991) and MEN-3k (Bruni et al., 2014). Each dataset consists of pairs of words along with an averaged similarity score obtained from several human annotators. For example an item in the WS-353 dataset is "book, paper $\rightarrow$ 7.46". We use standard cosine similarity to assign a score to word pairs in single-sense VSMs, and the following average similarity score to multi-sense variants, as proposed by Reisinger and Mooney (2010):

$$avgSim(w_i, w_{i'}) = \frac{1}{k_i k_j} \sum_{j,j'} cos(v_{ij}, v_{i'j'}) \quad (8)$$

The output of systems is evaluated against the gold standard using Spearman's rank correlation coefficient.

**Synonym Selection:** In this task, VSMs are used to select the semantically closest word to a target from a list of candidates. We use the following 3 standard datasets in this evaluation: ESL-50 (Turney, 2001), RD-300 (Jarmasz and Szpakowicz, 2004) and TOEFL-80 (Landauer and Dumais, 1997). These datasets consist of a list of target words that appear with several candidate lexical items. An example from the TOEFL dataset is "rug $\rightarrow$ sofa, ottoman, carpet, hallway", with "carpet" being the most synonym-like candidate to the target. We begin by scoring all pairs composed of the target and one of the candidates. We use cosine similarity for single-sense VSMs, and max similarity for multi-sense models[7]:

$$maxSim(w_i, w_{i'}) = \max_{j,j'} cos(v_{ij}, v_{i'j'}) \quad (9)$$

These scores are then sorted in descending order, with the top-ranking score yielding the semantically closest candidate to the target. Systems are evaluated on the basis of their accuracy at discriminating the top-ranked candidate.

The results for similarity scoring and synonym selection are presented in table 1. On both tasks and on all datasets, with the partial exception of WS-353 and MEN-3k, our vectors (RETRO & EM+RETRO) consistently yield better results than other VSMs. Notably, both our techniques perform better than preprocessing a corpus with WSD information in unsupervised or supervised fashion (SG-WSD & SG-IMS). Simple EM without an ontological prior to ground the vectors (SG-EM) also performs poorly.

We investigated the observed drop in performance on WS-353 and found that this dataset consists of two parts: a set of *similar* word pairs (e.g. "tiger" and "cat") and another set of *related* word pairs (e.g. "weather" and "forecast"). The synonym, hypernym and hyponym relations we use tend to encourage *similarity* to the detriment of *relatedness*.

We ran an auxiliary experiment to show this. SG-EM+RETRO training also learns vectors for context words – which can be thought of as a proxy for relatedness. Using this VSM we scored a word pair by the average similarity of all the sense vectors of

[7] Here we are specifically looking for synonyms, so the max makes more sense than taking an average.

| | | Word Similarity ($\rho$) | | | | Synonym Selection (%) | | |
|---|---|---|---|---|---|---|---|---|
| | | WS-353 | RG-65 | MC-30 | MEN-3k | ESL-50 | RD-300 | TOEFL-80 |
| GC | SINGLE | **0.623** | 0.629 | 0.657 | 0.314 | 47.73 | 45.07 | 60.87 |
| | MULTI | 0.535 | 0.510 | 0.309 | 0.359 | 27.27 | 47.89 | 52.17 |
| | **RETRO** | 0.543 | **0.661** | **0.714** | **0.528** | **63.64** | **66.20** | **71.01** |
| SG | SINGLE | **0.639** | 0.546 | 0.627 | **0.646** | 52.08 | 55.66 | 66.67 |
| | EM | 0.194 | 0.278 | 0.167 | 0.228 | 27.08 | 33.96 | 40.00 |
| | WSD | 0.481 | 0.298 | 0.396 | 0.175 | 16.67 | 49.06 | 42.67 |
| | IMS | 0.549 | 0.579 | 0.606 | 0.591 | 41.67 | 53.77 | 66.67 |
| | **RETRO** | 0.552 | 0.673 | 0.705 | 0.560 | 56.25 | 65.09 | **73.33** |
| | **EM+RETRO** | 0.321 | **0.734** | **0.758** | 0.428 | **62.22** | **66.67** | 68.63 |

Table 1: Similarity scoring and synonym selection in English across several datasets involving different VSMs. Higher scores are better; best scores within each category are in bold. In most cases our models consistently and significantly outperform the other VSMs.

one word to the context vector of the other word, averaged over both words. With this scoring function the correlation $\rho$ jumped from 0.321 to 0.493. While still not as good as some of the other VSMs, it should be noted that this scoring function negatively influences the *similar* word pairs in the dataset.

The MEN-3k dataset is crowd-sourced and contains much diversity, with word pairs evidencing similarity as well as relatedness. However, we aren't sure why the performance for GC-RETRO improves greatly over GC-SINGLE for this dataset, while that of SG-RETRO and SG-RETRO+EM drops in relation to SG-SINGLE.

**Similarity Scoring in Context:** As outlined by Reisinger and Mooney (2010), multi-sense VSMs can be used to consider context when computing similarity between words. We use the SCWS dataset (Huang et al., 2012) in these experiments. This dataset is similar to the similarity scoring datasets, except that they additionally are presented in context. For example an item involving the words "bank" and "money", gives the words in their respective contexts, "along the east **bank** of the Des Moines River" and "the basis of all **money** laundering" with a low averaged similarity score of 2.5 (on a scale of 1.0 to 10.0). Following Reisinger and Mooney (2010) we use the following function to assign a score to word pairs in their respective contexts, given a multi-sense VSM:

$$avgSimC(w_i, c_i, w_{i'}, c_{i'}) = \sum_{j,j'} p(s_{ij}|c_i, w_i)p(s_{i'j'}|c_{i'}, w_{i'})cos(v_{ij}, v_{i'j'}) \quad (10)$$

| Vectors | SCWS ($\rho$) |
|---|---|
| SG-WSD | 0.343 |
| SG-IMS | 0.528 |
| SG-RETRO | 0.417 |
| GC-RETRO | 0.420 |
| SG-EM | 0.613 |
| SG-EM+RETRO | 0.587 |
| GC-MULTI | **0.657** |

Table 2: Contextual word similarity in English. Higher scores are better.

As with similarity scoring, the output of systems is evaluated against gold standard using Spearman's rank correlation coefficient.

The results are presented in table 2. Preprocessing a corpus with WSD information in an unsupervised fashion (SG-WSD) yields poor results. In comparison, the retrofitted vectors (SG-RETRO & GC-RETRO) already perform better, even though they do not have access to context vectors, and thus do not take contextual information into account. Supervised sense vectors (SG-IMS) are also competent, scoring better than both retrofitting techniques. Our EM vectors (SG-EM & SG-EM+RETRO) yield even better results and are able to capitalize on contextual information, however they still fall short of the pretrained GC-MULTI vectors. We were surprised that SG-EM+RETRO actually performed worse than SG-EM, given how poorly SG-EM performed in the other evaluations. However, an analysis again revealed that this was due to the kind of similarity encouraged by WordNet rather than an inability of the model to learn useful vectors. The SCWS dataset, in addition to containing related

| Method | CPU Time |
|---|---|
| RETRO | ~20 secs |
| EM+RETRO | ~4 hours |
| IMS | ~3 days |
| WSD | ~1 year |

Table 3: Training time associated with different methods of generating sense-specific VSMs.

words – which we showed, hurt our performance on WS-353 – also contains word pairs with different POS tags. WordNet synonymy, hypernymy and hyponymy relations are exclusively defined between lemmas of the same POS tag, which adversely affects performance further.

### 3.3 Discussion

While both our approaches are capable of integrating ontological information into VSMs, an important question is which one should be preferred? From an empirical point of view, the EM+RETRO framework yields better performance than RETRO across most of our semantic evaluations. Additionally EM+RETRO is more powerful, allowing to adapt more expressive models that can jointly learn other useful parameters – such as context vectors in the case of skip-gram. However, RETRO is far more generalizable, allowing it to be used for *any* VSM, not just predictive MLE models, and is also empirically competitive. Another consideration is computational efficiency, which is summarized in table 3.

Not only is RETRO much faster, but it scales linearly with respect to the vocabulary size, unlike EM+RETRO, WSD, and IMS which are dependent on the input training corpus. Nevertheless, both our techniques are empirically superior as well as computationally more efficient than both unsupervised and supervised word-sense disambiguation paradigms.

Both our approaches are sensitive to the structure of the ontology. Therefore, an important consideration is the relations we use and the weights we associate with them. In our experiments we selected the simplest set of relations and assigned weights heuristically, showing that our methods can effectively integrate ontological information into VSMs. A more exhaustive selection procedure with weight tuning on held-out data would almost certainly lead to better performance on our evaluation suite.

### 3.4 Qualitative Analysis

We qualitatively attempt to address the question of whether the vectors are truly sense specific. In table 4 we present the three most similar words of an ambiguous lexical item in a standard VSM (SG-SINGLE) in comparison with the three most similar words of different lemma senses of the same lexical item in grounded sense VSMs (SG-RETRO & SG-EM+RETRO).

| Word or Sense | Top 3 Most Similar |
|---|---|
| hanging | hung dangled hangs |
| hanging (suspending) | shoring support suspension |
| hanging (decoration) | tapestry braid smock |
| climber | climbers skier Loretan |
| climber (sportsman) | lifter swinger sharpshooter |
| climber (vine) | woodbine brier kiwi |

Table 4: The top 3 most similar words for two polysemous types. Single sense VSMs capture the most frequent sense. Our techniques effectively separates out the different senses of words, and are grounded in WordNet.

The sense-agnostic VSMs tend to capture only the most frequent sense of a lexical item. On the other hand, the disambiguated vectors capture sense specificity of even less frequent senses successfully. This is probably due to the nature of WordNet where the nearest neighbors of the words in question are in fact these rare words. A careful tuning of weights will likely optimize the trade-off between ontologically rare neighbors and distributionally common words.

In our analyses, we noticed that lemma senses that had many neighbors (i.e. synonyms, hypernyms and hyponyms), tended to have more clearly sense specific vectors. This is expected, since it is these neighborhoods that disambiguate and help to distinguish the vectors from their single sense embeddings.

## 4 Related Work

Since Reisinger and Mooney (2010) first proposed a simple context clustering technique to generate multi-prototype VSMs, a number of related efforts have worked on adaptations and improvements relying on the same clustering principle. Huang et al. (2012) train their vectors with a neural network and additionally take global context into account. Neelakantan et al. (2014) extend the popular skip-gram model (Mikolov et al., 2013a) in a non-parametric fashion to allow for different number of senses for words. Guo et al. (2014) exploit bilingual alignments to perform better context clustering during training. Tian et al. (2014) propose a probabilistic extension to skip-gram that treats the different prototypes as latent variables. This is similar to our second EM training framework, and turns out to be a special case of our general model. In all these papers, however, the multiple senses remain abstract and are not grounded in an ontology.

Conceptually, our work is also similar to Yu and Dredze (2014) and Faruqui et al. (2014), who treat lexicons such as the paraphrase database (PPDB) (Ganitkevitch et al., 2013) or WordNet (Miller, 1995) as an auxiliary thesaurus to improve VSMs. However, they do not model senses in any way. Pilehvar et al. (2013) do model senses from an ontology by performing random-walks on the Wordnet graph, however their approach does not take distributional information from VSMs into account.

Thus, to the best of our knowledge, our work presents the first attempt at producing sense grounded VSMs that are symbolically tied to lexical ontologies. From a modelling point of view, it is also the first to outline a unified, principled and extensible framework that effectively combines the symbolic and distributional paradigms of semantics.

Both our models leverage the graph structure of ontologies to effectively ground the senses of a VSM. This ties into previous research (Das and Smith, 2011; Das and Petrov, 2011) that propagates information through a factor graph to perform tasks such as frame-semantic parsing and POS-tagging across languages. More generally, this approach can be viewed from the perspective of semi-supervised learning, with an optimization over a graph loss function defined on smoothness properties (Corduneanu and Jaakkola, 2002; Zhu et al., 2003; Subramanya and Bilmes, 2009).

Related to the problem of polysemy is the issue of different shades of meaning a word assumes based on context. The space of research on this topic can be divided into three broad categories: models for computing contextual lexical semantics based on composition (Mitchell and Lapata, 2008; Erk and Padó, 2008; Thater et al., 2011), models that use fuzzy exemplar-based contexts without composing them (Erk and Padó, 2010; Reddy et al., 2011), and models that propose latent variable techniques (Dinu and Lapata, 2010; Séaghdha and Korhonen, 2011; Van de Cruys et al., 2011). Our work, which tackles the stronger form of lexical ambiguity in polysemy falls into the latter two of three categories.

## 5 Conclusion and Future Work

We have presented two general and flexible approaches to producing sense-specific VSMs grounded in an ontology. The first technique is applicable to any VSM as an efficient post-processing step while the second provides a framework to integrate ontological information with existing MLE-based predictive models. We presented an evaluation of 3 semantic tasks on 7 datasets. Our results show that our proposed methods are effectively able to capture the different senses in an ontology. In most cases this results in significant improvements over baselines. We have also discussed the trade-offs between the two techniques from several different perspectives. Finally, we have presented a qualitative analysis investigating the nature of the sense-specific vectors, and shown that they capture the semantics of different senses.

Our findings suggest several avenues for future research. We propose to use sense-specific vectors as features in downstream applications such a Word Sense Disambiguation. Our current approach assumes a fixed ontology, but we hope to explore a more bi-directional relationship between ontology and VSM in future work. In particularly we envisage simultaneously incrementing ontologies with structure learning in addition to improving VSMs. We also hope to extend our research to the multi-lingual domain. We are particularly excited by the idea of using multi-lingual WordNets to learn sense specific semantic vectors that generalize across languages.

## Acknowledgments

The authors would like to thank Manaal Faruqui, Jesse Dodge and Noah Smith for their insight and feedback. Thanks also go to the anonymous reviewers for their valuable comments and suggestions to improve the quality of the paper. This work was supported in part by the following grants: NSF grant IIS-1143703, NSF award IIS-1147810, DARPA grant FA87501220342.

## References


Elia Bruni, Nam-Khanh Tran, and Marco Baroni. 2014. Multimodal distributional semantics. *Journal of Artificial Intelligence Research (JAIR)*, 49:1–47.

Bob Carpenter. 2008. Lazy sparse stochastic gradient descent for regularized multinomial logistic regression. technical report, alias-i. available at http://lingpipe-blog.com/ lingpipe-white-papers.

Ronan Collobert and Jason Weston. 2008. A unified architecture for natural language processing: deep neural networks with multitask learning. In *Proceedings of the 25th international conference on Machine learning*, ICML '08, pages 160–167, New York, NY, USA. ACM.

Adrian Corduneanu and Tommi Jaakkola. 2002. On information regularization. In *Proceedings of the Nineteenth conference on Uncertainty in Artificial Intelligence*, pages 151–158. Morgan Kaufmann Publishers Inc.

Dipanjan Das and Slav Petrov. 2011. Unsupervised part-of-speech tagging with bilingual graph-based projections. In *Proc. of ACL*.

Dipanjan Das and Noah A. Smith. 2011. Semi-supervised frame-semantic parsing for unknown predicates. In *Proc. of ACL*.

S. C. Deerwester, S. T. Dumais, T. K. Landauer, G. W. Furnas, and R. A. Harshman. 1990. Indexing by latent semantic analysis. *Journal of the American Society for Information Science*.

Georgiana Dinu and Mirella Lapata. 2010. Measuring distributional similarity in context. In *Proceedings of the 2010 Conference on Empirical Methods in Natural Language Processing*, pages 1162–1172. Association for Computational Linguistics.

Katrin Erk and Sebastian Padó. 2008. A structured vector space model for word meaning in context. In *Proceedings of the Conference on Empirical Methods in Natural Language Processing*, EMNLP '08, pages 897–906, Stroudsburg, PA, USA. Association for Computational Linguistics.

Katrin Erk and Sebastian Padó. 2010. Exemplar-based models for word meaning in context. In *Proceedings of the ACL 2010 Conference Short Papers*, pages 92–97. Association for Computational Linguistics.

Manaal Faruqui, Jesse Dodge, Sujay K Jauhar, Chris Dyer, Eduard Hovy, and Noah A Smith. 2014. Retrofitting word vectors to semantic lexicons. *arXiv preprint arXiv:1411.4166*.

Lev Finkelstein, Evgeniy Gabrilovich, Yossi Matias, Ehud Rivlin, Zach Solan, Gadi Wolfman, and Eytan Ruppin. 2002. Placing search in context: The concept revisited. In *ACM Transactions on Information Systems*, volume 20, pages 116–131, January.

Juri Ganitkevitch, Benjamin Van Durme, and Chris Callison-Burch. 2013. PPDB: The paraphrase database. In *Proceedings of NAACL-HLT*, pages 758–764, Atlanta, Georgia, June. Association for Computational Linguistics.

Jiang Guo, Wanxiang Che, Haifeng Wang, and Ting Liu. 2014. Learning sense-specific word embeddings by exploiting bilingual resources. In *Proceedings of COLING*, pages 497–507.

Eric H Huang, Richard Socher, Christopher D Manning, and Andrew Y Ng. 2012. Improving word representations via global context and multiple word prototypes. In *Proceedings of the 50th ACL: Long Papers-Volume 1*, pages 873–882.

Mario Jarmasz and Stan Szpakowicz. 2004. Roget's thesaurus and semantic similarity. *Recent Advances in Natural Language Processing III: Selected Papers from RANLP*, 2003:111.

Mark Johnson. 2007. Why doesn't em find good hmm pos-taggers? In *EMNLP-CoNLL*, pages 296–305. Citeseer.

Adam Kilgarriff. 1997. I don't believe in word senses. *Computers and the Humanities*, 31(2):91–113.

Thomas K Landauer and Susan T. Dumais. 1997. A solution to plato's problem: The latent semantic analysis theory of acquisition, induction, and representation of knowledge. *Psychological review*, pages 211–240.

Christopher D. Manning, Prabhakar Raghavan, and Hinrich Schütze. 2008. *Introduction to Information Retrieval*. Cambridge University Press, New York, NY, USA.

Tomas Mikolov, Kai Chen, Greg Corrado, and Jeffrey Dean. 2013a. Efficient estimation of word representations in vector space. *arXiv preprint arXiv:1301.3781*.

Tomas Mikolov, Wen-tau Yih, and Geoffrey Zweig. 2013b. Linguistic regularities in continuous space word representations. In *Proceedings of the 2013 Conference of the NAACL: Human Language Technologies*, pages 746–751, Atlanta, Georgia, June.

George Miller and Walter Charles. 1991. Contextual correlates of semantic similarity. In *Language and Cognitive Processes*, pages 1–28.

George A Miller. 1995. Wordnet: a lexical database for english. *Communications of the ACM*, 38(11):39–41.

Jeff Mitchell and Mirella Lapata. 2008. Vector-based models of semantic composition. In *Proceedings of ACL-08: HLT*, pages 236–244.

Andriy Mnih and Yee Whye Teh. 2012. A fast and simple algorithm for training neural probabilistic language models. In *Proceedings of the 29th International Conference on Machine Learning*, pages 1751–1758.

Arvind Neelakantan, Jeevan Shankar, Alexandre Passos, and Andrew McCallum. 2014. Efficient non-parametric estimation of multiple embeddings per word in vector space. In *Proceedings of EMNLP*.

Ted Pedersen and Varada Kolhatkar. 2009. Wordnet:: Senserelate:: Allwords: a broad coverage word sense tagger that maximizes semantic relatedness. In *Proceedings of human language technologies: The 2009 annual conference of the north american chapter of the association for computational linguistics, companion volume: Demonstration session*, pages 17–20. Association for Computational Linguistics.

Mohammad Taher Pilehvar, David Jurgens, and Roberto Navigli. 2013. Align, disambiguate and walk: A unified approach for measuring semantic similarity. In *ACL (1)*, pages 1341–1351.

Siva Reddy, Ioannis P Klapaftis, Diana McCarthy, and Suresh Manandhar. 2011. Dynamic and static prototype vectors for semantic composition. In *IJCNLP*, pages 705–713.

Joseph Reisinger and Raymond J. Mooney. 2010. Multi-prototype vector-space models of word meaning. In *Proceedings of the 11th Annual Conference of the North American Chapter of the Association for Computational Linguistics (NAACL-2010)*, pages 109–117.

Herbert Rubenstein and John B. Goodenough. 1965. Contextual correlates of synonymy. *Commun. ACM*, 8(10):627–633, October.

Diarmuid Ó Séaghdha and Anna Korhonen. 2011. Probabilistic models of similarity in syntactic context. In *Proceedings of the Conference on Empirical Methods in Natural Language Processing*, EMNLP '11, pages 1047–1057, Stroudsburg, PA, USA. Association for Computational Linguistics.

Amarnag Subramanya and Jeff A Bilmes. 2009. Entropic graph regularization in non-parametric semi-supervised classification. In *NIPS*, pages 1803–1811.

Stefanie Tellex, Boris Katz, Jimmy J. Lin, Aaron Fernandes, and Gregory Marton. 2003. Quantitative evaluation of passage retrieval algorithms for question answering. In *SIGIR*, pages 41–47.

Stefan Thater, Hagen Fürstenau, and Manfred Pinkal. 2011. Word meaning in context: A simple and effective vector model. In *IJCNLP*, pages 1134–1143.

Fei Tian, Hanjun Dai, Jiang Bian, Bin Gao, Rui Zhang, Enhong Chen, and Tie-Yan Liu. 2014. A probabilistic model for learning multi-prototype word embeddings. In *Proceedings of COLING*, pages 151–160.

Peter D. Turney. 2001. Mining the web for synonyms: Pmi-ir versus lsa on toefl. In *Proceedings of the 12th European Conference on Machine Learning*, EMCL '01, pages 491–502, London, UK, UK. Springer-Verlag.

Peter D. Turney. 2006. Similarity of semantic relations. *Comput. Linguist.*, 32(3):379–416, September.

Peter D Turney. 2013. Distributional semantics beyond words: Supervised learning of analogy and paraphrase. *Transactions of the Association for Computational Linguistics*, 1:353–366.

Tim Van de Cruys, Thierry Poibeau, and Anna Korhonen. 2011. Latent vector weighting for word meaning in context. In *Proceedings of the Conference on Empirical Methods in Natural Language Processing*, pages 1012–1022. Association for Computational Linguistics.

Mo Yu and Mark Dredze. 2014. Improving lexical embeddings with semantic knowledge. In *Proceedings of the 52nd Annual Meeting of the Association for Computational Linguistics*.

Zhi Zhong and Hwee Tou Ng. 2010. It makes sense: A wide-coverage word sense disambiguation system for free text. In *Proceedings of the ACL 2010 System Demonstrations*, pages 78–83. Association for Computational Linguistics.

Xiaojin Zhu, Zoubin Ghahramani, John Lafferty, et al. 2003. Semi-supervised learning using gaussian fields and harmonic functions. In *ICML*, volume 3, pages 912–919.

# Subsentential Sentiment on a Shoestring: A Crosslingual Analysis of Compositional Classification

**Michael Haas** and **Yannick Versley**
Institute for Computational Linguistics
University of Heidelberg
{haas,versley}@cl.uni-heidelberg.de

## Abstract

Sentiment analysis has undergone a shift from *document-level* analysis, where labels expresses the sentiment of a whole document or whole sentence, to subsentential approaches, which assess the contribution of individual phrases, in particular including the *composition* of sentiment terms and phrases such as negators and intensifiers.

Starting from a small sentiment treebank modeled after the Stanford Sentiment Treebank of Socher et al. (2013), we investigate suitable methods to perform compositional sentiment classification for German in a data-scarce setting, harnessing cross-lingual methods as well as existing general-domain lexical resources.

## 1 Introduction

In sentiment classification, we find a general tendency from document-level classification towards more fine-grained approaches that yield a more detailed appraisal of the judgement performed in the text - in particular, using composition over syntactic structure to get a more detailed approach over phrases.

For English movie reviews, work using the Stanford Sentiment Treebank (SSTb) has shown that such subsentential sentiment information can yield approaches with both very high accuracy (Socher et al., 2013; Dong et al., 2014; Hall et al., 2014) and precise information about the role of each phrase – information which can subsequently used for extracting or summarizing the sentiment expressed in the text.

The effort for creating a sentiment treebank such as the SSTb, however, seems prohibitive if we wanted to create such a resource for each pair of relevant domain and language: Compared to document-level annotations for sentiment, which are easy to come by (e.g., star ratings), annotating individual syntactic phrases requires considerable effort.

The main focus of this paper is the question if and how it is possible to reach sensible performance for compositional sentiment classification when we only have limited resources to spend on an in-language, in-domain sentiment treebank. For this goal, we use a new resource, the *Heidelberg Sentiment Treebank* (HeiST), which is a German-language counterpart to the Stanford Sentiment Treebank in the sense that it makes explicit the composition of sentiment expression over syntactic phrases. Our experiments on HeiST provide a direct comparison of different techniques for harnessing cross-lingual, cross-domain, or cross-task information, and are the first of this kind to specifically target *compositional* sentiment analysis.

Figure 1 (next page) shows a schematic overview of the experiments: beyond supervised baseline experiments using SVM classification and a supervised RNTN model (section 3), we evaluated cross-lingual projection (section 4), lexicon-based approaches (section 5), as well as semi-supervised approaches based on word clusters (section 6).

## 2 Related Work

The starting point for our research is the idea that the sentiment of larger stretches of text can be calculated through composition over smaller stretches of text, which was investigated in a learning framework by both Yessenalina and Cardie (2011) and Socher et al. (2011, 2012), both learning in a compositional



*Human Language Technologies: The 2015 Annual Conference of the North American Chapter of the ACL*, pages 694–704,
Denver, Colorado, May 31 – June 5, 2015. 

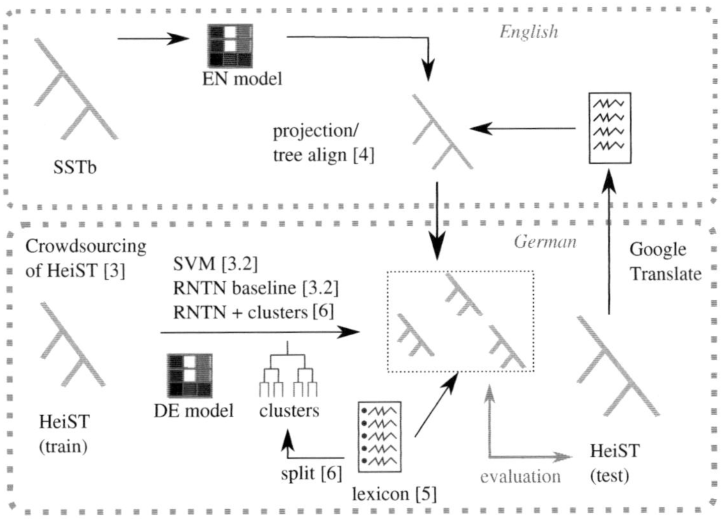


Figure 1: Plan to the experiments described in this paper

fashion from datasets that only have document-level sentiment annotation.

On the same dataset as Socher et al., Wang and Manning (2012) later demonstrated that unigram and bigram features in an SVM-based classification framework can reach a greater accuracy than the earlier recursive neural network approach of Socher et al. (2011, 2012), which calls into question the assumption that sentiment composition can be learned purely from sentence-level annotations.

**Compositionality through Tensors** In subsequent work, Socher et al. (2013) introduce the Stanford Sentiment Treebank, which contains detailed annotations of sentiment values for individual syntactic phrases in a binarized tree, and an approach based on recursive neural tensor networks (RNTN) which yields significant improvements over the earlier approaches using token-level features.

The RNTN represents the contribution of individual nodes as vectors of reals and achieves its precision by using a tensor $V^{[1:d]} \in \mathbb{R}^{2d \times 2d \times d}$ as well as a matrix $W \in \mathbb{R}^{2d \times d}$ to capture second-order dependencies between the two children of a node in the tree (with vectors $a$, $b$), yielding first a vector $h$ by

$$h_i = \begin{bmatrix} a \\ b \end{bmatrix}^T V^{[i]} \begin{bmatrix} a \\ b \end{bmatrix} + W_i \begin{bmatrix} a \\ b \end{bmatrix}$$

then using a monotonic nonlinear function on $h$ (here: *tanh*) to yield the vector for this node. The sentiment label of a node is then gained by multiplying these *hidden vectors* by a matrix $W_s$, yielding a five-dimensional vector with the classification. Using hidden vectors for each node and capturing second-order interaction between the two child vectors $a$ and $b$, the RNTN model achieves descriptive power greater than that of TreeCRFs (Nakagawa et al., 2010), and similar to latent-variable models that have been very successful in syntactic parsing (Petrov et al., 2006).

In later work, Zhu et al. (2014) show that the RNTN's lexicalized modeling of negators and their behaviour leads to increased descriptive power of the model, which results in an improved treatment of negation. Dong et al. (2014) introduce an approach that chooses between multiple composition tensors (AdaMC-RNTN), which yields further gains with respect to RNTN performance.

In contrast to the lexicalized and high-dimensional RNTN model, there are several lines of work that attempt to work in a more data-scarce setting.

**Lexicon-based approaches** The classical approach for performing sentiment classification in a setting where training data is sparse can be seen in the SO-CAL approach of Taboada et al. (2011): Using a manually curated dictionary with sentiment values for multiple parts of speech, and a set of heuristics that predict how intensifiers, negators/shifters as well as nonveridical moods affect the sentiment of a phrase, they show that it is possible to reach good results across different domains.

Choi and Cardie (2009) show that it is possible to adapt an existing general-domain sentiment lexicon to a specific domain using an approach that optimizes a joint objective of classification loss, sparsity of the changes made to the lexicon, and ambiguity of lexicon entries. Their approach yields appreciable gains over the general-domain lexicon, both with CRF-based machine learning classification and with a simpler "vote & flip" algorithm that is based on majority voting and negators.

**Crosslingual Sentiment Analysis** involves the usage of a dataset in one language to perform sentiment analysis in another language; in their work, Banea et al. (2013) show that translating text in the target language to the source language and applying a well-tuned sentiment classification system works better than either translating the training corpus or the lexicon used by the system.

In research by other groups, Wan (2009) advocates a bootstrapping approach that combines source-side and target-side features in one classifier; Duh et al. (2011) note that crosslingual sentiment analysis techniques always incur a loss due to the shift in language from the source language texts to the target language even though the general domain is the same. Popat et al. (2013) argue that full machine translation is not useful for resource-scarce languages, and propose to use cross-lingual clustering both to improve the generalization capability within a single language as well as for crosslingual projection, which works better than machine translation with the English-Hindi language pair.

It should be noted that most of the work presented in the last two paragraph works with document-level sentiment, or (in the case of Choi and Cardie) with shallower annotations, and offers additional challenges in the case of sentiment composition.

## 3 Low-Budget Treebanking for Sentiment

For both supervised training and for evaluation, we created a German dataset that is close in domain to the Stanford Sentiment treebank (Socher et al., 2013), covering opinionated sentences from movie reviews with phrase-level sentiment annotations.

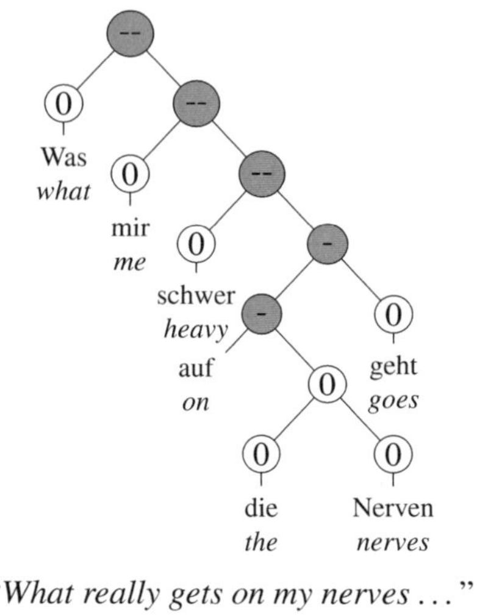


Figure 2: A multiword expression in HeiST

The original Stanford Sentiment Treebank is based on the dataset of Pang and Lee (2005), which includes 10,662 sentences from excerpts of movie reviews published on `rottentomatoes.com`. It should be noted that these excerpts are much more likely to express an opinion than general text or even the main body of a movie review since they contain precisely a summary of the opinion.

In order to match both domain and role of these sentences most precisely, we collected creative-commons-licensed reviews from a German movie review site, `filmrezensionen.de`, and used only the summary part of these documents, yielding 1184 sentences, for which we crowdsourced annotation for each individual phrase in the binary tree (see Figure 2 for an example tree fragment).

For the purpose of getting binary phrase trees, sentences were processed with the Berkeley Parser (Petrov et al., 2006), NP nodes were added inside PPs (Samuelsson and Volk, 2004) and the resulting parse trees binarized using the head table in CoreNLP (Rafferty and Manning, 2008), yielding 14,321 unique phrases.

Annotation was outsourced via the CrowdFlower service, which collects three judgements for each phrase and computes an end result through voting, using unambiguous test items (which we composed from strongly positive or strongly negative adjective-noun combinations) to filter out annotators lacking the requisite understanding of German.

| *Experiment A: Features, Confidence* | Prec | Recl |
|---|---|---|
| SentiWS | 0.882 | 0.959 |
| SentiWS+Regression | 0.894 | 0.967 |
| SentiWS+Regression, @50% | 0.935 | 0.985 |
| SentiWS+Regression+POS | 0.912 | 0.960 |
| SentiWS+Regression+POS, @50% | 0.978 | 0.997 |
| *Experiment B: Classifier (@50%)* | Prec | Recl |
| Linear SVM | 0.975 | 0.980 |
| Random Forest | 0.984 | 0.992 |
| Gradient Boosting | 0.978 | 0.997 |

Table 1: Filtering out objective phrases

The HeiST treebank, as well as the code used in these experiments, are available for research purposes.[1]

### 3.1 Selecting Subjective Phrases

One possible approach to reduce annotation effort would be to annotate only those phrases that a classification model deems to have sentiment content in the first place. As a more extreme example of such an approach, consider the MLSA sentiment dataset for German, where 270 sentences were selected that already contained two words from an existing sentiment lexicon (Clematide et al., 2012), with the goal of getting sentences with interesting interactions between sentiment words. Given the potential benefits (getting more data for the same annotation effort), an approach that filters out non-interesting (confidently objective) phrases would be highly appealing.

For the pre-classification experiment, we used cross-validation on 20 to assess the potential impact of strategies for saving. For the corresponding classifier, we used features from a German general-domain sentiment lexicon, a regression model for document-level sentiment (see section 5.2), as well as part-of-speech tag features in a gradient boosting classifier. As seen in table 1, the sentiment lexicon, especially in conjunction with the regression model and a POS-based filter, would allow to detect uninteresting (objective) phrases with high accuracy. We limit ourselves to the 50% of most confident classifications, and as a measure of caution, the filter is bypassed for any phrase that contains a word in one of several sentiment dictionaries (see section 5). The classifier has a precision of 96.5% for objective

[1] `http://www.cl.uni-heidelberg.de/~versley/HeiST/`

| System | Node Acc. | Root Acc. |
|---|---|---|
| **HeiST, only pos+neg sentences** | | |
| *supervised* | | |
| RNTN (tuned) | 0.776 | 0.687 |
| SVM (unigrams, coarse) | **0.850**** | **0.774**** |
| SVM (unigrams, fine) | 0.835** | 0.735 |
| *cross-lingual* | | |
| CLSA (simple feat.) | 0.823** | 0.737 |
| CLSA (complex feat.) | 0.810** | 0.738* |
| **Comparison: HeiST, all sentences** | | |
| *supervised* | | |
| RNTN (tuned) | 0.803 | 0.703 |

*/**: significantly better than RNTN ($p < 0.05$ / $p < 0.005$)

Table 2: HeiST baseline, cross-lingual projection, SVM.

| System | Node Acc. | Root Acc. |
|---|---|---|
| **Comparison: SSTb sample, pos+neg sentences** | | |
| *lexicon-based* | | |
| General Inquirer | 0.824 | 0.715 |
| SubjectivityClues | 0.820 | 0.695 |
| *supervised* | | |
| RNTN, 500 sent. | 0.704 | 0.526 |
| RNTN, 1000 sent. | 0.738 | 0.539 |
| RNTN, 1500 sent. | 0.756 | 0.569 |
| SVM, 500 sent. | 0.803 | 0.652 |
| SVM, 1000 sent. | 0.814 | 0.675 |
| SVM, 1500 sent. | 0.823 | 0.683 |
| RNTN, 6920 sent.[a] | 0.876 | 0.854 |
| SVM, 6920 sent.[a] | 0.846 | 0.794 |

[a]: published figures from Socher et al. (2013)

Table 3: Comparison figures on subsets of the Stanford Sentiment Treebank

phrases while catching about 66.7% of all objective nodes. While this would correspond to substantial savings (about a quarter of all nodes would be assigned the "neutral" label and not annotated), we would also lose a fraction of non-neutral phrase and introduce an unwanted bias (towards lexicon-based resources) into our dataset.

### 3.2 Baseline results

We use the existing RNTN implementation of Socher et al. (2013) to train and test supervised learning for sentiment composition, using cross-validation. For parameter tuning, we varied the number of vector dimensions as well as the size of the minibatches used in training, and found that the resulting classifier yields very sensible results compared to a similarly-sized sample from SSTb (see

Tables 2 and 3). We evaluate our results as in Socher et al. (2013): we consider the recall of positive and negative nodes while ignoring both neutral nodes and the difference between positive (+) and strongly positive (++) or between negative (-) and strongly negative (--) nodes, respectively. Socher et al. remove sentences with neutral overall sentiment in training as well as in testing, which seems to worsen the RNTN performance on our dataset (see Table 2), although other methods seem to be less affected by it. For comparability reasons, all other reported figures are based on Socher's non-neutral-sentences-only setting. In comparison results on SSTb (see Table 3), classification experiments from the English data also show poor results for the RNTN classifier at small data sizes, in parallel with anecdotal evidence on recurrent neural networks having trouble with small dataset sizes.[2]

## 4 Crosslingual Projection for Compositional Sentiment

Our crosslingual approach follows Banea et al. (2013) in assuming that machine translation of the target documents to the source language, then applying a source-language sentiment analysis, and finally projecting the result back to the target side will yield usable sentiment classification. In difference to previous approaches for cross-lingual sentiment analysis, however, our annotation transfer concerns not just analysis results for the complete sentence, but for individual syntactic nodes.

After translating the target-language trees using the Google Translate API, we parsed the sentences using the English model of the Stanford parser, and applied the RNTN model of Socher et al. (2013) trained on the English Stanford Sentiment Treebank, yielding a labeling for each syntactic node with a sentiment value. We then performed word alignment using the PostCAT word aligner (Ganchev et al., 2008) with a model trained on the OPUS version of the EuroParl corpus (Tiedemann, 2012), and alignment of syntactic nodes using the `Lingua::Align` toolbox for tree alignment Tiedemann (2010) with a model trained on the Smultron parallel treebank (Volk et al., 2010).

[2]Alec Radford (2015): *General Sequence Learning using Recurrent Neural Nets*, https://indico.io/blog/general-sequence-learning-using-recurrent-neural-nets/

| System | Node Acc. | Root Acc. |
|---|---|---|
| *Vote-only* | | |
| Klenner *et al.* | 0.769 | 0.646 |
| GermanPolarityClues | **0.815** | 0.648 |
| SentiWS | **0.815** | **0.711** |
| SentiMerge [0.0] | 0.660 | 0.577 |
| SentiMerge [0.23] | 0.718 | 0.604 |
| SentiMerge [0.4] | 0.724 | 0.604 |
| Amazon+Lasso | 0.499 | 0.426 |
| *Vote-and-flip* | | |
| Klenner *et al.* | 0.780 | 0.646 |
| GermanPolarityClues | 0.802 | **0.680** |
| SentiWS | **0.807** | 0.665 |
| SentiMerge [0.0] | 0.653 | 0.582 |
| SentiMerge [0.23] | 0.717 | 0.607 |
| SentiMerge [0.4] | 0.723 | 0.603 |
| Amazon+Lasso | 0.471 | 0.413 |

Table 4: Lexicon-based phrase labeling

Using the word alignment and our `Lingua::Align` model, we are able to map 98.6% of the target-language nodes to a corresponding node on the source (English) side, whereas the remaining nodes are assigned the same sentiment label as the root. As can be seen in table 2, a model that uses simpler features for `Lingua::Align` works less well than the full feature model. Considering that the RNTN on the Stanford Sentiment Treebank reaches 87.6% node accuracy and 85.4% root accuracy, we see that the crosslingual projection step induces a loss in accuracy, but still performs well in comparison to the approaches that use the HeiST training data.

## 5 Lexicon-based Approaches

Considering that the size of HeiST creates a sparse data problem for the RNTN learner, it is natural to ask whether we can improve the generalization capabilities of the system by either using a less-supervised approach or by generalizing over individual word forms to alleviate the sparse data problem.

### 5.1 General-domain lexicon

Several general-domain sentiment lexicons exist for German, including those of Klenner et al. (2009), Waltinger (2010a), Remus et al. (2010), and Emerson and Declerck (2014).

Klenner et al. (2009) created their polarity lexicon by semiautomatic extension of an existing one: starting from a set of 2866 adjective seeds, they looked for adjectives that often co-occur in coordinations with known sentiment-bearing adjectives, which were added to the lexicon after a manual filtering step. The current version of Klenner et al.'s PolArt lexicon also contains other parts of speech, and a list of *shifters* and *intensifiers* that interact with subjective terms.

The GermanPolarityClues lexicon of Waltinger (2010a) combines translation from English lexicons with a semi-automatic approach for merging and manually correcting lexicon entries.

The SentiWS lexicon (Remus et al., 2010) contains translations of the English General Inquirer (Stone et al., 1966), which have been translated via Google Translate, as well as a small number of terms that were mined from positive and negative product reviews, expanded using a collocation dictionary.

Finally, the SentiMerge lexicon (Emerson and Declerck, 2014) has been constructed as a Bayesian combination (i.e., averaging with imputation for missing entries) of the three resources above together with the *German SentiSpin* resource of Waltinger (2010b), which contains automatic (dictionary-based) translations of the SentiSpin lexicon of Tamura et al. (2005).

We tested all lexicons using two approaches: In the **vote-only** approach, the sentiment of a phrase is determined by the sum of the scores of the words in that phrase as they are assigned in the sentiment lexicon. In the **vote-and-flip** approach, we consider the average of the sentiment terms, but invert the sentiment value whenever a term from the *shifter* category of Klenner et al.'s lexicon is found within the yield of the node. A similar strategy was used in many papers on sentiment composition, usually with a performance rather close to the best system (see e.g. the CompoMC baseline in Choi and Cardie, 2008, or the Vote-and-Flip baseline in Choi and Cardie, 2009).

### 5.2 Near-domain lexicon construction

While the *filmrezensionen* web site offers a good number of reviews, the final collection is rather small. To complement our small in-domain dataset we use the most common way of getting text with document-level annotations, namely customer-written reviews from the movies section of `amazon.de` web site.

Perhaps expectedly, customer reviews do not focus exclusively on the film and its performance. Rather, it often occurs that customer reviews include a discussion of the physical (or other) medium that the film came on:[3]

(1) *I am with Lovefilm (now Prime) and tried to stream the series. Terrible! Always [issues with] loading time and loss of the stream. It seems that Amazon hasn't come to terms with the technology yet.*

Other reviews on Amazon match our domain fairly well, as in the following:

(2) *If this is truly a sequel to "Speed", it only shows in the second hour of the film. It's only then that deBont shows why he would be an action [film] specialist. Admittedly, even then we don't get the same tension as in the predecessor, but in any case it's better than the first hour of the film.*

While we found that a small quantity of data (20+20 hand-classified sentences) together with a 300-class LDA representation was sufficient to reach 100% accuracy in separating content-related versus media-related text, we found that filtering out the irrelevant texts made no difference for the mean square error, in sharp contrast to L1/Lasso regularization, which allows to learn a sparse lexicon.

## 6 Variants of the RNTN Model

While the RNTN model certainly performs well on the full Stanford Sentiment Treebank, it is likely that its performance on HeiST is suffering from sparse data problems, and that both words and particular constructions can be novel and unseen.

In syntactic parsing, Koo et al. (2008) and Candito and Seddah (2010) have shown that using Brown clusters can be beneficial for alleviating sparse data problems in parsing. In a similar vein, Popat et al. (2013) have successfully applied crosslingual clustering to generalizing over potentially unseen words

[3]German original text has been omitted for space reasons

| System | Node Acc. | Root Acc. |
|---|---|---|
| *supervised baseline* | | |
| RNTN, supervised | 0.776 | 0.687 |
| *RNTN + clusters* | | |
| newspaper text+Brown | 0.708 | 0.649 |
| movie reviews+Brown | **0.780** | **0.677** |
| features+k-means | 0.755 | 0.674 |
| *RNTN + split movie-review clusters* | | |
| split *SentiWS* | 0.774 | 0.676 |
| split *GermanPolarityClues* | **0.807** | **0.689** |
| *RNTN + lexicon-based replacement* | | |
| *replace-gold* | *0.844* | *0.730* |
| repl-GermanPolarityClues | 0.789** | 0.681 |
| repl-SentiMerge[0.23] | 0.780* | 0.648 |

Table 5: Incorporating additional information

in (document-level) sentiment analysis for English, Hindi and Marathi.

In our experiments, we follow Candito and Seddah (2010) in simply replacing words by clusters: in their experiments, even this simple procedure can yield an improvement, with improved results when the unlabeled data stems from the target domain. Since Brown clusters are mostly syntactic/semantic in nature and do not automatically distinguish positive or negative sentiment, we additionally performed multiple experiments to use clusters while incorporating additional sentiment information:

On one hand, we try to incorporate the judgements on the Amazon near-domain dataset more directly into the clusters by using the repeated bisecting K-Means algorithm as implemented in CLUTO (Zhao and Karypis, 2005), with previous/next word, part-of-speech tag, and the score of the containing review as features. On the other hand, we split the Brown clusters according to the sentiment value that they have in a particular sentiment lexicon (e.g. SentiMerge), yielding three clusters *01101+*, *01101-* and *01101?* instead of the original cluster *01101*.

As a final experiment, we consider replacing *only sentiment words* by a concatenation of their part-of-speech and the sentiment class (turning "*a great film*" into "*a JJ++ film*"), and leaving neutral words intact. As an upper baseline for this approach, we can get words' sentiment polarity directly from training and testing data, which yields the *replace-gold* entry in table 5.

| *rule type* | # in SSTb | # in HeiST |
|---|---|---|
| AVG | 119468 | 19228 |
| INV | 2158 | 289 |
| INT | 6614 | 646 |
| MWE | 18235 | 1936 |

Table 6: Rule types in SSTb and HeiST

## 7 Results and Error analysis

Looking at the results in tables 2, 4 and 5, we see that simple support vector machine classification is very effective for reproducing the positive/negative sentiment of nodes and complete sentences, followed by crosslingual projection and a simple averaging approach; we also see that handling negation in the *vote-and-flip* approach seems to lower the score, just as the best model with word clusters and splitting (using the *GermanPolarityClues* lexicon) performs better than the word-based RNTN approach, but less well than the lexicon by itself. Even the *replace-gold* upper baseline – replacing sentiment-carrying words by their sentiment label, which raises the performance substantially – gives results below the simpler SVM approach, which is counterintuitive.

### 7.1 Is it about Compositionality?

One motivation for using sub-sentence structure both in approaches for rule-based composition (as, e.g. in Taboada et al. (2011) and other lexicon-based approaches) as well as in more complex learning approaches such as RNN (Socher et al., 2011) and RNTN (Socher et al., 2013) is the idea that such approaches are able to model the interaction between sentiment-bearing words and sentiment-modifying words. An example for investigations based on this assumption is the work by Zhu et al. (2014), who contrast different lexicon-based approaches for handling negation with an RNTN model of negation and a modification of said model.

Given the results using a lexicon-based approach implementing the *vote-and-flip* heuristic in comparison to the *vote-only* heuristic, we found it worth investigating what specific types of interaction exist in compositional sentiment treebanks, also considering that Zhu et al.'s investigations yielded a more precise picture of the sentiment-shifting action of negators as a highly lexicalized phenomenon.

For our analysis, we grouped the production rules $s_p \rightarrow s_l s_r$ in a sentiment treebank into one of the following categories:

**AVG** A production is said to be *averaging* if the parent category is within the range of either daughter category. (e.g. *mind-numbingly good* would be the composition of a negative term and a positive term to a positive term, which still fits the averaging heuristic).

**INV** A production is said to be *inverting* if one daughter category is neutral and the other daughter category is on the other side on the spectrum (e.g. "not great" landing on the negative side)

**INT** A production is said to be *intensifying* if the parent category is on the same side of the scale as the daughters but more extreme.

**MWE** A production is said to be a *multi-word* production if the daughter categories are classified as neutral while the parent category is not.[4]

As can be seen in table 6, the number of *inverting* and *intensifying* productions is dwarfed, both for the SST and for HeiST, by the number of *multi-word* rules. While it is likely that these counts are slightly distorted by noise in the annotation (as both datasets are the product of crowdsourcing), this fact is remarkable and merits further investigation.

**Types of multiword expressions** If we try to group the nodes with a "multiword" production, we can distinguish at least the following categories:

- **aspect descriptions**: In some cases, an adjective is specifically used to describe a (positive or negative) aspect of the movie, such as an *elaborate continuation*, or an *expanded vision*, where individual words have a neutral sentiment label (and conceivable could have been used in a non-aspect-specific way to convey a neutral or negative sentiment, such as an *elaborate perversion*, or an *expanded nightshift*) Similarly, *wenig Handlung* (not much action) has a negative meaning as a construction despite "*wenig*" (few/not much) not having a negative meaning itself.
- **expression strengthening** is a phenomenon that occurs when a term is judged as neutral by annotators by itself, but gains a sentiment value when paired with an intensifier or negator. For example, *intrusive* was labeled as neutral in SSTb, but *simply intrusive* as negative.
- **comparatives** are a very regular construction where too much of something is almost always bad: *too long, too insistent, too much, too many* are all negative in SSTb, just as *zu viel* (too many) and *zu wenig* (not enough) and other counterparts in HeiST are negative.
- **true constructions** such as *plot holes* or *historically significant* in SSTB, or *ruhigen Gewissens* (with a calm conscience) and *Finger weg* (don't touch it) in HeiST are both a problem for approaches relying purely on composition and not regular enough that we would expect to model it as a regular construction.

Some of the neutral-to-positive or neutral-to-negative transitions don't seem well-motivated and may be regarded as artifacts from the crowdsourcing, as *does n't, is n't* and *are n't* are negative in SSTb whereas *'s not, do n't* and *did n't* get a neutral label. In HeiST, *nicht immer* (not always) as well as *nicht ganz* (not quite) are negative, whereas *auch nicht* (neither) and *nicht so* (not as) or *nicht unbedingt* (not necessarily) are neutral.

The MWE productions seem to overlap with well-known linguistic phenomena – consider Fahrni and Klenner (2008) and their claim that most adjectives have a polarity that is dependent on the target they modify instead of having a '*prior*' polarity that holds independently of the target, or the observation of Su and Markert (2009) that sentiment should be dependent on word senses instead of word forms (which would capture a large number of examples within the *expression strengthening* category). Yet, others may be idiosyncracies introduced by the crowdsourcing process, and powerful learners such as RNTN or the approach of Hall et al. (2014) will gain performance from simply memorizing the idiosyncracies of the data when there is

[4]The MWE category also contains a small number – about 5% of total MWE productions – of positive-to-neutral and negative-to-neutral productions, which we found to be predominantly noise from the crowdsourcing process.

| | | SVM | | CLSA | | RNTN | | *+replace-gold* | |
|---|---|---|---|---|---|---|---|---|---|
| Type | Total | Corr | Prec | Corr | Prec | Corr | Prec | Corr | Prec |
| AVG | 6341 | 3408 | 0.546 | 3158 | 0.506 | 3604 | 0.577 | 4309 | 0.690 |
| MWE | 1638 | 369 | 0.225 | 538 | 0.328 | 538 | 0.359 | 546 | 0.333 |
| INT | 612 | 370 | 0.605 | 362 | 0.592 | 413 | 0.675 | 470 | 0.768 |
| ID | 392 | 283 | 0.722 | 269 | 0.686 | 286 | 0.730 | 323 | 0.824 |
| INV | 259 | 76 | 0.293 | 65 | 0.251 | 93 | 0.359 | 79 | 0.305 |

Table 7: Precision of rules with non-neutral parent label (ID: daughters and parent have identical labels)

enough of it – because of the way the Stanford Sentiment Treebank is constructed, phrases always have the same (context-independent) label, while we may get a more accurate (and possibly different) picture from introducing additional means of quality control (which in turn increases the necessary investment for such a sentiment treebank).

### 7.2 Contrasting SVM and RNTN behaviour

In table 7, we tabulated the classification accuracy for the parent node in different types of productions in HeiST. In this evaluation, we counted a production as correct whenever the parent node has the right sentiment label (in parallel with the *labeled recall* in syntactic evaluation), ignoring for the moment the question whether the production produced by a system falls into the same category. It is easy to see that AVG-type productions are the least error-prone for all classifiers, whereas MWE and INV productions pose a significant challenge for the models. We also see that on these challenging production, the RNTN performs better than the other methods.

## 8 Summary

We presented a novel dataset for subsentential sentiment classification, which uses the same conventions as the Stanford Sentiment Treebank (SSTb), which is the only German resource of this type besides the smaller (270 sentences) MLSA corpus (Clematide et al., 2012). We performed a systematic exploration into supervised, cross-lingual, and lexicon-based approaches on this dataset and found that, paradoxically, the performance of the state-of-the-art recursive neural tensor network (RNTN) models are severely impeded in this data-sparse situation, unlike latent-variable models for syntax which can deal with such conditions quite well: Lavelli and Corazza (2009), for example, reports that the best results for parsing on the very small TUT treebank (slightly more than 2000 sentences) can be achieved using a PCFG-LA model.

We showed that a wide variety of models – from lexicon-based sentiment prediction over SVM with unigram features to crosslingual classification – performs better than the RNTN, and that methods to improve RNTN performance that work in other settings (syntax) do not offer any easy fix.

In a second step, we took a closer look at the crowdsourced data in order to explain certain counterintuitive results (such as the fact that most sentiment lexicons do not benefit from negation handling, or that the *upper* baseline achievable with the RNTN by getting gold-standard information on positive and negative words is at about the same level as our SVM classifier), and found that SSTb-type resources show marked differences from e.g., the MLSA dataset as they incorporate *multiword* items, but seem to be challenging for the study of compositionality due to noise that is not present in expert-annotated resources.

## References


Banea, C., Mihalcea, R., and Wiebe, J. (2013). Porting multilingual subjectivity resources across languages. *IEEE Transactions on Affective Computing*, 2(4):211–225.

Candito, M.-H. and Seddah, D. (2010). Parsing word clusters. In *Proceedings of the First Workshop on Statistical Parsing of Morphologically-Rich Languages (SPMRL 2010)*.

Choi, Y. and Cardie, C. (2008). Learning with compositional semantics as structural inference for subsentential sentiment analysis. In *Proceedings of the 2008 Conference on Empirical Methods in Natural Language Processing (EMNLP 2008)*.

Choi, Y. and Cardie, C. (2009). Adapting a polarity lexicon using integer linear programming for domain-specific sentiment classification. In *Proceedings of the 2009 Conference on Empirical Methods in Natural Language Processing*.

Clematide, S., Gindl, S., Klenner, M., Petrakis, S., Remus, R., Ruppenhofer, J., Waltinger, U., and Wiegand, M. (2012). MLSA – a multi-layered reference corpus for german sentiment analysis. In *Proceedings of the Eigth International Conference on Language Resources and Evaluation (LREC 2012)*.

Dong, L., Wei, F., Zhou, M., and Xu, K. (2014). Adaptive multi-compositionality for recursive neural models with applications to sentiment analysis. In *AAAI 2014*.

Duh, K., Fujino, A., and Nagata, M. (2011). Is machine translation ripe for cross-lingual sentiment classification. In *Proceedings of the 49th Annual Meeting of the Association for Computational Linguistics:shortpapers*.

Emerson, G. and Declerck, T. (2014). SentiMerge: Combining sentiment lexicons in a Bayesian framework. In *Proceedings of the Workshop on Lexical and Grammatical Resources for Language Processing*.

Fahrni, A. and Klenner, M. (2008). Old wine or warm beer: Target-specific sentiment analysis of adjectives. In *Affective Language in Human and Machine (AISB 2008)*.

Ganchev, K., Graca, J., and Taskar, B. (2008). Better alignments = better translations? In *Procecedings of the 46th Annual Meeting of the Association of Computational Linguistics (ACL 2008)*.

Hall, D., Durrett, G., and Klein, D. (2014). Less grammar, more features. In *ACL 2014*.

Klenner, M., Petrakis, S., and Fahrni, A. (2009). PolArt: A robust tool for sentiment analysis. In *NODALIDA 2009*.

Koo, T., Carreras, X., and Collins, M. (2008). Simple semi-supervised dependency parsing. In *ACL 2008*.

Lavelli, A. and Corazza, A. (2009). The Berkeley Parser at the EVALITA constituency parsing task. In *Proceedings of the Workshop on Evaluation of NLP Tools for Italian (EVALITA 2009)*.

Nakagawa, T., Inui, K., and Kurohashi, S. (2010). Dependency tree-based sentiment classification using crfs with hidden variables. In *Human Language Technologies: The 2010 Annual Conference of the North American Chapter of the ACL*.

Pang, B. and Lee, L. (2005). Seeing stars: Exploiting class relationships for sentiment categorization with respect to rating scales. In *ACL 2005*.

Petrov, S., Barett, L., Thibaux, R., and Klein, D. (2006). Learning accurate, compact, and interpretable tree annotation. In *COLING-ACL 2006*.

Popat, K., Balamurali, A. R., Bhattacharyya, P., and Haffari, G. (2013). The haves and the have-nots: Leveraging unlabelled corpora for sentiment analysis. In *Proceedings of ACL 2013*.

Rafferty, A. and Manning, C. D. (2008). Parsing three German treebanks: Lexicalized and unlexicalized baselines. In *ACL'08 workshop on Parsing German*.

Remus, R., Quasthoff, U., and Heyer, G. (2010). SentiWS - a publicly-available German-language resource for sentiment analysis. In *Proceedings of the 7th International Language Resources and Evaluation Conference (LREC 2010)*.

Samuelsson, Y. and Volk, M. (2004). Automatic node insertion for treebank deepening. In *Proceedings of the 3rd Workshop on Treebanks and Linguistic Theories (TLT 2004)*.

Socher, R., Hurval, B., Manning, C. D., and Ng, A. Y. (2012). Semantic compositionality through recursive matrix-vector spaces. In *EMNLP 2012*.

Socher, R., Pennington, J., Huang, E. H., Ng, A. Y., and Manning, C. D. (2011). Semi-supervised recursive autoencoders for predicting sentiment distributions. In *EMNLP 2011*.

Socher, R., Perelygin, A., Wu, J., Chuang, J., Manning, C., Ng, A., and Potts, C. (2013). Recursive deep models for semantic compositionality over a sentiment treebank. In *Conference on Empirical Methods in Natural Language Processing (EMNLP 2013)*.

Stone, P. J., Dunphy, D. C., and Smith, M. S. (1966).

*The General Inquirer: A Computer Approach to Content Analysis*. MIT Press.

Su, F. and Markert, K. (2009). Subjectivity recognition on word senses via semi-supervised mincuts. In *Proceedings of NAACL 2009*.

Taboada, M., Brooke, J., Tofilofski, M., Voll, K., and Stede, M. (2011). Lexicon-based methods for sentiment analysis. *Computational Linguistics*, 37(2):267–307.

Tamura, H., Inui, T., and Okumura, M. (2005). Extracting semantic orientation of words using spin model. In *Proceedings of the 43rd Annual Meeting of the Association for Computational Linguistics (ACL 2005)*.

Tiedemann, J. (2010). Lingua-align: An experimental toolbox for automatic tree-to-tree alignment. In *Proceedings of LREC 2010*.

Tiedemann, J. (2012). Parallel data, tools and interfaces in OPUS. In *Proceedings of the 8th International Conference on Language Resources and Evaluation (LREC'2012)*.

Volk, M., Göhring, A., Marek, T., and Samuelsson, Y. (2010). SMULTRON (version 3.0) – The Stockholm MULtilingual parallel TReebank. `http://www.cl.uzh.ch/research/parallelcorpora/paralleltreebanks_en.html`.

Waltinger, U. (2010a). GermanPolarityClues: A lexical resource for German sentiment analysis. In *Proceedings of the 7th International Language Resources and Evaluation Conference (LREC 2010)*.

Waltinger, U. (2010b). Sentiment analysis reloaded - an empirical study on machine learning.based sentiment classification using polarity clues. In *Proceedings of the 6th International Conference on Web Information Systems and Technologies (WEBIST 2010)*.

Wan, X. (2009). Co-training for cross-lingual sentiment classification. In *Proceedings of the 47th Annual Meeting of the ACL and the 4th IJCNLP of the AFNLP (ACL-IJCNLP 2009)*.

Wang, S. and Manning, C. D. (2012). Baselines and bigrams: Simple, good sentiment and topic classification. In *Proceedings of ACL 2012*.

Yessenalina, A. and Cardie, C. (2011). Compositional matrix-space models for sentiment analysis. In *EMNLP 2011*.

Zhao, Y. and Karypis, G. (2005). Hierarchical clustering algorithms for document datasets. *Data Mining and Knowledge Discovery*, 10:141–168.

Zhu, X., Guo, H., Mohammad, S., and Kiritchenko, S. (2014). An empirical study on the effect of negation words on sentiment. In *ACL 2014*.

# Cost Optimization for Crowdsourcing Translation

**Mingkun Gao, Wei Xu** and **Chris Callison-Burch**
Computer and Information Science Department
University of Pennsylvania, Philadelphia, PA, USA
{gmingkun, xwe, ccb}@seas.upenn.edu

## Abstract

Crowdsourcing makes it possible to create translations at much lower cost than hiring professional translators. However, it is still expensive to obtain the millions of translations that are needed to train statistical machine translation systems. We propose two mechanisms to reduce the cost of crowdsourcing while maintaining high translation quality. First, we develop a method to reduce redundant translations. We train a linear model to evaluate the translation quality on a sentence-by-sentence basis, and fit a threshold between acceptable and unacceptable translations. Unlike past work, which always paid for a fixed number of translations for each source sentence and then chose the best from them, we can stop earlier and pay less when we receive a translation that is good enough. Second, we introduce a method to reduce the pool of translators by quickly identifying bad translators after they have translated only a few sentences. This also allows us to rank translators, so that we re-hire only good translators to reduce cost.

## 1 Introduction

Crowdsourcing is a promising new mechanism for collecting large volumes of annotated data at low cost. Many NLP researchers have started creating speech and language data through crowdsourcing (for example, Snow et al. (2008), Callison-Burch and Dredze (2010) and others). One NLP application that has been the focus of crowdsourced data collection is statistical machine translation (SMT) which requires large bilingual sentence-aligned parallel corpora to train translation models. Crowdsourcing's low cost has made it possible to hire people to create sufficient volumes of translation in order to train SMT systems (for example, Ambati and Vogel (2010), Zbib et al. (2012), Post et al. (2012), Zbib et al. (2013)).

However, crowdsourcing is not perfect, and one of its most pressing challenges is how to ensure the quality of the data that is created by it. Unlike in more traditional employment scenarios, where annotators are pre-vetted and their skills are clear, in crowdsourcing very little is known about the annotators. They are not professional translators, and there are no built-in mechanisms for testing their language skills. They complete tasks without any oversight. Thus, translations produced via crowdousrcing may be low quality. Previous work has addressed this problem, showing that non-professional translators hired on Amazon Mechanical Turk (MTurk) can achieve professional-level quality, by soliciting multiple translations of each source sentence and then choosing the best translation (Zaidan and Callison-Burch, 2011).

In this paper we focus on a different aspect of crowdsourcing than Zaidan and Callison-Burch (2011). We attempt to achieve the same high quality while **minimizing the associated costs**. We propose two complementary methods: (1) We reduce the number of translations that we solicit for each source sentence. Instead of soliciting a fixed number of translations for each foreign sentence, we stop soliciting translations after we get an acceptable one. We do so by building models to distinguish between



*Human Language Technologies: The 2015 Annual Conference of the North American Chapter of the ACL*, pages 705–713,
Denver, Colorado, May 31 – June 5, 2015. ©2015 Association for Computational Linguistics

acceptable translations and unacceptable ones. (2) We reduce the number of workers we hire, and retain only high quality translators by quickly identifying and filtering out workers who produce low quality translations. Our work stands in contrast with Zaidan and Callison-Burch (2011) who always solicited and paid for a fixed number of translations for each source sentence, and who had no model of annotator quality.

In this paper we demonstrate that:

- Our model can predict whether a given translation is acceptable with high accuracy, substantially reducing the number of redundant translations needed for every source segment.
- Translators can be ranked well even when observing only small amounts of data. Compared with a gold standard ranking, we achieve a correlation of 0.94 after seeing the translations of only 20 sentences from each worker. Therefore, bad workers can be filtered out quickly.
- We can achieve a similar BLEU score as Zaidan and Callison-Burch (2011) at half the cost using our cost optimizing methods.

## 2 Problem Setup

We start with a corpus of source sentences to be translated, and we may solicit one or more translation for every sentence in the corpus. Our targeted task is to assemble a single high quality translation for each source sentence while minimizing the associated cost. This process can be repeated to obtain multiple high quality translations.

We study the data collected by Zaidan and Callison-Burch (2011) through Amazon's Mechanical Turk. They hired Turkers to translate 1792 Urdu sentences from the 2009 NIST Urdu-English Open Machine Translation Evaluation set[1]. A total of 52 Turkers contributed translations. Turkers also filled out a survey about their language skills and their countries of origin. Each Urdu sentence was translated by 4 non-professional translators (the Turkers) and 4 professional translators hired by the LDC. The cost of non-professional translation was $0.10 per sentence and we estimate the cost of professional translation to be approximately $0.30 per word (or $6 per sentence, with 20 words on average).

Following Zaidan and Callison-Burch (2011), we use BLEU (Papineni et al., 2002) to gauge the quality of human translations. We can compute the expected quality of professional translation by comparing each of the professional translators against the other 3. This results in an average BLEU score of 42.38. In comparison, the average Turker translations score only 28.13 without quality control. Zaidan and Callison-Burch trained a MERT (Och, 2003; Zaidan, 2009) model to select one non-professional translation out of the four and pushed the quality of crowdsourcing translation to 38.99, closer to the expected quality of professional translation. They used a small amount of professional translations (10%) as calibration data to estimate the goodness of the non-professional translation. The component costs of their approach are the 4 non-professional translations for each source sentence, and the professional translations for the calibration data.

Although Zaidan and Callison-Burch demonstrated that non-professional translation was significantly cheaper than professionals, we are interested in further reducing the costs. Cost reduction plays an important role if we want to assemble a large enough parallel corpus to train a statistical machine translation system which typically require millions of translated sentences. Here, we introduce several methods for reducing the number of non-professional translations while still maintaining high quality.

## 3 Estimating Translation Quality

We use a linear regression model[2] to predict a quality score ($score(t) \in \mathbb{R}$) for an input translation $t$.

$$score(t) = \vec{w} \cdot \vec{f}(t)$$

where $\vec{w}$ is the associated weight vector and $\vec{f}(t)$ is the feature vector of the translation $t$.

We replicate the feature set used by Zaidan and Callison-Burch (2011) in their MERT model:

- Sentence-level features: 9 features based on

[1]LDC Catalog number LDC2010T23

[2]We used WEKA package: http://www.cs.waikato.ac.nz/ml/weka/

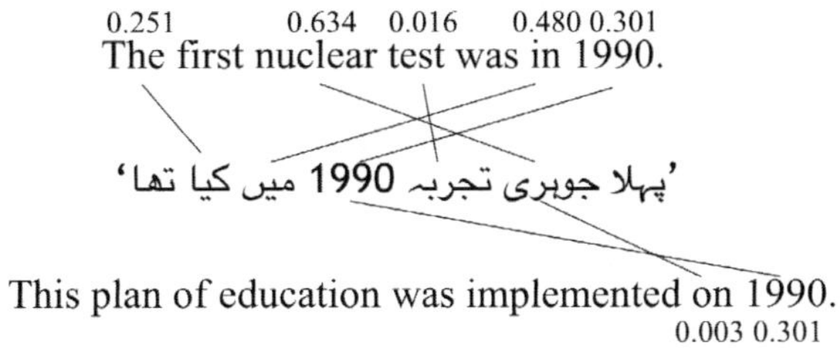


Figure 1: Example bilingual features for two crowd-sourced translations of an Urdu sentence. The numbers are alignment probabilities for each aligned word. The bilingual feature is the average of these probabilities, thus 0.240 for the good translation and 0.043 for the bad translation. Some words are not aligned if potential word pairs don't exist in bilingual training corpus.

language model, sentence length and edit distance to other translations.

- Worker-level features: 15 features based on worker's language ability, location and average sentence-level scores.
- Ranking features: 3 features based on the judgments of monolingual English speakers' ranking the translations from best to worst.
- Calibration features: 1 feature based on the average BLEU score of a worker's translations provided is computed against professional references.

We additionally introduce a new bilingual feature based on IBM Model 1. We align words between each candidate translation and its corresponding source sentence. The bilingual feature is the average of its alignment probabilities between words in the source sentence and words in the Turker's translation. In Figure 1, we show how the bilingual feature allows us to distinguish between a valid translation (top) and an invalid/spammy translation (bottom).

## 4 Reducing the Number of Translations

The first way that we optimize cost is to solicit fewer redundant translations. The strategy is to recognize when we have got a good translation of a source sentence and to immediately stop purchasing additional translations of that sentence. The crux of this method is to decide whether a translation is 'good enough,' in which case we do not gain any benefit from paying for another redundant translation.

---

**Algorithm 1** How good is good enough

**Input**: $\delta$, the allowable deviation from the expected upper bound on BLEU score (using all redundant translations); $\alpha$, the upper bound BLEU score; a training set $S = \{\vec{f}^s_{i,j}, y^s_{i,j})^{j=1..m}_{i=1..n}\}$ and a validation set $V = \{(\vec{f}^v_{i,j}, y^v_{i,j})^{j=1..m}_{i=1..n}\}$ where $\vec{f}_{i,j}$ is the feature vector for $t_{i,j}$ which is the $jth$ translation of the source sentence $s_i$ and $y_{i,j}$ is the label for $\vec{f}_{i,j}$.

**Output**: $\theta$, the threshold between acceptable and unacceptable translations; $\vec{w}$, a linear regression model parameter.

```
initialize θ ← 0, w ← ∅
w' ← train a linear regression model on S
maxbleu ← select best translations for each
    s_i ∈ S based on the model parameter w' and
    record the highest model predicted BLEU score
while θ ≠ maxbleu do
    for i ← 1 to n do
        for j ← 1 to m do
            if w' · f^v_{i,j} > θ ∧ j < m then select
    t^v_{i,j} for s_i and break
            if j == m then select t^v_{i,m} for s_i
    q ← calculate translation quality for V
    if q > δ · α then break
    else θ = θ + stepsize
w ← train a linear regression model on S ∪ V
Return: θ and model parameter w
```

---

Our translation reduction method allows us to set an empirical definition of 'good enough'. We define an Oracle upper bound $\alpha$ to be the estimated BLEU score using the full set of non-professional translations. We introduce a parameter $\delta$ to set the allowable degradation in translation quality. We train a model to search for a threshold $\theta$ between acceptable and unacceptable translations for a specific value of $\delta$. For instance, we may fix $\delta$ at 95%, meaning that the resulting BLEU score should not drop below 95% of the $\alpha$ after reducing the number of translations.

For a new translation, our model scores it, and if its score is higher than $\theta$, then we do not solicit another translation. Otherwise, we continue to so-

| $\delta(\%)$ | BLEU Score | # Trans. |
|---|---|---|
| 90 | 36.26 | 1.63 |
| 91 | 36.66 | 1.69 |
| 92 | 36.93 | 1.78 |
| 93 | 37.23 | 1.85 |
| 94 | 37.48 | 1.93 |
| 95 | 38.05 | 2.21 |
| 96 | 38.16 | 2.30 |
| 97 | 38.48 | 2.47 |
| 98 | 38.67 | 2.59 |
| 99 | 38.95 | 2.78 |
| 100 | 39.54 | 3.18 |

Table 1: The relationship between $\delta$ (the allowable deviation from the expected upper bound on BLEU score), the BLEU score for translations selected by models from partial sets and the average number of translation candidates set for each source sentence (*# Trans*).

licit translations. Algorithm 1 details the process of model training and searching for $\theta$.

### 4.1 Experiments

We divide data into a training set (10%), a validation set (10%) and a test set (80%). Each source sentence has four translations in total. We use the validation set to search for $\theta$. The Oracle upper bound on BLEU is set to be 40.13 empirically. We then vary the value of $\delta$ from 90% to 100%, and sweep values of $\theta$ by incrementing it in step sizes of 0.01. We report results based on a five-fold cross validation, rotating the training, validation and test sets.

#### 4.1.1 Baseline and upper bound

The baseline selection method of randomly picking one translation for each source sentence achieves a BLEU score of 29.56. To establish an upper bound on translation quality, we perform an oracle experiment to select best translation for each source segment from full sets of candidates. It reaches a BLEU score of 40.13.

#### 4.1.2 Translation reducing method

Table 1 shows the results for translation reducing method. The $\delta$ variable correctly predicts the deviation in BLEU score when compared to using the full set of translations. If we set $\delta < 0.95$ then we lose 2 BLEU points, but we cut the cost of translations in half, since we pay for only two translations of each source segment on average.

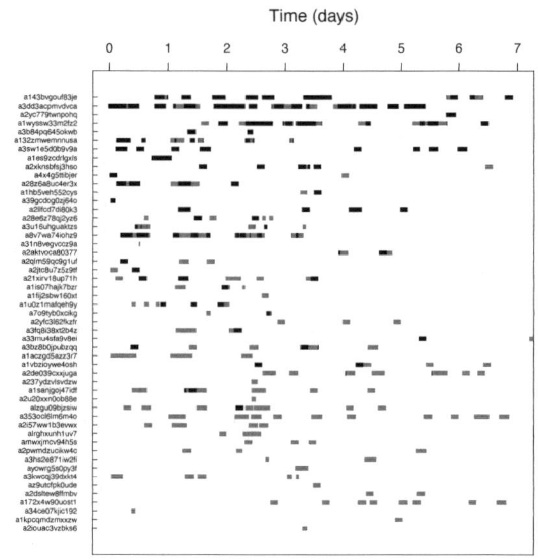


Figure 2: A time-series plot of all of the translations produced by Turkers (identified by their WorkerID serial number). Turkers are sorted with the best translator at the top of the y-axis. Each tick represent a single translation and black means better than average quality.

## 5 Choosing Better Translators

The second mechanism that we use to optimize cost is to reduce the number of non-professional translators that we hire. Our goal is to quickly identify whether Turkers are good or bad translators, so that we can continue to hire only the good translators and stop hiring the bad translators after they are identified as such. Before presenting our method, we first demonstrate that Turkers produce consistent quality translations over time.

### 5.1 Turkers' behavior in translating sentences

Do Turkers produce good (or bad) translations consistently or not? Are some Turkers consistent and others not? We used the professional translations as a gold-standard to analyze the individual Turkers, and we found that most Turkers' performance stayed surprisingly consistent over time.

Figure 2 illustrates the consistency of workers' quality by plotting quality of their individual translations on a timeline. The translation quality is computed based on the BLEU against professional translations. Each tick represent a single translation and depicts the BLEU score using two colors. The tick is black if its BLEU score is higher than the median and it is red otherwise. Good translators tend to produce consistently good translations and bad translators rarely produce good translations.

### 5.2 Evaluating Rankings

We use weighted Pearson correlation (Pozzi et al., 2012) to evaluate our ranking of workers against gold standard ranking. Since workers translated different number of sentences, it is more important to rank the workers who translated more sentences correctly. Taking the importance of workers into consideration, we set a weight to each worker using the number of translations he or she submitted when calculating the correlation. Given two lists of worker scores *x* and *y* and the weight vector *w*, the weighted Pearson correlation $\rho$ can be calculated as:

$$\rho(x, y; w) = \frac{cov(x, y; w)}{\sqrt{cov(x, x; w) cov(y, y; w)}} \quad (1)$$

where $cov$ is weighted covariance:

$$cov(x, y; w) = \frac{\sum_i w_i (x_i - m(x; w))(y_i - m(y; w))}{\sum_i w_i} \quad (2)$$

and $m$ is weighted mean:

$$m(x; w) = \frac{\sum_i w_i x_i}{\sum_i w_i} \quad (3)$$

### 5.3 Automatically Ranking Translators

We introduce two approaches to rank workers using a small portion of the work that they submitted. The strategy is to filter out bad workers, and to select the best translation from translations provided by the remaining workers. We propose two different ranking methods:

**Ranking workers using their first $k$ translations** We rank the Turkers using their first few translations by comparing their translations against the professional translations of those sentences. Ranking workers on gold standard data would allow us to discard bad workers. This is similar to the idea of a qualification test in MTurk.

**Ranking workers using a model** In addition to ranking workers by comparing them against a gold standard, we also attempt to automatically predict their ranks with a model. We use the linear regression model to score each translation and rank workers by their model predicted performance. The model predicted performance of the worker $w$ is:

$$performance(w) = \frac{\sum_{t \in T_w} score(t)}{|T_w|} \quad (4)$$

where $T_w$ is the set of translations completed by the worker $w$ and $score(t)$ is the model predicted score for translation $t$.

### 5.4 Experiments

After we rank workers, we keep top-ranked workers and select the best translation only from their translations. For both ranking approaches, we vary the number of good workers that we retain.

We report both rankings' correlation with the gold standard ranking. Since the top worker threshold is varied and since we change the value of $k$ in first $k$ sentence ranking, we have a different test set in different settings. Each test set excludes any items which were used to rank the workers, or which did not have any translations from the top workers according to our rankings.

#### 5.4.1 Gold standard and Baseline

We evaluate ranking quality using the weighted Pearson correlation ($\rho$) compared with the gold standard ranking of workers. To establish the gold standard ranking, we score each Turker based on the BLEU score comparing all of his or her translations to the corresponding professional references.

We use the ranking by the MERT model developed by Zaidan and Callison-Burch (2011) as baseline. It achieves a correlation of 0.73 against the gold standard ranking.

#### 5.4.2 Ranking workers using their first $k$ translations

Without using any model, we rank workers using their first $k$ translations. We select best translation of each source sentence from the top ranked worker who translated that sentence.

Table 2 shows the results of Pearson correlations for different value of $k$. As $k$ increases, our rankings

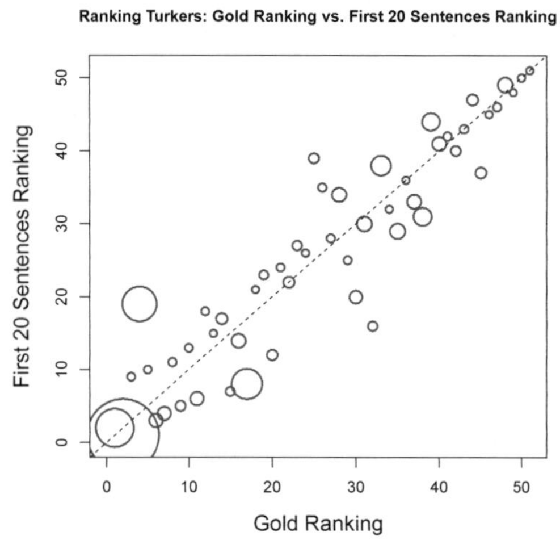


Figure 3: Correlation between gold standard ranking and ranking computed using the first 20 sentences as calibration. Each bubble represents a worker. The radius of each bubble shows the relative volume of translations completed by the worker. The weighted correlation is 0.94.

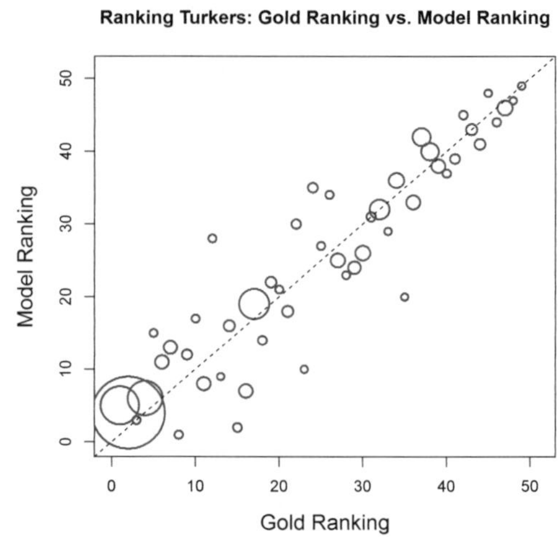


Figure 4: Correlation between gold standard ranking and our model's ranking. The corresponding weighted correlation is 0.95.

fit the gold ranking better. Consequently, we can decide whether to continue to hire a worker in a very short time after analyzing the first $k$ sentences ($k \leq 20$) provided by each worker. Figure 3 shows the correlation of gold ranking and the ranking based on workers' first 20 sentences.

### 5.4.3 Ranking workers using a model

We train a linear regression model on 10% of the data to rank workers. We use the model to select the best translation in one of two ways:

- Using the model's prediction of workers' rank, and selecting the translation from the best worker.
- Using the model's score for each translation and selecting the highest scoring translation of each source sentence.

Table 3 shows that the model trained on all features achieves a very high correlation with the gold standard ranking (Pearson's $\rho$ = 0.95), and a BLEU score of 39.80.

Figure 4 presents a visualization of the gold ranking and model ranking. The workers who produce the largest number of translations (large bubbles in the figure) are ranked extremely well.

### 5.5 Filtering out bad workers

Ranking translators would allow us to reduce costs by only re-hiring top workers. Table 4 shows what happens when we vary the percentage of top ranked workers we retain. In general, the model does a good job of picking the best translations from the remaining good translators. Compared to actually knowing the gold ranking, the model loses only 0.55 BLEU when we filter out 75% of the workers. In this case we only need to solicit two translations for each source sentence on average.

## 6 Cost Analysis

We have introduced several ways of significantly lowering the costs associated with crowdsourcing translations when a large amount of data are solicited (on the order of millions of samples):

- We show that after we have collected one translation of a source sentence, we can consult a model that predicts whether its quality is sufficiently high or whether we should pay to have the sentence re-translated. The cost savings for non-professionals here comes from reducing the number of redundant translations. We

| Proportion of Calibration Data | | $\rho$ |
|---|---|---|
| First k sentences | Percentage | |
| 1 | 0.7% | 0.21 |
| 2 | 1.3% | 0.38 |
| 3 | 2.0% | 0.41 |
| 4 | 2.7% | 0.56 |
| 5 | 3.3% | 0.70 |
| 10 | 6.6% | 0.81 |
| 20 | 13.3% | 0.94 |
| 30 | 19.9% | 0.96 |
| 40 | 26.6% | 0.98 |
| 50 | 33.2% | 0.98 |
| 60 | 39.8% | 0.98 |

Table 2: Pearson Correlations for calibration data in different proportion. The percentage column shows what proportion of the whole data set is used for calibration.

| Feature Set | $\rho$ | BLEU | |
|---|---|---|---|
| | | rank | score |
| (S)entence features | 0.80 | 36.66 | 37.84 |
| (W)orker features | 0.78 | 36.92 | 36.92 |
| (R)anking features | 0.81 | 36.94 | 35.69 |
| Calibration features | 0.93 | 38.27 | 38.27 |
| S+W+R features | 0.86 | 37.39 | 38.69 |
| S+W+R+Bilingual features | 0.88 | 37.59 | 39.23 |
| All features | **0.95** | **38.37** | **39.80** |
| Baseline (MERT) | 0.73 | - | 38.99 |

Table 3: Correlation ($\rho$) and translation quality for the various features used by our model. Translation quality is computed by selecting best translations based on model-predicted ranking for workers (rank) and model-predicted scores for translations (score). Here we do not filter out bad workers when selecting the best translation.

can save almost half of the cost associated with non-professional translations to get 95% of the translation quality using the full set of redundant translations.

- We show that we can quickly identify bad translators, either by having them first translate a small number of sentences to be tested against professional translations, or by estimating their performance using a feature-based linear regression model. The cost savings for non-professionals here comes from not hiring

| Top (%) | BLEU | | | | # Trans |
|---|---|---|---|---|---|
| | random | model | gold | $\Delta$ | |
| 25 | 29.85 | 38.53 | 39.08 | 0.55 | 1.95 |
| 50 | 29.80 | 38.40 | 39.00 | 0.60 | 2.73 |
| 75 | 29.76 | 38.37 | 38.98 | 0.61 | 3.48 |
| 100 | 29.83 | 38.37 | 38.99 | 0.62 | 4.00 |

Table 4: A comparison of the translation quality when we retain the top translators under different rankings. The rankings shown are random, the model's ranking (using all features from Table 3) and the gold ranking. $\Delta$ is the difference between the BLEU scores for the gold ranking and the model ranking. # Trans is the average number of translations needed for each source sentence.

bad workers. Similarly, we reduce the non-professional translation cost to the half of the original cost.

- In both cases we need some amount of professionally translated materials to use as a gold standard for calibration. Although the unit cost for each reference is much higher than the unit cost for each non-professional translation, the cost associated with non-professional translations can dominate the total cost since the large amount of data need to be collected. Thus, we focus on reducing cost associated with non-professional translations.

## 7 Related Work

Sheng et al. (2008) focused on training a machine learning model from noisy labels. We cannot always get high-quality labeled data from crowdsourcing, but we can still ensure that a model trained on the data is accurate by redundantly labeling the data. Sheng et al. (2008) proposed a framework for repeated-labeling that resolves the uncertainty in labeling via majority voting. The experimental results show that a model's accuracy is improved even if labels in its training data are noisy and imperfect. As long as the integrated quality (the probability of the integrated labeling being correct) is higher than 0.5, repeated labeling benefits model training.

Passonneau and Carpenter (2013) created a Bayesian model of annotation. They applied it to the problem of word sense annotation. Passonneau and Carpenter (2013) also proposed an approach to detect and avoid spam workers. They measured the performance of worker by comparing worker's labels to the current majority labels. Workers with bad performance can be identified and blocked.

Lin et al. (2014) examined the relationship between worker accuracy and budget in the context of using crowdsourcing to train a machine learning classifier. They show that if the goal is to train a classifier on the labels, that the properties of the classifier will determine whether it is better to re-label data (resulting in higher quality labels) or get more single labeled items (of lower quality). They showed that classifiers with weak inductive bias benefit more from relabeling, and that relabeling is more important when worker accuracy is low.

Novotney and Callison-Burch (2010) showed a similar result for training an automatic speech recognition (ASR) system. When creating training data for an ASR system, given a fixed budget, their system's accuracy was higher when it is trained on more low quality transcription data compared to when it was trained on fewer high quality transcriptions.

## 8 Conclusion

In this paper, we propose two mechanisms to optimize cost: a translation reducing method and a translator reducing method. They have different applicable scenarios for large corpus construction. The translation reducing method works if there exists a specific requirement that the quality must reach a certain threshold. This model is most effective when reasonable amounts of pre-existing professional translations are available for setting the model's threshold. The translator reducing method is very simple and easy to implement. This approach is inspired by the intuition that workers' performance is consistent. The translator reducing method is suitable for crowdsourcing tasks which do not have specific requirements about the quality of the translations, or when only very limited amounts of gold standard data is available.

## Acknowledgements

This material is based on research sponsored by a DARPA Computer Science Study Panel phase 3 award entitled "Crowdsourcing Translation" (contract D12PC00368). The views and conclusions contained in this publication are those of the authors and should not be interpreted as representing official policies or endorsements by DARPA or the U.S. Government. This research was supported by the Johns Hopkins University Human Language Technology Center of Excellence and through gifts from Microsoft, Google and Facebook.

## References

Vamshi Ambati and Stephan Vogel. 2010. Can crowds build parallel corpora for machine translation systems? In *Proceedings of the NAACL HLT 2010 Workshop on Creating Speech and Language Data with Amazon's Mechanical Turk*, pages 62–65.

Chris Callison-Burch and Mark Dredze. 2010. Creating speech and language data with Amazon's Mechanical Turk. In *Proceedings of the NAACL HLT 2010 Workshop on Creating Speech and Language Data with Amazon's Mechanical Turk*, pages 1–12.

Christopher H Lin, Mausam, and Daniel S Weld. 2014. To re (label), or not to re (label). In *Proceedings of the 2014 AAAI Conference on Human Computation and Crowdsourcing*.

Scott Novotney and Chris Callison-Burch. 2010. Cheap, fast and good enough: Automatic speech recognition with non-expert transcription. In *Human Language Technologies: The 2010 Annual Conference of the North American Chapter of the Association for Computational Linguistics (NAACL-HLT)*, pages 207–215.

Franz Josef Och. 2003. Minimum error rate training in statistical machine translation. In *Proceedings of the 41st Annual Meeting on Association for Computational Linguistics-Volume 1(ACL)*, pages 160–167.

Kishore Papineni, Salim Roukos, Todd Ward, and Wei-Jing Zhu. 2002. Bleu: a method for automatic evaluation of machine translation. In *Proceedings of the 40th Annual Meeting on Association for Computational Linguistics (ACL)*, pages 311–318.

Rebecca J Passonneau and Bob Carpenter. 2013. The benefits of a model of annotation. In *Proceedings of the 7th Linguistic Annotation Workshop and Interoperability with Discourse*, pages 187–195.

Matt Post, Chris Callison-Burch, and Miles Osborne. 2012. Constructing parallel corpora for six indian languages via crowdsourcing. In *Proceedings of the Seventh Workshop on Statistical Machine Translation*, pages 401–409.

F Pozzi, T Di Matteo, and T Aste. 2012. Exponential smoothing weighted correlations. *The European Physical Journal B-Condensed Matter and Complex Systems*, 85(6):1–21.

Victor S Sheng, Foster Provost, and Panagiotis G Ipeirotis. 2008. Get another label? Improving data quality and data mining using multiple, noisy labelers. In *Proceedings of the 14th ACM SIGKDD international conference on Knowledge discovery and data mining*, pages 614–622.

Rion Snow, Brendan O'Connor, Daniel Jurafsky, and Andrew Y Ng. 2008. Cheap and fast—but is it good?: Evaluating non-expert annotations for natural language tasks. In *Proceedings of the Conference on Empirical Methods in Natural Language Processing (EMNLP)*, pages 254–263.

Omar F. Zaidan and Chris Callison-Burch. 2011. Crowdsourcing translation: Professional quality from non-professionals. In *Proceedings of the 49th Annual Meeting of the Association for Computational Linguistics: Human Language Technologies (ACL-HLT)*, pages 1220–1229.

Omar F. Zaidan. 2009. Z-MERT: A fully configurable open source tool for minimum error rate training of machine translation systems. *The Prague Bulletin of Mathematical Linguistics*, 91:79–88.

Rabih Zbib, Erika Malchiodi, Jacob Devlin, David Stallard, Spyros Matsoukas, Richard Schwartz, John Makhoul, Omar F Zaidan, and Chris Callison-Burch. 2012. Machine translation of arabic dialects. In *Proceedings of the 2012 Conference of the North American Chapter of the Association for Computational Linguistics: Human Language Technologies (NAACL-HLT)*, pages 49–59.

Rabih Zbib, Gretchen Markiewicz, Spyros Matsoukas, Richard M Schwartz, and John Makhoul. 2013. Systematic comparison of professional and crowdsourced reference translations for machine translation. In *Proceedings of the 2013 Conference of the North American Chapter of the Association for Computational Linguistics: Human Language Technologies (NAACL-HLT)*, pages 612–616.

# Multitask Learning for Adaptive Quality Estimation of Automatically Transcribed Utterances

José G. C. de Souza[⋆†], Hamed Zamani[‡], Matteo Negri[†], Marco Turchi[†], Daniele Falavigna[†]
[⋆]University of Trento, Italy
[†]Fondazione Bruno Kessler, Italy
[‡]School of ECE, College of Engineering, University of Tehran, Iran
{desouza, negri, turchi, falavi}@fbk.eu
h.zamani@ut.ac.ir

## Abstract

We investigate the problem of predicting the quality of automatic speech recognition (ASR) output under the following rigid constraints: *i)* reference transcriptions are not available, *ii)* confidence information about the system that produced the transcriptions is not accessible, and *iii)* training and test data come from multiple domains. To cope with these constraints (typical of the constantly increasing amount of automatic transcriptions that can be found on the Web), we propose a domain-adaptive approach based on multitask learning. Different algorithms and strategies are evaluated with English data coming from four domains, showing that the proposed approach can cope with the limitations of previously proposed single task learning methods.

## 1 Introduction

The variety of applications for large vocabulary speech recognition technology (LVCSR) is rapidly growing. For instance, automatic transcriptions are now used, either *as-is* or as rough material to be checked and corrected by humans, for captioning and subtitling DVD movies, Youtube videos, TV programs and recordings in noisy environments such as meetings and teleconferences. To enable further integration in these and other scenarios, the improvement of the core automatic speech recognition (ASR) technology should go hand in hand with the development of evaluation methods adequate to address new needs and constraints. Indeed, the standard evaluation protocol, based on computing the word error rate of transcription hypotheses against reference transcripts,[1] is not always a viable solution.

In terms of *needs*, the aforementioned applications call for efficient and replicable evaluation methods suitable for real-time processing. While the availability of manually-created reference transcripts is a core ingredient for system development, tuning and lab testing, their use for on-field evaluation (*i.e.* during the actual use) is impractical for obvious reasons (*i.e.* the need of a quick response).

In terms of *constraints*, the problem is that ASR technology is often used as a black-box, that is, without any knowledge of how the transcriptions are generated.[2] This calls for techniques capable to estimate ASR output quality under the rigid constraint of having, as a basic source of information, only the spoken utterance (the acoustic signal) and the transcription itself. Indeed, the invaluable information provided by current confidence estimation methods (*e.g.* word posterior probabilities (Evermann and Woodland, 2000; Wessel et al., 2001), consensus decoding (Mangu et al., 2000) and minimum Bayes-risk decoding (Xu et al., 2010)) is not accessible when evaluating the output of an unknown system.

[1]The word error rate (WER) is the minimum edit distance between an hypothesis and the reference transcription. Edit distance is calculated as the number of edits (word insertions, deletions, substitutions) divided by the number of words in the reference.

[2]For instance, as announced by Google, in 2012 about 157 million YouTube videos in 10 languages already featured captions generated by a black-box ASR system (source: http://techcrunch.com/2012/06/15/youtube-launches-auto-captions-in-spanish/).



*Human Language Technologies: The 2015 Annual Conference of the North American Chapter of the ACL*, pages 714–724,
Denver, Colorado, May 31 – June 5, 2015. 

To cope with these issues, Negri et al. (2014) proposed a reference-free ASR *quality estimation* (QE) method capable to operate both in a glass-box (*i.e.* having access to confidence information) and in a black-box fashion (*i.e.* without any knowledge about the ASR system's inner workings). According to the authors, despite the promising evaluation results, the supervised learning approach adopted has a main limitation: the degradation in performance when models are trained on non-homogeneous data that comes from different domains, speakers, or systems. However, although empirical evidence of this limitation is provided, the robustness of ASR QE systems to the heterogeneity of training and test data is left as an open issue.

Filling this gap, which is the goal of this paper, would be a significant step towards real-time ASR output evaluation, and its seamless integration in a number of application frameworks. Along this direction, we propose and evaluate a supervised domain adaptation technique based on *multitask learning* (Caruana, 1997). Our approach aims to exploit training data coming from different "domains" (in a broad sense, *e.g.* different genres, speakers, topics, styles, etc.) and to obtain ASR QE models that are robust to differences with respect to the test data. Experiments are carried out with English data coming from four domains, and by comparing different algorithms and strategies.

Overall, our contributions can be summarized as follows:

- Multitask learning (MTL) is investigated for the first time in the ASR QE scenario, as a way to cope with the dissimilarity between training and test data coming from multiple domains.

- The QE problem is approached both as a regression (assignment of real-valued quality labels) and as a binary classification task (assignment of 'good'/'bad' labels according to a given, arbitrary WER threshold). The latter task is introduced as a preliminary study.

- Results are thoroughly analyzed, considering both the amount of training data coming from the different domains and the relative distance between their distributions.

## 2 Related Work

In the ASR field, most prior works that address the reference-free estimation of output quality fall into the confidence estimation (CE) framework. In this framework, the reliability of a transcription is estimated from the system's standpoint, that is, as a function of the process that generated the transcription (Sukkar and Lee, 1996; Evermann and Woodland, 2000; Wessel et al., 2001; Sanchis et al., 2012; Seigel, 2013, *inter alia*). In CE, the information available to the estimator covers all the aspects of the decoding process (*e.g.* word posterior probabilities, n-best lists, hypotheses density, language model scores). Although related to our problem, CE hence builds on a strong assumption (*i.e.* the ASR system is known), which does not hold in many situations.

Quality estimation, instead, operates in the least favorable condition in which, besides the lack of references, the ASR system is regarded as a "black-box". To our knowledge, the study proposed in (Negri et al., 2014) is the most relevant related work along this direction. In their investigation, the authors run a set of experiments aimed to predict the WER of automatically transcribed utterances in different testing conditions (by varying the distance between training and test data), with different state-of-the-art learning algorithms (all for regression), and with different groups of features (the so called "black-box" and "glass-box" feature groups). The major problem emphasized in their analysis is the strong dependency between QE models and the degree of homogeneity of training and test data. From the application perspective, this is a severe limitation since (as in any other supervised learning setting) the similarity of training and test sets is a strong requirement that should be bypassed (possibly with minimal loss in performance). This issue, which has not been addressed yet, is the starting point of our investigation.

Another aspect that so far has been disregarded concerns the type of estimates that a model should return. Indeed, while ASR QE has been explored as a regression task (*i.e.* aiming to return real-valued quality estimates), nothing has been done to approach it as a classification problem (*i.e.* assigning quality estimates chosen from two or more classes). In classification mode, we return explicit good/bad labels based on a fixed, application-dependent quality criterion defined a priori (a threshold set on training data). Since the way to present the quality estimates can have interesting effects on their practical use, the impact of the aforementioned learning problem on a supervised classification setting is another aspect that deserves investigation and motivates our work.

## 3 Multitask Learning for Adaptive ASR Quality Estimation

The problem of dealing with different distributions between training and test data is broadly investigated by the machine learning community. In particular, approaches for dealing with domain drift are proposed within the scope of *transfer learning*, whose aim is to explore knowledge from one or more source tasks (henceforth, we use the terms domain and task interchangeably) and apply it to a target task (Pan and Yang, 2010). In this paper we use a transfer learning technique called *multitask learning* (MTL), which explores domain-specific training signals of related tasks to improve model generalization (Caruana, 1997).

MTL is an inductive transfer method that assumes that the tasks are related and share a certain structure that allows knowledge transfer. In early works, for instance, these shared structures are the hidden layers of a neural network (Caruana, 1997).[3] The authors showed that MTL improves over learning each task in isolation (called single task learning, STL henceforth) for different problems. Several approaches to MTL have been proposed and each makes different assumptions about the structure shared among the tasks. In this work we explore three different MTL algorithms that deal with task relatedness in different ways.

Before defining each one of the three approaches, we introduce some basic notation previously used by Chen et al. (2011). In MTL there are $K \in \mathbb{N}$ tasks and each task $k \in [1, K]$ has $m_k$ training instances $\{(\mathbf{x}_1, y_1), \ldots, (\mathbf{x}_{m_k}, y_{m_k})\}$, with $\mathbf{x}_i \in \mathbb{R}^d$ where $d$ is the number of features and $y_i \in \mathbb{R}$ is the output (the response variable or label). For each task, the input features and labels form two different matrices $\mathbf{X}_{(k)} = [\mathbf{x}_{1,(k)}, \ldots, \mathbf{x}_{m_k,(k)}]$ and $\mathbf{Y}_{(k)} = [y_{1,(k)}, \ldots, y_{m_k,(k)}]$, respectively. The weights of the features for all tasks are represented by matrix $\mathbf{W}$, where each column corresponds to a task and each row corresponds to a feature. The function $\mathcal{L}(\mathbf{W}, \mathbf{X}, \mathbf{Y})$ is the loss function defined for each algorithm. We work with two loss functions:

- Least squares (for regression), defined as $(\mathbf{X}_{(k)}^T \mathbf{W}_k - \mathbf{Y}_{(k)})^2$, where $k$ is the task identifier and $\mathbf{W}_k$ is the $k$-th column of $\mathbf{W}$;
- Logistic Regression (for classification), defined as $\log(1 + \exp(-\mathbf{Y}_{(k)} \mathbf{X}_{(k)}^T \mathbf{W}_k))$.

**MTL Lasso.** This algorithm extends the idea of the Lasso (Tibshirani, 1996) to the MTL setting. In MTL Lasso the $\ell_1$-norm (the sum of the absolute values of the weights vector, given by $\sum_{i=1}^{d} |w_i|$) is applied to all the tasks at once (the $||\mathbf{W}||_1$ component in Eq. 1). The $\lambda \in [0, 1]$ parameter controls the level of regularization applied to the model. In other words, the sparsity of the predicted model is controlled via $\lambda$ which weights the $\ell_1$-norm across all tasks.

$$\min_{W} \sum_{k=1}^{K} \mathcal{L}(\mathbf{W}_k, \mathbf{X}_{(k)}, \mathbf{Y}_{(k)}) + \lambda ||\mathbf{W}||_1 \qquad (1)$$

**MTL L21.** This algorithm (Argyriou et al., 2007) learns a low-dimensional representation of the features across tasks, and induces sparsity on the feature weights for all the tasks at the same time. This is achieved through the use of a group regularizer that penalizes the weights matrix $\mathbf{W}$ with the $\ell_{2,1}$-norm (Eq. 2). This norm is defined as $||\mathbf{W}||_{2,1} = \sum_{i=1}^{d} ||\mathbf{W}_i||_2$, where $d$ is the number of features and $\mathbf{W}_i$ is the $i$-th row of $\mathbf{W}$. It is obtained by first computing the 2-norm of each row in $\mathbf{W}$ (the features) and then computing the 1-norm over the resulting vector. The 2-norm of a vector is given by $||\mathbf{x}||_2 = \sqrt{\sum_i x_i^2}$. The parameter $\lambda \in [0, 1]$ controls the regularization applied to the model. MTL L21 assumes that all tasks share the same feature representation.

[3] Another intuitive example of transferable knowledge is the fact that, for some domains, a fraction of the extracted features can show a correlated behavior.

$$\min_{W} \sum_{k=1}^{K} \mathcal{L}(\mathbf{W}_k, \mathbf{X}_{(k)}, \mathbf{Y}_{(k)}) + \lambda ||\mathbf{W}||_{2,1} \quad (2)$$

**Robust MTL.** This algorithm does not assume that all the tasks share the same feature representation as the previous two algorithms do (Chen et al., 2011). Moreover, RMTL uses two different structures: one for grouping related tasks to share knowledge; the other for identifying irrelevant tasks and keeping them in a different group that does not share information with the first one. This is to cope with situations in which, since tasks are not related, negative transfer of information across tasks might occur, thus harming the generalization of the model. The algorithm approximates task relatedness via a low-rank structure and identifies outlier tasks using a group-sparse structure (column-sparse, at task level). RMTL minimizes the expression described in 3. It employs a non-negative linear combination of the trace norm (the task relatedness component $\mathbf{L}$) and a column-sparse structure induced by the $\ell_{1,2}$-norm (the outlier task detection component $\mathbf{S}$). If a task is an outlier it will have non-zero entries in $\mathbf{S}$.

$$\min_{W} \sum_{k=1}^{K} \mathcal{L}(\mathbf{W}_k, \mathbf{X}_{(k)}, \mathbf{Y}_{(k)}) + \lambda_l ||\mathbf{L}||_* + \lambda_s ||\mathbf{S}||_{1,2} \quad (3)$$

In Eq. 3 $\mathbf{W}$ is subject to $\mathbf{L} + \mathbf{S}$, where $||.||_*$ is the trace norm, given by the sum of the singular values $\sigma_i$ of $\mathbf{W}$, and $||\mathbf{S}||_{1,2}$ is the group regularizer that induces sparsity on the tasks. It is obtained by first computing the $\ell_1$-norm over the columns of $\mathbf{W}$ and then applying the $\ell_2$-norm over the resulting vector. The $\lambda_l$ and $\lambda_s$ parameters control the level of regularization of $\mathbf{L}$ and $\mathbf{S}$, respectively.

All the MTL algorithms presented in this section are linear, with different regularization terms. While RMTL is only defined for regression, the other algorithms are defined for both regression and classification.

## 4 Experimental Setting

Our experiments aim to measure the capability of MTL methods to learn across different domains. To this aim, the algorithms[4] previously described are compared with the STL baseline, both in regression and in binary classification. Given a set of *(signal, transcription, WER)* tuples as training instances, our task is to label new unseen *(signal, transcription)* test pairs with a WER prediction (regression models) or with a good/bad tag (classification models) depending on the quality of the transcription.

In classification, the class boundary is defined a priori, according to an arbitrary threshold $\tau$ set on the WER of the instances: those with a $WER \leq \tau$ will be considered as positive examples while the others will be considered as negative examples. Different thresholds can be set to experiment with testing conditions that reflect a variety of application-oriented requirements. We work at one extreme, in which a value of $\tau$ close to zero ($0.05$) emphasizes systems' ability to precisely identify high-quality transcriptions (those with $WER \leq \tau$). Any application that requires precise judgments to isolate high-quality ASR output can potentially benefit of such optimization (*e.g.* data selection for acoustic modeling using a QE-based active learning model). The investigation of other thresholding schemes, however, is certainly an aspect that we want to explore in the future.

The small value of $\tau$ selected produces a skewed distribution of classes, with a ratio of good to bad labels across the four domains of about 75% "good" and 25% "bad". To cope with this issue, we use a sample weighting technique while training the classification models (Veropoulos et al., 1999). We assign a weight $w$ to each of the training instances, computed as the inverse of its class frequency in the training set. In other words, $w$ is obtained by dividing the total number of training samples by the number of training samples belonging to the class of the given utterance.

### 4.1 Data

Our datasets include English audio recordings from four different domains: broadcast news (henceforth News), political speeches (Legal), weather reports (Weather) and talks of single speakers in the context of the TED talks (TED). All datasets (see Table 1 for details) were used in past ASR evaluation campaigns, and are provided with manual reference transcriptions associated to each audio recording.

[4] In our experiments we used the implementations available in the Malsar toolkit (Zhou et al., 2012)

| | News | Legal | Weather | TED |
|---|---|---|---|---|
| **Total dur. (min)** | 150 | 338 | 108 | 340 |
| **# running words** | 26,282 | 53,846 | 23,722 | 41,545 |
| **# utterances** | 737 | 2,922 | 1,290 | 2,245 |
| **# speakers** | 178 | 95 | 36 | 28 |
| **Avg. utt. dur. (s)** | 12.2 | 6.9 | 5.0 | 9.1 |
| **WER** | 17.7 | 20.4 | 11.9 | 22.9 |

Table 1: Some characteristics of the four domains.

**News.** We use the HUB4[5] corpus, which contains 104 hours of broadcasts from different television and radio networks. We selected the 1999 test set of the DARPA Hub-4 evaluation, consisting of two recordings acquired in TV studios and containing speech of professional speakers reading news.

**Legal.** This audio database[6] contains recordings of European Parliament members speaking in plenary sessions, as well as recordings of interpreters (non-native speakers). Speech is hence quite spontaneous, and a relevant level of reverberation is present due to the usage of table-mounted microphones. The data that we used for our experiments are both the English EPPS development (dev06) and evaluation (eval07) sets of the 2007 TC-STAR ASR evaluation campaign (Hamon et al., 2007).

**Weather.** This dataset is formed by recordings of weather reports broadcasted by the BBC English TV channel, and contains both national and local weather forecasts. There are roughly 50 native speakers and the speech is delivered very quickly. Although the speakers are native and the recordings are performed in a controlled environment, there are some hesitations, grammar errors or lengthy formulations in the recordings which are corrected in the captions (which can thus be considered as loose reference transcripts (Mohr et al., 2013)).

**TED.** This dataset contains audio recordings of English speakers (28 different talks) and was used within the IWSLT 2013 evaluation campaign (Cettolo et al., 2013). This domain presents large variability of topics (hence a large, unconstrained vocabulary), presence of non-native speakers, and a rather informal speaking style.

Given their diverse nature, the four domains present a big challenge both for ASR and QE systems. From Table 1 it is possible to grasp several differences among them. One aspect that reflects such differences is the WER of the ASR system we used to transcribe the utterances (described in Section 4.2). The lowest WER is for Weather, a domain in which the speech is planned. This is also the domain with the shortest average utterance duration (5 sec.), the lowest number of speakers (36) and the lowest number of running words (23,722). The higher WER achieved on the other domains is due to the more challenging conditions posed by each of them. TED and News include speeches about unconstrained topics, and their average utterance durations tend to be longer than for the other two domains. News is the shortest domain in duration and the smallest in number of utterances (150 min. for 737 utterances), but has the highest number of speakers. This means that there are very few utterances for each speaker, in average, and that both the ASR and the QE system must cope with the differences in speech for all these subjects. Legal presents the second largest number of speakers, both native and non-native, using a specific terminology on a varied number of topics.

### 4.2 ASR System

The ASR engine used in our experiments makes use of Hidden Markov Models (HMMs) of triphone units and of 4-gram back-off language models (LMs). HMMs are trained on domain-specific sets of audio data. The HUB4 training corpus is released with "verbatim" transcriptions of the audio signals while, for the other three domains (*i.e.* Legal, Weather and TED), training data have only associated captions, which are not always exact transcriptions of the corresponding audio recordings. To extract audio segments with reliable transcriptions we hence applied a lightly supervised training procedure (Lamel et al., 2001). This resulted in 67 hours of recordings for the Weather domain, 144 hours for TED, 164 hours for News and 100 hours for Legal. For LM training, first, a general purpose LM is trained on the Gigaword text corpus (5th ed.) (Parker et al., 2011) then, it is adapted to all domains, using domain specific text data. Each auto-

[5]distributed by the Linguistic Data Consortium and available at https://catalog.ldc.upenn.edu/docs/LDC2000S88/

[6]http://catalog.elra.info/product_info.php?products_id=1032

matic transcription of the data presented in Table 1 is generated with the corresponding word and time boundaries that are aligned with the reference utterances. This allows us to compute the utterance WER and the features for the various prediction models.

### 4.3 Features

Our models are trained with the same 52 *"black-box"* features proposed by Negri et al. (2014), which can be categorized in three groups: Signal, Hybrid and Textual. The first group aims to capture the difficulty to transcribe the input and is extracted by looking at the signal segment as a whole. Hybrid features provide a more fine-grained way to capture the transcription difficulty, by linking the signal to the output transcription. Textual features aim to capture the plausibility/fluency of a transcription considering its surface word information.

### 4.4 Evaluation Metrics

**Regression.** Our regression models are evaluated in terms of mean absolute error (MAE). The MAE, a standard error measure for regression, is the average of the absolute difference between the prediction $\hat{y}_i$ of a model and the gold standard response $y_i$ for all instances in the test set. As it is an error measure, lower values indicate better performance.

**Classification.** To handle the imbalanced class distribution, and equally reward the correct classification on both classes, our evaluation is carried out in terms of balanced accuracy (BA – the higher the better), which is computed as the average of the accuracies on the two classes (Brodersen et al., 2010). When the distribution of classes is balanced, BA is equal to the accuracy metric.

### 4.5 Baselines

**Regression.** We compare the MTL methods against two baselines. The first one, simple but often hard to beat for regression models, is computed by labeling all the test instances with the *Mean* WER value calculated on the training set. The second baseline is an STL algorithm trained on data from the target domain. The algorithm that we used (STL Elastic henceforth) is the elastic net (Zou and Hastie, 2005). Parameter estimation is performed with 5-fold cross-validation.

**Classification.** In this setting we also consider two baselines. The first one (*Majority*) is computed by labeling all the test instances with the most frequent label in the training set and, by definition, corresponds to a score of 0.5 in terms of balanced accuracy. The second classification baseline is the logistic regression (STL LogReg henceforth), also known as maximum entropy algorithm (Hastie et al., 2009). We perform parameter optimization for LogReg using stratified 5-fold cross-validation in a randomized search process (Bergstra and Bengio, 2012).

For both STL baselines we selected algorithms[7] that induce linear models and use the same loss functions (least squares for regression and logistic regression for classification) of the MTL methods.

## 5 Results and Discussion

To mitigate the effect of having considerably different amounts of training data in the four domains, and equally weight their contribution to the learning task, all our models (STL and MTL) are trained using the same number of instances from all the domains and, at most, half of the data available for the smallest domain, News (*i.e.* 362 instances). To analyze performance variations with different amounts of data, we create subsets of the 362 instances, for 10 different sizes ranging from 10% to 100% of the instances for each domain.[8] We repeat this process 30 times by randomly shuffling all the data available for each domain. For each of the resulting learning curves, the plots in this section present the confidence intervals[9] (at 95%) for the 30 different train/test splits.

In addition to the STL model trained only on in-domain data, we also experiment with an STL model trained on the concatenation of the training data of all domains. Its results are, on average, statistically comparable to, or worse than, STL in-domain for both regression and classification.

**Regression.** Among the three MTL regression algorithms, RMTL achieves the best results in all our

[7]We used the implementations available in Scikit-learn (Pedregosa et al., 2011).

[8]That is, for instance, with 10% of training data from four domains, the total amount of instances is 144 (36*4).

[9]The confidence intervals are used to show whether there are statistically significant differences in performance among the models.

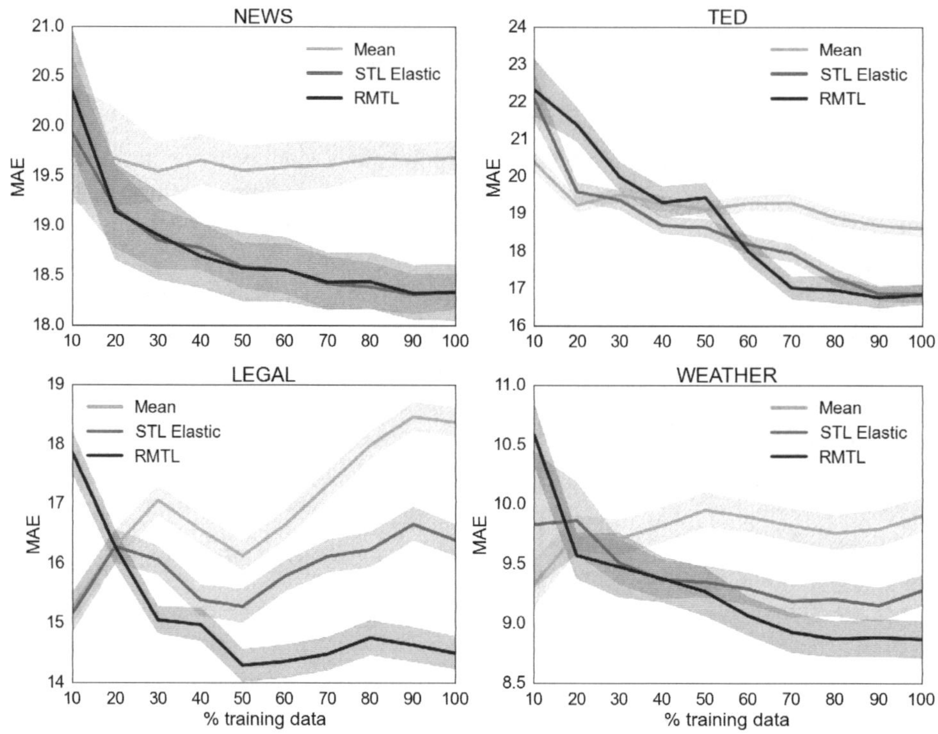


Figure 1: Learning curves for the regression models evaluated on the four domains. The evaluation metric is MAE (↓).

tests. This suggests that its capability to handle domain divergence, thus avoiding negative transfer, is required to increase performance. For the sake of visualization, in the plots in Figure 1 we hence omit the curves of the other MTL methods, keeping only those of RMTL and the two baselines.

As shown in the figure, for the Legal domain, RMTL results are better than those of both the baselines (lower MAE) even with 30% of the data and, except in one case (40% of the data), the improvement over STL (always the stronger baseline) is statistically significant. For Weather and TED, the improvement is less evident: more data are required to outperform the STL baseline (respectively 50% and 60%), the improvements are not always statistically significant and, for TED, the MAE results converge to those of STL with 100% of the data. For the News domain RMTL's performance is always comparable to STL. An interesting behavior can be observed in the Legal domain, in which the Mean baseline degrades as we add training data. This suggests that, even internally to the domain, training and test labels have very different distributions. A smaller degradation is observed for the STL model, which improves over the Mean baseline as it also uses the information captured by the features. The two baselines, however, assume that both training and test data come from similar distributions. Instead, by taking advantage also of the knowledge transferred from the other domains, RMTL allows to cope with the differences between training and test.

**Classification.** In this setting we compare the MTL algorithms (L21 and Lasso) with the STL (LogReg) and Majority baselines. As shown in Figure 2, the two MTL models (which significantly outperform the Majority baseline in all conditions) always achieve a higher balanced accuracy than single task learning in three domains (TED, Legal and Weather). In the Weather domain, the performance improvement over the STL baseline is always statistically significant when using from 20% to 100% of the training data. For TED and Legal, MTL performance tends to converge to the results of STL when the models are trained on 100% of the data (around 65% BA), with an improvement that remains statis-

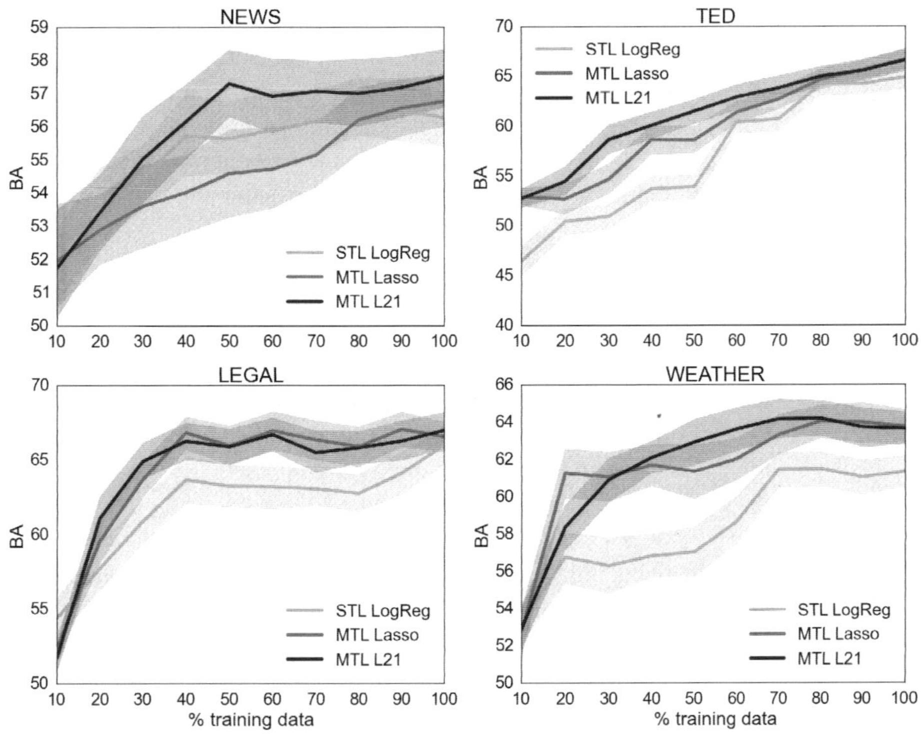


Figure 2: Learning curves for the classification models evaluated on four domains for WER scores with threshold at 0.05. Evaluation is calculated with balanced accuracy (↑).

tically significant only for TED. For the News domain, similar to the regression setting, the improvement of MTL over STL is less evident. Indeed, only L21 outperforms the single task baseline but the difference is not statistically significant.

Our classification results can be explained taking into consideration the distribution of positive and negative instances in each domain. Weather, for which MTL always outperforms STL, has the most balanced distribution (35% good and 65% bad). In the other three domains, instead, the proportion of negative samples is always above 77%. Although in this penalized condition all algorithms are supported by sample weighting, MTL seems to better exploit this technique when the target domain is balanced.

The challenging nature of the data we are using (described in Section 4.1) is corroborated by the moderate performance achieved by STL. Although it is trained with in-domain data, the best STL classification model (for the Legal domain) does not exceed a BA of 66%. In this difficult scenario, the usefulness of MTL is demonstrated by its capability of reaching the best performance of STL with smaller amounts of data in most of the cases (*e.g.* 30% of the data for the Legal domain).

**Domains divergence.** To further analyze the performance of MTL in regression and classification, following previous works on MTL and domain adaptation in computer vision (Costante et al., 2014; Samanta et al., 2014), we use maximum mean discrepancy (MMD) as a measure of divergence between domains. MMD is an effective way to compare two multivariate distributions $p$ and $q$ by minimizing the difference in Reproducing Kernel Hilbert Space (RKHS) between the means of the projected distributions (Gretton et al., 2012). It is defined as $\sup_{f \in \mathbb{F}} \mathbb{E}_p[f(p)] - \mathbb{E}_q[f(q)]$ where $p$ and $q$ are points sampled i.i.d. from two domains and $f(.)$ is a continuous bounded function on $p$ and $q$ (usually a unit ball function). We measure the pairwise divergences among the domains described in Section 4.1 using the features extracted and a radial basis function kernel. The divergences are presented in Figure 3.

According to the pairwise MMD, the most divergent pair is News-Weather, which is followed by News-Legal. The distance between News and the other domains indicates that, when it is used as target, knowledge transfer from the other domains might be problematic. In fact, looking at the results obtained by classification and regression models for News, we notice that none of the MTL methods achieves significant improvements over the STL baselines. Furthermore, the RMTL regression learning curve (Figure 1) for News shows that RMTL follows the same curve of STL, meaning that it is able to handle the high divergence between News and the other domains and hence, it learns mostly from in-domain data.

In general, the divergence measurements between the domains are relatively high (the values are closer to 1 than to 0). This is not surprising given the intra- and inter-domain variability of speakers and topics, the different conditions in which speech was recorded, and the WER differences across domains. However, the interesting aspect evidenced by the measurements is that MMD allows to successfully approximate such domain differences (and, likely, other more implicit diversity indicators), thus being a useful instrument to measure domain relatedness.

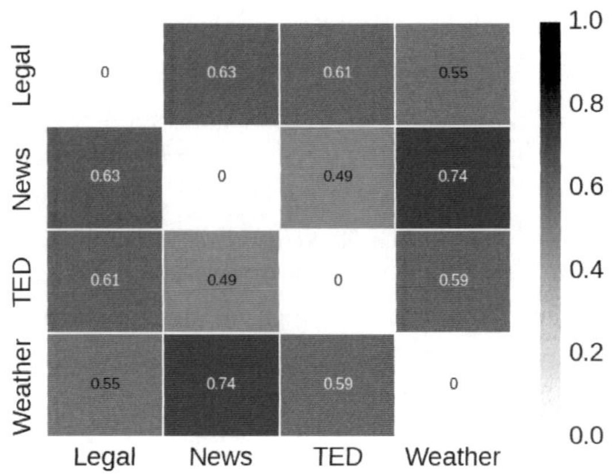


Figure 3: Domains divergence given by MMD (0 means similar and 1 means dissimilar).

## 6 Conclusion

We presented a supervised approach to ASR quality estimation aimed to cope with large differences between training and test data. To achieve robustness and adaptability to such differences, we exploited the capability of multitask learning, which allows QE models to make the best use of training data coming from multiple domains by transferring knowledge across them. The MTL learning paradigm was applied both in regression mode (WER prediction) and, in a preliminary investigation, for binary classification (assignment of 'good'/'bad' quality labels). In both settings, we experimented with different amounts of English data coming from four very diverse domains (different genres, speakers, topics, and styles).

Our results indicate that MTL, which we used for the first time in ASR QE[10], is able to take advantage of data coming from such heterogeneous domains and to significantly improve over single-task learning baselines both in regression and in classification. Although the extent of the improvement depends on the divergence between the domains (a major issue for any supervised learning task), our results show that in the worst case MTL performance converges to the results of single-task learning. Overall, by suggesting a way to overcome the main limitations of previous approaches, our study opens interesting research avenues towards reference-free, system-agnostic and real-time ASR output evaluation.

## Acknowledgments

The work of Hamed Zamani was supported by the FBK-HLT Summer Internship Program 2014.

## References

[Argyriou et al.2007] Andreas Argyriou, Theodoros Evgeniou, and Massimiliano Pontil. 2007. Multi-task feature learning. In *Advances in Neural Information Processing Systems 19*, pages 41–48.

[Bergstra and Bengio2012] James Bergstra and Yoshua Bengio. 2012. Random Search for Hyper-Parameter Optimization. *Journal of Machine Learning Research*, 13:281–305.

[Brodersen et al.2010] Kay Henning Brodersen, Cheng Soon Ong, Klaas Enno Stephan, and

[10]Previous works (Cohn and Specia, 2013; C. de Souza et al., 2014b) successfully applied similar methods to QE for machine translation (Specia et al., 2009; Mehdad et al., 2012; C. de Souza et al., 2014a; Turchi et al., 2014).

Joachim M. Buhmann. 2010. The balanced accuracy and its posterior distribution. In *Proceedings of the 2010 20th International Conference on Pattern Recognition*, ICPR '10, pages 3121–3124.

[C. de Souza et al.2014a] José G. C. de Souza, Jesús González-Rubio, Christian Buck, Marco Turchi, and Matteo Negri. 2014a. FBK-UPV-UEdin participation in the WMT14 Quality Estimation shared-task. In *Proceedings of the Ninth Workshop on Statistical Machine Translation*, pages 322–328.

[C. de Souza et al.2014b] José G. C. de Souza, Marco Turchi, and Matteo Negri. 2014b. Machine Translation Quality Estimation Across Domains. In *Proceedings of the 25th International Conference on Computational Linguistics*, COLING '14, pages 409–420.

[Caruana1997] Rich Caruana. 1997. Multitask Learning. *Machine learning*, 28(28):41–75.

[Cettolo et al.2013] Mauro Cettolo, Jan Niehues, Sebastian Stuker, Luisa Bentivogli, and Marcello Federico. 2013. Report on the 10th IWSLT Evaluation Campaign. In *Proceedings of the International Workshop on Spoken Language Translation*.

[Chen et al.2011] Jianhui Chen, Jiayu Zhou, and Jieping Ye. 2011. Integrating Low-rank and Group-sparse Structures for Robust Multi-task Learning. In *Proceedings of the 17th ACM SIGKDD International Conference on Knowledge Discovery and Data Mining*, KDD '11, pages 42–50.

[Cohn and Specia2013] Trevor Cohn and Lucia Specia. 2013. Modelling Annotator Bias with Multi-task Gaussian Processes: An application to Machine Translation Quality Estimation. In *Proceedings of the 51st Annual Meeting of the Association for Computational Linguistics*, pages 32–42.

[Costante et al.2014] G. Costante, E. Bellocchio, P. Valigi, and E. Ricci. 2014. Personalizing Vision-based Gestural Interfaces for HRI with UAVs: a Transfer Learning Approach. In *Proceedings of the 2014 International Conference on Intelligent Robots and Systems*, IROS '14, pages 3319–3326.

[Evermann and Woodland2000] G. Evermann and P. C. Woodland. 2000. Large vocabulary decoding and confidence estimation using word posterior probabilities. In *Proceedings of the 2000 International Conference on Acoustics, Speech, and Signal Processing*, ICASSP '00, pages 1655–1658.

[Gretton et al.2012] Arthur Gretton, Karsten M. Borgwardt, Malte J. Rasch, Bernhard Scholkopf, and Alexander Smola. 2012. A kernel two-sample test. *Journal of Machine Learning Research*, 13:723–773.

[Hamon et al.2007] Olivier Hamon, Djamel Mostefa, and Khalid Choukri. 2007. End-to-End Evaluation of a Speech-to-Speech Translation System in TC-STAR. In *Proceedings of Machine Translation Summit XI*, pages 223–230.

[Hastie et al.2009] Trevor Hastie, Robert Tibshirani, and Jerome Friedman. 2009. *The Elements of Statistical Learning*.

[Lamel et al.2001] Lori Lamel, Jean-Luc Gauvain, and Gilles Adda. 2001. Investigating lightly supervised acoustic model training. In *Proceedings of the 2001 International Conference on Acoustics, Speech, and Signal Processing*, volume 1 of *ICASSP '01*, pages 477–480. IEEE.

[Mangu et al.2000] Lidia Mangu, Eric Brill, and Andreas Stolcke. 2000. Finding consensus in speech recognition: word error minimization and other applications of confusion networks. *Computer Speech & Language*, 14(4):373–400.

[Mehdad et al.2012] Yashar Mehdad, Matteo Negri, and Marcello Federico. 2012. Match without a Referee: Evaluating MT Adequacy without Reference Translations. In *Proceedings of the Seventh Workshop on Statistical Machine Translation*, pages 171–180, Montréal, Canada, June. Association for Computational Linguistics.

[Mohr et al.2013] Christian Mohr, Christian Saam, Kevin Kilgour, Jonas Gehring, Sebastian Stüker, and Alex Waibel. 2013. Slightly supervised adaptation of acoustic models on captioned bbc weather forecasts. In *Proceedings of the First Workshop on Speech, Language and Audio in Multimedia (SLAM)*, pages 32–36.

[Negri et al.2014] Matteo Negri, Marco Turchi, José G. C. de Souza, and Daniele Falavina. 2014. Quality Estimation for Automatic Speech Recognition. In *Proceedings of the 25th International Conference on Computational Linguistics*, COLING '14, pages 1813–1823.

[Pan and Yang2010] Sinno Jialin Pan and Qiang Yang. 2010. A Survey on Transfer Learning. *IEEE Transactions on Knowledge and Data Engineering*, 22(10):1345–1359.

[Parker et al.2011] Robert Parker, David Graff, Junbo Kong, Ke Chen, and Kazuaki Maeda. 2011. English gigaword fifth edition, june. *Linguistic Data Consortium, LDC2011T07*.

[Pedregosa et al.2011] Fabian Pedregosa, Gaël Varoquaux, Alexandre Gramfort, Vincent Michel, Bertrand Thirion, Olivier Grisel, Mathieu Blondel, Peter Prettenhofer, Ron Weiss, Vincent Dubourg, Jake Vanderplas, Alexandre Passos, David Cournapeau, Mathieu Brucher, Mathieu Perrot, and Édouard Duchesnay. 2011. Scikit-learn : Machine Learning in Python. *Journal of Machine Learning Research*, 12:2825–2830.

[Samanta et al.2014] Suranjana Samanta, Tirumarai A. Selvan, and Sukhendu Das. 2014. Modeling Sequential Domain Shift through Estimation of Optimal Subspaces for Categorization. In *Proceedings of the 2014 British Machine Vision Conference*.

[Sanchis et al.2012] Alberto Sanchis, Alfons Juan, and Enrique Vidal. 2012. A Word-Based Naïve Bayes Classifier for Confidence Estimation in Speech Recognition. *IEEE Transactions on Audio, Speech and Language Processing*, 20(2):565–574.

[Seigel2013] Mathew Stephen Seigel. 2013. *Confidence Estimation for Automatic Speech Recognition Hypotheses*. Ph.D. thesis, University of Cambridge.

[Specia et al.2009] Lucia Specia, Nicola Cancedda, Marc Dymetman, Marco Turchi, and Nello Cristianini. 2009. Estimating the Sentence-Level Quality of Machine Translation Systems. In *Proceedings of the 13th Annual Conference of the EAMT*, number May, pages 28–35.

[Sukkar and Lee1996] Rafid A. Sukkar and Chin-Hui Lee. 1996. Vocabulary independent discriminative utterance verification for nonkeyword rejection in subword based speech recognition. *IEEE Transactions on Audio, Speech and Language Processing*, 4(6):420–429.

[Tibshirani1996] Rob Tibshirani. 1996. Regression shrinkage and selection via the lasso. *Journal of the Royal Statistical Society. Series B (Methodological)*, 58(1):267–288.

[Turchi et al.2014] Marco Turchi, Antonios Anastasopoulos, José G. C. de Souza, and Matteo Negri. 2014. Adaptive Quality Estimation for Machine Translation. In *Proceedings of the 52nd Annual Meeting of the Association for Computational Linguistics (Volume 1: Long Papers)*, pages 710–720, Baltimore, Maryland, June. Association for Computational Linguistics.

[Veropoulos et al.1999] K. Veropoulos, C. Campbell, and N. Cristianini. 1999. Controlling the sensitivity of support vector machines. In *Proceedings of the International Joint Conference on Artificial Intelligence*, IJCAI '99, pages 55–60.

[Wessel et al.2001] Frank Wessel, Ralf Schluter, Klaus Macherey, and Hermann Ney. 2001. Confidence measures for large vocabulary continuous speech recognition. *IEEE Transactions on Audio, Speech and Language Processing*, 9(3):288–298.

[Xu et al.2010] Haihua Xu, Dan Povey, Lidia Mangu, and Jie Zhu. 2010. An improved consensus-like method for Minimum Bayes Risk decoding and lattice combination. In *Proceedings of the 2010 International Conference on Acoustics Speech and Signal Processing*, ICASSP '10, pages 4938–4941.

[Zhou et al.2012] Jiayu Zhou, Jianhui Chen, and Jieping Ye. 2012. MALSAR: Multi-tAsk Learning via StructurAl Regularization.

[Zou and Hastie2005] Hui Zou and Trevor Hastie. 2005. Regularization and variable selection via the elastic net. *Journal of the Royal Statistical Society: Series B (Statistical Methodology)*, 67(2):301–320.

# Incorporating Word Correlation Knowledge into Topic Modeling

**Pengtao Xie**
School of Computer Science
Carnegie Mellon University
Pittsburgh, PA 15213, USA
pengtaox@cs.cmu.edu

**Diyi Yang**
School of Computer Science
Carnegie Mellon University
Pittsburgh, PA 15213, USA
diyiy@cs.cmu.edu

**Eric P. Xing**
School of Computer Science
Carnegie Mellon University
Pittsburgh, PA 15213, USA
epxing@cs.cmu.edu

## Abstract

This paper studies how to incorporate the external word correlation knowledge to improve the coherence of topic modeling. Existing topic models assume words are generated independently and lack the mechanism to utilize the rich similarity relationships among words to learn coherent topics. To solve this problem, we build a Markov Random Field (MRF) regularized Latent Dirichlet Allocation (LDA) model, which defines a MRF on the latent topic layer of LDA to encourage words labeled as similar to share the same topic label. Under our model, the topic assignment of each word is not independent, but rather affected by the topic labels of its correlated words. Similar words have better chance to be put into the same topic due to the regularization of MRF, hence the coherence of topics can be boosted. In addition, our model can accommodate the subtlety that whether two words are similar depends on which topic they appear in, which allows word with multiple senses to be put into different topics properly. We derive a variational inference method to infer the posterior probabilities and learn model parameters and present techniques to deal with the hard-to-compute partition function in MRF. Experiments on two datasets demonstrate the effectiveness of our model.

## 1 Introduction

Probabilistic topic models (PTM), such as probabilistic latent semantic indexing(PLSI) (Hofmann, 1999) and latent Dirichlet allocation(LDA) (Blei et al., 2003) have shown great success in documents modeling and analysis. Topic models posit document collection exhibits multiple latent semantic topics where each topic is represented as a multinomial distribution over a given vocabulary and each document is a mixture of hidden topics. To generate a document $d$, PTM first samples a topic proportion vector, then for each word $w$ in $d$, samples a topic indicator $z$ and generates $w$ from the topic-word multinomial corresponding to topic $z$.

A key limitation of the existing PTMs is that words are assumed to be uncorrelated and generated independently. The topic assignment for each word is irrelevant to all other words. While this assumption facilitates computational efficiency, it loses the rich correlations between words. In many applications, users have external knowledge regarding word correlation, which can be taken into account to improve the semantic coherence of topic modeling. For example, WordNet (Miller, 1995a) presents a large amount of synonym relationships between words, Wikipedia[1] provides a knowledge graph by linking correlated concepts together and named entity recognizer identifies the categories of entity mentions. All of these external knowledge can be leveraged to learn more coherent topics if we can design a mechanism to encourage similar words, correlated concepts, entities of the same category to be assigned to the same topic.

Many approaches (Andrzejewski et al., 2009; Petterson et al., 2010; Newman et al., 2011) have attempted to solve this problem by enforcing hard and topic-independent rules that similar words should have similar probabilities in all topics, which is

[1] https://www.wikipedia.org/



*Human Language Technologies: The 2015 Annual Conference of the North American Chapter of the ACL*, pages 725–734,
Denver, Colorado, May 31 – June 5, 2015. 

questionable in that two words with similar representativeness of one topic are not necessarily of equal importance for another topic. For example, in the *fruit* topic, the words *apple* and *orange* have similar representativeness, while in an *IT company* topic, *apple* has much higher importance than *orange*. As another example, $church$ and $bible$ are similarly relevant to a $religion$ topic, whereas their relevance to an $architecture$ topic are vastly different. Exiting approaches are unable to differentiate the subtleties of word sense across topics and would falsely put irrelevant words into the same topic. For instance, since *orange* and *microsoft* are both labeled as similar to *apple* and are required to have similar probabilities in all topics as *apple* has, in the end, they will be unreasonably allocated to the same topic.

The existing approaches fail to properly use the word correlation knowledge, which is usually a list of word pairs labeled as *similar*. The similarity is computed based on statistics such as co-occurrence which are unable to accommodate the subtlety that whether two words labeled as similar are truly similar depends on which topic they appear in, as explained by the aforementioned examples. Ideally, the knowledge would be word $A$ and $B$ are similar under topic $C$. However, in reality, we only know two words are similar, but not under which topic. In this paper, we aim to abridge this gap. Gaining insights from (Verbeek and Triggs, 2007; Zhao et al., 2010; Zhu and Xing, 2010), we design a Markov Random Field regularized LDA model (MRF-LDA) which utilizes the external knowledge in a soft and topic-dependent manner to improve the coherence of topic modeling. We define a MRF on the latent topic layer of LDA to encode word correlations. Within a document, if two words are labeled as similar according to the external knowledge, their latent topic nodes will be connected by an undirected edge and a binary potential function is defined to encourage them to share the same topic label. This mechanism gives correlated words a better chance to be put into the same topic, thereby, improves the coherence of the learned topics. Our model provides a mechanism to automatically decide under which topic, two words labeled as similar are truly similar. We encourage words labeled as similar to share the same topic label, but do not specify which topic label they should share, and leave this to be decided by data. In the above mentioned *apple*, *orange*, *microsoft* example, we encourage *apple* and *orange* to share the same topic label A and try to push *apple* and *microsoft* to the same topic B. But A and B are not necessarily the same and they will be inferred according to the fitness of data. Different from the existing approaches which directly use the word similarities to control the topic-word distributions in a hard and topic-independent way, our method imposes constraints on the latent topic layer by which the topic-word multinomials are influenced indirectly and softly and are topic-aware.

The rest of the paper is organized as follows. In Section 2, we introduce related work. In Section 3, we propose the MRF-LDA model and present the variational inference method. Section 4 gives experimental results. Section 5 concludes the paper.

## 2 Related Work

Different from purely unsupervised topics models that often result in incoherent topics, knowledge based topic models enable us to take prior knowledge into account to produce more meaningful topics. Various approaches have been proposed to exploit the correlations and similarities among words to improve topic modeling instead of purely relying on how often words co-occur in different contexts (Heinrich, 2009). For instance, Andrzejewski et al. (2009) imposes Dirichlet Forest prior over the topic-word multinomials to encode the Must-Links and Cannot-Links between words. Words with Must-Links are encouraged to have similar probabilities within all topics while those with Cannot-Links are disallowed to simultaneously have large probabilities within any topic. Similarly, Petterson et al. (2010) adopted word information as features rather than as explicit constraints and defined a prior over the topic-word multinomials such that similar words share similar topic distributions. Newman et al. (2011) proposed a quadratic regularizer and a convolved Dirichlet regularizer over topic-word multinomials to incorporate the correlation between words. All of these methods directly incorporate the word correlation knowledge into the topic-word distributions in a hard and topic-independent way, which ignore the fact that whether two words are correlated depends on which topic they appear in.

There are several works utilizing knowledge with more complex structure to improve topic modeling. Boyd-Graber et al. (2007) incorporate the synset structure in WordNet (Miller, 1995b) into LDA for word sense disambiguation, where each topic is a random process defined over the synsets. Hu et al. (2011) proposed interactive topic modeling, which allows users to iteratively refine the discovered topics by adding constraints such as certain set of words must appear together in the same topic. Andrzejewski et al. (2011) proposed a general framework which uses first order logic to encode various domain knowledge regarding documents, topics and side information into LDA. The vast generality and expressivity of this model makes its inference to be very hard. Chen et al. (2013) proposed a topic model to model multi-domain knowledge, where each document is an admixture of latent topics and each topic is a probability distribution over domain knowledge. Jagarlamudi et al. (2012) proposed to guide topic modeling by setting a set of seed words in the beginning that user believes could represent certain topics. While these knowledge are rich in structure, they are hard to acquire in the real world applications. In this paper, we focus on pairwise word correlation knowledge which are widely attainable in many scenarios.

In the domain of computer vision, the idea of using MRF to enforce topical coherence between neighboring patches or superpixels has been exploited by several works. Verbeek and Triggs (2007) proposed Markov field aspect model where each image patch is modeled using PLSA (Hofmann, 1999) and a Potts model is imposed on the hidden topic layer to enforce spatial coherence. Zhao et al. (2010) proposed topic random field model where each superpixel is modeled using a combination of LDA and mixture of Gaussian model and a Potts model is defined on the topic layer to encourage neighboring superpixels to share the same topic. Similarly, Zhu and Xing (2010) proposed a conditional topic random field to incorporate features about words and documents into topic modeling. In their model, the MRF is restricted to be a linear chain, which can only capture the dependencies between neighboring words and is unable to incorporate long range word correlations. Different from these works, the MRF in our model is not restricted to Potts or chain structure. Instead, its structure is decided by the word correlation knowledge and can be arbitrary.

## 3 Markov Random Field Regularized Latent Dirichlet Allocation

In this section, we present the MRF-LDA model and the variational inference technique.

### 3.1 MRF-LDA

We propose the MRF-LDA model to incorporate word similarities into topic modeling. As shown in Figure 1, MRF-LDA extends the standard LDA model by imposing a Markov Random Field on the latent topic layer. Similar to LDA, we assume a document possesses a topic proportion vector $\theta$ sampled from a Dirichlet distribution. Each topic $\boldsymbol{\beta}_k$ is a multinomial distribution over words. Each word $w$ has a topic label $z$ indicating which topic $w$ belongs to.

In many scenarios, we have access to external knowledge regarding the correlations between words, such as *apple* and *orange* are similar, *church* and *bible* are semantically related. These similarity relationships among words can be leveraged to improve the coherence of learned topics. To do this, we define a Markov Random Field over the latent topic layer. Given a document $d$ containing $N$ words $\{w_i\}_{i=1}^N$, we examine each word pair $(w_i, w_j)$. If they are correlated according to the external knowledge, we create an undirected edge between their topic labels $(z_i, z_j)$. In the end, we obtain an undirected graph $G$ where the nodes are latent topic labels $\{z_i\}_{i=1}^N$ and edges connect topic labels of correlated words. In the example shown in Figure 1, $G$ contains five nodes $z_1, z_2, z_3, z_4, z_5$ and four edges connecting $(z_1, z_3), (z_2, z_5), (z_3, z_4), (z_3, z_5)$.

Given the undirected graph $G$, we can turn it into a Markov Random Field by defining unary potentials over nodes and binary potentials over edges. We define the unary potential for $z_i$ as $p(z_i|\boldsymbol{\theta})$, which is a multinomial distribution parameterized by $\boldsymbol{\theta}$. In standard LDA, this is how a topic is sampled from the topic proportion vector. For binary potential, with the goal to encourage similar words to have similar topic assignments, we define the edge potential between $(z_i, z_j)$ as $\exp\{\mathbb{I}(z_i = z_j)\}$, where $\mathbb{I}(\cdot)$ is the indicator function. This potential function yields a larger value if the two topic labels are the same and a smaller value if the two topic labels are different. Hence, it encourages similar words to be assigned to the same topic. Under the MRF model, the joint probability of all topic assignments $\mathbf{z} = \{z_i\}_{i=1}^N$ can be written as

$$p(\mathbf{z}|\boldsymbol{\theta},\lambda) = \frac{1}{A(\boldsymbol{\theta},\lambda)} \prod_{i=1}^{N} p(z_i|\boldsymbol{\theta}) \exp\{\lambda \sum_{(m,n)\in\mathcal{P}} \mathbb{I}(z_m = z_n)\} \tag{1}$$

where $\mathcal{P}$ denotes the edges in $G$ and $A(\boldsymbol{\theta},\lambda)$ is the partition function

$$A(\boldsymbol{\theta}) = \sum_{\mathbf{z}} \prod_{i=1}^{N} p(z_i|\boldsymbol{\theta}) \exp\{\lambda \sum_{(m,n)\in\mathcal{P}} \mathbb{I}(z_m = z_n)\} \tag{2}$$

We introduce $\lambda \geq 0$ as a trade-off parameter between unary potential and binary potential. In standard LDA, topic label $z_i$ only depends on topic proportion vector $\boldsymbol{\theta}$. In MRF-LDA, $z_i$ not only depends on $\boldsymbol{\theta}$, but also depends on the topic labels of similar words. If $\gamma$ is set to zero, the correlation between words is ignored and MRF-LDA is reduced to LDA. Given the topic labels, the generation of words is the same as LDA. $w_i$ is generated from the topic-words multinomial distribution $\boldsymbol{\beta}_{z_i}$ corresponding to $z_i$.

In MRF-LDA, the generative process of a document is summarized as follows:

- Draw a topic proportion vector $\boldsymbol{\theta} \sim Dir(\boldsymbol{\alpha})$
- Draw topic labels $\mathbf{z}$ for all words from the joint distribution defined in Eq.(1)
- For each word $w_i$, drawn $w_i \sim multi(\boldsymbol{\beta}_{z_i})$

Accordingly, the joint distribution of $\boldsymbol{\theta}, \mathbf{z}$ and $\mathbf{w}$ can be written as

$$p(\boldsymbol{\theta},\mathbf{z},\mathbf{w}|\boldsymbol{\alpha},\boldsymbol{\beta},\lambda) = p(\boldsymbol{\theta}|\boldsymbol{\alpha})p(\mathbf{z}|\boldsymbol{\theta},\lambda) \prod_{i=1}^{N} p(w_i|z_i,\boldsymbol{\beta}) \tag{3}$$

### 3.2 Variational Inference and Parameter Learning

The key inference problem we need to solve in MRF-LDA is to compute the posterior $p(\boldsymbol{\theta},\mathbf{z}|\mathbf{w})$ of latent variables $\boldsymbol{\theta},\mathbf{z}$ given observed data $\mathbf{w}$. As in LDA (Blei et al., 2003), exact computation is intractable. What makes things even challenging in

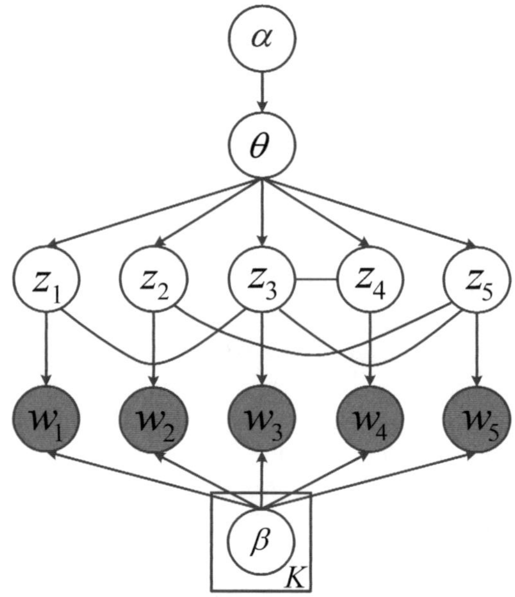


Figure 1: Markov Random Field Regularized Latent Dirichlet Allocation Model

MRF-LDA is that, an undirected MRF is coupled with a directed LDA and the hard-to-compute partition function of MRF makes the posterior inference and parameter learning very difficult. To solve this problem, we resort to variational inference (Wainwright and Jordan, 2008), which uses a easy-to-handle variational distribution to approximate the true posterior of latent variables. To deal with the partition function in MRF, we seek lower bound of the variational lower bound to achieve tractability. We introduce a variational distribution

$$q(\boldsymbol{\theta},\mathbf{z}) = q(\boldsymbol{\theta}|\boldsymbol{\eta}) \prod_{i=1}^{N} q(z_i|\boldsymbol{\phi}_i) \tag{4}$$

where Dirichlet parameter $\boldsymbol{\eta}$ and multinomial parameters $\{\boldsymbol{\phi}_i\}_{i=1}^N$ are free variational parameters. Using Jensen's inequality (Wainwright and Jordan, 2008), we can obtain a variational lower bound

$$\begin{aligned}\mathcal{L} &= \mathbb{E}_q[\log p(\boldsymbol{\theta}|\boldsymbol{\alpha})] + \mathbb{E}_q[\log p(\mathbf{z}|\boldsymbol{\theta},\lambda)] \\ &+ \mathbb{E}_q[\log \prod_{i=1}^{N} p(w_i|z_i,\boldsymbol{\beta})] - \mathbb{E}_q[\log q(\boldsymbol{\theta}|\boldsymbol{\eta})] \\ &- \mathbb{E}_q[\log \prod_{i=1}^{N} q(z_i|\boldsymbol{\phi}_i)]\end{aligned} \tag{5}$$

in which $\mathbb{E}_q[\log p(\mathbf{z}|\boldsymbol{\theta},\lambda)]$ can be expanded as

$$\begin{aligned}&\mathbb{E}_q[\log p(\mathbf{z}|\boldsymbol{\theta},\lambda)]\\&=-\mathbb{E}_q[\log A(\boldsymbol{\theta},\lambda)]+\lambda\sum_{(m,n)\in\mathcal{P}}\sum_{k=1}^{K}\phi_{mk}\phi_{nk}\\&+\sum_{i=1}^{N}\sum_{k=1}^{K}\phi_{ik}(\Psi(\eta_k)-\Psi(\sum_{j=1}^{K}\eta_j))\end{aligned}\tag{6}$$

The item $\mathbb{E}_q[\log A(\boldsymbol{\theta},\lambda)]$ involves the hard-to-compute partition function, which has no analytical expressions. We discuss how to deal with it in the sequel. With Taylor expansion, we can obtain an upper bound of $\mathbb{E}_q[\log A(\boldsymbol{\theta},\lambda)]$

$$\mathbb{E}_q[\log A(\boldsymbol{\theta},\lambda)]\leq c^{-1}\mathbb{E}_q[A(\boldsymbol{\theta},\lambda)]-1+\log c \tag{7}$$

where $c \geq 0$ is a new variational parameter. $\mathbb{E}_q[A(\boldsymbol{\theta},\lambda)]$ can be further upper bounded as

$$\begin{aligned}\mathbb{E}_q[\log A(\boldsymbol{\theta},\lambda)]\leq\exp\{\sum_{(m,n)\in\mathcal{P}}\lambda\}\\\sum_{n_1,n_2,\cdots,n_K}\mathbb{E}_q[\prod_{k=1}^{K}\boldsymbol{\theta}^{n_k}]\end{aligned}\tag{8}$$

where $n_k$ denotes the number of words assigned with topic label $k$ and $\sum_{k=1}^{K} n_k = N$. We further bound $\sum_{n_1,n_2,\cdots,n_K}\mathbb{E}_q[\prod_{k=1}^{K}\boldsymbol{\theta}^{n_k}]$ as follows

$$\begin{aligned}&\sum_{n_1,n_2,\cdots,n_K}\mathbb{E}_q[\prod_{k=1}^{K}\boldsymbol{\theta}^{n_k}]\\&=\sum_{n_1,n_2,\cdots,n_K}\frac{\Gamma(\sum_{k=1}^{K}\eta_k)}{\prod_{k=1}^{K}\Gamma(\eta_k)}\int\prod_{k=1}^{K}\theta^{n_k+\eta_k-1}d\boldsymbol{\theta}\\&=\sum_{n_1,n_2,\cdots,n_K}\frac{\Gamma(\sum_{k=1}^{K}\eta_k)\prod_{k=1}^{K}\Gamma(n_k+\eta_k)}{\prod_{k=1}^{K}\Gamma(\eta_k)\Gamma(\sum_{k=1}^{K}n_k+\eta_k)}\\&=\sum_{n_1,n_2,\cdots,n_K}\frac{\prod_{k=1}^{K}(\eta_k)_{n_k}}{(\sum_{k=1}^{K}\eta_k)_N}\\&\leq\sum_{n_1,n_2,\cdots,n_K}\frac{\prod_{k=1}^{K}(n_k)!}{(N)!}\end{aligned}\tag{9}$$

where $(a)_n$ denotes the Pochhammer symbol, which is defined as $(a)_n = a(a+1)\dots(a+n-1)$ and $\sum_{n_1,n_2,\cdots,n_K}\frac{\prod_{k=1}^{K}(n_k)!}{(N)!}$ is a constant. Setting $c = c/\sum_{n_1,n_2,\cdots,n_K}\frac{\prod_{k=1}^{K}(n_k)!}{(N)!}$, we get

$$\mathbb{E}_q[\log A(\boldsymbol{\theta},\lambda)]\ \leq\ c^{-1}\exp\{\sum_{(i,j)\in\mathcal{P}}\lambda\}-1+\log c \tag{10}$$

Given this upper bound, we can obtain a lower bound of the variational lower bound defined in Eq.(5). Variational parameters and model parameters can be learned by maximizing the lower bound using iterative EM algorithm. In E-step, we fix the model parameters and compute the variational parameters by setting the derivatives of the lower bound w.r.t the variational parameters to zero

$$\eta_k=\alpha_k+\sum_{i=1}^{N}\phi_{ik},c=\exp\{\sum_{(m,n)\in\mathcal{P}}\lambda\} \tag{11}$$

$$\begin{aligned}&\phi_{ik}\propto\exp\{\Psi(\eta_k)-\Psi(\sum_{j=1}^{K}\eta_j)+\lambda\sum_{j\in\mathcal{N}(i)}\phi_{jk}\\&+\sum_{v=1}^{V}w_{iv}\log\beta_{kv}\}\end{aligned}\tag{12}$$

In Eq.(12), $\mathcal{N}(i)$ denotes the words that are labeled to be similar to $i$. As can be seen from this equation, the probability $\phi_{ik}$ that word $i$ is assigned to topic $k$ depends on the probability $\phi_{jk}$ of $i$'s correlated words $j$. This explains how our model can incorporate word correlations in topic assignments. In M-step, we fix the variational parameters and update the model parameters by maximizing the lower bound defined on the set of documents $\{\mathbf{w}_d\}_{d=1}^{D}$

$$\beta_{kv}\propto\sum_{d=1}^{D}\sum_{i=1}^{N_d}\phi_{d,i,k}w_{d,i,v} \tag{13}$$

$$\lambda=\frac{1}{|P|}\log\frac{\sum_{d=1}^{D}\sum_{(m,n)\in P_d}\sum_{k=1}^{K}\phi_{d,m,k}\phi_{d,n,k}}{|P|\sum_{d=1}^{D}\frac{1}{c_d}} \tag{14}$$

## 4 Experiment

In this section, we corroborate the effectiveness of our model by comparing it with three baseline methods on two datasets.

| dataset | 20-Newsgroups | NIPS |
|---|---|---|
| # documents | 18846 | 1500 |
| # words | 40343 | 12419 |

Table 1: Dataset Statistics

### 4.1 Experiment Setup

- **Dataset**: We use two datasets in the experiments: 20-Newsgroups[2] and NIPS[3]. Their statistics are summarized in Table 1.

- **External Knowledge**: We extract word correlation knowledge from Web Eigenwords[4], where each word has a real-valued vector capturing the semantic meaning of this word based on distributional similarity. Two words are regarded as correlated if their representation vectors are similar enough. It is worth mentioning that, other sources of external word correlation knowledge, such as Word2Vec (Mikolov et al., 2013) and Glove (Pennington et al., 2014), can be readily incorporated into MRF-LDA.

- **Baselines**: We compare our model with three baseline methods: LDA (Blei et al., 2003), DF-LDA (Andrzejewski et al., 2009) and Quad-LDA (Newman et al., 2011). LDA is the most widely used topic model, but it is unable to incorporate external knowledge. DF-LDA and Quad-LDA are two models designed to incorporate word correlation to improve topic modeling. DF-LDA puts a Dirichlet Forest prior over the topic-word multinomials to encode the Must-Links and Cannot-Links between words. Quad-LDA regularizes the topic-word distributions with a structured prior to incorporate word relation.

- **Parameter Settings:** For all methods, we learn 100 topics. LDA parameters are set to their default settings in (Andrzejewski et al., 2009). For DF-LDA, we set its parameters as $\alpha = 1$, $\beta = 0.01$ and $\eta = 100$. The Must/Cannot links between words are generated based on the cosine similarity of words' vector representations in Web Eigenwords. Word pairs with similarity higher than 0.99 are set as Must-Links, and pairs with similarity lower than 0.1 are put into Cannot-Link set. For Quad-LDA, $\beta$ is set as 0.01; $\alpha$ is defined as $\frac{0.05 \cdot N}{D \cdot T}$, where N is the total occurrences of all words in all documents, D is the number of documents and T is topic number. For MRF-LDA, word pairs with similarity higher than 0.99 are labeled as correlated.

[2]http://qwone.com/ jason/20Newsgroups/

[3]http://archive.ics.uci.edu/ml/datasets/Bag+of+Words

[4]http://www.cis.upenn.edu/ ungar/eigenwords/

### 4.2 Results

We compare our model with the baseline methods both qualitatively and quantitatively.

#### 4.2.1 Qualitative Evaluation

Table 2 shows some exemplar topics learned by the four methods on the 20-Newsgroups dataset. Each topic is visualized by the top ten words. Words that are noisy and lack representativeness are highlighted with bold font. Topic 1 is about crime and guns. Topic 2 is about sex. Topic 3 is about sports and topic 4 is about health insurance. As can be seen from the table, our method MRF-LDA can learn more coherent topics with fewer noisy and meaningless words than the baseline methods. LDA lacks the mechanism to incorporate word correlation knowledge and generates the words independently. The similarity relationships among words cannot be utilized to imporve the coherence of topic modeling. Consequently, noise words such as *will*, *year*, *used* which cannot effectively represent a topic, show up due to their high frequency. DF-LDA and Quad-LDA proposed to use word correlations to enhance the coherence of learned topics. However, they improperly enforce words labeled as similar to have similar probabilities in all topics, which violates the fact that whether two words are similar depend on which topic they appear in. As a consequence, the topics extracted by these two methods are unsatisfactory. For example, topic 2 learned by DF-LDA mixed up a *sex* topic and a *reading* topic. Less relevant words such as *columbia*, *year*, *write* show up in the health insurance topic (topic 4) learned by Quad-LDA. Our method MRF-LDA incorporates the word correlation knowledge by imposing a MRF over the latent topic layer to encourage correlated words to share the same topic label, hence similar words have better chance to be put into the same topic. Conse-

Table 2: Topics Learned from 20-Newsgroups Dataset

| LDA | | | | DF-LDA | | | |
|---|---|---|---|---|---|---|---|
| Topic 1 (Crime) | Topic 2 (Sex) | Topic 3 (Sports) | Topic 4 (Health) | Topic 1 (Crime) | Topic 2 (Sex) | Topic 3 (Sports) | Topic 4 (Health) |
| gun | sex | team | government | gun | **book** | game | money |
| guns | men | game | money | police | men | games | pay |
| weapons | homosexuality | hockey | private | carry | **books** | players | insurance |
| control | homosexual | season | people | kill | homosexual | hockey | policy |
| firearms | gay | **will** | **will** | killed | homosexuality | baseball | tax |
| crime | sexual | **year** | health | weapon | **reference** | fan | companies |
| police | **com** | play | tax | cops | gay | league | **today** |
| **com** | homosexuals | nhl | care | warrant | **read** | played | plan |
| weapon | people | games | insurance | deaths | male | season | health |
| **used** | **cramer** | teams | program | control | homosexuals | ball | jobs |

| Quad-LDA | | | | MRF-LDA | | | |
|---|---|---|---|---|---|---|---|
| Topic 1 (Crime) | Topic 2 (Sex) | Topic 3 (Sports) | Topic 4 (Health) | Topic 1 (Crime) | Topic 2 (Sex) | Topic 3 (Sports) | Topic 4 (Health) |
| gun | homosexuality | game | money | gun | men | game | care |
| guns | sex | team | insurance | guns | sex | team | insurance |
| crime | homosexual | play | **columbia** | weapons | women | hockey | private |
| police | sin | games | pay | child | homosexual | players | cost |
| weapons | marriage | hockey | health | police | homosexuality | play | health |
| firearms | **context** | season | tax | control | child | player | costs |
| criminal | people | **rom** | **year** | kill | ass | fans | company |
| criminals | sexual | **period** | private | deaths | sexual | teams | companies |
| **people** | gay | goal | care | death | gay | fan | tax |
| law | homosexuals | player | **write** | **people** | homosexuals | best | public |

quently, the learned topics are of high coherence. As shown in Table 2, the topics learned by our method are largely better than those learned by the baseline methods. The topics are of high coherence and contain fewer noise and irrelevant words.

Our method provides a mechanism to automatically decide under which topic, two words labeled as similar are truly similar. The decision is made flexibly by data according to their fitness to the model, rather than by a hard rule adopted by DF-LDA and Quad-LDA. For instance, according to the external knowledge, the word *child* is correlated with *gun* and with *men* simultaneously. Under a *crime* topic, *child* and *gun* are truly correlated because they co-occur a lot in youth crime news, whereas, *child* and *men* are less correlated in this topic. Under a *sex* topic, *child* and *men* are truly correlated whereas *child* and *gun* are not. Our method can differentiate this subtlety and successfully put *child* and *gun* into the *crime* topic and put *child* and *men* into the *sex* topic. This is because our method encourages *child* and *gun* to be put into the same topic $A$ and encourages *child* and *men* to be put into the same topic $B$, but does not require $A$ and $B$ to be the same. $A$ and $B$ are freely decided by data.

Table 3 shows some topics learned on NIPS dataset. The four topics correspond to vision, neural network, speech recognition and electronic circuits respectively. From this table, we observe that the topics learned by our method are better in coherence than those learned from the baseline methods, which again demonstrates the effectiveness of our model.

#### 4.2.2 Quantitative Evaluation

We also evaluate our method in a quantitative manner. Similar to (Xie and Xing, 2013), we use the coherence measure (CM) to assess how coherent the learned topics are. For each topic, we pick up the top 10 candidate words and ask human annotators to judge whether they are relevant to the topic. First, annotators needs to judge whether a topic is interpretable or not. If not, the ten candidate words in this

Table 3: Topics Learned from NIPS Dataset

| LDA | | | | DF-LDA | | | |
|---|---|---|---|---|---|---|---|
| Topic 1 (Vision) | Topic 2 (Neural Net) | Topic 3 (Speech) | Topic 4 (Circuits) | Topic 1 (Vision) | Topic 2 (Neural Net) | Topic 3 (Speech) | Topic 4 (Circuits) |
| image | network | hmm | chip | images | network | speech | analog |
| images | neural | **mlp** | analog | pixel | system | context | chip |
| pixel | feedforward | hidden | **weight** | view | connection | speaker | vlsi |
| vision | architecture | context | digital | recognition | application | frame | implement |
| segment | **research** | model | **neural** | face | artificial | continuous | digital |
| visual | **general** | recognition | hardware | ica | input | processing | hardware |
| scene | **applied** | probabilities | bit | vision | **obtained** | **number** | voltage |
| texture | **vol** | training | **neuron** | system | **department** | **dependent** | bit |
| contour | **paper** | markov | implement | **natural** | **fixed** | frames | transistor |
| edge | **introduction** | system | vlsi | faces | techniques | spectral | design |
| **Quad-LDA** | | | | **MRF-LDA** | | | |
| Topic 1 (Vision) | Topic 2 (Neural Net) | Topic 3 (Speech) | Topic 4 (Circuits) | Topic 1 (Vision) | Topic 2 (Neural Net) | Topic 3 (Speech) | Topic 4 (Circuits) |
| image | training | speech | circuit | image | network | hmm | chip |
| images | set | hmm | analog | images | model | speech | **synapse** |
| pixel | network | speaker | chip | pixel | learning | acoustic | digital |
| region | learning | acoustic | voltage | disparity | function | context | analog |
| vision | net | phonetic | current | color | input | word | board |
| scene | number | vocabulary | vlsi | intensity | neural | phonetic | charge |
| surface | algorithm | phone | **neuron** | stereo | set | frames | **synaptic** |
| texture | **class** | utterance | gate | scene | algorithm | speaker | hardware |
| **local** | input | utterances | **input** | camera | system | phone | vlsi |
| contour | **examples** | frames | transistor | **detector** | data | vocabulary | programmable |

topic are automatically labeled as irrelevant. Otherwise, annotators are asked to identify words that are relevant to this topic. Coherence measure (CM) is defined as the ratio between the number of relevant words and total number of candidate words. In our experiments, four graduate students participated the labeling. For each dataset and each method, 10% of topics were randomly chosen for labeling.

Table 4 and 5 summarize the coherence measure of topics learned on 20-Newsgroups dataset and NIPS dataset respectively. As shown in the table, our method significantly outperforms the baseline methods with a large margin. On the 20-Newsgroups dataset, our method achieves an average coherence measure of 60.8%, which is two times better than LDA. On the NIPS dataset, our method is also much better than the baselines. In summary, we conclude that MRF-LDA produces much better results on both datasets compared to baselines, which demonstrates the effectiveness of our model in exploiting word correlation knowledge to improve the quality of topic modeling. To assess the consistency of the labelings made by different annotators, we computed the intraclass correlation coefficient (ICC). The ICCs on 20-Newsgroups and NIPS dataset are 0.925 and 0.725 respectively, which indicate good agreement between different annotators.

## 5 Conclusion

In this paper, we propose a MRF-LDA model, aiming to incorporate word correlation knowledge to improve topic modeling. Our model defines a MRF over the latent topic layer of LDA, to encourage correlated words to be put into the same topic. Our model provides the flexibility to enable a word to be similar to different words under different topics, which is more plausible and allows a word to show up in multiple topics properly. We evaluate our model on two datasets and corroborate its effectiveness both qualitatively and quantitatively.

| Method | Annotator1 | Annotator2 | Annotator3 | Annotator4 | Mean | Standard Deviation |
|---|---|---|---|---|---|---|
| LDA | 30 | 33 | 22 | 29 | 28.5 | 4.7 |
| DF-LDA | 35 | 41 | 35 | 27 | 36.8 | 2.9 |
| Quad-LDA | 32 | 36 | 33 | 26 | 31.8 | 4.2 |
| MRF-LDA | **60** | **60** | **63** | **60** | **60.8** | **1.5** |

Table 4: CM (%) on 20-Newsgroups Dataset

| Method | Annotator1 | Annotator2 | Annotator3 | Annotator4 | Mean | Standard Deviation |
|---|---|---|---|---|---|---|
| LDA | 75 | 74 | 74 | 69 | 73 | 2.7 |
| DF-LDA | 65 | 74 | 72 | 47 | 66 | 9.5 |
| Quad-LDA | 40 | 40 | 38 | 25 | 35.8 | 7.2 |
| MRF-LDA | **86** | **85** | **87** | **84** | **85.8** | **1.0** |

Table 5: CM (%) on NIPS Dataset

## References


David Andrzejewski, Xiaojin Zhu, and Mark Craven. 2009. Incorporating domain knowledge into topic modeling via dirichlet forest priors. In *Proceedings of the 26th Annual International Conference on Machine Learning*, pages 25–32. ACM.

David Andrzejewski, Xiaojin Zhu, Mark Craven, and Benjamin Recht. 2011. A framework for incorporating general domain knowledge into latent dirichlet allocation using first-order logic. In *Proceedings of the Twenty-Second international joint conference on Artificial Intelligence-Volume Volume Two*, pages 1171–1177. AAAI Press.

David M Blei, Andrew Y Ng, and Michael I Jordan. 2003. Latent dirichlet allocation. *the Journal of machine Learning research*, 3:993–1022.

Jordan L Boyd-Graber, David M Blei, and Xiaojin Zhu. 2007. A topic model for word sense disambiguation. In *EMNLP-CoNLL*, pages 1024–1033.

Zhiyuan Chen, Arjun Mukherjee, Bing Liu, Meichun Hsu, Malu Castellanos, and Riddhiman Ghosh. 2013. Leveraging multi-domain prior knowledge in topic models. In *Proceedings of the Twenty-Third International Joint Conference on Artificial Intelligence*, IJCAI'13, pages 2071–2077.

Gregor Heinrich. 2009. A generic approach to topic models. In *Machine Learning and Knowledge Discovery in Databases*, pages 517–532. Springer.

Thomas Hofmann. 1999. Probabilistic latent semantic indexing. In *Proceedings of the 22nd annual international ACM SIGIR conference on Research and development in information retrieval*, pages 50–57. ACM.

Yuening Hu, Jordan L Boyd-Graber, and Brianna Satinoff. 2011. Interactive topic modeling. In *ACL*, pages 248–257.

Jagadeesh Jagarlamudi, Hal Daumé, III, and Raghavendra Udupa. 2012. Incorporating lexical priors into topic models. In *Proceedings of the 13th Conference of the European Chapter of the Association for Computational Linguistics*, EACL '12, pages 204–213.

Tomas Mikolov, Ilya Sutskever, Kai Chen, Greg S Corrado, and Jeff Dean. 2013. Distributed representations of words and phrases and their compositionality. In *Advances in Neural Information Processing Systems*, pages 3111–3119.

George A Miller. 1995a. Wordnet: a lexical database for english. *Communications of the ACM*, 38(11):39–41.

George A. Miller. 1995b. Wordnet: A lexical database for english. *Commun. ACM*, 38(11):39–41, November.

David Newman, Edwin V Bonilla, and Wray Buntine. 2011. Improving topic coherence with regularized topic models. In *Advances in Neural Information Processing Systems*, pages 496–504.

Jeffrey Pennington, Richard Socher, and Christopher D Manning. 2014. Glove: Global vectors for word representation. *Proceedings of the Empiricial Methods in Natural Language Processing (EMNLP 2014)*, 12.

James Petterson, Wray Buntine, Shravan M Narayanamurthy, Tibério S Caetano, and Alex J Smola. 2010. Word features for latent dirichlet allocation. In *Advances in Neural Information Processing Systems*, pages 1921–1929.

Jakob Verbeek and Bill Triggs. 2007. Region classification with markov field aspect models. In *Computer Vision and Pattern Recognition, 2007. CVPR'07. IEEE Conference on*, pages 1–8. IEEE.

Martin J Wainwright and Michael I Jordan. 2008. Graphical models, exponential families, and variational inference. *Foundations and Trends® in Machine Learning*, 1(1-2):1–305.

Pengtao Xie and Eric P Xing. 2013. Integrating document clustering and topic modeling. *Proceedings of the 30th Conference on Uncertainty in Artificial Intelligence*.

Bin Zhao, Li Fei-Fei, and Eric Xing. 2010. Image segmentation with topic random field. *Computer Vision–ECCV 2010*, pages 785–798.

Jun Zhu and Eric P Xing. 2010. Conditional topic random fields. In *Proceedings of the 27th International Conference on Machine Learning (ICML-10)*, pages 1239–1246.

# The Unreasonable Effectiveness of Word Representations for Twitter Named Entity Recognition

**Colin Cherry** and **Hongyu Guo**
National Research Council Canada
first.last@nrc-cnrc.gc.ca

## Abstract

Named entity recognition (NER) systems trained on newswire perform very badly when tested on Twitter. Signals that were reliable in copy-edited text disappear almost entirely in Twitter's informal chatter, requiring the construction of specialized models. Using well-understood techniques, we set out to improve Twitter NER performance when given a small set of annotated training tweets. To leverage unlabeled tweets, we build Brown clusters and word vectors, enabling generalizations across distributionally similar words. To leverage annotated newswire data, we employ an importance weighting scheme. Taken all together, we establish a new state-of-the-art on two common test sets. Though it is well-known that word representations are useful for NER, supporting experiments have thus far focused on newswire data. We emphasize the effectiveness of representations on Twitter NER, and demonstrate that their inclusion can improve performance by up to 20 F1.

## 1 Introduction

Named entity recognition (NER) is the task of finding rigid designators as they appear in free text and classifying them into coarse categories such as *person* or *location* (Nadeau and Sekine, 2007). NER enables many other information extraction tasks such as relation extraction (Bunescu and Mooney, 2005) and entity linking (Ratinov et al., 2011).

There is considerable excitement at the prospect of porting information extraction technology to social media platforms such as Twitter. Social media reacts to world events faster than traditional news sources, and its sub-communities pay close attention to topics that other sources might ignore. An early example of the potential inherent in social information extraction is the Twitter Calendar (Ritter et al., 2012), which detects upcoming events (concerts, elections, video game releases, etc.) based on the anticipatory chatter of Twitter users. Unfortunately, processing social media text presents a unique set of challenges, especially for technologies designed for newswire: Twitter posts are short, the language is informal, capitalization is inconsistent at best, and spelling variations and abbreviations run rampant.

Armed with an affordable training set of 1,000 annotated tweets, we establish a strong baseline for Twitter NER using well-understood techniques. We build two unsupervised word representations in order to leverage a large collection of unannotated tweets, while a data-weighting technique allows us to benefit from annotated newswire data. Taken together, these two simple ideas establish a new state-of-the-art for both our test sets. We rigorously test the impact of both continuous and cluster-based word representations on Twitter NER, emphasizing the dramatic improvement that they bring. We also bring the experimental methodology of the domain adaptation community to Twitter NER, testing in-domain, out-of-domain and combined training scenarios, and revealing that it is not trivial to benefit from out-of-domain training data. Finally, an error analysis helps us begin to understand which social media challenges are being addressed by our adaptations, and which problems persist.

## 2 Background

Our work builds on a long line of research in discriminative tagging (Collins, 2002), and its application to named entity recognition (McCallum and Li, 2003). Our baseline tagger draws inspiration from Sarawagi and Cohen (2004), who introduce the no-



*Human Language Technologies: The 2015 Annual Conference of the North American Chapter of the ACL*, pages 735–745,
Denver, Colorado, May 31 – June 5, 2015. 

tion of semi-Markov tagging for NER, and from de Bruijn et al. (2011), who apply a similar tagger to clinical information extraction.

A number of previous studies have closely examined the use of word representations in NER, where one leverages unlabeled data to build features that help the tagger generalize across similar words. Miller et al. (2004) introduce this idea and provide the framework to build representation features from word clusters, while Lin and Wu (2009) extend this technique with phrases and sheer masses of unlabeled data. Turian et al. (2010) introduce continuous vectors as alternative word representations, and provide several experiments comparing these with clusters. Recently, Passos et al. (2014) have shown how continuous representations can be tailored to NER with a combination of context- and gazetteer-aware objectives. All of these studies employ representations only in newswire scenarios. Ratinov and Roth (2009) investigate cluster representations in a Web NER task, but the performance of their baseline indicates that it is not nearly so drastic a domain shift as our Twitter task.

### 2.1 Adapting to Social Media

There has been much recent activity in adapting NLP tools for social media. Ritter et al. (2011) collect training data and adapt tools for a number of tasks, including part-of-speech (POS) tagging, shallow parsing and NER. Owoputi et al. (2013) extends a line of research on building robust POS taggers for Twitter, and share our focus on the utility of word representations in this domain.

Liu et al. (2011) carry out the first study to specifically examine NER on Twitter. They use a nearest-neighbour word classifier stacked with a CRF, along with a boot-strapping scheme for semi-supervised learning. Interestingly, they find no utility in using cluster-based word representations, perhaps because their model directly accounts for a type's global context with bag-of-word features. Ritter et al. (2011) also examine Twitter NER, developing a semi-supervised technique that uses labeled LDA to project information from Freebase gazetteers onto unlabeled tweets. Plank et al. (2014) suggest a distant-supervision scheme, creating artificial training data by projecting reliable NER tags from web pages onto the tweets that link to those pages.

Fromreide et al. (2014) and Plank et al. (2014) point out that NER performance can be over-estimated when a system is tested on data extracted from the same pool as its training data. Temporal effects and annotation biases can result in gains that disappear when shifting to another test set. We follow their lead by testing on data that was annotated independently from our training data.

## 3 Methods

Our named entity recognizer is a discriminative, semi-Markov tagger, trained online using large-margin updates. It differs from word-based CRF systems in three ways: its inference algorithm, its tag structure, and its learning algorithm. This tagger allows us to develop new systems quickly, but it is important to emphasize that the adaptation strategies described later in this section can just as easily be applied to word-based CRFs.

#### Semi-Markov Inference

Sarawagi and Cohen (2004) describe a straightforward extension to the Viterbi algorithm that enables the tagging of contiguous phrases instead of words. Because each phrasal entity is tagged as a unit, we can recover entity boundaries without distinguishing between *Begin* and *Inside* tags, leaving the tagger to track only entity classes and *Outside* tags. This in turn allows us to run our tagger without Markov features. Since most entities are surrounded by *Outside* tags, conditioning on previous tag assignments has only limited utility. Finally, our phrasal tags enable useful features that consider entire entities, such as phrase-identity indicators.

#### Phrasal and Word-level Tags

In word-based models, it is beneficial to not only identify words that *Begin* entities, but also those that are in the middle (*Inside*) or at the end of entities (*Last*), as well as entities that consist of exactly one *Unique* word (Ratinov and Roth, 2009). Since we tag entire phrases at once, we can easily assign each word in the phrase to one of these four entity-relative positions. Therefore, even though our tagger tracks only entity class, its word-level features are annotated as if we maintained a full *BILUO* tag set.

**Passive-Aggressive Learning**

We train our model with a structured version of the Passive-Aggressive (PA) algorithm (Crammer et al., 2006). The benefits of using PA in place of a CRF are that we require only Viterbi inference, and memory requirements are minimized, as we update the model one training sentence at a time.

PA is an online, large-margin learning algorithm that attempts to separate correct sequences from incorrect ones by a margin of 1. For each update to the weight vector $w$, we select a training sentence $x$ and its gold-standard tag sequence $y$. We use dynamic programming to search for a response $\hat{y}$ that maximizes the structured hinge loss:[1]

$$\hat{y} = \operatorname*{arg\,max}_{y' \neq y} = \left[1 + w^{\mathrm{T}}\big(\Phi(x, y') - \Phi(x, y)\big)\right] \tag{1}$$

where $\Phi()$ maps an $(x, y)$ pair to a feature vector. If the loss is greater than 0, we update our model:

$$w = w + \tau\big(\Phi(x, y) - \Phi(x, \hat{y})\big) \tag{2}$$

where $\tau$ is an adaptive learning rate that scales the update to the smallest step size that achieves 0 loss:

$$\tau = \min\left(C, \frac{1 + w^{\mathrm{T}}\big(\Phi(x, \hat{y}) - \Phi(x, y)\big)}{||\Phi(x, y) - \Phi(x, \hat{y})||}\right) \tag{3}$$

$C$ is a hyper-parameter that truncates large steps to prevent over-fitting. It is related to the $C$-parameter of an SVM (Martins et al., 2010). To further guard against over-fitting, we use the average of all vectors $w$ seen during training when tagging new text (Collins, 2002).

**Features**

The feature function $\Phi(x, y)$ must decompose into the semi-Markov dynamic program:

$$\Phi(x, y) = \sum_{(s,t,y_j) \in D(x,y)} \phi(s, t, y_j, x) \tag{4}$$

where $D$ is a derivation decomposing $(x, y)$ into $J$ entity-tag assignments $(s, t, y_j)$, each asserting that the phrase $x_s \ldots x_{t-1}$ is assigned the tag $y_j$. Tagged spans are non-overlapping, and to eliminate spurious ambiguity, constrained so that *Outside* can tag only single-word spans ($t = s + 1$).

[1] This can be done by running a 2-best tagger. If the 1-best answer is not correct ($y' \neq y$), then it maximizes the loss, otherwise, the 2-best answer maximizes the loss.

| Phrase: |
|---|
| $[y_j]$, $[y_j, x_s \ldots x_{t-1}]$, $[y_j, lc(x_s \ldots x_{t-1})]$, $[y_j, ss(x_s \ldots x_{t-1})]$ |

| Word, for each $i$ s.t. $s \leq i < t$: |
|---|
| $\{[y_j, x_{i+k}, k]\}_{k=-2}^{2}$, $\{[y_j, er_{s,t}(i), x_{i+k}, k]\}_{k=-2}^{2}$, $\{[y_j, lc(x_{i+k}), k]\}_{k=-2}^{2}$, $\{[y_j, er_{s,t}(i), lc(x_{i+k}), k]\}_{k=-2}^{2}$, $\{[y_j, ss(x_{i+k}), k]\}_{k=-2}^{2}$, $\{[y_j, er_{s,t}(i), ss(x_{i+k}), k]\}_{k=-2}^{2}$, $\{[y_j, pf(n, x_i)]\}_{n=1}^{3}$, $\{[y_j, er_{s,t}(i), pf(n, x_i)]\}_{n=1}^{3}$, $\{[y_j, sf(n, x_i)]\}_{n=1}^{3}$, $\{[y_j, er_{s,t}(i), sf(n, x_i)]\}_{n=1}^{3}$ |

Table 1: Baseline features $\phi(s, t, y_j, x)$. [*str*] stands for an indicator feature with the name *str*; *lc*() maps a string onto its lowercased form; *ss*() maps a string onto its word shape ("Apple Inc." becomes "Aa Aa."); $pf(n, x_i)$ and $sf(n, x_i)$ are $n$-character prefixes and suffixes of $x_i$; and $er_{s,t}(i)$ maps an absolute sentence position $i$ ($s \leq i < t$) to a relative entity position drawn from $\{B, I, L, U\}$.

Our baseline feature set, shown in Table 1, closely mimics the set proposed by Ratnaparkhi (1996), covering word identity, prefixes, suffixes and surrounding words. It has been augmented with phrase-identity indicators and hierarchical word-level tags. These conjoin the entity class $y_j$ with the word's entity-relative position, backing off to $y_j$ alone. Most features look only at a single word $x_i$, which improves efficiency by allowing the tagger to re-use word-level scores across many phrasal tags.

There are some standard NER features that we chose not to include. We follow Lin and Wu (2009) in omitting POS tags and gazetteers in order to reduce our dependence on linguistic resources. We expect similar information to be provided by unsupervised word representations, and we test this assumption in Section 5.2. We omit context aggregation, which accounts for the repetition of entities (Ratinov and Roth, 2009), because Twitter's short message length reduces the utility of document-level features.

### 3.1 Word Representations

Our primary tool for domain adaptation will be unsupervised word representations, which convey information about a word's distributional profile.

| Brown clusters, for each $i$ s.t. $s \leq i < t$: |
|---|
| $\{[y_j, brn(n, x_i), n]\}_{n \in \{2,4,8,12\}}$, |
| $\{[y_j, er_{s,t}(i), brn(n, x_i), n]\}_{n \in \{2,4,8,12\}}$ |
| Word vectors, for each $i$ s.t. $s \leq i < t$: |
| $\{[y_j, n] = w2v(n, x_i)\}_{n=1}^{300}$, |
| $\{[y_j, er_{s,t}(i), n] = w2v(n, x_i)\}_{n=1}^{300}$ |

Table 2: Word representation features in $\phi(s, t, y_j, x)$. $brn(n, x_i)$ maps a word $x_i$ to the first $n$ bits of its Brown cluster bit sequence. $w2v(n, x_i)$ maps $x_i$ to the $n^{th}$ component of its word vector, and $[str] = v$ stands for a real-valued feature with name *str* and value $v$.

**Brown Clusters**

The Brown clustering algorithm assigns types to a deterministic, hierarchical clustering, which has been trained to optimize the likelihood of a first-order, class-based language model (Brown et al., 1992). The clusters capture both syntactic and semantic regularities, and have been shown to perform well as unsupervised part-of-speech taggers (Blunsom and Cohn, 2011).

The clusters are organized into a binary tree structure; therefore, each cluster can be represented as a bit string that encodes the branching decisions required to reach its leaf from the root. By truncating the bit string at different prefix lengths, one can access different granularities of clusters. Cluster membership can then be used to create indicators similar to the baseline's word identity features. This results in two feature templates, shown in Table 2.[2]

This technique has been previously applied to both newswire NER (Miller et al., 2004; Turian et al., 2010; Passos et al., 2014) and Twitter NER (Ritter et al., 2011; Plank et al., 2014). But previous work on Twitter NER has not directly tested the impact of Brown clusters; instead, they generally appear as part of an adapted baseline.

**Word Vectors**

An alternative word representation maps each word type deterministically to a low-dimensional continuous vector space. This technique was originally used as the bottom layer for continuous-space language models (Bengio et al., 2003), where the type-to-vector mapping can be learned with back-propagation. However, Mikolov et al. (2013) have shown that useful vector representations can be learned more efficiently by eschewing the language-modeling objective. Their skip-gram model, which we adopt here, optimizes for each token, the likelihood of the tokens in a window surrounding it. This training process creates a linear classifier that predicts words conditioned on the central token's vector representation. The classifier and the word vectors are learned simultaneously, but once training is complete, the classifier is usually discarded, leaving only the vectors.

These continuous representations project words into a low-dimensional space. Words that tend to have similar contexts, and therefore similar syntactic and semantic properties, will tend to be near one another in this space. We incorporate these representations into our NER system as real-valued features of each word $x_i$, as shown in Table 2.

### 3.2 Data Weighting

Our next tool for domain adaptation is a small pool of in-domain, annotated data. The easiest way to make use of this data is to append it to our large pool of out-of-domain training data, which is what has been done in previous work on Twitter NER (Ritter et al., 2011; Plank et al., 2014). However, we have the strong intuition that greater weight should be placed on the in-domain data.

Assume that for each training pair $(x, y)$ we also have an importance weight $\eta$. In our case, all out-of-domain pairs will share one value for $\eta$, and all in-domain pairs will share another, higher $\eta$. We modify our PA learner to calculate $\tau$ using a version of Equation 3 that replaces $C$ with $\eta C$. Unlike scaling $\tau$ directly, scaling $C$ has the desirable property of having even high-$\eta$ examples stop updating at precisely 0 loss, just as if we had duplicated that training example $\eta$ times (Karampatziakis and Langford, 2010). If we view $C$ as a regularization term, then this modification can also be interpreted as implementing example-specific regularization. Importance weights can also be incorporated into CRFs by modifying their training objective; however, this is not a standard feature of most CRF packages.

[2] We also experimented with templates over clusters and vectors for surrounding words, to no benefit.

| Data | Lines | Types | Tokens | # PER | # LOC | # ORG |
|---|---|---|---|---|---|---|
| Fin10 (Train) | 1,000 | 4,865 | 17,276 | 192 | 143 | 172 |
| Fin10Dev (Test) | 1,975 | 7,734 | 33,770 | 325 | 279 | 287 |
| Rit11 (Test) | 2,394 | 8,686 | 46,469 | 454 | 377 | 280 |
| Fro14 (Test) | 1,545 | 5,392 | 20,666 | 390 | 163 | 200 |
| CoNLL (Train) | 14,041 | 20,752 | 203,621 | 6,601 | 7,142 | 6,322 |
| Unlabeled Tweets | 98M | 57M | 1,995M | – | – | – |

Table 3: Details of our NER-annotated corpora. A *line* is a tweet in Twitter and a sentence in newswire.

## 4 Experimental Design

Vital statistics for all of our data sets are shown in Table 3. For in-domain NER data, we use three collections of annotated tweets: Fin10 was originally crowd-sourced by Finin et al. (2010), and was manually corrected by Fromreide et al. (2014), while Rit11 (Ritter et al., 2011) and Fro14 (Fromreide et al., 2014) were built by expert annotators. We divide Fin10 temporally into a training set and a development set, and we consider Rit11 and Fro14 to be our test sets. This reflects a plausible training scenario, with train and dev drawn from the same pool, but with distinct tests drawn from later in time. These three data sets were collected and unified by Plank et al. (2014), who normalized the tags into three entity classes: *person* (PER), *location* (LOC) and *organization* (ORG). The source text has also been normalized; notably, all numbers are normalized to NUMBER, and all URLs and Twitter @user names have been normalized to URL and @USER respectively. In the gold-standard, we choose to reverse a tagging normalization performed by Plank et al. (2014), who had post-processed the data so that all @user names are tagged as PER. These tags are trivial to replicate, and we found that they inflate scores quite dramatically. Therefore, all @user names are untagged in both the gold standard and our system outputs.

We use the CoNLL 2003 newswire training set as a source of out-of-domain NER annotations (Tjong Kim Sang and De Meulder, 2003). The source text has been normalized to match the Twitter NER data, and we have removed the MISC tag from the gold standard, leaving PER, LOC and ORG.

Finally, we also use a large corpus of unannotated tweets, collected from between May 2011 and April 2012. It has been tokenized by the CMU Twokenizer,[3] but is otherwise unnormalized.

### 4.1 Hyper-parameter Configuration

Our NER system is trained for 10 epochs with its regularization parameter $C$ set to 0.01.

We train our word vectors with an in-house implementation of word2vec (Mikolov et al., 2013), with vector size set to 300, a hierarchical soft-max objective, down-sampling frequent words at a rate of 0.001, a window-size of 10 tokens, and a minimum frequency count of 10. When run on our unannotated tweets, this produces vector representations for 2.5M types. We generate a random vector, with each component sampled from the standard normal, to use as the representation for any word that did not occur in our unlabeled data, including begin- and end-of-sentence markers. We do not scale the vectors before using them as NER features.

We train Brown clusters on the same data using the implementation by Liang (2005), with 1,000 clusters and a minimum frequency of 10, resulting in cluster assignments for the same 2.5M types.

## 5 Results

We evaluate our various NER taggers using the CoNLL 2003 metrics: phrase-level precision, recall, and balanced F-measure (F1).

We begin by testing our system on the CoNLL newswire task, both to confirm that our implementation is reasonable, and to help situate the Twitter results that appear later. We train on the unmodified CoNLL training corpus, and report F1 on the CoNLL development and test sets. We compare our baseline to the baseline from Ratinov and Roth (2009) (RR09), and we compare our representation-enhanced system (*+Reps*) to their "All External

[3]http://www.ark.cs.cmu.edu/TweetNLP/

| System | Dev F1 | Test F1 |
|---|---|---|
| RR09 Baseline | 89.2 | 83.6 |
| Our Baseline | 90.4 | 84.3 |
| RR09 Base + All External | 92.5 | 88.6 |
| Our Base + Reps | 91.6 | 88.0 |

Table 4: Performance on newswire (CoNLL) data.

| System | Fin10Dev | Rit11 | Fro14 | Avg |
|---|---|---|---|---|
| CoNLL | 27.3 | 27.1 | 29.5 | 28.0 |
| + Brown | 38.4 | 39.4 | 42.5 | 40.1 |
| + Vector | 40.8 | 40.4 | 42.9 | 41.4 |
| + Reps | 42.4 | 42.2 | 46.2 | 43.6 |
| Fin10 | 36.7 | 29.0 | 30.4 | 32.0 |
| + Brown | 59.9 | 53.9 | 56.3 | 56.7 |
| + Vector | 61.5 | 56.4 | 58.4 | 58.8 |
| + Reps | 64.0 | 58.5 | 60.2 | 60.9 |
| CoNLL+Fin10 | 44.7 | 39.9 | 44.2 | 42.9 |
| + Brown | 54.9 | 52.9 | 58.5 | 55.4 |
| + Vector | 58.9 | 55.2 | 59.9 | 58.0 |
| + Reps | 58.9 | 56.4 | 61.8 | 59.0 |
| + Weights | 64.4 | 59.6 | 63.3 | 62.4 |

Table 5: Impact of our components on Twitter NER performance, as measured by F1, under 3 data scenarios.

Knowledge" system. Both use Brown clusters, but RR09 uses Wikipedia gazetteers where we use word vectors. Results are shown in Table 4.

We achieve broadly comparable scores in both settings. Our external knowledge features are not as useful as theirs, which may be due to our lack of Wikipedia gazetteers, or due to a domain mismatch in our unannotated training data. Their clusters are trained on the 1996 Reuters corpus, a superset of the CoNLL data, matching it in both era and domain. Conversely, our clusters and vectors are both trained on tweets from 2011, so it is somewhat surprising that they help to the extent that they do.

### 5.1 Performance on Twitter

Our primary results are shown in Table 5, where we compare our word representation and data weighting techniques under three scenarios: training on out-of-domain data only (*CoNLL*), on in-domain data only (*Fin10*), and on both. Our data weighting technique (*+Weights*, see Section 3.2) only applies when we use both training sets. We used Fin10Dev to determine our importance weights, selecting $\eta = 0.01$ for CoNLL and $\eta = 1$ for Fin10. For these experiments, we test Brown clusters (*+Brown*), word vectors (*+Vector*), and both together (*+Reps*).

| System | Prec | Rec | F1 |
|---|---|---|---|
| CoNLL | 43.0 | 49.8 | 46.2 |
| Fin10 | 75.3 | 50.2 | 60.2 |
| CoNLL+Fin10 | 66.0 | 58.0 | 61.8 |
| +Weights | 73.8 | 55.4 | 63.3 |

Table 6: Precision, recall and F1 on the *Fro14* test set with the *Base+All Reps* feature set.

Our Twitter NER results are much lower than the newswire results from Table 4, with our best Twitter system scoring more than 25 F1 below our best CoNLL system. But the picture would look much worse without word representations, which boost performance in every training scenario. Our best representation-free system lags nearly 20 F1 behind our best system that uses representations.

Looking across scenarios, we note that *CoNLL+Reps* outperforms *CoNLL+Fin10* on 2 out of 3 tests. This is interesting, as it shows that, given the hypothetical choice between collecting 100 million unannotated tweets for word representations, and collecting one thousand annotated tweets for NER training, we are better served by the unannotated data. Of course, it is even better to use both; their combined benefit in *CoNLL+Fin10+Reps* is more than additive.

Across all data scenarios and test sets, Brown clusters help less than word vectors. This contradicts the observations from Turian et al. (2010), who generally found Brown clusters to perform best. This may be because of our domain adaptation scenario, or it could be due to our use of word2vec, which did not exist at the time of the Turian study. The combination of Brown clusters and word vectors is consistently better than using either alone. The two representations track different sorts of information: our use of a large window leads word2vec to build topic-focused vectors (Turney, 2012), while Brown clustering is naturally more local, creating very syntactic, part-of-speech-like clusters. It is easy to see how both types of information can be useful to NER.

Ritter et al. (2011) report that including out-of-

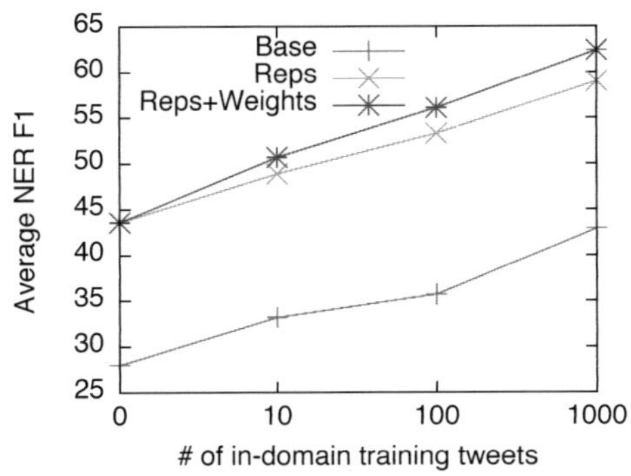


Figure 1: F1 averaged over all 3 test sets as we add Fin10 training data to CoNLL.

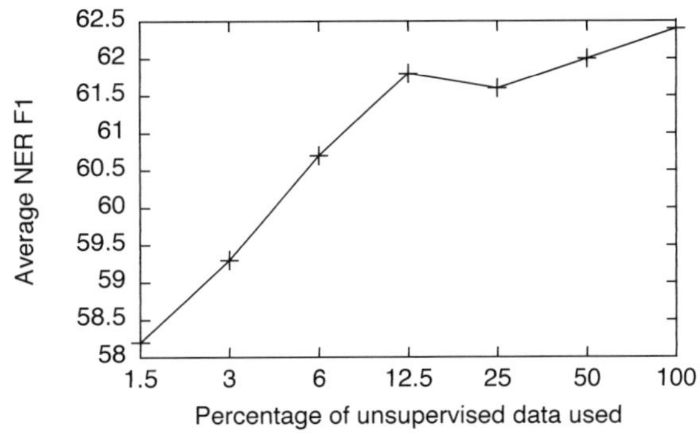


Figure 2: F1 averaged over all 3 test sets as we increase the percentage of tweets used to build representations.

| Test Set | PER | LOC | ORG |
|---|---|---|---|
| Fin10Dev | 71.3 | 72.4 | 48.8 |
| Rit11 | 70.8 | 61.9 | 36.9 |
| Fro14 | 69.4 | 70.2 | 42.6 |

Table 7: F1 for our *All Data+Reps+Weights* system, organized by entity class.

domain data hurts NER performance. Focusing on the lines *Fin10+Reps* and *CoNLL+Fin10+Reps*, we see the same problem. In the presence of word representations, unweighted CoNLL data hurts performance when added to a *Fin10* system. Fortunately, the inclusion of importance weights (+*Weights*) reverses this trend, giving us our best result on each test. We saw no consistent improvement from importance weights on the representation-free system.

To better understand the benefits of importance weights, Table 6 reports detailed scores for the Fro14 test set under the *Base+Reps* feature set, as we vary training scenarios. Results on the other test sets are similar. The *Fin10* system achieves high precision but low recall, while the *CoNLL+Fin10* does the opposite. This is because the CoNLL data is much more entity-dense than the Twitter data, which biases systems trained on CoNLL to return too many entities. By down-weighting the CoNLL data, we reduce this bias and gain 6.8 points of precision at the cost of only 2.6 points of recall.

Figure 1 gives learning curves as we add *Fin10* data to *CoNLL* across several feature sets. There is a steady improvement for all systems as the in-domain data grows, and importance weighting increases the impact of in-domain data even at very low quantities. Though the curves shows no sign of flattening out, note that the x-axis is log-scaled.

We have access to roughly 100 million tweets for unsupervised representation learning. Figure 2 provides a learning curve for our *Reps+Weights* system as we increase the percentage of unlabeled tweets used to train both Brown clusters and word vectors from 1.5% to 100% of that data, doubling the amount with each step. With only 1.5 million tweets, average performance is already very good, and we can see that the benefits of scale are starting to level off after we clear 12.5 million.

Table 7 reports our best system's performance by entity class. For all three test sets, ORG is the most difficult. ORG is perhaps the broadest entity class, but we suspect it is also the most likely to be annotated inconsistently, as it is rife with subtle distinctions: bands (ORG) versus musicians (PER); companies (ORG) versus their products (O); and teams (ORG) versus their home cities (LOC). During an inspection of 25 incorrect ORG predictions by our best system, drawn from a test on *Fin10Dev*, we found 10 cases where the gold standard was questionable. Two of these incorrectly placed "the" inside a chunk, ("[the Mariners]" is wrong; "the [Mariners]" is right), while the remaining 8 involved company-product distinctions, which are tricky even for human annotators. The NER task is not always as intuitive as we would like, and *organizations* tend to highlight these difficulties.

### 5.2 Comparison with Linguistic Resources

Thus far, we have restricted ourselves to a setting without access to linguistic resources, but for some

|  | Base +X | Reps +X |
|---|---|---|
| $\emptyset$ | 42.9 | 62.4 |
| [P]OS Tags | 47.1 | 63.0 |
| [G]azetteers | 52.8 | 63.2 |
| [P]+[G] | 55.6 | 63.5 |

Table 8: Adding linguistic resources to our baseline and representation-enabled systems, as measured by F1 averaged over 3 test sets. All systems are trained on CoNLL+Fin10, and all but Base+$\emptyset$ use data weighting.

languages, such as English, rich resources exist and can be very useful. We now examine how word representations compare and interact with gazetteers and POS taggers.

For gazetteers, we use those included with the Illinois NER system (Ratinov and Roth, 2009), generating features that indicate when a word appears as part of a phrase found in a gazetteer. For POS tags, we use the CMU Twitter Tagger (Owoputi et al., 2013), and generate POS tag indicators for the current word and for tags within a 2-word window. For some of our corpora, notably CoNLL and Rit11, the corpus tokenization did not match the POS tagger's tokenization. We resolve mismatches by allowing the POS tagger to further tokenize the input sentence to better match its assumptions. After POS tagging, we merge any split tokens back to the original tokenization, picking a representative tag from among merged tags according to a priority list (verb > noun > adjective, etc.). The POS tags may have performed better if we had used the tagger's native tokenization throughout.[4]

Results of our comparison are shown in Table 8. Comparing *Base+*$\emptyset$ and *Base+[P]+[G]*, we see that linguistic resources boost the baseline's performance considerably. Turning to *Reps+[P]+[G]*, we see that adding word representations to linguistic resources provides another substantial boost of 7.9 F1. Conversely, adding linguistic resources to a system that already has representations increases F1 by only 1.1 points, indicating that not much new information is being added. The per-feature analysis indicates that much of this boost comes from the gazetteers.

[4]Inconsistent tokenization also hinders the word representations, which were constructed from a corpus tokenized by the CMU Twokenizer.

| System | Rit11 | Fro14 |
|---|---|---|
| PHMS14 Baseline | 77.4 | 82.1 |
| PHMS14 Dict $\prec$ Web | 78.5 | 83.9 |
| All Data+Reps+Weights | 82.3 | 86.4 |
| All Data+Ling+Reps+Weights | 82.6 | 86.9 |

Table 9: Comparison with the state-of-the-art, reporting test F1. Both the gold-standard and the system outputs have `@user` names deterministically tagged as PER.

### 5.3 Comparison with the State-of-the-Art

In Table 9, we compare our best system, including linguistic resources, to the state-of-the-art results reported by Plank et al. (2014).[5] In order to create a fair comparison, we post-process both our system output and the gold-standard to tag all @user names as PER, just as they do.

Like our system, their baseline includes CoNLL and Twitter data, and uses Brown clusters trained on a comparable number of unlabeled tweets. Their strongest system uses distant supervision over linked web-pages to create artificial training data. But we are able to outperform it with our vector representations and importance weights. Note that this comparison is not perfect, as they train on a much larger pool of crowd-sourced, NER-annotated tweets, consisting of 170k tokens compared to our 17k. The size of their training data is balanced by the fact that its annotations were automatically correctly using MACE (Hovy et al., 2013), where ours were corrected manually, making it unclear which group has the advantage. Nonetheless, our results establish a new state-of-the-art for both test sets, and they do so using only 1k annotated tweets.

## 6 Analysis

We inspected 100 tweets from the Rit11 test set, focusing on the output from our primary system, *Base+Reps+Weights*, and our baseline, *Base*, both trained on the *CoNLL+Fin10* data. We noted cases where the primary system improved upon the baseline, and cases where it failed to achieve the gold-standard, and placed the phenomena we observed into bins. In general, the baseline was observed

[5]We omit the Fin10 test set from this comparison, as Plank et al. (2014) test on the entirety of Fin10, while we have divided it into training and development sets.

($a$) RT @USER : [Christmas:PER] was so much better when there was a santa :( #allteensthings
RT @USER : Christmas was so much better when there was a santa :( #allteensthings

($b$) Lmao . I have a feeling [Imma:ORG] get yelled at tomorrow . Big time . XD Ehh oh well
Lmao . I have a feeling Imma get yelled at tomorrow . Big time . XD Ehh oh well

($c$) I pray an give God glory even when im in pain , hurting , or crying .
I pray an give [God:PER] glory even when im in pain , hurting , or crying .

($d$) Anyone know what days/times that you can smoke hookah at the mix ( cma center ) in [corbin:PER] .
Anyone know what days/times that you can smoke hookah at the mix ( cma center ) in [corbin:LOC] .

Figure 3: (a,b): examples where the baseline (top) is improved by our final system (bottom)
(c,d): examples where our final system (top) falls short of the gold-standard (bottom)

to rely heavily on local context and capitalization, while the primary system has a much stronger global prior on a given type's entity assignment.

*Reps+Weights* improved the baseline in 54 out of 100 tweets. There were 31 cases where the primary system corrected a baseline error caused by a misleading capitalization cue. Some of these, such as Figure 3(a) are patched by world knowledge provided by word representations, but many simply reflect a reduced reliance on capitalization. We were surprised to find only 11 cases where Twitter's informal language led to an error, often due to a vaguely name-shaped colloquialism, such as in 3(b). 6 of these 11 cases were fixed by the primary system.

*Reps+Weights* fell short of the gold-standard in 62 of 100 tweets. We observed 39 recall errors that were difficult to divide into smaller bins. These entities were often missed despite clear capitalization cues, as in Figure 3(c). This particular example is actually a symptom of inconsistent annotation: CoNLL and Rit11 consistently annotate *God* as a person, while our Fin10 training data leaves *God* untagged. The next largest class of errors consists of 11 problems caused by uniform casing (all caps or all lowercase). We also have 5 remaining errors due to informal language, which are interesting, as they highlight gaps in our representations. These include cases where the system generates false entities for variants of rare words (*Tidying* $\rightarrow$ *Tidyin*), or unusual lengthenings (*Yayaayayay*, as opposed to the well-attested *Yayayayay*). We also saw cases where entities were missed due to creative punctuation (*Go V-I-K-I-N-G-S!*). Finally, we found 4 cases where the system actually over-relies on its word representations, such as in 3(d), where the global PER interpretation of *corbin* overrides a fairly strong LOC signal provided by the local context word *in*.

## 7 Discussion

We have shown that the combination of Brown clusters, word vectors, and a simple data weighting scheme is sufficient to establish a new state-of-the-art on two Twitter NER test sets, using only 1,000 annotated tweets. We have designed our experiments to emphasize the dramatic impact of word representations in this domain, and to clarify the effects of in- and out-of-domain training sets.

Word representations learned on a large, unlabeled Twitter corpus have addressed a surprising number of issues with inconsistent capitalization and informal language. However, our continuing problems with uncased tweets and unusual colloquialisms demonstrate that there are still many human-readable words that remain a mystery to our system. In response to these observations, we would like to investigate more flexible representations, perhaps similar to those of Botha and Blunsom (2014), who use a linear combination of morpheme vectors to create representations that can generalize across words with similar forms.

## Acknowledgments

Thanks to the anonymous reviewers for their helpful comments, to Alan Ritter for providing us with our corpus of unlabeled tweets, and to Barbara Plank for providing us with our three labeled corpora.

## References


Yoshua Bengio, Réjean Ducharme, Pascal Vincent, and Christian Jauvin. 2003. A neural probabilistic language model. *Journal of Machine Learning Research*, 3:1137–1155.

Phil Blunsom and Trevor Cohn. 2011. A hierarchical pitman-yor process hmm for unsupervised part of speech induction. In *ACL*, pages 865–874, Portland, Oregon, USA, June.

Jan A. Botha and Phil Blunsom. 2014. Compositional Morphology for Word Representations and Language Modelling. In *ICML*, Beijing, China.

Peter F Brown, Peter V Desouza, Robert L Mercer, Vincent J Della Pietra, and Jenifer C Lai. 1992. Class-based n-gram models of natural language. *Computational linguistics*, 18(4):467–479.

Razvan C Bunescu and Raymond J Mooney. 2005. A shortest path dependency kernel for relation extraction. In *EMNLP*, pages 724–731.

M. Collins. 2002. Discriminative training methods for hidden markov models: Theory and experiments with perceptron algorithms. In *EMNLP*.

Koby Crammer, Ofer Dekel, Joseph Keshet, Shai Shalev-Shwartz, and Yoram Singer. 2006. Online passive-aggressive algorithms. *Journal of Machine Learning Research*.

Berry de Bruijn, Colin Cherry, Svetlana Kiritchenko, Joel Martin, and Xiaodan Zhu. 2011. Machine-learned solutions for three stages of clinical information extraction: the state of the art at i2b2 2010. *Journal of the American Medical Informatics Association*, 18(5):557–562.

Tim Finin, Will Murnane, Anand Karandikar, Nicholas Keller, Justin Martineau, and Mark Dredze. 2010. Annotating named entities in twitter data with crowdsourcing. In *Proceedings of the NAACL HLT 2010 Workshop on Creating Speech and Language Data with Amazon's Mechanical Turk*, pages 80–88.

Hege Fromreide, Dirk Hovy, and Anders Søgaard. 2014. Crowdsourcing and annotating NER for Twitter #drift. In *LREC*, pages 2544–2547, Reykjavik, Iceland.

Dirk Hovy, Taylor Berg-Kirkpatrick, Ashish Vaswani, and Eduard Hovy. 2013. Learning whom to trust with mace. In *HLT-NAACL*, pages 1120–1130, Atlanta, Georgia, June.

Nikos Karampatziakis and John Langford. 2010. Online importance weight aware updates. *arXiv preprint arXiv:1011.1576.*

Percy Liang. 2005. *Semi-supervised learning for natural language*. Ph.D. thesis, Massachusetts Institute of Technology.

Dekang Lin and Xiaoyun Wu. 2009. Phrase clustering for discriminative learning. In *Proceedings of the Joint Conference of the ACL and the AFNLP*, pages 1030–1038, Singapore, August.

Xiaohua Liu, Shaodian Zhang, Furu Wei, and Ming Zhou. 2011. Recognizing named entities in tweets. In *ACL*, pages 359–367, Portland, Oregon, USA, June.

André F. T. Martins, Kevin Gimpel, Noah A. Smith, Eric P. Xing, Pedro M. Q. Aguiar, and Mário A. T. Figueiredo. 2010. Learning structured classifiers with dual coordinate descent. Technical Report CMU-ML-10-109, Carnegie Mellon University.

Andrew McCallum and Wei Li. 2003. Early results for named entity recognition with conditional random fields, feature induction and web-enhanced lexicons. In *CoNLL*, pages 188–191. Association for Computational Linguistics.

Tomas Mikolov, Kai Chen, Greg Corrado, and Jeffrey Dean. 2013. Efficient estimation of word representations in vector space. In *ICLR Workshop*.

Scott Miller, Jethran Guinness, and Alex Zamanian. 2004. Name tagging with word clusters and discriminative training. In *HLT-NAACL*, pages 337–342.

David Nadeau and Satoshi Sekine. 2007. A survey of named entity recognition and classification. *Lingvisticae Investigationes*, 30(1):3–26.

Olutobi Owoputi, Brendan O'Connor, Chris Dyer, Kevin Gimpel, Nathan Schneider, and Noah A Smith. 2013. Improved part-of-speech tagging for online conversational text with word clusters. In *HLT-NAACL*, pages 380–390.

Alexandre Passos, Vineet Kumar, and Andrew McCallum. 2014. Lexicon infused phrase embeddings for named entity resolution. In *CoNLL*, pages 78–86.

Barbara Plank, Dirk Hovy, Ryan McDonald, and Anders Søgaard. 2014. Adapting taggers to Twitter with not-so-distant supervision. In *COLING*, pages 1783–1792, Dublin, Ireland.

Lev Ratinov and Dan Roth. 2009. Design challenges and misconceptions in named entity recognition. In *CoNLL*, pages 147–155.

Lev Ratinov, Dan Roth, Doug Downey, and Mike Anderson. 2011. Local and global algorithms for disambiguation to wikipedia. In *ACL*, pages 1375–1384.

Adwait Ratnaparkhi. 1996. A maximum entropy model for part-of-speech tagging. In *EMNLP*, pages 133–142.

Alan Ritter, Sam Clark, Mausam, and Oren Etzioni. 2011. Named entity recognition in tweets: An experimental study. In *EMNLP*, pages 1524–1534, Edinburgh, Scotland, UK.

Alan Ritter, Oren Etzioni, Sam Clark, et al. 2012. Open domain event extraction from twitter. In *KDD*, pages 1104–1112.

Sunita Sarawagi and William W Cohen. 2004. Semi-markov conditional random fields for information extraction. In *NIPS*, pages 1185–1192.

Erik F. Tjong Kim Sang and Fien De Meulder. 2003. Introduction to the CoNLL-2003 shared task: Language-independent named entity recognition. In *CoNLL*, pages 142–147.

Joseph Turian, Lev Ratinov, and Yoshua Bengio. 2010. Word representations: a simple and general method for semi-supervised learning. In *ACL*, pages 384–394.

Peter D Turney. 2012. Domain and function: A dual-space model of semantic relations and compositions. *Journal of Artificial Intelligence Research*, pages 533–585.

# Is Your Anchor Going Up or Down? Fast and Accurate Supervised Topic Models

**Thang Nguyen**
iSchool and UMIACS
University of Maryland
and National Library of Medicine,
National Institutes of Health
daithang@umiacs.umd.edu

**Jordan Boyd-Graber**
Computer Science
University of Colorado Boulder
Jordan.Boyd.Graber
@colorado.edu

**Jeff Lund,**
**Kevin Seppi, Eric Ringger**
Computer Science
Brigham Young University
{jefflund,kseppi}@byu.edu
ringger@cs.byu.edu

## Abstract

Topic models provide insights into document collections, and their supervised extensions also capture associated document-level metadata such as sentiment. However, inferring such models from data is often slow and cannot scale to big data. We build upon the "anchor" method for learning topic models to capture the relationship between metadata and latent topics by extending the vector-space representation of word-cooccurrence to include metadata-specific dimensions. These additional dimensions reveal new anchor words that reflect specific combinations of metadata and topic. We show that these new latent representations predict sentiment as accurately as supervised topic models, and we find these representations more quickly without sacrificing interpretability.

Topic models were introduced in an unsupervised setting (Blei et al., 2003), aiding in the discovery of topical structure in text: large corpora can be distilled into human-interpretable themes that facilitate quick understanding. In addition to illuminating document collections for humans, topic models have increasingly been used for automatic downstream applications such as sentiment analysis (Titov and McDonald, 2008; Paul and Girju, 2010; Nguyen et al., 2013).

Unfortunately, the structure discovered by unsupervised topic models does not necessarily constitute the best set of features for tasks such as sentiment analysis. Consider a topic model trained on Amazon product reviews. A topic model might discover a topic about vampire romance. However, we often want to go deeper, discovering facets of a topic that reflect topic-specific sentiment, e.g., "buffy" and "spike" for positive sentiment vs. "twilight" and "cullen" for negative sentiment. Techniques for discovering such associations, called supervised topic models (Section 2), both produce interpretable topics and predict metadata values. While unsupervised topic models now have scalable inference strategies (Hoffman et al., 2013; Zhai et al., 2012), supervised topic model inference has not received as much attention and often scales poorly.

The anchor algorithm is a fast, scalable unsupervised approach for finding "anchor words"—precise words with unique co-occurrence patterns that can define the topics of a collection of documents. We augment the anchor algorithm to find supervised sentiment-specific anchor words (Section 3). Our algorithm is faster and just as effective as traditional schemes for supervised topic modeling (Section 4).

## 1 Anchors: Speedy Unsupervised Models

The anchor algorithm (Arora et al., 2013) begins with a $V \times V$ matrix $\bar{Q}$ of word co-occurrences, where $V$ is the size of the vocabulary. Each word type defines a vector $\bar{Q}_{i,\cdot}$ of length $V$ so that $\bar{Q}_{i,j}$ encodes the conditional probability of seeing word $j$ given that word $i$ has already been seen. Spectral methods (Anandkumar et al., 2012) and the anchor algorithm are fast alternatives to traditional topic model inference schemes because they can discover topics via these summary statistics (quadratic in the number of *types*) rather than examining the whole dataset (proportional to the much larger number of *tokens*).

The anchor algorithm takes its name from the idea



*Human Language Technologies: The 2015 Annual Conference of the North American Chapter of the ACL*, pages 746–755,
Denver, Colorado, May 31 – June 5, 2015. 

of anchor words—words which unambiguously identify a particular topic. For instance, "wicket" might be an anchor word for the cricket topic. Thus, for any anchor word $a$, $\bar{Q}_{a,\cdot}$ will look like a topic distribution. $\bar{Q}_{\text{wicket},\cdot}$ will have high probability for "bowl", "century", "pitch", and "bat"; these words are related to cricket, but they cannot be anchor words because they are also related to other topics.

Because these other non-anchor words could be topically ambiguous, their co-occurrence must be explained through some combination of anchor words; thus for non-anchor word $i$,

$$\bar{Q}_{i,\cdot} = \sum_{g_k \in \mathcal{G}} C_{i,k} \bar{Q}_{g_k,\cdot}, \tag{1}$$

where $\mathcal{G} = \{g_1, g_2, \ldots, g_K\}$ is the set of $K$ anchor words. The coefficients $C_{i,k}$ of this linear combination correspond to the probability of seeing a topic *given a word*, from which we can recover the probability of a word *given a topic* (represented in a matrix $A$) using Bayes' rule. In our experiments, we follow Arora et al. (2013) to first estimate $\bar{Q}$ based on the training data and then recover the $C$ matrix

$$C^*_{i,\cdot} = argmin_{C_{i,\cdot}} D_{KL}(\bar{Q}_{i,\cdot} \,||\, \sum_{g_k \in \mathcal{G}} C_{i,k} \bar{Q}_{g_k,\cdot}),$$

where $D_{KL}(x, y)$ denotes the Kullback-Leibler divergence between $x$ and $y$.

In addition to discovering topics from a given set of anchor words as described above, Arora et al. (2013) also provide a geometric interpretation of a process for finding the needed anchor words. If we view the rows of $\bar{Q}$ as points in a high-dimensional space, the convex hull of those points provides the anchor words.[1]

Equation 1 linearly combines anchor words' co-occurrence vectors $\bar{Q}_{g_k,\cdot}$ to create the representation of other words. The convex hull corresponds to the perimeter of the space of all possible co-occurrence vectors that can be formed from the set of basis anchor vectors. However, the convex hull only encodes

[1]As discussed by Arora et al. (2013), this is a slight simplification, since the most extreme points will be words that only appear infrequently. Thus, there is some nuance to choosing the anchor words. For instance, a key step for effective topic modeling is choosing a minimum number of documents a word must appear in before it can be considered an anchor word. (c.f. Figure 3).

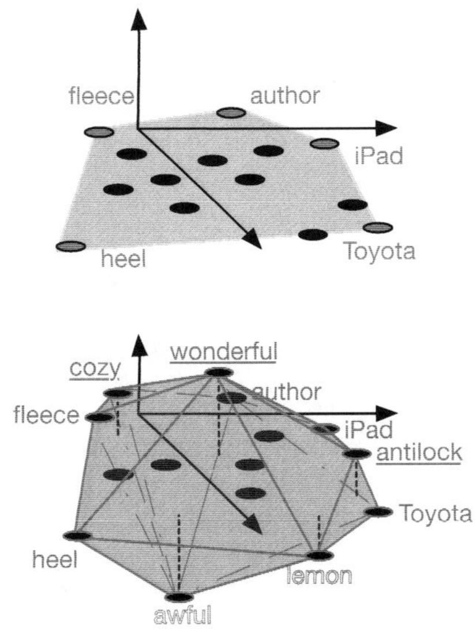


Figure 1: Graphical intuition behind supervised anchor words. Anchor words (in gold) form the convex hull of word co-occurrence probabilities in unsupervised topic modeling (top). Adding an additional dimension to capture metadata, such as sentiment, changes the convex hull: positive words appear above the original 2D plane (underlined) and negative words appear below (in outline).

an unsupervised view of the data. To capture topics informed by metadata such as sentiment, we need to explicitly represent the combination of words and metadata.

One problem inherited by the anchor method from parametric topic models is the determination of the number of anchor words (and thus topics) to use. Because word co-occurrence statistics live in an extremely high-dimensional space, the number of anchor words needed to cover all of the data will be quite high. Thus, Arora et al. (2013) require a user to specify the number of anchor words *a priori* (just as for parametric topic models). They use a form of the Gram-Schmidt process to find the best words that enclose the maximum volume of points.

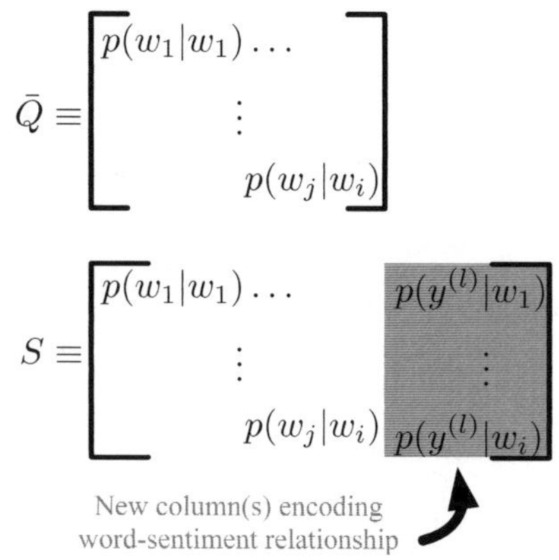


Figure 2: We form a new column to capture the relationship between words *and* each sentiment level: per entry is the conditional probability of observing a sentiment level $y^{(l)}$ given an observation of the word $w_i$. Adding all of these columns to $\bar{Q}$ to form an augmented matrix $S$.

## 2 Supervised Topics: Effective but Slow

Topic models discover a set of topics $A$. Each topic is a distribution over the $V$ word types in the corpus. $A_{i,t}$ is the probability of seeing word $i$ in topic $t$. Supervised topic models relate those topics with predictions of document metadata such as sentiment by discovering a vector of regression parameters $\vec{\mu}$ that connects topics to per-document observations $y_d$ (Blei and McAuliffe, 2007). Blei and McAuliffe (2007) treat this as a regression: seeing one word with topic $k$ in document $d$ means that prediction of $y_d$ should be adjusted by $\mu_k$. Given a document's distribution over topics $\bar{z}_d$, the response $y_d$ is normally distributed with mean $\vec{\mu}^\top \bar{z}_d$.[2]

Typically, the topics are discovered through a process of probabilistic inference, either variational EM (Wang et al., 2009) or Gibbs sampling (Boyd-Graber and Resnik, 2010). However, these methods scale poorly to large datasets. Variational inference requires dozens of expensive passes over the entire dataset, and Gibbs sampling requires multiple Markov chains (Nguyen et al., 2014b).

[2]We are eliding some details in the interest of a more compact presentation. The topics used by a document, $\bar{z}_d$, are based on per-token inference of topic assignments; this detail is not relevant to our contribution, and in Section 4.2 we use existing techniques to discover documents' topics.

## 3 Supervised Anchor Words

Because the anchor algorithm scales so well compared to traditional probabilistic inference, we now unify the supervised topic models of Section 2 with the anchor algorithm discussed in Section 1. We do so by augmenting the matrix $\bar{Q}$ with an additional dimension for each metadata attribute, such as sentiment. We provide the geometric intuition in Figure 1.

Picture the anchor words projected down to two dimensions (Lee and Mimno, 2014): each word is a point, and the anchor words are the vertices of a polygon encompassing every point. Every non-anchor word can be approximated by a convex combination of the anchor words (Figure 1, top).

Now add an additional dimension as a column to $\bar{Q}$ (Figure 2). This column encodes the metadata specific to a word. For example, we have encoded sentiment metadata in a new dimension (Figure 1, bottom). Neutral sentiment words will stay in the plane inhabited by the other words, positive sentiment words will move up, and negative sentiment words will move down. For simplicity, we only show a single additional dimension, but in general we can add as many dimensions as needed to encode the metadata.

In this new space some of the original anchor words may still be anchor words ("author"). Other words that were near the convex hull boundary in the unaugmented representation may become anchor words in the augmented representation because they capture both topic and sentiment ("anti-lock" vs. "lemon"). Finally, extreme sentiment words might become anchor words in the new higher-dimensional space because they are so important for explaining extreme sentiment values ("wonderful" vs. "awful").

### 3.1 Words to Sentiment

Having explained how a word is connected to sentiment, we now elaborates on how to model that connection using the conditional probability of sentiment given a particular word. Assume that sentiment is discretized into a finite set of $L$ sentiment levels $\{y^{(1)}, y^{(2)}, \ldots, y^{(L)}\}$ and that each document is assigned to one of these levels. We define a matrix $S$ of size $V \times (V + L)$. The first $V$ columns are the same as $\bar{Q}$ and the $L$ additional columns capture the relationship of a word to each discrete sentiment level.

For each additional column $l$, $S_{i,(V+l)} \equiv p(y = y^{(l)} \mid w = i)$ is the conditional probability of observing a sentiment level $y^{(l)}$ given an observation of word $i$. We compute the conditional probability of a sentiment level $y^{(l)}$ given word $i$

$$S_{i,(V+l)} \equiv \frac{\sum_d (\mathbb{1}\left[i \in d\right] \cdot \mathbb{1}\left[y_d = y^{(l)}\right])}{\sum_d \mathbb{1}\left[i \in d\right]}, \quad (2)$$

where the numerator is the number of documents that contain word type $i$ and have sentiment level $y^{(l)}$ and the denominator is the number of documents containing word $i$.

Given this augmented matrix, we again want to find the set of anchor words $\mathcal{G}$ and coefficients $C_{i,k}$ that best capture the relationship between words and sentiment (c.f. Equation 1)

$$S_{i,\cdot} = \sum_{g_k \in \mathcal{G}} C_{i,k} S_{g_k,\cdot}. \quad (3)$$

Because we retain the property that non-anchor words are explained through a linear combination of the anchor words, our method retains the same theoretical guarantees of sampling complexity and robustness as the original anchor algorithm.

To facilitate direct comparisons, we keep the number of anchor words fixed in our experiments. Even so, the introduction of metadata forces the anchor method to select the words that best capture this metadata-augmented view of the data. Consequently, some of the original anchor words will remain, and some will be replaced by sentiment-specific anchor words.

## 4 Quantitative Comparison of Supervised Topic Models

In this section, we evaluate the effectiveness of our new method on a binary sentiment classification problem. Because the supervised anchor algorithm (**SUP ANCHOR**) finds anchor words (and thus different topics) which capture the sentiment metadata, we evaluate the degree to which its latent representation improves upon the original unsupervised anchor algorithm (Arora et al., 2013, **ANCHOR**) for classification in terms of both accuracy and speed.

### 4.1 Sentiment Datasets

We use three common sentiment datasets for evaluation: AMAZON product reviews (Jindal and Liu, 2008), YELP restaurant reviews (Jo and Oh, 2011), and TRIPADVISOR hotel reviews (Wang et al., 2010). For each dataset, we preprocess by tokenizing and removing all non-alphanumeric words and stopwords. As very short reviews are often inscrutable and lack cues to connect to the sentiment, we only consider documents with at least thirty words. We also reduce the vocabulary size by keeping only words that appear in a sufficient number of documents: 50 for AMAZON and YELP datasets, and 150 for TRIPADVISOR (Table 1).

### 4.2 Documents to Labels

Our goal is to perform binary classification of sentiment. Due to a positive skew of the datasets, the median for all datasets is four out of five. All 5-star reviews are assigned to $y^+$ and the rest of the reviews are assigned to $y^-$. Table 1 summarizes the composition of each dataset and the percentage of documents with high positive sentiment.[3]

We compare the effectiveness of different representations in predicting high-sentiment documents: unsupervised topic models (**LDA**), traditional supervised topic models (**SLDA**), the unmodified anchor algorithm (**ANCHOR**), our supervised anchor algorithm (**SUP ANCHOR**), and a traditional TF-IDF (Salton, 1968, **TF-IDF**) representation of the words.

The anchor algorithm only provides the topic distribution over words; it does not provide the per-document assignment of topics needed to represent the document in a low-dimensional space necessary for producing a prediction $y_d$. Fortunately, this requires a very quick—because the topics are fixed—pass over the documents using a traditional topic model inference algorithm. We use the variational inference implementation for **LDA** of Blei et al. (2003)[4] to obtain $\bar{z}_d$, the topic distribution for document $d$.[5]

[3] Multiclass labeling for each sentiment label also works well, but binary classification simplifies the analysis and presentation.

[4] http://www.cs.princeton.edu/~blei/lda-c/

[5] For other inference schemes, we use native inference to apply pre-trained topics to extract DEV and TEST topic proportions.

| Corpus | Train Documents | Test Documents | Tokens | Types | Percentage with Positive Sentiment |
|---|---|---|---|---|---|
| AMAZON | 13,300 | 3,314 | 1,031,659 | 2,662 | 52.2% |
| TRIPADVISOR | 115,384 | 28,828 | 12,752,444 | 4,867 | 41.5% |
| YELP | 13,955 | 3,482 | 1,142,555 | 2,585 | 27.7% |

Table 1: Statistics for the datasets employed in the experiments.

**Classifiers** Given a low-dimensional representation of a test document, we predict the document's sentiment $y_d$. We have already inferred the topic distribution $\bar{z}_d$ for each document, and we use $log(\bar{z}_d)$ as the features for a classifier. Feature vectors from training data are used to train the classifiers, and feature vectors from the development or test set are used to evaluate the classifiers.

We run three standard machine learning classifiers: decision trees (Quinlan, 1986), logistic regression (Friedman et al., 1998), and a discriminative classifier. For decision trees (hence TREE) and logistic regression (hence LOGISTIC), we use SKLEARN.[6] For the discriminative classifier, we use a linear classifier with hinge loss (hence HINGE) in Vowpal Wabbit.[7] Because HINGE outputs a regression value in $[0, 1]$, we use a threshold 0.5 to make predictions.

**Parameter Tuning** Parameter tuning is important in topic models, so we cross-validate: each sentiment dataset is split randomly into five folds. We used four folds to form the TRAIN set and reserved the last fold for the TEST set. All cross-validation results are averaged over the four held out DEV sets; the best cross-validation result provides the parameter settings we use on the TEST set.

For **ANCHOR** and **SUP ANCHOR**, the parameter for the document-level Dirichlet prior $\alpha$ is required for inferring document-topic distributions given learned topics. Despite selecting this parameter using grid search, $\alpha$ does not affect our final results. The same is also true for **SLDA**: its predictive performance does not significantly vary as $\alpha$ varies, given a fixed number of topics $K$.[8]

Anchor algorithms are sensitive to the value of anchor threshold $M$ (the minimum document frequency for a word to be considered an anchor word). For each number of topics $K$, we perform a grid search to find the best value of $M$. Figure 3 shows the performance trends.

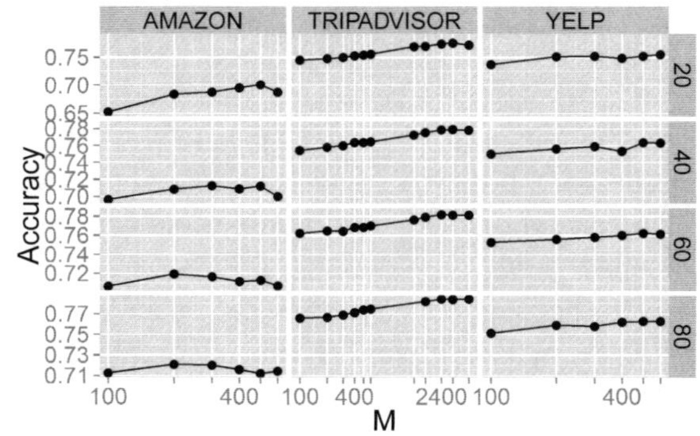


Figure 3: Grid search for selecting the word-document threshold $M$ for **SUP ANCHOR** based on development set accuracy.

For **LDA**, we use the Gibbs sampling implementation in Mallet.[9] For training the model, we run **LDA** with 5,000 iterations; and for inference (on DEV and TEST) of document topic distribution we iterate 100 times, with lag 5 and 50 burn-in iterations. As Mallet accepts $\sum \alpha_i$ as a parameter, we always initialize $\sum \alpha_i = 1$ and only perform a grid search over different values of $\beta$, the hyper-parameter for Dirichlet prior over the per-topic topic-word distribution, starting from 0.01 and doubling until reaching 0.5.

### 4.3 SUP ANCHOR Outperforms ANCHOR

Learning topics that jointly reflect words and metadata improves subsequent prediction. The results for both **SUP ANCHOR** and **ANCHOR** on the TEST set are shown in Figure 4. **SUP ANCHOR** outperforms **ANCHOR** on all datasets. This trend holds consistently for LOGISTIC, TREE, and HINGE methods for sentiment prediction. For example, with twenty topics on the AMAZON dataset, **SUP ANCHOR** gives an

[6] `http://scikit-learn.org/stable/`

[7] `http://hunch.net/~vw/`

[8] We use the SLDA implementation by Chong Wang: `http://www.cs.cmu.edu/~chongw/slda/` to estimate $\alpha$.

[9] `http://mallet.cs.umass.edu/topics.php`

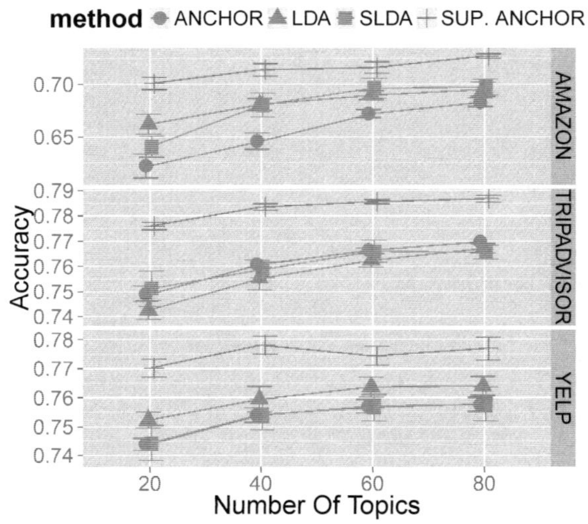


Figure 4: Results on TEST fold, **SUP ANCHOR** outperforms **ANCHOR**, **LDA**, and **SLDA** on all three datasets. We report the results based on LOGISTIC as it produces the best accuracy consistently for **ANCHOR**, **SUP ANCHOR**, and **LDA**.

accuracy of 0.71 in comparison to only 0.62 from **ANCHOR**. Similarly, with twenty topics on the YELP dataset, **SUP ANCHOR** has 0.77 accuracy while **ANCHOR** has 0.74. Our **SUP ANCHOR** model is able to incorporate metadata to learn better representations for predicting sentiment. Moreover, in Section 5 we show that **SUP ANCHOR** does not need to sacrifice topic quality to gain predictive power.

### 4.4 SUP ANCHOR Outperforms SLDA

More surprising is that **SUP ANCHOR** also outperforms **SLDA**. Like **SUP ANCHOR**, **SLDA** jointly learns topics and their relation to metadata such as sentiment. Figure 4 shows that this trend is consistent on all sentiment datasets. On average, **SUP ANCHOR** is 2.2 percent better than **SLDA** on AMAZON, and 2.0 percent better on both YELP and TRIPADVISOR. Furthermore, **SUP ANCHOR** is much faster than **SLDA**.

**SLDA** performs worse than **SUP ANCHOR** in part because **SUP ANCHOR** is able to jointly find specific lexical terms that improve prediction. Nguyen et al. (2013) show that this improves supervised topic models; forming anchor words around the same strong lexical cues could discover better topics. In contrast, **SLDA** must discover the relationship through the proxy of topics.

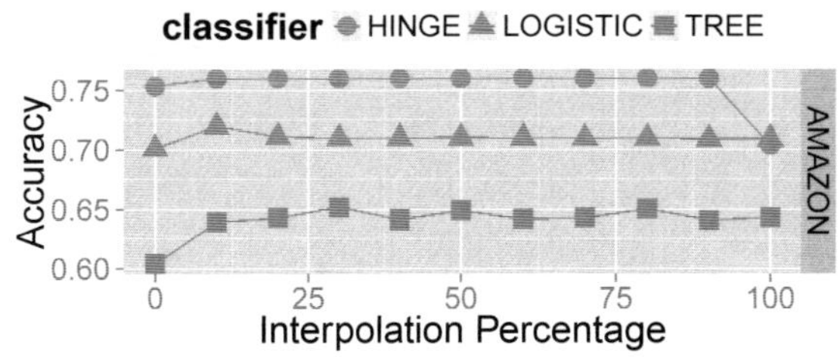


Figure 5: Accuracy on AMAZON with twenty topics. **SUP ANCHOR** produces good representations for sentiment classification that can be improved by interpolating with lexical **TF-IDF** features. The interpolation ($x$-axis) ranges from zero (all **TF-IDF** features) to one hundred (all **SUP ANCHOR** topic features).

### 4.5 Lexical Features

Ramage et al. (2010) show that interpolating topic and lexical features often provides better classification than either alone. Here, we take the same approach and show how different interpolations of topic and lexical features create better classifiers. We first select an interpolation value $\lambda$ in $\{0, 0.1, 0.2, \ldots, 1\}$, and we then form a new feature vector by concatenating $\lambda$-weighted topic features with $(1-\lambda)$-weighted lexical features. Figure 5 shows the interplay between topic features and **TF-IDF** features[10] as the weight of topic features increases from zero (all **TF-IDF**) to one hundred (all **SUP ANCHOR** topic features) percent on the AMAZON dataset (other datasets are similar). Combining both feature sets is better than either alone, although the interpolation depends on the classifier.

### 4.6 Runtime Analysis

Having shown that **SUP ANCHOR** outperforms both **ANCHOR** and **SLDA**, in this section we show that **SUP ANCHOR** also inherits the runtime efficiency from **ANCHOR**. Table 2 summarizes the runtimes on both AMAZON and TRIPADVISOR; these results were obtained using a six-core 2.8GHz Intel Xeon X5660. On the small dataset AMAZON, **SUP ANCHOR** finishes the training within one minute, and for the larger TRIPADVISOR dataset it completes the

[10]As before, we do parameter selection on DEV data and report final TEST results.

| Dataset | Measure | **SUP ANCHOR** | **LDA** | **SLDA** |
|---|---|---|---|---|
| AMAZON | Preprocessing | 32 | 32 | 32 |
| | Generating $\bar{Q}/S$ | 29 | | |
| | Training | 33 | 886 | 4,762 |
| | LDAC inference | 38 (train), 13 (dev/test) | | |
| | Classification | <5 | <5 | |
| TRIPADVISOR | Preprocessing | 305 | 305 | 305 |
| | Generating $\bar{Q}/S$ | 262 | | |
| | Training | 181 | 8,158 | 71,967 |
| | LDAC inference | 830 (train), 280 (dev/test) | | |
| | Classification | <5 | <5 | |

Table 2: Runtime statistics (in seconds) for the AMAZON and TRIPADVISOR datasets. Blank cells indicate a timing which does not apply to a particular model. **SUP ANCHOR** is significantly faster than conventional methods.

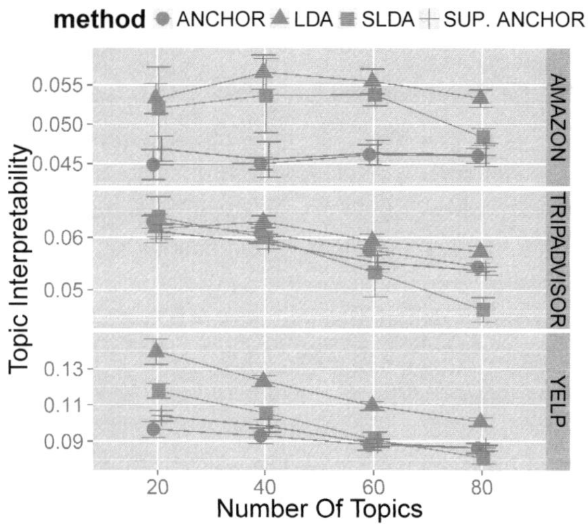


Figure 6: **SUP ANCHOR** and **ANCHOR** produce the same topic quality. **LDA** outperforms all other models and produces the best topics. Performance of **SLDA** degrades significantly as the number of topic increases.

learning in around three minutes. The main bottleneck for **SUP ANCHOR** is learning the document distributions over topics, although even this stage is fast for known topic distributions. This result is far better than the twenty hours required by **SLDA** to train on TRIPADVISOR.

## 5 Inspecting Anchors and their Topics

One important evaluation for topic models is how easy it is for a human reader to understand the topics. In this section, we evaluate topics produced by each model using topic interpretability (Chang et al., 2009). Topic interpretability measures how human users understand topics presented by a topic modeling algorithm. We use an automated approximation of interpretability that uses a reference corpus as a proxy for which words belong together (Newman et al., 2010). Using half a million documents from Wikipedia, we compute the induced normalized pairwise mutual information (Lau et al., 2014, NPMI) on the top ten words in topics as a proxy for interpretability.

Figure 6 shows the NPMI scores for each model. Unsurprisingly, unsupervised models (**LDA**) produce the best topic quality. In contrast, supervised models must balance metadata (i.e., response variable) prediction against capturing word meaning. Consequently, **SLDA** does slightly worse with respect to topic interpretability.

**SUP ANCHOR** and **ANCHOR** produce the same topic quality consistently on all datasets. Since **SUP ANCHOR** and **ANCHOR** have nearly identical runtime, **SUP ANCHOR** is better suited for supervised tasks because it improves classification without sacrificing interpretability. It is possible that regularization would improve the interpretability of these topics; Nguyen et al. (2014a) show that adding regularization removes overly frequent words from anchor-discovered topics.

The topics produced by the **ANCHOR** and **SUP ANCHOR** algorithms have many similarities. In Table 3, nearly all of the anchor words discovered by **ANCHOR** are also used by **SUP ANCHOR**. These anchor words tend to describe general food types, such as

| Model | Anchor Words and Top Words in Topics | |
|---|---|---|
| ANCHOR and SUP ANCHOR | **pizza burger sushi ice garlic hot amp chicken pork french sandwich coffee cake steak beer fish** | |
| ANCHOR | **wine** | wine restaurant dinner menu nice night bar table meal experience |
| | **hour** | wait hour people minutes line long table waiting worth order |
| | **late** | night late ive people pretty love youre friends restaurant open |
| SUP ANCHOR | **favorite** | love favorite ive amazing delicious restaurant eat menu fresh awesome |
| | **decent** | pretty didnt restaurant ordered decent wasnt nice night bad stars |
| | **line** | line wait people long tacos worth order waiting minutes taco |

Table 3: Comparing topics generated for the YELP dataset: anchor words shared by both **ANCHOR** and **SUP ANCHOR** are listed. Unique anchor words for each algorithm are listed along with the top ten words for that topic. For clarity, we pruned words which appear in more than 3000 documents as these words appear in every topic. The distinct anchor words reflect positive ("favorite") and negative ("line") sentiment rather than less sentiment-specific qualities of restaurants (e.g., restaurants open "late").

"pizza" or "burger", and characterize the YELP dataset well. The similarity of these shared topics explains why both **ANCHOR** and **SUP ANCHOR** achieve similar topic interpretability scores.

To explain the predictive power of **SUP ANCHOR** we must examine the anchor words and topics unique to both algorithms. The anchor words which are unique to **ANCHOR** include a general topic about wine, and two somewhat coherent topics related to time. By adding supervision to the model we get three new anchor words which identify sentiment ranging from extremely positive reviews mentioning a favorite restaurant to extremely negative reviews complaining about long waits.

This general trend is seen across each of the datasets. For example, **ANCHOR** and **SUP ANCHOR** both discover shared topics describing consumer goods, but **SUP ANCHOR** replaces two topics discussing headphones with topics describing "frustrating" products and "great" products. Similarly, in the TRIPADVISOR data, both **ANCHOR** and **SUP ANCHOR** share topics about specific destinations, but only **SUP ANCHOR** discovers a topic describing "disgusting" hotel rooms.

## 6 Related Work

Improving the scalability of statistical learning has taken many forms: creating online approximations of large batch algorithms (Hoffman et al., 2013; Zhai et al., 2014) or improving the efficiency of sampling (Yao et al., 2009; Hu and Boyd-Graber, 2012; Li et al., 2014).

These insights have also improved supervised topic models. For example, Zhu et al. (2013) train the max-margin supervised topic models **MEDLDA** (Zhu et al., 2009) by reformulating the model such that the hinge loss is included inside a collapsed Gibbs sampler, rather than being applied externally on the sampler using costly SVMs. Using insights from Smola and Narayanamurthy (2010), the samplers run in parallel to train the model. While these advancements improve the scalability of max-margin supervised topic models, the improvement is limited by the fact that the sampling algorithm grows with the number of tokens.

In contrast, this paper explores a different vein of research that focuses on using efficient representations of summary statistics to estimate statistical models. While this has seen great success in unsupervised models (Cohen and Collins, 2014), it has increasingly also been applied to supervised models. Wang and Zhu (2014) show how to use tensor decomposition to estimate the parameters of **SLDA** instead of sampling to find maximum likelihood estimates. In contrast, anchor-based methods rely on non-negative matrix factorization.

We found that a discriminative classifier did not always perform best on the downstream classification task. Zhu et al. (2009) make a comprehensive comparison between **MEDLDA**, **SLDA**, and SVM+LDA, and they show that SVM+LDA performs worse than **MEDLDA** and **SLDA** on binary classification. It could be that better feature preprocessing could improve our performance.

Bag-of-words representations are not ideal for sentiment tasks. Rubin et al. (2012) introduce Dependency LDA which associates individual word tokens with different labels; their model also outperforms linear SVMs on a very large multi-labeled corpus. Latent variable models that consider grammatical structure (Sayeed et al., 2012; Socher et al., 2011; Iyyer et al., 2014) could also be improved through efficient inference (Cohen and Collins, 2014).

## 7 Discussion

Supervised anchor word topic modeling provides a general framework for learning better topic representations by taking advantage of both word-cooccurrence and metadata. Our straightforward extension (Equation 2) places each word in a vector space that not only captures co-occurrence with other terms but also the interaction of the word and its sentiment, in contrast to algorithms that only consider raw words.

While our experiments focus on binary classification, the same extension is also applicable to multi-class classification.

Moreover, supervised anchor word topic modeling is fast: it inherits the polynomial-time efficiency from the original unsupervised anchor word algorithm. It is also effective: it is better at providing features for classification than unsupervised topic models and also better than supervised topic models with conventional inference.

Our supervised anchor word algorithm offers the ability to quickly analyze datasets without the overhead of Gibbs sampling or variational inference, allowing users to more quickly understand big data and to make decisions. Combining bag-of-words analysis with metadata through efficient, low-latency topic analysis allows users to have deep insights more quickly.

**Acknowledgments** We thank Daniel Petersen, Jim Martin, and the anonymous reviewers for their insightful comments. This work was supported by the collaborative NSF Grant IIS-1409287 (UMD) and IIS-1409739 (BYU). Boyd-Graber is also supported by NSF grants IIS-1320538 and NCSE-1422492.

## References

Anima Anandkumar, Dean P. Foster, Daniel Hsu, Sham Kakade, and Yi-Kai Liu. 2012. A spectral algorithm for latent Dirichlet allocation. In *Proceedings of Advances in Neural Information Processing Systems.*

Sanjeev Arora, Rong Ge, Yoni Halpern, David M. Mimno, Ankur Moitra, David Sontag, Yichen Wu, and Michael Zhu. 2013. A practical algorithm for topic modeling with provable guarantees. In *Proceedings of the International Conference of Machine Learning.*

David M. Blei and Jon D. McAuliffe. 2007. Supervised topic models. In *Proceedings of Advances in Neural Information Processing Systems.*

David M. Blei, Andrew Ng, and Michael Jordan. 2003. Latent Dirichlet allocation. *Journal of Machine Learning Research*, 3.

Jordan Boyd-Graber and Philip Resnik. 2010. Holistic sentiment analysis across languages: Multilingual supervised latent Dirichlet allocation. In *Proceedings of Empirical Methods in Natural Language Processing.*

Jonathan Chang, Jordan Boyd-Graber, Chong Wang, Sean Gerrish, and David M. Blei. 2009. Reading tea leaves: How humans interpret topic models. In *Proceedings of Advances in Neural Information Processing Systems.*

Shay B. Cohen and Michael Collins. 2014. A provably correct learning algorithm for latent-variable PCFGs. In *Proceedings of the Association for Computational Linguistics.*

Jerome Friedman, Trevor Hastie, and Robert Tibshirani. 1998. Additive logistic regression: a statistical view of boosting. *Annals of Statistics*, 28:2000.

Matthew Hoffman, David M. Blei, Chong Wang, and John Paisley. 2013. Stochastic variational inference. In *Journal of Machine Learning Research.*

Yuening Hu and Jordan Boyd-Graber. 2012. Efficient tree-based topic modeling. In *Proceedings of the Association for Computational Linguistics.*

Mohit Iyyer, Peter Enns, Jordan Boyd-Graber, and Philip Resnik. 2014. Political ideology detection using recursive neural networks. In *Proceedings of the Association for Computational Linguistics.*

Nitin Jindal and Bing Liu. 2008. Opinion spam and analysis. In *Proceedings of First ACM International Conference on Web Search and Data Mining.*

Yohan Jo and Alice H. Oh. 2011. Aspect and sentiment unification model for online review analysis. In *Proceedings of ACM International Conference on Web Search and Data Mining.*

Jey Han Lau, David Newman, and Timothy Baldwin. 2014. Machine reading tea leaves: Automatically evaluating topic coherence and topic model quality. In *Proceedings of the European Chapter of the Association for Computational Linguistics.*

Moontae Lee and David Mimno. 2014. Low-dimensional embeddings for interpretable anchor-based topic inference. In *Proceedings of Empirical Methods in Natural Language Processing*.

Aaron Q Li, Amr Ahmed, Sujith Ravi, and Alexander J Smola. 2014. Reducing the sampling complexity of topic models. In *Proceedings of the 20th ACM SIGKDD international conference on Knowledge discovery and data mining*, pages 891–900. ACM.

David Newman, Jey Han Lau, Karl Grieser, and Timothy Baldwin. 2010. Automatic evaluation of topic coherence. In *Conference of the North American Chapter of the Association for Computational Linguistics*.

Viet-An Nguyen, Jordan Boyd-Graber, and Philip Resnik. 2013. Lexical and hierarchical topic regression. In *Proceedings of Advances in Neural Information Processing Systems*.

Thang Nguyen, Yuening Hu, and Jordan Boyd-Graber. 2014a. Anchors regularized: Adding robustness and extensibility to scalable topic-modeling algorithms. In *Proceedings of the Association for Computational Linguistics*.

Viet-An Nguyen, Jordan Boyd-Graber, and Philip Resnik. 2014b. Sometimes average is best: The importance of averaging for prediction using MCMC inference in topic modeling. In *Proceedings of Empirical Methods in Natural Language Processing*.

Michael Paul and Roxana Girju. 2010. A two-dimensional topic-aspect model for discovering multi-faceted topics. In *Association for the Advancement of Artificial Intelligence*.

J. R. Quinlan. 1986. Induction of decision trees. 1(1):81–106, March.

Daniel Ramage, Susan T. Dumais, and Daniel J. Liebling. 2010. Characterizing microblogs with topic models. In *International Conference on Weblogs and Social Media*.

Timothy N. Rubin, America Chambers, Padhraic Smyth, and Mark Steyvers. 2012. Statistical topic models for multi-label document classification. *Journal of Machine Learning Research*, 88(1-2):157–208, July.

Gerard Salton. 1968. *Automatic Information Organization and Retrieval.* McGraw Hill Text.

Asad B. Sayeed, Jordan Boyd-Graber, Bryan Rusk, and Amy Weinberg. 2012. Grammatical structures for word-level sentiment detection. In *North American Association of Computational Linguistics*.

Alexander Smola and Shravan Narayanamurthy. 2010. An architecture for parallel topic models. *International Conference on Very Large Databases*, 3(1-2):703–710.

Richard Socher, Jeffrey Pennington, Eric H. Huang, Andrew Y. Ng, and Christopher D. Manning. 2011. Semi-supervised recursive autoencoders for predicting sentiment distributions. In *Proceedings of Empirical Methods in Natural Language Processing*.

Ivan Titov and Ryan McDonald. 2008. A joint model of text and aspect ratings for sentiment summarization. In *Proceedings of the Association for Computational Linguistics*.

Yining Wang and Jun Zhu. 2014. Spectral methods for supervised topic models. In *Proceedings of Advances in Neural Information Processing Systems*.

Chong Wang, David Blei, and Li Fei-Fei. 2009. Simultaneous image classification and annotation. In *Computer Vision and Pattern Recognition*.

Hongning Wang, Yue Lu, and Chengxiang Zhai. 2010. Latent aspect rating analysis on review text data: a rating regression approach. In *Knowledge Discovery and Data Mining*.

Limin Yao, David Mimno, and Andrew McCallum. 2009. Efficient methods for topic model inference on streaming document collections. In *Knowledge Discovery and Data Mining*.

Ke Zhai, Jordan Boyd-Graber, Nima Asadi, and Mohamad Alkhouja. 2012. Mr. LDA: A flexible large scale topic modeling package using variational inference in mapreduce. In *Proceedings of World Wide Web Conference*.

Ke Zhai, Jordan Boyd-Graber, and Shay B. Cohen. 2014. Online adaptor grammars with hybrid inference.

Jun Zhu, Amr Ahmed, and Eric P. Xing. 2009. MedLDA: maximum margin supervised topic models for regression and classification. In *Proceedings of the International Conference of Machine Learning*.

Jun Zhu, Xun Zheng, Li Zhou, and Bo Zhang. 2013. Scalable inference in max-margin topic models. In *Knowledge Discovery and Data Mining*.

# Grounded Semantic Parsing for Complex Knowledge Extraction


**Ankur P. Parikh**[*]
School of Computer Science
Carnegie Mellon University
apparikh@cs.cmu.edu

**Hoifung Poon** **Kristina Toutanova**
Microsoft Research
Redmond, WA, USA
hoifung,kristout@microsoft.com



## Abstract

Recently, there has been increasing interest in learning semantic parsers with indirect supervision, but existing work focuses almost exclusively on question answering. Separately, there have been active pursuits in leveraging databases for distant supervision in information extraction, yet such methods are often limited to binary relations and none can handle nested events. In this paper, we generalize distant supervision to complex knowledge extraction, by proposing the first approach to learn a semantic parser for extracting nested event structures without annotated examples, using only a database of such complex events and unannotated text. The key idea is to model the annotations as latent variables, and incorporate a prior that favors semantic parses containing known events. Experiments on the GENIA event extraction dataset show that our approach can learn from and extract complex biological pathway events. Moreover, when supplied with just five example words per event type, it becomes competitive even among supervised systems, outperforming 19 out of 24 teams that participated in the original shared task.


## 1 Introduction

The goal of semantic parsing is to map text into a complete and detailed meaning representation (Mooney, 2007). Supervised approaches for learning a semantic parser require annotated examples, which are expensive and time-consuming to acquire (Zelle and Mooney, 1993; Zettlemoyer and Collins, 2005; Zettlemoyer and Collins, 2007). As a result, there has been rising interest in learning semantic parsers from indirect supervision. Examples include unsupervised approaches that leverage distributional similarity by recursive clustering (Poon and Domingos, 2009; Poon and Domingos, 2010; Titov and Klementiev, 2011), semi-supervised approaches that learn from dialog context (Artzi and Zettlemoyer, 2011), grounded approaches that learn from annotated question-answer pairs (Clarke et al., 2010; Liang et al., 2011) or virtual worlds (Chen and Mooney, 2011; Artzi and Zettlemoyer, 2013).

Information Extraction: (NEG-REG,BCL,RFLAT) (NEG-REG,IL-10,RFLAT)

Complex Event: (POS-REG,BCL,(NEG-REG,IL-10,RFLAT))

GENIA Event Annotation:

| ID | TYPE | CAUSE | THEME | TRIGGER |
|---|---|---|---|---|
| T1 | PROTEIN | - | - | BCL |
| T2 | PROTEIN | - | - | RFLAT |
| T3 | PROTEIN | - | - | IL-10 |
| E1 | POS-REG | T1 | E2 | stimulates |
| E2 | NEG-REG | T3 | T2 | inhibition |

Figure 1: Given sentence "BCL stimulates inhibition of RFLAT by IL-10", information extraction focuses on classifying simple relations among entities (top), whereas ideally we want to extract the complex event that captures important contextual information (middle), as exemplified by the GENIA event annotation (bottom).

Such progress is exciting, but most applications focus on question answering, where the semantic parser is used to convert natural-language questions into formal queries. In contrast, complex knowledge extraction represents a relatively untapped ap-

[*] This research was conducted during the author's internship at Microsoft Research.




*Human Language Technologies: The 2015 Annual Conference of the North American Chapter of the ACL*, pages 756–766,
Denver, Colorado, May 31 – June 5, 2015.

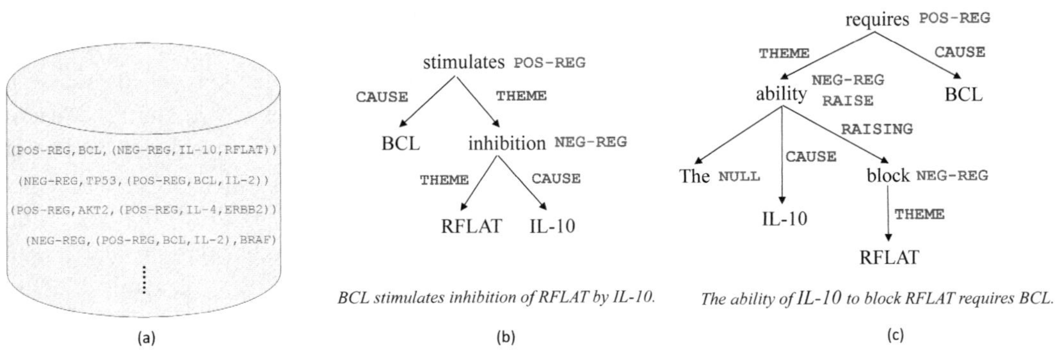


Figure 2: Grounded semantic parsing for complex knowledge extraction: (a) input database of complex events, without textual annotation; (b) event extraction as semantic parsing; (c) a complex sentence that requires RAISING.

plication area for semantic parsing, with great potential. Text with valuable information has been undergoing rapid growth across scientific and business disciplines alike. A prominent example is PubMed (www.ncbi.nlm.nih.gov/pubmed), which contains over 24 million biomedical research articles and grows by over one million each year. Research on information extraction abounds, but it tends to focus on classifying simple relations among entities, so is incapable of extracting the prevalent complex knowledge with nested event structures. Figure 1 illustrates this problem with an example sentence "BCL stimulates inhibition of RFLAT by IL-10". Traditional information extraction would be content with extracting two binary relation instances (NEG-REG,BCL,RFLAT) and (NEG-REG,IL-10,RFLAT), where NEG-REG represents a negative regulation (i.e., inhibition). However, the sentence also discloses important contextual information, i.e., BCL regulates RFLAT by stimulating the inhibitive effect of IL-10, and likewise the inhibition of RFLAT by IL-10 is controlled by BCL. Such context-specific knowledge is crucial in translational medicine: imagine a targeted therapy that tries to suppress RFLAT by inducing either BCL or IL-10, without taking into account their interdependency. As Figure 1 shows, this knowledge can be represented by events with nested structures (e.g., the THEME argument of E1 is an event E2), as exemplified by the GENIA event extraction dataset (Kim et al., 2009).

Complex knowledge extraction can be naturally framed as a semantic parsing problem, with the event structure represented by a semantic parse; see Figure 2. However, annotating example sentences is expensive and time-consuming. GENIA is the only corpus of its kind by far; its annotation took years and its scope is limited to the narrow domain of transcription in human blood cells. In contrast, databases are usually available. For example, due to the central importance of biological pathways in understanding diseases and developing drug targets, there exist many pathway databases (Schaefer et al., 2009; Kanehisa, 2002; Cerami et al., 2011). Limited by manual curation, they are incomplete and not up-to-date, thereby the need for automated extraction. But compared to question answering, knowledge extraction can derive more leverage from such databases via distant supervision (Craven and Kumlien, 1999; Mintz et al., 2009). The key insight is that databases can be used to automatically annotate sentences with a relation if the arguments of a known instance co-occur in the sentence. This learning paradigm, however, has never been applied to extracting nested events.

In this paper, we propose the first approach to learn a semantic parser from a database of complex events and unannotated text, by generalizing distant supervision to complex knowledge extraction. The key idea is to recover the latent annotations via EM, guided by a structured prior that favors semantic parses containing known events in the database, in the form of virtual evidence (Pearl, 1988; Subramanya and Bilmes, 2007). Experiments on the GENIA dataset demonstrate the promise of this direction. Our GUSPEE (*GroUnded Semantic Parsing for Event Extraction*) system can successfully learn from and extract complex events, without requiring textual annotations (Figure 2). Moreover, after incorporating prototype-driven learning using just five example words for each event type, GUSPEE becomes competitive even among supervised systems, outperforming 19 out of 24 teams that participated in the GENIA event extraction shared task. With significant information loss (skipping event triggers and, most importantly, the nested event structures), it is possible to reduce GENIA events to binary relations so that existing distant-supervision methods are applicable. Yet even in such an evaluation tailored for existing methods, our system still outperformed them by a wide margin.

## 2 Related Work

Existing approaches for GENIA event extraction are supervised methods that either used a carefully engineered classification pipeline (Bjorne et al., 2009; Quirk et al., 2011) or applied joint inference (Riedel et al., 2009; Poon and Vanderwende, 2010; Riedel and McCallum, 2011). Poon and Vanderwende (2010) used a dependency-based formulation that resembled our semantic parsing one, but learned from supervised data. Classification approaches first need to classify words into event triggers, where distant supervision is not directly applicable.

In distant supervision (Craven and Kumlien, 1999; Mintz et al., 2009), if two entities are known to have a binary relation in the database, their cooccurrence in a sentence justifies labeling the instance with the relation. This assumption is often incorrect, and Riedel et al. (2010) introduced latent variables to model the uncertainty; the model was later improved by Hoffmann et al. (2011). GUSPEE generalizes this idea to structured prediction where the latent annotations are not simple classification decisions, but nested events. Krishnamurthy and Mitchell (2012) and Reddy et al. (2014) took an important step toward this direction, by learning a semantic parser based on combinatorial categorial grammar (CCG) from Freebase and web sentences. However, Krishnamurthy and Mitchell (2012) still learned from binary relations, using only simple sentences (of length ten or less). Reddy et al. (2014) learned from n-ary relations as well, yet their formulation only allows relations between entities, not relations between relations. Thus their approach cannot represent nested events, let alone extracting them. And like Krishnamurthy and Mitchell (2012), Reddy et al. (2014) focused on simple text and excluded sentences where entities were not dependency neighbors (i.e., not directly connected in the ungrounded graph), as well as sentences with unknown entities. While such restrictions do not impede parsing simple questions in their evaluation, their approach is not directly applicable to complex knowledge extraction. Reschke et al. (2014) also generalized distant supervision to n-ary relations for extracting template-based events, but similar to Reddy et al. (2014), they did not consider nested events.

Distant supervision can be viewed as a special case of the more general paradigm of *grounded learning* from a database. Clarke et al. (2010) and Liang et al. (2011) used the database to determine if a candidate semantic parse would yield the annotated answer, whereas distant supervision uses the database to determine if a relation instance is contained therein. Our GUSPEE system is inspired by grounded unsupervised semantic parsing (GUSP) (Poon, 2013) and shares a similar semantic representation. GUSP, like most grounded learning approaches, applied to question answering and did not leverage distant supervision. GUSPEE can thus be viewed as an extension of GUSP to leverage distant supervision for complex knowledge extraction.

Grounding in GUSPEE is materialized by virtual evidence favoring semantic structures that conform with the database. The idea of virtual evidence was first introduced by Pearl (1988) and later applied in several applications such as Subramanya and Bilmes (2007). Unlike in prior work, the virtual evidence in GUSPEE involves non-local factors (comparing a semantic parse with complex events in the database) and presents a major challenge to efficient learning.

Existing semantic parsers often adopt highly expressive formalisms such as CCG (Steedman, 2000). Such formalisms are extremely powerful, but also difficult to learn. We instead adopted a dependency-based formalism (Poon and Domingos, 2009; Liang et al., 2011; Poon, 2013). Moreover, following Poon and Domingos (2009), Krishnamurthy and Mitchell (2012), Poon (2013), we started with syntactic dependency parses, and focused on annotating nodes and edges with semantic states.

## 3 Grounded Semantic Parsing for Event Extraction

We use the GENIA event extraction task (Kim et al., 2009) as a representative example of complex knowledge extraction. The goal is to identify biological events from text, including the trigger words and arguments (Figure 1, bottom). There are nine event types, including simple ones such as `Expression` and `Transcription` that can only have one `THEME` argument, `Binding` that can have more than one `THEME` argument, and regulations that can have both `THEME` and `CAUSE` arguments. Protein annotations are given as input.

We formulate this task as semantic parsing and present our GUSPEE system (Figure 2). The core of GUSPEE is a tree HMM (Section 3.1), which extracts events from a sentence by annotating its syntactic dependency tree with event and argument states. In training, GUSPEE takes as input unannotated text and a database of complex events, and learns the tree HMM using EM, guided by grounded learning from the database via virtual evidence.

### 3.1 Problem Formulation

Let $t$ be a syntactic dependency tree for a sentence, with nodes $n_i$ and dependency edges $d_{i,j}$ ($n_j$ is a child of $n_i$). A semantic parse of $t$ is an assignment $z$ that maps each node to an event state and each dependency to an argument state. The semantic state of a protein word is fixed to that protein annotation. Basic event states are the nine event types and `NULL` (signifying a non-event, e.g., "The" in Figure 2 (c)). Basic argument states are `THEME`, `CAUSE`, and `NULL`. Additional states will be introduced later in Section 3.2 and 3.4.

GUSPEE models $z, t$ by a tree HMM:

$$P_\theta(z,t) = \prod_m P_{\texttt{EMIT}}(t_m|z_m,\theta) \cdot P_{\texttt{TRANS}}(z_m|z_{\pi(m)},\theta)$$

where $\theta$ are the emission and transition parameters, $m$ ranges over the nodes and dependency edges, $\pi(n_j) = d_{i,j}$ and $\pi(d_{i,j}) = n_i$. Note that this formulation implicitly assumes a fixed underlying directed tree, while the words and dependencies may vary.

Semantic parsing finds the most probable semantic assignment given the dependency tree:

$$z^* = \arg\max_z \log P_\theta(z|t) = \arg\max_z \log P_\theta(z,t)$$

In training, GUSPEE takes as input a set of complex events (database $K$) and syntactic dependency trees (unannotated text $T$), and maximizes the likelihood of $T$ augmented by virtual evidence $\phi_K(z)$.

$$\begin{aligned}\theta^* &= \arg\max_\theta \quad \log P_\theta(T|K) \\ &= \arg\max_\theta \quad \sum_{t \in T} \log \sum_z P_\theta(z,t) \cdot \phi_K(z)\end{aligned}$$

Virtual evidence is analogous to a Bayesian prior, but applies to variable states rather than model parameters (Subramanya and Bilmes, 2007).

### 3.2 Handling Syntax-Semantics Mismatch

For simple sentences such as the one in Figure 2(b), the complex event can be represented by a semantic parse using only basic states. In general, however, syntax and semantics often diverge. For example, in Figure 2(c), "requires" triggers the top `POS-NEG` event that has a `THEME` argument triggered by "block", but "ability" stands in between the two; likewise for "block" and "IL-10". Additionally, mismatch could stem from errors in the syntactic parse. In such cases, the correct semantic parse can no longer be represented by basic states alone. Following GUSP (Poon, 2013), we introduced a new argument state `RAISING` which, if assigned to a dependency, would require that the parent and child be assigned the same basic event state. We also introduce a corresponding `RAISE` version for each non-null event state, to signify that the word derives its basic state from `RAISING` of a child. `RAISING` is related to but not identical with type raising in CCG and other grammars. For simplicity, we did not use other complex states explored in Poon (2013).

### 3.3 Virtual Evidence for Grounded Learning

Grounded learning in GUSPEE is attained by incorporating the virtual evidence $\phi_K(z)$, which favors the $z$'s containing known events in $K$ and penalizes those containing unknown events. Intuitively, this can be accomplished by identifying events in $z$ and comparing them with events in $K$. But this is not robust as individual events and mentions may be fragmental and incomplete. Insisting on matching an event in full would miss partial matches that still convey valuable supervision. Proteins are given as input and can be mapped to event arguments a priori. Matching sub-events with only one protein argument would be too noisy without direct supervision on triggers. We thus consider matching minimum sub-events with two protein arguments.

Specifically, we preprocessed complex events in $K$ to identify minimum logical forms containing two protein arguments from each complex event, where arguments not directly leading to either protein are skipped. For example, the complex event in Figure 1 would generate three sub-events: (NEG-REG, IL-10, RFLAT), (POS-REG, BCL, (NEG-REG, -, RFLAT)), (POS-REG, BCL, (NEG-REG, IL-10, -)), where - signifies underspecification. We denote the set of such sub-events as $S(K)$.

Likewise, given a semantic parse $z$, for every protein pair in $z$, we would convert the minimum semantic parse subtree spanning the two proteins into the canonical logical form and compare it with elements in $S(K)$. If the minimum subtree contains NULL, either in an event or argument state, it signifies a non-event and would be ignored. Otherwise, the canonical form is derived by collapsing RAISING states. For example, in both Figure 2 (b) and (c), the minimum subtree spanning the proteins IL-10 and RFLAT is converted into the same logical form of (NEG-REG, IL-10, RFLAT). We denote the set of such logical forms as $E(z)$.

Formally, the virtual evidence in GUSPEE are:

$$\phi_K(z) = \exp \sum_{e \in E(z)} \sigma(e, K)$$

where

$$\sigma(e, K) = \begin{cases} \kappa & : e \in S(K) \\ -\kappa & : e \notin S(K) \end{cases}$$

In distant supervision, where $z$ is simply a binary relation, it is trivial to evaluate $\phi_K(z)$. (In fact, the original distant supervision algorithm is exactly equivalent to this form, with $\kappa = \infty$.) In GUSPEE, however, $z$ is a semantic parse and evaluating $E(z)$ and $\sigma(e, K)$ involves a global factor that does not decompose into local dependencies as the tree HMM $P_\theta(z, t)$. The naive way to compute the augmented likelihood (Section 3.1) is thus intractable.

### 3.4 Efficient Learning with Virtual Evidence

To render learning tractable, the key idea is to augment the local event and argument states so that they contain sufficient information for evaluating $\phi_K(z)$. Specifically, the semantic state $z(n_i)$ needs to represent not only the semantic assignment to $n_i$ (e.g., a NEG-REG event trigger), but also the set of (possibly incomplete) sub-events in the subtree under $n_i$. We accomplished this by representing the semantic paths from $n_i$ to proteins in the subtree. For example, in Figure 2 (b), the augmented state of "inhibition" would be (NEG-REG→THEME→RFLAT, NEG-REG→CAUSE→IL-10). To facilitate canonicalization and sub-event comparison, a path containing NULL will be skipped, and RAISING will be collapsed. E.g., in Figure 2(c), the augmented state of "ability" would become (NEG-REG→THEME→RFLAT, NEG-REG→CAUSE→IL-10).

With these augmented states, $\phi_K(z)$ decomposes into local factors. The proteins under $n_i$ are known a priori, as well as the children containing them. Semantic paths from $n_i$ to proteins can thus be computed by imposing consistency constraints for each child. Namely, for child $n_j$ that contains protein $p$, the semantic path from $n_i$ to $p$ should result from combining $z(n_i)$, $z(d_{i,j})$, and the semantic path from $n_j$ to $p$. The minimum sub-events spanning two proteins under $n_i$, if any, can be derived from the semantic paths in the augmented state. Note that if both proteins come from the same child $n_j$, the pair needs not be considered at $n_i$, as their minimum spanning sub-event, if any, would be under $n_j$ and already be factored in there.

The number of augmented states is $O(s^p)$, and the number of sub-event evaluations is $O(s \cdot p^2)$, where $s$ is the number of distinct semantic paths, and $p$ is the number of proteins in the subtree. Below, we show how $s, p$ can be constrained to reasonable ranges to make computation efficient.

First, consider $s$. The number of semantic paths is theoretically unbounded since a path can be arbitrarily long. However, semantic paths contained in a database event are bounded in length and can be precomputed from the database (the maximum in GENIA is four). Longer paths can be represented by a special dummy path signifying that they would not match any database events. Likewise, certain sub-paths would not occur in database events. E.g., in GENIA, simple events cannot take events as arguments, so paths containing sub-paths such as `Expression` $\rightarrow$ `Transcription` are also illegitimate and can be represented same as the above. We also notice that for regulation events with other regulation events as arguments, the semantics can be compressed into a single regulation event, e.g., POS-REG$\rightarrow$NEG-REG is semantically equivalent with NEG-REG, as the collective effect of a positive regulation on top of a negative one is negative. Therefore, when evaulating the semantic path from $n_i$ to a protein during dynamic programming, we would collapse consecutive regulation events in the child path, if any. This further reduces the length of semantic paths to at most three (regulation - regulation - simple event - protein).

Next, we notice that $p$ is bounded to begin with, but it could be quite large. When a sentence contains many proteins (i.e., large $p$), it often stems from conjunction of proteins, as in "TP53 regulates many downstream targets such as ABCB1, AFP, APC, ATF3, BAX". All proteins in the conjunct play a similar role in their respective events, such as THEME in the above example among "ABCB1, AFP, APC, ATF3, BAX", and so share the same semantic paths. Therefore, prior to learning, we preprocessed the sentences to condense each conjunct into a single *effective* protein node. We identified conjunction by Stanford dependencies (`conj_*`). In GENIA, this reduces the maximum number of effective protein nodes to two for the vast majority of sentences (over 90%). Both representation and evaluation are now reasonably efficient. To further speed up learning, in our experiments we only trained on sentences with at most two effective protein nodes, as this already performed quite well. Training on GENIA took 1.5 hours and semantic parsing of a sentence took less than a second (with one i7 core at 2.4 GHz).

Unlike RAISING, the augmented states introduced in this section are specific to GENIA events. However, the rules to canonicalize states are general and can potentially be adapted to other domains. An alternative strategy to combat state explosion is by embedding the discrete states in a low-dimensional vector space (Socher et al., 2013), which is a direction for future research.

### 3.5 Features

The GUSPEE model uses log-linear models for the emission and transition probabilities and trains using feature-rich EM (Berg-Kirkpatrick et al., 2010). The features are:

**Word emission** $\mathbb{I}[\text{lemma} = l, z_m = n]$;

**Dependency emission** $\mathbb{I}[\text{dependency} = d, z_m = e]$ where $e \notin \{\texttt{NULL}, \texttt{RAISE}\}$;

**Transition** $\mathbb{I}[z_m = a, z_{\pi(m)} = b]$ where $a, b \notin \{\texttt{NULL}, \texttt{RAISE}\}$.

To modulate the model complexity, GUSPEE imposes a standard $L_2$ prior on the weights, and includes the following features with fixed weights:

- $W_{\texttt{NULL}}$: apply to NULL states;
- $W_{\texttt{RAISE}-P}$: apply to protein RAISING;
- $W_{\texttt{RAISE}-E}$: apply to event RAISING.

The advantage of a feature-rich representation is flexibility in feature engineering. Here, we excluded NULL and RAISE in dependency emission and transition features, and regulated them separately to enable parameter tying for better generalization.

## 4 Experiments

### 4.1 Evaluation on GENIA Event Extraction

In principle, we can learn GUSPEE from any pathway database. However, evaluation is challenging as these databases do not contain textual annotations. Prior work on distant supervision resorted to sampling and annotating new extractions. This is effective for comparing among distant-supervision systems, but it cannot be used to compare them with supervised learning. Moreover, as annotation is conducted by the authors or crowdsourcing, consistency and quality are hard to control.

We thus adopted a novel approach to evaluation by simulating a grounded learning scenario using the GENIA event extraction dataset (Kim et al., 2009). Specifically, we generated a set of complex events from the annotations of training sentences as the database. The annotations were discarded afterwards and GUSPEE learned from the database and unannotated text alone. The learned model was then applied to semantic parsing of test sentences and evaluated on event precision, recall, and F1. This

| Event Type | Rec. | Prec. | F1 |
|---|---|---|---|
| Expression | 50.8 | 41.9 | 45.9 |
| Transcription | 18.3 | 14.0 | 15.9 |
| Catabolism | 0 | 0 | 0 |
| Phosphorylation | 36.2 | 43.6 | 39.5 |
| Localization | 0 | 0 | 0 |
| Binding | 24.0 | 42.6 | 30.7 |
| Regulation | 2.5 | 5.0 | 3.3 |
| Positive_regulation | 11.4 | 21.4 | 14.9 |
| Negative_regulation | 4.4 | 16.4 | 6.9 |
| Total Event F1 | 19.1 | 29.4 | 23.2 |

Table 1: GENIA event extraction results of GUSPEE

| Event Type | Rec. | Prec. | F1 |
|---|---|---|---|
| Expression | 76.4 | 81.5 | 78.8 |
| Transcription | 49.4 | 73.6 | 59.1 |
| Catabolism | 65.6 | 80.0 | 74.4 |
| Phosphorylation | 73.9 | 84.5 | 78.9 |
| Localization | 74.6 | 75.8 | 75.2 |
| Binding | 48.0 | 50.9 | 49.4 |
| Regulation | 32.5 | 47.1 | 38.6 |
| Positive_regulation | 38.7 | 51.7 | 44.3 |
| Negative_regulation | 35.9 | 54.9 | 43.9 |
| Total Event F1 | 50.2 | 62.6 | 55.7 |

Table 2: GENIA event extraction results of state-of-the-art supervised system MSR11 (Quirk et al., 2011).

evaluation methodology enables us to assess the true accuracy and compare head-to-head with supervised methods.

GENIA contains 800 abstracts for training and 150 for development. It also has a test set, but its annotation is not made public. Therefore, we used the training set for grounded learning and development, and reserved the development set for testing. The majority events are Regulation (including Positive_regulation, Negative_regulation). See Kim et al. (2009) for details. We processed all sentences using SPLAT (Quirk et al., 2012), to conduct tokenization, part-of-speech tagging, and constituency parsing. We then postprocessed the parses to obtain Stanford dependencies (de Marneffe et al., 2006). During development on the training data, we found the following parameters (Section 3) to perform quite well and used them in all subsequent experiments: $\kappa = 20$, $W_{\texttt{NULL}} = 4$, $W_{\texttt{RAISE}-P} = 2$, $W_{\texttt{RAISE}-E} = -6$, $L_2$ prior $= 0.1$. Interestingly, we found that encouraging protein RAISING is beneficial, which probably stems from the fact that proteins are often separated from event triggers by noun modifiers, such as "the BCL gene", "IL-10 protein".

Table 1 shows GUSPEE's results on GENIA event extraction. Note that this event-based evaluation is rather stringent, as it considers an event incorrect if one of its argument events is not completely correct, thus an incorrect event will render all its upstream events incorrect. See Kim et al. (2009) for details. For comparison, Table 2 shows the results of MSR11, a state-of-the-art supervised system. MSR11 also provides a upper bound for the supervised version of GUSPEE, as the latter is much less engineered.

Not surprisingly, grounded learning with GUSPEE still lags behind supervised learning. MSR11 used a rich set of features, including POS tags, linear and dependency n-grams, etc. Also, it is expected that indirect supervision do not provide as effective signals as direct supervision. However, the comparison reveals a particularly interesting contrast. Event types such as Expression, Catabolism, Phosphorylation, and Localization are relatively easy, yet GUSPEE performed rather poorly on them. Simple events do not admit multiple arguments, so they appear less often in the virtual evidence, and grounded learning has difficulty learning these event types, especially their triggers. In light of this, it's actually remarkable that GUSPEE still learned a substantial portion of them.

### 4.2 Prototype-Driven Learning

While full-blown annotations are undoubtedly expensive and time-consuming to generate, it is rather easy for a domain expert to provide a few trigger words per event type, such as "expression", "expressed" for Expression. This motivates us to explore prototype-driven learning (Haghighi and Klein, 2006) in combination with grounded learning. Specifically, we simulated expert selection by picking the top five most frequent trigger words for each event type from training data. We then augmented grounded learning in GUSPEE by incorporating word emission features for each prototype word and the corresponding event state, e.g., $\mathbb{I}[\text{lemma} = \text{express}, z_m = \texttt{Expression}]$. The weights are fixed to a large number (five in our case). Table 3 shows the results with prototypes, which improved substantially. Not surprisingly, simple

| Event Type | Rec. | Prec. | F1 |
|---|---|---|---|
| Expression | 55.3 | 88.3 | 68.0 |
| Transcription | 50.0 | 39.1 | 43.9 |
| Catabolism | 52.4 | 100.0 | 68.9 |
| Phosphorylation | 61.7 | 82.9 | 70.7 |
| Localization | 52.8 | 100.0 | 69.1 |
| Binding | 20.2 | 92.7 | 33.2 |
| Regulation | 24.1 | 64.0 | 35.0 |
| Positive_regulation | 17.4 | 63.8 | 27.4 |
| Negative_regulation | 8.4 | 52.8 | 14.5 |
| Total Event F1 | 27.9 | 72.2 | 40.2 |

Table 3: GENIA event extraction results of GUSPEE with five prototype words per event type

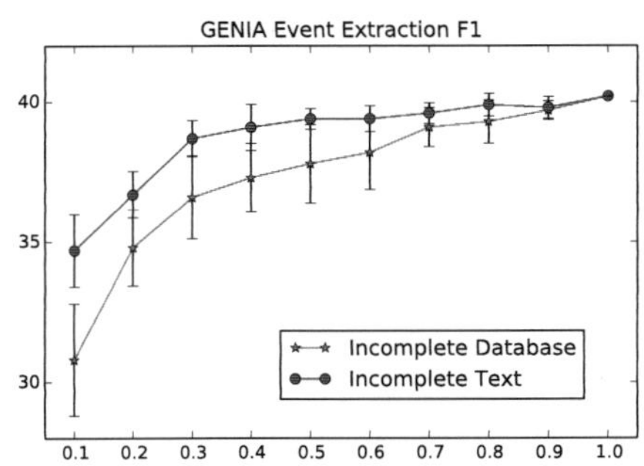


Figure 3: GENIA Event F1 of GUSPEE with prototypes, using incomplete database or text.

events such as Catabolism benefited the most from prototypes, as they have fewer variations in triggers. While the F1 score 40.2 still lags behind the supervised state of the art, it would have been competitive compared to the 24 teams participating in the original shared task, outperforming 19 of them (the top 5th system scored an F1 of 40.5, see www.nactem.ac.uk/tsujii/GENIA/SharedTask /results/results-master.html, Task 1).

### 4.3 Database-Text Mismatch

In our simulation of grounded learning, every event in the database is mentioned in some text and vice versa. In practice, however, there is usually a mismatch between database and text: the unannotated text generally contains more facts than are already populated in the database; conversely, a database fact may not be explicitly mentioned in the text.

The GENIA dataset offers an excellent opportunity to study the robustness of grounded learning in light of such mismatch. Specifically, we simulated a grounded learning scenario with an incomplete database by populating events from the annotations of a random fraction of training text, and then learning GUSPEE with this database and all training text. Likewise, we simulated a scenario with incomplete text using the training event database in full, but only a fraction of unannotated text.

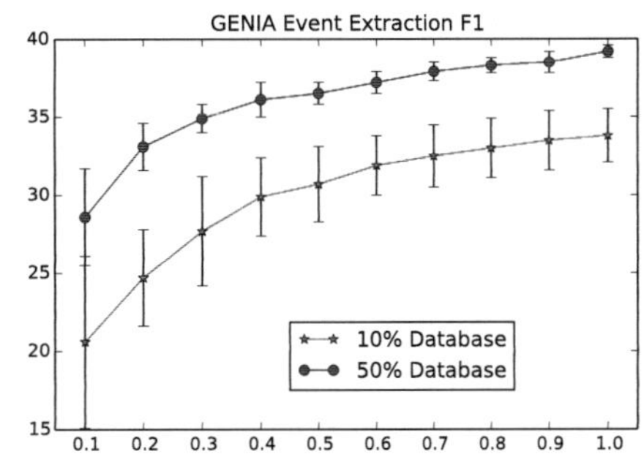


Figure 4: GENIA Event F1 of GUSPEE with prototypes, using a fraction of database and increasing amount of unannotated text.

Figure 3 shows the results of GUSPEE with prototypes as the fraction varies between 0.1 and 1, by averaging five random runs. In both scenarios, the F1 score degrades smoothly as the fraction gets smaller. Precision stays roughly the same while recall gradually degrades (curves not shown). This shows that GUSPEE is reasonably robust. Not surprisingly, the degradation is steeper with incomplete database than with incomplete text.

To further investigate the effect of unannotated text, we also randomly sampled a fraction of database events for grounded supervision, and evaluated GUSPEE with increasing amounts of unannotated text. Figure 4 shows the results by averaging nine random runs. The F1 increases steadily with additional unannotated text, mainly due to rising recall (curves not shown). This suggests that GUSPEE could potentially benefit from more unannotated text and is reasonably robust even when some text is not relevant to the available events. As expected, more grounded supervision (50% vs. 10% database) led to substantially better F1 and lower variation.

### 4.4 Error Analysis

Upon manual inspection, we found that syntactic errors considerably affect performance. Poon (2013) introduced complex states such as `Sinking` and `Implicit` to combat syntax-semantics mismatch, which could also be incorporated into GUSPEE. Improving syntactic parsing, either separately by adapting to the biomedical domain, or jointly along with semantic parsing, is another important future direction. GUSPEE achieved better precision than recall, especially when learning with prototypes, and might benefit from augmenting prototypes by distributional similarity (Haghighi and Klein, 2006).

### 4.5 Comparison with Existing Distant Supervision Approaches

Existing distant supervision approaches are not directly applicable to extracting nested events. However, we can convert the extraction task into classifying minimum sub-events between proteins, for which existing methods can be applied. Specifically, we used binary sub-events in $S(K)$ (Section 3.3) for distant supervision, and evaluated on classifying test sentences. This would enable an interesting comparison with GUSPEE, as the latter also derived indirect supervision from $S(K)$ alone. Textual annotations of triggers and nested event structures in GUSPEE output were ignored, and prototypes were not used to enable a fair comparison. For distant supervision, we used the state-of-the-art MultiR system (Hoffmann et al., 2011) with standard lexical and syntactic features (Mintz et al., 2009). MultiR can be used for supervised learning by fixing relations according to the sentence-level annotations, which provides a supervised upper bound.

Table 4 shows the results. GUSPEE outperformed MultiR by a wide margin, improving F1 by 24%. Surprisingly, GUSPEE even surpassed the supervised upper bound of MultiR. This suggests that our semantic parsing formulation not only is superior in representation power, but also facilitates better learning. We also experimented with sharing parameters among related sub-events in a MultiR-like model, but it did not improve the performance. Upon close inspection, we found that MultiR mainly scored on `Binding` events and failed almostly entirely on the more difficult `Regulation` events. GUSPEE was able to extract `Regulation` events, but incurred some precision errors.

| Method | Rec. | Prec. | F1 (Class.) |
|---|---|---|---|
| MultiR | 11.2 | 21.7 | 14.8 |
| MultiR (Super.) | 12.1 | 24.4 | 16.2 |
| GUSPEE | 22.9 | 15.3 | 18.4 |

Table 4: Classification results on GENIA when events are simplified to binary relations for distant supervision.

## 5 Summary

We generalize distant supervision to complex knowledge extraction and propose the first approach to learn a semantic parser from a database of nested events and unannotated text. Experiments on GENIA event extraction showed that our GUSPEE system could learn from and extract such complex events, and was competitive even among supervised systems after incorporating a few easily-obtainable prototype event trigger words.

Future directions include: PubMed-scale pathway extraction; application to other domains; incorporating additional complex states to address syntax-semantics mismatch; learning vector-space representations for complex states; joint syntactic-semantic parsing; incorporating reasoning and other sources of indirect supervision.

## References


Yoav Artzi and Luke Zettlemoyer. 2011. Bootstrapping semantic parsers from conversations. In *Proceedings of the 2011 Conference on Empirical Methods in Natural Language Processing*.

Yoav Artzi and Luke Zettlemoyer. 2013. Weakly supervised learning of semantic parsers for mapping instructions to actions. *Transactions of the Association for Computational Linguistics*, 1:49–62.

Taylor Berg-Kirkpatrick, John DeNero, and Dan Klein. 2010. Painless unsupervised learning with features. In *Proceedings of Human Language Technologies: The 2010 Annual Conference of the North American Chapter of the Association for Computational Linguistics*.

Jari Bjorne, Juho Heimonen, Filip Ginter, Antti Airola, Tapio Pahikkala, and Tapio Salakoski. 2009. Extracting complex biological events with rich graph-based feature sets. In *Proceedings of the BioNLP Workshop*.

Ethan G Cerami, Benjamin E Gross, Emek Demir, Igor Rodchenkov, Özgün Babur, Nadia Anwar, Nikolaus Schultz, Gary D Bader, and Chris Sander. 2011. Pathway commons, a web resource for biological pathway data. *Nucleic acids research*, 39(suppl 1):D685–D690.

David Chen and Ray Mooney. 2011. Learning to interpret natural language navigation instructions from observations. In *Proceedings of the Twenty Sixth National Conference on Artificial Intelligence*.

James Clarke, Dan Goldwasser, Ming-Wei Chang, and Dan Roth. 2010. Driving semantic parsing from world's response. In *Proceedings of the 2010 Conference on Natural Language Learning*.

M. Craven and J. Kumlien. 1999. Constructing biological knowledge bases by extracting information from text sources. In *Proceedings of the 7th International Conference on Intelligent Systems for Molecular Biology*, pages 77–86. AAAI Press.

Marie-Catherine de Marneffe, Bill MacCartney, and Christopher D. Manning. 2006. Generating typed dependency parses from phrase structure parses. In *Proceedings of the Fifth International Conference on Language Resources and Evaluation*, pages 449–454, Genoa, Italy. ELRA.

Aria Haghighi and Dan Klein. 2006. Prototype-driven learning for sequence models. In *Proceedings of the Forty Fourth Annual Meeting of the Association for Computational Linguistics*.

Raphael Hoffmann, Congle Zhang, Xiao Ling, Luke Zettlemoyer, and Daniel S. Weld. 2011. Knowledge-based weak supervision for information extraction of overlapping relations. In *Proceedings of the Forty Ninth Annual Meeting of the Association for Computational Linguistics*.

Minoru Kanehisa. 2002. The kegg database. *Silico Simulation of Biological Processes*, 247:91–103.

Jin-Dong Kim, Tomoko Ohta, Sampo Pyysalo, Yoshinobu Kano, and Junichi Tsujii. 2009. Overview of BioNLP-09 Shared Task on event extraction. In *Proceedings of the BioNLP Workshop*.

Jayant Krishnamurthy and Tom M. Mitchell. 2012. Weakly supervised training of semantic parsers. In *EMNLP-12*.

Percy Liang, Michael Jordan, and Dan Klein. 2011. Learning dependency-based compositional semantics. In *Proceedings of the Forty Ninth Annual Meeting of the Association for Computational Linguistics*.

Mike Mintz, Steven Bills, Rion Snow, and Dan Jurafsky. 2009. Distant supervision for relation extraction without labeled data. In *Proceedings of the Forty Seventh Annual Meeting of the Association for Computational Linguistics*.

Raymond J. Mooney. 2007. Learning for semantic parsing. In *Proceedings of the Eighth International Conference on Computational Linguistics and Intelligent Text Processing*, pages 311–324, Mexico City, Mexico. Springer.

J. Pearl. 1988. *Probabilistic Reasoning in Intelligent Systems: Networks of Plausible Inference*. Morgan Kaufmann, San Francisco, CA.

Hoifung Poon and Pedro Domingos. 2009. Unsupervised semantic parsing. In *Proceedings of the 2009 Conference on Empirical Methods in Natural Language Processing*, pages 1–10, Singapore. ACL.

Hoifung Poon and Pedro Domingos. 2010. Unsupervised ontological induction from text. In *Proceedings of the Forty Eighth Annual Meeting of the Association for Computational Linguistics*, pages 296–305, Uppsala, Sweden. ACL.

Hoifung Poon and Lucy Vanderwende. 2010. Joint inference for knowledge extraction from biomedical literature. In *Proceedings of Human Language Technologies: The 2010 Annual Conference of the North American Chapter of the Association for Computational Linguistics*.

Hoifung Poon. 2013. Grounded unsupervised semantic parsing. In *Proceedings of the Fifty First Annual Meeting of the Association for Computational Linguistics*.

Chris Quirk, Pallavi Choudhury, Michael Gamon, and Lucy Vanderwende. 2011. Msr-nlp entry in bionlp shared task 2011. In *Proc. BioNLP*.

Chris Quirk, Pallavi Choudhury, Jianfeng Gao, Hisami Suzuki, Kristina Toutanova, Michael Gamon, Wentau Yih, and Lucy Vanderwende. 2012. MSR SPLAT, a language analysis toolkit. In *Proceedings of NAACL HLT Demonstration Session*.

Siva Reddy, Mirella Lapata, and Mark Steedman. 2014. Large-scale semantic parsing without question-answer pairs. *Transactions of the Association for Computational Linguistics*.

Kevin Reschke, Martin Jankowiak, Mihai Surdeanu, Christopher D Manning, and Daniel Jurafsky. 2014. Event extraction using distant supervision. In *Language Resources and Evaluation Conference (LREC)*.

Sebastian Riedel and Andrew McCallum. 2011. Fast and robust joint models for biomedical event extraction. In *Proceedings of the Conference on Empirical Methods in Natural Language Processing*.

Sebastian Riedel, Hong-Woo Chun, Toshihisa Takagi, and Jun'ichi Tsujii. 2009. A markov logic approach to bio-molecular event extraction. In *Proc. BioNLP*.

Sebastian Riedel, Limin Yao, and Andrew McCallum. 2010. Modeling relations and their mentions without labeled text. In *Proceedings of the Sixteen European Conference on Machine Learning*.

Carl F. Schaefer, Kira Anthony, Shiva Krupa, Jeffrey Buchoff, Matthew Day, Timo Hannay, and Kenneth H. Buetow. 2009. PID: The pathway interaction database. *Nucleic Acids Research*, 37:674–679.

Richard Socher, John Bauer, Christopher D. Manning, and Andrew Y. Ng. 2013. Parsing with compositional vector grammars. In *Proceedings of the Fifty First Annual Meeting of the Association for Computational Linguistics*.

Mark Steedman. 2000. *The syntactic process*, volume 35. MIT Press.

Amarnag Subramanya and Jeff Bilmes. 2007. Virtual evidence for training speech recognizers using partially labeled data. In *Proceedings of Human Language Technologies: The 2007 Annual Conference of the North American Chapter of the Association for Computational Linguistics*.

Ivan Titov and Alexandre Klementiev. 2011. A bayesian model for unsupervised semantic parsing. In *Proceedings of the Forty Ninth Annual Meeting of the Association for Computational Linguistics*.

John M. Zelle and Ray Mooney. 1993. Learning semantic grammars with constructive inductive logic programming. In *Proceedings of the Eleventh National Conference on Artificial Intelligence*.

Luke S. Zettlemoyer and Michael Collins. 2005. Learning to map sentences to logical form: Structured classification with probabilistic categorial grammers. In *Proceedings of the Twenty First Conference on Uncertainty in Artificial Intelligence*, pages 658–666, Edinburgh, Scotland. AUAI Press.

Luke S. Zettlemoyer and Michael Collins. 2007. Online learning of relaxed ccg grammars for parsing to logical form. In *Proceedings of the Joint Conference on Empirical Methods in Natural Language Processing and Computational Natural Language Learning*.

# Sentiment after Translation: A Case-Study on Arabic Social Media Posts

**Mohammad Salameh**
University of Alberta
msalameh@ualberta.ca

**Saif M. Mohammad and Svetlana Kiritchenko**
National Research Council Canada
{saif.mohammad,svetlana.kiritchenko}@nrc-cnrc.gc.ca

## Abstract

When text is translated from one language into another, sentiment is preserved to varying degrees. In this paper, we use Arabic social media posts as stand-in for source language text, and determine loss in sentiment predictability when they are translated into English, manually and automatically. As benchmarks, we use manually and automatically determined sentiment labels of the Arabic texts. We show that sentiment analysis of English translations of Arabic texts produces competitive results, w.r.t. Arabic sentiment analysis. We discover that even though translation significantly reduces the human ability to recover sentiment, automatic sentiment systems are still able to capture sentiment information from the translations.

## 1 Introduction

Automatic sentiment analysis of text, especially social media posts, has a number of applications in commerce, public health, and public policy development. However, a vast majority of prior research on automatic sentiment analysis has been on English texts. Furthermore, many sentiment resources essential to automatic sentiment analysis (e.g., sentiment lexicons) exist only in English. Thus there is a growing need for effective methods for analyzing text from other languages such as Arabic and Chinese, especially posts on social media. There has also been marked progress in automatic translation of texts, especially from other languages into English. Thus, instead of building source-language specific sentiment analysis systems, one can translate the texts into English and use an English sentiment analysis system. However, it is widely believed that aspects of sentiment may be lost in translation, especially in automatic translation. Though, the extent of this loss, in terms of drop in accuracy of automatic sentiment systems remains undetermined.

This paper analyzes several methods available in annotating non-English texts for sentiment:

- Use a source-language sentiment analysis system.
- Run an English sentiment analysis system on manually created English translations of source language text.
- Run an English sentiment analysis system on automatically generated English translations of source language text.

In our experiments, we use Arabic social media posts as a specific instance of the source language text. We use state-of-the-art Arabic and English sentiment analysis systems as well as a state-of-the-art Arabic-to-English translation system. We outline the advantages and disadvantages of each of the methods listed above, and more importantly conduct experiments to determine accuracy of sentiment labels obtained using each of these methods. As benchmarks we use manually and automatically determined sentiment labels of the Arabic tweets.

These results will help users determine methods best suited for their particular needs. Along the way, we answer several research questions such as:

1. What sentiment prediction accuracy is expected when Arabic blog posts and tweets are



*Human Language Technologies: The 2015 Annual Conference of the North American Chapter of the ACL*, pages 767–777,
Denver, Colorado, May 31 – June 5, 2015. 

translated into English (using the current state-of-art techniques), and then run through a state-of-the-art English sentiment analysis system?

2. How does this performance compare with that of a current state-of-the-art Arabic sentiment system?
3. What is the loss in sentiment predictability when translating Arabic text into English automatically vs. manually?
4. How difficult is it for humans to determine sentiment of automatically translated text?
5. When dealing with translated text, which is more accurate at determining the sentiment of Arabic text: (1) automatic sentiment analysis of the translated text, or (2) human annotation of the translated text for sentiment?

The inferences drawn from these experiments do not necessarily apply to language pairs other than Arabic–English. Languages can differ significantly in terms of characteristics that impact accuracy of an automatic sentiment analysis system. Our goal here specifically is to understand sentiment predictability of Arabic dialectal text on translation. However, a similar set of experiments can be used for other language pairs as well to determine the impact of translation on sentiment.

Through our experiments on two different datasets, we show that sentiment analysis of English translations of Arabic texts produces competitive results, w.r.t. Arabic sentiment analysis. We also show that translation (both manual and automatic) introduces marked changes in sentiment carried by the text; positive and negative texts can often be translated into texts that are neutral. We also find that certain attributes of automatically translated text that mislead humans with regards to the true sentiment of the source text, do not seem to affect the automatic sentiment analysis system.

In the process of developing these experiments to study how translation alters sentiment, we created a state-of-the-art Arabic sentiment analysis system by porting NRC-Canada's competition winning system (Kiritchenko et al., 2014) to Arabic. We also created a substantial amount of sentiment labeled data pertaining to Arabic social media texts and their English translations which is made freely available.[1]

[1]http://www.purl.com/net/ArabicSentiment

This is the first such resource where text in one language and its translations into another language (both manually and automatically produced) are each manually labeled for sentiment.

## 2 Related Work

### 2.1 Sentiment Analysis of English Social Media

Sentiment analysis systems have been applied to many different kinds of texts including customer reviews, newspaper headlines (Bellegarda, 2010), novels (Boucouvalas, 2002; Mohammad and Yang, 2011), emails (Liu et al., 2003; Mohammad and Yang, 2011), blogs (Neviarouskaya et al., 2011), and tweets (Mohammad, 2012). Often these systems have to cater to the specific needs of the text such as formality versus informality, length of utterances, etc. Sentiment analysis systems developed specifically for tweets include those by Go et al. (2009), Pak and Paroubek (2010), Agarwal et al. (2011), and Thelwall et al. (2011). A survey by Martínez-Cámara et al. (2012) provides an overview of the research on sentiment analysis of tweets. In the last two years, several shared tasks on sentiment analysis were organized by the Conference on Semantic Evaluation Exercises (SemEval), which allowed for comparison of different approaches on common datasets from different domains (Wilson et al., 2013; Rosenthal et al., 2014; Pontiki et al., 2014). The NRC-Canada system (Kiritchenko et al., 2014) ranked first in these competitions, and we use it in our experiments. Details of the system are described in Section 6.

### 2.2 Sentiment Analysis of Arabic Social Media

Sentiment analysis of Arabic social media texts has several challenges. The text is often in a regional Arabic dialect rather than Modern Standard Arabic (MSA). Unlike MSA which is a standardized form of Arabic, dialectal Arabic is the spoken form of Arabic and lacks strict writing standards. The text often includes words from languages other than Arabic and multiple scripts may be used to express Arabic and foreign words. In addition, Arabic is a morphologically complex language, thus having a lexicon of word-sentiment associations that covers all different surface forms becomes a cumbersome task. Negation in MSA is expressed through negation particles, but in some dialects (Egyptian) it is expressed using suffixes at the end of the word. We refer the reader to Mourad and Darwish (2013) for more details on these issues.

There have been a few studies tackling sentiment analysis of Arabic texts (Ahmad et al., 2006; Badaro et al., 2014). The ones most closely related to our work are the studies of sentiment analysis of Arabic social media (Al-Kabi et al., 2013; El-Beltagy and Ali, 2013; Mourad and Darwish, 2013; Abdul-Mageed et al., 2014). Here we review existing Arabic sentiment analysis systems that were designed specifically for Arabic social media datasets. Abdul-Mageed et al. (2014) trained an SVM classifier on a manually labeled dataset and applied a two-stage classification that first separates subjective from objective sentences and then classifies the subjective into positive or negative instances. The authors have compiled several datasets from multiple social media resources that include chatroom messages, tweets, forum posts, and Wikipedia Talk pages. However, these resources have not been made publicly available yet.

Mourad and Darwish (2013) trained SVM and Naive Bayes classifiers on Arabic tweets annotated by two native Arabic speakers. We compare our system's performance to theirs in Section 7.

Refaee and Rieser (2014b) manually annotated tweets for sentiment by two native Arabic speakers. They used an SVM to classify tweets in a two-stage approach, polar vs neutral, then positive vs. negative. The authors shared their data with us and we test our system on their dataset. However, the dataset they provided us is a larger superset than the one they had originally used (Refaee and Rieser, 2014a). Thus, the results of sentiment systems on the two sets are not directly comparable.

### 2.3 Multilingual Sentiment Analysis

Work on multilingual sentiment analysis has mainly addressed mapping sentiment resources from English into morphologically complex languages. Mihalcea et al. (2007) used English resources to automatically generate a Romanian subjectivity lexicon using an English–Romanian dictionary. The generated lexicon is then used to classify Romanian text. Wan (2008) translated Chinese customer reviews to English using a machine translation system. The translated reviews are then classified with a rule-based system that relies on English lexicons. A higher accuracy is achieved by using ensemble methods and combining knowledge from Chinese and English resources. Balahur and Turchi (2014) conducted a study to assess the performance of statistical sentiment analysis techniques on machine-translated texts. Opinion-bearing phrases from the *New York Times* text corpus (2002–2005) were automatically translated using publicly available machine-translation engines (Google, Bing, and Moses). Then, the accuracy of a sentiment analysis system trained on original English texts was compared to the accuracy of the system trained on automatic translations to German, Spanish, and French. The authors concluded that the quality of machine translation is sufficient for sentiment analysis to be performed on automatically translated texts without a substantial loss in accuracy. Contrary to that work, our study uses both manual and automatic translations as well as both manual and automatic sentiment assignments to systematically examine the effect of translation on sentiment. Additionally, we deal with noisy social media texts as opposed to more polished news media texts. There exists research on using sentiment analysis to improve machine translation (Chen and Zhu, 2014), but that is beyond the scope of this paper.

## 3 Method for Determining Sentiment Predictability on Translation

In order to systematically study the impact of translation on sentiment analysis, we propose the following experimental setup:

- Identify or compile an Arabic social media dataset. We will refer to it as *Ar*. (*Ar* comes from the first two letter of Arabic.)
- Manually translate *Ar* into English. We will refer to these English translations as *En(Manl.Trans.)* [*Manl.* is for manual, and *Trans.* is for translations.]
- Automatically translate *Ar* into English. We will refer to these English translations as *En(Auto.Trans.)* [*Auto.* is for automatic.]
- Manually annotate Ar. for sentiment. We will refer to the sentiment-labeled dataset as *Ar(Manl.Sent.)*

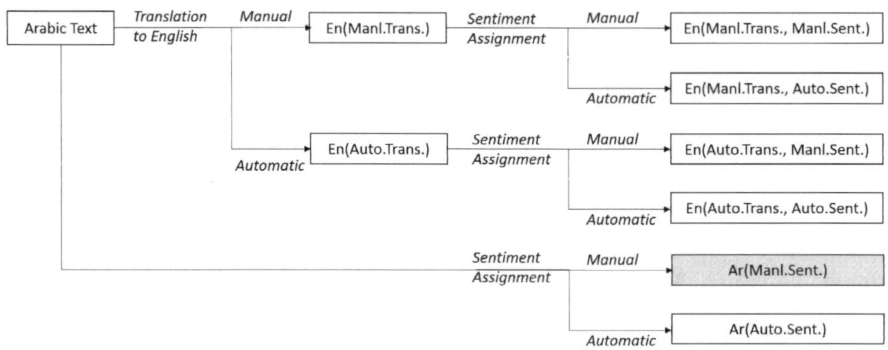


Figure 1: Experimental setup to determine the impact of translation on sentiment. We compare sentiment labels between Ar(Manl.Sent.) (shown in a shaded box) and other datasets shown on the right side of the figure. Ar(Manl.Sent.) is the original Arabic text manually annotated for sentiment.

- Manually annotate all English datasets [*En(Manl.Trans.)* and *En(Auto.Trans.)*] for sentiment, creating *En(Manl.Trans., Manl.Sent.)* and *En(Auto.Trans., Manl.Sent.)*, respectively.
- Run a state-of-the-art Arabic sentiment analysis system on *Ar*, creating *Ar(Auto.Sent.)*
- Run a state-of-the-art English sentiment analysis system on all the English datasets [*En(Manl.Trans.)* and *En(Auto.Trans.)*], creating *En(Manl.Trans., Auto.Sent.)* and *En(Auto.Trans., Auto.Sent.)*, respectively.

Figure 1 depicts this setup. Once the various sentiment-labeled datasets are created, we can compare pairs of datasets to draw inferences. For example, comparing the labels for *Ar(Manl.Sent.)* and *En(Manl.Trans., Manl.Sent.)* will show how different the sentiment labels tend to be when text is translated from Arabic to English. The comparison will also show, for example, whether positive tweets tend to often be translated into neutral tweets, and to what extent. The results will also show how feasible it is to first translate Arabic text into English and then use automatic sentiment analysis (*Ar(Manl.Sent.)* vs. *En(Auto.Trans., Auto.Sent.)*). In Section 8, we provide an analysis of several such comparisons for two different Arabic social media datasets.

**DATA:** Since manual translation of text from Arabic to English is a costly exercise, we chose, for our experiments, an existing Arabic social media dataset that has already been translated – the BBN Arabic-Dialect/English Parallel Text (Zbib et al., 2012).[2] It contains about 3.5 million tokens of Arabic dialect sentences and their English translations. We use a randomly chosen subset of 1200 Levantine dialectal sentences, which we will refer to as the *BBN posts* or *BBN dataset*, in our experiments. Additionally, we also conduct experiments on a dataset of 2000 tweets originating from Syria (a country where Levantine dialectal Arabic is commonly spoken). These tweets were collected in May 2014 by polling the Twitter API. We will refer to this dataset as the *Syrian tweets* or *Syrian dataset*. Note, however, that manual translations of the Syrian dataset are not available.

The experimental setup described above involves several component tasks: generating translations manually and automatically (Section 4), manually annotating Arabic and English texts for sentiment (Section 5), automatic sentiment analysis of English texts (Section 6), and automatic sentiment analysis of Arabic texts (Section 7).

## 4 Generating English Translations

The BBN dialectal Arabic dataset comes with manual translations into English. We generate automatic translations of the Arabic BBN posts and the Syrian tweets, by training a multi-stack phrase-based machine translation system to translate from Arabic to English. Our in-house system is quite similar to Cherry and Foster (2012). This statistical machine translation (SMT) system is trained on data from OpenMT 2012. We preprocess the training data by

[2]https://catalog.ldc.upenn.edu/LDC2012T09

segmenting the Arabic source side of the training data with MADA 3.2 (Habash et al., 2009), using Penn Arabic Treebank (PATB) segmentation scheme as recommended by El Kholy and Habash (2012). The Arabic script is further normalized by converting different forms of Alif إ أ آ ا and Ya ى ي to bare Alif ا and dotless Ya ى. The different forms are used interchangeably, and normalization decreases the sparcity of Arabic tokens and improves translation. The English side of the training data is lowercased and tokenized by stripping punctuation marks. We set the decoder's stack size to 10000 and distortion limit to 7. We replace the *out-of-vocabulary* words in the translated text with *UNKNOWN* token (which is shown to the annotators). The decoder's log-linear model is tuned with MIRA (Chiang et al., 2008; Cherry and Foster, 2012). A KN-smoothed 5-gram language model is trained on the English Gigaword and the target side of the parallel data.

## 5 Creating sentiment labeled data in Arabic and English

Manual sentiment annotations were performed on the crowdsourcing platform CrowdFlower[3] for three BBN datasets and two Syrian datasets:

1. Original Arabic posts (BBN and Syria datasets), annotated by Arabic speakers.
2. Manual English translations of Arabic posts, annotated by English speakers (only for BBN dataset).
3. Automatic English translations of Arabic posts (BBN and Syria datasets), annotated by English speakers.

Each post was annotated by at least ten annotators and the majority sentiment label was chosen. Table 1 shows the class distribution of sentiment labels in various datasets. Observe from rows *a* and *d* that neutral tweets constitute only about 10% of the data in both BBN and Syria datasets. The Syrian tweets have a much higher percentage of negative posts, whereas in the BBN data, the percentages of positive and negative posts are comparable. (Arabic tweets in general tend to be much more skewed to the negative class than Arabic blog post sentences.) Rows b, c, and e show that translated texts tend to lose some of the sentiment information and there is a relatively higher percentage of neutral instances in the translated text than in the original text.

For each post, we determine the count of the most frequent annotation divided by the total number of annotations. This score is averaged for all posts to determine the inter-annotator agreement shown in the last column of Table 1. We use this agreement score as benchmark to compare performance of automatic sentiment systems (described below).

## 6 English Sentiment Analysis

We use the English-language sentiment analysis system developed by NRC-Canada (Kiritchenko et al., 2014) in our experiments. This system obtained highest scores in two recent international competitions on sentiment analysis of tweets –SemEval-2013 Task 2 and SemEval-2014 Task 9 (Wilson et al., 2013; Rosenthal et al., 2014). We briefly describe the system below; for more details, we refer the reader to Kiritchenko et al. (2014).

A linear-kernel Support Vector Machine (Chang and Lin, 2011) classifier is trained on the available training data. The classifier leverages a variety of surface-form, semantic, and sentiment lexicon features described below. The sentiment lexicon features are derived from existing, general-purpose, manual lexicons, namely NRC Emotion Lexicon (Mohammad and Turney, 2010; Mohammad and Turney, 2013), Bing Liu's Lexicon (Hu and Liu, 2004), and MPQA Subjectivity Lexicon (Wilson et al., 2005), as well as automatically generated, tweet-specific lexicons, Hashtag Sentiment Lexicon and Sentiment140 Lexicon (Kiritchenko et al., 2014).[4]

### 6.1 Generating English Sentiment Lexicon

Ablation experiments in Mohammad et al. (2013) showed that their sentiment system benefited most from the use of the Hashtag Sentiment Lexicon. The lexicon was created as follows. A list of 77 seed words, which are synonyms of *positive* and *negative*, was compiled from the Roget's Thesaurus. Then, the Twitter API was polled to collect tweets that had these words as hashtags. A tweet is considered positive if it has a positive hashtag and negative if it

[3]http://www.crowdflower.com

[4]http://www.purl.com/net/lexicons

| | positive | negative | neutral | agreement |
|---|---|---|---|---|
| *BBN data* | | | | |
| a. Ar(Manl.Sent) | 41.50 | 47.92 | 10.58 | 73.80 |
| b. En(Manl.Trans., Manl.Sent) | 35.00 | 43.25 | 21.75 | 68.00 |
| c. En(Auto.Trans., Manl.Sent) | 36.17 | 36.50 | 27.34 | 65.70 |
| *Syria data* | | | | |
| d. Ar(Manl.Sent) | 22.40 | 67.50 | 10.10 | 79.00 |
| e. En(Auto.Trans., Manl.Sent) | 14.25 | 66.15 | 19.60 | 76.10 |

Table 1: Class distribution (in percentage) of the sentiment annotated datasets.

has a negative hashtag. For each term in the tweet set, a sentiment score is computed by measuring the PMI (pointwise mutual information) between the term and the positive and negative categories:

$$SenScore\,(w) = PMI(w, pos) - PMI(w, neg) \quad (1)$$

where $w$ is a term in the lexicon. $PMI(w, pos)$ is the PMI score between $w$ and the positive class, and $PMI(w, neg)$ is the PMI score between $w$ and the negative class. A positive *SenScore* (w) suggests that the word is associated with positive sentiment and a negative score suggests that the word is associated with negative sentiment. The magnitude indicates the strength of the association.

### 6.2 Pre-processing and Feature Generation

The following pre-processing steps are performed. URLs and user mentions are normalized to http://someurl and @someuser, respectively. Tweets are tokenized and part-of-speech tagged with the CMU Twitter NLP tool (Gimpel et al., 2011). Then, each tweet is represented as a feature vector.

**The features:**

- Word and character ngrams;
- POS: # occurrences of each part-of-speech tag;
- Negation: # negated contexts. Negation also affects the ngram features: a word $w$ becomes $w\_NEG$ in a negated context;
- Automatic sentiment lexicons: For each token $w$ occurring in a tweet, its sentiment score $score(w)$ is used to compute: # tokens with $score(w) \neq 0$; the total score = $\sum_{w \in tweet} score(w)$; the maximal score = $max_{w \in tweet} score(w)$; the score of the last token in the tweet.
- Manually created sentiment lexicons: For each of the three manual sentiment lexicons, the following features are computed: the sum of positive and the sum of negative scores for tweet tokens in affirmative contexts and in negated contexts, separately.

## 7 Arabic Sentiment Analysis

### 7.1 Building an Arabic Sentiment System

We built an Arabic sentiment analysis system by reconstructing the NRC-Canada English system to deal with Arabic text. It extracts the same feature set as described in Section 6.2. We also generated a word-sentiment association lexicon as described in Section 6.1, but for Arabic words from Arabic tweets (more details in sub-section below). We pre-process Arabic text by tokenizing with CMU Twitter NLP tool to deal with specific tokens such as URLs, usernames, and emoticons. Then we use MADA to generate lemmas. Finally, we normalize different forms of Alif and Ya to bare Alif and dotless Ya to decrease token sparcity in Arabic datasets.

#### 7.1.1 Generating Arabic Sentiment Lexicon

We translated 77 positive and negative seed words used to generate the English NRC Hashtag Sentiment Lexicon into Arabic using Google Translate. Among the several translations provided by it, we chose words that were less ambiguous and tended to have strong sentiment in Arabic texts. To increase the coverage of our seed list, we manually added different inflections for these translations.

We polled the Twitter API for the period of June to August 2014 and collected tweets with *#(keyword)*. After filtering out duplicate tweets and retweets, we ended up with 163,944 positive unique tweets and 37,848 negative unique tweets. Then for each word $w$, *SenScore* (w) was calculated just as described in Section 6.1.

| Arabic Sentiment Labeled Dataset | MD | RR | BBN | Syria |
|---|---|---|---|---|
| sentiment classes | pos, neg | pos,neg | pos, neg, neu | pos, neg, neu |
| number of instances | 1111 | 2681 | 1199 | 2000 |
| Most frequent class baseline | 66.06 | 68.92 | 47.95 | 67.50 |
| Human agreement benchmark | - | - | 73.82 | 79.05 |
| Mourad and Darwish Arabic SA system | 72.50 | - | - | - |
| Our Arabic SA system | 74.62 | 85.23 | 63.89 | 78.65 |

Table 2: Accuracy (in percentage) of sentiment analysis (SA) systems on various Arabic social media datasets.

| | pos | neg | neu |
|---|---|---|---|
| *BBN data* | | | |
| a. Ar(Auto.Sent) | 39.78 | 60.05 | 0.17 |
| b. En(Manl.Trans., Auto.Sent) | 43.12 | 55.63 | 1.25 |
| c. En(Auto.Trans., Auto.Sent) | 42.87 | 56.05 | 1.08 |
| *Syria data* | | | |
| d. Ar(Auto.Sent) | 20.60 | 75.30 | 4.10 |
| e. En(Auto.Trans., Auto.Sent) | 24.75 | 69.75 | 5.50 |

Table 3: Class distribution (in percentage) resulting from automatic sentiment analysis.

### 7.2 Evaluation

We tested the Arabic sentiment system on two existing Arabic datasets (Mourad and Darwish (2013) (MD) and Refaee and Rieser (2014a) (RR)) and two newly sentiment-annotated Arabic datasets (BBN and Syria). Table 2 shows results of ten-fold cross-validation experiments on each of the datasets. For MD and RR, the presented results are for the two-class problem (positive vs. negative) to allow for comparison with prior published results. For BBN and Syria, the results are shown for the case where the system has to identify one of three classes: positive, negative, or neutral. Human agreement scores are shown where available.

Note that the accuracy of our system is higher than previously published results on the MD dataset. The only previously published results on the RR dataset are on a small subset (about 1000 instances) for which Refaee and Rieser (2014a) obtained an accuracy of 87%. The results in Table 2 are for a larger dataset and so not directly comparable.

## 8 Sentiment After Translation

Using the methods and systems described in Sections 4, 5, 6, and 7, we generated all the manually and automatically labeled datasets mentioned in Section 3's Experimental Setup. Table 3 shows the distribution of positive, negative, and neutral classes in datasets that have been automatically labeled with sentiment. These percentages can be compared with those in Table 1 (rows a and d) which show the true sentiment distribution in the BBN and Syria datasets. Observe that the automatic system has difficulty in assigning neutral class to posts. This is probably because of the small percentage (about 10%) of neutral tweets in the training data. Also notice that the system predominantly guesses negative, which is also a reflection of the distribution in the training data. The strong bias to negatives is lessened in the English translations.

**Main Result:** Tables 4 and 5 show how similar the sentiment labels are across various pairs of datasets for the BBN posts and the Syrian posts, respectively. For example, row a. in Table 4 shows the comparison between Arabic tweets that were manually annotated for sentiment and those that were automatically labeled for sentiment by our Arabic sentiment analysis system. Column 2 shows the percentage of instances where the sentiment labels match across the two datasets being compared. For row a. the match percentage of 63.89% represents the accuracy of the automatic sentiment analysis system on the Arabic BBN posts.

Row b. shows the difference in labels when text is manually translated from Arabic to English, even though sentiment labeling in both Arabic and English is done manually. Observe that the two labels match only 71.31% of the time. However, the agreement among human sentiment annotators on original Arabic texts was only 73.8%. So, the English translation does affect sentiment, but not dramatically.

Row c. shows results for when the manually translated text is run through an English sentiment analysis system and the labels are compared against *Ar(Manl.Sent.)* Observe that the match for this pair is 68.65%, which is not too much lower than 71.31% obtained by manual sentiment labeling. This shows

| Data Pair | Match % |
|---|---|
| a. Ar(Manl.Sent) - Ar(Auto.Sent) | 63.89 |
| b. Ar(Manl.Sent) - En(Manl.Trans., Manl.Sent) | 71.31 |
| c. Ar(Manl.Sent) - En(Manl.Trans., Auto.Sent) | 68.65 |
| d. Ar(Manl.Sent) - En(Auto.Trans., Manl.Sent) | 57.21 |
| e. Ar(Manl.Sent) - En(Auto.Trans., Auto.Sent) | 62.49 |
| f. En(Manl.Trans., Manl.Sent) - En(Auto.Trans., Manl.Sent) | 60.08 |
| g. En(Manl.Trans., Manl.Sent) - En(Manl.Trans., Auto.Sent) | 66.51 |
| h. En(Auto.Trans., Manl.Sent) - En(Auto.Trans., Auto.Sent) | 69.58 |

Table 4: Match percentage between pairs of sentiment labelled BBN datasets.

| Data Pair | Match % |
|---|---|
| a. Ar(Manl.Sent) - Ar(Auto.Sent) | 78.65 |
| b. Ar(Manl.Sent) - En(Auto.Trans., Manl.Sent) | 71.05 |
| c. Ar(Manl.Sent) - En(Auto.Trans.-Auto.Sent) | 78.11 |
| d. En(Auto.Trans, Manl.Sent) - En(Auto.Trans., Auto.Sent) | 78.80 |

Table 5: Match percentage between pairs of sentiment labelled Syria datasets.

that the English sentiment system is performing rather well. (One would not expect it to get a match greater than 71.31%.) More importantly, the English sentiment system shows a competitive result of 62.49% when run on the automatically translated text (row e.), which makes this choice a viable option for sentiment analysis of non-English texts. This result is inline with previous findings in Information Retrieval (Nie et al., 1999) and Text Classification (Amini and Goutte, 2010).

Rows d. and e. compare *Ar(Manl.Sent.)* with manual and automatic sentiment labeling of automatic translations. Since automatic translation from Arabic to English is fairly difficult, we expect these match percentages to be lower than those in rows b. and c., and that is exactly what we observe. However, it is unexpected to find the number for row e. to be higher than that of row d. We find the same pattern for corresponding data pairs in the Syrian tweets as well (rows b. and c. in Table 6). This suggests that certain attributes of automatically translated text mislead humans with regards to the true sentiment of the source text. However, these same attributes do not seem to affect the automatic sentiment analysis system as much. Since the NRC sentiment analysis system is largely reliant on word-sentiment associations and does not use syntax-based features, it is possible that syntactic abnormalities introduced by automatic translation impact human perception of sentiment. However, this supposition needs to be validated by future work.

Row f. shows that manual and automatic translation lead to only about 60% match in manually annotated sentiment labels with each other. Row g. shows accuracy of the English automatic sentiment analysis system on the manually translated text (assuming the English sentiment labels as gold). The result of 66.51% is very close to human agreement on manually translated data (68%), which demonstrates the high quality of the English sentiment analysis system. Row h. shows accuracy of the English automatic sentiment analysis system on the automatically translated text (assuming the English sentiment labels as gold). In this case, the system's accuracy of 69.58% is higher than the human agreement on automatically translated text (65.7%), which again shows that automatic translation greatly impacts sentiment perceived by humans.

We manually examined several tweets from the BBN dataset to understand why humans incorrectly annotate a tweet's automatic translation. Most of the cases were due to bad translation where sentiment words either disappeared or were replaced with words of opposite sentiment. In some cases, the translation was affected by typos on the Arabic side. Table 6 shows some examples. Often the mistranslations occurred due to word sense ambiguity. For example, عقارب has two meanings: *scorpions* and *clock arms*. In example 1 (metaphorically stating that relatives can hurt like scorpion bites), the word is mistranslated, leading to neutral (instead of negative) sentiment.

| | | |
|---|---|---|
| ***1. Bad auto. translation: mistranslation of ambiguous words*** | | |
| Post | الدنيا علمتني ان اكثر الاقارب عقارب | negative |
| Auto.Trans. | the minimum taught me that more relatives clock | neutral |
| Manl.Trans. | Life has taught me that most of the relatives are scorpions | negative |
| ***2. Bad auto. translation: mistranslation of ambiguous words*** | | |
| Post | ليتنى اعيش في مكان لا تنقطع عنه الثلوج | positive |
| Auto.Trans. | i wish i live in a place not cut off by snow | negative |
| Manl.Trans. | I wish I live in a place where snow never stops falling | positive |
| ***3. Bad auto. translation: sarcasm is hard to translate*** | | |
| Post | لسه الخير لقدام تسرب المي موجودة من زمان | negative |
| Auto.Trans. | you're still good in front of the leakage of water existed from time | positive |
| Manl.Trans. | Expect more good to come, water has been leaking since a long time | negative |

Table 6: Examples where the automatic translation was annotated a sentiment different from the sentiment of the original Arabic tweet, but whose original sentiment was correctly predicted by the English sentiment system. The manual translations are also listed for reference.

One reason why the automatic sentiment analysis system correctly annotates several automatically translated instances (where manual annotations of the translation may fail), is that the system can learn an appropriate model even from mistranslated text — especially when automatic translation makes consistent errors. For example, اللهم انصر (*Oh God grant victory to*) has been consistently translated to *God forsake*. All tweets having this phrase are correctly annotated as positive by our system, but were marked negative by the human annotators.

**Caveats:** The automatic systems employed in these experiments, i.e., Arabic sentiment analysis, English sentiment analysis, and SMT systems, exhibit state-of-the-art performance; nevertheless, further improvements are possible. The Arabic sentiment system will benefit from extended sentiment lexicons and features derived specifically for the Arabic language. The English sentiment analysis system can be further adapted to the peculiarities of machine-translated texts, which are notably different from regular English. The current translation system has been trained on non-tweet data that results in a high percentage of out-of-vocabulary words on our datasets. In our experiments, we assumed that all texts are written in Levantine dialect of the Arabic language. However, tweets can have a mixture of dialects or even a mixture of languages (e.g., Arabic and English). Addressing these factors will give even more insight on how sentiment is altered on translation, in specific contexts.

## 9 Conclusions

We presented a set of experiments to systematically study the impact of English translation (manual and automatic) on sentiment analysis of Arabic social media posts. Our experiments show that automatic sentiment analysis of English translations (even of automatic translations) can lead to competitive results—results that are similar to that obtained by current state-of-the-art Arabic sentiment analysis systems. Our results also show that automatic sentiment analysis of automatic translations outperforms the manual sentiment annotations of the automatically translated text. This suggests that SMT errors impact human perception of sentiment markedly more than automatic sentiment systems. This is an interesting avenue for future exploration. We also show that translated texts tend to lose some of the sentiment information and there is a relatively higher percentage of neutral instances in the translated text than in the original dataset. The resources created as part of this project (Arabic sentiment lexicons, Arabic sentiment annotations of social media posts, and English sentiment annotations of their translations) are made freely available.[5]

## Acknowledgments

Thanks to Kareem Darwish and Eshrag Refaee for sharing their data. We thank Colin Cherry, Samuel Larkin, and Marine Carpuat for helpful discussions.

[5]http://www.purl.com/net/ArabicSentiment

## References


Muhammad Abdul-Mageed, Mona Diab, and Sandra Kübler. 2014. SAMAR: Subjectivity and sentiment analysis for Arabic social media. *Computer Speech & Language*, 28(1):20 – 37.

Apoorv Agarwal, Boyi Xie, Ilia Vovsha, Owen Rambow, and Rebecca Passonneau. 2011. Sentiment analysis of Twitter data. In *Proceedings of the Workshop on Languages in Social Media*, LSM '11, pages 30–38, Portland, Oregon.

Khurshid Ahmad, David Cheng, and Yousif Almas. 2006. Multi-lingual sentiment analysis of financial news streams. In *Proceedings of the 1st International Conference on Grid in Finance*.

Mohammed Al-Kabi, Amal Gigieh, Izzat Alsmadi, Heider Wahsheh, and Mohamad Haidar. 2013. An opinion analysis tool for colloquial and standard Arabic. In *Proceedings of the 4th International Conference on Information and Communication Systems*, ICICS '13.

Massih-Reza Amini and Cyril Goutte. 2010. A co-classification approach to learning from multilingual corpora. *Machine learning*, 79(1-2):105–121.

Gilbert Badaro, Ramy Baly, Hazem Hajj, Nizar Habash, and Wassim El-Hajj. 2014. A large scale Arabic sentiment lexicon for Arabic opinion mining. In *Proceedings of the EMNLP Workshop on Arabic Natural Language Processing (ANLP)*, pages 165–173. Association for Computational Linguistics.

Alexandra Balahur and Marco Turchi. 2014. Comparative experiments using supervised learning and machine translation for multilingual sentiment analysis. *Computer Speech & Language*, 28(1):56–75.

Jerome Bellegarda. 2010. Emotion analysis using latent affective folding and embedding. In *Proceedings of the NAACL-HLT Workshop on Computational Approaches to Analysis and Generation of Emotion in Text*, pages 1–9, Los Angeles, California.

Anthony C. Boucouvalas. 2002. Real time text-to-emotion engine for expressive Internet communication. *Emerging Communication: Studies on New Technologies and Practices in Communication*, 5:305–318.

Chih-Chung Chang and Chih-Jen Lin. 2011. LIBSVM: A library for support vector machines. *ACM Transactions on Intelligent Systems and Technology*, 2(3):27:1–27:27.

Boxing Chen and Xiaodan Zhu. 2014. Bilingual sentiment consistency for statistical machine translation. In *Proceedings of the 14th Conference of the European Chapter of the Association for Computational Linguistics*, pages 607–615, Gothenburg, Sweden, April. Association for Computational Linguistics.

Colin Cherry and George Foster. 2012. Batch tuning strategies for statistical machine translation. In *Proceedings of the Conference of the North American Chapter of the Association for Computational Linguistics: Human Language Technologies*, pages 427–436. Association for Computational Linguistics.

David Chiang, Yuval Marton, and Philip Resnik. 2008. Online large-margin training of syntactic and structural translation features. In *Proceedings of the Conference on Empirical Methods in Natural Language Processing*, EMNLP '08, pages 224–233. Association for Computational Linguistics.

Samhaa R El-Beltagy and Ahmed Ali. 2013. Open issues in the sentiment analysis of Arabic social media: A case study. In *Proceedings of the 9th International Conference on Innovations in Information Technology*, pages 215–220. IEEE.

Ahmed El Kholy and Nizar Habash. 2012. Orthographic and morphological processing for English–Arabic statistical machine translation. *Machine Translation*, 26(1-2):25–45, March.

Kevin Gimpel, Nathan Schneider, Brendan O'Connor, Dipanjan Das, Daniel Mills, Jacob Eisenstein, Michael Heilman, Dani Yogatama, Jeffrey Flanigan, and Noah A. Smith. 2011. Part-of-speech tagging for Twitter: Annotation, features, and experiments. In *Proceedings of the Annual Meeting of the Association for Computational Linguistics*, ACL '11, pages 42–47.

Alec Go, Richa Bhayani, and Lei Huang. 2009. Twitter sentiment classification using distant supervision. Technical report, Stanford University.

Nizar Habash, Owen Rambow, and Ryan Roth. 2009. MADA+TOKAN: A toolkit for Arabic tokenization, diacritization, morphological disambiguation, POS tagging, stemming and lemmatization. In *Proceedings of the 2nd International Conference on Arabic Language Resources and Tools*, pages 102–109, Cairo, Egypt, April. The MEDAR Consortium.

Minqing Hu and Bing Liu. 2004. Mining and summarizing customer reviews. In *Proceedings of the 10th ACM SIGKDD International Conference on Knowledge Discovery and Data Mining*, KDD '04, pages 168–177, New York, NY, USA. ACM.

Svetlana Kiritchenko, Xiaodan Zhu, and Saif M. Mohammad. 2014. Sentiment analysis of short informal texts. *Journal of Artificial Intelligence Research*, 50:723–762.

Hugo Liu, Henry Lieberman, and Ted Selker. 2003. A model of textual affect sensing using real-world knowledge. In *Proceedings of the 8th International Conference on Intelligent User Interfaces*, IUI '03, pages 125–132, New York, NY. ACM.

Eugenio Martínez-Cámara, M Teresa Martín-Valdivia, L Alfonso Ureñalópez, and A Rturo Montejoráez.

2012. Sentiment analysis in Twitter. *Natural Language Engineering*, pages 1–28.

Rada Mihalcea, Carmen Banea, and Janyce Wiebe. 2007. Learning multilingual subjective language via cross-lingual projections. In *Proceedings of the 45th Annual Meeting of the Association of Computational Linguistics*, page 976.

Saif M. Mohammad and Peter D. Turney. 2010. Emotions evoked by common words and phrases: Using Mechanical Turk to create an emotion lexicon. In *Proceedings of the NAACL-HLT Workshop on Computational Approaches to Analysis and Generation of Emotion in Text*, pages 26–34, LA, California.

Saif M. Mohammad and Peter D. Turney. 2013. Crowdsourcing a word-emotion association lexicon. *Computational Intelligence*, 29(3):436–465.

Saif M. Mohammad and Tony (Wenda) Yang. 2011. Tracking sentiment in mail: How genders differ on emotional axes. In *Proceedings of the ACL Workshop on Computational Approaches to Subjectivity and Sentiment Analysis*, WASSA '11, pages 70–79, Portland, OR, USA.

Saif M. Mohammad, Svetlana Kiritchenko, and Xiaodan Zhu. 2013. NRC-Canada: Building the state-of-the-art in sentiment analysis of tweets. In *Proceedings of the 7th International Workshop on Semantic Evaluation Exercises*, SemEval '13, Atlanta, Georgia, USA, June.

Saif M. Mohammad. 2012. #Emotional tweets. In *Proceedings of the First Joint Conference on Lexical and Computational Semantics*, *SEM '12, pages 246–255, Montréal, Canada.

Ahmed Mourad and Kareem Darwish. 2013. Subjectivity and sentiment analysis of modern standard Arabic and Arabic microblogs. In *Proceedings of the 4th Workshop on Computational Approaches to Subjectivity, Sentiment and Social Media Analysis*, WASSA '13, pages 55–64.

Alena Neviarouskaya, Helmut Prendinger, and Mitsuru Ishizuka. 2011. Affect analysis model: novel rule-based approach to affect sensing from text. *Natural Language Engineering*, 17:95–135, 1.

Jian-Yun Nie, Michel Simard, Pierre Isabelle, and Richard Durand. 1999. Cross-language information retrieval based on parallel texts and automatic mining of parallel texts from the Web. In *Proceedings of the 22nd Annual International ACM SIGIR Conference on Research and Development in Information Retrieval*, pages 74–81. ACM.

Alexander Pak and Patrick Paroubek. 2010. Twitter as a corpus for sentiment analysis and opinion mining. In *Proceedings of the 7th Conference on International Language Resources and Evaluation*, LREC '10, pages 1320–1326, Valletta, Malta, May.

Maria Pontiki, Dimitrios Galanis, John Pavlopoulos, Harris Papageorgiou, Ion Androutsopoulos, and Suresh Manandhar. 2014. SemEval-2014 Task 4: Aspect based sentiment analysis. In *Proceedings of the International Workshop on Semantic Evaluation*, SemEval '14, pages 27–35, Dublin, Ireland, August.

Eshrag Refaee and Verena Rieser. 2014a. An Arabic Twitter corpus for subjectivity and sentiment analysis. In *Proceedings of the 9th International Conference on Language Resources and Evaluation*, LREC '14, Reykjavik, Iceland, May. European Language Resources Association.

Eshrag Refaee and Verena Rieser. 2014b. Subjectivity and sentiment analysis of Arabic Twitter feeds with limited resources. In *Proceedings of the Workshop on Free/Open-Source Arabic Corpora and Corpora Processing Tools*, page 16.

Sara Rosenthal, Alan Ritter, Preslav Nakov, and Veselin Stoyanov. 2014. SemEval-2014 Task 9: Sentiment analysis in Twitter. In *Proceedings of the 8th International Workshop on Semantic Evaluation*, SemEval '14, pages 73–80, Dublin, Ireland, August.

Mike Thelwall, Kevan Buckley, and Georgios Paltoglou. 2011. Sentiment in Twitter events. *Journal of the American Society for Information Science and Technology*, 62(2):406–418.

Xiaojun Wan. 2008. Using bilingual knowledge and ensemble techniques for unsupervised Chinese sentiment analysis. In *Proceedings of the Conference on Empirical Methods in Natural Language Processing*, EMNLP '08, pages 553–561, Stroudsburg, PA, USA. Association for Computational Linguistics.

Theresa Wilson, Janyce Wiebe, and Paul Hoffmann. 2005. Recognizing contextual polarity in phrase-level sentiment analysis. In *Proceedings of the Conference on Human Language Technology and Empirical Methods in Natural Language Processing*, HLT '05, pages 347–354, Stroudsburg, PA, USA.

Theresa Wilson, Zornitsa Kozareva, Preslav Nakov, Sara Rosenthal, Veselin Stoyanov, and Alan Ritter. 2013. SemEval-2013 Task 2: Sentiment analysis in Twitter. In *Proceedings of the International Workshop on Semantic Evaluation*, SemEval '13, Atlanta, Georgia, USA, June.

Rabih Zbib, Erika Malchiodi, Jacob Devlin, David Stallard, Spyros Matsoukas, Richard Schwartz, John Makhoul, Omar F Zaidan, and Chris Callison-Burch. 2012. Machine translation of Arabic dialects. In *Proceedings of the Conference of the North American Chapter of the Association for Computational Linguistics: Human Language Technologies*, pages 49–59. Association for Computational Linguistics.

# Using External Resources and Joint Learning for Bigram Weighting in ILP-Based Multi-Document Summarization

**Chen Li[1], Yang Liu[1], Lin Zhao[2]**
[1] Computer Science Department, The University of Texas at Dallas
Richardson, Texas 75080, USA
[2] Research and Technology Center, Robert Bosch LLC
Palo Alto, California 94304, USA
{chenli,yangl@hlt.utdallas.edu}
{lin.zhao@us.bosch.com}

## Abstract

Some state-of-the-art summarization systems use integer linear programming (ILP) based methods that aim to maximize the important concepts covered in the summary. These concepts are often obtained by selecting bigrams from the documents. In this paper, we improve such bigram based ILP summarization methods from different aspects. First we use syntactic information to select more important bigrams. Second, to estimate the importance of the bigrams, in addition to the internal features based on the test documents (e.g., document frequency, bigram positions), we propose to extract features by leveraging multiple external resources (such as word embedding from additional corpus, Wikipedia, Dbpedia, WordNet, SentiWordNet). The bigram weights are then trained discriminatively in a joint learning model that predicts the bigram weights and selects the summary sentences in the ILP framework at the same time. We demonstrate that our system consistently outperforms the prior ILP method on different TAC data sets, and performs competitively compared to other previously reported best results. We also conducted various analyses to show the contributions of different components.

## 1 Introduction

Extractive summarization is a sentence selection problem: identifying important summary sentences from one or multiple documents. Many methods have been developed for this problem, including supervised approaches that use a classifier to predict whether or not a sentence is in the summary, or unsupervised methods such as graph-based approaches to rank the sentences. Recently global optimization methods such as integer linear programming (ILP) have been shown to be quite powerful for this task. For example, Gillick et al. (2009) used ILP to achieve the best result in the TAC 09 summarization task. The core idea of this summarization method is to select the summary sentences by maximizing the sum of the weights of the language concepts that appear in the summary. Bigrams are often used as these language concepts because Gillick et al. (2009) stated that the bigrams gave consistently better performance than unigrams or trigrams for a variety of ROUGE measures. The association between the language concepts and sentences serves as the constraints. This ILP method is formally represented as below (see (Gillick et al., 2009) for more details):

$$\max \quad \textstyle\sum_i w_i c_i \tag{1}$$
$$s.t. \quad s_j Occ_{ij} \le c_i \tag{2}$$
$$\textstyle\sum_j s_j Occ_{ij} \ge c_i \tag{3}$$
$$\textstyle\sum_j l_j s_j \le L \tag{4}$$
$$c_i \in \{0,1\}\ \forall i \tag{5}$$
$$s_j \in \{0,1\}\ \forall j \tag{6}$$

$c_i$ and $s_j$ are binary variables that indicate the presence of a concept and a sentence respectively. $l_j$ is the sentence length and $L$ is maximum length of the generated summary. $w_i$ is a concept's weight and $Occ_{ij}$ means the occurrence of concept $i$ in sentence $j$. Inequalities (2)(3) associate the sentences



*Human Language Technologies: The 2015 Annual Conference of the North American Chapter of the ACL*, pages 778–787,
Denver, Colorado, May 31 – June 5, 2015. ©2015 Association for Computational Linguistics

and concepts. They ensure that selecting a sentence leads to the selection of all the concepts it contains, and selecting a concept only happens when it is present in at least one of the selected sentences.

In such ILP-based summarization methods, how to determine the concepts and measure their weights is the key factor impacting the system performance. Intuitively, if we can successfully identify the important key bigrams to use in the ILP system, or assign large weights to those important bigrams, the system generated summary sentences will contain as many important bigrams as possible. The oracle experiment in (Gillick et al., 2008) showed that if they just use the bigrams extracted from human generated summaries as the input of the ILP system, much better ROUGE scores can be obtained than using the automatically selected bigrams.

In this paper, we adopt the ILP summarization framework, but make improvement from three aspects. First, we use the part-of-speech tag and constituent parse information to identify important bigram candidates: bigrams from base NP (noun phrases) and bigrams containing verbs or adjectives. This bigram selection method allows us to keep the important bigrams and filter useless ones. Second, to estimate the bigrams' weights, in addition to using information from the test documents, such as document frequency, syntactic role in a sentence, etc., we utilize a variety of external resources, including a corpus of news articles with human generated summaries, Wiki documents, description of name entities from DBpedia, WordNet, and SentiWordNet. Discriminative features are computed based on these external resources with the goal to better represent the importance of a bigram and its semantic similarity with the given query. Finally, we propose to use a joint bigram weighting and sentence selection process to train the feature weights. Our experimental results on multiple TAC data sets show the competitiveness of our proposed methods.

## 2 Related Work

Optimization methods have been widely used in extractive summarization lately. McDonald (2007) first introduced the sentence level ILP for summarization. Later Gillick et al. (2009) revised it to concept-based ILP, which is similar to the Budgeted Maximal Coverage problem in (Khuller et al., 1999). The concept-based ILP system performed very well in the TAC 2008 and 2009 summarization task (Gillick et al., 2008; Gillick et al., 2009). After that, the global optimization strategy attracted increasing attention in the summarization task. Lin and Bilmes (2010) treated the summarization task as a maximization problem of submodular functions. Davis et al. (2012) proposed an optimal combinatorial covering algorithm combined with LSA to measure the term weight for extractive summarization. Takamura and Okumura (2009) also defined the summarization problem as a maximum coverage problem and used a branch-and-bound method to search for the optimal solution. Li et al. (2013b) used the same ILP framework as (Gillick et al., 2009), but incorporated a supervised model to estimate the bigram frequency in the final summary.

Similar optimization methods are also widely used in the abstractive summarization task. Martins and Smith (2009) leveraged ILP technique to jointly select and compress sentences for multi-document summarization. A novel summary guided sentence compression was proposed by (Li et al., 2013a) and it successfully improved the summarization performance. Woodsend and Lapata (2012) and Li et al. (2014) both leveraged constituent parser trees to help sentence compression, which is also modeled in the optimization framework. But these kinds of work involve using complex linguistic information, often based on syntactic analysis.

Since the language concepts (or bigrams) can be considered as key phrases of the documents, the other line related to our work is how to extract and measure the importance of key phrases from documents. In particular, our work is related to key phrase extraction by using external resources. A survey by (Hasan and Ng, 2014) showed that using external resources to extract and measure key phrases is very effective. In (Medelyan et al., 2009), Wikipedia-based key phrases are determined based on a candidate's document frequency multiplied by the ratio of the number of Wikipedia articles containing the candidate as a link to the number of articles containing the candidate. Query logs were also used as another external resource by (Yih et al., 2006) to exploit the observation that a candidate is potentially important if it was used as a search query. Similarly terminological databases have been exploited to encode the salience of candidate key phrases in scientific papers (Lopez and Romary, 2010). In summarization, external information has also been used to measure word salience. Some TAC systems like (Kumar et al., 2010; Jia et al., 2010) used Wiki as an important external resource to measure the words' importance, which helped improve the summarization results. Hong and Nenkova (2014) introduced a supervised model for predicting word importance that incorporated a rich set of features. Tweets information is leveraged by (Wei and Gao, 2014) to help generate news highlights.

In this paper our focus is on choosing useful bigrams and estimating accurate weights to use in the concept-based ILP methods. We explore many external resources to extract features for bigram candidates, and more importantly, propose to estimate the feature weights in a joint process via structured perceptron learning that optimizes summary sentence selection.

## 3 Summarization System

In this study we use the ILP-based summarization framework (Formulas 1-6) that tries to maximize the weights of the selected concepts (bigrams) under the summary length constraint. Our focus is on better selection of the bigrams and estimation of the bigram weights. We use syntax tree and POS of tokens to help filter some useless bigrams. Then supervised methods are applied to predict the bigram weights. The rich set of features we use is introduced in Section 4. In the following we describe how to select important bigrams and how the feature weights are trained.

### 3.1 Bigram Selection

In (Gillick et al., 2009), bigrams whose document frequency is higher than a predefined threshold (df=3 in previous work) are used as the concepts in the ILP model. The weight for these bigrams in the ILP optimization objective function (Formula 1) is simply set as their document frequency. Although this setting has been demonstrated to be quite effective, its gap with the oracle experiment (using bigrams that appear in the human summaries) is still very large, suggesting potential gains by using better bigrams/concepts in the ILP optimization method. Details are described in (Gillick et al., 2009).

In this paper, rather than considering all the bigrams, we propose to utilize syntactic information to help select important bigrams. Intuitively bigrams containing content words carry more topic related information. As proven in (Klavans and Kan, 1998), nouns, verbs, and adjectives were indeed beneficial in document analysis. Therefore we focus on choosing bigrams containing these words. First, we use a bottom-up strategy to go through the constituent parse tree and identify the 'NP' nodes in the lowest level of the tree. Then all the bigrams in these base NPs are kept as candidates. Second, we find the verbs and adjectives from the sentence based on the POS tags, and construct bigrams by concatenating the previous or the next word of that verb or adjective. If these bigrams are not included in those already found from the base NPs, they are added to the bigram candidates. After the above filtering, we further drop bigrams if both words are stop words, as previous work in (Gillick et al., 2009).

### 3.2 Weight Training

We propose to train the feature weights in a joint learning fashion. In the ILP summarization framework, we use the following new objective function:

$$\max \quad \textstyle\sum_i (\theta \cdot \mathbf{f}(b_i)) c_i \qquad (7)$$

We replace the $w_i$ in Formula 1 with a vector inner product of bigram features and their corresponding weights. Constraints remain the same as those in Formula 2 to 6.

To train the model (feature weights), we leverage structured perceptron strategy (Collins, 2002) to update the feature weights whenever the hypothesis offered by the ILP decoding process is incorrect. Binary class labels are used for bigrams in the learning process, that is, we only consider whether a bigram is in the system generated summary or human summaries, not their term or document frequency. During perceptron training, a fixed learning rate is used and parameters are averaged to prevent overfitting.

## 4 Features for Bigrams

We use a rich set of features to represent each bigram candidate, including internal features based on the test documents, and features extracted from external resources. The goal is to better predict the importance of a bigram, which we expect will help the ILP module better determine whether to include the bigram in the summary.

### 4.1 Internal Features

These features are generated from the provided test documents (note our task is multi-document summarization, and there is a given query topic. See Section 5 for the description of tasks and data).

- Frequency of the bigram in the entire set.
- Frequency of the bigram in related sentences.[1]
- Document frequency of the bigram in the entire set.
- Is this bigram in the first 1/2/3 sentence?
- Is this bigram in the last 1/2/3 sentence?
- Similarity with the topic title, calculated by the number of common tokens in these two strings, divided by the length of the longer string.

### 4.2 Importance Score based on Language Models

The idea is to train two language models (LMs), one from the original documents, and the other one from the summaries, and compare the likelihood of a bigram generated by these two LMs, which can indicate how often a bigram is used in a summary. Similar to previous work in (Hong and Nenkova, 2014), we leveraged The New York Times Annotated Corpus (LDC Catalog No: LDC2008T19), which has the original news articles and human generated abstracts. We build two language models, from the news articles and the corresponding summaries respectively. We used about 160K abstract-original pairs. The KL scores for a bigram are defined as follows:

$$KL(LM_A|LM_O)(b) = Pr_A(b) * ln\frac{Pr_A(b)}{Pr_O(b)} \quad (8)$$

$$KL(LM_O|LM_A)(b) = Pr_O(b) * ln\frac{Pr_O(b)}{Pr_A(b)} \quad (9)$$

where $(LM_A)$ and $(LM_O)$ are the LMs from the abstracts and the original news articles. Note that one difference from (Hong and Nenkova, 2014) is that we calculate these scores for a bigram, not a word. As (Hong and Nenkova, 2014) showed, a higher value from the score in Formula 8 means the words are favored in the summaries, and vice verse in Formula 9. In addition to the above features, we also include the likelihood $Pr_A(b)$ and $Pr_O(b)$ based on the two LMs, and the absolute and relative difference between them: $Pr_A(b) - Pr_O(b), Pr_A(b)/Pr_O(b)$.

### 4.3 Similarity based on Word Embedding Representation

Given the recent success of the continuous representation for words, we propose to use an unsupervised method to induce dense real-valued low dimensional word embedding, and then use the inner product as a measure of semantic similarity between two strings. In the word embedding model, every word can be represented by a vector $\vec{w}$. We define the similarity between two sequences $S1 = x_1, x_2, ...x_k$ and sequence $S2 = y_1, y_2, ...y_l$ as the average pairwise similarity between any two words in them:

$$Sim(S1, S2) = \frac{\sum_{i=1}^{k}\sum_{j=1}^{l} \vec{x}_i \cdot \vec{y}_j}{k * l} \quad (10)$$

Based on such word embedding models, we derive two similarity features: (1) similarity between a bigram and the topic query, and (2) similarity between a bigram and top-k most frequent unigrams in this topic. We trained two word embedding models, from the abstract and news article collections in the New York Times Annotated Corpus, and thus have two sets of the above similarity features. We use the continuous bag-of-words model introduced by (Mikolov et al., 2013), and the tool word2vec[2] to obtain the word embeddings.

### 4.4 Similarity based on WordNet[3]

Similar to the above method, here we still focus on measuring the similarity between a bigram and the topic query, but based on WordNet. We use WordNet to identify the synonyms of nouns, verbs,

[1]Note that we do not use all the sentences in the ILP module. The 'relevant' sentences are those that have at least one bigram with document frequency larger than or equal to three.

[2]https://code.google.com/p/word2vec/

[3]http://wordnet.princeton.edu/

and adjectives from each bigram and the query of the topic. Then every bigram and sentence can be represented as a bag of synonyms of the original words. Finally based on these synonyms we leverage the following four similarity measurements: Lin Similarity (Lin, 1998), Wu-Palmer Similarity (Wu and Palmer, 1994), Jiang-Conrath Similarity (Jiang and Conrath, 1997), and Resnik Similarity (Resnik, 1995). These four similarity measurements are all implemented in the NLTK toolkit[4]. We expect that these features would improve the estimation accuracy because they can overcome the ambiguity and the diversity of the vocabulary.

### 4.5 Importance based on Wikipedia

Wikipedia is a very popular resource used in many different tasks. In order to obtain more precise external information from Wikipedia for our task, we collect the articles from Wikipedia by two steps. If the query is already the title of a wiki page, we will not further gather other wiki pages for this topic. Otherwise, we first search for the wiki pages for the given topic query and description (if available) using Google advanced search function to find pages from http://en.wikipedia.org/. For each returned wiki page, we further calculate its similarity between its abstract and the test documents' top k frequent words. We select 3 most similar pages as the external Wiki resource for this topic. For these wikipages, we split into two parts: abstract and content.[5] The features are the following: For each bigram, we collect its tf*idf score from the abstract and content part respectively, and the average tf*idf value of the unigrams in the bigram candidate. In addition, we design two boolean features that represent whether a bigram is the top-k most frequent ones in the abstract or the content part of the Wikepages.

### 4.6 DBpedia[6] for Extending Name Entity

DBpedia is a crowd-sourced community effort to extract structured information from Wikipedia and its Spotlight Service[7] is an entity linking tool to connect free text to DBpedia through the recognition and disambiguation of entities and concepts from the DBpedia Knowledge Base. We use this service to extract the entity from each sentence, and if the recognized entity is also identified as a named entity by Stanford CoreNLP[8], we use this entity's DBpedia abstract content to extend the bigrams. For example, in the bigram 'Kashmir area', the word 'Kashmir' is recognized as an entity by both (Stanford CoreNLP and DBpedia Spotlight service), then we use the description for 'Kashmir' from DBpedia[9] to extend this bigram, and calculate the cosine similarity between this description and the topic query and top-k most frequent unigrams in the documents.

### 4.7 Sentiment Feature from SentiWordNet[10]

SentiWordNet (Baccianella et al., 2010) is an extension on WordNet and it further assigns to each synset of WordNet three sentiment scores: positivity, negativity, objectivity. The sentiment score of a bigram is the average score of the two words in the bigram.

To sum up, the features we use include the internal features, and external ones derived from various resources: news article corpus with summaries, Wikipeida, DBpedia, WordNet and SentiWordNet. Some external features represent the inherent importance of bigrams. For example, features extracted from the news article corpus and wikipedia are used to represent how often bigrams are used in summary/abstract compared to the entire document. Some external features are used to better compute semantic similarity, for example, features from the word embedding methods, DBpedia, and WordNet.

## 5 Experiments

### 5.1 Data and Experiment Setup

We evaluate our methods using several recent TAC data sets, from 2008 to 2011. The TAC summarization task is to generate at most 100 words summaries from 10 documents for a given topic query

[4]http://www.nltk.org/

[5]Every Wikipage has a table of contents. The part before that is considered as abstract and the part after that is the content of that page.

[6]http://dbpedia.org/About

[7]http://blog.dbpedia.org/2014/07/21/dbpedia-spotlight-v07-released/

[8]http://nlp.stanford.edu/software/corenlp.shtml

[9]The Indian subcontinent is a southerly region of Asia, mostly situated on the Indian Plate and projecting southward into the Indian Ocean. Definitions of the extent of the Indian subcontinent differ but it usually includes the core lands of India, Pakistan, and Bangladesh

[10]http://sentiwordnet.isti.cnr.it/

consisting of a title and more detailed description (this is unavailable in 2010 and 2011 data). When evaluating on one TAC data set, we use the data from the other three years as the training set. All the summaries are evaluated using ROUGE (Lin, 2004; Owczarzak et al., 2012). In all of our experiments, we use Stanford CoreNLP toolkit to tokenize the sentences, extract name entities and POS tags. Berkeley Parser (Petrov et al., 2006) is used to get the constituent parse tree for every sentence. An academic free solver [11] does all the ILP decoding.

## 5.2 Results and Analysis

### 5.2.1 Summarization Results

Table 1 shows the ROUGE-2 results of our proposed joint system, the ICSI system (which uses document frequency threshold to select bigram concepts and uses df as weights), the best performing system in the NIST TAC evaluation, and the state of the art performance we could find. The result of our proposed method is statistically significantly better than that of ICSI ILP ($p < 0.05$ based on paired t-test). It is also statistically significantly ($p < 0.05$) better than that of TAC Rank1 except 2011, and previous best in 2008 and 2010. The 2011 previous best results from (Ng et al., 2012) involve some rule-based sentence compression, which improves the ROUGE value. If we apply the same or similar rule-based sentence compression on our results, and the ROUGE-2 of our proposed method improves to 14.38.

| | 2008 | 2009 | 2010 | 2011 |
|---|---|---|---|---|
| ICSI ILP | 10.23 | 11.60 | 10.03 | 12.71 |
| TAC Rank1 | 10.38 | 12.16 | 9.57 | 13.44 |
| Previous Best | 10.76† | 12.46† | 10.8‡ | 13.93∗ |
| Proposed Method | **11.84** | **12.77** | **11.78** | **13.97** |

Table 1: ROUGE-2 summarization results.† is from (Li et al., 2013b), ‡ is from (Davis et al., 2012), and ∗ is from (Ng et al., 2012).

### 5.2.2 The Effect of Bigram Selection

In our experiments, the document frequency threshold used to filter the bigrams is 3, the same as that in (Gillick et al., 2009), in order to make a better comparison with previous work. Figure 1 shows the percentage of the correct bigrams (those in the human reference summaries) by our proposed selection method and the original ICSI system which just used document frequency based selection. We can see that our selection method yields a higher percent of the correctly chosen bigrams. Since our proposed method is slightly aggressive when filtering bigrams, the absolute number of the correct bigrams decreased. However, our filtering method successfully removes more useless bigrams, resulting in a higher percentage of the correct bigrams.

Table 2 shows the summarization results when using different bigrams: the method used in the ICSI ILP system, that is, document frequency based selection/filtering and our selection method. Both of them use document frequency as the bigram weight in the ILP summarization module. The results show that just by changing the input bigrams, our method has already outperformed the ICSI system, which means the selection of bigram indeed has an impact on summarization results.

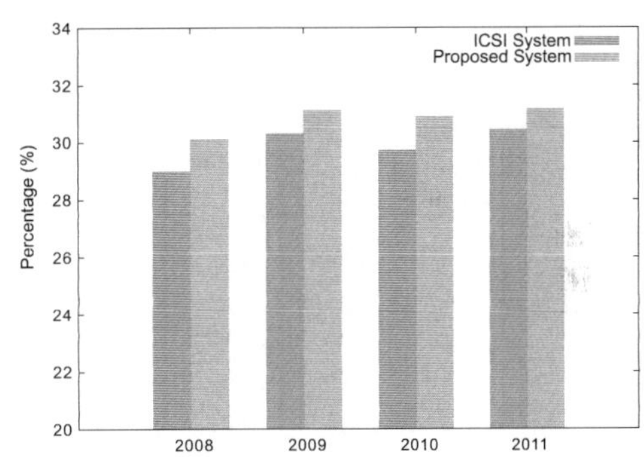


Figure 1: Percentage of correct bigrams in the selected bigrams from ICSI and our proposed system.

| | 2008 | 2009 | 2010 | 2011 |
|---|---|---|---|---|
| ICSI ILP | 10.23 | 11.60 | 10.03 | 12.71 |
| Ours | 10.26 | 11.65 | 10.25 | 12.75 |

Table 2: ROUGE-2 summarization results when using different bigrams, both using document frequencies as weights.

[11] http://www.gurobi.com

#### 5.2.3 The Effect of Features

Next we evaluate the contributions of different features. We show results for four experiments: (i) use just one type of features; (ii) combine the internal features with features from just one external resource; (iii) incrementally add external resources one by one; (iv) leave out each feature type.

Table 3 shows the ROUGE-2 results when we only apply one type of features. First, we can see that the system with the internal features has already outperformed the baseline which used document frequency as the weight. It shows that the other chosen internal features (beyond document frequency) are useful. Second, when we use the features from only one external resource, the results from some resources are competitive compared to that from the system using internal features. In particular, when using the LM scores, Wiki or Word Embedding features, the results are slightly better than the internal features. Using DBpedia or SentiWordNet has worse results than the internal features. This is because the SentiWordNet features themselves are not very discriminative. For DBpedia, since it only has feature values for the bigrams containing name entities, it will only assign weights for those bigrams. Therefore, only considering DBpedia features means that the ILP decoder would prefer to choose bigrams that are name entities with positive weights.

| | 2008 | 2009 | 2010 | 2011 |
|---|---|---|---|---|
| Internal | 10.40 | 11.76 | 10.42 | 12.91 |
| LM | 10.58 | 11.86 | 10.48 | 12.94 |
| Word Embedding | 10.67 | 11.96 | 10.58 | 13.02 |
| Wikipedia | 10.61 | 11.90 | 10.52 | 13.00 |
| DBpedia | 8.35 | 9.85 | 9.46 | 11.00 |
| WordNet | 10.39 | 11.76 | 10.40 | 12.86 |
| SentiwordNet | 9.90 | 10.80 | 10.08 | 12.50 |

Table 3: ROUGE-2 results using one feature type.

Table 4 shows the results when combining the internal features with features from one external resource. We can see that the features from Word Embedding model outperform others, suggesting the effectiveness of this semantic similarity measure. Features from the LM scores and Wiki are also quite useful. Wiki pages are extracted for the test topic itself, therefore they provide topic relevant background information. The LM score features are extracted from large amounts of news article data, and are good representation of the general importance of bigrams for the test domain. In contrast, WordNet information is collected from a more general aspect, which may not be a very good choice for this task. Also notice that even though the features from DBpedia and sentiwordnet do not perform well by themselves, after the combination with internal features, there is significant improvement. This proves that the features from DBpedia and sentiwordnet provide additional information not captured by the internal features from the documents.

| | 2008 | 2009 | 2010 | 2011 |
|---|---|---|---|---|
| Internal | 10.40 | 11.76 | 10.42 | 12.91 |
| +LM | 10.76 | 12.03 | 10.80 | 13.11 |
| +Word Embedding | 10.92 | 12.12 | 10.85 | 13.24 |
| +Wikipedia | 10.81 | 12.08 | 10.76 | 13.17 |
| +WordNet | 10.68 | 11.96 | 10.71 | 12.99 |
| +SentiwordNet | 10.60 | 11.96 | 10.63 | 12.96 |
| +DBpedia | 10.69 | 12.00 | 10.70 | 13.07 |

Table 4: ROUGE-2 results using internal features combined with features from just one external resource.

Table 5 shows the results when adding features one by one. The order is based on its individual impact when combined with internal features. The results show that Wiki, LM and DBpedia features give more improvement than WordNet and SentiWordNet features. This shows the different impact of the external resources. We can see there is consistent improvement when more features are added.

| | 2008 | 2009 | 2010 | 2011 |
|---|---|---|---|---|
| 1: Internal +Word Embedding | 10.92 | 12.12 | 10.85 | 13.24 |
| 2: 1+Wiki | 11.22 | 12.25 | 11.15 | 13.47 |
| 3: 2+LM | 11.41 | 12.41 | 11.37 | 13.68 |
| 4: 3+DBpedia | 11.65 | 12.60 | 11.61 | 13.77 |
| 5: 4+WordNet | 11.75 | 12.67 | 11.70 | 13.90 |
| 6: 5+SentiWordNet | 11.84 | 12.77 | 11.78 | 13.97 |

Table 5: ROUGE-2 results using features incrementally combined.

Table 6 shows the feature ablation results, that is, each row means that the corresponding features are excluded and the system uses all the other features. This set of experiments again shows that the external features like Word Embedding model based on large corpus and Wiki resource are very useful. Without using them, the system has the biggest performance degradation compared to the best result.

| | 2008 | 2009 | 2010 | 2011 |
|---|---|---|---|---|
| -Internal | 11.34 | 12.41 | 11.42 | 13.71 |
| -Word Embedding | 11.29 | 12.25 | 11.36 | 13.55 |
| -Wiki | 11.35 | 12.38 | 11.38 | 13.58 |
| -LM | 11.40 | 12.39 | 11.42 | 13.61 |
| -DBpedia | 11.50 | 12.47 | 11.47 | 13.71 |
| -WordNet | 11.67 | 12.64 | 11.64 | 13.80 |
| -SentiWordNet | 11.75 | 12.67 | 11.70 | 13.90 |

Table 6: ROUGE-2 results when leaving out each feature type.

#### 5.2.4 Distribution of Correct Bigrams After Feature Weighting

In the next experiment we analyze the distribution of the correct bigrams from the ranked bigrams using different features in order to better evaluate their impact on bigram weighting. We rank all the bigrams in descending order according to the estimated weight, then calculate the number of correct bigrams (i.e., the bigrams in human generated summary) in Top10, 30, 50 and 80. The more correct bigrams appear on the top of the list, the better our features estimate the importance of the bigrams. We conducted this experiment using four systems: the system only with internal features, only with Word Embedding features, with combination of internal and Word Embedding features, and with all the features. Figure 2 shows the results of this experiment on TAC 2008 data. The pattern is similar on the other three years' data. The results show that systems with better ROUGE-2 value indeed can assign higher weights to correct bigrams, allowing the ILP decoding process to select these bigrams, which leads to a better sentence selection.

#### 5.2.5 Joint Learning Results

Finally we evaluate the effectiveness of our proposed joint learning approach. For comparison, we implement a pipeline method, where we use the bigram's document frequency as the target value to train a regression model, and during testing use the

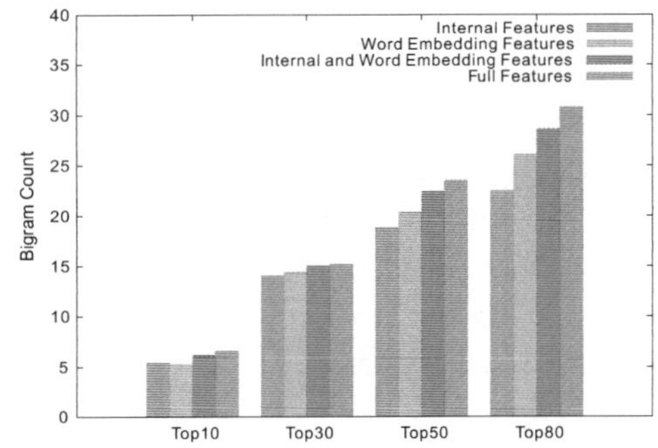


Figure 2: Distribution of correct bigrams in Top-n weighted bigrams from four systems.

model's predicted value as the weight in the ILP framework. Table 7 compares the results using the joint learning method and this pipeline approach. We only show the results using the system with all the features due to limited space. We can see that our joint method outperforms the pipeline system based on ROUGE-2 measurement, indicating that weights are better learned in the joint process that takes into account both bigram and sentence selection.

| System | 2008 | 2009 | 2010 | 2011 |
|---|---|---|---|---|
| Pipeline System | 11.60 | 12.64 | 11.56 | 13.65 |
| Joint Model | 11.84 | 12.77 | 11.78 | 13.97 |

Table 7: ROUGE-2 results using different training strategies.

## 6 Conclusions

In this paper, we adopt the ILP based summarization framework, and propose methods to improve bigram concept selection and weighting. We use syntactic information to filter and select bigrams, various external resources to extract features, and a joint learning process for weight training. Our experiments in the TAC data sets demonstrate that our proposed methods outperform other state-of-the-art results. Through the analysis, we found the external resources are helpful to estimate the bigram importance and thus improve the summarization performance. While in summarization research, optimization-based methods have already rivaled other approaches in performance, the task is far from being solved. Our analysis revealed that there are at least three points worth mentioning. First, using external resources contributes to the improved performance of our method compared to others that only use internal features. Second, employing and designing sophisticated features, especially those that encode background knowledge or semantic relationship like the word embedding features from a large corpus we used, will enable language concepts to be distinguished more easily in the presence of a large number of candidates. Third, one limitation of the use of the external resources is that they are not always available, such as the pairwise news articles along with the human generated summaries, and the relevant Wiki pages. While much recent work has focused on algorithmic development, the summarization task needs to have a deeper "understanding" of a document in order to reach the next level of performance. Such an understanding can be facilitated by the incorporation of background knowledge, which can lead to significant summarization performance improvement, as demonstrated in this study.

## Acknowledgments

We thank the anonymous reviewers for their detailed and insightful comments on earlier drafts of this paper. The work is partially supported by NSF award IIS-0845484 and DARPA Contract No. FA8750-13-2-0041. Any opinions, findings, and conclusions or recommendations expressed are those of the authors and do not necessarily reflect the views of the funding agencies.

## References

Stefano Baccianella, Andrea Esuli, and Fabrizio Sebastiani. 2010. Sentiwordnet 3.0: An enhanced lexical resource for sentiment analysis and opinion mining. In *Proceedings of LREC*.

Michael Collins. 2002. Discriminative training methods for hidden markov models: Theory and experiments with perceptron algorithms. In *Proceedings of EMNLP*.

Sashka T. Davis, John M. Conroy, and Judith D. Schlesinger. 2012. Occams - an optimal combinatorial covering algorithm for multi-document summarization. In *Proceedings of ICDM*.

Dan Gillick, Benoit Favre, and Dilek Hakkani-Tur. 2008. The ICSI summarization system at tac 2008. In *Proceedings of TAC*.

Dan Gillick, Benoit Favre, Dilek Hakkani-Tur, Berndt Bohnet, Yang Liu, and Shasha Xie. 2009. The ICSI/UTD summarization system at tac 2009. In *Proceedings of TAC*.

Kazi Saidul Hasan and Vincent Ng. 2014. Automatic keyphrase extraction: A survey of the state of the art. In *Proceedings of ACL*.

Kai Hong and Ani Nenkova. 2014. Improving the estimation of word importance for news multi-document summarization. In *Proceedings of EACL*.

Houping Jia, Xiaojiang Huang, Tengfei Ma, Xiaojun Wan, and Jianguo Xiao. 2010. Pkutm participation at tac 2010 rte and summarization track. In *Proceedings of TAC*.

Jay J Jiang and David W Conrath. 1997. Semantic similarity based on corpus statistics and lexical taxonomy. *arXiv preprint cmp-lg/9709008*.

Samir Khuller, Anna Moss, and Joseph Seffi Naor. 1999. The budgeted maximum coverage problem. *Information Processing Letters*.

Judith L. Klavans and Min-Yen Kan. 1998. Role of verbs in document analysis. In *Proceedings of the ACL*.

Niraj Kumar, Kannan Srinathan, and Vasudeva Varma. 2010. An effective approach for aesop and guided summarization task. In *Proceedings of TAC*.

Chen Li, Fei Liu, Fuliang Weng, and Yang Liu. 2013a. Document summarization via guided sentence compression. In *Proceedings of the EMNLP*.

Chen Li, Xian Qian, and Yang Liu. 2013b. Using supervised bigram-based ilp for extractive summarization. In *Proceedings of ACL*.

Chen Li, Yang Liu, Fei Liu, Lin Zhao, and Fuliang Weng. 2014. Improving multi-documents summarization by sentence compression based on expanded constituent parse trees. In *Proceedings of EMNLP*.

Hui Lin and Jeff Bilmes. 2010. Multi-document summarization via budgeted maximization of submodular functions. In *Proceedings of NAACL*.

Dekang Lin. 1998. An information-theoretic definition of similarity. In *Proceedings of ICML*.

Chin-Yew Lin. 2004. Rouge: a package for automatic evaluation of summaries. In *Proceedings of ACL*.

Patrice Lopez and Laurent Romary. 2010. Humb: Automatic key term extraction from scientific articles in grobid. In *Proceedings of the international workshop on semantic evaluation*.

Andre F. T. Martins and Noah A. Smith. 2009. Summarization with a joint model for sentence extraction and compression. In *Proceedings of the ACL Workshop on Integer Linear Programming for Natural Language Processing*.

Ryan McDonald. 2007. A study of global inference algorithms in multi-document summarization. In *Proceedings of ECIR*.

Olena Medelyan, Eibe Frank, and Ian H Witten. 2009. Human-competitive tagging using automatic keyphrase extraction. In *Proceedings of the EMNLP*.

Tomas Mikolov, Kai Chen, Greg Corrado, and Jeffrey Dean. 2013. Efficient estimation of word representations in vector space. *Proceedings of Workshop at ICLR*.

Jun-Ping Ng, Praveen Bysani, Ziheng Lin, Min-Yen Kan, and Chew-Lim Tan. 2012. Exploiting category-specific information for multi-document summarization. In *Proceedings of COLING*.

Karolina Owczarzak, John M. Conroy, Hoa Trang Dang, and Ani Nenkova. 2012. An assessment of the accuracy of automatic evaluation in summarization. In *Proceedings of Workshop on Evaluation Metrics and System Comparison for Automatic Summarization*.

Slav Petrov, Leon Barrett, Romain Thibaux, and Dan Klein. 2006. Learning accurate, compact, and interpretable tree annotation. In *Proceedings of COLING-ACL*.

Philip Resnik. 1995. Using information content to evaluate semantic similarity in a taxonomy. *arXiv preprint cmp-lg/9511007*.

Hiroya Takamura and Manabu Okumura. 2009. Text summarization model based on maximum coverage problem and its variant. In *Proceedings of EACL*.

Zhongyu Wei and Wei Gao. 2014. Utilizing microblogs for automatic news highlights extraction. In *Proceedings of COLING*.

Kristian Woodsend and Mirella Lapata. 2012. Multiple aspect summarization using integer linear programming. In *Proceedings of EMNLP-CoNLL*.

Zhibiao Wu and Martha Palmer. 1994. Verbs semantics and lexical selection. In *Proceedings of ACL*.

Wen-Tau Yih, Joshua Goodman, and Vitor R Carvalho. 2006. Finding advertising keywords on web pages. In *Proceedings of international conference on World Wide Web*.

# Transforming Dependencies into Phrase Structures

**Lingpeng Kong**
School of Computer Science
Carnegie Mellon University
Pittsburgh, PA, USA
lingpenk@cs.cmu.edu

**Alexander M. Rush**
Facebook AI Research
New York, NY, USA
srush@seas.harvard.edu

**Noah A. Smith**
School of Computer Science
Carnegie Mellon University
Pittsburgh, PA, USA
nasmith@cs.cmu.edu

## Abstract

We present a new algorithm for transforming dependency parse trees into phrase-structure parse trees. We cast the problem as structured prediction and learn a statistical model. Our algorithm is faster than traditional phrase-structure parsing and achieves 90.4% English parsing accuracy and 82.4% Chinese parsing accuracy, near to the state of the art on both benchmarks.

## 1 Introduction

Natural language parsers typically produce phrase-structure (constituent) trees or dependency trees. These representations capture some of the same syntactic phenomena, and the two can be produced jointly (Klein and Manning, 2002; Hall and Nivre, 2008; Carreras et al., 2008; Rush et al., 2010). Yet it appears to be completely unpredictable which will be preferred by a particular subcommunity or used in a particular application. Both continue to receive the attention of parsing researchers.

Further, it appears to be a historical accident that phrase-structure syntax was used in annotating the Penn Treebank, and that English dependency annotations are largely derived through mechanical, rule-based transformations (reviewed in Section 2). Indeed, despite extensive work on direct-to-dependency parsing algorithms (which we call *d-parsing*), the most accurate dependency parsers for English still involve phrase-structure parsing (which we call *c-parsing*) followed by rule-based extraction of dependencies (Kong and Smith, 2014).

What if dependency annotations had come first? Because d-parsers are generally much faster than c-parsers, we consider an alternate pipeline (Section 3): d-parse first, then transform the dependency representation into a phrase-structure tree constrained to be consistent with the dependency parse. This idea was explored by Xia and Palmer (2001) and Xia et al. (2009) using hand-written rules. Instead, we present a data-driven algorithm using the structured prediction framework (Section 4). The approach can be understood as a specially-trained coarse-to-fine decoding algorithm where a d-parser provides "coarse" structure and the second stage refines it (Charniak and Johnson, 2005; Petrov and Klein, 2007).

Our lexicalized phrase-structure parser, PAD, is asymptotically faster than parsing with a lexicalized context-free grammar: $O(n^2)$ plus d-parsing, vs. $O(n^5)$ worst case runtime in sentence length $n$, with the same grammar constant. Experiments show that our approach achieves linear observable runtime, and accuracy similar to state-of-the-art phrase-structure parsers without reranking or semi-supervised training (Section 7).

## 2 Background

We begin with the conventional development by first introducing c-parsing and then defining d-parses through a mechanical conversion using head rules. In the next section, we consider the reverse transformation.

### 2.1 CFG Parsing

The phrase-structure trees annotated in the Penn Treebank are derivation trees from a context-free grammar. Define a binary[1] context-free grammar

[1]For notational simplicity, we defer discussion of non-binary rules to Section 3.3.



*Human Language Technologies: The 2015 Annual Conference of the North American Chapter of the ACL*, pages 788–798,
Denver, Colorado, May 31 – June 5, 2015. 

(CFG) as a 4-tuple $(\mathcal{N}, \mathcal{G}, \mathcal{T}, r)$ where $\mathcal{N}$ is a set of nonterminal symbols (e.g. NP, VP), $\mathcal{T}$ is a set of terminal symbols, consisting of the words in the language, $\mathcal{G}$ is a set of binary rules of the form $A \rightarrow \beta_1\ \beta_2$, and $r \in \mathcal{N}$ is a distinguished root nonterminal symbol.

Given an input sentence $x_1, \ldots, x_n$ of terminal symbols from $\mathcal{T}$, define the set of c-parses for the sentence as $\mathcal{Y}(x)$. This set consists of all binary ordered trees with fringe $x_1, \ldots, x_n$, internal nodes labeled from $\mathcal{N}$, all tree productions $A \rightarrow \beta_1\ \beta_2$ consisting of members of $\mathcal{G}$, and root label $r$.

For a c-parse $y \in \mathcal{Y}(x)$, we further associate a span $\langle v_{\Leftarrow}, v_{\Rightarrow}\rangle$ with each vertex in the tree. This specifies the subsequence $\{x_{v_{\Leftarrow}}, \ldots, x_{v_{\Rightarrow}}\}$ of the sentence covered by this vertex.

## 2.2 Dependency Parsing

Dependency parses provide an alternative, and in some sense simpler, representation of sentence structure. These d-parses can be derived through mechanical transformation from context-free trees. There are several popular transformations in wide use; each provides a different representation of a sentence's structure (Collins, 2003; De Marneffe and Manning, 2008; Yamada and Matsumoto, 2003; Johansson and Nugues, 2007).

We consider the class of transformations that are defined through local *head rules*. For a binary CFG, define a collection of head rules as a mapping from each CFG rule to a head preference for its left or right child. We use the notation $A \rightarrow \beta_1^*\ \beta_2$ and $A \rightarrow \beta_1\ \beta_2^*$ to indicate a left- or right-headed rule, respectively.

The head rules can be used to map a c-parse to a dependency tree (d-parse). In a d-parse, each word in the sentence is assigned as a dependent to a head word, $h \in \{0, \ldots, n\}$, where 0 is a special symbol indicating the pseudo-root of the sentence. For each $h$ we define $\mathcal{L}(h) \subset \{1, \ldots, h-1\}$ as the set of left dependencies of $h$, and $\mathcal{R}(h) \subset \{h+1, \ldots, n\}$ as the set of right dependencies.

A d-parse can be constructed recursively from a c-parse and the head rules. For each c-parse vertex $v$ with potential children $v_{\text{L}}$ and $v_{\text{R}}$ in bottom-up order, we apply the following procedure to both assign heads to the c-parse and construct the d-parse:

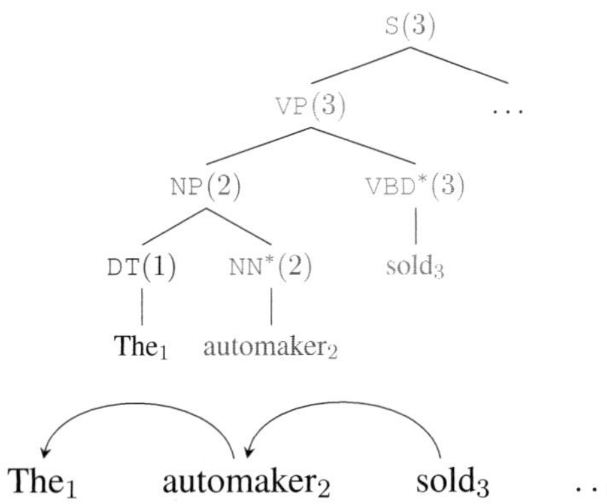


Figure 1: Illustration of c-parse to d-parse conversion with head rules $\{\texttt{VP} \rightarrow \texttt{NP VBD}^*, \texttt{NP} \rightarrow \texttt{DT NN}^*, \ldots\}$. The c-parse is an ordered tree with fringe $x_1, \ldots, x_n$. Each vertex is annotated with a terminal or nonterminal symbol and a derived head index. The blue and red vertices have the words $\texttt{automaker}_2$ and $\texttt{sold}_3$ as heads respectively. The vertex VP(3) implies that $\texttt{automaker}_2$ is a left-dependent of $\texttt{sold}_3$, and that $2 \in \mathcal{L}(3)$ in the d-parse.

1. If the vertex is leaf $x_m$, then $\text{head}(v) = m$.
2. If the next rule is $A \rightarrow \beta_1^*\ \beta_2$ then $\text{head}(v) = \text{head}(v_{\text{L}})$ and $\text{head}(v_{\text{R}}) \in \mathcal{R}(\text{head}(v))$, i.e. the head of the right-child is a dependent of the head word.
3. If the next rule is $A \rightarrow \beta_1\ \beta_2^*$ then $\text{head}(v) = \text{head}(v_{\text{R}})$ and $\text{head}(v_{\text{L}}) \in \mathcal{L}(\text{head}(v))$, i.e. the head of the left-child is a dependent of the head word.

Figure 1 shows an example conversion of a c-parse to d-parse using this procedure.

By construction, these dependencies form a directed tree with arcs $(h, m)$ for all $h \in \{0, \ldots, n\}$ and $m \in \mathcal{L}(h) \cup \mathcal{R}(h)$. While this tree differs from the original c-parse, we can relate the two trees through their spans. Define the dependency tree span $\langle h_{\Leftarrow}, h_{\Rightarrow}\rangle$ as the contiguous sequence of words reachable from word $h$ in this tree.[2] This span is equivalent to the maximal span $\langle v_{\Leftarrow}, v_{\Rightarrow}\rangle$ of any c-parse vertex with $\text{head}(v) = h$. This property will be important for the parsing algorithm presented in the next section.

[2]The conversion from a standard CFG tree to a d-parse preserves this sequence property, known as *projectivity*. We leave the question of non-projective d-parses and the related question of traces and co-indexation in c-parses to future work.

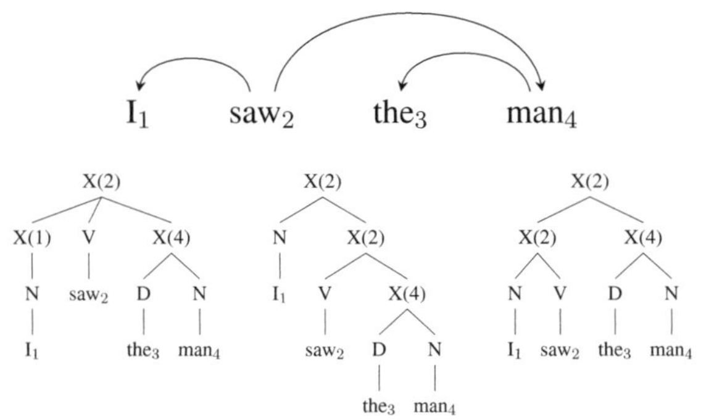


Figure 2: [Adapted from (Collins et al., 1999).] A d-parse (left) and several c-parses consistent with it (right). Our goal is to select the best parse from this set.

## 3 Parsing Dependencies

Now we consider flipping this setup. There has been significant progress in developing efficient direct-to-dependency parsers. These d-parsers are trained only on dependency annotations and do not require full phrase-structure trees.[3] Some prefer this setup, since it allows easy selection of the specific dependencies of interest in a downstream task (e.g., information extraction), and perhaps even training specifically for those dependencies. Other applications make use of phrase structures, so c-parsers enjoy wide use as well.

With these latter applications in mind, we consider the problem of converting a fixed d-parse into a c-parse, with the intent of using off-the-shelf d-parsers for constructing phrase-structure parses. Since this problem is more challenging than its inverse, we use a structured prediction setup: we learn a function to score possible c-parse conversions, and then generate the highest-scoring c-parse given a d-parse. A toy example of the problem is shown in Figure 2.

### 3.1 Parsing Algorithm

Consider the classical problem of predicting the best c-parse under a CFG with head rules, known as lexicalized context-free parsing. Assume that we are given a binary CFG defining a set of valid c-parses $\mathcal{Y}(x)$. The parsing problem is to find the highest-scoring parse in this set, i.e. $\arg\max_{y\in\mathcal{Y}(x)} s(y;x)$ where $s$ is a scoring function that factors over lexicalized tree productions.

This problem can be solved by extending the CKY algorithm to propagate head information. The algorithm can be compactly defined by the productions in Figure 3 (left). For example, one type of production is of the form

$$\frac{(\langle i,k\rangle, m, \beta_1) \quad (\langle k+1,j\rangle, h, \beta_2)}{(\langle i,j\rangle, h, A)}$$

for all rules $A \rightarrow \beta_1\ \beta_2^* \in \mathcal{G}$ and spans $i \leq k < j$. This particular production indicates that rule $A \rightarrow \beta_1\ \beta_2^*$ was applied at a vertex covering $\langle i,j\rangle$ to produce two vertices covering $\langle i,k\rangle$ and $\langle k+1,j\rangle$, and that the new head is index $h$ has dependent index $m$. We say this production "completes" word $m$ since it can no longer be the head of a larger span.

Running the algorithm consists of bottom-up dynamic programming over these productions. However, applying this version of the CKY algorithm requires $O(n^5|\mathcal{G}|)$ time (linear in the number of productions), which is not practical to run without heavy pruning. Most lexicalized parsers therefore make further assumptions on the scoring function which can lead to asymptotically faster algorithms (Eisner and Satta, 1999).

Instead, we consider the same objective, but constrain the c-parses to be consistent with a given d-parse, $d$. By "consistent," we mean that the c-parse will be converted by the head rules to this exact d-parse.[4] Define the set of consistent c-parses as $\mathcal{Y}(x,d)$ and the constrained search problem as $\arg\max_{y\in\mathcal{Y}(x,d)} s(y;x,d)$.

Figure 3 (right) shows the algorithm for this new problem. The algorithm has several nice properties. All rules now must select words $h$ and $m$ that are consistent with the dependency parse (i.e., there is an arc $(h,m)$) so these variables are no longer free. Furthermore, since we have the full d-parse, we can precompute the dependency span of each word $\langle m_{\Leftarrow}, m_{\Rightarrow}\rangle$. By our definition of consistency, this gives us the c-parse span of $m$ before it is completed, and fixes two more free variables. Finally the head item must have its alternative side index match

[3] For English these parsers are still often trained on trees converted from c-parses; however, for other languages, dependency-only treebanks of directly-annotated d-parses are common.

[4] An alternative, soft version of consistency, might enforce that the c-parse is close to the d-parse. While this allows the algorithm to potentially correct d-parse mistakes, it is much more computationally expensive.

**Premise:**

$$(\langle i,i\rangle, i, A) \quad \forall i \in \{1 \dots n\}, A \in \mathcal{N}$$

**Rules:**
For $i \le h \le k < m \le j$, and rule $A \rightarrow \beta_1^* \ \beta_2$,

$$\frac{(\langle i,k\rangle, h, \beta_1) \quad (\langle k+1, j\rangle, m, \beta_2)}{(\langle i,j\rangle, h, A)}$$

For $i \le m \le k < h \le j$, rule $A \rightarrow \beta_1 \ \beta_2^*$,

$$\frac{(\langle i,k\rangle, m, \beta_1) \quad (\langle k+1, j\rangle, h, \beta_2)}{(\langle i,j\rangle, h, A)}$$

**Goal:**

$$(\langle 1,n\rangle, m, r) \text{ for any } m$$

**Premise:**

$$(\langle i,i\rangle, i, A) \quad \forall i \in \{1 \dots n\}, A \in \mathcal{N}$$

**Rules:**
For all $h$, $m \in \mathcal{R}(h)$, rule $A \rightarrow \beta_1^* \ \beta_2$,
and $i \in \{m'_{\Leftarrow} : m' \in \mathcal{L}(h)\} \cup \{h\}$,

$$\frac{(\langle i, m_{\Leftarrow} - 1\rangle, h, \beta_1) \quad (\langle m_{\Leftarrow}, m_{\Rightarrow}\rangle, m, \beta_2)}{(\langle i, m_{\Rightarrow}\rangle, h, A)}$$

For all $h$, $m \in \mathcal{L}(h)$, rule $A \rightarrow \beta_1 \ \beta_2^*$,
and $j \in \{m'_{\Rightarrow} : m' \in \mathcal{R}(h)\} \cup \{h\}$,

$$\frac{(\langle m_{\Leftarrow}, m_{\Rightarrow}\rangle, m, \beta_1) \quad (\langle m_{\Rightarrow} + 1, j\rangle, h, \beta_2)}{(\langle m_{\Leftarrow}, j\rangle, h, A)}$$

**Goal:**

$$(\langle 1,n\rangle, m, r) \text{ for any } m \in \mathcal{R}(0)$$

Figure 3: The two algorithms written as deductive parsers. Starting from the *premise*, any valid application of *rules* that leads to a *goal* is a valid parse. Left: lexicalized CKY algorithm for CFG parsing with head rules. For this algorithm there are $O(n^5|\mathcal{G}|)$ rules where $n$ is the length of the sentence. Right: the constrained CKY parsing algorithm for $\mathcal{Y}(x,d)$. The algorithm is nearly identical except that many of the free indices are now fixed given the dependency parse. Finding the optimal c-parse with the new algorithm now requires $O\left((\sum_h |\mathcal{L}(h)||\mathcal{R}(h)|)|\mathcal{G}|\right)$ time where $\mathcal{L}(h)$ and $\mathcal{R}(h)$ are the left and right dependents of word $h$.

a valid dependency span. For example, if for a word $h$ there are $|\mathcal{L}(h)| = 3$ left dependents, then when taking the next right-dependent there can only be 4 valid left boundary indices.

The runtime of the final algorithm reduces to $O(\sum_h |\mathcal{L}(h)||\mathcal{R}(h)||\mathcal{G}|)$. While the terms $|\mathcal{L}(h)|$ and $|\mathcal{R}(h)|$ could in theory make the runtime quadratic, in practice the number of dependents is almost always constant in the length of the sentence. This leads to linear observed runtime in practice as we will show in Section 7.

### 3.2 Pruning

In addition to constraining the number of c-parses, the d-parse also provides valuable information about the labeling and structure of the c-parse. We can use this information to further prune the search space. We employ two pruning methods:

Method 1 uses the part-of-speech tag of $x_h$, $\text{tag}(h)$, to limit the possible rule productions at a given span. We build tables $\mathcal{G}_{\text{tag}(h)}$ and restrict the search to rules seen in training for a particular part-of-speech tag.

Method 2 prunes based on the order in which dependent words are added. By the constraints of the algorithm, a head word $x_h$ must combine with each of its left and right dependents. However, the order of combination can lead to different tree structures (as illustrated in Figure 2). In total there are $|\mathcal{L}(h)| \times |\mathcal{R}(h)|$ possible orderings of dependents.

In practice, though, it is often easy to predict which side, left or right, will come next. We do this by estimating the distribution,

$$p(\text{side} \mid \text{tag}(h), \text{tag}(m), \text{tag}(m')),$$

where $m \in \mathcal{L}(h)$ is the next left dependent and $m' \in \mathcal{R}(h)$ is the next right dependent. If the conditional probability of left or right is greater than a threshold parameter $\gamma$, we make a hard decision to combine with that side next. This pruning further reduces the impact of outliers with multiple dependents on both sides.

We empirically measure how these pruning methods affect observed runtime and oracle parsing performance (i.e., how well a perfect scoring function could do with a pruned $\mathcal{Y}(x,d)$). Table 1 shows a comparison of these pruning methods on development data. The constrained parsing algorithm is much faster than standard lexicalized parsing, and

| Model | Complexity | Sent./s. | Ora. $F_1$ |
|---|---|---|---|
| LEX CKY* | $n^5\|\mathcal{G}\|$ | 0.25 | 100.0 |
| DEP CKY | $\sum_h \|\mathcal{L}(h)\|\|\mathcal{R}(h)\|\|\mathcal{G}\|$ | 71.2 | 92.6 |
| PRUNE1 | $\sum_h \|\mathcal{L}(h)\|\|\mathcal{R}(h)\|\|\mathcal{G}_T\|$ | 336.0 | 92.5 |
| PRUNE2 | – | 96.6 | 92.5 |
| PRUNE1+2 | – | 425.1 | 92.5 |

Table 1: Comparison of three parsing setups: LEX CKY* is the complete lexicalized c-parser on $\mathcal{Y}(x)$, but limited to only sentences less than 20 words for tractability, DEP CKY is the constrained c-parser on $\mathcal{Y}(x, d)$, PRUNE1, PRUNE2, and PRUNE1+2 are combinations of the pruning methods described in Section 3.2. The oracle is the best labeled $F_1$ achievable on the development data (§22, see Section 7).

pruning contributes even greater speed-ups. The oracle experiments show that the d-parse constraints do contribute a large drop in oracle accuracy, while pruning contributes a relatively small one. Still, this upper-bound on accuracy is high enough to make it possible to still recover c-parses at least as accurate as state-of-the-art c-parsers. We will return to this discussion in Section 7.

### 3.3 Binarization and Unary Rules

We have to this point developed the algorithm for a strictly binary-branching grammar; however, we need to produce trees have rules with varying size. In order to apply the algorithm, we binarize the grammar and add productions to handle unary rules.

Consider a non-binarized rule of the form $A \rightarrow \beta_1 \dots \beta_m$ with head child $\beta_k^*$. Relative to the head child $\beta_k$ the rule has left-side $\beta_1 \dots \beta_{k-1}$ and right-side $\beta_{k+1} \dots \beta_m$. We replace this rule with new binary rules and non-terminal symbols to produce each side independently as a simple chain, left-side first. The transformation introduces the following new rules:[5] $A \rightarrow \beta_1\ \bar{A}^*$, $\bar{A} \rightarrow \beta_i\ \bar{A}^*$ for $i \in \{2, \dots, k\}$, and $\bar{A} \rightarrow \bar{A}^*\ \beta_i$ for $i \in \{k, \dots, m\}$.

As an example consider the transformation of a rule with four children:

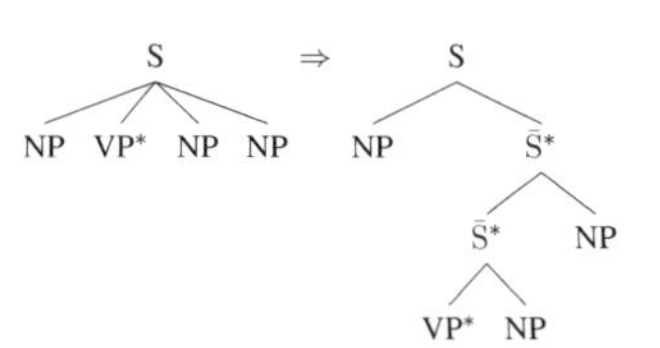


These rules can then be reversed deterministically to produce a non-binary tree.

[5]These rules are slightly modified when $k = 1$.

We also explored binarization using horizontal and vertical markovization to include additional context of the tree, as found useful in unlexicalized approaches (Klein and Manning, 2003). Preliminary experiments showed that this increased the size of the grammar, and the runtime of the algorithm, without leading to improvements in accuracy.

Phrase-structure trees also include unary rules of the form $A \rightarrow \beta_1^*$. To handle unary rules we modify the parsing algorithms in Figure 3 to include a unary completion rule,

$$\frac{(\langle i, j\rangle, h, \beta_1)}{(\langle i, j\rangle, h, A)}$$

for all indices $i \leq h \leq j$ that are consistent with the dependency parse. In order to avoid unary recursion, we limit the number of applications of this rule at each span (preserving the runtime of the algorithm). Preliminary experiments looked at collapsing the unary rules into the nonterminal symbols, but we found that this hurt performance compared to explicit unary rules.

## 4 Structured Prediction

We learn the d-parse to c-parse conversion using a standard structured prediction setup. Define the linear scoring function $s$ for a conversion as $s(y; x, d, \theta) = \theta^\top f(x, d, y)$ where $\theta$ is a parameter vector and $f(x, d, y)$ is a feature function that maps parse productions to sparse feature vectors. While the parser only requires a d-parse at prediction time, the parameters of this scoring function are learned directly from a treebank of c-parses and a set of head rules. The structured prediction model, in effect, learns to invert the head rule transformation.

### 4.1 Features

The scoring function requires specifying a set of parse features $f$ which, in theory, could be directly adapted from existing lexicalized c-parsers. However, the structure of the dependency parse greatly limits the number of decisions that need to be made, and allows for a smaller set of features.

We model our features after two bare-bones parsing systems. The first set is the basic arc-factored features used by McDonald (2006). These features include combinations of: rule and top nonterminal,

For a production $\dfrac{(\langle i,k\rangle, m, \beta_1) \quad (\langle k+1,j\rangle, h, \beta_2)}{(\langle i,j\rangle, h, A)}$

| Nonterm Features |
|---|
| $(A, \beta_1)$ $(A, \beta_1, \text{tag}(m))$ |
| $(A, \beta_2)$ $(A, \beta_2, \text{tag}(h))$ |

| Span Features |
|---|
| $(\text{rule}, x_i)$ $(\text{rule}, x_{i-1})$ |
| $(\text{rule}, x_j)$ $(\text{rule}, x_{j+1})$ |
| $(\text{rule}, x_k)$ $(\text{rule}, x_{k+1})$ |
| $(\text{rule}, \text{bin}(j-i))$ |

| Rule Features |
|---|
| (rule) |
| $(\text{rule}, x_h, \text{tag}(m))$ |
| $(\text{rule}, \text{tag}(h), x_m)$ |
| $(\text{rule}, \text{tag}(h), \text{tag}(m))$ |
| $(\text{rule}, x_h)$ |
| $(\text{rule}, \text{tag}(h))$ |
| $(\text{rule}, x_m)$ |
| $(\text{rule}, \text{tag}(m))$ |

Figure 4: The feature templates used in the function $f(x, d, y)$. For the span features, the symbol rule is expanded into both $A \rightarrow B\ C$ and backoff symbol $A$. The function $\text{bin}(i)$ partitions a span length into one of 10 bins.

| | PTB §22 | | |
|---|---|---|---|
| Model | Prec. | Rec. | $F_1$ |
| Xia et al. (2009) | 88.1 | 90.7 | 89.4 |
| PAD (§19) | 95.9 | 95.9 | 95.9 |
| PAD (§2–21) | 97.5 | 97.8 | 97.7 |

Table 2: Comparison with the rule-based system of Xia et al. (2009). Results are shown using gold-standard tags and dependencies. Xia et al. report results consulting only §19 in development and note that additional data had little effect. We show our system's results using §19 and the full training set.

modifier word and part-of-speech, and head word and part-of-speech.

The second set of features is modeled after the span features described in the X-bar-style parser of Hall et al. (2014). These include conjunctions of the rule with: first and last word of current span, preceding and following word of current span, adjacent words at split of current span, and binned length of the span.

The full feature set is shown in Figure 4. After training, there are a total of around 2 million nonzero features. For efficiency, we use lossy feature hashing. We found this had no impact on parsing accuracy but made the parsing significantly faster.

### 4.2 Training

The parameters $\theta$ are estimated using a structural support vector machine (Taskar et al., 2004). Given a set of gold-annotated c-parse examples, $(x^1, y^1), \dots, (x^D, y^D)$, and d-parses $d^1 \dots d^D$ induced from the head rules, we estimate the parameters to minimize the regularized empirical risk

$$\min_\theta \sum_{i=1}^{D} \ell(x^i, d^i, y^i, \theta) + \lambda ||\theta||_1$$

where we define $\ell$ as $\ell(x, d, y, \theta) = -s(y) + \max_{y' \in \mathcal{Y}(x,d)} (s(y') + \Delta(y, y'))$ and where $\Delta$ is a problem specific cost-function. In experiments, we use a Hamming loss $\Delta(y, y') = |y - y'|$ where $y$ is an indicator for production rules firing over pairs of adjacent spans (i.e., $i, j, k$).

The objective is optimized using AdaGrad (Duchi et al., 2011). The gradient calculation requires computing a loss-augmented max-scoring c-parse for each training example which is done using the algorithm of Figure 3 (right).

## 5 Related Work

The problem of converting dependency to phrase-structured trees has been studied previously from the perspective of building multi-representational treebanks. Xia and Palmer (2001) and Xia et al. (2009) develop a rule-based system for the conversion of human-annotated dependency parses. This work focuses on modeling the conversion decisions made and capturing how researchers annotate specific phenomena. Our work focuses on a different problem of learning a data-driven structured prediction model that is also able to handle automatically predicted dependency parses as input. While the aim is different, Table 2 does give a direct comparison of our system to that of Xia et al. (2009) on gold d-parse data.

An important line of previous work also uses dependency parsers to produce phrase-structure trees. In particular Hall et al. (2007) and Hall and Nivre (2008) develop a specialized dependency label set to encode phrase-structure information in the d-parse. After predicting a d-parse this label information can be used to assemble a predicted c-parse. Our work differs in that it does not make any assumptions on the labeling of the dependency tree used and it uses structured prediction to produce the final c-parse.

Very recently, Fernández-González and Martins (2015) also show that an off-the-shelf, trainable, dependency parser is enough to build a highly-competitive constituent parser. They proposed a new intermediate representation called "head-ordered dependency trees", which encode head ordering information in dependeny labels. Their algorithm is based on a reduction of the constituent parsing to dependency parsing of such trees.

There has been successful work combining dependency and phrase-structure information to build accurate c-parsers. Klein and Manning (2002) construct a factored generative model that scores both context-free syntactic productions and semantic dependencies. Carreras et al. (2008) construct a state-of-the-art parser that uses a dependency parsing model both for pruning and within a richer lexicalized parser. Similarly, Rush et al. (2010) use dual decomposition to combine a powerful dependency parser with a lexicalized phrase-structure model. This work differs in that we treat the dependency parse as a hard constraint, hence largely reduce the runtime of a fully lexicalized phrase structure parsing model while maintaining the ability, at least in principle, to generate highly accurate phrase-structure parses.

Finally there have also been several papers that use ideas from dependency parsing to simplify and speed up phrase-structure prediction. Zhu et al. (2013) build a high-accuracy phrase-structure parser using a transition-based system. Hall et al. (2014) use a stripped down parser based on a simple X-bar grammar and a small set of lexicalized features.

## 6 Methods

We ran a series of experiments to assess the accuracy, efficiency, and applicability of our parser, PAD, to several tasks. These experiments use the following setup.

For English experiments we use the standard Penn Treebank (PTB) experimental setup (Marcus et al., 1993). Training is done on §2–21, development on §22, and testing on §23. We use the development set to tune the regularization parameter, $\lambda = 1e-8$, and the pruning threshold, $\gamma = 0.95$.

For Chinese experiments, we use version 5.1 of the Penn Chinese Treebank 5.1 (CTB) (Xue et al., 2005). We followed previous work and used articles 001–270 and 440–1151 for training, 301–325 for development, and 271–300 for test. We also use the development set to tune the regularization parameter, $\lambda = 1e-3$.

Part-of-speech tagging is performed for all models using TurboTagger (Martins et al., 2013). Prior to training the d-parser, the training sections are automatically processed using 10-fold jackknifing (Collins and Koo, 2005) for both dependency and phrase structure trees. Zhu et al. (2013) found this simple technique gives an improvement to dependency accuracy of 0.4% on English and 2.0% on Chinese in their system.

During training, we use the d-parses induced by the head rules from the gold c-parses as constraints. There is a slight mismatch here with test, since these d-parses are guaranteed to be consistent with the target c-parse. We also experimented with using 10-fold jacknifing of the d-parser during training to produce more realistic parses; however, we found that this hurt performance of the parser.

Unless otherwise noted, in English the test d-parsing is done using the RedShift implementation[6] of the parser of Zhang and Nivre (2011), trained to follow the conventions of Collins head rules (Collins, 2003). This parser is a transition-based beam search parser, and the size of the beam $k$ controls a speed/accuracy trade-off. By default we use a beam of $k = 16$. We found that dependency labels have a significant impact on the performance of the RedShift parser, but not on English dependency conversion. We therefore train a labeled parser, but discard the labels.

For Chinese, we use the head rules compiled by Ding and Palmer (2005)[7]. For this data-set we trained the d-parser using the YaraParser implementation[8] of the parser of Zhang and Nivre (2011), because it has a better Chinese implementation. We use a beam of $k = 64$. In experiments, we found that Chinese labels were quite helpful, and added four additional features templates conjoining the label with the non-terminals of a rule.

Evaluation for phrase-structure parses is performed using the `evalb`[9] script with the standard setup. We report labeled $F_1$ scores as well as recall and precision. For dependency parsing, we report

[6] https://github.com/syllog1sm/redshift
[7] http://stp.lingfil.uu.se/~nivre/research/chn_headrules.txt
[8] https://github.com/yahoo/YaraParser
[9] http://nlp.cs.nyu.edu/evalb

| Model | PTB §23 $F_1$ | Sent./s. |
|---|---|---|
| Charniak (2000) | 89.5 | – |
| Stanford PCFG (2003) | 85.5 | 5.3 |
| Petrov (2007) | 90.1 | 8.6 |
| Zhu (2013) | 90.3 | 39.0 |
| Carreras (2008) | 91.1 | – |
| CJ Reranking (2005) | 91.5 | 4.3 |
| Stanford RNN (2013) | 90.0 | 2.8 |
| PAD | 90.4 | 34.3 |
| PAD (Pruned) | 90.3 | 58.6 |

| Model | CTB $F_1$ |
|---|---|
| Charniak (2000) | 80.8 |
| Bikel (2004) | 80.6 |
| Petrov (2007) | 83.3 |
| Zhu (2013) | 83.2 |
| PAD | 82.4 |

Table 3: Accuracy and speed on PTB §23 and CTB 5.1 test split. Comparisons are to state-of-the-art non-reranking supervised phrase-structure parsers (Charniak, 2000; Klein and Manning, 2003; Petrov and Klein, 2007; Carreras et al., 2008; Zhu et al., 2013; Bikel, 2004), and semi-supervised and reranking parsers (Charniak and Johnson, 2005; Socher et al., 2013).

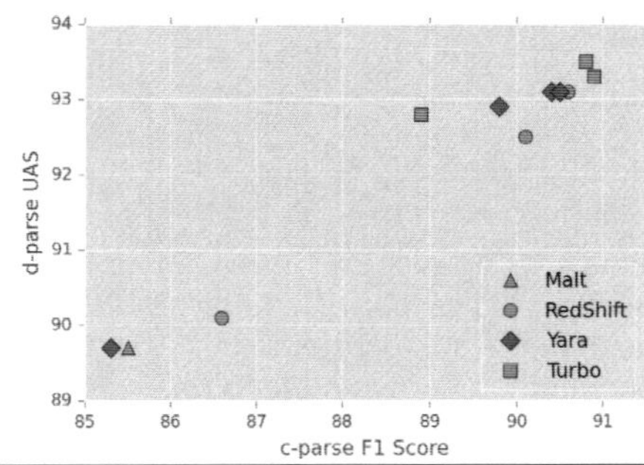


| Model | UAS | $F_1$ | Sent./s. | Oracle |
|---|---|---|---|---|
| MALTPARSER | 89.7 | 85.5 | 240.7 | 87.8 |
| RS-K1 | 90.1 | 86.6 | 233.9 | 87.6 |
| RS-K4 | 92.5 | 90.1 | 151.3 | 91.5 |
| RS-K16 | 93.1 | 90.6 | 58.6 | 92.5 |
| YARA-K1 | 89.7 | 85.3 | 1265.8 | 86.7 |
| YARA-K16 | 92.9 | 89.8 | 157.5 | 91.7 |
| YARA-K32 | 93.1 | 90.4 | 48.3 | 92.0 |
| YARA-K64 | 93.1 | 90.5 | 47.3 | 92.2 |
| TP-BASIC | 92.8 | 88.9 | 132.8 | 90.8 |
| TP-STANDARD | 93.3 | 90.9 | 27.2 | 92.6 |
| TP-FULL | 93.5 | 90.8 | 13.2 | 92.9 |

Table 4: The effect of d-parsing accuracy (PTB §22) on PAD and an oracle converter. Runtime includes d-parsing and c-parsing. Inputs include MaltParser (Nivre et al., 2006), the RedShift and the Yara implementations of the parser of Zhang and Nivre (2011) with various beam size, and three versions of TurboParser trained with projective constraints (Martins et al., 2013).

unlabeled accuracy score (UAS).

We implemented the grammar binarization, head rules, and pruning tables in Python, and the parser, features, and training in C++. Experiments are performed on a Lenovo ThinkCentre desktop computer with 32GB of memory and Core i7-3770 3.4GHz 8M cache CPU.

## 7 Experiments

We ran experiments to assess the accuracy of the method, its runtime efficiency, the effect of dependency parsing accuracy, and the effect of the amount of annotated phrase-structure data.

**Parsing Accuracy** Table 3 compares the accuracy and speed of the phrase-structure trees produced by the parser. For these experiments we treat our system and the Zhang-Nivre parser as an independently trained, but complete end-to-end c-parser. Runtime for these experiments includes both the time for d-parsing and conversion. Despite the fixed dependency constraints, the English results show that the parser is comparable in accuracy to many widely-used systems, and is significantly faster. The parser most competitive in both speed and accuracy is that of Zhu et al. (2013), a fast shift-reduce phrase-structure parser.

Furthermore, the Chinese results suggest that, even without making language-specific changes in the feature system we can still achieve competitive parsing accuracy.

**Effect of Dependencies** Table 4 shows experiments comparing the effect of different input d-parses. For these experiments we used the same version of PAD with 11 different d-parsers of varying quality and speed. We measure for each parser: its UAS, speed, and labeled $F_1$ when used with PAD and with an oracle converter.[10] The paired figure

[10]For a gold parse $y$ and predicted dependencies $\hat{d}$, define the oracle parse as $y' = \arg\min_{y' \in \mathcal{Y}(x,\hat{d})} \Delta(y, y')$

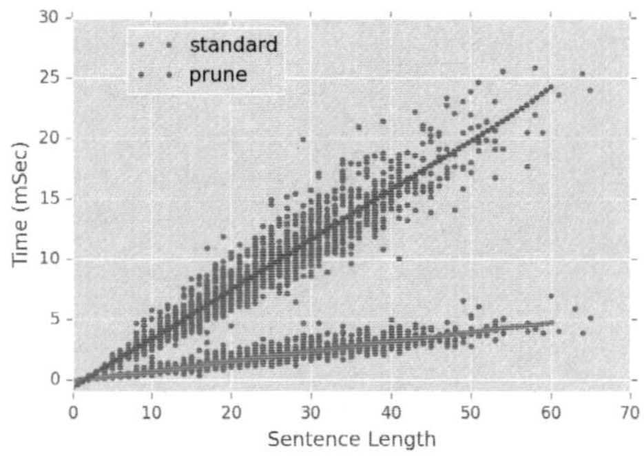


Figure 5: Empirical runtime of the parser on sentences of varying length, with and without pruning. Despite a worst-case quadratic complexity, observed runtime is linear.

| Class | | | Results | |
|---|---|---|---|---|
| Dep. $(h, m)$ | Span $\langle i, j\rangle$ | Split $k$ | Count | Acc. $A$ |
| + | + | + | 32853 | 97.9 |
| – | + | + | 381 | 69.3 |
| + | + | – | 802 | 83.3 |
| – | + | – | 496 | 85.9 |
| + | – | – | 1717 | 0.0 |
| – | – | – | 1794 | 0.0 |

Table 5: Error analysis of binary CFG rules. Rules used are split into classes based on correct (+) identification of dependency $(h, m)$, span $\langle i, j\rangle$, and split $k$. "Count" is the size of each class. "Acc." is the accuracy of span nonterminal identification.

shows that there is a direct correlation between the UAS of the inputs and labeled $F_1$.

**Runtime** In Section 3 we considered the theoretical complexity of the parsing model and presented the main speed results in Table 1. Despite having a quadratic theoretical complexity, the practical runtime was quite fast. Here we consider the empirical complexity of the model by measuring the time spent on individual sentences. Figure 5 shows parser speed for sentences of varying length for both the full algorithm and with pruning. In both cases the observed runtime is linear.

**Recovering Phrase-Structure Treebanks** Annotating phrase-structure trees is often more expensive and slower than annotating unlabeled dependency trees (Schneider et al., 2013). For low-resource languages, an alternative approach to developing fully annotated phrase-structure treebanks might be to label a small amount of c-parses and a large amount of cheaper d-parses. Assuming this setup, we ask how many c-parses would be necessary to obtain reasonable performance?

For this experiment, we train PAD on only 5% of the PTB training set and apply it to predicted d-parses from a fully-trained model. Even with this small amount of data, we obtain a parser with development score of $F_1 = 89.1\%$, which is comparable to Charniak (2000) and Stanford PCFG (Klein and Manning, 2003) trained on the complete c-parse training set. Additionally, if the gold dependencies are available, PAD with 5% training achieves $F_1 = 95.8\%$ on development, demonstrating a strong ability to recover the phrase-structure trees from dependency annotations.

**Analysis** Finally we consider an internal error analysis of the parser. For this analysis, we group each binary rule production selected by the parser by three properties: Is its dependency $(h, m)$ correct? Is its span $\langle i, j\rangle$ correct? Is its split $k$ correct? The first property is fully determined by the input d-parse, the others are partially determined by PAD itself.

Table 5 shows the breakdown. The conversion is almost always accurate ($\sim$98%) when the parser has correct span and dependency information. As expected, the difficult cases come when the dependency was fully incorrect, or there is a propagated span mistake. As dependency parsers improve, the performance of PAD should improve as well.

## 8 Conclusion

With recent advances in statistical dependency parsing, we find that fast, high-quality phrase-structure parsing is achievable using dependency parsing first, followed by a statistical conversion algorithm to fill in phrase-structure trees. Our implementation is available as open-source software at `https://github.com/ikekonglp/PAD`.

**Acknowledgments** The authors thank the anonymous reviewers and André Martins, Chris Dyer, and Slav Petrov for helpful feedback. This research was supported in part by NSF grant IIS-1352440 and computing resources provided by Google and the Pittsburgh Supercomputing Center.

## References


Daniel M Bikel. 2004. *On the parameter space of generative lexicalized statistical parsing models*. Ph.D. thesis, University of Pennsylvania.

Xavier Carreras, Michael Collins, and Terry Koo. 2008. Tag, dynamic programming, and the perceptron for efficient, feature-rich parsing. In *Proceedings of the Twelfth Conference on Computational Natural Language Learning*, pages 9–16. Association for Computational Linguistics.

Eugene Charniak and Mark Johnson. 2005. Coarse-to-fine n-best parsing and maxent discriminative reranking. In *Proceedings of the 43rd Annual Meeting on Association for Computational Linguistics*, pages 173–180. Association for Computational Linguistics.

Eugene Charniak. 2000. A maximum-entropy-inspired parser. In *Proceedings of the 1st North American chapter of the Association for Computational Linguistics conference*, pages 132–139. Association for Computational Linguistics.

Michael Collins and Terry Koo. 2005. Discriminative reranking for natural language parsing. *Computational Linguistics*, 31(1):25–70.

Michael Collins, Lance Ramshaw, Jan Hajič, and Christoph Tillmann. 1999. A statistical parser for czech. In *Proceedings of the 37th annual meeting of the Association for Computational Linguistics on Computational Linguistics*, pages 505–512. Association for Computational Linguistics.

Michael Collins. 2003. Head-driven statistical models for natural language parsing. *Computational linguistics*, 29(4):589–637.

Marie-Catherine De Marneffe and Christopher D Manning. 2008. The stanford typed dependencies representation. In *Coling 2008: Proceedings of the workshop on Cross-Framework and Cross-Domain Parser Evaluation*, pages 1–8. Association for Computational Linguistics.

Yuan Ding and Martha Palmer. 2005. Machine translation using probabilistic synchronous dependency insertion grammars. In *Proceedings of the 43rd Annual Meeting on Association for Computational Linguistics*, pages 541–548. Association for Computational Linguistics.

John Duchi, Elad Hazan, and Yoram Singer. 2011. Adaptive subgradient methods for online learning and stochastic optimization. *The Journal of Machine Learning Research*, 12:2121–2159.

Jason Eisner and Giorgio Satta. 1999. Efficient parsing for bilexical context-free grammars and head automaton grammars. In *Proceedings of the 37th annual meeting of the Association for Computational Linguistics on Computational Linguistics*, pages 457–464. Association for Computational Linguistics.

Daniel Fernández-González and André FT Martins. 2015. Parsing as reduction. *arXiv preprint arXiv:1503.00030*.

Johan Hall and Joakim Nivre. 2008. A dependency-driven parser for german dependency and constituency representations. In *Proceedings of the Workshop on Parsing German*, pages 47–54. Association for Computational Linguistics.

Johan Hall, Joakim Nivre, and Jens Nilsson. 2007. A hybrid constituency-dependency parser for swedish. In *Proceedings of NODALIDA*, pages 284–287.

David Hall, Greg Durrett, and Dan Klein. 2014. Less grammar, more features. In *ACL*.

Richard Johansson and Pierre Nugues. 2007. Extended constituent-to-dependency conversion for english. In *16th Nordic Conference of Computational Linguistics*, pages 105–112. University of Tartu.

Dan Klein and Christopher D Manning. 2002. Fast exact inference with a factored model for natural language parsing. In *Advances in neural information processing systems*, pages 3–10.

Dan Klein and Christopher D Manning. 2003. Accurate unlexicalized parsing. In *Proceedings of the 41st Annual Meeting on Association for Computational Linguistics-Volume 1*, pages 423–430. Association for Computational Linguistics.

Lingpeng Kong and Noah A Smith. 2014. An empirical comparison of parsing methods for stanford dependencies. *arXiv preprint arXiv:1404.4314*.

Mitchell P Marcus, Mary Ann Marcinkiewicz, and Beatrice Santorini. 1993. Building a large annotated corpus of english: The penn treebank. *Computational linguistics*, 19(2):313–330.

André FT Martins, Miguel Almeida, and Noah A Smith. 2013. Turning on the turbo: Fast third-order non-projective turbo parsers. In *ACL (2)*, pages 617–622.

Ryan McDonald. 2006. *Discriminative learning and spanning tree algorithms for dependency parsing*. Ph.D. thesis, University of Pennsylvania.

Joakim Nivre, Johan Hall, and Jens Nilsson. 2006. Maltparser: A data-driven parser-generator for dependency parsing. In *Proceedings of LREC*, volume 6, pages 2216–2219.

Slav Petrov and Dan Klein. 2007. Improved inference for unlexicalized parsing. In *HLT-NAACL*, pages 404–411. Citeseer.

Alexander M Rush, David Sontag, Michael Collins, and Tommi Jaakkola. 2010. On dual decomposition and linear programming relaxations for natural language processing. In *Proceedings of the 2010 Conference on Empirical Methods in Natural Language Processing*, pages 1–11. Association for Computational Linguistics.

Nathan Schneider, Brendan O'Connor, Naomi Saphra, David Bamman, Manaal Faruqui, Noah A Smith, Chris Dyer, and Jason Baldridge. 2013. A framework for (under) specifying dependency syntax without overloading annotators. *arXiv preprint arXiv:1306.2091*.

Richard Socher, John Bauer, Christopher D Manning, and Andrew Y Ng. 2013. Parsing with compositional vector grammars. In *In Proceedings of the ACL conference*.

Ben Taskar, Carlos Guestrin, and Daphne Koller. 2004. Max-margin Markov networks. In *Advances in Neural Information Processing Systems 16*.

Fei Xia and Martha Palmer. 2001. Converting dependency structures to phrase structures. In *Proceedings of the first international conference on Human language technology research*, pages 1–5. Association for Computational Linguistics.

Fei Xia, Owen Rambow, Rajesh Bhatt, Martha Palmer, and Dipti Misra Sharma. 2009. Towards a multi-representational treebank. In *The 7th International Workshop on Treebanks and Linguistic Theories. Groningen, Netherlands*.

Naiwen Xue, Fei Xia, Fu-Dong Chiou, and Martha Palmer. 2005. The penn chinese treebank: Phrase structure annotation of a large corpus. *Natural language engineering*, 11(02):207–238.

Hiroyasu Yamada and Yuji Matsumoto. 2003. Statistical dependency analysis with support vector machines. In *Proceedings of IWPT*, volume 3.

Yue Zhang and Joakim Nivre. 2011. Transition-based dependency parsing with rich non-local features. In *Proceedings of the 49th Annual Meeting of the Association for Computational Linguistics: Human Language Technologies: short papers-Volume 2*, pages 188–193. Association for Computational Linguistics.

Muhua Zhu, Yue Zhang, Wenliang Chen, Min Zhang, and Jingbo Zhu. 2013. Fast and accurate shift-reduce constituent parsing. In *ACL (1)*, pages 434–443.

# Improving the Inference of Implicit Discourse Relations via Classifying Explicit Discourse Connectives

**Attapol T. Rutherford**
Department of Computer Science
Brandeis University
Waltham, MA 02453, USA
tet@brandeis.edu

**Nianwen Xue**
Department of Computer Science
Brandeis University
Waltham, MA 02453, USA
xuen@brandeis.edu

## Abstract

Discourse relation classification is an important component for automatic discourse parsing and natural language understanding. The performance bottleneck of a discourse parser comes from implicit discourse relations, whose discourse connectives are not overtly present. Explicit discourse connectives can potentially be exploited to collect more training data to collect more data and boost the performance. However, using them indiscriminately has been shown to hurt the performance because not all discourse connectives can be dropped arbitrarily. Based on this insight, we investigate the interaction between discourse connectives and the discourse relations and propose the criteria for selecting the discourse connectives that can be dropped independently of the context without changing the interpretation of the discourse. Extra training data collected only by the freely omissible connectives improve the performance of the system without additional features.

## 1 Introduction

The analysis of discourse-level structure has received increasing attention from the field in recent years (Feng and Hirst, 2012; Patterson and Kehler, 2013; Li et al., 2014). Discourse-level analysis is typically concerned with relations between clauses and sentences, linguistic units that go beyond sentence boundaries. There are a few conceptions of the discourse structure representation of a text such as a tree (Mann and Thompson, 1988), or a graph (Wolf et al., 2005). In the work we describe here, we adopt the view of the Penn Discourse Treebank (PDTB) (Prasad et al., 2008), which views a text as a series of local discourse relations, each of which consists of a discourse connective as a predicate taking two arguments. Syntactically, these two arguments are typically realized as clauses or sentences. The discourse connective (underlined) can either be *explicit*, as in (1), or *implicit*, as in (2):

(1) [The city's Campaign Finance Board has refused to pay Mr Dinkins $95,142 in matching funds]$_{Arg1}$ <u>because</u> [his campaign records are incomplete]$_{Arg2}$.

(2) [So much of the stuff poured into its Austin, Texas, offices that its mail rooms there simply stopped delivering it]$_{Arg1}$. <u>Implicit=so</u> [Now, thousands of mailers, catalogs and sales pitches go straight into the trash]$_{Arg2}$.

Determining the sense of an explicit discourse relation such as (1) is straightforward since "because" is a strong indicator that the relation between the two arguments is CONTINGENCY.CAUSE. This task effectively amounts to disambiguating the sense of discourse connective, which can be done with high accuracy (Pitler et al., 2008).

However, in the absence of an explicit discourse connective, inferring the sense of a discourse relation has proved to a very challenging task (Park and Cardie, 2012; Rutherford and Xue, 2014). The sense is no longer localized on one or two discourse connectives and must now be inferred solely based on its two textual arguments. Given the limited amount of annotated data in comparison to the number of features needed, the process of building a classifier is plagued by the data sparsity problem (Li and Nenkova, 2014). As a result, the classification accuracy of implicit discourse relations remains much



*Human Language Technologies: The 2015 Annual Conference of the North American Chapter of the ACL*, pages 799–808,
Denver, Colorado, May 31 – June 5, 2015. 

lower than that of explicit discourse relations (Pitler et al., 2008).

One potential method for reducing the data sparsity problem is through a distantly supervised learning paradigm, which is the direction we take in this work. Distant supervision approaches make use of prior knowledge or heuristics to cheaply obtain *weakly labeled data*, which potentially contain a small number of false labels. Weakly labeled data can be collected from unannotated data and incorporated in the model training process to supplement manually labeled data. For our task, we can collect instances of explicit discourse relations from unannotated data by some simple heuristics. After dropping the discourse connectives, we should be able to treat them as additional implicit discourse relations.

The approach assumes that when the discourse connective is omitted, the discourse relation remains the same, which is a popular assumption in discourse analysis (Fraser, 2006; Schourup, 1999). This assumption turns out to be too strong in many cases as illustrated in (3):

(3) [I want to go home for the holiday]$_{Arg1}$. Nonetheless, [I will book a flight to Hawaii]$_{Arg2}$.

If "Nonetheless" is dropped in (3), one can no longer infer the COMPARISON relation. Instead, one would naturally infer a CONTINGENCY relation. Dropping the connective and adding the relation as a training sample adds noise to the training set and can only hurt the performance. In addition, certain types of explicit discourse relations have no corresponding implicit discourse relations. For example, discourse relations of the type CONTINGENY.CONDITION are almost always expressed with an explicit discourse connective and do not exist in implicit relations. We believe this also explains the lack of success in previous attempts to boost the performance of implicit discourse relation detection with this approach. (Biran and McKeown, 2013; Pitler et al., 2009). This suggests that in order for this approach to work, we need to identify instances of explicit discourse relations that closely match the characteristics of implicit discourse relations.

In this paper, we propose two criteria for selecting such explicit discourse relation instances: *omission rate* and *context differential*. Our selection criteria first classify discourse connectives by their distributional properties and suggest that not all discourse connectives are truly optional and not all implicit and explicit discourse relations are equivalent, contrary to commonly held beliefs in previous studies of discourse connectives. We show that only the freely omissible discourse connectives gather additional training instances that lead to significant performance gain against a strong baseline. Our approach improves the performance of implicit discourse relations without additional feature engineering in many settings and opens doors to more sophisticated models that require more training data.

The rest of the paper is structured as follows. In Section 2, we describe the discourse connective selection criteria. In Section 3, we present our discourse connective classification method and experimental results that demonstrate its impact on inferring implicit discourse relations. We discuss related work and conclude our findings in Section 4 and 5 respectively.

## 2 Discourse Connective Classification and Discourse Relation Extraction

### 2.1 Datasets used for selection

We use two datasets for the purposes of extracting and selecting weakly labeled explicit discourse relation instances: the Penn Discourse Treebank 2.0 (Prasad et al., 2008) and the English Gigaword corpus version 3 (Graff et al., 2007).

The Penn Discourse Treebank (PDTB) is the largest manually annotated corpus of discourse relations on top of one million word tokens from the Wall Street Journal (Prasad et al., 2008; Prasad et al., 2007). Each discourse relation in the PDTB is annotated with a semantic sense in the PDTB sense hierarchy, which has three levels: CLASS, TYPE and SUBTYPE. In this work, we are primarily concerned with the four top-level CLASS senses: EXPANSION, COMPARISON, CONTINGENCY, and TEMPORAL. The distribution of top-level senses of implicit discourse relations is shown in Table 2. The spans of text that participate in the discourse relation are also explicitly annotated. These are called ARG1 or ARG2, depending on its relationship with the discourse connective.

The PDTB is our corpus of choice for its lexical

groundedness. The existence of a discourse relation must be linked or grounded to a discourse connective. More importantly, this applies to not only explicit discourse connectives that occur naturally as part of the text but also to implicit discourse relations where a discourse connective is added by annotators during the annotation process. This is crucial to the work reported here in that it allows us to compare the distribution of the same connective in explicit and implicit discourse relations. In the next subsection, we will explain in detail how we compute the comparison measures and apply them to the selection of explicit discourse connectives that can be used for collecting good weakly labeled data.

We use the Gigaword corpus, a large unannotated newswire corpus, to extract and select instances of explicit discourse discourse relations to supplement the manually annotated instances from the PDTB. The Gigaword corpus is used for its large size of 2.9 billion words and its similarity to the Wall Street Journal data from the PDTB. The source of the corpus is drawn from six distinct international sources of English newswire dating from 1994 - 2006. We use this corpus to extract weakly labeled data for the experiment.

## 2.2 Discourse relation extraction pattern

We extract instances of explicit discourse relations from the Gigaword Corpus that have the same patterns as the implicit discourse relations in the PDTB, using simple regular expressions. We first sentence-segment the Gigaword Corpus using the NLTK sentence segmenter (Bird, 2006). We then write a set of rules to prevent some common erroneous cases such as *because* vs *because of* from being included.

If a discourse connective is a subordinating conjunction, then we use the following pattern:

```
(Clause 1) (connective) (clause 2).
```

Clause 1 and capitalized clause 2 are then used as *Arg1* and *Arg2* respectively.

If a discourse connective is a coordinating conjunction or discourse adverbial, we use the following pattern:

```
(Sentence 1). (Connective),(clause 2).
```

Sentence 1 and Clause 2 with the first word capitalized are used as *Arg1* and *Arg2* respectively.

Although there are obviously many other syntactic patterns associated with explicit discourse connectives, we use these two patterns because these are the only patterns that are also observed in the implicit discourse relations. We want to select instances of explicit discourse relations that match the argument patterns of implicit discourse relations as much as possible. As restrictive as this may seem, these two patterns along with the set of rules allow us to extract more than 200,000 relation instances from the Gigaword corpus, so the coverage is not an issue.

## 2.3 Discourse connective selection and classification criteria

We hypothesize that connectives that are omitted often and in a way that is insensitive to the semantic context are our ideal candidates for extracting good weakly labeled data. We call this type of connectives *freely omissible discourse connectives*. To search for this class of connectives, we need to characterize connectives by the rate at which they are omitted and by the similarity between their context, in this case their arguments, in explicit and implicit discourse relations. This is possible because implicit discourse connectives are inserted during annotation in the PDTB. For each discourse connective, we can compute *omission rate* and *context differential* from annotated explicit and implicit discourse relation instances in the PDTB and use those measures to classify and select discourse connectives.

### 2.3.1 Omission rate (OR)

We use *omission rates* (OR) to measure the level of optionality of a discourse connective. The omission rate of a type of discourse connective (DC) is defined as:

$$\frac{\text{\# occurrences of DC in implicit relations}}{\text{\# total occurrences of DC}}$$

Our intuition is that the discourse connectives that have a high level of omission rate are more suitable as supplemental training data to infer the sense of implicit discourse relations.

### 2.3.2 Context differential

The omission of a freely omissible discourse connective should also be context-independent. If the omission of a discourse connective leads to a different interpretation of the discourse relation, this means that the explicit and implicit discourse relations bound by this discourse connective are not equivalent, and the explicit discourse relation instance cannot be used to help infer the sense of the implicit discourse relation. Conversely, if the contexts for the discourse connective in explicit and implicit discourse relations do not significantly differ, then the explicit discourse relation instance can be used as weakly labeled data.

To capture this intuition, we must quantify the context differential of explicit and implicit discourse relations for each discourse connective. We represent the semantic context of a discourse connective through a unigram distribution over words in its two arguments, with Arg1 and Arg2 combined. We use Jensen-Shannon Divergence (JSD) as a metric for measuring the difference between the contexts of a discourse connective in implicit and explicit discourse relations. Computing a context differential of the discourse connective therefore involves fitting a unigram distribution from all implicit discourse relations bound by that discourse connective and fitting another from all explicit discourse relations bound by the same discourse connective. We choose this method because it has been shown to be exceptionally effective in capturing similarities of discourse connectives (Hutchinson, 2005) and statistical language analysis in general (Lee, 2001; Ljubesic et al., 2008).

The Jensen-Shannon Divergence (JSD) metric for difference between $P_o$, the semantic environments (unigram distribution of words in Arg1 and Arg2 combined) in implicit discourse relations, and $P_r$, the semantic environments in explicit discourse relations, is defined as:

$$JSD(P_o||P_r) = \frac{1}{2}D(P_o||M) + \frac{1}{2}D(P_r||M)$$

where $M = \frac{1}{2}(P_o + P_r)$ is a mixture of the two distributions and $D(.||.)$ is Kullback-Leibler divergence function for discrete probability distributions:

$$D(P||Q) = \sum_i \ln(\frac{P(i)}{Q(i)})P(i)$$

### 2.4 Discourse Connective Classification

Using the two metrics, we can classify discourse connectives into the following classes:

1. Freely omissible: High OR and low JSD
2. Omissible: Low non-zero OR and low JSD.
3. Alternating I: High OR and high JSD.
4. Alternating II: Low non-zero OR and high JSD.
5. Non-omissible: Zero OR. JSD cannot be computed because the connectives are never found in any implicit discourse relations.

Classifying the connectives into these classes allow us to empirically investigate which explicit discourse relations are useful as supplemental training data for determining the sense of implicit discourse relations. We discuss each type of connectives below.

#### 2.4.1 Freely omissible discourse connectives

These are connectives whose usage in implicit and explicit discourse relations is indistinguishable and therefore suitable as a source of supplemental training data. These connectives are defined as having high omission rate and low context differential. This definition implies that the omission is frequent and insensitive to the context. "Because" and "in particular" in (4) and (5) are such connectives. Dropping them has minimal impact on the understanding the discourse relation between their two arguments and one might argue they even make the sentences sound more natural.

(4) We cleared up questions and inconsistencies very quickly because the people who had the skills and perspective required to resolve them were part of the task team. (WSJ0562)

(5) Both companies are conservative marketers that rely on extensive market research. P&G, in particular, rarely rolls out a product nationally before extensive test-marketing. (WSJ0589)

#### 2.4.2 Omissible discourse connectives

They are connectives whose usage in implicit and explicit discourse relations is indistinguishable, yet they are not often omitted because the discourse relation might be hard to interpret without them. These connectives are defined as having low omission rate and low context differential. For example,

(6) Such problems will require considerable skill to resolve. However, neither Mr. Baum nor Mr. Harper has much international experience. (WSJ0109)

One can infer from the discourse that the problems require international experience, but Mr. Baum and Mr. Harper don't have that experience even without the discourse connective "however". In other words, the truth value of this proposition is not affected by the presence or absence of this discourse connective. The sentence might sound a bit less natural, and the discourse relation seems a bit more difficult to infer if "however" is omitted.

#### 2.4.3 Alternating discourse connectives

They are connectives whose usage in implicit and explicit discourse relations is substantially different and they are defined as having high context differential. Having high context differential means that the two arguments of an explicit discourse connective differ substantially from those of an implicit discourse. An example of such discourse connectives is "nevertheless" in (7). If the discourse connective is dropped, one might infer EXPANSION or CONTINGENCY relation instead of COMPARISON indicated by the connective.

(7) Plant Genetic's success in creating genetically engineered male steriles doesn't automatically mean it would be simple to create hybrids in all crops. Nevertheless, he said, he is negotiating with Plant Genetic to acquire the technology to try breeding hybrid cotton. (WSJ0209)

We hypothesize that this type of explicit discourse relations would not be useful as extra training instances for inferring implicit discourse relations because they will only add noise to the training set.

#### 2.4.4 Non-omissible discourse connectives

They are defined as discourse connectives whose omission rate is close to zero as they are never found in implicit discourse relations. For example, conditionals can not be easily expressed without the use of an explicit discourse connective like "if". We hypothesize that instances of explicit discourse relations with such discourse connectives would not be useful as additional training data for inferring implicit discourse relations because they represent discourse relation senses that do not exist in the implicit discourse relations.

## 3 Experiments

### 3.1 Partitioning the discourse connectives

We only include the discourse connectives that appear in both explicit and implicit discourse connectives in the PDTB to make the comparison and classification possible. As a result, we only analyze 69 out of 134 connectives for the purpose of classification. We also leave out 15 connectives whose most frequent sense acccounts for less than 90% of their instances. For example, *since* can indicate a TEMPORAL sense or a CONTINGENCY sense of almost equal chance, so it is not readily useful for gathering weakly labeled data. Ultimately, we have 54 connectives as our candidates for freely omissible discourse connectives.

We first classify the discourse connectives based on their omission rates and context differentials as discussed in the previous section and partition all of the explicit discourse connective instances based on this classification. The distributions of omission rates and context differentials show substantial amount of variation among different connectives. Many connectives are rarely omitted and naturally form its own class of non-omissible discourse connectives (Figure 1). We run the agglomerative hierchical clustering algorithm using Euclidean distance on the rest of the connectives to divide them into two groups: high omission and low omission rates. The boundary between the two groups is around 0.65.

The distribution of discourse connectives with respect to the context differential suggests two distinct groups across the two corpora (Figure 2). The analysis only includes connectives that are omitted at least twenty times in the PDTB corpus, so that JSD can be computed. The hierarchical clustering algorithm divides the connectives into two groups with the boundary at around 0.32, as should be apparent from the histogram. The JSD's computed from the explicit discourse relations from the two corpora are highly correlated ($\rho = 0.80$, $p < 0.05$), so we can safely use the Gigaword corpus for the analysis and evaluation.

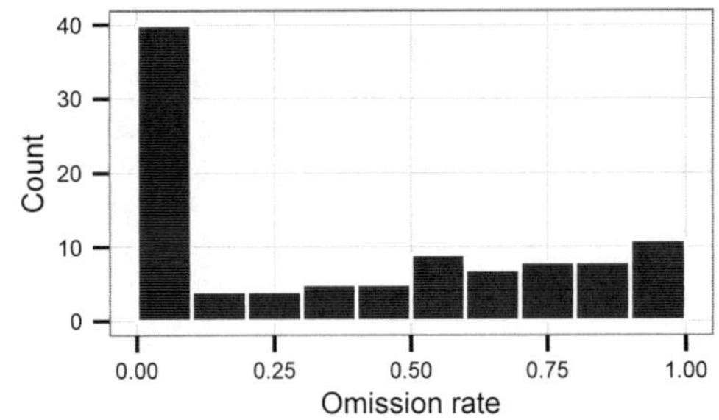


Figure 1: Omission rates of the discourse connective types vary drastically, suggesting that connectives vary in their optionality. Some connectives are never omitted.

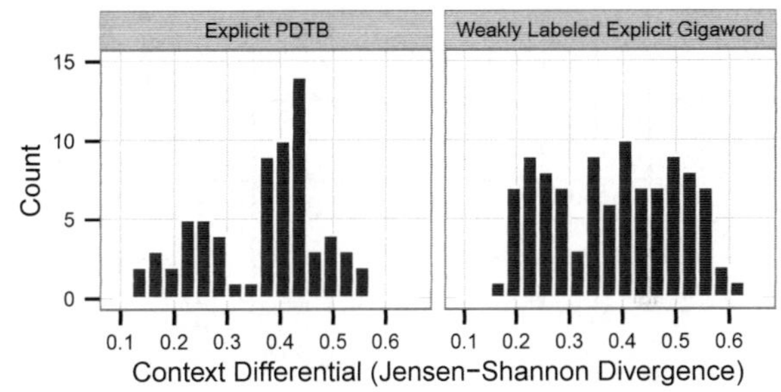


Figure 2: The distributions of Jensen-Shannon Divergence from both corpora shows two potential distinct clusters of discourse connectives.

The omission rate boundary and context differential boundary together classify the discourse connectives into four classes in addition to the non-omissible connectives. When plotted against each other, omission rates and context differential together group the discourse connectives nicely into clusters (Figure 3). For the purpose of evaluation, we combine Alternating I and II into one class because each individual class is too sparse on its own. The complete discourse connective classification result is displayed in Table 1.

| Sense | Train | Dev | Test |
|---|---|---|---|
| Comparison | 1855 | 189 | 145 |
| Contingency | 3235 | 281 | 273 |
| Expansion | 6673 | 638 | 538 |
| Temporal | 582 | 48 | 55 |
| Total | 12345 | 1156 | 1011 |

Table 2: The distribution of senses of implicit discourse relations in the PDTB

| Class Name | OR | JSD | Connectives |
|---|---|---|---|
| Alternating I | High | High | further, in sum, in the end, overall, similarly, whereas |
| Alternating II | Low | High | earlier, in turn, nevertheless, on the other hand, ultimately |
| Freely Omissible | High | Low | accordingly, as a result, because, by comparison, by contrast, consequently, for example, for instance, furthermore, in fact, in other words, in particular, in short, indeed, previously, rather, so, specifically, therefore, |
| Omissible | Low | Low | also, although, and, as, but, however, in addition, instead, meanwhile, moreover, rather, since, then, thus, while |
| Non-omissible | zero | NA | as long as, if, nor, now that, once, otherwise, unless, until |

Table 1: Classification of discourse connectives based on omission rate (OR) and Jensen-Shannon Divergence context differential (JSD).

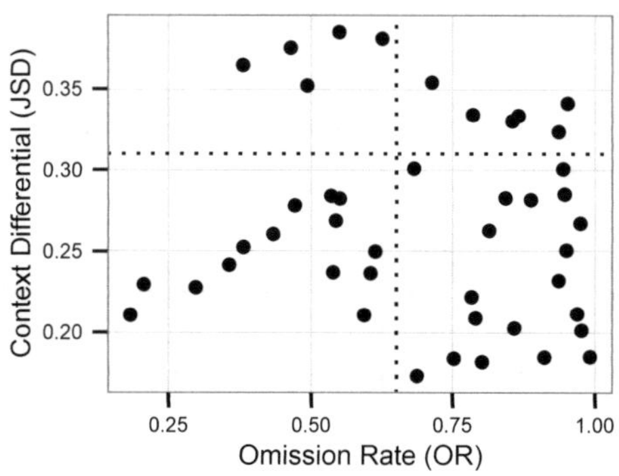


Figure 3: The scattergram of the discourse connectives suggest three distinct classes. Each dot represents a discourse connective.

### 3.2 Evaluation results

We formulate the implicit relation classification task as a 4-way classification task in a departure from previous practice where the task is usually set up as four *one vs other* binary classification tasks so that the effect of adding the distant supervision from the weakly labeled data can be more easily studied. We also believe this setup is more natural in realistic settings. Each classification instance consists of the two arguments of an implicit discourse relation, typically adjacent pairs of sentences in a text. The distribution of the sense labels is shown in Table 2. We follow the data split used in previous work for a consistent comparison (Rutherford and Xue, 2014). The PDTB corpus is split into a training set, development set, and test set. Sections 2 to 20 are used to train classifiers. Sections 0 and 1 are used for developing feature sets and tuning models. Section 21 and 22 are used for testing the systems.

To evaluate our method for selecting explicit discourse relation instances, we extract weakly labeled discourse relations from the Gigaword corpus for each class of discourse connective such that the discourse connectives are equally represented within the class. We train and test Maximum Entropy classifiers by adding varying number (1000, 2000, ..., 20000) of randomly selected explicit discourse discourse relation instances to the manually annotated implicit discourse relations in the PDTB as training data. We do this for each class of discourse connectives as presented in Table 1. We perform 30 trials of this experiment and compute average accuracy rates to smooth out the variation from random shuffling of the weakly labeled data.

The statistical models used in this study are from the MALLET implementation with its default setting (McCallum, 2002). Features used in all experiments are taken from the state-of-the-art implicit discourse relation classification system (Rutherford and Xue, 2014). The feature set consists of combinations of various lexical features, production rules, and Brown cluster pairs. These features are described in greater detail by Pitler et al. (2009) and Rutherford and Xue (2014).

Instance reweighting is required when using weakly labeled data because the training set no longer represents the natural distribution of the labels. We reweight each instance such that the sums of the weights of all the instances of the same label are equal. More precisely, if an instance $i$ is from class $j$, then the weight for the instance $w_{ij}$ is equal to the inverse proportion of class $j$:

$$w_{ij} = \frac{\text{Number of total instances}}{\text{Size of class } j \cdot \text{Number of classes}} = \frac{\sum_{j'}^{k} c_{j'}}{c_j \cdot k} = \frac{n}{c_j \cdot k}$$

where $c_j$ is the total number of instances from class $j$ and $k$ is the number of classes in the dataset of size $n$. It is trivial to show that the sum of the weights for all instances from class $j$ is exactly $\frac{n}{k}$ for all classes.

The impact of different classes of weakly labeled explicit discourse connective relations is illustrated in Figure 4. The results show that expicit discourse relations with freely omissible discourse connectives (high OR and low JSD) improve the performance on the standard test set and outperform the other classes of discourse connectives and the naive approach where all of the discourse

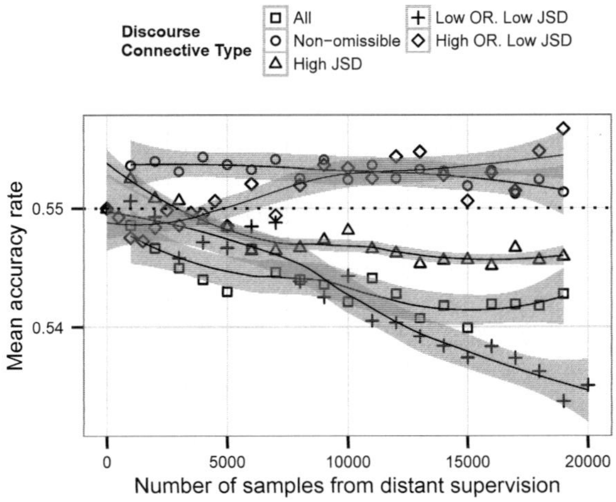


Figure 4: Discourse connectives with high omission rates and low context differentials lead to highest performance boost over the state-of-the-art baseline (dotted line). Each point is an average over multiple trials. The solid lines are LOESS smoothing curves.

connectives are used. In addition, it shows that on average, the system with weakly labeled data from freely omissible discourse connectives continues to rise as we increase the number of samples unlike the other classes of discourse connectives, which show the opposite trend. This suggests that discourse connectives must have both high omission rates and low context differential between implicit and explicit use of the connectives in order to be helpful to the inference of implicit discourse relations.

Table 3 presents results that show, overall, our best performing system, the one using distant supervision from freely omissible discourse connectives, raises the accuracy rate from 0.550 to 0.571 ($p < 0.05$; bootstrap test) and the macro-average $F_1$ score from 0.384 to 0.405. We achieve such performance after we tune the subset of weakly labeled data to maximize the performance on the development set. Our distant supervision approach improves the performance by adding more weakly labeled data and no additional features.

For a more direct comparison with previous results, we also replicated the state-of-the-art system described in Rutherford and Xue (2014), who follows the practice of the first work on this topic (Pitler et al., 2009) in setting up the task as four binary one vs. other classifiers. The results are presented in Table 4. The results show that the extra data extracted from the Gigaword Corpus is particularly helpful for minority classes such as *Comparison vs. Others* and *Temporal vs Others*, where our current system significantly outperforms that of Rutherford and Xue (2014). Interestingly, the *Expansion vs. Others* classifier did not improve as the *Expansion* class in the four-way classification (Table 3).

| | | Baseline features | Baseline + extra data |
|---|---|---|---|
| Expansion | Precision | 0.608 | 0.614 |
| | Recall | 0.751 | 0.788 |
| | $F_1$ | 0.672 | 0.691 |
| Comparison | Precision | 0.398 | 0.449 |
| | Recall | 0.228 | 0.276 |
| | $F_1$ | 0.290 | 0.342 |
| Contingency | Precision | 0.465 | 0.493 |
| | Recall | 0.418 | 0.396 |
| | $F_1$ | 0.440 | 0.439 |
| Temporal | Precision | 0.263 | 0.385 |
| | Recall | 0.091 | 0.091 |
| | $F_1$ | 0.135 | 0.147 |
| Accuracy | | 0.550 | **0.571** |
| Macro-Average $F_1$ | | 0.384 | **0.405** |

Table 3: Our current 4-way classification system outperforms the baseline overall. The difference in accuracy is statistically significant ($p < 0.05$; bootstrap test).

| | R&X (2014) | Baseline + extra data | Baseline |
|---|---|---|---|
| Comparison vs Others | 0.397 | **0.410** | 0.380 |
| Contingency vs Others | 0.544 | 0.538 | 0.539 |
| Expansion vs Others | 0.702 | 0.694 | 0.679 |
| Temporal vs Others | 0.287 | **0.333** | 0.246 |

Table 4: The performance of our approach on the binary classification task formulation.

### 3.3 Just how good is the weakly labeled data?

We performed additional experiments to get a sense of just how good the weakly labeled data extracted from an unlabeled corpus are. Table 5 presents four-way classification results using just the weakly labeled data from the Gigaword Corpus. The results show that the same trend holds when the implicit relations from the PDTB are not included in the training process. The freely omissible discourse connectives achieves the accuracy rate of 0.505, which is significantly higher than the other classes, but they are weaker than the manually labeled data, which achieves the accuracy rate of 0.550 for the same number of training instances.

Weakly labeled data are not perfectly equivalent to the true implicit discourse relations, but they do provide strong enough additional signal. Figure 5 presents experimental results that compare the impact of weakly labeled data from Gigaword Corpus vs gold standard data from the PDTB for the freely omissible class. The mean accuracy rates from the PDTB data are significantly higher than those from the Gigaword Corpus ($p$ <0.05; $t$-test

| Class | Gigaword only | Gigaword + Implicit PDTB |
|---|---|---|
| Freely omissible | **0.505** | **0.571** |
| Omissible | 0.313 | 0.527 |
| Alternating I + II | 0.399 | 0.546 |
| Non-Omissible | 0.449 | 0.554 |
| All of above | 0.490 | 0.547 |

Table 5: The accuracy rates for the freely omissible class are higher than the ones for the other classes both when using the Gigaword data alone and when using it in conjunction with the implicit relations in the PDTB.

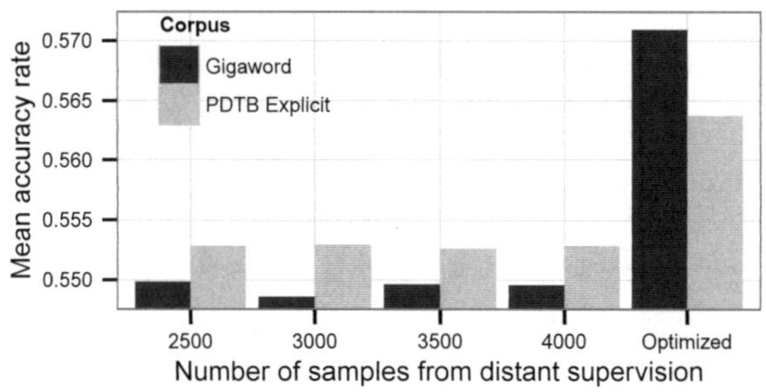


Figure 5: The PDTB corpus leads to more improvement for the same amount of the data. However, Gigaword corpus achieves significantly better performance ($p < 0.05$; bootstrap test) when both models are tuned on the developement set.

and bootstrap test) for the same number of training instances combined with the implicit discourse relations. However, when the number of introduced weakly labeled data exceeds a certain threshold of around 12,000 instances, the performance of the Gigaword corpus rises significantly above the baseline and the explicit PDTB (Figure 4).

The relative superiority of our approach derives precisely from the two selection criteria that we propose. The performance gain does not come from the fact that freely omissible discourse connectives have better coverage of all four senses (Table 6). When all classes are combined equally, the system performs worse as we add more samples although all four senses are covered. The coverage of all four senses is not sufficient for a class of discourse connectives to boost the performance. The two selection criteria are both necessary for the success of this paradigm.

## 4 Related work

Previous work on implicit discourse relation classification have focused on supervised learning approaches (Lin et al., 2010; Rutherford and Xue, 2014), and the distantly supervised approach using explicit discourse relations

| Class | Sense Comp. | Cont. | Exp. | Temp. |
|---|---|---|---|---|
| Freely omissible | 2 | 6 | 10 | 1 |
| Omissible | 4 | 2 | 5 | 3 |
| Alternating I | 1 | 0 | 5 | 0 |
| Alternating II | 2 | 0 | 0 | 3 |
| Non-omissible | 0 | 3 | 3 | 2 |

Table 6: The sense distribution by connective class.

has not shown satisfactory results (Pitler et al., 2009; Park and Cardie, 2012; Wang et al., 2012; Sporleder and Lascarides, 2008) Explicit discourse relations have been used to remedy the sparsity problem or gain extra features with limited success (Biran and McKeown, 2013; Pitler et al., 2009). Our heuristics for extracting discourse relations has been explored in the unsupervised setting (Marcu and Echihabi, 2002), but it has never been evaluated on the gold standard data to show its true efficacy. Our distant supervision approach chooses only certain types of discourse connectives to extract weakly labeled data and is the first of its kind to improve the performance in this task tested on the manually annotated data.

Distant supervision approaches have recently been explored in the context of natural language processing due to the recent capability to process large amount of data. These approaches are known to be particularly useful for relation extraction tasks because training data provided do not suffice for the task and are difficult to obtain (Riloff et al., 1999; Yao et al., 2010). For example, Mintz et al. (2009) acquire a large amount of weakly labeled data based on the Freebase knowledge base and improves the performance of relation extraction. Distantly supervised learning has also recently been demonstrated to be useful for text classification problems (Speriosu et al., 2011; Marchetti-Bowick and Chambers, 2012). For example, Thamrongrattanarit et al. (2013) use simple heuristics to gather weakly labeled data to perform text classification with no manually annotated training data.

Discourse connectives have been studied and classified based on their syntactic properties such subordinating conjunction, adverbials, etc. (Fraser, 2006; Fraser, 1996). While providing a useful insight into how discourse connectives fit into utterances, the syntactic classification does not seem suitable for selecting useful discourse connectives for our purposes of distant supervision for our task.

## 5 Conclusion and Future Directions

We propose two selection criteria for discourse connectives that can be used to gather weakly labeled data for implicit discourse relation classifiers and improve the performance of the state-of-the-art system without further feature engineering. As part of this goal, we classify discourse connectives based on their distributional semantic properties and found that certain classes of discourse connectives cannot be omitted in every context, which plague the weakly labeled data used in previous studies. Our discourse connective classification allows for the better selection of data points for distant supervision.

More importantly, this work presents a new direction in distantly supervised learning paradigm for implicit discourse relation classification. This virtual dramatic increase in the training set size allows for more feature engineering and more sophisticated models. Implicit discourse relation classification is now no longer limited to strictly supervised learning approaches.

## Acknowledgments

This work was funded partially by the National Science Foundation via Grant No. 0910532 entitled "Richer Representations for Machine Translation". All views expressed in this paper are those of the authors and do not necessarily represent the view of the National Science Foundation. We also would like to thank Karl Pichotta and Gary Patterson for feedback on the manuscript and the three anonymous reviewers for their suggestions and comments.

## References

Or Biran and Kathleen McKeown. 2013. Aggregated word pair features for implicit discourse relation disambiguation. In *Proceedings of the 51st Annual Meeting of the Association for Computational Linguistics*, pages 69–73. The Association for Computational Linguistics.

Steven Bird. 2006. Nltk: the natural language toolkit. In *Proceedings of the COLING/ACL on Interactive presentation sessions*, pages 69–72. Association for Computational Linguistics.

Vanessa Wei Feng and Graeme Hirst. 2012. Text-level discourse parsing with rich linguistic features. In *Proceedings of the 50th Annual Meeting of the Association for Computational Linguistics: Long Papers-Volume 1*, pages 60–68. Association for Computational Linguistics.

Bruce Fraser. 1996. Pragmatic markers. *Pragmatics*, 6:167–190.

Bruce Fraser. 2006. Towards a theory of discourse markers. *Approaches to discourse particles*, 1:189–204.

D Graff, J Kong, K Chen, and K Maeda. 2007. English gigaword third edition, 2007, ldc 2007t07.

Ben Hutchinson. 2005. Modelling the similarity of discourse connectives. In *Proceedings of the the 27th Annual Meeting of the Cognitive Science Society (CogSci2005)*.

Lillian Lee. 2001. On the effectiveness of the skew divergence for statistical language analysis. In *Artificial Intelligence and Statistics*, volume 2001, pages 65–72.

Junyi Jessy Li and Ani Nenkova. 2014. Reducing sparsity improves the recognition of implicit discourse relations. In *Proceedings of the 15th Annual Meeting of the Special Interest Group on Discourse and Dialogue (SIGDIAL)*, pages 199–207, Philadelphia, PA, U.S.A., June. Association for Computational Linguistics.

Jiwei Li, Rumeng Li, and Eduard Hovy. 2014. Recursive deep models for discourse parsing. In *Proceedings of the 2014 Conference on Empirical Methods in Natural Language Processing (EMNLP)*, pages 2061–2069.

Ziheng Lin, Hwee Tou Ng, and Min-Yen Kan. 2010. A PDTB-Styled End-to-End Discourse Parser. *arXiv.org*, November.

N Ljubesic, Damir Boras, Nikola Bakaric, and Jasmina Njavro. 2008. Comparing measures of semantic similarity. In *Information Technology Interfaces, 2008. ITI 2008. 30th International Conference on*, pages 675–682. IEEE.

William C Mann and Sandra A Thompson. 1988. Rhetorical structure theory: Toward a functional theory of text organization. *Text*, 8(3):243–281.

Micol Marchetti-Bowick and Nathanael Chambers. 2012. Learning for microblogs with distant supervision: Political forecasting with twitter. In *Proceedings of the 13th Conference of the European Chapter of the Association for Computational Linguistics*, pages 603–612. Association for Computational Linguistics.

Daniel Marcu and Abdessamad Echihabi. 2002. An unsupervised approach to recognizing discourse relations. In *Proceedings of the 40th Annual Meeting on Association for Computational Linguistics*, pages 368–375. Association for Computational Linguistics.

Andrew Kachites McCallum. 2002. Mallet: A machine learning for language toolkit. http://www.cs.umass.edu/ mccallum/mallet.

Mike Mintz, Steven Bills, Rion Snow, and Dan Jurafsky. 2009. Distant supervision for relation extraction without labeled data. In *Proceedings of the Joint Conference of the 47th Annual Meeting of the ACL and the 4th International Joint Conference on Natural Language Processing of the AFNLP: Volume 2-Volume 2*, pages 1003–1011. Association for Computational Linguistics.

Joonsuk Park and Claire Cardie. 2012. Improving implicit discourse relation recognition through feature set optimization. In *Proceedings of the 13th Annual Meeting of the Special Interest Group on Discourse and Dialogue*, pages 108–112. Association for Computational Linguistics.

Gary Patterson and Andrew Kehler. 2013. Predicting the presence of discourse connectives. In *Proceedings of the Conference on Empirical Methods in Natural Language Processing*. Association for Computational Linguistics.

Emily Pitler, Mridhula Raghupathy, Hena Mehta, Ani Nenkova, Alan Lee, and Aravind K Joshi. 2008. Easily identifiable discourse relations. *Technical Reports (CIS)*, page 884.

Emily Pitler, Annie Louis, and Ani Nenkova. 2009. Automatic sense prediction for implicit discourse relations in text. In *Proceedings of the Joint Conference of the 47th Annual Meeting of the ACL and the 4th International Joint Conference on Natural Language Processing of the AFNLP: Volume 2-Volume 2*, pages 683–691. Association for Computational Linguistics.

Rashmi Prasad, Eleni Miltsakaki, Nikhil Dinesh, Alan Lee, Aravind Joshi, Livio Robaldo, and Bonnie L Webber. 2007. The penn discourse treebank 2.0 annotation manual.

Rashmi Prasad, Nikhil Dinesh, Alan Lee, Eleni Miltsakaki, Livio Robaldo, Aravind K Joshi, and Bonnie L Webber. 2008. The penn discourse treebank 2.0. In *LREC*. Citeseer.

Ellen Riloff, Rosie Jones, et al. 1999. Learning dictionaries for information extraction by multi-level bootstrapping. In *AAAI/IAAI*, pages 474–479.

Attapol T. Rutherford and Nianwen Xue. 2014. Discovering implicit discourse relations through brown cluster pair representation and coreference patterns. In *Proceedings of the 14th Conference of the European Chapter of the Association for Computational Linguistics (EACL 2014)*, Gothenburg, Sweden, April.

Lawrence Schourup. 1999. Discourse markers. *Lingua*, 107(3):227–265.

Michael Speriosu, Nikita Sudan, Sid Upadhyay, and Jason Baldridge. 2011. Twitter polarity classification with label propagation over lexical links and the follower graph. In *Proceedings of the First workshop on Unsupervised Learning in NLP*, pages 53–63. Association for Computational Linguistics.

Caroline Sporleder and Alex Lascarides. 2008. Using automatically labelled examples to classify rhetorical relations: An assessment. *Natural Language Engineering*, 14(03):369–416.

Attapol Thamrongrattanarit, Colin Pollock, Benjamin Goldenberg, and Jason Fennell. 2013. A distant supervision approach for identifying perspectives in unstructured user-generated text. In *Proceedings of the Sixth International Joint Conference on Natural Language Processing*, pages 922–926, Nagoya, Japan, October. Asian Federation of Natural Language Processing.

Xun Wang, Sujian Li, Jiwei Li, and Wenjie Li. 2012. Implicit discourse relation recognition by selecting typical training examples. In *Proceedings of COLING 2012*, pages 2757–2772, Mumbai, India, December. The COLING 2012 Organizing Committee.

Florian Wolf, Edward Gibson, Amy Fisher, and Meredith Knight. 2005. The discourse graphbank: A database of texts annotated with coherence relations. *Linguistic Data Consortium*.

Limin Yao, Sebastian Riedel, and Andrew McCallum. 2010. Collective cross-document relation extraction without labelled data. In *Proceedings of the 2010 Conference on Empirical Methods in Natural Language Processing*, pages 1013–1023. Association for Computational Linguistics.

# Solving Hard Coreference Problems

**Haoruo Peng*** and **Daniel Khashabi*** and **Dan Roth**
University of Illinois, Urbana-Champaign
Urbana, IL, 61801
{hpeng7,khashab2,danr}@illinois.edu

## Abstract

Coreference resolution is a key problem in natural language understanding that still escapes reliable solutions. One fundamental difficulty has been that of resolving instances involving pronouns since they often require deep language understanding and use of background knowledge. In this paper we propose an algorithmic solution that involves a new representation for the knowledge required to address hard coreference problems, along with a constrained optimization framework that uses this knowledge in coreference decision making. Our representation, Predicate Schemas, is instantiated with knowledge acquired in an unsupervised way, and is compiled automatically into constraints that impact the coreference decision. We present a general coreference resolution system that significantly improves state-of-the-art performance on hard, *Winograd*-style, pronoun resolution cases, while still performing at the state-of-the-art level on standard coreference resolution datasets.

## 1 Introduction

Coreference resolution is one of the most important tasks in *Natural Language Processing* (NLP). Although there is a plethora of works on this task (Soon et al., 2001a; Ng and Cardie, 2002a; Ng, 2004; Bengtson and Roth, 2008; Pradhan et al., 2012; Kummerfeld and Klein, 2013; Chang et al., 2013), it is still deemed an unsolved problem due to intricate and ambiguous nature of natural language text. Existing methods perform particularly poorly on pronouns, specifically when gender or plurality information cannot help. In this paper, we aim to improve coreference resolution by addressing these hard problems. Consider the following examples:

Ex.1 *[A bird]$_{e_1}$ perched on the [limb]$_{e_2}$ and [it]$_{pro}$ bent.*

Ex.2 *[Robert]$_{e_1}$ was robbed by [Kevin]$_{e_2}$, and [he]$_{pro}$ is arrested by police.*

In both examples, one cannot resolve the pronouns based on only gender or plurality information. Recently, Rahman and Ng (2012) gathered a dataset containing 1886 sentences of such challenging pronoun resolution problems (referred to later as the *Winograd* dataset, following Winograd (1972) and Levesque et al. (2011)). As an indication to the difficulty of these instances, we note that a state-of-the-art coreference resolution system (Chang et al., 2013) achieves precision of 53.26% on it. A special purpose classifier (Rahman and Ng, 2012) trained on this data set achieves 73.05%. The key contribution of this paper is a general purpose, state-of-the-art coreference approach which, at the same time, achieves precision of 76.76% on these hard cases.

Addressing these hard coreference problems requires significant amounts of background knowledge, along with an inference paradigm that can make use of it in supporting the coreference decision. Specifically, in Ex.1 one needs to know that "a limb bends" is more likely than "a bird bends". In Ex.2 one needs to know that the *subject* of the verb "rob" is more likely to be the *object* of "arrest" than the *object* of the verb "rob" is. The knowledge required is, naturally, centered around

*These authors contributed equally to this work.



*Human Language Technologies: The 2015 Annual Conference of the North American Chapter of the ACL*, pages 809–819,
Denver, Colorado, May 31 – June 5, 2015. 

the key predicates in the sentence, motivating the central notion proposed in this paper, that of *Predicate Schemas*. In this paper, we develop the notion of *Predicate Schemas*, instantiate them with automatically acquired knowledge, and show how to compile it into constraints that are used to resolve coreference within a general *Integer Linear Programming* (ILP) driven approach to coreference resolution. Specifically, we study two types of Predicate Schemas that, as we show, cover a large fraction of the challenging cases. The first specifies one predicate with its subject and object, thus providing information on the subject and object preferences of a given predicate. The second specifies two predicates with a semantically shared argument (either subject or object), thus specifies role preferences of one predicate, among roles of the other. We instantiate these schemas by acquiring statistics in an unsupervised way from multiple resources including the Gigaword corpus, Wikipedia, Web Queries and polarity information.

A lot of recent work has attempted to utilize similar types of resources to improve coreference resolution (Rahman and Ng, 2011a; Ratinov and Roth, 2012; Bansal and Klein, 2012; Rahman and Ng, 2012). The common approach has been to inject knowledge as features. However, these pieces of knowledge provide relatively strong evidence that loses impact in standard training due to sparsity. Instead, we compile our Predicate Schemas knowledge automatically, at inference time, into constraints, and make use of an ILP driven framework (Roth and Yih, 2004) to make decisions. Using constraints is also beneficial when the interaction between multiple pronouns is taken into account when making global decisions. Consider the following example:

Ex.3 *[Jack]*$_{e_1}$ *threw the bags of [John]*$_{e_2}$ *into the water since [he]*$_{pro_1}$ *mistakenly asked [him]*$_{pro_2}$ *to carry [his]*$_{pro_3}$ *bags.*

In order to correctly resolve the pronouns in Ex.3, one needs to have the knowledge that "*he* asks *him*" indicates that *he* and *him* refer to different entities (because they are subject and object of the same predicate; otherwise, *himself* should be used instead of *him*). This knowledge, which can be easily represented as constraints during inference, then impacts other pronoun decisions in a global decision with respect to all pronouns: $pro_3$ is likely to be different from $pro_2$, and is likely to refer to $e_2$. This type of inference can be easily represented as a constraint during inference, but hard to inject as a feature.

We then incorporate all constraints into a general coreference system (Chang et al., 2013) utilizing the mention-pair model (Ng and Cardie, 2002b; Bengtson and Roth, 2008; Stoyanov et al., 2010). A classifier learns a pairwise metric between mentions, and during inference, we follow the framework proposed in Chang et al. (2011) using ILP.

The main contributions of this paper can be summarized as follows:

1. We propose the Predicate Schemas representation and study two specific schemas that are important for coreference.
2. We show how, in a given context, Predicate Schemas can be automatically compiled into constraints and affect inference.
3. Consequently, we address hard pronoun resolution problems as a standard coreference problem and develop a system[1] which shows significant improvement for hard coreference problems while achieving the same state-of-the-art level of performance on standard coreference problems.

The rest of the paper is organized as follows. We describe our Predicate Schemas in Section 2 and explain the inference framework and automatic constraint generation in Section 3. A summary of our knowledge acquisition steps is given in Section 4. We report our experimental results and analysis in Section 5, and review related work in Section 6.

## 2 Predicate Schema

In this section we present multiple kinds of knowledge that are needed in order to improve hard coreference problems. Table 1 provides two example sentences for each type of knowledge. We use $m$ to refer to a mention. A mention can either be an entity $e$ or a pronoun $pro$. $pred_m$ denotes the predicate of $m$ (similarly, $pred_{pro}$ and $pred_e$ for pronouns and entities, respectively). For instance, in sentence 1.1 in Table 1, the predicate of $e_1$ and $e_2$

[1] Available at http://cogcomp.cs.illinois.edu/page/software_view/Winocoref

| Category | # | Sentence |
|---|---|---|
| 1 | 1.1 | *[The bird]$_{e_1}$ perched on the [limb]$_{e_2}$ and [it]$_{pro}$ bent.* |
| | 1.2 | *[The bee]$_{e_1}$ landed on [the flower]$_{e_2}$ because [it]$_{pro}$ had pollen.* |
| 2 | 2.1 | *[Bill]$_{e_1}$ was robbed by [John]$_{e_2}$, so the officer arrested [him]$_{pro}$.* |
| | 2.2 | *[Jimbo]$_{e_1}$ was afraid of [Bobbert]$_{e_2}$ because [he]$_{pro}$ gets scared around new people.* |
| 3 | 3.1 | *[Lakshman]$_{e_1}$ asked [Vivan]$_{e_2}$ to get him some ice cream because [he]$_{pro}$ was hot.* |
| | 3.2 | *Paula liked [Ness]$_{e_1}$ more than [Pokey]$_{e_2}$ because [he]$_{pro}$ was mean to her.* |

Table 1: Example sentences for each schema category. The annotated entities and pronouns are hard coreference problems.

| Type | Schema form | Explanation of examples from Table 1 |
|---|---|---|
| 1 | $pred_m(m, a)$ | Example 1.2: It is enough to know that: $\mathcal{S}(\text{have}(m = [\text{the flower}], a = [\text{pollen}])) >$ $\mathcal{S}(\text{have}(m = [\text{the bee}], a = [\text{pollen}]))$ |
| 2 | $pred_m(m, a) \vert \widehat{pred}_m(m, \widehat{a}), cn$ | Example 2.2: It is enough to know that: $\mathcal{S}(\textit{be afraid of}(m = *, a = *) \vert \textit{get scared}(m = *, \widehat{a} = *), \text{because}) >$ $\mathcal{S}(\textit{be afraid of}(a = *, m = *) \vert \textit{get scared}(m = *, \widehat{a} = *), \text{because})$ |

Table 2: Predicate Schemas and examples of the logic behind the schema design. Here $*$ indicates that the argument is dropped, and $\mathcal{S}(.)$ denotes the scoring function defined in the text.

| | |
|---|---|
| Type 1 | $\mathcal{S}(pred_m(m, a))$<br>$\mathcal{S}(pred_m(a, m))$<br>$\mathcal{S}(pred_m(m, *))$<br>$\mathcal{S}(pred_m(*, m))$ |
| Type 2 | $\mathcal{S}\left(pred_m(m, a) \vert \widehat{pred}_m(m, \widehat{a}), cn\right)$<br>$\mathcal{S}\left(pred_m(a, m) \vert \widehat{pred}_m(m, \widehat{a}), cn\right)$<br>$\mathcal{S}\left(pred_m(m, a) \vert \widehat{pred}_m(\widehat{a}, m), cn\right)$<br>$\mathcal{S}\left(pred_m(a, m) \vert \widehat{pred}_m(\widehat{a}, m), cn\right)$<br>$\mathcal{S}\left(pred_m(m, *) \vert \widehat{pred}_m(m, *), cn\right)$<br>⋮ |

Table 3: Possible variations for scoring function statistics. Here $*$ indicates that the argument is dropped.

is $pred_{e_1} = pred_{e_2} =$"perch on". $cn$ refers to the discourse connective ($cn$="and" in sentence 1.1). $a$ denotes an argument of $pred_m$ other than $m$. For example, in sentence 1.1, assuming that $m = e_1$, the corresponding argument is $a = e_2$.

We represent the knowledge needed with two types of Predicate Schemas (as depicted in Table 2). To solve the assignment of [it]$_{pro}$ in sentence 1.1, as mentioned in Section 1, we need the knowledge that "a limb bends" is more reasonable than "a bird bends". Note that the predicate of the pronoun is playing a key role here. Also the entity mention itself is essential. Similarly, for sentence 1.2, to resolve [it]$_{pro}$, we need the knowledge that "bee had pollen" is more reasonable than "flower had pollen". Here, in addition to entity mention and the predicate (of the pronoun), we need the argument which shares the predicate with the pronoun. To formally define the type of knowledge needed we denote it with "$\boldsymbol{pred_m(m, a)}$" where $m$ and $a$ are a mention and an argument, respectively[2]. We use $\mathcal{S}(.)$ to denote the score representing how likely the combination of the predicate-mention-argument is. For each schema, we use several variations by either changing the order of the arguments (*subj.* vs *obj.*) or dropping either of them. We score the various Type 1 and Type 2 schemas (shown in Table 3) differently. The first row of Table 2 shows how Type 1 schema is being used in the case of Sentence 1.2.

For sentence 2.2, we need to have the knowledge that the *subject* of the verb phrase "be afraid of" is more likely than the *object* of the verb phrase "be afraid of" to be the *subject* of the verb phrase "get scared". The structure here is more complicated than that of Type 1 schema. To make it clearer, we analyze sentence 2.1. In this sentence, the *object* of "be robbed by" is more likely than the *subject*

[2]Note that the order of $m$ and $a$ relative to the predicate is a critical issue. To keep things general in the schemas definition, we do not show the ordering; however, when using scores in practice the order between a mention and an argument is a critical issue.

of the verb phrase "be robbed by" to be the *object* of "the officer arrest". We can see in both examples (and for the Type 2 schema in general), that both predicates (the entity predicate and the pronoun predicate) play a crucial role. Consequently, we design the Type 2 schema to capture the interaction between the entity predicate and the pronoun predicate. In addition to the predicates, we may need mention-argument information. Also, we stress the importance of the discourse connective between entity mention and pronoun; if in either sentence 2.1 or 2.2, we change the discourse connective to "although", the coreference resolution will completely change. Overall, we can represent the knowledge as "$\boldsymbol{pred}_m\left(m, a\right) | \widehat{\boldsymbol{pred}_m}\left(m, \widehat{a}\right), \boldsymbol{cn}$". Just like for Type 1 schema, we can represent Type 2 schema with a score function for different variations of arguments (lower half of Table 3). In Table 2, we exhibit this for sentence 2.2.

Type 3 contains the set of instances which cannot be solved using schemas of Type 1 or 2. Two such examples are included in Table 1. In sentence 3.1 and 3.2, the context containing the necessary information goes beyond our triple representation and therefore this instance cannot be resolved with either of the two schema types. It is important to note that the notion of Predicate Schemas is more general than the Type 1 and Type 2 schemas introduced here. Designing more informative and structured schemas will be essential to resolving additional types of hard coreference instances.

## 3 Constrained ILP Inference

*Integer Linear Programming* (ILP) based formulations of NLP problems (Roth and Yih, 2004) have been used in a board range of NLP problems and, particularly, in coreference problems (Chang et al., 2011; Denis and Baldridge, 2007). Our formulation is inspired by Chang et al. (2013). Let $\mathcal{M}$ be the set of all mentions in a given text snippet, and $\mathcal{P}$ the set of all pronouns, such that $\mathcal{P} \subset \mathcal{M}$. We train a coreference model by learning a pairwise mention scoring function. Specifically, given a mention-pair $(u, v) \in \mathcal{M}$ ($u$ is the antecedent of $v$), we learn a left-linking scoring function $f_{u,v} = \mathbf{w}^\top \phi(u, v)$, where $\phi(u, v)$ is a pairwise feature vector and $\mathbf{w}$ is the weight vector. We then follow the *Best-Link* approach (Section 2.3 from Chang et al. (2011)) for inference. The ILP problem that we solve is formally defined as follows:

$$\begin{cases} \arg\max_y \sum_{u \in \mathcal{M}, v \in \mathcal{M}} f_{u,v} y_{u,v} \\ \text{s.t. } y_{u,v} \in \{0, 1\}, \quad \forall u, v \in \mathcal{M} \\ \quad \sum_{u<v, u \in \mathcal{M}} y_{u,v} \leq 1, \quad \forall v \in \mathcal{M} \\ \quad \text{Constraints from Predicate Schemas Knowledge} \\ \quad \text{Constraints between pronouns.} \end{cases}$$

Here, $u, v$ are mentions and $y_{u,v}$ is the decision variable to indicate whether or not mention $u$ and mention $v$ are coreferents. As the first constraint shows, $y_{u,v}$ is a binary variable. $y_{u,v}$ equals 1 if $u, v$ are coreferents and 0 otherwise. The second constraint indicates that we only choose at most one antecedent to be coreferent with each mention $v$. ($u < v$ represents that $u$ appears beore $v$, thus $u$ is an antecedent of $v$.) In this work, we add constraints from Predicate Schemas Knowledge and between pronouns.

The Predicate Schemas knowledge provides a vector of score values $\mathcal{S}(u, v)$ for mention pairs $\{(u, v) | (u \in \mathcal{M}, v \in \mathcal{P}\}$, which concatenates all the schemas involving $u$ and $v$. Entries in the score vector are designed so that the larger the value is, the more likely $u$ and $v$ are to be coreferents. We have two ways to use the score values: 1) Augumenting the feature vector $\phi(u, v)$ with these scores. 2) Casting the scores as constraints for the coreference resolution ILP in one of the following forms:

$$\begin{cases} \text{if } s_i(u, v) \geq \alpha_i s_i(w, v) \Rightarrow y_{u,v} \geq y_{w,v}, \\ \text{if } s_i(u, v) \geq s_i(w, v) + \beta_i \Rightarrow y_{u,v} \geq y_{w,v}, \end{cases} \tag{1}$$

where $s_i(.)$ is the $i$-th dimension of the score vector $\mathcal{S}(.)$ corresponding to the $i$-th schema represented for a given mention pair. $\alpha_i$ and $\beta_i$ are threshold values which we tune on a development set.[3] If an inequality holds for all relevant schemas (that is, all the dimensions of the score vector), we add an inequality between the corresponding indicator variables inside the ILP.[4] As we increase the value of a

[3]For the $i_{\text{th}}$ dimension of the score vector, we choose either $\alpha_i$ or $\beta_i$ as the threshold.

[4]If the constraints dictated by any two dimensions of $\mathcal{S}$ are contradictory, we ignore both of them.

threshold, the constraints in (1) become more conservative, thus it leads to fewer but more reliable constraints added into the ILP. We tune the threshold values such that their corresponding scores attain high enough accuracy, either in the multiplicative form or the additive form.[5] Note that, given a pair of mentions and context, we automatically instantiate a collection of relevant schemas, and then generate and evaluate a set of corresponding constraints. To the best of our knowledge, this is the first work to use such automatic constraint generation and tuning method for coreference resolution with ILP inference. In Section 4, we describe how we acquire the score vectors $\mathcal{S}(u,v)$ for the Predicate Schemas in an unsupervised fashion.

We now briefly explain the pre-processing step required in order to extract the score vector $\mathcal{S}(u,v)$ from a pair of mentions. Define a triple structure $t_m \triangleq pred_m(m, a_m)$ for any $m \in \mathcal{M}$. The subscript $m$ for *pred* and $a$, emphasizes that they are extracted as a function of the mention $m$. The extraction of triples is done by utilizing the dependency parse tree from the Easy-first dependency parser (Goldberg and Elhadad, 2010). We start with a mention $m$, and extract its related predicate and the other argument based on the dependency parse tree and part-of-speech information. To handle multiword predicates and arguments, we use a set of hand-designed rules. We then get the score vector $\mathcal{S}(u,v)$ by concatenating all scores of the Predicate Schemas given two triples $t_u$, $t_v$. Thus, we can expand the score representation for each type of Predicate Schemas given in Table 2: 1) For Type 1 schema, $\mathcal{S}(u,v) \equiv \mathcal{S}(pred_v(m=u, a=a_v))$ [6] 2) For Type 2 schema, $\mathcal{S}(u,v) \equiv \mathcal{S}(pred_u(m=u, a=a_u)|\widehat{pred}_v(m=v, a=a_v), cn)$.

In additional to schema-driven constraints, we also apply constraints between pairs of pronouns within a fixed distance[7]. For two pronouns that are semantically different (e.g. *he* vs. *it*), they must refer to different antecedents. For two non-possesive pronouns that are related to the same predicate (e.g. *he saw him*), they must refer to different antecedents.[8]

## 4 Knowledge Acquisition

One key point that remains to be explained is how to acquire the knowledge scores $\mathcal{S}(u,v)$. In this section, we propose multiple ways to acquire these scores. In the current implementation, we make use of four resources. Each of them generates its own score vector. Therefore, the overall score vector is the concatenation of the score vector from each resource: $\mathcal{S}(u,v) = [\mathcal{S}_{giga}(u,v)\ \mathcal{S}_{wiki}(u,v)\ \mathcal{S}_{web}(u,v)\ \mathcal{S}_{pol}(u,v)]$.

### 4.1 Gigaword Co-occurence

We extract triples $t_m \triangleq pred_m(m, a_m)$ (explained in Section 3) from Gigaword data (4,111,240 documents). We start by extracting noun phrases using the Illinois-Chunker (Punyakanok and Roth, 2001). For each noun phrase, we extract its head noun and then extract the associated predicate and argument to form a triple.

We gather the statistics for both schema types after applying lemmatization on the predicates and arguments. Using the extracted triples, we get a score vector from each schema type: $\mathcal{S}_{giga} = [\mathcal{S}^{(1)}_{giga}\ \mathcal{S}^{(2)}_{giga}]$.

To extract scores for Type 1 Predicate Schemas, we create occurence counts for each schema instance. After all scores are gathered, our goal is to query $\mathcal{S}^{(1)}_{giga}(u,v) \equiv \mathcal{S}(pred_v(m=u, a=a_v))$ from our knowledge base. The returned score is the $log(.)$ of the number of occurences.

For Type 2 Predicate Schemas, we gather the statistics of triple co-occurence. We count the co-occurrence of neighboring triples that share at least one linked argument. We consider two triples to be neighbors if they are within a distance of three sentences. We use two heuristic rules to decide whether a pair of arguments between two neighboring triples are coreferents or not: 1) If the head noun of two arguments can match, we consider them coreferents. 2) If one argument in the first triple is a person name and there is a compatible pronoun (based on its gender and plurality information) in the second triple, they are also labeled as coreferents. We also extract the discourse connectives between triples (*because*,

[5]The choice is made based on the performance on the development set.

[6]In $pred_v(m=u, a=a_v)$ the argument and the predicate are extracted relative to $v$ but the mention $m$ is set to be $u$.

[7]We set the distance to be 3 sentences.

[8]Three cases are considered: *he-him*, *she-her*, *they-them*

$$s_{pol}(u,v) = \begin{bmatrix} \mathbf{1}\{Po(p_u) = + \text{ AND } Po(p_v) = +\} \quad \text{OR} \quad \mathbf{1}\{Po(p_u) = - \text{ AND } Po(p_v) = -\} \\ \mathbf{1}\{Po(p_u) = + \text{ AND } Po(p_v) = +\} \\ \mathbf{1}\{Po(p_u) = - \text{ AND } Po(p_v) = -\} \end{bmatrix}$$

Table 4: Extrating the polarity score given polarity information of a mention-pair $(u, v)$. To be brief, we use the shorthand notation $p_v \triangleq pred_v$ and $p_u \triangleq pred_u$. $\mathbf{1}\{\cdot\}$ is an indicator function. $s_{pol}(u, v)$ is a binary vector of size three.

*therefore*, etc.) if there are any. To avoid sparsity, we only keep the mention roles (only *subj* or *obj*; no exact strings are kept). Two triple-pairs are considered different if they have different predicates, different roles, different coreferred argument-pairs, or different discourse connectives. The co-occurrence counts extracted in this form correspond to Type 2 schemas in Table 2. During inference, we match a Type 2 schema for $\mathcal{S}^{(2)}_{giga}(u, v) \equiv \mathcal{S}(pred_u(m = u, a = a_u)|\widehat{pred_v}(m = u, a = a_v), cn)$.

Our method is related, but different from the proposal in Balasubramanian et al. (2012), who suggested to extract triples using an OpenIE system (Mausam et al., 2012). We extracted triples by starting from a mention, then extract the predicate and the other argument. An OpenIE system does not easily provide this ability. Our Gigaword counts are gathered also in a way similar to what has been proposed in Chambers and Jurafsky (2009), but we gather much larger amounts of data.

### 4.2 Wikipedia Disambiguated Co-occurence

One of the problems with blindly extracting triple counts is that we may miss important semantic information. To address this issue, we use the publicly avaiable Illinois Wikifier (Cheng and Roth, 2013; Ratinov et al., 2011), a system that disambiguates mentions by mapping them into correct Wikipedia pages, to process the Wikipedia data. We then extract from the Wikipedia text all entities, verbs and nouns, and gather co-occurrence statistics with these syntactic *variations*: 1) *immediately after* 2) *immediately before* 3) *before* 4) *after*. For each of these variations, we get the probability and count[9] of a pair of words (e.g. probability[10]/count for "bend" *immediately following* "limb") as separate dimensions of the score vector.

[9] We use the $log(.)$ of the counts here.

[10] Conditional probability of "limb" immediately following the given verb "bend".

Given the co-occurrence information, we get a score vector $\mathcal{S}_{wiki}(u, v)$ corresponding to Type 1 Predicate Schemas, and hence $\mathcal{S}(u, v)_{wiki} \equiv \mathcal{S}(pred_v(m = u, a = a_v))$.

### 4.3 Web Search Query Count

Our third source of score vectors is web queries that we implement using Google queries. We extract a score vector $\mathcal{S}_{web}(u, v) \equiv \mathcal{S}(pred_v(m = u, a = a_v))$ (Type 1 Predicate Schemas) by querying for 1) "$u$ $a_v$" 2) "$u$ $pred_v$" 3) "$u$ $pred_v$ $a_v$" 4) "$a_v$ $u$"[11]. For each variation of nouns (plural and singular) and verbs (different tenses) we create a different query and average the counts over all queries. Concatenating the counts (each is a separate dimension) would give us the score vector $\mathcal{S}_{web}(u, v)$.

### 4.4 Polarity of Context

Another rich source of information is the polarity of context, which has been previously used for Winograd schema problems (Rahman and Ng, 2012). Here we use a slightly modified version. The polarity scores are used for Type 1 Predicate Schemas and therefore we want to get $\mathcal{S}_{pol}(u, v) \equiv \mathcal{S}(pred_v(m = u, a = a_v))$. We first extract polarity values for $Po(pred_u)$ and $Po(pred_v)$ by repeating the following procedures for each of them:

- We extract initial polarity information given the predicate (using the data provided by Wilson et al. (2005)).
- If the role of the mention is *object*, we negate its polarity.
- If there is a polarity-reversing discourse connective (such as "but") preceding the predicate, we reverse the polarity.
- If there is a negative comparative adverb (such as "less", "lower") we reverse the polarity.

[11] We query this only when $a_v$ is an adjective and $pred_v$ is a to-be verb.

| | # Doc | # Train | # Test | # Mention | # Pronoun | # Predictions for Pronoun |
|---|---|---|---|---|---|---|
| Winograd | 1886 | 1212 | 674 | 5658 | 1886 | 1348 |
| WinoCoref | 1886 | 1212 | 674 | 6404 | 2595 | 2118 |
| ACE | 375 | 268 | 107 | 23247 | 3862 | 13836 |
| OntoNotes | 3150 | 2802 | 348 | 175324 | 58952 | 37846 |

Table 5: Statistics of *Winograd*, *WinoCoref*, *ACE* and *OntoNotes*. We give the total number of mentions and pronouns, while the number of predictions for pronoun is specific for the test data. We added 746 mentions (709 among them are pronouns) to *WinoCoref* compared to *Winograd*.

Given the polarity values $Po(pred_u)$ and $Po(pred_v)$, we construct the score vector $\mathcal{S}_{pol}(u, v)$ following Table 4.

## 5 Experiments

In this section, we evaluate our system for both hard coreference problems and general coreference problems, and provide detailed anaylsis on the impact of our proposed Predicate Schemas. Since we treat resolving hard pronouns as part of the general coreference problems, we extend the *Winograd* dataset with a more complete annotation to get a new dataset. We evaluate our system on both datasets, and show significant improvemnt over the baseline system and over the results reported in Rahman and Ng (2012). Moreover, we show that, at the same time, our system achieves the state-of-art performance on standard coreference datasets.

### 5.1 Experimental Setup

**Datasets:** Since we aim to solve hard coreference problems, we choose to test our system on the *Winograd* dataset[12] (Rahman and Ng, 2012). It is a challenging pronoun resolution dataset which consists of sentence pairs based on Winograd schemas. The original annotation only specifies one pronoun and two entites in each sentence, and it is considered as a binary decision for each pronoun. As our target is to model and solve them as general coreference problems, we expand the annotation to include all pronouns and their linked entities as mentions (We call this new re-annotated dataset *WinoCoref*[13]). Ex.3 in Section 1 is from the *Winograd* dataset. It originally only specifies *he* as the pronoun in question, and we added *him* and *his* as additional target pronouns. We also use two standard coreference resolution datasets *ACE*(2004) (NIST, 2004) and *OntoNotes-5.0* (Pradhan et al., 2011) for evaluation. Statistics of the datasets are provided in Table 5.

| Systems | Learning Method | Inference Method |
|---|---|---|
| Illinois | BLMP | BLL |
| IlliCons | BLMP | ILP |
| KnowFeat | BLMP+SF | BLL |
| KnowCons | BLMP | ILP+SC |
| KnowComb | BLMP+SF | ILP+SC |

Table 6: Summary of learning and inference methods for all systems. SF stands for schema features while SC represents constraints from schema knowledge.

**Baseline Systems:** We use the state-of-art Illinois coreference system as our baseline system (Chang et al., 2013). It includes two different versions. One employs *Best-Left-Link* (BLL) inference method (Ng and Cardie, 2002b), and we name it *Illinois*[14]; while the other uses ILP with constraints for inference, and we name it *IlliCons*. Both systems use *Best-Link Mention-Pair* (BLMP) model for training. On *Winograd* dataset, we also treat the reported result from Rahman and Ng (2012) as a baseline.

**Developed Systems:** We present three variations of the Predicate Schemas based system developed here. We inject Predicate Schemas knowledge as mention-pair features and retrain the system (*KnowFeat*). We use the original coreference model and Predicate Schemas knowledge as constraints during inference (*KnowCons*). We also have a combined system (*KnowComb*), which uses the schema knowledge to add features for learning as well as constraints for inference. A summary of all systems is provided in Table 6.

[12] Available at http://www.hlt.utdallas.edu/~vince/data/emnlp12/

[13] Available at http://cogcomp.cs.illinois.edu/page/data/

[14] In implementation, we use the $L^3M$ model proposed in Chang et al. (2013), which is slightly different. It can be seen as an extension of BLL inference method.

| Dataset | Metric | Illinois | IlliCons | Rahman and Ng (2012) | KnowFeat | KnowCons | KnowComb |
|---|---|---|---|---|---|---|---|
| *Winograd* | Precision | 51.48 | 53.26 | 73.05 | 71.81 | 74.93 | **76.41** |
| *WinoCoref* | AntePre | 68.37 | 74.32 | — | 88.48 | 88.95 | **89.32** |

Table 7: Performance results on *Winograd* and *WinoCoref* datasets. All our three systems are trained on *WinoCoref*, and we evaluate the predictions on both datasets. Our systems improve over the baselines by over than 20% on *Winograd* and over 15% on *WinoCoref*.

**Evaluation Metrics:** When evaluating on the full datasets of *ACE* and *OntoNotes*, we use the widely recoginzed metrics MUC (Vilain et al., 1995), BCUB (Bagga and Baldwin, 1998), Entity-based CEAF ($\text{CEAF}_e$) (Luo, 2005) and their average. As *Winograd* is a pronoun resolution dataset, we use precision as the evaluation metric. Although *WinoCoref* is more general, each coreferent cluster only contains 2-4 mentions and all are within the same sentence. Since traditional coreference metrics cannot serve as good metrics, we extend the precision metric and design a new one called *AntePre*. Suppose there are $k$ pronouns in the dataset, and each pronoun has $n_1, n_2, \cdots, n_k$ antecedents, respectively. We can view predicted coreference clusters as binary decisions on each antecedent-pronoun pair (linked or not). The total number of binary decisions is $\sum_{i=1}^{k} n_i$. We then meaure how many binary decisions among them are correct; let $m$ be the number of correct decisions, then *AnrePre* is computed as: $\frac{m}{\sum_{i=1}^{k} n_i}$.

### 5.2 Results for Hard Coreference Problems

Performance results on *Winograd* and *WinoCoref* datasets are shown in Table 7. The best performing system is *KnowComb*. It improves by over 20% over a state-of-art general coreference system on *Winograd* and also outperforms Rahman and Ng (2012) by a margin of 3.3%. On the *WinoCoref* dataset, it improves by 15%. These results show significant performance improvement by using Predicate Schemas knowledge on hard coreference problems. Note that the system developed in Rahman and Ng (2012) cannot be used on the *WinoCoref* dataset. The results also show that it is better to compile knowledge into constraints when the knowledge quality is high than add them as features.

### 5.3 Results for Standard Coreference Problems

Performance results on standard *ACE* and *OntoNotes* datasets are shown in Table 8. Our *KnowComb* system achieves the same level of performance as does the state-of-art general coreference system we base it on. As hard coreference problems are rare in standard coreference datasets, we do not have significant performance improvement. However, these results show that our additional Predicate Schemas do not harm the predictions for regular mentions.

| System | MUC | BCUB | CEAFe | AVG |
|---|---|---|---|---|
| ACE | | | | |
| IlliCons | **78.17** | 81.64 | **78.45** | **79.42** |
| KnowComb | 77.51 | **81.97** | 77.44 | 78.97 |
| OntoNotes | | | | |
| IlliCons | 84.10 | **78.30** | **68.74** | **77.05** |
| KnowComb | **84.33** | 78.02 | 67.95 | 76.76 |

Table 8: Performance results on *ACE* and *OntoNotes* datasets. Our system gets the same level of performance compared to a state-of-art general coreference system.

| Category | Cat1 | Cat2 | Cat3 |
|---|---|---|---|
| Size | 317 | 1060 | 509 |
| Portion | 16.8% | 56.2% | 27.0% |

Table 9: Distribution of instances in *Winograd* dataset of each category. Cat1/Cat2 is the subset of instances that require Type 1/Type 2 schema knowledge, respectively. All other instances are put into Cat3. Cat1 and Cat2 instances can be covered by our proposed Predicate Schemas.

### 5.4 Detailed Analysis

To study the coverage of our Predicate Schemas knowledge, we label the instances in *Winograd* (which also applies to *WinoCoref*) with the type of Predicate Schemas knowledge required. The distribution of the instances is shown in Table 9. Our proposed Predicate Schemas cover 73% of the instances.

We also provide an ablation study on the

| Schema | AntePre(Test) | AntePre(Train) |
|---|---|---|
| Type 1 | 76.67 | 86.79 |
| Type 2 | 79.55 | 88.86 |
| Type 1 (Cat1) | 90.26 | 93.64 |
| Type 2 (Cat2) | 83.38 | 92.49 |

Table 10: Ablation Study of Knowledge Schemas on *WinoCoref*. The first line specifies the preformance for *KnowComb* with only Type 1 schema knowledge tested on all data while the third line specifies the preformance using the same model but tested on Cat1 data. The second line specifies the preformance results for *KnowComb* system with only Type 2 schema knowledge on all data while the fourth line specifies the preformance using the same model but tested on Cat2 data.

*WinoCoref* dataset in Table 10. These results use the best performing *KnowComb* system. They show that both Type 1 and Type 2 schema knowledge have higher precision on Category 1 and Category 2 data instances, respectively, compared to that on full data. Type 1 and Type 2 knowledge have similiar performance on full data, but the results show that it is harder to solve instances in category 2 than those in category 1. Also, the performance drop between Cat1/Cat2 and full data indicates that there is a need to design more complicated knowledge schemas and to refine the knowledge acquisition for further performance improvement.

## 6 Related Work

**Winograd Schema:** Winograd (1972) showed that small changes in context could completely change coreference decisions. Levesque et al. (2011) proposed to assemble a set of sentences which comply with Winograd's schema. Specifically, there are pairs of sentences which are identical except for minor differences which lead to different references of the same pronoun in both sentences. These references can be easily solved by humans, but are hard, he claimed, for computer programs.

**Anaphora Resolution:** There has been a lot of work on anaphora resolution in the past two decades. Many of the early rule-based systems like Hobbs (1978) and Lappin and Leass (1994) gained considerable popularity. The early designs were easy to understand and the rules were designed manually. With the development of machine learning based models (Connolly et al., 1994; Soon et al., 2001b; Ng and Cardie, 2002a), attention shifted to solving standard coreference resolution problems. However, many hard coreference problems involve pronouns. As Winograd's schema shows, there is still a need for further investigation in this subarea.

**World Knowledge Acquisition:** Many tasks in NLP (such as Textual Entailment, Question Answering, etc.) require *World Knowledge*. Although there are many existing works on acquiring them (Schwartz and Gomez, 2009; Balasubramanian et al., 2013; Tandon et al., 2014), there is still no consensus on how to represent, gather and utilize high quality *World Knowledge*. When it comes to coreference resolution, there are a handful of works which either use web query information or apply alignment to an external knowledge base (Rahman and Ng, 2011b; Kobdani et al., 2011; Ratinov and Roth, 2012; Bansal and Klein, 2012; Zheng et al., 2013). With the introduction of Predicate Schema, our goal is to bring these different approaches together and provide a coherent view.

## Acknowledgments

The authors would like to thank Kai-Wei Chang, Alice Lai, Eric Horn and Stephen Mayhew for comments that helped to improve this work. This work is partly supported by NSF grant #SMA 12-09359 and by DARPA under agreement number FA8750-13-2-0008. The U.S. Government is authorized to reproduce and distribute reprints for Governmental purposes notwithstanding any copyright notation thereon. The views and conclusions contained herein are those of the authors and should not be interpreted as necessarily representing the official policies or endorsements, either expressed or implied, of DARPA or the U.S. Government.

## References

A. Bagga and B. Baldwin. 1998. Algorithms for scoring coreference chains. In *The First International Conference on Language Resources and Evaluation Workshop on Linguistics Coreference*, pages 563–566.

N. Balasubramanian, S. Soderland, O. Etzioni, et al. 2012. Rel-grams: a probabilistic model of relations in text. In *Proceedings of the Joint Workshop on Au-*

*tomatic Knowledge Base Construction and Web-scale Knowledge Extraction*, pages 101–105. Association for Computational Linguistics.

N. Balasubramanian, S. Soderland, Mausam, and O. Etzioni. 2013. Generating coherent event schemas at scale. In *EMNLP*, pages 1721–1731.

M. Bansal and D. Klein. 2012. Coreference semantics from web features. In *Proceedings of the Annual Meeting of the Association for Computational Linguistics (ACL)*, Jeju Island, South Korea, July.

E. Bengtson and D. Roth. 2008. Understanding the value of features for coreference resolution. In *Proceedings of the Conference on Empirical Methods for Natural Language Processing (EMNLP)*, pages 294–303, Oct.

N. Chambers and D. Jurafsky. 2009. Unsupervised learning of narrative schemas and their participants. In *Proceedings of the Joint Conference of the 47th Annual Meeting of the ACL and the 4th International Joint Conference on Natural Language Processing of the AFNLP*, volume 2, pages 602–610. Association for Computational Linguistics.

K. Chang, R. Samdani, A. Rozovskaya, N. Rizzolo, M. Sammons, and D. Roth. 2011. Inference protocols for coreference resolution. In *Proceedings of the Annual Conference on Computational Natural Language Learning (CoNLL)*, pages 40–44, Portland, Oregon, USA. Association for Computational Linguistics.

K. Chang, R. Samdani, and D. Roth. 2013. A constrained latent variable model for coreference resolution. In *Proceedings of the 2013 Conference on Empirical Methods in Natural Language Processing*, pages 601–612. Association for Computational Linguistics.

X. Cheng and D. Roth. 2013. Relational inference for wikification. In *Proceedings of the 2013 Conference on Empirical Methods in Natural Language Processing*, pages 1787–1796. Association for Computational Linguistics.

D. Connolly, J. D. Burger, and D. S. Day. 1994. A machine learning approach to anaphoric reference. In *Proceedings of the International Conference on New Methods in Language Processing (NeMLaP)*. ACL.

P. Denis and J. Baldridge. 2007. Joint determination of anaphoricity and coreference resolution using integer programming. In *Proceedings of the Annual Meeting of the North American Association of Computational Linguistics (NAACL)*.

Y. Goldberg and M. Elhadad. 2010. An efficient algorithm for easy-first non-directional dependency parsing. In *Human Language Technologies: The 2010 Annual Conference of the North American Chapter of the Association for Computational Linguistics*, pages 742–750. Association for Computational Linguistics.

J. R Hobbs. 1978. Resolving pronoun references. *Lingua*, 44(4):311–338.

H. Kobdani, H. Schuetze, M. Schiehlen, and H. Kamp. 2011. Bootstrapping coreference resolution using word associations. In *Proceedings of the 49th Annual Meeting of the Association for Computational Linguistics: Human Language Technologies*, pages 783–792. Association for Computational Linguistics.

K. J. Kummerfeld and D. Klein. 2013. Error-driven analysis of challenges in coreference resolution. In *Proceedings of the 2013 Conference on Empirical Methods in Natural Language Processing*, pages 265–277. Association for Computational Linguistics.

S. Lappin and H. J. Leass. 1994. An algorithm for pronominal anaphora resolution. *Computational linguistics*, 20(4):535–561.

H. J. Levesque, E. Davis, and L. Morgenstern. 2011. The winograd schema challenge. In *AAAI Spring Symposium: Logical Formalizations of Commonsense Reasoning*.

X. Luo. 2005. On coreference resolution performance metrics. In *Proceedings of the Conference on Empirical Methods for Natural Language Processing (EMNLP)*.

Mausam, M. Schmitz, R. Bart, S. Soderland, and O. Etzioni. 2012. Open language learning for information extraction. In *Proceedings of Conference on Empirical Methods in Natural Language Processing and Computational Natural Language Learning (EMNLP-CoNLL)*.

V. Ng and C. Cardie. 2002a. Identifying anaphoric and non-anaphoric noun phrases to improve coreference resolution. In *Proceedings of the 19th international conference on Computational linguistics-Volume 1*, pages 1–7. Association for Computational Linguistics.

V. Ng and C. Cardie. 2002b. Improving machine learning approaches to coreference resolution. In *Proceedings of the 40th Annual Meeting of the Association for Computational Linguistics*.

V. Ng. 2004. Learning noun phrase anaphoricity to improve conference resolution: Issues in representation and optimization. In *Proceedings of the 42nd Annual Meeting of the Association for Computational Linguistics (ACL-04)*.

NIST. 2004. The ACE evaluation plan.

S. Pradhan, L. Ramshaw, M. Marcus, M. Palmer, R. Weischedel, and N. Xue. 2011. Conll-2011 shared task: Modeling unrestricted coreference in ontonotes. In *Proceedings of the Annual Conference on Computational Natural Language Learning (CoNLL)*.

S. Pradhan, A. Moschitti, N. Xue, O. Uryupina, and Y. Zhang. 2012. CoNLL-2012 shared task: Modeling multilingual unrestricted coreference in OntoNotes. In *Proceedings of the Annual Conference on Computational Natural Language Learning (CoNLL)*.

V. Punyakanok and D. Roth. 2001. The use of classifiers in sequential inference. In *The Conference on Advances in Neural Information Processing Systems (NIPS)*, pages 995–1001. MIT Press.

A. Rahman and V. Ng. 2011a. Coreference resolution with world knowledge. In *Proceedings of the 49th Annual Meeting of the Association for Computational Linguistics: Human Language Technologies*, pages 814–824. Association for Computational Linguistics.

A. Rahman and V. Ng. 2011b. Coreference resolution with world knowledge. In *ACL*, pages 814–824.

A. Rahman and V. Ng. 2012. Resolving complex cases of definite pronouns: the winograd schema challenge. In *Proceedings of the 2012 Joint Conference on Empirical Methods in Natural Language Processing and Computational Natural Language Learning*, pages 777–789. Association for Computational Linguistics.

L. Ratinov and D. Roth. 2012. Learning-based multi-sieve co-reference resolution with knowledge. In *Proceedings of the Conference on Empirical Methods for Natural Language Processing (EMNLP)*.

Lev Ratinov, Dan Roth, Doug Downey, and Mike Anderson. 2011. Local and global algorithms for disambiguation to wikipedia. In *Proceedings of the 49th Annual Meeting of the Association for Computational Linguistics: Human Language Technologies*, pages 1375–1384, Portland, Oregon, USA, June. Association for Computational Linguistics.

D. Roth and W. Yih. 2004. A linear programming formulation for global inference in natural language tasks. In Hwee Tou Ng and Ellen Riloff, editors, *Proceedings of the Annual Conference on Computational Natural Language Learning (CoNLL)*, pages 1–8. Association for Computational Linguistics.

H. A. Schwartz and F. Gomez. 2009. Acquiring applicable common sense knowledge from the web. In *Proceedings of the Workshop on Unsupervised and Minimally Supervised Learning of Lexical Semantics*, UMSLLS '09, pages 1–9, Stroudsburg, PA, USA. Association for Computational Linguistics.

W. M. Soon, D. C. Y. Lim, and H. T. Ng. 2001a. A machine learning approach to coreference resolution of noun phrases. *Computational Linguistics, Volume 27, Number 4, December 2001*.

Wee Meng Soon, Hwee Tou Ng, and Daniel Chung Yong Lim. 2001b. A machine learning approach to coreference resolution of noun phrases. *Computational linguistics*, 27(4):521–544.

V. Stoyanov, C. Cardie, N. Gilbert, E. Riloff, D. Buttler, and D. Hysom. 2010. Coreference resolution with reconcile. In *Proceedings of the ACL 2010 Conference Short Papers*, pages 156–161. Association for Computational Linguistics.

N. Tandon, G. de Melo, and G. Weikum. 2014. Acquiring comparative commonsense knowledge from the web. In *Proceedings of AAAI Conference on Artificial Intelligence*. AAAI.

M. Vilain, J. Burger, J. Aberdeen, D. Connolly, and L. Hirschman. 1995. A model-theoretic coreference scoring scheme. In *Proceedings of the 6th conference on Message understanding*.

T. Wilson, P. Hoffmann, S. Somasundaran, J. Kessler, J. Wiebe, Y. Choi, C. Cardie, E. Riloff, and S. Patwardhan. 2005. Opinionfinder: A system for subjectivity analysis. In *Proceedings of HLT/EMNLP on interactive demonstrations*, pages 34–35. Association for Computational Linguistics.

T. Winograd. 1972. Understanding natural language. *Cognitive psychology*, 3(1):1–191.

J. Zheng, L. Vilnis, S. Singh, J. D. Choi, and A. McCallum. 2013. Dynamic knowledge-base alignment for coreference resolution. In *Proceedings of the Seventeenth Conference on Computational Natural Language Learning (CoNLL)*, pages 153–162, Sofia, Bulgaria, August. Association for Computational Linguistics.

# Author Index

# Conference of the North American Chapter of the Association for Computational Linguistics: Human Language Technologies

# (NAACL HLT 2015)

**Denver, Colorado, USA**
**31 May – 5 June 2015**

**Volume 2 of 2**

**ISBN: 978-1-5108-0445-6**

**Printed from e-media with permission by:**

Curran Associates, Inc.
57 Morehouse Lane
Red Hook, NY 12571

CURRAN ASSOCIATES INC.
proceedings
.com

**Some format issues inherent in the e-media version may also appear in this print version.**



Printed by Curran Associates, Inc. (2015)



Association for Computational Linguistics
209 N. Eighth Street
Stroudsburg, Pennsylvania 18360

Phone: 1-570-476-8006
Fax: 1-570-476-0860

acl@aclweb.org

**Additional copies of this publication are available from:**

Curran Associates, Inc.
57 Morehouse Lane
Red Hook, NY 12571 USA
Phone: 845-758-0400
Fax: 845-758-2634
Email: curran@proceedings.com
Web: www.proceedings.com

NAACL HLT 2015

# The 2015 Conference of the North American Chapter of the Association for Computational Linguistics: Human Language Technologies

## Proceedings of the Conference

May 31 – June 5, 2015
Denver, Colorado, USA

**Platinum**

**Gold**

**Silver**

**Bronze**

**Supporters**

**Overseas student fellowship sponsors**

# Message from the General Chair

Welcome to NAACL-HLT 2015 – at its $14^{th}$ edition! Computational Linguistics has grown into one of the most exciting and diverse research communities, with an ever increasing number of researchers, many big and small companies, and a vibrant community of learners eager to get prepared to take on some of the fun and exciting challenges in the field. This year's NAACL-HLT conference is a testimony to the vibrancy and vitality of this community.

Some of the highlights of this year's program include two excellent invited speakers – Lillian Lee from Cornell and Fei-fei Li from Stanford – who will talk about the exciting research going on at the intersection of our field with social sciences and computer vision; many interesting paper presentations on cutting-edge research in computational linguistics, culminating with three best paper awards that will be presented in a plenary session during the last day of the conference; several excellent student-authored papers and dissertation proposals as part of the student research workshop; many exciting demos showing the latest in terms of developed systems available in our field; six tutorials on some of the most up-and-coming research topics in computational linguistics; several workshops on diverse topics ranging from multiword expressions and metaphors to clinical psychology and educational applications, including thirteen (!) one-day workshops and SEMEVAL as a two-day workshop; the fourth joint conference on lexical and computational semantics *SEM as a collocated conference; and, last but not least: a country line dance lesson!

As with any event of this scale, it would have not been possible without the hard work of a wonderful group of people. I would like to thank Priscilla Rasmussen for the zillions of bits and pieces that she has been doing on an everyday basis, to make sure that every single logistical detail of the forthcoming NAACL-HLT was ironed out. It is no overstatement to say that the success (and fun!) of this year's conference is in large part due to Priscilla.

I am also grateful to Hal Daumé III for getting us started on this "NAACL-HLT 2015" journey, and being always willing to help with advice and information from his experience from previous years. Lucy Vanderwende and Daniel Marcu have also graciously agreed to "pass the baton" conversations that were very helpful and informative.

I was extremely fortunate to have the chance to work with the best committee ever: Joyce Chai and Anoop Sarkar (program chairs); Cornelia Caragea and Bing Liu (workshop co-chairs); Yang Liu and Thamar Solorio (tutorial co-chairs); Shibamouli Lahiri, Karen Mazidi and Alisa Zhila (student co-chairs) and Diana Inkpen and Smaranda Muresan (faculty advisors) for the student research workshop; Matt Gerber, Catherine Havasi, and Finley Lacatusu (demo co-chairs); Annie Louise (student volunteer coordinator); Kevin Cohen (local sponsorship chair); Saif Mohammad (publicity chair); Matt Post and Adam Lopez (publication co-chairs); Peter Ljunglöf (website chair); Aurelia Bunescu (handbook cover designer); Graeme Hirst and Joel Tetreault (treasurers); Asli Celikyilmaz and Julia Hockenmaier (sponsorship co-chairs).

I am also grateful to our sponsors for their generous contributions, which made the conference possible: A9, Baobab, Bloomberg, Digital Roots, Goldman Sachs, Google, IBM, Information Sciences Institute, National Science Foundation, Nuance, SDL, University of Washington Computational Linguistics, Yahoo Labs.

Finally, my gratitude goes to everyone else who contributed to the success of the conference: area chairs, workshop organizers, tutorial presenters, student mentors, and reviewers. And of course my deepest thanks to you, the attendees: you are the life and spirit of this entire conference.

Here is to an enjoyable NAACL-HLT 2015, and many more exciting conferences to come!

Rada Mihalcea, University of Michigan
NAACL 2015 General Chair

# Message from the Program Chairs

Welcome to the 2015 Conference of the North American Chapter of the Association for Computational Linguistics – Human Language Technologies or NAACL HLT 2015 for short.

This year, we received the largest number of submissions in the history of NAACL: a total of 714 submissions with 402 long paper submissions and 312 short papers submissions. From these, 117 long papers (62 oral presentations and 55 poster presentations) and 69 short papers (24 oral presentations and 45 poster presentations) were accepted to appear at the conference.

The submissions to NAACL HLT 2015 were assigned to 18 technical areas including a new topic area called *Language and Vision*. This track was introduced with an intent to broaden research on natural language processing that is situated in a rich visual and perceptual context. We received 16 submissions for this area and seven of them will be presented at the conference.

For NAACL HLT 2015 we initiated a meta review process, where each paper received an analysis of the merits of the paper from the area chair's perspective that was based on the reviewer comments, the reviewer discussion and the author rebuttal. We found the meta reviews very helpful in consolidating the reviews and providing justifications for final decisions. As this was an experiment this year, the meta reviews were not sent to the authors.

Based on comments from reviewers, nominations from area chairs, and rankings from the best paper committee, three papers were selected to receive the best paper awards at the conference.

Continuing the tradition, NAACL HLT 2015 will feature 19 papers which were accepted for publication in the Transactions of the Association for Computational Linguistics (TACL). The TACL papers were split into 10 oral presentations and 9 poster presentatons.

We are very pleased to have two exciting keynote talks: one by Professor Lillian Lee (Cornell University) and the other by Professor Fei-fei Li (Stanford University).

There are many people to thank for who have worked diligently to make NAACL HLT 2015 possible. Thanks to the 32 area chairs for their hard work on recruiting reviewers, managing reviews, leading discussions, and making recommendations. All the area chairs are listed in the Program Committee section of the Front Matter. Thanks to Chris Callison-Burch, David Mimno, Sameer Pradhan, and Philip Resnik for stepping in to serve as area co-chairs at the last minute when we were faced with an unexpectedly large number of submissions in some tracks.

Following what was done in the last NAACL conference, we used the paper assignment tool developed by Mark Dredze to assign papers to reviewers. Thanks to Mark Dredze and Jiang Guo for their hard work on assigning papers to reviewers based on their preferences. We had to especially rely on this tool this year because the distribution of submissions across areas was very different from past trends.

This program certainly would not be possible without the help of the 460 reviewers. Their names are listed in the Program Committee section. In particular, 116 reviewers from this list were recognized by the area chairs as best reviewers who have turned in exceptionally well-written and constructive reviews and who have actively engaged in the post-rebuttal discussions. The names of the best reviewers are marked with * in the list of reviewers.

We are also indebted to the best paper award committee which consists of Claire Cardie, Daniel Gildea, Daniel Marcu, and Fernando Pereira. Their time and effort in recommending the best paper awards is much appreciated.

We also would like to thank Hal Daumé III, Kristina Toutanova, and Lucy Vanderwende for generously sharing their experience in organizing prior NAACL/ACL conferences and for their advice. We are grateful for the guidance and the support of the NAACL president Hal Daumé III, and the NAACL board. We also would like to thank the publication co-chairs Matt Post and Adam Lopez for putting together the proceedings and the conference handbook; and Paolo Gai and Rich Gerber from Softconf for always being responsive to our requests.

We would like to thank the ACL Business Manager Priscilla Rasmussen. She was our *go to* person who knew all details of the conference in and out. We are very grateful for her help.

Finally, this conference could not have happened without the efforts of the general chair, Rada Mihalcea. She made sure the various sections of NAACL organization worked well together. Her monthly newsletters informed all the organizers about what was being done by everyone else. We are very thankful for her leadership in the organization of NAACL HLT 2015.

We hope you will enjoy NAACL HLT 2015!

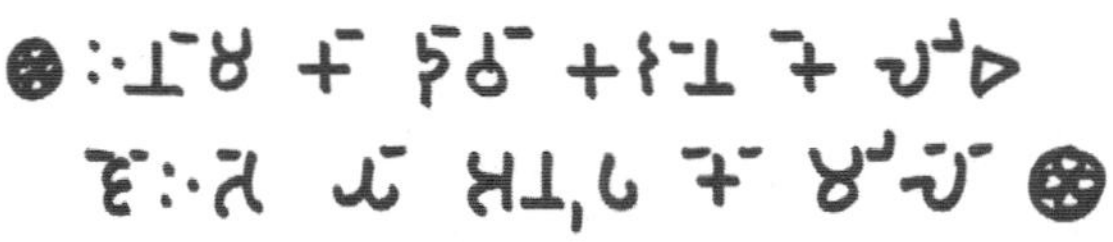

NAACL HLT 2015 Program Co-Chairs
Joyce Chai, Michigan State University
Anoop Sarkar, Simon Fraser University

# Organizing Committee

**General Chair**
Rada Mihalcea, University of Michigan, USA

**Local Arrangements Chair**
Priscilla Rasmussen, ACL Business Manager

**Program Committee Co-chairs**
Joyce Chai, Michigan State University, USA
Anoop Sarkar, Simon Fraser University, Canada

**Workshop Co-chairs**
Cornelia Caragea, University of North Texas, USA
Bing Liu, University of Illinois at Chicago, USA

**Tutorial Co-chairs**
Yang Liu, University of Texas at Dallas, USA
Thamar Solorio, University of Alabama at Birmingham, USA

**Student Research Workshop Co-chairs**
*Student Co-chairs*
Shibamouli Lahiri, University of Michigan, USA
Karen Mazidi, University of North Texas, USA
Alisa Zhila, Instituto Politécnico Nacional (National Polytechnic Institute), Mexico
*Faculty Advisors*
Diana Inkpen, University of Ottawa, Canada
Smaranda Muresan, Columbia University, USA

**Demo Co-chairs**
Matt Gerber, University of Virginia, USA
Catherine Havasi, Massachusetts Institute of Technology, USA
Finley Lacatusu, Language Computer Corporation, USA

**Student Volunteer Coordinator**
Annie Louis, University of Edinburgh, UK

**Reviewing Coordinators**
Mark Dredze, Johns Hopkins University
Jiang Guo, Harbin Institute of Technology

**Local Sponsorship Chair**
Kevin B. Cohen, University of Colorado, USA

**Publicity Chair**
Saif M. Mohammad, National Research Council Canada

**Publication Co-chairs**
Matt Post, John Hopkins University, USA
Adam Lopez, University of Edinburgh, UK

**Conference Handbook Editor**
Matt Post, Johns Hopkins University

**Website Chair**
Peter Ljunglöf, University of Gothenburg and Chalmers University of Technology, Sweden

**Business Manager**
Priscilla Rasmussen

# Program Committee

**Program Committee Co-chairs**
Joyce Chai, Michigan State University, USA
Anoop Sarkar, Simon Fraser University, Canada

**Area Chairs**
*Dialogue and Interactive Systems*
Jason D. Williams, Microsoft Research

*Discourse and Pragmatics*
Ani Nenkova, University of Pennsylvania
Vincent Ng, University of Texas at Dallas

*Generation and Summarization*
Chris Callison-Burch, University of Pennsylvania
Fei Liu, Carnegie Mellon University

*Information Extraction and Question Answering*
Alan Ritter, The Ohio State University
Bowen Zhou, IBM Research

*Information Retrieval*
David Smith, Northeastern University

*Language and Vision*
Julia Hockenmaier, University of Illinois at Urbana-Champaign

*Language Resources and Evaluation*
Will Lewis, Microsoft Research
Sameer Pradhan, Harvard University

*Linguistic and Psycholinguistic Aspects of CL*
William Schuler, The Ohio State University

*Machine Learning for NLP*
Amarnag Subramanya, Google Research
Tong Zhang, Baidu Inc. and Rutgers University

*Machine Translation*
Bill Byrne, Cambridge University
Hany Hassan, Microsoft Research
Kevin Knight, Information Sciences Institute, University of Southern California
Haitao Mi, IBM Research

*NLP for Web, Social Media and Social Sciences*
Brendan O'Connor, University of Massachusetts
Philip Resnik, University of Maryland

*NLP-enabled Technology*
Richard Socher, Stanford University

*Phonology, Morphology, and Word Segmentation*
Sami Virpioja, Lingsoft and Aalto University

*Semantics*
Dipanjan Das, Google
William Dolan, Microsoft Research
Luke Zettlemoyer, University of Washington

*Sentiment Analysis and Opinion Mining*
Saif M. Mohammad, National Research Council Canada
Jerry Zhu, University of Wisconsin-Madison

*Spoken Language Processing*
Xiaodong He, Microsoft Research

*Tagging, Chunking, Syntax, and Parsing*
Noah Smith, Carnegie Mellon University
Yue Zhang, Singapore University of Technology and Design

*Text Categorization and Topic Models*
Jordan Boyd-Graber, University of Colorado at Boulder
David Mimno, Cornell University

### Primary Reviewers

The list of all reviewers for NAACL HLT 2015. The area chairs also picked the best reviewers in their track. These best reviewers are marked with an asterisk in the list which is alphabetical on the last name. Multiple asterisks mean that multiple area chairs chose that reviewer to be the best in their track.

Amjad Abu-Jbara, Mikhail Ageev, Eneko Agirre, *Gregory Aist, Jan Alexandersson, *James Allan, Jesse Anderton, Jacob Andreas, Nicholas Andrews, Gabor Angeli, *Yoav Artzi, Nicholas Asher, Javed Aslam, Michael Auli, amittai axelrod.

Anton Bakalov, Kirk Baker, *Timothy Baldwin, Miguel Ballesteros, David Bamman, *Srinivas Bangalore, *Mohit Bansal, *Marco Baroni, Roberto Basili, Daniel Bauer, Beata Beigman Klebanov, *Emily M. Bender, Michael Bendersky, Jonathan Berant, Taylor Berg-Kirkpatrick, Sabine Bergler, Delphine Bernhard, Pushpak Bhattacharyya, *Klinton Bicknell, Dan Bikel, Steven Bird, Anders Björkelund, *Graeme Blackwood, Eduardo Blanco, John Blitzer, Nathan Bodenstab, Bernd Bohnet, Johan Bos, Alexandre Bouchard, Kristy Boyer, Chris Brew, *Chris Brockett, Paul Buitelaar, Wray Buntine, *David Burkett, *Benjamin Börschinger.

Aoife Cahill, Nicoletta Calzolari, Marine Carpuat, Xavier Carreras, Marc-Allen Cartright, Damir Cavar, Asli Celikyilmaz, *Daniel Cer, Nathanael Chambers, Ming-Wei Chang, Wanxiang Che, Boxing Chen, Hsin-Hsi Chen, Chen Chen, Wenliang Chen, *Colin Cherry, *Jackie Chi Kit Cheung, *David Chiang, Christian Chiarcos, Jinho D. Choi, *Yejin Choi, Jennifer Chu-Carroll, Christopher Cieri, Philipp Cimiano, *Stephen Clark, *Jonathan Clark, Martin Cmejrek, Shay B. Cohen, Trevor Cohn, *John Conroy, Paul Cook, Dan Cristea, Peter Culicover, Aron Culotta.

Robert Daland, Jeff Dalton, Pradipto Das, *Hal Daumé III, Adrià de Gispert, Vera Demberg, *Steve DeNeefe, Pascal Denis, Leon Derczynski, David DeVault, *Jacob Devlin, *Barbara Di Eugenio, Mona Diab, *Laura Dietz, *Doug Downey, Gabriel Doyle, Eduard Dragut, Mark Dredze, Markus Dreyer, Lan Du, *Kevin Duh, Ewan Dunbar, *Greg Durrett, Chris Dyer.

Sauleh Eetemadi, Markus Egg, Koji Eguchi, Patrick Ehlen, Andreas Eisele, Jacob Eisenstein, Jason Eisner, Desmond Elliott, Tamer Elsayed, *Micha Elsner, Ahmad Emami, *Katrin Erk.

Anthony Fader, James Fan, *Manaal Faruqui, Afsaneh Fazly, Marcello Federico, *Christian Federmann, Yang Feng, Vanessa Wei Feng, Minwei Feng, *Katja Filippova, Nicholas FitzGerald, Jeffrey Flanigan, Radu Florian, Sandiway Fong, *George Foster, Jennifer Foster, Diego Frassinelli.

**Michel Galley, Michael Gamon, Sudeep Gandhe, Juri Ganitkevitch, *Qin Gao, *Claire Gardent, Milica Gasic, Niyu Ge, George Giannakopoulos, Daniel Gildea, *Kevin Gimpel, Filip Ginter, *Roxana Girju, Peter B. Golbus, Yoav Goldberg, Dan Goldwasser, Sharon Goldwater, Jeff Good, Kyle Gorman, Cyril Goutte, Joao Graca, Stephan Greene, Edward Grefenstette, Stig-Arne Grönroos, Weiwei Guo, Iryna Gurevych, *Carlos Gómez-Rodríguez.

Nizar Habash, Eva Hajicova, John Hale, Keith Hall, *David Hall, Michael Hammond, *Sanda Harabagiu, *Eva Hasler, Claudia Hauff, Kenneth Heafield, John Henderson, Aurélie Herbelot, Jack Hessel, Derrick Higgins, Julia Hirschberg, *Graeme Hirst, Anna Hjalmarsson, Micah Hodosh, *Dirk Hovy, Eduard Hovy, *Yuening Hu, Zhongqiang Huang, Minlie Huang, Liang Huang, Ruihong Huang, *Mans Hulden, Rebecca Hwa.

Gonzalo Iglesias, Ryu Iida, Diana Inkpen, Amy Isard, Abe Ittycheriah.

Jagadeesh Jagarlamudi, *Jing Jiang, Richard Johansson, Mark Johnson, *Michael Johnston, Shafiq Joty, Dan Jurafsky, *David Jurgens.

*Min-Yen Kan, Pallika Kanani, *Saurabh Kataria, Daisuke Kawahara, *Andrew Kehler, *Frank Keller, Svetlana Kiritchenko, Alexandre Klementiev, Alistair Knott, Philipp Koehn, Oskar Kohonen, Kazunori Komatani, Terry Koo, Anna Korhonen, Alexander Kotov, Zornitsa Kozareva, Jayant Krishnamurthy, Kriste Krstovski, Canasai Kruengkrai, Lun-Wei Ku, *Marco Kuhlmann, *Roland Kuhn, Shankar Kumar, Jonathan K. Kummerfeld, *Tom Kwiatkowski.

Igor Labutov, D Terence Langendoen, *Guy Lapalme, **Mirella Lapata, Jey Han Lau, *Alon Lavie, *Hung-yi Lee, Sungjin Lee, Yoong Keok Lee, Moontae Lee, Maider Lehr, Tao Lei, Alessandro Lenci, *Omer Levy, Shoushan Li, Fangtao Li, Jiwei Li, Junyi Jessy Li, Jinyu Li, Percy Liang, Mark Liberman, *Shou-de Lin, *Chin-Yew Lin, Xiao Ling, *Yang Liu, Lemao Liu, Jingjing Liu, Qun Liu, *Yang Liu, Adam Lopez, *Annie Louis, Bin Lu, Xiaoqiang Luo, Thang Luong.

Wei-Yun Ma, *Andrew Maas, Wolfgang Macherey, Nitin Madnani, Suresh Manandhar, Gideon Mann, *Christopher D. Manning, *Daniel Marcu, Katja Markert, André F. T. Martins, Yuval Marton, Sameer Maskey, *Michael Maxwell, Diana Maynard, Diana McCarthy, David McClosky, Ryan McDonald, *Bridget McInnes, Louise McNally, *Arul Menezes, Florian Metze, Timothy Miller, Eleni Miltsakaki, *Margaret Mitchell, Yusuke Miyao, Samaneh Moghaddam, Karo Moilanen, Christof Monz, *Taesun Moon, *Robert Moore, Roser Morante, Alessandro Moschitti, *Robert Munro, Brian Murphy.

Mikio Nakano, Preslav Nakov, Roberto Navigli, *Graham Neubig, Guenter Neumann, Hwee Tou Ng, Viet-An Nguyen, Malvina Nissim, Joakim Nivre.

Alice Oh, *Manabu Okumura, Miles Osborne, Myle Ott, Karolina Owczarzak.

Ulrike Pado, *Alexis Palmer, *Martha Palmer, Sinno J. Pan, Siddharth Patwardhan, Michael J. Paul, Virgil Pavlu, *Ted Pedersen, Gerald Penn, Jose Manuel Perea-Ortega, Slav Petrov, Olivier Pietquin, Tommi Pirinen, Emily Pitler, Massimo Poesio, Hoifung Poon, *Andrei Popescu-Belis, Matt Post, Emily Prud'hommeaux, Stephen Pulman, Matthew Purver.

Xian Qian, *Chris Quirk.

Altaf Rahman, Owen Rambow, Antoine Raux, Sujith Ravi, Kyle Rawlins, Siva Reddy, Roi Reichart, David Reitter, Sebastian Riedel, Jason Riesa, Stefan Riezler, German Rigau, *Ellen Riloff, *Laura Rimell, *Eric Ringger, *Brian Roark, Kirk Roberts, Hannah Rohde, Carolyn Rose, Andrew Rosenberg, Sara Rosenthal, Paolo Rosso, *Michael Roth, Teemu Ruokolainen, Irene Russo.

*Kenji Sagae, Alicia Sagae, Saurav Sahay, Rajhans Samdani, *Murat Saraclar, *Giorgio Satta, Asad Sayeed, David Schlangen, Nathan Schneider, Alexandra Schofield, *Lane Schwartz, H. Andrew Schwartz, Holger Schwenk, Hendra Setiawan, Izhak Shafran, Ekaterina Shutova, Khalil Sima'an, Sameer Singh, *Kairit Sirts, Gabriel Skantze, Linfeng Song, Caroline Sporleder, Vivek Srikumar, Manfred Stede, Mark Steedman, Amanda Stent, Brandon Stewart, Veselin Stoyanov, Weiwei Sun, *Mihai Surdeanu, Anders Søgaard.

Partha P. Talukdar, *Joel Tetreault, *Kapil Thadani, Jörg Tiedemann, Christoph Tillmann, Ivan Titov,

*Kristina Toutanova, David Traum, Reut Tsarfaty, Oren Tsur, Yoshimasa Tsuruoka, *Peter Turney, *Oscar Täckström.

Jakob Uszkoreit.

Tim Van de Cruys, *Benjamin Van Durme, **Lucy Vanderwende, Yannick Versley, Aline Villavicencio.

*Xiaojun Wan, *Stephen Wan, Haifeng Wang, Lidan Wang, Lu Wang, Zhiguo Wang, *William Yang Wang, *Taro Watanabe, Andy Way, *Bonnie Webber, David Weir, David Weiss, *Michael White, Janyce Wiebe, Michael Wiegand, Shuly Wintner, Andreas Witt, *Kam-Fai Wong, Kristian Woodsend.

*Fei Xia, Yunqing Xia, Bing Xiang, Tong Xiao, Peng Xu, Wei Xu, Jia Xu, Nianwen Xue.

Hui Yang, Bishan Yang, Muyun Yang, Yi Yang, *Xuchen Yao, Mahsa Yarmohammadi, *Wen-tau Yih, Dani Yogatama, Jianxing Yu, *François Yvon.

Fabio Massimo Zanzotto, Alessandra Zarcone, *Rabih Zbib, Richard Zens, Ke Zhai, Min Zhang, Lei Zhang, Hao Zhang, Hai Zhao, Guodong Zhou, Xiaodan Zhu, Chengqing Zong, *Geoffrey Zweig.

# Invited Talk: "Big data pragmatics!", or, "Putting the ACL in computational social science", or, if you think these title alternatives could turn people on, turn people off, or otherwise have an effect, this talk might be for you.

**Lillian Lee**

Cornell University

## Abstract

What effect does language have on people?

You might say in response, "Who are you to discuss this problem?" and you would be right to do so; this is a Major Question that science has been tackling for many years. But as a field, I think natural language processing and computational linguistics have much to contribute to the conversation, and I hope to encourage the community to further address these issues.

This talk will focus on the effect of phrasing, emphasizing aspects that go beyond just the selection of one particular word over another. The issues we'll consider include: Does the way in which something is worded in and of itself have an effect on whether it is remembered or attracts attention, beyond its content or context? Can we characterize how different sides in a debate frame their arguments, in a way that goes beyond specific lexical choice (e.g., "pro-choice" vs. "pro-life")? The settings we'll explore range from movie quotes that achieve cultural prominence; to posts on Facebook, Wikipedia, Twitter, and the arXiv; to framing in public discourse on the inclusion of genetically-modified organisms in food.

Joint work with Lars Backstrom, Justin Cheng, Eunsol Choi, Cristian Danescu-Niculescu-Mizil, Jon Kleinberg, Bo Pang, Jennifer Spindel, and Chenhao Tan.

## Biography

Lillian Lee is a professor of computer science and of information science at Cornell University, and the co-Editor-in-Chief, together with Michael Collins, of Transactions of the ACL. Her research interests include natural language processing and computational social science. She is the recipient of the inaugural Best Paper Award at HLT-NAACL 2004 (joint with Regina Barzilay), a citation in "Top Picks: Technology Research Advances of 2004" by Technology Research News (also joint with Regina Barzilay), and an Alfred P. Sloan Research Fellowship; and in 2013, she was named a Fellow of the Association for the Advancement of Artificial Intelligence (AAAI). Her group's work has received several mentions in the popular press, including The New York Times, NPR's All Things Considered, and NBC's The Today Show, and one of her co-authored papers was publicly called "boring" by Youtubers Rhett and Link, in a video viewed over 1.8 million times.

# Invited Talk: A Quest for Visual Intelligence in Computers

**Fei-Fei Li**

Stanford University

## Abstract

More than half of the human brain is involved in visual processing. While it took mother nature billions of years to evolve and deliver us a remarkable human visual system, computer vision is one of the youngest disciplines of AI, born with the goal of achieving one of the loftiest dreams of AI. The central problem of computer vision is to turn millions of pixels of a single image into interpretable and actionable concepts so that computers can understand pictures just as well as humans do, from objects, to scenes, activities, events and beyond. Such technology will have a fundamental impact in almost every aspect of our daily life and the society as a whole, ranging from e-commerce, image search and indexing, assistive technology, autonomous driving, digital health and medicine, surveillance, national security, robotics and beyond. In this talk, I will give an overview of what computer vision technology is about and its brief history. I will then discuss some of the recent work from my lab towards large scale object recognition and visual scene story telling. I will particularly emphasize on what we call the "three pillars" of AI in our quest for visual intelligence: data, learning and knowledge. Each of them is critical towards the final solution, yet dependent on the other. This talk draws upon a number of projects ongoing at the Stanford Vision Lab.

## Biography

Dr. Fei-Fei Li is an Associate Professor in the Computer Science Department at Stanford, and the Director of the Stanford Artificial Intelligence Lab and the Stanford Vision Lab. Her research areas are in machine learning, computer vision and cognitive and computational neuroscience, with an emphasis on Big Data analysis. Dr. Fei-Fei Li has published more than 100 scientific articles in top-tier journals and conferences, including Nature, PNAS, Journal of Neuroscience, CVPR, ICCV, NIPS, ECCV, IJCV, IEEE-PAMI, etc. Dr. Fei-Fei Li obtained her B.A. degree in physics from Princeton in 1999 with High Honors, and her PhD degree in electrical engineering from California Institute of Technology (Caltech) in 2005. She joined Stanford in 2009 as an assistant professor, and was promoted to associate professor with tenure in 2012. Prior to that, she was on faculty at Princeton University (2007-2009) and University of Illinois Urbana-Champaign (2005-2006). Dr. Fei-Fei Li is a speaker at TED2015 main conference, a recipient of the 2014 IBM Faculty Fellow Award, 2011 Alfred Sloan Faculty Award, 2012 Yahoo Labs FREP award, 2009 NSF CAREER award, the 2006 Microsoft Research New Faculty Fellowship and a number of Google Research awards. Work from Fei-Fei's lab have been featured in a number of popular press magazines and newspapers including New York Times, Wired Magazine, and New Scientists.

# Table of Contents

# Conference Program

**Monday, June 1, 2015**

**07:30–08:45** ***Registration and Breakfast***

08:45–09:00 *Welcome to NAACL HLT 2015*
Rada Mihalcea

09:00–10:10 *Invited Talk: "Big data pragmatics!", or, "Putting the ACL in computational social science", or, if you think these title alternatives could turn people on, turn people off, or otherwise have an effect, this talk might be for you*
Lillian Lee

**10:10–10:40** ***Break***

**10:40–12:20** **Session 1A: Semantics (Long Papers)**

10:40–11:05 *Unsupervised Induction of Semantic Roles within a Reconstruction-Error Minimization Framework*
Ivan Titov and Ehsan Khoddam

11:05–11:30 *Predicate Argument Alignment using a Global Coherence Model*
Travis Wolfe, Mark Dredze and Benjamin Van Durme

11:30–11:55 *Improving unsupervised vector-space thematic fit evaluation via role-filler prototype clustering*
Clayton Greenberg, Asad Sayeed and Vera Demberg

11:55–12:20 *A Compositional and Interpretable Semantic Space*
Alona Fyshe, Leila Wehbe, Partha P. Talukdar, Brian Murphy and Tom M. Mitchell

**10:40–12:20 Session 1B: Tagging, Chunking, Syntax and Parsing (Long + TACL Papers)**

10:40–11:05 *Randomized Greedy Inference for Joint Segmentation, POS Tagging and Dependency Parsing*
Yuan Zhang, Chengtao Li, Regina Barzilay and Kareem Darwish

11:05–11:30 *An Incremental Algorithm for Transition-based CCG Parsing*
Bharat Ram Ambati, Tejaswini Deoskar, Mark Johnson and Mark Steedman

11:30–11:55 *Because Syntax Does Matter: Improving Predicate-Argument Structures Parsing with Syntactic Features*
Corentin Ribeyre, Eric Villemonte de la Clergerie and Djamé Seddah

11:55–12:20 *[TACL] Exploring Compositional Architectures and Word Vector Representations for Prepositional Phrase Attachment*
Yonatan Belinkov, Tao Lei, Regina Barzilay, Amir Globerson

**10:40–12:20 Session 1C: Information Retrieval, Text Categorization, Topic Modeling (Long Papers)**

10:40–11:05 *A Hybrid Generative/Discriminative Approach To Citation Prediction*
Chris Tanner and Eugene Charniak

11:05–11:30 *Weakly Supervised Slot Tagging with Partially Labeled Sequences from Web Search Click Logs*
Young-Bum Kim, Minwoo Jeong, Karl Stratos and Ruhi Sarikaya

11:30–11:55 *Not All Character N-grams Are Created Equal: A Study in Authorship Attribution*
Upendra Sapkota, Steven Bethard, Manuel Montes and Thamar Solorio

11:55–12:20 *Effective Use of Word Order for Text Categorization with Convolutional Neural Networks*
Rie Johnson and Tong Zhang

**12:20–14:00** ***Lunch***

**Monday, June 1, 2015 (continued)**

**14:00–15:15 Session 2A: Generation and Summarization (Long Papers)**

14:00–14:25 *Transition-Based Syntactic Linearization*
Yijia Liu, Yue Zhang, Wanxiang Che and Bing Qin

14:25–14:50 *Extractive Summarisation Based on Keyword Profile and Language Model*
Han Xu, Eric Martin and Ashesh Mahidadia

14:50–15:15 *HEADS: Headline Generation as Sequence Prediction Using an Abstract Feature-Rich Space*
Carlos A. Colmenares, Marina Litvak, Amin Mantrach and Fabrizio Silvestri

**14:00–15:15 Session 2B: Language and Vision (Long Papers)**

14:00–14:25 *What's Cookin'? Interpreting Cooking Videos using Text, Speech and Vision*
Jonathan Malmaud, Jonathan Huang, Vivek Rathod, Nicholas Johnston, Andrew Rabinovich and Kevin Murphy

14:25–14:50 *Combining Language and Vision with a Multimodal Skip-gram Model*
Angeliki Lazaridou, Nghia The Pham and Marco Baroni

14:50–15:15 *Discriminative Unsupervised Alignment of Natural Language Instructions with Corresponding Video Segments*
Iftekhar Naim, Young C. Song, Qiguang Liu, Liang Huang, Henry Kautz, Jiebo Luo and Daniel Gildea

**14:00–15:15 Session 2C: NLP for Web, Social Media and Social Sciences (Long Papers)**

14:00–14:25 *TopicCheck: Interactive Alignment for Assessing Topic Model Stability*
Jason Chuang, Margaret E. Roberts, Brandon M. Stewart, Rebecca Weiss, Dustin Tingley, Justin Grimmer and Jeffrey Heer

14:25–14:50 *Inferring latent attributes of Twitter users with label regularization*
Ehsan Mohammady Ardehaly and Aron Culotta

14:50–15:15 *A Neural Network Approach to Context-Sensitive Generation of Conversational Responses*
Alessandro Sordoni, Michel Galley, Michael Auli, Chris Brockett, Yangfeng Ji, Margaret Mitchell, Jian-Yun Nie, Jianfeng Gao and Bill Dolan

**Monday, June 1, 2015 (continued)**

**15:15–16:00 Session 3A: Generation and Summarization (Short Papers)**

15:15–15:30 *How to Make a Frenemy: Multitape FSTs for Portmanteau Generation*
Aliya Deri and Kevin Knight

15:30–15:45 *Aligning Sentences from Standard Wikipedia to Simple Wikipedia*
William Hwang, Hannaneh Hajishirzi, Mari Ostendorf and Wei Wu

15:45–16:00 *Inducing Lexical Style Properties for Paraphrase and Genre Differentiation*
Ellie Pavlick and Ani Nenkova

**15:15–16:00 Session 3B: Information Extraction and Question Answering (Short Papers)**

15:15–15:30 *Entity Linking for Spoken Language*
Adrian Benton and Mark Dredze

15:30–15:45 *Spinning Straw into Gold: Using Free Text to Train Monolingual Alignment Models for Non-factoid Question Answering*
Rebecca Sharp, Peter Jansen, Mihai Surdeanu and Peter Clark

15:45–16:00 *Personalized Page Rank for Named Entity Disambiguation*
Maria Pershina, Yifan He and Ralph Grishman

**15:15–16:00 Session 3C: Machine Learning for NLP (Short Papers)**

15:15–15:30 *When and why are log-linear models self-normalizing?*
Jacob Andreas and Dan Klein

15:30–15:45 *Deep Multilingual Correlation for Improved Word Embeddings*
Ang Lu, Weiran Wang, Mohit Bansal, Kevin Gimpel and Karen Livescu

15:45–16:00 *Disfluency Detection with a Semi-Markov Model and Prosodic Features*
James Ferguson, Greg Durrett and Dan Klein

**16:00–16:30** ***Break***

**16:30–18:00 One minute madness (Long + TACL papers)**

**Session P1A: 18:00–19:30 Poster session 1A: Long + TACL papers**

*The Geometry of Statistical Machine Translation*
Aurelien Waite and Bill Byrne

*Data-driven sentence generation with non-isomorphic trees*
Miguel Ballesteros, Bernd Bohnet, Simon Mille and Leo Wanner

*Latent Domain Word Alignment for Heterogeneous Corpora*
Hoang Cuong and Khalil Sima'an

*Extracting Human Temporal Orientation from Facebook Language*
H. Andrew Schwartz, Gregory Park, Maarten Sap, Evan Weingarten, Johannes Eichstaedt, Margaret Kern, David Stillwell, Michal Kosinski, Jonah Berger, Martin Seligman and Lyle Ungar

*An In-depth Analysis of the Effect of Text Normalization in Social Media*
Tyler Baldwin and Yunyao Li

*Using Summarization to Discover Argument Facets in Online Idealogical Dialog*
Amita Misra, Pranav Anand, Jean E. Fox Tree and Marilyn Walker

*Active Learning with Rationales for Text Classification*
Manali Sharma, Di Zhuang and Mustafa Bilgic

*Inferring Temporally-Anchored Spatial Knowledge from Semantic Roles*
Eduardo Blanco and Alakananda Vempala

*A Dynamic Programming Algorithm for Tree Trimming-based Text Summarization*
Masaaki Nishino, Norihito Yasuda, Tsutomu Hirao, Shin-ichi Minato and Masaaki Nagata

*Modeling Word Meaning in Context with Substitute Vectors*
Oren Melamud, Ido Dagan and Jacob Goldberger

*Corpus-based discovery of semantic intensity scales*
Chaitanya Shivade, Marie-Catherine de Marneffe, Eric Fosler-Lussier and Albert M. Lai

*Dialogue focus tracking for zero pronoun resolution*
Sudha Rao, Allyson Ettinger, Hal Daumé III and Philip Resnik

*Déjà Image-Captions: A Corpus of Expressive Descriptions in Repetition*
Jianfu Chen, Polina Kuznetsova, David Warren and Yejin Choi

**Session P1B: 19:30–21:00 Poster session 1B: Long + TACL papers**

**Monday, June 1, 2015 (continued)**

*Constraint-Based Models of Lexical Borrowing*
Yulia Tsvetkov, Waleed Ammar and Chris Dyer

*Model Invertibility Regularization: Sequence Alignment With or Without Parallel Data*
Tomer Levinboim, Ashish Vaswani and David Chiang

*Jointly Modeling Inter-Slot Relations by Random Walk on Knowledge Graphs for Unsupervised Spoken Language Understanding*
Yun-Nung Chen, William Yang Wang and Alexander Rudnicky

*Expanding Paraphrase Lexicons by Exploiting Lexical Variants*
Atsushi Fujita and Pierre Isabelle

*Diamonds in the Rough: Event Extraction from Imperfect Microblog Data*
Ander Intxaurrondo, Eneko Agirre, Oier Lopez de Lacalle and Mihai Surdeanu

*Unsupervised Dependency Parsing: Let's Use Supervised Parsers*
Phong Le and Willem Zuidema

*A Linear-Time Transition System for Crossing Interval Trees*
Emily Pitler and Ryan McDonald

*Unsupervised Multi-Domain Adaptation with Feature Embeddings*
Yi Yang and Jacob Eisenstein

*Ontologically Grounded Multi-sense Representation Learning for Semantic Vector Space Models*
Sujay Kumar Jauhar, Chris Dyer and Eduard Hovy

*Subsentential Sentiment on a Shoestring: A Crosslingual Analysis of Compositional Classification*
Michael Haas and Yannick Versley

*Cost Optimization in Crowdsourcing Translation: Low cost translations made even cheaper*
Mingkun Gao, Wei Xu and Chris Callison-Burch

*Multitask Learning for Adaptive Quality Estimation of Automatically Transcribed Utterances*
José G. C. de Souza, Hamed Zamani, Matteo Negri, Marco Turchi and Falavigna Daniele

*Incorporating Word Correlation Knowledge into Topic Modeling*
Pengtao Xie, Diyi Yang and Eric Xing

*The Unreasonable Effectiveness of Word Representations for Twitter Named Entity Recognition*
Colin Cherry and Hongyu Guo

*Is Your Anchor Going Up or Down? Fast and Accurate Supervised Topic Models*
Thang Nguyen, Jordan Boyd-Graber, Jeffrey Lund, Kevin Seppi and Eric Ringger

*Grounded Semantic Parsing for Complex Knowledge Extraction*
Ankur P. Parikh, Hoifung Poon and Kristina Toutanova

*Sentiment after Translation: A Case-Study on Arabic Social Media Posts*
Mohammad Salameh, Saif Mohammad and Svetlana Kiritchenko

*Using External Resources and Joint Learning for Bigram Weighting in ILP-Based Multi-Document Summarization*
Chen Li, Yang Liu and Lin Zhao

*Transforming Dependencies into Phrase Structures*
Lingpeng Kong, Alexander M. Rush and Noah A. Smith

*Improving the Inference of Implicit Discourse Relations via Classifying Explicit Discourse Connectives*
Attapol Rutherford and Nianwen Xue

*Solving Hard Coreference Problems*
Haoruo Peng, Daniel Khashabi and Dan Roth

*Pragmatic Neural Language Modelling in Machine Translation*
Paul Baltescu and Phil Blunsom

*Key Female Characters in Film Have More to Talk About Besides Men: Automating the Bechdel Test*
Apoorv Agarwal, Jiehan Zheng, Shruti Kamath, Sriramkumar Balasubramanian and Shirin Ann Dey

*[TACL] Dense Event Ordering with a Multi-Pass Architecture*
Nathanael Chambers, Taylor Cassidy, Bill McDowell, and Steven Bethard

*[TACL] Locally Non-Linear Learning for Statistical Machine Translation via Discretization and Structured Regularization*
Jonathan H. Clark, Chris Dyer, and Alon Lavie

*[TACL] SPRITE: Generalizing Topic Models with Structured Priors*
Michael J. Paul and Mark Dredze

**Monday, June 1, 2015 (continued)**

*[TACL] Reasoning about Quantities in Natural Language*
Subhro Roy, Tim Vieira, and Dan Roth

*[TACL] A sense-topic model for WSI with unsupervised data enrichment*
Jing Wang, Mohit Bansal, Kevin Gimpel, Brian D. Ziebart, and Clement T. Yu

**Tuesday, June 2, 2015**

**07:30–09:00** ***Registration and Breakfast***

**09:00–10:40** **Session 4A: Dialogue and Spoken Language Processing (Long Papers)**

09:00–09:25 *Semantic Grounding in Dialogue for Complex Problem Solving*
Xiaolong Li and Kristy Boyer

09:25–09:50 *Learning Knowledge Graphs for Question Answering through Conversational Dialog*
Ben Hixon, Peter Clark and Hannaneh Hajishirzi

09:50–10:15 *Sentence segmentation of aphasic speech*
Kathleen C. Fraser, Naama Ben-David, Graeme Hirst, Naida Graham and Elizabeth Rochon

10:15–10:40 *Semantic parsing of speech using grammars learned with weak supervision*
Judith Gaspers, Philipp Cimiano and Britta Wrede

**09:00–10:40 Session 4B: Machine Learning for NLP (Long Papers)**

09:00–09:25 *Early Gains Matter: A Case for Preferring Generative over Discriminative Crowd-sourcing Models*
Paul Felt, Kevin Black, Eric Ringger, Kevin Seppi and Robbie Haertel

09:25–09:50 *Optimizing Multivariate Performance Measures for Learning Relation Extraction Models*
Gholamreza Haffari, Ajay Nagesh and Ganesh Ramakrishnan

09:50–10:15 *Convolutional Neural Network for Paraphrase Identification*
Wenpeng Yin and Hinrich Schütze

10:15–10:40 *Representation Learning Using Multi-Task Deep Neural Networks for Semantic Classification and Information Retrieval*
Xiaodong Liu, Jianfeng Gao, Xiaodong He, Li Deng, Kevin Duh and Ye-Yi Wang

**09:00–10:40 Session 4C: Phonology, Morphology and Word Segmentation (Long Papers)**

09:00–09:25 *Inflection Generation as Discriminative String Transduction*
Garrett Nicolai, Colin Cherry and Grzegorz Kondrak

09:25–09:50 *Penalized Expectation Propagation for Graphical Models over Strings*
Ryan Cotterell and Jason Eisner

09:50–10:15 *Joint Generation of Transliterations from Multiple Representations*
Lei Yao and Grzegorz Kondrak

10:15–10:40 *Prosodic boundary information helps unsupervised word segmentation*
Bogdan Ludusan, Gabriel Synnaeve and Emmanuel Dupoux

**10:40–11:15** ***Break***

**Tuesday, June 2, 2015 (continued)**

**11:15–12:30 Session 5A: Semantics (Short Papers)**

11:15–11:30 *So similar and yet incompatible: Toward the automated identification of semantically compatible words*
Germán Kruszewski and Marco Baroni

11:30–11:45 *Do Supervised Distributional Methods Really Learn Lexical Inference Relations?*
Omer Levy, Steffen Remus, Chris Biemann and Ido Dagan

11:45–12:00 *A Word Embedding Approach to Predicting the Compositionality of Multiword Expressions*
Bahar Salehi, Paul Cook and Timothy Baldwin

12:00–12:15 *Word Embedding-based Antonym Detection using Thesauri and Distributional Information*
Masataka Ono, Makoto Miwa and Yutaka Sasaki

12:15–12:30 *A Comparison of Word Similarity Performance Using Explanatory and Non-explanatory Texts*
Lifeng Jin and William Schuler

**11:15–12:30 Session 5B: Machine Translation (Short Papers)**

11:15–11:30 *Morphological Modeling for Machine Translation of English-Iraqi Arabic Spoken Dialogs*
Katrin Kirchhoff, Yik-Cheung Tam, Colleen Richey and Wen Wang

11:30–11:45 *Continuous Adaptation to User Feedback for Statistical Machine Translation*
Frédéric Blain, Fethi Bougares, Amir Hazem, Loïc Barrault and Holger Schwenk

11:45–12:00 *Normalized Word Embedding and Orthogonal Transform for Bilingual Word Translation*
Chao Xing, Dong Wang, Chao Liu and Yiye Lin

12:00–12:15 *Fast and Accurate Preordering for SMT using Neural Networks*
Adrià de Gispert, Gonzalo Iglesias and Bill Byrne

12:15–12:30 *APRO: All-Pairs Ranking Optimization for MT Tuning*
Markus Dreyer and Yuanzhe Dong

**11:15–12:30 Session 5C: Morphology, Syntax, Multilinguality, and Applications (Short Papers)**

11:15–11:30 *Paradigm classification in supervised learning of morphology*
Malin Ahlberg, Markus Forsberg and Mans Hulden

11:30–11:45 *Shift-Reduce Constituency Parsing with Dynamic Programming and POS Tag Lattice*
Haitao Mi and Liang Huang

11:45–12:00 *Unsupervised Code-Switching for Multilingual Historical Document Transcription*
Dan Garrette, Hannah Alpert-Abrams, Taylor Berg-Kirkpatrick and Dan Klein

12:00–12:15 *Matching Citation Text and Cited Spans in Biomedical Literature: a Search-Oriented Approach*
Arman Cohan, Luca Soldaini and Nazli Goharian

12:15–12:30 *Effective Feature Integration for Automated Short Answer Scoring*
Keisuke Sakaguchi, Michael Heilman and Nitin Madnani

**12:30–14:00 *Lunch***

**14:00–15:15 Session 6A: Generation and Summarization (Long Papers)**

14:00–14:25 *Socially-Informed Timeline Generation for Complex Events*
Lu Wang, Claire Cardie and Galen Marchetti

14:25–14:50 *Movie Script Summarization as Graph-based Scene Extraction*
Philip John Gorinski and Mirella Lapata

14:50–15:15 *Toward Abstractive Summarization Using Semantic Representations*
Fei Liu, Jeffrey Flanigan, Sam Thomson, Norman Sadeh and Noah A. Smith

**14:00–15:15 Session 6B: Discourse and Coreference (Long Papers)**

14:00–14:25 *Encoding World Knowledge in the Evaluation of Local Coherence*
Muyu Zhang, Vanessa Wei Feng, Bing Qin, Graeme Hirst, Ting Liu and Jingwen Huang

14:25–14:50 *Chinese Event Coreference Resolution: An Unsupervised Probabilistic Model Rivaling Supervised Resolvers*
Chen Chen and Vincent Ng

14:50–15:15 *Removing the Training Wheels: A Coreference Dataset that Entertains Humans and Challenges Computers*
Anupam Guha, Mohit Iyyer, Danny Bouman and Jordan Boyd-Graber

**14:00–15:15 Session 6C: Information Extraction and Question Answering (Long Papers)**

14:00–14:25 *Injecting Logical Background Knowledge into Embeddings for Relation Extraction*
Tim Rocktäschel, Sameer Singh and Sebastian Riedel

14:25–14:50 *Unsupervised Entity Linking with Abstract Meaning Representation*
Xiaoman Pan, Taylor Cassidy, Ulf Hermjakob, Heng Ji and Kevin Knight

14:50–15:15 *Idest: Learning a Distributed Representation for Event Patterns*
Sebastian Krause, Enrique Alfonseca, Katja Filippova and Daniele Pighin

**15:15–15:45 *Break***

**15:45–17:00 Session 7A: Semantics (Long + TACL Papers)**

15:45–16:10 *High-Order Low-Rank Tensors for Semantic Role Labeling*
Tao Lei, Yuan Zhang, Lluís Màrquez, Alessandro Moschitti and Regina Barzilay

16:10–16:35 *[TACL] Large-scale Semantic Parsing without Question-Answer Pairs*
Siva Reddy, Mirella Lapata, and Mark Steedman

16:35–17:00 *[TACL] A Large Scale Evaluation of Distributional Semantic Models: Parameters, Interactions and Model Selection*
Gabriella Lapesa and Stefan Evert

**15:45–17:00 Session 7B: Information Extraction and Question Answering (Long + TACL Papers)**

15:45–16:10 *Lexical Event Ordering with an Edge-Factored Model*
Omri Abend, Shay B. Cohen and Mark Steedman

16:10–16:35 *[TACL] Entity disambiguation with web links*
Andrew Chisholm and Ben Hachey

16:35–17:00 *[TACL] A Joint Model for Entity Analysis: Coreference, Typing, and Linking*
Greg Durrett and Dan Klein

**15:45–17:00 Session 7C: Machine Translation (Long Papers)**

15:45–16:10 *Bag-of-Words Forced Decoding for Cross-Lingual Information Retrieval*
Felix Hieber and Stefan Riezler

16:10–16:35 *Accurate Evaluation of Segment-level Machine Translation Metrics*
Yvette Graham, Timothy Baldwin and Nitika Mathur

16:35–17:00 *Leveraging Small Multilingual Corpora for SMT Using Many Pivot Languages*
Raj Dabre, Fabien Cromieres, Sadao Kurohashi and Pushpak Bhattacharyya

**Session P2B: 18:30–20:00 Poster session 2B: Short papers**

**Wednesday, June 3, 2015**

**07:30–09:00** ***Registration and Breakfast***

09:00–10:10 *Invited Talk: A Quest for Visual Intelligence in Computers*
Fei-fei Li

**10:10–10:40** ***Break***

**10:40–11:55** **Session 8A: NLP for Web, Social Media and Social Sciences (Long + TACL Papers)**

10:40–11:05 *Testing and Comparing Computational Approaches for Identifying the Language of Framing in Political News*
Eric Baumer, Elisha Elovic, Ying Qin, Francesca Polletta and Geri Gay

11:05–11:30 *[TACL] Extracting Lexically Divergent Paraphrases from Twitter*
Wei Xu, Alan Ritter, Chris Callison-Burch, William B. Dolan, and Yangfeng Ji

11:30–11:55 *Echoes of Persuasion: The Effect of Euphony in Persuasive Communication*
Marco Guerini, Gözde Özbal and Carlo Strapparava

**10:40–11:55** **Session 8B: Language and Vision (Long + TACL Papers)**

10:40–11:05 *Translating Videos to Natural Language Using Deep Recurrent Neural Networks*
Subhashini Venugopalan, Huijuan Xu, Jeff Donahue, Marcus Rohrbach, Raymond Mooney and Kate Saenko

11:05–11:30 *[TACL] A Bayesian Model of Grounded Color Semantics*
Brian McMahan and Matthew Stone

11:30–11:55 *Learning to Interpret and Describe Abstract Scenes*
Luis Gilberto Mateos Ortiz, Clemens Wolff and Mirella Lapata

**10:40–11:55 Session 8C: Machine Translation (Long + TACL Papers)**

10:40–11:05 *A Comparison of Update Strategies for Large-Scale Maximum Expected BLEU Training*
Joern Wuebker, Sebastian Muehr, Patrick Lehnen, Stephan Peitz and Hermann Ney

11:05–11:30 *[TACL] Gappy Pattern Matching on GPUs for On-Demand Extraction of Hierarchical Translation Grammars*
Hua He, Jimmy Lin, and Adam Lopez

11:30–11:55 *Learning Translation Models from Monolingual Continuous Representations*
Kai Zhao, Hany Hassan and Michael Auli

**11:55–13:00** ***Lunch***

**13:00–14:00 NAACL Business Meeting**

**14:00–15:15 Session 9A: Lexical Semantics and Sentiment Analysis (Long Papers)**

14:00–14:25 *A Corpus and Model Integrating Multiword Expressions and Supersenses*
Nathan Schneider and Noah A. Smith

14:25–14:50 *Good News or Bad News: Using Affect Control Theory to Analyze Readers' Reaction Towards News Articles*
Areej Alhothali and Jesse Hoey

14:50–15:15 *Do We Really Need Lexical Information? Towards a Top-down Approach to Sentiment Analysis of Product Reviews*
Yulia Otmakhova and Hyopil Shin

**14:00–15:15 Session 9B: NLP-enabled Technology (Long + TACL Papers)**

14:00–14:25 *How to Memorize a Random 60-Bit String*
Marjan Ghazvininejad and Kevin Knight

14:25–14:50 *[TACL] Building a State-of-the-Art Grammatical Error Correction System*
Alla Rozovskaya and Dan Roth

14:50–15:15 *[TACL] Predicting the Difficulty of Language Proficiency Tests*
Lisa Beinborn, Torsten Zesch, and Iryna Gurevych

**14:00–15:15 Session 9C: Linguistic and Psycholinguistic Aspects of CL (Long Papers)**

14:00–14:25 *A Bayesian Model for Joint Learning of Categories and their Features*
Lea Frermann and Mirella Lapata

14:25–14:50 *Shared common ground influences information density in microblog texts*
Gabriel Doyle and Michael Frank

14:50–15:15 *Hierarchic syntax improves reading time prediction*
Marten van Schijndel and William Schuler

**15:15–15:45 *Break***

**Wednesday, June 3, 2015 (continued)**

**15:45–17:15 Best Paper Plenary Session**

15:45–16:15 *Retrofitting Word Vectors to Semantic Lexicons*
Manaal Faruqui, Jesse Dodge, Sujay Kumar Jauhar, Chris Dyer, Eduard Hovy and Noah A. Smith

16:15–16:45 *"You're Mr. Lebowski, I'm the Dude": Inducing Address Term Formality in Signed Social Networks*
Vinodh Krishnan and Jacob Eisenstein

16:45–17:15 *Unsupervised Morphology Induction Using Word Embeddings*
Radu Soricut and Franz Och

**17:15–17:30** ***Best paper awards and Closing Remarks***

# Pragmatic Neural Language Modelling in Machine Translation

**Paul Baltescu**
University of Oxford
paul.baltescu@cs.ox.ac.uk

**Phil Blunsom**
University of Oxford
Google DeepMind
phil.blunsom@cs.ox.ac.uk

## Abstract

This paper presents an in-depth investigation on integrating neural language models in translation systems. Scaling neural language models is a difficult task, but crucial for real-world applications. This paper evaluates the impact on end-to-end MT quality of both new and existing scaling techniques. We show when explicitly normalising neural models is necessary and what optimisation tricks one should use in such scenarios. We also focus on scalable training algorithms and investigate noise contrastive estimation and diagonal contexts as sources for further speed improvements. We explore the trade-offs between neural models and back-off n-gram models and find that neural models make strong candidates for natural language applications in memory constrained environments, yet still lag behind traditional models in raw translation quality. We conclude with a set of recommendations one should follow to build a scalable neural language model for MT.

## 1 Introduction

Language models are used in translation systems to improve the fluency of the output translations. The most popular language model implementation is a back-off n-gram model with Kneser-Ney smoothing (Chen and Goodman, 1999). Back-off n-gram models are conceptually simple, very efficient to construct and query, and are regarded as being extremely effective in translation systems.

Neural language models are a more recent class of language models (Bengio et al., 2003) that have been shown to outperform back-off n-gram models using intrinsic evaluations of heldout perplexity (Chelba et al., 2013; Bengio et al., 2003), or when used in addition to traditional models in natural language systems such as speech recognizers (Mikolov et al., 2011a; Schwenk, 2007). Neural language models combat the problem of data sparsity inherent to traditional n-gram models by learning distributed representations for words in a continuous vector space.

It has been shown that neural language models can improve translation quality when used as additional features in a decoder (Vaswani et al., 2013; Botha and Blunsom, 2014; Baltescu et al., 2014; Auli and Gao, 2014) or if used for n-best list rescoring (Schwenk, 2010; Auli et al., 2013). These results show great promise and in this paper we continue this line of research by investigating the trade-off between speed and accuracy when integrating neural language models in a decoder. We also focus on how effective these models are when used as the sole language model in a translation system. This is important because our hypothesis is that most of the language modelling is done by the n-gram model, with the neural model only acting as a differentiating factor when the n-gram model cannot provide a decisive probability. Furthermore, neural language models are considerably more compact and represent strong candidates for modelling language in memory constrained environments (e.g. mobile devices, commodity machines, etc.), where back-off n-gram models trained on large amounts of data do not fit into memory.

Our results show that a novel combination of noise contrastive estimation (Mnih and Teh, 2012)



*Human Language Technologies: The 2015 Annual Conference of the North American Chapter of the ACL*, pages 820–829,
Denver, Colorado, May 31 – June 5, 2015. 

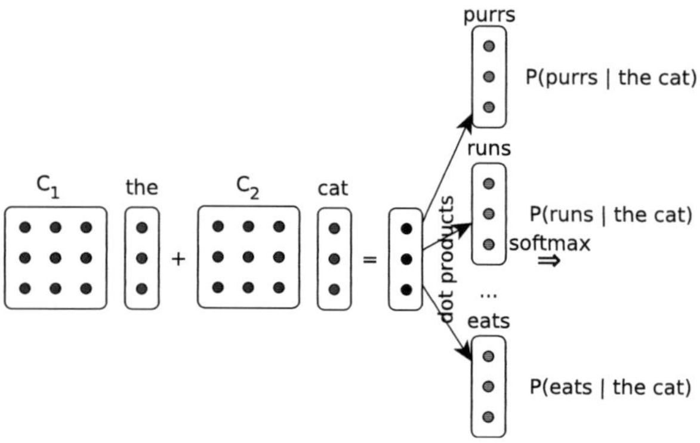


Figure 1: A 3-gram neural language model is used to predict the word following the context *the cat*.

and factoring the softmax layer using Brown clusters (Brown et al., 1992) provides the most pragmatic solution for fast training and decoding. Further, we confirm that when evaluated purely on BLEU score, neural models are unable to match the benchmark Kneser-Ney models, even if trained with large hidden layers. However, when the evaluation is restricted to models that match a certain memory footprint, neural models clearly outperform the n-gram benchmarks, confirming that they represent a practical solution for memory constrained environments.

## 2 Model Description

As a basis for our investigation, we implement a probabilistic neural language model as defined in Bengio et al. (2003).[1] For every word $w$ in the vocabulary $V$, we learn two distributed representations $\mathbf{q}_w$ and $\mathbf{r}_w$ in $\mathbb{R}^D$. The vector $\mathbf{q}_w$ captures the syntactic and semantic role of the word $w$ when $w$ is part of a conditioning context, while $\mathbf{r}_w$ captures its role as a prediction. For some word $w_i$ in a given corpus, let $h_i$ denote the conditioning context $w_{i-1}, \ldots, w_{i-n+1}$. To find the conditional probability $P(w_i|h_i)$, our model first computes a context projection vector:

$$\mathbf{p} = f\left(\sum_{j=1}^{n-1} \mathrm{C}_j \mathbf{q}_{h_{ij}}\right),$$

where $\mathrm{C}_j \in \mathbb{R}^{D\times D}$ are context specific transformation matrices and $f$ is a component-wise *rectified*

[1]Our goal is to release a scalable neural language modelling toolkit at the following URL: `http://www.example.com`.

| Model | Training | Exact Decoding |
|---|---|---|
| Standard | $O(\|V\| \times D)$ | $O(\|V\| \times D)$ |
| Class Factored | $O(\sqrt{\|V\|} \times D)$ | $O(\sqrt{\|V\|} \times D)$ |
| Tree Factored | $O(\log \|V\| \times D)$ | $O(\log \|V\| \times D)$ |
| NCE | $O(k \times D)$ | $O(\|V\| \times D)$ |

Table 1: Training and decoding complexities for the optimization tricks discussed in section 2.

*linear* activation. The model computes a set of similarity scores measuring how well each word $w \in V$ matches the context projection of $h_i$. The similarity score is defined as $\phi(w, h_i) = \mathbf{r}_w^{\mathrm{T}}\mathbf{p} + b_w$, where $b_w$ is a bias term incorporating the prior probability of the word $w$. The similarity scores are transformed into probabilities using the softmax function:

$$P(w_i|h_i) = \frac{\exp(\phi(w_i, h_i))}{\sum_{w\in V}\exp(\phi(w, h_i))},$$

The model architecture is illustrated in Figure 1. The parameters are learned with gradient descent to maximize log-likelihood with $L_2$ regularization.

Scaling neural language models is hard because any forward pass through the underlying neural network computes an expensive softmax activation in the output layer. This operation is performed during training and testing for all contexts presented as input to the network. Several methods have been proposed to alleviate this problem: some applicable only during training (Mnih and Teh, 2012; Bengio and Senecal, 2008), while others may also speed up arbitrary queries to the language model (Morin and Bengio, 2005; Mnih and Hinton, 2009).

In the following subsections, we present several extensions to this model, all sharing the goal of reducing the computational cost of the softmax step. Table 1 summarizes the complexities of these methods during training and decoding.

### 2.1 Class Based Factorisation

The time complexity of the softmax step is $O(|V| \times D)$. One option for reducing this excessive amount of computation is to rely on a class based factorisation trick (Goodman, 2001). We partition the vocabulary into $K$ classes $\{\mathcal{C}_1, \ldots, \mathcal{C}_K\}$ such that $V = \bigcup_{i=1}^{K} \mathcal{C}_i$ and $\mathcal{C}_i \cap \mathcal{C}_j = \varnothing, \forall 1 \leq i < j \leq K$.

We define the conditional probabilities as:

$$P(w_i|h_i) = P(c_i|h_i)P(w_i|c_i, h_i),$$

where $c_i$ is the class the word $w_i$ belongs to, i.e. $w_i \in \mathcal{C}_{c_i}$. We adjust the model definition to also account for the class probabilities $P(c_i|h_i)$. We associate a distributed representation $\mathbf{s}_c$ and a bias term $t_c$ to every class $c$. The class conditional probabilities are computed reusing the projection vector $\mathbf{p}$ with a new scoring function $\psi(c, h_i) = \mathbf{s}_c^{\mathrm{T}}\mathbf{p} + t_c$. The probabilities are normalised separately:

$$P(c_i|h_i) = \frac{\exp(\psi(c_i, h_i))}{\sum_{j=1}^{K} \exp(\psi(c_j, h_i))}$$

$$P(w_i|c_i, h_i) = \frac{\exp(\phi(w_i, h_i))}{\sum_{w \in \mathcal{C}_{c_i}} \exp(\phi(w, h_i))}$$

When $K \approx \sqrt{|V|}$ and the word classes have roughly equal sizes, the softmax step has a more manageable time complexity of $O(\sqrt{|V|} \times D)$ for both training and testing.

## 2.2 Tree Factored Models

One can take the idea presented in the previous section one step further and construct a tree over the vocabulary $V$. The words in the vocabulary are used to label the leaves of the tree. Let $n_1, \ldots, n_k$ be the nodes on the path descending from the root ($n_1$) to the leaf labelled with $w_i$ ($n_k$). The probability of the word $w_i$ to follow the context $h_i$ is defined as:

$$P(w_i|h_i) = \prod_{j=2}^{k} P(n_j|n_1, \ldots, n_{j-1}, h_i).$$

We associate a distributed representation $\mathbf{s}_n$ and bias term $t_n$ to each node in the tree. The conditional probabilities are obtained reusing the scoring function $\psi(n_j, h_i)$:

$$P(n_j|n_1, \ldots, n_{j-1}, h_i) = \frac{\exp(\psi(n_j, h_i))}{\sum_{n \in \mathcal{S}(n_j)} \exp(\psi(n, h_i))},$$

where $\mathcal{S}(n_j)$ is the set containing the siblings of $n_j$ and the node itself. Note that the class decomposition trick described earlier can be understood as a tree factored model with two layers, where the first layer contains the word classes and the second layer contains the words in the vocabulary.

The optimal time complexity is obtained by using balanced binary trees. The overall complexity of the normalisation step becomes $O(\log |V| \times D)$ because the length of any path is bounded by $O(\log |V|)$ and because exactly two terms are present in the denominator of every normalisation operation.

Inducing high quality binary trees is a difficult problem which has received some attention in the research literature (Mnih and Hinton, 2009; Morin and Bengio, 2005). Results have been somewhat unsatisfactory, with the exception of Mnih and Hinton (2009), who did not release the code they used to construct their trees. In our experiments, we use Huffman trees (Huffman, 1952) which do not have any linguistic motivation, but guarantee that a minimum number of nodes are accessed during training. Huffman trees have depths that are close to $\log |V|$.

## 2.3 Noise Contrastive Estimation

Training neural language models to maximise data likelihood involves several iterations over the entire training corpus and applying the backpropagation algorithm for every training sample. Even with the previous factorisation tricks, training neural models is slow. We investigate an alternative approach for training language models based on noise contrastive estimation, a technique which does not require normalised probabilities when computing gradients (Mnih and Teh, 2012). This method has already been used for training neural language models for machine translation by Vaswani et al. (2013).

The idea behind noise contrastive training is to transform a density estimation problem into a classification problem, by learning a classifier to discriminate between samples drawn from the data distribution and samples drawn for a known noise distribution. Following Mnih and Teh (2012), we set the unigram distribution $P_n(w)$ as the noise distribution and use $k$ times more noise samples than data samples to train our models. The new objective is:

$$J(\theta) = \sum_{i=1}^{m} \log P(C = 1|\theta, w_i, h_i) + \sum_{i=1}^{m} \sum_{j=1}^{k} \log P(C = 0|\theta, n_{ij}, h_i),$$

where $n_{ij}$ are the noise samples drawn from $P_n(w)$. The posterior probability that a word is generated

| Language pairs | # tokens | # sentences |
|---|---|---|
| fr→en | 113M | 2M |
| en→cs | 36.5M | 733.4k |
| en→de | 104.9M | 1.95M |

Table 2: Statistics for the parallel corpora.

| Language | # tokens | Vocabulary |
|---|---|---|
| English (en) | 2.05B | 105.5k |
| Czech (cs) | 566M | 214.9k |
| German (de) | 1.57B | 369k |

Table 3: Statistics for the monolingual corpora.

from the data distribution given its context is:

$$P(C = 1|\theta, w_i, h_i) = \frac{P(w_i|\theta, h_i)}{P(w_i|\theta, h_i) + kP_n(w_i)}.$$

Mnih and Teh (2012) show that the gradient of $J(\theta)$ converges to the gradient of the log-likelihood objective when $k \to \infty$.

When using noise contrastive estimation, additional parameters can be used to capture the normalisation terms. Mnih and Teh (2012) fix these parameters to 1 and obtain the same perplexities, thereby circumventing the need for explicit normalisation. However, this method does not provide any guarantees that the models are normalised at test time. In fact, the outputs may sum up to arbitrary values, unless the model is explicitly normalised.

Noise contrastive estimation is more efficient than the factorisation tricks at training time, but at test time one still has to normalise the model to obtain valid probabilities. We propose combining this approach with the class decomposition trick resulting in a fast algorithm for both training and testing. In the new training algorithm, when we account for the class conditional probabilities $P(c_i|h_i)$, we draw noise samples from the class unigram distribution, and when we account for $P(w_i|c_i, h_i)$, we sample from the unigram distribution of only the words in the class $\mathcal{C}_{c_i}$.

## 3 Experimental Setup

In our experiments, we use data from the 2014 ACL Workshop in Machine Translation.[2] We train standard phrase-based translation systems for French → English, English → Czech and English → German using the `Moses` toolkit (Koehn et al., 2007).

We used the `europarl` and the `news commentary` corpora as parallel data for training the translation systems. The parallel corpora were tokenized, lowercased and sentences longer than 80 words were removed using standard text processing tools.[3] Table 2 contains statistics about the training corpora after the preprocessing step. We tuned the translation systems on the `newstest2013` data using minimum error rate training (Och, 2003) and we used the `newstest2014` corpora to report uncased BLEU scores averaged over 3 runs.

The monolingual training data used for training language models consists of the `europarl`, `news commentary` and the `news crawl 2007-2013` corpora. The corpora were tokenized and lowercased using the same text processing scripts and the words not occuring the in the target side of the parallel data were replaced with a special `<unk>` token. Statistics for the monolingual data after the preprocessing step are reported in Table 3.

Throughout this paper we report results for 5-gram language models, regardless of whether they are back-off n-gram models or neural models. To construct the back-off n-gram models, we used a compact trie-based implementation available in `KenLM` (Heafield, 2011), because otherwise we would have had difficulties with fitting these models in the main memory of our machines. When training neural language models, we set the size of the distributed representations to 500, we used diagonal context matrices and we used 10 negative samples for noise contrastive estimation, unless otherwise indicated. In cases where we perform experiments on only one language pair, the reader should assume we used French→English data.

## 4 Normalisation

The key challenge with neural language models is scaling the softmax step in the output layer of the

[2]The data is available here: `http://www.statmt.org/wmt14/translation-task.html`.

[3]We followed the first two steps from `http://www.cdec-decoder.org/guide/tutorial.html`.

| Model | fr→en | en→cs | en→de |
|---|---|---|---|
| KenLM | 33.01 (120.446) | 19.11 | 19.75 |
| NLM | 31.55 (115.119) | 18.56 | 18.33 |

Table 4: A comparison between standard back-off n-gram models and neural language models. The perplexities for the English language models are shown in parentheses.

| Normalisation | fr→en | en→cs | en→de |
|---|---|---|---|
| Unnormalised | 33.89 | 20.06 | 20.25 |
| Class Factored | 33.87 | 19.96 | 20.25 |
| Tree Factored | 33.69 | 19.52 | 19.87 |

Table 5: Qualitative analysis of the proposed normalisation schemes *with* an additional back-off n-gram model.

| Normalisation | fr→en | en→cs | en→de |
|---|---|---|---|
| Unnormalised | 30.98 | 18.57 | 18.05 |
| Class Factored | 31.55 | 18.56 | 18.33 |
| Tree Factored | 30.37 | 17.19 | 17.26 |

Table 6: Qualitative analysis of the proposed normalisation schemes *without* an additional back-off n-gram model.

network. This operation is especially problematic when the neural language model is incorporated as a feature in the decoder, as the language model is queried several hundred thousand times for any sentence of average length.

Previous publications on neural language models in machine translation have approached this problem in two different ways. Vaswani et al. (2013) and Devlin et al. (2014) simply ignore normalisation when decoding, albeit Devlin et al. (2014) alter their training objective to learn self-normalised models, i.e. models where the sum of the values in the output layer is (hopefully) close to 1. Vaswani et al. (2013) use noise contrastive estimation to speed up training, while Devlin et al. (2014) train their models with standard gradient descent on a GPU.

The second approach is to explicitly normalise the models, but to limit the set of words over which the normalisation is performed, either via class-based factorisation (Botha and Blunsom, 2014; Baltescu et al., 2014) or using a shortlist containing only the most frequent words in the vocabulary and scoring the remaining words with a back-off n-gram model (Schwenk, 2010). Tree factored models follow the same general approach, but to our knowledge, they have never been investigated in a translation system before. These normalisation techniques can be successfully applied both when training the models and when using them in a decoder.

Table 4 shows a side by side comparison of out of the box neural language models and back-off n-gram models. We note a significant drop in quality when neural language models are used (roughly 1.5 BLEU for fr→en and en→de and 0.5 BLEU for en→ cs). This result is in line with Zhao et al. (2014) and shows that by default back-off n-gram models are much more effective in MT. An interesting observation is that the neural models have lower perplexities than the n-gram models, implying that BLEU scores and perplexities are only loosely correlated.

Table 5 and Table 6 show the impact on translation quality for the proposed normalisation schemes with and without an additional n-gram model. We note that when `KenLM` is used, no significant differences are observed between normalised and unnormalised models, which is again in accordance with the results of Zhao et al. (2014). However, when the n-gram model is removed, class factored models perform better (at least for fr→en and en→de), despite being only an approximation of the fully normalised models. We believe this difference in not observed in the first case because most of the language modelling is done by the n-gram model (as indicated by the results in Table 4) and that the neural models only act as a differentiating feature when the n-gram models do not provide accurate probabilities. We conclude that some form of normalisation is likely to be necessary whenever neural models are used alone. This result may also explain why Zhao et al. (2014) show, perhaps surprisingly, that normalisation is important when reranking n-best lists with recurrent neural language models, but not in other cases. (This is the only scenario where they use neural models without supporting n-gram models.)

Table 5 and Table 6 also show that tree factored models perform poorly compared to the other candidates. We believe this is likely to be a result of the artificial hierarchy imposed by the tree over the vocabulary.

| Normalisation | Clustering | BLEU |
|---|---|---|
| Class Factored | Brown clustering | 31.55 |
| Class Factored | Frequency binning | 31.07 |
| Tree Factored | Huffman encoding | 30.37 |

Table 7: Qualitative analysis of clustering strategies on fr→en data.

| Model | Average decoding time |
|---|---|
| KenLM | 1.64 s |
| Unnormalised NLM | 3.31 s |
| Class Factored NLM | 42.22 s |
| Tree Factored NLM | 18.82 s |

Table 8: Average decoding time per sentence for the proposed normalisation schemes.

Table 7 compares two popular techniques for obtaining word classes: Brown clustering (Brown et al., 1992; Liang, 2005) and frequency binning (Mikolov et al., 2011b). From these results, we learn that the clustering technique employed to partition the vocabulary into classes can have a huge impact on translation quality and that Brown clustering is clearly superior to frequency binning.

Another thing to note is that frequency binning partitions the vocabulary in a similar way to Huffman encoding. This observation implies that the BLEU scores we report for tree factored models are not optimal, but we can get an insight on how much we expect to lose in general by imposing a tree structure over the vocabulary (on the fr→en setup, we lose roughly 0.7 BLEU points). Unfortunately, we are not able to report BLEU scores for factored models using Brown trees because the time complexity for constructing such trees is $O(|V|^3)$.

We report the average time needed to decode a sentence for each of the models described in this paper in Table 8. We note that factored models are slow compared to unnormalised models. One option for speeding up factored models is using a GPU to perform the vector-matrix operations. However, GPU integration is architecture specific and thus against our goal of making our language modelling toolkit usable by everyone.

| Training | Perplexity | BLEU | Duration |
|---|---|---|---|
| SGD | 116.596 | 31.75 | 9.1 days |
| NCE | 115.119 | 31.55 | 1.2 days |

Table 9: A comparison between stochastic gradient descent (SGD) and noise contrastive estimation (NCE) for class factored models on the fr→en data.

| Model | Training time |
|---|---|
| Unnormalised NCE | 1.23 days |
| Class Factored NCE | 1.20 days |
| Tree Factored SGD | 1.4 days |

Table 10: Training times for neural models on fr→en data.

## 5 Training

In this section, we are concerned with finding scalable training algorithms for neural language models. We investigate noise contrastive estimation as a much more efficient alternative to standard maximum likelihood training via stochastic gradient descent. Class factored models enable us to conduct this investigation at a much larger scale than previous results (e.g. the WSJ corpus used by Mnih and Teh (2012) has slightly over 1M tokens), thereby gaining useful insights on how this method truly performs at scale. (In our experiments, we use a 2B words corpus and a 100k vocabulary.) Table 9 summarizes our findings. We obtain a slightly better BLEU score with stochastic gradient descent, but this is likely to be just noise from tuning the translation system with MERT. On the other hand, noise contrastive training reduces training time by a factor of 7.

Table 10 reviews the neural models described in this paper and shows the time needed to train each one. We note that noise contrastive training requires roughly the same amount of time regardless of the structure of the model. Also, we note that this method is at least as fast as maximum likelihood training even when the latter is applied to tree factored models. Since tree factored models have lower quality, take longer to query and do not yield any substantial benefits at training time when compared to unnormalised models, we conclude they represent a suboptimal language modelling choice

| Contexts | Perplexity | BLEU | Training time |
|---|---|---|---|
| Full | 114.113 | 31.43 | 3.64 days |
| Diagonal | 115.119 | 31.55 | 1.20 days |

Table 11: A side by side comparison of class factored models with and without diagonal contexts trained with noise contrastive estimation on the fr→en data.

for machine translation.

## 6 Diagonal Context Matrices

In this section, we investigate diagonal context matrices as a source for reducing the computational cost of calculating the projection vector. In the standard definition of a neural language model, this cost is dominated by the *softmax* step, but as soon as tricks like noise contrastive estimation or tree or class factorisations are used, this operation becomes the main bottleneck for training and querying the model. Using diagonal context matrices when computing the projection layer reduces the time complexity from $O(D^2)$ to $O(D)$. A similar optimization is achieved in the backpropagation algorithm, as only $O(D)$ context parameters need to be updated for every training instance.

Devlin et al. (2014) also identified the need for finding a scalable solution for computing the projection vector. Their approach is to cache the product between every word embedding and every context matrix and to look up these terms in a table as needed. Devlin et al. (2014)'s approach works well when decoding, but it requires additional memory and is not applicable during training.

Table 11 compares diagonal and full context matrices for class factored models. Both models have similar BLEU scores, but the training time is reduced by a factor of 3 when diagonal context matrices are used. We obtain similar improvements when decoding with class factored models, but the speed up for unnormalised models is over 100x!

## 7 Quality vs. Memory Trade-off

Neural language models are a very appealing option for natural language applications that are expected to run on mobile phones and commodity computers, where the typical amount of memory available is limited to 1-2 GB. Nowadays, it is becoming more and more common for these devices to include reasonably powerful GPUs, supporting the idea that further scaling is possible if necessary. On the other hand, fitting back-off n-gram models on such devices is difficult because these models store the probability of every n-gram in the training data. In this section, we seek to gain further understanding on how these models perform under such conditions.

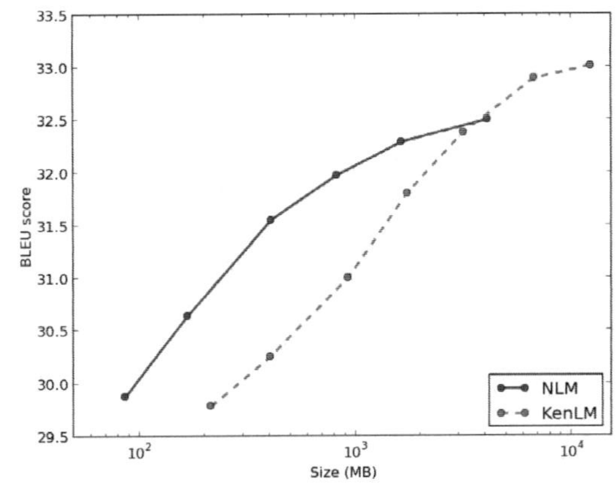


Figure 2: A graph highlighting the quality vs. memory trade-off between traditional n-gram models and neural language models.

In this analysis, we used Heafield (2011)'s trie-based implementation with quantization for constructing memory efficient back-off n-gram models. A 5-gram model trained on the English monolingual data introduced in section 3 requires 12 GB of memory. We randomly sampled sentences with an acceptance ratio ranging between 0.01 and 1 to construct smaller models and observe their performance on a larger spectrum. The BLEU scores obtained using these models are reported in Figure 2. We note that the translation quality improves as the amount of training data increases, but the improvements are less significant when most of the data is used.

The neural language models we used to report results throughout this paper are roughly 400 MB in size. Note that we do not use any compression techniques to obtain smaller models, although this is technically possible (e.g. quantization). We are interested to see how these models perform for various memory thresholds and we experiment with setting the size of the word embeddings between 100 and 5000. More importantly, these experiments are meant to give us an insight on whether very large neural language models have any chance of achieving the same performance as back-off n-gram models in translation tasks. A positive result would imply that significant gains can be obtained by scaling these models further, while a negative result signals a possible inherent inefficiency of neural language models in MT. The results are shown in Figure 2.

From Figure 2, we learn that neural models perform significantly better (over 1 BLEU point) when there is under 1 GB of memory available. This is exactly the amount of memory generally available on mobile phones and ordinary computers, confirming the potential of neural language models for applications designed to run on such devices. However, at the other end of the scale, we can see that back-off models outperform even the largest neural language models by a decent margin and we can expect only modest gains if we scale these models further.

## 8 Conclusion

This paper presents an empirical analysis of neural language models in machine translation. The experiments presented in this paper help us draw several useful conclusions about the ideal usage of these language models in MT systems.

The first problem we investigate is whether normalisation has any impact on translation quality and we survey the effects of some of the most frequently used techniques for scaling neural language models. We conclude that normalisation is not necessary when neural models are used in addition to back-off n-gram models. This result is due to the fact that most of the language modelling is done by the n-gram model. (Experiments show that out of the box n-gram models clearly outperform their neural counterparts.) The MT system learns a smaller weight for neural models and we believe their main use is to correct the inaccuracies of the n-gram models.

On the other hand, when neural language models are used in isolation, we observe that normalisation does matter. We believe this result generalizes to other neural architectures such as neural translation models (Sutskever et al., 2014; Cho et al., 2014). We observe that the most effective normalisation strategy in terms of translation quality is the class-based decomposition trick. We learn that the algorithm used for partitioning the vocabulary into classes has a strong impact on the overall quality and that Brown clustering (Brown et al., 1992) is a good choice. Decoding with class factored models can be slow, but this issue can be corrected using GPUs, or if a comprise in quality is acceptable, unnormalised models represent a much faster alternative. We also conclude that tree factored models are not a strong candidate for translation since they are outperformed by unnormalised models in every aspect.

We introduce noise contrastive estimation for class factored models and show that it performs almost as well as maximum likelihood training with stochastic gradient descent. To our knowledge, this is the first side by side comparison of these two techniques on a dataset consisting of a few billions of training examples and a vocabulary with over 100k tokens. On this setup, noise contrastive estimation can be used to train standard or class factored models in a little over 1 day.

We explore diagonal context matrices as an optimization for computing the projection layer in the neural network. The trick effectively reduces the time complexity of this operation from $O(D^2)$ to $O(D)$. Compared to Devlin et al. (2014)'s approach of caching vector-matrix products, diagonal context matrices are also useful for speeding up training and do not require additional memory. Our experiments show that diagonal context matrices perform just as well as full matrices in terms of translation quality.

We also explore the trade-off between neural language models and back-off n-gram models. We observe that in the memory range that is typically available on a mobile phone or a commodity computer, neural models outperform n-gram models with more than 1 BLEU point. On the other hand, when memory is not a limitation, traditional n-gram models outperform even the largest neural models by a sizable margin (over 0.5 BLEU in our experiments).

Our work is important because it reviews the most important scaling techniques used in neural language modelling for MT. We show how these methods compare to each other and we combine them to obtain neural models that are fast to both train and test. We conclude by exploring the strengths and weaknesses of these models into greater detail.

## Acknowledgments

This work was supported by a Xerox Foundation Award and EPSRC grant number EP/K036580/1.

## References

Michael Auli and Jianfeng Gao. Decoder integration and expected bleu training for recurrent neural network language models. In *Proceedings of the 52nd Annual Meeting of the Association for Computational Linguistics (ACL '14)*, pages 136–142, Baltimore, Maryland, June 2014. Association for Computational Linguistics.

Michael Auli, Michel Galley, Chris Quirk, and Geoffrey Zweig. Joint language and translation modeling with recurrent neural networks. In *Proceedings of the 2013 Conference on Empirical Methods in Natural Language Processing*, pages 1044–1054, Seattle, Washington, USA, October 2013. Association for Computational Linguistics.

Paul Baltescu, Phil Blunsom, and Hieu Hoang. Oxlm: A neural language modelling framework for machine translation. *The Prague Bulletin of Mathematical Linguistics*, 102(1):81–92, October 2014.

Yoshua Bengio and Jean-Sbastien Senecal. Adaptive importance sampling to accelerate training of a neural probabilistic language model. *IEEE Transactions on Neural Networks*, 19(4):713–722, 2008.

Yoshua Bengio, Réjean Ducharme, Pascal Vincent, and Christian Janvin. A neural probabilistic language model. *Journal of Machine Learning Research*, 3:1137–1155, 2003.

Jan A. Botha and Phil Blunsom. Compositional morphology for word representations and language modelling. In *Proceedings of the 31st International Conference on Machine Learning (ICML '14)*, Beijing, China, 2014.

Peter F. Brown, Peter V. deSouza, Robert L. Mercer, Vincent J. Della Pietra, and Jenifer C. Lai. Class-based n-gram models of natural language. *Computational Linguistics*, 18(4):467–479, 1992.

Ciprian Chelba, Tomas Mikolov, Mike Schuster, Qi Ge, Thorsten Brants, and Phillipp Koehn. One billion word benchmark for measuring progress in statistical language modeling. *CoRR*, 2013.

Stanley F. Chen and Joshua Goodman. An empirical study of smoothing techniques for language modeling. *Computer Speech & Language*, 13(4): 359–393, 1999.

KyungHyun Cho, Bart van Merrienboer, Dzmitry Bahdanau, and Yoshua Bengio. On the properties of neural machine translation: Encoder-decoder approaches. *CoRR*, 2014.

Jacob Devlin, Rabih Zbib, Zhongqiang Huang, Thomas Lamar, Richard M. Schwartz, and John Makhoul. Fast and robust neural network joint models for statistical machine translation. In *Proceedings of the 52nd Annual Meeting of the Association for Computational Linguistics (ACL'14)*, Baltimore, MD, USA, June 2014.

Joshua Goodman. Classes for fast maximum entropy training. *CoRR*, 2001.

Kenneth Heafield. Kenlm: Faster and smaller language model queries. In *Proceedings of the Sixth Workshop on Statistical Machine Translation (WMT '11)*, pages 187–197, Edinburgh, Scotland, July 2011. Association for Computational Linguistics.

David A. Huffman. A method for the construction of minimum-redundancy codes. *Proceedings of the Institute of Radio Engineers*, 40(9):1098–1101, September 1952.

Philipp Koehn, Hieu Hoang, Alexandra Birch, Chris Callison-Burch, Marcello Federico, Nicola Bertoldi, Brooke Cowan, Wade Shen, Christine Moran, Richard Zens, Chris Dyer, Ondrej Bojar, Alexandra Constantin, and Evan Herbst. Moses: Open source toolkit for statistical machine translation. In *Proceedings of the 45th Annual Meeting of the Association for Computational Linguistics (ACL '07)*, pages 177–180, Prague, Czech Republic, June 2007. Association for Computational Linguistics.

P. Liang. Semi-supervised learning for natural language. Master's thesis, Massachusetts Institute of Technology, 2005.

Tomas Mikolov, Anoop Deoras, Daniel Povey, Lukas Burget, and Jan Cernocky. Strategies for training large scale neural network language models. In *Proceedings of the 2011 Automatic Speech*

*Recognition and Understanding Workshop*, pages 196–201. IEEE Signal Processing Society, 2011a.

Tom Mikolov, Stefan Kombrink, Luk Burget, Jan ernock, and Sanjeev Khudanpur. Extensions of recurrent neural network language model. In *Proceedings of the 2011 IEEE International Conference on Acoustics, Speech, and Signal Processing, ICASSP 2011*, pages 5528–5531. IEEE Signal Processing Society, 2011b.

Andriy Mnih and Geoffrey Hinton. A scalable hierarchical distributed language model. In *Advances in Neural Information Processing Systems*, volume 21, pages 1081–1088, 2009.

Andriy Mnih and Yee Whye Teh. A fast and simple algorithm for training neural probabilistic language models. In *Proceedings of the 29th International Conference on Machine Learning (ICML '12)*, pages 1751–1758, Edinburgh, Scotland, 2012.

Frederic Morin and Yoshua Bengio. Hierarchical probabilistic neural network language model. In *Proceedings of the 10th International Workshop on Artificial Intelligence and Statistics (AISTATS '05)*, pages 246–252. Society for Artificial Intelligence and Statistics, 2005.

Franz Josef Och. Minimum error rate training in statistical machine translation. In *Proceedings of the 41st Annual Meeting on Association for Computational Linguistics (ACL'03)*, pages 160–167. Association for Computational Linguistics, 2003.

Holger Schwenk. Continuous space language models. *Computer Speech & Language*, 21(3):492–518, 2007.

Holger Schwenk. Continuous-space language models for statistical machine translation. *Prague Bulletin of Mathematical Linguistics*, 93:137–146, 2010.

Ilya Sutskever, Oriol Vinyals, and Quoc V. Le. Sequence to sequence learning with neural networks. *CoRR*, 2014.

Ashish Vaswani, Yinggong Zhao, Victoria Fossum, and David Chiang. Decoding with large-scale neural language models improves translation. In *Proceedings of the 2013 Conference on Empirical Methods in Natural Language Processing*, pages 1387–1392, Seattle, Washington, USA, October 2013. Association for Computational Linguistics.

Yinggong Zhao, Shujian Huang, Huadong Chen, and Jiajun Chen. An investigation on statistical machine translation with neural language models. In *Chinese Computational Linguistics and Natural Language Processing Based on Naturally Annotated Big Data - 13th China National Conference, CCL 2014, and Second International Symposium, NLP-NABD*, pages 175–186, Wuhan, China, October 2014.

# Key Female Characters in Film Have More to Talk About Besides Men: Automating the Bechdel Test

**Apoorv Agarwal**
Computer Science Department
Columbia University
NY, USA
apoorv@cs.columbia.edu

**Jiehan Zheng**[†]
Trinity College of Arts and Sciences
Duke University
NC, USA
jiehan.zheng@duke.edu

**Shruti Vasanth Kamath**[†]
Columbia University
NY, USA
svk2113@columbia.edu

**Sriram Balasubramanian**[†]
Facebook
CA, USA
grambler@fb.com

**Shirin Ann Dey**
Columbia University
NY, USA
sad2166@columbia.edu

## Abstract

The *Bechdel test* is a sequence of three questions designed to assess the presence of women in movies. Many believe that because women are seldom represented in film as strong leaders and thinkers, viewers associate weaker stereotypes with women. In this paper, we present a computational approach to automate the task of finding whether a movie passes or fails the Bechdel test. This allows us to study the key differences in language use and in the importance of roles of women in movies that pass the test versus the movies that fail the test. Our experiments confirm that in movies that fail the test, women are in fact portrayed as less-central and less-important characters.

## 1 Introduction

The Bechdel test is a series of three questions, which originated from Alison Bechdel's comic "Dykes to Watch Out For" (Bechdel, 1986). The three questions (or tests) are as follows: (T1) are there at least two named women in the movie? (T2) do these women talk to each other? and (T3) do these women talk to each other about something besides a man? If after watching a movie, the viewers answer "yes" to all three questions, that movie is said to pass the Bechdel test.

The test was designed to assess the presence of women in movies. Some researchers have embraced the test as an effective primary detector for male bias (Scheiner-Fisher and Russell III, 2012). Due to its generality, the Bechdel test has also been used to assess the presence of women in dialogues held on social media platforms such as MySpace and Twitter (Garcia et al., 2014). Several researchers have noted that gender inequality roots itself in both the subconscious of individuals and the culture of society as a whole (Žižek, 1989; Michel et al., 2011; García and Tanase, 2013). Therefore, combining the Bechdel test with computational analysis can allow for the exposure of gender inequality over a large body of films and literature, thus having the potential to alert society of the necessity to challenge the status quo of male dominance.

In this paper, we investigate the task of automating the Bechdel test. In doing so, we aim to study the effectiveness of various linguistic and social network analysis features developed for conducting this task. Our results show that the features based on social network analysis metrics (such as betweenness centrality) are most effective. More specifically, in movies that fail the test, women are significantly less centrally connected as compared to movies that pass the test. This finding provides support for the long held belief that women are seldom portrayed as strong leaders and thinkers in popular media. Our results also show that word unigrams, topic modeling features, and features that capture mentions of men in conversations are less effective. This may look like a rather surprising result since the question,

[†]These authors contributed equally. The work was done while Jiehan Zheng was at Peddie School and Sriram Balasubramanian was at Columbia University.



*Human Language Technologies: The 2015 Annual Conference of the North American Chapter of the ACL*, pages 830–840,
Denver, Colorado, May 31 – June 5, 2015. 

*(T3) do these women talk to each other about something besides a man?* seems to be one that linguistic features should be able to answer. A closer analysis suggests why this may be the case. Consider the screenplay excerpt in Figure 1 (on the next page). This excerpt is from the movie *Hannah and Her Sisters*, which passes the Bechdel test. Even though the conversation between named women *Mickey* and *Gail* mentions a man (*He*), the conversation is not *about* a man. The conversation is about *Mickey's* brain tumor. Now consider the following (contrived) conversation between the same characters:

> *Mickey*: Ssssss, if i'm in love, I don't know what I'm gonna do.
> *Gail*: You're not in love. Didn't he tell you that it was over.
> *Mickey*: No, naturally

This conversation is clearly about a man (or being in love with a man). Much like the original conversation, this conversation mentions a man only once. The linguistic phenomena that allows us to infer that this contrived conversation is about a man is quite complex; it requires a deeper semantic analysis and world knowledge. First, we need to infer that *it being over* refers to a relationship. Relationships typically have two participants. In order to identify the participants, we need to use world knowledge that relationships can end and that the person ending the relationship was once part of the relationship, and so on. Eventually, we are able to conclude that one of the main participants of the conversation or the event being discussed is a man.

As a first attempt to automate the test, we only experiment with basic linguistic features. However, we believe that the task itself offers an opportunity for the development of— and subsequent evaluation of— rich linguistic features that may be better equipped for determining the *aboutness* of conversations.

The rest of the paper is structured as follows. Section 2 reviews the related literature. Section 3 introduces the terminology regarding movie screenplays that we use throughout the paper. Section 4 describes the data and gold standard used for the purposes of automating the test. Sections 5, 6, and 7 present our approach, evaluation and results for the three Bechdel tests, respectively. We conclude and present future direction for research in Section 8.

## 2 Related

There has been much work in the computational sciences community on studying gender differences in the way language is used by men versus women (Peersman et al., 2011; Mohammad and Yang, 2011; Bamman et al., 2012; Schwartz et al., 2013; Bamman et al., 2014; Prabhakaran et al., 2014). In fact, researchers have proposed linguistic features for supervised classifiers that predict the gender of authors given their written text (Koppel et al., 2002; Corney et al., 2002; Cheng et al., 2011). There has also been a growth in research that utilizes computational techniques and big data for quantifying existing gender biases in society (Sugimoto et al., 2013; Garcia et al., 2014; Wagner et al., 2015).

More closely related to our application is the ongoing work in the social sciences community regarding the study of gender biases in movie scripts and books (Weitzman et al., 1972; Clark et al., 2003; Gooden and Gooden, 2001; McCabe et al., 2011; Chick and Corle, 2012; Smith et al., 2013). This work has largely depended on manual effort. McCabe et al. (2011) analyzed the presence of male and female characters in titles, and their centralities, in 5,618 children's books. The authors employed multiple human coders for obtaining the relevant annotations. Smith et al. (2013) employed 71 research assistants to evaluate 600 films to study gender prevalence in their scripts. Our work offers computational techniques that may help reduce the manual effort involved in carrying out similar social science studies.

Recently, Garcia et al. (2014) used 213 movie screenplays for evaluating the correlation of two novel scores with whether or not movies passed the Bechdel test. However, the main focus of their work was not to automate the test. The focus of their work was to study gender biases in MySpace and Twitter (using these scores). Nonetheless, we experiment with these scores and in fact they provide a strong baseline for automating the task. Furthermore, we use our previous work (Agarwal et al., 2014b) to *clean* noisy screenplays found on the web and carry out the study on a larger data-set of 457 screenplays.

```
M|                                                          CUT TO:
 |
S|           INT. MICKEY'S OFFICE - NIGHT
 |
N|           Gail, wearing her glasses, stands behind a crowded but well-
N|           ordered desk.  Two assistants, a man and a woman, stand around
N|           her.
 |
C|                                 MICKEY
M|                          (turning to Gail,
M|                          gesturing nervously)
D|                     Sssss, if I have a brain tumor, I
D|                     don't know what I'm gonna do.
M|                          (sighing)
 |
C|                                 GAIL
D|                     You don't have a brain tumor.  He
D|                     didn't say you had a brain tumor.
 |
C|                                 MICKEY
M|                          (sighing)
D|                     No, naturally
```

Figure 1: A scene from the movie *Hannah and Her Sisters*. The scene shows *one* conversation between two *named women Mickey* and *Gail*. Tag S denotes scene boundary, C denotes character mention, D denotes dialogue, N denotes scene description, and M denotes meta-data.

Researchers in the Natural Language Processing (NLP) community have used movie screenplays for a number of different applications. Ye and Baldwin (2008) used movie screenplays for evaluating word sense disambiguation in an effort to automatically generate animated storyboards. Danescu-Niculescu-Mizil and Lee (2011) utilized movie screenplays for studying the coordination of linguistic styles in dialogues. Bamman et al. (2013) used movie plot summaries for finding personas of film characters. Agarwal et al. (2014c) used screenplays for automatically creating the *xkcd* movie narrative charts. In this paper, we use movie screenplays for yet another novel NLP task: automating the Bechdel test.

## 3 Terminology Related to Screenplays

Turetsky and Dimitrova (2004) described the structure of a movie screenplay as follows: a screenplay describes a story, characters, action, setting and dialogue of a film. The content of a screenplay follows a (semi) regular format. Figure 1 shows a snippet of a screenplay from the film *Hannah and Her Sisters*. A scene (tag "S") starts with what is called the *slug line* (or scene boundary). The slug line indicates whether the scene is to take place inside or outside (INT, EXT), the name of the location ("MICKEY'S OFFICE"), and can potentially specify the time of day (e.g. DAY or NIGHT). Following the scene boundary, is a scene description (tag "N"). A scene description is followed by a character name (tag "C"), which is followed by dialogues (tag "D"). Screenplays also have directions for the camera, such as "CUT TO:, DISSOLVE TO:". For lack of a better name, we refer to these as meta-data (tag "M").

Screenplays are expected to conform to a strict grammar – scene boundaries should be capitalized and start with markers such as INT./EXT., character names should be capitalized with an optional (V.O.) for "Voice Over" or (O.S.) for "Off-screen.", dialogues and scene descriptions should be *indented*[1] at a unique level (i.e. nothing else in the screenplay is indented at this level). However, screenplays found on the web have *anomalies* in their structures (Gil et al., 2011). In order to parse screenplays found on the web, we presented a supervised machine learning approach in Agarwal et al. (2014b). By parsing we mean assigning each line of the screenplay one of the following five tags: {S, N, C, D, M}. We showed that a rule based system, often used in

[1]By level of indentation we mean the number of spaces from the start of the line to the first non-space character.

the literature (Turetsky and Dimitrova, 2004; Weng et al., 2009; Gil et al., 2011), is not well equipped to handle anomalies in the structure of screenplays. Our supervised models outperformed the regular expressions based baseline by a large and significant margin (0.69 versus 0.96 macro-F1 measure for the five classes). We use these parsed screenplays for the purposes of this paper.

Many of our features designed to automate the Bechdel test rely on the definition of a scene and a conversation. We define them here:
Scene: A scene is the span of screenplay that lies between two scene boundaries (tag "S").
Conversation: A conversation between two or more characters is defined as their dialogue exchange in *one* scene.

## 4 Data

The website bechdeltest.com has reviewed movies from as long ago as 1892 and as recent as 2015. Over the years, thousands of people have visited the website and assigned ratings to thousands of movies: movies that fail the first test are assigned a rating of 0, movies that pass the first test but fail the second test are assigned a rating of 1, movies that pass the second test but fail the third test are assigned a rating of 2, and movies that pass all three tests are assigned a rating of 3. Any visitor who adds a new movie to the list gets the opportunity to rate the movie. Subsequent visitors who disagree with the rating may leave comments stating the reason for their disagreement. The website has a *webmaster* with admin rights to update the visitor ratings. If the webmaster is unsure or the visitor comments are inconclusive, she sets a flag (called the "dubious" flag) to *true*. For example, *niel (webmaster)* updated the rating for the movie *3 Days to Kill* from 1 to 3.[2] The dubious flag does not show up on the website interface but is available as a meta-data field. Over the course of the project, we noticed that the dubious flag for the movie *Up in the Air* changed from false to true.[3] This provided evidence that the website is actively maintained and moderated by its owners.

| | Train & Dev. Set | | Test Set | |
|---|---|---|---|---|
| | Fail | Pass | Fail | Pass |
| B. Test 1 | 26 | 341 | 5 | 85 |
| B. Test 2 | 128 | 213 | 32 | 53 |
| B. Test 3 | 60 | 153 | 15 | 38 |
| Overall | 214 | 153 | 52 | 38 |

Table 1: Distribution of movies for the three tests over the training/development and test sets. B. stands for Bechdel.

We crawled a total of 964 movie screenplays from the Internet Movie Script Database (IMSDB). Out of these, only 457 were assigned labels on bechdeltest.com. We decided to use 367 movies for training and development and 90 movies (about 20%) for testing. Table 1 presents the distribution of movies that pass/fail the three tests in our training and test sets. The distribution shows that a majority of movies fail the test. In our collection, 266 fail while only 191 pass the Bechdel test.

## 5 Test 1: are there at least two named women in the movie?

A movie passes the first test if there are two or more *named women* in the movie. We experiment with several name-to-gender resources for finding the character's gender. If, after analyzing all the characters in a movie, we find there are two or more *named women*, we say the movie passes the first test, otherwise it does not.

### 5.1 Resources for Determining Gender

IMDB_GMAP: The Internet Movie Database (IMDB) provides a full list of the cast and crew for movies. This list specifies a one-to-one mapping from character names to the actors who perform that role. Actors are associated with their gender through a meta-data field. Using this information, we created an individual dictionary for each movie that mapped character names to their genders.
SSA_GMAP: The Social Security Administration (SSA) of the United States has created a publicly available list of first names given to babies born in a given year, with counts, separated by gender.[4] Sugimoto et al. (2013) used this resource for assigning genders to authors of scientific articles. Prabhakaran

[2] http://bechdeltest.com/view/5192/3_days_to_kill/
[3] http://bechdeltest.com/view/578/up_in_the_air/
[4] http://www.ssa.gov/oact/babynames/limits.html

| | Fail Test 1 | | | Pass Test 1 | | | |
|---|---|---|---|---|---|---|---|
| Gender Resource | P | R | F1 | P | R | F1 | Macro-F1 |
| IMDB_GMAP | 0.35 | 0.63 | 0.45 | 0.97 | 0.91 | 0.94 | 0.71 |
| SSA_GMAP | 0.26 | 0.21 | 0.24 | 0.94 | 0.95 | 0.94 | 0.59 |
| STAN_GMAP | 0.22 | 0.96 | 0.36 | 0.996 | 0.74 | 0.85 | 0.71 |
| STAN_GMAP+ IMDB_GMAP | 0.52 | 0.55 | **0.54** | 0.97 | 0.96 | **0.96** | **0.75** |

Table 2: Results for **Test 1**: "are there at least two named women in the movie".

et al. (2014) used this resource for assigning gender to sender and recipients of emails in the Enron email corpus. The authors noted that a first name may appear several times with conflicting genders. For example, the first name *Aidyn* appears 15 times as a male and 15 times as a female. For our purposes, we removed such names from the original list. The resulting resource had 90,000 names, 33,000 with the gender male and 57,000 with the gender female.

STAN_GMAP: In our experiments, we found both IMDB_GMAP and SSA_GMAP to be insufficient. We therefore devised a simple technique for assigning genders to named entities using the context of their appearance. This technique is general (not specific to movie screenplays) and may be used for automatically assigning genders to named characters in literary texts. The technique is as follows: (1) run a named entity coreference resolution system on the text, (2) collect all third person pronouns (*she, her, herself, he, his, him, himself*) that are resolved to each entity, and (3) assign a gender based on the gender of the third person pronouns.

We used Stanford's named entity coreference resolution system (Lee et al., 2013) for finding coreferences. Note that the existing coreference systems are not equipped to resolve references within a conversation. For example, in the conversation between *Mickey* and *Gail* (see Figure 1) "He" refers to *Mickey's* doctor, *Dr. Wilkes*, who is mentioned by name in an earlier scene (almost 100 lines before this conversation). To avoid incorrect coreferences, we therefore ran the coreference resolution system only on the scene descriptions of screenplays.

### 5.2 Results and Discussion

Table 2 presents the results for using various name to gender mapping resources for the first test. Since it is important for us to perform well on both classes (fail and pass), we report the macro-F1 measure; macro-F1 measure weights the classes equally unlike micro-F1 measure (Yang, 1999).

The results show that SSA_GMAP performs significantly[5] worse than all the other name-to-gender resources. One reason is that movies have a number of named characters that have gender different from the common gender associated with their names. For example, the movie *Frozen* (released in 2010) has two named women: *Parker* and *Shannon*. According to SSA_GMAP, *Parker* is a male, which leads to an incorrect prediction (fail when the movie actually passes the first test).

The results show that a combination of STAN_GMAP and IMDB_GMAP outperforms all the individual resources by a significant margin. We combined the resources by taking their union. If a name appeared in both resources with conflicting genders, we retained the gender recorded in IMDB_GMAP. Note that the precision of IMDB_GMAP is significantly higher than the precision of STAN_GMAP for the class Fail (0.35 versus 0.22). This has to do with coverage: STAN_GMAP is not able to determine the gender of a number of characters and predicts fail when the movie actually passes the test. We expected this behavior as a result of being able to run the coreference resolution tool only on the scene descriptions. Not all characters are mentioned in scene descriptions.

Also note that the precision of IMDB_GMAP is significantly lower than the precision of STAN_GMAP for the class Pass (0.97 versus 0.996). Error analysis revealed two problems with IMDB_GMAP. First, it lists non-named characters (such as *Stewardess*) along with the named characters in the credit list. So while the movie *A*

[5]We use McNemars test with $p < 0.05$ to report significance throughout the paper.

| | Fail Test 2 | | | Pass Test 2 | | | |
|---|---|---|---|---|---|---|---|
| Network | P | R | F1 | P | R | F1 | Macro-F1 |
| CLIQUE | 0.55 | 0.20 | 0.29 | 0.65 | 0.92 | 0.76 | 0.57 |
| CONSECUTIVE | 0.63 | 0.28 | **0.39** | 0.67 | 0.90 | **0.77** | **0.62** |

Table 3: Results for **Test 2**: "do these women talk to each other?"

*Space Odyssey* actually fails the test (it has only one named woman, *Elena*), IMDB_GMAP incorrectly detects *Stewardess* as another named woman and makes an incorrect prediction. Second, certain characters are credited with a name different from the way they appear in the screenplay. Following is a user comment from bechdeltest.com on the movie *Up in the Air* that highlights this second limitation:

> Natalie refers to Karen Barnes as "Miss Barnes" when they first meet. She is also named later. Despite the fact that she's credited as "Terminated employee", she's definitely a named female character.

The methodology used for finding named women directly impacts the performance of our classifiers on the next two tests. For instance, if a methodology under-predicts the number of named women in a movie, its chances of failing the next two tests increase. In fact, we experimented with all combinations and found the combination STAN_GMAP+ IMDB_GMAP to outperform other gender resources for the next two tests. Due to space limitations, we do not present these results in the paper. We use the lists of named women and named men generated by STAN_GMAP+ IMDB_GMAP for the next two tests.

## 6 Test 2: Do these women talk to each other?

So far, we have parsed screenplays for identifying character mentions, scene boundaries, and other elements of a screenplay (see Figure 1). We have also identified the gender of named characters. For automating the second test (*do these women talk to each other?*) we experimented with two techniques for creating *interaction* networks of characters. Consider the following sequence of tagged lines in a screenplay: {S1, C1, C2, C3, S2, C1, ...}. S1 denotes the first scene boundary, C1 denotes the first speaking character in the first scene, C2 the second speaking character, and so on. One way of creating an *interaction* network is to connect all the characters that appear between two scene boundaries (Weng et al., 2009). Since the characters C1, C2, and C3 appear between two scene boundaries (S1 and S2), we connect all the three characters with pair-wise links. We call this the CLIQUE approach. Another way of connecting speaking characters is to connect only the ones that appear consecutively (C1 to C2 and C2 to C3, no link between C1 and C3). We call this the CONSECUTIVE approach.

Results presented in Table 3 show that the CONSEQUITIVE approach performs significantly better than the CLIQUE approach.

We investigated the reason for an overall low performance for this test. One reason was the over-prediction of named women by our gender resource (labeling *Stewardess* as a named woman). Another reason was the inconsistent use of scene descriptions in screenplays. Consider the sequence of scene boundaries, characters, and scene descriptions: {S1, N1, C1, C2, N2, C3, C4, S2, ...}. While for some screenplays N2 divided the scene between S1 and S2 into two scenes (S1-N2 and N2-S2), for other screenplays it did not. For the screenplays that it did, our CONSECUTIVE approach incorrectly connected the characters C2 and C3, which led to an over-prediction of characters that talk to each other. Both these reasons contributed to the low recall for the Fail class.

## 7 Test 3: Do these women talk to each other about something besides a man?

For the third Bechdel test, we experimented with machine learning models that utilized linguistic features as well as social network analysis features derived from the interaction network of characters.

### 7.1 Feature Set

We considered four broad categories of features: word unigrams (BOW), distribution of conversations over topics (TOPIC), linguistic features that captured mentions of *men* in dialogue (LING), and social network analysis features (SNA). We additionally experimented with the two scores proposed by Garcia et al. (2014).

For BOW, we collected all the words that appeared in conversations between pairs of women and normalized the binary vector by the number of pairs of named women and by the number of conversations they had in a screenplay. BOW was a fixed feature vector of length 18,889.

The feature set LING consisted of the following features: (1) the average length of conversations between each pair of named women (2) the number of conversations between each pair of named women, (3) a binary feature that recorded if *all* conversations between a particular pair of named women mentioned a man, and (4) a binary feature that recorded if *any* conversation between a particular pair of named women mentioned a man. Let us denote these feature vectors by $\{v_1, v_2, v_3, v_4\}$. Note that the length of these features vectors ($|v_i| \leq \binom{n}{2}$, where $n$ is the number of named women in a movie) may vary from one movie to the other. We converted these variable length vectors into fixed length vectors of length four by using a function, GET_MIN_MAX_MEAN_STD(VECTOR), that returned the minimum, maximum, mean, and standard deviation for each vector. In all, we had $4 * 4 = 16$ LING features for each movie.

We found multiple instances of conversations that were about men but did not explicitly mention a man. For example, *don't we all fall for those pricks?* and *which one did you fall in love with?*. We also found conversations that mentioned a man explicitly and were around the same topic (say, *love*). For example, *I'm not in love with him, okay!*. In an attempt to capture possible correlations between general topics and conversations in which women talked about men, we decided to experiment with features derived from topic models. We trained a topic model on all the conversations between named women (Blei et al., 2003; McCallum, 2002). Before training the topic model, we converted all the mentions of men to a fixed tag "MALE" and all the mentions of women to a fixed tag "FEMALE". For each conversation between every pair of women, we queried the topic model for its distribution over the $k$ topics. Since the number of pairs of women and the number of conversations between them could vary from one movie to the other, we took the average of the $k$-length topic distributions. We experimented with $k = 2$, 20, and 50. Thus the length of the TOPIC feature vector was 72.

While the Bechdel test was originally designed to assess the presence of women, it has subsequently been used to comment on the importance of roles of women in movies. But does *talking about men* correlate with the importance of their roles? To study this correlation we designed the following set of SNA features. We created variable length feature vectors (length equal to number of women) for several social network analysis metrics (Wasserman and Faust, 1994), all appropriately normalized: (1) degree centrality, (2) closeness centrality, (3) betweenness centrality, (4) the number of men a woman was connected to, and (5) the number of other women a woman was connected to. We created two other variable length feature vectors (length equal to the number of pairs of women) that recorded (6) the number of men in common between two women and (7) the number of women in common between two women. We converted these variable length feature vectors to fixed length vectors of length four by using the GET_MIN_MAX_MEAN_STD(VECTOR) function described above. This constituted $7 * 4 = 28$ of our SNA features. We additionally experimented with the following features: (8) the ratio of the number of women to the number of men, (9) the ratio of the number of women to the total number of characters, (10) the percentage of women that formed a 3-clique with a man and another woman, (11, 12, 13) the percentage of women in the list of five *main* characters (main based on each of the three notions of centralities), (14, 15, 16) three boolean features recording whether the main character was a women, (17, 18, 19) three boolean features recording whether any woman connected another woman to the main man, and (20, 21, 23) the percentage of women that connected the main man to another woman. In all we had 28 + 15 = 43 SNA features.

As a baseline, we experimented with the features proposed by Garcia et al. (2014). The authors proposed two scores: $B_F$ and $B_M$. $B_F$ was the ratio of {dialogues between female characters that did not contain mentions of men} over {the total num-

| | | | Fail Test 3 | | | Pass Test 3 | | | Macro |
|---|---|---|---|---|---|---|---|---|---|
| Row # | Kernel | Feature Set | P | R | F1 | P | R | F1 | F1 |
| 1 | Linear | Garcia et al. (2014) | 0.39 | 0.70 | 0.50 | 0.84 | 0.57 | 0.67 | 0.62 |
| 2 | Linear | BOW | 0.40 | 0.37 | 0.38 | 0.74 | 0.76 | **0.75** | 0.57 |
| 3 | Linear | LING | 0.39 | 0.37 | 0.37 | 0.75 | 0.76 | **0.75** | 0.57 |
| 4 | Linear | TOPIC | 0.28 | 0.29 | 0.27 | 0.71 | 0.70 | 0.70 | 0.50 |
| 5 | RBF | SNA | 0.42 | 0.84 | **0.56** | 0.90 | 0.55 | 0.68 | **0.68** |

Table 4: Results for **Test 3**: "do these women talk to each other about something besides a man?" Column two specifies the kernel used with the SVM classifier.

| | | Fail Test 3 | | | Pass Test 3 | | | Macro |
|---|---|---|---|---|---|---|---|---|
| Kernel | Feature | P | R | F1 | P | R | F1 | Macro-F1 |
| Linear | Garcia et al. (2014) | 0.72 | 0.93 | 0.81 | 0.81 | 0.47 | 0.60 | 0.73 |
| RBF | SNA | 0.80 | 0.91 | **0.85** | 0.83 | 0.66 | **0.73** | **0.80** |

Table 5: Results on the unseen test set on the end task: does a movie passes the Bechdel Test?

ber of dialogues in a movie}. $B_M$ was the ratio of {dialogues between male characters that did not contain mentions of women} over {the total number of dialogues in a movie}.

### 7.2 Evaluation and Results

There were 60 movies that failed and 153 movies that passed the third test (see Table 1). We experimented with Logistic Regression and Support Vector Machines (SVM) with the linear and RBF kernels. Out of these SVM with linear and RBF kernels performed the best. Table 4 reports the averaged 5-fold cross-validation F1-measures for the best combinations of classifiers and feature sets. For each fold, we penalized a mistake on the minority class by a factor of 2.55 (153/60), while penalizing a mistake on the majority class by a factor of 1. This was an important step and as expected had a significant impact on the results. A binary classifier that uses a 0-1 loss function optimizes for accuracy. In a skewed data distribution scenario where F1-measure is a better measure to report, classifiers optimizing for accuracy tend to learn a trivial function that classifies all examples into the same class as the majority class. By penalizing mistakes on the minority class more heavily, we forced the classifier to learn a non-trivial function that achieved a higher F1-measure.

Results in Table 4 show that the features derived from social network analysis metrics (SNA) outperform linguistic features (BOW, LING, and TOPIC) by a significant margin. SNA features also outperform the features proposed by Garcia et al. (2014) by a significant margin (0.68 versus 0.62). Various feature combinations did not outperform the SNA features. In fact, all the top feature combinations that performed almost as well as the SNA features included SNA as one of the feature sets.

### 7.3 Evaluation on the End Task

We used the IMDB_GMAP + STAN_GMAP gender resource for the first test, the CONSECUTIVE approach for creating an interaction network for the second test, and compared the performance of the baseline versus the best feature set for the third test. Table 5 presents the results for the evaluation on our unseen test set of 52 movies that failed and 38 movies that passed the Bechdel test. As the results show, our best feature and classifier combination outperforms the baseline by a significant margin (0.73 versus 0.80). Note that the end evaluation is easier than the evaluation of each individual test. Consider a movie that fails the first test (and thus fails the Bechdel test). At test time, lets say, the movie is mis-predicted and passes the first two tests. However, the classifier for the third test correctly predicts the movie to fail the Bechdel test. Even though the errors propagated all the way to the third level, these errors are not penalized for the purposes of evaluating on the end task.

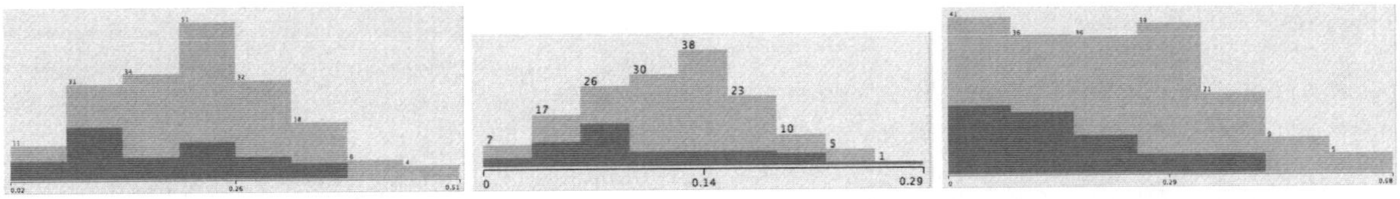


Figure 2: Distribution of three SNA features (left to right): mean degree centrality, mean closeness centrality, and mean betweenness centrality of named women. Red histogram is for movies that fail and the Blue histogram is for movies that pass the third Bechdel Test. The histograms show that the average centralities of women are higher for movies that pass the Bechdel test.

### 7.4 Discussion

We studied the correlation of our SNA features and the features proposed by Garcia et al. (2014) with the gold class on the set of 183 movies that pass or fail the third test in our training set. The most correlated SNA feature was the one that calculated the percentage of women who formed a 3-clique with a man and another woman ($r = 0.34$). Another highly correlated SNA feature was the binary feature that was true when the main character was a woman in terms of betweenness centrality ($r = 0.32$). Several other SNA features regarding the different notions of centralities of women were among the top. The feature suggested by Garcia et al. (2014), $B_F$ and $B_M$, were also significantly correlated, with $r = 0.27$ and $r = -0.23$ respectively.

Figure 2 shows the distribution of three of our SNA features: mean degree centrality, mean closeness centrality, and mean betweenness centrality of named women. As the distributions show, most of the mass for movies that fail the test is towards the left of the plot, while most of the mass for movies that pass is towards the right. So movies that fail the test tend to have lower centrality measures as compared to movies that pass the test. Using our classification results, correlation analysis, and visualizations of the distributions of the SNA features, we conclude that in fact, movies that fail the test are highly likely to have less centrally connected women.

## 8 Conclusion and Future Work

In this paper, we introduced a novel NLP task of automating the Bechdel test. We utilized and studied the effectiveness of a wide range of linguistic features and features derived from social network analysis metrics for the task. Our results revealed that the question, *do women talk to each other about something other than a man*, is best answered by network analysis features derived from the interaction networks of characters in screenplays. We were thus able to show a significant correlation between the importance of roles of women in movies with the Bechdel test. Indeed, movies that fail the test tend to portray women as less-important and peripheral characters.

To the best of our knowledge, there is no large scale empirical study on quantifying the percentage of children's books and novels that fail the Bechdel test. In the future, we hope to combine some of the ideas from this work with our past work on social network extraction from literary texts (Agarwal and Rambow, 2010; Agarwal et al., 2012; Agarwal et al., 2013a; Agarwal et al., 2013b; Agarwal et al., 2014a) for presenting a large scale study on children's book and novels.

## Acknowledgments

We would like to thank anonymous reviewers for their insightful comments. We would also like to thank Owen Rambow, Caronae Howell, Kapil Thadani, Daniel Bauer, and Evelyn Rajan for their helpful comments. We thank Noura Farra for suggesting the title for the paper. The idea originated from a class project (Agarwal, 2013). We credit Michelle Adriana Marguer Cheripka and Christopher I. Young for the initial idea. This paper is based upon work supported in part by the DARPA DEFT Program. The views expressed are those of the authors and do not reflect the official policy or position of the Department of Defense or the U.S. Government.

## References


Apoorv Agarwal and Owen Rambow. 2010. Automatic detection and classification of social events. In *Proceedings of the 2010 Conference on Empirical Methods in Natural Language Processing*, pages 1024–1034, Cambridge, MA, October. Association for Computational Linguistics.

Apoorv Agarwal, Augusto Corvalan, Jacob Jensen, and Owen Rambow. 2012. Social network analysis of alice in wonderland. In *Proceedings of the NAACL-HLT 2012 Workshop on Computational Linguistics for Literature*, pages 88–96, Montréal, Canada, June. Association for Computational Linguistics.

Apoorv Agarwal, Anup Kotalwar, and Owen Rambow. 2013a. Automatic extraction of social networks from literary text: A case study on alice in wonderland. *In the Proceedings of the 6th International Joint Conference on Natural Language Processing (IJCNLP 2013).*

Apoorv Agarwal, Anup Kotalwar, Jiehan Zheng, and Owen Rambow. 2013b. Sinnet: Social interaction network extractor from text. In *Sixth International Joint Conference on Natural Language Processing*, page 33.

Apoorv Agarwal, Sriramkumar Balasubramanian, Anup Kotalwar, Jiehan Zheng, and Owen Rambow. 2014a. Frame semantic tree kernels for social network extraction from text. *14th Conference of the European Chapter of the Association for Computational Linguistics.*

Apoorv Agarwal, Sriramkumar Balasubramanian, Jiehan Zheng, and Sarthak Dash. 2014b. Parsing screenplays for extracting social networks from movies. *EACL-CLFL 2014*, pages 50–58.

Apoorv Agarwal, Sarthak Dash, Sriramkumar Balasubramanian, and Jiehan Zheng. 2014c. Using determinantal point processes for clustering with application to automatically generating and drawing xkcd movie narrative charts. *Academy of Science and Engineering (ASE).*

Apoorv Agarwal. 2013. Teaching the basics of nlp and ml in an introductory course to information science. In *Proceedings of the Fourth Workshop on Teaching NLP and CL*, pages 77–84, Sofia, Bulgaria, August. Association for Computational Linguistics.

David Bamman, Jacob Eisenstein, and Tyler Schnoebelen. 2012. Gender in twitter: Styles, stances, and social networks. *arXiv preprint arXiv:1210.4567.*

David Bamman, Brendan O'Connor, and Noah A. Smith. 2013. Learning latent personas of film characters. In *Proceedings of the 51st Annual Meeting of the Association for Computational Linguistics*, pages 352–361, Sofia, Bulgaria, August. Association for Computational Linguistics.

David Bamman, Jacob Eisenstein, and Tyler Schnoebelen. 2014. Gender identity and lexical variation in social media. *Journal of Sociolinguistics*, 18(2):135–160.

Alison Bechdel. 1986. *Dykes to watch out for.* Firebrand Books.

David M Blei, Andrew Y Ng, and Michael I Jordan. 2003. Latent dirichlet allocation. *the Journal of machine Learning research*, 3:993–1022.

Na Cheng, Rajarathnam Chandramouli, and KP Subbalakshmi. 2011. Author gender identification from text. *Digital Investigation*, 8(1):78–88.

Kay Chick and Stacey Corle. 2012. A gender analysis of ncss notable trade books for the intermediate grades. *Social Studies Research and Practice*, 7(2):1–14.

Roger Clark, Jessica Guilmain, Paul Khalil Saucier, and Jocelyn Tavarez. 2003. Two steps forward, one step back: The presence of female characters and gender stereotyping in award-winning picture books between the 1930s and the 1960s. *Sex roles*, 49(9-10):439–449.

Malcolm Corney, Olivier de Vel, Alison Anderson, and George Mohay. 2002. Gender-preferential text mining of e-mail discourse. In *Computer Security Applications Conference, 2002. Proceedings. 18th Annual*, pages 282–289. IEEE.

Cristian Danescu-Niculescu-Mizil and Lillian Lee. 2011. Chameleons in imagined conversations: A new approach to understanding coordination of linguistic style in dialogs. In *Proceedings of the 2nd Workshop on Cognitive Modeling and Computational Linguistics*, pages 76–87. Association for Computational Linguistics.

David García and Dorian Tanase. 2013. Measuring cultural dynamics through the eurovision song contest. *Advances in Complex Systems*, 16(08).

David Garcia, Ingmar Weber, and Venkata Rama Kiran Garimella. 2014. Gender asymmetries in reality and fiction: The bechdel test of social media. *International Conference on Weblogs and Social Media (ICWSM).*

Sebastian Gil, Laney Kuenzel, and Suen Caroline. 2011. Extraction and analysis of character interaction networks from plays and movies. Technical report, Stanford University.

Angela M Gooden and Mark A Gooden. 2001. Gender representation in notable children's picture books: 1995–1999. *Sex Roles*, 45(1-2):89–101.

Moshe Koppel, Shlomo Argamon, and Anat Rachel Shimoni. 2002. Automatically categorizing written texts by author gender. *Literary and Linguistic Computing*, 17(4):401–412.

Heeyoung Lee, Angel Chang, Yves Peirsman, Nathanael Chambers, Mihai Surdeanu, and Dan Jurafsky. 2013. Deterministic coreference resolution based on entity-centric, precision-ranked rules. *MIT Press.*

Janice McCabe, Emily Fairchild, Liz Grauerholz, Bernice A Pescosolido, and Daniel Tope. 2011. Gender in twentieth-century childrens books patterns of disparity in titles and central characters. *Gender & Society*, 25(2):197–226.

Andrew Kachites McCallum. 2002. Mallet: A machine learning for language toolkit. http://mallet.cs.umass.edu.

Jean-Baptiste Michel, Yuan Kui Shen, Aviva Presser Aiden, Adrian Veres, Matthew K Gray, Joseph P Pickett, Dale Hoiberg, Dan Clancy, Peter Norvig, Jon Orwant, et al. 2011. Quantitative analysis of culture using millions of digitized books. *science*, 331(6014):176–182.

Saif M Mohammad and Tony Wenda Yang. 2011. Tracking sentiment in mail: how genders differ on emotional axes. In *Proceedings of the 2nd Workshop on Computational Approaches to Subjectivity and Sentiment Analysis (ACL-HLT 2011*, pages 70–79.

Claudia Peersman, Walter Daelemans, and Leona Van Vaerenbergh. 2011. Predicting age and gender in online social networks. In *Proceedings of the 3rd international workshop on Search and mining user-generated contents*, pages 37–44. ACM.

Vinodkumar Prabhakaran, Emily E Reid, and Owen Rambow. 2014. Gender and power: How gender and gender environment affect manifestations of power. In *Proceedings of the 2014 Conference on Empirical Methods in Natural Language Processing, Doha, Qatar, October. Association for Computational Linguistics*.

Cicely Scheiner-Fisher and William B Russell III. 2012. Using historical films to promote gender equity in the history curriculum. *The Social Studies*, 103(6):221–225.

H. Andrew Schwartz, Johannes C. Eichstaedt, Margaret L. Kern, Lukasz Dziurzynski, Stephanie M. Ramones, Megha Agrawal, Achal Shah, Michal Kosinski, David Stillwell, Martin E. P. Seligman, and Lyle H. Ungar. 2013. Personality, gender, and age in the language of social media: The open-vocabulary approach. *PLoS ONE*.

S.L. Smith, M. Choueiti, E. Scofield, and K. Pieper. 2013. Gender inequality in 500 popular films: Examining onscreen portrayals and behindthescenes employment patterns in motion pictures released between 2007 and 2012. *Media, Diversity, and Social Change Initiative: Annenberg School for Communication and Journalism, USC*.

Cassidy R Sugimoto, Vincent Lariviere, CQ Ni, Yves Gingras, and Blaise Cronin. 2013. Global gender disparities in science. *Nature*, 504(7479):211–213.

Robert Turetsky and Nevenka Dimitrova. 2004. Screenplay alignment for closed-system speaker identification and analysis of feature films. In *Multimedia and Expo, 2004. ICME'04. 2004 IEEE International Conference on*, volume 3, pages 1659–1662. IEEE.

Claudia Wagner, David Garcia, Mohsen Jadidi, and Markus Strohmaier. 2015. It's a man's wikipedia? assessing gender inequality in an online encyclopedia. Arxiv preprint arXiv:1501.06307.

Stanley Wasserman and Katherine Faust. 1994. *Social Network Analysis: Methods and Applications*. New York: Cambridge University Press.

Lenore J Weitzman, Deborah Eifler, Elizabeth Hokada, and Catherine Ross. 1972. Sex-role socialization in picture books for preschool children. *American journal of Sociology*, pages 1125–1150.

Chung-Yi Weng, Wei-Ta Chu, and Ja-Ling Wu. 2009. Rolenet: Movie analysis from the perspective of social networks. *Multimedia, IEEE Transactions on*, 11(2):256–271.

Yiming Yang. 1999. An evaluation of statistical approaches to text categorization. *Information retrieval*, 1(1-2):69–90.

Patrick Ye and Timothy Baldwin. 2008. Towards automatic animated storyboarding. In *AAAI*, pages 578–583.

Slavoj Žižek. 1989. *The sublime object of ideology*. Verso.

# Semantic Grounding in Dialogue for Complex Problem Solving

**Xiaolong Li**
Department of Computer Science
North Carolina State University
Raleigh, NC, 27695
xli30@ncsu.edu

**Kristy Elizabeth Boyer**
Department of Computer Science
North Carolina State University
Raleigh, NC, 27695
keboyer@ncsu.edu

## Abstract

Dialogue systems that support users in complex problem solving must interpret user utterances within the context of a dynamically changing, user-created problem solving artifact. This paper presents a novel approach to semantic grounding of noun phrases within tutorial dialogue for computer programming. Our approach performs joint segmentation and labeling of the noun phrases to link them to attributes of entities within the problem-solving environment. Evaluation results on a corpus of tutorial dialogue for Java programming demonstrate that a Conditional Random Field model performs well, achieving an accuracy of 89.3% for linking semantic segments to the correct entity attributes. This work is a step toward enabling dialogue systems to support users in increasingly complex problem-solving tasks.

## 1 Introduction

In the dialogue systems research community, there is growing recognition that dialogue systems need to support users in increasingly complex tasks. To move in this direction, dialogue systems must perform natural language understanding within richer and richer contexts, and this understanding includes semantic interpretation of user utterances (Traum, et al., 2012, Rudnicky, et al., 1999). Previous approaches for semantic interpretation include domain-specific grammars (Lemon et al., 2001) and open-domain parsers together with a domain-specific lexicon (Rosé, 2000). However, existing techniques are not sufficient to support increasingly complex problem-solving dialogues due to several challenges. For example, domain-specific grammars become intractable when applied to more ill-formed domains, and open-domain parsers may not perform well across domains (McClosky et al., 2010).

The call for addressing these limitations is particularly strong for dialogue systems that help people learn, such as *tutorial dialogue systems*. Today's tutorial dialogue systems engage in natural language dialogue in support of tasks such as solving qualitative physics problems (VanLehn et al., 2002), understanding computer architecture and physics (Graesser et al., 2004), and predicting behavior of electrical circuits (Dzikovska et al., 2011). Although these systems differ in many ways, they have an important commonality: in order to semantically interpret user dialogue utterances, these systems ground the utterances in a fixed domain description that is an integral part of the engineered system. This characteristic is shared by most dialogue systems, which ground their dialogue in manually defined domain-specific ontologies, such as for the task of booking flights (Allen, et al., 2001), checking bus schedules (Raux, 2004), and finding restaurants (Young et al., 2007).

These task-oriented domains, though they present a rich set of research challenges, stand in stark contrast to a *complex problem-solving* domain in which the user is creating an artifact to solve a problem. Yet the psychology literature tells us that complex problem solving is an essential activity in human learning (Greiff et al., 2013; Mayer et al., 2006; Funke, 2010). In such a domain, understanding user dialogue utterances involves grounding them within an infinite set of possible user-created



*Human Language Technologies: The 2015 Annual Conference of the North American Chapter of the ACL*, pages 841–850,
Denver, Colorado, May 31 – June 5, 2015. 

artifacts, not within a system ontology. This paper focuses on the complex problem-solving domain of introductory computer programming. In this domain the user might say, for example, "Is `myVariable` supposed to be an `int`?" where `myVariable` refers to the name of a variable within the computer program that the user has created. The semantic interpretation task in this case is akin to situated dialogue where user utterances must be grounded within a physical environment (Liu et al., 2014, Gorniak et al., 2007). However, even these situated dialogue models typically rely on a world defined by a limited number of entities (e.g., a chair or a cup).

To address these challenges, this paper presents a step toward semantic grounding for complex problem-solving dialogues, in which the number of potential entities (e.g., a Java variable or a piece of code) is infinite. The present work focuses on the semantic understanding of *noun phrases*, which tend to bear significant semantic information for each utterance. Although noun phrases are typically small in their number of tokens, their complexity and semantics vary in important ways. For example, in the domain of computer programming, two similar noun phrases such as "the 2 dimensional array" and "the 3 dimensional array" refer to two different entities within the problem-solving artifact. Inferring the semantic structure of the noun phrases is necessary to differentiate these two references within a dialogue, to ground them in the task, and to respond to them appropriately.

This noun phrase grounding task is similar to coreference resolution, which discovers the relationship between pairs of noun phrases in a piece of natural language text (Culotta, Wick, & Mccallum, 2007; Lappin & Leass, 1994). However, different from coreference resolution, noun phrase grounding links natural language expressions to entities in a real world environment. The current approach leverages the structure of noun phrases, mapping their segments to attributes of entities to which they should be semantically linked. In order to overcome the limitation of needing to fully enumerate the entities in the environment, we represent the entities as automatically extracted vectors of attributes. We then perform joint segmentation and labeling of the noun phrases in user utterances to map them to the entity vectors (used to describe entities within the environment). This mapping of noun phrases to real-world attributes is the grounding task focused on in this work. The results show that a Conditional Random Field performs well for this task, achieving 89.3% accuracy. Moreover, even in the absence of lexical features (using only dependency parse features and parts of speech), the model achieves 71.3% accuracy, indicating that it may be tolerant to unseen words. The flexibility of this approach is due in part to the fact that it does not rely on a syntactic parser's ability to accurately segment within noun phrases, but rather includes parse features as just one type of feature among several made available to the model. Finally, in contrast to methods based on bag-of-words such as latent semantic analysis, the proposed approach models the structure of noun phrases to facilitate specific grounding within an artifact.

The remainder of this paper is structured as follows. Section 2 presents related work on semantic interpretation and on natural language interpretation for tutorial dialogue. Section 3 describes the corpus and highlights some of the characteristics of dialogue for complex problem solving. The semantic interpretation approach is introduced in Section 4, with the experiments and results presented in Section 5. Section 6 concludes with important directions for future work.

## 2 Related Work

The approach presented in this paper draws upon a rich foundation of research in semantic interpretation and specifically upon dialogue interpretation for tutorial dialogues. Each of these areas of related work is discussed in turn.

### 2.1 Semantic Interpretation

The current work is closely related to several well-established research directions within the computational linguistics literature: semantic role labeling, semantic parsing, and language grounding. Semantic tagging assigns a semantic role label to text segments in a sentence (Pradhan, et. al, 2004). The set of semantic roles are relatively coarse-grained, not mapping to specific entities within the world. In contrast, the approach used in this paper does perform semantic role labeling, but the semantic grounding of these text segments are extracted at the same time. Semantic parsing addresses a more complex problem than semantic role labeling: interpreting the semantic structure of a sentence. Supervised semantic parsing requires a target logical form for each sentence, which is costly (Zettlemoyer et. al, 2012). Unsupervised methods rely on accurate dependency parsing, and the semantics learned with unsupervised methods are not directly grounded in a domain (Poon et al., 2009). Our approach does not require a logical form or accurate parse in order to train the model.

Another aspect of semantic interpretation involves language grounding, which links natural language to representations of entities in the (often physical) world directly. Matuszek et al. (2012) propose a joint language/perception model to learn attribute names in a physical environment. Barnard et al. (2003) learn interpretation of segments of images in words with a number of models. Liu et al. (2014) label the referential entities in a collaborative discourse with graph mapping. All of these approaches work in scenarios in which the number of entities is limited. This is different from the case of a complex problem-solving domain in which there could be infinitely many combinations of entities and surface forms of the problem-solving artifact. Thus, building an entity graph to model the relationships between entities would be intractable. Grounding based on semantic interpretation using our approach will address this problem since it first narrows down the category of entity for a noun phrase and then grounds within a family of factorized vectors.

### 2.2 Language Understanding in Tutorial Dialogue Systems

All dialogue systems employ some form of semantic interpretation. Within tutorial dialogue, some dialogue interpretation relies on a manually defined domain-specific grammar and lexicon (Lemon et al., 2001, Evens et al., 2005). CIRCSIM-Tutor (Evens et al., 2005), a tutorial dialogue system in the domain of cardiovascular physiology, uses a set of finite state transducers and a domain-specific lexicon. Such domain-specific grammars are successful within well-formed domains but become unwieldy in larger or ill-defined domains.

Another approach is to employ an open-domain parser in combination with domain-specific knowledge. CARMEL (Rosé, 2000) is a natural language understanding component that has been used in multiple dialogue systems (Zinn et al., 2000; Litman, 2004; VanLehn et al., 2002). CARMEL uses a semantic interpretation framework that performs semantic interpretation with semantic constructor functions during syntactic parsing. The semantic interpretation employs encoded domain-specific semantic knowledge and a frame-based representation.

Dzikovska et al. (2007) proposed an approach that divides the logical form representation of utterances and the knowledge representation ontology in order to make a NLU component adaptable for multiple domains. The logical form representation contains high-level word sense and semantic role labels. Then, a contextual interpreter is employed for mapping between the logical form and the domain ontology. This work still relies on an open domain parser to generate the logical forms.

Different from all of the approaches mentioned above, AutoTutor (Graesser et al., 2004) uses latent semantic analysis (LSA) to evaluate students' utterances by comparing them to a handcrafted expected answer. LSA represents semantics as a high-dimensional vector and computes similarity between pieces of text. As a bag-of-words approach, LSA does not capture the kind of semantic structure that facilitates specific language grounding in an environment.

## 3 Corpus of Complex Problem Solving Dialogue

Complex problem solving is defined within the psychology literature as the process of reaching a goal state by applying multiple problem solving skills, when the desired goal state cannot simply be reached by applying one from a set of existing solution patterns (Greiff et al., 2013; Mayer et al., 2006; Funke, 2010). Dialogue surrounding complex problem solving is therefore grounded within a problem-solving artifact that could have infinitely many surface forms. The complex problem-solving domain that is the focus of this paper is computer programming, specifically Java programming, and the corpus under consideration reflects textual tutorial dialogue exchanged between two humans in support of that problem solving.

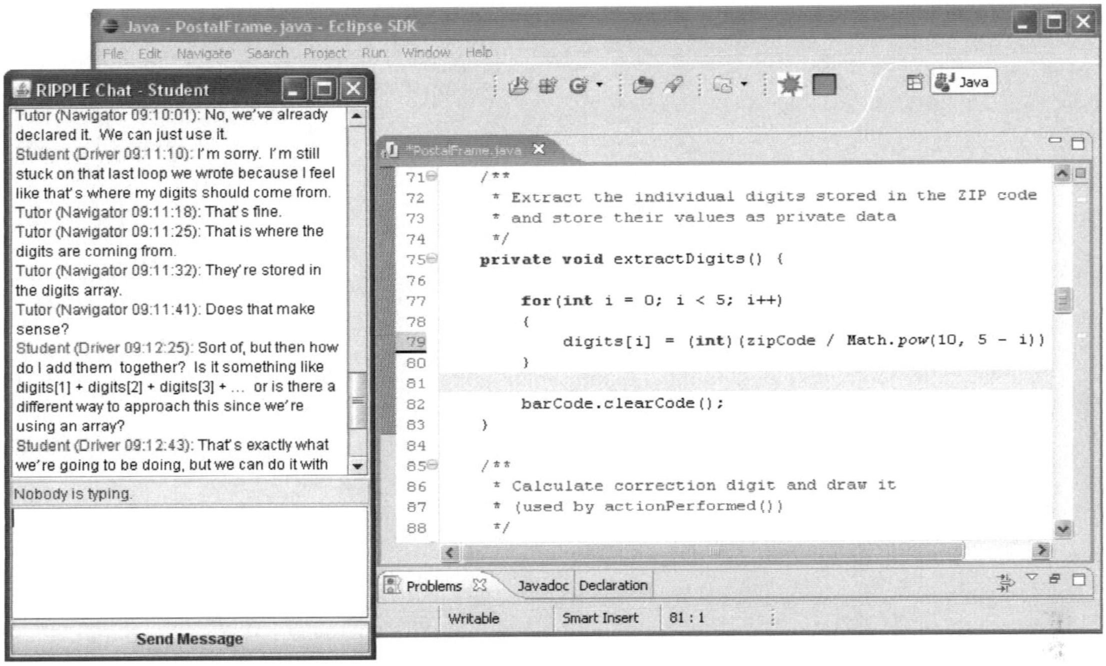


Figure 1. Tutorial dialogue interface.

The corpus was collected within a tutorial dialogue study in which human tutors and students interacted through a tutorial dialogue interface that supported remote textual communication (Boyer et al., 2011) The tutorial dialogue interface (Figure 1) consists of two windows that display interactive components: the student's Java code, the compilation or execution output associated with the code, and the textual dialogue messages between the student and tutor. All of the information in these two windows was synchronized between the student's screen and tutor's screen in real time.

The corpus contains 45 Java programming tutorial sessions from student-tutor pairs, with a total of 4857 utterances, an average of 108 utterances per session. For the current work, six of these tutorial sessions were manually annotated for their semantic grounding (as described in Section 5), a total of 758 utterances. The problem students solved during this tutorial dialogue involved creating, traversing, and modifying parallel arrays. This task was challenging for students and represented a complex problem-solving effort since the students were novices who were enrolled in an introductory computer programming class.

The dialogues within this domain are characterized by situated features that pertain to the programming task. A portion of user utterances refer to general Java knowledge, and in these cases semantic interpretation can be accomplished by mapping to a domain-specific ontology (e.g., Dzikovska et al., 2007). In contrast, many utterances refer to concrete entities within the dynamically changing, user-created programing artifact. Identifying these entities correctly is crucial for generating specific tutorial dialogue moves. A dialogue excerpt is shown in Figure 2.

## 4 Methodology

To ground the dialogue utterances as described in the previous section, our approach focuses first upon noun phrases, which contain rich semantic information. This section introduces the approach, based on Conditional Random Fields, to jointly segment the noun phrases and link those segments to entities within the domain.

### 4.1 Noun Phrases in Domain Language

A noun phrase is defined as "a phrase which has a noun (or indefinite pronoun) as its head word, or which performs the same grammatical function as such a phrase" (Crystal, 1997). The syntactic structure of a noun phrase consists of dependents which could include determiners, adjectives, prepositional phrases, or even a clause. For example, let us con-

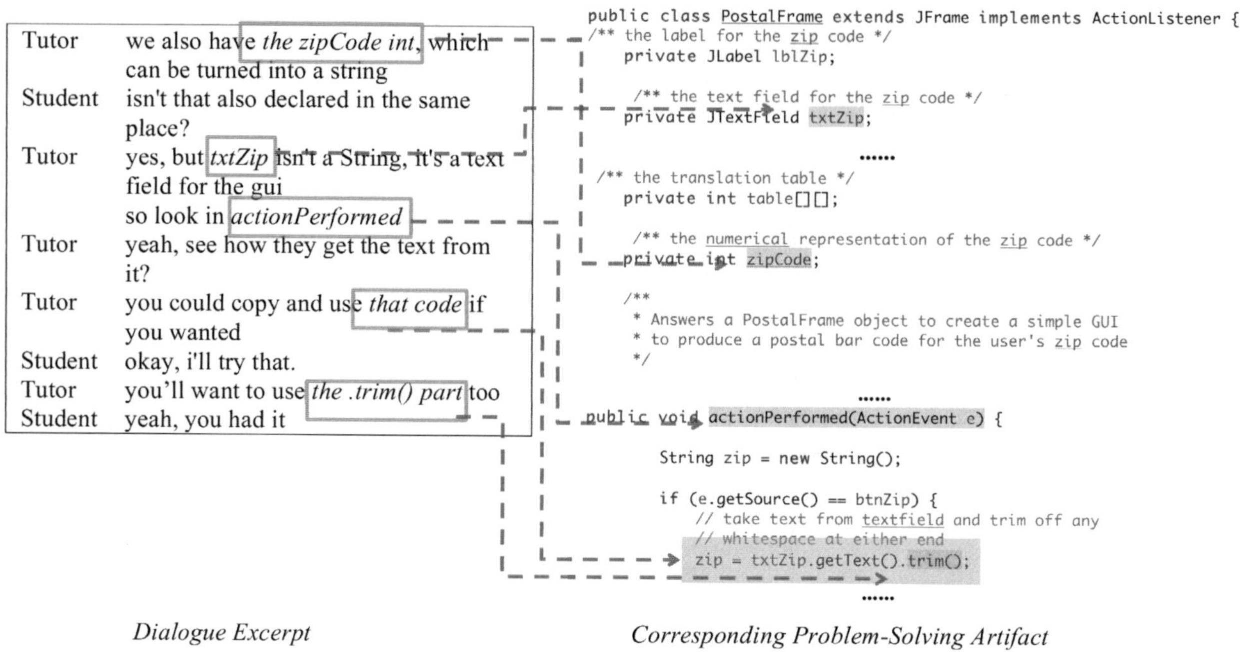


Figure 2. Dialogue excerpt from the corpus.

sider the noun phrase *"a 2 dimensional array"*. Its head is *"array"* and its dependents are *"a"* as the determiner and "2 dimensional" as an adjective phrase. In this simple case the syntactic boundaries also indicate semantic segments, as these dependents indicate one or more attributes of the head. If this relationship were always true, the semantic structure understanding task would be a labeling task that only requires assigning a semantic tag to each syntactic segment of the noun phrase. But this is not always true, in part because a syntactic parser trained on an open-domain corpus will not necessarily perform well on domain language (McClosky et al., 2010). For example, in the noun phrase *"the outer for loop,"* which also occurs in the Java programming corpus, the head of the noun phrase is *"for loop,"* but the syntactic parse (generated by the Stanford parser) of this noun phrase understandably (but incorrectly) identifies this head as part of a prepositional phrase (Figure 3).

To address this challenge, this paper utilizes a joint segmentation and semantic labeling approach that does not rely on accurate syntactic parsing within noun phrases. In this approach the head and dependents of each noun phrase are each referred to as a *segment,* with exactly one segment per dependent, and one or more words per segment. Identifying these segments correctly is essential to correct assignment of semantic tags. Pipeline methods for semantic segmentation rely on stable performance of an open domain parser, but as described above, this assumption is not desirable for grounding some domain language. We therefore utilize joint segmentation and labeling and apply a Conditional Random Field approach (Lafferty, 2001), a natural choice for the sequential data segmentation and labeling problem.

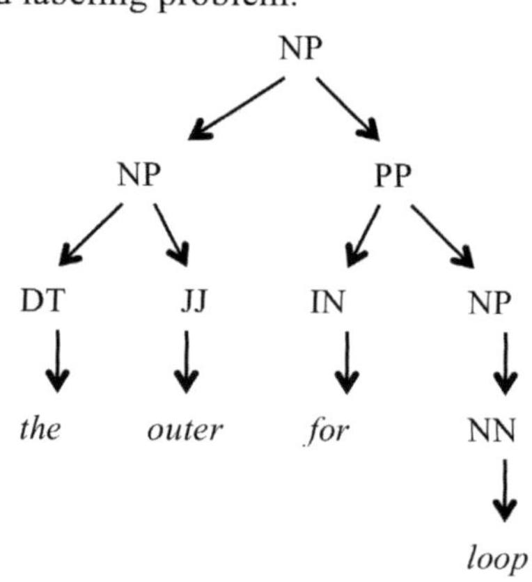


Figure 3. A parse of *"the outer for loop"* from Stanford Parser.

### 4.2 Description Vector

The goal is to ground each noun phrase to attributes of entities within the problem-solving artifact, which constitutes the "world" in this domain. To do this, we will link each semantic segment in a noun phrase to an attribute of an entity in the world. Because the world can contain any of an infinite set of user-created entities, representation cannot rely upon exhaustively enumerating the entities. To represent an entity in the domain, we define a description vector $V$ which defines the attribute types for entities in the domain. Then, an entity $O$ in the domain is represented uniquely by an instance of $V$. The values of each $V_i$ indicate the value of the attribute $i$ of $O$, as illustrated in Table 1. This definition of the description vector relies upon the structure of the domain by factorizing the attributes of entities.

With this representation, grounding a noun phrase involves linking each segment of the noun phrase to an attribute in the description vector. Formally, we represent a noun phrase as a series of segments:

$$NP = < s_1, s_2, \ldots, s_k >$$

where $s_i$ is the $i_{th}$ segment in this noun phrase. A noun phrase is also a sequence of words:

$$NP = < w_1, w_2, \ldots, w_n >$$

where each $w_j$ is the $j^{th}$ word in the noun phrase. Therefore each segment is a series of words:

$$s_i = < w_j, w_{j+1}, \ldots, w_{j+l-1} >$$

where $l$ is the length of semantic segment $i$.

Given a noun phrase, the segmentation problem is thus choosing a segmentation that maximizes the following conditional probability:

$$p(< s_1, s_2, \ldots, s_k > \ \mid \ < w_1, w_2, \ldots, w_n >)$$

Complementary to the segmentation problem is the semantic linking problem, which is to link $s_i$ to an attribute $a_i$, which is the label of the $i^{th}$ attribute in the entity description vector. That is, we wish to maximize the probability of the attribute label sequence $a$ given the segments of the noun phrase:

$$p(< a_1, a_2, \ldots, a_k > \ \mid \ < s_1, s_2, \ldots, s_k >)$$

Taking consecutive words with the same attribute label as the same semantic segment, the noun phrase segmentation and semantic linking problem is then:

$$\underset{a}{argmax}\, p(< a_1, a_2, \ldots, a_n > \ \mid \ < w_1, w_2, \ldots, w_n >)$$

In the tag sequence $<a_1, a_2, \ldots, a_n>$, if $a_i$ and $a_{i+1}$ are the same, then $w_i$ and $w_{i+1}$ are assigned to the same semantic segment with tag $a_i$. The process of segmentation and semantic linking is illustrated in Figure 4.

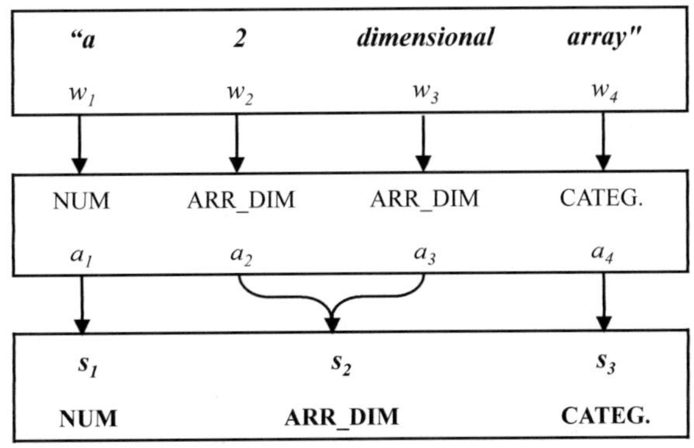


Figure 4. Segmentation and semantic linking of NP *"a 2 dimensional array."*

### 4.3 Joint Segmentation and Labeling

In order to perform this joint segmentation and labeling, we utilize a Conditional Random Field (CRF), which is a classic approach for sequence segmentation and labeling (Lafferty et al., 2001). Given the linear nature of our data, we employ a linear chain CRF. Specifically, given a sequence of words $w$, the probability of a label sequence $a$ is defined as

$$p(a \mid w) = \frac{1}{Z(w)} \exp\left(\sum_{i=1}^{n} \sum_{j=1}^{m} \lambda_j f_j(i, w, a_i, a_{i-1})\right)$$

where $f_j(i,w,a_i,a_{i-1})$ is a feature function. The weights $\lambda_j$ of this feature function are learned within the training process. The normalization function $Z(w)$ is the sum over the weighted feature function for all possible label sequences:

$$Z(w) = \sum_{a} \exp\left(\sum_{i=1}^{n} \sum_{j=1}^{m} \lambda_j f_j(i, w, a_i, a_{i-1})\right)$$

The optimal labeling $\hat{a}$ is the one that maximizes the likelihood of the training set, where $K$ is the number of noun phrases in the corpus.

$$\hat{a} = argmax\left(\sum_{i=1}^{K} \log P(a^{(i)} \mid w^{(i)})\right)$$

### 4.4 Features

Next, we introduce the features used to train the CRF. The feature function $f_j(i,w,a_i,a_{i-1})$ was defined as a binary function, in which $w$ is a feature value. We use both lexical and syntactic features. In a trained CRF model, the value of $f_i(i,w,a_i,a_{i-1})$ is known given a combination of parameters $(i,w,a_i,a_{i-1})$. The features used in the CRF model include words themselves, word lemmas, parts of speech, and dependency relationships from the syntactic parse. The word itself, lemmatized words and parts-of-speech have all been shown useful within segmentation and labeling tasks, so they are made available here (Xue et al., 2004). Each of these features is represented as categorical data. For example, a word is represented as its index in a list of all of the words that appeared in the corpus.

The dependency structure of natural language has also been shown to be important in semantic interpretation (Poon et al., 2009). This paper employs a dependency feature vector extracted from dependency parses. The head word of each noun phrase is the root of the dependency tree. Each dependent is a sub-tree directly under the head. We design the dependency feature as a sequence of dependency labels as follows.

Given a dependency tree, words in each semantic segment of the noun phrase are assigned a tag according to the relationship between them and the head. The relationship between each segment and head is defined by the dependency type in the dependency tree. For example, the dependency tree of *"a 2 dimensional array"* is shown in Figure 5. The dependency features are *<det,amod,amod,root>*. In this way, the dependency information from an open-domain parser is encoded as a feature to the semantic grounding model.

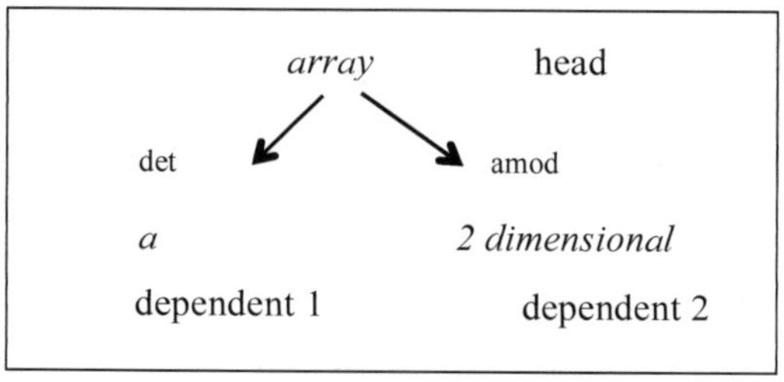


Figure 5. Dependency structure of *"a 2 dimensional array."*

## 5 Experiments & Results

The goal of the experiments is to determine how well the trained CRF can segment noun phrases and link these segments to the correct attribute of entities in the world. This section presents the experiments using CRFs trained and tested on the Java programming tutorial dialogue corpus. As described below, the results were evaluated by comparing with manually labeled data.

Noun phrases from the tutorial dialogues were first manually extracted and annotated as to their slots in the description vector described in Section

| **Attributes** | **Meaning (in Java programming)** | **Example** |
|---|---|---|
| CATEGORY | Category of an entity | `Method, Variable, etc.` |
| NAME | Variable name; often user-created | `extractDigit` |
| VAR_TYPE | Type of variable | `int, String, etc.` |
| NUMBER | Number of entities | `2` |
| IN_CLASS | The class that contains this entity | `postalFrame` |
| IN_METHOD | The method that contains this entity | `actionPerformed` |
| DIR_PARENT | Direct parent entity | `For_Statement, Method` |
| LINE_NUMBER | Line number | `67` |
| SUPER_CLASS | Superclass of this entity | `JFrame` |
| MODIFIER | Access modifier | `public, private, etc.` |
| ARRAY_TYPE | Type of Array | `int, char, etc.` |
| ARRAY_DIMENSION | Dimension of array | `2, 1` |
| OBJ_CLASS | The class an object instantiates | `PostalBarCode` |
| RETURN_TYPE | Return type | `String, int, etc.` |
| OTHER | Other attributes | `the, extra, etc.` |

Table 1. Elements of entity description vector to which noun phrases are mapped.

4.2. There were 364 grounded noun phrases extracted manually from the six tutorial dialogue sessions used in the current work. Each of these noun phrases extracted has one or multiple corresponding entities in the programming artifact. Since each word in a noun phrase is linked to an element in the description vector, the indices in this vector were used as the label for each word. Annotation of all 346 noun phrases was performed by one annotator, and 20% of the noun phrases (70 noun phrases) were doubly annotated by an independent second annotator. The percent agreement was 85.3% and the Kappa was 0.765.

To extract features, the lemmatization and syntactic parsing were performed with the Stanford CoreNLP toolkit (Manning et al., 2014). Then, a CRF was trained to predict the label for each word in a new noun phrase. The training was performed with the crfChain toolbox (Schmidt, 2008).

We use ten-fold cross-validation to evaluate the performance of the CRF in this problem. Results with different feature combinations are shown in Table 2. Manually labeled data were taken as ground truth for computing accuracy, which is defined as the percentage of segments correctly labeled.

Recall that consecutive words with the same label in a noun phrase are treated as a segment. Therefore, if a segment $s_{CRF}$ identified by the CRF has the same boundary and the same label as a segment $s_{Human}$ in the noun phrase containing $s_{CRF}$, this segment $s_{CRF}$ will be counted as a correct segment. Otherwise, $s_{CRF}$ will be counted as incorrect. The accuracy is then calculated as the number of correct segments identified by the CRF divided by the number of segments annotated manually. As can be seen in Table 2, all of the models perform substantially better than a minimal majority class baseline of 43%, which would result from taking each word as a segment and assigning it with the most frequent attribute label.

The results demonstrate important characteristics of the segmentation and labeling model. First, unlike most previous semantic interpretation work, our semantic interpretation of noun phrases does not rely on accurate syntactic parse within noun phrases. Rather, we use a dependency parse from an open-domain parser as only one of several types of features provided to the model. These dependency features improved the model in most feature combinations (Table 2). The feature combination of words, lemmas, and dependency parses achieved the best accuracy, which is 4.8% higher than the model that only used word features. This difference is statistically significant (Wilcoxon rank-sum test; $n$=10; $p$=0.02).

| features | accuracy |
|---|---|
| *word* | 84.5% |
| *word + lemma* | 85.5% |
| *Word + Dep* | 87.22% |
| *lemma + Dep* | 89.1% |
| ***word + lemma + Dep*** | **89.3%** |
| *word + lemma + POS* | 86.9% |
| *word + lemma + POS + Dep* | 88.7% |
| *POS + Dep* | 71.3% |

Table 2. Labeling accuracy.

Notably, the combination of part-of-speech features and dependency parse features still performed at 71.3% accuracy, indicating that to some extent, the method may be tolerant to unseen words.

## 6 Conclusion and Future Work

This paper has presented a technique for semantic grounding of noun phrases in a complex problem-solving domain, tutorial dialogue for computer programming. By performing joint segmentation and labeling of noun phrases from user utterances, and mapping those segments to attributes of entities within the problem solving artifact, we have made a first step toward grounding complex problem-solving dialogue within a dynamically changing artifact from a potentially infinite set of surface forms. While trained on a small subset of the corpus, the high accuracy of this model indicates that it may be successfully applied to the larger corpus without extensive additional manual annotations.

Several directions of future work are very promising. In order to fully support users in complex problem-solving dialogues, the field must move toward richer grounding of natural language utterances within complex artifacts across many domains. Additionally, generating specific and tailored dialogue feedback grounded in the artifact is a complementary area of research that holds the potential to increase the effectiveness of dialogue systems for supporting problem solving. It is hoped that this line of investigation will lead to dialogue systems that smoothly support a much broader range of human endeavors.

## Acknowledgments

The authors wish to thank the members of the LearnDialogue group, especially Joseph Wiggins, at North Carolina State University for their helpful input. This work is supported in part by the National Science Foundation through grants IIS-1409639 and the STARS Alliance, CNS-1042468. Any opinions, findings, conclusions, or recommendations expressed in this report are those of the authors, and do not necessarily represent the official views, opinions, or policy of the National Science Foundation.

## References

Allen, J. F., Byron, D. K., Dzikovska, M., Ferguson, G., Galescu, L., & Stent, A. (2001). Toward Conversational Human-Computer Interaction. *AI Magazine*, 22(4), 27.

Barnard, K., Forsyth, D., & Jordan, M. I. (2003). Matching Words and Pictures. *Journal of Machine Learning Research*, 3, 1107–1135.

Boyer, K. E., Phillips, R., Ingram, A., Ha, E. Y., Wallis, M. D., Vouk, M. A., & Lester, J. C. (2011). Investigating the Relationship Between Dialogue Structure and Tutoring Effectiveness: A Hidden Markov Modeling Approach. *International Journal of Artificial Intelligence in Education (IJAIED)*, 21(1), 65–81.

Crystal, D. (1997). *A Dictionary of Linguistics and Phonetics* ($4^{th}$ ed.). Oxford University Press.

Culotta, A., Wick, M., & Mccallum, A. (2007). First-Order Probabilistic Models for Coreference Resolution. *In Proceedings of the 2007 Annual Conference of the North American Chapter of the Association for Computational Linguistics (NAACL)* (pp. 81–88).

Dzikovska, M. O., Allen, J. F., & Swift, M. D. (2007). Linking Semantic and Knowledge Representations in a Multi-Domain Dialogue System. *Journal of Logic and Computation*, 18(3), 405–430. Retrieved from http://logcom.oxfordjournals.org/cgi/doi/10.1093/logcom/exm067

Dzikovska, M. O., Isard, A., Bell, P., Moore, J. D., Steinhauser, N., & Campbell, G. (2011). BEETLE II: An Adaptable Tutorial Dialogue System. *Proceedings of the 12th Annual SIGdial Meeting on Discourse and Dialogue*, 338–340.

Evens, M., & Michael, J. (2005). *One-on-One Tutoring by Humans and Computers.* Psychology Press.

Funke, J. (2010). Complex problem solving: A case for complex cognition? *Cognitive Processing*, 11(2), 133–142.

Gorniak, P., & Roy, D. (2007). Situated Language Understanding as Filtering Perceived Affordances. *Cognitive Science*, 31(2), 197–231.

Graesser, A. C., Lu, S., Jackson, G. T., Mitchell, H. H., Ventura, M., Olney, A., & Louwerse, M. M. (2004). AutoTutor: A Tutor with Dialogue in Natural Language. *Behavior Research Methods, Instruments, & Computers*, 36(2), 180–192.

Greiff, S., Wüstenberg, S., Holt, D. V., Goldhammer, F., & Funke, J. (2013). Computer-based Assessment of Complex Problem Solving: Concept, Implementation, and Application. *Educational Technology Research and Development*, 61(3), 407–421.

Lafferty, J., McCallum, A., & Pereira, F. C. (2001). Conditional Random Fields: Probabilistic Models for Segmenting and Labeling Sequence Data. *In Proceedings of the International Conference on Machine Learning* (pp. 282–289).

Lappin, S., & Leass, H. J. (1994). An Algorithm for Pronominal Anaphora Resolution. *Computational Linguistics*, 20(4), 535–561.

Lemon, O., Bracy, A., Gruenstein, A., & Peters, S. (2001). The WITAS Multi-Modal Dialogue System I. *In Proceedings of INTERSPEECH* (pp. 1559–1562).

Litman, D. J. (2004). ITSPOKE : An Intelligent Tutoring Spoken Dialogue System. *In Demonstration Papers at the 2004 Annual Conference of the North American Chapter of the Association for Computational Linguistics (HLT-NAACL)* (pp. 5–8).

Liu, C., She, L., Fang, R., & Chai, J. Y. (2014). Probabilistic Labeling for Efficient Referential Grounding Based On Collaborative Discourse. *In Proceedings of the 52nd Annual Meeting of the Association for Computational Linguistics (ACL)* (pp. 13–18).

Manning, C. D., Bauer, J., Finkel, J., & Bethard, S. J. (2014). The Stanford CoreNLP Natural Language Processing Toolkit. *In the 52nd Annual Meeting of the Association for Computational Linguistics: System Demonstrations* (pp. 55–60).

Matuszek, C., Fitzgerald, N., Zettlemoyer, L., Bo, L., & Fox, D. (2012). A Joint Model of Language and Perception for Grounded Attribute Learning. *In Proceedings of the 29th International Conference on Machine Learning.*

Mayer, R. E., & Wittrock, M. C. (2006). Problem Solving. *Handbook of Educational Psychology*, 2, 287–303.

McClosky, D., Charniak, E., & Johnson, M. (2010). Automatic Domain Adaptation for Parsing. *In Proceedings of the 2010 Annual Conference of the North American Chapter of the Association for Computational Linguistics (HLT-NAACL)* (pp. 28–36).

Poon, H., & Domingos, P. (2009). Unsupervised Semantic Parsing. *In Proceedings of the 2009 Conference on Empirical Methods in Natural Language Processing (EMNLP)* (pp. 1–10).

Pradhan, S. S., Ward, W., Hacioglu, K., Martin, J. H., & Jurafsky, D. (2004). Shallow Semantic Parsing using Support Vector Machines. *In Proceedings of the 2004 Annual Conference of the North American Chapter of the Association for Computational Linguistics (NAACL)* (pp. 233–240).

Raux, A., & Eskenazi, M. (2004). Non-Native Users in the Let's Go!! Spoken Dialogue System: Dealing with Linguistic Mismatch. *In Proceedings of the 2004 North American Chapter of the Association for Computational Linguistics (HLT-NAACL)* (pp. 217–224).

Rosé, C. P. (2000). A Framework for Robust Semantic Interpretation. *In Proceedings of the 1st North American Chapter of the Association for Computational Linguistics Conference (NAACL)* (pp. 311–318).

Rudnicky, A., Thayer, E., Constantinides, P., Tchou, C., Shern, R., Lenzo, K., … Oh, A. (1999). Creating Natural Dialogs in the Carnegie Mellon Communicator System. *In Proceedings of the Sixth European Conference on Speech Communication and Technology, (EUROSPEECH)* (Vol. 4, pp. 1531–1534).

Schmidt, M., & Swersky, K. (2008). http://www.cs.ubc.ca/~schmidtm/Software/crfChain.html.

Traum, D., Devault, D., Lee, J., Wang, Z., & Marsella, S. (2012). Incremental Dialogue Understanding and Feedback for Multiparty, Multimodal Conversation. *Intelligent Virtual Agents*, 7502, 275–288.

VanLehn, K., Jordan, P. W., Rosé, C. P., Bhembe, D., Bottner, M., Gaydos, A., … Roque, A. (2002). The Architecture of Why2-Atlas: A Coach for Qualitative Physics Essay Writing. *In Proceedings of the Sixth International Conference on Intelligent Tutoring Systems* (Vol. 2363, pp. 158–167). Springer.

Xue, N., & Palmer, M. (2004). Calibrating Features for Semantic Role Labeling. *In Proceedings of the 2004 Conference on Empirical Methods in Natural Language Processing (EMNLP)* (pp. 88–94).

Young, S., Schatzmann, J., Weilhammer, K., & Ye, H. (2007). The Hidden Information State Approach to Dialog Management. *Acoustics, Speech and Signal Processing* (Vol. 4, pp. 149-152).

Zettlemoyer, L. S., & Collins, M. (2012). Learning to Map Sentences to Logical Form: Structured Classification with Probabilistic Categorial Grammars. *In Proceedings of the Twenty First Conference on Uncertainty in Artificial Intelligence* (pp. 658–666).

Zinn, C., Moore, J. D., Core, M. G., & Varges, S. (2000). The BE&E Tutorial Learning Environment ( BEETLE ). *In Proceedings of the Seventh Workshop on the Semantics and Pragmatics of Dialogue.*

# Learning Knowledge Graphs for Question Answering through Conversational Dialog

**Ben Hixon**
University of Washington
Computer Science & Engineering
Seattle, WA, USA
bhixon@cs.washington.edu

**Peter Clark**
Allen Institute for AI
Seattle, WA, USA
peterc@allenai.org

**Hannaneh Hajishirzi**
University of Washington
Electrical Engineering
Seattle, WA, USA
hannaneh@washington.edu

## Abstract

We describe how a question-answering system can learn about its domain from conversational dialogs. Our system learns to relate concepts in science questions to propositions in a fact corpus, stores new concepts and relations in a knowledge graph (KG), and uses the graph to solve questions. We are the first to acquire knowledge for question-answering from open, natural language dialogs without a fixed ontology or domain model that predetermines what users can say. Our relation-based strategies complete more successful dialogs than a query expansion baseline, our task-driven relations are more effective for solving science questions than relations from general knowledge sources, and our method is practical enough to generalize to other domains.

## 1 Introduction

Our goal is a question-answering (QA) system that learns about its domain from users in open, natural language dialogs. Dialog learning interfaces built on top of existing QA systems can complement and refine knowledge acquired from other sources. Even large QA systems such as Watson (Ferrucci et al., 2010) that utilize heavy domain engineering could benefit from focused dialogs to dynamically improve their knowledge.

A successful QA system requires domain knowledge. For example, 4th grade science questions are difficult since they often exclude knowledge necessary to relate answers to known facts. The question in Figure 1 asks if an *iron nail* conducts electricity;

S1: Here's the question: Which object is the best conductor of electricity? (A) a wax crayon (B) a plastic spoon (C) a rubber eraser (D) an iron nail. I'm not sure of the answer. What do you think the answer is?
U1: iron nail
S2: Why do you think the answer is (D) an iron nail?
U2: electricity goes through metal
S3: I know "metals are shiny and good conductors of electricity and heat," does that mean that the answer is (D) an iron nail?
U3: yeah
S4: Okay, great. What's the relationship between 'electricity' and 'iron', if any?
U4: iron conducts electricity because its metal
S5: Okay, great, I get it! The answer is (D) an iron nail

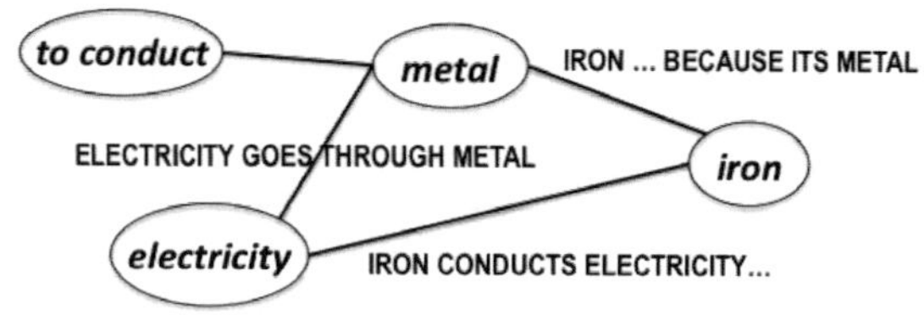


Figure 1: Top: A successful real user dialog. Open-ended prompts (S1&S2) encourage conversational explanations. Focused prompts (S4) target particular relations. Bottom: Corresponding knowledge graph consisting of relations between concepts.

the system only knows that *metal* conducts electricity, and it needs to learn that *iron* is a *metal* in order to answer the question with the relevant fact.

Our dialog system, KNOWBOT, conducts dialogs about science questions and learns how concepts in each question relate to propositions in a corpus of science facts. KNOWBOT presents its user with a question (line S1 in Figure 1), prompts them to choose and explain their answer, and extracts *relations* – any semantic relationship between two con-



*Human Language Technologies: The 2015 Annual Conference of the North American Chapter of the ACL*, pages 851–861,
Denver, Colorado, May 31 – June 5, 2015. 

cepts, such as *metal* to *iron* (line U4 in Figure 1) – that increase its confidence in the user's answer.

Relation extraction systems such as NELL (Carlson et al., 2010) use ontologies to predetermine valid relation types and arguments, then scan text to fill the ontology with facts. Open Information Extraction (Etzioni et al., 2011) avoids fixed ontologies with domain-independent linguistic features, distant supervision, and redundancy, but requires web-scale text and doesn't improve with interaction. Like Open IE, we extract relations without predetermined types, but are the first to do so from dialog.

KNOWBOT is an *open* dialog system, which means a user utterance may progress the dialog task even if its underlying action is not explicitly represented in a dialog model. This lets KNOWBOT quickly bootstrap domain knowledge from users without significant engineering overhead. Dialog-driven extraction produces effective relations without annotation, improves after each interaction, acquires relations useful on a particular task, and embeds relations in a rich dialog context.

Users successfully correct the system in approximately 50% of dialogs even without a predetermined dialog model. A baseline query expansion (Bast et al., 2007) strategy that bases decisions on the acquisition of new keywords instead of new relations results in only a 5% success rate. In comparison to paraphrase relations from general knowledge bases, relations acquired by our method are more effective as domain knowledge, demonstrating that we successfully learn from real users.

Our contributions include:

1. The first end-to-end system to construct knowledge graphs for question-answering through conversational dialog.

2. A generalizable method to represent the meaning of user utterances without a dialog model when task progression can be computed as a function of extracted relations.

3. A novel data set of real user dialogs in which users correct a QA system's answer, together with knowledge graphs representing the important concepts and relations in each question, labeled with rich dialog features.

## 2 Conversational extraction for QA

Our QA task consists of 107 science questions from the 4th grade New York Regents exam (Clark et al., 2014).[1] Each question has four possible answers. We convert each of the four question-answer pairs into a true/false *question-answer statement* using a small number of pattern-based transformation rules.

Just as 4th graders read their textbooks for answers, we collect SCITEXT (Clark et al., 2014), a corpus of unlabeled true-false natural language sentences from science textbooks, study guides, and Wikipedia Science. Each question-answer statement is associated with a subset of true/false support sentences from SCITEXT based on positive word overlap between the question-answer pair and the support sentence. The degree to which a SCITEXT sentence supports a question-answer pair is the sentence's *alignment score* (section 2.3).

Initially, the alignment score depends on keyword overlap alone, but SCITEXT needs domain knowledge to answer our questions. For example, the correct question-answer statement to *What form of energy causes an ice cube to melt? (A) mechanical (B) magnetic (C) sound (D) heat* is $Q_{(D)}$, "Heat is a form of energy and heat causes an ice cube to melt." To better align $Q_{(D)}$ to the SCITEXT sentence "A snowball melting in your hand is an example of heat energy," we need to know that *snowballs* are made of *ice*. Figure 2 illustrates this example.

To construct a knowledge base with which to use SCITEXT, we extract *concepts* (section 2.1) from questions and SCITEXT sentences, then use *relations* (section 2.2) between concepts to determine which question-answer statement $Q_i$ is most highly aligned with a supporting SCITEXT sentence.

### 2.1 Concepts

A *concept keyword* in a sentence or user utterance is any non-stopword of at least three characters. Stopwords are domain-independent, low-information words such as "the."

A *concept* is a set of concept keywords with a common root, e.g. {*melts, melted, melting*} or {*heat, heats, heated*}. We use the Porter algorithm for stemming (Porter, 1997). *Question concepts* ap-

[1]Our dialogs, extractions, and tools are available at www.cs.washington.edu/research/nlp/knowbot

pear in a question-answer statement, and *support concepts* appear in a SCITEXT support sentence.

### 2.2 Relations

A *relation* is any pair of concepts that represents a semantic correspondence. In general, relations can be labeled with any feature that describes the correspondence, such as a particular *type*. For example, the relation between *Obama* and *Hawaii* can be labeled with the type *born-in*.

A predetermined ontology is typically required to label relations with their type. In this work we label acquired relations with dialog-specific features. Our thesis is that user explanations intend to relate concepts together, and the system's task is to determine the user's intent. For example, the user utterance `U: it's melting because of heat` relates the concepts represented by *melt[ing]* and *heat*, with the words `because of` appearing between the two concept keywords. We refer to `because of` as the relation's *intext*.

Relations can be intuitively arranged as a *knowledge graph*, which in this work is any graph whose nodes are concepts and whose edges are relations between those concepts, in the spirit of semantic networks such as ConceptNet (Havasi et al., 2007).

### 2.3 Sentence alignment

We calculate the alignment score $\alpha$ between the $i$th question-answer statement $Q_i$ and its $j$th supporting SCITEXT sentence $S_{i,j}$ as the normalized number of relations between their concepts,

$$\alpha(Q_i, S_{i,j}) = \frac{\|R_{Q_i,S_{i,j}}\|}{\|C_{Q_i} \cup C_{S_{i,j}}\|}, \quad (1)$$

where $C_{Q_i}$ is the set of concepts in $Q_i$, $C_{S_{i,j}}$ is the set of concepts in $S_{i,j}$, and $\|R_{Q_i,S_{i,j}}\|$ is the number of relations between $C_{Q_i}$ and $C_{S_{i,j}}$.

Normalized relation count is a practical semantic similarity score that generalizes to different knowledge representations. The dialog in Figure 2 aligns $Q_{(D)}$ with the SCITEXT fact $S$ by learning from the user that, for example, *heat* is related to *melting*.

## 3 The KNOWBOT dialog system

KNOWBOT grows a knowledge graph of commonsense semantic relations in open, conversational dialog. Figure 2 traces the growth of a knowledge graph over a single dialog. Section 3.1 details how knowledge is extracted from user explanations without a dialog model. Section 3.2 describes dialog strategies that elicit natural language explanations.

KNOWBOT uses task progress to drive natural language understanding. It assumes the user intends to provide one or more novel relations, and uses the constraints described in section 3.1.1 to disambiguate noisy relations. This way, KNOWBOT knows when the dialog progresses because its confidence in the user's chosen answer increases.

### 3.1 Building knowledge graphs from dialog

KNOWBOT builds KGs at three levels: per utterance, per dialog, and globally over all dialogs. An *utterance-level knowledge graph* (uKG) (Figure 2a) is a fully connected graph whose nodes are all concepts in an utterance. After aggressive pruning (section 3.1.1), remaining edges update a *dialog-level knowledge graph* (dKG) (Figure 2b; section 3.1.2).

Upon dialog termination, the dKG updates the *global knowledge graph* (gKG), which stores relations acquired from all dialogs (section 3.1.3).

#### 3.1.1 Utterance-level KGs

KNOWBOT initially relates every pair of concepts in an utterance, then prunes them based on two constraints: *alignment* and *adjacency*.

Each user explanation is first converted into a fully-connected utterance-level knowledge graph. This uKG is noisy because users don't intend relations between every pair of keywords in their utterance. For example, a typical utterance `U: freezes means it changes water from a liquid to a solid` mentions six concepts, *freezing, meaning, change, water, liquid, solid*, with $\binom{6}{2}$ potential binary relations. Not every relation is salient to the question. To remove noisy relations, edges in the uKG are aggressively pruned with two simple, rational constraints:

1. *Alignment.* An edge can only relate a question concept to a support concept.

2. *Adjacency.* Edges can't relate concepts whose keywords are adjacent in the utterance.

The intuition for the alignment constraint is that the user intends each explanation to relate the question

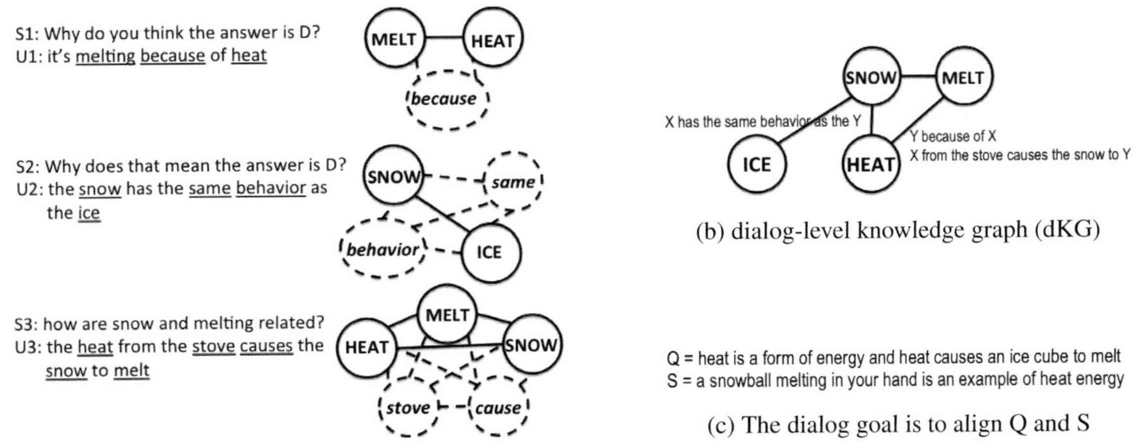


(a) utterance-level knowledge graph (uKG)

(b) dialog-level knowledge graph (dKG)

(c) The dialog goal is to align Q and S

Figure 2: Every pair of concepts in each user utterance is related then aggressively pruned. (a) Utterance-level knowledge graphs represent individual utterances. Concepts (underlined, inset in nodes) are obtained by removing stopwords and stemming. An edge that either doesn't connect a question and support concept or else which connects concepts whose keywords in the user utterance have no intervening words (*intexts*) are pruned, indicated here with dashed lines. (b) The four remaining relations are stored in a dialog-level dKG.

to a known fact, and other relations in the utterance are unintentional. For example, in the uKG for the first utterance in Figure 2(a), the edge between *melt[ing]* and *heat* is an alignment relation because *melt[ing]* is a concept in S and *heat* is a concept in Q. But the edge between *because* and *heat* is pruned (dashed lines) since *because* is not a concept in S.

Adjacency is a simple, practical syntactic feature to reduce spurious relations. Users typically put words or *intexts* between concepts they intend to relate. The edge between *melt[ing]* and *because* is pruned since their keywords are adjacent in `U1: it's melting because of heat`, while `U2` relates *snow* and *ice* with the intext `has the same behavior as the`.

We find these constraints effective in practice, but at this point other pruning constraints can be deployed. A strength of our approach is that it welcomes aggressive pruning: just as in human-human interaction, users who initially fail to communicate their intention can try again later in the dialog.

#### 3.1.2 Dialog-level KGs

Each dialog focuses on a single question. KNOWBOT starts with an empty dialog-level knowledge graph (dKG). After each user turn, edges from that turn's uKG are added to the dKG, and KNOWBOT rescores each of the four answers according to equation (1) where the set of relations $R_{Q_i,S_{i,j}}$ is exactly the set of edges in the dKG. The dialog successfully terminates when the user's answer has the highest alignment score, indicating the "missing knowledge" has been successfully provided by the user.

#### 3.1.3 The global knowledge graph

The *global knowledge graph* (gKG) includes every relation learned from every KNOWBOT dialog.

Because we do not use a fixed ontology or comprehensive dialog model, individual dialogs can result in noisy relations even after aggressive pruning. However, as KNOWBOT conducts more dialogs about the same problem, relations that more often re-occur are more likely to be salient to the problem.

In this work, KNOWBOT takes advantage of redundancy with a simple filter: it ignores *singleton* relations originating in a single user utterance. We find even this simple filter increases performance. As KNOWBOT accumulates more dialogs, frequency can be incorporated in more sophisticated models.

### 3.2 Dialog strategies for knowledge acquisition

We've described how a user's free text explanations are converted into knowledge graphs. Each user explanation is uttered in response to a system prompt. A dialog system's *dialog manager* chooses the prompt to say next according to its *dialog strategy*, which maps each system state to an action. An effective dialog strategy guides users to informative explanations that provide novel relations which let KNOWBOT successfully answer the question.

We compare two different strategies. A *user-initiative* strategy always asks open-ended questions to prompt the user for new explanations, e.g. line S2 in Figure 1. These prompts let users introduce salient concepts on their own.

In contrast, a *mixed-initiative* strategy utilizes focused prompts (line S4 in Figure 1) to introduce potentially related concepts. KNOWBOT chooses what pair of concepts to ask about based on how *discriminative* they are. The most discriminative concepts are the pair of question and support concepts that (1) don't already have an edge between them, (2) satisfies the alignment constraint for the user's answer, and (3) satisfies the alignment constraint for the fewest alternative answers. By proposing relations that would lead to a swift completion of the dialog task, KNOWBOT shares the burden of knowledge acquisition with the user.

Both dialog strategies are question-independent, but because we don't use a comprehensive dialog model to represent the state space, we rely on hand built rules instead of optimizing with respect to a reward function. For example, KNOWBOT always starts by asking the user for their answer, and if a new support sentence is found will always immediately present it to the user for confirmation.

## 4 Evaluation of dialog strategies

Our first experiment compares mixed-initiative and user-initiative strategies (section 3.2) to a baseline interactive query expansion (section 4.1). The purpose of this experiment is to investigate whether users can successfully complete our complex dialog task even though we don't use a trained semantic parser for natural language understanding.

Dialogs were conducted through a web browser. Users were colleagues and interns at the Allen Institute for Artificial Intelligence, and so were familiar with the question-answering task but were not expert annotators. Users were invited to converse with the system of their choice, and to move on to a new question if they felt the dialog was not progressing. Individual dialog sessions were anonymous.

The system starts each dialog with an empty knowledge graph, using only *identity* relations to select its answer. This default answer is correct on 44 of the 107 questions, and an additional 10 questions have no associated supporting sentence for the correct answer in SCITEXT. We run dialogs for the remaining 53 questions, for which each answer candidate has 80 supporting sentences in SCITEXT on average. A successful dialog terminates when the system extracts enough novel relations from the user that the correct answer has the highest alignment score with one of its supporting sentences.

### 4.1 Baseline: Interactive query expansion

To evaluate whether task-driven relation extraction is an effective method for knowledge acquisition in the absence of an explicit dialog model, we also implement a baseline dialog strategy based on interactive *query expansion* (IQE). This baseline is similar to the recent knowledge acquisition dialog system of Rudnicky and Pappu (2014a; 2014b).

In IQE, new knowledge is learned in the form of novel keywords that are appended to the question-answer statement. For example, the dialog in Figure 1 shows the user teaching KNOWBOT how *metal* relates to *electricity*. KNOWBOT understands that the user intends that relation because it drives the dialog forward. IQE, in contrast, treats the user utterance as an unstructured bag of keywords. The unrecognized word "metal" is added to the bag of keywords representing each of the four alternative answers to form four *augmented* queries, and new overlap scores against sentences from SCITEXT are computed. The dialog progresses whenever a new vocabulary word increases the score for the augmented query for the user's chosen answer.

The intuition behind query expansion is that users will explain their answers with salient keywords missing from the original question sentence. The expanded query will overlap with and uprank a support sentence that contains the acquired keywords.

### 4.2 Performance metrics

*Task completion* is the proportion of dialogs that end in agreement. Higher task completion indicates that the dialog system is more successful in acquiring enough knowledge by the end of the dialog to change its answer from incorrect to correct.

*Dialog length* is the number of system and user turns. Shorter dialogs are more efficient.

*Acquisition rate* is the number of edges in the dKG at the end of each dialog. Acquisition rate measures two contrasting system features:

(1) how much new knowledge is acquired, and

(2) how much *explanatory effort* users expend.

From the perspective of raw knowledge acquisition, higher acquisition rate is better because each dialog adds more edges to the knowledge graph. From the perspective of usability, lower acquisition rate is better provided it doesn't negatively affect dialog success, because it indicates the user is able to successfully correct the system's answer with a fewer number of explanatory relations.

### 4.3 Results

Our results (Table 1) show both strategies dramatically outperform the baseline and have comparable success rate and dialog length to each other. User-initiative strategies acquire more knowledge per dialog but require more user effort.

| | IQE | U.I. | M.I. |
|---|---|---|---|
| Total dialogs | 35 | 27 | 57 |
| Task completion rate | 5.7% | 55.6% | 49.1% |
| Mean Dialog Length | 14.1 | 10.6 | 10.9 |
| Mean acquisition Rate | N/A | 13.5 | 7.4 |

Table 1: Comparison of knowledge acquisition strategies. Interactive query expansion (IQE)'s poor task completion indicates keywords can't bridge the knowledge gap. Relations are more successful. User-initiative (U.I.) and mixed-initiative (M.I.) strategies have comparable task completion and dialog length, but U.I. extracts twice the relations before getting the correct answer: more knowledge acquired but at the cost of more explanatory effort. User comments indicate M.I. is more satisfying.

We find that the baseline has a very low completion rate of 5%, and longer dialog lengths of 14 turns on average. Interactive query expansion is a poor knowledge acquisition dialog strategy for our task.

In contrast, users were able to successfully correct our system using both strategies about 50% of the time, even though no in-domain ontology guides extractions and no comprehensive dialog model classifies explanations. The average dialog lengths and completion rate for User Initiative (U.I.) and Mixed Initiative (M.I.) strategies was approximately the same, so that choice of strategy had little impact on overall task success. However, strategy has a great effect on acquisition rate. M.I. cuts the knowledge acquisition rate nearly in half when compared to U.I (7.4 novel relations per dialog to 13.5). M.I. learns fewer new relations per dialog with comparable task success, which means each dialog succeeds with much less explanatory effort by the user but also contributes less to the knowledge graph.

User comments indicated that the mixed-initiative strategy was the most enjoyable system to use. We find that open-ended, user-initiative strategies can acquire more helpful relations in a single dialog but guided, mixed-initiative strategies may be more appropriate when usability is taken into account. Because our goal is lifelong interactive knowledge acquisition, the impact of a single dialog on the total knowledge graph is less important than the individual user effort required, and we conclude that the mixed-initiative strategy is preferable.

## 5 Evaluation of knowledge quality

Experiment 1 evaluated whether users could successfully complete our dialog task. Next, we evaluate whether the total output of our system, all relations acquired during all 431 conducted dialogs, represents useful domain knowledge on this task. We evaluate on questions for which dialogs have been held to investigate whether it's possible to learn any domain knowledge from natural language conversation without a dialog model, irrespective of overfitting. We then use cross-validation to test if knowledge transfers between questions.

As described in section 2, our QA system decomposes each question/answer pair into a true/false statement and chooses as its answer the statement among the four that has the best supporting sentence in a text corpus. Equation (1) scores each question-answer statement by using domain relations to align question concepts to support concepts. The next section describes sources of domain relations.

### 5.1 Sources of domain knowledge

We compare relations from five sources:

IDENTITY: An edgeless knowledge graph. The only relations are between identical concepts, equivalent to Jaccard overlap of concept keyword roots.

WORDNET: Paraphrase relations from Wordnet. Wordnet (Fellbaum, 1998) is a lexical database of synonyms and hypernyms common in NLP tasks. For example, Snow et al (2006) use Wordnet as training data for ontology induction. To build WORDNET, we draw an edge between every pair of Wordnet concepts $(w_s, w_q)$ for which the Wu-Palmer Similarity (WUP) (Wu and Palmer, 1994) of the first sense in each concept's synset exceeds 0.9, the best-performing WUP threshold we found. Concepts in the Wordnet hierarchy have a higher WUP when they have a closer common ancestor. If a known fact is *Heat energy causes snow to melt*, but a question asks if *ice* melts, then Wordnet should provide the missing knowledge that *ice* acts like *snow*.

PPDB: Paraphrase relations from PPDB (Ganitkevitch et al., 2013) are derived by aligning bilingual parallel texts. PPDB is divided into subsets where the larger subsets have more paraphrases with less precision. We tried all subsets and found the smallest to give the best results, which we report here. The largest performed the worst of all relation sets we tested. We use the lexical paraphrases, which relates unigrams. Concepts are related when at least one concept keyword for each are paraphrases in PPDB. We obtained better performance by stemming PPDB words: for example, if *snows* and *iced* are paraphrases in PPDB then we also considered *snowing* and *icy* to be in PPDB.

KNOWBOT: Each question is answered using relations pooled from all dialogs about all questions. The goal in each dialog is to acquire knowledge helpful to answer the question. If KNOWBOT leads to an increase in QA accuracy over IDENTITY, then we can successfully use open dialog with a human in the loop to learn knowledge that solves a question.

LEAVE-ONE-OUT: Each question is answered only with relations learned during dialogs for every other question. While KNOWBOT uses relations learned from dialogs about the questions on those same questions, LEAVE-ONE-OUT tests whether knowledge generalizes to questions without dialogs. Generalization is only possible when there are at least two questions involving the same concepts. Due to our small number of questions, in the best case we expect only slight improvement.

| | %correct |
|---|---|
| IDENTITY | 41% |
| WORDNET | 34% |
| PPDB | 39% |
| KNOWBOT | **57%** |
| LEAVE-ONE-OUT | 45% |

Table 2: QA accuracy on the 107 questions with different sources of domain knowledge. IDENTITY: identity relations only, e.g. "heats" to "heating." WORDNET: Wordnet-derived pseudo-synonyms, e.g. "eagle" to "owl." KNOWBOT: the full, unablated global KG. LEAVE-ONE-OUT: answers each question while ignoring relations acquired during dialogs on that question.

## 5.2 Results

The results of QA using the different domain knowledge is shown in Table 2. IDENTITY achieves 41% accuracy on this difficult reasoning task, showing that some questions are answerable by searching SCITEXT for supporting sentences with the same concepts as in the question-answer statement. WORDNET works surprisingly poorly. Examination found WORDNET's relations to be of good quality, yet underperform IDENTITY. PPDB performed better but still underperformed IDENTITY. We conclude that general paraphrase bases introduce too much noise to apply directly without manual curation to our science domain, underscoring the need for domain-specific knowledge acquisition.

KNOWBOT achieves accuracy of 57%, a dramatic improvement over both baselines. Importantly, this value does not test *generalization* to unseen questions, since KNOWBOT has held dialogs on these questions. However, it does show that our system can effectively learn about its domain: a poor dialog extraction system will fail to extract any helpful knowledge from users during a training dialog. This is a significant result because it shows that we successfully acquire knowledge to solve many question through conversational interaction without the overhead of a closed dialog model or fixed ontology.

We also tested how well knowledge generalizes with LEAVE-ONE-OUT. Our question set is less suited to evaluate generalization because it covers a wide range of topics with little overlap between questions. We still found LEAVE-ONE-OUT to be the second-best performer with accuracy of 45%, a 10% relative improvement versus IDENTITY. Redundancy is an effective noise reduction constraint: when LEAVE-ONE-OUT ignores redundancy and includes singleton relations (those originating in a single dialog utterance), its accuracy reduces to 32%.

## 6 Related work

Knowledge acquisition in dialog has long been a central goal of AI research. Early dialog systems acquired knowledge through ambitious interaction, but were brittle, required hand-defined dialog models and did not scale. Terry Winograd (1972) presented the first dialog system that acquires knowledge about the block world. TEIRESIAS (Davis, 1977) refines inference rules from terse interaction with experts. CONVINCE (Kim and Pearl, 1987) and its prototypes (Leal and Pearl, 1977) learn decision structures through stylized but conversational dialogs. An interactive interface for CYC (Witbrock et al., 2003) learns from experts but don't use natural language. Fernández et al (2011) argue the importance of interactive language learning for conversational agents. Williams et al (2015) combine active learning and dialog to efficiently label training data for dialog act classifiers.

Relatively little work integrates relation extraction and dialog systems. Attribute-value pairs from restaurant reviews can generate system prompts (Reschke et al., 2013), and single-turn exchanges with search engines can populate a knowledge graph (Hakkani-Tur et al., 2014). Dependency relations extracted from individual dialog utterances by a parser also make effective features for dialog act classification (Klüwer et al., 2010).

The work closest to our own, Pappu and Rudnicky (2014a; 2014b), investigates knowledge acquisition strategies for academic events. Their system asks its users open-ended questions in order to elicit information about academic events of interest. They compare strategies by how many new vocabulary words are acquired, so that the best strategy prompts the user to mention the most OOV words. In their most recent work (2014b), they group the acquired researcher names by their interests to form a bipartite graph, and use acquired keywords for query expansion in a simple information retrieval task. Our present contribution builds on this general idea, but we learn an unlimited number of relations and concepts from open dialogs, whereas they learn a small number of relations belonging to a fixed ontology from closed dialogs. We also show the acquired knowledge is objectively useful for QA.

In *closed* dialog systems, the system's dialog model explicitly represents the meaning of every potential user utterance. Any utterance not represented by this comprehensive model is rejected and the user asked to rephrase. Closed dialog systems work well in practice. For example, in the well-studied *slot-filling* or *frame-filling* model, users fill slots to constrain their goal, and an NLU module decomposes user utterances to known actions, slots, and values. A slot-filling system to find flights might map the utterance `U: Show me a flight from Nashville to Seattle on Sunday` to the action *find-flight* and the filled slots *origin* = *Nashville, destination* = *Seattle*, and *time* = *Sunday*. However, for our domain, each distinct question warrants its own actions, slots, and values. Such a complex model would require abundant training data or laboriously handcrafted interpretation rules.

In contrast, an *open* dialog system can usefully interpret, learn from, and respond to user utterances without a comprehensive dialog model. Domain-independent dialog systems with the flexibility to accept novel user utterances are a longstanding goal in dialog research (Polifroni et al., 2003). Recent work to address more open dialog includes bootstrapping a semantic parser from unlabeled dialogs (Artzi and Zettlemoyer, 2011), extracting potential user goals and system responses from backend databases (Hixon and Passonneau, 2013), and inducing slots and slot-fillers from a corpus of human-human dialogs with the use of FrameNet (Chen et al., 2014). These works focus on systems that learn about their domain prior to any human-system dialog. Our system learns about its domain *during* the dialog. While we rely on a limited number of templates to generate system responses, unscripted user utterances can usefully progress the dialog. This allows relation extraction from complex natural language utterances without a closed set of recognized actions and known slot-value decompositions.

## 7 Discussion and Future Work

KNOWBOT acquires helpful, task-driven relations from conversational dialogs in a difficult QA domain. A dialog is a success when it produces knowledge to solve the question. Extractions increase QA accuracy on questions for which dialogs have been held, indicating that knowledge acquisition dialogs can succeed without a closed dialog model by using task progress and careful pruning to drive natural language understanding. Our method is general enough to scale to any task in which alternative dialog goals can be presented to a user and the system's confidence in each alternative computed from semantic relations between concepts.

Our focus is on facilitated knowledge acquisition rather than question-answering, so we purposefully keep inference simple. The alignment score is a Jaccard overlap modified to use relations, which makes it fast and practical, but results in many ties which we score as incorrect, and also ignores word order. For example, the bag-of-keywords is identical for contradicting answers "changing from liquid to solid" and "changing from solid to liquid." To make this distinction, we could use an alignment score that is sensitive to word order such as an edit distance. We could expand our simple pruning constraints to take more advantage of syntax, for example by using dependency parsers optimized for conversational language (Kong et al., 2014).

The relational model for reasoning is both flexible and powerful (Liu and Singh, 2004). However, in a small number of cases, relations that align known facts with question-answer statements are unlikely to lead to the correct answer. For example, our question set contains a single math problem, *How long does it take for Earth to rotate on its axis seven times? (A) one day (B) one week (C) one month (D) one year*. The multiplication operation necessary to infer the answer from the SCITEXT fact "The Earth rotates, or spins, on its axis once every 24 hours" is not easily represented by our model and requires other techniques (Hosseini et al., 2014).

We observed only slight transfer of knowledge between questions. A larger question set with multiple questions per topic will allow us to better evaluate knowledge transfer. Our long-term goal is learning through any conversational interaction in a completely open domain, but because the fundamental trick that enables model-free NLU is computing progress towards an explicit dialog goal as a function of possible extractions, our current method is limited to tasks with explicit goals.

The simple redundancy filter we use effectively distinguishes salient from noisy relations, but could be improved with a model of relation frequency. We consider all acquired relations equally salient, but future work will examine how to rank relation saliency. We will also examine how dialog features can help distinguish between paraphrase, entailment, and negative relations.

Our open system acquires relations from a wide variety of user explanations without the bottleneck of a hand-built dialog model, but the tradeoff is that we use relatively simple, templated system prompts. However, our collected corpus of real human-system dialogs can be used to improve our system in further iterations. For example, the knowledge graphs we produce are targeted, question-specific semantic networks, which could be used in lieu of FrameNet to induce domain-specific dialog models (Chen et al., 2014). With a dialog model to represent the state space, reinforcement learning could then be employed to optimize our strategies.

While most question-answering systems focus on factoid questions, reasoning tasks such as ours require different techniques. Our method generalizes to other non-factoid QA tasks which could usefully employ relations, such as arithmetic word problems (Hosseini et al., 2014) and biology reading comprehension questions (Berant et al., 2014).

## Acknowledgments

This research was conducted at the Allen Institute for Artificial Intelligence. We'd like to thank Luke Zettlemoyer, Mark Yatskar, Rik Koncel-Kedziorski, Eric Gribkoff, Oren Etzioni and the anonymous reviewers for helpful comments, and AI2 interns and colleagues for their support and participation in the user studies. The first author was supported by the National Science Foundation Graduate Research Fellowship Program under Grant Number DGE-1256082. The third author was supported by grants from the Allen Institute for AI (66-9175) and the NSF (IIS-1352249).

## References


Yoav Artzi and Luke Zettlemoyer. 2011. Bootstrapping semantic parsers from conversations. In *Proceedings of the 2011 Conference on Empirical Methods in Natural Language Processing*, pages 421–432, Edinburgh, Scotland, UK., July. Association for Computational Linguistics.

Holger Bast, Debapriyo Majumdar, and Ingmar Weber. 2007. Efficient interactive query expansion with complete search. In *Proceedings of the Sixteenth ACM Conference on Conference on Information and Knowledge Management*, CIKM '07, pages 857–860, New York, NY, USA. ACM.

Jonathan Berant, Vivek Srikumar, Pei-Chun Chen, Abby Vander Linden, Brittany Harding, Brad Huang, Peter Clark, and Christopher D. Manning. 2014. Modeling biological processes for reading comprehension. In *Proceedings of EMNLP*.

Andrew Carlson, Justin Betteridge, Bryan Kisiel, Burr Settles, Estevam Hruschka, and Tom Mitchell. 2010. Toward an architecture for never-ending language learning. In *AAAI Conference on Artificial Intelligence*.

Yun-Nung Chen, William Yang Wang, and Alexander I. Rudnicky. 2014. Leveraging frame semantics and distributional semantics for unsupervised semantic slot induction in spoken dialogue systems. In *2014 IEEE Spoken Language Technology Workshop (SLT 2014)*.

Peter Clark, Niranjan Balasubramanian, Sumithra Bhakthavatsalam, Kevin Humphreys, Jesse Kinkead, Ashish Sabharwal, and Oyvind Tajford. 2014. Automatic construction of inference-supporting knowledge bases. In *4th Workshop on Automated Knowledge Base Construction (AKBC)*.

Randall Davis. 1977. Interactive transfer of expertise: Acquisition of new inference rules. In *Proceedings of the 5th International Joint Conference on Artificial Intelligence. Cambridge, MA, August 1977*, pages 321–328.

Oren Etzioni, Anthony Fader, Janara Christensen, Stephen Soderland, and Mausam Mausam. 2011. Open information extraction: The second generation. In *Proceedings of the Twenty-Second International Joint Conference on Artificial Intelligence - Volume Volume One*, IJCAI'11, pages 3–10. AAAI Press.

Christiane Fellbaum. 1998. *WordNet: An Electronic Lexical Database*. Bradford Books.

Raquel Fernández, Staffan Larsson, Robin Cooper, Jonathan Ginzburg, and David Schlangen. 2011. Reciprocal learning via dialogue interaction: Challenges and prospects. Proceedings of the IJCAI 2011 Workshop on Agents Learning Interactively from Human Teachers (ALIHT 2011).

David Ferrucci, Eric Brown, Jennifer Chu-Carroll, James Fan, David Gondek, Aditya A Kalyanpur, Adam Lally, J William Murdock, Eric Nyberg, John Prager, et al. 2010. Building watson: An overview of the deepqa project. *AI magazine*, 31(3):59–79.

Juri Ganitkevitch, Benjamin Van Durme, and Chris Callison-Burch. 2013. PPDB: The paraphrase database. In *Proceedings of NAACL-HLT*, pages 758–764, Atlanta, Georgia, June. Association for Computational Linguistics.

Dilek Hakkani-Tur, Asli Celikyilmaz, Larry Heck, Gokhan Tur, and Geoff Zweig. 2014. Probabilistic enrichment of knowledge graph entities for relation detection in conversational understanding. In *Proceedings of Interspeech*. ISCA - International Speech Communication Association, September.

Catherine Havasi, Robert Speer, and Jason Alonso. 2007. Conceptnet 3: a flexible, multilingual semantic network for common sense knowledge. In *Recent Advances in Natural Language Processing*, Borovets, Bulgaria, September.

Ben Hixon and Rebecca J. Passonneau. 2013. Open dialogue management for relational databases. In *Proceedings of the 2013 Conference of the North American Chapter of the Association for Computational Linguistics: Human Language Technologies*, pages 1082–1091, Atlanta, Georgia, June. Association for Computational Linguistics.

Javad Mohammad Hosseini, Hannaneh Hajishirzi, Oren Etzioni, and Nate Kushman. 2014. Learning to solve arithmetic word problems with verb categorization. In *Proceedings of the 2014 Conference on Empirical Methods in Natural Language Processing (EMNLP)*, pages 523–533. Association for Computational Linguistics.

Jin H. Kim and Judea Pearl. 1987. Convince: A conversational inference consolidation engine. *IEEE Trans. Syst. Man Cybern.*, 17(2):120–132, March.

Tina Klüwer, Hans Uszkoreit, and Feiyu Xu. 2010. Using syntactic and semantic based relations for dialogue act recognition. In *Proceedings of the 23rd International Conference on Computational Linguistics: Posters*, COLING '10, pages 570–578, Stroudsburg, PA, USA.

Lingpeng Kong, Nathan Schneider, Swabha Swayamdipta, Archna Bhatia, Chris Dyer, and A. Noah Smith. 2014. A dependency parser for tweets. In *Proceedings of the 2014 Conference on Empirical Methods in Natural Language Processing (EMNLP)*, pages 1001–1012. Association for Computational Linguistics.

Antonio Leal and Judea Pearl. 1977. An interactive program for conversational elicitation of decision structures. *IEEE Transactions on Systems, Man, and Cybernetics*, 7(5):368–376.

Hugo Liu and Push Singh. 2004. Commonsense reasoning in and over natural language. In *Proceedings of the 8th International Conference on Knowledge-Based Intelligent Information and Engineering Systems (KES-2004*. Springer.

Aasish Pappu and Alexander Rudnicky. 2014a. Knowledge acquisition strategies for goal-oriented dialog systems. In *Proceedings of the 15th Annual Meeting of the Special Interest Group on Discourse and Dialogue (SIGDIAL)*, pages 194–198, Philadelphia, PA, U.S.A., June.

Aasish Pappu and Alexander Rudnicky. 2014b. Learning situated knowledge bases through dialog. In *Proceedings of Interspeech*, September.

Joseph Polifroni, Grace Chung, and Stephanie Seneff. 2003. Towards automatic generation of mixed-initiative dialog systems from web content. In *Eurospeech*.

M. F. Porter. 1997. Readings in information retrieval. chapter An Algorithm for Suffix Stripping, pages 313–316. Morgan Kaufmann Publishers Inc., San Francisco, CA, USA.

Kevin Reschke, Adam Vogel, and Dan Jurafsky. 2013. Generating recommendation dialogs by extracting information from user reviews. In *Proceedings of the 51st Annual Meeting of the Association for Computational Linguistics (Volume 2: Short Papers)*, pages 499–504, Sofia, Bulgaria, August. Association for Computational Linguistics.

Rion Snow, Daniel Jurafsky, and Andrew Y Ng. 2006. Semantic taxonomy induction from heterogenous evidence. In *Proceedings of the 21st International Conference on Computational Linguistics and the 44th annual meeting of the Association for Computational Linguistics*, pages 801–808. Association for Computational Linguistics.

Jason D. Williams, Nobal B. Niraula, Pradeep Dasigi, Aparna Lakshmiratan, Carlos Garcia Jurado Suarez, Mouni Reddy, and Geoff Zweig. 2015. Rapidly scaling dialog systems with interactive learning. In *2015 International Workshop Series on Spoken Dialogue Systems Technology (IWSDS)*, January.

T. Winograd. 1972. *Understanding natural language*. Academic Press.

Michael Witbrock, David Baxter, Jon Curtis, Dave Schneider, Robert Kahlert, Pierluigi Miraglia, Peter Wagner, Kathy Panton, Gavin Matthews, and Amanda Vizedom. 2003. An interactive dialogue system for knowledge acquisition in cyc. In *Proceedings of the IJCAI-2003 Workshop on Mixed-Initiative Intelligent Systems.*, pages 138–145.

Zhibiao Wu and Martha Palmer. 1994. Verbs semantics and lexical selection. In *Proceedings of the 32Nd Annual Meeting on Association for Computational Linguistics*, ACL '94, pages 133–138, Stroudsburg, PA, USA. Association for Computational Linguistics.

# Sentence segmentation of aphasic speech

**Kathleen C. Fraser[1,3], Naama Ben-David[1], Graeme Hirst[1], Naida L. Graham[2,3], Elizabeth Rochon[2,3]**
[1]Department of Computer Science, University of Toronto, Toronto, Canada
[2]Department of Speech-Language Pathology, University of Toronto, Toronto, Canada
[3]Toronto Rehabilitation Institute, Toronto, Canada
{kfraser,naama,gh}@cs.toronto.edu, {naida.graham,elizabeth.rochon}@utoronto.ca

## Abstract

Automatic analysis of impaired speech for screening or diagnosis is a growing research field; however there are still many barriers to a fully automated approach. When automatic speech recognition is used to obtain the speech transcripts, sentence boundaries must be inserted before most measures of syntactic complexity can be computed. In this paper, we consider how language impairments can affect segmentation methods, and compare the results of computing syntactic complexity metrics on automatically and manually segmented transcripts. We find that the important boundary indicators and the resulting segmentation accuracy can vary depending on the type of impairment observed, but that results on patient data are generally similar to control data. We also find that a number of syntactic complexity metrics are robust to the types of segmentation errors that are typically made.

## 1 Introduction

The automatic analysis of speech samples is a promising direction for the screening and diagnosis of cognitive impairments. For example, recent studies have shown that machine learning classifiers trained on speech and language features can detect, with reasonably high accuracy, whether a speaker has mild cognitive impairment (Roark et al., 2011), frontotemporal lobar degeneration (Pakhomov et al., 2010b), primary progressive aphasia (Fraser et al., 2014), or Alzheimer's disease (Orimaye et al., 2014; Thomas et al., 2005). These studies used manually transcribed samples of patient speech; however, it is clear that for such systems to be practical in the real world they must use automatic speech recognition (ASR). One issue that arises with ASR is the introduction of word recognition errors: insertions, deletions, and substitutions. This problem as it relates to impaired speech has been considered elsewhere (Jarrold et al., 2014; Fraser et al., 2013; Rudzicz et al., 2014), although more work is needed. Another issue, which we address here, is how ASR transcripts are divided into sentences.

| |
|---|
| turning to politics for al gore and george w bush another day of rehearsal in just over forty eight hours the two men will face off in their first of three debates for the first time voters will get a live unfiltered view of them together |

| |
|---|
| Turning to politics, for Al Gore and George W Bush another day of rehearsal. In just over forty-eight hours the two men will face off in their first of three debates. For the first time, voters will get a live, unfiltered view of them together. |

Figure 1: ASR text before and after processing.

The raw output from an ASR system is generally a stream of words, as shown in Figure 1. With some effort, it can be transformed into a format which is more readable by both humans and machines. Many algorithms exist for the segmentation of the raw text stream into sentences. However, there has been no previous work on how those algorithms might be applied to impaired speech.

This problem must be addressed for two reasons: first, sentence boundaries are important when analyzing the syntactic complexity of speech, which can be a strong indicator of potential impairment.



*Human Language Technologies: The 2015 Annual Conference of the North American Chapter of the ACL*, pages 862–871,
Denver, Colorado, May 31 – June 5, 2015. 

Many measures of syntactic complexity are based on properties of the syntactic parse tree (e.g. Yngve depth, tree height), which first require the demarcation of individual sentences. Even very basic measures of syntactic complexity, such as the mean length of sentence, require this information. Secondly, there are many reasons to believe that existing algorithms might not perform well on impaired speech, since assumptions about normal speech do not hold true in the impaired case. For example, in normal speech, pausing is often used to indicate a boundary between syntactic units, whereas in some types of dementia or aphasia a pause may indicate word-finding difficulty instead. Other indicators of sentence boundaries, such as prosody, filled pauses, and discourse markers, can also be affected by cognitive impairments (Emmorey, 1987; Bridges and Van Lancker Sidtis, 2013).

Here we explore whether we can apply standard approaches to sentence segmentation to impaired speech, and compare our results to the segmentation of broadcast news. We then extract syntactic complexity features from the automatically segmented text, and compare the feature values with measurements taken on manually segmented text. We assess which features are most robust to the noisy segmentation, and thus could be appropriate features for future work on automatic diagnostic interfaces.

## 2 Background

### 2.1 Automatic sentence segmentation

Many approaches to the problem of segmenting recognized speech have been proposed. One popular way of framing the problem is to treat it as a sequence tagging problem, where each interword boundary must be labelled as either a sentence boundary (B) or not (NB) (Liu and Shriberg, 2007).

Liu et al. (2005) showed that using a conditional random field (CRF) classifier for this problem resulted in a lower error rate than using a hidden Markov model or maximum entropy classifier. They stated that the CRF approach combined the benefits of these two other popular approaches, since it is discriminative, can handle correlated features, and uses a globally optimal sequence decoding.

The features used to train such classifiers fall broadly into two categories: word features and prosodic features. Word features can include word or part-of-speech $n$-grams, keyword identification, and filled pauses (Stevenson and Gaizauskas, 2000; Stolcke and Shriberg, 1996; Gavalda et al., 1997). Prosodic features include measures of pitch, energy, and duration of phonemes around the boundary, as well as the length of the silent pause between words (Shriberg et al., 2000; Wang et al., 2003).

The features which are most discriminative to the segmentation task can change depending on the nature of the speech. One important factor can be whether the speech is prepared or spontaneous. Cuendet et al. (2007) explored three different genres of speech: broadcast news, broadcast conversations, and meetings. They analyzed the effectiveness of different feature sets on each type of data. They found that pause features were the most discriminative across all groups, although the best results were achieved using a combination of lexical and prosodic features. Kolář et al. (2009) also looked at genre effects on segmentation, and found that prosodic features were more useful for segmenting broadcast news than broadcast conversations.

### 2.2 Primary progressive aphasia

There are many different forms of language impairment that could affect how sentence boundaries are placed in a transcript. Here, we focus on the syndrome of primary progressive aphasia (PPA). PPA is a form of frontotemporal dementia which is characterized by progressive language impairment without other notable cognitive impairment. In particular, we consider two subtypes of PPA: semantic dementia (SD) and progressive nonfluent aphasia (PNFA). SD is typically marked by fluent but empty speech, obvious word finding difficulties, and spared grammar (Gorno-Tempini et al., 2011). In contrast, PNFA is characterized by halting and sometimes agrammatic speech, reduced syntactic complexity, and relatively spared single-word comprehension (Gorno-Tempini et al., 2011). Because syntactic impairment, including reduced syntactic complexity, is a core feature of PNFA, we expect that measures of syntactic complexity would be important for a downstream screening application. Fraser et al. (2013) presented an automatic system for classifying PPA subtypes from ASR transcripts, but they were not able to include any syntactic complexity metrics because their transcripts did not contain sentence boundaries.

## 3 Data

### 3.1 PPA data

Twenty-eight patients with PPA (11 with SD and 17 with PNFA) were recruited through three memory clinics, and 23 age- and education-matched healthy controls were recruited through a volunteer pool. All participants were native speakers of English, or had completed some of their education in English.

To elicit a sample of narrative speech, participants were asked to tell the well-known story of *Cinderella*. They were given a wordless picture book to remind them of the story; then the book was removed and they were asked to tell the story in their own words. This procedure, described in full by Saffran et al. (1989), is commonly used in studies of connected speech in aphasia.

The narrative samples were transcribed by trained research assistants. The transcriptions include filled pauses, repetitions, and false starts. Sentence boundaries were marked by a single annotator according to semantic, syntactic, and prosodic cues. We removed capitalization and punctuation, keeping track of original sentence boundaries for training and evaluation, to simulate a high-quality ASR transcript.

### 3.2 Broadcast news data

For the broadcast news data, we use a 804,064 word subset of the English section of the TDT4 Multilingual Broadcast News Speech Corpus[1]. Using the annotations in the transcripts, we extracted news stories only (ignoring teasers, miscellaneous text, and under-transcribed segments). The transcriptions were generated by closed captioning services and commercial transcription agencies (Strassel, 2005), and so they are of high but not perfect quality. Again, we remove capitalization and punctuation to simulate the output from an ASR system.

Since the TDT4 corpus is much larger than our PPA data set, we also construct a small news data set by randomly selecting 20 news stories from the TDT4 corpus. This allows us to determine which effects are due to differences in genre and which are due to having a smaller training set.

[1] `catalog.ldc.upenn.edu/LDC2005S11`

## 4 Methods

### 4.1 Lexical and POS features

The lexical features are simply the unlemmatized word tokens. We do not consider word $n$-grams due to the small size of our PPA data set. To extract our part-of-speech (POS) features, we first tag the transcripts using the NLTK POS tagger (Bird et al., 2009). We use the POS of the current word, the next word, and the previous word as features.

### 4.2 Prosodic features

To calculate the prosodic features, we first perform automatic alignment of the transcripts to the audio files. This provides us with a phone-level transcription, with the start and end of each phone linked to a time in the audio file. Using this information, we are able to calculate the length of the pauses between words, which we bin into three categories based on previous work by Pakhomov et al. (2010a). Each interword boundary either contains no pause, a short pause (<400 ms), or a long pause (>400 ms).

We calculate the pitch (Talkin, 1995; Brookes, 1997), energy, and duration of the last vowel before an interword boundary. For each measurement, we compare the value to the average value for that speaker, as well as to the values for the last vowel before the next and previous interword boundaries.

We perform the automatic alignment using the HTK toolkit (Young et al., 1997). Our pronunciation dictionary is based on the CMU dictionary[2], augmented with estimated pronunciations of out-of-vocabulary words using the "g2p" grapheme-to-phoneme toolkit (Bisani and Ney, 2008). We use a generic acoustic model that has been trained on Wall Street Journal text (Vertanen, 2006).

### 4.3 Classification

We use a conditional random field (CRF) to label each interword boundary as either a sentence boundary (B) or not (NB). We use a CRF implementation called CRFsuite (Okazaki, 2007) with the passive-aggressive learning algorithm. To avoid overfitting, we set the minimum feature frequency cut-off to 20.

To evaluate the performance of our system, we compare the hypothesized sentence boundaries with

[2] `www.speech.cs.cmu.edu/cgi-bin/cmudict`

the manually annotated sentence boundaries and report the $F$ score, where $F$ is the harmonic mean of recall and precision. For the PPA data and the small news data, we assess the system using a leave-one-out cross validation framework, in which each narrative is sequentially held out as test data while the system is trained on the remaining narratives. For the large TDT4 corpus, we randomly hold out 10% of the corpus as test data, and train on the remaining 90%.

### 4.4 Assessment of syntactic complexity

Once we have segmented the transcripts, we want to assess how the (presumably noisy) segmentation affects our measures of syntactic complexity. Here we consider a number of syntactic complexity metrics that have been previously used in the study of PPA speech (Fraser et al., 2014). The metrics are defined in the first column of Table 3. For the first four metrics, we generated the parse tree for each sentence using the Stanford parser (Klein and Manning, 2003). The Yngve depth is a well-known measure of how left-branching a parse tree is (Sampson, 1997; Yngve, 1960). The remaining metrics in Table 3 were calculated using Lu's Syntactic Complexity Analyzer (SCA) (Lu, 2010). We follow Lu's definitions for the various syntactic units: a *clause* is a structure consisting of at least a subject and a finite verb, a *dependent clause* is a clause which could not form a sentence on its own, a *verb phrase* is a phrase consisting of at least a verb and its dependents, a *complex nominal* is a noun phrase, clause, or gerund that stands in for a noun, a *coordinate phrase* is an adjective, adverb, noun, or verb phrase immediately dominated by a coordinating conjunction, a *T-unit* is a clause and all of its dependent clauses, and a *complex T-unit* is a T-unit which contains a dependent clause.

## 5 Segmentation results

### 5.1 Comparison between data sets

Table 1 shows the performance on the different data sets when trained using different combinations of feature types. We also report the chance baseline for comparison.

We first consider the differences in results observed between the two news data sets. The best results are similar in both groups, although, as would be expected, the larger training sample performs better. However, the difference is small, which suggests that the small size of the PPA data set should not greatly hurt the performance. When we compare the performance of these two groups with different sets of training features, we notice that the difference in performance is greatest when training on lexical features. In a small random sample from the TDT4 corpus, it is unlikely that two stories will cover the same topic, and so there will be little overlap in vocabulary. This is reflected in the results showing that lexical features hurt the performance in this small news sample.

| **Feature set** | **TDT4** | **TDT4 (small)** | **Controls** | **SD** | **PNFA** |
|---|---|---|---|---|---|
| **Chance baseline** | 0.07 | 0.07 | 0.05 | 0.07 | 0.06 |
| **All** | **0.61** | 0.57 | **0.51** | **0.43** | **0.47** |
| **Lexical+prosody** | 0.57 | 0.50 | 0.44 | 0.30 | 0.33 |
| **Lexical+POS** | 0.48 | 0.36 | 0.36 | 0.36 | 0.40 |
| **POS+prosody** | **0.61** | **0.59** | 0.45 | 0.39 | 0.45 |
| **POS** | 0.45 | 0.39 | 0.28 | 0.35 | 0.39 |
| **Prosody** | 0.50 | 0.48 | 0.24 | 0.23 | 0.25 |
| **Lexical** | 0.26 | 0.14 | 0.18 | 0.17 | 0.18 |

Table 1: $F$ score for the automatic segmentation method on each data set. Boldface indicates best in column.

Performance on the news corpus is better than on the PPA data (including the control group). Comparing the small news sample to the PPA controls, we see that this is not simply due to the size of the training set, so we instead attribute the effect to the fact that speech in broadcast news is often prepared, while in the PPA data sets it is spontaneous.

A closer look at the effect of prosodic features in our training data further shows the difference we observe between prepared and spontaneous speech. When trained on the prosodic features alone, the news data set performs relatively well, while performance on the control data is much worse. These results are consistent with the findings of Kolár et al. (2009) regarding the effect of prosodic features in prepared and spontaneous speech.

When comparing the performance on the control group and on the PPA data, we see that generally, the results are better on the controls. This is to be expected, as the speech in the control group has more complete sentences and fewer disfluencies. However, it is interesting to note that performance on the PNFA and SD groups is not much worse. All three data sets achieved the best results when trained with all feature types. This suggests that standard methods of sentence segmentation for spontaneous speech can be effective on PPA speech as well.

Looking at the PPA and control groups with other feature sets, we see that POS features are more important in the PNFA and SD groups than they are for the control data. A closer look at the transcripts shows us that the PPA participants tend to connect independent clauses with a conjunction more frequently than control participants, and independent clauses are often separated in the manual segmentation. This means that many sentence boundaries in the PPA data are marked by conjunctions. This is discussed further in the next section.

When considering the prosodic and lexical feature sets individually, we see that performance is similar in all three cases (control, SD, and PNFA). However, when we combine prosodic and lexical features together, the performance in the control case increases by a much larger margin than in the two aphasic cases. This suggests that control participants combine words and prosody in a manner that is more predictive of sentence boundaries than in the aphasic case.

## 5.2 Important features

In Table 2, we report the 10 features in each data set which are most strongly associated with a boundary or a non-boundary. We consider only the small news corpus, for a fair comparison with the PPA data.

The POS tags shown are the output of the NLTK part of speech tagger, which uses the Penn Treebank Tag Set. We append '_next' and '_prev' to indicate that this is the POS tag of the next and previous word respectively. Italicized words represent lexical items.

We first consider the features that indicate a sentence boundary (see Table 2a). In general, we observe that our minimum frequency cut-off removes many of the lexical features from the top 10. (In the absence of such a cut-off, we observed that very low frequency words can be given deceptively high weights.) The exceptions to this are the words *go* and *her* in the control set. When we look at the data, there are indeed many occurrences of *go* and *her* at the end of sentences, for example, *she was not allowed to go* or *she couldn't go*, and *very mean to her* or *so in love with her*. While these lexical items are not specific to the *Cinderella* story, it seems unlikely that these features would generalize to other story-telling tasks (although we note that the Cinderella story is very widely used in the assessment of aphasia and some types of dementia).

| **TDT-4 (small)** | **Control** | **SD** | **PNFA** |
|---|---|---|---|
| PRP_next | long pause | CC_next | long pause |
| DT_next | *go* | NNS | CC_next |
| RB | *her* | RB | NN |
| NNS | NNS | NN | RB_next |
| long pause | CC_next | RB_next | NNS |
| pitch<ave | RB | PRP_next | RB |
| NN | RB_next | energy<ave | short pause |
| CC_next | PRP_next | RB_prev | PRP_next |
| energy<ave | IN | VB | no pause |
| IN_prev | short pause | IN_prev | RB_prev |

(a) Features associated with a boundary

| **TDT-4 (small)** | **Control** | **SD** | **PNFA** |
|---|---|---|---|
| VBD_next | TO_next | *the* | TO_next |
| *the* | *so* | PRP$_next | *then* |
| IN | CC | *and* | *the* |
| MD_next | NNS_next | *then* | *she* |
| CC | *the* | VBD_next | VBP_next |
| VBG_next | *she* | VBZ_next | *and* |
| VBN_next | *and* | TO_next | *uh* |
| CD_prev | VBD_next | *'s* | VB_next |
| *a* | *of* | *I* | VBD_next |
| *to* | *uh* | *a* | *a* |

(b) Features associated with a non-boundary

Table 2: The 10 features with the highest weights in each CRF model, indicating either that the following interword boundary is or is not a sentence boundary.

The POS of the given word and its neighbours are generally important features. In all four cases, the next word being a coordinating conjunction or a pronoun is indicative of a boundary. In the three PPA cases, but not the news case, the next word being an adverb is also indicative. Looking at the data, we observe that this very often corresponds to the use of words like *so*, *then*, *well*, *anyway*, etc. This would seem to reflect a difference between the frequent use of discourse markers in spontaneous speech and their relative sparsity in prepared speech.

The POS of the current word is also important. In

all cases, a boundary is associated with the current word being an adverb or a noun. In the control data only, the tag IN, representing either a preposition or a subordinating clause, is also associated with a boundary. Although this seems counter-intuitive, an examination of the data reveals that in almost every case, this corresponds to the phrase *happily ever after*. The fact that this feature does not occur in the other PPA groups could indicate that the patients are less likely to use this phrase, but could also be due to our relatively high frequency cut-off.

Another anomalous result is that the tag VB (verb, base form) is associated with a sentence boundary in the SD case only. Again, examples from the data suggest a probable explanation. In many cases, sentences ending with VB are actually statements about the difficulty of the task, rather than narrative content; e.g., *that's all I can say*, *I can't recall*, or *I don't know*. These statements are consistent with the word-finding difficulties that are a hallmark of SD.

In the prosodic features, we see that long pauses and decreases in pitch and energy are associated with sentence boundaries in the news corpus. However, the results are mixed in the PPA data. This finding is consistent with our results in Section 5.1, and supports the conclusion of Cuendet et al. (2007) and Kolář et al. (2009) that prosodic features are more useful in prepared than spontaneous speech.

We now look briefly at the features which are associated with a non-boundary (Table 2b). Here we see more lexical features in the top 10, mostly function words and filled pauses. These features reflect the reasonable assumption that most sentences do not end with determiners, conjunctions, or subjective pronouns. One feature which occurs in the news data but not the PPA data is the next word being a modal verb (MD). This seems to be a result of the more frequent use of the future tense in the news stories (e.g. *the senator will serve another term*), in contrast to the Cinderella stories, which are generally told in the present or simple past tense.

## 6 Complexity results

We first compare calculating the syntactic complexity metrics on the manually segmented transcripts and the automatically segmented transcripts. The results are given in Table 3. Metrics for which there is no significant difference between the manual and automatic segmentation are marked with "NS". Of course, we do not claim that there is actually no difference between the values, as can be seen in the table, but we use this as a threshold to determine which features are less affected by the automatic segmentation.

All the features relating to Yngve depth and height of the parse trees are significantly different (in at least one of the three clinical groups). However, of the eight primary syntactic units calculated by Lu's SCA, six show no significant difference when measured on the automatically segmented transcripts. To examine this effect further, we will discuss how each of the eight is affected by the segmentation process.

Although the number of sentences (S) is different, the number of clauses (C) is not significantly affected by the automatic segmentation, which implies that the boundaries are rarely placed within clauses, but rather between clauses. An example of this phenomenon is given in Example 1:

**Manual:** And then they go off to the ball and then she comes I dunno how she meets up with this um fairy godmother whatever.

**Auto:** And then they go off to the ball. And then she comes I dunno how she meets up with this um fairy godmother whatever.

Our automatic method inserts a sentence boundary before the second *and*, breaking one sentence into two but not altering the number of clauses. In fact, the proposed boundary seems quite reasonable, although it does not agree with the human annotator. The correlation between the number of clauses counted in the manual and automatic transcripts is 0.99 in all three clinical groups. The counts for dependent clauses (DC) are also relatively unaffected by the automatic segmentation, for similar reasons.

The T-unit count (T) is also not significantly affected by the automatic segmentation. Since a T-unit only contains one independent clause as well as any attached dependent clauses, this suggests that the segmentation generally does not separate dependent clauses from their independent clauses. This also helps explain the lack of difference on complex T-units (CT).

Table 3 also indicates that the number of verb phrases (VP) and complex nominals (CN) is not significantly different in the automatically segmented

| Metric | Diff? | Controls | | SD | | PNFA | |
|---|---|---|---|---|---|---|---|
| | | Manual | Auto | Manual | Auto | Manual | Auto |
| **Max YD** maximum Yngve depth | | 5.10 | 4.53 | 4.45 | 3.87 | 4.66 | 3.83 |
| **Mean YD** mean Yngve depth | | 2.97 | 2.72 | 2.68 | 2.44 | 2.77 | 2.41 |
| **Total YD** total sum of the Yngve depths | | 66.92 | 53.41 | 42.48 | 32.95 | 49.95 | 32.57 |
| **Tree height** average parse tree height | | 12.56 | 11.30 | 10.79 | 9.81 | 11.25 | 9.88 |
| **S** number of sentences | | 24.35 | 31.22 | 27.73 | 37.36 | 18.82 | 25.47 |
| **T** number of T-units | NS | 31.43 | 35.13 | 32.55 | 39.27 | 23.29 | 27.41 |
| **C** number of clauses | NS | 61.48 | 64.48 | 57.73 | 62.45 | 42.94 | 46.65 |
| **DC** number of dependent clauses | NS | 24.70 | 27.30 | 26.27 | 26.09 | 16.59 | 18.88 |
| **CN** number of complex nominals | NS | 41.39 | 43.52 | 38.73 | 39.64 | 27.12 | 27.88 |
| **VP** number of verb phrases | NS | 77.00 | 79.65 | 72.09 | 77.00 | 51.76 | 55.24 |
| **CP** number of coordinate phrases | | 12.39 | 10.30 | 11.55 | 6.91 | 7.82 | 4.18 |
| **CT** number of complex T-units | NS | 14.30 | 13.52 | 12.00 | 11.82 | 9.29 | 8.71 |
| **MLS** mean length of sentence | | 19.79 | 16.22 | 14.04 | 11.25 | 15.86 | 11.60 |
| **MLT** mean length of T-unit | | 14.92 | 13.72 | 12.19 | 10.46 | 12.78 | 10.66 |
| **MLC** mean length of clause | | 7.55 | 7.21 | 7.13 | 6.58 | 6.89 | 6.39 |
| **T/S** T-units per sentence | | 1.34 | 1.17 | 1.15 | 1.06 | 1.23 | 1.08 |
| **C/S** clauses per sentence | | 2.64 | 2.25 | 1.96 | 1.70 | 2.28 | 1.82 |
| **DC/T** dependent clauses per T-unit | NS | 0.80 | 0.78 | 0.73 | 0.63 | 0.73 | 0.69 |
| **VP/T** verb phrases per T-unit | | 2.47 | 2.34 | 2.11 | 1.92 | 2.23 | 1.98 |
| **CP/T** coordinate phrases per T-unit | | 0.40 | 0.33 | 0.35 | 0.17 | 0.35 | 0.15 |
| **CN/T** complex nominals per T-unit | NS | 1.32 | 1.26 | 1.18 | 1.10 | 1.17 | 1.01 |
| **C/T** clauses per T-unit | | 1.99 | 1.91 | 1.71 | 1.58 | 1.86 | 1.68 |
| **CT/T** complex T-units per T-unit | NS | 0.46 | 0.40 | 0.37 | 0.32 | 0.39 | 0.32 |
| **DC/C** dependent clauses per clause | NS | 0.39 | 0.41 | 0.42 | 0.40 | 0.38 | 0.41 |
| **CP/C** coordinate phrases per clause | | 0.20 | 0.17 | 0.20 | 0.10 | 0.19 | 0.09 |
| **CN/C** complex nominals per clause | NS | 0.65 | 0.65 | 0.70 | 0.71 | 0.63 | 0.61 |

Table 3: Mean values of syntactic complexity metrics for the different patient groups. Features which show no significant difference between the manual and automatic segmentation on all three clinical groups are marked as "NS" (not significant).

transcripts. Since these syntactic units are typically sub-clausal, this is not unexpected given the arguments above.

The remaining primary syntactic unit, the coordinate phrase (CP), *is* different in the automatic transcripts. This represents a weakness of our method; namely, it has a tendency to insert a boundary before all coordinating conjunctions, as in Example 2:

**Manual:** So she is very upset and she's crying and with her fairy godmother who then uh creates a carriage and horses and horsemen and and driver and beautiful dress and magical shoes.

**Auto:** So she is very upset. And she's crying and with her. Fairy godmother who then uh creates a carriage. And horses and horsemen and and driver. And beautiful dress. And magical shoes.

In this case, the manual transcript has five coordinate phrases, while the automatic transcript has only two.

The mean lengths of sentence (MLS), clause (MLC), and T-unit (MLT) are all significantly different in the automatically segmented transcripts. We ascribe this to the fact that a small change in C or T can lead to a large change in MLC or MLT. The remaining metrics in Table 3 are simply combinations of the primary units discussed above.

Our analysis so far suggests that some syntactic units are relatively impervious to the automatic sentence segmentation, while others are more susceptible to error. However, when we examine the mean values given in Table 3, we observe that even in cases when the complexity metrics are significantly different in the automatic transcripts, the differences appear to be systematic. For example, we know that our segmentation method tends to produce more sentences than appear in the manual transcripts (i.e., S is always greater in the automatic transcripts). If we look at the differences across clinical groups, the same pattern emerges in both the man-

| Metric | SD vs controls | | PNFA vs controls | | SD vs PNFA | |
|---|---|---|---|---|---|---|
| | manual | auto | manual | auto | manual | auto |
| **Max YD** | * | * | * | * | | |
| **Mean YD** | * | | * | * | | |
| **Total YD** | * | * | * | * | | |
| **Tree height** | * | * | * | * | | |
| **S** | | | | | | |
| **T** | | | * | * | | |
| **C** | | | * | * | | |
| **DC** | | | * | * | | |
| **CN** | | | * | * | | |
| **VP** | | | * | * | | |
| **CP** | | | * | * | | |
| **CT** | | | * | * | | |
| **MLS** | * | * | * | * | | |
| **MLT** | * | * | * | * | | |
| **MLC** | | * | * | * | | |
| **T/S** | * | | | | | |
| **C/S** | * | * | * | | * | |
| **DC/T** | | | | | | |
| **VP/T** | * | | | * | | |
| **CP/T** | | * | | * | | |
| **CN/T** | | | | * | | |
| **C/T** | * | | | | | |
| **CT/T** | * | * | | | | |
| **DC/C** | | | | | | |
| **CP/C** | | * | | * | | |
| **CN/C** | | | | | | |

Table 4: Difference between syntactic complexity metrics for each pair of patient groups. A significant difference ($p < 0.05$) is marked with an asterisk.

ual and automatic transcripts: participants with SD produce the most sentences, followed by controls, followed by participants with PNFA. In most applications of these syntactic complexity metrics, what matters most is not the absolute value of the metric, but the relative differences between groups. So, we now ask: which features distinguish between clinical groups in the manually segmented transcripts, and do they still distinguish between the groups in the automatically segmented transcripts?

Our results for this experiment are reported in Table 4. In the case of SD vs. controls, there are 11 features which are significantly different between the two groups in the manual transcripts. Seven of these features are also significantly different between groups in the automatic transcripts, while an additional three features are significant only in the automatic transcripts. In the PNFA vs. controls case, there are 15 distinguishing features in the manual transcripts, and 14 of those are also significantly different in the automatic transcripts. There are four features which are significant only in the automatic case. Finally, in the case of SD vs. PNFA, there is only one distinguishing feature in the manual transcripts, and none in the automatic transcript.

These findings suggest that automatically segmented transcripts can still be useful, even if the complexity metrics have different values from the manual transcripts. Importantly, a comparison of the mean feature values in Table 3 reveals that in 92% of cases, and in every case marked as significant in Table 4 4, the direction of the trend is the same in the manual and automatic transcripts.

For example, in the first column of Table 4, maximum Yngve depth is significantly different between SD participants and controls. In both the manual and automatic transcripts, the controls have a greater maximum depth than SD participants. This is true for every metric that is significant in both the manual and automatic transcripts. This indicates that the metrics are not only significantly different, and therefore useful for machine learning classification or some other downstream application, but that they are interpretable in relation to the specific language impairments that we expect to observe in the patient groups.

## 7 Discussion

We have introduced the issue of sentence segmentation of impaired speech, and tested the effectiveness of standard segmentation methods on PPA speech samples. We found that, as expected, performance was best on prepared speech from broadcast news, then on healthy controls, and worst on speech samples from PPA patients. However, the results on the PPA data are promising, and suggest that similar methods could be effective for impaired speech. Future work will look at adapting the standard algorithms to improve performance in the impaired case. This would include an evaluation of the forced alignment on impaired speech data, as well as the exploration of new features for the boundary classification.

One limitation of this study is the use of manually transcribed data with capitalization and punctuation removed to simulate perfect ASR data. We expect that real ASR data will contain recognition errors, and it is not clear how these errors will affect the segmentation process. As well, our PPA data set is relatively small from a machine learning perspective, due to the inherent difficulties associated with collecting clinical data. Furthermore, we assumed that the diagnostic group is known *a priori*, allowing us to train and test on each group separately.

We analyzed our results to see how the noise introduced by our segmentation affects various syntactic complexity measures. Some measures (e.g. T-units) were robust to the noise, while others (e.g. Yngve depth) were not. When using such automatic methods for the analysis of speech data, researchers should be aware of the unequal effects on different complexity metrics.

For the more practical goal of distinguishing between different patient groups, we found that most measures that were significant for this task using the manual transcripts remained so when using the automatically segmented ones, and the direction of the difference was the same in the manual and automatic transcripts. In all cases where a significant difference between the groups was detected, the direction of the difference was the same in the manual and automatic transcripts. These results indicate that imperfect segmentation methods might still be useful for some applications, since they affect the data in a systematic way.

Although we evaluated our methods against human-annotated data, there is some uncertainty about whether a single gold standard for the sentence segmentation of speech truly exists. Miller and Weinert (1998), among others, argue that the concept of a sentence as defined in written language does not necessarily exist in spoken language. In future work, it would useful to compare the inter-annotator agreement between trained human annotators to determine an upper bound for the accuracy.

## Acknowledgments

Many thanks to Bruna Seixas Lima for providing the manual annotations. This work was supported by the Canadian Institutes of Health Research (CIHR), Grant #MOP-82744, and the Natural Sciences and Engineering Research Council of Canada (NSERC).

## References

Steven Bird, Ewan Klein, and Edward Loper. 2009. *Natural language processing with Python.* " O'Reilly Media, Inc.".

Maximilian Bisani and Hermann Ney. 2008. Joint-sequence models for grapheme-to-phoneme conversion. *Speech Communication*, 50(5):434–451.

Kelly Ann Bridges and Diana Van Lancker Sidtis. 2013. Formulaic language in Alzheimer's disease. *Aphasiology*, pages 1–12.

Michael Brookes. 1997. Voicebox: Speech processing toolbox for Matlab. `www.ee.ic.ac.uk/hp/staff/dmb/voicebox/voicebox.html`.

Sebastien Cuendet, Elizabeth Shriberg, Benoit Favre, James Fung, and Dilek Hakkani-Tür. 2007. An analysis of sentence segmentation features for broadcast news, broadcast conversations, and meetings. *Searching Spontaneous Conversational Speech*, pages 43–49.

Karen D. Emmorey. 1987. The neurological substrates for prosodic aspects of speech. *Brain and Language*, 30(2):305–320.

Kathleen Fraser, Frank Rudzicz, Naida Graham, and Elizabeth Rochon. 2013. Automatic speech recognition in the diagnosis of primary progressive aphasia. In *Proceedings of the Fourth Workshop on Speech and Language Processing for Assistive Technologies*, pages 47–54.

Kathleen C. Fraser, Jed A. Meltzer, Naida L. Graham, Carol Leonard, Graeme Hirst, Sandra E. Black, and Elizabeth Rochon. 2014. Automated classification of primary progressive aphasia subtypes from narrative speech transcripts. *Cortex*, 55:43–60.

Marsal Gavalda, Klaus Zechner, et al. 1997. High performance segmentation of spontaneous speech using part of speech and trigger word information. In *Proceedings of the Fifth Conference on Applied Natural Language Processing*, pages 12–15. Association for Computational Linguistics.

M. L. Gorno-Tempini, A. E. Hillis, S. Weintraub, A. Kertesz, M. Mendez, S. F. Cappa, J. M. Ogar, J. D. Rohrer, S. Black, B. F. Boeve, F. Manes, N. F. Dronkers, R. Vandenberghe, K. Rascovsky, K. Patterson, B. L. Miller, D. S. Knopman, J. R. Hodges, M. M. Mesulam, and M. Grossman. 2011. Classification of primary progressive aphasia and its variants. *Neurology*, 76:1006–1014.

William Jarrold, Bart Peintner, David Wilkins, Dimitra Vergryi, Colleen Richey, Maria Luisa Gorno-Tempini, and Jennifer Ogar. 2014. Aided diagnosis of dementia type through computer-based analysis of spontaneous speech. In *Proceedings of the ACL Workshop on Computational Linguistics and Clinical Psychology*, pages 27–36.

Dan Klein and Christopher D. Manning. 2003. Accurate unlexicalized parsing. In *Proceedings of the 41st Meeting of the Association for Computational Linguistics*, pages 423–430.

Jáchym Kolár, Yang Liu, and Elizabeth Shriberg. 2009. Genre effects on automatic sentence segmentation of speech: A comparison of broadcast news and broadcast conversations. In *Proceedings of the IEEE International Conference on Acoustics, Speech and Signal Processing (ICASSP)*, pages 4701–4704. IEEE.

Yang Liu and Elizabeth Shriberg. 2007. Comparing evaluation metrics for sentence boundary detection. In *Proceedings of the IEEE International Conference on Acoustics, Speech and Signal Processing (ICASSP)*, volume 4, pages 182–185. IEEE.

Yang Liu, Andreas Stolcke, Elizabeth Shriberg, and Mary Harper. 2005. Using conditional random fields for sentence boundary detection in speech. In *Proceedings of the 43rd Annual Meeting on Association for Computational Linguistics*, ACL '05, pages 451–458, Stroudsburg, PA, USA. Association for Computational Linguistics.

Xiaofei Lu. 2010. Automatic analysis of syntactic complexity in second language writing. *International Journal of Corpus Linguistics*, 15(4):474–496.

Jim Miller and Regina Weinert. 1998. *Spontaneous spoken language*. Clarendon Press.

Naoaki Okazaki. 2007. CRFsuite: a fast implementation of conditional random fields (CRFs).

Sylvester Olubolu Orimaye, Jojo Sze-Meng Wong, and Karen Jennifer Golden. 2014. Learning predictive linguistic features for Alzheimer's disease and related dementias using verbal utterances. In *Proceedings of the 1st Workshop on Computational Linguistics and Clinical Psychology (CLPsych)*, pages 78–87, Baltimore, Maryland. Association for Computational Linguistics.

S. V. Pakhomov, G. E. Smith, D. Chacon, Y. Feliciano, N. Graff-Radford, R. Caselli, and D. S. Knopman. 2010a. Computerized analysis of speech and language to identify psycholinguistic correlates of frontotemporal lobar degeneration. *Cognitive and Behavioral Neurology*, 23:165–177.

Serguei V.S. Pakhomov, Glen E. Smith, Susan Marino, Angela Birnbaum, Neill Graff-Radford, Richard Caselli, Bradley Boeve, and David D. Knopman. 2010b. A computerized technique to assess language use patterns in patients with frontotemporal dementia. *Journal of Neurolinguistics*, 23:127–144.

Brian Roark, Margaret Mitchell, John-Paul Hosom, Kristy Hollingshead, and Jeffery Kaye. 2011. Spoken language derived measures for detecting mild cognitive impairment. *IEEE Transactions on Audio, Speech, and Language Processing*, 19(7):2081–2090.

Frank Rudzicz, Rosalie Wang, Momotaz Begum, and Alex Mihailidis. 2014. Speech recognition in Alzheimer's disease with personal assistive robots. In *Proceedings of the 5th Workshop on Speech and Language Processing for Assistive Technologies (SLPAT)*, pages 20–28. Association for Computational Linguistics.

Eleanor M. Saffran, Rita Sloan Berndt, and Myrna F. Schwartz. 1989. The quantitative analysis of agrammatic production: Procedure and data. *Brain and Language*, 37(3):440–479.

Geoffrey Sampson. 1997. Depth in English grammar. *Journal of Linguistics*, 33:131–51.

Elizabeth Shriberg, Andreas Stolcke, Dilek Hakkani-Tür, and Gökhan Tür. 2000. Prosody-based automatic segmentation of speech into sentences and topics. *Speech Communication*, 32(1):127–154.

Mark Stevenson and Robert Gaizauskas. 2000. Experiments on sentence boundary detection. In *Proceedings of the Sixth Conference on Applied Natural Language Processing*, pages 84–89. Association for Computational Linguistics.

Andreas Stolcke and Elizabeth Shriberg. 1996. Automatic linguistic segmentation of conversational speech. In *Proceedings of the Fourth International Conference on Spoken Language Processing*, volume 2, pages 1005–1008. IEEE.

Stephanie Strassel, 2005. *Topic Detection and Tracking Annotation Guidelines: Task Definition to Support the TDT2002 and TDT2003 Evaluations in English, Chinese and Arabic*. Linguistic Data Consortium, 1.5 edition.

David Talkin. 1995. A robust algorithm for pitch tracking (RAPT). *Speech Coding and synthesis*, 495:495–518.

Calvin Thomas, Vlado Keselj, Nick Cercone, Kenneth Rockwood, and Elissa Asp. 2005. Automatic detection and rating of dementia of Alzheimer type through lexical analysis of spontaneous speech. In *Proceedings of the IEEE International Conference on Mechatronics and Automation*, pages 1569–1574.

Keith Vertanen. 2006. Baseline WSJ acoustic models for HTK and Sphinx: Training recipes and recognition experiments. Technical report, Cavendish Laboratory, University of Cambridge.

Dong Wang, Lie Lu, and Hong-Jiang Zhang. 2003. Speech segmentation without speech recognition. In *Proceedings of the IEEE International Conference Acoustics, Speech, and Signal Processing (ICASSP)*, volume 1, pages 468–471. IEEE.

Victor Yngve. 1960. A model and hypothesis for language structure. *Proceedings of the American Physical Society*, 104:444–466.

Steve Young, Gunnar Evermann, Dan Kershaw, Gareth Moore, Julian Odell, Dave Ollason, Valtcho Valtchev, and Phil Woodland. 1997. *The HTK book*, volume 2. Entropic Cambridge Research Laboratory Cambridge.

# Semantic parsing of speech using grammars learned with weak supervision

**Judith Gaspers**
Semantic Computing Group
CITEC
Bielefeld University

**Philipp Cimiano**
Semantic Computing Group
CITEC
Bielefeld University

**Britta Wrede**
Applied Informatics
Faculty of Technology
Bielefeld University

{jgaspers|cimiano|bwrede}@cit-ec.uni-bielefeld.de

## Abstract

Semantic grammars can be applied both as a language model for a speech recognizer and for semantic parsing, e.g. in order to map the output of a speech recognizer into formal meaning representations. Semantic speech recognition grammars are, however, typically created manually or learned in a supervised fashion, requiring extensive manual effort in both cases. Aiming to reduce this effort, in this paper we investigate the induction of semantic speech recognition grammars under weak supervision. We present empirical results, indicating that the induced grammars support semantic parsing of speech with a rather low loss in performance when compared to parsing of input without recognition errors. Further, we show improved parsing performance compared to applying n-gram models as language models and demonstrate how our semantic speech recognition grammars can be enhanced by weights based on occurrence frequencies, yielding an improvement in parsing performance over applying unweighted grammars.

## 1 Motivation

Semantic parsers map natural language utterances (*NL*) into formal meaning representations (*MR*), and are applied for both parsing of textual input and in Spoken Language Understanding (SLU). In data-driven SLU research, typically pipeline-based systems are applied in which first an automatic speech recognizer (ASR) is applied to transcribe speech input, and subsequently a semantic parser is applied to map the transcriptions into some semantic form (Deoras et al., 2013). Such systems typically use different models for recognition and understanding. Since ASR yields recognition errors, parsing performance can degrade rapidly compared to parsing performance on written text. While the performance of ASR and parsing components are often optimized independently of each other, in particular in case of the ASR to minimize recognitions errors, research has shown that ASR transcriptions with a lower error rate can in fact yield worse understanding performance (Wang et al., 2003; Bayer and Riccardi, 2012) and that joint approaches to recognition and understanding can yield improved performance (Wang and Acero, 2006b; Deoras et al., 2013). In particular, Wang and Acero (2006b) have shown that applying the same grammar for speech recognition and understanding can yield improved understanding performance compared to applying a standard n-gram model with the ASR, since dependencies between acoustics and semantics can be captured. Their grammars are, however, learned in a supervised setting. In fact, while semantic grammars are often applied for speech recognition and/or understanding, they are often created manually or – as mentioned previously – learned from data containing semantic annotations, which are time-consuming to produce.

In the field of Natural Language Processing (NLP), the development of semantic parsers has received considerable attention. While some researchers have considered fully supervised settings (Wong and Mooney, 2006; Zettlemoyer and Collins, 2007), requiring accurate and complete semantic annota-



*Human Language Technologies: The 2015 Annual Conference of the North American Chapter of the ACL*, pages 872–881,
Denver, Colorado, May 31 – June 5, 2015. 

tions, others have developed weakly supervised approaches exploiting ambiguous representations of the context in which an utterance is produced instead of accurate and complete annotations (Chen et al., 2010; Börschinger et al., 2011; Chen and Mooney, 2008). In this line, in this paper we explore how an approach that induces semantic parsers in the form of a (semantic) grammar from ambiguous training data can be applied to acquire a language model (LM) for speech recognition as well as a semantic parser for the understanding task at the same time. Making use of a semantic parser as a language model for speech recognition also comes with the advantage that no separate language model must be trained. In our experiments, we compare performance of the induced grammars to the performance of different language models, in particular n-gram models, and we investigate the impact of enhancing induced semantic grammars with weights based on the training data. We present empirical results showing that it is possible to induce semantic grammars with weak supervision that can be applied successfully both as an LM for a speech recognizer and for semantic parsing. We show that with respect to parsing performance, our joint approach in which the same grammar is used for parsing and as an LM yields a higher $F_1$ (84.46%) compared to an approach in which a standard n-gram based model is used as an LM (78.36%). In addition, our results indicate that enhancing speech recognition grammar rules with weights based on occurrence frequencies can yield improved performance over unweighted grammars (84.46% vs 82.37% for weighted vs unweighted grammars, respectively).

## 2 Background & related work

In principle, two different types of language models can be applied with an ASR: stochastic LMs – typically n-gram models – and speech recognition grammars. While n-gram models estimate probabilities of word sequences, speech recognition grammars explicitly specify rules defining which words and patterns a user may utter. Further, semantic information can be directly included within the rules. Thus, when applied with an ASR, spoken utterances can be directly transformed into a corresponding semantic representation without producing a sequence of words as intermediate step. This approach is typically taken when building commercial systems (Wang et al., 2011). Such grammars are, however, typically created manually, which is time-consuming and error-prone. Hence, data-driven approaches to automatic grammar induction have been explored (Wang and Acero, 2006b; Wang and Acero, 2005; Wang and Acero, 2003). However, they often rely on fully supervised settings, requiring training data which is annotated at the utterance- or word level, which is costly and time-consuming to produce. In contrast, aiming to reduce the required manual effort, in this paper we explore the utility of weak supervision in the form of ambiguous context information for the induction of grammars applicable for both speech recognition and understanding.
The utility of this kind of weak supervision has been explored previously in the field of semantic parsing (Chen et al., 2010; Börschinger et al., 2011; Chen and Mooney, 2008), and unsupervised approaches to semantic parsing have been proposed as well (Poon and Domingos, 2009; Goldwasser et al., 2011). While such approaches may be applied as parsing components for SLU systems – notice though that the SLU task differs from parsing of written text in that recognition errors and phenomena of spoken language must be handled, and that not all SLU models can be applied as an LM (Wang et al., 2011) – we are not aware of work aiming to transform these parsers into speech recognition grammars or investigating their performance with respect to different LMs applied with an ASR.
Semantic parsers applied in pipeline-based SLU systems are in general usually learned in a supervised fashion. Other than semantic grammar-based approaches, probabilistic models and machine learning techniques have been applied in SLU for conceptual tagging due to their robustness to noise, e.g. Conditional Random Fields (Lafferty et al., 2001) have been applied (e.g. Wang and Acero (2006a; Dinarelli et al. (2012)); He and Young (2005) present an approach based on Hidden Markos Models. However, evaluations have shown that even in case of applying machine learning techniques or probabilistic models, semantic parsing of ASR transcriptions is affected by much more errors compared to parsing of correct transcriptions (De Mori, 2011). In order to reduce annotation costs, work has,

for instance, focused on providing annotation tools (Wang and Acero, 2006b; Wang and Acero, 2005), exploring supervised learning in combination with active learning (Wu et al., 2010) and gaining additional training data, for instance, from the Web using queries generated from a (small) existing grammar (Klasinas et al., 2013). These approaches, however, still assume manual effort and may be somewhat complementary to the one investigated here. Further, data-driven SLU parsers are often based on rather local features, e.g. n-grams, while we explore template-based grammars which can capture long-distance linguistic dependencies.

Several approaches have addressed unsupervised (Solan et al., 2005; van Zaanen and Adriaans, 2001) and semi-supervised (Wong and Meng, 2001; Siu and Meng, 1999; Meng and Siu, 2002) induction of grammars, where the latter may comprise manual post-processing of automatically induced rules. In particular, in order to be applicable as an SLU model, semantic information must be added manually, since only syntactic structures can be induced automatically in this case.

While in data-driven SLU research typically pipeline-based systems are applied, a few joint approaches have been proposed (Deoras et al., 2013; Wang and Acero, 2006b; Bayer and Riccardi, 2012). Specifically, the work presented here is most similar to the approach presented by Wang and Acero (2006b). In particular, we also attempt to learn grammars applicable for both speech recognition and understanding. However, Wang and Acero (2006b) explore a supervised setting based on word-level annotations for slots and induce rather local rules, i.e. based on preambles and postambles for slots, while we explore a template-based approach, capturing long-distance linguistic dependencies.

## 3 Methodology

In this paper, we explore the induction of semantic grammars under weak supervision provided in the form of ambiguous representations of the semantic context as explored in the NLP field of Semantic Parsing (Chen et al., 2010). In particular, the training data comprises of a set of textual utterances coupled with symbolic context information from which we induce semantic parsers and derive different LMs for application with an ASR. LMs are then applied to transcribe speech data, and the resulting transcriptions are in turn mapped into meaning representations by the learned semantic parsers. In the following, we will first describe the input data and learning scenario and subsequently the semantic parsing approach as well as the creation of language models.

### 3.1 Learning scenario and input data

Our experiments were performed on the RoboCup soccer corpus (Chen and Mooney, 2008), which is a standard dataset used for the evaluation of semantic parsing algorithms taking written natural language utterances as input. The corpus comprises four RoboCup games. Game events are represented by predicate logic formulas, which represent the ambiguous contextual representations from which semantic parsers are trained in a weakly supervised fashion. The games were commented by humans, yielding examples for *written* natural language utterances (*NL*). In the corpus, each *NL* is paired with a set of possible meaning representations $mr_i \in MR$, each expressing a game action, and *NL* corresponds to at most one them. For example, *pass(purple10,purple7)* represents an *mr* for a passing event which might be commented as "purple10 kicks to purple7". However, there is no direct correspondence between the *NL* comments and their corresponding *mr*s; thus, these correspondences have to be learned.

The corpus also contains a gold standard comprising *NL*s annotated with their correct *mr*s. Several semantic parsers have been evaluated using this dataset by applying the evaluation schema introduced by Chen et al. (2010). The authors performed 4-fold cross-validation on the four games. Training was done on the ambiguous training data, while the gold standard for a fourth game was used for testing. Results were presented by means of the $F_1$ score. Precision and recall were computed as the percentage of *mr*s produced by the system that were correct and the percentage of *mr*s that the system produced correctly, respectively. A parse was considered as correct if it matched the gold standard exactly (Chen et al., 2010). Recently, this task has been extended to consider speech data, both in learning and applying a parser. In particular, the approach of Gaspers and Cimiano (2014) relied on transcriptions made by a task-independent phoneme recognizer as input. For this purpose, *NL* comments contained in the dataset were read by a speaker. By contrast, in this paper we explore how grammars for speech recognition and understanding can be built from textual input in a weakly supervised setting, and subsequently be applied for recognition and parsing of speech input. Hence, we explore a 4-fold cross-validation scenario in which for each fold learning is performed using the *written* ambiguous training data for three games, while the *spoken* gold standard of the forth game is used for testing, i.e. for performing both speech recognition and subsequent parsing of the resulting ASR transcriptions; spoken data are the same as in Gaspers and Cimiano (2014). For application with the ASR we normalized training data which mainly comprised lowercasing and replacement of numbers in player names, e.g. "pink4" → "pink four". Some statistics for the normalized dataset are presented in Table 1.[1]

Table 1: Dataset statistics.

| | |
|---|---|
| Total number of comments | 1,872 |
| Comments having correct $mr$ | 1,539 |
| Average number of events per comment | 2.5 |
| Maximum number of events per comment | 12 |
| SD in number of events per comment | 1.8 |
| Mean utterance length | 7.39 |
| # Types | 355 |
| # Tokens | 13,838 |

### 3.2 The applied semantic parsing algorithm

For semantic parser induction we applied the algorithm presented in Gaspers and Cimiano (2014), which is mainly designed to work with the output of a phoneme recognizer. The algorithm is also applicable to textual input and has been shown to achieve state-of-the-art performance on written input (cf. Gaspers and Cimiano (2014)). The induced parser is represented in the form of a lexicon and an inventory containing syntactic constructions and thus well-suited to be transformed into a rule-based speech recognition grammar. The learned lexicon comprises lexical units, i.e. words or short sequences of words, along with their mapping to semantic referents, e.g. "pink goalie" → $pink1$. Each syntactic construction consists of a syntactic pattern, e.g. "$X_1$ kicks to $X_2$", along with an associated semantic frame, e.g. $pass(ARG_1, ARG_2)$, and a mapping which maps slots in the syntactic pattern to argument slots in the semantic frame, e.g. $X_1 \rightarrow ARG_1, X_2 \rightarrow ARG_2$. Slots in syntactic patterns represent positions in which a lexical unit from the parser's lexicon can be inserted. For instance, in the previous pattern "pink goalie" can be inserted at position $X_1$ or $X_2$. When applied to written text, parser induction is performed by applying the following learning steps:

1. acquisition of an initial lexicon
2. computation of alignments between *NL*s and ambiguous context representations, and
3. estimation of co-occurrence frequencies at different levels.

This work flow is illustrated in Fig 1.

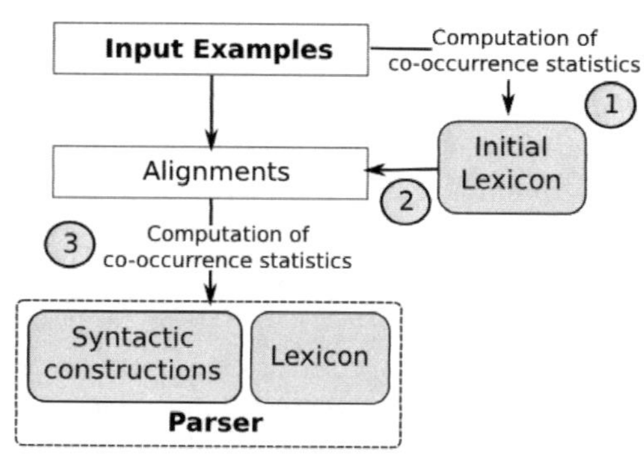


Figure 1: The algorithm's work flow.

In step 1, initial lexical knowledge is learned by computing co-occurrence frequencies between all bi- and unigrams appearing in the *NL* data and all semantic referents appearing in the *MR* data. In step 2, this knowledge is used to compute alignments for each example between its *NL* and all $mr_i \in MR$ observed with it, i.e. lexical knowledge is used to segment *NL* such that all semantic referents observed in an *mr* are expressed by individual sequences, and hypotheses concerning a mapping between *NL* and

[1]Numbers for mean utterance length and number of tokens and types are computed only for comments included in the training dataset. Regarding the total number of comments we use one more per game than Chen et al. (2010) in line with Börschinger et al. (2011).

semantics are created. For instance, given an input example

(1)

| *NL*: | purple eight kicks to purple seven |
|---|---|
| $mr_1$: | $playmode(play\_on)$ |
| $mr_2$: | $pass(purple8, purple7)$ |
| $mr_3$: | $pass(purple2, purple5)$ |

the following alignment might be created:

(2)

| *NL* | $X_1$ kicks to $X_2$ |
|---|---|
| $mr$ | $pass(ARG_1, ARG_2)$<br>Mapping: $X_1 \rightarrow ARG_1$, $X_2 \rightarrow ARG_2$ |
| $nl \rightarrow ref$ | purple eight $\rightarrow$ *purple8*<br>purple seven $\rightarrow$ *purple7* |

That is, assuming that the algorithm has learned in step 1 that "purple eight" and "purple seven" refer to $purpl8$ and $purple7$, respectively, it may use this knowledge to hypothesize that *NL* is an instantiation of a pattern "$X_1$ kicks to $X_2$", which in turn refers to the predicate $pass(ARG_1, ARG_2)$ with a mapping $X_1 \rightarrow ARG_1$, $X_2 \rightarrow ARG_2$.
Alignments are rated, and for each example only those having maximal scores are used for parser induction. By this, lexical knowledge is used to pre-disambiguate the training data. Given the alignments induced in step 3, a parser is estimated by computing co-occurrence frequencies at different levels. In particular, association scores are computed at three different levels, i.e.

1. $nl \rightarrow ref$: between all lexical units, e.g. "purple eight", and semantic referents, e.g. *purple8*, appearing in alignments,

2. *NL* $\rightarrow mr$: between all syntactic patterns, e.g. "$X_1$ kicks to $X_2$", and semantic frames, e.g. $pass(ARG_1, ARG_2)$, appearing in alignments, and

3. mapping: between all slots in a syntactic pattern, e.g. $X_1$, and argument slots, e.g. $ARG_1$, specific for each pattern and semantic frame.

Then, the parser's lexicon consists of rules of the form $nl \rightarrow ref$, while the syntactic constructions have the form *NL* $\rightarrow mr$, each coupled with its individual mapping.
Parsing is performed by searching for an appropriate syntactic construction given an input *NL*, and the arguments matching the elements at the slots in the syntactic pattern are inserted into the appropriate argument slots in the associated semantic frame. Approximate matching can be applied during parsing of *NL*s for which no pattern can be found otherwise. In this paper, we always perform approximate matching by searching for a matching syntactic pattern with a Levenshtein distance of 1 if no matching pattern can be found directly, which allows us to parse utterances containing a recognition error. Even though – of course – more than one recognition error might be contained in a given utterance, we do not use greater distance values because this would likely yield parsing errors, as utterances are rather short and most of the words are important for detecting the meaning; leaving out too many words will in general increase the likelihood of matching wrong patterns, thus yielding spurious interpretations. Using the algorithm, for each fold of the RoboCup data set we created a semantic parser using the written training data of three games.

### 3.3 Creation of language models

Based on the written training data we created different LMs. In particular, we created rule-based recognition grammars using the algorithm and further LMs, such as trigram models, for comparison.

#### 3.3.1 Recognition grammars

We built semantic speech recognition grammars given a semantic parser by transforming all rules with an occurrence greater than one into JSpeech Grammar Format (JSGF)[2]. The resulting grammars consisted of rules representing the parser's inventory of syntactic constructions as well as its lexicon. In case of the inventory of syntactic constructions, alternative expansions of learned syntactic patterns were defined, and in case of the lexicon, alternative expansions of learned lexical units were defined. In particular, with respect to the lexicon we defined a rule <ref> which comprises the learned lexical units. With respect to syntactic constructions we defined a rule <utterance> which comprises the patterns. Further, syntactic slots in patterns were replaced by <ref>, allowing lexical units to appear at those positions. In grammar creation, we also investigated the influence of occurrence frequencies of

[2]http://www.w3.org/TR/jsgf/

syntactic patterns and lexical units to enhance grammatical rules with weights. In particular, we created both weighted and unweighted grammars. When using weights, rules were weighted by using occurrence frequencies, i.e. the frequency which was observed for pattern or lexical unit as aligned by the algorithm during training. Hence, weights for patterns and lexical units aligned less frequently in the training data were smaller, indicating that they were less likely to be spoken. An example illustrating a subset of two (weighted) rules is illustrated in Fig. 2.

Notice that resulting JSGF grammars do not explicitly contain semantic information, but their induction was driven by semantic information. This is the case because a mapping to semantics was not needed during recognition as we explore a two-stage approach where parsing is performed after recognition, allowing the inclusion of further LMs during recognition. However, because both parsing and understanding are performed using the same grammar – where semantic information is ignored by the LM – it would also be possible to induce a semantic grammar that directly maps ASR output into semantic representations.

#### 3.3.2 Baseline language models

We computed different language models for comparison; these were mainly stochastic LMs. In particular, we created standard trigram language models from the written training data without making use of concurrent perceptual context information using SRILM (Stolcke, 2002). Since the RoboCup corpus is rather small and n-gram models are typically learned from large amounts of data, in addition we interpolated the trigram models trained solely on the in-domain RoboCup corpus each with a large background language model trained on a broadcast news corpus, i.e. the HUB4 dataset (Fiscus et al., 1998). We also experimented with class-based models, but automatic induction of classes in an unsupervised fashion did not appear promising and we refrained from manually creating classes since the focus of this paper is on the automatic creation of ASR resources without requiring extensive manual effort. However, an interesting experiment would be to utilize the semantic classes induced by our algorithm in order to create class-based language models.

Moreover, in order to evaluate the utility of ambiguous perceptual context for speech recognition grammar induction, as a fully unsupervised grammar-based baseline, we induced syntactic grammars relying on the ADIOS algorithm (Solan et al., 2005). Notice, however, that it is not common to apply grammars learned in an unsupervised fashion directly for SLU. In particular, with respect to semantic parsing, automatically induced grammars are typically post-processed manually, which we refrained from doing, since the focus of this paper is on the automatic creation of speech recognition and understanding components.

## 4 Experiments & Results

We evaluated the word error rate (WER) as well as parsing accuracy for different language models and combinations thereof. In particular, in case of applying recognition grammars we applied these also in combination with an n-gram back off LM. In particular, the n-gram model was applied in case of utterances which were rejected by the recognizer as out of grammar (OOG), as these might still be parsed subsequently by applying approximate matching. Notice, however, that for our experiments we did not apply both LMs at a time but combined the output of two recognizers for further processing. Notice further that most speech recognizers can only be applied using either a recognition grammar or an n-gram model at a time, but one can assume that two recognizers might be configured to run in parallel. As mentioned previously, we performed 4-fold cross-validation on the four RoboCup games. For each fold, learning semantic parsers and creation of language models was performed using the ambiguous *written* training data for three games and the *spoken* gold standard for the forth game for testing. In the following, we will discuss results for applying our induced grammars as an LM compared to using standard trigrams models (solely trained on the in-domain data) as a baseline, since these yielded the best results. In particular, we do not discuss the results achieved by the grammars induced in a purely syntactic manner as they performed worse than semantic grammars in all experiments, and we do not discuss the experiments for the interpolated/adapted

Figure 2: A subset of weighted speech recognition grammar rules

```
public <utterance> = /6/ <ref> again passes to <ref> | /199/ <ref> kicks to <ref> | ...
<ref> =  /15/ pink goalie | /132/ pink nine | /10/ pink one | ...
```

trigram models as they performed worse than the in-domain trigram models with the exception of a very slight improvement when applied as a back off model for SLU.[3]

### 4.1 Speech recognition

Speech recognition was performed using different (combinations of) LMs individually; lexicon and acoustic models were the same in all cases.[4] Speech recognition results with respect to the word error rate averaged over all folds are presented in Table 2.

Table 2: speech recognition results

| **Applied language model(s)** | **WER (%)** |
|---|---|
| Semantic grammar w/o weights | 15.55 |
| Semantic grammar w/o weights + trigram back off | 12.63 |
| Semantic grammar inc. weights | 17.15 |
| Semantic grammar inc. weights + trigram back off | 10.88 |
| Trigram (baseline) | **7.1** |

As can be seen, with a rather low error rate of 7.1%, applying trigram language models yields the best results. While in case of applying semantically motivated recognition grammars the WER increases, it must be noted that in cases in which no back off models were applied this is to some extent due to OOG utterances (as these yield several deletions compared to the reference data). Yet, the OOG-rate is rather low, i.e. averaged over all folds 8.6% and 4.1% when using grammars with and without weights, respectively. However, even in cases where OOG utterances are recognized by applying trigram language models, the WER is higher compared to applying trigram language models only. Notably, these results were not consistent across folds. For two folds, the WER actually decreased when combining a semantically motivated grammar including weights with a trigram language model compared to applying the trigram language model only, thus indicating that combining semantically motivated grammars learned with weak supervision with trigram models can also yield improved recognition performance over applying trigram models only in some cases.

### 4.2 Semantic parsing

For each fold, ASR transcriptions were parsed using the semantic parser learned on the training data for that fold. For comparison, as an upper baseline we computed parsing performance on normalized gold standard data, since typically performance degrades – and often to a large extent – when a semantic parser is applied to ASR transcriptions of speech; recall that the applied algorithm achieves state-of-the-art performance on the dataset.[5] Results are presented in Table 3.

Table 3: Semantic parsing results on written text and on speech transcribed using different language models

| **Written text (reference)** | | | |
|---|---|---|---|
| | **$F_1$** | **Prec.** | **Recall** |
| Normalized text | 87.26 | 94.28 | 81.42 |
| **Speech** | | | |
| **Applied language model(s)** | **$F_1$** | **Prec.** | **Recall** |
| Semantic grammar inc. weights | 84.18 | 88.7 | 80.18 |
| Semantic grammar inc. weights + trigram back off | **84.46** | 87.53 | 81.64 |
| Semantic grammar w/o weights | 82.24 | 84.83 | 79.84 |
| Semantic grammar w/o weights + trigram back off | 82.37 | 84.67 | 80.21 |
| Trigram (baseline) | 78.36 | 90.34 | 69.4 |

[3]The results were: interpolated/adapted LM: WER: 13.43%, $F_1$: 71.22%, semantic grammar + interpolated/adapted LM backoff: WER: 13.85, $F_1$: 84.6%, syntactic recognition grammar: WER: 18.98%, $F_1$: 70.86%, syntactic recognition grammar + trigram back off: WER: 13.98%, $F_1$: 71.27%.

[4]We applied Sphinx4 (Walker et al., 2004) using lexicon and acoustic models trained on the HUB4 dataset (Fiscus et al., 1998), which contains broadcast news speech matching our RoboCup data with respect to acoustics in that in both cases read speech is addressed; these resources are available online. We added phonetic transcriptions for out of vocabulary (OOV) to the vocabulary; only two were OOV along with some typos.

[5]While comparison with a manually created gold standard grammar would be interesting as well, a manually created grammar for the utilized dataset is unfortunately not available.

The results reveal that in case of applying trigram LMs $F_1$ degrades about 9% absolute compared to parsing written text (reference), yielding 78.36% in $F_1$, even though the WER is rather low with a value of 7.1%. Thus, the trigram seems to "destroy" semantically meaningful sequences while restoring sequences that contain no meaning. By contrast, in case of applying a semantically motivated recognition grammar including weights, performance improves by 6% absolute over the trigram model, even though the WER is higher in this case. Moreover, including weights in the recognition grammars yields improved performance compared to using unweighted grammars.

Notably, the decrease in performance in case of applying a weighted semantically motivated recognition grammar (+ trigram back off) compared to performance on the reference data is mainly due to a decrease in precision. Here it must be noted that the high values in $F_1$ are achieved without performing any optimization of (recognition) parameters. In the performed experiments, the probability for OOG utterances was rather low, and thus utterances were matched incorrectly by the ASR which were actually not covered by the grammar, yielding both recognition and subsequent parsing errors. However, these parameters can be tuned, likely increasing precision and $F_1$ even further (and probably also the WER).

Applying a back off trigram model yields only little improvement in parsing performance, although this may to some extent be due to not tuning recognition parameters. That is, if the ASR would be tuned to reject more OOG utterances correctly, these utterances might instead be recognized by a trigram model and probably parsed correctly by applying approximate matching.

## 5 Discussion

When applying trigram models, even with a rather low error rate of 7.1%, semantic parsing performance degraded about 9% absolute in $F_1$. Here it must be noted that due to the evaluation schema a single recognition error can yield a completely incorrect parse. Recall that evaluation is performed on the basis of fully correct *mr*s, i.e. all referents and the predicate must be determined correctly in order to yield a correct parse. For instance, if any of the words "purple", "pink", "two" or "five" is deleted or substituted in an utterance "purple two passes to pink five", one of the referents may not be identified (correctly). Similarly, deleting or substituting "passes" may yield an incorrect predicate or no parse at all. Hence, parsing performance can degrade rapidly even on ASR transcriptions containing only few recognition errors.

The results show that, in line with previous research (Wang et al., 2003; Bayer and Riccardi, 2012), a lower WER may not yield better understanding results, i.e. in our case parsing performance is not directly dependent on the WER but rather on the type of errors made. In particular, with respect to semantic parsing it is important that words carrying important meaning are recognized correctly. For instance, a spoken utterance "pink nine passes the ball to pink seven" in which "seven" is incorrectly recognized as "eleven" likely yields a parsing error while a recognition error which substitutes "backward" by "forward" may not prevent correct parsing. This is the case because "forward" and "backward" do not carry any semantics in the data set at hand, while correct identification of numbers is in most cases essential for detecting the correct semantic referents.

Applying the semantically motivated grammars may have been beneficial in recognizing the semantic referents correctly because the system can explicitly learn them and their appearances in certain patterns in contrast to the trigram model. In particular, if an utterance "pink nine passes the ball to pink seven" appears during recognition and "pink seven" has not been observed in the context of the preceding words during training, then the n-gram model would assign a low probability, likely leading to a recognition error such as "pink eleven". By contrast, in case of semantic grammars the system can learn that the utterance is an instantiation of a pattern "*player* passes the ball to *player*" and that all players can appear at the contained slots, thus making the appearance of the example utterance more likely. Notably, semantic classes such as *player* can in principle also be modeled in stochastic language models, in particular by applying class-based models, or in syntactically motivated grammars. Recall that we also experimented with syntactically motivated grammars and with class-based models and that neither classes which were auto-induced on the raw text data nor syntactically motivated grammars yielded promising results. Thus, using weak supervision in the form of perceptual context information appears to be beneficial for detecting semantic classes compared to working with raw text. An interesting point for future work might be to explore whether using semantic groupings induced by our algorithm in a class-based model yields reasonable results, in particular when applied as a back-off model in combination with a semantically motivated recognition grammar. Further, we have also investigated weighting rules for semantically meaningful lexical units, i.e. in this example the probability for the occurrence of players like "pink nine" and "pink seven" can be increased according to their occurrence frequencies, thus making recognizing them more likely. Our results indicate that by weighting semantically meaningful sequences, performance is improved, possibly because more words carrying semantics are recognized correctly, even though words carrying no semantics like "forward" or "backward" might be confused, which, however, may not prevent correct parsing. In general, while in SLU research mainly cascading systems are explored, in line with previous work (Wang et al., 2003; Bayer and Riccardi, 2012), our results indicate that joint models yield improved parsing performance, even though word recognition performance may decrease. Yet, our results indicate that a combination of a semantic grammar with a standard trigram model during speech recognition can also reduce the word error rate in some cases compared to applying the trigram model only. Furthermore, the results emphasize that capturing semantic information in a language model applied during ASR is beneficial for subsequent semantic parsing, since the ASR can be tuned towards recognizing words carrying semantics more precisely, which is important with respect to parsing performance.

## 6 Conclusion

This work investigated the induction of semantic grammars applicable for both speech recognition and understanding in a weakly supervised setting, i.e. using ambiguous context information. In doing so, we compared parsing the output of speech recognizers applied with different language models. Our results indicate that by applying the same semantically motivated grammar learned with weak supervision for both recognition and parsing, speech can be parsed into formal meaning representations with a rather low loss in performance compared to parsing of data without recognition errors, that is, textual data or manual transcriptions of speech. An improvement in parsing performance was obtained over a cascading approach in which a standard n-gram model is used, and we have shown how learning weights for grammatical rules applied in speech recognition can yield improved subsequent parsing results compared to applying unweighted grammars.

## Acknowledgments

This work has been funded by the DFG within the CRC 673 and the Cognitive Interaction Technology Excellence Center.

## References

Ali Orkan Bayer and Giuseppe Riccardi. 2012. Joint language models for automatic speech recognition and understanding. In *Proceedings of the IEEE/ACL Workshop on Spoken Language Technology (SLT)*.

Benjamin Börschinger, Bevan K. Jones, and Mark Johnson. 2011. Reducing grounded learning tasks to grammatical inference. In *Proceedings of the 2011 Conference on Empirical Methods in Natural Language Processing (EMNLP)*.

David L. Chen and Raymond J. Mooney. 2008. Learning to sportscast: A test of grounded language acquisition. In *Proceedings of the 25th International Conference on Machine Learning (ICML)*.

David L. Chen, Joohyun Kim, and Raymond J. Mooney. 2010. Training a multilingual sportscaster: Using perceptual context to learn language. *Journal of Artificial Intelligence Research*, 37(1):397–435.

Renato De Mori, 2011. *History of Knowledge and Processes for Spoken Language Understanding*, pages 11–40. John Wiley & Sons.

Anoop Deoras, Gokhan Tur, Ruhi Sarikaya, and Dilek Hakkani-Tur. 2013. Joint discriminative decoding of words and semantic tags for spoken language understanding. *IEEE Transactions on Audio, Speech and Language Processing*.

Marco Dinarelli, Alessandro Moschitti, and Giuseppe Riccardi. 2012. Discriminative reranking for spoken language understanding. *IEEE Transactions on Audio Speech and Language Processing*, 20(2):526–539.

Jonathan Fiscus, John Garofolo, Mark Przybocki, William Fisher, and David Pallett. 1998. 1997 english broadcast news speech (hub4). Linguistic Data Consortium.

Judith Gaspers and Philipp Cimiano. 2014. Learning a semantic parser from spoken utterances. In *Proceedings of the IEEE International Conference on Acoustics, Speech and Signal Processing (ICASSP)*.

Dan Goldwasser, Roi Reichart, James Clarke, and Dan Roth. 2011. Confidence driven unsupervised semantic parsing. In *Proceedings of the Annual Meeting of the Association for Computational Linguistics (ACL)*.

Yulan He and Steve Young. 2005. Semantic processing using the hidden vector state model. *Computer Speech and Language*, 19:85–106.

Ioannis Klasinas, Alexandros Potamianos, Elias Iosif, Spiros Georgiladakis, and Gianluca Mameli. 2013. Web data harvesting for speech understanding grammar induction. In *Proceedings INTERSPEECH*.

J. Lafferty, A. McCallum, and F. Pereira. 2001. Conditional random fields: Probabilistic models for segmenting and labeling sequence data. In *Proceedings of the International Conference on Machine Learning (ICML)*.

Helen M. Meng and Kai-Chung Siu. 2002. Semiautomatic acquisition of semantic structures for understanding domain-specific natural language queries. *IEEE Trans. Knowl. Data Eng.*, 14(1):172–181.

Hoifung Poon and Pedro Domingos. 2009. Unsupervised semantic parsing. In *Proceedings of the Conference on Empirical Methods in Natural Language Processing (EMNLP)*.

Kai-chung Siu and Helen M. Meng. 1999. Semiautomatic acquisition of domain-specific semantic structures. In *Proceedings EUROSPEECH*.

Zach Solan, David Horn, Eytan Ruppin, and Shimon Edelman. 2005. Unsupervised learning of natural languages. *Proceedings of the National Academy of Sciences*, 102(33):11629–11634.

Andreas Stolcke. 2002. SRILM - An Extensible Language Modeling Toolkit. In *Proceedings of the International Conference on Spoken Language Processing*, pages 901–904.

Menno van Zaanen and Pieter Adriaans. 2001. Alignment-Based Learning versus EMILE: A Comparison. In *Proceedings of the Belgian-Dutch Conference on Artificial Intelligence*.

Willie Walker, Paul Lamere, Philip Kwok, Bhiksha Raj, Rita Singh, Evandro Gouvea, Peter Wolf, and Joe Woelfel. 2004. Sphinx-4: A flexible open source framework for speech recognition. Technical report, Sun Microsystems.

Ye-Yi Wang and Alex Acero. 2003. Combination of CFG and N-gram Modeling in Semantic Grammar Learning. In *Proceedings EUROSPEECH*.

Ye-Yi Wang and Alex Acero. 2005. Sgstudio: Rapid semantic grammar development for spoken language understanding. In *Proceedings of the European Conference on Speech Communication and Technology*.

Ye-Yi Wang and Alex Acero. 2006a. Discriminative models for spoken language understanding. In *Proceedings of the International Conference on Spoken Language Processing*.

Ye-Yi Wang and Alex Acero. 2006b. Rapid development of spoken language understanding grammars. *Speech Communication*, 48 (3-4):390–416.

Ye-Yi Wang, Alex Acero, and Ciprian Chelba. 2003. Is word error rate a good indicator for spoken language understanding accuracy. In *IEEE Workshop on Automatic Speech Recognition and Understanding*.

Ye-Yi Wang, Li Deng, and Alex Acero, 2011. *Semantic Frame-based Spoken Language Understanding*, pages 41–92. John Wiley & Sons.

Chin-Chung Wong and Helen Meng. 2001. Improvements on a semi-automatic grammar induction framework. In *Proceedings of the IEEE Automatic Speech Recognition and Understanding Workshop*.

Yuk Wah Wong and Raymond J. Mooney. 2006. Learning for semantic parsing with statistical machine translation. In *Proceedings of the Human Language Technology Conference of the North American Chapter of the Association for Computational Linguistics*.

Wei-Lin Wu, Ru-Zhan Lu, Jian-Yong Duan, Hui Liu, Feng Gao, and Yu-Quan Chen. 2010. Spoken language understanding using weakly supervised learning. *Computer*, 24:358–382.

Luke S. Zettlemoyer and Michael Collins. 2007. Online Learning of Relaxed CCG Grammars for Parsing to Logical Form. In *Empirical Methods in Natural Language Processing and Computational Natural Language Learning (EMNLP)*.

# Early Gains Matter: A Case for Preferring Generative over Discriminative Crowdsourcing Models

**Paul Felt, Eric Ringger, Kevin Seppi, Kevin Black, Robbie Haertel**
Brigham Young University
Provo, UT 84602, USA
{paul_felt,kevin_black}@byu.edu, {ringger,kseppi}@cs.byu.edu, robbie.haertel@gmail.com

## Abstract

In modern practice, labeling a dataset often involves aggregating annotator judgments obtained from crowdsourcing. State-of-the-art aggregation is performed via inference on probabilistic models, some of which are data-aware, meaning that they leverage features of the data (e.g., words in a document) in addition to annotator judgments. Previous work largely prefers discriminatively trained conditional models. This paper demonstrates that a data-aware crowdsourcing model incorporating a generative multinomial data model enjoys a strong competitive advantage over its discriminative log-linear counterpart in the typical crowdsourcing setting. That is, the generative approach is better except when the annotators are highly accurate in which case simple majority vote is often sufficient. Additionally, we present a novel mean-field variational inference algorithm for the generative model that significantly improves on the previously reported state-of-the-art for that model. We validate our conclusions on six text classification datasets with both human-generated and synthetic annotations.

## 1 Introduction

The success of supervised machine learning has created an urgent need for manually-labeled training datasets. Crowdsourcing allows human label judgments to be obtained rapidly and at relatively low cost. Micro-task markets such as Amazon's Mechanical Turk and CrowdFlower have popularized crowdsourcing by reducing the overhead required to distribute a job to a community of annotators (the "crowd"). However, crowdsourced judgments often suffer from high error rates. A common solution to this problem is to obtain multiple redundant human judgments, or annotations,[1] relying on the observation that, in aggregate, the ability of non-experts often rivals or exceeds that of experts by averaging over individual error patterns (Surowiecki, 2005; Snow et al., 2008; Jurgens, 2013).

For the purposes of this paper a *crowdsourcing model* is a model that infers, at a minimum, class labels $y$ based on the evidence of one or more imperfect annotations $a$. A common baseline method aggregates annotations by *majority vote* but by so doing ignores important information. For example, some annotators are more reliable than others, and their judgments ought to be weighted accordingly. State-of-the-art crowdsourcing methods formulate probabilistic models that account for such side information and then apply standard inference techniques to the task of inferring ground truth labels from imperfect annotations.

Data-aware crowdsourcing models additionally account for the features $x$ comprising each data instance (e.g., words in a document). The data can be modeled generatively by proposing a joint distribution $p(y,x,a)$. However, because of the challenge of accurately modeling complex data $x$, most previous work uses a discriminatively trained conditional model $p(y,a|x)$, hereafter referred to as a discriminative model. As Ng and Jordan (2001) explain, maximizing conditional log likelihood is a compu-

[1] We use the term *annotation* to identify human judgments and distinguish them from gold standard class *labels*.



*Human Language Technologies: The 2015 Annual Conference of the North American Chapter of the ACL*, pages 882–891,
Denver, Colorado, May 31 – June 5, 2015. ©2015 Association for Computational Linguistics

tationally convenient approximation to minimizing a discriminative 0-1 loss objective, giving rise to the common practice of referring to conditional models as discriminative.

**Contributions**. This paper challenges the popular preference for discriminative data models in the crowdsourcing literature by demonstrating that in typical crowdsourcing scenarios a generative model enjoys a strong advantage over its discriminative counterpart. We conduct, on both real and synthetic annotations, the first empirical comparison of structurally comparable generative and discriminative crowdsourcing models. The comparison is made fair by developing similar mean-field variational inference algorithms for both models. The generative model is considerably improved by our variational algorithm compared with the previously reported state-of-the-art for that model.

## 2 Previous Work

Dawid and Skene (1979) laid the groundwork for modern annotation aggregation by proposing the *item-response* model: a probabilistic crowdsourcing model $p(y,a|\gamma)$ over document labels $y$ and annotations $a$ parameterized by confusion matrices $\gamma$ for each annotator. A growing body of work extends this model to account for such things as correlation among annotators, annotator trustworthiness, item difficulty, and so forth (Bragg et al., 2013; Hovy et al., 2013; Passonneau and Carpenter, 2013; Pasternack and Roth, 2010; Smyth et al., 1995; Welinder et al., 2010; Whitehill et al., 2009; Zhou et al., 2012).

Of the crowdsourcing models that are data-aware, most model the data discriminatively (Carroll et al., 2007; Liu et al., 2012; Raykar et al., 2010; Yan et al., 2014). A smaller line of work models the data generatively (Lam and Stork, 2005; Simpson and Roberts, In Press). We are aware of no papers that compare a generative crowdsourcing model with a similar discriminative model. In the larger context of supervised machine learning, Ng and Jordan (2001) observe that generative models parameters tend to converge with fewer training examples than their discriminatively trained counterparts, but to lower asymptotic performance levels. This paper explores those insights in the context of crowdsourcing models.

## 3 Models

At a minimum, a probabilistic crowdsourcing model predicts ground truth labels $y$ from imperfect annotations $a$ (i.e., $\text{argmax}_y\, p(y|a)$). In this section we review the specifics of two previously-proposed data-aware crowdsourcing models. These models are best understood as extensions to a Bayesian formulation of the item-response model that we will refer to as ITEMRESP. ITEMRESP, illustrated in Figure 1a, is defined by the joint distribution

$$p(\theta,\gamma,y,a) \tag{1}$$
$$= p(\theta)\Big[\prod_{j\in J}\prod_{k\in K} p(\gamma_{jk})\Big]\prod_{i\in N} p(y_i|\theta)\prod_{j\in J} p(a_{ij}|\gamma_j,y_i)$$

where $J$ is the set of annotators, $K$ is the set of class labels, $N$ is the set of data instances in the corpus, $\theta$ is a stochastic vector in which $\theta_k$ is the probability of label class $k$, $\gamma_j$ is a matrix of stochastic vector rows in which $\gamma_{jkk'}$ is the probability that annotator $j$ annotates with $k'$ items whose true label is $k$, $y_i$ is the class label associated with the $i$th instance in the corpus, and $a_{ijk}$ is the number of times that instance $i$ was annotated by annotator $j$ with label $k$. The fact that $a_{ij}$ is a count vector allows for the general case where annotators express their uncertainty over multiple class values. Also, $\theta \sim Dirichlet(b^{(\theta)})$, $\gamma_{jk} \sim Dirichlet(b^{(\gamma)}_{jk})$, $y_i|\theta \sim Categorical(\theta)$, and $a_{ij}|y_i,\gamma_j \sim Multinomial(\gamma_{jy_i}, M_i)$ where $M_i$ is the number of times annotator $j$ annotated instance $i$. We need not define a distribution over $M_i$ because in practice $M_i = |a_{ij}|_1$ is fixed and known during posterior inference. A special case of this model formulates $a_{ij}$ as a categorical distribution assuming that annotators will provide at most one annotation per item. All hyperparameters are designated $b$ and are disambiguated with a superscript (e.g., the hyperparameters for $p(\theta)$ are $b^{(\theta)}$). When ITEMRESP parameters are set with uniform $\theta$ values and diagonal confusion matrices $\gamma$, majority vote is obtained.

Inference in a crowdsourcing model involves a corpus with an annotated portion $N^A = \{i : |a_i|_1 > 0\}$ and also potentially an unannotated portion $N^U = \{i : |a_i|_1 = 0\}$. ITEMRESP can be written as $p(\gamma,y,a) = p(\gamma,y^A,y^U,a)$ where $y^A = \{y_i : i \in N^A\}$ and $y^U = \{y_i : i \in N^U\}$. However, because ITEMRESP has no model of the data $x$, it receives no benefit from unannotated data $N^U$.

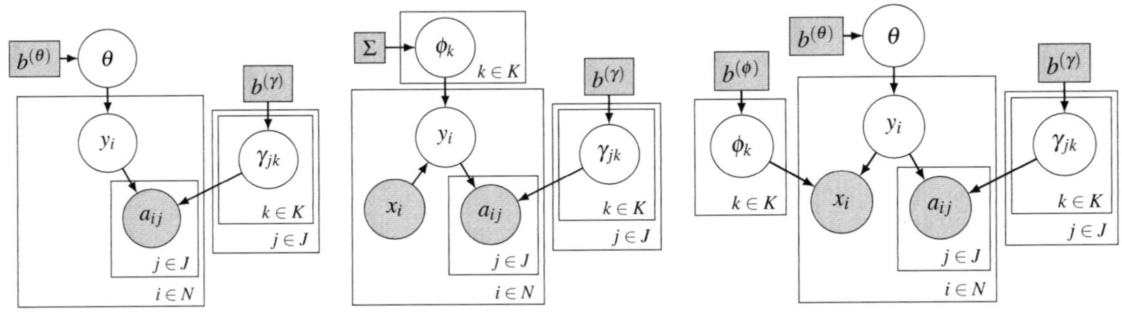

(a) ITEMRESP (b) LOGRESP (c) MOMRESP

Figure 1: Directed graphical model depictions of the models discussed in this paper. Round nodes are variables with distributions. Rectangular nodes are hyperparameters (without distributions). Shaded nodes have known values (although some $a$ values may be unobserved).

### 3.1 Log-linear data model (LOGRESP)

One way to make ITEMRESP data-aware is by adding a discriminative log-linear data component (Raykar et al., 2010; Liu et al., 2012). For short, we refer to this model as LOGRESP, illustrated in Figure 1b. Concretely,

$$p(\gamma,\phi,y,a|x) = \Big[\prod_{j\in J}\prod_{k\in K} p(\gamma_{jk})\Big] \prod_{k\in K} p(\phi_k)\prod_{i\in N} p(y_i|x_i,\phi)\prod_{j\in J} p(a_{ij}|\gamma_j,y_i) \quad (2)$$

where $x_{if}$ is the value of feature $f$ in data instance $i$ (e.g., a word count in a text classification problem), $\phi_{kf}$ is the probability of feature $f$ occurring in an instance of class $k$, $\phi_k \sim Normal(0,\Sigma)$, and $y_i|x_i,\phi \sim LogLinear(x_i,\phi)$. That is, $p(y_i|x_i,\phi) = \exp[\phi_{y_i}^T x_i]/\sum_k \exp[\phi_k^T x_i]$.

In the special case that each $\gamma_j$ is the identity matrix (each annotator is perfectly accurate), LOGRESP reduces to a multinomial logistic regression model. Because it is a conditional model, LOGRESP lacks any built-in capacity for semi-supervised learning.

### 3.2 Multinomial data model (MOMRESP)

An alternative way to make ITEMRESP data-aware is by adding a generative multinomial data component (Lam and Stork, 2005; Felt et al., 2014). We refer to the model as MOMRESP, shown in Figure 1c.

$$p(\theta,\gamma,\phi,y,x,a) = p(\theta)\Big[\prod_{j\in J}\prod_{k\in K} p(\gamma_{jk})\Big] \prod_{k\in K} p(\phi_k)\prod_{i\in N} p(y_i|\theta)p(x_i|y_i,\phi)\prod_{j\in J} p(a_{ij}|\gamma_j,y_i) \quad (3)$$

where $\phi_{kf}$ is the probability of feature $f$ occurring in an instance of class $k$, $\phi_k \sim Dirichlet(b_k^{(\phi)})$, $x_i \sim Multinomial(\phi_{y_i}, T_i)$, and $T_i$ is a number-of-trials parameter (e.g., for text classification $T_i$ is the number of words in document $i$). $T_i = |x_i|_1$ is observed during posterior inference $p(\theta,\gamma,\phi,y|x,a)$.

Because MOMRESP is fully generative over the data features $x$, it naturally performs semi-supervised learning as data from unannotated instances $N^U$ inform inferred class labels $y^A$ of annotated instances via $\phi$. This can be seen by observing that $p(x)$ terms prevent terms involving $y^U$ from summing out of the marginal distribution $p(\theta,\gamma,\phi,y^A,x,a) = \sum_{y^U} p(\theta,\gamma,\phi,y^A,y^U,x,a) = p(\theta,\gamma,\phi,y^A,x^A,a)\sum_{y^U} p(y^U|\theta)p(x^U|y^U)$.

When $N = N^U$ (the unsupervised setting) the posterior distribution $p(\theta,\gamma,\phi,y^U|x,a) = p(\theta,\phi,y^U|x)$ is a mixture of multinomials clustering model. Otherwise, the model resembles a semi-supervised naïve Bayes classifier (Nigam et al., 2006). However, naïve Bayes is supervised by trustworthy labels whereas MOMRESP is supervised by imperfect annotations mediated by inferred annotator error characteristic $\gamma$. In the special case that $\gamma$ is the identity matrix (each annotator is perfectly accurate), MOMRESP reduces to a possibly semi-supervised naïve

Bayes classifier where each annotation is a fully trusted label.

### 3.3 A Generative-Discriminative Pair

MOMRESP and LOGRESP are a generative-discriminative pair, meaning that they belong to the same parametric model family but with parameters fit to optimize joint likelihood and conditional likelihood, respectively. This relationship is seen via the equivalence of the conditional probability of LOGRESP $p_L(y,a|x)$ and the same expression according to MOMRESP $p_M(y,a|x)$. For simplicity in this derivation we omit priors and consider $\phi$, $\theta$, and $\gamma$ to be known values. Then

$$p_M(y,a|x) = \frac{p(y)p(x|y)p(a|y)}{\sum_{y'}\sum_{a'} p(y')p(x|y')p(a'|y')} \quad (4)$$

$$= \frac{p(y)p(x|y)}{\sum_{y'} p(y')p(x|y')} \cdot p(a|y) \quad (5)$$

$$= \frac{\exp[e^{w_y^T x+z}]}{\sum_k \exp[e^{w_k^T x+z}]} \cdot p(a|y) \quad (6)$$

$$= p_L(y,a|x) \quad (7)$$

Equation 4 follows from Bayes Rule and conditional independence in the model. In Equation 5 $p(a'|y)$ sums to 1. The first term of Equation 6 is the posterior $p(y|x)$ of a naïve Bayes classifier, known to have the same form as a logistic regression classifier where parameters $w$ and $z$ are constructed from $\phi$ and $\theta$.[2]

## 4 Mean-field Variational Inference (MF)

In this section we present novel mean-field (MF) variational algorithms for LOGRESP and MOMRESP. Note that Liu et al. (2012) present (in an appendix) variational inference for LOGRESP based on belief propagation (BP). They do not test their algorithm for LOGRESP; however, their comparison of MF and BP variational inference for the ITEMRESP model indicates that the two flavors of variational inference perform very similarly. Our MF algorithm for LOGRESP has not been designed with the idea of outperforming its BP analogue, but rather with the goal of ensuring that the generative and discriminative model use the same inference algorithm. We expect that we would achieve the same results if our comparison used variational BP algorithms for both MOMRESP and LOGRESP, although such an additional comparison is beyond the scope of this work.

Broadly speaking, variational approaches to posterior inference transform inference into an optimization problem by searching within some family of tractable approximate distributions $Q$ for the distribution $q \in Q$ that minimizes distributional divergence from an intractable target posterior $p^*$. In particular, under the mean-field assumption we confine our search to distributions $Q$ that are fully factorized.

### 4.1 LOGRESP Inference

We approximate LOGRESP's posterior $p^*(\gamma,\phi,y|x,a)$ using the fully factorized approximation $q(\gamma,\phi,y) = \left[\prod_j \prod_k q(\gamma_{jk})\right] \prod_k q(\phi_k) \prod_i q(y_i)$. Approximate marginal posteriors $q$ are disambiguated by their arguments.

**Algorithm.** Initialize each $q(y_i)$ to the empirical distribution observed in the annotations $a_i$. The Kullback-Leibler divergence $KL(q||p^*)$ is minimized by iteratively updating each variational distribution in the model as follows:

$$q(\gamma_{jk}) \propto \prod_{k' \in K} \gamma_{jkk'}^{b^{(\gamma)}_{jkk'} + \sum_{i \in N} a_{ijk'} q(y_i=k) - 1} = Dirichlet(\alpha^{(\gamma)}_{jk})$$

$$q(\phi_k) \propto \exp\left[\phi_k^T \Sigma^{-1} \phi_k + \sum_{i \in N} q(y_i = k)\phi_k^T x_i\right]$$

$$q(y_i) \propto \prod_{k \in K} \exp\Big[\sum_{j \in J}\sum_{k' \in K} a_{ijk'} E_{q(\gamma_{jk})}[\log \gamma_{jkk'}] + \sum_{f \in F} x_{if} E_{q(\phi_k)}[\phi_{kf}]\Big]^{\mathbb{1}(y_i=k)}$$

$$\propto \prod_{k \in K} \alpha_{ik}^{(y)\mathbb{1}(y_i=k)} = Categorical(\alpha_i^{(y)})$$

Approximate distributions are updated by calculating variational parameters $\alpha^{(\cdot)}$, disambiguated by a superscript. Because $q(\gamma_{jk})$ is a Dirichlet distribution the term $E_{q(\gamma_{jk})}[\log \gamma_{jkk'}]$ appearing in $q(y_i)$ is computed analytically as $\psi(\alpha^{(\gamma)}_{jkk'}) - \psi(\sum_{k'} \alpha^{(\gamma)}_{jkk'})$ where $\psi$ is the digamma function.

The distribution $q(\phi_k)$ is a logistic normal distribution. This means that the expectations $E_{q(\phi_k)}[\phi_{kf}]$ that appear in $q(y_i)$ cannot be computed analytically. Following Liu et al. (2012), we approximate the distribution $q(\phi_k)$ with the point estimate

[2] http://cs.cmu.edu/~tom/mlbook/NBayesLogReg.pdf gives a proof of this property in the continuous case and hints about the discrete case proof.

$\hat{\phi}_k = \text{argmax}_{\phi_k} q(\phi_k)$ which can be calculated using existing numerical optimization methods for log-linear models. Such maximization can be understood as embedding the variational algorithm inside of an outer EM loop such as might be used to tune hyperparameters in an empirical Bayesian approach (where $\phi$ are treated as hyperparameters).

### 4.2 MomResp Inference

MomResp's posterior $p^*(y, \theta, \gamma, \phi | x, a)$ is approximated with the fully factorized distribution $q(y, \theta, \gamma, \phi) = q(\theta) \left[ \prod_j \prod_k q(\gamma_{jk}) \right] \prod_k q(\phi_k) \prod_i q(y_i)$.

**Algorithm**. Initialize each $q(y_i)$ to the empirical distribution observed in the annotations $a_i$. The Kullback-Leibler divergence $KL(q||p^*)$ is minimized by iteratively updating each variational distribution in the model as follows:

$$q(\theta) \propto \prod_{k \in K} \theta_k^{b_k^{(\theta)} + \sum_{i \in N} q(y_i=k) - 1} = Dirichlet(\alpha^{(\theta)})$$

$$q(\gamma_{jk}) \propto \prod_{k' \in K} \gamma_{jkk'}^{b_{jkk'}^{(\gamma)} + \sum_{i \in N} a_{ijk'} q(y_i=k) - 1} = Dirichlet(\alpha_{jk}^{(\gamma)})$$

$$q(\phi_k) \propto \prod_{f \in F} \phi_{kf}^{b_{kf}^{(\phi)} + \sum_{i \in N} x_{if} q(y_i=k) - 1} = Dirichlet(\alpha_k^{(\phi)})$$

$$\begin{aligned} q(y_i) \propto \prod_{k \in K} \exp \Big[ & \sum_{j \in J} \sum_{k' \in K} a_{ijk'} E_{q(\gamma_{jk})}[\log \gamma_{jkk'}] + \\ & E_{q(\theta_k)}[\log \theta_k] + \sum_{f \in F} x_{if} E_{q(\phi_k)}[\log \phi_{kf}] \Big]^{\mathbb{1}(y_i=k)} \\ \propto \prod_{k \in K} & \alpha_{ik}^{(y) \mathbb{1}(y_i=k)} = Categorical(\alpha_i^{(y)}) \end{aligned}$$

Approximate distributions are updated by calculating the values of variational parameters $\alpha^{(\cdot)}$, disambiguated by a superscript. The expectations of log terms in the $q(y_i)$ update are all with respect to Dirichlet distributions and so can be computed analytically as explained previously.

### 4.3 Model priors and implementation details

Computing a lower bound on the log likelihood shows that in practice the variational algorithms presented above converge after only a dozen or so updates. We compute $\text{argmax}_{\phi_k} q(\phi_k)$ for LogResp using the L-BFGS algorithm as implemented in MALLET (McCallum, 2002). We choose uninformed priors $b_k^{(\theta)} = 1$ for MomResp and identity matrix $\Sigma = \mathbb{1}$ for LogResp. We set $b_{kf}^{(\phi)} = 0.1$ for MomResp to encourage sparsity in per-class word distributions. Liu et al. (2012) argue that a uniform prior over the entries of each confusion matrix $\gamma_j$ can lead to degenerate performance. Accordingly, we set the diagonal entries of each $b_j^{(\gamma)}$ to a higher value $b_{jkk}^{(\gamma)} = \frac{1+\delta}{K+\delta}$ and off-diagonal entries to a lower value $b_{jkk'}^{(\gamma)} = \frac{1}{K+\delta}$ with $\delta = 2$.

Both MomResp and LogResp are given full access to all instances in the dataset, annotated and unannotated. However, as explained in Section 3.1, LogResp is conditioned on the data and thus is structurally unable to make use of unannotated data. We experimented briefly with self-training for LogResp but it had little effect. With additional effort one could likely settle on a heuristic scheme that allowed LogResp to benefit from unannotated data. However, since such an extension is external to the model itself, it is beyond the scope of this work.

## 5 Experiments with Simulated Annotators

Models which learn from error-prone annotations can be challenging to evaluate in a systematic way. Simulated annotations allow us to systematically control annotator behavior and measure the performance of our models in each configuration.

### 5.1 Simulating Annotators

We simulate an annotator by corrupting ground truth labels according to that annotator's accuracy parameters. Simulated annotators are drawn from the annotator quality pools listed in Table 1. Each row is a named pool and contains five annotators A1–A5, each with a corresponding accuracy parameter (the number five is chosen arbitrarily). In the pools HIGH, MED, and LOW, annotator errors are distributed uniformly across the incorrect classes. Because there are no patterns among errors, these settings approximate situations in which annotators are ultimately in agreement about the task they are doing, although some are better at it than others. The HIGH pool represents a corpus annotation project with high quality annotators. In the MED and LOW pools annotators are progressively less reliable.

The CONFLICT annotator pool in Table 1 is special in that annotator errors are made systematically rather than uniformly. Systematic errors are

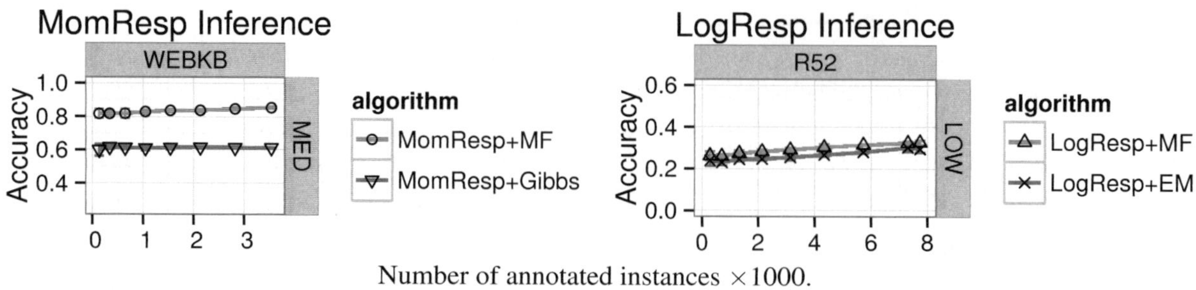


Figure 2: Mean field (MF) variational inference outperforms previous inference methods for both models. *Left*: MOMRESP with MF (MOMRESP+MF) versus with Gibbs sampling (MOMRESP+Gibbs) on the WebKB dataset using annotators from the MED pool. *Right*: LOGRESP with MF (LOGRESP+MF) versus with EM (LOGRESP+EM) on the Reuters52 dataset using annotators from the LOW pool.

produced at simulation time by constructing a per-annotator confusion matrix (similar to $\gamma_j$) whose diagonal is set to the desired accuracy setting, and whose off-diagonal row entries are sampled from a symmetric Dirichlet distribution with parameter 0.1 to encourage sparsity and then scaled so that each row properly sums to 1. These draws from a sparse Dirichlet yield consistent error patterns. The CONFLICT pool approximates an annotation project where annotators understand the annotation guidelines differently from one another. For the sake of example, annotator A5 in the CONFLICT setting will annotate documents with the true class $B$ as $B$ exactly 10% of the time but might annotate $B$ as $C$ 85% of the time. On the other hand, annotator A4 might annotate $B$ as $D$ most of the time. We choose low agreement rates for CONFLICT to highlight a case that violates majority vote's assumption that annotators are basically in agreement.

| | A1 | A2 | A3 | A4 | A5 |
|---|---|---|---|---|---|
| HIGH | 90 | 85 | 80 | 75 | 70 |
| MED | 70 | 65 | 60 | 55 | 50 |
| LOW | 50 | 40 | 30 | 20 | 10 |
| CONFLICT | 50† | 40† | 30† | 20† | 10† |

Table 1: For each simulated annotator quality pool (HIGH, MED, LOW, CONFLICT), annotators A1-A5 are assigned an accuracy. † indicates that errors are systematically in conflict as described in the text.

### 5.2 Datasets and Features

We simulate the annotator pools from Table 1 on each of six text classification datasets. The datasets 20 Newsgroups, WebKB, Cade12, Reuters8, and Reuters52 are described by Cardoso-Cachopo (2007). The LDC-labeled Enron emails dataset is described by Berry et al. (2001). Each dataset is preprocessed via Porter stemming and by removal of the stopwords from MALLET's stopword list. Features occurring fewer than 5 times in the corpus are discarded. Features are fractionally scaled so that $|x_i|_1$ is equal to the average document length since document scaling has been shown to be beneficial for multinomial document models (Nigam et al., 2006).

Each dataset is annotated according to the following process: an instance is selected at random (without replacement) and annotated by three annotators selected at random (without replacement). Because annotation simulation is a stochastic process, each simulation is repeated five times.

### 5.3 Validating Mean-field Variational Inference

Figure 2 compares mean-field variational inference (MF) with alternative inference algorithms from previous work. For variety, the left and right plots are calculated over arbitrarily chosen datasets and annotator pools, but these trends are representative of other settings. MOMRESP using MF is compared with MOMRESP using Gibbs sampling estimating $p(y|x,a)$ from several hundred samples (an improvement to the method used by Felt et al. (2014)).

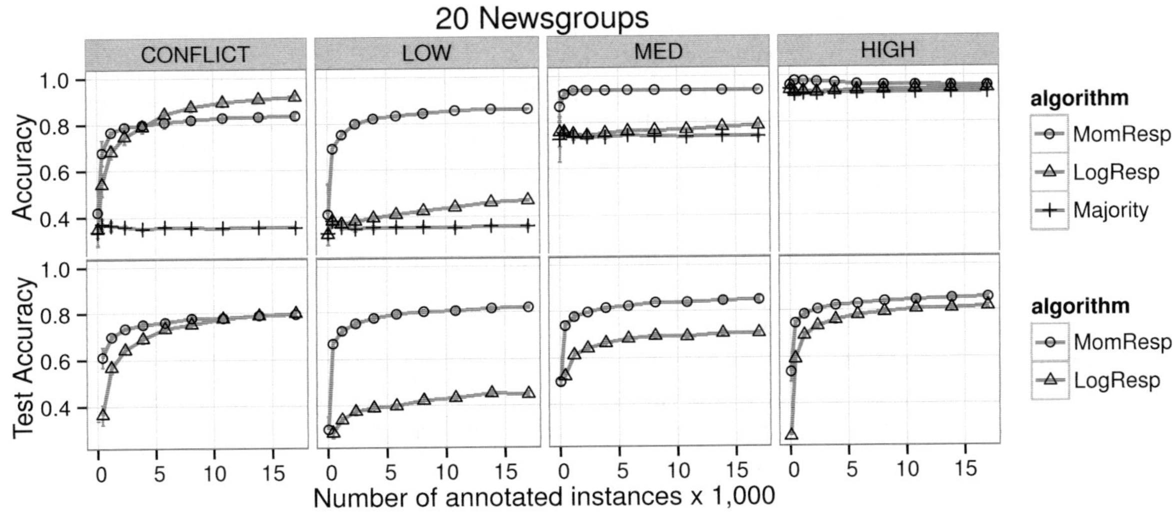


Figure 3: *Top row*: Inferred label accuracy on three-deep annotations. A majority vote baseline is shown for reference. *Bottom row*: Generalization accuracy on a test set. Majority vote is not shown since it does not generate test set predictions. Each column uses the indicated simulated annotator pool.

MOMRESP benefits significantly from MF. We suspect that this disparity could be reduced via hyperparameter optimization as indicated by Asuncion et al. (2009). However, that investigation is beyond the scope of the current work. LOGRESP using MF is compared with LOGRESP using expectation maximization (EM) as in (Raykar et al., 2010). LOGRESP with MF displays minor improvements over LOGRESP with EM. This is consistent with the modest gains that Liu et al. (2012) reported when comparing variational and EM inference for the ITEMRESP model.

### 5.4 Discriminative (LOGRESP) versus Generative (MOMRESP)

We run MOMRESP and LOGRESP with MF inference on the cross product of datasets and annotator pools. Inferred label accuracy on items that have been annotated is the primary task of crowdsourcing; we track this measure accordingly. However, the ability of these models to generalize on unannotated data is also of interest and allows better comparison with traditional non-crowdsourcing models. Figure 3 plots learning curves for each annotator pool on the 20 Newsgroups dataset; results on other datasets are summarized in Table 2. The first row of Figure 3 plots the accuracy of labels inferred from annotations. The second row of Figure 3 plots generalization accuracy using the inferred model parameters $\phi$ (and $\theta$ in the case of MOMRESP) on held-out test sets with no annotations. The generalization accuracy curves of MOMRESP and LOGRESP may be compared with those of naïve Bayes and logistic regression, respectively. Recall that in the special case where annotations are both flawless and trusted (via diagonal confusion matrices $\gamma$) then MOMRESP and LOGRESP simplify to semi-supervised naïve Bayes and logistic regression classifiers, respectively.

Notice that MOMRESP climbs more steeply than LOGRESP in all cases. This observation is in keeping with previous work in supervised learning. Ng and Jordan (2001) argue that generative and discriminative models have complementary strengths: generative models tend to have steeper learning curves and converge in terms of parameter values after only $\log n$ training examples, whereas discriminative models tend to achieve higher asymptotic levels but converge more slowly after $n$ training examples. The second row of Figure 3 shows that even after training on three-deep annotations over the entire 20 newsgroups dataset, LOGRESP's data model does not approach its asymptotic level of performance. The early steep slope of the generative model is more desirable in this setting than the eventually superior performance of the discriminative model given large numbers of annotations. Figure 4 additionally plots MOMRESPA, a variant of MOMRESP deprived of all unannotated documents, showing that the early generative advantage is not attributable entirely to semi-supervision.

The generative model is more robust to annotation noise than the discriminative model, seen by comparing the LOW, MED, and HIGH columns in Figure 3. This robustness is significant because crowdsourcing tends to yield noisy annotations, making the LOW and MED annotator pools of greatest practical interest. This assertion is borne out by an experiment with CrowdFlower, reported in Section 6.

To validate that LOGRESP does, indeed, asymptotically surpass MOMRESP we ran inference on datasets with increasing annotation depths. Crossover does not occur until 20 Newsgroups is annotated nearly 12-deep for LOW, 5-deep for MED, and 3.5-deep (on average) for HIGH. Additionally, for each combination of dataset and annotator pool except those involving CONFLICT, by the time LOGRESP surpasses MOMRESP, the majority vote baseline is extremely competitive with LOGRESP. The CONFLICT setting is the exception to this rule: CONFLICT annotators are particularly challenging for majority vote since they violate the implicit assumption that annotators are basically aligned with the truth. The CONFLICT setting is of practical interest only when annotators have dramatic deep-seated differences of opinion about what various labels should mean. For most crowdsourcing projects this issue may be avoided with sufficient up-front orientation of the annotators. For reference, in Figure 4 we show that a less extreme variant of CONFLICT behaves more similarly to LOW.

Table 2 reports the percent of the dataset that must be annotated three-deep before LOGRESP's inferred label accuracy surpasses that of MOMRESP. Crossover tends to happen later when annotation quality is low and earlier when annotator quality is high. Cases reported as *NA* were too close to call; that is, the dominating algorithm changed depending on the random run.

Unsurprisingly, MOMRESP is not well suited to all classification datasets. The 0% entries in Table 2 mean that LOGRESP dominates the learning curve for that annotator pool and dataset. These cases are likely the result of the MOMRESP model making the same strict inter-feature independence assumptions as naïve Bayes, rendering it tractable and effective for many classification tasks but ill-suited for datasets where features are highly correlated or for tasks in which class identity is not informed by document vocabulary. The CADE12 dataset, in particular, is known to be challenging. A supervised naïve Bayes classifier achieves only 57% accuracy on this dataset (Cardoso-Cachopo, 2007). We would expect MOMRESP to perform similarly poorly on sentiment classification data. Although we assert that generative models are inherently better suited to crowdsourcing than discriminative models, a sufficiently strong mismatch between model assumptions and data can negate this advantage.

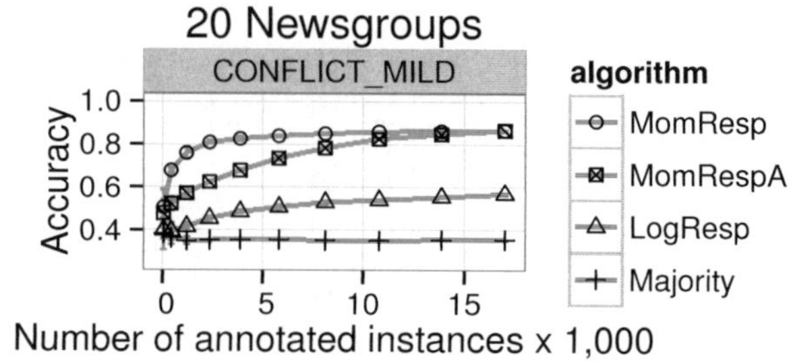


Figure 4: Inferred label accuracy for a variant of the CONFLICT annotator pool in which the off-diagonals of each annotator confusion matrix are drawn from a Dirichlet parameterized by 1 rather than 0.1. Also adds the algorithm MOMRESPA to show the effect of removing MOMRESP's access to unannotated documents.

## 6 Experiments with Human Annotators

In the previous section we used simulations to control annotator error. In this section we relax that control. To assess the effect of real-world annotation error on MOMRESP and LOGRESP, we selected 1000 instances at random from 20 Newsgroups and paid annotators on CrowdFlower to annotate them with the 20 Newsgroups categories, presented as human-readable names (e.g., “Atheism” for alt.atheism). Annotators were allowed to express uncertainty by

| | CONFLICT | LOW | MED | HIGH |
|---|---|---|---|---|
| 20 News | 21% | ✓ | ✓ | ✓ |
| WebKB | *NA* | ✓ | ✓ | 0% |
| Reuters8 | *NA* | ✓ | ✓ | ✓ |
| Reuters52 | ✓ | ✓ | ✓ | ✓ |
| CADE12 | 0% | ✓ | 0% | 0% |
| Enron | ✓ | ✓ | ✓ | 18% |

Table 2: The percentage of the dataset that must be annotated (three-deep) before the generative model MOMRESP is surpassed by LOGRESP. ✓indicates that MOMRESP dominates the entire learning curve; 0% indicates that LOGRESP dominates. *NA* indicates high variance cases that were too close to call.

selecting up to three unique categories per document. During the course of a single day we gathered 7,265 annotations, with each document having a minimum of 3 and a mean of 7.3 annotations.[3] Figure 5 shows learning curves for the CrowdFlower annotations. The trends observed previously are unchanged. MOMRESP enjoys a significant advantage when relatively few annotations are available. Presumably LOGRESP would still dominate if we were able to explore later portions of the curve or curves with greater annotation depth.

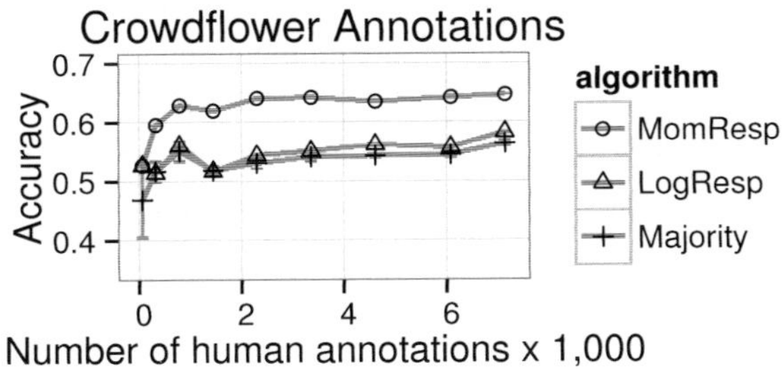


Figure 5: Inferred label accuracy on annotations gathered from CrowdFlower over a subset of 1000 instances of the 20 Newsgroups dataset. At the last plotted point there are $7{,}265/1{,}000 \approx 7.3$ annotations per instance.

[3] This dataset and the scripts that produced it are available via git at git://nlp.cs.byu.edu/plf1/crowdflower-newsgroups.git

## 7 Conclusions and Future Work

We have argued that generative models are better suited than discriminative models to the task of annotation aggregation since they tend to be more robust to annotation noise and to approach their asymptotic performance levels with fewer annotations. Also, in settings where a discriminative model would usually shine, there are often enough annotations that a simple baseline of majority vote is sufficient.

In support of this argument, we developed comparable mean-field variational inference for a generative-discriminative pair of crowdsourcing models and compared them on both crowdsourced and synthetic annotations on six text classification datasets. In practice we found that on classification tasks for which generative models of the data work reasonably well, the generative model greatly outperforms its discriminative log-linear counterpart.

The generative multinomial model we employed makes inter-feature independence assumptions ill suited to some classification tasks. Document topic models (Blei, 2012) could be used as the basis of a more sophisticated generative crowdsourcing model. One might also transform the data to make it more amenable to a simple model using documents assembled from distributed word representations (Mikolov et al., 2013). Finally, although we expect these results to generalize, we have only experimented with text classification. Similar experiments could be performed on other commonly crowdsourced tasks such as sequence labeling.

## Acknowledgments

We thank Alex Smola and the anonymous reviewers for their insightful comments. This work was supported by the collaborative NSF Grant IIS-1409739 (BYU) and IIS-1409287 (UMD).

## References

[Asuncion et al.2009] A. Asuncion, M. Welling, P. Smyth, and Y. W. Teh. 2009. On smoothing and inference for topic models. In *Proceedings of the Twenty-Fifth Conference on Uncertainty in Artificial Intelligence*, pages 27–34. AUAI Press.

[Berry et al.2001] M. W. Berry, M. Browne, and

B. Signer. 2001. Topic annotated Enron email data set. *Linguistic Data Consortium, Philadelphia*.

[Blei2012] D. Blei. 2012. Probabilistic topic models. *Communications of the ACM*, 55(4):77–84.

[Bragg et al.2013] J. Bragg, Mausam, and D. Weld. 2013. Crowdsourcing multi-label classification for taxonomy creation. In *First AAAI Conference on Human Computation and Crowdsourcing*.

[Cardoso-Cachopo2007] A. Cardoso-Cachopo. 2007. *Improving Methods for Single-label Text Categorization*. Ph.D. thesis, Universidade Tecnica de Lisboa.

[Carroll et al.2007] J. Carroll, R. Haertel, P. McClanahan, E. Ringger, and K. Seppi. 2007. Modeling the annotation process for ancient corpus creation. In *Proceedings of ECAL 2007*, pages 25–42. Charles University.

[Dawid and Skene1979] A.P. Dawid and A.M. Skene. 1979. Maximum likelihood estimation of observer error-rates using the EM algorithm. *Applied Statistics*, pages 20–28.

[Felt et al.2014] P. Felt, R. Haertel, E. Ringger, and K. Seppi. 2014. MomResp: A Bayesian model for multi-annotator document labeling. In *Proceedings of LREC*.

[Hovy et al.2013] D. Hovy, T. Berg-Kirkpatrick, A. Vaswani, and E. Hovy. 2013. Learning whom to trust with MACE. In *Proceedings of HLT-NAACL 2013*, pages 1120–1130.

[Jurgens2013] D. Jurgens. 2013. Embracing ambiguity: A comparison of annotation methodologies for crowdsourcing word sense labels. In *Proceedings of NAACL-HLT 2013*, pages 556–562.

[Lam and Stork2005] C. P. Lam and D. G. Stork. 2005. Toward optimal labeling strategy under multiple unreliable labelers. In *AAAI Spring Symposium: Knowledge Collection from Volunteer Contributors*.

[Liu et al.2012] Q. Liu, J. Peng, and A. Ihler. 2012. Variational inference for crowdsourcing. In *NIPS*, pages 692–700.

[McCallum2002] Andrew Kachites McCallum. 2002. Mallet: A machine learning for language toolkit. http://mallet.cs.umass.edu.

[Mikolov et al.2013] T. Mikolov, I. Sutskever, K. Chen, G. Corrado, and J. Dean. 2013. Distributed representations of words and phrases and their compositionality. In *Advances in Neural Information Processing Systems*, pages 3111–3119.

[Ng and Jordan2001] A. Ng and M. Jordan. 2001. On discriminative vs. generative classifiers: A comparison of logistic regression and naive Bayes. *NIPS*, 14:841–848.

[Nigam et al.2006] K. Nigam, A. McCallum, and T. Mitchell. 2006. Semi-supervised text classification using EM. *Semi-Supervised Learning*, pages 33–56.

[Passonneau and Carpenter2013] R. Passonneau and B. Carpenter. 2013. The benefits of a model of annotation. In *Proceedings of the 7th Linguistic Annotation Workshop and Interoperability with Discourse*, pages 187–195. Citeseer.

[Pasternack and Roth2010] J. Pasternack and D. Roth. 2010. Knowing what to believe (when you already know something). In *COLING*, Beijing, China.

[Raykar et al.2010] V. Raykar, S. Yu, L. Zhao, G. Valadez, C. Florin, L. Bogoni, and L. Moy. 2010. Learning from crowds. *The Journal of Machine Learning Research*, 11:1297–1322.

[Simpson and RobertsIn Press] E. Simpson and S. Roberts. In Press. Bayesian methods for intelligent task assignment in crowdsourcing systems. In *Decision Making: Uncertainty, Imperfection, Deliberation and Scalability*. Springer.

[Smyth et al.1995] P. Smyth, U. Fayyad, M. Burl, P. Perona, and P. Baldi. 1995. Inferring ground truth from subjective labelling of Venus images. *NIPS*, pages 1085–1092.

[Snow et al.2008] R. Snow, B. O'Connor, D. Jurafsky, and A. Ng. 2008. Cheap and fast—but is it good?: Evaluating non-expert annotations for natural language tasks. In *Proceedings of EMNLP*. ACL.

[Surowiecki2005] J. Surowiecki. 2005. *The Wisdom of Crowds*. Random House LLC.

[Welinder et al.2010] P. Welinder, S. Branson, P. Perona, and S. Belongie. 2010. The multidimensional wisdom of crowds. In *NIPS*, pages 2424–2432.

[Whitehill et al.2009] J. Whitehill, P. Ruvolo, T. Wu, J. Bergsma, and J. Movellan. 2009. Whose vote should count more: Optimal integration of labels from labelers of unknown expertise. *NIPS*, 22:2035–2043.

[Yan et al.2014] Y. Yan, R. Rosales, G. Fung, R. Subramanian, and J. Dy. 2014. Learning from multiple annotators with varying expertise. *Machine Learning*, 95(3):291–327.

[Zhou et al.2012] D. Zhou, J. Platt, S. Basu, and Y. Mao. 2012. Learning from the wisdom of crowds by minimax entropy. In *NIPS*, volume 25, pages 2204–2212.

# Optimizing Multivariate Performance Measures for Learning Relation Extraction Models

**Gholamreza Haffari**
[2]Faculty of IT, Monash University
gholamreza.haffari@monash.edu

**Ajay Nagesh**[1,2,3]
[1]IITB-Monash Research Academy
ajaynagesh@cse.iitb.ac.in

**Ganesh Ramakrishnan**
[3]Dept. of CSE, IIT Bombay
ganesh@cse.iitb.ac.in

## Abstract

We describe a novel max-margin learning approach to optimize non-linear performance measures for distantly-supervised relation extraction models. Our approach can be generally used to learn latent variable models under multivariate non-linear performance measures, such as $F_\beta$-score. Our approach interleaves Concave-Convex Procedure (CCCP) for populating latent variables with dual decomposition to factorize the original hard problem into smaller independent sub-problems. The experimental results demonstrate that our learning algorithm is more effective than the ones commonly used in the literature for distant supervision of information extraction models. On several data conditions, we show that our method outperforms the baseline and results in up to 8.5% improvement in the $F_1$-score.

## 1 Introduction

Rich models with latent variables are popular for many problems in natural language processing. In information extraction, for example, one needs to predict the relation labels $\mathbf{y}$ that an entity-pair $\mathbf{x}$ can have based on the hidden relation mentions $\mathbf{h}$, *i.e.*, the relation labels for occurrences of the entity-pair in a given corpus. However, these models are often trained by optimizing performance measures (such as conditional log-likelihood or error rate) that are not directly related to the task-specific non-linear performance measure, *e.g.*, the $F_1$-score. However, better models may be trained by optimizing the task-specific performance measure while allowing latent variables to adapt their values accordingly.

We present a large-margin method to learn parameters of latent variable models for a wide range of non-linear multivariate performance measures such as $F_\beta$. Our method can be applied to learning graphical models that incorporate inter-dependencies among the output variables either directly, or indirectly through hidden variables.

Large-margin methods have been shown to be a compelling approach to learn rich models detailing the inter-dependencies among the output variables, via optimizing loss functions decomposable over the *training instances* (Taskar et al., 2003; Tsochantaridis et al., 2004) or non-decompasable loss functions (Ranjbar et al., 2013; Tarlow and Zemel, 2012; Rosenfeld et al., 2014; Keshet, 2014). They have also been shown to be powerful when applied to latent variable models when optimizing for decomposable loss functions (Wang and Mori, 2011; Felzenszwalb et al., 2010; Yu and Joachims, 2009).

Our large-margin method learns latent variable models via optimizing non-decomposable loss functions. It interleaves the Concave-Convex Procedure (CCCP) (Yuille and Rangarajan, 2001) for populating latent variables with dual decomposition (Komodakis et al., 2011; Rush and Collins, 2012). The latter factorizes the hard optimization problem (encountered in learning) into smaller independent sub-problems over the training instances. We then present linear programming and local search methods for effective optimization of the sub-problems encountered in the dual decomposition. Our local search algorithm leads to a speed up of 7,000 times compared to the exhaustive search used in the literature (Joachims, 2005; Ranjbar et al., 2012).

Our work is the first to make use of max-margin training in distant supervision of relation extraction models. We demonstrate the effectiveness of our proposed method compared to two strong baseline systems which optimize for the error rate and conditional likelihood, including a state-of-the-art system by Hoffmann et al. (2011). On several data conditions, we show that our method outperforms the baseline and results in up to 8.5% improvement in the $F_1$-score.



*Human Language Technologies: The 2015 Annual Conference of the North American Chapter of the ACL*, pages 892–900,
Denver, Colorado, May 31 – June 5, 2015. 

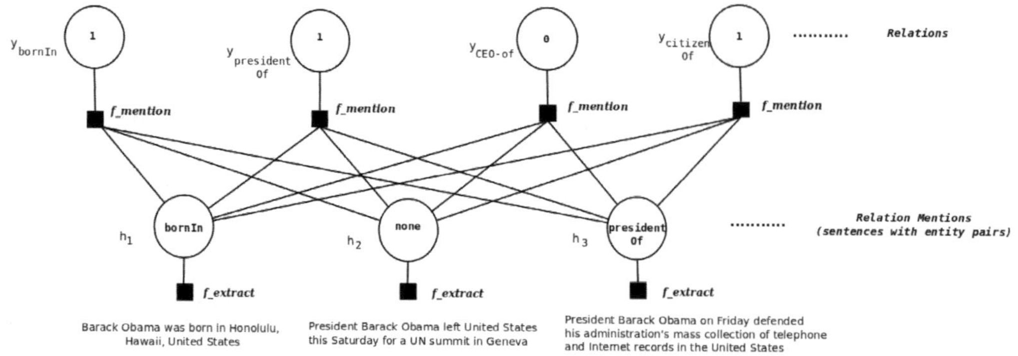


Figure 1: Graphical model instantiated for entity pair $\mathbf{x} :=$ (Barack Obama, United States)

## 2 Preliminaries

### 2.1 Distant Supervision for Relation Extraction

Our framework is motivated by distant supervision for learning relation extraction models (Mintz et al., 2009). The goal is to learn relation extraction models by aligning facts in a database to sentences in a large unlabeled corpus. Since the individual sentences are not hand labeled, the facts in the database act as "weak" or "distant" labels, hence the learning scenario is termed as distantly supervised.

Prior work casts this problem as a multi-instance multi-label learning problem (Hoffmann et al., 2011; Surdeanu et al., 2012). It is multi-instance since for a given entity-pair, only the label of the bag of sentences containing both entities (aka mentions) is given. It is multi-label since a bag of mentions can have multiple labels. The inter-dependencies between relation labels and (hidden) mention labels are modeled by a Markov Random Field (Figure 1) (Hoffmann et al., 2011). The learning algorithms used in the literature for this problem optimize the (conditional) likelihood, but the evaluation measure is commonly the $F$-score.

Formally, the training data is $\mathcal{D} := \{(\mathbf{x}_i, \mathbf{y}_i)\}_{i=1}^N$ where $\mathbf{x}_i \in \mathcal{X}$ is the entity-pair, $\mathbf{y}_i \in \mathcal{Y}$ denotes the relation labels, and $\mathbf{h}_i \in \mathcal{H}$ denotes the *hidden* mention labels. The possible relation labels for the entity pair are observed from a given knowledge-base. If there are $L$ candidate relation labels in the knowledge-base, then $\mathbf{y}_i \in \{0,1\}^L$, (e.g. $y_{i,\ell}$ is 1 if the relation $\ell$ is licensed by the knowledge-base for the entity-pair) and $\mathbf{h}_i \in \{1, .., L, nil\}^{|\mathbf{x}_i|}$ (i.e. each mention realizes one of the relation labels or *nil*).

**Notation.** In the rest of the paper, we denote the collection of all entity-pairs $\{\mathbf{x}_i\}_{i=1}^N$ by $\mathbf{X} \in \boldsymbol{\mathcal{X}} := \mathcal{X} \times .. \times \mathcal{X}$, the collection of mention relations $\{\mathbf{h}_i\}_{i=1}^N$ by $\mathbf{H} \in \boldsymbol{\mathcal{H}} := \mathcal{H} \times .. \times \mathcal{H}$, and the collection of relation labels $\{\mathbf{y}_i\}_{i=1}^N$ by $\mathbf{Y} \in \boldsymbol{\mathcal{Y}} := \mathcal{Y} \times .. \times \mathcal{Y}$.

The aim is to learn a parameter vector $\mathbf{w} \in \mathbb{R}^d$ by which the relation labels for a new entity-pair $\mathbf{x}$ can be predicted

$$f_{\mathbf{w}}(\mathbf{x}) := \arg\max_{\mathbf{y}} \max_{\mathbf{h}} \mathbf{w} \cdot \Phi(\mathbf{x}, \mathbf{h}, \mathbf{y}) \qquad (1)$$

where $\Phi \in \mathbb{R}^d$ is a feature vector defined according to the Markov Random Field, modeling the inter-dependencies between $\mathbf{x}$ and $\mathbf{y}$ through $\mathbf{h}$ (Figure 1). In training, we would like to minimize the loss function $\Delta$ by which the model will be assessed at test time. For the relation extraction task, the loss can be considered to be the negative of the $F_\beta$ score:

$$F_\beta = \frac{1}{\frac{\beta}{\text{Precision}} + \frac{1-\beta}{\text{Recall}}} \qquad (2)$$

where $\beta = 0.5$ results in optimizing against $F_1$-score. Our proposed learning method optimizes those loss functions $\Delta$ which cannot be decomposed over individual training instances. For example, $F_\beta$ depends non-linearly on Precision and Recall which in turn require the predictions for *all* the entity pairs in the training set, hence it cannot be decomposed over individual training instances.

### 2.2 Structured Prediction Learning

The goal of our learning problem is to find $\mathbf{w} \in R^d$ which minimizes the expected loss, aka *risk*, over a new sample $\mathcal{D}'$ of size $N'$:

$$R^{\Delta}_{f_{\mathbf{w}}} := \int \Delta\Big(\big(f_{\mathbf{w}}(\mathbf{x}'_1), .., f_{\mathbf{w}}(\mathbf{x}'_{N'})\big), \big(\mathbf{y}'_1, .., \mathbf{y}'_{N'}\big)\Big) dPr(\mathcal{D}') \tag{3}$$

Generally, the loss function $\Delta$ cannot be decomposed into a linear combination of a loss function $\delta$ over individual training samples. However, most discriminative large-margin learning algorithms assume for simplicity that the loss function is decomposable and the samples are i.i.d. (independent and identically distributed), which simplifies the sample risk $R^{\Delta}_{f_{\mathbf{w}}}$ as:

$$R^{\delta}_{f_{\mathbf{w}}} := \int \delta(f_{\mathbf{w}}(\mathbf{x}'), \mathbf{y}') dPr(\mathbf{x}', \mathbf{y}') \tag{4}$$

Often learning algorithms make use of the empirical risk as an approximation of the sample risk:

$$\hat{R}^{\delta}_{f_{\mathbf{w}}} := \frac{1}{N} \sum_{i=1}^{N} \delta(f_{\mathbf{w}}(\mathbf{x}_i), \mathbf{y}_i) \tag{5}$$

For non-decomposable loss functions, such as $F_\beta$, $\Delta$ cannot be expressed in terms of instance-specific loss function $\delta$ to construct the empirical risk of the kind in Eq. (5). Instead, we need to optimize the empirical risk constructed based on the sample loss:

$$\hat{R}^{\Delta}_{f_{\mathbf{w}}} := \Delta\Big(\big(f_{\mathbf{w}}(\mathbf{x}_1), .., f_{\mathbf{w}}(\mathbf{x}_N)\big), \big(\mathbf{y}_1, .., \mathbf{y}_N\big)\Big) \tag{6}$$

or equivalently

$$\hat{R}^{\Delta}_{f_{\mathbf{w}}} := \Delta(f_{\mathbf{w}}(\mathbf{X}), \mathbf{Y}) \tag{7}$$

where $f_{\mathbf{w}}(\mathbf{X}) := (f_{\mathbf{w}}(\mathbf{x}_1), .., f_{\mathbf{w}}(\mathbf{x}_N))$.

Having defined the empirical risk in Eq (7), we formulate the learning problem as a structured prediction problem. Instead of learning a mapping function $f_{\mathbf{w}} : \mathcal{X} \rightarrow \mathcal{Y}$ from an individual instance $\mathbf{x} \in \mathcal{X}$ to its label $\mathbf{y} \in \mathcal{Y}$, let us learn a mapping function $\mathbf{f} : \boldsymbol{\mathcal{X}} \rightarrow \boldsymbol{\mathcal{Y}}$ from all instances $\mathbf{X} \in \boldsymbol{\mathcal{X}}$ to their labels $\mathbf{Y} \in \boldsymbol{\mathcal{Y}}$. We then define the best labeling using a linear discriminant function:

$$\mathbf{f}(\mathbf{X}) := \arg\max_{\mathbf{Y}' \in \boldsymbol{\mathcal{Y}}} \max_{\mathbf{H} \in \boldsymbol{\mathcal{H}}} \Big\{ \mathbf{w} \cdot \Psi(\mathbf{X}, \mathbf{H}, \mathbf{Y}') \Big\} \tag{8}$$

where $\Psi(\mathbf{X}, \mathbf{H}, \mathbf{Y}') := \sum_{i=1}^{N} \Phi(\mathbf{x}_i, \mathbf{h}_i, \mathbf{y}'_i)$. Based on the margin re-scaling formulation of structured prediction problems (Tsochantaridis et al., 2004), the training objective can be written as the following unconstrained optimization problem:

$$\min_{\mathbf{w}} \frac{1}{2}||\mathbf{w}||_2^2 + C \max_{\mathbf{Y}'} \Big\{ \max_{\mathbf{H}} \mathbf{w} \cdot \Psi(\mathbf{X}, \mathbf{H}, \mathbf{Y}') - \max_{\mathbf{H}} \mathbf{w} \cdot \Psi(\mathbf{X}, \mathbf{H}, \mathbf{Y}) + \Delta(\mathbf{Y}', \mathbf{Y}) \Big\} \tag{9}$$

which is similar to the training objective for the latent SVMs (Yu and Joachims, 2009), with the difference that instance-dependent loss function $\delta$ is replaced by the sample loss function $\Delta$. Learning $\mathbf{w}$ by optimizing the above objective function is challenging, and is the subject of the next section.

## 3 Optimizing the Training Objective

In this section we present our method to learn latent SVMs with non-decomposable loss functions. Our training objective is Eq (9), which can be equivalently expressed as:

$$\min_{\mathbf{w}} \frac{1}{2}||\mathbf{w}||_2^2 + C \max_{\mathbf{y}'_1, \dots, \mathbf{y}'_N} \Big\{ \Delta\Big((\mathbf{y}_1, .., \mathbf{y}_N), (\mathbf{y}'_1, .., \mathbf{y}'_N)\Big) + \sum_{i=1}^{N} \max_{\mathbf{h}} \mathbf{w} \cdot \Phi(\mathbf{x}_i, \mathbf{h}, \mathbf{y}'_i) - \sum_{i=1}^{N} \max_{\mathbf{h}} \mathbf{w} \cdot \Phi(\mathbf{x}_i, \mathbf{h}, \mathbf{y}_i) \Big\} \tag{10}$$

The training objective is non-convex, since it is the difference of two convex functions. In this section we make use of the CCCP to populate the hidden variables (Yu and Joachims, 2009; Yuille and Rangarajan, 2001), and interleave it with dual decomposition (DD) to solve the resulting intermediate loss-augmented inference problems (Ranjbar et al., 2012; Rush and Collins, 2012; Komodakis et al., 2011).

### 3.1 Concave-Convex Procedure (CCCP)

The CCCP (Yuille and Rangarajan, 2001) gives a general iterative method to optimize those non-convex objective functions which can be written as the difference of two convex functions $g_1(\mathbf{w}) - g_2(\mathbf{w})$. The idea is to iteratively lowerbound $g_2$ with a linear function $g_2(\mathbf{w}^{(t)}) + \mathbf{v} \cdot (\mathbf{w} - \mathbf{w}^{(t)})$, and take the following step to update $\mathbf{w}$:

$$\mathbf{w}^{(t+1)} := \arg\min_{\mathbf{w}} \big\{ g_1(\mathbf{w}) - \mathbf{w} \cdot \mathbf{v}^{(t)} \big\} \tag{11}$$

In our case, the training objective Eq (10) is the difference of two convex functions, where the second function $g_2$ is $C \sum_{i=1}^{N} \max_{\mathbf{h}} \big\{ \mathbf{w} \cdot \Phi(\mathbf{x}_i, \mathbf{h}, \mathbf{y}_i) \big\}$. The

**Algorithm 1** The Training Algorithm (Optimizing Eq 10)

**procedure** OPT-LATENTSVM($\mathbf{X}, \mathbf{Y}$)
  Initialize $\mathbf{w}^{(0)}$ and set $t = 0$
  **repeat**
    **for** $i := 1$ to $N$ **do**
      $\mathbf{h}_i^* := \arg\max_{\mathbf{h}} \mathbf{w}^{(t)} \cdot \Phi(\mathbf{x}_i, \mathbf{h}, \mathbf{y}_i)$
    // Optimizing Eq 12
    $\mathbf{w}^{(t+1)} :=$ optSVM($\mathbf{X}, \mathbf{H}^*, \mathbf{Y}$)
    $t := t + 1$
  **until** some stopping condition is met
  **return** $\mathbf{w}^{(t)}$

lowerbound of $g_2(\mathbf{w})$ involves populating the hidden variables by:

$$\mathbf{h}_i^* := \arg\max_{\mathbf{h}} \{\mathbf{w}^{(t)} \cdot \Phi(\mathbf{x}_i, \mathbf{h}, \mathbf{y}_i)\}.$$

Therefore, in each iteration of our CCCP-based algorithm we need to optimize Eq (12), which is reminiscent of the standard structural SVM without latent variables:

$$\min_{\mathbf{w}} \frac{1}{2}||\mathbf{w}||_2^2 + C \max_{\mathbf{y'}_1,..,\mathbf{y'}_N} \Big\{\Delta\Big((\mathbf{y}_1,..,\mathbf{y}_N),(\mathbf{y'}_1,..,\mathbf{y'}_N)\Big) + \sum_{i=1}^{N} \max_{\mathbf{h}} \mathbf{w} \cdot \Phi(\mathbf{x}_i, \mathbf{h}, \mathbf{y}'_i) - \sum_{i=1}^{N} \mathbf{w} \cdot \Phi(\mathbf{x}_i, \mathbf{h}_i^*, \mathbf{y}_i)\Big\} \quad (12)$$

The above objective function can be optimized using the standard cutting-plane algorithms for structural SVM (Tsochantaridis et al., 2004; Joachims, 2005). The cutting-plane algorithm in turn needs to solve the *loss-augmented inference*, which is the subject of the next sub-section. The CCCP-based training algorithm is summarized in Algorithm 1.

### 3.2 Loss-Augmented Inference

To be able to optimize the training objective Eq (12) encountered in each iteration of Algorithm 1, we need to solve (the so-called) loss-augmented inference:

$$\max_{\mathbf{y}'_1,..,\mathbf{y}'_N} \Delta\Big((\mathbf{y}_1,..,\mathbf{y}_N),(\mathbf{y}'_1,..,\mathbf{y}'_N)\Big) + \sum_{i=1}^{N} \max_{\mathbf{h}} \mathbf{w} \cdot \Phi(\mathbf{x}_i, \mathbf{h}, \mathbf{y}'_i) \quad (13)$$

We make use of the dual decomposition (DD) technique to decouple the two terms of the above objective function, and efficiently find an approximate solution. DD is shown to be an effective technique for loss-augmented inference in structured prediction models *without* hidden variables (Ranjbar et al., 2012).

To apply DD to the loss-augmented inference (13), let us rewrite it as a constrained optimization problem:

$$\max_{\mathbf{y}'_1,...,\mathbf{y}'_N,\mathbf{y}''_1,...,\mathbf{y}''_N} \Delta\Big((\mathbf{y}_1,\dots,\mathbf{y}_N),(\mathbf{y}'_1,\dots,\mathbf{y}'_N)\Big) + \sum_{i=1}^{N} \max_{\mathbf{h}} \mathbf{w} \cdot \Phi(\mathbf{x}_i, \mathbf{h}, \mathbf{y}_i'')$$

subject to

$$\forall i \in \{1,\dots,N\}, \forall \ell \in \{1,\dots,L\}, \quad y'_{i,\ell} = y''_{i,\ell}$$

Introduction of the new variables $(\mathbf{y}''_1,..,\mathbf{y}''_N)$ decouples the two terms in the objective function, and as we will see, leads to an effective optimization algorithm. After forming the Lagrangian, the dual objective function is derived as:

$$L(\mathbf{\Lambda}) := \max_{\mathbf{Y}'} \Delta(\mathbf{Y}, \mathbf{Y}') + \sum_i \sum_\ell \lambda_i(\ell) y'_{i,\ell} + \max_{\mathbf{Y}''} \sum_{i=1}^{N} \max_{\mathbf{h}} \mathbf{w} \cdot \Phi(\mathbf{x}_i, \mathbf{h}, \mathbf{y}_i'') - \sum_i \sum_\ell \lambda_i(\ell) y''_{i,\ell}$$

where $\mathbf{\Lambda} := (\boldsymbol{\lambda}_1,..,\boldsymbol{\lambda}_N)$, and $\boldsymbol{\lambda}_i$ is a vector of Lagrange multipliers for $L$ binary variables each of which represent a relation label. The two optimization problems involved in the dual $L(\mathbf{\Lambda})$ are independent and can be solved separately. The dual is an upperbound on the loss-augmented objective function for any value of $\mathbf{\Lambda}$; therefore, we can find the tightest upperbound as an approximate solution:

$$\min_{\mathbf{\Lambda}} L(\mathbf{\Lambda})$$

The dual is non-differentiable at those points $\mathbf{\Lambda}$ where either of the two optimisation problems has multiple optima. Therefore, it is optimized using the subgradient descent method:

$$\Lambda^{(t)} := \Lambda^{(t-1)} - \eta^{(t)}(\mathbf{Y}'_* - \mathbf{Y}''_*)$$

where $\eta^{(t)} = \frac{1}{\sqrt{t}}$ is the step size[1], and

$$\mathbf{Y}'_* := \arg\max_{\mathbf{Y}'} \Delta(\mathbf{Y}, \mathbf{Y}') + \sum_i \sum_\ell \lambda_i^{(t-1)}(\ell) y'_{i,\ell} \quad (14)$$

$$\mathbf{Y}''_* := \arg\max_{\mathbf{Y}''} \sum_{i=1}^{N} \max_{\mathbf{h}} \mathbf{w} \cdot \Phi(\mathbf{x}_i, \mathbf{h}, \mathbf{y}_i'') - \sum_i \sum_\ell \lambda_i^{(t-1)}(\ell) y''_{i,\ell} \quad (15)$$

[1] Other (non-increasing) functions of the iteration number $t$ are also plausible, as far as they satisfy the following conditions (Komodakis et al., 2011) needed to guarantee the convergence to the optimal solution in the subgradient descent method: $\eta^{(t)} \geq 0, \lim_{t\to\infty} \eta^{(t)} = 0, \sum_{t=1}^{\infty} \eta^{(t)} = \infty$

**Algorithm 2** Loss-Augmented Inference

**procedure** OPT-LOSSAUG($\mathbf{w}, \mathbf{X}, \mathbf{Y}$)
  Initialize $\mathbf{\Lambda}^{(0)}$ and set $t = 0$
  **repeat**
    $\mathbf{Y}'_* :=$ opt-LossLag($\mathbf{\Lambda}, \mathbf{Y}$) // Eq (14)
    $\mathbf{Y}''_* :=$ opt-ModelLag($\mathbf{\Lambda}, \mathbf{X}$) // Eq (15)
    **if** $\mathbf{Y}'_* = \mathbf{Y}''_*$ **then**
      **return** $\mathbf{Y}'_*$
    **for** $i := 1$ to $N$ **do**
      **for** $\ell := 1$ to $L$ **do**
        $\lambda_i^{(t+1)}(\ell) := \lambda_i^{(t)}(\ell) - \eta^{(t)}(y'_{i,\ell} - y''_{i,\ell})$
  **until** some stopping condition is met
  **return** $\mathbf{Y}'_*$

The DD algorithm to compute the loss-augmented inference is outlined in Algorithm 2. Now the challenge is how to solve the above two optimization problems, which is the subject of the following section.

### 3.3 Effective Optimization of the Dual

The two optimization problems involved in the dual are hard in general. More specifically, the optimization of the affine-augmented model score (in Eq. 15) is as difficult as the MAP inference in the underlying graphical model, which can be challenging for loopy graphs. For the graphical model underlying distant supervision of relation extraction (Fig 1), we formulate the inference as an ILP (integer linear program). Furthermore, we relax the ILP to LP to speed up the inference, in the expense of trading exact solutions with approximate solutions[2].

Likewise, the optimization of the affine-augmented multivariate loss (in Eq. 14) is difficult. This is because we have to search over the entire space of $\mathbf{Y}' \in \mathcal{Y}$, which is exponentially large $\mathcal{O}(2^{N*L})$. However, if the loss term $\Delta$ can be expressed in terms of some aggregate statistics over $\mathbf{Y}'$, such as false positives (FPs) and false negatives (FNs), the optimization can be performed efficiently. This is due to the fact that the number of FPs can range from zero to the size of negative labels, and the number of FNs can range from zero to the number of positive labels. Therefore, the loss term can take $\mathcal{O}(N^2L^2)$ different values which can

[2] We observed in our experiments that relaxing the ILP to LP does not hurt the performance, but significantly speeds up the inference.

**Algorithm 3** Finding $\mathbf{Y}'_*$ : Local Search

**procedure** OPT-LOSSLAG($\mathbf{\Lambda}, \mathbf{Y}$)
  $(idx_1^n \dots idx_{\#neg}^n) \leftarrow$ Sort $\downarrow (\lambda_i(\ell))$ // FPs
  $(idx_1^n \dots idx_{\#pos}^n) \leftarrow$ Sort $\uparrow (\lambda_i(\ell))$ // FNs
  Initialise $(fp, fn)$ on the grid
  **repeat**
    **for** $((fp', fn') \in$ `Neigbours`$(fp, fn)$ **do**
      $loss_{(fp',fn')} = \Delta(fp', fn') + \mathbf{\Lambda}_{sorted}$[3]
    $loss_{(fp'',fn'')} = \arg\max_{(fp',fn')} loss_{(fp',fn')}$
    **if** $loss_{(fp,fn)} > loss_{(fp'',fn'')}$ **then**
      break
    **else**
      $(fp, fn) = (fp'', fn'')$
  **until** $loss_{(fp,fn)} \leq loss_{(fp'',fn'')}$
**return** { $\mathbf{Y}'$ corresponding to $(fp, fn)$ }

be represented on a two-dimensional grid. Fixing FPs and FNs to a grid point, $\mathbf{\Lambda} \cdot \mathbf{Y}'$ is maximized with respect to $\mathbf{Y}'$. The grid point which has the best value for $\Delta(\mathbf{Y}, \mathbf{Y}') + \mathbf{\Lambda} \cdot \mathbf{Y}'$ will then give the optimal solution for Eq (14).

Exhaustive search in the space of all possible grid points is not efficient as soon as the grid becomes large. Therefore, we have to adapt the techniques proposed in previous work (Ranjbar et al., 2012; Joachims, 2005). We propose a simple but effective *local search* strategy for this purpose. The procedure is outlined in Algorithm 3. We start with a random grid point, and move to the best neighbour. We keep hill climbing until there is no neighbour better than the current point. We define the neighbourhood by a set of exponentially-spaced points in all directions around the current point, to improve the exploration of the search space. We present some analysis on the benefits of using this search strategy vis-a-vis the exhaustive search in the Experiments section.

## 4 Experiments

**Dataset:** We use the challenging benchmark dataset created by Riedel et al. (2010) for distant supervision of relation extraction models. It is created by aligning relations from *Freebase*[4] with the sentences in *New York Times* corpus (Sandhaus, 2008). The labels for the datapoints come from the Freebase

[3] For a given $(fp, fn)$, we set $\mathbf{y}'$ by picking the sorted unary terms that maximize the score according to $\mathbf{y}$.

[4] `www.freebase.com`

database but Freebase is incomplete (Ritter et al., 2013). So a data point is labeled *nil* when either no relation exists or the relation is absent in Freebase. To avoid this ambiguity we train and evaluate the baseline and our algorithms on a subset of this dataset which consists of only non-nil relation labeled datapoints (termed as *positive dataset*). For the sake of completeness, we do report the accuracies of the various approaches on the entire evaluation dataset.

**Systems and Baseline:** Hoffmann et al. (2011) describe a state-of-the-art approach for this task. They use a perceptron-style parameter update scheme adapted to handle latent variables; their training objective is the conditional likelihood. Out of the two implementations of this algorithm, we use the better[5] of these two[6], as our baseline (denoted by `Hoffmann`). For a fair comparison, the training dataset and the set of features defined over it are common to all the experiments.

We discuss the results of two of our approaches. One, is the LatentSVM max-margin formulation with the simple decomposable Hamming loss function which minimizes the error rate (denoted by `MM-hamming`). The other is the LatentSVM max-margin formulation with the non-decomposable loss function which minimizes the negative of $F_\beta$ score (denoted by `MM-F-loss`)[7].

**Evaluation Measure:** The performance measure is $F_\beta$ which can be expressed in terms of false positives (FP) and false negatives (FN) as:

$$F_\beta = \frac{N_p - FN}{\beta(FP - FN) + N_p}$$

where $\beta$ is the weight assigned to precision (and $1 - \beta$ to recall). $FP$, $FN$ and $N_p$ are defined as :

$$\begin{aligned} FP &= \sum_i \sum_\ell y'_{i,\ell}(1 - y_{i,l}) \\ FN &= \sum_i \sum_\ell y_{i,\ell}(1 - y'_{i,l}) \\ N_p &= \sum_i \sum_\ell y_{i,\ell} \end{aligned}$$

[5]It is not quite clear why the performance of the two implementations are different.

[6]`nlp.stanford.edu/software/mimlre.shtml`

[7]We use a combination of F1 loss and hamming loss, as using only F1-loss overfits the training dataset, as observed from the experiments.

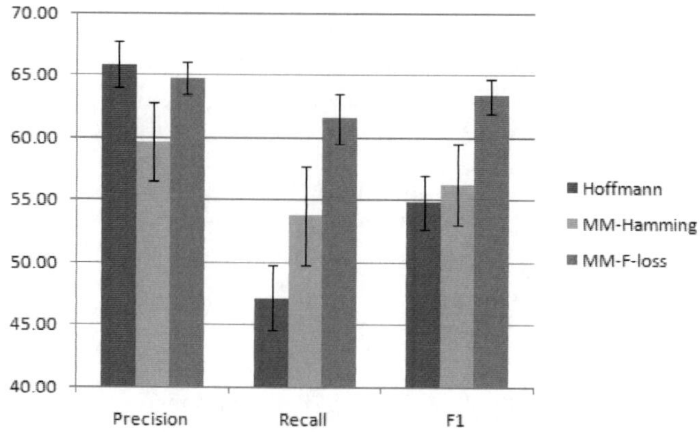


Figure 2: Experiments on 10% Riedel datasets.

| | *Precision* | *Recall* | $F_1$ |
|---|---|---|---|
| *Hoffmann* | 65.93 | 47.22 | 54.91 |
| *MM-Hamming* | 59.74 | 53.81 | 56.32 |
| *MM-F-loss* | 64.81 | 61.63 | 63.44 |

Table 1: Average results on 10% Riedel datasets.

We use $1 - F_\beta$ as the expression for the multivariate-loss.

### 4.1 Training on Sub-samples of Data

We performed a number of experiments using different randomized subsets of the Riedel dataset (10% of the positive dataset) for training the max-margin approaches. This was done in order to empirically determine a good set of parameters for training. We also compare the results of the approaches with `Hoffmann` trained on the same sub-samples.

**Comparison with the Baseline:** We report the average over 15 subsets of the dataset with a 90% confidence interval (using student-t distribution). The results of these experiments are shown in Figure 2 and Table 1. We observe that both `MM-hamming` and `MM-F-loss` have higher $F_1$-score compared to the baseline. There is a significant improvement in $F_1$-score to the tune of 8.52% for the multivariate performance measure over `Hoffmann`. There is also an improvement of $F_1$-score of 7.12% compared to `MM-Hamming`. This highlights the importance of using non-linear loss functions compared to simple loss functions like error rate during training.

However, `Hoffmann` has a marginally higher precision of about 1.13%. We noticed that this was

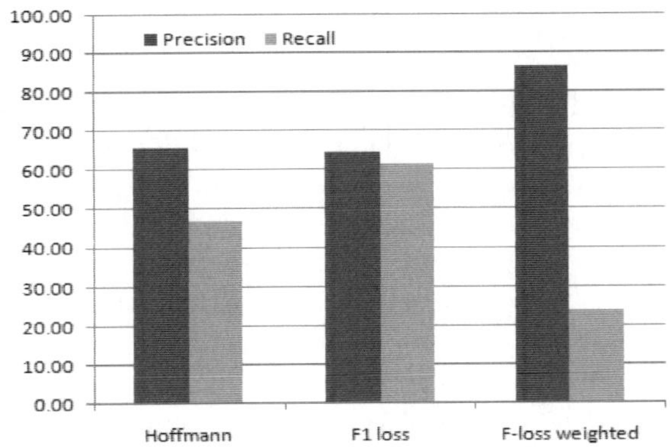


Figure 3: Weighting of Precision and Recall ($\beta = 0.833$)

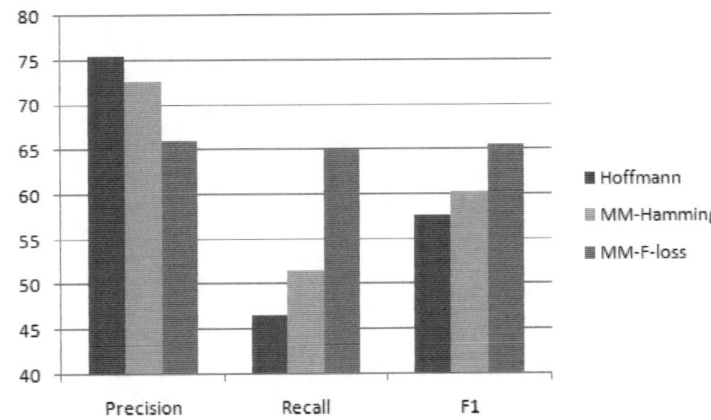


Figure 4: Overall accuracies Riedel dataset

due to over-fitting the data, as the performance on the training datasets were very high. One more interesting observation of `MM-F-loss` is that it is fairly balanced w.r.t both precision and recall which the other approaches do not exhibit.

**Tuning towards Precision/Recall:** Often we come across situations where either precision or recall is important for a given application. This is modeled by the notion of $F_\beta$ (van Rijsbergen, 1979). One of the main advantages of using a non-decomposable loss function like $F_\beta$ is the ability to vary the learning algorithm to factor such situations. For instance we can tune the objective to favor precision more than recall by "up-weighting" precision in the $F_\beta$-score.

For instance, in the previous case we observed that `MM-F-loss` has a marginally poorer precision compared to `Hoffmann`. Suppose we increase the weight of precision, $\beta = 0.833$, we observe a dramatic increase in precision from 65.83% to 86.59%. As expected, due to the precision-recall trade-off, we observe a decrease in recall. The results are shown in Figure 3.

**Local vs. Exhaustive Grid Search:** As we described in Section 3.3, we devise a simple yet efficient local search strategy to search the space of $(FP, FN)$ grid-points. This enables a speed up of three orders of magnitude in solving the dual-optimization problem. In Table 2, we compare the average time per iteration and the $F_1$-score when each of these techniques is used for training on a sub-sample dataset. We observe that there is a significant decrease in training time when we use local search (almost 7000 times faster), with a negligible decrease in $F_1$-score (0.073%).

| | *avg. time per iter.* | $F_1$ |
|---|---|---|
| *Local Search* | 0.09s | 58.322 |
| *Exhaustive Search* | 630s | 58.395 |

Table 2: Local vs. Exhaustive Search.

### 4.2 The Overall Results

Figure 4 and Table 3 present the overall results of our approaches compared to the baseline on the *positive* dataset. We observe that `MM-F-loss` has an increase in $F_1$-score to the tune of $\sim$8% compared to the baseline. This confirms our observation on the sub-sample datasets we saw earlier.

By assigning more weight to precision, we are able to improve over the precision of `Hoffmann` by $\sim$1.6% (Table 4). When precision is tuned with a higher weight during training of `MM-F-loss`, we see an improvement in precision without much dip in recall.

| | *Precision* | *Recall* | $F_1$ |
|---|---|---|---|
| *Hoffmann* | 75.436 | 46.615 | 57.623 |
| *MM-Hamming* | 76.839 | 50.462 | 60.918 |
| *MM-F-loss* | 65.991 | 65.211 | 65.598 |

Table 3: Overal results on the *positive* dataset.

| | *Precision* | *Recall* | $F_\beta$ |
|---|---|---|---|
| *Hoffmann* | 75.44 | 46.62 | 57.62 |
| *MM-F-loss-wt* | 77.04 | 53.44 | 63.11 |

Table 4: Increasing weight on Precision in $F_\beta$.

### 4.3 Discussion

So far we have discussed the performance of various approaches on the *positive* evaluation dataset. Our approach is shown to improve overall $F_\beta$-score having better recall than the baseline. By suitably tweaking the $F_\beta$ we show an improvement in precision as well.

The performance of the approaches when evaluated on the entire test dataset (consisting of both nil and non-nil datapoints) is shown in Table 5. Max-margin based approaches generally perform well when trained only on the *positive* dataset compared to `Hoffmann`. However, our $F_1$-scores are $\sim$8% less when we train on the entire dataset consisting of both nil and non-nil datapoints.

| ***Trained On*** $\rightarrow$ | *entire dataset* | *positive dataset* |
|---|---|---|
| *Hoffmann* | 23.14 | 3.269 |
| *MM-Hamming* | 13.20 | 16.26 |
| *MM-F-loss* | 13.94 | 21.93 |

Table 5: $F_1$-scores on the entire test set.

In a recent work, Xu et al. (2013) provide some statistics about the incompleteness of the Riedel dataset. Out of the sampled 1854 sentences from NYTimes corpus most of the entity pairs expressing a relation in Freebase correspond to false negatives. This is one of the reasons why we do not consider nil labeled datapoints during training and evaluation.

MIMLRE (Surdeanu et al., 2012) is another state-of-the-art system which is based on the EM algorithm. Since that system uses an additional set of features for the relation variables $\mathbf{y}$, it is not our primary baseline. On the *positive* dataset, our model `MM-F-loss` achieves a $F_1$-score of 65.598% compared to 65.341% of MIMLRE. As part of the future work, we would like to incorporate the additional features present in MIMLRE into our approach.

## 5 Conclusion

In this paper, we described a novel max-margin approach to optimize non-linear performance measures, such as $F_\beta$, in distant supervision of information extraction models. Our approach is general and can be applied to other latent variable models in NLP. Our approach involves solving the hard-optimization problem in learning by interleaving Concave-Convex Procedure with dual decomposition. Dual decomposition allowed us to solve the hard sub-problems independently. A key aspect of our approach involves a local-search algorithm which has led to a speed up of 7,000 times in our experiments. We have demonstrated the efficacy of our approach in distant supervision of relation extraction. Under several conditions, we have shown our technique outperforms very strong baselines, and results in up to 8.5% improvement in $F_1$-score.

For future work, we would like to maximize other performance measures, such as area under the curve, for information extraction models. Furthermore, we would like to explore our approach for other latent variable models in NLP, such as those in machine translation.

## Acknowledgements

Gholamreza Haffari is grateful to National ICT Australia (NICTA) for their generous funding, as part of the Machine Learning Collaborative Research Projects. Ajay Nagesh acknowledges Xerox Research Centre India (XRCI) for their travel support in the form of International Student Travel grant.

## References

Pedro F. Felzenszwalb, Ross B. Girshick, David A. McAllester, and Deva Ramanan. 2010. Object detection with discriminatively trained part-based models. *IEEE Trans. Pattern Anal. Mach. Intell.*, 32(9):1627–1645.

Raphael Hoffmann, Congle Zhang, Xiao Ling, Luke Zettlemoyer, and Daniel S. Weld. 2011. Knowledge-based weak supervision for information extraction of overlapping relations. In *Proceedings of the 49th Annual Meeting of the Association for Computational Linguistics: Human Language Technologies - Volume 1*, HLT '11, pages 541–550, Stroudsburg, PA, USA. Association for Computational Linguistics.

T. Joachims. 2005. A support vector method for multivariate performance measures. In *International Conference on Machine Learning (ICML)*, pages 377–384.

Joseph Keshet. 2014. Optimizing the measure of performance in structured prediction. In Jeremy Jancsary Sebastian Nowozin, Peter V. Gehler and Christoph H. Lampert, editors, *Advanced Structured Prediction*. The MIT Press.

Nikos Komodakis, Nikos Paragios, and Georgios Tziritas. 2011. Mrf energy minimization and beyond via dual decomposition. *IEEE Transactions on Pattern Analysis and Machine Intelligence*, 33(3):531–552.

Mike Mintz, Steven Bills, Rion Snow, and Dan Jurafsky. 2009. Distant supervision for relation extraction without labeled data. In *Proceedings of the Joint Conference of the 47th Annual Meeting of the ACL and the 4th International Joint Conference on Natural Language Processing of the AFNLP: Volume 2 - Volume 2*, ACL '09, pages 1003–1011, Stroudsburg, PA, USA. Association for Computational Linguistics.

Mani Ranjbar, Arash Vahdat, and Greg Mori. 2012. Complex loss optimization via dual decomposition. In *2012 IEEE Conference on Computer Vision and Pattern Recognition, Providence, RI, USA, June 16-21, 2012*, pages 2304–2311.

Mani Ranjbar, Tian Lan, Yang Wang, Stephen N. Robinovitch, Ze-Nian Li, and Greg Mori. 2013. Optimizing nondecomposable loss functions in structured prediction. *IEEE Trans. Pattern Anal. Mach. Intell.*, 35(4):911–924.

Sebastian Riedel, Limin Yao, and Andrew McCallum. 2010. Modeling relations and their mentions without labeled text. In *Proceedings of the 2010 European conference on Machine learning and knowledge discovery in databases: Part III*, ECML PKDD'10, pages 148–163, Berlin, Heidelberg. Springer-Verlag.

Alan Ritter, Luke Zettlemoyer, Mausam, and Oren Etzioni. 2013. Modeling missing data in distant supervision for information extraction. *TACL*, 1:367–378.

Nir Rosenfeld, Ofer Meshi, Amir Globerson, and Daniel Tarlow. 2014. Learning structured models with the auc loss and its generalizations. In *Proceedings of the 17th International Conference on Artificial Intelligence and Statistics (AISTATS)*.

Alexander M. Rush and Michael Collins. 2012. A tutorial on dual decomposition and lagrangian relaxation for inference in natural language processing. *J. Artif. Intell. Res. (JAIR)*, 45:305–362.

E. Sandhaus. 2008. The new york times annotated corpus.

Mihai Surdeanu, Julie Tibshirani, Ramesh Nallapati, and Christopher D. Manning. 2012. Multi-instance multi-label learning for relation extraction. In *Proceedings of the 2012 Joint Conference on Empirical Methods in Natural Language Processing and Computational Natural Language Learning*, EMNLP-CoNLL '12, pages 455–465, Stroudsburg, PA, USA. Association for Computational Linguistics.

Daniel Tarlow and Richard S Zemel. 2012. Structured output learning with high order loss functions. In *Proceedings of the 15th Conference on Artificial Intelligence and Statistics*.

Benjamin Taskar, Carlos Guestrin, and Daphne Koller. 2003. Max-margin markov networks. In *NIPS*.

I. Tsochantaridis, T. Hofmann, T. Joachims, and Y. Altun. 2004. Support vector machine learning for interdependent and structured output spaces. In *International Conference on Machine Learning (ICML)*, pages 104–112.

C. J. van Rijsbergen. 1979. *Information retrieval*. Butterworths, London, 2 edition.

Yang Wang and Greg Mori. 2011. Hidden part models for human action recognition: Probabilistic versus max margin. *IEEE Trans. Pattern Anal. Mach. Intell.*, 33(7):1310–1323.

Wei Xu, Raphael Hoffmann, Le Zhao, and Ralph Grishman. 2013. Filling knowledge base gaps for distant supervision of relation extraction. In *Proceedings of the 51st Annual Meeting of the Association for Computational Linguistics (Volume 2: Short Papers)*, pages 665–670, Sofia, Bulgaria, August. Association for Computational Linguistics.

Chun-Nam John Yu and Thorsten Joachims. 2009. Learning structural svms with latent variables. In *Proceedings of the 26th Annual International Conference on Machine Learning, ICML 2009, Montreal, Quebec, Canada, June 14-18, 2009*, page 147.

Alan L. Yuille and Anand Rangarajan. 2001. The concave-convex procedure (cccp). In *NIPS*, pages 1033–1040.

# Convolutional Neural Network for Paraphrase Identification

**Wenpeng Yin** and **Hinrich Schütze**
Center for Information and Language Processing
University of Munich, Germany
wenpeng@cis.uni-muenchen.de

## Abstract

We present a new deep learning architecture Bi-CNN-MI for paraphrase identification (PI). Based on the insight that PI requires comparing two sentences *on multiple levels of granularity*, we learn multigranular sentence representations using convolutional neural network (CNN) and model interaction features at each level. These features are then the input to a logistic classifier for PI. All parameters of the model (for embeddings, convolution and classification) are directly optimized for PI. To address the lack of training data, we pretrain the network in a novel way using a language modeling task. Results on the MSRP corpus surpass that of previous NN competitors.

## 1 Introduction

In this paper, we address the problem of paraphrase identification. It is usually formalized as a binary classification task: for two sentences $(S_1, S_2)$, determine whether they roughly have the same meaning.

Inspired by recent successes of deep neural networks (NNs) in fields like computer vision (Neverova et al., 2014), speech recognition (Deng et al., 2013) and natural language processing (Collobert and Weston, 2008), we adopt a deep learning approach to paraphrase identification in this paper.

The key observation that motivates our NN architecture is that the identification of a paraphrase relationship between $S_1$ and $S_2$ requires an analysis *at multiple levels of granularity*.

(A1) "Detroit manufacturers have raised vehicle prices by ten percent." – (A2) "GM, Ford and Chrysler have raised car prices by five percent."

Example A1/A2 shows that paraphrase identification requires comparison *at the word level*. A1 cannot be a paraphrase of A2 because the numbers "ten" and "five" are different.

(B1) "Mary gave birth to a son in 2000." – (B2) "He is 14 years old and his mother is Mary."

PI for B1/B2 can only succeed *at the sentence level* since B1/B2 express the same meaning using very different means.

Most work on paraphrase identification has focused on only one level of granularity: either on low-level features (e.g., Madnani et al. (2012)) or on the sentence level (e.g., ARC-I, Hu et al. (2014)).

An exception is the RAE model (Socher et al., 2011). It computes representations on all levels of a parse tree: each node – including nodes corresponding to words, phrases and the entire sentence – is represented as a vector. RAE then computes a $n_1 \times n_2$ comparison matrix of the two trees derived from $S_1$ and $S_2$ respectively, where $n_1, n_2$ are the number of nodes and each comparison is the Euclidean distance between two vectors. This is then the basis for paraphrase classification.

RAE (Socher et al., 2011) is one of three prior NN architectures that we draw on to design our system. It embodies the key insight that paraphrase identification involves analysis of information at multiple levels of granularity. However, relying on parsing has limitations for noisy text and for other applications in which highly accurate parsers are not available. We extend the basic idea of RAE by exploring stacked convolution layers which on one hand use sliding windows to split sentences into flexible phrases, furthermore, higher layers are able to ex-



*Human Language Technologies: The 2015 Annual Conference of the North American Chapter of the ACL*, pages 901–911,
Denver, Colorado, May 31 – June 5, 2015. ©2015 Association for Computational Linguistics

tract more abstract features of longer-range phrases by combining phrases in lower layers.

A representative way of doing this in deep learning is the work by Kalchbrenner et al. (2014), the second prior NN architecture that we draw on. They use convolution to learn representations at multiple levels (Collobert and Weston, 2008). The motivation for convolution is that natural language consists of long sequences in which many short subsequences contribute in a stable way to the structure and meaning of the long sequence *regardless of the position of the subsequence within the long sequence*. Thus, it is advantageous to learn convolutional filters that detect a particular feature regardless of position. Kalchbrenner et al. (2014)'s architecture extends this idea in two important ways. First, k-max pooling extracts the $k$ top values from a sequence of convolutional filter applications and guarantees a fixed length output. Second, they stack several levels of convolutional filters, thus achieving multigranularity. We incorporate this architecture as the part that analyzes an individual sentence.

The third prior NN architecture we draw on is ARC proposed by Hu et al. (2014) who also attempt to exploit convolution for paraphrase identification. Their key insight is that *we want to be able to directly optimize the entire system for the task we are addressing,* i.e., for paraphrase identification. Hu et al. (2014) do this by adopting a Siamese architecture: their NN consists of two shared-weight sentence analysis NNs that feed into a binary classifier that is directly trained on labeled sentence pairs. As we will show below, this is superior to separating the two steps: first learning sentence representations, then training binary classification for fixed, learned sentence representations as Bromley et al. (1993), Socher et al. (2011) and many others do.

We can now give an overview of our NN architecture (Figure 1). We call it Bi-CNN-MI: "Bi-CNN" stands for double CNNs used in Siamese framework, "MI" for *multigranular interaction* features. Bi-CNN-MI has three parts: (i) the sentence analysis network CNN-SM, (ii) the sentence interaction model CNN-IM and (iii) a logistic regression on top of the network that performs paraphrase identification. We now describe these three parts in detail.

(i) Following Kalchbrenner et al. (2014), we design CNN-SM, a convolutional sentence analysis NN that computes representations at four different levels: word, short ngram, long ngram and sentence. This multigranularity is important because paraphrase identification benefits from analyzing sentences at multiple levels.

(ii) Following Socher et al. (2011), CNN-IM, the interaction model, computes interaction features as $s_1 \times s_2$ matrices, where $s_i$ is the number of items of a certain granularity in $S_i$. In contrast to Socher et al. (2011), CNN-IM computes these features at fixed levels and only for comparable units; e.g., we do not compare single words with entire sentences.

(iii) Following Hu et al. (2014), we integrate two copies of CNN-SM into a Siamese architecture that allows to optimize all parameters of the NN for paraphrase identification. In our case, these parameters include parameters for word embedding, for convolution filters, and for the classification of paraphrase candidate pairs. In contrast to Hu et al. (2014), the inputs to the final paraphrase candidate pair classification layer are *interaction feature matrices at multiple levels* – as opposed to *single-level features* that do not directly *compare an element of $S_1$ with a potentially corresponding element of $S_2$*.

There is one other problem we have to address to get good performance. Training sets for paraphrase identification are small in comparison with the high complexity of the task. Training a complex network like Bi-CNN-MI with a large number of parameters on a small training set is not promising due to sparseness and likely overfitting.

In order to make full use of the training data, we propose a new unsupervised training scheme CNN-LM (CNN Language Model) to pretrain the largest part of the model, the sentence analysis network CNN-SM. The key innovation is that we use a language modeling task in a setup similar to autoencoding for pretraining (see below for details). This means that embedding and convolutional parameters can be pretrained on very large corpora since no human labels are required for pretraining.

We will show below that this pretraining is critical for getting good performance in the paraphrase task. However, the general design principle of this type of unsupervised pretraining should be widely applicable given that next-word prediction training is possible in many NLP applications. Thus, this new way of unsupervised pretraining could be an important contribution of the paper independent of paraphrase identification.

Section 2 discusses related work. Sections 3 and 4 introduce the sentence model CNN-SM and the sentence interaction model CNN-IM. Section 5 describes the training regime. The experiments are presented in Section 6. Section 7 concludes.

## 2 Related work

Bi-CNN-MI is closely related to NN models for sentence representations and for text matching.

A pioneering work using CNN to model sentences is (Collobert and Weston, 2008). They conducted convolutions on sliding windows of a sentence and finally use max pooling to form a sentence representation. Kalchbrenner et al. (2014) introduce k-max pooling and stacking of several CNNs as discussed in Section 1.

Lu and Li (2013) developed a deep NN to match short texts, where interactions between components within the two objects were considered. These interactions were obtained via LDA (Blei et al., 2003). A two-dimensional interaction space is formed, then those local decisions will be sent to the corresponding neurons in upper layers to get rounds of fusion, finally logistic regression in the output layer produces the final matching score. Drawbacks of this approach are that LDA parameters are not optimized for the paraphrase task and that the interactions are formed on the level of single words only.

Gao et al. (2014) model *interestingness* between two documents with deep NNs. They map source-target document pairs to feature vectors in a latent space in such a way that the distance between the source document and its corresponding interesting target in that space is minimized. Interestingness is more like topic relevance, based mainly on the aggregate meaning of lots of keywords. Additionally, their model is a document-level model and is not multigranular.

Madnani et al. (2012) treated paraphrase relationship as a kind of mutual translation, hence combined eight kinds of machine translation metrics including BLEU (Papineni et al., 2002), NIST (Doddington, 2002), TER (Snover et al., 2006), TERp (Snover et al., 2009), METEOR (Denkowski and Lavie, 2010), SEPIA (Habash and Elkholy, 2008), BADGER (Parker, 2008) and MAXSIM (Chan and Ng, 2008). These features are not multigranular; rather they are low-level only; high-level features – e.g., a representation of the entire sentence – are not considered.

Bach et al. (2014) claimed that elementary discourse units obtained by segmenting sentences play an important role in paraphrasing. Their conclusion also endorses Socher et al. (2011)'s and our work, for both take similarities between component phrases into account.

We discussed Socher et al. (2011)'s RAE and Hu et al. (2014)'s ARC-I in Section 1. In addition to similarity matrices there are two other important aspects of (Socher et al., 2011). First, the similarity matrices are converted to a fixed size feature vector by *dynamic pooling*. We adopt this approach in Bi-CNN-MI; see Section 4.2 for details.

Second, (Socher et al., 2011) is partially based on parsing as is some other work on paraphrase identification (e.g., Wan et al. (2006), Ji and Eisenstein (2013)). Parsing is a potentially powerful tool for identifying the important meaning units of a sentence, which can then be the basis for determining meaning equivalence. However, reliance on parsing makes these approaches less flexible. For example, there are no high-quality parsers available for some domains and some languages. Our approach is in principle applicable for any domain and language. It is also unclear how we would identify comparable units in the parse trees of $S_1$ and $S_2$ if the parse trees have different height and the sentences different lengths. A key property of Bi-CNN-MI is that it is designed to produce units at fixed levels and only units at the same level are compared with each other.

## 3 Convolution sentence model CNN-SM

Our network Bi-CNN-MI for paraphrase detection (Figure 1) consists of four parts. On the left and on the right there are two multilayer NNs with seven layers, from "initialized word embeddings: sentence 1/2" to "k-max pooling". The weights of these two NNs are shared. This part of Bi-CNN-MI is based on (Kalchbrenner et al., 2014) and we refer to it as convolutional sentence model CNN-SM.

Between the two CNN-SMs there is the interaction model CNN-IM, consisting of four feature ma-

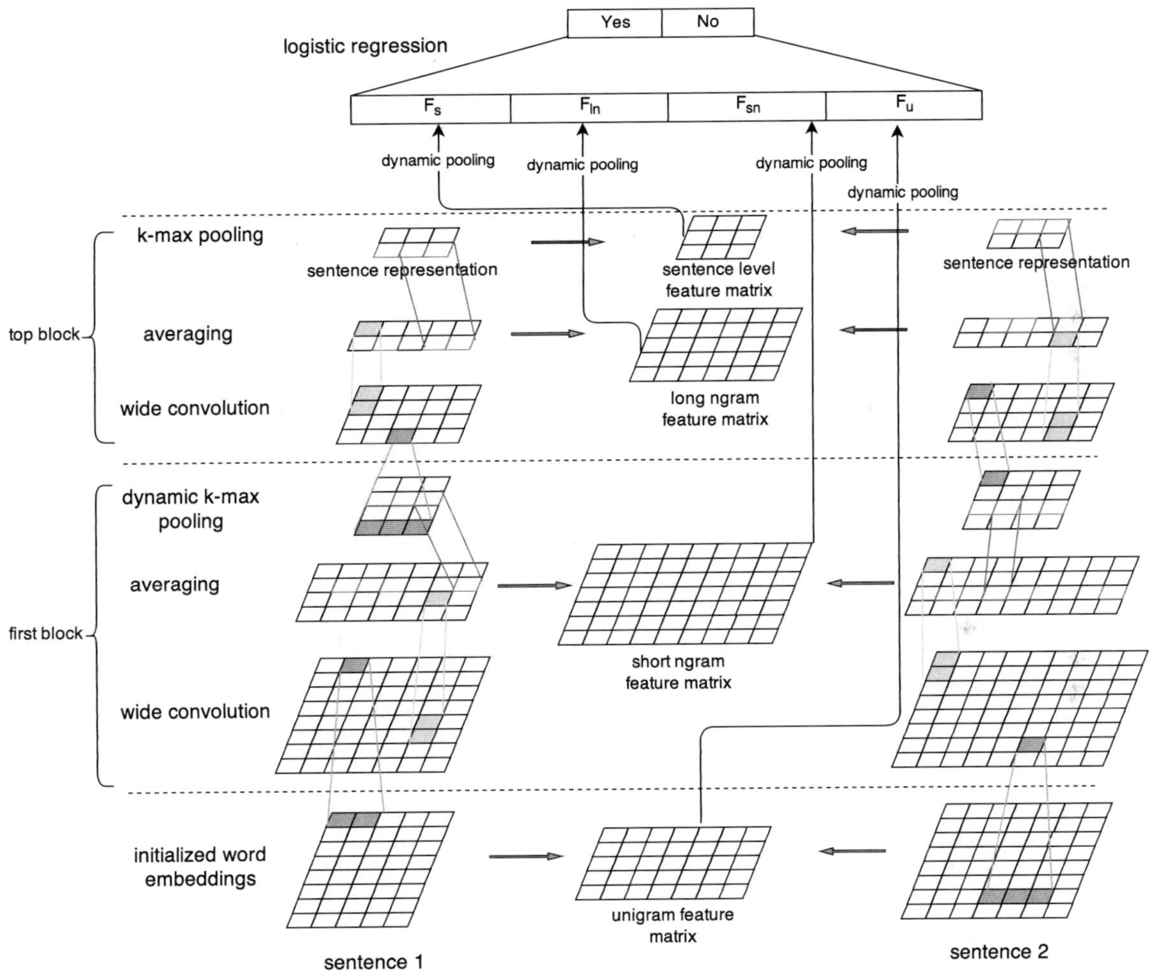


Figure 1: The paraphrase identification architecture Bi-CNN-MI

trices (unigram, short ngram, long ngram, sentence). CNN-IM feeds into a logistic classifier that performs paraphrase detection. See Sections 4 and 5 for these two parts of Bi-CNN-MI.

### 3.1 Wide convolution

We use Kalchbrenner et al. (2014)'s **wide one-dimensional convolution**. Denoting the number of tokens of $S_i$ as $|S_i|$, we convolve weight matrix $\mathbf{M} \in \mathbb{R}^{d \times m}$ over sentence representation matrix $\mathbf{S} \in \mathbb{R}^{d \times |S_i|}$ and generate a matrix $\mathbf{C} \in \mathbb{R}^{d \times (|S_i|+m-1)}$ each column of which is the representation of an $m$-gram. $d$ is the dimension of word (and also ngram) embeddings. $m$ is filter width.

Our motivation for using convolution is that after training, a convolutional filter corresponds to a feature detector that learns to recognize a class of $m$-grams that is useful for paraphrase detection.

### 3.2 Averaging

After convolution, to build simple relations across rows, each odd row and the row behind immediately are *averaged*, generating matrix $\mathbf{A} \in \mathbb{R}^{\frac{d}{2} \times (|S_i|+m-1)}$. Namely:

$$\mathbf{A} = (\mathbf{C}_{\text{odd}} + \mathbf{C}_{\text{even}})/2 \tag{1}$$

where $\mathbf{C}_{\text{odd}}$, $\mathbf{C}_{\text{even}}$ denote the odd and even rows of $\mathbf{C}$, respectively. Finally, this convolution layer will output matrix $\mathbf{B}$ whose $j$th column is defined thus:

$$\mathbf{B}_{:,j} = \tanh(\mathbf{A}_{:,j} + \mathbf{b}^T) \quad 0 \leq j < (|S_i| + m - 1) \tag{2}$$

$\mathbf{b}$ is a bias vector with dimension $d/2$, same for each column.

### 3.3 Dynamic k-max pooling

We use Kalchbrenner et al. (2014)'s **dynamic k-max pooling** to extract features for variable-length sentences. It extracts $k_{\text{dy}}$ top values from each dimension after the first layer of averaging and $k_{\text{top}} = 4$ top values after the top layer of averaging. We set

$$k_{\text{dy}} = \max(k_{\text{top}}, |S_i|/2 + 1) \tag{3}$$

Thus, $k_{\text{dy}}$ depends on the length of $S_i$.

The sequence of layers in (Kalchbrenner et al., 2014) is convolution, folding, k-max pooling, $\tanh$. We experimented with this sequence and found that after k-max pooling many $\tanh$ units had an input close to 1, in the nondynamic range of the function (since the input is the addition of several values). This makes learning difficult. We therefore changed the sequence to convolution, averaging, $\tanh$, k-max pooling. This makes it less likely that $\tanh$ units will be saturated.

We have described convolution, averaging and k-max pooling. We can stack several blocks of these three layers to form deep architectures, as the two blocks (marked "first block" and "top block") in Figure 1.

## 4 Convolution interaction model CNN-IM

After the introduction in the previous section of the CNN-SM part of our architecture for processing an *individual sentence*, we now turn to the CNN-IM interaction model that computes the four feature matrices in Figure 1 to assess the *interactions between the two sentences.*

### 4.1 Feature matrices

One key innovation of our approach is multigranularity: we compute similarity between the two paraphrase candidates on multiple levels. Specifically, we compute similarity at four levels in this paper: unigram, short ngram, long ngram and sentence. We use notation $l \in \{\text{u}, \text{sn}, \text{ln}, \text{s}\}$ to refer to the four levels, and use $\mathbf{S}^{i,l}$ to denote the matrix representing sentence $S_i$ at level $l$. For level $l$, we compute feature matrices $\hat{\mathbf{F}}_l$ as follows:

$$\hat{\mathbf{F}}_l^{ij} = \exp(\frac{-||\mathbf{S}_{:,i}^{1,l} - \mathbf{S}_{:,j}^{2,l}||^2}{2\beta}) \tag{4}$$

where $||\mathbf{S}_{:,i}^{1,l} - \mathbf{S}_{:,j}^{2,l}||^2$ is the Euclidean distance between the representations of the $i$th item of $S_1$ and the $j$th item of $S_2$ on level $l$. We set $\beta = 2$ (cf. Wu et al. (2013)).

We do not use cosine because the magnitude of the activations of hidden units is important, not just the overall direction; e.g., if $\mathbf{S}_{:,i}^{1,l}$ and $\mathbf{S}_{:,j}^{2,l}$ point in the same direction, but activations are much larger in $\mathbf{S}_{:,j}^{2,l}$, then the two vectors are very dissimilar.

The lowest level feature matrix ($l = \text{u}$) is the unigram similarity matrix $\hat{\mathbf{F}}_{\text{u}}$. It has size $|S_1| \times |S_2|$. The feature entry $\hat{\mathbf{F}}_{\text{u}}{}^{ij}$ is the similarity between the $i$th word of $S_1$ and the $j$th word of $S_2$ where each word is represented by a $d$-dimensional word embedding ($d = 100$ in our experiments).

The next level feature matrix is the short ngram similarity matrix $\hat{\mathbf{F}}_{\text{sn}}$. It has size $(|S_1| + m_{\text{sn}} - 1) \times (|S_2| + m_{\text{sn}} - 1)$ where $m_{\text{sn}} = 3$ is the filter width in this convolution layer and $|S_i| + m_{\text{sn}} - 1$ is the number of short ngrams in $S_i$. The feature entry $\hat{\mathbf{F}}_{\text{sn}}{}^{ij}$ is the similarity between two $d/2$-dimensional vectors representing two short ngrams from $S_1$ and $S_2$.

We use multiple feature maps to improve the system performance. Different feature maps are expected to extract different kinds of sentence features, and can be implemented in the same convolution layer in parallel. Specifically, we use $f_{\text{sn}} = 6$ feature maps on this level following Kalchbrenner et al. (2014). Thus, we actually compute six feature matrices $\hat{\mathbf{F}}_{\text{sn},i}$ ($i = 1, \cdots, f_{\text{sn}}$), one for each pair of feature maps that share convolution weights while derived from $S_1$ and $S_2$ respectively. (Figure 1 only shows one of those six matrices.)

The next level feature matrix is the long ngram similarity matrix $\hat{\mathbf{F}}_{\text{ln}}$. It has size $(k_{\text{dy},1} + m_{\text{ln}} - 1) \times (k_{\text{dy},2} + m_{\text{ln}} - 1)$ where $k_{\text{dy},i}$ (Equation 3) is the $k$ value in dynamic k-max pooling for sentence $i$, $k_{\text{dy},i} + m_{\text{ln}} - 1$ is the number of long ngrams in $S_i$ and $m_{\text{ln}} = 5$ is the filter width in this convolution layer. The feature entry $\hat{\mathbf{F}}_{\text{ln}}{}^{ij}$ is the similarity between two $d/4$-dimensional vectors representing two long ngrams from $S_1$ and $S_2$.

We use $f_{\text{ln}} = 14$ feature maps on this level following Kalchbrenner et al. (2014). Thus, we compute 14 feature matrices $\hat{\mathbf{F}}_{\text{ln},i}$ ($i = 1, \cdots, f_{\text{ln}}$), in a way analogous to the $f_{\text{sn}} = 6$ feature maps $\hat{\mathbf{F}}_{\text{sn},i}$.

The last feature matrix is the sentence similarity matrix $\hat{\mathbf{F}}_{\text{s}}$. It has size $k_{\text{top}} \times k_{\text{top}}$ where $k_{\text{top}} = 4$ is the parameter in k-max pooling at the last max pooling layer. The feature entry $\hat{\mathbf{F}}_{\text{s}}{}^{ij}$ is the similarity between two $d/4$-dimensional vectors computed by max pooling from $S_1$ and $S_2$.

For $l = \text{s}$, there are also $f_{\text{ln}} = 14$ feature matrices $\hat{\mathbf{F}}_{\text{s},i}$ ($i = 1, \cdots, f_{\text{ln}}$), analogous to the $f_{\text{ln}} = 14$ feature matrices $\hat{\mathbf{F}}_{\text{ln},i}$.

A general design principle of the architecture is that we compute each interaction feature matrix between two feature maps that share the same convolution weights. Two feature maps learned with the same filter will contain the same kinds of features derived from the input.

### 4.2 Dynamic pooling of feature matrices

As sentence lengths vary, feature matrices $\hat{\mathbf{F}}_l$ have different sizes, which makes it impossible to use them directly as input of the last layer.

That means we need to map $\hat{\mathbf{F}}_l \in \mathbb{R}^{r \times c}$ into a matrix $\mathbf{F}_l$ of fixed size $r' \times c'$ ($l \in \{\text{u}, \text{sn}, \text{ln}, \text{s}\}$; $r'$, $c'$ are parameters and are the same for all sentence pairs while $r, c$ depend on $|S_1|$ and $|S_2|$). Dynamic pooling divides $\hat{\mathbf{F}}_l$ into $r' \times c'$ nonoverlapping *(dynamic) pools* and copies the maximum value in each dynamic pool to $\mathbf{F}_l$. Our method is similar to (Socher et al., 2011), but preserves locality better.

$\hat{\mathbf{F}}_l$ can be split into equal regions only if $r$ (resp. $c$) is divisible by $r'$ (resp. $c'$). Otherwise, for $r > r'$ and if $r \bmod r' = b$, the dynamic pools in the first $r' - b$ splits each have $\lfloor \frac{r}{r'} \rfloor$ rows while the remaining $b$ splits each have $\lfloor \frac{r}{r'} \rfloor + 1$ rows. In Figure 2, a $r \times c = 4 \times 5$ matrix (left) is split into $r' \times c' = 3 \times 3$ dynamic pools (middle): each row is split into [1, 1, 2] and each column is split into [1, 2, 2].

If $r < r'$, we first repeat all rows until no fewer than $r'$ rows remain. Then first $r'$ rows are kept and split into $r'$ dynamic pools. The same principle applies to the partitioning of columns. In Figure 2 (right), the areas with dashed lines and dotted lines are repeated parts for rows and columns, respectively; each cell is its own dynamic pool.

## 5 Training

### 5.1 Supervised training

Dynamic pooling gives us fixed size interaction feature matrices for sentence, ngram and unigram levels. As shown in Figure 1, the concatenation of these features ($\mathbf{F}_{\text{s}}$, $\mathbf{F}_{\text{ln}}$, $\mathbf{F}_{\text{sn}}$ and $\mathbf{F}_{\text{u}}$) is the input to a logistic regression layer for paraphrase classification. We have now described all three parts of Bi-CNN-MI: CNN-SM, CNN-IM and logistic regression.

Bi-CNN-MI with all its parameters – including word embeddings and convolution weights – is trained on MSRP. We initialize embeddings with those provided by Turian et al. (2010)[1] (based on Collobert and Weston (2008)). For layer sn, we have $f_{\text{sn}} = 6$ feature maps and set filter width $m_{\text{sn}} = 3$. For layer ln, we have $f_{\text{ln}} = 14$ feature maps and set filter width $m_{\text{ln}} = 5$ and $k_{\text{top}} = 4$. Dynamic pooling

[1] `metaoptimize.com/projects/wordreprs/`

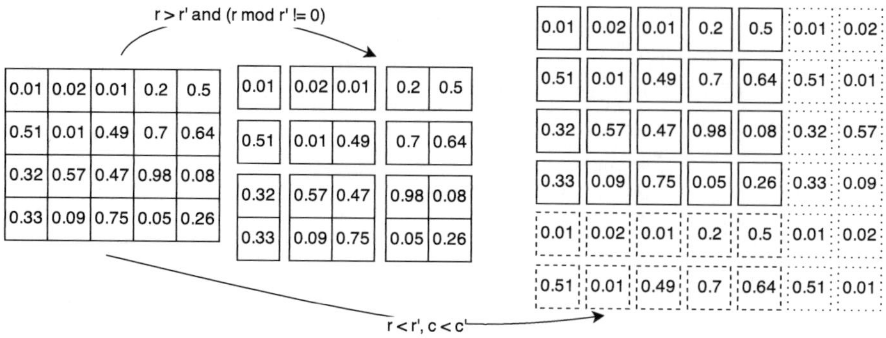


Figure 2: Partition methods in dynamic pooling. Original matrix with size $4 \times 5$ is mapped into matrix with size $3 \times 3$ and matrix with size $6 \times 7$, respectively. Each dynamic pool is distinguished by a border of empty white space around it.

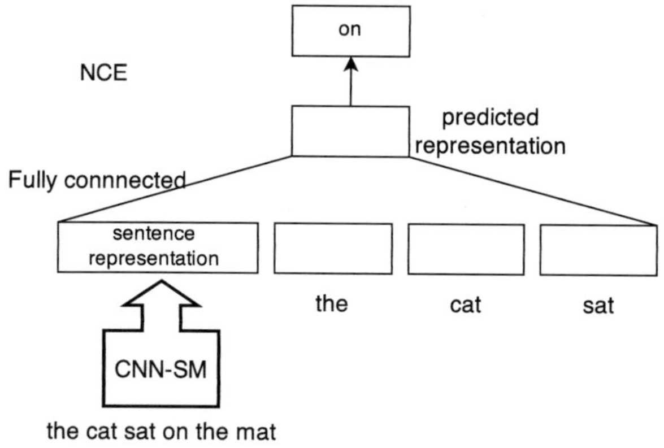


Figure 3: Unsupervised architecture: CNN-LM

sizes are $10 \times 10$, $10 \times 10$, $6 \times 6$, $2 \times 2$ for unigram, short ngram, long ngram and sentence, respectively. For training, we employ mini-batch of size 70, $L_2$ regularization with weight $5 \times 10^{-4}$ and Adagrad (Duchi et al., 2011).

### 5.2 Unsupervised pretraining

One of the key contributions of this paper is the architecture CNN-LM shown in Figure 3. CNN-LM is used to pretrain the convolutional filters on unlabeled data. This addresses sparseness and limited training data for paraphrase identification.

The convolution sentence model CNN-SM (Section 3) is part of CNN-LM ("CNN-SM" in Figure 3). The input to CNN-SM is the entire sentence ("the cat sat on the mat"); its output ("sentence representation" in the leftmost rectangle in Figure 3 and the two grids labeled "sentence representation" in the top layer of the top block in Figure 1) is concatenated with a history consisting of the embeddings of the $h = 3$ preceding words ("the", "cat", "sat") as the input of a fully connected layer to generate a predicted representation for the next word ("on"). We employ noise-contrastive estimation (NCE) (Mnih and Teh, 2012; Mnih and Kavukcuoglu, 2013) to compute the cost: the model learns to discriminate between true next words and noise words. NCE allows us to fit unnormalized models making the training time effectively independent of the vocabulary size.

In experiments, CNN-LM is trained on unlabeled MSRP data and an additional 100,000 sentences from English Gigaword (Graff et al., 2003). In principle, sentences from any source, not just English Gigaword, can be used to train this model. In NCE, 20 noise words are sampled for each true example.

So training has two parts: unsupervised, CNN-LM (Figure 3) and supervised, Bi-CNN-MI (Figure 1). In the first phase, the unsupervised training phase, we adopt a language modeling approach because it does not require human labels and can use large corpora to pretrain word embeddings and convolution weights. The goal is to learn sentence features that are unbiased and reflect useful attributes of the input sentence. More importantly, pretraining is useful to relieve overfitting, which is a severe problem when building deep NNs on small corpora like MSRP (cf. Hu et al. (2014)).

In the second phase, the supervised training phase, pretrained word embeddings and convolution weights are tuned for optimal performance on PI.

In CNN-LM, we have combined several architectural elements to pretrain a high-quality sentence analysis NN despite the lack of training data. (i) Similar to PV-DM (Le and Mikolov, 2014), we integrate global context (CNN-SM) and local context (the history of size $h$) into one model – although our global context consists only of a sentence, not of a paragraph or document. (ii) Similar to work on autoencoding (Vincent et al., 2010), the output that is to be predicted is part of the input. Autoencoding is a successful approach to learning representations and we adapt it here to pretrain good sentence representations. (iii) A second successful approach to learning embeddings is neural network language modeling (Bengio et al., 2003; Mikolov, 2012). Again, we adopt this by including in CNN-LM an ngram language modeling part to predict the next word. The great advantage of this type of embedding learning is that no labels are needed. (iv) CNN-LM only adds one hidden layer over CNN-SM. It keeps simple architecture like PV-DM (Le and Mikolov, 2014), CBOW (Mikolov et al., 2013) and LBL (Mnih and Teh, 2012), enabling the CNN-SM as main training target.

In summary, the key contribution of CNN-LM is that we pretrain convolutional filters. Architectural elements from the literature are combined to support effective pretraining of convolutional filters.

## 6 Experiments

### 6.1 Data set and evaluation metrics

We use the Microsoft Research Paraphrase Corpus (MSRP) (Dolan et al., 2004; Das and Smith, 2009). The training set contains 2753 true and 1323 false paraphrase pairs; the test set contains 1147 and 578 pairs, respectively. For each triple (label, $S_1$, $S_2$) in the training set we also add (label, $S_2$, $S_1$) to make best use of the training data; these additions are nonredundant because the interaction feature matrices (Section 4.1) are asymmetric. Systems are evaluated by accuracy and $F_1$.

### 6.2 Paraphrase detection systems

Since we want to show that Bi-CNN-MI performs better than previous NN work, we compare with three NN approaches: NLM, ARC and RAE (Table 1).[2] We also include the majority baseline ("baseline") and MT (Madnani et al., 2012). **RAE** (Socher et al., 2011) and **MT** were discussed in Sections 1 and 2. We now briefly describe the other prior work.

Blacoe and Lapata (2012) compute the vector representation of a sentence from the neural language model (NLM) embeddings (computed based on (Collobert and Weston, 2008)) of the words of the sentence as the sum of the word embeddings (**NLM+**), as the element-wise multiplication of the word embeddings (**NLM**$\odot$), or by means of the recursive autoencoder (**NLM_RAE**, Socher et al. (2011)). The representations of the two paraphrase candidates are then concatenated as input to an SVM classifier. See Blacoe and Lapata (2012) for details.

The ARC model (Hu et al., 2014) is a convolutional architecture similar to (Collobert and Weston, 2008). **ARC-I** is a Siamese architecture in which two shared-weight convolutional sentence models are trained on the binary paraphrase detection task. Hu et al. (2014) find that ARC-I is suboptimal in that it defers the interaction between $S_1$ and $S_2$ to the very end of processing: only after the vectors representing $S_1$ and $S_2$ have been computed does an interaction occur. To remedy this problem, they propose **ARC-II** in which the Siamese architecture is replaced by a multilayer NN that processes a single representation produced by interleaving $S_1$ and $S_2$.

We also evaluate **Bi-CNN-MI–**, an NN identical to Bi-CNN-MI, except that it is not pretrained in unsupervised training.

### 6.3 Results

Table 1 shows that Bi-CNN-MI outperforms all other systems. The comparison with Bi-CNN-MI– indicates that this is partly due to one major innovation we introduced: unsupervised pretraining. Bi-CNN-MI–, the model without unsupervised pretraining, performs badly. Thus, unsupervised training is helpful to pretrain parameters in paraphrase

[2] A reviewer suggests an additional experiment to directly evaluate the importance of multigranularity: a "system that puts all unigrams, short ngrams, long ngrams, and sentence representations into one interaction matrix." This would indeed be an interesting baseline, but there is no obvious way to conduct this experiment since vectors from different levels are not comparable; e.g., they have different dimensionality.

| method | acc | $F_1$ |
|---|---|---|
| baseline | 66.5 | 79.9 |
| NLM+ | 69.0 | 80.1 |
| NLM⊙ | 67.8 | 79.3 |
| NLM_RAE | 70.3 | 81.3 |
| ARC-I | 69.6 | 80.3 |
| ARC-II | 69.9 | 80.9 |
| RAE | 76.7 | 83.6 |
| MT | 77.4 | 84.1 |
| Bi-CNN-MI– | 72.5 | 81.4 |
| Bi-CNN-MI | **78.1** | **84.4** |

Table 1: Performance of different systems on MSRP

| | features used | acc | $F_1$ |
|---|---|---|---|
| 1 | no features | 66.5 | 79.9 |
| 2 | + u: unigram | 68.4 | 79.7 |
| 3 | + sn: short ngram | 75.3 | 82.8 |
| 4 | + ln: long ngram | 76.2 | 83.1 |
| 5 | + s: sentence | 73.4 | 82.3 |
| 6 | – u: unigram | 77.8 | 84.3 |
| 7 | – sn: short ngram | 76.3 | 83.5 |
| 8 | – ln: long ngram | 75.6 | 83.2 |
| 9 | – s: sentence | 77.6 | 84.2 |
| 10 | all features | 78.1 | 84.4 |

Table 2: Analysis of impact of the four feature classes. Line 1: majority baseline. Line 10: Bi-CNN-MI result from Table 1. Lines 2–5: Bi-CNN-MI when only one feature class is used. Line 6–9: ablation experiment: on each line one feature class is removed.

detection, especially when the training set is small. RAE also uses pretraining, but not as effectively as Bi-CNN-MI as Table 1 indicates. Hu et al. (2014) also suggest that training complex NNs only with supervised training runs the risk of overfitting on the small MSRP corpus.

Table 2 looks at the relative importance of the four feature matrices shown in Figure 1. (The unsupervised part of the training regime is not changed for this experiment.) The results indicate that levels sn and ln are most informative: $F_1$ scores are highest if only these two levels are used (lines 3&4: 82.8, 83.1) and performance drops most when they are removed (lines 7&8: 83.5, 83.2).

Unigrams contribute little to overall performance (lines 2&6), probably because the paraphrases in the corpus typically do not involve individual words (replacing one word by its synonym); rather, the paraphrase relationship involves larger context, which can only be judged by the higher-level features.

Just using the sentence matrix by itself performs well (line 5), but less well than using only levels sn or ln (lines 3&4). Most prior NN work on PI has taken the sentence-level approach. Our results indicate that combining this with the more fine-grained comparison on the ngram-level is superior.

Removing the sentence matrix results in a small drop in performance (line 9). The reason is that sentence representations are computed by k-max pooling from level ln. Thus, we can roughly view the sentence-level feature matrix $\mathbf{F}_s$ as a subset of $\mathbf{F}_{ln}$.

Adding (Madnani et al., 2012)'s MT metrics as input to the Bi-CNN-MI logistic regression further improves performance: accuracy of 78.4 and $F_1$ of 84.6.

## 7 Conclusion and future work

We presented the deep learning architecture Bi-CNN-MI for paraphrase identification (PI). Based on the insight that PI requires comparing two sentences *on multiple levels of granularity*, we learn multigranular sentence representations using convolution and compute interaction feature matrices at each level. These matrices are then the input to a logistic classifier for PI. All parameters of the model (for embeddings, convolution and classification) are directly optimized for PI. To address the lack of training data, we pretrain the network in a novel way for a language modeling task. Results on MSRP are state of the art.

In the future, we plan to apply Bi-CNN-MI to sentence matching, question answering and other tasks.

## Acknowledgments

We are grateful to Thang Vu, Irina Sergienya and Sebastian Ebert for comments on earlier versions of this paper. This work was supported by Baidu (through a Baidu scholarship awarded to Wenpeng Yin) and by Deutsche Forschungsgemeinschaft (grant DFG SCHU 2246/8-2, SPP 1335).

## References


Ngo Xuan Bach, Nguyen Le Minh, and Akira Shimazu. 2014. Exploiting discourse information to identify paraphrases. *Expert Systems with Applications*, 41(6):2832–2841.

Yoshua Bengio, Réjean Ducharme, Pascal Vincent, and Christian Jauvin. 2003. A neural probabilistic language model. *Journal of Machine Learning Research*, 3:1137–1155.

William Blacoe and Mirella Lapata. 2012. A comparison of vector-based representations for semantic composition. In *Proceedings of the 2012 Joint Conference on Empirical Methods in Natural Language Processing and Computational Natural Language Learning*, pages 546–556.

David M Blei, Andrew Y Ng, and Michael I Jordan. 2003. Latent dirichlet allocation. *the Journal of machine Learning research*, 3:993–1022.

Jane Bromley, James W Bentz, Léon Bottou, Isabelle Guyon, Yann LeCun, Cliff Moore, Eduard Säckinger, and Roopak Shah. 1993. Signature verification using a "siamese" time delay neural network. *International Journal of Pattern Recognition and Artificial Intelligence*, 7(04):669–688.

Yee Seng Chan and Hwee Tou Ng. 2008. Maxsim: A maximum similarity metric for machine translation evaluation. In *ACL*, pages 55–62.

Ronan Collobert and Jason Weston. 2008. A unified architecture for natural language processing: Deep neural networks with multitask learning. In *Proceedings of the 25th international conference on Machine learning*, pages 160–167.

Dipanjan Das and Noah A Smith. 2009. Paraphrase identification as probabilistic quasi-synchronous recognition. In *Proceedings of the Joint Conference of the 47th Annual Meeting of the ACL and the 4th International Joint Conference on Natural Language Processing of the AFNLP: Volume 1-Volume 1*, pages 468–476.

Li Deng, Geoffrey Hinton, and Brian Kingsbury. 2013. New types of deep neural network learning for speech recognition and related applications: An overview. In *Acoustics, Speech and Signal Processing (ICASSP), 2013 IEEE International Conference on*, pages 8599–8603.

Michael Denkowski and Alon Lavie. 2010. Extending the meteor machine translation evaluation metric to the phrase level. In *Human Language Technologies: The 2010 Annual Conference of the North American Chapter of the Association for Computational Linguistics*, pages 250–253.

George Doddington. 2002. Automatic evaluation of machine translation quality using n-gram co-occurrence statistics. In *Proceedings of the second international conference on Human Language Technology Research*, pages 138–145.

Bill Dolan, Chris Quirk, and Chris Brockett. 2004. Unsupervised construction of large paraphrase corpora: Exploiting massively parallel news sources. In *Proceedings of the 20th international conference on Computational Linguistics*, page 350.

John Duchi, Elad Hazan, and Yoram Singer. 2011. Adaptive subgradient methods for online learning and stochastic optimization. *The Journal of Machine Learning Research*, 12:2121–2159.

Jianfeng Gao, Patrick Pantel, Michael Gamon, Xiaodong He, Li Deng, and Yelong Shen. 2014. Modeling interestingness with deep neural networks. In *Proceedings of the 2013 Conference on Empirical Methods in Natural Language Processing*.

David Graff, Junbo Kong, Ke Chen, and Kazuaki Maeda. 2003. English gigaword. *Linguistic Data Consortium, Philadelphia*.

Nizar Habash and Ahmed Elkholy. 2008. Sepia: surface span extension to syntactic dependency precision-based mt evaluation. In *Proceedings of the NIST metrics for machine translation workshop at the association for machine translation in the Americas conference, AMTA-2008. Waikiki, HI*.

Baotian Hu, Zhengdong Lu, Hang Li, and Qingcai Chen. 2014. Convolutional neural network architectures for matching natural language sentences. In *Advances in Neural Information Processing Systems*.

Yangfeng Ji and Jacob Eisenstein. 2013. Discriminative improvements to distributional sentence similarity. In *Proceedings of the Conference on Empirical Methods in Natural Language Processing*.

Nal Kalchbrenner, Edward Grefenstette, and Phil Blunsom. 2014. A convolutional neural network for modelling sentences. In *Proceedings of the 52nd Annual Meeting of the Association for Computational Linguistics*.

Quoc V Le and Tomas Mikolov. 2014. Distributed representations of sentences and documents. In *Proceedings of the 31th international conference on Machine learning*.

Zhengdong Lu and Hang Li. 2013. A deep architecture for matching short texts. In *Advances in Neural Information Processing Systems*, pages 1367–1375.

Nitin Madnani, Joel Tetreault, and Martin Chodorow. 2012. Re-examining machine translation metrics for paraphrase identification. In *Proceedings of the 2012 NAACL-HLT*, pages 182–190.

Tomas Mikolov, Kai Chen, Greg Corrado, and Jeffrey Dean. 2013. Efficient estimation of word representations in vector space. In *Proceedings of Workshop at ICLR*.

Tomáš Mikolov. 2012. *Statistical language models based on neural networks*. Ph.D. thesis, Ph. D. thesis, Brno University of Technology.

Andriy Mnih and Koray Kavukcuoglu. 2013. Learning word embeddings efficiently with noise-contrastive estimation. In *Advances in Neural Information Processing Systems*, pages 2265–2273.

Andriy Mnih and Yee Whye Teh. 2012. A fast and simple algorithm for training neural probabilistic language models. In *Proceedings of the 29th International Conference on Machine Learning*, pages 1751–1758.

N Neverova, C Wolf, GW Taylor, and F Nebout. 2014. Multi-scale deep learning for gesture detection and localization. In *European Conference on Computer Vision (ECCV) 2014 ChaLearn Workshop. Zurich*.

Kishore Papineni, Salim Roukos, Todd Ward, and Wei-Jing Zhu. 2002. Bleu: a method for automatic evaluation of machine translation. In *Proceedings of the 40th ACL*, pages 311–318.

Steven Parker. 2008. Badger: A new machine translation metric. *Metrics for Machine Translation Challenge*.

Matthew Snover, Bonnie Dorr, Richard Schwartz, Linnea Micciulla, and John Makhoul. 2006. A study of translation edit rate with targeted human annotation. In *Proceedings of association for machine translation in the Americas*, pages 223–231.

Matthew G Snover, Nitin Madnani, Bonnie Dorr, and Richard Schwartz. 2009. Ter-plus: paraphrase, semantic, and alignment enhancements to translation edit rate. *Machine Translation*, 23(2-3):117–127.

Richard Socher, Eric H Huang, Jeffrey Pennin, Christopher D Manning, and Andrew Y Ng. 2011. Dynamic pooling and unfolding recursive autoencoders for paraphrase detection. In *Advances in Neural Information Processing Systems*, pages 801–809.

Joseph Turian, Lev Ratinov, and Yoshua Bengio. 2010. Word representations: a simple and general method for semi-supervised learning. In *Proceedings of the 48th Annual Meeting of the Association for Computational Linguistics*, pages 384–394.

Pascal Vincent, Hugo Larochelle, Isabelle Lajoie, Yoshua Bengio, and Pierre-Antoine Manzagol. 2010. Stacked denoising autoencoders: Learning useful representations in a deep network with a local denoising criterion. *The Journal of Machine Learning Research*, 11:3371–3408.

Stephen Wan, Mark Dras, Robert Dale, and Cécile Paris. 2006. Using dependency-based features to take the "para-farce" out of paraphrase. In *Proceedings of the Australasian Language Technology Workshop*, volume 2006.

Pengcheng Wu, Steven CH Hoi, Hao Xia, Peilin Zhao, Dayong Wang, and Chunyan Miao. 2013. Online multimodal deep similarity learning with application to image retrieval. In *Proceedings of the 21st ACM international conference on Multimedia*, pages 153–162. ACM.

# Representation Learning Using Multi-Task Deep Neural Networks for Semantic Classification and Information Retrieval

**Xiaodong Liu**[†,*] **Jianfeng Gao**[‡], **Xiaodong He**[‡], **Li Deng**[‡], **Kevin Duh**[†] **and Ye-yi Wang**[‡]
[†]Nara Institute of Science and Technology, 8916-5 Takayama, Ikoma, Nara 630-0192, Japan
[‡]Microsoft Research, One Microsoft Way, Redmond, WA 98052, USA
xiaodong-l@is.naist.jp, {jfgao,xiaohe,deng}@microsoft.com
kevinduh@is.naist.jp, yeyiwang@microsoft.com

## Abstract

Methods of deep neural networks (DNNs) have recently demonstrated superior performance on a number of natural language processing tasks. However, in most previous work, the models are learned based on either unsupervised objectives, which does not directly optimize the desired task, or single-task supervised objectives, which often suffer from insufficient training data. We develop a multi-task DNN for learning representations across multiple tasks, not only leveraging large amounts of cross-task data, but also benefiting from a regularization effect that leads to more general representations to help tasks in new domains. Our multi-task DNN approach combines tasks of multiple-domain classification (for query classification) and information retrieval (ranking for web search), and demonstrates significant gains over strong baselines in a comprehensive set of domain adaptation.

## 1 Introduction

Recent advances in deep neural networks (DNNs) have demonstrated the importance of learning vector-space representations of text, e.g., words and sentences, for a number of natural language processing tasks. For example, the study reported in (Collobert et al., 2011) demonstrated significant accuracy gains in tagging, named entity recognition, and semantic role labeling when using vector space word representations learned from large corpora. Further, since these representations are usually in a low-dimensional vector space, they result in more compact models than those built from surface-form features. A recent successful example is the parser by (Chen and Manning, 2014), which is not only accurate but also fast.

However, existing vector-space representation learning methods are far from optimal. Most previous methods are based on unsupervised objectives such as word prediction for training (Mikolov et al., 2013c; Pennington et al., 2014). Other methods use supervised training objectives on a single task, e.g. (Socher et al., 2013), and thus are often constrained by limited amounts of training data. Motivated by the success of multi-task learning (Caruana, 1997), we propose in this paper a multi-task DNN approach for representation learning that leverages supervised data from many tasks. In addition to the benefit of having more data for training, the use of multi-task also profits from a regularization effect, i.e., reducing overfitting to a specific task, thus making the learned representations universal across tasks.

Our contributions are of two-folds: First, we propose a multi-task deep neural network for representation learning, in particular focusing on semantic classification (query classification) and semantic information retrieval (ranking for web search) tasks. Our model learns to map arbitrary text queries and documents into semantic vector representations in a low dimensional latent space. While the general concept of multi-task neural nets is not new, our model is novel in that it successfully combines tasks as disparate as operations necessary for classifica-

*This research was conducted during the author's internship at Microsoft Research.



*Human Language Technologies: The 2015 Annual Conference of the North American Chapter of the ACL*, pages 912–921,
Denver, Colorado, May 31 – June 5, 2015. 

tion or ranking.

Second, we demonstrate strong results on query classification and web search. Our multi-task representation learning consistently outperforms state-of-the-art baselines. Meanwhile, we show that our model is not only compact but it also enables agile deployment into new domains. This is because the learned representations allow domain adaptation with substantially fewer in-domain labels.

## 2 Multi-Task Representation Learning

### 2.1 Preliminaries

Our multi-task model combines classification and ranking tasks. For concreteness, throughout this paper we will use query classification as the classification task and web search as the ranking task. These are important tasks in commercial search engines:

**Query Classification:** Given a search query $Q$, the model classifies in the binary fashion as to whether it belongs to one of the domains of interest. For example, if the query $Q$ is "Denver sushi", the classifier should decide that it belongs to the "Restaurant" domain. Accurate query classification enables a richer personalized user experience, since the search engine can tailor the interface and results. It is however challenging because queries tend to be short (Shen et al., 2006). Surface-form word features that are common in traditional document classification problems tend to be too sparse for query classification, so representation learning is a promising solution. In this study, we classify queries into four domains of interest: ("Restaurant", "Hotel", "Flight", "Nightlife"). Note that one query can belong to multiple domains. Therefore, a set of binary classifiers are built, one for each domain, to perform the classification. We frame the problem as four binary classification tasks. Thus, for domain $C_t$, our goal is binary classification based on $P(C_t|\ Q)$ ($C_t = \{0, 1\}$ ). For each domain $t$, we assume supervised data ($Q, y_t = \{0, 1\}$ with $y_t$ as binary labels.[1]

**Web Search:** Given a search query $Q$ and a document list **L**, the model ranks documents in the order of relevance. For example, if the query $Q$ is "Denver sushi", model returns a list of documents that satisfies such information need. Formally, we estimate $P(D_1|Q), P(D_2|Q), \ldots$ for each document $D_n$ and rank according to these probabilities. We assume that supervised data exist; I.e., there is at least one relevant document $D_n$ for each query $Q$.

### 2.2 The Proposed Multi-Task DNN Model

Briefly, our proposed model maps any arbitrary queries $Q$ or documents $D$ into fixed low-dimensional vector representations using DNNs. These vectors can then be used to perform query classification or web search. In contrast to existing representation learning methods which employ either unsupervised or single-task supervised objectives, our model learns these representations using multi-task objectives.

The architecture of our multi-task DNN model is shown in Figure 1. The lower layers are shared across different tasks, whereas the top layers represent task-specific outputs. Importantly, the input $X$ (either a query or document), initially represented as a bag of words, is mapped to a vector ($l_2$) of dimension 300. This is the shared semantic representation that is trained by our multi-task objectives. In the following, we elaborate the model in detail:

**Word Hash Layer** ($l_1$): Traditionally, each word is represented by a one-hot word vector, where the dimensionality of the vector is the vocabulary size. However, due to the large size of vocabulary in real-world tasks, it is very expensive to learn such kind of models. To alleviate this problem, we adopt the *word hashing* method (Huang et al., 2013). We map a one-hot word vector, with an extremely high dimensionality, into a limited letter-trigram space (e.g., with the dimensionality as low as 50k). For example, word *cat* is hashed as the bag of letter trigram {*#-c-a, c-a-t, a-t-#*}, where # is a boundary symbol. Word hashing complements the one-hot vector representation in two aspects: 1) out of vocabulary words can be represented by letter-trigram vectors; 2) spelling variations of the same word can be mapped to the points that are close to each other in the letter-trigram space.

**Semantic-Representation Layer** ($l_2$): This is a shared representation learned across different tasks. this layer maps the letter-trigram inputs into a 300-

[1]One could frame the problem as a a single multi-class classification task, but our formulation is more practical as it allows adding new domains without retraining existing classifiers. This will be relevant in domain adaptation (§3.3).

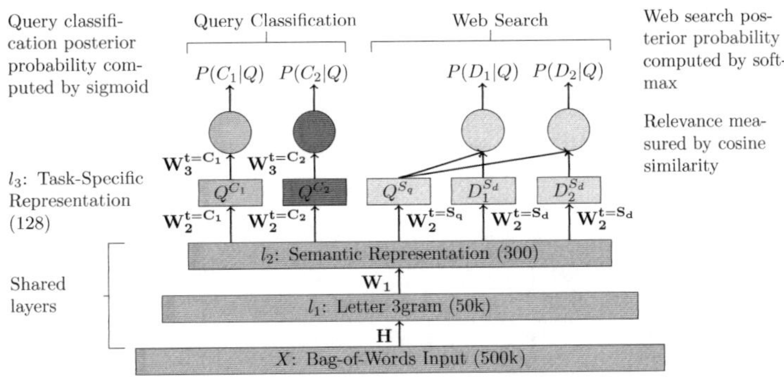


Figure 1: **Architecture of the Multi-task Deep Neural Network (DNN) for Representation Learning:** The lower layers are shared across all tasks, while top layers are task-specific. The input $X$ (either a query or document, with vocabulary size 500k) is first represented as a bag of words, then hashed into letter 3-grams $l_1$. Non-linear projection $W_1$ generates the shared semantic representation, a vector $l_2$ (dimension 300) that is trained to capture the essential characteristics of queries and documents. Finally, for each task, additional non-linear projections $W_2^t$ generate task-specific representations $l_3$ (dimension 128), followed by operations necessary for classification or ranking.

dimensional vector by

$$l_2 = f(\mathbf{W_1} \cdot l_1) \quad (1)$$

where $f(\cdot)$ is the tanh nonlinear activation $f(z) = \frac{1-e^{-2z}}{1+e^{-2z}}$. This 50k-by-300 matrix $\mathbf{W_1}$ is responsible for generating the cross-task semantic representation for arbitrary text inputs (e.g., $Q$ or $D$).

**Task-Specific Representation** ($l_3$): For each task, a nonlinear transformation maps the 300-dimension semantic representation $l_2$ into the 128-dimension task-specific representation by

$$l_3 = f(\mathbf{W}_2^t \cdot l_2) \quad (2)$$

where, $t$ denotes different tasks (query classification or web search).

**Query Classification Output**: Suppose $Q^{C_1} \equiv l_3 = f(\mathbf{W}_2^{t=C_1} \cdot l_2)$ is the 128-dimension task-specific representation for a query $Q$. The probability that $Q$ belongs to class $C_1$ is predicted by a logistic regression, with sigmoid $g(z) = \frac{1}{1+e^{-z}}$:

$$P(C_1|Q) = g(\mathbf{W}_3^{t=C_1} \cdot Q^{C_1}) \quad (3)$$

**Web Search Output**: For the web search task, both the query $Q$ and the document $D$ are mapped into 128-dimension task-specific representations $Q^{S_q}$ and $D^{S_d}$. Then, the relevance score is computed by cosine similarity as:

$$R(Q, D) = cos(Q^{S_q}, D^{S_d}) = \frac{Q^{S_q} \cdot D^{S_d}}{||Q^{S_q}||||D^{S_d}||} \quad (4)$$

**Algorithm 1:** Training a Multi-task DNN

Initialize model $\Theta$ : $\{\mathbf{W_1}, \mathbf{W_2^t}, \mathbf{W_3^t}\}$ randomly
**for** *iteration in* $0...\infty$ **do**
1. Pick a task $t$ randomly
2. Pick sample(s) from task $t$
   $(Q, y_t = \{0, 1\})$ for query classification
   $(Q, \mathbf{L})$ for web search
3. Compute loss: $L(\Theta)$
   $L(\Theta)$=Eq. 5 for query classification
   $L(\Theta)$=Eq. 6 for web search
4. Compute gradient: $\nabla(\Theta)$
5. Update model: $\Theta = \Theta - \epsilon\nabla(\Theta)$

**end**

The task $t$ is one of the query classification tasks or web search task, as shown in Figure 1. For query classification, each training sample includes one query and its category label. For web search, each training sample includes query and document list.

## 2.3 The Training Procedure

In order to learn the parameters of our model, we use mini-batch-based stochastic gradient descent (SGD) as shown in Algorithm 1. In each iteration, a task $t$ is selected randomly, and the model is updated according to the task-specific objective. This approximately optimizes the sum of all multi-task objectives. For query classification of class $C_t$, we use the cross-entropy loss as the objective:

$$-\{y_t \ln P(C_t|Q) + (1 - y_t) \ln(1 - P(C_t|Q))\} \quad (5)$$

where $y_t = \{0, 1\}$ is the label and the loss is summed over all samples in the mini-batch (1024 samples in experiments).

The objective for web search used in this paper follows the pair-wise learning-to-rank paradigm outlined in (Burges et al., 2005). Given a query $Q$, we obtain a list of documents $\mathbf{L}$ that includes a clicked document $D^+$ (positive sample), and $J$ randomly-sampled non-clicked documents $\{D_j^-\}_{j=1,.,J}$. We then minimize the negative log likelihood of the clicked document (defined in Eq. 7) given queries across the training data

$$-\log \prod_{(Q,D^+)} P(D^+|Q) \quad (6)$$

where the probability of a given document $D^+$ is computed

$$P(D^+|Q) = \frac{\exp(\gamma R(Q, D^+))}{\sum_{D' \in \mathbf{L}} \exp(\gamma R(Q, D'))} \quad (7)$$

here, $\gamma$ is a tuning factor determined on held-out data.

**Additional training details**: (1) Model parameters are initialized with uniform distribution in the range $(-\sqrt{6/(fan_{in} + fan_{out})}, \sqrt{6/(fan_{in} + fan_{out})})$ (Montavon et al., 2012). Empirically, we have not observed better performance by initialization with layer-wise pre-training. (2) Moment methods and AdaGrad training (Duchi et al., 2011) speed up the convergence speed but gave similar results as plain SGD. The SGD learning rate is fixed at $\epsilon = 0.1/1024$. (3) We run Algorithm 1 for 800K iterations, taking 13 hours on an NVidia K20 GPU.

### 2.4 An Alternative View of the Multi-Task Model

Our proposed multi-task DNN (Figure 1) can be viewed as a combination of a standard DNN for classification and a Deep Structured Semantic Model (DSSM) for ranking, shown in Figure 2. Other ways to merge the models are possible. Figure 3 shows an alternative multi-task architecture, where only the query part is shared among all tasks and the DSSM

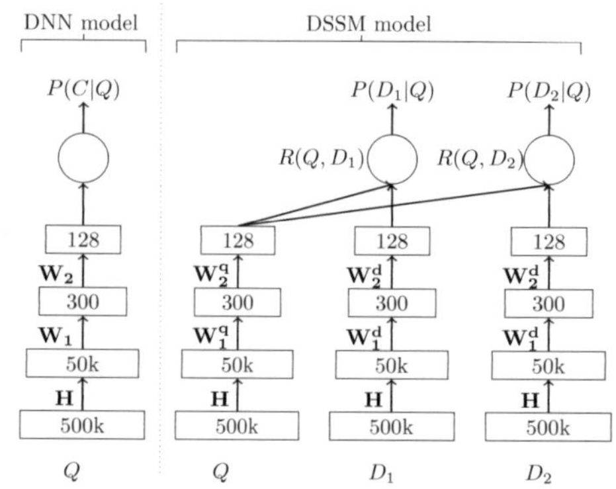


Figure 2: A DNN model for classification and a DSSM model (Huang et al., 2013) for ranking.

retains independent parameters for computing the document representations. This is more similar to the original DSSM. We have attempted training this model using Algorithm 1, but it achieves good results on query classification at the expense of web search. This is likely due to unbalanced updates (i.e. parameters for queries are updated more often than that of documents), and implying that the amount of sharing is an important design choice in multi-task models.

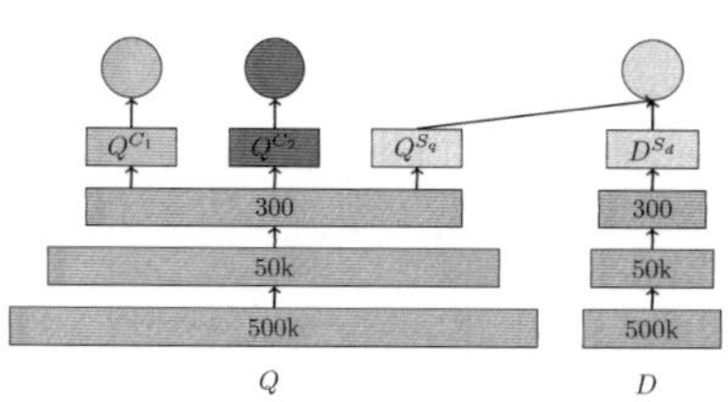


Figure 3: An alternative multi-task architecture. Compared with Figure 1, only the query part is shared across tasks here.

## 3 Experimental Evaluation

### 3.1 Data Sets and Evaluation Metrics

We employ large-scale, real data sets in our evaluation. See Table 1 for statistics. The test data for query classification were sampled from one-year log files of a commercial search engine with labels (yes or no) judged by humans. The test data for web search contains 12,071 English queries, where each query-document pair has a relevance label manually annotated on a 5-level relevance scale: *bad*, *fair*,

| Task | Query Classification | | | | Web Search |
|---|---|---|---|---|---|
| | Restaurant | Hotel | Flight | Nightlife | |
| Training | 1,585K | 2,131K | 1,880K | 1,214K | 4,084K queries & click-through documents |
| Test | 3,074 | 6,307 | 6,199 | 298 | 12,071 queries / 897,770 documents |

Table 1: Statistics of the data sets used in the experiments.

*good*, *excellent* and *perfect*. The evaluation metric for query classification is the Area under of Receiver Operating Characteristic (ROC) curve (AUC) score (Bradley, 1997). For web search, we employ the Normalized Discounted Cumulative Gain (NDCG) (Järvelin and Kekäläinen, 2000).

### 3.2 Results on Accuracy

First, we evaluate whether our model can robustly improve performance, measured as accuracy across multiple tasks.

Table 2 summarizes the AUC scores for query classification, comparing the following classifiers:

- SVM-Word: a SVM model[2] with unigram, bigram and trigram surface-form word features.
- SVM-Letter: a SVM model with letter trigram features (i.e. $l_1$ in Figure 1 as input to SVM).
- DNN: single-task deep neural net (Figure 2).
- MT-DNN: our multi-task proposal (Figure 1).

The results show that the proposed MT-DNN performs best in all four domains. Further, we observe:

1. MT-DNN outperforms DNN, indicating the usefulness of the multi-task objective (that includes web search) over the single-task objective of query classification.
2. Both DNN and MT-DNN outperform SVM-Letter, which initially uses the same input features ($l_1$). This indicates the importance of learning a semantic representation $l_2$ on top of these letter trigrams.
3. Both DNN and MT-DNN outperform a strong SVM-Word baseline, which has a large feature set that consists of 3 billion features.

Table 3 summarizes the NDCG results on web search, comparing the following models:

| System | Query Classification | | | |
|---|---|---|---|---|
| | Restaurant | Hotel | Flight | Nightlife |
| SVM-Word | 90.91 | 75.82 | 91.17 | 91.27 |
| SVM-Letter | 88.75 | 69.65 | 85.51 | 87.71 |
| DNN | 97.38 | 76.81 | 95.58 | 93.24 |
| MT-DNN | **97.57** | **78.56** | **96.21** | **94.20** |

Table 2: Query Classification AUC results.

- Popular baselines in the web search literature, e.g. BM25, Language Model, PLSA
- DSSM: single-task ranking model (Figure 2)
- MT-DNN: our multi-task proposal (Figure 1)

Again, we observe that MT-DNN performs best. For example, MT-DNN achieves NDCG@1=0.334, outperforming the current state-of-the-art single-task DSSM (0.327) and the classic methods like PLSA (0.308) and BM25 (0.305). This is a statistically significant improvement ($p < 0.05$) over DSSM and other baselines.

To recap, our MT-DNN robustly outperforms strong baselines across all web search and query classification tasks. Further, due to the use of larger training data (from different domains) and the regularization effort as we discussed in Section 1, we confirm the advantage of multi-task models over than single-task ones.[3]

### 3.3 Results on Model Compactness and Domain Adaptation

Important criteria for building practical systems are agility of deployment and small memory footprint and fast run-time. Our model satisfies both with

[2]In this paper, we use the liblinear to build SVM classifiers and optimize the corresponding parameter $C$ by using 5-fold cross-validation in training data. http://www.csie.ntu.edu.tw/ cjlin/liblinear/

[3]We have also trained SVM using Word2Vec (Mikolov et al., 2013b; Mikolov et al., 2013a) features. Unfortunately, the results are poor at 60-70 AUC, indicating the sub-optimality of unsupervised representation learning objectives for actual prediction tasks. We optimized the Word2Vec features in the SVM baseline by scaling and normalizing as well, but did not observe much improvement.

| Models | NDCG@1 | NDCG@3 | NDCG@10 |
|---|---|---|---|
| TF-IDF model (BM25) | 0.305 | 0.328 | 0.388 |
| Unigram Language Model (Zhai and Lafferty, 2001) | 0.304 | 0.327 | 0.385 |
| PLSA(Topic=100) (Hofmann, 1999; Gao et al., 2011) | 0.305 | 0.335 | 0.402 |
| PLSA(Topic=500) (Hofmann, 1999; Gao et al., 2011) | 0.308 | 0.337 | 0.402 |
| Latent Dirichlet Allocation (Topic=100) (Blei et al., 2003) | 0.308 | 0.339 | 0.403 |
| Latent Dirichlet Allocation (Topic=500) (Blei et al., 2003) | 0.310 | 0.339 | 0.405 |
| Bilingual Topic Model (Gao et al., 2011) | 0.316 | 0.344 | 0.410 |
| Word based Machine Translation model (Gao et al., 2010) | 0.315 | 0.342 | 0.411 |
| DSSM, J=50 (Figure 2, (Huang et al., 2013)) | 0.327 | 0.359 | 0.432 |
| MT-DNN (Proposed, Figure 3) | **0.334*** | **0.363** | **0.434** |

Table 3: Web Search NDCG results. Here, * indicates statistical significance improvement compared to the best baseline (DSSM) measured by $t$-test at $p$-value of 0.05.

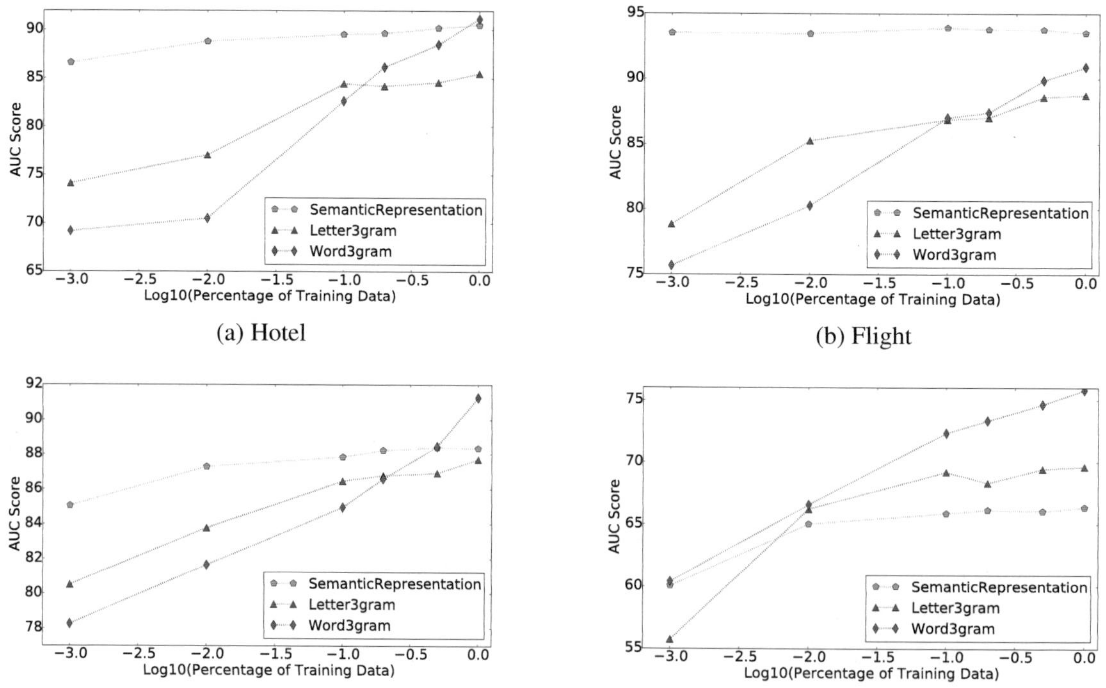


Figure 4: Domain Adaption in Query Classification: Comparison of features using SVM classifiers. The X-axis indicates the amount of labeled samples used in training the SVM. Intuitively, the three feature representations correspond to different layers in Figure 1. **SemanticRepresentation** is the $l_2$ layer trained by MT-DNN. **Word3gram** is input $X$ and **Letter3gram** is word hash layer ($l_1$), both not trained/adapted. Generally, **SemanticRepresentation** performs best for small training labels, indicating its usefulness in domain adaptation. Note that the numbers -3.0, -2.0, -1.0 and 0.0 in x-axis denote 0.1, 1, 10 and 100 percent training data in each domain, respectively.

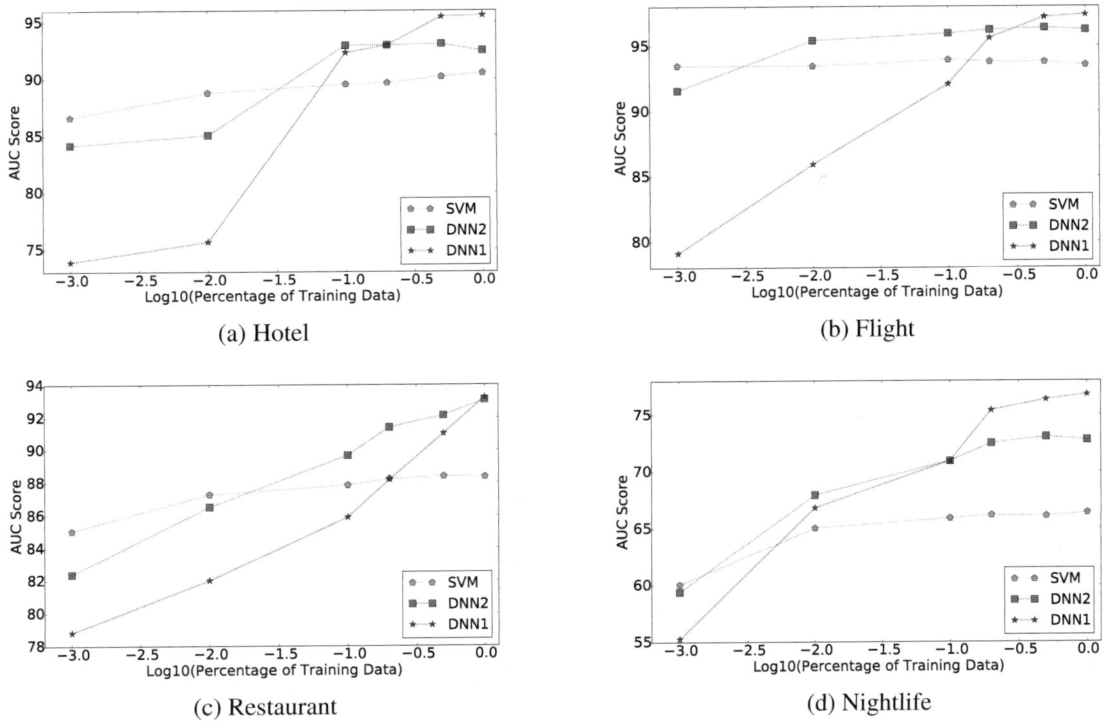


(a) Hotel (b) Flight

(c) Restaurant (d) Nightlife

Figure 5: Domain Adaptation in Query Classification. Comparison of different DNNs.

high model compactness. The key to the compactness is the aggressive compression from the 500k-dimensional bag-of-words input to 300-dimensional semantic representation $l_2$. This significantly reduces the memory/run-time requirements compared to systems that rely on surface-form features. The most expensive portion of the model is storage of the 50k-by-300 $W_1$ and its matrix multiplication with $l_1$, which is sparse: this is trivial on modern hardware. Our multi-task DNN takes $<$ 150KB in memory whereas e.g. SVM-Word takes about 200MB.

Compactness is particularly important for query classification, since one may desire to add new domains after discovering new needs from the query logs of an operational system. On the other hand, it is prohibitively expensive to collect labeled training data for new domains. Very often, we only have very small training data or even no training data.

To evaluate the models using the above criteria, we perform domain adaptation experiments on query classification using the following procedure: (1) Select one query classification task $t^*$. Train MT-DNN on the remaining tasks (including Web Search task) to obtain a semantic representation ($l_2$); (2) Given a fixed $l_2$, train an SVM on the training data $t^*$, using varying amounts of labels; (3) Evaluate the AUC on the test data of $t^*$

We compare three SVM classifiers trained using different feature representations: (1) **SemanticRepresentation** uses the $l_2$ features generated according to the above procedure. (2) **Word3gram** uses unigram, bigram and trigram word features. (3) **Letter3gram** uses letter-trigrams. Note that **Word3gram** and **Letter3gram** correspond to SVM-Word and SVM-Letter respectively in Table 2.

The AUC results for different amounts of $t^*$ training data are shown in Figure 4. In the Hotel, Flight and Restaurant domains, we observe that our semantic representation dominated the other two feature representations (**Word3gram** and **Letter3gram**) in all cases except the extremely large-data regime (more than 1 million training samples in domain $t^*$). Given sufficient labels, SVM is able to train well on **Word3gram** sparse features, but for most cases **Se-**

**manticRepresentation** is recommended.[4]

In a further experiment, we compare the following two DNNs using the same domain adaptation procedure: (1) **DNN1**: DNN where $\mathbf{W}_1$ is randomly initialized and parameters $\mathbf{W}_1, \mathbf{W}_2, \mathbf{W}_3^{t^*}$ are trained on varying amounts of data in $t^*$; (2) **DNN2**: DNN where $\mathbf{W}_1$ is obtained from other tasks (i.e. **SemanticRepresentation**) and fixed, while parameters $\mathbf{W}_2, \mathbf{W}_3^{t^*}$ are trained on varying amounts of data in $t^*$. The purpose is to see whether shared semantic representation is useful even under a DNN architecture. Figure 5 show the AUC results of DNN1 vs. DNN2 (the results **SVM** denotes the same system as **SemanticRepresentation** in Figure 4, plotted here for reference). We observe that when the training data is extremely large (millions of samples), one does best by training all parameters from scratch (DNN1). Otherwise, one is better off using a shared semantic representation trained by multitask objectives. Comparing DNN2 and SVM with **SemanticRepresentation**, we note that SVM works best for training data of several thousand samples; DNN2 works best in the medium data range.

## 4 Related Work

There is a large body of work on representation learning for natural language processing, sometimes using different terminologies for similar concepts; e.g., feature generation, dimensionality reduction, and vector space models. The main motivation is similar: to abstract away from surface forms in words, sentences, or documents, in order to alleviate sparsity and approximate semantics. Traditional techniques include LSA (Deerwester et al., 1990), ESA (Gabrilovich and Markovitch, 2007), PCA (Karhunen, 1998), and non-linear kernel variants (Schölkopf et al., 1998). Recently, learning-based approaches inspired by neural networks, especially DNNs, have gained in prominence, due to their favorable performance (Huang et al., 2013; Baroni et al., 2014; Milajevs et al., 2014).

Popular methods for learning *word* representations include (Collobert et al., 2011; Mikolov et al., 2013c; Mnih and Kavukcuoglu, 2013; Pennington et al., 2014): all are based on unsupervised objectives of predicting words or word frequencies from raw text. End-to-end neural network models for specific tasks (e.g. parsing) often use these word representations as initialization, which are then iteratively improved by optimizing a supervised objective (e.g. parsing accuracy). A selection of successful applications of this approach include sequence labeling (Turian et al., 2010), parsing (Chen and Manning, 2014), sentiment (Socher et al., 2013), question answering (Iyyer et al., 2014) and translation modeling (Gao et al., 2014a).

Our model takes queries and documents as input, so it learns *sentence/document* representations. This is currently an open research question, the challenge being how to properly model semantic compositionality of words in vector space (Huang et al., 2013; M. Baroni and Zamparelli, 2013; Socher et al., 2013). While we adopt a bag-of-words approach for practical reasons (memory and run-time), our multi-task framework is extensible to other methods for sentence/document representations, such as those based on convolutional networks (Kalchbrenner et al., 2014; Shen et al., 2014; Gao et al., 2014b), parse tree structure (Irsoy and Cardie, 2014), and run-time inference (Le and Mikolov, 2014).

The synergy between multi-task learning and neural nets is quite natural; the general idea dates back to (Caruana, 1997). The main challenge is in designing the tasks and the network structure. For example, (Collobert et al., 2011) defined part-of-speech tagging, chunking, and named entity recognition as multiple tasks in a single sequence labeler; (Bordes et al., 2012) defined multiple data sources as tasks in their relation extraction system. While conceptually similar, our model is novel in that it combines tasks as disparate as classification and ranking. Further, considering that multi-task models often exhibit mixed results (i.e. gains in some tasks but degradation in others), our accuracy improvements across all tasks is a very satisfactory result.

## 5 Conclusion

In this work, we propose a robust and practical representation learning algorithm based on multi-task objectives. Our multi-task DNN model successfully combines tasks as disparate as classification and ranking, and the experimental results demon-

[4]The trends differ slightly in the Nightlife domain. We believe this may be due to data bias on test data (only 298 samples).

strate that the model consistently outperforms strong baselines in various query classification and web search tasks. Meanwhile, we demonstrated compactness of the model and the utility of the learned query/document representation for domain adaptation.

Our model can be viewed as a general method for learning semantic representations beyond the word level. Beyond query classification and web search, we believe there are many other knowledge sources (e.g. sentiment, paraphrase) that can be incorporated either as classification or ranking tasks. A comprehensive exploration will be pursued as future work.

## Acknowledgments

We thank Xiaolong Li, Yelong Shen, Xinying Song, Jianshu Chen, Byungki Byun, Bin Cao and the anonymous reviewers for valuable discussions and comments.

## References

Marco Baroni, Georgiana Dinu, and Germán Kruszewski. 2014. Don't count, predict! a systematic comparison of context-counting vs. context-predicting semantic vectors. In *Proceedings of the 52nd Annual Meeting of the Association for Computational Linguistics (Volume 1: Long Papers)*, pages 238–247, Baltimore, Maryland, June. Association for Computational Linguistics.

David M Blei, Andrew Y Ng, and Michael I Jordan. 2003. Latent dirichlet allocation. *the Journal of machine Learning research*, 3:993–1022.

Antoine Bordes, Xavier Glorot, Jason Weston, and Yoshua Bengio. 2012. Joint learning of words and meaning representations for open-text semantic parsing. In *AISTATS*.

Andrew P Bradley. 1997. The use of the area under the roc curve in the evaluation of machine learning algorithms. *Pattern recognition*, 30(7):1145–1159.

Chris Burges, Tal Shaked, Erin Renshaw, Ari Lazier, Matt Deeds, Nicole Hamilton, and Greg Hullender. 2005. Learning to rank using gradient descent. In *Proceedings of the 22nd international conference on Machine learning*, pages 89–96. ACM.

Rich Caruana. 1997. Multitask learning. *Machine Learning*, 28.

Danqi Chen and Christopher Manning. 2014. A fast and accurate dependency parser using neural networks. In *Proceedings of the 2014 Conference on Empirical Methods in Natural Language Processing (EMNLP)*, pages 740–750, Doha, Qatar, October. Association for Computational Linguistics.

R. Collobert, J. Weston, L. Bottou, M. Karlen, K. Kavukcuoglu, and P. Kuksa. 2011. Natural language processing (almost) from scratch. *Journal of Machine Learning Research*, 12:2493–2537.

Scott Deerwester, Susan T. Dumais, George W. Furnas, Thomas K. Landauer, and Richard Harshman. 1990. Indexing by latent semantic analysis. *Journal of the American Society for Information Science*, 41(6).

John Duchi, Elad Hazan, and Yoram Singer. 2011. Adaptive subgradient methods for online learning and stochastic optimization. *The Journal of Machine Learning Research*, 12:2121–2159.

E. Gabrilovich and S. Markovitch. 2007. Computing semantic relatedness using wikipedia-based explicit semantic analysis. In *IJCAI*.

Jianfeng Gao, Xiaodong He, and Jian-Yun Nie. 2010. Clickthrough-based translation models for web search: from word models to phrase models. In *Proceedings of the 19th ACM international conference on Information and knowledge management*, pages 1139–1148. ACM.

Jianfeng Gao, Kristina Toutanova, and Wen-tau Yih. 2011. Clickthrough-based latent semantic models for web search. In *Proceedings of the 34th international ACM SIGIR conference on Research and development in Information Retrieval*, pages 675–684. ACM.

Jianfeng Gao, Xiaodong He, Wen-tau Yih, and Li Deng. 2014a. Learning continuous phrase representations for translation modeling. In *Proceedings of the 52nd Annual Meeting of the Association for Computational Linguistics (Volume 1: Long Papers)*, pages 699–709, Baltimore, Maryland, June. Association for Computational Linguistics.

Jianfeng Gao, Patrick Pantel, Michael Gamon, Xiaodong He, and Li Deng. 2014b. Modeling interestingness with deep neural networks. In *Proceedings of the 2014 Conference on Empirical Methods in Natural Language Processing (EMNLP)*, pages 2–13, Doha, Qatar, October. Association for Computational Linguistics.

Thomas Hofmann. 1999. Probabilistic latent semantic indexing. In *Proceedings of the 22nd annual international ACM SIGIR conference on Research and development in information retrieval*, pages 50–57. ACM.

Po-Sen Huang, Xiaodong He, Jianfeng Gao, Li Deng, Alex Acero, and Larry Heck. 2013. Learning deep structured semantic models for web search using clickthrough data. In *Proceedings of the 22nd ACM international conference on Conference on information & knowledge management*, pages 2333–2338. ACM.

Ozan Irsoy and Claire Cardie. 2014. Deep recursive neural networks for compositionality in language. In *NIPS*.

Mohit Iyyer, Jordan Boyd-Graber, Leonardo Claudino, Richard Socher, and Hal Daumé III. 2014. A neural network for factoid question answering over paragraphs. In *Proceedings of the 2014 Conference on Empirical Methods in Natural Language Processing (EMNLP)*, pages 633–644, Doha, Qatar, October. Association for Computational Linguistics.

Kalervo Järvelin and Jaana Kekäläinen. 2000. Ir evaluation methods for retrieving highly relevant documents. In *Proceedings of the 23rd annual international ACM SIGIR conference on Research and development in information retrieval*, pages 41–48. ACM.

Nal Kalchbrenner, Edward Grefenstette, and Phil Blunsom. 2014. A convolutional neural network for modelling sentences. In *Proceedings of the 52nd Annual Meeting of the Association for Computational Linguistics (Volume 1: Long Papers)*, pages 655–665, Baltimore, Maryland, June. Association for Computational Linguistics.

Juha Karhunen. 1998. Principal component neural networkstheory and applications. *Pattern Analysis & Applications*, 1(1):74–75.

Quoc Le and Tomas Mikolov. 2014. Distributed representations of sentences and documents. In *Proceedings of the International Conference on Machine Learning (ICML)*.

R. Bernardi M. Baroni and R. Zamparelli. 2013. Frege in space: A program for compositional distributional semantics. *Linguistic Issues in Language Technologies*.

Tomas Mikolov, Ilya Sutskever, Kai Chen, Greg S Corrado, and Jeff Dean. 2013a. Distributed representations of words and phrases and their compositionality. In *Advances in Neural Information Processing Systems*, pages 3111–3119.

Tomas Mikolov, Wen-tau Yih, and Geoffrey Zweig. 2013b. Linguistic regularities in continuous space word representations. In *Proceedings of the 2013 Conference of the North American Chapter of the Association for Computational Linguistics: Human Language Technologies*, pages 746–751, Atlanta, Georgia, June. Association for Computational Linguistics.

Tomáš Mikolov, Ilya Sutskever, Kai Chen, Greg Corrado, and Jeffrey Dean. 2013c. Distributed representations of words and phrases and their compositionality. In *NIPS*.

Dmitrijs Milajevs, Dimitri Kartsaklis, Mehrnoosh Sadrzadeh, and Matthew Purver. 2014. Evaluating neural word representations in tensor-based compositional settings. In *Proceedings of the 2014 Conference on Empirical Methods in Natural Language Processing (EMNLP)*, pages 708–719, Doha, Qatar, October. Association for Computational Linguistics.

Andriy Mnih and Koray Kavukcuoglu. 2013. Learning word embeddings efficiently with noise-contrastive estimation. In *Advances in Neural Information Processing Systems 26 (NIPS 2013)*.

Gregoire Montavon, Genevieve Orr, and Klaus-Robert Muller. 2012. *Neural Networks: Tricks of the Trade 2nd ed.* springer.

Jeffrey Pennington, Richard Socher, and Christopher Manning. 2014. Glove: Global vectors for word representation. In *Proceedings of the 2014 Conference on Empirical Methods in Natural Language Processing (EMNLP)*, pages 1532–1543, Doha, Qatar, October. Association for Computational Linguistics.

B. Schölkopf, A. Smola, and K.-R. Müller. 1998. Nonlinear component analysis as kernel eigenvalue problem. *Neural Computation*, 10.

Dou Shen, Rong Pan, Jian-Tao Sun, Jeffrey Junfeng Pan, Kangheng Wu, Jie Yin, and Qiang Yang. 2006. Query enrichment for web-query classification. *ACM Trans. Inf. Syst.*, 24(3):320–352, July.

Yelong Shen, Xiaodong He, Jianfeng Gao, Li Deng, and Grégoire Mesnil. 2014. A latent semantic model with convolutional-pooling structure for information retrieval. In *Proceedings of the 23rd ACM International Conference on Conference on Information and Knowledge Management*, pages 101–110. ACM.

Richard Socher, Alex Perelygin, Jean Wu, Jason Chuang, Christopher D. Manning, Andrew Ng, and Christopher Potts. 2013. Recursive deep models for semantic compositionality over a sentiment treebank. In *Proceedings of the 2013 Conference on Empirical Methods in Natural Language Processing*, pages 1631–1642, Seattle, Washington, USA, October. Association for Computational Linguistics.

Joseph Turian, Lev-Arie Ratinov, and Yoshua Bengio. 2010. Word representations: A simple and general method for semi-supervised learning. In *Proceedings of the 48th Annual Meeting of the Association for Computational Linguistics*, pages 384–394, Uppsala, Sweden, July.

Chengxiang Zhai and John Lafferty. 2001. A study of smoothing methods for language models applied to ad hoc information retrieval. In *Proceedings of the 24th annual international ACM SIGIR conference on Research and development in information retrieval*, pages 334–342. ACM.

# Inflection Generation as Discriminative String Transduction

**Garrett Nicolai**[†] **Colin Cherry**[‡] **Grzegorz Kondrak**[†]

[†]Department of Computing Science
University of Alberta
Edmonton, AB, T6G 2E8, Canada
{nicolai,gkondrak}@ualberta.ca

[‡]National Research Council Canada
1200 Montreal Road
Ottawa, ON, K1A 0R6, Canada
Colin.Cherry@nrc-cnrc.gc.ca

## Abstract

We approach the task of morphological inflection generation as discriminative string transduction. Our supervised system learns to generate word-forms from lemmas accompanied by morphological tags, and refines them by referring to the other forms within a paradigm. Results of experiments on six diverse languages with varying amounts of training data demonstrate that our approach improves the state of the art in terms of predicting inflected word-forms.

| | | |
|---|---|---|
| infinitive | | atmen |
| present participle | | atmend |
| past participle | | geatmet |
| auxiliary | | haben |
| | indicative | |
| present | ich atme | wir **atmen** |
| | du atmest | ihr atmet |
| | er atmet | sie **atmen** |
| preterite | ich atmete | wir atmeten |
| | du atmetest | ihr atmetet |
| | er atmete | sie atmeten |

Figure 1: A partial inflection table for the German verb *atmen* "to breathe" in Wiktionary.

## 1 Introduction

Word-forms that correspond to the same lemma can be viewed as paradigmatically related instantiations of the lemma. For example, *take, takes, taking, took,* and *taken* are the word-forms of the lemma *take*. Many languages have complex morphology with dozens of different word-forms for any given lemma: verbs inflect for tense, mood, and person; nouns can vary depending on their role in a sentence, and adjectives agree with the nouns that they modify. For such languages, many forms will not be attested even in a large corpus. However, different lemmas often exhibit the same inflectional patterns, called *paradigms*, which are based on phonological, semantic, or morphological criteria. The paradigm of a given lemma can be identified and used to generate unseen forms.

Inflection prediction has the potential to improve Statistical Machine Translation (SMT) into morphologically complex languages. In order to address data sparsity in the training bitext, Clifton and Sarkar (2011) and Fraser et al. (2012) reduce diverse inflected forms in the target language into the corresponding base forms, or lemmas. At test time, they predict an abstract inflection tag for each translated lemma, which is then transformed into a proper word-form. Unfortunately, hand-crafted morphological generators such as the ones that they use for this purpose are available only for a small number of languages, and are expensive to create from scratch. The supervised inflection generation models that we investigate in this paper can instead be trained on publicly available inflection tables.

The task of an inflection generator is to produce an inflected form given a base-form (e.g., an infinitive) and desired inflection, which can be specified as an abstract inflectional tag. The generator is trained on a number of inflection tables, such as the one in Figure 1, which enumerate inflection forms for a given lemma. At test time, the generator predicts inflections for previously unseen base-forms. For example, given the input *atmen* + *1SIA*, where the tag stands for "first person singular indicative preterite," it should output *atmete*.

Recently, Durrett and DeNero (2013) and Ahlberg



*Human Language Technologies: The 2015 Annual Conference of the North American Chapter of the ACL*, pages 922–931,
Denver, Colorado, May 31 – June 5, 2015. 

et al. (2014) have proposed to model inflection generation as a two-stage process: an input base-form is first matched with rules corresponding to a paradigm seen during training, which is then used to generate all inflections for that base-form simultaneously. Although their methods are quite different, both systems account for paradigm-wide regularities by creating rules that span all inflections within a paradigm. We analyze both approaches in greater detail in Section 2.

In this paper, we approach the task of supervised inflection generation as discriminative string transduction, in which character-level operations are applied to transform a lemma concatenated with an inflection tag into the correct surface word-form. We carefully model the transformations carried out for a single inflection, taking into account source characters surrounding a rule, rule sequence patterns, and the shape of the resulting inflected word. To take advantage of paradigmatic regularities, we perform a subsequent reranking of the top $n$ word-forms produced by the transducer. In the reranking model, soft constraints capture similarities between different inflection slots within a table. Where previous work leveraged large, rigid rules to span paradigms, our work is characterized by small, flexible rules that can be applied to any inflection, with features determining what rule sequence works best for each pairing of a base-form with an inflection.

Since our target application is machine translation, we focus on maximizing inflection form accuracy, rather than complete table accuracy. Unlike previous work, which aims at learning linguistically-correct paradigms from crowd-sourced data, our approach is designed to be robust with respect to incomplete and noisy training data, which could be extracted from digital lexicons and annotated corpora. We conduct a series of experiments which demonstrate that our method can accurately learn complex morphological rules in languages with varying levels of morphological complexity. In each experiment we either match or improve over the state of the art reported in previous work. In addition to providing a detailed comparison of the available inflection prediction systems, we also contribute four new inflection datasets composed of Dutch and French verbs, and Czech verbs and nouns, which are made available for future research.

## 2 Inflection generation

Durrett and DeNero (2013) formulate the specific task of supervised generation of inflected forms for a given base-form based on a large number of training inflection tables, while Ahlberg et al. (2014) test their alternative method on the same Wiktionary dataset. In this section, we compare their work to our approach with respect to the following three subtasks:

1. character-wise alignment of the word-forms in an inflection table (Section 2.1),
2. extraction of rules from aligned forms (2.2),
3. matching of rules to new base-forms (2.3).

### 2.1 Table alignment

The first step in supervised paradigm learning is the alignment of related inflected forms in a table. Though technically a multiple-alignment problem, this can also be addressed by aligning each inflected form to a base-form. Durrett & DeNero do exactly this, aligning each inflection to the base with a paradigm-aware, position-dependent edit distance. Ahlberg et al. use finite-state-automata to implement a multiple longest-common-subsequence (LCS) alignment, avoiding the use of an explicit base-form. Both systems leverage the intuition that character alignment is mostly a problem of aligning those characters that remain unchanged throughout the inflection table.

Our alignment approach differs from previous work in that we use an EM-driven, many-to-many aligner. Instead of focusing on unchanged characters within a single paradigm, we look for small multi-character operations that have statistical support across all paradigms. This includes operations that simply copy their source into the target, leaving the characters unchanged.

### 2.2 Rule extraction

The second step involves transforming the character alignments into inflection rules. Both previous efforts begin addressing this problem in the same way: by finding maximal, contiguous spans of changed characters, in the base-form for Durrett & DeNero, and in the aligned word-forms for Ahlberg et al. Given those spans, the two methods diverge quite substantially. Durrett & DeNero extract a rule for

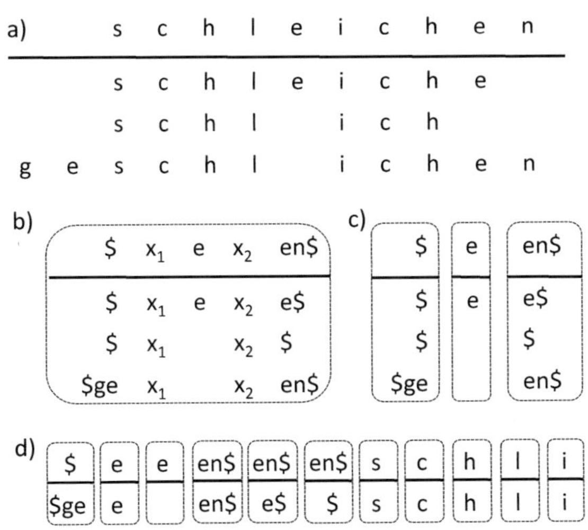


Figure 2: Competing strategies for rule extraction: (a) an aligned table; (b) a table-level rule; (c) vertical rules; (d) atomic rules. $ is a word boundary marker.

each *changed* span, with the rule specifying transformations to perform for each inflection. Ahlberg et al. instead replace each *unchanged* span with a variable, creating a single rule that specifies complete inflections for the entire table. The latter approach creates larger rules, which are easier to interpret for a linguist, but are less flexible, and restrict information sharing across paradigms.

We move in the opposite direction by extracting a rule for each minimal, multi-character transformation identified by our aligner, with no hard constraint on what rules travel together across different inflections. We attempt to learn atomic character transformations, which extends the flexibility of our rules at the cost of reduced interpretability.

The differences in rule granularity are illustrated on the German verb *schleichen* "to sneak" in Figure 2. The single rule of Ahlberg et al. comprises three vertical rules of Durrett & DeNero, which in turn correspond to eleven atomic rules in our system. Note that this is a simplification, as alignments and word boundary markers vary across the three systems.

### 2.3 Rule selection

The final component of an inflection generation system is a mechanism to determine what rules to apply to a new base-form, in order to generate the inflected forms. The strongest signal for this task comes from learning how the training base-forms use the rules. With their highly restrictive rules, Ahlberg et al. can afford a simple scheme, keeping an index that associates rules with base-forms, and employing a longest suffix match against this index to assign rules to new base-forms. They also use the corpus frequency of the inflections that would be created by their rules as a rule-selection feature. Durrett & DeNero have much more freedom, both in what rules can be used together and in where each rule can be applied. Therefore, they employ a more complex semi-Markov model to assign rules to spans of the base-form, with features characterizing the $n$-gram character context surrounding the source side of each rule.

Since our rules provide even greater flexibility, we model rule application very carefully. Like Durrett & DeNero, we employ a discriminative semi-Markov model that considers source character context, and like Ahlberg et al., we use a corpus to reevaluate predictions. In addition, we model rule sequences, and the character-shape of the resulting inflected form. Note that our rules are much more general than those of our predecessors, which makes it easy to get statistical support for these additional features. Finally, since our rules are not bound by paradigm structure, we employ a reranking step to account for intra-paradigm regularities.

## 3 Discriminative Transduction

In this section, we describe the details of our approach, including the affix representation, the string alignment and transduction, and the paradigm reranking.

### 3.1 Affix representation

Our inflection generation engine is a discriminative semi-Markov model, similar to a monotonic phrase-based decoder from machine translation (Zens and Ney, 2004). This system cannot insert characters, except as a part of a phrasal substitution, so when inflecting a base form, we add an abstract affix representation to both provide an insertion site and to indicate the desired inflection.

Abstract tags are separated from their lemmas with a single '+' character. Marking the morpheme boundary in such a way allows the transducer to generalize the context of a morpheme boundary. For example, the third person singular indicative present of the verb *atmen* is represented as *atmen+3SIE*. We use readable tags throughout this paper, but they are presented to the transducer as indivisible units; it cannot translate them character-by-character.

German and Dutch past participles, as well as several Czech inflections, are formed by circumfixation, a special process of simultaneous prefixation and suffixation. We represent such inflections with separate copies of the circumfix tag before and after the lemma. For example, the past participle *gebracht* "brought" is represented as *PPL+bringen+PPL*. In the absence of language-specific information regarding the set of inflections that involve circumfixation, the system can learn to transduce particular affixes into empty strings.

During development, we experimented with an alternative method, in which affixes are represented by a default allomorph. Allomorphic representations have the potential advantage of reducing the complexity of transductions by the virtue of being similar to the correct form of the affix. However, we found that allomorphic affixes tend to obfuscate differences between distinct inflections, so we decided to employ abstract tags instead.

### 3.2 String transduction

We perform string transduction adapting the tool DIRECTL+, originally designed for grapheme-to-phoneme conversion (Jiampojamarn et al., 2010). DIRECTL+ is a feature-rich, discriminative character transducer, which searches for a model-optimal sequence of character transformation rules for its input. The core of the engine is a dynamic programming algorithm capable of transducing many consecutive characters in a single operation, also known as a semi-Markov model. Using a structured version of the MIRA algorithm (McDonald et al., 2005), training attempts to assign weights to each feature so that its linear model separates the gold-standard derivation from all others in its search space.

DIRECTL+ uses a number of feature templates to assess the quality of a rule: source context, target $n$-gram, and joint $n$-gram features. Context features conjoin the rule with indicators for all source character $n$-grams within a fixed window of where the rule is being applied. Target $n$-grams provide indicators on target character sequences, describing the shape of the target as it is being produced, and may also be conjoined with our source context features. Joint $n$-grams build indicators on rule sequences, combining source and target context, and memorizing frequently-used rule patterns. Durrett & DeNero also use source context features, but we are the first group to account for features that consider rule sequences or target word shape.

Following Toutanova and Cherry (2009), we modify the out-of-the-box version of DIRECTL+ by implementing an abstract copy feature that indicates when a rule simply copies its source characters into the target, e.g. $p \rightarrow p$. The copy feature has the effect of biasing the transducer towards preserving the base-form within the inflected form.

In addition to the general model that is trained on all inflected word-forms, we derive tag-specific models for each type of inflection. Development experiments showed the general model to be slightly more accurate overall, but we use both types of models in our reranker.

### 3.3 String alignment

DIRECTL+ training requires a set of aligned pairs of source and target strings. The alignments account for every input and output character without the use of insertion. Derivations that transform the input substrings into the desired output substrings are then extracted from the alignments.

We induce the alignments by adapting the M2M aligner of (Jiampojamarn et al., 2007), which uses Expectation-Maximization to maximize the joint likelihood of its input under a pairwise alignment scheme. Previous work creates alignments based upon entire inflection tables, while ours considers each inflection paired with its base form independently. M2M goes beyond linking single characters by aligning entire substrings instead. In practice, the base-form serves as a pivot for the entire inflection table, leading to consistent multiple alignments.

We modify the M2M aligner to differentiate between stems and affixes. The alignments between stem letters rarely require more than a 2-2 alignment. A single tag, however, must align to an entire affix, which may be composed of four or more letters. The distinction allows us to set different substring length limits for the two types.

In order to encourage alignments between identical letters, we augment the training set by pairing each inflected form with itself. In addition, we modify the aligner to generalize the identity alignments into a single operation, which corresponds to the copy feature described in Section 3.2.

### 3.4 Reranking

Morphological processes such as stem changes tend to be similar across different word-forms of the same lemma. In order to take advantage of such paradigmatic consistency, we perform a reranking of the $n$-best word-forms generated by DIRECTL+. The correct form is sometimes included in the $n$-best list, but with a lower score than an incorrect form. We propose to rerank such lists on the basis of features extracted from the 1-best word-forms generated for other inflection slots, the majority of which are typically correct.

We perform reranking with the Liblinear SVM (Fan et al., 2008), using the method of Joachims (2002). An initial inflection table, created to generate reranking features, is composed of 1-best predictions from the general model. For each inflection, we then generate lists of candidate forms by taking the intersection of the $n$-best lists from the general and the tag-specific models.

In order to generate features from our initial inflection table, we make pairwise comparisons between a prediction and each form in the initial table. We separate stems from affixes using the alignment. Our three features indicate whether the compared forms share the same stem, the same affix, and the same surface word-form, respectively. We generate a feature vector for each aligned pair of related word-forms, such as past participle vs. present participle. In addition, we include as features the confidence scores generated by both models.

Two extra features are designed to leverage a large corpus of raw text. A binary indicator feature fires if the generated form occurs in the corpus. In order to model the phonotactics of the language, we also derive a 4-gram character language model from the same corpus, and include as a feature the normalized log-likelihood of the predicted form.

| Language / POS | Set | Base forms | Infl. |
|---|---|---|---|
| German Nouns | DE-N | 2764 | 8 |
| German Verbs | DE-V | 2027 | 27 |
| Spanish Verbs | ES-V | 4055 | 57 |
| Finnish Nouns | FI-N | 6400[1] | 28 |
| Finnish Verbs | FI-V | 7249 | 53 |
| Dutch Verbs | NL-V | 11200 | 9 |
| French Verbs | FR-V | 6957 | 48 |
| Czech Nouns | CZ-N | 21830 | 17 |
| Czech Verbs | CZ-V | 4435 | 54 |

Table 1: The number of base forms and inflections for each dataset.

## 4 Experiments

We perform five experiments that differ with respect to the amount and completeness of training data, and whether the training is performed on individual word-forms or entire inflection tables. We follow the experimental settings established by previous work, as much as possible.

The parameters of our transducer and aligner were established on a development set of German nouns and verbs, and kept fixed in all experiments. We limit stem alignments to 2-2, affix alignments to 2-4, source context to 8 characters, joint n-grams to 5 characters, and target Markov features to 2 characters.

### 4.1 Inflection data

We adopt the Wiktionary inflection data made available by Durrett and DeNero (2013), with the same training, development, and test splits. The development and test sets contain 200 inflection tables each. and the training sets consist of the remaining data. Table 1 shows the total number of tables in each language set. We convert their inflectional information to abstract tags for input to our transducer.

We augment the original five datasets with four new sets: Dutch verbs from the CELEX lexical database (Baayen et al., 1995), French verbs from Verbiste, an online French conjugation dictionary[2], and Czech nouns and verbs from the Prague Dependency Treebank (Böhmová et al., 2003). For each of

[1]Durrett & DeNero report 40589 forms, but only use 6000 for training, and 200 each for development and testing

[2]http://perso.b2b2c.ca/sarrazip/dev/verbiste.html

| Case | Singular | Plural |
|---|---|---|
| Nominative | Buch | Bücher |
| Accusative | Buch | Bücher |
| Dative | Buch | Büchern |
| Genitive | Buches | Bücher |

Table 2: All word-forms of the German noun *Buch*.

| Set | DDN | Ours | 10-best |
|---|---|---|---|
| DE-V | 94.8 | **97.5** | 99.8 |
| DE-N | 88.3 | **88.6** | 98.6 |
| ES-V | 99.6 | **99.8** | 100 |
| FI-V | 97.2 | **98.1** | 99.9 |
| FI-N | 92.1 | **93.0** | 99.0 |
| NL-V | 90.5* | **96.1** | 99.4 |
| FR-V | 98.8* | **99.2** | 99.7 |

Table 3: Prediction accuracy of models trained and tested on individual inflections.

these sets, the training data is restricted to 80% of the inflection tables listed in Table 1, with 10% each for development and testing. Each lemma inflects to a finite number of forms that vary by part-of-speech and language (Table 1); German nouns inflect for number and case (Table 2), while French, Spanish, German, and Dutch verbs inflect for number, person, mood, and tense.

We extract Czech data from the Prague Dependency Treebank, which is fully annotated for morphological information. This dataset contains few complete inflection tables, with many lemmas represented by a small number of word-forms. For this reason, it is only suitable for one of our experiments, which we describe in Section 4.5.

Finnish has a morphological system that is unlike any of the Indo-European languages. There are 15 different grammatical cases for nouns and adjectives, while verbs make a number of distinctions, such as conditional vs. potential, and affirmative vs. negative. We derive separate models for two noun classes (singular and plural), and six verb classes (infinitive, conditional, potential, participle, imperative, and indicative). This is partly motivated by the number of individual training instances for Finnish, which is much larger than the other languages, but also to take advantage of the similarities within classes.

For the reranker experiments, we use the appropriate Wikipedia language dump. The number of tokens in the corpora is approximately 77M for Czech, 200M for Dutch, 6M for Finnish, 425M for French, 550M for German, and 400M for Spanish.

### 4.2 Individual inflections

In the first experiment, we test the accuracy of our basic model which excludes our reranker, and therefore has no access to features based on inflection tables or corpus counts. Table 3 compares our results against the Factored model of Durrett & DeNero (DDN), which also makes an independent prediction for each inflection. The numbers marked with an asterisk were not reported in the original paper, but were generated by running their publicly-available code on our new Dutch and French datasets. For the purpose of quantifying the effectiveness of our reranker, we also include the percentage of correct answers that appear in our 10-best lists.

Our basic model achieves higher accuracy on all datasets, which shows that our refined transduction features are consistently more effective than the source-context features employed by the other system. Naturally, their system, as well as the system of Ahlberg et al., is intended for whole-table scenarios, which we test next.

### 4.3 Complete paradigms

In this experiment, we assume the access to complete inflection tables, as well as to raw corpora. We compare our reranking system to the Joint model of Durrett & DeNero (DDN), which is trained on complete tables, and the full model of Ahlberg et al. (AFH), which is trained on complete tables, and matches forms to rules with aid of corpus counts. Again, we calculated the numbers marked with an asterisk by running the respective implementations on our new datasets.

The results of the experiment are shown in Table 4. Our reranking model outperforms the Joint model of DDN on all sets, and the full model of AFH on most verb sets. Looking across tables to Table 3, we can see that reranking improves upon our independent model on 5 out of 7 sets, and is equivalent on the remaining two sets. However, accord-

| Set | DDN | AFH | Ours |
|---|---|---|---|
| DE-V | 96.2 | **97.9** | **97.9** |
| DE-N | 88.9 | **91.8** | 89.9 |
| ES-V | 99.7 | 99.6 | **99.9** |
| FI-V | 96.4 | 96.6 | **98.1** |
| FI-N | 93.4 | **93.8** | 93.6 |
| NL-V | 94.4* | 87.7* | **96.6** |
| FR-V | 96.8* | 98.1* | **99.2** |

Table 4: Individual form accuracy of models trained on complete inflection tables.

| Set | DDN | AFH | Ours |
|---|---|---|---|
| DE-V | 85.0 | 76.5 | **90.5** |
| DE-N | 79.5 | **82.0** | 76.5 |
| ES-V | 95.0 | 98.0 | **99.0** |
| FI-V | 87.5 | 92.5 | **94.5** |
| FI-N | 83.5 | **88.0** | 82.0 |
| NL-V | 79.5* | 37.7* | **82.1** |
| FR-V | 92.1* | 96.0* | **97.1** |

Table 5: Complete table accuracy of models trained on complete inflection tables.

ing to single-form accuracy, neither our system nor DDN benefits too much from joint predictions. Table 5 shows the same results evaluated with respect to complete table accuracy.

### 4.4 Incomplete paradigms

In this experiment, we consider a scenario where, instead of complete tables, we have access to some but not all of the possible word-forms. This could occur for example if we extracted our training data from a morphologically annotated corpus. We simulate this by only including in our training tables the forms that are observed in the corresponding raw corpus. We then test our ability to predict the same test forms as in the previous experiments, regardless of whether or not they were observed in the corpus. We also allow a small held-out set of complete tables, which corresponds to the development set. For Durrett & DeNero's method, we include this held-out set in the training data, while for our system, we use it to train the reranker.

The Joint method of DDN and the methods of AFH are incapable of training on incomplete tables, and thus, we can only compare our results against the Factored model of DDN. However, unlike their Factored model, we can then still take advantage of paradigmatic and corpus information, by applying our reranker to the predictions made by our simple model.

The results are shown in Table 6, where we refer to our independent model as *Basic*, and to our reranked system as *Reranked*. The latter outperforms DDN on all sets. Furthermore, even with only partial tables available during training, reranking improves upon our independent model in every case.

### 4.5 Partial paradigms

We run a separate experiment for Czech, as the data is substantially less comprehensive than for the other languages. Although the number of 13.0% observed noun forms is comparable to the Finnish case, the percentages in Table 6 refer only to the training set: the test and held-out sets are complete. For Czech, the percentage includes the testing and held-out sets. Thus, the method of Durrett & DeNero and our reranker have access to less training data than in the experiment of Section 4.4.

The results of this experiment are shown in Table 7. Our Basic model outperforms DDN for both nouns and verbs, despite training on less data. However, reranking actually decreases the accuracy of our system on Czech nouns. It appears that the reranker is adversely affected by the lack of complete target paradigms. We leave the full investigation into the effectiveness of the reranker on incomplete data to future work.

### 4.6 Seed paradigms

Dreyer and Eisner (2011) are particularly concerned with situations involving limited training data, and approach inflection generation as a semi-supervised task. In our last experiment we follow their experimental setup, which simulates the situation where we obtain a small number of complete tables from an expert. We use the same training, development, and test splits to test our system. Due to the nature of our model, we need to set aside a hold-out set for reranking. Thus, rather than training on 50 and 100 tables, we train on 40 and 80, but compare the results

| Set | % of Total | DDN | Ours | |
|---|---|---|---|---|
| | | | Basic | Reranked |
| DE-V | 69.2 | 90.2 | 96.2 | **97.9** |
| DE-N | 92.7 | 88.3 | 88.4 | **89.8** |
| ES-V | 36.1 | 97.1 | 95.9 | **99.6** |
| FI-V | 15.6 | 73.8 | 78.7 | **85.6** |
| FI-N | 15.2 | 71.6 | 78.2 | **80.4** |
| DU-V | 50.5 | 89.8 | 94.9 | **96.0** |
| FR-V | 27.6 | 94.6 | 96.6 | **98.9** |

Table 6: Prediction accuracy of models trained on observed forms.

with the models trained on 50 and 100, respectively. For reranking, we use the same German corpus as in our previous experiments, but limited to the first 10M words.

The results are shown in Table 8. When trained on 50 seed tables, the accuracy of our models is comparable to both the basic model of Dreyer and Eisner (DE) and the Factored model of DDN, and matches the best system when we add reranking. When trained on 100 seed tables, our full reranking model outperforms the other models.

## 5 Error analysis

In this section, we analyze several types of errors made by the various systems. Non-word predictions are marked with an asterisk.

German and Dutch are closely-related languages that exhibit similar errors. Many errors involve the past participle, which is often created by circumfixation. For the German verb *verfilmen* "to film," we predict the correct *verfilmt*, while the other systems have *verfilmen**, and *geverfilmt**, respectively. DDN simply select an incorrect rule for the past participle. AFH choose paradigms through suffix analysis, which fails to account for the fact that verbs that begin with a small set of prefixes, such as *ver-*, do not take a *ge-* prefix. This type of error particularly affects the accuracy of AFH on Dutch because of a number of verbs in our test set that involve infixation for the past participle. Our system uses its source and target-side $n$-gram features to match these prefixes with their correct representation.

The second type of error is an over-correction by the corpus. The past participle of the verb *dimmen* is

| Set | % of Total | DDN | Ours | |
|---|---|---|---|---|
| | | | Basic | Reranked |
| CZ-N | 13.0 | 91.1 | **97.7** | 93.5 |
| CZ-V | 6.8 | 82.5 | 83.6 | **85.8** |

Table 7: Prediction accuracy of models trained on observed Czech forms.

*gedimmt*, but AFH predict *dimmt**, and then change it to *dummen* with the corpus. *Dummen* is indeed a valid word in German, but unrelated to the verb *dimmen*. It is also far more common, with 181 occurrences in the corpus, compared with only 28 for *gedimmt*. Since AFH use corpus frequencies, mistakes like this can occur. Our system is trained to balance transducer confidence against a form's existence in a corpus (as opposed to log frequency), which helps it ignore the bias of common, but incorrect, forms.

The German verb *brennen* "to burn" has an irregular past participle: *gebrannt*. It involves both a stem vowel change and a circumfix, two processes that only rarely co-occur. AFH predict the form *brannt**, using the paradigm of the similar *bekennen*. The flexibility of DDN allows them to predict the correct form. Our basic model predicts *gebrennt**, which follows the regular pattern of applying a circumfix, while maintaining the stem vowel. The reranker is able to correct this mistake by relating it to the form *gebrannt* in the corpus, whose stem is identical to the stem of the preterite forms, which is a common paradigmatic pattern.

Our system can also over-correct, such as with the second person plural indicative preterite form for the verb *reisen*, which should be *reistet*, and which our basic model correctly predicts. The reranker, however, changes the prediction to *rist*. This is a nominal form that is observed in the corpus, while the verbal form is not.

An interesting example of a mistake made by the Factored model of DDN involves the Dutch verb *aandragen*. Their model learns that stem vowel *a* should be doubled, and that an *a* should be included as part of the suffix *-agt*, which results in an incorrect form *aandraaagt**. Thanks to the modelling of phonotactics, our model is able to correctly rule out the tripling of a vowel.

| Seed Tables | DE | | DDN | | Ours | |
|---|---|---|---|---|---|---|
| | Basic | Full | Factored | Joint | Basic | Full |
| 50 | 89.9 | **90.9** | 89.6 | 90.5 | 89.7 | **90.9** |
| 100 | 91.5 | 92.2 | 91.4 | 92.3 | 92.0 | **92.6** |

Table 8: Prediction accuracy on German verb forms after training on a small number of seed inflection tables.

Finnish errors tend to fall into one of three types. First, words that involve harmonically neutral vowels, such as "e" and "i" occasionally cause errors in vowel harmony. Second, all three systems have difficulty identifying syllable and compound boundaries, and make errors predicting vowels near boundaries. Finally, consonant gradation, which alternates consonants in open and closed syllables, causes a relatively large number of errors; for example, our system predicts **heltempien*, instead of the correct *hellempien* as the genitive singular of the comparative adjective *hellempi* "more affectionate".

## 6 Conclusion

We have proposed an alternative method of generating inflected word-forms which is based on discriminative string transduction and reranking. We have conducted a series of experiments on nine datasets involving six languages, including four new datasets that we created. The results demonstrate that our method is not only highly accurate, but also robust against incomplete or limited inflection data. In the future, we would like to apply our method to non-European languages, with different morphological systems. We also plan to investigate methods of extracting morphological tags from a corpus, including differentiating syncretic forms in context.

## Acknowledgments

We thank Mans Hulden and Aki-Juhani Kyröläinen for their assistance in analyzing Finnish errors..

This research was supported by the Natural Sciences and Engineering Research Council of Canada, and the Alberta Innovates Technology Futures.

## References

Malin Ahlberg, Markus Forsberg, and Mans Hulden. 2014. Semi-supervised learning of morphological paradigms and lexicons. In *Proceedings of the 14th Conference of the European Chapter of the Association for Computational Linguistics*, pages 569–578, Gothenburg, Sweden, April. Association for Computational Linguistics.

Harald R. Baayen, Richard Piepenbrock, and Leon Gulikers. 1995. *The CELEX Lexical Database. Release 2 (CD-ROM)*. Linguistic Data Consortium, University of Pennsylvania, Philadelphia, Pennsylvania.

Alena Böhmová, Jan Hajič, Eva Hajičová, and Barbora Hladká. 2003. The Prague dependency treebank. In *Treebanks*, pages 103–127. Springer.

Ann Clifton and Anoop Sarkar. 2011. Combining morpheme-based machine translation with post-processing morpheme prediction. In *Proceedings of the 49th Annual Meeting of the Association for Computational Linguistics: Human Language Technologies-Volume 1*, pages 32–42. Association for Computational Linguistics.

Markus Dreyer and Jason Eisner. 2011. Discovering morphological paradigms from plain text using a dirichlet process mixture model. In *Proceedings of the Conference on Empirical Methods in Natural Language Processing*, pages 616–627. Association for Computational Linguistics.

Greg Durrett and John DeNero. 2013. Supervised learning of complete morphological paradigms. In *Proceedings of NAACL-HLT*, pages 1185–1195.

Rong-En Fan, Kai-Wei Chang, Cho-Jui Hsieh, Xiang-Rui Wang, and Chih-Jen Lin. 2008. LIBLINEAR: A library for large linear classification. *The Journal of Machine Learning Research*, 9:1871–1874.

Alexander Fraser, Marion Weller, Aoife Cahill, and Fabienne Cap. 2012. Modeling inflection and word-formation in SMT. In *Proceedings of the 13th Conference of the European Chapter of the Association for Computational Linguistics*, pages 664–674. Association for Computational Linguistics.

Sittichai Jiampojamarn, Grzegorz Kondrak, and Tarek Sherif. 2007. Applying many-to-many alignments and hidden markov models to letter-to-phoneme conversion. In *Human Language Technologies 2007: The Conference of the North American Chapter of the Association for Computational Linguistics; Proceedings of the Main Conference*, pages 372–379, Rochester, New York, April. Association for Computational Linguistics.

Sittichai Jiampojamarn, Colin Cherry, and Grzegorz Kondrak. 2010. Integrating joint n-gram features into a discriminative training framework. In *Proceedings of NAACL-2010*, Los Angeles, CA, June. Association for Computational Linguistics.

Thorsten Joachims. 2002. Optimizing search engines using clickthrough data. In *Proceedings of the eighth ACM SIGKDD international conference on Knowledge discovery and data mining*, pages 133–142. ACM.

Ryan McDonald, Koby Crammer, and Fernando Pereira. 2005. Online large-margin training of dependency parsers. In *Proceedings of the Annual Meeting of the Association for Computational Linguistics*.

Kristina Toutanova and Colin Cherry. 2009. A global model for joint lemmatization and part-of-speech prediction. In *Proceedings of the Joint Conference of the 47th Annual Meeting of the ACL and the 4th International Joint Conference on Natural Language Processing of the AFNLP: Volume 1-Volume 1*, pages 486–494. Association for Computational Linguistics.

Richard Zens and Hermann Ney. 2004. Improvements in phrase-based statistical machine translation. In *HLT-NAACL 2004: Main Proceedings*, pages 257–264, Boston, USA, May.

# Penalized Expectation Propagation for Graphical Models over Strings*

**Ryan Cotterell** and **Jason Eisner**
Department of Computer Science, Johns Hopkins University
{ryan.cotterell,jason}@cs.jhu.edu

## Abstract

We present penalized expectation propagation (PEP), a novel algorithm for approximate inference in graphical models. Expectation propagation is a variant of loopy belief propagation that keeps messages tractable by projecting them back into a given family of functions. Our extension, PEP, uses a structured-sparsity penalty to encourage simple messages, thus balancing speed and accuracy. We specifically show how to instantiate PEP in the case of string-valued random variables, where we adaptively approximate finite-state distributions by variable-order $n$-gram models. On phonological inference problems, we obtain substantial speedup over previous related algorithms with no significant loss in accuracy.

## 1 Introduction

Graphical models are well-suited to reasoning about linguistic structure in the presence of uncertainty. Such models typically use discrete random variables, where each variable ranges over a finite set of values such as words or tags. But a variable can also be allowed to range over an *infinite* space of discrete *structures*—in particular, the set of all strings, a case first explored by Bouchard-Côté et al. (2007).

This setting arises because human languages make use of many word forms. These strings are systematically related in their spellings due to linguistic processes such as morphology, phonology, abbreviation, copying error and historical change. To analyze or predict novel strings, we can model the joint distribution of many related strings at once. Under a graphical model, the joint probability of an assignment tuple is modeled as a product of potentials on sub-tuples, each of which is usually modeled in turn by a weighted finite-state machine.

In general, we wish to infer the values of unknown strings in the graphical model. Deterministic approaches to this problem have focused on belief propagation (BP), a message-passing algorithm that is exact on acyclic graphical models and approximate on cyclic ("loopy") ones (Murphy et al., 1999). But in both cases, further heuristic approximations of the BP messages are generally used for speed.

In this paper, we develop a more principled and flexible way to approximate the messages, using variable-order $n$-gram models.

We first develop a version of expectation propagation (EP) for string-valued variables. EP offers a principled way to approximate BP messages by distributions from a *fixed* family—e.g., by trigram models. Each message update is found by minimizing a certain KL-divergence (Minka, 2001a).

Second, we generalize to variable-order models. To do this, we augment EP's minimization problem with a novel penalty term that keeps the number of $n$-grams finite. In general, we advocate penalizing more "complex" messages (in our setting, large finite-state acceptors). Complex messages are slower to construct, and slower to use in later steps.

Our penalty term is formally similar to regularizers that encourage structured sparsity (Bach et al., 2011; Martins et al., 2011). Like a regularizer, it lets us use a more expressive family of distributions, secure in the knowledge that we will use only as many of the parameters as we really need for a "pretty good" fit. But *why* avoid using more parameters? Regularization seeks better *generalization* by not overfitting the model to the data. By contrast, we already have a model and are merely doing inference. We seek better *runtime* by not over-fussing about capturing the model's marginal distributions.

Our "penalized EP" (PEP) inference strategy is applicable to any graphical model with complex messages. In this paper, we focus on strings, and show how PEP speeds up inference on the computational phonology model of Cotterell et al. (2015).

We provide further details, tutorial material, and results in the appendices (supplementary material).

*This material is based upon work supported by the National Science Foundation under Grant No. 1423276, and by a Fulbright Research Scholarship to the first author.



*Human Language Technologies: The 2015 Annual Conference of the North American Chapter of the ACL*, pages 932–942,
Denver, Colorado, May 31 – June 5, 2015. 

## 2 Background

Graphical models over strings are in fairly broad use. Linear-chain graphical models are equivalent to cascades of finite-state transducers, which have long been used to model stepwise derivational processes such as speech production (Pereira and Riley, 1997) and transliteration (Knight and Graehl, 1998). Tree-shaped graphical models have been used to model the evolution and speciation of word forms, in order to reconstruct ancient languages (Bouchard-Côté et al., 2007; Bouchard-Côté et al., 2008) and discover cognates in related languages (Hall and Klein, 2010; Hall and Klein, 2011). Cyclic graphical models have been used to model morphological paradigms (Dreyer and Eisner, 2009; Dreyer and Eisner, 2011) and to reconstruct phonological underlying forms (Cotterell et al., 2015). All of these graphical models, except Dreyer's, happen to be *directed* ones. And all of these papers, except Bouchard-Côté's, use *deterministic* inference methods—based on BP.

### 2.1 Graphical models over strings

A directed or undirected graphical model describes a joint probability distribution over a set of random variables. To perform inference *given* a setting of the model parameters *and* observations of some variables, it is convenient to construct a *factor graph* (Kschischang et al., 2001). A factor graph is a finite bipartite graph whose vertices are the random variables $\{V_1, V_2, \ldots\}$ and the factors $\{F_1, F_2, \ldots\}$. Each factor $F$ is a function of the variables that it is connected to; it returns a non-negative real number that depends on the values of those variables. We define our factor graph so that the posterior probability $p(V_1 = v_1, V_2 = v_2, \ldots \mid \text{observations})$, as defined by the original graphical model, can be computed as proportional to the product of the numbers returned by all the factors when $V_1 = v_1, V_2 = v_2, \ldots$.

In a graphical model *over strings*, each random variable $V$ is permitted to range over the strings $\Sigma^*$ where $\Sigma$ is a fixed alphabet. As in previous work, we will assume that each factor $F$ connected to $d$ variables is a $d$-way rational relation, i.e., a function that can be computed by a $d$-tape weighted finite-state acceptor (Elgot and Mezei, 1965; Mohri et al., 2002; Kempe et al., 2004). The weights fall in the semiring $(\mathbb{R}, +, \times)$: $F$'s return value is the *total* weight of all paths that accept the $d$-tuple of strings, where a path's weight is the *product* of its arcs' weights. So our model marginalizes over possible paths in $F$.

### 2.2 Inference by (loopy) belief propagation

Inference seeks the posterior marginal probabilities $p(V_i = v \mid \text{observations})$, for each $i$. BP is an iterative procedure whose "normalized beliefs" converge to exactly these marginals if the factor graph is acyclic (Pearl, 1988). In the cyclic case, the normalized beliefs still typically converge and can be used as approximate marginals (Murphy et al., 1999).

A full presentation of BP for graphical models over strings can be found in Dreyer and Eisner (2009). We largely follow their notation. $\mathcal{N}(X)$ represents the set of neighbors of $X$ in the factor graph.

For each edge in the factor graph, between a factor $F$ and a variable $V$, BP maintains two *messages*, $\mu_{V \to F}$ and $\mu_{F \to V}$. Each of these is a function over the possible values $v$ of variable $V$, mapping each $v$ to a non-negative score. BP also maintains another such function, the *belief* $b_V$, for each variable $V$.

In general, each message or belief should be regarded as giving only *relative* scores for the different $v$. Rescaling it by a positive constant would only result in rescaling other messages and beliefs, which would not change the final normalized beliefs. The *normalized belief* is the probability distribution $\hat{b}_V$ such that each $\hat{b}_V(v)$ is proportional to $b_V(v)$.

The basic BP algorithm is just to repeatedly select and update a function until convergence. The rules for updating $\mu_{V \to F}$, $\mu_{F \to V}$, and $b_V$, given the set of "neighboring" messages in each case, can be found as equations (2)–(4) of Dreyer and Eisner (2009). (We will give the EP variants in section 4.)

Importantly, that paper shows that for graphical models over strings, each BP update can be implemented via standard finite-state operations of composition, projection, and intersection. Each message or belief is represented as a weighted finite-state acceptor (WFSA) that scores all strings $v \in \Sigma^*$.

### 2.3 The need for approximation

BP is generally only used directly for short cascades of finite-state transducers (Pereira and Riley, 1997; Knight and Graehl, 1998). Alas, in other graphical models over strings, the BP messages—which are acceptors—become too large to be practical.

In cyclic factor graphs, where exact inference for strings can be *undecidable*, the WFSAs can become *unboundedly* large as they are iteratively updated around a cycle (Dreyer and Eisner, 2009). Even in an acyclic graph (where BP is exact), the finite-state operations quickly lead to large WFSAs. Each intersection or composition is a Cartesian product construction, whose output's size (number of automaton states) may be as large as the *product* of its inputs' sizes. Combining many of these operations leads to exponential blowup.

## 3 Variational Approximation of WFSAs

To address this difficulty through EP (section 4), we will need the ability to approximate any probability distribution $p$ that is given by a WFSA, by choosing a "simple" distribution from a family $\mathcal{Q}$.

Take $\mathcal{Q}$ to be a family of log-linear distributions

$$q_{\boldsymbol{\theta}}(v) \stackrel{\text{def}}{=} \exp(\boldsymbol{\theta} \cdot \boldsymbol{f}(v)) \,/\, Z_{\boldsymbol{\theta}} \qquad (\forall v \in \Sigma^*) \tag{1}$$

where $\boldsymbol{\theta}$ is a weight vector, $\boldsymbol{f}(v)$ is a feature vector that describes $v$, and $Z_{\boldsymbol{\theta}} \stackrel{\text{def}}{=} \sum_{v \in \Sigma^*} \exp(\boldsymbol{\theta} \cdot \boldsymbol{f}(v))$ so that $\sum_v q_{\boldsymbol{\theta}}(v) = 1$. Notice that the featurization function $\boldsymbol{f}$ specifies the family $\mathcal{Q}$, while the variational parameters $\boldsymbol{\theta}$ specify a particular $q \in \mathcal{Q}$.[1]

We project $p$ into $\mathcal{Q}$ via inclusive KL divergence:

$$\boldsymbol{\theta} = \operatorname{argmin}_{\boldsymbol{\theta}} \mathrm{D}(p \,||\, q_{\boldsymbol{\theta}}) \tag{2}$$

Now $q_{\boldsymbol{\theta}}$ approximates $p$, and has support everywhere that $p$ does. We can get finer-grained approximations by expanding $\boldsymbol{f}$ to extract more features: however, $\boldsymbol{\theta}$ is then larger to store and slower to find.

### 3.1 Finding $\boldsymbol{\theta}$

Solving (2) reduces to maximizing $-H(p, q_{\boldsymbol{\theta}}) = \mathbb{E}_{v \sim p}[\log q_{\boldsymbol{\theta}}(v)]$, the log-likelihood of $q_{\boldsymbol{\theta}}$ on an "infinite sample" from $p$. This is similar to fitting a log-linear model to data (without any regularization: we want $q_{\boldsymbol{\theta}}$ to fit $p$ as well as possible). This objective is concave and can be maximized by following its gradient $\mathbb{E}_{v \sim p}[\boldsymbol{f}(v)] - \mathbb{E}_{v \sim q_{\boldsymbol{\theta}}}[\boldsymbol{f}(v)]$. Often it is also possible to optimize $\boldsymbol{\theta}$ in closed form, as we will see later. Either way, the optimal $q_{\boldsymbol{\theta}}$ matches $p$'s *expected* feature vector: $\mathbb{E}_{v \sim q_{\boldsymbol{\theta}}}[\boldsymbol{f}(v)] = \mathbb{E}_{v \sim p}[\boldsymbol{f}(v)]$. This inspired the name "expectation propagation."

### 3.2 Working with $\boldsymbol{\theta}$

Although $p$ is defined by an arbitrary WFSA, we can represent $q_{\boldsymbol{\theta}}$ quite simply by just storing the parameter vector $\boldsymbol{\theta}$. We will later take sums of such vectors to construct product distributions: observe that under (1), $q_{\boldsymbol{\theta}_1 + \boldsymbol{\theta}_2}(v)$ is proportional to $q_{\boldsymbol{\theta}_1}(v) \cdot q_{\boldsymbol{\theta}_2}(v)$.

We will also need to construct WFSA versions of these distributions $q_{\boldsymbol{\theta}} \in \mathcal{Q}$, and of other log-linear functions (messages) that may not be normalizable into distributions. Let ENCODE($\boldsymbol{\theta}$) denote a WFSA that accepts each $v \in \Sigma^*$ with weight $\exp(\boldsymbol{\theta} \cdot \boldsymbol{f}(v))$.

### 3.3 Substring features

To obtain our family $\mathcal{Q}$, we must design $\boldsymbol{f}$. Our strategy is to choose a set of "interesting" substrings $\mathcal{W}$. For each $w \in \mathcal{W}$, define a feature function "How many times does $w$ appear as a substring of $v$?" Thus, $\boldsymbol{f}(v)$ is simply a vector of counts (non-negative integers), indexed by the substrings in $\mathcal{W}$.

A natural choice of $\mathcal{W}$ is the set of all $n$-grams for fixed $n$. In this case, $\mathcal{Q}$ turns out to be equivalent to the family of $n$-gram language models.[2] Already in previous work ("variational decoding"), we used (2) with this family to approximate WFSAs or weighted hypergraphs that arose at runtime (Li et al., 2009).

Yet a fixed $n$ is not ideal. If $\mathcal{W}$ is the set of bigrams, one might do well to add the trigram `the`—perhaps because `the` is "really" a bigram (counting the digraph `th` as a single consonant), or because the bigram model fails to capture how common `the` is under $p$. Adding `the` to $\mathcal{W}$ ensures that $q_{\boldsymbol{\theta}}$ will now match $p$'s expected count for this trigram. Doing this should not require adding all $|\Sigma|^3$ trigrams.

By including strings of mixed lengths in $\mathcal{W}$ we get *variable-order* Markov models (Ron et al., 1996).

### 3.4 Arbitrary FSA-based features

More generally, let $\mathcal{A}$ be any *unambiguous and complete* finite-state acceptor: that is, any $v \in \Sigma^*$ has exactly one accepting path in $\mathcal{A}$. For each arc or final state $a$ in $\mathcal{A}$, we can define a feature function "How

[1] To be precise, we take $\mathcal{Q} = \{q_{\boldsymbol{\theta}} : Z_{\boldsymbol{\theta}} \text{ is finite}\}$. For example, $\boldsymbol{\theta} = \mathbf{0}$ is excluded because then $Z_{\boldsymbol{\theta}} = \sum_{v \in \Sigma^*} \exp 0 = \infty$. Aside from this restriction, $\boldsymbol{\theta}$ may be any vector over $\mathbb{R} \cup \{-\infty\}$. We allow $-\infty$ since it is a feature's optimal weight if $p(v) = 0$ for all $v$ with that feature: then $q_{\boldsymbol{\theta}}(v) = 0$ for such strings as well. (Provided that $\boldsymbol{f}(v) \geq \mathbf{0}$, as we will ensure.)

[2] Provided that we include special $n$-grams that match at the boundaries of $v$. See Appendix B.2 for details.

many times is $a$ used when $\mathcal{A}$ accepts $v$?" Thus, $\boldsymbol{f}(v)$ is again a vector of non-negative counts.

Section 6 gives algorithms for this general setting. We implement the previous section as a special case, constructing $\mathcal{A}$ so that its arcs essentially correspond to the substrings in $\mathcal{W}$. This encodes a variable-order Markov model as an FSA similarly to (Allauzen et al., 2003); see Appendix B.4 for details.

In this general setting, ENCODE($\boldsymbol{\theta}$) just returns a *weighted* version of $\mathcal{A}$ where each arc or final state $a$ has weight $\exp \theta_a$ in the $(+, \times)$ semiring. Thus, this WFSA accepts each $v$ with weight $\exp(\boldsymbol{\theta} \cdot \boldsymbol{f}(v))$.

### 3.5 Adaptive featurization

How do we choose $\mathcal{W}$ (or $\mathcal{A}$)? Expanding $\mathcal{W}$ will allow better approximations to $p$—but at greater computational cost. We would like $\mathcal{W}$ to include just the substrings needed to approximate a *given* $p$ well. For instance, if $p$ is concentrated on a few high-probability strings, then a good $\mathcal{W}$ might contain those full strings (with positive weights), plus some shorter substrings that help model the rest of $p$.

To select $\mathcal{W}$ at runtime in a way that adapts to $p$, let us say that $\boldsymbol{\theta}$ is actually an infinite vector with weights for *all possible* substrings, and define $\mathcal{W} = \{w \in \Sigma^* : \theta_w \neq 0\}$. Provided that $\mathcal{W}$ stays finite, we can store $\boldsymbol{\theta}$ as a map from substrings to *nonzero* weights. We keep $\mathcal{W}$ small by replacing (2) with

$$\boldsymbol{\theta} = \operatorname{argmin}_{\boldsymbol{\theta}} \mathrm{D}(p \mid\mid q_{\boldsymbol{\theta}}) + \lambda \cdot \Omega(\boldsymbol{\theta}) \quad (3)$$

where $\Omega(\boldsymbol{\theta})$ measures the complexity of this $\mathcal{W}$ or the corresponding $\mathcal{A}$. Small WFSAs ensure fast finite-state operations, so ideally, $\Omega(\boldsymbol{\theta})$ should measure the size of ENCODE($\boldsymbol{\theta}$). Choosing $\lambda > 0$ to be large will then emphasize speed over accuracy.

Section 6.1 will extend section 6's algorithms to approximately minimize the new objective (3). Formally this objective resembles regularized log-likelihood. However, $\Omega(\boldsymbol{\theta})$ is not a regularizer—as section 1 noted, we have no statistical reason to avoid "overfitting" $\hat{p}$, only a computational one.

## 4 Expectation Propagation

Recall from section 2.2 that for each variable $V$, the BP algorithm maintains several nonnegative functions that score $V$'s possible values $v$: the messages $\mu_{V \to F}$ and $\mu_{F \to V}$ ($\forall F \in \mathcal{N}(V)$), and the belief $b_V$.

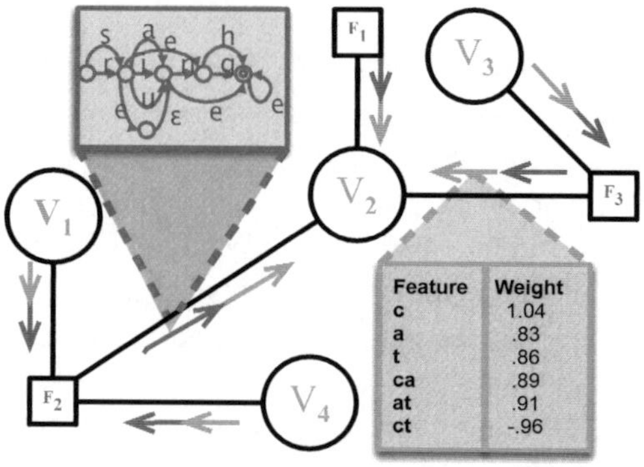


Figure 1: Information flowing toward $V_2$ in EP (reverse flow not shown). The factors work with purple $\mu$ messages represented by WFSAs, while the variables work with green $\boldsymbol{\theta}$ messages represented by log-linear weight vectors. The green table shows a $\boldsymbol{\theta}$ message: a sparse weight vector that puts high weight on the string `cat`.

EP is a variant in which all of these are forced to be log-linear functions from the same family, namely $\exp(\boldsymbol{\theta} \cdot \boldsymbol{f}_V(v))$. Here $\boldsymbol{f}_V$ is the featurization function we've chosen for variable $V$.[3] We can represent these functions by their parameter vectors—let us call those $\boldsymbol{\theta}_{V \to F}$, $\boldsymbol{\theta}_{F \to V}$, and $\boldsymbol{\theta}_V$ respectively.

### 4.1 Passing messages through variables

What happens to BP's update equations in this setting? According to BP, the belief $b_V$ is the pointwise product of all "incoming" messages to $V$. But as we saw in section 3.2, pointwise products are *far easier* in EP's restricted setting! Instead of intersecting several WFSAs, we can simply add several vectors:

$$\boldsymbol{\theta}_V = \sum_{F' \in \mathcal{N}(V)} \boldsymbol{\theta}_{F' \to V} \quad (4)$$

Similarly, the "outgoing" message from $V$ to factor $F$ is the pointwise product of all "incoming" messages *except* the one from $F$. This message $\boldsymbol{\theta}_{V \to F}$ can be computed as $\boldsymbol{\theta}_V - \boldsymbol{\theta}_{F \to V}$, which adjusts (4).[4] We never store this but just compute it on demand.

[3] A single graphical model might mix categorical variables, continuous variables, orthographic strings over (say) the Roman alphabet, and phonological strings over the International Phonetic Alphabet. These different data types certainly require different featurization functions. Moreover, even when two variables have the same type, we could choose to approximate their marginals differently, e.g., with bigram vs. trigram features.

[4] If features can have $-\infty$ weight (footnote 1), this trick might need to subtract $-\infty$ from $-\infty$ (the log-space version of $0/0$). That gives an undefined result, but it turns out that any result will do—it makes no difference to the subsequent beliefs.

### 4.2 Passing messages through factors

Our factors are weighted finite-state machines, so their messages still require finite-state computations, as shown by the purple material in Figure 1. These computations are just as in BP. Concretely, let $F$ be a factor of degree $d$, given as a $d$-tape machine. We can compute a belief *at this factor* by joining $F$ with $d$ WFSAs that represent its $d$ incoming messages, namely $\text{ENCODE}(\boldsymbol{\theta}_{V' \to F})$ for $V' \in \mathcal{N}(F)$. This gives a new $d$-tape machine, $b_F$. We then obtain each outgoing message $\mu_{F \to V}$ by projecting $b_F$ onto its $V$ tape, but removing (dividing out) the weights that were contributed (multiplied in) by $\boldsymbol{\theta}_{V \to F}$.[5]

### 4.3 Getting from factors back to variables

Finally, we reach the only tricky step. Each resulting $\mu_{F \to V}$ is a possibly large WFSA, so we must *force it back into our log-linear family* to get an updated approximation $\boldsymbol{\theta}_{F \to V}$. One cannot directly employ the methods of section 3, because KL divergence is only defined between probability distributions. ($\mu_{F \to V}$ might not be normalizable into a distribution, nor is its best approximation necessarily normalizable.)

The EP trick is to use section 3 to instead approximate the belief at $V$, which *is* a distribution, and *then* reconstruct the approximate message to $V$ that would have produced this approximated belief. The "unapproximated belief" $\hat{p}_V$ resembles (4): it multiplies the unapproximated message $\mu_{F \to V}$ by the current values of all *other* messages $\boldsymbol{\theta}_{F' \to V}$. We know the product of those *other* messages, $\boldsymbol{\theta}_{V \to F}$, so

$$\hat{p}_V := \mu_{F \to V} \odot \mu_{V \to F} \tag{5}$$

where the pointwise product $\odot$ is carried out by WFSA intersection and $\mu_{V \to F} \stackrel{\text{def}}{=} \text{ENCODE}(\boldsymbol{\theta}_{V \to F})$.

We now apply section 3 to choose $\boldsymbol{\theta}_V$ such that $q_{\boldsymbol{\theta}_V}$ is a good approximation of the WFSA $\hat{p}_V$. Finally, to preserve (4) as an invariant, we reconstruct

$$\boldsymbol{\theta}_{F \to V} := \boldsymbol{\theta}_V - \boldsymbol{\theta}_{V \to F} \tag{6}$$

In short, EP combines $\mu_{F \to V}$ with $\boldsymbol{\theta}_{V \to F}$, then approximates the result $\hat{p}_V$ by $\boldsymbol{\theta}_V$ before removing $\boldsymbol{\theta}_{V \to F}$ again. Thus EP is approximating $\mu_{F \to V}$ by

$$\boldsymbol{\theta}_{F \to V} := \underset{\boldsymbol{\theta}}{\operatorname{argmin}} \, \mathrm{D}(\underbrace{\mu_{F \to V} \odot \mu_{V \to F}}_{=\hat{p}_V} \,||\, \underbrace{q_{\boldsymbol{\theta}} \odot \mu_{V \to F}}_{=\boldsymbol{\theta}_V}) \tag{7}$$

in a way that updates not only $\boldsymbol{\theta}_{F \to V}$ but also $\boldsymbol{\theta}_V$.

Wisely, this objective focuses on approximating the message's scores for the *plausible* values $v$. Some values $v$ may have $\hat{p}_V(v) \approx 0$, perhaps because *another* incoming message $\boldsymbol{\theta}_{F' \to V}$ rules them out. It does not much harm the objective (7) if these $\mu_{F \to V}(v)$ are poorly approximated by $q_{\boldsymbol{\theta}_{F \to V}}(v)$, since the overall belief is still roughly correct.

Our *penalized* EP simply adds $\lambda \cdot \Omega(\boldsymbol{\theta})$ into (7).

### 4.4 The EP algorithm: Putting it all together

To run EP (or PEP), initialize all $\boldsymbol{\theta}_V$ and $\boldsymbol{\theta}_{F \to V}$ to $\mathbf{0}$, and then loop repeatedly over the nodes of the factor graph. When visiting a factor $F$, ENCODE its incoming messages $\boldsymbol{\theta}_{V \to F}$ (computed on demand) as WFSAs, construct a belief $b_F$, and update the outgoing WFSA messages $\mu_{F \to V}$. When visiting a variable $V$, iterate $K \geq 1$ times over its incoming WFSA messages: for each incoming $\mu_{F \to V}$, compute the unapproximated belief $\hat{p}_V$ via (5), then update $\boldsymbol{\theta}_V$ to approximate $\hat{p}_V$, then update $\boldsymbol{\theta}_{F \to V}$ via (6).

For possibly faster convergence, one can alternate "forward" and "backward" sweeps. Visit the factor graph's nodes in a fixed order (given by an approximate topological sort). At a factor, update the outgoing WFSA messages to *later* variables only. At a variable, approximate only those incoming WFSA messages from *earlier* factors (all the outgoing messages $\boldsymbol{\theta}_{V \to F}$ will be recomputed on demand). Note that both cases examine all incoming messages. After each sweep, reverse the node ordering and repeat.

If gradient ascent is used to find the $\boldsymbol{\theta}_V$ that approximates $\hat{p}_V$, it is wasteful to optimize to convergence. After all, the optimization problem will keep changing as the messages change. Our implementation improves $\boldsymbol{\theta}_V$ by only a single gradient step on each visit to $V$, since $V$ will be visited repeatedly.

See Appendix A for an alternative view of EP.

## 5 Related Approximation Methods

We have presented EP as a method for simplifying a variable's incoming messages during BP. The vari-

[5] This is equivalent to computing each $\mu_{F \to V}$ by "generalized composition" of $F$ with the $d-1$ messages to $F$ from its *other* neighbors $V'$. The operations of join and generalized composition were defined by Kempe et al. (2004).

In the simple case $d = 2$, $F$ is just a weighted finite-state transducer mapping $V'$ to $V$, and computing $\mu_{F \to V}$ reduces to composing $\text{ENCODE}(\boldsymbol{\theta}_{V' \to F})$ with $F$ and projecting the result onto the output tape. In fact, one can assume WLOG that $d \leq 2$, enabling the use of popular finite-state toolkits that handle at most 2-tape machines. See Appendix B.10 for the construction.

able's outgoing messages are pointwise products of the incoming ones, so they become simple too. Past work has used approximations with a similar flavor.

Hall and Klein (2011) heuristically predetermine a short, fixed list of plausible values for $V$ that were observed elsewhere in their dataset. This list is analogous to our $\boldsymbol{\theta}_V$. After updating $\mu_{F\to V}$, they force $\mu_{F\to V}(v)$ to 0 for all $v$ outside the list, yielding a *finite* message that is analogous to our $\boldsymbol{\theta}_{F\to V}$.

Our own past papers are similar, except they *adaptively* set the "plausible values" list to $\bigcup_{F'\in\mathcal{N}(V)} k\text{-BEST}(\mu_{F'\to V})$. These strings are favored by at least one of the *current* messages to $V$ (Dreyer and Eisner, 2009; Dreyer and Eisner, 2011; Cotterell et al., 2015). Thus, simplifying one of $V$'s incoming messages considers all of them, as in EP.

The above methods *prune* each message, so may prune correct values. Hall and Klein (2010) avoid this: they fit a full bigram model by inclusive KL divergence, which refuses to prune *any* values (see section 3). Specifically, they minimized $\mathrm{D}(\mu_{F\to V}\odot\tau \,||\, q_{\boldsymbol{\theta}}\odot\tau)$, where $\tau$ was a simple fixed function (a 0-gram model) included so that they were working with distributions (see section 4.3). This is very similar to our (7). Indeed, Hall and Klein (2010) found their procedure "reminiscent of EP," hinting that $\tau$ was a surrogate for a real $\mu_{V\to F}$ term. Dreyer and Eisner (2009) had also suggested EP as future work.

EP has been applied only twice before in the NLP community. Daumé III and Marcu (2006) used EP for query summarization (following Minka and Lafferty (2003)'s application to an LDA model with fixed topics) and Hall and Klein (2012) used EP for rich parsing. However, these papers inferred a single structured variable connected to all factors (as in the traditional presentation of EP—see Appendix A), rather than inferring many structured variables connected in a sparse graphical model.

We regard EP as a generalization of loopy BP for just this setting: graphical models with large or unbounded variable domains. Of course, we are not the first to use such a scheme; e.g., Qi (2005, chapter 2) applies EP to linear-chain models with both continuous and discrete hidden states. We believe that EP should also be broadly useful in NLP, since it naturally handles joint distributions over the kinds of structured variables that arise in NLP.

## 6 Two Methods for Optimizing $\boldsymbol{\theta}$

We now fill in details. If the feature set is defined by an unambiguous FSA $\mathcal{A}$ (section 3.4), two methods exist to max $\mathbb{E}_{v\sim p}[\log q_{\boldsymbol{\theta}}(v)]$ as section 3.1 requires.

**Closed-form.** Determine how often $\mathcal{A}$ would traverse each of its arcs, in expectation, when reading a random string drawn from $p$. We would obtain an optimal $\text{ENCODE}(\boldsymbol{\theta})$ by, at each state of $\mathcal{A}$, setting the weights of the arcs from that state to be proportional to these counts while summing to 1.[6] Thus, the logs of these arc weights give an optimal $\boldsymbol{\theta}$.

For example, in a trigram model, the probability of the `c` arc from the `ab` state is the expected count of `abc` (according to $p$) divided by the expected count of `ab`. Such expected substring counts can be found by the method of Allauzen et al. (2003). For general $\mathcal{A}$, we can use the method sketched by Li et al. (2009, footnote 9): intersect the WFSA for $p$ with the unweighted FSA $\mathcal{A}$, and then run the forward-backward algorithm to determine the posterior count of each arc in the result. This tells us the expected total number of traversals of each arc in $\mathcal{A}$, if we have kept track of which arcs in the intersection of $p$ with $\mathcal{A}$ were derived from which arcs in $\mathcal{A}$. That bookkeeping can be handled with an expectation semiring (Eisner, 2002), or simply with backpointers.

**Gradient ascent.** For any given $\boldsymbol{\theta}$, we can use the WFSAs $p$ and $\text{ENCODE}(\boldsymbol{\theta})$ to exactly compute $\mathbb{E}_{v\sim p}[\log q_{\boldsymbol{\theta}}(v)] = -H(p, q_{\boldsymbol{\theta}})$ (Cortes et al., 2006). We can tune $\boldsymbol{\theta}$ to globally maximize this objective.

The technique is to intersect $p$ with $\text{ENCODE}(\boldsymbol{\theta})$, after lifting their weights into the expectation semiring via the mappings $k \mapsto \langle k, 0\rangle$ and $k \mapsto \langle 0, \log k\rangle$ respectively. Summing over all paths of this intersection via the forward algorithm yields $\langle Z, r\rangle$ where $Z$ is the normalizing constant for $p$. We also sum over paths of $\text{ENCODE}(\boldsymbol{\theta})$ to get the normalizing constant $Z_{\boldsymbol{\theta}}$. Now the desired objective is $r/Z - \log Z_{\boldsymbol{\theta}}$. Its *gradient* with respect to $\boldsymbol{\theta}$ can be found by back-propagation, or equivalently by the forward-backward algorithm (Li and Eisner, 2009).

An overlarge gradient step can leave the feasible space (footnote 1) by driving $Z_{\boldsymbol{\theta}_V}$ to $\infty$ and thus driving (2) to $\infty$ (Dreyer, 2011, section 2.8.2). In this case, we try again with reduced stepsize.

[6] This method always yields a probabilistic FSA, i.e., the arc weights are locally normalized probabilities. This does not sacrifice any expressiveness; see Appendix B.7 for discussion.

## 6.1 Optimizing $\theta$ with a penalty

Now consider the penalized objective (3). Ideally, $\Omega(\boldsymbol{\theta})$ would count the number of nonzero weights in $\boldsymbol{\theta}$—or better, the number of arcs in ENCODE($\boldsymbol{\theta}$). But it is not known how to efficiently minimize the resulting discontinuous function. We give two approximate methods, based on the two methods above.

**Proximal gradient.** Leaning on recent advances in sparse estimation, we replace this $\Omega(\boldsymbol{\theta})$ with a convex surrogate whose partial derivative with respect to each $\theta_w$ is undefined at $\theta_w = 0$ (Bach et al., 2011). Such a penalty tends to create sparse optima.

A popular surrogate is an $\ell_1$ penalty, $\Omega(\boldsymbol{\theta}) \stackrel{\text{def}}{=} \sum_w |\boldsymbol{\theta}_w|$. However, $\ell_1$ would not recognize that $\boldsymbol{\theta}$ is simpler with the features $\{\texttt{ab}, \texttt{abc}, \texttt{abd}\}$ than with the features $\{\texttt{ab}, \texttt{pqr}, \texttt{xyz}\}$. The former leads to a smaller WFSA encoding. In other words, it is cheaper to add abd once abc is already present, as a state already exists that represents the context ab.

We would thus like the penalty to be the number of distinct *prefixes* in the set of nonzero features,

$$|\{u \in \Sigma^* : (\exists x \in \Sigma^*)\, \theta_{ux} \neq 0\}|, \qquad (8)$$

as this is the number of ordinary arcs in ENCODE($\boldsymbol{\theta}$) (see Appendix B.4). Its convex surrogate is

$$\Omega(\boldsymbol{\theta}) \stackrel{\text{def}}{=} \sum_{u \in \Sigma^*} \sqrt{\sum_{x \in \Sigma^*} \theta_{ux}^2} \qquad (9)$$

This *tree-structured group lasso* (Nelakanti et al., 2013) is an instance of group lasso (Yuan and Lin, 2006) where the string $w = \texttt{abd}$ belongs to four groups, corresponding to its prefixes $u = \epsilon, u = \texttt{a}, u = \texttt{ab}, u = \texttt{abd}$. Under group lasso, moving $\theta_w$ away from 0 increases $\Omega(\boldsymbol{\theta})$ by $\lambda|\theta_w|$ (just as in $\ell_1$) *for each group in which $w$ is the only nonzero feature*. This penalizes for the new WFSA arcs needed for these groups. There are also increases due to $w$'s other groups, but these are smaller, especially for groups with many strongly weighted features.

Our objective (3) is now the sum of a differentiable convex function (2) and a *particular* non-differentiable convex function (9). We minimize it by proximal gradient (Parikh and Boyd, 2013). At each step, this algorithm first takes a gradient step as in section 6 to improve the differentiable term, and then applies a "proximal operator" to jump to a nearby point that improves the non-differentiable term. The proximal operator for tree-structured group lasso (9) can be implemented with an efficient recursive procedure (Jenatton et al., 2011).

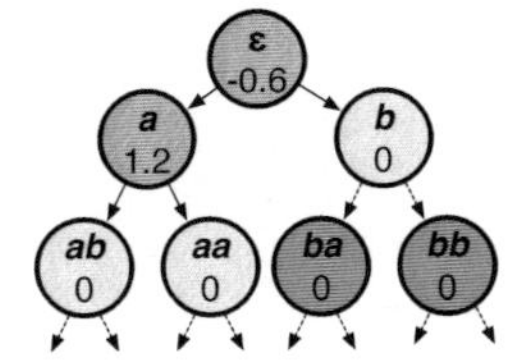


Figure 2: Active set method, showing the infinite tree of all features for the alphabet $\Sigma = \{a, b\}$. The green nodes currently have non-zero weights. The yellow nodes are on the frontier and are *allowed* to become non-zero, but the penalty function is still keeping them at 0. The red nodes are not yet considered, forcing them to remain at 0.

What if $\boldsymbol{\theta}$ is $\infty$-dimensional because we allow all $n$-grams as features? Paul and Eisner (2012) used just this feature set in a dual decomposition algorithm. Like them, we rely on an *active set* method (Schmidt and Murphy, 2010). We fix abcd's weight at 0 until abc's weight becomes nonzero (if ever);[7] only then does feature abc become "active." Thus, at a given step, we only have to compute the gradient with respect to the currently nonzero features (green nodes in Figure 2) and their immediate children (yellow nodes). This hierarchical inclusion technique ensures that we only consider a small, finite subset of all $n$-grams at any given iteration of optimization.

**Closed-form with greedy growing.** There are existing methods for estimating variable-order $n$-gram language models from data, based on either "shrinking" a high-order model (Stolcke, 1998) or "growing" a low-order one (Siivola et al., 2007).

We have designed a simple "growing" algorithm to estimate such a model from a WFSA $p$. It approximately minimizes the objective (3) where $\Omega(\boldsymbol{\theta})$ is given by (8). We enumerate all $n$-grams $w \in \Sigma^*$ in decreasing order of expected count (this can be done efficiently using a priority queue). We add $w$ to $\mathcal{W}$ if we *estimate* that it will decrease the objective. Every so often, we measure the *actual* objective (just as in the gradient-based methods), and we stop if it is no longer improving. Algorithmic details are given in Appendices B.8–B.9.

[7] Paul and Eisner (2012) also required bcd to have nonzero weight, observing that abcd is a *conjunction* abc$\wedge$bcd (McCallum, 2003). This added test would be wise for us too.

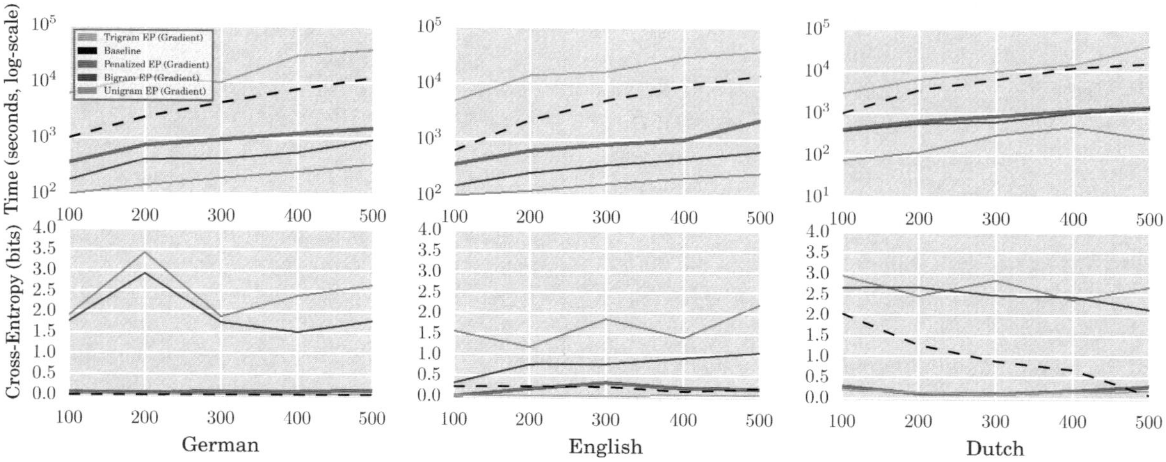


Figure 3: Inference on 15 factor graphs (3 languages $\times$ 5 datasets of different sizes). The first row shows the total runtime (logscale) of each inference method. The second row shows the accuracy, as measured by the negated log-probability that the inferred belief at a variable assigns to its gold-standard value, averaged over "underlying morpheme" variables. At this penalty level ($\lambda = 0.01$), PEP [thick line] is faster than the pruning baseline of Cotterell et al. (2015) [dashed line] and much faster than trigram EP, yet is about as accurate. (For Dutch with sparse observations, it is considerably more accurate than baseline.) Indeed, PEP is nearly as fast as bigram EP, which has terrible accuracy. An ideal implementation of PEP would be faster yet (see Appendix B.5). Further graphs are in Appendix C.

## 7 Experiments and Results

Our experimental design aims to answer three questions. (1) Is our algorithm able to beat a strong baseline (adaptive pruning) in a non-trivial model? (2) Is PEP actually better than ordinary EP, given that the structured sparsity penalty makes it more algorithmically complex? (3) Does the $\lambda$ parameter successfully trade off between speed and accuracy?

All experiments took place using the graphical model over strings for the discovery of underlying phonological forms introduced in Cotterell et al. (2015). They write: "Comparing `cats` ([kæts]), `dogs` ([dɔgz]), and `quizzes` ([kwɪzɪz]), we see the English plural morpheme evidently has at least three pronunciations." Cotterell et al. (2015) sought a unifying account of such variation in terms of phonological underlying forms for the morphemes.

In their Bayes net, morpheme underlying forms are latent variables, while word surface forms are observed variables. The factors model underlying-to-surface phonological changes. They learn the factors by Expectation Maximization (EM). Their first E step presents the hardest inference problem because the factors initially contribute no knowledge of the language; so that is the setting we test on here.

Their data are surface phonological forms from the CELEX database (Baayen et al., 1995). For each of 3 languages, we run 5 experiments, by observing the surface forms of 100 to 500 words and running EP to infer the underlying forms of their morphemes. Each of the 15 factor graphs has $\approx$ 150–700 latent variables, joined by 500–2200 edges to 200–1200 factors of degree 1–3. Variables representing suffixes can have extremely high degree ($> 100$).

We compare PEP with other approximate inference methods. As our main baseline, we take the approximation scheme actually used by Cotterell et al. (2015), which restricts the domain of a belief to that of the union of 20-best strings of its incoming messages (section 5).We also compare to unpenalized EP with unigram, bigram, and trigram features.

We report both speed and accuracy for all methods. Speed is reported in seconds. Judging accuracy is a bit trickier. The best metric would to be to measure our beliefs' distance from the true marginals or even from the beliefs computed by vanilla loopy BP. Obtaining these quantities, however, would be extremely expensive—even Gibbs sampling is infeasible in our setting, let alone 100-way WFSA intersections. Luckily, Cotterell et al. (2015) provide gold-standard values for the latent variables (underlying forms). Figure 3 shows the negated log-probabilities of these gold strings according to our beliefs, averaged over variables in a given factor graph. Our accuracy is weaker than Cotterell et al. (2015) because we are doing inference with their *initial* (untrained) parameters, a more challenging problem.

Each update to $\boldsymbol{\theta}_V$ consisted of a single step of (proximal) gradient descent: starting at the current value, improve (2) with a gradient step of size $\eta = 0.05$, then (in the adaptive case) apply the proximal operator of (9) with $\lambda = 0.01$. We chose these values by preliminary exploration, taking $\eta$ small enough to avoid backtracking (section 6.1).

We repeatedly visit variables and factors (section 4.4) in the forward-backward order used by Cotterell et al. (2015). For the first few iterations, when we visit a variable we make $K = 20$ passes over its incoming messages, updating them iteratively to ensure that the high probability strings in the initial approximations are "in the ballpark". For subsequent iterations of message passing we take $K = 1$. For similar reasons, we constrained PEP to use only unigram features on the first iteration, when there are still many viable candidates for each morph.

### 7.1 Results

The results show that PEP is much faster than the baseline pruning method, as described in Figure 3 and its caption. It mainly achieves better cross-entropy on English and Dutch, and even though it loses on German, it still places almost all of its probability mass on the gold forms. While EP with unigram and bigram approximations are both faster than PEP, their accuracy is poor. Trigram EP is nearly as accurate but even slower than the baseline. The results support the claim that PEP has achieved a "Goldilocks number" of $n$-grams in its approximation—just enough $n$-grams to approximate the message well while retaining speed.

Figure 4 shows the effect of $\lambda$ on the speed-accuracy tradeoff. To compare apples to apples, this experiment fixed the set of $\mu_{F\to V}$ messages for each variable. Thus, we held the set of beliefs fixed, but measured the size and accuracy of different approximations to these beliefs by varying $\lambda$.

These figures show only the results from gradient-based approximation. Closed-form approximation is faster and comparably accurate: see Appendix C.

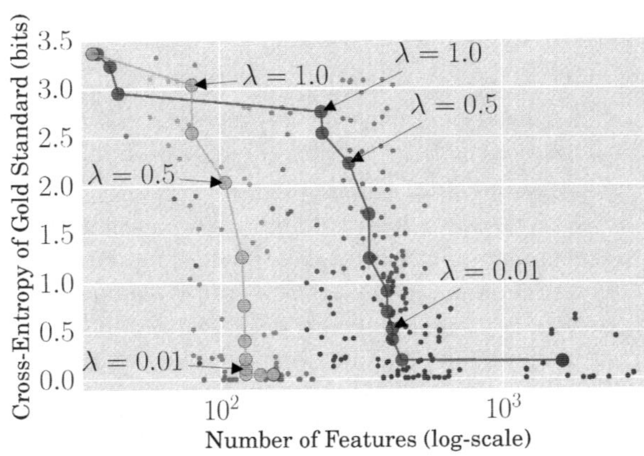


Figure 4: Increasing $\lambda$ will greatly reduce the number of selected features in a belief—initially without harming accuracy, and then accuracy degrades gracefully. (Number of features has 0.72 correlation with runtime, and is shown on a *log scale* on the $x$ axis.)

Each point shows the result of using PEP to approximate the belief at some latent variable $V$, using $\mu_{F\to V}$ messages from running the baseline method on German. Lighter points use larger $\lambda$. Orange points are affixes (shorter strings), blue are stems (longer strings). Large circles are averages over all points for a given $\lambda$.

## 8 Conclusion and Future Work

We have presented penalized expectation propagation (PEP), a novel approximate inference algorithm for graphical models, and developed specific techniques for string-valued random variables. Our method integrates structured sparsity directly into inference. Our experiments show large speedups over the strong baseline of Cotterell et al. (2015).

In future, instead of choosing $\lambda$, we plan to reduce $\lambda$ as PEP runs. This serves to gradually refine the approximations, yielding an *anytime algorithm* whose beliefs approach the BP beliefs. Thanks to (7), the coarse messages from early iterations guide the choice of finer-grained messages at later iterations. In this regard, "Anytime PEP" resembles other coarse-to-fine architectures such as generalized A* search (Felzenszwalb and McAllester, 2007).

As NLP turns its attention to lower-resource languages and social media, it is important to model the rich phonological, morphological, and orthographic processes that interrelate words. We hope that the introduction of faster inference algorithms will increase the use of graphical models over strings. We are releasing our code package (see Appendix D).

## References


Cyril Allauzen, Mehryar Mohri, and Brian Roark. 2003. Generalized algorithms for constructing statistical language models. In *Proceedings of ACL*, pages 40–47.

Cyril Allauzen, Michael Riley, Johan Schalkwyk, Wojciech Skut, and Mehryar Mohri. 2007. OpenFst: A general and efficient weighted finite-state transducer library. In *Proceedings of the 12th International Conference on Implementation and Application of Automata*, volume 4783 of *Lecture Notes in Computer Science*, pages 11–23. Springer.

R. Harald Baayen, Richard Piepenbrock, and Leon Gulikers. 1995. The CELEX lexical database on CD-ROM.

Francis Bach, Rodolphe Jenatton, Julien Mairal, Guillaume Obozinski, et al. 2011. Convex optimization with sparsity-inducing norms. In S. Sra, S. Nowozin, and S. J. Wright, editors, *Optimization for Machine Learning*. MIT Press.

Alexandre Bouchard-Côté, Percy Liang, Thomas L Griffiths, and Dan Klein. 2007. A probabilistic approach to diachronic phonology. In *Proceedings of EMNLP-CoNLL*, pages 887–896.

Alexandre Bouchard-Côté, Percy Liang, Thomas Griffiths, and Dan Klein. 2008. A probabilistic approach to language change. In *Proceedings of NIPS*.

Victor Chahuneau. 2013. PyFST. `https://github.com/vchahun/pyfst`.

Corinna Cortes, Mehryar Mohri, Ashish Rastogi, and Michael D Riley. 2006. Efficient computation of the relative entropy of probabilistic automata. In *LATIN 2006: Theoretical Informatics*, pages 323–336. Springer.

Ryan Cotterell, Nanyun Peng, and Jason Eisner. 2014. Stochastic contextual edit distance and probabilistic FSTs. In *Proceedings of ACL*, pages 625–630.

Ryan Cotterell, Nanyun Peng, and Jason Eisner. 2015. Modeling word forms using latent underlying morphs and phonology. *Transactions of the Association for Computational Linguistics*. To appear.

Hal Daumé III and Daniel Marcu. 2006. Bayesian query-focused summarization. In *Proceedings of ACL*, pages 305–312.

Markus Dreyer and Jason Eisner. 2009. Graphical models over multiple strings. In *Proceedings of EMNLP*, pages 101–110, Singapore, August.

Markus Dreyer and Jason Eisner. 2011. Discovering morphological paradigms from plain text using a Dirichlet process mixture model. In *Proceedings of EMNLP*, pages 616–627, Edinburgh, July.

Markus Dreyer. 2011. *A Non-Parametric Model for the Discovery of Inflectional Paradigms from Plain Text Using Graphical Models over Strings*. Ph.D. thesis, Johns Hopkins University, Baltimore, MD, April.

Jason Eisner. 2002. Parameter estimation for probabilistic finite-state transducers. In *Proceedings of ACL*, pages 1–8.

C.C. Elgot and J.E. Mezei. 1965. On relations defined by generalized finite automata. *IBM Journal of Research and Development*, 9(1):47–68.

Gal Elidan, Ian Mcgraw, and Daphne Koller. 2006. Residual belief propagation: Informed scheduling for asynchronous message passing. In *Proceedings of UAI*.

P. F. Felzenszwalb and D. McAllester. 2007. The generalized A* architecture. *Journal of Artificial Intelligence Research*, 29:153–190.

David Hall and Dan Klein. 2010. Finding cognate groups using phylogenies. In *Proceedings of ACL*.

David Hall and Dan Klein. 2011. Large-scale cognate recovery. In *Proceedings of EMNLP*.

David Hall and Dan Klein. 2012. Training factored PCFGs with expectation propagation. In *Proceedings of EMNLP*.

Rodolphe Jenatton, Julien Mairal, Guillaume Obozinski, and Francis Bach. 2011. Proximal methods for hierarchical sparse coding. *The Journal of Machine Learning Research*, 12:2297–2334.

André Kempe, Jean-Marc Champarnaud, and Jason Eisner. 2004. A note on join and auto-intersection of $n$-ary rational relations. In Loek Cleophas and Bruce Watson, editors, *Proceedings of the Eindhoven FASTAR Days (Computer Science Technical Report 04-40)*, pages 64–78. Department of Mathematics and Computer Science, Technische Universiteit Eindhoven, Netherlands, December.

Kevin Knight and Jonathan Graehl. 1998. Machine transliteration. *Computational Linguistics*, 24(4).

F. R. Kschischang, B. J. Frey, and H. A. Loeliger. 2001. Factor graphs and the sum-product algorithm. *IEEE Transactions on Information Theory*, 47(2):498–519, February.

Zhifei Li and Jason Eisner. 2009. First- and second-order expectation semirings with applications to minimum-risk training on translation forests. In *Proceedings of EMNLP*, pages 40–51.

Zhifei Li, Jason Eisner, and Sanjeev Khudanpur. 2009. Variational decoding for statistical machine translation. In *Proceedings of ACL*, pages 593–601.

André F. T. Martins, Noah A. Smith, Pedro M. Q. Aguiar, and Mário A. T. Figueiredo. 2011. Structured sparsity in structured prediction. In *Proceedings of EMNLP*, pages 1500–1511.

Andrew McCallum. 2003. Efficiently inducing features of conditional random fields. In *Proceedings of UAI*.

Thomas Minka and John Lafferty. 2003. Expectation-propagation for the generative aspect model. In *Proceedings of UAI*.

Thomas P Minka. 2001a. Expectation propagation for approximate Bayesian inference. In *Proceedings of UAI*, pages 362–369.

Thomas P. Minka. 2001b. *A Family of Algorithms for Approximate Bayesian Inference*. Ph.D. thesis, Massachusetts Institute of Technology, January.

Thomas Minka. 2005. Divergence measures and message passing. Technical Report MSR-TR-2005-173, Microsoft Research, January.

Mehryar Mohri, Fernando Pereira, and Michael Riley. 2002. Weighted finite-state transducers in speech recognition. *Computer Speech & Language*, 16(1):69–88.

Mehryar Mohri. 2000. Minimization algorithms for sequential transducers. *Theoretical Computer Science*, 324:177–201, March.

Mehryar Mohri. 2005. Local grammar algorithms. In Antti Arppe, Lauri Carlson, Krister Lindèn, Jussi Piitulainen, Mickael Suominen, Martti Vainio, Hanna Westerlund, and Anssi Yli-Jyrä, editors, *Inquiries into Words, Constraints, and Contexts: Festschrift in Honour of Kimmo Koskenniemi on his 60th Birthday*, chapter 9, pages 84–93. CSLI Publications, Stanford University.

Kevin P. Murphy, Yair Weiss, and Michael I. Jordan. 1999. Loopy belief propagation for approximate inference: An empirical study. In *Proceedings of UAI*, pages 467–475.

Anil Nelakanti, Cédric Archambeau, Julien Mairal, Francis Bach, Guillaume Bouchard, et al. 2013. Structured penalties for log-linear language models. In *Proceedings of EMNLP*, pages 233–243.

Neal Parikh and Stephen Boyd. 2013. Proximal algorithms. *Foundations and Trends in Optimization*, 1(3):123–231.

Michael Paul and Jason Eisner. 2012. Implicitly intersecting weighted automata using dual decomposition. In *Proceedings of NAACL-HLT*, pages 232–242, Montreal, June.

Judea Pearl. 1988. *Probabilistic Reasoning in Intelligent Systems: Networks of Plausible Inference*. Morgan Kaufmann, San Mateo, California.

Fernando C. N. Pereira and Michael Riley. 1997. Speech recognition by composition of weighted finite automata. In Emmanuel Roche and Yves Schabes, editors, *Finite-State Language Processing*. MIT Press, Cambridge, MA.

Slav Petrov, Leon Barrett, Romain Thibaux, and Dan Klein. 2006. Learning accurate, compact, and interpretable tree annotation. In *Proceedings of COLING-ACL*, pages 433–440, July.

Yuan Qi. 2005. *Extending Expectation Propagation for Graphical Models*. Ph.D. thesis, Massachusetts Institute of Technology, February.

Dana Ron, Yoram Singer, and Naftali Tishby. 1996. The power of amnesia: Learning probabilistic automata with variable memory length. *Machine Learning*, 25(2-3):117–149.

Mark W Schmidt and Kevin P Murphy. 2010. Convex structure learning in log-linear models: Beyond pairwise potentials. In *Proceedings of AISTATS*, pages 709–716.

Vesa Siivola, Teemu Hirsimäki, and Sami Virpioja. 2007. On growing and pruning Kneser-Ney smoothed $n$-gram models. *IEEE Transactions on Audio, Speech, and Language Processsing*, 15(5):1617–1624.

Andreas Stolcke. 1998. Entropy-based pruning of backoff language models. In *Proceedings of the DARPA Broadcast News Transcription and Understanding Workshop*, pages 270–274.

Ming Yuan and Yi Lin. 2006. Model selection and estimation in regression with grouped variables. *Journal of the Royal Statistical Society: Series B (Statistical Methodology)*, 68(1):49–67.

# Joint Generation of Transliterations from Multiple Representations

**Lei Yao** and **Grzegorz Kondrak**
Department of Computing Science
University of Alberta
Edmonton, AB, Canada
{lyao1,gkondrak}@ualberta.ca

## Abstract

Machine transliteration is often referred to as phonetic translation. We show that transliterations incorporate information from both spelling and pronunciation, and propose an effective model for joint transliteration generation from both representations. We further generalize this model to include transliterations from other languages, and enhance it with reranking and lexicon features. We demonstrate significant improvements in transliteration accuracy on several datasets.

## 1 Introduction

Transliteration is the conversion of a text from one script to another. When a new name like *Eyjafjallajökull* appears in the news, it needs to be promptly transliterated into dozens of languages. Computer-generated transliterations can be more accurate than those created by humans (Sherif and Kondrak, 2007). When the names in question originate from languages that use the same writing script as the target language, they are likely to be copied verbatim; however, their pronunciation may still be ambiguous. Existing transliterations and transcriptions can help in establishing the correct pronunciation (Bhargava and Kondrak, 2012).

Transliteration is often defined as *phonetic translation* (Zhang et al., 2012). In the idealized model of Knight and Graehl (1997), a bilingual expert pronounces a name in the source language, modifies the pronunciation to fit the target language phonology, and writes it down using the orthographic rules of the target script. In practice, however, it may be difficult to guess the correct pronunciation of an unfamiliar name from the spelling.

Phonetic-based models of transliteration tend to achieve suboptimal performance. Al-Onaizan and Knight (2002) report that a spelling-based model outperforms a phonetic-based model even when pronunciations are extracted from a pronunciation dictionary. This can be attributed to the importance of the source orthography in the transliteration process. For example, the initial letters of the Russian transliterations of the names *Chicano* ([tʃɪkɑno]) and *Chicago* ([ʃɪkɑgo]) are identical, but different from *Shilo* ([ʃɪlo]). The contrast is likely due to the idiosyncratic spelling of *Chicago*.

Typical transliteration systems learn direct orthographic mapping between the source and the target languages from parallel training sets of word pairs (Zhang et al., 2012). Their accuracy is limited by the fact that the training data is likely to contain names originating from different languages that have different romanization rules. For example, the Russian transliterations of *Jedi*, *Juan*, *Jenins*, *Jeltoqsan*, and *Jecheon* all differ in their initial letters. In addition, because of inconsistent correspondences between letters and phonemes in some languages, the pronunciation of a word may be difficult to derive from its orthographic form.

We believe that transliteration is not simply phonetic translation, but rather a process that combines both phonetic and orthographic information. This observation prompted the development of several hybrid approaches that take advantage of both types of information, and improvements were reported on some test corpora (Al-Onaizan and Knight, 2002; Bilac and Tanaka, 2004; Oh and Choi, 2005). These models, which we discuss in more detail in Section 2.1, are well behind the current state of the art in machine transliteration.



*Human Language Technologies: The 2015 Annual Conference of the North American Chapter of the ACL*, pages 943–952,
Denver, Colorado, May 31 – June 5, 2015. 

In this paper, we conduct experiments that show the relative importance of spelling and pronunciation. We propose a new hybrid approach of joint transliteration generation from both orthography and pronunciation, which is based on a discriminative string transduction approach. We demonstrate that our approach results in significant improvements in transliteration accuracy. Because phonetic transcriptions are rarely available, we propose to capture the phonetic information from supplemental transliterations. We show that the most effective way of utilizing supplemental transliterations is to directly include their original orthographic representations. We show improvements of up to 30% in word accuracy when using supplemental transliterations from several languages.

The paper is organized as follows. We discuss related work in Section 2. Section 3 describes our hybrid model and a generalization of this model that leverages supplemental transliterations. Section 4 and 5 present our experiments of joint generation with supplemental transcriptions and transliterations, respectively. Section 6 presents our conclusions and future work.

## 2 Related work

In this section, we focus on hybrid transliteration models, and on methods of leveraging supplemental transliterations.

### 2.1 Hybrid models

Al-Onaizan and Knight (2002) present a hybrid model for Arabic-to-English transliteration, which is a linear combination of phoneme-based and grapheme-based models. The hybrid model is shown to be superior to the phoneme-based model, but inferior to the grapheme-based model.

Bilac and Tanaka (2004) propose a hybrid model for Japanese-to-English back-transliteration, which is also based on linear interpolation, but the interpolation is performed during the transliteration generation process, rather than after candidate target words have been generated. They report improvement over the two component models on some, but not all, of their test corpora.

Oh and Choi (2005) replace the fixed linear interpolation approach with a more flexible model that takes into account the correspondence between the phonemes and graphemes during the transliteration generation process. They report superior performance of their hybrid model over both component models. However, their model does not consider the coherence of the target word during the generation process, nor other important features that have been shown to significantly improve machine transliteration (Li et al., 2004; Jiampojamarn et al., 2010).

Oh et al. (2009) report that their hybrid models improve the accuracy of English-to-Chinese transliteration. However, since their focus is on investigating the influence of Chinese phonemes, their hybrid model is again a simple linear combination of basic models.

### 2.2 Leveraging supplemental transliterations

Previous work that explore the idea of taking advantage of data from additional languages tend to employ supplemental transliterations indirectly, rather than to incorporate them directly into the generation process.

Khapra et al. (2010) propose a bridge approach of transliterating low-resource language pair $(X, Y)$ by pivoting on an high-resource language $Z$, with the assumption that the pairwise data between $(X, Z)$ and $(Y, Z)$ is relatively large. Their experiments show that pivoting on $Z$ results in lower accuracy than directly transliterating $X$ into $Y$. Zhang et al. (2010) and Kumaran et al. (2010) combine the pivot model with a grapheme-based model, which works better than either of the two approaches alone. However, their model is not able to incorporate more than two languages.

Bhargava and Kondrak (2011) propose a reranking approach that uses supplemental transliterations to improve grapheme-to-phoneme conversion of names. Bhargava and Kondrak (2012) generalize this idea to improve transliteration accuracy by utilizing either transliterations from other languages, or phonetic transcriptions in the source language. Specifically, they apply an SVM reranker to the top-$n$ outputs of a base spelling-based model. However, the post-hoc property of reranking is a limiting factor; it can identify the correct transliteration only if the base model includes it in its output candidate list.

## 3 Joint Generation

In this section, we describe our approach of the joint transduction of a transliteration $T$ from a source orthographic string $S$ and a source phonemic string $P$ (Figure 1). We implement our approach by modifying the DIRECTL+ system of Jiampojamarn et al. (2010), which we describe in Section 3.1. In the following sections, we discuss other components of our approach, namely alignment (3.2), scoring (3.3), and search (3.4). In Section 3.5 we generalize the joint model to accept multiple input strings.

### 3.1 DirecTL+

DIRECTL+ (Jiampojamarn et al., 2010) is a discriminative string transducer which learns to convert source strings into target strings from a set of parallel training data. It requires pairs of strings to be aligned at the character level prior to training. M2M-ALIGNER (Jiampojamarn et al., 2007), an unsupervised EM-based aligner, is often used to generate such alignments. The output is a ranked list of candidate target strings with their confidence scores. Below, we briefly describe the scoring model, the training process, and the search algorithm.

The scoring model assigns a score to an aligned pair of source and target strings $(S, T)$. Assuming there are $m$ aligned substrings, such that the $i$th source substring generates the $i$th target substring, the score is computed with the following formula:

$$\sum_{i}^{m} \alpha \cdot \Phi(i, S, T) \quad (1)$$

where $\alpha$ is the weight vector, and $\Phi$ is the feature vector.

There are four sets of features. *Context* features are character n-grams within the source word. *Transition* features are character n-grams within the target word. *Linear-chain* features combine context features and transition features. *Joint n-gram* features further capture the joint information on both sides.

The feature weights $\alpha$ are learned with the Maximum Infused Relaxed Algorithm (MIRA) of Crammer and Singer (2003). MIRA aims to find the smallest change in current weights so that the new weights separate the correct target strings from incorrect ones by a margin defined by a loss function. Given the training instance $(S, T)$ and the current feature weights $\alpha_{k-1}$, the update of the feature weights can be described as the following optimization problem:

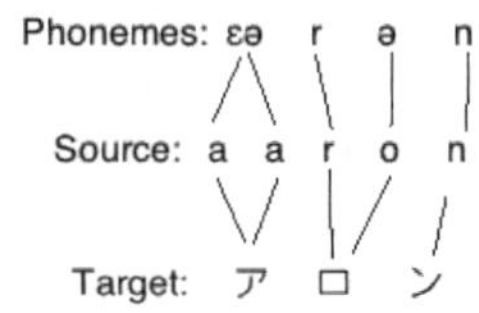


Figure 1: Triple alignment between the source phonemes, source graphemes, and the target graphemes アロン (A-RO-N).

$$\min_{\alpha_k} \|\alpha_k - \alpha_{k-1}\| \;\; s.t. \;\; \forall \hat{T} \in T_n :$$

$$\alpha_k \cdot (\Phi(S, T) - \Phi(S, \hat{T})) \geq loss(T, \hat{T})$$

where $\hat{T}$ is a candidate target in the $n$-best list $T_n$ found under the current model parameterized by $\alpha_{k-1}$. The loss function is the Levenshtein distance between $T$ and $\hat{T}$.

Given an unsegmented source string, the search algorithm finds a target string that achieves the highest score according to the scoring model. It searches through all the possible segmentations of the source string and all possible target substrings using the following dynamic programming formulation:

$$Q(0, \$) = 0$$
$$Q(j, t) = \max_{t', t, j-N \leq j' < j} \alpha \cdot \phi(S_{j'+1}^{j}, t', t) + Q(j', t')$$
$$Q(J+1, \$) = \max_{t'} \alpha \cdot \phi(\$, t', \$) + Q(J, t')$$

$Q(j, t)$ is defined as the maximum score of the target sequence ending with target substring $t$, generated by the letter sequence $S_1...S_j$. $\phi$ describes the features extracted from the current generator substring $S_{j'+1}^{j}$ of target substring $t$, with $t'$ to be the last generated target substring. $N$ specifies the maximum length of the source substring. The \$ symbols are used to represent both the start and the end of a string. Assuming that the source string contains $J$ characters, $Q(J+1, \$)$ gives the score of the highest scoring target string, which can be recovered through backtracking.

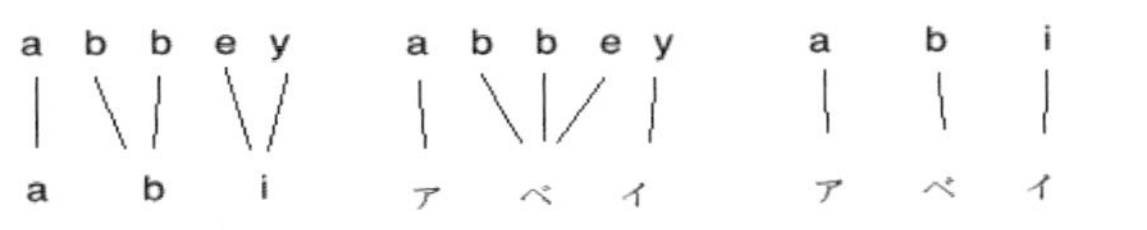


Figure 2: Three pairwise alignments between the English word *abbey*, its transcription [*abi*], and the Japanese transliteration アペイ (A-BE-I).

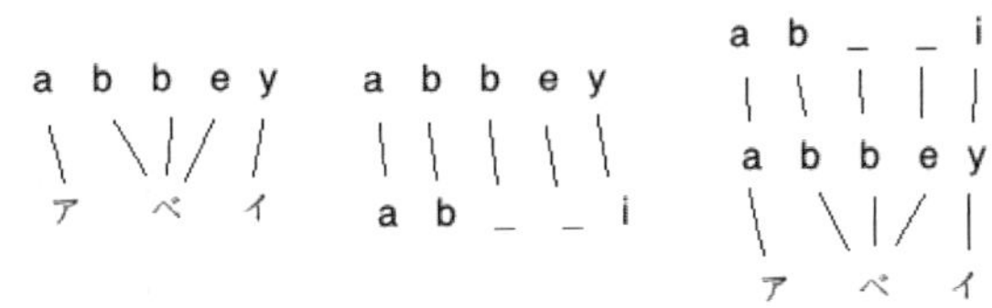


Figure 3: Obtaining a triple alignment by pivoting on the source word.

### 3.2 Multi-alignment

M2M-ALIGNER applies the EM algorithm to align sets of string pairs. For the purpose of joint generation, we need to align triples $S$, $P$ and $T$ prior to training. The alignment of multiple strings is a challenging problem (Bhargava and Kondrak, 2009). In general, there is no obvious way of merging three pairwise alignments. Figure 2 shows an example of three pairwise alignments that are mutually inconsistent: the English letter *e* is aligned to the phoneme [i] and to the grapheme ペ*(BE)*, which are not aligned to each other

Our solution is to select one of the input strings as the *pivot* for aligning the remaining two strings. Specifically, we align the pivot string to each of the other two strings through one-to-many alignments, where the maximum length of aligned substrings in the pivot string is set to one. Then we merge these two pairwise alignments according to the pivot string. Since the source phoneme string may or may not be available for a particular training instance, we use the source orthographic string as the pivot. The one-to-many pairwise alignments between the graphemes and phonemes, and between the graphemes and the transliterations are generated with M2M-ALIGNER. Figure 3 provides an example of this process.

An alternative approach is to pivot on the target string. However, because the target string is not available at test time, we need to search for the highest-scoring target string, given an unsegmented source string $S$ and the corresponding unsegmented phoneme string $P$. We can generalize the original search algorithm by introducing another dimension into the dynamic-programming table for segmenting $P$, but it substantially increases the time complexity of the decoding process. Our development experiments indicated that pivoting on the target string not only requires more time, but also results in less accurate transliterations.

### 3.3 Scoring Model

The scoring formula (1) is extended to compute a linear combination of features of three aligned strings $(S, P, T)$:

$$\sum_{i}^{m} \alpha \cdot [\Phi(i, S, T), \Phi(i, P, T)] \tag{2}$$

The transition features on $T$ are only computed once, because they are independent of the input strings. We observed no improvement by including features between $S$ and $P$ in our development experiments.

### 3.4 Search

Our search algorithm finds the highest-scoring target string, given a source string and a phoneme string. Since we pivot on the source string to achieve multiple alignment, the input to the search algorithm is actually one-to-many aligned pair of the source string and the phoneme string. The search space is therefore the same as that of DirecTL+, i.e. the product of all possible segmentations of the source string and all possible target substrings. However, since we apply one-to-many alignment, there is only one possible segmentation of the source string, which is obtained by treating every letter as a substring. We apply the same dynamic programming search as DirecTL+, except that we extend the feature extraction function $\phi(S_{j'+1}^{j}, t', t)$ in the original formulation to $[\phi(S_{j'+1}^{j}, t', t), \phi(P_{k'+1}^{k}, t', t)]$ so that features between the current phoneme substring $P_{k'+1}^{k}$ and the target substrings are taken into consideration. The time complexity of this search is only double of the complexity of DIRECTL+, and is independent of the length of the phoneme string.

### 3.5 Generalization

Since we may need to leverage information from other sources, e.g., phonemes of supplemental transliterations, each training instance can be composed of a source word, a target word, and a list of supplemental strings. The size of the list is not fixed because we may not have access to some of the supplemental strings for certain source words.

We first align all strings in each training instance by merging one-to-many pairwise alignments between the source word and every other string in the instance, as described in Section 3.2. The generalization of training is straightforward. For the scoring model, we extract the same set of features as before by pairing each supplemental string with the target word. Since the alignment is performed beforehand, the time complexity of the generalized search only increases linearly in the number of input strings with respect to the original complexity.

## 4 Leveraging transcriptions

In this section, we describe experiments that involve generating transliterations jointly from the source orthography and pronunciation. We test our method on the English-to-Hindi and English-to-Japanese transliteration data from the NEWS 2010 Machine Transliteration Shared Task (Li et al., 2010). We extract the corresponding English pronunciations from the Combilex Lexicon (Richmond et al., 2009). We split each transliteration dataset into 80% for training, 10% for development, 10% for testing. We limit the datasets to contain only transliterations that have phonetic transcriptions in Combilex, so that each entry is composed of a source English word, a source transcription, and a target Japanese or Hindi word. The final results are obtained by joining the training and development sets as the final training set. The final training/test sets contain 8,264/916 entries for English-to-Japanese, and 3,503/353 entries for English-to-Hindi.

### 4.1 Gold transcriptions

We compare three approaches that use different sources of information: (a) graphemes only; (b) phonemes only; and (c) both graphemes and phonemes. The first two approaches use DIRECTL+, while the last approach uses our joint model described in Section 3. We evaluate each approach by computing the word accuracy.

| Model | En→Ja | En→Hi |
|---|---|---|
| Graphemes only | 58.0 | 42.6 |
| Phonemes only | 52.4 | 39.4 |
| Joint | **63.6** | **46.1** |

Table 1: Transliteration word accuracy depending on the source information.

Table 1 presents the transliteration results. Even with gold-standard transcriptions, the phoneme-based model is worse than the grapheme-based model. This demonstrates that it is incorrect to refer to the process of transliteration as phonetic translation. On the other hand, our joint generation approach outperforms both single-source models on both test sets, which confirms that transliteration requires a joint consideration of orthography and pronunciation.

It is instructive to look at a couple of examples where outputs of the models differ. Consider the name *Marlon*, pronounced [mɑrlən], which is transliterated into Japanese as マロン *(MA-RO-N)* (correct), and マレン *(MA-RE-N)* (incorrect), by the orthographic and phonetic approaches, respectively. The letter bigram *lo* is always transliterated into ロ in the orthographic training data, while the phoneme bigram /lə/ has multiple correspondences in the phonetic training data. In this case, the unstressed vowel reduction process in English causes a loss of the orthographic information, which needs to be preserved in the transliteration.

In the joint model, the phonetic information sometimes helps disambiguate the pronunciation of the source word, thus benefiting the transliteration process. For example, the outputs of the three models for *haddock*, pronounced [hadək], are ハダク *(HA-DA-KU)* (phonetic), ハドドック *(HA-DO-DO-K-KU)* (orthographic), and ハドック *(HA-DO-K-KU)* (joint, correct). The phonetic model is again confused by the reduced vowel [ə], while the orthographic model mistakenly replicates the rendering of the consonant *d*, which is pronounced as a single phoneme.

| Model | En→Ja | En→Hi |
|---|---|---|
| Graphemes only | 63.1 | 43.5 |
| Joint (gold phon.) | **67.4** | **48.0** |
| Joint (generated phon.) | 65.8 | 46.1 |

Table 2: Transliteration accuracy improvement with gold and generated phonetic transcriptions.

| Model | En→Ja | En→Hi |
|---|---|---|
| Graphemes only | 53.3 | 46.4 |
| Phonemes only | 19.2 | 10.4 |
| Joint (suppl. phonemes) | **54.8** | **50.0** |

Table 3: Transliteration accuracy with transcriptions generated from third-language transliterations.

### 4.2 Generated Transcriptions

The training entries that have no corresponding transcriptions in our pronunciation lexicon were excluded from the experiment described above. When we add those entries back to the datasets, we can no longer apply the phonetic approach, but we can still compare the orthographic approach to our joint approach, which can handle the lack of a phonetic transcription in some of the training instances. The training sets are thus larger in the experiments described in this section: 30,190 entries for English-to-Japanese, and 12,070 for English-to-Hindi. The test sets are the same as in Section 4.1. The results in the first two rows in Table 2 show that the joint approach outperforms the orthographic approach even when most training entries lack the pronunciation information.[1]

Gold transcriptions are not always available, especially for names that originate from other languages. Next, we investigate whether we can replace the gold transcriptions with transcriptions that are automatically generated from the source orthography. We adopt DIRECTL+ as a grapheme-to-phoneme (G2P) converter, train it on the entire Combilex lexicon, and include the generated transcriptions instead of the gold transcriptions in the transliteration training and test sets for the joint model. The test sets are unchanged.

The third row in Table 2 shows the result of leveraging generated transcriptions. We still see improvement over the orthographic approach, albeit smaller than with the gold transcriptions. However, we need to be careful when interpreting these results. Since our G2P converter is trained on Combilex, the generated transcriptions of words in the test set are quite accurate. When we test the joint approach only on words that are *not* found in Combilex, the improvement over the orthographic approach largely disappears. We interpret this result as an indication that the generated transcriptions help mostly by capturing consistent grapheme-to-phoneme correspondences in the pronunciation lexicon.

## 5 Leveraging transliterations

In the previous section, we have shown that phonetic transcriptions can improve the accuracy of the transliteration process by disambiguating the pronunciation of the source word. Unfortunately, phonetic transcriptions are rarely available, especially for words which originate from other languages, and generating them on the fly is less likely to help. However, transliterations from other languages constitute another potential source of information that could be used to approximate the pronunciation in the source language. In this section, we present experiments of leveraging such supplemental transliterations through our joint model.

### 5.1 Third-language transcriptions

An intuitive way of employing transliterations from another language is to convert them into phonetic transcriptions using a G2P model, which are then provided to our joint model together with the source orthography. We test this idea on the data from the NEWS 2010 shared task. We select Thai as the third language, because it has the largest number of the corresponding transliterations. We restrict the training and test sets to include only words for which Thai transliterations are available. The resulting English-to-Japanese and English-to-Hindi training/test sets contain 12,889/1,009, and 763/250 entries, respectively. We adopt DIRECTL+ as a G2P converter, and train it on 911 Thai spelling-pronunciation pairs extracted from Wiktionary. Be-

[1]The improvement is statistically significant according to the McNemar test with $p < 0.05$. The differences in the baseline results between Table 1 and Table 2 are due to the differences in the training sets. The matching value of 46.1 across both tables is a coincidence. The comparison of results within any given table column is fair.

| Language | Acc. | Data size |
|---|---|---|
| Thai | 15.2 | 911 |
| Hindi | 25.9 | 819 |
| Hebrew | 21.3 | 475 |
| Korean | 40.9 | 3181 |

Table 4: Grapheme-to-phoneme word accuracy on the Wiktionary data.

| Model | En→Ja | En→Hi |
|---|---|---|
| Graphemes only | 54.5 | 46.1 |
| Joint (suppl. phonemes) | **58.6** | **46.4** |

Table 5: Transliteration accuracy with transcriptions generated from multiple transliterations.

cause of the small size of the training data, it can only achieve about 15% word accuracy in our G2P development experiment.

Table 3 shows the transliteration results. The accuracy of the model that uses only supplemental transcriptions (row 2) is very low, but the joint model obtains an improvement even with such inaccurate third-language transcriptions. Note that the Thai pronunciation is often quite different from English. For instance, the phoneme sequence [waj] obtained from the Thai transliteration of *Whyte*, helps the joint model correctly transliterate the English name into Japanese ホワイト *(HO-WA-I-TO)*, which is better than ホイト *(HO-I-TO)* produced by the orthographic model.

### 5.2 Multi-lingual transcriptions

Transcriptions obtained from a third language are not only noisy because of the imperfect G2P conversion, but often also lossy, in the sense of missing some phonetic information present in the source pronunciation. In addition, supplemental transliterations are not always available in a given third language. In this section, we investigate the idea of extracting phonetic information from multiple languages, with the goal of reducing the noise of generated transcriptions.

We first train G2P converters for several languages on the pronunciation data collected from Wiktionary. Table 4 shows the sizes of the G2P datasets, and the corresponding G2P word accuracy numbers, which are obtained by using 90% of the data for training, and the rest for testing.[2] For the highly-regular Japanese Katakana, we instead create a rule-based converter. Then we convert supplemental transliterations from those languages into noisy phonetic transcriptions. In order to obtain representative results, we also include transliteration pairs without supplemental transliterations, which results in different datasets than in the previous experiments. The sets for English-to-Japanese and English-to-Hindi now contain 30,190/17,557/1,886 and 12,070/3,777/380 entries, where the sizes refer to (1) the entire training set, (2) the subset of training entries that have at least one supplemental transcription, and (3) the test set (in which all entries have supplemental transcriptions).

An interlingual approach holds the promise of ultimately replacing $n^2$ pairwise grapheme-grapheme transliteration models involving $n$ languages with $2n$ grapheme-phoneme and phoneme-grapheme models based on a unified phonetic representation. In our implementation, we merge different phonetic transcriptions of a given word into a single abstract vector representation. Specifically, we replace each phoneme with a phonetic feature vector according to a phonological feature chart, which includes features such as *labial, voiced*, and *tense*. After merging the vectors by averaging their weights, we incorporate them into the joint model described in Section 3.3 by modifying $\Phi(i, P, T)$. Unfortunately, the results are disappointing. It appears that the vector merging process compounds the information loss, which offsets the advantage of incorporating multiple transcriptions.

Another way of utilizing supplemental transcriptions is to provide them directly to our generalized joint model described in Section 3.5, which can handle multiple input strings. Table 5 presents the results on leveraging transcriptions generated from supplemental transliterations. We see that the joint generation from multiple transcriptions significantly boosts the accuracy on English-to-Japanese, but the improvement on English-to-Hindi is minimal.

[2] We use the entire datasets to train G2P converters for the transliteration experiments, but their accuracy is unlikely to improve much due to a small increase in the training data.

| Model | En→Ja | Ja→En | En→Hi | Hi→En |
|---|---|---|---|---|
| DIRECTL+ | 51.5 | 19.7 | 43.4 | 42.6 |
| Reranking | 56.8 | 30.3 | 50.8 | 48.9 |
| Joint | 56.4 | 38.8 | 51.6 | 51.1 |
| Joint + Reranking | **57.0** | 44.6 | **53.0** | 57.2 |
| + Lexicon | - | **53.1** | - | **61.7** |

Table 6: Transliteration accuracy with supplemental information.

### 5.3 Multi-lingual transliterations

The generated transcriptions of supplemental transliterations discussed in the previous section are quite inaccurate because of small and noisy G2P training data. In addition, we are prevented from taking advantage of supplemental transliterations from other languages by the lack of the G2P training data. In order to circumvent these limitations, we propose to directly incorporate supplemental transliterations into the generation process. Specifically, we train our generalized joint model on the graphemes of the source word, as well as on the graphemes of supplemental transliterations.

The experiments that we have conducted so far suggest two additional methods of improving the transliteration accuracy. We have observed that $n$-best lists produced by our joint model contain the correct transliteration more often than the baseline models. Therefore, we follow the joint generation with a reranking step, in order to boost the top-1 accuracy. We apply the reranking algorithm of Bhargava and Kondrak (2011), except that our joint model is the base system for reranking. In order to ensure fair comparison, the held-out sets for training the rerankers are subtracted from the original training sets.

Another observation that we aim to exploit is that a substantial number of the outputs generated by our joint model are very close to gold-standard transliterations. In fact, news writers often use slightly different transliterations of the same name, which makes the model's task more difficult. Therefore, we rerank the model outputs using a target-language lexicon, which is a list of words together with their frequencies collected from a raw corpus. We follow Cherry and Suzuki (2009) in extracting lexicon features for a given word according to coarse bins, i.e., $[< 2000]$, $[< 200]$, $[< 20]$, $[< 2]$, $[< 1]$. For example, a word with the frequency 194 will cause the features $[< 2000]$ and $[< 200]$ to fire.

We conduct our final experiment on forward and backward transliteration. We utilize supplemental transliterations from all eight languages in the NEWS 2010 dataset. The English-Japanese and English-Hindi datasets contain 33,540 and 13,483 entries, of which 23,613 and 12,131 have at least one supplemental transliteration, respectively. These sets are split into training/development/test sets. The entries that have no supplemental transliterations are removed from the test sets, which results in 2,321 and 1,226 test entries. In addition, we extract an English lexicon comprising 7.5M word types from the English gigaword monolingual corpus (LDC2012T21) for the back-transliteration experiments.

We evaluate the following models: (1) the baseline DIRECTL+ model trained on source graphemes; (2) the reranking model of Bhargava and Kondrak (2011)[3], with DIRECTL+ as the base system; (3) our joint model described in Section 3.5; (4) "combination", which is a reranking model with our joint model as the base system; and (5) a reranking model that uses the English target lexicon and model (4) as the base system.

Table 6 present the results. We see that our joint model performs much better by directly incorporating the supplemental transliterations than by using the corresponding phonetic transcriptions. This is consistent with our experiments in Section 4 that show the importance of the orthographic information. We also observe that our joint model achieves substantial improvements over the baseline on the back-transliteration tasks from Japanese and Hindi into English. This result suggests the orthographic information from the supplemental transliterations is

[3]Code from http://www.cs.toronto.edu/~aditya/g2p-tl-rr/

particularly effective in recovering the information about the pronunciation of the original word which is often obfuscated by the transliteration into a different language.

Our joint model is more effective in utilizing supplemental transliterations than the reranking approach of Bhargava and Kondrak (2011), except on English-to-Japanese. The combination of these two approaches works better than either of them, particularly on the back-transliteration tasks. Finally, the incorporation of a target-lexicon brings additional gains.

Back-transliteration from Japanese to English is more challenging than in the forward direction, which was already noted by Knight and Graehl (1997). Most of the names in the dataset originate from English, and Japanese phonotactics require introduction of extra vowels to separate consonant clusters. During back-transliteration, it is often unclear which vowels should be removed and which preserved. Our approach is able to dramatically improve the quality of the results by recovering the original information from multiple supplemental transliterations.

## 6 Conclusion

We have investigated the relative importance of the orthographic and phonetic information in the transliteration process. We have proposed a novel joint generation model that directly utilizes both sources of information. We have shown that a generalized joint model is able to achieve substantial improvements over the baseline represented by a state-of-the-art transliteration tool by directly incorporating multiple supplemental transliterations. In the future, we would like to further explore the idea of using interlingual representations for transliteration without parallel training data.

## Acknowledgements

We thank Adam St Arnaud for help in improving the final version of this paper.

This research was supported by the Natural Sciences and Engineering Research Council of Canada (NSERC).

## References

Yaser Al-Onaizan and Kevin Knight. 2002. Machine transliteration of names in Arabic texts. In *Proceedings of the ACL-02 Workshop on Computational Approaches to Semitic Languages*, Philadelphia, Pennsylvania, USA, July. Association for Computational Linguistics.

Aditya Bhargava and Grzegorz Kondrak. 2009. Multiple word alignment with Profile Hidden Markov Models. In *Proceedings of Human Language Technologies: The 2009 Annual Conference of the North American Chapter of the Association for Computational Linguistics, Companion Volume: Student Research Workshop and Doctoral Consortium*, pages 43–48, Boulder, Colorado, June. Association for Computational Linguistics.

Aditya Bhargava and Grzegorz Kondrak. 2011. How do you pronounce your name? Improving G2P with transliterations. In *Proceedings of the 49th Annual Meeting of the Association for Computational Linguistics: Human Language Technologies*, pages 399–408, Portland, Oregon, USA, June. Association for Computational Linguistics.

Aditya Bhargava and Grzegorz Kondrak. 2012. Leveraging supplemental representations for sequential transduction. In *Proceedings of the 2012 Conference of the North American Chapter of the Association for Computational Linguistics: Human Language Technologies*, pages 396–406, Montréal, Canada, June. Association for Computational Linguistics.

Slaven Bilac and Hozumi Tanaka. 2004. A hybrid back-transliteration system for Japanese. In *Proceedings of Coling 2004*, pages 597–603, Geneva, Switzerland, Aug 23–Aug 27. COLING.

Colin Cherry and Hisami Suzuki. 2009. Discriminative substring decoding for transliteration. In *Proceedings of the 2009 Conference on Empirical Methods in Natural Language Processing*, pages 1066–1075, Singapore, August. Association for Computational Linguistics.

Koby Crammer and Yoram Singer. 2003. Ultraconservative online algorithms for multiclass problems. *J. Mach. Learn. Res.*, 3:951–991, March.

Sittichai Jiampojamarn, Grzegorz Kondrak, and Tarek Sherif. 2007. Applying many-to-many alignments and hidden Markov models to letter-to-phoneme conversion. In *Human Language Technologies 2007: The Conference of the North American Chapter of the Association for Computational Linguistics; Proceedings of the Main Conference*, pages 372–379, Rochester, New York, April. Association for Computational Linguistics.

Sittichai Jiampojamarn, Colin Cherry, and Grzegorz Kondrak. 2010. Integrating joint n-gram features into a discriminative training framework. In *Human Language Technologies: The 2010 Annual Conference of the North American Chapter of the Association for Computational Linguistics*, pages 697–700, Los Angeles, California, June. Association for Computational Linguistics.

Mitesh M. Khapra, A Kumaran, and Pushpak Bhattacharyya. 2010. Everybody loves a rich cousin: An empirical study of transliteration through bridge languages. In *Human Language Technologies: The 2010 Annual Conference of the North American Chapter of the Association for Computational Linguistics*, pages 420–428, Los Angeles, California, June. Association for Computational Linguistics.

Kevin Knight and Jonathan Graehl. 1997. Machine transliteration. In *Proceedings of the 35th Annual Meeting of the Association for Computational Linguistics*, pages 128–135, Madrid, Spain, July. Association for Computational Linguistics.

A. Kumaran, Mitesh M. Khapra, and Pushpak Bhattacharyya. 2010. Compositional machine transliteration. *ACM Transactions on Asian Language Information Processing (TALIP)*, 9(4):13:1–13:29, December.

Haizhou Li, Min Zhang, and Jian Su. 2004. A joint source-channel model for machine transliteration. In *Proceedings of the 42Nd Annual Meeting on Association for Computational Linguistics*, ACL '04, Stroudsburg, PA, USA. Association for Computational Linguistics.

Haizhou Li, A Kumaran, Min Zhang, and Vladimir Pervouchine. 2010. Report of NEWS 2010 transliteration generation shared task. In *Proceedings of the 2010 Named Entities Workshop*, pages 1–11, Uppsala, Sweden, July. Association for Computational Linguistics.

Jong-Hoon Oh and Key-Sun Choi. 2005. Machine learning based English-to-Korean transliteration using grapheme and phoneme information. *IEICE - Trans. Inf. Syst.*, E88-D(7):1737–1748, July.

Jong-Hoon Oh, Kiyotaka Uchimoto, and Kentaro Torisawa. 2009. Can Chinese phonemes improve machine transliteration?: A comparative study of English-to-Chinese transliteration models. In *Proceedings of the 2009 Conference on Empirical Methods in Natural Language Processing: Volume 2 - Volume 2*, EMNLP '09, pages 658–667, Stroudsburg, PA, USA. Association for Computational Linguistics.

Korin Richmond, Robert Clark, and Sue Fitt. 2009. Robust LTS rules with the Combilex speech technology lexicon. In *Proceedings of Interspeech*, pages 1259–1298, Brighton, UK, September.

Tarek Sherif and Grzegorz Kondrak. 2007. Substring-based transliteration. In *Proceedings of the 45th Annual Meeting of the Association of Computational Linguistics*, pages 944–951, Prague, Czech Republic, June. Association for Computational Linguistics.

Min Zhang, Xiangyu Duan, Vladimir Pervouchine, and Haizhou Li. 2010. Machine transliteration: Leveraging on third languages. In *Coling 2010: Posters*, pages 1444–1452, Beijing, China, August. Coling 2010 Organizing Committee.

Min Zhang, Haizhou Li, A Kumaran, and Ming Liu. 2012. Whitepaper of NEWS 2012 shared task on machine transliteration. In *Proceedings of the 4th Named Entity Workshop*, pages 1–9, Jeju, Korea, July. Association for Computational Linguistics.

# Prosodic boundary information helps unsupervised word segmentation

**Bogdan Ludusan, Gabriel Synnaeve and Emmanuel Dupoux**
Laboratoire de Sciences Cognitives et Psycholinguistique
EHESS / ENS / CNRS
29 rue d'Ulm, 75005 Paris, France
bogdan.ludusan@ens.fr, gabriel.synnaeve@gmail.com,
emmanuel.dupoux@gmail.com

## Abstract

It is well known that prosodic information is used by infants in early language acquisition. In particular, prosodic boundaries have been shown to help infants with sentence and word-level segmentation. In this study, we extend an unsupervised method for word segmentation to include information about prosodic boundaries. The boundary information used was either derived from oracle data (hand-annotated), or extracted automatically with a system that employs only acoustic cues for boundary detection. The approach was tested on two different languages, English and Japanese, and the results show that boundary information helps word segmentation in both cases. The performance gain obtained for two typologically distinct languages shows the robustness of prosodic information for word segmentation. Furthermore, the improvements are not limited to the use of oracle information, similar performances being obtained also with automatically extracted boundaries.

## 1 Introduction

Prosodic information is thought to play a fundamental role in early language acquisition, and provide infants with rich structural information about their language (Christophe et al., 1997). In particular, prosody has been claimed to help infants find word boundaries (Christophe and Dupoux, 1996). Newborns are able discriminate between disyllables that contains vs. does not contain a phonological phrase boundary (Christophe et al., 1994; Christophe et al., 2001), showing that they are able to encode the corresponding prosodic cues. Nine-month olds show evidence of parsing utterances into prosodic units, and show 'surprise' when a pause is inappropriately inserted inside as opposed to between these units (Jusczyk et al., 1992; Gerken et al., 1994). Ten to 13 month olds show evidence of using prosodic units to parse utterances into words, as they fail to recognize a familiar word if it appears to straddle a prosodic boundary (Gout et al., 2004).

Curiously enough, however, prosody is not used very much in unsupervised models of language acquisition, and in particular, in models of word segmentation. Most such models use text as input, and apply some form of lexical optimization. For instance, Brent and Cartwright (1996) used a Minimal Description Length Principle to optimize the size of the description of a corpus. State of the art systems use hierarchical Bayesian models (Goldwater et al., 2009) which parse a corpus into words or other linguistic units with a bias to reuse previously parsed elements. Adaptor Grammars is a generic framework which enables to formulate such Bayesian models within an overarching architecture based on probabilistic context free grammars (Johnson et al., 2007). Such models have been used to study the role of linguistic information such as syllabic structure (Johnson and Goldwater, 2009), morphology (Johnson, 2008), function words (Johnson et al., 2014), as well as the role of non-linguistic context (Synnaeve et al., 2014). To our knowledge, only one paper studied the role of prosodic information (Börschinger and Johnson, 2014). In this study, the authors used the role of word stress in constraining word segmentation (as in stress languages, there is only one main stress per word).



*Human Language Technologies: The 2015 Annual Conference of the North American Chapter of the ACL*, pages 953–963,
Denver, Colorado, May 31 – June 5, 2015. 

Here, we test whether prosodic boundaries could directly help symbolic word segmentation by providing some word boundaries 'for free', as this was already shown to be true in the case of signal-based term discovery systems (Ludusan et al., 2014). Being a feasibility study, we will use gold prosodic boundaries in order to quantify what is the maximum gain we can expect using this type of information. In addition to that, we test whether prosodic boundaries automatically derived from the speech signal (Ludusan and Dupoux, 2014) could also provide a performance gain. As this study relies on the existence of prosodic information (either gold, or derived from speech), we did not use the standard corpora used in these studies (the Bernstein-Ratner corpus), but introduced three new corpora, two in English and one in Japanese.

The paper is structured as follows: In the next sections we introduce the systems employed in this study - the prosodic boundary detection system in section 2 and the word segmentation procedure in section 3. Next, we present the datasets used in the experiments, with the results obtained being illustrated in section 5. The paper will conclude with a general discussion and some final remarks.

## 2 Prosodic annotation

There are numerous studies in the speech processing literature focusing on the detection of prosodic boundaries (e.g. Wightman and Ostendorf (1991), Ananthakrishnan and Narayanan (2008), Huang et al. (2008), Jeon and Liu (2009), just to name a few). While the approaches taken vary between these studies, they tend to use either supervised learning, thus needing large, prosodically annotated corpora, or higher level information (syntactic, lexical, etc) which would also require further annotations. Since unsupervised word segmentation is a process that requires low resources (only symbolic transcription), we have decided to use for the automatic detection of prosodic boundaries a previously proposed method which employs only acoustic cues that can be extracted from the speech signal (Ludusan and Dupoux, 2014).

The algorithm takes into consideration four acoustic cues which had been shown, in the language acquisition literature, to be used by young infants for the recognition of prosodic boundaries. The cues correspond to the following phenomena that occur next to prosodic breaks: silent pauses, final lengthening, initial strengthening and F0 reset. The acoustic cues were extracted at the syllable level and they include: the duration of the pause following the syllable (pause cue), the syllable nucleus duration (nucleus cue), the distance between the nucleus onset of the current syllable and that of the following one (onset cue) and the difference between the F0 end value of the current syllable and the F0 beginning value of the following syllable (F0 reset cue). The nucleus and onset cues are computed for all the syllables, the later being a combination of the nucleus cue, pause cue and the onset of the following syllable, which is the domain of the initial strengthening phenomenon. The pause cue is set to 0 for syllables not followed by a silence pause, while F0 reset is only computed for syllables which are at a local minimum for F0, otherwise it is set to 0. Then, for each individual cue function except pause, we considered only the values which were local maxima, the other values being set to 0.

Once a numerical value for each of the cues is obtained, they are standardized between 0 and 1 and combined in a detector function, by summing them up. The local maxima of the detector function are then obtained and the syllables corresponding to the maxima will be considered as prosodic boundary candidates. Next, a thresholding of these values is applied and all the right-hand boundaries of the syllables greater or equal to this threshold are marked as prosodic boundaries. This operation is followed by a second step in which prosodic boundaries are marked based on a different rule, rule that we would call conjunction of cues. This rule was inspired by the results of several studies in the infant literature (Seidl, 2007; Wellmann et al., 2012) showing that most prosodic boundaries tend to be marked by more than one acoustic cue. Taking these findings into account, we could also mark as prosodic boundaries all syllables which are signalled by at least two different cues, regardless of the value of these cues. Thus, by employing the conjunction of cues we can give a higher weight to a group of cues which, by appearing together, mark more reliably the presence of a boundary, in the hope that it would increase recall without decreasing too much the precision.

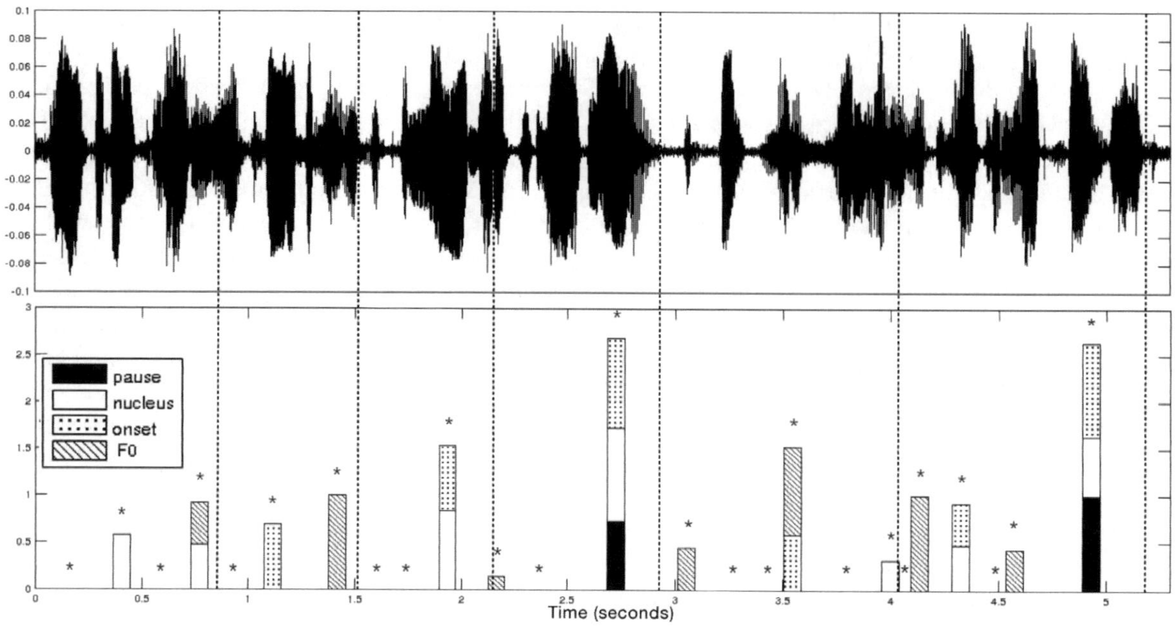


Figure 1: Speech waveform and corresponding detector function employed for prosodic boundary detection of the phrase: "My tape machine records well, but the knobs are too small, the buttons are flimsy and the counter misplaced" (for details, see (Ludusan and Dupoux, 2014)).

The parameters of the algorithm: the combination of cues, the cut-off threshold and the combination of conjunction of cues are obtained on a hold-out set, by aiming to maximize the performance of the system on that particular set.

The prosodic boundary detection procedure is illustrated in Figure 1 for the following utterance: "My tape machine records well, but the knobs are too small, the buttons are flimsy and the counter misplaced". The waveform of the speech signal is shown in the upper panel, with prosodic boundaries marked with dashed lines. In the lower panel are the values of the computed detector function, for each syllable, and the contribution of each of the cues towards the value of the function (the asterisk denotes the position of the syllable nucleus). The syllables corresponding to local maxima of the detector function (syllables 2, 4, 7, 10, 13, 17, 19, 21 and 25) would be considered as possible candidates for the position of a prosodic boundary. Provided that their value is higher than the decision threshold, they will be marked as actual boundaries. For example, if the threshold is set to the first percentile of the function, all the candidates will be kept, for the 50th percentile only syllables 10, 13, 17 and 25 will be considered, while a threshold equal to the value of the 100th percentile will leave only syllable 13 to be marked as a boundary. If we also use what we called conjunction of cues, and we set the cues to be the nucleus and the onset, syllables 10, 13, 22 and 25 will be marked as boundary placeholders, regardless of the fact they are or not a local maximum or they pass or not over the decision threshold.

## 3 Word segmentation models

### 3.1 Adaptor grammars

Adaptor Grammars (AGs) are an extension of probabilistic context-free grammars (PCFGs) that learn probability of entire subtrees as well as probabilities of rules (Johnson et al., 2007). A PCFG $(N, W, R, S, \theta)$ consists of a start symbol $S$, $N$ and $W$ disjoints sets of nonterminals and terminal symbols respectively. $R$ is a set of rules producing elements of $N$ or $W$. Finally, $\theta$ is a set of distributions over the rules $R_X, \forall X \in N$ ($R_X$ are the rules that expand $X$). An AG $(N, W, R, S, \theta, A, C)$ extends the above PCFG with a subset $(A \subseteq N)$ of adapted nonterminals, each of them $(X \in A)$ having an associated adaptor $(C_X \in C)$. An AG defines a distribution over trees $G_X, \forall X \in N \cup W$. If $X \notin A$, then $G_X$ is defined exactly as for a PCFG:

$$G_X = \sum_{\substack{X \to Y_1 \ldots Y_n \\ \in R_X}} \theta_{X \to Y_1 \ldots Y_n} \mathrm{TD}_X(G_{Y_1} \ldots G_{Y_n})$$

With $\mathrm{TD}_X(G_1 \ldots G_n)$ the distribution over trees with root node $X$ and each subtree $t_i \sim G_i$ i.i.d. If $X \in A$, then there is an additional indirection (composition) with the distribution $H_X$:

$$G_X = \sum_{\substack{X \to Y_1 \ldots Y_n \\ \in R_X}} \theta_{X \to Y_1 \ldots Y_n} \mathrm{TD}_X(H_{Y_1} \ldots H_{Y_n})$$

$$H_X \sim C_X(G_X)$$

We used $C_X$ adaptors following the Pitman-Yor process (PYP) (Perman et al., 1992; Teh, 2006) with parameters $a$ and $b$. The PYP generates (Zipfian) type frequencies that are similar to those that occur in natural language (Goldwater et al., 2011). Metaphorically, if there are $n$ customers and $m$ tables, the $n + 1$th customer is assigned to table $z_{n+1}$ according to ($\delta_k$ is the Kronecker delta function):

$$z_{n+1} | z_1 \ldots z_n \sim \frac{ma + b}{n + b} \delta_{m+1} + \sum_{k=1}^{m} \frac{n_k - a}{n + b} \delta_k$$

For an AG, this means that adapted non-terminals ($X \in A$) either expand to a previously generated subtree ($T(X)_k$) with probability proportional to how often it was visited ($n_k$), or to a new subtree ($T(X)_{m+1}$) generated through the PCFG with probability proportional to $ma + b$.

### 3.2 Grammars including prosodic information

The *baseline* that we are using is commonly called the "Colloc3-Syll" model (Johnson and Goldwater, 2009) and is reported at 87% token F-score on the standard Brent version of the Bernstein-Ratner corpus corpus. It posits that sentences are composed of 3 hierarchical levels of collocations, the lower level being collocations of words, and words are composed of syllables. Goldwater et al. (2009) showed how an assumption of independence between words (a unigram model) led to under-segmentation. So, above the $Word$ level, we take the collocations (co-occurring sequences) of words into account.

$$\begin{aligned} &Sentence \to Colloc3^{+} \\ &\underline{Colloc3} \to Colloc2^{+} \\ &\underline{Colloc2} \to Colloc1^{+} \\ &\underline{Colloc1} \to Word^{+} \\ &\underline{Word} \to StructSyll \end{aligned}$$

where the rule $\underline{Colloc2} \to Colloc1^{+}$ is implemented by:

$$\begin{aligned} &\underline{Colloc2} \to Collocs1 \\ &Collocs1 \to Colloc1 \\ &Collocs1 \to Colloc1\ Collocs1 \end{aligned}$$

$Word$ splits into general syllables and initial- or final- specific syllables in $StructSyll$. In English, syllables consist of onsets or codas (producing consonants), and nuclei (vowels). Onsets, nuclei and codas are adapted, thus allowing this model to memorize sequences or consonants or sequences of vowels, dependent on their position in the word. Consonants and vowels are the pre-terminals, their derivation is specified in the grammar into phonemes of the language. In Japanese, syllables are adapted and are composed either of (Consonant-)Vowel(-Nasal) or Nasal. Phonemes are annotated either as consonant, vowel, or nasal (the moraic nasal /N/).

To allow for these grammars to use the prosodic information, we modify them so that prosodic boundaries are considered as breaks at a given level of collocations (or words). For instance we describe below how we change a Colloc3-Syll grammar to make use of the prosodic boundaries information at the lower level of collocations (Colloc1), by using the terminal symbols "|" (the rest is unchanged):

$$\begin{aligned} &\underline{Colloc2} \to Collocs1 \\ &Collocs1 \to Colloc1 \\ &Collocs1 \to Colloc1 \mid Collocs1 \\ &Collocs1 \to Colloc1\ Collocs1 \\ &\underline{Colloc1} \to Word^{+} \end{aligned}$$

We produced and tested grammars which incorporated these prosodic boundary annotations at different levels, from $Collocs3$ down to $Word$ level.

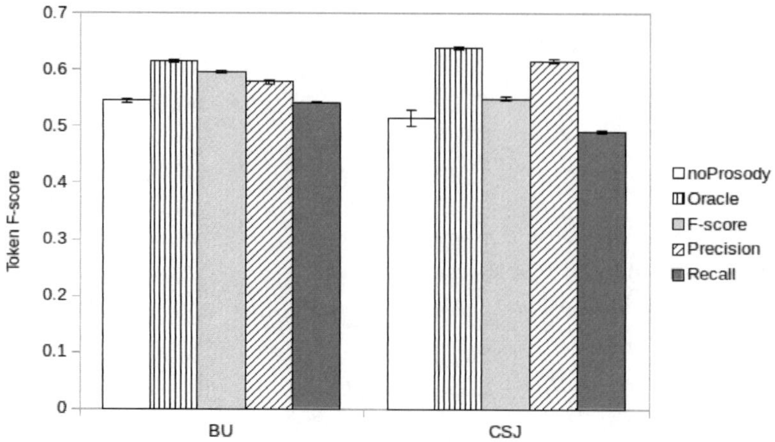


Figure 2: Colloc3-Syll based grammars scores on the BU and CSJ datasets. We show the best results without prosodic annotation, with hand-annotated prosody information (oracle), and with automatically derived annotations that maximize either F-score, precision, or recall of prosodic boundaries.

## 4 Materials

The experiments were performed on two distinct languages: English and Japanese. For English, we have chosen the Boston University radio news (BU) corpus (Ostendorf et al., 1995) and the LUCID corpus (Baker and Hazan, 2010). The first one, the BU corpus, consists of broadcast news recorded by professional speakers and is widely used in speech prosody research. Here, we only used the prosody annotated portion of the corpus, containing about 3 hours of recordings, labelled for accent tones and prosodic breaks following the ToBI standard for American English (Silverman et al., 1992). Level 3 and level 4 break indices, corresponding to intermediate and intonational phrase boundaries, were considered in this work. The recordings belonging to 6 speakers were used for the experiments, while those belonging to one speaker were employed as a development set, for setting the parameters of the automatic boundary detection algorithm. The evaluation set was divided into utterances, at pauses longer or equal to 200 ms, giving in total 2,273 utterances having 27,980 tokens.

While the BU corpus has the advantage of being annotated for prosodic boundaries, and thus being able to provide us with an upper bound of the performance increase that the prosodic information could bring, it is not large enough to give state-of-the-art results using AG. For this, we have taken a large corpus of spontaneous interactions, the LUCID corpus, and used it in connection to automatically detected prosodic boundaries. Due to the more spontaneous nature of these materials, we have defined utterances as being stretches of speech bounded by pauses at least 500 ms long. Since durational information is needed for the detection of the prosodic boundaries, the corpus was force aligned using the UPenn aligner (Yuan and Liberman, 2008). From the utterances obtained we have excluded all utterances containing hesitations or words not present in the dictionary of the aligner. Thus, a total of 21,649 utterances were eventually used in the experiments, corresponding to 118,640 tokens.

For Japanese, a subpart of the core of the Corpus of Spontaneous Japanese (CSJ) was used (Maekawa, 2003). It contains more than 18 hours of academic recordings from 70 speakers and it was annotated for prosodic boundaries using the X-JToBI standard (Maekawa et al., 2002). Oracle level 2 and level 3 prosodic breaks (accentual and intonational phrases) were used in this study as well as automatically obtained boundaries. The data set aside for the setting of parameters belongs to 5 speakers, with the recordings of the rest of the speakers used for the evaluation. We used the utterance markings provided with the corpus, the evaluation set containing 21,974 utterances and 195,744 tokens.

While previous studies on word segmentation have focused on infant-directed speech (IDS), we employ here corpora of adult-directed speech. The reason behind this choice is the fact that IDS corpora

| Model | F-score | Precision | Recall |
|---|---|---|---|
| maxFscore | **.608** | .705 | .535 |
| maxPrecision | .391 | **.986** | .244 |
| maxRecall | .496 | .377 | **.724** |

Table 1: Automatic prosodic boundary annotation performance on the BU corpus.

are not, generally, annotated for prosody. We would expect that experiments on ADS would improve less over the baseline, when compared to those run on IDS, due to its less exaggerated prosody and its reduced number of prosodic boundaries. Thus, any improvement found on ADS, would be found also on IDS.

The corpora used have all been transcribed phonetically, but, for the purpose of this paper, we have transformed this phonetic annotation into a phonemic one. For the English databases the mappings proposed by Lee and Hon (1989) were employed, with two notable exceptions: vowels /er/ and /axr/ were mapped to the phonemes /ah/ and /r/, while the syllabic consonants /el/, /em/ and /en/ were mapped to the label /ah/ and their corresponding consonant (/l/, /m/ or /n/). For Japanese, we employed the same mappings used by Boruta (2011).

## 5 Results

The prosodic boundary procedure on the BU and the CSJ used oracle segmental (phonetic) information, while phonemes were force-aligned from word-level annotation for the LUCID. The prosodic boundaries were evaluated with the classic measurements: precision, recall and F-score. The word segmentation token F-scores were obtained every 10 epochs (for less correlation due to the sampler) during the 100 epochs (BU corpus), or the 200 epochs (LUCID and CSJ corpora) centered around the point of convergence, and their mean and standard deviation computed. The convergence point was determined by smoothing the prior probability of the grammar with a sliding window and choosing the epoch where the negative log probability was the lowest.

### 5.1 English

The best parameters of the prosodic boundary detection system were searched for on the development set left aside for this purpose. The F-score of the system was maximized and the best combination of cues and conjunction of cues were $pause{+}onset$ and $pause + nucleus$, respectively. For these settings, we then determined the threshold values which gave the best F-score, precision and recall for boundary detection, which were further used to run the algorithm on the evaluation set. The results obtained on the evaluation set for the systems trying to maximize F-score ($maxFscore$), precision ($maxPrecision$) or recall ($maxRecall$) are presented in Table 1.

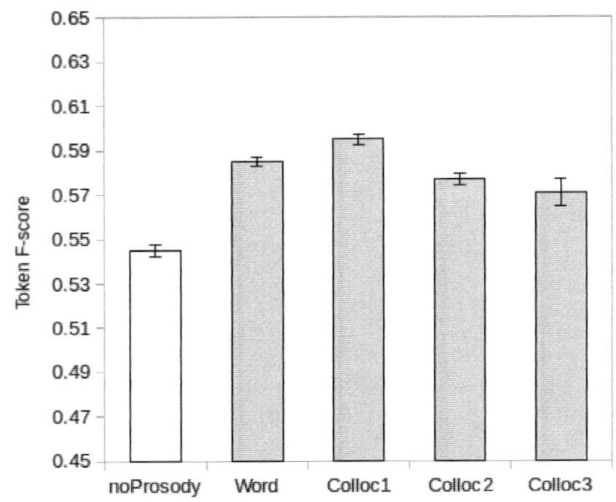


Figure 3: Colloc3-Syll based grammars scores on the BU dataset, comparing results without prosodic annotation, with those obtained by automatic prosodic boundaries that maximize F-score, added at different levels in the grammar.

The word segmentation method was then run with the grammars defined in section 3.2, with and without prosodic boundary information. For the prosody enhanced cases, both oracle and automatic boundaries were employed. The best results obtained on the BU corpus, for each of the five settings, are illustrated on the left side of Figure 2. It appears that all cases that employ prosodic information improve over the baseline, with oracle boundaries giving a $7\%$ absolute performance gain.

Next, we looked in more detail at the behaviour of the best system that uses automatic boundaries ($maxFscore$). We present the token F-score obtained by this system for the different levels of the grammar where the prosodic information is added.

Although we obtained improvements on the BU corpus, for all cases when prosodic information was used, the overall results are far from state-of-the art

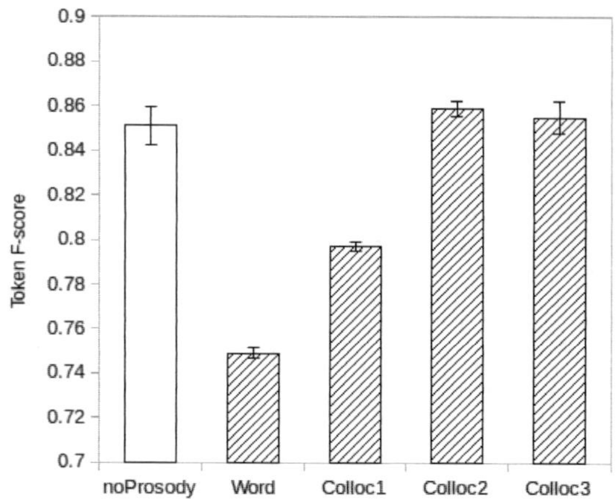


Figure 4: Colloc3-Syll based grammars scores on the LUCID dataset, comparing results without prosodic annotation, with those obtained by automatic prosodic boundaries that maximize precision, added at different levels in the grammar.

performance, due to the relatively small size of the corpus. For this reason, we chose to test on a bigger English corpus, LUCID. While this corpus is indeed larger, it has the disadvantage of not being prosodically annotated. Thus, we investigated only the cases when automatically determined prosodic boundaries are employed. The detection of prosodic boundaries used the same parameters obtained on the BU corpus but, since no prosodic annotation exists, we were not able to perform the same evaluation of the boundaries, as we did for BU.

The token F-scores for the best prosodic boundary setting ($maxPrecision$) are displayed in Figure 4. These results are closer to the state-of-the-art for English, which stand at 87% token F-score. Contrary to the results on the BU corpus, the prosody enhanced system improves over the baseline only when the boundary information is added at $Colloc2$ or $Colloc3$ level (best gain: 0.8% absolute value). While the improvements brought here tend to be quite small, compared to those obtained for BU, we are closer to ceiling value on LUCID and also the quality of the automatic boundaries might be lower, due to the different type of speech on which the parameters of the model were found.

With the Adaptor Grammar tending to slightly over-segment the results, the inclusion of prosody at $Word$ or $Colloc1$ has increased the precision slightly, at the expense of a significantly lower recall, and thus a lower overall F-score. This over-segmentation trait was instead much more pronounced for the BU corpus, where the increase in precision was accompanied only by a slight decrease in recall, brought the two measures closer together, and thus has maximized the F-score.

| Model | F-score | Precision | Recall |
|---|---|---|---|
| maxFscore | **.469** | .533 | .418 |
| maxPrecision | .398 | **.781** | .267 |
| maxRecall | .431 | .353 | **.552** |

Table 2: Automatic prosodic boundary annotation performance on the CSJ corpus.

## 5.2 Japanese

The same procedure for parameter detection as for the BU corpus was applied and the best cues obtained were $pause + onset$, while the best combination of conjunction of cues was $pause + f0Reset$. Table 2 illustrates the prosodic boundary results obtained on the CSJ evaluation set, for the systems maximizing F-score, precision and recall, respectively.

Since oracle prosodic information was available for this corpus, we were able to compare the performance of the baseline to that of the oracle and automatic boundaries enhanced system. This comparison is displayed in Figure 2, right hand side. Having a sizable corpus, the results are more similar to the state-of-the-art for Japanese, reported in (Fourtassi et al., 2013) (55%). Increases in performance can be observed when hand-labelled prosody is introduced (12.3% absolute value), and also when automatic boundaries ($maxPrecision$) are employed (10% absolute value).

Similarly to the previous experiments, we display in Figure 5 the comparison between the baseline and the best system employing automatic boundaries ($maxPrecision$), for the different levels where the information is added. It shows that prosody helps, regardless of the level where prosody is used, although it appears to favour the lower collocation levels.

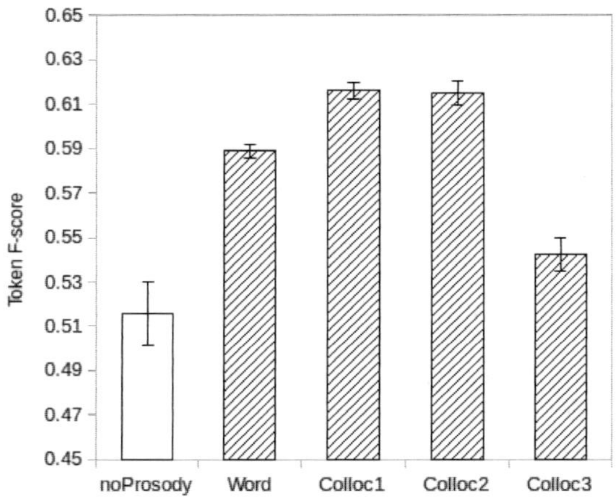


Figure 5: Colloc3-Syll based grammars scores on the CSJ dataset, comparing results without prosodic annotation, with those obtained by automatic prosodic boundaries that maximize precision, added at different levels in the grammar.

## 6 Discussion and Conclusions

We have investigated the use of prosodic boundary information for unsupervised word discovery in a multilingual setting. We showed that prosodic boundaries can improve word segmentation across both languages even when automatically determined boundaries are used. We also illustrated that the way in which to integrate prosody into word segmentation is not homogeneous across corpora, both in terms of the level of collocation where these boundaries are introduced, and in terms of the balance between precision and recall, when it comes to using automatic boundaries.

For the first issue, the results on BU suggest that $Word$ or $Colloc1$ would be the best level, those on LUCID show that either $Colloc2$ or $Colloc3$ would give the best performance, while the scores on CSJ favors $Colloc1$ or $Colloc2$. But, if we were to discard the results on BU, due to its heavy over-segmentation and its small size, and use the collocation level giving the most balanced scores on the other two datasets, it appears that $Colloc2$ would be the common denominator. Besides giving the most balanced token scores it also gives the most balanced boundary scores, striking a good compromise between the under-segmentation produced by adding the prosody at lower levels and the over-segmentation tendency for boundaries introduced at higher levels.

To investigate the second issue, a closer look to the tables presenting the evaluation of the automatic boundaries (Table 1 and Table 2) is needed. The best word segmentation scores on BU were obtained for the $maxFscore$ system, but we can observe that the condition also has a high precision (.705). At the same time, the best score on CSJ was obtained for the $maxPrecision$ system, the $maxFscore$ system (with a precision of .533) giving no improvement over the baseline (see Figure 2). Furthermore, $maxRecall$, which has very low precisions, seems to behave similar to, or below the baseline, for both datasets. Thus, it appears that a relatively high precision for the prosodic boundaries is needed to obtain improvements in word segmentation and, once this condition is fulfilled, any increase in recall would increase the gain over the baseline.

Further evidence supporting this can be found when performing a word-based evaluation of the automatic prosodic boundaries obtained. For the BU and CSJ corpora, we computed the percentage of word boundaries found, out of the total word boundaries in the corpora, and the proportion of incorrect word boundaries from the total number of boundaries found (see Table 3). It shows that the systems that bring improvements over the baseline ($maxFscore$ and $maxPrecision$ for BU, and $maxPrecision$ for CSJ) have a relatively low rate of false alarms (lower than 6%). At the same time, the increase in performance can be obtained even without a high coverage of the corpus, the $maxPrecision$ models achieving this with a coverage lower than 10%.

Since all the resuls reported in this paper were obtained using the state-of-the-art Adaptor Grammar model, $Colloc3-Syll$, we also verified that our results are generalizable across different models. We created several AG models, by varying the following settings in the grammar: using either one or three collocation levels, and having knowledge or not of the syllabic structure. This gave us, besides the already tested $Colloc3-Syll$ model, three new models: $Colloc3-noSyll$, $Colloc-Syll$ and $Colloc-noSyll$, which were all tested on the CSJ. When evaluating the token F-score obtained using these models, we can see improvements for all the models, regardless of the nature of the prosodic

| Corpus | Model | % found | % incorr |
|---|---|---|---|
| BU | oracle | 100 | 0 |
| | maxPrecision | 7.0 | 0.1 |
| | maxFscore | 20.3 | 5.7 |
| | maxRecall | 40.4 | 34.2 |
| CSJ | oracle | 100 | 0 |
| | maxPrec | 9.9 | 0.04 |
| | maxFscore | 21.0 | 23.5 |
| | maxRecall | 32.8 | 51.3 |

Table 3: Word boundary-based evaluation of the three systems used for prosodic boundary detection. We report the percentage of correct word boundaries found and the number of incorrect boundaries found, as a percentage of all boundaries found.

boundaries used.

Before closing, we note that prosody seem to helps differentially the segmentation of the two languages we tested. In Japanese we found improvements reaching 10 percentage points in F-score, whereas the improvements in English were more modest (5 points for the BU, 1 point for the LUCID), when automatic boundaries are used. This could be due to differences in the segmentation problem across these two languages. Indeed, words in Japanese are in their majority composed of several syllables, and many words contain embedded words, making the segmentation problem intrinsically more difficult than in English, for which the large majority of words are monosyllabic (Fourtassi et al., 2013). It is possible that prosody particularly helps those languages with a polysyllabic lexicon, by helping prevent over-segmentation.

While the current work examined the use of prosodic boundaries for word segmentation in two languages, we would like to extend the study to more languages. We would expect a similar behaviour also for other languages, but it would be interesting to investigate the interaction between boundary information and collocation level for other typologically distinct languages. Also, we have employed here oracle segmental information for the automatic detection of prosodic boundaries. In the future we plan to completely automatize the process, by employing segmental durations obtained with signal-based methods for speech segmentation. Finally, prosody was introduced here by way of a discrete symbol, forcing us to make a binary decision. A more integrated model would enable to associate prosodic break with a probability distribution, over acoustic features, thereby achieving the joint learning of segmentation and prosody.

## Acknowledgments

The authors would like to thank the three anonymous reviewers for their insightful comments. The research leading to these results was funded by the European Research Council (ERC-2011-AdG-295810 BOOTPHON). It was also supported by the Agence Nationale pour la Recherche (ANR-10-LABX-0087 IEC, ANR-10-IDEX-0001-02 PSL*), the Fondation de France, the École des Neurosciences de Paris, and the Région Île-de-France (DIM cerveau et pensée).

## References

Sankaranarayanan Ananthakrishnan and Shrikanth Narayanan. 2008. Automatic prosodic event detection using acoustic, lexical, and syntactic evidence. *Audio, Speech, and Language Processing, IEEE Transactions on*, 16(1):216–228.

Rachel Baker and Valerie Hazan. 2010. LUCID: a corpus of spontaneous and read clear speech in British English. In *Proceedings of DiSS-LPSS Joint Workshop*, pages 3–6.

Benjamin Börschinger and Mark Johnson. 2014. Exploring the role of stress in Bayesian word segmentation using Adaptor Grammars. *Transactions of the Association for Computational Linguistics*, 2:93–104.

Luc Boruta. 2011. *Indicators of allophony and phonemehood*. Ph.D. thesis, Paris-Diderot University.

Michael Brent and Timothy Cartwright. 1996. Distributional regularity and phonotactics are useful for segmentation. *Cognition*, 61:3–125.

Anne Christophe and Emmanuel Dupoux. 1996. Bootstrapping lexical acquisition: The role of prosodic structure. *The Linguistic Review*, 13(3-4):383–412.

Anne Christophe, Emmanuel Dupoux, Josiane Bertoncini, and Jacques Mehler. 1994. Do infants perceive word boundaries? An empirical study of the bootstrapping of lexical acquisition. *Journal of the Acoustical Society of America*, 95:1570–1580.

Anne Christophe, Teresa Guasti, Marina Nespor, Emmanuel Dupoux, and Brit van Ooyen. 1997. Reflections on prosodic bootstrapping: its role for lexical and syntactic acquisition. *Language and Cognitive Processes*, 12:585–612.

Anne Christophe, Jacques Mehler, and Núria Sebastián-Gallés. 2001. Perception of prosodic boundary correlates by newborn infants. *Infancy*, 2(3):385–394.

Abdellah Fourtassi, Benjamin Börschinger, Mark Johnson, and Emmanuel Dupoux. 2013. Whyisenglishsoeasytosegment? In *CMCL 2013*.

LouAnn Gerken, Peter Jusczyk, and Denise Mandel. 1994. When prosody fails to cue syntactic structure: 9-month-olds' sensitivity to phonological versus syntactic phrases. *Cognition*, 51(3):237–265.

Sharon Goldwater, Thomas Griffiths, and Mark Johnson. 2009. A Bayesian framework for word segmentation: Exploring the effects of context. *Cognition*, 112(1):21–54.

Sharon Goldwater, Thomas Griffiths, and Mark Johnson. 2011. Producing power-law distributions and damping word frequencies with two-stage language models. *Journal of Machine Learning Research*, 12:2335–2382.

Ariel Gout, Anne Christophe, and James Morgan. 2004. Phonological phrase boundaries constrain lexical access II. Infant data. *Journal of Memory and Language*, 51(4):548–567.

Jui-Ting Huang, Mark Hasegawa-Johnson, and Chilin Shih. 2008. Unsupervised prosodic break detection in Mandarin speech. In *Proc. of Speech Prosody*, pages 165–168.

Je Hun Jeon and Yang Liu. 2009. Semi-supervised learning for automatic prosodic event detection using co-training algorithm. In *Proceedings of the Joint Conference of the 47th Annual Meeting of the ACL and the 4th International Joint Conference on Natural Language Processing of the AFNLP*, pages 540–548.

Mark Johnson and Sharon Goldwater. 2009. Improving nonparameteric Bayesian inference: experiments on unsupervised word segmentation with adaptor grammars. In *Proceedings of Human Language Technologies: The 2009 Annual Conference of the North American Chapter of the Association for Computational Linguistics*, pages 317–325.

Mark Johnson, Thomas Griffiths, and Sharon Goldwater. 2007. Adaptor grammars: A framework for specifying compositional nonparametric bayesian models. *Advances in neural information processing systems*, 19:641.

Mark Johnson, Anne Christophe, Emmanuel Dupoux, and Katherine Demuth. 2014. Modelling function words improves unsupervised word segmentation. In *Proceedings of the 52nd Annual Meeting of the Association for Computational Linguistics (Volume 1: Long Papers)*, pages 282–292.

Mark Johnson. 2008. Unsupervised word segmentation for Sesotho using adaptor grammars. In *Proceedings of the Tenth Meeting of ACL Special Interest Group on Computational Morphology and Phonology*, pages 20–27.

Peter Jusczyk, Kathy Hirsh-Pasek, Deborah Kemler-Nelson, Lori Kennedy, Amanda Woodward, and Julie Piwoz. 1992. Perception of acoustic correlates of major phrasal units by young infants. *Cognitive Psychology*, 24(2):252–293.

Kai-Fu Lee and Hsiao-Wuen Hon. 1989. Speaker-independent phone recognition using hidden Markov models. *Acoustics, Speech and Signal Processing, IEEE Transactions on*, 37(11):1641–1648.

Bogdan Ludusan and Emmanuel Dupoux. 2014. Towards low-resource prosodic boundary detection. In *Proceedings of SLTU*, pages 231–237.

Bogdan Ludusan, Guillaume Gravier, and Emmanuel Dupoux. 2014. Incorporating prosodic boundaries in unsupervised term discovery. In *Proceedings of Speech Prosody*, pages 939–943.

Kikuo Maekawa, Hideaki Kikuchi, Yosuke Igarashi, and Jennifer Venditti. 2002. X-JToBI: an extended J-ToBI for spontaneous speech. In *Proceedings of INTERSPEECH*, pages 1545–1548.

Kikuo Maekawa. 2003. Corpus of Spontaneous Japanese: Its design and evaluation. In *ISCA & IEEE Workshop on Spontaneous Speech Processing and Recognition*.

Mari Ostendorf, Patti Price, and Stefanie Shattuck-Hufnagel. 1995. The Boston University radio news corpus. *Linguistic Data Consortium*, pages 1–19.

Mihael Perman, Jim Pitman, and Marc Yor. 1992. Size-biased sampling of Poisson point processes and excursions. *Probability Theory and Related Fields*, 92(1):21–39.

Amanda Seidl. 2007. Infants use and weighting of prosodic cues in clause segmentation. *Journal of Memory and Language*, 57:24–48.

Kim Silverman, Mary Beckman, John Pitrelli, Mari Ostendorf, Colin Wightman, Patti Price, Janet Pierrehumbert, and Julia Hirschberg. 1992. TOBI: a standard for labeling English prosody. In *Proceedings of ICSLP*, pages 867–870.

Gabriel Synnaeve, Isabelle Dautriche, Benjamin Börschinger, Mark Johnson, and Emmanuel Dupoux. 2014. Unsupervised word segmentation in context. In *Proceedings of COLING 2014, the 25th International Conference on Computational Linguistics: Technical Papers*, pages 2326–2334.

Yee Whye Teh. 2006. A hierarchical Bayesian language model based on Pitman-Yor processes. In *Proceedings of the 21st International Conference on Computational Linguistics and the 44th annual meeting of the Association for Computational Linguistics*, pages 985–992.

Caroline Wellmann, Julia Holzgrefe, Hubert Truckenbrodt, Isabell Wartenburger, and Barbara Höhle. 2012. How each prosodic boundary cue matters: evidence from German infants. *Frontiers in psychology*, 3.

Colin Wightman and Mari Ostendorf. 1991. Automatic recognition of prosodic phrases. In *Proceedings of Acoustics, Speech, and Signal Processing, 1991 International Conference on*, pages 321–324.

Jiahong Yuan and Mark Liberman. 2008. Speaker identification on the SCOTUS corpus. In *Proceedings of Acoustics '08*.

# So similar and yet incompatible: Toward automated identification of semantically compatible words

**Germán Kruszewski** and **Marco Baroni**
Center for Mind/Brain Sciences (University of Trento, Italy)
(german.kruszewski|marco.baroni)@unitn.it

## Abstract

We introduce the challenge of detecting *semantically compatible* words, that is, words that can potentially refer to the same thing (*cat* and *hindrance* are compatible, *cat* and *dog* are not), arguing for its central role in many semantic tasks. We present a publicly available data-set of human compatibility ratings, and a neural-network model that takes distributional embeddings of words as input and learns alternative embeddings that perform the compatibility detection task quite well.

## 1 Introduction

Vectors encoding distributional information extracted from large text corpora provide very effective estimates of semantic similarity or, more generally, relatedness between words (Clark, 2015; Erk, 2012; Turney and Pantel, 2010). Semantic relatedness is undoubtedly a core property of word understanding, and indeed current vector-based *distributional semantic models* (DSMs) provide an impressive approximation to human judgments in many tasks (Baroni et al., 2014). However, relatedness alone is too general a notion to truly capture the nuances of human conceptual knowledge. The terms *animal*, *puppy*, and *cat* are all closely related to *dog*, but the nature of their relation is very different, each affording different inferences: If you tell me that Fido is a dog, I will also conclude that he's an animal, that he is not a cat, and that he might or might not be a puppy.

The previous examples hint at a fundamental semantic property that is only partially linked to relatedness, namely *compatibility*, that we define, for our current purposes, as follows: *Linguistic expressions $w_1$ and $w_2$ are compatible iff, in a reasonably normal state of affairs, they can both truthfully refer to the same thing. If they cannot, then they are incompatible.* We realize that the notion of a "reasonably normal sate of affairs" is dangerously vague, but we want to exclude science-fiction scenarios in which dogs mutate into cats. And we use *thing* as a catch-all term for anything words (or other linguistic expressions) can refer to (entities, events, collections, etc.).

The notions of compatibility and incompatibility have been introduced in theoretical semantics before (Cruse, 1986; Murphy, 2010). The definition that we give here for compatibility is related, but different from the one by Cruse. For example, subsuming pairs are out of the scope of compatibility under his definition, whereas we include them. Murphy defines incompatibility similarly to us, but she does not define compatibility. We are not aware, on the other hand, of any earlier systematic attempt to study the phenomenon empirically, nor to model it computationally.

In general, compatible terms will be semantically related (*dog* and *animal*). However, relatedness does not suffice: many semantically related, even very similar terms are not compatible (*dog* and *cat*). Relatedness is not even a necessary condition: A *husband* can be a *hindrance* in an all-too-normal state of affairs, but the concepts of husband and hindrance are not semantically close. Moreover, compatibility does not reduce to (a set of) more commonly studied semantic relations. While it relates to hy-



*Human Language Technologies: The 2015 Annual Conference of the North American Chapter of the ACL*, pages 964–969,
Denver, Colorado, May 31 – June 5, 2015. 

pernymy, synonymy and co-hyponymy, there are cases, such as *husband/hindrance*, that do not naturally map to any of these relations. Also, although many incompatibles among closely related pairs are co-hyponyms, this is not necessarily the case: You cannot be both a *dog* and a *cat*, but you can be a *violinist* and a *drummer*.

We argue that, since knowing what's compatible plays a central role in human semantic reasoning, algorithms that determine compatibility automatically will help in many domains that require human-like semantic knowledge. Most obviously, compatibility is a necessary (although not sufficient) prerequisite for coreference. *Dog* and *puppy* could belong to the same coreference chain, whereas *dog* and *cat* do not. We conjecture that the relatively disappointing performance of DSMs in support of coreference resolution (Poesio et al., 2010) is at least partially due to the inability of standard DSMs to distinguish compatible and incompatible terms. Compatibility is also central to recognizing entailment (and contradiction): Standard DSMs are of relatively little use in recognizing entailment as they treat antonymous, contradictory words such as *dead* and *alive* as highly related (Adel and Schütze, 2014; Mohammad et al., 2013), with catastrophic results for the inferences that can be drawn (antonyms are just the tip of the incompatibility iceberg: *dog* and *cat* are not antonyms, but one still contradicts the other). Knowing what's compatible might also help in tasks that require recognizing (distant) paraphrases, such as question answering, document summarization or even machine translation (*the violinist also played the drum* might corefer with *the drummer also played the violin*, whereas *the dog was killed* and *the cat was killed* must refer to different events). Other applications could include modeling semantic plausibility of a nominal phrase (Vecchi et al., 2011; Lynott and Connell, 2009), where the goal is to accept expressions like *coastal mosquito*, but reject *parlamentary tomato*. Finally, the notion of incompatibility relates to (certain kinds of) negation. Negation is notoriously difficult to model with DSMs (Hermann et al., 2013), and compatibility might offer a new angle into it.

In this paper, we introduce a new, large benchmark to evaluate computational models on compatibility detection. We then present a supervised neural-network based model that takes distributional semantic vectors as input and embeds them into a space that is optimized for compatibility detection. The model performs significantly better than direct DSM relatedness, and achieves high scores in absolute terms.

## 2 The compatibility benchmark

We started the benchmark construction by manually assembling a list of 299 words including mostly concrete, basic-level concepts picked from categories where taxonomically close terms tend to be incompatible (e.g., biological classes such as animals and vegetables), as well as from categories that are more compatibility-prone (kinship terms, professions), or somewhere in the middle (tools, places). The list also included category names at different levels of abstraction (*creature*, *animal*, *carnivore*...), as well as some terms that were expected to be of high general compatibility (*hindrance*, *expert*, *companion*...). By randomly coupling words from this list, we generated pairs that should reflect a wide range of compatibility patterns (compatible and incompatible coordinate terms, words in an entailment relation, dissimilar but compatible, dissimilar and incompatible, etc.).[1] We generated about 18K such random pairs.

We used a subset of about 3K pairs in a pilot study on the CrowdFlower[2] crowd-sourcing platforms, in which we asked participants to annotate them for compatibility either as a yes/no judgment accompanied by a confidence rating, or on a 7-point scale. Correlation between mean binary and ordinal ratings was extremely high (>0.95), so we decided to adopt the potentially more precise, albeit more noisy, 7-point scale. Confidence judgments (median: 6.6/7), participant agreement and sanity checks on obvious cases confirmed that the raters understood the task well and produced the expected judgments consistently.

We thus launched a larger CrowdFlower survey,

[1] We realize that the resulting pairs might not resemble the natural distribution of compatibility decisions that an average person might encounter in daily life. However, the fact that (as we show below) subjects were highly consistent in judging the items proves that the data reflect genuine shared semantic knowledge a computational model should be able to capture.

[2] http://www.crowdflower.com

asking participants to rate pairs on a 7-point scale by answering the following question: "How much do you agree with the statement that <*word1*> and <*word2*> can refer to the same thing, animal or person?" We asked the judges to consider real-life scenarios and fairly ordinary circumstances; in case of ambiguity, they were asked to choose the sense that would make the pair compatible, as long as it was sufficiently common. 20 control items with obvious choices (e.g. *drummer/ant - writer/father*) were inserted to exclude raters that did not perform the task seriously. We paid close attention to contributors' feedback, correcting dubious controls. For example, we removed *bucket/chair*, since one contributor pointed out that you could turn a bucket upside down and use it as a chair.[3] In this way, we obtained usable annotation for 17973 pairs, each rated by 10 participants[4]. The average standard deviation was as as low as 0.70, compared to the standard deviation of a uniformly distributed multinomial distribution, which amounts to 1.8. As expected, ratings were highly skewed as most random pairs are incompatible: the median is 1.10 (with a standard deviation of 1.81). Yet, the overall distribution is bimodal, peaking at the two ends of the scale.

In order to be able to phrase (in)compatibility detection not only in continuous terms, but also as dichotomous tasks, we further produced a list of unambiguously (in)compatible pairs from the ends of the rating scale. Specifically, we manually inspected a subset of the list (before any computational simulation was run), and picked a mean 3.7 rating (exclusive) as minimum value for compatible pairs, and 1.6 (inclusive) as maximum score for incompatible ones. The number of problematic cases above/below these thresholds was absolutely negligible. We thus coded the data set by classifying the 2,933 pairs above the first threshold as compatible (e.g., *expert/criminal*, *hill/obstacle*, *snake/vermin*), the 12,669 pairs below the second as incompatible (e.g., *bottle/plate*, *cheetah/queen*), and the remainder as neither.

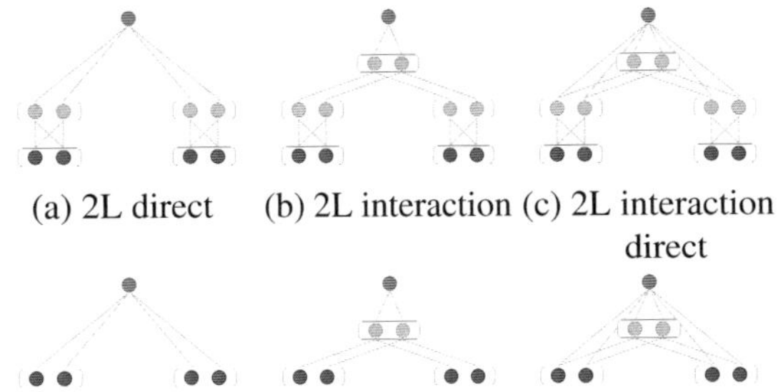

(a) 2L direct (b) 2L interaction (c) 2L interaction direct

(d) 1L direct (e) 1L interaction (f) 1L interaction direct

Figure 1: Schematic representation of the models

## 3 Models

We take DSM vectors as input, since they provide us with semantically rich word representations, and seek to induce a compatibility measure by learning the parameters of a model in a supervised manner. In particular, we used the word vectors publicly available at `http://clic.cimec.unitn.it/composes/semantic-vectors.html`. These vectors, extracted with the word2vec toolkit (Mikolov et al., 2013) from a 3B token corpus, were shown by Baroni et al. (2014) to produce near-state-of-the-art performance on a variety of semantic tasks.

We hypothesized that the interaction between a simple set of features (induced from the distributional ones) should account for a large portion of compatibility patterns. For example, human roles would typically be compatible (*classmate/friend*), whereas two animals would probably be incompatible (*iguana/zebra*). The model should thus be able to learn features associated to such classes, and compatibility rules associated to their interaction (e.g., if both $w_1$ and $w_2$ have large values for a *human* feature, compatibility is more likely). We incorporated this insight into the **2L interaction** neural network illustrated in Figure 1b. This network takes the distributional representations of the words in a pair, transforms them into new feature vectors by means of a mapping that is shared by both inputs, constructs the vector of pairwise interactions between the induced features, and finally uses the weighted combination of the latter to produce a real-number

[3]We also were surprised to learn that drummer ants actually exist. Yet, in that case we decided to keep the control item since, under the most common sense of *drummer*, and in ordinary circumstances, ants cannot be drummers.

[4]The guidlienes provided to the participants and the collected data set are available at: `http://clic.cimec.unitn.it/composes/`

score.

We considered then some variations of the 2L interaction model, to investigate the importance of each of its components. In **2L direct** (Figure 1a), we removed the interaction layer, making the model score a weighted combination of the mapped vectors. The **2L interaction direct** model (Figure 1c) computes the final score through a weighted combination of both the mapped representations and their interaction vector. The **1L** models (Figures 1d, 1e and 1f) are analogous to the corresponding 2L models, but removing the feature mapping layer, thus operating directly on the distributional vectors.

## 4 Experiments

Since compatibility is a symmetric relation, we first duplicated each pair in the benchmark by swapping the two words. We then split it into training, testing and development sections. To make the task more challenging, we enforced disjoint vocabularies in each of them. For example, *drummer* only occurs in the training set, while *ant*, only in the test set. We use about 1/10th of the vocabulary (29 words) on the development set and the rest was split equally between train and test (135 words each). The resulting partitions contain 7,228 (train), 7,336 (test) and 312 (development) pairs, respectively.

To train the models, we used the scores they generate in three sub-tasks: approximation of average ratings, classification of compatibles and classification of incompatibles. We used mean square error as cost function for the first sub-task, cross-entropy for the latter two.

We implemented the models in Torch7 (Collobert et al., 2011).[5] We trained them for 120 epochs with adagrad, with a batch size of 150 items and adopting an emphasizing scheme (LeCun et al., 2012), where compatibles, incompatibles and middle-ground items appear in equal proportions. We fixed hidden-layer size to 100 dimensions, while we tuned a coefficient for a L2-norm regularization term on the development data.

We evaluated the models ability to predict human compatibility ratings as well as to detect compatible and incompatible items.

[5]We make the code available at `https://github.com/germank/compatibility-naacl2015`

| | corr. | comp. | | | incomp. | | |
|---|---|---|---|---|---|---|---|
| Model | $r$ | P | R | F1 | P | R | F1 |
| 1L direct | 50 | 59 | 55 | 57 | 80 | 83 | 72 |
| 1L interaction | 51 | 50 | 61 | 55 | 80 | 77 | 79 |
| 1L int. direct | 49 | 52 | 57 | 54 | 80 | 79 | 80 |
| 2L direct | 49 | 51 | 58 | 54 | 81 | 79 | 80 |
| **2L interaction** | **72** | 76 | 58 | **66** | 84 | 90 | **87** |
| 2L int. direct | 67 | 71 | 58 | 64 | 82 | 85 | 84 |
| 1L mono | 35 | 31 | 57 | 41 | 79 | 77 | 78 |
| 2L mono | 35 | 32 | 64 | 43 | 80 | 72 | 76 |
| Cosine | 36 | 29 | 58 | 38 | 78 | 71 | 74 |

Table 1: Experimental results. Correlation with human ratings measured by Pearson $r$. (In)compatibility detection scored by the F1 measure.

We compared the supervised measures to the cosine of pairs directly represented by their DSM vectors (with thresholds tuned on the training set). We expected this baseline to fare relatively well on incompatibility detection, since many of our randomly generated pairs were both incompatible and dissimilar (e.g., *bag/bus*).

Also, we controlled for the portion of the data that can be accounted just by looking at one of the words of the relation (for example, the presence of a word might indicate that the relation is incompatible). To this end, we included two models that look at only one of the words in the pair. **1L mono** is a logistic regression model that only looks at the first word of the pair while **2L mono** is an analogous neural network with one hidden layer.

Results are reported in Table 1. As it can be seen, all the supervised models from Figure 1 strongly outperform the cosine (that, as expected, is nevertheless quite good at detecting incompatibles). Also, they outperform the mono models (with the only exception of 1L direct on incompatibility), showing that the data they account for cannot be reduced to properties of individual lexical items. Importantly, the 2L interaction model is way ahead of all other models, confirming our expectations.

To gain some insight into the features learned by the best model, we labeled the words of our input vocabulary with one of the following general category tags: *animal*, *artefact*, *general-function*, *human*, *organic-and-food* and *place*. The distribution

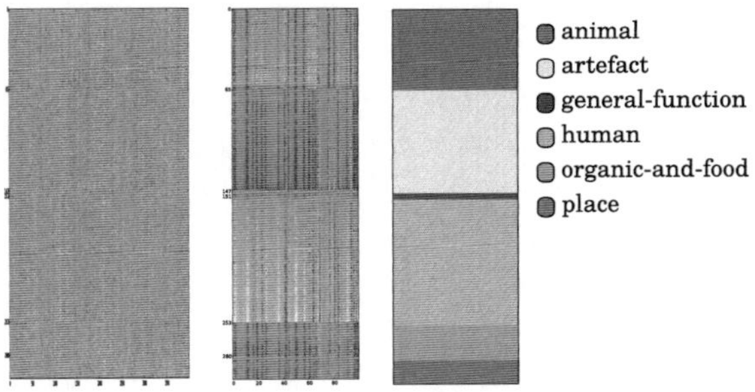


(a) Input vectors (b) Mapped vectors (c) Categories

Figure 2: Heatmap visualization of original DSM features and features learned by the mapping function of the 2L interaction model.

of the vocabulary across the labels is shown in Figure 2c. If we plot the input distributional vectors so that words tagged with the same category are adjacent to each other, and categories arranged as in Figure 2c, we obtain the heatmap in Figure 2a, where no obvious pattern emerges. If instead we plot the output vectors of 2L interaction mapping in the same way, we obtain the heatmap in Figure 2b. It is evident that the mapping produces vectors that are similar within most categories, and very different across them. Thus, the 2L interaction model clearly learned the relevance of general categories in capturing compatibility judgments. The fact that this model produced the best results hints at the importance of exploiting this source of information, confirming the intuition we used in designing it, that compatibility can be characterized by a combination of general relatedness and category-specific cues.

Finally, we explored to what extent the data can be accounted by co-hyponymy, an idea briefly introduced in the introductory discussion of Section 1. For simplicity purposes, we take the same category tags we just introduced as a word's hypernym. Classifying co-hyponyms as incompatibles and non-cohyponyms as compatibles performs very poorly (7 and 18 F1-scores for compatibility and incompatibility, respectively). On the other hand, the opposite strategy – co-hyponyms as compatibles and non-cohyponyms as incompatibles – works much better (62 and 84 F1), even outperforming many supervised models. Yet, this strategy does not suffice. For example, all animal pairs would be treated as compatibles, whereas 54% of them are actually incompatible. By contrast the L2 interaction model gets 78% of these incompatible pairs right.

## 5 Conclusion

We have introduced the challenge of modeling compatibility to the computational linguistics community. To this end, we collected a data set, and produced a model that satisfactorily captures a large portion of the data, that cannot be accounted for by simple semantic relatedness. Finally, we have explored the features learned by the model, confirming that high-order category information is relevant for producing compatibility judgements.

Computational models of compatibility could help in many semantic tasks, such as coreference resolution, question answering, modeling plausibility and negation. Future lines of research will explore the contributions that accounting for compatibility can make to these tasks.

## Acknowledgments

We thank Denis Paperno for the interesting discussions that motivated this paper and the three anonymous reviewers for useful comments. We acknowledge ERC 2011 Starting Independent Research Grant n. 283554 (COMPOSES).

## References

Heike Adel and Hinrich Schütze. 2014. Using mined coreference chains as a resource for a semantic task. In *Proceedings of EMNLP*, pages 1447–1452, Doha, Qatar.

Marco Baroni, Georgiana Dinu, and Germán Kruszewski. 2014. Don't count, predict! a systematic comparison of context-counting vs. context-predicting semantic vectors. In *Proceedings of ACL*, pages 238–247, Baltimore, MD.

Stephen Clark. 2015. Vector space models of lexical meaning. In Shalom Lappin and Chris Fox, editors, *Handbook of Contemporary Semantics, 2nd ed.* Blackwell, Malden, MA. In press; http://www.cl.cam.ac.uk/~sc609/pubs/sem_handbook.pdf.

Ronan Collobert, Koray Kavukcuoglu, and Clément Farabet. 2011. Torch7: A matlab-like environment for machine learning. In *BigLearn, NIPS Workshop*.

D. Alan Cruse. 1986. *Lexical Semantics*. Cambridge University Press, Cambridge, UK.

Katrin Erk. 2012. Vector space models of word meaning and phrase meaning: A survey. *Language and Linguistics Compass*, 6(10):635–653.

Karl Moritz Hermann, Edward Grefenstette, and Phil Blunsom. 2013. "Not not bad" is not "bad": A distributional account of negation. In *Proceedings of ACL Workshop on Continuous Vector Space Models and their Compositionality*, pages 74–82, Sofia, Bulgaria.

Yann A LeCun, Léon Bottou, Genevieve B Orr, and Klaus-Robert Müller. 2012. Efficient backprop. In *Neural networks: Tricks of the trade*, pages 9–48. Springer, Berlin.

Dermot Lynott and Louise Connell. 2009. Embodied conceptual combination. *Frontiers in Psychology*, 1:212.

Tomas Mikolov, Kai Chen, Greg Corrado, and Jeffrey Dean. 2013. Efficient estimation of word representations in vector space. http://arxiv.org/abs/1301.3781/.

Saif Mohammad, Bonnie Dorr, Graeme Hirst, and Peter Turney. 2013. Computing lexical contrast. *Computational Linguistics*, 39(3):555–590.

M. Lynne Murphy. 2010. Antonymy and incompatibility. In Keith Allan, editor, *Concise Encyclopedia of Semantics*. Elsevier, Amsterdam.

Massimo Poesio, Simone Ponzetto, and Yannick Versley. 2010. Computational models of anaphora resolution: A survey. http://clic.cimec.unitn.it/massimo/Publications/lilt.pdf.

Peter Turney and Patrick Pantel. 2010. From frequency to meaning: Vector space models of semantics. *Journal of Artificial Intelligence Research*, 37:141–188.

Eva Maria Vecchi, Marco Baroni, and Roberto Zamparelli. 2011. (Linear) maps of the impossible: Capturing semantic anomalies in distributional space. In *Proceedings of the ACL Workshop on Distributional Semantics and Compositionality*, pages 1–9, Portland, OR.

# Do Supervised Distributional Methods Really Learn Lexical Inference Relations?

**Omer Levy**† **Steffen Remus**§ **Chris Biemann**§ **Ido Dagan**†

† Natural Language Processing Lab
Bar-Ilan University
Ramat-Gan, Israel
{omerlevy,dagan}@cs.biu.ac.il

§ Language Technology Lab
Technische Universität Darmstadt
Darmstadt, Germany
{remus,biem}@cs.tu-darmstadt.de

## Abstract

Distributional representations of words have been recently used in supervised settings for recognizing lexical inference relations between word pairs, such as hypernymy and entailment. We investigate a collection of these state-of-the-art methods, and show that they do not actually learn a relation between two words. Instead, they learn an independent property of a single word in the pair: whether that word is a "prototypical hypernym".

## 1 Introduction

Inference in language involves recognizing inference relations between two words ($x$ and $y$), such as causality ($flu \rightarrow fever$), hypernymy ($cat \rightarrow animal$), and other notions of lexical entailment. The distributional approach to automatically recognize these relations relies on representing each word $x$ as a vector $\vec{x}$ of *contextual features*: other words that tend to appear in its vicinity. Such features are typically used in word similarity tasks, where cosine similarity is a standard similarity measure between two word vectors: $sim(x, y) = cos(\vec{x}, \vec{y})$.

Many unsupervised distributional methods of recognizing lexical inference replace cosine similarity with an asymmetric similarity function (Weeds and Weir, 2003; Clarke, 2009; Kotlerman et al., 2010; Santus et al., 2014). Supervised methods, reported to perform better, try to learn the asymmetric operator from a training set. The various supervised methods differ by the way they represent each candidate pair of words $(x, y)$: Baroni et al. (2012) use concatenation $\vec{x} \oplus \vec{y}$, others (Roller et al., 2014; Weeds et al., 2014; Fu et al., 2014) take the vectors' difference $\vec{y} - \vec{x}$, and more sophisticated representations, based on contextual features, have also been tested (Turney and Mohammad, 2014; Rimell, 2014).

In this paper, we argue that these supervised methods do not, in fact, learn to recognize lexical inference. Our experiments reveal that much of their previously perceived success stems from lexical memorizing. Further experiments show that these supervised methods learn whether $y$ is a "prototypical hypernym" (i.e. a category), regardless of $x$, rather than learning a concrete relation between $x$ and $y$.

Our mathematical analysis reveals that said methods ignore the interaction between $x$ and $y$, explaining our empirical findings. We modify them accordingly by incorporating the similarity between $x$ and $y$. Unfortunately, the improvement in performance is incremental. We suspect that methods based solely on contextual features of single words are not learning lexical inference relations because contextual features might lack the necessary information to deduce how one word relates to another.

## 2 Experiment Setup

Due to various differences (e.g. corpora, train/test splits), we do not list previously reported results, but apply a large space of state-of-the-art supervised methods and review them comparatively. We observe similar trends to previously published results, and make the dataset splits available for replication.[1]

[1] http://u.cs.biu.ac.il/~nlp/resources/downloads/



*Human Language Technologies: The 2015 Annual Conference of the North American Chapter of the ACL*, pages 970–976,
Denver, Colorado, May 31 – June 5, 2015. 

| Dataset | #Instances | #Positive | #Negative |
|---|---|---|---|
| Kotlerman 2010 | 2,940 | 880 | 2,060 |
| Bless 2011 | 14,547 | 1,337 | 13,210 |
| Baroni 2012 | 2,770 | 1,385 | 1,385 |
| Turney 2014 | 1,692 | 920 | 772 |
| Levy 2014 | 12,602 | 945 | 11,657 |

Table 1: Datasets evaluated in this work.

### 2.1 Word Representations

We built 9 word representations over Wikipedia (1.5 billion tokens) using the cross-product of 3 types of contexts and 3 representation models.

#### 2.1.1 Context Types

**Bag-of-Words** Uses 5 tokens to each side of the target word (10 context words in total). It also employs subsampling (Mikolov et al., 2013a) to increase the impact of content words.

**Positional** Uses only 2 tokens to each side of the target word, and decorates them with their position (relative to the target word); e.g. $the_{-1}$ is a common positional context of *cat* (Schütze, 1993).

**Dependency** Takes all words that share a syntactic connection with the target word (Lin, 1998; Padó and Lapata, 2007; Baroni and Lenci, 2010). We used the same parsing apparatus as in (Levy and Goldberg, 2014).

#### 2.1.2 Representation Models

**PPMI** A word-context positive pointwise mutual information matrix $M$ (Niwa and Nitta, 1994).

**SVD** We reduced $M$'s dimensionality to $k = 500$ using Singular Value Decomposition (SVD).[2]

**SGNS** Skip-grams with negative sampling (Mikolov et al., 2013b) with 500 dimensions and 5 negative samples. SGNS was trained using a modified version of `word2vec` that allows different context types (Levy and Goldberg, 2014).[3]

### 2.2 Labeled Datasets

We used 5 labeled datasets for evaluation. Each dataset entry contains two words $(x, y)$ and a label whether $x$ entails $y$. Note that each dataset was created with a slightly different goal in mind, affecting word-pair generation and annotation. For example, both of Baroni's datasets are designed to capture hypernyms, while other datasets try to capture broader notions of lexical inference (e.g. causality). Table 1 provides metadata on each dataset, and the description below explains how each one was created.

**(Kotlerman et al., 2010)** Manually annotated lexical entailment of distributionally similar nouns.

**(Baroni and Lenci, 2011)** a.k.a. BLESS. Created by selecting unambiguous word pairs and their semantic relations from WordNet. Following Roller et al. (2014), we labeled noun hypernyms as positive examples and used meronyms, noun cohyponyms, and random noun pairs as negative.

**(Baroni et al., 2012)** Created in a similar fashion to BLESS. Hypernym pairs were selected as positive examples from WordNet, and then permutated to generate negative examples.

**(Turney and Mohammad, 2014)** Based on a crowdsourced dataset of 79 semantic relations (Jurgens et al., 2012). Each semantic relation was linguistically annotated as entailing or not.

**(Levy et al., 2014)** Based on manually annotated entailment graphs of subject-verb-object tuples (propositions). Noun entailments were extracted from entailing tuples that were identical except for one of the arguments, thus propagating the existence/absence of proposition-level entailment to the noun level. This dataset is the most realistic dataset, since the original entailment annotations were made in the context of a complete proposition.

### 2.3 Supervised Methods

We tested 4 compositions for representing $(x, y)$ as a feature vector: **concat** ($\vec{x} \oplus \vec{y}$) (Baroni et al., 2012), **diff** ($\vec{y} - \vec{x}$) (Roller et al., 2014; Weeds et al., 2014; Fu et al., 2014), **only x** ($\vec{x}$), and **only y** ($\vec{y}$). For each composition, we trained two types of classifiers, tuning hyperparameters with a validation set: logistic regression with $L_1$ or $L_2$ regularization, and SVM with a linear kernel or quadratic kernel.

## 3 Negative Results

Based on the above setup, we present three negative empirical results, which challenge the claim that the methods presented in §2.3 are learning a relation between $x$ and $y$. In addition to our setup, these results were also reproduced in preliminary exper-

[2]Following Caron (2001), we used the square root of the eigenvalue matrix $\Sigma_k$ for representing words: $M_k = U_k\sqrt{\Sigma_k}$.

[3]`http://bitbucket.org/yoavgo/word2vecf`

| Dataset | Lexical | +Contextual | $\Delta$ |
|---|---|---|---|
| Kotlerman 2010 | .346 | .437 | .091 |
| Bless 2011 | .960 | .960 | .000 |
| Baroni 2012 | .638 | .802 | .164 |
| Turney 2014 | .644 | .747 | .103 |
| Levy 2014 | .302 | .370 | .068 |

Table 2: The performance ($F_1$) of lexical versus contextual feature classifiers on a random train/test split with lexical overlap.

| Dataset | Best Supervised | Only $\vec{y}$ | Unsupervised |
|---|---|---|---|
| Kotlerman 2010 | .408 | .375 | **.461** |
| Bless 2011 | **.665** | .637 | .197 |
| Baroni 2012 | .774 | .663 | **.788** |
| Turney 2014 | **.696** | .649 | .642 |
| Levy 2014 | **.324** | **.324** | .231 |

Table 3: A comparison of each dataset's best supervised method with: (a) the best result using **only y** composition; (b) unsupervised cosine similarity $cos(\vec{x}, \vec{y})$. Performance is measured by $F_1$. Uses lexical train/test splits.

iments by applying the JoBimText framework[4] for scalable distributional thesauri (Biemann and Riedl, 2013) using Google's syntactic N-grams (Goldberg and Orwant, 2013) as a corpus.

**Lexical Memorization** is the phenomenon in which the classifier learns that a specific word in a specific slot is a strong indicator of the label. For example, if a classifier sees many positive examples where $y = animal$, it may learn that anything that appears with $y = animal$ is likely to be positive, effectively *memorizing* the word $animal$.

The following experiment shows that supervised methods with contextual features are indeed memorizing words from the training set. We randomly split each dataset into 70% train, 5% validation, and 25% test, and train lexical-feature classifiers, using a one-hot vector representation of $y$ as input features. By definition, these classifiers memorize words from the training set. We then add contextual-features (as described in §2.1), on top of the lexical features, and train classifiers analogously. Table 2 compares the best lexical- and contextual-feature classifiers on each dataset. The performance difference is under 10 points in the larger datasets, showing that much of the contextual-feature classifiers' success is due to lexical memorization. Similar findings were also reported by Roller et al. (2014) and Weeds et al. (2014), supporting our memorization argument.

To prevent lexical memorization in our following experiments, we split each dataset into train and test sets with zero lexical overlap. We do this by randomly splitting the vocabulary into "train" and "test" words, and extract train-only and test-only subsets of each dataset accordingly. About half of each original dataset contains "mixed" examples (one train-word and one test-word); these are discarded.

[4] `http://jobimtext.org`

**Supervised vs Unsupervised** While supervised methods were reported to perform better than unsupervised ones, this is not always the case. As a baseline, we measured the "vanilla" cosine similarity of $x$ and $y$, tuning a threshold with the validation set. This unsupervised symmetric method outperforms all supervised methods in 2 out of 5 datasets (Table 3).

**Ignoring $x$'s Information** We compared the performance of **only y** to that of the best configuration in each dataset (Table 3). In 4 out of 5 datasets, the difference in performance is less than 5 points. This means that the classifiers are *ignoring* most of the information in $x$. Furthermore, they might be overlooking the compatibility (or incompatibility) of $x$ to $y$. Weeds et al. (2014) reported a similar result, but did not address the fundamental question it beckons: if the classifier *cannot* capture a relation between $x$ and $y$, then what is it learning?

## 4 Prototypical Hypernyms

We hypothesize that the supervised methods examined in this paper are learning whether $y$ is a likely "category" word – a *prototypical hypernym* – and, to a lesser extent, whether $x$ is a likely "instance" word. This hypothesis is consistent with our previous observations (§3).

Though the terms "instance" and "category" pertain to hypernymy, we use them here in the broader sense of entailment, i.e. as "tends to entail" and "tends to be entailed", respectively. We later show (§4.2) that this phenomenon indeed extends to other inference relations, such as meronymy.

### 4.1 Testing the Hypothesis

To test our hypothesis, we measure the performance of a trained classifier on *mismatched* instance-

| Dataset | Top Positional Contexts of $y$ |
|---|---|
| Kotlerman 2010 | grave$_{-1}$, substances$_{+2}$, lend-lease$_{-1}$, poor$_{-2}$, bureaucratic$_{-1}$, physical$_{-1}$, dry$_{-1}$, air$_{-1}$, civil$_{-1}$ |
| Bless 2011 | other$_{-1}$, resembling$_{+1}$, such$_{+1}$, assemblages$_{+1}$, magical$_{-1}$, species$_{+1}$, any$_{-2}$, invertebrate$_{-1}$ |
| Baroni 2012 | any$_{-1}$, any$_{-2}$, social$_{-1}$, every$_{-1}$, this$_{-1}$, kinds$_{-2}$, exotic$_{-1}$, magical$_{-1}$, institute$_{-2}$, important$_{-1}$ |
| Turney 2014 | of$_{+1}$, inner$_{-1}$, including$_{+1}$, such$_{+1}$, considerable$_{-1}$, their$_{-1}$, extra$_{-1}$, types$_{-2}$, different$_{-1}$, other$_{-1}$ |
| Levy 2014 | psychosomatic$_{-1}$, unidentified$_{-1}$, auto-immune$_{+2}$, specific$_{-1}$, unspecified$_{-1}$, treatable$_{-2}$, any$_{-1}$ |

Table 4: Top positional features learned with logistic regression over **concat**. Displaying positive features of $y$.

category pairs, e.g. $(banana, animal)$. For each dataset, we generate a set of such synthetic examples $S$, by taking the positive examples from the test portion $T^+$, and extracting all of its instance words $T_x^+$ and category words $T_y^+$.

$$T_x^+ = \{x|(x,y) \in T^+\} \quad T_y^+ = \{y|(x,y) \in T^+\}$$

We then define $S$ as all the in-place combinations of instance-category word pairs that did not appear in $T^+$, and are therefore likely to be false.

$$S = \left(T_x^+ \times T_y^+\right) \setminus T^+$$

Finally, we test the classifier on a sample of $S$ (due to its size). Since all examples are assumed to be false, we measure the false positive rate as *match error* – the error of classifying a mismatching instance-category pair as positive.

According to our hypothesis, the classifier cannot differentiate between matched and mismatched examples ($T^+$ and $S$, respectively). We therefore expect it to classify a similar proportion of $T^+$ and $S$ as positive. We validate this by comparing *recall* (proportion of $T^+$ classified as positive) to *match error* (proportion of $S$ classified as positive). Figure 1 plots these two measures across all configurations and datasets, and finds them to be extremely close (regression curve: $match\ error = 0.935 \cdot recall$), thus confirming our hypothesis.

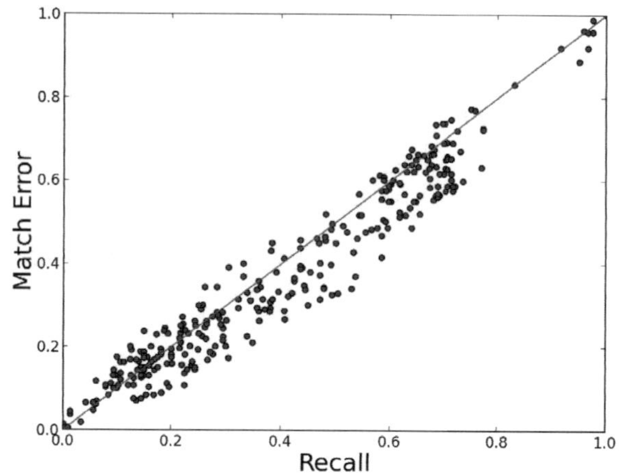


Figure 1: The correlation of recall (positive rate on $T^+$) with match error (positive rate on $S$) compared to perfect correlation (green line).

### 4.2 Prototypical Hypernym Features

A qualitative way of analyzing our hypothesis is to look at which features the classifiers tend to consider. Since SVD and SGNS features are not easily interpretable, we used PPMI with positional contexts as our representation, and trained a logistic regression model with $L_1$ regularization using **concat** over the entire dataset (no splits). We then observed the features with the highest weights (Table 4).

Many of these features describe dataset-specific category words. For example, in Levy's medical-domain dataset, many words entail "symptom", which is captured by the discriminative feature $psychosomatic_{-1}$. Other features are domain-independent indicators of category, e.g. $any_{-1}$, $every_{-1}$, and $kinds_{-2}$. The most striking features, though, are those that occur in Hearst (1992) patterns: $other_{-1}$, $such_{+1}$, $including_{+1}$, etc. These features appear in all datasets, and their analogues are often observed for $x$ (e.g. $such_{-2}$). Even qualitatively, many of the dominant features capture prototypical or dataset-specific hypernyms.

As mentioned, the datasets examined in this work also contain inference relations other than hypernymy. In Turney's dataset, for example, 77 % of positive pairs are non-hypernyms, and $y$ is often a quality ($coat \rightarrow warmth$) or a component ($chair \rightarrow legs$) of $x$. Qualities and components can often be detected via possessives, e.g. $of_{+1}$ and $their_{-1}$. Other prominent features, such as $extra_{-1}$

and $exotic_{-1}$, may also indicate qualities. These examples suggest that our hypothesis extends beyond hypernymy to other inference relations as well.

## 5 Analysis of Vector Composition

Our empirical findings show that **concat** and **diff** are clearly ignoring the relation between $x$ and $y$. To understand why, we analyze these compositions in the setting of a linear SVM. Given a test example, $(x, y)$ and a training example that is part of the SVM's support $(x_s, y_s)$, the linear kernel function yields Equations (1) for **concat** and (2) for **diff**.

$$K(\vec{x} \oplus \vec{y}, \vec{x_s} \oplus \vec{y_s}) = \vec{x} \cdot \vec{x_s} + \vec{y} \cdot \vec{y_s} \quad (1)$$

$$K(\vec{y} - \vec{x}, \vec{y_s} - \vec{x_s}) = \vec{x} \cdot \vec{x_s} + \vec{y} \cdot \vec{y_s} - \vec{x} \cdot \vec{y_s} - \vec{y} \cdot \vec{x_s} \quad (2)$$

Assuming all vectors are normalized (as in our experiments), the kernel function of **concat** is actually the similarity of the $x$-words plus the similarity of the $y$-words. Two dis-similarity terms are added to **diff**'s kernel, preventing the $x$ of one pair from being too similar to the other pair's $y$ (and vice versa).

Notice the absence of the term $\vec{x} \cdot \vec{y}$. This means that the classifier has no way of knowing if $x$ and $y$ are even related, let alone entailing. This flaw makes the classifier believe that any instance-category pair $(x, y)$ is in an entailment relation, even if they are unrelated, as seen in §4. Polynomial kernels also lack $\vec{x} \cdot \vec{y}$, and thus suffer from the same flaw.

## 6 Adding Intra-Pair Similarity

Using an RBF kernel with **diff** slightly mitigates this issue, as it factors in $\vec{x} \cdot \vec{y}$, among other similarities:

$$K_{RBF}(\vec{y} - \vec{x}, \vec{y_s} - \vec{x_s}) = e^{-\frac{1}{\sigma^2}|(\vec{y}-\vec{x})-(\vec{y_s}-\vec{x_s})|^2}$$
$$= e^{-\frac{1}{\sigma^2}(\vec{x}\vec{y}+\vec{x_s}\vec{y_s}+\vec{x}\vec{x_s}+\vec{y}\vec{y_s}-\vec{x}\vec{y_s}-\vec{y}\vec{x_s}-2)} \quad (3)$$

A more direct approach of incorporating $\vec{x} \cdot \vec{y}$ is to create a new kernel, which balances intra-pair similarities with inter-pair ones:

$$K_{SIM}((\vec{x}, \vec{y}), (\vec{x_s}, \vec{y_s})) = (\vec{x}\vec{y} \cdot \vec{x_s}\vec{y_s})^{\frac{\alpha}{2}} (\vec{x}\vec{x_s} \cdot \vec{y}\vec{y_s})^{\frac{1-\alpha}{2}} \quad (4)$$

While these methods reduce match error – $match\ error = 0.618 \cdot recall$ versus the previous regression curve of $match\ error = 0.935 \cdot recall$ – their overall performance is only incrementally better than that of linear methods (Table 5). This improvement is also, partially, a result of the nonlinearity introduced in these kernels.

| Dataset | LIN(concat) | LIN(diff) | RBF(diff) | SIM |
|---|---|---|---|---|
| Kotlerman 2010 | .367 | .187 | **.407** | .332 |
| Bless 2011 | .634 | .665 | .636 | **.687** |
| Baroni 2012 | .745 | .769 | .848 | **.859** |
| Turney 2014 | **.696** | .694 | .691 | .641 |
| Levy 2014 | .229 | .219 | **.252** | .244 |

Table 5: Performance ($F_1$) of SVM across kernels. **LIN** refers to the linear kernel (equations (1) and (2)), **RBF** to the Gaussian kernel (equation (3)), and **SIM** to our new kernel (equation (4)). Uses lexical train/test splits.

## 7 The Limitations of Contextual Features

In this work, we showed that state-of-the-art supervised methods for recognizing lexical inference appear to be learning whether $y$ is a prototypical hypernym, regardless of its relation with $x$. We tried to factor in the similarity between $x$ and $y$, yet observed only marginal improvements. While more sophisticated methods might be able to extract the necessary relational information from contextual features alone, it is also possible that this information simply *does not exist* in those features.

A (de)motivating example can be seen in §4.2. A typical $y$ often has $such_{+1}$ as a dominant feature, whereas $x$ tends to appear with $such_{-2}$. These features are relics of the Hearst (1992) pattern "$y$ such as $x$". However, contextual features of single words cannot capture the *joint* occurrence of $x$ and $y$ in that pattern; instead, they record only this observation as two independent features of different words. In that sense, contextual features are inherently handicapped in capturing relational information, requiring supervised methods to harness complementary information from more sophisticated features, such as textual patterns that connect $x$ with $y$ (Snow et al., 2005; Turney, 2006).

## Acknowledgements

This work was supported by the Adolf Messer Foundation, the Google Research Award Program, and the German Research Foundation through the German-Israeli Project Cooperation (DIP, grant DA 1600/1-1). We thank Stephen Roller for his valuable insights.

## References


Marco Baroni and Alessandro Lenci. 2010. Distributional memory: A general framework for corpus-based semantics. *Computational Linguistics*, 36(4):673–721.

Marco Baroni and Alessandro Lenci. 2011. How we blessed distributional semantic evaluation. In *Proceedings of the GEMS 2011 Workshop on GEometrical Models of Natural Language Semantics*, pages 1–10, Edinburgh, UK.

Marco Baroni, Raffaella Bernardi, Ngoc-Quynh Do, and Chung-chieh Shan. 2012. Entailment above the word level in distributional semantics. In *Proceedings of the 13th Conference of the European Chapter of the Association for Computational Linguistics*, pages 23–32, Avignon, France.

Chris Biemann and Martin Riedl. 2013. Text: Now in 2D! A framework for lexical expansion with contextual similarity. *Journal of Language Modelling*, 1(1):55–95.

John Caron. 2001. Experiments with LSA scoring: Optimal rank and basis. In *Proceedings of the SIAM Computational Information Retrieval Workshop*, pages 157–169.

Daoud Clarke. 2009. Context-theoretic semantics for natural language: an overview. In *Proceedings of the Workshop on Geometrical Models of Natural Language Semantics*, pages 112–119, Athens, Greece.

Ruiji Fu, Jiang Guo, Bing Qin, Wanxiang Che, Haifeng Wang, and Ting Liu. 2014. Learning semantic hierarchies via word embeddings. In *Proceedings of the 52nd Annual Meeting of the Association for Computational Linguistics (Volume 1: Long Papers)*, pages 1199–1209, Baltimore, Maryland.

Yoav Goldberg and Jon Orwant. 2013. A dataset of syntactic-ngrams over time from a very large corpus of english books. In *Second Joint Conference on Lexical and Computational Semantics (*SEM), Volume 1: Proceedings of the Main Conference and the Shared Task: Semantic Textual Similarity*, pages 241–247, Atlanta, Georgia, USA.

Marti A Hearst. 1992. Automatic acquisition of hyponyms from large text corpora. In *COLING 1992 Volume 2: The 15th International Conference on Computational Linguistics*, pages 529–545, Nantes, France.

David A Jurgens, Peter D Turney, Saif M Mohammad, and Keith J Holyoak. 2012. Semeval-2012 task 2: Measuring degrees of relational similarity. In **SEM 2012: The First Joint Conference on Lexical and Computational Semantics – Volume 1: Proceedings of the main conference and the shared task, and Volume 2: Proceedings of the Sixth International Workshop on Semantic Evaluation (SemEval 2012)*, pages 356–364, Montréal, Quebec, Canada.

Lili Kotlerman, Ido Dagan, Idan Szpektor, and Maayan Zhitomirsky-Geffet. 2010. Directional distributional similarity for lexical inference. *Natural Language Engineering*, 4(16):359–389.

Omer Levy and Yoav Goldberg. 2014. Dependency-based word embeddings. In *Proceedings of the 52nd Annual Meeting of the Association for Computational Linguistics (Volume 2: Short Papers)*, pages 302–308, Baltimore, Maryland.

Omer Levy, Ido Dagan, and Jacob Goldberger. 2014. Focused entailment graphs for open ie propositions. In *Proceedings of the Eighteenth Conference on Computational Natural Language Learning*, pages 87–97, Baltimore, Maryland.

Dekang Lin. 1998. Automatic retrieval and clustering of similar words. In *Proceedings of the 36th Annual Meeting of the Association for Computational Linguistics and 17th International Conference on Computational Linguistics, Volume 2*, pages 768–774, Montréal, Quebec, Canada.

Tomas Mikolov, Kai Chen, Greg Corrado, and Jeffrey Dean. 2013a. Efficient estimation of word representations in vector space. In *Proceedings of the International Conference on Learning Representations (ICLR)*.

Tomas Mikolov, Ilya Sutskever, Kai Chen, Gregory S Corrado, and Jeffrey Dean. 2013b. Distributed representations of words and phrases and their compositionality. In *Advances in Neural Information Processing Systems*, pages 3111–3119.

Yoshiki Niwa and Yoshihiko Nitta. 1994. Co-occurrence vectors from corpora vs. distance vectors from dictionaries. In *COLING 1994 Volume 1: The 15th International Conference on Computational Linguistics*, Kyoto, Japan.

Sebastian Padó and Mirella Lapata. 2007. Dependency-based construction of semantic space models. *Computational Linguistics*, 33(2):161–199.

Laura Rimell. 2014. Distributional lexical entailment by topic coherence. In *Proceedings of the 14th Conference of the European Chapter of the Association for Computational Linguistics*, pages 511–519, Gothenburg, Sweden.

Stephen Roller, Katrin Erk, and Gemma Boleda. 2014. Inclusive yet selective: Supervised distributional hypernymy detection. In *Proceedings of COLING 2014, the 25th International Conference on Computational Linguistics: Technical Papers*, pages 1025–1036, Dublin, Ireland.

Enrico Santus, Alessandro Lenci, Qin Lu, and Sabine Schulte im Walde. 2014. Chasing hypernyms in vector spaces with entropy. In *Proceedings of the 14th*

*Conference of the European Chapter of the Association for Computational Linguistics, volume 2: Short Papers*, pages 38–42, Gothenburg, Sweden.

Hinrich Schütze. 1993. Part-of-speech induction from scratch. In *Proceedings of the 31st Annual Meeting of the Association for Computational Linguistics*, pages 251–258, Columbus, Ohio, USA.

Rion Snow, Daniel Jurafsky, and Andrew Y Ng. 2005. Learning syntactic patterns for automatic hypernym discovery. In *Advances in Neural Information Processing*.

Peter D Turney and Saif M Mohammad. 2014. Experiments with three approaches to recognizing lexical entailment. *Natural Language Engineering*, pages 1–40.

Peter D Turney. 2006. Similarity of semantic relations. *Computational Linguistics*, 32(3):379–416.

Julie Weeds and David Weir. 2003. A general framework for distributional similarity. In *Proceedings of the 2003 Conference on Empirical Methods in Natural Language Processing*, pages 81–88, Sapporo, Japan.

Julie Weeds, Daoud Clarke, Jeremy Reffin, David Weir, and Bill Keller. 2014. Learning to distinguish hypernyms and co-hyponyms. In *Proceedings of COLING 2014, the 25th International Conference on Computational Linguistics: Technical Papers*, pages 2249–2259, Dublin, Ireland.

# A Word Embedding Approach to Predicting the Compositionality of Multiword Expressions

**Bahar Salehi,♠ Paul Cook♡ and Timothy Baldwin♠**
♠ NICTA Victoria Research Laboratory
Department of Computing and Information Systems
The University of Melbourne
Victoria 3010, Australia

♡ Faculty of Computer Science
University of New Brunswick
Fredericton, NB E3B 5A3, Canada

bsalehi@student.unimelb.edu.au, paul.cook@unb.ca, tb@ldwin.net

## Abstract

This paper presents the first attempt to use word embeddings to predict the compositionality of multiword expressions. We consider both single- and multi-prototype word embeddings. Experimental results show that, in combination with a back-off method based on string similarity, word embeddings outperform a method using count-based distributional similarity. Our best results are competitive with, or superior to, state-of-the-art methods over three standard compositionality datasets, which include two types of multiword expressions and two languages.

## 1 Introduction

Multiword expressions (MWEs) are word combinations that display some form of idiomaticity (Baldwin and Kim, 2009), including semantic idiomaticity, wherein the semantics of the MWE (e.g. *ivory tower*) cannot be predicted from the semantics of the component words (e.g. *ivory* and *tower*). Recent NLP work on semantic idiomaticity has focused on the task of "compositionality prediction", in the form of a regression task whereby a given MWE is mapped onto a continuous-valued compositionality score, either for the MWE as a whole or for each of its component words (Reddy et al., 2011; Schulte im Walde et al., 2013; Salehi et al., 2014b).

Separately in NLP, there has been a recent surge of interest in learning distributed representations of word meaning, in the form of "word embeddings" (Collobert and Weston, 2008; Mikolov et al., 2013a) and composition over distributed representations (Socher et al., 2012; Baroni et al., 2014).

This paper is the first attempt to bring together the work on word embedding-style distributional analysis with compositionality prediction of MWEs. In the context of compositionality prediction, our primary research questions here are:

RQ1: Are word embeddings superior to conventional count-based models of distributional similarity?
RQ2: How sensitive to parameter optimisation are different word embedding approaches?
RQ3: Are multi-prototype word embeddings empirically superior to single-prototype word embeddings?

We explore these questions relative to three compositionality prediction datasets spanning two MWE construction types (noun compounds and verb particle constructions) and two languages (English and German), and arrive at the following conclusions: (1) consistent with recent work over other NLP tasks, word embeddings are superior to count–based models of distributional similarity (and also translation-based string similarity); (2) the results are relatively stable under parameter optimisation for a given word embedding learning approach; and (3) based on two simple approaches to composition, single word embeddings are empirically slightly superior to multi-prototype word embeddings overall.



*Human Language Technologies: The 2015 Annual Conference of the North American Chapter of the ACL*, pages 977–983,
Denver, Colorado, May 31 – June 5, 2015. 

## 2 Related Work

Recent work on distributed approaches to distributional semantics has demonstrated their utility in a wide range of NLP tasks, including identifying various morphosyntactic and semantic relations (Mikolov et al., 2013a), dependency parsing (Bansal et al., 2014), sentiment analysis (Socher et al., 2013), named-entity recognition (Collobert and Weston, 2008; Passos et al., 2014), and machine translation (Zou et al., 2013; Devlin et al., 2014). Despite the wealth of research applying word embeddings within NLP, they have not yet been considered for predicting the compositionality of MWEs.

Much prior work on MWEs has been tailored to specific kinds of MWEs in particular languages (e.g. English verb–noun combinations (Fazly et al., 2009)). There has however been recent interest in approaches to MWEs that are more broadly applicable to a wider range of languages and MWE types (Brooke et al., 2014; Salehi et al., 2014b; Schneider et al., 2014). Word embeddings could form the basis for such an approach to predicting MWE compositionality.

## 3 Methodology

In this work, we estimate the compositionality of an MWE based on the similarity between the expression and its component words in vector space. We use three different vector-space models: (1) a simple count-based model of distributional similarity; (2) word embeddings based on WORD2VEC; and (3) a multi-sense skip-gram model that, unlike the previous two models, is able to learn multiple embeddings per target word (or MWE). For all three models, we first greedily pre-tokenise the corpus to represent each MWE as a single token, similarly to Baldwin et al. (2003). In this, we apply the constraint that no language-specific pre-processing can be applied to the training corpus, in order to make the method maximally language independent. As such, we cannot perform any form of lemmatisation, and MWE identification takes the form of simple string match for concatenated instances of the component words, naively assuming that all occurrences of that word combination are MWEs. We detail each of the distributional similarity methods below.

### 3.1 Count-Based Distributional Similarity

Our first method for building vectors is that of Salehi et al. (2014b): the top 50 most-frequent words in the training corpus are considered to be stopwords and discarded, and words with frequency rank 51–1051 are considered to be the content-bearing words, which form the dimensions for our vectors, in the manner of Schütze (1997). To measure the similarity of the MWE vector and the component word vectors, we considered two different approaches.

The first approach is based on Reddy et al. (2011) and Schulte im Walde et al. (2013). The similarity between the MWE and each of its components is measured, and the overall compositionality of the MWE is computed by combining the similarity scores for the two components as follows:

$$comp_1(\mathbf{MWE}) = \alpha sim(\mathbf{MWE}, \mathbf{C}_1) \\ +(1-\alpha) sim(\mathbf{MWE}, \mathbf{C}_2)$$

where $\mathbf{MWE}$ is the vector associated with the MWE, $\mathbf{C}_i$ is the vector associated with the $i$th component word of the MWE, $sim$ is a vector similarity function, and $\alpha \in [0, 1]$ is a weight parameter.

We also experimented with the approach from Mitchell and Lapata (2010), where $\mathbf{MWE}$ is compared directly with a composed vector of the component words, based on vector addition:[1]

$$comp_2(\mathbf{MWE}) = sim(\mathbf{MWE}, \mathbf{C}_1 + \mathbf{C}_2)$$

For both $comp_1$ and $comp_2$, we used cosine similarity as our similarity measure $sim$.

### 3.2 WORD2VEC

Our second method is based on the recurrent neural network language model (RNNLM) approach to learning word embeddings of Mikolov et al. (2013a) and Mikolov et al. (2013b), using the WORD2VEC package.[2] WORD2VEC uses a log-linear model inspired by the original RNNLM approach of Mikolov et al. (2010), in two forms: (1) a continuous bag-of-words ("CBOW") model, whereby all words in a context window are averaged in a single projection layer; and (2) a continuous skip-gram model

[1] We also experimented with vector multiplication, but found it to perform poorly compared to the other approaches.

[2] https://code.google.com/p/word2vec/

("C-SKIP"), whereby a given word in context is projected onto a projection layer, and used to predict its immediate context (preceding and following words). WORD2VEC generates a vector of fixed dimensionality $d$ for each pre-tokenised word/MWE type with frequency above a certain threshold in the training corpus. We again use $comp_1$ and $comp_2$ to estimate compositionality from these vectors.

### 3.3 Multi-Sense Skip-gram Model

One potential shortcoming of WORD2VEC is that it generates a single word embedding for each word, irrespective of the relative polysemy of the word. Neelakantan et al. (2014) proposed a method motivated by WORD2VEC, which efficiently learns multiple embeddings per word/MWE. We refer to this approach as the multi-sense skip-gram (MSSG) model. We once again compose the resultant vectors with $comp_1$ and $comp_2$, but modify the formulation slightly to handle the variable number of vectors for each word/MWE, by searching over the cross-product of vectors in each $sim$ calculation and taking the maximum in each case. We initially set the number of embeddings to 2 in our MSSG experiments — in keeping with the findings in Neelakantan et al. (2014) — but come back to examine the impact of the number of embeddings on compositionality prediction in Section 5.

## 4 Datasets

We evaluate our methods over three datasets:[3] (1) English noun compounds ("ENCs", e.g. *spelling bee* and *swimming pool*); (2) English verb particle constructions ("EVPCs", e.g. *stand up* and *give away*); and (3) German noun compounds ("GNCs", e.g. *ahornblatt* "maple leaf" and *eidechse* "lizard").

The ENC dataset consists of 90 binary English noun compounds, and is annotated on a continuous $[0, 5]$ scale for both overall compositionality and the component-wise compositionality of each of the modifier and head noun (Reddy et al., 2011). The state-of-the-art method for this dataset (Salehi et al., 2014b) is a supervised support vector regression model, trained over the distributional method from Section 3.1 as applied to both English and 51 target languages (under word and MWE translation).

The EVPC dataset consists of 160 English verb particle constructions, and is manually annotated for compositionality on a binary scale for each of the head verb and particle (Bannard, 2006). In order to translate the dataset into a regression task, we calculate the overall compositionality as the number of annotations of entailment for the verb, divided by the total number of verb annotations for that VPC. The state-of-the-art method for this dataset (Salehi et al., 2014b) is a linear combination of: (1) the distributional method from Section 3.1; (2) the same method applied to 10 target languages (under word and MWE translation, selecting the languages using supervised learning); and (3) the string similarity method of Salehi and Cook (2013).

The GNC dataset consists of 246 German noun compounds, and is annotated on a continuous $[1, 7]$ scale (von der Heide and Borgwaldt, 2009; Schulte im Walde et al., 2013). The state-of-the-art method for this dataset is a distributional similarity method applied to part-of-speech tagged and lemmatised data (Schulte im Walde et al., 2013).

## 5 Experiments

For all experiments, we train our models over raw text Wikipedia corpora for either English or German, depending on the language of the dataset. The raw English and German corpora were preprocessed using the WP2TXT toolbox[4] to eliminate XML and HTML tags and hyperlinks, and punctuation was removed. Finally, word-tokenisation was performed based on simple whitespace delimitation, after which we greedily identified all string occurrences of the MWEs in each of our datasets and combined them into a single token.[5]

The word embedding approaches are unable to generate vector representations for tokens which occur with frequency below a fixed cutoff.[6] In order to

[3] We also considered using the dataset from the DisCo shared task (Biemann and Giesbrecht, 2011), but ultimately excluded it because it includes different types of MWEs without indication of the syntactic type of a given MWE, preventing us from carrying out construction-specific parameter tuning.

[4] `http://wp2txt.rubyforge.org/`

[5] For English, a single model was trained over a corpus containing both ENC and EVPC tokens.

[6] For a frequency threshold of 15, the total numbers of ENCs, EVPCs and GNCs for which we were unable to generate word embeddings were 3, 0 and 25, respectively, in the latter case, largely as a result of our simple tokenisation strategy and

| Dataset | Method | | $comp_1$ | $comp_1$ +SS | $comp_2$ | $comp_2$ +SS |
|---|---|---|---|---|---|---|
| ENC | WORD2VEC | ($d = 500$, C-SKIP) | .628 | .761 | .632 | .761 |
| | | ($d = 500$, CBOW) | .696 | .786 | .710 | .791 |
| | | ($d = 1000$, C-SKIP) | .636 | .764 | .648 | .767 |
| | | ($d = 1000$, CBOW) | .717 | .789 | .736 | **.796** |
| | MSSG | ($d = 300, w = 5$) | .640 | .764 | .624 | .759 |
| | | ($d = 600, w = 5$) | .615 | .758 | .594 | .758 |
| | | ($d = 600, w = 10$) | .614 | .749 | .631 | .756 |
| | Distributional similarity | | .714 | | | |
| | String similarity | | .644 | | | |
| | State-of-the-art | | .744 | | | |
| EVPC | WORD2VEC | ($d = 500$, C-SKIP) | .289 | .496 | — | — |
| | | ($d = 500$, CBOW) | .293 | .486 | — | — |
| | | ($d = 1000$, C-SKIP) | .289 | .504 | — | — |
| | | ($d = 1000$, CBOW) | .289 | .489 | — | — |
| | MSSG | ($d = 300, w = 5$) | .309 | **.506** | — | — |
| | | ($d = 600, w = 5$) | .294 | .498 | — | — |
| | | ($d = 600, w = 10$) | .273 | .494 | — | — |
| | Distributional similarity | | .165 | | | |
| | String similarity | | .385 | | | |
| | State-of-the-art | | .417 | | | |
| GNC | WORD2VEC | ($d = 500$, C-SKIP) | .393 | .442 | .321 | .415 |
| | | ($d = 500$, CBOW) | .400 | .439 | .361 | .423 |
| | | ($d = 1000$, C-SKIP) | .341 | .411 | .282 | .394 |
| | | ($d = 1000$, CBOW) | .371 | .414 | .349 | .411 |
| | MSSG | ($d = 300, w = 5$) | .181 | .320 | .122 | .295 |
| | | ($d = 600, w = 5$) | .202 | .335 | .146 | .303 |
| | | ($d = 600, w = 10$) | .155 | .310 | .101 | .282 |
| | Distributional Similarity | | .140 | | | |
| | String Similarity | | .372 | | | |
| | State-of-the-art | | **.450** | | | |

Table 1: Pearson's correlation ($r$) for the different methods over the three datasets; the state-of-the-art for each dataset is described in Section 4

generate a compositionality prediction back-off for the small numbers of MWEs in this category, we assign a default value, which is the mean of computed compositionality scores for other instances.[7]

As a baseline, we use the translation string similarity approach of Salehi and Cook (2013), including the cross-validation-based method for selecting the 10 best languages to use for each dataset. We further include a linear combination of the string similarity method with each of the various approaches based on word embeddings.

Table 1 shows the results for the various methods, over a range of hyper-parameter settings for each of WORD2VEC (vector dimensionality $d$; we also present results for CBOW vs. C-SKIP) and MSSG (vector dimensionality $d$ and window size $w$), informed by the experimental results in the respective publications. Note that for EVPC, we don't use the vector for the particle, in keeping with Salehi et al. (2014b); as such, there are no results for $comp_2$. For $comp_1$, $\alpha$ is set to 1.0 for EVPC, and 0.7 for both ENC and GNC, also based on the findings of Salehi et al. (2014b).

The results indicate that the approaches using both WORD2VEC and MSSG outperform simple distributional and string similarity by a substantial margin. Further, over a variety of parameteriza-

lack of lemmatisation.

[7]We also experimented with using the string similarity approach as a back-off, which resulted in marginally lower results than what is reported in Table 1.

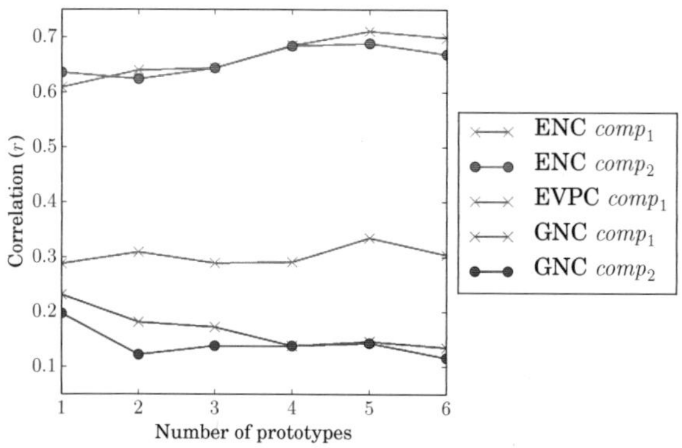


Figure 1: The effect of the number of prototypes on the results with MSSG

tions, they surpass the state-of-the-art methods for ENC and EVPC; in the case of GNC, the best-performing method (WORD2VEC with $d = 500$ and C-SKIP) roughly matches the state-of-the-art. Note that in each case, the state-of-the-art is achieved using varying levels of supervision over labelled data (ENC and EVPC) or language-specific pre-processing (GNC), whereas the word embedding methods use no labelled data. As such, the answer to RQ1 would appear to be a resounding yes.

Looking to RQ2, the models are remarkably insensitive to hyper-parameter optimisation for EVPC, but there are slight deviations in the results for ENC and GNC. Having said that, they are largely between the different word embedding approaches, and the results for a given approach under different parameter settings is relatively stable. A large part of the cause of the drop in results and greater parameter sensitivity over GNC is the lower token frequencies, through a combination of the Wikipedia corpus being markedly smaller and our naive tokenisation strategy having low recall over German due to the richer morphology. As such, the answer would appear to be a tentative "relatively insensitive, assuming high token frequencies".

Finally, looking to RQ3, there was little separating WORD2VEC and MSSG over ENC, but over the other two datasets, WORD2VEC had a clear advantage. Given the high levels of polysemy observed in high frequency English verb particle constructions (Salehi et al., 2014a), this result for EVPC was particularly surprising, and suggests that, at least under our two basic forms of composition, multi-prototype word embeddings are at best equal to, and in many cases, inferior to, single-prototype word embeddings.

According to the results, the string similarity approach complements all word-embedding approaches. We hypothesise that this is because it is not based on any corpus, and is thus not biased by the frequency of token instances in the corpus.

In Table 1, the number of embeddings for MSSG was set to 2 prototypes, based on the default recommendations of Neelakantan et al. (2014). To investigate the impact of this parameter on our results, we retrained MSSG over the range $[1, 6]$ and reran our experiments for each set of embeddings over the three datasets (without string similarity, to isolate the effect of the number of embeddings), as shown in Figure 1. For both English datasets (ENC and EVPC), setting the number of prototypes to a value higher than 2 boosts the results slightly, with 5 prototypes appearing to be the optimal value. For the German dataset (GNC), on the other hand, the best results are actually achieved for a single prototype. Further research is required to better understand this effect.

## 6 Conclusions

We presented the first approach to using word embeddings to predict the compositionality of MWEs. We showed that this approach, in combination with information from string similarity, surpassed, or was competitive with, the current state-of-the-art on three compositionality datasets. In future work we intend to explore the contribution of information from word embeddings of a target expression and its component words under translation into many languages, along the lines of Salehi et al. (2014b).


### Acknowledgements

We thank the anonymous reviewers for their insightful comments and valuable suggestions. NICTA is funded by the Australian government as represented by Department of Broadband, Communication and Digital Economy, and the Australian Research Council through the ICT Centre of Excellence programme.

## References

Timothy Baldwin and Su Nam Kim. 2009. Multiword expressions. In Nitin Indurkhya and Fred J. Damerau, editors, *Handbook of Natural Language Processing*. CRC Press, Boca Raton, USA, 2nd edition.

Timothy Baldwin, Colin Bannard, Takaaki Tanaka, and Dominic Widdows. 2003. An empirical model of multiword expression decomposability. In *Proceedings of the ACL-2003 Workshop on Multiword Expressions: Analysis, Acquisition and Treatment*, pages 89–96, Sapporo, Japan.

Colin James Bannard. 2006. *Acquiring Phrasal Lexicons from Corpora*. Ph.D. thesis, University of Edinburgh.

Mohit Bansal, Kevin Gimpel, and Karen Livescu. 2014. Tailoring continuous word representations for dependency parsing. In *Proceedings of the 52nd Annual Meeting of the Association for Computational Linguistics (Volume 2: Short Papers)*, pages 809–815, Baltimore, USA.

Marco Baroni, Georgiana Dinu, and Germán Kruszewski. 2014. Don't count, predict! a systematic comparison of context-counting vs. context-predicting semantic vectors. In *Proceedings of the 52nd Annual Meeting of the Association for Computational Linguistics (ACL 2014)*, pages 238–247, Baltimore, USA.

Chris Biemann and Eugenie Giesbrecht. 2011. Distributional semantics and compositionality 2011: Shared task description and results. In *Proceedings of the workshop on distributional semantics and compositionality*, pages 21–28, Portland, Oregon, USA.

Julian Brooke, Vivian Tsang, Graeme Hirst, and Fraser Shein. 2014. Unsupervised multiword segmentation of large corpora using prediction-driven decomposition of $n$-grams. In *Proceedings of COLING 2014, the 25th International Conference on Computational Linguistics: Technical Papers*, pages 753–761, Dublin, Ireland.

Ronan Collobert and Jason Weston. 2008. A unified architecture for natural language processing: Deep neural networks with multitask learning. In *Proceedings of the 25th International Conference on Machine Learning (ICML 2008)*, pages 160–167, Helsinki, Finland.

Jacob Devlin, Rabih Zbib, Zhongqiang Huang, Thomas Lamar, Richard Schwartz, and John Makhoul. 2014. Fast and robust neural network joint models for statistical machine translation. In *Proceedings of the 52nd Annual Meeting of the Association for Computational Linguistics (ACL 2014)*, pages 1370–1380, Baltimore, USA.

Afsaneh Fazly, Paul Cook, and Suzanne Stevenson. 2009. Unsupervised type and token identification of idiomatic expressions. *Computational Linguistics*, 35(1):61–103.

Tomas Mikolov, Martin Karafiát, Lukas Burget, Jan Cernockỳ, and Sanjeev Khudanpur. 2010. Recurrent neural network based language model. In *Proceedings of the 11th Annual Conference of the International Speech Communication Association (INTERSPEECH 2010)*, pages 1045–1048, Makuhari, Japan.

Tomas Mikolov, Kai Chen, Greg Corrado, and Jeffrey Dean. 2013a. Efficient estimation of word representations in vector space. In *Proceedings of Workshop at the International Conference on Learning Representations, 2013*, Scottsdale, USA.

Tomas Mikolov, Ilya Sutskever, Kai Chen, Greg S Corrado, and Jeff Dean. 2013b. Distributed representations of words and phrases and their compositionality. In *Advances in Neural Information Processing Systems*, pages 3111–3119.

Jeff Mitchell and Mirella Lapata. 2010. Composition in distributional models of semantics. *Cognitive Science*, 34(8):1388–1429.

Arvind Neelakantan, Jeevan Shankar, Alexandre Passos, and Andrew McCallum. 2014. Efficient non-parametric estimation of multiple embeddings per word in vector space. In *Proceedings of the 2014 Conference on Empirical Methods in Natural Language Processing (EMNLP 2014)*, pages 1059–1069, Doha, Qatar.

Alexandre Passos, Vineet Kumar, and Andrew McCallum. 2014. Lexicon infused phrase embeddings for named entity resolution. In *Proceedings of the Eighteenth Conference on Computational Natural Language Learning*, pages 78–86, Baltimore, USA.

Siva Reddy, Diana McCarthy, and Suresh Manandhar. 2011. An empirical study on compositionality in compound nouns. In *Proceedings of IJCNLP*, pages 210–218, Chiang Mai, Thailand.

Bahar Salehi and Paul Cook. 2013. Predicting the compositionality of multiword expressions using translations in multiple languages. In *Second Joint Conference on Lexical and Computational Semantics (*SEM), Volume 1: Proceedings of the Main Conference and the Shared Task: Semantic Textual Similarity*, pages 266–275, Atlanta, Georgia, USA, June.

Bahar Salehi, Paul Cook, and Timothy Baldwin. 2014a. Detecting non-compositional MWE components using Wiktionary. In *Proceedings of the 2014 Conference on Empirical Methods in Natural Language Processing (EMNLP)*, pages 1792–1797, Doha, Qatar, October.

Bahar Salehi, Paul Cook, and Timothy Baldwin. 2014b. Using distributional similarity of multi-way translations to predict multiword expression compositionality. In *Proceedings of the 14th Conference of the European Chapter of the Association for Computational Linguistics*, pages 472–481, Gothenburg, Sweden, April.

Nathan Schneider, Emily Danchik, Chris Dyer, and Noah A. Smith. 2014. Discriminative lexical semantic segmentation with gaps: Running the mwe gamut. *Transactions of the Association of Computational Linguistics*, 2:193–206.

Sabine Schulte im Walde, Stefan Müller, and Stephen Roller. 2013. Exploring vector space models to predict the compositionality of German noun-noun compounds. In *Proceedings of the Second Joint Conference on Lexical and Computational Semantics*, pages 255–265, Atlanta, USA.

Hinrich Schütze. 1997. *Ambiguity Resolution in Language Learning*. CSLI Publications, Stanford, USA.

Richard Socher, Brody Huval, Christopher D. Manning, and Andrew Y. Ng. 2012. Semantic compositionality through recursive matrix-vector spaces. In *Proceedings of the Joint Conference on Empirical Methods in Natural Language Processing and Computational Natural Language Learning 2012 (EMNLP-CoNLL 2012)*, pages 1201–1211, Jeju Island, Korea.

Richard Socher, Alex Perelygin, Jean Wu, Jason Chuang, Christopher D. Manning, Andrew Ng, and Christopher Potts. 2013. Recursive deep models for semantic compositionality over a sentiment treebank. In *Proceedings of the 2013 Conference on Empirical Methods in Natural Language Processing (EMNLP 2013)*, pages 1631–1642, Seattle, USA.

Claudia von der Heide and Susanne Borgwaldt. 2009. Assoziationen zu Unter, Basis und Oberbegriffen. Eine explorative Studie. In *Proceedings of the 9th Norddeutsches Linguistisches Kolloquium*, pages 51–74.

Will Y. Zou, Richard Socher, Daniel Cer, and Christopher D. Manning. 2013. Bilingual word embeddings for phrase-based machine translation. In *Proceedings of the 2013 Conference on Empirical Methods in Natural Language Processing*, pages 1393–1398, Seattle, USA.

# Word Embedding-based Antonym Detection using Thesauri and Distributional Information

**Masataka Ono, Makoto Miwa, Yutaka Sasaki**
Department of Advanced Science and Technology
Toyota Technological Institute
2-12-1 Hisakata, Tempaku-ku, Nagoya, Japan
{sd12412, makoto-miwa, yutaka.sasaki}@toyota-ti.ac.jp

## Abstract

This paper proposes a novel approach to train word embeddings to capture antonyms. Word embeddings have shown to capture synonyms and analogies. Such word embeddings, however, cannot capture antonyms since they depend on the distributional hypothesis. Our approach utilizes supervised synonym and antonym information from thesauri, as well as distributional information from large-scale unlabelled text data. The evaluation results on the GRE antonym question task show that our model outperforms the state-of-the-art systems and it can answer the antonym questions in the F-score of 89%.

## 1 Introduction

Word embeddings have shown to capture synonyms and analogies (Mikolov et al., 2013b; Mnih and Kavukcuoglu, 2013; Pennington et al., 2014). Word embeddings have also been effectively employed in several tasks such as named entity recognition (Turian et al., 2010; Guo et al., 2014), adjectival scales (Kim and de Marneffe, 2013) and text classification (Le and Mikolov, 2014). Such embeddings trained based on *distributional hypothesis* (Harris, 1954), however, often fail to recognize antonyms since antonymous words, e.g. *strong* and *weak*, occur in similar contexts. Recent studies focuses on learning word embeddings for specific tasks, such as sentiment analysis (Tang et al., 2014) and dependency parsing (Bansal et al., 2014; Chen et al., 2014). These motivate a new approach to learn word embeddings to capture antonyms.

Recent studies on antonym detection have shown that thesauri information are useful in distinguishing antonyms from synonyms. The state-of-the-art systems achieved over 80% in F-score on GRE antonym tests. Yih et al. (2012) proposed a Polarity Inducing Latent Semantic Analysis (PILSA) that incorporated polarity information in two thesauri in constructing a matrix for latent semantic analysis. They additionally used context vectors to cover the out-of-vocabulary words; however, they did not use word embeddings. Recently, Zhang et al. (2014) proposed a Bayesian Probabilistic Tensor Factorization (BPTF) model to combine thesauri information and existing word embeddings. They showed that the usefulness of word embeddings but they used pretrained word embeddings.

In this paper, we propose a novel approach to construct word embeddings that can capture antonyms. Unlike the previous approaches, our approach directly trains word embeddings to represent antonyms. We propose two models: a Word Embedding on Thesauri information (WE-T) model and a Word Embeddings on Thesauri and Distributional information (WE-TD) model. The WE-T model receives supervised information from synonym and antonym pairs in thesauri and infers the relations of the other word pairs in the thesauri from the supervised information. The WE-TD model incorporates corpus-based contextual information (distributional information) into the WE-T model, which enables the calculation of the similarities among in-vocabulary and out-of-vocabulary words.



*Human Language Technologies: The 2015 Annual Conference of the North American Chapter of the ACL*, pages 984–989,
Denver, Colorado, May 31 – June 5, 2015. 

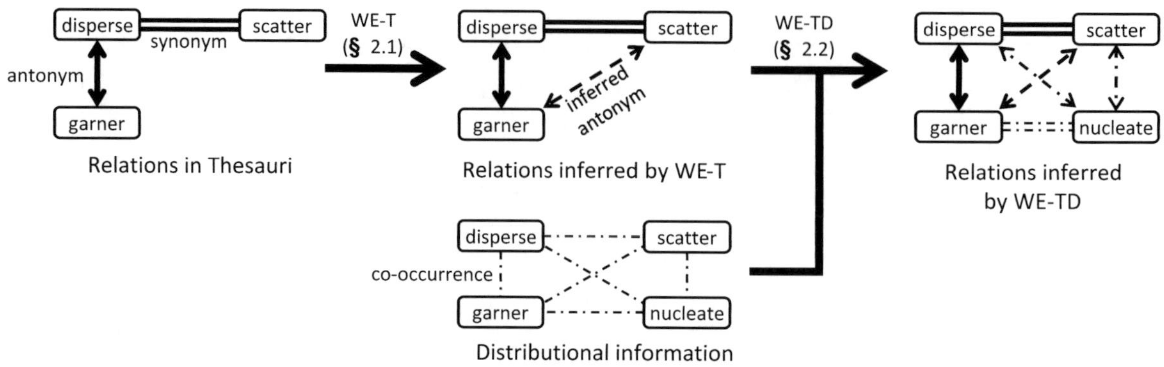


Figure 1: Overview of our approach. When we use the thesauri directly, *disperse* and *garner* are known to be antonymous and *disperse* and *scatter* are known to be synonymous, but the remaining relations are unknown. WE-T infers indirect relations among words in thesauri. Furthermore, WE-TD incorporates distributional information, and the relatedness among in-vocabulary and out-of-vocabulary words (*nucleate* here) are obtained.

## 2 Word embeddings for antonyms

This section explains how we train word embeddings from synonym and antonym pairs in thesauri. We then explain how to incorporate distributional information to cover out-of-vocabulary words. Figure 1 illustrates the overview of our approach.

### 2.1 Word embeddings using thesauri information

We first introduce a model to train word embeddings using thesauri information alone, which is called the WE-T model. We embed vectors to words in thesauri and train vectors to represent synonym and antonym pairs in the thesauri. More concretely, we train the vectors by maximizing the following objective function:

$$\sum_{w \in V} \sum_{s \in S_w} \log \sigma(sim(w, s)) + \alpha \sum_{w \in V} \sum_{a \in A_w} \log \sigma(-sim(w, a)) \quad (1)$$

$V$ is the vocabulary in thesauri. $S_w$ is a set of synonyms of a word $w$, and $A_w$ is a set of antonyms of a word $w$. $\sigma(x)$ is the sigmoid function $\frac{1}{1+e^{-x}}$. $\alpha$ is a parameter to balance the effects of synonyms and antonyms. $sim(w_1, w_2)$ is a scoring function that measures a similarity between two vectors embedded to the corresponding words $w_1$ and $w_2$. We use the following asymmetric function for the scoring function:

$$sim(w_1, w_2) = \mathbf{v}_{w_1} \cdot \mathbf{v}_{w_2} + b_{w_1} \quad (2)$$

$\mathbf{v}_w$ is a vector embedded to a word $w$ and $b_w$ is a scalar bias term corresponding to $w$. This similarity score ranges from minus infinity to plus infinity and the sigmoid function in Equation (1) scales the score into the $[0, 1]$ range.

The first term of Equation (1) denotes the sum of the similarities between synonym pairs. The second term of Equation (1) denotes the sum of the dissimilarities between antonym pairs. By maximizing this objective, synonym and antonym pairs are tuned to have high and low similarity scores respectively, and indirect antonym pairs, e.g., synonym of antonym, will also have low similarity scores since the embeddings of the words in the pairs will be dissimilar. We use AdaGrad (Duchi et al., 2011) to maximize this objective function. AdaGrad is an online learning method using a gradient-based update with automatically-determined learning rate.

### 2.2 Word embeddings using thesauri and distributional information

Now we explain a model to incorporate corpus-based distributional information into the WE-T model, which is called the WE-TD model.

We hereby introduce Skip-Gram with Negative Sampling (SGNS) (Mikolov et al., 2013a), which the WE-TD model bases on. Levy and Goldberg (2014) shows the objective function for SGNS can be rewritten as follows.

$$\sum_{w\in V}\sum_{c\in V}\{\#(w,c)\log\sigma(sim(w,c)) + k\#(w)P_0(c)\log\sigma(-sim(w,c))\} \quad (3)$$

The first term represents the co-occurrence pairs within a context window of $C$ words preceding and following target words. $\#(w,c)$ stands for the number of appearances of a target word $w$ and its context $c$. The second term represents the negative sampling. $k$ is a number of negatively sampled words for each target word. $\#_p(w)$ is the number of appearances of $w$ as a target word, and its negative context $c$ is sampled from a modified unigram distribution $P_0$ (Mikolov et al., 2013a). We employ the subsampling (Mikolov et al., 2013a), which discards words according to the probability of $P(w) = 1 - \sqrt{\frac{t}{p(w)}}$. $p(w)$ is the proportion of occurrences of a word $w$ in the corpus, and $t$ is a threshold to control the discard. When we use a large-scale corpus directly, the effects of rare words are dominated by the effects of frequent words. Subsampling alleviates this problem by discarding frequent words more often than rare words.

To incorporate the distributional information into the WE-T model, we propose the following objective function, which simply adds this objective function to Equation 1 with an weight $\beta$:

$$\begin{aligned}&\beta\{\sum_{w\in V}\sum_{s\in S_w}\log\sigma(sim(w,s))\\&+\alpha\sum_{w\in V}\sum_{a\in A_w}\log\sigma(-sim(w,a))\}\\&+\sum_{w\in V}\sum_{c\in V}\{\#(w,c)\log\sigma(sim(w,c))\\&+k\#(w)P_0(c)\log\sigma(-sim(w,c))\}\end{aligned} \quad (4)$$

This function can be further arranged as

$$\sum_{w\in V}\sum_{c\in V}\{A_{w,c}\log\sigma(sim(w,c)) + B_{w,c}\log\sigma(-sim(w,c))\} \quad (5)$$

Here, the coefficients $A_{w,c}$ and $B_{w,c}$ are sums of corresponding coefficients in Equation 4. These terms can be pre-calculated by using the number of appearances of contextual word pairs, unigram distributions, and synonym and antonym pairs in thesauri.

The objective is maximized by using AdaGrad. We skip some updates according to the coefficients $A_{w,c}$ and $B_{w,c}$ to speed up the computation; we ignore the terms with extremely small coefficients ($< 10^{-5}$) and we sample the terms according to the coefficients when the coefficients are less than 1.

## 3 Experiments

### 3.1 Evaluation settings

This section explains the task setting, resource for training, parameter settings, and evaluation metrics.

#### 3.1.1 GRE antonym question task

We evaluate our models and compare them with other existing models using GRE antonym question dataset originally provided by Mohammad et al. (2008). This dataset is widely used to evaluate the performance of antonym detection. Each question has a target word and five candidate words, and the system has to choose the most contrasting word to the target word from the candidate words (Mohammad et al., 2013). All the words in the questions are single-token words. This dataset consists of two parts, development and test, and they have 162 and 950 questions, respectively. Since the test part contains 160 development data set, We will also report results on 790 (950-160) questions following Mohammad et al. (2013).

In evaluating our models on the questions, we first calculated similarities between a target word and its candidate words. The similarities were calculated by averaging asymmetric similarity scores using the similarity function in Equation 2. We then chose a word which had the lowest similarity among them. When the model did not contain any words in a question, the question was left unanswered.

#### 3.1.2 Resource for training

For supervised dataset, we used synonym and antonym pairs in two thesauri: WordNet (Miller, 1995) and Roget (Kipfer, 2009). These pairs were provided by Zhang et al. (2014)[1]. There were 52,760 entries (words), each of which had 11.7 synonyms on average, and 21,319 entries, each of which had 6.5 antonyms on average.

[1] https://github.com/iceboal/word-representations-bptf

| | Dev. Set | | | Test Set (950) | | | Test Set (790) | | |
|---|---|---|---|---|---|---|---|---|---|
| | Prec. | Rec. | F | Prec. | Rec. | F | Prec. | Rec. | F |
| Encarta lookup† | 0.65 | 0.61 | 0.63 | 0.61 | 0.56 | 0.59 | — | — | — |
| WordNet & Roget lookup¶ | 1.00 | 0.49 | 0.66 | 0.98 | 0.45 | 0.62 | 0.98 | 0.45 | 0.61 |
| WE-T | 0.92 | 0.71 | 0.80 | 0.90 | 0.72 | 0.80 | 0.90 | 0.72 | 0.80 |
| WordNet + Affix heuristics + Adjacent category annotation§ | 0.79 | 0.66 | 0.72 | — | — | — | 0.77 | 0.63 | 0.69 |
| WE-D | 0.09 | 0.08 | 0.09 | 0.08 | 0.07 | 0.07 | 0.07 | 0.07 | 0.07 |
| Encarta PILSA + S2Net + Embedding† | 0.88 | 0.87 | 0.87 | 0.81 | 0.80 | 0.81 | — | — | — |
| WordNet & Roget BPTF‡ | 0.88 | 0.88 | 0.88 | 0.82 | 0.82 | 0.82 | — | — | — |
| WE-TD | 0.92 | 0.91 | 0.91 | 0.90 | 0.88 | 0.89 | 0.89 | 0.87 | 0.88 |

Table 1: Results on the GRE antonym question task. † is from Yih et al. (2012), ‡ is from Zhang et al. (2014), and § is from Mohammad et al. (2013). ¶ slightly differs from the result in Zhang et al. (2014) since thesauri can contain multiple candidates as antonyms and the answer is randomly selected for the candidates.

| Error Type | Description | # Errors | Example Target | Example Gold | Example Predicted |
|---|---|---|---|---|---|
| Contrasting | Predicted answer is contrasting, but not antonym. | 7 | reticence<br>dussuade | loquaciousness<br>exhort | storm<br>extol |
| Degree | Both answers are antonyms, but gold has a higher degree of contrast. | 3 | postulate | verify | reject |
| Incorrect gold | Gold answer is incorrect. | 2 | flinch | extol | advance |
| Wrong expansion | Gold and predicted answers are both in the expanded thesauri. | 1 | hapless | fortunate | happy |
| Incorrect | Predicted answer is not contrasting. | 1 | sessile | obile | ceasing |
| Total | | 14 | — | — | — |

Table 2: Error types by WE-TD on the development set.

We obtained raw texts from Wikipedia on November 2013 for unsupervised dataset. We lowercased all words in the text.

### 3.1.3 Parameter settings

The parameters were tuned using the development part of the dataset. In training the WE-T model, the dimension of embeddings was set to 300, the number of iteration of AdaGrad was set to 20, and the initial learning rate of AdaGrad was set to 0.03. $\alpha$ in Equation 1 were set to 3.2, according to the proportion of the numbers of synonym and antonym pairs in the thesauri. In addition to these parameters, when we trained the WE-TD model, we added the top 100,000 frequent words appearing in Wikipedia into the vocabulary. The parameter $\beta$ was set to 100, the number of negative sampling $k$ was set as 5, the context window size $C$ was set to 5, the threshold for subsampling[2] was set to $10^{-8}$.

### 3.1.4 Evaluation metrics

We used the *F-score* as a primary evaluation metric following Zhang et al. (2014). The *F-score* is the harmonic mean of *precision* and *recall*. *Precision* is the proportion of correctly answered questions over answered questions. *Recall* is the proportion of correctly answered questions over the questions.

[2]This small threshold is because this was used to balance the effects of supervised and unsupervised information.

### 3.2 Results

Table 1 shows the results of our models on the GRE antonym question task. This table also shows the results of previous systems (Yih et al., 2012; Zhang et al., 2014; Mohammad et al., 2013) and models trained on Wikipedia without thesauri (WE-D) for the comparison.

The low performance of WE-D illuminates the problem of distributional hypothesis. Word embeddings trained by using distributional information could not distinguish antonyms from synonyms.

Our WE-T model achieved higher performance than the baselines that only look up thesauri. In the thesauri information we used, the synonyms and antonyms have already been extended for the original thesauri by some rules such as ignoring part of speech (Zhang et al., 2014). This extension contributes to the larger coverage than the original synonym and antonym pairs in the thesauri. This improvement shows that our model not only captures the information of synonyms and antonyms provided by the supervised information but also infers the relations of other word pairs more effectively than the rule-based extension.

Our WE-TD model achieved the highest score among the models that use both thesauri and distributional information. Furthermore, our model has small differences in the results on the development and test parts compared to the other models.

### 3.3 Error Analysis

We analyzed the 14 errors on the development set, and summarized the result in Table 2.

Half of the errors (i.e., seven errors) were caused in the case that the predicted word is contrasting to some extent but not antonym ("Contrasting"). This might be caused by some kind of semantic drift. In order to predict these gold answers correctly, constraints of the words, such as part of speech and selectional preferences, need to be used. For example, "venerate" usually takes "person" as its object, while "magnify" takes "god." Three of the errors were caused by the degree of contrast of the gold and the predicted answers ("Degree"). The predicted word can be regarded as an antonym but the gold answer is more appropriate. This is because our model does not consider the degree of antonymy, which is out of our focus. One of the questions in the errors had an incorrect gold answer ("Incorrect gold"). We found that in one case both gold and predicted answers are in the expanded antonym dictionary ("Wrong expansion"). In expanding dictionary entries, the gold and predicted answers were both included in the word list of an antonym entries. In one case, the predicted answer was simply wrong ("Incorrect").

## 4 Conclusions

This paper proposed a novel approach that trains word embeddings to capture antonyms. We proposed two models: WE-T and WE-TD models. WE-T trains word embeddings on thesauri information, and WE-TD incorporates distributional information into the WE-T model. The evaluation on the GRE antonym question task shows that WE-T can achieve a higher performance over the thesauri lookup baselines and, by incorporating distributional information, WE-TD showed 89% in F-score, which outperformed the conventional state-of-the-art performances. As future work, we plan to extend our approaches to obtain word embeddings for other semantic relations (Gao et al., 2014).

## References

Mohit Bansal, Kevin Gimpel, and Karen Livescu. 2014. Tailoring continuous word representations for dependency parsing. In *Proceedings of the 52nd Annual Meeting of the Association for Computational Linguistics (Volume 2: Short Papers)*, pages 809–815, Baltimore, Maryland, June. Association for Computational Linguistics.

Wenliang Chen, Yue Zhang, and Min Zhang. 2014. Feature embedding for dependency parsing. In *Proceedings of COLING 2014, the 25th International Conference on Computational Linguistics: Technical Papers*, pages 816–826, Dublin, Ireland, August. Dublin City University and Association for Computational Linguistics.

John Duchi, Elad Hazan, and Yoram Singer. 2011. Adaptive subgradient methods for online learning and stochastic optimization. *Journal of Machine Learning Research*, 12:2121–2159, July.

Bin Gao, Jiang Bian, and Tie-Yan Liu. 2014. Wordrep: A benchmark for research on learning word representations. *ICML 2014 Workshop on Knowledge-Powered Deep Learning for Text Mining*.

Jiang Guo, Wanxiang Che, Haifeng Wang, and Ting Liu. 2014. Revisiting embedding features for simple semi-supervised learning. In *Proceedings of the 2014 Conference on Empirical Methods in Natural Language Processing (EMNLP)*, pages 110–120, Doha, Qatar, October. Association for Computational Linguistics.

Zellig S Harris. 1954. Distributional structure. *Word*, 10(23):146–162.

Joo-Kyung Kim and Marie-Catherine de Marneffe. 2013. Deriving adjectival scales from continuous space word representations. In *Proceedings of the 2013 Conference on Empirical Methods in Natural Language Processing*, pages 1625–1630, Seattle, Washington, USA, October. Association for Computational Linguistics.

Barbara Ann Kipfer. 2009. *Roget's 21st Century Thesaurus*. Philip Lief Group, third edition edition.

Quoc Le and Tomas Mikolov. 2014. Distributed representations of sentences and documents. In Tony Jebara and Eric P. Xing, editors, *Proceedings of the 31st International Conference on Machine Learning (ICML-14)*, pages 1188–1196. JMLR Workshop and Conference Proceedings.

Omer Levy and Yoav Goldberg. 2014. Neural word embedding as implicit matrix factorization. In Z. Ghahramani, M. Welling, C. Cortes, N.D. Lawrence, and K.Q. Weinberger, editors, *Advances in Neural Information Processing Systems 27*, pages 2177–2185. Curran Associates, Inc.

Tomas Mikolov, Ilya Sutskever, Kai Chen, Greg S Corrado, and Jeff Dean. 2013a. Distributed representations of words and phrases and their compositionality. In C.J.C. Burges, L. Bottou, M. Welling, Z. Ghahramani, and K.Q. Weinberger, editors, *Advances in Neural Information Processing Systems 26*, pages 3111–3119. Curran Associates, Inc.

Tomas Mikolov, Wen-tau Yih, and Geoffrey Zweig. 2013b. Linguistic regularities in continuous space word representations. In *Proceedings of the 2013 Conference of the North American Chapter of the Association for Computational Linguistics: Human Language Technologies*, pages 746–751, Atlanta, Georgia, June. Association for Computational Linguistics.

George A. Miller. 1995. Wordnet: A lexical database for english. *Commun. ACM*, 38(11):39–41, November.

Andriy Mnih and Koray Kavukcuoglu. 2013. Learning word embeddings efficiently with noise-contrastive estimation. In Z. Ghahramani, M. Welling, C. Cortes, N.D. Lawrence, and K.Q. Weinberger, editors, *Advances in Neural Information Processing Systems 26*, pages 2265–2273. Curran Associates, Inc.

Saif Mohammad, Bonnie Dorr, and Graeme Hirst. 2008. Computing word-pair antonymy. In *Proceedings of the 2008 Conference on Empirical Methods in Natural Language Processing*, pages 982–991, Honolulu, Hawaii, October. Association for Computational Linguistics.

Saif M. Mohammad, Bonnie J. Dorr, Graeme Hirst, and Peter D. Turney. 2013. Computing lexical contrast. *Computational Linguistics*, 39(3):555–590, September.

Jeffrey Pennington, Richard Socher, and Christopher Manning. 2014. Glove: Global vectors for word representation. In *Proceedings of the 2014 Conference on Empirical Methods in Natural Language Processing (EMNLP)*, pages 1532–1543, Doha, Qatar, October. Association for Computational Linguistics.

Duyu Tang, Furu Wei, Nan Yang, Ming Zhou, Ting Liu, and Bing Qin. 2014. Learning sentiment-specific word embedding for twitter sentiment classification. In *Proceedings of the 52nd Annual Meeting of the Association for Computational Linguistics (Volume 1: Long Papers)*, pages 1555–1565, Baltimore, Maryland, June. Association for Computational Linguistics.

Joseph Turian, Lev Ratinov, and Yoshua Bengio. 2010. Word representations: A simple and general method for semi-supervised learning. In *Proceedings of the 48th Annual Meeting of the Association for Computational Linguistics*, ACL '10, pages 384–394, Stroudsburg, PA, USA. Association for Computational Linguistics.

Wen-tau Yih, Geoffrey Zweig, and John Platt. 2012. Polarity inducing latent semantic analysis. In *Proceedings of the 2012 Joint Conference on Empirical Methods in Natural Language Processing and Computational Natural Language Learning*, pages 1212–1222, Jeju Island, Korea, July. Association for Computational Linguistics.

Jingwei Zhang, Jeremy Salwen, Michael Glass, and Alfio Gliozzo. 2014. Word semantic representations using bayesian probabilistic tensor factorization. In *Proceedings of the 2014 Conference on Empirical Methods in Natural Language Processing (EMNLP)*, pages 1522–1531. Association for Computational Linguistics.

# A Comparison of Word Similarity Performance Using Explanatory and Non-explanatory Texts

**Lifeng Jin**
Department of Linguistics
The Ohio State University
jin@ling.osu.edu

**William Schuler**
Department of Linguistics
The Ohio State University
schuler@ling.osu.edu

## Abstract

Vectorial representations of words derived from large current events datasets have been shown to perform well on word similarity tasks. This paper shows vectorial representations derived from substantially smaller explanatory text datasets such as English Wikipedia and Simple English Wikipedia preserve enough lexical semantic information to make these kinds of category judgments with equal or better accuracy.

## 1 Introduction

Vectorial representations derived from large current events datasets such as Google News have been shown to perform well on word similarity tasks (Mikolov, 2013; Levy & Goldberg, 2014). This paper shows vectorial representations derived from substantially smaller explanatory text datasets such as English Wikipedia and Simple English Wikipedia preserve enough lexical semantic information to make these kinds of category judgments with equal or better accuracy. Analysis shows these results may be driven by a prevalence of commonsense facts in explanatory text. These positive results for relatively small datasets suggest vectors derived from slower but more accurate analyses of these resources may be practical for lexical semantic applications.

## 2 Background

### 2.1 Wikipedia

Wikipedia is a free Internet encyclopedia website and the largest general reference work over the Internet.[1] As of December 2014, Wikipedia contained over 4.6 million articles[2] and 1.6 billion words. Wikipedia as a corpus has been heavily used to train various NLP models. Features of Wikipedia are well exploited in research like semantic web (Lehmann et al, 2014) and topic modeling (Dumais, 1988; Gabrilovich, 2007), but more importantly Wikipedia has been a reliable source for word embedding training because of its sheer size and coverage (Qiu, 2014), as recent word embedding models (Mikolov et al, 2013; Pennington et al, 2014) all use Wikipedia as an important corpus to build and evaluate their algorithms for word embedding creation.

### 2.2 Simple English Wikipedia

Simple English Wikipedia[3] is a Wikipedia database where all articles are written using simple English words and grammar. It is created to help adults and children who are learning English to look for encyclopedic information. Compared with full English Wikipedia, Simple English Wikipedia is much smaller. It contains around 120,000 articles and 20 million words, which is almost one fortieth the number of articles and one eightieth the number of words compared to full English Wikipedia, so the average length of articles is also shorter. Simple English Wikipedia is often used in simplification research (Coster, 2011; Napoles, 2010) where sentences from full English Wikipedia are matched to sentences from Simple English Wikipedia to explore techniques to simplify sentences. It would be

[1] See https://en.wikipedia.org/wiki/Wikipedia
[2] See http://en.wikipedia.org/wiki/Wikipedia:Size_of_Wikipedia
[3] See http://simple.wikipedia.org/wiki/Main_Page



*Human Language Technologies: The 2015 Annual Conference of the North American Chapter of the ACL*, pages 990–994,
Denver, Colorado, May 31 – June 5, 2015. 

reasonable to expect that the small vocabulary size of Simple English Wikipedia may be disadvantageous when trying to create word embeddings using co-occurrence information, but it may also be true that despite the much smaller vocabulary size and overall size, because of the explanatory nature of its text, Simple English Wikipedia would still preserve enough information to allow the performance of models trained with Simple English Wikipedia to be comparable to models trained on full Wikipedia, and perform equally well or better than non-explanatory texts like the Google News corpus.

### 2.3 Word2Vec

The distributed representation of words, or word embeddings, has gained significant attention in the research community, and one of the more discussed works is Mikolov's (2013) word representation estimation research. Mikolov proposed two neusral network based models for word representation: Continuous Bag-of-Words (CBOW) and Skip-gram. CBOW takes advantage of context words surrounding a given word to predict the word by summing all the context word vectors together to represent the word; whereas Skip-gram uses the word to predict the context word vectors for skip-gram positions, therefore making the model sensitive to positions of context words. Both of the models scale well to large quantities of training data, however it is noted by Mikolov that Skip-gram works well with small amounts of training data and provides good representations for rare words, and CBOW would perform better and have higher accuracy for frequent words if trained on larger corpora. The purpose of this paper is not to compare the models, but to use the models to compare training corpora to see how different arrangement of information may impact the quality of the word embeddings.

## 3 Task Description

To evaluate the effectiveness of full English Wikipedia and Simple English Wikipedia as training corpora for word embeddings, the word similarity-relatedness task described by Levy & Goldberg (2014) is used. As pointed out by Agirre et al (2009) and Levy & Goldberg (2014), relatedness may actually be measuring topical similarity and be better predicted by a bag-of-words model, and similarity may be measuring functional or syntactic similarity and be better predicted by a context-window model. However, when the models are constant, the semantic information of the test words in the training corpora is crucial to allowing the model to build semantic representations for the words. It may be argued that when the corpus is explanatory, more semantic information about the target words is present; whereas when the corpus is non-explanatory, information around the words is merely related to the words. The WordSim353 (Agirre, 2009) dataset is used as the test dataset. This dataset contains pairs of words that are decided by human annotators to be either similar or related, and a similarity or relatedness gold standard score is also given to every pair of words. There are 100 similar word pairs, 149 related pairs and 104 pairs of words with very weak or no relation. In the evaluation task, the unrelated word pairs are discarded from the dataset.

The objective of the task is to rank the similar word pairs higher than related ones. The retrieval/ranking procedure is as follows. First, the cosine similarity scores are calculated using word embeddings from a certain model; then the scores are sorted from the highest to the lowest. The retrieval step is then carried out by locating the last pair of the first $n\%$ of the pairs of similar words in the sorted list of scores and determining the percentage of similar word pairs in the sub-list delimited by the last pair of similar words. In other words, the procedure treats similar word pairs as successful retrievals and determines the accuracy rate when the recall rate is $n\%$. Because the accuracy rate would always fall to the percentage of similar word pairs in all word pairs, it is expected that the later and more suddenly it falls, the better the model is performing in this task.

## 4 Models

The word2vec python implementation provided by gensim (Rehurek et al, 2010) package is used to train all the word2vec models. For Skip-gram and CBOW, a 5-word window size is used to allow them to get the same amount of raw information, also words appearing 5 times or fewer are filtered out. The dimensions of the word embeddings from Skip-gram and CBOW are all 300. Both full English Wikipedia and Simple English Wikipedia are used as training corpora with minimal preprocessing procedures: XML tags are removed and infoboxes are filtered out, thus yielding four models: Full English Wikipedia – CBOW(FW-CBOW), Full English Wikipedia – Skip-gram(FW-SG), Simple English Wikipedia – CBOW(SW-CBOW) and Simple English Wikipedia – Skip-gram(SW-SG). The pre-trained Google News skip-gram model with 300-dimensional vectors (GN-SG) is also downloaded from the Google word2vec website for comparison. This model is trained on the Google News dataset with 100 billion words, which is 30 times as large as the full English Wikipedia and 240 times as large as Simple English Wikipedia.

## 5 Results

Table 1 shows the accuracy rate at every recall rate point, with the sum of all the accuracy rates as the cumulative score. It is shown that GN-SG, although not far behind, is not giving the best performance despite being trained on the largest dataset. In fact, it is clear that it never excels at any given recall rate point. It outperforms various models at certain recall rate points by a small margin, but there is no obvious advantage gained from training using a much larger corpus even when compared with the models trained on Simple English Wikipedia, despite the greater risk of sparse data problems on this smaller data set.

For models trained on Simple English Wikipedia and full English Wikipedia, it is also interesting to see that the models almost perform equally well. The FW-CBOW trained on full English Wikipedia performs the best among the models overall, but for the first few recall rate points, it performs equally well or slightly worse than either SW-CBOW or SW-SG trained on Simple English Wikipedia. At the later points, it is also clear that although FW-CBOW is generally better than all the other models most of the time, the margin could be considered narrow and furthermore it is equally as good as SW-CBOW at the first two recall points.

Comparing FW-SG with SW-SG and SW-CBOW, there is almost no sign of performance gain from training using full Wikipedia instead of the much smaller Simple Wikipedia. FW-SG performs equally well or often slightly worse than both Simple Wikipedia models.

The main observation in this paper is that Google News is not out-performing other systems substantially and that full Wikipedia systems are not out-performing Simple Wikipedia substantially (that is, comparing the CBOW models to one another and the Skip-gram models to one another). The main result from the table is not that smaller training datasets yield better systems, but that systems trained using significantly smaller training datasets of explanatory text have very close performances in this task compared with systems trained on very large datasets, despite the big training data size difference.

## 6 Analysis

As mentioned previously, similarity may be better predicted by a context-window model because it measures functional or syntactic similarity. However, it is not clear in these models that the syntactic information is a major component in the word embeddings. Instead, it may be that the main factor for the performance level of the models is the general explanatory content of the Wikipedia articles, as opposed to the current events content of Google News.

For similar words such as synonyms or hyponyms, the crucial information making them similar is shared general semantic features of the words. For example, for the word pair *physics : chemistry*, the shared semantic features might be that they are both academic subjects, both studied in institutions and both composed of different subfields, as shown in Table 2. The '@' sign in table 2 connects a context word with its position relative to the word in the center of the window. These shared properties

| Model | 10% Recall Rate | 20% Recall Rate | 30% Recall Rate | 40% Recall Rate | 50% Recall Rate | 60% Recall Rate | 70% Recall Rate | 80% Recall Rate | 90% Recall Rate | 100% Recall Rate | Cumulative Score |
|---|---|---|---|---|---|---|---|---|---|---|---|
| FW-CBOW | **0.91** | **0.95** | 0.89 | **0.83** | **0.72** | **0.74** | **0.61** | **0.51** | **0.46** | 0.40 | **7.03** |
| SW-CBOW | **0.91** | **0.95** | 0.78 | 0.75 | **0.72** | 0.70 | 0.56 | 0.50 | **0.46** | 0.40 | 6.74 |
| FW-SG | **0.91** | **0.95** | 0.79 | 0.75 | 0.63 | 0.61 | 0.53 | 0.49 | 0.43 | 0.40 | 6.50 |
| SW-SG | **0.91** | **0.95** | **0.91** | 0.70 | 0.62 | 0.57 | 0.54 | 0.45 | 0.42 | 0.40 | 6.47 |
| GN-SG | 0.85 | 0.84 | 0.82 | 0.79 | 0.70 | 0.64 | 0.57 | 0.48 | 0.43 | 0.40 | 6.51 |

Table 1: Performance of Different Models at Different Recall Rate Points

of the core semantic identities for these words may contribute greatly to the similarity judgments for humans and machines alike, and these shared properties may be considered general knowledge about the words. For the related words, for example *computer : keyboard*, it may be difficult to pinpoint the semantic overlap between the components which build up the core semantic identities of these words, and none is observed in the data.

General knowledge of a certain word may be found in explanatory texts about the word like dictionaries or encyclopedias, but rarely found in texts other than that. It would be assumed by the writers of informative non-explanatory texts like news articles that the readers are well acquainted with all the basic semantic information about the words, therefore repetition of such information would be unnecessary. For a similarity/relatedness judgment task where basic and compositional semantic information may prove to be useful, using a corpus like Google News, where information or context for a particular word assumes one is already conversant with it, would not be as effective as using a corpus like Wikipedia where general knowledge about a word may be available and repeated. Also, the smaller vocabulary size of Wikipedia compared with Google News would suggest that general knowledge may be conveyed more efficiently with less data sparsity.

In the Simple Wikipedia vs. full Wikipedia case, both corpora are explanatory texts. Despite the much smaller size, the general semantic overlap between each pair of similar words seems as evident in Simple Wikipedia as in full Wikipedia. For measurements like cosine similarity where large values in the same dimensions are favored, the basic semantic components which contribute to the similarity judgments for the words are the same comparatively across two different corpora. This may not be surprising because although more information may be present in full Wikipedia, because of its explanatory nature, the core semantic components which make a concept distinct still dominate over new and sparser information added to it. In Simple Wikipedia, the size of the articles

| Word Pair | COAST | SHORE | PHYSICS | CHEMISTRY |
|---|---|---|---|---|
| Simple Wikipedia | east@-1 164 | Lake@2 39 | particle@-1 34 | organic@-1 86 |
| | **west@-1 137** | **eastern@-1 25** | chemistry@2 29 | physics@-2 29 |
| | **south@-1 75** | **north@-1 17** | **quantum@-1 28** | physical@-1 21 |
| | **north@-1 64** | **south@-1 17** | nuclear@-1 23 | used@-3 20 |
| | Africa@2 63 | **Sea@4 14** | **theoretical@-1 21** | supramolecular@-1 18 |
| | **Sea@4 55** | **western@-1 14** | **University@3 21** | chemistry@3 17 |
| | Atlantic@-1 53 | **northern@-1 12** | laws@-2 21 | chemistry@-3 17 |
| | **western@-1 52** | **southern@-1 11** | mathematical@-1 16 | **theoretical@-1 16** |
| | **northern@-1 52** | lake@3 10 | chemistry@-2 16 | physics@2 16 |
| | **eastern@-1 50** | River@4 8 | **professor@-2 14** | placed@3 14 |
| | North@2 46 | close@-2 7 | mathematics@2 13 | biology@2 14 |
| | Australia@2 43 | Michigan@3 6 | mathematics@-2 13 | analytical@-1 12 |
| | **southern@-1 40** | washed@-3 5 | classical@-1 13 | **University@3 12** |
| | Pacific@-1 37 | **west@-1 5** | atomic@-1 13 | **quantum@-1 12** |
| | America@3 33 | **island@3 5** | modern@-1 11 | Organic@-1 11 |
| | city@-4 33 | sea@-1 5 | Nobel@-3 10 | computational@-1 11 |
| | **island@3 30** | Texas@-1 4 | physics@3 10 | **professor@-2 11** |
| Full Wikipedia | **west@-1 16279** | Lake@2 3700 | particle@-1 2898 | organic@-1 2733 |
| | **east@-1 13662** | **north@-1 2718** | theoretical@-1 2366 | physics@-2 1864 |
| | **south@-1 4574** | **eastern@-1 2567** | **University@3 2053** | **University@3 1267** |
| | Atlantic@-1 3741 | along@-3 2229 | mathematics@-2 1929 | physics@2 1192 |
| | **north@-1 3497** | **western@-1 2163** | chemistry@2 1864 | physical@-1 1080 |
| | Pacific@-1 3383 | **located@-4 1955** | nuclear@-1 1745 | **professor@-2 977** |
| | **western@-1 2802** | **south@-1 1908** | laws@-2 1686 | biology@-2 886 |
| | **southern@-1 2783** | **southern@-1 1810** | **quantum@-1 1443** | biology@2 756 |
| | **eastern@-1 2771** | Lake@3 1645 | chemistry@-2 1192 | **studied@-1 667** |
| | Sea@-1 2463 | **northern@-1 1628** | **professor@-2 1192** | analytical@-1 633 |
| | America@3 2446 | batteries@1 1162 | mathematical@-1 1136 | inorganic@-1 575 |
| | **northern@-1 2383** | lake@3 1121 | mathematics@2 1032 | **degree@-2 559** |
| | Island@3 2333 | Bay@3 1050 | matter@-1 786 | **quantum@-1 554** |
| | North@2 2280 | River@4 875 | **degree@-2 741** | **University@4 517** |
| | Africa@2 2254 | **east@-1 800** | state@-1 737 | chemistry@3 418 |
| | **located@-4 2177** | **west@-1 785** | **University@4 706** | chemistry@-3 418 |
| | island@3 1966 | bombardment@1 664 | **studied@-1 679** | computational@-1 396 |

Table 2: Top 17 Context Words that Co-occur with the Sample Similar Word Pairs

and vocabulary may restrict it to be basic and precise to explain a certain concept with fewer presumptions of what the readers already know, and it is suggested by the analysis that such style is also reflected in full Wikipedia, leading to the domination of general knowledge over specific facts.

## 7 Conclusion

This paper has shown vectorial representations derived from substantially smaller explanatory text datasets such as Wikipedia and Simple Wikipedia preserve enough lexical semantic information to make these kinds of category judgments with equal or better accuracy than news corpora. Analysis shows these results may be driven by a prevalence of commonsense facts in explanatory text. These positive results for small datasets suggest vectors derived from slower but more accurate analysis of these resources may be practical for lexical semantic applications, and we hope by providing this result, future researchers may be more aware of the viability of smaller-scale resources like Simple English Wikipedia (or presumably Wikipedia in other languages which are substantially smaller in size than English Wikipedia), that can still produce high quality vectors despite a much smaller size.

## References


Agirre, E., Alfonseca, E., Hall, K., Kravalova, J., Pasca, M., & Soroa, A. (2009). A study on similarity and relatedness using distributional and WordNet-based approaches (pp. 19–27). Association for Computational Linguistics.

Coster, W., & Kauchak, D. (2011). Learning to simplify sentences using Wikipedia (pp. 1–9). Association for Computational Linguistics.

Dumais, S. T., Furnas, G. W., Landauer, T. K., Deerwester, S., & Harshman, R. (1988). Using latent semantic analysis to improve access to textual information. the SIGCHI conference (pp. 281–285). New York, New York, USA: ACM. doi:10.1145/57167.57214

Gabrilovich, E., & Markovitch, S. (2007). Computing Semantic Relatedness Using Wikipedia-based Explicit Semantic Analysis. IJCAI.

Lehmann, J., Isele, R., Jakob, M., & Jentzsch, A. (2014). DBpedia–A large-scale, multilingual knowledge base extracted from Wikipedia. Semantic Web.

Levy, O., & Goldberg, Y. (2014). Dependency-Based Word Embeddings. Association for Computational Linguistics.

Mikolov, T., Chen, K., Corrado, G., & Dean, J. (2013). *Efficient estimation of word representations in vector space*. ICLR Workshop Papers

Napoles, C., & Dredze, M. (2010). Learning simple Wikipedia: A cogitation in ascertaining abecedarian language. NAACL HLT

Pennington, J., & Socher, R. (2014). Glove: Global vectors for word representation. EMNLP.

Qiu, L., Cai, Y., Nie, Z., & Rui, Y. (2014). Learning Word Representation Considering Proximity and Ambiguity (pp. 1572–1578). AAAI Conference on Artificial Intelligence.

Rehurek, R., & Sojka, P. (2010). Software Framework for Topic Modelling with Large Corpora. LREC Workshop on New Challenges for NLP Frameworks, 45–50.

# Morphological Modeling for Machine Translation of English-Iraqi Arabic Spoken Dialogs

**Katrin Kirchhoff**
Department of
Electrical Engineering
University of Washington
Seattle, WA, USA
kk2@u.washington.edu

**Wilson Tam**
Microsoft Corporation
wilson.yctam@gmail.com

**Colleen Richey, Wen Wang**
SRI International
Menlo Park, CA, USA
colleen@speech.sri.com
wwang@speech.sri.com

## Abstract

This paper addresses the problem of morphological modeling in statistical speech-to-speech translation for English to Iraqi Arabic. An analysis of user data from a real-time MT-based dialog system showed that generating correct verbal inflections is a key problem for this language pair. We approach this problem by enriching the training data with morphological information derived from source-side dependency parses. We analyze the performance of several parsers as well as the effect on different types of translation models. Our method achieves an improvement of more than a full BLEU point and a significant increase in verbal inflection accuracy; at the same time, it is computationally inexpensive and does not rely on target-language linguistic tools.

## 1 Introduction

SMT from a morphologically poor language like English into a language with richer morphology continues to be a problem, in particular when training data is sparse and/or the SMT system has insufficient modeling capabilities for morphological variation in the target language. Most previous approaches to this problem have utilized a translate-and-inflect method, where a first-pass SMT system is trained on lemmatized forms, and the correct inflection for every word is predicted in a second pass by statistical classifiers trained on a combination of source and target language features. This paper looks at morphological modeling from a different perspective, namely to improve SMT in a real-time speech-to-speech translation system. Our focus is on resolving those morphological translation errors that are most likely to cause confusions and misunderstandings in machine-translation mediated human-human dialogs. Due to the constraints imposed by a real-time system, previous approaches that rely on elaborate feature sets and multi-pass processing strategies are unsuitable for this problem. The language pair of interest in this study is English and Iraqi Arabic (IA). The latter is a spoken dialect of Arabic with few existing linguistic resources. We therefore develop a low-resource approach that relies on source-side dependency parses only. We analyze its performance in combination with different types of parsers and different translation models. Results show a significant improvement in translation performance in both automatic and manual evaluations. Moreover, the proposed method is sufficiently fast for a real-time system.

## 2 Prior Work

Much work in SMT has addressed the issue of translating from morphologically-rich languages by preprocessing the source and/or target data by e.g., stemming and morphological decomposition (Popovic and Ney, 2004; Goldwater and McClosky, 2005), compound splitting (Koehn and Knight, 2003), or various forms of tokenization (Lee, 2004; Habash and Sadat, 2006). In (Minkov et al., 2007; Toutanova et al., 2008) morphological generation was applied as a postprocessing step for translation *into* morphologically-rich languages. A maximum-entropy Markov model was trained to predict the correct inflection for every stemmed word in the



*Human Language Technologies: The 2015 Annual Conference of the North American Chapter of the ACL*, pages 995–1000,
Denver, Colorado, May 31 – June 5, 2015. 

machine translation output from a first-pass system, conditioned on a set of lexical, morphological and syntactic features. More recently, (Chahuneau et al., 2013) applied a similar translate-and-inflect approach, utilizing unsupervised in addition to supervised morphological analyses. Inflection generation models were also used by (Fraser et al., 2012; Weller et al., 2013) for translation into German, and by (El Kholy and Habash, 2012) for Modern Standard Arabic. (Sultan, 2011) added both syntactic information on the source side that was used in filtering the phrase table, plus postprocessing on the target side for English-Arabic translation. Still other approaches enrich the translation system with morphology-aware feature functions or specific agreement models (Koehn and Hoang, 2007; Green and DeNero, 2012; Williams and Koehn, 2011).

In contrast to the above studies, which have concentrated on text translation, this paper focuses on spoken language translation within a bilingual human-human dialog system. Thus, our main goal is not to predict the correct morphological form of every word, but to prevent communication errors resulting from the mishandling of morphology. The intended use in a real-time dialog system imposes additional constraints on morphological modeling: any proposed approach should not add a significant computational burden to the overall system that might result in delays in translation or response generation. Our goal is also complicated by the fact that our target language is a spoken dialect of Arabic, for which few linguistic resources (training data, lexicons, morphological analyzers) exist. Lastly, Arabic written forms are morphologically highly ambiguous due to the lack of short vowel markers that signal grammatical categories.

## 3 Dialog System and Analysis

The first step in the dialog system used for this study consists of an automatic speech recognition (ASR) component that produces ASR hypotheses for the user's speech input. Several error detection modules then identify likely out-of-vocabulary and misrecognized words. This information is used by a clarification module that asks the user to rephrase these error segments; another module then combines the user's answers into a merged, corrected representation before sending it to the translation engine. A machine translation error detection module analyzes the translation to check for errors, such as unknown words. If an error is found, another clarification subdialog is initiated; otherwise, the translation is sent to a text-to-speech engine to produce the acoustic output in the other language. A schematic representation is shown in Figure 1. More details about the system can be found in (et al., 2013). The system was evaluated in live mode with native IA speakers as part of the DARPA BOLT Phase-II benchmark evaluations. The predefined scenarios included military and humanitarian assistance/disaster relief scenarios as well as general topics. All system interactions were logged and evaluated by bilingual human assessors.

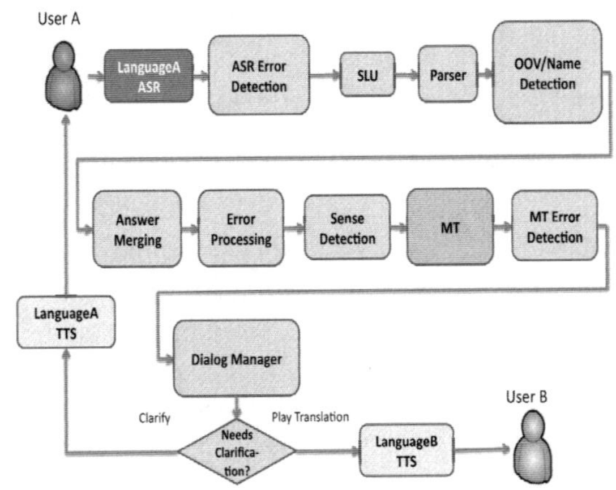


Figure 1: Dialog system used in this work.

During debriefing sessions with the users, some users voiced dissatisfaction with the translation quality, and a subsequent detailed error analysis was conducted on the logs of 30 interactions. Similar to previous studies (Condon et al., 2010) we found that a frequently recurring problem was wrong morphological verb forms in the IA output. Some examples are shown in Table 1. In Example 1, *to make sure* should be translated by a first-person plural verb but it is translated by a second-person plural form, changing the meaning to (*you (pl.) make sure*). The desired verb form would be *ntAkd*. Similarly, in Example 2 the translation of *transport* should agree with the translations of *someone* and the preceding

| | |
|---|---|
| 1 | *you need to tell the locals to evacuate the area so we can secure the area* **to make sure** *no one gets hurt*<br>*lAzm tqwl Alhm AhAly AlmnTqp bAlAxlA' AlmnTqp HtY nqdr nwmn AlmnTqp Elmwd* **ttAkdwn** *Anh mHd ytAY* |
| 2 | *do you have someone that can* **transport you** *to the nearest american base*<br>*Endk wAHd yqdr* **nqlk** *lAqrb qAEdp Amrykyp* |

Table 1: Examples of mistranslated morphology: English ASR hypotheses and IA translation hypotheses.

auxiliary verb *can* (*yqdr*). The correct form would be *yqlk* (*he/she transports you*) instead of *nqlk* (*we transport you*). Such translation errors are confusing to users as they affect the understanding of basic semantic roles. They tend to occur when translating English infinitival constructions (*to*+verb) or other syntactic constructions where English base verb forms need to be translated by a finite verb in IA. In these cases, explicit morphological features like person and number are required in Arabic but they are lacking in the English input.

## 4 Approach

An analysis of the SMT component showed that morphological translation errors primarily occur when a head word and its dependent (such as a verbal head and its subject noun dependent) are translated as part of different phrases or rules. In that case, insufficient context is available to produce the correct translation. Our approach is to annotate syntactic dependencies on the source side using a statistical parser. Based on the resulting dependency structures the source-side data is then tagged with explicit morphological verbal features using deterministic rules (e.g., subject nouns assign their person/number features to their verbal heads), and a new translation model is trained on this data. Our assumption is that words tagged with explicit morphological features will be aligned with their correct translations during training and will thus produce correctly inflected forms during testing even when the syntactic context is not available in the same phrase/rule. For instance, the input sentence in Example 1 in Table 1 would be annotated as:
*you need-2sg to tell-2sg the locals to evacuate-3pl the area so we can-1pl secure-1pl the area to make-1pl sure no one gets-3sg hurt.*
This approach avoids the costly extraction of multiple features, subsequent statistical classification, and inflection generation during run time; moreover, it does not require target-side annotation tools, an advantage when dealing with under-resourced spoken dialects. There are, however, several potential issues with this approach. First, introducing tags fragments the training data: the same word may receive multiple different tags, either due to genuine ambiguity or because of parser errors. As a result, word alignment and phrase extraction may suffer from data sparsity. Second, new word-tag combinations in the test data that were not observed in the training data will not have an existing translation. Third, the performance of the model is highly dependent on the accuracy of the parser. Finally, we make the assumption that the expression of person and number categories are matched across source and target language – in practice, we have indeed seen very few mismatched cases where e.g., a singular noun phrase in English is translated by a plural noun phrase in IA (see Section 6 below).

To address the first point the morph-tagged translation model can be used in a backoff procedure rather than as an alternative model. In this case the baseline model is used by default, and the morph-tagged model is only used whenever heads and dependents are translated as part of different phrases. Unseen translations for particular word-tag combinations in the test set could in principle be addressed by using a morphological analyzer to generate novel word forms with the desired inflections. However, this would require identifying the correct stem for the word in question, generating all possible morphological forms, and either selecting one or providing all options to the SMT system, which again increases system load. We analyzed unseen word-tag combination in the test data but found that their percentage was very small ($< 1\%$). Thus, for these forms we back off to the untagged counterparts rather than generating new inflected forms. To obtain better insight into the effect of parsing accuracy we compared the performance of two parsers in our annotation pipeline: the Stanford parser (de Marneffe et al., 2006) (version 3.3.1) and the Macaon parser (Nasr et al., 2014). The latter is an implementation of graph-based parsing (McDonald et al., 2005) where a projective dependency tree maximizing a score function is sought in the graph of all possible trees using dynamic programming. It uses a 1st-order decoder, which is more robust to speech input as well as out-of-domain training data. The features implemented reflect those of (Bohnet, 2010) (based on lexemes and part-of-speech tags). The parser was trained on Penn-Treebank data transformed to match speech (lower-cased, no punctuation), with one iteration of self-training on the Transtac training set. We also use the combination of both parsers, where source words are only tagged if the tags derived independently from each parser agree with each other.

## 5 Data and Baseline Systems

Development experiments were carried out on the Transtac corpus of dialogs in the military and medical domain. The number of sentence pairs is 762k for the training set, 6.9k for the dev set, 2.8k for eval set 1, and 1.8k for eval set 2. Eval set 1 has one reference per sentence, eval set 2 has four references. For the development experiments we used a phrase-based Moses SMT system with a hierarchical reordering model, tested on Eval set 1. The language model was a backoff 6-gram model trained using Kneser-Ney discounting and interpolation of higher- and lower-order n-grams. In addition to automatic evaluation we performed manual analyses of the accuracy of verbal features in the IA translations on a subset of 65 sentences (containing 143 verb forms) from the live evaluations described above. This analysis counts a verb form as correct if its morphological features for person and number are correct, although it may have the wrong lemma (e.g., wrong word sense). The development experiments were designed to identify the setup that produces the highest verbal inflection accuracy. For final testing we used a more advanced SMT engine on Eval set 2.This system is the one used in the real-time dialog system; it contains a hierarchical phrase-based translation model, sparse features, and a neural network joint model (NNJM) (Devlin et al., 2014).

| | BLEU | | Acc (%) | |
|---|---|---|---|---|
| Parser | std | bo | std | bo |
| Baseline | 16.8 | N/A | 37.1 | N/A |
| Stanford | 16.9 | 17.0 | 60.1 | 59.4 |
| Macaon | 17.0 | 17.1 | **67.1** | 62.9 |
| Combined | 17.1 | 17.1 | 59.4 | 57.3 |

Table 2: BLEU scores on Transtac eval set 1 and accuracy of verbal morphological features on manual eval set. *std* = standard, *bo* = backed-off system.

## 6 Experiments and Results

Results in Table 2 show the comparison between the baseline, different parsers, and the combined system. We see that verbal inflection accuracy increases substantially from the baseline performance and is best for the Macaon parser. Improvements over the baseline system without morphology are statistically significant; differences between the individual parsers are not (not, however, that the sample size for manual evaluation was quite small).

BLEU is not affected negatively but even increases slightly - thus, data fragmentation does not seem to be a problem overall. This may be due to the nature of the task and domain, which is results in fairly short, simple sentence constructions that can be adequately translated by a concatenation of shorter phrases rather than requiring longer phrases. Back-off systems (indicated by *bo*) and the combined system improve BLEU only trivially while decreasing verbal inflection accuracy by varying amounts. For testing within the dialog system we thus choose the Macaon parser and utilize a standard translation model rather than a backoff model. An added benefit is that the Macaon parser is already used in other components in the dialog system. Using this setup we ran two experiments with dialog system's SMT engine: first, we re-extracted phrases and rules based on the morph-tagged data and reoptimized the feature weights. In the second experiment, we additionally applied the NNJM to the morph-tagged source text. To this end we include all the morphological variants of the original vocabulary that was used for the NNJM in the untagged baseline system. Table 3 shows the results. The morph-tagged data improves the BLEU score under both conditions: in Experiment 1, the improvement is almost a full BLEU point (0.91); in Experiment 2 the improvement is even larger (1.13), even though the baseline performance is stronger. Both results are statistically significant at p = 0.05, using a paired bootstrap resampling test. The combination of morph-tagged data and the more advanced modeling options (sparse features, NNJM) in this system seem to be beneficial. Improved translation performance may also be captured by the four reference translations as opposed to one in Eval set 1. In order to assess the added computation cost

| System | no NNJM | with NNJM |
|---|---|---|
| Baseline | 34.38 | 36.17 |
| Morph tags | **35.29** | **37.30** |

Table 3: BLEU on Eval set 2 using dialog system's SMT engine.

of our procedure we computed the decoding speed of the MT component in the dialog system for both the baseline and the morpho-tag systems. In the baseline MT system (with NNJM) without morpho-tags, decoding takes 0.01572 seconds per word or 0.15408 seconds per sentence – these numbers were obtained on a Dell Precision M4800 Laptop with a quad-core Intel i7-4930MX Processor and 32GB of RAM. Morpho-tagging only adds 0.00031 seconds per word or 0.0024 seconds per sentence. Thus, our procedure is extremely efficient.

An analysis of the remaining morphological translation errors not captured by our approach showed that in about 34% of all cases these were due to part-of-speech tagging or parser errors, i.e. verbs were mistagged as nouns rather than verbs and thus did not receive any morphological tags, or the parser hypothesized wrong dependency relations. In 53% of the cases the problem is the lack of more extensive discourse or contextual knowledge. This includes constructions where there is no overt subject for a verb in the current utterance, and the appropriate underlying subject must be inferred from the preceding discourse or from knowledge of the situational context. This is an instance of the more general problem of control (see e.g.,(Landau, 2013) for an overview of research in this area). It is exemplified by cases such as the following:

1. *The first step is to make sure that all personnel are in your debrief.*

Here, the underlying subject of "to make sure" could be a range of different candidates (*I*, *you*, *we*, etc.) and must be inferred from context.

2. *I can provide up to one platoon to help you guys cordon off the area.*

In this case the statistical parser identified *I* as the subject of *help*, but *platoon* is more likely to be the controller and was in fact identified as the underlying subject by the annotator. Such cases could potentially be resolved during the parsing step by integrating semantic information, e.g. as in (Bansal et al., 2014). However, initial investigations with semantic features in the Macaon parser resulted in a significant slow-down of the parser. In other cases, more sophisticated modeling of the entities and their relationships in the situational context will be required. This clearly is an area for future study.

Finally, in 13% of the cases, mistranslations are caused by a mismatch of number features across languages (e.g. number features for nouns such as *family* or *people*).

## 7 Conclusion

We have shown that significant gains in BLEU and verbal inflection accuracy in speech-to-speech translation for English-IA can be achieved by incorporating morphological tags derived from dependency parse information in the source language. The proposed method is fast, low-resource, and can easily be incorporated into a real-time dialog system. It adds negligible computational cost and does not require any target-language specific annotation tools. Possible areas for future study include the use of discourse or and other contextual information to determine morphological agreement, application to other languages pairs/morphological agreement types, and learning the annotation rules from data.

**Acknowledgments**

This study was funded by the Defense Advanced Research Projects Agency (DARPA) under contract HR0011-12-C-0016 - subcontract 19-000234.

## References

M. Bansal, K. Gimpel, and K. Livescu. 2014. Tailoring continuous word representations for dependency parsing. In *Proc. of ACL*.

B. Bohnet. 2010. Very high accuracy and fast dependency parsing is not a contradiction. In *Proceedings of COLING*, pages 89–97.

V. Chahuneau, E. Schlinger, N. Smith, and C. Dyer. 2013. Translating into morphologically rich languages with synthetic phrases. In *Proceedings of EMNLP*.

S. Condon, D. Parvaz, J. Aberdeen, C. Doran, A. Freeman, and M. Awad. 2010. Evaluation of machine translation errors in English and Iraqi Arabic. In *Proceedings of LREC*.

M.-C. de Marneffe, B. MacCartney, and C.D. Manning. 2006. Generating typed dependency parses from phrase structure parses. In *Proceedings of LREC*.

J. Devlin et al. 2014. Fast and robust neural network joint models for statistical machine translation. In *Proceedings of ACL*, pages 1370–1380.

A. El Kholy and N. Habash. 2012. Translate, predict or generate: modeling rich morphology in statistical machine translation. In *Proceedings of EAMT*.

N.F. Ayan et al. 2013. Can you give me another word for hyperbaric? - improving speech translation using targeted clarification questions. In *Proceedings of ICASSP*.

A. Fraser, M. Weller, A. Cahill, and F. Cap. 2012. Modeling inflection and word-formation in SMT. In *Proceedings of EACL*, pages 664–674.

S. Goldwater and D. McClosky. 2005. Improving statistical MT through morphological analysis. In *Proceedings of EMNLP*, pages 676–683.

S. Green and J. DeNero. 2012. A class-based agreement model for generating accuractely inflected translation. In *Proceedings of ACL*, pages 146–155.

N. Habash and F. Sadat. 2006. Arabic preprocessing schemes for statistical machine translation. In *Proceedings of NAACL*.

P. Koehn and H. Hoang. 2007. Factored translation models. In *Proceedings of EMNLP*, pages 868–876.

P. Koehn and K. Knight. 2003. Empirical methods for compound splitting. In *Proceedings of EACL*.

I. Landau. 2013. *Control in Generative Grammar: A Research Companion*. Cambridge University Press, Cambridge, UK.

Y.S. Lee. 2004. Morphological analysis for statistical machine translation. In *Proceedings of HLT-NAACL*.

R. McDonald, F. Pereira, K. Ribarov, and J. Hajič. 2005. Non-projective dependency parsing using spanning tree algorithms. In *Proceedings of HLT/EMNLP*, pages 523–530.

E. Minkov, K. Toutanova, and H. Suzuki. 2007. Generating complex morphology for machine translation. In *Proceedings of ACL*, pages 128–135.

A. Nasr, F. Bechet, B. Favre, T. Bazillon, J. Deulofeu, and A. Valli. 2014. Automatically enriching spoken corpora with syntactic information for linguistic studies. In *Proceedings of LREC*.

M. Popovic and H. Ney. 2004. Towards the use of word stems and suffixes for statistical machine translation. In *Proceedings of LREC*.

S. Sultan. 2011. *Applying Morphology to English-Arabic Statistical Machine Translation*. Ph.D. thesis, Department of Computer Science, ETH Zürich.

K. Toutanova, H. Suzuki, and A. Ruopp. 2008. Applying morphology generation models to machine translation. In *Proceedings of ACL*, pages 514–522.

M. Weller, A. Fraser, and S. Schulte im Walde. 2013. Using subcategorization knowledge to improve case prediction for translation to German. In *Proceedings of ACL*, pages 593–603.

P. Williams and P. Koehn. 2011. Agreement constraints for statistical machine translation into German. In *Proceedings of WMT*.

# Continuous Adaptation to User Feedback for Statistical Machine Translation

**Frédéric Blain, Fethi Bougares, Amir Hazem, Loïc Barrault and Holger Schwenk**
LIUM - University of Le Mans (France)
firstname.surname@lium.univ-lemans.fr

## Abstract

This paper gives a detailed experiment feedback of different approaches to adapt a statistical machine translation system towards a targeted translation project, using only small amounts of parallel in-domain data. The experiments were performed by professional translators under realistic conditions of work using a computer assisted translation tool. We analyze the influence of these adaptations on the translator productivity and on the overall post-editing effort. We show that significant improvements can be obtained by using the presented adaptation techniques.

## 1 Introduction

Language service providers (LSP) and human professional translators currently use machine translation (MT) technology as a tool to increase their productivity. For this, MT is closely integrated into computer-assisted translation (CAT) tool. The MT system suggests an automatic translation of the input sentence which is then post-edited by the human professional translators. They generally work on a project-based pace, *i.e.* a set of documents (the project) have to be translated in a certain period of time. It is well know that an MT system has to be adapted to the target task and domain in order to achieve the best performances. This process of adaptation can be separated into two different steps. First, an adaptation is performed before the beginning of the translation process,. This aims to specialize the system to the targeted domain: we will to this adaptation as *domain adaptation*.

Then, another adaptation is performed during the translation process with the aim of iteratively integrating users' feedback into the MT system. The adaptation can be performed at two different frequencies: (i) the system can continuously learn from post-edited segments, the models being immediately updated, or (ii) all the available project-specific data is used after each day of work to adapt the MT engine. This scheme is more related to document level adaptation; we will refer to it as *project adaptation*. The experimental work described in this paper fits into the latter adaptation scheme.

As part of the MateCat project[1], we analyze project adaptation performed over several days. All experiments were performed with professional human translators under realistic conditions of work. The motivations of this work are detailed in section 2 and related work is discussed. In sections 3 and 4 we present both the experimental protocol and framework before presenting the corresponding results in section 5.

## 2 Motivations

This work is a continuation of earlier research on adaptation of a statistical MT (SMT) system Cettolo et al., 2014). More precisely, it was motivated by remaining opened questions. First, what does the learning curve look like for an iterative usage of the daily adaptation procedure? Even if the efficiency of the project adaptation scheme has been established, it has not been tested yet over multiple days. Does it reaches a plateau or do the translation

[1] www.matecat.com



*Human Language Technologies: The 2015 Annual Conference of the North American Chapter of the ACL*, pages 1001–1005,
Denver, Colorado, May 31 – June 5, 2015. 

quality continue to improve? What are the causes for the observed gains? Are they due to the familiarization of the users with both the system and the task, or are they due to real efficiency of the adaptation scheme? In previous work, the protocol did not allow to clearly measure the adaptation performance. In order to avoid this issue, a specific experimental protocol has been defined as described in section 3. Moreover, in addition to answer these new questions, we assessed a project adaptation scheme which take advantage of continuous space language modeling (CSLM) as explained in section 4. As far as we know, this is the first time that a neural network LM is integrated into a professional environment workflow, and that adaptation in such an approach is considered.

## 3 Evaluation Protocol

We defined an adaptation protocol with the goal to assess the same task with and without adaptation procedure. Like in (Guerberof, 2009; Plitt and Masselot, 2010), three professional translators were involved in a two parts experiment: during the first part, translators receive MT suggestions from a state-of-the-art domain-adapted engine built with the Moses toolkit (Koehn et al., 2007), without being adapted with the data generated during the translation of the project.For the second part, the MT suggestions are provided by a MT system which was previously adapted to the current project using the human translations of prior working days. Since we asked the same translators to post-edit the same document twice (*i.e.* with and without MT adaptation), the second run was launched after a sufficient delay: the human memory impact is reduced since translators worked on other projects in between.

To measure the user productivity, we considered two performance indicators: (i) the post-editing effort measured with TER (Snover et al., 2006) which corresponds to the number of edits made individually by each translator, (ii) the time-to-edit rate expressed in number of translated words per hour. In addition to these two key indicators, we evaluated the translation quality using an automatic measure, namely BLEU score (Papineni et al., 2002). This measure is used to make sure that no regression in the translation quality is observed after several days of work due to overfitting of the project adaptation (since previous working days are used to adapt the models).

Moreover, in order to respect realistic working conditions, we decided to set up a unique user-specific Moses engine per translator. By these means, any inter-user side-effects due to personal choices or stylistic edits are avoided. In addition, we obtain multiple references for assessing the results of the test. Consequently, it was required for the assessment that human translators work in a synchronized manner, *i.e.* the same amount of data is translated every day by each translator. The systems are then adapted, individually for each translator, using previous days of work, and used by the translators during the next day, and so on.

## 4 Experimental framework

We ran contrastive experiments by asking the translators to post-edit translations of a Legal document from English into French (about 15k words) over five days (*i.e.* about 3k words/day). An in-domain adapted (DA) system was used as baseline system for the first day, before project adapted (PA) systems have taken over.

### 4.1 Domain adapted system

Before the human translator starts working, our DA system is trained using an extracted subset of bilingual training data that is mostly relevant to our specific domain. The extraction process, widely known as *data selection*, is applied using cross-entropy difference algorithm proposed by (Axelrod et al., 2011)[2]. In order to augment the amount of training data[3] (about 22M words) we also select a bilingual subset from *Europarl*, *JRC-Acquis*, *news commentary*, *software manuals of the OPUS corpus*, *translation memories* and the *United Nations corpus*. About 700M additional newspaper monolingual data selected from WMT evaluation campaign are also used for language modeling.

### 4.2 Project adapted system

Our project-adaptation scenario, which is repeated iteratively during the lifetime of the translation

[2]We used the XenC tool for data selection

[3]DGT+ECB corpora (see http://opus.lingfil.uu.se)

project, is achieved as follows: the new daily amount of specific data is added to the development set, and new monolingual and bilingual data selections are performed with it. The new SMT system built on these selected data is then optimized on the new development set.

When performing project adaptation of an SMT system, we assume that the documents of a project are quite close and then, adapting the SMT system using the $n$-th days could be helpful to translate the $n + 1$ day. However, we need to be careful to not overfit to a particular day of the project. This is particularly risky since the daily amount of specific data is relatively small (about 3k words). Therefore, we chose to add three times the daily data to our existing in-domain development set. This factor of three was empirically determined during prior lab tests. Also, all the previous days are used, *i.e.* when we adapt after three days of work, we used all the data from the first three days.

### 4.3 Continuous Space Language Model

Over the last years, there has been significantly increasing interest in using neural networks in SMT. As mentioned above, we used this technology into our project adaptation scheme. Fully integrated to the MT systems, it was used by our three SMT systems dedicated to the translators.

A continuous space LM (CSLM) (Schwenk, 2010; Schwenk, 2013) is trained on the same data than a classical $n$-gram back-off LM and is used to rescore the $n$-best list. In our case, and after each day of work, the daily generated data (3k words) is used to perform the adaptation of the CSLM by continuing its training (see (Ter-Sarkisov et al., 2014) for details). An important advantage of this approach is that the adaptation can be performed in a couple of minutes.

## 5 Experimental results and discussion

All the results presented in this section have been extracted from the edit logs provided by the MATECAT CAT tool.

### 5.1 Post-editing effort

In terms of post-editing effort, the results for each translator according to several SMT systems are shown in Table 1. Several TER scores are computed between the SMT system output and various sets of references. This score reveals the number of edits performed by the translator in order to obtain a suitable translation. The first column indicates the day of the experiment. The second column represents three SMT systems, namely: the baseline system adapted to the domain (DA), the same system with a CSLM (DA+CSLM) and the project adapted system (all models were updated, including the CSLM) noted "PA+CSLM-adapt". The third, fourth and fifth columns represent respectively the TER scores for the three translators. The first score is calculated using the reference produced by the translator himself. It could be considered as HTER (Snover et al., 2009). The second score (in parenthesis) is calculated using the three references produced by the translators. The third score (in brackets) is calculated according to an official "generic" reference provided by the European Commission. By these additional results, we aim to assess whether their is a tendency of the systems to adapt strongly to the particular style of one translator, or whether they still perform well with respect to independent references. On day 1, only the DA and DA+CSLM systems are presented since the project adaptation can only start after the first working day.

First of all, we can notice that the use of CSLM significantly decrease the TER scores for all translators. We can also remark that the third translator has a much higher TER than the two other translators during the first two days. Then, the system seems to learn his style and the TER reaches a comparable level at day 3. We can observe that project adaptation always lowers the TER with respect to the individual reference. The only exception can be observed for the first translator for days 2, 4 and 5. However, the project-adapted system is better or identical in most cases when multiple references are used. It is also interesting to note that our adaptation procedure improves the post-editing effort with respect to the independent reference translation in nine out of twelve cases. Overall, it can be clearly seen that the adaptation scheme is very effective. The difference between the baseline system (DA+CSLM) and the fully adapted system (PA+CSLM-adapt) reaches 9 TER points in some conditions.

A quite similar tendency can be observed when

| day | method | translator 1 | translator 2 | translator 3 |
|---|---|---|---|---|
| 1 | **DA** | 33.34 (28.10) **[54.59]** | 32.99 (28.10) **[54.59]** | 48.62 (28.10) **[54.59]** |
| | **DA+CSLM** | **31.13 (25.73)** [54.94] | **31.43 (25.73)** [54.94] | **48.50 (25.73)** [54.94] |
| 2 | **DA** | 35.33 (30.73) [56.63] | 37.44 (30.73) [56.63] | 49.03 (30.73) [56.63] |
| | **DA+CSLM** | **33.06 (28.86)** [56.30] | 36.24 (28.86) **[56.30]** | 49.12 **(28.86) [56.30]** |
| | **PA+CSLM-adapt** | 34.31 (29.07) **[56.18]** | **30.48 (27.21) [56.30]** | **47.29** (29.62) [56.53] |
| 3 | **DA** | 30.76 (26.68) [55.49] | 35.09 (26.68) [55.49] | 38.05 (26.68) [55.49] |
| | **DA+CSLM** | 27.87 (24.70) [55.09] | 33.86 (24.70) [55.09] | 36.72 (24.70) [55.09] |
| | **PA+CSLM-adapt** | **25.24 (20.04) [54.13]** | **27.48 (20.40) [54.16]** | **27.42 (20.99) [53.77]** |
| 4 | **DA** | 33.01 (29.07) [55.90] | 38.31 (29.07) **[55.90]** | 41.96 (29.07) [55.90] |
| | **DA+CSLM** | **29.79** (27.12) [56.78] | 37.92 (27.12) [56.78] | 41.03 (27.12) [56.78] |
| | **PA+CSLM-adapt** | 30.47 **(25.87) [55.21]** | **30.15 (25.53)** [56.12] | **32.70 (24.03) [55.86]** |
| 5 | **DA** | 31.34 (26.31) [54.78] | 34.38 (26.31) [54.78] | 39.41 (26.31) [54.78] |
| | **DA+CSLM** | **29.52** (24.88) **[52.59]** | 33.94 (24.88) [54.74] | 38.85 (24.88) [54.74] |
| | **PA+CSLM-adapt** | 31.52 **(24.43)** [53.08] | **26.19 (22.34) [53.16]** | **30.46 (23.71) [54.31]** |

Table 1: TER scores for English-French data of the Legal domain for the three translators over 5 days. Parenthesized scores are calculated using the references of all three translators, while scores in brackets are calculated using a generic reference provided by the European Commission.

analyzing translation quality in terms of BLEU score (results not presented here). Like for the prior TER results, the BLEU scores for translator 3 are much worse than the scores of the two other ones. After the third day, the scores reach the same level. Again, this could indicate that the adaptation process has learned his particular style.

### 5.2 Translation speed

Table 2 reports, for each translator, the translation speed, expressed in number of post-edited words per hour. The results are given for the two conditions of our experiment, along with the percentage of relative improvement. We can observe a very high productivity gain for all translators between the two sessions of our test, from 18.5% to 38.3%. The huge gain for translator T3 could be biased by the low working speed of the translator, even if we had confirmed that all the translators are experts with the post-editing process. We assume that either T3 had some difficulties with the legal domain or he had just taken his time to perform the test, or both. This could partially explain the huge improvement in productivity which is doubled.

| User ID | Translation speed (words/hour) DA+CSLM | PA+CSLM-adapt | Δ |
|---|---|---|---|
| T1 | 928 | 1283 | 38.3% |
| T2 | 1533 | 1816 | 18.5 % |
| T3 | 308 | 704 | 128.5% |

Table 2: Overall translation speed for all translators. Measurements are taken on post-edits performed with the domain-adapted MT system (DA+CSLM) and the project-adapted MT system (PA+CSLM-adapt).

## 6 Conclusion

Several studies have also shown that the close integration of MT into a CAT tool can increase the productivity of human translators. In this work, we extended these works in several aspects. We have observed systematic improvements of the translation quality and speed when adapting the systems with data generated during the translation project (spanning several days). The MT system does not only adapt to the style of the human translator who post-edit the automatic translations. In all cases, we observed improved translation quality with respect to an independent reference translation. Finally, we have shown that neural network LMs can be used in an operational SMT system and that they can be adapted very quickly to small amount of data. Although the use of neural networks in SMT is drawing a lot of attention, we are not aware at any other deployment in real applications.

## Acknowledgments

We thank the post-editors who took part to this experiment, as well as our anonymous reviewers for their feedback and suggestions. This work has been partially supported by the EC-funded project MATECAT (ICT-2011.4.2-287688).

## References

Axelrod, A., He, X., and Gao, J. (2011). Domain adaptation via pseudo in-domain data selection. In *Proceedings of the 2011 Conference on Empirical Methods in Natural Language Processing (EMNLP)*, pages 355–362.

Cettolo, M., Bertoldi, N., Federico, M., Schwenk, H., Barrault, L., and Servan, C. (2014). Translation project adaptation for mt-enhanced computer assisted translation. *Machine Translation*, 28(2):127–150.

Guerberof, A. (2009). Productivity and quality in mt post-editing. *MT Summit XII-Workshop: Beyond Translation Memories: New Tools for Translators MT*.

Koehn, P., Hoang, H., Birch, A., Callison-Burch, C., Federico, M., Bertoldi, N., Cowan, B., Shen, W., Moran, C., Zens, R., et al. (2007). Moses: Open source toolkit for statistical machine translation. In *Proceedings of the 45th Annual Meeting of the ACL on Interactive Poster and Demonstration Sessions*, pages 177–180. Association for Computational Linguistics.

Papineni, K., Roukos, S., Ward, T., and Zhu, W.-J. (2002). BLEU: a method for automatic evaluation of machine translation. In *Proceedings of the 40th Annual Meeting on Association for Computational Linguistics*, pages 311–318.

Plitt, M. and Masselot, F. (2010). A productivity test of statistical machine translation post-editing in a typical localisation context. *The Prague Bulletin of Mathematical Linguistics*, 93(-1):7–16.

Schwenk, H. (2010). Continuous space language models for statistical machine translation. In *The Prague Bulletin of Mathematical Linguistics*, number 93, pages 137–146.

Schwenk, H. (2013). Cslm - a modular open-source continuous space language modeling toolkit. *Interspeech*.

Snover, M., Dorr, B., Schwartz, R., Micciulla, L., and Makhoul, J. (2006). A study of translation edit rate with targeted human annotation. In *Proceedings of the 7th Conference of the Association for Machine Translation in the Americas (AMTA)*, pages 223–231.

Snover, M., Madnani, N., Dorr, B., and Schwartz, R. (2009). Fluency, adequacy, or HTER? exploring different human judgments with a tunable MT metric. In *Proceedings of the Fourth Workshop on Statistical Machine Translation*, pages 259–268.

Ter-Sarkisov, A., Schwenk, H., Bougares, F., and Barrault, L. (2014). Incremental adaptation strategies for neural network language models. *Available at http://arxiv.org/abs/1412.6650.*

# Normalized Word Embedding and Orthogonal Transform for Bilingual Word Translation

**Chao Xing**
CSLT, Tsinghua University
Beijing Jiaotong University
Beijing, P.R. China

**Dong Wang***
CSLT, RIIT, Tsinghua University
TNList, China
Beijing, P.R. China

**Chao Liu**
CSLT, RIIT, Tsinghua University
CS Department, Tsinghua University
Beijing, P.R. China

**Yiye Lin**
CSLT, RIIT, Tsinghua University
Beijing Institute of Technology
Beijing, P.R. China

## Abstract

Word embedding has been found to be highly powerful to translate words from one language to another by a simple linear transform. However, we found some inconsistence among the objective functions of the embedding and the transform learning, as well as the distance measurement. This paper proposes a solution which normalizes the word vectors on a hypersphere and constrains the linear transform as an orthogonal transform. The experimental results confirmed that the proposed solution can offer better performance on a word similarity task and an English-to-Spanish word translation task.

## 1 Introduction

Word embedding has been extensively studied in recent years (Bengio et al., 2003; Turian et al., 2010; Collobert et al., 2011; Huang et al., 2012). Following the idea that the meaning of a word can be determined by 'the company it keeps' (Baroni and Zamparelli, 2010), i.e., the words that it co-occurs with, word embedding projects discrete words to a low-dimensional and continuous vector space where co-occurred words are located close to each other. Compared to conventional discrete representations (e.g., the one-hot encoding), word embedding provides more robust representations for words, particulary for those that infrequently appear in the training data. More importantly, the embedding encodes syntactic and semantic content implicitly, so that relations among words can be simply computed as the distances among their embeddings, or word vectors. A well-known efficient word embedding approach was recently proposed by (Mikolov et al., 2013a), where two log-linear models (CBOW and skip-gram) are proposed to learn the neighboring relation of words in context. A following work proposed by the same authors introduces some modifications that largely improve the efficiency of model training (Mikolov et al., 2013c).

An interesting property of word vectors learned by the log-linear model is that the relations among relevant words seem linear and can be computed by simple vector addition and substraction (Mikolov et al., 2013d). For example, the following relation approximately holds in the word vector space: Paris - France + Rome = Italy. In (Mikolov et al., 2013b), the linear relation is extended to the bilingual scenario, where a linear transform is learned to project semantically identical words from one language to another. The authors reported a high accuracy on a bilingual word translation task.

Although promising, we argue that both the word embedding and the linear transform are ill-posed, due to the inconsistence among the objective function used to learn the word vectors (maximum likelihood based on inner product), the distance measurement for word vectors (cosine distance), and the objective function used to learn the linear transform (mean square error). This inconsistence may lead to



*Human Language Technologies: The 2015 Annual Conference of the North American Chapter of the ACL*, pages 1006–1011,
Denver, Colorado, May 31 – June 5, 2015. 

suboptimal estimation for both word vectors and the bilingual transform, as we will see shortly.

This paper solves the inconsistence by normalizing the word vectors. Specifically, we enforce the word vectors to be in a unit length during the learning of the embedding. By this constraint, all the word vectors are located on a hypersphere and so the inner product falls back to the cosine distance. This hence solves the inconsistence between the embedding and the distance measurement. To respect the normalization constraint on word vectors, the linear transform in the bilingual projection has to be constrained as an orthogonal transform. Finally, the cosine distance is used when we train the orthogonal transform, in order to achieve full consistence.

## 2 Related work

This work largely follows the methodology and experimental settings of (Mikolov et al., 2013b), while we normalize the embedding and use an orthogonal transform to conduct bilingual translation.

Multilingual learning can be categorized into projection-based approaches and regularization-based approaches. In the projection-based approaches, the embedding is performed for each language individually with monolingual data, and then one or several projections are learned using multilingual data to represent the relation between languages. Our method in this paper and the linear projection method in (Mikolov et al., 2013b) both belong to this category. Another interesting work proposed by (Faruqui and Dyer, 2014) learns linear transforms that project word vectors of all languages to a common low-dimensional space, where the correlation of the multilingual word pairs is maximized with the canonical correlation analysis (CCA).

The regularization-based approaches involve the multilingual constraint in the objective function for learning the embedding. For example, (Zou et al., 2013) adds an extra term that reflects the distances of some pairs of semantically related words from different languages into the objective funtion. A similar approach is proposed in (Klementiev et al., 2012), which casts multilingual learning as a multitask learning and encodes the multilingual information in the interaction matrix.

All the above methods rely on a multilingual lexicon or a word/pharse alignment, usually from a machine translation (MT) system. (Blunsom et al., 2014) proposed a novel approach based on a joint optimization method for word alignments and the embedding. A simplified version of this approach is proposed in (Hermann and Blunsom, 2014), where a sentence is represented by the mean vector of the words involved. Multilingual learning is then reduced to maximizing the overall distance of the parallel sentences in the training corpus, with the distance computed upon the sentence vectors.

## 3 Normalized word vectors

Taking the skip-gram model, the goal is to predict the context words with a word in the central position. Mathematically, the training process maximizes the following likelihood function with a word sequence $w_1, w_2 ... w_N$:

$$\frac{1}{N}\sum_{i=1}^{N}\sum_{-C\leq j\leq C, j\neq 0} logP(w_{i+j}|w_i) \quad (1)$$

where $C$ is the length of the context in concern, and the prediction probability is given by:

$$P(w_{i+j}|w_i) = \frac{\exp(c_{w_{i+j}}^T c_{w_i})}{\sum_w \exp(c_w^T c_{w_i})} \quad (2)$$

where $w$ is any word in the vocabulary, and $c_w$ denotes the vector of word $w$. Obviously, the word vectors learned by this way are not constrained and disperse in the entire $M$-dimensional space, where $M$ is the dimension of the word vectors. An inconsistence with this model is that the distance measurement in the training is the inner product $c_w^T c_{w'}$, however when word vectors are applied, e.g., to estimate word similarities, the metric is often the cosine distance $\frac{c_w^T c_{w'}}{||c_w|| ||c_{w'}||}$. A way to solve this consistence is to use the inner product in applications, however using the cosine distance is a convention in natural language processing (NLP) and this measure does show better performance than the inner product in our experiments.

We therefore perform in an opposite way, i.e., enforcing the word vectors to be unit in length. Theoretically, this changes the learning of the embedding to an optimization problem with a quadratic constraint. Solving this problem by Lagrange multipliers is possible, but here we simply divide a vector by its $l$-2 norm whenever the vector is updated. This does not involve much code change and is efficient enough.[1]

The consequence of the normalization is that all the word vectors are located on a hypersphere, as illustrated in Figure 1. In addition, by the normalization, the inner product falls back to the cosine distance, hence solving the inconsistence between the embedding learning and the distance measurement.

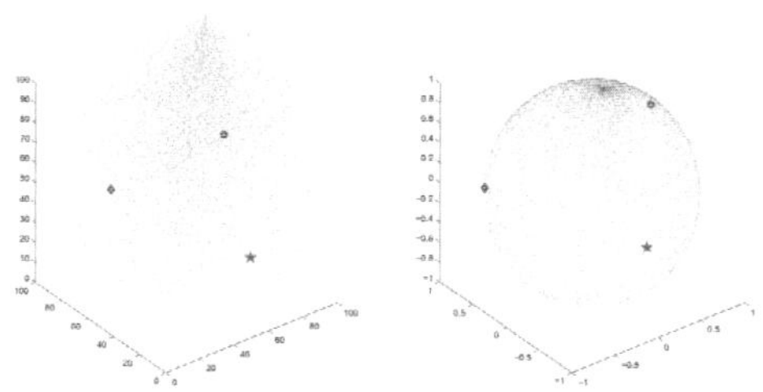

Figure 1: The distributions of unnormalized (left) and normalized (right) word vectors. The red circles/stars/diamonds represent three words that are embedded in the two vector spaces respectively.

## 4 Orthogonal transform

The bilingual word translation provided by (Mikolov et al., 2013b) learns a linear transform from the source language to the target language by the linear regression. The objective function is as follows:

$$\min_W \sum_i ||Wx_i - z_i||^2 \tag{3}$$

[1]For efficiency, this normalization can be conducted every $n$ mini-batches. The performance is expected to be not much impacted, given that $n$ is not too large.

where $W$ is the projection matrix to be learned, and $x_i$ and $z_i$ are word vectors in the source and target language respectively. The bilingual pair $(x_i, z_i)$ indicates that $x_i$ and $z_i$ are identical in semantic meaning. A high accuracy was reported on a word translation task, where a word projected to the vector space of the target language is expected to be as close as possible to its translation (Mikolov et al., 2013b). However, we note that the 'closeness' of words in the projection space is measured by the cosine distance, which is fundamentally different from the Euler distance in the objective function (3) and hence causes inconsistence.

We solve this problem by using the cosine distance in the transform learning, so the optimization task can be redefined as follows:

$$\max_W \sum_i (Wx_i)^T z_i. \tag{4}$$

Note that the word vectors in both the source and target vector spaces are normalized, so the inner product in (4) is equivalent to the cosine distance. A problem of this change, however, is that the projected vector $Wx_i$ has to be normalized, which is not guaranteed so far.

To solve the problem, we first consider the case where the dimensions of the source and target vector spaces are the same. In this case, the normalization constraint on word vectors can be satisfied by constraining $W$ as an orthogonal matrix, which turns the unconstrained problem (4) to a constrained optimization problem. A general solver such as SQP can be used to solve the problem. However, we seek a simple approximation in this work. Firstly, solve (4) by gradient descendant without considering any constraint. A simple calculation shows that the gradient is as follows:

$$\bigtriangledown_W = \sum_i x_i y_i^T, \tag{5}$$

and the update rule is simply given by:

$$W = W + \alpha \bigtriangledown_W \tag{6}$$

where $\alpha$ is the learning rate. After the update, $W$ is orthogonalized by solving the following constrained quadratic problem:

$$\min_{\bar{W}} ||W - \bar{W}|| \quad s.t. \ \bar{W}^T\bar{W} = I. \qquad (7)$$

One can show that this problem can be solved by taking the singular value decomposition (SVD) of $W$ and replacing the singular values to ones.

For the case where the dimensions of the source and target vector spaces are different, the normalization constraint upon the projected vectors is not easy to satisfy. We choose a pragmatic solution. First, we extend the low-dimensional vector space by padding a small tunable constant at the end of the word vectors so that the source and target vector spaces are in the same dimension. The vectors are then renormalized after the padding to respect the normalization constraint. Once this is done, the same gradient descendant and orthognalization approaches are ready to use to learn the orthogonal transform.

## 5 Experiment

We first present the data profile and configurations used to learn monolingual word vectors, and then examine the learning quality on the word similarity task. Finally, a comparative study is reported on the bilingual word translation task, with Mikolov's linear transform and the orthogonal transform proposed in this paper.

### 5.1 Monolingual word embedding

The monolingual word embedding is conducted with the data published by the EMNLP 2011 SMT workshop (WMT11)[2]. For an easy comparison, we largely follow Mikolov's settings in (Mikolov et al., 2013b) and set English and Spanish as the source and target language, respectively. The data preparation involves the following steps. Firstly, the text was tokenized by the standard scripts provided by WMT11[3], and then duplicated sentences were removed. The numerical expressions were tokenized as 'NUM', and special characters (such as !?,:) were removed.

The word2vector toolkit[4] was used to train the word embedding model. We chose the skip-gram model and the text window was set to 5. The training resulted in embedding of 169k English tokens and 116k Spanish tokens.

### 5.2 Monolingual word similarity

The first experiment examines the quality of the learned word vectors in English. We choose the word similarity task, which tests to what extent the word similarity computed based on word vectors agrees with human judgement. The WordSimilarity-353 Test Collection[5] provided by (Finkelstein et al., 2002) is used. The dataset involves 154 word pairs whose similarities are measured by 13 people and the mean values are used as the human judgement. In the experiment, the correlation between the cosine distances computed based on the word vectors and the humane-judged similarity is used to measure the quality of the embedding. The results are shown in Figure 2, where the dimension of the vector space varies from 300 to 1000. It can be observed that the normalized word vectors offer a high correlation with human judgement than the unnormalized counterparts.

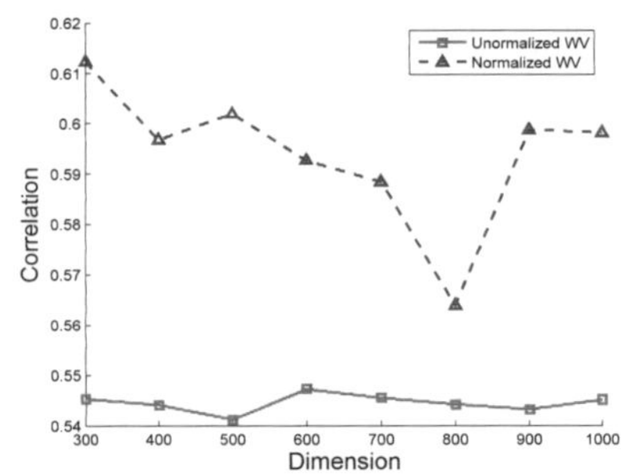


Figure 2: Results on the word similarity task with the normalized and unnormalized word vectors. A higher correlation indicates better quality.

[2]http://www.statmt.org/wmt11/

[3]http://www.statmt.org

[4]https://code.google.com/p/word2vec

[5]http://www.cs.technion.ac.il/ gabr/resources/data/wordsim353/

### 5.3 Bilingual word translation

The second experiment focuses on bilingual word translation. We select 6000 frequent words in English and employ the online Google's translation service to translate them to Spanish. The resulting 6000 English-Spanish word pairs are used to train and test the bilingual transform in the way of cross validation. Specifically, the 6000 pairs are randomly divided into 10 subsets, and at each time, 9 subsets are used for training and the rest 1 subset for testing. The average of the results of the 10 tests is reported as the final result. Note that not all the words translated by Google are in the vocabulary of the target language; the vocabulary coverage is 99.5% in our test.

#### 5.3.1 Results with linear transform

We first reproduce Mikolov's work with the linear transform. A number of dimension settings are experimented with and the results are reported in Table 1. The proportions that the correct translations are in the top 1 and top 5 candidate list are reported as P@1 and P@5 respectively. As can be seen, the best dimension setting is 800 for English and 200 for Spanish, and the corresponding P@1 and P@5 are 35.36% and 53.96%, respectively. These results are comparable with the results reported in (Mikolov et al., 2013b).

| D-EN | D-ES | P@1 | P@5 |
|---|---|---|---|
| 300 | 300 | 30.43% | 49.43% |
| 500 | 500 | 25.76% | 44.29% |
| 700 | 700 | 20.69% | 39.12% |
| 800 | 200 | 35.36% | 53.96% |

Table 1: Performance on word translation with unnormalized embedding and linear transform. 'D-EN' and 'D-ES' denote the dimensions of the English and Spanish vector spaces, respectively.

#### 5.3.2 Results with orthogonal transform

The results with the normalized word vectors and the orthogonal transform are reported in Table 2. It can be seen that the results with the orthogonal transform are consistently better than those reported in Table1 which are based on the linear transform. This confirms our conjecture that bilingual translation can be largely improved by the normalized embedding and the accompanied orthogonal transform.

| D-EN | D-ES | P@1 | P@5 |
|---|---|---|---|
| 300 | 300 | 38.99% | 59.16% |
| 500 | 500 | 39.91% | 59.82% |
| 700 | 700 | 41.04% | 59.38% |
| 800 | 200 | 40.06% | 60.02% |

Table 2: Performance on word translation with normalized embedding and orthogonal transform. 'D-EN' and 'D-ES' denote the dimensions of the English and Spanish vector spaces, respectively.

## 6 Conclusions

We proposed an orthogonal transform based on normalized word vectors for bilingual word translation. This approach solves the inherent inconsistence in the original approach based on unnormalized word vectors and a linear transform. The experimental results on a monolingual word similarity task and an English-to-Spanish word translation task show clear advantage of the proposal. This work, however, is still preliminary. It is unknown if the normalized embedding works on other tasks such as relation prediction, although we expect so. The solution to the orthogonal transform between vector spaces with mismatched dimensions is rather ad-hoc. Nevertheless, locating word vectors on a hypersphere opens a door to study the properties of the word embedding in a space that is yet less known to us.

## Acknowledgement

This work was conducted when CX & YYL were visiting students in CSLT, Tsinghua University. This research was supported by the National Science Foundation of China (NSFC) under the project No. 61371136, and the MESTDC PhD Foundation Project No. 20130002120011. It was also supported by Sinovoice and Huilan Ltd.

## References


Marco Baroni and Roberto Zamparelli. 2010. Nouns are vectors, adjectives are matrices: Representing adjective-noun constructions in semantic space. In *Proceedings of the 2010 Conference on Empirical Methods in Natural Language Processing*, pages 1183–1193.

Yoshua Bengio, Réjean Ducharme, Pascal Vincent, and Christian Janvin. 2003. A neural probabilistic language model. *J. Mach. Learn. Res.*, 3:1137–1155.

Phil Blunsom, Karl Moritz Hermann, Tomas Kocisky, et al. 2014. Learning bilingual word representations by marginalizing alignments. In *Proceedings of the 52nd Annual Meeting of the Association for Computational Linguistics*, pages 224–229.

Ronan Collobert, Jason Weston, Léon Bottou, Michael Karlen, Koray Kavukcuoglu, and Pavel Kuksa. 2011. Natural language processing (almost) from scratch. *J. Mach. Learn. Res.*, 12:2493–2537.

Manaal Faruqui and Chris Dyer. 2014. Improving vector space word representations using multilingual correlation. *Proceeding of EACL. Association for Computational Linguistics.*

Lev Finkelstein, Evgeniy Gabrilovich, Yossi Matias, Ehud Rivlin, Zach Solan, Gadi Wolfman, and Eytan Ruppin. 2002. Placing search in context: The concept revisited. In *Proceedings of The 2002 Conference of the North American Chapter of the Association for Computational Linguistics: Human Language Technologies*, pages 116–131.

Karl Moritz Hermann and Phil Blunsom. 2014. Multilingual distributed representations without word alignment. In *Proceedings of International Conference on Learning Representations (ICLR)*.

Eric H. Huang, Richard Socher, Christopher D. Manning, and Andrew Y. Ng. 2012. Improving word representations via global context and multiple word prototypes. In *Proceeding of Annual Meeting of the Association for Computational Linguistics (ACL)*.

Alexandre Klementiev, Ivan Titov, and Binod Bhattarai. 2012. Inducing crosslingual distributed representations of words. In *Proceedings of COLING*. Citeseer.

Tomas Mikolov, Kai Chen, Greg Corrado, and Jeffrey Dean. 2013a. Efficient estimation of word representations in vector space. In *International Conference on Learning Representations (ICLR)*.

Tomas Mikolov, Quoc V Le, and Ilya Sutskever. 2013b. Exploiting similarities among languages for machine translation. *arXiv preprint arXiv:1309.4168*.

Tomas Mikolov, Ilya Sutskever, Kai Chen, Greg S Corrado, and Jeff Dean. 2013c. Distributed representations of words and phrases and their compositionality. In *Advances in Neural Information Processing Systems*, pages 3111–3119.

Tomas Mikolov, Wen-tau Yih, and Geoffrey Zweig. 2013d. Linguistic regularities in continuous space word representations. In *Proceedings of The 2013 Conference of the North American Chapter of the Association for Computational Linguistics: Human Language Technologies*, pages 746–751. Citeseer.

Joseph Turian, Departement d'Informatique Et, Recherche Operationnelle (diro, Universite De Montreal, Lev Ratinov, and Yoshua Bengio. 2010. Word representations: A simple and general method for semisupervised learning. In *Proceeding of Annual Meeting of the Association for Computational Linguistics (ACL)*, pages 384–394.

Will Y Zou, Richard Socher, Daniel M Cer, and Christopher D Manning. 2013. Bilingual word embeddings for phrase-based machine translation. In *Proceeding of Conference on Empirical Methods on Natural Language Processing (EMNLP)*, pages 1393–1398.

# Fast and Accurate Preordering for SMT using Neural Networks

**Adrià de Gispert** **Gonzalo Iglesias** **Bill Byrne**
SDL Research
East Road, Cambridge CB1 1BH, U.K.
{agispert|giglesias|bbyrne}@sdl.com

## Abstract

We propose the use of neural networks to model source-side preordering for faster and better statistical machine translation. The neural network trains a logistic regression model to predict whether two sibling nodes of the source-side parse tree should be swapped in order to obtain a more monotonic parallel corpus, based on samples extracted from the word-aligned parallel corpus. For multiple language pairs and domains, we show that this yields the best reordering performance against other state-of-the-art techniques, resulting in improved translation quality and very fast decoding.

## 1 Introduction

Preordering is a pre-processing task in translation that aims to reorder the source sentence so that it best resembles the order of the target sentence. If done correctly, it has a doubly beneficial effect: it allows a better estimation of word alignment and translation models which results in higher translation quality for distant language pairs, *and* it speeds up decoding enormously as less word movement is required.

Preordering schemes can be automatically learnt from source-side parsed, word-aligned parallel corpora. Recently Jehl et al (2014) described a scheme based on a feature-rich logistic regression model that predicts whether a pair of sibling nodes in the source-side dependency tree need to be permuted. Based on the node-pair swapping probability predictions of this model, a branch-and-bound search returns the best ordering of nodes in the tree.

We propose using a neural network (NN) to estimate this node-swapping probability. We find that this straightforward change to their scheme has multiple advantages:

1. The superior modeling capabilities of NNs achieve better performance at preordering and overall translation quality when using the same set of features.
2. There is no need to manually define which feature combinations are to be considered in training.
3. Preordering is even faster as a result of the previous point. Our results in translating from English to Japanese, Korean, Chinese, Arabic and Hindi support these findings by comparing against two other preordering schemes.

### 1.1 Related Work

There is a strong research and commercial interest in preordering, as reflected by the extensive previous work on the subject (Collins et al., 2005; Xu et al., 2009; DeNero and Uszkoreit, 2011; Neubig et al., 2012). We are interested in practical, language-independent preordering approaches that rely only on automatic source-language parsers (Genzel, 2010). The most recent work in this area uses large-scale feature-rich discriminative models, effectively treating preordering either as a learning to rank (Yang et al., 2012), multi-classification (Lerner and Petrov, 2013) or logistic regression (Jehl et al., 2014) problem. In this paper we incorporate NNs into the latter approach.

Lately an increasing body of work that uses NNs for various NLP tasks has been published, including language modeling (Bengio et al., 2003), POS



*Human Language Technologies: The 2015 Annual Conference of the North American Chapter of the ACL*, pages 1012–1017,
Denver, Colorado, May 31 – June 5, 2015. 

tagging (Collobert et al., 2011), or dependency parsing (Chen and Manning, 2014). In translation, NNs have been used for improved word alignment (Yang et al., 2013; Tamura et al., 2014; Songyot and Chiang, 2014), to model reordering under an ITG grammar (Li et al., 2013), and to define additional feature functions to be used in decoding (Sundermeyer et al., 2014; Devlin et al., 2014). End-to-end translation systems based on NNs have also been proposed (Kalchbrenner and Blunsom, 2013; Sutskever et al., 2014; Bahdanau et al., 2014).

Despite the gains reported, only the approaches that do not dramatically affect decoding times can be directly applied to today's commercial SMT systems. Our paper is a step towards this direction, and to the best of our knowledge, it is the first one to describe the usage of NNs in preordering for SMT.

## 2 Preordering as node-pair swapping

Jehl et al (2014) describe a preordering scheme based on a logistic regression model that predicts whether a pair of sibling nodes in the source-side dependency tree need to be permuted in order to have a more monotonically-aligned parallel corpus. Their method can be briefly summarised by the pseudocode of Figure 1.

PREORDERPARSETREE

1 **for each** node $n \in N, |C_n| > 1$
2 $\quad F \leftarrow \text{GETFEATURES}(n)$
3 $\quad$**for each** pair of nodes $i, j \in C_n, i \neq j$
4 $\quad\quad F \leftarrow F \cup \text{GETFEATURES}(i)$
5 $\quad\quad F \leftarrow F \cup \text{GETFEATURES}(j)$
6 $\quad\quad F_c \leftarrow \text{FEATURECOMBINATIONS}(F)$
7 $\quad\quad p_n(i,j) = \text{LOGREGPREDICT}(F, F_c)$
8 $\quad$**end for**
9 $\quad \pi_n \leftarrow \text{SEARCHPERMUTATION}(p_n)$
10 $\quad \text{SORT}(C_n, \pi_n)$

Figure 1: Pseudocode for the preordering scheme of Jehl et al (2014)

Let $N$ be the set of nodes in the source tree, and let $C_n$ be the set of children nodes of node $n$. For each node with at least two children, first extract the node features (lines 1-2). Then, for each pair of its children nodes: extract their respective features (lines 4-5), produce all relevant feature combinations (line 6), and store the node-pair swapping probability predicted by a logistic regression model based on all available features (line 7). Once all pair-wise probabilities are stored, search for the best global permutation and sort $C_n$ accordingly (lines 9-10).

As features, Jehl et al (2014) use POS tags and dependency labels, as well as the identity and class of the head word (for the parent node) or the left/rightmost word (for children nodes). These are combined into *conjunctions* of 2 or 3 features to create new features. For logistic regression, they train a L1-regularised linear model using LIBLINEAR (Fan et al., 2008). The training samples are either positive/negative depending on whether swapping the nodes reduces/increases the number of crossed links in the aligned parallel corpus.

### 2.1 Applying Neural Networks

"A (feedforward) neural network is a series of logistic regression models stacked on top of each other, with the final layer being either another logistic regression model or a linear regression model" (Murphy, 2012).

Given this, we propose a straightforward alternative to the above framework: replace the linear logistic regression model by a neural network (NN). This way a superior modeling performance of the node-swapping phenomenon is to be expected. Additionally, feature combination need not be engineered anymore because that is *learnt* by the NN in training (line 6 in Figure 1 is skipped).

Training the neural network requires the same labeled samples that were used by Jehl et al (2014). We use the NPLM toolkit out-of-the-box (Vaswani et al., 2013). The architecture is a feed-forward neural network (Bengio et al., 2003) with four layers. The first layer $i$ contains the input embeddings. The next two hidden layers $(h_1, h_2)$ use rectified linear units; the last one is the softmax layer $(o)$. We did not experiment with deeper NNs.

For our purposes, the input vocabulary of the NN is the set of all possible feature indicator names that are used for preordering[1]. There are no OOVs. Given the sequence of $\sim$ 20 features seen by the

[1]Using a vocabulary of the 5K top-frequency English words, 50 word classes, approximately 40 POS tags and 50 dependency labels, the largest input vocabulary in our experiments is roughly 30,000.

preorderer, the NN is trained to predict whether the nodes should be reordered or not, i.e. $|o| = 2$. For the rest of the layers, we use $|i| = 50$, $|h_1| = 100$, $|h_2| = 50$. We set the learning rate to 1, the mini-batch size to 64 and the number of epochs to 20.

# 3 Experiments

## 3.1 Data and setup

We report translation results in English into Japanese, Korean, Chinese, Arabic and Hindi. For each language pair, we use generic parallel data extracted from the web. The number of words is about 100M for Japanese and Korean, 300M for Chinese, 200M for Arabic and 9M for Hindi.

We use two types of dev/test sets: in-domain and mix-domain. The in-domain sets have 2K sentences each and were created by randomly extracting parallel sentences from the corpus, ensuring no repetitions remained. The mix-domain sets have about 1K sentences each and were created to evenly represent 10 different domains, including world news, chat/SMS, health, sport, science, business, and others.

Additionally, we report results on the English-to-Hindi WMT 2014 shared task (Bojar et al., 2014a) using the data provided[2]. The dev and test sets have 520 and 2507 sentences each. All dev and test sets have one single reference. We use SVMTool (Giménez and Màrquez, 2004) for POS Tagging, and MaltParser (Nivre et al., 2007) for dependency parsing.

## 3.2 Intrinsic reordering evaluation

We evaluate the intrinsic preordering task on a random 5K-sentence subset of the training data which is excluded from model estimation. We report the normalized crossing score $c/s$, where $c$ is the number of crossing links (Genzel, 2010; Yang et al., 2012) in the aligned parallel corpus, and $s$ is the number of source (e.g. English) words. Ideally we would like this metric to be zero, meaning a completely monotonic parallel corpus[3]; the more monotonic the corpus, the better the translation models will be and the faster decoding will run as less distortion will be needed.

[2]HindEndCorp v0.5 (Bojar et al., 2014b)

[3]However this may not be achievable given the alignment links and parse tree available. In this approach, only permutations of sibling nodes in the single source parse tree are permitted.

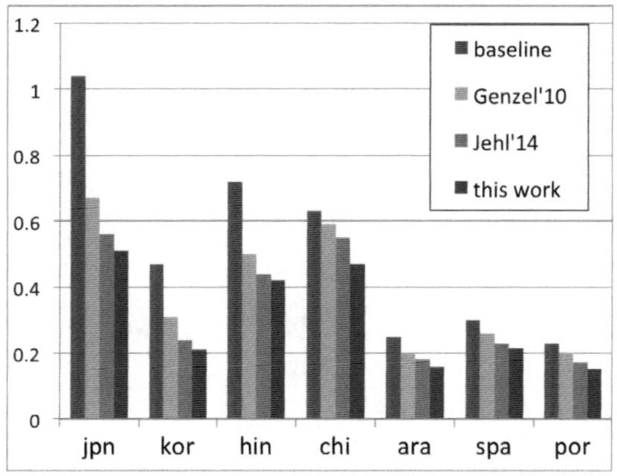


Figure 2: Normalized crossing score for English into Japanese, Korean, Hindi, Chinese, Arabic, Spanish and Portuguese.

Normalizing over the number of source words allows us to compare this metric across language pairs, and so the potential impact of preordering in translation performance becomes apparent. See Figure 2 for results across several language pairs. In all cases our proposed NN-based preorderer achieves the lowest normalized crossing score among all preordering schemes.

## 3.3 Translation performance

For translation experiments, we use a phrase-based decoder that incorporates a set of standard features and a hierarchical reordering model (Galley and Manning, 2008). The decoder stack size is set to 1000. Weights are tuned using MERT to optimize BLEU on the dev set. In English-to-Japanese and Chinese we use character-BLEU instead. To minimise optimization noise, we tune all our systems from flat parameters three times and report average BLEU score and standard deviation on the test set.

Table 1 contrasts the performance obtained by the system when using no preordering capabilities (baseline), and when using three alternative preordering schemes: the rule-based approach of Genzel (2010), the linear-model logistic-regression approach of Jehl et al (2014) and our NN-based preorderer. We report two baselines: one with distortion limit $d = 10$ and another with $d = 3$. For systems

| $d$ | system | speed ratio | eng-jpn in | eng-jpn mixed | eng-kor in | eng-kor mixed |
|---|---|---|---|---|---|---|
| 10 | baseline | 1x | 54.5 ±0.2 | 26.2 ±0.2 | **33.5** ±0.3 | 9.7 ±0.2 |
| 3 | baseline | 3.2x | 50.9 ±0.2 | 25.0 ±0.2 | 28.7 ±0.1 | 8.2 ±0.1 |
| 3 | Genzel (2010) | 2.7x | 54.0 ±0.1 | 26.4 ±0.2 | 30.5 ±0.2 | 9.8 ±0.2 |
| 3 | Jehl et al (2014) | 2.3x | 55.0 ±0.1 | 26.9 ±0.2 | 33.1 ±0.1 | 10.4 ±0.1 |
| 3 | *this work* | 2.7x | **55.6** ±0.2 | **27.2** ±0.1 | **33.4** ±0.1 | **10.6** ±0.2 |

| $d$ | system | eng-chi in | eng-chi mixed | eng-ara in | eng-ara mixed | eng-hin mixed | eng-hin wmt14 |
|---|---|---|---|---|---|---|---|
| 10 | baseline | **46.9** ±0.5 | 18.4 ±0.6 | 25.1 ±0.1 | **22.7** ±0.2 | 10.1 ±0.3 | 11.7 ±0.1 |
| 3 | baseline | 44.8 ±0.7 | 18.3 ±0.4 | 24.6 ±0.1 | 21.9 ±0.2 | 8.3 ±0.2 | 9.3 ±0.3 |
| 3 | Genzel (2010) | 45.4 ±0.2 | 17.9 ±0.2 | 24.8 ±0.1 | 21.6 ±0.3 | 9.6 ±0.2 | 11.4 ±0.3 |
| 3 | Jehl et al (2014) | 45.8 ±0.1 | 18.5 ±0.3 | 25.1 ±0.2 | 22.4 ±0.2 | 10.0 ±0.1 | **12.7** ±0.3 |
| 3 | *this work* | **46.5** ±0.4 | **19.2** ±0.2 | **25.5** ±0.2 | **22.6** ±0.1 | **10.6** ±0.1 | **12.6** ±0.3 |
| | | | | best WMT14 constrained system | | | 11.1 |

Table 1: Translation performance for various language pairs using no preordering (baseline), and three alternative preordering systems. Average test BLEU score and standard deviation across 3 independent tuning runs. Speed ratio is calculated with respect to the speed of the slower baseline that uses a $d = 10$. Stack size is 1000. For eng-jpn and eng-chi, character-based BLEU is used.

with preordering we only report $d = 3$, as increasing $d$ does not improve performance.

As shown, our preorderer obtains the best BLEU scores for all reported languages and domains, proving that the neural network is modeling the dependency tree node-swapping phenomenon more accurately, and that the reductions in crossing score reported in the previous section have a positive impact in the final translation performance.

The bottom right-most column reports results on the WMT 2014 English-to-Hindi task. Our system achieves better results than the best score reported for this task[4]. In this case, the two logistic regression preorderers perform similarly, as standard deviation is higher, possibly due to the small size of the dev set.

### 3.4 Decoding Speed

The main purpose of preordering is to find a better translation performance in fast decoding conditions. In other words, by preordering the text we expect to be able to decode with less distortion or phrase reordering, resulting in faster decoding. This is shown in Table 1, which reports the speed ratio between each system and the speed of the top-most baseline, as measured in English-to-Japanese in-domain[5]. We find that decoding with a $d = 3$ is about 3 times faster than for $d = 10$.

We now take this further by reducing the stack size from 1000 to 50; see results in Table 2. As expected, all systems accelerate with respect to our initial baseline. However, this usually comes at a cost in BLEU with respect to using a wider beam, *unless* preordering is used. In fact, the logistic regression preorderers achieve the same performance while decoding over 60 times faster than the baseline.

Interestingly, the NN-based preorderer turns out to be slightly faster than any of the other preordering approaches. This is because there is no need to explicitly create thousands of feature combinations for each node pair; simply performing the forward matrix multiplications given the input sequence of $\sim$20 features is more efficient. Similar observations have been noted recently in the context of dependency parsing with NNs (Chen and Manning, 2014). Note also that, on average, only 25 pair-wise probabilities are queried to the logistic regression model per source sentence. Overall, we incorporate the benefits of neural networks for preordering at no compu-

[4] Details at matrix.statmt.org/matrix/systems_list/1749

[5] Similar speed ratios were observed for other language pairs (not reported here for space)

| $d$ | system w/ stack=50 | speed ratio | eng-jpn | | eng-kor | | eng-chi |
|---|---|---|---|---|---|---|---|
| | | | in | mixed | in | mixed | mixed |
| 10 | baseline | 22x | 53.6 (-0.9) | 25.4 (-0.8) | 32.8 (-0.7) | 9.3 (-0.4) | 17.9 (-0.5) |
| 3 | baseline | 66x | 50.5 (-0.4) | 24.8 (-0.2) | 28.8 (+0.1) | 8.1 (-0.1) | 18.0 (-0.3) |
| 3 | Genzel (2010) | 64x | 53.8 (-0.2) | 26.3 (-0.1) | 30.4 (-0.1) | 9.8 (0.0) | 18.1 (+0.2) |
| 3 | Jehl et al (2014) | 61x | 55.0 (0.0) | 26.5 (-0.4) | 33.0 (-0.1) | 10.4 (0.0) | 18.3 (-0.2) |
| 3 | *this work* | 65x | **55.7** (+0.1) | **27.2** (0.0) | **33.2** (-0.2) | **10.8** (+0.2) | **19.1** (-0.1) |

Table 2: Translation performance for maximum stack size of 50. The figures in parentheses indicate the difference in BLEU scores due to using a smaller stack size, that is, compared to the same systems in Table 1. Speed ratio is calculated with respect to the speed of the slower baseline that uses a stack of 1000, eg. the first row in Table 1.

tational cost.

Currently, our preorderer takes 6.3% of the total decoding time (including 2.6% for parsing and 3.7% for actually preordering). We believe that further improvements in preordering will result in more translation gains and faster decoding, as the distortion limit is lowered.

## 4 Conclusions

To the best of our knowledge, this is the first paper to describe the usage of NNs in preordering for SMT. We show that simply replacing the logistic regression node-swapping model with an NN model improves both crossing scores and translation performance across various language pairs. Feature combination engineering is avoided, which also results in even faster decoding times.

## References


Dzmitry Bahdanau, Kyunghyun Cho, and Yoshua Bengio. 2014. Neural machine translation by jointly learning to align and translate. *CoRR*, abs/1409.0473.

Yoshua Bengio, Rjean Ducharme, Pascal Vincent, and Christian Jauvin. 2003. A neural probabilistic language model. *Machine Learning Research*, 3:1137–1155.

Ondrej Bojar, Christian Buck, Christian Federmann, Barry Haddow, Philipp Koehn, Johannes Leveling, Christof Monz, Pavel Pecina, Matt Post, Herve Saint-Amand, Radu Soricut, Lucia Specia, and Aleš Tamchyna. 2014a. Findings of the 2014 workshop on statistical machine translation. In *Proceedings of the Ninth Workshop on Statistical Machine Translation*, pages 12–58.

Ondřej Bojar, Vojtěch Diatka, Pavel Rychlý, Pavel Straňák, Vít Suchomel, Aleš Tamchyna, and Daniel Zeman. 2014b. HindEnCorp - Hindi-English and Hindi-only Corpus for Machine Translation. In *Proceedings of LREC*, pages 3550–3555.

Danqi Chen and Christopher Manning. 2014. A fast and accurate dependency parser using neural networks. In *Proceedings of EMNLP*, pages 740–750.

Michael Collins, Philipp Koehn, and Ivona Kucerova. 2005. Clause Restructuring for Statistical Machine Translation. In *Proceedings of ACL*, pages 531–540.

Ronan Collobert, Jason Weston, Léon Bottou, Michael Karlen, Koray Kavukcuoglu, and Pavel Kuksa. 2011. Natural language processing (almost) from scratch. *Journal of Machine Learning Research*, 12:2493–2537.

John DeNero and Jakob Uszkoreit. 2011. Inducing Sentence Structure from Parallel Corpora for Reordering. In *Proceedings of EMNLP*, pages 193–203.

Jacob Devlin, Rabih Zbib, Zhongqiang Huang, Thomas Lamar, Richard Schwartz, and John Makhoul. 2014. Fast and robust neural network joint models for statistical machine translation. In *Proceedings of ACL*, pages 1370–1380.

Rong-En Fan, Kai-Wei Chang, Cho-Jui Hsieh, Xiang-Rui Wang, and Chih-Jen Lin. 2008. LIBLINEAR: A Library for Large Linear Classification. *Journal of Machine Learning Research*, 9:1871–1874.

Michel Galley and Christopher D. Manning. 2008. A Simple and Effective Hierarchical Phrase Reordering Model. In *Proceedings of EMNLP*, pages 847–855.

Dmitriy Genzel. 2010. Automatically learning source-side reordering rules for large scale machine translation. In *Proceedings of COLING*, pages 376–384.

Jesús Giménez and Lluís Màrquez. 2004. SVMTool: A general POS tagger generator based on Support Vector Machines. In *Proceedings of LREC*, pages 43–46.

Laura Jehl, Adrià de Gispert, Mark Hopkins, and Bill Byrne. 2014. Source-side preordering for translation using logistic regression and depth-first branch-and-bound search. In *Proceedings of EACL*, pages 239–248.

Nal Kalchbrenner and Phil Blunsom. 2013. Recurrent continuous translation models. In *Proceedings of EMNLP*, pages 1700–1709.

Uri Lerner and Slav Petrov. 2013. Source-Side Classifier Preordering for Machine Translation. In *Proceedings of EMNLP*, pages 513–523.

Peng Li, Yang Liu, and Maosong Sun. 2013. Recursive autoencoders for ITG-based translation. In *Proceedings of EMNLP*, pages 567–577.

Kevin P. Murphy. 2012. *Machine Learning: A Probabilistic Perspective*. MIT Press, Cambridge, MA.

Graham Neubig, Taro Watanabe, and Shinsuke Mori. 2012. Inducing a Discriminative Parser to Optimize Machine Translation Reordering. In *Proceedings of EMNLP-CoNLL*, pages 843–853.

Joakim Nivre, Johan Hall, Jens Nilsson, Atanas Chanev, Glsen Eryigit, Sandra Kübler, Svetoslav Marinov, and Erwin Marsi. 2007. Maltparser: A language-independent system for data-driven dependency parsing. *Natural Language Engineering*, 13(2):95–135.

Theerawat Songyot and David Chiang. 2014. Improving word alignment using word similarity. In *Proceedings of EMNLP*, pages 1840–1845.

Martin Sundermeyer, Tamer Alkhouli, Joern Wuebker, and Hermann Ney. 2014. Translation modeling with bidirectional recurrent neural networks. In *Proceedings of EMNLP*, pages 14–25.

Ilya Sutskever, Oriol Vinyals, and Quoc V. Le. 2014. Sequence to sequence learning with neural networks. *CoRR*, abs/1409.3215.

Akihiro Tamura, Taro Watanabe, and Eiichiro Sumita. 2014. Recurrent neural networks for word alignment model. In *Proceedings of ACL*, pages 1470–1480.

Ashish Vaswani, Yinggong Zhao, Victoria Fossum, and David Chiang. 2013. Decoding with large-scale neural language models improves translation. In *Proceedings of EMNLP*, pages 1387–1392.

Peng Xu, Jaeho Kang, Michael Ringgaard, and Franz Och. 2009. Using a Dependency Parser to Improve SMT for Subject-Object-Verb Languages. In *Proceedings of HTL-NAACL*, pages 245–253.

Nan Yang, Mu Li, Dongdong Zhang, and Nenghai Yu. 2012. A ranking-based approach to word reordering for statistical machine translation. In *Proceedings of ACL*, pages 912–920.

Nan Yang, Shujie Liu, Mu Li, Ming Zhou, and Nenghai Yu. 2013. Word alignment modeling with context dependent deep neural network. In *Proceedings of ACL*, pages 166–175.

# APRO: All-Pairs Ranking Optimization for MT Tuning


**Markus Dreyer***
SDL Research
6060 Center Drive Suite 150
Los Angeles, CA 90045
markus.dreyer@gmail.com

**Yuanzhe Dong**
SDL Research
6060 Center Drive Suite 150
Los Angeles, CA 90045
ydong@sdl.com



## Abstract

We present APRO, a new method for machine translation tuning that can handle large feature sets. As opposed to other popular methods (e.g., MERT, MIRA, PRO), which involve randomness and require multiple runs to obtain a reliable result, APRO gives the same result on any run, given initial feature weights. APRO follows the pairwise ranking approach of PRO (Hopkins and May, 2011), but instead of ranking a small sampled subset of pairs from the $k$-best list, APRO efficiently ranks *all* pairs. By obviating the need for manually determined sampling settings, we obtain more reliable results. APRO converges more quickly than PRO and gives similar or better translation results.


## 1 Introduction

Machine translation tuning seeks to find feature weights that maximize translation quality. Recent efforts have focused on methods that scale to large numbers of features (Cherry and Foster, 2012), and among these, PRO has gained popularity (Pairwise Ranking Optimization, Hopkins and May (2011)).

PRO's goal is to find feature weights such that the resulting $k$-best list entries are ranked in the same way that an evaluation function (e.g., BLEU, Papineni et al. (2002)) ranks them. To do this, it labels pairs of translations for each sentence as *positive* or *negative*, depending on the gold ranking of the two pair elements given by BLEU. A binary classifier is trained on these labeled examples, resulting in new feature weights, and the procedure is iterated. This procedure would ordinarily be too expensive since there are $\mathcal{O}(k^2)$ pairs per sentence, where both $k$ and the number of sentences can be in the thousands, so billions of training examples would be produced per iteration. Therefore, Hopkins and May (2011) use subsampling to consider a small percentage of all pairs per sentence.

We present APRO (All-Pairs Ranking Optimization), a tuning approach that, like PRO, uses pairwise ranking for tuning. Unlike PRO, it is not limited to optimizing a small percentage of pairs per sentence. Based on an efficient ranking SVM formulation (Airola et al. (2011), Lee and Lin (2014)), we find, in each iteration, feature weights that minimize ranking errors for *all* pairs of translations per sentence. This tuning method inherits all the advantages of PRO—it is scalable, effective, easy to implement—and removes its limitations. It does not require meta-tuning of sampling parameters since no sampling is used; it does not need to be run multiple times to obtain reliable results, like MERT (Och, 2003), PRO, MIRA (Chiang et al., 2008) and others, since it uses global optimization and is deterministic given initial feature weights; and it converges quickly.

## 2 Notation and Definitions

For both PRO and APRO, we use the following definitions: A tuning dataset contains $S$ source sentences $x^1, \ldots, x^S$. Let $\mathcal{Y}^s$ be the space of all translations of $x^s$. It contains one or more known reference translations $\boldsymbol{y}_+^s$. Each translation $y_i^s \in \mathcal{Y}^s$ has a fea-

*Markus Dreyer is now at Amazon, Inc., Seattle, WA.



*Human Language Technologies: The 2015 Annual Conference of the North American Chapter of the ACL*, pages 1018–1023,
Denver, Colorado, May 31 – June 5, 2015. 

ture representation[1] $\boldsymbol{f}(x^s, y_i^s)$, or for short, $\boldsymbol{f}_i^s$, and a linear classification score $h_i^s = \mathbf{w}^T \boldsymbol{f}_i^s$, where $\mathbf{w}$ is a feature weight vector. Given a source sentence $x^s$, a translation decoder can search (often a subset of) $\mathcal{Y}^s$ and return the $k$ translations $y_1^s, \ldots, y_k^s$ with the highest classification scores. A $k$-best list is the list of $y_1^s, \ldots, y_k^s, \forall s$. For each translation $y_i^s$ we can obtain an evaluation score $b(y_i^s, \boldsymbol{y}_+^s)$, or for short, $b_i^s$, which can be the BLEU+1 score (Lin and Och, 2004).[2] For a given source sentence $x^s$, let $(i, j)$ denote a pair of translations $(y_i^s, y_j^s)$.

## 3 PRO

We now describe PRO, before constrasting it with our new approach, APRO. For each iteration $t$ from $t = 1 \ldots T$, PRO performs the following steps:

**1.** Given current feature weights $\mathbf{w}_t$, obtain a $k$-best list, as defined above, from the translation decoder. For each $x^s$, add to its $k$-best entries the $k$-best entries from previous iterations, so that $x^s$ now has $k_s$ translations; the overall list is called an *accumulated* $k$-best list.

**2.** For each source sentence $x^s$, first sample up to $\Gamma$ candidate pairs from its translations in the $k$-best list. Less similar pairs are more likely to become candidate pairs. Similarity in a pair $(i, j)$ here means a small absolute difference $d_{ij}^s$ between $b_i^s$ and $b_j^s$. The most similar pairs ($d_{ij}^s < \beta$) are discarded. Then select the $\Xi$ least similar pairs among the remaining candidate pairs.

**3.** For each pair $(i, j)$ from the $\Xi$ selected pairs, add the difference vector $(\boldsymbol{f}_i^s - \boldsymbol{f}_j^s)$ with class label 1 if $b_i^s > b_j^s$, otherwise add it with class label $-1$. Also add $(\boldsymbol{f}_j^s - \boldsymbol{f}_i^s)$ with the opposite label.

**4.** Train any classifier on the labeled data, resulting in a new weights vector $\mathbf{w}'$. Set $\mathbf{w}_{t+1} = \Psi \cdot \mathbf{w}' + (1 - \Psi) \cdot \mathbf{w}_t$.

Dependencies between tuning iterations are introduced by the use of accumulated $k$-best lists and the interpolation of weight vectors in step 4, using an interpolation factor $\Psi$. Translation quality varies with different choices for $\Gamma$, $\Xi$, $\beta$, $\Psi$, see Figure 1. The quality varies even when PRO is run multiple times with the *same* parameters, due to the sampling step. Practitioners would have to perform an expensive grid search multiple times to be sure to obtain good results. APRO seeks to remedy this problem. One could try to improve PRO by experimenting with other pair selection heuristics; APRO circumvents the problem by efficiently selecting *all* pairs.

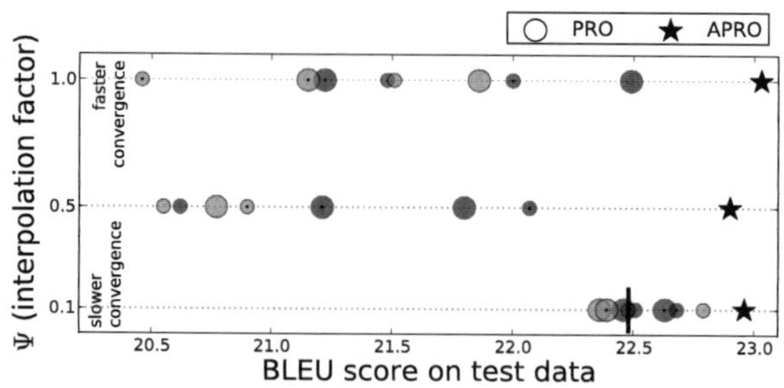


Figure 1: PRO versus APRO (eng-swe) for 3 settings of $\Psi$. PRO: 8 sampling settings per $\Psi$ setting.[4] APRO: no sampling. Vertical line indicates settings from H&M (2011). Not shown: PRO outlier with BLEU =7.9 at $\Psi = 0.5$.

## 4 APRO

Our method APRO is, like PRO, a ranking method. We believe that learning to rank is a suitable method for MT tuning because it matches the test-time requirements of correctly predicting the best translations or correctly ranked $k$-best lists of translations.

Compared to PRO, we simplify the procedure by removing sampling and labeling steps 2 and 3, thereby removing some of PRO's implementation complexity and manually set parameters. We run only two steps, corresponding to PRO's steps 1 and 4: In each tuning iteration, we obtain an accumulated $k$-best list, then directly find a new $\mathbf{w}'$ that minimizes the loss on that $k$-best list, which corresponds to PRO's running of a classifier. APRO's classification model is an efficient ranking SVM (Airola et al. (2011), Lee and Lin (2014)), described as follows.

### 4.1 Model

For each sentence $x^s$, we define the set of preference pairs as the set of ordered translation pairs for which the evaluation score prefers the first element:

$$\mathcal{P}^s = \{(i, j) \; : \; b_i^s > b_j^s\} \tag{1}$$

[1] For simplicity, we leave out nuisance variables like alignments, segmentations, or parse trees, from this description, which may be part of the feature space.

[2] But see Nakov et al. (2013) for variants.

[4] PRO settings: $\Gamma = \{5k, 8k\} = \{\text{small, large}\}$, $\Xi = \{50, 100\} = \{\text{light, dark}\}$, $\beta = \{.03, .05\} = \{\text{no dot, dot}\}$.

Following Lee and Lin (2014), we define the loss (or, error) of any sentence $s$ as the sum of its pairwise squared hinge losses:

$$L^s_{\mathbf{w}} = \sum_{(i,j)\in\mathcal{P}^s} \max(0, 1-h^s_i+h^s_j)^2 \tag{2}$$

That is, no loss is contributed by preference pairs for which the classification score correctly prefers the first element by a large-enough margin, i.e., $h^s_i \geq h^s_j+1$; all other preference pairs contribute some loss. We seek to find a weight vector that minimizes the regularized overall loss:

$$\mathbf{w}' = \operatorname*{argmin}_{\mathbf{w}} R_{\mathbf{w}} + C \cdot \frac{1}{N} \sum_s L^s_{\mathbf{w}} \tag{3}$$

where $R_{\mathbf{w}} = \frac{1}{2}\mathbf{w}^T\mathbf{w}$ is a Gaussian regularizer to prevent overfitting and $C$ a constant controlling the relative regularization amount. We divide by $N = \sum_s k_s$ to account for the increasing sizes of accumulated $k$-best lists between tuning iterations, which leads to increased sentence losses. If this were not done, the relative amount of regularization would decrease in subsequent iterations of tuning.

Any gradient-based optimization method can be used to find $\mathbf{w}'$. Since the loss is convex, the weights we find given a particular $k$-best list are optimal. This is different from PRO and Bazrafshan et al. (2012), where the resulting weights depend on the pairs sampled; MIRA, where they depend on the order of sentences processed; and MERT, where optimization is greedy and depends on initial weights.

### 4.2 Efficient Computation

How do we efficiently compute $L^s_{\mathbf{w}}$ per sentence? In this and the following subsection, we leave out all sentence indices $s$ for ease of notation; it is understood that we operate on a given sentence.

A straightforward algorithm to compute $L_{\mathbf{w}}$ would iterate over all preference pairs $(i, j) \in \mathcal{P}$ and add up their losses (Joachims, 2002). However, since there are $\mathcal{O}(k^2)$ pairs per sentence, with potentially thousands of sentences, this would be extremely inefficient. PRO's solution to this problem is subsampling. The alternative solution we apply is to make the sums over translation pairs efficient by carefully rearranging the terms of the sentence loss, making use of quantities that can be precomputed efficiently (Airola et al. (2011), Lee and Lin (2014)).

**Definitions.** Let us define those quantities. For a given sentence $s$, let the set $\mathcal{Q}$ contain all members of $\mathcal{P}$ that contribute a positive loss to the overall loss term:

$$\mathcal{Q} = \{(i,j) : (i,j) \in \mathcal{P} \wedge (1-h_i+h_j > 0)\} \tag{4}$$

We also define an index notation into $\mathcal{Q}$:

$$\mathcal{Q}_{i\bullet} = \{(i,j) \in \mathcal{Q}, \forall j\} \quad q_{i\bullet} = |\mathcal{Q}_{i\bullet}| \tag{5}$$

$$\mathcal{Q}_{\bullet j} = \{(i,j) \in \mathcal{Q}, \forall i\} \quad q_{\bullet j} = |\mathcal{Q}_{\bullet j}| \tag{6}$$

$$r_{i\bullet} = \sum_{(i,j)\in\mathcal{Q}_{i\bullet}} h_j \tag{7}$$

The bullet ($\bullet$) can be read as *any*. Example: $\mathcal{Q}_{\bullet 3}$ contains pairs $\in \mathcal{Q}$ whose second element is translation 3. $q_{i\bullet}$ and $q_{\bullet j}$ denote corresponding set sizes.

**Rearrangement.** We use these definitions to express the loss as a sum over only $\mathcal{O}(k)$ elements.

First, we simplify the loss expression by summing only over elements from $\mathcal{Q}$, i.e., pairs from $\mathcal{P}$ that contribute a positive loss, so the max becomes unnecessary:

$$L_{\mathbf{w}} = \sum_{(i,j)\in\mathcal{P}} \max(0, 1-h_i+h_j)^2 \tag{8}$$

$$= \sum_{(i,j)\in\mathcal{Q}} (1-h_i+h_j)^2 \tag{9}$$

$$= \sum_{(i,j)\in\mathcal{Q}} h_i^2-2h_i+1+h_j^2+2h_j-2h_ih_j \tag{10}$$

We then use the precomputed quantities defined above to rewrite the sum over $\mathcal{O}(k^2)$ pairs to a sum over just $\mathcal{O}(k)$ elements:

$$L_{\mathbf{w}} = \sum_{i=1}^{k} q_{i\bullet}(h_i^2-2h_i+1)+q_{\bullet i}(h_i^2+2h_i) - 2\, r_{i\bullet}\, h_i \tag{11}$$

This step is described in detail below. Our new formulation is simpler but equivalent to Lee and Lin

(2014). Using order statistics trees (Cormen et al., 2001), the quantities $q_{i\bullet}$, $q_{\bullet i}$, and $r_{i\bullet}$ can be precomputed in $\mathcal{O}(k \log k)$ time (see details in Lee and Lin (2014)). This precomputation, together with the rearranged loss, allows APRO to make efficient weight updates without having to subsample.

**Detailed derivation.** We explain how to derive Equation 11 from Equation 10.
First, let us define the following equalities:

$$\sum_{(1,j)\in\mathcal{Q}} h_1 = q_{1\bullet} \cdot h_1$$

$$\sum_{(2,j)\in\mathcal{Q}} h_2 = q_{2\bullet} \cdot h_2$$

$$\ldots$$

If we do not fix the first pair element to a particular value, we have:

$$\sum_{(i,j)\in\mathcal{Q}} h_i = \sum_i q_{i\bullet} \cdot h_i \qquad (12)$$

Similarly:

$$\sum_{(j,1)\in\mathcal{Q}} h_1 = q_{\bullet 1} \cdot h_1$$

$$\sum_{(j,2)\in\mathcal{Q}} h_2 = q_{\bullet 2} \cdot h_2$$

$$\ldots$$

If we do not fix the second element of each pair to a particular value, we have:

$$\sum_{(j,i)\in\mathcal{Q}} h_i = \sum_i q_{\bullet i} \cdot h_i \qquad (13)$$

We split Equation 10 into separate sums and perform a change of variables in the second sum:

$$L_{\mathbf{w}} = \sum_{(i,j)\in\mathcal{Q}} h_i^2 - 2h_i + 1 + \sum_{(j,i)\in\mathcal{Q}} h_i^2 + 2h_i \\ -2 \sum_{(i,j)\in\mathcal{Q}} h_i h_j \qquad (14)$$

We introduce one more equality, where (16) follows from the definition of $r_{i\bullet}$ in Equation 7:

$$\sum_{(i,j)\in\mathcal{Q}} h_i h_j = \sum_i h_i \left( \sum_{(i,j)\in\mathcal{Q}_{i\bullet}} h_j \right) \qquad (15)$$

$$= \sum_i h_i \; r_{i\bullet} \qquad (16)$$

| Lang. | Train | Dev | Test |
|---|---|---|---|
| Ara-Eng | 14.4M | 66K | 37K |
| Chi-Eng | 142.9M | 61K | 29K |
| Eng-Swe | 100.1M | 21K | 22K |
| Eng-Fra | 100.0M | 63K | 20K |
| Ita-Eng | 102.8M | 21K | 20K |
| Pol-Eng | 90.5M | 21K | 19K |

Table 1: Number of words in the used data sets.

We now use equalities 12, 13, and 16 to arrive at Equation 11:

$$L_{\mathbf{w}} = \sum_i q_{i\bullet}(h_i^2 - 2h_i + 1) + \sum_i q_{\bullet i}(h_i^2 + 2h_i) \\ -2 \sum_i r_{i\bullet} \; h_i \\ = \sum_i q_{i\bullet}(h_i^2 - 2h_i + 1) + q_{\bullet i}(h_i^2 + 2h_i) \\ -2 r_{i\bullet} \; h_i$$

## 5 Experiments

### 5.1 Experimental Setup

We validate APRO on 6 diverse language pairs. For each one, we perform HMM-based word alignment (Vogel et al., 1996) and phrase rule extraction on the training data. We use 20 standard features, incl. 8 reordering features, plus the sparse features listed for PBTM systems in Hopkins and May (2011).[5]

For Ara-Eng and Chi-Eng, we use BOLT Y2 data sets.[6] For all other languages, we sample train, dev, and test sets from in-house data. Table 1 describes the different data set sizes. We use 5-gram LMs trained on the target side of the training data; for Ara-Eng and Chi-Eng, we add 2 LMs trained on English Gigaword and other sources.

We tune on dev data. In each tuning run, we use $k = 500$, except for Ara-Eng ($k = 1500$). We use the same weight initialization for every tuning run, where most features are initialized to 0 and some dense features are initialized to 1 or -1. During tuning, we use case-insensitive BLEU+1. We tune for

[5]We use the 500 most frequent words for word pair features.

[6]For ara-eng, a subset of the training data was chosen whose source side has maximum similarity to the test source side.

| | Pro | | Apro | |
|---|---|---|---|---|
| | Bleu | LR | Bleu | LR |
| Ara-Eng | (29.3) 30.7 | (0.93) 0.97 | (30.3) 30.8 | (0.98) 0.99 |
| Chi-Eng | (15.4) 20.8 | (0.78) 0.98 | (19.2) 20.8 | (1.01) 0.98 |
| Eng-Fra | (30.9) 33.0 | (0.95) 0.97 | (32.7) 33.3 | (1.00) 0.99 |
| Eng-Swe | (22.2) 22.4 | (1.00) 1.01 | (23.1) 23.0 | (1.00) 1.00 |
| Ita-Eng | (25.6) 25.3 | (1.00) 1.00 | (25.2) 25.6 | (1.00) 1.00 |
| Pol-Eng | (22.4) 23.0 | (0.95) 0.99 | (23.3) 23.3 | (1.00) 0.99 |

Table 2: PRO versus APRO after 10 iterations (small in parentheses) and at convergence ($\leq$ 30 iterations). Good results after 10 iterations indicate fast convergence. PRO: mean over 2 runs (average BLEU standard deviation was 0.1); APRO: single run. LR: length ratio.

up to 30 iterations,[7] where we reset the accumulated $k$-best list after 10 iterations.[8] For PRO, we use $\Gamma$=5000, $\Xi$=50, $\beta$=0.05, $\Psi$=0.1, and (MegaM) regularization strength $\lambda$=1 as described in Hopkins and May (2011). For APRO, we use regularization strength $C$=0.01 and $\Psi$=1, which effectively removes the weight interpolation step. We repeat each PRO tuning twice and report the mean of length ratios and case-sensitive BLEU scores on test data. For APRO, no repeated runs are necessary; it gives the same result on any run given initial feature weights.

For APRO, we optimize using the implementation by Lee and Lin, which uses a truncated Newton method.[9]

### 5.2 Results

We measure the runtime of PRO and APRO. For an accumulated $k$-best list containing $s$=2,748 sentences with an average $k_s$=3,600 translation, PRO and APRO take 13 and 8 minutes, respectively. Table 2 shows translation quality after 10 iterations and at convergence. We observe that APRO converges quickly: After running for 10 iterations, it gives higher BLEU scores and better length ratios than PRO for five out of six language pairs. At convergence, PRO has caught up, but for all language pairs APRO performs similar or better.

One of APRO's advantages are stable results: Figure 1 compares PRO and APRO for 3 values of $\Psi$: For each value, we run PRO eight times with different sampling settings and APRO once. We observe that the different PRO settings result in different BLEU scores. Cherry and Foster (2012) report that they could not find one PRO setting that worked across all language pairs. This suggests that practitioners may have to run expensive grid searches to find optimal PRO performance; this is not necessary with APRO. While PRO performs best with $\Psi = 0.1$, APRO gets good results for $\Psi$=1, which is the reason for its fast convergence (Table 2).

[7] Like Hopkins and May (2011), we stop earlier when the accumulated $k$-best list does not change anymore.

[8] This removes bad translations from early iterations and provides good initial weights for the last 20 iterations. This did not decrease but sometimes increase final performance.

[9] See `http://goo.gl/CVmnoZ`. No change to the software is necessary; but in each iteration it must be called with $C' = \frac{C}{N}$, see Equation 3. We have also experimented with a change to the software that scales the loss of each sentence by the number of translation pairs for that sentence; this did not give reliable BLEU improvements over Equation 3.

## 6 Conclusions

We have presented APRO, a new tuning method for machine translation. Like PRO, APRO is a batch pairwise ranking method, and as such, it inherits PRO's advantages of being effective, scalable to large feature sets and easy to fit into the standard batch MT tuning framework. We remove PRO's sampling step and learn a pairwise ranking over the whole $k$-best list in $\mathcal{O}(k \log k)$ time. We have shown that PRO's different sampling settings result in different final results; by removing these settings we get more reliable results. We find that PRO's weight interpolation is not necessary for APRO, resulting in faster convergence. At convergence, APRO's translation quality was found to be similar or better than PRO's. APRO's use of global optimization and the lack of randomness lead to more stable tuning with deterministic results.

## Acknowledgments

We thank Jonathan May, Mark Hopkins, Bill Byrne, Adria Gispert, Gonzalo Iglesias, Steve DeNeefe and the anonymous reviewers for their valuable comments and suggestions.

## References

Antti Airola, Tapio Pahikkala, and Tapio Salakoski. 2011. Training linear ranking SVMs in linearithmic time using red-black trees. *Pattern Recognition Letters*, 32(9):1328–1336.

Marzieh Bazrafshan, Tagyoung Chung, and Daniel Gildea. 2012. Tuning as linear regression. In *Pro-*

*ceedings of the 2012 Conference of the North American Chapter of the Association for Computational Linguistics: Human Language Technologies*, pages 543–547. Association for Computational Linguistics.

Colin Cherry and George Foster. 2012. Batch tuning strategies for statistical machine translation. In *Proceedings of the 2012 Conference of the North American Chapter of the Association for Computational Linguistics: Human Language Technologies*, pages 427–436. Association for Computational Linguistics.

David Chiang, Yuval Marton, and Philip Resnik. 2008. Online large-margin training of syntactic and structural translation features. In *Proceedings of the Conference on Empirical Methods in Natural Language Processing*, pages 224–233. Association for Computational Linguistics.

Thomas H Cormen, Charles E Leiserson, Ronald L Rivest, Clifford Stein, et al. 2001. *Introduction to algorithms*. MIT press Cambridge, 2nd edition.

Mark Hopkins and Jonathan May. 2011. Tuning as ranking. In *Proceedings of the 2011 Conference on Empirical Methods in Natural Language Processing*, pages 1352–1362. Association for Computational Linguistics.

Thorsten Joachims. 2002. Optimizing search engines using clickthrough data. In *Proceedings of the eighth ACM SIGKDD international conference on Knowledge discovery and data mining*, pages 133–142. ACM.

Ching-Pei Lee and Chih-Jen Lin. 2014. Large-scale linear RankSVM. *Neural computation*, 26(4):781–817.

Chin-Yew Lin and Franz Josef Och. 2004. ORANGE: a method for evaluating automatic evaluation metrics for machine translation. In *Proceedings of Coling 2004*, pages 501–507, Geneva, Switzerland, Aug 23–Aug 27. COLING.

Preslav Nakov, Francisco Guzmán, and Stephan Vogel. 2013. A tale about PRO and monsters. In *Proceedings of the 51st Annual Meeting of the Association for Computational Linguistics (Volume 2: Short Papers)*, pages 12–17, Sofia, Bulgaria, August. Association for Computational Linguistics.

Franz Josef Och. 2003. Minimum error rate training in statistical machine translation. In *Proceedings of the 41st Annual Meeting on Association for Computational Linguistics-Volume 1*, pages 160–167. Association for Computational Linguistics.

K. Papineni, S. Roukos, T. Ward, and W. J Zhu. 2002. BLEU: a method for automatic evaluation of machine translation. In *Proceedings of the 40th annual meeting on association for computational linguistics*, pages 311–318.

Stephan Vogel, Hermann Ney, and Christoph Tillmann. 1996. HMM-based word alignment in statistical translation. In *Proceedings of the 16th conference on Computational linguistics-Volume 2*, pages 836–841. Association for Computational Linguistics.

# Paradigm classification in supervised learning of morphology

**Malin Ahlberg**
Språkbanken
University of Gothenburg
malin.ahlberg@gu.se

**Markus Forsberg**
Språkbanken
University of Gothenburg
markus.forsberg@gu.se

**Mans Hulden**
Department of Linguistics
University of Colorado Boulder
mans.hulden@colorado.edu

## Abstract

Supervised morphological paradigm learning by identifying and aligning the longest common subsequence found in inflection tables has recently been proposed as a simple yet competitive way to induce morphological patterns. We combine this non-probabilistic strategy of inflection table generalization with a discriminative classifier to permit the reconstruction of complete inflection tables of unseen words. Our system learns morphological paradigms from labeled examples of inflection patterns (inflection tables) and then produces inflection tables from unseen lemmas or base forms. We evaluate the approach on datasets covering 11 different languages and show that this approach results in consistently higher accuracies vis-à-vis other methods on the same task, thus indicating that the general method is a viable approach to quickly creating high-accuracy morphological resources.

## 1 Introduction

Use of detailed and sophisticated morphological features has been found to be crucial for many downstream NLP tasks, including part-of-speech tagging and parsing (Tseng et al., 2005; Spoustová et al., 2007). However, creating an accurate wide-coverage morphological analyzer for a new language that can be used in tandem with other higher-level analyses is an arduous task.

Learning word inflection patterns by organizing related word-forms into morphological paradigms based on the longest common subsequence (LCS) found in an inflection table has recently been proposed as a method for supervised and semi-supervised induction of morphological processing tools from labeled data (Ahlberg et al., 2014). Also, the argument that the LCS shared by different inflected forms of a word—even if discontinuous within a word—corresponds strongly to a cross-linguistic notion of a 'stem' has later been advanced independently on grounds of descriptive economy and minimum description length (Lee and Goldsmith, 2014).

We used this idea in (Ahlberg et al., 2014) to create a relatively simple-to-implement system that learns paradigms from example inflection tables and is then able to reconstruct inflection tables for unseen words by comparing suffixes of new base forms to base forms seen during training. The system performs well on available datasets and results in human-readable and editable output. The longest common subsequence strategy itself shows little bias toward any specific morphological process such as prefixation, suffixation, or infixation. Using the model, we argued, a selection of ready-inflected tables could be quickly provided by a linguist, allowing rapid development of morphological resources for languages for which few such resources exist.

Potentially, however, the model's commitment to a simple suffix-based learner is a weakness. To assess this, we evaluate a similar LCS-based generalization system with a more refined discriminative classifier that takes advantage of substrings in the example data and performs careful feature selection. We show that much higher accuracies can be achieved by combining the LCS paradigm generalization strategy with such a feature-based classi-



*Human Language Technologies: The 2015 Annual Conference of the North American Chapter of the ACL*, pages 1024–1029,
Denver, Colorado, May 31 – June 5, 2015. 

fier that assigns unknown words to the LCS-learned paradigm based on substring features taken from word edges. This holds in particular for languages where paradigmatic behavior is triggered by material in the beginning of a word (e.g. German verbs).

We present experiments on 18 datasets in 11 languages varying in morphological complexity. In all the experiments, the task is to reconstruct a complete inflection table from a base form, which usually corresponds to the lemma or dictionary form of a noun, verb, or adjective. The experiments are divided into two sets. In the first, we use an earlier dataset (Durrett and DeNero, 2013) of Finnish, German, and Spanish to compare against other methods of paradigm learning. In the second, we use a more comprehensive and complex dataset we have developed for 8 additional languages. This new dataset is less regular and intended to be more realistic in that it also features defective or incomplete inflection tables and inflection tables containing various alternate forms, naturally making the classification task substantially more difficult.[1]

Overall, supervised and semi-supervised learning of morphology by generalizing patterns from inflection tables is an active research field. Recent work sharing our goals includes Toutanova and Cherry (2009), Dreyer and Eisner (2011), which works with a fully Bayesian model, Dinu et al. (2012), Eskander et al. (2013), which attempts to learn lexicons from morphologically annotated corpora, and Durrett and DeNero (2013), who train a discriminative model that learns transformation rules between word forms. We directly compare our results against the last using the same dataset.

The paper is organized as follows: section 2 contains the experimental setup, section 3 the datasets, and section 4 the results and discussion.

## 2 Method

As a first step, our system converts inflection tables into paradigms using a procedure given in Hulden (2014). The system generalizes concrete inflection tables by associating the common symbol subsequences shared by the words (the LCS) with vari-

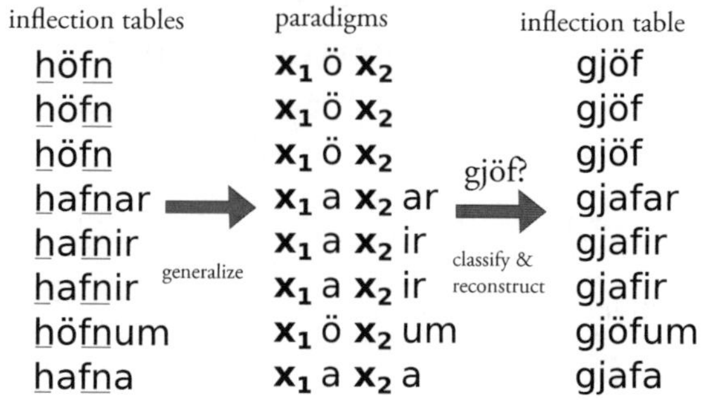


Figure 1: General overview of the system, exemplified using Icelandic nouns. First, a large number of inflection tables are generalized into a smaller number of paradigms; the generalization of the table for **höfn** 'harbor' into a paradigm is illustrated here. At classification time, an unknown base form is classified into one of the learned paradigms and its inflection table is reconstructed, illustrated here by **gjöf** 'present'.

ables. These variables represent abstractions that at table reconstruction time can correspond to any sequence of one or more symbols. As many inflection tables of different words are identical after assigning the common parts to 'variables,' this procedure results in a comparatively small number of paradigms after being input a large number of inflection tables. The process is illustrated in Figure 1. During generalization, the forms that gave rise to a particular paradigm are stored and later used for training a classifier to assign unknown base forms to paradigms. Having a number of paradigms at our disposal by this generalization method, the task of reconstructing an inflection table for an unseen base form in effect means picking the correct paradigm from among the ones generalized, a standard classification task of choosing the right/best paradigm.

After seeing a number of inflection tables generalized into abstract paradigms as described above, the task we evaluate is how well complete inflection tables can be reconstructed from only seeing an unknown base form. To this end, we train a "one-vs-the-rest" linear multi-class support vector machine (SVM).[2] For each example base form $wb_i$ that is a member of paradigm $p_j$, we extract all substrings from $wb_i$ from the left and right edges, and use those as binary features corresponding to the paradigm $p_j$.

[1]The data and the code is available at our website `https://svn.spraakbanken.gu.se/clt/naacl/2015/extract`

[2]Using LIBLINEAR (Fan et al., 2008) with L2-regularization.

For example, during training, the German verb **lesen** would have the following binary features activated: {#l, #le, #les, #lese, #lesen, #lesen#, lesen#, esen#, sen#, en#, n#}.

Before applying the classifier to an unseen base form and reconstructing the corresponding inflection table, many competing paradigms can be ruled out as being ill-matched simply by inspecting the base form. For example, the infinitive for the paradigm containing the English verb **sing** is generalized as $x_1$+**i**+$x_2$. At classification time of a verb like **run**, this paradigm can be ruled out due to incompatibility, as there is no **i** in **run**, and so the infinitive cannot be generated. Likewise, the Icelandic paradigm seen in Figure 1 can be ruled out for the base form **hest** 'horse', as the base form does not contain **ö**. The SVM-classifier may indeed suggest such paradigm assignments, but such classifications are ignored and the highest scoring compatible paradigm is selected instead. These additional constraints on possible base form-paradigm pairings are a general feature of the LCS-strategy and are not at all tied to the classification method here.

### 2.1 Feature selection

In order to eliminate noise features, we performed feature selection using the development set. We simultaneously tuned the SVM soft-margin penalty parameter $C$, as well as the length and type (prefix/suffix) of substrings to include as features. More concretely, we explored the values using a grid search over $C = 0.01 \ldots 5.0$, with a growing sequence gap (Hsu et al., 2003), as well as tuning the maximum length of anchored substring features to use $(3 \ldots 9)$, and whether to include prefix-anchored substrings at all $(0/1)$. In the second experiment, where cross-validation was used, we performed the same tuning procedure on each fold's development set.

## 3 Data

For the first experiment, we use the datasets provided by Durrett and DeNero (2013). This dataset contains complete inflection tables for German nouns and verbs (DE-NOUNS, DE-VERBS), Finnish verbs and nouns combined with adjectives (FI-VERBS, FI-NOUNADJ), and Spanish verbs (ES-VERBS). The number of inflection tables in this set ranges from 2,027 (DE-VERBS) to 7,249 (FI-VERBS). From these tables, 200 were held out for development and 200 for testing, following the splits that previous authors have used (Durrett and DeNero, 2013; Ahlberg et al., 2014) to ensure a fair baseline.[3]

For the second experiment, we collected additional inflection tables from Catalan (CA), English (EN), French (FR), Galician (GL), Italian (IT), Portuguese (PT), Russian (RU) (all from the FreeLing project (Padró and Stanilovsky, 2012)) and Maltese (MT) (Camilleri, 2013).[4] These inflection tables are often incomplete or defective and some contain very rarely occurring grammatical forms. Many alternate forms are also given. To avoid having to account for rare or historical forms, we filtered out grammatical forms (slots) that occur in less than $\sim$1% of all inflection tables. We also performed an independent cross-check with Wiktionary and removed some inflection table slots that did not appear in that resource. We further limited the number of inflection tables to 5,000. In the second experiment, we also split each dataset into 5 folds for cross-validation (maximally 4,000 tables for training, 500 for development and 500 for testing for each fold).

## 4 Results and discussion

In the main results tables 1, 2, and 3 we report the per table accuracy and per form accuracy in reconstructing complete inflection tables from unseen base forms. The per table accuracy is the percentage of inflection tables that are perfectly reconstructed from the base form. The per form accuracy is the percentage of correct forms in the reconstructed table. The associated oracle scores, which independently provide a measure of generalization power of the LCS-method, represent the maximal percentage achievable by an oracle classifier that always picks

[3]The development and test data for the first experiment had been filtered to not contain any of the 200 most frequently occurring forms in the language (Durrett and DeNero, 2013); this may result in an easier classification task because the maneuver in effect ensures that words belonging to irregular paradigms—i.e. those which would otherwise be difficult to classify correctly—are never evaluated against.

[4]The FreeLing data also included Russian verbs. However, this data set was deemed too incomplete to be useful and was left out.

| Data | Per table accuracy | | | Per form accuracy | | | Oracle acc. per form (table) |
|---|---|---|---|---|---|---|---|
| | SVM | AFH14 | D&DN13 | SVM | AFH14 | D&DN13 | |
| DE-VERBS | **91.5** | 68.0 | 85.0 | **98.11** | 97.04 | 96.19 | 99.70 (198/200) |
| DE-NOUNS | **80.5** | 76.5 | 79.5 | **89.88** | 87.81 | 88.94 | 100.00 (200/200) |
| ES-VERBS | **99.0** | 96.0 | 95.0 | **99.92** | 99.52 | 99.67 | 100.00 (200/200) |
| FI-VERBS | **94.0** | 92.5 | 87.5 | **97.14** | 96.36 | 96.43 | 99.00 (195/200) |
| FI-NOUNS-ADJS | **85.5** | 85.0 | 83.5 | **93.68** | 91.91 | 93.41 | 100.00 (200/200) |

Table 1: Results on experiment 1. Here AFH14 stands for Ahlberg et al. (2014) and D&DN for Durrett and DeNero (2013). The SVM-columns show the results of the current method.

the best learned paradigm for an unseen base form. In experiment 2, where the correct forms may consist of several alternatives, we only count a form as correct if all alternatives are given and all are correct. For example, the verb **dream** in English lists two alternative past participles, **dreamed** and **dreamt**, which both must be reconstructed for the past participle form to count as being correct.

### Experiment 1

The accuracies obtained on the first three-language comparison experiment are shown in Table 1. Here, we see a consistent improvement upon the *max-suff*-strategy (AFH14) that simply picks the longest matching suffix among the base forms seen and assigns the unseen word to the same paradigm (breaking ties by paradigm frequency), as well as improvement over other learning strategies (D&DN13). Particularly marked is the improved accuracy on German verbs. We assume that this is because German verb prefixes, which are ignored in a suffix-based classifier, contain information that is useful in classifying verb behavior. German verbs that contain so-called inseparable prefixes like **miss-, ver-, wider-** do not prefix a **ge-** in the past participle form. For example: **kaufen** ~ **gekauft**, **brauchen** ~ **gebraucht**, **legen** ~ **gelegt**, but **verkaufen** ~ **verkauft**, **widerlegen** ~ **widerlegt**, **missbrauchen** ~ **missbraucht**, reflecting the replacement of the standard **ge-** by the inseparable prefix. There are many such inseparable prefixes that immediately trigger this behavior (although some prefixes only occasionally show inseparable behavior), yet this information is lost when only looking at suffixes at classification time. This analysis is supported by the fact that, during feature selection, German verbs was the only dataset in this first experiment where word prefixes were not removed by the feature selection process.

### Experiment 2

The results of the second experiment are given in tables 2 (per table accuracy) and 3 (per form accuracy). The tables contain information about how many inflection tables were input on average over 5 folds to the learner (**#tbl**), how many paradigms this reduced to (**#par**), and how many forms (slots) each paradigm has (**#forms**). The **mfreq** column is a baseline where the classifier always picks the most populated paradigm, i.e. the paradigm that resulted from combining the largest number of different inflection tables by the LCS process. The **AFH14** shows the performance of a maximal suffix matching classifier, identical to that used in Ahlberg et al. (2014).

### Discussion

Overall, the results support earlier claims that the LCS-generalization appears to capture paradigmatic behavior well, especially if combined with careful classification into paradigms. There is a clear and consistent improvement over baselines that use the same data sets. In addition, the SVM-classifier yields results comparable, and in many cases better, to using a maximum suffix classifier and additionally having access to raw corpus data in the language, a semi-supervised experiment reported separately in Ahlberg et al. (2014). In this work we have not attempted to extend the current method to such a semi-supervised scenario, although such an extension seems both interesting and possible.

| Data | #tbl | #par | mfreq | AFH14 | SVM | Oracle |
|---|---|---|---|---|---|---|
| DE-N | 2,210 | 66 | 18.99 | 76.09 | **77.68** | 98.99 |
| DE-V | 1,621 | 125 | 52.77 | 65.02 | **83.59** | 95.45 |
| ES-V | 3,243 | 90 | 70.42 | 92.25 | **93.48** | 96.59 |
| FI-N&A | 4,000 | 233 | 26.52 | **83.20** | 82.84 | 98.12 |
| FI-V | 4,000 | 204 | 43.04 | **91.88** | 91.64 | 94.76 |
| MT-V | 826 | 200 | 10.68 | 18.83 | **38.64** | 85.63 |
| CA-N | 4,000 | 49 | 44.12 | 94.00 | **94.92** | 99.44 |
| CA-V | 4,000 | 164 | 60.44 | 90.76 | **93.40** | 98.48 |
| EN-V | 4,000 | 161 | 77.12 | 89.40 | **90.00** | 97.40 |
| FR-N | 4,000 | 57 | 92.16 | 91.60 | **93.96** | 98.72 |
| FR-V | 4,000 | 95 | 81.52 | 93.72 | **96.48** | 98.80 |
| GL-N | 4,000 | 24 | 88.36 | 90.48 | **95.08** | 99.80 |
| GL-V | 3,212 | 101 | 45.21 | 58.92 | **60.87** | 98.95 |
| IT-N | 4,000 | 39 | 83.84 | 92.32 | **93.76** | 99.40 |
| IT-V | 4,000 | 115 | 63.96 | 89.68 | **91.56** | 98.68 |
| PT-N | 4,000 | 68 | 74.52 | 88.12 | **90.88** | 99.04 |
| PT-V | 4,000 | 92 | 62.00 | 76.96 | **80.20** | 99.20 |
| RU-N | 4,000 | 260 | 15.76 | 64.12 | **66.36** | 96.80 |

Table 2: Per table accuracy results on the second experiment. 5-fold cross-validation is used throughout. The **#tbl**-column shows the number of inflection tables input to the LCS-learner and the **#par** column shows the number of resulting unique paradigms. The **mfreq**-column illustrates a baseline of simply picking the most frequent paradigm, while **AFH14** is the strategy of finding the longest suffix match to the base forms in the training data (Ahlberg et al., 2014). The **SVM**-column shows the results discussed in this paper.

| Data | #forms | mfreq | AFH14 | SVM | Oracle |
|---|---|---|---|---|---|
| DE-N | 8 | 57.36 | 89.72 | **90.25** | 99.69 |
| DE-V | 27 | 87.35 | **96.12** | 95.28 | 99.20 |
| ES-V | 57 | 93.80 | 98.72 | **98.83** | 99.47 |
| FI-N&A | 233 | 52.15 | 91.03 | **91.06** | 98.95 |
| FI-V | 54 | 70.38 | **95.27** | 95.22 | 96.76 |
| MT-V | 16 | 39.75 | 54.66 | **61.15** | 95.49 |
| CA-N | 2 | 71.30 | 96.89 | **97.33** | 97.93 |
| CA-V | 53 | 86.89 | 98.18 | **98.89** | 99.77 |
| EN-V | 6 | 91.43 | 95.93 | **96.16** | 99.28 |
| FR-N | 2 | 93.24 | 92.48 | **94.68** | 99.08 |
| FR-V | 51 | 91.47 | 97.09 | **98.33** | 99.02 |
| GL-N | 2 | 91.92 | 92.82 | **95.38** | 99.78 |
| GL-V | 70 | 94.89 | **98.48** | 98.32 | 99.67 |
| IT-N | 3 | 89.36 | 93.38 | **94.59** | 97.44 |
| IT-V | 51 | 89.51 | 97.76 | **98.21** | 99.64 |
| PT-N | 4 | 83.35 | 89.78 | **91.97** | 98.60 |
| PT-V | 65 | 92.62 | 96.81 | **97.20** | 99.68 |
| RU-N | 12 | 25.16 | 88.19 | **89.35** | 99.15 |

Table 3: Per form accuracy results on the second experiment. 5-fold cross-validation is used throughout. The **#forms**-column shows the number of different slots in the paradigms. Other columns are as in table 2.

In some cases, we see a significant drop between the per-form and the per-table accuracy. For example, in the case of Russian nouns, per table accuracy is at 66.36%, while the per-form accuracy is 89.35%. This effect is explained—not only in the Russian case but in many others—by the existence of similar paradigms that differ only in very few forms. If the classifier picks an incorrect, but closely related paradigm, most forms may be produced correctly although the entire reconstructed table counts as wrong if even a single form is incorrect.

A few outliers remain. The Maltese verbs, which exhibit Semitic interdigitation in some paradigms, seem to generalize fairly well, and have a per form oracle score of 95.49 (shown in table 3). However, this is not reflected in the relatively low per form accuracy (61.15), which warrants further analysis. It may be an indication of that the correct paradigm is simply difficult to ascertain based only on the lemma form, or that additional features could be developed, perhaps ones that are discontinuous in the word.

An obvious extension to the current method is to inspect a suggested reconstructed table holistically, i.e., not relying only on base form features. That is, one could avoid making a commitment to a particular paradigm based solely on the features of the base form, and instead also include features from all the forms that a paradigm would generate. Such features are of course available in the training data in the various forms in an inflection table. Features from the seen forms could be used to rate compatibility since an incorrect reconstruction of an inflection table may likely be identified by its tendency to produce phonotactic patterns rarely or never seen in the training data.

With relatively few paradigms learned from collections of word forms, one can achieve fairly high coverage on unseen data. In principle, for example, the 13 most frequently used paradigms of Spanish verbs suffice to cover 90% of all verbs (per token). A useful application of this is rapid language resource development—one can elicit from a speaker a small number of well-chosen inflection tables, e.g. all forms of specific nouns, verbs, adjectives; generalize these inflection tables into paradigms; and use this information to deduce the possible morphological classes for a majority of unseen word forms.

## References


Malin Ahlberg, Markus Forsberg, and Mans Hulden. 2014. Semi-supervised learning of morphological paradigms and lexicons. In *Proceedings of the 14th Conference of the European Chapter of the Association for Computational Linguistics*, pages 569–578, Gothenburg, Sweden. Association for Computational Linguistics.

John J. Camilleri. 2013. A computational grammar and lexicon for Maltese. Master's thesis, Chalmers University of Technology. Gothenburg, Sweden.

Liviu P Dinu, Vlad Niculae, and Octavia-Maria Şulea. 2012. Learning how to conjugate the Romanian verb: rules for regular and partially irregular verbs. In *Proceedings of the 13th Conference of the European Chapter of the Association for Computational Linguistics*, pages 524–528. Association for Computational Linguistics.

Markus Dreyer and Jason Eisner. 2011. Discovering morphological paradigms from plain text using a Dirichlet process mixture model. In *Proceedings of the Conference on Empirical Methods in Natural Language Processing*, pages 616–627. Association for Computational Linguistics.

Greg Durrett and John DeNero. 2013. Supervised learning of complete morphological paradigms. In *Proceedings of NAACL-HLT*, pages 1185–1195.

Ramy Eskander, Nizar Habash, and Owen Rambow. 2013. Automatic extraction of morphological lexicons from morphologically annotated corpora. In *Proceedings of the 2013 Conference on Empirical Methods in Natural Language Processing*, pages 1032–1043. Association for Computational Linguistics.

Rong-En Fan, Kai-Wei Chang, Cho-Jui Hsieh, Xiang-Rui Wang, and Chih-Jen Lin. 2008. LIBLINEAR: A library for large linear classification. *Journal of Machine Learning Research*, 9:1871–1874.

Chih-Wei Hsu, Chih-Chung Chang, Chih-Jen Lin, et al. 2003. A practical guide to support vector classification.

Mans Hulden. 2014. Generalizing inflection tables into paradigms with finite state operations. In *Proceedings of the 2014 Joint Meeting of SIGMORPHON and SIGFSM*, pages 29–36. Association for Computational Linguistics.

Jackson L Lee and John A Goldsmith. 2014. Complexity across morphological paradigms: a minimum description length approach to identifying inflectional stems. In *Poster at the MorphologyFest: Symposium on Morphological Complexity, Indiana University, Bloomington*.

Lluís Padró and Evgeny Stanilovsky. 2012. Freeling 3.0: Towards wider multilinguality. In *Proceedings of the Language Resources and Evaluation Conference (LREC 2012)*, Istanbul, Turkey, May. ELRA.

Drahomíra Spoustová, Jan Hajič, Jan Votrubec, Pavel Krbec, and Pavel Květoň. 2007. The best of two worlds: Cooperation of statistical and rule-based taggers for Czech. In *Proceedings of the Workshop on Balto-Slavonic Natural Language Processing*, pages 67–74.

Kristina Toutanova and Colin Cherry. 2009. A global model for joint lemmatization and part-of-speech prediction. In *Proceedings of the Joint Conference of the 47th Annual Meeting of the ACL and the 4th International Joint Conference on Natural Language Processing of the AFNLP: Volume 1-Volume 1*, pages 486–494. Association for Computational Linguistics.

Huihsin Tseng, Daniel Jurafsky, and Christopher Manning. 2005. Morphological features help POS tagging of unknown words across language varieties. In *Proceedings of the fourth SIGHAN workshop on Chinese language processing*, pages 32–39.

# Shift-Reduce Constituency Parsing with Dynamic Programming and POS Tag Lattice

**Haitao Mi**[†]
[†]T.J. Watson Research Center
IBM
hmi@us.ibm.com

**Liang Huang**[‡†]
[‡]Queens College & Graduate Center
City University of New York
liang.huang.sh@gmail.com

## Abstract

We present the first dynamic programming (DP) algorithm for shift-reduce constituency parsing, which extends the DP idea of Huang and Sagae (2010) to context-free grammars. To alleviate the propagation of errors from part-of-speech tagging, we also extend the parser to take a tag lattice instead of a fixed tag sequence. Experiments on both English and Chinese treebanks show that our DP parser significantly improves parsing quality over non-DP baselines, and achieves the best accuracies among empirical linear-time parsers.

## 1 Introduction

Incremental parsing has gained popularity in both dependency (Nivre, 2004; Zhang and Clark, 2008) and constituency parsing (Zhu et al., 2013; Wang and Xue, 2014). However, the greedy or beam search algorithms used in these parsers can only explore a tiny fraction of trees among exponentially many candidates. To alleviate this problem, Huang and Sagae (2010) propose a dynamic programming (DP) algorithm, reducing the search space to a polynomial size by merging equivalent states. This idea has been extended by Kuhlmann et al. (2011) and Cohen et al. (2011) to other dependency parsing paradigms.

In constituency parsing, however, DP has not yet been applied to incremental parsing, and the bigger search space in constituency parsing suggests a potentially even bigger advantage by DP. However, with unary rules and more-than-binary branchings, constituency parsing presents challenges not found in dependency parsing that must be addressed before applying DP. Thus, we first present an odd-even shift-reduce constituency parser which always finishes in same number of steps, eliminating the complicated asynchronicity issue in previous work (Zhu et al., 2013; Wang and Xue, 2014), and then develop dynamic programming on top of that. Secondly, to alleviate the error propagation from POS tagging, we also extends the algorithm to take a tagging sausage lattice as input, which is a compromise between pipeline and joint approaches (Hatori et al., 2011; Li et al., 2011; Wang and Xue, 2014).

Our DP parser achieves state-of-the-art performances on both Chinese and English treebanks (at 90.8% on PTB and 83.9% on CTB, the latter being the highest in literature).

## 2 Odd-Even Shift-Reduce CFG Parser

One major challenge in constituency parsing is unary rules. Unlike dependency parsing where shift-reduce always finishes in $2n-1$ steps, existing incremental constituency parsers (Zhu et al., 2013; Wang and Xue, 2014) reach the goal state (full parse tree) in different steps due to different number of unary rules. So we propose a new, synchronized, "odd-even" system to reach the goal in the same $4n-2$ steps. A *state* is notated $p = \langle S, Q \rangle$, where $S$ is a stack of trees ..., $s_1, s_0$, and $Q$ is a queue of word-tag pairs. At even steps (when step index is even) we can choose one of the three standard actions

- sh: shift the head of $Q$, a word-tag pair $(t, w)$, onto $S$ as a singleton tree $t(w)$;
- $\mathsf{re}^x_{\curvearrowleft}$: combine the top two trees on the stack and replace them with a new tree $x(s_1, s_0)$, $x$ being the root nonterminal, headed on $s_0$;
- $\mathsf{re}^x_{\curvearrowright}$: similar to $\mathsf{re}^x_{\curvearrowleft}$ but headed on $s_1$;

and at odd steps we can choose two new actions:



*Human Language Technologies: The 2015 Annual Conference of the North American Chapter of the ACL*, pages 1030–1035,
Denver, Colorado, May 31 – June 5, 2015. ©2015 Association for Computational Linguistics

input $(t_1, w_1) \dots (t_n, w_n)$

axiom $0 : \langle \epsilon, (t_1, w_1) \dots (t_n, w_n) \rangle : 0$

$$\textsf{sh} \quad \frac{l : \langle S, (t,w)|Q \rangle : c}{l{+}1 : \langle S|t(w), Q \rangle : c{+}c_{\textsf{sh}}} \; l \text{ is even}$$

$$\textsf{re}^x_{\curvearrowleft} \quad \frac{l : \langle S|s_1|s_0, Q \rangle : c}{l{+}1 : \langle S|x(s_1, s_0), Q \rangle : c{+}c_{\textsf{re}^x_{\curvearrowleft}}} \; l \text{ is even}$$

$$\textsf{un}^x \quad \frac{l : \langle S|s_0, Q \rangle : c}{l{+}1 : \langle S|x(s_0), Q \rangle : c{+}c_{\textsf{un}^x}} \; l \text{ is odd}$$

$$\textsf{st} \quad \frac{l : \langle S|s_0, Q \rangle : c}{l{+}1 : \langle S|s_0, Q \rangle : c{+}c_{\textsf{st}}} \; l \text{ is odd}$$

goal $2(2n-1) : \langle s_0, \epsilon \rangle : c$

Figure 1: Shift-reduce system, omitting $\textsf{re}^x_{\curvearrowright}$. $c$ is the model score, and $c_{\textsf{sh}}$, $c_{\textsf{re}^x_{\curvearrowleft}}$, etc. are the action scores.

- $\textsf{un}^x$: replace $s_0$ with a new tree $x(s_0)$ with $x$ being the root nonterminal;
- $\textsf{st}$: no action.

Figure 1 shows the deductive system. Note that we alternate between standard shift-reduce actions in even steps and unary actions ($\textsf{un}^x$ or $\textsf{st}$) in odd steps, and the first action must be $\textsf{sh}$, followed by a $\textsf{un}^x$ or $\textsf{st}$, and followed by another $\textsf{sh}$. Continuing this procedure, we can always achieve the goal in $2(2n-1)$ steps.

In practice, we have larger than two-way rules and multi-level unary rules, so we binarize them and collapse multi-level unary rules into one level, for example,

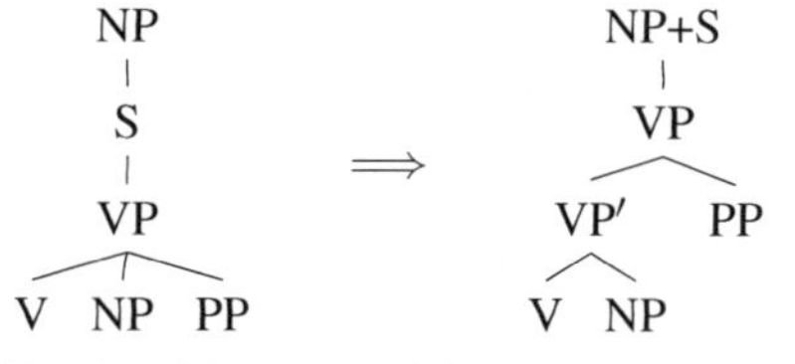


Following Huang and Sagae (2010), we represent **feature templates** as functions $\mathbf{f}(\cdot,\cdot)$ on stack $S$ and queue $Q$. Table 1 shows the 43 feature templates we use in this paper, all adopted from Zhu et al. (2013). They are combinations of the 32 **atomic features** $\tilde{\mathbf{f}}(S, Q)$ (e.g. $s_0$.t and $s_0$.c denote the head tag and syntactic category of tree $s_0$, resp., and $s_0$.lc.w is the head word of its leftmost child).

$$\textsf{sh} \quad \frac{l : \langle S, (t,w)|Q \rangle : (c, v)}{l{+}1 : \langle S|t(w), Q \rangle : (c{+}c_{\textsf{sh}}, 0)} \; l \text{ is even}$$

$$\textsf{re}^x_{\curvearrowleft} \quad \frac{\overset{\text{state } p:}{l' : \langle S'|s'_1, Q' \rangle : (c', v')} \quad \overset{\text{state } q:}{l : \langle S|s_1|s_0, Q \rangle : (c, v)}}{l{+}1 : \langle S'|x(s'_1, s_0), Q \rangle : (c'{+}v{+}\delta, v'{+}v{+}\delta)} \; l \text{ and } l' \text{ are even, } p \in \pi(q)$$

$$\textsf{un}^x \quad \frac{l : \langle S|s_0, Q \rangle : (c, v)}{l{+}1 : \langle S|x(s_0), Q \rangle : (c{+}c_{\textsf{un}^x}, v + c_{\textsf{un}^x})} \; l \text{ is odd}$$

Figure 2: DP shift-reduce, omitting $\textsf{re}^x_{\curvearrowright}$ and $\textsf{st}$. $c$ and $v$ are prefix and inside scores, and $\delta = c_{\textsf{sh}}(p) + c_{\textsf{re}^x_{\curvearrowleft}}(q)$. State equivalence is defined below in Section 3.

## 3 Dynamic Programming

The key idea towards DP is the merging of equivalent states, after which the stacks are organized in a "graph-structured stack" (GSS)(Tomita, 1988). Following Huang and Sagae (2010), "equivalent states" $\sim$ in a same beam are defined by the atomic features $\tilde{\mathbf{f}}(S, Q)$ and the span of $s_0$:

$$\langle S, Q \rangle \sim \langle S', Q' \rangle$$
$$\Leftrightarrow \tilde{\mathbf{f}}(S, Q) = \tilde{\mathbf{f}}(S', Q') \text{ and } s_0.span = s'_0.span.$$

Similarly, for each state $p$, $\pi(p)$ is a set of **predictor states**, each of which can be combined with $p$ in a $\textsf{re}^x_{\curvearrowleft}$ or $\textsf{re}^x_{\curvearrowright}$ action. For each action, we have different operations on $\pi(p)$. If a state $p$ makes a $\textsf{sh}$ action and generates a state $p'$, then $\pi(p') = \{p\}$. If two shifted states $p'$ and $p''$ are equivalent, $p' \sim p''$, we merge $\pi(p')$ and $\pi(p'')$. If a state $p$ makes a reduce ($\textsf{re}^x_{\curvearrowleft}$ or $\textsf{re}^x_{\curvearrowright}$) action, $p$ tries to combine with every $p' \in \pi(p)$, and each combination generates a state $r$ with $\pi(r) = \pi(p')$. If two reduced states are equivalent, we only keep one predictor states, as their predictor states are identical. If a state $p$ fires an $\textsf{un}^x$ or a $\textsf{st}$ action resulting in a state $u$, we copy the predictor states $\pi(u) = \pi(p)$. Similar to reduce actions, if two resulting states after applying an $\textsf{un}^x$ or a $\textsf{st}$ action are equivalent, we only keep the best one with highest score (the recombined ones are only useful for searching $k$-best trees).

| feature templates $\mathbf{f}(S, Q)$ | | | | | | |
|---|---|---|---|---|---|---|
| unigrams | $s_0.\mathsf{t} \circ s_0.\mathsf{c}$ | $s_0.\mathsf{w} \circ s_0.\mathsf{c}$ | $s_1.\mathsf{t} \circ s_1.\mathsf{c}$ | $s_1.\mathsf{w} \circ s_1.\mathsf{c}$ | $s_2.\mathsf{t} \circ s_2.\mathsf{c}$ | $s_2.\mathsf{w} \circ s_2.\mathsf{c}$ |
| | $s_3.\mathsf{t} \circ s_3.\mathsf{c}$ | $q_0.\mathsf{w} \circ q_0.\mathsf{t}$ | $q_1.\mathsf{w} \circ q_1.\mathsf{t}$ | $q_2.\mathsf{w} \circ q_2.\mathsf{t}$ | $q_3.\mathsf{w} \circ q_3.\mathsf{t}$ | $s_0.\mathsf{lc.w} \circ s_0.\mathsf{lc.c}$ |
| | $s_0.\mathsf{rc.w} \circ s_0.\mathsf{rc.c}$ | $s_0.\mathsf{u.w} \circ s_0.\mathsf{u.c}$ | $s_1.\mathsf{lc.w} \circ s_1.\mathsf{lc.c}$ | $s_1.\mathsf{rc.w} \circ s_1.\mathsf{rc.c}$ | $s_1.\mathsf{u.w} \circ s_1.\mathsf{u.c}$ | |
| bigrams | $s_0.\mathsf{w} \circ s_1.\mathsf{w}$ | $s_0.\mathsf{w} \circ s_1.\mathsf{c}$ | $s_0.\mathsf{c} \circ s_1.\mathsf{w}$ | $s_0.\mathsf{c} \circ s_1.\mathsf{c}$ | $s_0.\mathsf{w} \circ q_0.\mathsf{w}$ | $s_0.\mathsf{w} \circ q_0.\mathsf{t}$ |
| | $s_0.\mathsf{c} \circ q_0.\mathsf{w}$ | $s_0.\mathsf{c} \circ q_0.\mathsf{t}$ | $q_0.\mathsf{w} \circ q_1.\mathsf{w}$ | $q_0.\mathsf{w} \circ q_1.\mathsf{t}$ | $q_0.\mathsf{t} \circ q_1.\mathsf{w}$ | $q_0.\mathsf{t} \circ q_1.\mathsf{t}$ |
| | $s_1.\mathsf{w} \circ q_0.\mathsf{w}$ | $s_1.\mathsf{w} \circ q_0.\mathsf{t}$ | $s_1.\mathsf{c} \circ q_0.\mathsf{w}$ | $s_1.\mathsf{c} \circ q_0.\mathsf{t}$ | | |
| | $s_0.\mathsf{c} \circ s_0.\mathsf{lc.c} \circ s_0.\mathsf{rc.c} \circ s_1.\mathsf{c}$ | | $s_0.\mathsf{c} \circ s_0.\mathsf{lc.c} \circ s_0.\mathsf{rc.c} \circ s_1.\mathsf{c}$ | | | |
| trigrams | $s_0.\mathsf{c} \circ s_1.\mathsf{c} \circ s_2.\mathsf{c}$ | | $s_0.\mathsf{w} \circ s_1.\mathsf{c} \circ s_2.\mathsf{c}$ | | $s_0.\mathsf{c} \circ s_1.\mathsf{w} \circ q_0.\mathsf{t}$ | |
| | $s_0.\mathsf{c} \circ s_1.\mathsf{c} \circ s_2.\mathsf{w}$ | | $s_0.\mathsf{c} \circ s_1.\mathsf{c} \circ q_0.\mathsf{t}$ | | $s_0.\mathsf{w} \circ s_1.\mathsf{c} \circ q_0.\mathsf{t}$ | |
| | $s_0.\mathsf{c} \circ s_1.\mathsf{w} \circ q_0.\mathsf{t}$ | | $s_0.\mathsf{c} \circ s_1.\mathsf{c} \circ q_0.\mathsf{w}$ | | | |

Table 1: All feature templates (43 templates based on 32 atomic features), taken from Zhu et al. (2013). $s_i$.c, $s_i$.w and $s_i$.t denote the syntactic label, the head word, and the head tag of $s_i$. $s_i$.lc.w means the head word of the left child of $s_i$. $s_i$.u.w means the head word of the unary root $s_i$. $q_i$.w and $q_i$.t denote the word and the tag of $q_i$.

input $(T_1, w_1)...(T_n, w_n)$

axioms $0 : \langle \epsilon, (t, w_1)...(T_n, w_n)(\{\text{</s>}\}, \text{</s>}) \rangle : 0, \forall\, t \in T_1$

$$\mathsf{sh}\ \frac{l : \langle S,\ (t, w)|(T', w')|Q \rangle : (c, v)}{l{+}1 : \langle S|t(w),\ (t', w')|Q \rangle : (c{+}c_{\mathsf{sh}}, 0)}\ \begin{array}{l} t' \in T', \\ l \text{ is even} \end{array}$$

Figure 3: Extended shift-reduce deductive system with tagging sausage lattice, only showing sh.

In order to compute all the scores in GSS, for each state $p$, we calculate the prefix score, $c$, which is the total cost of the best action sequence from the initial state to the end of state $p$, and the inside score $v$, which is the score since the last shift (Figure 2).

The new mechanism beyond Huang and Sagae (2010) is the non-trivial dynamic programming treatment of unary actions ($\mathsf{un}^x$ and st), which is not found in dependency parsing. Note that the score calculation is quite different from shift in the sense that unary actions are more like reduces.

## 4 Incorporating Tag Lattices

It is easy to extend our deductive system to take tagging sausage lattices as input. The key difference is that the tag $t$ associated with each word in the input sequence becomes a set of tags $T$. Thus, in the sh action, we split the state with all the possible tags $t'$ in the tagset $T'$ for the **second** word on the queue. Figure 3 shows the deductive system, where we only change the sh action, input and axiom. For simplicity reasons we only present one word look ahead (we just need to know the tag of the first word on the queue), but in practice, we use a look ahead of 4 words ($q_0..q_3$, see Table 1), so each shift actually splits the tagset of the 5th word on the queue ($q_4$).

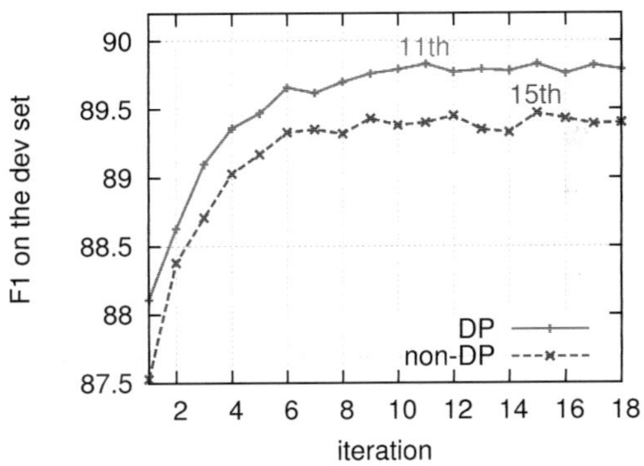


Figure 4: The learning curves of non-DP and DP parsers on the development set. DP achieves the best performance at 11th iteration with 89.8%, while non-DP gets its optimal iteration at 15th with a lower F1 89.5%.

## 5 Experiments

We evaluate our parsers on both Penn English Treebank (PTB) and Chinese Treebank (CTB). For PTB, we use sections 02-21 as the training, section 24 as the dev set, and section 23 as the test. For CTB, we use the version of 5.1, articles 001-270 and 440-1151 as the training data, articles 301-325 as the dev set, and articles 271-300 as the test set.

Besides training with gold POS tags, we add $k$-best automatic tagging results to the training set using a MaxEnt model with ten-way jackknifing (Collins, 2000). And we automatically tag the dev and test sets with $k$-best tagging sequences us-

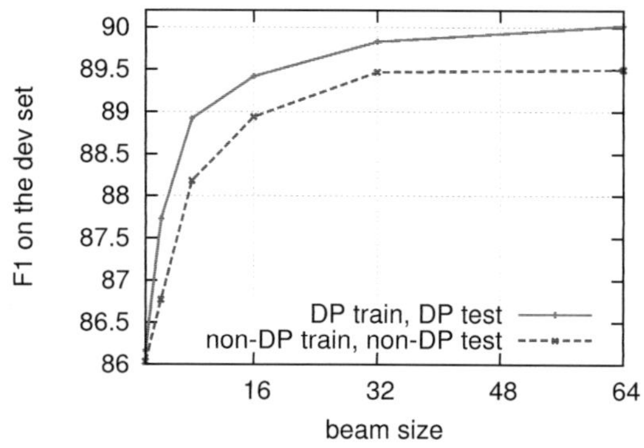


Figure 5: The F1 curves of non-DP and DP parsers (train and test consistently) on the dev set.

| | LR | LP | F1 | comp. |
|---|---|---|---|---|
| Collins (1999) | 88.1 | 88.3 | 88.2 | $O(n^5)$ |
| Charniak (2000) | 89.5 | 89.9 | 89.5 | $O(n^5)$ † |
| Carreras (2008) | 90.7 | 91.4 | 91.1 | $O(n^4)$ ‡ |
| Petrov (2007) | 90.1 | 90.2 | 90.1 | $O(n^3)$ † |
| Ratnaparkhi (1997) | 86.3 | 87.5 | 86.9 | |
| Sagae (2006) | 87.8 | 88.1 | 87.9 | $O(n)$ |
| Zhu (2013) | 90.2 | 90.7 | 90.4 | |
| **non-DP** | 90.3 | 90.4 | 90.3 | $O(n)$ |
| **DP** | **90.7** | **90.9** | **90.8** | |

Table 2: Final Results on English (PTB) test set (sec23). †The empirical complexities for Charniak and Petrov are $O(n^{2.5})$ and $O(n^{2.4})$, resp., ‡but Carreras is exact $O(n^4)$.

| | LR | LP | F1 | POS |
|---|---|---|---|---|
| Charniak (2000) | 79.6 | 82.1 | 80.8 | - |
| Petrov (2007) | 81.9 | 84.8 | 83.3 | - |
| Zhu (2013) | 82.1 | 84.3 | 83.2 | - |
| Wang (2014) (1-best POS) | 80.3 | 80.0 | 80.1 | 94.0 |
| Wang (2014) (joint) | 82.9 | 84.2 | 83.6 | 95.5 |
| **non-DP** (1-best POS) | 80.7 | 80.5 | 80.6 | 94.5 |
| **non-DP** (20-best POS) | 83.3 | 83.2 | 83.2 | 95.5 |
| **DP** (20-best POS) | **83.6** | **84.2** | **83.9** | **95.6** |

Table 3: Results on Chinese (CTB) 5.1 test set.

ing the MaxEnt POS tagger (at 97.1% accuracy on English, and 94.5% on Chinese) trained on the training set. We set $k$ to 20 for English. And we run two sets of experiments, 1-best vs. 20-best, for Chinese to address the tagging issue. We train our parsers using "max-violation perceptron" (Huang et al., 2012) (which has been shown to converge much faster than "early-update" of Collins and Roark (2004)) with minibatch parallelization (Zhao and Huang, 2013) on the head-out binarized and unary-collapsed training set. We finally debinarize the trees to recover the collapsed unary rules.

We evaluate parser performance with EVALB including labeled precision (LP), labeled recall (LR), and bracketing F1. We use a beam size of 32, and pick the optimal iteration number based on the performances on the dev set.

Our baseline is the shift-reduce parser without state recombination (henceforth "non-DP"), and our dynamic programming parser (henceforth "DP") is the extension of the baseline.

### 5.1 Learning Curves and Search Quality

Figure 4 shows the learning curves on the PTB dev set. With a same beam width, DP parser achieves a better performance (89.8%, peaking at the 11th iteration) and converges faster than non-DP. Picking the optimal iterations for DP and non-DP models, we test each with various beam size, and plot the F1 curves in Figure 5. Again, DP is always better than non-DP, with 0.5% difference at beam of 64.

### 5.2 Final Results on English

Table 2 shows the final results on the PTB test set. The last column shows the empirical time complexity. Our baseline parser achieves a competitive score, which is higher than Berkeley even with a linear time complexity, and is comparable to Zhu et al. (2013). Our DP parser improves the F1 score by 0.5 points over the non-DP, and achieves the best F1 score among empirical linear-time parsers.

### 5.3 Sausage Lattice Parsing

To alleviate the propagation of errors from POS tagging, we run sausage lattice parsing on both Chinese and English, where Chinese tagging accuracy significantly lag behind English.

Table 3 shows the F1 score and POS tagging accuracy of all parsing models on the Chinese 5.1 test set. Our MaxEnt POS tagger achieves an accuracy of 94.5% on 1-best outputs, and an oracle score of 97.1% on 20-best results. The average number of tags for each word in the 20-best list is 1.1.

The joint tagging and parsing approach of Wang and Xue (2014) improves the F1 score from 80.1% to 83.6% (see lines 4 and 5). We instead use sausage lattices, a much cheaper way. The non-DP (1-best POS) and non-DP (20-best POS) lines show the effectiveness of using sausage lattices (+1.1 for tagging and +2.6 for parsing). As Wang and Xue (2014) is a non-DP model, it is comparable to our non-DP results. With the help of 20-best tagging lattices, we achieve the same tagging accuracy at 95.5%, but still 0.4 worse on the F1 score than the joint model. It suggests that we need a larger $k$ to catch up the gap. But our DP model boosts the performance further to the best score at 83.9% with a similar set of features.

The last two lines (non-DP and DP) in Table 2 show our English lattice parsing results. So we run another baseline with the non-DP English parser on 1-best POS tags, and the baseline achieves a tagging accuracy at 97.11 and an F1 score at 90.1. Comparing to the tagging accuracy (97.15) and F1 score (90.3) of our non-DP lattice parser, sausage lattice parsing doesn't help the tagging accuracy, but helps parsing a little by 0.2 points. The statistics show that 2 percent of POS tags in the lattice parsing result are different from the baseline, and those differences lead to a slight improvement on parsing.

## 6 Conclusions

In this paper, we present a dynamic programming algorithm based on graph-structured stack (GSS) for shift-reduce constituency parsing, and extend the algorithm to take tagging sausage lattices as input. Experiments on both English and Chinese treebanks show that our DP parser outperforms almost all other parsers except of Carreras et al. (2008), which runs in a much higher time complexity.

## Acknowledgment

We thank the anonymous reviewers for comments. Haitao Mi is supported by DARPA HR0011-12-C-0015 (BOLT), and Liang Huang is supported by DARPA FA8750-13-2-0041 (DEFT), NSF IIS-1449278, and a Google Faculty Research Award. The views and findings in this paper are those of the authors and are not endorsed by the DARPA.

## References

Xavier Carreras, Michael Collins, and Terry Koo. 2008. Tag, dynamic programming, and the perceptron for efficient, feature-rich parsing. In *Proceedings of CoNLL 2008*.

Eugene Charniak. 2000. A maximum-entropy-inspired parser. In *Proceedings of NAACL*.

Shay B. Cohen, Carlos Gómez-Rodríguez, and Giorgio Satta. 2011. Exact inference for generative probabilistic non-projective dependency parsing. In *Proceedings of the Conference on Empirical Methods in Natural Language Processing*.

Michael Collins and Brian Roark. 2004. Incremental parsing with the perceptron algorithm. In *Proceedings of ACL*.

Michael Collins. 1999. *Head-Driven Statistical Models for Natural Language Parsing*. Ph.D. thesis, University of Pennsylvania.

Michael Collins. 2000. Discriminative reranking for natural language parsing. In *Proceedings of ICML*, pages 175–182.

Jun Hatori, Takuya Matsuzaki, Yusuke Miyao, and Jun'ichi Tsujii. 2011. Incremental joint pos tagging and dependency parsing in chinese. In *IJCNLP*.

Liang Huang and Kenji Sagae. 2010. Dynamic programming for linear-time incremental parsing. In *Proceedings of ACL 2010*.

Liang Huang, Suphan Fayong, and Yang Guo. 2012. Structured perceptron with inexact search. In *Proceedings of NAACL*.

Marco Kuhlmann, Carlos Gmez-Rodrguez, and Giorgio Satta. 2011. Dynamic programming algorithms for transition-based dependency parsers. In *Proceedings of ACL*.

Zhenghua Li, Min Zhang, Wanxiang Che, Ting Liu, Wenliang Chen, and Haizhou Li. 2011. Joint models for chinese pos tagging and dependency parsing. In *Proceedings of EMNLP*, pages 1180–1191.

Joakim Nivre. 2004. Incrementality in deterministic dependency parsing. In *Incremental Parsing: Bringing Engineering and Cognition Together. Workshop at ACL-2004*, Barcelona.

Slav Petrov and Dan Klein. 2007. Improved inference for unlexicalized parsing. In *Proceedings of HLT-NAACL*.

Adwait Ratnaparkhi. 1997. A linear observed time statistical parser based on maximum entropy models. In *Proceedings of EMNLP*, pages 1–10.

Kenji Sagae and Alon Lavie. 2006. A best-first probabilistic shift-reduce parser. In *Proceedings of ACL (poster)*.

Masaru Tomita. 1988. Graph-structured stack and natural language parsing. In *Proceedings of the 26th annual meeting on Association for Computational Linguistics*, pages 249–257, Morristown, NJ, USA. Association for Computational Linguistics.

Zhiguo Wang and Nianwen Xue. 2014. Joint pos tagging and transition-based constituent parsing in chinese with non-local features. In *Proceedings of ACL*.

Yue Zhang and Stephen Clark. 2008. A tale of two parsers: investigating and combining graph-based and transition-based dependency parsing using beam-search. In *Proceedings of EMNLP*.

Kai Zhao and Liang Huang. 2013. Minibatch and parallelization for online large margin structured learning. In *Proceedings of NAACL 2013*.

Muhua Zhu, Yue Zhang, Wenliang Chen, Min Zhang, and Jingbo Zhu. 2013. Fast and accurate shift-reduce constituent parsing. In *Proceedings of ACL 2013*.

# Unsupervised Code-Switching for Multilingual Historical Document Transcription

**Dan Garrette*** **Hannah Alpert-Abrams†** **Taylor Berg-Kirkpatrick‡** **Dan Klein‡**

*Department of Computer Science, University of Texas at Austin, dhg@cs.utexas.edu
†Comparative Literature Program, University of Texas at Austin, halperta@gmail.com
‡Computer Science Division, University of California at Berkeley, {tberg, klein}@cs.berkeley.edu

## Abstract

Transcribing documents from the printing press era, a challenge in its own right, is more complicated when documents interleave multiple languages—a common feature of 16th century texts. Additionally, many of these documents precede consistent orthographic conventions, making the task even harder. We extend the state-of-the-art historical OCR model of Berg-Kirkpatrick et al. (2013) to handle word-level code-switching between multiple languages. Further, we enable our system to handle spelling variability, including now-obsolete shorthand systems used by printers. Our results show average relative character error reductions of 14% across a variety of historical texts.

## 1 Introduction

Transcribing documents printed on historical printing presses poses a number of challenges for OCR technology. Berg-Kirkpatrick et al. (2013) presented an unsupervised system, called *Ocular*, that handles the types of noise that are characteristic of pre-20th century documents and uses a fixed monolingual language model to guide learning. While this approach is highly effective on English documents from the 18th and 19th centuries, problems arise when it is applied to older documents that feature code-switching between multiple languages and obsolete orthographic characteristics.

In this work, we address these issues by developing a new language model for *Ocular*. First, to handle multilingual documents, we replace *Ocular's* simple $n$-gram language model with an unsupervised model of intrasentential code-switching that allows joint transcription and word-level language identification. Second, to handle orthographic variation, we provide an interface that allows individuals familiar with relevant languages to guide the language model with targeted orthographic information. As a result, our system handles inconsistent spelling, punctuation, and diacritic usage, as well as now-obsolete shorthand conventions used by printers.

We evaluate our model using documents from the *Primeros Libros* project, a digital archive of books printed in the Americas prior to 1601 (Dolan, 2012). These texts, written in European and indigenous languages, often feature as many as three languages on a single page, with code-switching occurring on the chapter, sentence, and word level. Orthographic variations are pervasive throughout, and are particularly difficult with indigenous languages, for which writing systems were still being developed.

Our results show improvements across a range of documents, yielding an average 14% relative character error reduction over the previous state-of-the-art, with reductions as high as 27% on particular texts.

## 2 Data

Writing during the early modern period in Europe was characterized by increasing use of vernacular languages alongside Latin, Greek, and Hebrew. In the colonies, this was matched by the development of grammars and alphabetic writing systems for indigenous languages (see Eisenstein (1979) and Mignolo (1995)). In all cases, orthographies were regionally variable and subject to the limited resources of the printing houses; this is particularly true in the Americas, where resources were scarce,



*Human Language Technologies: The 2015 Annual Conference of the North American Chapter of the ACL*, pages 1036–1041,
Denver, Colorado, May 31 – June 5, 2015. 

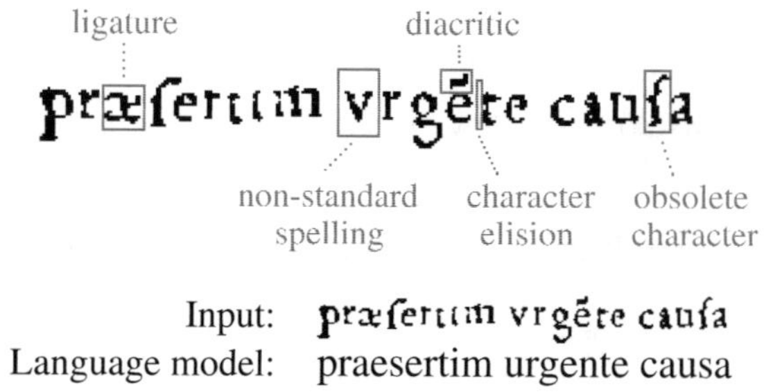


Figure 1: An example OCR input showing the original image and an example of an equivalent modernized text similar to data used to train the LM.

and where indigenous-language orthographies were first being developed (Baddeley and Voeste, 2013).

The 349 digital facsimiles in the *Primeros Libros* collection are characteristic of this trend. Produced during the first century of Spanish colonization, they represent the introduction of printing technology into the Americas, and reflect the (sometimes conflicted) priorities of the nascent colony, from religious orthodoxy to conversion and education.

For our experiments, we focus on multilingual documents in three languages: Spanish, Latin, and Nahuatl. As Berg-Kirkpatrick et al. (2013) show, a language model built on contemporaneous data will perform better than modern data. For this reason, we collected 15–17th century texts from Project Gutenberg,[1] producing Spanish and Latin corpora of more than one million characters each. Due to its relative scarcity, we augmented the Nahuatl corpus with a private collection of transcribed colonial documents.

## 3 Baseline System

The starting point for our work is the *Ocular* system described by Berg-Kirkpatrick et al. (2013). The fonts used in historical documents are usually unknown and can vary drastically from document to document. *Ocular* deals with this problem by learning the font in an unsupervised fashion – directly from the input historical document. In order to accomplish this, the system uses a specialized generative model that reasons about the main sources of variation and noise in historical printing. These include the shapes of the character glyphs, the horizontal spacing between characters, and the vertical offset of each character from a common baseline. Additionally, since documents exhibit variable inking levels (where individual characters are often faded or smeared with blotched ink) the system also models the amount of ink applied to each type piece.

The generative process operates as follows. First, a sequence of character tokens is generated by a character $n$-gram language model. Then, bounding boxes for each character token are generated, conditioned on the character type, followed by vertical offsets and inking levels. Finally, the pixels in each bounding box are generated, conditioned on the character types, vertical offsets, and inking levels. In this work, we focus on improving the language model, and leave the rest of the generative process untouched.

## 4 Language Model

We present a new language model for *Ocular* that is designed to handle issues that are characteristic of older historical documents: code-switching and orthographic variability. We extend the conventional character $n$-gram language model and its training procedure to deal with each of these problems in turn.

### 4.1 Code-Switching

Because *Ocular*'s character $n$-gram language model (LM) is fixed and monolithic, even when it is trained on corpora from multiple languages, it treats all text as a single "language"—a multilingual blur at best. As a result, the system cannot model the fact that different contiguous blocks of text correspond to specific languages and thus follow specific statistical patterns. In order to transcribe documents that feature intrasentential code-switching, we replace *Ocular*'s simple $n$-gram LM with one that directly models code-switching by representing language segmentation as a latent variable.

Our code-switching LM generates a sequence of pairs $(e_i, \ell_i)$ where $e_i$ is the current character and $\ell_i$ is the current language. The sequence of languages $\ell_i$ specifies the segmentation of generated text into language regions. Our LM is built from several component models: First, for each language type $\ell$, we incorporate a standard monolingual character $n$-gram model trained on data from language $\ell$. The com-

[1] http://www.gutenberg.org/

ponent model corresponding to language $\ell$ is called $P_\ell^{\text{CHAR}}$. Second, our LM also incorporates a model that governs code-switching between languages. We call this model $P^{\text{LANG}}$. The generative process for our LM works as follows. For the $i$th character position, we first generate the current language $\ell_i$ conditioned on the previous character $e_{i-1}$ and the previous language $\ell_{i-1}$ using $P^{\text{LANG}}$. Then, conditioned on the current language $l_i$ and the previous $n-1$ characters, we generate the current character $e_i$ using $P_{\ell_i}^{\text{CHAR}}$. This means that the probability of pair $(e_i, \ell_i)$ given its context is computed as:

$$P^{\text{LANG}}(\ell_i \mid e_{i-1}, \ell_{i-1}) \cdot P_{\ell_i}^{\text{CHAR}}(e_i \mid e_{i-1} \dots e_{i-n+1})$$

We parameterize $P^{\text{LANG}}$ in a way that enforces two constraints. First, to ensure that each word is assigned a single language, we only allow language transitions for characters directly following whitespace (a space character or a page margin, unless the character follows a line-end hyphen). Second, to resist overly frequent code-switching (and encourage longer spans), we let a Bernoulli parameter $\kappa$ specify the probability of choosing to draw a new language at a word boundary (instead of deterministically staying in the same language). By setting $\kappa$ low, we indicate a strong belief that language switches should be infrequent, while still allowing a switch if sufficient evidence is found in the image.[2] Finally, we parameterize the frequency of each language in the text. Specifically, for each language $\ell$, a multinomial parameter $\theta_\ell$ specifies the probability of transitioning to $\ell$ when you draw a new language. We learn this group of multinomial parameters, $\theta_\ell$ for each language, in an unsupervised fashion, and in doing so, adapt to the proportions of languages found in the particular input document. Thus, using our parameterization, the probability of transitioning from language $\ell$ to $\ell'$, given previous character $e$, is:

$$P^{\text{LANG}}(\ell' \mid e, \ell) = \begin{cases} (1-\kappa) + \kappa \cdot \theta_{\ell'} & \text{if } e = \textit{space} \text{ and } \ell = \ell' \\ \kappa \cdot \theta_{\ell'} & \text{if } e = \textit{space} \text{ and } \ell \neq \ell' \\ 1 & \text{if } e \neq \textit{space} \text{ and } \ell = \ell' \\ 0 & \text{if } e \neq \textit{space} \text{ and } \ell \neq \ell' \end{cases}$$

[2] We use $\kappa = 10^{-6}$ across all experiments.

| original | → | replacement |
|---|---|---|
| à | | a |
| á | | a |
| que | | q̃ |
| per | | p̃ |
| ce | | ze |
| x | | j |
| j | | x |
| an | | ã |
| ⟨space⟩h | | ⟨space⟩ |
| be | | ve |
| u | | v |
| v | | u |
| oracion | | or̃on |

Table 1: An example subset of the orthographic replacement rules for Spanish.

Finally, because our code-switching LM uses multiple separate language-specific $n$-gram models $P_\ell^{\text{CHAR}}$, we are able to maintain a distinct set of valid characters for each language. By restricting each language's model to the set of characters in the corpus for that language, we can push the model away from incompatible languages during transcription if it is confident about certain rare characters, and limit the search space by reducing the number of character combinations considered for any given position. We also include, for all languages, a set of punctuation symbols such as ¶ and § that appear in printed books but not in the LM training data.

### 4.2 Orthographic Variability

The component monolingual $n$-gram LMs must be trained on monolingual corpora in their respective languages. However, due to the lack of codified orthographic conventions concerning spelling, diacritic usage, and spacing, compounded by the liberal use of now-obsolete shorthand notations by printers, statistics gleaned from available modern corpora provide a poor representation of the language used in the printed documents. Even 16th century texts on Project Gutenberg tend to be written, for the benefit of the reader, using modern spellings. The disconnect between the orthography of the original documents and modern texts can be seen in Figure 1. To address these issues, we introduced an interface for

| author<br>pub. year | *Gante*<br>1553 | | *Anunciación*<br>1565 | | *Sahagún*<br>1583 | | *Rincón*<br>1595 | | *Bautista*<br>1600 | | **Macro Average** | | |
|---|---|---|---|---|---|---|---|---|---|---|---|---|---|
| | CER | WER | CER | WER | CER | WER | CER | WER | CER | WER | CER | WER | WER w.p. |
| *Ocular* | 13.7 | 55.9 | 15.7 | 53.6 | 10.8 | 44.3 | 11.6 | 38.4 | 9.7 | 25.7 | 12.3 | 43.6 | 56.6 |
| +code-switch | **12.8** | **55.0** | 14.6 | 53.8 | 9.6 | 38.7 | 10.7 | 35.4 | 8.8 | 24.5 | 11.3 | 41.5 | 53.5 |
| +orth. var. | 13.5 | 55.3 | **14.1** | **51.6** | **8.4** | **34.9** | **9.5** | **31.0** | **7.1** | **18.2** | **10.5** | **38.2** | **51.0** |

Table 2: Experimental results for each book, and average across all books. Columns show Character Error Rate (CER) or Word Error Rate (WER; excluding punctuation). The final column gives the average WER *including* punctuation (*w.p.*). The *Ocular* row is the previous state-of-the-art: Berg-Kirkpatrick et al. (2013). The second row uses our code-switching model, and the third additionally handles orthographic variability.

| | |
|---|---|
| *Gan.* (1553) | mõtlacatilia:ynica facramento Baptif- |
| *Anu.* (1565) | ¶ Aicnoneltoquitia ynoios |
| *Sah.* (1583) | Yoan oquilhui in Emperador, in tlaça |
| *Rin.* (1595) | ction.v.g.tetlaçotlaliztli.amatio, vel, |
| *Bau.* (1600) | ſſimo, hæc fupra dictus doctor Medina. Mas |

Table 3: An example line from each test book.

incorporating orthographic variability into the training procedure for the component LMs.

For our experiments, we built Latin, Nahuatl, and Spanish variability rulebanks by asking language experts to identify spelling anomalies from among several sample pages from *Primeros Libros* documents, and specify *rewrite rules* that map modern spellings back to variant spellings; we also drew on data from paleographic textbooks. Example rules can be seen in Table 1. These rules are used to rewrite corpus text before the LMs are trained; for instance, every $n$th occurrence of *en* in the Spanish corpus might be rewritten as *ẽ*. This approach reintroduces historically accurate orthographic variability into the LM.

## 5 Experiments

We compare to *Ocular*, the state of the art for historical OCR.[3] Since *Ocular* only supports monolingual English OCR, we added support for alternative alphabets, including diacritics and ligatures, and trained a single mixed-language model on a combined Spanish/Latin/Nahuatl corpus.

We evaluate our model on five different books from the *Primeros Libros* collection, representing a variety of printers, presses, typefaces, and authors (Table 3). Each book features code-switching between Spanish, Latin, and Nahuatl. For each book, a font was trained on ten (untranscribed) pages using unsupervised learning procedure described by Berg-Kirkpatrick et al. (2013). The font was evaluated on a separate set of ten pages, manually transcribed.[4]

## 6 Results and Analysis

Our overall results (Table 2) show improvements on every book in our evaluation, achieving as high as 29% relative word-error (WER) reduction.

Replacing *Ocular*'s single mixed-language LM with our unsupervised code-switch model results in immediate improvements. An example of transcription output, including the language-assignments made by the model, can be seen in Figure 2.

Further improvements are seen by handling orthographic variation. Figure 3 gives an example of how a single spelling variation can lead to a cascade of transcription errors. Here, the baseline system, confused by the elision of the letter *n* in the word *mẽtira* (from *mentira*, "lie"), transcribed it with an entirely different word (*merita*, "merit"). When our handling of alternate spellings is employed, the LM has good statistics for character sequences including the character *ẽ*, and is able to decode the word correctly.

There are several explanations for the differences in results among the five evaluation books. First, the two oldest texts, *Gante* and *Anunciación*, use Gothic fonts that are more difficult to read and feature capital letters that are nearly impossible for the model to recognize (see Table 3). This contributes to the high character error rates for those books.

Second, the word error rate metric is complicated by the inconsistent use of spaces in Nahuatl writ-

[3] http://nlp.cs.berkeley.edu/projects/ocular.shtml

[4] Hyperparameters were set to be consistent with Berg-Kirkpatrick et al. (2013).

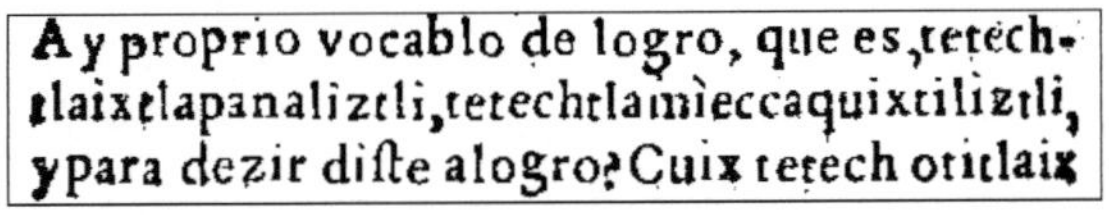
Ay proprio vocablo de logro, que es tetech-
tlaixtlapanaliztli, tetechtlamieccaquixtiliztli,
ypara dezir difte alogro? Cuix tetech otitlaix

Ay proprio vocablo de logró, que es *tetech -*
*tlaixtlapanaliztli, tetechtla miec caquixtiliztli,*
y para dezir difte a *logro? Cuix tetech otitlaix-*

Figure 2: A passage with Spanish/Nahuatl code-switching, and our model's language-coded output. (Spanish in blue; Nahuatl in red/italics.)

| | mentira | mẽtira |
|---|---|---|
| no variation handling | mentira | merita |
| handling variation | mentira | mẽtira |

Figure 3: Two variants of the same word (*mentira*), pulled from the same page of text. The form *mentira* appears in the LM training corpus, but the shorthand *mẽtira* does not. Without special handling, the model does not know that *mẽtira* is valid.

ing, falsely claiming "word" errors when all *characters* are correct. Use of spaces is not standardized across the printed books, or across the digitized LM training corpora, and is still in fact a contested issue among modern Nahuatl scholars. While it is important for the transcription process to insert spaces appropriately into the Spanish and Latin text (even when the printer left little, as with *ypara* in Figure 2), it is difficult to assess what it means for a space to be "correctly" inserted into Nahuatl text. *Rincón* and *Bautista* contain relatively less Nahuatl text and are affected less by this problem.

A final source of errors arises when our model "corrects" the original document to match modern conventions, as with diacritics, whose usages were less conventionalized at the time these books were printed. For example, the string *numero* is often transcribed as *número*, the correct modern spelling.

## 7 Conclusions and Future Work

We have demonstrated an unsupervised OCR model that improves upon Berg-Kirkpatrick et al. (2013)'s state-of-the-art *Ocular* system in order to effectively handle the code-switching and orthographic variability prevalent in historical texts. In addition to transcribing documents, our system also implicitly assigns language labels to words, allowing their usage in downstream tasks. We have also presented a new corpus, with transcriptions, for the evaluation of multilingual historical OCR systems.

Our system, as currently designed, attempts to faithfully transcribe text. However, for the purposes of indexability and searchability of these documents, it may be desirable to also produce *canonicalized* transcriptions, for example collapsing spelling variants to their modern forms. Fortunately, this can be done in our approach by running the variability rewrite rules "backward" as a post-processing step.

Further technical improvements may be made by having the system automatically attempt to bootstrap the identification of spelling variants, a process that could complement our approach through an active learning setup. Additionally, since even our relatively simple unsupervised code-switch language modeling approach yielded improvements to OCR performance, it may be justified to attempt the adaptation of more complex code-switch recognition techniques (Solorio et al., 2014).

The automatic transcription of the *Primeros Libros* collection has significant implications for scholars of the humanities interested in the role that inscription and transmission play in colonial history. For example, there are parallels between the way that the Spanish transformed indigenous languages into Latin-like writing systems (removing "noise" like phonemes that do not exist in Latin), and the way that the OCR tool transforms historical printed documents into unicode (removing "noise" like artifacts of the printing process and physical changes to the pages); in both instances, arguably important information is lost. We present some of these ideas at the American Comparative Literature Association's annual meeting, where we discuss the relationship between sixteenth century indigenous orthography and *Ocular*'s code-switching language models (Alpert-Abrams and Garrette, 2015).


## Acknowledgements

We would like to thank Stephanie Wood, Kelly McDonough, Albert Palacios, Adam Coon, and Sergio Romero, as well as Kent Norsworthy for their input, advice, and assistance on this project.

## References

Hannah Alpert-Abrams and Dan Garrette. 2015. Reading *Primeros Libros*: From archive to OCR. In *Proceedings of The Annual Meeting of the American Comparative Literature Association*.

Susan Baddeley and Anja Voeste. 2013. *Orthographies in Early Modern Europe*. De Gruyter.

Taylor Berg-Kirkpatrick and Dan Klein. 2014. Improved typesetting models for historical OCR. In *Proceedings of ACL*.

Taylor Berg-Kirkpatrick, Greg Durrett, and Dan Klein. 2013. Unsupervised transcription of historical documents. In *Proceedings of ACL*.

Thomas G. Dolan. 2012. The Primeros Libros Project. *The Hispanic Outlook in Higher Education*, 22:20–22, March.

Elizabeth L. Eisenstein. 1979. *The printing press as an agent of change*. Cambridge University Press.

Walter Mignolo. 1995. *The Darker Side of the Renaissance*. University of Michigan Press.

Thamar Solorio, Elizabeth Blair, Suraj Maharjan, Steven Bethard, Mona Diab, Mahmoud Gohneim, Abdelati Hawwari, Fahad AlGhamdi, Julia Hirschberg, Alison Chang, and Pascale Fung. 2014. Overview for the first shared task on language identification in code-switched data. In *Proceedings of The First Workshop on Computational Approaches to Code Switching*.

# Matching Citation Text and Cited Spans in Biomedical Literature: a Search-Oriented Approach

**Arman Cohan, Luca Soldaini, Nazli Goharian**
Georgetown University, Information Retrieval Lab, Computer Science Department
{arman, luca, nazli}@ir.cs.georgetown.edu

## Abstract

Citation sentences (citances) to a reference article have been extensively studied for summarization tasks. However, citances might not accurately represent the content of the cited article, as they often fail to capture the context of the reported findings and can be affected by epistemic value drift. Following the intuition behind the TAC (Text Analysis Conference) 2014 Biomedical Summarization track, we propose a system that identifies text spans in the reference article that are related to a given citance. We refer to this problem as citance-reference spans matching. We approach the problem as a retrieval task; in this paper, we detail a comparison of different citance reformulation methods and their combinations. While our results show improvement over the baseline (up to 25.9%), their absolute magnitude implies that there is ample room for future improvement.

## 1 Introduction

The size of scientific literature has increased dramatically during recent decades. In biomedical domain for example, PubMed – the largest repository of biomedical literature – contains more than 24 million articles. Thus, there is a need for concise presentation of important findings in the scientific articles being published. Text summarization of scientific articles is a method for such presentation. One obvious form of scientific summaries, is the abstract of the articles. Another type of scientific summaries relates to citance-based summaries which are summaries created using the set of citations to a reference article. This kind of summary covers some aspects of the reference article which might not be present in its abstract (Elkiss et al., 2008).

Citances often cover important and novel insights about findings or aspects of a paper that others have found interesting; thus, they capture contributions that had an impact on the research community (Elkiss et al., 2008; Qazvinian and Radev, 2008).

**Reference Article**

(Voorhoeve et al., 2006): *"These miRNAs neutralize p53-mediated CDK inhibition,* ***possibly*** *through direct inhibition of the expression of the tumor suppressor LATS2."*

**Citing Article**

(Okada et al., 2011): *"Two oncogenic miRNAs, miR-372 and miR-373,* ***directly inhibit*** *the expression of Lats2,* ***thereby*** *allowing tumorigenic growth in the presence of p53 (Voorhoeve et al., 2006)."*

Figure 1: Example of epistemic value drift from (De Waard and Maat, 2012). The claim in (Voorhoeve et al., 2006) becomes fact in (Okada et al., 2011).

In the past, many have focused on citance extraction and citance-based summarization. Example of citance extraction include (Siddharthan and Teufel, 2007), who used a machine learning approach with linguistic, lexical, statistical and positional features, and (Kaplan et al., 2009), who studied a coreference resolution based approach. Citance extraction has been also studied in the context of automatic summarization. For example, (Qazvinian and Radev, 2010) proposed a framework based on probabilistic inference to identify citances, while (Abu-Jbara and Radev, 2011) approached the problem as a classification task. In the biomedical domain, the use of citances was first studied by (Nakov et al., 2004).

While useful, citances by themselves lack the appropriate evidence to capture the exact content of the original paper, such as circumstances, data and assumptions under which certain findings were obtained. Citance-based summaries might also modify the epistemic value of a claim presented in the cited work (De Waard and Maat, 2012); that is, they might report a preliminary result or a claim as a definite fact (example in figure 1).

Recently, a new track at TAC has been introduced to explore ways to generate better citance-based



*Human Language Technologies: The 2015 Annual Conference of the North American Chapter of the ACL*, pages 1042–1048, Denver, Colorado, May 31 – June 5, 2015. 

summaries[1]. One way to achieve this, is to link citances to text spans in the reference article to obtain a more informative collection of sentences representing the reference article (figure 2). A framework designed to solve such problem requires two components: (*i*) a method to identify the most relevant spans of text in the reference text and (*ii*) a system to automatically generate a summary given a set of citances and reference spans.

In this paper, we propose an information retrieval approach designed to address the first task. We explore the impact of several query reformulation techniques – some domain independent, others tailored to biomedical literature – on the performance of the system. Furthermore, we apply combined reformulations, which yields an additional improvement over any single method (25% over the baseline).

As a related area, passage retrieval in biomedical articles has been studied in the context of the genomics track (Hersh et al., 2006; Hersh et al., 2007) and in following efforts (Urbain et al., 2008; Urbain et al., 2009; Chen et al., 2011). In these works, the goal is to find passages that relate to a given term or keyword (e.g. GeneRIF). In contrast, our system considers citances as queries, which are substantially longer than keyword-based queries and have a syntactical structure.

In summary, our contributions are: (*i*) A search-based, unsupervised (thus easily scalable to other domains) approach to citance-reference spans matching and (*ii*) adaptation of various query reformulation techniques for the citatnce-refrence span matching.

# 2 Methodology

The goal of the proposed system is to retrieve text spans from the reference paper that match the finding(s) each citance is referring to. We approach this problem as a search task. That is we consider the citance as a query and the reference text spans as documents. Then, using a retrieval model along with query reformulation, we find the most relevant text spans to a given citance. Our methodology consist of the following steps:

1. Create sentence level index from the reference article.

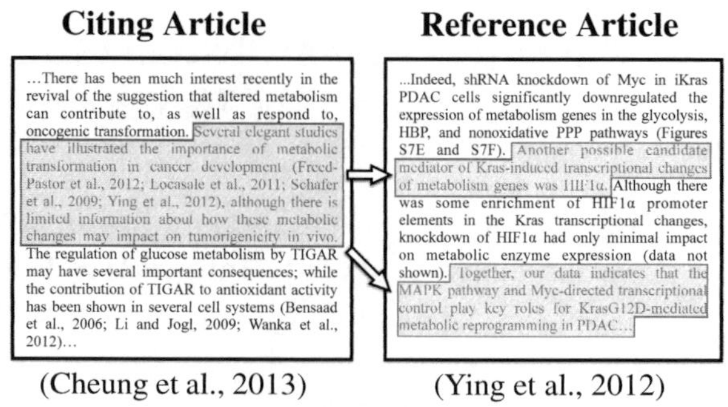


Figure 2: Example of a citance/reference article pair from the TAC training set[1]. The text in the red box on the left is referred to as the citance text, while the text in the green boxes on the right is referred to as the reference text.

2. Apply query reformulation to the given citance and retrieve the most relevant spans.
3. Rerank and merge the retrieved spans that correctly describe the citance.

We will describe each step in the following sections.

## 2.1 Creating the index

To create an index of spans, each reference article is tokenized at a sentence level using the Punkt tokenize (Kiss and Strunk, 2006). Because each relevant reference span in the reference text can be formed by several consecutive sentences (according to the annotation guidelines, each span can consist of one up to five consecutive sentences), we index text spans comprised of one up to five sentences.

## 2.2 Retrieval model

We evaluated the performance of several retrieval models during experimentation, i.e. vector space model (Salton et al., 1975), probabilistic BM25 (Robertson and Zaragoza, 2009), divergence from randomness (DFR) (Amati and Van Rijsbergen, 2002), and language models (Ponte and Croft, 1998) with Dirichlet priors. All models showed very similar performances (with only DFR constantly underperforming all other models) and we did not observe any statistically significant differences between each set of runs. Therefore, we opted for the vector space model as our retrieval model.

## 2.3 Query reformulation

We apply several query reformulation techniques to the citance to better retrieve the related text spans. We leverage both general and domain specific query reformulations for this purpose. Specifically,

[1] http://www.nist.gov/tac/2014/BiomedSumm/

we use biomedical concepts, ontology information, keyphrases and the syntactic structure of the citance.

**2.3.1. Unmodified query (*baseline*):** The citance after removing stop words, numeric values and citation markers (i.e. the actual indicator of the citation) serves as our baseline.

**2.3.2. Biomedical concepts (UMLS-*reduce*):** We remove from the query those terms that do not map to any medical concept in the UMLS[1] metathesaurus. We use MetaMap (Aronson, 2001) to map biomedical expressions in the citances to UMLS concepts. More specifically, our heuristic greedily matches the longest expressions in the citance to concepts in the UMLS metathesaurus; such strategy was deemed the most appropriate after experimenting with various matching approaches. We limited the scope of UMLS-reduce to SNOMED Clinical Terms (Bos et al., 2006) collection of UMLS and the "preferred concepts" (i.e., concepts that are determined by the National Library of Medicine to provide the best representation for a concept); terms that are not mapped to any UMLS concept were removed.

**2.3.3. Noun phrases (*NP*):** Citances include many important biological concepts, often appearing as noun phrases. For this reason, we reformulate citance by only keeping noun phrases and filtering out other parts of speech. We retain noun phrases that consist of up to 3 terms, as longer phrases were empirically determined to be too specific. Stopwords are removed from noun phrases.

**2.3.4. Keyword based (*KW*):** We consider a statistical measure for identifying key terms in the citance. Specifically, we computed the *idf*[2] of the terms in the citance in a domain-specific corpus to evaluate their importance. Given the domain of our dataset, we used the Open Access Subset of PubMed Central[3]. We filter out the terms whose *idf* value is less than a fixed threshold (after empirical evaluation, this threshold was set to 2.5).

**2.3.5. Biomedical expansion (UMLS-*expand*):** The terminology used by the citing author and the referenced author is not necessarily identical. Multiple terms or multi-word expressions can be mapped to the same concepts and each author might use their own choice of terms for describing a concept. In this approach, we add related terminology to the important concepts in the citance to solve this issue. Since our dataset consists of articles from biomedical literature, we took advantage of the UMLS metathesaurus to expand terms or multi-word expressions with their synonyms. We did not enforce any threshold for the number of terms added by UMLS-*expand*. However, in order to prevent query drift, we expanded citances using only UMLS's "preferred concepts" and concepts from the "SNOMED Clinical Terms" (SNOMED CT) terminology.

**2.3.6. Combined reformulation:** Due to the narrative structure of citances and their relative long length, using all citance terms for expansion is likely to cause query drift. Therefore, we first reduce the citance using one of previously described reduction approaches and then apply query expansion. In detail, we evaluated the combination of noun phrases and UMLS expansion, as well as UMLS reduction and expansion.

## 2.4 Combining retrieved spans

Due to our indexing strategy described in section 2.1, some text spans retrieved by the search engine could overlap with each other. Intuitively, if a span containing multiple contiguous sentences $\{s_1, \ldots, s_l\}$ is retrieved alongside any of its constituent sentences $s_i$, its relevance score should be increased to account for the relevance of $s_i$.

We exploited such intuition by adding the score of each span with the score of any of the constituent sentences or sub-spans retrieved alongside it. After the score is updated, the constituent sentences or sub-spans are removed from the list of retrieved results. Finally, because the number of reference spans indicated by the annotators in our data set is at most three, the system returns the top three results.

It is worth mentioning that we also looked at some other query reformulation approaches such as pseudo relevance feedback (Buckley et al., 1995) and Wikipedia based biomedical term filtering (Cohan et al., 2014); however, our experimentations should that these methods performed substantially worse than the baseline, consequently, we do not report those results nor their relevant discussions.

[1] http://www.nlm.nih.gov/research/umls/

[2] Inverted Document Frequency

[3] http://www.ncbi.nlm.nih.gov/pmc/

| Type of agreement | Count | Average overlap |
|---|---|---|
| Full agreement | 2 | 100% |
| Partial agreement between all annotators | 66 | $21.7 \pm 15.4\%$ |
| Partial agreement between a majority of annotators | 121 | $19.2 \pm 11.4\%$ |
| Partial agreement between a minority of annotators | 113 | $27.0 \pm 15.9\%$ |
| No agreement at all | 11 | 0% |

Table 1: Levels of agreement between annotators. The 4 annotators fully agree on just 2 of the 313 annotations. In most cases, a majority (3 annotators) or a minority (2 annotators) agrees on a portion of reference spans, indicating that the task is not trivial even for domain experts.

## 3 Evaluation and Dataset

The system was evaluated on TAC 2014 Biomedical Summarization track training dataset. It consists of 20 topics, each of which contains between 10 to 20 citing articles and 1 reference article. For each topic, four domain experts were asked to identify the appropriate reference spans for each citance in the reference text. To better understand the dataset, we analyzed the agreement between annotators (table 1). This table shows that the overall agreement is relatively low.

We used two sets of metrics for evaluation of the task. The first one is based on the weighted overlaps between the retrieved spans and the correct spans designated by annotators and is meant to reward spans overlapping with the ground truth. Weighted recall and precision for a system returning span $S$ with respect to a set of $M$ annotators, consisting of gold spans $G_1$, ..., $G_M$ are defined as follows:

$$\text{Recall} \stackrel{\text{def}}{=} \frac{\sum_{i=1}^{M} |S \cap G_i|}{\sum_{i=1}^{M} |G_i|} \quad \text{Prec} \stackrel{\text{def}}{=} \frac{\sum_{i=1}^{M} |S \cap G_i|}{M \times |S|} \qquad (1)$$

The overall score of the system is the mean F-1 (harmonic mean of the weighted precision and recall) over all the topics.

Based on the weighted F-1 score, a method could be penalized for retrieving any spans that are not indicated as gold spans by the annotators. Even if those spans are semantically similar to the gold spans, they will not receive any score. This is not ideal because, as the high disagreement shown in table 1 implies, gold spans by offset locations are highly controversial. For this reason, we also considered ROUGE-L (Lin, 2004) as another evaluation metric, as it rewards a method for retrieving spans that are similar to the gold spans. Specifically, ROUGE-L, takes into account the sentence similarity by considering the longest in sequence n-grams between the retrieved spans and gold spans.

## 4 Results and discussion

The problem of matching citations with cited spans in scientific articles is a new task and to the best of our knowledge, there is no prior work on this task. Thus to evaluate the effectiveness of our different methods, we compared the performance of our proposed approaches against the unmodified query baseline. The results are shown in Table 2.

Interestingly, we observe that UMLS-*reduce* performs worse than the baseline in terms of F-1. This can be attributed to the fact that multiple expressions in the biomedical literature can be used to refer to the same concept. Such diversity is not captured by UMLS-*reduce*, as it only performs query reduction. Moreover, a citance often contains expressions that, while not mapping to any biomedical concepts, provide useful context and therefore are fundamental in conveying the meaning of the citance (we will refer to such expressions as *supporting expressions* in the reminder of the paper). These supporting expressions are not captured by UMLS-*reduce*.

*NP* outperforms the baseline (+18.8% F-1). This outcome is expected, as most important biomedical concepts in the citance are noun phrases. Moreover, supporting expressions are also captured, as most of them are noun phrases.

*KW* also shows promising results (+11.5% F-1 and +15.2% ROUGE-L F-1 improvement), proving that the *idf* of the terms in citance over a large biomedical corpus is a valid measure of their informativeness for this task.

When comparing *KW* and *NP*, we notice that the former obtains higher precision values than the latter; this outcome is reversed with respect to recall (i.e., *NP*'s recall is higher than *KW*'s). Such behavior can be motivated by the fact that *NP*, as it extracts noun phrases that are likely to appear in the gold reference span, has a higher chance of retrieving relevant sections of the reference text. However, *NP* is more likely to retrieve non-relevant spans, as the extracted noun phrases, which are often describing the main findings of the cited paper, are preva-

| | Recall | Precision | F-1 | ROUGE-L Recall | ROUGE-L Prec | ROUGE-L F-1 |
|---|---|---|---|---|---|---|
| *baseline* | 0.169 | 0.152 | 0.156 | 0.496 | 0.200 | 0.280 |
| UMLS-*reduce* | 0.132 (-22.0%) | 0.146 (-4.08%) | 0.136 (-12.5%) | 0.496 (0.0%) | 0.224* (12.0%) | 0.293 (4.8%) |
| *KW* | 0.173* (3.0%) | 0.193** (27.6%) | 0.174** (11.5%) | 0.491 (-0.1%) | 0.273** (36.3%) | 0.323** (15.2%) |
| *NP* | 0.199** (18.3%) | 0.178** (17.6%) | 0.185** (18.8%) | 0.550** (11.1 %) | 0.211* (5.5 %) | 0.280 (0.0%) |
| UMLS-*expand* | 0.182** (8.1%) | 0.148 (-2.1%) | 0.160* (3.2 %) | 0.498 (0.5%) | 0.245** (22.2%) | 0.315** (12.3%) |
| UMLS-*reduce* + UMLS-*expand* | **0.201** (19.6%)** | 0.179** (18.0%) | 0.187** (20.0%) | **0.558** (12.6 %)** | 0.209** (4.4 %) | 0.293* (4.4%) |
| *NP* + UMLS-*expand* | 0.180* (7.1%) | **0.224** (47.8%)** | **0.196** (25.9%)** | 0.501 (1.13%) | **0.280** (39.9%)** | **0.333** (18.8%)** |

Table 2: Results for reference span matching; *KW*: reduction using KeyWords; *NP*: reduction using Noun Phrases; UMLS-*expand*: expansion using UMLS; UMLS-*reduce*: reduction using UMLS; * (**) indicates statistical significance at $p < 0.05$ ($p < 0.01$) using student's t-test over the baseline.

lent throughout the reference article. On the other hand, *KW* selects highly discriminative terms which are highly effective in retrieving some relevant reference spans, but might not appear in others.

We observe that UMLS-*expand*, by adding related concepts to the query, achieves significant improvement over the baseline in terms of recall (+8.1%). Such improvement is expected, as UMLS-*expand* augments the citance with all possible formulations of the detected biomedical concepts. However, its precision is only comparable with the baseline, as it does not remove any noisy terms from the citance. Interestingly, we notice that its ROUGE-L precision greatly outperforms the baseline (+22.2%). This behavior is motivated by the fact that UMLS-*expand*, even when not retrieving all the correct reference spans, extracts certain parts of the reference articles that share many biomedical concepts with the gold spans, thus achieving high structural similarity.

The two combined methods (*NP* + UMLS-*expand* and UMLS-*reduce* + UMLS-*expand*) obtain the best overall performance compared to the baseline. UMLS-*reduce* + UMLS-*expand* obtains the highest recall among all methods. This outcome directly depends on the fact that all the synonyms of a certain biomedical concept are captured using UMLS-*expand*. However, unlike UMLS-*expand*, this combined method also achieves statistically significant improvement in terms of precision, as UMLS-*reduce* removes terms that can cause query drift.

*NP* + UMLS-*expand* has the highest overall performance, achieving a 25.9% increase over the baseline in terms of F-1, and an 18.8% increase in terms of ROUGE-L F-1. As previously mentioned, noun phrases are highly effective in identifying relevant biomedical concepts, as well as supporting expressions. Given the addition of UMLS-*expand*, synonyms of the extracted noun phrases are also considered, further increasing the chance of retrieving relevant reference spans.

The limited performance of all methods in terms of the overall weighted F-1 and ROUGE-L scores is expected due to the difficulty of the task, as further corroborated by the low agreement between annotators. As previously stated, this makes the task particularly challenging for any system, as identifying the most appropriate reference spans is highly nontrivial even for domain experts. Nevertheless, while full agreement between domain experts is not present, as it is shown in table 1, more than 60% of the time, annotators agree – at least partially – on the position of the reference spans. This makes the task worth exploring.

## 5 Conclusion

In this paper, we propose an information retrieval approach for the problem of matching reference text spans with citances. Our approach takes advantage of several general and domain specific query reformulation techniques. Our best performing method obtains a significant increase over the baseline (25.9% F-1). However, as the absolute performance of the system indicates, the task of identifying matching reference spans to a given citance is highly non trivial. This fact is also reflected by the high disagreement between domain experts annotations and suggests that further exploration of the task is needed.


## Acknowledgments

This work was partially supported by NSF (grant CNS-1204347).

## References


Abu-Jbara, A. and Radev, D. (2011). Coherent citation-based summarization of scientific papers. In *Proceedings of the 49th Annual Meeting of the Association for Computational Linguistics: Human Language Technologies-Volume 1*, pages 500–509. Association for Computational Linguistics.

Amati, G. and Van Rijsbergen, C. J. (2002). Probabilistic models of information retrieval based on measuring the divergence from randomness. *ACM Transactions on Information Systems (TOIS)*, 20(4):357–389.

Aronson, A. R. (2001). Effective mapping of biomedical text to the umls metathesaurus: the metamap program. In *Proceedings of the AMIA Symposium*, page 17. American Medical Informatics Association.

Bos, L. et al. (2006). Snomed-ct: The advanced terminology and coding system for ehealth. *Stud Health Technol Inform*, 121:279–290.

Buckley, C., Singhal, A., Mitra, M., and Salton, G. (1995). New retrieval approaches using smart: Trec 4. In *Proceedings of the Fourth Text REtrieval Conference (TREC-4)*, pages 25–48.

Chen, R., Lin, H., and Yang, Z. (2011). Passage retrieval based hidden knowledge discovery from biomedical literature. *Expert Systems with Applications*, 38(8):9958–9964.

Cheung, E. C., Athineos, D., Lee, P., Ridgway, R. A., Lambie, W., Nixon, C., Strathdee, D., Blyth, K., Sansom, O. J., and Vousden, K. H. (2013). Tigar is required for efficient intestinal regeneration and tumorigenesis. *Developmental cell*, 25(5):463–477.

Cohan, A., Soldaini, L., and Goharian, N. (2014). Towards citation-based summarization of biomedical literature. Proceedings of the Text Analysis Conference (TAC '14).

De Waard, A. and Maat, H. P. (2012). Epistemic modality and knowledge attribution in scientific discourse: A taxonomy of types and overview of features. In *Proceedings of the Workshop on Detecting Structure in Scholarly Discourse*, pages 47–55. Association for Computational Linguistics.

Elkiss, A., Shen, S., Fader, A., Erkan, G., States, D., and Radev, D. (2008). Blind men and elephants: What do citation summaries tell us about a research article? *Journal of the American Society for Information Science and Technology*, 59(1):51–62.

Hersh, W. R., Cohen, A. M., Roberts, P. M., and Rekapalli, H. K. (2006). Text retrieval conference 2006 genomics track overview. In *TREC*.

Hersh, W. R., Cohen, A. M., Ruslen, L., and Roberts, P. M. (2007). Text retrieval conference 2007 genomics track overview. In *TREC*.

Kaplan, D., Iida, R., and Tokunaga, T. (2009). Automatic extraction of citation contexts for research paper summarization: A coreference-chain based approach. In *Proceedings of the 2009 Workshop on Text and Citation Analysis for Scholarly Digital Libraries*, pages 88–95. Association for Computational Linguistics.

Kiss, T. and Strunk, J. (2006). Unsupervised multilingual sentence boundary detection. *Computational Linguistics*, 32(4):485–525.

Lin, C.-Y. (2004). Rouge: A package for automatic evaluation of summaries. In *Text Summarization Branches Out: Proceedings of the ACL-04 Workshop*, pages 74–81.

Nakov, P. I., Schwartz, A. S., and Hearst, M. (2004). Citances: Citation sentences for semantic analysis of bioscience text. In *Proceedings of the SIGIR'04 workshop on Search and Discovery in Bioinformatics*, pages 81–88.

Okada, N., Yabuta, N., Suzuki, H., Aylon, Y., Oren, M., and Nojima, H. (2011). A novel chk1/2–lats2–14-3-3 signaling pathway regulates p-body formation in response to uv damage. *Journal of cell science*, 124(1):57–67.

Ponte, J. M. and Croft, W. B. (1998). A language modeling approach to information retrieval. In *Proceedings of the 21st annual international ACM SIGIR conference on Research and development in information retrieval*, pages 275–281. ACM.

Qazvinian, V. and Radev, D. R. (2008). Scientific paper summarization using citation summary networks. In *Proceedings of the 22Nd International Conference on Computational Linguistics - Volume 1*, COLING '08, pages 689–696, Stroudsburg, PA, USA. Association for Computational Linguistics.

Qazvinian, V. and Radev, D. R. (2010). Identifying non-explicit citing sentences for citation-based summarization. In *Proceedings of the 48th annual meeting of the association for computational linguistics*, pages 555–564. Association for Computational Linguistics.

Robertson, S. and Zaragoza, H. (2009). *The probabilistic relevance framework: BM25 and beyond*. Now Publishers Inc.

Salton, G., Wong, A., and Yang, C.-S. (1975). A vector space model for automatic indexing. *Communications of the ACM*, 18(11):613–620.

Siddharthan, A. and Teufel, S. (2007). Whose idea was this, and why does it matter? attributing scientific work to citations. In *HLT-NAACL*, pages 316–323. Citeseer.

Urbain, J., Frieder, O., and Goharian, N. (2009). Passage relevance models for genomics search. *BMC bioinformatics*, 10(Suppl 3):S3.

Urbain, J., Goharian, N., and Frieder, O. (2008). Probabilistic passage models for semantic search of genomics literature. *Journal of the American Society for Information Science and Technology*, 59(12).

Voorhoeve, P. M., Le Sage, C., Schrier, M., Gillis, A. J., Stoop, H., Nagel, R., Liu, Y.-P., Van Duijse, J., Drost, J., Griekspoor, A., et al. (2006). A genetic screen implicates mirna-372 and mirna-373 as oncogenes in testicular germ cell tumors. *Cell*, 124(6):1169–1181.

Ying, H., Kimmelman, A. C., Lyssiotis, C. A., Hua, S., Chu, G. C., Fletcher-Sananikone, E., Locasale, J. W., Son, J., Zhang, H., Coloff, J. L., et al. (2012). Oncogenic kras maintains pancreatic tumors through regulation of anabolic glucose metabolism. *Cell*, 149(3):656–670.

# Effective Feature Integration for Automated Short Answer Scoring*

**Keisuke Sakaguchi**
CLSP, Johns Hopkins University
Baltimore, MD
keisuke@cs.jhu.edu

**Michael Heilman** **Nitin Madnani**
Educational Testing Service
Princeton, NJ
{mheilman,nmadnani}@ets.org

## Abstract

A major opportunity for NLP to have a real-world impact is in helping educators score student writing, particularly content-based writing (i.e., the task of automated short answer scoring). A major challenge in this enterprise is that scored responses to a particular question (i.e., labeled data) are valuable for modeling but limited in quantity. Additional information from the scoring guidelines for humans, such as exemplars for each score level and descriptions of key concepts, can also be used. Here, we explore methods for integrating scoring guidelines and labeled responses, and we find that stacked generalization (Wolpert, 1992) improves performance, especially for small training sets.

## 1 Introduction

Educational applications of NLP have considerable potential for real-world impact, particularly in helping to score responses to assessments, which could allow educators to focus more on instruction.

We focus on the task of analyzing short, content-focused responses from an assessment of reading comprehension, following previous work on short answer scoring (Leacock and Chodorow, 2003; Mohler et al., 2011; Dzikovska et al., 2013). This task is typically defined as a text regression or classification problem: we label student responses that consist of one or more sentences with scores on an ordinal scale (e.g. correct, partially correct, or incorrect; 1–5 score range, etc.). Importantly, in addition to the student response itself, we may also have available other information such as reference answers or descriptions of key concepts from the scoring guidelines for human scorers. Such information can be cheap to acquire since it is often generated as part of the assessment development process.

Generally speaking, most work on short answer scoring takes one of the following approaches:

- A **response-based** approach uses detailed features extracted from the student response itself (e.g., word $n$-grams, etc.) and learns a scoring function from human-scored responses.
- A **reference-based** approach compares the student response to reference texts, such as exemplars for each score level, or specifications of required content from the assessment's scoring guidelines. Various text similarity methods (Agirre et al., 2013) can be used.

These two approaches can, of course, be combined. However, to our knowledge, the issues of how to combine the approaches and when that is likely to be useful have not been thoroughly studied.

A challenge in combining the approaches is that the response-based approach produces a large set of sparse features (e.g., word $n$-gram indicators), while the reference-based approach produces a small set of continuous features (e.g., similarity scores between the response and exemplars for different score levels). A simple combination method is to train a model on the union of the feature sets (§3.3). However, the dense reference features may be lost among the many sparse response features.

*Work done when Keisuke Sakaguchi was an intern at ETS. Michael Heilman is now a data scientist at Civis Analytics.



*Human Language Technologies: The 2015 Annual Conference of the North American Chapter of the ACL*, pages 1049–1054,
Denver, Colorado, May 31 – June 5, 2015. 

Therefore, we apply stacked generalization (i.e. stacking) (Wolpert, 1992; Sakkis et al., 2001; Torres Martins et al., 2008) to build an ensemble of the response- and reference-based approaches. To our knowledge, there is little if any research investigating the value of stacking for NLP applications such as automated scoring.[1]

The contributions of this paper are as follows: (1) we investigate various reference-based features for short answer scoring, (2) we apply stacking (Wolpert, 1992) in order to combine the reference- and response-based methods, and (3) we demonstrate that the stacked combination outperforms other models, especially for small training sets.

## 2 Task and Dataset

We conduct our experiments on short-answer questions that are developed under the *Reading for Understanding* (RfU) assessment framework. This framework is designed to measure the reading comprehension skills of students from grades 6 through 9 by attempting to assess whether the reader has formed a coherent mental model consistent with the text discourse. A more detailed description is provided by Sabatini and O'Reilly (2013).

We use 4 short-answer questions based on two different reading passages. The first passage is a 1300-word short story. A single question ("Q1" hereafter) asks the reader to read the story and write a 5–7 sentence synopsis in her own words that includes all the main characters and action from the story but does *not* include any opinions or information from outside the story. The second passage is a 700-word article that describes the experiences of European immigrants in the late 19th and early 20th centuries. There are 3 questions associated with this passage: two that ask the reader to summarize one section each in the article ("Q2" and "Q4") and a third that asks to summarize the entire article ("Q3"). These 3 questions ask the reader to restrict his or her responses to 1–2 sentences each.

Each question includes the following:

- **scored responses**: short responses written by students, scored on a 0 to 4 scale for the first question, and 0 to 3 for the other 3.
- **exemplars**: one or two exemplar responses for each score level, and
- **key concepts**: several ($\leq$ 10) sentences briefly expressing key concepts in a correct answer.

The data for each question is split into a training and testing sets. For each question, we have about 2,000 scored student responses.

Following previous work on automatic scoring (Shermis and Burstein, 2013), we evaluate performance using the quadratically weighted $\kappa$ (Cohen, 1968) between human and machine scores (rounded and trimmed to the range of the training scores).

## 3 Models for Short Answer Scoring

Next, we describe our implementations of the response- and reference-based scoring methods. All models use support vector regression (SVR) (Smola and Schölkopf, 2004), with the complexity parameter tuned by cross-validation on the training data.[2]

### 3.1 Response-based

Our implementation of the response-based scoring approach ("resp" in §4) uses SVR to estimate a model to predicts human scores for text responses. Various sparse binary indicators of linguistic features are used:

- binned response length (e.g. the `length-7` feature fires when the character contains 128-255 characters.)
- word $n$-grams from $n = 1$ to 2
- character $n$-grams from $n = 2$ to 5, which is more robust than word $n$-gram regarding spelling errors in student responses
- syntactic dependencies in the form of Parent-Label-Child (e.g. `boy-det-the` for "the boy")
- semantic roles in the form of PropBank[3] style (e.g. `say.01-A0-boy` for "(the) boy said")

[1]Some applications have used stacking but not analyzed its value. For example, many participants used stacking in the ASAP2 competition `http://http://www.kaggle.com/c/asap-sas`. Also, Heilman and Madnani (2013) used stacking for Task 7 of SemEval 2013.

[2]We used the implementation of SVR in scikit-learn (Pedregosa et al., 2011) via SKLL (`https://github.com/EducationalTestingService/skll`) version 0.27.0. Other than the complexity parameter, we used the defaults.

[3]`http://verbs.colorado.edu/~mpalmer/projects/ace.html`

The syntactic and semantic features were extracted using the ClearNLP parser.[4] We used the default models and options for the parser. We treat this model as a strong baseline to which we will add reference-based features.

### 3.2 Reference-based

Our implementation of the reference-based approach ("ref" in §4) uses SVR to estimate a model to predict human scores from various measures of the similarity between the response and information from the scoring guidelines provided to the human scorers. Specifically, we use the following information from §2: (a) sentences expressing key concepts that should be present in correct responses, and (b) small sets of exemplar responses for each score level. For each type of reference, we use the following similarity metrics:

- **BLEU**: the BLEU machine translation metric (Papineni et al., 2002), with the student response as the translation hypothesis. When using BLEU to compare the student response to the (much shorter) sentences containing key concepts, we ignore the brevity penalty.
- **word2vec cosine**: the cosine similarity between the averages of the word2vec vectors (Mikolov et al., 2013) of content words in the response and reference texts (e.g., exemplar), respectively.[5,6]
- **word2vec alignment**: the alignment method below with word2vec word similarities.
- **WordNet alignment**: the alignment method below with the Wu and Palmer (1994) WordNet (Miller, 1995) similarity score.

The WordNet and word2vec alignment metrics are computed as follows, where $S$ is a student response, $R$ is one of a set of reference texts, $W_s$ and $W_r$ are content words in $S$ and $R$, respectively, and $Sim(W_s, W_r)$ is the word similarity function:

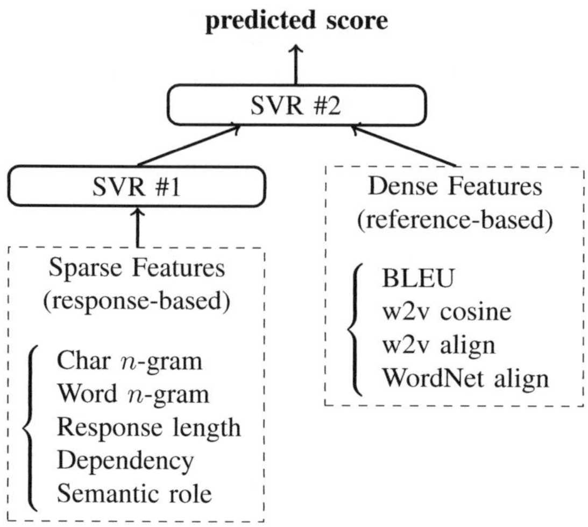


Figure 1: Stacking model for short answer scoring

$$\frac{1}{len(S)} \sum_{W_s} \max_{W_r \in R} Sim(W_s, W_r) \quad (1)$$

When $R$ is one of a set of reference texts (e.g., one of multiple exemplars available for a given score point), we use the maximum similarity over available values of $R$. In our data, there are multiple exemplars per score point, but only one text (usually, a single sentence) per key concept. In other words, we select the most similar exemplar response for each score level.

### 3.3 Simple Model Combination

One obvious way to combine the response- and reference-based models is to simply train a single model that uses both the sparse features of the student response and the dense, real-valued similarity features. Our experiments (§4) include such a model as a strong baseline, using SVR to estimate feature weights.

### 3.4 Model Combination with Stacking

In preliminary experiments with the training data, we observed no gains for the simple combination model over the component models. One potential challenge of combining the two scoring approaches is that the weights for the dense, reference-based features may be difficult to properly esti-

[4] http://www.clearnlp.com, v2.0.2

[5] The word2vec model was trained on the English Wikipedia as of June 2012, using gensim (http://radimrehurek.com/gensim/) with 100 dimensions, a context window of 5, a minimum count of 5 for vocabulary items, and the default skip-gram architecture.

[6] We define content words as ones whose POS tags begin with "N" (nouns), "V" (verbs), "J" (adjectives), or "R" (adverbs).

mate due to regularization[7] and the large number of sparse, mostly irrelevant linguistic features from the response-based approach. In fact, the reference-based sparse features constitute almost 90% of the entire feature set, while the response-based dense features constitute the remaining 10%.

This leads us to explore stacking (Wolpert, 1992), an ensemble technique where a top-layer model makes predictions based on predictions from lower-layer models. Here, we train a lower-layer model to aggregate the sparse response-based features into a single "response-based prediction" feature, and then train an upper-layer SVR model that includes that feature along with all of the reference-based features. Figure 1 shows the details.[8]

For training our stacking model, we first train the response-based regression model (SVR #1 in Figure 1), and then train the reference-based regression model (SVR #2) with an additional prediction feature value from the response-based model. Specifically, the lower-layer model concentrates sparse and binary features into a single continuous value, which accords with reference-based dense features in the upper-layer model. In training the lower-layer SVR on the training data, computing the response-based prediction feature (i.e., output of the lower-layer SVR) from the sparse features is similar to $k$-fold cross-validation ($k = 10$ here): the prediction feature values are computed for each fold by response-based SVR models trained on the remaining folds. In training the upper-layer SVR on the testing data, this prediction feature is computed by a single model trained on the entire training set.

## 4 Experiments

This section describes two experiments: an evaluation of reference-based similarity metrics, and an evaluation of methods for combining the reference- and response-based features by stacking. As mentioned in §2, we evaluate performance using quadratically weighted $\kappa$ between the human and predicted scores.

| | Q1 | Q2 | Q3 | Q4 |
|---|---|---|---|---|
| BLEU | .72 | .45 | .60 | .52 |
| word2vec cosine | .75 | .45 | .61 | .52 |
| word2vec alignment | .76 | .47 | .61 | .51 |
| WordNet alignment | .73 | .49 | .59 | .51 |
| All ("ref") | .78 | .52 | .66 | .59 |
| length | .68 | .42 | .59 | .51 |
| response-based ("resp") | .82 | .72 | .75 | .74 |

Table 1: Training set cross-validation performance of reference-based models, in quadratically weighted $\kappa$, with baselines for comparison. The response-based ("resp") model is a stronger baseline as described in §3.3. Note that each reference-based model includes the length bin features for a fair comparison to "resp".

### 4.1 Similarity Metrics

We first evaluate the similarity metrics from §3.2 using 10-fold cross-validation on the training data. We evaluated SVR models for each metric individually as well as a model combining all features from all metrics. In all models, we included the response length bin features (§3.1) as a proxy for response-based features. We compare to the response-based model (§3.1) and to a model consisting of only the response length bin feature.

The results are shown in Table 1. Each similarity metric by itself does not always improve the performance remarkably from the baseline (i.e., the response length bin features). However, when we incorporate all the similarity features, we obtained substantial gain in all 4 questions. In the subsequent model combination experiment, therefore, we used all similarity features to represent the reference-based approach because it outperformed the other similarity models.

### 4.2 Model Combination

Next, we tested models that use both response- and reference-based features on a held-out test set, which contains 400 responses per question. We evaluated the response-based ("resp", §3.1) and reference-based ("ref", §3.2) individual models as well as the two combination methods ("ref+resp", §3.3 and "ref+resp stacking", §3.4). We also eval-

[7] Another possible combination approach would be to use the combination method from §3.3 but apply less regularization to the reference-based features, or, equivalently, scale them by a large constant. We only briefly explored this through training set cross-validation. The stacking approach seemed to perform at least as well in general.

[8] It would also be possible to also make a lower-layer model for the reference-based features, though doing this did not show benefits in preliminary experiments.

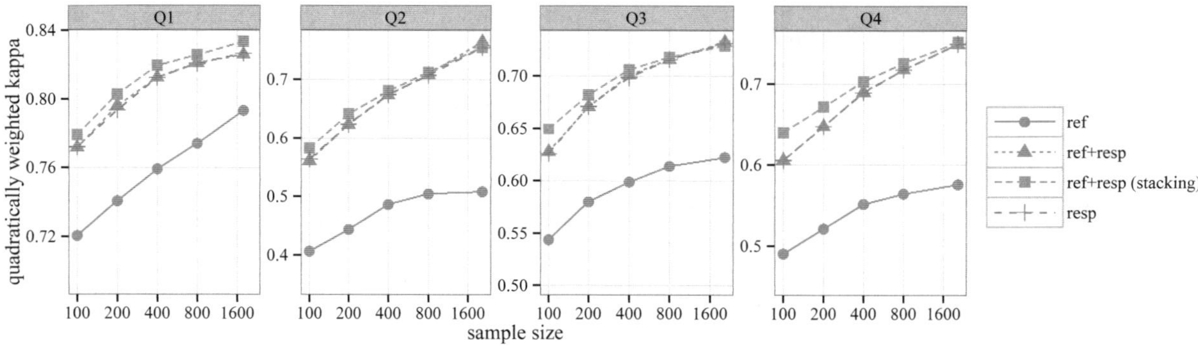


Figure 2: Test set results for various models trained on differently sized random samples of the training data. Each point represents an average over 20 runs, except for the rightmost points for each question, which correspond to training on the full training set. Note that the "resp" and "ref+resp" lines mostly overlap.

uated models trained on differently sized subsets of the training data. For each subset size, we averaged over 20 samples. The results are in Figure 2.

The performance of all models increased as training data grew, though there were diminishing returns (note the logarithmic scale). Also, the models with response-based features outperform those with just reference-based features, as observed previously by Heilman and Madnani (2013).

Most importantly, while all models with response-based features perform about the same with 1,000 training examples or higher, the stacked model tended to outperform the other models for cases where the number of training examples was very limited.[9] This indicates that stacking enables learning better feature weights than a simple combination when the feature set contains a mixture of sparse as well as dense features, particularly for smaller data sizes.

## 5 Conclusion

In this paper, we explored methods for using different sources of information for automatically scoring short, content-based assessment responses. We combined a response-based method that uses sparse features (e.g., word and character $n$-grams) with a reference-based method that uses a small number of features for the similarity between the response and information from the scoring guidelines (exemplars and key concepts).

On four reading comprehension assessment questions, we found that a combined model using stacking outperformed a non-stacked combination, particularly for the most practically relevant cases where training data was limited. We believe that such an approach may be useful for dealing with diverse feature sets in other automated scoring tasks as well as other NLP tasks.

As future work, it might be interesting to explore a more sophisticated model where the regression models in different layers are trained simultaneously by back-propagating the error of the upper-layer, as in neural networks.

[9] We are not aware of an appropriate significance test for experiments where subsets of the training data are used. However, the benefits of stacking seem unlikely to be due to chance. For all 4 items, stacking outperformed the non-stacking combination for 18 or more of the 20 200-response training subsets (note that under a binomial test, this would be significant with $p < 0.001$). Also, for the 100-response training subsets, stacking was better for 16 or more of the 20 subsets ($p < 0.01$).

## Acknowledgments

We would like to thank John Sabatini and Kietha Biggers for providing us with the RfU datasets. We would also like to thank Dan Blanchard, Aoife Cahill, Swapna Somasundaran, Anastassia Loukina, Beata Beigman Klebanov, and the anonymous reviewers for their help.

## References

Eneko Agirre, Daniel Cer, Mona Diab, Aitor Gonzalez-Agirre, and Weiwei Guo. 2013. *SEM 2013 shared task: Semantic textual similarity. In *Second Joint Conference on Lexical and Computational Semantics (*SEM), Volume 1: Proceedings of the Main Conference and the Shared Task: Semantic Textual Similarity*, pages 32–43, Atlanta, Georgia, USA, June.

J. Cohen. 1968. Weighted kappa: Nominal scale agreement with provision for scaled disagreement or partial credit. *Psychological Bulletin*, 70(4).

Myroslava Dzikovska, Rodney Nielsen, Chris Brew, Claudia Leacock, Danilo Giampiccolo, Luisa Bentivogli, Peter Clark, Ido Dagan, and Hoa Trang Dang. 2013. SemEval-2013 task 7: The joint student response analysis and 8th recognizing textual entailment challenge. In *Second Joint Conference on Lexical and Computational Semantics (*SEM), Volume 2: Proceedings of the Seventh International Workshop on Semantic Evaluation (SemEval 2013)*, pages 263–274, Atlanta, Georgia, USA, June.

Michael Heilman and Nitin Madnani. 2013. ETS: Domain adaptation and stacking for short answer scoring. In *Second Joint Conference on Lexical and Computational Semantics (*SEM), Volume 2: Proceedings of the Seventh International Workshop on Semantic Evaluation (SemEval 2013)*, pages 275–279, Atlanta, Georgia, USA, June.

C. Leacock and M. Chodorow. 2003. c-rater: Scoring of short-answer questions. *Computers and the Humanities*, 37.

Tomas Mikolov, Ilya Sutskever, Kai Chen, Greg S Corrado, and Jeff Dean. 2013. Distributed representations of words and phrases and their compositionality. In C.J.C. Burges, L. Bottou, M. Welling, Z. Ghahramani, and K.Q. Weinberger, editors, *Advances in Neural Information Processing Systems 26*, pages 3111–3119.

George A. Miller. 1995. WordNet: a lexical database for english. *Communications of the ACM*, 38(11):39–41.

Michael Mohler, Razvan Bunescu, and Rada Mihalcea. 2011. Learning to grade short answer questions using semantic similarity measures and dependency graph alignments. In *Proceedings of ACL:HLT*, pages 752–762, Portland, Oregon, USA, June.

Kishore Papineni, Salim Roukos, Todd Ward, and Wei-Jing Zhu. 2002. BLEU: A method for automatic evaluation of machine translation. In *Proceedings of ACL*, pages 311–318.

F. Pedregosa, G. Varoquaux, A. Gramfort, V. Michel, B. Thirion, O. Grisel, M. Blondel, P. Prettenhofer, R. Weiss, V. Dubourg, J. Vanderplas, A. Passos, D. Cournapeau, M. Brucher, M. Perrot, and E. Duchesnay. 2011. Scikit-learn: Machine learning in python. *Journal of Machine Learning Research*, 12:2825–2830.

J. Sabatini and T. O'Reilly. 2013. Rationale for a new generation of reading comprehension assessments. In B. Miller, L. Cutting, and P. McCardle, editors, *Unraveling Reading Comprehension: Behavioral, Neurobiological and Genetic Components*. Paul H. Brooks Publishing Co.

Georgios Sakkis, Ion Androutsopoulos, Georgios Paliouras, Vangelis Karkaletsis, Constantine D. Spyropoulos, and Panagiotis Stamatopoulos. 2001. Stacking classifiers for anti-spam filtering of e-mail. In L. Lee and D. Harman, editors, *Proceedings of the 6th Conference on Empirical Methods in Natural Language Processing (EMNLP 2001)*, pages 44–50.

Mark D. Shermis and Jill Burstein. 2013. *Handbook of automated essay evaluation: Current applications and new directions*. Routledge.

Alex J. Smola and Bernhard Schölkopf. 2004. A tutorial on support vector regression. *Statistics and Computing*, 14(3):199–222.

André Filipe Torres Martins, Dipanjan Das, Noah A. Smith, and Eric P. Xing. 2008. Stacking dependency parsers. In *Proceedings of the 2008 Conference on Empirical Methods in Natural Language Processing*, pages 157–166, Honolulu, Hawaii, October.

David H. Wolpert. 1992. Stacked generalization. *Neural Networks*, 5(2):241 – 259.

Zhibiao Wu and Martha Palmer. 1994. Verbs semantics and lexical selection. In *Proceedings of the 32Nd Annual Meeting on Association for Computational Linguistics*, ACL '94, pages 133–138, Stroudsburg, PA, USA. Association for Computational Linguistics.

# Socially-Informed Timeline Generation for Complex Events

**Lu Wang Claire Cardie Galen Marchetti**
Department of Computer Science
Cornell University
Ithaca, NY 14853
{luwang, cardie}@cs.cornell.edu gjm97@cornell.edu

## Abstract

Existing timeline generation systems for complex events consider only information from traditional media, ignoring the rich social context provided by user-generated content that reveals representative public interests or insightful opinions. We instead aim to generate socially-informed timelines that contain both news article summaries and selected user comments. We present an optimization framework designed to balance topical cohesion between the article and comment summaries along with their informativeness and coverage of the event. Automatic evaluations on real-world datasets that cover four complex events show that our system produces more informative timelines than state-of-the-art systems. In human evaluation, the associated comment summaries are furthermore rated more insightful than editor's picks and comments ranked highly by users.

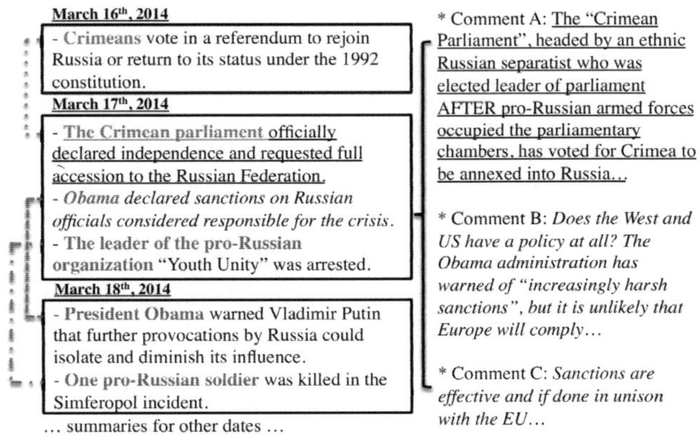


Figure 1: A snippet of the event timeline on Ukraine Crisis is displayed on the left. On the right, we display a set of representative comments addressing the article summary of March $17^{th}$. Comment A (underlined) brings a perspective on "Crimean parliament passes declaration of independence" (the article sentence is also underlined on the left). Comments B and C focus on Obama's sanctions on Ukrainian and Russian officials. Sentences linked by edges belong to the same event thread, which is centered on the entities with the same color.

## 1 Introduction

Social media sites on the Internet provide increasingly more, and increasingly popular, means for people to voice their opinions on trending events. Traditional news media — the New York Times and CNN, for example — now provide online mechanisms that allow and encourage readers to share reactions, opinions, and personal experiences relevant to a news story. For complex emerging events, in particular, user comments can provide relevant, interesting and insightful information beyond the facts reported in the news. But their large volume and tremendous variation in quality make it impossible for readers to efficiently digest the user-generated content, much less integrate it with reported facts from the dozens or hundreds of news reports produced on the event each day.

In this work, we present a *socially-informed timeline generation system* that jointly generates a news article summary and a user comment summary for each day of an ongoing complex event. A sample (gold standard) timeline snippet for Ukraine Crisis is shown in Figure 1. The event timeline is on the left; the comment summary for March $17^{th}$ is on the right.



*Human Language Technologies: The 2015 Annual Conference of the North American Chapter of the ACL*, pages 1055–1065,
Denver, Colorado, May 31 – June 5, 2015. 

While generating timelines from news articles and summarizing user comments have been studied as separate problems (Yan et al., 2011; Ma et al., 2012), their joint summarization for timeline generation raises new challenges. Firstly, there should be a tight connection between the article and comment portion of the timeline. By definition, users comment on socially relevant events. So the important part of articles and insightful comments should both cover these events. Moreover, good reading experience requires that the article summary and comment summary demonstrate evident connectivity. For example, Comment C in Figure 1 ("Sanctions are effective and if done in unison with the EU") is obscure without knowing the context that "sanctions are imposed by U.S". Simply combining the outputs from a timeline generation system and a comment summarization system may lead to timelines that lack cohesion. On the other hand, articles and comments are from intrinsically different genres of text: articles emphasize facts and are written in a professional style; comments reflect opinions in a less formal way. Thus, it could be difficult to recognize the connections between articles and comments. Finally, it is also challenging to enforce continuity in timelines with many entities and events.

To address the challenges mentioned above, we formulate the timeline generation task as an optimization problem, where we maximize topic cohesion between the article and comment summaries while preserving their ability to reflect *important* concepts and subevents, adequate *coverage* of mentioned topics, and *continuity* of the timeline as it is updated with new material each day. We design a novel alternating optimizing algorithm that allows the generation of a high quality article summary and comment summary via mutual reinforcement. We demonstrate the effectiveness of our algorithm on four disparate complex event datasets collected over months from the New York Times, CNN, and BBC. Automatic evaluation using ROUGE (Lin and Hovy, 2003) and gold standard timelines indicates that our system can effectively leverage user comments to outperform state-of-the-art approaches on timeline generation. In a human evaluation via Amazon Mechanical Turk, the comment summaries generated by our method were selected as the best in terms of informativeness and insightfulness in 66.7% and 51.7% of the evaluations (vs. 26.7% and 30.0% for randomly selected editor's-picks).

Especially, our optimization framework relies on two scoring functions that estimate the importance of including individual article sentences and user comments in the timeline. Based on the observation that entities or events frequently discussed in the user comments can help with identify summary-worthy content, we show that the scoring functions can be learned jointly by utilizing graph-based regularization. Experiments show that our joint learning model outperforms state-of-the-art ranking algorithms and other joint learning based methods when evaluated on sentence ranking and comment ranking. For example, we achieve an NDCG@3 of 0.88 on the Ukraine crisis dataset, compared to 0.77 from Yang et al. (2011) which also conducts joint learning between articles and social context using factor graphs.

Finally, to encourage continuity in the generated timeline, we propose an entity-centered event threading algorithm. Human evaluation demonstrates that users who read timelines with event threads write more informative answers than users who do not see the threads while answering the same questions. This implies that our system constructed threads can help users better navigate the timelines and collect relevant information in a short time.

For the rest of the paper, we first describe data collection (Section 2). We then introduce the joint learning model for importance prediction (Section 3). The full timeline generation system is presented in Section 4, which is followed by evaluations (Section 5). Related work and conclusion are in Sections 6 and 7.

## 2 Data Collection and Preprocessing

We crawled news articles from New York Times (NYT), CNN, and BBC on four trending events: the missing Malaysia Airlines Flight MH370 (MH370), the political unrest in Ukraine (Ukraine), the Israel-Gaza conflict (Israel-Gaza), and the NSA surveillance leaks (NSA). For each event, we select a set of key words (usually entities' name), which are used to filter out irrelevant articles. We collect comments for NYT articles through NYT community API, and comments for CNN articles via Disqus

API. [1] NYT comments come with information on whether a comment is an editor's-pick. The statistics on the four datasets are displayed in Table 1.[2]

| | Time Span | # Articles | # Comments |
|---|---|---|---|
| MH370 | 03/08 - 06/30 | 955 | 406,646 |
| Ukraine | 03/08 - 06/30 | 3,779 | 646,961 |
| Israel-Gaza | 07/20 - 09/30 | 909 | 322,244 |
| NSA | 03/23 - 06/30 | 145 | 60,481 |

Table 1: Statistics on the four event datasets.

We extract parse trees, dependency trees, and coreference resolution results of articles and comments with Stanford CoreNLP (Manning et al., 2014). Sentences in articles are labeled with timestamps using SUTime (Chang and Manning, 2012).

We also collect all articles with comments from NYT in 2013 (henceforth NYT2013) to form a training set for learning importance scoring functions on articles sentences and comments (see Section 3). NYT2013 contains $3,863$ articles and $833,032$ comments.

## 3 Joint Learning for Importance Scoring

We first introduce a joint learning method that uses *graph-based regularization* to simultaneously learn two functions — a SENTENCE scorer and a COMMENT scorer — that predict the importance of including an individual news article sentence or a particular user comment in the timeline.

We train the model on the aforementioned NYT2013 dataset, where 20% of the articles and their comments are reserved for parameter tuning. Formally, the training data consists of a set of articles $D = \{d_i\}_{i=0}^{|D|-1}$. Each article $d_i$ contains a set of sentences $x_{s_{d_i}} = \{x_{s_{d_i},j}\}_{j=0}^{|s_{d_i}|-1}$ and a set of associated comments $x_{c_{d_i}} = \{x_{c_{d_i},k}\}_{k=0}^{|c_{d_i}|-1}$, where $|s_{d_i}|$ and $|c_{d_i}|$ are the numbers of sentences and comments for $d_i$. For simplicity, we use $x_s$ or $x_c$ to denote a sentence or a comment wherever there is no ambiguity.

In addition, each article has a human-written abstract. We use the ROUGE-2 (Lin and Hovy, 2003) score of each sentence computed against the associated abstract as its gold-standard importance score. Each comment is assigned a gold-standard value of 1.0 if it is an editor's pick, or 0.0 otherwise.

The SENTENCE and COMMENT scorers rely on two classifiers, each designed to handle the special characteristics of news and user comments, respectively; and a graph-based regularizing constraint that encourages similarity between selected sentences and comments. We describe each component below.

**Article** SENTENCE **Importance.** Each sentence $x_s$ in a news article is represented as a $k$-dimensional feature vector $\mathbf{x_s} \in \mathbb{R}^k$, with a gold-standard label $y_s$. We denote the training set as a feature matrix $\tilde{\mathbf{X}}_\mathbf{s}$, with a label vector $\tilde{\mathbf{Y}}_\mathbf{s}$. To produce the SENTENCE scoring function $f_s(x_s) = \mathbf{x_s} \cdot \mathbf{w_s}$, we use ridge regression to learn a vector $\mathbf{w_s}$ that minimizes $||\tilde{\mathbf{X}}_\mathbf{s}\mathbf{w_s} - \tilde{\mathbf{Y}}_\mathbf{s}||_2^2 + \beta_s \cdot ||\mathbf{w_s}||_2^2$. Features used in the model are listed in Table 2. We also impose the following *position-based regularizing constraint* to encode the fact that the first sentence in a news article usually conveys the most essential information: $\lambda_s \cdot \sum_{d_i} \sum_{x_{s_{d_i},j}, j \neq 0} ||(\mathbf{x_{s_{d_i},0}} - \mathbf{x_{s_{d_i},j}}) \cdot \mathbf{w_s} - (y_{s_{d_i},0} - y_{s_{d_i},j})||_2^2$ , where $x_{s_{d_i},j}$ is the $j$-th sentence in document $d_i$. Term $(\mathbf{x_{s_{d_i},0}} - \mathbf{x_{s_{d_i},j}}) \cdot \mathbf{w_s}$ measures the difference in predicted scores between the first sentence and any other sentence. This value is expected be close to the true difference. We further construct $\tilde{\mathbf{X}}'_\mathbf{s}$ to contain all difference vectors $(\mathbf{x_{s_{d_i},0}} - \mathbf{x_{s_{d_i},j}})$, with $\tilde{\mathbf{Y}}'_\mathbf{s}$ as label difference vector. The objective function to minimize becomes

$$J_s(\mathbf{w_s}) = \\ ||\tilde{\mathbf{X}}_\mathbf{s}\mathbf{w_s} - \tilde{\mathbf{Y}}_\mathbf{s}||_2^2 + \lambda_s \cdot ||\tilde{\mathbf{X}}'_\mathbf{s}\mathbf{w_s} - \tilde{\mathbf{Y}}'_\mathbf{s}||_2^2 + \beta_s \cdot ||\mathbf{w_s}||_2^2 \quad (1)$$

**User** COMMENT **Importance.** Similarly, each comment $x_c$ is represented as an $l$−dimensional feature vector $\mathbf{x_c} \in \mathbb{R}^l$, with label $y_c$. Comments in the training data are denoted with a feature matrix $\tilde{\mathbf{X}}_\mathbf{c}$ with a label vector $\tilde{\mathbf{Y}}_\mathbf{c}$. Likewise, we learn $f_c(x_c) = \mathbf{x_c} \cdot \mathbf{w_c}$ by minimizing $||\tilde{\mathbf{X}}_\mathbf{c}\mathbf{w_c} - \tilde{\mathbf{Y}}_\mathbf{c}||_2^2 + \beta_c \cdot ||\mathbf{w_c}||_2^2$. Features are listed in Table 3. We apply a *pairwise preference-based regularizing constraint* (Joachims, 2002) to incorporate a bias toward editor's picks: $\lambda_c \cdot \sum_{d_i} \sum_{x_{c_{d_i},j} \in \mathbf{E_{d_i}}, x_{c_{d_i},k} \notin \mathbf{E_{d_i}}} ||(\mathbf{x_{c_{d_i},j}} - \mathbf{x_{c_{d_i},k}}) \cdot \mathbf{w_c} - 1||_2^2$ , where $\mathbf{E_{d_i}}$ are the editor's picks for $d_i$. Term $(\mathbf{x_{c_{d_i},j}} - \mathbf{x_{c_{d_i},k}}) \cdot \mathbf{w_c}$ enforces the separation of editor's picks from regular comments. We further construct $\tilde{\mathbf{X}}'_\mathbf{c}$ to contain all the pairwise differences

[1] BBC comment volume is low, so we do not collect it.

[2] The datasets are available at `http://www.cs.cornell.edu/~luwang/data.html`.

$(\mathbf{x_{c_{d_i},j}} - \mathbf{x_{c_{d_i},k}})$. $\tilde{\mathbf{Y}}'_\mathbf{c}$ is a vector of same size as $\tilde{\mathbf{X}}'_\mathbf{c}$ with each element as 1. Thus, the objective function to minimize is:

$$J_c(\mathbf{w_c}) = \\ ||\tilde{\mathbf{X}}_\mathbf{c}\mathbf{w_c} - \tilde{\mathbf{Y}}_\mathbf{c}||_2^2 + \lambda_c \cdot ||\tilde{\mathbf{X}}'_\mathbf{c}\mathbf{w_c} - \tilde{\mathbf{Y}}'_\mathbf{c}||_2^2 + \beta_c \cdot ||\mathbf{w_c}||_2^2 \quad (2)$$

**Graph-Based Regularization.** The regularizing constraint is based on two mutually reinforcing hypotheses: (1) the importance of a sentence depends partially on the availability of sufficient insightful comments that touch on topics in the sentence; (2) the importance of a comment depends partially on whether it addresses notable events reported in the sentences. For example, we want our model to bias $\mathbf{w_s}$ to predict a high score for a sentence with high similarity to numerous insightful comments.

We first create a bipartite graph from sentences and comments on the same articles, where edge *weights* are based on the content similarity between a sentence and a comment (TF-IDF similarity is used). Let $\tilde{\mathbf{R}}$ be an $N \times M$ adjacency matrix, where $N$ and $M$ are the numbers of sentences and comments. $R_{sc}$ is the similarity between sentence $x_s$ and comment $x_c$. We normalize $\tilde{\mathbf{R}}$ by $\tilde{\mathbf{Q}} = \tilde{\mathbf{D}}^{-\frac{1}{2}}\tilde{\mathbf{R}}\tilde{\mathbf{D}}'^{-\frac{1}{2}}$, where $\tilde{\mathbf{D}}$ and $\tilde{\mathbf{D}}'$ are diagonal matrices: $\tilde{\mathbf{D}} \in \mathbb{R}^{N\times N}$, $D_{i,i} = \sum_{j=1}^{M} R_{i,j}$; $\tilde{\mathbf{D}}' \in \mathbb{R}^{M\times M}$, $D'_{j,j} = \sum_{i=1}^{N} R_{i,j}$. The interplay between the two types of data is encoded in the following regularizing constraint:

$$J_{s,c}(\mathbf{w_s}, \mathbf{w_c}) = \\ \lambda_{sc} \cdot \sum_{d_i} \sum_{x_s \in x_{s_{d_i}}, x_c \in x_{c_{d_i}}} Q_{x_s,x_c} \cdot (\mathbf{x_s} \cdot \mathbf{w_s} - \mathbf{x_c} \cdot \mathbf{w_c})^2 \quad (3)$$

**Full Objective Function.** Thus, the full objective function consists of the three parts discussed above:

$$J(\mathbf{w_s}, \mathbf{w_c}) = J_s(\mathbf{w_s}) + J_c(\mathbf{w_c}) + J_{s,c}(\mathbf{w_s}, \mathbf{w_c}) \quad (4)$$

Furthermore, using the following notation,

$$\tilde{\mathbf{X}} = \begin{bmatrix} \tilde{\mathbf{X}}_\mathbf{s} & 0 \\ 0 & \tilde{\mathbf{X}}_\mathbf{c} \end{bmatrix} \; \tilde{\mathbf{Y}} = \begin{bmatrix} \tilde{\mathbf{Y}}_\mathbf{s} \\ \tilde{\mathbf{Y}}_\mathbf{c} \end{bmatrix} \; \tilde{\mathbf{X}}' = \begin{bmatrix} \tilde{\mathbf{X}}'_\mathbf{s} & 0 \\ 0 & \tilde{\mathbf{X}}'_\mathbf{c} \end{bmatrix} \; \tilde{\mathbf{Y}}' = \begin{bmatrix} \tilde{\mathbf{Y}}'_\mathbf{s} \\ \tilde{\mathbf{Y}}'_\mathbf{c} \end{bmatrix}$$

$$\tilde{\boldsymbol{\beta}} = \begin{bmatrix} \beta_s \mathbf{I_k} & 0 \\ 0 & \beta_c \mathbf{I_l} \end{bmatrix} \quad \tilde{\boldsymbol{\lambda}} = \begin{bmatrix} \lambda_s \mathbf{I}_{|\mathbf{X}'_s|} & 0 \\ 0 & \lambda_c \mathbf{I}_{|\mathbf{X}'_c|} \end{bmatrix}$$

$$\tilde{\mathbf{L}} = \begin{bmatrix} \lambda_{sc}\mathbf{I}_{|\mathbf{X_s}|} & -\lambda_{sc}\tilde{\mathbf{Q}} \\ -\lambda_{sc}\tilde{\mathbf{Q}}^\mathbf{T} & \lambda_{sc}\mathbf{I}_{|\mathbf{X_c}|} \end{bmatrix} \quad \mathbf{w} = \begin{bmatrix} \mathbf{w_s} \\ \mathbf{w_c} \end{bmatrix}$$

we can show a **closed form solution** to Equation 4 as follows:

$$\hat{\mathbf{w}} = \\ (\tilde{\mathbf{X}}^\mathbf{T}\tilde{\mathbf{L}}\tilde{\mathbf{X}} + \tilde{\mathbf{X}}^\mathbf{T}\tilde{\mathbf{X}} + \tilde{\mathbf{X}}'^\mathbf{T}\tilde{\boldsymbol{\lambda}}\tilde{\mathbf{X}}' + \tilde{\boldsymbol{\beta}})^{-1}(\tilde{\mathbf{X}}^\mathbf{T}\tilde{\mathbf{Y}} + \tilde{\mathbf{X}}'^\mathbf{T}\tilde{\boldsymbol{\lambda}}\tilde{\mathbf{Y}}') \quad (5)$$

| Basic Features | Social Features |
|---|---|
| - num of words<br>- absolute/relative position<br>- overlaps with headline<br>- avg/sum TF-IDF scores<br>- num of NEs | - avg/sum frequency of words appearing in comment<br>- avg/sum frequency of dependency relations appearing in comment |

Table 2: Features used for sentence importance scoring.

| Basic Features | Readability Features |
|---|---|
| - num of words<br>- num of sentences<br>- avg num of words per sentence<br>- num of NEs<br>- num/proportion of capitalized words<br>- avg/sum TF-IDF<br>- contains URL<br>- user rating (pos/neg) | - Flesch-Kincaid Readability<br>- Gunning-Fog Readability<br>**Discourse Features**<br>- num/proportion of connectives<br>- num/proportion of hedge words<br>**Article Features**<br>- TF/TF-IDF simi with article<br>- TF/TF-IDF simi with comments<br>- JS/KL divergence (div) with article<br>- JS/KL div with comments |
| **Sentiment Features**<br>- num /proportion of positive/negative/neutral words (MPQA (Wilson et al., 2005), General Inquirer (Stone et al., 1966))<br>- num /proportion of sentiment words | |

Table 3: Features used for comment importance scoring.

## 4 Timeline Generation

Now we present an optimization framework for timeline generation. Formally, for each day, our system takes as input a set of sentences $V_s$ and a set of comments $V_c$ to be summarized, and the (automatically generated) timeline $\mathcal{T}$ (represented as threads) for days prior to the current day. It then identifies a subset $S \subseteq V_s$ as the article summary and a subset $C \subseteq V_c$ as the comment summary by maximizing the following function:

$$\mathcal{Z}(S, C; \mathcal{T}) = \mathcal{S}_{qual}(S; \mathcal{T}) + \mathcal{C}_{qual}(C) + \delta\mathcal{X}(S, C) \quad (6)$$

where $\mathcal{S}_{qual}(S; \mathcal{T})$ measures the quality of the article summary $S$ in the context of the historical timeline represented as event threads $\mathcal{T}$; $\mathcal{C}_{qual}(C)$ computes the quality of the comment summary $C$; and $\mathcal{X}(S, C)$ estimates the connectivity between $S$ and $C$.

We solve this maximization problem using an alternating optimization algorithm which is outlined in Section 4.4. In general, we alternately search for a better article summary $S$ with hill climbing search and a better comment summary $C$ with Ford-Fulkerson algorithm until convergence.

In the rest of this section, we first describe an *entity-centered event threading* algorithm to construct event threads $\mathcal{T}$ which are used to boost article timeline continuity. Then we explain how to compute $\mathcal{S}_{qual}(S;\mathcal{T})$ and $\mathcal{C}_{qual}(C)$ in Section 4.2, followed by $\mathcal{X}(S,C)$ in Section 4.3.

### 4.1 Entity-Centered Event Threading

We present an event threading process where each thread connects sequential events centered on a set of relevant *entities*. For instance, the following thread connects events about *Obama*'s action towards the annexation of Crimea by *Russia*:

Day 1: *Obama* declared sanctions on *Russian officials*.
Day 2: *President Obama* warned *Russian*.
Day 3: *Obama* urges *Russian* to move back its troops.
Day 4: *Obama* condemns *Russian* aggression in Ukraine.

We first collect relation extractions as *(entity, relation, entity)* triples from OLLIE (Mausam et al., 2012), a dependency relation based open information extraction system. We retain extractions with confidence scores higher than 0.5. We further design syntactic patterns based on Fader et al. (2011) to identify relations expressed as a combination of a verb and nouns. Each relation contains at least one event-related word (Ritter et al., 2012).

The *entity-centered event threading* algorithm works as follows: on the first day, each sentence in the summary becomes an individual cluster; thereafter, each sentence in the current day's article summary either gets attached to an existing thread or starts a new thread. The updated threads then become the input to next day's summary generation process. On day $n$, we have a set of threads $\mathcal{T} = \{\tau : \mathbf{s_1}, \mathbf{s_2}, \cdots, \mathbf{s_{n-1}}\}$ constructed from previous $n-1$ days, where $\mathbf{s_i}$ represents the set of sentences attached to thread $\tau$ from day $i$. The *cohesion* between a new sentence $s \in S$ and a thread $\tau$ is denoted as $cohn(s,\tau)$. $s$ is attached to $\hat{\tau}$ if there exists $\hat{\tau} = \max_{\tau \in \mathcal{T}} cohn(s,\tau)$ and $cohn(s,\hat{\tau}) > 0.0$. Otherwise, $s$ becomes a new thread. We define $cohn(s,\tau) = \min_{\mathbf{s_i} \in \tau, \mathbf{s_i} \neq \emptyset} tfsimi(\mathbf{s_i}, s)$, where $tfsimi(\mathbf{s_i}, s)$ measures the TF similarity between $\mathbf{s_i}$ and $s$. We consider unigrams/bigrams/trigrams generated from the entities of our event extractions.

### 4.2 Summary Quality Measurement

Recall that we learned two separate importance scoring functions for sentences and comments, which will be denoted here as $imp_s(s)$ and $imp_c(c)$. With an article summary $S$ and threads $\mathcal{T} = \{\tau_i\}$, the **article summary quality** function $\mathcal{S}_{qual}(S;\mathcal{T})$ has the following form:

$$\mathcal{S}_{qual}(S;\mathcal{T}) = \sum_{s \in S} imp(s)$$
$$+\theta_{cov} \sum_{s' \in V_s} \min(\sum_{s \in S} tfidf(s,s'), \alpha \sum_{\hat{s} \in V_s} tfidf(\hat{s},s'))$$
$$+\ \theta_{cont} \sum_{\tau \in \mathcal{T}} \max_{s_k \in S} cohn(s_k,\tau)$$

$tfidf(\cdot,\cdot)$ is the TF-IDF similarity function. $\mathcal{S}_{qual}(S;\mathcal{T})$ captures three desired qualities of an article summary: *importance* (first item), *coverage* (second item), and the *continuity* of the current summary to previously generated summaries. The coverage function has been used to encourage summary diversity and reduce redundancy (Lin and Bilmes, 2011; Wang et al., 2014). The continuity function considers how well article summary $S$ can be attached to each event thread, thus favors summaries that can be connected to multiple threads.

Parameters $\theta_{cov}$ and $\alpha$ are tuned on multi-document summarization dataset DUC 2003 (Over and Yen, 2003). Experiments show that system performance peaks and is stable for $\theta_{cont} \in [1.0, 5.0]$. We thus fix $\theta_{cont}$ to 1.0. We discard sentences with more than 80% of content words covered by historical summaries. We use BASIC to denote a system that only optimizes on importance and coverage (i.e. first two items in $\mathcal{S}_{qual}(S;\mathcal{T})$). The system optimizing $\mathcal{S}_{qual}(S;\mathcal{T})$ is henceforth called THREAD.

The **comment summary quality** function simply takes the form $\mathcal{C}_{qual}(C) = \sum_{c \in C} imp_c(c)$.

### 4.3 Connectivity Measurement

We encode two objectives in the connectivity function $\mathcal{X}(S,C)$: (1) encouraging topical cohesion (i.e. connectivity) between article summary and comment summary; and (2) favoring comments that cover diversified events.

Let $conn(s,c)$ measure content similarity between a sentence $s \in S$ and a comment $c \in C$. Connectivity between article summary $S$ and comment summary $C$ is computed as follows. We build a bipartite graph $\mathcal{G}$ between $S$ and $C$ with edge weight as $conn(s,c)$.

We then find an edge set $\mathcal{M}$, the best matching of $\mathcal{G}$. $\mathcal{X}(S, C)$ is defined as the sum over edge weights in $\mathcal{M}$, i.e. $\mathcal{X}(S, C) = \sum_{e \in \mathcal{M}} weight(e)$. An example is illustrated in Figure 2.

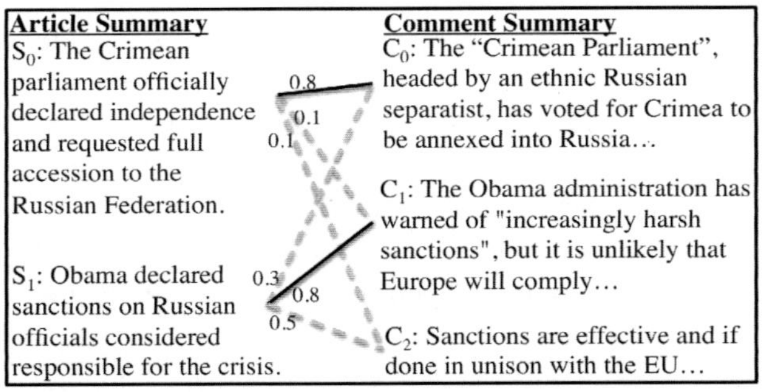


Figure 2: An example on computing the connectivity between an article summary (left) and a comment summary (right) via best matching in bipartite graph. Number on each edge indicates the content similarity between a sentence and a comment. Solid lines are edges in the best matching graph. For this example, the connectivity $\mathcal{X}(S, C)$ is $0.8 + 0.8 = 1.6$.

We consider two options for $conn(s, c)$. One is *lexical similarity* which is based on TF-IDF vectors. Another is *semantic similarity*. Let $R_s = \{(a_s, r_s, b_s)\}$ and $R_c = \{(a_c, r_c, b_c)\}$ be the sets of dependency relations in $s$ and $c$. $conn(s, c)$ is calculated as:

$$\sum_{(a_s, r_s, b_s) \in R_s} \max_{\substack{(a_c, r_c, b_c) \in R_c \\ r_s = r_c}} simi(a_s, a_c) \times simi(b_s, b_c)$$

where $simi(\cdot, \cdot)$ is a word similarity function. We experiment with shortest path based similarity defined on WordNet (Miller, 1995) and Cosine similarity with word vectors trained on Google news (Mikolov et al., 2013). Systems using the three metrics that optimize $\mathcal{Z}(S, C; \mathcal{T})$ are henceforth called THREAD+OPT$_{\texttt{TFIDF}}$, THREAD+OPT$_{\texttt{WordNet}}$ and THREAD+OPT$_{\texttt{WordVec}}$.

### 4.4 An Alternating Optimization Algorithm

To maximize the full objective function $\mathcal{Z}(S, C; \mathcal{T})$, we design a novel alternating optimization algorithm (Alg. 1) where we alternately find better $S$ and $C$.

We initialize $S_0$ by a greedy algorithm (Lin and Bilmes, 2011) with respect to $\mathcal{S}_{qual}(S; \mathcal{T})$. Notice that $\mathcal{S}_{qual}(S; \mathcal{T})$ is a submodular function, so that the greedy solution is a $1 - 1/e$ approximation to the optimal solution of $\mathcal{S}_{qual}(S; \mathcal{T})$. Fixing $S_0$, we model the problem of finding $C_0$ that maximizes $\mathcal{C}_{qual}(C) + \delta\mathcal{X}(S_0, C)$ as a maximum-weight bipartite graph matching problem. This problem can be reduced to a maximum network flow problem, and then be solved by Ford-Fulkerson algorithm (details are discussed in (Kleinberg and Tardos, 2005)). Thereafter, for each iteration, we alternately find a better $S_t$ with regard to $\mathcal{S}_{qual}(S; \mathcal{T}) + \delta\mathcal{X}(S, C_{t-1})$ using hill climbing, and an exact solution $C_t$ to $\mathcal{C}_{qual}(C) + \delta\mathcal{X}(S_t, C)$ with Ford-Fulkerson algorithm. Iteration stops when the increase of $\mathcal{Z}(S, C)$ is below threshold $\epsilon$ (set to 0.01). System performance is stable when we vary $\delta \in [1.0, 10.0]$, so we set $\delta = 1.0$.

**Input** : sentences $V_s$, comments $V_c$, threads $\mathcal{T}$, $\delta$, threshold $\epsilon$, functions $\mathcal{Z}(S, C; \mathcal{T})$, $\mathcal{S}_{qual}(S; \mathcal{T})$, $\mathcal{C}_{qual}(C)$, $\mathcal{X}(S, C)$
**Output**: article summary $S$, comment summary $C$

/* Initialize $S$ and $C$ by greedy algorithm and Ford-Fulkerson algorithm */
$S_0 \leftarrow \max_S \mathcal{S}_{qual}(S; \mathcal{T})$;
$C_0 \leftarrow \max_C \mathcal{C}_{qual}(C) + \delta\mathcal{X}(S_0, C)$;
$t \leftarrow 1$;
$\Delta\mathcal{Z} \leftarrow \infty$;
**while** $\Delta\mathcal{Z} > \epsilon$ **do**
  /* Step 1: Hill climbing algorithm */
  $S_t \leftarrow \max_S \mathcal{S}_{qual}(S; \mathcal{T}) + \delta\mathcal{X}(S, C_{t-1})$;
  /* Step 2: Ford-Fulkerson algorithm */
  $C_t \leftarrow \max_C \mathcal{C}_{qual}(C) + \delta\mathcal{X}(S_t, C)$;
  $\Delta\mathcal{Z} = \mathcal{Z}(S_t, C_t; \mathcal{T}) - \mathcal{Z}(S_{t-1}, C_{t-1}; \mathcal{T})$;
  $t \leftarrow t + 1$;
**end**

**Algorithm 1:** Generate article summary and comment summary for a given day via alternating optimization .

Algorithm 1 is guaranteed to find a solution at least as good as $S_0$ and $C_0$. It progresses only if Step 1 finds $S_t$ that improves upon $\mathcal{Z}(S_{t-1}, C_{t-1}; \mathcal{T})$, and Step 2 finds $C_t$ where $\mathcal{Z}(S_t, C_t; \mathcal{T}) \geq \mathcal{Z}(S_t, C_{t-1}; \mathcal{T})$.

## 5 Experimental Results

### 5.1 Evaluation of SENTENCE and COMMENT Importance Scorers

We test importance scorers (Section 3) on single document *sentence ranking* and *comment ranking*.

For both tasks, we compare with two previous systems on joint ranking and summarization of news articles and tweets. *Yang et al. (2011)* employ supervised learning based on factor graphs to model content similarity between the two types of data. We use the same features for this model. *Gao et al. (2012)* summarize by including the complementary information between articles and tweets, which is estimated by an unsupervised topic model.[3] We also consider two state-of-the-art rankers: *RankBoost* (Freund et al., 2003) and *LambdaMART* (Burges, 2010). Finally, we use a *position baseline* that ranks sentences based on their position in the article, and a *rating baseline* that ranks comments based on positive user ratings.

We evaluate using normalized discounted cumulative gain at top 3 returned results (NDCG@3). Sentences are considered relevant if they have ROUGE-2 scores larger than 0.0 (computed against human abstracts), and comments are considered relevant if they are editor's picks.[4] Figure 3 demonstrates that our joint learning model uniformly outperforms all the other comparisons for both ranking tasks. In general, supervised learning based approaches (e.g. our method, Yang et al. (2011), RankBoost, and LambdaMART) produce better results than unsupervised method (e.g. Gao et al. (2012)).[5]

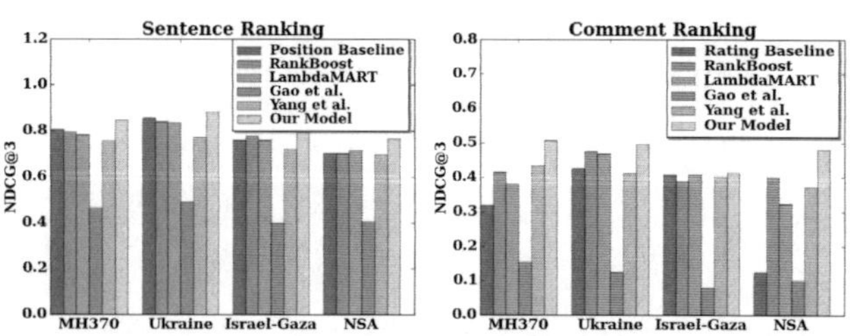


Figure 3: Evaluation of sentence and comment ranking on the four datasets by using normalized discounted cumulative gain at top 3 returned results (NDCG@3). Our joint learning based approach uniformly outperforms all the other comparisons.

## 5.2 Leveraging User Comments

In this section, we test if our system can leverage comments to produce better article-based summaries for event timelines. We collect **gold-standard timelines** for each of the four events from the corresponding Wikipedia page(s), NYT topic page, or BBC news page.

We consider two existing timeline creation systems that only utilize news articles, and a timeline generated from single-article human abstracts: (1) CHIEU AND LEE (2004) select sentences with high "interestingness" and "burstiness" using a likelihood ratio test to compare word distributions of sentences with articles in neighboring days. (2) YAN ET AL. (2011) design an evolutionary summarization system that selects sentences based on on coverage, coherence, and diversity. (3) We construct a timeline from the human ABSTRACTs provided with each article: we sort them chronologically according to article timestamps and add abstract sentences into each daily summary until reaching the word limit.

We test on five variations of our system. The first two systems generate article summaries with no comment information by optimizing $S_{qual}(S;T)$ using a greedy algorithm: BASIC ignores event threading; THREAD considers the threads. THREAD+OPT$_{\texttt{TFIDF}}$, THREAD+OPT$_{\texttt{WordNet}}$ and THREAD+OPT$_{\texttt{WordVec}}$ (see Section 4.3) leverage user comments to generate article summaries as well as comment summaries based on alternating optimization of Equation 3. Although comment summaries are generated, they are not used in the evaluation.

For all systems, we generate daily article summaries of at most 100 words, and select 5 comments for the corresponding comment summary. We employ ROUGE (Lin and Hovy, 2003) to automatically evaluate the content coverage (in terms of ngrams) of the article-based timelines vs. gold-standard timelines. ROUGE-2 (measures bigram overlap) and ROUGE-SU4 (measures unigram and skip-bigrams separated by up to four words) scores are reported in Table 4. As can be seen, under the alternating optimization framework, our systems, employing both articles and comments, consistently yield better ROUGE scores than the three baseline systems and our systems that do not leverage comments. Though constructed from single-article abstracts, baseline ABSTRACT is found to contain redundant information and thus limited in content coverage. This is due to the fact that different media tend to report on the same important events.

## 5.3 Evaluating Socially-Informed Timelines

We evaluate the full article+comment-based timelines on Amazon Mechanical Turk. Turkers are presented with a timeline consisting of five consecutive days' article summaries and four variations of the accompanying comment summary:

[3]We thank Zi Yang and Peng Li for providing the code.

[4]We experiment with all articles for sentence ranking, and NYT comments (with editor's picks) for comment ranking.

[5]Similar results are obtained with mean reciprocal rank.

| | MH370 | | Ukraine | | Israel-Gaza | | NSA | |
|---|---|---|---|---|---|---|---|---|
| | *R-2* | *R-SU4* | *R-2* | *R-SU4* | *R-2* | *R-SU4* | *R-2* | *R-SU4* |
| CHIEU AND LEE | 6.43 | 10.89 | 4.64 | 8.87 | 3.38 | **7.32** | 6.14 | 9.73 |
| YAN ET AL. | 6.37 | 10.35 | 4.57 | 8.67 | 2.39 | 5.78 | 3.99 | 7.73 |
| ABSTRACT | 6.16 | 10.62 | 3.85 | 8.40 | 2.21 | 5.42 | 7.03 | 8.65 |
| *- Greedy Algorithm* | | | | | | | | |
| BASIC | 6.59 | 9.80 | 5.31 | 9.23 | 3.15 | 6.20 | 3.81 | 7.58 |
| THREAD | 6.55 | 10.86 | 5.73 | 9.75 | 3.16 | 6.16 | 6.29 | 10.09 |
| *- Alternating Optimization (leveraging comments)* | | | | | | | | |
| THREAD+OPT$_{\texttt{TFIDF}}$ | *8.74* | 11.63 | *9.10* | *12.59* | 3.78 | 6.45 | *8.07* | *10.31* |
| THREAD+OPT$_{\texttt{WordNet}}$ | *8.73* | ***11.87*** | *8.67* | *12.10* | **4.11** | 6.64 | ***8.63*** | ***11.12*** |
| THREAD+OPT$_{\texttt{WordVec}}$ | ***9.29*** | 11.63 | ***9.16*** | ***12.72*** | 3.75 | 6.38 | *8.29* | *10.36* |

Table 4: ROUGE-2 (R-2) and ROUGE-SU4 (R-SU4) scores (multiplied by 100) for different timeline generation approaches on four event datasets. Systems that statistically significantly outperform the three baselines ($p < 0.05$, paired $t-$test) are in *italics*. Numbers in **bold** are the highest score for each column.

RANDOMly selected comments, USER'S-PICKS (ranked by positive user ratings), *randomly* selected EDITOR'S-PICKS and timelines produced by the THREAD+OPT$_{\texttt{WordVec}}$ version of OUR SYSTEM. We also include one noisy comment summary (i.e. irrelevant to the question) to avoid spam. We display two comments per day for each system.[6]

Turkers are asked to rank the comment summary variations according to *informativeness* and *insightfulness*. For informativeness, we ask the Turkers to judge based only on knowledge displayed in the timeline, and to rate each comment summary based on how much relevant information they learn from it. For insightfulness, Turkers are required to focus on insights and valuable opinions. They are requested to leave a short explanation of their ranking.

15 five-day periods are randomly selected. We solicit four distinct Turkers located in the U.S. to evaluate each set of timelines. An inter-rater agreement of Krippendorff's $\alpha$ of 0.63 is achieved for informativeness ranking and $\alpha$ is 0.50 for insightfulness ranking.

Table 5 shows the percentage of times a particular method is selected as producing the best comment portion of the timeline, as well as the micro-average rank of each method, for both informativeness and insightfulness. Our system is selected as the best in 66.7% of the evaluations for informativeness and 51.7% for insightfulness. In both cases, we statistically significantly outperform ($p < 0.05$ using a Wilcoxon signed-rank test) the editor's-picks

| | Informativeness | | Insightfulness | |
|---|---|---|---|---|
| | % Best | Avg Rank | % Best | Avg Rank |
| Random | 1.7% | 3.67 | 3.3% | 3.58 |
| User's-picks | 5.0% | 2.83 | 15.0% | 2.55 |
| Editor's-picks | 26.7% | 2.05 | 30.0% | 2.22 |
| Our system | **66.7%** | **1.45** | **51.7%** | **1.65** |

Table 5: Human evaluation results on the comment portion of socially-informed timelines. **Boldface** indicates statistical significance vs. other results in the same column using a Wilcoxon signed-rank test ($p < 0.05$). On average, the output from our system is ranked higher than all other alternatives.

and user's-picks. Turkers' explanations indicate that they prefer our comment summaries mainly because they are "very informative and insightful to what was happening", and "show the sharpness of the commenter". Turkers sometimes think the summaries randomly selected from editor's-picks "lack connection", and characterize user's-picks as "the information was somewhat limited".

Figure 4 shows part of the timeline generated by our system for the Ukraine crisis.

| Article Summary | Comment Summary |
|---|---|
| 2014-03-17 Obama administration froze the U.S. assets of seven Russian officials, while similar sanctions were imposed on four Ukrainian officials. . . . | Theodore Roosevelt said that the worst possible thing you can do in diplomacy is "soft hitting". That is what the US and the EU are doing in these timid "sanctions" against people without any overseas accounts. . . |
| 2014-03-18 Ukraine does not recognize a treaty signed in Moscow on Tuesday making its Crimean peninsula a part of Russia. . . | Though there were many in Crimea who supported annexation, there were certainly some who did not. what about those people?. . . |
| 2014-03-19 The head of NATO warned on Wednesday that Russian President Vladimir Putin may not stop with the annexation of Crimea . . . | If you look at a real map , Crimea is an island and has always been more connected to Russia than to Ukraine. . . |
| 2014-03-20 The United States on Thursday expanded its sanctions on Russians. . . | The US and EU should follow up economic sanctions with concrete steps to strengthen NATO. . . |

Figure 4: A snippet of timeline generated by our system THREAD+OPT$_{\texttt{WordVec}}$ for the Ukraine crisis. Due to space limitations, we only display partial summaries.

### 5.4 Human Evaluation of Event Threading

Here we evaluate on the utility of event threads for high-level information access guidance: *can event threads allow users to easily locate and absorb information with a specific interest in mind?*

We first sample a 10-day timeline for each dataset from those produced by the THREAD+OPT$_{\texttt{WordVec}}$

[6]For our system, we select the two comments with highest importance scores from the comment summary.

variation of our system. We designed one question for each timeline. Sample questions are: "describe the activities for searching for the missing flight MH370", and "describe the attitude and action of Russian Government on Eastern Ukraine". We recruited 10 undergraduate and graduate students who are native speakers of English. Each student first read one question and its corresponding timeline for 5 minutes. The timeline was then removed, and the student wrote down an answer for the question. We asked each student to answer the question for each of four timelines (one for each event dataset). Two timelines are displayed with threads, and two without threads. We presented threads by adding a thread number in front of each sentence.

We then used Amazon Mechanical Turk to evaluate the informativeness of students' answers. Turkers were asked to read all 10 answers for the same question, with five answers based on timelines with threads and five others based on timelines without threads. After that, they rated each answer with an informativeness score on a 1-to-5 rating scale (1 as "not relevant to the query", and 5 as "very informative"). We also added two quality control questions. Table 6 shows that the average rating for answers written after reading timelines *with threads* is 3.29 (43% are rated $\geq 4$), higher than the 2.58 for the timelines with *no thread* exhibited (30% are rated $\geq 4$).

| Answer Type | Avg $\pm$ STD | Rated 5 (%) | Rated 4 (%) |
|---|---|---|---|
| No Thread | $2.58 \pm 1.20$ | 7% | 23% |
| With Threads | $3.29 \pm 1.28$ | 17% | 26% |

Table 6: Human evaluation on the informativeness of answers written after reading timelines *with threads* vs. with *no thread*. Answers written with access to threads are rated higher (3.29) than the ones with no thread (2.58).

## 6 Related Work

There is a growing interest in generating article summaries informed by social context. Existing work focuses on learning users' interests from comments and incorporates the learned information into a news article summarization system (Hu et al., 2008). Zhao et al. (2013) instead estimate word distributions from tweets, and bias a Page Rank algorithm to give higher restart probability to sentences with similar distributions. Generating tweet+article summaries has been recently investigated in Yang et al. (2011). They propose a factor graph to allow sentences and tweets to mutually reinforce each other. Gao et al. (2012) exploit a co-ranking model to identify sentence-tweet pairs with complementary information estimated from a topic model. These efforts handle a small number of documents and tweets, while we target a larger scale of data.

In terms of timeline summarization, the Chieu and Lee (2004) system ranks sentences according to "burstiness" and "interestingness" estimated by a likelihood ratio test. Yan et al. (2011) explore an optimization framework that maximizes the relevance, coverage, diversity, and coherence of the timeline. Neither system has leveraged the social context. Our event threading algorithm is also inspired by work on topic detection and tracking (TDT) (Allan et al., 1998), where efforts are made for document-level link detection and topic tracking. Similarly, Nallapati et al. (2004) investigate event threading for articles, where they predict linkage based on causal and temporal dependencies. Shahaf et al. (2012) instead seek for connecting articles into one coherent graph. To the best of our knowledge, we are the first to study sentence-level event threading.

## 7 Conclusion

We presented a socially-informed timeline generation system, which constructs timelines consisting of article summaries and comment summaries. An alternating optimization algorithm is designed to maximize the connectivity between the two sets of summaries as well as their importance and information coverage. Automatic and human evaluations showed that our system produced more informative timelines than state-of-the-art systems. Our comment summaries were also rated as very insightful.

## Acknowledgments

We thank John Hessel, Lillian Lee, Moontae Lee, David Lutz, Karthik Raman, Vikram Rao, Yiye Ruan, Xanda Schofield, Adith Swaminathan, Chenhao Tan, Bishan Yang, other members of Cornell NLP group, and the NAACL reviewers for valuable suggestions and advice on various aspects of this work. This work was supported in part by DARPA DEFT Grant FA8750-13-2-0015.

## References


J. Allan, J. Carbonell, G. Doddington, J. Yamron, and Y. Yang. 1998. Topic detection and tracking pilot study: Final report. In *Proceedings of the DARPA Broadcast News Transcription and Understanding Workshop*, pages 194–218, Lansdowne, VA, USA, February. 007.

Christopher J. C. Burges. 2010. From RankNet to LambdaRank to LambdaMART: An Overview. Technical report, Microsoft Research.

Angel X. Chang and Christopher Manning. 2012. Sutime: A library for recognizing and normalizing time expressions. In Nicoletta Calzolari (Conference Chair), Khalid Choukri, Thierry Declerck, Mehmet Uur Doan, Bente Maegaard, Joseph Mariani, Asuncion Moreno, Jan Odijk, and Stelios Piperidis, editors, *Proceedings of the Eight International Conference on Language Resources and Evaluation (LREC'12)*, Istanbul, Turkey, may. European Language Resources Association (ELRA).

Hai Leong Chieu and Yoong Keok Lee. 2004. Query based event extraction along a timeline. In *Proceedings of the 27th Annual International ACM SIGIR Conference on Research and Development in Information Retrieval*, SIGIR '04, pages 425–432, New York, NY, USA. ACM.

Anthony Fader, Stephen Soderland, and Oren Etzioni. 2011. Identifying relations for open information extraction. In *Proceedings of the Conference on Empirical Methods in Natural Language Processing*, EMNLP '11, pages 1535–1545, Stroudsburg, PA, USA. Association for Computational Linguistics.

Yoav Freund, Raj Iyer, Robert E. Schapire, and Yoram Singer. 2003. An efficient boosting algorithm for combining preferences. *J. Mach. Learn. Res.*, 4:933–969, December.

Wei Gao, Peng Li, and Kareem Darwish. 2012. Joint topic modeling for event summarization across news and social media streams. In *Proceedings of the 21st ACM International Conference on Information and Knowledge Management*, CIKM '12, pages 1173–1182, New York, NY, USA. ACM.

Meishan Hu, Aixin Sun, and Ee-Peng Lim. 2008. Comments-oriented document summarization: Understanding documents with readers' feedback. In *Proceedings of the 31st Annual International ACM SIGIR Conference on Research and Development in Information Retrieval*, SIGIR '08, pages 291–298, New York, NY, USA. ACM.

Thorsten Joachims. 2002. Optimizing search engines using clickthrough data. In *Proceedings of the Eighth ACM SIGKDD International Conference on Knowledge Discovery and Data Mining*, KDD '02, pages 133–142, New York, NY, USA. ACM.

Jon Kleinberg and Eva Tardos. 2005. *Algorithm Design*. Addison-Wesley Longman Publishing Co., Inc., Boston, MA, USA.

Hui Lin and Jeff Bilmes. 2011. A class of submodular functions for document summarization. In *Proceedings of the 49th Annual Meeting of the Association for Computational Linguistics: Human Language Technologies - Volume 1*, HLT '11, pages 510–520, Stroudsburg, PA, USA. Association for Computational Linguistics.

Chin-Yew Lin and Eduard Hovy. 2003. Automatic evaluation of summaries using n-gram co-occurrence statistics. In *Proceedings of the 2003 Conference of the North American Chapter of the Association for Computational Linguistics on Human Language Technology - Volume 1*, pages 71–78.

Zongyang Ma, Aixin Sun, Quan Yuan, and Gao Cong. 2012. Topic-driven reader comments summarization. In *Proceedings of the 21st ACM International Conference on Information and Knowledge Management*, CIKM '12, pages 265–274, New York, NY, USA. ACM.

Christopher Manning, Mihai Surdeanu, John Bauer, Jenny Finkel, Steven Bethard, and David McClosky. 2014. The stanford corenlp natural language processing toolkit. In *Proceedings of 52nd Annual Meeting of the Association for Computational Linguistics: System Demonstrations*, pages 55–60, Baltimore, Maryland. Association for Computational Linguistics.

Mausam, Michael Schmitz, Robert Bart, Stephen Soderland, and Oren Etzioni. 2012. Open language learning for information extraction. In *Proceedings of the 2012 Joint Conference on Empirical Methods in Natural Language Processing and Computational Natural Language Learning*, EMNLP-CoNLL '12, pages 523–534, Stroudsburg, PA, USA. Association for Computational Linguistics.

Tomas Mikolov, Kai Chen, Greg Corrado, and Jeffrey Dean. 2013. Efficient estimation of word representations in vector space. *CoRR*, abs/1301.3781.

George A. Miller. 1995. Wordnet: A lexical database for english. *Commun. ACM*, 38(11):39–41, November.

Ramesh Nallapati, Ao Feng, Fuchun Peng, and James Allan. 2004. Event threading within news topics. In *Proceedings of the Thirteenth ACM International Conference on Information and Knowledge Management*, CIKM '04, pages 446–453, New York, NY, USA. ACM.

P. Over and J. Yen. 2003. An introduction to DUC 2003: Intrinsic evaluation of generic news text summarization systems.

Alan Ritter, Mausam, Oren Etzioni, and Sam Clark. 2012. Open domain event extraction from twitter. In *Proceedings of the 18th ACM SIGKDD International Conference on Knowledge Discovery and Data Mining*, KDD '12, pages 1104–1112, New York, NY, USA. ACM.

Dafna Shahaf, Carlos Guestrin, and Eric Horvitz. 2012. Trains of thought: Generating information maps. In *Proceedings of the 21st International Conference on World Wide Web*, WWW '12, pages 899–908, New York, NY, USA. ACM.

Philip J. Stone, Dexter C. Dunphy, Marshall S. Smith, and Daniel M. Ogilvie. 1966. *The General Inquirer: A Computer Approach to Content Analysis*. MIT Press, Cambridge, MA.

Lu Wang, Hema Raghavan, Claire Cardie, and Vittorio Castelli. 2014. Query-focused opinion summarization for user-generated content. In *Proceedings of COLING 2014, the 25th International Conference on Computational Linguistics: Technical Papers*, pages 1660–1669, Dublin, Ireland, August. Dublin City University and Association for Computational Linguistics.

Theresa Wilson, Janyce Wiebe, and Paul Hoffmann. 2005. Recognizing contextual polarity in phrase-level sentiment analysis. In *Proceedings of the Conference on Human Language Technology and Empirical Methods in Natural Language Processing*, HLT '05, pages 347–354, Stroudsburg, PA, USA. Association for Computational Linguistics.

Rui Yan, Xiaojun Wan, Jahna Otterbacher, Liang Kong, Xiaoming Li, and Yan Zhang. 2011. Evolutionary timeline summarization: A balanced optimization framework via iterative substitution. In *Proceedings of the 34th International ACM SIGIR Conference on Research and Development in Information Retrieval*, SIGIR '11, pages 745–754, New York, NY, USA. ACM.

Zi Yang, Keke Cai, Jie Tang, Li Zhang, Zhong Su, and Juanzi Li. 2011. Social context summarization. In *Proceedings of the 34th International ACM SIGIR Conference on Research and Development in Information Retrieval*, SIGIR '11, pages 255–264, New York, NY, USA. ACM.

Xin Wayne Zhao, Yanwei Guo, Rui Yan, Yulan He, and Xiaoming Li. 2013. Timeline generation with social attention. In *Proceedings of the 36th International ACM SIGIR Conference on Research and Development in Information Retrieval*, SIGIR '13, pages 1061–1064, New York, NY, USA. ACM.

# Movie Script Summarization as Graph-based Scene Extraction

**Philip John Gorinski** and **Mirella Lapata**
Institute for Language, Cognition and Computation
School of Informatics, University of Edinburgh
10 Crichton Street, Edinburgh EH8 9AB
P.J.Gorinski@sms.ed.ac.uk, mlap@inf.ed.ac.uk

## Abstract

In this paper we study the task of movie script summarization, which we argue could enhance script browsing, give readers a rough idea of the script's plotline, and speed up reading time. We formalize the process of generating a shorter version of a screenplay as the task of finding an optimal chain of scenes. We develop a graph-based model that selects a chain by jointly optimizing its logical progression, diversity, and importance. Human evaluation based on a question-answering task shows that our model produces summaries which are more informative compared to competitive baselines.

## 1 Introduction

Each year, about 50,000 screenplays are registered with the WGA[1], the Writers Guild of America. Only a fraction of these make it through to be considered for production and an even smaller fraction to the big screen. How do producers and directors navigate through this vast number of scripts available? Typically, production companies, agencies, and studios hire script readers, whose job is to analyze screenplays that come in, sorting the hopeful from the hopeless. Having read the script, a reader will generate a coverage report consisting of a logline (one or two sentences describing the story in a nutshell), a synopsis (a two- to three-page long summary of the script), comments explaining its appeal or problematic aspects, and a final verdict as to whether the script merits further consideration. A script excerpt

```
We can't get a good glimpse of his face, but
his body is plump, above average height; he
is in his mid 30's.  Together they easily
lift the chair into the truck.
                  MAN (O.S.)
        Let's slide it up, you mind?
CUT TO:
INT. THE PANEL TRUCK - NIGHT
He climbs inside the truck, ducking under a
small hand winch, and grabs the chair.  She
hesitates again, but climbs in after him.
                     MAN
          Are you about a size 14?
                  CATHERINE
                 (surprised)
                    What?
Suddenly, in the shadowy dark, he clubs her
over the back of her head with his cast.
```

Figure 1: Excerpt from "The Silence of the Lambs". The scene heading `INT. THE PANEL TRUCK - NIGHT` denotes that the action takes place inside the panel truck at night. Character cues (e.g., `MAN`, `CATHERINE`) preface the lines the actors speak. Action lines describe what the camera sees (e.g., `We can't get a good glimpse of his face, but his body...`).

from "Silence of the Lambs", an American thriller released in 1991, is shown in Figure 1.

Although there are several screenwriting tools for authors (e.g., Final Draft is a popular application which automatically formats scripts to industry standards, keeps track of revisions, allows insertion of notes, and writing collaboratively online), there is a lack of any kind of script reading aids. Features of such a tool could be to automatically grade the quality of the script (e.g., thumbs up or down), generate

[1] The WGA is a collective term representing US TV and film writers.



*Human Language Technologies: The 2015 Annual Conference of the North American Chapter of the ACL*, pages 1066–1076,
Denver, Colorado, May 31 – June 5, 2015. ©2015 Association for Computational Linguistics

synopses and loglines, identify main characters and their stories, or facilitate browsing (e.g., "show me every scene where there is a shooting"). In this paper we explore whether current NLP technology can be used to address some of these tasks. Specifically, we focus on script summarization, which we conceptualize as the process of generating a shorter version of a screenplay, ideally encapsulating its most informative scenes. The resulting summaries can be used to enhance script browsing, give readers a rough idea of the script's content and plotline, and speed up reading time.

So, what makes a good script summary? According to modern film theory, "all films are about nothing — nothing but character" (Monaco, 1982). Beyond characters, a summary should also highlight major scenes representative of the story and its progression. With this in mind, we define a script summary as a *chain of scenes* which conveys a narrative and smooth transitions from one scene to the next. At the same time, a good chain should incorporate some *diversity* (i.e., avoid redundancy), and focus on *important* scenes and characters. We formalize the problem of selecting a good summary chain using a graph-theoretic approach. We represent scripts as (directed) bipartite graphs with vertices corresponding to scenes and characters, and edge weights to their strength of correlation. Intuitively, if two scenes are connected, a random walk starting from one would reach the other frequently. We find a chain of highly connected scenes by jointly optimizing logical progression, diversity, and importance.

Our contributions in this work are three-fold: we introduce a novel summarization task, on a new text genre, and formalize scene selection as the problem of finding a chain that represents a film's story; we propose several novel methods for analyzing script content (e.g., identifying important characters and their interactions); and perform a large-scale human evaluation study using a question-answering task. Experimental results show that our method produces summaries which are more informative compared to several competitive baselines.

## 2 Related Work

Computer-assisted analysis of literary text has a long history, with the first studies dating back to the 1960s (Mosteller and Wallace, 1964). More recently, the availability of large collections of digitized books and works of fiction has enabled researchers to observe cultural trends, address questions about language use and its evolution, study how individuals rise to and fall from fame, perform gender studies, and so on (Michel et al., 2010). Most existing work focuses on low-level analysis of word patterns, with a few notable exceptions. Elson et al. (2010) analyze 19th century British novels by constructing a conversational network with vertices corresponding to characters and weighted edges corresponding to the amount of conversational interaction. Elsner (2012) analyzes characters and their emotional trajectories, whereas Nalisnick and Baird (2013) identify a character's enemies and allies in plays based on the sentiment of their utterances. Other work (Bamman et al., 2013, 2014) automatically infers latent character types (e.g., villains or heroes) in novels and movie plot summaries.

Although we are not aware of any previous approaches to summarize screenplays, the field of computer vision is rife with attempts to summarize video (see Reed 2004 for an overview). Most techniques are based on visual information and rely on low-level cues such as motion, color, or audio (e.g., Rasheed et al. 2005). Movie summarization is a special type of video summarization which poses many challenges due to the large variety of film styles and genres. A few recent studies (Weng et al., 2009; Lin et al., 2013) have used concepts from social network analysis to identify lead roles and role communities in order to segment movies into scenes (containing one or more shots) and create more informative summaries. A surprising fact about this line of work is that it does not exploit the movie script in any way. Characters are typically identified using face recognition techniques and scene boundaries are presumed unknown and are automatically detected. A notable exception are Sang and Xu (2010) who generate video summaries for movies, while taking into account character interaction features which they estimate from the corresponding screenplay.

Our own approach is inspired by work in egocentric video analysis. An egocentric video offers a first-person view of the world and is captured from a wearable camera focusing on the user's activities,

| | # Movies | AvgLines | AvgScenes | AvgChars |
|---|---|---|---|---|
| Drama | 665 | 4484.53 | 79.77 | 60.94 |
| Thriller | 451 | 4333.10 | 91.84 | 52.59 |
| Comedy | 378 | 4303.02 | 66.13 | 57.51 |
| Action | 288 | 4255.56 | 101.82 | 59.99 |

Figure 2: ScriptBase corpus statistics. Movies can have multiple genres, thus numbers do not add up to 1,276.

social interactions, and interests. Lu and Grauman (2013) present a summarization model which extracts subshot sequences while finding a balance of important subshots that are both diverse and provide a natural progression through the video, in terms of prominent visual objects (e.g., bottle, mug, television). We adapt their technique to our task, and show how to estimate character-scene correlations based on linguistic analysis. We also interpret movies as social networks and extract a rich set of features from character interactions and their sentiment which we use to guide the summarization process.

## 3 ScriptBase: A Movie Script Corpus

We compiled ScriptBase, a collection of 1,276 movie scripts, by automatically crawling web-sites which host or link entire movie scripts (e.g., `imsdb.com`). The retrieved scripts were then cross-matched against Wikipedia[2] and IMDB[3] and paired with corresponding user-written summaries, plot sections, loglines and taglines (taglines are short snippets used by marketing departments to promote a movie). We also collected meta-information regarding the movie's genre, its actors, the production year, etc. ScriptBase contains movies comprising 23 genres; each movie is on average accompanied by 3 user summaries, 3 loglines, and 3 taglines. The corpus spans years 1909–2013. Some corpus statistics are shown in Figure 2.

The scripts were further post-processed with the Stanford CoreNLP pipeline (Manning et al., 2014) to perform tagging, parsing, named entity recognition and coreference resolution. They were also annotated with semantic roles (e.g., ARG0, ARG1), using the MATE tools (Björkelund et al., 2009). Our summarization experiments focused on comedies and thrillers. We randomly selected 30 movies for training/development and 65 movies for testing.

[2]`http://en.wikipedia.org`

[3]`http://www.imdb.com/`

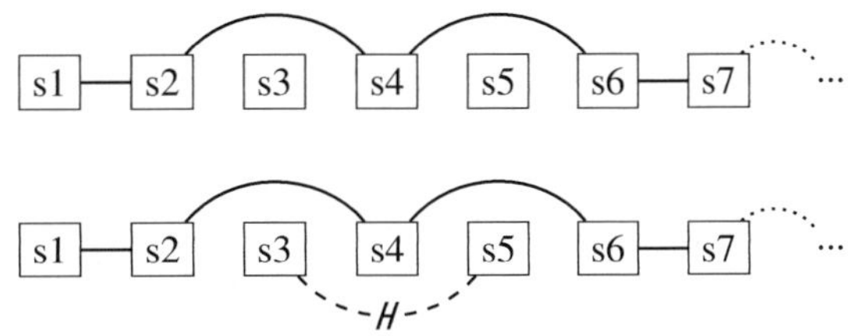


Figure 3: Example of consecutive chain (top). Squares represent scenes in a screenplay. The bottom chain would not be allowed, since the connection between $s3$ and $s5$ makes it non-consecutive.

## 4 The Scene Extraction Model

As mentioned earlier, we define script summarization as the task of selecting a chain of scenes representing the movie's most important content. We interpret the term scene in the screenplay sense. A scene is a unit of action that takes place in one location at one time (see Figure 1). We therefore need not be concerned with scene segmentation; scene boundaries are clearly marked, and constitute the basic units over which our model operates.

Let $M = (S, C)$ represent a screenplay consisting of a set $S = \{s_1, s_2, \dots, s_n\}$ of scenes, and a set $C = \{c_1, \dots, c_m\}$ of characters. We are interested in finding a list $S' = \{s_i, \dots s_k\}$ of *ordered, consecutive* scenes subject to a compression rate $m$ (see the example in Figure 3). A natural interpretation of $m$ in our case is the percentage of scenes from the original script retained in the summary. The extracted chain should contain (a) *important* scenes (i.e., critical for comprehending the story and its development); (b) *diverse* scenes that cover different aspects of the story; and (c) scenes which highlight the story's *progression* from beginning to end. We therefore find the chain $S'$ maximizing the objective function $Q(S')$ which is the weighted sum of three terms: the story progression $P$, scene diversity $D$, and scene importance $I$:

$$S^* = \underset{S' \subset S}{arg\,max}\, Q(S') \quad (1)$$

$$Q(S') = \lambda_P P(S') + \lambda_D D(S') + \lambda_I I(S') \quad (2)$$

In the following, we define each of the three terms.

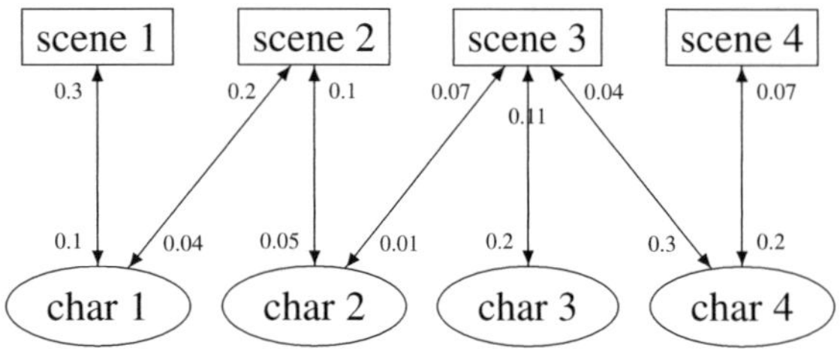


Figure 4: Example of a bipartite graph, connecting a movie's scenes with participating characters.

**Scene-to-scene Progression** The first term in the objective is responsible for selecting chains representing a logically coherent story. Intuitively, this means that if our chain includes a scene where a character commits an action, then scenes involving affected parties or follow-up actions should also be included. We operationalize this idea of progression in a story in terms of how strongly the characters in a selected scene $s_i$ influence the transition to the next scene $s_{i+1}$:

$$P(S') = \sum_{i=0}^{|S'|-1} \sum_{c \in C_i} INF(s_i, s_{i+1}|c) \tag{3}$$

We represent screenplays as weighted, bipartite graphs connecting scenes and characters:

$$B = (V, E) : V = C \cup S$$

$$E = \{(s, c, w_{s,c}) | s \in S, c \in C, w_{s,c} \in [0,1]\} \cup$$
$$\{(c, s, w_{c,s}) | c \in C, s \in S, w_{c,s} \in [0,1]\}$$

The set of vertices $V$ corresponds to the union of characters $C$ and scenes $S$. We therefore add to the bipartite graph one node per scene and one node per character, and two directed edges for each scene-character and character-scene pair. An example of a bipartite graph is shown in Figure 4. We further assume that two scenes $s_i$ and $s_{i+1}$ are tightly connected in such a graph if a random walk with restart (RWR; Tong et al. 2006; Kim et al. 2014) which starts in $s_i$ has a high probability of ending in $s_{i+1}$.

In order to calculate the random walk stationary distributions, we must estimate the weights between a character and a scene. We are interested in how important a character is generally in the movie, and specifically in a particular scene. For $w_{c,s}$, we consider the probability of a character being important, i.e., of them belonging to the set of main characters:

$$w_{c,s} = P(c \in main(M)), \; \forall (c, s, w_{c,s}) \in E \tag{4}$$

where $P(c \in main(M))$ is some probability score associated with $c$ being a main character in script $M$. For $w_{s,c}$, we take the number of interactions a character is involved in relative to the total number of interactions in a specific scene as indicative of the character's importance in that scene. Interactions refer to conversational interactions as well as relations between characters (e.g., who does what to whom):

$$w_{s,c} = \frac{\sum_{c' \in C_s} inter(c, c')}{\sum_{c_1, c_2 \in C_s} inter(c_1, c_2)}, \; \forall (s, c, w_{s,c}) \in E \tag{5}$$

We defer discussion of how we model probability $P(c \in Main(M))$ and obtain interaction counts to Section 5. Weights $w_{s,c}$ and $w_{c,s}$ are normalized:

$$w_{s,c} = \frac{w_{s,c}}{\sum_{(s,c',w'_{s,c})} w'_{s,c}}, \; \forall (s, c, w_{s,c}) \in E \tag{6}$$

$$w_{c,s} = \frac{w_{c,s}}{\sum_{(c,s',w'_{c,s})} w'_{c,s}}, \; \forall (c, s, w_{c,s}) \in E \tag{7}$$

We calculate the stationary distributions of a random walk on a transition matrix $T$, enumerating over all vertices $v$ (i.e., characters *and* scenes) in the bipartite graph $B$:

$$T(i,j) = \begin{cases} w_{i,j} \text{ if } (v_i, v_j, w_{i,j} \in E^B) \\ 0 \text{ otherwise} \end{cases} \tag{8}$$

We measure the *influence* individual characters have on scene-to-scene transitions as follows. The stationary distribution $r_k$ for a RWR walker starting at node $k$ is a vector that satisfies:

$$r_k = (1 - \varepsilon) T r_k + \varepsilon e_k \tag{9}$$

where $T$ is the transition matrix of the graph, $e_k$ is a *seed vector*, with all elements 0, except for element $k$ which is set to 1, and $\varepsilon$ is a restart probability parameter. In practice, our vectors $r_k$ and $e_k$ are indexed by the scenes and characters in a movie, i.e., they have length $|S| + |C|$, and their $n_{th}$ element corresponds either to a known scene or character. In cases where graphs are relatively small, we can compute $r$ directly[4] by solving:

$$r_k = \varepsilon(I - (1-\varepsilon)T)^{-1} e_k \quad (10)$$

The $l$th element of $r$ then equals the probability of the random walker being in state $l$ in the stationary distribution. Let $r_k^c$ be the same as $r_k$, but with the character node $c$ of the bipartite graph being turned into a sink, i.e., all entries for $c$ in the transition matrix $T$ are 0. We can then define how a single character influences the transition between scenes $s_i$ and $s_{i+1}$ as:

$$INF(s_i, s_{i+1}|c) = r_{s_i}[s_{i+1}] - r_{s_i}^c[s_{i+1}] \quad (11)$$

where $r_{s_i}[s_{i+1}]$ is shorthand for that element in the vector $r_{s_i}$ that corresponds to scene $s_{i+1}$. We use the $INF$ score directly in Equation (3) to determine the progress score of a candidate chain.

**Diversity** The diversity term $D(S')$ in our objective should encourage chains which consist of more dissimilar scenes, thereby avoiding redundancy. The diversity of chain $S'$ is the sum of the diversities of its successive scenes:

$$D(S') = \sum_{i=1}^{|S'|-1} d(s_i, s_{i+1}) \quad (12)$$

The diversity $d(s_i, s_{i+1})$ of two scenes $s_i$ and $s_{i+1}$ is estimated taking into account two factors: (a) do they have any characters in common, and (b) does the sentiment change from one scene to the next:

$$d(s_i, s_{i+1}) = \frac{d_{char}(s_i, s_{i+1}) + d_{sen}(s_i, s_{i+1})}{2} \quad (13)$$

where $d_{char}(s_i, s_{i+1})$ and $d_{sen}(s_i, s_{i+1})$ respectively denote character and sentiment similarity between scenes. Specifically, $d_{char}(s_i, s_{i+1})$ is the relative character overlap between scenes $s_i$ and $s_{i+1}$:

$$d_{char}(s_i, s_{i+1}) = 1 - \frac{|C_{s_i} \cap C_{s_{i+1}}|}{|C_{s_i} \cup C_{s_{i+1}}|} \quad (14)$$

$d_{char}$ will be 0 if two scenes share the same characters and 1 if no characters are shared. Analogously, we define $d_{sen}$, the sentiment overlap between two scenes as:

$$d_{sen}(s_i, s_{i+1}) = 1 - \frac{k \cdot dif(s_i, s_{i+1})}{k - k \cdot dif(s_i, s_{i+1}) + 1} \quad (15)$$

$$dif(s_i, s_{i+1}) = \frac{1}{1 + |sen(s_i) - sen(s_{i+1})|} \quad (16)$$

where the sentiment $sen(s)$ of scene $s$ is the aggregate sentiment score of all interactions in $s$:

$$sen(s) = \sum_{c,c' \in C_s} sen(inter(c, c')) \quad (17)$$

We explain how interactions and their sentiment are computed in Section 5. Again, $d_{sen}$ is larger if two scenes have a less similar sentiment. $dif(s_i, s_{i+1})$ becomes 1 if the sentiments are identical, and increasingly smaller for more dissimilar sentiments. The sigmoid-like function in Equation (15) scales $d_{sen}$ within range $[0, 1]$ to take smaller values for larger sentiment differences (factor $k$ adjusts the curve's smoothness).

**Importance** The score $I(S')$ captures whether a chain contains important scenes. We define $I(S')$ as the sum of all scene-specific importance scores $imp(s_i)$ of scenes contained in the chain:

$$I(S') = \sum_{i=1}^{|S'|} imp(s_i) \quad (18)$$

The importance $imp(s_i)$ of a scene $s_i$ is the ratio of lead to support characters within that scene:

$$imp(s_i) = \frac{\sum_{c:\, c \in C_{s_i} \wedge c \in main(M)} 1}{\sum_{c:\, c \in C_{s_i}} 1} \quad (19)$$

where $C_{s_i}$ is the set of characters present in scene $s_i$, and $main(M)$ is the set of main characters in the movie.[5] $I(s_i)$ is 0 if a scene does not contain any main characters, and 1 if it contains only main characters (see Section 5 for how $main(M)$ is inferred).

**Optimal Chain Selection** We use Linear Programming to efficiently find a good chain. The objective is to maximize Equation (2), i.e., the sum of the terms for progress, diversity and importance,

[4] We could also solve for $r$ recursively which would be preferable for large graphs, since the performed matrix inversion is computationally expensive.

[5] Whether scenes are important if they contain many main characters is an empirical question in its own right. For our purposes, we assume that this relation holds.

subject to their weights $\lambda$. We add a constraint corresponding to the compression rate, i.e., the number of scenes to be selected and enforce their linear order by disallowing non-consecutive combinations. We use GLPK[6] to solve the linear problem.

## 5 Implementation

In this section we discuss several aspects of the implementation of the model presented in the previous section. We explain how interactions are extracted and how sentiment is calculated. We also present our method for identifying main characters and estimating the weights $w_{s,c}$ and $w_{c,s}$ in the bipartite graph.

**Interactions** The notion of interaction underlies many aspects of the model defined in the previous section. For instance, interaction counts are required to estimate the weights $w_{s,c}$ in the bipartite graph of the progression term (see Equation (5)), and in defining diversity (see Equations (15)–(17)). As we shall see below, interactions are also important for identifying main characters in a screenplay.

We use the term interaction to refer to *conversations* between two characters, as well as their *relations* (e.g., if a character kills another). For conversational interactions, we simply need to identify the *speaker* generating an utterance and the *listener*. Speaker attribution comes for free in our case, as speakers are clearly marked in the text (see Figure 1). Listener identification is more involved, especially when there are multiple characters in a scene. We rely on a few simple heuristics. We assume that the previous speaker in the same scene, who is different from the current speaker, is the listener. If there is no previous speaker, we assume that the listener is the closest character mentioned in the speaker's utterance (e.g., via a coreferring proper name or a pronoun). In cases where we cannot find a suitable listener, we assume the current speaker is the listener.

We obtain character relations from the output of a semantic role labeler. Relations are denoted by verbs whose ARG0 and ARG1 roles are character names. We extract relations from the dialogue but also from scene descriptions. For example, in Figure 1 the description `Suddenly, [...] he clubs her over the head` contains the relation `clubs(MAN,CATHERINE)`. Pronouns are resolved to their antecedent using the Stanford coreference resolution system (Lee et al., 2011).

**Sentiment** We labeled lexical items in screenplays with sentiment values using the AFINN-96 lexicon (Nielsen, 2011), which is essentially a list of words scored with sentiment strength within the range $[-5,+5]$. The list also contains obscene words (which are often used in movies) and some Internet slang. By summing over the sentiment scores of individual words, we can work out the sentiment of an interaction between two characters, the sentiment of a scene (see Equation (17)), and even the sentiment between characters (e.g., who likes or dislikes whom in the movie in general).

**Main Characters** The progress term in our summarization objective crucially relies on characters and their importance (see the weight $w_{c,s}$ in Equation (4)). Previous work (Weng et al., 2009; Lin et al., 2013) extracts social networks where nodes correspond to roles in the movie, and edges to their co-occurrence. Leading roles (and their communities) are then identified by measuring their centrality in the network (i.e., number of edges terminating in a given node).

It is relatively straightforward to obtain a social network from a screenplay. Formally, for each movie we define a *weighted* and *undirected* graph:

$$G=\{C,E\},: C=\{c_1,\dots c_n\},$$
$$E=\{(c_i,c_j,w)|c_i,c_j\in C,\, w\in\mathbb{N}_{>0}\}$$

where vertices correspond to movie characters[7], and edges denote character-to-character interactions. Figure 5 shows an example of a social network for "The Silence of the Lambs". Due to lack of space, only main characters are displayed, however the actual graph contains *all* characters (42 in this case). Importantly, edge weights are not normalized, but directly reflect the strength of association between different characters.

We do not solely rely on the social network to identify main characters. We estimate $P(c\in main(M))$, the probability of $c$ being a leading character in movie $M$, using a Multi Layer

[6]https://www.gnu.org/software/glpk/

[7]We assume one node per *speaking role* in the script.

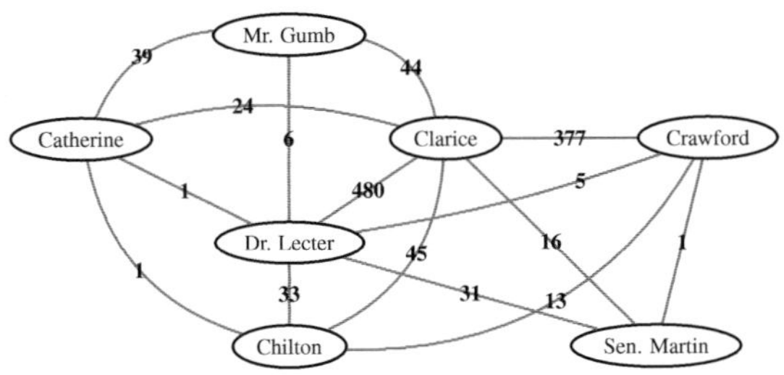


Figure 5: Social network for "The Silence of the Lambs"; edge weights correspond to absolute number of interactions between nodes.

Perceptron (MLP) and several features pertaining to the structure of the social network and the script text itself. A potential stumbling block in treating character identification as a classification task is obtaining training data, i.e., a list of main characters for each movie. We generate a gold-standard by assuming that the characters listed under Wikipedia's *Cast* section (or an equivalent section, e.g., *Characters*) are the main characters in the movie.

Examples of the features we used for the classification task include the barycenter of a character (i.e., the sum of its distance to all other characters), PageRank (Page et al., 1999), an eigenvector-based centrality measure, absolute/relative interaction weight (the sum of all interactions a character is involved in, divided by the sum of all interactions in the network), absolute/relative number of sentences uttered by a character, number of times a character is described by other characters (e.g., `He is a monster` or `She is nice`), number of times a character talks about other characters, and type-token-ratio of sentences uttered by the character (i.e., rate of unique words in a character's speech). Using these features, the MLP achieves an F1 of 79.0% on the test set. It outperforms other classification methods such as Naive Bayes or logistic regression. Using the full-feature set, the MLP also obtains performance superior to any individual measure of graph connectivity.

Aside from Equation (4), lead characters also appear in Equation (19), which determines scene importance. We assume a character $c \in main(M)$ if it is predicted by the MLP with a probability $\geq 0.5$.

## 6 Experimental Setup

**Gold Standard Chains** The development and tuning of the chain extraction model presented in Section 4 necessitates access to a gold standard of key scene chains representing the movie's most important content. Our experiments concentrated on a sample of 95 movies (comedies and thrillers) from the ScriptBase corpus (Section 3). Performing the scene selection task for such a big corpus manually would be both time consuming and costly. Instead, we used distant supervision based on Wikipedia to automatically generate a gold standard.

Specifically, we assume that Wikipedia plots are representative of the most important content in a movie. Using the alignment algorithm presented in Nelken and Shieber (2006), we align script sentences to Wikipedia plot sentences and assume that scenes with at least one alignment are part of the *gold chain* of scenes. We obtain many-to-many alignments using features such as lemma overlap and word stem similarity. When evaluated on four movies[8] (from the training set) whose content was manually aligned to Wikipedia plots, the aligner achieved a precision of .53 at a recall rate of .82 at deciding whether a scene should be aligned. Scenes are ranked according to the number of alignments they contain. When creating gold chains at different compression rates, we start with the best-ranked scenes and then successively add lower ranked ones until we reach the desired compression rate.

**System Comparison** In our experiments we compared our scene extraction model (SceneSum) against three baselines. The first baseline was based on the *minimum* overlap (MinOv) of characters in consecutive scenes and corresponds closely to the diversity term in our objective. The second baseline was based on the *maximum* overlap (MaxOv) of characters and approximates the importance term in our objective. The third baseline selects scenes at random (averaged over 1,000 runs). Parameters for our models were tuned on the training set, weights for the terms in the objective were optimized to the following values: $\lambda_P = 1.0$, $\lambda_D = 0.3$, and $\lambda_I = 0.1$. We set the restart probability of our random walker

[8] "Cars 2", "Shrek", "Swordfish", and "The Silence of the Lambs".

| | |
|---|---|
| 1. | Why does Trevor leave New York and where does he move to? |
| 2. | What is KOS, who is their leader, and why is he attending high school? |
| 3. | What happened to Cesar's finger, how did he eventually die? |
| 4. | Who killed Benny and how does Ellen find out? |
| 5. | Who is Rita and what becomes of her? |

Table 1: Questions for the movie "One Eight Seven".

to $\varepsilon = 0.5$, and the sigmoid scaling factor in our diversity term to $k = -1.2$.

**Evaluation** We assessed the output of our model (and comparison systems) automatically against the gold chains described above. We performed experiments with compression rates in the range of 10% to 50% and measured performance in terms of F1. In addition, we also evaluated the quality of the extracted scenes as perceived by humans, which is necessary, given the approximate nature of our gold standard. We adopted a question-answering (Q&A) evaluation paradigm which has been used previously to evaluate summaries and document compression (Morris et al., 1992; Mani et al., 2002; Clarke and Lapata, 2010). Under the assumption that the summary is to function as a replacement for the full script, we can measure the extent to which it can be used to find answers to questions which have been derived from the entire script and are representative of its core content. The more questions a hypothetical system can answer, the better it is at summarizing the script as a whole.

Two annotators were independently instructed to read scripts (from our test set) and create Q&A pairs. The annotators generated questions relating to the plot of the movie and the development of its characters, requiring an unambiguous answer. They compared and revised their Q&A pairs until a common agreed-upon set of five questions per movie was reached (see Table 1 for an example). In addition, for every movie we asked subjects to name the main characters, and summarize its plot (in no more than four sentences). Using Amazon Mechanical Turk (AMT)[9], we elicited answers for eight scripts (four comedies and thrillers) in four summarization conditions: using our model, the two baselines based on minimum and maximum character overlap, and the random system. All models were assessed at the same compression rate of 20% which seems realistic in an actual application environment, e.g., computer aided summarization. The scripts were preselected in an earlier AMT study where participants were asked to declare whether they had seen the movies in our test set (65 in total). We chose the screenplays which had received the least viewings so as to avoid eliciting answers based on familiarity with the movie. A total of 29 participants, all self-reported native English speakers, completed the Q&A task. The answers provided by the subjects were scored against an answer key. A correct answer was marked with a score of one, and zero otherwise. In cases where more answers were required per question, partial scores were awarded to each correct answer (e.g., 0.5). The score for a summary is the average of its question scores.

[9]https://www.mturk.com/

| | 10% | 20% | 30% | 40% | 50% |
|---|---|---|---|---|---|
| MaxOv | 0.40 | 0.50 | 0.58 | 0.64 | 0.71 |
| MinOv | 0.13 | 0.27 | 0.40 | 0.53 | 0.66 |
| SceneSum | 0.23 | 0.37 | 0.50 | 0.60 | 0.68 |
| Random | 0.10 | 0.20 | 0.30 | 0.40 | 0.50 |

Table 2: Model performance on automatically generated gold standard (test set) at different compression rates.

## 7 Results

Table 2 shows the performance of SceneSum, our scene extraction model, and the three comparison systems (MaxOv, MinOv, Random) on the automatic gold standard at five compression rates. As can be seen, MaxOv performs best in terms of F1, followed by SceneSum. We believe this is an artifact due to the way the gold standard was created. Scenes with large numbers of main characters are more likely to figure in Wikipedia plot summaries and will thus be more frequently aligned. A chain based on maximum character overlap will focus on such scenes and will agree with the gold standard better compared to chains which take additional script properties into account.

We further analyzed the scenes selected by SceneSum and the comparison systems with respect to their position in the script. Table 3 shows the av-

| | Beginning | Middle | End |
|---|---|---|---|
| MaxOv | 33.95 | 34.89 | 31.16 |
| MinOv | 34.30 | 33.91 | 31.80 |
| SceneSum | 35.30 | 33.54 | 31.16 |
| Random | 34.30 | 33.91 | 31.80 |

Table 3: Average percentage of scenes taken from the beginning, middle and ends of movies, on automatic gold standard test set.

erage percentage of scenes selected from the beginning, middle, and end of the movie (based on an equal division of the number of scenes in the screenplay). As can be seen, the number of selected scenes tends to be evenly distributed across the entire movie. SceneSum has a slight bias towards the beginning of the movie which is probably natural, since leading characters appear early on, as well as important scenes introducing essential story elements (e.g., setting, points of view).

The results of our human evaluation study are summarized in Table 4. We observe that SceneSum summaries are overall more informative compared to those created by the baselines. In other words, AMT participants are able to answer more questions regarding the story of the movie when reading SceneSum summaries. In two instances ("A Nightmare on Elm Street 3" and "Mumford"), the overlap models score better, however, in this case the movies largely consist of scenes with the same characters and relatively little variation ("A Nightmare on Elm Street 3"), or the camera follows the main lead in his interactions with other characters ("Mumford"). Since our model is not so character-centric, it might be thrown off by non-character-based terms in its objective, leading to the selection of unfavorable scenes. Table 4 also presents a break down of the different types of questions answered by our participants. Again, we see that in most cases a larger percentage is answered correctly when reading SceneSum summaries.

Overall, we observe that SceneSum extracts chains which encapsulate important movie content across the board. We should point out that although our movies are broadly classified as comedies and thrillers, they have very different structure and content. For example, "Little Athens" has a very loose plotline, "Living in Oblivion" has multiple dream sequences, whereas "While She was Out" contains only a few characters and a series of important scenes towards the end. Despite this variety, SceneSum performs consistently better in our task-based evaluation.

| Movies | MaxOv | MinOv | SceneSum | Random |
|---|---|---|---|---|
| Nightmare 3 | 69.18 | **74.49** | 60.24 | 56.33 |
| Little Athens | 34.92 | 31.75 | **36.90** | 33.33 |
| Living in Oblivion | 40.95 | 35.00 | **60.00** | 30.24 |
| Mumford | **72.86** | 60.00 | 30.00 | 54.29 |
| One Eight Seven | 47.30 | 38.89 | **67.86** | 30.16 |
| Anniversary Party | 45.39 | 56.35 | **62.46** | 37.62 |
| We Own the Night | 28.57 | 32.14 | **52.86** | 28.57 |
| While She Was Out | 72.86 | 75.71 | **85.00** | 45.71 |
| All Questions | 51.51 | 50.54 | **56.91** | 39.53 |
| Five Questions | 51.00 | 53.13 | **57.38** | 36.88 |
| Plot Question | 60.00 | 56.88 | **73.75** | 55.00 |
| Characters Question | **45.54** | 37.34 | 37.75 | 31.29 |

Table 4: Percentage of questions answered correctly.

## 8 Conclusions

In this paper we have developed a graph-based model for script summarization. We formalized the process of generating a shorter version of a screenplay as the task of finding an optimal chain of scenes, which are diverse, important, and exhibit logical progression. A large-scale evaluation based on a question-answering task revealed that our method produces more informative summaries compared to several baselines. In the future, we plan to explore model performance in a wider range of movie genres as well as its applicability to other NLP tasks (e.g., book summarization or event extraction). We would also like to automatically determine the compression rate which should presumably vary according to the movie's length and content. Finally, our long-term goal is to be able to generate loglines as well as movie plot summaries.

**Acknowledgments** We would like to thank Rik Sarkar, Jon Oberlander and Annie Louis for their valuable feedback. Special thanks to Bharat Ambati, Lea Frermann, and Daniel Renshaw for their help with system evaluation.

## References

Bamman, David, Brendan O'Connor, and Noah A. Smith. 2013. Learning Latent Personas of

Film Characters. In *Proceedings of the 51st Annual Meeting of the Association for Computational Linguistics*. Sofia, Bulgaria, pages 352–361.

Bamman, David, Ted Underwood, and A. Noah Smith. 2014. A Bayesian Mixed Effects Model of Literary Character. In *Proceedings of the 52nd Annual Meeting of the Association for Computational Linguistics*. Baltimore, MD, USA, pages 370–379.

Björkelund, Anders, Love Hafdell, and Pierre Nugues. 2009. Multilingual Semantic Role Labeling. In *Proceedings of the 13th Conference on Computational Natural Language Learning: Shared Task*. Boulder, Colorado, pages 43–48.

Clarke, James and Mirella Lapata. 2010. Discourse Constraints for Document Compression. *Computational Linguistics* 36(3):411–441.

Elsner, Micha. 2012. Character-based kernels for novelistic plot structure. In *Proceedings of the 13th Conference of the European Chapter of the Association for Computational Linguistics*. Avignon, France, pages 634–644.

Elson, David K., Nicholas Dames, and Kathleen R. McKeown. 2010. Extracting Social Networks from Literary Fiction. In *Proceedings of the 48th Annual Meeting of the Association for Computational Linguistics*. Uppsala, Sweden, pages 138–147.

Kim, Jun-Seong, Jae-Young Sim, and Chang-Su Kim. 2014. Multiscale Saliency Detection Using Random Walk With Restart. *IEEE Transactions on Circuits and Systems for Video Technology* 24(2):198–210.

Lee, Heeyoung, Yves Peirsman, Angel Chang, Nathanael Chambers, Mihai Surdeanu, and Dan Jurafsky. 2011. Stanford's Multi-Pass Sieve Coreference Resolution System at the CoNLL-2011 Shared Task. In *Proceedings of the 15th Conference on Computational Natural Language Learning: Shared Task*. Portland, OR, USA, pages 28–34.

Lin, C., C. Tsai, L. Kang, and Weisi Lin. 2013. Scene-Based Movie Summarization via Role-Community Networks. *IEEE Transactions on Circuits and Systems for Video Technology* 23(11):1927–1940.

Lu, Zheng and Kristen Grauman. 2013. Story-Driven Summarization for Egocentric Video. In *Proceedings of the 2013 IEEE Conference on Computer Vision and Pattern Recognition*. Portland, OR, USA, pages 2714–2721.

Mani, Inderjeet, Gary Klein, David House, Lynette Hirschman, Therese Firmin, and Beth Sundheim. 2002. SUMMAC: A Text Summarization Evaluation. *Natural Language Engineering* 8(1):43–68.

Manning, Christopher, Mihai Surdeanu, John Bauer, Jenny Finkel, Steven Bethard, and David McClosky. 2014. The Stanford CoreNLP Natural Language Processing Toolkit. In *Proceedings of 52nd Annual Meeting of the Association for Computational Linguistics: System Demonstrations*. pages 55–60.

Michel, Jean-Baptiste, Yuan Kui Shen, aviva Presser Aiden, Adrian Veres, Matthew K. Gray, The Google Books Team, Joseph P. Pickett, Dale Hoiberg, Dan Clancy, Peter Norvig, Jon Orwant, Steven Pinker, Martin A. Nowak, and Erez Lieberman Aiden. 2010. Quantitative Analysis of Culture Using Millions of Digitized Books. *Science* 331(6014):176–182.

Monaco, James. 1982. *How to Read a Film: The Art, Technology, Language, History and Theory of Film and Media*. OUP, New York, NY, USA.

Morris, A., G. Kasper, and D. Adams. 1992. The Effects and Limitations of Automated Text Condensing on Reading Comprehension Performance. *Information Systems Research* 3(1):17–35.

Mosteller, Frederick and David Wallace. 1964. *Inference and Dispituted Authorship: The Federalists*. Addison-Wesley, Boston, MA, USA.

Nalisnick, T. Eric and S. Henry Baird. 2013. Character-to-Character Sentiment Analysis in Shakespeare's Plays. In *Proceedings of the 51st Annual Meeting of the Association for Computational Linguistics*. Sofia, Bulgaria, pages 479–483.

Nelken, Rani and Stuart Shieber. 2006. Towards Robust Context-Sensitive Sentence Alignment for Monolingual Corpora. In *Proceedings of the 11th Conference of the European Chapter of the Association for Computational Linguistics*. Trento, Italy, pages 161–168.

Nielsen, Finn Arup. 2011. A new ANEW: Evaluation of a word list for sentiment analysis in microblogs. In *Proceedings of the ESWC2011 Workshop on 'Making Sense of Microposts': Big Things Come in Small Packages*. Heraklion, Crete, pages 93–98.

Page, Lawrence, Sergey Brin, Rajeev Motwani, and Terry Winograd. 1999. The pagerank citation ranking: Bringing order to the web. Technical Report 1999-66, Stanford InfoLab. Previous number SIDL-WP-1999-0120.

Rasheed, Z., Y. Sheikh, and M. Shah. 2005. On the Use of Computable Features for Film Classification. *IEEE Transactions on Circuits and Systems for Video Technology* 15(1):52–64.

Reed, Todd, editor. 2004. *Digital Image Sequence Processing*. Taylor & Francis.

Sang, Jitao and Changsheng Xu. 2010. Character-based Movie Summarization. In *Proceedings of the International Conference on Multimedia*. Firenze, Italy, pages 855–858.

Tong, Hanghang, Christos Faloutsos, and Jia-Yu Pan. 2006. Fast Random Walk with Restart and Its Applications. In *Proceedings of the Sixth International Conference on Data Mining*. Hong Kong, pages 613–622.

Weng, Chung-yi, Wei-Ta Chu, and Ja ling Wu. 2009. Rolenet: Movie Analysis from the perspective of Social Networks. *IEEE Transactions on Multimedia* 11(2):256–271.

# Toward Abstractive Summarization Using Semantic Representations

**Fei Liu  Jeffrey Flanigan  Sam Thomson  Norman Sadeh  Noah A. Smith**
School of Computer Science
Carnegie Mellon University
Pittsburgh, PA 15213, USA
{feiliu, jflanigan, sthomson, sadeh, nasmith}@cs.cmu.edu

## Abstract

We present a novel abstractive summarization framework that draws on the recent development of a treebank for the Abstract Meaning Representation (AMR). In this framework, the source text is parsed to a set of AMR graphs, the graphs are transformed into a summary graph, and then text is generated from the summary graph. We focus on the graph-to-graph transformation that reduces the source semantic graph into a summary graph, making use of an existing AMR parser and assuming the eventual availability of an AMR-to-text generator. The framework is data-driven, trainable, and not specifically designed for a particular domain. Experiments on gold-standard AMR annotations and system parses show promising results. Code is available at: `https://github.com/summarization`

## 1 Introduction

Abstractive summarization is an elusive technological capability in which textual summaries of content are generated *de novo*. Demand is on the rise for high-quality summaries not just for lengthy texts (e.g., books; Bamman and Smith, 2013) and texts known to be prohibitively difficult for people to understand (e.g., website privacy policies; Sadeh et al., 2013), but also for non-textual media (e.g., videos and image collections; Kim et al., 2014; Kuznetsova et al., 2014; Zhao and Xing, 2014), where extractive and compressive summarization techniques simply do not suffice. We believe that the challenge of abstractive summarization deserves renewed attention and propose that recent developments in semantic analysis have an important role to play.

We conduct the first study exploring the feasibility of an abstractive summarization system based on transformations of semantic representations such as the Abstract Meaning Representation (AMR; Banarescu et al., 2013). Example sentences and their AMR graphs are shown in Fig. 1. AMR has much in common with earlier formalisms (Kasper, 1989; Dorr et al., 1998); today an annotated corpus comprised of over 20,000 AMR-analyzed English sentences (Knight et al., 2014) and an automatic AMR parser (JAMR; Flanigan et al., 2014) are available.

In our framework, summarization consists of three steps illustrated in Fig. 1: (1) parsing the input sentences to individual AMR graphs, (2) combining and transforming those graphs into a single summary AMR graph, and (3) generating text from the summary graph. This paper focuses on step 2, treating it as a structured prediction problem. We assume text documents as input[1] and use JAMR for step 1. We use a simple method to read a bag of words off the summary graph, allowing evaluation with ROUGE-1, and leave full text generation from AMR (step 3) to future work.

The graph summarizer, described in §4, first merges AMR graphs for each input sentence through a *concept merging* step, in which coreferent nodes of the graphs are merged; a *sentence conjunction* step, which connects the root of each sentence's AMR graph to a dummy "ROOT" node; and an optional

[1] In principle, the framework could be applied to other inputs, such as image collections, if AMR parsers became available for them.



*Human Language Technologies: The 2015 Annual Conference of the North American Chapter of the ACL*, pages 1077–1086,
Denver, Colorado, May 31 – June 5, 2015. 

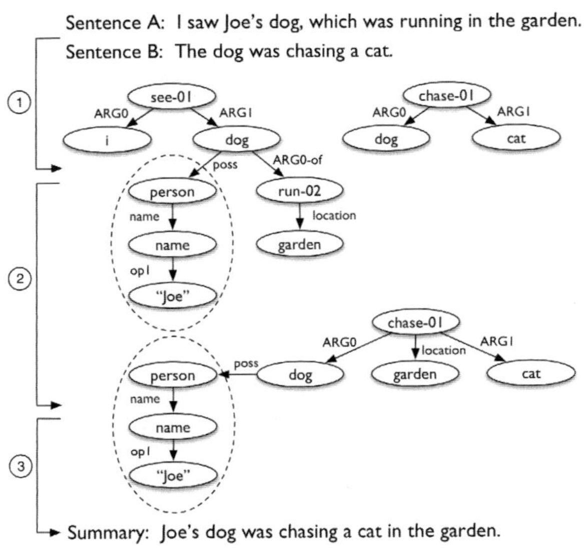


Figure 1: A toy example. Sentences are parsed into individual AMR graphs in step 1; step 2 conducts graph transformation that produces a single summary AMR graph; text is generated from the summary graph in step 3.

*graph expansion* step, where additional edges are added to create a fully dense graph on the sentence-level. These steps result in a single connected *source graph*. A subset of the nodes and arcs from the source graph are then selected for inclusion in the *summary graph*. Ideally this is a condensed representation of the most salient semantic content from the source.

We briefly review AMR and JAMR (§2), then present the dataset used in this paper (§3). The main algorithm is presented in §4, and we discuss our simple generation step in §5. Our experiments (§6) measure the intrinsic quality of the graph transformation algorithm as well as the quality of the terms selected for the summary (using ROUGE-1). We explore variations on the transformation and the learning algorithm, and show oracle upper bounds of various kinds.

## 2 Background: Abstract Meaning Representation and JAMR

AMR provides a whole-sentence semantic representation, represented as a rooted, directed, acyclic graph (Fig. 1). Nodes of an AMR graph are labeled with *concepts*, and edges are labeled with *relations*. Concepts can be English words ("dog"), PropBank event predicates ("chase-01," "run-02"), or special keywords ("person"). For example, "chase-01" represents a PropBank roleset that corresponds to the first sense of "chase". According to Banarescu et al. (2013), AMR uses approximately 100 relations. The rolesets and core semantic relations (e.g., ARG0 to ARG5) are adopted from the PropBank annotations in OntoNotes (Hovy et al., 2006). Other semantic relations include "location," "mode," "name," "time," and "topic." The AMR guidelines[2] provide more detailed descriptions. Banarescu et al. (2013) describe AMR Bank, a 20,341-sentence corpus annotated with AMR by experts.

Step 1 of our framework converts input document sentences into AMR graphs. We use a statistical semantic parser, JAMR (Flanigan et al., 2014), which was trained on AMR Bank. JAMR's current performance on our test dataset is 63% $F$-score.[3] We will analyze the effect of AMR parsing errors by comparing JAMR output with gold-standard annotations of input sentences in the experiments (§6).

In addition to predicting AMR graphs for each sentence, JAMR provides alignments between spans of words in the source sentence and fragments of its predicted graph. For example, a graph fragment headed by "date-entity" could be aligned to the tokens "April 8, 2002." We use these alignments in our simple text generation module (step 3; §5).

## 3 Dataset

To build and evaluate our framework, we require a dataset that includes inputs and summaries, each with gold-standard AMR annotations.[4] This allows us to use a statistical model for step 2 (graph summarization) and to separate its errors from those in step 1 (AMR parsing), which is important in determining whether this approach is worth further investment.

Fortunately, the "proxy report" section of the AMR Bank (Knight et al., 2014) suits our needs. A

[2] `http://www.isi.edu/~ulf/amr/help/amr-guidelines.pdf`

[3] AMR parse quality is evaluated using smatch (Cai and Knight, 2013), which measures the accuracy of concept and relation predictions. JAMR was trained on the in-domain training portion of LDC2014T12 for our experiments.

[4] Traditional multi-document summarization datasets, such as the ones used in DUC and TAC competitions, do not have gold-standard AMR annotations.

|  | # Docs. | Ave. # Sents. |  | Source Graph |  |  |
|---|---|---|---|---|---|---|
|  |  | Summ. | Doc. | Nodes | Edges | Expand |
| Train | 298 | 1.5 | 17.5 | 127 | 188 | 2,670 |
| Dev. | 35 | 1.4 | 19.2 | 143 | 220 | 3,203 |
| Test | 33 | 1.4 | 20.5 | 162 | 255 | 4,002 |

Table 1: Statistics of our dataset. "Expand" shows the number of edges after performing graph expansion. The numbers are averaged across all documents in the split. We use the official split, dropping one training document for which no summary sentences were annotated.

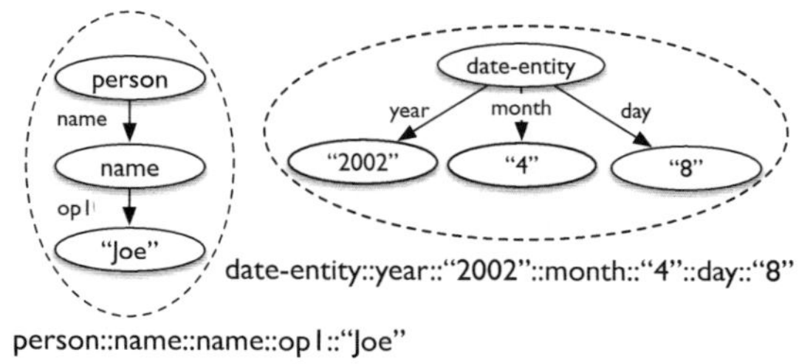


Figure 2: Graph fragments are collapsed into a single concept and assigned a new concept label.

proxy report is created by annotators based on a single newswire article, selected from the English Gigaword corpus. The report header contains metadata about date, country, topic, and a short summary. The report body is generated by editing or rewriting the content of the newswire article to approximate the style of an analyst report. Hence this is a single document summarization task. All sentences are paired with gold-standard AMR annotations. Table 1 provides an overview of our dataset.

## 4 Graph Summarization

Given AMR graphs for all of the sentences in the input (step 1), graph summarization transforms them into a single summary AMR graph (step 2). This is accomplished in two stages: source graph construction (§4.1); and subgraph prediction (§4.2).

### 4.1 Source Graph Construction

The "source graph" is a single graph constructed using the individual sentences' AMR graphs by merging identical concepts. In the AMR formalism, an entity or event is canonicalized and represented by a single graph fragment, regardless of how many times it is referred to in the sentence. This principle can be extended to multiple sentences, ideally resulting in a source graph with no redundancy. Because repeated mentions of a concept in the input can signal its importance, we will later encode the frequency of mentions as a feature used in subgraph prediction.

Concept merging involves collapsing certain graph fragments into a single concept, then merging all concepts that have the same label. We collapse the graph fragments that are headed by either a date-entity ("date-entity") or a named entity ("name"), if the fragment is a flat structure. A collapsed named entity is further combined with its parent (e.g., "person") into one concept node if it is the only child of the parent. Two such graph fragments are illustrated in Fig. 2. We choose named and date entity concepts since they appear frequently, but most often refer to different entities (e.g., "April 8, 2002" vs. "Nov. 17"). No further collapsing is done. A collapsed graph fragment is assigned a new label by concatenating the consisting concept and edge labels. Each fragment that is collapsed into a new concept node can then only be merged with other identical fragments. This process won't recognize coreferent concepts like "Barack Obama" = "Obama" and "say-01" = "report-01," but future work may incorporate both entity coreference resolution and event coreference resolution, as concept nodes can represent either.

Due to the concept merging step, a pair of concepts may now have multiple labeled edges between them. We merge all such edges between a given pair of concepts into a single unlabeled edge. We remember the two most common labels in such a group, which are used in the edge "Label" feature (Table 3).

To ensure that the source graph is connected, we add a new "ROOT" node and connect it to every concept that was originally the root of a sentence graph (see Fig. 3). When we apply this procedure to the documents in our dataset (§3), source graphs contain 144 nodes and 221 edges on average.

We investigated how well these automatically constructed source graphs cover the gold-standard summary graphs produced by AMR annotators. Ideally, a source graph should cover all of the gold-standard edges, so that summarization can be accomplished by selecting a subgraph of the source

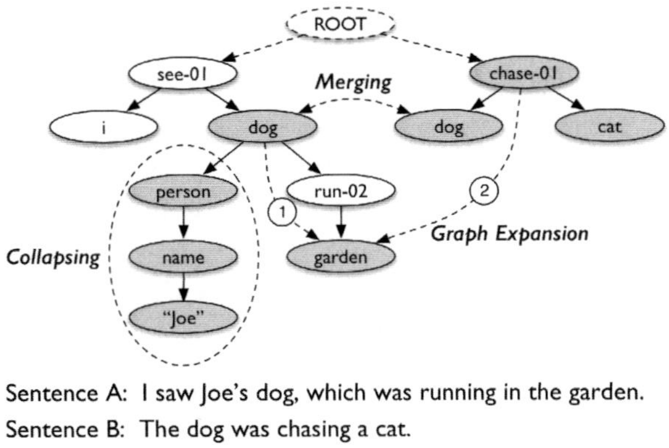


Figure 3: A source graph formed from two sentence AMR graphs. Concept collapsing, merging, and graph expansion are demonstrated. Edges are unlabeled. A "ROOT" node is added to ensure connectivity. (1) and (2) are among edges added through the optional expansion step, corresponding to sentence- and document-level expansion, respectively. Concept nodes included in the summary graph are shaded.

| | Summary Edge Coverage (%) | | | |
|---|---|---|---|---|
| | | | Expand | |
| | Labeled | Unlabeled | Sent. | Doc. |
| Train | 64.8 | 67.0 | 75.5 | 84.6 |
| Dev. | 77.3 | 78.6 | 85.4 | 91.8 |
| Test | 63.0 | 64.7 | 75.0 | 83.3 |

Table 2: Percentage of summary edges that can be covered by an automatically constructed source graph.

graph (§4.2). In Table 2, columns one and two report labeled and unlabeled edge coverage. 'Unlabeled' counts edges as matching if both the source and destination concepts have identical labels, but ignores the edge label.

In order to improve edge coverage, we explore expanding the source graph by adding every possible edge between every pair of concepts within the same sentence. We also explored adding every possible edge between every pair of concepts in the entire source graph. Edges that are newly introduced during expansion receive a default label 'null'. We report unlabeled edge coverage in Table 2, columns three and four, respectively. Subgraph prediction became infeasable with the document-level expansion, so we conducted our experiments using only sentence-level expansion. Sentence-level graph expansion increases the average number of edges by a factor of 15, to 3,292. Fig. 3 illustrates the motivation. Document-level expansion covers the gold-standard summary edge "chase-01" $\rightarrow$ "garden," yet the expansion is computationally prohibitive; sentence-level expansion adds an edge "dog" $\rightarrow$ "garden," which enables the prediction of a structure with similar semantic meaning: "Joe's dog was in the garden chasing a cat."

## 4.2 Subgraph Prediction

We pose the selection of a summary subgraph from the source graph as a structured prediction problem that trades off among including important information without altering its meaning, maintaining brevity, and producing fluent language (Nenkova and McKeown, 2011). We incorporate these concerns in the form of features and constraints in the statistical model for subgraph selection.

Let $G = (V, E)$ denote the merged source graph, where each node $v \in V$ represents a unique concept and each directed edge $e \in E$ connects two concepts. $G$ is a connected, directed, node-labeled graph. Edges in this graph are unlabeled, and edge labels are not predicted during subgraph selection. We seek to maximize a score that factorizes over graph nodes and edges that are included in the summary graph. For subgraph $(V', E')$:

$$score(V', E'; \boldsymbol{\theta}, \boldsymbol{\psi}) = \sum_{v \in V'} \boldsymbol{\theta}^\top \mathbf{f}(v) + \sum_{e \in E'} \boldsymbol{\psi}^\top \mathbf{g}(e) \quad (1)$$

where $\mathbf{f}(v)$ and $\mathbf{g}(e)$ are the feature representations of node $v$ and edge $e$, respectively. We describe node and edge features in Table 3. $\boldsymbol{\theta}$ and $\boldsymbol{\psi}$ are vectors of empirically estimated coefficients in a linear model.

We next formulate the selection of the subgraph using integer linear programming (ILP; §4.2.1) and describe supervised learning for the parameters (coefficients) from a collection of source graphs paired with summary graphs (§4.2.2).

### 4.2.1 Decoding

We cast decoding as an ILP whose constraints ensure that the output forms a connected subcomponent of the source graph. We index source graph concept nodes by $i$ and $j$, giving the "ROOT" node

| | | |
|---|---|---|
| Node Features | Concept | Identity feature for concept label |
| | Freq | Concept freq in the input sentence set; one binary feature defined for each frequency threshold $\tau = 0/1/2/5/10$ |
| | Depth | Average and smallest depth of node to the root of the sentence graph; binarized using 5 depth thresholds |
| | Position | Average and foremost position of sentences containing the concept; binarized using 5 position thresholds |
| | Span | Average and longest word span of concept; binarized using 5 length thresholds; word spans obtained from JAMR |
| | Entity | Two binary features indicating whether the concept is a named entity/date entity or not |
| | Bias | Bias term, 1 for any node |
| Edge Features | Label | First and second most frequent edge labels between concepts; relative freq of each label, binarized by 3 thresholds |
| | Freq | Edge frequency (w/o label, non-expanded edges) in the document sentences; binarized using 5 frequency thresholds |
| | Position | Average and foremost position of sentences containing the edge (without label); binarized using 5 position thresholds |
| | Nodes | Node features extracted from the source and target nodes (all above node features except the bias term) |
| | IsExpanded | A binary feature indicating the edge is due to graph expansion or not; edge freq (w/o label, all occurrences) |
| | Bias | Bias term, 1 for any edge |

Table 3: Node and edge features (all binarized).

index 0. Let $N$ be the number of nodes in the graph. Let $v_i$ and $e_{i,j}$ be binary variables. $v_i$ is 1 iff source node $i$ is included; $e_{i,j}$ is 1 iff the directed edge from node $i$ to node $j$ is included.

The ILP objective to be maximized is Equation 1, rewritten here in the present notation:

$$\sum_{i=1}^{N} v_i \underbrace{\boldsymbol{\theta}^\top \mathbf{f}(i)}_{\text{node score}} + \sum_{(i,j)\in E} e_{i,j} \underbrace{\boldsymbol{\psi}^\top \mathbf{g}(i,j)}_{\text{edge score}} \quad (2)$$

Note that this objective is linear in $\{v_i, e_{i,j}\}_{i,j}$ and that features and coefficients can be folded into node and edge scores and treated as constants during decoding.

Constraints are required to ensure that the selected nodes and edges form a valid graph. In particular, if an edge $(i,j)$ is selected ($e_{i,j}$ takes value of 1), then both its endpoints $i, j$ must be included:

$$v_i - e_{i,j} \geq 0, \quad v_j - e_{i,j} \geq 0, \quad \forall i,j \leq N \quad (3)$$

Connectivity is enforced using a set of single-commodity flow variables $f_{i,j}$, each taking a non-negative integral value, representing the flow from node $i$ to $j$. The root node sends out up to $N$ units of flow, one to reach each included node (Equation 4). Each included node consumes one unit of flow, reflected as the difference between incoming and outgoing flow (Equation 5). Flow may only be sent over an edge if the edge is included (Equation 6).

$$\sum_i f_{0,i} - \sum_i v_i = 0, \quad (4)$$

$$\sum_i f_{i,j} - \sum_k f_{j,k} - v_j = 0, \quad \forall j \leq N, \quad (5)$$

$$N \cdot e_{i,j} - f_{i,j} \geq 0, \quad \forall i,j \leq N. \quad (6)$$

The AMR representation allows graph reentrancies (concept nodes having multiple parents), yet reentrancies are rare; about 5% of edges are reentrancies in our dataset. In this preliminary study we force the summary graph to be tree-structured, requiring that there is at most one incoming edge for each node:

$$\sum_j e_{i,j} \leq 1, \quad \forall j \leq N. \quad (7)$$

Interestingly, the formulation so far equates to an ILP for solving the prize-collecting Steiner tree problem (PCST; Segev, 1987), which is known to be NP-complete (Karp, 1972). Our ILP formulation is modified from that of Ljubić et al. (2006). Flow-based constraints for tree structures have also previously been used in NLP for dependency parsing (Martins et al., 2009) and sentence compression (Thadani and McKeown, 2013). In our experiments, we use an exact ILP solver,[5] though many approximate methods are available.

Finally, an optional constraint can be used to fix the size of the summary graph (measured by the number of edges) to $L$:

$$\sum_i \sum_j e_{i,j} = L \quad (8)$$

The performance of summarization systems depends strongly on their compression rate, so systems are only directly comparable when their compression rates are similar (Napoles et al., 2011). $L$ is supplied to the system to control summary graph size.

[5]http://www.gurobi.com

#### 4.2.2 Parameter Estimation

Given a collection of input and output pairs (here, source graphs and summary graphs), a natural starting place for learning the coefficients $\boldsymbol{\theta}$ and $\boldsymbol{\psi}$ is the structured perceptron (Collins, 2002), which is easy to implement and often performs well. Alternatively, incorporating factored cost functions through a structured hinge loss leads to a structured support vector machine (SVM; Taskar et al., 2004) which can be learned with a very similar stochastic optimization algorithm. In our scenario, however, the gold-standard summary graph may not actually be a subset of the source graph. In machine translation, *ramp loss* has been found to work well in situations where the gold-standard output may not even be in the hypothesis space of the model (Gimpel and Smith, 2012). The structured perceptron, hinge, and ramp losses are compared in Table 4.

We explore learning by minimizing each of the perceptron, hinge, and ramp losses, each optimized using Adagrad (Duchi et al., 2011), a stochastic optimization procedure. Let $\beta$ be one model parameter (coefficient from $\boldsymbol{\theta}$ or $\boldsymbol{\psi}$). Let $g^{(t)}$ be the subgradient of the loss on the instance considered on the $t^{th}$ iteration with respect to $\beta$. Given an initial step size $\eta$, the update for $\beta$ on iteration $t$ is:

$$\beta^{(t+1)} \leftarrow \beta^{(t)} - \frac{\eta}{\sqrt{\sum_{\tau=1}^{t}(g^{(\tau)})^2}} g^{(t)} \tag{9}$$

## 5 Generation

Generation from AMR-like representations has received some attention, e.g., by Langkilde and Knight (1998) who described a statistical method. Though we know of work in progress driven by the goal of machine translation using AMR, there is currently no system available.

We therefore use a heuristic approach to generate a bag of words. Given a predicted subgraph, a system summary is created by finding the most frequently aligned word span for each concept node. (Recall that the JAMR parser provides these alignments; §2). The words in the resulting spans are generated in no particular order. While this is not a natural language summary, it is suitable for unigram-based summarization evaluation methods like ROUGE-1.

## 6 Experiments

In Table 5, we report the performance of subgraph prediction and end-to-end summarization on the test set, using gold-standard and automatic AMR parses for the input. Gold-standard AMR annotations are used for model training in all conditions. During testing, we apply the trained model to source graphs constructed using either gold-standard or JAMR parses. In all of these experiments, we use the number of edges in the gold-standard summary graph to fix the number of edges in the predicted subgraph, allowing direct comparison across conditions.

Subgraph prediction is evaluated against the gold-standard AMR graphs on summaries. We report precision, recall, and $F_1$ for nodes, and $F_1$ for edges.[6]

Oracle results for the subgraph prediction stage are obtained using the ILP decoder to minimize the cost of the output graph, given the gold-standard. We assign wrong nodes and edges a score of $-1$, correct nodes and edges a score of 0, then decode with the same structural constraints as in subgraph prediction. The resulting graph is the best summary graph in the hypothesis space of our model, and provides an upper bound on performance achievable within our framework. Oracle performance on node prediction is in the range of 80% when using gold-standard AMR annotations, and 70% when using JAMR output. Edge prediction has lower performance, yielding 52.2% for gold-standard and 31.1% for JAMR parses. When graph expansion was applied, the numbers increased to 64% and 46.7%, respectively. The uncovered summary edge (i.e., those not covered by source graph) is a major source for low recall values on edge prediction (see Table 2); graph expansion slightly alleviates this issue.

Summarization is evaluated by comparing system summaries against reference summaries, using ROUGE-1 scores (Lin, 2004)[7]. System summaries are generated using the heuristic approach presented in §5: given a predicted subgraph, the approach finds the most frequently aligned word span for each concept node, and then puts them together as a bag of words. ROUGE-1 is particularly usefully for eval-

[6] Precision, recall, and $F_1$ are equal since the number of edges is fixed.

[7] ROUGE version 1.5.5 with options '-e data -n 4 -m -2 4 -u -c 95 -r 1000 -f A -p 0.5 -t 0 -a -x'

| | | |
|---|---|---|
| Structured perceptron loss: | $-score(G^*)$ | $+ \max_G score(G)$ |
| Structured hinge loss: | $-score(G^*)$ | $+ \max_G(score(G) + cost(G; G^*))$ |
| Structured ramp loss: | $-\max_G(score(G) - cost(G; G^*))$ | $+ \max_G(score(G) + cost(G; G^*))$ |

Table 4: Loss functions minimized in parameter estimation. $G^*$ denotes the gold-standard summary graph. $score(\cdot)$ is as defined in Equation 1. $cost(G; G^*)$ penalizes each vertex or edge in $G \cup G^* \setminus (G \cap G^*)$. Since $cost$ factors just like the scoring function, each $\max$ operation can be accomplished using a variant of ILP decoding (§4.2.1) in which the cost is incorporated into the linear objective while the constraints remain the same.

| | | Subgraph Prediction | | | | Summarization | | |
|---|---|---|---|---|---|---|---|---|
| | | Nodes | | | Edges | ROUGE-1 | | |
| | | P (%) | R (%) | F (%) | F (%) | P (%) | R (%) | F (%) |
| gold-standard parses | Perceptron | 39.6 | 46.1 | 42.6 | 24.7 | 41.4 | 27.1 | 32.3 |
| | Hinge | 41.2 | 47.9 | 44.2 | 26.4 | 42.6 | 28.3 | 33.5 |
| | Ramp | **54.7** | **63.5** | **58.7** | **39.0** | **51.9** | **39.0** | **44.3** |
| | Ramp + Expand | 53.0 | 61.3 | 56.8 | 36.1 | 50.4 | 37.4 | 42.8 |
| | Oracle | 75.8 | 86.4 | 80.7 | 52.2 | 89.1 | 52.8 | 65.8 |
| | Oracle + Expand | 78.9 | 90.1 | 83.9 | 64.0 | | | |
| JAMR parses | Perceptron | 42.2 | 48.9 | 45.2 | 14.5 | 46.1 | 35.0 | 39.5 |
| | Hinge | 41.7 | 48.3 | 44.7 | 15.8 | 44.9 | 33.6 | 38.2 |
| | Ramp | **48.1** | **55.6** | **51.5** | **20.0** | 50.6 | 40.0 | 44.4 |
| | Ramp + Expand | 47.5 | 54.6 | 50.7 | 19.0 | **51.2** | **40.0** | **44.7** |
| | Oracle | 64.1 | 74.8 | 68.9 | 31.1 | 87.5 | 43.7 | 57.8 |
| | Oracle + Expand | 66.9 | 76.4 | 71.2 | 46.7 | | | |

Table 5: Subgraph prediction and summarization (to bag of words) results on test set. Gold-standard AMR annotations are used for model training in all conditions. "+ Expand" means the result is obtained using source graph with expansion; edge performance is measured ignoring labels.

uating such less well-formed summaries, such as those generated from speech transcripts (Liu and Liu, 2013).

Oracle summaries are produced by taking the gold-standard AMR parses of the reference summary, obtaining the most frequently aligned word span for each unique concept node using the JAMR aligner (§2), and then generating a bag of words summary. Evaluation of oracle summaries is performed in the same manner as for system summaries. The above process does not involve graph expansion, so summarization performance is the same for the two conditions "Oracle" and "Oracle + Expand."

We find that JAMR parses are a large source of degradation of edge prediction performance, and a smaller but still significant source of degradation for concept prediction. Surprisingly, using JAMR parses leads to slightly improved ROUGE-1 scores. Keep in mind, though, that under our bag-of-words generator, ROUGE-1 scores only depend on concept prediction and are unaffected by edge prediction. The oracle summarization results, 65.8% and 57.8% $F_1$ scores for gold-standard and JAMR parses, respectively, further suggest that improved graph summarization models (step 2) might benefit from future improvements in AMR parsing (step 1).

Across all conditions and both evaluations, we find that incorporating a cost-aware loss function (hinge vs. perceptron) has little effect, but that using ramp loss leads to substantial gains.

In Table 5, we show detailed results with and without graph expansion. "+ Expand" means the results are obtained using the expanded source graph. We find that graph expansion only marginally affects system performance. Graph expansion slightly hurts the system performance on edge prediction. For example, using ramp loss with JAMR parser as input, we obtained 50.7% and 19.0% for node and edge prediction with graph expansion; 51.5% and 20.0%

without edge expansion. On the other hand, it increases the oracle performance by a large margin. This suggests that with more training data, or a more sophisticated model that is able to better discriminate among the enlarged output space, graph expansion still has promise to be helpful.

## 7 Related and Future Work

According to Dang and Owczarzak (2008), the majority of competitive summarization systems are extractive, selecting representative sentences from input documents and concatenating them to form a summary. This is often combined with sentence compression, allowing more sentences to be included within a budget. ILPs and approximations have been used to encode compression and extraction (McDonald, 2007; Martins and Smith, 2009; Gillick and Favre, 2009; Berg-Kirkpatrick et al., 2011; Almeida and Martins, 2013; Li et al., 2014). Other decoding approaches have included a greedy method exploiting submodularity (Lin and Bilmes, 2010), document reconstruction (He et al., 2012), and graph cuts (Qian and Liu, 2013), among others.

Previous work on abstractive summarization has explored user studies that compare extractive with NLG-based abstractive summarization (Carenini and Cheung, 2008). Ganesan et al. (2010) propose to construct summary sentences by repeatedly searching the highest scored graph paths. (Gerani et al., 2014) generate abstractive summaries by modifying discourse parse trees. Our work is similar in spirit to Cheung and Penn (2014), which splices and recombines dependency parse trees to produce abstractive summaries. In contrast, our work operates on semantic graphs, taking advantage of the recently developed AMR Bank.

Also related to our work are graph-based summarization methods (Vanderwende et al., 2004; Erkan and Radev, 2004; Mihalcea and Tarau, 2004). Vanderwende et al. (2004) transform input to logical forms, score nodes using PageRank, and grow the graph from high-value nodes using heuristics. In Erkan and Radev (2004) and Mihalcea and Tarau (2004), the graph connects surface terms that co-occur. In both cases, the graphs are constructed based on surface text; it is not a representation of propositional semantics like AMR. However, future work might explore similar graph-based calculations to contribute features for subgraph selection in our framework.

Our constructed source graph can easily reach ten times or more of the size of a sentence dependency graph. Thus more efficient graph decoding algorithms, e.g., based on Lagrangian relaxation or approximate algorithms, may be explored in future work. Other future directions may include jointly performing subgraph and edge label prediction; exploring a full-fledged pipeline that consists of an automatic AMR parser, a graph-to-graph summarizer, and a AMR-to-text generator; and devising an evaluation metric that is better suited to abstractive summarization.

Many domains stand to eventually benefit from summarization. These include books, audio/video segments, and legal texts.

## 8 Conclusion

We have introduced a statistical abstractive summarization framework driven by the Abstract Meaning Representation. The centerpiece of the approach is a structured prediction algorithm that transforms semantic graphs of the input into a single summary semantic graph. Experiments show the approach to be promising and suggest directions for future research.

## Acknowledgments

The authors thank three anonymous reviewers for their insightful input. We are grateful to Nathan Schneider, Kevin Gimpel, Sasha Rush, and the ARK group for valuable discussions. The research was supported by NSF grant SaTC-1330596, DARPA grant FA8750-12-2-0342 funded under the DEFT program, the U. S. Army Research Laboratory and the U. S. Army Research Office under contract/grant number W911NF-10-1-0533, and by IARPA via DoI/NBC contract number D12PC00337. The views and conclusions contained herein are those of the authors and should not be interpreted as necessarily representing the official policies or endorsements, either expressed or implied, of the sponsors.

## References

Miguel B. Almeida and Andre F. T. Martins. 2013. Fast and robust compressive summarization with dual decomposition and multi-task learning. In *Proceedings of ACL*.

David Bamman and Noah A. Smith. 2013. New alignment methods for discriminative book summarization. In *arXiv:1305.1319*.

Laura Banarescu, Claire Bonial, Shu Cai, Madalina Georgescu, Kira Griffitt, Ulf Hermjakob, Kevin Knight, Philipp Koehn, Martha Palmer, and Nathan Schneider. 2013. Abstract meaning representation for sembanking. In *Proceedings of Linguistic Annotation Workshop*.

Taylor Berg-Kirkpatrick, Dan Gillick, and Dan Klein. 2011. Jointly learning to extract and compress. In *Proceedings of ACL*.

Shu Cai and Kevin Knight. 2013. Smatch: an evaluation metric for semantic feature structures. In *Proceedings of ACL*.

Giuseppe Carenini and Jackie Chi Kit Cheung. 2008. Extractive vs. NLG-based abstractive summarization of evaluative text: The effect of corpus controversiality. In *Proceedings of the Fifth International Natural Language Generation Conference (INLG)*.

Jackie Chi Kit Cheung and Gerald Penn. 2014. Unsupervised sentence enhancement for automatic summarization. In *Proceedings of EMNLP*.

Michael Collins. 2002. Discriminative training methods for hidden Markov models: Theory and experiments with perceptron algorithms. In *Proceedings of EMNLP*.

Hoa Trang Dang and Karolina Owczarzak. 2008. Overview of the TAC 2008 update summarization task. In *Proceedings of Text Analysis Conference (TAC)*.

Bonnie Dorr, Nizar Habash, and David Traum. 1998. A thematic hierarchy for efficient generation from lexical-conceptual structure. In David Farwell, Laurie Gerber, and Eduard Hovy, editors, *Machine Translation and the Information Soup: Proceedings of the Third Conference of the Association for Machine Translation in the Americas*, Lecture Notes in Computer Science. Springer.

John Duchi, Elad Hazan, and Yoram Singer. 2011. Adaptive subgradient methods for online learning and stochastic optimization. *Journal of Machine Learning Research*.

Günes Erkan and Dragomir R. Radev. 2004. LexRank: Graph-based lexical centrality as salience in text summarization. *Journal of Artificial Intelligence Research*.

Jeffrey Flanigan, Sam Thomson, Jaime Carbonell, Chris Dyer, and Noah A. Smith. 2014. A discriminative graph-based parser for the abstract meaning representation. In *Proceedings of ACL*.

Kavita Ganesan, ChengXiang Zhai, and Jiawei Han. 2010. Opinosis: A graph-based approach to abstractive summarization of highly redundant opinions. In *Proceedings of COLING*.

Shima Gerani, Yashar Mehdad, Giuseppe Carenini, Raymond T. Ng, and Bita Nejat. 2014. Abstractive summarization of product reviews using discourse structure. In *Proceedings of EMNLP*.

Dan Gillick and Benoit Favre. 2009. A scalable global model for summarization. In *Proceedings of the NAACL Workshop on Integer Linear Programming for Natural Langauge Processing*.

Kevin Gimpel and Noah A. Smith. 2012. Structured ramp loss minimization for machine translation. In *Proceedings of NAACL-HLT*.

Zhanying He, Chun Chen, Jiajun Bu, Can Wang, Lijun Zhang, Deng Cai, and Xiaofei He. 2012. Document summarization based on data reconstruction. In *Proceedings of AAAI*.

Eduard Hovy, Mitchell Marcus, Martha Palmer, Lance Ramshaw, and Ralph Weischedel. 2006. OntoNotes: The 90% solution. In *Proceedings of NAACL*.

Richard M. Karp. 1972. Reducibility Among Combinatorial Problems. In *Complexity of Computer Computations*, pages 85–103. Springer US.

Robert T. Kasper. 1989. A flexible interface for linking applications to Penman's sentence generator. In *Proceedings of the DARPA Speech and Natural Language Workshop*.

Gunhee Kim, Leonid Sigal, and Eric P. Xing. 2014. Joint summarization of large-scale collections of web images and videos for storyline reconstruction. In *Proceedings of CVPR*.

Kevin Knight, Laura Baranescu, Claire Bonial, Madalina Georgescu, Kira Griffitt, Ulf Hermjakob, Daniel Marcu, Martha Palmer, and Nathan Schneider. 2014. Abstract meaning representation (AMR) annotation release 1.0 LDC2014T12. Web Download. Philadelphia: Linguistic Data Consortium.

Polina Kuznetsova, Vicente Ordonez, Tamara L. Berg, and Yejin Choi. 2014. TREETALK: Composition and compression of trees for image descriptions. *Transactions of ACL*.

Irene Langkilde and Kevin Knight. 1998. Generation that exploits corpus-based statistical knowledge. In *Proceedings of COLING*.

Chen Li, Yang Liu, Fei Liu, Lin Zhao, and Fuliang Weng. 2014. Improving multi-documents summarization by sentence compression based on expanded constituent parse tree. In *Proceedings of EMNLP*.

Hui Lin and Jeff Bilmes. 2010. Multi-document summarization via budgeted maximization of submodular functions. In *Proceedings of NAACL*.

Chin-Yew Lin. 2004. ROUGE: a package for automatic evaluation of summaries. In *Proceedings of ACL Workshop on Text Summarization Branches Out*.

Fei Liu and Yang Liu. 2013. Towards abstractive speech summarization: Exploring unsupervised and supervised approaches for spoken utterance compression. *IEEE Transactions on Audio, Speech, and Language Processing*.

Ivana Ljubić, René Weiskircher, Ulrich Pferschy, Gunnar W. Klau, Petra Mutzel, and Matteo Fischetti. 2006. An Algorithmic Framework for the Exact Solution of the Prize-Collecting Steiner Tree Problem. In *Mathematical Progamming, Series B*.

Andre F. T. Martins and Noah A. Smith. 2009. Summarization with a joint model for sentence extraction and compression. In *Proceedings of the ACL Workshop on Integer Linear Programming for Natural Language Processing*.

Andre F. T. Martins, Noah A. Smith, and Eric P. Xing. 2009. Concise integer linear programming formulations for dependency parsing. In *Proceedings of ACL*.

Ryan McDonald. 2007. A study of global inference algorithms in multi-document summarization. In *Proceedings of ECIR*.

Rada Mihalcea and Paul Tarau. 2004. TextRank: Bringing order into text. In *Proceedings of EMNLP*.

Courtney Napoles, Benjamin Van Durme, and Chris Callison-Burch. 2011. Evaluating Sentence Compression: Pitfalls and Suggested Remedies. In *Proceedings of the Workshop on Monolingual Text-To-Text Generation*, MTTG '11, pages 91–97, Stroudsburg, PA, USA. Association for Computational Linguistics.

Ani Nenkova and Kathleen McKeown. 2011. Automatic summarization. *Foundations and Trends in Information Retrieval*.

Xian Qian and Yang Liu. 2013. Fast joint compression and summarization via graph cuts. In *Proceedings of EMNLP*.

Norman Sadeh, Alessandro Acquisti, Travis D. Breaux, Lorrie Faith Cranor, Aleecia M. McDonald, Joel R. Reidenberg, Noah A. Smith, Fei Liu, N. Cameron Russell, Florian Schaub, and Shomir Wilson. 2013. The usable privacy policy project. *Technical Report, CMU-ISR-13-119, Carnegie Mellon University*.

Arie Segev. 1987. The Node-Weighted Steiner Tree Problem. *Networks*, 17(1):1–17.

Ben Taskar, Carlos Guestrin, and Daphne Koller. 2004. Max-margin Markov networks. In *Advances in Neural Information Processing Systems 16*.

Kapil Thadani and Kathleen McKeown. 2013. Sentence compression with joint structural inference. In *Proceedings of CoNLL*.

Lucy Vanderwende, Michele Banko, , and Arul Menezes. 2004. Event-centric summary generation. In *Proceedings of DUC*.

Bin Zhao and Eric P. Xing. 2014. Quasi real-time summarization for consumer videos. In *Proceedings of CVPR*.

# Encoding World Knowledge in the Evaluation of Local Coherence

**Muyu Zhang**[1,*], **Vanessa Wei Feng**[2], **Bing Qin**[1], **Graeme Hirst**[2], **Ting Liu**[1] **and Jingwen Huang**[1]
[1]Research Center for Social Computing and Information Retrieval
Harbin Institute of Technology, Harbin, China
[2]Department of Computer Science, University of Toronto, Toronto, ON, Canada
{myzhang,qinb,tliu,jwhuang}@ir.hit.edu.cn
{weifeng,gh}@cs.toronto.edu

## Abstract

Previous work on text coherence was primarily based on matching multiple mentions of the same entity in different parts of the text; therefore, it misses the contribution from semantically related but not necessarily coreferential entities (e.g., ***Gates*** and ***Microsoft***). In this paper, we capture such semantic relatedness by leveraging world knowledge (e.g., ***Gates*** *is the person who created* ***Microsoft***), and use two existing evaluation frameworks. First, in the unsupervised framework, we introduce semantic relatedness as an enrichment to the original graph-based model of Guinaudeau and Strube (2013). In addition, we incorporate semantic relatedness as additional features into the popular entity-based model of Barzilay and Lapata (2008). Across both frameworks, our enriched model with semantic relatedness outperforms the original methods, especially on short documents.

## 1 Introduction

In a well-written document, sentences are organized and presented in a logical and coherent form, which makes the text fluent and easily understood. Therefore, coherence is a fundamental aspect of high text quality, and the evaluation of coherence is a crucial component of many NLP applications, such as essay scoring (Miltsakaki and Kukich, 2004), story generation (McIntyre and Lapata, 2010), and document summarization (Barzilay et al., 2002).

A particularly popular model for evaluating text coherence is the entity-based local coherence model of Barzilay and Lapata (2008) (B&L), which extracts mentions of entities in adjacent sentences, and captures local coherence in terms of the transitions in the grammatical role of each mention. Following this direction, a number of extensions have been proposed (Elsner and Charniak, 2008; Elsner and Charniak, 2011; Lin et al., 2011; Feng et al., 2014), the majority of which focus on enriching the original entity features. An exception is the unsupervised model of Guinaudeau and Strube (2013) (G&S), which converts the document into a graph of sentences, and evaluates the text coherence by computing the average out-degree over the entire graph.

However, despite the apparent success of these methods, they rely merely on matching mentions of the same entity, but neglect the contribution from semantically related but not necessarily coreferential entities. For example, the text in Figure 1a[1] has no common entity in $s_2$ and $s_3$. However, the transition between them is perfectly coherent, because there exists close semantic relatedness between two distinct entities, ***Gates*** in $s_2$ and ***Microsoft*** in $s_3$, which can be captured by the world knowledge that ***Gates*** *is the person who created* ***Microsoft*** (represented by ***Gates-create-Microsoft***). In fact, the issue of absence of common entities between adjacent sentences is quite prevalent. Analyzing the CoNLL 2012 dataset (Pradhan et al., 2012), we found that 42.34% of the time, adjacent sentences do not share common entities. As a result, methods which rely on strict entity matching would fail on these cases.

[*] This work was partly done while the first author was visiting University of Toronto.

[1] Based on a news item: http://www.cnbc.com/id/101576926



*Human Language Technologies: The 2015 Annual Conference of the North American Chapter of the ACL*, pages 1087–1096,
Denver, Colorado, May 31 – June 5, 2015. 

$s_1$: In 1980, [ Gates ]$_S$ licensed [ 86-DOS ]$_O$ from [ Tim Paterson ]$_X$ for $50,000, which marketed it as [ PC-DOS ]$_X$.
$s_2$: [ Gates' smartest move ]$_S$ was retaining [ ownership of the source code ]$_O$ of what he and [ Allen ]$_X$ would develop as [ MS-DOS ]$_X$.
$s_3$: [ Microsoft ]$_S$ got a [ licensing fee ]$_O$ every time [ IBM ]$_S$ sold a [ PC ]$_O$.

(a) A fragment of news text

| | Gates | 86-DOS | Paterson | PC-DOS | Move | Ownership | Source | Code | MS-DOS | Microsoft | Fee | Time | IBM | PC |
|---|---|---|---|---|---|---|---|---|---|---|---|---|---|---|
| $s_1$ | S | O | X | X | - | - | - | - | - | - | - | - | - | - |
| $s_2$ | S | - | - | - | S | O | O | O | O | - | - | - | - | - |
| $s_3$ | - | - | - | - | - | - | - | - | - | S | O | X | S | O |

(b) The corresponding entity grid

Figure 1: A news text fragment with its corresponding entity grid constructed following B&L (2008). Although $s_2$ and $s_3$ share no entity, their transition is still coherent, because ***Gates*** and ***Microsoft*** are semantically related by the knowledge ***Gates-create-Microsoft***.

We wish to incorporate semantic relatedness between different entities into existing models to tackle the problem described above. In particular, we propose to capture such semantic relatedness between different entities with world knowledge represented as triples, e.g., ***Gates-create-Microsoft***. Given a text to be evaluated, we first retrieve relevant world knowledge from multiple sources. For the unsupervised framework of G&S, we integrate knowledge into the original graph-based document representation, in which sentences are the nodes and edges are formed by shared entities and our world knowledge. Then, we adopt a dynamic programming algorithm to produce a coherence score for the text. For the supervised framework of B&L, we incorporate the world knowledge as a novel set of features into the original entity-based model, and train a model to discriminate different degrees of text coherence.

To evaluate the impact of incorporating semantic relatedness, we conduct experiments on two datasets, each of which resembles a real sub-task in the text coherence modeling: **sentence ordering** and **summary coherence rating**. On both tasks, across two frameworks, supervised and unsupervised, we perform a direct comparison between our enhanced model and the original one. On both tasks, our models are shown to be more powerful than the models relying on entity matching only. Moreover, for sentence ordering, world knowledge is shown to be especially useful on short documents.

## 2 Background

### 2.1 Entity-based local coherence modeling

The initial entity-based model was developed by B&L. It is based on the intuition that there exists a canonical order of how entities occur in the text. Therefore, we can model text coherence by measuring how mentions of various entities are distributed within the text. Specifically, for a given document $d$, an entity grid is constructed in which the rows represent the sentences and the columns represent entities. Each grid cell $r_{ij}$ corresponds to the syntactic role of entity $e_j$ in sentence $s_i$: subject ($S$), object ($O$), other ($X$), or nothing ($-$). For example, Figure 1b shows the entity grid of the text shown in Figure 1a. If an entity serves multiple syntactic roles in a sentence, its grammatical role is resolved according to the priority order: $S > O > X > -$.

Based on the entity grid representation, a local coherence transition is defined as a sequence $\{S, O, X, -\}^n$, representing the grammatical roles or absence of a particular entity across $n$ adjacent sentences. Then, the document is encoded as a feature vector $\Phi(d) = (p_1(d), p_2(d), \ldots, p_m(d))$, where $p_t(d)$ is the normalized frequency of the transition $t$ in the entity grid, and $m$ is the number of predefined transitions. $p_t(d)$ is computed as the number of occurrences of transition $t$ among all entities in the entity grid, divided by the total number of transitions of the same length. Using this feature encoding, the model is then trained as a preference ranking problem between documents of different degrees of coherence.

### 2.2 Graph-based local coherence modeling

As mentioned previously, most extensions to the entity-based local coherence model focus on enriching the feature set (Filippova and Strube, 2007; Elsner and Charniak, 2011; Lin et al., 2011; Feng et al., 2014), all of which follow a supervised learning framework. To the best of our knowledge, the only exception is the unsupervised method proposed by

G&S, which transforms the entity grid into a sentence graph and measures text coherence by computing the average out-degree of the graph. For a document $d$, its entity grid is constructed first, following the method described in Section 2.1. Then, a bipartite graph $G = (V_s, V_e, L, W)$ is constructed, where $V_s$ is the set of nodes representing sentences in the text; $V_e$ is the set of nodes representing entities; $L$ is the set of edges associated with a weight $w \in W$. An edge exists between a sentence $s_x$ and an entity $e$, if and only if $e$ occurs in $s_x$. Each edge is further associated with a weight $w(e, s_x)$, determined by the grammatical role of the entity $e$ in sentence $s_x$: 3 for subject ($S$), 2 for object ($O$), 1 for other ($X$), and 0 for nothing ($-$). Note that graph $G$ consists of both sentence nodes and entity nodes.

Then, $G$ is converted to another graph $P$, which consists of sentence nodes only, where an edge connects two sentence nodes if and only if at least one entity is shared between these two sentences. In $P$, the weight of each edge is computed by aggregating the edge weights in the original bipartite graph $G$:

$$w^{(P)}(s_x, s_y) = \sum\nolimits_{e \in E_{xy}} w^{(G)}(e, s_x) * w^{(G)}(e, s_y), \quad (1)$$

where $E_{xy}$ is the set of entities shared by two sentences $s_x$ and $s_y$, and $w^{(G)}(e, s_x)$ is the weight of edge between entity $e$ and sentence $s_x$ as illustrated before. The coherence of the document is thus measured by the average out-degree of graph $P$.

Although this method is purely unsupervised, it achieves a performance comparable with its supervised counterparts, e.g., B&L. However, since this method still relies on matching multiple mentions of the same entity, it misses the important contribution from those semantically related yet distinct entities, e.g. ***Gates*** and ***Microsoft*** in Figure 1a.

## 3 Finding relevant world knowledge

To supplement existing models with information derived from semantic relatedness, given a document $d$ to be evaluated, we first retrieve all world knowledge related to $d$. There are two major issues for this process: (1) **knowledge sources**: where can we obtain this knowledge?, and (2) **knowledge selection**: how do we pinpoint the most relevant ones?

**Knowledge sources** There are two main kinds of knowledge sources: (1) manually edited knowledge bases, such as YAGO (Hoffart et al., 2013), which consists of about 4 million human-edited instances from on-line encyclopedias such as WikiPedia (Denoyer and Gallinari, 2007) and FreeBase (Bollacker et al., 2008), and (2) automatically constructed knowledge bases, such as Reverb (Fader et al., 2011), which covers about 20 million instances extracted from raw texts. Generally speaking, manually edited knowledge bases have better accuracy but lower coverage, while automatically extracted knowledge bases are the opposite. To seek a good balance, we use both YAGO and Reverb as our knowledge sources. In addition, the automatically constructed knowledge bases can be extracted from raw texts of any domain, which makes our method adaptable. Both sources are presented in triples, *argument*$_1$*-predicate-argument*$_2$, (e.g., ***Gates-create-Microsoft***), where the two arguments are usually entities and the predicate is the relation between them (Zhang et al., 2014).

**Knowledge selection** For each document $d$, we then select the subset of relevant knowledge instances, in the sense that they represent relations between the entities in $d$. In particular, we extract all entities in $d$, and query the knowledge bases to obtain all the knowledge instances in which both of the two arguments, *argument*$_1$ and *argument*$_2$, match some of the entities in $d$.

One issue in knowledge selection is whether to retrieve knowledge instances using exact or partial matching. For a given pair of entities in the text, the chance is rather low to find instances in the knowledge bases where the two arguments perfectly match the pair of entities, because entities in the source document might appear in aliases or abbreviations. In contrast, partial matching between arguments and entities usually increases coverage but at risk of introducing more noise. In our work, to balance accuracy and coverage, when retrieving world knowledge, we use partial matching and form queries only for those entities realized as noun phrases in the text.

## 4 World knowledge encoding

### 4.1 Unsupervised graph-based framework

As described in Section 2.2, G&S represents the text as a graph and measures the coherence by the average out-degree of the graph. In this part, we describe

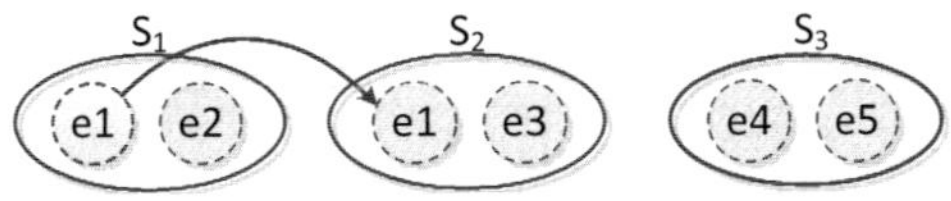


(a) Traditional entity graph relying on entity matching

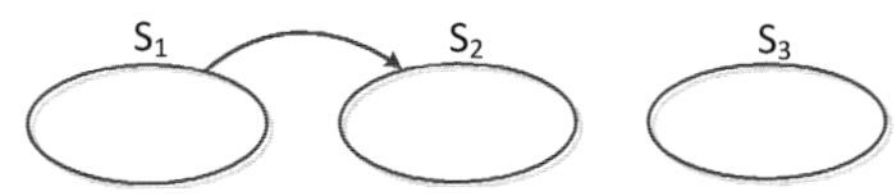


(b) Traditional sentence graph converted from (a)

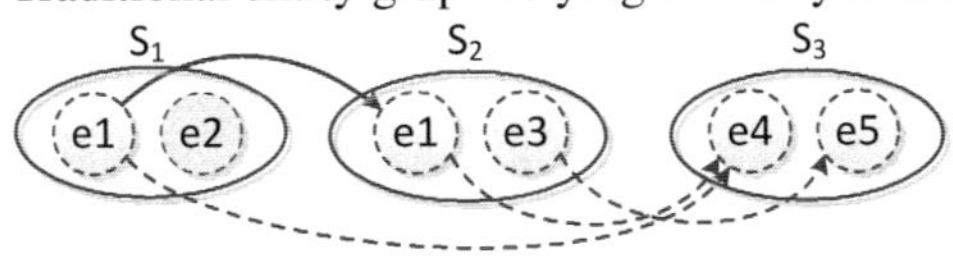


(c) Our entity graph encoding relatedness between entities

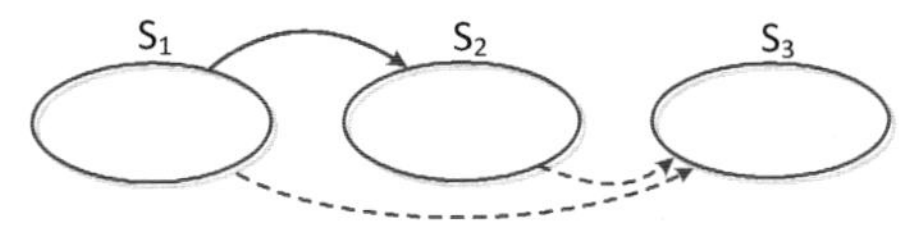


(d) Our sentence graph converted from (c)

Figure 2: (a) and (b) show the traditional entity and sentence graph based on matching multiple mentions of the same entity; while (c) and (d) represent our entity and sentence graph encoding semantic relatedness between those semantically related but not necessarily coreferential entities (e.g., ***Gates*** and ***Microsoft***) by adding *world-knowledge edges* (dashed lines) accroding to world knowledge (e.g., ***Gates-create-Microsoft***).

how we capture semantic relatedness by encoding world knowledge to the graph-based model. The outline of our method is as follows. Given a document $d$, we first retrieve relevant world knowledge from multiple sources (see Section 3). Then, we construct an *entity graph* with world knowledge to capture both the distribution information and semantic relatedness between entities (see Section 4.1.1). After that, we convert the entity graph into a *sentence graph* (see Section 4.1.2), in which two sentences are connected not only through common entities but also through world knowledge. Finally, we apply our novel *reachability score computation* **over the sentence graph** to produce a coherence score for the text to be evaluated (see Section 4.1.3).

### 4.1.1 Entity graph

As shown in Figure 2c, there are two kinds of edges in our *entity graph*: (1) *common-entity edges* (solid lines), which connect different mentions of the same entity, such as ***Gates*** in $s_1$ and ***Gates*** in $s_2$; (2) *world-knowledge edges* (dashed lines), which connect different entities through certain world knowledge, such as ***Gates*** in $s_2$ and ***Microsoft*** in $s_3$ related by ***Gates-create-Microsoft***. This representation captures not only the distribution information of individual entities but also the semantic relatedness between different entities. In contrast, the original graph-based model by G&S (Figures 2a and 2b) includes common-entity edges only and misses the semantic relatedness information. Formally, for a document $d$, we define its entity graph as $G = (V, L_m, L_k, W_m, W_k)$, where $V$ denotes the nodes of entities; $L_m$ denotes the set of common-entity edges and $L_k$ denotes the set of world-knowledge edges; and $W_m$ and $W_k$ are the two sets of weights associated with $L_m$ and $L_k$ respectively.

Following G&S, for each common-entity edge $l_m \in L_m$, which connects two mentions of the same entity $e$ appearing in different sentences $s_x$ and $s_y$, we compute its weight as $w(e, s_x) \times w(e, s_y)$, where the value of $w(e, s_x)$ is based on the grammatical role of the entity $e$ in the sentence $s_x$ as follows: 3 for subject ($S$), 2 for object ($O$), 1 for other ($X$), and 0 for nothing($-$). When multiple mentions of the same entity appear with different grammatical roles in the same sentence, the role with the highest weight is chosen to represent the entity. For each world-knowledge edge $l_k \in L_k$, which connects two different entities $e_{ix}$ and $e_{jy}$ appearing in sentence $s_x$ and $s_y$ respectively, we consider three factors when assigning the weight to the edge: (1) semantic relatedness between $e_{ix}$ and $e_{jy}$: higher relatedness leads to a higher weight; (2) the grammatical roles of $e_{ix}$ and $e_{jy}$ in $s_x$ and $s_y$: different roles correspond to different weights; and (3) textual distance between $e_{ix}$ and $e_{jy}$: longer distance results in a lower weight. Therefore we compute the weight of $l_k$ between $e_{ix}$ and $e_{jy}$ as below:

$$w_k(e_{ix}, e_{jy}) = \frac{r(e_i, e_j) \times w(e_{ix}, s_x) \times w(e_{jy}, s_y)}{d(e_{ix}, e_{jy}) \times 2}, \quad (2)$$

where $w(e_{ix}, s_x)$ is associated to the grammatical role of $e_{ix}$ in $s_x$ as illustrated before; $d(e_{ix}, e_{jy})$ is the distance between $e_{ix}$ and $e_{jy}$; and $r(e_i, e_j)$ is the semantic relatedness between $e_{ix}$ and $e_{jy}$ as shown in Formula 3 below. Note that the value of $r(e_i, e_j)$ is independent of the sentence in which $e_i$ and $e_j$ appear, so we denote it as $r(e_i, e_j)$ instead of $r(e_{ix}, e_{jy})$.

$$r(e_i, e_j) = \begin{cases} \dfrac{\log n(e_i, e_j)}{\max\limits_{l_{mn} \in L_k} \log n(e_m, e_n)} & \text{if } n(e_i, e_j) > 2, \\ 0 & \text{otherwise.} \end{cases} \tag{3}$$

where $n(e_i, e_j)$ corresponds to the number of world knowledge instances relating $e_i$ and $e_j$. For instance, Figure 1a contains an edge between ***Gates*** ($e_1$ in $s_1$) and ***Microsoft*** ($e_2$ in $s_3$), in which $w(e_{11}, s_1)$ and $w(e_{23}, s_3)$ are 3, and $d(e_{11}, e_{23})$ is 2. Note that we consider the grammatical roles in both common edges and background knowledge edges because we treat them independently from each other. The grammatical information is important to both of these two kinds of edges.

#### 4.1.2 Sentence graph

Figure 2d shows the sentence graph converted from the entity graph in Figure 2c. In our work, in order to incorporate world knowledge, we adopt an enriched representation of sentence graph, $G' = (V', L'_m, L'_k, W'_m, W'_k)$, where $V'$ is the sentence nodes; $L'_m$ denotes the set of common-entity edges (solid lines); $L'_k$ denotes the set of world-knowledge edges (dashed lines), and $W'_m$ and $W'_k$ correspond to the weights associated with the edges in $L'_m$ and $L'_k$.

Intuitively, the semantic relatedness between two sentences can be measured as the total relatedness of each entity pair in the two sentences. Therefore, in our enhanced sentence graph representation, for a pair of sentences $s_x$ and $s_y$, the weight of their common-entity edge, $w'_m(s_x, s_y)$, is computed as $w'_m(s_x, s_y) = \sum_{e_i \in V_{xy}} w_m(e_{ix}, e_{iy})$, where $V_{xy}$ is the set of entities shared by two sentences $s_x$ and $s_y$, and $w_m(e_{ix}, e_{iy})$ is the weight of the corresponding common-entity edge in the entity graph (see Section 4.1.1). Similarly, the weight of their world-knowledge edge, $w'_k(s_x, s_y)$, is computed as $w'_k(s_x, s_y) = \sum_{e_i \in V_x, e_j \in V_y} w_k(e_{ix}, e_{jy})$, where $V_x$ and $V_y$ denote the set of entities in $s_x$ and $s_y$ respectively, and $w_k(e_{ix}, e_{jy})$ is the weight of the corresponding world-knowledge edge in the entity graph.

**Algorithm 1:** Reachability score computation.

**Input**: $G' = (V', L'_m, L'_k, W'_m, W'_k)$.
**Output**: The final reachability score $S$.

$n \leftarrow |V'|$
**for** $j = 1 \rightarrow n$ **do**
  $score(v'_j) \leftarrow 0$
**for** $j = 1 \rightarrow n$ **do**
  **for** $i = 0 \rightarrow j-1$ **do**
    **if** $l'_m(i, j) \in L'_m$ **then**
      $score(v'_j) \leftarrow score(v'_i) + w'_m(i, j)$
    **if** $l'_k(i, j) \in L'_k$ **then**
      $score(v'_j) \leftarrow score(v'_i) + w'_k(i, j)$
**return** $S = \dfrac{\sum_{v'_j \in V' \wedge out(v'_j)=0} score(v'_j)}{|\{v'_j : v'_j \in V' \wedge out(v'_j) = 0\}|}$

#### 4.1.3 Reachability score computation

Based on our sentence graph representation, we compute a reachability score for each sentence node. To produce a final coherence score for the text, we compute the ***average reachability score*** among those nodes whose out-degree is equal to 0 in the graph, rather than among all nodes, because of the intuition that, if a sentence node has no subsequent nodes, their reachability score therefore reflects the tightness between this sentence and the preceding part of the text. For a certain sentence node $v'_j$, its reachability score is defined as the sum of edge weights on all paths from the starting node (i.e., the first sentence) to $v'_j$, and the contribution of each path to the final reachability score depends on the total weight of that path as shown in Equation 4.

$$score(v'_j) = \sum_{v'_i \in V', v'_i \neq v'_j} (score(v'_i) + w'_m(i, j) + w'_k(i, j)) \tag{4}$$

where $score(v'_i)$ denotes the reachability score of $v'_i$, and $w'_m(i, j)$ and $w'_k(i, j)$ are the weights of the common-entity edge and the world-knowledge edge between $v'_i$ and $v'_j$; if there is no such edge in the graph, the corresponding weight is set to 0.

Algorithm 1 summarizes our reachability score computation, in which the reachability score of each node is initially 0, and iteratively updated.

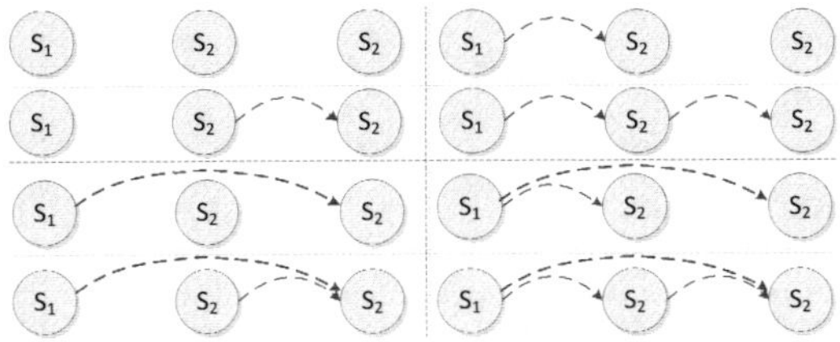

Figure 3: Eight patterns of how world knowledge is distributed among three adjacent sentences.

### 4.2 Supervised entity-based framework

As mentioned previously, numerous extensions have been proposed to the original entity-based model of B&L. However, those extensions mostly rely on entity matching and thus fail to incorporate the information from semantically related yet distinct entities. We propose a novel extension by introducing world knowledge to capture entity-wise relatedness.

Inspired by the original entity-based model, in which local coherence is reflected by the patterns of how entities act grammatically from one sentence to the next, we believe that local coherence can also be characterized by the patterns of how world knowledge relates a pair of sentences. Specifically, given a set of sentences, there are different patterns of how knowledge instances are distributed among them. We consider modeling those patterns within a window of 3 sentences, in which there are $2^3 = 8$ different distribution patterns, as shown in Figure 3. We then use the frequencies of these distribution patterns over the entire document as additional features into the entity-based model. In particular, for each particular distribution pattern $b_k$, its corresponding frequency $p(b_k) = \frac{|b_k|}{|V'| - 2}$, where $|b_k|$ is the number of occurrences of $b_k$ in the sentence graph.

In addition to $p(b_k)$, we also compute another feature, $p(E)$, which is the frequency that two nodes are connected by certain world knowledge over the sentence graph, reflecting the overall semantic relatedness within the graph. $p(E)$ is computed as $p(E) = \frac{|L'_k|}{|V'|}$. With these world knowledge features incorporated into the original entity-based model, we obtain an enhanced model with an emphasis on semantic relatedness between different entities.

## 5 Experiments

To evaluate the impact of incorporating semantic relatedness, we conduct experiments on two datasets, each of which resembles a real sub-task in modeling text coherence: **sentence ordering** and **summary coherence rating**. Since text coherence is a relative concept rather than a binary distinction, in both tasks, we formulate the problem as pairwise preference ranking. Specifically, given a set of texts with different degrees of coherence, we train a ranker to prefer the more coherent text over the less coherent one. Performance is therefore measured as the fraction of correct pairwise rankings as recognized by the ranker. We use SVM$^{light}$ (Joachims, 2002) with the ranking configuration to train and evaluate our models, with all parameters set to default values.

On both tasks, across two frameworks, supervised and unsupervised, we directly compare our modified model against the original one, i.e., B&L in the supervised framework and G&S in the unsupervised framework. In our experiments, we use the Stanford parser (Marneffe et al., 2006) to automatically extract the grammatical role for each entity mention.

### 5.1 Sentence ordering

The task of sentence ordering attempts to simulate the situation where, given a predefined set of information-bearing items, we need to determine the best order to arrange those items.

In this paper, we follow G&S and introduce CoNLL 2012[2] (Pradhan et al., 2012) as our dataset, which is composed of documents from multiple news sources. For each text, we randomly shuffle its sentences to generate 20 permutations with incorrect sentence order. For a fair comparison, we also evaluate our model on a filtered subset of documents with an average length of 31.8 sentences. Therefore, our dataset contains 72 documents and $72 \times 20 = 1440$ permutations, among which the shortest one contains 25 sentences. For our enhanced graph-based model (introduced in Section 4.1), which is purely unsupervised, we evaluate our model over the entire dataset. For our enhanced entity-based model (introduced in Section 4.2), which is purely supervised, we use half of the complete CoNLL dataset for training (237 documents plus permutations) and use half

[2] http://conll.cemantix.org/2012/data.html

of the filtered subset (36 documents plus permutations). The training and test sets do not overlap.

In this task, each training and test instance is composed of a pair of a source document and one of its permutations, and the source document is always considered more coherent than its permutation.

### 5.2 Summary coherence rating

The second task is summary coherence rating, in which, given a pair of summaries about the same set of source documents, we determine the ranking of these two summaries based on their degrees of coherence. The performance of the model is assessed by comparing model-induced rankings against the rankings given by human judges. We use the same dataset (DUC 2003) as B&L and G&S did, which consists of summaries generated either by human writers or by automatic summarization systems. Each summary was given a coherence score by averaging among seven judges. Often, machine-generated summaries receive low coherence scores because they contain sentences taken out of context and thus display problems with respect to coherence.

This dataset consists of 16 input document clusters, each of which is associated with five machine-generated summaries along with a human-written summary. In total, we have 96 summaries (for more details, see B&L). We form pairwise rankings by taking any two summaries originating from the same document cluster, given that the two summaries receive different coherence scores: 144 of the resulting rankings are used for training and 80 are for testing.

### 5.3 Experiment results

In this section, we demonstrate the performance of our models with world knowledge encoded in one of the two ways: paths in a sentence graph or features in an entity grid. We compare our models against the original graph-based model (G&S) and entity-based model (B&L). The evaluation is conducted on the two tasks, sentence ordering and summary coherence rating, and the accuracy is the fraction of correct pairwise rankings.

Table 1 shows the performance of various models on both tasks. The first section shows the results of G&S's graph-based local coherence model, including the performance reported in their original paper and that achieved by our re-implementation, representing the effect with no world knowledge encoded. The second section shows the performance of our two graph-based models with world knowledge encoded. *Graph model + K* is the basic model with world knowledge encoded, but coherence is simply measured as the average out-degree as in G&S's approach. *Graph model + K + Avg_R* replaces the out-degree measurement by our *average reachability score* (described in Section 4.1.3), which measures coherence in a more sophisticated way. The third section shows the results of B&L's entity-based local coherence model, including the originally reported performance and that obtained by our re-implementation, in which no world knowledge features are included. The last section, *Entity model + K*, shows the result of entity-based model with our world knowledge features encoded. Note that the random baseline of both tasks is 50%.

| Model | SO | SCR |
|---|---|---|
| Graph model (G&S) | 88.9 | 80.0 |
| Graph model (Implemented) | 89.6 | 48.8 |
| Graph model + K | 91.3** | 50.0 |
| **Graph model + K + Avg_R** | **93.4****| **55.0*** |
| Entity model (B&L) | 88.9 | 83.8 |
| Entity model (Implemented) | 93.7 | 90.0 |
| **Entity model + K** | **95.1**** | **91.3** |

Table 1: Accuracies (%) of various models on the two tasks, sentence ordering (*SO*) and summary coherence rating (*SCR*). Models that perform significantly better than their corresponding re-implemented basic models are denoted by ** ($p < .01$) or * ($p < .05$), verified using paired $t$-test.

Firstly, for graph-based models, our *Graph model + K* outperforms the original models, suggesting that world knowledge is truly helpful for capturing more coherence information[3]. Moreover, by intro-

[3]The large discrepancy between the performance reported by G&S and that of our re-implementation in *Task 2* is due to the fact that G&S experimented with a set of specially formed summary pairs (see their paper for detail), which we have no access to. They also did not give sufficient details about how they constructed those summary pairs, which has a great impact on the final result. This made it difficult for us to fully re-implement their experiment. So we use B&L's set of summary pairs, which are generated randomly and are more difficult to distinguish, which explains our differing results from theirs.

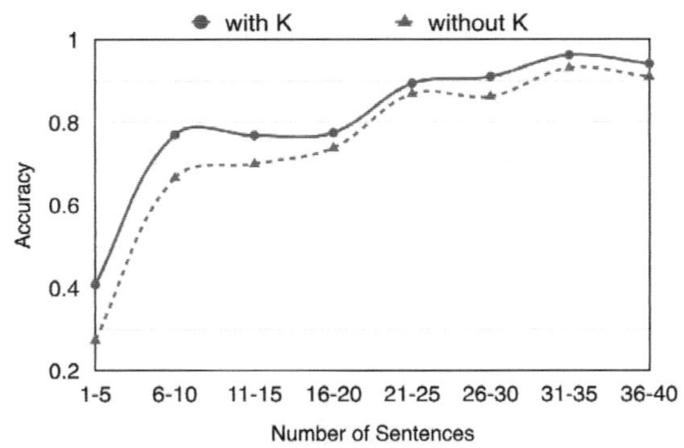


Figure 4: Graph-based models, with and without world knowledge (labeled as *With K* and *Without K*), tested on sets with different numbers of sentences.

ducing the scoring scheme of *average reachability score*, our *Graph model + K + Avg_R* achieves the best performance among all graph-based models.

Secondly, for entity-based models, our enhanced model with knowledge features encoded also achieves superior performance than our re-implemented model, again confirming the usefulness of world knowledge. Interestingly, we observe that our re-implementation obtains higher accuracy compared to the performance reported by B&L. This is partly due to the fact that the documents in our dataset have an average length of 31.5 sentences, which are longer than those used in B&L's experiments. We will further discuss this problem in Section 5.4 and show that document length is an important factor to the overall performance.

However, on the task of summary coherence rating, the difference between our extended models and the original ones is generally not significant, primarily due to the fact that the sample size for this task is too small, i.e., 80 pairwise rankings.

## 5.4 Effect of document length

### 5.4.1 Effect of document length on the overall performance

We further analyze the impact of document length on the task of sentence ordering. We partition our original dataset, which consists of 214 documents and their permutations, into 8 non-overlapping subsets, according to the length of documents: 1-5, 6-10,..., and 36-40 sentences. To illustrate the correlation between the performance and the length of document, we test our models with and without world knowledge encoded on each subset separately. Since the size of the available training data in each subset is relatively small, the supervised entity-based model suffers from sparsity. Therefore, we focus on the unsupervised graph-based models only.

Figure 4 shows the performance on different subsets. We can see that the performance of both models generally improves as the number of sentences increases. This observation is quite intuitive, because the longer a document is, the higher the chance is that, after being shuffled, adjacent sentences in the resulting permutation would be completely irrelevant to each other. Therefore, for longer documents, it is much easier for the model to distinguish a permutation from its source document.

| Model | Accuracy (%) |
|---|---|
| Graph Model | 27.4 |
| **Graph Model + K** | **44.2** |
| Entity Model | 65.8 |
| **Entity Model + K** | **71.1** |

Table 2: Performance of various models with and without world knowledge in the sentence ordering task, tested on short documents with 1–5 sentences.

### 5.4.2 Effect of document length on the model with world knowledge

Moreover, we also observe that the document length has a non-universal effect, in terms of how the model could benefit from incorporating world knowledge. Specifically, we find that world knowledge has a greater effect on short documents, as demonstrated in Table 2. Evaluated on a set of documents composed of 30 extremely short documents only (1–5 sentences), we see that our enhanced graph-based model is able to improve the performance by 16.8% over the basic model, and our enhanced entity-based model achieves 5.3% improvement (both differences are significant at $p < .01$). We postulate that it is primarily because a document with fewer sentences tends to shift to another subtopic immediately without elaborating on the previous one, and strict entity matching would find it difficult to establish coherent transitions between them. Therefore, the contribution from semantic relatedness tends to dominate the overall performance.

## 6 Conclusions and future work

In this paper, for the evaluation of text coherence, we go beyond strict entity matching and model the semantic relatedness between distinct entities through the use of world knowledge. Specifically, we incorporate world knowledge into two existing frameworks: (1) the unsupervised graph-based model (G&S), and (2) the supervised entity-grid model (B&L). Across the two frameworks, on both of our evaluation tasks, sentence ordering and summary coherence rating, our enhanced models with world knowledge encoded are shown to be stronger than the corresponding basic models, confirming that semantic relatedness is truly important for coherence modeling and such relatedness can be effectively captured by world knowledge. Moreover, we observe that world knowledge is particularly useful for short documents in sentence ordering, as it provides additional clues to relate sub-topics in the text.

In our future work, we wish to explore the effect of our world knowledge in conjunction with discourse relations. Specifically, we plan to incorporate world knowledge into the framework of discourse role matrix (Lin et al., 2011; Feng et al., 2014). In addition, we also plan to develop a more sophisticated feature encoding by distinguishing different types of predicates in world knowledge triples.

## Acknowledgments

We would like to thank Mao Zheng and Yanyan Zhao for their great help. This work was partly supported by National Natural Science Foundation of China via grant 61133012, the National 863 Leading Technology Research Project via grant 2012AA011102 and the National Natural Science Foundation of China Surface Project via grant 61273321.

## References

Regina Barzilay and Mirella Lapata. 2008. Modeling local coherence: An entity-based approach. *Computational Linguistics*, 34(1):1–34.

Regina Barzilay, Noemie Elhadad, and Kathleen R. McKeown. 2002. Inferring strategies for sentence ordering in multidocument news summarization. *Journal of Artificial Intelligence Research*, 17(1):35–55.

Kurt Bollacker, Colin Evans, Praveen Paritosh, Tim Sturge, and Jamie Taylor. 2008. Freebase: a collaboratively created graph database for structuring human knowledge. In *Proceedings of the 2008 ACM SIGMOD international conference on Management of data*, pages 1247–1250. ACM.

Ludovic Denoyer and Patrick Gallinari. 2007. The Wikipedia XML corpus. In *Comparative Evaluation of XML Information Retrieval Systems*, pages 12–19. Springer.

Micha Elsner and Eugene Charniak. 2008. Coreference-inspired coherence modeling. In *Proceedings of the 46th Annual Meeting of the Association for Computational Linguistics on Human Language Technologies: Short Papers*, pages 41–44. Association for Computational Linguistics.

Micha Elsner and Eugene Charniak. 2011. Extending the entity grid with entity-specific features. In *Proceedings of the 49th Annual Meeting of the Association for Computational Linguistics: Human Language Technologies: short papers-Volume 2*, pages 125–129. Association for Computational Linguistics.

Anthony Fader, Stephen Soderland, and Oren Etzioni. 2011. Identifying relations for open information extraction. In *Proceedings of the Conference on Empirical Methods in Natural Language Processing*, pages 1535–1545. Association for Computational Linguistics.

Vanessa Wei Feng, Ziheng Lin, and Graeme Hirst. 2014. The impact of deep hierarchical discourse structures in the evaluation of text coherence. In *Proceedings of the 25th International Conference on Computational Linguistics*, pages 940–949.

Katja Filippova and Michael Strube. 2007. Extending the entity-grid coherence model to semantically related entities. In *Proceedings of the Eleventh European Workshop on Natural Language Generation*, pages 139–142. Association for Computational Linguistics.

Camille Guinaudeau and Michael Strube. 2013. Graph-based local coherence modeling. In *Proceedings of the 51st Annual Meeting of the Association for Computational Linguistics*, pages 93–103.

Johannes Hoffart, Fabian M Suchanek, Klaus Berberich, and Gerhard Weikum. 2013. Yago2: a spatially and temporally enhanced knowledge base from Wikipedia. *Artificial Intelligence*, 194:28–61.

Thorsten Joachims. 2002. Optimizing search engines using clickthrough data. In *Proceedings of the Eighth ACM SIGKDD International Conference on Knowledge Discovery and Data Mining*, pages 133–142. ACM.

Ziheng Lin, Hwee Tou Ng, and Min-Yen Kan. 2011. Automatically evaluating text coherence using discourse relations. In *Proceedings of the 49th Annual Meeting of the Association for Computational Linguistics: Human Language Technologies-Volume 1*, pages 997–1006. Association for Computational Linguistics.

M. Marneffe, B. Maccartney, and C. Manning. 2006. Generating typed dependency parses from phrase structure parses. In *Proceedings of the 5th International Conference on Language Resources and Evaluation*, volume 6, pages 449–454. European Language Resources Association (ELRA).

Neil McIntyre and Mirella Lapata. 2010. Plot induction and evolutionary search for story generation. In *Proceedings of the 48th Annual Meeting of the Association for Computational Linguistics*, pages 1562–1572. Association for Computational Linguistics.

Eleni Miltsakaki and Karen Kukich. 2004. Evaluation of text coherence for electronic essay scoring systems. *Natural Language Engineering*, 10(1):25–55.

Sameer Pradhan, Alessandro Moschitti, Nianwen Xue, Olga Uryupina, and Yuchen Zhang. 2012. CoNLL-2012 shared task: Modeling multilingual unrestricted coreference in ontonotes. In *Joint Conference on EMNLP and CoNLL-Shared Task*, pages 1–40. Association for Computational Linguistics.

Muyu Zhang, Bing Qin, Ting Liu, and Mao Zheng. 2014. Triple based background knowledge ranking for document enrichment. In *Proceedings of the 25th International Conference on Computational Linguistics*, pages 917–927.

# Chinese Event Coreference Resolution: An Unsupervised Probabilistic Model Rivaling Supervised Resolvers

**Chen Chen** and **Vincent Ng**
Human Language Technology Research Institute
University of Texas at Dallas
Richardson, TX 75083-0688
{yzcchen,vince}@hlt.utdallas.edu

## Abstract

Recent work has successfully leveraged the semantic information extracted from lexical knowledge bases such as WordNet and FrameNet to improve English event coreference resolvers. The lack of comparable resources in other languages, however, has made the design of high-performance non-English event coreference resolvers, particularly those employing unsupervised models, very difficult. We propose a generative model for the under-studied task of Chinese event coreference resolution that rivals its supervised counterparts in performance when evaluated on the ACE 2005 corpus.

## 1 Introduction

Event coreference resolution is the task of determining which event mentions in a text refer to the same real-world event. Compared to entity coreference, event coreference is not only much less studied, but it is arguably more challenging. Recall that for two event mentions to be coreferent, both their *triggers* (i.e., the words realizing the occurrence of the events) and their corresponding *arguments* (e.g., the times, places, and people involved in them) have to be compatible. However, identifying potential arguments (which is typically performed by an entity extraction system), linking arguments to their event mentions (which is typically performed by an event extraction system), and determining the compatibility between two event arguments (which is the job of an entity coreference resolver), are all non-trivial tasks. In other words, end-to-end event coreference resolution is complicated in part by the fact that an event coreference resolver has to rely on the noisy outputs produced by its upstream components in the standard information extraction (IE) pipeline.

In this paper, we examine Chinese event coreference resolution. While English event coreference is under-investigated, Chinese event coreference is much less studied than English event coreference. In terms of task definition, there is no difference between English and Chinese event coreference. However, the design of high-performance Chinese event coreference resolvers is complicated in part by the lack of large-scale lexical knowledge bases. Recent work by Bejan and Harabagiu (2010; 2014) has shown that the semantic information extracted from WordNet (Fellbaum, 1998) and FrameNet (Baker et al., 1998) significantly contributed to the performance of their English event coreference resolver.

While the lack of comparable lexical knowledge bases in Chinese can be mitigated in part by the use of event coreference annotated data, we focus on a challenging version of the task --- *unsupervised* Chinese event coreference resolution. Specifically, our goal is to learn an event coreference model *without* using data annotated with event coreference links. When evaluated on the Chinese portion of the ACE 2005 corpus, our unsupervised probabilistic model for event coreference resolution rivals its state-of-the-art supervised counterpart in performance. This, together with the fact that its underlying generative process is not language-dependent and does not rely on features extracted from lexical knowledge bases, potentially enables it to be applied to languages where neither annotated data nor large-scale



*Human Language Technologies: The 2015 Annual Conference of the North American Chapter of the ACL*, pages 1097–1107, knowledge bases are available.

Another feature of our model that deserves mention is that it performs joint event coreference resolution and anaphoricity determination. Anaphoricity determination, the task of determining whether a mention is anaphoric and hence needs to be resolved, is an issue common to both entity and event coreference resolution. However, determining the anaphoricity of an event mention is arguably more difficult than determining the anaphoricity of a pronoun. The reason is that while there exist lexical and syntactic cues that can be used to reliably identify pleonastic pronouns (Bergsma and Yarowsky, 2011), the lack of such cues in event mentions makes the identification of anaphoric event mentions challenging even in a supervised manner, let alone in an unsupervised manner. Note that ignoring anaphoricity determination and having our model attempt to resolve every event mention is not a viable option, as only 24.4% of the Chinese event mentions in our evaluation corpus (ACE 2005) are anaphoric. Our decision to jointly model anaphoricity determination and event coreference resolution was inspired by the difficulty of designing a standalone system for determining the anaphoricity of event mentions.

## 2 Related Work

Almost all existing approaches to event coreference are developed for English. These approaches can broadly be divided into three categories.

**Within-document coreference** is the most popularly investigated and arguably the most important event coreference task. While early work in MUC (e.g., Humphreys et al. (1997)) is limited to several scenarios, ACE takes a further step towards processing more fine-grained events. Most ACE event coreference resolvers are supervised, training a pairwise model to determine whether two event mentions are coreferent (e.g., Ahn (2006)).

Improvements to this standard approach include the use of *feature weighting* to train a better model (McConky et al., 2012), and *graph-based clustering algorithms* to produce event coreference clusters (Chen and Ji, 2009; Sangeetha and Arock, 2012). Chen et al. (2011) train multiple classifiers to handle coreference between event mentions of different syntactic types (e.g., verb-noun coreference, noun-noun coreference) on the OntoNotes corpus (Pradhan et al., 2007). However, OntoNotes is only partially annotated with event coreference links, and Chen et al. further make the simplifying assumption that event coreference chains are all and only those coreference chains that involve at least one verb.

More recently, Cybulska and Vossen (2012) and Goyal et al. (2013) have performed event coreference using semantic relations (e.g., hyponymy relations extracted from WordNet) and distributional semantic information, respectively, on the Intelligence Community (IC) corpus (Hovy et al., 2013). The IC corpus, which at the time of writing is not yet publicly available, is different from the MUC and ACE corpora in that it is annotated with not only *full* event coreference relations but also *partial* event coreference relations. Partial coreference is a term coined by Hovy et al. to refer to event relations that exhibit subtle deviation from the perfect identity of events (e.g., the subset relation, the membership relation). While all of the aforementioned work addresses the full event coreference task, a two-stage approach is recently proposed by Araki et al. (2014) to identify subevent relations from the IC corpus.

**Cross-document coreference** is first investigated by Bagga and Baldwin (1999), who represent an event mention as a vector of its context words and determine whether two event mentions are coreferent based on the cosine similarity of their vectors. Bejan and Harabagiu (2010; 2014) and Lee et al. (2012) propose nonparametric models and a joint entity and event coreference model respectively for within- and cross-document event coreference, evaluating their models on the ECB corpus. However, ECB "is annotated mainly for cross-document coreference" and many difficult cases of within-document coreference are not annotated (Liu et al., 2014).

Naughton (2009) and Elkhlifi and Faiz (2009) have worked on **sentence-level event coreference**, where the goal is to determine whether two sentences containing event mentions are coreferent. Somewhat unfortunately, simplifying assumptions have to be made when a sentence containing multiple non-coreferent event mentions is encountered.

Compared to English event coreference, there has been much less work on Chinese event coreference. SinoCoreferencer (Chen and Ng, 2014), a publicly-available ACE-style within-document event coreference resolver for Chinese that achieves state-of-the-art results, employs a supervised approach where a classifier is trained to determine whether two event mentions are coreferent. We will compare our unsupervised model against this supervised resolver.

## 3 ACE Event Coreference

In this section, we overview the ACE 2005 event coreference task, which is the version of the within-document event coreference task we focus on.

The ACE 2005 event coreference task requires that an event coreference resolver perform coreference on event mentions belonging to one of the ACE event types. More specifically, an event mention is composed of a *trigger* (i.e., the word realizing the event's occurrence) and a set of *arguments* (i.e., the event's participants). Each event trigger has a *type* and a *subtype*. In ACE 2005, eight event types are defined, which are further subcategorized into 33 subtypes. Each event argument has a semantic *role*. In ACE 2005, a set of argument roles is defined for each event type. That is, an event's type determines what roles its mentions' arguments can assume. Not surprisingly, two event mentions cannot be coreferent if their triggers have different subtypes or they have incompatible arguments (e.g., their dates or locations are different).

To better understand the ACE 2005 event coreference task, consider the sentence in Figure 1, which is taken from the ACE 2005 corpus. This example contains three event mentions belonging to the ACE event types. Specifically, these three mentions are triggered by the words 离 (leaving), 暗杀 (assassinated) and 攻击 (attack). 暗杀 and 攻击 have type LIFE and subtype DIE, whereas 离 has type MOVEMENT and subtype TRANSPORT. Note that 暗杀 and 攻击 refer to the same real-world event and are therefore coreferent.

## 4 The Generative Model

In this section, we present our generative model.

### 4.1 Notation

We begin by introducing the notation that we use in the rest of this paper. We denote $e$ to be the current event mention to be resolved (henceforth the *active* event mention). $C$, the set of candidate antecedents

---

沙米里与其子在上午交通尖峰时间 [离] 家时，遭到 [暗杀]。这次 [攻击] 再次显示叛乱分子能力。

Shameri and his son were [assassinated] during morning rush hour when [leaving] home. This [attack] once again demonstrated the insurgents' ability.

---

Figure 1: An excerpt from a Chinese document in the ACE 2005 corpus with the corresponding English translation. The event mentions are bracketed.

of $e$, contains all the event mentions preceding $e$ in the associated text as well as a dummy candidate antecedent $d$ (to which $e$ will be resolved if it is non-anaphoric). Also, we define $k$ to be the context surrounding $e$ as well as every candidate antecedent $c$ in $C$, and $k_c$ to be the context surrounding $e$ and candidate antecedent $c$. Moreover, we define $l$ to be a binary variable indicating whether $c$ is the correct antecedent of $e$. Finally, $e_t$ and $c_t$ denote $e$ and $c$'s respective trigger words.

### 4.2 Training

Our model estimates $P(e, k, c, l)$, the probability of seeing (1) the active event mention $e$; (2) the context $k$ surrounding $e$ and its candidate antecedents; (3) a candidate antecedent $c$ of $e$; and (4) $l$, a binary value indicating whether $c$ is $e$'s correct antecedent. Since we estimate this probability from a raw, unannotated corpus, we are effectively treating $e$, $k$, and $c$ as observed data and $l$ as hidden data.

Owing to the presence of hidden data, we estimate the model parameters using the Expectation-Maximization (EM) algorithm (Dempster et al., 1977). Specifically, we use EM to iteratively estimate the model parameters from data in which each event mention is labeled with the probability that it corefers with each of its candidate antecedents, and apply the resulting model to relabel each event mention with the probability that it corefers with each of its candidate antecedents. Below we describe the details of the E-step and the M-step.

#### 4.2.1 E-Step

The goal of the E-step is to compute $P(l=1|e, k, c)$, the probability that a candidate antecedent $c$ is the correct antecedent of $e$ given context $k$. Assuming that exactly one of the $e$'s candidate antecedents is its correct antecedent, we can rewrite $P(l{=}1|e,k,c)$ as follows:

$$P(l{=}1|e,k,c) = \frac{P(e,k,c,l{=}1)}{\sum_{c' \in C} P(e,k,c',l{=}1)} \quad (1)$$

As we can see from Equation (1), to compute $P(l{=}1|e,k,c)$, we need to compute $P(e,k,c,l{=}1)$, which can be rewritten using Chain Rule:

$$P(e,k,c,l{=}1) = P(e|k,c,l{=}1) * P(l{=}1|k,c) * P(c|k) * P(k) \quad (2)$$

Next, given $l = 1$ (i.e., $c$ is the antecedent of $e$), we assume that we can generate $e$ from $c$ without looking at the context. Using this assumption and approximating $e$ and $c$ by their trigger words, we can rewrite $P(e|k,c,l{=}1)$ as follows:

$$P(e|k,c,l{=}1) \approx P(e_t|c_t,l{=}1) \quad (3)$$

Moreover, we assume that (1) given $e$ and $c$'s context, the probability of $c$ being the antecedent of $e$ is not affected by the context of the other candidate antecedents; and (2) $k_c$ is sufficient for determining whether $c$ is the antecedent of $e$. So,

$$P(l{=}1|k,c) \approx P(l{=}1|k_c,c) \approx P(l{=}1|k_c) \quad (4)$$

Next, applying Bayes Rule to $P(l{=}1|k_c)$, we get:

$$\frac{P(k_c|l{=}1)P(l{=}1)}{P(k_c|l{=}1)P(l{=}1) + P(k_c|l{=}0)P(l{=}0)} \quad (5)$$

Representing $k_c$ as a set of $n$ features $f_c^1, \ldots f_c^n$ and assuming that each $f_c^i$ is conditionally independent given $l$, we can approximate Expression (5) as:

$$\frac{\prod_i P(f_c^i|l{=}1)P(l{=}1)}{\prod_i P(f_c^i|l{=}1)P(l{=}1) + \prod_i P(f_c^i|l{=}0)P(l{=}0)} \quad (6)$$

Given Equations (2), (3), (4) and (6), we can rewrite $P(l{=}1|e,k,c)$ as follows:

$$P(l{=}1|e,k,c) = \frac{P(e,k,c,l{=}1)}{\sum_{c' \in C} P(e,k,c',l{=}1)} \approx \frac{P(e_t|c_t,l{=}1) * \frac{\prod_i P(f_c^i|l=1)}{Z_c} * P(c|k)}{\sum_{c' \in C} P(e_t|c'_t,l{=}1) * \frac{\prod_i P(f_{c'}^i|l=1)}{Z_{c'}} * P(c'|k)} \quad (7)$$

where

$$Z_x = \prod_i P(f_x^i|l{=}1)P(l{=}1) + \prod_i P(f_x^i|l{=}0)P(l{=}0) \quad (8)$$

As we can see from Equation (7), our model has four groups of parameters, namely $P(e_t|c_t,l{=}1)$, $P(f_c^i{=}1|l)$, $P(l)$ and $P(c|k)$. With these four groups of parameters, we can apply Equation (7) to efficiently compute $P(l{=}1|e,k,c)$.

Two points deserve mention before we describe our M-step. First, among the four groups of parameters, $P(e_t|c_t,l{=}1)$ and $P(f_c^i|l)$ are estimated in the M-step described below; $P(l)$ is estimated in parameter initialization and used throughout the EM iterations (details on parameter initialization appear after the M-step); and $P(c|k)$ is computed heuristically. Intuitively, $P(c|k)$ is the prior probability of a candidate antecedent $c$ given context $k$. The simplest way to model $P(c|k)$ is to assume that every candidate antecedent is equally likely given the context. In practice, however, some candidate antecedents are implausible given the context. To identify such candidate antecedents, we employ a simple heuristic, which considers a candidate antecedent implausible if its event subtype is different from that of $e$. Consequently, we model $P(c|k)$ as follows: if $c$ is implausible, we set $P(c|k)$ to 0 and distribute the probability mass uniformly over all and only the plausible candidate antecedents. Since this heuristic is not applicable to dummy candidates, we assume for simplicity that they are all plausible.

Second, by including $d$ as a dummy candidate antecedent for each $e$, we model anaphoricity determination and event coreference in a joint fashion. If the model resolves $e$ to $d$, it means that the model posits $e$ as non-anaphoric; on the other hand, if the model resolves $e$ to a non-dummy candidate antecedent $c$, it means that the model posits $e$ as anaphoric and $c$ as $e$'s correct antecedent. This joint modeling method has proven effective in earlier work on supervised entity coreference resolution (e.g., Rahman and Ng (2009; 2011)).

### 4.2.2 M-Step

Given $P(l{=}1|e,k,c)$, the goal of the M-step is to (re)estimate two of the four groups of parameters mentioned above, namely $P(e_t|c_t,l{=}1)$ and $P(f_c^i|l)$, using maximum likelihood estimation.

Specifically, $P(e_t|c_t, l{=}1)$ is estimated as follows:

$$P(e_t|c_t, l{=}1) = \frac{Count(e_t, c_t, l{=}1) + \theta}{Count(c_t, l{=}1) + \theta * |t|} \quad (9)$$

where $Count(c_t, l{=}1)$ is the expected number of times $c$ has trigger word $c_t$ when it is the antecedent of an event mention; and $|t|$ is the number of possible trigger words in the training data (we treat the "trigger word" of a dummy candidate antecedent as an unseen word). Also, $\theta$ is the Laplace smoothing parameter, which we set to 1, and $Count(e_t, c_t, l{=}1)$ is the expected number of times $e$ has $e_t$ as its trigger when its antecedent $c$ has trigger $c_t$. Given trigger words $e'_t$ and $c'_t$, we compute $Count(e'_t, c'_t, l{=}1)$ as follows:

$$Count(e'_t, c'_t, l{=}1) = \sum_{e,c:e_t=e'_t, c_t=c'_t} P(l{=}1|e, k, c) \quad (10)$$

The remaining group of parameters, $P(f^i_c|l)$, can be estimated in a similar fashion.

To start the induction process, we initialize all parameters with uniform values. Specifically, $P(e_t|c_t, l{=}1)$ is set to $\frac{1}{|t|}$, and $P(l{=}1|k_c)$ is set to 0.5. As noted before, $P(l)$ is also initialized here and used throughout the EM iterations. Recall that $P(l{=}1)$ is the fraction of event pairs that are coreferent. Since we assumed earlier that each event mention has exactly one (dummy or non-dummy) antecedent, $P(l{=}1)$ can be computed as the number of event mentions divided by the total number of event pairs. After initialization, we iteratively run the E-step and the M-step until convergence.

There is an important question we have not addressed: what features $f^i_c$ should we use to represent context $k_c$, which we need to estimate $P(f^i_c|l)$? We defer the discussion of this question to Section 5.

### 4.3 Inference

After training, we can apply the resulting model to resolve event mentions. Given an event mention $e$, we determine its antecedent as follows:

$$\hat{c} = \arg\max_{c \in C} P(l{=}1|e, k, c) \quad (11)$$

where $C$ is the set of candidate antecedents of $e$. In other words, we apply Equation (11) to each of $e$'s candidate antecedents, and select the one that yields the largest probability. If $c$ is a non-dummy candidate antecedent, we posit $c$ as the antecedent of $e$; otherwise, we posit $e$ as non-anaphoric.

## 5 Context Features

As mentioned at the end of Section 4.2.2, to fully specify our model, we need to describe the features $f^i_c$ used to represent $k_c$, which is needed to compute $P(f^i_c|l)$. Recall that $k_c$ encodes the context surrounding candidate antecedent $c$ and active event mention $e$. We represent $k_c$ using six features that encode the relationship between $c$ and $e$, some of which are motivated by previous work on supervised event coreference resolution (e.g., Chen and Ji (2009)). Below we describe these six features, which can be broadly divided into three categories.

### 5.1 Trigger-Based Features

We employ two trigger-based features (Features 1 and 2), both of which are binary-valued and are computed based on $e$'s and $c$'s triggers.

Feature 1 encodes whether $c_t$ and $e_t$, the trigger words of $c$ and $e$, satisfy any of the following three conditions:

1. $c_t$ and $e_t$ are lexically identical;
2. $c_t$ and $e_t$ contain the same basic verb (BV) and their verb structures are compatible;
3. the similarity between $c_t$ and $e_t$ is greater than a certain threshold (which we set to 0.8 in our experiments).

Intuitively, Feature 1 is a recall-enhancing feature: it encodes a condition whose satisfaction can help discover many event coreference links. However, it is not designed to be precision-oriented, as it is computed based solely on the triggers and not their surrounding contexts. Below we explain conditions 2 and 3 in more detail.

Recall that condition 2 encodes our observation that an event coreference relation may exist between two non-identical trigger words having the same BV if their verb structures are compatible. To understand this condition, let us explain the notion of BVs and how we determine the compatibility of two verb structures. A BV is a single-character Chinese verb, which is the building block of all Chinese verbs.

Specifically, Li et al. (2012) observe that, with a few exceptions, a Chinese verb constructed out of a basic verb $bv$ possesses one of six main *verb structures*: (1) $bv$ (e.g., 逮 (arrest)); (2) $bv$ + verb (e.g., 送到 (deliver), where $bv$ is 送); (3) verb + $bv$ (e.g., 离开 (leave), where $bv$ is 开); (4) $bv$ + complementation (e.g., 进了 (enter), where $bv$ is 进); (5) $bv$ + noun/adjective (e.g., 开枪 (shoot), where $bv$ is 开); (6) noun/adjective + $bv$ (e.g., 轻伤 (slight wound), where $bv$ is 伤). Now, assuming that $t_1$ and $t_2$ are two lexically different trigger words containing the same BV ($bv$), we say that their verb structures (denoted as $vs_1$ and $vs_2$) are incompatible if one of the following conditions is satisfied: (1) $bv$ appears in different positions in $t_1$ and $t_2$ (e.g., 开枪 (shoot) and 离开 (leave), where $bv$ is 开); (2) both $vs_1$ and $vs_2$ have $bv$ + verb or verb + $bv$ as their verb structure (e.g., 送到 (deliver) and 赶到 (reach), where $bv$ is 到); or (3) both $vs_1$ and $vs_2$ have noun/adjective + $bv$ or $bv$ + noun/adjective as their verb structure (e.g., 轻伤 (slight wound) and 重伤 (severe wound), where $bv$ is 伤). Note that these three incompatibility conditions encode our commonsense knowledge of when two Chinese verbs having the same BV cannot have the same meaning.

Next, we explain how we compute the similarity between two trigger words in condition 3. To capture their semantic similarity, we first apply word2vec (Mikolov et al., 2013) to the Chinese Gigaword corpus (Parker et al., 2009) to obtain a vector representation of each word and then compute the cosine similarity between the two word vectors.

Feature 2, our second trigger-based feature, encodes whether two nominal event mentions are incompatible w.r.t. number. Specifically, its value is True if and only if (1) $c$ and $e$ are both nouns, and (2) one is singular and the other is plural. Intuitively, this feature encodes a non-coreference condition.

### 5.2 Argument-Based Features

We employ three argument-based features (Features 3−5), all of which are binary-valued and are computed based on $c$'s and $e$'s arguments.

Feature 3 encodes whether $c$ and $e$ possess two arguments that have the same semantic role but different semantic classes.[1] Intuitively, Feature 3 encodes a non-coreference condition: $c$ and $e$ cannot be coreferent if such arguments exist.

Feature 4 can be viewed as a generalized version of Feature 3, encoding whether $c$ and $e$ possess two arguments that have the same semantic role but are not coreferent.

Feature 5 encodes whether $c$ and $e$ possess two named entity (NE) arguments that both have VALUE as their NE type but are lexically different. Such event mentions have a good chance of being not coreferent.

### 5.3 Distance Feature

We employ one distance feature (Feature 6) that encodes how far $c$ and $e$ are apart from each other in terms of the number of event mentions. To reduce data sparseness during parameter estimation, however, we quantize the distance as follows. Let $d$ be the distance between the first event mention and the last event mention in the document for which the distance feature will be computed. Note that the distance between an arbitrary pair of event mentions in this document will be between 0 and $d$. We divide the interval $[0,d]$ into four equal-sized regions, and set the value of the distance feature based on which of the four bins it falls into.

### 5.4 Features for Dummy Candidates

Now that we can compute the aforementioned six features for a non-dummy candidate antecedent, we next specify how we compute these features for a dummy candidate antecedent $d$ of active event mention $e$. For Feature 1, we set the feature value of $d$ to True, whereas for Features 2−5, we set the feature value of $d$ to False. To understand why these values are chosen, note that for each of these features the opposite value could be a strong indicator of non-coreference, potentially causing the model to have an overly strong bias against selecting $d$ as the antecedent of $e$.

Finally, to compute Feature 6, we assume that $d$ is the zero-th event mention of the associated document, and then compute the distance feature in the same way as described above. By letting $d$ be the zero-th event mention, we make the probability of picking $d$ as the correct antecedent (the probability of

[1] The possible semantic classes are the ACE 2005 entity types, i.e., PERSON, ORGANIZATION, GPE, FACILITY, and LOCATION.

classifying $e$ as non-anaphoric) depend on $e$'s position in the associated text. This makes sense because in general, the probability of $e$ being non-anaphoric tends to be larger (smaller) when it appears earlier (later) in the document.

## 6 Evaluation

### 6.1 Experimental Setup

**Dataset.** For evaluation, we conduct five-fold cross-validation experiments on the 633 Chinese documents of the ACE 2005 training corpus. Statistics on the corpus are shown in Table 1.

**Evaluation measures.** We report results in terms of recall (R), precision (P), and F-score (F) using the commonly-used coreference evaluation measures given by the CoNLL scorer, namely the link-based MUC scorer (Vilain et al., 1995), the mention-based $B^3$ scorer (Bagga and Baldwin, 1998), the entity-based version of the CEAF scorer (Luo, 2005), and the Rand index-based BLANC scorer (Recasens and Hovy, 2011), after singleton event mentions are removed from the coreference partitions produced by our resolver. We use the latest version (version 8) of the CoNLL scorer[2], which fixes a bug in previous versions (Pradhan et al., 2014). In addition, we report the CoNLL score (Pradhan et al., 2011), which is the unweighted average of the MUC, $B^3$, and CEAF F-scores.

**Evaluation setting.** We perform an end-to-end evaluation, as it can more accurately reflect the performance of an event coreference resolver when it is used in practice.

More specifically, to extract the event mentions used in our evaluation, we employ SinoCoreferencer[3], which, as mentioned before, is an end-to-end ACE-style Chinese IE system that achieves state-of-the-art event coreference results. Specifically, the event triggers needed to compute the trigger-based context features are extracted using SinoCoreferencer's event extraction subsystem. The event subtypes needed to identify and filter out implausible candidate antecedents are also provided by its event extraction subsystem. The event arguments needed to compute the argument-based context features are first extracted and typed by its entity extraction subsystem, and then linked to their triggers by its event extraction subsystem. Finally, the entity coreference links and the semantic roles needed to compute Feature 4 are provided by its entity coreference subsystem and its event extraction subsystem, respectively.[4] Details of each of these subsystems can be found in Chen and Ng (2014).

| | |
|---|---|
| Documents | 633 |
| Sentences | 9,967 |
| Event mentions | 3,333 |
| Event coreference chains | 2,521 |

Table 1: Statistics on the ACE 2005 Chinese corpus.

### 6.2 Results

We employ two supervised resolvers as baseline systems. The first baseline employs rote learning, simply positing two event mentions as coreferent if their corresponding triggers are annotated as coreferent in the training data. The second baseline is SinoCoreferencer, which has produced the best Chinese event coreference results to date on the ACE corpus.

Row 1 of Table 2 shows the results of the baseline that employs rote learning. As we can see, this baseline achieves a CoNLL score of 37.9. Row 2 shows the results of SinoCoreferencer. It performs significantly better than the rote-learning baseline w.r.t. all five scoring measures[5], achieving a CoNLL score of 39.2. Finally, row 3 shows the results of our model. Despite being unsupervised, it significantly outperforms the better baseline, SinoCoreferencer, w.r.t. all five scoring measures, achieving a CoNLL score of 41.5, which is 2.3 points higher than that of SinoCoreferencer. These results suggest that a generative approach to unsupervised event coreference holds promise.

### 6.3 Ablation Experiments

Recall that in our model eight probability terms play a major role: $P(e_t|c_t)$, $P(c|k)$, and $P(f_c^i|l)$ for each

[2] conll.github.io/reference-coreference-scorers/

[3] Downloadable from http://www.hlt.utdallas.edu/~yzcchen/coreference/

[4] We employ only those semantic roles that can be reliably determined by SinoCoreferencer's event extraction subsystem, namely, AGENT, ADJUDICATOR, DEFENDANT, GIVER, PERSON, PLACE, POSITION, ORGANIZATION, ORIGIN, and RECIPIENT.

[5] All significance tests are paired $t$-tests, with $p < 0.05$.

| System | MUC | | | B$^3$ | | | CEAF$_e$ | | | BLANC | | | CoNLL |
|---|---|---|---|---|---|---|---|---|---|---|---|---|---|
| | R | P | F | R | P | F | R | P | F | R | P | F | F |
| Rote learning | 42.6 | 36.4 | 39.3 | 41.4 | 32.3 | 36.3 | 37.0 | 39.7 | 38.3 | 27.4 | 20.0 | 23.1 | 37.9 |
| SinoCoreferencer | 42.7 | 38.3 | 40.4 | 41.5 | 34.7 | 37.8 | 39.9 | 39.2 | 39.5 | 28.1 | 23.7 | 25.7 | 39.2 |
| Our model | 43.1 | 42.4 | 42.8 | 41.4 | 39.1 | 40.2 | 40.7 | 42.6 | 41.6 | 27.5 | 26.4 | 26.9 | 41.5 |

Table 2: Five-fold cross-validation event coreference results on the ACE 2005 corpus.

of the six context features. To investigate the contribution of each probability term to overall performance, we conduct ablation experiments. Specifically, in each ablation experiment, we remove exactly one term from the model and retrain it.

Ablation results are shown in Table 3. Each row contains the F-scores obtained via the five evaluation measures. To facilitate comparison, the scores of the model in which all eight probability terms are used is shown in row 1. As we can see, Feature 1 is the most useful feature: its removal causes the CoNLL score to drop significantly by 5.3 points. A closer examination reveals that the drop in the CoNLL score is caused by a significant drop in recall w.r.t. all scorers. Recall that this feature encodes the conditions under which two triggers are likely to be coreferent. It is perhaps not surprising that its removal causes a significant drop in recall.

The second most useful feature is $P(c|k)$, which places zero probability mass on candidate antecedents whose event subtypes are different from that of the active event mention. Its removal causes the CoNLL score to drop significantly by 1.6 points. The removal of each other feature resulted in a small, insignificant drop in the CoNLL score.

| System | MUC | B$^3$ | CEAF$_e$ | BLANC | CoNLL |
|---|---|---|---|---|---|
| Full model | 42.8 | 40.2 | 41.6 | 26.9 | 41.5 |
| $-$ $P(e_t\|c_t)$ | 42.9 | 39.8 | 40.9 | 26.9 | 41.2 |
| $-$ $P(c\|k)$ | 41.2 | 38.6 | 39.8 | 24.9 | 39.9 |
| $-$ Feature 1 | 37.5 | 32.9 | 38.2 | 20.8 | 36.2 |
| $-$ Feature 2 | 42.5 | 39.9 | 41.4 | 26.6 | 41.3 |
| $-$ Feature 3 | 42.4 | 40.0 | 41.3 | 26.9 | 41.2 |
| $-$ Feature 4 | 42.5 | 40.1 | 41.7 | 27.0 | 41.4 |
| $-$ Feature 5 | 42.4 | 40.0 | 41.4 | 26.5 | 41.3 |
| $-$ Feature 6 | 42.3 | 39.6 | 40.9 | 26.8 | 40.9 |

Table 3: Ablation results in terms of F-scores.

## 6.4 Error Analysis

It is somewhat surprising that our unsupervised event coreference model outperforms the better supervised baseline, SinoCoreferencer. To understand why, we analyze the errors made by the two resolvers.

Our analysis proceeds as follows. First, to gain insights into the differences between the two resolvers, we examine those candidate event mentions that are correctly handled by one model but not the other (Section 6.4.1). Specifically, we consider a candidate event mention $e$ correctly handled if (1) $e$ is a correctly resolved anaphoric event mention; (2) $e$ is an unresolved singleton event mention; or (3) $e$ is an unresolved non-event mention (i.e., not a true event mention). Second, to understand how to improve event coreference, we identify the major sources of error made by both resolvers (Section 6.4.2).

### 6.4.1 Common Sources of Disagreement

There are 323 candidate event mentions that are correctly handled by one model but not the other in our dataset. Among these 323 cases, 205 (50 anaphoric + 79 singletons + 76 non-event) are correctly handled by the unsupervised model, and 118 (42 anaphoric + 52 singletons + 24 non-event) are correctly handled by SinoCoreferencer.

From these numbers, we can see that the unsupervised model performs far better than SinoCoreferencer in *not* resolving the singletons and the non-event mentions. This is perhaps not surprising given the unsupervised model's relatively stricter conditions on resolving a candidate event mention. Specifically, it is unlikely to posit two candidate event mentions as coreferent unless (1) their triggers have a BV match or a large word2vec similarity value and (2) none of the non-coreference conditions are satisfied. Overall, these results explain why the unsupervised model has a much higher precision than SinoCoreferencer.

Not only does the unsupervised model perform much better in not resolving singletons and non-event mentions, but it is also slightly more accurate in resolving the anaphoric event mentions, which ultimately enables it to achieve a higher recall than SinoCoreferencer. In particular, it correctly resolves 50 anaphoric mentions that are incorrectly handled by SinoCoreferencer. The successful resolution of these anaphoric mentions can be attributed largely to its use of BV and word2vec, neither of which is exploited by SinoCoreferencer. However, while a BV match or a high word2vec similarity value is a good indicator of event coreference, they are by no means perfect. This partly explains why there are singletons and non-event mentions that are correctly handled by SinoCoreferencer but not the unsupervised model.

Despite the fact that SinoCoreferencer slightly lags behind the unsupervised model in resolving anaphoric mentions, it correctly resolves 42 anaphoric event mentions that are incorrectly handled by the unsupervised model. These are cases that cannot be handled simply by relying on BV match or word2vec similarity. More specifically, two of the unique features of SinoCoreferencer are primarily responsible for its successful resolution of these event mentions. First, it learns coreferent trigger pairs from the training data. These pairs proved to be useful for event coreference, as we saw from the competitive results provided by the rote-learning baseline. Second, unlike the unsupervised model, SinoCoreferencer can posit two event mentions as coreferent *without* considering their triggers. More specifically, SinoCoreferencer may posit two event mentions as coreferent if the corresponding arguments of the two event mentions (i.e., arguments having the same role) are coreferent. Neither of these two recall-enhancing features of SinoCoreferencer is a precise indicator of event coreference. In other words, employing them widens the precision gap between the two resolvers.

#### 6.4.2 Common Sources of Error

Next, we discuss the major sources of error made by both our unsupervised model and SinoCoreferencer. Broadly, the errors can be divided into two categories, precision errors and recall errors.

Precision errors arise primarily from erroneous coreference links established between (1) one or more candidate event mentions that are not true event mentions; (2) two event mentions with incompatible latent attributes such as MODALITY, POLARITY, GENERICITY, and TENSE, since these attributes are not exploited by the two resolvers; (3) two event mentions with incompatible arguments, since these arguments fail to be extracted by the argument identification component; (4) two mentions representing events that occur at different times, since the event mentions are not timestamped[6]; and (5) two event mentions whose corresponding arguments are incorrectly posited by the entity coreference subsystem as coreferent.

On the other hand, recall errors arise primarily from missing coreference links attributed to (1) the trigger identification component's failure to detect one or both of the triggers involved in an event coreference link; (2) the entity coreference subsystem's failure to establish the link(s) between the corresponding arguments of two coreferent event mentions; (3) the lack of positive evidence of event coreference, such as BV match, high word2vec similarity, and coreferent arguments; and (4) the argument identification component's failure to extract one or more arguments of an event mention.

## 7 Conclusions

We presented a generative model for the relatively under-studied task of unsupervised Chinese event coreference resolution whose parameters were learned using EM from an unannotated corpus. When evaluated on the ACE 2005 corpus, our model significantly outperforms SinoCoreferencer, a state-of-the-art Chinese event coreference resolver.

Since the performance of our resolver is limited in part by the errors made by SinoCoreferencer's subsystems, we plan to mitigate this problem by performing joint inference for entity coreference, event extraction and event coreference in future work.

## Acknowledgments

We thank the three anonymous reviewers for their detailed and insightful comments on an earlier draft of this paper. This work was supported in part by NSF Grants IIS-1147644 and IIS-1219142.

[6]Not all of these errors can be fixed by exploiting the TENSE attribute, as TENSE is only a crude approximation of time. For instance, in the phrases 首度被捕 (arrested for the first time) and 再度被捕 (arrested again), the two occurrences of 被捕 (arrested) are associated with different timestamps despite the fact that they have the same TENSE.

## References


David Ahn. 2006. The stages of event extraction. In *Proceedings of the Workshop on Annotating and Reasoning about Time and Events*, pages 1--8.

Jun Araki, Zhengzhong Liu, Eduard Hovy, and Teruko Mitamura. 2014. Detecting subevent structure for event coreference resolution. In *Proceedings of the Ninth International Conference on Language Resources and Evaluation*, pages 4553--4558.

Amit Bagga and Breck Baldwin. 1998. Algorithms for scoring coreference chains. In *Proceedings of the Linguistic Coreference Workshop at the First International Conference on Language Resources and Evaluation*, page 563--566.

Amit Bagga and Breck Baldwin. 1999. Cross-document event coreference: Annotation, experiments, and observations. In *Proceedings of the ACL Workshop on Coreference and Its Applications*, pages 1--9.

Collin F. Baker, Charles J. Fillmore, and John B. Lowe. 1998. The Berkeley FrameNet project. In *Proceedings of the 36th Annual Meeting of the Association for Computational Linguistics and the 17th International Conference on Computational Linguistics, Volume 1*, pages 86--90.

Cosmin Bejan and Sanda Harabagiu. 2010. Unsupervised event coreference resolution with rich linguistic features. In *Proceedings of the 48th Annual Meeting of the Association for Computational Linguistics*, pages 1412--1422.

Cosmin Bejan and Sanda Harabagiu. 2014. Unsupervised event coreference resolution. *Computational Linguistics*, 40(2):311--347.

Shane Bergsma and David Yarowsky. 2011. NADA: A robust system for non-referential pronoun detection. In *Proceedings of the 8th Discourse Anaphora and Anaphor Resolution Colloquium*, pages 12--23.

Zheng Chen and Heng Ji. 2009. Graph-based event coreference resolution. In *Proceedings of the 2009 Workshop on Graph-based Methods for Natural Language Processing (TextGraphs-4)*, pages 54--57.

Chen Chen and Vincent Ng. 2014. SinoCoreferencer: An end-to-end Chinese event coreference resolver. In *Proceedings of the Ninth International Conference on Language Resources and Evaluation*, pages 4532--4538.

Bin Chen, Jian Su, Sinno Jialin Pan, and Chew Lim Tan. 2011. A unified event coreference resolution by integrating multiple resolvers. In *Proceedings of the 5th International Joint Conference on Natura Language Processing*, pages 102--110.

Agata Cybulska and Piek Vossen. 2012. Using semantic relations to solve event coreference in text. In *Proceedings of the LREC Workshop on Semantic Relations-II Enhancing Resources and Applications (SemRel 2012)*, pages 60--67.

Arthur P. Dempster, Nan M. Laird, and Donald B. Rubin. 1977. Maximum likelihood from incomplete data via the EM algorithm. *Journal of the Royal Statistical Society. Series B (Methodological)*, 39:1--38.

Aymen Elkhlifi and Rim Faiz. 2009. Automatic annotation approach of events in news articles. *International Journal of Computing and Information Sciences*, 7(1):40--50.

Christiane Fellbaum. 1998. *WordNet: An Electronic Lexical Database*. MIT Press, Cambridge, MA.

Kartik Goyal, Sujay Kumar Jauhar, Huiying Li, Mrinmaya Sachan, Shashank Srivastava, and Eduard Hovy. 2013. A structured distributional semantic model for event co-reference. In *Proceedings of the 51st Annual Meeting of the Association for Computational Linguistics: Volume 2 (Short Papers)*, pages 467--473.

Eduard Hovy, Teruko Mitamura, Felisa Verdejo, Jun Araki, and Andrew Philpot. 2013. Events are not simple: Identity, non-identity, and quasi-identity. In *Proceedings of the NAACL-HLT Workshop on Events: Definition, Detection, Coreference, and Representation*, pages 21--28.

Kevin Humphreys, Robert Gaizauskas, and Saliha Azzam. 1997. Event coreference for information extraction. In *Proceedings of the ACL/EACL Workshop on Operational Factors in Practical, Robust Anaphora Resolution for Unrestricted Texts*, pages 75--81.

Heeyoung Lee, Marta Recasens, Angel Chang, Mihai Surdeanu, and Dan Jurafsky. 2012. Joint entity and event coreference resolution across documents. In *Proceedings of the 2012 Joint Conference on Empirical Methods in Natural Language Processing and Computational Natural Language Learning*, pages 489--500.

Peifeng Li, Guodong Zhou, Qiaoming Zhu, and Libin Hou. 2012. Employing compositional semantics and discourse consistency in Chinese event extraction. In *Proceedings of the 2012 Joint Conference on Empirical Methods in Natural Language Processing and Computational Natural Language Learning*, pages 1006--1016.

Zhengzhong Liu, Jun Araki, Eduard Hovy, and Teruko Mitamura. 2014. Supervised within-document event coreference using information propagation. In *Proceedings of the Ninth International Conference on Language Resources and Evaluation*, pages 4539--4544.

Xiaoqiang Luo. 2005. On coreference resolution performance metrics. In *Proceedings of Human Language Technology Conference and Conference on Empirical Methods in Natural Language Processing*, pages 25--32.

Katie McConky, Rakesh Nagi, Moises Sudit, and William Hughes. 2012. Improving event co-reference by context extraction and dynamic feature weighting. In *Proceedings of the 2012 IEEE International Multi-Disciplinary Conference on Cognitive Methods in Situation Awareness and Decision Support*, pages 38--43.

Tomas Mikolov, Ilya Sutskever, Kai Chen, Greg S Corrado, and Jeff Dean. 2013. Distributed representations of words and phrases and their compositionality. In *Proceedings of the Advances in Neural Information Processing Systems*, pages 3111--3119.

Martina Naughton. 2009. *Sentence Level Event Detection and Coreference Resolution.* Ph.D. thesis, National University of Ireland, Dublin, Ireland.

Robert Parker, David Graff, Ke Chen, Junbo Kong, and Kazuaki Maeda. 2009. Chinese Gigaword fourth edition. Linguistic Data Consortium, Philadelphia, PA.

Sameer Pradhan, Lance Ramshaw, Ralph Weischedel, Jessica MacBride, and Linnea Micciulla. 2007. Unrestricted coreference: Identifying entities and events in OntoNotes. In *Proceedings of the International Conference on Semantic Computing*, pages 446--453.

Sameer Pradhan, Lance Ramshaw, Mitchell Marcus, Martha Palmer, Ralph Weischedel, and Nianwen Xue. 2011. CoNLL-2011 Shared Task: Modeling unrestricted coreference in OntoNotes. In *Proceedings of the Fifteenth Conference on Computational Natural Language Learning: Shared Task*, pages 1--27.

Sameer Pradhan, Xiaoqiang Luo, Marta Recasens, Eduard Hovy, Vincent Ng, and Michael Strube. 2014. Scoring coreference partitions of predicted mentions: A reference implementation. In *Proceedings of the 52nd Annual Meeting of the Association for Computational Linguistics (Volume 2: Short Papers)*, pages 30--35.

Altaf Rahman and Vincent Ng. 2009. Supervised models for coreference resolution. In *Proceedings of the 2009 Conference on Empirical Methods in Natural Language Processing*, pages 968--977.

Altaf Rahman and Vincent Ng. 2011. Narrowing the modeling gap: A cluster-ranking approach to coreference resolution. *Journal of Artificial Intelligence Research*, 40:469--521.

Marta Recasens and Eduard Hovy. 2011. BLANC: Implementing the Rand Index for coreference evaluation. *Natural Language Engineering*, 17(4):485--510.

S. Sangeetha and Michael Arock. 2012. Event coreference resolution using mincut based graph clustering. In *Proceedings of the Fourth International Workshop on Computer Networks & Communications*, pages 253--260.

Marc Vilain, John Burger, John Aberdeen, Dennis Connolly, and Lynette Hirschman. 1995. A model-theoretic coreference scoring scheme. In *Proceedings of the Sixth Message Understanding Conference*, pages 45--52.

# Removing the Training Wheels: A Coreference Dataset that Entertains Humans and Challenges Computers

**Anupam Guha,**[1] **Mohit Iyyer,**[1] **Danny Bouman,**[1] **Jordan Boyd-Graber**[2]
[1]University of Maryland, Department of Computer Science and UMIACS
[2]University of Colorado, Department of Computer Science
aguha@cs.umd.edu, miyyer@umiacs.umd.edu, dannybb@gmail.com,
Jordan.Boyd.Graber@colorado.edu

## Abstract

Coreference is a core NLP problem. However, newswire data, the primary source of existing coreference data, lack the richness necessary to truly solve coreference. We present a new domain with denser references—quiz bowl questions—that is challenging and enjoyable to humans, and we use the quiz bowl community to develop a new coreference dataset, together with an annotation framework that can tag any text data with coreferences and named entities. We also successfully integrate active learning into this annotation pipeline to collect documents maximally useful to coreference models. State-of-the-art coreference systems underperform a simple classifier on our new dataset, motivating non-newswire data for future coreference research.

## 1 Introduction

Coreference resolution—adding annotations to an input text where multiple strings refer to the same entity—is a fundamental problem in computational linguistics. It is challenging because it requires the application of syntactic, semantic, and world knowledge (Ng, 2010).

For example, in the sentence *Monsieur Poirot assured Hastings that he ought to have faith in him*, the strings *Monsieur Poirot* and *him* refer to the same person, while *Hastings* and *he* refer to a different character.

There are a panoply of sophisticated coreference systems, both data-driven (Fernandes et al., 2012; Durrett and Klein, 2013; Durrett and Klein, 2014; Björkelund and Kuhn, 2014) and rule-based (Pradhan et al., 2011; Lee et al., 2011). Recent CoNLL shared tasks provide the opportunity to make a fair comparison between these systems. However, because all of these shared tasks contain strictly newswire data,[1] it is unclear how existing systems perform on more diverse data.

We argue in Section 2 that to truly solve coreference resolution, the research community needs high-quality datasets that contain many challenging cases such as nested coreferences and coreferences that can only be resolved using external knowledge. In contrast, newswire is deliberately written to contain few coreferences, and those coreferences should be easy for the reader to resolve. Thus, systems that are trained on such data commonly fail to detect coreferences in more expressive, non-newswire text.

Given newswire's imperfect range of coreference examples, can we do better? In Section 3 we present a specialized dataset that specifically tests a *human's* coreference resolution ability. This dataset comes from a community of trivia fans who also serve as enthusiastic annotators (Section 4). These data have denser coreference mentions than newswire text and present hitherto unexplored questions of what is coreferent and what is not. We also incorporate active learning into the annotation process. The result is a small but highly dense dataset of 400 documents with 9,471 mentions.

[1]We use "newswire" as an umbrella term that encompasses all forms of edited news-related data, including news articles, blogs, newsgroups, and transcripts of broadcast news.



*Human Language Technologies: The 2015 Annual Conference of the North American Chapter of the ACL*, pages 1108–1118,
Denver, Colorado, May 31 – June 5, 2015. 

We demonstrate in Section 5 that our dataset is significantly different from newswire based on results from the effective, widely-used Berkeley system (Durrett and Klein, 2013). These results motivate us to develop a very simple end-to-end coreference resolution system consisting of a CRF-based mention detector and a pairwise classifier. Our system outperforms the Berkeley system when both have been trained on our new dataset. This result motivates further exploration into complex coreference types absent in newswire data, which we discuss at length in Section 7.

## 2 Newswire's Limitations for Coreference

Newswire text is widely used as training data for coreference resolution systems. The standard datasets used in the MUC (MUC-6, 1995; MUC-7, 1997), ACE (Doddington et al., 2004), and CoNLL shared tasks (Pradhan et al., 2011) contain only such text. In this section we argue why this monoculture, despite its many past successes, offer diminishing results for advancing the coreference subfield.

First, newswire text has sparse references, and those that it has are mainly identity coreferences and appositives. In the CoNLL 2011 shared task (Pradhan et al., 2007) based on OntoNotes 4.0 (Hovy et al., 2006),[2] there are 2.1 mentions per sentence; in the next section we present a dataset with 3.7 mentions per sentence.[3] In newswire text, most nominal entities (not including pronouns) are singletons; in other words, they do not corefer to anything. OntoNotes 4.0 development data contains 25.4K singleton nominal entities (Durrett and Klein, 2013), compared to only 7.6K entities which corefer to something (anaphora). On the other hand, most pronominals are anaphoric, which makes them easy to resolve as pronouns are single token entities. While it is easy to obtain a lot of newswire data, the amount of coreferent-heavy mention clusters in such text is not correspondingly high.

Second, coreference resolution in news text is trivial for humans because it rarely requires world knowledge or semantic understanding. Systems trained on news media data for a related problem—entity extraction—falter on non-journalistic texts (Poibeau and Kosseim, 2001). This discrepancy in performance can be attributed to the stylistic conventions of journalism. Journalists are instructed to limit the number of entities mentioned in a sentence, and there are strict rules for referring to individuals (Boyd et al., 2008). Furthermore, writers cannot assume that their readers are familiar with all participants in the story, which requires that each entity is explicitly introduced in the text (Goldstein and Press, 2004). These constraints make for easy reading and, as a side effect, easy coreference resolution. Unlike this simplified "journalistic" coreference, everyday coreference relies heavily on inferring the identities of people and entities in language, which requires substantial world knowledge.

While news media contains examples of coreference, the primary goal of a journalist is to convey information, not to challenge the reader's coreference resolution faculty. Our goal is to evaluate coreference systems on data that taxes even human coreference.

## 3 Quiz Bowl: A Game of Human Coreference

One example of such data comes from a game called *quiz bowl*. Quiz bowl is a trivia game where questions are structured as a series of sentences, all of which indirectly refer to the answer. Each question has multiple clusters of mutually-coreferent terms, and one of those clusters is coreferent with the answer. Figure 1 shows an example of a quiz bowl question where all answer coreferences have been marked.

A player's job is to determine[4] the entity ref-

[2]As our representative for "newswire" data, the English portion of the Ontonotes 4.0 contains professionally-delivered weblogs and newsgroups (15%), newswire (46%), broadcast news (15%), and broadcast conversation (15%).

[3]Neither of these figures include singleton mentions, as OntoNotes does not have gold tagged singletons. Our dataset has an even higher density when singletons are included.

[4]In actual competition, it is a race to see which team can identify the coreference faster, but we ignore that aspect here.

| | |
|---|---|
| **NW** | Later, [they]$_1$ all met with [President Jacques Chirac]$_2$. [Mr. Chirac]$_2$ said an important first step had been taken to calm tensions. |
| **NW** | Around the time of the [Macau]$_1$ handover, questions that were hot in [the Western media]$_2$ were "what is Macaense"? And what is native [Macau]$_1$ culture? |
| **NW** | [MCA]$_1$ said that [it]$_1$ expects [the proposed transaction]$_2$ to be completed no later than November 10th. |
| **QB** | As a child, [this character]$_1$ reads [[his]$_1$ uncle]$_2$ [the column]$_3$ [*That Body of Yours*]$_3$ every Sunday. |
| **QB** | At one point, [these characters]$_1$ climb into barrels aboard a ship bound for England. Later, [one of [these characters]$_1$]$_2$ stabs [the Player]$_3$ with a fake knife. |
| **QB** | [One poet from [this country]$_2$]$_1$ invented the haiku, while [another]$_3$ wrote the [*Tale of Genji*]$_4$. Identify [this homeland]$_2$ of [Basho]$_1$ and [Lady Murasaki]$_3$. |

Table 1: Three newswire sentences and three quiz bowl sentences with annotated coreferences and singleton mentions. These examples show that quiz bowl sentences contain more complicated types of coreferences that may even require world knowledge to resolve.

[The Canadian rock band by [this name]] has released such albums as Take A Deep Breath, Young Wild and Free, and Love Machine and had a 1986 Top Ten single with Can't Wait For the Night. [The song by [this name]] is [the first track on Queen's Sheer Heart Attack]. [The novel by [this name]] concerns Fred Hale, who returns to town to hand out cards for a newspaper competition and is murdered by the teenage gang member Pinkie Brown, who abuses [the title substance]. [The novel] was adapted into [a 1947 film starring Richard Attenborough]; [this] was released in the US as Young Scarface. FTP, identify [the shared name of, most notably, [a novel by Graham Greene]].

Figure 1: An example quiz bowl question about the novel *Brighton Rock*. Every mention referring to the answer of the question has been marked; note the variety of mentions that refer to the same entity.

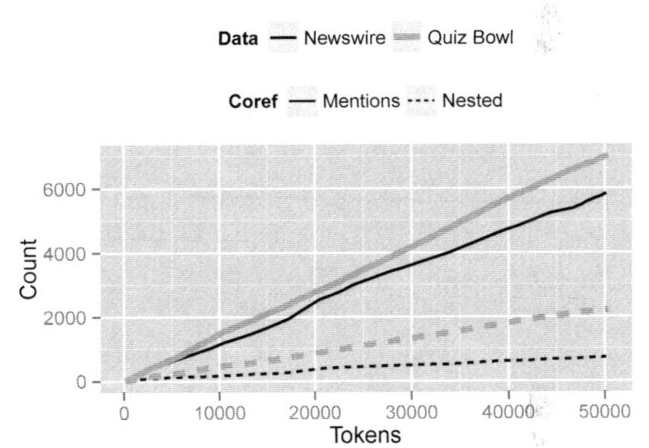


Figure 2: Density of quiz bowl vs. CoNLL coreference both for raw and nested mentions.

erenced by the question. Each sentence contains progressively more informative references and more well-known clues. For example, a question on Sherlock Holmes might refer to him as "he", "this character", "this housemate of Dr. Watson", and finally "this detective and resident of 221B Baker Street". While quiz bowl has been viewed as a classification task (Iyyer et al., 2014), previous work has ignored the fundamental task of coreference. Nevertheless, quiz bowl data are dense and diverse in coreference examples. For example, nested mentions, which are difficult for both humans and machines, are very rare in the newswire text of OntoNotes—0.25 mentions per sentence—while quiz bowl contains 1.16 mentions per sentence (Figure 2). Examples of nested mentions can be seen in in Table 1. Since quiz bowl is a game, it makes the task of solving coreference interesting and *challenging* for an annotator. In the next section, we use the intrinsic fun of this task to create a new annotated coreference dataset.

## 4 Intelligent Annotation

Here we describe our annotation process. Each document is a single quiz bowl question containing an average of 5.2 sentences. While quiz bowl covers all areas of academic knowledge, we focus on questions about literature from Boyd-Graber et al. (2012), as annotation standards are more straightforward.

Our webapp (Figure 3) allows users to annotate a question by highlighting a phrase using their mouse and then pressing a number corresponding to the coreference group to which it belongs. Each group is highlighted with a single color in the interface. The webapp displays a single question at a time, and for some questions, users can compare their answers against gold annotations by the authors. We provide annotators the ability to see if their tags match the gold labels for a few documents as we need to provide a mechanism to help them learn the annotation guidelines as the annotators are crowdsourced volunteers. This improves inter-annotator agreement.

The webapp was advertised to quiz bowl players before a national tournament and attracted passionate, competent annotators preparing for the tournament. A leaderboard was implemented to encourage competitiveness, and prizes were given to the top five annotators.

Users are instructed to annotate all authors, characters, works, and the answer to the question (even if the answer is not one of the previously specified types of entities). We consider a coreference to be the maximal span that can be replaced by a pronoun.[5] As an example, in the phrase *this folk sermon by James Weldon Johnson*, the entire phrase is marked, not just *sermon* or *this folk sermon*. Users are asked to consider appositives as separate coreferences to the same entity. Thus, *The Japanese poet Basho* has two phrases to be marked, *The Japanese poet* and *Basho*, which both refer to the same group.[6] Users annotated prepositional phrases attached to a noun to capture entire noun phrases.

Titular mentions are mentions that refer to entities with similar names or the same name as a title, e.g., "The titular doctor" refers to the person "Dr. Zhivago" while talking about the book with the same name. For our purposes, all titular mentions refer to the same coreference group. We also encountered a few mentions that refer to multiple groups; for example, in the sentence *Romeo met Juliet at a fancy ball, and they get married the next day*, the word *they* refers to both *Romeo* and *Juliet*. Currently, our webapp cannot handle such mentions.

To illustrate how popular the webapp proved to be among the quiz bowl community, we had 615 documents tagged by seventy-six users within a month. The top five annotators, who between them tagged 342 documents out of 651, have an agreement rate of 87% with a set of twenty author-annotated questions used to measure tagging accuracy.

We only consider documents that have either been tagged by four or more users with a predetermined degree of similarity and verified by one or more author (150 documents), or documents tagged by the authors in committee (250 documents). Thus, our gold dataset has 400 documents.

Both our quiz bowl dataset and the OntoNotes dataset are summarized in Table 2. If coreference resolution is done by pairwise classification, our dataset has a total of 116,125 possible mention pairs. On average it takes about fifteen minutes to tag a document because often the annotator will not know which mentions co-refer

| Number of ... | Quiz bowl | OntoNotes |
|---|---|---|
| **documents**[7] | 400 | 1,667 |
| **sentences** | 1,890 | 44,687 |
| **tokens** | 50,347 | 955,317 |
| **mentions** | 9,471 | 94,155 |
| **singletons**[8] | 2,461 | 0 |
| **anaphora** | 7,010 | 94,155 |
| **nested ment.** | 2,194 | 11,454 |

Table 2: Statistics of both our quiz bowl dataset and the OntoNotes training data from the CoNLL 2011 shared task.

[5] We phrased the instruction in this way to allow our educated but linguistically unsavvy annotators to approximate a noun phrase.

[6] The datasets, full annotation guide, and code can be found at `http://www.cs.umd.edu/~aguha/qbcoreference`.

[7] This number is for the OntoNotes training split only.

[8] OntoNotes is not annotated for singletons.

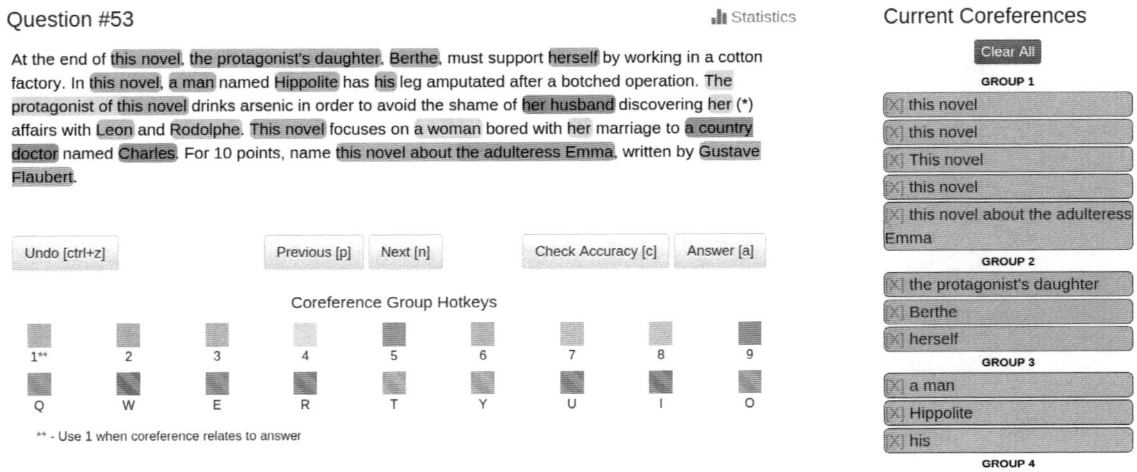


Figure 3: The webapp to collect annotations. The user highlights a phrase and then assigns it to a group (by number). Showing a summary list of coreferences on the right significantly speeds up user annotations.

to what group without using external knowledge. OntoNotes is 18.97 larger than our dataset in terms of tokens but only 13.4 times larger in terms of mentions.[9] Next, we describe a technique that allows our webapp to choose which documents to display for annotation.

### 4.1 Active Learning

*Active learning* is a technique that alternates between training and annotation by selecting instances or documents that are maximally useful for a classifier (Settles, 2010). Because of the large sample space and amount of diversity present in the data, active learning helps us build our coreference dataset. To be more concrete, the original corpus contains over 7,000 literature questions, and we want to tag only the useful ones. Since it can take a quarter hour to tag a single document and we want at least four annotators to agree on every document that we include in the final dataset, annotating all 7,000 questions is infeasible.

We follow Miller et al. (2012), who use active learning for document-level coreference rather than at the mention level. Starting from a seed set of a hundred documents and an evaluation set of fifty documents[10] we sample 250 more documents from our set of 7,000 quiz bowl questions. We use the Berkeley coreference system (described in the next section) for the training phase. In Figure 4 we show the effectiveness of our iteration procedure. Unlike the result shown by Miller et al. (2012), we find that for our dataset voting sampling beats random sampling, which supports the findings of Laws et al. (2012).

Voting sampling works by dividing the seed set into multiple parts and using each to train a model. Then, from the rest of the dataset we select the document that has the most variance in results after predicting using all of the models. Once that document gets tagged, we add it to the seed set, retrain, and repeat the procedure. This process is impractical with instance-level active learning methods, as there are 116,125 mention pairs (instances) for just 400 documents. Even with document-level sampling, the procedure of training on all documents in the seed set and then testing every document in the sample space is a slow task. Batch learning can speed up this process at the cost of increased document redundancy; we choose not to use it because we want a diverse collection of annotated documents. Active learning's advantage is that new documents are more likely to contain diverse

[9]These numbers do not include singletons as OntoNotes does not have them tagged, while ours does.

[10]These were documents tagged by the quiz bowl community, so we didn't have to make them wait for the active learning process to retrain candidate models.

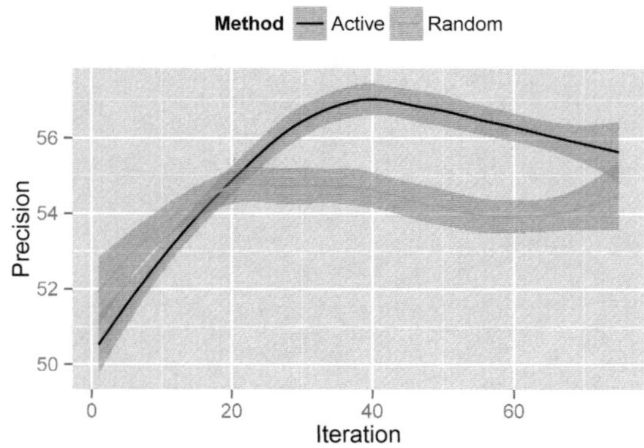


Figure 4: Voting sampling active learning works better than randomly sampling for annotation.

(and thus interesting) combinations of entities and references, which annotators noticed during the annotation process. Documents selected by the active learning process were dissimilar to previously-selected questions in both content and structure.

## 5 Experimental Comparison of Coreference Systems

We evaluate the widely used Berkeley coreference system (Durrett and Klein, 2013) on our dataset to show that models trained on newswire data cannot effectively resolve coreference in quiz bowl data. Training and evaluating the Berkeley system on quiz bowl data also results in poor performance. [11] This result motivates us to build an end-to-end coreference resolution system that includes a data-driven mention detector (as opposed to Berkeley's rule-based one) and a simple pairwise classifier. Using our mentions and only six feature types, we are able to outperform the Berkeley system on our data. Finally, we explore the linguistic phenomena that make quiz bowl coreference so hard and draw insights from our analysis that may help to guide the next generation of coreference systems.

[11] We use default options, including hyperparameters tuned on OntoNotes

### 5.1 Evaluating the Berkeley System on Quiz Bowl Data

We use two publicly-available pretrained models supplied with the Berkeley coreference system, *Surface* and *Final*, which are trained on the entire OntoNotes dataset. The difference between the two models is that *Final* includes semantic features. We report results with both models to see if the extra semantic features in *Final* are expressive enough to capture quiz bowl's inherently difficult coreferences. We also train the Berkeley system on quiz bowl data and compare the performance of these models to the pretrained newswire ones in Table 3. Our results are obtained by running a five-fold cross-validation on our dataset. The results show that newswire is a poor source of data for learning how to resolve quiz bowl coreferences and prompted us to see how well a pairwise classifier does in comparison. To build an end-to-end coreference system using this classifier, we first need to know which parts of the text are "mentions", or spans of a text that refer to real world entities. In the next section we talk about our mention detection system.

### 5.2 A Simple Mention Detector

Detecting mentions is done differently by different coreference systems. The Berkeley system does rule-based mention detection to detect every NP span, every pronoun, and every named entity, which leads to many spurious mentions. This process is based on an earlier work of Kummerfeld et al. (2011), which assumes that every maximal projection of a noun or a pronoun is a mention and uses rules to weed out spurious mentions. Instead of using such a rule-based mention detector, our system detects mentions via sequence labeling, as detecting mentions is essentially a problem of detecting start and stop points in spans of text. We solve this sequence tagging problem using the MALLET (McCallum, 2002) implementation of conditional random fields (Lafferty et al., 2001). Since our data contain nested mentions, the sequence labels are BIO markers (Ratinov and Roth, 2009). The features we use, which are similar to those used in Kummerfeld et al. (2011), are:

| | | MUC | | |
|---|---|---|---|---|
| System | Train | P | R | $F_1$ |
| Surface | OntoN | 47.22 | 27.97 | 35.13 |
| Final | OntoN | 50.79 | 30.77 | 38.32 |
| Surface | QB | **60.44** | 31.31 | 41.2 |
| Final | QB | 60.21 | **33.41** | **42.35** |

Table 3: The top half of the table represents Berkeley models trained on OntoNotes 4.0 data, while the bottom half shows models trained on quiz bowl data. The MUC $F_1$-score of the Berkeley system on OntoNotes text is 66.4, which when compared to these results prove that quiz bowl coreference is significantly different than OntoNotes coreference.

- the token itself
- the part of speech
- the named entity type
- a dependency relation concatenated with the parent token[12]

Using these simple features, we obtain surprisingly good results. When comparing our detected mentions to gold standard mentions on the quiz bowl dataset using exact matches, we obtain 76.1% precision, 69.6% recall, and 72.7% $F_1$ measure. Now that we have high-quality mentions, we can feed each pair of mentions into a pairwise mention classifier.

### 5.3 A Simple Coref Classifier

We follow previous pairwise coreference systems (Ng and Cardie, 2002; Uryupina, 2006; Versley et al., 2008) in extracting a set of lexical, syntactic, and semantic features from two mentions to determine whether they are coreferent. For example, if *Sylvia Plath*, *he*, and *she* are all of the mentions that occur in a document, our classifier gives predictions for the pairs *he—Sylvia Plath*, *she—Sylvia Plath*, and *he—she*.

Given two mentions in a document, $m_1$ and $m_2$, we generate the following features and feed them to a logistic regression classifier:

- binary indicators for all tokens contained in $m_1$ and $m_2$ concatenated with their parts-of-speech
- same as above except for an $n$-word window before and after $m_1$ and $m_2$
- how many tokens separate $m_1$ and $m_2$
- how many sentences separate $m_1$ and $m_2$
- the cosine similarity of `word2vec` (Mikolov et al., 2013) vector representations of $m_1$ and $m_2$; we obtain these vectors by averaging the word embeddings for all words in each mention. We use publicly-available 300-dimensional embeddings that have been pre-trained on 100B tokens from Google News.
- same as above except with publicly-available 300-dimensional `GloVe` (Pennington et al., 2014) vector embeddings trained on 840B tokens from the Common Crawl

The first four features are standard in coreference literature and similar to some of the surface features used by the Berkeley system, while the word embedding similarity scores increase our F-measure by about 5 points on the quiz bowl data. Since they have been trained on huge corpora, the word embeddings allow us to infuse world knowledge into our model; for instance, the vector for *Russian* is more similar to *Dostoevsky* than *Hemingway*.

Figure 5 shows that our logistic regression model (LR) outperforms the Berkeley system on numerous metrics when trained and evaluated on the quiz bowl dataset. We use precision, recall, and $F_1$, metrics applied to MUC, BCUB, and CEAFE measures used for comparing coreference systems.[13] We find that our LR model outperforms Berkeley by a wide margin when both are trained on the mentions found by our mention detector (CRF). For four metrics, the CRF mentions actually improve over training on the gold mentions.

Why does the LR model outperform Berkeley

[12] These features were obtained using the Stanford dependency parser (De Marneffe et al., 2006).

[13] The MUC (Vilain et al., 1995) score is the minimum number of links between mentions to be inserted or deleted when mapping the output to a gold standard key set. BCUB (Bagga and Baldwin, 1998) computes the precision and recall for all mentions separately and then combines them to get the final precision and recall of the output. CEAFE (Luo, 2005) is an improvement on BCUB and does not use entities multiple times to compute scores.

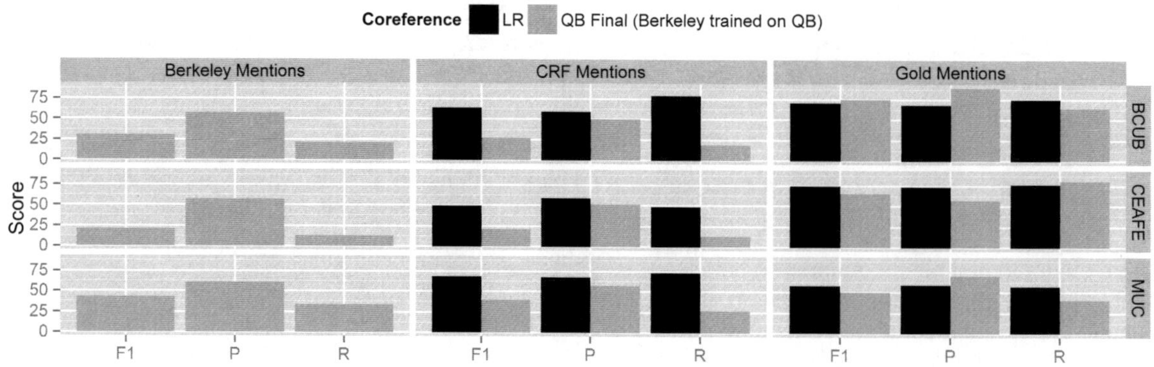


Figure 5: All models are trained and evaluated on quiz bowl data via five fold cross validation on $F_1$, precision, and recall. Berkeley/CRF/Gold refers to the mention detection used, LR refers to our logistic regression model and *QB Final* refers to the Berkeley model trained on quiz bowl data. Our model outperforms the Berkeley model on every metric when using our detected CRF mentions. When given gold mentions, LR outperforms Berkeley *QB Final* in five of nine metrics.

when both are trained on our quiz bowl dataset? We hypothesize that some of Berkeley's features, while helpful for sparse OntoNotes coreferences, do not offer the same utility in the denser quiz bowl domain. Compared to newswire text, our dataset contains a much larger percentage of complex coreference types that require world knowledge to resolve. Since the Berkeley system lacks semantic features, it is unlikely to correctly resolve these instances, whereas the pretrained word embedding features give our LR model a better chance of handling them correctly. Another difference between the two models is that the Berkeley system ranks mentions as opposed to doing pairwise classification like our LR model, and the mention ranking features may be optimized for newswire text.

## 5.4 Why Quiz Bowl Coreference is Challenging

While models trained on newswire falter on these data, is this simply a domain adaptation issue or something deeper? In the rest of this section, we examine specific examples to understand why quiz bowl coreference is so difficult. We begin with examples that *Final* gets wrong.

> *This writer* depicted a group of samurai's battle against an imperial. For ten points, name *this Japanese writer of A Personal Matter and The Silent Cry.*

While *Final* identifies most of pronouns associated with Kenzaburo Oe (the answer), it cannot recognize that the theme of the entire paragraph is building to the final reference, "this Japanese writer", despite the many Japanese-related ideas in the text of the question (e.g., Samurai and emperor). *Final* also cannot reason effectively about coreferences that are tied together by similar modifiers as in the below example:

> That *title character* plots to secure a "beautiful death" for Lovberg by burning his manuscript and giving him a pistol. For 10 points, name this play in which *the titular wife of George Tesman* commits suicide.

While a reader can connect "titular" and "title" to the same character, Hedda Gabler, the Berkeley system fails to make this inference. These data are a challenge for all systems, as they require extensive world knowledge. For example, in the following sentence, a model must know that the story referenced in the first sentence is about a dragon and that dragons can fly.

> The protagonist of *one of this man's works* erects a sign claiming that that story's title figure will fly to heaven from a pond. Identify this author of *Dragon: the Old Potter's Tale*

Humans solve cases like these using a vast amount of external knowledge, but existing models lack information about worlds (both real and imaginary) and thus cannot confidently mark these coreferences. We discuss coreference work that incorporates external resources such as Wikipedia in the next section; our aim is to provide a dataset that benefits more from this type of information than newswire does.

## 6 Related Work

We describe relevant data-driven coreference research in this section, all of which train and evaluate on only newswire text. Despite efforts to build better rule-based (Luo et al., 2004) or hybrid statistical systems (Haghighi and Klein, 2010), data-driven systems currently dominate the field. The 2012 CoNLL shared task led to improved data-driven systems for coreference resolution that finally outperformed both the Stanford system (Lee et al., 2011) and the IMS system (Björkelund and Farkas, 2012), the latter of which was the best available publicly-available English coreference system at the time. The recently-released Berkeley coreference system (Durrett and Klein, 2013) is especially striking: it performs well with only a sparse set of carefully-chosen features. Semantic knowledge sources—especially WordNet (Miller, 1995) and Wikipedia—have been used in coreference engines (Ponzetto and Strube, 2006). A system by Ratinov and Roth (2012) demonstrates good performance by using Wikipedia knowledge to strengthen a multi-pass rule based system. In a more recent work, Durrett and Klein (2014) outperform previous systems by building a joint model that matches mentions to Wikipedia entities while doing named entity resolution and coreference resolution simultaneously. We take a different approach by approximating semantic and world knowledge through our word embedding features. Our simple classifier yields a binary decision for each mention pair, a method that had been very popular before the last five years (Soon et al., 2001; Bengtson and Roth, 2008; Stoyanov et al., 2010). Recently, better results have been obtained with mention-ranking systems (Luo et al., 2004; Haghighi and Klein, 2010; Durrett and Klein, 2013; Björkelund and Kuhn, 2014). However, on quiz bowl data, our experiments show that binary classifiers can outperform mention-ranking approaches.

## 7 Embracing Harder Coreference

This paper introduces a new, naturally-occuring coreference dataset that is easy to annotate but difficult for computers to solve. We show that active learning allows us to create a dataset that is rich in different types of coreference. We develop an end-to-end coreference system using very simple mention detection and pairwise classification models that outperforms traditional systems on our dataset. The next challenge is to incorporate the necessary world knowledge to solve these harder coreference problems. Systems should be able to distinguish who is likely to marry whom, identify the titles of books from roundabout descriptions, and intuit family relationships from raw text. These are coreference challenges not found in newswire but that do exist in the real world. Unlike other AI-complete problems like machine translation, coreference in challenging datasets is easy to both annotate and evaluate. This paper provides the necessary building blocks to create and evaluate those systems.

## 8 Acknowledgments

We thank the anonymous reviewers for their insightful comments. We also thank Dr. Hal Daumé III and the members of the "feetthinking" research group for their advice and assistance. We also thank Dr. Yuening Hu and Mossaab Bagdouri for their help in reviewing the draft of this paper. This work was supported by NSF Grant IIS-1320538. Boyd-Graber is also supported by NSF Grants CCF-1018625 and NCSE-1422492. Any opinions, findings, results, or recommendations expressed here are of the authors and do not necessarily reflect the view of the sponsor.

## References


Amit Bagga and Breck Baldwin. 1998. Algorithms for scoring coreference chains. In *International Language Resources and Evaluation*. Citeseer.

Eric Bengtson and Dan Roth. 2008. Understanding the value of features for coreference resolution. In *Proceedings of Emperical Methods in Natural Language Processing*. Association for Computational Linguistics.

Anders Björkelund and Richárd Farkas. 2012. Data-driven multilingual coreference resolution using resolver stacking. In *Conference on Computational Natural Language Learning*.

Anders Björkelund and Jonas Kuhn. 2014. Learning structured perceptrons for coreference resolution with latent antecedents and non-local features. In *Proceedings of the Association for Computational Linguistics*.

A. Boyd, P. Stewart, and R. Alexander. 2008. *Broadcast Journalism: Techniques of Radio and Television News*. Taylor & Francis.

Jordan Boyd-Graber, Brianna Satinoff, He He, and Hal Daume III. 2012. Besting the quiz master: Crowdsourcing incremental classification games. In *Proceedings of Emperical Methods in Natural Language Processing*.

Marie-Catherine De Marneffe, Bill MacCartney, Christopher D Manning, et al. 2006. Generating typed dependency parses from phrase structure parses. In *International Language Resources and Evaluation*.

George R Doddington, Alexis Mitchell, Mark A Przybocki, Lance A Ramshaw, Stephanie Strassel, and Ralph M Weischedel. 2004. The automatic content extraction (ACE) program-tasks, data, and evaluation. In *International Language Resources and Evaluation*.

Greg Durrett and Dan Klein. 2013. Easy victories and uphill battles in coreference resolution. In *Proceedings of Emperical Methods in Natural Language Processing*.

Greg Durrett and Dan Klein. 2014. A joint model for entity analysis: Coreference, typing, and linking. *Transactions of the Association for Computational Linguistics*.

Eraldo Rezende Fernandes, Cícero Nogueira Dos Santos, and Ruy Luiz Milidiú. 2012. Latent structure perceptron with feature induction for unrestricted coreference resolution. In *Proceedings of Emperical Methods in Natural Language Processing*.

N. Goldstein and A. Press. 2004. *The Associated Press Stylebook and Briefing on Media Law*. Associated Press Stylebook and Briefing on Media Law. Basic Books.

Aria Haghighi and Dan Klein. 2010. Coreference resolution in a modular, entity-centered model. In *Conference of the North American Chapter of the Association for Computational Linguistics*.

Eduard Hovy, Mitchell Marcus, Martha Palmer, Lance Ramshaw, and Ralph Weischedel. 2006. Ontonotes: the 90% solution. In *Conference of the North American Chapter of the Association for Computational Linguistics*.

Mohit Iyyer, Jordan Boyd-Graber, Leonardo Claudino, Richard Socher, and Hal Daumé III. 2014. A neural network for factoid question answering over paragraphs. In *Proceedings of Emperical Methods in Natural Language Processing*.

Jonathan K Kummerfeld, Mohit Bansal, David Burkett, and Dan Klein. 2011. Mention detection: heuristics for the ontonotes annotations. In *Conference on Computational Natural Language Learning*.

John Lafferty, Andrew McCallum, and Fernando CN Pereira. 2001. Conditional random fields: Probabilistic models for segmenting and labeling sequence data.

Florian Laws, Florian Heimerl, and Hinrich Schütze. 2012. Active learning for coreference resolution. In *Conference of the North American Chapter of the Association for Computational Linguistics*.

Heeyoung Lee, Yves Peirsman, Angel Chang, Nathanael Chambers, Mihai Surdeanu, and Dan Jurafsky. 2011. Stanford's multi-pass sieve coreference resolution system at the conll-2011 shared task. In *Conference on Computational Natural Language Learning*.

Xiaoqiang Luo, Abe Ittycheriah, Hongyan Jing, Nanda Kambhatla, and Salim Roukos. 2004. A mention-synchronous coreference resolution algorithm based on the bell tree. In *Proceedings of the Association for Computational Linguistics*.

Xiaoqiang Luo. 2005. On coreference resolution performance metrics. In *Proceedings of Emperical Methods in Natural Language Processing*.

Andrew Kachites McCallum. 2002. Mallet: A machine learning for language toolkit. http://mallet.cs.umass.edu.

Tomas Mikolov, Kai Chen, Greg Corrado, and Jeffrey Dean. 2013. Efficient estimation of word representations in vector space. *arXiv preprint arXiv:1301.3781*.

Timothy A Miller, Dmitriy Dligach, and Guergana K Savova. 2012. Active learning for coreference resolution. In *Proceedings of the 2012 Workshop on*

*Biomedical Natural Language Processing*. Proceedings of the Association for Computational Linguistics.

George A Miller. 1995. Wordnet: a lexical database for english. *Communications of the ACM*, 38(11):39–41.

MUC-6. 1995. Coreference task definition (v2.3, 8 sep 95). In *Proceedings of the Sixth Message Understanding Conference (MUC-6)*.

MUC-7. 1997. Coreference task definition (v3.0, 13 jun 97). In *Proceedings of the Seventh Message Understanding Conference (MUC-7)*.

Vincent Ng and Claire Cardie. 2002. Improving machine learning approaches to coreference resolution. In *Proceedings of the Association for Computational Linguistics*.

Vincent Ng. 2010. Supervised noun phrase coreference research: The first fifteen years. In *Proceedings of the Association for Computational Linguistics*.

Jeffrey Pennington, Richard Socher, and Christopher Manning. 2014. Glove: Global vectors for word representation. In *Proceedings of Emperical Methods in Natural Language Processing*.

Thierry Poibeau and Leila Kosseim. 2001. Proper name extraction from non-journalistic texts. *Language and computers*, 37(1):144–157.

Simone Paolo Ponzetto and Michael Strube. 2006. Exploiting semantic role labeling, WordNet and Wikipedia for coreference resolution. In *Conference of the North American Chapter of the Association for Computational Linguistics*.

Sameer S Pradhan, Eduard Hovy, Mitch Marcus, Martha Palmer, Lance Ramshaw, and Ralph Weischedel. 2007. Ontonotes: A unified relational semantic representation. *International Journal of Semantic Computing*, 1(04).

Sameer Pradhan, Lance Ramshaw, Mitchell Marcus, Martha Palmer, Ralph Weischedel, and Nianwen Xue. 2011. CoNLL-2011 shared task: Modeling unrestricted coreference in Ontonotes. In *Conference on Computational Natural Language Learning*.

Lev Ratinov and Dan Roth. 2009. Design challenges and misconceptions in named entity recognition. In *Conference on Computational Natural Language Learning*.

Lev Ratinov and Dan Roth. 2012. Learning-based multi-sieve co-reference resolution with knowledge. In *Proceedings of Emperical Methods in Natural Language Processing*.

Burr Settles. 2010. Active learning literature survey. *University of Wisconsin, Madison*, 52:55–66.

Wee Meng Soon, Hwee Tou Ng, and Daniel Chung Yong Lim. 2001. A machine learning approach to coreference resolution of noun phrases. *Computational linguistics*, 27(4).

Veselin Stoyanov, Claire Cardie, Nathan Gilbert, Ellen Riloff, David Buttler, and David Hysom. 2010. Coreference resolution with reconcile. In *Proceedings of the Association for Computational Linguistics*.

Olga Uryupina. 2006. Coreference resolution with and without linguistic knowledge. In *International Language Resources and Evaluation*.

Yannick Versley, Simone Paolo Ponzetto, Massimo Poesio, Vladimir Eidelman, Alan Jern, Jason Smith, Xiaofeng Yang, and Alessandro Moschitti. 2008. Bart: A modular toolkit for coreference resolution. In *Proceedings of the Association for Computational Linguistics*.

Marc Vilain, John Burger, John Aberdeen, Dennis Connolly, and Lynette Hirschman. 1995. A model-theoretic coreference scoring scheme. In *Proceedings of the conference on Message understanding*, pages 45–52.

# Injecting Logical Background Knowledge into Embeddings for Relation Extraction

**Tim Rocktäschel**
University College London
London, UK

**Sameer Singh**
University of Washington
Seattle, WA

**Sebastian Riedel**
University College London
London, UK

## Abstract

Matrix factorization approaches to relation extraction provide several attractive features: they support distant supervision, handle open schemas, and leverage unlabeled data. Unfortunately, these methods share a shortcoming with all other distantly supervised approaches: they cannot learn to extract target relations without existing data in the knowledge base, and likewise, these models are inaccurate for relations with sparse data. Rule-based extractors, on the other hand, can be easily extended to novel relations and improved for existing but inaccurate relations, through first-order formulae that capture auxiliary domain knowledge. However, usually a large set of such formulae is necessary to achieve generalization.

In this paper, we introduce a paradigm for learning low-dimensional embeddings of entity-pairs and relations that combine the advantages of matrix factorization with first-order logic domain knowledge. We introduce simple approaches for estimating such embeddings, as well as a novel training algorithm to jointly optimize over factual and first-order logic information. Our results show that this method is able to learn accurate extractors with little or no distant supervision alignments, while at the same time generalizing to textual patterns that do not appear in the formulae.

## 1 Introduction

Relation extraction, the task of identifying relations between named entities, is a crucial component for information extraction. A recent successful approach (Riedel et al., 2013) relies on two ideas: (a) unifying traditional canonical relations, such as those of the Freebase schema, with OpenIE surface form patterns in a *universal schema*, and (b) completing a knowledge base of such a schema using matrix factorization. This approach has several attractive properties. First, for canonical relations it effectively performs distant supervision (Bunescu and Mooney, 2007; Mintz et al., 2009; Yao et al., 2011; Hoffmann et al., 2011; Surdeanu et al., 2012) and hence requires no textual annotations. Second, in the spirit of OpenIE, a universal schema can use textual patterns as novel relations and thus increases the coverage of traditional schemas (Riedel et al., 2013; Fan et al., 2014). Third, matrix factorization learns better embeddings for entity-pairs for which only surface form patterns are observed, and these can also lead to better extractions of canonical relations.

Unfortunately, populating a universal schema knowledge base using matrix factorization suffers from a problem all distantly-supervised techniques share: you can only reliably learn relations that appear frequently enough in the knowledge base. In particular, for relations that do not appear in the knowledge base or for which no facts are known we cannot learn a predictor at all. One way to overcome this problem is to incorporate additional domain knowledge, either specified manually or bootstrapped from auxiliary sources. In fact, domain knowledge encoded as simple logic formulae over patterns and relations has been used in practice to directly specify relation extractors (Reiss et al., 2008; Chiticariu et al., 2013; Akbik et al., 2014). However, these extractors can be brittle and obtain poor recall, since they are unable to generalize to textual patterns that are not



*Human Language Technologies: The 2015 Annual Conference of the North American Chapter of the ACL*, pages 1119–1129,
Denver, Colorado, May 31 – June 5, 2015. 

found in given formulae. Hence, there is a need for learning extractors that are able to combine logical knowledge with benefits of factorization techniques to facilitate precise extractions and generalization to novel relations.

In this paper, we propose a paradigm for learning universal schema extractors by combining matrix factorization based relation extraction with additional information in the form of first-order logic knowledge. Our contributions are threefold: (i) We introduce simple baselines that enforce logic constraints through deterministic inference before and after matrix factorization (§3.1). (ii) We propose a novel joint training algorithm that learns vector embeddings of relations and entity-pairs using both distant supervision and first-order logic formulae such that the factorization captures these formulae (§3.2). (iii) We present an empirical evaluation using automatically mined rules that demonstrates the benefits of incorporating logical knowledge in relation extraction, in particular that joint factorization of distant and logic supervision is efficient, accurate, and robust to noise (§5).

## 2 Matrix Factorization and Logic

In this section we provide background on matrix factorization for universal schema relation extraction, and describe its connections to first-order logic.

### 2.1 Notation

In order to later unify observed facts and logical background knowledge, we first represent given factual data in terms of first-order logic. We have a set $\mathcal{E}$ of *constants* that refer to entities, and a set of *predicates* $\mathcal{R}$ that refer to relations between these entities. In the following we will focus on binary relations in a *universal schema* that contains both structured relations from one (or more) knowledge bases, and surface-form relations. Further, with $\mathcal{P} \subseteq \mathcal{E} \times \mathcal{E}$ we denote the domain over entity-pairs of interest.

In function-free first-order logic a *term* is defined as a constant or a variable, and the most basic form of a formula is an *atom* such as $\texttt{professorAt}(x, y)$ that applies a predicate to a pair of terms. More complex formulae such as $\forall x, y : \texttt{professorAt}(x, y) \Rightarrow \texttt{employeeAt}(x, y)$ can be constructed by combining atoms with logical connectives (such as $\neg$ and $\wedge$) and quantifiers ($\exists x$, $\forall x$).

The simplest form of first-order formulae are *ground atoms*: predicates applied to constants, such as $\texttt{directorOf}$(NOLAN,INTERSTELLAR). A *possible world* is a set of ground atoms. *Ground literals* are either ground atoms or negated ground atoms such as $\neg\texttt{bornIn}$(NOLAN,BERLIN), and correspond to positive or negative *facts*. Training data for distant supervision can now be viewed as a knowledge base of such ground literals. Our goal is to extend the class of formulae from such facts to rules such as the first-order formula above.

### 2.2 Matrix Factorization with Ground Atoms

Given the notation presented above, matrix factorization can now be seen as a learning task in which low-dimensional embeddings are estimated for all constant pairs in $\mathcal{P}$ and predicates (relations) in $\mathcal{R}$, given a collection of ground atoms (facts) as supervision. We represent constant-pairs as rows and predicates as columns of a $|\mathcal{P}| \times |\mathcal{R}|$ binary matrix, and each atom in the training data represents an observed cell in this matrix. As introduced in Riedel et al. (2013), we seek to find a low-rank factorization into a $|\mathcal{P}| \times k$ matrix of embeddings of constant-pairs and a $k \times |\mathcal{R}|$ matrix of predicate embeddings such that they approximate the observed matrix.

More precisely, let $\mathbf{v}_{(\cdot)}$ denote the mapping from constant-pairs and predicates to their corresponding embedding. That is, $\mathbf{v}_{r_m}$ is the embedding for predicate $r_m$, and $\mathbf{v}_{(e_i,e_j)}$ is the embedding for the pair of constants $(e_i, e_j)$. Let $\mathbf{w}$ be a possible world (*i.e.* a set of ground atoms), and $\mathbf{V}$ be the set of all entity-pair and relation embeddings. Further, let $\pi_m^{e_i,e_j} = \sigma(\mathbf{v}_{r_m} \cdot \mathbf{v}_{e_i,e_j})$ where $\sigma$ is the sigmoid function and $\mathbf{v}_{r_m} \cdot \mathbf{v}_{(e_i,e_j)}$ denotes the vector dot-product between the embeddings of relation $r_m$ and entity-pair $(e_i, e_j)$. We define the conditional probability of a possible world $\mathbf{w}$ given embeddings $\mathbf{V}$ as

$$p(\mathbf{w}|\mathbf{V}) = \prod_{r_m(e_i,e_j)\in w} \pi_m^{e_i,e_j} \prod_{r_m(e_i,e_j)\notin w} \left(1 - \pi_m^{e_i,e_j}\right).$$

The embeddings can be estimated by maximizing the likelihood of a set of observed ground atoms with $\ell_2$ regularization (Collins et al., 2001), optimized using stochastic gradient descent. In summary, with atomic formulae (*i.e.* factual knowledge) we learn entity-pair and relation embeddings that reconstruct known facts and are able to generalize to unknown facts.

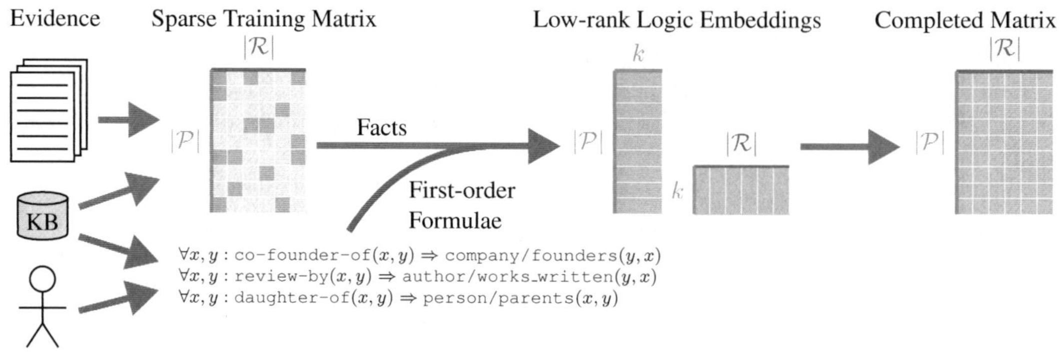


Figure 1: **Injecting Logic into Matrix Factorization:** Given a sparse binary matrix consisting of observed facts over entity-pairs $\mathcal{P}$ and predicates/relations $\mathcal{R}$, matrix factorization is used to learn $k$-dimensional relation and entity-pair embeddings that approximate the observed matrix. In this paper we use additional first-order logic formulae over entities and relations to learn the embeddings such that the predictions (completed matrix) also satisfy these formulae.

## 3 Injecting Logic Into Factorization

Matrix factorization is capable of learning complex dependencies between relations, but requires observed facts as training signal. However, often we either do not have this signal because the relations of interest do not have pre-existing facts, or this signal is noisy due to alignment errors or mismatches when linking knowledge base entities to mentions in text.

To overcome this problem we investigate the use of first-order logic background knowledge (*e.g.* implications) to aid relation extraction. One option is to rely on a fully symbolic approach that exclusively uses first-order logic (Bos and Markert, 2005; Baader et al., 2007; Bos, 2008). In this case incorporating additional background knowledge is trivial. However, it is difficult to generalize and deal with noise and uncertainty in language when relying only on manual rules. In contrast, matrix factorization methods can overcome these shortcomings, but it is not clear how they can be combined with logic formulae.

In this section, we propose to inject formulae into the embeddings of relations and entity-pairs, *i.e.*, estimate the embeddings such that predictions based on them conform to given logic formulae (see Figure 1 for an overview). We refer to such embeddings as *low-rank logic embeddings*. Akin to matrix factorization, inference of a fact at test time still amounts to an efficient dot product of the corresponding relation and entity-pair embeddings, and logical inference is not needed. We present two techniques for injecting logical background knowledge, *pre-factorization inference* (§3.1) and *joint optimization* (§3.2), and demonstrate in subsequent sections that they generalize better than direct logical inference, even if such inference is performed on the *predictions* of the matrix factorization model.

### 3.1 Pre-Factorization Inference

Background knowledge in form of first-order formulae can be seen as *hints* that can be used to generate additional training data (Abu-Mostafa, 1990). For *pre-factorization inference* we first perform logical inference on the training data and add inferred facts as additional training data. For example, for a formula $\mathcal{F} = \forall x, y : r_s(x, y) \Rightarrow r_t(x, y)$, we add an additional observed cell $r_t(x, y)$ for any $(x, y)$ for which $r_s(x, y)$ is observed in the distant supervision training data. This is repeated until no further facts can be inferred. Subsequently, we run matrix factorization on the extended set of observed cells.

The intuition is that the additional training data generated by the formulae provide evidence of the logical dependencies between relations to the matrix factorization model, while at the same time allowing the factorization to generalize to unobserved facts and to deal with ambiguity and noise in the data. No further logical inference is performed during or after training of the factorization model as we expect that the learned embeddings encode the given formulae.

### 3.2 Joint Optimization

One drawback of pre-factorization inference is that the formulae are enforced only on observed atoms, *i.e.*, first-order dependencies on *predicted* facts are ignored. Instead we would like to include a loss term for the logical formulae directly in the matrix factorization objective, thus jointly optimizing embeddings to reconstruct factual training data as well as obeying to first-order logical background knowledge.

#### 3.2.1 Training Objective

Here we first present a learning objective that unifies ground atoms (facts) and logical background knowledge by treating both as logic formulae (atomic or complex), and define a loss function over this general representation. We then define the loss function for ground atoms and simple implications, along with a brief sketch of how the loss can be defined for arbitrarily complex logic formulae.

As introduced in §2.1, let $\mathcal{R}$ be the set of all relations/predicates and $\mathcal{P}$ be the set of all entity-pairs/constants. Furthermore, let $\mathfrak{F}$ be a training set of logic formulae $\mathcal{F}$, and $\mathcal{L}$ a loss function. The training objective (omitting $\ell_2$ regularization on $\mathbf{v}_{(\cdot)}$ for simplicity) is

$$\min_{\mathbf{V}} \sum_{\mathcal{F}\in\mathfrak{F}} \mathcal{L}([\mathcal{F}]) \quad (1)$$

where $\mathbf{V}$ is the set of all relation and entity-pair embeddings, and $[\mathcal{F}]$ is the marginal probability $p(w|\mathbf{V})$ that the formula $\mathcal{F}$ is true under the model. In this paper we use the logistic loss: $\mathcal{L}([\mathcal{F}]) := -\log([\mathcal{F}])$. The objective thus prefers embeddings that assign formulae a high marginal probability.

To optimize this function we need the marginal probabilities $[\mathcal{F}]$, and the gradients of the losses $\mathcal{L}([\mathcal{F}])$ for every $\mathcal{F} \in \mathfrak{F}$ with respect to entity-pair and relation embeddings, *i.e.*, $\partial\mathcal{L}([\mathcal{F}])/\partial\mathbf{v}_{r_m}$ and $\partial\mathcal{L}([\mathcal{F}])/\partial\mathbf{v}_{(e_i,e_j)}$. Below we discuss how these quantities can be computed or approximated for arbitrary first-order logic formulae, with details provided for ground atoms and implications.

**Ground Atoms** Due to the conditional independence of ground atoms in the distribution $p(\mathbf{w}|\mathbf{V})$, the marginal probability of a ground atom $\mathcal{F} = r_m(e_i, e_j)$ is $[\mathcal{F}] = \pi_m^{e_i,e_j} = \sigma(\mathbf{v}_{r_m} \cdot \mathbf{v}_{e_i,e_j})$. Hence when only ground atoms (or literals) are used, objective (1) reduces to the standard log-likelihood loss. The gradients of the loss for the entity-pair embedding $\mathbf{v}_{(e_i,e_j)}$ and relation embedding $\mathbf{v}_{r_m}$ are

$$\partial[\mathcal{F}]/\partial\mathbf{v}_{(e_i,e_j)} = [\mathcal{F}](1-[\mathcal{F}])\mathbf{v}_{r_m} \quad (2)$$

$$\partial[\mathcal{F}]/\partial\mathbf{v}_{r_m} = [\mathcal{F}](1-[\mathcal{F}])\mathbf{v}_{(e_i,e_j)} \quad (3)$$

$$\partial\mathcal{L}([\mathcal{F}])/\partial\mathbf{v}_{(e_i,e_j)} = -[\mathcal{F}]^{-1}\partial[\mathcal{F}]/\partial\mathbf{v}_{(e_i,e_j)} \quad (4)$$

$$\partial\mathcal{L}([\mathcal{F}])/\partial\mathbf{v}_{r_m} = -[\mathcal{F}]^{-1}\partial[\mathcal{F}]/\partial\mathbf{v}_{r_m}. \quad (5)$$

**First-order Logic** Crucially, and in contrast to the log-likelihood loss for matrix factorization, we can inject more expressive logic formulae than just ground atoms. We briefly outline how to recursively compute the probability of the formula $[\mathcal{F}]$ and the gradients of the loss $\mathcal{L}([\mathcal{F}])$ for any first-order formula $\mathcal{F}$. Again, note that the probabilities of ground atoms in our model are independent conditioned on embeddings. This means that for any two formulae $\mathcal{A}$ and $\mathcal{B}$, the marginal probability of $[\mathcal{A} \wedge \mathcal{B}]$ can be computed as $[\mathcal{A}][\mathcal{B}]$ (known as *product t-norm*), provided both formula concern non-overlapping sets of ground atoms. In combination with $[\neg\mathcal{A}] := 1 - [\mathcal{A}]$ and the $[\ ]$ operator as defined for ground atoms earlier, we can compute the probability of *any* propositional formula recursively, *e.g.*,

$$[\mathcal{A} \vee \mathcal{B}] = [\mathcal{A}] + [\mathcal{B}] - [\mathcal{A}][\mathcal{B}]$$

$$[\mathcal{A} \Rightarrow \mathcal{B}] = [\mathcal{A}]([\mathcal{B}] - 1) + 1$$

$$[\mathcal{A} \wedge \neg\mathcal{B} \Rightarrow \mathcal{C}] = ([\mathcal{A}](1-[\mathcal{B}]))([\mathcal{C}] - 1) + 1.$$

Note that for statements $[\mathcal{F}] \in \{0, 1\}$, we directly recover logical semantics. First-order formulae in finite domains can be embedded through explicit grounding. For universal quantification we can get $[\forall x, y : \mathcal{F}(x, y)] = [\bigwedge_{x,y} \mathcal{F}(x, y)]$. If we again assume non-overlapping ground atoms in each of the arguments of the conjunction, we can simplify this to $\prod_{x,y}[\mathcal{F}(x, y)]$. When arguments do overlap we can think of this simplification as an approximation.

Since $[\mathcal{F}(x, y)]$ is defined recursively, we can back-propagate the training signal through the structure of $[\mathcal{F}]$ to compute $\partial[\mathcal{F}(x, y)]/\partial\mathbf{v}_{r_m}$ and $\partial[\mathcal{F}(x, y)]/\partial\mathbf{v}_{e_i,e_j}$ for any nested formula.

**Implications** A particularly useful family of formulae for relation extraction are universally quantified first-order formula over a knowledge base such as $\mathcal{F} = \forall x, y : r_s(x, y) \Rightarrow r_t(x, y)$. Assuming a finite domain, such a formula can be unrolled into a conjunction of propositional statements of the form $\mathcal{F}_{ij} = r_s(e_i, e_j) \Rightarrow r_t(e_i, e_j)$, one for each entity-pair $(e_i, e_j)$ in the domain. Specifically, $[\mathcal{F}] = \prod_{(e_i,e_j)\in\mathcal{P}}[\mathcal{F}_{ij}]$, and therefore $\mathcal{L}([\mathcal{F}]) = \sum_{(e_i,e_j)\in\mathcal{P}}\mathcal{L}([\mathcal{F}_{ij}])$. The gradients are derived as:

$$[\mathcal{F}_{ij}] = [r_s(e_i, e_j)]\,([r_t(e_i, e_j)] - 1) + 1 \quad (6)$$

$$\frac{\partial\mathcal{L}([\mathcal{F}_{ij}])}{\partial\mathbf{v}_{r_s}} = -[\mathcal{F}_{ij}]^{-1}\,([r_t(e_i, e_j)] - 1)\,\frac{\partial[r_s(e_i, e_j)]}{\partial\mathbf{v}_{r_s}}$$

$$\frac{\partial\mathcal{L}([\mathcal{F}_{ij}])}{\partial\mathbf{v}_{r_t}} = -[\mathcal{F}_{ij}]^{-1}[r_s(e_i, e_j)]\frac{\partial[r_t(e_i, e_j)]}{\partial\mathbf{v}_{r_t}} \quad (7)$$

$$\frac{\partial\mathcal{L}([\mathcal{F}_{ij}])}{\partial\mathbf{v}_{e_i,e_j}} = -[\mathcal{F}_{ij}]^{-1}\,([r_t(e_i, e_j)] - 1)\,\frac{\partial[r_s(e_i, e_j)]}{\partial\mathbf{v}_{e_i,e_j}} - [\mathcal{F}_{ij}]^{-1}[r_s(e_i, e_j)]\frac{\partial[r_t(e_i, e_j)]}{\partial\mathbf{v}_{e_i,e_j}}. \quad (8)$$

Following such a derivation, one can obtain gradients for other first-order logic formulae as well.

### 3.2.2 Learning

We learn the embeddings by minimizing Eq. 1 with $\ell_2$-regularization using AdaGrad (Duchi et al., 2011). Since we have no negative training facts, we follow Riedel et al. (2013) by sampling unobserved facts that we assume to be false. Specifically, in every epoch and for every true training fact $r_m(e_i, e_j)$ we sample an $(e_p, e_q)$ such that $r_m(e_p, e_q)$ is unobserved. Subsequently, we perform two kinds of updates: $\mathcal{F} = r_m(e_i, e_j)$ and $\mathcal{F} = \neg r_m(e_p, e_q)$. For every non-atomic first-order formula in $\mathfrak{F}$ we iterate over all entity-pairs for which at least one atom in the formula is observed (in addition to as many sampled entity-pairs for which *none* of the atoms have been observed) and add corresponding grounded propositional formulae to the training objective. At test time, predicting a score for any unobserved statement $r_m(e_i, e_j)$ is done efficiently by calculating $[r_m(e_i, e_j)]$. Note that this does not involve any explicit logical inference, instead we expect that the predictions from the learned embeddings already respect the provided formulae.

## 4 Experimental Setup

There are two orthogonal question when evaluating the effectiveness of low-rank logic embeddings: a) does injection of logic formulae into the embeddings of entity-pairs and relations provide any benefits, and b) where do the background formulae come from? The latter is a well-studied problem (Hipp et al., 2000; Schoenmackers et al., 2010; Völker and Niepert, 2011). In this paper we focus the evaluation on the ability of various approaches to benefit from formulae that we directly extract from the training data using a simple method.

**Distant Supervision Evaluation** We follow the procedure as used in Riedel et al. (2013) for evaluating knowledge base completion of Freebase (Bollacker et al., 2008) with textual data from the NYTimes corpus (Sandhaus, 2008). The training matrix consists of 4 111 columns, representing 151 Freebase relations and 3 960 textual patterns, 41 913 rows (entity-pairs) and 118 781 training facts of which 7 293 belong to Freebase relations. The entity-pairs are divided into train and test, and we hide all Freebase relations for the test pairs from training. Our primary evaluation measure is average and (weighted) mean average precision, **MAP** and **wMAP** respectively (see Riedel et al. (2013) for details).

**Formulae Extraction and Annotation** We use a simple technique for extracting formulae from the matrix factorization model. We first run matrix factorization over the complete training data to learn accurate relation and entity-pair embeddings. After training, we iterate over all pairs of relations $(r_s, r_t)$ where $r_t$ is a Freebase relation. For every relation-pair we iterate over all training atoms $r_s(e_i, e_j)$, evaluate the score $[r_s(e_i, e_j) \Rightarrow r_t(e_i, e_j)]$ as described in §3.2.1, and calculate the average to arrive at a score for the formula. Finally, we rank all formulae by their score and manually filter the top 100 formulae, which resulted in 36 annotated high-quality formulae (see Table 1 for examples). Note that our formula extraction approach does not observe the relations for test entity-pairs. All models used in our experiments have access to these formulae, except for the matrix factorization baseline.

**Methods** Our proposed methods for injecting logic into relation embeddings are *pre-factorization inference* (**Pre**; §3.1) which performs regular matrix factorization after propagating the logic formulae in a deterministic manner, and *joint optimization* (**Joint**; §3.2) which maximizes an objective that combines terms from factual and first-order logic knowledge. Additionally, we use the following three baselines. The *matrix factorization* (**MF**; §2.2) model uses only ground atoms to learn relation and entity-pair embed-

| Formula | Score |
|---|---|
| $\forall x, y$ : #2-unit-of-#1$(x, y) \Rightarrow$ org/parent/child$(x, y)$ | 0.97 |
| $\forall x, y$ : #2-city-of-#1$(x, y) \Rightarrow$ location/containedby$(x, y)$ | 0.97 |
| $\forall x, y$ : #2-minister-#1$(x, y) \Rightarrow$ person/nationality$(x, y)$ | 0.97 |
| $\forall x, y$ : #2-executive-#1$(x, y) \Rightarrow$ person/company$(x, y)$ | 0.96 |
| $\forall x, y$ : #2-co-founder-of-#1$(x, y) \Rightarrow$ company/founders$(y, x)$ | 0.96 |

Table 1: **Sample Extracted Formulae:** Top implications of textual patterns to five different Freebase relations. These implications were extracted from the matrix factorization model and manually annotated. The premises of these implications are dependency paths, but we present a simplified version to make them more readable.

| Relation | # | MF | Inf | Post | Pre | Joint |
|---|---|---|---|---|---|---|
| person/company | 102 | 0.07 | 0.03 | 0.15 | 0.31 | **0.35** |
| location/containedby | 72 | 0.03 | 0.06 | 0.14 | 0.22 | **0.31** |
| author/works_written | 27 | 0.02 | 0.05 | 0.18 | **0.31** | 0.27 |
| person/nationality | 25 | 0.01 | *0.19* | 0.09 | 0.15 | *0.19* |
| parent/child | 19 | 0.01 | 0.01 | 0.48 | 0.66 | **0.75** |
| person/place_of_birth | 18 | 0.01 | 0.43 | 0.40 | 0.56 | **0.59** |
| person/place_of_death | 18 | 0.01 | 0.24 | 0.23 | **0.27** | 0.23 |
| neighborhood/neighborhood_of | 11 | 0.00 | 0.00 | 0.60 | 0.63 | **0.65** |
| person/parents | 6 | 0.00 | 0.17 | 0.19 | 0.37 | **0.65** |
| company/founders | 4 | 0.00 | 0.25 | 0.13 | 0.37 | **0.77** |
| film/directed_by | 2 | 0.00 | 0.50 | 0.50 | 0.36 | **0.51** |
| film/produced_by | 1 | 0.00 | *1.00* | *1.00* | *1.00* | *1.00* |
| MAP | | 0.01 | 0.23 | 0.34 | 0.43 | **0.52** |
| Weighted MAP | | 0.03 | 0.10 | 0.21 | 0.33 | **0.38** |

Table 2: **Zero-shot Relation Learning:** Average and (weighted) mean average precisions with relations that do not appear in any of the annotated formulae omitted from the evaluation. The difference between "Pre" and "Joint" is significant according to the sign-test ($p < 0.05$).

dings (*i.e.* it has no access to any formulae). Furthermore, we consider pure *logical inference* (**Inf**). Our final approach, *post-factorization inference* (**Post**), first runs matrix factorization and then performs logical inference on the known and predicted facts. Post-inference is computationally expensive, since for all premises of formulae we have to iterate over *all* rows (entity-pairs) in the matrix to assess whether the premise is true or not.

**Parameters** For every matrix factorization based method we use $k = 100$ as the dimension for the embeddings, $\lambda = 0.01$ as parameter of $\ell_2$-regularization and $\alpha = 0.1$ as initial learning rate for AdaGrad, which we run for 200 epochs.

**Complexity** Each AdaGrad update is defined over a single cell of the matrix, and thus training data can be streamed one ground atom at a time. For matrix factorization, each AdaGrad epoch touches all the observed atoms once, and as many sampled negative atoms. With given formulae, it additionally revisits all the observed atoms that appear as an atom in the formula (and as many sampled negative atoms), and thus more general formulae will be more expensive. However the updates over atoms are performed independently and thus not all the data needs to be stored in memory. All presented models take less than 15 minutes to train on a 2.8 GHz Intel Core i7 machine.

## 5 Results and Discussion

To evaluate the utility of injecting logic formulae into embeddings, we present a comparison on a variety of benchmarks. First, in §5.1 we study the scenario of learning extractors for relations for which we do not have any Freebase alignments, evaluating how the approaches are able to generalize only from logic formulae and textual patterns. In §5.2 we then describe an experiment where the amount of Freebase alignments is varied in order to assess the effect of combining distant supervision and background knowledge on the accuracy of predictions. Although the methods presented in this paper target relations with insufficient alignments, we also provide a comparison on the complete distant supervision dataset in §5.3. We conclude in §5.4 with a brief analysis of the reasoning capacity of the learned embeddings.

### 5.1 Zero-shot Relation Learning

We start with the scenario of learning extractors for relations that do not appear in the knowledge base schema, *i.e.*, those that do not have any textual alignments. Such a scenario occurs in practice when a new relation needs to be added to a knowledge base for which there are no facts that connect the new relation to existing relations or surface patterns. For accurate extractions of such relations, the model needs to rely primarily on background domain knowledge to identify relevant textual alignments, but at the same time it also needs to utilize correlations between textual patterns for generalization. To simulate this setup, we remove all alignments between all entity-pairs and Freebase relations from the distant supervision data, use the extracted logic formulae (§4) as background knowledge, and evaluate on the ability of the different methods to recover the lost alignments.

Table 2 provides detailed results. Unsurprisingly,

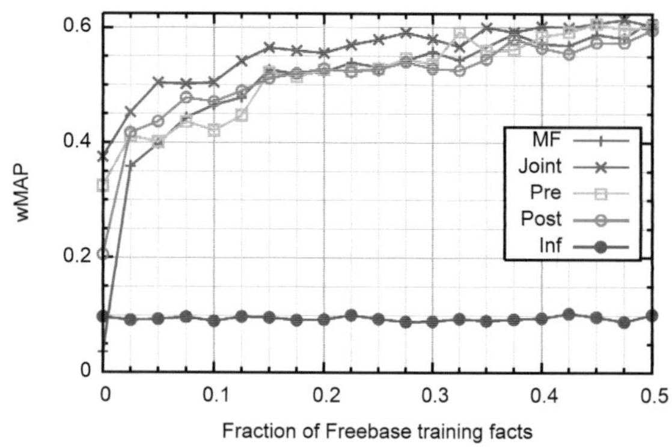


Figure 2: **Relations with Few Distant Labels:** Weighted mean average precisions of the various methods as the fraction of Freebase training facts is varied. For 0% Freebase training facts we get the zero-shot relation learning results presented in Table 2.

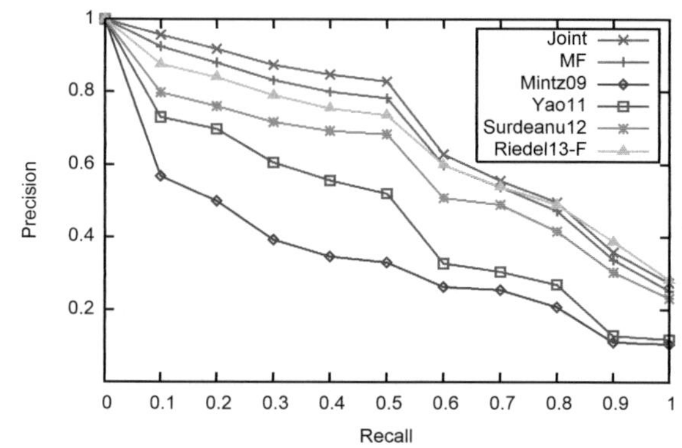


Figure 3: **Comparison on Complete Data:** Averaged precision/recall curve demonstrating that the "Joint" method outperforms existing factorization approaches ("MF" and "Riedel13-F"). The formulae used by our approach have been extracted only from the training data.

matrix factorization (**MF**) performs poorly since embeddings cannot be learned for the Freebase relations without any observed cells. Scores higher than zero for matrix factorization are caused by random predictions. Logical inference (**Inf**) is limited by the number of known facts that appear as premise in one of the implications. Although post-factorization inference (**Post**) is able to achieve a large improvement over logical inference, explicitly injecting logic formulae into the embeddings (*i.e.* learning low-rank logic embeddings) using pre-factorization inference (**Pre**) or joint optimization (**Joint**) gives superior results. Last, we observe that joint optimization is able to best combine logic formulae and textual patterns for accurate, zero-shot learning of relation extractors.

## 5.2 Relations with Few Distant Labels

In this section we study the scenario of learning relations that have only a few distant supervision alignments, in particular, we observe the behavior of the various methods as the amount of distant supervision is varied. We run all methods on training data that contains different fractions of Freebase training facts (and therefore different degrees of relation/text pattern alignment), but keep all textual patterns in addition to the set of extracted formulae.

Figure 2 summarizes the results. The performance of pure logical inference does not depend on the amount of distant supervision data, since it does not take advantage of the correlations in the data. Matrix factorization ignores logic formulae, and thus is the baseline performance when only using distant supervision. For the factorization based methods, only a small fraction (15%) of the training data is needed to achieve around 0.50 wMAP performance, thus demonstrating that they are efficiently exploiting correlations and generalizing to unobserved facts.

Pre-factorization inference, however, does not outperform post-factorization inference, and is on par with matrix factorization for most of the curve. This suggests that it is not an effective way of injecting logic into embeddings when ground facts are also available. In contrast, joint optimization leads to low-rank logic embeddings that outperform all other methods in the 0 to 30% Freebase training data interval. Beyond 30% there seem to be sufficient Freebase facts for matrix factorization to encode these formulae, thus yielding diminishing returns.

## 5.3 Comparison on Complete Data

Although the focus of this paper is injection of logical knowledge for relations without sufficient alignments to the knowledge base, we also present an evaluation on the complete distant supervision data as used by Riedel et al. (2013). Compared to the Riedel et al.'s "F" model, our matrix factorization implementation ("MF") achieves a lower wMAP (64% vs 68%) and a higher MAP (66% vs 64%). We attribute this difference to the different loss function (logistic loss in our case vs. ranking loss). We show the PR curve in Figure 3, demonstrating that joint optimization provides benefits over the existing factorization and distant supervision techniques even on the complete dataset, and obtains 66% wMAP and 69% MAP. This improvement over the matrix factorization model can be explained by reinforcement of high-quality annotated formulae via the joint model.

### 5.4 Analysis of Asymmetry in the Predictions

Since the injected formulae are of the form $\forall x, y : r_s(x, y) \Rightarrow r_t(x, y)$, it is worthwhile to study the extent to which these rules are captured, and which approaches are in fact capturing the asymmetric nature of the implication. To this end, we compute the probabilities that the formulae and their inverse hold, averaged over all annotated formulae and cells. The degree to which $r_s \Rightarrow r_t$ is captured is quite high for all models (0.94, 0.96, and 0.97 for matrix factorization, pre-factorization inference, and joint optimization respectively). On the other hand, the probability of $r_t \Rightarrow r_s$ is also relatively high for matrix factorization and pre-factorization inference (0.81 and 0.83 respectively), suggesting that these methods are primarily capturing symmetric similarity between relations. Joint optimization, however, produces much more asymmetric predictions (probability of $r_t \Rightarrow r_s$ is 0.49), demonstrating that it is appropriate for encoding logic in the embeddings.

## 6 Related Work

**Embeddings for Knowledge Base Completion** Embedding predicates and constants (or pairs of constants) based on factual knowledge for knowledge base completion has for instance been investigated by Bordes et al. (2011), Nickel et al. (2012), Socher et al. (2013), Riedel et al. (2013) and Fan et al. (2014). Our work goes further in that we learn embeddings that follow not only factual but also first-order logic knowledge, and the ideas presented in this paper can be incorporated with any embedding-based method that uses a per-atom loss.

**Logical Inference** A common alternative that directly incorporates first-order logic knowledge is to perform logical inference (Bos and Markert, 2005; Baader et al., 2007; Bos, 2008), however such purely symbolic approaches cannot deal with the uncertainty inherent to natural language, and generalize poorly.

**Probabilistic Inference** To ameliorate some of the drawbacks of symbolic logical inference, probabilistic logic based approaches have been proposed (Schoenmackers et al., 2008; Garrette et al., 2011; Beltagy et al., 2013; Beltagy et al., 2014). Since logical connections between relations are modeled explicitly, such approaches are generally hard to scale. Specifically, approaches based on Markov Logic Networks (MLNs) (Richardson and Domingos, 2006) encode logical knowledge in dense, loopy graphical models, making structure learning, parameter estimation, and inference hard for the scale of our data. In contrast, in our model the logical knowledge is captured directly in the embeddings, leading to efficient inference. Furthermore, as our model is based on matrix factorization, we have a natural way to deal with linguistic ambiguities and label errors.

**Weakly Supervised Learning** Our work is also inspired by weakly supervised approaches (Ganchev et al., 2010) that use structural constraints as a source of indirect supervision, and have been used for several NLP tasks (Chang et al., 2007; Mann and McCallum, 2008; Druck et al., 2009; Singh et al., 2010). Carlson et al. (2010) in particular is similar since they use common sense constraints to jointly train multiple information extractors. In this work, however, we are training a matrix factorization model, and allowing for arbitrarily complex logic formulae.

**Combining Symbolic and Distributed Representations** There have been a number of recent approaches that combine distributed representations with symbolic knowledge. Grefenstette (2013) describes an isomorphism between first-order logic and tensor calculus, using full-rank matrices to exactly *memorize* facts. Based on this isomorphism, Rocktäschel et al. (2014) combine logic with matrix factorization for learning low-dimensional embeddings that approximately satisfy given formulae and generalize to unobserved facts on toy data. Our work extends this workshop paper by proposing a simpler formalism without tensor-based logical connectives, presenting results on a real-world task, and demonstrating the utility of this approach for learning relations with few textual alignments.

Chang et al. (2014) use Freebase entity types as hard constraints in a tensor factorization objective for universal schema relation extraction. In contrast, our approach is imposing soft constraints that are formulated as universally quantified first-order formula.

de Lacalle and Lapata (2013) combine first-order logic knowledge with a topic model to improve surface pattern clustering for relation extraction. Since these formulae only specify which relations can be clustered and which not, they do not capture the variety of dependencies embeddings can model, such as asymmetry. Lewis and Steedman (2013) use distributed representations to cluster predicates before logical inference. Again, this approach is not as powerful as factorizing the relations, as it makes symmetry assumptions for the predicates.

Several studies have investigated the use of symbolic representations (such as dependency trees) to guide the composition of distributed representations (Clark and Pulman, 2007; Mitchell and Lapata, 2008; Coecke et al., 2010; Hermann and Blunsom, 2013). Instead we are using symbolic representations (first-order logic) as prior domain knowledge to directly learn better embeddings.

Combining symbolic information with neural networks has also been an active area of research. Towell and Shavlik (1994) introduce Knowledge-Based Artificial Neural Networks whose topology is isomorphic to a knowledge base of facts and inference formulae. There, facts are input units, intermediate conclusions hidden units, and final conclusions (inferred facts) output units. Unlike our work, there is no latent representation of predicates and constants. Hölldobler et al. (1999) and Hitzler et al. (2004) prove that for every logic program theoretically there exists a recurrent neural network that approximates the semantics of that program. Finally, Bowman (2014) recently demonstrated that a neural tensor network can accurately learn natural logic reasoning.

## 7 Conclusions

Inspired by the benefits of logical background knowledge that can lead to precise extractors, and of distant supervision based matrix factorization that can utilize dependencies between textual patterns to generalize, in this paper we introduced a novel training paradigm for learning embeddings that combine matrix factorization with logic formulae. Along with a deterministic approach to enforce the formulae a priori, we propose a joint objective that rewards predictions that satisfy given logical knowledge, thus learning embeddings that do not require logical inference at test time. Experiments show that the proposed approaches are able to learn extractors for relations with little to no observed textual alignments, while at the same time benefiting more common relations. The source code of the methods presented in this paper and the annotated formulae used for evaluation are available at `github.com/uclmr/low-rank-logic`.

This research has thrown up many questions in need of further investigation. As opposed to our approach that modifies both relation and entity-pair embeddings, further work needs to explore training methods that only modify relation embeddings in order to encode logical dependencies explicitly, and thus avoid *memorization*. Although we obtain significant gains by using implications, our approach facilitates the use of arbitrary formulae; it would be worthwhile to pursue this direction by following the steps outlined in §3.2.1. Furthermore, we are interested in combining relation extraction with models that learn *entity type* representations (*e.g.* tensor factorization or neural models) to allow for expressive logical statements such as $\forall x, y$ : $\texttt{nationality}(x, y) \Rightarrow \texttt{country}(y)$. Since such common sense formulae are often not directly observed in distant supervision, they can go a long way in fixing common extraction errors. Finally, we will investigate methods to automatically mine commonsense knowledge for injection into embeddings from additional resources such as Probase (Wu et al., 2012) or directly from text using a semantic parser (Zettlemoyer and Collins, 2005).

## Acknowledgments

The authors want to thank Mathias Niepert for proposing pre-factorization inference as alternative to joint optimization. We thank Edward Grefenstette, Luke Zettlemoyer, and Guillaume Bouchard for comments on the manuscript, and the reviewers for very helpful feedback. This work was supported in part by Microsoft Research through its PhD Scholarship Programme and in part by the TerraSwarm Research Center, one of six centers supported by the STARnet phase of the Focus Center Research Program (FCRP) a Semiconductor Research Corporation program sponsored by MARCO and DARPA.

## References


Yaser S Abu-Mostafa. 1990. Learning from hints in neural networks. *Journal of complexity*, 6(2):192–198.

Alan Akbik, Thilo Michael, and Christoph Boden. 2014. Exploratory relation extraction in large text corpora. In *International Conference on Computational Linguistics (COLING)*, pages 2087–2096.

Franz Baader, Bernhard Ganter, Baris Sertkaya, and Ulrike Sattler. 2007. Completing description logic knowledge bases using formal concept analysis. In *IJCAI*, pages 230–235.

Islam Beltagy, Cuong Chau, Gemma Boleda, Dan Garrette, Katrin Erk, and Raymond Mooney. 2013. Montague meets markov: Deep semantics with probabilistic logical form. In *2nd Joint Conference on Lexical and Computational Semantics: Proceeding of the Main Conference and the Shared Task, Atlanta*, pages 11–21.

Islam Beltagy, Katrin Erk, and Raymond J. Mooney. 2014. Probabilistic soft logic for semantic textual similarity. In *Proceedings of the 52nd Annual Meeting of the Association for Computational Linguistics (ACL-14)*, Baltimore, MD.

Kurt Bollacker, Colin Evans, Praveen Paritosh, Tim Sturge, and Jamie Taylor. 2008. Freebase: a collaboratively created graph database for structuring human knowledge. In *Proceedings of the 2008 ACM SIGMOD international conference on Management of data*, pages 1247–1250. ACM.

Antoine Bordes, Jason Weston, Ronan Collobert, and Yoshua Bengio. 2011. Learning structured embeddings of knowledge bases. In *AAAI*.

Johan Bos and Katja Markert. 2005. Recognising textual entailment with logical inference. In *Proceedings of the conference on Human Language Technology and Empirical Methods in Natural Language Processing*, pages 628–635. Association for Computational Linguistics.

Johan Bos. 2008. Wide-coverage semantic analysis with boxer. In Johan Bos and Rodolfo Delmonte, editors, *Semantics in Text Processing. STEP 2008 Conference Proceedings*, Research in Computational Semantics, pages 277–286. College Publications.

Samuel R Bowman. 2014. Can recursive neural tensor networks learn logical reasoning? In *ICLR'14*.

Razvan C. Bunescu and Raymond J. Mooney. 2007. Learning to Extract Relations from the Web using Minimal Supervision. In *Annual Meeting of the Association for Computational Linguistics (ACL)*, Prague, Czech Republic, June.

Andrew Carlson, Justin Betteridge, Richard C. Wang, Estevam R. Hruschka, Jr., and Tom M. Mitchell. 2010. Coupled semi-supervised learning for information extraction. In *International conference on Web search and data mining (WSDM)*.

Ming-Wei Chang, Lev Ratinov, and Dan Roth. 2007. Guiding semi-supervision with constraint-driven learning. In *Annual Meeting of the Association for Computational Linguistics (ACL)*, pages 280–287.

Kai-Wei Chang, Wen-tau Yih, Bishan Yang, and Christopher Meek. 2014. Typed tensor decomposition of knowledge bases for relation extraction.

Laura Chiticariu, Yunyao Li, and Frederick R. Reiss. 2013. Rule-based information extraction is dead! long live rule-based information extraction systems! In *Empirical Methods in Natural Language Processing (EMNLP)*, pages 827–832.

Stephen Clark and Stephen Pulman. 2007. Combining symbolic and distributional models of meaning. In *AAAI Spring Symposium: Quantum Interaction*, pages 52–55.

Bob Coecke, Mehrnoosh Sadrzadeh, and Stephen Clark. 2010. Mathematical foundations for a compositional distributional model of meaning. *CoRR*, abs/1003.4394.

Michael Collins, Sanjoy Dasgupta, and Robert E Schapire. 2001. A generalization of principal components analysis to the exponential family. In *Advances in neural information processing systems*, pages 617–624.

Oier Lopez de Lacalle and Mirella Lapata. 2013. Unsupervised relation extraction with general domain knowledge. In *EMNLP*, pages 415–425.

Gregory Druck, Gideon Mann, and Andrew McCallum. 2009. Semi-supervised learning of dependency parsers using generalized expectation criteria. In *Joint Conference of the Annual Meeting of the ACL and the International Joint Conference on Natural Language Processing of the AFNLP*.

John Duchi, Elad Hazan, and Yoram Singer. 2011. Adaptive subgradient methods for online learning and stochastic optimization. *The Journal of Machine Learning Research*, 12:2121–2159.

Miao Fan, Deli Zhao, Qiang Zhou, Zhiyuan Liu, Thomas Fang Zheng, and Edward Y Chang. 2014. Distant supervision for relation extraction with matrix completion. In *Proceedings of the 52nd Annual Meeting of the Association for Computational Linguistics*, volume 1, pages 839–849.

Kuzman Ganchev, Joao Graca, Jennifer Gillenwater, and Ben Taskar. 2010. Posterior regularization for structured latent variable models. *Journal of Machine Learning Research (JMLR)*, July.

Dan Garrette, Katrin Erk, and Raymond Mooney. 2011. Integrating logical representations with probabilistic information using markov logic. In *Proceedings of the Ninth International Conference on Computational Semantics*, pages 105–114. Association for Computational Linguistics.

Edward Grefenstette. 2013. Towards a formal distributional semantics: Simulating logical calculi with tensors. In *Proceedings of the Second Joint Conference on Lexical and Computational Semantics*, pages 1–10.

Karl Moritz Hermann and Phil Blunsom. 2013. The role of syntax in vector space models of compositional semantics. In *Proc. of ACL*, pages 894–904.

Jochen Hipp, Ulrich Güntzer, and Gholamreza Nakhaeizadeh. 2000. Algorithms for association rule mininga general survey and comparison. *ACM sigkdd explorations newsletter*, 2(1):58–64.

Pascal Hitzler, Steffen Hölldobler, and Anthony Karel Seda. 2004. Logic programs and connectionist networks. *Journal of Applied Logic*, 2(3):245–272.

Raphael Hoffmann, Congle Zhang, Xiao Ling, Luke Zettlemoyer, and Daniel S. Weld. 2011. Knowledge-based weak supervision for information extraction of overlapping relations. In *Annual Meeting of the Association for Computational Linguistics (ACL)*.

Steffen Hölldobler, Yvonne Kalinke, and Hans-Peter Störr. 1999. Approximating the semantics of logic programs by recurrent neural networks. *Appl. Intell.*, 11(1):45–58.

Mike Lewis and Mark Steedman. 2013. Combined distributional and logical semantics. In *Transactions of the Association for Computational Linguistics*, volume 1, pages 179–192.

Gideon S. Mann and Andrew McCallum. 2008. Generalized expectation criteria for semi-supervised learning of conditional random fields. In *Annual Meeting of the Association for Computational Linguistics (ACL)*, pages 870–878.

Mike Mintz, Steven Bills, Rion Snow, and Daniel Jurafsky. 2009. Distant supervision for relation extraction without labeled data. In *Association for Computational Linguistics (ACL)*.

Jeff Mitchell and Mirella Lapata. 2008. Vector-based models of semantic composition. In *Proc. of ACL*, pages 236–244.

Maximilian Nickel, Volker Tresp, and Hans-Peter Kriegel. 2012. Factorizing yago: scalable machine learning for linked data. In *Proc. of WWW*, pages 271–280.

Frederick Reiss, Sriram Raghavan, Rajasekar Krishnamurthy, Huaiyu Zhu, and Shivakumar Vaithyanathan. 2008. An algebraic approach to rule-based information extraction. In *International Conference on Data Engineering (ICDE)*, pages 933–942, April.

Matthew Richardson and Pedro Domingos. 2006. Markov logic networks. *Machine Learning*, 62(1-2):107–136.

Sebastian Riedel, Limin Yao, Andrew McCallum, and Benjamin M Marlin. 2013. Relation extraction with matrix factorization and universal schemas. In *Proceedings of NAACL-HLT*, pages 74–84.

Tim Rocktäschel, Matko Bosnjak, Sameer Singh, and Sebastian Riedel. 2014. Low-Dimensional Embeddings of Logic. In *ACL Workshop on Semantic Parsing (SP'14)*.

Evan Sandhaus. 2008. The New York Times annotated corpus. *Linguistic Data Consortium*.

Stefan Schoenmackers, Oren Etzioni, and Daniel S. Weld. 2008. Scaling textual inference to the web. In *Empirical Methods in Natural Language Processing (EMNLP)*.

Stefan Schoenmackers, Jesse Davis, Oren Etzioni, and Daniel Weld. 2010. Learning first-order horn clauses from web text. In *Empirical Methods in Natural Language Processing (EMNLP)*.

Sameer Singh, Dustin Hillard, and Chris Leggetter. 2010. Minimally-supervised extraction of entities from text advertisements. In *North American Chapter of the Association for Computational Linguistics - Human Language Technologies (NAACL HLT)*.

Richard Socher, Danqi Chen, Christopher D. Manning, and Andrew Y. Ng. 2013. Reasoning with neural tensor networks for knowledge base completion. In *NIPS*, pages 926–934.

Mihai Surdeanu, Julie Tibshirani, Ramesh Nallapati, and Christopher D. Manning. 2012. Multi-instance multi-label learning for relation extraction. In *Empirical Methods in Natural Language Processing (EMNLP)*.

Geoffrey G Towell and Jude W Shavlik. 1994. Knowledge-based artificial neural networks. *Artificial intelligence*, 70(1):119–165.

Johanna Völker and Mathias Niepert. 2011. Statistical schema induction. In *The Semantic Web: Research and Applications*, pages 124–138. Springer.

Wentao Wu, Hongsong Li, Haixun Wang, and Kenny Q Zhu. 2012. Probase: A probabilistic taxonomy for text understanding. In *Proceedings of the 2012 ACM SIGMOD International Conference on Management of Data*, pages 481–492. ACM.

Limin Yao, Aria Haghighi, Sebastian Riedel, and Andrew McCallum. 2011. Structured relation discovery using generative models. In *Proceedings of the Conference on Empirical methods in natural language processing (EMNLP '11)*, July.

Luke S Zettlemoyer and Michael Collins. 2005. Learning to map sentences to logical form: Structured classification with probabilistic categorial grammars. In *Uncertainty in Artifical Intelligence (UAI)*.

# Unsupervised Entity Linking with Abstract Meaning Representation

**Xiaoman Pan[1], Taylor Cassidy[2], Ulf Hermjakob[3], Heng Ji[1], Kevin Knight[3]**
[1]Computer Science Department, Rensselaer Polytechnic Institute
{panx2,jih}@rpi.edu
[2]IBM Research & Army Research Laboratory
taylor.cassidy.civ@mail.mil
[3]Information Sciences Institute, University of Southern California
{ulf,knight}@isi.edu

## Abstract

Most successful Entity Linking (EL) methods aim to link mentions to their referent entities in a structured Knowledge Base (KB) by comparing their respective contexts, often using similarity measures. While the KB structure is given, current methods have suffered from impoverished information representations on the mention side. In this paper, we demonstrate the effectiveness of Abstract Meaning Representation (AMR) (Banarescu et al., 2013) to select high quality sets of entity "collaborators" to feed a simple similarity measure (Jaccard) to link entity mentions. Experimental results show that AMR captures contextual properties discriminative enough to make linking decisions, without the need for EL training data, and that system with AMR parsing output outperforms hand labeled traditional semantic roles as context representation for EL. Finally, we show promising preliminary results for using AMR to select sets of "coherent" entity mentions for collective entity linking [1].

## 1 Introduction

The Entity Linking (EL) task (Ji et al., 2010; Ji et al., 2011; Ji et al., 2014) aims at automatically linking each named entity mention appearing in a *source* text document to its unique referent in a *target* knowledge base (KB). For example, consider the following sentence posted to a discussion forum during the 2012 U.S. presidential election: "*Where would McCain be without Sarah?*". An Entity Linker should link the entity mentions "*McCain*" and "*Sarah*" to the entities `John McCain` and `Sarah Palin`, respectively, which serve as unique identifiers for the real people.

A typical EL system works as follows. Given a mention $m$ (a string in a source document), the top $N$ most likely entity referents from the KB are enumerated based on prior knowledge about which entities are most likely referred to using $m$. The candidate entities are re-ranked to ultimately link each mention to the top entity in its candidate list. Re-ranking consists of two key elements: *context representation* and *context comparison*. For a given mention, candidate entities are re-ranked based on a comparison of information obtained from the context of $m$ with known structured and/or unstructured information associated with the top $N$ KB entities, which can be considered the "context" of the KB entity[2]. The basic intuition is that the entity referents of $m$ and related mentions should be similarly connected in the KB.

However, there might be many entity mentions in the context of a target entity mention that could potentially be leveraged for disambiguation. In this paper, we show that a deeper semantic knowledge representation - including the Abstract Meaning Representation (AMR) (Banarescu et al., 2013) - can capture contextual properties that are discriminative enough to disambiguate entity mentions that current state-of-the-art systems cannot handle, without the need for EL training data. Specifically, for a given

[1]The web service of this EL system is at: blender02.cs.rpi.edu:3300 and some related AMR tools are at: github.com/panx27/amr-reader

[2]Most work uses Wikipedia and related resources to derive the KB, prior link likelihood, and entity information (e.g., Wikipedia article text and infoboxes).



*Human Language Technologies: The 2015 Annual Conference of the North American Chapter of the ACL*, pages 1130–1139,
Denver, Colorado, May 31 – June 5, 2015. 

entity mention, using AMR provides a rich context representation, facilitating the selection of an optimal set of *collaborator* entity mentions, i.e., those co-occurring mentions most useful for disambiguation. In previous approaches, collaborator sets have tended to be too narrow or too broad, introducing noise. We then use unsupervised graph inference for context comparison, achieving results comparable with state-of-the-art supervised methods and substantially outperforming context representation based on traditional Semantic Role Labeling.

In addition, most state-of-the-art EL approaches now rely on *collective inference*, where a set of *coherent mentions* are linked simultaneously by choosing an "optimal" or maximally "coherent" set of named entity targets - one target entity for each mention in the coherent set. We show preliminary results suggesting that AMR is effective for the partitioning of all mentions in a document into coherent sets for collective linking.

We evaluate our approach using both human and automatic AMR annotation, limiting target named entity types to person (PER), organization (ORG), and geo-political entities (GPE) [3].

## 2 Related Work

In most recent collective inference methods for EL (e.g., (Kulkarni et al., 2009; Pennacchiotti and Pantel, 2009; Fernandez et al., 2010; Radford et al., 2010; Cucerzan, 2011; Guo et al., 2011; Han and Sun, 2011; Ratinov et al., 2011; Chen and Ji, 2011; Kozareva et al., 2011; Dalton and Dietz, 2013)), the target entity mention's "collaborators" may simply include all mentions which co-occur in the same discourse (sentence, paragraph or document) (Ratinov et al., 2011; Nguyen et al., 2012). But this approach usually introduces many irrelevant mentions, and it's very difficult to automatically determine the scope of discourse. In contrast, some recent work exploited more restricted measures by only choosing those mentions which are topically related (Cassidy et al., 2012; Xu et al., 2012), bear a relation from a fixed set (Cheng and Roth, 2013), coreferential (Nguyen et al., 2012; Huang et al., 2014), socially related (Cassidy et al., 2012; Huang et al., 2014), dependent (Ling et al., 2014), or a combination of these through meta-paths (Huang et al., 2014). These measures can collect more precise collaborators but suffer from low coverage of predefined information templates and the unsatisfying quality of state-of-the-art coreference resolution, relation and event extraction.

In this paper, we demonstrate that AMR is an appropriate and elegant way to acquire, select, represent and organize deeper knowledge in text. Together with our novel utilization of the rich structures in merged KBs, the whole framework carries rich enough evidence for effective EL, without the need for any labeled data, collective inference, or sophisticated similarity.

## 3 Knowledge Network Construction from Source

Abstract Meaning Representation (AMR) (Banarescu et al., 2013) is a sembanking language that captures whole sentence meanings in a rooted, directed, labeled, and (predominantly) acyclic graph structure. AMR utilizes multi-layer linguistic analysis such as PropBank frames, non-core semantic roles, coreference, named entity annotation, modality and negation to represent the semantic structure of a sentence. AMR strives for a more logical, less syntactic representation. Compared to traditional dependency parsing and semantic role labeling, the nodes in AMR are entities instead of words, and the edge types are much more fine-grained[4]. AMR thus captures deeper meaning compared with other representations more commonly used to represent mention context in EL.

We use AMR to represent semantic information about entity mentions expressed in their textual context. Specifically, given an entity mention $m$, we use a rule based method to construct a Knowledge Network, which is a star-shaped graph with $m$ at the hub, with leaf nodes obtained from entity mentions reachable by AMR graph traversal from $m$, as well as AMR node attributes such as entity type. A subset of the leaf nodes are selected as $m$'s collaborators using rules presented in the following subsec-

[3]The mapping from AMR entity types to these three main types is at: amr.isi.edu/lib/ne-type-sc.txt

[4]AMR distinguishes between entities and concepts, the former being instances of the latter. We consider AMR concepts as entity mentions, and use AMR entity annotation for coreference resolution.

tions. Note that while we only evaluate linking of PER, ORG, and GPE entities, collaborators may be of any type. We also outline preliminary efforts to use AMR to create sets of coherent entity mentions.

In each of the following subsections we describe elements of AMR useful for context representation in EL. For each element we explain how our current system makes use of it (primarily, by using it to add entity mentions to a particular entity mention's set of collaborators). In doing so, we mainly refer to several examples from political discussion forums about "*Mitt Romney*", "*Ron Paul*" and "*Gary Johnson*". Their AMR graphs are depicted in Figure 1.

### 3.1 Entity Nodes

Each AMR node represents an entity mention, and contains its canonical name as inferred from sentential context. This property is called *name expansion*. Consider the following sentence: "*Indonesia lies in a zone where the* ***Eurasian***, ***Philippine*** *and* ***Pacific*** *plates meet and occasionally shift, causing earthquakes and sometimes generating tsunamis.*". Here, the nodes representing the three plates will be labeled as "*Eurasian Plate*", "*Philippine Plate*" and "*Pacific Plate*" respectively, even though these strings do not occur in the sentence. Note that these labels may be recovered primarily by appealing to syntactic reasoning, without consulting a KB. In our implementation we consider these expanded names as mentions (these strings supersede raw mentions as input to the salience based candidate enumeration (Section 5.2)). Because the initial enumeration of entity candidates depends heavily on the mention's surface form, independent of context, name expansion will help us link "*Philippine*" to "`Philippine Sea Plate`" as opposed to the country.

An AMR node also contains an entity type. AMR defines 8 main entity types (Person, Organization, Location, Facility, Event, Product, Publication, Natural object, Other) and over one hundred fine-grained subtypes. For example, company, government organization, military, criminal organization, political party, school, university, research institute, team and league are subtypes of organization. The fine-grained entity types defined in AMR help us restrict KB entity candidates for a given mention by encouraging entity type matching. For example, in "*The* ***Yuri dolgoruky*** *is the first in a series of new nuclear submarines to be commissioned this*

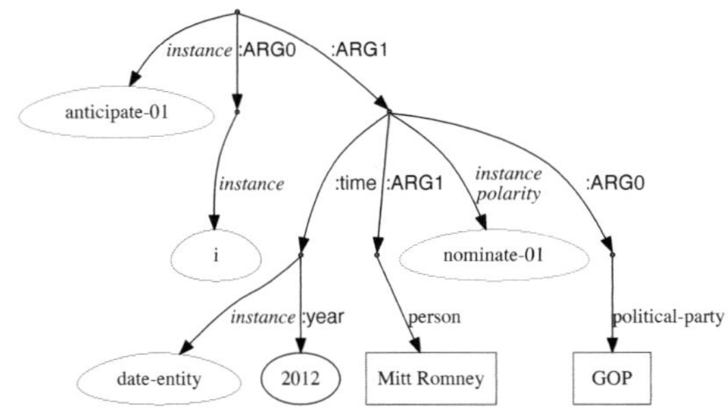


(a) *I am cautiously anticipating the GOP nominee in 2012 not to be* ***Mitt Romney***.

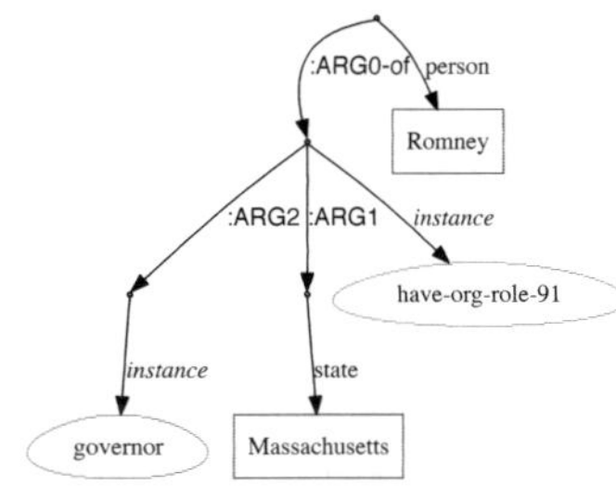


(b) ***Romney*** *was the Governor of Massachusetts...*

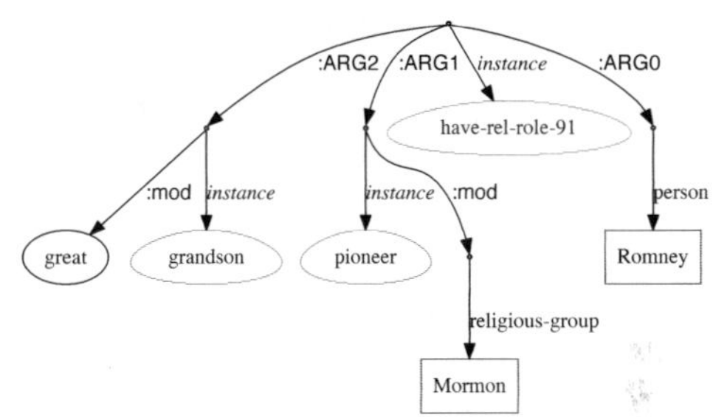


(c) ***Romney*** *is the great-great-grandson of a Mormon pioneer...*

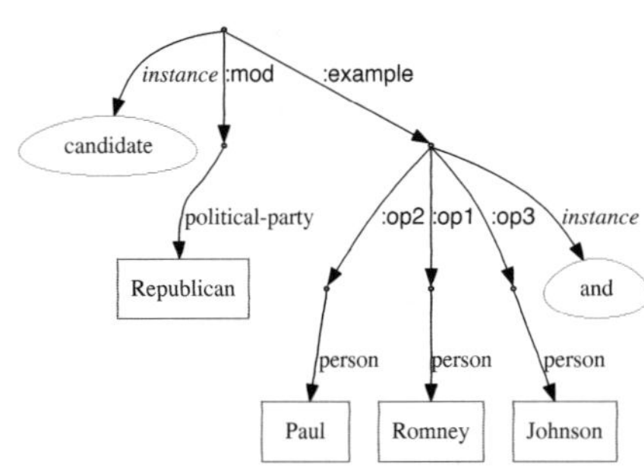


(d) *Republican candidates like* ***Romney***, ***Paul***, *and* ***Johnson***...

Figure 1: AMR for the Walk-through Example

*year but the bulava nuclear-armed missile developed to equip the submarine has failed tests and the deployment prospects are uncertain.*", AMR labels "*Yuri dolgoruky*" as a product instead of a person. We manually mapped AMR entity types to equivalent DBpedia types to inform type matching restrictions [5]. However, to make our context comparison algorithm less dependent on the quality of this mapping, and on automatic AMR name type assignment, we add a mention's type to its collaborators [6]. In future work we plan to investigate the effects of different type matching techniques, varying degrees of strictness.

### 3.2 Semantic Roles

AMR defines core roles based on the OntoNotes (Hovy et al., 2006) semantic role layer. Each predicate is associated with a sense and frame description. If a target entity mention $m$ and a context entity mention $n$ are both playing core roles for the same predicate, we consider $n$ as a collaborator of $m$. Consider the following post: "*Did **Palin** apologize to **Giffords**? He needs to conduct a beer summit between **Palin** and **NBC**.*". We add "*Giffords*" and "*NBC*" as collaborators of "*Palin*", because they play core roles in both the "*apologize-01*" and "*meet-03*" events.

AMR defines new core semantic roles which did not exist in PropBank (Palmer et al., 2005), NomBank (Meyers et al., 2004), or Ontonotes (Hovy et al., 2006). Intuitively, the following special roles should provide discriminative collaborators:

- The ARG2 role of the *have-org-role-91* frame indicates the title held by an entity (ARG0), such as President and Governor, within a particular organization (ARG1).
- ARG2 and ARG3 of *have-rel-role-91* are used to describe two related entities of the same type, such as family members.

AMR defines a rich set of general semantic relations through non-core semantic roles. We choose the following subset of non-core roles to provide collaborators for entity mentions: *domain*, *mod*, *cause*, *concession*, *condition*, *consist-of*, *extent*, *part*, *purpose*, *degree*, *manner*, *medium*, *instrument*, *ord*, *poss*, *quant*, *subevent*, *subset*, *topic*.

[5]The mapping from three main types and AMR entity types to Dbpedia types is at: nlp.cs.rpi.edu/amrel/dbtype.txt

[6]A more strict approach might disallow type mismatches between entity mentions and their target KB entities outright.

### 3.3 Background Time and Location

AMR provides rich temporal and spatial information about entities and events. Types instantiated in AMR include time, year, month, day, source, destination, path and location. We exploit time and location entities as collaborators for entity mentions when they each play a role in the same predicate. For example, in the following post, the time role of the "*die-01*" event is "*2008*": "*I just Read of Clark's death in 2008*". We can link "*Clark*" to `Arthur C Clark` in the KB, which contains the triple: <`Arthur C Clark`, *date-of-death*, 2008-03-19> (see Section 4). Similarly, it's very challenging to link the abbreviation "*BMKG*", in the following sentence, to the correct target entity `Indonesian Agency for Meteorology, Climatology and Geophysics`, whose headquarters are listed as `Jakarta` in the KB: "*It keeps on shaking. **Jakarta** BMKG spokesman Mujuhidin said*". Here, "*Jakarta*" is added as a collaborator of "*BMKG*" since AMR labels it as the location of the organization, which facilitates the correct link because in DBpedia `Jakarta` is listed as its headquarter.

Authors often assume that readers will infer implicit temporal information about events. In fact, half of the events extracted by information extraction (IE) systems lack time arguments (Ji et al., 2009). Therefore if an AMR parse includes no time information, we use the document creation time as an additional collaborator for mention in question. For example, knowing the document creation time "*2005-06-05*" can help us link "*Hsiung Feng*" in the following sentence "*The BBC reported that Taiwan has successfully test fired the **Hsiung Feng**, its first cruise missile.*" to `Hsiung Feng IIE`, which was deployed in 2005. Similarly, we include document creation location as a global collaborator.

### 3.4 Coreference

For linking purposes, we treat a coreferential chain of mentions as a single "mention". In doing so, the collaborator set for the entire chain is computed as the union over all of the chain's mentions' collaborator sets. From here on we refer to a coreferential chain of mentions as simply a "mention".

AMR currently only represents sentence-level coreference resolution. In order to construct a knowledge network across sentences, we use the following heuristic rules. If two names have a substring match (on a token-wise basis with stop words removed), or one name consists of the initials of another in all capital letters, then we mark them as coreferential. We replace all names in a coreferential chain with their canonical name, which may have been derived via name expansion (Section 3.1): full names for people and abbreviations for organizations.

### 3.5 Knowledge Networks for Coherent Mentions

AMR defines a rich set of conjunction relations: "*and*", "*or*", "*contrast-01*", "*either*", "*compared to*", "*prep along with*", "*neither*", "*slash*", "*between*" and "*both*". These relations are often expressed between entities that have other relations in common. We therefore group mentions connected by conjunction relations into sets of coherent mentions. This representation is used only in preliminary experiments on collective entity linking.

Figure 2 shows the expanded knowledge network that includes results from individual networks for each of the coherent mentions from the walk-through example. For each coherent set, we merge the knowledge networks of all of its mentions [7].

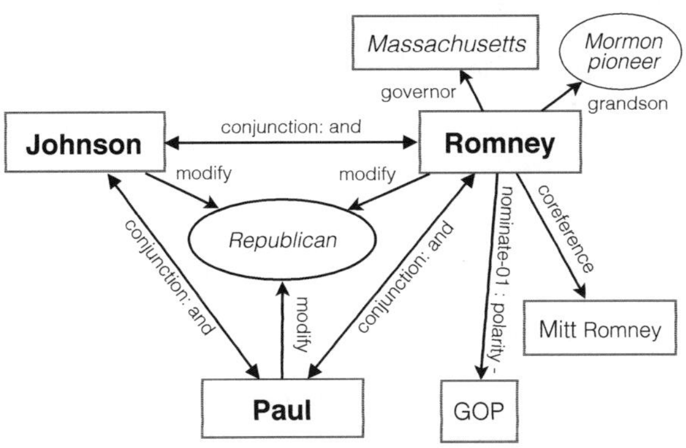


Figure 2: Knowledge Network for Mentions in Source

[7]recall that by mention, we mean a coreferential chain of mentions that may extend across sentences

## 4 Knowledge Network Construction from KB

We combine Wikipedia with derivative resources to create the KB. The KB is a single knowledge network in which nodes are entities (Wikipedia articles) or constant values (e.g. a dollar amount or date), and the edges represent relations. We use this structure for context representation for entities, which together with context representation for mentions (Section 3) feeds re-ranking based on context comparison.

The KB is formally represented by triples:

$$< Entity, EdgeLabel, Node >$$

where *Entity* is the entity's unique identifier, *EdgeLabel* is relation type, and *Node* is the corresponding relation value - either another Entity or a constant. These triples are derived from typed relations expressed within Wikipedia infoboxes, Templates, and Categories, untyped hyperlinks within Wikipedia article text, typed relations within DBpedia (dbpedia.org) and Freebase (www.freebase.com), and Google's "people also searched for" list [8]. Figure 3 shows a portion of the KB pertaining to the example in Figure 1.

In order to merge nodes from multiple KBs, we use the Wikipedia title as a primary key, and then use DBpedia *wikiPageID* and Freebase *Key* relations.

## 5 Linking Knowledge Networks

### 5.1 Overview

In this section we present our detailed algorithm to link each mention to a KB entity using a simple similarity measure over knowledge networks. Recall that a rule-based method has already been employed to construct star-shaped knowledge networks for individual mentions and entities (see sections 3 and 4; A KB knowledge network is the subnetwork of the entire KB centered at a candidate entity).

For each mention to be linked, an initial list of candidate entities are enumerated based on entity salience with respect to the mention, independent of mention context (Section 5.2)[9]. *Context collaborator* re-ranking proceeds in an unsupervised fashion

[8]In response to a query entity Google provides a list of entities that "people also search for" - we add them to the entity's network.

[9]Here, "mention" means coreferential chain of mentions.

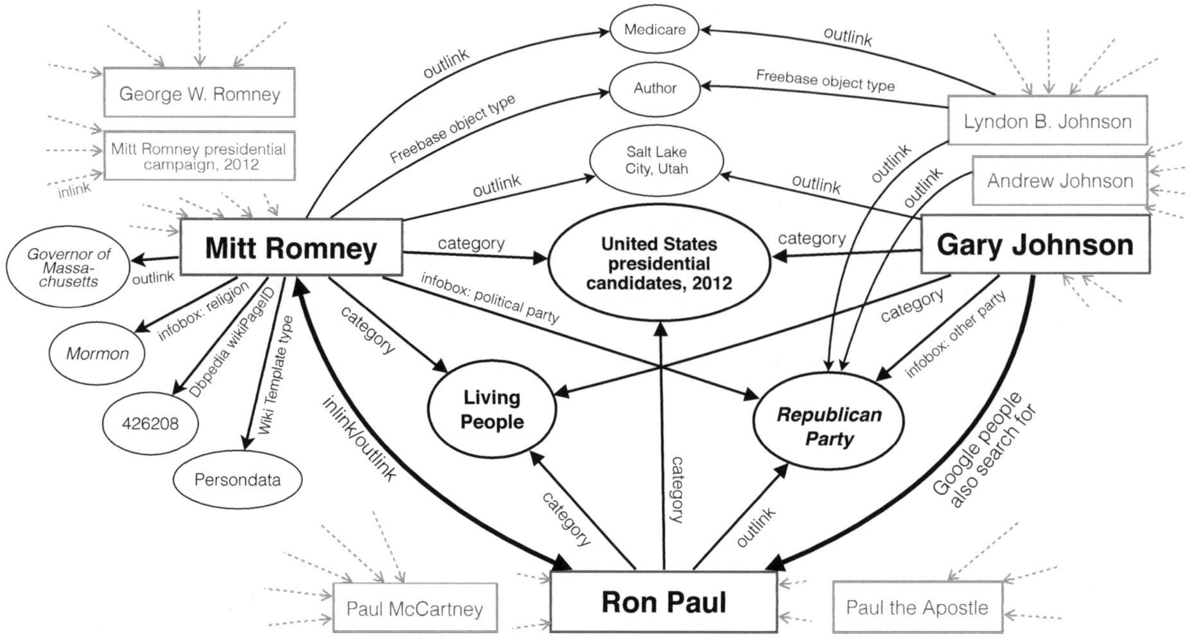


Figure 3: Knowledge Network for Entities in KB

agnostic to knowledge network edge labels using the Jaccard similarity measure computed between the mention and each entity, by taking their collaborator sets as inputs (Section 5.3).

We also describe *Context Coherence* re-ranking in terms of KB knowledge networks only, which constitutes preliminary steps toward unsupervised collective entity linking in section 5.4 based on the notion of coherence described in section 3.5. We leave a combination of the two re-ranking approaches to future work.

### 5.2 Salience

We use commonness (Medelyan and Legg, 2008) as a measure of context independent salience for each mention $m$, to generate an initial ranked list of candidate entities $E = (e_1, ..., e_N)$ where $N$ is the cutoff for number of candidates. In all experiments, we used N = 15 which can give us an oracle accuracy score 97.58%.

$$Commonness(m, e) = \frac{count(m, e)}{\sum_{e'} count(m, e')}$$

Here, $count(m, e)$ is the number of hyperlinks with anchor text $m$ and entity $e$ within all of Wikipedia. As illustrated in Figure 3, using this salience measure "*Romney*" is successfully linked to `Mitt Romney`. For the mention "*Paul*", the politician `Ron Paul` is ranked at top 2 (less popular than the musician `Paul McCartney`). For the mention "*Johnson*", the correct entity `Gary Johnson` is ranked at top 9, after more popular entities such as `Lyndon B. Johnson` and `Andrew Johnson`.

### 5.3 Context Collaborator Based Re-ranking

Context collaborator based re-ranking is driven by the similarity between mention and entity knowledge networks. We construct knowledge network $g(m)$ for each mention $m$, and knowledge network $g(e_i)$ for each entity candidate $e_i$ in $m$'s entity candidate list $E$. We re-rank $E$ according to Jaccard Similarity, which computes the similarity between $g(m)$ and $g(e_i)$:

$$J(g(m), g(e_i)) = \frac{|g(m) \cap g(e_i)|}{|g(m) \cup g(e_i)|}$$

Note that the edge labels (e.g., *nominate-01* for a mention, or *infobox: religion* for an entity) are ignored, as the similarity metric operates over sets of collaborators (leaf nodes in the knowledge networks). For set intersection and union computation, elements are treated as lists of lower-cased tokens with stop words removed, and two elements are considered equal if and only if they have one or more token in common. Due to the support from their neighbor Republican in the KB (Figure 3) which matches the neighbor "*Republican*" of mentions "*Paul*" and "*Johnson*" (Figure 2), Ron Paul and Gary Johnson are promoted to top 1 and top 3 respectively. Gary Johnson is still behind two former U.S. presidents Andrew Johnson and Lyndon B. Johnson who also shares the neighbor Republican in the KB.

### 5.4 Context Coherence Based Re-ranking

Context coherence based re-ranking is driven by the similarity among KB entities. Let $R_m$ be a set of coherent entity mentions, and $R_E$ be the set of corresponding entity candidate lists, which are generated according to salience. Given $R_E$, we generate every combination of possible top candidate lists for the mentions in $R_m$, and denote the set of these combinations $C_m$. Formally, $C_m$ is the Cartesian product of all candidate lists $E \in R_E$. In the walk-through example, $R_m$ contains ["*Romney*", "*Paul*", "*Johnson*"], and $C_m$ contains [Mitt Romney, Ron Paul, Gary Johnson], [Mitt Romney, Paul McCartney, Lyndon Johnson], etc. We compute coherence for each combination $c \in C_m$ as Jaccard Similarity, by applying a form of Equation 5.3 generalized to take any number of arguments to the set of knowledge networks for all entities in $c$, i.e., $\{g(e)|e \in c\}$. The highest similarity combination is selected, yielding a top candidate for each $m \in R_m$. For example, compared to Andrew Johnson and Lyndon Johnson, Gary Johnson is more coherently connected with Mitt Romney and Ron Paul, therefore it is promoted to top 1 with the coherence measure.

## 6 Experiments

### 6.1 Data And Scoring Metric

For our experiments we use a publicly available AMR R3 corpus (LDC2013E117) that includes manual EL annotations for all entity mentions (LDC2014E15) [10].

For evaluation we used all the discussion forum posts (DF), and news documents (News) that were sorted according to alphabetic order of document IDs and taken as a tenth. The detailed data statistics are presented in Table 1 [11].

| | PER | ORG | GPE | All |
|---|---|---|---|---|
| News | 159 | 187 | 679 | 1,025 |
| DF | 235 | 129 | 224 | 588 |
| All | 394 | 316 | 903 | 1,613 |

Table 1: Total # of Entity Mentions in Test Set

For each mention, we check whether the KB entity returned by an approach is correct or not. We compute accuracy for an approach as the proportion of mentions correctly linked.

### 6.2 Experiment Results

We focus primarily on context collaborator based reranking results. We compare our results with several baseline and state-of-the-art approaches in Table 2. In Table 3 we present preliminary results for collective linking.

Our Unsupervised Context Collaborator Approach substantially outperforms the popularity based methods. More importantly, we see that AMR provides the best context representation for collaborator selection. Even system AMR outperformed not only baseline co-occurrence based collaborator selection methods, but also outperforms the collaborator selection method based on human annotated core semantic roles. Figure 4 depicts accuracy increases as more AMR annotation is used in selecting collaborators. From the commonness baseline, additional knowledge about individual names leads to substantial gains followed by additional gains after incorporating links denoting semantic roles. Note that coreference here includes cross-sentence co-reference not based on AMR (Section 3.4). Furthermore, the results using human annotated AMR outperform the state-of-the-art supervised methods trained from a large scale EL training corpus, which rely on collective inference[12]. These results all verify the importance of incorporating a wider range of deep knowledge. Finally, Table 2 presents results in which our

[10]EL annotations are available to KBP shared task registrants (nlp.cs.rpi.edu/kbp/2014) via Linguistic Data Consortium (www.ldc.upenn.edu).

[11]The list of document IDs in the test set is at: nlp.cs.rpi.edu/amrel/testdoc.txt

[12]Note that the ground-truth EL annotation for the test set was created by correcting the output from supervised methods, so it may even favor these methods.

| Approach | | Definition | News | DF | Total |
|---|---|---|---|---|---|
| Popularity | Commonness | based on the popularity measure as described in section 5.2. | 89.76 | 68.99 | 82.20 |
| | Google Search | use the top Wikipedia page returned by Google search using the mention as a key word. | 88.10 | 77.17 | 84.12 |
| Supervised | State-of-the-art | supervised re-ranking using multi-level linguistic features for collaborators and collective inference, trained from 20,000 entity mentions from TAC-KBP2009-2014. We combined two systems (Chen and Ji, 2011; Cheng and Roth, 2013) using rules to highlight their strengths. | 93.07 | 87.41 | **91.01** |
| Unsupervised Context Collaborator Approach | Sen. Level Cooccurrence | sentence-level co-occurrence based collaborator selection | 93.17 | 73.25 | 85.92 |
| | | (collaborators limited to human AMR-labeled named entities) | 90.77 | 70.31 | 83.31 |
| | Doc. Level Cooccurrence | document-level co-occurrence based collaborator selection | 90.05 | 69.86 | 82.69 |
| | | (collaborators limited to human AMR-labeled named entities) | 87.51 | 69.37 | 80.90 |
| | Human AMR | using human annotated AMR nodes and edges. | 93.56 | 86.88 | **91.13** |
| | System AMR | using AMR nodes and edges automatically generated by an AMR parser (Flanigan et al., 2014). | 90.15 | 85.69 | **88.52** |
| | Human SRL | using human annotated core semantic roles defined in PropBank (Palmer et al., 2005) and NomBank (Meyers et al., 2004): ARG0, ARG1, ARG2, ARG4 and ARG5. | 93.27 | 71.21 | 85.24 |
| Unsupervised Combined Approach | Human AMR | coherence approach used where possible (215 mentions), collaborator approach elsewhere (remaining 1398 mentions), using human annotated AMR nodes and edges. | 94.34 | 88.25 | **92.12** |

Table 2: Accuracy (%) on Test Set (1613 mentions)

context coherence method is used where possible (i.e., those 215 mentions that are members of coherent sets according to our criteria as described in Section 3.5), and the context collaborator approach based on human AMR annotation is applied elsewhere.

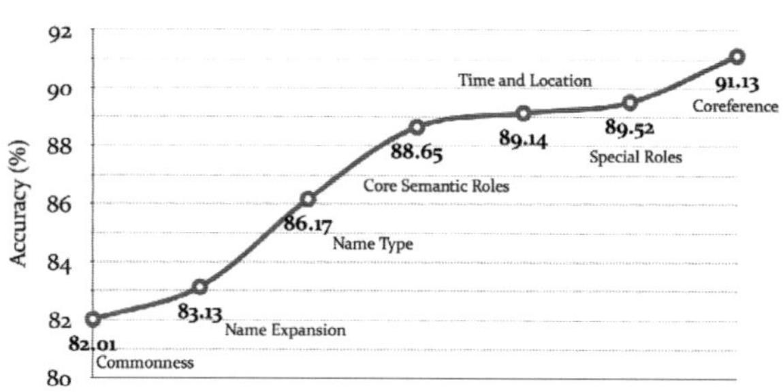


Figure 4: AMR Annotation Layers Effects on Accuracy

Table 3 focuses on the 215 mentions that met our narrow criteria for forming a coherent set of mentions. We applied the context coherence based re-ranking method (Section 5.4) to collectively link those mentions. This approach substantially outperforms the co-occurrence baseline, and even outperforms the context collaborator approach applied to those 215 mentions, especially for discussion forum data.

| Approach Description | News | DF | All |
|---|---|---|---|
| **Coherence**: coherence set built from within-sentence collaborators limited to human AMR-labeled Named Entities. | 72.64 | 76.85 | 75.47 |
| **Coherence**: coherence set built from human AMR conjunctions (Sec. 3.5) | 96.73 | 95.16 | **96.28** |
| **Collaborator**: used coherent set based on human AMR as collaborators. | 91.50 | 82.26 | 88.84 |

Table 3: Context Coherence Accuracy (%) on 215 Mentions which Can Form Coherent Sets

### 6.3 Remaining Error Analysis and Discussion

A challenging source of errors pertains to the *knowledge gap* between the source text and KB. News and social media are source text genres that tend to focus on new information, trending topics, breaking events, or even mundane details about the entity. In contrast, the KB usually provides a snapshot summarizing only the entity's most representative and important facts. A source-KB similarity driven approach alone will not suffice when a mention's context differs substantially from anything on the KB side. AMR annotation's synthesis of words and phrases from the surface texts into concepts only provides a first step toward bridging the knowledge gap. Successful linking may require (1) reasoning using general knowledge, or (2) retrieval of other sources that contain additional useful linking information. Table 4 illustrates two relevant examples

| Type | Source | Knowledge Base |
|---|---|---|
| General Knowledge | **[Christies]m** denial of ***marriage*** privledges to ***gays*** will alienate independents and his "I wanted to have the people ***vote*** on it" will ring hollow. | **[Chris Christie]e** has said that he favoured New Jersey's law allowing ***same-sex*** couples to form civil unions, but would veto any bill legalizing ***same-sex marriage*** in New Jersey. |
| External Knowledge | Translation out of hype-speak: some kook made ***threatening*** noises at **[Brownback]m** and go ***arrested***. | **[Samuel Dale "Sam" Brownback]e** (born September 12, 1956) is an American politician, the 46th and current ***Governor*** of Kansas. |

Table 4: Examples of Knowledge Gap

that our system does not correctly link. In the first example, if we don't already know that Christie is the topic of discussion, as humans we might use our general knowledge that "governors veto bills" to pick the correct entity. Using this type of knowledge presents interesting challenges (e.g., governors don't always veto bills, nor are they the only ones who can do so). In the second example, the rumor about this politician is not important enough to be reported in his Wikipedia page. We might first figure out, using cross-document coreference techniques, that a news article with the headline "*Man Accused Of Making Threatening Phone Call To Kansas Gov.* ***Sam Brownback*** *May Face Felony Charge...*" is talking about the same rumor. Then we might use biographical facts (e.g., Brownback is the governor of Kansas) from the article to enrich Brownback's knowledge network on the source side.

Sometimes helpful neighbor concepts are omitted because the current collaborator selection criteria are too restricted. For example, "*armed*" and "*conflicts*" are informative words for linking "*The Stockholm Institute*" to `Stockholm International Peace Research Institute` in the following sentence "***The Stockholm Institute*** *stated that 23 of 25 major armed conflicts in the world in 2000 occurred in impoverished nations.*", but they were not selected as context collaborators. In addition, our cross-sentence coreference resolution is currently limited to proper names. Expanding it to include nominals could further enrich context collaborators to overcome some remaining errors. For example, in the sentence, "*The first woman to serve on* ***SCOTUS***", if we know "*The first woman*" is coreferential with "*Sandra Day O'Connor*" in the previous sentence, we can link "*SCOTUS*" to `Supreme Court of the United States` instead of `Scotus College`.

## 7 Conclusions and Future Work

EL requires a representation of the relations among entities in text. We showed that the Abstract Meaning Representation (AMR) can better capture and represent the contexts of entity mentions for EL than previous approaches. We plan to improve AMR representation as well as automatic annotation. We showed that AMR enables EL performance comparable to the supervised state of the art using an unsupervised, non-collective approach. We plan to combine collaborator and coherence methods into a unified approach, and to use edge labels in knowledge networks for context comparison (note that the last of these is quite challenging due to normalization, polysemy, and semantic distance issues). We have only applied a subset of AMR representations to the EL task, but we aim to explore how more AMR knowledge can be used for other more challenging Information Extraction and Knowledge Base Population tasks.

## Acknowledgments

This work was supported by the U.S. DARPA DEFT Program No. FA8750-13-2-0041 and FA8750-13-2-0045, DARPA BOLT Program No. HR0011-12-C-0014, ARL NS-CTA No. W911NF-09-2-0053, NSF Awards IIS-0953149 and IIS-1523198, AFRL DREAM project, DHS CCICADA, gift awards from IBM, Google, Disney and Bosch. The views and conclusions contained in this document are those of the authors and should not be interpreted as representing the official policies, either expressed or implied, of the U.S. Government. The U.S. Government is authorized to reproduce and distribute reprints for Government purposes notwithstanding any copyright notation here on.

## References


L. Banarescu, C. Bonial, S. Cai, M. Georgescu, K. Griffitt, U. Hermjakob, K. Knight, P. Koehn, M. Palmer, and N. Schneider. 2013. Abstract meaning representation for sembanking. In *Proc. ACL 2013 Workshop on Linguistic Annotation and Interoperability with Discourse*.

T. Cassidy, H. Ji, L. Ratinov, A. Zubiaga, and H. Huang. 2012. Analysis and enhancement of wikification for microblogs with context expansion. In *Proc. International Conference on Computational Linguistics (COLING 2012)*.

Z. Chen and H. Ji. 2011. Collaborative ranking: A case study on entity linking. In *Proc. Empirical Methods in Natural Language Processing (EMNLP 2011)*.

X. Cheng and D. Roth. 2013. Relational inference for wikification. In *Proc. Empirical Methods in Natural Language Processing (EMNLP 2013)*.

S. Cucerzan. 2011. Tac entity linking by performing full-document entity extraction and disambiguation. In *Proc. Text Analysis Conference (TAC 2011)*.

J. Dalton and L. Dietz. 2013. A neighborhood relevance model for entity linking. In *Proc. Open Research Areas in Information Retrieval (OAIR 2013)*.

N. Fernandez, J. A. Fisteus, L. Sanchez, and E. Martin. 2010. Webtlab: A cooccurence-based approach to kbp 2010 entity-linking task. In *Proc. Text Analysis Conference (TAC 2010)*.

J. Flanigan, S. Thomson, J. Carbonell, C. Dyer, and N. A. Smith. 2014. A discriminative graph-based parser for the abstract meaning representation. In *Proc. Association for Computational Linguistics (ACL 2014)*.

Y. Guo, W. Che, T. Liu, and S. Li. 2011. A graph-based method for entity linking. In *Proc. International Joint Conference on Natural Language Processing (IJCNLP 2011)*.

X. Han and L. Sun. 2011. A generative entity-mention model for linking entities with knowledge base. In *Proc. Association for Computational Linguistics: Human Language Technologies (ACL-HLT 2011)*.

E.d Hovy, M. Marcus, M. Palmer, L. Ramshaw, and R. Weischedel. 2006. Ontonotes: The 90% solution. In *Proc. Human Language Technology conference - North American chapter of the Association for Computational Linguistics (HLT-NAACL 2006)*.

H. Huang, Y. Cao, X. Huang, H. Ji, and C. Lin. 2014. Collective tweet wikification based on semi-supervised graph regularization. In *Proc. Association for Computational Linguistics (ACL 2014)*.

H. Ji, R. Grishman, Z. Chen, and P. Gupta. 2009. Cross-document event extraction and tracking: Task, evaluation, techniques and challenges. In *Proc. Recent Advances in Natural Language Processing (RANLP 2009)*.

H. Ji, R. Grishman, H. T. Dang, K. Griffitt, and J. Ellis. 2010. Overview of the tac 2010 knowledge base population track. In *Proc. Text Analysis Conference (TAC 2010)*.

H. Ji, R. Grishman, and H. T. Dang. 2011. Overview of the tac 2011 knowledge base population track. In *Proc. Text Analysis Conference (TAC 2011)*.

H. Ji, J. Nothman, and H. Ben. 2014. Overview of tac-kbp2014 entity discovery and linking tasks. In *Proc. Text Analysis Conference (TAC 2014)*.

Z. Kozareva, K. Voevodski, and S. Teng. 2011. Class label enhancement via related instances. In *Proc. Empirical Methods in Natural Language Processing (EMNLP 2011)*.

S. Kulkarni, A. Singh, G. Ramakrishnan, and S. Chakrabarti. 2009. Collective annotation of wikipedia entities in web text. In *Proc. Knowledge Discovery and Data Mining (KDD 2009)*.

X. Ling, S. Singh, and D. S. Weld. 2014. Context representation for named entity linking. In *Proc. Pacific Northwest Regional NLP Workshop (NW-NLP 2014)*.

O. Medelyan and C. Legg. 2008. Integrating cyc and wikipedia: Folksonomy meets rigorously defined common-sense. In *Proc. AAAI 2008 Workshop on Wikipedia and Artificial Intelligence*.

A. Meyers, R. Reeves, C. Macleod, R. Szekely, V. Zielinska, B. Young, and R. Grishman. 2004. The nombank project: An interim report. In *Proc. HLT-NAACL 2004 Workshop on Frontiers in Corpus Annotation*.

H. Nguyen, H. Minha, T. Cao, and T. Nguyenb. 2012. Jvn-tdt entity linking systems at tac-kbp2012. In *Proc. Text Analysis Conference (TAC 2012)*.

M. Palmer, D. Gildea, and P. Kingsbury. 2005. The proposition bank: An annotated corpus of semantic roles. *Computational Linguistics*, 31(1):71–106.

M. Pennacchiotti and P. Pantel. 2009. Entity extraction via ensemble semantics. In *Proc. Empirical Methods in Natural Language Processing (EMNLP 2009)*.

W. Radford, B. Hachey, J. Nothman, M. Honnibal, and J. R. Curran. 2010. Cmcrc at tac10: Document-level entity linking with graph-based re-ranking. In *Proc. Text Analysis Conference (TAC 2010)*.

L. Ratinov, D. Roth, D. Downey, and M. Anderson. 2011. Local and global algorithms for disambiguation to wikipedia. In *Proc. Association for Computational Linguistics: Human Language Technologies (ACL-HLT 2011)*.

J. Xu, Q. Lu, J. Liu, and R. Xu. 2012. Nlpcomp in tac 2012 entity linking and slot-filling. In *Proc. Text Analysis Conference (TAC 2012)*.

# IDEST: Learning a Distributed Representation for Event Patterns

**Sebastian Krause***
LT Lab, DFKI
Alt-Moabit 91c
10559 Berlin, Germany
skrause@dfki.de

**Enrique Alfonseca Katja Filippova Daniele Pighin**
Google Research
Brandschenkestrasse 110
8810 Zurich, Switzerland
{ealfonseca,katjaf,biondo}@google.com

## Abstract

This paper describes IDEST, a new method for learning paraphrases of event patterns. It is based on a new neural network architecture that only relies on the weak supervision signal that comes from the news published on the same day and mention the same real-world entities. It can generalize across extractions from different dates to produce a robust paraphrase model for event patterns that can also capture meaningful representations for rare patterns. We compare it with two state-of-the-art systems and show that it can attain comparable quality when trained on a small dataset. Its generalization capabilities also allow it to leverage much more data, leading to substantial quality improvements.

## 1 Introduction

Most Open Information Extraction (Open-IE) systems (Banko et al., 2007) extract textual relational patterns between entities automatically (Fader et al., 2011; Mausam et al., 2012) and optionally organize them into paraphrase clusters. These pattern clusters have been found to be useful for Question Answering (Lin & Pantel, 2001; Fader et al., 2013) and relation extraction (Moro & Navigli, 2012; Grycner & Weikum, 2014), among other tasks.

A related Open-IE problem is that of automatically extracting and paraphrasing **event patterns**: those that describe changes in the state or attribute values of one or several entities. An existing approach lo learn paraphrases of event patterns is to build on the following weak supervision signal: news articles that were published on the same day and mention the same entities should contain good paraphrase candidates. Two state-of-the-art event paraphrasing systems that are based on this assumption are NEWSSPIKE (Zhang & Weld, 2013) and HEADY (Alfonseca et al., 2013; Pighin et al., 2014).

These two systems have a lot in common, yet they have never been compared with each other. They have specific weak and strong points, and there are many ways in which they are substantially different:

- *Scope of generalization.* In NEWSSPIKE the paraphrase clusters are learned separately for each publication day and entity set, and the system cannot generalize across events of the same type involving different entities occurring on the same or on different days. For example, if the event verbs *has married* and *wed* appear in news about two entities $A$ and $B$ marrying, and *has married* and *tied the knot with* appear in news involving two different entities $C$ and $D$, NEWSSPIKE is not able to infer that *wed* and *tied the knot with* are also paraphrases, unless a post-processing is done.

  HEADY overcomes this limitation thanks to a global model that learns event representations across different days and sets of entities. However, the global nature of the learning problem can incur into other drawbacks. First, training a global model is more costly and more difficult to parallelize. Second, relatively frequent patterns that erroneously co-occur with other patterns may have a negative impact on the final models, potentially resulting in noisier clusters. Lastly, low-frequency patterns are likely to be

*Work performed during an internship at Google



*Human Language Technologies: The 2015 Annual Conference of the North American Chapter of the ACL*, pages 1140–1149,
Denver, Colorado, May 31 – June 5, 2015. 

discarded as noisy in the final model. Overall, HEADY is better at capturing paraphrases from the head of the pattern distribution, and is likely to ignore most of the long tail where useful paraphrases can still be found.

- *Simplifying assumptions.* We already mentioned that the two systems share a common underlying assumption, i.e., that good paraphrase candidates can be found by looking at news published on the same day and mentioning the same entities. On top of this, NEWSSPIKE also assumes that better paraphrases are reported around spiky entities, verb tenses may not differ, there is one event mention per discourse, and others. These restrictions are not enforced by HEADY, where the common assumption is indeed even relaxed across days and entity sets.

- *Annotated data.* NEWSSPIKE requires hand-annotated data to train the parameters of a supervised model that combines the different heuristics, whereas HEADY does not need annotated data.

This paper describes IDEST, a new method for learning paraphrases of event patterns that is designed to combine the advantages of these two systems and compensate for their weaknesses. It is based on a new neural-network architecture that, like HEADY, only relies on the weak supervision signal that comes from the news published on the same day, requiring no additional heuristics or training data. Unlike NEWSSPIKE, it can generalize across different sets of extracted patterns, and each event pattern is mapped into a low-dimensional embedding space. This allows us to define a neighborhood around a pattern to find the ones that are closer in meaning.

IDEST produces a robust global model that can also capture meaningful representations for rare patterns, thus overcoming one of HEADY's main limitations. Our evaluation of the potential trade-off between local and global paraphrase models shows that comparably good results to NEWSSPIKE can be attained without relying on supervised training. At the same time, the ability of IDEST to produce a global model allows it to benefit from a much larger news corpus.

## 2 Related work

**Relational Open-IE** In an early attempt to move away from domain-specific, supervised IE systems, Riloff (1996) attempted to automatically find relational patterns on the web and other unstructured resources in an open domain setting. This idea has been further explored in more recent years by Brin (1999), Agichtein & Gravano (2000), Ravichandran & Hovy (2002) and Sekine (2006), among the others. Banko et al. (2007) introduced Open-IE and the TEXTRUNNER system, which extracted binary patterns using a few selection rules applied on the dependency tree. More recent systems such as REVERB (Fader et al., 2011) and OLLIE (Mausam et al., 2012) also define linguistically-motivated heuristics to find text fragments or dependency structures that can be used as relational patterns.

A natural extension to the previous work is to automatically identify which of the extracted patterns have the same meaning, by producing either a hard or a soft clustering. Lin & Pantel (2001) use the mutual information between the patterns and their observed slot fillers. Resolver (Yates & Etzioni, 2007) introduces a probabilistic model called the Extracted Shared Property (ESP) where the probability that two instances or patterns are paraphrases is based on how many properties or instances they share. USP (Poon & Domingos, 2009) produces a clustering by greedily merging the extracted relations. Yao et al. (2012) employ topic models to learn a probabilistic model that can capture also the ambiguity of polysemous patterns. More recent work also organizes patterns in clusters or taxonomies using distributional methods on the pattern contexts or entities extracted (Moro & Navigli, 2012; Nakashole et al., 2012), or implicitly clusters relational text patterns via the learning of latent feature vectors for entity tuples and relations, in a setting similar to knowledge-base completion (Riedel et al., 2013).

A shared difficulty for systems that cluster patterns based on the arguments they select is that it is very hard for them to distinguish between identity and entailment. If one pattern entails another, both are likely to be observed in the corpus involving the same entity sets. A typical example illustrating this problem is the two patterns $e_1$ *married* $e_2$ and $e_1$

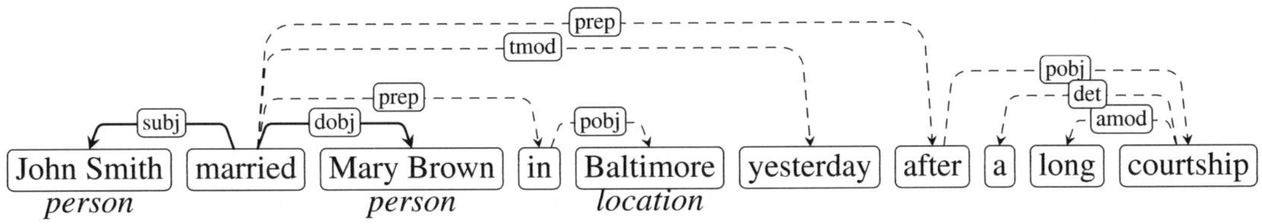


Figure 1: Example sentence, and extraction (the nodes connected through solid dependency edges).

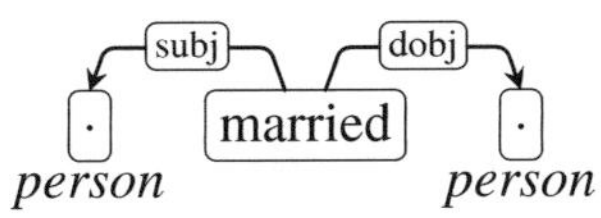


Figure 2: Example pattern that encodes a wedding event between two people.

*dated* $e_2$, which can be observed involving the same pairs of entities, but which carry a different meaning. As discussed below, relying on the temporal dimension (given by the publication date of the input documents) is one way to overcome this problem.

**Event patterns and Open-IE** Although some earlier work uses the temporal dimension of text as filters to improve precision of relational pattern clusters, NEWSSPIKE (Zhang & Weld, 2013) and HEADY (Alfonseca et al., 2013; Pighin et al., 2014) fully rely on it as its main supervision signal. In order to compare the two approaches, we will start by defining some terms:

- An **event pattern** encodes an expression that describes an event. It can be either a linear surface pattern or a lexico-syntactic pattern, and can possibly include entity-type restrictions on the arguments. For example, Figure 2 represents a binary pattern that corresponds to a wedding event between two people.

- An **extraction** is a pattern instance obtained from an input sentence, involving specific entities. For example, the subgraph represented with solid dependency edges in Figure 1 is an extraction corresponding to the pattern in Figure 2.

- An **Extracted Event Candidate Set** (EEC-Set (Zhang & Weld, 2013), or just EEC for brevity) is the set of extractions obtained from news articles published on the same day, and involving the same set of entities.

- Two extractions are **co-occurrent** if there is at least one EEC that contains both of them.

NEWSSPIKE produces extractions from the input documents using REVERB (Fader et al., 2011). The EECs are generated from the titles and all the sentences of the first paragraph of the documents published on the same day. From each EEC, potentially one paraphrase cluster may be generated. The model is a factor graph that captures several additional heuristics. Integer Lineal Programming (ILP) is then used to find the Maximum a Posteriori (MAP) solution for each set of patterns, and model parameters are trained using a labeled corpus that contains 500 of these sets.

Regarding HEADY, it only considers titles and first sentences for pattern extraction and trains a two-layer Noisy-OR Bayesian Network, in which the hidden nodes represent possible event types, and the observed nodes represent the textual patterns. A maximum-likelihood model is the one in which highly co-occurring patterns are generated by the same latent events. The output is a global soft clustering, in which two patterns may also be clustered together even if they never co-occur in any EEC, as long as there is a chain of co-occurring patterns generated by the same hidden node. HEADY was evaluated using three different extraction methods: a heuristic-based pattern extractor, a sentence compression algorithm and a memory-based method.

While this model produces a soft clustering of patterns, HEADY was evaluated only on a *headline generation* task and not intrinsically w.r.t. the quality of the clustering itself.

**Neural networks and distributed representations** Another related field aims to learn continuous vector representations for various abstraction levels of natural language. In particular the creation of so-called word embeddings has attracted a lot of attention in the past years, often by implementing neural-network language models. Prominent examples include the works by Bengio et al. (2003) and Mikolov et al. (2013), with the skip-gram model of the latter providing a basis for the vector representations learned in our approach.

Also closely related to IDEST are approaches which employ neural networks capable of handling word sequences of variable length. For example, Le & Mikolov (2014) extend the architectures of Mikolov et al. (2013) with artificial paragraph tokens, which accumulate the meaning of words appearing in the respective paragraphs.

In contrast to these shallow methods, other approaches employ deep multi-layer networks for the processing of sentences. Examples include Kalchbrenner et al. (2014), who employ convolutional neural networks for analyzing the sentiment of sentences, and Socher et al. (2013), who present a special kind of recursive neural network utilizing tensors to model the semantics of a sentence in a compositional way, guided by the parse tree.

A frequent issue with the deeper methods described above is the high computational complexity coming with the large numbers of parameters in a multi-layer neural network or in the value propagation in unfolded recursive neural networks. To circumvent this problem, our model is inspired by Mikolov's simpler skip-gram model, as described below.

# 3 Proposed model

Similarly to HEADY and NEWSSPIKE, our model is also based on the underlying assumption that if sentences from two news articles were published on the same day and mention the same entity set, then they are good paraphrase candidates. The main novelty is in the way we train the paraphrase model from the source data. We propose a new neural-network architecture which is able to learn meaningful distributed representations of full patterns.

## 3.1 Skip-gram neural network

The original Skip-gram architecture (Mikolov et al., 2013) is a feed-forward neural network that is trained on distributional input examples, by assuming that each word should be able to predict to some extent the other words in its context. A skip-gram architecture consists of:

1. An input layer, usually represented as a *one-of-V* or *one-hot-spot* layer. This layer type has as many input nodes as the vocabulary size. Each training example will activate exactly one input node corresponding to the current word $w_i$, and all the other input nodes will be set to zero.

2. A first hidden layer, the embedding or projection layer, that will learn a distributed representation for each possible input word.

3. Zero or more additional hidden layers.

4. An output layer, expected to predict the words in the context of $w_i$: $w_{i-K}, ..., w_{i-1}, w_{i+1}, ..., w_{i+K}$.

In practice, when training based on this architecture, the network converges towards representing words that appear in similar contexts with vectors that are close to each other, as close vectors will produce a similar distribution of output labels in the network.

## 3.2 IDEST neural network

Figure 3 shows the network architecture we use for training our paraphrase model in IDEST. In our case, the input vocabulary is the set of $N$ unique event patterns extracted from text, and our supervision signal is the co-occurrence of event patterns in EECs. We set the input to be a *one-hot-spot* layer with a dimensionality of $N$, and for each pair of patterns that belong to the same EECs, we will have these patterns predict each other respectively, in two separate training examples. The output layer is also a *one-of-V* layer, because for each training example only one output node will be set to 1, corresponding to a co-occurring pattern.

After training, if two patterns $P_i$ and $P_j$ have a large overlap in the set of entities they co-occur with, then they should be mapped onto similar internal representations. Note that the actual entities are only used for EEC construction, but they do not play a role in the training itself, thus allowing the network to generalize over specific entity instantiations. To exemplify, given the two EECs {"*[Alex] married [Leslie]*", "*[Leslie] tied the knot with*

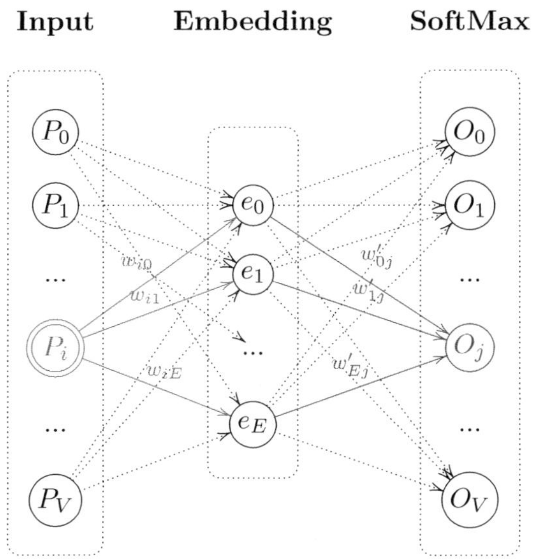


Figure 3: Model used for training. $V$ is the total number of unique patterns, which are used both in the *one-of-V* input and output. $E$ is the dimensionality of the embedding space.

*[Alex]"*} and {*"[Carl] and [Jane] wed"*, *"[Carl] married [Jane]"*}, IDEST could learn an embedding space in which *"[Per] tied the know with [Per]"* and *"[Per] and [Per] wed"* are relatively close, even though the two patterns never co-occur in the same EEC. This is possible because both patterns have been trained to predict the same pattern {*"[Per] married [Per]"*}.

Reported representations of word embeddings typically use between 50 and 600 dimensions (Mikolov et al., 2013; Levy & Goldberg, 2014). For our pattern embeddings we have opted for an embedding layer size of 200 nodes. We also experimented with larger sizes and with adding more intermediate hidden layers, but while the added cost in terms of training time was substantial we did not observe a significant difference in the results.

## 4 Experimental settings

### 4.1 Pattern extraction methods used

In previous work we can find three different pattern extraction methods from a sentence:

- *Heuristic-based*, where a number of handwritten rules or regular expressions based on part-of-speech tags or dependency trees are used to select the most likely pattern from the source sentence (Fader et al., 2011; Mausam et al., 2012; Alfonseca et al., 2013).
- *Sentence compression*, which takes as input the original sentence and the entities of interest and produces a shorter version of the sentence that still includes the entities (Pighin et al., 2014).
- *Memory-based*, that tries to find the shortest reduction of the sentence that still includes the entities, with the constraint that its lexico-syntactic structure has been seen previously as a full sentence in a high-quality corpus (Pighin et al., 2014).

It is important to note that the final purpose of the system may impact the decision of which extraction method to choose. Pighin et al. (2014) use the event models to generate headlines, and using the memory-based method resulted in more grammatical headlines at the cost of coverage. If the purpose of the patterns is information extraction for knowledge base population, then the importance of having well-formed complete sentences as patterns becomes less obvious, and higher coverage methods become more attractive. For these reasons, in this paper we focus on the first two approaches, which are very well-established and can produce high-coverage output. More specifically, we use REVERB extractions and a statistical compression model trained on (sentence, compression) pairs implemented after Filippova & Altun (2013).

### 4.2 Generating clusters from the embedding vectors

IDEST does not produce a clustering like NEWSSPIKE and HEADY, so in order to be able to compare against them we have used the algorithm described in Figure 4 to build paraphrase clusters from the pattern embeddings. Given a similarity threshold on the cosine similarity of embedding vectors, we start by sorting the patterns by extraction frequency and proceed in order along the sorted vector by keeping the most similar pattern of each. Used patterns are removed from the original set to make sure that a pattern is not added to two clusters at the same time.

```
function COMPUTECLUSTERS(P, θ)
    Result = {}
    SORTBYFREQUENCY(P)
    while |P| > 0 do
        p = POP(P)                    ▷ Take highest-frequency pattern
        C_p = {p}                     ▷ Initialize cluster around p
        N = NEIGHBORS(p, P, θ)        ▷ n ∈ P, sim(n, p) > θ
        for all n ∈ N do
            C_p = C_p ∪ {n}
            REMOVE(P, n)              ▷ Remember n has been used
        Result = Result ∪ {C_p}
    return Result
```

Figure 4: Pseudocode of the algorithm for producing a clustering from the distributed representation of the extracted patterns. $P$ is the set of extracted patterns, and $\theta$ is the similarity threshold to include two patterns in the same cluster.

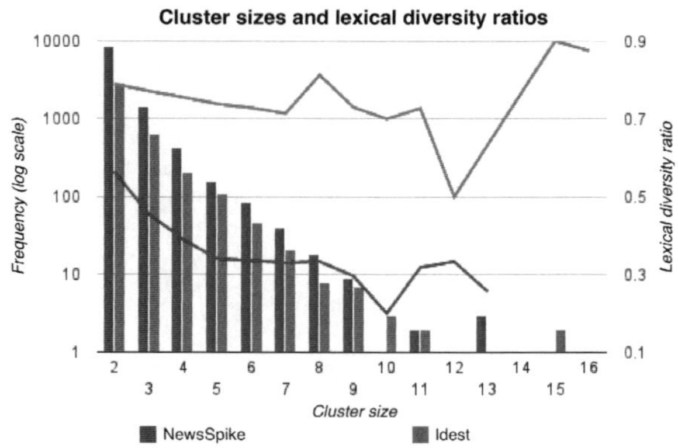


Figure 5: Cluster size (log-scale) and ratio of unique verb lemmas in the clusters generated from NEWSSPIKE and IDEST with the REVERB extractions as input.

## 5 Evaluation results

This section opens with a quantitative look at the clusterings obtained with the different methods to understand their implications with respect to the distribution of event clusters and their internal diversity. In 5.2, we will complement these figures with the results of a manual quality evaluation.

### 5.1 Quantitative analysis

#### 5.1.1 NEWSSPIKE vs. IDEST-ReV-NS

This section compares the clustering models that were output by NEWSSPIKE and IDEST when using the same set of extractions, to evaluate the performance of the factor graph-based method and the neural-network method on exactly the same EECs. We have used as input the dataset released by Zhang & Weld (2013)[1], which contains 546,713 news articles, from which 2.6 million REVERB extractions were reportedly produced. 84,023 of these are grouped into the 23,078 distributed EECs, based on mentions of the same entities on the same day. We compare here the released output clusters from NEWSSPIKE and a clustering obtained from a IDEST-based distributed representation trained on the same EECs.

Figure 5 shows a comparative analysis of the two sets of clusters. As can be seen, IDEST generates somewhat fewer clusters for every cluster size than NEWSSPIKE. We have also computed a *lexical diversity ratio*, defined as the percentage of root-verb lemmas in a cluster that are unique. This metric captures whether a cluster mainly contains the same verb with different inflections or modifiers, or whether it contains different predicates. The figure shows that IDEST generates clusters with much more lexical diversity. These results make sense intuitively, as a global model should be able to produce more aggregated clusters by merging patterns originating from different EECs, resulting in fewer clusters with a higher lexical diversity. A higher lexical diversity may be a signal of richer paraphrases or noisier clusters. The manual evaluation in Section 5.2 will address this issue by comparing the quality of the clusterings.

[1] http://www.cs.washington.edu/node/9473

#### 5.1.2 NEWSSPIKE vs. IDEST-Comp-NS

Figure 6 compares NEWSSPIKE's clusters against IDEST clusters obtained using sentence compression instead of REVERB for extracting patterns. Both systems were trained on the same set of input news. Using sentence compression, the total number of extracted patterns was 321,130, organized in 41,740 EECs. We can observe that IDEST produced larger clusters than NEWSSPIKE. For cluster sizes larger or equal to 4, this configuration of IDEST produced more clusters than NEWSSPIKE. At the same time, lexical diversity remained consistently on much higher levels, well over 60%.

#### 5.1.3 IDEST-Comp-NS vs. IDEST-Comp-All

In order to evaluate the impact of the size of training data, we produced a clustering from embedding vectors trained from a much larger dataset. We used

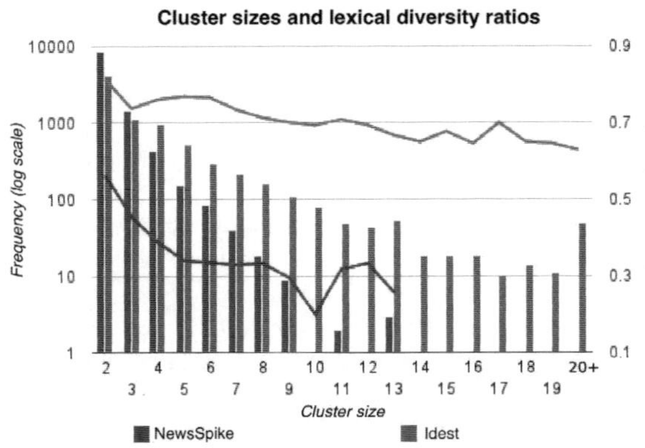


Figure 6: Cluster size (log-scale) and ratio of unique verb lemmas in the clusters generated from NEWSSPIKE and IDEST with compression-based pattern extraction.

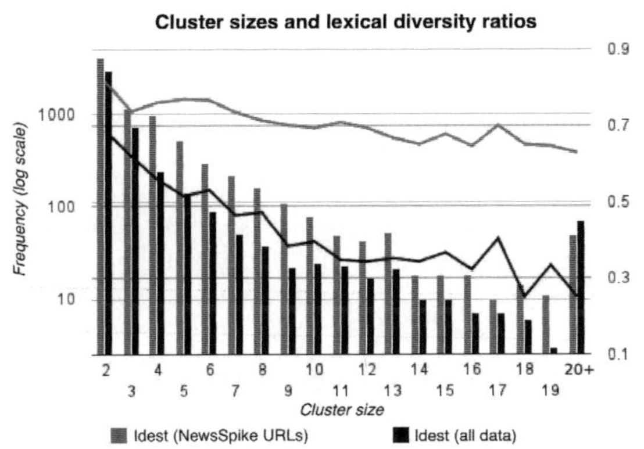


Figure 7: Cluster size (log-scale) and ratio of unique verb lemmas in the clusters generated from IDEST with compression-based pattern extraction, using only the 500,000 NEWSSPIKE articles, or the large dataset.

our own crawl of news collected between 2008 and 2014. Using sentence compression, hundreds of millions of extractions have been produced.

In order to keep the dataset at a reasonable size, and aiming at producing a model of comparable size to the other approaches, we applied a filtering step in which we removed all the event patterns that were not extracted at least five times from the dataset. After this filtering, 28,014,423 extractions remained, grouped in 8,340,162 non-singleton EECs.

Figure 7 compares the resulting clusterings. In the all-data setting, clusters were generally smaller and showed less lexical variability. We believe that this is due to the removal of the long tail of low-frequency and noisy patterns. Indeed, while high lexical variability is desirable it can also be a sign of noisy, unrelated patterns in the clusters. The cohesiveness of the clusters, which we will evaluate in Section 5.2, must also be considered to tell constructive and destructive lexical variability apart.

#### 5.1.4 HEADY

HEADY produces a soft-clustering from a generative model, and expects the maximum number of clusters to be provided beforehand. The model then tries to approximate this number. In our experiments, 5,496 clusters were finally generated. One weak point of HEADY, mentioned above, is that low-frequency patterns do not have enough evidence and Noisy-OR Bayesian Networks tend to discard them; in our experiments, only 4.3% of the unique extracted patterns actually ended up in the final model.

### 5.2 Qualitative analysis

The clusters obtained with different systems and dataset have been evaluated by five expert raters with respect to three metrics, according to the following rating workflow:

1. The rater is shown the cluster, and is asked to annotate which patterns are meaningless or unreadable[2]. This provides us with a **Readability** score, which measures at the same time the quality of the extraction algorithm and the ability of the method to filter out noise.

2. The rater is asked whether there is a majority theme in the cluster, defined as having at least half of the readable patterns refer to the same real-world event happening. If the answer is *No*, the cluster is annotated as noise. We call this metric **Cohesiveness**.

3. If a cluster is cohesive, the rater is finally asked to indicate which patterns are expressing the main theme, and which ones are unrelated to it. The third metric, **Relatedness**, is defined as the percentage of patterns that are related to the main cluster theme. All the patterns in a non-cohesive cluster are automatically marked as unrelated.

[2]In the data released by NewsSpike, REVERB patterns are lemmatized, but the original inflected sentences are also provided. We have restored the original inflection of all the words to make those patterns more readable for the raters.

The inter-annotator agreement on the three metrics, measured as the intraclass correlation (ICC), was strong (Cicchetti, 1994; Hallgren, 2012). More precisely, the observed ICC scores (with 0.95 confidence intervals) were 0.71 [0.70, 0.72] for cohesiveness, 0.71 [0.70, 0.73] for relatedness and 0.66 [0.64, 0.67] for readability.

For the evaluation, from each model we selected enough clusters to achieve an overall size (number of distinct event patterns) comparable to NEWSSPIKE's. For HEADY and IDEST, the stopping condition in Figure 4 was modified accordingly.

Table 1 shows the outcome of the annotation. As expected, using a global model (that can merge patterns from different EECs into single clusters) and using the whole news dataset both led to larger clusters. At the same time, we observe that using REVERB extractions generally led to smaller clusters. This is probably because REVERB produced fewer extractions than sentence compression from the same input documents.

On REVERB extractions, NEWSSPIKE outperformed IDEST in terms of cohesiveness and relatedness, but NEWSSPIKE's lowest cluster size and lexical diversity makes it difficult to prefer any of the two models only w.r.t. the quality of the clusters. On the other hand, the patterns retained by IDEST-ReV-NS were generally more readable (65.16 vs. 56.66).

On the same original news data, using IDEST with sentence compression produced comparable results to IDEST-ReV-NS, Cohesiveness being the only metric that improved significantly.

More generally, in terms of readability all the models that rely on global optimization (i.e., all but NEWSSPIKE) showed better readability than NEWSSPIKE, supporting the intuition that global models are more effective in filtering out noisy extractions. Also, the more data was available to IDEST, the better the quality across all metrics. IDEST model using all data, i.e, IDEST-Comp-All, was significantly better (with 0.95 confidence) than all other configurations in terms of cluster size, cohesiveness and pattern readability. Pattern relatedness was higher, though not significantly better, than NEWSSPIKE, whose clusters were on average more than ten times smaller.

We did not evaluate NEWSSPIKE on the whole news dataset. Being a local model, extending the dataset to cover six years of news would only lead to many more EECs, but it would not affect the reported metrics as each final cluster would still be generated from one single EEC.

| System | Ext | Data | Size | Coh(%) | Rel(%) | Read(%) |
|---|---|---|---|---|---|---|
| HEADY | Comp | All | $12.66^{bcd}$ | $34.40^{!}$ | $27.70^{!}$ | 60.70 |
| NEWSSPIKE | ReV | NS | $3.40^{!}$ | $56.20^{ac}$ | $66.42^{acd}$ | 56.66 |
| IDEST | ReV | NS | $3.62^{b}$ | 40.00 | $47.10^{a}$ | $65.16^{b}$ |
| IDEST | Comp | NS | $5.54^{bc}$ | $50.31^{ac}$ | $46.58^{a}$ | $66.04^{b}$ |
| IDEST | Comp | All | $44.09^{*}$ | $87.93^{*}$ | $68.28^{acd}$ | $80.13^{*}$ |

Table 1: Results of the manual evaluation, averaged over all the clusters produced by each configuration listed. **Extraction algorithms**: *ReV* = REVERB; *Comp* = Compression; **Data sets**: *NS* = NewsSpike URLs; *All* = news 2008-2014. **Quality metrics**: *Size*: average cluster size; *Coh*: cohesiveness; *Rel*: relatedness; *Read*: readability. **Statistical significance**: $^{a}$: better than HEADY; $^{b}$: better than NEWSSPIKE; $^{c}$: better than IDEST-ReV-NS; $^{d}$: better than IDEST-Comp-NS; $^{*}$: better than all others; $^{!}$: worse than all others (0.95 confidence intervals, bootstrap resampling).

It is interesting to see that, even though they were trained on the same data, IDEST outperformed HEADY significantly across all metrics, sometimes by a very large margin. Given the improvements on cluster quality, it would be interesting to evaluate IDEST performance on the headline-generation task for which HEADY was initially designed, but we leave this as future work.

## 6 Conclusions

We described IDEST, a new approach based on neural networks to map event patterns into an embedding space. We show that it can be used to construct high quality pattern clusters based on neighborhood in the embedding space. On a small dataset, IDEST produces comparable results to NEWSSPIKE, but its main strength is in its ability to generalize extractions into a single global model. It scales to hundreds of millions of news, leading to larger clusters of event patterns with significantly better coherence and readability. When compared to HEADY, IDEST outperforms it significantly on all the metrics tried.

## Acknowledgments

The first author was partially supported by the German Federal Ministry of Education and Research, project ALL SIDES (contract 01IW14002).

## References


Agichtein, E. & L. Gravano (2000). Snowball: Extracting relations from large plain-text collections. In *Proceedings of the fifth ACM conference on Digital libraries*, pp. 85–94.

Alfonseca, E., D. Pighin & G. Garrido (2013). HEADY: News headline abstraction through event pattern clustering. In *Proc. of ACL-13*, pp. 1243–1253.

Banko, M., M. J. Cafarella, S. Soderland, M. Broadhead & O. Etzioni (2007). Open information extraction from the Web. In *Proc. of IJCAI-07*, pp. 2670–2676.

Bengio, Y., R. Ducharme & P. Vincent (2003). A neural probabilistic language model. *Journal of Machine Learning Research*, 3:1137–1155.

Brin, S. (1999). Extracting patterns and relations from the world wide web. In *The World Wide Web and Databases*, pp. 172–183. Springer.

Cicchetti, D. V. (1994). Guidelines, criteria, and rules of thumb for evaluating normed and standardized assessment instruments in psychology. *Psychological Assessment*, 6(4):284.

Fader, A., S. Soderland & O. Etzioni (2011). Identifying relations for open information extraction. In *Proc. of EMNLP-11*, pp. 1535–1545.

Fader, A., L. S. Zettlemoyer & O. Etzioni (2013). Paraphrase-driven learning for open question answering. In *Proc. of ACL-13*, pp. 1608–1618.

Filippova, K. & Y. Altun (2013). Overcoming the lack of parallel data in sentence compression. In *Proc. of EMNLP-13*, pp. 1481–1491.

Grycner, A. & G. Weikum (2014). Harpy: Hypernyms and alignment of relational paraphrases. In *Proc. of COLING-14*, pp. 2195–2204.

Hallgren, K. A. (2012). Computing inter-rater reliability for observational data: An overview and tutorial. *Tutorials in quantitative methods for psychology*, 8(1):23.

Kalchbrenner, N., E. Grefenstette & P. Blunsom (2014). A convolutional neural network for modelling sentences. In *Proc. of ACL-14*.

Le, Q. & T. Mikolov (2014). Distributed representations of sentences and documents. In *Proc. of ICML-14*.

Levy, O. & Y. Goldberg (2014). Linguistic regularities in sparse and explicit word representations. In *Proc. of CoNLL-14*.

Lin, D. & P. Pantel (2001). Discovery of inference rules for question-answering. *Natural Language Engineering*, 7(4):343–360.

Mausam, M. Schmitz, R. Bart, S. Soderland & O. Etzioni (2012). Open language learning for information extraction. In *Proc. of EMNLP-12*, pp. 523–534.

Mikolov, T., I. Sutskever, K. Chen, G. S. Corrado & J. Dean (2013). Distributed representations of words and phrases and their compositionality. In *Advances in Neural Information Processing Systems*, pp. 3111–3119.

Moro, A. & R. Navigli (2012). Wisenet: Building a wikipedia-based semantic network with ontologized relations. In *Proc. of CIKM-12*, pp. 1672–1676.

Nakashole, N., G. Weikum & F. Suchanek (2012). Patty: a taxonomy of relational patterns with semantic types. In *Proc. of EMNLP-12*, pp. 1135–1145.

Pighin, D., M. Colnolti, E. Alfonseca & K. Filippova (2014). Modelling events through memory-based, Open-IE patterns for abstractive summarization. In *Proc. of ACL-14*, pp. 892–901.

Poon, H. & P. Domingos (2009). Unsupervised semantic parsing. In *Proc. of EMNLP-09*, pp. 1–10.

Ravichandran, D. & E. H. Hovy (2002). Learning surface text patterns for a question answering system. In *Proc. of ACL-02*, pp. 41–47.

Riedel, S., L. Yao, B. M. Marlin & A. McCallum (2013). Relation extraction with matrix factorization and universal schemas. In *Proc. of HLT-NAACL-13*.

Riloff, E. (1996). Automatically generating extraction patterns from untagged text. In *Proc. of AAAI-96*, pp. 1044–1049.

Sekine, S. (2006). On-demand information extraction. In *Proc. of COLING-ACL-06 Poster Session*, pp. 731–738.

Socher, R., A. Perelygin, J. Wu, J. Chuang, C. Manning, A. Ng & C. Potts (2013). Recursive deep models for semantic compositionality over a sentiment treebank. In *Proc. of EMNLP-13*.

Yao, L., S. Riedel & A. McCallum (2012). Unsupervised relation discovery with sense disambiguation. In *Proc. of ACL-12*, pp. 712–720.

Yates, A. & O. Etzioni (2007). Unsupervised resolution of objects and relations on the Web. In *Proc. of NAACL-HLT-07*, pp. 121–130.

Zhang, C. & D. S. Weld (2013). Harvesting parallel news streams to generate paraphrases of event relations. In *Proc. of EMNLP-13*, pp. 1776–1786.

# High-Order Low-Rank Tensors for Semantic Role Labeling

**Tao Lei**[1], **Yuan Zhang**[1], **Lluís Màrquez**[2], **Alessandro Moschitti**[2], **and Regina Barzilay**[1]
[1]Computer Science and Artificial Intelligence Laboratory, Massachusetts Institute of Technology
[2]ALT Research Group, Qatar Computing Research Institute
[1]{taolei, yuanzh, regina}@csail.mit.edu
[2]{lmarquez, amoschitti}@qf.org.qa

## Abstract

This paper introduces a tensor-based approach to semantic role labeling (SRL). The motivation behind the approach is to automatically induce a compact feature representation for words and their relations, tailoring them to the task. In this sense, our dimensionality reduction method provides a clear alternative to the traditional feature engineering approach used in SRL. To capture meaningful interactions between the argument, predicate, their syntactic path and the corresponding role label, we compress each feature representation first to a lower dimensional space prior to assessing their interactions. This corresponds to using an overall cross-product feature representation and maintaining associated parameters as a four-way low-rank tensor. The tensor parameters are optimized for the SRL performance using standard online algorithms. Our tensor-based approach rivals the best performing system on the CoNLL-2009 shared task. In addition, we demonstrate that adding the representation tensor to a competitive tensor-free model yields 2% absolute increase in F-score.[1]

## 1 Introduction

The accuracy of Semantic Role Labeling (SRL) systems depends strongly on the features used by the underlying classifiers. For instance, the top performing system on the CoNLL–2009 shared task employs over 50 language-specific templates for feature generation (Che et al., 2009). The templates are manually created and thus offer specific means of incorporating prior knowledge into the method. However, finding compact, informative templates is difficult since the relevant signal may be spread over many correlated features. Moreover, the use of lexicalized features, which are inevitably sparse, leads to overfitting. In this case it is advantageous to try to automatically compress the feature set to use a small number of underlying co-varying dimensions. Dimensionality reduction of this kind can be incorporated into the classifier directly by utilizing tensor calculus. In this paper, we adopt this strategy.

We start by building high-dimensional feature vectors that are subsequently mapped into a low-dimensional representation. Since this high-dimensional representation has to reflect the interaction between different indicators of semantic relations, we construct it as a cross-product of smaller feature vectors that capture distinct facets of semantic dependence: *predicate*, *argument*, *syntactic path* and *role label*. By compressing this sparse representation into lower dimensions, we obtain dense representations for words (predicate, argument) and their connecting paths, uncovering meaningful interactions. The associated parameters are maintained as a four-way low-rank tensor, and optimized for SRL performance. Tensor modularity enables us to employ standard online algorithms for training.

Our approach to SRL is inspired by recent success of our tensor-based approaches in dependency parsing (Lei et al., 2014). Applying analogous techniques to SRL brings about new challenges, however. The scoring function needs to reflect the high-order interactions between the predicate, argument,

[1]Our code is available at https://github.com/taolei87/SRLParser.



*Human Language Technologies: The 2015 Annual Conference of the North American Chapter of the ACL*, pages 1150–1160,
Denver, Colorado, May 31 – June 5, 2015. 

their syntactic path and the corresponding role label. Therefore, we parametrize the scoring function as a four-way tensor. Generalization to high-order tensors also requires new initialization and update procedures. For instance, the SVD initialization used in our dependency parsing work results in memory explosion when extending to our 4-way tensor. Instead, we employ the power method (De Lathauwer et al., 1995) to build the initial tensor from smaller pieces, one rank-1 component at a time. For learning, in order to optimize an overall non-convex objective function with respect to the tensor parameters, we modify the passive-aggressive algorithm to update all the low-rank components in one step. The update strategy readily generalizes to any high-order tensor.

We evaluate our tensor-based approach for SRL on the CoNLL–2009 shared task benchmark datasets of five languages: English, German, Chinese, Catalan and Spanish (Surdeanu et al., 2008). As a baseline, we use a simple SRL model that relies on a minimal set of standard features. Our results demonstrate that the tensor-based model outperforms the original SRL model by a significant margin, yielding absolute improvements of 2.1% $F_1$ score. We also compare our results against the best performing system on this task (Zhao et al., 2009a). On three out of five languages, the tensor-based model outperforms this system. These results are particularly notable because the system of Zhao et al. (2009a) employs a rich set of language-specific features carefully engineered for this task. Finally, we demonstrate that using four-way tensor yields better performance than its three-way counterpart, highlighting the importance of modeling the relation between role labels and properties of the path.

## 2 Related Work

A great deal of SRL research has been dedicated to designing rich, expressive features. The initial work by Gildea and Jurafsky (2002) already identified a compact core set of features, which were widely adopted by the SRL community. These features describe the predicate, the candidate argument, and the syntactic relation between them (*path*). Early systems primarily extended this core set by including local context lexicalized patterns (e.g., $n$-grams), several extended representations of the *path* features, and some linguistically motivated syntactic patterns, as the *syntactic frame* (Surdeanu et al., 2003; Xue and Palmer, 2004; Pradhan et al., 2005).

More recent approaches explored a broader range of features. Among others, Toutanova et al. (2008), Martins and Almeida (2014) and Yang and Zong (2014) have explored high-order features involving several arguments and even pairs of sentence predicates. Other approaches have focused on semantic generalizations of lexical features using selectional preferences, neural network embeddings or latent word language models (Zapirain et al., 2013; Collobert et al., 2011; Deschacht and Moens, 2009; Roth and Woodsend, 2014). To avoid the intensive feature engineering inherent in SRL, Moschitti et al. (2008) employ kernel learning. Although attractive from this perspective, the kernel-based approach comes with a high computational cost. In contrast to prior work, our approach effectively learns low-dimensional representation of words and their roles, eliminating the need for heavy manual feature engineering. Finally, system combination approaches such as reranking typically outperform individual systems (Björkelund et al., 2010). Our method can be easily integrated as a component in one of those systems.

In technical terms, our work builds on our recent tensor-based approach for dependency parsing (Lei et al., 2014). In that work, we use a three-way tensor to score candidate dependency relations within a first-order scoring function. The tensor captures the interaction between words and their syntactic (head-modifier) relations. In contrast, the scoring function in SRL involves higher-order interactions between the path, argument, predicate and their associated role label. Therefore, we parametrized the scoring function with a four-way low-rank tensor. To help with this extension, we developed a new initialization and update strategy. Our experimental results demonstrate that the new representation tailored to SRL outperforms previous approaches.

## 3 Problem Formulation

Our setup follows the CoNLL–2009 shared task (Hajič et al., 2009). Each token in sentence $\mathbf{x}$ is annotated with a predicted POS tag and predicted

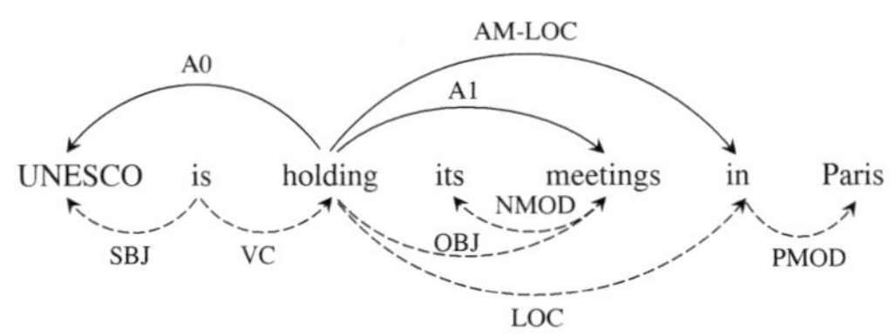


Figure 1: Example sentence from the CoNLL–2009 dataset annotated with syntactic and semantic dependencies. The lower graph is the syntactic dependency tree for the sentence. The upper part contains the semantic dependencies for the predicate "holding".

word lemma. Some tokens are also marked as predicates, i.e., argument-bearing tokens. The goal is to determine the semantic dependencies for each predicate $p_i$ (cf. upper part of Figure 1). These dependencies identify the arguments of each predicate and their role labels. In this work, we focus only on the semantic side – that is, identification and classification of predicate arguments. To this end, our system takes as input a syntactic dependency tree $\mathbf{y}_{\text{syn}}$ derived from a state-of-the-art parser (bottom part of Figure 1).

More formally, let $\{p_i\} \subset \mathbf{x}$ be the set of verbal and nominal predicates in the sentence. For each predicate $p_i$ (e.g., "holding"), our goal is to predict tuples $(p_i, a_{ij}, r_{ij})$ specifying the semantic dependency arcs, where $a_{ij} \in \mathbf{x}$ is one argument (e.g., "meetings"), and $r_{ij}$ is the corresponding semantic role label (e.g., A1). The semantic parse is then the collection of predicted arcs $\mathbf{z}_{\text{sem}} = \{(p_i, a_{ij}, r_{ij})\}$.

We decouple syntactic and semantic inference problems into two separate steps. We first run our syntactic dependency parser RBGParser[2] to obtain the syntactic dependency tree $\mathbf{y}_{\text{syn}}$. The semantic parse $\mathbf{z}_{\text{sem}}$ is then found conditionally on the syntactic part:

$$\mathbf{z}^*_{\text{sem}} = \arg\max_{\mathbf{z}_{\text{sem}}} S_{\text{sem}}(\mathbf{x}, \mathbf{y}_{\text{syn}}, \mathbf{z}_{\text{sem}}), \qquad (1)$$

Here $S_{\text{sem}}(\cdot)$ is the parametrized scoring function to be learned. We build our scoring function by combining a traditional feature scoring function with a tensor-based scoring function.

[2]https://github.com/taolei87/RBGParser

| | |
|---|---|
| Predicate word | Path |
| Predicate POS | Path + arg. POS |
| Argument word | Path + pred. POS |
| Argument POS | Path + arg. word |
| Pred. + arg. words | Path + pred. word |
| Pred. + arg. POS | Voice + pred. + arg. POS |
| Voice + pred. word | Voice + pred. POS |

Table 1: Templates for first-order semantic features. These features are also (optionally) combined with role labels.

### 3.1 Traditional Scoring Using Manually-designed Features

In a typical feature-based approach (Johansson, 2009; Che et al., 2009), feature templates give rise to rich feature descriptions of the semantic structure. The score $S_{\text{sem}}(\mathbf{x}, \mathbf{y}_{\text{syn}}, \mathbf{z}_{\text{sem}})$ is then defined as the inner product between the parameter vector and the feature vector. In the first-order arc-factored case,

$$\begin{aligned} S_{\text{sem}}(\mathbf{x}, \mathbf{y}_{\text{syn}}, \mathbf{z}_{\text{sem}}) &= \mathbf{w} \cdot \phi(\mathbf{x}, \mathbf{y}_{\text{syn}}, \mathbf{z}_{\text{sem}}) \\ &= \sum_{(p,a,r) \in \mathbf{z}_{\text{sem}}} \mathbf{w} \cdot \phi(p, a, r), \end{aligned}$$

where $\mathbf{w}$ are the model parameters and $\phi(p, a, r)$ is the feature vector representing a single semantic arc $(p, a, r)$ (we suppress its dependence on $\mathbf{x}$ and $\mathbf{y}_{\text{syn}}$). We also experiment with second order features, i.e., considering two arguments associated with the same predicate, or two predicates sharing the same token as argument.

For the arc-factored model, there are mainly four types of atomic information that define the arc features in $\phi(p, a, r)$:

(a) the predicate token $p$ (and its local context);
(b) the argument token $a$ (and its local context);
(c) the dependency label path that connects $p$ and $a$ in the syntactic tree;
(d) the semantic role label $r$ of the arc.

These pieces of atomic information are either used directly or combined as unigram up to 4-gram features into traditional models. To avoid heavy feature engineering and overfitting, we use a light and compact feature set derived from the information in (a)–(d). Table 1 shows the complete list of feature templates, used as our first-order semantic baseline in the experiments.

### 3.2 Low-rank Scoring via Projected Representations

Now, we describe the tensor-based scoring function. We characterize each semantic arc $(p, a, r)$ using the cross-product of atomic feature vectors associated with the four types of information described above: the predicate vector $\phi(p)$, the argument vector $\phi(a)$, the dependency path vector $\phi(path)$ and the semantic role label vector $\phi(r)$. For example, in the simplest case $\phi(p), \phi(a) \in [0,1]^n$ are one-hot indicator vectors, where $n$ is the size of the vocabulary. Similarly, $\phi(path) \in [0,1]^m$ and $\phi(r) \in [0,1]^l$ are indicator vectors where $m$ is the number of unique paths (seen in the training set) and $l$ is the number of semantic role labels. Of course, we can add other atomic information into these atomic vectors. For example, $\phi(p)$ will not only indicate the word form of the current predicate $p$, but also the word lemma, POS tag and surrounding tokens as well. The cross-product of these four vectors is an extremely high-dimensional rank-1 tensor,

$$\phi(p) \otimes \phi(a) \otimes \phi(path) \otimes \phi(r) \;\in\; \mathbb{R}^{n\times n\times m\times l}$$

in which each entry indicates the combination of four atomic features appearing in the semantic arc $(p, a, r)$[3]. The rank-1 tensor (cross-product) captures all possible combinations over atomic units, and therefore it is a full feature expansion over the manually selected feature set in Table 1. Similar to the traditional scoring, the semantic arc score is the inner product between a 4-way parameter tensor $A$ and this feature tensor:

$$A \in \mathbb{R}^{n\times n\times m\times l} :$$
$$vec(A) \cdot vec\left(\phi(p) \otimes \phi(a) \otimes \phi(path) \otimes \phi(r)\right), \quad (2)$$

where $vec(\cdot)$ denotes the vector representation of a matrix / tensor.

Instead of reducing and pruning possible feature concatenations (e.g., by manual feature template construction as in the traditional approach), this tensor scoring method avoids parameter explosion and overfitting by assuming a low-rank factorization of the parameters $A$. Specifically, A is decomposed into the sum of $k$ simple rank-1 components,

$$A = \sum_{i=1}^{k} P(i) \otimes Q(i) \otimes R(i) \otimes S(i). \quad (3)$$

Here $k$ is a small constant, $P, Q \in \mathbb{R}^{k\times n}$, $R \in \mathbb{R}^{k\times m}$ and $S \in \mathbb{R}^{k\times l}$ are parameter matrices, and $P(i)$ (and similarly $Q(i)$, $R(i)$ and $S(i)$) represents the $i$-th row vector of matrix $P$.

The advantages of this low-rank assumption are as follows. First, computing the score no longer requires maintaining and constructing extremely large tensors. Instead, we can project atomic vectors via $P$, $Q$, $R$ and $S$ obtaining small dense vectors, and subsequently calculating the arc score by

$$\sum_{i=1}^{k} [P\phi(p)]_i \, [Q\phi(a)]_i \, [R\phi(path)]_i \, [S\phi(r)]_i \, .$$

Second, projecting atomic units such as words, POS tags and labels into dense, low-dimensional vectors can effectively alleviate the sparsity problem, and it enables the model to capture high-order feature interactions between atomic units, while avoiding the parameter explosion problem.

### 3.3 Combined System

Similar to our low-rank syntactic dependency parsing model (Lei et al., 2014), our final scoring function $S_{\text{sem}}(\mathbf{x}, \mathbf{y}_{\text{syn}}, \mathbf{z}_{\text{sem}})$ is the combination of the traditional scoring and the low-rank scoring,

$$S_{\text{sem}}(\mathbf{x}, \mathbf{y}_{\text{syn}}, \mathbf{z}_{\text{sem}}) \quad = \quad \gamma \, \mathbf{w} \cdot \phi(\mathbf{x}, \mathbf{y}_{\text{syn}}, \mathbf{z}_{\text{sem}}) + (1-\gamma) \sum_{(p,a,r)\in \mathbf{z}_{\text{sem}}} \sum_{i=1}^{k} [P\phi(p)]_i \, [Q\phi(a)]_i \, [R\phi(path)]_i \, [S\phi(r)]_i \, .$$

where $\gamma \in [0, 1]$ is a hyper-parameter balancing the two scoring terms. We tune this value on the development set. Finally, the set of parameters of our model is denoted as $\boldsymbol{\theta} = \{\mathbf{w}, P, Q, R, S\}$. Our goal is to optimize the weight vector $\mathbf{w}$ as well as the four projection matrices given the training set.

[3] We always add a bias term into these atomic vectors (e.g., a fixed "1" attached to the beginning of every vector). Therefore, their cross-product will contain all unigram to 4-gram concatenations, not just 4-gram concatenations.

## 4 Learning

We now describe the learning method for our SRL model. Let $D = \{(\hat{\mathbf{x}}^{(i)}, \hat{\mathbf{y}_{\text{syn}}}^{(i)}, \hat{\mathbf{z}_{\text{sem}}}^{(i)})\}_{i=1}^{N}$ be the collection of $N$ training samples. The values of the set of parameters $\boldsymbol{\theta} = \{\mathbf{w}, P, Q, R, S\}$ are estimated on the basis of this training set. Following standard practice, we optimize the parameter values in a maximum soft-margin framework. That is, for the given sentence $\hat{\mathbf{x}}$ and the corresponding syntactic tree $\hat{\mathbf{y}_{\text{syn}}}$, we adjust parameter values to separate gold semantic parse and other incorrect alternatives:

$$\begin{aligned}
&\forall \mathbf{z}_{\text{sem}} \in \mathcal{Z}(\hat{\mathbf{x}}, \hat{\mathbf{y}_{\text{syn}}}) : \\
&\quad S_{sem}(\hat{\mathbf{x}}, \hat{\mathbf{y}_{\text{syn}}}, \hat{\mathbf{z}_{\text{sem}}}) \geq S_{sem}(\hat{\mathbf{x}}, \hat{\mathbf{y}_{\text{syn}}}, \mathbf{z}_{\text{sem}}) \\
&\quad + cost(\hat{\mathbf{z}_{\text{sem}}}, \mathbf{z}_{\text{sem}})
\end{aligned} \tag{4}$$

where $\mathcal{Z}(\hat{\mathbf{x}}, \hat{\mathbf{y}_{\text{syn}}})$ represent the set of all possible semantic parses, and $cost(\hat{\mathbf{z}_{\text{sem}}}, \mathbf{z}_{\text{sem}})$ is a non-negative function representing the structural difference between $\hat{\mathbf{z}_{\text{sem}}}$ and $\mathbf{z}_{\text{sem}}$. The cost is zero when $\mathbf{z}_{\text{sem}} = \hat{\mathbf{z}_{\text{sem}}}$, otherwise it becomes positive and therefore is the "margin" to separate the two parses. Following previous work (Johansson, 2009; Martins and Almeida, 2014), this cost function is defined as the sum of arc errors – we add 1.0 for each false-positive arc, 2.0 for each false-negative arc (a missing arc) and 0.5 if the predicate-argument pair $(p, a)$ is in both parses but the semantic role label $r$ is incorrect.

### 4.1 Online Update

The parameters are updated successively after each training sentence. Each update first checks whether the constraint (4) is violated. This requires "cost-augmented decoding" to find the maximum violation with respect to the gold semantic parse:

$$\begin{aligned}
\tilde{\mathbf{z}_{\text{sem}}} = \arg\max_{\mathbf{z}_{\text{sem}}} \; & S_{\text{sem}}(\hat{\mathbf{x}}, \hat{\mathbf{y}_{\text{syn}}}, \mathbf{z}_{\text{sem}}) \\
& + cost(\hat{\mathbf{z}_{\text{sem}}}, \mathbf{z}_{\text{sem}})
\end{aligned}$$

When the constraint (4) is violated (i.e. $\tilde{\mathbf{z}_{\text{sem}}} \neq \hat{\mathbf{z}_{\text{sem}}}$), we seek a parameter update $\Delta\boldsymbol{\theta}$ to fix this violation. In other words, we define the hinge loss for this example as follows,

$$\begin{aligned}
loss(\boldsymbol{\theta}) \quad = \quad & \max\{\, 0,\; S_{\text{sem}}(\hat{\mathbf{x}}, \hat{\mathbf{y}_{\text{syn}}}, \tilde{\mathbf{z}_{\text{sem}}}) \\
& + cost(\hat{\mathbf{z}_{\text{sem}}}, \tilde{\mathbf{z}_{\text{sem}}}) - S_{\text{sem}}(\hat{\mathbf{x}}, \hat{\mathbf{y}_{\text{syn}}}, \hat{\mathbf{z}_{\text{sem}}}) \,\}
\end{aligned}$$

and we revise the parameter values to minimize this loss function.

Since this loss function is neither linear nor convex with respect to the parameters $\boldsymbol{\theta}$ (more precisely the low-rank component matrices $P$, $Q$, $R$ and $S$), we can use the same alternating passive-aggressive (PA) update strategy in our previous work (Lei et al., 2014) to update one parameter matrix at one time while fixing the other matrices. However, as we demonstrated later, modifying the passive-aggressive algorithm slightly can give us a **joint** update over all components in $\boldsymbol{\theta}$. Our preliminary experiment shows this modified version achieves better results compared to the alternating PA.

### 4.2 Joint PA Update for Tensor

The original passive-aggressive parameter update $\Delta\theta$ is derived for a linear, convex loss function by solving a quadatic optimization problem. Although our scoring function $S_{\text{sem}}(\cdot)$ is not linear, we can simply approximate it with its first-order Taylor expansion:

$$S(\mathbf{x}, \mathbf{y}, \mathbf{z}; \boldsymbol{\theta} + \Delta\boldsymbol{\theta}) \approx S(\mathbf{x}, \mathbf{y}, \mathbf{z}; \boldsymbol{\theta}) + \frac{dS}{d\boldsymbol{\theta}} \cdot \Delta\boldsymbol{\theta}$$

In fact, by plugging this into the hinge loss function and the quadratic optimization problem, we get a joint closed-form update which can be simply described as,

$$\Delta\boldsymbol{\theta} = \max\left\{C,\; \frac{loss(\boldsymbol{\theta})}{\|g\boldsymbol{\theta}\|^2}\right\} g\boldsymbol{\theta}$$

where

$$g\boldsymbol{\theta} = \frac{dS}{d\boldsymbol{\theta}}(\hat{\mathbf{x}}, \hat{\mathbf{y}_{\text{syn}}}, \hat{\mathbf{z}_{\text{sem}}}) - \frac{dS}{d\boldsymbol{\theta}}(\hat{\mathbf{x}}, \hat{\mathbf{y}_{\text{syn}}}, \tilde{\mathbf{z}_{\text{sem}}}),$$

and $C$ is a regularization hyper-parameter controlling the maximum step size of each update. Note that $\boldsymbol{\theta}$ is the set of all parameters, the update jointly adjusts all low-rank matrices and the traditional weight vector. The PA update is "adaptive" in the sense that its step size is propotional to the $loss(\boldsymbol{\theta})$ of the current training sample. Therefore the step size is adaptively decreased as the model fits the training data.

### 4.3 Tensor Initialization

Since the scoring and loss function with high-order tensor components is highly non-convex, our model performance can be impacted by the initialization of the matrices $P$, $Q$, $R$ and $S$. In addition to intializing these low-rank components randomly, we also experiment with a strategy to provide a good guess of the low-rank tensor.

First, note that the traditional manually-selected feature set (i.e., $\phi(p, a, r)$ in our notation) is an expressive and informative subset of the huge feature expansion covered in the feature tensor. We can train our model using only the manual feature set and then use the corresponding feature weights $\mathbf{w}$ to intialize the tensor. Specifically, we create a sparse tensor $T \in \mathbb{R}^{n \times n \times m \times l}$ by putting each parameter weight in $\mathbf{w}$ into its corresponding entry in $T$. We then try to find a low-rank approximation of sparse tensor $T$ by approximately minimizing the squared error:

$$\min_{P,Q,R,S} \|T - \sum_i P(i) \otimes Q(i) \otimes R(i) \otimes S(i)\|_2^2$$

In the low-rank dependency parsing work (Lei et al., 2014), this is achieved by unfolding the sparse tensor $T$ into a $n \times nml$ matrix and taking the SVD to get the top low-rank components. Unfortunately this strategy does not apply in our case (and other high-order tensor cases) because even the number of columns in the unfolded matrix is huge, $nml > 10^{11}$, and simply taking the SVD would fail because of memory limits.

Instead, we adopt the generalized high-order power method, a.k.a. power iteration (De Lathauwer et al., 1995), to incrementally obtain the most important rank-1 component one-by-one – $P(i)$, $Q(i)$, $R(i)$ and $S(i)$ for each $i = 1..k$. This method is a very simple iterative algorithm and is used to find the largest eigenvalues and eigenvectors (or singular values and vectors in SVD case) of a matrix. Its generalization directly applies to our high-order tensor case.

**Input:** sparse tensor $T$, rank number $i$ and fixed rank-1 components $P(j)$, $Q(j)$, $R(j)$ and $S(j)$ for $j = 1..(i-1)$

**Output:** new component $P(i)$, $Q(i)$, $R(i)$ and $S(i)$.

---

Randomly initialize four unit vectors $p$, $q$, $r$ and $s$
$T' = T - \sum_j P(j) \otimes Q(j) \otimes R(j) \otimes S(j)$
**repeat**
  $p = \langle T', -, q, r, s \rangle$ and normalize it
  $q = \langle T', p, -, r, s \rangle$ and normalize it
  $r = \langle T', p, q, -, s \rangle$ and normalize it
  $s = \langle T', p, q, r, - \rangle$
  $norm = \|s\|_2^2$
**until** $norm$ converges
$P(i) = p$ and $Q(i) = q$
$R(i) = r$ and $S(i) = s$

Figure 2: The iterative power method for high-order tensor initialization. The operator $p = \langle T', -, q, r, s \rangle$ is the multiplication between the tensor and three vectors, defined as $p_i = \sum_{jkl} T_{ijkl} q_j r_k s_l$. Similarly, $q_j = \sum_{ikl} T_{ijkl} p_i r_k s_l$ etc.

## 5 Implementation Details

**Decoding** Following Lluís et al. (2013), the decoding of SRL is formulated as a bipartite maximum assignment problem, where we assign arguments to semantic roles for each predicate. We use the maximum weighted assignment algorithm (Kuhn, 1955). For syntactic dependency parsing, we employ the randomized hill-climbing algorithm from our previous work (Zhang et al., 2014).

**Features** Table 1 summarizes the first-order feature templates. These features are mainly drawn from previous work (Johansson, 2009). In addition, we extend each template with the argument label.

Table 2 summarizes the atomic features used in $\phi(p)$ and $\phi(a)$ for the tensor component. For each predicate or argument, the feature vector includes its word form and POS tag, as well as the POS tags of the context words. We also add unsupervised word embeddings learned on raw corpus.[4] For atomic vectors $\phi(path)$ and $\phi(r)$ representing the path and the semantic role label, we use the indicator feature and a bias term.

## 6 Experimental Setup

**Dataset** We evaluate our model on the English dataset and other 4 datasets in the CoNLL-2009 shared task (Surdeanu et al., 2008). We use the

[4] https://github.com/wolet/sprml13-word-embeddings

| | | |
|---|---|---|
| word | word-l | word-r |
| pos | pos-l | pos-r |
| pos-l + pos | pos + pos-r | pos + word |
| pos-l + pos + pos-r | voice | embeddings |

Table 2: Predicate/argument atomic features used by our tensor for SRL. `word` stands for the word form (and also lemma), `pos` stands for the predicted POS tag and `voice` stands for the voice of the predicate. The suffixes `-l` and `-r` refer to the left and right of the current token respectively. For example, `pos-l` means the POS tag to the left of the current word in the sentence.

official split for training, development and testing. For English, the data is mainly drawn from the Wall Street Journal. In addition, a subset of the Brown corpus is used as the secondary out-of-domain test set, in order to evaluate how well the model generalizes to a different domain. Following the official practice, we use predicted POS tags, lemmas and morphological analysis provided in the dataset across all our experiments. The predicates in each sentence are also given during both training and testing. However, we neither predict nor use the sense for each predicate.

**Systems for Comparisons** We compare against three systems that achieve the top average performance in the joint syntactic and semantic parsing track of the CoNLL-2009 shared task (Che et al., 2009; Zhao et al., 2009a; Gesmundo et al., 2009). All approaches extensively explored rich features for the SRL task. We also compare with the state-of-the-art parser (Björkelund et al., 2010) for English, an improved version of systems participated in CoNLL-2009. This system combines the pipeline of dependency parser and semantic role labeler with a global reranker. Finally, we compare with the recent approach which employs distributional word representations for SRL (Roth and Woodsend, 2014). We directly obtain the outputs of all these systems from the CoNLL-2009 website[5] or the authors.

**Model Variants** Our full model utilizes 4-way tensor component and a standard feature set from (Johansson, 2009). We also compare against our model without the tensor component, as well as a variant with a 3-way tensor by combining the path and semantic role label parts into a single mode (dimension).

**Evaluation Measures** Following standard practice in the SRL evaluation, we measure the performance using labeled F-score. To this end, we apply the evaluation script provided on the official website.[6] The standard evaluation script considers the predicate sense prediction as a special kind of semantic label.[7] Since we are neither predicting nor using the predicate sense information, we exclude this information in most of the evaluation. In addition, we combine the predicate sense classification output of (Björkelund et al., 2010) with our semantic role labeling output, to provide results directly comparable to previous reported numbers.

**Experimental Details** Across all experiments, we fix the rank of the tensor to 50 and train our model for a maximum of 20 epochs. Following common practice, we average parameters over all iterations. For each experimental setting, we tune the hyper-parameter $\gamma \in \{0.3, 0.5, 0.7, 0.9\}$ and $C \in \{0.01, 0.1, 1\}$ on the development set and apply the best model on the test set. Each model is evaluated on the development set after every epoch to pick the the best number of training epoch. For the experiments with random initialization on the tensor component, the vectors are initialized as random unit vectors. We combine our SRL model with our syntactic dependency parser, RBGParser v1.1 (Lei et al., 2014), for joint syntactic and semantic parsing. The labeled attachment score (LAS) of RBGParser is 90.4 on English, when we train the "standard" model type using the unsupervised word vectors.

## 7 Results

We first report the performance of our methods and other state-of-the-art SRL systems on English datasets (See Table 3). We single out performance

[5]`http://ufal.mff.cuni.cz/conll2009-st/results/results.php`

[6]`http://ufal.mff.cuni.cz/conll2009-st/scorer.html`

[7]Note that the original script includes such prediction in the F-score calculation, although the predicate sense is typically predicted in a separate step before semantic label classification.

| Model | Excluding predicate senses | | | Including predicate senses | |
|---|---|---|---|---|---|
| | WSJ-dev | WSJ-test | Brown-test | WSJ-test | Brown-test |
| 1st-order w/o tensor | 79.42 | 80.84 | 69.38 | 85.46 | 74.66 |
| + 3-way tensor | 80.77 | 82.19 | 69.76 | 86.34 | 74.94 |
| + 4-way tensor | **81.03** | **82.51*** | **70.77** | **86.58*** | **75.57** |
| CoNLL-2009 1st place | – | 82.08 | 69.84 | 86.15 | 74.58 |
| CoNLL-2009 2nd place | – | 81.20 | 68.86 | 85.51 | 73.82 |
| CoNLL-2009 3rd place | – | 78.66 | 65.89 | 83.24 | 70.65 |
| (Roth and Woodsend, 2014) | – | 80.87 | 69.33 | 85.50 | 74.67 |
| (Björkelund et al., 2010) | 78.85 | 81.35 | 68.34 | 85.80 | 73.92 |
| **Model + Reranker** | WSJ-dev | WSJ-test | Brown-test | WSJ-test | Brown-test |
| (Roth and Woodsend, 2014) + reranking | – | 82.10 | **71.12** | 86.34 | **75.88** |
| (Björkelund et al., 2010) + reranking | 80.50 | **82.87** | 70.91 | **86.86** | 75.71 |

Table 3: SRL labeled F-score of our model variants, and state-of-the-art systems on the CoNLL shared task. We consider a tensor-free variant of our model, and tensor-based variants that include first-order SRL features. For the latter, we consider implementations with 3-way and 4-way tensors. Winning systems (with and without a reranker) are marked in bold. Statistical significance with $p < 0.05$ is marked with $*$.

on English corpora because these datasets are most commonly used for system evalutation. As a single system without reranking, our model outperforms the five top performing systems (second block in Table 3) on both in-domain and out-of-domain datasets. The improvement from the F-score of 82.08% to our result 82.51% on the WSJ in-domain test set is significant with $p < 0.05$, which is computed using a randomized test tool[8] based on Yeh (2000). For comparison purposes, we also report F-score performance when predicate senses are included in evaluation. The relative performance between the systems is consistent independent of whether the predicate senses are included or excluded.

Table 4 shows the results of our system on other languages in the CoNLL-2009 shared task. Out of five languages, our model rivals the best performing system on three languages, achieving statistically significant gains on English and Chinese. Note that our model uses the same feature configuration for all the languages. In contrast, Zhao et al. (2009b) rely on language-specific configurations obtained via "huge feature engineering" (as noted by the authors).

Results in Table 3 and 4 also highlight the contribution of the tensor to the model performance, which is consistent across languages. Without the tensor component, our system trails the top two performing systems. However, adding the tensor component provides on average 2.1% absolute gain, resulting in competitive performance. The mode of the tensor also contributes to the performance – the 4-way tensor model performs better than the 3-way counterpart, demonstrating the importance of modeling the interactions between dependency paths and semantic role labels.

| | | WSJ-test | Brown-test |
|---|---|---|---|
| 1st-order w/o tensor | | 80.84 | 69.38 |
| + 3-way tensor | Rnd. Init. | 81.87 | 69.82 |
| | PM. Init. | 82.19 | 69.76 |
| + 4-way tensor | Rnd. Init. | 81.63 | 70.63 |
| | PM. Init. | 82.51 | 70.77 |

Table 5: SRL labeled F-score for different initialization strategies of the first order model. Rnd stands for the random initialization, and PM for the power method initialization.

Table 5 shows the impact of initialization on the performance of the tensor-based model. The initialization based on the power method yields superior results compared to random initialization, for both

[8] http://www.nlpado.de/~sebastian/software/sigf.shtml

| Language | Test set | | | |
|---|---|---|---|---|
| | Ours (4-way tensor) | Ours (no tensor) | CoNLL 1st | CoNLL 2nd |
| English | **82.51*** | 80.84 | 82.08 | 81.20 |
| Catalan | 74.67 | 71.86 | **76.78*** | 74.02 |
| Chinese | **69.16*** | 68.43 | 68.52 | 68.71 |
| German | **76.94** | 74.03 | 74.65 | 76.27 |
| Spanish | 75.58 | 72.85 | **77.33*** | 74.01 |
| Average | 75.77 | 73.60 | 75.87 | 74.84 |

Table 4: Semantic labeled F-score excluding predicate senses on 5 languages in the CoNLL-2009 shared task. Statistical significance with $p < 0.05$ is marked with $*$. Adding the tensor leads to more than 2% absolute gain on average F-score. Our method with the same feature configuration (a standard set + 4-way tensor) rivals the best CoNLL-2009 system which explores much richer feature sets, language-specific feature engineering, and n-best parse combination (Zhao et al., 2009a).

| Our method | WSJ-test | Gain |
|---|---|---|
| 1st order w/o tensor | 80.84 | – |
| + 4-way tensor | 82.51 | +1.67 |
| + 3-way tensor | 82.19 | +1.35 |

| (Roth and Woodsend) | WSJ-test | Gain |
|---|---|---|
| original baseline | 80.38 | – |
| + pred & arg | 80.23 | -0.15 |
| + deppath | 80.63 | +0.25 |
| + span | 80.87 | +0.49 |

Table 6: Comparision between our low-rank tensor method and (Roth and Woodsend, 2014) for leveraing word compositions.

3-way and 4-way tensors. However, random initialization still delivers reasonable performance, outperforming the tensor-free model by more than 1% in F-score.

Finally, we compare our tensor-based approach against a simpler model that captures interactions between predicate, argument and syntactic path using word embeddings (Roth and Woodsend, 2014). Table 6 demonstrates that modeling feature interactions using tensor yields higher gains than using word embeddings alone. For instance, the highest gain achieved by Roth and Woodsend (2014) when the embeddings of the arguments are averaged is 0.5%, compared to 1.6% obtained by our model.

## 8 Conclusions

In this paper we introduce a tensor-based approach to SRL that induces a compact feature representation for words and their relations. In this sense, our dimensionality reduction method provides a clear alternative to a traditional feature engineering approach used in SRL. Augmenting a simple, yet competitive SRL model with the tensor component yields significant performance gains. We demonstrate that our full model outperforms the best performing systems on the CoNLL-2009 shared task.

## Acknowledgments

The authors acknowledge the support of the MURI program (W911NF-10-1-0533) and the DARPA BOLT program. This research is developed in a collaboration of MIT with the Arabic Language Technologies (ALT) group at Qatar Computing Research Institute (QCRI) within the Interactive sYstems for Answer Search (IYAS) project. We are grateful to Anders Bjökelund and Michael Roth for providing the outputs of their systems. We thank Yu Xin, Tommi Jaakkola, the MIT NLP group and the ACL reviewers for their comments. Any opinions, findings, conclusions, or recommendations expressed in this paper are those of the authors, and do not necessarily reflect the views of the funding organizations.

## References


Anders Björkelund, Bernd Bohnet, Love Hafdell, and Pierre Nugues. 2010. A high-performance syntactic and semantic dependency parser. In *Proceedings of the 23rd International Conference on Computational Linguistics: Demonstrations*. Association for Computational Linguistics.

Wanxiang Che, Zhenghua Li, Yongqiang Li, Yuhang Guo, Bing Qin, and Ting Liu. 2009. Multilingual dependency-based syntactic and semantic parsing. In *Proceedings of the Thirteenth Conference on Computational Natural Language Learning (CoNLL 2009): Shared Task*, pages 49–54, Boulder, Colorado, June. Association for Computational Linguistics.

Ronan Collobert, Jason Weston, Léon Bottou, Michael Karlen, Koray Kavukcuoglu, and Pavel Kuksa. 2011. Natural language processing (almost) from scratch. *Journal of Machine Learning Research*, 11(Aug):2493–2537.

Lieven De Lathauwer, Pierre Comon, Bart De Moor, and Joos Vandewalle. 1995. Higher-order power method. *Nonlinear Theory and its Applications, NOLTA95*, 1.

Koen Deschacht and Marie-Francine Moens. 2009. Semi-supervised semantic role labeling using the Latent Words Language Model. In *Proceedings of the 2009 Conference on Empirical Methods in Natural Language Processing*, pages 21–29, Singapore, August. Association for Computational Linguistics.

Andrea Gesmundo, James Henderson, Paola Merlo, and Ivan Titov. 2009. A latent variable model of synchronous syntactic-semantic parsing for multiple languages. In *Proceedings of the Thirteenth Conference on Computational Natural Language Learning: Shared Task*. Association for Computational Linguistics.

Daniel Gildea and Daniel Jurafsky. 2002. Automatic labeling of semantic roles. *Computational Linguistics*, 28(3):245–288.

Jan Hajič, Massimiliano Ciaramita, Richard Johansson, Daisuke Kawahara, Maria Antònia Martí, Lluís Màrquez, Adam Meyers, Joakim Nivre, Sebastian Padó, Jan Štěpánek, Pavel Straňák, Mihai Surdeanu, Nianwen Xue, and Yi Zhang. 2009. The conll-2009 shared task: Syntactic and semantic dependencies in multiple languages. In *Proceedings of the Thirteenth Conference on Computational Natural Language Learning (CoNLL 2009): Shared Task*, pages 1–18, Boulder, Colorado, June. Association for Computational Linguistics.

Richard Johansson. 2009. Statistical bistratal dependency parsing. In *Proceedings of the 2009 Conference on Empirical Methods in Natural Language Processing*, pages 561–569, Singapore.

Harold W Kuhn. 1955. The hungarian method for the assignment problem. *Naval research logistics quarterly*, 2(1-2):83–97.

Tao Lei, Yu Xin, Yuan Zhang, Regina Barzilay, and Tommi Jaakkola. 2014. Low-rank tensors for scoring dependency structures. In *Proceedings of the 52nd Annual Meeting of the Association for Computational Linguistics (Volume 1: Long Papers)*, pages 1381–1391, Baltimore, Maryland, June. Association for Computational Linguistics.

Xavier Lluís, Xavier Carreras, and Lluís Màrquez. 2013. Joint arc-factored parsing of syntactic and semantic dependencies. *Transactions of the Association for Computational Linguistics*, 1.

André F. T. Martins and Mariana S. C. Almeida. 2014. Priberam: A turbo semantic parser with second order features. In *Proceedings of the 8th International Workshop on Semantic Evaluation (SemEval 2014)*, pages 471–476, Dublin, Ireland, August. Association for Computational Linguistics and Dublin City University.

Alessandro Moschitti, Daniele Pighin, and Roberto Basili. 2008. Tree kernels for semantic role labeling. *Computational Linguistics*, 34(2):193–224.

Sameer Pradhan, Kadri Hacioglu, Valerie Krugler, Wayne Ward, James H. Martin, and Daniel Jurafsky. 2005. Support vector learning for semantic argument classification. *Machine Learning*, 60(1):11–39.

Michael Roth and Kristian Woodsend. 2014. Composition of word representations improves semantic role labelling. In *Proceedings of the 2014 Conference on Empirical Methods in Natural Language Processing (EMNLP)*. Association for Computational Linguistics.

Mihai Surdeanu, Sanda Harabagiu, John Williams, and Paul Aarseth. 2003. Using predicate-argument structures for information extraction. In *Proceedings of the 41st Annual Meeting of the Association for Computational Linguistics*, pages 8–15, Sapporo, Japan.

Mihai Surdeanu, Richard Johansson, Adam Meyers, Lluís Màrquez, and Joakim Nivre. 2008. The conll-2008 shared task on joint parsing of syntactic and semantic dependencies. In *Proceedings of the Twelfth Conference on Computational Natural Language Learning*, pages 159–177. Association for Computational Linguistics.

Kristina Toutanova, Aria Haghighi, and Christopher Manning. 2008. A global joint model for semantic role labeling. *Computational Linguistics*, 34(2):161–191.

Nianwen Xue and Martha Palmer. 2004. Calibrating features for semantic role labeling. In Dekang Lin and Dekai Wu, editors, *Proceedings of EMNLP 2004*, pages 88–94, Barcelona, Spain, July. Association for Computational Linguistics.

Haitong Yang and Chengqing Zong. 2014. Multi-predicate semantic role labeling. In *Proceedings of the 2014 Conference on Empirical Methods in Natural Language Processing (EMNLP)*, pages 363–373, Doha, Qatar, October. Association for Computational Linguistics.

Alexander Yeh. 2000. More accurate tests for the statistical significance of result differences. In *Proceedings of the 18th conference on Computational linguistics-Volume 2*. Association for Computational Linguistics.

Benat Zapirain, Eneko Agirre, Lluís Màrquez, and Mihai Surdeanu. 2013. Selectional preferences for semantic role classification. *Computational Linguistics*, 39(3):631–664.

Yuan Zhang, Tao Lei, Regina Barzilay, and Tommi Jaakkola. 2014. Greed is good if randomized: New inference for dependency parsing. In *Proceedings of the 2014 Conference on Empirical Methods in Natural Language Processing (EMNLP)*. Association for Computational Linguistics.

Hai Zhao, Wenliang Chen, Jun'ichi Kazama, Kiyotaka Uchimoto, and Kentaro Torisawa. 2009a. Multilingual dependency learning: Exploiting rich features for tagging syntactic and semantic dependencies. In *Proceedings of the Thirteenth Conference on Computational Natural Language Learning: Shared Task*, pages 61–66. Association for Computational Linguistics.

Hai Zhao, Wenliang Chen, Chunyu Kity, and Guodong Zhou. 2009b. Multilingual dependency learning: A huge feature engineering method to semantic dependency parsing. In *Proceedings of the Thirteenth Conference on Computational Natural Language Learning (CoNLL 2009): Shared Task*. Association for Computational Linguistics.

# Lexical Event Ordering with an Edge-Factored Model

**Omri Abend, Shay B. Cohen and Mark Steedman**
School of Informatics, University of Edinburgh
Edinburgh EH8 9AB, United Kingdom
{oabend,scohen,steedman}@inf.ed.ac.uk

## Abstract

Extensive lexical knowledge is necessary for temporal analysis and planning tasks. We address in this paper a lexical setting that allows for the straightforward incorporation of rich features and structural constraints. We explore a *lexical event ordering* task, namely determining the likely temporal order of events based solely on the identity of their predicates and arguments. We propose an "edge-factored" model for the task that decomposes over the edges of the event graph. We learn it using the structured perceptron. As lexical tasks require large amounts of text, we do not attempt manual annotation and instead use the textual order of events in a domain where this order is aligned with their temporal order, namely cooking recipes.

## 1 Introduction

Temporal relations between events are often implicit, and inferring them relies on lexical and world knowledge about the likely order of events. For instance, to execute the instruction "fry the onion," the hearer should probably obtain oil beforehand, even if not instructed so explicitly. Lexical knowledge about the likely order of events is therefore necessary for any semantic task that requires temporal reasoning or planning, such as classifying temporal relations (Mani et al., 2006; Lapata and Lascarides, 2006; Yoshikawa et al., 2009; D'Souza and Ng, 2013; Mirza and Tonelli, 2014, *inter alia*), textual entailment (Dagan et al., 2013) or temporal information extraction (Ling and Weld, 2010). Lexical temporal knowledge is further important for modeling grammatical phenomena such as tense and aspect (Steedman, 2002).

In this paper we address the task of lexical event ordering, namely predicting the ordering of events based only on the identity of the words comprising their predicates and arguments. Concretely, the task is to predict the order of an unordered set of predicate-argument structures. Predicting the likely order of event types is a step towards more intricate planning and reasoning scenarios (see §3), and is useful in itself for tasks such as concept-to-text generation (Reiter et al., 2000), or in validating the correctness of instruction sets. A related idea can be found in modeling sentence coherence (Lapata, 2003; Barzilay and Lapata, 2008, *inter alia*), although here we focus on lexical relations between events, rather than coherence relations between complete sentences.

Compiling a resource of temporal tendencies between events can hardly be done manually, given the number and wealth of phenomena that have to be accounted for. Temporally annotated corpora, often annotated according to TimeML principles (Pustejovsky et al., 2003), are a useful resource for studying temporal relations. However, due to incurred costs, annotated corpora are too small for most lexical tasks. For instance, the TimeML annotated data used in the latest TempEval shared task contains only 100K words or so (UzZaman et al., 2013).

Previous work that does not rely on manually annotated data has had some success in discovering temporal lexical relations between predicates (Chklovski and Pantel, 2004; Chambers and Jurafsky, 2008b; Talukdar et al., 2012). However, despite their appeal, these methods have mostly fo-



*Human Language Technologies: The 2015 Annual Conference of the North American Chapter of the ACL*, pages 1161–1171,
Denver, Colorado, May 31 – June 5, 2015. 

cused on inducing simple event types, consisting of single words (e.g., "buy-own") or fixed expressions, and are hard to extend to include rich features (e.g., order-based and pattern-based features). Furthermore, measuring recall without annotated data is notoriously difficult, and evaluation is often precision-based or extrinsic.

We take a graph-based structured prediction approach to the task, motivated by the flexibility it allows in incorporating various feature sets and constraints. We use an edge-factored model, which decomposes over the edges in the graph of events comprising the recipe (§4). We estimate the model using the structured perceptron algorithm. We compare the structured perceptron approach to an approximate greedy baseline and to a locally normalized model reminiscent of common approaches for order learning, obtaining superior results (§8). The learning algorithm is of potential use in other ordering tasks such as machine translation reordering (Tromble and Eisner, 2009).

We focus on domains in which the order of events in the text is aligned with their temporal order. By doing so we avoid the costly and error-prone manual annotation of temporal relations by using the textual order of recipes to approximate their temporal order.[1] Specifically, we address the cooking recipes domain, which we motivate in §2.

In summary, the contribution of this paper is three-fold: (1) we explore the task of lexical event ordering and means for its evaluation; (2) we present an edge-factored model for the task, and show it can be used to predict the order of events well (77.7% according to standard measures for ordering evaluation); (3) we present a method for extracting events and create a dataset of ordered events using recipes extracted from the web.

## 2 Related Work

Temporal semantics is receiving increasing attention in recent years. Lexical features are in frequent use and rely in most part on external resources which are either manually compiled or automatically induced. The line of work most closely related to ours focuses on inducing lexical relations between event types. Most work has been unsupervised, often using pattern-based approaches relying on manually crafted (Chklovski and Pantel, 2004) or induced patterns (Davidov et al., 2007), that correlate with temporal relations (e.g., temporal discourse connectives). Talukdar et al. (2012) uses the textual order of events in Wikipedia biographical articles to induce lexical information. We use both textual order and discourse connectives to define our feature set, and explore a setting which allows for the straightforward incorporation of additional features.

Chambers and Jurafsky (2008b; 2009) addressed the unsupervised induction of partially ordered event chains (or schema) in the news domain, centered around a common protagonist. One of their evaluation scenarios tackles a binary classification related to event ordering, and seeks to distinguish ordered sets of events from randomly permuted ones, yielding an accuracy of 75%. Manshadi et al. (2008) used language models to learn event sequences and conducted a similar evaluation on weblogs with about 65% accuracy. The classification task we explore here is considerably more complex (see §8).

The task of script knowledge induction has been frequently addressed in recent years. Balasubramanian et al. (2013) and Pichotta and Mooney (2014) extended Chambers and Jurafsky's model to include events that have multiple arguments. Jans et al. (2012) use skip-grams to capture event-event relations between not necessarily consecutive events.

Regneri et al. (2010) constructed a temporal lexical knowledge base through crowd-sourcing. Their approach is appealing as it greatly reduces the costs incurred by manual annotation and can potentially be used in conjunction with lexical information obtained from raw text. Modi and Titov (2014) jointly learns the stereotypical order of events and their distributional representation, in order to capture paraphrased instances of the same event type. Frermann et al. (2014) models the joint task of inducing event paraphrases and their order using a Bayesian framework. All latter three works evaluated their induced temporal ordering knowledge on a binary prediction of whether a temporal relation between a pair of (not necessarily related) events holds, and not on the prediction of a complete permutation given an unordered event set as in this work. Their evaluation was conducted on 30 event pairs manually an-

[1] See Cassidy et al. (2014) for a discussion of inter-annotator agreement in TimeML-based schemes.

notated through crowd-sourcing, where Modi and Titov (2014) further included an evaluation on a large set of pairs automatically extracted from the Gigaword corpus.

The appeal of the cooking domain for studying various semantic phenomena has been recognized by several studies in NLP and AI (Tasse and Smith, 2008; Bollini et al., 2013; Cimiano et al., 2013; Regneri et al., 2013; Malmaud et al., 2014). The domain is here motivated by several considerations. First, recipes mostly describe concrete actions, rather than abstract relations, which are less relevant to temporal ordering. Second, from a practical point of view, many recipes are available online in computer-readable format. Third, the restrictiveness of the cooking domain can also be seen as an advantage, as it can reveal major conceptual challenges raised by the task, without introducing additional confounds.

## 3 Temporally Ordering Lexical Events

We formalize our task as follows. Let $U$ be a set of event types, namely actions or states (represented as predicates) and objects which these actions operate on (represented as arguments to the predicates; mostly ingredients or kitchenware). Formally, each $e \in U$ is a tuple $\langle a, c_1, \ldots, c_n \rangle$ where $a$ is the main verb or predicate describing the event (such as "stir" or "mix") and $c_1, \ldots, c_n$ is a list of arguments that the predicate takes (e.g., "salt" or "spoon"). Two additional marked events, $s$ and $f$, correspond to "start" and "finish" events. A recipe is a sequence of events in $U$, starting at $s$ and ending at $f$.

Given a recipe $R = \langle e_1, ..., e_m \rangle$, we wish to predict the order of the events just from the (multi)set $\{e_i\}_{i=1}^{m}$. In this work we use the textual order of events to approximate their temporal order (see, e.g., Talukdar et al. (2012) for a similar assumption). The validity of this assumption for cooking recipes is supported in §6.

Figure 1 gives an example of a set of events extracted from our dataset for the dish "Apple Crisp Ala [sic] Brigitte." Lexical information places quite a few limitations on the order of this recipe. For instance, in most cases serving is carried out at the end while putting the ingredients in is done prior to baking them. However, lexical knowledge in itself is unlikely to predict the exact ordering of the events as given in the recipe (e.g., spreading butter might be done before or after baking).

One of the major obstacles in tackling planning problems in AI is the knowledge bottleneck. Lexical event ordering is therefore a step towards more ambitious goals in planning. For instance, temporal relations may be used to induce planning operators (Mourão et al., 2012), which can in turn be used to generate a plan (recipe) given a specified goal and an initial set of ingredients.

## 4 Model, Inference and Learning

In this section we describe the main learning components that compose our approach to event ordering.

### 4.1 Edge-Factored Model for Event Ordering

We hereby detail the linear model we use for ordering events. Let $S = \{e_1, \ldots, e_m\} \subseteq U$ be a set of events as mentioned in §3. Let $G(S) = (S \cup \{s, f\}, E(S))$ be an almost-complete directed graph with $E(S) = (S \cup \{s\}) \times (S \cup \{f\}) \subseteq U \times U$. Every Hamiltonian path[2] in $G(S)$ that starts in $s$ and ends in $f$ defines an ordering of the events in $S$. The edge $(e_i, e_j)$ in such a path denotes that $e_i$ is the event that comes before $e_j$.

The modeling problem is to score Hamiltonian paths in a given directed graph $G(S)$. Here, we use an edge-factored model. Let $\phi\colon (U \times U) \to \mathbb{R}^d$ be a feature function for pairs of events, represented as directed edges. In addition, let $\theta \in \mathbb{R}^d$ be a weight vector. We define the score of a Hamiltonian path $h = (h_1, \ldots, h_{m+1})$ ($h_i \in E(S)$) as:

$$\mathrm{score}(h|S) = \sum_{i=1}^{m+1} \theta^\top \phi(h_i) \quad (1)$$

Given a weight vector $\theta$ and a set of events $S$, inference is carried out by computing the highest scoring Hamiltonian path in $G(S)$:

$$h^* = \arg \max_{h \in H(S)} \mathrm{score}(h|S) \quad (2)$$

where $H(S)$ is the set of Hamiltonian paths in $G(S)$ that start with $s$ and end with $f$. The path $h^*$ is the best temporal ordering of the set of events $S$ according to the model in Eq. 1 with weight vector $\theta$.

[2] A path in a graph that visits all nodes exactly once.

(a)
$e_1 = \langle \textit{butter, dish} \rangle$
$e_2 = \langle \textit{put, apples, water, ... flour, cinnamon, it} \rangle$
$e_3 = \langle \textit{mix, with spoon,} \rangle$
$e_4 = \langle \textit{spread, butter, salt, ... over mix} \rangle$
$e_5 = \langle \textit{bake, F} \rangle$
$e_6 = \langle \textit{serve, cream, cream} \rangle$

(b) Butter a deep baking dish, put apples, water, flour, sugar and cinnamon in it. Mix with spoon and spread butter and salt over the apple mix. Bake at 350 degrees F until the apples are tender and the crust brown, about 30 minutes. Serve with cream or whipped cream.

(c)
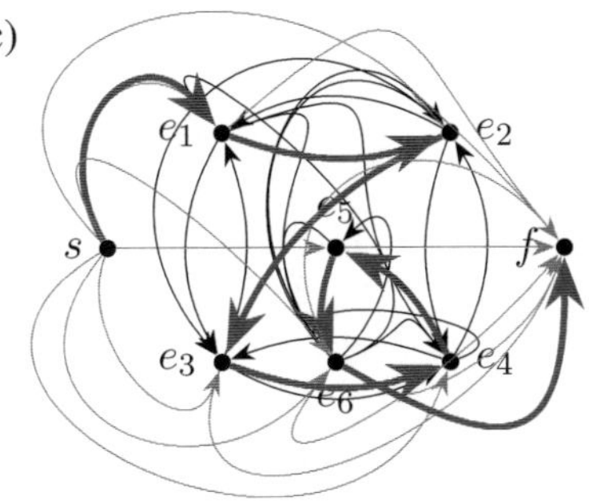


Figure 1: (a) The sequence of events representing the recipe for the dish "Apple Crisp Ala [sic] Brigitte." (b) The actual recipe for this dish. (c) A complete graph over the set of events with start and finish states. Each internal node in the graph is one of the events $e_i$ for $i \in \{1, \ldots, 6\}$. The path in blue bold denotes the correct Hamiltonian path describing the set of actions as ordered in the recipe. Red edges denote edges from the start state and to the end state. The edges, in practice, are weighted.

### 4.2 Inference

As mentioned above, inference with the edge-factored model requires solving the maximization problem in Eq. 2. This corresponds to finding a Hamiltonian path in a complete graph, which is generally an NP-hard problem. Reasonable approximations for this problem are also NP-hard. Still techniques are developed for specialized cases, due to the problem's importance in discrete optimization.

Despite its theoretical NP-hardness, this maximization problem can be represented as an Integer Linear Program (ILP), and then solved using generic techniques for ILP optimization. Due to the relatively short length of recipes (13.8 events on average in our corpus), the problem can be effectively solved in most cases.

The proposed algorithmic setting is appealing for its flexibility. The linear score formulation allows us to use rich features, while using ILP allows to easily incorporate structural constraints. Indeed, ILP has been proven valuable in various NLP tasks (Roth and Yih, 2007; Talukdar et al., 2012; Scaria et al., 2013). See Appendix A for our ILP formulation.

As a baseline, we experiment with an additional greedy inference algorithm, similar to the one described by Lapata (2003) for sentence ordering. The algorithm iteratively selects an outgoing edge (starting from the node $s$) that has the largest weight to a node that has not been visited so far, until all vertices are covered, at which point the path terminates by traveling to $f$.

### 4.3 Learning

The learning problem takes as input a dataset consisting of unordered sets of events, paired with a target ordering. We consider two types of learning algorithms for the edge-factored model in the previous section. The first learns in a global training setting using the averaged structured perceptron (Collins, 2002), with the decoding algorithm being either the one based on ILP (henceforth, GLOBAL-PRC), or the greedy one (GREEDY-PRC). Given a training instance $S$ and its correct label $h^c$, the structured perceptron calls the inference procedure as a subroutine and updates the weight vector $\theta$ according to the difference between the value of the feature function on the predicted path ($\sum_{h^*} \phi(h_i)$) and on the correct path ($\sum_{h^c} \phi(h_i)$).

The second learning algorithm we try is based on *factored* training. This algorithm maximizes the likelihood of a conditional log-linear model $p$:

$$p(e_2|e_1, \theta, S) = \frac{\exp\left(\theta^\top \phi(e_1, e_2)\right)}{Z(\theta, S, e_1)}$$

$$Z(\theta, S, e_1) = \sum_{e:\ (e_1, e) \in E(S)} \exp\left(\theta^\top \phi(e_1, e)\right)$$

where $e_1, e_2 \in S \cup \{s, f\}$. This is a locally normalized log-linear model that gives the probability of transitioning to node $e_2$ from node $e_1$. Maximizing the score in Eq. 1 has an interpretation of finding the highest scoring path according to an edge-factored Markovian model, such that:

$$p(h|\theta, S) = \prod_{i=1}^{m+1} p(e_i|e_{i-1}, \theta, S),$$

where $h = (h_1, \ldots, h_{m+1})$ is a Hamiltonian path with $h_i = (e_{i-1}, e_i)$ being a directed edge in the path. Initial experimentation suggested that greedy inference (henceforth, GREEDY-LOGLIN) works better in practice than the ILP formulation for the locally-normalized model. We therefore do not report results on global inference with this log-linear model. We suspect that greedy inference works better with the log-linear model because it is trained locally, while the perceptron algorithm includes a global inference step in its training, and therefore better matches global decoding.

GREEDY-LOGLIN closely resembles the learning model of Lapata (2003), as both are first-order Markovian and use the same (greedy) inference procedure. Lapata's model differs from GREEDY-LOGLIN in being a generative model, where each event is a tuple of features, and the transition probability between events is defined as the product of transition probabilities between feature pairs. GREEDY-LOGLIN is discriminative, so to be maximally comparable to the presented model.

## 5 The Feature Set

Table 1 presents the complete set of features. We consider three sets of features: Lexical encodes the written forms of the event pair predicates and objects; Brown uses Brown clusters (Brown et al., 1992) to encode similar information, but allows generalization between distributionally similar words; and Frequency encodes the empirical distribution of temporally-related phenomena.

The feature definitions make use of several functions. For brevity, we sometimes say that an event $e$ is $(a, c_1)$ if $e$'s predicate is $a$ and its first argument is $c_1$, disregarding its other arguments. Let C be a reference corpus of recipes for collecting statistics. The function $B(w)$ gives the Brown cluster of a word $w$, as determined by clustering C into 50 clusters $\{1, \ldots, 50\}$. The function $\mathrm{ORD}(a, c)$ returns the mean ordinal number of an $(a, c)$ event in C. The ordinal number of the event $e_i$ in a recipe $(e_1, ..., e_m)$ is defined as $i - \frac{m}{2}$.

| | Template | Example |
|---|---|---|
| Lexical | $(a^1, a^2)$ | *(fry, add)* |
| | $(a^1, c_1^2)$ | *(fry, oil)* |
| | $(a^2, c_1^1)$ | *(onions, add)* |
| | $(c_1^1, c_1^2)$ | *(onions, oil)* |
| Brown | $(B(a^1), B(a^2))$ | (1,3) |
| | $\forall (k, k') \in K.$ $\lvert\{(c_i^1, c_j^2) \colon B(c_i^1) = k, B(c_j^2) = k'\}\rvert$ | (5,4) : 2 |
| | $\forall k \in K. \lvert\{c_i^2 \colon B(c_i^2) = k\}\rvert$ | 12 : 1 |
| | $B(a^2)$ | 5 |
| Frequency | $\forall \ell \in L. \log(\epsilon + P_\ell[(a^2, c_1^2) \mid (a^1, c_1^1)])$ | -2.3 |
| | $\forall \ell \in L. \mathrm{PMI}_\ell((a^1, c_1^1), (a^2, c_1^2))$ | 3.1 |
| | $\forall \ell \in L. \mathrm{PMI}_\ell((a^2, c_1^2), (a^1, c_1^1))$ | -2.0 |
| | $\mathrm{ORD}(a^2, c_1^2)$ | 3.2 |

Table 1: Feature templates used for computing $\phi$. The templates operate on two events $\langle a^1, c_1^1, \ldots, c_{m_1}^1 \rangle$ and $\langle a^2, c_1^2, \ldots, c_{m_2}^2 \rangle$. $B(w)$ maps a word $w$ to its Brown cluster in $K = \{1, \ldots, 50\}$. $\mathrm{ORD}(e)$ returns the mean ordinal value of $e$. Feature templates which start with $\forall$ stand for multiple features, one for each element in the set quantified over. Non-numerical feature templates correspond to binary features. E.g., *(fry, add)* as an instance of $(a^1, a^2)$ is a binary feature indicating the appearance of an event with $a^1 =$ *fry* on one end of the edge and an event with $a^2 =$ *add* on the other end of it. $\epsilon = 10^{-3}$ in our experiments. See text for elaboration.

We further encode the tendency of two events to appear with temporal discourse connectives, such as "before" or "until." We define a linkage between two events as a triplet $(e_1, e_2, \ell) \in (U \times U \times L)$, where $L$ is the set of linkage types, defined according to their marker's written form. §6 details the extraction process of linkages from recipes. We further include a special linkage type *linear* based on the order of events in the text, and consider every pair of events $e_1$ and $e_2$ that follow one another in a recipe as linked under this linkage type.

For each linkage type $\ell \in L$, we define an empirical probability distribution $P_\ell((a, c_1), (a', c_1')) = P((a, c_1), (a', c_1')|\ell)$, based on simple counting. The function PMI gives the point-wise mutual information of two events and is defined as:

$$\mathrm{PMI}_\ell((a, c), (a', c')) = \log\left(\frac{P_\ell((a, c_1), (a', c_1'))}{P_\ell(a, c_1) \cdot P_\ell(a', c_1')}\right)$$

Frequency-based features encode the empirical estimate of the probabilities that various pairs of features would occur one after the other or linked with a discourse marker. They are equivalent to using probabilities extracted from maximum likelihood estimation according to a bigram model in the discriminative learning. While some of this information is implicitly found in the lexical features, collecting frequency counts from a large training set is much quicker than running costly structured optimization. Rather the discriminative training can weigh the different empirical probabilities according to their discriminative power. Indeed we find that these features are important in practice and can result in high accuracy even after training on a small training set.

## 6 The Recipe Dataset

**Data and Preprocessing.** The data is extracted from a recipe repository found on the web.[3] The recipes are given as free text. To extract event types we run the Stanford CoreNLP[4] pipeline of a tokenizer, POS tagger, a lexical constituency parser (the *englishPCFG* parsing model) and extract typed Stanford dependencies (de Marneffe and Manning, 2008). As is common with web extractions, the recipes contain occasional spelling, grammatical and formatting errors. The corpus consists of 139 files, 73484 recipes, 1.02M events (13.8 events per recipe on average) and 11.05M words.[5]

**Event Extraction.** We focus on verbal events and do not extract nominal and adjectival argument structures, which are not as well supported by current parsing technology. Any verb is taken to define an event, aside from modal verbs, auxiliaries and secondary verbs. A secondary verb (e.g., "let," "begin") does not describe an action in its own right, but rather modifies an event introduced by another verb. We identify these verbs heuristically using a list given in Dixon (2005, p. 490–491) and a few simple rules defined over parse trees. E.g., from the sentence "you should begin to chop the onion," we extract a single event with a predicate "chop." Arguments are taken to be the immediate dependents of the predicate that have an argument dependency type (such as direct or indirect objects) according to the extracted Stanford dependencies. For prepositional phrases, we include the preposition as part of the argument. Argument indices are determined by their order in the text. The order of events is taken to be the order of their verbs in the text.

**Linkage Extraction.** We focus on a subset of linkage relations, which are relevant for temporal relations. We use Pitler and Nenkova's (2009) explicit discourse connectives classifier to identify temporal discourse linkers, discarding all other discourse linkers. Once a discourse linker has been detected, we heuristically extract its arguments (namely the pair of verbs it links) according to a deterministic extraction rule defined over the parse tree. We find 28 distinct connectives in our training set, where the 5 most common linkers "until," "then," "before," "when" and "as" cover over 95% of the instances. We extract 36756 such linkages from the corpus, 0.5 linkages per recipe on average.

**Temporal and Textual Ordering.** In order to confirm that temporal and textual order of recipes are generally in agreement, we manually examine the first 20 recipes in our development set. One recipe was excluded as noise[6], resulting in 19 recipes and 353 events. We identify the sources of misalignment between the linear order and the temporal order of the events.[7] 13 events (3.7%) did not have any clear temporal orderings. These consisted of mostly negations and modalities (e.g., "do not overbrown!"), sub-section headings (e.g., "Preparation") or other general statements that do not constitute actions or states. For the remaining 340 events, we compare their linear and the temporal orderings.

We estimate the frequency of sub-sequences that contradict the temporal order and confirm that they occur only infrequently. We find that most disagreements fall into these two categories: (1) disjunctions between several events, only one of which will actually take place (e.g., "roll Springerle pin over dough, or press mold into top"); (2) a pair, or less commonly a triplet, of events are expressed in reverse order. For instance, "*place* on *greased* and *floured* cookie sheet," where greasing and flouring should occur before the placing action. We note that assuming the alignment of the temporal and textual order

[3] http://www.ffts.com/recipes.htm

[4] http://nlp.stanford.edu/software/corenlp.shtml

[5] Links to the original recipes, the preprocessed recipes and all extracted events can be found in http://homepages.inf.ed.ac.uk/oabend/event_order.html.

[6] This did not result from an extraction problem, but rather from the recipe text itself being too noisy to interpret.

[7] Events are parsed manually so to avoid confounding the results with the parser's performance.

of recipes does not suggest that the textual order is the only order of events that would yield the same outcome.

We compute the Kendall's Tau correlation, a standard measure for information ordering (Lapata, 2006), between the temporal and linear orderings for each recipe. In cases of several events that happen simultaneously (including disjunctions), we take their ordinals to be equal. For instance, for three events where the last two happen at the same time, we take their ordering to be (1,2,2) in our analysis. We find that indeed temporal and textual orderings are in very high agreement, with 6 recipes of the 19 perfectly aligned. The average Kendall's Tau between the temporal ordering and the linear one is 0.924.

## 7 Experimental Setup

**Evaluation.** We compute the accuracy of our algorithms by comparing the predicted order to the one in which the events are written. We first compute the number of exact matches, denoted with EXACT, namely the percentage of recipes in which the predicted and the textual orders are the same.

For a more detailed analysis of imperfect predictions, we compute the agreement between subsequences of the orderings. We borrow the notion of a "concordant pair" from the definition of Kendall's Tau and generalize it to capture agreement of longer sub-sequences. Two $k$-tuples of integers $(x_1, ..., x_k)$ and $(y_1, ..., y_k)$ are said to "agree in order" if for every $1 \leq i < j \leq k$, $x_i < x_j$ iff $y_i < y_j$. Given two orderings of the same recipe $O_1 = (e_{\tau(1)}, ..., e_{\tau(m)})$ and $O_2 = (e_{\sigma(1)}, ..., e_{\sigma(m)})$ (where $\tau$ and $\sigma$ are permutations over $[m] = \{1, \ldots, m\}$) and given a sequence of $k$ monotonically increasing indices $t = (i_1, ..., i_k)$, $t$ is said to be a "concordant $k$-tuple" of $O_1$ and $O_2$ if $(\tau(i_1), ..., \tau(i_k))$ and $(\sigma(i_1), ..., \sigma(i_k))$ agree in order, as defined above.

Denote the unordered recipes of the test data as $\{R_i\}_{i=1}^N$, where $R_i = \{e_1^i, ..., e_{m_i}^i\} \subset U$ for all $i$, and their target orderings $\Sigma = \{\sigma_i\}_{i=1}^N$, where $\sigma_i$ is a permutation over $[m_i]$. Assume we wish to evaluate a set of predicted orderings for this test data $\mathrm{T} = \{\tau_i\}_{i=1}^N$, where again $\tau_i$ is a permutation over $[m_i]$. Denote the number of concordant $k$-tuples of $\sigma_i$ and $\tau_i$ as $\mathrm{conc}(\sigma_i, \tau_i)$. The total number of of monotonically increasing $k$-tuples of indices is $\binom{m_i}{k}$. The $k$-wise (micro-averaged) accuracy of T with respect to $\Sigma$ is:

$$\mathrm{acc}_k(\Sigma, \mathrm{T}) = \frac{\sum_{i=1}^N \mathrm{conc}(\sigma_i, \tau_i)}{\sum_{i=1}^N \binom{m_i}{k}}$$

Any $k$-tuples containing the start node $s$ or the end node $f$ are excluded, as their ordering is trivial. Recipes of length less than $k$ are discarded when computing $\mathrm{acc}_k$. A micro-averaged accuracy measure is used so as not to disproportionately weigh short recipes. However, in order to allow comparison to mean Kendall's Tau, commonly used in works on order learning, we further report a macro-averaged $\mathrm{acc}_2$ by computing $\mathrm{acc}_2$ for each recipe separately, and taking the average of resulting accuracy levels. Average Kendall's Tau can now be computed by $2\mathrm{acc}_2 - 1$ for the macro-averaged $\mathrm{acc}_2$ score.

**Data.** We randomly partition the text into training, test and development sets, taking an 80-10-10 percent split. We do not partition the individual files so as to avoid statistical artifacts introduced by recipe duplications or near-duplications. The training, development and test sets contain 58038, 7667 and 7779 recipes respectively. The total number of feature template instantiations in the training data is 8.94M.

**Baselines and Algorithms.** We compare three learning algorithms. GLOBAL-PRC is the structured perceptron algorithm that uses ILP inference. GREEDY-PRC is a structured perceptron in which inference is done greedily. GREEDY-LOGLIN is the locally normalized log-linear model with greedy inference. RANDOM randomly (uniformly) selects a permutation of the recipe's events.

**Experimental Settings.** The structured perceptron algorithms, GLOBAL-PRC and GREEDY-PRC, are run with a learning rate of 0.1 for 3 iterations. To avoid exceedingly long runs, we set a time limit in seconds $\beta$ on the running time of each ILP inference stage used in GLOBAL-PRC. We consider two training scenarios: *4K*, which trains on the first 4K recipes of the training set, and *58K*, which trains on the full training data of 58K recipes. In GLOBAL-PRC we set $\beta$ to be 30 seconds for the 4K

| | Alg. | acc2 | | acc3 | acc4 | EXACT |
|---|---|---|---|---|---|---|
| | | MI | MA | | | |
| 4K | GLOBAL-PRC | **71.2** | **77.7** | **44.7** | **27.9** | **35.1** |
| | GREEDY-PRC | 60.8 | 68.0 | 30.6 | 15.0 | 20.4 |
| | GREEDY-LOGLIN | 65.6 | 71.5 | 35.8 | 18.7 | 21.0 |
| 58K | GLOBAL-PRC | 68.9 | 76.4 | 41.3 | 24.8 | 34.4 |
| | GREEDY-PRC | 60.7 | 67.8 | 30.6 | 15.2 | 20.5 |
| | GREEDY-LOGLIN | 66.3 | 72.4 | 36.6 | 19.4 | 21.3 |
| | RANDOM | 50.0 | 51.2 | 16.7 | 4.2 | 0.5 |

Table 2: Accuracy of the different models on the test data in percents. Columns correspond to evaluation measures, namely accuracy of sub-sequences of lengths 2 (micro and macro averages), 3 and 4, and exact match. The upper (lower) part presents results for a training set of 4K (58K) samples. GLOBAL-PRC is run with $\beta = 30$ for 4K and with $\beta = 5$ for 58K. In 58K, all models are run with the Full feature set. In 4K, following prior experimentation on the development set, we select the best performing feature sets (Full for GREEDY-LOGLIN and GREEDY-PRC; Fr + Lex for GLOBAL-PRC).

| $\beta$ | Set | acc2 | | acc3 | acc4 | EXACT |
|---|---|---|---|---|---|---|
| | | MI | MA | | | |
| 30 | FrLim | 55.9 | 61.5 | 21.6 | 6.9 | 8.2 |
| | Fr | 68.7 | 75.9 | 40.6 | **23.9** | 31.7 |
| | Fr + Le | **68.9** | **76.2** | **40.7** | 23.8 | **32.1** |
| | Full | 68.4 | 76.0 | 39.9 | 23.1 | 31.8 |
| 5 | FrLim | 55.1 | 60.9 | 20.9 | 6.5 | 8.2 |
| | Fr | 65.9 | 74.2 | 36.0 | 19.3 | 30.4 |
| | Fr + Le | 66.2 | 74.3 | 36.8 | 20.4 | 30.7 |
| | Full | 66.3 | 74.5 | 36.9 | 20.4 | 30.4 |

Table 3: The performance of GLOBAL-PRC on the development set in various settings (4K scenario). Columns correspond to evaluation measures, namely accuracy of sub-sequences of lengths 2 (micro and macro averages), 3 and 4, and exact match. The upper (lower) part of the table presents results for a time limit of $\beta$=30 (5). Fr includes the Frequency features estimated on 58K recipes. Fr + Le further includes Lexical features. Full includes all features. FrLim includes all features, where Frequency features are estimated only on 4K recipes.

scenario, and 5 seconds in the 58K scenario. The number of threads was limited to 3. Where the time limit is reached before an optimal solution is found, the highest scoring Hamiltonian path found up to that point is returned by the ILP solver. In the infrequent samples where no feasible solution is found during training, the sample is skipped over, while at test time, we perform greedy inference instead.

We define the following feature sets. Fr includes only features of class Frequency, while Fr + Lex includes features from both the Frequency and Lexical categories. Full includes all feature sets. All above feature sets take C, the reference corpus for computing FREQUENCY features, to be the entire 58K training samples in both scenarios. In the 4K scenario, we also experiment with FrLim, which includes all features, but takes C to contain only the 4K samples of the training data.

We use the Gurobi package for ILP.[8] Brown clusters are extracted from the 58K samples of the training data using Liang's implementation.[9] The convex log-likelihood function of GREEDY-LOGLIN is optimized using LBFGS. All features are selected and all parameters are tuned using the development set.

## 8 Results

Table 2 presents the results of the three major algorithms in the two main scenarios *58K* and *4K*. We find that the structured perceptron algorithm, GLOBAL-PRC, obtains the best results in both cases and under all evaluation measures. The importance of global optimization was also stressed in other works on event ordering (Chambers and Jurafsky, 2008a; Talukdar et al., 2012).

In order to assess the contribution of the different components of the model of the best scoring model, GLOBAL-PRC, we compare the performance of the different feature sets and settings of $\beta$ on the development set in 4K (Table 3). Results reveal the strong impact of the Frequency feature set on the results. Using this category set alone (Fr) yields slightly lower results than using the full feature set, while estimating the Frequency features on a small corpus (FrLim) lowers results dramatically. Adding Lexical and Brown features yields a small improvement over using Frequency alone.

While Table 3 demonstrates the importance of $\beta$ in the performance of GLOBAL-PRC, it also shows that on a limited time budget, a small training set and few features (4K, Fr) and a reasonably small $\beta$ (5) can yield competitive results. Increasing $\beta$ from 5 to 30 generally improves results by 2 to 3 percent absolute. The importance of $\beta$ is further demonstrated in Table 2, where performance with 4K training instances and $\beta = 30$ is better than with 58K training instances and $\beta = 5$. Preliminary experiments conducted on the development data with higher values of $\beta$ of 60 and 120 suggest that further increasing $\beta$

[8] http://www.gurobi.com

[9] https://github.com/percyliang/brown-cluster

yields no further improvement.

Previous studies evaluated their models on the related problem of distinguishing randomly permuted and correctly ordered chains of events (§2). In this paper we generalize this task to complete event ordering. In order to demonstrate the relative difficulty of the tasks, we apply our highest scoring model (4K, Fr + Le) to the binary task (without re-training it). We do so by computing the percentage of cases in which the correct ordering obtains a higher score than an average ordering. The high resulting accuracy of 93%, as opposed to considerably lower accuracies obtained under ordering evaluation measures, reflects the relative difficulty of the tasks.

The proposed edge-factored model can easily capture pair-wise ordering relations between events, but is more limited in accounting for relations between larger sets of events. A simple way of doing so is by adding the feature $\sum_e P(e_i|e)P(e|e_j)$ between events $e_i$ and $e_j$ (in addition to the regular transition probabilities $P(e_i|e_j)$). However, preliminary experimentation with this technique did not yield improved performance. Future work will address higher-order models that straightforwardly account for such long-distance dependencies.

To qualitatively assess what generalizations are learned by the model, we apply GLOBAL-PRC to the development data and look at what event pairs obtained either particularly high or particularly low results. For each pair of predicates and their first arguments ($a^1$,$c_1^1$), ($a^2$,$c_1^2$), we compute the average weight of an edge connecting events of these types, discarding pairs of frequency less than 20.

The 20 highest scoring edges contain pairs such as ("add," "mixing after addition"), ("beat whites," "fold into mixture") and ("cover for minutes," "cook"), in addition to a few noisy pairs resulting from parser errors. The 20 lowest scoring edges contain event pairs that are likely to appear in the opposite order. 11 of the cases include as a first argument the predicates "serve," "cool" or "chill," which are likely to occur at the end of a recipe. 3 other edges linked duplications (e.g., ("reduce heat," "reduce heat")), which are indeed unlikely to immediately follow one another. These findings suggest the importance of detecting both lexical pairs that are unlikely to follow one another, in addition to those that are likely to.

## 9 Conclusion

We addressed the problem of lexical event ordering, and developed an edge-factored model for tackling it. We rely on temporally aligned texts, using a new dataset of cooking recipes as a test case, thereby avoiding the need for costly and error-prone manual annotation. We present results of a pair-wise accuracy of over 70% using a basic set of features, and show the utility of the structured perceptron algorithm over simpler greedy and local approaches. The setup we explore, which uses a discriminative model and an ILP formulation, is easy to extend both in terms of features and in terms of more complex formal constraints and edge dependencies, as was done in graph-based dependency parsing (McDonald et al., 2005). Future work will address the extension of the feature set and model, and the application of this model to temporal semantics and planning tasks. We will further address the application of semi-supervised variants of the proposed techniques (e.g., self-training) to other domains, where no sizable corpora of temporally aligned data can be found.


## Acknowledgments

We would like to thank Nathan Schneider, Roy Schwartz, Bonnie Webber and the members of the Probmodels group at the University of Edinburgh for helpful comments. This work was supported by ERC Advanced Fellowship 249520 GRAMPLUS.


## Appendix A: Maximal Hamiltonian Path

Let $G(S) = (S \cup \{s, f\}, E(S))$ be an almost-complete directed graph with $E = E(S) = (S \cup \{s\}) \times (S \cup \{f\})$. Let $c_{ij} \in \mathbb{R}$ be weights for its edges ($(i, j) \in E$). A Hamiltonian path between $s, f \in V$ can be found by solving the following program, returning $P = \{(i, j)|x_{ij} = 1\}$.

$$\max_{\substack{x_{ij} \in \{0,1\}:\ (i,j) \in E \\ u_i \in \mathbb{Z}:\ i \in V}} \sum_{i \neq j}^{n} c_{ij} x_{ij}$$

$$\text{s.t.} \sum_{i=0, i \neq j}^{n} x_{ij} = 1\ \forall j \neq s; \quad \sum_{j=0, j \neq i}^{n} x_{ij} = 1\ \ \forall i \neq e;$$

$$u_i - u_j + |V| x_{ij} \leq |V| - 1\ \ \forall (i, j) \in E$$

## References


Niranjan Balasubramanian, Stephen Soderland, Mausam, and Oren Etzioni. 2013. Generating coherent event schemas at scale. In *EMNLP '13*, pages 1721–1731.

Regina Barzilay and Mirella Lapata. 2008. Modeling local coherence: An entity-based approach. *Computational Linguistics*, 34(1):1–34.

Mario Bollini, Stefanie Tellex, Tyler Thompson, Nicholas Roy, and Daniela Rus. 2013. Interpreting and executing recipes with a cooking robot. In *Experimental Robotics*, pages 481–495. Springer.

Peter F Brown, Peter V Desouza, Robert L Mercer, Vincent J Della Pietra, and Jenifer C Lai. 1992. Class-based n-gram models of natural language. *Computational Linguistics*, 18(4):467–479.

Taylor Cassidy, Bill McDowell, Nathanael Chambers, and Steven Bethard. 2014. An annotation framework for dense event ordering. In *ACL '14: Short Papers*, pages 501–506.

Nathanael Chambers and Dan Jurafsky. 2008a. Jointly combining implicit constraints improves temporal ordering. In *EMNLP '08*, pages 698–706.

Nathanael Chambers and Dan Jurafsky. 2008b. Unsupervised learning of narrative event chains. In *ACL-HLT '08*, pages 789–797.

Nathanael Chambers and Dan Jurafsky. 2009. Unsupervised learning of narrative schemas and their participants. In *ACL-IJCNLP '09*, pages 602–610, Suntec, Singapore, August.

Timothy Chklovski and Patrick Pantel. 2004. Verbocean: Mining the web for fine-grained semantic verb relations. In *EMNLP '04*, pages 33–40.

Philipp Cimiano, Janna Lüker, David Nagel, and Christina Unger. 2013. Exploiting ontology lexica for generating natural language texts from RDF data. In *European Workshop on Natural Language Generation*, pages 10–19.

Michael Collins. 2002. Discriminative training methods for hidden markov models: Theory and experiments with perceptron algorithms. In *EMNLP '02*, pages 1–8.

Ido Dagan, Dan Roth, Mark Sammons, and Fabio Massimo Zanzotto. 2013. Recognizing textual entailment: Models and applications. *Synthesis Lectures on Human Language Technologies*, 6(4):1–220.

Dmitry Davidov, Ari Rappoport, and Moshe Koppel. 2007. Fully unsupervised discovery of concept-specific relationships by web mining. In *ACL '07*, pages 232–239.

Marie-Catherine de Marneffe and Christopher D Manning. 2008. The Stanford typed dependencies representation. In *the COLING '08 workshop on Cross-Framework and Cross-Domain Parser Evaluation*, pages 1–8.

Robert M.W. Dixon. 2005. *A Semantic Approach To English Grammar*. Oxford University Press.

Jennifer D'Souza and Vincent Ng. 2013. Classifying temporal relations with rich linguistic knowledge. In *NAACL-HLT '13*, pages 918–927.

Lea Frermann, Ivan Titov, and Manfred Pinkal. 2014. A hierarchical bayesian model for unsupervised induction of script knowledge. In *EACL '14*, pages 49–57.

Bram Jans, Steven Bethard, Ivan Vulić, and Marie-Francine Moens. 2012. Skip n-grams and ranking functions for predicting script events. In *EACL '12*, pages 336–344.

Maria Lapata and Alex Lascarides. 2006. Learning sentence-internal temporal relations. *Journal of Artificial Intelligence Research (JAIR)*, 27:85–117.

Mirella Lapata. 2003. Probabilistic text structuring: Experiments with sentence ordering. In *ACL '03*, pages 545–552.

Mirella Lapata. 2006. Automatic evaluation of information ordering: Kendall's tau. *Computational Linguistics*, 32(4):471–484.

Xiao Ling and Daniel S Weld. 2010. Temporal information extraction. In *AAAI '10*, pages 1385 – 1390.

Jonathan Malmaud, Earl Wagner, Nancy Chang, and Kevin Murphy. 2014. Cooking with semantics. In *the ACL 2014 Workshop on Semantic Parsing*, pages 33–38.

Inderjeet Mani, Marc Verhagen, Ben Wellner, Chong Min Lee, and James Pustejovsky. 2006. Machine learning of temporal relations. In *ACL-COLING '06*, pages 753–760.

Mehdi Manshadi, Reid Swanson, and Andrew S. Gordon. 2008. Learning a probabilistic model of event sequences from internet weblog stories. In *FLAIRS '08*, pages 159–164.

Ryan McDonald, Koby Crammer, and Fernando Pereira. 2005. Online large-margin training of dependency parsers. In *ACL '05*, pages 91–98.

Paramita Mirza and Sara Tonelli. 2014. Classifying temporal relations with simple features. In *EACL '14*, pages 308–317, Gothenburg, Sweden, April.

Ashutosh Modi and Ivan Titov. 2014. Inducing neural models of script knowledge. In *CoNLL '14*, pages 49–57.

Kira Mourão, Luke Zettlemoyer, Ronald Petrick, and Mark Steedman. 2012. Learning STRIPS operators from noisy and incomplete observations. In *UAI '12*.

Karl Pichotta and Raymond Mooney. 2014. Statistical script learning with multi-argument events. In *EACL '14*, pages 220–229.

Emily Pitler and Ani Nenkova. 2009. Using syntax to disambiguate explicit discourse connectives in text. In *ACL-IJCNLP '09: Short Papers*, pages 13–16.

James Pustejovsky, José M Castano, Robert Ingria, Robert J Gaizauskas, Andrea Setzer, Graham Katz, and Dragomir R Radev. 2003. TimeML: Robust specification of event and temporal expressions in text. *New directions in question answering*, 3:28–34.

Michaela Regneri, Alexander Koller, and Manfred Pinkal. 2010. Learning script knowledge with web experiments. In *ACL '10*, pages 979–988.

Michaela Regneri, Marcus Rohrbach, Dominikus Wetzel, Stefan Thater, Bernt Schiele, and Manfred Pinkal. 2013. Grounding action descriptions in videos. *Transactions of the Association for Computational Linguistics (TACL)*, 1:25–36.

Ehud Reiter, Robert Dale, and Zhiwei Feng. 2000. *Building natural language generation systems*, volume 33. Cambridge: Cambridge university press.

Dan Roth and Wen-tau Yih. 2007. Global inference for entity and relation identification via a linear programming formulation. In Lise Getoor and Ben Taskar, editors, *Introduction to Statistical Relational Learning*. MIT Press.

Aju Thalappillil Scaria, Jonathan Berant, Mengqiu Wang, Christopher D Manning, Justin Lewis, Brittany Harding, and Peter Clark. 2013. Learning biological processes with global constraints. In *EMNLP '13*.

Mark Steedman. 2002. Plans, affordances, and combinatory grammar. *Linguistics and Philosophy*, 25(5-6):723–753.

Partha Pratim Talukdar, Derry Wijaya, and Tom Mitchell. 2012. Acquiring temporal constraints between relations. In *CIKM '12*, pages 992–1001.

Dan Tasse and Noah A Smith. 2008. SOUR CREAM: Toward semantic processing of recipes. Technical report, Technical Report CMU-LTI-08-005, Carnegie Mellon University, Pittsburgh, PA.

Roy Tromble and Jason Eisner. 2009. Learning linear ordering problems for better translation. In *EMNLP '09*, pages 1007–1016.

Naushad UzZaman, Hector Llorens, Leon Derczynski, James Allen, Marc Verhagen, and James Pustejovsky. 2013. Semeval-2013 task 1: Tempeval-3: Evaluating time expressions, events, and temporal relations. In **SEM-SemEval '13*, pages 1–9.

Katsumasa Yoshikawa, Sebastian Riedel, Masayuki Asahara, and Yuji Matsumoto. 2009. Jointly identifying temporal relations with markov logic. In *ACL-IJCNLP '09*, pages 405–413.

# Bag-of-Words Forced Decoding for Cross-Lingual Information Retrieval

**Felix Hieber**
Computational Linguistics
Heidelberg University
69120 Heidelberg, Germany
hieber@cl.uni-heidelberg.de

**Stefan Riezler**
Computational Linguistics
Heidelberg University
69120 Heidelberg, Germany
riezler@cl.uni-heidelberg.de

## Abstract

Current approaches to cross-lingual information retrieval (CLIR) rely on standard retrieval models into which query translations by statistical machine translation (SMT) are integrated at varying degree. In this paper, we present an attempt to turn this situation on its head: Instead of the retrieval aspect, we emphasize the translation component in CLIR. We perform search by using an SMT decoder in forced decoding mode to produce a bag-of-words representation of the target documents to be ranked. The SMT model is extended by retrieval-specific features that are optimized jointly with standard translation features for a ranking objective. We find significant gains over the state-of-the-art in a large-scale evaluation on cross-lingual search in the domains patents and Wikipedia.

## 1 Introduction

Approaches to CLIR have been plentiful and diverse. While simple word translation probabilities are easily integrated into term-based retrieval models (Berger and Lafferty, 1999; Xu et al., 2001), state-of-the-art SMT systems (Koehn, 2010; Chiang, 2007) are complex statistical models on their own. The use of established translation models for context-aware translation of query strings, effectively reducing the problem of CLIR to a pipeline of translation and monolingual retrieval, has been shown to work well in the past (Chin et al., 2008). Only recently, approaches have been presented to include (weighted) translation alternatives into the query structure to allow a more generalized term matching (Ture et al., 2012a; Ture et al., 2012b). However, this integration of SMT remains agnostic about its use for CLIR and is instead optimized to match fluent, human reference translations. In contrast, retrieval systems often use bag-of-word representations, stopword filtering, and stemming techniques during document scoring, and queries are rarely fluent, grammatical natural language queries (Downey et al., 2008). Thus, most of a translation's structural information is lost during retrieval, and lexical choices may not be optimal for the retrieval task. Furthermore, the nature of modeling translation and retrieval separately requires that a single query translation is selected, which is usually done by choosing the most probable SMT output.

Attempts to inform the SMT system about its use for retrieval by optimizing its parameters towards a retrieval objective have been presented in the form or re-ranking (Nikoulina et al., 2012) or ranking (Sokolov et al., 2014). In this paper, we take this idea a step further and directly integrate the task of scoring documents with respect to the query into the process of *translation decoding*. We make the full expressiveness of the translation search space available to the retrieval model, without enumerating all possible translation alternatives. This is done by augmenting the linear model of the SMT system with features that relate partial translation hypotheses to documents in the retrieval collection. These retrieval-specific features decompose over partial translation hypotheses and thus allow efficient decoding using standard dynamic programming techniques. Furthermore, we apply learning-to-rank to jointly optimize translation and retrieval for the ob-



*Human Language Technologies: The 2015 Annual Conference of the North American Chapter of the ACL*, pages 1172–1182,
Denver, Colorado, May 31 – June 5, 2015. 

jective of retrieving relevant documents, and use decoding over the weighted translation hypergraph directly to perform cross-lingual search. Since high weights on retrieval features for words in the bag-of-words (BOW) representation of documents *force* the decoder to prefer relevant documents with high probability, by a slight abuse of terminology, we call our approach *BOW Forced Decoding*.

One of the key features of our approach is the use of context-sensitive information such as the language model and reordering information. We show that the use of such a translation-benign search space is crucial to outperform state-of-the-art CLIR approaches. Our experimental evaluation of retrieval performance is done on Wikipedia cross-lingual article retrieval (Bai et al., 2010; Schamoni et al., 2014) and patent prior art search (Fujii et al., 2009; Guo and Gomes, 2009; Sokolov et al., 2013; Schamoni et al., 2014). On both datasets, we show substantial improvements over the CLIR baselines of direct translation (Chin et al., 2008) or Probabilistic Structured Queries (Ture et al., 2012b), with and without further parameter tuning using learning-to-rank techniques and extended feature sets. From our results we conclude, that, in spite of algorithmic complexity, it is central to model translation and retrieval jointly to create more powerful CLIR models.

## 2 Related Work

The framework of translation-model based retrieval has been introduced by Berger and Lafferty (1999). An extension to the cross-lingual case using context-free lexical translation tables has been given by Xu et al. (2001). While the industry standard to CLIR is a pipeline of SMT-based query translation feeding into monolingual retrieval (Chin et al., 2008), recent approaches include (weighted) SMT translation alternatives into the query structure to allow a more generalized term matching (Ture et al., 2012a; Ture et al., 2012b). Less work has been devoted to optimizing SMT towards a retrieval objective, for example in a re-ranking framework (Nikoulina et al., 2012) or by integrating a decomposable proxy for retrieval quality of query translations into discriminative ranking (Sokolov et al., 2014).

The idea of forced decoding has been employed recently to select better perceptron updates from the full SMT search space for discriminative parameter tuning of SMT systems (Yu et al., 2013; Zhao et al., 2014).

Most similar to our approach is the recent work of Dong et al. (2014) who use the `Moses` translation option lattices for translation retrieval, i.e., for mining comparable data. Their query lattices given by the translation options encode exponentially many queries and are used to retrieve the most probable translation candidate from a set of candidates. The approach is evaluated in the context of a parallel corpus mining system. We present a model that not only uses the full search space, including the language model and reordering information, but also evaluate the model specifically for the task of retrieval, rather than mate-finding only. We show that a forced decoding model using bag-of-word representations for documents and retrieval features that are decomposable over query terms significantly outperforms state-of-the-art CLIR baselines such as direct translation (Chin et al., 2008) or Probabilistic Structured Queries obtained from $n$-best list query translations (Darwish and Oard, 2003; Ture et al., 2012b). Additionally we find that the use of context-sensitive translation information such as language models or reordering information, greatly improves retrieval quality in these types of models. We furthermore show how to directly optimize the retrieval objective using large-scale retrieval data sets with automatically induced relevance judgments.

## 3 A Bag-of-Words Forced Decoding Model

**Model Definition.** SMT systems use a Viterbi approximation to find the output hypothesis $q_e^*$

$$q_e^* = \arg\max_{q_e} \max_{h \in \mathcal{E}_{q_f}} P(h, q_e | q_f). \tag{1}$$

over the search space of hypotheses or derivations $h \in \mathcal{E}_{q_f}$ for a given input $q_f$. The probability of a translation output $q_e$ under derivation $h$ given $q_f$ is usually modeled in a log-linear model

$$P(h, q_e | q_f; \mathbf{w}_{smt}) = \frac{e^{F_{smt}(h, q_e, q_f)}}{\sum_{q_e, h} e^{F_{smt}(h, q_e, q_f)}},$$

where $F(h, q_e, q_f)$ is a learned linear combination of input-output features, that is, the dot product between parameter column vector $\mathbf{w}_{smt}$ and feature column vector given by feature map $\mathbf{\Phi}_{smt}$,

$$F_{smt}(h, q_e, q_f) = \mathbf{w}_{smt}^T \mathbf{\Phi}_{smt}(h, q_e, q_f). \quad (2)$$

In CLIR, we seek to choose a derivation that is *both* an accurate translation of the input according to the translation model, and a well-formed discriminative query that matches relevant documents with high probability. We combine both objectives by directly modeling the probability of a document $d_e$ in target language $e$ given a query $q_f$ in source language $f$, factorized as follows:

$$P(d_e|q_f) = \sum_{h \in \mathcal{E}_{q_f}} \underbrace{P(h|q_f)}_{\text{translation}} \times \underbrace{P(d_e|h, q_f)}_{\text{retrieval}}.$$

Applying the same Viterbi approximation during inference as in (1), we choose the retrieval score of $d_e$ to be the score of the highest scoring hypothesis $h$,

$$score(q_f, d_e) = \max_{h \in \mathcal{E}_{q_f}} P(h|q_f) \times P(d_e|h, q_f), \quad (3)$$

where the product between both models can be interpreted as a conjunctive operation similar to a product of experts (Hinton, 2002): A high score is achieved if both experts, namely translation and retrieval models, assign high scores to a hypothesis. That is, the model attempts to produce a well-formed translation, but at the same time chooses lexical items present in the bag-of-words representation of the document. Similarly, we can interpret the inclusion of the retrieval component as a constraint to *force* the decoder to retrieve $d_e$ with high probability. By a slight abuse of terminology, we will henceforth call our approach Bag-of-Words Forced Decoding (BOW-FD).[1]

The translation term $P(h|q_f)$ is modeled as in (2) for standard hierarchical phrase-based SMT (Chiang, 2007) and left unchanged in our joint model. The retrieval term $P(d_e|h, q_f)$ is modeled in a similar form

$$F_{ir}(h, d_e) = \mathbf{w}_{ir}^T \mathbf{\Phi}_{ir}(h, d_e),$$

where IR features do not depend on $q_f$ (thus allowing us to drop this term) and decompose over derivation terms. This allows a bag-of-word vector representation of documents, and retrieval features are local to single edges in the search space for efficient Viterbi inference. The joint scoring model is defined as follows:

$$score(q_f, d_e; \mathbf{w}) = \max_{h \in \mathcal{E}_{q_f}} e^{F_{smt}(h, q_e, q_f) + F_{ir}(h, d_e)},$$

where the weight vector is defined by the vector concatenation $\mathbf{w} = \mathbf{w}_{smt} \| \mathbf{w}_{ir}$, and $q_e$ refers to the yield that is determined uniquely by derivation $h$.

Following the interpretation of our joint model as forced or constrained decoding, we can view pipeline approaches such as the direct translation baseline as instances of *unconstrained* decoding. That is, the SMT decoder yields a single translation output for every document and the assignment of document scores is deferred to a (monolingual) retrieval model given this single output structure. Other CLIR approaches such as probabilistic structured queries (Darwish and Oard, 2003; Ture et al., 2012b) try to mitigate this early disambiguation by keeping enumerated translation alternatives at retrieval time. However, they either use context-free word-based translation tables or select only terms from a small $n$-best fraction of the full search space.

**Dynamic Programming on Hypergraphs.** Decoding in a hierarchical phrase-based SMT (Chiang, 2007) is usually understood as a two-step process: Initially, an input sentence is parsed using a Weighted Synchronous Context-Free Grammar (WSCFG) in a bottom-up manner to construct an initial hypergraph $\mathcal{H}$ that compactly encodes the full search space ("translation forest") (Gallo et al., 1993; Klein and Manning, 2001; Huang and Chiang, 2005; Dyer et al., 2010). An ordered, directed hypergraph $\mathcal{H}$ is a tuple $\langle V, E, g, \mathcal{W} \rangle$, consisting of a finite set of nodes $V$, a finite set of hyperedges $E$, and weight function $\mathcal{W} : E \mapsto \mathbb{R}$ assigning real-valued weights to $e \in E$. Language models are typically added in a second rescoring phase that is carried out by approximate solutions, such as cube-pruning (Chiang, 2007; Huang and Chiang, 2007), limiting the number of derivations created at each node. A translation hypothesis $h \in \mathcal{E}$ corresponds

[1] Standardly, the term forced decoding is used to describe the search for only those derivations that exactly produce the reference translation. Our use of this terminology deviates from the standard in two respects: First, we do not require exact reachability of the reference, but only a BOW match. Second, our constraint on the decoder is not strict, but only applies with high probability.

to a sequence of nodes $S \subseteq V$ connected via hyperedges $e$ ending in goal node $g$. Each edge $e$ is associated with a synchronous grammar rule $r(e)$, and corresponding feature values $\mathbf{\Phi}(r(e))$. The weight of hyperedge $e$ is defined as $\mathcal{W}(e; \mathbf{w}) = \mathbf{w}^T \mathbf{\Phi}(r(e))$.

The quantity in (1) is efficiently computed using dynamic programming under the proper semiring. A commutative semiring $K$ is a tuple $\langle \mathbb{K}, \bigoplus, \bigotimes, \bar{0}, \bar{1} \rangle$, of a set $\mathbb{K}$, an associative and commutative addition operator $\bigoplus$, an associative multiplication operator $\bigotimes$, and their "neutral" elements $\bar{0}$ and $\bar{1}$, respectively (Dyer, 2010). The Inside algorithm over the topologically sorted, acyclic hypergraph $\mathcal{H}$ under the tropical $\langle \mathbb{R}, \max, \times, -\infty, 0 \rangle$ semiring (Goodman, 1999; Mohri, 2009) computes the inside score $\alpha$ of the Viterbi hypothesis, i.e. the weight of its sequence of nodes ending in goal node $g$:

$$\begin{aligned} \arg\max_{h \in \mathcal{E}_q} P(h|q) &\equiv \alpha(g) \\ &= \bigoplus_{h \in \mathcal{H}_q} \bigotimes_{e \in h} \mathcal{W}(e; \mathbf{w}_{smt}), \end{aligned}$$

where $\mathcal{W}(e; \mathbf{w}_{smt}) = \mathbf{w}_{smt}^T \mathbf{\Phi}_{smt}(r(e))$ assigns weights given parameters and features of the translation model.

For Bag-of-Words Forced Decoding, we extend $\mathcal{W}$ with another set of parameters $\mathbf{w}_{ir}$ for local IR features $\mathbf{\Phi}_{ir}$:

$$\begin{aligned} \arg\max_{h \in \mathcal{E}_q} P(h|q,d) &\equiv \alpha(g) \\ &= \bigoplus_{h \in \mathcal{H}_q} \bigotimes_{e \in h} \mathcal{W}'(e, d; \mathbf{w}_{smt}, \mathbf{w}_{ir}), \end{aligned} \quad (4)$$

with $\mathcal{W}'(e, d; \mathbf{w}_{smt}, \mathbf{w}_{ir}) = \mathbf{w}_{smt}^T \mathbf{\Phi}_{smt}(r(e)) + \mathbf{w}_{ir}^T \mathbf{\Phi}_{ir}(r(e), d)$. Note that $\mathbf{\Phi}_{ir}$ depends on both translation rule $r(e)$ and document $d$, while $\mathbf{\Phi}_{smt}$ solely depends on source and target side of $r(e)$.

**Decomposable Retrieval Features.** We use sparse, lexicalized, real-valuead IR features that relate derivations $h$ to document $d$ using *Okapi bm25 term weights* (Robertson and Zaragoza, 2009):

$$bm25(t, d) = rsj(t, \mathcal{C}) \cdot tf_{bm25}(t, d),$$

where $rsj(t, \mathcal{C}) = log\left(\frac{|\mathcal{C}| - df(t,\mathcal{C}) + 0.5}{df(t,\mathcal{C}) + 0.5}\right)$ is a constant term weight approximated on document frequencies for collection $\mathcal{C}$, and $tf_{bm25}(t, d) = tf(t,d)/(k_1((1-b) + b\frac{dl}{avdl}) + tf(t,d))$ a saturated term frequency weight of term $t$ in document $d$, taking into account (average) document lengths $dl$ and $avdl$[2]. We fire the Okapi $bm25$ term weight for each derivation term $t \in h$ w.r.t. document $d$ in collection $\mathcal{C}$. The sum of feature values for all derivation terms $t_i \in h$ equals the regular $BM25$ score $BM25(h, d) = \sum_{t \in h} bm25(t, d)$. Weights $\mathbf{w}_{ir}$ for this type of features are interpretable as additional, general term weights.

Additionally, we report experiments using sparse alignment features that fire an indicator for each alignment, insertion, or deletion of words in source and target. They allow the model to adapt lexical choice and dropping of function words for retrieval.

**Default Retrieval Weights & Self-Translation.** To enforce a ranking over documents, we define an *IR default weight* $v$, $\mathbf{w}_{ir} = \mathbf{1}v$. Intuitively, $v$ controls the model's disposition to diverge from the SMT Viterbi path. If IR features fire in other regions of the search space than the SMT Viterbi path, this weight compensates for the loss incurred for not producing the Viterbi hypothesis. Furthermore, the default weight allows the model to generalize to unseen data: If an unknown query word, for example a named entity, causes an IR feature to fire at test time, the decoder will simply *pass through* the source word to any derivation, and the IR feature can contribute to the retrieval score with $v > 0$.

**Multi-Sentence Queries.** Specialized retrieval tasks such as patent prior art search may exhibit long, coherent search queries that contain multiple sentences. If multiple sentences of query $q = (s_1, \ldots, s_m)$ are processed independently, we need to combine the sentence-wise rankings to obtain a final ranking. We model this task from a product of experts perspective (Hinton, 2002) and multiply scores $score(\cdot, d)$ of document $d$ in all $m$ sentence rankings, re-sorting the final output. If $d$ is not in the top-$k$ ranking of a sentence, we take the minimum score of that top-$k$ ranking as a smoothing value to prevent the product to become zero.

[2]bm25 parameters were fixed at $k_1 = 1.2$ and $b = 0.75$

**Implementation and Complexity Analysis.**[3] We implemented the above model on top of the hierarchical phrase-based decoder `cdec` (Dyer et al., 2010), but there are no limitations for applying this approach to phrase-based systems (Koehn et al., 2007). Procedurally, after `cdec` yields the translation forest, we compute the overlap of IR feature activations between edges in the forest and the document candidates. The Inside algorithm is only carried out for documents that activate at least one IR feature in the search space. For documents with no activation we can skip the computation of scores and assign the SMT Viterbi score, which constitutes a lower bound on the model score.

For a single query $q$, forced decoding requires a single pass over the topologically sorted search space to find IR feature activations along hyperedges, yielding a complexity of $O(|V| + |E|)$. The dynamic programming procedure that computes a score for a document requires another pass over the forest evaluating the extended edge weight (4) for every edge $e \in E$, where the dot product for translation features is already precomputed by `cdec` , and the retrieval part depends on the number of active IR features, $\omega := |\mathbf{\Phi}_{ir}(r(e), d)|$. Overall complexity for a single query and all documents $d \in \mathcal{C}$ is thus

$$O\Big(|V| + |E| + \big(|V| + |E| \cdot \omega\big) \cdot |\mathcal{C}|\Big).$$

As noted above, we can reduce the quantity $|\mathcal{C}|$ by checking if a document candidate shares any IR features with the search space and avoid superfluous executions of the Inside algorithm. In our experiments on Wikipedia data, we found that this check reduces $|\mathcal{C}|$ to about 64% of its original size. This pre-filtering is similar to the coarse query approach of Dong et al. (2014), who score only documents that contain at least one term in the query lattice. We further reduce runtime of the inference procedure by using approximate decoding. We experimented with using a beam search approach to limit the number of weight evaluations in (4) for incoming edges at each node. The $\max$ operation of the tropical semiring is discontinued once the number of considered incoming edges at a node exceeds the size of the beam.

[3]The complexity of the construction of the translation forest including the language model is common to BOW-FD and the other baselines and thus not included in the following analysis.

## 4 Learning to Decode for Retrieval

We now turn to the problem of learning parameter weights for the BOW-FD model. The objective is to prefer a relevant document $d^+$ over an irrelevant one $d^-$ by assigning a higher score to $d^+$ than to $d^-$,

$$score(q, d^+; \mathbf{w}) > score(q, d^-; \mathbf{w}).$$

We sample a set of preference pairs

$$\mathcal{P} = \{(d^+, d^-) | rl(d^+, q) > rl(d^-, q)\}$$

from relevance-annotated data where $rl(d, q)$ indicates the relevance level of a document given query. Furthermore, we require the difference of scores to satisfy a certain margin:

$$score(q, d^+; \mathbf{w}) > score(q, d^-; \mathbf{w}) + \Delta,$$

where the margin is defined as

$$\Delta = rl(d^+, q) - rl(d^-, q).$$

Our final objective is a margin-rescaled hinge-loss

$$L(\mathcal{P}) = \sum_{d^+, d^- \in \mathcal{P}} \big[score(q, d^-; \mathbf{w}) - score(q, d^+; \mathbf{w}) + \Delta\big]_+$$

where $[\cdot]_+ = max(0, \cdot)$.

We use stochastic (sub)gradient descent optimization using the *Adadelta* (Zeiler, 2012) update rule. Adadelta does not require manual tuning of a global learning rate and requires only two hyperparameters that have shown to be quite robust to changes: the sliding window decay rate $\rho = 0.95$ and a constant $\epsilon = 10^{-6}$ were set to the default parameters given in the original paper. We furthermore use the distributed learning technique of *Iterative Parameter Mixing* (McDonald et al., 2010), where multiple models on several shards of the training data are trained in parallel and parameters are averaged after each epoch. We perform incremental optimization using a *cyclic order* of the data sequence (Bertsekas, 2011), that is, the learner steps through a fixed sequence of pairs, query by query, and relevant document by relevant document, without randomization after epochs. This allows us to cache consecutive query search spaces and feature vectors for relevant documents. Regularization is done by early stopping where the best iteration is found on a held-out development set.

| | Wikipedia | | | patents | | |
|---|---|---|---|---|---|---|
| | MAP | NDCG | PRES | MAP | NDCG | PRES |
| DT | .3678 | .5691 | .7219 | .2554 | .5397 | .5680 |
| PSQ | .3642 | .5671 | .7165 | .2659 | .5508 | .5851 |
| BOW-FD | *.3880 | *.5911 | *.7417 | *.2825 | *.5721 | *.6072 |
| BOW-FD+LTR | †.3913 | †.5962 | †**.7543** | †.2870 | †.5807 | †**.6260** |
| BOW-FD+LEX+LTR | †**.3919** | †**.5963** | †.7528 | †**.2883** | †**.5819** | †.6251 |

Table 1: Retrieval results of baseline systems and BOW-FD with default weight $v = 1.6$ for Wikipedia and $v = 0.8$ for patents, respectively. Baseline and BOW-FD models use the same SMT system. Significant differences at $p = 10^{-4}$ with respect to baselines are indicated with *. Significant differences at $p = 10^{-6}$ of learning-to-rank-based models (LTR) with respect to BOW-FD are indicated with †.

| | Wikipedia | | | patents | | |
|---|---|---|---|---|---|---|
| | MAP | NDCG | PRES | MAP | NDCG | PRES |
| DT | $.3347^{(-.03)}$ | $.5368^{(-.03)}$ | $.6970^{(-.03)}$ | $.2315^{(-.02)}$ | $.5105^{(-.03)}$ | $.5420^{(-.03)}$ |
| PSQ | $.3464^{(-.02)}$ | $.5483^{(-.02)}$ | $.7006^{(-.02)}$ | $.2460^{(-.02)}$ | $.5290^{(-.02)}$ | $.5672^{(-.02)}$ |
| BOW-FD | $.3218^{(-.07)}$ | $.5315^{(-.06)}$ | $.7220^{(-.02)}$ | $.1651^{(-.12)}$ | $.4185^{(-.15)}$ | $.4959^{(-.11)}$ |

Table 2: SMT-based CLIR models without a language model. Numbers in superscripts denote the absolute loss with respect to equivalent systems in Table 1.

## 5 Evaluation

**Data and Systems.** We conducted experiments on two large-scale CLIR tasks, namely German-English Wikipedia cross-lingual article retrieval[4] (Bai et al., 2010; Schamoni et al., 2014), and patent prior art search with Japanese-English patent abstracts[5] (Fujii et al., 2009; Guo and Gomes, 2009; Sokolov et al., 2013; Schamoni et al., 2014), comparing retrieval performance of BOW-FD against the state-of-the-art SMT-based CLIR baselines of *Direct Translation* (DT) and cross-lingual *Probabilistic Structured Queries* (PSQ) (Ture et al., 2012a; Ture et al., 2012b). The SMT models, as well as baseline evaluation scores were taken from (Schamoni et al., 2014).

We present results for BOW-FD using a default weight $v$ optimized on the development sets, and for models with parameters trained using pairwise learning-to-rank. We compute MAP, NDCG (Manning et al., 2008) and PRES (Magdy and Jones, 2010) scores on the top 1,000 returned documents to provide an extensive evaluation across precision-, and recall-oriented measures. Differences in evaluation scores between two systems were tested for statistical significance using paired randomization tests (Smucker et al., 2007). Significance levels are either indicated as superscripts, or provided in the captions of the respective tables.

Baseline SMT systems and BOW-FD share the hierarchical phrase-based SMT systems built with `cdec` (Dyer et al., 2010). For German-English cross-lingual article retrieval on Wikipedia, we built a system analogously to Schamoni et al. (2014) from parallel training data (over 104M words) consisting of the Europarl corpus (Koehn, 2005) in version 7, the News Commentary corpus, and the Common Crawl corpus (Smith et al., 2013). Word alignments were created with `fast_align` (Dyer et al., 2013). The 4-gram language model was trained with the KenLM toolkit (Heafield, 2011) on the English side of the training data and the English Wikipedia articles. Language model scores are added to the search spaces using the cube pruning algorithm (Huang and Chiang, 2007) with $poplimit = 200$. SMT Model parameters were optimized using MIRA (Chiang et al., 2008) on the WMT2011 news test set (3003

[4] `http://www.cl.uni-heidelberg.de/statnlpgroup/wikiclir/`

[5] `http://www.cl.uni-heidelberg.de/statnlpgroup/boostclir/`

sentences). The parameters for the baseline PSQ model were found on a development set consisting of 10,000 German queries using 1,000-best lists: interpolation parameter $\lambda = 0.4$, lower threshold $L = 0$, and cumulative threshold $C = 1$.

For the task of Japanese-English patent prior-art search, we use a system analog to Sokolov et al. (2013) and Schamoni et al. (2014). Its SMT features are trained on 1.8M parallel sentences of NTCIR-7 data (Fujii et al., 2008) and weights were tuned on the NTCIR-8 test collection (2,000 sentences) using MIRA (Chiang et al., 2008). A 5-gram language model on the English side of the training data was trained with the KenLM toolkit (Heafield, 2011). The system uses a cube pruning poplimit of 30. Parameters for the baseline PSQ model were found on a development set of 2,000 patent abstract queries and set to $n$-best list size = 1000, $\lambda = 1.0$, $L = 0.005$, $C = 0.95$

**Experimental Results.** We first find a default weight $v$ using grid search within $v = [0, 3]$ and $v = [0, 2]$ on the development sets for Wikipedia and patents, respectively. $v$ controls the balance between the retrieval and translation features and with larger $v$, the model is more likely to produce query derivations diverging from the SMT 1-best translation. For Wikipedia, we sample 1,000 out of 10,000 queries to reduce the time of the grid search. For patents we use the full development set of 2,000 queries with 8,381 sentences. We combine rankings for single-sentence queries from multi-sentence patent abstracts using the product method as previously described. Well performing values were found at $v = 1.6$ for Wikipedia, and $v = 0.8$ for patents, respectively.

Table 1 shows test set performance of DT and PSQ baselines versus BOW-FD. Scores for DT and PSQ are as reported in Schamoni et al. (2014). We observe that BOW-FD significantly outperforms both baselines by over 2 points on Wikipedia and patents under all three evaluation measures. While the cube pruning poplimit was set to 200 for the Wikipedia experiments, it is set to 30 for patents. This may reduce the diversity of the search space considerably. Increasing the poplimit from 30 to 200 yielded another significant gain (MAP=0.2893, NDCG=0.5807, PRES=0.6172) on this dataset.

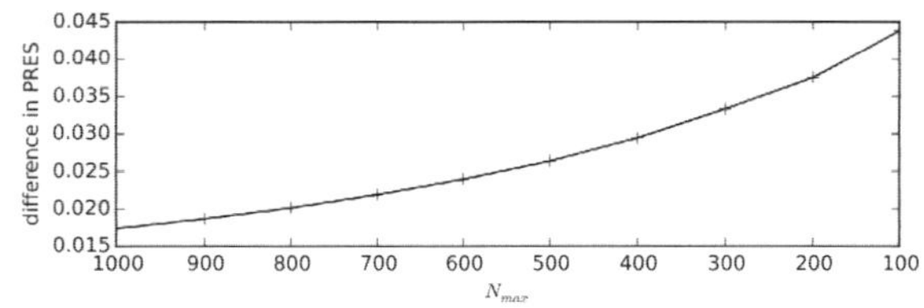


Figure 1: Difference in PRES scores on the Wikipedia development set as a function of PRES's $N_{max}$ parameter between BOW-FD +LM and -LM systems.

**Learning-to-rank results.** We learned the weights of the BOW-FD model starting from IR default weights optimized by grid search, and from SMT feature weights "pre-trained" on parallel data. We furthermore found improvements over BOW-FD in precision-oriented metrics (MAP and NDCG) by freezing SMT weights. Table 1 shows that BOW-FD+(LEX+)LTR models significantly outperform BOW-FD on both data sets, with the largest improvement for PRES. Differences between models with and without lexical alignment features are not statistically significant. We conjecture that LTR models mostly optimize recall rather than precision, i.e. placing more relevant document in the ranking. This is supported by the fact that BOW-FD+LTR retrieves 70.1% of the relevant documents in the test set, compared to 68.0% by BOW-FD, while Mean Reciprocal Rank (MRR) hardly differs (0.7344 vs. 0.7332). An experiment with no pre-trained SMT or default IR weights, performed worse, indicating the importance of translation-benign search spaces and IR default weights for generalization to unseen terms.

**Importance of Language Model for Retrieval.** Liu et al. (2012) and Dong et al. (2014) claim that computationally expensive SMT feature functions such as language models have only minor impact on CLIR performance of SMT-based models. We found that such context-sensitive information present in single 1-best query translations (DT), weighted translation alternatives from the $n$-best list (PSQ), and forced decoding in a "translation-benign" search space (BOW- FD) is crucial for retrieval performance in the experiments reported this paper. In order to investigate the question of the importance of context-sensitive information such as language model scores for retrieval we conducted an experiment in which the language model information is removed from all three SMT-based models. For the PSQ models, we also set the parameter $\lambda$ to 1.0 to disable interpolation with the context-free lexical translation table (Ture et al., 2012a). Table 2 shows that retrieval performance drops significantly for all models. The drop in performance for the two baseline models is comparable on both data sets. Removing the language model for BOW-FD hurts performance the most (with an average drop of 6 points in MAP and NDCG scores for Wikipedia, and over 11 points in all measures for patents). However, scores for recall-oriented PRES on Wikipedia remains relatively stable for BOW-FD with and without a language model. A closer analysis on the rankings for BOW-FD on Wikipedia shows that the -LM model returns 1,589 (out of 86,994) relevant documents less than the +LM model. However, only 2 documents with relevance level 3, i.e., directly linked cross-lingual "mates", were no longer retrieved, suggesting that excluding the language model from the system mostly affects the retrieval of "non-mates", i.e. documents that are linked by, or link to the cross-lingual mate. We explain this behavior as follows: Cross-lingual mates are likely to contain words that are close to an adequate query translation, since they constitute the beginning of a Wikipedia article with the same topic as the query. Derivations generated for these documents are such that both translation model features (with or without the LM) *and* retrieval features agree on a path close to the SMT Viterbi translation. In contrast, other relevant documents require more non-standard lexical choices that are harder to achieve in a +LM search space, since the strong weight on the language model, plus a language model-driven pruning technique, strongly favor lexical choices that agree with the language model's concept of fluency. In a -LM search space, disfluent derivations are easily reached by IR feature activations whose default weight is much larger in relation to the remaining SMT features. The use of "glue rules" allowing left-to-right concatenation of partial translations along with loosely extracted synchronous grammar rules give hierarchical MT models large degrees of freedom in producing very disfluent translations in the -LM space. If a language model is not ensuring a more or less "translation-benign" search space, the "reachability" of terms in irrelevant documents is increased causing them to interfere with the ranking of relevant documents that may be closer translations of the query. This behavior immediately affects precision-oriented scores such as MAP and NDCG, while PRES is only affected if its recall cutoff parameter, $N_{max}$, is lowered, as shown in Figure 1.

The major drop in performance for patent data may be explained with the way multiple sentence queries are evaluated: A language model limits diversity of translation options for multiple sentences. Without a language model, the sets of documents retrieved by each sentence are almost disjoint, i.e. the sentences do not agree on a common set of documents.

## 6 Conclusion

In this paper, we presented an approach to CLIR that shifts the focus from retrieval to translation by forcing a standard SMT decoder to produce a bag-of-words representation of the document repository. This is done by joint optimization of a linear model including both translation and retrieval features under a ranking objective. Highly weighted term-match features are then used to find a decoding path that gives highest score to the document that is optimal with respect to both relevance and translational adequacy. We showed in a large-scale evaluation on cross-lingual retrieval tasks in the domains of patents and Wikipedia pages that our approach significantly outperforms direct translation and Probabilistic Structured Query approaches under a variety of evaluation metrics. Furthermore, we investigated the role of context-sensitive information such as language model scores in retrieval. In contrast to previous claims about the minor impact of language models in retrieval performance in SMT-based CLIR, we found significant drops in MAP and NDCG across all models when removing language model information. This confirms the dual role of the language model to ensure fluency and to select the proper translation terms in the context of the neighboring target terms. The latter role of the language model makes it an indispensable ingredient of any SMT-based CLIR approach.

Open questions in our work regard further improvements in efficiency of retrieval. So far we could achieve substantial reductions in retrieval complexity by pre-filtering based on coarse term matches. The inherent complexity of SMT decoding is less of a problem in offline applications such as translation retrieval (Dong et al., 2014), but it becomes prohibitive in online applications such as cross-lingual web search. In future work, we would like to address efficiency, e.g. by investigating the possibility of incorporating an inverted index into online applications of forced decoding.

## Acknowledgments

This research was supported in part by DFG grant RI-2221/1-2 "Weakly Supervised Learning of Cross-Lingual Systems".

## References

Bing Bai, Jason Weston, David Grangier, Ronan Collobert, Kunihiko Sadamasa, Yanjun Qi, Olivier Chapelle, and Kilian Weinberger. 2010. Learning to rank with (a lot of) word features. *Information Retrieval*, 13(3):291–314.

Adam Berger and John Lafferty. 1999. Information retrieval as statistical translation. In *Proceedings of the 22Nd Annual International ACM SIGIR Conference on Research and Development in Information Retrieval (SIGIR'99)*, Berkeley, CA.

Dimitri P. Bertsekas. 2011. Incremental gradient, subgradient, and proximal methods for convex optimization: A survey. In Suvrit Sra, Sebastian Nowozin, and Stephen J. Wright, editors, *Optimization for Machine Learning*. MIT Press.

David Chiang, Yuval Marton, and Philip Resnik. 2008. Online large-margin training of syntactic and structural translation features. In *Proceedings of the Conference on Empirical Methods in Natural Language Processing (EMNLP'08)*, Honolulu, Hawaii.

David Chiang. 2007. Hierarchical phrase-based translation. *Computational Linguistics*, 33(2):201–228.

Jeffrey Chin, Maureen Heymans, Alexandre Kojoukhov, Jocelyn Lin, and Hui Tan. 2008. Cross-language information retrieval. Patent Application. US 2008/0288474 A1.

Kareem Darwish and Douglas W. Oard. 2003. Probabilistic structured query methods. In *Proceedings of the 26th annual international ACM SIGIR conference on Research and development in informaion retrieval (SIGIR'03)*, Toronto, Canada.

Meiping Dong, Yong Cheng, Yang Liu, Jia Xu, and Maosong Sun. 2014. Query lattice for translation retrieval. In *Proceedings of the 25th International Conference on Computational Linguistics (COLING'14)*, Dublin, Ireland.

Doug Downey, Susan Dumais, Dan Liebling, and Eric Horvitz. 2008. Understanding the relationship between searchers' queries and information goals. In *Proceedings of the 17th ACM conference on Information and knowledge management (CIKM'08)*, Napa Valley, California.

Christopher Dyer, Adam Lopez, Juri Ganitkevitch, Jonathan Weese, Ferhan Ture, Phil Blunsom, Hendra Setiawan, Vladimir Eidelman, and Philip Resnik. 2010. cdec: A decoder, alignment, and learning framework for finite-state and context-free translation models. In *Proceedings of the ACL-10 System Demonstrations (ACL'10)*, Uppsala, Sweden.

Christopher Dyer, Victor Chahuneau, and Noah Smith. 2013. A simple, fast, and effective reparameterization of IBM Model 2. In *Proceedings of the 2013 Conference of the North American Chapter of the Association for Computational Linguistics on Human Language Technologies (NAACL-HLT'13)*, Atlanta, Georgia.

Christopher Dyer. 2010. *A Formal Model of Ambiguity and Its Applications in Machine Translation*. Ph.D. thesis, University of Maryland, College Park, Maryland.

Atsushi Fujii, Masao Utiyama, Mikio Yamamoto, and Takehito Utsuro. 2008. Overview of the patent translation task at the NTCIR-7 workshop. In *Proceedings of the 7th NII Testbeds and Community for Information access Research Workshop (NTCIR-7'08)*, Tokyo, Japan.

Atsushi Fujii, Masao Utiyama, Mikio Yamamoto, and Takehito Utsuro. 2009. Evaluating effects of machine translation accuracy on cross-lingual patent retrieval. In *Proceedings of the 32rd international ACM SIGIR conference on Research and development in information retrieval (SIGIR'09)*, Boston, Massachusetts.

Giorgio Gallo, Giustino Longo, Stefano Pallottino, and Sang Nguyen. 1993. Directed hypergraphs and applications. *Discrete Applied Mathematics – Special issue: combinatorial structures and algorithms*, 42(2-3):177–201.

Joshua Goodman. 1999. Semiring parsing. *Computational Linguistics*, 25(4):573–605.

Yunsong Guo and Carla Gomes. 2009. Ranking structured documents: A large margin based approach for patent prior art search. In *Proc. of the International Joint Conference on Artificial Intelligence (IJCAI'09)*, Pasadena, CA.

Kenneth Heafield. 2011. KenLM: faster and smaller language model queries. In *Proceedings of the EMNLP 2011 Sixth Workshop on Statistical Machine Translation (WMT'11)*, Edinburgh, UK.

Geoffrey E. Hinton. 2002. Training products of experts by minimizing contrastive divergence. *Neural Computation*, 14(8):1771–1800.

Liang Huang and David Chiang. 2005. Better k-best parsing. In *Proceedings of the Ninth International Workshop on Parsing Technology (IWPT'05)*, Vancouver, Canada.

Liang Huang and David Chiang. 2007. Forest rescoring: Faster decoding with integrated language models. In *Proceedings of the 45th Annual Meeting of the Association of Computational Linguistics (ACL'07)*, Prague, Czech Republic.

Dan Klein and Christopher D. Manning. 2001. Parsing and hypergraphs. In *Proceedings of the Seventh International Workshop on Parsing Technologies (IWPT'01)*, Beijing, China.

Philipp Koehn, Hieu Hoang, Alexandra Birch, Chris Callison-Burch, Marcello Federico, Nicola Bertoldi, Brooke Cowan, Wade Shen, Christine Moran, Richard Zens, Christopher Dyer, Ondrej Bojar, Alexandra Constantin, and Evan Herbst. 2007. Moses: Open source toolkit for statistical machine translation. In *Proceedings of the ACL-07 2007 Demo and Poster Sessions (ACL'07)*, Prague, Czech Republic.

Philipp Koehn. 2005. Europarl: A parallel corpus for statistical machine translation. In *Proceedings of Machine Translation Summit X*, Phuket, Thailand.

Philipp Koehn. 2010. *Statistical Machine Translation*. Cambridge University Press, New York, New York, 1st edition.

Chunyang Liu, Qi Liu, Yang Liu, and Maosong Sun. 2012. Thutr: A translation retrieval system. In *Proceedings of COLING'12: Demonstration Papers*, Bombay, India.

Walid Magdy and Gareth Jones Jones. 2010. PRES: A score metric for evaluating recall-oriented information retrieval applications. In *Proceedings of the 33rd International ACM SIGIR Conference on Research and Development in Information Retrieval (SIGIR'10)*, Geneva, Switzerland.

Christopher D. Manning, Prabhakar Raghavan, and Hinrich Schütze. 2008. *Introduction to Information Retrieval*. Cambridge University Press, New York, New York.

Ryan McDonald, Keith Hall, and Gideon Mann. 2010. Distributed training strategies for the structured perceptron. In *Proceedings of the 2010 Annual Conference of the North American Chapter of the Association for Computational Linguistics on Human Language Technologies (NAACL-HLT'10)*, Los Angeles, California.

Mehryar Mohri. 2009. Weighted automata algorithms. In *Handbook of weighted automata*, pages 213–254. Springer Berlin Heidelberg.

Vassilina Nikoulina, Bogomil Kovachev, Nikolaos Lagos, and Christof Monz. 2012. Adaptation of statistical machine translation model for cross-lingual information retrieval in a service context. In *Proceedings of the 13th Conference of the European Chapter of the Association for Computational Linguistics (EACL'12)*, Avignon, France.

Stephen Robertson and Hugo Zaragoza. 2009. The probabilistic relevance framework: BM25 and beyond. *Foundations and Trends in Information Retrieval*, 3(4):333–389.

Shigehiko Schamoni, Felix Hieber, Artem Sokolov, and Stefan Riezler. 2014. Learning translational and knowledge-based similarities from relevance rankings for cross-language retrieval. In *Proceedings of the 52nd Annual Meeting of the Association for Computational Linguistics (ACL'14)*, Baltimore, USA.

Jason R. Smith, Herve Saint-Amand, Magdalena Plamada, Philipp Koehn, Chris Callison-Burch, and Adam Lopez. 2013. Dirt cheap web-scale parallel text from the common crawl. In *Proceedings of the 51st Annual Meeting of the Association for Computational Linguistics (ACL'13)*, Sofia, Bulgaria.

Mark D. Smucker, James Allan, and Ben Carterette. 2007. A comparison of statistical significance tests for information retrieval evaluation. In *Proceedings of the 16th ACM conference on Conference on Information and Knowledge Management (CIKM'07)*, New York, New York.

Artem Sokolov, Laura Jehl, Felix Hieber, and Stefan Riezler. 2013. Boosting cross-language retrieval by learning bilingual phrase associations from relevance rankings. In *Proceedings of the Conference on Empirical Methods in Natural Language Processing (EMNLP'13)*, Seattle, WA.

Artem Sokolov, Felix Hieber, and Stefan Riezler. 2014. Learning to translate queries for clir. In *Proceedings of the 37th Annual ACM SIGIR Conference (SIGIR'14)*, Gold Coast, Australia.

Ferhan Ture, Jimmy Lin, and Douglas W. Oard. 2012a. Combining statistical translation techniques for cross-language information retrieval. In *Proceedings of the International Conference on Computational Linguistics (COLING'12)*, Mumbai, India.

Ferhan Ture, Jimmy Lin, and Douglas W. Oard. 2012b. Looking inside the box: Context-sensitive translation for cross-language information retrieval. In *Proceedings of the ACM SIGIR Conference on Research and Development in Information Retrieval (SIGIR'12)*, Portland, Oregon.

Jinxi Xu, Ralph Weischedel, and Chanh Nguyen. 2001. Evaluating a probabilistic model for cross-lingual information retrieval. In *Proceedings of the 24th annual international ACM SIGIR conference on Research and development in information retrieval (SIGIR'01)*, New Orleans, Louisiana.

Heng Yu, Liang Huang, Haitao Mi, and Kai Zhao. 2013. Max-violation perceptron and forced decoding for scalable mt training. In *Proceedings of the Conference on Empirical Methods in Natural Language Processing (EMNLP'13)*, Seattle, Washington.

Matthew D. Zeiler. 2012. ADADELTA: An adaptive learning rate method. *Computing Research Repository (CoRR'2012)*, abs/1212.5701.

Kai Zhao, Liang Huang, Haitao Mi, and Abe Ittycheriah. 2014. Hierarchical mt training using max-violation perceptron. In *Proceedings of the 52nd Annual Meeting of the Association for Computational Linguistics (ACL'14)*, Baltimore, Maryland.

# Accurate Evaluation of Segment-level Machine Translation Metrics

**Yvette Graham**[†‡] **Nitika Mathur**[†] **Timothy Baldwin**[†]
[†]Department of Computing and Information Systems, The University of Melbourne
[‡]ADAPT Research Centre, Trinity College Dublin
ygraham@scss.tcd.ie, nmathur@student.unimelb.edu.au, tb@ldwin.net

## Abstract

Evaluation of segment-level machine translation metrics is currently hampered by: (1) low inter-annotator agreement levels in human assessments; (2) lack of an effective mechanism for evaluation of translations of equal quality; and (3) lack of methods of significance testing improvements over a baseline. In this paper, we provide solutions to each of these challenges and outline a new human evaluation methodology aimed specifically at assessment of segment-level metrics. We replicate the human evaluation component of WMT-13 and reveal that the current state-of-the-art performance of segment-level metrics is better than previously believed. Three segment-level metrics — METEOR, NLEPOR and SENTBLEU-MOSES — are found to correlate with human assessment at a level not significantly outperformed by any other metric in both the individual language pair assessment for Spanish-to-English and the aggregated set of 9 language pairs.

## 1 Introduction

Automatic segment-level machine translation (MT) metrics have the potential to greatly advance MT by providing more fine-grained error analysis, increasing efficiency of system tuning methods and leveraging techniques for system hybridization. However, a major obstacle currently hindering the development of segment-level metrics is their evaluation. Human assessment is the gold standard against which metrics must be evaluated, but when it comes to the task of evaluating translation quality, human annotators are notoriously inconsistent. For example, the main venue for evaluation of metrics, the annual Workshop on Statistical Machine Translation (WMT), reports disturbingly low inter-annotator agreement levels and highlights the need for better human assessment of MT. WMT-13, for example, report Kappa coefficients ranging from 0.075 to 0.324 for assessors from crowd-sourcing services, only increasing to between 0.315 and 0.457 for MT researchers (Bojar et al., 2013a). For evaluation of metrics that operate at the system or document-level such as BLEU, inconsistency in individual human judgments can, to some degree, be overcome by aggregation of individual human assessments over the segments within a document. However, for evaluation of segment-level metrics, there is no escaping the need to boost the consistency of human annotation of individual segments.

This motivates our analysis of current methods of human evaluation of segment-level metrics, and proposal of an alternative annotation mechanism. We examine the accuracy of segment scores collected with our proposed method by replicating components of the WMT-13 human evaluation (Bojar et al., 2013b), with the sole aim of optimizing agreement in segment scores to provide an effective gold standard for evaluating segment-level metrics. Our method also supports the use of significance testing of segment-level metrics, and tests applied to the WMT-13 metrics over nine language pairs reveal for the first time which segment-level metrics outperform others. We have made available code for acquiring accurate segment-level MT human evaluations from the crowd, in addition to significance



*Human Language Technologies: The 2015 Annual Conference of the North American Chapter of the ACL*, pages 1183–1191,
Denver, Colorado, May 31 – June 5, 2015. 

testing competing segment-level metrics, at:

`https://github.com/ygraham/segment-mteval`

## 2 WMT-style Evaluation of Segment-level MT Metrics

Since 2008, the WMT workshop series has included a shared task for automatic metrics, and as with the translation shared task, human evaluation remains the official gold standard for evaluation. In order to minimize the amount of annotation work and enforce consistency between the primary shared tasks in WMT, the same evaluations are used to evaluate MT systems in the shared translation task, as well as MT evaluation metrics in the document-level metrics and segment-level metrics tasks. Although WMT have trialled several methods of human evaluation over the years, the prevailing method takes the form of ranking a set of five competing translations for a single source language (SL) input segment from best to worst. A total of ten pairwise human relative preference judgments can be extracted from each set of five translations. Performance of a segment-level metric is assessed by the degree to which it corresponds with human judgment, measured by the number of metric scores for pairs of translations that are either concordant ($Con$) or discordant ($Dis$) with those of a human assessor, which the organizers describe as "Kendall's $\tau$":

$$\tau = \frac{|Con| - |Dis|}{|Con| + |Dis|}$$

Pairs of translations deemed equally good by a human assessor are omitted from evaluation of segment-level metrics (Bojar et al., 2014).

There is a mismatch between the human judgments data used to evaluate segment-level metrics and the standard conditions under which Kendall's $\tau$ is applied, however: Kendall's $\tau$ is used to measure the association between a set of observations of a single pair of joint random variables, $X$ (e.g. the human rank of a translation) and $Y$ (e.g. the metric score for the same translation). A conventional application of Kendall's $\tau$ would be comparison of all pairs of values within $X$ with each corresponding pair within $Y$. Since the human assessment data is, however, a large number of separately ranked sets of five competing translations and not a single ranking of all translations, it is not possible to compute a single Kendall's $\tau$ correlation.[1] The formula used to assess the performance of a metric in the task, therefore, is not what is ordinarily understood to be a Kendall's $\tau$ coefficient, but, in fact, equivalent to a weighted average of all Kendall's $\tau$ for each human-ranked set of five translations.

A more significant problem, however, lies in the inconsistency of human relative preference judgments within data sets. Since overall scores for metrics are described as correlations, possible values achievable by any metric could be expected to lie in the range $[-1, 1]$ (or "$\pm 1$"). This is not the case, and achievements of metrics are obscured by contradictory human judgments. Before any metric has provided scores for segments, for example, the maximum and minimum correlation achievable by a participating metric can be computed as, in the case of WMT-13:

- Russian-to-English: $\pm 0.92$
- Spanish-to-English: $\pm 0.90$
- French-to-English: $\pm 0.90$
- German-to-English: $\pm 0.92$
- Czech-to-English: $\pm 0.89$
- English-to-Russian: $\pm 0.90$
- English-to-Spanish: $\pm 0.90$
- English-to-French: $\pm 0.91$
- English-to-German: $\pm 0.90$
- English-to-Czech: $\pm 0.87$

If we are interested in the relative performance of metrics and take a closer look at the formula used to contribute a score to metrics, we can effectively ignore the denominator ($|Con| + |Dis|$), as it is constant for all metrics. The numerator ($|Con| - |Dis|$) is what determines our evaluation of the relative performance of metrics, and although the formula appears to be a straightforward subtraction of counts of concordant and discordant pairs, due to the large numbers of contradictory human relative preference judgments in data sets, what this number actually represents is not immediately obvious. If, for example, translations $A$ and $B$ were scored by a metric such that metric_score$(A)$ > metric_score$(B)$, one

[1] This would in fact require all (|MT systems| × |distinct segments|) translations included in the evaluation to be placed in a single rank order.

might expect an addition or subtraction of 1 depending on whether or not the metric's scores agreed with those of a human. Instead, however, the following is added:

$$(\max(|A > B|, |A < B|) \\ - \min(|A > B|, |A < B|)) \times d$$

where:

$$|A > B| = \text{\# human judgments where A was preferred over B}$$
$$|A < B| = \text{\# human judgments where B was preferred over A}$$
$$d = \begin{cases} 1 & \text{if } |A < B| > |A > B| \\ -1 & \text{if } |A < B| < |A > B| \end{cases}$$

For example, translations of segment 971 for Czech-to-English systems *uedin-heafield* and *uedin-wmt13* were compared by human assessors a total of 12 times: the first system was judged to be best 4 times, the second system was judged to be best 2 times, and the two systems were judged to be equal 6 times. This results in a score of $4-2$ for a system-level metric that scores the *uedin-heafield* translation higher than *uedin-wmt13* (tied judgments are omitted), or score of $2-4$ in the converse case.

Another challenge is how to deal with relative preference judgments where two translations are deemed equal quality (as opposed to strictly better or worse). In the current setup, tied translation pairs are excluded from the data, meaning that the ability for evaluation metrics to evaluate similar translations is not directly evaluated, and a metric that manages to score two equal quality translations closer, does not receive credit. A segment-level metric that can accurately predict not just disparities between translations but also similarities is likely to have high utility for MT system optimization, and is possibly the strongest motivation for developing segment-level metrics in the first place. In WMT-13, however, 24% of all relative preference judgments were omitted on the basis of ties, broken down as follows:

- Spanish-to-English: 28%
- French-to-English: 26%
- German-to-English: 27%
- Czech-to-English: 25%
- Russian-to-English: 24%
- English-to-Spanish: 23%
- English-to-French: 23%
- English-to-German: 20%
- English-to-Czech: 16%
- English-to-Russian: 27%

Although significance tests for evaluation of MT systems and document-level metrics have been identified (Koehn, 2004; Graham and Baldwin, 2014; Graham et al., 2014b), no such test has been proposed for segment-level metrics, and it is unfortunately common to conclude success without taking into account the fact that an increase in correlation can occur simply by chance. In the rare cases where significance tests have been applied, tests or confidence intervals for *individual* correlations form the basis for drawing conclusions (Aziz et al., 2012; Machacek and Bojar, 2014). However, such tests do not provide insight into whether or not a metric outperforms another, as all that's required for rejection of the null hypothesis with such a test is a likelihood that an individual metric's correlation with human judgment is not equal to zero. In addition, data sets for evaluation in both document and segment-level metrics are not independent and the correlation that exists between pairs of metrics should also be taken into account by significance tests.

## 3 Segment-Level Human Evaluation

Many human evaluation methodologies attempt to elicit precisely the same quality judgment for individual translations from all assessors, and inevitably produce large numbers of conflicting assessments in the process, including from the same individual human judge (Callison-Burch et al., 2007; Callison-Burch et al., 2008; Callison-Burch et al., 2009). An alternative approach is to take into account the fact that different judges may genuinely disagree, and allow assessments provided by individuals to each contribute to an overall estimate of the quality of a given translation.

In an ideal world in which we had access to assessments provided by the entire population of qualified human assessors, for example, the mean of those assessments would provide a statistic that, in theory at least, would provide a meaningful segment-level human score for translations. If it were possible to collect assessments from the entire population we could directly compute the *true mean score* for a translation segment. This is of course not possible, but thanks to the law of large numbers we can make the following assumption:

> Given a sufficiently large assessment sample for a given translation, the mean of assessments will provide a very good estimate of the true mean score of the translation sourced from the entire assessor population.

What the law of large numbers does not tell us, however, is, for our particular case of translation quality assessment, precisely how large the sample of assessments needs to be, so that the mean of scores provides a close enough estimate to the true mean score for any translation. For a sample mean for which the variance is known, the required sample size can be computed for a specified standard error. However, due to the large number of distinct translations we deal with, the variance in sample score distributions may change considerably from one translation to the next. In addition, the choice as to what exactly is an acceptable standard error in sample means would be somewhat arbitrary. On the one hand, if we specify a standard error that's lower than is required, and subsequently collect more repeat assessments than is needed, we would be wasting resources that could, for example, be targeted at the annotation of additional translation segments.

Our solution is to empirically investigate the impact on sample size of repeat assessments on the mean score for a given segment, and base our determination of sample size on the findings. Since we later motivate the use of Pearson's correlation to measure the linear association between human and metric scores (see Section 4), we base our investigation on Pearson's correlation.

We collect multiple assessments per segment to create score distributions for segments for a fixed set per language pair. This is repeated twice over the same set of segments to generate two distinct sets of annotations: one set is used to estimate the true mean score, and the second set is randomly downsampled to simulate a set of assessments of fixed sample size. We measure the Pearson correlation between the true mean score and different numbers of assessments for a given assessment, to ask the question: how many assessments must be collected for a given segment to obtain mean segment scores that truly reflects translation quality? Scores are sampled according to annotation time to simulate a realistic setting.

| Language pair | # translations | # assessments per translation |
|---|---|---|
| es-en | 280 | 40 |
| en-es | 140 | 19 |
| en-ru | 140 | 15 |
| en-de | 140 | 14 |

Table 1: Datasets used to assess translation assessment sample size

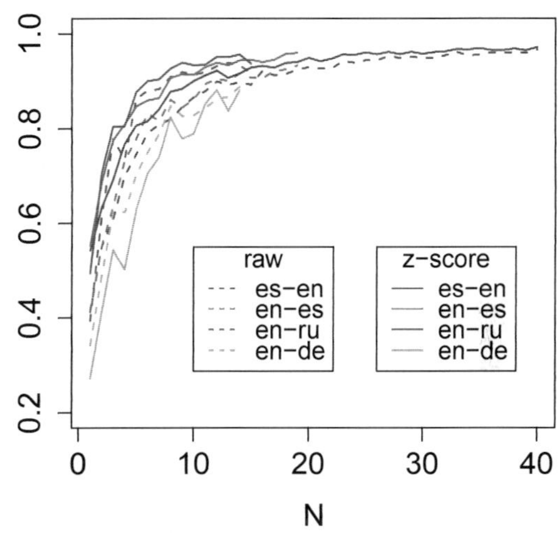


Figure 1: Correlation ($r$) of translation quality estimates between the initial and repeat experiment runs for each of the four language pairs from WMT-13, for sample size $N$ and based on raw and standardized ($z$) scores.

### 3.1 Translation Assessment Sample Size

MTurk was used to collect large numbers of translation assessments, in sets of 100 translations per assessment task (or "HIT" in MTurk parlance). The HITS were structured to include degraded translations and repeat translations, and rated on a continuous Likert scale with a single translation assessment displayed to the assessor at one time (Graham et al., 2014a; Graham et al., 2013). This supports accurate quality-control as well as normalisation of translation scores for each assessor. The assessment

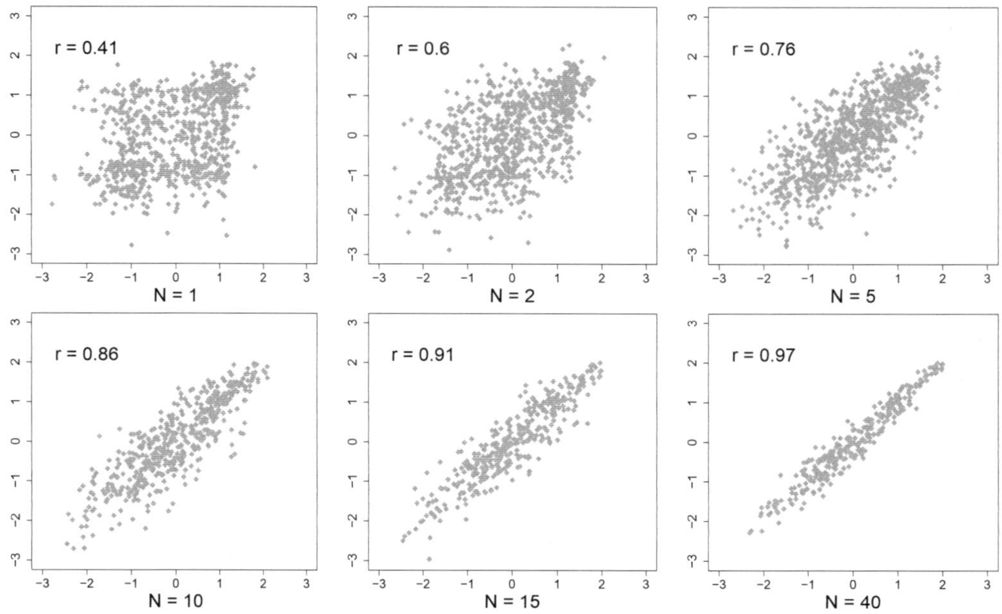


Figure 2: Plots and correlation ($r$) of translation quality assessments in the initial ($x$-axis) and replicate experiments ($y$-axis) for Spanish-to-English over WMT-13, where each point represents a standardized segment-level score computed as the mean of the $N$ individual assessments for that plot.

task was posed as a monolingual task, where assessors were asked to rate the degree to which the MT system output adequately expressed the meaning of the corresponding reference translation. Translations were sampled at random from the WMT-13 data sets for the four language pairs, as detailed in Table 1. Due to low-quality assessors on MTurk and the need for assessments solely for quality assurance purposes, the exercise required a substantial number of individual assessments. For Spanish-to-English, for example, a total of (280 translations + 120 translations for quality-control purposes) $\times$ 40 assessments per translation $\times$ 2 separate data collections $\times$ $\sim$2 to allow for filtering of low-quality assessors = $\sim$64k assessments were collected; after quality control filtering and removing the quality-control translations, around 22k assessments were used for the actual experiment.

Figure 1 shows the Pearson correlation between mean segment-level scores calculated for varying numbers of assessments ($N$), and the full set of assessments for the second set of assessments. For each language pair, we calculate the correlation first over the raw segment scores and second over standardized scores, based on the method of Graham et al. (2014a).[2] For all language pairs, although the correlation is relatively low for single assessments, as the sample size increases, it increases, and by approximately $N = 15$ assessments, for all four language pairs, the correlation reaches $r = 0.9$. For Spanish-to-English, for which most assessments were collected, when we increase the number of assessments to $N = 40$ per translation, the correlation reaches $r = 0.97$. Figure 2 is a set of scatter plots for mean segment-level scores for Spanish-to-English rising, for varying sample sizes $N$.

As expected, the larger the sample size of assessments, the greater the agreement with the true mean score, but what is more surprising is that with as few as 15 assessments, the scores collected in the two separate experiments correlate extremely well, and provide what we believe to be a sufficient stability to evaluate segment-level metrics.

[2]Standardized segment scores are computed by standardizing individual raw scores according to the mean and standard deviation of individual assessors, and then combined into mean segment scores.

## 4 Segment-level Metric Evaluation

Since the scores generated by our method are continuous and segment-level metrics are also required to output continuous-valued scores, we can now compare the scores directly using Pearson's correlation. Pearson's correlation has three main advantages for this purpose. Firstly, the measure is unit-free, so metrics do not have to produce scores on the same scale as the human assessments. Secondly, scores are absolute as opposed to relative and therefore more intuitive and ultimately more powerful; for example, we are able to evaluate metrics over the 20% of translations of highest or lowest quality in the test set. Finally, the use of Pearson's correlation facilitates the measurement of statistical significance in correlation differences.

It is important to point out, however, that moving from Kendall's $\tau$ over relative preference judgments to Pearson's $r$ over absolute scores does, in fact, change the task required of metrics in one respect: previously, there was no direct evaluation of the scores generated by a metric, nor indeed did the evaluation ever directly compare translations for different source language inputs (as relative preference judgments were always relative to other translations for the same input). Pearson's correlation, on the other hand, compares scores across the entire test set.

### 4.1 Significance Testing of Segment-level Metrics

With the move to Pearson's correlation, we can also test statistical significance in differences between metrics, based on the Williams test (Williams, 1959),[3] which evaluates significance in a difference in dependent correlations (Steiger, 1980). As suggested by Graham and Baldwin (2014), the test is appropriate for evaluation of document-level MT metrics since the data is not independent, and for similar reasons, the test can also be used for evaluation of segment-level metrics.

### 4.2 Spanish-to-English Segment-level Metrics

We first carry out tests for Spanish-to-English segment-level metrics from WMT-13. In our experiments in Section 3.1, we used only a sub-sample of segments, so the first thing is to collect assessments for the remaining Spanish-to-English translation segments using MTurk, based on a sample of at least 15 assessments. A total of 24 HITs of 100 translations each were posted on MTurk; after removal of low quality workers (~50%) and quality control items (a further 30%), this resulted in 840 translation segments with 15 or more assessments each. The scores were standardized and combined into mean segment scores.

| Metric | $r$ | $\tau$ |
|---|---|---|
| METEOR | 0.484 | 0.324 |
| NLEPOR | 0.483 | 0.281 |
| SENTBLEU-MOSES | 0.465 | 0.266 |
| DEP-REF-EX | 0.453 | 0.307 |
| DEP-REF-A | 0.453 | 0.312 |
| SIMPBLEUP | 0.450 | 0.287 |
| SIMPBLEUR | 0.444 | 0.388 |
| LEPOR | 0.408 | 0.236 |
| UMEANT | 0.353 | 0.202 |
| MEANT | 0.342 | 0.202 |
| TERRORCAT | 0.313 | 0.313 |

Table 2: Pearson's correlation and Kendall's $\tau$ between WMT-13 segment-level metrics and human assessment for Spanish-to-English (ES-EN). Note that Kendall's $\tau$ is based on the WMT-13 formulation, and the preference judgments from WMT-13.

Table 2 shows the Pearson's correlation for each metric that participated in the WMT-13 Spanish-to-English evaluation task, along with the Kendall's $\tau$ based on the original WMT-13 methodology and relative preference assessments. Overall, when we compare correlations using the new evaluation methodology to those from the original evaluation, even though we have raised the bar by assessing the raw numeric outputs rather than translating them into preference judgments relative to other translations for the same SL input, all metrics achieve higher correlation with human judgment than reported in the original evaluation. This indicates that the new evaluation setup is by no means unrealistically difficult, and that even though it was not required of the metrics in the original task setup, the metrics are doing a relatively good job of absolute scoring of translation adequacy. In addition,

[3] Also sometimes referred to as the Hotelling–Williams test.

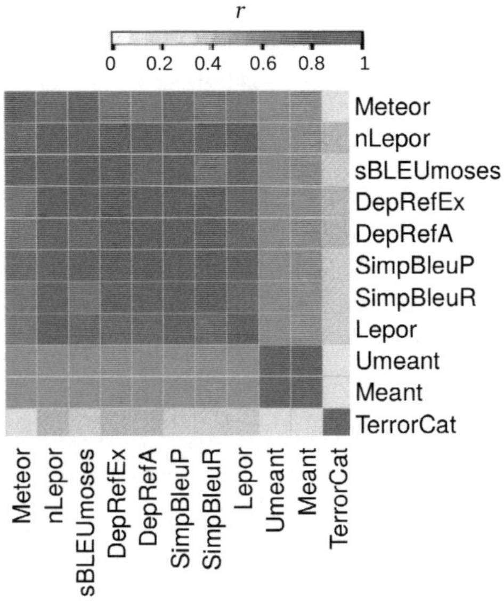


Figure 3: Pearson's correlation between every pair of segment-level metric competing in the WMT-13 Spanish-to-English task.

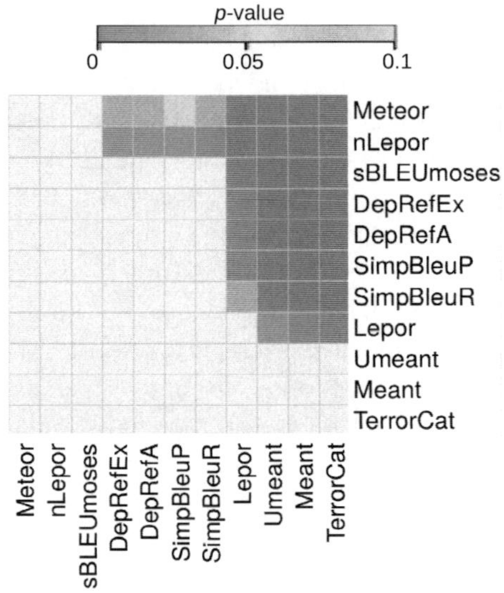


Figure 5: Evaluation of significance of increase in correlation with human judgment between every pair of segment-level metrics competing in the Spanish-to-English WMT-13 metrics task. A colored cell $(i,j)$ indicates that system named in row $i$ significantly outperforms system named in column $j$ at $p < 0.1$, and green cells at $p < 0.05$.

the new assessment reflects how well metrics score translations of very close or equal quality, and, as described in Section 2, ameliorates the issue of low inter-annotator agreement as well as resolving the original mismatch between discrete human relative preference judgments and continuous metric scores.

Figure 3 is a heat map of the Pearson's correlation between each pair of segment-level metrics for Spanish-to-English from WMT-13, and Figure 4 shows correspondence between scores of three segment-level metrics with our human evaluation data. Figure 5 displays the outcome of the Williams significance test as applied to each pairing of competing metrics. Since the power of Williams test increases with the strength of correlation between a pair of metrics, it is important *not* to conclude the best system by the number of other metrics it outperforms. Instead, the best choice of metric for that language pair is any metric that is *not significantly outperformed by any other metric*. Three metrics prove not to be significantly outperformed by any other metric for Spanish-to-English, and tie for best performance: METEOR (Denkowski and Lavie, 2011), NLEPOR (Han et al., 2013) and SENTBLEU-MOSES (sBLEU-moses).

| **Metric** | $r$ |
|---|---|
| METEOR | 0.441 |
| NLEPOR | 0.416 |
| SENTBLEU-MOSES | 0.422 |
| SIMPBLEUP | 0.418 |
| SIMPBLEUR | 0.404 |
| LEPOR | 0.326 |

Table 3: Pearson's correlation between each WMT-13 segment-level metric and human assessment for the combined set of nine language pairs.

### 4.3 9 Language Pairs

Since human assessments are now absolute, scores effectively have the same meaning across language pairs, facilitating the combination of data across multiple language pairs. Since many approaches to MT are language-pair independent, the ability to know what segment-level metric works best across all language pairs is useful for choosing an appropriate default metric or simply avoiding having to swap and change metrics across different language

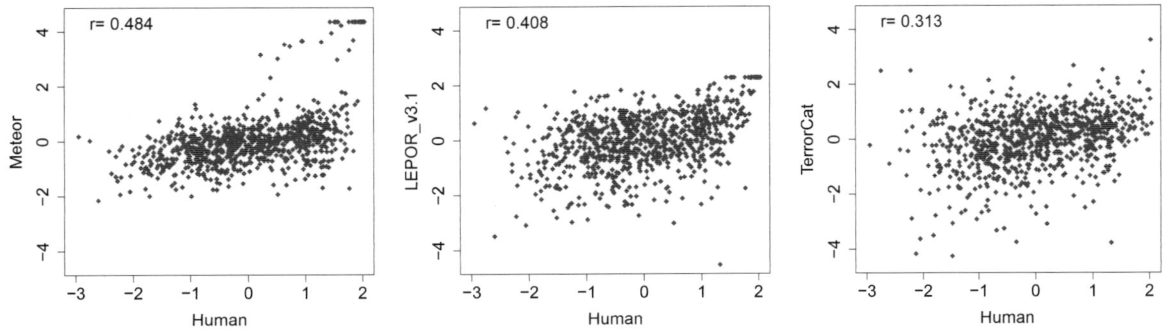


Figure 4: Standardized segment-level scores for human vs. metric over the WMT-13 Spanish-to-English segment-level metric task, for a metric achieving highest, mid-range and lowest Pearson's correlation with human judgment.

pairs.

Assessments of translations were crowd-sourced for nine language pairs used in the WMT-13 shared metrics task: Russian-to-English, Spanish-to-English, French-to-English, German-to-English, Czech-to-English, English-to-Russian, English-to-Spanish, English-to-French and English-to-German.[4] Again, we obtain a minimum of 15 assessments per translation, and collect scores for 100 translations per language pair. After removal of quality control items, this leaves 70 distinct translations per language pair, combined into a cross-lingual test set of 630 distinct translations spanning nine language pairs.

Table 3 shows Pearson's correlation with human assessment for the six segment-level metrics that competed across all language pairs in WMT-13, and Figure 6 shows the outcomes of Williams test for statistical significance between different pairings of metrics. Results reveal that the same three metrics as before (METEOR, SENTBLEU-MOSES and NLEPOR), in addition to SIMPBLEUP and SIMPBLEUR are not significantly outperformed by any other metric at $p$<0.05. However, since the latter two were shown to be outperformed for Spanish-to-English, all else being equal, METEOR, SENTBLEU-MOSES and NLEPOR are still a superior choice of default metric.

[4]We were regrettably unable to include English-to-Czech, due to a lack of Czech-speaking MTurk workers.

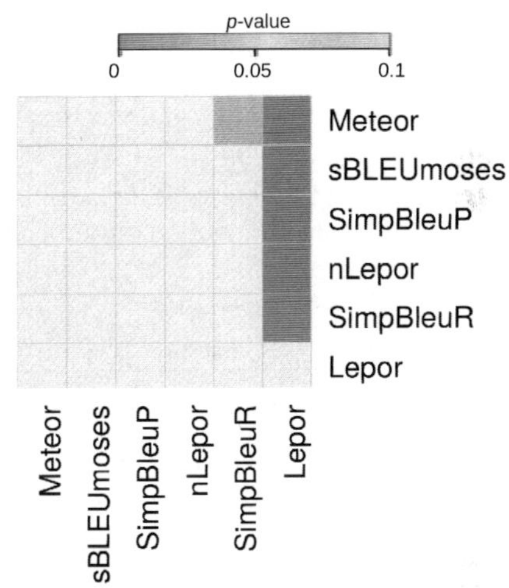


Figure 6: Evaluation of significance of increase in correlation with human judgment between every pair of segment-level metrics competing in all nine in WMT-13 metrics task. A colored cell $(i,j)$ indicates that system named in row $i$ significantly outperforms system named in column $j$ at $p < 0.1$ and green cells specifically $p < 0.05$.

## 5 Conclusion

We presented a new evaluation methodology for segment-level metrics that overcomes the issue of low inter-annotator agreement levels in human assessments, includes evaluation of very close and equal quality translations, and provides a significance test that supports system comparison with confidence. Our large-scale human evaluation reveals three metrics to not be significantly outperformed by any other metric in both Spanish-to-

English and a combined evaluation across nine language pairs, namely: METEOR, NLEPOR and SENTBLEU-MOSES.

### Acknowledgements

We wish to thank the anonymous reviewers for their valuable comments. This research was supported by funding from the Australian Research Council and Science Foundation Ireland (Grant 12/CE/12267).

## References

W. Aziz, S. Castilho, and L. Specia. 2012. PET: a tool for post-editing and assessing machine translation. In *Proc. of the 8th International Conference on Language Resources and Evaluation (LREC 2012)*, pages 3982–3987, Istanbul, Turkey.

O. Bojar, C. Buck, C. Callison-Burch, C. Federmann, B. Haddow, P. Koehn, C. Monz, M. Post, R. Soricut, and L. Specia. 2013a. Findings of the 2013 Workshop on Statistical Machine Translation. In *Proceedings of the Eighth Workshop on Statistical Machine Translation*, pages 1–44, Sofia, Bulgaria.

O. Bojar, C. Buck, C. Callison-Burch, C. Federmann, B. Haddow, P. Koehn, C. Monz, M. Post, R. Soricut, and L. Specia. 2013b. Findings of the 2013 Workshop on Statistical Machine Translation. In *Proc. 8th Wkshp. Statistical Machine Translation*, pages 1–44, Sofia, Bulgaria.

O. Bojar, C. Buck, C. Federmann, B. Haddow, P. Koehn, J. Leveling, C. Monz, P. Pecina, M. Post, H. Saint-Amand, R. Soricut, L. Specia, and A. Tamchyna. 2014. Findings of the 2014 Workshop on Statistical Machine Translation. In *Proc. 9th Wkshp. Statistical Machine Translation*, pages 12–58, Baltimore, USA.

C. Callison-Burch, C. Fordyce, P. Koehn, C. Monz, and J. Schroeder. 2007. (Meta-) evaluation of machine translation. In *Proc. 2nd Wkshp. Statistical Machine Translation*, pages 136–158, Prague, Czech Republic.

C. Callison-Burch, C. Fordyce, P. Koehn, C. Monz, and J. Schroeder. 2008. Further meta-evaluation of machine translation. In *Proc. 3rd Wkshp. Statistical Machine Translation*, pages 70–106, Columbus, USA.

C. Callison-Burch, P. Koehn, C. Monz, and J. Schroeder. 2009. Findings of the 2009 Workshop on Statistical Machine Translation. In *Proc. 4th Wkshp. Statistical Machine Translation*, pages 1–28, Athens, Greece.

M. Denkowski and A. Lavie. 2011. Meteor 1.3: Automatic metric for reliable optimization and evaluation of machine translation systems. In *Proc. 6th Wkshp. Statistical Machine Translation*, pages 85–91, Edinburgh, Scotland.

Y. Graham and T. Baldwin. 2014. Testing for significance of increased correlation with human judgment. In *Proceedings of the Conference on Empirical Methods in Natural Language Processing*, pages 172–176, Doha, Qatar.

Y. Graham, T. Baldwin, A. Moffat, and J. Zobel. 2013. Continuous measurement scales in human evaluation of machine translation. In *Proc. 7th Linguistic Annotation Wkshp. & Interoperability with Discourse*, pages 33–41, Sofia, Bulgaria.

Y. Graham, T. Baldwin, A. Moffat, and J. Zobel. 2014a. Is machine translation getting better over time? In *Proceedings of the European Chapter of the Association of Computational Linguistics*, pages 443–451, Gothenburg, Sweden.

Y. Graham, N. Mathur, and T. Baldwin. 2014b. Randomized significance tests in machine translation. In *Proc. Ninth ACL Wkshp. Statistical Machine Translation*, pages 266–74, Baltimore, MD.

A.L. Han, D.F. Wong, L.S. Chao, Y. Lu, L. He, Y. Wang, and J. Zhou. 2013. A description of tunable machine translation evaluation systems in WMT13 metrics task. In *Proceedings of the Eight Workshop on Statistical Machine Translation*, pages 414–421, Sofia, Bulgaria.

P. Koehn. 2004. Statistical significance tests for machine translation evaluation. In *Proc. of Empirical Methods in Natural Language Processing*, pages 388–395, Barcelona, Spain.

M. Machacek and O. Bojar. 2014. Results of the wmt14 metrics shared task. In *Proceedings of the Ninth Workshop on Statistical Machine Translation*, pages 293–301, Baltimore, USA.

J.H. Steiger. 1980. Tests for comparing elements of a correlation matrix. *Psychological Bulletin*, 87(2):245.

E.J. Williams. 1959. *Regression analysis*, volume 14. Wiley, New York, USA.

# Leveraging Small Multilingual Corpora for SMT Using Many Pivot Languages

**Raj Dabre**
Graduate School of Informatics
Kyoto University
Kyoto 606-8501
prajdabre@gmail.com

**Fabien Cromieres**
Japan Science and Technology Agency
Kawaguchi-shi
Saitama 332-0012
fabien@pa.jst.jp

**Sadao Kurohashi**
Graduate School of Informatics
Kyoto University
Kyoto 606-8501
kuro@i.kyoto-u.ac.jp

**Pushpak Bhattacharyya**
CFILT
IIT Bombay, Powai
India 400076
pushpakbh@gmail.com

## Abstract

We present our work on leveraging multilingual parallel corpora of small sizes for Statistical Machine Translation between Japanese and Hindi using multiple pivot languages. In our setting, the source and target part of the corpus remains the same, but we show that using several different pivot to extract phrase pairs from these source and target parts lead to large BLEU improvements. We focus on a variety of ways to exploit phrase tables generated using multiple pivots to support a direct source-target phrase table. Our main method uses the Multiple Decoding Paths (MDP) feature of Moses, which we empirically verify as the best compared to the other methods we used. We compare and contrast our various results to show that one can overcome the limitations of small corpora by using as many pivot languages as possible in a multilingual setting. Most importantly, we show that such pivoting aids in learning of additional phrase pairs which are not learned when the direct source-target corpus is small. We obtained improvements of up to 3 BLEU points using multiple pivots for Japanese to Hindi translation compared to when only one pivot is used. To the best of our knowledge, this work is also the first of its kind to attempt the simultaneous utilization of 7 pivot languages at decoding time.

## 1 Introduction

With the increasing size of parallel corpora it has become possible to achieve very high quality translation. However, not all language pairs are blessed with the availability of large parallel corpora in the sizes of millions of lines. With the exception of the major European languages and a few Asian languages like Chinese and Japanese, other languages have parallel corpora in the sizes of a few thousands of lines. Since translation quality is related to the size of the parallel corpus, it is impossible to achieve the same level of translation quality as that in the case of resource rich languages. To remedy this scenario, an intermediate resource rich language can be exploited. Although, finding a direct parallel corpus between source and target languages might be difficult, there are higher odds of finding a pair of parallel corpora: one between the source language and an intermediate resource rich language (henceforth called pivot[1]) and one between that pivot and the target language.

Using the methods developed for Pivot Based SMT (Wu and Wang, 2007) (Utiyama and Isahara, 2007) one can use the source-pivot and pivot-target parallel corpora to develop a source-target translation system (henceforth called as pivot based system [2]) . Moreover, if there exists a small source-target parallel corpus then the resulting system (henceforth called as direct system[3]) can be supported by the pivot based source-target system to significantly improve the translation quality. Note that in this paper we use the terms "translation system" and "phrase table" interchangeably since the phrase table is the

[1] In most cases this is English.

[2] The phrase table will be known as the pivot phrase table.

[3] The phrase table will be called as direct phrase table and the corpus will be the direct parallel corpus.



*Human Language Technologies: The 2015 Annual Conference of the North American Chapter of the ACL*, pages 1192–1202,
Denver, Colorado, May 31 – June 5, 2015. 

main component of the translation system. Reordering tables are supplementary and can usually be replaced by a simple distortion model.

Major problems arise when source-pivot and pivot-target corpora belong to different domains leading to rather poor quality translations. Even if the individual corpora are large, one will run into domain adaptation problems. In such a scenario the availability of a small size multilingual corpus of a few thousand lines belonging to a single domain can be beneficial. The setting of this paper is:

1. We suppose the existence of a multilingual corpus with sentences aligned across $N$[4] different languages.

2. We show using the other languages as additional pivots leads to the construction of better phrase tables and better translation results.

Note that this setting is realistic and differs from the majority of existing work on pivot languages, in which the source-pivot and pivot-target corpora are unrelated (or at least do not have equivalent sentences). In addition to the well-known Europarl corpus, many other similar multilingual corpora exist. For example, a multilingual parallel corpus for 9 major Indian Languages belonging to the Health and Tourism domain of approximately 50000 lines was used to develop basic SMT systems (Kunchukuttan et al., 2014). For our experiments we will use a recently released Bible domain multilingual parallel corpus (Resnik et al., 1999) for a large number (over 25) of languages (other than Indian) including Japanese and Hindi (Japanese to Hindi translation being our focus) of approximately 30000 lines. We chose this setting because we feel that this multilingual approach is especially important for low-resource language pairs.

Typically system combination methods like linear interpolation are used to combine the direct and pivot phrase tables by modifying the probabilities of phrase pairs leading to the modification of the underlying distribution which affects the resultant translation quality. The Multiple Decoding Paths (Birch and Osborne, 2007) (MDP) feature has been used to combine two source-target phrase tables of different domains for domain adaptation (Koehn and Schroeder, 2007) but not so extensively in a pivot language scenario, especially when multiple pivots are involved (7 in our case). Our work is different from other previous works in the following ways:

- We work on a realistic low resource setting for translation between Japanese and Hindi in which we use small sized multilingual corpora containing translations of a sentence in multiple languages.
- We focus on the impact of using a relatively large number of pivot languages (7 to be precise) to improve the translation quality and compare this to when only one pivot language is used.
- Most works focus on obtaining pivot based phrase tables on relatively larger corpora than the ones used for the direct phrase table. We use the same corpora sizes for the pivot as well as direct tables.
- We verify that Multiple Decoding Paths (MDP) feature of Moses is much more effective than plain linear interpolation, especially when more pivot languages are used together.
- We show that simply varying the pivot language leads to additional phrase pairs being acquired that impact translation quality.

Section 2 contains the related work. Section 3 begins with a basic description about the languages involved, followed by the corpora details and the experimental methodology. Section 4 consists of results, observations and discussions. The paper ends with conclusions and future work.

## 2 Related Work

Utiyama and Isahara (2007) developed a method (sentence translation strategy) for cascading a source-pivot and a pivot-target system to translate from source to target using a pivot language. Since this results in multiplicative error propagation Wu and Wang (2009) developed a method (triangulation) in which they combined the source-pivot and pivot-target phrase tables to get a source-target

[4]The construction of a multilingual corpus has already the benefit that each new language added to it will allow direct translation with a SMT system for $N$ new language pairs.

phrase table. They then combine the pivoted and direct tables by linear interpolation whose weights were manually specified. There is a method to automatically learn the weights (Sennrich, 2012) but it requires reference phrase pairs not easily available in resource constrained scenarios like ours. Work on translation from Indonesian to English using Malay and Spanish to English using Portuguese (Nakov and Ng, 2009) as pivot languages worked well since the pivots had substantial similarity to the source languages. This is one of the first works to use MDP in the pivot based SMT scenario.

(Paul et al., 2013) and (Paul et al., 2009) showed that English is not the best pivot language for many language pairs, including Japanese and Hindi. This was reason enough for us to not consider English as a pivot in our experiments. None of the above works focus on the utilization and impact of more than 2 pivots in their experiments which was one of our main objectives. Related to multilingual translation are works by Habash and Hu (2009), El Kholy et al. (2013), Salloum et al. (2014) and Koehn et al. (2009). Work on multi source translation (Och and Ney, 2001) which is complementary to our work must also be noted.

In the related field of information retrieval, pivot languages were employed to translate queries in cross-language information retrieval (CLIR) (Gollins and Sanderson, 2001) (Kishida and Kando, 2003). Chinnakotla et al. (2010) retrieved feedback terms from documents written in the pivot languages (after translating back from the pivot), and augmented source queries leading to improvements in information retrieval. We now talk about the languages, corpora and experiments conducted.

## 3 Description of Languages, Corpora and Experiments

We first describe the pivot languages and the corpora we use. We follow this with a description of the triangulation method which we use to construct phrase tables using the pivot languages, the methods used to combine the constructed tables and then the experiments that use them.

### 3.1 Languages involved

We performed experiments on translation between Japanese and Hindi which do not belong to the same language group but exhibit many similarities: Japanese (J) and Hindi (H) both have SOV order and are morphologically rich. For pivots we considered languages like Chinese, Korean (East-Asian languages of which Korean is closer to source), Marathi, Kannada, Telugu (Indian languages closer to target), Paite (Sino-Tibetian) and Esperanto (relatively distant from both source and target). Increasing the number of languages reduced the size of multilingual parallel translations available[5]. Our choice of languages was initially random but led to interesting observations as will be seen later.

### 3.2 Corpora Details

The corpora used comes from the freely available multilingual Bible corpus[6] stored in XML files. After sentence aligning all 9 languages we got 29780 sentence tuples. A tuple contains 9 sentences: 1 for each language. This we divided into 29000 training tuples, 280 tuning tuples and 500 testing tuples. The Japanese sentences were segmented using JUMAN (Kurohashi et al., 1994). The Chinese and Korean (Hangul blocks were space separated) sentences were directly available in their character segmented form. The corpora of the other languages were left morphologically and syntactically unprocessed.

### 3.3 Phrase Table Triangulation

We implemented the phrase table triangulation method (Wu and Wang, 2007) using JAVA as the programming language. The phrase table has 4 main scores: forward and inverse phrase translation probabilities (equations 1 and 2) accompanied by forward and inverse lexical translation probabilities (equations 3 and 4). The formulae for generating them using pivots are:

$$\Theta(f|e) = \sum_{p_i} \Theta(f|p_i) * \Theta(p_i|e) \qquad (1)$$

[5]It must be noted that Hebrew and Greek are most likely the languages from which the Bible sentences were translated into the other languages.

[6]http://homepages.inf.ed.ac.uk/s0787820/bible/

$$\Theta(e|f) = \sum_{p_i} \Theta(e|p_i) * \Theta(p_i|f) \quad (2)$$

$$P_w(f|e,a) = \sum_{p_i} P_w(f|p_i,a_1) * P_w(p_i|e,a_2) \quad (3)$$

$$P_w(e|f,a) = \sum_{p_i} P_w(e|p_i,a_2) * P_w(p_i|f,a_1) \quad (4)$$

Here $a_1$ is the alignment between phrases $f$ (source) and $p_i$ (pivot), $a_2$, the alignment between $p_i$ and $e$ (target) and $a$ the alignment between $e$ and $f$. Note that the lexical translation probabilities are calculated in the same way as the phrase probabilities. Our results might improve even more if we used more sophisticated approaches like crosslanguage similarity method or the method which uses pivot induced alignments (Wu and Wang, 2007).

### 3.4 Phrase Table Combination

There are 3 ways to combine phrase tables: linear interpolation, fillup interpolation and multiple decoding paths. Linear interpolation is performed by merging the tables and computing a weighted sum of phrase pair probabilities from each phrase table giving a final single table. Typically, the direct phrase table is given a significantly higher weight than the pivot based table.

$$\Theta(f|e) = \alpha_0 * \Theta_{direct}(f|e) + \sum_{l_i} \alpha_{l_i} * \Theta_{l_i}(f|e)$$
$$subject\ to\ \alpha_0 + \sum_{l_i} \alpha_{l_i} = 1 \quad (5)$$

Typically $\alpha_0$ is 0.9 (Wu and Wang, 2009) and the pivot languages are collectively given a weight of 0.1. $\Theta_{l_i}(f|e)$ is the inverse translation probability for language $l_i$. In our experiments we set the $\alpha$'s according to the ratio of the BLEU scores, on the test set, of the translations using the individual phrase tables. It is possible to learn optimal weights but this requires a collection of reference phrase pairs which would not be readily available in a resource constrained scenario.

Fillup interpolation does not modify phrase probabilities but selects phrase pair entries from the next table if they are not present in the current table. The priority of the phrase tables should be specified which we do by ranking them according to the BLEU scores on a test set.

Multiple Decoding Paths (MDP) method of Moses which uses all the tables simultaneously while decoding ensures that each pivot table is kept separate and translation options are collected from all the tables. Increasing the number of pivot languages slows the decoding process drastically but the existence of powerful machines negates this limitation. For the sake of completeness we also experimented with a combination of both, linear and MDP, methods by: Firstly, combining the pivot based phrase tables into a single table using equation 5 (using the ratio of BLEU scores as interpolation weights) followed by using this table to support the direct phrase table by MDP. Note that the right way would be to use the BLEU scores on the tuning set but our objective was to show that even in the best case scenario (also called Oracle[7] scenario) this method is still inferior compared to only using the MDP method.

### 3.5 Descriptions of Experiments

Our experiments were centered around Phrase Based SMT (PBSMT). We used the open source Moses decoder (Hoang et al., 2007) package (including Giza++) for word alignment, phrase table extraction and decoding for sentence translation. We also used the Moses scripts for linear and fillup interpolation along with the multiple decoding paths (MDP) setting (by modifying the moses.ini files). We performed MERT (Och, 2003) based tuning using the MIRA algorithm. We used BLEU (Papineni et al., 2002) as our evaluation criteria and the bootstrapping method (Koehn, 2004) for significance testing. For the sake of comparison with previous methods, we experimented with sentence translation strategy (Utiyama and Isahara, 2007) using 10 as the n-best list size for intermediate and target language translations. The experiments we performed are given below. Each experiment involves either the creation of a phrase tables or combination of phrase tables. We tune, test and evaluate these tables or combinations.

1. A src (source) to tgt (target) direct phrase table.
2. For piv in Pivot_Languages_Set; the set of pivot languages to be used (Tables 1 and 2):

[7] By Oracle scenario we mean that we already know the performance on the test sets and exploit this information to "unfairly" boost the translation scores.

(a) src to piv and piv to tgt phrase tables. Translate the src test sentences to tgt using the sentence translation strategy and evaluate. (Column 2)
(b) Triangulate the src-piv and piv-tgt phrase tables to get the src-piv-tgt phrase table. (Column 3)
(c) Perform linear interpolation of the src-tgt and src-piv-tgt table using 9:1 weight ratio in equation 5 to get a combined table. (Column 4)
(d) Perform linear interpolation of the src-tgt and src-piv-tgt table using the ratio of their BLEU scores as weights in equation 5 to get a combined table. (Column 5)
(e) Perform fillup interpolation of the src-tgt (main) and src-piv-tgt table (secondary) to get a combined table. (Column 6)
(f) Combine the src-tgt and src-piv-tgt phrase table using MDP (2 paths, 1 for direct and 1 for pivot). (Column 7)

3. Combine **all** the src-piv-tgt tables into a single table using linear (weights are ratios of BLEU scores) and fillup interpolation independently, giving the phrase tables: linear_interp_all and fill_interp_all respectively. Table 3, rows 4 and 5.

4. Perform linear interpolation of the src-tgt and linear_interp_all tables using 9:1 weight ratio in equation 5 to get a combined table. Table 3, row 6.

5. Perform linear interpolation of the src-tgt and **all** src-piv-tgt phrase tables using the ratio of their BLEU scores as weights in equation 5 to get a combined table. Table 3, row 7.

6. Perform fillup interpolation of the src-tgt and **all** src-piv-tgt phrase tables. The priority of the tables is given by the descending order of BLEU scores. Table 3, row 8.

7. Combine the linear_interp_all with the src-tgt phrase table using MDP. Repeat this for fill_interp_all. Table 3, rows 9 and 10.

8. Combine **all** the src-piv-tgt phrase tables with the src-tgt phrase table using MDP (8 paths, 1 for direct and 1 for each of the 7 pivots). Table 3, row 11.

9. Combine the **top 3** pivot phrase tables with the src-piv-tgt phrase tables with the src-tgt phrase table using MDP (4 paths, 1 for direct and 1 for each of the 3 pivots). The pivot tables with the 3 highest[8] standalone BLEU scores are selected. Table 3, row 12.

## 4 Results and Discussions

BLEU scores obtained after testing the tuned tables are reported. Scores in bold are statistically significant ($p<0.05$) over the baseline which is the system trained using a direct src-tgt parallel corpus.

### 4.1 Results

The Japanese-Hindi direct translation system gave a BLEU of 33.86 whereas the Hindi-Japanese one gave 37.47. For the rest of the paper these will be the baselines, unless mentioned otherwise.

The evaluation scores are split into 3 tables. Table 1 contains the scores for Japanese to Hindi (Table 2 for Hindi to Japanese) translation using each pivot separately and has 7 columns whose details are given in section 3.5 from 2.a to 2.f. Table 3 contains the scores for Japanese to Hindi (and vice versa) translation using all 7 pivots together in various ways. Each row is self explanatory. In row 6, we mean that the direct phrase table has a weight of 0.9 and the remainder 0.1 is distributed amongst the pivot phrase tables in the ratio of their standalone BLEU scores which can be seen in column 3 of tables 1 and 2. It is quite clear that sentence translation strategy is the most inferior technique.

### 4.2 Observations

Below, we give an explanation of the observed scores from various points of views.

#### 4.2.1 On the Pivots Used

It is logical to consider that the closeness of a pivot language to the source or target is an important factor in the improvement of translation quality, since Korean helps Japanese-Hindi translation.

[8]We chose 3 since our evaluation showed that the BLEU scores for the 3 pivot languages were much larger than the remaining ones.

| Pivot Language | Sentence Strategy | Standalone | Linear Interpolate (1) With Direct | Linear Interpolate (2) With Direct | Fill Interpolate With Direct | MDP With Direct |
|---|---|---|---|---|---|---|
| **1. Direct** | **33.86** | | | | | |
| **2. Chinese** | 23.53 | 28.89 | 34.03 | **34.61** | 34.31 | **35.66** |
| **3. Korean** | 26.30 | 28.92 | **34.65** | 34.18 | 34.64 | **35.60** |
| **4. Esperanto** | 22.43 | 28.73 | **34.63** | **34.55** | 35.32 | **35.74** |
| **5. Paite** | 19.40 | 26.64 | 34.17 | 34.40 | **34.66** | **35.22** |
| **6. Marathi** | 15.68 | 21.80 | 33.88 | 33.80 | 33.83 | 34.03 |
| **7. Kannada** | 16.94 | 24.15 | 33.74 | 34.13 | **34.87** | **35.52** |
| **8. Telugu** | 14.15 | 21.31 | 33.81 | 33.85 | 34.04 | **34.57** |

Table 1: Japanese-Hindi Results Using Single Pivots

| Pivot Language | Sentence Strategy | Standalone | Linear Interpolate (1) With Direct | Linear Interpolate (2) With Direct | Fill Interpolate With Direct | MDP With Direct |
|---|---|---|---|---|---|---|
| **1. Direct** | **37.47** | | | | | |
| **2. Chinese** | 27.93 | 30.97 | 35.90 | **38.47** | **38.41** | **39.49** |
| **3. Korean** | 30.68 | 32.67 | 35.99 | **38.72** | **38.55** | **39.49** |
| **4. Esperanto** | 26.67 | 30.80 | 36.07 | 37.82 | 37.85 | **39.14** |
| **5. Paite** | 23.37 | 29.17 | 35.89 | 37.73 | 37.39 | **38.19** |
| **6. Marathi** | 20.59 | 26.21 | 35.89 | 37.57 | 37.72 | **38.30** |
| **7. Kannada** | 23.21 | 26.96 | 35.84 | 38.05 | 37.79 | **38.05** |
| **8. Telugu** | 19.01 | 25.22 | 37.25 | 36.98 | 37.11 | 37.04 |

Table 2: Hindi-Japanese Results Using Single Pivots

Of all the scores, the ones obtained using Korean and Chinese as pivots stand out as the best and it is known that Korean and Japanese share many similarities. Although this gives reason to believe that languages belonging to the same language group should act as good choices of pivots, the languages Kannada, Telugu and (especially) Marathi should have helped improve Hindi to Japanese translation. Moreover, languages like Paite and Esperanto which are relatively distant from both Hindi and Japanese gave better performance than the Indian Languages. Remember that the Chinese and Korean corpora were character segmented[9] and that Esperanto and Paite are not so morphologically rich. The Indian pivot languages have agglutinative features which is one of the main causes of poor quality SMT. This clearly indicates that morphological similarity to source and target is another equally important aspect that affects the translation quality. Had this not been the case, the Indian Languages would have acted as good pivots. This shows that experiments involving forcing the morpheme to morpheme ratio, of the source to pivot to target sentences, to be the same, must be conducted. Henceforth, it is to be expected that the most significant improvements will be obtained when Chinese, Korean and Esperanto (in a number of cases) are used as pivots.

[9]Hangul blocks were space separated in the Korean case.

#### 4.2.2 On the Linear and Fill Interpolation Methods

**Single pivots:** All the interpolation methods (columns 4, 5 and 6 of Tables 1 and 2) gave small improvements in BLEU in most cases compared to the baselines for both language pairs. The results do not show drastic improvements, which is expected since the baseline and pivots based phrase tables are constructed from the same multilingual

| Combination Type | Jap-Hin | Hin-Jap |
|---|---|---|
| 1. Direct phrase table (baseline) | 33.86 | 37.47 |
| 2. Best result using single pivot | 35.74 (Esp.) | 39.49 (Kor.) |
| 3. Combine All Pivots using MDP | 34.49 | 37.02 |
| 4. A - Linear Interpolate All Pivot tables (BLEU score ratio) | 32.50 | 35.65 |
| 5. B - Fill Interpolate All Pivot tables (Priority according to BLEU score) | 32.12 | 34.44 |
| 6. Linear Interpolate (9:1 ratio) Direct with All Pivot tables | **34.56** | **38.60** |
| 7. Linear Interpolate (BLEU score ratio) Direct with All Pivots | **35.24** | **39.08** |
| 8. Fill Interpolate Direct with All Pivots (Priority according to BLEU score) | **35.28** | **38.70** |
| 9. Combine Direct and A using MDP | **36.40** | **39.85** |
| 10. Combine Direct and B using MDP | **36.67** | **40.07** |
| 11. Combine Direct and All Pivots tables using MDP | **38.42** | **40.19** |
| 12. Combine Direct and Top 3 (BLEU) pivot tables using MDP (Oracle) | **38.22** | **41.09** |

Table 3: Results Using Multiple Pivots With Different Combination Methods

training instances (29000 tuples - see section 3.2). Typically the interpolation methods are shown to give substantial performance boosts when the direct source-target phrase table is obtained using relatively smaller corpora sizes compared to those used for the source-pivot and pivot-target tables. In case of linear interpolation with a 9:1 weight ratio, the scores improve slightly in some cases for Japanese-Hindi but degrade in case of Hindi-Japanese. However, in the case of linear interpolation where the BLEU score ratio is used as the weight ratio, the improvements are much better[10].

Fill based interpolation also gives improvements in some cases, mostly when Chinese and Korean are used as pivots. An overall comparison shows that there is no consistency when a single pivot language is used and no conclusive comment can be made on the efficacy of these interpolation methods.

**Multiple Pivots:** However in Table 3, rows 6 to 8 show that using all the pivots together, result in a significant improvement over the direct phrase tables. Linear interpolation with BLEU score ratio gives 35.24 BLEU (33.86 for direct phrase table) for Japanese-Hindi and 39.08 BLEU (37.47 for direct phrase table). Rows 4 and 5 show the scores of the linear and fill interpolation of only the pivot based phrase tables. It is interesting to see that in case of Japanese-Hindi the BLEU scores rival that of the direct phrase table (32.50/32.12 v.s. 33.86). This is similar in the case of Hindi-Japanese: 35.65/34.44 v.s. 37.47. The following points must be noted:

**a.** Since the setting is multilingual and improvements, however slight, are observed in some cases it must be the case that, through pivoting, additional (and possibly improved) phrase pairs are induced which are not extracted using the direct source-target parallel corpus. This also gives reason to believe that every pivot induces a different set of phrase pairs thereby overcoming the limitations of poor alignment (and effectively phrase extraction) on small corpora. Even if there is no alignment error, pivoting still introduces new phrase pairs which improves MT performance.

**b.** The pivot based phrase tables already have an incomplete probability space with respect to the phrase pair distribution. Linear interpolation tends to violate the overall probability mass since the phrase pair distribution gets changed. Fill interpolation just adds additional phrase pairs from the next phrase table when not available in the current one which leads to poor mixing of different probability models giving poorer performance in-spite of additional phrase pairs being available.

**c.** Since some pivot languages are obviously bad, their probability scores would drastically affect the overall probability mass. They should be excluded or given low weights, which we do by considering the BLEU score ratio. However, this is not a good idea because the scores for Telugu, a bad pivot for Hindi-Japanese translation, degraded to a lesser ex-

[10]Expected as we use test set evaluation information.

tent when the Telugu based phrase table was linearly combined with the direct phrase table. Sennrich (2012) gave a method to learn these weights, but in a resource constrained scenario such a method is difficult to apply.

This motivated us to try the Multiple Decoding Paths (MDP) feature of Moses.

#### 4.2.3 On using MDP

**Single pivots:** Since log linear combination does not modify the probability space it should lead to definitive increase in translation scores. This claim is validated by the last columns of Tables 1 and 2. For Japanese-Hindi: barring Marathi, the combination of the direct and pivot phrase table leads to significant improvement over the direct phrase tables. A similar situation occurs for Hindi-Japanese except that Telugu behaves as a bad pivot.

**Multiple pivots:** Row 3 of Table 3 indicates that the log linear combination of all the pivot tables using MDP for Japanese-Hindi gives a BLEU of 34.49, an improvement ($p<0.05$) over the direct table (BLEU 33.86). For Hindi-Japanese, although the equivalent BLEU score (37.02) is not an improvement over that of the direct table (37.47), it does show that multiple pivots can be used to achieve translation quality similar to the quality obtained by a direct table.

Since it was observed that the interpolation of all the pivot tables into a single one gave scores close to the direct tables we decided to try the combination of the all pivots interpolated table with the direct table using MDP. Rows 9 and 10 show that there is a significant improvement compared to the scores of the direct tables alone. But this method of linear + log linear combination would still suffer from the limitation of linear interpolation which led to the final 2 experiments which use only log linear combination.

Row 11 shows that the method of combining the direct and all the pivot tables using MDP (one for each table) outperforms all the methods so far. The reason is simple: Only good translation options are collected from all tables during hypothesis expansion, the bad ones are automatically pruned. For Japanese-Hindi the BLEU is 38.42 which is an improvement of 4.56 (13% relative) over the BLEU of the direct phrase table (33.86). For Hindi-Japanese the BLEU of 40.19 is an improvement of 2.72 (7.25% relative) over that of the direct table (37.47). The increment is lesser because of the premise we established in section 4.2.1. This points to an interesting observation that pivot languages induce better phrase pairs in a multilingual setting which are not present in the direct phrase table. This is quite beneficial when the corpora sizes are small which lead to poor quality phrase tables.

To test whether exclusion of bad performing pivots leads to improvements in BLEU we performed another oracle experiment in which we only included the pivot phrase tables having significant standalone BLEU difference compared to the others. Korean, Chinese and Esperanto were the ones that stood out. The last row shows that for Japanese-Hindi the BLEU (38.22) does not significantly increase over the situation when all pivots are used together (38.42). However for Hindi-Japanese the BLEU is 41.09 which is a significant ($p<0.05$) increase compared to when all the pivots are used together (40.19 - 2.2% relative). Note that this leads to an absolute BLEU difference of 3.62 (9.66% relative) compared to the BLEU of the direct phrase table. The improvements for Japanese-Hindi were already so large (13%) that more significant improvements would need deeper inspection and improved methods. We believe that further significant improvements are possible and advanced methods to effectively select multiple pivots need to be studied and implemented.

#### 4.2.4 On the number of new phrase pairs induced

Based on the cutoff of 0.001 for the inverse translation probability, Table 4 contains the statistics of the unique phrase pairs in each pivot table (Columns 4 to 10) and the direct table (Column 3) along with the number of phrase pairs common (Column 2) to all. It is quite obvious that each pivot[11] induces its own set of unique phrase pairs.

#### 4.2.5 On the improvement in translations

Table 5 gives the count of improved translations, out of 500 tested sentences, over the direct using sentence level BLEU difference at various cutoffs. On an average 50% of the sentences showed increase

[11]For each language we use their first 3 characters of their names as the shortened versions.

| Direction | Common | Direct | Chi | Kor | Esp | Pai | Kan | Mar | Tel |
|---|---|---|---|---|---|---|---|---|---|
| 1. Jap-Hin | 0.032 | 1.404 | 20.74 | 18.65 | 16.06 | 23.85 | 26.56 | 30.92 | 26.84 |
| 2. Hin-Jap | 0.034 | 1.528 | 26.20 | 20.26 | 18.06 | 28.83 | 29.90 | 36.98 | 31.23 |

Table 4: Unique phrase pairs in each table (in millions of pairs)

| Direction | >0 | >0.1 | >0.2 | >0.3 | >0.4 | >0.5 | >0.6 | >0.7 |
|---|---|---|---|---|---|---|---|---|
| 1. Jap-Hin | 267 | 108 | 36 | 12 | 6 | 4 | 2 | 0 |
| 2. Hin-Jap | 275 | 124 | 60 | 24 | 12 | 4 | 1 | 1 |

Table 5: Number of improved translations (out of 500) using sentence level BLEU difference at various cutoffs

in BLEU and the number of improved sentences decreases with increasing cutoff. We manually verified a random sample and found that the improvements were commensurate with the reported differences. Finally, consider an example of improvement in Japanese to Hindi translation.

**Input:** それ から 、 ヨハネ の 弟子 たち が きる 、 死体 を 引き取る 葬る 。 そして 、 イエス の ところ に 行く 報告 する 。 (Sore kara, Yohane no deshi-tachi ga kiru, shitai o hikitoru homuru. Soshite, iesu no tokoro ni iku hokoku suru.)

**English equivalent:** After that, John's disciples came and took his corpse away, buried it and then went to Jesus to give him the news.

**Direct translation:** तब यूहन्ना के चेलों ने आकर उस की लोथ ले गया और उसके पास जाकर बता दिया (Tab yohanna ke chelo ne aakar uss ki lotha le gaya; aura uske paas jaakar bata diya)

**Best translation using MDP:** तब यूहन्ना के चेलों ने आकर उस की लोथ को ले जाकर गाढ दिया और जाकर यीशु को समाचार दिया (Tab yohanna ke chelo ne aakar usa ki lotha ko le jaakar gaad diya aura jakar yesu ko samachara diya)

**Analysis:** Note that in the direct translation the part about "burying the corpse" (gaad diya) and "Jesus" (yesu) is missing which is present in the MDP translation. Also the verb forms indicating the sequence of actions like "came and" (aakar) and "took his corpse away" (usa ki lotha ko le jaakar) are much better in the MDP translation. Instead of "samachara diya" (gave news) the preferred translation is "samachara di".

## 5 Conclusions and Future Work

We have presented our work on leveraging a small sized multilingual parallel corpus using 7 pivot languages for SMT between Japanese and Hindi. Our main objective was to augment a phrase table on direct parallel corpus using many pivot language based phrase tables constructed from the same multilingual corpus. We confirm that this induces additional and improved phrase pairs which, under the Multiple Decoding Paths setting (MDP), leads to substantial improvements over the direct phrase tables. More importantly, we show that using multiple pivot languages simultaneously lead to large improvements in BLEU compared to the when a single pivot is used; which is the novel aspect of our work. This opens up many further research directions like **a.** How can one choose a set of good pivot languages amongst available choices? **b.** Does this multilingual leveraging help in a situation where we have large size corpora like Europarl corpora? **c.** How much of an impact can treatment (morphological or syntactic) of the pivot language help in improving translation quality? **d.** Can good reordering information be extracted by pivoting? **e.** Can multi source and multi pivot setting further enhance quality? **f.** How can the noise induced by pivoting be controlled by methods other than probability cutoffs? and finally **g.** Can simpler but more effective methods compared to triangulation be exploited in a multilingual scenario? The last 4 questions have long been ignored and deserve to be answered. We will pursue these directions in the future and attempt to provide satisfactory answers.

## References


Alexandra Birch and Miles Osborne. 2007. Ccg supertags in factored statistical machine translation. In *In ACL Workshop on Statistical Machine Translation*, pages 9–16.

Manoj K. Chinnakotla, Karthik Raman, and Pushpak Bhattacharyya. 2010. Multilingual pseudo-relevance feedback: Performance study of assisting languages. In *Proceedings of the 48th Annual Meeting of the Association for Computational Linguistics*, ACL '10, pages 1346–1356, Stroudsburg, PA, USA. Association for Computational Linguistics.

Ahmed El Kholy, Nizar Habash, Gregor Leusch, Evgeny Matusov, and Hassan Sawaf. 2013. Selective combination of pivot and direct statistical machine translation models. In *Proceedings of the Sixth International Joint Conference on Natural Language Processing*, pages 1174–1180. Asian Federation of Natural Language Processing.

Tim Gollins and Mark Sanderson. 2001. Improving cross language retrieval with triangulated translation. In *Proceedings of the 24th Annual International ACM SIGIR Conference on Research and Development in Information Retrieval*, SIGIR '01, pages 90–95, New York, NY, USA. ACM.

Nizar Habash and Jun Hu. 2009. Improving arabic-chinese statistical machine translation using english as pivot language.

Hieu Hoang, Alexandra Birch, Chris Callison-burch, Richard Zens, Marcello Federico, Nicola Bertoldi, Chris Dyer, Brooke Cowan, Wade Shen, Christine Moran, Ondřej Bojar, Alexandra Constantin, and Evan Herbst. 2007. Moses: Open source toolkit for statistical machine translation". acl-2007.

Kazuaki Kishida and Noriko Kando. 2003. Two-stage refinement of query translation in a pivot language approach to cross-lingual information retrieval: An experiment at clef 2003. In Carol Peters, Julio Gonzalo, Martin Braschler, and Michael Kluck, editors, *CLEF*, volume 3237 of *Lecture Notes in Computer Science*, pages 253–262. Springer.

Philipp Koehn and Josh Schroeder. 2007. Experiments in domain adaptation for statistical machine translation. In *Proceedings of the Second Workshop on Statistical Machine Translation*, StatMT '07, pages 224–227, Stroudsburg, PA, USA. Association for Computational Linguistics.

Philipp Koehn, Alexandra Birch, and Ralf Steinberger, 2009. *462 Machine Translation Systems for Europe*, pages 65–72. Association for Machine Translation in the Americas, AMTA.

Philipp Koehn. 2004. Statistical significance tests for machine translation evaluation. In *EMNLP*, pages 388–395.

Anoop Kunchukuttan, Abhijit Mishra, Rajen Chatterjee, Ritesh Shah, and Pushpak Bhattacharyya. 2014. Shata-anuvadak: Tackling multiway translation of indian languages. In *Proceedings of the Ninth International Conference on Language Resources and Evaluation (LREC'14)*, pages 1781–1787, Reykjavik, Iceland, May. European Language Resources Association (ELRA). ACL Anthology Identifier: L14-1355.

Sadao Kurohashi, Toshihisa Nakamura, Yuji Matsumoto, and Makoto Nagao. 1994. Improvements of japanese morphological analyzer juman. In *Proceedings of The International Workshop on Sharable Natural Language*, pages 22–28.

Preslav Nakov and Hwee Tou Ng. 2009. Improved statistical machine translation for resource-poor languages using related resource-rich languages. In *Proceedings of the 2009 Conference on Empirical Methods in Natural Language Processing: Volume 3 - Volume 3*, EMNLP '09, pages 1358–1367, Stroudsburg, PA, USA. Association for Computational Linguistics.

Franz Josef Och and Hermann Ney. 2001. Statistical multi-source translation. In *In MT Summit 2001*, pages 253–258.

Franz Josef Och. 2003. Minimum error rate training in statistical machine translation. In *Proceedings of the 41st Annual Meeting on Association for Computational Linguistics - Volume 1*, ACL '03, pages 160–167, Stroudsburg, PA, USA. Association for Computational Linguistics.

Kishore Papineni, Salim Roukos, Todd Ward, and Wei-Jing Zhu. 2002. Bleu: A method for automatic evaluation of machine translation. In *Proceedings of the 40th Annual Meeting on Association for Computational Linguistics*, ACL '02, pages 311–318, Stroudsburg, PA, USA. Association for Computational Linguistics.

Michael Paul, Hirofumi Yamamoto, Eiichiro Sumita, and Satoshi Nakamura. 2009. On the importance of pivot language selection for statistical machine translation. In *Proceedings of Human Language Technologies: The 2009 Annual Conference of the North American Chapter of the Association for Computational Linguistics, Companion Volume: Short Papers*, NAACL-Short '09, pages 221–224, Stroudsburg, PA, USA. Association for Computational Linguistics.

Michael Paul, Andrew Finch, and Eiichrio Sumita. 2013. How to choose the best pivot language for automatic translation of low-resource languages. 12(4):14:1–14:17, October.

Philip Resnik, MariBroman Olsen, and Mona Diab. 1999. The bible as a parallel corpus: Annotating the 'book of 2000 tongues'. *Computers and the Humanities*, 33(1-2):129–153.

Wael Salloum, Heba Elfardy, Linda Alamir-Salloum, Nizar Habash, and Mona Diab. 2014. Sentence level dialect identification for machine translation system selection. In *Proceedings of the 52nd Annual Meeting of the Association for Computational Linguistics (Volume 2: Short Papers)*, pages 772–778. Association for Computational Linguistics.

Rico Sennrich. 2012. Perplexity minimization for translation model domain adaptation in statistical machine translation. In *Proceedings of the 13th Conference of the European Chapter of the Association for Computational Linguistics*, EACL '12, pages 539–549, Stroudsburg, PA, USA. Association for Computational Linguistics.

Masao Utiyama and Hitoshi Isahara. 2007. A comparison of pivot methods for phrase-based statistical machine translation. In *in Proceedings of the conference on Human Language Technology Conference of the North American Chapter of the Association of Computational Linguistics (NAACL-HLT*, pages 484–491.

Hua Wu and Haifeng Wang. 2007. Pivot language approach for phrase-based statistical machine translation. *Machine Translation*, 21(3):165–181, September.

Hua Wu and Haifeng Wang. 2009. Revisiting pivot language approach for machine translation. In *Proceedings of the Joint Conference of the 47th Annual Meeting of the ACL and the 4th International Joint Conference on Natural Language Processing of the AFNLP: Volume 1 - Volume 1*, ACL '09, pages 154–162, Stroudsburg, PA, USA. Association for Computational Linguistics.

# Why Read if You Can Scan? Trigger Scoping Strategy for Biographical Fact Extraction

**Dian Yu and Heng Ji**
Computer Science Department
Rensselaer Polytechnic Institute
Troy, NY, USA
{yud2, jih}@rpi.edu

**Sujian Li**
Peking University
Key Laboratory of
Computational Linguistics
Beijing, China
lisujian@pku.edu.cn

**Chin-Yew Lin**
Microsoft Research Asia
Beijing, China
cyl@microsoft.com

## Abstract

The rapid growth of information sources brings a unique challenge to biographical information extraction: how to find specific facts without having to read all the words. An effective solution is to follow the human scanning strategy which keeps a specific keyword in mind and searches within a specific scope. In this paper, we mimic a scanning process to extract biographical facts. We use event and relation *triggers* as keywords, identify their scopes and apply type constraints to extract answers within the scope of a trigger. Experiments demonstrate that our approach outperforms state-of-the-art methods up to 26% absolute gain in F-score without using any syntactic analysis or external knowledge bases.

## 1 Introduction

Extracting biographical information is an important task because it can help readers understand an ongoing event more easily by providing the background biographical information of participants in this event. In fact, this task has been part of the Text Analysis Conference (TAC) - Knowledge Base Population (KBP) Slot Filling (SF) Track (Ji et al., 2010; Ji et al., 2011; Surdeanu, 2013; Surdeanu and Ji, 2014) for years.

Overall, state-of-the-art research still needs improvement. A typical approach is based on patterns which include triggers (*e.g.*, (Sun et al., 2011; Li et al., 2012)). Here *trigger* is defined as the smallest extent of a text which most clearly expresses an event occurrence or indicates a relation type. High-quality patterns yield quite high precision but relatively low recall. In addition, it's relatively expensive to maintain and update a set of extraction patterns.

Furthermore, we carefully investigated the TAC-KBP SF 2012 ground truth corpus and find that 94.36% of the biographical facts are mentioned in a sentence containing indicative fact-specific triggers. For example, *born* is a trigger for extracting birth-related facts. Triggers are crucial in predicting the type of facts (Aguilar et al., 2014). However, most previous studies only focused on using triggers to create more patterns (*e.g.*, (Li et al., 2013)). Therefore the critical problem is how to make the most of triggers in biographical fact extraction?

We observe that people tend to scan a document when they want to quickly find a biographical fact within limited time. According to Douglas and Frazier (2001), *scanning* is a strategy for quickly finding specific information (keywords or ideas) in a text while ignoring its broader meaning. Scanning involves skipping words, but the emphasis is that the reader knows what to look for and rapidly scans until words are found and closer reading can occur (Phipps, 1983).

There are five steps in implementing scanning strategy according to Arnold (1999):

1. Keep in mind what you are searching for.
2. Anticipate in what form the information is likely to appear – number, proper nouns, etc.
3. Analyze the organization of the content before starting to scan.



*Human Language Technologies: The 2015 Annual Conference of the North American Chapter of the ACL*, pages 1203–1208,
Denver, Colorado, May 31 – June 5, 2015. 

4. Let your eyes run rapidly over several lines of print at a time.

5. When you find the sentence that has the information you seek, read the entire sentence.

Educators have verified that scanning is an effective strategy in enhancing reading comprehension (Motallebzadeh and Mamdoohi, 2011). There are two important aspects in the scanning strategy: keywords and their corresponding scopes. For biographical fact extraction, triggers can easily act as the keywords used by human during scanning and thus we focus on identifying the scopes of triggers.

Given a sentence that contains one or more triggers, we define *trigger scope* as the shortest fragment that is related to a trigger. Based on our observation, each fact-specific trigger has its own scope and its corresponding facts seldom appear outside of its scope. In the following sentence, if we can identify the scope of *graduated*, a trigger for education-related facts, we can skip the rest of the sentence after *1965* even though *Chesterbrook Academy* is an educational organization.

*She [<**graduated**> from **Barnard** in 1965] and soon began teaching English at **Chesterbrook Academy** in Pennsylvania.*[1]

In this paper, we study the effect of triggers by learning their linguistic scopes at the sentence level and apply this strategy to extract 11 types of biographical facts, namely, *birth date, death date, birth place, death place, residence place, education, parents, spouse, children, siblings* and *other family* as described in the KBP SF task.

We design our extraction process following the scanning steps corresponding to Arnold's scanning theory.

1. Let the computer know the query and the fact type to be extracted.

2. Let the computer know what form or entity type the candidate answer is likely to appear – person, organization, phrase, time, etc.

3. Locate all the triggers of the given fact type and recognize their respective scopes.

4. Within each scope, extract candidate answers which satisfy the entity type constraint in 2.

The contributions of our paper are as follows.

- We are the first to study the application of trigger scoping in biographical fact extraction.

- Our approach does not rely on any external knowledge bases for training or manually created fact-specific rules, and yet dramatically advances state-of-the-art.

## 2 Approach

In this section, we present the detailed approach of applying trigger scoping to biographical fact extraction. In Section 2.1, we first introduce the annotation methods of constructing the gold-standard dataset for evaluating scope identification. We use the sentence in Figure 1 as our illustrative example.

> *Paul Francis Conrad* and his [twin <**brother**>, James], were [<**born**> in Cedar Rapids, Iowa, on June 27, 1924], [<**sons**> of Robert H. Conrad and Florence Lawler Conrad].

Figure 1: Trigger and scope annotation example.

### 2.1 Trigger and Scope Annotation

#### 2.1.1 Basic issues

In a text, the sentences containing biographical facts (e.g., birth, death, family, residence or education) are considered for annotation. We discard a sentence if it expresses a biographical fact without surface cues.

During annotation, triggers are marked by angle brackets (*e.g.*, <*resident*>), and the scope boundaries of a trigger are denoted by square brackets as shown in Figure 1.

#### 2.1.2 Trigger Tagging

We mined fact-specific trigger lists from existing patterns (Chen et al., 2010; Min et al., 2012; Li et al., 2012) and ground truth sentences from KBP 2012

[1]The scope is marked with [] and the trigger is marked with <>.

SF corpus. In our experiment, we use 343 triggers and 38 triggers on average for each fact type[2].

We examine all the sentences containing any possible triggers. The presence of a word in one trigger list does not necessarily mean that the sentence contains an event or a relation. For instance, the second *child* in the following sentence is part of an organization's name.

*He and his wife, Ann McGarry Buchwald moved to Washington in 1963 with their [<**child**>], who was adopted from orphanages and [<**child**> welfare agencies] in Ireland, Spain and France.*

We also keep such sentences and annotate their trigger scopes without distinction.

Note that we only mark the syntactic head of a trigger phrase. For example, we mark *child* for the noun phrase *the second child.*

#### 2.1.3 Scope Tagging

During the scope annotation, we first include the trigger within its own scope and then mark its left and right boundaries. Usually the left boundary is the trigger itself.

When there are multiple triggers in the same sentence, we annotate each trigger's scope separately since it is possible that the scopes of different triggers are overlapped or nested as shown in the following instance (the scope of *daughters* covers the scope of *wife*):

*Pavarotti had three [<**daughters**> with his first wife, Lorenza, Cristina and Giuliana; and one, Alice, with his second wife].*

*Pavarotti had three daughters with his first [<**wife**>], Lorenza, Cristina and Giuliana; and one, Alice, with his second [<**wife**>].*

The scope of a word is not transitive. In the phrase *"his [<**son**>'s home] in Washington"*, *home* is within *son*'s scope and *in Washington* is within *home*'s scope, however, the last prepositional phrase is outside of *son*'s scope.

### 2.2 Scope Identification

We will introduce two methods for identifying trigger scopes.

[2]The trigger lists are publicly available for research purposes at: http://nlp.cs.rpi.edu/data/triggers.zip

#### 2.2.1 Rule-based Method

This method is used to investigate the performance of trigger scoping strategy when we do not have any labeled data. We use trigger as the left scope boundary. A verb or trigger with other fact types is regarded as the right boundary.

The rule-based scoping result of the walk-through example is as follows:

*Paul Francis Conrad* and his twin [<**brother**>, James, were] [<**born**> in Cedar Rapids, Iowa, on June 27, 1924,] [<**sons**> of Robert H. Conrad and Florence Lawler Conrad.]

#### 2.2.2 Supervised Classification

Alternatively we regard scope identification as a classification task. For each detected trigger, scope identification is performed as a binary classification of each token in the sentence as to whether it is within or outside of a trigger's scope.

We apply the Stanford CoreNLP toolkit (Manning et al., 2014) to annotate part-of-speech tags and names in each document. We design the following features to train a classifier.

- Position: The feature takes value 1 if the word appears before the trigger, and 0 otherwise.
- Distance: The distance (in words) between the word and the trigger.
- POS: POS tags of the word and the trigger.
- Name Entity: The name entity type of the word.
- Interrupt: The feature takes value 1 if there is a verb or a trigger with other fact type between the trigger and the word, and 0 otherwise. Verbs and triggers with other fact types can effectively change the current topic or continue in another way.

Note that the trained classifier can make predictions that result in nonconsecutive blocks of scope tokens. In this case, we aggregate the labels of all the words of an entity to assign a global label, which means that we assign the entity the majority label of the words it contains.

| Fact Type | Recall (%) | | | Precision (%) | | | F-score (%) | | |
|---|---|---|---|---|---|---|---|---|---|
| | 1 | 2 | 3 | 1 | 2 | 3 | 1 | 2 | 3 |
| per:place_of_birth | 59.4 | 88.2 | 88.2 | 76.0 | 87.0 | 88.2 | 66.7 | 87.6 | **88.2** |
| per:date_of_birth | 59.1 | 94.4 | 100.0 | 100.0 | 94.4 | 100.0 | 74.3 | 94.4 | **100.0** |
| per:place_of_death | 55.4 | 92.4 | 86.1 | 86.1 | 58.9 | 63.6 | 67.4 | 71.9 | **73.1** |
| per:date_of_death | 46.4 | 98.2 | 96.5 | 81.3 | 48.3 | 53.4 | 59.1 | 64.7 | **68.8** |
| per:place_of_residence | 60.0 | 68.9 | 68.9 | 40.4 | 64.2 | 61.3 | 48.3 | **66.5** | 64.9 |
| per:school_attended | 54.3 | 65.8 | 68.4 | 86.4 | 67.6 | 76.5 | 66.7 | 66.7 | **72.2** |
| per:parents | 41.9 | 75.7 | 73.0 | 68.4 | 31.8 | 50.0 | 52.0 | 44.8 | **59.3** |
| per:sibling | 50.0 | 76.2 | 76.2 | 61.5 | 59.3 | 55.2 | 55.2 | **66.7** | 64.0 |
| per:spouse | 36.0 | 63.3 | 81.7 | 78.3 | 54.3 | 49.5 | 49.3 | 58.5 | **61.6** |
| per:children | 39.5 | 61.8 | 76.4 | 73.2 | 58.5 | 71.6 | 51.3 | 60.1 | **73.9** |
| per:other_family | 23.1 | 66.7 | 71.4 | 75.0 | 53.9 | 53.6 | 35.3 | 59.6 | **61.2** |
| overall | 47.7 | 77.4 | 80.6 | 75.1 | 61.7 | 65.7 | 56.9 | 67.4 | **71.6** |

Table 1: performance on KBP 2013 (1:state-of-the-art; 2:rule-based; 3: SVMs).

### 2.3 Biographical Fact Extraction

For each relevant document of a given query, we use Stanford CoreNLP to find the coreferential mentions of the query and then return all the sentences which contain at least one query entity mention. For each trigger in a sentence, we extract the entities which satisfy fact-specific constraints within its s-cope. As shown in Figure 1, *brother* is the trigger for *per:siblings* and the candidate fact should be a person name. Thus we return all the person names (*e.g.*, *James*) within *brother*'s scope as the query *Paul*'s siblings.

## 3 Experiments and Discussion

### 3.1 Data

We use the KBP 2012 and 2013 SF corpora as the development and testing data sets respectively. There are 50 person queries each year.

From the KBP 2012 SF corpus, we annotated 2,806 sentences in formal writing from news reports as the gold-standard trigger scoping data set. We randomly partitioned the labeled data and performed ten-fold cross-validation using LIBSVM toolkit (Chang and Lin, 2011). We employ the classification model trained from all the labeled sentences to classify tokens in the unlabeled sentences.

### 3.2 Results

#### 3.2.1 Scope Identification

The scope identification evaluation results of the rule-based method and the SVMs with the RBF kernel are presented in Table 2. We can see that the supervised classification method performs better since it incorporates the weights of different features rather than simply applying hard constraints. In addition, it allows the answers to appear before a trigger as shown in the following sentence. Our rule-based method fails to extract *Fred* since it appears before the trigger *married*:

*She was a part of a group of black intellectuals who included philosopher and poet [**Fred Clifton**, whom she <**married**> in 1958].*

| Fact Group | Accuracy (%) | | F-score (%) | |
|---|---|---|---|---|
| | Rule | SVMs | Rule | SVMs |
| Birth | 85.97 | **96.66** | 80.01 | **94.21** |
| Death | 92.31 | **94.56** | 82.16 | **89.01** |
| Residence | 90.67 | **95.67** | 76.11 | **83.25** |
| Family | 92.49 | **94.11** | 75.30 | **77.31** |
| Education | 91.51 | **93.87** | 88.46 | **90.65** |

Table 2: Scope identification results.

#### 3.2.2 Biographical Fact Extraction

The fact extraction results in Table 1 demonstrate our trigger scoping strategy can outperform state-of-the-art methods. For a certain fact type, we choose the SF system which has the best performance for comparison. Specifically, we compare with two successful approaches: (1) the combination of distant supervision and rules (*e.g.*, (Grishman, 2013; Roth et al., 2013)); (2) patterns based on dependency paths (*e.g.*, (Li et al., 2013; Yu et al., 2013)).

The advantage of our method lies in trigger-driven

exploration. The positions of facts in the sentence can be very flexible and therefore difficult to be captured using a limited number of patterns. For example, the patterns in table 2[3] fail to extract *James* in Figure 1. However, the ways in which we express the trigger and words it dominated tend to be relatively fixed. For example, all the following patterns contain a fact-specific trigger and also facts usually appear within its scope.

| **PER:SIBLING** |
|---|
| **[Q]** poss$^{-1}$ **brother** appos **[A]** |
| **[Q]** appos$^{-1}$ **brother** appos **[A]** |
| **[Q]** appos **brother** appos-1 **[A]** |
| **[Q]** nsubjpass$^{-1}$ survived agent **brother** appos **[A]** |
| **[Q]** poss$^{-1}$ **sister** appos **[A]** |
| **[Q]** appos$^{-1}$ **sister** appos **[A]** |
| **[Q]** appos **sister** appos$^{-1}$ **[A]** |
| **[Q]** nsubjpass$^{-1}$ survived agent **sister** appos **[A]** |

Table 3: Patterns used for extracting sibling facts (Li et al., 2013). Q: Query, A: Answer.

The limitation of our method is that we assume a sentence centers around only one person thus every biographical fact mentioned should be related to the centroid person. For example, our method mistakenly extracted *February* as the death-date fact for both *Reina* and *Orlando* in the following case.

*Also at the mass was **Reina Tamayo**, the mother of **Orlando Zapata**, who [<**died**> in February] after an 85-day hunger strike to protest the fate of political prisoners here.*

In order to solve this problem, we need to further analyze the relation between the query entity mention and the trigger so that we can identify *Orlando Zapata* is irrelevant to the death-related fact.

## 4 Related Work

Previous successful approaches to construct the biographical knowledge base are relatively expensive: Distant Supervision (Surdeanu et al., 2010) relies upon external knowledge bases and it is time-consuming to manually write or edit patterns (Sun et al., 2011; Li et al., 2012). The main impact of our trigger scoping strategy is to narrow down the text span of searching for facts, from sentence-level to fragment-level. We only focus on analyzing the content which is likely to contain an answer.

Our trigger scoping method is also partially inspired from the negation scope detection work (*e.g.*, (Szarvas et al., 2008; Elkin et al., 2005; Chapman et al., 2001; Morante and Daelemans, 2009; Agarwal and Yu, 2010)) and reference scope identification in citing sentences (Abu-Jbara and Radev, 2011; Abu-Jbara and Radev, 2012).

[3]*A poss$^{-1}$ B* means there is a possession modifier relation (poss) between B and A.

## 5 Conclusions and Future Work

In this paper we explore the role of triggers and their scopes in biographical fact extraction. We implement the trigger scoping strategy using two simple but effective methods. Experiments demonstrate that our approach outperforms state-of-the-art without any syntactic analysis and external knowledge bases.

In the future, we will aim to explore how to generate a trigger list for a "surprise" new fact type within limited time.

## Acknowledgement

This work was supported by the U.S. DARPA Award No. FA8750-13-2-0045 in the Deep Exploration and Filtering of Text (DEFT) Program, the U.S. Army Research Laboratory under Cooperative Agreement No. W911NF-09-2-0053 (NS-CTA), U.S. NSF CAREER Award under Grant IIS-0953149, U.S. AFRL DREAM project, IBM Faculty Award, Google Research Award, Disney Research Award, Bosch Research Award, and RPI faculty start-up grant. The views and conclusions contained in this document are those of the authors and should not be interpreted as representing the official policies, either expressed or implied, of the U.S. Government. The U.S. Government is authorized to reproduce and distribute reprints for Government purposes notwithstanding any copyright notation here on.

## References

A. Abu-Jbara and D. Radev. 2011. Coherent citation-based summarization of scientific papers. In *Proc. Association for Computational Linguistics (ACL2011)*. Association for Computational Linguistics.

A. Abu-Jbara and D. Radev. 2012. Reference scope identification in citing sentences. In *Proc. Human*

*Language Technologies conference - North American Chapter of the Association for Computational Linguistics (HLT-NAACL 2012).*

S. Agarwal and H. Yu. 2010. Biomedical negation scope detection with conditional random fields. *Journal of the American medical informatics association*, 17(6):696–701.

J. Aguilar, C. Beller, P. McNamee, and B. Van Durme. 2014. A comparison of the events and relations across ace, ere, tac-kbp, and framenet annotation standards. *ACL 2014 Workshop on Events.*

Arnold. 1999. Skimming and scanning. In *Reading and Study Skills Lab.*

C. Chang and C. Lin. 2011. Libsvm: a library for support vector machines. *ACM Transactions on Intelligent Systems and Technology (TIST)*, 2(3):27.

W. Chapman, W. Bridewell, P. Hanbury, G. Cooper, and B. Buchanan. 2001. A simple algorithm for identifying negated findings and diseases in discharge summaries. *Journal of biomedical informatics*, 34(5):301–310.

Z. Chen, S. Tamang, A. Lee, X. Li, W. Lin, M. Snover, J. Artiles, M. Passantino, and H. Ji. 2010. Cuny-blender tac-kbp2010 entity linking and slot filling system description. In *Proc. Text Analysis Conference (TAC 2012).*

D. Douglas and S. Frazier. 2001. Teaching by principles: An interactive approach to language pedagogy (2nd ed.). *TESOL Quarterly*, 35(2):341–342.

P. Elkin, S. Brown, B. Bauer, C. Husser, W. Carruth, L. Bergstrom, and D. Wahner-Roedler. 2005. A controlled trial of automated classification of negation from clinical notes. *BMC medical informatics and decision making*, 5(1):13.

R. Grishman. 2013. Off to a cold start: New york universitys 2013 knowledge base population systems. In *Proc. Text Analysis Conference (TAC 2013).*

H. Ji, R. Grishman, H. Dang, K. Griffitt, and J. Ellis. 2010. Overview of the tac 2010 knowledge base population track. In *Proc. Text Analysis Conference (TAC 2010).*

H. Ji, R. Grishman, and H. Dang. 2011. An overview of the tac2011 knowledge base population track. In *Proc. Text Analysis Conference (TAC 2011).*

Y. Li, S. Chen, Z. Zhou, J. Yin, H. Luo, L. Hong, W. Xu, G. Chen, and J. Guo. 2012. Pris at tac2012 kbp track. In *Proc. of Text Analysis Conference (TAC 2012).*

Y. Li, Y. Zhang, D. Li, X. Tong, J. Wang, N. Zuo, Y. Wang, W. Xu, G. Chen, and J. Guo. 2013. Pris at tac2013 kbp track. In *Proc. Text Analysis Conference (TAC 2013).*

C. Manning, M. Surdeanu, J. Bauer, J. Finkel, S. Bethard, and D. McClosky. 2014. The Stanford CoreNLP natural language processing toolkit. In *Proc. Association for Computational Linguistics (ACL2014).*

B. Min, X. Li, R. Grishman, and A. Sun. 2012. New york university 2012 system for kbp slot filling. *Proc. Text Analysis Conference (TAC 2012).*

R. Morante and W. Daelemans. 2009. Learning the scope of hedge cues in biomedical texts. In *Proc. ACL 2009 Workshop on Current Trends in Biomedical Natural Language Processing.*

K. Motallebzadeh and N. Mamdoohi. 2011. Language learning strategies: A key factor to improvement of toefl candidates reading comprehension ability. *International Journal of Linguistics*, 3(1):E26.

R. Phipps. 1983. *The Successful Student's handbook: A Step-By-Step Guide to Study, Reading, and Thinking Skills.* Seattle and London: University of Washington Press.

B. Roth, T. Barth, M. Wiegand, M. Singh, and D. Klakow. 2013. Effective slot filling based on shallow distant supervision methods. *Proc. Text Analysis Conference (TAC 2013).*

A. Sun, R. Grishman, W. Xu, and B. Min. 2011. New york university 2011 system for kbp slot filling. In *Proc. Text Analysis Conference (TAC 2011).*

M. Surdeanu and H. Ji. 2014. Overview of the english slot filling track at the tac2014 knowledge base population evaluation. In *Proc. Text Analysis Conference (TAC2014).*

M. Surdeanu, D. McClosky, J. Tibshirani, J. Bauer, A. Chang, V. Spitkovsky, and C. Manning. 2010. A simple distant supervision approach for the tac-kbp slot filling task. In *Proc. Text Analysis Conference (TAC 2010).*

M. Surdeanu. 2013. Overview of the tac2013 knowledge base population evaluation: English slot filling and temporal slot filling. In *Proc. Text Analysis Conference (TAC 2013).*

G. Szarvas, V. Vincze, R. Farkas, and J. Csirik. 2008. The bioscope corpus: annotation for negation, uncertainty and their scope in biomedical texts. In *Proc. ACL Workshop on Current Trends in Biomedical Natural Language Processing.*

D. Yu, H. Li, T. Cassidy, Q. Li, H. Huang, Z. Chen, H. Ji, Y. Zhang, and D. Roth. 2013. Rpi-blender tac-kbp2013 knowledge base population system. In *Proc. Text Analysis Conference (TAC 2013).*

# Lachmannian Archetype Reconstruction for Ancient Manuscript Corpora

**Armin Hoenen**
Goethe University
Robert- Mayer Strasse 10
60486 Frankfurt, Germany
hoenen@em.uni-frankfurt.de

## Abstract

Two goals are targeted by computer philology for ancient manuscript corpora: firstly, making an edition, that is roughly speaking one text version representing the whole corpus, which contains variety induced through copy errors and other processes and secondly, producing a stemma. A stemma is a graph-based visualization of the copy history with manuscripts as nodes and copy events as edges. Its root, the so-called archetype, is the supposed original text or *urtext* from which all subsequent copies are made. Our main contribution is to present one of the first computational approaches to automatic archetype reconstruction and to introduce the first text-based evaluation for automatically produced archetypes. We compare a philologically generated archetype with one generated by bio-informatic software.

## 1 Introduction

In philology, oftentimes more than one single manuscript of the same *tradition* (that is, the same text) has survived. These manuscripts often differ in their wording in various places since copy errors, corrections, and other processes have led to deviation from the original text. This causes two problems: uncertainty about the original wording and uncertainty about which manuscript has been copied from which other.

The reconstruction of the copy history of manuscript texts is largely similar to that of DNA, which is why phylogenetic approaches have been adopted (Robinson and O'Hara, 1996; Robinson et al., 1998; van Reenen et al., 1996; van Reenen et al., 2004; Spencer et al., 2004; Roos and Heikkilä, 2009; Roelli and Bachmann, 2010; Andrews and Macé, 2013). However, the main goal of the philological work on ancient manuscripts is not the reconstruction of the copy history but compiling an edition of a historical text. This entails reducing the variation encountered so that one single main text as the prototypical representation of the manuscript corpus emerges. Ideally, this text is believed to be the author's original or closest possible to it. Two model approaches to making an edition are most widespread. The earlier one by Lachmann (see for instance Lachmann (1853)) opts for reconstructing an urtext actively, that is if needed by means of *emendation*, which refers to inferring the original (authorial) wording from the extant variants even if the so-inferred form is not itself extant and thus not attested in any of the manuscripts. The later approach after Bédier (see for instance Bédier (1928)) bases the edition directly on the text of the best available manuscript.

In this paper, we will present a first automatic implementation of the earlier approach. Additionally, an algorithm for evaluation of a so-reconstructed text will be presented and applied to artificial benchmark data sets (gold standard). First, we will introduce the data sets. Then, two methods, rule-based (using philological principles) and statistical (likelihood-based using bio-informatic software) will be explained in detail before the results are being presented, followed by a general discussion, a field specific discussion, and a conclusion and outlook.



*Human Language Technologies: The 2015 Annual Conference of the North American Chapter of the ACL*, pages 1209–1214,
Denver, Colorado, May 31 – June 5, 2015. ©2015 Association for Computational Linguistics

| Text | Lang | MS | Tok |
|---|---|---|---|
| Parzival | English | 21 | 957 |
| Notre Besoin | French | 13 | 1029 |

Table 1: The artificial traditions. MS = number of manuscripts, Tok = number of tokens, Lang = language

## 2 Artificial Traditions

An *artificial tradition* is a fully digitized set of manuscripts which have been produced through manual copying in recent times whilst recording the true copy history/genealogical relationships. Three of these corpora have been published to date, *Parzival* by (Spencer et al., 2004), *Notre Besoin* by (Baret et al., 2004), and *Heinrichi* by (Roos and Heikkilä, 2009). They are provided in a fully word-aligned tabular version by the authors, so that collation must not be performed anymore. We excluded the Heinrichi tradition from computation as Old Finnish data could not be interpreted by us. Table 1 displays the composition of the artificial traditions we used.

## 3 Method

Contrasting a rule-based and a statistical approach, we automatically reconstruct the archetype text for the two aforementioned traditions. To the best of our knowledge, this paper treats automatic archetype reconstruction in connection with evaluation for the first time and applies suitable bio-informatic programs for the first time. While the transfer of biological software to philology, especially in stemmatics, is done since the 1990ies, (O'Hara, 1996), purely philological automatic reconstructions are a recent development. As input for both reconstruction methods, we use the same tree, generated by bio-informatic software. Corresponding to this tree, we reconstruct the archetype using a) a philological rule-based majority-vote bottom-up algorithm and b) statistical bio-informatic software.

### 3.1 Philological Reconstruction

A lost manuscript text can be reconstructed in different ways given a precomputed stemma. The key question is how to resolve variation. Depending on a concrete decision rule for disambiguation of variation among the direct descendents of a lost manuscript node, there are several possible reconstructions, which means one stemma can correspond to several possible archetype texts (depending on the decision rule). We implement the majority-vote decision rule as referred to frequently in philological discourse, see for instance (West, 1973). The algorithm simply assigns the most frequent variant of all direct descendents. If more than one variant is most frequent, our reconstruction retains all for later disambiguation either through majority-vote in subsequent recursion steps or for manual disambiguation through the expert if more than one variants end undisambiguated in the reconstructed archetype. Lost text of leaf nodes should be pruned since their texts are more corrupt than the one of their ancestors, thus unnecessarily corrupting the tradition. This pruning roughly parallels the philological practice of *recensio*, the prior exclusion of uninformative manuscripts.

In mathematical terms, let $S$ be a rooted stemmatic tree (directed acyclic) consisting of a set of vertices $V$, a set of edges $E$, and one root node $v_0$; Each vertex has an indegree of 1, only $v_0$ has no incoming edges. Let each vertex $v_i$ be associated with a text $T_i \in T_{all}$, which is its textual content, $|V| = |T_{all}|$. While $T_{all}$ is the set of all texts that really existed in the tradition, $T'$ initially is the set of surviving texts, $T' \subseteq T_{all}$. The texts in $T_{all}$ are aligned, that is each text consists of a sequence of tokens or reconstructed tokens $\{T_{i_i}, .., T_{i_n}\}$ and all $T_i$ have the same length. A recontructed token can be a set of to be disambiguated tokens. For each $T_j \in T_{all} \setminus T'$, we reconstruct the lost text in the following way:

1. Collect all texts $\{T_k, .., T_m\}, 1 \leq (k, m) \leq |T_{all}| - 1; k, m \neq j$ associated with the vertices $\{v_k, .., v_m\}$ which are direct descendents of vertex $v_j$, which is associated with $T_j$. If one of the texts in $\{T_k, .., T_m\}$ is itself not in $T'$, delay the actual reconstruction and start a new reconstruction for the next unreconstructed text until all texts $\{T_k, .., T_m\}$ are reconstructed

2. Text reconstruction for each token $T_{j_i}$: $T_{j_i} = majority(\{T_{k_i}, .., T_{m_i}\})$; in case $|majority(\{T_{k_i}, .., T_{m_i}\})| > 1$ assign all variants to $T_j$ (using a separator), if one of $\{T_{k_i}, .., T_{m_i}\}$ does already carry multiple variants, treat each one as one variant

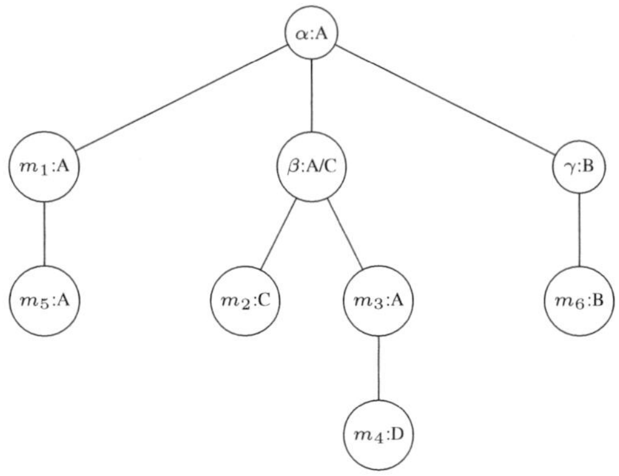


Figure 1: A simple stemma of a one word tradition, Greek letters denoting lost (hype)archetype(s). The Roman upper case letters refer to the observed variant (manuscripts $m_i$) or to the reconstructed variant ((hype)archetype(s)) inferred bottom-up.

| $m_1$ | $m_2$ | $m_3$ | $m_4$ | **Variants** |
|---|---|---|---|---|
| this | t' | it | dis | A-D |
| is | is | is | is | A |
| a | an | a | | A-C |
| text | text | text | text | A |
| AAAA | BABA | CAAA | DACA | **PseudoDNA** |

Table 2: Conversion of a word-aligned example tradition to a pseudo-DNA.

and compute the majority variant (example: $\{T_{2_i}, T_{5_i}\} = \{this/tis, tis\}$ then $majority(\{T_{2_i}, T_{5_i}\}) = tis$)

3. $T' = T' \cup T_j$; if $T' = T_{all}$ end else start next reconstruction

For an example see Figure 1.

### 3.2 Bio-informatic Reconstruction

In bio-informatics, reconstruction of ancestral genomes has been undertaken. The most famous case is presumably that of the mammoths, (Miller et al., 2008). However, bacterial asexual reproduction is generally more similar to manuscript copying than mammalian sexual reproduction. Therefore and for other methodological reasons, it is more appropriate to transfer bacteriological reconstruction to philology. Bacteriologists sucessfully reconstructed the predecessors of yeast, (Voordeckers et al., 2012). Given a pregenerated tree, they used Bayesian marginal and joint probabilities to generate the sequences best explaining the tree. A program performing this is PAML, (Yang, 2007).

We converted the already word-aligned traditions into sequences of letters for each manuscript, see Table 2. Each letter encodes the variant the current manuscript carries at the current position. For the so-produced pseudo-DNA sequences, the PAML software generates a stemmatic tree using the maximum likelihood (ML) criterion without resolving variation at inferred internodes. This ML tree or any other can be used as input to generate ancestral sequences at the internodes and the root node using an optimization with a) marginal probabilities, for details see (Yang et al., 1995) and b) an optimization with joint probabilities, for details see (Pupko et al., 2000). Yang (2007) states that the results of a) and b) differ only in borderline cases. Indeed we found, that the respectively produced archetypes were identical in our case.

The ML tree is usually bifurcating, generating many internodes and an extra-corporal root. Although in our context, it challenges performance of automatic reconstruction, bifurcations are not a circumstance necessarily paralleling philology closely, (Howe et al., 2012).

## 4 Evaluation

For each position of the alignment, a produced archetype (PA) is compared to the original archetype present in the benchmark data sets. Whenever the PA has at least one variant at the current position corresponding to the archetype, an agreement score is incremented by one divided through the number of current variants in the PA. This assumes implicitly that manual disambiguation is at random and represents therefore a baseline evaluation. The agreement score is divided by the number of positions in the alignment to give the total precision of the PA text. This evaluation is called whole text evaluation (WTE). It serves as an orientation point towards the overall reliability of the reconstructed text as a whole. A second evaluation concerns the proportion of correctly disambiguated positions of variation. That agreement score is produced in the same way as described above, but only for positions where the corpus had variation. This evaluation is called po-

| Tradition | WTE | PVE | ASD |
|---|---|---|---|
| Parzival(PAML) | 0.91 | 0.73 | 51.38 |
| Parzival(MV) | 0.96 | 0.88 | |
| Notre Besoin(PAML) | 0.95 | 0.9 | 54.95 |
| Notre Besoin(MV) | 0.97 | 0.94 | |

Table 3: Evaluation of the archetypes by PAML and majority-vote (MV). ML trees evaluated with ASD.

sition of variation evaluation (PVE). Formally, both WTE and PVE can be represented by

$$\frac{\sum_{i=0}^{n} \frac{\mathbb{1}_{C_i}(a_i)}{|C_i|}}{n}, \mathbb{1}_{C_i}(a_i) = \begin{cases} 1 & \text{if } a_i \in C_i \\ 0 & \text{if } a_i \notin C_i \end{cases} \quad (1)$$

where $n$ is either the number of words in the alignment (WTE) or the number of positions of variation (PVE), $a$ is the archetype, $a_i$ the i-th token in the archetype, and $C_i$ the set of variants of the PA at the i-th position.

## 5 Results

We evaluated the PAs (rule-based and statistical) with WTE and PVE and additionally evaluated the initial ML trees against the true stemma by means of the graph-based Average Sign Distance (ASD),[1] a measure of distance of genealogical trees using vertex triple distances as described in (Roos and Heikkilä, 2009). In order to achieve this, we converted the stemmas automatically from the Newick output format by PAML into the required format of the ASD. Results are displayed in Table 3. The philological reconstruction outperformed the PAML one in both cases.

In order to assess the quality of these results, we produced the majority archetype (MA), which at each position carried the majority variant. Additionally, we produced a random archetype (RA), where a randomizer as implemented in the Java programming language chose one variant at random for every place of variation. The RA was then evaluated. This procedure was repeated 1000 times and then we averaged over the RA evaluation results. As a point of orientation, we additionally provide the evaluation score of the maximally wrong archetype (MW), which is the one archetype that has a non-archetypical variant at each position where variation occurred. Note that none of these automatically produced archetypes requires a stemma beforehand. The results are displayed in Table 4. The RAs are considerably better than the MWs, but are clearly outperformed by both reconstructions and the MAs.

[1]For details, data sets and evaluation scripts, browse `http://www.cs.helsinki.fi/u/ttonteri/casc`.

| $\alpha$(P/NB) | WTE | PVE |
|---|---|---|
| MW(P) | 0.68 | 0 |
| RA(P) | 0.8 | 0.38 |
| MA(P) | 0.96 | 0.87 |
| MW(NB) | 0.52 | 0 |
| RA(NB) | 0.76 | 0.49 |
| MA(NB) | 0.98 | 0.95 |

Table 4: Evaluation of archetypes. $\alpha$ as used in philology denotes the archetype. We evaluated the majority archetypes (MA), the averaged random archetypes (RA) and the maximally wrong archetypes (MW) for the Parzival (P) and Notre Besoin (NB) traditions.

## 6 Discussion

The MA and MV archetypes are the most accurate ones. Hence, the true distribution of variants considering all manuscripts is such that the majority variant in the majority of cases is the archetypical one. Whether this conclusion holds for historical corpora remains to be shown. The PAML-generated archetypes performed well and were considerably better than the random condition. Note that the ML tree's ASD score was relatively low as compared to other algorithms evaluated in (Roos and Heikkilä, 2009). The limitation of the current reconstruction is that at each position the reconstructed text can only carry one of the variants of the extant manuscripts. This makes any reconstruction with many reconstructed internodes, such as the MVs or the PAML reconstructions by definition quite similar to the MAs.

### 6.1 Comparing Stemma and Archetype Production

From a bad stemma, disambiguation rules can nevertheless produce an accurate archetype and vice versa. One stemma can correspond to several possible archetypes and one archetype can be consistent with several different stemmas. The two tasks and evaluations should therefore be considered separately. This is of utter importance as it points to an imbalance of computational effort in the field.

### 6.2 Implications for Computer Philology

In biology the establishment of genealogical relations is in its own rights a primary goal, reconstruction of ancestral sequences being rather secondary. On the contrary in philology, compiling an edition is not only historically preceeding stemmatology, but can be considered the main target of dealing with manuscript corpora. Stemma construction is rather a secondary goal.[2] Despite this imbalance between the fields, the technological emphasis is on genealogical trees in both. This may be seen as a computer philological co-loan from bio-informatics. On the other hand it might correspond to a more Bédierian edition practise, where stemmatology is emphasized because it can point to the most important manuscript, which is however implicit and unlikely. Another reason for a benefit resulting from a shifting focus onto automatic archetype reconstruction is the problem of having two vorlages for one copy called *contamination*. Whilst especially excessive contamination is a bad problem for stemmatology, (Maas, 1960), considering automatic archetype reconstruction, on a word level it doesn't increase diversity and should therefore be a less severe problem.

For both traditions, the produced archetype was reasonably accurate. The automatisation of this process could thus accelerate the production of editions, making them most dependent on the indispensable digitization of corpora.

### 6.3 Implications for Bio-Informatics

In biology, reconstructive algorithms such as the one by Yang (2007) have been developed alongside biological benchmark data sets enumerated by Linder et al. (2010). However, in stemmatology, the probability to have a manuscript and its copy in the corpus at the same time is disproportionately higher than in the biological case making archetype production more transparent here. The resulting algorithmic conclusions from philology could therefore enrich the field of ancestral sequence reconstruction.

[2]For more details, consider for instance Pasquali (1988), Timpanaro (2005), and Reynolds & Wilson (2013).

## 7 Conclusion and Outlook

We have presented an automated reconstruction of an archetypical text through philological rules and phylogenetic software. Additionally, we invented an evaluation for the produced archetypes, where we found the reconstruction to produce results considerably above chance level.

The inversion of the process is implicit. From a (manually or automatically) constructed archetype, all possible corresponding stemmas on the given set of manuscript digitizations can be computed and evaluated, which would be a new approach to stemmatology. Both tasks could thus profit from each other provided they are understood as separate and developed each in its own right.

Many issues remain unaddressed. The phenomena encountered in manuscripts are much more varied than word substitutions as modelled in this paper; an enumeration of some of the phenomena will corroborate this: word deletions, word separation errors, whole passages missing, text on the margins, unreadable or destructed text, crossing out of sections, oral variation, contamination. Trovato (2009) claims that manuscript loss of far more than 90% is realistic. In linguistics, historical-comparative studies have engaged in using bio-informatic software for instance in connection with the recontruction of language family trees. For automatic emendation these studies as well as the reconstruction of unattested word forms are a valuable source. Stemmatology itself offers ever new algorithms, artificial traditions and tools for electronic editing.

In the light of these manifold possibilities for elaboration and cooperation, the current study presents but one entry point into automatic archetype reconstruction.

## Acknowledgments

We greatfully acknowledge the financial support of the Goethe University, the Federal State of Hesse and the Federal Ministry of Education and Research BMBF. We express our gratitude to our colleagues of the Texttechnology Lab for valuable comments, help and advice.

## References


T. L. Andrews and C. Macé. 2013. Beyond the tree of texts: Building an empirical model of scribal variation through graph analysis of texts and stemmas. *Literary and Linguistic Computing*, 28(4):504–521, December.

P. Baret, C. Macé, and P. Robinson (eds.). 2004. Testing methods on an artificially created textual tradition. In *Linguistica Computationale XXIV-XXV*, volume XXIV-XXV, pages 255–281, Pisa-Roma. Instituti Editoriali e Poligrafici Internationali.

Joseph Bédier. 1928. La tradition manuscrite du 'Lai de l'Ombre': Réflexions sur l'Art d'Éditer les Anciens Textes. *Romania*, 394:161–196, 321–356.

C. Howe, R. Connoly, and H. Windram. 2012. Responding to criticism of phylogenetic methods in stemmatology. *SEL studies in English Literature*, 52:51–67.

Karl Lachmann. 1853. *In T. Lucretii Cari De rerum natura libros commentarius: Index*. Georg Reimer.

C. Randal Linder, Rahul Suri, Kevin Liu, and Tandy Warnow. 2010. Benchmark datasets and software for developing and testing methods for large-scale multiple sequence alignment and phylogenetic inference. *PLoS Currents*, 2.

P. Maas. 1960. *Textkritik*. B. G. Teubner.

Webb Miller, Daniela I. Drautz, Aakrosh Ratan, Barbara Pusey, Ji Qi, Arthur M. Lesk, Lynn P. Tomsho, Michael D. Packard, Fangqing Zhao, Andrei Sher, Alexei Tikhonov, Brian Raney, Nick Patterson, Kerstin Lindblad-Toh, Eric S. Lander, James R. Knight, Gerard P. Irzyk, Karin M. Fredrikson, Timothy T. Harkins, Sharon Sheridan, Tom Pringle, and Stephan C. Schuster. 2008. Sequencing the nuclear genome of the extinct woolly mammoth. *Nature*, 456(7220):387–390.

R. J. O'Hara. 1996. Trees of history in systematics and philology. *Memorie della Società Italiana di Scienze Naturali e del Museo Civico di Storia Naturale di Milano*, 27(1):81–88.

Giorgo Pasquali. 1988. *Storia della tradizione e critica del testo*. Casa editrice Le lettere, Firenze.

Tal Pupko, Itsik Pe'er, Ron Shamir, and Dan Graur. 2000. A fast algorithm for joint reconstruction of ancestral amino acid sequences. *Mol. Biol. Evol.*, 17(6):890–896.

L.D. Reynolds and N.G. Wilson. 2013. *Scribes and Scholars, A Guide to the Transmission of Greek & Roman literatures*. Oxford University Press.

P. Robinson and R. J. O'Hara. 1996. Cladistic Analysis of an Old Norse Manuscript Tradition. *Research in Humanities Computing (4)*.

P. Robinson, A. Barbrook, N. Blake, and C. Howe. 1998. The Phylogeny of The Canterbury Tales. *Nature*, 394:839.

Philipp Roelli and Dieter Bachmann. 2010. Towards Generating a Stemma of Complicated Manuscript Traditions: Petrus Alfonsis Dialogus. *Revue dhistoire des textes*, 5(4):307–321.

Teemu Roos and Tuomas Heikkilä. 2009. Evaluating methods for computer-assisted stemmatology using artificial benchmark data sets. *Literary and Linguistic Computing*, 24:417–433.

M. Spencer, E. Davidson, A. Barbrook, and C. Howe. 2004. Phylogenetics of artificial manuscripts. *Journal of Theoretical Biology*, 227:503–511.

Sebastiano Timpanaro. 2005. *The Genesis of Lachmann's Method*. University of Chicago, Chicago.

Paolo Trovato. 2009. *Everything You Always Wanted to Know about Lachmann's Method, A Non-Standard Handbook of Genealogical Textual Criticism in the Age of Post-Structuralism, Cladistics, and Copy-Text*. libreriauniversitaria.it.

P. T. van Reenen, M. van Mulken, and J. Dyk. 1996. *Studies in Stemmatology I*. Studies in Stemmatology. John Benjamins Publishing Company.

P. T. van Reenen, A. A. den Hollander, and M. van Mulken. 2004. *Studies in Stemmatology II*. Studies in Stemmatology. John Benjamins Publishing Company.

K. Voordeckers, C.A. Brown, K. Vanneste, E. van der Zande, A. Voet, S. Maere, and K. J. Verstrepen. 2012. Reconstruction of ancestral metabolic enzymes reveals molecular mechanisms underlying evolutionary innovation through gene duplication. *PLoS Biol*, 10(12).

Martin L. West. 1973. *Textual Criticism and Editorial Technique: Applicable to Greek and Latin texts*. Teubner, Stuttgart.

Ziheng Yang, Sudhir Kumar, and Masatoshi Nei. 1995. A new method of inference of ancestral nucleotide and amino acid sequences. *Genetics*, 141:1641–1650.

Ziheng Yang. 2007. PAML 4: phylogenetic analysis by maximum likelihood. *Mol. Biol. Evol.*, 24(8):1586–1591.

# Distributed Representations of Words to Guide Bootstrapped Entity Classifiers

**Sonal Gupta**
Department of Computer Science
Stanford University
sonal@cs.stanford.edu

**Christopher D. Manning**
Department of Computer Science
Stanford University
manning@stanford.edu

## Abstract

Bootstrapped classifiers iteratively generalize from a few seed examples or prototypes to other examples of target labels. However, sparseness of language and limited supervision make the task difficult. We address this problem by using distributed vector representations of words to aid the generalization. We use the word vectors to expand entity sets used for training classifiers in a bootstrapped pattern-based entity extraction system. Our experiments show that the classifiers trained with the expanded sets perform better on entity extraction from four online forums, with 30% $F_1$ improvement on one forum. The results suggest that distributed representations can provide good directions for generalization in a bootstrapping system.

## 1 Introduction

Bootstrapped or distantly-supervised learning is a form of semi-supervised learning, in which supervision is provided by seed examples. Supervised machine learning systems, on the other hand, require hand-labeling sufficient data to train a model, which can be costly and time consuming. Bootstrapped information extraction (IE) has become even more pertinent with the ever-growing amount of data coupled with the emergence of open IE systems (Carlson et al., 2010; Fader et al., 2011) and shared tasks like TAC-KBP.[1]

Limited supervision provided in bootstrapped systems, though an attractive quality, is also one of its main challenges. When seed sets are small, noisy, or do not cover the label space, the bootstrapped classifiers do not generalize well.

We use a major guiding inspiration of deep learning: we can learn a lot about syntactic and semantic similarities between words in an unsupervised fashion and capture this information in word vectors. This distributed representation can inform an inductive bias to generalize in a bootstrapping system.

In this paper, we present a simple approach of using the distributed vector representations of words to expand training data for entity classifiers in a bootstrapped system (see Algorithm 1). To improve the step of learning an entity classifier, we first learn vector representation of entities using the continuous bag of words model (Mikolov et al., 2013a). We then use $k$NN to expand the training set of the classifier by adding unlabeled entities close to seed entities in the training set. The key insight is to use the word vector similarity indirectly by enhancing training data for the entity classifier. We do not directly label the unlabeled entities using the similarity between word vectors, which we show extracts many noisy entities. We show that classifiers trained with expanded sets of entities perform better on extracting drug-and-treatment entities from four online health forums from MedHelp.[2]

## 2 Related Work

Bootstrapping has many variants, such as self-training, co-training, and label propagation. Yarowsky's style of self-training algo-

[1] http://www.nist.gov/tac/2014/KBP

[2] http://www.medhelp.org



*Human Language Technologies: The 2015 Annual Conference of the North American Chapter of the ACL*, pages 1215–1220,
Denver, Colorado, May 31 – June 5, 2015. 

rithms (Yarowsky, 1995) have been shown to be successful at bootstrapping (Collins and Singer, 1999). Co-training (Blum and Mitchell, 1998) and its boostrapped adaptation (Collins and Singer, 1999) require disjoint views of the features of the data. Whitney and Sarkar (2012) proposed a modified Yarowsky algorithm that used label propagation on graphs, inspired by Subramanya et al. (2010) algorithm that used a large labeled data for domain adaptation.

In this paper, we use the setting of bootstrapped pattern-based entity extraction (Riloff, 1996; Thelen and Riloff, 2002). This can be viewed as a form of the Yarowsky algorithm, with pattern learning as an additional step. Pattern based approaches have been widely used for IE (Chiticariu et al., 2013; Fader et al., 2011; Etzioni et al., 2005). Patterns are useful in two ways: they are good features, and they identify promising candidate entities. Recently, Gupta and Manning (2014) improved pattern scoring (Step 2 in Algorithm 1) using predicted labels of unlabeled entities. For entity scoring (Step 3), they used an average of feature values to predict the scores. We use the same framework but focus on improving the entity classifiers.

In most IE systems, including ours, word classes or word vectors are used as features in a classifier (Haghighi and Klein, 2006; Ratinov and Roth, 2009).

To the best of our knowledge, our work is the first to use distributed representations of words to improve a bootstrapped system by expanding the training set.

## 3 Background

In a bootstrapped pattern-based entity learning system, seed dictionaries and/or patterns provide weak supervision to label data. The system iteratively learns new entities belonging to a specific label from unlabeled text (Riloff, 1996; Collins and Singer, 1999) using patterns, such as lexico-syntactic surface word patterns (Hearst, 1992) and dependency tree patterns (Yangarber et al., 2000). We use lexico-syntactic surface word patterns to extract entities from unlabeled text starting with seed dictionaries for multiple classes. Algorithm 1 gives an overview. In this paper, we focus on improving the entity classifier (Step 3) by expanding its training data using distributed vector representations of words.

**Algorithm 1** Bootstrapped Pattern-based Entity Extraction

Given: Text $D$, labels $L$, seed entities $E_l$ $\forall l \in$ L
**while** not-terminating-condition (e.g. precision is high) **do**
 **for** $l \in L$ **do**
  1. Label $D$ with $E_l$
  2. Create patterns around labeled entities. Learn good patterns and use them to extract candidate entities $C_l$.
  3. Learn an entity classifier and classify $C_l$. Add new classified entities to $E_l$.

**Labeling known entities**: The text is labeled using the label dictionaries, starting with the seed dictionaries in the first iteration.
**Creating and Learning Patterns**: Patterns are then created using the context around the labeled entities to create candidate patterns for label $l$. Candidate patterns are scored using a pattern scoring measure and the top ones are added to the list of learned patterns for label $l$. In our experiments, we use a widely used pattern scoring measure, RlogF (Riloff, 1996; Thelen and Riloff, 2002). Top ranked patterns with scores above a certain threshold are used to extract candidate entities $C_l$ from text.
**Learning entities**: An entity classifier predicts the labels of $C_l$ and adds the newly classified entities to label $l$'s dictionary, $E_l$. We discard common words, negative entities, and those containing non-alphanumeric characters from the set.
**Entity Classifier** We build a one-vs-all entity classifier using logistic regression. In each iteration, for label $l$, the entity classifier is trained by treating $l$'s dictionary entities (seed and learned in previous iterations) as positive and entities belonging to all other labels as negative. To improve generalization, we also sample the unlabeled entities that are not function words as negative. To train with a balanced dataset, we randomly sub-sample the negatives such that the number of negative instances is equal to the number of positive instances. The features for the entities are similar to Gupta and Manning (2014): edit distances from positive and negative entities, relative frequency of the entity words

in the seed dictionaries, word classes computed using the Brown clustering algorithm (Brown et al., 1992; Liang, 2005), and pattern TF-IDF score. The last feature gives higher scores to entities that are extracted by many learned patterns and have low frequency in the dataset. In our experiments, we call this classifier as *NotExpanded*.

## 4 Approach

The lack of labeled data to train a good entity classifier is one of the challenges in bootstrapped learning. We use distributed representations of words, in the form of word vectors, to guide the entity classifier by expanding its training set. As explained in the previous section, we train a one-vs-all entity classifier in each iteration of the bootstrapped entity extraction for each label. We use unlabeled entities that are similar to the seed entities of the label as positive examples, and use unlabeled entities that are similar to seed entities of other labels as negative examples.[3]

To compute similarity of an unlabeled entity to the positive entities, we find $k$ most similar positive entities, measured by cosine similarity between the word vectors, and average the scores. Similarly, we compute similarity of the unlabeled entity to the negative entities. If the entity's positive similarity score is above a given threshold $\theta$ and is higher than its negative similarity score, it is added to the training set with positive label. We expand the negative entities similarly.[4]

An alternative to our approach is to directly label the entities using the vector similarities. Our experimental results suggest that even though exploiting similarities between word vectors is useful for guiding the classifier by expanding the training set, it is not robust enough to use for labeling entities directly. For example, for our development dataset, when $\theta$ was set as 0.4, 16 out of 41 unlabeled entities that were expanded into the training set as positive entities were false positives.[5] Thus, labeling entities solely based on similarity scores resulted in lower performance. A classifier, on the other hand, can use other sources of information as features to predict an entity's label.

We compute the distributed vector representations using the continuous bag-of-words model (Mikolov et al., 2013a; Mikolov et al., 2013b) implemented in the word2vec toolkit.[6] We train 200-dimensional vector representations on a combined dataset of a 2014 Wikipedia dump (1.6 billion tokens), a sample of 50 million tweets from Twitter (200 million tokens), and an in-domain dataset of all MedHelp forums (400 million tokens). We removed words that occurred less than 20 times, resulting in a vocabulary of 89k words. We call this dataset Wiki+Twit+MedHelp. We used the parameters suggested in Pennington et al. (2014): negative sampling with 10 samples and a window size of 10. We ran the model for 3 iterations.

## 5 Experimental Setup

We present results on the same experimental setup, dataset, and seed lists as used in Gupta and Manning (2014). The task is to extract drug-and-treatment (DT) entities in sentences from four forums on the MedHelp user health discussion website: 1. Asthma, 2. Acne, 3. Adult Type II Diabetes (called Diabetes), and 4. Ear Nose & Throat (called ENT). A DT entity is defined as a pharmaceutical drug, or any treatment or intervention mentioned that may help a symptom or a condition. The output of all systems were judged by the authors, following the guidelines in (Gupta and Manning, 2014). We used Asthma as the development forum for parameter and threshold tuning. We used threshold $\theta$ as 0.4 and use $k$ (number of nearest neighbors) as 2 when expanding the seed sets.

We evaluate systems by their precision and recall. Precision is defined as the fraction of correct entities among the entities extracted. Similar to (Gupta and Manning, 2014), we present the precision and recall curves for precision above 75% to compare systems when they extract entities with reasonably

[3]We take the cautious approach of finding similar entities only to the seed entities and not the learned entities. The algorithm can be modified to find similar entities to learned entities as well. Cautious approaches have been shown to be better for bootstrapped learning (Abney, 2004).

[4]We tried expanding just the positive entities and just the negative entities. Their relative performance, though higher than the baselines, varied between the datasets. Thus, for conciseness, we present results only for expanding both positives and negatives.

[5]Increasing $\theta$ extracted far fewer entities. $\theta = 0.5$ extracted only 5 entities, all true positives, and $\theta = 0.6$ extracted none.

[6]`http://code.google.com/p/word2vec/`

| Forum | Expanded | Expanded-M | NotExpanded | Average |
|---|---|---|---|---|
| Asthma | **77.01** | 75.68 | 74.48 | 65.42 |
| Acne | 73.84 | **75.41** | 71.65 | 65.05 |
| Diabetes | **82.37** | 44.25 | 48.75 | 21.82 |
| ENT | **80.66** | 80.04 | 77.02 | 59.50 |

Table 1: Area under Precision-Recall curve for all the systems. Expanded is our system when word vectors are learned using the Wiki+Twit+MedHelp data and Expanded-M is when word vectors are learning using the MedHelp data.

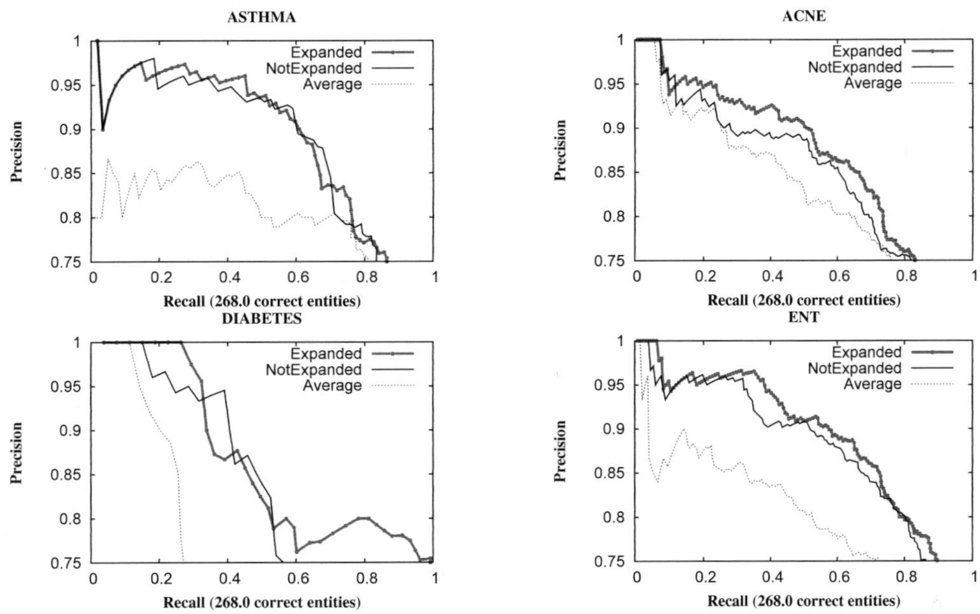


Figure 1: Precision vs. Recall curves of our system and the baselines for the four forums.

high precision. Recall is defined as the fraction of correct entities among the total unique correct entities pooled from all systems.[7] We calculate the area under the precision-recall curves (AUC-PR) to compare the systems.

We call our system *Expanded* in the experiments. To compare the effects of word vectors learned using different types of datasets, we also study our system when the word vectors are learned using just the in-domain MedHelp data, called *Expanded-M*. We compare against two baselines: *NotExpanded* as explained in Section 3, and *Average*, in which we average the feature values, similar to (Gupta and Manning, 2014).

[7]Note that calculating lower precisions or true recall is very hard to compute. Our dataset is unlabeled and manually labeling all entities is expensive. Pooling is a common evaluation strategy in such situations (such as, TAC-KBP shared task).

## 6 Results and Discussion

Table 1 shows AUC-PR of various systems and Figure 1 shows the precision-recall curves. Our systems *Expanded* and *Expanded-M*, which used similar entities for training, improved the scores for all four forums. We believe the improvement for the Diabetes forum was much higher than other forums because the baseline's performance on the forum degraded quickly in later iterations (see the figure), and improving the classifier helped in adding more cor rect entities. Additionally, Diabetes DT entities are more lifestyle-based and hence occur frequently in web text, making the word vectors trained using the Wiki+Twit+MedHelp dataset better suited.

In three out of four forums, word vectors trained

| Positives | Negatives |
|---|---|
| Asthma | |
| pranayama, sterilizing, expectorants, inhalable, sanitizers, ayurvedic | block, yougurt, medcine, exertion, hate, virally |
| Diabetes | |
| quinoa, vinegars, vegatables, threadmill, possilbe, asanas, omegas | nicely, chiropracter, exhales, paralytic, metabolize, fluffy |

Table 2: Examples of unlabeled entities that were expanded into the training sets. Gray colored entities were judged by the authors as falsely labeled.

using a large corpus perform better than those trained using the smaller in-domain corpus. For the Acne forum, where brand name DT entities are more frequent, the entities expanded by MedHelp vectors had fewer false positives than those expanded by Wiki+Twit+MedHelp.

Table 2 shows some examples of unlabeled entities that were included as positive/negative entities in the entity classifiers. Even though some entities were included in the training data with wrong labels, overall the classifiers benefited from the expansion.

## 7 Conclusion

We improve entity classifiers in bootstrapped entity extraction systems by enhancing the training set using unsupervised distributed representations of words. The classifiers learned using the expanded seed sets extract entities with better $F_1$ score. This supports our hypothesis that generalizing labels to entities that are similar according to unsupervised methods of word vector learning is effective in improving entity classifiers, notwithstanding that the label generalization is quite noisy.

## References


S. Abney. 2004. Understanding the Yarowsky algorithm. *Computational Linguistics*, 30:365–395.

A. Blum and T. Mitchell. 1998. Combining labeled and unlabeled data with co-training. In *Conference on Learning Theory (COLT)*.

P. F. Brown, V. J. D. Pietra, P. V. deSouza, J. C. Lai, and R. L. Mercer. 1992. Class-based n-gram models of natural language. *Computational Linguistics*, 18:467–479.

A. Carlson, J. Betteridge, R. C. Wang, Jr. E. R. Hruschka, and T. M. Mitchell. 2010. Coupled semi-supervised learning for information extraction. In *Web Search and Data Mining (WSDM)*, pages 101–110.

L. Chiticariu, Y. Li, and F. R. Reiss. 2013. Rule-based information extraction is dead! long live rule-based information extraction systems! In *Empirical Methods in Natural Language Processing (EMNLP)*, pages 827–832.

M. Collins and Y. Singer. 1999. Unsupervised models for named entity classification. In *Empirical Methods in Natural Language Processing (EMNLP)*.

O. Etzioni, M. Cafarella, D. Downey, A. Popescu, T. Shaked, S. Soderland, D. S. Weld, and A. Yates. 2005. Unsupervised named-entity extraction from the web: An experimental study. *Artificial Intelligence*, 165(1):91–134.

A. Fader, S. Soderland, and O. Etzioni. 2011. Identifying relations for open information extraction. In *Empirical Methods in Natural Language Processing (EMNLP)*.

S. Gupta and C. D. Manning. 2014. Improved pattern learning for bootstrapped entity extraction. In *Computational Natural Language Learning (CoNLL)*.

A. Haghighi and D. Klein. 2006. Prototype-driven learning for sequence models. In *North American Association for Computational Linguistics (NAACL)*, pages 320–327.

M. A. Hearst. 1992. Automatic acquisition of hyponyms from large text corpora. In *Interational Conference on Computational linguistics*, pages 539–545.

P. Liang. 2005. Semi-supervised learning for natural language. Master's thesis, Massachusetts Institute of Technology.

T. Mikolov, K. Chen, G. Corrado, and J. Dean. 2013a. Efficient estimation of word representations in vector space. Technical Report 1301.3781, arXiv.

T. Mikolov, I. Sutskever, K. Chen, G. Corrado, and J. Dean. 2013b. Distributed representations of words and phrases and their compositionality. In *Advances in Neural Information Processing Systems (NIPS)*.

J. Pennington, R. Socher, and C. D. Manning. 2014. Glove: Global vectors for word representation. In *Empirical Methods in Natural Language Processing (EMNLP)*.

L. Ratinov and D. Roth. 2009. Design challenges and misconceptions in named entity recognition. In *Computational Natural Language Learning (CoNLL)*.

E. Riloff. 1996. Automatically generating extraction patterns from untagged text. In *Association for the Advancement of Artificial Intelligence (AAAI)*, pages 1044–1049.

A. Subramanya, S. Petrov, and F. Pereira. 2010. Efficient graph-based semi-supervised learning of structured tagging models. In *Empirical Methods in Natural Language Processing (EMNLP)*.

M. Thelen and E. Riloff. 2002. A bootstrapping method for learning semantic lexicons using extraction pattern contexts. In *Empirical Methods in Natural Language Processing (EMNLP)*, pages 214–221.

M. Whitney and A. Sarkar. 2012. Bootstrapping via graph propagation. In *Association for Computational Linguistics (ACL)*.

R. Yangarber, R. Grishman, and P. Tapanainen. 2000. Automatic acquisition of domain knowledge for information extraction. In *International Conference on Computational Linguistics (COLING)*, pages 940–946.

D. Yarowsky. 1995. Unsupervised word sense disambiguation rivaling supervised methods. In *Association for Computational Linguistics (ACL)*.

# Multi-Task Word Alignment Triangulation for Low-Resource Languages

**Tomer Levinboim** and **David Chiang**
Department of Computer Science and Engineering
University of Notre Dame
{levinboim.1,dchiang}@nd.edu

## Abstract

We present a multi-task learning approach that jointly trains three word alignment models over disjoint bitexts of three languages: source, target and pivot. Our approach builds upon model triangulation, following Wang et al., which approximates a source-target model by combining source-pivot and pivot-target models. We develop a MAP-EM algorithm that uses triangulation as a prior, and show how to extend it to a multi-task setting. On a low-resource Czech-English corpus, using French as the pivot, our multi-task learning approach more than doubles the gains in both F- and B scores compared to the interpolation approach of Wang et al. Further experiments reveal that the choice of pivot language does not significantly affect performance.

## 1 Introduction

Word alignment (Brown et al., 1993; Vogel et al., 1996) is a fundamental task in the machine translation (MT) pipeline. To train good word alignment models, we require access to a large parallel corpus. However, collection of parallel corpora has mostly focused on a small number of widely-spoken languages. As such, resources for almost any other pair are either limited or non-existent.

To improve word alignment and MT in a low-resource setting, we design a multitask learning approach that utilizes parallel data of a third language, called the *pivot* language (§3). Specifically, we derive an efficient and easy-to-implement MAP-EM-like algorithm that jointly trains source-target, source-pivot and pivot-target alignment models, each on its own bitext, such that each model benefits from observations made by the other two.

Our method subsumes the model interpolation approach of Wang et al. (2006), who independently train these three models and then interpolate the source-target model with an approximate source-target model, constructed by combining the source-pivot and pivot-target models.

Pretending that Czech-English is low-resource, we conduct word alignment and MT experiments (§4). With French as the pivot, our approach significantly outperforms the interpolation method of Wang et al. (2006) on both alignment F- and B scores. Somewhat surprisingly, we find that our approach is insensitive to the choice of pivot language.

## 2 Triangulation and Interpolation

Wang et al. (2006) focus on learning a word alignment model without a source-target corpus. To do so, they assume access to both source-pivot and pivot-target bitexts on which they independently train a source-pivot word alignment model $\Theta_{\mathtt{sp}}$ and a pivot-target model $\Theta_{\mathtt{pt}}$. They then combine the two models by marginalizing over the pivot language, resulting in an approximate source-target model $\Theta_{\widetilde{\mathtt{st}}}$. This combination process is referred to as *triangulation* (see §5).

In particular, they construct the triangulated source-target t-table $\mathtt{t}_{\widetilde{\mathtt{st}}}$ from the source-pivot and pivot-target t-tables $\mathtt{t}_{\mathtt{sp}}, \mathtt{t}_{\mathtt{pt}}$ using the following approximation:

$$\begin{aligned} \mathtt{t}_{\widetilde{\mathtt{st}}}(t \mid s) &= \sum_{p} \mathtt{t}(t \mid p, s) \cdot \mathtt{t}(p \mid s) \\ &\approx \sum_{p} \mathtt{t}_{\mathtt{pt}}(t \mid p) \cdot \mathtt{t}_{\mathtt{sp}}(p \mid s) \end{aligned} \qquad (1)$$

Subsequently, if a source-target corpus is available, they train a standard source-target model $\Theta_{\mathtt{st}}$, and tune the interpolation

$$\hat{\mathtt{t}}_{\mathtt{st}} = \lambda_{\text{interp}} \mathtt{t}_{\mathtt{st}} + (1 - \lambda_{\text{interp}}) \mathtt{t}_{\widetilde{\mathtt{st}}}$$

with respect to $\lambda_{\text{interp}}$ to reduce alignment error rate (Koehn, 2005) over a hand-aligned development set.



*Human Language Technologies: The 2015 Annual Conference of the North American Chapter of the ACL*, pages 1221–1226,
Denver, Colorado, May 31 – June 5, 2015. 

Wang et al. (2006) propose triangulation heuristics for other model parameters; however, in this paper, we consider only t-table triangulation.

## 3 Our Method

We now discuss two approaches that better exploit model triangulation. In the first, we use the triangulated t-table to construct a prior on the source-target t-table. In the second, we place a prior on each of the three models and train them jointly.

### 3.1 Triangulation as a Fixed Prior

We first propose to better utilize the triangulated t-table $\mathtt{t}_{\widetilde{\mathtt{st}}}$ (Eq. 1) by using it to construct an informative prior for the source-target t-table $\mathtt{t}_{\mathtt{st}} \in \Theta_{\mathtt{st}}$.

Specifically, we modify the word alignment generative story by placing Dirichlet priors on each of the multinomial t-table distributions $\mathtt{t}_{\mathtt{st}}(\cdot \mid s)$:

$$\mathtt{t}_{\mathtt{st}}(\cdot \mid s) \sim \text{Dirichlet}(\alpha_s) \qquad \text{for all } s. \tag{2}$$

Here, each $\alpha_s = (\ldots, \alpha_{st}, \ldots)$ denotes a hyperparameter vector which will be defined shortly.

Fixing this prior, we optimize the model posterior likelihood $P(\Theta_{\mathtt{st}} \mid \mathtt{bitext}_{\mathtt{st}})$ to find a maximum-*a-posteriori* (MAP) estimate. This is done according the MAP-EM framework (Dempster et al., 1977), which differs slightly from standard EM. The E-step remains as is: fixing the model $\Theta_{\mathtt{st}}$, we collect expected counts $E[\mathtt{c}(s,t)]$ for each decision in the generative story. The M-step is modified to maximize the *regularized* expected complete-data log-likelihood with respect to the model parameters $\Theta_{\mathtt{st}}$, where the regularizer corresponds to the prior.

Due to the conjugacy of the Dirichlet priors with the multinomial t-table distributions, the sole modification to the regular EM implementation is in the M-step update rule of the t-table parameters:

$$\mathtt{t}_{\mathtt{st}}(t \mid s) = \frac{E[\mathtt{c}(s,t)] + \alpha_{st} - 1}{\sum_t (E[\mathtt{c}(s,t)] + \alpha_{st} - 1)} \tag{3}$$

where $E[\mathtt{c}(s,t)]$ is the expected number of times source word $s$ aligns with target word $t$ in the source-target bitext. Moreover, through Eq. 3, we can view $\alpha_{st} - 1$ as a pseudo-count for such an alignment.

To define the hyperparameter vector $\alpha_s$ we decompose it as follows:

$$\alpha_s = C_s \cdot m_s + 1 \tag{4}$$

where $C_s > 0$ is a scalar parameter, $m_s$ is a probability vector, encoding the mode of the Dirichlet and 1 denotes an all-one vector. Roughly, when $C_s$ is high, samples drawn from the Dirichlet are likely to concentrate near the mode $m_s$. Using this decomposition, we set for all $s$:

$$m_s = \mathtt{t}_{\widetilde{\mathtt{st}}}(\cdot \mid s) \tag{5}$$

$$C_s = \lambda \cdot \mathtt{c}(s)^\gamma \cdot \frac{\sum_{s'} \mathtt{c}(s')}{\sum_{s'} \mathtt{c}(s')^\gamma} \tag{6}$$

where $\mathtt{c}(s)$ is the count of source word $s$ in the source-target bitext, and the scalar hyperparameters $\lambda, \gamma > 0$ are to be tuned (We experimented with completely eliminating the hyperparameters $\gamma, \lambda$ by directly learning the parameters $C_s$. To do so, we implemented the algorithm of Minka (2000) for learning the Dirichlet prior, but only learned the parameters $C_s$ while keeping the means $m_s$ fixed to the triangulation. However, preliminary experiments showed performance degradation compared to simple hyperparameter tuning). Thus, the distribution $\mathtt{t}_{\mathtt{st}}(\cdot \mid s)$ arises from a Dirichlet with mode $\mathtt{t}_{\widetilde{\mathtt{st}}}(\cdot \mid s)$ and will tend to concentrate around this mode as a function of the frequency of $s$.

The hyperparameter $\lambda$ linearly controls the strength of all priors. The last term in Eq. 6 keeps the sum of $C_s$ insensitive to $\gamma$, such that $\sum_s C_s = \lambda \sum_s \mathtt{c}(s)$. In all our experiments we fixed $\gamma = 0.5$. Setting $\gamma < 1$ down-weights the parameter $C_s$ of frequent words $s$ compared to rare ones. This makes the Dirichlet prior relatively weaker for frequent words, where we can let the data speak for itself, and relatively stronger for rare ones, where a good prior is needed.

Finally, note that this EM procedure reduces to an interpolation method similar to that of Wang et al. by applying Eq. 3 only at the very last M-step, with $\alpha_s$, $m_s$ as above and $C_s = \lambda \sum_t E[\mathtt{c}(s,t)]$.

### 3.2 Joint Training

Next, we further exploit the triangulation idea in designing a multi-task learning approach that jointly trains the three word alignment models $\Theta_{\mathtt{st}}$, $\Theta_{\mathtt{sp}}$, and $\Theta_{\mathtt{pt}}$.

To do so, we view each model's t-table as originating from Dirichlet distributions defined by the triangulation of the other two t-tables. We then train

**Algorithm 1** Joint training of $\Theta_{\mathtt{st}}, \Theta_{\mathtt{sp}}, \Theta_{\mathtt{pt}}$

**Parameters**: $\lambda, \gamma > 0$

- Initialize $\left\{\Theta_{\mathtt{st}}^{(0)}, \Theta_{\mathtt{sp}}^{(0)}, \Theta_{\mathtt{pt}}^{(0)}\right\}$
- Initialize $\{C_{\mathtt{s}}\}, \{C_{\mathtt{p}}\}, \{C_{\mathtt{t}}\}$ as in Eq. 6
- For each EM iteration $i$:

  **Estimate hyperparameters** $\alpha$:
  1. Compute $\mathtt{t}_{\widetilde{\mathtt{st}}}^{(i)}$ from $\mathtt{t}_{\mathtt{sp}}^{(i-1)}$ and $\mathtt{t}_{\mathtt{pt}}^{(i-1)}$ (Eq. 1)
  2. Set $\alpha_{st}^{(i)} := C_s \cdot \mathtt{t}_{\widetilde{\mathtt{st}}}^{(i)}(t \mid s) + 1$

  **E:** collect expected counts $E[\mathtt{c}(\cdot)]^{(i)}$ from $\Theta_{\mathtt{st}}^{(i-1)}$

  **M:** Update $\Theta_{\mathtt{st}}^{(i)}$ using $E[\mathtt{c}(\cdot)]^{(i)}$ and $\alpha_{\mathtt{st}}^{(i)}$ (Eq. 3)

  **Repeat** for $\Theta_{\mathtt{sp}}^{(i)}, \Theta_{\mathtt{pt}}^{(i)}$ using Eq. 7 as required

the models in a MAP-EM like manner, updating both the model parameters and their prior hyperparameters at each iteration. Roughly, this approach aims at maximizing the posterior likelihood of the three models with respect to both model parameters and their hyperparameters (see Appendix).

Procedurally, the idea is simple: In the E-step, expected counts $E[\mathtt{c}(\cdot)]$ are collected from each model as usual. In the M-step, each t-table is updated according to Eq. 3 using the current expected counts $E[\mathtt{c}(\cdot)]$ and an estimate of $\alpha$ from the triangulation of the *most recent* version of the other two models. See Algorithm 1.

Note, however, that we cannot obtain the triangulated t-tables $\mathtt{t}_{\widetilde{\mathtt{sp}}}, \mathtt{t}_{\widetilde{\mathtt{pt}}}$ by simply applying the triangulation equation (Eq. 1). For example, to construct $\mathtt{t}_{\widetilde{\mathtt{sp}}}$ we need both source-to-target and target-to-pivot distributions. While we have the former in $\mathtt{t}_{\mathtt{st}}$, we do not have $\mathtt{t}_{\mathtt{tp}}$. To resolve this issue, we simply approximate $\mathtt{t}_{\mathtt{tp}}$ from the reverse t-table $\mathtt{t}_{\mathtt{pt}} \in \Theta_{\mathtt{pt}}$ as follows:

$$\mathtt{t}_{\mathtt{tp}}(p \mid t) := \frac{\mathtt{c}(p)\mathtt{t}_{\mathtt{pt}}(t \mid p)}{\sum_p \mathtt{c}(p)\mathtt{t}_{\mathtt{pt}}(t \mid p)} \tag{7}$$

where $\mathtt{c}(p)$ denotes the unigram frequency of the word p. A similar transformation is done on $\mathtt{t}_{\mathtt{sp}}$ to obtain $\mathtt{t}_{\mathtt{ps}}$, which is then used in computing $\mathtt{t}_{\widetilde{\mathtt{pt}}}$.

### 3.3 Adjustment of the t-table

Note that a t-table resulting from the triangulation equation (Eq. 1) is both noisy and dense. To see why, consider that $\mathtt{t}_{\widetilde{\mathtt{st}}}(t \mid s)$ is non-zero whenever there is a pivot word $p$ that co-occurs with both $s$ and $t$. This is very likely to occur, for example, if $p$ is a function word.

To adjust for both density and noise, we propose a simple product-of-experts re-estimation that relies on the available source-target parallel data. The two experts are the triangulated t-table as defined by Eq. 1 and the exponentiated pointwise mutual information (PMI), derived from simple token co-occurrence statistics of the source-target bitext. That is, we adjust:

$$\mathtt{t}_{\widetilde{\mathtt{st}}}(t \mid s) \quad := \quad \mathtt{t}_{\widetilde{\mathtt{st}}}(t \mid s) \cdot \frac{p(s,t)}{p(s)p(t)}$$

and normalize the result to form valid conditional distributions.

Note that the sparsity pattern of the adjusted t-table matches that of a co-occurrence t-table. We applied this adjustment in all of our experiments.

## 4 Experimental Results

Pretending that Czech-English is a low-resource pair, we conduct two experiments. In the first, we set French as the pivot language and compare our fixed-prior (Sec. §3.1) and joint training (Sec. §3.2) approaches against the interpolation method of Wang et al. and a baseline HMM word alignment model (Vogel et al., 1996).

In the second, we examine the effect of the pivot language identity on our joint training approach, varying the pivot language over French, German, Greek, Hungarian, Lithuanian and Slovak.

### 4.1 Data

For word alignment, we use the Czech-English News Commentary corpus, along with a development set of 460 hand aligned sentence pairs. For the MT experiments, we use the WMT10 tuning set (2051 parallel sentences), and both WMT09/10 shared task test sets. See Table 1.

For each of the 6 pivot languages, we created Czech-pivot and pivot-English bitexts of roughly the same size (ranging from 196k sentences for English-Greek to 223k sentences for Czech-Lithuanian). Each bitext was created by forming a Czech-pivot-English tritext, consisting of about 500k sentences from the Europarl corpus (Koehn, 2005) which was then split into two disjoint Czech-pivot and pivot-English bitexts of equal size. Sentences of length greater than 40 were filtered out from all training corpora.

### 4.2 Experiment 1: Method Comparison

We trained word alignment models in both source-to-target and target-to-source directions. We used 5 iterations of IBM Model 1 followed by 5 iterations of HMM. We tuned hyperparameters to maximize alignment F-score of the hand-aligned development set. Both interpolation parameters $\lambda_{\text{interp}}$ and $\lambda$ were tuned over the range [0, 1]. For our methods, we fixed $\gamma = 0.5$, which we found effective during preliminary experiments. Alignment F-scores using grow-diag-final-and (gdfa) symmetrization (Koehn, 2010) are reported in Table 2, column 2.

We conducted MT experiments using the Moses translation system (Koehn, 2005). We used a 5-gram LM trained on the Xinhua portion of English Gigaword (LDC2007T07). To tune the decoder, we used the WMT10 tune set. MT B scores are reported in Table 2, columns 3–4.

Both our methods outperform the baseline and the interpolation approach. In particular, the joint training approach more than doubles the gains obtained by the interpolation approach, on both F- and B .

We also evaluated the Czech-French and French-English alignments produced as a by-product of our joint method. While our French-to-English MT experiments showed no improvement in B , we saw a +0.6 (25.6 to 26.2) gain in B on the Czech-to-French translation task. This shows that joint training may lead to some improvements even on high-resource bitexts.

### 4.3 Other Pivot Languages

We examined how the choice of pivot language affects the joint training approach by varying it over 6 languages (French, German, Greek, Hungarian, Lithuanian and Slovak), while keeping the size of the pivot language resources roughly the same.

Somewhat surprisingly, all models achieved an F-score of about 70%, which resulted in B scores comparable to those reported with French (Table 2). Subsequently, we combined all pivot languages by simply concatenating the aligned parallel texts across pairs, triples and all pivot languages. Combining all pivots yielded modest B score improvements of +0.2 and +0.1 on the test datasets (Table 3).

Considering the low variance in F- and B scores across pivot languages, we computed the pairwise F-scores between the predicted alignments: All scores ranged around 97–98%, indicating that the choice of pivot language had little effect on the joint training procedure.

To further verify, we repeated this experiment over Greek-English and Lithuanian-English as the source-target task (85k parallel sentences), using the same pivot languages as above, and with comparable amounts of parallel data (~200k sentences). We obtained similar results: In all cases, pairwise F-scores were above 97%.

| | train | dev | WMT09 | WMT10 |
|---|---|---|---|---|
| sentences | 85k | 460 | 2525 | 2489 |
| cz tokens | 1.63M | 9.7k | 55k | 53k |
| en tokens | 1.78M | 10k | 66k | 62k |

Table 1: Czech-English sentence and token statistics.

| | F | B | |
|---|---|---|---|
| **method/dataset** | **dev** | **WMT09** | **WMT10** |
| baseline | 63.8 | 16.2 | 16.6 |
| interpolation (Wang) | 66.2 | 16.6 | 17.1 |
| fixed-prior (§3.1) | 67.3 | 16.9 | 17.3 |
| joint (§3.2) | **70.1** | **17.2** | **17.7** |

Table 2: F- and B scores for Czech-English via French. The joint training method outperforms all other methods tested.

| | fr | fr, sk | fr, el | fr, sk, el | all 6 |
|---|---|---|---|---|---|
| Tune | 16.1 | 16.4 | 16.4 | 16.4 | 16.4 |
| WMT09 | 17.2 | 17.2 | 17.2 | 17.3 | 17.4 |
| WMT10 | 17.7 | 17.8 | 17.8 | 17.8 | 17.8 |

Table 3: Czech-English B scores over pivot language combinations. Key: fr=French, sk=Slovak, el=Greek.

## 5 Related Work

The term "triangulation" comes from the *phrase-table* triangulation literature (Cohn and Lapata, 2007; Razmara and Sarkar, 2013; Dholakia and

Sarkar, 2014), in which source-pivot and pivot-target phrase tables are triangulated according to Eq. 1 (with words replaced by phrases). The resulting triangulated phrase table can then be combined with an existing source-target phrase table, and is especially useful in increasing the source language vocabulary coverage, reducing OOVs. In our case, since word alignment is a closed vocabulary task, OOVs are never an issue.

In word alignment, Kumar et al. (2007) uses *multilingual* parallel data to compute better source-target alignment posteriors. Filali and Bilmes (2005) tag each source token and target token with their most likely translation in a pivot language, and then proceed to align (source word, source tag) tuple sequences to (target word, target tag) tuple sequences. In contrast, our word alignment method can be applied without multilingual parallel data, and does not commit to hard decisions.

## 6 Conclusion and Future Work

We presented a simple multi-task learning algorithm that jointly trains three word alignment models over disjoint bitexts. Our approach is a natural extension of a mathematically sound MAP-EM algorithm we originally developed to better utilize the model triangulation idea. Both algorithms are easy to implement (with closed-form solutions for each step) and require minimal effort to integrate into an EM-based word alignment system.

We evaluated our methods on a low-resource Czech-English word alignment task using additional Czech-French and French-English corpora. Our multi-task learning approach significantly improves F- and B scores compared to both baseline and the interpolation method of Wang et al. (2006). Further experiments showed our approach is insensitive to the choice of pivot language, producing roughly the same alignments over six different pivot language choices.

For future work, we plan to improve word alignment and translation quality in a more data restricted case where there are very weak source-pivot resources: for example, word alignment of Malagasy-English via French, using only a Malagasy-French dictionary, or Pashto-English via Persian.

## Acknowledgements

The authors would like to thank Kevin Knight, Daniel Marcu and Ashish Vaswani for their comments and insights as well as the anonymous reviewers for their valuable feedback. This work was partially supported by DARPA grants DOI/NBC D12AP00225 and HR0011-12-C-0014 and a Google Faculty Research Award to Chiang.

## Appendix: Joint Training Generative Story

We argue that our joint training procedure can be seen as optimizing the posterior likelihood of the three models. Specifically, suppose we place Dirichlet priors on each of the t-tables $\mathtt{t}_{\mathtt{st}}, \mathtt{t}_{\mathtt{sp}}, \mathtt{t}_{\mathtt{pt}}$ as before, but define the prior parameterization using a single hyperparameter $\alpha = \{\alpha_{spt}\}$ and its marginals such that:

$$\begin{aligned} \mathtt{t}_{\mathtt{st}}(\cdot \mid s) &\sim D(\ldots, \alpha_{s\cdot t}, \ldots) & \alpha_{s\cdot t} &= \textstyle\sum_p \alpha_{spt} \\ \mathtt{t}_{\mathtt{sp}}(\cdot \mid s) &\sim D(\ldots, \alpha_{sp\cdot}, \ldots) & \alpha_{sp\cdot} &= \textstyle\sum_t \alpha_{spt} \\ \mathtt{t}_{\mathtt{pt}}(\cdot \mid p) &\sim D(\ldots, \alpha_{\cdot pt}, \ldots) & \alpha_{\cdot pt} &= \textstyle\sum_s \alpha_{spt} \end{aligned}$$

Intuitively, $\alpha_{spt}$ represents the number of times a source-pivot-target triplet $(s, p, t)$ was observed.

With this prior, we can maximize the posterior likelihood of the three models given the three bitexts (denoted $\mathtt{data} = \{\mathtt{bitext}_{\mathtt{st}}, \mathtt{bitext}_{\mathtt{sp}}, \mathtt{bitext}_{\mathtt{pt}}\}$) with respect to all parameters and hyperparameters:

$$\begin{aligned} &\arg\max_{\Theta,\alpha} P(\Theta \mid \alpha, \mathtt{data}) = \\ &\quad \arg\max_{\Theta,\alpha} \textstyle\prod_{d \in \{\mathtt{st},\mathtt{sp},\mathtt{pt}\}} P(\mathtt{bitext}_d \mid \Theta_d) P(\Theta_d \mid \alpha) \end{aligned}$$

Under the generative story, we need only observe the marginals $\alpha_{s\cdot t}, \alpha_{sp\cdot}, \alpha_{\cdot pt}$ of $\alpha$. Therefore, instead of explicitly optimizing over $\alpha$, we can optimize over the marginals while keeping them consistent (via constraints such as $\sum_t \alpha_{s\cdot t} = \sum_p \alpha_{sp\cdot}$ for all $s$).

In our joint training algorithm (Algorithm 1) we abandon these consistency constraints in favor of closed form estimates of the marginals $\alpha_{s\cdot t}, \alpha_{sp\cdot}, \alpha_{\cdot pt}$.

## References

Peter F. Brown, Vincent J.Della Pietra, Stephen A. Della Pietra, and Robert. L. Mercer. 1993. The mathematics of statistical machine translation: Parameter estimation. *Computational Linguistics*, 19:263–311.

Trevor Cohn and Mirella Lapata. 2007. Machine translation by triangulation: Making effective use of multi-parallel corpora. In *Proc. ACL 2007*.

A. P. Dempster, N. M. Laird, and D. B. Rubin. 1977. Maximum likelihood from incomplete data via the EM algorithm. *Journal of the Royal Statistical Society, Series B*, 39(1):1–38.

Rohit Dholakia and Anoop Sarkar. 2014. Pivot-based triangulation for low-resource languages. In *Proc. AMTA*.

Karim Filali and Jeff Bilmes. 2005. Leveraging multiple languages to improve statistical MT word alignments. In *Proc. IEEE Automatic Speech Recognition and Understanding Workshop (ASRU)*.

P. Koehn. 2005. Europarl: A parallel corpus for statistical machine translation. In *Proc. Machine Translation Summit X*, pages 79–86.

Philipp Koehn. 2010. *Statistical Machine Translation*. Cambridge University Press, New York, NY, USA, 1st edition.

Shankar Kumar, Franz Och, and Wolfgang Macherey. 2007. Improving word alignment with bridge languages. In *Proc. EMNLP-CoNLL*.

Thomas P. Minka. 2000. Estimating a Dirichlet distribution. Technical report, MIT.

Majid Razmara and Anoop Sarkar. 2013. Ensemble triangulation for statistical machine translation. In *Proc. IJCNLP*, pages 252–260.

Stephan Vogel, Hermann Ney, and Christoph Tillmann. 1996. HMM-based word alignment in statistical translation. In *Proc. COLING*, pages 836–841.

Haifeng Wang, Hua Wu, and Zhanyi Liu. 2006. Word alignment for languages with scarce resources using bilingual corpora of other language pairs. In *Proc. COLING/ACL*, pages 874–881.

# Automatic cognate identification with gap-weighted string subsequences.

**Taraka Rama**
Språkbanken
University of Gothenburg
Box 200, Gothenburg, Sweden
taraka.rama.kasicheyanula@gu.se

## Abstract

In this paper, we describe the problem of cognate identification in NLP. We introduce the idea of gap-weighted subsequences for discriminating cognates from non-cognates. We also propose a scheme to integrate phonetic features into the feature vectors for cognate identification. We show that subsequence based features perform better than state-of-the-art classifier for the purpose of cognate identification. The contribution of this paper is the use of subsequence features for cognate identification.

## 1 Introduction

Cognates are words across languages whose origin can be traced back to a common ancestral language. For example, English ~ German *night* ~ *Nacht* 'night' and English *hound* ~ German *Hund* 'dog' are cognates whose origin can be traced back to Proto-Germanic. Sometimes, cognates are not revealingly similar but have changed substantially over time such that they do not share form similarity. An example of such a cognate pair is the English *wheel* and Sanskrit *chakra* 'wheel', which can be traced back to Proto-Indo-European (PIE) $*k^wek^welo$.

Automatic cognate identification, in NLP, refers to the application of string similarity or phonetic similarity algorithms either independently, or in tandem with machine learning algorithms for determining if a given word pair is cognate or not (Inkpen et al., 2005). In NLP, even borrowed words (*loanwords*) are referred to as cognates. In contrast, historical linguistics makes a stark distinction between loanwords and cognates. For example, English *beef* is a loanword from Norman French.

In this paper, we use cognates to refer to those words whose origin can be traced back to a common ancestor. We use string subsequence based features (motivated from string kernels) for automatic cognate identification. We show that subsequence-based features outperform word similarity measures at the task of automatic cognate identification. We motivate the use of subsequence based features in terms of linguistic examples and then proceed to formulate the subsequence based features that can be derived from string kernels (Shawe-Taylor and Cristianini, 2004). In information retrieval literature, string subsequences go under the name of skip-grams (Järvelin et al., 2007).

## 2 Related work

The approaches developed by Kondrak and Sherif (2006) and Inkpen et al. (2005) supply different string distances between a pair of words as features to a linear classifier. Usually, a linear classifier such as SVM is trained on labeled positive ("cognates") and negative ("non-cognates") examples and tested on a held-out dataset. Basic vocabulary lists such as the ones devised by Morris Swadesh (Swadesh, 1952), provide a suitable testing ground for applying machine learning algorithms to automatically identify cognates. Some standardized word lists come with cognate information and, subsequently, can used to infer the relationship between the languages (Dyen et al., 1992).



*Human Language Technologies: The 2015 Annual Conference of the North American Chapter of the ACL*, pages 1227–1231,
Denver, Colorado, May 31 – June 5, 2015. 

Ellison and Kirby (2006) use scaled edit distance (normalized by average length) to measure the intra-lexical divergence in a language. The inter-language distance matrix is supplied to a clustering algorithm to infer a tree for the Indo-European language family. The authors only perform a qualitative evaluation of the inferred tree. The authors mention string kernels but do not pursue this line of research further.

Bouchard-Côté et al. (2013) employ a graphical model to reconstruct the proto-word forms from the synchronic word-forms for the Austronesian language family. They compare their automated reconstructions with the ones reconstructed by historical linguists and find that their model beats an edit-distance baseline. However, their model has a requirement that the tree structure between the languages under study has to be known beforehand.

Hauer and Kondrak (2011) – referred to as HK – supply different string similarity scores as features to a SVM classifier for determining if a given word pair is a cognate or not. The authors also employ an additional binary language-pair feature – that is used to weigh the language distance – and find that the additional feature assists the task of semantic clustering of cognates. In this task, the cognacy judgments given by a linear classifier is used to flat cluster the lexical items belonging to a single concept. The clustering quality is evaluated against the gold standard cognacy judgments. Unfortunately, the experiments of these scholars cannot be replicated since the partitioning details of their training and test datasets is not available.

In our experiments, we compare our system's performance with the performance of the classifiers trained from HK-based features. In the next section, we will describe string similarity measures, subsequences features, dataset, and results.

# 3 Cognate identification

## 3.1 String similarity features and issues

Edit distance counts the minimum number of insertions, deletions, and substitutions required to transform one word into another word. Identical words have 0 edit distance. For example, the edit distance between two cognates English *hound* and German *hund* is 1. Similarly, the edit distance between Swedish *i* and Russian *v* 'in', which are cognates, is 1. The edit distance treats both of the cognates at the same level and does not reflect the amount of change which has occurred in the Swedish and Russian words from the PIE word.

Dice is another string similarity measure that defines similarity between two strings as the ratio between the number of common bigrams to the total number of bigrams. The similarity between Lusatian *dolhi* and Czech *dluhe* 'long' is 0 since they do not share any common bigrams and the edit distance between the two strings is 3. Although the two words share all the consonants, the Dice score is 0 due to the intervening vowels.

Another string similarity measure, Longest Common Subsequence (LCS) measures the length of the longest common subsequence between the two words. The LCS is 4 (*hund*), 0 (*i* and *v*), and 3 (*dlh*) for the above examples. One can put forth a number of examples which are problematical for the commonly-used string similarity measures. Alternatively, string kernels in machine learning research offer a way to exploit the similarities between two words without any restrictions on the length and character similarity.

## 3.2 Subsequence features

Subsequences as formulated below weigh the similarity between two words based on the number of dropped characters and combine phoneme classes seamlessly. Having motivated why subsequences seems to be a good idea, we formulate subsequences below.

We follow the notation given in Shawe-Taylor and Cristianini (2004) to formulate our representation of a string (word). Let $\Sigma$ denote the set of phonetic alphabet. Given a string $s$ over $\Sigma$, the subsequence vector $\mathbf{\Phi(s)}$ is defined as follows. The string $s$ can be decomposed as $s_1, \ldots, s_{|s|}$ where $|s|$ denotes the length of the string. Let $\overrightarrow{I}$ denote a sequence of indices $(i_1, \ldots, i_{|u|})$ where, $1 \leq i_1 < \ldots < i_{|u|} \leq |s|$. Then, a subsequence $u$ is a sequence of characters $s[\overrightarrow{I}]$. Note that a subsequence can occur multiple times in a string. Then, the weight of $u$, $\phi_u(s)$ is defined as $\sum_{\overrightarrow{I}:u=s[\overrightarrow{I}]} \lambda^{l(\overrightarrow{I})}$ where, $l(\overrightarrow{I}) = i_{|u|} - i_1 + 1$ and $\lambda \in (0, 1)$ is a decay factor.

The subsequence vector $\Phi(s)$ is composed of

$\phi_u(s)\ \forall u \in \bigcup_{n=1}^{p} \Sigma^n$, where $1 \leq n \leq p$ is the length of $u$ and $p$ is the maximum length of the subsequences. As $\lambda \rightarrow 0$, a subsequence is constrained to a substring. As $\lambda \rightarrow 1$, $\phi_u(s)$ counts the frequency of $u$ in $s$. We also experiment with different values of $\lambda$ in this paper.

The $\lambda$ factor is exponential and penalizes $u$ over long gaps in a string. Due to the above formulation, the frequency of a subsequence $u$ in a single string is also taken into account. The subsequence formulation also allows for the incorporation of a class-based features easily. For instance, each $\sigma$ in $u$ can be mapped to its **Consonant/Vowel** class: $\sigma \mapsto \{C, V\}$. The subsequence formulation also allows us to map each phonetic symbol (for example, from International Phonetic Alphabet [IPA]) to an intermediary phonetic alphabet also. Unfortunately, the current dataset is not transcribed in IPA to convert it into an intermediary broader format. In this paper, we map each string $s$ into its $C, V$ sequence $s_{cv}$ and then compute the subsequence weights.[1]

A combined subsequence vector $\Phi(s + s_{cv})$ is further normalized by its norm, $\|\Phi(s + s_{cv})\|$, to transform into a unit vector. The common subsequence vector $\Phi(s_1, s_2)$ is composed of all the common subsequences between $s_1$ and $s_2$. The weight of a common subsequence is $\phi_u(s_1) + \phi_u(s_2)$.

Moschitti et al. (2012) list the features of the above weighting scheme.

- Longer subsequences receive lower weights.
- Characters can be omitted (called *gaps*).
- The exponent of $\lambda$ penalizes recurring subsequences with longer gaps.

For a string of length $m$ and subsequence length $n$, the computational complexity is in the order of $\mathcal{O}(mn)$.

On a linguistic note, gaps are consistent with the prevalent sound changes such as sound loss, sound gain, and assimilation,[2] processes which alter word forms in an ancestral language causing the daughter languages to have different surface forms. The $\lambda$ factor weighs the number of gaps found in a subsequence. For instance, the Sardinian word form for 'fish' *pissi* has the subsequence *ps* occurring twice but with different weights: $\lambda^3, \lambda^4$. Hence, *ps*'s weight is $\lambda^3 + \lambda^4$. On another note, the idea of gap subsequences subsumes the definitions of different $n$-gram similarities introduced by Kondrak (2005).

The combined feature vector, for a word pair, is used to train a SVM classifier. In our experiments, we use the LIBLINEAR package (Fan et al., 2008) to solve the primal problem with $L_2$-regularization and $L_2$-loss. The next subsection describes the makeup of the dataset. We use the default SVM parameters since we did not observe any difference in our development experiments.

### 3.3 Dataset and results

In this section, we will present the dataset, HK features, and results of our experiments.

**Dataset.** We used the publicly available[3] Indo-European dataset (Dyen et al., 1992) for our experiments. The dataset has $16,520$ lexical items for 200 concepts and 84 language varieties. Each word form is assigned to a unique CCN (Cognate Class Number). There are more than 200 identical non-cognate pairs in the dataset. For the first experiment, we extracted all word pairs for a concept and assigned a positive label if the word pair has an identical CCN; a negative label, if the word pair has different CCNs. We extracted a total of $619,635$ word pairs out of which $145,145$ are cognates. The dataset is transcribed in a broad romanized phonetic alphabet.

We explored if we could use two other word list databases: ASJP (Brown et al., 2008) and Ringe et al. (2002) for our experiments. Although the ASJP database has word lists for more than half of the world's languages, it has cognacy judgments for few selected languages and is limited to 40 concepts. Moreover, the ASJP database does not have cognacy judgments for Indo-European family. The other dataset of Ringe et al. (2002) has items for 24 Indo-European languages which are transcribed in an orthographic format and not in a uniform phonetic alphabet.[4] Moreover, there are a number of missing items for some of the languages. Hence, we did not use Ringe et al.'s dataset in our experiments. In contrast, Dyen's dataset is much larger and transcribed in an uniform format. Now, we proceed to

[1] $V = \{a, e, i, o, u, y\}, C = \Sigma \setminus V$.

[2] A sound can assimilate to a neighboring sound. Sanskrit *agni* > Prakrit *aggi* 'fire'. Compare the Latin form *ignis* with the Sanskrit form.

[3] http://www.wordgumbo.com/ie/cmp/iedata.txt

[4] http://www.cs.rice.edu/ nakhleh/CPHL/ie-wordlist-07.pdf

describe the previous best-performing system.

**HK's system.** We compare the performance of subsequence features against the SVM classifier system trained on the following word-similarity features from Hauer and Kondrak (2011):

- Edit distance.
- Length of longest common prefix.
- Number of common bigrams.
- Lengths of individual words.
- Absolute difference between the lengths of the words.

**Cross-Validation experiment.** As a first step, we perform a random ten-fold cross-validation of the dataset and report the accuracies for various values of $\lambda$ and $p$. The results of this experiment are

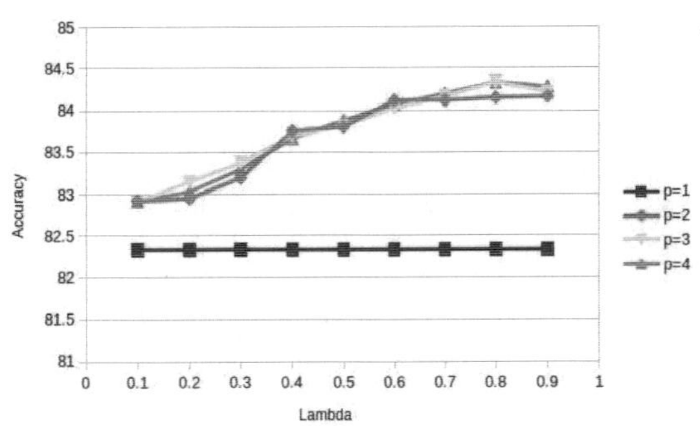


Figure 1: Ten-fold cross-validation accuracy for incremental $\lambda$ and $p$. The accuracy of the system of HK is 82.61%.

shown in figure 1. The best results are obtained at $\lambda = 0.8, p = 3$. The accuracies increase with an increment in the value of $\lambda$ until 0.8 for all $p > 1$ (non-unigram models). This experiment is mainly designed to test the robustness of subsequence features against random splits in the dataset which turns out to be robust. The subsequence features outperform HK-based classifier in this experiment.

| | positive | negative |
|---|---|---|
| training | 111,918 | 353,957 |
| test | 33,227 | 120,533 |

Table 1: Number of positive and negative examples in the training and test sets. The ratio of positive to negative examples is 1 : 3.62.

**Concepts experiment.** In this experiment, we split our dataset into two sets by concepts; and train on one set and test on the other. To replicate our dataset, we performed an alphabetical sort of the concepts and split the concepts into training and testing datasets with a ratio of 3 : 1. Now, we extract positive and negative examples from each subset of concepts; and train and test on each concepts' subset. We also performed a 3-fold cross-validation on the training set to tune $c$ (SVM hyperparameter). We observed that the value of $c$ did not effect the cross-validation accuracy on the training dataset. Hence we fixed $c$ at 1. We also experimented with radial-basis function kernel and polynomial kernels but did not find any improvement over the linear kernel classifier. The composition of the training and test sets is given in table 1.

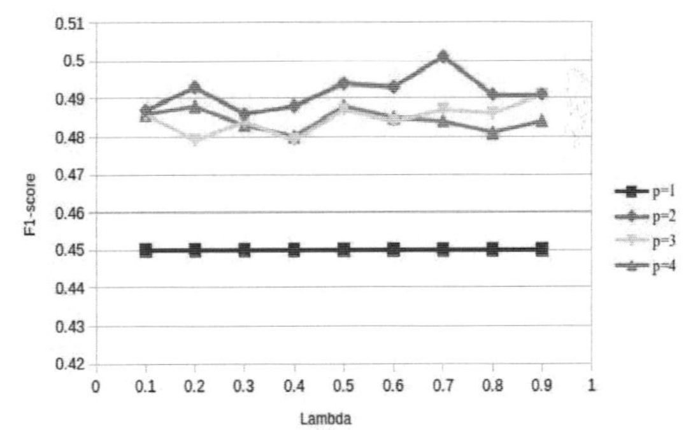


Figure 2: $F_1$-score for different values of $p$ and $\lambda$. The $F_1$-score of the system of HK is 0.46.

In this experiment, we report the $F_1$-score, defined as $\frac{2PR}{P+R}$ (**P**recision and **R**ecall), for different values of $\lambda$ and $p$. The results of this experiment are shown in figure 2. The $F_1$-score of the system of HK is 0.46 whereas the best performing subsequence system ($\lambda = 0.7, p = 2$) has a score of 0.5. Our system performs better than the system of HK in terms of cross-validation accuracy as well as $F_1$-score. Overall, all non-unigram models perform better than the system of HK at cross-validation and concepts experiments.

## 4 Conclusion

In this paper, we proposed a string kernel based approach for the purpose of cognate identification. We formulated an approach to integrate phonetic features of a phonetic symbol into the feature vector and showed that it beats the system of HK at cognate identification at cross-validation and concepts subsets experiments.

In future, we plan to make a larger dataset of cognacy judgments for other language families in a richer phonetic transcription and integrate articulatory phonetic features into the feature vectors for the purpose of cognate identification. We also plan on testing with different feature vector combinations.

## Acknowledgments

I thank the three anonymous reviewers for the comments that helped improve the paper. I thank Søren Wichmann, Richard Johansson, Gerlof Bouma, Prasanth Kolachina, and Johann-Mattis List for all the discussions and comments that helped improve the paper. This research was supported by University of Gothenburg through its support of the Centre for Language Technology and Språkbanken.

## References

Alexandre Bouchard-Côté, David Hall, Thomas L. Griffiths, and Dan Klein. 2013. Automated reconstruction of ancient languages using probabilistic models of sound change. *Proceedings of the National Academy of Sciences*, 110(11):4224–4229.

Cecil H. Brown, Eric W. Holman, Søren Wichmann, and Viveka Velupillai. 2008. Automated classification of the world's languages: A description of the method and preliminary results. *Sprachtypologie und Universalienforschung*, 61(4):285–308.

Isidore Dyen, Joseph B. Kruskal, and Paul Black. 1992. An Indo-European classification: A lexicostatistical experiment. *Transactions of the American Philosophical Society*, 82(5):1–132.

T. Mark Ellison and Simon Kirby. 2006. Measuring language divergence by intra-lexical comparison. In *Proceedings of the 21st International Conference on Computational Linguistics and 44th Annual Meeting of the Association for Computational Linguistics*, pages 273–280, Sydney, Australia, July. Association for Computational Linguistics.

Rong-En Fan, Kai-Wei Chang, Cho-Jui Hsieh, Xiang-Rui Wang, and Chih-Jen Lin. 2008. Liblinear: A library for large linear classification. *The Journal of Machine Learning Research*, 9:1871–1874.

Bradley Hauer and Grzegorz Kondrak. 2011. Clustering semantically equivalent words into cognate sets in multilingual lists. In *Proceedings of 5th International Joint Conference on Natural Language Processing*, pages 865–873, Chiang Mai, Thailand, November. Asian Federation of Natural Language Processing.

Diana Inkpen, Oana Frunza, and Grzegorz Kondrak. 2005. Automatic identification of cognates and false friends in French and English. In *Proceedings of the International Conference Recent Advances in Natural Language Processing*, pages 251–257.

Anni Järvelin, Antti Järvelin, and Kalervo Järvelin. 2007. s-grams: Defining generalized n-grams for information retrieval. *Information Processing & Management*, 43(4):1005–1019.

Grzegorz Kondrak and Tarek Sherif. 2006. Evaluation of several phonetic similarity algorithms on the task of cognate identification. In *Proceedings of ACL Workshop on Linguistic Distances*, pages 43–50. Association for Computational Linguistics.

Grzegorz Kondrak. 2005. N-gram similarity and distance. In *String Processing and Information Retrieval*, pages 115–126. Springer.

Alessandro Moschitti, Qi Ju, and Richard Johansson. 2012. Modeling topic dependencies in hierarchical text categorization. In *Proceedings of the 50th Annual Meeting of the Association for Computational Linguistics: Long Papers-Volume 1*, pages 759–767. Association for Computational Linguistics.

Don Ringe, Tandy Warnow, and Ann Taylor. 2002. Indo-European and computational cladistics. *Transactions of the Philological Society*, 100(1):59–129.

John Shawe-Taylor and Nello Cristianini. 2004. *Kernel methods for pattern analysis*. Cambridge university press.

Morris Swadesh. 1952. Lexico-statistic dating of prehistoric ethnic contacts: with special reference to North American Indians and Eskimos. *Proceedings of the American philosophical society*, 96(4):452–463.

# Short Text Understanding by Leveraging Knowledge into Topic Model

**Shansong Yang, Weiming Lu*, Dezhi Yang, Liang Yao, Baogang Wei**
Zhejiang University
Hangzhou, Zhejiang 310000, China
{yangshansong, luwm, deathyyoung, yaoliang, wbg}@zju.edu.cn

## Abstract

In this paper, we investigate the challenging task of understanding short text (*STU* task) by jointly considering topic modeling and knowledge incorporation. Knowledge incorporation can solve the content sparsity problem effectively for topic modeling. Specifically, the phrase topic model is proposed to leverage the auto-mined knowledge, i.e., the phrases, to guide the generative process of short text. Experimental results illustrate the effectiveness of the mechanism that utilizes knowledge to improve topic modeling's performance.

## 1 Introduction

The explosion of online text content, such as twitter messages, text advertisements, QA community messages and product reviews has given rise to the necessity of understanding these prevalent short texts.

Conventional topic modeling, like PLSA (Hofmann, 1999) and LDA (Blei et al., 2003) are widely used for uncovering the hidden topics from text corpus. However, the sparsity of content in short texts brings new challenges to topic modeling.

In fact, short texts usually do not contain sufficient statistical signals to support many state-of-the-art approaches for text processing such as topic modeling (Hua et al., 2015). Knowledge is indispensable to *STU* task, where knowledge-based topic model (Andrzejewski et al., 2009; Hu et al., 2011; Jagarlamudi et al., 2012; Mukherjee and Liu, 2012; Chen et al., 2013; Yan et al., 2013) has attracted more attention recently.

*Corresponding author

We consider, in the *STU* task, the available knowledge can be divided into two classes: self-contained knowledge and external knowledge. Self-contained knowledge, which is focused in this paper, is extracted from the short text itself, such as key-phrase. External knowledge is constructed without special purpose, such as WordNet (Miller, 1995), KnowItAll (Etzioni et al., 2005), Wikipedia (Gabrilovich and Markovitch, 2007), Yago (Suchanek et al., 2007), NELL (Carlson et al., 2010) and Probase (Wu et al., 2012).

PLSA and LDA are the typical unsupervised topic models, that is non-knowledgeable model. In contrast, Biterm topic model (BTM) (Yan et al., 2013) leverages self-contained knowledge into semantic analysis. BTM learns topics over short texts by modeling the generation of biterms in the whole corpus. A biterm is an unordered word-pair co-occurring in short contexts. BTM posits that the two words in a biterm share the same topic drawn from a mixture of topics over the whole corpus. The major advantage of BTM is that BTM explicitly model the word co-occurrences in the local context, which well captures the short-range dependencies between words.

External knowledge-based models incorporate expert domain knowledge to help guide the models. DF-LDA (Andrzejewski et al., 2009) model incorporates domain knowledge in the form of *must-link* and *cannot link*. *Must link* states that two words should belong to the same topic, while *cannot-link* states that two words should not be in the same topic. GK-LDA (Chen et al., 2013) leverages lexical semantic relations of words such as synonyms, antonyms and adjective attributes in topic models. A



*Human Language Technologies: The 2015 Annual Conference of the North American Chapter of the ACL*, pages 1232–1237,
Denver, Colorado, May 31 – June 5, 2015. 

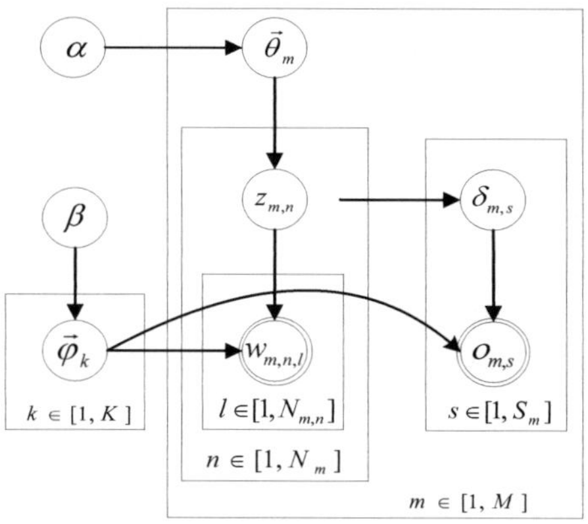


Figure 1: The phrase topic model proposed in this paper.

vast amount of lexical knowledge about words and their relationships, denoted as *LR-sets*, available in online dictionaries or other resources can be exploited by this model to generate more coherent topics.

However, for external knowledge-based models, the incorporated knowledge is too general to be consistent with the short text in the semantic space. On the other hand, BTM, as a typical self-contained knowledge-based model, makes rough assumption on the generated biterms. The generated biterms are inundated with noise, for not any two terms in short text share same topic. Based on the above analysis, we first identify key-phrases from short text, which can be deemed as self-contained knowledge, then propose phrase topic model (PTM), which constrains same topic for terms in key-phrase and sample topics for non-phrase terms from mixture of key-phrase's topic.

## 2 Phrase Topic Model

### 2.1 Model

A phrase is defined as a consecutive sequence of terms, or unigrams. In this paper, we focus on self-contained knowledge in short text, i.e., the key-phrases. Key-phrase extraction is a fundamental component in our work. We use CRF++[1] to identify key-phrases in a short text. The training data is built manually, and the features contain the word itself, the part of speech tagged by Stanford Log-linear Part-Of-Speech Tagger (Toutanova et al., 2003). Sample identified key-phrases are shown in Table 2.

In this paper, our phrase topic model is proposed based on three assumptions:

- Key-phrases are the key points of interest in the short text, which should be the focus.
- Terms consisting of the same key-phrase will share common topic.
- Non-phrase term's topic assignment should depend on that of key-phrases in the same text.

Our assumptions is indeed similar to other models (Gruber et al., 2007), for example each sentence is assumed to be assigned to one topic, however this assumption is too general, in many cases, different words should be assigned different topics even in short text. Our model is more refined to distinguish key-phrase and non-phrase. In addition, if two or more key-phrases exist in the same short text, they are probably assigned different topics.

The graphical representation of PTM is illustrated in Figure 1. $\alpha$ and $\beta$ are hyper-parameters, which are experienced tuned. $\varphi$ is corpus-level parameter, while $\theta$ is document-level parameter. The hidden variables consist of $z_{m,n}$ and $\delta_{m,s}$. The generative process of phrase topic model is presented as follows.

- For each topic $k \in [1, K]$
  - draw a topic-specific word distribution $\varphi_k \sim Dir(\beta)$
- For each document $m \in [1, M]$
  - draw a topic distribution $\theta_m \sim Dir(\alpha)$
  - For each key-phrase $n \in [1, N_m]$
    * draw topic assignment $z_{m,n} \sim Multi(\theta_m)$
    * For each word $l \in [1, N_{m,n}]$
      · draw $w_{m,n,l} \sim Multi(\varphi_{z_{m,n}})$
  - For each non-phrase word $s \in [1, S_m]$
    * draw a topic assignment $\delta_{m,s} \sim Uniform(z_{m,1}, \ldots, z_{m,N_m})$
    * draw word $o_{m,s} \sim Multi(\varphi_{\delta_{m,s}})$

From this process, we can see the generation of key-phrases and non-phrases are distinguished and non-phrase's generation is based on the topic assignment of key-phrases in the same document.

[1] http://crfpp.googlecode.com/svn/trunk/doc/index.html

## 2.2 Inference By Gibbs Sampling

Similarly with LDA, collapsed Gibbs sampling (Griffiths and Steyvers, 2004) can be utilized to perform approximate inference. In our model, the hidden variables are key-phrase's topic assignment $\boldsymbol{z}$ and non-phrase word's topic assignment $\boldsymbol{\delta}$. To perform Gibbs sampling, we first randomly initialize the hidden variables. Then we sample the topic assignment based on the conditional distribution $p(z_{m,n} = k|\mathbf{z}_{\neg(m,n)}, \mathbf{w}, \mathbf{o}, \delta)$ and $p(\delta_{m,s} = k|\mathbf{z}, \mathbf{w}, \mathbf{o}, \delta_{\neg(m,s)})$.

We can derive the conditional probability for $z_{m,n}$ following Equation 1, where $n^{k}_{m,\neg(m,n)}$ denotes the number of key-phrases whose topic assignment are $k$ in document $m$ without consideration of key-phrase $\{m,n\}$, which is similar to $n^{k'}_{m,\neg(m,n)}$. $n^{w_{m,n,l}}_{k,\neg(m,n)}$ denotes the number of times key-phrase term $w_{m,n,l}$ assigned to topic $k$ without consideration of key-phrase $\{m,n\}$, which is similar to $n^{w}_{k,\neg(m,n)}$. $n^{o_{m,s}}_{k,\neg m}$ denotes the number of times non-phrase term $o_{m,s}$ assigned to topic $k$ without consideration of document $m$, which is similar to $n^{w}_{k,\neg m}$.

Similarly, we can derive the conditional probability for $\delta_{m,s}$ following Equation 2, where $n^{o_{m,s}}_{k,\neg(m,s)}$ denotes the number of times non-phrase term $o_{m,s}$ assigned to topic $k$ without consideration of non-phrase term $\{m,s\}$, which is similar to $n^{w}_{k,\neg(m,s)}$. $L_m$ denotes the number of topics assigned to key-phrases in document $m$.

Finally, we can easily estimate the topic distribution $\theta_{m,k}$ and topic-word distribution $\varphi_{k,w}$ following Equation 3 and 4.

$$\theta_{m,k} = \frac{n^{k}_{m} + \alpha}{\sum_{k'=1}^{K} n^{k'}_{m} + K\alpha} \quad (3)$$

$$\varphi_{k,w} = \frac{n^{w}_{k} + \beta}{\sum_{w'=1}^{V} n^{w'}_{k} + V\beta} \quad (4)$$

## 3 Experiments and Results

Online reviews dataset (Chen et al., 2013), which consists of four domains, is utilized to evaluate our model, where each domain collection contains 500 reviews. Each review's average length is 20.42. The statistics of each domain are presented in Table 1. It's worth noting that the ***Phrase*** is auto-identified by the key-phrase extraction method. And the ***Word*** represents the whole distinct words for those identified key-phrases.

In our paper, we assumed each domain has a single topic model. For different domain, we think the semantic space is quite different. So we performed the proposed topic model with respect to different domain. The number of topics is usually determined by experience, in our experiment, each domain collection contains 500 reviews, we think the number of topics ranging from 2 to 20 is appropriate, and these reviews are sufficient to train a topic model.

Table 1: Statistic information of the dataset.

| Dataset | ***Phrase*** | ***Word*** | Vocabulary |
|---|---|---|---|
| Computer | 1439 | 1423 | 5109 |
| Cellphone | 1110 | 1109 | 4184 |
| Camera | 2962 | 2620 | 8366 |
| Food | 1235 | 1350 | 4488 |

Recent research (Chang et al., 2009; Newman et al., 2010) shows that the models which achieve better predictive perplexity often have less interpretable latent spaces. So the *Topic Coherence Metric* (Mimno et al., 2011) is utilized to assess topic quality, which is consistent with human labeling.

We compare our model with four baseline models: non-knowledgeable model LDA, self-contained knowledgeable model BTM, external knowledge-based model GK-LDA (Chen et al., 2013) and DF-LDA (Andrzejewski et al., 2009). Those identified key-phrases are used as *must-links* in DF-LDA and *LR-sets* in GK-LDA. This can ensure the incorporated knowledge upon different models are equal.

Table 2 illustrates the auto-identified phrases from cellphone dataset. From this result, we can see key-phrase extraction method can efficiently identify mostly phrases. More than one phrase, for example *warranty service* and *android phone*, may appear in a single sentence, and their topic assignments are probably different. Our proposed phrase topic model(PTM) can well handle this case, which is more well-defined than the assumption of all words within a sentence share one topic. Our phrase topic model assumes non-phrase term's topic assignment should depend on that of key-phrases in the same text. This assumption can be clearly confirmed by Table 2, for example, *Nokia N97 mini* is semantic dependent *US-*

$$p(z_{m,n} = k|\mathbf{z}_{\neg(m,n)}, \mathbf{w}, \mathbf{o}, \delta) = \frac{n^{k}_{m,\neg(m,n)} + \alpha}{\sum_{k'=1}^{K} n^{k'}_{m,\neg(m,n)} + K\alpha} \cdot \frac{\prod_{l=1}^{N_{m,n}} (n^{w_{m,n,l}}_{k,\neg(m,n)} + \beta)}{\prod_{l=1}^{N_{m,n}} (\sum_{w=1}^{V} n^{w}_{k,\neg(m,n)} + V\beta)} \cdot \frac{\prod_{s=1}^{S_m} (n^{o_{m,s}}_{k,\neg m} + \beta)}{\prod_{s=1}^{S_m} (\sum_{w=1}^{V} n^{w}_{k,\neg m} + V\beta)} \quad (1)$$

$$p(\delta_{m,s} = k|\mathbf{z}, \mathbf{w}, \mathbf{o}, \delta_{\neg(m,s)}) = \frac{n^{o_{m,s}}_{k,\neg(m,s)} + \beta}{\sum_{w=1}^{V} n^{w}_{k,\neg(m,s)} + V\beta} \cdot \frac{1}{L_m} \quad (2)$$

*B charge cable*, the same as *company* and *warranty service*.

For all models, posterior inference was drawn after 1000 Gibbs iterations with an initial burn-in of 800 iterations. For all models, we set the hyperparameters $\alpha = 2$ and $\beta = 0.5$.

The evaluation results over *Topic Coherence Metric* are presented in Figure 2 and Figure 3. This figure indicates our model and BTM can get higher topic coherence score than GK-LDA and DF-LDA, which means the self-defined knowledge and the mechanism of knowledge incorporation are effective to topic model. LDA's performance is acceptable but not stable. Our model performs better than BTM, which is probably because the rough assumption of BTM on generated biterms. From the above analysis, we can see our proposed model can get the best performance.

T-test results show that the performance improvement of our model over baselines is statistically significant on *Topic Coherence Metric*. All p-values for t-test are less than 0.00001.

Figure 4 presents the fluctuation of topic coherence when tuning the hyper-parameter $\alpha$ and $\beta$. We can see that the performance fluctuates within a limited range as we vary $\alpha$ and $\beta$. The topic coherence fluctuates between $-550$ and $-950$ other than food dataset, which gets less fluctuation range.

Table 3 shows example topics for each domain, where inconsistent words are highlighted in red. From this results, we can see the number of errors in phrase topic model(PTM) is significantly less than LDA, which indicates our proposed topic model is more suitable than LDA for short text.

## 4 Conclusions and Future Work

In this paper, we present a topic model to achieve *STU* task starting from key-phrases. The terms in key-phrases identified from the short texts are supposed to share a common topic respectively. And those key-phrases are assumed to be the central focus in the generative process of documents. In the future work, the self-contained knowledge, such as those identified key-phrases, and the external knowledge-base should be integrated to guide topic modeling.


## Acknowledgements

This work is supported by the National Natural Science Foundation of China No.61103099, the Fundamental Research Funds for the Central Universities(2014QNA5008), Chinese Knowledge Center of Engineering Science and Technology(CKCEST) and Specialized Research Fund for the Doctoral Program of Higher Education(SRFDP)(No.20130101110136).


## References


[Andrzejewski et al.2009] David Andrzejewski, Xiaojin Zhu, and Mark Craven. 2009. Incorporating domain knowledge into topic modeling via dirichlet forest priors. In *Proceedings of the 26th Annual International Conference on Machine Learning, ICML 2009*, pages 25–32.

[Blei et al.2003] David M Blei, Andrew Y Ng, and Michael I Jordan. 2003. Latent dirichlet allocation. *the Journal of machine Learning research*, 3:993–1022.

[Carlson et al.2010] Andrew Carlson, Justin Betteridge, Bryan Kisiel, Burr Settles, Estevam R. Hruschka Jr.,

Table 2: Identified Key-phrase in Cellphone dataset

[1] Both sites list compatible devices including the *Samsung Galaxy Tab*.
[2] My Dell Streak needed more power than any normal *USB car adapter* could give me.
[3] This actually comes with a micro *USB charge cable* which fits and works perfectly for my Nokia N97 mini.
[4] I contacted the company for *warranty service*. On my *android phone* I paired ...
[5] Everything from pulling it out of the box to syncing it with both my IPhone and *Ipod touch* 4g were effortless.

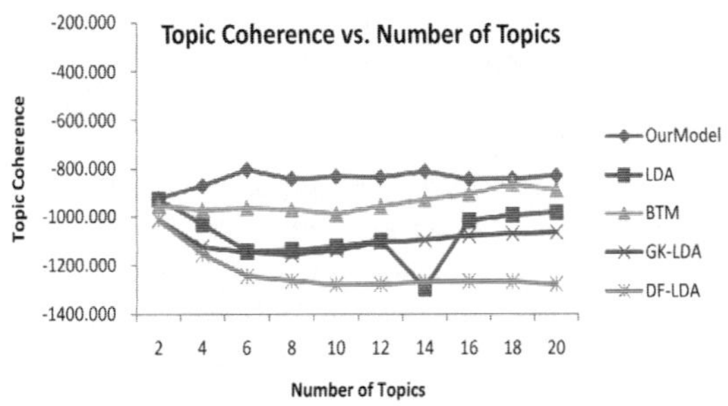


Figure 2: Average Topic Coherence score of each model.

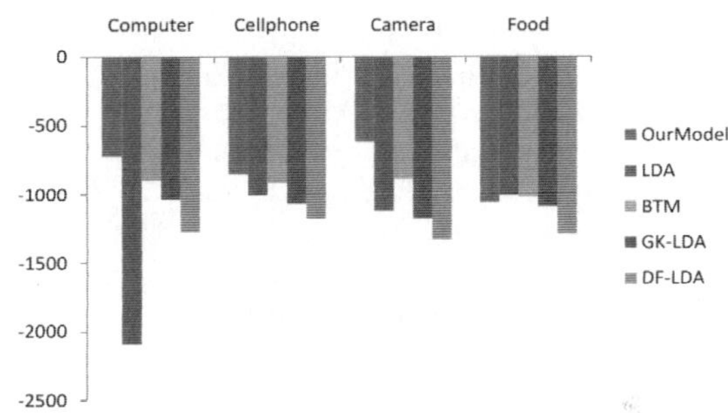


Figure 3: Detailed Topic Coherence score of $T = 15$.

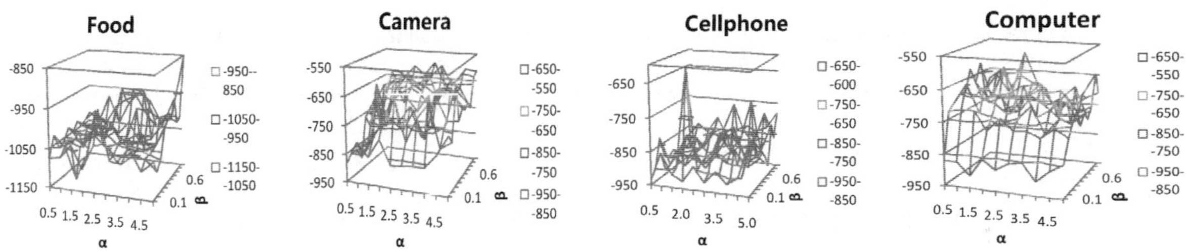


Figure 4: Parameter influences with fixed topic number $T = 15$.

Table 3: Example topics. First row: domain, Second row: inferred topic tag. Errors are highlighted in red.

| Cellphone | | Computer | | Food | | Camera | |
|---|---|---|---|---|---|---|---|
| music | | game | | dinner | | buy | |
| LDA | PTM | LDA | PTM | LDA | PTM | LDA | PTM |
| phone | phone | *buy* | fps | coffee | soup | camera | camera |
| music | music | *make* | disruption | *product* | good | bought | bought |
| iphone | car | games | *dips* | *found* | bread | wanted | pictures |
| *calls* | radio | *time* | playable | *love* | mix | *year* | video |
| play | device | fast | wars | *amazon* | popcorn | *time* | sony |
| bluetooth | sound | play | age | bread | taste | *happy* | *back* |
| hear | quality | people | *pretty* | popcorn | great | purchase | canon |
| *free* | iphone | *thing* | update | eating | *bag* | *day* | battery |
| cell | volume | card | star | *ordered* | flavor | *month* | *time* |
| listen | bluetooth | *full* | empires | *bought* | make | love | price |
| *hands* | *easy* | *product* | laggy | good | coffee | *ago* | lens |
| *charge* | good | *read* | unplayable | taste | eat | *week* | quality |

and Tom M. Mitchell. 2010. Toward an architecture for never-ending language learning. In *Proceedings of the Twenty-Fourth AAAI Conference on Artificial Intelligence, AAAI 2010.*

[Chang et al.2009] Jonathan Chang, Jordan L. Boyd-Graber, Sean Gerrish, Chong Wang, and David M. Blei. 2009. Reading tea leaves: How humans interpret topic models. In *23rd Annual Conference on Neural Information Processing Systems 2009*, pages 288–296.

[Chen et al.2013] Zhiyuan Chen, Arjun Mukherjee, Bing Liu, Meichun Hsu, Malu Castellanos, and Riddhiman Ghosh. 2013. Discovering coherent topics using general knowledge. In *Proceedings of the 22nd ACM international conference on Conference on information & knowledge management*, pages 209–218. ACM.

[Etzioni et al.2005] Oren Etzioni, Michael J. Cafarella, Doug Downey, Ana-Maria Popescu, Tal Shaked, Stephen Soderland, Daniel S. Weld, and Alexander Yates. 2005. Unsupervised named-entity extraction from the web: An experimental study. *Artif. Intell.*, 165(1):91–134.

[Gabrilovich and Markovitch2007] Evgeniy Gabrilovich and Shaul Markovitch. 2007. Computing semantic relatedness using wikipedia-based explicit semantic analysis. In *Proceedings of the 20th International Joint Conference on Artificial Intelligence*, pages 1606–1611.

[Griffiths and Steyvers2004] Thomas L Griffiths and Mark Steyvers. 2004. Finding scientific topics. *Proceedings of the National academy of Sciences of the United States of America*, 101(Suppl 1):5228–5235.

[Gruber et al.2007] Amit Gruber, Yair Weiss, and Michal Rosen-Zvi. 2007. Hidden topic markov models. In *Proceedings of the Eleventh International Conference on Artificial Intelligence and Statistics, AISTATS 2007, San Juan, Puerto Rico, March 21-24, 2007*, pages 163–170.

[Hofmann1999] Thomas Hofmann. 1999. Probabilistic latent semantic indexing. In *Proceedings of the 22nd Annual International ACM SIGIR Conference on Research and Development in Information Retrieval*, pages 50–57.

[Hu et al.2011] Yuening Hu, Jordan L. Boyd-Graber, and Brianna Satinoff. 2011. Interactive topic modeling. In *The 49th Annual Meeting of the Association for Computational Linguistics: Human Language Technologies*, pages 248–257.

[Hua et al.2015] Wen Hua, Zhongyuan Wang, Haixun Wang, Kai Zheng, and Xiaofang Zhou. 2015. Short text understanding through lexical-semantic analysis. In *International Conference on Data Engineering (ICDE).*

[Jagarlamudi et al.2012] Jagadeesh Jagarlamudi, Hal Daum III, and Raghavendra Udupa. 2012. Incorporating lexical priors into topic models. In *13th Conference of the European Chapter of the Association for Computational Linguistics*, pages 204–213.

[Miller1995] George A. Miller. 1995. Wordnet: A lexical database for english. *Commun. ACM*, 38(11):39–41.

[Mimno et al.2011] David M. Mimno, Hanna M. Wallach, Edmund M. Talley, Miriam Leenders, and Andrew McCallum. 2011. Optimizing semantic coherence in topic models. In *Proceedings of the 2011 Conference on Empirical Methods in Natural Language Processing, EMNLP 2011*, pages 262–272.

[Mukherjee and Liu2012] Arjun Mukherjee and Bing Liu. 2012. Aspect extraction through semi-supervised modeling. In *The 50th Annual Meeting of the Association for Computational Linguistics*, pages 339–348.

[Newman et al.2010] David Newman, Youn Noh, Edmund M. Talley, Sarvnaz Karimi, and Timothy Baldwin. 2010. Evaluating topic models for digital libraries. In *Proceedings of the 2010 Joint International Conference on Digital Libraries*, pages 215–224.

[Suchanek et al.2007] Fabian M. Suchanek, Gjergji Kasneci, and Gerhard Weikum. 2007. Yago: a core of semantic knowledge. In *Proceedings of the 16th International Conference on World Wide Web, WWW 2007, Banff, Alberta, Canada, May 8-12, 2007*, pages 697–706.

[Toutanova et al.2003] Kristina Toutanova, Dan Klein, Christopher D. Manning, and Yoram Singer. 2003. Feature-rich part-of-speech tagging with a cyclic dependency network. In *HLT-NAACL 2003, Human Language Technology Conference of the North American Chapter of the Association for Computational Linguistics.*

[Wu et al.2012] Wentao Wu, Hongsong Li, Haixun Wang, and Kenny Qili Zhu. 2012. Probase: a probabilistic taxonomy for text understanding. In *Proceedings of the ACM SIGMOD International Conference on Management of Data, SIGMOD 2012, Scottsdale, AZ, USA, May 20-24, 2012*, pages 481–492.

[Yan et al.2013] Xiaohui Yan, Jiafeng Guo, Yanyan Lan, and Xueqi Cheng. 2013. A biterm topic model for short texts. In *22nd International World Wide Web Conference*, pages 1445–1456.

# Unsupervised Most Frequent Sense Detection using Word Embeddings

**Sudha Bhingardive Dhirendra Singh Rudra Murthy V**
**Hanumant Redkar and Pushpak Bhattacharyya**
Department of Computer Science and Engineering,
Indian Institute of Technology Bombay.
{sudha, dhirendra, rudra, pb}@cse.iitb.ac.in
{hanumantredkar}@gmail.com

## Abstract

An acid test for any new Word Sense Disambiguation (WSD) algorithm is its performance against the Most Frequent Sense (MFS). The field of WSD has found the MFS baseline very hard to beat. Clearly, if WSD researchers had access to MFS values, their striving to better this heuristic will push the WSD frontier. However, getting MFS values requires sense annotated corpus in enormous amounts, which is out of bounds for most languages, even if their WordNets are available. In this paper, we propose an unsupervised method for MFS detection from the untagged corpora, which exploits word embeddings. *We compare the word embedding of a word with all its sense embeddings and obtain the predominant sense with the highest similarity.* We observe significant performance gain for Hindi WSD over the WordNet First Sense (WFS) baseline. As for English, the SemCor baseline is bettered for those words whose frequency is greater than 2. Our approach is language and domain independent.

## 1 Introduction

The MFS baseline is often hard to beat for any WSD system and it is considered as the strongest baseline in WSD (Agirre and Edmonds, 2007). It has been observed that supervised WSD approaches generally outperform the MFS baseline, whereas unsupervised WSD approaches fail to beat this baseline. The MFS baseline can be easily created if we have a large amount of sense annotated corpora. The frequencies of word senses are obtained from the available sense annotated corpora. Creating such a costly resource for all languages is infeasible, looking at the amount of time and money required. Hence, unsupervised approaches have received widespread attention as they do not use any sense annotated corpora.

In this paper, we propose an unsupervised method for MFS detection. We explore the use of word embeddings for finding the most frequent sense. We have restricted our approach only to nouns. Our approach can be easily ported to various domains and across languages.

The roadmap of the paper is as follows. Section 2 describes our approach - 'UMFS-WE'. Experiments are given in Section 3. Results and Discussions are given in Section 4. Section 5 mentions the related work. Finally, Section 6 concludes the paper and points to future work.

## 2 Our Approach: UMFS-WE

Word Embeddings have recently gained popularity among Natural Language Processing community (Bengio et al., 2003; Collobert et al., 2011). They are based on Distributional Hypothesis which works under the assumption that similar words occur in similar contexts (Harris, 1954). Word Embeddings represent each word with a low-dimensional real valued vector with similar words occurring closer in that space.

In our approach, we use the word embedding of a given word and compare it with all its sense embeddings to find the most frequent sense of that word. Sense embeddings are created using the WordNet based features in the light of the extended Lesk algorithm (Banerjee and Pedersen, 2003) as described



*Human Language Technologies: The 2015 Annual Conference of the North American Chapter of the ACL*, pages 1238–1243,
Denver, Colorado, May 31 – June 5, 2015. 

later in this paper.

## 2.1 Training of Word Embeddings

Word embeddings for English and Hindi have been trained using *word2vec*[1] tool (Mikolov et al., 2013). This tool provides two broad techniques for creating word embeddings: Continuous Bag of Words (CBOW) and Skip-gram model. The CBOW model predicts the current word based on the surrounding context, whereas, the Skip-gram model tries to maximize the probability of a word based on other words in the same sentence (Mikolov et al., 2013).

**Word Embeddings for English**

We have used publicly available pre-trained word embeddings for English which were trained on Google News dataset[2] (about 100 billion words). These word embeddings are available for around 3 million words and phrases. Each of these word embeddings have 300-dimensions.

**Word Embeddings for Hindi**

Word embeddings for Hindi have been trained on Bojar's (2014) corpus. This corpus contains 44 million sentences. Here, the Skip-gram model is used for obtaining word embeddings. The dimensions are set as 200 and the window size as 7 (i.e. $w = 7$).

We used the test of similarity to establish the correctness of these word embeddings. We observed that given a word and its embedding, the list of words ranked by similarity score had at the top of the list those words which were actually similar to the given word.

## 2.2 Sense Embeddings

Sense embeddings are similar to word embeddings which are low dimensional real valued vectors. Sense embeddings are obtained by taking the average of word embeddings of each word in the sense-bag. The sense-bag for each sense of a word is obtained by extracting the context words from the WordNet such as synset members (S), content words in the gloss (G), content words in the example sentence (E), synset members of the hypernymy-hyponymy synsets (HS), content words in the gloss of the hypernymy-hyponymy synsets (HG) and content words in the example sentence of the hypernymy-hyponymy synsets (HE).

We consider word embeddings of all words in the sense-bag as a cluster of points and choose the sense embedding as the centroid of this cluster.

Consider a word $w$ with $k$ senses $w_{S_1}, w_{S_2}, ....w_{S_k}$ taken from the WordNet. Sense embeddings are created using the following formula,

$$\texttt{vec}(w_{S_i}) = \frac{\sum_{x \in \texttt{SB}(w_{S_i})} \texttt{vec}(x)}{N} \quad (1)$$

where, $\texttt{N}$ is the number of words present in the sense-bag $\texttt{SB}(w_{S_i})$ and $\texttt{SB}(w_{S_i})$ is the sense-bag for the sense $w_{S_i}$ which is given as,

$$\texttt{SB}(w_{S_i}) = \{x | x \in \texttt{Features}(w_{S_i})\}$$

where, $\texttt{Features}(w_{S_i})$ includes the WordNet based features for $w_{S_i}$ which are mentioned earlier in this section.

As we can see in Figure 1, consider the sense-bag created for the senses of a word *table*. Here, the word *table* has three senses, $S_1$ {*a set of data arranged in rows and columns*}, $S_2$ {*a piece of furniture having a smooth flat top that is usually supported by one or more vertical legs*} and $S_3$ {*a company of people assembled at a table for a meal or game*}. The corresponding word embeddings of all words in the sense-bag will act as a cluster as shown in the Figure. Here, there are three clusters with centroids $C_1$, $C_2$, $C_3$ which corresponds to the three sense embeddings of the word *table*.

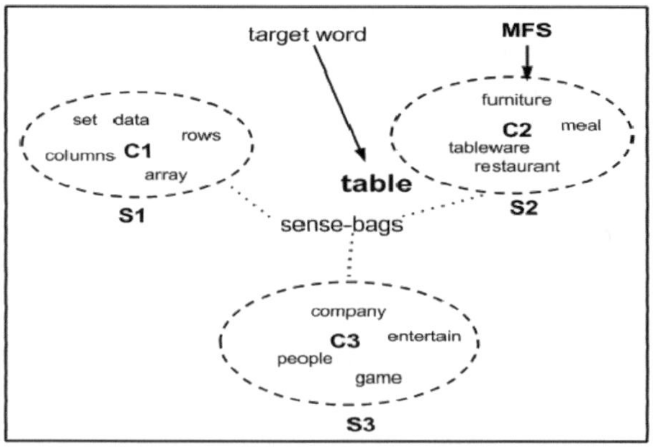


Figure 1: Most Frequent Sense (MFS) detection using Word Embeddings and Sense Embeddings

[1] https://code.google.com/p/word2vec/

[2] Downloaded from https://code.google.com/p/word2vec/

### 2.3 Most Frequent Sense Identification

For a given word $w$, we obtain its word embedding and sense embeddings as discussed earlier. We treat the most frequent sense identification problem as finding the closest cluster centroid (i.e. sense embedding) with respect to a given word. We use the cosine similarity as the similarity measure. The most frequent sense is obtained by using the following formulation,

$$\texttt{MFS}_w = \underset{ws_i}{\arg\max}\ \cos(\texttt{vec}(w), \texttt{vec}(ws_i))$$

where, $\texttt{vec}(w)$ is the word embedding for word $w$, $ws_i$ is the $i^{th}$ sense of word $w$ and $\texttt{vec}(ws_i)$ is the sense embedding for $ws_i$.

As seen in Figure 1, the word embedding of the word *table* is more closer to the centroid $C_2$ as compared to the centroids $C_1$ and $C_3$. Therefore, the MFS of the word *table* is chosen as $S_2$ $\{$*a piece of furniture having a smooth flat top that is usually supported by one or more vertical legs*$\}$.

## 3 Experiments

We have performed several experiments to compare the accuracy of UMFS-WE for Hindi and English WSD. The experiments are restricted to only polysemous nouns. For Hindi, a newspaper sense-tagged dataset of around 80,000 polysemous noun entries was used. This is an in-house data. For English, SENSEVAL-2 and SENSEVAL-3 datasets[3] were used. The accuracy of WSD experiments was measured in terms of precision (P), recall (R) and F-Score (F-1).

To compare the performance of UMFS-WE approach, we have used the WFS baseline for Hindi, while the SemCor[4] baseline is used for English. In the WFS baseline, the first sense in the WordNet is used for WSD. For Hindi, the WFS is manually determined by a lexicographer based on his/her intuition. In SemCor baseline, the most frequent sense obtained from the SemCor sense tagged corpus is used for WSD. For English, the SemCor is considered as the most powerful baseline for WSD.

[3]SENSEVAL-2 and SENSEVAL-3 datasets are downloaded from http://web.eecs.umich.edu/ mihalcea/downloads.html

[4]http://web.eecs.umich.edu/m̃ihalcea/downloads.html#semcor

## 4 Results and Discussions

In this section, we present and discuss results of the experiments performed on Hindi and English WSD. Results of Hindi WSD on the newspaper dataset are given in Table 1, while English WSD results on SENSEVAL-2 and SENSEVAL-3 datasets are given in Table 2 and Table 3 respectively. The UMFS-WE approach achieves F-1 of 62% for the Hindi dataset and 52.34%, 43.28% for English SENSEVAL-2, SENSEVAL-3 datasets respectively.

| System | P | R | F-1 |
|---|---|---|---|
| UMFS-WE | 62.43 | 61.58 | 62.00 |
| WFS | 61.73 | 59.31 | 60.49 |

Table 1: Results of Hindi WSD on the newspaper dataset

| System | P | R | F-1 |
|---|---|---|---|
| UMFS-WE | 52.39 | 52.27 | 52.34 |
| SemCor | 61.72 | 58.16 | 59.88 |

Table 2: Results of English WSD on the SENSEVAL-2 dataset

| System | P | R | F-1 |
|---|---|---|---|
| UMFS-WE | 43.34 | 43.22 | 43.28 |
| SemCor | 66.57 | 64.89 | 65.72 |

Table 3: Results of English WSD on the SENSEVAL-3 dataset

We have performed several tests using various combinations of WordNet based features (refer Section 2.2) for Hindi and English WSD, as shown in Table 4 and Table 5 respectively. We study its impact on the performance of the system for Hindi and English WSD and present a detailed analysis below.

### 4.1 Hindi

Our approach, UMFS-WE achieves better performance for Hindi WSD as compared to the WFS baseline. We have used various WordNet based features for comparing results. It is observed that synset members alone are not sufficient for identifying the most frequent sense. This is because some of synsets have a very small number of synset members. Synset members along with gloss members improve results as gloss members are more direct in

| WordNet Features | P | R | F-1 |
|---|---|---|---|
| S | 51.73 | 38.13 | 43.89 |
| S+G | 53.31 | 52.39 | 52.85 |
| S+G+E | 56.61 | 55.84 | 56.22 |
| S+G+E+HS | 59.53 | 58.72 | 59.12 |
| S+G+E+HG | 60.57 | 59.75 | 60.16 |
| S+G+E+HE | 60.12 | 59.3 | 59.71 |
| S+G+E+HS+HG | 57.59 | 56.81 | 57.19 |
| S+G+E+HS+HE | 58.93 | 58.13 | 58.52 |
| S+G+E+HG+HE | **62.43** | **61.58** | **62.00** |
| S+G+E+HS+HG+HE | 58.56 | 57.76 | 58.16 |

Table 4: UMFS-WE accuracy on Hindi WSD with various WordNet features

defining the sense. The other reason is to bring down the impact of topic drift which may have occurred because of polysemous synset members. Similarly, it is observed that adding hypernym/hyponym gloss members gives better performance compared to hypernym/hyponym synset members. Example sentence members also provide additional information in determining the MFS of a word, which further improves the results.

On the whole, we achieve the best performance when S, G, E, HG and HE features are used together. This is shown in Table 4.

| WordNet Features | P | R | F-1 |
|---|---|---|---|
| S | 22.89 | 22.82 | 22.85 |
| S+G | 32.72 | 32.64 | 32.68 |
| S+G+E | 30.87 | 30.79 | 30.84 |
| S+G+E+HS | 33.46 | 33.37 | 33.42 |
| S+G+E+HG | 39.36 | 39.26 | 39.31 |
| S+G+E+HE | 29.77 | 29.69 | 29.73 |
| S+G+E+HS+HG | 46.00 | 45.89 | 45.95 |
| S+G+E+HS+HE | 39.11 | 39.02 | 39.06 |
| S+G+E+HG+HE | 41.82 | 41.72 | 41.77 |
| S+G+E+HS+HG+HE | **52.39** | **52.27** | **52.34** |
| S+G+HS+HG | 51.17 | 51.04 | 51.11 |

Table 5: UMFS-WE accuracy on English WSD with various WordNet features

### 4.2 English

We achieve good performance for English WSD on the SENSEVAL-2 dataset, whereas the performance on the SENSEVAL-3 dataset is comparatively poor. Here also, synset members alone perform badly. However, adding gloss members improves results. The same is observed for hypernym/hyponym gloss members. Using example sentence members of either synsets or their hypernymy/hyponymy synsets bring down the performance of the system. This is also justified when we consider only synset members, gloss members, hypernym/hyponym synset members, hypernym/hyponym gloss members which give a score close to the best obtained score. All the features (S, G, E, HS, HG & HE), when used together, give the best performance as shown in Table 5.

Also, we have calculated the F-1 score for Hindi and English WSD for increasing thresholds on the frequency of nouns appearing in the corpus. This is depicted in Figure 2 and Figure 3 for Hindi and English WSD respectively. Here, in both plots, it is clearly shown that, as the frequency of nouns in the corpus increases our approach outperforms baselines for both Hindi and English WSD. On the other hand, SemCor baseline accuracy decreases for those words which occur more than 8 times in the test corpus. This is depicted in Figure 3. There are 15 such frequent word types. The main reason for low SemCor accuracy is that these words occur very few times with their MFS as listed by the SemCor baseline. For example, the word *cell* never appears with its MFS (as listed by SemCor baseline) in the SENSEVAL-2 dataset.

As opposed to baselines, our approach gives a feasible way to extract predominant senses in an unsupervised setup. Our approach is domain independent sothat it can be very easily adapted to a domain specific corpus. To get the domain specific word embeddings, we simply have to run the *word2vec* program on the domain specific corpus. The domain specific word embeddings can be used to get the MFS for the domain of interest. Our approach is language independent. However, due to time and space constraints we have performed our experiments on only Hindi and English languages.

## 5 Related Work

McCarthy et al. (2007) proposed an unsupervised approach for finding the predominant sense using an automatic thesaurus. They used WordNet similarity for identifying the predominant sense. Their approach outperforms the SemCor baseline for words

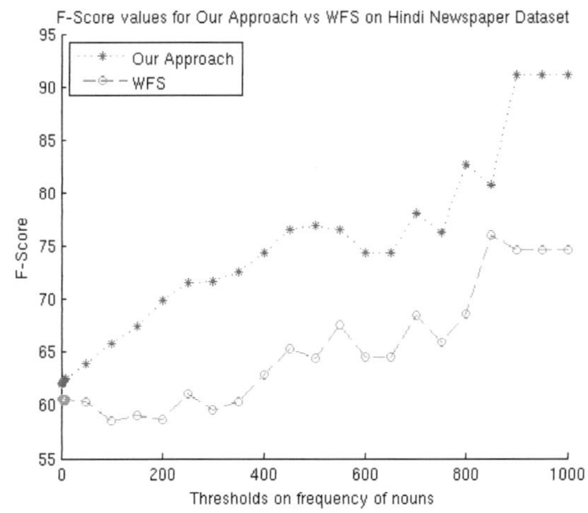


Figure 2: UMFS-WE accuracy on Hindi WSD for words with various frequency thresholds in Newspaper dataset

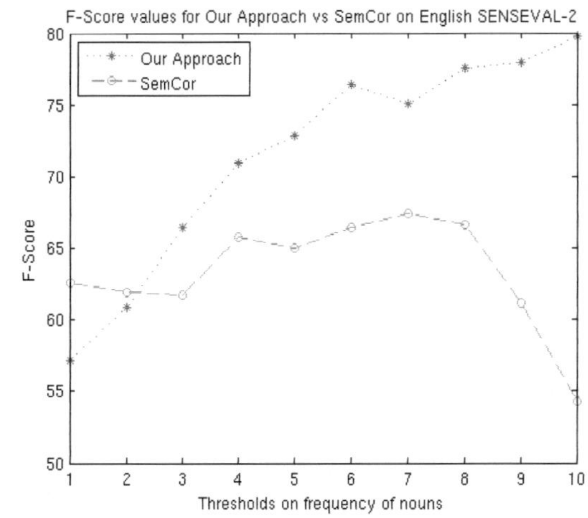


Figure 3: UMFS-WE accuracy on English WSD for words with various frequency thresholds in SENSEVAL-2 dataset

with SemCor frequency below five. Buitelaar et al. (2001) presented the knowledge based approach for ranking GermaNet synsets on specific domains. Lapata et al. (2004) worked on detecting the predominant sense of verbs where verb senses are taken from the Levin classes. Our approach is similar to that of McCarthy et al. (2007) as we are also learning predominant senses from the untagged text.

## 6 Conclusion and Future Work

In our paper, we presented an unsupervised approach for finding the most frequent sense for nouns by exploiting word embeddings. Our approach is tested on Hindi and English WSD. It is found that our approach outperforms the WFS baseline for Hindi. As the frequency of noun increases in the corpus, our approach outperforms the baseline for both Hindi and English WSD. Our approach can be easily ported to various domains and across languages. In future, we plan to improve on the performance of our model for English, even for infrequent words. Also, we will explore this approach for other languages and for other parts-of-speech.

## 7 Acknowledgments

We would like to thank Mrs. Rajita Shukla, Mrs. Jaya Saraswati and Mrs. Laxmi Kashyap for their enormous efforts in the creation of the WordNet First Baseline for the Hindi WordNet. We also thank TDIL, DeitY for their continued support.

## References

Satanjeev Banerjee and Ted Pedersen. 2003. *Extended Gloss Overlaps as a Measure of Semantic Relatedness.* In Proceedings of the Eighteenth International Joint Conference on Artificial Intelligence, pp 805-810.

Mohit Bansal, Kevin Gimpel and Karen Livescu. 2014. *Tailoring Continuous Word Representations for Dependency Parsing.* Proceedings of ACL 2014.

Ondřej Bojar, Diatka Vojtěch, Rychlý Pavel, Straňák Pavel, Suchomel Vít, Tamchyna Aleš and Zeman Daniel. 2014. *HindEnCorp - Hindi-English and Hindi-only Corpus for Machine Translation.* Proceedings of the Ninth International Conference on Language Resources and Evaluation (LREC'14).

Paul Buitelaar and Bogdan Sacaleanu. 2001. *Ranking and selecting synsets by domain relevance.* Proceedings of WordNet and Other Lexical Resources, NAACL 2001 Workshop.

Xinxiong Chen, Zhiyuan Liu and Maosong Sun. 2014. *A Unified Model for Word Sense Representation and Disambiguation.* Proceedings of ACL 2014.

Ronan Collobert, Jason Weston, Léon Bottou, Michael Karlen, Koray Kavukcuoglu, Pavel P. Kuksa. 2011. *Natural Language Processing (almost) from Scratch.* CoRR, http://arxiv.org/abs/1103.0398.

Agirre Eneko and Edmonds Philip. 2007. *Word Sense Disambiguation: Algorithms and Applications.* Springer Publishing Company, Incorporated, ISBN:1402068700 9781402068706.

Z. Harris. 1954. *Distributional structure.* Word 10(23):146-162.

Tomas Mikolov, Chen Kai, Corrado Greg and Dean Jeffrey. 2013. *Efficient Estimation of Word Representations in Vector Space.* In Proceedings of Workshop at ICLR, 2013.

Diana McCarthy, Rob Koeling, Julie Weeds and John Carroll. 2007. *Unsupervised Acquisition of Predominant Word Senses.* Computational Linguistics, 33 (4) pp 553-590.

Mirella Lapata and Chris Brew. 2004. *Verb class disambiguation using informative priors.* Computational Linguistics, 30(1):45-75.

Bengio Yoshua, Ducharme Réjean, Vincent Pascal and Janvin Christian. 2003. *A Neural Probabilistic Language Model.* J. Mach. Learn. Res., issn = 1532-4435, pp 1137-1155.

# Chain based RNN for Relation Classification

**Javid Ebrahimi** and **Dejing Dou**
Department of Computer and Information Science, University of Oregon
Eugene, Oregon 97403, USA
{javid,dou}@cs.uoregon.edu

## Abstract

We present a novel approach for relation classification, using a recursive neural network (RNN), based on the shortest path between two entities in a dependency graph. Previous works on RNN are based on constituency-based parsing because phrasal nodes in a parse tree can capture compositionality in a sentence. Compared with constituency-based parse trees, dependency graphs can represent relations more compactly. This is particularly important in sentences with distant entities, where the parse tree spans words that are not relevant to the relation. In such cases RNN cannot be trained effectively in a timely manner. However, due to the lack of phrasal nodes in dependency graphs, application of RNN is not straightforward. In order to tackle this problem, we utilize dependency constituent units called *chains*. Our experiments on two relation classification datasets show that Chain based RNN provides a shallower network, which performs considerably faster and achieves better classification results.

## 1 Introduction

Relation extraction is the task of finding relations between entities in text, which is useful for several tasks such as information extraction, summarization, and question answering (Wu and Weld, 2010). For instance, in the sentence: those "cancers" were caused by radiation "exposures," the two entities have a *cause-effect* relation. As reported in detail (SaraWagi, 2008), one approach to the problem involves supervised methods where the models rely on lexical, syntactic, and semantic features to classify relations between pairs of entities. The downside of this approach is that one has to retrain the model for other domains with different target relations. Thus it is not scalable to the web, where thousands of (previously-unseen) relations exist (Banko et al., 2007). To address this problem, Open Information Extraction is proposed, which does not require supervision. In these systems (Banko et al., 2007; Mausam et al., 2012), patterns based on lexical, syntactic, POS, and dependency features are extracted. While these patterns give good precision, they suffer from low recall (Banko and Etzioni, 2008). This is because they fail to extract patterns which have not been pre-specified, and thereby are unable to generalize.

Recursive Neural Network (RNN) has proven to be highly successful in capturing semantic compositionality in text and has improved the results of several Natural Language Processing tasks (Socher et al., 2012; Socher et al., 2013). Previous applications of Recursive Neural Networks (RNN) to supervised relation extraction (Socher et al., 2012; Hashimoto et al., 2013; Khashabi, 2013) are based on constituency-based parsers. These RNNs may span words that do not contribute to the relation. We investigate the incorporation of dependency parsing into RNN that can give a more compact representation of relations.

Our contribution is introducing a compositional account of dependency graphs that can match RNN's recursive nature, and can be applied to relation classification. We study different data structures that incorporate dependency trees into RNNs.



*Human Language Technologies: The 2015 Annual Conference of the North American Chapter of the ACL*, pages 1244–1249,
Denver, Colorado, May 31 – June 5, 2015. 

One of these structures produces a compact full binary tree that compared with the constituency-based RNN, has higher classification accuracy and saves up to 70% in the training time.

## 2 Related Work

At the core of deep learning techniques for NLP, lies the vector based word representation, which maps words to an n-dimensional space. Having word vectors as parameters makes neural models flexible in finding different word embeddings for separate tasks (Collobert and Weston, 2008). Recursive Neural Network (RNN) is a recursive deep architecture that can learn feature representation of words, phrases and sentences.

As an example, in (Socher et al., 2010), each node in the parse tree is associated with a vector and at each internal node $p$, there exists a composition function that takes its input from its children $c_1 \in \mathbb{R}^n$ and $c_2 \in \mathbb{R}^n$.

$$p = f(c_1, c_2) = tanh(W\begin{bmatrix} c_1 \\ c_2 \end{bmatrix} + b) \quad (1)$$

The matrix $W \in \mathbb{R}^{n \times 2n}$ is the global composition parameter, $b$ is the bias term, and the output of the function $p \in \mathbb{R}^n$ is another vector in the space of inputs. Socher et al. (2012) propose Matrix-Vector Recursive Neural Network (MV-RNN), where instead of using only vectors for words, an additional matrix for each word is used to capture operator semantics in language. To apply RNN to relation classification, they find the path in the parse tree between the two entities and apply compositions bottom up. Hashimoto et al. (2013) follow the same design but introduce a different composition function. They make use of word-POS pairs and use untied weights based on phrase categories of the pair.

Socher et al. (2014) introduce a dependency-based RNN that extracts features from a dependency graph whose composition function has major differences from ours. Their function consists of a linear sum of unary compositions, while our function is a binary composition of children. Our work is also related to (Bunescu and Mooney, 2005), where the similarity between the words on the path connecting two entities in the dependency graph is used to devise a Kernel function.

## 3 Chain based RNN

While constituency-based parsing seems to be a reasonable choice for compositionality in general, it may not be the best choice for all NLP tasks. In particular, for relation classification, one may prefer to use a structure that encodes more information about the relations between the words in a sentence. To this end, we use dependency-based parsing that provides a one-to-one correspondence between nodes in a dependency graph (DG).

DGs are significantly different from constituency parse trees since they lack phrasal nodes. More precisely, the internal nodes where the nonlinear combinations take place, do not exist in DGs. Therefore, we modify the original RNN and present a dependency-based RNN for relation classification. In our experiments, we restrict ourselves to trees where each dependent has only one head. We also use the example in Figure 1 for better illustration; in this example the arguments of the relation are *child* and *cradle*.

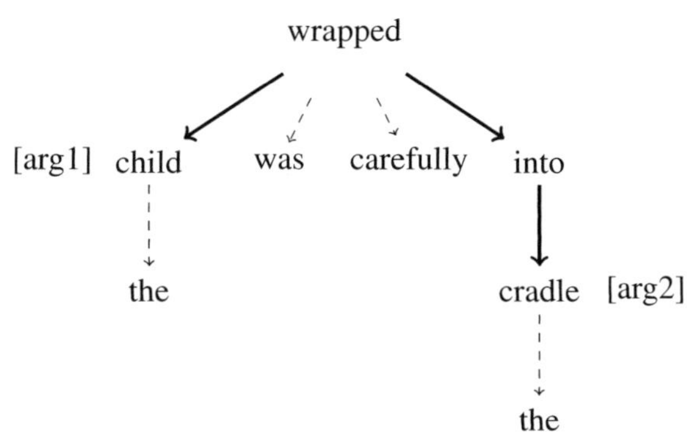


Figure 1: DG: the child was carefully wrapped into the cradle.

We apply compositions on the words on the shortest path between entities. From a linguistic point of view, this type of composition is related to the concept of *chain* or dependency constituent unit in DGs (Osborne, 2005).

> **Chain**: The words A ... B ... C ... (order irrelevant) form a chain iff A immediately dominates (is the parent of) B and C, or if A immediately dominates B and B immediately dominates C.

Based on this definition, *child wrapped, into cradle, wrapped into cradle, child wrapped into cradle* all qualify as a chain while *child was* does not. To illustrate the motivation to use dependency parsing, consider the sentence:

> The hidden "camera," found by a security guard, was hidden in a business card-sized "box" placed at an unmanned ATM.

The shortest path between entities is:

camera $\rightarrow$ found $\leftarrow$ hidden $\leftarrow$ in $\leftarrow$ box

Using dependency parsing, we only need four compositions for this chain, which results in 86% decrease against constituency-based parsing.

Now with all words represented as vectors, we need to find a reduced dimensional representation of the chain in fixed size. To this end, we transform this chain to a data structure, the root of which represents the extracted features.

### 3.1 Fixed Structure

We cannot use an off-the-shelf syntax parser to create a tree for the chain because the chain may not necessarily be a coherent English statement. Thus, we build two Directed Acyclic Graph (DAG) structures by heuristics. The idea is to start from argument(s) and recursively combine dependent-head pairs to the (common) ancestor i.e., each head is combined with the subtree below itself. In the simplest case: $a \rightarrow b$ results in $p = f(a, b)$.

The subtlety of this approach lies in the treatment of the word with two dependents. We use two methods to handle such a node: 1) including it in only one composition as in Figure 2 or 2) including it in two compositions and sum their results as in Figure 3.

Both structures produce a DAG where each internal node has two children and there is only one node with two non-leaf children. We now prove that this greedy algorithm results in a full binary tree for the first case. We skip the proof of the algorithm for the second case which produces a full binary DAG.

**Lemma**: *There is at most one node with exactly two none-leaf children in the tree.*

*Proof.* If one of the arguments is an ancestor of the other argument e.g., arg1 $\rightarrow$ ... $\rightarrow$ arg2, then

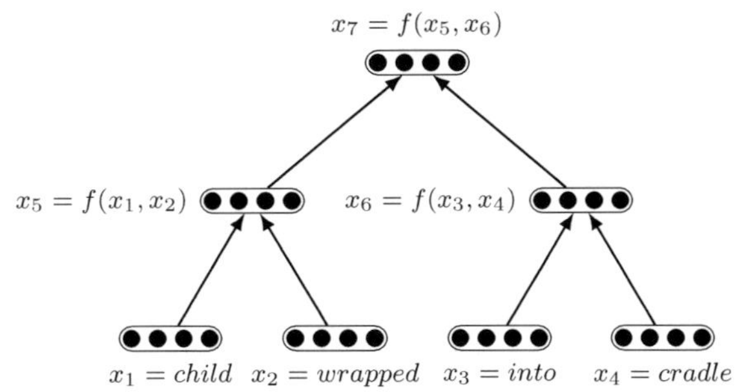


Figure 2: a fixed tree example

obviously every head on the chain has exactly one dependent. Combination of each head and its subtree's output vector results in a full binary node in the tree. If the arguments have a common ancestor $p$ e.g., arg1 $\rightarrow$ ... $p$ ... $\leftarrow$ arg2, then that particular node has two dependents. In this case, the parent is combined with either its left or right subtrees, and its result is combined with the output of the other child. No other head has this property; otherwise, $p$ is not the common ancestor.

**Theorem**: *The algorithm converts a chain to a full binary tree.*

*Proof.* The leaves of the tree are words of the chain. By applying the lemma, there exists one root and all internal nodes have exactly two children.

Note that we only consider dependency trees as the input; so each pair of arguments has a unique common ancestor. Concretely, having a connected graph leads to at least one such ancestor and having only one head for each node (being a tree) leads to exactly one such ancestor.

### 3.2 Predicted Tree Structure

Instead of using a deterministic approach to create the tree, we can use Recursive Autoencoders (RAE) to find the best representation of the chain. This model is similar to (Socher et al., 2011) with some modification in implementation. Socher et al. (2011) use a semi supervised method where the objective function is a weighted sum of the supervised and unsupervised error. We achieved better results with a pipeline where first, during pre-training, the unsupervised autoencoder predicts the structure of RNN and then during training, the supervised cross entropy error is minimized.

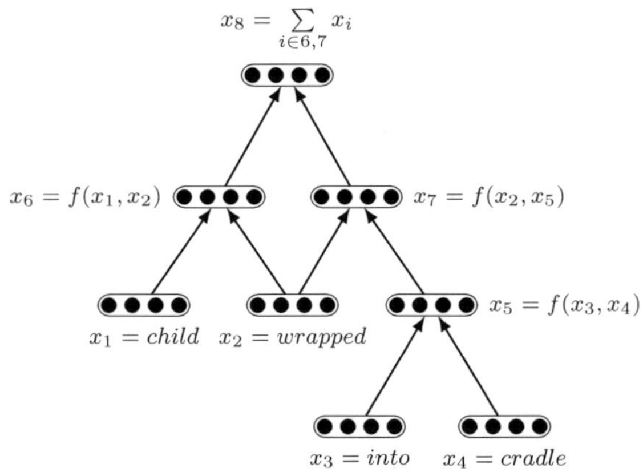


Figure 3: a fixed DAG example

## 4 Learning

To predict the label of the relation, a softmax classifier is added on top of the tree. i.e., $y_i = softmax(P_n^T W^{label})$ where $L \in \mathbb{R}^k$, $k$ is the number of classes, and $P_n$ is the final vector on top of the tree for sentence $n$. The objective function is the sum of cross entropy error at all the nodes, for all the sentences in the training set.

$$E(\theta) = -\sum_n \sum_k t_n^k \log y_n^k + \frac{\lambda}{2} \parallel \theta \parallel^2 \quad (2)$$

The vectors for target, predicted labels, and regularization parameters are denoted by $t_n$, $y_n$ and $\lambda$ respectively. We initialize the word vectors with pretrained 50-dimensional words from (Collobert and Weston, 2008) and initialize other parameters by a normal distribution with mean of 0 and standard deviation of 0.01. Derivatives are computed by backpropagation through structure (Goller and Kuchler, 1996) and L-BFGS is used for optimization.

## 5 Experiments

In this section we discuss our experimental results on two datasets for relation classification. To derive the dependency tree for each sentence, we use arc-eager MaltParser (Goldberg and Nivre, 2012). We set the hyper-parameters through a validation set for the first dataset and use them for the second dataset too. Similar to the previous works, a few internal features were also added e.g., depth of the tree, distance between entities, context words, and the type of dependencies in our model. We found that using dependency types inside the composition function as in typed functions worsens the results.

### 5.1 SemEval-2010 Task 8

This data set consists of 10017 sentences and nine types of relations between nominals (Hendrickx et al., 2010). Table 1 compares the results of our tree based chain RNN (C-RNN), DAG based chain RNN (DC-RNN) and the autoencoder based one (C-RNN-RAE) with other RNN models and the best system participating (Rink and Harabagiu, 2010) in the task. Evaluation of the systems is done by comparing the F-measure of their best runs. The best system (Rink and Harabagiu, 2010) uses SVM with many sets of features. We add some external features using supersense sequence tagger (Ciaramita and Altun, 2006). Adding POS tags, WordNet hypernyms, and named entity tags (NER) of the two arguments helps C-RNN improve the results.

We implement SDT-RNN (Socher et al., 2014) which has similar complexity as our model but has significantly lower F-measure. SDT-RNN also performs much better when considering only the words on the path between entities; confirming our hypothesis about the effectiveness of chains. This can be attributed to the intuitive advantage of dependency trees where the shortest path between entities captures most of the information about the relation (Bunescu and Mooney, 2005).

As it can bee seen in Table 1, C-RNN achieves the best results. The baseline RNN, uses a global composition function and $\mathbb{R}^{50}$ vectors for each word. We also use the same number of model parameters.

The advantage of our approach is that our models are computationally less expensive compared with other RNN models. MV-RNN (Socher et al., 2012) uses an additional matrix $\mathbb{R}^{50\times 50}$ for each word, resulting in a 50 fold increase in the number of model parameters. POS-RNN (Hashimoto et al., 2013) uses untied weight matrices and POS based word vectors that results in about 100% increase in the number of model parameters compared with C-RNN.

Relations with long distances between entities are harder to classify. This is illustrated in Figure 4 where MV-RNN and C-RNN are compared. Considering three bins for the distance between two en-

| Method | F-measure | Feature sets |
|---|---|---|
| RNN | 74.8 | - |
| SDT-RNN | 75.12 | - |
| MV-RNN | 79.1 | - |
| POS-RNN | 79.4 | - |
| DC-RNN | 77.36 | - |
| C-RNN-RAE | 78.78 | - |
| C-RNN | **79.68** | - |
| SVM | 82.2 | POS, WordNet, Levine classes, PropBank, FrameNet, TextRunner, paraphrases, Google *n*-grams, NormLex-Plus, morphological features, dependency parse features |
| MV-RNN | 82.4 | POS, NER, WordNet |
| C-RNN | **82.66** | POS, NER, WordNet |

Table 1: Results on SemEval 2010 relation classification task with the feature sets used. C-RNN outperforms all RNN based models. By including three extra features, it achieves the state-of-the-art performance.

tities, the figure shows what fraction of test instances are misclassified in each bin. Both classifiers make more errors when the distance between entities is longer than 10. The performance of the two classifiers for distances less than five is quite similar while C-RNN has the advantage in classifying more relations correctly when the distance increases.

### 5.2 SemEval-2013 Task 9.b

To further illustrate the advantage of C-RNN over MV-RNN, we evaluate our work on another data set. See Table 2. In this task, the goal is to extract interactions between drug mentions in text. The corpus (Segura-Bedmar et al., 2013) consists of 1,017 texts that were manually annotated with a total of 5021 drug-drug interactions of four types: *mechanism, effect, advise* and *int.*

| Method | Precision | Recall | F=measure |
|---|---|---|---|
| MV-RNN | 74.07 | 65.53 | 67.84 |
| C-RNN | **75.31** | **66.19** | **68.64** |

Table 2: Results on SemEval 2013 Drug-Drug Interaction task

### 5.3 Training Time

Dependency graphs can represent relations more compactly by utilizing only the words on the shortest path between entities. C-RNN uses a sixth of neural computations of MV-RNN. More precisely, there is an 83% decrease in the number of *tanh* evaluations. Consequently, as demonstrated by Figure 5, C-RNN runs 3.21 and 1.95 times faster for SemEval 2010 and SemEval 2013 respectively.

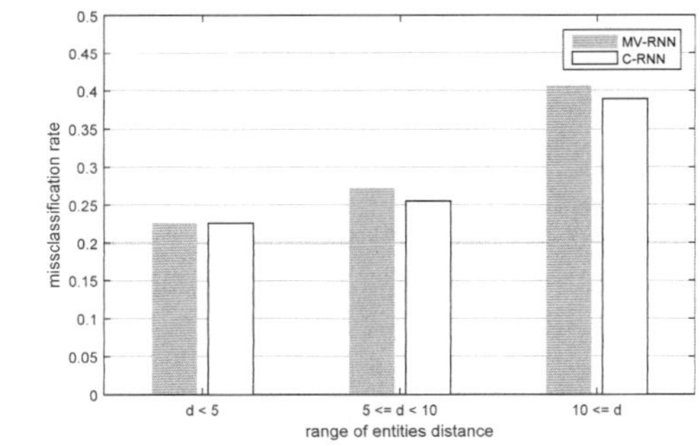


Figure 4: Misclassification based on entities distance in three bins. More errors occur with entities separated by more than ten words. C-RNN performs better in bottleneck long distances.

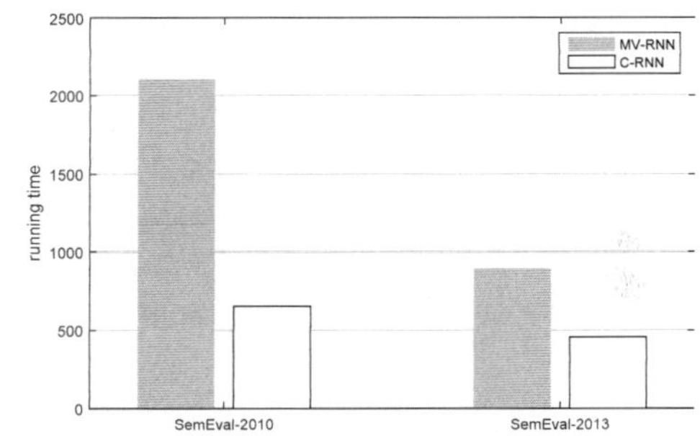


Figure 5: Training time measured by seconds. Experiments were run on a cluster node with 6 core 2.66GHz cpu.

## 6 Conclusions

Recently, Recursive Neural Network (RNN) has found a wide appeal in the Machine Learning community. This deep architecture has been applied in several NLP tasks including relation classification. We present an RNN architecture based on a compositional account of dependency graphs. The proposed RNN model is based on the shortest path between entities in a dependency graph. The resulting shallow network is superior for supervised learning in terms of speed and accuracy. We improve the classification results and save up to 70% in training time compared with a constituency-based RNN . The limitation of our Chain based RNN is that it assumes the named entities to be known in advance. This requires a separate named entity recognizer and cannot extract the entities jointly with the relation classifier.

## Acknowledgment

This work is partially supported by the NIH grant R01GM103309.

## References


Michele Banko and Oren Etzioni. 2008. The tradeoffs between open and traditional relation extraction. In *Proceedings of ACL*, pages 28–36.

Michele Banko, Michael J Cafarella, Stephen Soderland, Matt Broadhead, and Oren Etzioni. 2007. Open information extraction from the web. In *Proceedings of IJCAI*, pages 2670–2676.

Razvan Bunescu and Raymond J. Mooney. 2005. A Shortest Path Dependency Kernel for Relation Extraction . In *Proceedings of HLT/EMNLP*, pages 724–731.

Massimiliano Ciaramita and Yasemin Altun. 2006. Broad-coverage sense disambiguation and information extraction with a supersense sequence tagger. In *Proceedings of EMNLP*, pages 594–602.

R. Collobert and J. Weston. 2008. A unified architecture for natural language processing: Deep neural networks with multitask learning. In *Proceedings of ICML*, pages 160–167.

Yoav Goldberg and Joakim Nivre. 2012. A dynamic oracle for arc-eager dependency parsing. In *Proceedings of COLING*, pages 959–976.

Christoph Goller and Andreas Kuchler. 1996. Learning task-dependent distributed representations by backpropagation through structure. In *Proceedings of ICNN*, pages 347–352.

Kazuma Hashimoto, Makoto Miwa, Yoshimasa Tsuruoka, and Takashi Chikayama. 2013. Simple customization of recursive neural networks for semantic relation classification. In *Proceedings of EMNLP*, pages 1372–1376.

Iris Hendrickx, Su Nam Kim, Zornitsa Kozareva, Preslav Nakov, Diarmuid Ó Séaghdha, Sebastian Padó, Marco Pennacchiotti, Lorenza Romano, and Stan Szpakowicz. 2010. Semeval-2010 task 8: Multi-way classification of semantic relations between pairs of nominals. In *Proceedings of SemEval*, pages 33–38.

Daniel Khashabi. 2013. On the recursive neural networks for relation extraction and entity recognition. Technical report, UIUC.

Mausam, Michael D Schmitz, Robert E. Bart, Stephen Soderland, and Oren Etzioni. 2012. Open Language Learning for Information Extraction . In *Proceedings of EMNLP*, pages 523–534.

Timothy Osborne. 2005. Beyond the constituent: a dependency grammar analysis of chains. *Folia Linguistica*, 39(3-4):251–297.

Bryan Rink and Sanda Harabagiu. 2010. Utd: Classifying semantic relations by combining lexical and semantic resources. In *Proceedings of SemaEval*, pages 256–259.

Sunita SaraWagi. 2008. Information Extraction. In *Foundations and Trends in Databases,Volume 1 Issue 3*, pages 261–377.

Isabel Segura-Bedmar, Paloma Martínez, and María Herrero Zazo. 2013. Semeval-2013 task 9 : Extraction of drug-drug interactions from biomedical texts (DDIExtraction 2013). In *Proceedings of SemEval*, pages 341–350.

Richard Socher, Christopher D. Manning, and Andrew Y. Ng. 2010. Learning Continuous Phrase Representations and Syntactic Parsing with Recursive Neural Networks. In *Deep Learning and Unsupervised Feature Learning Workshop, NIPS*, pages 1–9.

Richard Socher, Jeffrey Pennington, Eric H. Huang, Andrew Y. Ng, and Christopher D. Manning. 2011. Semi-Supervised Recursive Autoencoders for Predicting Sentiment Distributions. In *Proceedings of EMNLP*, pages 151–161.

Richard Socher, Brody Huval, Christopher D. Manning, and Andrew Y. Ng. 2012. Semantic Compositionality Through Recursive Matrix-Vector Spaces. In *Proceedings of EMNLP*, pages 1201–1211.

Richard Socher, Alex Perelygin, Jean Wu, Jason Chuang, Christopher D. Manning, Andrew Y. Ng, and Christopher Potts. 2013. Recursive Deep Models for Semantic Compositionality Over a Sentiment Treebank. In *Proceedings of EMNLP*, pages 1631–1642.

Richard Socher, Andrej Karpathy, Quoc V. Le, Christopher D. Manning, and Andrew Y. Ng. 2014. Grounded compositional semantics for finding and describing images with sentences. *TACL*, 2:207–218.

Fei Wu and Daniel S. Weld. 2010. Open information extraction using wikipedia. In *Proceeding of ACL*, pages 118–127.

# LR Parsing for LCFRS

**Laura Kallmeyer** and **Wolfgang Maier**
Institute for Language and Information
University of Düsseldorf
Düsseldorf, Germany
{kallmeyer,maierwo}@phil.hhu.de

**Abstract**

LR parsing is a popular parsing strategy for variants of Context-Free Grammar (CFG). It has also been used for mildly context-sensitive formalisms, such as Tree-Adjoining Grammar. In this paper, we present the first LR-style parsing algorithm for Linear Context-Free Rewriting Systems (LCFRS), a mildly context-sensitive extension of CFG which has received considerable attention in the last years.

## 1 Introduction

LR parsing is an incremental shift-reduce parsing strategy in which the transitions between parser states are guided by an automaton which is compiled offline. LR parsers were first introduced for deterministic context-free languages (Knuth, 1965) and later generalized to context-free languages (Tomita, 1984) and tree-adjoining languages (Nederhof, 1998; Prolo, 2003).

Linear Context-Free Rewriting System (LCFRS) (Vijay-Shanker et al., 1987) is an immediate extension of CFG in which each non-terminal can cover more than one continuous span of the input string. LCFRS and equivalent formalisms have been used for the modeling of discontinuous constituents (Maier and Lichte, 2011) and non-projective dependencies (Kuhlmann, 2013), as well as for data-driven parsing of such structures (Maier and Kallmeyer, 2010; Kallmeyer and Maier, 2013; van Cranenburgh, 2012; Angelov and Ljunglöf, 2014). They have also been used for modeling non-concatenative morphology (Botha and Blunsom, 2013), for grammar engineering (Ranta, 2011), and for modeling alignments in machine translation (Søgaard, 2008; Kaeshammer, 2013). To our knowledge, so far, no LR strategy for LCFRS has been presented in the literature. In this paper, we present an LR-style parser for LCFRS. It is based on the incremental parsing strategy implemented by Thread Automata (Villemonte de la Clergerie, 2002).

The remainder of the article is structured as follows. In the following section, we introduce LCFRS and thread automata. Section 3 presents the algorithm along an example. In particular, section 3.2 gives the algorithms for automaton and parse table constructions, and section 3.3 presents the parsing algorithm. Section 4 concludes the article.

## 2 Preliminaries

### 2.1 LCFRS

In this paper, we restrict ourselves to string rewriting LCFRS and omit the more general definition (Weir, 1988).

In LCFRS, a single non-terminal can span $k \geq 1$ continuous blocks of a string. A CFG is simply a special case of an LCFRS in which $k = 1$. $k$ is called the *fan-out* of the non-terminal. We notate LCFRS with the syntax of Simple Range Concatenation Grammars (SRCG) (Boullier, 1998), a formalism equivalent to LCFRS.

An LCFRS[1] (Vijay-Shanker et al., 1987; Seki et al., 1991) is a tuple $G = (N, T, V, P, S)$ where $N$

[1]Note that for purposes of exposition, we limit ourselves to $\varepsilon$-free LCFRS.



*Human Language Technologies: The 2015 Annual Conference of the North American Chapter of the ACL*, pages 1250–1255,
Denver, Colorado, May 31 – June 5, 2015. 

is a finite set of non-terminals with a function $dim$: $N \to \mathbb{N}$ determining the *fan-out* of each $A \in N$; $T$ and $V$ are disjoint finite sets of terminals and variables; $S \in N$ is the start symbol with $dim(S) = 1$.

$P$ is a finite set of rewriting rules with *rank* $m \geq 0$. All $\gamma \in P$ have the form

$$A(\alpha_0, \dots, \alpha_{dim(A)-1}) \to A_1(X_0^{(1)}, \dots, X_{dim(A_1)-1}^{(1)}) \\ \cdots A_m(X_0^{(m)}, \dots, X_{dim(A_m)-1}^{(m)})$$

where $A, A_1, \dots, A_m \in N$, $X_j^{(l)} \in V$ for $1 \leq l \leq m, 0 \leq j < dim(A_i)$ and $\alpha_i \in (V \cup T)^+$ for $0 \leq i < dim(A)$. All $\alpha_i$ and $X_j^{(l)}$ are called *arguments* (or sometimes *components*); the elements in $\alpha_i$ are called *argument elements*. $\mathcal{A}_\gamma$ is the set of all argument elements of $\gamma$. Variable occurrences in the arguments of the non-terminals of $\gamma$ are ordered by a strict total order $\prec$. For all $X_1, X_2 \in V$ occurring in arguments of a non-terminal of $\gamma$, it holds that $X_1 \prec X_2$ iff either $X_1$ precedes $X_2$ in an argument of the non-terminal or the argument $X_1$ occurs in precedes the argument $X_2$ occurs in.

For all $\gamma \in P$, every variable $X$ occurring in $\gamma$ occurs exactly once in the left-hand side (LHS) and exactly once in the right-hand side (RHS). Furthermore, if for two variables $X_1, X_2 \in V$, it holds that $X_1 \prec X_2$ on the RHS, then also $X_1 \prec X_2$ on the LHS. The *rank* of $G$ is the maximal rank of any of its rules, its *fan-out* is the maximal fan-out of any of its non-terminals.

We use the following additional notation: For a rule $\gamma \in P$, $lhs(\gamma)$ gives the LHS non-terminal; $lhs(\gamma, i)$ gives the $i$th argument of the LHS and $lhs(\gamma, i, j)$ its $j$th symbol; $rhs(\gamma, k)$ gives the $k$th RHS non-terminal; and $rhs(\gamma, k, l)$ gives the $l$th component of the $k$th RHS element (starting with index 0 in all four cases). These function have value $\perp$ whenever there is no such element. Furthermore, in the sense of dotted productions, we define for each $\gamma \in P$ a set of symbols denoting computation points of $\gamma$, $\mathcal{C}_\gamma = \{\gamma_{i.j} \mid 0 \leq i < dim_A, 0 \leq j \leq |\alpha_i|\}$, as well as the set $\mathcal{C} = \bigcup_{\gamma \in P} \mathcal{C}_\gamma$.

A non-terminal $A \in N$ can be *instantiated* w.r.t. an input string $w_1 \cdots w_{|w|}$ and a rule $\gamma \in P$ with $lhs(\gamma) = A$. An instantiation maps all argument elements of $\gamma$ to spans of $w$ ($(i-1, j)^w$ denotes the span $w_i \cdots w_j$, $1 \leq i \leq j \leq n$). All instantiations are given by a function $\sigma : \mathcal{A}_\gamma \to \mathbb{N} \times \mathbb{N}$ where for all $x, y \in \mathcal{A}_\gamma$ with $x \neq y$, $\sigma(x) = (i, j)^w$ and $\sigma(y) = (k, l)^w$ it holds that $i, k \geq 0$; $j, l \leq |w|$; if $x$ ($y$) is a terminal, then $j = i + 1$ ($l = k + 1$), otherwise $j > i$ ($k > l$). Iff $x \prec y$ in $\gamma$, then $j \leq k$. A derivation rewrites strings of instantiated non-terminals, i.e., given an instantiated clause, the instantiated LHS non-terminal may be replaced with the sequence of instantiated RHS terminals. The language of the grammar is the set of strings which can be reduced to the empty word, starting with $S$ instantiated to the input string.

$$\alpha : S(xy) \to A(x, y) \quad \gamma : A(a, b) \to \varepsilon$$
$$\beta : A(ax, ya) \to A(x, y)$$

Figure 1: LCFRS for $\{a^n aba^n \mid n \geq 0\}$

See figure 1 for a sample LCFRS.

## 2.2 Thread Automata

Thread automata (TA) (Villemonte de la Clergerie, 2002) are a generic automaton model which can be parametrized to recognize different mildly context-sensitive languages. The TA for LCFRS (LCFRS-TA) implements a prefix-valid top-down incremental parsing strategy similar to the ones of Kallmeyer and Maier (2009) and Burden and Ljunglöf (2005).

An LCFRS-TA for some LCFRS $G = (N, T, V, P, S)$ works as follows. The processing of a single rule is handled by a single *thread* which will traverse the LHS arguments of the rule. A thread is given by a pair $p : X$, where $p \in \{1, \dots, m\}^*$ with $m$ the rank of $G$ is the *address*, and $X \in N \cup \{ret\} \cup \mathcal{C}$ where $ret \notin N$ is the *content* of the thread. An automaton state is given by a tuple $\langle i, p, \mathcal{T} \rangle$ where $\mathcal{T}$ is a set of threads, the *thread store*, $p$ is the address of the active thread, and $i \geq 0$ indicates that $i$ tokens have been recognized. We introduce a new start symbol $S' \notin N$ that expands to $S$ and use $\langle 0, \varepsilon, \{\varepsilon : S'\} \rangle$ as start state.

The specific TA for a given LCFRS $G = (N, T, V, P, S)$ can be defined as tuple $\langle N', T, S', ret, \delta, \Theta \rangle$ with $N' = N \cup \mathcal{C} \cup \{S', ret\}$; $\delta$ is a function from $\mathcal{C}$ to $\{1, \dots, m\} \cup \{\perp\}$ such that $\delta(\gamma_{k,i}) = j$ if there is a $l$ such that $lhs(\gamma, k, i) = rhs(\gamma, j-1, l)$, and $\delta(\gamma_{k,i}) = \perp$ if $lhs(\gamma, k, i) \in T \cup \{\perp\}$ (intuitively, a $\delta$ value $j$ tells us that the next symbol to process is a variable that

| | | | | |
|---|---|---|---|---|
| Call: | $S' \to [S']S$ | $\alpha_{0,0} \to [\alpha_{0,0}]A$ | $\beta_{0,1} \to [\beta_{0,1}]A$ | |
| Predict: | $S \to \alpha_{0,0}$ | $A \to \beta_{0,0}$ | $A \to \gamma_{0,0}$ | |
| Scan: | $\beta_{0,0} \xrightarrow{a} \beta_{0,1}$ | $\beta_{1,1} \xrightarrow{a} \beta_{1,2}$ | $\gamma_{0,0} \xrightarrow{a} \gamma_{0,1}$ | $\gamma_{1,0} \xrightarrow{b} \gamma_{1,1}$ |
| Publish: | $\alpha_{0,2} \to ret$ | $\beta_{1,2} \to ret$ | $\gamma_{1,1} \to ret$ | |
| Suspend: | $[\alpha_{0,1}]ret \to \alpha_{0,2}$ | $[\beta_{1,0}]ret \to \beta_{1,1}$ | | |
| | $[\alpha_{0,0}]\beta_{0,2} \to \alpha_{0,1}[\beta_{0,2}]$ | $[\alpha_{0,0}]\gamma_{0,1} \to \alpha_{0,1}[\gamma_{0,1}]$ | $[\beta_{0,1}]\beta_{0,2} \to \beta_{0,2}[\beta_{0,2}]$ | $[\beta_{0,1}]\gamma_{0,1} \to \beta_{0,2}[\gamma_{0,1}]$ |
| Resume: | $\alpha_{0,1}[\beta_{0,2}] \to [\alpha_{0,1}]\beta_{1,0}$ | $\alpha_{0,1}[\gamma_{0,1}] \to [\alpha_{0,1}]\gamma_{1,0}$ | $\beta_{1,0}[\beta_{0,2}] \to [\beta_{1,0}]\beta_{1,0}$ | $\beta_{1,0}[\gamma_{0,1}] \to [\beta_{1,0}]\gamma_{1,0}$ |

Figure 2: TA transitions for the LCFRS from figure 1

is an argument of the $j$th RHS non-terminal); and $\Theta$ is a finite set of transitions. Every transition has the form $\alpha \xrightarrow{a} \beta$ with $a \in T \cup \{\varepsilon\}$ and they roughly indicate that in the thread store, $\alpha$ can be replaced with $\beta$ while scanning $a$. Square brackets in $\alpha$ and $\beta$ indicate parts that do not belong to the active thread. This will be made more precise below. $\Theta$ contains the following transitions (see figure 2):

- **Call** transitions start a new thread, either for the start symbol or for a daughter non-terminal. They move down in the parse tree.
  $S' \to [S']S$ (initial call), $\gamma_{k,i} \to [\gamma_{k,i}]A$ if $A = rhs(\gamma, j-1)$ and $lhs(\gamma, k, i) = rhs(\gamma, j-1, 0)$ where $j = \delta(\gamma_{k,i})$.
- **Predict** transitions predict a new rule for a non-terminal $A$: $A \to \gamma_{0,0}$ if $A = lhs(\gamma)$.
- **Scan** reads a LHS terminal while scanning the next input symbol:
  $\gamma_{k,i} \xrightarrow{lhs(\gamma,k,i)} \gamma_{k,i+1}$ if $lhs(\gamma, k, i) \in T$.
- **Publish** marks the completion of a production, i.e., its full recognition:
  $\gamma_{k,j} \to ret$ if $dim(lhs(\gamma)) = k+1$ and $j = |lhs(\gamma, k)|$.
- **Suspend** suspends a daughter thread and resumes the parent. i.e., moves up in the parse tree. There are two cases:
  (i) The daughter is completely recognized: $[\gamma_{k,i}]ret \to \gamma_{k,i+1}$ if $lhs(\gamma, k, i) = rhs(\gamma, \delta(\gamma_{k,i})-1, dim(rhs(\delta(\gamma_{k,i})-1))-1)$.
  (ii) The daughter is not yet completely recognized, we have only finished one of its components: $[\gamma_{k,i}]\beta_{l,j} \to \gamma_{k,i+1}[\beta_{l,j}]$ if $dim(lhs(\beta)) > l+1$, $|lhs(\beta, l)| = j$, $lhs(\gamma, k, i) = rhs(\gamma, \delta(\gamma_{k,i}) - 1, l)$ and $rhs(\gamma, \delta(\gamma_{k,i}) - 1) = lhs(\beta)$.
- **Resume** resumes an already present daughter thread, i.e., moves down into some daughter that has already been partly recognized.
  $\gamma_{k,i}[\beta_{l,j}] \to [\gamma_{k,i}]\beta_{l+1,0}$ if $lhs(\gamma, k, i) = rhs(\gamma, \delta(\gamma_{k,i}) - 1, l+1)$, $rhs(\gamma, \delta(\gamma_{k,i}) - 1) = lhs(\beta)$ and $\beta_{l,j+1} \notin \mathcal{C}$.

This is not exactly the TA for LCFRS proposed in Villemonte de la Clergerie (2002) but rather the one from Kallmeyer (2010), which is close to the Earley parser from Burden and Ljunglöf (2005).

The set of configurations for a given input $w \in T^*$ is then defined by the deduction rules in figure 3 (the use of set union $\mathcal{S}_1 \cup \mathcal{S}_2$ in these rules assumes that $\mathcal{S}_1 \cap \mathcal{S}_2 = \emptyset$). The accepting state of the automaton for some input $w$ is $\langle |w|, 1, \{\varepsilon : S', 1 : ret\}\rangle$.

### 2.3 LR Parsing

In an LR parser, the parser actions are guided by an automaton, resp. a *parse table* which is compiled offline. Consider the context-free case. An LR parser for CFG is a guided shift-reduce parser, in which we first build the LR automaton. Its states are sets of dotted productions closed under prediction, and its transitions correspond to having recognized a part of the input, e.g., to moving the dot over a RHS element after having scanned a terminal or recognized a non-terminal. Given an automaton with $n$ states, we build the *parse table* with $n$ rows. Each row $i$, $0 \leq i < n$, describes the possible parser actions associated with the state $q_i$, i.e., for each state and each possible shift or reduce operation, it tells us in which state to go after the operation.

## 3 LR for LCFRS

### 3.1 Intuition

The states in the automaton are predict and resume closures of TA thread stores. In order to keep them finite, we allow the addresses to be regular expressions. A configuration of the parser consists of a

$$\text{Initial configuration: } \frac{}{\langle 0, \varepsilon, \{\varepsilon : S'\}\rangle} \qquad \text{Initial call: } \frac{\langle 0, \varepsilon, \{\varepsilon : S'\}\rangle}{\langle 0, 1, \{\varepsilon : S', 1 : S\}\rangle}$$

$$\text{Further calls: } \frac{\langle i, p, \mathcal{S} \cup p : \gamma_{k,i}\rangle}{\langle i, pj, \mathcal{S} \cup p : \gamma_{k,i} \cup pj : A\rangle} \; \begin{array}{l}\gamma_{k,i} \to [\gamma_{k,i}]A \in \Theta, \\ A \in N, \delta(\gamma_{k,i}) = j+1\end{array} \qquad \text{Predict: } \frac{\langle i, p, \mathcal{S} \cup p : A\rangle}{\langle i, p, \mathcal{S} \cup p : \gamma_{0,0}\rangle} \; \begin{array}{l}A \in N, \\ A \to \gamma_{1,0} \in \Theta\end{array}$$

$$\text{Scan: } \frac{\langle j, p, \mathcal{S} \cup p : \gamma_{k,i}\rangle}{\langle j+1, p, \mathcal{S} \cup p : \gamma_{k,i+1}\rangle} \; \gamma_{k,i} \stackrel{w_{j+1}}{\to} \gamma_{k,i+1} \in \Theta \qquad \text{Publish: } \frac{\langle i, p, \mathcal{S} \cup \{p : \gamma_{k,i}\}\rangle}{\langle i, p, \mathcal{S} \cup \{p : ret\}\rangle} \; \gamma_{k,j} \to ret \in \Theta$$

$$\text{Suspend 1: } \frac{\langle i, pj, \mathcal{S} \cup \{p : \gamma_{k,i}, pj : ret\}\rangle}{\langle i, p, \mathcal{S} \cup \{p : \gamma_{k,i+1}\}\rangle} \; [\gamma_{k,i}]ret \to \gamma_{k,i+1} \in \Theta$$

$$\text{Suspend 2: } \frac{\langle i, pj, \mathcal{S} \cup \{p : \gamma_{k,i}, pj : \beta_{l,m}\}\rangle}{\langle i, p, \mathcal{S} \cup \{p : \gamma_{k,i+1}, pj : \beta_{l,m}\}\rangle} \; [\gamma_{k,i}]\beta_{l,m} \to \gamma_{k,i+1}[\beta_{l,m}] \in \Theta$$

$$\text{Resume: } \frac{\langle i, p, \mathcal{S} \cup \{p : \gamma_{k,i}, p\delta(\gamma_{k,i}) : \beta_{l,j}\}\rangle}{\langle i, p\delta(\gamma_{k,i}), \mathcal{S} \cup \{p : \gamma_{k,i}, p\delta(\gamma_{k,i}) : \beta_{l+1,0}\}\rangle} \; \gamma_{k,i}[\beta_{l,j}] \to [\gamma_{k,i}]\beta_{l+1,0} \in \Theta$$

Figure 3: Deduction rules for TA configurations

stack, a set of completed components and the remaining input. The completed components are of the form $p : \gamma_i$ where $p$ is an address and $\gamma_i$ the component of a rule. The stack has the form $\Gamma_1 x_1 \Gamma_2 \ldots x_{n-1} \Gamma_n$ where $\Gamma_i$ is an address followed by a state and $x_i \in T \cup \{A_k \,|\, A \in N, 1 \leq k \leq dim(A)\}$.

**Shift**: Whenever we have $p : q$ on top of the stack and an edge from $q$ to $q'$ labeled with the next input symbol and an address $p'$, we add the input symbol followed by $pp' : q'$ to the stack.

**Suspend**: Whenever the top of the stack is $p_1 : q$ such that there is a $\gamma_{i-1,k} \in q$ with $k = |lhs(\gamma, i-1)|$ and $i < dim(\gamma)$, we can suspend. If $i = 1$, we add $p_1 : \gamma_i$ to the set of completed components and we remove $|lhs(\gamma, i)|$ terminals/component nonterminals and their preceding states from the stack. If $i \geq 1$, we check whether there is a $p_2 : \gamma_{i-1}$ in the set of completed components such that the intersection $L(p_1) \cap L(p_2)$ is not empty.[2] We then remove $p_2 : \gamma_{i-1}$ from the set of complete components and we add $p : \gamma_i$ to it where $p$ is a regular expression denoting $L(p_1) \cap L(p_2)$. Suppose the topmost state on the stack is now $p' : q'$. We then have to follow the edge leading from $q'$ to some $q''$ labeled $A_i : p''$ where $A = lhs(\gamma)$. This means that we push $A_i$ followed by $p'p'' : q''$ on the stack.

[2]Note that the corresponding finite state automata can be deterministic; in this case the intersection is quadratic in the size of the two automata.
In LCFRS without left recursion in any of the components, the intersection is trivial since the regular expressions denote only a single path each.

**Reduce**: Whenever there is a $\gamma_{i-1,k}$ in our current state with $k = |lhs(\gamma, i-1)|$ and $i = dim(\gamma)$, we can reduce, which is like suspend except that nothing is added to the set of completed components.

### 3.2 Automaton and parse table construction

The states of the LR-automaton are sets of pairs $p : X$ where $p$ is a regular expression over $\{1, \ldots, m\}$, $m$ the rank of $G$, and $X \in \mathcal{C} \cup \{S'\}$. They represent predict and resume closures.The predict/resume closure $\overline{q}$ of some set $q$ is described by the deduction rules in figure 4. This closure is not always finite.

$$\frac{\varepsilon : S'}{1 : \alpha_{0,0}} \; lhs(\alpha) = S$$

$$\frac{p : \gamma_{i,j}}{pk : \gamma'_{l,0}} \; \begin{array}{l} lhs(\gamma, i, j) = rhs(\gamma, k-1, l), \\ rhs(\gamma, k) = lhs(\gamma') \end{array}$$

Figure 4: Predict/resume closure

However, if it is not, we obtain a set of items that can be represented by a finite set of pairs $r : \gamma_{i,j}$ plus eventually $\varepsilon : S'$ such that $r$ is a regular expression denoting a set of possible addresses. As an example for such a case, see $q_3$ in figure 5.

The reason why we can represent these closures by finite sets using regular expressions for paths is the following: There is a finite number of possible elements $\gamma_{i,j}$. For each of these, the set of possible addresses it might be combined with in a state that is the closure of $\{\varepsilon : X_1, \varepsilon : X_2, \ldots, \varepsilon : X_n\}$ is generated by the CFG $\langle \mathcal{C} \cup \{S'\} \cup \{S_{new}\}, \{1, \ldots, m\}, P, S_{new}\rangle$ with $S_{new} \to X_i \in P$ for all $1 \leq i \leq n$, $X \to Yk \in P$ for all instances $\frac{p:X}{pk:Y}$ of deduction rules and $\gamma_{i,j} \to \varepsilon$. This is a regular grammar, its string language can thus be characterized by a regular expression.

The construction of the set of states starts with $q_0 = \overline{\{\varepsilon : S'\}}$. For every state $q$, every non-terminal $A$ and every $1 \leq i \leq dim(A)$, we define $read(q, A_i, p) = \{\varepsilon : \gamma_{j,k+1} \,|\, p : \gamma_{j,k} \in q$ and there is some $l$ such that $rhs(\gamma, l) = A$ and $lhs(\gamma, j, k) = rhs(\gamma, l, i-1)\}$ and $\overline{read}(q, A_i, p) = \overline{read(q, A_i, p)}$. Similarly, for every such $q$ and every $a \in T$, we define $read(q, a, p) = \{\varepsilon : \gamma_{j,k+1} \,|\, p : \gamma_{j,k} \in q$ and $lhs(\gamma, j, k) = a\}$ and $\overline{read}(q, a, p) = \overline{read(q, a, p)}$. The set of states of our automaton is then the closure of $\{q_0\}$ under the application of the $\overline{read}$-functions. The edges in our automaton correspond to $\overline{read}$-transitions, where each edge is labeled with the corresponding pair $A_i, p$ or $a, p$ respectively. The automaton we obtain for the grammar in figure 1 is shown in figure 5. The number of possible states

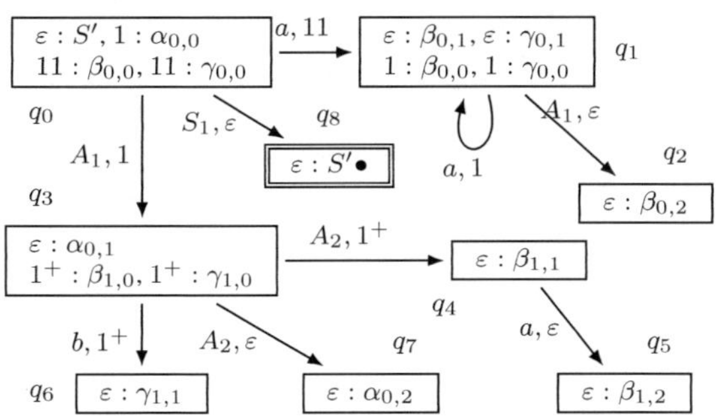


Figure 5: The automaton

is necessarily finite since each state is the closure of some set containing only items with address $\varepsilon$. There are only finitely many such sets.

In the parse table, our operations are $s(p, q)$ for shifting some terminal $a$ followed by the old address concatenated with $p$ and state $q$ and $r(\alpha, i)$ for reducing the $i$th component of rule $\alpha$. The two reduce operations can be distinguished by the component indices. Furthermore, the goto-part of the table tells where to go when traversing a component edge and which address to add then. The parse table can be read off the automaton as follows: $action(q, a) = s(p, q')$ iff $\overline{read}(q, a, p) = q'$; $action(q, -) = r(\gamma, i)$ iff there is some $p : \gamma_{i,k} \in q$ such that $k = |lhs(\gamma, i)|$. Concerning the goto part of the table, we have $goto(q, A_i) = \langle p, q' \rangle$ iff $\overline{read}(q, A_i, p) = q'$. Figure 6 shows the parse table

| | $a$ | $b$ | | $A_1$ | $A_2$ | $S_1$ |
|---|---|---|---|---|---|---|
| 0 | $s(11, 1)$ | | | $\langle 1, 3\rangle$ | | $\langle \varepsilon, 8\rangle$ |
| 1 | $s(1, 1)$ | | $r(\gamma, 1)$ | $\langle \varepsilon, 2\rangle$ | | |
| 2 | | | $r(\beta, 1)$ | | | |
| 3 | | $s(1^+, 6)$ | | | $\langle 1^+, 4\rangle$, $\langle \varepsilon, 7\rangle$ | |
| 4 | $s(\varepsilon, 5)$ | | | | | |
| 5 | | | $r(\beta, 2)$ | | | |
| 6 | | | $r(\gamma, 2)$ | | | |
| 7 | | | $r(\alpha, 1)$ | | | |
| 8 | | | acc | | | |

Figure 6: The parse table

| **stack** | **completed** | **input** | **operation** |
|---|---|---|---|
| $\varepsilon{:}q_0$ | [ ] | $aaba$ | initial state |
| $\varepsilon{:}q_0\ a\ 11{:}q_1$ | [ ] | $aba$ | shift $a$,11 |
| $\varepsilon{:}q_0\ a\ 11{:}q_1\ a\ 111{:}q_1$ | [ ] | $ba$ | shift $a$,1 |
| $\varepsilon{:}q_0\ a\ 11{:}q_1\ A_1\ 11{:}q_2$ | [111:$\gamma_1$] | $ba$ | suspend $\gamma_{0,1}$ |
| $\varepsilon{:}q_0\ A_1\ 1{:}q_3$ | [111:$\gamma_1$,11:$\beta_1$] | $ba$ | suspend $\beta_{0,2}$ |
| $\varepsilon{:}q_0\ A_1\ 1{:}q_3\ b\ 11^+{:}q_6$ | [111:$\gamma_1$,11:$\beta_1$] | $a$ | shift $b$,$1^+$ |
| $\varepsilon{:}q_0\ A_1\ 1{:}q_3\ A_2\ 11^+{:}q_4$ | [11:$\beta_1$] | $a$ | reduce $\gamma_{1,1}$ |
| $\varepsilon{:}q_0\ A_1\ 1{:}q_3\ A_2\ 11^+{:}q_4\ a\ 11^+{:}q_5$ | [11:$\beta_1$] | $\varepsilon$ | shift $a$,$\varepsilon$ |
| $\varepsilon{:}q_0\ A_1\ 1{:}q_3\ A_2\ 1{:}q_4$ | [ ] | $\varepsilon$ | reduce $\beta_{1,2}$ |
| $\varepsilon{:}q_0\ S_1\ \varepsilon{:}q_8$ | [ ] | $\varepsilon$ | reduce $\alpha_{0,2}$ |

Figure 7: Sample run with $w = aaba$

for our example.

### 3.3 Parsing

We run the automaton with $\langle \varepsilon : q_0, [\ ], w\rangle$ and input $w = aaba$. The trace is shown in figure 7. We start in $q_0$, and shift two $a$s, which leads to $q_1$. We have then fully recognized the first components of $\gamma$ and $\beta$: We suspend them and keep them in the set of completed components, which takes us to $q_3$. Shifting the $b$ takes us to $q_6$, from where we can reduce, which finally takes us to $q_4$. From there, we can shift the remaining $a$ (to $q_5$), with which we have fully recognized $\beta$. We can now reduce both $\beta$ and with that, $\alpha$, which takes us to the accepting state $q_8$.

## 4 Conclusion

We presented the first LR style algorithm for LCFRS parsing. It offers a convenient factorization of predict/resume operations. We are currently exploring the possibility to use it in data-driven parsing.


## Acknowledgments

The work presented in this paper was partly funded by the German Research Foundation (DFG). We wish to thank three anonymous reviewers for their valuable comments.

## References


Krasimir Angelov and Peter Ljunglöf. 2014. Fast statistical parsing with parallel multiple context-free grammars. In *Proceedings of the 14th Conference of the European Chapter of the Association for Computational Linguistics*, pages 368–376, Gothenburg, Sweden.

Jan A. Botha and Phil Blunsom. 2013. Adaptor grammars for learning non-concatenative morphology. In *Proceedings of the 2013 Conference on Empirical Methods in Natural Language Processing*, pages 345–356, Seattle, WA.

Pierre Boullier. 1998. Proposal for a Natural Language Processing syntactic backbone. Research Report 3342, INRIA-Rocquencourt, Rocquencourt, France.

Håkan Burden and Peter Ljunglöf. 2005. Parsing linear context-free rewriting systems. In *Proceedings of the Ninth International Workshop on Parsing Technology*, pages 11–17, Vancouver, BC.

Miriam Kaeshammer. 2013. Synchronous linear context-free rewriting systems for machine translation. In *Proceedings of the Seventh Workshop on Syntax, Semantics and Structure in Statistical Translation*, pages 68–77, Atlanta, GA.

Laura Kallmeyer and Wolfgang Maier. 2009. An incremental Earley parser for simple range concatenation grammar. In *Proceedings of the 11th International Conference on Parsing Technologies (IWPT'09)*, pages 61–64, Paris, France.

Laura Kallmeyer and Wolfgang Maier. 2013. Data-driven parsing using probabilistic linear context-free rewriting systems. *Computational Linguistics*, 39(1):87–119.

Laura Kallmeyer. 2010. *Parsing beyond Context-Free Grammar*. Springer, Heidelberg.

Donald E. Knuth. 1965. On the translation of languages from left to right. *Information and Control*, 8(6):607–639, July.

Marco Kuhlmann. 2013. Mildly non-projective dependency grammar. *Computational Linguistics*, 39(2):355–387.

Wolfgang Maier and Laura Kallmeyer. 2010. Discontinuity and non-projectivity: Using mildly context-sensitive formalisms for data-driven parsing. In *Proceedings of the Tenth International Workshop on Tree Adjoining Grammar and Related Formalisms (TAG+10)*, pages 119–126, New Haven, CT.

Wolfgang Maier and Timm Lichte. 2011. Characterizing discontinuity in constituent treebanks. In *Formal Grammar. 14th International Conference, FG 2009. Bordeaux, France, July 25-26, 2009. Revised Selected Papers*, volume 5591 of *Lecture Notes in Artificial Intelligence*, pages 167–182, Berlin, Heidelberg, New York. Springer-Verlag.

Mark-Jan Nederhof. 1998. An alternative LR algorithm for TAGs. In *Proceedings of the 36th Annual Meeting of the Association for Computational Linguistics and 17th International Conference on Computational Linguistics*, volume 1, pages 946–952, Montreal, QC.

Carlos A. Prolo. 2003. *LR Parsing for Tree Adjoining Grammars and its Application to Corpus-based Natural Language Parsing*. Ph.D. thesis, Department of Computer and Information Science, University of Pennsylvania, Philadelphia, PA.

Aarne Ranta. 2011. *Grammatical Framework: Programming with Multilingual Grammars*. CSLI Publications, Stanford.

Hiroyuki Seki, Takashi Matsumura, Mamoru Fujii, and Tadao Kasami. 1991. On multiple context-free grammars. *Theoretical Computer Science*, 88(2):191–229.

Anders Søgaard. 2008. Range concatenation grammars for translation. In *The 22nd International Conference on Computational Linguistics (COLING)*, pages 103–106, Manchester, England.

Masaru Tomita. 1984. LR parsers for natural languages. In *Proceedings of COLING 1984: The 10th International Conference on Computational Linguistics*, pages 354–357, Stanford University.

Andreas van Cranenburgh. 2012. Efficient parsing with linear context-free rewriting systems. In *Proceedings of the 13th Conference of the European Chapter of the Association for Computational Linguistics*, pages 460–470, Avignon, France.

K. Vijay-Shanker, David Weir, and Aravind K. Joshi. 1987. Characterising structural descriptions used by various formalisms. In *Proceedings of the 25th Annual Meeting of the Association for Computational Linguistics*, pages 104–111, Stanford, CA.

Éric Villemonte de la Clergerie. 2002. Parsing mildly context-sensitive languages with thread automata. In *Proceedings of COLING 2002: The 19th International Conference on Computational Linguistics*, Taipei, Taiwan.

David Weir. 1988. *Characterizing Mildly Context-Sensitive Grammar Formalisms*. Ph.D. thesis, University of Pennsylviania, Philadelphia, PA.

# Mining for unambiguous instances to adapt part-of-speech taggers to new domains

**Dirk Hovy, Barbara Plank, Héctor Martínez Alonso, Anders Søgaard**
Center for Language Technology
University of Copenhagen, Denmark
Njalsgade 140
{dirk|bplank}@cst.dk,{alonso|soegaard}@hum.ku.dk

## Abstract

We present a simple, yet effective approach to adapt part-of-speech (POS) taggers to new domains. Our approach only requires a dictionary and large amounts of unlabeled target data. The idea is to use the dictionary to mine the unlabeled target data for unambiguous word sequences, thus effectively collecting *labeled* target data. We add the mined instances to available labeled newswire data to train a POS tagger for the target domain. The induced models significantly improve tagging accuracy on held-out test sets across three domains (Twitter, spoken language, and search queries). We also present results for Dutch, Spanish and Portuguese Twitter data, and provide two novel manually-annotated test sets.

## 1 Introduction

Part-of-speech (POS) taggers are typically trained on newswire and exhibit severe out-of-domain performance drops (Blitzer et al., 2006; Daume III, 2007; Foster et al., 2011). When faced with a new domain, one option is to try to leverage available unlabeled data. However, rather than resorting to pure self-training approaches (self-labeling), we here resort to another source of information. One way to address the annotation problem is to use collaboratively created resources such as Wikipedia for *distant supervision* (Mintz et al., 2009), or the automatically derived dictionaries called *Wiktionary* (Li et al., 2012). We show how to leverage these resources to create labeled training data. It turns out that many entries in Wiktionary are actually *unambiguous*, i.e., there is only *one* possible tag for the word. In fact, for English Wiktionary (Li et al., 2012), we find that 93% of the unigram types are unambiguous (cf. Table 2).

Our idea here is simple: we mine for *unlabeled* sentences that contain only unambiguous items (according to Wiktionary), and use the resulting data as additional, *labeled* training material. Concretely, we mine unannotated corpora of tweets, transcribed speech, and search queries for sentences that contain only unambiguous tokens, and combine those instances with newswire data to train POS models that adapt better to the respective domains. We show that adding unambiguous data leads to considerable improvements over both unadapted and weakly-supervised baselines (Li et al., 2012).

Since Wiktionary has relatively low coverage for some of these domains, we also explore the use of Brown clusters to extend the coverage. This enables us to generalize across spelling variations and synonyms. Additionally, we evaluate our approach on Dutch, Portuguese and Spanish Twitter and present tow novel data sets for the latter two languages.

## 2 Data

### 2.1 Wiktionary

In our experiments, we use the (unigram) tag dictionaries from Wiktionary, as collected by Li et al. (2012).[1] The size and quality of our tag dictionaries crucially influence how much unambiguous data we can extract, and for some languages, the number of dictionary entries is small.

We can resort to normalization dictionaries to extend Wiktionary's coverage. We do so for English (Han and Baldwin, 2011). It replaces some

[1] https://code.google.com/p/wikily-supervised-pos-tagger/



*Human Language Technologies: The 2015 Annual Conference of the North American Chapter of the ACL*, pages 1256–1261, Denver, Colorado, May 31 – June 5, 2015. 

| | | |
|---|---|---|
| NEWSWIRE | Spielberg took the helm of this big budget live action project with Robin Williams playing an adult Peter and Dustin Hoffman as the dastardly Captain Hook. |
| TWITTER | Rooofiii Oooooo, didn't think ppl<3the movie as much as me, this movie will always b the peter pan story2me #robin #williams #hook |
| SPOKEN | I loved that movie... Uhm... You know, Hook. With Robin Williams, uh. |
| QUERIES | peter pan williams movie |

Table 1: Examples from source (top row) and target domains (bottom rows)

spelling variations with the standard form (*youuuu-uuuu* $\rightarrow$ *you*), which reduces the vocabulary size.

For languages where no such normalization dictionary is available, we use word clusterings based on Brown clusters (Brown et al., 1992) to generalize tags from unambiguous words to previously unseen words in the same class.

| CLUSTER | TOKEN | TAG $\in D$ | PROJ. TAG |
|---|---|---|---|
| 01011110 | offish | ADJ | — |
| 01011110 | alreadyyy | ??? | ADV |
| 01011110 | finali | ??? | ADV |
| 01011110 | aleady | ??? | ADV |
| 01011110 | previously | ADV | — |
| 01011110 | already | ADV | — |
| 01011110 | recently | ADV | — |

Figure 1: Example of a Brown cluster with unambiguous tokens, as well as projected tags for new tokens (tokens marked "—" are unchanged in $D'$).

In particular, to extend the dictionary $D$ to $D'$ using clusters, we first run clustering on the unlabeled data $T$, using Brown clustering.[2] We then assign to each unambiguous word in the cluster its tag from dictionary $D$. For all remaining tokens in the same cluster, we assign them the most frequently observed tag in the cluster, provided that label occurred at least twice as often as the second most frequent one, and the token itself was not already in Wiktionary.

As an example, consider the cluster in Figure 1. Since three tokens were unambiguously tagged as ADV in the original dictionary (*previously*, *already*, *recently*), we project ADV to all tokens in the cluster that were not already in $D$ (here: *alreadyyy*, *finali*, *aleady*), and finally add all words to $D'$. The token *offish* remains an ADJ.

[2]https://github.com/percyliang/brown-cluster

## 2.2 Unlabeled data

For each domain and language, given dictionary $D$, we extract unambiguous sentences/tweets. User names and URLs are assumed to be nouns. If all words are unambiguous according to the dictionary, we include the sentence/tweet in our training data. For hashtags on Twitter, we remove the "#" sign and check the remainder against the dictionary. We exclude tweets that *only* contain users and URLs.

The unambiguous subsets of the unlabeled data represent very biased samples of the various domains. The ratio of unambiguous English tweets, for example, is only about 0.012 (or 1 in 84), and the distribution of tags in the Twitter data set is heavily skewed towards nouns, while several other labels are under-represented.

**Twitter** We collect the unlabeled data from the Twitter streaming API.[3] We collected 57m tweets for English, 8.2m for Spanish, 4.1m for Portuguese, and 0.5m for Dutch. We do not perform sentence splitting on tweets, but take them as unit sequences.

**Spoken language** We use the Switchboard corpus of transcribed telephone conversations (Godfrey et al., 1992), sections 2 and 3, as well as the English section of EuroParl (Koehn, 2005) and CHILDES (MacWhinney, 1997). We removed all meta-data and inline annotations (gestures, sounds, etc.), as well as dialogue markers. The final joint corpus contains transcriptions of 570k spoken sentences.

**Search queries** For search queries, we use a combination of queries from Yahoo[4] and AOL. We only use the search terms and ignore any additional information, such as user ID, time, and linked URLs. The resulting data set contains 10m queries.

[3]https://github.com/saffsd/langid.py
[4]http://webscope.sandbox.yahoo.com/

### 2.3 Labeled data

We train our models on newswire, as well as mined unambiguous instances. For English, we use the OntoNotes release of the WSJ section of the Penn Treebank as training data for Twitter, spoken data, and queries.[5] For Dutch, we use the training section of the Alpino treebank from the CoNLL task.[6] For Portuguese, we use the training section of the Bosque treebank.[7] For Spanish, we use the training section of the Cast3LB treebank.[8] In order to map between Wiktionary and the treebanks, we need a common coarse tag set. We thus map all data to the universal tag set (Petrov et al., 2012).

**Dev and test sets** Our approach is basically parameter free. However, we did experiment with different ways of extending Wiktionary and hence used an average over three English Twitter dev sections as development set (Ritter et al., 2011; Gimpel et al., 2011; Foster et al., 2011), all mapped and normalized following Hovy et al. (2014).

For evaluation, we use three domains: tweets, spoken data and queries. For Twitter, we performed experiments in four languages: English, Portuguese, Spanish and Dutch. The Spanish and Portuguese tweets were annotated in-house, which will be made available.[9] For the other languages, we use preexisting datasets for English (Hovy et al., 2014) and Dutch (Avontuur et al., 2012). Table 2 lists the complete statistics for the different language data sets.

For the other two domains, we use the manually labeled data from Switchboard section 4 as spoken data test set. For queries, we use manually labeled data from Bendersky et al. (2010).

## 3 Experiments

### 3.1 Model

We use a CRF[10] model (Lafferty et al., 2001) with the same features as Owoputi et al. (2013) and default parameters. As baselines we consider a) a CRF model trained only on newswire; b) available off-the-shelf systems (TOOLS); and c) a weakly supervised model (LI10). For English, the off-the-shelf tagger is the Stanford tagger (Toutanova et al., 2003), for the other languages we use TreeTagger (Schmid, 1994) with pre-trained models.

The weakly supervised model trained is on the unannotated data. It is a second-order HMM model (Mari et al., 1997; Thede and Harper, 1999) (SOHMM) using logistic regression to estimate the emission probabilities. This method allows us to use feature vectors rather than just word identity, as in standard HMMs. In addition, we constrain the inference space of the tagger using type-level tag constraints derived from Wiktionary. This model, called LI10 in Table 3, was originally proposed by Li et al. (2012). We extend the model by adding continuous word representations, induced from the unlabeled data using the skip-gram algorithm (Mikolov et al., 2013), to the feature representations. Our logistic regression model thus works over a combination of discrete and continuous variables when estimating emission probabilities. This extended model is called $\text{LI10}^{+}$. For both models, we do 50 passes over the data as in Li et al. (2012).

## 4 Results

Table 3 presents results for various models on several languages. Our results show that our newswire-trained CRF model with target-specific Brown clusters already does better than *all* our other baseline models (TOOLS and weakly LI10) , with the exception of QUERIES, where the Stanford tagger does remarkably well. All improvements are statistically significant ($p < 0.005$, calculated using approximate randomization with 10k iterations).

Adding the unambiguous unlabeled data leads to further improvements, with error reductions (over CRF) of up to 20%. The exceptions here are Portuguese tweets and SPOKEN. For SPOKEN, this is due to the small amounts of unlabeled data, so we re-used the clusters induced on Twitter, reasoning that language use in these two domains is similar to each other. Despite this conjecture, we see small improvements. For English, Portuguese, and Spanish TWITTER, as well as QUERIES, we see further

[5] LDC2011T03.

[6] http://www.let.rug.nl/~vannoord/trees/

[7] http://www.linguateca.pt/floresta/info_floresta_English.html

[8] http://www.iula.upf.edu/recurs01_tbk_uk.htm

[9] http://lowlands.ku.dk/results

[10] https://code.google.com/p/crfpp/

| | TWITTER | | | | SPOKEN | QUERIES |
|---|---|---|---|---|---|---|
| | EN | ES | PT | NL | EN | EN |
| NEWSWIRE | 762k | 93k | 216k | 217k | 762k | 762k |
| UNLABELED | 57m | 9m | 4.5m | 0.5m | 0.6m | 10.1m |
| TEST | 3,064 | 1,524 | 1,593 | 16,725 | 205k | 7,671 |
| words in $D$ | 380k | 240k | 43k | 55k | 380k | 380k |
| % unamb. | 93% | 97% | 98% | 94% | 93% | 93% |
| unamb. inst. | 1.1m | 148k | 134k | 10k | 98k | 1.5m |
| words in $D'$ | 458k | 279k | 332k | 129k | 381k | 388k |
| unamb. inst. | 2.7m | 613k | 892k | 55k | 113k | 2.3m |

Table 2: Characteristics of data sets used in this paper

| DOMAIN | LANG | TOOLS | LI10 | LI10$^+$ | CRF | CRF+$D$ | +CRF+$D'$ |
|---|---|---|---|---|---|---|---|
| TWITTER | en | 80.55 | 81.72 | 83.26 | 86.72 | 87.50 | **87.76** |
| | es | 75.66 | 71.40 | 73.20 | 78.48 | 82.74 | **82.87** |
| | nl | 84.79 | 74.00 | 80.50 | 89.15 | **89.29** | 89.08 |
| | pt | 67.17 | 64.90 | 72.50 | 80.04 | 79.16 | **80.10** |
| SPOKEN | en | 89.02 | 38.72 | 87.86 | 90.53 | **90.54** | * |
| QUERIES | en | 88.06 | 65.96 | 84.39 | 85.52 | 88.06 | **88.28** |

Table 3: Tagging accuracies. TOOLS are off-the-shelf taggers (Stanford and TreeTagger), LI10/LI10$^+$ the weakly supervised models with and without embeddings, and CRF the model trained on newswire with in-domain word clusters. Last two columns show results when extending with unambiguous data. *: Unlabeled data too small to generate clusters with cut-off 100.

considerable improvements by using our extended tag dictionaries.

The most obvious reason this approach should work is the decrease in unseen words in the in-domain evaluation data. Since the unambiguous data is in-domain, the out-of-vocabulary (OOV) rate goes down when we add the unambiguous data to the newswire training data. In fact, for English Twitter, the OOV rate is reduced by half, and for Portuguese and Spanish, it is reduced by about 40%. For Dutch Twitter, the reduction in OOV rate is much smaller, which probably explains the small gain for this dataset. The difference in reduction of OOV rates are due to sample biases in our unlabeled data. This probably also explains the difference in gains between SPEECH and QUERIES. For search queries, the OOV rate is reduced by 66%, whereas it stays roughly the same for speech transcripts.

## 5 Discussion

We have presented a simple, yet effective approach to adapt POS taggers to a new domain. It requires a) the availability of large amounts of unlabeled data and b) a lexicon to mine unambiguous sentences. As sentence length increases, the likelihood of being completely unambiguous drops. For this reason, our approach works well for domains with shorter average sentence length, such as Twitter, spoken language, and search queries.

We also experimented with allowing up to one ambiguous item per sentence, i.e., we include a sentence in our training data if it contains exactly one item that either a) has more than one licensed tag in the dictionary or b) is not in the dictionary. In the first case, we choose the tag randomly at training time from the set of licensed ones. In the second case, we assume the unknown word to be a NOUN, since unknown words mostly tend to be proper names. When added to newswire, this data results in worse models, presumably by introducing too much noise. However, for low-resource languages or domains with longer sentences and no available newswire data, this might be a viable alternative.

## 6 Related Work

Our approach is similar to mining high-precision items. However, previous approaches on this in NLP have mainly focused on well-defined *classification* tasks, such as PP attachment (Pantel and Lin, 2000; Kawahara and Kurohashi, 2005), or discourse connective disambiguation (Marcu and Echihabi, 2002). In contrast, we mine for *sequences* of unambiguous tokens in a structured prediction task.

While we use the same dictionaries as in Li et al. (2012) and Täckström et al. (2013), our approach differs in several respects. First, we use Wiktionary to mine for *training data*, rather than as type constraints, and second, we use Brown clusters to extend Wiktionary. We did experiment with different ways of doing this, including using various forms of word embeddings, leading to models similar to the baseline models in Socher et al. (2013), but the approach based on Brown clusters led to the best results on our development data.

**?**) use a different approach to distant supervision to improve tagging accuracy for Twitter. They use hyperlinks to fetch additional un-annotated training data that can be used in a self-training loop. Our approach differs in that it produces annotated data and is more readily applicable to various domains.

## 7 Conclusion

We have presented a domain adaptation approach to POS tagging by augmenting newswire data with automatically mined unambiguous instances. We demonstrate our approach on Twitter (in several languages), spoken language transcripts, and search queries. We use dictionaries extended with Brown clusters to collect labeled training data from unlabeled data, saving additional annotation work.

Our models perform significantly better on held-out data than both off-the-shelf taggers and models trained on newswire data only. Improvements hold across several languages (English, Spanish, Portuguese, and Dutch). For spoken language transcripts and search queries, we see some improvements, but find that extending the dictionaries with clusters has less of an effect than for Twitter. Our method can provide a viable alternative to costly annotation when adapting to new domains where unlabeled data and dictionaries are available.

## Acknowledgements

We would like to thank the anonymous reviewers for valuable comments and feedback, as well as Chris Biemann for help with the Twitter data, and Hector Martinez Alonso for the annotation. This research is funded by the ERC Starting Grant LOWLANDS No. 313695.

## References

Tetske Avontuur, Iris Balemans, Laura Elshof, Nanne van Noord, and Menno van Zaanen. 2012. Developing a part-of-speech tagger for dutch tweets. *Computational Linguistics in the Netherlands Journal*, 2:34–51.

Michael Bendersky, Bruce Croft, and David Smith. 2010. Structural annotation of search queries using pseudo-relevance feedback. In *CIKM*.

John Blitzer, Ryan McDonald, and Fernando Pereira. 2006. Domain adaptation with structural correspondence learning. In *EMNLP*.

P.F. Brown, P.V. Desouza, R.L. Mercer, V.J. DellaPietra, and J.C. Lai. 1992. Class-based n-gram models of natural language. *Computational linguistics*, 18(4):467–479.

Hal Daume III. 2007. Frustratingly easy domain adaptation. In *ACL*.

Jennifer Foster, Ozlem Cetinoglu, Joachim Wagner, Josef Le Roux, Joakim Nivre, Deirde Hogan, and Josef van Genabith. 2011. From news to comments: Resources and benchmarks for parsing the language of Web 2.0. In *IJCNLP*.

Kevin Gimpel, Nathan Schneider, Brendan O'Connor, Dipanjan Das, Daniel Mills, Jacob Eisenstein, Michael Heilman, Dani Yogatama, Jeffrey Flanigan, and Noah A. Smith. 2011. Part-of-Speech Tagging for Twitter: Annotation, Features, and Experiments. In *ACL*.

John J Godfrey, Edward C Holliman, and Jane McDaniel. 1992. Switchboard: Telephone speech corpus for research and development. In *Acoustics, Speech, and Signal Processing, 1992. ICASSP-92., 1992 IEEE International Conference on*, volume 1, pages 517–520. IEEE.

Bo Han and Timothy Baldwin. 2011. Lexical normalisation of short text messages: Makn sens a# twitter. In *ACL*.

Dirk Hovy, Barbara Plank, and Anders Søgaard. 2014. When pos datasets don't add up: Combatting sample bias. In *LREC*.

Daisuke Kawahara and Sadao Kurohashi. 2005. Pp-attachment disambiguation boosted by a gigantic volume of unambiguous examples. In *IJCNLP*, pages 188–198. Springer.

Philipp Koehn. 2005. Europarl: A parallel corpus for statistical machine translation. In *MT summit*, volume 5, pages 79–86.

John Lafferty, Andrew McCallum, and Fernando Pereira. 2001. Conditional random fields: probabilistic models for segmenting and labeling sequence data. In *ICML*.

Shen Li, João Graça, and Ben Taskar. 2012. Wiki-ly supervised part-of-speech tagging. In *EMNLP*.

B. MacWhinney. 1997. *The CHILDES Database. 5th Edition*. Dublin, OH, Discovery Systems.

Daniel Marcu and Abdessamad Echihabi. 2002. An unsupervised approach to recognizing discourse relations. In *ACL*.

Jean-Francois Mari, Jean-Paul Haton, and Abdelaziz Kriouile. 1997. Automatic word recognition based on second-order hidden Markov models. *IEEE Transactions on Speech and Audio Processing*, 5(1):22–25.

Tomas Mikolov, Ilya Sutskever, Kai Chen, Gregory Corrado, and Jeffrey Dean. 2013. Distributed representations of words and phrases and their compositionality. In *NIPS*.

Mike Mintz, Steven Bills, Rion Snow, and Dan Jurafsky. 2009. Distant supervision for relation extraction without labeled data. In *ACL*.

Olutobi Owoputi, Brendan O'Connor, Chris Dyer, Kevin Gimpel, Nathan Schneider, and Noah A Smith. 2013. Improved part-of-speech tagging for online conversational text with word clusters. In *NAACL*.

Patrick Pantel and Dekang Lin. 2000. An unsupervised approach to prepositional phrase attachment using contextually similar words. In *ACL*.

Slav Petrov, Dipanjan Das, and Ryan McDonald. 2012. A universal part-of-speech tagset. In *LREC*.

Barbara Plank, Dirk Hovy, Ryan McDonald, and Anders Søgaard. 2014. Adapting taggers to twitter with not-so-distant supervision. COLING.

Alan Ritter, Sam Clark, Oren Etzioni, et al. 2011. Named entity recognition in tweets: an experimental study. In *EMNLP*.

Helmut Schmid. 1994. Probabilistic part-of-speech tagging using decision trees. In *Proceedings of international conference on new methods in language processing*, volume 12, pages 44–49. Manchester, UK.

Richard Socher, Danqi Chen, Chris Manning, and Andrew Ng. 2013. Reasoning with neural tensor networks for knowledge base completion. In *NIPS*.

Oscar Täckström, Dipanjan Das, Slav Petrov, Ryan McDonald, and Joakim Nivre. 2013. Token and type constraints for cross-lingual part-of-speech tagging. *TACL*, 1:1–12.

Scott Thede and Mary Harper. 1999. A second-order hidden Markov model for part-of-speech tagging. In *ACL*.

Kristina Toutanova, Dan Klein, Christopher D Manning, and Yoram Singer. 2003. Feature-rich part-of-speech tagging with a cyclic dependency network. In *NAACL*.

# Clustering Sentences with Density Peaks for Multi-document Summarization

**Yang Zhang**
Shenzhen Graduate School
Peking University, China
ecezhangy@sz.pku.edu.cn

**Yunqing Xia**
Dept. of Comp. Sci. and Tech.
Tsinghua University, China
yqxia@tsinghua.edu.cn

**Yi Liu**
IMSL, PKU-HKUST Shenzhen
Hong Kong Institution, China
yi.liu@imsl.org.cn

**Wenmin Wang**
Shenzhen Graduate School
Peking University, China
wangwm@ece.pku.edu.cn

## Abstract

Multi-document Summarization (MDS) is of great value to many real world applications. Many scoring models are proposed to select appropriate sentences from documents to form the summary, in which the clustering-based methods are popular. In this work, we propose a unified sentence scoring model which measures representativeness and diversity at the same time. Experimental results on DUC04 demonstrate that our MDS method outperforms the DUC04 best method and the existing clustering-based methods, and it yields close results compared to the state-of-the-art generic MDS methods. Advantages of the proposed MDS method are two-fold: (1) The density peaks clustering algorithm is firstly adopted, which is effective and fast. (2) No external resources such as Wordnet and Wikipedia or complex language parsing algorithms is used, making reproduction and deployment very easy in real environment.

## 1 Introduction

Document summarization is the process of generating a generic or topic-focused summary by reducing documents in size while retaining the main characteristics of original documents(Wang et al., 2011). The summary may be formed in a variety of different ways, which are generally categorized as abstractive and extractive(Shen et al., 2007). In this paper, we address the problem of generic multi-document summarization (MDS). An effective summarization method should properly consider the following three important issues: representativeness, diversity, conciseness.

Many scoring models are proposed to select appropriate sentences from documents to form the summary, in which the clustering-based methods are popular. Some researchers address the sentence scoring task in an *isolation* manner(Radev et al., 2004; Wang et al., 2008; Wan and Yang, 2008) (i.e., clustering and ranking are two independent steps). Others handle the sentence ranking task in a *mutuality* manner(Cai and Li, 2013; Cai et al., 2010; Wang et al., 2011) (i.e., clustering improves ranking and vice versa). Two drawbacks of the existing clustering-based methods are worth noting. First, extra algorithms are required to determine the number of clusters beforehand. Second, models are required to rank or score sentences within and across the clusters after clustering.

Our proposed MDS method is inspired by the recent work on density peaks clustering (DPC) algorithm published on *Science* (Rodriguez and Laio, 2014). The underlying assumption is that *cluster centers are characterized by a higher density than their neighbors and by a relatively large distance from points with higher densities.* In this paper, we adapt the density peaks clustering algorithm(Rodriguez and Laio, 2014) to simultaneously cluster sentences and rank them in the *mutuality* manner. Thanks to the density peaks clustering algorithm, we *do not* need to set the number of clusters and *do not* need a post-processing module to reduce redundancy. From the view of summarization task, *DPC* is superior to other clustering methods because it can not only find the best cluster centers, but also do rank all data points, including



*Human Language Technologies: The 2015 Annual Conference of the North American Chapter of the ACL*, pages 1262–1267,
Denver, Colorado, May 31 – June 5, 2015. 

cluster centers, within and across clusters at the same time. Experimental results on the DUC2004 demonstrate that our method outperforms the best method in DUC04 and yields close results compared to the state-of-the-art unsupervised MDS methods.

The major contributions of this work are two-fold: Firstly, a unified sentence scoring model is proposed to consider representativeness, diversity and conciseness at the same time. Secondly, the density peaks clustering algorithm is first applied in the MDS task. We further revise the clustering algorithm to address the summary length constraint.

## 2 Related Work

A vast number of methods are reported in literatures on MDS. The MDS methods can be generally categorized into abstractive and extractive. The extractive MDS can be also categorised into supervised and unsupervised. Several supervised learning methods have been developed for training accurate model for extract-based summarization. The unsupervised methods, on the other hand, also contribute a lot to MDS. In this work, we put our contributions in context of the sentence ranking-based extractive MDS under the unsupervised framework.

Several clustering-based MDS methods have also been proposed. For example, ClusterHITS is proposed to incorporate the cluster-level information into the process of sentence ranking(Wan and Yang, 2008). RankClus is proposed to update sentence ranking and clustering interactively and iteratively with frequency relationships between two sentences, or sentences and terms (Cai et al., 2010). Some kinds of matrix factorization methods are also explored in MDS methods(Gong and Liu, 2001; Lee et al., 2009; Wang et al., 2008; Wang et al., 2011; Shen et al., 2011). For example, matrix factorization methods is adopted to generate sentence clusters, in which non-negative factorization is performed on the term-document matrix using the term-sentence matrix as the base so that the document-topic and sentence-topic matrices could be constructed(Wang et al., 2008).

We follow the idea of clustering-based sentence ranking. Different from the previous work, we attempt to design a unified sentence scoring model to rank sentences and reduce redundancy at the same time.

## 3 Method

In this work, the density peaks sentence clustering (DPSC) method is designed for multi-document summarization.

### 3.1 Density Peaks Sentence Clustering

The density peaks clustering (DPC) algorithm is achieved upon the object similarity matrix. Objects are finally assigned density values and mini-distance values. In this work, we consider sentences as objects and follow the framework to calculate representativeness score and diversity score of each sentence in a unified model.

To construct the sentence similarity matrix for the DPC algorithm, we first segment documents into sentences and remove the non-stop words in the sentences. We then represent the sentences using bag-of-words vector space model, thus the cosine equation is applicable to calculate sentence similarity. The terms can be weighted with different schemes such as $boolean$ (occurring or not), $tf$ (term frequency) and $tf * isf$ (term frequency inverse sentence frequency). We finally choose the boolean scheme in our experiments because it performs best in our empirical study.

### 3.2 Representativeness Scoring

For document summarization, we need a representative score to quantify the degree how much a sentence is important in the documents. Enlightened by the DPC algorithm, we assume that when a sentence has more similar sentences (i.e., higher density), it will be considered more important or more representative. Thus we define the following function to calculate the representativeness score $s^{\text{REP}}(i)$ for each sentence $s_i$:

$$s^{\text{REP}}(i) = \frac{1}{K} \sum_{j=1, j \neq i}^{K} \chi(sim_{ij} - \delta), \quad (1)$$

$$\chi(x) = \begin{cases} 1 & \text{if } x > 0 \\ 0 & \text{otherwise} \end{cases} \quad (2)$$

where $sim_{ij}$ denotes the similarity value between the $i$-th and $j$-th sentence, and $K$ denotes the number of sentences in the datasets. $\delta$ denotes a predefined density threshold. Note that we set the density threshold following (Rodriguez and Laio, 2014), which attempts to exclude the sentences holding lower similarity with the current sentence.

### 3.3 Diversity Scoring

Most of the previous work handles diversity via reduce redundancy in a post processing module after the sentences are ranked. In this work, we measure diversity in the ranking model.

Diversity score of a sentence is measured by computing the minimum distance between the sentence $s_i$ and any other sentences with higher density score.

In order to reflect the above observation, we define the following function to calculate the diversity score $s^{\text{DIV}}(i)$:

$$s^{\text{DIV}}(i) = 1 - \max_{j:s^{\text{REP}}(j)>s^{\text{REP}}(i)} sim_{ij}. \quad (3)$$

For the sentence with the highest density, we conventionally take

$$s^{\text{DIV}}(i) = 1 - \min_{j \neq i} sim_{ij}. \quad (4)$$

The proposed diversity score looks similar to the famous *Maximum Marginal Relevance* (MMR) (Carbonell and Goldstein, 1998), which is widely used in removing redundancy by using a greedy algorithm to remove sentences that are too similar to the already selected ones. The difference lies that MMR selects a sentence by comparing it to those selected sentences while we compare it to all the other sentences in the dataset, thus it can enhance the diversity globally.

### 3.4 Length Scoring

It is widely accepted that summarization task has an important constraint, i.e., summary length. In order to satisfy this constraint, the length of selected sentences should be as short as possible. Based on this analysis, we propose the length score, which has relationship with the *effective length* and *real length*. The *real length* is defined as the number of word occurrences that a sentence contains. We then define the *effective length* as how many unique non-stop terms a sentence contains. We finally define the following function to calculate the length score $s^{\text{LEN}}(i)$.

The motivation to propose the length score is, shorter sentences with better representativeness score and diversity score are more favorable for the final summaries. Furthermore, as we use the Boolean scheme to measure sentence similarity, we only count unique words as effective sentence length.

$$s^{\text{LEN}}(i) = \frac{el(s_i)}{\max_{j=1}^{K} el(s_j)} \times \log \frac{\left(\max_{j=1}^{K} rl(s_j)\right)}{rl(s_i)}, \quad (5)$$

where $el(s_i)$ returns the *effective length* of sentence $s_i$, and $rl(s_i)$ the *real length* of sentence $s_i$.

### 3.5 Unified Sentence Scoring

Now we integrate representativeness score, diversity score and length score in the following unified sentence scoring function:

$$s^{\text{DPSC}}(i) = s^{\text{REP}}(i) \times s^{\text{DIV}}(i) \times s^{\text{LEN}}(i). \quad (6)$$

The assumption is obviously that we need those sentences which are as representative, diversified as possible and contain unique terms as many as possible within a limited length.

In calculation, we simply apply logarithm since:

$$s^{\text{DPSC}}(i) \sim \log s^{\text{REP}}(i) + \log s^{\text{DIV}}(i) + \log s^{\text{LEN}}(i) \quad (7)$$

### 3.6 Summary Generation

As three scores above including the representativeness, diversity and length constraint are measured in a unified sentence scoring model, generating a summary with out method is basically achieved by selecting the higher ranking sentences. In other words, our summary contains more representative and diversified information in the limited length.

**Complexity Analysis**: Suppose $K$ is the total number of sentences in the document collection. The complexity in calculating the sentence similarity matrix is $O(K^2)$. As the complexity in the function of representativeness scoring, diversity scoring and length scoring are all $O(K)$, the total time complexity of our DPSC method is $O(K^2) + O(K) + O(K) \sim O(K^2)$.

## 4 Evaluation

Two experiments are reported in this paper: comparing the MDS methods and tuning the density threshold. For both experiments, we use the DUC2004(task 2)[1] dataset, which is annotated manually for generic MDS. We adopted ROUGE (Lin, 2004) version 1.5.5[2] and take F-measure of ROUGE-1, ROUGE-2 and ROUGE-SU as our evaluation metrics. In pre-processing, we use the Porter Stemmer[3] in sentence segmenting, stop-word removing and word stemming. Note that our MDS method is purely unsupervised, and uses no training or development data.

### 4.1 The MDS Methods

We selected three categories of baselines[4]:

(1) DUC04 MDS methods: *DUC04Best* (Conroy et al., 2004).

(2) Clustering-based MDS methods: *Centroid* (Radev et al., 2004), *ClusterHITS* (Wan and Yang, 2008), *SNMF* (Wang et al., 2008), *RTC* (Cai and Li, 2013), *FGB* (Wang et al., 2011), and *AASum* (Canhasi and Kononenko, 2013).

(3) Other state-of-the-art MDS methods: *LexRank* (graph-based method) (Erkan and Radev, 2004), *CSFO* (optimization-oriented method) (Lin and Bilmes, 2011) and *WCS* (aggregation-oriented method) (Wang and Li, 2012).

For our *DPSC* method, we adopt the following settings: (1) Density threshold is set 0.22 as it is empirically found as optimal in Section 4.2 in the DUC04 dataset. (2) Term weighting scheme is set *Boolean*. In our experiments, *Boolean* is found outperforming *tf* and *tfisf* in sentence representation, this is because term repetition happens less frequently in short text units like sentences than that in documents. Experimental results of the MDS methods are presented in Table 1. Note the ROUGE values of some MDS methods are not reported in the literatures and marked with $'-'$ in Table 1.

According to Table 1, *DPSC* outperforms *DUC04Best*, which ignores the cross-sentence information to solve the diversity problem. *DPSC* outperforms most clustering-based methods except for *AASum*, which performs slightly better than *DPSC* on ROUGE-1. *AASum* is a very complex MDS method which fully exploits the advantages of clustering and the flexibility of matrix factorization. A weakness of the approach is that the number of archetypes must be predefined, and a post-processing module is required to reduce redundancy (Canhasi and Kononenko, 2013).

Table 1: Experimental results of the MDS methods on DUC04.

| System | ROUGE-1 | ROUGE-2 | ROUGE-SU |
|---|---|---|---|
| DUC04Best | 0.38224 | 0.09216 | 0.13233 |
| Centroid | 0.36728 | 0.07379 | 0.12511 |
| ClusterHITS | 0.36463 | 0.07632 | – |
| SNMF | – | 0.08400 | 0.12660 |
| RTC | 0.37475 | 0.08973 | – |
| FGB | 0.38724 | 0.08115 | 0.12957 |
| AASum | **0.41150** | 0.09340 | 0.13760 |
| LexRank | 0.37842 | 0.08572 | 0.13097 |
| CSFO | 0.38900 | – | – |
| WCS | 0.39872 | **0.09611** | 0.13532 |
| DPSC | 0.39075 | 0.09376 | **0.14000** |

*DPSC* also outperforms *LexRank* and *CSFO*, and yields close results compared with *WCS*. According to Table 1, *DPSC* performs slightly worse than *WCS*. The marginal performance gain of *WCS* comes from the aggregation strategy, namely, multiple MDS systems are required. As a comparison, *DPSC* is a pure and simple MDS method, exhibiting much lower complexity.

*DPSC* method is also advantageous on usability, because it does not involve any external resources such as Wordnet and Wikipedia or very complex natural language processing algorithms such as sentence parsing. Moreover, DPSC is a very fast MDS method. Thus it can be easily reproduced and deployed in real environment.

### 4.2 Density Threshold

Following (Rodriguez and Laio, 2014), we design an experiment on DUC04 dataset to investigate how the density threshold influences quality of the summaries. We tune the density threshold by varying it from 0.10 to 0.40(see the X-axis in Figure 1).

Figure 1 shows that on the specific dataset (i.e., DUC04), *DPSC* reaches the best ROUGE score

[1] http://duc.nist.gov/duc2004/tasks.html

[2] Options used: -a -c 95 -b 665 -m -n 4 -w 1.2

[3] http://tartarus.org/martin/PorterStemmer/

[4] Interested readers can refer to details in the references.

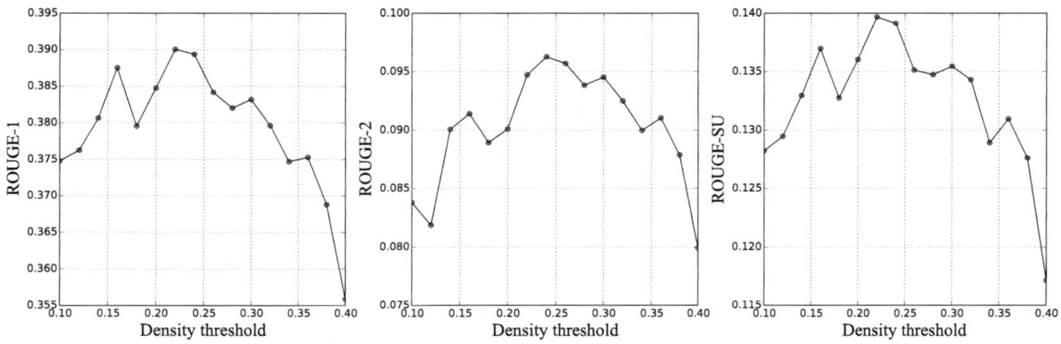


Figure 1: ROUGE curves of DPSC method varying the density threshold.

when the density threshold is set around 0.22 while starts to drop significantly after 0.30. This indicates that 0.22 is a good setting for the density threshold on DUC04.

## 5 Conclusion and Future Work

In this paper we report the density peaks sentence clustering (DPSC) method for multi-document summarization. Different from the prior work which deals with representativeness and redundancy independently, a unified sentence scoring model is designed in DPSC to combine the representativeness score, the diversity score and the length score of each sentence. Experimental results on DUC04 dataset show that DPSC outperforms the DUC04 best method and the existing clustering-based methods. Meanwhile, it yields close results when compared with the state-of-the-art generic MDS methods. It is thus verified that density peaks clustering algorithm is able to handle MDS effectively.

However, this work is still preliminary. We will study semantic text similarity to improve the sentence similarity matrix. We will then apply the proposed method in query-based multi-document summarization.

## Acknowledgement

This work is partially supported by Natural Science Foundation of China (61272233, 61373056, 61433018) and Shenzhen Peacock Scheme(183003656). We thank the reviewers for the insightful comments.

## References

Xiaoyan Cai and Wenjie Li. 2013. Ranking through clustering: An integrated approach to multi-document summarization. *Audio, Speech, and Language Processing, IEEE Transactions on*, 21(7):1424–1433.

Xiaoyan Cai, Wenjie Li, You Ouyang, and Hong Yan. 2010. Simultaneous ranking and clustering of sentences: a reinforcement approach to multi-document summarization. In *Proceedings of the 23rd International Conference on Computational Linguistics*, pages 134–142. Association for Computational Linguistics.

Ercan Canhasi and Igor Kononenko. 2013. Multi-document summarization via archetypal analysis of the content-graph joint model. *Knowledge and Information Systems*, pages 1–22.

Jaime Carbonell and Jade Goldstein. 1998. The use of mmr, diversity-based reranking for reordering documents and producing summaries. In *Proceedings of the 21st annual international ACM SIGIR conference on Research and development in information retrieval*, pages 335–336. ACM.

John M Conroy, Judith D Schlesinger, Jade Goldstein, and Dianne P Oleary. 2004. Left-brain/right-brain multi-document summarization. In *Proceedings of the Document Understanding Conference (DUC 2004)*.

Günes Erkan and Dragomir R Radev. 2004. Lexrank: Graph-based lexical centrality as salience in text summarization. *J. Artif. Intell. Res.(JAIR)*, 22(1):457–479.

Yihong Gong and Xin Liu. 2001. Generic text summarization using relevance measure and latent semantic analysis. In *Proceedings of the 24th annual international ACM SIGIR conference on Research and development in information retrieval*, pages 19–25. ACM.

Ju-Hong Lee, Sun Park, Chan-Min Ahn, and Daeho Kim. 2009. Automatic generic document summarization based on non-negative matrix factorization. *Information Processing & Management*, 45(1):20–34.

Hui Lin and Jeff Bilmes. 2011. A class of submodular functions for document summarization. In *Proceedings of the 49th Annual Meeting of the Association for Computational Linguistics: Human Language Technologies-Volume 1*, pages 510–520. Association for Computational Linguistics.

Chin-Yew Lin. 2004. Rouge: A package for automatic evaluation of summaries. In *Text Summarization Branches Out: Proceedings of the ACL-04 Workshop*, pages 74–81.

Dragomir R Radev, Hongyan Jing, Małgorzata Styś, and Daniel Tam. 2004. Centroid-based summarization of multiple documents. *Information Processing & Management*, 40(6):919–938.

Alex Rodriguez and Alessandro Laio. 2014. Clustering by fast search and find of density peaks. *Science*, 344(6191):1492–1496.

Dou Shen, Jian-Tao Sun, Hua Li, Qiang Yang, and Zheng Chen. 2007. Document summarization using conditional random fields. In *IJCAI*, volume 7, pages 2862–2867.

Chao Shen, Tao Li, and Chris HQ Ding. 2011. Integrating clustering and multi-document summarization by bi-mixture probabilistic latent semantic analysis (plsa) with sentence bases. In *AAAI*.

Xiaojun Wan and Jianwu Yang. 2008. Multi-document summarization using cluster-based link analysis. In *Proceedings of the 31st annual international ACM SIGIR conference on Research and development in information retrieval*, pages 299–306. ACM.

Dingding Wang and Tao Li. 2012. Weighted consensus multi-document summarization. *Information Processing & Management*, 48(3):513–523.

Dingding Wang, Tao Li, Shenghuo Zhu, and Chris Ding. 2008. Multi-document summarization via sentence-level semantic analysis and symmetric matrix factorization. In *Proceedings of the 31st annual international ACM SIGIR conference on Research and development in information retrieval*, pages 307–314. ACM.

Dingding Wang, Shenghuo Zhu, Tao Li, Yun Chi, and Yihong Gong. 2011. Integrating document clustering and multidocument summarization. *ACM Transactions on Knowledge Discovery from Data (TKDD)*, 5(3):14.

# Development of the Multilingual Semantic Annotation System

**Scott Piao**
Lancaster University
Lancaster
UK
s.piao@lancaster.ac.uk

**Francesca Bianchi**
University of the Salento
Lecce
Italy
francesca.bianchi@unisalento.it

**Carmen Dayrell**
Lancaster University
Lancaster
UK
c.dayrell@lancaster.ac.uk

**Angela D'Egidio**
University of the Salento
Lecce
Italy
angela.degidio@unisalento.it

**Paul Rayson**
Lancaster University
Lancaster
UK
p.rayson@lancaster.ac.uk

## Abstract

This paper reports on our research to generate multilingual semantic lexical resources and develop multilingual semantic annotation software, which assigns each word in running text to a semantic category based on a lexical semantic classification scheme. Such tools have an important role in developing intelligent multilingual NLP, text mining and ICT systems. In this work, we aim to extend an existing English semantic annotation tool to cover a range of languages, namely Italian, Chinese and Brazilian Portuguese, by bootstrapping new semantic lexical resources via automatically translating existing English semantic lexicons into these languages. We used a set of bilingual dictionaries and word lists for this purpose. In our experiment, with minor manual improvement of the automatically generated semantic lexicons, the prototype tools based on the new lexicons achieved an average lexical coverage of 79.86% and an average annotation precision of 71.42% (if only precise annotations are considered) or 84.64% (if partially correct annotations are included) on the three languages. Our experiment demonstrates that it is feasible to rapidly develop prototype semantic annotation tools for new languages by automatically bootstrapping new semantic lexicons based on existing ones.

## 1 Introduction

In this paper, we report on an experiment to develop prototype semantic annotation tools for Italian, Chinese and Brazilian Portuguese based on an existing English annotation tool. Over the last twenty years, semantic lexical resources and semantic annotation tools, such as EuroWordNet (Vossen, 1998) and USAS (Rayson et al., 2004), have played an important role in developing intelligent NLP and HLT systems. Various applications of semantic annotation systems and annotated corpus resources have been reported, including empirical language studies at the semantic level (Rayson et al. 2004; Ooi et al., 2007; Beigman Klebanov et al., 2008; Potts and Baker, 2013) and studies in information technology (Volk, et al., 2002; Nakano et al, 2005; Doherty et al., 2006; Chitchyan et al., 2006; Taiani et al., 2008; Gacitua et al., 2008) among others.

While various semantic annotation tools are available for monolingual analysis, particularly for English, there are few such systems that can carry out semantic analysis of multiple languages with a unified semantic annotation scheme. We aim to address this issue by extending an existing English semantic annotation tool (Rayson et al., 2004) to cover a range of languages.

The USAS semantic annotation tool mentioned above adopts a lexical semantic classification scheme derived from Tom McArthur's Longman Lexicon of Contemporary English (McArthur, 1981), which consists of 21 main discourse fields and 232 sub-fields, such as "social actions, states and processes" and "emotion" etc. It also uses a set



*Human Language Technologies: The 2015 Annual Conference of the North American Chapter of the ACL*, pages 1268–1274,
Denver, Colorado, May 31 – June 5, 2015. 

of auxiliary codes, such as ***m/f*** (male/female), +/- (positive/negative) etc. For example, it tags "happy" and "sad" with "E4.1+" and "E4.1-" respectively, indicating positive and negative sentiment. It also identifies many types of multi-word expressions, such as phrasal verbs, noun phrases, named entities and true non-compositional idioms, and annotates them with single semantic tags since this is highly significant for identifying contextual meaning. Recent applications of the USAS tagger include analysis of literary language (Balossi, 2014), the language of psychopaths (Hancock et al, 2013) and scientific deception (Markowitz and Hancock, 2014). There would be obvious benefits if such a semantic tool could cover a wide range of languages. Efforts have been made to port the existing semantic annotation system to other languages (Finnish and Russian) (Löfberg et al., 2005; Mudraya et al., 2006), so a prototype software framework could be used. However, manually developing semantic lexical resources for new languages from scratch is a time consuming task. In this experiment, we examine the feasibility of rapidly bootstrapping semantic lexical resources for new languages by automatically translating existing English semantic lexicons using bilingual dictionaries. We developed prototype semantic annotation tools for Italian, Chinese and Brazilian Portuguese based on automatically generated semantic lexicons. Our evaluation of the tools shows that it is feasible to rapidly develop prototype semantic tools via the aforementioned automatic method, which can be improved and refined manually to achieve a high performance.

## 2 Related Work

There exist various tools that can semantically annotate multilingual texts, including GATE (Cunningham et al., 2011) and KIM (Popov et al., 2003) which, combined together, provide multilingual semantic annotation functionalities based on ontologies. Freeling (Padró et al., 2012) provides multilingual annotations such as named entity recognition and WordNet sense tagging. Recent developments in this area include Zhang and Rettinger's work (2014) in which they tested a toolkit for Wikipedia-based annotation (wikification) of multilingual texts. However, in the work described here we employ a lexicographically-informed semantic classification scheme and we perform *all-words* annotation. In terms of porting tools from one language to another by translating lexicons, Brooke et al. (2009) obtained poor results from a small dictionary in cross-linguistic sentiment analysis.

## 3 Generating Multilingual Semantic Lexicons by Automatic Mapping

The USAS tagger relies heavily on the semantic dictionary as its knowledge source, so the main task in the development of our prototype semantic annotation tools for new languages was to generate semantic lexicons, both for single word and multiword expressions (MWE), in which words and MWEs can be associated with appropriate semantic tags. For this purpose, our approach involves mapping existing English semantic lexicons into target languages in order to transfer the semantic tags across translation equivalents. The entries of the English semantic lexicons are classified under the USAS semantic annotation scheme (Archer et al., 2004), which consists of 21 major semantic categories that are further divided into 232 subcategories.

In order to translate the English semantic lexicons into other languages, we needed a bilingual lexicon for each of the target languages, Italian, Chinese and Portuguese in our particular case. For this purpose, we first used two corpus-based frequency dictionaries compiled for Chinese (Xiao et al., 2009) and Portuguese (Davies and Preto-Bay, 2007), which cover the 5,000 most frequent Chinese and Portuguese words respectively. These dictionaries provided high-quality manually edited word translations. In addition, we used large English-Italian and English-Portuguese bilingual lexicons available from FreeLang site (http://www.freelang.net/dictionary) as well as an English-Chinese bilingual word list available from LDC (Linguistic Data Consortium). Compiled without professional editing, these bilingual word lists contain errors and inaccurate translations, and hence they introduced noise into the mapping process. However, they provided wider lexical coverage of the languages involved and complemented the limited sizes of the high-quality dictionaries used in our experiment. Table 1 lists the bilingual lexical resources employed for translating the English lexicons into each of the three languages involved in our experiment.

| Language | Lexical resources |
|---|---|
| Italian | English-Italian FreeLang wordlist (33,700 entries); |
| Chinese | Chinese/English dictionary (5,000 entries);<br>LDC Eng-Chi bilingual wordlist (110,800 entries) |
| Portuguese | Portuguese/English dictionary (5,000 entries);<br>English-Portuguese (Brazilian version) FreeLang wordlist (20,980 entries) |

Table 1: Bilingual lexical resources used.

The semantic lexicon translation process mainly involves transferring semantic tags from an English lexeme to its translation equivalent/s. For instance, given a pair of word/MWE translations, one of which is English, if the English headword is found in the English semantic lexicon, its semantic categories are passed to its translation equivalents. For the high-quality formal dictionaries, this approach worked very well in our experiment, thanks to the accurate translations and explicit part-of-speech (POS) information provided by such resources.

With the bilingual word lists from FreeLang and LDC, however, this translation process was not straightforward. Firstly, most of the entries of the word lists do not contain any POS information. To avoid losing any potentially relevant semantic tags, we have to consider all possible POS categories of each English headword, and the same applies to their translation equivalents. For example, the English headword "advance" has four possible *C7* POS tags (*JJ*-adjective, *NN1*-singular noun, *VV0*-base form of verb, *VVI*-infinitive verb) in the English semantic lexicon with different semantic categories including *N4* (linear order), *A9-* (giving), *M1* (moving, coming and going), *A5.1* (evaluation: good/bad), *A2.1* (affect: modify, change), Q2.2 (speech acts), *S8+* (helping), *Q2.1* (speech etc: communicative), although with some overlap, as shown below (in each line, the first code is a POS tag and the following ones denote USAS semantic categories[1]):

*advance JJ N4*
*advance NN1 A9- M1 A5.1+/A2.1*
*advance VV0 M1 A9- Q2.2 A5.1+/A2.1*
*advance VVI M1 S8+ A9- A5.1+/A2.1 Q2.1*

In such a case, for each of the possible translation equivalents of the word "advance", these four types of POS tags and their corresponding semantic tags need to be assigned to their corresponding translations in the target languages. Obviously this would lead to passing wrong and redundant semantic tags to the translation equivalents. Nevertheless, we have to accept such noise in order to increase the chances of obtaining correct semantic tags, as it would be easier to remove redundant/incorrect semantic tags than searching for missing ones in the manual improvement stage.

Another major challenge in the translation process was the mapping between the POS tagsets employed by different lexical resources and tools. Even for the same language, different lexicons and tools can employ different POS tagsets. For example, different Portuguese POS tagsets are used by the Portuguese frequency dictionary and the POS TreeTagger (Schmid, 1994). To bridge between the different POS tagsets, we designed a simplified common POS tagset for each language, into which other tags can be mapped. For example, the Portuguese POS tagset was simplified into 12 categories "adj, adv, det, noun, pnoun, verb, pron, conj, intj, prep, num, punc". Because a single semantic category tends to span similar POS categories, e.g. present/past/progressive tense of verbs, simplification of POS tagsets generally does not affect semantic annotation accuracy.

After applying all the resources and automatic mapping described above, we obtained approximately 38,720, 83,600 and 15,700 semantic lexicon entries for Italian, Chinese and Portuguese respectively. Our initial evaluation involved direct manual checking of these bootstrapped lexicons. For example, 5,622 Italian MWE entries and 1,763 Italian single word entries have been manually corrected. For the Chinese lexicon, the most frequent words were identified using the Chinese word frequency list of Internet Corpus (Sharoff, 2006), and the semantic tags of about 560 entries related to the most frequent words were manually corrected. For Portuguese, about 900 lexicon entries were manually checked.

The manual improvement mainly involves three processes: a) filtering lexicon entries having wrong POS tags, b) selecting correct semantic tags from candidates, c) adding missing semantic tags. The amount of effort needed depends on the quality of the bilingual dictionaries. For example, from the automatically generated 900 Chinese entries containing the most frequent (also highly ambiguous) words, 505 entries were selected after the POS filtering. In addition, 145 of them were improved by

[1] For definitions of the POS and semantic tags, see websites http://ucrel.lancs.ac.uk/claws7tags.html and http://ucrel.lancs.ac.uk/usas/USASSemanticTagset.pdf

adding missing semantic tags. Table 2 shows the sizes of the current lexicons.

| Language | Single word entries | MWE entries |
|---|---|---|
| Italian | 33,100 | 5,622 |
| Chinese | 64,413 | 19,039 |
| Portuguese | 13,942 | 1,799 |

Table 2: Sizes of current semantic lexicons.

## 4 Architecture of Annotation System

Based on the multilingual semantic lexicons described in the previous section, prototype semantic taggers were built for the three languages by deploying the lexicons into the existing software architecture, which employs disambiguation methods reported by Rayson et al. (2004). A set of POS tagging tools were incorporated to pre-process texts from the target languages. The TreeTagger (Schmid, 1994) was used for Italian and Portuguese, and the Stanford POS tagger (Toutanova et al., 2003) was used for Chinese. These tools and semantic lexicon look-up components form pipelines to annotate words in running texts. Figure 1 shows the architecture of the software framework.

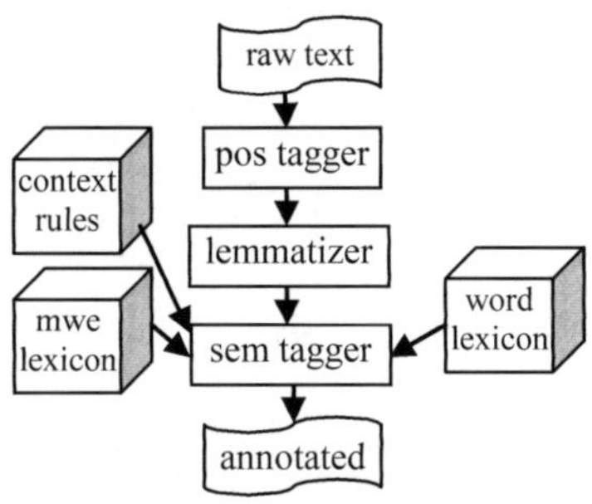


Figure 1: Architecture of the semantic tagger.

## 5 Evaluation of Prototype System

Following the initial manual evaluation of the prototype semantic taggers described in section 3, we then carried out larger scale automatic evaluations using a set of sample corpora. We conducted two complementary types of evaluations: lexical coverage and annotation precision. The lexical coverage is a particularly interesting metric for our evaluation, as we expect this is where an automatic approach can make significant contribution to the development of annotation systems. On the other hand, high annotation precision normally entails manual improvement of the lexical resources or a period of training on manually tagged corpora.

For the lexical coverage evaluation, three reference corpora were chosen: PAISÀ Italian corpus (Borghetti et al., 2011), LCMC Corpus (Lancaster Corpus of Mandarin Chinese) (McEnery and Xiao, 2004) and Lacio-Ref Portuguese corpus (Aluisio et al., 2003). Because PAISÀ and Lacio-Ref corpora are too large for our purpose, we extracted subsections of about 1.5 million Italian words and 1.7 million Portuguese words from them.

For the evaluation, we annotated the corpus data using the annotation tools of the corresponding target languages, and examined what percentage of the words were assigned with semantic tags. Punctuation marks were excluded in this evaluation process. Table 3 shows the statistics of the evaluation for each language.

| Language | Number of words | Tagged words | Lexicon coverage (%) |
|---|---|---|---|
| Italian | 1,479,394 | 1,265,399 | 85.53 |
| Chinese | 975,482 | 786,663 | 80.64 |
| Portuguese | 1,705,184 | 1,251,579 | 73.40 |
| Average | | | 79.86 |

Table 3: Lexical coverage of the semantic taggers.

As shown in the table, the annotation tools achieved an average lexical coverage of 79.86% over the three languages, with Italian having the highest coverage of 85.53% and Portuguese the lowest coverage of 73.40%. Due to the different types of data in the three sample corpora, this result is not conclusive. Homogeneous corpus data from all of the three languages will be needed to make more reliable comparison of the lexical coverage. Considering that the tools were built based on only three bilingual lexical resources over a short period of time, such lexical coverage is encouraging. This result also demonstrates that, if sufficiently large bilingual lexicons become available; our approach can potentially achieve high lexical coverage.

Next we conducted an evaluation of the precision of the prototype tools. We randomly selected sample texts for each language as follows. Italian sample texts were selected from domains of press, contemporary literature and blogs; Chinese sample texts from press, reviews and fiction; Portuguese sample texts from press and fiction. In the evaluation, we annotated the sample texts using the prototype annotation tools and manually checked the precision among the annotated words. We used two metrics: correctly tagged and partially correctly tagged. With the current tools, a word can be assigned with multiple candidate semantic tags. The first evaluation metric refers to the cases where the first candidate tag is correct, whereas the other metric refers to the cases where the other tags in the list are correct or closely related to the true word sense. Table 4 shows the statistics of the evaluation.

| Lan. | Sample text size | Tagged words | Correct | Partially correct |
|---|---|---|---|---|
| Ita | 4,510 | 3,266 | 1,826 (55.91%) | 672 (20.58%) |
| Chi | 1,053 | 813 | 616 (75.76%) | 97 (11.93%) |
| Port | 1,231 | 953 | 787 (82.58%) | 68 (7.14%) |
| Avg | | | 71.42% | 13.22% |

Table 4: Evaluation of precision.

As shown in the table, the Portuguese tagger obtained the highest first-tag precision (82.58%), while the Italian tagger produced a precision (55.91%) significantly lower than others. However, if we include the partially correct annotations, the precision scores become more consistent: 76.49%, 87.69% and 89.72% for the three languages respectively, with an average precision of 84.64%. We also estimated recall based on the numbers of tokens of the sample texts and those tagged correctly/partially correctly, obtaining 55.39%, 67.71% and 69.46% for Italian, Chinese and Portuguese respectively. Such a fairly close range of the precision and recall values indicates that our approach to developing prototype semantic annotation tools can be expected to achieve stable results across various languages, although we need larger-scale evaluations to draw a conclusion. It is worth noting that, although the recall is still low, these taggers are starting to approach the precision of the English system at 91% (Rayson et al., 2004).

Our further error analysis revealed that the main causes of the errors include the homonym translations (e.g. *bank* as river bank vs. money bank), translation errors and missing of the translation words in the English semantic lexicons. For example, the Chinese word "爸爸" (father) has a number of synonymous English translation equivalents in the bilingual lexicon: *dad* (with semantic tag *S4m*), *baba, da, dada, daddy* (*S4m*), *father* (*S4m S9/S2m*), *papa* (*S4m*). It is also translated into *presence* (*M6, A3+, S1.1.3+, S1.2, S9*) by mistake. Among the correct English translations, *baba, da, dada* (transliteration) are not included in the English semantic lexicons. Making things worse, *da* is a homonym which is classified as a discourse marker of exclamation (*Z4*) in English lexicons. Our current automatic process collects all the semantic tags derived from the English translation counterparts found in the bilingual lexicon and assigns them to the Chinese word "爸爸", resulting in an erroneous entry as shown below:

爸爸 *noun* *M6 A3+ S1.1.3+ S1.2 S9 S4/B1 S4m S9/S2.2m Z4*

In order to resolve such cases, we will need to consider contexts of each translation word pairs' usage via parallel or comparable corpora.

## 6 Conclusion and Future Work

In this paper, we have investigated the feasibility of rapidly bootstrapping semantic annotation tools for new target languages[2] by mapping an existing semantic lexicon and software architecture. In particular, we tested the possibility of automatically translating existing English semantic lexicons into other languages, Italian, Chinese and Brazilian Portuguese in this particular case. Our experiment demonstrates that, if appropriate high-quality bilingual lexicons are available, it is feasible to rapidly generating prototype systems with a good lexical coverage with our automatic approach. On the other hand, our experiment also shows that, in order to achieve a high precision, parallel/comparable corpus based disambiguation is needed for identifying precise translation equivalents, and a certain amount of manual cleaning and improvement of the automatically generated semantic lexicons is indispensible. We are continuing to improve the multilingual semantic taggers and extend them to cover more languages, such as Spanish and Dutch, aiming to develop a large-scale multilingual semantic annotation and analysis system. We also intend to perform task-based evaluation of the manually checked versus automatically generated lexicons.

## Acknowledgments

We would like to thank Prof. Elena Semino, Prof. Yufang Qian and Dr. Richard Xiao for their contributions to our research. This work is supported by the UCREL research centre and the ESRC Centre for Corpus Approaches to Social Science (CASS), ESRC grant reference ES/K002155/1, both at Lancaster University, UK.

[2] The results are available at http://ucrel.lancs.ac.uk/usas/

## References


Aluisio, Sandra M., Gisele Pinheiro, Marcelo Finger, Maria das Graças V. Nunes and Stella E. Tagnin (2003). The Lacio-Web Project: overview and issues in Brazilian Portuguese corpora creation. In Proceedings of Corpus Linguistics 2003 Conference (CL2003), Lancaster, UK.

Archer, Dawn, Paul Rayson, Scott Piao, Tony McEnery (2004). Comparing the UCREL Semantic Annotation Scheme with Lexicographical Taxonomies. In Williams G. and Vessier S. (eds.) Proceedings of the 11th EURALEX (European Association for Lexicography) International Congress (Euralex 2004), Lorient, France. Volume III, pp. 817-827.

Balossi, Giuseppina (2014) A Corpus Linguistic Approach to Literary Language and Characterization: Virginia Woolf's The Waves. Benjamins.

Borghetti, Claudia, Sara Castagnoli and Marco Brunello (2011). I testi del web: una proposta di classificazione sulla base del corpus PAISÀ. In Cerruti, M., E. Corino and C. Onesti (eds.): Scritto e parlato, formale e informale: La comunicazione mediata dalla rete., Roma: Carocci, pp. 147-170.

Brooke, Julian, Milan Tofiloski, and Maite Taboada (2009). Cross-linguistic sentiment analysis: From English to Spanish. In Proceedings of the International Conference on Recent Advances in Natural Language Processing (RANLP), pp. 50-54.

Chitchyan, Ruzanna, Américo Sampaio, Awais Rashid and Paul Rayson (2006). Evaluating EA-Miner: Are Early Aspect Mining Techniques Effective? In proceedings of Towards Evaluation of Aspect Mining (TEAM 2006). Workshop Co-located with ECOOP 2006, European Conference on Object-Oriented Programming, 20th edition, Nantes, France, pp. 5-8.

Cunningham, Hamish, Diana Maynard, Kalina Bontcheva (2011). Text Processing with GATE. Gateway Press CA. ISBN: 0956599311 9780956599315.

Davies, Mark and Ana Preto-Bay (2007). A Frequency Dictionary of Portuguese. Routledge. ISBN-10: 0415419972.

Doherty, Neil, Nigel Lockett, Paul Rayson and Stuart Riley (2006). Electronic-CRM: a simple sales tool or facilitator of relationship marketing? The 29th Institute for Small Business & Entrepreneurship Conference. International Entrepreneurship - from local to global enterprise creation and development, Cardiff-Caerdydd, UK.

Gacitua, Ricardo, Pete Sawyer, Paul Rayson (2008). A flexible framework to experiment with ontology learning techniques. In Knowledge-Based Systems, 21(3), pp. 192-199.

Hancock, Jeffrey, T., Michael T. Woodworth and Stephen Porter (2013) Hungry like the wolf: A word-pattern analysis of the language of psychopaths. Legal and Criminological Psychology. 18 (1) pp. 102-114.

Hermann, Karl Moritz and Phil Blunsom (2013). A Simple Model for Learning Multilingual Compositional Semantics. arXiv:1312.6173 [cs.CL]. URL: http://arxiv.org/abs/1312.6173.

Klebanov, Beigman B., Daniel Diermeier and Eyal Beigman (2008). Automatic annotation of semantic fields for political science research. Journal of Language Technology and Politics 5(1), pp. 95-120.

Löfberg, Laura, Scott Piao, Asko Nykanen, Krista Varantola, Paul Rayson, and Jukka-Pekka Juntunen (2005). A semantic tagger for the Finnish language. In the Proceedings of the Corpus Linguistics Conference 2005, Birmingham, UK.

McArthur, Tom (1981). Longman Lexicon of Contemporary English. Longman London.

McEnery, Tony and Zhonghua. Xiao (2004). The Lancaster corpus of Mandarin Chinese: a corpus for monolingual and contrastive language study. In Proceedings of LREC 2004. pp. 1175-1178.

Markowitz DM, Hancock JT (2014) Linguistic Traces of a Scientific Fraud: The Case of Diederik Stapel. PLoS ONE 9(8): e105937.

Mudraya, Olga, Bogdan Babych, Scott Piao, Paul Rayson and Andrew Wilson (2006). Developing a Russian semantic tagger for automatic semantic annotation. In Proceedings of the International Conference "Corpus Linguistics - 2006", St.-Petersburg, Russia, pp. 290-297.

Nakano, Tomofumi and Yukie Koyama (2005). e-Learning Materials Development Based on Abstract Analysis Using Web Tools. Knowledge-Based Intelligent Information and Engineering Systems. In Proceedings of KES 2005, Melbourne, Australia, LNCS 3681, Springer, pp. 794-800. DOI 10.1007/11552413_113.

Nasiruddin, Mohammad (2013). A State of the Art of Word Sense Induction: A Way Towards Word Sense Disambiguation for Under-Resourced Languages. arXiv:1310.1425 [cs.CL]. URL: http://arxiv.org/abs/1310.1425.

Ooi, Vincent B.Y., Peter K.W. Tan and Andy K. L. Chiang (2007). Analyzing personal weblogs in Singapore English: the Wmatrix approach. Studies in Variation, Contacts and Change in English. Volume 2. Research Unit for Variation, Contacts and Change in English (VARIENG), University of Helsinki.

Padró, Lluís and Evgeny Stanilovsky (2012). FreeLing 3.0: Towards Wider Multilinguality. In Proceedings of the Language Resources and Evaluation Conference (LREC 2012). Istanbul, Turkey. May, 2012.

Popov, Borislav, Atanas Kiryakov, Angel Kirilov, Dimitar Manov, Damyan Ognyanoff and Miroslav

Goranov (2003). KIM - Semantic Annotation Platform. In Proceedings of 2nd International Semantic Web Conference (ISWC2003), Florida, USA, pp. 834-849.

Potts, Amanda and Paul Baker (2013). Does semantic tagging identify cultural change in British and American English?, International Journal of Corpus Linguistics 17(3): 295-324.

Rayson, Paul, Dawn Archer, Scott Piao, Tony McEnery (2004). The UCREL semantic analysis system. In proceedings of the workshop on Beyond Named Entity Recognition Semantic labelling for NLP tasks in association with 4th International Conference on Language Resources and Evaluation (LREC 2004), Lisbon, Portugal, pp. 7-12.

Reeve, Lawrence and Hyoil Han (2005). Survey of Semantic Annotation Platforms. Proceedings of the 2005 ACM Symposium on Applied Computing, pp. 1634—1638.

Schmid, Helmut (1994). Probabilistic Part-of-Speech Tagging Using Decision Trees. Proceedings of International Conference on New Methods in Language Processing, Manchester, UK.

Sharoff, Serge. (2006). Creating general-purpose corpora using automated search engine queries. In M. Baroni and S. Bernardini (eds.), WaCky! Working papers on the Web as Corpus. Bologna, Italy: Gedit.

Taiani, Francois, Paul Grace, Geoff Coulson and Gordon Blair (2008). Past and future of reflective middleware: Towards a corpus-based impact analysis. The 7th Workshop On Adaptive And Reflective Middleware (ARM'08) December 1st 2008, Leuven, Belgium, collocated with Middleware 2008.

Toutanova, Kristina, Dan Klein, Christopher Manning, and Yoram Singer (2003). Feature-Rich Part-of-Speech Tagging with a Cyclic Dependency Network. In Proceedings of HLT-NAACL 2003, pp. 252-259.

Volk, Martin, Bärbel Ripplinger, Spela Vintar, Paul Buitelaar , Diana Raileanu , Bogdan Sacaleanu (2002). Semantic Annotation for Concept-Based Cross-Language Medical Information Retrieval. International Journal of Medical Informatics 67(1-3), pp. 97-112.

Vossen, Piek (ed) (1998). EuroWordNet: a multilingual database with lexical semantic networks, Kluwer Academic Publishers. ISBN 0792352955.

Xiao, Richard, Paul Rayson and Tony McEnery (2009). A Frequency Dictionary of Mandarin Chinese: Core Vocabulary for Learners. Routledge. ISBN-10: 0415455863.

Zhang, Lei and Achim Rettinger (2014). Semantic Annotation, Analysis and Comparison: A Multilingual and Cross-lingual Text Analytics Toolkit. In Proceedings of the Demonstrations at the EACL 2014, Gothenburg, Sweden, pp. 13-16.

# Unsupervised Sparse Vector Densification for Short Text Similarity

**Yangqiu Song and Dan Roth**
Department of Computer Science
University of Illinois at Urbana-Champaign
Urbana, IL 61801, USA
{yqsong,danr}@illinois.edu

## Abstract

Sparse representations of text such as bag-of-words models or extended explicit semantic analysis (ESA) representations are commonly used in many NLP applications. However, for short texts, the similarity between two such s-parse vectors is not accurate due to the small term overlap. While there have been multiple proposals for dense representations of words, measuring similarity between short texts (sentences, snippets, paragraphs) requires combining these token level similarities. In this paper, we propose to combine ESA representations and word2vec representations as a way to generate denser representations and, consequently, a better similarity measure between short texts. We study three densification mechanisms that involve aligning sparse representation via many-to-many, many-to-one, and one-to-one mappings. We then show the effectiveness of these mechanisms on measuring similarity between short texts.

## 1 Introduction

Bag-of-words model has been used for many applications as the state-of-the-art method for tasks such as document classifications and information retrieval. It represents each text as a bag-of-words, and computes the similarity, e.g., cosine value, between two sparse vectors in the high-dimensional space. When the contextual information is insufficient, e.g., due to the short length of the document, explicit semantic analysis (ESA) has been used as a way to enrich the text representation (Gabrilovich and Markovitch, 2006; Gabrilovich and Markovitch, 2007). Instead of using only the words in a document, ESA uses a bag-of-concepts retrieved from Wikipedia to represent the text. Then the similarity between two texts can be computed in this enriched concept space.

Both bag-of-words and bag-of-concepts model-s suffer from the sparsity problem. Because both models use sparse vectors to represent text, when comparing two pieces of texts, the similarity can be zero even when the text snippets are highly related, but make use of different vocabulary. We can expect that these two texts are related but the similarity val-ue does not reflect that. ESA, despite augmenting the lexical space with relevant Wikipedia concepts, still suffers from the sparsity problem. We illustrate this problem with the following simple experiment, done by choosing a documents from the "rec.autos" group in the 20-newsgroups data set[1]. For both documents and the label description "cars" (here we follow the description shown in (Chang et al., 2008; Song and Roth, 2014)), we computed 500 concepts using ESA. Then we identified the concepts that appear both in the document ESA representation and in the label ESA representation. The average sizes of this intersection (number of overlapping concepts in the document and label representation) are shown in Table 1. In addition to the original documents, we also split each document into 2, 4, 8, 16 equal length parts, computed the ESA representation of each, and then the intersection with the ESA representation of the label. Table 1 shows that the number of concepts shared by the label and the document representation decreases significantly, even if not as significantly

[1] http://qwone.com/~jason/20Newsgroups/



*Human Language Technologies: The 2015 Annual Conference of the North American Chapter of the ACL*, pages 1275–1280,
Denver, Colorado, May 31 – June 5, 2015. ©2015 Association for Computational Linguistics

Table 1: Average sizes of the intersection between the ESA concept representations of documents and labels. Both documents and label are represented with 500 Wikipedia concepts. Documents are split into different lengths.

| # of split | Avg. # of words per doc. | Avg. # of concepts |
|---|---|---|
| 1 | 209.6 | 23.1 |
| 2 | 104.8 | 18.1 |
| 4 | 52.4 | 13.8 |
| 8 | 26.2 | 10.6 |
| 16 | 13.1 | 8.4 |

as the drop in the document size. For example, there are on average 8 concepts in the intersection of two vectors with 500 non-zero concepts when we split each document into 16 parts.

When there are fewer overlapping terms between two pieces of texts, it can cause mismatch or biased match and result in less accurate comparison. In this paper, we propose to use unsupervised approaches to improve the representation, along with a corresponding similarity approach between these representations. Our contribution is twofold. First, we incorporate the popular word2vec (Mikolov et al., 2013a; Mikolov et al., 2013b) representations into ESA representation, and show that incorporating semantic relatedness between Wikipedia titles can indeed help the similarity measure between short texts. Second, we propose and evaluate three mechanisms for comparing the resulting representations. We verify the superiority of the proposed methods using three different NLP tasks.

## 2 Sparse Vector Densification

In this section, we introduce a way to compute the similarity between two sparse vectors by augmenting the original similarity measure, i.e., cosine similarity. Suppose we have two vectors $\mathbf{x} = (x_1, \ldots, x_V)^T$ and $\mathbf{y} = (y_1, \ldots, y_V)^T$ where $V$ is the vocabulary size. Traditional cosine similarity computes the dot product between these two vectors and normalizes it by their norms: $\cos(\mathbf{x}, \mathbf{y}) = \frac{\mathbf{x}^T\mathbf{y}}{||\mathbf{x}|| \cdot ||\mathbf{y}||}$. This requires each dimension of $\mathbf{x}$ to be aligned with the same dimension of $\mathbf{y}$. Note that for sparse vectors $\mathbf{x}$ and $\mathbf{y}$, most of the the elements can be zero. Aligning the indices can result in zero similarity even though the two pieces of texts are related. Thus, we propose to align different indices of $\mathbf{x}$ and $\mathbf{y}$ together to increase the similarity value.

We can rewrite the vectors $\mathbf{x}$ and $\mathbf{y}$ as $\mathbf{x} = \{x_{a_1}, \ldots, x_{a_{n_x}}\}$ and $\mathbf{y} = \{y_{b_1}, \ldots, y_{b_{n_y}}\}$, where $a_i$ and $b_j$ are indices of the non-zero terms in $\mathbf{x}$ and $\mathbf{y}$ $(1 \leq a_i, b_j \leq V)$. $x_{a_i}$ and $y_{b_i}$ are the weights associated to the terms in the vocabulary. Suppose there are non-zero terms $n_x$ and $n_y$ in $\mathbf{x}$ and $\mathbf{y}$ respectively. Then cosine similarity can be rewritten as:

$$\cos(\mathbf{x}, \mathbf{y}) = \frac{\sum_{i=1}^{n_x} \sum_{j=1}^{n_y} \delta(a_i - b_j) x_{a_i} y_{b_j}}{||\mathbf{x}|| \cdot ||\mathbf{y}||}, \quad (1)$$

where $\delta(\cdot)$ is the Dirac function $\delta(0) = 1$ and $\delta(\text{other}) = 0$. Suppose we can compute the similarity between terms $a_i$ and $b_j$, which is denoted as $\phi(a_i, b_j)$, then the problem is how to aggregate the similarities between all $a_i$'s and $b_j$'s to augment the original cosine similarity.

### 2.1 Similarity Augmentation

The most intuitive way to integrate the similarities between terms is averaging them:

$$S_A(\mathbf{x}, \mathbf{y}) = \frac{1}{n_x||\mathbf{x}|| \cdot n_y||\mathbf{y}||} \sum_{i=1}^{n_x} \sum_{j=1}^{n_y} x_{a_i} y_{b_j} \phi(a_i, b_j). \quad (2)$$

This similarity averages all the pairwise similarities between terms $a_i$'s and $b_j$'s. However, we can expect a lot of the similarities $\phi(a_i, b_j)$ to be close to zero. In this case, instead of introducing the relatedness between nonidentical terms, it will also introduce noise. Therefore, we also consider an alignment mechanism that we implement greedily via a maximum matching mechanism:

$$S_M(\mathbf{x}, \mathbf{y}) = \frac{1}{||\mathbf{x}|| \cdot ||\mathbf{y}||} \sum_{i=1}^{n_x} x_{a_i} y_{b_j} \max_j \phi(a_i, b_j). \quad (3)$$

We choose $j$ as $\text{argmax}_{j'} \phi(a_i, b_{j'})$ and substitute the similarity $\phi(a_i, b_j)$ between terms $a_i$ and $b_j$ into the final similarity between $\mathbf{x}$ and $\mathbf{y}$. Note that this similarity is not symmetric. Thus, if one needs a symmetric similarity, the similarity can be computed by averaging two similarities $S_M(\mathbf{x}, \mathbf{y})$ and $S_M(\mathbf{y}, \mathbf{x})$.

The above two similarity measurements are simple and intuitive. We can think about $S_A(\mathbf{x}, \mathbf{y})$ as leveraging term many-to-many mapping, while

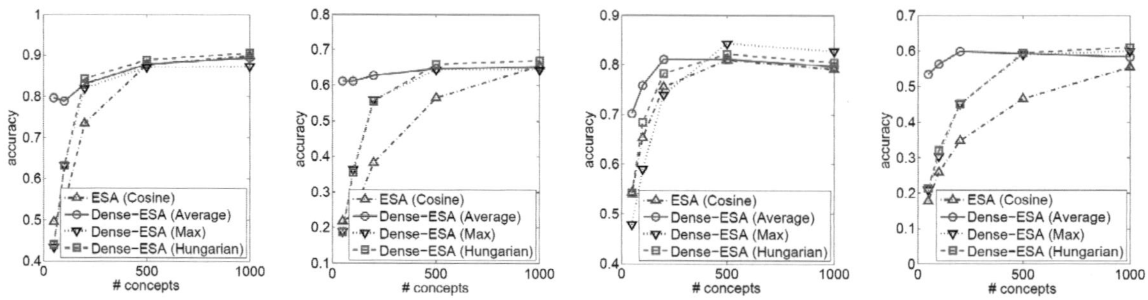


(a) rec.autos vs. sci.electronics (full doc.) (b) rec.autos vs. sci.electronics (1/16 doc.) (c) rec.autos vs. rec.motorcycles (full doc.) (d) rec.autos vs. rec.motorcycles (1/16 doc.)

Figure 1: Accuracy of dataless classification using ESA and Dense-ESA with different numbers of concepts.

$S_M(\mathbf{x}, \mathbf{y})$ uses only one-to-many term mapping. $S_A(\mathbf{x}, \mathbf{y})$ can introduce small and noisy similarity values between terms. While $S_M(\mathbf{x}, \mathbf{y})$ essentially aligns each term in $\mathbf{x}$ with it's best match in $\mathbf{y}$, we run the risk that multiple components of $\mathbf{x}$ will select the same element in $\mathbf{y}$. To ensure that all the non-zero terms in $\mathbf{x}$ and $\mathbf{y}$ are matched, we propose to constrain this metric by disallowing many-to-one mapping. We do that by using a similarity metric based on the Hungarian method (Papadimitriou and Steiglitz, 1982). The Hungarian method is a combinatorial optimization algorithm that solves the bipartite graph matching problem by finding an optimal assignment matching the two sides of the graph on a one-to-one basis. Assume that we run the Hungarian method on the the pair $\{\mathbf{x}, \mathbf{y}\}$, and let $h(a_i) = b_j$ denote the outcome of the algorithm, that is $a_i$ is aligned with $b_j$. (We assume here, for simplicity, that $n_x = n_y$; we can always achieve that by adding some zero weighted terms that are not aligned). The we define the similarity as:

$$S_H(\mathbf{x}, \mathbf{y}) = \frac{1}{||\mathbf{x}|| \cdot ||\mathbf{y}||} \sum_{i=1}^{n_x} x_{a_i} y_{h(a_i)} \phi(a_i, h(a_i)). \tag{4}$$

### 2.2 Term Similarity Measure

To evaluate the term similarity $\phi(\cdot, \cdot)$, we use local contextual similarity based on distributed representations. We adopt the word2vec (Mikolov et al., 2013a; Mikolov et al., 2013b) approach to obtain a dense representation of words. The representation of each word is predicted based on the context word distribution in a window around it. We trained word2vec on the Wikipedia dump data using the default parameters (CBOW model with window size as five). For each word, we finally obtained a 200 dimensional vector. If the term is a phrase, we simply average words' vectors of each phrase to obtain the representation following the original word2vec approach (Mikolov et al., 2013a; Mikolov et al., 2013b). We use two vectors $\mathbf{a}$ and $\mathbf{b}$ to represent the vectors for the two terms. To evaluate the similarity between two terms, for the average approach as Eq. (2), we use the RBF kernel over the two vectors $\exp\{-||\mathbf{a} - \mathbf{b}||^2/(0.03 \cdot ||\mathbf{a}|| \cdot ||\mathbf{b}||)\}$ as the similarity for all the experiments, since this will have a good property to cut the terms with small similarities. For the max and Hungarian approach as Eqs. (3) and (4), we simply use the cosine similarity between the two word2vec vectors. In addition, we cut off all similarities below threshold $\gamma$ and map them to zero.

## 3 Experiments

We experiment on three data sets. We use dataless classification (Chang et al., 2008; Song and Roth, 2014) over 20-newsgroups data set to verify the correctness of our argument of short text problems, and use two short text data sets to evaluate document similarity measurement and event classification for sentences.

### 3.1 Dataless Classification

Dataless classification uses the similarity between documents and labels in an enriched "semantic" space to determine in which category the given document is. In this experiment, we used the label descriptions provided by (Chang et al., 2008). It has been shown that ESA outperforms other representations for dataless classification (Chang et al., 2008; Song and Roth, 2014). Thus, we chose ESA as our

Table 2: Accuracy of dataless classification using ESA and Dense-ESA with 500 dimensions.

| | rec.autos vs. sci.electronics (easy) | | rec.autos vs. rec.motorcycles (difficult) | |
|---|---|---|---|---|
| Method | Full document | Short (1/16 doc.) | Full document | Short (1/16 doc.) |
| ESA (Cosine) | 87.75% | 56.55% | 80.95% | 46.64% |
| Dense-ESA (Average) | 87.80% | 64.67% | 81.11% | 59.38% |
| Dense-ESA (Max) | 87.10% | 64.34% | **84.30%** | 59.11% |
| Dense-ESA (Hungarian) | **88.85%** | **65.95%** | 82.15% | **59.65%** |

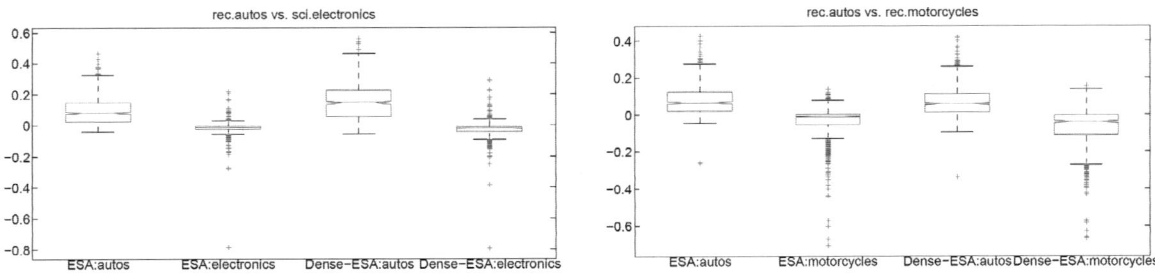


Figure 2: Boxplot of similarity scores for "rec.autos vs. sci.electronics" (easy, left) and "rec.autos vs. rec.motorcycles" (difficult, right). For each method of ESA and Dense-ESA with max matching in Eq. (3), we compute $S(d, l_1)$ and $S(d, l_2)$ between a document $d$ and the labels $l_1$ and $l_2$. Then we compute $S(d) = S(d, l_1) - S(d, l_2)$. For each ground truth label, we draw the distribution of $S(\cdot)$ with outliers in the figures. For example, "ESA:autos" shows the $S(\cdot)$'s distribution of the data with label "rec.autos." The t-test results show that the distributions of different labels are significantly different (99%). We can see that Dense-ESA pulls apart the distributions of different labels and that the separation is more significant for the more difficult problem (right).

baseline method. To demonstrate how the length of documents affects the classification result, we used both full documents and the 16 split parts (the parts are associated with the same label as the original document). To demonstrate the impact of densification, we selected two problems as an illustration: "rec.autos vs. sci.electronics" and "rec.autos vs. rec.motorcycles." While the former problem is relatively easy since they belong to different super-classes, the latter problem is more difficult since they are under the same super-class. The value of threshold $\gamma$ for max matching and Hungarian based densification is set to 0.85 empirically.

Figure 1 shows the results of the dataless classification using ESA and ESA with densification (Dense-ESA) with different numbers of Wikipedia concepts as the representation dimensionality. We can see that Dense-ESA significantly improves the dataless classification results. As shown in Table 2, while the max matching and Hungarian matching based methods are typically the best metrics the most significant results, the improvements are more significant for shorter documents, and for more difficult problems. Figure 2 highlights this observation.

Table 3: Spearman's correlation of document similarity using ESA and Dense-ESA with 500 concepts.

| Method | Spearman's correlation |
|---|---|
| ESA (Cosine) | 0.5665 |
| Dense-ESA (Average) | 0.5814 |
| Dense-ESA (Max) | 0.5888 |
| Dense-ESA (Hungarian) | **0.6003** |

### 3.2 Document Similarity

We used the data set provided by Lee et al.[2] (Lee et al., 2005) to evaluate pairwise short document similarity. There are 50 documents and the average number of words is 80.2. We averaged all the human annotations for the same document pair as the similarity score. After computing the scores for pairs of documents, we used Spearman's correlation to evaluate the results. Larger correlation score means that the similarity is more consistent with human annotation. The best word level based similarity result is close to 0.5 (Lee et al., 2005). We tried the cosine similarity between ESA representations and

[2]http://faculty.sites.uci.edu/mdlee/similarity-data/

Table 4: $F_1$ of sentence event type classification using ESA and Dense-ESA with 500 concepts.

| Method | $F_1$ (mean±std) |
|---|---|
| ESA (Cosine) | 0.469±0.011 |
| Dense-ESA (Average) | 0.451±0.010 |
| Dense-ESA (Max) | **0.481±0.008** |
| Dense-ESA (Hungarian) | 0.475±0.016 |

also Dense-ESA. The value of $\gamma$ for max matching based densification is set to 0.95, and for Hungarian based densification it is set to 0.89. We can see that from Table 3, ESA is better than the word based method, and that all versions of Dense-ESA outperform the original ESA.

### 3.3 Event Classification

In this experiment, we chose the ACE2005[3] data set to test how well we can classify sentences into event types without any training. There are eight types of events: life, movement, conflict, contact, etc. We chose all the sentences that contain event information as the data set. Following the dataless classification protocol, we compare the similarity between sentences and label descriptions to determine the event types. There are 3,644 unique sentences with events, including 2,712 sentences having only one event type, 421 having two event types, and 30 having three event types. The average length of the sentences is 23.71. Thus, this is a multi-label classification problem. To test the approaches, we used five-fold cross validation to select the thresholds for each class to classify whether the sentence belongs to an event type. The value of threshold $\gamma$ for both max matching and Hungarian based densification is also set to 0.85 empirically. Then we report the mean and standard derivation over five runs. The results are shown in Table 4. We can see that Dense-ESA also outperforms ESA.

## 4 Related Work

ESA (Gabrilovich and Markovitch, 2006; Gabrilovich and Markovitch, 2007) and distributed word representations (Ratinov and Roth, 2009; Turian et al., 2010; Collobert et al., 2011; Mikolov et al., 2013a; Mikolov et al., 2013b; Pennington et al., 2014) are popular text representations that encode world knowledge. Recently, several representations were proposed to extend word representations for phrases or sentences (Lu and Li, 2013; Hermann and Blunsom, 2014; Passos et al., 2014; Kalchbrenner et al., 2014; Le and Mikolov, 2014; Hu et al., 2014; Sutskever et al., 2014; Zhao et al., 2015). In this paper, we evaluate how to combine two off-the-shelf representations to densify the similarity between text data.

Yih et al. also used average matching and a different maximum matching for QA problem (Yih et al., 2013). However, their sparse representation is still at the word level while ours is based on ESA. Interestingly, related ideas to our average matching mechanism have been proposed also in the computer vision community, which is the set kernel (or set similarity) (Smola et al., 2007; Gretton et al., 2012; Xiong et al., 2013).

## 5 Conclusion

In this paper, we study the mechanisms of combining two popular representations of text, i.e., ESA and word2vec, to enhance computing short text similarity. Furthermore, we proposed three different mechanisms to compute the similarity between these representations, and demonstrated, using three different data sets that the proposed method outperforms the traditional ESA.

## Acknowledgments

This work is supported by the Multimodal Information Access & Synthesis Center at UIUC, part of CCICADA, a DHS Science and Technology Center of Excellence, by the Army Research Laboratory (ARL) under agreement W911NF-09-2-0053, and by DARPA under agreement number FA8750-13-2-0008. The views and conclusions contained herein are those of the authors and should not be interpreted as necessarily representing the official policies or endorsements, either expressed or implied by these agencies or the U.S. Government.

[3]http://www.itl.nist.gov/iad/mig/tests/ace/2005/

## References


M. Chang, L. Ratinov, D. Roth, and V. Srikumar. 2008. Importance of semantic representation: Dataless classification. In *AAAI*, pages 830–835.

R. Collobert, J. Weston, L. Bottou, M. Karlen, K. Kavukcuoglu, and P. P. Kuksa. 2011. Natural language processing (almost) from scratch. *J. Mach. Learn. Res.*, 12:2493–2537.

E. Gabrilovich and S. Markovitch. 2006. Overcoming the brittleness bottleneck using Wikipedia: Enhancing text categorization with encyclopedic knowledge. In *AAAI*, pages 1301–1306.

E. Gabrilovich and S. Markovitch. 2007. Computing semantic relatedness using Wikipedia-based explicit semantic analysis. In *IJCAI*, pages 1606–1611.

A. Gretton, K. M. Borgwardt, M. J. Rasch, B. Schölkopf, and A. Smola. 2012. A kernel two-sample test. *J. Mach. Learn. Res.*, 13:723–773.

K. M. Hermann and P. Blunsom. 2014. Multilingual models for compositional distributed semantics. In *A-CL*, pages 58–68.

B. Hu, Z. Lu, H. Li, and Q. Chen. 2014. Convolutional neural network architectures for matching natural language sentences. In *NIPS*, pages 2042–2050.

N. Kalchbrenner, E. Grefenstette, and P. Blunsom. 2014. A convolutional neural network for modelling sentences. In *ACL*, pages 655–665.

Q. V. Le and T. Mikolov. 2014. Distributed representations of sentences and documents. In *ICML*, pages 1188–1196.

M. D. Lee, B. Pincombe, and M. Welsh. 2005. An empirical evaluation of models of text document similarity. In *CogSci*, pages 1254–1259.

Z. Lu and H. Li. 2013. A deep architecture for matching short texts. In *NIPS*, pages 1367–1375.

T. Mikolov, I. Sutskever, K. Chen, G. S. Corrado, and J. Dean. 2013a. Distributed representations of words and phrases and their compositionality. In *NIPS*, pages 3111–3119.

T. Mikolov, W.-t. Yih, and G. Zweig. 2013b. Linguistic regularities in continuous space word representations. In *HLT-NAACL*, pages 746–751.

C. H. Papadimitriou and K. Steiglitz. 1982. *Combinatorial Optimization: Algorithm und Complexity*. Englewood Cliffs, NJ: Prentice-Hall.

A. Passos, V. Kumar, and A. McCallum. 2014. Lexicon infused phrase embeddings for named entity resolution. In *CoNLL*, pages 78–86.

J. Pennington, R. Socher, and C. D. Manning. 2014. Glove: Global vectors for word representation. In *EMNLP*, pages 1532–1543.

L. Ratinov and D. Roth. 2009. Design challenges and misconceptions in named entity recognition. In *CoNLL*, pages 147–155.

A. J. Smola, A. Gretton, L. Song, and B. Schölkopf. 2007. A hilbert space embedding for distributions. In *ALT*, pages 13–31.

Y. Song and D. Roth. 2014. On dataless hierarchical text classification. In *AAAI*, pages 1579–1585.

I. Sutskever, O. Vinyals, and Q. V. Le. 2014. Sequence to sequence learning with neural networks. In *NIPS*, pages 3104–3112.

J. Turian, L. Ratinov, and Y. Bengio. 2010. Word representations: A simple and general method for semi-supervised learning. In *ACL*, pages 384–394.

L. Xiong, B. Póczos, and J. G. Schneider. 2013. Efficient learning on point sets. In *ICDM*, pages 847–856.

W. Yih, M. Chang, C. Meek, and A. Pastusiak. 2013. Question answering using enhanced lexical semantic models. In *ACL*, pages 1744–1753.

Y. Zhao, Z. Liu, and M. Sun. 2015. Phrase type sensitive tensor indexing model for semantic composition. In *AAAI*.

# #WhyIStayed, #WhyILeft: Microblogging to Make Sense of Domestic Abuse

**Nicolas Schrading**[1] **Cecilia O. Alm**[2] **Ray Ptucha**[1] **Christopher M. Homan**[3]
[1] Kate Gleason College of Engineering, Rochester Institute of Technology
[2] College of Liberal Arts, Rochester Institute of Technology
[3] Golisano College of Computing and Information Sciences, Rochester Institute of Technology
$\{jxs8172^{\S}|coagla^{\S}|rwpeec^{\S}|cmh^{\dagger}\}@\{^{\S}rit.edu|^{\dagger}cs.rit.edu\}$

## Abstract

In September 2014, Twitter users unequivocally reacted to the Ray Rice assault scandal by unleashing personal stories of domestic abuse via the hashtags `#WhyIStayed` or `#WhyILeft`. We explore at a macro-level firsthand accounts of domestic abuse from a substantial, balanced corpus of tweeted instances designated with these tags. To seek insights into the reasons victims give for staying in vs. leaving abusive relationships, we analyze the corpus using linguistically motivated methods. We also report on an annotation study for corpus assessment. We perform classification, contributing a classifier that discriminates between the two hashtags exceptionally well at 82% accuracy with a substantial error reduction over its baseline.

## 1 Introduction

Domestic abuse is a problem of pandemic proportions; nearly 25% of females and 7.6% of males have been raped or physically assaulted by an intimate partner (Tjaden and Thoennes, 2000). These numbers only include physical violence; psychological abuse and other forms of domestic abuse may be even more prevalent. There is thus an urgent need to better understand and characterize domestic abuse, in order to provide resources for victims and efficiently implement preventative measures.

Survey methods exploring domestic abuse involve considerable time and investment, and may suffer from under-reporting, due to the taboo and stressful nature of abuse. Additionally, many may not have the option of directly seeking clinical help. Social media may provide a less intimidating and more accessible channel for reporting, collectively processing, and making sense of traumatic and stigmatizing experiences (Homan et al., 2014; Walther, 1996). Such data has been used for analyzing and predicting distinct societal and health issues, aimed at improving the understanding of wide-reaching societal concerns. For instance, Choudhury et al. (2013) predicted the onset of depression from user tweets, while other studies have modeled distress (Homan et al., 2014; Lehrman et al., 2012). Xu et al. (2013) used Twitter data to identify bullying language, then analyzed the characteristics of these tweets, and forecasted if a tweet would be deleted out of regret.

In September 2014, in the wake of the Ray Rice assault scandal[1] and the negative public reaction to the victim's decision to stay and support her abuser, Twitter users unequivocally reacted in a viral discussion of domestic abuse, defending the victim using the hashtag #WhyIStayed and contrasting those with #WhyILeft. Such narrative sharing may have a cathartic and therapeutic effect, extending the viral reach of the trend.

Analysis of the linguistic structures embedded in these tweet instances provides insight into the critical reasons that victims of domestic abuse report for choosing to stay or leave. Trained classifiers agree with these linguistic structures, adding evidence that these social media texts provide valuable insights into domestic abuse.

[1] `http://www.sbnation.com/nfl/2014/5/23/5744964/ray-rice-arrest-assault-statement-apology-ravens.`



*Human Language Technologies: The 2015 Annual Conference of the North American Chapter of the ACL*, pages 1281–1286,
Denver, Colorado, May 31 – June 5, 2015. 

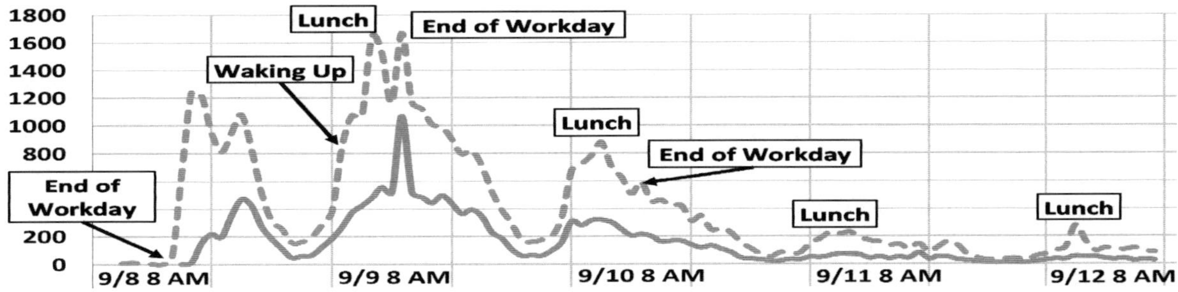


Figure 1: Tweet count per hour with #WhyIStayed (dotted) or #WhyILeft (solid) from 9/8 to 9/12. Times in EST, vertical lines mark 12 hour periods, with label corresponding to its left line. Spam removed, includes meta tweets.

## 2 Data

We collected a new corpus of tweets using the Twitter and Topsy[2] application programming interfaces. The corpus spans the beginning of September (the start of the trend) to the beginning of October, 2014. We fully rehydrated the tweets (to update the retweet count, etc.) at the end of the collection period. Figure 1 displays the behavior from the initial days of this trend. Due to its viral nature, the majority of tweets are from the first week of the trend's creation.

### 2.1 Preprocessing

We removed spam tweets based on the usernames of the most prevalent spammers, as well as key spam hashtags.[3] We also removed tweets related to a key controversy, in which the Twitter account for DiGiorno Pizza (ignorant of the trend's meaning) tweeted *#WhyIStayed You had pizza.*[4] This resulted in over 57,000 unique tweets in the corpus.

Many tweets in the dataset were reflections on the trend itself or contained messages of support to the users sharing their stories, for example, *Not usually a fan of hashtag trends, but #WhyIStayed is incredibly powerful. #NFL #RayRice.*[5] These tweets, here denoted *meta-tweets*, were often retweeted, but they rarely contained reasons for staying or leaving (our interest), so we filtered them out by keyword.[6] In section 2.3 we empirically explore the remaining instances.

[2]For outside Twitter's history, `http://topsy.com/`

[3]Such as *#MTVEMA, #AppleWatch, #CMWorld.*

[4]Removed by keywords *pizza, digiorno.*

[5]Illustrative tweet examples were anonymized and we purposefully attempted to minimize inclusion of sensitive content.

[6]Including *janay/ray rice, football, tweets, trend, video, etc.*

### 2.2 Extracting Gold Standard Labels

Typically, users provided reasons for staying and leaving, with the reasons prefixed by or appended with the hashtags #WhyIStayed or #WhyILeft as in this example: *#WhyIStayed because he told me no one else would love me. #WhyILeft because I gained the courage to love myself.* Regular expressions matched these structures and for tweets marked by both tags, split them into multiple instances, labeled with their respective tag. If the tweet contained only one of the target hashtags, the instance was labeled with that hashtag. If the tweet contained both hashtags but did not match with any of the regular expressions, it was excluded to ensure data quality.

The resulting corpus comprised 24,861 #WhyIStayed and 8,767 #WhyILeft labeled datapoints. The class imbalance may be a result of the origins of the trend rather than an indicator that more victims stay than leave. The tweet that started the trend contained only the hashtag #WhyIStayed, and media reporting on the trend tended to refer to it as the "#WhyIStayed phenomenon." As Figure 1 shows, the first #WhyILeft tweet occurred hours after the #WhyIStayed trend had taken off, and never gained as much use. By this reasoning, we concluded that an even set of data would be appropriate, and enable us to use the ratio metric in experiments discussed in this paper, as well as compare themes in the two sets. By random sampling of #WhyIStayed, a balanced set of 8,767 examples per class was obtained, resulting in a binary 50% baseline. From this set, 15% were held out as a final testset, to be considered after a tuning procedure with the remaining 85% devset.

### 2.3 Annotation Study

Four people (co-authors) annotated a random sample of 1000 instances from the devset, to further characterize the filtered corpus and to assess the automated extraction of gold standard labels. This random subset is composed of 47% #WhyIStayed and 53% #WhyILeft gold standard samples. Overall agreement overlap was 77% and Randolph's free-marginal multirater kappa (Warrens, 2010) score was 0.72. According to the annotations in this random sample, on average 36% of the instances are reasons for staying (S), 44% are reasons for leaving (L), 12% are meta comments (M), 2% are jokes (J), 2% are ads (A), and 4% do not match prior categories (O). Table 1 shows that most related directly to S or L, with annotators identifying more clearly L. Of interest are examples in which annotators did not agree, as these are indicative of problems in the data, and are samples that a classifier will likely label incorrectly. The tweet *because i was slowly dying anyway* was marked by two annotators as S and two annotators as L. Did the victim have no hope left and decide to stay? Or did the victim decide that since they were "slowly dying anyway" they could attempt to leave despite the possibility of potentially being killed in the attempt? The ground truth label is #WhyILeft. Another example with two annotators labeling as S and two as L is *two years of bliss, followed by uncertainty and fear*. This tweet's label is #WhyIStayed. The limited context from these samples makes it difficult to interpret fully, and causes human annotators to fail; however, most cases contain clear enough reasoning to interpret correctly.

| | | A | J | L | M | O | S |
|---|---|---|---|---|---|---|---|
| A1 | #L | .01 | .01 | .78 | .11 | .03 | .07 |
| | #S | .01 | .03 | .10 | .21 | .02 | .63 |
| A2 | #L | .02 | .01 | .72 | .06 | .09 | .10 |
| | #S | .03 | .01 | .07 | .16 | .10 | .63 |
| A3 | #L | .00 | .02 | .77 | .09 | 0 | .11 |
| | #S | .01 | .04 | .06 | .21 | 0 | .68 |
| A4 | #L | .02 | .01 | .75 | .05 | .04 | .14 |
| | #S | .03 | .01 | .16 | .12 | .05 | .63 |

Table 1: Confusion matrices of all 4 annotators, compared to the gold standard. Annotators mostly identified reasons for staying or leaving, and only a small fraction were unrelated. #L=#WhyILeft, #S=#WhyIStayed.

## 3 Methods for Exploring Reasons

### 3.1 Cleaning and Classifier Tuning

All experiments used the same cleaned data: removing hashtags, replacing URLs with the token *url* and user mentions with *@mention*, and replacing common emoticons with a sentiment indicator: *emotsent*$\{p|n|neut\}$ for positive/negative/neutral. Informal register was expanded to standard English forms using a slang dictionary.[7] Classifier tuning involved 5-fold cross-validation and selecting the best parameters based on the mean accuracy. For held-out data testing the full devset was used for training.

### 3.2 Analysis of Vocabulary

We examined the vocabulary in use in the data of the two hashtag sets by creating a frequency distribution of all unigrams after stoplisting and lowercasing. The wordcloud unigrams in Figure 2 are weighted by their relative frequency. These wordclouds hint at the reasons; however, decontextualized unigrams lead to confusion. For example, why does *left* appear in both? Other experiments were done to provide context and expand analysis.

Figure 2: A wordcloud of unigrams, weighted by unigram frequencies, for (top) #WhyIStayed instances and (bottom) #WhyILeft instances.[8]

[7] `http://www.noslang.com/`

[8] Created using `http://amueller.github.io/word_cloud/`

| Most discriminative *abuser onto victim* verbs | | | | | | | | | Legend |
|---|---|---|---|---|---|---|---|---|---|
| convince | find | isolate | kick | kill | love | manipulate | promise | want | #WhyIStayed |
| 0.96 | 1 | 0.93 | 1 | 0.91 | 0.95 | 1 | 0.83 | 0.93 | #WhyILeft |
| Most discriminative *victim as subject* verbs | | | | | | | | | |
| believe | choose | decide | felt | know | learn | realize | think | want | |
| 0.81 | 1 | 1 | 0.79 | 0.82 | 1 | 0.99 | 0.93 | 0.83 | |

Table 2: Discriminative verbs for *abuser onto victim* and *victim as subject* structures.

### 3.3 Analysis of Subject-Verb-Object Structures

Data inspection suggested that many users explained their reasons using a Subject-Verb-Object (SVO) structure, in which the abuser is doing something to the victim, or the victim is explaining something about the abuser or oneself.[9] We used the open-source tools Tweeboparser (Kong et al., 2014) and TurboParser (Martins et al., 2013) to heuristically extract syntactic dependencies, constrained by pronomial usage. Both parsers performed similarly, most likely due to the well-formed English in the corpus. While tweets are known for non-standard forms, the seriousness of the discourse domain may have encouraged more standard writing conventions.

Using TurboParser, we conducted an analysis for both male and female genders acting as the abuser in the subject position. Starting at the lemmatized predicate verb in each dependency parse, if the predicate verb followed an abuser subject word[10] per the dependency links, and preceded a victim object word,[11] it was added to a conditional frequency distribution, with the two classes as conditions. These structures are here denoted *abuser onto victim*. We used similar methods to extract structures in which the victim is the subject. Instances with female abusers were rare, and statistical gender differences could not be pursued. Accordingly, both genders' frequency counts were combined. Discriminative predicates from these conditional frequency distributions were determined by equation (1). In Table 2 we report on those where the ratio is greater than 0.75 and the total count exceeds a threshold to avoid bias towards lower frequency verbs.

$$ratio = \frac{count_{largerOfCounts}}{count_{left} + count_{stayed}} \quad (1)$$

[9]Example: *He hurt my child* S: *He*, V: *hurt*, O: *my child*.

[10]Male abuser: *he, his, my bf,* etc. Female: *she, her*, etc.

[11]Male victim: *me, my, him*, etc. *Female: me, my, her*, etc.

### 3.4 Classification Experiments

We examined the usefulness of the SVO structures, using subsets of the devset and testset having SVO structures (10% of the instances in total). While 10% is not a large proportion overall, given the massive number of possible dependency structures, it is a pattern worth examining – not only for corpus analytics but also classification, particularly as these SVO structures provide insight into the abuser-victim relationship. A linear SVM using boolean SVO features performed best (C=1), obtaining 70% $\pm$ 2% accuracy on the devset and 73% accuracy on the testset. The weights assigned to features by a Linear SVM are indicative of their importance (Guyon et al., 2002). Here, the top features presented as (S,V,O) for #WhyIStayed were: *(he, introduce, me)*, *(i, think, my)*, *(he, convince, me)*, *(i, believe, his)*, and *(he, beat, my)*. For #WhyILeft they were *(he, choke, me)*, *(i, beg, me)*, *(he, want, my)*, *(i, realize, my)*, and *(i, listen, my)*.

The SVO structures capture meaning related to staying and leaving, but are limited in their data coverage. Another experiment explored an extended feature set including uni-, bi-, and trigrams in sublinear $tf \times idf$ vectors, tweet instance character length, its retweet count, and SVO structures. We compared Naïve Bayes, Linear SVM, and RBF SVM classifiers from the Scikit-learn package (Pedregosa et al., 2011). The RBF SVM performed slightly better than the others, achieving a maximum accuracy of 81% $\pm$ .3% on the devset and 82% on the testset.[12,13] Feature ablation, following the procedure in Fraser et al. (2014), was utilized to determine the most important features for the classifier, the results

[12]Tuned parameters: max df = 11%, C=10, gamma=1.

[13]Dimensionality reduction with Supervised Locality Preserving Projections (SLPP) (Ptucha and Savakis, 2014) was attempted, but this did not improve results.

of which can be seen in Table 3.

| Removed | Remaining Features | % Acc |
|---|---|---|
| | NG+E+IR+TL+RT+SVO | 81.90 |
| SVO | NG+E+IR+TL+RT | 82.09 |
| TL | NG+E+IR+RT | 82.21 |
| E | NG+IR+RT | 82.21 |
| RT | NG+IR | 82.13 |
| IR | NG | 81.48 |

Table 3: Feature ablation study with an RBF SVM and no dimensionality reduction. NG = ngrams, E = emoticon replacement, IR = informal register replacement, TL = tweet length, RT = retweet count, SVO = subject-verb-object structures. % Acc is accuracy on the testset.

Interestingly, the SVO features combined with n-grams worsened performance slightly, perhaps due to trigrams capturing the majority of SVO cases. The highest accuracy, 82.21% on the testset, could be achieved with a combination of ngrams, informal register replacement, and retweet count. However the vast majority of cases can be classified accurately with ngrams alone. Emoticons may not have contributed to performance since they were rare in the corpus. Standardizing non-standard forms presumably helped the SVM slightly by boosting the frequency counts of ngrams while removing non-standard ngrams. Tweet length reduced accuracy slightly, while the number of retweets helped.

## 4 Discussion

From the analyses of SVO structures, word-clouds, and Linear SVM weights, interesting micro-narratives of staying and leaving emerge. Victims report staying in abusive relationships due to cognitive manipulation, as indicated by a predominance of verbs including *manipulate, isolate, convince, think, believe, felt* while report leaving when experiencing or fearing physical violence, via predicates such as *kill* and *kick*. They also report staying when in dire financial straits (*money*), when attempting to keep the nuclear family united (*family, marriage*) or when experiencing shame about their situation (*ashamed, shame*). They report leaving when threats are made towards loved-ones (*son, daughter*), gain agency (*choose, decide*), realize their situation or self-worth (*realize, learn, worth, deserve, finally, better*), or gain support from friends or family (*courage, support, help*). Importantly, such reasons for staying are validated in the clinical literature (Buel, 1999).

## 5 Conclusion

We discuss and analyze a filtered, balanced corpus having the hashtags #WhyIStayed or #WhyILeft. Our analysis reveals micro-narratives in tweeted reasons for staying vs. leaving. Our findings are consistent across various methods, correspond to observations in the clinical literature, and affirm the relevance of NLP for exploring issues of social importance in social media. Future work will focus on improving SVO extraction, especially adding consideration for negations of predicate verbs. In addition we will analyse other hashtags in use in the trend and perform further analysis of the trend itself, implement advanced text normalization rather than relying on a dictionary, and determine the roles features from linked webpages and FrameNet or other semantic resources play in making sense of domestic abuse.

## 6 Acknowledgement

This work was supported in part by a Golisano College of Computing and Information Sciences Kodak Endowed Chair Fund Health Information Technology Strategic Initiative Grant and NSF Award #SES-1111016.

## References

Sarah M. Buel. 1999. Fifty obstacles to leaving, a.k.a, why abuse victims stay. *The Colorado Lawyer*, 28(10):19–28, Oct.

Munmun De Choudhury, Scott Counts, Eric Horvitz, and Michael Gamon. 2013. Predicting depression via social media. In *Proceedings of the 7th International AAAI Conference on Weblogs and Social Media (ICWSM)*, Cambridge, Massachusetts, July. Association for the Advancement of Artificial Intelligence.

Kathleen C. Fraser, Graeme Hirst, Naida L. Graham, Jed A. Meltzer, Sandra E. Black, and Elizabeth Rochon. 2014. Comparison of different feature sets for identification of variants in progressive aphasia. In *Proceedings of the Workshop on Computational Linguistics and Clinical Psychology: From Linguistic Signal to Clinical Reality*, pages 17–26, Baltimore, Maryland, USA, June. Association for Computational Linguistics.

Isabelle Guyon, Jason Weston, Stephen Barnhill, and Vladimir Vapnik. 2002. Gene selection for cancer classification using support vector machines. *Machine Learning*, 46(1-3):389–422, March.

Christopher Homan, Ravdeep Johar, Tong Liu, Megan Lytle, Vincent Silenzio, and Cecilia Ovesdotter Alm. 2014. Toward macro-insights for suicide prevention: Analyzing fine-grained distress at scale. In *Proceedings of the Workshop on Computational Linguistics and Clinical Psychology: From Linguistic Signal to Clinical Reality*, pages 107–117, Baltimore, Maryland, USA, June. Association for Computational Linguistics.

Lingpeng Kong, Nathan Schneider, Swabha Swayamdipta, Archna Bhatia, Chris Dyer, and Noah A. Smith. 2014. A dependency parser for tweets. In *Proceedings of the Conference on Empirical Methods in Natural Language Processing (EMNLP)*, pages 1001–1012, Doha, Qatar, October. Association for Computational Linguistics.

Michael Thaul Lehrman, Cecilia Ovesdotter Alm, and Rubén A. Proaño. 2012. Detecting distressed and non-distressed affect states in short forum texts. In *Proceedings of the Second Workshop on Language in Social Media*, LSM '12, pages 9–18, Stroudsburg, PA, USA. Association for Computational Linguistics.

Andre Martins, Miguel Almeida, and Noah A. Smith. 2013. Turning on the turbo: Fast third-order non-projective turbo parsers. In *Proceedings of the 51st Annual Meeting of the Association for Computational Linguistics (Volume 2: Short Papers)*, pages 617–622, Sofia, Bulgaria, August. Association for Computational Linguistics.

Fabian Pedregosa, Gaël Varoquaux., Alexandre Gramfort, Vincent Michel, Bertrand Thirion, Olivier Grisel, Mathieu Blondel, Peter Prettenhofer, Ron Weiss, Vincent Dubourg, Jake Vanderplas, Alexandre Passos, David Cournapeau, Matthieu Brucher, Matthieu Perrot, and Édouard Duchesnay. 2011. Scikit-learn: Machine learning in Python. *Journal of Machine Learning Research*, 12:2825–2830.

Raymond Ptucha and Andreas Savakis. 2014. LGE-KSVD: Robust sparse representation classification. *IEEE Transactions on Image Processing*, 23(4):1737–1750, April.

Patricia Tjaden and Nancy Thoennes. 2000. Extent, nature, and consequences of intimate partner violence: Findings from the national violence against women survey. Technical Report NCJ 181867, National Institute of Justice, Centers for Disease Control and Prevention, Washington, DC.

Joseph Walther. 1996. Computer-mediated communication: Impersonal, interpersonal, and hyperpersonal interaction. *Communication Research*, 23(1):3–43, Feb.

Matthijs J. Warrens. 2010. Inequalities between multi-rater kappas. *Advances in Data Analysis and Classification*, 4(4):271–286.

Jun-Ming Xu, Benjamin Burchfiel, Xiaojin Zhu, and Amy Bellmore. 2013. An examination of regret in bullying tweets. In *Proceedings of the 2013 Conference of the North American Chapter of the Association for Computational Linguistics: Human Language Technologies*, pages 697–702, Atlanta, Georgia, June. Association for Computational Linguistics.

# Morphological Word-Embeddings

**Ryan Cotterell**[1,2]
Department of Computer Science[1]
Johns Hopkins University, USA
ryan.cotterell@jhu.edu

**Hinrich Schütze**[2]
Center for Information and Language Processing[2]
University of Munich, Germany
inquiries@cislmu.org

## Abstract

Linguistic similarity is multi-faceted. For instance, two words may be similar with respect to semantics, syntax, or morphology *inter alia*. Continuous word-embeddings have been shown to capture most of these shades of similarity to some degree. This work considers guiding word-embeddings with morphologically annotated data, a form of semi-supervised learning, encouraging the vectors to encode a word's morphology, i.e., words close in the embedded space share morphological features. We extend the log-bilinear model to this end and show that indeed our learned embeddings achieve this, using German as a case study.

## 1 Introduction

Word representation is fundamental for NLP. Recently, continuous word-embeddings have gained traction as a general-purpose representation framework. While such embeddings have proven themselves useful, they typically treat words holistically, ignoring their internal structure. For morphologically impoverished languages, i.e., languages with a low morpheme-per-word ratio such as English, this is often not a problem. However, for the processing of morphologically-rich languages exploiting word-internal structure is necessary.

Word-embeddings are typically trained to produce representations that capture linguistic similarity. The general idea is that words that are close in the embedding space should be close in meaning. A key issue, however, is that meaning is a multi-faceted concept and thus there are multiple axes, along which two words can be similar. For example, `ice` and `cold` are *topically* related, `ice` and `fire` are *syntactically* related as they are both nouns, and `ice` and `icy` are *morphologically* related as they are both derived from the same root. In this work, we are interested in distinguishing between these various axes and guiding the embeddings such that similar embeddings are morphologically related.

We augment the log-bilinear model (LBL) of Mnih and Hinton (2007) with a multi-task objective. In addition to raw text, our model is trained on a corpus annotated with morphological tags, encouraging the vectors to encode a word's morphology. To be concrete, the first task is language modeling—the traditional use of the LBL—and the second is akin to unigram morphological tagging. The LBL, described in section 3, is fundamentally a language model (LM)—word-embeddings fall out as low dimensional representations of context used to predict the next word. We extend the model to jointly predict the next morphological tag along with the next word, encouraging the resulting embeddings to encode morphology. We present a novel metric and experiments on German as a case study that demonstrates that our approach produces word-embeddings that better preserve morphological relationships.

## 2 Related Work

Here we discuss the role morphology has played in language modeling and offer a brief overview of various approaches to the larger task of computational morphology.

### 2.1 Morphology in Language Modeling

Morphological structure has been previously integrated into LMs. Most notably, Bilmes and Kirch-



*Human Language Technologies: The 2015 Annual Conference of the North American Chapter of the ACL*, pages 1287–1292,
Denver, Colorado, May 31 – June 5, 2015. 

| ARTICLE | ADJECTIVE | NOUN |
|---|---|---|
| ART.DEF.NOM.SG.FEM | ADJ.NOM.SG.FEM | N.NOM.SG.FEM |
| `die` | `größte` | `Stadt` |
| the | biggest | city |

Table 1: A sample German phrase in TIGER (Brants et al., 2004) annotation with an accompanying English translation. Each word is annotated with a complex morphological tag and its corresponding coarse-grained POS tag. For instance, `Stadt` is annotated with N.NOM.SG.FEM indicating that it is a *noun* in the *nominative* case and also both *singular* and *feminine*. Each tag is composed of meaningful *sub-tag units* that are shared across whole tags, e.g., the feature NOM fires on both adjectives and nouns.

hoff (2003) introduced *factored LMs*, which effectively add tiers, allowing easy incorporation of morphological structure as well as part-of-speech (POS) tags. More recently, Müller and Schütze (2011) trained a class-based LM using common suffixes—often indicative of morphology—achieving state-of-the-art results when interpolated with a Kneser-Ney LM. In neural probabilistic modeling, Luong et al. (2013) described a recursive neural network LM, whose topology was derived from the output of MORFESSOR, an unsupervised morphological segmentation tool (Creutz and Lagus, 2005). Similarly, Qiu et al. (2014) augmented WORD2VEC (Mikolov et al., 2013) to embed morphs as well as whole words—also taking advantage of MORFESSOR. LMs were tackled by dos Santos and Zadrozny (2014) with a convolutional neural network with a $k$-best max-pooling layer to extract character level $n$-grams, efficiently inserting orthographic features into the LM—use of the vectors in down-stream POS tagging achieved state-of-the-art results in Portuguese. Finally, most similar to our model, Botha and Blunsom (2014) introduced the additive log-bilinear model (LBL++). Best summarized as a neural factored LM, the LBL++ created separate embeddings for each constituent morpheme of a word, summing them to get a single word-embedding.

### 2.2 Computational Morphology

Our work is also related to morphological tagging, which can be thought of as ultra-fine-grained POS tagging. For morphologically impoverished languages, such as English, it is natural to consider a small tag set. For instance, in their universal POS tagset, Petrov et al. (2011) propose the coarse tag NOUN to represent all substantives. In inflectionally-rich languages, like German, considering other nominal attributes, e.g., case, gender and number, is also important. An example of an annotated German phrase is found in table 1. This often leads to a large tag set; e.g., in the morphological tag set of Hajič (2000), English had 137 tags whereas morphologically-rich Czech had 970 tags!

Clearly, much of the information needed to determine a word's morphological tag is encoded in the word itself. For example, the suffix `ed` is generally indicative of the past tense in English. However, distributional similarity has also been shown to be an important cue for morphology (Yarowsky and Wicentowski, 2000; Schone and Jurafsky, 2001). Much as contextual signatures are reliably exploited approximations to the semantics of the lexicon (Harris, 1954)—*you shall know the meaning of the word by the company it keeps* (Firth, 1957)—they can be similarly exploited for morphological analysis. This is not an unexpected result—in German, e.g., we would expect nouns that follow an adjective in the genitive case to also be in the genitive case themselves. Much of what our model is designed to accomplish is the isolation of the components of the contextual signature that are indeed predictive of morphology.

## 3 Log-Bilinear Model

The LBL is a generalization of the well-known log-linear model. The key difference lies in how it deals with features—instead of making use of hand-crafted features, the LBL *learns* the features along with the weights. In the language modeling setting, we define the following model,

$$p(w \mid h) \stackrel{\text{def}}{=} \frac{\exp\left(s_\theta(w, h)\right)}{\sum_{w'} \exp\left(s_\theta(w', h)\right)}, \qquad (1)$$

where $w$ is a word, $h$ is a history and $s_\theta$ is an energy function. Following the notation of Mnih and Teh (2012), in the LBL we define

$$s_\theta(w, h) \stackrel{\text{def}}{=} \left(\sum_{i=1}^{n-1} C_i r_{h_i}\right)^T q_w + b_w, \qquad (2)$$

where $n-1$ is history length and the parameters $\theta$ consist of $C$, a matrix of context specific weights, $R$, the context word-embeddings, $Q$, the target word-embeddings, and $b$, a bias term. Note that a sub-scripted matrix indicates a vector, e.g., $q_w$ indicates the target word-embedding for word $w$ and $r_{h_i}$ is the embedding for the $i$th word in the history. The gradient, as in all energy-based models, takes the form of the difference between two expectations (LeCun et al., 2006).

## 4 Morph-LBL

We propose a multi-task objective that jointly predicts the next word $w$ and its morphological tag $t$ given a history $h$. Thus we are interested in a joint probability distribution defined as

$$p(w, t \mid h) \propto \exp((f_t^T S + \sum_{i=1}^{n-1} C_i r_{h_i})^T q_w + b_w), \tag{3}$$

where $f_t$ is a hand-crafted feature vector for a morphological tag $t$ and $S$ is an additional weight matrix. Upon inspection, we see that

$$p(t \mid w, h) \propto \exp(f_t S^T q_w). \tag{4}$$

Hence given a fixed embedding $q_w$ for word $w$, we can interpret $S$ as the weights of a conditional log-linear model used to predict the tag $t$.

Morphological tags lend themselves to easy featurization. As shown in table 1, the morphological tag ADJ.NOM.SG.FEM decomposes into sub-tag units ADJ, NOM, SG and FEM. Our model includes a binary feature for each sub-tag unit in the tag set and only those present in a given tag fire; e.g., $F_{\text{ADJ.NOM.SG.FEM}}$ is a vector with exactly four non-zero components.

### 4.1 Semi-Supervised Learning

In the fully supervised case, the method we proposed above requires a corpus annotated with morphological tags to train. This conflicts with a key use case of word-embeddings—they allow the easy incorporation of large, unannotated corpora into supervised tasks (Turian et al., 2010). To resolve this, we train our model on a partially annotated corpus. The key idea here is that we only need a partial set of labeled data to steer the embeddings to ensure they capture morphological properties of the words. We marginalize out the tags for the subset of the data for which we do not have annotation.

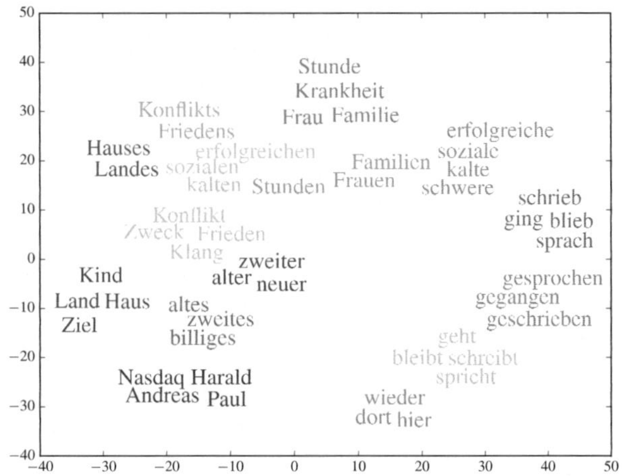


Figure 1: Projections of our 100 dimensional embeddings onto $\mathbb{R}^2$ through t-SNE (Van der Maaten and Hinton, 2008). Each word is given a distinct color determined by its morphological tag. We see clear clusters reflecting morphological tags and coarse-grained POS—verbs are in various shades of green, adjectives in blue, adverbs in grey and nouns in red and orange. Moreover, we see similarity across coarse-grained POS tags, e.g., the genitive adjective `sozialen` lives near the genitive noun `Friedens`, reflecting the fact that "sozialen Friedens" 'social peace' is a frequently used German phrase.

## 5 Evaluation

In our evaluation, we attempt to intrinsically determine whether it is indeed true that words similar in the embedding space are morphologically related. Qualitative evaluation, shown in figure 1, indicates that this is the case.

### 5.1 MorphoDist

We introduce a new evaluation metric for morphologically-driven embeddings to quantitatively score models. Roughly, the question we want to evaluate is: are words that are similar in the embedded space also morphologically related? Given a word $w$ and its embedding $q_w$, let $\mathcal{M}_w$ be the set of morphological tags associated with $w$ represented by bit vectors. This is a set because words may have several morphological parses. Our

| | Morph-LBL | LBL | WORD2VEC |
|---|---|---|---|
| All Types | 81.5% | 22.1% | 10.2% |
| No Tags | 44.8% | 15.3% | 14.8% |

Table 2: We examined to what extent the individual embeddings store morphological information. To quantify this, we treated the problem as supervised multi-way classification with the embedding as the input and the morphological tag as the output to predict. Note that "All Types" refers to all types in the training corpus and "No Tags" refers to the subset of types, whose morphological tag was *not* seen by Morph-LBL at training time.

measure is then defined below,

$$\textsc{MorphoDist}(w) \stackrel{\text{def}}{=} -\sum_{w' \in \mathcal{K}_w} \min_{m_w, m_{w'}} d_h(m_w, m_{w'}),$$

where $m_w \in \mathcal{M}_w$, $m_{w'} \in \mathcal{M}_{w'}$, $d_h$ is the Hamming distance and $\mathcal{K}_w$ is a set of words close to $w$ in the embedding space. We are given some freedom in choosing the set $\mathcal{K}_w$—in our experiments we take $\mathcal{K}_w$ to be the $k$-nearest neighbors ($k$-NN) in the embedded space using cosine distance. We report performance under this evaluation metric for various $k$. Note that MORPHODIST can be viewed as a soft version of $k$-NN—we measure not just whether a word has the same morphological tag as its neighbors, but rather has a *similar* morphological tag.

Metrics similar to MORPHODIST have been applied in the speech recognition community. For example, Levin et al. (2013) had a similar motivation for their evaluation of fixed-length acoustic embeddings that preserve linguistic similarity.

## 6 Experiments and Results

To show the potential of our approach, we chose to perform a case study on German, a morphologically-rich language. We conducted experiments on the TIGER corpus of newspaper German (Brants et al., 2004). To the best of our knowledge, no previous word-embedding techniques have attempted to incorporate *morphological tags* into embeddings in a supervised fashion. We note again that there has been recent work on incorporating *morphological segmentations* into embeddings—generally in a pipelined approach using a segmenter, e.g., MORFESSOR, as a preprocessing step, but we distinguish our model through its use of a different view on morphology.

We opted to compare Morph-LBL with two fully unsupervised models: the original LBL and WORD2VEC (`code.google.com/p/word2vec/`, Mikolov et al. (2013)). All models were trained on the first 200k words of the train split of the TIGER corpus; Morph-LBL was given the correct morphological annotation for the first 100k words. The LBL and Morph-LBL models were implemented in Python using THEANO (Bastien et al., 2012). All vectors had dimensionality 200. We used the Skip-Gram model of the WORD2VEC toolkit with context $n = 5$. We initialized parameters of LBL and Morph-LBL randomly and trained them using stochastic gradient descent (Robbins and Monro, 1951). We used a history size of $n = 4$.

### 6.1 Experiment 1: Morphological Content

We first investigated whether the embeddings learned by Morph-LBL do indeed encode morphological information. For each word, we selected the most frequently occurring morphological tag for that word (ties were broken randomly). We then treated the problem of labeling a word-embedding with its most frequent morphological tag as a multi-way classification problem. We trained a $k$ nearest neighbors classifier where $k$ was optimized on development data. We used the `scikit-learn` library (Pedregosa et al., 2011) on all types in the vocabulary with 10-fold cross-validation, holding out 10% of the data for testing at each fold and an additional 10% of training as a development set. The results displayed in table 2 are broken down by whether MorphLBL observed the morphological tag at training time or not. We see that embeddings from Morph-LBL do store the proper morphological analysis at a much higher rate than both the vanilla LBL and WORD2VEC.

Word-embeddings, however, are often trained on massive amounts of unlabeled data. To this end, we also explored on how WORD2VEC itself encodes morphology, when trained on an order of magnitude more data. Using the same experimental setup as above, we trained WORD2VEC on the *union* of the TIGER German corpus and German section of Europarl (Koehn, 2005) for a total of $\approx$ 45 million tokens. Looking only at those types found in TIGER, we found that the $k$-NN classifier predicted the cor-

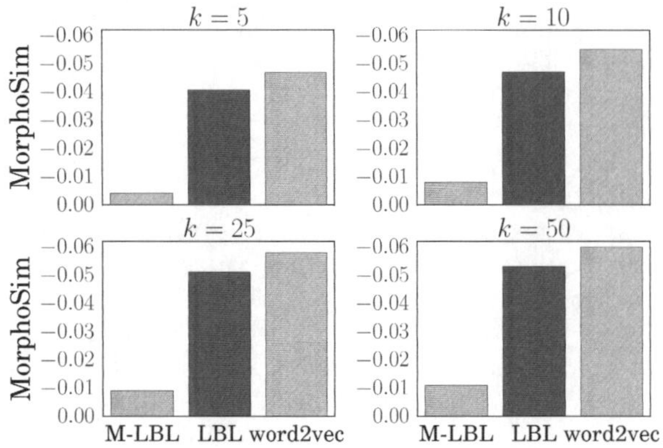


Figure 2: Results for the MORPHODIST measure for $k \in \{5, 10, 25, 50\}$. Lower MORPHODIST values are better—they indicate that the nearest neighbors of each word are closer morphologically.

rect tag with $\approx 22\%$ accuracy (not shown in the table).

### 6.2 Experiment 2: MORPHODIST

We also evaluated the three types of embeddings using the MORPHODIST metric introduced in section 5.1. This metric roughly tells us how similar each word is to its neighbors, where distance is measured in the Hamming distance between morphological tags. We only evaluated on words that MorphLBL did *not* observe at training time to get a fair idea of how well our model has managed to encode morphology purely from the contextual signature. Figure 2 reports results for $k \in \{5, 10, 25, 50\}$ nearest neighbors. We see that the values of $k$ studied do not affect the metric—the closest 5 words are about as similar as the closest 50 words. We see again that the Morph-LBL embeddings generally encode morphology better than the baselines.

### 6.3 Discussion

The superior performance of Morph-LBL over both the original LBL and WORD2VEC under both evaluation metrics is not surprising as we provide our model with annotated data at training time. That the LBL outperforms WORD2VEC is also not surprising. The LBL looks at a local history thus making it more amenable to learning syntactically-aware embeddings than WORD2VEC, whose skip-grams often look at non-local context.

What is of interest, however, is Morph-LBL's ability to robustly maintain morphological relationships only making use of the distributional signature, *without* word-internal features. *This result shows that in large corpora, a large portion of morphology can be extracted through contextual similarity.*

## 7 Conclusion and Future Work

We described a new model, Morph-LBL, for the semi-supervised induction of morphologically guided embeddings. The combination of morphologically annotated data with raw text allows us to train embeddings that preserve morphological relationships among words. Our model handily outperformed two baselines trained on the same corpus.

While contextual signatures provide a strong cue for morphological proximity, orthographic features are also requisite for a strong model. Consider the words `loving` and `eating`. Both are likely to occur after `is/are` and thus their local contextual signatures are likely to be similar. However, perhaps an equally strong signal is that the two words end in the same substring `ing`. Future work will handle such integration of character-level features.

We are interested in the application of our embeddings to morphological tagging and other tasks. Word-embeddings have proven themselves as useful features in a variety of tasks in the NLP pipeline. Morphologically-driven embeddings have the potential to leverage raw text in a way state-of-the-art morphological taggers cannot, improving tagging performance downstream.

## Acknowledgements

This material is based upon work supported by a Fulbright fellowship awarded to the first author by the German-American Fulbright Commission and the National Science Foundation under Grant No. 1423276. The second author was supported by Deutsche Forschungsgemeinschaft (grant DFG SCHU 2246/10-1). We thank Thomas Müller for several insightful discussions on morphological tagging and Jason Eisner for discussions about experimental design. Finally, we thank the anonymous reviewers for their many helpful comments.

## References


Frédéric Bastien, Pascal Lamblin, Razvan Pascanu, James Bergstra, Ian J. Goodfellow, Arnaud Bergeron, Nicolas Bouchard, and Yoshua Bengio. 2012. Theano: new features and speed improvements. Deep Learning and Unsupervised Feature Learning NIPS 2012 Workshop.

Jeff A Bilmes and Katrin Kirchhoff. 2003. Factored language models and generalized parallel backoff. In *HLT-NAACL*.

Jan A. Botha and Phil Blunsom. 2014. Compositional Morphology for Word Representations and Language Modelling. In *ICML*.

Sabine Brants, Stefanie Dipper, Peter Eisenberg, Silvia Hansen-Schirra, Esther König, Wolfgang Lezius, Christian Rohrer, George Smith, and Hans Uszkoreit. 2004. TIGER: Linguistic interpretation of a German corpus. *Research on Language and Computation*, 2(4):597–620.

Mathias Creutz and Krista Lagus. 2005. Unsupervised Morpheme Segmentation and Morphology Induction from Text Corpora using Morfessor. *Publications in Computer and Information Science, Report A*, 81.

Cıcero Nogueira dos Santos and Bianca Zadrozny. 2014. Learning character-level representations for part-of-speech tagging. In *ICML*.

John Rupert Firth. 1957. *Papers in linguistics, 1934–1951*. Oxford University Press.

Jan Hajič. 2000. Morphological tagging: Data vs. dictionaries. In *HLT-NAACL*.

Zellig Harris. 1954. Distributional Structure. *Word*.

Philipp Koehn. 2005. Europarl: A parallel corpus for statistical machine translation. In *MT Summit*, volume 5, pages 79–86.

Yann LeCun, Sumit Chopra, Raia Hadsell, M Ranzato, and F Huang. 2006. A Tutorial on Energy-based Learning. *Predicting Structured Data*.

Keith Levin, Katharine Henry, Aren Jansen, and Karen Livescu. 2013. Fixed-dimensional acoustic embeddings of variable-length segments in low-resource settings. In *Automatic Speech Recognition and Understanding (ASRU)*, pages 410–415. IEEE.

Minh-Thang Luong, Richard Socher, and C Manning. 2013. Better word representations with recursive neural networks for morphology. In *CoNLL*, volume 104.

Tomas Mikolov, Kai Chen, Greg Corrado, and Jeffrey Dean. 2013. Efficient estimation of word representations in vector space. In *ICRL*.

Andriy Mnih and Geoffrey Hinton. 2007. Three new graphical models for statistical language modelling. In *ICML*.

Andriy Mnih and Yee Whye Teh. 2012. A fast and simple algorithm for training neural probabilistic language models. In *ICML*.

Thomas Müller and Hinrich Schütze. 2011. Improved modeling of out-of-vocabularly words using morphological classes. In *ACL*.

Fabian Pedregosa, Gaël Varoquaux, Alexandre Gramfort, Vincent Michel, Bertrand Thirion, Olivier Grisel, Mathieu Blondel, Peter Prettenhofer, Ron Weiss, Vincent Dubourg, et al. 2011. Scikit-learn: Machine learning in Python. *The Journal of Machine Learning Research*, 12:2825–2830.

Slav Petrov, Dipanjan Das, and Ryan McDonald. 2011. A universal part-of-speech tagset. In *LREC*.

Siyu Qiu, Qing Cui, Jiang Bian, Bin Gao, and Tie-Yan Liu. 2014. Co-learning of word representations and morpheme representations. In *COLING*.

Herbert Robbins and Sutton Monro. 1951. A Stochastic Approximation Method. *The Annals of Mathematical Statistics*, pages 400–407.

Patrick Schone and Daniel Jurafsky. 2001. Knowledge-free induction of inflectional morphologies. In *ACL*.

Joseph Turian, Lev Ratinov, and Yoshua Bengio. 2010. Word representations: A simple and general method for semi-supervised learning. In *ACL*.

Laurens Van der Maaten and Geoffrey Hinton. 2008. Visualizing Data using t-SNE. *Journal of Machine Learning Research*, 9(2579-2605):85.

David Yarowsky and Richard Wicentowski. 2000. Minimally supervised morphological analysis by multimodal alignment. In *ACL*.

# Recognizing Social Constructs from Textual Conversation

**Somak Aditya** and **Chitta Baral** and **Nguyen H. Vo** and **Joohyung Lee** and **Jieping Ye,**
**Zaw Naung** and **Barry Lumpkin** and **Jenny Hastings**
Dept. of Computer Science, Arizona State University

**Richard Scherl**
Dept. of Computer Science,
Monmouth University

**Dawn M. Sweet**
Dept. of Psychology,
Iowa State University

**Daniela Inclezan**
Dept. of Computer Science,
Miami University

## Abstract

In this paper we present our work on recognizing high level social constructs such as *Leadership* and *Status* from textual conversation using an approach that makes use of the background knowledge about social hierarchy and integrates statistical methods and symbolic logic based methods. We use a stratified approach in which we first detect lower level language constructs such as politeness, command and agreement that help us to infer intermediate constructs such as deference, closeness and authority that are observed between the parties engaged in conversation. These intermediate constructs in turn are used to determine the social constructs *Leadership* and *Status*. We have implemented this system successfully in both English and Korean languages and achieved considerable accuracy.

## 1 Introduction and Related Works

The traditional information extraction paradigm has seen success in extracting simplistic behaviors or emotions from text. However, to detect high-level social constructs such as leadership or status, we require robustly defined notions about language constructs that cannot always be directly inferred from text. Hence, in this paper we focus on extracting information from text that requires additional background knowledge and inference. There are a few works in this direction, such as (Tari et al., 2010), however our focus in this paper is to extract information pertaining to different social constructs from textual conversation. The earlier research in analyzing conversations includes developing annotated chat corpuses (Shaikh et al., 2010), and developing a socio-cultural phenomena model from discourse with a small-scale implementation (Strzalkowski et al., 2010). Other researchers have focused on automatically annotating social behavior in conversation using statistical approaches (Mayfield et al., 2013). The discourse structure of a conversation is modeled as a Hidden Markov Model in (Stolcke, 2000) to determine dialogue acts such as Statement, Question and Agreement. In (Prabhakaran et al., 2012) annotated email threads are presented for facilitating detection of social relations.

Among recent works, (Gilbert, 2012) uses linguistic cues to discover workplace hierarchy from emails. The use of phrases to detect *language use* such as "commands" is motivating. However, due to the lack of logical explanation and robust definition, the effectiveness of this method decreases in the semi-formally moderated Wikipedia community, which has interplay of several different *LU*s such as command, politeness and informal language. In (Danescu-Niculescu-Mizil et al., 2012), the authors explain how reflection of linguistic styles can shed light on power differentials; though, a social community like Wikipedia might not always conform to the *lingustic style coordination assumption*. For example, two friends who are coordinating on writing an article may have the same status socially, but difference in their expertise will drive the conversation. Other works such as (Gupte et al., 2011) have concentrated more on other features of the persons involved in social network, than linguistic cues. Also, we feel that, the hierarchy depends on the task or the context. In other words, one person could as-



*Human Language Technologies: The 2015 Annual Conference of the North American Chapter of the ACL*, pages 1293–1298,
Denver, Colorado, May 31 – June 5, 2015. 

sume different roles in different context. The above works do not seem to address this. (Prabhakaran et al., 2012) achieves a commendable accuracy in detecting overt display of "power". However, by our definitions, this is a lower level attribute and is similar to *authoritative behavior* which is a lower level concept than Leadership or Status. Hence, their results are not directly comparable to ours.

In this paper, we use a mixture of logic-based and statistical approaches which better encodes the domain knowledge and infers higher-level constructs from indirect textual cues. The aim of this paper is to formalize the theory behind our work, highlight the advantages of integration of statistical and logic-based approaches and present results from an empirical study.

## 2 Motivation by a use-case

We start our discussion by presenting a use-case and explain how results of other traditional methods inspired us to come up with an integrated approach.

Consider the following conversation from Wikipedia where the participants discuss about a misleading animation that is used under the topic *Convolution*.

*{D: Put a message on the talk page of the guy who made it. You're right; g(t) should be g(tau - t), and (f*g)(t) should be (f*g)(tau).*

*T: I don't think he has a talk page. He's provided the code so I can reproduce it. I think he's right with (f*g)(t), though?*

*D: Actually, I think we're both wrong. You need a variable of integration running opposite directions ....*

*T: I've updated ... I guess it's not important, but would be kind of cool. Feel free to suggest improvements to the animations.}*

As we understand, these conversations suggest that participant $D$ is supposed to hold a higher rank/status than $T$. If we analyze manually, we understand that phrases like *Put a message*, *You're right*, *I think we're both wrong* together supports our conclusion. Considered separately, the above phrases might be misleading. To conclude the example, our system outputs :

*D has a higher status than T because D demonstrates more language uses associated with status than T. Confidence: high.*

The above example illustrates the degree of context-sensitivity of our problem. The current statistical literature suggests methods such as Decision Trees, Boosting methods comprising of a collection of Weak classifiers (basically rules) and probabilistic generative models (Medhat et al., 2014), (Hutto and Gilbert, 2014), (Vanzo et al., 2014) and (Saif et al., 2012). While their accuracy on some datasets is quite satisfactory, it is not clear how well they do on completely unseen data.

From our experience on such classifiers, we believe that a higher level of accuracy with explainability can be achieved by imposing a structure that encodes background knowledge about the social hierarchy that is observed in nature. With this motivation, we built a system whose hierarchical architecture robustly defines the social constructs, the "hidden" concepts that induce them and their inter-connections. We define notions of intermediate *Language Use (LU)* and lower level *Language Indicator (LI)* categories[1]. With the help of these robust definitions, our system properly explains how different emotions and behaviors interact to express status and leadership among individuals.

## 3 Social Constructs

Our framework supports determination of various important *Social Constructs* such as *Leadership*, *Status*, *Group Cohesion* and *Sub-Group Formation*. However, due to the length constraints of the paper, we will only discuss **Leadership** and **Status**.

### 3.1 Definitions and Architecture

We begin by first formally defining the two Social Constructs and the different Language Use categories.

**Leadership:** A leader is someone who guides a group toward outcomes, controls the group actions, manages interactions between members and members usually recognize the leader.

**Status:** Status is defined as the social position of one person with respect to another in a group.

The principal *Language Use* categories that we detect are: Deference, Closeness, Authoritative Behavior and Motivational Behavior. The following intuitions are used to infer such *LU*s from text:

**Deference** is understood when one uses language that shows respect to another conversational participant or defers to another's expertise or knowledge or authority.

**Closeness** is understood when one uses language that shows familiarity with another conversationalist. It is also indicated by dialogues where conversationalists refer to similar events, experiences etc.

**Authoritative Behavior** is understood when one uses language that shows power, dominance and control over a situation.

**Motivational Behavior** is understood when one uses language that moves conversational participants toward

[1]These definitions were proposed as part of the IARPA Socio-Cultural Content In Language(SCIL) program.

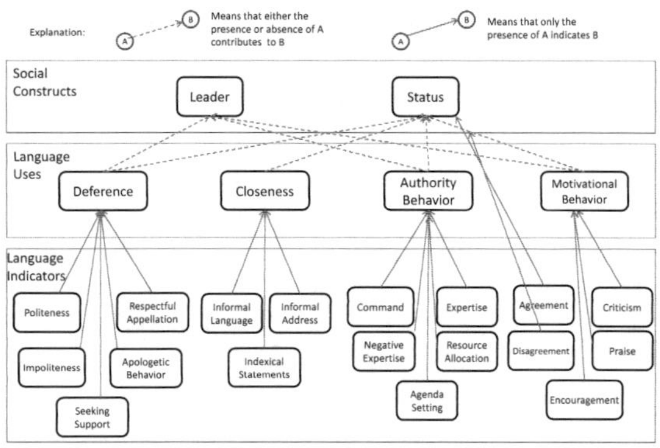


Figure 1: Social Construct-Language Use-Language Indicator hierarchy for English Language

sharing a common goal, collaboration, problem solving and solidarity.

In Figure 1, we present the entire hierarchy and how the categories are connected among each other. The arrows in the figure show which of the *LI* categories are used to infer a particular type of *LU*. It also demonstrates how each of the *LU* contributes to the Social Constructs.

## 4 Behind the Curtain: Our Intuitions

One of the fundamental contributions in this paper is formally describing the hierarchy to determine the Social Constructs, as shown in Figure 1. To come up with these interconnections and each of the different *pieces of the puzzle*, we went through an iterative process of discussions with many social scientists and linguists to analyze a large number of example conversations. In this process, we came up with the aforementioned hierarchy, definitions of *SC*, *LU* and *LI*s and most importantly, the following understanding:

- The *Language Indicators* as shown in the Figure 1, suffice for the detection of *Leadership* and *Status*.
- Each detected *LI* is associated with an *Intensity Level* that helps us to encode the dissimilar effects of different words in inferring *LI*s.
- Each *LI* is associated with a **Signed Language Use**. For example, the *LI politeness* is associated with the signed *LU positive deference*.
- Indicators of an *LU* with a certain sign are **counter-indicators** of the same *LU* with the opposite sign.
- A signed *LU* may contribute either **favorably or unfavorably** towards its associated *SC*. For example, positive authoritative behavior contributes favorably towards higher status.
- The signed *LU*s that contribute towards the *SC Status* are **ordered** based on their importance. We assume the following ordering exists: authoritative behavior > motivational behavior > negative deference > positive deference in the opposite direction > closeness. However, we do not assume such an ordering for the *SC Leadership*.

Our extensive research and successful implementation of our system for different natural languages leads us to believe that these notions are universal in application.

## 5 Fundamentals of the implementation

After we parse each sentence using Stanford Dependency parser to get the POS tags and mutual dependencies, the detection of individual *LI*s and the mapping of *LI*s, *LU*s to *SC*s are achieved using a combination of statistical and logic based approach. Many of the ideas and insights about the detection of *LI*s and their relations with the *LU*s are motivated from (Simon, 1946), (Pennebaker et al., 2003) , (Bernstein, 2010) , (Brown and Levinson, 1988) and a few others. Some of our ideas for textual inference have been inspired by (Scherl et al., 2010).

### 5.1 Determining the Language Indicators

The process of detection of language indicators from sentences uses a huge ensemble of complex rules. To create these rules, we borrowed ideas from the researchers of social science and psychology (Simon, 1946; Pennebaker et al., 2003).

With the help of POS tags, mutual dependencies and regular expressions, we create a framework where we detect individual events, verbs, other sentence constituents and their positive and negative sense. On top of this framework, we use two different methods to detect language indicators. The ideas are similar for all the LIs. We will only present a few examples for the LI "Command".

#### 5.1.1 Using Regular Expressions Alone

We use regular expressions of the form "*.*\b[wW]hy don'?t (you|YOU) (start|read|submit|make|write|get)\s*\b.**" to detect LIs such as "Command". We employ a collection of such expressions to cover several different linguistic styles which indicates "Command" by an individual.

We achieved a very high recall (close to 1.0) for most indicators with these rules on test data. However, in few cases, the frequency of such indicators (such as politeness) were very low deeming the set of regular expressions as incomplete. This observation led us to refine the regular expressions with Logical rules so that we can incorporate our domain knowledge and remove such bias to the training set.

#### 5.1.2 Using Logical rules on Regular Expression output and Sentence constituents

One example of the rules we use to detect "Command" is: *if the subject of the verb is second person and the verb is associated with a modal verb which indicates a question that suggests command, then the LI "Command" is detected.*

Examples of such verbs are "Would you" and "Could you" etc. It is to be noted that such a verb will denote both politeness and command depending on the rest of the sentence. This fascinating inter-dependency is one reason why we have to collect all such *Language Indicators* before we infer the higher level *Language Uses*.

### 5.2 Mapping of LIs to LUs and LUs to Social Constructs

**Input:** To encode one conversation we use a collection of facts of the form *participant(X)* and *addresses(X, Y, LI, Level)*.

These facts essentially encode the identity of the participants and the *Language Indicators* observed in the overall conversation among a pair of participants.

**Output:** The module outputs a collection of claim, evidence and confidence mappings.

For example one such mapping is: *claim_mapping(X, "is the leader", "because", X, "demonstrates <language use>","(Confidence: <confidence level>)")*. Here <language use> is one of the language uses, <confidence level> is either low, medium, or high.

**Algorithm:** We employ statistical and logic-based procedure in parallel to get the above output. On the statistical side, we adopt a regression technique to learn a function that can map the scores associated with *LI*s to individual *LUs* based on annotated training data and this function is then applied to test data to get confidence score on *LU*s. The same procedure is adopted for mapping *LU*s to *SC*s.

In parallel to this procedure, we also employ a rule-based technique that uses quantized confidence scores and outputs confidence levels along with explanations. As we are able to get the explanation from logical reasoning, we use the output confidence scores as votes from statistical learning to output the final confidence level.

The rules for logical reasoning are explained as definitions and intuitions in the following paragraphs.

**Mapping LIs into LUs:** A signed *LU* is said to be exhibited by participant X towards participant Y with a certain degree of confidence based on the number of indicators(*LI*) and counter-indicators(*LI*) of the signed *LU* used by X when addressing Y. The **confidence** in *LU* is directly proportional to the difference between the number of indicators and counter-indicators.

We categorize *LU*s according to the number of indicators and apply slight variation to the above rules for each such category. Also, there are a few *LI*s that, when used, automatically **override** the computed **confidence level** for an *LU* and increase it to high. For example, "criticism" increases confidence level of positive "motivational behavior" to high.

**Mapping LUs to SCs:** The relative status of two participants is determined based on i) the number of relevant signed LUs exhibited by each participant towards the other, ii) the ordering of relevant signed LUs and iii) the confidence level in each exhibited signed LU.

The leader is determined based on the number of exhibited relevant LUs (both favorable and unfavorable).

**Mapping LIs to SCs:** As shown in Figure 1, we directly associate some of the LIs to Social Constructs. For such an association, we again adopt the regression technique mentioned previously. In this case, the confidence scores from *LI*s are directly mapped to the confidence scores of *SC*s. We combine this confidence with the above confidence levels using simplistic rules to output final social constructs.

It should be noted *that the constants used in the rules are obtained from statistics on annotated conversations.* The annotation process involves labels about SCs, LUs and LIs for each conversation data.

### 5.3 Brief Details and Results of the Regression Technique

In this sub-section, we provide few details of the Sparse Logistic Regression technique we have used alongside the logical formulation and present few results from our experiments with relevant statistical methods. We have used a similar formulations for mapping LIs to LUs and LUs to SCs. Here, we provide the example of formulating the entire problem of detection of Social Constructs directly in the Classification paradigm.

Status and Leadership can be formulated as a three-class and two-class problem respectively. For Status, we had $102$ samples with the $38(higher)$, $26(equal)$ and $38(lower)$ samples each for three classes. For Leadership, we had $149$ samples with $108$(not-leader) and $41$(leader) samples for the two classes. For both the tasks, we extracted $28$ textual features. We used the one-vs-rest scheme for multi-class problem. For each task, we evaluated the framework as follows: i. First, we randomly separate the dataset into training set(p) and test set(1-p). ii. In the training set, we use 10-fold cross validation to select proper parameters. iii. We iterate the above procedure for 100 times, and accuracy is evaluated on the predictions in all iterations. iv. We select different p (from 0.25 to 0.9) and observe the change of accuracy.

We compared the accuracy achieved using Sparse Logistic Regression with SVM(with RBF Kernel) among

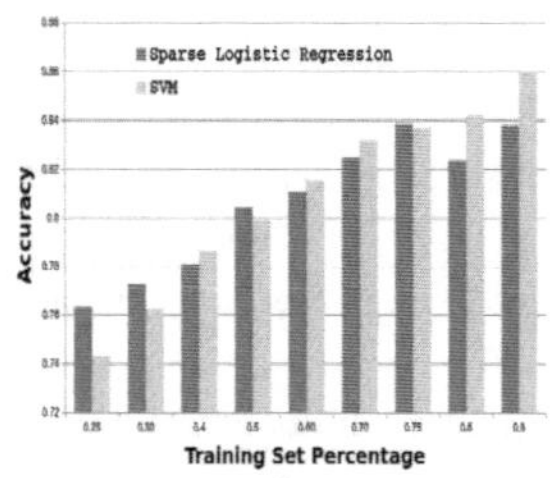


(a)

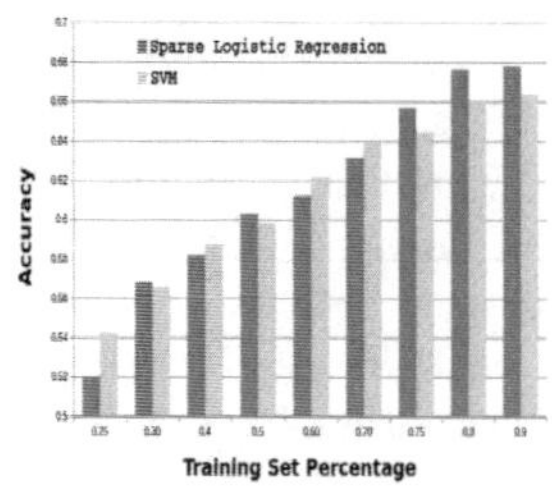


(b)

Figure 2: (a) Training set percentage vs Accuracy graph for Leadership problem, (b) Training set percentage vs Accuracy graph for Status classification problem.

others. The accuracy comparison of the SVM(with RBF kernel) and sparse Logistic Regression is provided in Figure 2. As we can observe, though the two methods are comparable, in most cases Sparse Logistic regression performs better.

## 5.4 Advantages from the integrated approach

The primary advantages are the following:

In general, statistical approaches need a "lot of data" to attain a certain level of accuracy. As the rules we use are quite universal and compact, we can achieve a comparable(or higher) accuracy with much less training data.

Using the *evidence* and *claim* mappings, we give an "explanation" as to why we detected such a particular SC in the dialogue. Knowldege of such depth is very hard to achieve with only statistical approaches.

Explicit representation of "context" specific information via rules results in improved accuracy in detection of LIs such as criticism, praise, command etc.

Statistical modules complement the rule-based approach where our domain knowledge is "incomplete".

We use ASP as the Logic Programming language of our choice as its ability to represent defaults and exceptions eases the implementation procedure.

# 6 Results

We have implemented this system using ASP(Gelfond and Lifschitz, 1988) and Java. The Wikipedia conversations are obtained by parsing the wiki dump from `http://dumps.wikimedia.org/`. We also evaluated on the NWTRB (US Nuclear Waste Technical Review Board) dataset. The accuracy and F1 measure are summarized in Table 1 for approximately two thousand English and one thousand Korean Wikipedia conversations. We evaluated two types of questions - i. *Yes-No* indicates questions like *Is John the leader?* and ii. *List* indicates questions such as *List all the leaders.*. Our work is perhaps unique in determining such social constructs and evaluating on familiar and unfamiliar datasets. Table 1 reports evaluations on wikipedia dump. These values are computed by comparing the results of our systems with annotated data. Note, in our experiments, we have performed strict evaluations. For example, the results are only marked positive if the complete list of leaders matches with a human-annotated list. Also, we consider the "explanation" too while performing the evaluation. The results are true positive only when the detected construct is correct alongwith the explanation provided by the reasoning module. In general, the previous research achieves an accuracy of 0.45 in comparable tasks such as dialog act tagging (Stolcke, 2000).

Table 1: Results

| SC | Q-Type | Language | Accuracy | F1 |
|---|---|---|---|---|
| Task Leader | Y-N | EN | 0.8900 | 0.6700 |
| Task Leader | List | EN | 0.6700 | 0.9900 |
| Status | Y-N | EN | 0.4700 | 0.3457 |
| Status | List | EN | 0.6923 | 0.5200 |
| Task Leader | Y-N | KO | 0.5667 | 0.4338 |
| Status | Y-N | KO | 0.4074 | 0.3900 |

# 7 Conclusion

In this paper, we have proposed a novel approach for logically recognizing social constructs from textual conversations. We have used both statistical classification and logical reasoning to robustly detect status and leadership as observed in virtual social networks. From our experiments, we show empirically how our approach achieves a significant accuracy and provides logical explanation of construct detection.

This research shows the merits of using logical rules along with statistical techniques to determine Social Constructs. As per our understanding, this level of accuracy and explainability needs integration of both statistical and logic based methods. Our observations suggest that there is an increasing need for such integration in various domains. We believe that this work is one of the early steps in that direction.

# 8 Acknowledgement

We thank the IARPA SCIL program for supporting this research. We also thank NSF for the DataNet Federation Consortium grant OCI-0940841 and ONR for their grant N00014-13-1-0334 for partially supporting this research.

## References


[Bernstein2010] Basil Bernstein. 2010. A public language: some sociological implications of a linguistic form. *British Journal of Sociology*, pages 53–69.

[Brown and Levinson1988] Penelope Brown and STEPHEN C. Levinson. 1988. *Politeness: Some Universals in Language Usage (Studies in Interactional Sociolinguistics 4)*. Cambridge University Press.

[Danescu-Niculescu-Mizil et al.2012] Cristian Danescu-Niculescu-Mizil, Lillian Lee, Bo Pang, and Jon Kleinberg. 2012. Echoes of power: Language effects and power differences in social interaction. In *Proceedings of the 21st International Conference on World Wide Web*, WWW '12, pages 699–708, New York, NY, USA. ACM.

[Gelfond and Lifschitz1988] Michael Gelfond and Vladimir Lifschitz. 1988. The stable model semantics for logic programming. pages 1070–1080. MIT Press.

[Gilbert2012] Eric Gilbert. 2012. Phrases that signal workplace hierarchy. In *Proceedings of the ACM 2012 Conference on Computer Supported Cooperative Work*, CSCW '12, pages 1037–1046, New York, NY, USA. ACM.

[Gupte et al.2011] Mangesh Gupte, Pravin Shankar, Jing Li, S. Muthukrishnan, and Liviu Iftode. 2011. Finding hierarchy in directed online social networks. In *Proceedings of the 20th International Conference on World Wide Web*, WWW '11, pages 557–566, New York, NY, USA. ACM.

[Hutto and Gilbert2014] C. J. Hutto and Eric Gilbert. 2014. Vader: A parsimonious rule-based model for sentiment analysis of social media text. In *ICWSM*.

[Mayfield et al.2013] Elijah Mayfield, David Adamson, and Carolyn Penstein Rosé. 2013. Recognizing rare social phenomena in conversation: Empowerment detection in support group chatrooms. pages 104–113.

[Medhat et al.2014] W. Medhat, A. Hassan, and H. Korashy. 2014. Sentiment analysis algorithms and applications: A survey. *Ain Shams Engineering Journal*, 5(4):1093 – 1113.

[Pennebaker et al.2003] James W. Pennebaker, Matthias R. Mehl, and Kate G. Niederhoffer. 2003. Psychological aspects of natural language use: Our words, our selves. *Annual Review of Psychology*, 54(1):547.

[Prabhakaran et al.2012] Vinodkumar Prabhakaran, Huzaifa Neralwala, Owen Rambow, and Mona Diab. 2012. Annotations for power relations on email threads. In *Proceedings of the Eight International Conference on Language Resources and Evaluation (LREC'12)*, Istanbul, Turkey, may. European Language Resources Association (ELRA).

[Saif et al.2012] Hassan Saif, Yulan He, and Harith Alani. 2012. Semantic sentiment analysis of twitter. In *Proceedings of the 11th International Conference on The Semantic Web - Volume Part I*, ISWC'12, pages 508–524, Berlin, Heidelberg. Springer-Verlag.

[Scherl et al.2010] R. Scherl, D. Inclezan, and M. Gelfond. 2010. Automated inference of socio-cultural information from natural language conversations. In *IEEE International Conference on Social Computing*, pages 480–487, Aug.

[Shaikh et al.2010] Samira Shaikh, Tomek Strzalkowski, Aaron Broadwell, Jennifer Stromer-Galley, Sarah Taylor, and Nick Webb. 2010. Mpc: A multi-party chat corpus for modeling social phenomena in discourse. In *Proceedings of the Seventh International Conference on LREC*, may.

[Simon1946] Herbert A. Simon. 1946. The proverbs of administration. *Public Administration Review*, 6(1):53–67.

[Stolcke2000] Andreas Stolcke. 2000. Dialogue act modeling for automatic tagging and recognition of conversational speech.

[Strzalkowski et al.2010] Tomek Strzalkowski, George Aaron Broadwell, Jennifer Stromer-Galley, Samira Shaikh, Sarah M. Taylor, and Nick Webb. 2010. Modeling socio-cultural phenomena in discourse. In *COLING 2010, 23rd International Conference on Computational Linguistics*, pages 1038–1046.

[Tari et al.2010] Luis Tari, Saadat Anwar, Shanshan Liang, James Cai, and Chitta Baral. 2010. Discovering drug-drug interactions: a text-mining and reasoning approach based on properties of drug metabolism. *Bioinformatics*, 26(18).

[Vanzo et al.2014] Andrea Vanzo, Danilo Croce, and Roberto Basili. 2014. A context based model for sentiment analysis in twitter. In *Proceedings of COLING 2014*, pages 2345–2354, Dublin, Ireland. Dublin City University and Association for Computational Linguistics.

# Two/Too Simple Adaptations of Word2Vec for Syntax Problems

**Wang Ling Chris Dyer Alan Black Isabel Trancoso**
L[2]F Spoken Systems Lab, INESC-ID, Lisbon, Portugal
Language Technologies Institute, Carnegie Mellon University, Pittsburgh, PA, USA
Instituto Superior Técnico, Lisbon, Portugal
{lingwang,cdyer,awb}@cs.cmu.edu
isabel.trancoso@inesc-id.pt

## Abstract

We present two simple modifications to the models in the popular Word2Vec tool, in order to generate embeddings more suited to tasks involving syntax. The main issue with the original models is the fact that they are insensitive to word order. While order independence is useful for inducing semantic representations, this leads to suboptimal results when they are used to solve syntax-based problems. We show improvements in part-of-speech tagging and dependency parsing using our proposed models.

## 1 Introduction

Word representations learned from neural language models have been shown to improve many NLP tasks, such as part-of-speech tagging (Collobert et al., 2011), dependency parsing (Chen and Manning, 2014; Kong et al., 2014) and machine translation (Liu et al., 2014; Kalchbrenner and Blunsom, 2013; Devlin et al., 2014; Sutskever et al., 2014). These low-dimensional representations are learned as parameters in a language model and trained to maximize the likelihood of a large corpus of raw text. They are then incorporated as features along side hand-engineered features (Turian et al., 2010), or used to initialize the parameters of neural networks targeting tasks for which substantially less training data is available (Hinton and Salakhutdinov, 2012; Erhan et al., 2010; Guo et al., 2014).

One of the most widely used tools for building word vectors are the models described in (Mikolov et al., 2013), implemented in the Word2Vec tool, in particular the "skip-gram" and the "continuous bag-of-words" (CBOW) models. These two models make different independence and conditioning assumptions; however, both models discard word order information in how they account for context. Thus, embeddings built using these models have been shown to capture semantic information between words, and pre-training using these models has been shown to lead to major improvements in many tasks (Collobert et al., 2011). While more sophisticated approaches have been proposed (Dhillon et al., 2011; Huang et al., 2012; Faruqui and Dyer, 2014; Levy and Goldberg, 2014; Yang and Eisenstein, 2015), Word2Vec remains a popular choice due to their efficiency and simplicity.

However, as these models are insensitive to word order, embeddings built using these models are suboptimal for tasks involving syntax, such as part-of-speech tagging or dependency parsing. This is because syntax defines "what words go where?", while semantics than "what words go together". Obviously, in a model where word order is discarded, the many syntactic relations between words cannot be captured properly. For instance, while most words occur with the word *the*, only nouns tend to occur exactly afterwords (e.g. *the cat*). This is supported by empirical evidence that suggests that order-insensitivity does indeed lead to substandard syntactic representations (Andreas and Klein, 2014; Bansal et al., 2014), where systems using pre-trained with Word2Vec models yield slight improvements while the computationally far more expensive which use word order information embeddings of Collobert et al. (2011) yielded much better results.



*Human Language Technologies: The 2015 Annual Conference of the North American Chapter of the ACL*, pages 1299–1304,
Denver, Colorado, May 31 – June 5, 2015. 

In this work, we describe two simple modifications to `Word2Vec`, one for the skip-gram model and one for the CBOW model, that improve the quality of the embeddings for syntax-based tasks[1]. Our goal is to improve the final embeddings while maintaining the simplicity and efficiency of the original models. We demonstrate the effectiveness of our approaches by training, on commodity hardware, on datasets containing more than 50 million sentences and over 1 billion words in less than a day, and show that our methods lead to improvements when used in state-of-the-art neural network systems for part-of-speech tagging and dependency parsing, relative to the original models.

## 2 Word2Vec

The work in (Mikolov et al., 2013) is a popular choice for pre-training the projection matrix $W \in \Re^{d\times|V|}$ where $d$ is the embedding dimension with the vocabulary $V$. As an unsupervised task that is trained on raw text, it builds word embeddings by maximizing the likelihood that words are predicted from their context or vice versa. Two models were defined, the skip-gram model and the continuous bag-of-words model, illustrated in Figure 1.

The skip-gram model's objective function is to maximize the likelihood of the prediction of contextual words given the center word. More formally, given a document of $T$ words, we wish to maximize

$$\mathcal{L} = \frac{1}{T}\sum_{t=1}^{T}\sum_{\substack{-c\leq j\leq c,\\ j\neq 0}} \log p(w_{t+j} \mid w_t) \qquad (1)$$

Where $c$ is a hyperparameter defining the window of context words. To obtain the output probability $p(w_o|w_i)$, the model estimates a matrix $O \in \Re^{|V|\times d_w}$, which maps the embeddings $r_{w_i}$ into a $|V|$-dimensional vector $o_{w_i}$. Then, the probability of predicting the word $w_o$ given the word $w_i$ is defined as:

$$p(w_o \mid w_i) = \frac{e^{o_{w_i}(w_o)}}{\sum_{w\in V} e^{o_{w_i}(w)}} \qquad (2)$$

This is referred as the softmax objective. However, for larger vocabularies it is inefficient to compute $o_{w_i}$, since this requires the computation of a $|V|\times d_w$ matrix multiplication. Solutions for problem are addressed in the `Word2Vec` by using the hierarchical softmax objective function or resorting to negative sampling (Goldberg and Levy, 2014).

The CBOW model predicts the center word $w_o$ given a representation of the surrounding words $w_{-c},...,w_{-1},w_1,w_c$. Thus, the output vector $o_{w_{-c},...,w_{-1},w_1,w_c}$ is obtained from the product of the matrix $O \in \Re^{|V|\times d_w}$ with the sum of the embeddings of the context words $\sum_{-c\leq j\leq c, j\neq 0} r_{w_j}$.

We can observe that in both methods, the *order of the context words does not influence the prediction output*. As such, while these methods may find similar representations for semantically similar words, they are less likely to representations based on the syntactic properties of the words.

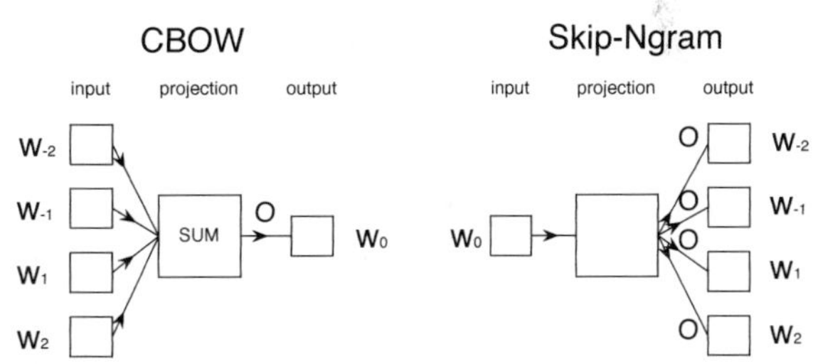


Figure 1: Illustration of the Skip-gram and Continuous Bag-of-Word (CBOW) models.

## 3 Structured Word2Vec

To account for the lack of order-dependence in the above models, we propose two simple modifications to these methods that include ordering information, which we expect will lead to more syntactically-oriented embeddings. These models are illustrated in Figure 2.

### 3.1 Structured Skip-gram Model

The skip-gram model uses a single output matrix $O \in \Re^{|V|\times d}$ to predict every contextual word $w_{-c},...,w_{-1},w_1,...,w_c$, given the embeddings of the center word $w_0$. Our approach adapts the model so that it is sensitive to the positioning of the words. It defines a set of $c \times 2$ output predictors $O_{-c},...,O_{-1},O_1,O_c$, with size $O \in \Re^{(|V|)\times d}$. Each of the output matrixes is dedicated to predicting the

[1]The code developed in this work is made available in https://github.com/wlin12/wang2vec.

output for a specific relative position to the center word. When making a prediction $p(w_o \mid w_i)$, we select the appropriate output matrix $O_{o-i}$ to project the word embeddings to the output vector. Note, that the number of operations that must be performed for the forward and backward passes in the network remains the same, as we are simply switching the output layer $O$ for each different word index.

### 3.2 Continuous Window Model

The Continuous Bag-Of-Words words model defines a window of words $w_{-c}, ..., w_c$ with size $c$, where the prediction of the center word $w_0$ is conditioned on the remaining words $w_{-c}, ..., w_{-1}, w_1, ..., w_c$. The prediction matrix $O \in \Re^{(|V|) \times d}$ is fed with the sum of the embeddings of the context words. As such, the order of the contextual words does not influence the prediction of the center word. Our approach defines a different output predictor $O \in \Re^{(|V| \times 2cd}$ which receives as input a $(2c \times d)$-dimensional vector that is the concatenation of the embeddings of the context words in the order they occur $[e(w_{-c}), \ldots, e(w_{-1}), e(w_1), \ldots, e(w_c)]$. As matrix $O$ defines a parameter for the word embeddings for each relative position, this allows the words to be treated differently depending on where they occur. This model, denoted as CWindow, is essentially the window-based model described in (Collobert et al., 2011), with the exception that we do not project the vector of word embeddings into a window embedding before making the final prediction.

In both models, we are increasing the number of parameters of matrix $O$ by a factor of $c \times 2$, which can lead to sparcity problems when training on small datasets. However, these models are generally trained on datasets in the order of 100 millions of words, where these issues are not as severe.

## 4 Experiments

We conducted experiments in two mainstream syntax-based tasks part-of-speech Tagging and Dependency parsing. Part-of-speech tagging is a word labeling task, where each word is to be labelled with its corresponding part-of-speech. In dependency parsing, the goal is to predict a tree built of syntactic relations between words. In both tasks, it has been

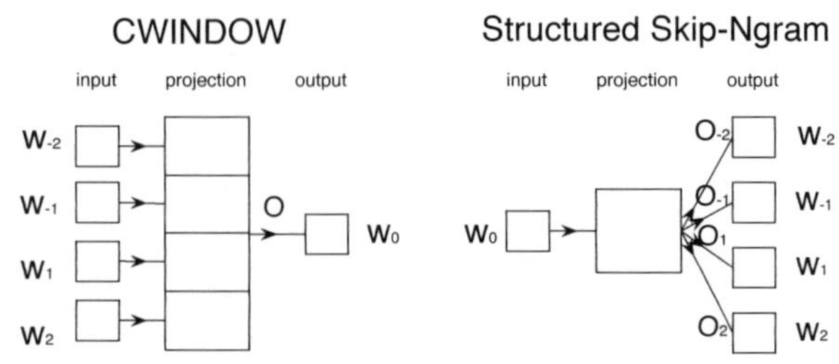


Figure 2: Illustration of the Structured Skip-gram and Continuous Window (CWindow) models.

shown that pre-trained embeddings can be used to achieve better generalization (Collobert et al., 2011; Chen and Manning, 2014).

### 4.1 Building Word Vectors

We built vectors for English in two very different domains. Firstly, we used an English Wikipedia dump containing 1,897 million words (60 million sentences), collected in September of 2014. We built word embeddings using the original and our proposed methods on this dataset. These embeddings will be denoted as *WIKI(L)*. Then, we took a sample of 56 million English tweets with 847 million words collected in (Owoputi et al., 2013), and applied the same procedure to build the *TWITTER* embeddings. Finally, we also use the Wikipedia documents, with 16 million words, provided in the `Word2Vec` package for contrastive purposes, denoted as *WIKI(S)*. As preprocessing, the text was lowercased and groups of contiguous digits were replaced by a special word. For all corpora, we trained the network with a $c = 5$, with a negative sampling value of 10 and filter out words with less than 40 instances. WIKI(L) and TWITTER have a vocabulary of 424,882 and 216,871 types, respectively, and embeddings of 50 dimensions.

Table 1 shows the similarity for a few selected keywords for each of the different embeddings. We can see hints that our models tend to group words that are more syntactically related. In fact, for the word *breaking*, the CWindow model's top five words are exclusively composed by verbs in the continuous form, while the Structured Skip-gram model tends to combine these with other forms of the verb break. The original models tend to be less keen on

| Embeddings | WIKI(S) | TWITTER | WIKI(L) |
|---|---|---|---|
| query | *breaking* | *amazing* | *person* |
| CBOW | breaks | incredible | someone |
| | turning | awesome | anyone |
| | broke | fantastic | oneself |
| | break | phenomenal | woman |
| | stumbled | awsome | if |
| Skip-gram | break | incredible | harasser |
| | breaks | awesome | themself |
| | broke | fantastic | declarant |
| | down | phenominal | someone |
| | broken | phenomenal | right-thinking |
| CWindow (this work) | putting | incredible | woman |
| | turning | amaaazing | man |
| | sticking | awesome | child |
| | pulling | amzing | grandparent |
| | picking | a-mazing | servicemember |
| Structured Skip-gram (this work) | break | incredible | declarant |
| | turning | awesome | circumstance |
| | putting | amaaazing | woman |
| | out | ah-mazing | schoolchild |
| | breaks | amzing | someone |

Table 1: Most similar words using different word embedding models for the words *breaking*, *amazing* and *person*. Each word is queried in a different dataset.

preserving such properties. As for the TWITTER embeddings, we can observe that our adapted embeddings are much better at finding lexical variations of the words, such as *a-mazing*, resembling the results obtained using brown clusters (Owoputi et al., 2013). Finally, for the query *person*, we can see that our models tend to associate this term to other words in the same class, such as *man*, *woman* and *child*, while original models tend to include unrelated words, such as *if* and *right-thinking*.

In terms of computation speed, the Skip-gram and CBOW models, achieve a processing rate of 71.35k and 342.17k words per second, respectively. The Structured Skip-gram and CWindow models can process 34.64k and 124.43k words per second, respectively. There is a large drop in computational speed in the CWindow model compared to the CBOW model, as it uses a larger output matrix, which grows with the size of the window. The Structured Skip-gram model processes words at almost half the speed of the Skip-gram model. This is explained by the fact that the Skip-gram model subsamples context words, varying the size of the window size stochastically, so that words closer to the center word are sampled more frequently. That is, when defining a window size of 5, the actual window size used for each sample is a random value between 1 and 5. As we use a separate output layer for each position, we did not find this property to be useful as it provides less training samples for output matrixes with higher indexes. While our models are slower they are still suitable for processing large datasets as all the embeddings we use were all built within a day.

## 4.2 Part-Of-Speech Tagging

We reimplemented the window-based model proposed in (Collobert et al., 2011), which defines a 3-layer perceptron. In this network, words are first projected into embeddings, which are concatenated and projected into a window embedding. These are finally projected into an output layer with size of the POS tag vocabulary, followed by a softmax. In our experiments, we used a window size of 5, word embeddings of size 50 and window embeddings of size 500. Word embeddings were initialized using the pre-trained vectors and these parameters are updated as the rest of the network. Additionally, we also add a capitalization feature which indicates whether the first letter of the work is uppercased, as all word features are lowercased words. Finally, for words unseen in the training set and in the pre-trained embeddings, we replace them with a special unknown token, which is also modelled as a word type with a set of 50 parameters. At training time, we stochastically replace word types that only occur once in the training dataset with the unknown token. Evaluation is performed with the part-of-speech tag accuracy, which denotes the percentage of words labelled correctly.

Experiments are performed on two datasets, the English Penn Treebank (PTB) dataset using the standard train, dev and test splits, and the ARK dataset (Gimpel et al., 2011), with 1000 training, 327 dev and 500 labelled English tweets from Twitter. For the PTB dataset, we use the WIKI(L) embeddings and use TWITTER embeddings for the ARK dataset. Finally, the set of parameters with the highest accuracy in the dev set are used to report the score for the test set.

Results are shown in Table 2, where we observe that our adapted models tend to yield better re-

| | PTB | | Twitter | |
|---|---|---|---|---|
| | Dev | Test | Dev | Test |
| CBOW | 95.89 | 96.13 | 87.85 | 87.54 |
| Skip-gram | 96.62 | 96.68 | 88.84 | 88.73 |
| CWindow | **96.99** | 97.01 | **89.72** | 89.63 |
| Structured Skip-gram | 96.62 | **97.05** | 89.69 | **89.79** |
| SENNA | 96.54 | 96.58 | 84.96 | 84.85 |

Table 2: Results for part-of-speech tagging using different word embeddings (rows) on different datasets (PTB and Twitter). Cells indicate the part-of-speech accuracy of each experiment.

| | Dev | | Test | |
|---|---|---|---|---|
| | UAS | LAS | UAS | LAS |
| CBOW | 91.74 | 88.74 | 91.52 | 88.93 |
| Skip-gram | 92.12 | 89.30 | 91.90 | 89.55 |
| CWindow | 92.38 | 89.62 | 92.00 | 89.70 |
| Structured Skip-gram | **92.49** | **89.78** | **92.24** | **89.92** |
| SENNA | 92.24 | 89.30 | 92.03 | 89.51 |

Table 3: Results for dependency parsing on PTB using different word embeddings (rows). Columns UAS and LAS indicate the labelled attachment score and the unlabelled parsing scores, respectively.

sults than the original models in both datasets. In the Twitter dataset, our results slightly higher than the accuracy reported using only Brown clusters in (Owoputi et al., 2013), which was 89.50. We also try initializing our embeddings with those in (Collobert et al., 2011), which are in the "Senna" row. Even though results are higher in our models, we cannot conclude that our method is better as they are trained crawls from Wikipedia in different time periods. However, it is a good reference to show that our embeddings are on par with those learned using more sophisticated models.

### 4.3 Dependency Parsing

The evaluation on dependency parsing is performed on the English PTB, with the standard train, dev and test splits with Stanford Dependencies. We use neural network defined in (Chen and Manning, 2014), with the default hyper-parameters[2] and trained for 5000 iterations. The word projections are initialized using WIKI(L) embeddings. Evaluation is performed with the labelled (LAS) and unlabeled (UAS) attachment scores.

In Table 3, we can observe that results are consistent with those in part-of-speech tagging, where our models obtain higher scores than the original models and with competitive results compared to Senna embeddings. This suggests that our models are suited at learning syntactic relations between words.

## 5 Conclusions

In this work, we present two modifications to the original models in Word2Vec that improve the word embeddings obtained for syntactically motivated tasks. This is done by introducing changes that make the network aware of the relative positioning of context words. With these models we obtain improvements in two mainstream NLP tasks, namely part-of-speech tagging and dependency parsing, and results generalize in both clean and noisy domains.

[2]Found in http://nlp.stanford.edu/software/nndep.shtml

## Acknowledgements

This work was partially supported by FCT (INESC-ID multiannual funding) through the PIDDAC Program funds, and also through projects CMU-PT/HuMach/0039/2008 and CMU-PT/0005/2007. The PhD thesis of Wang Ling is supported by FCT grant SFRH/BD/51157/2010. The authors also wish to thank the anonymous reviewers for many helpful comments.

## References

Jacob Andreas and Dan Klein. 2014. How much do word embeddings encode about syntax. In *Proceedings of ACL*.

Mohit Bansal, Kevin Gimpel, and Karen Livescu. 2014. Tailoring continuous word representations for dependency parsing. In *Proceedings of the Annual Meeting of the Association for Computational Linguistics*.

Danqi Chen and Christopher D Manning. 2014. A fast and accurate dependency parser using neural networks. In *Proceedings of the 2014 Conference on Empirical Methods in Natural Language Processing (EMNLP)*, pages 740–750.

Ronan Collobert, Jason Weston, Léon Bottou, Michael Karlen, Koray Kavukcuoglu, and Pavel Kuksa. 2011. Natural language processing (almost) from scratch. *The Journal of Machine Learning Research*, 12:2493–2537.

Jacob Devlin, Rabih Zbib, Zhongqiang Huang, Thomas Lamar, Richard Schwartz, and John Makhoul. 2014.

Fast and robust neural network joint models for statistical machine translation. In *52nd Annual Meeting of the Association for Computational Linguistics, Baltimore, MD, USA, June*.

Paramveer Dhillon, Dean P Foster, and Lyle H Ungar. 2011. Multi-view learning of word embeddings via cca. In *Advances in Neural Information Processing Systems*, pages 199–207.

Dumitru Erhan, Yoshua Bengio, Aaron Courville, Pierre-Antoine Manzagol, Pascal Vincent, and Samy Bengio. 2010. Why does unsupervised pre-training help deep learning? *The Journal of Machine Learning Research*, 11:625–660.

Manaal Faruqui and Chris Dyer. 2014. Improving vector space word representations using multilingual correlation. In *Proceedings of EACL*.

Kevin Gimpel, Nathan Schneider, Brendan O'Connor, Dipanjan Das, Daniel Mills, Jacob Eisenstein, Michael Heilman, Dani Yogatama, Jeffrey Flanigan, and Noah A Smith. 2011. Part-of-speech tagging for twitter: Annotation, features, and experiments. In *Proceedings of the 49th Annual Meeting of the Association for Computational Linguistics: Human Language Technologies: short papers-Volume 2*, pages 42–47. Association for Computational Linguistics.

Yoav Goldberg and Omer Levy. 2014. word2vec explained: deriving mikolov et al.'s negative-sampling word-embedding method. *arXiv preprint arXiv:1402.3722*.

Jiang Guo, Wanxiang Che, Haifeng Wang, and Ting Liu. 2014. Revisiting embedding features for simple semi-supervised learning. In *Proceedings of EMNLP*.

Geoffrey E Hinton and Ruslan Salakhutdinov. 2012. A better way to pretrain deep boltzmann machines. In *Advances in Neural Information Processing Systems*, pages 2447–2455.

Eric H Huang, Richard Socher, Christopher D Manning, and Andrew Y Ng. 2012. Improving word representations via global context and multiple word prototypes. In *Proceedings of the 50th Annual Meeting of the Association for Computational Linguistics: Long Papers-Volume 1*, pages 873–882. Association for Computational Linguistics.

Nal Kalchbrenner and Phil Blunsom. 2013. Recurrent continuous translation models. In *EMNLP*, pages 1700–1709.

Lingpeng Kong, Nathan Schneider, Swabha Swayamdipta, Archna Bhatia, Chris Dyer, and Noah A. Smith. 2014. A dependency parser for tweets. In *Proc. of EMNLP*, pages 1001–1012, Doha, Qatar, October.

Omer Levy and Yoav Goldberg. 2014. Dependency-based word embeddings. In *Proceedings of the 52nd Annual Meeting of the Association for Computational Linguistics*, volume 2.

Shujie Liu, Nan Yang, Mu Li, and Ming Zhou. 2014. A recursive recurrent neural network for statistical machine translation. In *Proceedings of ACL*, pages 1491–1500.

Tomas Mikolov, Ilya Sutskever, Kai Chen, Greg S Corrado, and Jeff Dean. 2013. Distributed representations of words and phrases and their compositionality. In *Advances in Neural Information Processing Systems*, pages 3111–3119.

Olutobi Owoputi, Brendan O'Connor, Chris Dyer, Kevin Gimpel, Nathan Schneider, and Noah A Smith. 2013. Improved part-of-speech tagging for online conversational text with word clusters. In *HLT-NAACL*, pages 380–390.

Ilya Sutskever, Oriol Vinyals, and Quoc VV Le. 2014. Sequence to sequence learning with neural networks. In *Advances in Neural Information Processing Systems*, pages 3104–3112.

Joseph Turian, Lev Ratinov, and Yoshua Bengio. 2010. Word representations: A simple and general method for semi-supervised learning. In *Proceedings of the 48th Annual Meeting of the Association for Computational Linguistics*, ACL '10, pages 384–394, Stroudsburg, PA, USA. Association for Computational Linguistics.

Yi Yang and Jacob Eisenstein. 2015. Unsupervised multi-domain adaptation with feature embeddings. In *Proceedings of the 2015 Conference of the North American Chapter of the Association for Computational Linguistics: Human Language Technologies*. Association for Computational Linguistics.

# Estimating Numerical Attributes by Bringing Together Fragmentary Clues

**Hiroya Takamura** and **Jun'ichi Tsujii**
Tokyo Institute of Technology   Microsoft Research Asia
takamura@pi.titech.ac.jp   jtsujii@microsoft.com

## Abstract

This work is an attempt to automatically obtain numerical attributes of physical objects. We propose representing each physical object as a feature vector and representing sizes as linear functions of feature vectors. We train the function in the framework of the combined regression and ranking with many types of fragmentary clues including absolute clues (e.g., $A$ is 30cm long) and relative clues (e.g., $A$ is larger than $B$).

## 1 Introduction

We know how large surfboards usually are and also that an inner pocket of any jacket is much smaller than a surfboard. Since we know about these numerical attributes, nobody of sound mind has probably ever tried to vainly put a surfboard into an inner pocket of a jacket. However, computers do not have comprehensive knowledge of this sort. This lack of comprehensive knowledge of the numerical attributes is one obstacle to flexible and natural man-machine communication. This work is an attempt to automatically obtain knowledge on numerical attributes so that computers can use it.

The knowledge on numerical attributes is also very useful on many other occasions. For example, it enables computers to alert their users when the users input incorrect numbers that are outside of the normal range of the attribute. In image recognition, a large red object will unlikely be recognized as a strawberry if the computer knows its normal size. In natural language processing, QA systems can use numerical knowledge to eliminate the out-of-range answer candidates to numerical questions.

A number of attempts similar to the current work have been made in some other fields such as psychology or fuzzy theory. However, such attempts heavily rely on costly experiments such as giving questionnaires to human subjects and have a problem in their scalability. In contrast, the current work attempts to use NLP techniques on large text data both online and offline in order to obtain such knowledge without relying on costly experiments such as questionnaires. A possible criticism of this project is that simply examining an existing knowledge source such as Wikipedia might accomplish this purpose without much effort. Indeed Wikipedia provides numerical information of some physical objects, but not all. For example, the Wikipedia page for *watches* provides descriptions on their function and their history, but no information on their size.

Clues to the numerical attributes are rather scattered over corpora and other linguistic resources. In a corpus, we can find informative descriptions such as "*X is 35cm tall*". We can also find text fragments suggesting an order relation between two physical objects with regard to the size as in "*X is larger than Y*", as well as implicit clues such as "*I put X into Y*", which usually means $X$ is smaller than $Y$. Holonymy relations ($X$ is a part of $Y$) in a thesaurus suggest an order relation in size ($X$ is smaller than $Y$). Glosses in a dictionary also provide subtle clues to the sizes of entry words. Each of these clues alone is not sufficient for precisely determining the size, so we have to bring them together. We have therefore developed a mathematical model that uses these



*Human Language Technologies: The 2015 Annual Conference of the North American Chapter of the ACL*, pages 1305–1310,
Denver, Colorado, May 31 – June 5, 2015. 

clues and determines the sizes of many physical objects simultaneously. The approach consists of two steps: (i) many different types of clues to the numerical attribute are collected from various linguistics resources, and (ii) those collected clues are brought together by a combined regression and ranking.

## 2 Related Work

Hovy et al. (2002) pointed out the importance of the knowledge on the numerical attributes in question answering. They hand-coded the possible range of a numerical attribute. Akiba et al. (2004), Fujihata et al. (2001), Aramaki et al. (2007), and Bakalov et al. (2011) made similar attempts. Their target, however, is the fixed numerical attributes of the named entities, while our target is the numerical attributes of general physical objects, not restricted to the named entities.

Davidov and Rappoport (2010) collected various types of text fragments indicating values of numerical attributes of physical objects. Our work differs from theirs in that we explore more subtle linguistic clues in addition to those used in the previous work, by using a global mathematical model that brings together all the clues.

Narisawa et al. (2013) tried to determine whether a given amount is large, small, or normal as a size of an object, making good use of clue words such as *only*; The sentence "*This laptop weighs only 0.7kg*" means that laptops are usually heavier than 0.7kg.

## 3 Fragmentary clues to sizes

### 3.1 Physical objects

We first collect physical objects, i.e., objects for which the size can be defined. However, the numerical attribute of a word depends on the sense in which the word is being used. We will therefore determine the size of each sense instead of each word. Specifically, we determine the size of each noun synset in the Japanese WordNet (Bond et al., 2009). We basically regard as physical objects the synsets that are descendants of the synset corresponding to "physical objects" (00002684-n). We filter out the physical objects that are descendants of any of the following synsets ( 09334396-n, 00027167-n, 09239740-n, 09287968-n, 09277686-n, 09335240-n, 04564698-n, and 03670849-n), since their sizes would be hard to define (e.g., earth, location, soil).

We further filter out approximately 400 synsets for various reasons such as ambiguity.[1]

### 3.2 Collecting absolute clues

We collect *absolute clues*, which indicate a value of a physical object without reference to other physical objects.

We used a search engine[2] with a query such as '"*the size of A*" AND *meter*' (AND represents a logical conjunction) and decompose the retrieved snippets into text fragments with "..." as a delimiter. We used only the first 1,000 pages (the maximum amount allowed by the terms of use for API users) for the query comprising a pattern ("*the size of A*", "*the length of A*", or "*the height of A*") and a length unit (millimeter, centimeter, meter, or kilometer).

Note that absolute clues are corpus-based.

### 3.3 Collecting relative clues

We also collect *relative clues*, which suggest a numerical order relation between two physical objects, i.e., $A$ should be larger than $B$. Note that holonymy and comparative sentences below are explicit relative clues as opposed to implicit relative clues that follow. Note also that holonymy is WordNet-based while comparative sentences and implicit relative clues are corpus-based.

#### 3.3.1 Holonymy

If $A$ is a part of $B$, it usually means that $A$ is smaller than $B$. We can obtain such part-of (holonymy) relations from the WordNet. Specifically, for each physical object obtained in Section 3.1, we retrieve its holonymy synsets. If a synset is a holonym of another synset, it suggests that the former is larger than the latter.

#### 3.3.2 Comparative sentences

The sentence "*the middle finger is longer than the ring finger*" suggests that the relation 'middle finger $>$ ring finger' holds for the size attribute. We collect such comparative sentences. Specifically, we search

[1]The list of those synsets and textual patterns and Japanese search keywords used in this work are available from `http://www.lr.pi.titech.ac.jp/~takamura/core9.html`.

[2]Yahoo!JAPAN API.

an $n$-gram corpus (Kudo and Kazawa, 2007) for the textual patterns including "*A is longer than B*".[3]

### 3.3.3 Implicit relative clues

People tend not to write out clues explicitly when most readers are expected to have the relevant knowledge. Since absolute clues and comparative sentences are explicit, we cannot expect a sufficient amount of such clues.

We argue that people unintentionally put many pieces of common knowledge into some specific textual patterns. The sentence "*I put my wallet into the pocket*" suggests that 'pocket > wallet' holds for the numerical attribute. We collect from the $n$-gram corpus such textual patterns (*A in B, put A in B, take A out of B, store A in B, put A on B, drop A from B, A go into B, and A go out of B*).

## 4 Bringing together the clues

### 4.1 Feature representation and linear model

To bring together the clues introduced in Section 3, we first represent physical objects with feature vectors and employ a linear model in which the size $f(\boldsymbol{w}, \boldsymbol{x})$ is represented as the inner product $\boldsymbol{w} \cdot \boldsymbol{x}$ of feature vector $\boldsymbol{x}$ and weight vector $\boldsymbol{w}$.

We use the following features: the synsets that are ancestors of the target synset (i.e., synsets that can be found by traversing up through hypernym-hyponym relations or instance-of relations), the synsets that the target synset is a member of (hmem in WordNet), the hypernym synsets of the target synset (hype in WordNet), the synsets that the target synset is an instance of (inst in WordNet), the synsets that the target synset has as a component (mprt in WordNet), the synsets that the target synset is a component of (hprt in WordNet), the head word in the gloss in a dictionary, and the synonyms in the target synset.

### 4.2 Formalization

We discuss how to estimate weight vector $\boldsymbol{w}$.

Some physical objects are given absolute clues. If multiple absolute clues are found for an object, we regard their average (actually, its logarithm) as the approximate size used for training. Since the size is a real number, the machine learning framework to be employed should be regression. Additionally, relative clues are incorporated into the training by means of ranking framework. We henceforth use the combined regression and ranking.

Our formalization is similar to the combined regression and ranking model developed by Sculley (2010). Let $D_a$ and $D_r$ denote respectively the training datasets consisting of absolute clues and relative clues. Each element in $D_a$ is represented as a pair of a feature vector $\boldsymbol{x}$ and its average size $y$. Each element in $D_r$ is represented as a tuple of feature vectors $\boldsymbol{x}_1$ and $\boldsymbol{x}_2$, and the order relation $z$; $z$ indicates whether $\boldsymbol{x}_1$ is larger ($z = +1$), or $\boldsymbol{x}_2$ is larger ($z = -1$). We minimize the following function:

$$(1-\alpha)L_a(\boldsymbol{w}, D_a) + \alpha L_r(\boldsymbol{w}, D_r) + \frac{\lambda}{2}||\boldsymbol{w}||^2, \quad (1)$$

where $\alpha$ is a trade-off parameter between regression loss $L_a(\boldsymbol{w}, D_a)$ and pairwise loss $L_r(\boldsymbol{w}, D_r)$. $(\lambda/2)||\boldsymbol{w}||^2$ is the regularization term.

The regression loss $L_a(\boldsymbol{w}, D_a)$ is decomposed as

$$\frac{1}{|D_a|} \sum_{(\boldsymbol{x},y)\in D_a} l_a(y, f(\boldsymbol{w}, \boldsymbol{x})), \quad (2)$$

where $l_a(y, f(\boldsymbol{w}, \boldsymbol{x}))$ is the loss of the pair $(\boldsymbol{x}, y)$ under the model $\boldsymbol{w}$, and is represented by *squared loss* $(y - f(\boldsymbol{w}, \boldsymbol{x}))^2$, indicating the difference between the target value and the model output.

The pairwise loss $L_r(\boldsymbol{w}, D_r)$, is decomposed as

$$\frac{1}{|D_r|} \sum_{(\boldsymbol{x}_1,\boldsymbol{x}_2,z)\in D_r} l_r(z, \boldsymbol{x}_1, \boldsymbol{x}_2, \boldsymbol{w}), \quad (3)$$

where $l_r(z, \boldsymbol{x}_1, \boldsymbol{x}_2, \boldsymbol{w})$ is the loss of the tuple $(\boldsymbol{x}_1, \boldsymbol{x}_2, z)$ under the model $\boldsymbol{w}$, and is represented by *hinge loss*, $\max(0, 1 - z \cdot f(\boldsymbol{w}, \boldsymbol{x}_1 - \boldsymbol{x}_2))$.

While a single type of loss function was used for the regression loss and the pairwise loss in the previous work (Sculley, 2010), the current framework relies on two different types of loss functions, i.e., squared loss and hinge loss, so that both absolute and relative clues can be used in the model.

## 5 Experiments

### 5.1 Experimental setting

We followed the process in Section 3.1 and eliminated infrequent ones from the obtained synsets. For

[3] We also used "shorter", "larger", and "smaller".

the remaining synsets, we performed a search for absolute and relative clues and obtained 1,329 absolute clues and 7,335 relative clues. This set of relative clues stems from 848 WordNet-based clues and 6,496 corpus-based clues with a small overlap. We note that fewer than 1% of these 6,496 corpus-based clues are explicit. The synsets for which no clues are found are removed from the following process, leaving 3,598 synsets. Thoroughly using the web data might provide a larger overall amount, but the current result suggests that there are fewer absolute clues than relative ones and fewer explicit clues than implicit ones.

We evaluate the methods in two different ways. One is the difference: the sizes of the 262 randomly sampled synsets without absolute clues are manually determined, and we calculated the difference between the estimated size and the manually determined size for each of those synsets. The other is the order relation classification: the size relations of 1,152 randomly sampled pairs of synsets are manually annotated, and we employ as an evaluation metric the accuracy indicating how many of those relations are correctly predicted.

We implemented our combined regression and ranking method by modifying a package.[4] We used the logarithms of sizes as the target value. We tuned $\lambda$ in Equation (1) to the value that optimizes the accuracy out of 11 values[5]: $10^{-7}, 10^{-6}, \cdots, 10^{3}$.

We tested different numbers of absolute clues in training (namely, 300, 500, 800, 1,000) in order to examine its effect.

### 5.2 Results

Figure 1 shows how the average difference for each number of absolute clues changes as $\alpha$ in Equation (1) is varied. All types of clues and features are used for Figure 1 (a), while the clues and features extracted from WordNet except for glosses are excluded for Figure 1 (b). The latter emulates the situation where the dictionary is available, but the large-scale thesaurus such as WordNet is not. The left-most point ($\alpha = 0$) for each figure corresponds to simple regression. The curves show that the difference can be reduced by using the combined regression and ranking. The improvement is more remarkable when fewer absolute clues are used.

| Size (cm) | Synset | Example word |
|---|---|---|
| $1.35\times10^{-1}$ | 11678768-n | ovum |
| $2.68\times10^{0}$ | 02312744-n | silkworm |
| $3.26\times10^{0}$ | 02206856-n | bee |
| $7.16\times10^{0}$ | 04453037-n | tooth of gear |
| $9.09\times10^{0}$ | 03209910-n | floppy disk |
| $1.14\times10^{1}$ | 03378442-n | foot |
| $3.01\times10^{1}$ | 04586225-n | wind chime |
| $3.35\times10^{1}$ | 03485794-n | hand towel |
| $4.57\times10^{1}$ | 04590553-n | windshield |
| $1.56\times10^{2}$ | 09189157-n | nest of hawk or eagle |
| $1.65\times10^{2}$ | 04152829-n | screen |
| $4.31\times10^{4}$ | 02687992-n | airport |

Table 1: Sample of the estimated sizes

Similarly, Figure 2 shows how the accuracy of the order relation classification for each number of absolute clues changes as $\alpha$ is varied. The accuracy of the order relation classification was around 70 to 80 %. The benefit of using combined regression and ranking is more remarkable in Figure 2 (b), i.e., when the thesaurus is not available.

Table 1 shows a sample of physical objects and their estimated sizes. We can see that the overall trend of the size has been successfully captured.

We also examine some features with small or large weights in Table 2. Very small weights are given to, for example, elementary particles in the field of particle physics, hydrons, and bacteria.[6]

| Feature | Weight |
|---|---|
| Synset for baryon, as ancestor | -7.75 |
| Hydron as synonym | -7.75 |
| Synset for fermion, as ancestor | -7.13 |
| Electron, as synonym | -6.06 |
| Bacteria, as synonym | -6.06 |
| Bell tower, hprt feature | +7.15 |
| Railroad as synonym, | +8.16 |
| Means of transportation as ancestor | +8.38 |

Table 2: Features with large absolute weights. Note that baryon is a heavy particle in the field of particle physics.

[4] http://code.google.com/p/sofia-ml/

[5] In the actual application, we would be able to use development data for tuning.

[6] More comprehensive results are available from http://www.lr.pi.titech.ac.jp/~takamura/core9.html.

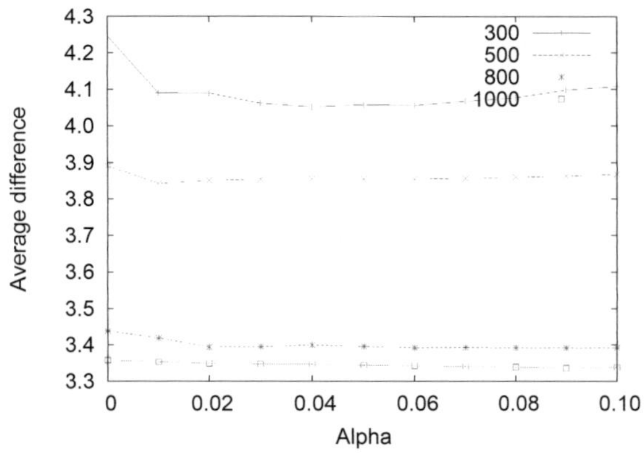

(a) All types of clues and features are used

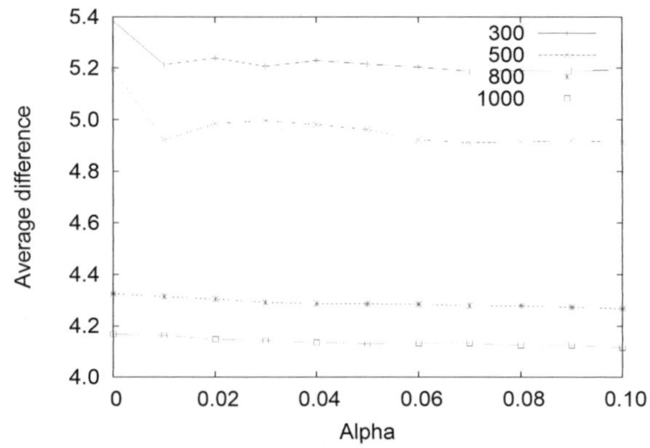

(b) WordNet-based clues and features are excluded except for the glosses

Figure 1: Average difference between the estimated size and the manually determined size (log of centimeter).

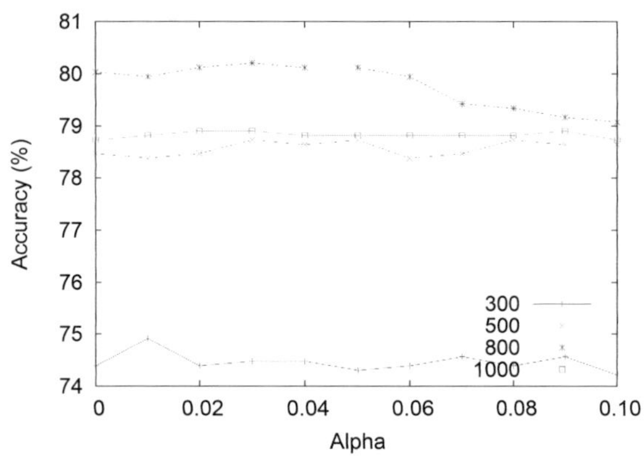

(a) All types of clues and features are used

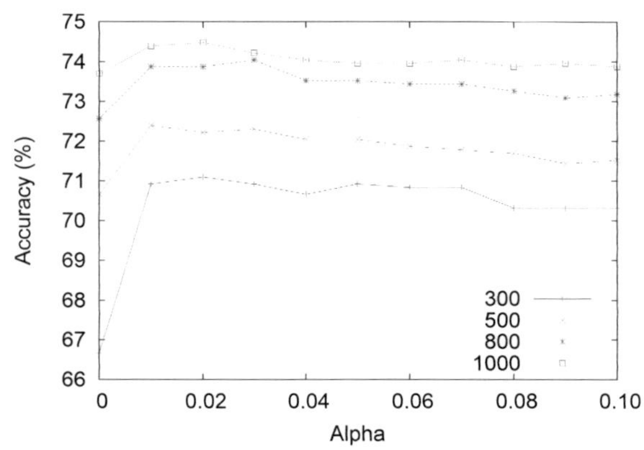

(b) WordNet-based clues and features are excluded except for the glosses

Figure 2: Accuracy of order relation classification

## 6 Conclusion

We addressed the task of automatically extracting numerical attributes of physical objects. We propose representing the sizes of objects using a linear function. We used the combined regression and ranking model with both absolute and relative clues.

Currently, many features are extracted from a thesaurus WordNet. If we can extract effective features from other resources, we would be able to apply our method to the objects that are not in the thesaurus. Future work also includes the following:
· more accurately collecting physical objects,
· sense disambiguation of words in clues,
· use of superlative sentences,
· filtering out descriptions of rare events,
· a more effective way of using glosses,
· application to other attributes, e.g., weight,
· handling idioms.

**Acknowledgment**
This work was partially supported by Microsoft Research (CORE Project 9).

## References


Tomoyosi Akiba, Katunobu Itou, and Atsushi Fujii. 2004. Question answering using common sense and utility maximization principle. In *Proceedings of the Fourth NTCIR Workshop on Research in Information Access Technologies Information Retrieval, Question Answering and Summarization*, pages 297–303.

Eiji Aramaki, Takeshi Imai, Kengo Miyo, and Kazuhiko Ohe. 2007. UTH: SVM-based semantic relation classification using physical sizes. In *Proceedings of the 4th International Workshop on Semantic Evaluations*, SemEval '07, pages 464–467, Stroudsburg, PA, USA. Association for Computational Linguistics.

Anton Bakalov, Ariel Fuxman, Partha Pratim Talukdar, and Soumen Chakrabarti. 2011. SCAD: Collective discovery of attribute values. In *Proceedings of the 20th International Conference on World Wide Web (WWW'11)*, pages 447–456.

Francis Bond, Hitoshi Isahara, Sanae Fujita, Kiyotaka Uchimoto, Takayuki Kuribayashi, and Kyoko Kanzaki. 2009. Enhancing the japanese wordnet. In *Proceedings of the 7th Workshop on Asian Language Resources (in conjunction with ACL-IJCNLP 2009)*.

Dmitry Davidov and Ari Rappoport. 2010. Extraction and approximation of numerical attributes from the web. In *Proceedings of the 48th Annual Meeting of the Association for Computational Linguistics*, pages 1308–1317.

Katsuyuki Fujihata, Masahiro Shiga, and Tatsuro Mori. 2001. Extraction of numerical expressions by constraints and default rules of dependency structure. In *Special Interest Group of Information Processing Society of Japan, 2001-NL-145 (in Japanese)*.

Eduard Hovy, Ulf Hermjakob, Chin-Yew Lin, and Deepak Ravichandran. 2002. Using knowledge to facilitate factoid answer pinpointing. In *Proceedings of the 19th International Conference on Computational Linguistics*, pages 369–375.

Taku Kudo and Hideto Kazawa. 2007. Japanese web n-gram corpus, version 1.

Katsuma Narisawa, Yotaro Watanabe, Junta Mizuno, Naoaki Okazaki, and Kentaro Inui. 2013. Is a 204 cm man tall or small? acquisition of numerical common sense from the web. In *Proceedings of the 51st Annual Meeting of the Association for Computational Linguistics (ACL 2013)*, pages 382–391.

David Sculley. 2010. Combined regression and ranking. In *Proceedings of the 16th ACM SIGKDD international conference on Knowledge discovery and data mining*, KDD '10, pages 979–988, New York, NY, USA. ACM.

# Unsupervised POS Induction with Word Embeddings

**Chu-Cheng Lin** **Waleed Ammar** **Chris Dyer** **Lori Levin**
School of Computer Science
Carnegie Mellon University
{chuchenl,wammar,cdyer,lsl}@cs.cmu.edu

## Abstract

Unsupervised word embeddings have been shown to be valuable as features in supervised learning problems; however, their role in unsupervised problems has been less thoroughly explored. In this paper, we show that embeddings can likewise add value to the problem of unsupervised POS induction. In two representative models of POS induction, we replace multinomial distributions over the vocabulary with multivariate Gaussian distributions over word embeddings and observe consistent improvements in eight languages. We also analyze the effect of various choices while inducing word embeddings on "downstream" POS induction results.

## 1 Introduction

Unsupervised POS induction is the problem of assigning word tokens to syntactic categories given only a corpus of untagged text. In this paper we explore the effect of replacing words with their vector space embeddings[1] in two POS induction models: the classic first-order HMM (Kupiec, 1992) and the newly introduced conditional random field autoencoder (Ammar et al., 2014). In each model, instead of using a conditional multinomial distribution[2] to generate a word token $w_i \in V$ given a POS tag $t_i \in T$, we use a conditional Gaussian distribution and generate a $d$-dimensional word embedding $\mathbf{v}_{w_i} \in \mathbb{R}^d$ given $t_i$.

[1]Unlike Yatbaz et al. (2014), we leverage easily obtainable and widely used embeddings of word types.

[2]Also known as a categorical distribution.

Our findings suggest that, in both models, substantial improvements are possible when word embeddings are used rather than opaque word types. However, the independence assumptions made by the model used to induce embeddings strongly determines its effectiveness for POS induction: embedding models that model short-range context are more effective than those that model longer-range contexts. This result is unsurprising, but it illustrates the lack of an evaluation metric that measures the syntactic (rather than semantic) information in word embeddings. Our results also confirm the conclusions of Sirts et al. (2014) who were likewise able to improve POS induction results, albeit using a custom clustering model based on the the distance-dependent Chinese restaurant process (Blei and Frazier, 2011).

Our contributions are as follows: (i) reparameterization of token-level POS induction models to use word embeddings; and (ii) a systematic evaluation of word embeddings with respect to the syntactic information they contain.

## 2 Vector Space Word Embeddings

Word embeddings represent words in a language's vocabulary as points in a $d$-dimensional space such that nearby words (points) are similar in terms of their distributional properties. A variety of techniques for learning embeddings have been proposed, e.g., matrix factorization (Deerwester et al., 1990; Dhillon et al., 2011) and neural language modeling (Mikolov et al., 2011; Collobert and Weston, 2008).

For the POS induction task, we specifically need embeddings that capture syntactic similarities. Therefore we experiment with two types of embeddings



*Human Language Technologies: The 2015 Annual Conference of the North American Chapter of the ACL*, pages 1311–1316,
Denver, Colorado, May 31 – June 5, 2015. 

that are known for such properties:

- **Skip-gram embeddings** (Mikolov et al., 2013) are based on a log bilinear model that predicts an unordered set of context words given a target word. Bansal et al. (2014) found that smaller context window sizes tend to result in embeddings with more syntactic information. We confirm this finding in our experiments.
- **Structured skip-gram embeddings** (Ling et al., 2015) extend the *standard* skip-gram embeddings (Mikolov et al., 2013) by taking into account the relative positions of words in a given context.

We use the tool `word2vec`[3] and Ling et al. (2015)'s modified version[4] to generate both plain and structured skip-gram embeddings in nine languages.

## 3 Models for POS Induction

In this section, we briefly review two classes of models used for POS induction (HMMs and CRF autoencoders), and explain how to generate word embedding observations in each class. We will represent a sentence of length $\ell$ as $\boldsymbol{w} = \langle w_1, w_2, \ldots, w_\ell \rangle \in V^\ell$ and a sequence of tags as $\boldsymbol{t} = \langle t_1, t_2, \ldots, t_\ell \rangle \in T^\ell$. The embeddings of word type $w \in V$ will be written as $\mathbf{v}_w \in \mathbb{R}^d$.

### 3.1 Hidden Markov Models

The hidden Markov model with multinomial emissions is a classic model for POS induction. This model makes the assumption that a latent Markov process with discrete states representing POS categories emits individual words in the vocabulary according to state (i.e., tag) specific emission distributions. An HMM thus defines the following joint distribution over sequences of observations and tags:

$$p(\boldsymbol{w}, \boldsymbol{t}) = \prod_{i=1}^{\ell} p(t_i \mid t_{i-1}) \times p(w_i \mid t_i) \qquad (1)$$

where distributions $p(t_i \mid t_{i-1})$ represents the transition probability and $p(w_i \mid t_i)$ is the emission probability, the probability of a particular tag generating the word at position $i$.[5]

We consider two variants of the HMM as baselines:

- $p(w_i \mid t_i)$ is parameterized as a "naïve multinomial" distribution with one distinct parameter for each word type.
- $p(w_i \mid t_i)$ is parameterized as a multinomial logistic regression model with hand-engineered features as detailed in (Berg-Kirkpatrick et al., 2010).

**Gaussian Emissions.** We now consider incorporating word embeddings in the HMM. Given a tag $t \in T$, instead of generating the observed word $w \in V$, we generate the (pre-trained) embedding $\mathbf{v}_w \in \mathbb{R}^d$ of that word. The conditional probability density assigned to $\mathbf{v}_w \mid t$ follows a multivariate Gaussian distribution with mean $\boldsymbol{\mu}_t$ and covariance matrix $\boldsymbol{\Sigma}_t$:

$$p(\mathbf{v}_w; \boldsymbol{\mu}_t, \boldsymbol{\Sigma}_t) = \frac{\exp\left(-\frac{1}{2}(\mathbf{v}_w - \boldsymbol{\mu}_t)^\top \boldsymbol{\Sigma}_t^{-1} (\mathbf{v}_w - \boldsymbol{\mu}_t)\right)}{\sqrt{(2\pi)^d |\boldsymbol{\Sigma}_t|}} \qquad (2)$$

This parameterization makes the assumption that embeddings of words which are often tagged as $t$ are concentrated around some point $\boldsymbol{\mu}_t \in \mathbb{R}^d$, and the concentration decays according to the covariance matrix $\boldsymbol{\Sigma}_t$.[6]

Now, the joint distribution over a sequence of observations $\mathbf{v} = \langle \mathbf{v}_{w_1}, \mathbf{v}_{w_2} \ldots, \mathbf{v}_{w_\ell} \rangle$ (which corresponds to word sequence $\boldsymbol{w} = \langle w_1, w_2, \ldots, w_\ell, \rangle$) and a tag sequence $\boldsymbol{t} = \langle t_1, t_2 \ldots, t_\ell \rangle$ becomes:

$$p(\mathbf{v}, \boldsymbol{t}) = \prod_{i=1}^{\ell} p(t_i \mid t_{i-1}) \times p(\mathbf{v}_{w_i}; \boldsymbol{\mu}_{t_i}, \boldsymbol{\Sigma}_{t_i})$$

We use the Baum–Welch algorithm to fit the $\boldsymbol{\mu}_t$ and $\boldsymbol{\Sigma}_{t_i}$ parameters. In every iteration, we update $\boldsymbol{\mu}_{t^*}$ as follows:

$$\boldsymbol{\mu}_{t^*}^{new} = \frac{\sum_{\mathbf{v} \in \mathcal{T}} \sum_{i=1\ldots\ell} p(t_i = t^* \mid \mathbf{v}) \times \mathbf{v}_{w_i}}{\sum_{\mathbf{v} \in \mathcal{T}} \sum_{i=1\ldots\ell} p(t_i = t^* \mid \mathbf{v})} \qquad (3)$$

where $\mathcal{T}$ is a data set of word embedding sequences $\mathbf{v}$ each of length $|\mathbf{v}| = \ell$, and $p(t_i = t^* \mid \mathbf{v})$ is the posterior probability of label $t^*$ at position $i$ in the sequence $\mathbf{v}$. Likewise the update to $\boldsymbol{\Sigma}_{t^*}$ is:

$$\boldsymbol{\Sigma}_{t^*}^{new} = \frac{\sum_{\mathbf{v} \in \mathcal{T}} \sum_{i=1\ldots\ell} p(t_i = t^* \mid \mathbf{v}) \times \boldsymbol{\delta}\boldsymbol{\delta}^\top}{\sum_{\mathbf{v} \in \mathcal{T}} \sum_{i=1\ldots\ell} p(t_i = t^* \mid \mathbf{v})} \qquad (4)$$

where $\boldsymbol{\delta} = \mathbf{v}_{w_i} - \boldsymbol{\mu}_{t^*}^{new}$.

[3] https://code.google.com/p/word2vec/

[4] https://github.com/wlin12/wang2vec/

[5] Terms for the starting and stopping transition probabilities are omitted for brevity.

[6] *"Essentially, all models are wrong, but some are useful."* — George E. P. Box

### 3.2 Conditional Random Field Autoencoders

The second class of models this work extends is called CRF autoencoders, which we recently proposed in (Ammar et al., 2014). It is a scalable family of models for feature-rich learning from unlabeled examples. The model conditions on one copy of the structured input, and generates a reconstruction of the input via a set of interdependent latent variables which represent the linguistic structure of interest. As shown in Eq. 5, the model factorizes into two distinct parts: the encoding model $p(\boldsymbol{t} \mid \boldsymbol{w})$ and the reconstruction model $p(\hat{\boldsymbol{w}} \mid \boldsymbol{t})$; where $\boldsymbol{w}$ is the structured input (e.g., a token sequence), $\boldsymbol{t}$ is the linguistic structure of interest (e.g., a sequence of POS tags), and $\hat{\boldsymbol{w}}$ is a generic reconstruction of the input. For POS induction, the encoding model is a linear-chain CRF with feature vector $\boldsymbol{\lambda}$ and local feature functions $\mathbf{f}$.

$$p(\hat{\boldsymbol{w}},\boldsymbol{t} \mid \boldsymbol{w}) = p(\boldsymbol{t} \mid \boldsymbol{w}) \times p(\hat{\boldsymbol{w}} \mid \boldsymbol{t}) \\ \propto p(\hat{\boldsymbol{w}} \mid \boldsymbol{t}) \times \exp \boldsymbol{\lambda} \cdot \sum_{i=1}^{|\boldsymbol{w}|} \mathbf{f}(t_i, t_{i-1}, \boldsymbol{w}) \quad (5)$$

In (Ammar et al., 2014), we explored two kinds of reconstructions $\hat{\boldsymbol{w}}$: surface forms and Brown clusters (Brown et al., 1992), and used "stupid multinomials" as the underlying distributions for re-generating $\hat{\boldsymbol{w}}$.

**Gaussian Reconstruction.** In this paper, we use $d$-dimensional word embedding reconstructions $\hat{w}_i = \mathbf{v}_{w_i} \in \mathbb{R}^d$, and replace the multinomial distribution of the reconstruction model with the multivariate Gaussian distribution in Eq. 2. We again use the Baum–Welch algorithm to estimate $\boldsymbol{\mu}_{t^*}$ and $\boldsymbol{\Sigma}_{t^*}$ similar to Eq. 3. The only difference is that posterior label probabilities are now conditional on both the input sequence $\boldsymbol{w}$ and the embeddings sequence $\mathbf{v}$, i.e., replace $p(t_i = t^* \mid \mathbf{v})$ in Eq. 2 with $p(t_i = t^* \mid \boldsymbol{w}, \mathbf{v})$.

## 4 Experiments

In this section, we attempt to answer the following questions:

- §4.1: Do syntactically-informed word embeddings improve POS induction? Which model performs best?
- §4.2: What kind of word embeddings are suitable for POS induction?

### 4.1 Choice of POS Induction Models

Here, we compare the following models for POS induction:

- Baseline: HMM with multinomial emissions (Kupiec, 1992),
- Baseline: HMM with log-linear emissions (Berg-Kirkpatrick et al., 2010),
- Baseline: CRF autoencoder with multinomial reconstructions (Ammar et al., 2014),[7]
- Proposed: HMM with Gaussian emissions, and
- Proposed: CRF autoencoder with Gaussian reconstructions.

**Data.** To train the POS induction models, we used the plain text from the training sections of the CoNLL-X shared task (Buchholz and Marsi, 2006) (for Danish and Turkish), the CoNLL 2007 shared task (Nivre et al., 2007) (for Arabic, Basque, Greek, Hungarian and Italian), and the Ukwabelana corpus (Spiegler et al., 2010) (for Zulu). For evaluation, we obtain the corresponding gold-standard POS tags by deterministically mapping the language-specific POS tags in the aforementioned corpora to the corresponding universal POS tag set (Petrov et al., 2012). This is the same set up we used in (Ammar et al., 2014).

**Setup.** In this section, we used skip-gram (i.e., `word2vec`) embeddings with a context window size = 1 and with dimensionality $d = 100$, trained with the largest corpora for each language in (Quasthoff et al., 2006), in addition to the plain text used to train the POS induction models.[8] In the proposed models, we only show results for estimating $\boldsymbol{\mu}_t$, assuming a diagonal covariance matrix $\boldsymbol{\Sigma}_t(k,k) = 0.45 \forall k \in \{1, \ldots, d\}$.[9] While the CRF autoencoder with multinomial reconstructions were carefully initialized as

[7]We use the configuration with best performance which reconstructs Brown clusters.

[8]We used the `corpus/tokenize-anything.sh` script in the cdec decoder (Dyer et al., 2010) to tokenize the corpora from (Quasthoff et al., 2006). The other corpora were already tokenized. In Arabic and Italian, we found a lot of discrepancies between the tokenization used for inducing word embeddings and the tokenization used for evaluation. We expect our results to improve with consistent tokenization.

[9]Surprisingly, we found that estimating $\boldsymbol{\Sigma}_t$ significantly degrades the performance. This may be due to overfitting (Shinozaki and Kawahara, 2007). Possible remedies include using a prior (Gauvain and Lee, 1994).

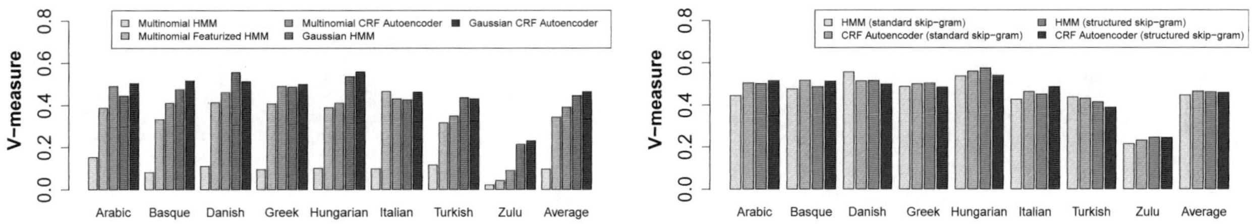


Figure 1: POS induction results. (V-measure, higher is better.) Window size is 1 for all word embeddings. **Left**: Models which use standard skip-gram word embeddings (i.e., Gaussian HMM and Gaussian CRF Autoencoder) outperform all baselines on average across languages. **Right**: comparison between standard and structured skip-grams on Gaussian HMM and CRF Autoencoder.

discussed in (Ammar et al., 2014), CRF autoencoder with Gaussian reconstructions were initialized uniformly at random in $[-1, 1]$. All HMM models were also randomly initialized. We tuned all hyperparameters on the English PTB corpus, then fixed them for all languages.

**Evaluation.** We use the V-measure evaluation metric (Rosenberg and Hirschberg, 2007) to evaluate the predicted syntactic classes at the token level.[10]

**Results.** The results in Fig. 1 clearly suggest that we can use word embeddings to improve POS induction. Surprisingly, the feature-less Gaussian HMM model outperforms the strong feature-rich baselines: Multinomial Featurized HMM and Multinomial CRF Autoencoder. One explanation is that our word embeddings were induced using larger unlabeled corpora than those used to train the POS induction models. The best results are obtained using both word embeddings and feature-rich models using the Gaussian CRF autoencoder model. This set of results suggest that word embeddings and hand-engineered features play complementary roles in POS induction. It is worth noting that the CRF autoencoder model with Gaussian reconstructions did not require careful initialization.[11]

### 4.2 Choice of Embeddings

**Standard skip-gram vs. structured skip-gram.** On Gaussian HMMs, structured skip-gram embeddings score moderately higher than standard skip-grams. And as context window size gets larger, the gap widens (as shown in Fig. 2.) The reason may be that structured skip-gram embeddings give each position within the context window its own project matrix, so the smearing effect is not as pronounced as the window grows when compared to the standard embeddings. However the best performance is still obtained when window size is small.[12]

**Dimensions = 20 vs. 200.** We also varied the number of dimensions in the word vectors ($d \in \{20, 50, 100, 200\}$). The best V-measure we obtain is 0.504 ($d = 20$) and the worst is 0.460 ($d = 100$). However, we did not observe a consistent pattern as shown in Fig. 3.

**Window size = 1 vs. 16.** Finally, we varied the window size for the context surrounding target words ($w \in \{1, 2, 4, 8, 16\}$). $w = 1$ yields the best average V-measure across the eight languages as shown in Fig. 2. This is true for both standard and structured

[10]We found the V-measure results to be consistent with the many-to-one evaluation metric (Johnson, 2007). We only show one set of results for brevity.

[11]In (Ammar et al., 2014), we found that careful initialization for the CRF autoencoder model with multinomial reconstructions is necessary.

[12]In preliminary experiments, we also compared standard skip-gram embeddings to SENNA embeddings (Collobert et al., 2011) (which are trained in a semi-supervised multi-task learning setup, with one task being POS tagging) on a subset of the English PTB corpus. As expected, the induced POS tags are much better when using SENNA embeddings, yielding a V-measure score of 0.57 compared to 0.51 for skip-gram embeddings. Since SENNA embeddings are only available in English, we did not include it in the comparison in Fig. 1.

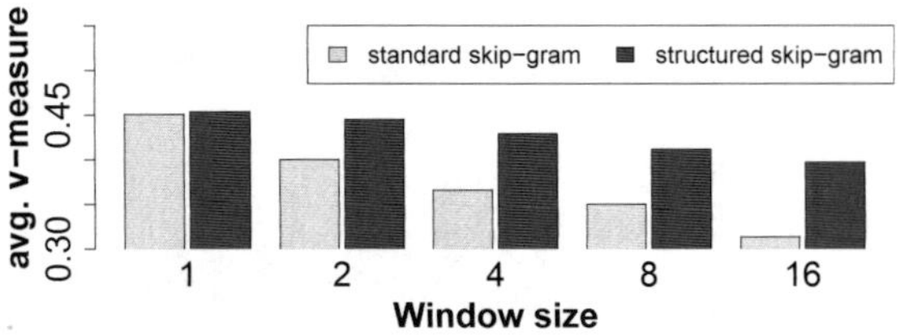


Figure 2: Effect of window size and embeddings type on POS induction over the languages in Fig. 1. $d = 100$. The model is HMM with Gaussian emissions.

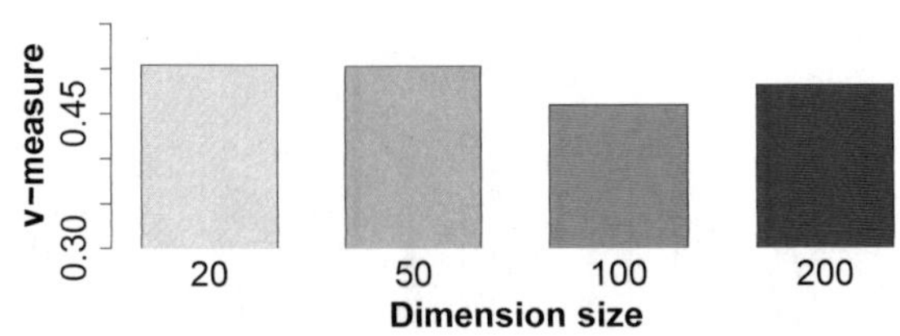


Figure 3: Effect of dimension size on POS induction on a subset of the English PTB corpus. $w = 1$. The model is HMM with Gaussian emissions.

skip-gram models. Notably, larger window sizes appear to produce word embeddings with less syntactic information. This result confirms the observations of Bansal et al. (2014).

### 4.3 Discussion

We have shown that (re)generating word embeddings does much better than generating opaque word types in unsupervised POS induction. At a high level, this confirms prior findings that unsupervised word embeddings capture syntactic properties of words, and shows that different embeddings capture more syntactically salient information than others. As such, we contend that unsupervised POS induction can be seen as a diagnostic metric for assessing the syntactic quality of embeddings.

To get a better understanding of what the multivariate Gaussian models have learned, we conduct a hill-climbing experiment on our English dataset. We seed each POS category with the average vector of 10 randomly sampled words from that category and train the model. Seeding unsurprisingly improves tagging performance. We also find words that are the nearest to the centroids generally agree with the correct category label, which validate our assumption that syntactically similar words tend to cluster in the high-dimensional embedding space. It also shows that careful initialization of model parameters can bring further improvements.

However we also find that words that are close to the centroid are not necessarily representative of what linguists consider to be prototypical. For example, Hopper and Thompson (1983) show that physical, telic, past tense verbs are more prototypical with respect to case marking, agreement, and other syntactic behavior. However, the verbs nearest our centroid all seem rather abstract. In English, the nearest 5 words in the verb category are *entails, aspires, attaches, foresees, deems*. This may be because these words seldom serve functions other than verbs; and placing the centroid around them incurs less penalty (in contrast to physical verbs, e.g. *bite*, which often also act as nouns). Therefore one should be cautious in interpreting what is prototypical about them.

## 5 Conclusion

We propose using a multivariate Gaussian model to generate vector space representations of observed words in generative or hybrid models for POS induction, as a superior alternative to using multinomial distributions to generate categorical word types. We find the performance from a simple Gaussian HMM competitive with strong feature-rich baselines. We further show that substituting the emission part of the CRF autoencoder can bring further improvements. We also confirm previous findings which suggest that smaller context windows in skip-gram models result in word embeddings which encode more syntactic information. It would be interesting to see if we can apply this approach to other tasks which require generative modeling of textual observations such as language modeling and grammar induction.

## Acknowledgements

This work was sponsored by the U.S. Army Research Laboratory and the U.S. Army Research Office under contract/grant numbers W911NF-11-2-0042 and W911NF-10-1-0533. The statements made herein are solely the responsibility of the authors.

## References


Waleed Ammar, Chris Dyer, and Noah A. Smith. 2014. Conditional random field autoencoders for unsupervised structured prediction. In *NIPS*.

Mohit Bansal, Kevin Gimpel, and Karen Livescu. 2014. Tailoring continuous word representations for dependency parsing. In *Proc. of ACL*.

Taylor Berg-Kirkpatrick, Alexandre Bouchard-Côté, John DeNero, and Dan Klein. 2010. Painless unsupervised learning with features. In *Proc. of NAACL*.

David M. Blei and Peter I. Frazier. 2011. Distance dependent Chinese restaurant processes. *JMLR*.

Peter F. Brown, Peter V. deSouza, Robert L. Mercer, Vincent J. Della Pietra, and Jenifer C. Lai. 1992. Class-based n-gram models of natural language. *Computational Linguistics*.

Sabine Buchholz and Erwin Marsi. 2006. CoNLL-X shared task on multilingual dependency parsing. In *CoNLL-X*.

Ronan Collobert and Jason Weston. 2008. A unified architecture for natural language processing: Deep neural networks with multitask learning. In *Proc. of ICML*.

Ronan Collobert, Jason Weston, Léon Bottou, Michael Karlen, Koray Kavukcuoglu, and Pavel Kuksa. 2011. Natural language processing (almost) from scratch. *JMLR*, 12:2493–2537, November.

Scott Deerwester, Susan T. Dumais, George W. Furnas, Thomas K. Landauer, and Richard Harshman. 1990. Indexing by latent semantic analysis. *Journal of the American society for information science*, 41(6):391–407.

Paramveer S. Dhillon, Dean Foster, and Lyle Ungar. 2011. Multi-view learning of word embeddings via CCA. In *NIPS*, volume 24.

Chris Dyer, Adam Lopez, Juri Ganitkevitch, Johnathan Weese, Ferhan Ture, Phil Blunsom, Hendra Setiawan, Vladimir Eidelman, and Philip Resnik. 2010. cdec: A decoder, alignment, and learning framework for finite-state and context-free translation models. In *Proc. of ACL*.

J. Gauvain and Chin-Hui Lee. 1994. Maximum a posteriori estimation for multivariate Gaussian mixture observations of Markov chains. *Speech and Audio Processing, IEEE Transactions on*, 2(2):291–298, Apr.

Paul Hopper and Sandra Thompson. 1983. The iconicity of the universal categories "noun" and "verb". In John Haiman, editor, *Iconicity in Syntax: Proceedings of a symposium on iconicity in syntax*.

Mark Johnson. 2007. Why doesn't EM find good HMM POS-taggers? In *Proc. of EMNLP*.

Julian Kupiec. 1992. Robust part-of-speech tagging using a hidden Markov model. *Computer Speech and Language*, 6:225–242.

Wang Ling, Chris Dyer, Alan Black, and Isabel Trancoso. 2015. Two/too simple adaptations of word2vec for syntax problems. In *Proc. of NAACL*.

Tomas Mikolov, Stefan Kombrink, Anoop Deoras, Lukar Burget, and J Cernocky. 2011. RNNLM — recurrent neural network language modeling toolkit. In *Proc. of the 2011 ASRU Workshop*, pages 196–201.

Tomas Mikolov, Kai Chen, Greg Corrado, and Jeffrey Dean. 2013. Efficient estimation of word representations in vector space. *ArXiv e-prints*, January.

Joakim Nivre, Johan Hall, Sandra Kubler, Ryan McDonald, Jens Nilsson, Sebastian Riedel, and Deniz Yuret. 2007. The CoNLL 2007 shared task on dependency parsing. In *Proc. of CoNLL*.

Slav Petrov, Dipanjan Das, and Ryan McDonald. 2012. A universal part-of-speech tagset. In *Proc. of LREC*, May.

Uwe Quasthoff, Matthias Richter, and Christian Biemann. 2006. Corpus portal for search in monolingual corpora. In *Proc. of LREC*, pages 1799–1802.

Andrew Rosenberg and Julia Hirschberg. 2007. V-measure: A conditional entropy-based external cluster evaluation measure. In *EMNLP-CoNLL*.

T. Shinozaki and T. Kawahara. 2007. HMM training based on CV-EM and CV gaussian mixture optimization. In *Proc. of the 2007 ASRU Workshop*, pages 318–322, Dec.

Kairit Sirts, Jacob Eisenstein, Micha Elsner, and Sharon Goldwater. 2014. POS induction with distributional and morphological information using a distance-dependent Chinese restaurant process. In *Proc. of ACL*.

Sebastian Spiegler, Andrew van der Spuy, and Peter A. Flach. 2010. Ukwabelana: An open-source morphological Zulu corpus. In *Proc. of COLING*, pages 1020–1028.

Mehmet Ali Yatbaz, Enis Rıfat Sert, and Deniz Yuret. 2014. Unsupervised instance-based part of speech induction using probable substitutes. In *Proc. of COLING*.

# Improving Update Summarization via Supervised ILP and Sentence Reranking

**Chen Li[1], Yang Liu[1], Lin Zhao[2]**
[1] Computer Science Department, The University of Texas at Dallas
Richardson, Texas 75080, USA
[2] Research and Technology Center, Robert Bosch LLC
Palo Alto, California 94304, USA
{chenli,yangl@hlt.utdallas.edu}
{lin.zhao@us.bosch.com}

## Abstract

Integer Linear Programming (ILP) based summarization methods have been widely adopted recently because of their state-of-the-art performance. This paper proposes two new modifications in this framework for update summarization. Our key idea is to use discriminative models with a set of features to measure both the salience and the novelty of words and sentences. First, these features are used in a supervised model to predict the weights of the concepts used in the ILP model. Second, we generate preliminary sentence candidates in the ILP model and then rerank them using sentence level features. We evaluate our method on different TAC update summarization data sets, and the results show that our system performs competitively compared to the best TAC systems based on the ROUGE evaluation metric.

## 1 Introduction

Update summarization has attracted significant research focus recently. Different from generic extractive summarization, update summarization assumes that users already have some information about a given topic from an old data set, and thus for a new data set the system aims to generate a summary that contains as much novel information as possible. This task was first introduced at DUC 2007 and then continued until TAC 2011. It is very useful to chronological events in real applications.

Most basic update summarization methods are variants of multi-document summarization methods, with some consideration of the difference between the earlier and later document sets (Boudin et al., 2008; Fisher and Roark, 2008; Long et al., 2010; Bysani, 2010). One important line is to use graph-based co-ranking. They rank the sentences in the earlier and later document sets simultaneously by considering the sentence relationship. For example, Li et al. (2008) was inspired by the intuition that "a sentence receives a positive influence from the sentences that correlate to it in the same collection, whereas receives a negative influence from the sentences that correlates to it in the different (or previously read) collection', and proposed a graph based sentence ranking algorithm for update summarization. Wan (2012) integrated two co-ranking processes by adding some strict constraints, which led to more accurate computation of sentences' scores for update summarization. A similar method was also applied earlier by (Wan et al., 2011) for multilingual news summarization. In addition, generative models, such as topic models, have also been adopted for this task. For example, Delort and Alfonseca (2012) proposed a novel nonparametric Bayesian approach, a variant of Latent Dirichlet Allocation (LDA), aiming to distinguish between common information and novel information. Li et al. (2012) borrowed the idea of evolutionary clustering and proposed a three-level HDP (Hierarchical Dirichlet Process) model to represent the diversity and commonality between aspects discovered from two different document data sets.

One of the most competitive summarization methods is based on Integer Linear Programming (ILP). It has been widely adopted in the generic summarization task (Martins and Smith, 2009; Berg-Kirkpatrick et al., 2011; Woodsend and Lapata, 2012; Li et al., 2013a; Li et al., 2013b; Li et al., 2014). In this paper, we use the ILP summarization



*Human Language Technologies: The 2015 Annual Conference of the North American Chapter of the ACL*, pages 1317–1322, framework for the update summarization task, and make improvement from two aspects, with the goal to more discriminatively represent both the salience and novelty of words and sentences. First, we use supervised models and a rich set of features to learn the weights for the bigram concepts used in the ILP model. Second, we design a sentence reranking component to score the summary candidate sentences generated by the ILP model. This second reranking approach allows us to explicitly model a sentence's importance and novelty, which complements the bigram centric view in the first step of ILP sentence selection. Our experimental results on multiple TAC data sets demonstrate the effectiveness of our proposed method.

## 2 Proposed Update Summarization System

### 2.1 ILP Framework for Summarization

The core idea of the ILP based summarization method is to select the summary sentences by maximizing the sum of the weights of the language concepts that appear in the summary. Bigrams are often used as the language concepts in this method. Gillick et al. (2009) stated that the bigrams gave consistently better performance than unigrams or trigrams for a variety of ROUGE measures. The association between the language concepts and sentences serves as the constraints. This ILP method is formally represented as below (see (Gillick et al., 2009) for more details):

$$\begin{aligned} \max \quad & \textstyle\sum_i w_i c_i \qquad (1) \\ s.t. \quad & c_i \in \{0,1\}\ \forall i \quad s_j \in \{0,1\}\ \forall j \\ & s_j Occ_{ij} \leq c_i \quad \sum_j s_j Occ_{ij} \geq c_i \\ & \textstyle\sum_j l_j s_j \leq L \end{aligned}$$

where $c_i$ and $s_j$ are binary variables that indicate the presence of a concept and a sentence respectively. $l_j$ is the sentence length and $L$ is the maximum length (word number) of the generated summary. $w_i$ is a concept's weight and $Occ_{ij}$ means the occurrence of concept $i$ in sentence $j$. The first two inequalities associate the sentences and concepts. They ensure that selecting a sentence leads to the selection of all the concepts it contains, and selecting a concept only happens when it is present in at least one of the selected sentences.

### 2.2 Bigrams Weighting for Salience and Novelty

In the above ILP-based summarization method, how to determine the concepts and measure their weights is the key factor impacting the system performance. Intuitively, if we can successfully identify the important key bigrams used in the ILP system, or assign large weights to those important bigrams, the generated summary sentences will contain as many important bigrams as possible, and thus resulting in better summarization performance. The oracle experiment in (Gillick et al., 2008) showed that if they use the bigrams extracted from the human written summaries as the input of the ILP system, much better ROUGE scores can be obtained than using the automatically selected bigrams, suggesting the importance of using the right concepts. (Gillick et al., 2009) used document frequency as the weight of a bigram. They also provided some justification for document frequency as a weighting function in that paper.

For update summarization, intuitively we need to not only identify the salience of the bigram, but also incorporate bigrams' novelty in their weights. Therefore, only using the document frequency as the weight in the objective function is insufficient. We thus propose to use a supervised framework for the bigram weight estimation in the ILP model. The new objective function is:

$$\max \quad \textstyle\sum_i (\theta \cdot \mathbf{f}(b_i))\, c_i \qquad (2)$$

We replace the heuristic $w_i$ in Formula (1) with a feature based one: $f(b_i)$ represents the features for a bigram $b_i$, and $\theta$ is a weight vector for these features. Constraints remain the same as before in the ILP method.

There are two kinds of features for each bigram: one set is related to the bigrams themselves; the other set is related to the sentences containing the bigram. Table 1 shows the features we design. For both the bigram and the sentence level features, we separate the features based on whether they represent the importance or the novelty. For

Feature 8 and 17, the summary is generated by a general unsupervised ILP-based summarization system from the given old data set. The idea of Feature 9 and 10 was first introduced by (Bysani, 2010); here we applied it to bigrams. $df_{max}$ is the number of documents in the data set (10 in the TAC data), which can be thought of the maximum value of document frequency for a bigram. Feature 11 is interpolated n-gram document frequency, which was first introduced by (Ng et al., 2012): $\frac{\alpha \sum_{w_u \in S} df_{new}(w_u) + (1-\alpha) \sum_{w_b \in S} df_{new}(w_b)}{|S|}$, where $w_u$ and $w_b$ are unigrams and bigrams respectively in sentence $S$. Feature 18 and 19 are variants of Features 11, where instead of document frequency (*df* in the formula above), bigram and unigram's novelty and uniqueness values are used. Among these features, the feature values of feature 4, 5 and 6 are discrete. In this study, we discretized all the other continuous values into ten categories according to the value range in the training data.

To train the model (feature weights), we use the average perceptron strategy (Collins, 2002) to update the feature weights whenever the hypothesis by the ILP decoding process is incorrect. Binary class labels are used for bigrams in the learning process, that is, we only consider whether a bigram is in the system generated summary or human summaries, not their term or document frequency. We use a fixed learning rate (0.1) in training.

### 2.3 Sentence Reranking on ILP Results

In the ILP method, sentence selection is done by considering the concepts that a sentence contains. It is difficult to add indicative features in this framework to explicitly represent the sentence's salience, and more importantly, its novelty for the update summarization task. This information is only captured by the weights of the bigrams using the method described above. Therefore, we propose to use a two-step approach, where an initial ILP module first selects some sentences and then a reranking module uses sentence level features to rerank them to generate the final summary. We expect this step of modeling sentences directly can complement the bigram centric view in the first ILP summarization module.

| **Bigram Level Features** |
|---|
| **Importance Related Features** |
| 1. $df_{new}(b)$: document frequency in new data set |
| 2. normalized term frequency in all filtered relevant sentences[1] |
| 3. sentence frequency in all relevant sentences |
| 4. do bigram words appear in topic's query ? |
| 5. is the bigram in the first 1/2/3 position of that sentence? |
| 6. is the bigram in the last 1/2/3 position of that sentence? |
| **Novelty Related Features** |
| 7. $df_{old}(b)$: document frequency in old data set |
| 8. normalized term frequency in the summary from old data set |
| 9. bigram novelty value $n(b) = \frac{df_{new}(b)}{df_{old}(b)+df_{max}}$ |
| 10. bigram uniqueness value $u(b) = 0$ if $df_{old}(b) > 0$; otherwise $u(b) = \frac{df_{new}(b)}{df_{max}}$ |
| **Sentence Level Features** |
| **Importance Related Features** |
| 11. interpolated n-gram document frequency |
| 12. sentence position in that document |
| 13. is the sentence in the first 1/2/3 position in that document? |
| 14. is the sentence in the last 1/2/3 position in that document? |
| 15. sentence length |
| 16. sentence similarity with topic's query |
| **Novelty Related Features** |
| 17. sentence similarity with the summary from old data set |
| 18. interpolated n-gram novelty |
| 19. interpolated n-gram uniqueness |

Table 1: Features in the supervised ILP model for weighting bigrams.

For the first step, we use the ILP framework with our supervised bigram weighting method to obtain a summary of $N$ words ($N$ is greater than the required summary length $L$). Note that the ILP model selects these output sentences as a set that optimizes the objective function, and there are no scores for each individual sentence. Second, we use sentence level features listed in Table 1 to rerank the can-

[1]Note that we do not use all the sentences in the ILP module. The 'relevant' sentences are those that have at least one bigram with document frequency larger than or equal to three.

didate sentences. This is expected to better evaluate the salience and the novelty of the sentences. We use a regression model (SVR) for this reranking purpose. When training the model, a sentence's ROUGE2 score compared with the human generated summary is used as the regression target. After reranking, we just select the top sentences that satisfy the length constraint to form the final summary. In this work we do not use any redundancy removal (e.g., MMR method). This is because the ILP decoding process tries to find a global optimal set maximizing the concept coverage, subject to the length constraint, and thus already considers redundancy among sentences. Typically when the initial set (i.e., the output from the first ILP step) is not too big, redundancy is not a big problem.

## 3 Experiments and Results

### 3.1 Data and Experiment Setup

We evaluate our methods using several recent TAC data sets, from 2008 to 2011. Every topic has two sets of 10 documents (Set A and B). The update task aims to create a 100-word summary from Set B given a topic query and Set A. When evaluating on one year's data, we use the data from the other three years as the training set. This applies to both the supervised ILP method and the sentence reranking regression model. All the summaries are evaluated using ROUGE (Lin, 2004). An academic free solver[2] does all the ILP decoding and libsvm[3] is used for SVR implementation.

### 3.2 Results

Table 2 and Table 3 show the R2 and R-SU4 values on different TAC data sets for the following systems.

- ILP baseline. This is the unsupervised ILP-based summarization system (Gillick et al., 2009), in which only bigrams with document frequency greater than 2 are used in the ILP summarization process, and weight $w_i$ is the document frequency of that bigram.
- TAC best. This is the best result in the TAC update summarization evaluation.[4] Note that there is limited research on update summarization and we cannot find better published results for these data sets than the TAC best systems.
- Supervised ILP. This is our supervised ILP method where bigram weights are learned discriminately. It is the one-step system that generates the summary with the target length. We use the same bigram set as the ILP baseline system. For this method, we show results using different features: only using the importance features; and using all the features. This is used to evaluate the impact of the novelty features on the update summarization task.
- Two-step method: supervised ILP followed by sentence reranking. We generate 200 (value of $N$) words summary in the ILP system. Two different configurations are also used: with and without the sentence novelty features in the sentence ranking module. All the features (including the novelty features) are used in the ILP pre-selection step.
- Sentence ranking without ILP. In this experiment, we do not use the ILP summarization module to generate candidate sentences first, but just apply sentence ranking to the entire data set. Then MMR is leveraged to select the final summary sentences. Again, we present results using different feature sets.

We can see from the tables that the supervised ILP model outperforms the unsupervised one. After including the novelty related features, the model can assign higher weights for the bigrams with novel information, resulting in improved summarization performance. There is further improvement when using our 2-step approach with the sentence reranking model. Our proposed method (ILP followed by sentence reranking, and using all the features) outperforms the TAC best result in 2010 and 2011, and also yields competitive results in the other data sets. The gain of ROUGE-2 of our proposed system compared with the ILP baseline is statistically significant based on ROUGE's 95% confidence. When using sentence ranking on the entire document set, without the ILP pre-selection step, its performance is worse than our proposed method. This shows the benefit of doing pre-selection using the ILP module. Finally,

[2]http://www.gurobi.com

[3]http://www.csie.ntu.edu.tw/čjlin/libsvm/

[4]The ID of the TAC best system from 2008 to 2011 is 14,40,16 and 43.

| | 2008 | 2009 | 2010 | 2011 |
|---|---|---|---|---|
| ILP Baseline | 8.55 | 8.84 | 7.04 | 8.63 |
| TAC Best | 10.10 | 10.41 | 8.00 | 9.58 |
| Supervised ILP | | | | |
| w/o novelty features | 9.18 | 9.06 | 7.39 | 9.20 |
| w all features | 9.4 | 9.28 | 7.76 | 9.46 |
| 2-step: Supervised ILP + Sentence Ranking | | | | |
| w/o novelty features | 9.65 | 9.47 | 7.97 | 9.70 |
| w all features | 9.99 | 9.61 | 8.11 | 9.99 |
| Sentence Ranking w/o ILP | | | | |
| w/o novelty features | 9.25 | 9.10 | 7.41 | 9.18 |
| w all features | 9.42 | 9.32 | 7.70 | 9.43 |

Table 2: ROUGE-2 results on TAC 2008-2011 data.

| | 2008 | 2009 | 2010 | 2011 |
|---|---|---|---|---|
| ILP Baseline | 12.17 | 12.54 | 10.57 | 12.01 |
| NIST Best | 13.66 | 13.95 | 11.97 | 13.08 |
| Supervised ILP | | | | |
| w/o novelty features | 12.57 | 12.94 | 11.01 | 12.76 |
| w all features | 12.78 | 13.21 | 11.61 | 12.95 |
| 2-step: Supervised ILP + Sentence Ranking | | | | |
| w/o novelty features | 13.10 | 13.65 | 11.98 | 13.24 |
| w all features | 13.61 | 13.77 | 12.20 | 13.42 |
| Sentence Ranking w/o ILP | | | | |
| w/o novelty features | 12.60 | 12.99 | 11.25 | 12.73 |
| w all features | 12.85 | 13.31 | 11.50 | 12.90 |

Table 3: ROUGE-SU4 results on TAC 2008-2011 data.

for all the methods, adding the novelty related features always performs better than that without them, proving the effect of our novelty features for update summarization.

Lastly we evaluate the effect of the summary length from the ILP module on the two-step summarization systems. Figure 1 shows the performance when $N$ changes from 150 to 400. We can see that there is some difference in the patterns for different data sets, and the best results are obtained when $N$ is around 150 to 250. When the first ILP module produces many sentence candidates, it is likely that there is redundancy among them. In this case, redundancy removal approaches such as MMR need to be used to generate the final summary. In addition, for a large candidate set, our current regression model also faces some challenges due to its limited features used in sentence reranking. Addressing these problems is our future work.

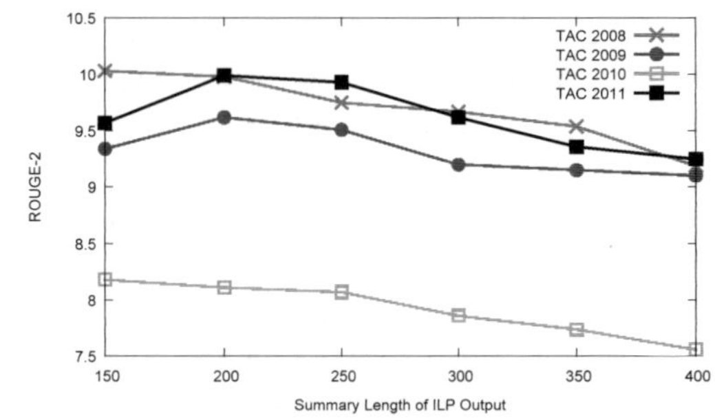


Figure 1: ROUGE-2 results when varying the output length for the first ILP selection step.

## 4 Conclusions

In this paper, we adopt the supervised ILP framework for the update summarization task. A set of rich features are used to measure the importance and novelty of the bigram concepts used in the ILP model. In addition, we proposed a re-selection component to rank candidate sentences generated by the ILP model based on sentence level features. Our experiment results show that our features and the reranking procedure both help improve the summarization performance. This pilot research points out new directions for generic or update summarization based on the ILP framework.

## Acknowledgments

We thank the anonymous reviewers for their detailed and insightful comments on earlier drafts of this paper. The work is partially supported by NSF award IIS-0845484 and DARPA Contract No. FA8750-13-2-0041. Any opinions, findings, and conclusions or recommendations expressed are those of the author and do not necessarily reflect the views of the funding agencies.

## References

Taylor Berg-Kirkpatrick, Dan Gillick, and Dan Klein. 2011. Jointly learning to extract and compress. In *Proceedings of ACL*.

Florian Boudin, Marc El-Bèze, and Juan-Manuel Torres-Moreno. 2008. The LIA update summarization systems at tac-2008. In *Proceedings of TAC*.

Praveen Bysani. 2010. Detecting novelty in the context of progressive summarization. In *Proceedings of the NAACL Student Research Workshop*.

Michael Collins. 2002. Discriminative training methods for hidden markov models: Theory and experiments with perceptron algorithms. In *Proceedings of EMNLP*.

Jean-Yves Delort and Enrique Alfonseca. 2012. Dualsum: a topic-model based approach for update summarization. In *Proceedings of EACL*.

Seeger Fisher and Brian Roark. 2008. Query-focused supervised sentence ranking for update summaries. In *Proceeding of TAC*.

Dan Gillick, Benoit Favre, and Dilek Hakkani-tur. 2008. The ICSI summarization system at tac 2008. In *Proceedings of TAC*.

Dan Gillick, Benoit Favre, Dilek Hakkani-Tur, Berndt Bohnet, Yang Liu, and Shasha Xie. 2009. The ICSI/UTD summarization system at tac 2009. In *Proceedings of TAC*.

Wenjie Li, Furu Wei, Qin Lu, and Yanxiang He. 2008. PNR2: Ranking sentences with positive and negative reinforcement for query-oriented update summarization. In *Proceedings of Coling*.

Jiwei Li, Sujian Li, Xun Wang, Ye Tian, and Baobao Chang. 2012. Update summarization using a multi-level hierarchical dirichlet process model. In *Proceedings of COLING*.

Chen Li, Fei Liu, Fuliang Weng, and Yang Liu. 2013a. Document summarization via guided sentence compression. In *Proceedings of the EMNLP*.

Chen Li, Xian Qian, and Yang Liu. 2013b. Using supervised bigram-based ilp for extractive summarization. In *Proceedings of ACL*.

Chen Li, Yang Liu, Fei Liu, Lin Zhao, and Fuliang Weng. 2014. Improving multi-documents summarization by sentence compression based on expanded constituent parse trees. In *Proceedings of EMNLP*.

Chin-Yew Lin. 2004. Rouge: a package for automatic evaluation of summaries. In *Proceedings of ACL*.

Chong Long, Minlie Huang, and Xiaoyan Zhu. 2010. Summarizing multidocuments by information distance. In *Proceedings of TAC*.

Andre F. T. Martins and Noah A. Smith. 2009. Summarization with a joint model for sentence extraction and compression. In *Proceedings of the ACL Workshop on Integer Linear Programming for Natural Language Processing*.

Jun-Ping Ng, Praveen Bysani, Ziheng Lin, Min-Yen Kan, and Chew-Lim Tan. 2012. Exploiting category-specific information for multi-document summarization. In *Proceedings of COLING*.

Xiaojun Wan, Houping Jia, Shanshan Huang, and Jianguo Xiao. 2011. Summarizing the differences in multilingual news. In *Proceedings of SIGIR*.

Xiaojun Wan. 2012. Update summarization based on co-ranking with constraints. In *Proceedings of COLING*.

Kristian Woodsend and Mirella Lapata. 2012. Multiple aspect summarization using integer linear programming. In *Proceedings of EMNLP-CoNLL*.

# MPQA 3.0: An Entity/Event-Level Sentiment Corpus

**Lingjia Deng**
Intelligent Systems Program
University of Pittsburgh
lid29@pitt.edu

**Janyce Wiebe**
Intelligent Systems Program
Department of Computer Science
University of Pittsburgh
wiebe@cs.pitt.edu

## Abstract

This paper presents an annotation scheme for adding entity and event target annotations to the MPQA corpus, a rich span-annotated opinion corpus. The new corpus promises to be a valuable new resource for developing systems for entity/event-level sentiment analysis. Such systems, in turn, would be valuable in NLP applications such as Automatic Question Answering. We introduce the idea of entity and event targets (*eTargets*), describe the annotation scheme, and present the results of an agreement study.

## 1 Introduction

Much work in sentiment analysis and opinion mining is at the document level (Pang et al., 2002; Turney, 2002). There is increasing interest in more fine-grained levels - sentence-level (Yu and Hatzivassiloglou, 2003; McDonald et al., 2007), phrase-level (Choi and Cardie, 2008), aspect-level (Hu and Liu, 2004; Titov and McDonald, 2008), etc. We specifically address sentiments toward entities and events (i.e., *eTargets*) expressed in data such as blogs, newswire, and editorials. A system that could recognize sentiments toward entities and events would be valuable in an application such as Automatic Question Answering, to support answering questions such as "Toward whom/what is $X$ negative/positive?" "Who is negative/positive toward $X$?" (Stoyanov et al., 2005). Or, to augment an automatic wikification system (Ratinov et al., 2011) – in addition to relationships such as *spouse* and *parents*, the system could include information about whom or what the subject supports or opposes. A recent NIST evaluation – The Knowledge Base Population (KBP) Sentiment track[1] — aims at using corpora to collect information regarding sentiments expressed toward or by named entities.

Annotated corpora of reviews (e.g., (Hu and Liu, 2004; Titov and McDonald, 2008)), widely used in NLP, often include target annotations. Such targets are often aspects or features of products or services, and as such are somewhat limited.[2]

Recently, to create the Sentiment Treebank (Socher et al., 2013), researchers crowdsourced annotations of movie review data and then overlaid the annotations onto syntax trees. Thus, the targets are not limited to aspects of products/services. However, annotators were asked to annotate small and then increasingly larger segments of the sentence. Thus, the annotations are mixed in the degree to which context was considered when making the judgements. Previously, we (Deng et al., 2013) annotated a corpus of non-review data with sentiments toward entities, but only for those that participate in certain types of events. In all of the above corpora, the only sentiments considered are those of the writer, excluding sentiments attributed to other entities.

The MPQA opinion annotated corpus (Wiebe et al., 2005; Wilson, 2007) is entirely span-based, and contains no eTarget annotations. However, it provides an infrastructure for sentiment annotation that is not provided by other sentiment NLP corpora, and

[1] http://www.nist.gov/tac/2014/KBP/Sentiment/index.html

[2] For example, as stated in SemEval-2014: "We annotate only aspect terms naming particular aspects."



*Human Language Technologies: The 2015 Annual Conference of the North American Chapter of the ACL*, pages 1323–1328,
Denver, Colorado, May 31 – June 5, 2015. 

is much more varied in topic, genre, and publication source. This paper addresses adding eTarget annotations to the MPQA corpus; we believe that the result will be a valuable new resource for the community.

## 2 From MPQA 2.0 to MPQA 3.0

To create MPQA 3.0, entity-target and event-target (*eTarget*) annotations are added to the MPQA 2.0 annotations.[3] The MPQA annotations consist of *private states*, which are states of *sources* holding *attitudes* toward *targets*. In the MPQA 2.0 annotations, the top-level annotations are *direct subjective* (*DS*) and *objective speech event* annotations. DS annotations are for private states, and objective speech event annotations are for objective statements attributed to a source. An important property of sources is that they are nested, reflecting the fact that private states and speech events are often embedded in one another.

As shown in Figure 1, one DS may contain links to multiple *attitude* annotations, meaning that all of the attitudes share the same nested source. The attitudes differ from one another in their attitude types, polarities, and/or targets. There are several types of attitudes included in MPQA 2.0 (Wilson, 2007; Somasundaran et al., 2007), including sentiment and arguing. This work focuses on sentiments, which are defined in (Wilson, 2007) as positive and negative evaluations, emotions, and judgements.

MPQA 2.0 also contains *expressive subjective element* (*ESE*) annotations, which pinpoint specific expressions used to express subjectivity (Wiebe et al., 2005). An ESE also has a nested-source annotation. Since we focus on sentiments, we only consider ESEs whose polarity is positive or negative (excluding those marked neutral).

The *target-span* annotations in MPQA 2.0 are linked to from the attitudes. More than one target may be linked to from an attitude, but most attitudes have only one target. The MPQA 2.0 annotators identified the main/most important target(s) they perceive in the sentence. If there is no target, the target-span annotation is "none". However, there are many other eTargets to be identified. First, while ESE annotations have nested sources, they do not have any target annotations. Second, there are many

[3] Available at http://mpqa.cs.pitt.edu

- DS
  - nested-source
  - attitude
    - attitude type
    - target
      - *eTarget*
      - *eTarget*
    - target
      - *eTarget*
    - *eTarget*
- ESE
  - nested-source
  - polarity
  - *eTarget*
  - *eTarget*
- objective speech event
  - nested-source
  - target

Figure 1: Structure in MPQA 3.0.

more targets that may be marked than the major ones identified in MPQA 2.0. In Figure 1, the eTargets are what we add in MPQA 3.0. We identify the blue (orange) eTargets that are in the span of a blue (orange) target in MPQA 2.0. We also identify the green eTargets that are not in the scope of any target.

Since our priority was to add eTargets to sentiments, no eTargets have yet been added to objective speech events, as shown in Figure 1.

To create MPQA 3.0, the corpus is first parsed, and *potential* eTarget annotations are automatically created from the heads of NPs and VPs. The annotators then consider each sentiment attitude and each polar ESE, and decide for each which eTargets to add. By adding eTargets to the existing annotations, the information in MPQA 2.0 is retained. Before presenting the scheme, we first give some examples.

### 2.1 Examples

For each example, a subset of the annotations are shown. The phrase in blue is an attitude span, the phrase in red is a target span, the tokens in yellow are the eTargets which are newly annotated in MPQA 3.0. The underlined phrases are ESE spans. Each example is followed by the MPQA structure of the annotations.

In Ex(1), a negative attitude is shown, *issued the fatwa against*. The source is *the Imam*. The target is the event *Rushdie insulting the Prophet*. However, the assertion that the Imam is negative toward the insult event is within the scope of this article. This is captured by an objective speech event annotation (not shown) whose target span includes the insult event, and whose source is the writer (*w*). Thus, the complete interpretation of this negative attitude is, according to the writer, the Imam is negative toward the insult event. And, the nested source is *w, imam*.

> Ex(1) When the Imam issued the fatwa against Salman Rushdie for insulting the Prophet ...
>
> **DS**: issued the fatwa
> **nested-source**: w, imam
> **attitude**: issued the fatwa against
> **attitude-type**: sentiment-negative
> **target**: Salman...insult...Prophet
> **eTarget** : Rushdie, insulting

We find two eTargets in the target-span: "Rushdie" himself plus his act of "insulting."

In the same sentence, there is another negative attitude, *insulting*, as shown in Ex(2). The source is *Salman Rushdie* and the target is *the Prophet*. Note that the span covering this event is the target span of the attitude in Ex(1) — the private state of Ex(2) is nested in the private state of Ex(1). Thus, the complete interpretation of the negative attitude in Ex(2) is: according to the writer, the Imam is negative toward Rushdie insulting the Prophet. The nested source is *w, Imam, Rushdie*.

> Ex(2) When the Imam issued the fatwa against Salman Rushdie for insulting the Prophet ...
>
> **DS**: insulting
> **nested-source**: w, imam, rushdie
> **attitude**: insulting
> **attitude-type**: sentiment-negative
> **target**: the Prophet
> **eTarget** : Prophet

We add an eTarget for the Prophet, anchored to the head "Prophet." Interestingly, "Prophet" is an eTarget for *w,Iman,Rushdie* (i.e., Rushdie is negative toward the Prophet), but not for *w,Imam* (i.e., the Imam is not negative toward the Prophet).

In the following example, the target span is short.

> Ex(3) He is therefore planning to trigger wars ...
>
> **DS**: (entire sentence)
> **nested-source**: w
> **attitude**: planning to trigger wars
> **attitude-type**: sentiment-negative
> **target**: He
> **eTarget** : He
> **eTarget** : planning, trigger, wars

"He" is George W. Bush; this article appeared in the early 2000s. The writer is negative toward Bush because (the writer claims) he is planning to trigger wars. As shown in the example, the MPQA 2.0 target span is only "He," for which we do create an eTarget. But there are three additional eTargets, which are not included in the target span. The writer is negative toward Bush planning to trigger wars; we make sense of this by inferring that the writer is negative toward the idea of triggering wars and thus toward war itself.

> Ex(4) Three leading international organisations warned jointly Thursday that the international fight against terrorism should not be a pretext for the violation of human rights.
>
> **DS**: warned
> **nested-source**: w, threeint
> **attitude**: warned
> **attitude-type**: sentiment-negative
> **target**: the international ... rights
> **eTarget** :be, pretext, violation
> **ESE**: pretext
> **nested-source**: w, threeint
> **polarity**: negative
> **eTarget** : pretext

The viewpoints in the article of Ex(4) are not against fighting terrorism (another sentence begins "While we recognize that the threat of terrorism requires specific measures ...") but against doing so in certain ways. Here the three organizations are against the fight being used as a pretext for civil rights violations. Thus, "be", "pretext", and "violation" are eTargets, but "fight" and "terrorism" are not. We mark "be" as an eTarget because the source is negative toward the **state** of the fight being a pretext for the violation of human rights. This makes sense with the source also being negative toward "pretext" and "violation." The fact that "pretext" is identified as a negative ESE annotation in the MPQA 2.0 supports this as well.

There is a difference between ESE and attitude eTarget annotations. Since ESE annotations pinpoint specific wording used to express subjectivity, ESE eTargets are annotated more narrowly than attitude eTargets. For ESEs, the eTargets are the entities and events that are directly evaluated by the expression, while, for attitudes, the eTargets include all entities and events toward which the attitude holds (as we saw in the examples above). For example:

> Ex(5) ... because the hard-line wing in the US administration comprising Vice President Dick Cheney ...

**DS**: (entire sentence)
  **nested-source**: w
  **attitude**: hard-line
    **attitude-type**: sentiment-negative
    **target**: wing in the .. Dick Cheney
      **eTarget** : wing, Cheney
**ESE**: hard-line wing
  **nested-source**: w
  **polarity**: negative
  **eTarget** : wing

The ESE has only one eTarget, "wing," while the attitude has two: "wing" and "Cheney."

### 2.2 MPQA 3.0 Annotation Scheme

An **eTarget** is an entity or event that is the target of a sentiment (identified in MPQA 2.0 by a sentiment attitude or polar ESE span). The eTarget annotation is anchored to the head word of the NP or VP that refers to the entity or event, and has **three slots**: *id* (unique within the document), *isNegated* (*yes* or *no*), and *type* (*entity* or *event*; note that *event* includes both states and events). The *isNegated* = *yes* option is for the case where the eTarget is the negation of the event referred to by the head word, for example, when the source is positive toward someone **not** doing something.

An **attitude** has one or more target-span annotations in MPQA 2.0. We provide two slots for the $k^{th}$ target annotation. *k-targetSpan* shows the $k^{th}$ target span. *k-eTarget-link* is to be filled with a list of ids of eTargets whose text anchors are within the $k^{th}$ target span. An additional slot *new-eTarget-link* is to be filled with a list of ids of other eTargets.

Each eTarget of an **ESE** has two slots, one for the eTarget id, and one for an attribute, *isReferedInSpan* (*yes*, or *no*). The value is *yes* if the eTarget is referred to in the ESE span.

## 3 Agreement Study

We developed the manual via iterative annotation, discussion, and revision. Once the manual was developed, we participated in an agreement study.

For the formal agreement study, one document was randomly selected from each of the four topics of the OPQA subset (Stoyanov et al., 2005) of the MPQA corpus. They were not any of the documents used to develop the manual. We then independently annotated the four documents. There are 292 eTargets in the four documents in total.

To evaluate the results, the same agreement measure is used for both attitude and ESE eTargets. Given an attitude or ESE, let set $A$ be the set of eTargets annotated by annotator $X$, and set $B$ be the set of eTargets annotated by annotator $Y$. Following (Wilson and Wiebe, 2003; Johansson and Moschitti, 2013), which treat each set $A$ and $B$ in turn as the gold-standard, we calculate the average F-measure, denoted $agr(A, B)$. The $agr(A, B)$ is 0.82 on average over the four documents, showing good agreement: $agr(A, B) = (|A \cap B|/|B| + |A \cap B|/|A|)/2$.

## 4 Disagreement Analysis

One issue is whether an attitude toward an entity or event is indeed communicated in the sentence. Consider this sentence: "President **Mugabe**'s **reelection** has been *praised by* OAU." The *OAU* is positive toward "reelection," which is an eTarget both annotators mark. The question is whether it is also communicated in this sentence that the OAU is also positive toward "Mugabe." $X$ did not mark Mugabe as an eTarget, whereas $Y$ did. During the subsequent discussion, $X$ now agrees that it should be marked. In general, $X$ was using what we now consider to be a too conservative policy. Overall, 29% of all disagreements are of this type of borderline case.

8% of the disagreements arise when there are multiple attitudes with overlapping spans, the same source, the same polarity, but different targets and intensities[4]. When there are new eTargets which are not in any target span, annotator $X$ splits the new eTargets into different attitudes based on the intensity, while annotator $Y$ adds the new eTargets to all the attitudes regardless of intensity. Later the annotators discuss to decide which attitude each new eTarget should be linked to in the final version.

31% of the disagreements are caused by negligence, meaning an annotator realized, during later discussion, that she should have included an eTarget when she saw that the other annotator had included it.

The remaining disagreements are due to annotator mistakes such as filling in the wrong id.

## 5 Current Corpus

The current corpus consists of 70 documents, including the subset of the documents in MPQA 2.0 that come from English-language sources (i.e., that are not translations) and a subset of the OPQA subset in MPQA 2.0. A subset contains consensus annotations of $X$ and $Y$ and the rest were annotated by $Y$. The 70 documents have 1,029 ESEs, 1,287 attitudes, and 1,213 target spans of attitudes (excluding the target span that are marked as "none") from MPQA 2.0; they have 4,459 eTargets in total. We added 1,366 eTargets to the ESEs and 1,608 eTargets to the target spans. We added 1,485 eTargets which are not in any target span.

## 6 An Example

In this section, we present an example from the OPQA subset (Stoyanov et al., 2005) to demonstrate how eTargets could help to automatically answer a question. There are opinion and fact questions for each document in the OPQA subset. The sentence below is annotated in MPQA 2.0 to answer the question, "Is the US Annual Human Rights Report received with universal approval around the world?" Here the writer is negative toward the report.

> It is due to this hegemony, which the United States wants to maintain, that its State Department makes an assessment of the human rights situation in different countries and prepares a report on their violations all over the world.

The annotations in MPQA 2.0:
S1: ⟨writer-US, positive, hegemony⟩
S2: ⟨writer, negative, the United States⟩
ESE1: ⟨writer, negative, N/A⟩

First, it is possible for a state-of-the-art system to be trained to recognize the sentiment S1, by the *maintaining* phrase and syntax information. But it would be difficult to find S2. There is no direct sentiment modifying the US, nor is there any sentiment or ESE annotation toward *maintain* or *hegemony* in MPQA 2.0. Now, in MPQA 3.0, we add the eTarget of the ESE1, so that it becomes ⟨writer, negative, hegemony⟩. This is a critical step, because the complete ESE bridges the two sentiments together.

Second, even though we have the two sentiments and the ESE, there is still a gap between *the United States* in the sentence and *report* in the question. One of the eTargets we add is "report." It is more feasible for a co-reference system to recognize *report* in both the sentence and the question as the same thing, than recognizing that *the United States* and *report* refer to the same concept.

Third, in this sentence, according to the newly added eTargets, the system knows the writer is negative toward both *the United States* and *State Department*. When building a knowledge base about the human rights report, this reveals that the two entities have the same stance toward this topic, even without any world knowledge.

## 7 Conclusion

This paper presents an annotation scheme for adding entity and event target annotations to the MPQA corpus. A subset of MPQA has already been annotated according to the new scheme. We believe that the corpus will be a valuable new resource for developing entity/event-level sentiment analysis systems to facilitate NLP applications such as Automatic Question Answering.

**Acknowledgements.** This work was supported in part by DARPA-BAA-12-47 DEFT grant #12475008. We thank the anonymous reviewers for their helpful comments.

[4] In MPQA 2.0, an attitude is marked with an intensity (low, medium, or high) representing the intensity.

## References


Yejin Choi and Claire Cardie. 2008. Learning with compositional semantics as structural inference for subsentential sentiment analysis. In *Proceedings of the Conference on Empirical Methods in Natural Language Processing*, pages 793–801. Association for Computational Linguistics.

Lingjia Deng, Yoonjung Choi, and Janyce Wiebe. 2013. Benefactive/malefactive event and writer attitude annotation. In *ACL (2)*, pages 120–125.

Minqing Hu and Bing Liu. 2004. Mining and summarizing customer reviews. In *Proceedings of the tenth ACM SIGKDD international conference on Knowledge discovery and data mining*, pages 168–177. ACM.

Richard Johansson and Alessandro Moschitti. 2013. Relational features in fine-grained opinion analysis. *Computational Linguistics*, 39(3):473–509.

Ryan McDonald, Kerry Hannan, Tyler Neylon, Mike Wells, and Jeff Reynar. 2007. Structured models for fine-to-coarse sentiment analysis. In *Annual Meeting-Association For Computational Linguistics*, volume 45, page 432. Citeseer.

Bo Pang, Lillian Lee, and Shivakumar Vaithyanathan. 2002. Thumbs up?: sentiment classification using machine learning techniques. In *Proceedings of the ACL-02 conference on Empirical methods in natural language processing-Volume 10*, pages 79–86. Association for Computational Linguistics.

Lev Ratinov, Dan Roth, Doug Downey, and Mike Anderson. 2011. Local and global algorithms for disambiguation to wikipedia. In *Proceedings of the 49th Annual Meeting of the Association for Computational Linguistics: Human Language Technologies-Volume 1*, pages 1375–1384. Association for Computational Linguistics.

Richard Socher, Alex Perelygin, Jean Y Wu, Jason Chuang, Christopher D Manning, Andrew Y Ng, and Christopher Potts. 2013. Recursive deep models for semantic compositionality over a sentiment treebank. In *Proceedings of the Conference on Empirical Methods in Natural Language Processing (EMNLP)*, pages 1631–1642. Citeseer.

Swapna Somasundaran, Theresa Wilson, Janyce Wiebe, and Veselin Stoyanov. 2007. Qa with attitude: Exploiting opinion type analysis for improving question answering in on-line discussions and the news. In *International Conference on Weblogs and Social Media*, Boulder, CO.

Veselin Stoyanov, Claire Cardie, and Janyce Wiebe. 2005. Multi-Perspective Question Answering using the OpQA corpus. In *Proceedings of the Human Language Technologies Conference/Conference on Empirical Methods in Natural Language Processing (HLT/EMNLP-2005)*, pages 923–930, Vancouver, Canada.

Ivan Titov and Ryan T McDonald. 2008. A joint model of text and aspect ratings for sentiment summarization. In *ACL*, volume 8, pages 308–316. Citeseer.

Peter D Turney. 2002. Thumbs up or thumbs down?: semantic orientation applied to unsupervised classification of reviews. In *Proceedings of the 40th annual meeting on association for computational linguistics*, pages 417–424. Association for Computational Linguistics.

Janyce Wiebe, Theresa Wilson, and Claire Cardie. 2005. Annotating expressions of opinions and emotions in language ann. *Language Resources and Evaluation*, 39(2/3):164–210.

Theresa Wilson and Janyce Wiebe. 2003. Annotating opinions in the world press. In *Proceedings of the 4th ACL SIGdial Workshop on Discourse and Dialogue (SIGdial-03)*, pages 13–22.

Theresa Wilson. 2007. *Fine-grained Subjectivity and Sentiment Analysis: Recognizing the Intensity, Polarity, and Attitudes of private states*. Ph.D. thesis, Intelligent Systems Program, University of Pittsburgh.

Hong Yu and Vasileios Hatzivassiloglou. 2003. Towards answering opinion questions: Separating facts from opinions and identifying the polarity of opinion sentences. In *Proceedings of the 2003 conference on Empirical methods in natural language processing*, pages 129–136. Association for Computational Linguistics.

# Everyone Likes Shopping!
# Multi-class Product Categorization for e-Commerce

**Zornitsa Kozareva**
Yahoo! Labs
701 First Avenue
Sunnyvale, CA 94089
zornitsa@kozareva.com

## Abstract

Online shopping caters the needs of millions of users on a daily basis. To build an accurate system that can retrieve relevant products for a query like "*MB252 with travel bags*" one requires product and query categorization mechanisms, which classify the text as *Home&Garden>Kitchen&Dining>Kitchen Appliances>Blenders*. One of the biggest challenges in e-Commerce is that providers like Amazon, e-Bay, Google, Yahoo! and Walmart organize products into different product taxonomies making it hard and time-consuming for sellers to categorize goods for each shopping platform.

To address this challenge, we propose an automatic product categorization mechanism, which for a given product title assigns the correct product category from a taxonomy. We conducted an empirical evaluation on $445,408$ product titles and used a rich product taxonomy of $319$ categories organized into $6$ levels. We compared performance against multiple algorithms and found that the best performing system reaches $.88$ f-score.

## 1 Introduction and Related Work

Over the past decade, e-Commerce has rapidly grown enabling customers to purchase any product with a click of a button. A key component for the success of such online shopping platforms is their ability to quickly and accurately retrieve the desired products for the customers. To be able to do so, shopping platforms use taxonomies (Kanagal et al., 2012), which hierarchically organize products from general to more specific classes. Taxonomies support keyword search and guarantee consistency of the categorization of similar products, which further enables product recommendation (Ziegler et al., 2004; Weng et al., 2008) and duplicate removal.

Shopping platforms like Amazon, e-Bay, Google, Yahoo!, Walmart among others use different taxonomies to organize products making it hard and labor-intensive for sellers to categorize the products. Sometimes sellers are encouraged to find similar products to those they sell and adopt this category to their products. However, this mechanism leads to two main problems: (1) it takes a lot of time for a merchant to categorize items and (2) such taggings can be inconsistent since different sellers might categorize the same product differently. To solve these problems, ideally one would like to have an automated procedure, which can classify any product title into a product taxonomy. Such process will both alleviate human labor and further improve product categorization consistency in e-Commerce websites.

Recently, a lot of interest has been developed around the induction of taxonomies using hierarchal LDA models (Zhang et al., 2014) and the categorization of products using product descriptions (Chen and Warren, 2013). Despite these efforts, yet no study focuses on classifying products using only titles. The question we address in this paper is: *Given a product title and a product taxonomy, can we accurately identify the corresponding category (root-to-leaf path in the taxonomy) that the title belongs to?*

The main contributions of the paper are:

- We built multi-class classification algorithm that classifies product titles into 319 distinct classes organized in 6 levels.
- We conducted an empirical evaluation with $445,408$ product titles and reach $.88$ f-score.



*Human Language Technologies: The 2015 Annual Conference of the North American Chapter of the ACL*, pages 1329–1333,
Denver, Colorado, May 31 – June 5, 2015. 

- During the error analysis we found out that our algorithm predicted more specific and fine-grained categories compared to those provided by humans.

## 2 Product Categorization Task Definition

We define our task as:

**Task Definition**: Given a set of titles describing products and a product taxonomy of 319 nodes organized into 6 levels, the goal is to build a multi-class classifier, which can accurately predict the product category of a new unlabeled product title.

The algorithm takes as input a product title "*MB22B 22 piece with bonus travel/storage bag*" and returns as output the whole product category hierarchy "*Home and Garden >Kitchen&Dining>Kitchen Appliances>Blenders*" as illustrated in Figure 1.

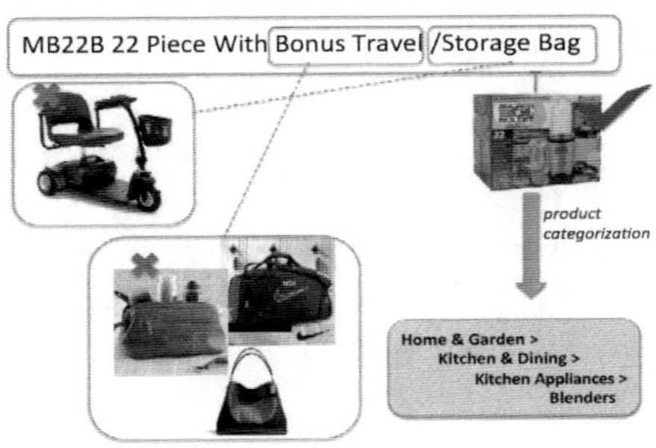


Figure 1: Example of Product Title Categorization.

## 3 Classification Methods

We model the product categorization task as classification problem, where for a given collection of labeled training examples $P$, the objective is to learn a classification function $f : p_i \rightarrow c_i$. Here, $p_i$ is a product title and $c_i \in \{1, ..., K\}$ is its corresponding category (one of 319 product taxonomy classes).

We learn a linear classifier model $f$ (parametrized by a weight vector $\mathbf{w}$) that minimizes the misclassification error on the training corpus $P$:

$$\min_{\mathbf{w}} \sum_{p_i \in P} \delta(c_i \neq f(\mathbf{w}, p_i)) + \lambda ||\mathbf{w}||_2^2$$

where, $\delta(.)$ is an indicator function which is 1 iff the prediction matches the true class and $\lambda$ is a regularization parameter.

For our experiments, we used two multi-classification algorithms from the large scale machine learning toolkit Vowpal Wabbit (Beygelzimer et al., 2009): one-against-all (OAA) and error correction tournament (ECT). OAA reduces the K-way multi-classification problem into multiple binary classification tasks by iteratively classifying each product title for category $K$ and comparing it against all other categories. ECT also reduces the problem to binary classification but employs a single-elimination tournament strategy to compare a set of $K$ players and repeats this process for $O(\log K)$ rounds to determine the multi-class label.

## 4 Feature Modeling

Next we describe the set of features we used to train our model.

### 4.1 Lexical Information

N-grams are commonly used features in text classification. As a baseline system, we use unigram and bigram features.

### 4.2 Mutual Information Dictionary

Lexical features require very large amount of training data to produce accurate predictions. To generalize the categorization models, we use semantic dictionaries, which capture the presence of a term with a product category. Ideally, we would like to use existing dictionaries for each product category, however such information is not available. For instance, WordNet provides at most synonyms/hyponyms/hypernyms for a given category name, but it does not provide products, brand names and the meaning of abbreviations.

We decided to generate our own dictionaries, by taking all product titles and estimating the mutual information $MI(w, C_i) = log\frac{f(w,C_i)}{(f(w,*).f(*,C_i)}$ of every word $w$ and product category $C_i$. For the dictionary, we keep all word-category pairs with MI above 5. During feature generation, for each title we estimate the percentage of words found with each category $C_i$ according to our automatically generated dictionary. The dimensions of the feature vector is equal to the total number of categories. The size of the generated lexicon is $34,337$ word-category pairs.

### 4.3 LDA Topics

We also incorporate latent information associated with product titles using topic modeling techniques.

We learn latent topics corresponding to terms occurring in the titles using Latent Dirichlet Allocation (David Blei and Jordan, 2003). We capture the meaning of a title using the learned topic distribution. For our experimental setting, we use the MALLET (McCallum, 2002) implementation of LDA and build it in the following manner.

**Method:** Given a set of titles and descriptions $D$ of products from different categories, find $K$ latent topics. The generative story is modeled as follows:

**for** each product category $s_k$ where $k \in \{1, ..., K\}$ **do**
  Generate $\beta_{s_k}$ according to $Dir(\eta)$
**end for**
**for** each title $i$ in the corpus $D$ **do**
  Choose $\theta_i \sim Dir(\alpha)$
  **for** each word $w_{i,j}$ where $j \in \{1, ..., N_i\}$ **do**
    Choose a topic $z_{i,j} \sim Multinomial(\theta_i)$
    Choose a word $w_{i,j} \sim Multinomial(\beta_{z_{i,j}})$
  **end for**
**end for**

**Inference:** We perform inference on this model using collapsed Gibbs sampling, where each of the hidden sense variables $z_{i,j}$ are sampled conditioned on an assignment for all other variables, while integrating over all possible parameter settings (Griffiths and Steyvers, 2002). We set the hyperparameter $\eta$ to the default value of 0.01 and $\alpha$=50. During feature generation, we take all words in the title and estimate the percentage of words associated with each topic $s_k$. The topic-word mapping is constructed from the word distribution learnt for a given topic. The number of features is equal to the number of topics.

Figure 2 shows an example of the different topics associated with the word *bag* for different product titles.

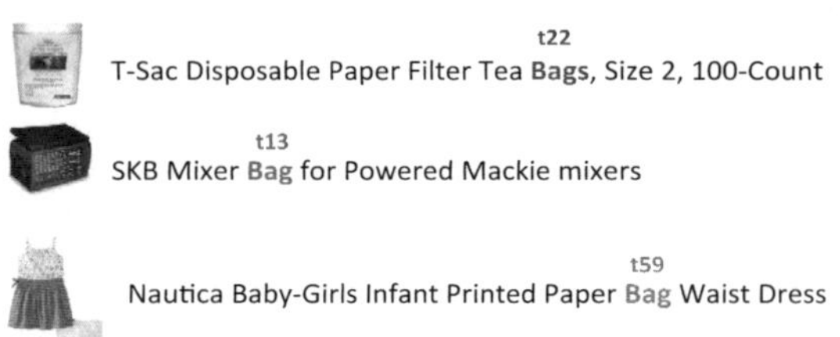


Figure 2: Learnt Topic Assignments for *bag*.

### 4.4 Neural Network Embeddings

While LDA allows us to capture the latent topics of the product titles, recent advances in unsupervised algorithms have demonstrated that deep neural network architectures can be effective in learning semantic representation of words and phrases from large unlabeled corpora.

To model the semantic representations of product titles, we learn embeddings over the corpus $P$ using the technique of (Mikolov et al., 2013a; Mikolov et al., 2013b). We use a feedforward neural network architecture in which the training objective is to find word (vector) representations that are useful for predicting the current word in a product title based on the context. Formally, given a sequence of training words $w_1, w_2, ..., w_T$ the objective is to maximize the average log probability

$$\frac{1}{T}\sum_{t=1}^{T} \sum_{-n \leq j \leq n, j \neq 0} \log p(w_t|w_{t+j})$$

where $n$ is the size of the training context and $p(w_t|w_{t+j})$ predicts the current position $w_t$ using the surrounding context words $w_{t+j}$ and learned with hierarchical softmax algorithm.

Since word2vec provides embeddings only for words or at most two word phrases, to represent a product title $p$ containing a sequence of $M$ word tokens $(w_1, ..., w_M)$, we retrieve the embeddings of all words and take the average score.

$$\begin{aligned} p &= [e^1, ..., e^d] \\ where, e^i &= \frac{1}{M}\sum_{j=1}^{M} e^i_{w_j} \end{aligned}$$

Here, $d$ is the embedding vector size, $e^i$ and $e^i_{w_j}$ are the vector values at position $i$ for the product $p$ and word $w_j$ in $p$, respectively.

To build the embeddings, we use a vector size of 200 and context of 5 consecutive words in our experiments. We then use the new vector representation $[e^1, ..., e^d]$ ($d$ features per title) to train and test the machine learning model.

## 5 Data Description

To conduct our experimental studies, we have used and manually annotated product titles from Yahoo's shopping platform. For each title, we asked two annotators to provide the whole product category from the root to the leaf and used these annotations as a gold standard.

We split the data into a training set of $353,809$ examples and a test set of $91,599$ examples. Our product taxonomy consists of 6 hierarchical levels. Figure 3 shows the total number of categories per level. The highest density is at levels 3 and 4.

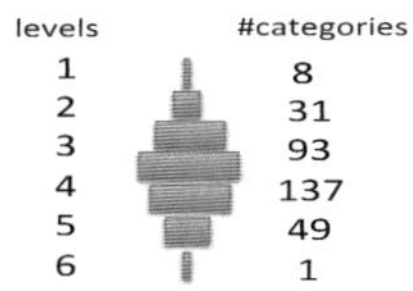


Figure 3: Product Taxonomy.

## 6 Experiments and Results

In this section, we describe the evaluation metric and the sets of experiments we have conducted.

### 6.1 Evaluation Metric

To evaluate the performance of the product categorization algorithms, we calculate *f-score* on the test set. The results are on exact match from top-to-leaf path of the gold and predicted categories.

### 6.2 Results

Table 1 shows the obtained results. For each feature we report the performance of the two machine learning algorithms one-against-all (OAA) and error correcting tournament (ECT).

| features | OAA | ECT |
|---|---|---|
| unigram | .72 | .63 |
| unigram+bigram | .67 | .58 |
| MI Dictionary | .85 | .77 |
| LDA Dictionary | .79 | .67 |
| NN-Embeddings | **.88** | .80 |

Table 1: *Results on Product Categorization.*

The highest performance is achieved with the neural network embedding representation. Between the two classifiers one-against-all consistently achieved the highest scores for all different feature sets. We also studied various feature combinations, however embeddings reached the highest performance.

### 6.3 Error Analysis

We analyzed the produced outputs and noticed that sometimes the predicted category could be different from the gold one, but often the predicted category was semantically similar or more descriptive than those provided by humans. Figure 4 shows some examples of the errors we discovered.

Figure 4: Examples of Categorized Products.

For instance, the title *cabela's tipped beer como comfy cup* was classified as *Small Animal Bedding*, while the gold standard category was *Dog Beds*. In our case we penalized such predictions, but still the two top level categories of *Animals* and *Pet Supplies* are similar. The major difference between the prediction and gold label is that the humans annotated *bed* as belonging to *Dog Beds*, while our algorithm predicted it as *Small Animal Bedding*. During manual inspection, we also noticed that often our classifier produces more descriptive categories compared to humans. For example, *flat slat sleigh crib espresso 8022n* had gold category *Baby & Toddler*, while our algorithm correctly identified the more descriptive category *Cribs and Toddler Beds*.

## 7 Conclusions

In this paper we have presented the first product categorization algorithm which operates on product title level. We classified products into a taxonomy of 319 categories organized into a 6 level taxonomy. We collected data for our experiments and conducted multiple empirical evaluations to study the effect of various features. Our experiments showed that neural network embeddings lead to the best performance reaching .88 f-score. We manually inspected the produced classification outputs and found that often the predicted categories are more specific and fine-grained compared to those provided by humans.

## Acknowledgments

We would like to thank the anonymous reviewers for their useful feedback and suggestions.

## References

Alina Beygelzimer, John Langford, and Pradeep Ravikumar. 2009. Error-correcting tournaments. In *Proceedings of the 20th International Conference on Algorithmic Learning Theory*, ALT'09, pages 247–262.

Jianfu Chen and David Warren. 2013. Cost-sensitive learning for large-scale hierarchical classification. In *Proceedings of the 22Nd ACM International Conference on Conference on Information & Knowledge Management*, CIKM '13, pages 1351–1360.

Andrew Ng David Blei and Michael Jordan. 2003. Latent dirichlet allocation. *Journal of Machine Leaning*, 3:993–1022.

Thomas L Griffiths and Mark Steyvers. 2002. A probabilistic approach to semantic representation. In *Proceedings of the Twenty-Fourth Annual Conference of Cognitive Science Society*.

Bhargav Kanagal, Amr Ahmed, Sandeep Pandey, Vanja Josifovski, Jeff Yuan, and Lluis Garcia-Pueyo. 2012. Supercharging recommender systems using taxonomies for learning user purchase behavior. *Proc. VLDB Endow.*, 5(10):956–967, June.

Andrew Kachites McCallum. 2002. Mallet: A machine learning for language toolkit. http://mallet.cs.umass.edu.

Tomas Mikolov, Kai Chen, Greg Corrado, and Jeff Dean. 2013a. Efficient estimation of word representations in vector space. *CoRR*.

Tomas Mikolov, Ilya Sutskever, Kai Chen, Greg Corrado, and Jeffrey Dean. 2013b. Distributed representations of words and phrases and their compositionality. *CoRR*, abs/1310.4546.

Li-Tung Weng, Yue Xu, Yuefeng Li, and Richi Nayak. 2008. Exploiting item taxonomy for solving cold-start problem in recommendation making. In *ICTAI (2)*, pages 113–120. IEEE Computer Society.

Yuchen Zhang, Amr Ahmed, Vanja Josifovski, and Alexander Smola. 2014. Taxonomy discovery for personalized recommendation. In *Proceedings of the 7th ACM International Conference on Web Search and Data Mining*, WSDM '14, pages 243–252.

Cai-Nicolas Ziegler, Georg Lausen, and Lars Schmidt-Thieme. 2004. Taxonomy-driven computation of product recommendations. In *Proceedings of the Thirteenth ACM International Conference on Information and Knowledge Management*, CIKM '04, pages 406–415.

# GPU-Friendly Local Regression for Voice Conversion

**Taylor Berg-Kirkpatrick** **Dan Klein**
Computer Science Division
University of California, Berkeley
{tberg,klein}@cs.berkeley.edu

## Abstract

Voice conversion is the task of transforming a source speaker's voice so that it sounds like a target speaker's voice. We present a GPU-friendly local regression model for voice conversion that is capable of converting speech in real-time and achieves state-of-the-art accuracy on this task. Our model uses a new approximation for computing local regression coefficients that is explicitly designed to preserve memory locality. As a result, our inference procedure is amenable to efficient implementation on the GPU. Our approach is more than 10X faster than a highly optimized CPU-based implementation, and is able to convert speech 2.7X faster than real-time.

## 1 Introduction

Voice conversion is the task of transforming an utterance from a source speaker's voice into a target speaker's voice. The primary setup in recent work has been to learn this transformation from a parallel corpus consisting of recordings of the same sequence of sentences read by both source and target speakers (Stylianou et al., 1998). The converted speech is evaluated by how well its spectral properties match those of the target voice.

While various models have been proposed (Stylianou et al., 1998; Toda et al., 2007; Toda et al., 2005), the most accurate ones are non-parametric because the mapping between two voices' spectra can be highly non-linear (Helander et al., 2012; Popa et al., 2012). Unfortunately, while non-parametric methods are accurate, they are also slow – current non-parametric approaches to voice conversion are too compute-intensive for the real-time speed required by many voice conversion applications. In this paper, we begin with the state-of-the-art local linear regression (LLR) model used by by Popa et al. (2012) for voice conversion, and present a new GPU-based inference approach that greatly accelerates it, to much faster than real-time.

LLR, in principle, requires each new model prediction to be a function of the entire set of training examples. In practice, LLR depends most strongly on nearby points, so a standard CPU implementation will skip distant points, with limited loss of accuracy. A GPU cannot exploit sparsity in the same way (scan and skip) without suffering from memory bottlenecks, but even a GPU will be relatively slow if all training points are included in each computation. Our primary algorithmic change is to make use of a new sparsity structure that allows the GPU to skip major sections of the training data while still using dense memory access patterns on the points it does process. In experiments, this inference technique is more than 10X faster than a highly-optimized CPU-based implementation, operates almost three times faster than real-time, and is only slightly less accurate than the CPU-based method.

## 2 Background and Model

Most representations of speech that are useful for speech processing break the acoustic signal into separate components that represent the sound source (the lungs and vocal folds) and sound filter (the vocal tract) portions of the vocal apparatus. Work on voice conversion is generally focused on transforming the representation of the vocal tract. We follow this approach and learn a transformation of a mel-cepstral representation of the acoustic signal (Kawahara, 2006).

We treat the task as a multiple regression problem. In order to produce the transformed signal, we break the source signal into a sequence of frames, each of which is a 24-dimensional vector of mel-



*Human Language Technologies: The 2015 Annual Conference of the North American Chapter of the ACL*, pages 1334–1338,
Denver, Colorado, May 31 – June 5, 2015. 

cepstral coefficients. We denote a single frame of input mel-cepstral coefficients as $x$. In order to produce the transformed signal, we simply predict frame-by-frame. Specifically, for a frame $x$ of the input we predict a transformed frame $\hat{y}$ as the mode of density $p(y|x)$, which we estimate from training data. A naive approach would be to use a linear model:

$$y = Ax + \epsilon$$

Here, $\epsilon$ is a Gaussian noise term, and the model is parameterized by the transformation matrix, $A$. For now, we assume training data are already frame-aligned (see Section 4). Let $y_i$ be frame $i$ of the target signal in the training data. Similarly, let $x_i$ be the corresponding frame of the source signal in the training data. Thus, using this linear model, we would estimate the transformation as:

$$\hat{A} = \underset{A}{\text{argmin}} \sum_i \|y_i - Ax_i\|^2$$

This very simple approach works, to some extent, but, because it cannot capture important non-linear relationships between $x$ and $y$, it is far from state-of-the-art. A more popular approach is to use a Gaussian mixture model (GMM) to jointly generate both source and target cepstral features (Stylianou et al., 1998; Toda et al., 2007; Toda et al., 2005). This approach essentially learns different linear transformations for different regions of the input space, capturing some non-linearity. However, the GMM introduces a new problem: the posterior over the latent clusters learned by the GMM can be highly peaked (Popa et al., 2012) and as a result distortion is introduced by discontinuities at cluster boundaries. Thus, we adopt neither the simple linear approach nor the GMM. We instead the state-of-the-art fully non-parametric approach introduced by Popa et al. (2012). This method, described in the next section, learns transformations that capture non-linearity but vary smoothly as the input changes.

### 2.1 Local Regression

Like Popa et al. (2012), we use local linear regression (LLR) (Cleveland, 1979) to estimate $p(y|x)$. LLR is a non-parametric method that estimates $p(y|x)$ as a linear transformation that varies slowly with the input $x$. Specifically, $p(y|x)$ is estimated as follows:

$$y = A(x) \cdot x + \epsilon$$
$$\hat{A}(x) = \underset{A}{\text{argmin}} \sum_i \left[ w(x, x_i) \cdot \|y_i - Ax_i\|^2 \right]$$

The transformation $\hat{A}$ is a function of $x$, and is computed by solving a weighted least squares problem that depends on $x$. $w$ is a kernel function that measures similarity between the current input, $x$, and each of the source training frames, $x_i$. We use a Gaussian kernel:

$$w(x, x_i) = \exp\left(\frac{-\|x - x_i\|^2}{2\sigma^2}\right)$$

Intuitively, for each input frame $x$ we solve a separate least squares regression where each training datum is weighted by its similarity to the input. As the input varies, so will the weighting, and thus so will the linear transformation.

## 3 Inference

Exact inference using LLR is too computationally expensive for most applications since it means solving a least squares problem over the entire training set for each input frame $x$. A common approach is to define a neighborhood function that, for each input frame $x$, selects $K$ training frames $x_i$ that are most relevant to $x$. Then, $\hat{A}(x)$ is computed by only solving the least squares problem over this neighborhood. This approach can work well in practice since the support for each local least squares problem is relatively sparse. By choosing the right neighborhood function, work can be skipped without substantially impacting learning.

### 3.1 Inference on the CPU

The standard approach when using a CPU is to let the neighborhood function pick out the indices of the $K$ training frames $x_i$ that maximize $w(x, x_i)$. We let this particular neighborhood function be called $g(x)$, depicted in Figure 1. Using this approach, for input frame $x$, $\hat{A}(x)$ has the following closed form expression:

$$\hat{A}(x) = H(x)^\top W(x) G(x) \Big( G(x)^\top W(x) G(x) \Big)^{-1}$$

$G(x)$ is a matrix formed by appending the training source vectors in the neighborhood of $x$. More specifically, $G(x)$ is a matrix that has the vectors $x_i^\top$ s.t. $i \in g(x)$ as its rows. Similarly, $H(x)$ is a matrix that has the vectors $y_i^\top$ s.t. $i \in g(x)$ as its rows (in the corresponding order). $W(x)$ is a matrix that has the weights $w(x, x_i)$ s.t. $i \in g(x)$ along its diagonal (also in the corresponding order).

This approach is much faster than the exhaustive method, but at typical audio sampling frequencies, inferring the transformation of the signal for an entire sentence can take over 30 seconds on a modern CPU, which is too slow for real-time conversion. In order to transform the signal for a new sentence, $\hat{A}(x)$ must be computed for each frame. This means that for each frame $x$, the distance to all training source frames must be computed, neighborhood matrices $G(x)$ and $H(x)$ must be formed, followed by several matrix multiplies, an LU decomposition, and a triangular solve operation.

### 3.2 Inference on the GPU

The computation of $\hat{A}(x)$ for a block of multiple input frames can be done in parallel if a fixed amount of lag is tolerated in the conversion process. The parallel computation of large number of small dense matrix operations (multiply, LU decomposition, triangular solve) is a perfect fit for implementation a GPU, which can achieve vastly more throughput than modern CPUs can. However, using the CPU's neighborhood structure on the GPU has a crippling bottleneck. The extraction of the neighborhood matrices $G(x)$ and $H(x)$ from the training data requires a large number of memory accesses that are effectively random. The indices of the closest $K$ training source vectors to an input $x$ are generally non-contiguous. As a result, the $K$ vectors in each of the neighborhood matrices must be copied with separate memory accesses, and since random access time on modern GPUs is very slow, extraction becomes a bottleneck. In initial experiments, we found that when this approach is implemented on a GPU it is even slower than the CPU-based implementation.

In contrast, memory bandwidth is extremely high on modern GPUs. Thus, if it were possible to order the training vectors $x_i$ and $y_i$ in GPU memory such that neighborhood matrices $G(x)$ and $H(x)$ were composed of contiguous blocks of training vectors,

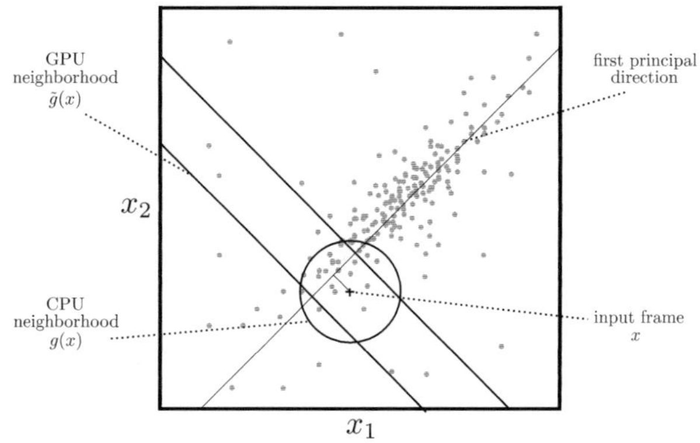

Figure 1: Depiction of standard neighborhood function $g(x)$ used for local regression on the CPU and surrogate neighborhood function $\tilde{g}(x)$ used for inference on the GPU, plotted for two-dimensional input data.

extraction on the GPU could be made very efficient. Unfortunately, with the current definition of the neighborhood function, $g$, such an ordering does not exist. Therefore, we define a new GPU-friendly neighborhood function, $\tilde{g}$, for which an ordering that permits contiguous extraction does exist.

Let $u(x)$ be the projection of source vector $x$ onto the first principal component resulting from running PCA on the source side of the training data. Now, we define $\tilde{g}$ as follows: $\tilde{g}(x)$ is the set of $K$ indices for which $|u(x) - u(x_i)|$ is the smallest, or, in other words, the set of training indices with source projections closest to the projection of the input frame. By ordering the training data by their projection onto the first principal component, we can ensure that $G(x)$ and $H(x)$ are contiguous in memory.

The hope is that this approach yields substantial speedups on the GPU without negatively impacting the learned transformation (see Section 4). Figure 1 depicts the difference between the CPU neighborhood function $g$ and the GPU function $\tilde{g}$. Intuitively, when most of the variance in the training data occurs along the first principal direction, the CPU and GPU neighborhood functions may be similar since the distance between projections is a good proxy for distance in the original space. The weighting function, $w$, is still computed in the original space, so distant training vectors that are inadvertently included in the neighborhood will be severely down-weighted. The potential pitfall is that for a fixed neighborhood size, $\tilde{g}$ may be less efficient at collecting training points that are relevant to the input.

| System | Scottish Male to US Female | | | US Female to Scottish Male | | |
|---|---|---|---|---|---|---|
| | CD | Time | Frac. RT | CD | Time | Frac. RT |
| GMM | 7.05 | 1.1 | 3.7X | 7.01 | 0.7 | 3.9X |
| CPU LLR | 5.99 | 12.2 | 0.3X | 6.51 | 8.75 | 0.3X |
| GPU LLR | 5.98 | 1.4 | 2.7X | 6.55 | 0.9 | 2.9X |

Table 1: Voice conversion results for the GMM baseline system, CPU-based local linear regression baseline system, and the GPU-based local linear regression method. The cepstral distortion (CD), average inference time per sentence in seconds (Time), and fraction of real-time (Frac. RT) are shown. Smaller cepstral distortion corresponds to more accurate transformations and fractions of real-time that exceed one imply faster than real-time operation.

## 4 Experiments

We run a series of experiments to determine whether our GPU-based inference technique offers speeds-ups and at what cost to accuracy.

**Baselines** We compare our LLR-based conversion system that performs inference on the GPU (using the GPU-friendly neighborhood function) with two different baseline systems. The first baseline system also uses LLR, but performs inference on the CPU using the standard neighborhood function. The second baseline is the GMM model of Toda et al. (2007), which is known to be fast and is widely used in practice. The size, $K$, of both CPU and GPU neighborhoods was set on a development data to the smallest value that did not show degraded performance compared to exact local regression.

**Implementation** We implemented our GPU-based LLR technique using the CUDA API (Nickolls et al., 2008), and the CUBLAS API which contains bindings for GPU BLAS routines. We ran the system using an NVIDIA Tesla K40c GPU. We built a multi-threaded implementation of CPU-based inference for local regression using calls to CPU BLAS routines, and ran this system on a 4.4GHz 4-core Intel CPU.

**Data** We train and test on a portion of the CMU Arctic database. The training data consists of 70 sentences spoken by both a US female speaker and a Scottish male speaker. The testing data consists of 20 sentences spoken by the same two speakers. We give results for converting in both directions, from the female voice to the male voice, and from the male voice to the female voice.

**Frame Alignment** Since the source and target speakers speak at slightly different rates, our training data consist of different numbers of frames for each training sentence. We use dynamic time warping to induce the frame alignment. Specifically, we find the minimum cost monotonic alignment from source frames into target frames where the cost of each alignment edge is the L2 distance between the corresponding vectors. We use a distortion limit of 2, and a linear distortion cost.

**Analysis and Synthesis** We use the CMU implementation of the STRAIGHT analysis and synthesis methods introduced by Kawahara (2006). This is the same method used many state-of-the-art voice conversion systems, included our GMM baseline of Toda et al. (2007). We transform the top 24 cepstral coefficients using our system, but process the power coefficient and fundamental frequency separately, using simple transformations for the latter two components.

**Evaluation** In order to evaluate the accuracy of our model we measure the cepstral distortion between the predicted ceptstral frames $\hat{y}$ and the actual cepstral frames for the target voice $y$. The cepstral distortion is calculated as follows:

$$\text{distortion}(\hat{y}, y) \propto \|\hat{y} - y\|$$

We using dynamic time warping to align the predicted frame sequence to the target frame sequence.

### 4.1 Results

The results of our experiments are displayed in Table 1. For the Scottish male to US female and the US female to Scottish male transformations the systems that use local regression outperform the parametric

GMM baseline in terms of average cepstral distortion. The GMM baseline, is however, the fastest of the compared systems. For both experiments, it is able to produce transformations substantially faster than real-time. The CPU-based local regression baseline achieves the best overall cepstral distortion, but is also the slowest method. In both experiments, it operates at 0.3X real-time speed. The GPU-based local regression method performs only slightly worse overall than the exact method in terms of cepstral distortion, yet in both experiments it operates substantially faster than real-time, nearly as fast as the parametric baseline.

## 5 Conclusion

We have demonstrated a method for substantially speeding-up inference using a non-parametric estimator for spectral voice conversion. Related approaches may prove useful for making non-parametric estimators more efficient in other areas of speech and language processing.

## Acknowledgements

This work was partially supported by BBN under DARPA contract HR0011-12-C-0014 and by an NSF fellowship for the first author. Thanks to the anonymous reviewers for their insightful comments. We further gratefully acknowledge a hardware donation by NVIDIA Corporation.

## References

William S Cleveland. 1979. Robust locally weighted regression and smoothing scatterplots. *Journal of the American statistical association*, 74(368):829–836.

E. Helander, H. Silen, T. Virtanen, and M. Gabbouj. 2012. Voice conversion using dynamic kernel partial least squares regression. *IEEE transactions on audio, speech, and language processing*, 20(3):806–817.

H. Kawahara. 2006. Straight, exploitation of the other aspect of vocoder: Perceptually isomorphic decomposition of speech sounds. *Acoustical science and technology*, 27(6):349–353.

John Nickolls, Ian Buck, Michael Garland, and Kevin Skadron. 2008. Scalable parallel programming with cuda. *Queue*, 6(2):40–53.

Victor Popa, Hanna Silen, Jani Nurminen, and Moncef Gabbouj. 2012. Local linear transformation for voice conversion. In *Acoustics, Speech and Signal Processing (ICASSP), 2012 IEEE International Conference on*, pages 4517–4520. IEEE.

Yannis Stylianou, Olivier Cappé, and Eric Moulines. 1998. Continuous probabilistic transform for voice conversion. *Speech and Audio Processing, IEEE Transactions on*, 6(2):131–142.

Tomoki Toda, Alan W Black, and Keiichi Tokuda. 2005. Spectral conversion based on maximum likelihood estimation considering global variance of converted parameter. In *ICASSP (1)*, pages 9–12.

T. Toda, A.W. Black, and K. Tokuda. 2007. Voice conversion based on maximum-likelihood estimation of spectral parameter trajectory. *Audio, Speech, and Language Processing, IEEE Transactions on*, 15(8):2222–2235.

# Response-based Learning for Machine Translation of Open-domain Database Queries

**Carolin Haas**
Computational Linguistics
Heidelberg University
69120 Heidelberg, Germany
haas1@cl.uni-heidelberg.de

**Stefan Riezler**
Computational Linguistics
Heidelberg University
69120 Heidelberg, Germany
riezler@cl.uni-heidelberg.de

## Abstract

Response-based learning allows to adapt a statistical machine translation (SMT) system to an extrinsic task by extracting supervision signals from task-specific feedback. In this paper, we elicit response signals for SMT adaptation by executing semantic parses of translated queries against the Freebase database. The challenge of our work lies in scaling semantic parsers to the lexical diversity of open-domain databases. We find that parser performance on incorrect English sentences, which is standardly ignored in parser evaluation, is key in model selection. In our experiments, the biggest improvements in F1-score for returning the correct answer from a semantic parse for a translated query are achieved by selecting a parser that is carefully enhanced by paraphrases and synonyms.

## 1 Introduction

In response-based learning for SMT, supervision signals are extracted from an extrinsic response to a machine translation, in contrast to using human-generated reference translations for supervision. We apply this framework to a scenario in which a semantic parse of a translated database query is executed against the Freebase database. We view learning from such task-specific feedback as adaptation of SMT parameters to the task of translating open-domain database queries, thereby grounding SMT in the task of multilingual database access. The success criterion for this task is F1-score in returning the correct answer from a semantic parse of the translated query, rather than BLEU. Since the semantic parser provides feedback to the response-based learner and defines the final evaluation criterion, the challenge of the presented work lies in scaling the semantic parser to the lexical diversity of open-domain databases such as Freebase. Riezler et al. (2014) showed how to use response-based learning to adapt an SMT system to a semantic parser for the Geoquery domain. The state-of-the-art in semantic parsing on Geoquery achieves a parsing accuracy of over 82% (see Andreas et al. (2013) for an overview), while the state-of-the-art in semantic parsing on the Free917 data (Cai and Yates, 2013) achieves 68.5% accuracy (Berant and Liang, 2014). This is due to the lexical variability of Free917 (2,036 word types) compared to Geoquery (279 word types).

In this paper, we compare different ways of scaling up state-of-the-art semantic parsers for Freebase by adding synonyms and paraphrases. First, we consider Berant and Liang (2014)'s own extension of the semantic parser of Berant et al. (2013) by using paraphrases. Second, we apply WordNet synonyms (Miller, 1995) for selected parts of speech to the queries in the Free917 dataset. The new pairs of queries and logical forms are added to the dataset on which the semantic parsers are retrained. We find that both techniques of enhancing the lexical coverage of the semantic parsers result in improved parsing performance, and that the improvements add up nicely. However, improved parsing performance does not correspond to improved F1-score in answer retrieval when using the respective parser in a response-based learning framework. We show that in order to produce helpful feedback for response-based learning, parser performance on incorrect En-



*Human Language Technologies: The 2015 Annual Conference of the North American Chapter of the ACL*, pages 1339–1344,
Denver, Colorado, May 31 – June 5, 2015. 

glish queries needs to be taken into account, which is standardly ignored in parser evaluation. That is, for the purpose of parsing translated queries, a parser should retrieve correct answers for correct English queries (true positives), and must not retrieve correct answers for incorrect translations (false positives). In order to measure false discovery rate, we prepare a test set of manually verified incorrect English in addition to a standard test set of original English queries. We show that if false discovery rate on incorrect English queries is taken into account in model selection, the semantic parser that yields best results for response-based learning in SMT can be found reliably.

## 2 Related Work

Our work is most closely related to Riezler et al. (2014). We extend their application of response-based learning for SMT to a larger and lexically more diverse dataset and show how to perform model selection in the environment from which response signals are obtained. In contrast to their work where a monolingual SMT-based approach (Andreas et al., 2013) is used as semantic parser, our work builds on existing parsers for Freebase, with a focus on exploiting paraphrasing and synonym extension for scaling semantic parsers to open-domain database queries.

Response-based learning has been applied in previous work to semantic parsing itself (Kwiatowski et al. (2013), Berant et al. (2013), Goldwasser and Roth (2013), *inter alia*). In these works, extrinsic responses in form of correct answers from a database are used to alleviate the problem of manual data annotation in semantic parsing. Saluja et al. (2012) integrate human binary feedback on the quality of an SMT system output into a discriminative learner.

Further work on learning from weak supervision signals has been presented in the machine learning community, e.g., in form of coactive learning (Shivaswamy and Joachims, 2012), reinforcement learning (Sutton and Barto, 1998), or online learning with limited feedback (Cesa-Bianchi and Lugosi, 2006).

## 3 Response-based Online SMT Learning

We denote by $\phi(x, y)$ a joint feature representation of input sentences $x$ and output translations $y \in Y(x)$, and by $s(x, y; w) = \langle w, \phi(x, y) \rangle$ a linear scoring function for predicting a translation $\hat{y}$. A response signal is denoted by a binary function $\mathrm{e}(y) \in \{1, 0\}$ that executes a semantic parse against the database and checks whether it receives the same answer as the gold standard parse. Furthermore, a cost function $\mathrm{c}(y^{(i)}, y) = (1 - \mathrm{BLEU}(y^{(i)}, y))$ based on sentence-wise BLEU (Nakov et al., 2012) is used. Algorithm 1, called "Response-based Online Learning" in Riezler et al. (2014), is based on contrasting a "positive" translation $y^+$ that receives positive feedback, has a high model score, and a low cost of predicting $y$ instead of $y^{(i)}$, with a "negative" translation $y^-$ that leads to negative feedback, has a high model score, and a high cost:

**Algorithm 1** Response-based Online Learning

**repeat**
  **for** $i = 1, \ldots, n$ **do**
    Receive input string $x^{(i)}$
    Predict translation $\hat{y}$
    Receive task feedback $\mathrm{e}(\hat{y}) \in \{1, 0\}$
    **if** $\mathrm{e}(\hat{y}) = 1$ **then**
      $y^+ \leftarrow \hat{y}$
      Store $\hat{y}$ as reference $y^{(i)}$ for $x^{(i)}$
      Compute $y^-$
    **else**
      $y^- \leftarrow \hat{y}$
      Receive reference $y^{(i)}$
      Compute $y^+$
    **end if**
    $w \leftarrow w + \eta(\phi(x^{(i)}, y^+) - \phi(x^{(i)}, y^-))$
  **end for**
**until** Convergence

$$y^+ = \operatorname*{arg\,max}_{y \in Y(x^{(i)}):\mathrm{e}(y)=1} \left( \mathrm{s}(x^{(i)}, y; w) - \mathrm{c}(y^{(i)}, y) \right),$$
$$y^- = \operatorname*{arg\,max}_{y \in Y(x^{(i)}):\mathrm{e}(y)=0} \left( \mathrm{s}(x^{(i)}, y; w) + \mathrm{c}(y^{(i)}, y) \right).$$

The central algorithm operates as follows: The SMT system predicts translation $\hat{y}$, and in case of positive task feedback, the prediction is accepted and stored as positive example by setting $y^+ \leftarrow \hat{y}$. In that case, $y^-$ needs to be computed in order to perform the stochastic gradient descent update of the weight vector. If the feedback is negative, the prediction is treated as $y^-$ and $y^+$ needs to be computed for the update. If either $y^+$ or $y^-$ cannot be computed, the example is skipped.

## 4 Scaling Semantic Parsing to Open-domain Database Queries

The main challenge of grounding SMT in semantic parsing for Freebase lies in scaling the semantic parser to the lexical diversity of the open-domain database. Our baseline system is the parser of Berant et al. (2013), called SEMPRE. We first consider the approach presented by Berant and Liang (2014) to scale the baseline to open-domain database queries: In their system, called PARASEMPRE, pairs of logical forms and utterances are generated from a given query and the database, and the pair whose utterance best paraphrases the input query is selected. These new pairs of queries and logical forms are added as ambiguous labels in training a model from query-answer pairs.

Following a similar idea of extending parser coverage by paraphrases, we extend the training set with synonyms from WordNet. This is done by iterating over the queries in the FREE917 dataset. To ensure that the replacement is sensible, each sentence is first POS tagged (Toutanova et al., 2003) and WordNet lookups are restricted to matching POS between synonym and query words, for nouns, verbs, adjectives and adverbs. Lastly, in order to limit the number of retrieved words, a WordNet lookup is performed by carefully choosing from the first three synsets which are ordered from most common to least frequently used sense. Within a synset all words are taken. The new training queries are appended to the training portion of FREE917.

## 5 Model Selection

The most straightforward strategy to perform model selection for the task of response-based learning for SMT is to rely on parsing evaluation scores that are standardly reported in the literature. However, as we will show experimentally, if precision is taken as the percentage of correct answers out of instances for which a parse could be produced, recall as the percentage of total examples for which a correct answer could be found, and F1 score as their harmonic mean, the metrics are not appropriate for model selection in our case. This is because for our goal of learning the language of correct English database queries from positive and negative parsing feedback, the semantic parser needs to be able to parse and retrieve correct answers for correct database queries, but it must not do so for incorrect queries.

However, information about incorrect queries is ignored in the definition of the metrics given above. In fact, retrieving correct answers for incorrect database queries hurts response-based learning for SMT. The problem lies in the incomplete nature of semantic parsing databases, where terms that are not parsed into logical forms in one context make a crucial difference in another context. For example in Geoquery, the gold standard queries "People in Boulder?" and "Number of people in Boulder?" parse into the same logical form, however, the queries "Give me the cities in Virginia" and "Give me the number of cities in Virginia" have different parses and different answers. While in the first case, for example in German-to-English translation of database queries, the German "Anzahl" may be translated incorrectly without consequences, it is crucial to translate the term into "number" in the second case. On an example from Free917, the SMT system translates the German "Steinformationen" into "kind of stone", which is incorrect in the geological context, where it should be "rock formations". If during response-based learning, the error slips through because of an incomplete parse leading to the correct answer, it might hurt on the test data. Negative parser feedback for incorrect translations is thus crucial for learning how to avoid these cases in response-based SMT.

In order to evaluate parsing performance on incorrect translations, we need to extend standard evaluation data of correct English database queries with evaluation data of incorrect English database queries. For this purpose, we took translations of an out-of-domain SMT system that were judged either grammatically or semantically incorrect by the authors to create a dataset of negative examples. On this dataset, we can define *true positives (TP)* as correct English queries that were given a correct answer by the semantic parser, and *false positives (FP)* as wrong English queries that obtained the correct answer. The crucial evaluation metric is the *false*

| Model | #data | F1 | FDR |
|---|---|---|---|
| S | 620 | 56.8 | 28.00 |
| P | 620 | 66.54 | 25.22 |
| P1 | 3,982 | 65.38 | **24.89** |
| P2 | 6,740 | **66.92** | 26.38 |
| P3 | 8,465 | 66.15 | 25.97 |

Table 1: Parsing F1 scores and False Discovery Rate (FDR) for SEMPRE (S), PARASEMPRE (P), and extensions of the latter with synonyms from first one (P1), first two (P2) and first three (P3) synsets, evaluated on the FREE917 test set of correct database queries for F1 and including the test set of incorrect database queries for FDR, and trained on #data training queries. Best results are indicated in **bold face**.

*discovery rate (FDR)* (Murphy, 2012), defined as *FP/FP+TP*, i.e., as the ratio of false positives out of all positive answer retrieval events.

## 6 Experiments

We use a data dump of Freebase[1] which was has been indexed by the Virtuoso SPARQL engine[2] as our knowledge base. The corpus used in the experiments is the FREE917 corpus as assembled by Cai and Yates (2013) and consists of 614 training and 276 test queries in English and corresponding logical forms.[3] The dataset of negative examples, i.e., incorrect English database queries that should receive incorrect answers, consists of 166 examples that were judged either grammatically or semantically incorrect by the authors.

The translation of the English queries in FREE917 into German, in order to provide a set of source sentences for SMT, was done by the authors. The SMT framework used is CDEC (Dyer et al., 2010) with standard dense features and additional sparse features as described in Simianer et al. (2012)[4]. Training of the baseline SMT system was performed on the COMMON CRAWL[5] (Smith et al., 2013) dataset consisting of 7.5M parallel English-German segments extracted from the web. Response-based learning for SMT uses the code described in Riezler et al. (2014)[6].

For semantic parsing we use the SEMPRE and PARASEMPRE tools of Berant et al. (2013) and Berant and Liang (2014) which were trained on the training portion of the FREE917 corpus[7]. Further models use the training data enhanced with synonyms from WordNet as described in Section 4. Following Jones et al. (2012), we evaluate semantic parsers according to *precision*, defined as the percentage of correctly answered examples out of those for which a parse could be produced, *recall*, defined as the percentage of total examples answered correctly, and *F1-score*, defined as harmonic mean of precision and recall. Furthermore, we report *false discovery rate (FDR)* on the combined set of 276 correct and 166 incorrect database queries.

Table 1 reports standard parsing evaluation metrics for the different parsers SEMPRE (S), PARASEMPRE (P), and extensions of the latter with synonyms from the first one (P1), first two (P2) and first three (P3) synsets which are ordered according to frequency of use of the sense. As shown in the second column, the size of the training data is increased up to 10 times by using various synonym extensions. As shown in the third column, PARASEMPRE improves F1 by nearly 10 points over SEMPRE. Another 0.5 points are added by extending the training data using two synsets. The third column shows that the system P1 that scored second-worst in terms of F1 score, scores best under the FDR metric[8].

Table 2 shows an evaluation of the use of different parsing models to retrieve correct answers from the FREE917 test set of correct database queries. The systems are applied to translated queries, but evaluated in terms of standard parsing metrics. Statistical significance is measured using an Approximate Randomization test (Noreen, 1989; Riezler and Maxwell, 2005). The baseline system is CDEC as described above. It never sees the FREE917 data during training. As a second baseline method we use a stochastic (sub)gradient descent variant of RAMPION (Gimpel and Smith, 2012). This system is

[1] http://www.freebase.com/

[2] http://virtuoso.openlinksw.com/

[3] Note that we filtered out 33 questions (21 from the training set and 12 from the test set) because their logical forms only returned an empty string as an answer.

[4] https://github.com/pks/cdec-dtrain

[5] http://www.statmt.org/wmt13/training-parallel-commoncrawl.tgz

[6] https://github.com/pks/rebol

[7] www-nlp.stanford.edu/software/sempre

[8] Note that in case of FDR, smaller is better.

| | 1 CDEC | 2 RAMPION | 3 REBOL |
|---|---|---|---|
| S | 40.0 | 40.36 | 42.92[12] |
| P | 42.92 | 44.59 | 45.85 |
| P1 | 42.92 | 46.36[1] | **48.8**[1] |
| P2 | 43.81 | 45.92 | 47.06 |
| P3 | 43.36 | 45.92 | 47.49 |

Table 2: Parsing F1 score on FREE917 test set of translated database queries using different parser models to provide response for translated queries. Best results are indicated in **bold face**. Statistical significance of result differences at $p < 0.05$ are indicated by algorithm number in superscript.

| | CDEC | RAMPION | REBOL |
|---|---|---|---|
| F1 | 0.85 | 0.29 | 0.1 |
| FDR | -0.21 | -0.58 | -0.7 |

Table 3: Spearman correlation between F1 / FDR from Table 1 and CDEC / RAMPION / REBOL F1 from Table 2.

trained by using the correct English queries in the FREE917 training data as references. Neither CDEC nor RAMPION use parser feedback in training. REBOL (**Re**sponse-**b**ased **O**nline **L**earning) is an implementation of Algorithm 1 described in Section 3. This algorithm makes use of positive parser feedback to convert predicted translation into references, in addition to using the original English queries as references. Training for both RAMPION and REBOL is performed for 10 epochs over the FREE917 training set, using a constant learning rate $\eta$ that was chosen via cross-validation. All methods then proceed to translate the FREE917 test set. Best results in Table 2 are obtained by using an extension of PARASEMPRE with one synset as parser in response-based learning with REBOL. This parsing system scored best under the FDR metric in Table 1.

Table 3 shows the Spearman rank correlation (Siegel and Castellan, 1988) between the F1 / FDR ranking of semantic parsers from Table 1 and their contribution to F1 scores in Table 2 for parsing query translations of CDEC, RAMPION or REBOL. The system CDEC cannot learn from parser performance based on query translations, thus best results on translated queries correlate positively with good parsing F1 score per se. RAMPION can implicitly take advantage of parsers with good FDR score since learning to move away from translations dissimilar to the reference is helpful if they do not lead to correct answers. REBOL can make the best use of parsers with low FDR score since it can learn to prevent incorrect translations from hurting parsing performance at test time.

## 7 Conclusion

We presented an adaptation of SMT to translating open-domain database queries by using feedback of a semantic parser to guide learning. Our work highlights an important aspect that is often overlooked in parser evaluation, namely that parser model selection in real-world applications needs to take the possibility of parsing incorrect language into account. We found that for our application of response-based learning for SMT, the key is to learn to prevent cases where the correct answer is retrieved despite the translation being incorrect. This can be avoided by performing model selection on semantic parsers that parse and retrieve correct answers for correct database queries, but do not do retrieve correct answers for incorrect queries.

In our experiments, we found that the parser that contributes most to response-based learning in SMT is one that is carefully extended by paraphrases and synonyms. In future work, we would like to investigate additional techniques for paraphrasing and synonym extension. For example, a good fit for our task of response-based learning for SMT might be Bannard and Callison-Burch (2005)'s approach to paraphrasing via pivoting on SMT phrase tables.

## Acknowledgments

This research was supported in part by DFG grant RI-2221/2-1 "Grounding Statistical Machine Translation in Perception and Action".

## References

Jacob Andreas, Andreas Vlachos, and Stephen Clark. 2013. Semantic parsing as machine translation. In *Proceedings of the 51st Annual Meeting of the Association for Computational Linguistics (ACL'13)*, Sofia, Bulgaria.

Colin Bannard and Chris Callison-Burch. 2005. Paraphrasing with bilingual parallel corpora. In *Proceed-*

*ings of the 43rd Annual Meeting of the Association for Computational Linguistics (ACL'05)*, Ann Arbor, MI.

Jonathan Berant and Percy Liang. 2014. Semantic parsing via paraphrasing. In *Proceedings of the 52nd Annual Meeting of the Association for Computational Linguistics (ACL 2014)*, Baltimore, MD.

Jonathan Berant, Andrew Chou, Roy Frostig, and Percy Liang. 2013. Semantic parsing on freebase from question-answer pairs. In *Proceedings of the 2013 Conference on Empirical Methods in Natural Language Processing (EMNLP'13)*, Seattle, WA.

Qingqing Cai and Alexander Yates. 2013. Large-scale semantic parsing via schema matching and lexicon extenstion. In *Proceedings of the 51st Annual Meeting of the Association for Computational Linguistics (ACL'13)*, Sofia, Bulgaria.

Nicolò Cesa-Bianchi and Gàbor Lugosi. 2006. *Prediction, Learning, and Games*. Cambridge University Press.

Chris Dyer, Adam Lopez, Juri Ganitkevitch, Johnathan Weese, Ferhan Ture, Phil Blunsom, Hendra Setiawan, Vladimir Eidelman, and Philip Resnik. 2010. cdec: A decoder, alignment, and learning framework for finite-state and context-free translation models. In *Proceedings of the 48th Annual Meeting of the Association for Computational Linguistics (ACL'10)*, Uppsala, Sweden.

Kevin Gimpel and Noah A. Smith. 2012. Structured ramp loss minimization for machine translation. In *Proceedings of the 2012 Conference of the North American Chapter of the Association for Computational Linguistics: Human Language Technologies (HLT-NAACL'12)*, Stroudsburg, PA.

Dan Goldwasser and Dan Roth. 2013. Learning from natural instructions. *Machine Learning*, 94(2):205–232.

Bevan K. Jones, Mark Johnson, and Sharon Goldwater. 2012. Semantic parsing with bayesion tree transducers. In *Proceedings of the 50th Annual Meeting of the Association for Computational Linguistics (ACL'12)*, Jeju Island, Korea.

Tom Kwiatowski, Eunsol Choi, Yoav Artzi, and Luke Zettlemoyer. 2013. Scaling semantic parsers with on-the-fly ontology matching. In *Proceedings of the 2013 Conference on Empirical Methods in Natural Language Processing (EMNLP'13)*, Seattle, WA.

George A. Miller. 1995. Wordnet: A lexical database for english. *Communications of the ACM*, 38(11):39–41.

Kevin P. Murphy. 2012. *Machine Learning. A Probabilistic Perspective*. The MIT Press.

Preslav Nakov, Francisco Guzmán, and Stephan Vogel. 2012. Optimizing for sentence-level bleu+1 yields short translations. In *Proceedings of the 24th International Conference on Computational Linguistics (COLING 2012)*, Bombay, India.

Eric W. Noreen. 1989. *Computer Intensive Methods for Testing Hypotheses: An Introduction*. Wiley, New York.

Stefan Riezler and John Maxwell. 2005. On some pitfalls in automatic evaluation and significance testing for MT. In *Proceedings of the ACL-05 Workshop on Intrinsic and Extrinsic Evaluation Measures for MT and/or Summarization*, Ann Arbor, MI.

Stefan Riezler, Patrick Simianer, and Carolin Haas. 2014. Response-based learning for grounded machine translation. In *Proceedings of the 52nd Annual Meeting of the Association for Computational Linguistics (ACL 2014)*, Baltimore, MD.

Avneesh Saluja, Ian Lane, and Ying Zhang. 2012. Machine translation with binary feedback: A large-margin approach. In *Proceedings of the 10th Biennial Conference of the Association for Machine Translation in the Americas (AMTA'12)*, San Diego, CA.

Pannaga Shivaswamy and Thorsten Joachims. 2012. Online structured prediction via coactive learning. In *Proceedings of the 29th International Conference on Machine Learning (ICML'12)*, Scotland, UK.

Sidney Siegel and John Castellan. 1988. *Nonparametric Statistics for the Behavioral Sciences. Second Edition*. MacGraw-Hill, Boston, MA.

Patrick Simianer, Stefan Riezler, and Chris Dyer. 2012. Joint feature selection in distributed stochastic learning for large-scale discriminative training in SMT. In *Proceedings of the 50th Annual Meeting of the Association for Computational Linguistics (ACL'12)*, Jeju Island, South Korea.

Jason Smith, Herve Saint-Amand, Magdalena Plamada, Philipp Koehn, Chris Callison-Burch, and Adam Lopez. 2013. Dirt cheap web-scale parallel text from the Common Crawl. In *Proceedings of the 51st Annual Meeting of the Association for Computational Linguistics (ACL'13)*, Sofia, Bulgaria.

Richard S. Sutton and Andrew G. Barto. 1998. *Reinforcement Learning. An Introduction*. The MIT Press.

Kristina Toutanova, Dan Klein, Christopher Manning, and Yoram Singer. 2003. Feature-rich part-of-speech tagging with a cyclic dependency network. In *Proceedings of the 2003 Conference of the North American Chapter of the Association for Computational Linguistics: Human Language Technologies (HLT-NAACL'03)*. Edmonton, Canada.

# Context-Dependent Automatic Response Generation Using Statistical Machine Translation Techniques

**Andrew Shin** **Ryohei Sasano** **Hiroya Takamura** **Manabu Okumura**
Tokyo Institute of Technology
shin@lr.pi.titech.ac.jp {sasano,takamura,oku}@pi.titech.ac.jp

## Abstract

Developing a system that can automatically respond to a user's utterance has recently become a topic of research in natural language processing. However, most works on the topic take into account only a single preceding utterance to generate a response. Recent works demonstrate that the application of statistical machine translation (SMT) techniques towards monolingual dialogue setting, in which a response is treated as a translation of a stimulus, has a great potential, and we exploit the approach to tackle the context-dependent response generation task. We attempt to extract relevant and significant information from the wider contextual scope of the conversation, and incorporate it into the SMT techniques. We also discuss the advantages and limitations of this approach through our experimental results.

## 1 Introduction

Various approaches have been applied to the response generation task, each with its own merits and drawbacks. While one of the main concerns on the topic has been the semantic relevance of the response, it has mostly been discussed in terms of a limited conversational scope, mostly a single utterance. This provides us with a room for research on a wider scope of conversation, which reflects not only a single preceding utterance, but the overall context of the current conversation.

SMT-based data-driven approach to the response generation task was recently introduced by Ritter et al. (2011). They demonstrated that it was better-suited for response generation than some of the previous approaches, including information retrieval approach. We exploit this model to address the above-mentioned problem of reflecting a wider scope of conversation.

We present a context-dependent model where we attempt to generate more semantically relevant and diverse responses by adding the semantically important words from previous utterances to the most recent one. By doing so, we hope not only to diversify the responses, but also to be able to take semantics from broader scope of the conversation into account.

## 2 Response Generation using SMT

### 2.1 Overview

Ritter et al. (2011) remarked that stimulus-response pairs in the same language often have a strong structural resemblance, as shown in the example conversation below, that may be exploited in SMT platforms. In the usual SMT setting, a string $f$ in a source language is translated into a string $e$ in a target language according to probability distribution $p(e|f)$ (Brown et al., 1993). Ritter et al. applied the SMT techniques to monolingual conversation setting, and treated the response as the *translation* of the stimulus.

**Stimulus:** What is your hobby?
**Response:** My hobby is hiking.

### 2.2 Challenges

Although the application of SMT to the response generation task demonstrates potentials, it has a few drawbacks due to its nature.



*Human Language Technologies: The 2015 Annual Conference of the North American Chapter of the ACL*, pages 1345–1350,
Denver, Colorado, May 31 – June 5, 2015. 

First, the lengths of the source and target utterances are not correlated in the conversational setting, and there is hardly any general tendency towards the relative length of the utterances, as shown in the example conversation below. SMT usually works on the data in which the ratio between the lengths of the source and target utterances stays relatively constant (Och and Ney, 2000). However, conversational setting, in which such constant ratio is absent, jeopardizes the functionality of the usual SMT models to make alignments. Although it is highly probable that some of the semantic elements in the source utterance are reflected in the target utterance, it is rarely on a one-to-one basis.

**A:** Is something going on today? ($S_1$)
**B:** Of course, it's dad's birthday. ($S_2$)
**A** (most recent stimulus) **:** What?! ($S_3$)
**B** (target) **:** Oh, you didn't know? ($S_4$)

Second, it cannot take into account what was previously discussed in the conversation. Unless the most recent utterance brings a completely new topic, or it has sufficient information in itself, such problem is evident.

Both problems regarding the context and the alignment become more pronounced especially in cases where the source utterance is short as shown in the above example. Clearly, no meaningful response can be derived from the most recent stimulus alone, and it is highly unclear how the alignments should be made. Indeed, the response generated by applying SMT to the most recent stimulus "What?" in this example is "that," which only mimics the syntactic structure but fails to deliver any meaningful content.

## 3 Context-Dependent Model

### 3.1 Overview

In order to deal with the issues of context and the lengths of the utterances without correlation, we work on building a context-dependent model, in which we balance the utterance lengths by selecting contextually important words from the previous part of the conversation, and adding them to the source utterance. For example, applying one of our models to the most recent stimulus ($S_3$) of the previous example conversation results in the following utterance, where the words in the parenthesis are newly added:

**A:** (today birthday) What?!

The rationale behind this approach is that the topic of a conversation can be characterized by a number of contextually important words, which provide semantic information to be reflected in the response generation process.

This approach seemingly reduces the grammatical integrity of the source utterance, and it may seem as if we risk confusing the translation model and losing grammaticality of the output. However, grammaticality of the output is handled by the language model, and the language model is constructed upon the target language only, which in our case corresponds to the target utterances that remain untouched. Also, the newly added words are of high relevance to the topic, so the new source utterance frequently demonstrates high semantic coherence both within itself, and in parallel with the target utterance.

The question now is how to determine which words are contextually important throughout the conversation. Since finding such contextually important words is our main concern, we find simple statistical significance test models more suitable than conventional methods from discourse modeling or dialogue systems (Oh et al., 2002). We examine two approaches, namely the pair-based approach, and the token-based approach. The pair-based approach uses Fisher's Exact Test (Moore, 2004), which is reported to give more accurate *p*-values than $\chi^2$ or $G^2$ when the counts are small (Ritter et al., 2011). This approach takes advantage of the proximity of utterances, and assumes that a utterance whose distance to the source utterance is shorter is likely to be more contextually related to the source utterance, i.e. $S_{n-1}$ is more likely than $S_{n-2}$ to be semantically relevant to $S_n$. The token-based approach considers at the entire conversation, and selects the words most characteristic of the conversation, using the most widely used term weighting algorithm, *tf-idf*.

### 3.2 Pair-Based Model

Given a conversation consisting of utterances $S_1$,...,$S_{n+1}$, where $S_n$ is the source utterance and $S_{n+1}$ is the target utterance, we start by computing the *p*-value from Fisher's Exact Test for every possible word pair between $S_n$ and $S_{n-1}$. If the *p*-value is less than the threshold, implying a significant relevance between the words constituting the pair, we store the words. We then add the stored words to the source utterance, avoiding duplicates with words already in the source utterance, until its length is the same as that of the target utterance. Words are added in a reversed order of their appearance, i.e., we give priority to words that appeared in the later part of the discourse, in light of the previously mentioned assumption. If, after adding all stored words to the source utterance, the length of the source utterance is still less than the length of the target utterance, we repeat the process with word pairs between $S_{n-1}$ and $S_{n-2}$, and so forth. This "crawling-up" is necessary because $S_n$ is often short or semantically trivial that further comparison of $S_n$ with other previous utterances fails to capture the contextually important words that are continuously discussed in the previous part of the conversation. The procedure ends when there are no more pairs whose $p$-value is less than the threshold, or the source utterance has the same length as the target utterance.

Note that, for training, we limit the application of our model only to the cases where source utterances are shorter than target utterances, since adding words in the opposite case will exacerbate the difficulty of alignment. In the test setting, however, we do not know the length of the actual target utterance, and thus selectively apply our model based on the absolute length of the source utterance, where the threshold is set to the average length of the source utterance throughout the training data. Also, since it is evident that we are not dealing with grammatically well-formed utterances whose ordering should matter, we opt not to use the reordering table (Bisazza et al., 2011).

### 3.3 Token-Based Model

The assumption behind the pair-based approach is that a topic of a conversation is something that continues to be discussed throughout the conversation, i.e. something that gets reflected/matched in the later part of the conversation. Finding collocated words using significant test does just that. However, there may be a trade-off here in terms of representing the diversity of context; for example, there may be a characteristic word that is not directly reflected/matched in the later part of the conversation. That provides the motivation for our token-based approach, using tf-idf.

This approach follows a similar manner of adding words to the source utterance until its length is equal to the target utterance, but differs in that it picks contextually important words by examining individual tokens, rather than pairs of words, using *tf-idf*. For *idf*, the total number of documents was set to the number of conversations in our training data.

Also, instead of crawling up the conversation from the source utterance, it scans through the entire conversation and selects characteristic words within the given scope of the conversation. This is intended to reflect that there could be words that are highly relevant to the overall topic of the conversation, yet not very close to the current source utterance. For example, in the following conversation, both ($S_3$) and ($S_4$) lack any element characteristic of the conversation that leads to the final response ($S_5$), while "NBA" or "fans" in ($S_1$) and ($S_2$) is indicative of the topic of the conversation, and will be relevant to words like "LeBron" or "dominating" in the target utterance.

**A:** Well, the NBA season is near again.($S_1$)

**B:** Yeah! So excited for all the NBA fans!($S_2$)

**A:** I'm not. ($S_3$)

**B** (source) **:** How come? ($S_4$)

**A** (target) **:** It's just gonna be LeBron dominating again. ($S_5$)

Although we examine the entire conversation, words that are too far from the source utterance (for example, 50 utterances apart) will rarely have much semantic impact to the current topic. Thus, it is necessary to keep the size of the conversation reasonably small, and we restrict it to be at most 8 utterances.

## 4 Experiment

### 4.1 Setting

We first built our baseline model following the procedure proposed by Ritter et al. (2011). In accordance with the paper, we also filtered out the phrase table by Fisher's Exact Test. We then implemented our model using Moses (Koehn et al., 2007) toolkit with KenLM (Heafield, 2011) as the language model in 5-gram setting. In accordance with the baseline, we built our training, tuning, and test data set from

| Model A | Model B | A>B | A=B | A<B | p-value | Agreement |
|---|---|---|---|---|---|---|
| Pair | Baseline | 287 | 32 | 81 | 4.0e-28 | .488 |
| | Actual | 58 | 28 | 314 | 1.2e-43 | .543 |
| | Token | 175 | 52 | 173 | 0.96 | .373 |
| Token | Baseline | 280 | 35 | 85 | 2.0e-25 | .462 |
| | Actual | 62 | 35 | 303 | 3.2e-39 | .529 |

Table 1: Performances against Each Model

Twitter, except we collected conversations, consisting of a tweet and successive replies, rather than pairs of tweets. We also restricted each conversation to have 3 to 8 utterances with only two speakers taking turns, to make it more likely that the topic of the conversation is preserved. Although there were some cases in which the topic deviated, our validation of the dataset showed that the amount of such cases was negligible. We ended up having approximately 1.4M pairs of utterances in the training data, which constitute 425,547 conversations. The threshold $p$-value for Fisher's Exact Test was set to 0.0001, to well-balance the number of selected words with the lengths of the utterances.

### 4.2 Evaluation

One of the challenging aspects of the researches on conversation is its distinct nature in which there is an extremely wide range of acceptable candidate responses to a stimulus, unlike usual bilingual translation tasks where there are typically pre-set candidates to be referenced with high reliability. Using the automatic evaluation metrics, we obtained slight improvements; for example, BLEU score (Papineni et al., 2002), with the actual responses from Twitter as the gold standard, increased from 0.82 for baseline to 0.89 for the pair-based approach. For the above-mentioned reason, however, we found it dubious whether a higher score in these metrics corresponds to better responses, and we thus resort to human manual evaluation as our primary source of evaluation.

We performed a human evaluation on Amazon Mechanical Turk (Buhrmester et al., 2011). The evaluation task consisted of four different sets of 100 questions, each set of which was handled by 10 workers. Each question was a ranking task, and the workers were shown a part of conversation and were instructed to rank the responses that followed the conversation in consideration of their relevance to the topic of the conversation. For all questions, workers were given four responses; the actual response from Twitter, one generated by the baseline model, and two by each of our context-dependent models.

| Model | 1st | 2nd | 3rd | 4th | Avg. Rank |
|---|---|---|---|---|---|
| Actual | .664 | .129 | .087 | .120 | 1.66 |
| Baseline | .092 | .232 | .271 | .406 | 2.99 |
| Pair | .112 | .323 | .346 | .220 | 2.67 |
| Token | .134 | .315 | .297 | .255 | 2.67 |

Table 2: Rankings from Human Evaluation

The order of responses was randomized for each question. In addition, in order to filter out the workers who do not take the tasks seriously, generating noise answers, we selected 10 questions that had obvious answers, and rejected the answers by the workers who failed to achieve 70% or higher accuracy on those questions. As stated in Section 3.1, the threshold for length of source sentence to determine whether to add words or not was set to the average length of source sentences throughout the training data, which in our case was 10. In roughly half of 400 questions, no words were added to the source sentence, and 1 to 6 words were added for roughly 25 to 30 questions respectively. Beyond 6 words, the number of questions begins to decline.

### 4.3 Results

Table 1 shows how our models performed against the actual responses, the baseline model, and each other, in regards to the number of questions for which our models were ranked higher. Overall, the table shows that our models were preferred over the baseline model, but performed poorly against the actual responses as expected. Yet, it was able to perform better than the actual responses in roughly

| Conversation | Response* | Avg. Rank |
|---|---|---|
| **A:** if youre following today maybe follow me<br>**B:** lol ur off to an early start | **1:** im at the bus stop how was your night | 2.1 |
| | **2:** i dont fancy hame pass for | 3.6 |
| | **3:** lmao i got my second home | 3.2 |
| | **4:** updating haha I get u off too | 1.9 |
| **A:** like you're talking about the stupidest things ever. its annoying<br>**B:** who is this about | **1:** the ppl behind you | 1.9 |
| | **2:** I want tie you | 3.6 |
| | **3:** like I said Im talking seriously are you | 2.3 |
| | **4:** one of them is that you | 2.9 |
| **A:** Aww man happy birthday bro!! Lol you know you gotta die right?<br>**B:** What? Lol | **1:** you gotta damn near die from drinking today | 1.2 |
| | **2:** lol yea | 3.8 |
| | **3:** thank you man you know me | 2.4 |
| | **4:** lol I know I know | 2.8 |

* 1 is the actual response on Twitter, while 2,3 and 4 are responses generated by the baseline, pair-based, token-based models respectively.

Table 3: Examples of Responses

15% of the questions, especially when the actual responses were grammatically poor, or irrelevant to the topic of the conversation. There was no significant difference between the performances of our models. It also shows the $p$-value and mutual agreement between two models. Using S coefficient (Bennett et al., 1954) as a measurement of agreement yields the following result. Most of them fall into "moderate agreement" range of 0.4 to 0.6, except Token-based model against Pair-based model is slightly lower and falls into "fair agreement" range (Landis and Koch, 1977).

Table 2 shows the distribution of each model over each ranking and their average rankings. Our models outperform the baseline model in higher rankings. Table 3 features examples of responses generated by each model and the actual responses on Twitter, along with their average ranking in the final evaluation. In the first conversation, one of our models was ranked higher than both the baseline model and the actual response. In other conversations, our models were ranked higher than the baseline model, but lower than the actual response. Generally, our models have a wider range of topic-relevant vocabularies, and sound comparatively coherent than the baseline model, without too much grammatical violations.

## 5 Conclusion and Future Work

As we observed in the experimental results, our context-dependent model outperformed the baseline model when examined in a wider scope of conversations. Although its performance against the actual responses was not as satisfactory, it could outperform them when the actual responses diverted from the topic, or had poor coherence and grammaticality.

Possible applications include chatterbots or conversational agents. Most such applications are based on one-turn conversation, where user says something, system gives some response, and that is technically the end of the conversation of current topic, which will not be referred to in later conversations. Our work can, for example, provide the system with possible topics to talk about, especially when the input from the user is short or trivial. Diversity of the responses is obtained because, even when the system is given the same input, it will return completely different responses depending on what was previously talked about, as opposed to the applications where certain responses can be expected given an input.

An improvement is likely to come from attempting different methods to extract the core tokens from the past utterances. We relied on the Fisher's Exact Test and *tf-idf* throughout the research, but other approaches may perform better. Alternatively, we may try different weighting systems depending on whether a token is from the same speaker as the current utterance or a different speaker, since it would generally make more sense for a particular speaker not to repeat him/herself.

## References

Arianna Bisazza, Nick Ruiz, and Marcello Federico. 2011. *Fill-up versus Interpolation Methods for Phrase-based SMT Adaptation.* In *International Workshop on Spoken Language Translation*, pages 136–143.

E. M. Bennett, R. Alpert, and A.C. Goldstein 1954. *Communications through limited-response questioning.* In *Public Opinion Quarterly*, pages 303–308.

Peter Brown, Stephen A. Della Pietra, Vincent J. Della Piera, and Robert J. Mercer. 1993. *The Mathematics of Statistical Machine Translation: Parameter Estimation.* In *Computational Linguistics*, pages 263–311.

Michael Burhmester, Tracy Kwang, and Samuel D. Gosling 2011. *Amazon's Mechanical Turk: A New Source of Inexpensive, Yet High-Quality Data?* In *Perspectives on Psychological Science*, 6, pages 3–5.

Kenneth Heafield. 2011. *KenLM: Faster and Smaller Language Model Queries.* In Proceedeings of the *Sixth Workshop on Statistical Machine Trnaslation*, pages 187–197.

Philipp Koehn, Hieu Hoang, Alexandra Birch, Chris Callison-Burch, Marcello Federico, Nicola Bertoldi, Brooke Cowan, Wade Shen, Christine Moran, Richard Zens, Chris Dyer, Ondrej Bojar, Alexandra Constantin, and Evan Herbst. 2007. *Moses: Open Source Toolkit for Statistical Machine Translation.* In Proceedings of the *Association for Computational Linguistics*, pages 177–180.

J. R. Landis and G. G. Koch. 1977. *The Measurement of Observer Agreement for Categorical Data. Biometrics*, Vol. 33, No. 1, pages 159–174.

Robert C. Moore. 2004. *On Log-Likelihood Ratios and the Significance of Rare Events.* In Proceedings of the *Conference on Empirical Methods in Natural Language Processing*, pages 333–340.

Franz J. Och, and Hermann Ney. 2000. *A Comparison of Alignment Models for Statistical Machine Translation.* In the *18th International Conference on Computational Linguistics*, pages 1086–1090.

Alice H. Oh, and Alexander I. Rudnicky. 2002. *Stochastic Natural Language Generation for Spoken Dialogue Systems.* In *Computer Speech & Language*, pages 387–407.

Kishore Papineni, Salim Roukos, Todd Ward, and Wei-Jing Zhu. 2002. *BLEU: a Method for Automatic Evaluation of Machine Translation.* In Proceedings of the *Association for Computational Linguistics*, pages 311–318.

Alan Ritter, Colin Cherry, and William B. Dolan. 2011. *Data-Driven Response Generation in Social Media.* In Proceedings of the *Conference on Empirical Methods in Natural Language Processing*, pages 583–593.

# Multilingual Open Relation Extraction Using Cross-lingual Projection

**Manaal Faruqui**
Carnegie Mellon University
Pittsburgh, PA 15213
mfaruqui@cs.cmu.edu

**Shankar Kumar**
Google Inc.
New York, NY 10011
shankarkumar@google.com

## Abstract

Open domain relation extraction systems identify relation and argument phrases in a sentence without relying on any underlying schema. However, current state-of-the-art relation extraction systems are available only for English because of their heavy reliance on linguistic tools such as part-of-speech taggers and dependency parsers. We present a cross-lingual annotation projection method for language independent relation extraction. We evaluate our method on a manually annotated test set and present results on three typologically different languages. We release these manual annotations and extracted relations in ten languages from Wikipedia.

## 1 Introduction

Relation extraction (RE) is the task of assigning a semantic relationship between a pair of arguments. The two major types of RE are closed domain and open domain RE. While closed-domain RE systems (Bunescu and Mooney, 2005; Bunescu, 2007; Mintz et al., 2009; Yao and Van Durme, 2014; Berant and Liang, 2014) consider only a closed set of relationships between two arguments, open domain systems (Yates et al., 2007; Carlson et al., 2010; Fader et al., 2011; Mausam et al., 2012) use an arbitrary phrase to specify a relationship. In this paper, we focus on open-domain RE for multiple languages. Although there are advantages to closed domain RE (Banko and Etzioni, 2008), it is expensive to construct a closed set of relation types which would be meaningful across multiple languages.

Open RE systems extract patterns from sentences in a given language to identify relations. For learning these patterns, the sentences are analyzed using a part of speech tagger, a dependency parser and possibly a named-entity recognizer. In languages other than English, these tools are either unavailable or not accurate enough to be used. In comparison, it is easier to obtain parallel bilingual corpora which can be used to build machine translation systems (Resnik and Smith, 2003; Smith et al., 2013).

In this paper, we present a system that performs RE on a sentence in a source language by first translating the sentence to English, performing RE in English, and finally projecting the relation phrase back to the source language sentence. Our system assumes the availability of a machine translation system from a source language to English and an open RE system in English but no any other analysis tool in the source language. The main contributions of this work are:

- A pipeline to develop relation extraction system for any source language.
- Extracted open relations in ten languages based on Wikipedia corpus.
- Manual judgements for the projected relations in three languages.

We first describe our methodology for language independent cross-lingual projection of extracted relations (§2) followed by the relation annotation procedure and the results (§3). The manually annotated relations in 3 languages and the automatically extracted relations in 10 languages are available at: http://cs.cmu.edu/~mfaruqui/soft.html.



*Human Language Technologies: The 2015 Annual Conference of the North American Chapter of the ACL*, pages 1351–1356,
Denver, Colorado, May 31 – June 5, 2015. ©2015 Association for Computational Linguistics

Figure 1: RE in a Spanish sentence using the cross-lingual relation extraction pipeline.

## 2 Multilingual Relation Extraction

Our method of RE for a sentence $\mathbf{s} = \langle s_1, s_2, \dots s_N \rangle$ in a non-English language consists of three steps: (1) Translation of **s** into English, that generates a sentence $\mathbf{t} = \langle t_1, t_2, \dots t_M \rangle$ with word alignments **a** relative to **s**, (2) Open RE on **t**, and (3) Relation projection from **t** to **s**. Figure 1 shows an example of RE in Spanish using our proposed pipeline. We employ OLLIE[1] (Mausam et al., 2012) for RE in English and GOOGLE TRANSLATE[2] API for translation from the source language to English, although in principle, we could use any translation system to translate the language to English. We next describe each of these components.

### 2.1 Relation Extraction in English

Suppose $\mathbf{t} = \langle t_1, t_2, \dots, t_M \rangle$ is a tokenized English sentence. Open relation extraction computes triples of non-overlapping phrases (**arg1**; **rel**; **arg2**) from the sentence **t**. The two arguments **arg1** and **arg2** are connected by the relation phrase **rel**.

We utilized OLLIE (Mausam et al., 2012) to extract the relation tuples for every English sentence. We chose OLLIE because it has been shown to give a higher yield at comparable precision relative to other open RE systems such as REVERB and WOE$^{\text{parse}}$ (Mausam et al., 2012). OLLIE was trained by extracting dependency path patterns on annotated training data. This training data was bootstrapped from a set of high precision seed tuples extracted from a simpler RE system REVERB (Fader et al., 2011). In *Godse killed Gandhi*, the extracted relation (Godse; killed; Gandhi) can be expressed by the dependency pattern: **arg1** $\uparrow$ nsubj $\uparrow$ **rel**:postag=VBD $\downarrow$ dobj $\downarrow$ **arg2**.[3] OLLIE also normalizes the relation phrase for some of the phrases, for example *is president of* is normalized to *be president of.* [4]

[1] http://knowitall.github.io/ollie/

[2] https://developers.google.com/translate/

**Data**: **s**, **t**, **a**, $p_t$
**Result**: $p_s$
$P \leftarrow$ PhraseExtract(**s**, **t**, **a**)
$p_s = \emptyset$, $score = -\infty$, $overlap = 0$
**for** $(phr_s, phr_t) \in P$ **do**
  **if** $BLEU(phr_t, p_t) > score$ **then**
    **if** $phr_t \cap p_t \neq \emptyset$ **then**
      $p_t \leftarrow phr_t$
      $score \leftarrow \text{BLEU}(phr_t, p_t)$
      $overlap \leftarrow phr_t \cap p_t$
**if** $overlap \neq 0$ **then**
  $length = \infty$
  **for** $(phr_s, p_t) \in P$ **do**
    **if** $len(phr_s) < length$ **then**
      $length \leftarrow len(phr_s)$
      $p_s \leftarrow phr_s$;
**else**
  $p_s \leftarrow$ WordAlignmentProj(**s**, **t**, **a**, $p_t$);

**Algorithm 1:** Cross-lingual projection of phrase $p_t$ from a target sentence **t** to a source sentence **s** using word alignments **a** and parallel phrases $P$.

### 2.2 Cross-lingual Relation Projection

We next describe an algorithm to project the extracted relation tuples in English back to the source language sentence. Given a source sentence, the GOOGLE TRANSLATE API provides us its translation along with the word-to-word alignments relative to the source. If $\mathbf{s} = s_1^N$ and $\mathbf{t} = t_1^M$ denote the source and its English translation, then the alignment $\mathbf{a} = \{a_{ij} : 1 \leq i \leq N; 1 \leq j \leq M\}$ where, $a_{ij} = 1$ if $s_i$ is aligned to $t_j$, and is 0 otherwise. A

[3] Example borrowed from Mausam et al. (2012)

[4] For sentences where the veracity of a relation depends on a clause, OLLIE also outputs the clause. For example, in *Early astronomers believed that Earth is the center of the universe*, the relation (Earth; be center of; universe) is supplemented by an (*AttributedTo:* believe; Early astronomers) clause. We ignore this clausal information.

naive word-alignment based projection would map every word from a phrase extracted in English to the source sentence. This algorithm has two drawbacks: first, since the word alignments are many-to-many, each English word can be possibly mapped to more than one source word which leads to ambiguity in its projection; second, a word level mapping can produce non-contiguous phrases in the source sentence, which are hard to interpret semantically.

To tackle these problems, we introduce a novel algorithm that incorporates a BLEU score (Papineni et al., 2002) based phrase similarity metric to perform cross-lingual projection of relations. Given a source sentence, its translation, and the word-to-word alignment, we first extract phrase-pairs $P$ using the phrase-extract algorithm (Och and Ney, 2004). In each extracted phrase pair $(phr_s, phr_t) \in P$, $phr_s$ and $phr_t$ are contiguous word sequences in **s** and **t** respectively. We next determine the translations of **arg1**, **rel** and **arg2** from the extracted phrase-pairs.

For each English phrase $p \in \{\text{arg1}, \text{rel}, \text{arg2}\}$, we first obtain the phrase-pair $(phr_s, phr_t) \in P$ such that $phr_t$ has the highest BLEU score relative to $p$ subject to the condition that $p \cap phr_t \neq \emptyset$ i.e, there is at least one word overlap between the two phrases. This condition is necessary since we use BLEU score with smoothing and may obtain a non-zero BLEU score even with zero word overlap. If there are multiple phrase-pairs in $P$ that correspond to the same target phrase $phr_t$, we select the shortest source phrase ($phr_s$). However, if there is no word overlap between the target phrase $p$ and any of the target phrases in $P$, we project the phrase using the word-alignment based projection. The cross-lingual projection method is presented in Algorithm 1.

## 3 Experiments

Evaluation for open relations is a difficult task with no standard evaluation datasets. We first describe the construction of our multilingual relation extraction dataset and then present the experiments.

**Annotation.** The current approach to evaluation for open relations (Fader et al., 2011; Mausam et al., 2012) is to extract relations from a sentence and manually annotate each relation as either valid (1) or invalid (0) for the sentence. For example, in the sentence: *"Michelle Obama, wife of Barack Obama was born in Chicago"*, the following are possible annotations: a) (Michelle Obama; born in; Chicago): 1, b) (Barack Obama; born in; Chicago): 0. Such binary annotations are not available for languages apart from English. Furthermore, a binary 1/0 label is a coarse annotation that could unfairly penalize an extracted relation which has the correct semantics but is slightly ungrammatical. This could occur either when prepositions are dropped from the relation phrase or when there is an ambiguity in the boundary of the relation phrase.

Therefore to evaluate our multilingual relation extraction framework, we obtained annotations from professional linguists for three typologically different languages: French, Hindi, and Russian. The annotation task is as follows: *Given a sentence and a pair of arguments (extracted automatically from the sentence), the annotator identifies the most relevant contiguous relation phrase from the sentence that establishes a plausible connection between the two arguments.* If there is no meaningful contiguous relation phrase between the two arguments, the arguments are considered invalid and hence, the extracted relation tuple from the sentence is considered incorrect.

Given the human annotated relation phrase and the automatically extracted relation phrase, we can measure the similarity between the two, thus alleviating the problem of coarse annotation in binary judgments. For evaluation, we first report the percentage of valid arguments. Then for sentences with valid arguments, we use smoothed sentence-level BLEU score (max n-gram order = 3) to measure the similarity of the automatically extracted relation relative to the human annotated relation.[5]

**Results.** We extracted relations from the entire Wikipedia[6] corpus in Russian, French and Hindi from all sentences whose lengths are in the range of $10 - 30$ words. We randomly selected $1,000$ relations for each of these languages and annotated them. The results are shown in table 1. The percentage of valid extractions is highest in French ($81.6\%$)

[5]We obtained two annotations for $\approx 300$ Russian sentences. Between the two annotations, the perfect agreement rate was 74.5% and the average BLEU score was 0.85.

[6]`www.wikipedia.org`

| Language | Argument 1 | Relation phrase | Argument 2 |
|---|---|---|---|
| French | Il<br>*He* | fut enrôlé de force au<br>*was conscripted to* | RAD<br>*RAD* |
| Hindi | bahut se log<br>*Many people* | aaye<br>*came to* | cailifornia<br>*California* |
| Russian | Автокатастрофа<br>*Crash* | произошла<br>*occured* | Черногории<br>*Montenegro* |

Table 3: Examples of extracted relations in different languages with English translations (Hindi is transliterated).

| Language | % valid | BLEU | Relation length | |
|---|---|---|---|---|
| | | | Gold | Auto |
| French | 81.6% | 0.47 | 3.6 | 2.5 |
| Hindi | 64.9% | 0.38 | 4.1 | 2.8 |
| Russian | 63.5% | 0.62 | 1.8 | 1.7 |

Table 1: % of valid relations and BLEU score of the extracted relations across languages with the average relation phrase length (in words).

| Language | Size | Language | Size |
|---|---|---|---|
| French | 6,743 | Georgian | 497 |
| Hindi | 367 | Latvian | 491 |
| Russian | 7,532 | Tagalog | 102 |
| Chinese | 2,876 | Swahili | 114 |
| Arabic | 707 | Indonesian | 1,876 |

Table 2: Number of extracted relations (in thousands) from Wikipedia in multiple languages.

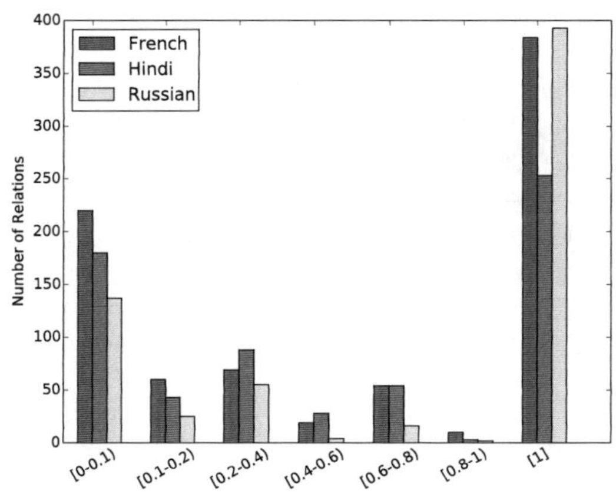


Figure 2: Number of automatically extracted relations binned by their BLEU scores computed relative to the manually annotated relations.

followed by Hindi and Russian (64.0%). Surprisingly, Russian obtains the lowest percentage of valid relations but has the highest BLEU score between the automatic and the human extracted relations. This could be attributed to the fact that the average relation length (in number of words) is the shortest for Russian. From table 1, we observe that the length of the relation phrase is inversely correlated with the BLEU score.

Figure 2 shows the distribution of the number of extracted relations across bins of similar BLEU scores. Interestingly, the highest BLEU score bin (1) contains the maximum number of relations in all three languages. This is an encouraging result since it implies that the majority of the extracted relation phrases are identical to the manually annotated relations. Table 2 lists the sizes of automatically extracted relations on 10 different languages from Wikipedia that we are going to make publicly available. These were selected to include a mixture of high-resource, low-resource, and typologically different languages. Table 3 shows examples of randomly selected relations in different languages along with their English translations.

## 4 Related Work

Cross-lingual projection has been used for transfer of syntactic (Yarowsky and Ngai, 2001; Hwa et al., 2005) and semantic information (Riloff et al., 2002; Padó and Lapata, 2009). There has been a growing interest in RE for languages other than English. Gamallo et al. (2012) present a dependency-parser based open RE system for Spanish, Portuguese and Galician. RE systems for Korean have been developed for both open-domain (Kim et al., 2011) and closed-domain (Kim and Lee, 2012; Kim et al., 2014) using annotation projection. These approaches use a Korean-English parallel corpus to project relations extracted in English to Korean. Following projection, a Korean POS-tagger and a dependency parser are employed to learn a RE system for Korean.

Tseng et al. (2014) describe an open RE for Chinese that employs word segmentation, POS-tagging, dependency parsing. Lewis and Steedman (2013) learn clusters of semantically equivalent relations across French and English by creating a semantic signature of relations by entity-typing. These relations are extracted using CCG parsing in English and dependency parsing in French. Blessing and Schütze (2012) use inter-wiki links to map relations from a relation database in a pivot language to the target language and use these instances for learning in a distant supervision setting. Gerber and Ngomo (2012) describe a multilingual pattern extraction system for RDF predicates that uses pre-existing knowledge bases for different languages.

## 5 Conclusion

We have presented a language independent open domain relation extraction pipeline and have evaluated its performance on three typologically different languages: French, Hindi and Russian. Our cross-lingual projection method utilizes OLLIE and GOOGLE TRANSLATE to extract relations in the language of interest. Our approach does not rely on the availability of linguistic resources such as POS-taggers or dependency parsers in the target language and can thus be extended to multiple languages supported by a machine translation system. We are releasing the manually annotated judgements for open relations in the three languages and the open relations extracted over the entire Wikipedia corpus in ten languages. The resources are available at: `http://cs.cmu.edu/~mfaruqui/soft.html`.

## Acknowledgment

This work was performed when the first author was an intern at Google. We thank Richard Sproat for providing comments on an earlier draft of this paper. We thank Hao Zhang for helping us with the relation extraction framework, and Richard Zens and Kishore Papineni for their feedback on this work. We are grateful to Bruno Cartoni, Vitaly Nikolaev and their teams for providing us annotations of multilingual relations.

## References

Michele Banko and Oren Etzioni. 2008. The tradeoffs between open and traditional relation extraction. In *Proceedings of ACL*.

J. Berant and P. Liang. 2014. Semantic parsing via paraphrasing. In *Proceedings of ACL*.

Andre Blessing and Hinrich Schütze. 2012. Crosslingual distant supervision for extracting relations of different complexity. In *Proceedings of CIKM*.

Razvan C. Bunescu and Raymond J. Mooney. 2005. A shortest path dependency kernel for relation extraction. In *Proceedings of EMNLP*.

Razvan C. Bunescu. 2007. Learning to extract relations from the web using minimal supervision. In *Proceedings of ACL*.

Andrew Carlson, Justin Betteridge, Bryan Kisiel, Burr Settles, Estevam R. Hruschka Jr., and Tom M. Mitchell. 2010. Toward an architecture for never-ending language learning. In *Proceedings of AAAI*.

Anthony Fader, Stephen Soderland, and Oren Etzioni. 2011. Identifying relations for open information extraction. In *Proceedings of EMNLP*.

Pablo Gamallo, Marcos Garcia, and Santiago Fernández-Lanza. 2012. Dependency-based open information extraction. In *Proceedings of ROBUS-UNSUP*.

Daniel Gerber and Axel-Cyrille Ngonga Ngomo. 2012. Extracting multilingual natural-language patterns for rdf predicates. In *Proceedings of the 18th International Conference on Knowledge Engineering and Knowledge Management*.

Rebecca Hwa, Philip Resnik, Amy Weinberg, Clara Cabezas, and Okan Kolak. 2005. Bootstrapping parsers via syntactic projection across parallel texts. *Natural Language Engineering*, 11:11–311.

Seokhwan Kim and Gary Geunbae Lee. 2012. A graph-based cross-lingual projection approach for weakly supervised relation extraction. In *Proceedings of ACL*.

Seokhwan Kim, Minwoo Jeong, Jonghoon Lee, and Gary Geunbae Lee. 2011. A cross-lingual annotation projection-based self-supervision approach for open information extraction. In *Proceedings of IJC-NLP*.

Seokhwan Kim, Minwoo Jeong, Jonghoon Lee, and Gary Geunbae Lee. 2014. Cross-lingual annotation projection for weakly-supervised relation extraction. *ACM Trans. Asian Lang. Inf. Process.*, pages 3–3.

Mike Lewis and Mark Steedman. 2013. Unsupervised induction of cross-lingual semantic relations. In *Proceedings of EMNLP*.

Mausam, Michael Schmitz, Robert Bart, Stephen Soderland, and Oren Etzioni. 2012. Open language learning for information extraction. In *Proceedings of EMNLP-CoNLL*.

Mike Mintz, Steven Bills, Rion Snow, and Dan Jurafsky. 2009. Distant supervision for relation extraction without labeled data. In *Proceedings of ACL*.

Franz Josef Och and Hermann Ney. 2004. The alignment template approach to statistical machine translation. *Comput. Linguist.*, pages 417–449.

Sebastian Padó and Mirella Lapata. 2009. Cross-lingual annotation projection of semantic roles. *Journal of Artificial Intelligence Research*, 36:307–340.

Kishore Papineni, Salim Roukos, Todd Ward, and Wei-Jing Zhu. 2002. Bleu: A method for automatic evaluation of machine translation. In *Proceedings of ACL*.

Philip Resnik and Noah A. Smith. 2003. The web as a parallel corpus. *Computational Linguistics*.

Ellen Riloff, Charles Schafer, and David Yarowsky. 2002. Inducing information extraction systems for new languages via cross-language projection. In *Proceedings of COLING*.

Jason R. Smith, Herve Saint-Amand, Magdalena Plamada, Philipp Koehn, Chris Callison-Burch, and Adam Lopez. 2013. Dirt cheap web-scale parallel text from the common crawl. In *Proceedings of ACL*.

Yuen-Hsien Tseng, Lung-Hao Lee, Shu-Yen Lin, Bo-Shun Liao, Mei-Jun Liu, Hsin-Hsi Chen, Oren Etzioni, and Anthony Fader. 2014. Chinese open relation extraction for knowledge acquisition. In *Proceedings of EACL*.

Xuchen Yao and Benjamin Van Durme. 2014. Information extraction over structured data: Question answering with freebase. In *Proceedings of ACL*.

David Yarowsky and Grace Ngai. 2001. Inducing multilingual pos taggers and np bracketers via robust projection across aligned corpora. In *Proceedings of NAACL*.

Alexander Yates, Michael Cafarella, Michele Banko, Oren Etzioni, Matthew Broadhead, and Stephen Soderland. 2007. Textrunner: Open information extraction on the web. In *Proceedings of NAACL: Demonstrations*.

# Learning to parse with IAA-weighted loss

**Héctor Martínez Alonso**[†] **Barbara Plank**[†] **Arne Skjærholt**[‡] **Anders Søgaard**[†]
[†]Njalsgade 140, Copenhagen (Denmark), University of Copenhagen
[‡]Gaustadalléen 23B, Oslo (Norway), University of Oslo
alonso@hum.ku.dk, bplank@cst.dk, arnskj@ifi.uio.no, soegaard@hum.ku.dk

## Abstract

Natural language processing (NLP) annotation projects employ guidelines to maximize inter-annotator agreement (IAA), and models are estimated assuming that there is one single ground truth. However, not all disagreement is noise, and in fact some of it may contain valuable linguistic information. We integrate such information in the training of a cost-sensitive dependency parser. We introduce five different factorizations of IAA and the corresponding loss functions, and evaluate these across six different languages. We obtain robust improvements across the board using a factorization that considers dependency labels and directionality. The best method-dataset combination reaches an average overall error reduction of 6.4% in labeled attachment score.

## 1 Introduction

Typically, NLP annotation projects employ guidelines to maximize inter-annotator agreement. Possible inconsistencies are resolved by adjudication, and models are induced assuming there is one single ground truth. However, there exist linguistically hard cases where there is no clear answer (Zeman, 2010; Manning, 2011), and incorporating such disagreements into the training of a model has proven helpful for POS tagging (Plank et al., 2014a; Plank et al., 2014b).

Inter-annotator agreement (IAA) is straightforward to calculate for POS, but not for dependency trees. There is no well-established standard for computing agreement on trees (Skjærholt, 2014). For a dependency tree, annotators can disagree in attachment, labeling, or both. We implement different strategies, i.e., *factorizations* (§2), to capture disagreement on specific syntactic phenomena.

Our hypothesis is that a dependency parser can be informed of disagreements to regularize over annotators' biases. Testing our hypothesis requires the availability of doubly-annotated data, and involves two steps: i) how to *factorize* attachment or labeling disagreements; and ii) how to *inform* the parser of them during learning (§3).

## 2 Factorizations

Assume a sample of sentences annotated by annotators $A_1$ and $A_2$. With such a sample we can estimate probabilities of the two annotators' disagreeing on the annotation of a word or span, relative to some dependency tree factorization. We factorize disagreement on dependency tree annotations relative to four properties of the annotated dependency edges: the POS of the dependent, the POS of the head, the label of the edge and the direction (left or right) of the head with regards to the dependent. This section describes the different factorizations.

We present five factorizations, depicted in Figure 1. With artificial root notes, all words in a dependency tree have one incoming edge. This means that in our sample, any word $w_i$ has two $\langle headId, label \rangle$ annotations, i.e., $\langle h_1, l_1 \rangle$ and $\langle h_2, l_2 \rangle$ given by $A_1$ and $A_2$, respectively, with POS$(\cdot)$ being a function from word indices to POS. The five factorizations are as follows:



*Human Language Technologies: The 2015 Annual Conference of the North American Chapter of the ACL*, pages 1357–1361,
Denver, Colorado, May 31 – June 5, 2015. 

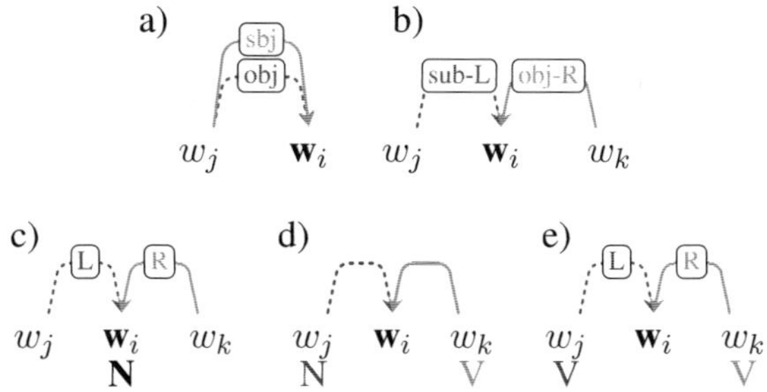


Figure 1: Factorizations: a) LABEL, b) LABELD; c) CHILDPOSD, d) HEADPOS and e) HEADPOSD. Red and green depict different choices by annotators $A_1$ and $A_2$.

a) LABEL: disagreement over label pairs, regardless of attachment ($h_1$,$h_2$). That is, $\langle h_1, l_1\rangle$ and $\langle h_2, l_2\rangle$ count as disagreement, iff $l_1 \neq l_2$.
b) LABELD, same as LABEL, but incorporating edge direction. That is, $\langle h_1, l_1\rangle$ and $\langle h_2, l_2\rangle$ count as disagreement, for any $j, k \in h_1, h_2$, iff $h_j < i < h_k$ *or* $l_1 \neq l_2$.
c) CHILDPOSD, i.e., disagreement on attachment direction given POS($i$). That is, for POS($i$), $\langle h_1, l_1\rangle$ and $\langle h_2, l_2\rangle$ count as disagreement, iff $h_j < i < h_k$.
d) HEADPOS: disagreement on head POS. That is, $\langle h_1, l_1\rangle$ and $\langle h_2, l_2\rangle$ count as disagreement, iff POS($h_1$)≠POS($h_2$).
e) HEADPOSD, i.e., HEADPOS, plus direction. That is, $\langle h_1, l_1\rangle$ and $\langle h_2, l_2\rangle$ count as disagreement, iff POS($h_1$)≠POS($h_2$) *or* $h_j < i < h_k$.

Each factorization yields a symmetric confusion matrix. In our Norwegian data (§4), for instance, for LABEL there are 834 words that have been labeled as ATR (attribute) by both annotators, while there are 44 cases where one annotator has given the ATR label and the other has given the ADV (adverbial) label. For LABELD, there are 968 words that have been labeled as ADV where both annotators agree on the head being on the left side of the word, whereas there are 9 cases where the annotators agree on ADV label but not on the direction of the head. These 9 cases count as disagreements for LABELD but not for LABEL.

| lang | train | test | *l* | *p* |
|---|---|---|---|---|
| NO | 13.7k/209k | 5.8k/96.7k | 29 | 19 |
| EN | 3.6k/70k | †1.0k/20.3k | 30 | 44 |
| DA | 4.2k/74k | †1.2k/23.4k | 31 | 25 |
| CA | 3.9k/73k | 1.7k/34.4k | 27 | 11 |
| HR | 3.1k/79k | 1.3k/35.5k | 26 | 27 |
| FI | 9.1k/123k | 3.9k/54.4k | 45 | 12 |

Table 1: Data statistics: number of sentences/tokens, dependency labels $l$, POS tags $p$ for NO (Norwegian), EN (English), DA (Danish), CA (Catalan), Croatian (HR) and Finnish (FI); †=canonical test split available.

## 3 Cost-sensitive updates

We use the cost-sensitive perceptron classifier, following Plank et al. (2014a), but extend it to transition-based dependency parsing, where the predicted values are transitions (Goldberg and Nivre, 2012). Given a gold $y_i$ and predicted label $\hat{y}_i$ (POS tags or transitions), the loss is weighted by $\gamma(\hat{y}_i, y_i)$:

$$L_{\mathbf{w}}(\hat{y}_i, y_i) = \gamma(\hat{y}_i, y_i) \max(0, -y_i \mathbf{w} \cdot \mathbf{x}_i)$$

Whenever a transition has been wrongly predicted, we retrieve the predicted edge and compare it to the gold dependency to calculate $\gamma$. $\gamma(y_i, y_j)$ is then the inverse of the confusion probability estimated from our sample of doubly-annotated data. For example, using the factorization LABEL, if the parser predicts $w_i$ to be SUBJECT and the gold annotation is OBJECT, the confusion probability is the number of times one annotator said SUBJECT while the other said OBJECT out of the times one annotator said one of them. In LABELD, $A_1$ and $A_2$ can disagree even if both say the grammatical function of some word $w_i$ is SUBJECT, namely if one says the subject is left of $w_i$, and the other says it is right of $w_i$. The confusion probability is then the count of disagreements over the total number of cases where both annotators said a word was SUBJECT.

In our baseline model, $\gamma(\hat{y}_i, y_i) = 1$. The values for our cost-sensitive systems (LABEL, LABELD, CHILDPOSD, HEADPOS, HEADPOSD) are never above 1, which means that we are selectively underfitting the parser for specific syntactic phenomena. In other words, we use the doubly-annotated data to regularize our model, hopefully preventing overfitting to annotators' biases.

## 4 Data

We use six treebanks (Buch-Kromann et al., 2003; Buch-Kromann et al., 2007; Arias et al., 2014; Solberg et al., 2014; Agić and Merkler, 2013; Haverinen et al., 2010) for which we could get a sample of doubly-annotated data. All these treebanks are directly developed as dependency treebanks, instead of being converted from constituent treebanks. Table 1 gives overview statistics of the treebanks, Table 2 lists the sizes of the doubly-annotated samples, as well as F1 scores between annotators and $\alpha$ values (Skjærholt, 2014). The doubly-annotated samples are solely used to estimate confusion probabilities, and not for training or testing. When a treebank had no canonical train/test split, we took the final 30% for testing.

| | | | between annotator: | | | |
|---|---|---|---|---|---|---|
| **lang** | **sents** | **tokens** | **LAS** | **UAS** | **LA** | **$\alpha$ plain** |
| NO | 400 | 5.3k | 94.70 | 96.47 | 96.62 | 0.984 |
| EN | 264 | 5.5k | 88.44 | 93.83 | 91.95 | 0.925 |
| DA | 162 | 2.4k | 90.43 | 96.12 | 92.40 | 0.957 |
| CA | 63 | 1.3k | 94.48 | 98.26 | 95.64 | 0.978 |
| HR | 100 | 2.4k | 78.89 | 89.16 | 84.07 | 0.939 |
| FI | 400 | 5.1k | 83.45 | 88.77 | 89.83 | 0.950 |

Table 2: Statistics of the doubly-annotated data.

## 5 Experiments

In our experiments, we use `redshift`,[1] a transition-based arc-eager dependency parser that implements the dynamic oracle (Goldberg and Nivre, 2012) with averaged perceptron training. We modified the parser[2] to read confusion matrices and weigh the updates with the respective $\gamma$. We compare the five (§2) factorized systems to a baseline system that does not take confusion probabilities into account, i.e., standard `redshift`. Throughout the experiments, we fix the number of iterations to 5, and we use pseudo-projectivization (Nivre and Nilsson, 2005).[3] The parser does not include morphological features, which lowers performance for morphological rich languages like FI. We report labeled attachment scores (LAS) incl. punctuation.

[1] `https://github.com/syllog1sm/redshift`

[2] The modified code, as well as the confusion matrices for all factorizations, is available at `https://bitbucket.org/lowlands/iaa-parsing`

[3] 15–33% of the sentences contain non-projectivities.

We use bootstrap sampling in all our experiments in order to get more reliable results. This method allows abstracting away from biases—in sampling and annotation—of training and test splits. We use two complementary evaluation methods: cross-validation within the training data, and learning curves against the test set. We calculate significance using the approximate randomization test (Noreen, 1989) with 10k iterations.

**Cross-validation** In this setup, we perform 50 runs of 5-fold cross validation on bootstrap-based samples of the training data. This allows us to gauge the effect of our factorization without committing to a certain test set. We report on the average of the total of 250 runs.

**Learning curve** To calculate the learning curves, we train the parser on increasing amounts of training data, bootstrap-sampled in steps of 10%, and evaluate against the test set. Each 10% increment is repeated $k = 50$ times. We finally report average overall error reduction over the baseline.

## 6 Results

**Cross-validation** The results for cross-validation are shown in Table 3. For 5 out of the 6 languages we get significant improvements over the baseline with some factorization. We obtain improvements on all treebanks using LABELD, and on five out of six using CHILDPOSD. For CA, with the smallest doubly-annotated sample, results are not as consistent across the two evaluation methods.

**Learning curve** Table 4 summarizes the overall average error reduction over the 10-step bootstrap-based learning curve (with 50 runs at each step). We get consistent improvements for languages for which we have a sample of 100+ sentences (Table 2). Again, the most robust factorization is LABELD. Figure 2 shows the learning curves for the system with the highest error reduction (NO with CHILDPOSD).

**Additional studies** In order to evaluate whether our results are meaningful and not just artifacts of random regularization, we performed a sanity check for the best performing system and factorization (i.e., NO with CHILDPOSD factorization). We

| | BASELINE | CHILDPOSD | LABEL | LABELD | HEADPOS | HEADPOSD |
|---|---|---|---|---|---|---|
| NO | 90.98 | **92.67**∗ | 91.16 | 91.34 | 92.08∗ | 90.48 |
| EN | 81.72 | 83.48∗ | 80.35 | 83.05∗ | 85.89∗ | **85.91**∗ |
| DA | 80.56 | 83.67∗ | 82.90∗ | 82.47∗ | 83.23∗ | **84.11**∗ |
| CA | 83.78 | 83.26 | **84.21**∗ | 83.79 | 82.84 | 82.61 |
| HR | 76.94 | 78.07 | 78.22 | 77.52 | **79.49**∗ | 78.71∗ |
| FI | 66.19 | 66.74 | 64.88 | **67.18** | 65.63 | 65.27 |

Table 3: Crossvalidation results (in LAS incl. punctuation). Gray: below baseline. Best factorization per language in boldface. Significance at $p < 0.01$ (computed over runs and wrt baseline) is indicated by $*$ .

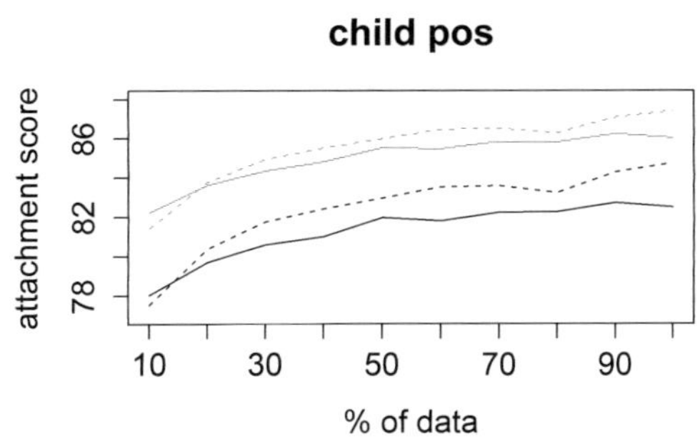


Figure 2: Bootstrap learning curve (k=50) for NO with CHILDPOSD. Black: LAS, green: UAS; solid line: baseline; dashed line: IAA-weighted model.

| | CHILDPOSD | LABEL | LABELD | HEADPOS | HEADPOSD |
|---|---|---|---|---|---|
| NO | **6.4%** | 0.6% | 0.7% | 3.3% | 1.2% |
| EN | 2.0% | 2.6% | 2.9% | **5.3%** | 3.8% |
| DA | 0.7% | 1.6% | 1.0% | **2.0%** | 1.0% |
| CA | -2.0% | -0.1% | -0.1% | -2.9% | -2.8% |
| HR | -0.2% | 0.3% | **0.7%** | 0.1% | 0.1% |
| FI | **0.4%** | -0.4% | 0.1% | -0.1% | -0.70% |

Table 4: Overall avg. error red. across learning curves.

shuffled the confusion matrix and ran the bootstrap learning curve with $k = 50$ repetitions, for five different shufflings. The mean over the five runs for the overall average error reductions is negative (-0.38%, compared to the 2.4% mean for the original, non-shuffled version). We thus conclude that our factorizations capture linguistically plausible information rather than random noise.

## 7 Related Work

Plank et al. (2014a) propose IAA-weighted cost-sensitive learning for POS tagging. We extend their line of work to dependency parsing.

A single sentence can have more than one plausible dependency annotation. Some researchers have proposed evaluation metrics that do not penalize disagreements (Schwartz et al., 2011; Tsarfaty et al., 2011), while others have argued that we should instead ensure the consistency of treebanks (Dickinson, 2010; Manning, 2011; McDonald et al., 2013). Others have claimed that because of these ambiguities, only downstream evaluations are meaningful (Elming et al., 2013).

Syntactic annotation disagreement has typically been studied in the context of treebank development. Haverinen et al. (2012), for example, analyze annotator disagreement for Finnish dependency syntax, and compare it against parser performance. Skjærholt (2014) use doubly-annotated data to evaluate various agreement metrics. Our paper differs from both lines of research in that we leverage disagreements from doubly-annotated data to obtain more robust models. While we agree that evaluation metrics should probably reflect disagreements, we show that our learning algorithms can indeed benefit from information about disagreement, also using standard performance metrics.

## 8 Conclusions

We have evaluated five different factorizations on six treebanks to evaluate the impact of IAA-weighted learning for dependency parsing, obtaining promising results. The findings support our hypothesis that annotator disagreement is informative for parsing. The LABELD factorization—which takes both labeling and word order into account—is the overall most robust factorization across all languages. However, the best factorization for each language varies. This variation can be a result of the morphosyntax of the language, but also of the dependency annotation formalisms, annotation method, training corpus and size of the doubly-annotated sample.

## Acknowledgements

We thank Jorge Vivaldi, Filip Ginter and Željko Agić for providing doubly-annotated data. This research is partially funded by the ERC Starting Grant LOWLANDS No. 313695.

## References

Željko Agić and Danijela Merkler. 2013. Three syntactic formalisms for data-driven dependency parsing of croatian. In *Text, Speech, and Dialogue*. Springer.

Blanca Arias, Nuria Bel, Mercè Lorente, Montserrat Marimón, Alba Milà, Jorge Vivaldi, Muntsa Padró, Marina Fomicheva, and Imanol Larrea. 2014. Boosting the creation of a treebank. In *LREC*.

Matthias Buch-Kromann, Line Mikkelsen, and Stine Kern Lynge. 2003. Danish dependency treebank. In *TLT*.

Matthias Buch-Kromann, Jürgen Wedekind, and Jakob Elming. 2007. The Copenhagen Danish-English Dependency Treebank v.2.0. *http://buch-kromann.dk/matthias/cdt2.0*.

Markus Dickinson. 2010. Detecting errors in automatically-parsed dependency relations. In *ACL*.

Jakob Elming, Anders Johannsen, Sigrid Klerke, Emanuele Lapponi, Hector Martinez, and Anders Søgaard. 2013. Down-stream effects of tree-to-dependency conversions. In *NAACL*.

Yoav Goldberg and Joakim Nivre. 2012. A dynamic oracle for arc-eager dependency parsing. In *COLING*.

Katri Haverinen, Timo Viljanen, Veronika Laippala, Samuel Kohonen, Filip Ginter, and Tapio Salakoski. 2010. Treebanking finnish. In *TLT*.

Katri Haverinen, Filip Ginter, Samuel Kohonen, Timo Viljanen, Jenna Nyblom, and Tapio Salakoski. 2012. A dependency-based analysis of treebank annotation errors. In *Computational Dependency Theory*. IOS Press.

Christopher D Manning. 2011. Part-of-speech tagging from 97% to 100%: is it time for some linguistics? In *Computational Linguistics and Intelligent Text Processing*. Springer.

Ryan McDonald, Joakim Nivre, Yvonne Quirmbach-Brundage, Yoav Goldberg, Dipanjan Das, Kuzman Ganchev, Keith Hall, Slav Petrov, Hao Zhang, Oscar Täckström, Claudia Bedini, Núria Bertomeu Castelló, and Jungmee Lee. 2013. Universal dependency annotation for multilingual parsing. In *ACL*.

Joakim Nivre and Jens Nilsson. 2005. Pseudo-projective dependency parsing. In *ACL*.

Eriw W. Noreen. 1989. *Computer-intensive methods for testing hypotheses: an introduction*. Wiley.

Barbara Plank, Dirk Hovy, and Anders Søgaard. 2014a. Learning part-of-speech taggers with inter-annotator agreement loss. In *EACL*.

Barbara Plank, Dirk Hovy, and Anders Søgaard. 2014b. Linguistically debatable or just plain wrong? In *ACL*.

Roy Schwartz, Omri Abend, Roi Reichart, and Ari Rappoport. 2011. Neutralizing linguistically problematic annotations in unsupervised dependency parsing evaluation. In *ACL*.

Arne Skjærholt. 2014. A chance-corrected measure of inter-annotator agreement for syntax. In *ACL*.

Per Erik Solberg, Arne Skjærholt, Lilja Øvrelid, Kristin Hagen, and Janne Bondi Johannessen. 2014. The Norwegian Dependency Treebank. In *LREC*.

Reut Tsarfaty, Joakim Nivre, and Evelina Ndersson. 2011. Evaluating dependency parsing: robust and heuristics-free cross-nnotation evaluation. In *EMNLP*.

Daniel Zeman. 2010. Hard problems of tagset conversion. In *Proceedings of the Second International Conference on Global Interoperability for Language Resources*.

# Exploiting Text and Network Context for Geolocation of Social Media Users

**Afshin Rahimi,**[1] **Duy Vu,**[2] **Trevor Cohn,**[1] and **Timothy Baldwin**[1]
[1]Department of Computing and Information Systems
[2]Department of Mathematics and Statistics
The University of Melbourne
arahimi@student.unimelb.edu.au
{duy.vu, t.cohn}@unimelb.edu.au
tb@ldwin.net

## Abstract

Research on automatically geolocating social media users has conventionally been based on the text content of posts from a given user or the social network of the user, with very little crossover between the two, and no benchmarking of the two approaches over comparable datasets. We bring the two threads of research together in first proposing a text-based method based on adaptive grids, followed by a hybrid network- and text-based method. Evaluating over three Twitter datasets, we show that the empirical difference between text- and network-based methods is not great, and that hybridisation of the two is superior to the component methods, especially in contexts where the user graph is not well connected. We achieve state-of-the-art results on all three datasets.

## 1 Introduction

There has recently been a spike in interest in the task of inferring the location of users of social media services, due to its utility in applications including location-aware information retrieval (Amitay et al., 2004), recommender systems (Noulas et al., 2012) and rapid disaster response (Earle et al., 2010). Social media sites such as Twitter and Facebook provide two primary means for users to declare their location: (1) through text-based metadata fields in the user's profile; and (2) through GPS-based geotagging of posts and check-ins. However, the text-based metadata is often missing, misleading or imprecise, and only a tiny proportion of users geotag their posts (Cheng et al., 2010). Given the small number of users with reliable location information, there has been significant interest in the task of automatically geolocating (predicting lat/long coordinates) of users based on their publicly available posts, metadata and social network information. These approaches are built on the premise that a user's location is evident from their posts, or through location homophily in their social network.

Our contributions in this paper are: *a*) the demonstration that network-based methods are generally superior to text-based user geolocation methods due to their robustness; *b*) the proposal of a hybrid classification method that backs-off from network- to text-based predictions for disconnected users, which we show to achieve state-of-the-art accuracy over all Twitter datasets we experiment with; and *c*) empirical evidence to suggest that text-based geolocation methods are largely competitive with network-based methods.

## 2 Related Work

Past work on user geolocation falls broadly into two categories: text-based and network-based methods. Common to both methods is the manner of framing the geolocation prediction problem. Geographic coordinates are real-valued, and accordingly this is most naturally modelled as (multiple) regression. However for modelling convenience, the problem is typically simplified to classification by first prepartitioning the regions into discrete sub-regions using either known city locations (Han et al., 2012; Rout et al., 2013) or a $k$-d tree partitioning (Roller et al., 2012; Wing and Baldridge, 2014). In the $k$-d tree methods, the resulting discrete regions are treated either as a flat list (as we do here) or a nested hierarchy.



*Human Language Technologies: The 2015 Annual Conference of the North American Chapter of the ACL*, pages 1362–1367,
Denver, Colorado, May 31 – June 5, 2015. 

### 2.1 Text-based Geolocation

Text-based approaches assume that language in social media is geographically biased, which is clearly evident for regions speaking different languages (Han et al., 2014), but is also reflected in regional dialects and the use of region specific terminology. Text based models have predominantly used bag of words features to learn per-region classifiers (Roller et al., 2012; Wing and Baldridge, 2014), including feature selection for location-indicative terms (Han et al., 2012).

Topic models have also been applied to model geospatial text usage (Eisenstein et al., 2010; Ahmed et al., 2013), by associating latent topics with locations. This has a benefit of allowing for prediction over continuous space, i.e., without the need to render the problem as classification. On the other hand, these methods have high algorithmic complexity and their generative formulation is unlikely to rival the performance of discriminative methods on large datasets.

### 2.2 Network-based Geolocation

Although online social networking sites allow for global interaction, users tend to befriend and interact with many of the same people online as they do off-line (Rout et al., 2013). Network-based methods exploit this property to infer the location of users from the locations of their friends (Jurgens, 2013; Rout et al., 2013). This relies on some form of friendship graph, through which location information can be propagated, e.g., using label propagation (Jurgens, 2013; Talukdar and Crammer, 2009). A significant caveat regarding the generality of these techniques is that friendship graphs are often not accessible, e.g., secured from the public (Facebook) or hidden behind a heavily rate-limited API (Twitter).

While the raw accuracies reported for network-based methods (e.g., Jurgens (2013) and Rout et al. (2013)) are generally higher than those reported for text-based methods (e.g., Wing and Baldridge (2014) and Han et al. (2014)), they have been evaluated over different datasets and spatial representations, making direct comparison uninformative. Part of our contribution in this paper is direct comparison between the respective methods over standard datasets. In this, we propose both text- and network-based methods, and show that they achieve state-of-the-art results on three pre-existing Twitter geolocation corpora. We also propose a new hybrid method incorporating both textual and network information, which also improves over the state-of-the-art, and outperforms the text-only or network-only methods over two of the three datasets.

## 3 Data

We evaluate on three Twitter corpora, each of which uses geotagged tweets to derive a geolocation for each user. Each user is represented by the concatenation of their tweets, and is assumed to come from a single location.

GEOTEXT: around 380K tweets from 9.5K users based in contiguous USA, of which 1895 is held out for development and testing (Eisenstein et al., 2010); the location of each user is set to the GPS coordinates of their first tweet.

TWITTER-US: around 39M tweets from 450K users based in the contiguous USA. 10K users are held out for each of development and testing (Roller et al., 2012); again users' locations are taken from their first tweet.

TWITTER-WORLD: around 12M English tweets from 1.4M users based around the world, of which 10K users are held out for each of development and testing (Han et al., 2012); users are geotagged with the centre of the closest city to their tweets.

In each case, we use the established training, development and testing partitions, and follow Cheng et al. (2010) and Eisenstein et al. (2010) in evaluating based on: (1) accuracy at 161km ("Acc@161"); (2) mean error distance, in kilometres ("Mean"); and (3) median error distance, in kilometres ("Median").

## 4 Methods

### 4.1 Text-based Classification

Our baseline method for text based geolocation is based on Wing and Baldridge (2014), who formulate the geolocation problem as classification using $k$-d trees. In summary, their approach first discretises the continuous space of geographical coordinates using a $k$-d tree such that each sub-region (leaf) has similar numbers of users. This results in many small regions for areas of high population density and fewer larger regions for country areas with low population density. Next, they use these regions as class labels to train a logistic regression model ("LR"). Our work is also subject to a sparse $l_1$ regularisation penalty (Tibshirani, 1996). In their work, Wing and Baldridge (2014) showed that hierarchical logistic regression with a beam search achieves higher results than logistic regression over a flat label set, but in this research, we use a flat representation, and leave experiments with hierarchical classification to future work.

For our experiments, the number of users in each region was selected from $\{300, 600, 900, 1200\}$ to optimise median error distance on the development set, resulting in values of 300, 600 and 600 for GEOTEXT, TWITTER-US and TWITTER-WORLD, respectively. The $l_1$ regularisation coefficient was also optimised in the same manner.

As features, we used a bag of unigrams (over both words and @-mentions) and removed all features that occurred in fewer than 10 documents, following Wing and Baldridge (2014). The features for each user were weighted using tf-idf, followed by per-user $l_2$ normalisation. The normalisation is particularly important because our 'documents' are formed from all the tweets of each user, which vary significantly in size between users; furthermore, this adjusts for differing degrees of lexical variation (Lee, 1995). The number of features was almost 10K for GEOTEXT and about 2.5M for the other two corpora. For evaluation we use the median of all training locations in the sub-region predicted by the classifier, from which we measure the error against a test user's gold standard location.

### 4.2 Network-based Label Propagation

Next, we consider the approach of Jurgens (2013) who used label propagation ("LP"; Zhu and Ghahramani (2002)) to infer user locations using social network structure. Jurgens (2013) defined an undirected network from interactions among Twitter users based on @-mentions in their tweets, a mechanism typically used for conversations between

| | GEOTEXT | TWITTER-US | TWITTER-WORLD |
|---|---|---|---|
| User mentions | 109K | 3.63M | 16.8M |
| Disconnected test users: | 23.5% | 27.7% | 2.36% |

Table 1: The graph size and proportion of test users disconnected from training users for each dataset.

friends. Consequently these links often correspond to offline friendships, and accordingly the network will exhibit a high degree of location homophily. The network is constructed by defining as nodes all users in a dataset (train and test), as well as other external users mentioned in their tweets. Unlike Jurgens (2013) who only created edges when both users mentioned one another, we created edges if either user mentioned the other. For the three datasets used in our experiments, bi-directional mentions were too rare to be useful, and we thus used the (weaker) uni-directional mentions as undirected edges instead. The edges between users are undirected and weighted by the number of @-mentions in tweets by either user.[1]

The mention network statistics for each of our datasets is shown in Table 1.[2] Following Jurgens (2013), we ran the label propagation algorithm to update the location of each non-training node to the weighted median of its neighbours. This process continues iteratively until convergence, which occurred at or before 10 iterations.

### 4.3 A Hybrid Method

Unfortunately many test users are not transitively connected to any training node (see Table 1), meaning that LP fails to assign them any location. This can happen when users don't use @-mentions, or when a set of nodes constitutes a disconnected component of the graph.

In order to alleviate this problem, we use the text for each test user in order to estimate their location, which is then used as an initial estimation during label propagation. In this hybrid approach, we first

[1]As our datasets don't have tweets for external users, these nodes do not contribute to the weight of their incident edges.

[2]Note that @-mentions were removed in the published TWITTER-US and TWITTER-WORLD datasets. To recover these we rebuilt the corpora from the Twitter archive.

| | GeoText | | | Twitter-US | | | Twitter-World | | |
|---|---|---|---|---|---|---|---|---|---|
| | Acc@161 | Mean | Median | Acc@161 | Mean | Median | Acc@161 | Mean | Median |
| LR (text-based) | 38.4 | 880.6 | 397.0 | 50.1 | 686.7 | 159.2 | **63.8** | **866.5** | **19.9** |
| LP (network-based) | 45.1 | 676.2 | 255.7 | 37.4 | 747.8 | 431.5 | 56.2 | 1026.5 | 79.8 |
| LP−LR (hybrid) | **50.2** | **653.9** | **151.2** | **50.2** | **620.0** | **157.1** | 59.2 | 903.6 | 53.7 |
| Wing and Baldridge (2014) (uniform) | — | — | — | 49.2 | 703.6 | 170.5 | 32.7 | 1714.6 | 490.0 |
| Wing and Baldridge (2014) ($k$-d) | — | — | — | 48.0 | 686.6 | 191.4 | 31.3 | 1669.6 | 509.1 |
| Han et al. (2012) | — | — | — | 45.0 | 814 | 260 | 24.1 | 1953 | 646 |
| Ahmed et al. (2013) | ??? | ??? | 298 | — | — | — | — | — | — |

Table 2: Geolocation accuracy over the three Twitter corpora comparing Logistic Regression (LR), Label Propagation (LP) and LP over LR initialisation (LP−LR) with the state-of-the-art methods for the respective datasets ("—" signifies that no results were published for the given dataset, and "???" signifies that no results were reported for the given metric).

estimate the location for each test node using the LR classifier described above, before running label propagation over the mention graph. This iteratively adjusts the locations based on both the known training users and guessed test users, while simultaneously inferring locations for the external users. In such a way, the inferred locations of test users will better match neighbouring users in their sub-graph, or in the case of disconnected nodes, will retain their initial classification estimate.

## 5 Results

Table 2 shows the performance of the three methods over the test set for the three datasets. The results are also compared with the state of the art for Twitter-US and Twitter-World (Wing and Baldridge, 2014), and GeoText (Ahmed et al., 2013).

Our methods achieve a sizeable improvement over the previous state of the art for all three datasets. LP−LR performs best over GeoText and Twitter-US, while LR performs best over Twitter-World; the reduction in median error distance over the state of the art ranges from around 40% to over 95%. Even for Twitter-World, the results for LP−LR are substantially better than the best-published results for that dataset.

Comparing LR and LP, no strong conclusion can be drawn — the text-based LP actually outperforms the network-based LR for two of the three datasets, but equally, the combination of the two (LP−LR) performs better than either component method over two of the three datasets. For the third (Twitter-World), LR outperforms LP−LR due to a combination of factors. First, unlike the other two datasets, the label set is pre-discretised (everything is aggregated at the city level), meaning that LP and LR use the same label set.[3] This annuls the representational advantage that LP has in the case of the other two datasets, in being able to capture a more fine-grained label set (i.e., all locations associated with training users). Second, there are substantially fewer disconnected test users in Twitter-World (see Table 1), meaning that the results for the hybrid LP−LR method are dominated by the empirically-inferior LP.

Although LR is similar to Wing and Baldridge (2014), we achieved large improvements over their reported results. This might be due to: (a) our use of @-mention features; (b) $l_1$ regularisation, which is essential to preventing overfitting for large feature sets; or (c) our use of $l_2$ normalisation of rows in the design matrix, which we found reduced errors by about 20% on GeoText, in keeping with results from text categorisation (Lee, 1995). Preliminary experiments also showed that lowering the term frequency threshold from 10 can further improve the LR results on all three datasets.

LP requires few hyper-parameters and is relatively robust. It converged on all datasets in fewer than 10 iterations, and geolocates not only the test users but all nodes in the mention graph. Another advantage of LP over LR is the relatively modest amount of memory and processing power it requires.

[3]For consistency, we learn a $k$-d tree for Twitter-World and use the merged representation for LR, but the $k$-d tree largely preserves the pre-existing city boundaries.

## 6 Conclusion

We proposed a series of approaches to social media user geolocation based on: (1) text-based analysis using logistic regression with regularisation; (2) network-based analysis using label propagation; and (3) a hybrid method based on network-based label propagation, and back-off to text-based analysis for disconnected users. We achieve state-of-the-art results over three pre-existing Twitter datasets, and find that, overall, the hybrid method is superior to the two component methods.The `LP-LR` method is a hybrid approach that uses the `LR` predictions as priors. It is not simply a backoff from network information to textual information in the sense that it propagates the `LR` geolocations through the network. That is, if a test node is disconnected from the training nodes but still has connections to other test nodes, the geolocation of the node is adjusted and propagated through the network. It is possible to add extra nodes to the graph after applying the algorithm and to geolocate only these nodes efficiently, although this approach is potentially less accurate than inferencing over the full graph from scratch.

Label propagation algorithms such as Modified Adsorption (Talukdar and Crammer, 2009) allow for different levels of influence between prior/known labels and propagated label distributions. These algorithms require a discretised output space for label propagation, while `LP` can work directly on continuous data. We leave label propagation over discritised output and allowing different influence levels between prior and propagated label distributions to future work.

There is no clear consensus on whether text- or network-based methods are empirically superior at the user geolocation task. Our results show that the network-based method (`LP`) is more robust than the text-based (`LR`) method as it requires a smaller number of hyper-parameters, uses less memory and computing resources, converges much faster and geolocates not only test users but all mentioned users. The drawback of `LP` is that it fails to geolocate disconnected test users. So for connected nodes – the majority of test nodes in all our datasets – `LP` is more robust than `LR`. Text-based methods are very sensitive to the regularisation settings and the types of textual features. That said, with thorough parameter tuning, they might outperform network-based method in terms of accuracy.

In future work, we hope to look at different types of network information for label propagation, more precise propagation methods to deal with non-local interactions, and also efficient ways of utilising both textual and network information in a joint model.


### Acknowledgements

We thank the anonymous reviewers for their insightful comments and valuable suggestions. This work was funded in part by the Australian Research Council.


## References


Amr Ahmed, Liangjie Hong, and Alexander J Smola. 2013. Hierarchical geographical modeling of user locations from social media posts. In *Proceedings of the 22nd International Conference on World Wide Web*, pages 25–36.

Einat Amitay, Nadav Har'El, Ron Sivan, and Aya Soffer. 2004. Web-a-where: geotagging web content. In *Proceedings of the 27th Annual International ACM SIGIR Conference on Research and Development in Information Retrieval*, pages 273–280.

Zhiyuan Cheng, James Caverlee, and Kyumin Lee. 2010. You are where you tweet: a content-based approach to geo-locating Twitter users. In *Proceedings of the 19th ACM International Conference on Information and Knowledge Management*, pages 759–768.

Paul Earle, Michelle Guy, Richard Buckmaster, Chris Ostrum, Scott Horvath, and Amy Vaughan. 2010. OMG earthquake! can Twitter improve earthquake response? *Seismological Research Letters*, 81(2):246–251.

Jacob Eisenstein, Brendan O'Connor, Noah A Smith, and Eric P Xing. 2010. A latent variable model for geographic lexical variation. In *Proceedings of the 2010 Conference on Empirical Methods in Natural Language Processing*, pages 1277–1287.

Bo Han, Timothy Baldwin, and Paul Cook. 2012. Geolocation prediction in social media data by finding location indicative words. *Proceedings of COLING 2012: Technical Papers*, pages 1045–1062.

Bo Han, Paul Cook, and Timothy Baldwin. 2014. Text-based Twitter user geolocation prediction. *Journal of Artificial Intelligence Research (JAIR)*, 49:451–500.

David Jurgens. 2013. That's what friends are for: Inferring location in online social media platforms based on social relationships. In *Proceedings of the 7th International Conference on Weblogs and Social Media (ICWSM 2013)*, pages 273–282.

Joon Ho Lee. 1995. Combining multiple evidence from different properties of weighting schemes. In *Proceedings of the 18th Annual International ACM SIGIR Conference on Research and Development in Information Retrieval*, pages 180–188.

Anastasios Noulas, Salvatore Scellato, Neal Lathia, and Cecilia Mascolo. 2012. A random walk around the city: New venue recommendation in location-based social networks. In *Privacy, Security, Risk and Trust (PASSAT), 2012 International Conference on and 2012 International Confernece on Social Computing (SocialCom)*, pages 144–153.

Stephen Roller, Michael Speriosu, Sarat Rallapalli, Benjamin Wing, and Jason Baldridge. 2012. Supervised text-based geolocation using language models on an adaptive grid. In *Proceedings of the 2012 Joint Conference on Empirical Methods in Natural Language Processing and Computational Natural Language Learning*, pages 1500–1510.

Dominic Rout, Kalina Bontcheva, Daniel Preoţiuc-Pietro, and Trevor Cohn. 2013. Where's @wally?: a classification approach to geolocating users based on their social ties. In *Proceedings of the 24th ACM Conference on Hypertext and Social Media*, pages 11–20.

Partha Pratim Talukdar and Koby Crammer. 2009. New regularized algorithms for transductive learning. In *Proceedings of the European Conference on Machine Learning (ECML-PKDD) 2009*, pages 442–457.

Robert Tibshirani. 1996. Regression shrinkage and selection via the lasso. *Journal of the Royal Statistical Society. Series B (Methodological)*, pages 267–288.

Benjamin P Wing and Jason Baldridge. 2014. Hierarchical discriminative classification for text-based geolocation. In *Proceedings of the 2014 Conference on Empirical Methods in Natural Language Processing (EMNLP 2014)*.

Xiaojin Zhu and Zoubin Ghahramani. 2002. Learning from labeled and unlabeled data with label propagation. Technical report, Technical Report CMU-CALD-02-107, Carnegie Mellon University.

# Discriminative Phrase Embedding for Paraphrase Identification

**Wenpeng Yin** and **Hinrich Schütze**
Center for Information and Language Processing
University of Munich, Germany
wenpeng@cis.lmu.de

## Abstract

This work, concerning paraphrase identification task, on one hand contributes to expanding deep learning embeddings to include continuous and discontinuous linguistic phrases. On the other hand, it comes up with a new scheme TF-KLD-KNN to learn the discriminative weights of words and phrases specific to paraphrase task, so that a weighted sum of embeddings can represent sentences more effectively. Based on these two innovations we get competitive state-of-the-art performance on paraphrase identification.

## 1 Introduction

This work investigates representation learning via deep learning in paraphrase identification task, which aims to determine whether two sentences have the same meaning. One main innovation of deep learning is that it learns distributed word representations (also called "word embeddings") to deal with various Natural Language Processing (NLP) tasks. Our goal is to use and refine embeddings to get competitive performance.

We adopt a supervised classification approach to paraphrase identification like most top performing systems. Our focus is representation learning of sentences. Following prior work (e.g., Blacoe and Lapata (2012)), we compute the vector of a sentence as the sum of the vectors of its components. But unlike prior work we use *single words, continuous phrases and discontinuous phrases* as the components, not just single words. Our rationale is that many semantic units are formed by multiple words – e.g., the continuous phrase "side effects" and the discontinuous phrase "pick … off". The better we can discover and represent such components, the better the compositional sentence vector should be. We use the term *unit* to refer to single words, continuous phrases and discontinuous phrases.

Ji and Eisenstein (2013) show that not all words are equally important for paraphrase identification. They propose TF-KLD, a discriminative weighting scheme to address this problem. While they do not represent sentences as vectors composed of other vectors, TF-KLD is promising for a vector-based approach as well since the insight that units are of different importance still applies. A shortcoming of TF-KLD is its failure to define weights for words that do not occur in the training set. We propose TF-KLD-KNN, an extension of TF-KLD that computes the weight of an unknown unit as the average of the weights of its $k$ nearest neighbors. We determine nearest neighbors by cosine measure over embedding space. We then represent a sentence as the sum of the vectors of its units, weighted by TF-KLD-KNN.

We use (Madnani et al., 2012) as our baseline system. They used simple features – eight different machine translation metrics – yet got good performance. Based on above new sentence representations, we compute three kinds of features to describe a pair of sentences – cosine similarity, element-wise sum and absolute element-wise difference – and show that combining them with the features from Madnani et al. (2012) gets state-of-the-art performance on the Microsoft Research Paraphrase (MSRP) corpus (Dolan et al., 2004).



*Human Language Technologies: The 2015 Annual Conference of the North American Chapter of the ACL*, pages 1368–1373,
Denver, Colorado, May 31 – June 5, 2015. 

In summary, our first contribution lies in embedding learning of continuous and discontinuous phrases. Our second contribution is the weighting scheme TF-KLD-KNN.

This paper is structured as follows. Section 2 reviews related work. Section 3 describes our method for learning embeddings of units. Section 4 introduces a measure of unit discriminativity that can be used for differential weighting of units. Section 5 presents experimental setup and results. Section 6 concludes.

## 2 Related work

The key for good performance in paraphrase identification is the design of good features. We now discuss relevant prior work based on the linguistic granularity of feature learning.

The first line is compositional semantics, which learns representations for words and then composes them to representations of sentences. Blacoe and Lapata (2012) carried out a comparative study of three word representation methods (the simple distributional semantic space (Mitchell and Lapata, 2010), distributional memory tensor (Baroni and Lenci, 2010) and word embedding (Collobert and Weston, 2008)), along with three composition methods (addition, point-wise multiplication, and recursive autoencoder (Socher et al., 2011)). They showed that addition over word embeddings is competitive, despite its simplicity.

The second category directly seeks sentence-level features. Ji and Eisenstein (2013) explored unigrams, bigrams and dependency pairs as sentence features. They proposed TF-KLD to weight features and used non-negative factorization to learn latent sentence representations. Our method TF-KLD-KNN is an extension of their work.

The third line directly computes features for sentence pairs. Wan et al. (2006) used N-gram overlap, dependency relation overlap, dependency tree-edit distance and difference of sentence lengths. Finch et al. (2005) and Madnani et al. (2012) combined several machine translation metrics. Das and Smith (2009) presented a generative model over two sentences' dependency trees, incorporating syntax, lexical semantics, and hidden loose alignments between the trees to model generating a paraphrase of a given sentence. Socher et al. (2011) used recursive autoencoders to learn representations for words and word sequences on each layer of the sentence parsing tree, and then proposed dynamic pooling layer to form a fixed-size matrix as the representation of the two sentences. Other work representative of this line is by Kozareva and Montoyo (2006), Qiu et al. (2006), Ul-Qayyum and Altaf (2012).

Our work, first learning unit embeddings, then adding them to form sentence representations, finally calculating pair features (cosine similarity, absolute difference and MT metrics) actually is a combination of above three lines.

## 3 Embedding learning for units

As explained in Section 1, "units" in this work include single words, continuous phrases and discontinuous phrases. Phrases have a larger linguistic granularity than words and thus will in general contain more meaning aspects for a sentence. For example, successful detection of continuous phrase "side effects" and discontinuous phrase "pick ··· off" is helpful to understand the sentence meaning correctly. This section focuses on how to detect phrases and how to represent them.

### 3.1 Phrase collection

Phrases defined by a lexicon have not been investigated extensively before in deep learning. To collect canonical phrase set, we extract two-word phrases defined in Wiktionary[1] and Wordnet (Miller and Fellbaum, 1998) to form a collection of size 95,218. This collection contains *continuous phrases* – phrases whose parts always occur next to each other (e.g., "side effects") – and *discontinuous phrases* – phrases whose parts more often occur separated from each other (e.g., "pick ... off").

### 3.2 Identification of phrase continuity

Wiktionary and WordNet do not categorize phrases as continuous or discontinuous. So we need a heuristic to determine this automatically.

For each phrase "A_B", we compute [$c_1$, $c_2$, $c_3$, $c_4$, $c_5$] where $c_i, 1 \leq i \leq 5$, indicates there are $c_i$ occurrences of A and B in that order with a distance

[1] http://en.wiktionary.org

of $i$. We compute these statistics for a corpus consisting of English Gigaword (Graff et al., 2003) and Wikipedia. We set the maximal distance to 5 because discontinuous phrases are rarely separated by more than 5 tokens.

If $c_1$ is 10 times higher than $(c_2+c_3+c_4+c_5)/4$, we classify "A_B" as *continuous*, otherwise as *discontinuous*. For example, $[c_1, \ldots, c_5]$ is [1121, 632, 337, 348, 4052] for "pick_off", so $c_1$ is smaller than the average 1342.25 and "pick_off" is set as "discontinuous"; $[c_1, \ldots, c_5]$ is [14831, 16, 177, 331, 3471] for "Cornell University", $c_1$ is 10 times larger than the average and this phrase is set to "continuous".

We found that that this heuristic for distinguishing between continuous and discontinuous phrases works well and leave the development of a more principled method for future work.

### 3.3 Sentence reformatting

Sentence "... A ... B ..." is

- reformatted as "... A_B ..." if A and B form a continuous phrase and no word intervenes between them and
- reformatted as "... A_B ... A_B ..." if A and B form a discontinuous phrase and are separated by 1 to 4 words. We replace each of the two component words with A_B to make the context of both constituents available to the phrase in learning.

This method of phrase detection will generate some false positives, e.g., if "pick" and "off" occur in a context like "she picked an island off the coast of Maine". However, our experimental results indicate that it is robust enough for our purposes.

We run word2vec (Mikolov et al., 2013) on the reformatted Wikipedia corpus to learn embeddings for all units. Embedding size is set to 200.

## 4 Measure of unit discriminativity

We will represent a sentence as the sum of the embeddings of its units. Building on Ji and Eisenstein (2013)'s TF-KLD, we want to weight units according to their ability to discriminate two sentences specific to the paraphrase task.

TF-KLD assumes a training set of sentence pairs in the form $\langle u_i, v_i, t_i\rangle$, where $u_i$ and $v_i$ denote the binary unit occurrence vectors for the sentences in the $i$th pair and $t_i \in \{0, 1\}$ is the gold tag. Then, we define $p_k$ and $q_k$ as follows.

- $p_k = P(u_{ik}|v_{ik} = 1, t_i = 1)$. This is the probability that unit $w_k$ occurs in sentence $u_i$ given that $w_k$ occurs in its counterpart $v_i$ and they are paraphrases.
- $q_k = P(u_{ik}|v_{ik} = 1, t_i = 0)$. This is the probability that unit $w_k$ occurs in sentence $u_i$ given that $w_k$ occurs in its counterpart $v_i$ and they are not paraphrases.

TF-KLD computes the discriminativity of unit $w_k$ as the Kullback-Leibler divergence of the Bernoulli distributions ($p_k$, 1-$p_k$) and ($q_k$, 1-$q_k$)

TF-KLD has a serious shortcoming for unknown units. Unfortunately, the test data of the commonly used MSPR corpus in paraphrase task has about 6% unknown words and 62.5% of its sentences contain unknown words. It motivates us to design an improved scheme TF-KLD-KNN to reweight the features.

TF-KLD-KNN weights are the same as TF-KLD weights for known units. For a unit that did not occur in training, TF-KLD-KNN computes its weight as the average of the weights of its $k$ nearest neighbors in embedding space, where unit similarity is calculated by cosine measure.[2]

Word2vec learns word embeddings based on the word context. The intuition of TF-KLD-KNN is that words with similar context have similar discriminativities. This enables us to transfer the weights of features in training data to the unknown features in test data, greatly helping to address problems of sparseness.

## 5 Experiments

### 5.1 Data and baselines

We use the MSRP corpus (Dolan et al., 2004) for evaluation. It consists of a training set of 2753 true paraphrase pairs and 1323 false paraphrase pairs and a test set of 1147 true and 578 false pairs.

[2]Unknown words without embeddings (only seven cases in our experiments) are ignored. This problem can be effectively relieved by training embedding on larger corpora.

For our new method, it is interesting to measure the improvement on the subset of those MSRP sentences that contain at least one phrase. In the standard MSRP corpus, 3027 training pairs (2123 true, 904 false) and 1273 test pairs (871 true, 402 false) contain phrases; we denote this subset as *subset*. We carry out experiments on *overall* (all MSRP sentences) as well as *subset* cases.

We compare six methods for paraphrase identification.

- **NOWEIGHT.** Following Blacoe and Lapata (2012), we simply represent a sentence as the unweighted sum of the embeddings of all its units.

- **MT** is the method proposed by Madnani et al. (2012): the sentence pair is represented as a vector of eight different machine translation metrics.

- **Ji and Eisenstein (2013)**. We reimplemented their "inductive" setup which is based on matrix factorization and is the top-performing system in paraphrasing task.[3]

  The following three methods not only use this vector of eight MT metrics, but use three kinds of additional features given two sentence representations $s_1$ and $s_2$: cosine similarity, element-wise sum $s_1 + s_2$ and element-wise absolute difference $|s_1 - s_2|$. We now describe how each of the three methods computes the sentence vectors.

- **WORD.** The sentence is represented as the sum of all single-word embeddings, weighted by TF-KLD-KNN.

- **WORD+PHRASE.** The sentence is represented as the sum of the embeddings of all its units (including phrases), weighted by TF-KLD-KNN.

- **WORD+GOOGLE.** Mikolov et al. (2013) use a data-driven method to detect statistical phrases which are mostly continuous bigrams. We implement their system by first exploiting word2phrase[4] to reformat Wikipedia, then using word2vec skip-gram model to train phrase embeddings.

We use the same weighting scheme TF-KLD-KNN for the three weighted sum approaches: WORD, WORD+PHRASE and WORD+GOOGLE. Note however that there is an interaction between representation space and nearest neighbor search. We limit the neighbor range of unknown words for WORD to single words; in contrast, we search the space of all single words and linguistic (resp. Google) phrases for WORD+PHRASE (resp. WORD+GOOGLE).

We use LIBLINEAR (Fan et al., 2008) as our linear SVM implementation. 20% training data is used as development data. Parameter $k$ is fine-tuned on development set and the best value 3 is finally used in following reported results.

### 5.2 Experimental results

Table 1 shows performance for the six methods as well as for the majority baseline. In the *overall* (resp. *subset*) setup, WORD+PHRASE performs best and outperforms (Ji and Eisenstein, 2013) by .009 (resp. .052) on accuracy. Interestingly, Ji and Eisenstein (2013)'s method obtains worse performance on *subset*. This can be explained by the effect of matrix factorization in their work: it works less well for smaller datasets like *subset*. This is a shortcoming of their approach. WORD+GOOGLE has a slightly worse performance than WORD+PHRASE; this suggests that linguistic phrases might be more effective than statistical phrases in identifying paraphrases.

Cases *overall* and *subset* both suggest that phrase embeddings improve sentence representations. The accuracy of WORD+PHRASE is lower on *overall* than on *subset* because WORD+PHRASE has no advantage over WORD for sentences without phrases.

### 5.3 Effectiveness of TF-KLD-KNN

The key contribution of TF-KLD-KNN is that it achieves full coverage of feature weights in the face of data sparseness. We now compare four weighting methods on overall corpus and with the combi-

[3]They report even better performance in a "transductive" setup that makes use of test data. We only address paraphrase identification for the case that the test data are not available for training the model in this paper.

[4]https://code.google.com/p/word2vec/

| method | overall acc | overall $F_1$ | subset acc | subset $F_1$ |
|---|---|---|---|---|
| baseline | .665 | .799 | .684 | .812 |
| NOWEIGHT | .708 | .809 | .713 | .823 |
| MT | .774 | .841 | .772 | .839 |
| Ji and Eisenstein (2013) | .778 | .843 | .749 | .827 |
| WORD | .775 | .839 | .776 | .843 |
| WORD+GOOGLE | .780 | .843 | .795 | .853 |
| WORD+PHRASE | **.787** | **.848*** | **.801** | **.857*** |

Table 1: Results on overall and subset corpus. Significant improvements over MT are marked with $*$ (approximate randomization test, Padó (2006), $p < .05$).

| method | acc | $F_1$ |
|---|---|---|
| NOWEIGHT | .746 | .815 |
| TF-IDF | .752 | .821 |
| TF-KLD | .774 | .842 |
| TF-KLD-KNN | **.787** | **.848** |

Table 2: Effects of different reweighting methods on overall.

nation of MT features: NOWEIGHT, TF-IDF, TF-KLD, TF-KLD

Table 2 suggests that task-specific reweighting approaches (including TF-KLD and TF-KLD-KNN) are superior to unspecific schemes (NOWEIGHT and TF-IDF). Also, it demonstrates the effectiveness of our weight learning solution for unknown units in paraphrase task.

### 5.4 Reweighting schemes for unseen units

We compare our reweighting scheme **KNN** (i.e., TF-KLD-KNN) with three other reweighting schemes. **Zero**: zero weight, i.e., ignore unseen units; **Type-average**: take the average of weights of all known unit types in test set; **Context-average**: average of the weights of the adjacent known units of the unknown unit (two, one or defaulting to Zero, depending on how many there are). Figure 1 shows that KNN performs best.

## 6 Conclusion

This work introduced TF-KLD-KNN, a new reweighting scheme that learns the discriminativities of known as well as unknown units effectively. We further improved paraphrase identification per-

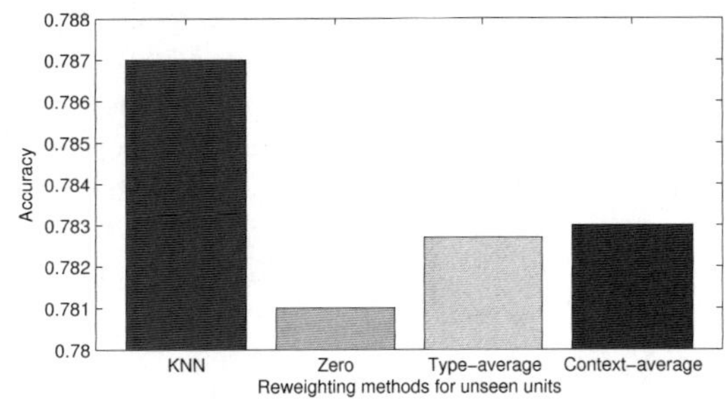


Figure 1: Performance of different reweighting schemes for unseen units on overall.

formance by the utilization of continuous and discontinuous phrase embeddings.

In future, we plan to do experiments in a cross-domain setup and enhance our algorithm for domain adaptation paraphrase identification.

## Acknowledgments

We are grateful to members of CIS for comments on earlier versions of this paper. This work was supported by Baidu (through a Baidu scholarship awarded to Wenpeng Yin) and by Deutsche Forschungsgemeinschaft (grant DFG SCHU 2246/8-2, SPP 1335).

## References

Marco Baroni and Alessandro Lenci. 2010. Distributional memory: A general framework for corpus-based semantics. *Computational Linguistics*, 36(4):673–721.

William Blacoe and Mirella Lapata. 2012. A comparison of vector-based representations for semantic composition. In *Proceedings of the 2012 Joint Conference on Empirical Methods in Natural Language Processing and Computational Natural Language Learning*, pages 546–556. Association for Computational Linguistics.

Ronan Collobert and Jason Weston. 2008. A unified architecture for natural language processing: Deep neural networks with multitask learning. In *Proceedings of the 25th international conference on Machine learning*, pages 160–167. ACM.

Dipanjan Das and Noah A Smith. 2009. Paraphrase identification as probabilistic quasi-synchronous recognition. In *Proceedings of the Joint Conference of the 47th Annual Meeting of the ACL and the 4th International Joint Conference on Natural Language Pro-*

*cessing of the AFNLP: Volume 1-Volume 1*, pages 468–476. Association for Computational Linguistics.

Bill Dolan, Chris Quirk, and Chris Brockett. 2004. Unsupervised construction of large paraphrase corpora: Exploiting massively parallel news sources. In *Proceedings of the 20th international conference on Computational Linguistics*, pages 350–356. Association for Computational Linguistics.

Rong-En Fan, Kai-Wei Chang, Cho-Jui Hsieh, Xiang-Rui Wang, and Chih-Jen Lin. 2008. Liblinear: A library for large linear classification. *The Journal of Machine Learning Research*, 9:1871–1874.

Andrew Finch, Young-Sook Hwang, and Eiichiro Sumita. 2005. Using machine translation evaluation techniques to determine sentence-level semantic equivalence. In *Proceedings of the Third International Workshop on Paraphrasing (IWP2005)*, pages 17–24.

David Graff, Junbo Kong, Ke Chen, and Kazuaki Maeda. 2003. English gigaword. *Linguistic Data Consortium, Philadelphia*.

Yangfeng Ji and Jacob Eisenstein. 2013. Discriminative improvements to distributional sentence similarity. In *Proceedings of the Conference on Empirical Methods in Natural Language Processing (EMNLP)*.

Zornitsa Kozareva and Andrés Montoyo. 2006. Paraphrase identification on the basis of supervised machine learning techniques. In *Advances in natural language processing*, pages 524–533. Springer.

Nitin Madnani, Joel Tetreault, and Martin Chodorow. 2012. Re-examining machine translation metrics for paraphrase identification. In *Proceedings of the 2012 Conference of the North American Chapter of the Association for Computational Linguistics: Human Language Technologies*, pages 182–190. Association for Computational Linguistics.

Tomas Mikolov, Ilya Sutskever, Kai Chen, Greg S Corrado, and Jeff Dean. 2013. Distributed representations of words and phrases and their compositionality. In *Advances in Neural Information Processing Systems*, pages 3111–3119.

George Miller and Christiane Fellbaum. 1998. Wordnet: An electronic lexical database.

Jeff Mitchell and Mirella Lapata. 2010. Composition in distributional models of semantics. *Cognitive science*, 34(8):1388–1429.

Sebastian Padó, 2006. *User's guide to* `sigf`*: Significance testing by approximate randomisation*.

Long Qiu, Min-Yen Kan, and Tat-Seng Chua. 2006. Paraphrase recognition via dissimilarity significance classification. In *Proceedings of the 2006 Conference on Empirical Methods in Natural Language Processing*, pages 18–26. Association for Computational Linguistics.

Richard Socher, Eric H Huang, Jeffrey Pennington, Andrew Y Ng, and Christopher D Manning. 2011. Dynamic pooling and unfolding recursive autoencoders for paraphrase detection. In *Advances in Neural Information Processing Systems*, volume 24, pages 801–809.

Zia Ul-Qayyum and Wasif Altaf. 2012. Paraphrase identification using semantic heuristic features. *Research Journal of Applied Sciences, Engineering and Technology*, 4(22):4894–4904.

Stephen Wan, Mark Dras, Robert Dale, and Cécile Paris. 2006. Using dependency-based features to take the para-farce out of paraphrase. In *Proceedings of the Australasian Language Technology Workshop*, volume 2006, pages 131–138.

# Combining Word Embeddings and Feature Embeddings for Fine-grained Relation Extraction

**Mo Yu** *
Machine Intelligence & Translation Lab
Harbin Institute of Technology
Harbin, China
gflfof@gmail.com

**Matthew R. Gormley, Mark Dredze**
Human Language Technology Center of Excellence
Center for Language and Speech Processing
Johns Hopkins University
Baltimore, MD, 21218
{mgormley, mdredze}@cs.jhu.edu

## Abstract

Compositional embedding models build a representation for a linguistic structure based on its component word embeddings. While recent work has combined these word embeddings with hand crafted features for improved performance, it was restricted to a small number of features due to model complexity, thus limiting its applicability. We propose a new model that conjoins features and word embeddings while maintaining a small number of parameters by learning feature embeddings jointly with the parameters of a compositional model. The result is a method that can scale to more features and more labels, while avoiding overfitting. We demonstrate that our model attains state-of-the-art results on ACE and ERE fine-grained relation extraction.

## 1 Introduction

Word embeddings represent words in some low-dimensional space, where each dimension might intuitively correspond to some syntactic or semantic property of the word.[1] These embeddings can be used to create novel features (Miller et al., 2004; Koo et al., 2008; Turian et al., 2010; Sun et al., 2011; Nguyen and Grishman, 2014; Roth and Woodsend, 2014), and can also be treated as model parameters to build representations for higher-level structures in some compositional embedding models (Collobert et al., 2011; Collobert, 2011; Socher et al., 2012; Socher et al., 2013b; Hermann et al., 2014). Applications of embedding have boosted the performance of many NLP tasks, including syntax (Turian et al., 2010; Collobert et al., 2011), semantics (Socher et al., 2012; Socher et al., 2013b; Hermann et al., 2014), question answering (Bordes et al., 2014) and machine translation (Devlin et al., 2014).

While compositional models aim to learn higher-level structure representations, composition of embeddings alone may not capture important syntactic or semantic patterns. Consider the task of relation extraction, where decisions require examining long-distance dependencies in a sentence. For the sentence in Figure 1, "*driving*" is a strong indicator of the "ART" (ACE) relation because it appears on the dependency path between a person and a vehicle. Yet such conjunctions of different syntactic/semantic annotations (dependency and NER) are typically not available in compositional models.

In contrast, hand-crafted features can easily capture this information, e.g. feature $f_{i3}$ (Figure 1). Therefore, engineered features should be combined with learned representations in compositional models. One approach is to use the features to select specific transformations for a sub-structure (Socher et al., 2013a; Hermann and Blunsom, 2013; Hermann et al., 2014; Roth and Woodsend, 2014), which can conjoin features and word embeddings, but is impractical as the numbers of transformations will exponentially increase with additional features. Typically, less than 10 features are used. A solution

* The work was done while the author was visiting JHU.

[1] Such embeddings have a long history in NLP, such as term co-occurrence frequency matrices and their low-dimensional counterparts obtained by linear algebra tools (LSA, PCA, CCA, NNMF) and word clusters. Recently, neural networks have become popular methods for obtaining such embeddings (Bengio et al., 2006; Collobert et al., 2011; Mikolov et al., 2013).



*Human Language Technologies: The 2015 Annual Conference of the North American Chapter of the ACL*, pages 1374–1379,
Denver, Colorado, May 31 – June 5, 2015. 

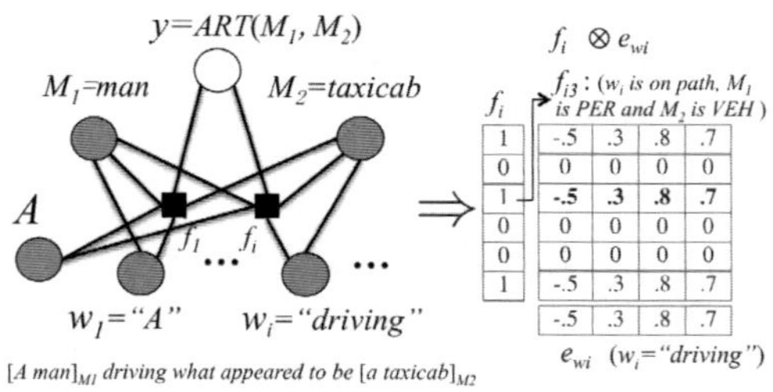


Figure 1: Example of input structure. Left: a sentence with target entities ($M_1, M_2$) and annotations $A$ (e.g. dependency tree). Right: outer product representation of a single word $w_i$ with an example of useful features $f_{i3}$.

is provided by the recent work of Yu et al. (2014), which reduces this complexity by using a tensor to transform the input feature vectors to a matrix transformation. The model is equivalent to treating the outer product between word embeddings and features as input to a parameter tensor, thus model parameters increase linearly with the number of features. Yet this model also uses too many parameters when a large number of features (e.g. over 1000) are used. This limits the applicability of their method to settings where there are a large number of training examples. For smaller training sets, the variance of their estimator will be high resulting in increased generalization error on test data. We seek to use many more features (based on rich annotations such as syntactic parsing and NER) and larger label sets, which further exacerbates the problem of overfitting.

We propose a new method of learning interactions between engineered features and word embeddings by combining the idea of the outer product in FCM (Yu et al., 2014) with learning feature embeddings (Collobert et al., 2011; Chen and Manning, 2014).[2] Our model jointly learns feature embeddings and a tensor-based classifier which relies on the outer product between features embeddings and word embeddings. Therefore, the number of parameters are dramatically reduced since features are only represented as low-dimensional embeddings, which alleviates problems with overfitting. The resulting model benefits from both approaches: conjunctions between feature and word embeddings allow model expressiveness, while keeping the number of parameters small. This is especially beneficial when considering tasks with many labels, such as fine-grained relation extraction. We demonstrate these advantages on two relation extraction tasks: the well studied ACE 2005 dataset and the new ERE relation extraction task. We consider both coarse and fine-grained relations, the latter of which has been largely unexplored in previous work.

## 2 Factor-based Compositional Embedding Models (FCM)

We begin by briefly summarizing the FCM model proposed by Yu et al. (2014) in the context of relation extraction. In relation extraction, for a pair of mentions in a given sentence, the task is to determine the type of relation that holds between the two entities, if any. For each pair of mentions in a sentence, we have a training instance $(\mathbf{x}, y)$; $\mathbf{x}$ is an annotated sentence, including target entity mentions $M_1$ and $M_2$, and a dependency parse. We consider directed relations: for relation type $Rel$, $y = Rel(M_1, M_2)$ and $y' = Rel(M_2, M_1)$ are different.

FCM has a log-linear form, which defines a particular utilization of the features and embeddings. FCM decomposes the structure of $\mathbf{x}$ into single words. For each word $w_i$, a binary feature vector $\mathbf{f_i}$ is defined, which considers the $i$th word and any other substructure of the annotated sentence $\mathbf{x}$. We denote the dense word embedding by $e_{w_i}$ and the label-specific model parameters by matrix $T_y$, e.g. in Figure 1, the gold label corresponds to matrix $T_y$ where $y$=*ART*$(M_1, M_2)$. FCM is then given by:

$$P(y|\mathbf{x}; T) \propto \exp(\textstyle\sum_i T_y \odot (\mathbf{f_i} \otimes e_{w_i})) \quad (1)$$

where $\otimes$ is the outer-product of the two vectors and $\odot$ is the 'matrix dot product' or Frobenious inner product of the two matrices. Here the model parameters form a tensor $T = [T_1 : ... : T_{|L|}]$, which transforms the input matrix to the labels.

The key idea in FCM is that it gives similar words (i.e. those with similar embeddings) with similar functions in the sentence (i.e. those with similar features) similar matrix representations. Thus, this model generalizes its model parameters across words with similar embeddings only when they share similar functions in the sentence. For the

[2] Collobert et al. (2011) and Chen and Manning (2014) also capture interactions between word embeddings and features by using deep convolutional networks with max-pooling or cube activate function, but they cannot directly express conjunctions of word embeddings and features.

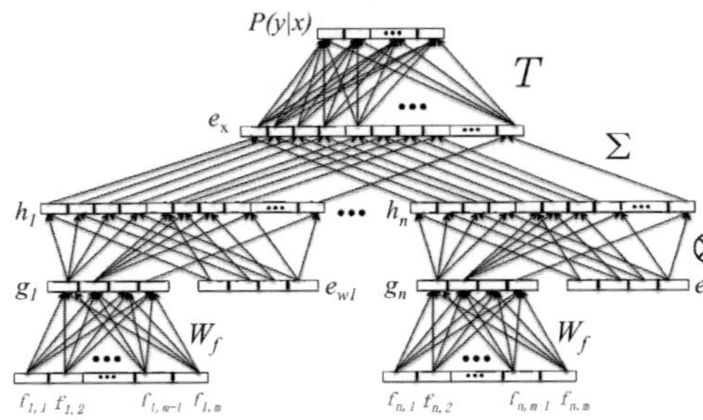

Figure 2: Neural network representation of LRFCM.

example in Figure 1, FCM can learn parameters which give words similar to "driving" with the feature $f_3 = 1$ (is-on-dependency-path $\wedge$ type($M_1$)=PER $\wedge$ type($M_2$)=VEH ) high weight for the *ART* label.

## 3 Low-Rank Approximation of FCM

FCM achieved state of the art performance on SemEval relation extraction (Yu et al., 2014), yet its generalization ability is limited by the size of the tensor $T$, which cannot easily scale to large number of features. We propose to replace features with feature embeddings (Chen and Manning, 2014), thereby reducing the dimensionality of the feature space, allowing for more generalization in learning the tensor. This will be especially beneficial with an increased number of output labels (i.e. more relation types), as this increases the number of parameters.

Our task is to determine the label $y$ (relation) given the instance $\mathbf{x}$. For each word $w_i \in \mathbf{x}$, there exists a list of $m$ associated features $\mathbf{f}_i = f_{i,1}, f_{i,2}, ..., f_{i,m}$. The model then transforms the feature vector into a $d_g$-dimensional ($d_g \ll m$) vector with a matrix (i.e. a lookup table) $\mathbf{W_f}$ as: $\mathbf{g}_i = \mathbf{f_i} \cdot \mathbf{W_f}$. Here we use a linear transformation for computational efficiency. We score label $y$ given $\mathbf{x}$ as (replacing Eq. 1):

$$P(y|\mathbf{x}; T, \mathbf{W_f}) \propto \exp(\textstyle\sum_i T_y \odot (\mathbf{g_i} \otimes e_{w_i})) \quad (2)$$

We call this model low-rank FCM (LRFCM). The result is a dramatic reduction in the number of model parameters, from $O(md|L|)$ to $O(d_g d|L| + d_g m)$, where $d$ is the size of the word embeddings. This reduction is intended to reduce the variance of our estimator, possibly at the expense of higher bias. Consider the case of 32 labels (fine-grained relations in §4), 3,000 features, and 200 dimensional word embeddings. For FCM, the size of $T$ is $1.92 \times 10^7$; potentially yielding a high variance estimator. However, for LRFCM with 20-dimensional feature embeddings, the size of $T$ is $1.28 \times 10^5$, significantly smaller with lower variance. Moreover, feature embeddings can capture correlations among features, further increasing generalization.

Figure 2 shows the *vectorized* form of LRFCM as a multi-layer perceptron. LRFCM constructs a dense low-dimensional matrix used as the input to Eq. 2. By contrast, FCM does not have a feature embedding layer and both feature vector $f$ and word embedding $e_w$ are feed forward directly to the outer product layer.

**Training** We optimize the following log-likelihood (of the probability in Eq. 2) objective with AdaGrad (Duchi et al., 2011) and compute gradients via back-propagation:

$$\mathcal{L}(T, \mathbf{W_f}) = \tfrac{1}{|D|} \textstyle\sum_{(y,\mathbf{x}) \in D} \log P(y|\mathbf{x}; T, \mathbf{W_f}), \quad (3)$$

where $D$ is the training set. For each instance $(y, \mathbf{x})$ we compute the gradient of the log-likelihood $\ell = \log P(y|\mathbf{x}; T, \mathbf{W_f})$. We define the vector $\mathbf{s} = [\sum_i T_y \odot (\mathbf{g_i} \otimes e_{w_i})]_{1 \le y \le L}$, which yields $\partial\ell/\partial\mathbf{s} = \left[(I[y = y'] - P(y'|\mathbf{x}; T, \mathbf{W_f}))_{1 \le y' \le L}\right]^T$, where $I[x]$ is the indicator function equal to 1 if $x$ is true and 0 otherwise. Then we have the following stochastic gradients, where $\circ$ is the tensor product:

$$\frac{\partial\ell}{\partial T} = \frac{\partial\ell}{\partial\mathbf{s}} \otimes \sum_{i=1}^{n} \mathbf{g}_i \otimes \mathbf{e}_{w_i}, \quad (4)$$

$$\frac{\partial\ell}{\partial\mathbf{W}_f} = \sum_{i=1}^{n} \frac{\partial\ell}{\partial\mathbf{g}_i}\frac{\partial\mathbf{g}_i}{\partial\mathbf{W}_f} = \sum_{i=1}^{n} \left(T \circ \frac{\partial\ell}{\partial\mathbf{s}} \circ \mathbf{e}_{w_i}\right) \otimes \mathbf{f_i}.$$

## 4 Experiments

**Datasets** We consider two relation extraction datasets: ACE2005 and ERE, both of which contain two sets of relations: coarse relation types and fine relation (sub-)types. Prior work on English ACE 2005 has focused only on coarse relations (Plank and Moschitti, 2013; Nguyen and Grishman, 2014; Li and Ji, 2014); to the best of our knowledge, this paper establishes the first baselines for the other datasets. Since the fine-grained relations require a large number of parameters, they will test the ability

| Model | ACE-bc (\|L\|=11) | | | ACE-bc (\|L\|=32) | | | ERE (\|L\|=9) | | | ERE (\|L\|=18) | | |
|---|---|---|---|---|---|---|---|---|---|---|---|---|
| | **P** | **R** | **F1** | **P** | **R** | **F1** | **P** | **R** | **F1** | **P** | **R** | **F1** |
| PM'13 (S) | 55.3 | 43.1 | 48.5 | - | - | - | - | - | - | - | - | - |
| FCM (S) | **62.3** | 45.1 | **52.3** | **59.7** | 41.6 | 49.0 | **68.3** | 52.6 | 59.4 | **67.1** | 51.5 | 58.2 |
| LRFCM(S) | 58.5 | **46.8** | 52.0 | 57.4 | **46.2** | **51.2** | 65.1 | **56.1** | **60.3** | 65.4 | **55.3** | **59.9** |
| BASELINE (ST) | **72.2** | 52.0 | **60.5** | 60.2 | **51.2** | 55.3 | **76.2** | 64.0 | 69.5 | 73.5 | 62.1 | 67.3 |
| FCM (ST) | 66.2 | 54.2 | 59.6 | 62.9 | 49.6 | 55.4 | 73.0 | 65.4 | 69.0 | **74.0** | 60.1 | 66.3 |
| LRFCM (ST) | 65.1 | **54.7** | 59.4 | **63.5** | 51.1 | **56.6** | 75.0 | **65.7** | **70.0** | 73.2 | **63.2** | **67.8** |

Table 1: Results on test for ACE and ERE where only the entity spans (S) are known (top) and where both the entity spans and types are known (ST). PM'13 is an embedding method. The sizes of relation sets are indicated by $|L|$.

of LRFCM to scale and generalize. As is standard, we report precision, recall, and F1 for all tasks.

**ACE 2005** We use the English portion of the ACE 2005 corpus (Walker et al., 2006). Following Plank and Moschitti (2013), we train on the union of the news domains (Newswire and Broadcast News), hold out half of the Broadcast Conversation (`bc`) domain as development data, and evaluate on the remainder of `bc`. There are 11 coarse types and 32 fine (sub-)type classes in total. In order to compare with traditional feature-based methods (Sun et al., 2011), we report results in which the gold entity spans *and* types are available at both train and test time. We train the models with all pairs of entity mentions in the training set to yield 43,518 classification instances. Furthermore, for comparison with prior work on embeddings for relation extraction (Plank and Moschitti, 2013), we report results using gold entity spans but no types, and generate negative relation instances from all pairs of entities within each sentence with three or fewer intervening entities.

**ERE** We use the third release of the ERE annotations from Phase 1 of DEFT (LDC, 2013) . We divided the proxy reports summarizing news articles (`pr`) into training (56,889 relations), development (6,804 relations) and test data (6,911 relations). We run experiments under both the settings with and without gold entity types, while generating negative relation instances just as in ACE with the gold entity types setting. To the best of our knowledge, we are the first to report results on this task.

Following the annotation guidelines of ERE relations, we treat all relations, except for "social.business", "social.family" and "social.unspecified", as asymmetric relations. For coarse relation task, we treat all relations as asymmetric, including the "social" relation. The reason is that the asymmetric subtype, "social.role", dominates the class: 679 of 834 total "social" relations.

**Setup** We randomly initialize the feature embeddings $W_f$ and pre-train 200-dimensional word embeddings on the NYT portion of Gigaword 5.0 (Parker et al., 2011) with word2vec (default setting of the toolkit) (Mikolov et al., 2013). Dependency parses are obtained from the Stanford Parser (De Marneffe et al., 2006). We use the same feature templates as Yu et al. (2014). When gold entity types are unavailable, we replace them with WordNet tags annotated by Ciaramita and Altun (2006). Learning rates, weights of L2-regularizations, the number of iterations and the size of the feature embeddings $d$ are tuned on dev sets. We selected $d$ from $\{12, 15, 20, 25, 30, 40\}$. We used $d$=30 for feature embeddings for fine-grained ACE without gold types, and $d$=20 otherwise. For ERE, we have $d$=15. The weights of L2 $\lambda$ was selected from {1e-3, 5e-4, 1e-4}. As in prior work (Yu et al., 2014), regularization did not significantly help FCM. However for LRFCM, $\lambda$=1e-4 slightly helps. We use a learning rate of 0.05.

We compare to two baselines. First, we use the features of Sun et al. (2011), who build on Zhou et al. (2005) with additional highly tuned features for ACE-style relation extraction from years of research. We implement these in a logistic regression model BASELINE, excluding country gazetteer and WordNet features. This baseline includes gold entity types and represents a high quality feature rich model. Second, we include results from Plank and Moschitti (2013) (PM'13), who obtained improve-

| ERE (\|L\|=18) | | LRFCM Correct | LRFCM Incorrect |
|---|---|---|---|
| FCM | Correct | 423 | 34 |
| | Incorrect | 57 | 246 |

Table 2: Confusion Matrix between the results of FCM and LRFCM on the test set of ERE fine relation task. Each item in the table shows the number of relations on which the two models make correct/incorrect predictions.

ments for coarse ACE relations with word embeddings (Brown clusters and LSA) without gold entity types. To demonstrate improvements of the low rank approximation of LRFCM, we compare to FCM [3].

**Results** Both FCM and LRFCM outperform Plank and Moschitti (2013) (no gold entities setting) (Table 1). With gold entity types, the feature-rich baseline beats both composition models for ACE coarse types. However, as we consider more labels, LRFCM improves over this baseline, as well as for ERE coarse types. Furthermore, LRFCM outperforms FCM on all tasks, save ACE coarse types, both with and without gold entity types. The fine-grained settings demonstrate that our model can better generalize by using relatively fewer parameters. Additionally, the gap between train and test F1 makes this clear. For coarse relations, FCM's train to test F1 gap was 35.2, compared to LRFCM with 25.4. On fine relations, the number increases to 40.2 for FCM but only 31.2 for LRFCM. In both cases, LRFCM does not display the same degree of overfitting.

**Analysis** To highlight differences in the results we provide the confusion matrix of the two models on ERE fine relations. Table 2 shows that the two models are complementary to each other to a certain degree. It indicates that the combination of FCM and LRFCM may further boost the performance. We leave the combination of FCM and LRFCM, as well as their combination with the baseline method, to future work.

## 5 Conclusion

Our LRFCM learns conjunctions between features and word embeddings and scales to many features and labels, achieving improved results for relation extraction tasks on both ACE 2005 and ERE.

To the best of our knowledge, we are the first to report relation extraction results on ERE. To make it easier to compare to our results on these tasks, we make the data splits used in this paper and our implementation available for general use[4].

**Acknowledgements** Mo Yu is supported by China Scholarship Council and by NSFC 61173073.

## References

Yoshua Bengio, Holger Schwenk, Jean-Sébastien Senécal, Fréderic Morin, and Jean-Luc Gauvain. 2006. Neural probabilistic language models. In *Innovations in Machine Learning*, pages 137–186. Springer.

Antoine Bordes, Sumit Chopra, and Jason Weston. 2014. Question answering with subgraph embeddings. *arXiv preprint arXiv:1406.3676*.

Danqi Chen and Christopher Manning. 2014. A fast and accurate dependency parser using neural networks. In *Proceedings of the 2014 Conference on Empirical Methods in Natural Language Processing (EMNLP)*, pages 740–750, Doha, Qatar, October. Association for Computational Linguistics.

Massimiliano Ciaramita and Yasemin Altun. 2006. Broad-coverage sense disambiguation and information extraction with a supersense sequence tagger. In *EMNLP2006*, pages 594–602, July.

Ronan Collobert, Jason Weston, Léon Bottou, Michael Karlen, Koray Kavukcuoglu, and Pavel Kuksa. 2011. Natural language processing (almost) from scratch. *JMLR*, 12:2493–2537.

Ronan Collobert. 2011. Deep learning for efficient discriminative parsing. In *International Conference on Artificial Intelligence and Statistics*.

Marie-Catherine De Marneffe, Bill MacCartney, Christopher D Manning, et al. 2006. Generating typed dependency parses from phrase structure parses. In *Proceedings of LREC*, volume 6, pages 449–454.

Jacob Devlin, Rabih Zbib, Zhongqiang Huang, Thomas Lamar, Richard Schwartz, and John Makhoul. 2014. Fast and robust neural network joint models for statistical machine translation. In *Proceedings of the 52nd Annual Meeting of the Association for Computational Linguistics (Volume 1: Long Papers)*, pages 1370–1380, Baltimore, Maryland, June. Association for Computational Linguistics.

[3]We used their implementation: https://github.com/Gorov/FCM_nips_workshop/

[4]https://github.com/Gorov/ERE_RE

John Duchi, Elad Hazan, and Yoram Singer. 2011. Adaptive subgradient methods for online learning and stochastic optimization. *The Journal of Machine Learning Research*, 12:2121–2159.

Karl Moritz Hermann and Phil Blunsom. 2013. The role of syntax in vector space models of compositional semantics. In *Association for Computational Linguistics*, pages 894–904.

Karl Moritz Hermann, Dipanjan Das, Jason Weston, and Kuzman Ganchev. 2014. Semantic frame identification with distributed word representations. In *Proceedings of ACL*. Association for Computational Linguistics, June.

Terry Koo, Xavier Carreras, and Michael Collins. 2008. Simple semi-supervised dependency parsing. In *Proceedings of ACL-08: HLT*, pages 595–603, Columbus, Ohio, June. Association for Computational Linguistics.

Linguistic Data Consortium (LDC). 2013. DEFT ERE Annotation Guidelines: Relations V1.1.

Qi Li and Heng Ji. 2014. Incremental Joint Extraction of Entity Mentions and Relations. In *Proceedings of the 52nd Annual Meeting of the Association for Computational Linguistics (Volume 1: Long Papers)*, pages 402–412, Baltimore, Maryland, June. Association for Computational Linguistics.

Tomas Mikolov, Ilya Sutskever, Kai Chen, Greg Corrado, and Jeffrey Dean. 2013. Distributed representations of words and phrases and their compositionality. *arXiv preprint arXiv:1310.4546*.

Scott Miller, Jethran Guinness, and Alex Zamanian. 2004. Name tagging with word clusters and discriminative training. In Susan Dumais, Daniel Marcu, and Salim Roukos, editors, *HLT-NAACL 2004: Main Proceedings*. Association for Computational Linguistics.

Thien Huu Nguyen and Ralph Grishman. 2014. Employing word representations and regularization for domain adaptation of relation extraction. In *Proceedings of the 52nd Annual Meeting of the Association for Computational Linguistics (Volume 2: Short Papers)*, pages 68–74, Baltimore, Maryland, June. Association for Computational Linguistics.

Robert Parker, David Graff, Junbo Kong, Ke Chen, and Kazuaki Maeda. 2011. English gigaword fifth edition, june. *Linguistic Data Consortium, LDC2011T07*.

Barbara Plank and Alessandro Moschitti. 2013. Embedding semantic similarity in tree kernels for domain adaptation of relation extraction. In *Proceedings of the 51st Annual Meeting of the Association for Computational Linguistics (Volume 1: Long Papers)*, pages 1498–1507, Sofia, Bulgaria, August. Association for Computational Linguistics.

Michael Roth and Kristian Woodsend. 2014. Composition of word representations improves semantic role labelling. In *EMNLP*.

Richard Socher, Brody Huval, Christopher D. Manning, and Andrew Y. Ng. 2012. Semantic compositionality through recursive matrix-vector spaces. In *Proceedings of the 2012 Joint Conference on Empirical Methods in Natural Language Processing and Computational Natural Language Learning*, pages 1201–1211, Jeju Island, Korea, July. Association for Computational Linguistics.

Richard Socher, John Bauer, Christopher D Manning, and Andrew Y Ng. 2013a. Parsing with compositional vector grammars. In *In Proceedings of the ACL conference*. Citeseer.

Richard Socher, Alex Perelygin, Jean Wu, Jason Chuang, Christopher D. Manning, Andrew Ng, and Christopher Potts. 2013b. Recursive deep models for semantic compositionality over a sentiment treebank. In *Empirical Methods in Natural Language Processing*, pages 1631–1642.

Ang Sun, Ralph Grishman, and Satoshi Sekine. 2011. Semi-supervised relation extraction with large-scale word clustering. In *Proceedings of the 49th Annual Meeting of the Association for Computational Linguistics: Human Language Technologies*, pages 521–529, Portland, Oregon, USA, June. Association for Computational Linguistics.

Joseph Turian, Lev Ratinov, and Yoshua Bengio. 2010. Word representations: a simple and general method for semi-supervised learning. In *Association for Computational Linguistics*, pages 384–394.

Christopher Walker, Stephanie Strassel, Julie Medero, and Kazuaki Maeda. 2006. ACE 2005 multilingual training corpus. *Linguistic Data Consortium, Philadelphia*.

Mo Yu, Matthew Gormley, and Mark Dredze. 2014. Factor-based compositional embedding models. In *NIPS Workshop on Learning Semantics*.

GuoDong Zhou, Jian Su, Jie Zhang, and Min Zhang. 2005. Exploring various knowledge in relation extraction. pages 427–434.

# CASSA: A Context-Aware Synonym Simplification Algorithm

**Ricardo Baeza-Yates**
Yahoo Labs &
Web Research Group
Universitat Pompeu Fabra,
Barcelona, Spain
rbaeza@acm.org

**Luz Rello**
Human-Computer Interaction Institute
Carnegie Mellon University
Pittsburgh, PA, USA
luzrello@acm.org

**Julia Dembowski**
Department of
Computational Linguistics
Saarland University, Germany
juliad@coli.uni-saarland.de

## Abstract

We present a new context-aware method for lexical simplification that uses two free language resources and real web frequencies. We compare it with the state-of-the-art method for lexical simplification in Spanish and the established simplification baseline, that is, the most frequent synonym. Our method improves upon the other methods in the detection of complex words, in meaning preservation, and in simplicity. Although we use Spanish, the method can be extended to other languages since it does not require alignment of parallel corpora.

## 1 Introduction

Simplified text is crucial for some populations to read effectively, especially for cognitively impaired people such as people with autism spectrum disorder (Evans et al., 2014; Orasan et al., 2013), aphasia (Carroll et al., 1999), dyslexia (Rello et al., 2013a), Down syndrome (Saggion et al., 2015; Saggion et al., 2011), or other intellectual disabilities (Huenerfauth et al., 2009).

In fact, the United Nations (1994) proposed a set of standard rules to leverage document accessibility for persons with disabilities. Text simplification attempts to solve this problem automatically by reducing the complexity of the lexicon, syntax, or semantics while attempting to preserve its meaning and information content (Siddharthan, 2006). Among all the types of text simplification this paper focuses on lexical simplification.

Lexical simplification methods require language resources, such as simplified corpora or synonyms dictionaries. For languages with less resources than English, *e.g.* no Simple Wikipedia (Biran et al., 2011; Yatskar et al., 2010) or less representation in WordNet, such as Spanish,[1] the creation of lexical simplification methods is more challenging.

Our approach makes use of two free resources, Google Books Ngram Corpus and the Spanish OpenThesaurus, as well as real web frequencies to create a lexical simplification system. Our system improves upon the state of the art for lexical simplification in Spanish and the established simplification baseline, *i.e.*, the most frequent synonym, in several aspects: complex word detection, meaning preservation, and simplicity. We also show the coverage of our technique in a collection of books in Spanish, as this is another relevant measure of a simplification algorithm. The method is language independent and given that these resources are available in other languages, it could be easily extended to other languages with similar language resources.

The rest of the paper is organized as follows. The next section presents related work. Then in Section 3 we present the simplification algorithm while in Sections 4 and 5 we present our experimental evaluation. Finally, in Section 6 we discuss our results, extensions to other languages, and outline future work.

[1]The Spanish part of EuroWordNet contains only 50,526 word meanings and 23,370 synsets, in comparison to 187,602 meanings and 94,515 synsets in the English WordNet 1.5. (Vossen, 2004).



*Human Language Technologies: The 2015 Annual Conference of the North American Chapter of the ACL*, pages 1380–1385,
Denver, Colorado, May 31 – June 5, 2015. 

## 2 Related Work

*Lexical simplification* is a kind of text simplification that aims at the word level. It can be performed through the substitution of words by simpler synonyms, by adding a definition, or by showing simpler synonyms. Most of the approaches aim at the substitution of complex words.

To find appropriate synonyms, many approaches use WordNet (Burstein et al., 2007; Carroll et al., 1999; Lal and Ruger, 2002). De Belder *et al.* (2010) apply explicit word sense disambiguation with a latent words language model. Devlin and Unthank (2006) use dictionaries. Aluisio and Gasperin (2010) use a thesaurus and lexical ontologies.

More recently, Biran *et al.* (2011) and Yatskar *et al.* (2010) used Simple English Wikipedia, in combination with the standard English Wikipedia for their lexical simplification algorithms using machine learning.

There are also machine translation based approaches (Coster and Kauchak, 2011; Specia, 2010) as well as hybrid approaches (Narayan and Gardent, 2014; Siddharthan and Angrosh, 2014) that are also able to handle lexical simplification, since the translation model maps words from the non-simplified language to words of the simplified language.

The closest algorithm to ours is LexSiS (Bott et al., 2012; Saggion et al., 2013), that uses the Spanish OpenThesaurus and a corpus that contains 6,595 words of original and 3,912 words of manually simplified news articles. To the best of our knowledge this is the first and only lexical simplification algorithm for Spanish. Hence, we use it here as the state-of-the-art in our evaluation.

To the best of our knowledge, our approach is novel in using the Google Books Ngram corpus for the word context, Open Thesaurus for the synonyms, and real web frequencies for disambiguating synonym candidates. However, Google Ngram have been previously used to find synonyms, for instance to expand user queries by including synonyms (Baker and Lamping, 2011).

## 3 Method

CASSA (Context-Aware Synonym Simplification Algorithm) is a method that generates simpler synonyms of a word. It takes into consideration the context and the web frequency of the complex word for disambiguation.

### 3.1 Resources

Our method uses the following two resources:

- **Spanish OpenThesaurus** (version 2): The thesaurus is freely available[2] to be used with OpenOffice.org. This thesaurus provides 21,378 target words (lemmas) with a total of 44,348 different word senses for them. The following is a part of the thesaurus entry for *farol*, which is ambiguous, as it could mean *'lie'*, *'lamp'*, or the adjective *'flashy'*, among others.

  `farol`
  - `embuste|mentira` *('lie')*
  - `luz|lámpara|fuego|bombilla` *('lamp')*
  - `ostentoso|jactancioso|farolero` *('flashy')*

- **Google Books Ngram Corpus for Spanish** (2012 edition): The corpus consists of n-grams and their usage frequency over time,[3] and is derived from 8,116,746 books, over 6% of all books ever published. The corpus has 854,649 volumes and 83,967,471,303 tokens (Lin et al., 2012).

### 3.2 Algorithm Description

First, we modified and enriched the Spanish OpenThesaurus and created our List of Senses. Instead of having a target word with different senses, we included the target word in each sense, and we kept a list of unique senses, including for each word its frequency in the Web using a large search engine index. The Spanish OpenThesaurus contains single-word and multi-word expressions. We only treated single-word units, which represent 98% of the cases, leaving out only 399 multi-word expressions, such as *de esta forma ('in this manner')*.

We lemmatized the words because the frequencies were all for inflected word forms as they appear in the Web while we were interested in the lemma frequencies for the synonyms, adding all the

[2] `http://openthes-es.berlios.de`
[3] `http://books.google.com/ngrams`

frequencies for each lemma. We take into account the frequency of the words, because previous studies have shown that less frequent words were found to be more challenging for people with and without the most frequent reading disorder, that is, dyslexia (Rello et al., 2013b).

Second, we use the 5-grams in the Google Books Ngram Corpus, where we use the third token of each 5-gram as our target words. The other tokens are the context of the target word. A context is considered valid if all words, including the target word, consist only of lowercase alphabetic characters, to filter for proper names, and is not a stop word, using a standard list of stop words in Spanish.

The lemmatized token is included in the list of target words only if it appears in our List of Senses. The remaining four tokens are the context, kept in a context list. We count the frequency of the target word appearing with that context in the corpus, as well as the frequency of the same context appearing with different target words. See two possible contexts for *noche* and *fortuna* in the examples below:

`era una` *noche* `oscura de` *('it was a dark night of')*
`de probar` *fortuna* `en el` *('to try fortune in the')*

Third, we define the complexity of a word using the relative frequency of the synonyms within the same sense in the List of Senses.

That is, our definition is tailored to web text. For this we use a parameter $k$ such that if a word is $k$ or more times less frequent than one or more of its synonyms, is considered a complex word. We used $k = 10$ as the default threshold to get that 27% of the words have simpler synonyms. We later show how this percentage changes with smaller $k$.

Finally, for each complex word and the contexts it appears in, we select as simpler synonym the most frequent synonym of the sense that appears most frequently for the n-gram corresponding to that $(word, context)$ pair. That is, to disambiguate the sense, our method uses the context where the target word appears. If the context is not found, we use the most frequent sense (baseline below).

# 4 Quality Evaluation

## 4.1 Comparison Points

**Baseline:** replaces a word with its most frequent synonym (presumed to be the simplest). This baseline has been broadly used in previous lexical simplification studies (Burstein et al., 2007; Carroll et al., 1999; Devlin and Unthank, 2006; Lal and Ruger, 2002), with the exception of (Bott et al., 2012) that used word frequency and length. It is very hard to beat this baseline for simpler synonyms generation. For instance, in SemEval task for English lexical simplification (Specia et al., 2012), only one system out of nine outperformed the frequency baseline. For the complexity part we use the same as our new method. That is, both algorithms consider the same words as complex.

| | |
|---|---|
| Original | Él **contemplaba** en silencio aquella cruz. |
| | *He was contemplating in silence that cross.* |
| Baseline | Él **veía** en silencio aquella cruz. |
| | *He was seeing in silence that cross.* |
| LexSis | Él **consideraba** en silencio aquella cruz. |
| | *He was considering in silence that cross.* |
| CASSA | Él **miraba** en silencio aquella cruz. |
| | *He was looking in silence that cross.* |

Figure 1: Example of substitutions performed by the three algorithms.

**LexSiS:** replaces a word with the output of the state-of-the-art method for Spanish lexical simplification (Bott et al., 2012).

## 4.2 Frequency Bands

We divided the selected complex words methods into two groups: [LOW], that includes very low frequency complex words, and [HIGH], that contains high frequency complex words. The word frequency ranges from 40 to 2,000 occurrences in Google Books Ngram Corpus for the [LOW] group, and from 2,001 to 1,300,000 for the [HIGH] group.

## 4.3 Evaluation Datasets

**Main dataset:** From a set of texts of scientific and literature genres (37,876 words), we randomly selected 20 [LOW] and 20 [HIGH] complex words within the sentence they appear, together with their corresponding candidate for substitution generated by the Baseline, LexSiS, and ours (a valid sentence must had at least 2 different substitutions). We had in total 120 simplification examples (composed by an original and a simplified sentence). Figure 1 shows a set of substitutions along with the original sentence.

Similar studies had smaller or slightly larger evaluation data sets. In Yatskar *et al.* (2010), 200 simplification examples were rated by six annotators (three native, three non-native speakers of English), although only the native speakers annotations were used for the results because they yielded higher inter-annotator agreement. Biran *et al.* (2011) used 130 examples that were judged by three annotators (native English speakers). In Bott *et al.* (2012), three annotators (native speakers of Spanish) rated 69 sentences each of the Spanish lexical simplification performed by LexSiS.

**Complexity dataset:** This dataset was created to evaluate the degree of complexity of the words selected by the algorithms. Using the same texts as before we extracted 40 random complex words according to LexSiS and 40 according to our method (recall that those also are complex for the baseline).

### 4.4 Judgment Guidelines

We presented the 200 examples in two different online tests, one for each evaluation dataset. The examples were presented in random order to three native Spanish speakers, frequent readers and non-authors of this paper. For the Main Dataset each annotator rated the simplification examples on two scales: Meaning Preservation –does the transformation preserve the original meaning of the sentence (yes/no); and Simplification –does the transformation result in a simpler sentence (more complex, same complexity or simpler). For the Complexity Dataset the annotators rated the examples on a three point scale (complex, neither complex or simple and simple).

We used Fleiss Kappa (Fleiss, 1971) to measure the inter-annotator agreement for multiple raters. We obtained a reasonable agreement: 0.46 for meaning preservation, 0.54 for simplicity ratings, and 0.41 for complexity. Hence, we have a moderate agreement (Landis and Koch, 1977), comparable with agreements in related literature (Biran et al., 2011; Bott et al., 2012; Yatskar et al., 2010).

### 4.5 Results

In Table 1 we show the results for the Main Dataset, where in the last column we consider only the simpler synonym substitutions (21 for Baseline, 16 for LexSiS, and 32 for ours) that preserved their meaning (agreement of 2 annotators). In this case, the simplicity performance improves for all the methods. In Table 2 we give the results for the two band frequencies for meaning preservation and simplicity. In the dataset our method overlaps in 15.79% with LexSiS candidates and in 65.79% with the baseline.

| **Type** | **Mean.** (%) | **Simp.** (%) | **SimpSyn.** (%) |
|---|---|---|---|
| Baseline | 49.17 | 60.00 | 65.08 |
| LexSiS | 42.50 | 35.83 | 45.83 |
| CASSA | **74.17** | **70.83** | **77.08** |

Table 1: Average percentage scores in meaning preservation (Mean.), simplification (Simp.), and simplification among the synonyms (SimpSyn.).

The results of LexSiS are consistent with the ones presented in Bott *et al.* (2012) for the news genre. In that study only for one dataset among three improved upon the frequency baseline in some measures (meaning preservation and global simplicity). As it can be observed from the frequency band results and the complexity measure, LexSiS offers better synonyms for high frequency and not for low frequency words. On the other hand, our method improves with low frequency complex words.

In the complexity evaluation, the prediction accuracy for complex words was only 13.33% for LexSis while was more than double, 34.17%, for ours (idem for the baseline as it used the same complexity criteria). The percentages for the complexity are low as the annotators were regular readers and non-impaired native speakers. For people with language difficulties or cognitive disabilities the accuracy should be higher because people which cognitive disabilities are more sensitive to text simplifications, such as people with Down Syndrome (Saggion et al., 2015), dyslexia (Rello and Baeza-Yates, 2014), or mild intellectual disabilities (Huenerfauth et al., 2009).

## 5 Coverage Evaluation

As not all possible contexts appear in Google Books Ngrams, we created a corpus made of 195 classic literature books from the 15th century to the 20th century of over 100Mb, to check the coverage of our

| Type | Freq. | Meaning (%) | Simp. (%) |
|---|---|---|---|
| Baseline | [HIGH] | 40.00 | 58.33 |
| LexSiS | [HIGH] | 41.67 | 36.67 |
| CASSA | [HIGH] | **73.33** | **70.00** |
| Baseline | [LOW] | 58.33 | 61.67 |
| LexSiS | [LOW] | 43.33 | 35.00 |
| CASSA | [LOW] | **75.00** | **71.67** |

Table 2: Average percentage scores by frequency band.

| Case | $k = 10$ | $k = 5$ | $k = 2$ | No $k$ |
|---|---|---|---|---|
| Comp. words | 27.16 | 38.80 | 54.24 | 100.00 |
| Baseline (abs.) | 24.07 | 35.32 | 50.14 | 84.43 |
| Baseline (rel.) | 88.62 | 91.03 | 92.04 | 84.43 |
| Comp. contexts | 27.95 | 40.03 | 55.84 | 100.00 |
| CASSA (abs.) | 2.67 | 4.14 | 6.44 | 12.14 |
| CASSA (rel.) | 9.55 | 10.34 | 11.53 | 12.14 |

Table 3: Coverage of the baseline and our method.

method. We included the books that are compulsory readings for secondary and high school in Spain. This corpus is composed by 16,495,885 tokens and 5,886,366 lexical words (without stop words, proper names and punctuation marks).[4]

The coverage of the Spanish Open Thesaurus in our corpus is 88.34%.[5] This is the maximum that any simplification algorithm that uses this resource can obtain. In Table 3 we present the coverage of the baseline and our method depending on the threshold $k$ used to decide what a complex word is and hence a complex content, including the absolute percentages as well as the relative percentages with respect to the complex words or contexts.

For smaller $k$, the coverage of the baseline increases significantly being the maximum possible 84.43% when all words are considered complex (more than three times the default coverage). On the other hand, our method does not increase much the coverage as that is limited by the context coverage reaching a maximum of 12.14%, only 27% more than the default case ($k = 10$). This maximum, compared with the baseline is a bit more than 14% of the cases, implying that our method is equal to the baseline around 85% of the time.

[4]All the book titles used for this corpus are given in the Appendix of Rello (2014).

[5]Note that this only applies to the corpus used in the coverage, not for the evaluation dataset.

Considering the maximum possible coverage of the baseline and assuming that all non covered sentences contain complex words (most probable case), the simplicity performance of the baseline drops to 53.1% while for ours would be 54.2% (that is, a 2.1% improvement). This should improve if any of the resources used grow.

## 6 Conclusions and Future Work

Our method improves upon LexSiS and the baseline for all the measures. As we mentioned earlier, even beating the baseline is very hard and we improve upon both other methods by more than 50% in meaning preservation and is 11.8% better than the baseline, the second best, for simplicity. Compared to the results for English of Biran *et al.* (2011) using WordNet, our method has better simplicity scores for low frequency words as well as is in meaning preservation, although they are not directly comparable as different resources are used.

Although Open Thesaurus is available in nine languages and Google Books Ngrams in seven, there are only two languages in both sets: Spanish and German. Hence our method should be easily extended to German. Other languages are also possible with language resources, in particular English.


## Acknowledgments

We thank Diego Saez-Trumper, Eduardo Graells and Miguel Ballesteros for their suggestions in the implementation of CASSA.


## References


S. M. Aluísio and C. Gasperin. 2010. Fostering digital inclusion and accessibility: the PorSimples project for simplification of Portuguese texts. In *Proc. NAACL HLT '10 Workshop YIWCALA '10*, pages 46–53, Stroudsburg, PA, USA.

S. D. Baker and J. O. Lamping. 2011. Identifying a synonym with n-gram agreement for a query phrase. US Patent 7,925,498.

O. Biran, S. Brody, and N. Elhadad. 2011. Putting it simply: a context-aware approach to lexical simplification. In *Proc. ACL'11*, pages 496–501, Portland, Oregon, USA.

S. Bott, L. Rello, B. Drndarevic, and H. Saggion. 2012. Can Spanish be simpler? LexSiS: Lexical simplification for Spanish. In *Proc. Coling '12*, Mumbay, India.

J. Burstein, J. Shore, J. Sabatini, Yong-Won Lee, and M. Ventura. 2007. The automated text adaptation tool. (demo). In *Proc. NAACL'07*, pages 3–4.

J. Carroll, G. Minnen, D. Pearce, Y. Canning, S. Devlin, and J. Tait. 1999. Simplifying text for language-impaired readers. In *Proc. EACL '09*, pages 269–270.

W. Coster and D. Kauchak. 2011. Learning to simplify sentences using wikipedia. In *Proceedings of the Workshop on Monolingual Text-To-Text Generation*, pages 1–9. Association for Computational Linguistics.

J. De Belder, K. Deschacht, and Marie-Francine Moens. 2010. Lexical simplification. In *Proceedings of LTEC 2010: 1st International Conference on Interdisciplinary Research on Technology, Education and Communication*.

S. Devlin and G. Unthank. 2006. Helping aphasic people process online information. In *Proc. ASSETS '06*, pages 225–226. ACM.

R. Evans, C. Orasan, and I. Dornescu. 2014. An evaluation of syntactic simplification rules for people with autism. In *Proceedings of the 3rd Workshop on Predicting and Improving Text Readability for Target Reader Populations (PITR) at EACL*, pages 131–140.

J. L. Fleiss. 1971. Measuring nominal scale agreement among many raters. *Psychological Bulletin*, 76(5):378–382.

M. Huenerfauth, L. Feng, and N. Elhadad. 2009. Comparing evaluation techniques for text readability software for adults with intellectual disabilities. In *Proc. ASSETS '09*, pages 3–10. ACM.

P. Lal and S. Ruger. 2002. Extract-based summarization with simplification. In *Proceedings of the ACL 2002 Automatic Summarization / DUC 2002 Workshop*.

J.R. Landis and G.G. Koch. 1977. The measurement of observer agreement for categorical data. *Biometrics*, pages 159–174.

Y. Lin, J-B. Michel, A. E. Lieberman, J. Orwant, W. Brockman, and S. Petrov. 2012. Syntactic annotations for the Google books ngram corpus. (demo). In *Proc. ACL'12*, pages 169–174.

S. Narayan and C. Gardent. 2014. Hybrid simplification using deep semantics and machine translation. In *ACL'14*, pages 435–445.

United Nations. 1994. Standard Rules on the Equalization of Opportunities for Persons with Disabilities.

C. Orasan, R. Evans, and I. Dornescu, 2013. *Towards Multilingual Europe 2020: A Romanian Perspective*, chapter Text Simplification for People with Autistic Spectrum Disorders, pages 287–312. Romanian Academy Publishing House, Bucharest.

L. Rello and R. Baeza-Yates. 2014. Evaluation of Dyswebxia: A reading app designed for people with dyslexia. In *Proc. W4A '14*, Seoul, Korea.

L. Rello, R. Baeza-Yates, S. Bott, and H. Saggion. 2013a. Simplify or help? Text simplification strategies for people with dyslexia. In *Proc. W4A '13*, Rio de Janeiro, Brazil.

L. Rello, R. Baeza-Yates, L. Dempere, and H. Saggion. 2013b. Frequent words improve readability and short words improve understandability for people with dyslexia. In *Proc. INTERACT '13*, Cape Town, South Africa.

L. Rello. 2014. *DysWebxia. A Text Accessibility Model for People with Dyslexia*. Ph.D. thesis, Universitat Pompeu Fabra.

H. Saggion, E. Gómez-Martínez, E. Etayo, A. Anula, and L. Bourg. 2011. Text Simplification in Simplext: Making Text More Accessible. *Revista de la Sociedad Española para el Procesamiento del Lenguaje Natural (Journal of the Spanish Society for Natural Language Processing)*, 47.

H. Saggion, S. Bott, and L. Rello. 2013. Comparing resources for Spanish lexical simplification. In *SLSP 2013: Statistical Language and Speech Processing*, volume 7978 of *Lecture Notes in Computer Science*, pages 236–247.

H. Saggion, S. Štajner, S. Bott, S. Mille, L. Rello, and B. Drndarevic. 2015. Making it simplext: Implementation and evaluation of a text simplification system for spanish. *ACM Transactions on Accessible Computing (TACCESS)*, In Press.

A. Siddharthan and M.A. Angrosh. 2014. Hybrid text simplification using synchronous dependency grammars with hand-written and automatically harvested rules. In *Proceedings of the 14th Conference of the European Chapter of the Association for Computational Linguistics (EACL), Gothenburg, Sweden,*, pages 722–731.

A. Siddharthan. 2006. Syntactic simplification and text cohesion. *Research on Language and Computation*, 4(1):77–109.

L. Specia, S. K. Jauhar, and R. Mihalcea. 2012. Semeval-2012 task 1: English lexical simplification. In *Proceedings of the First Joint Conference on Lexical and Computational Semantics*, pages 347–355.

L. Specia. 2010. Translating from Complex to Simplified Sentences. In *PROPOR*, pages 30–39.

P. Vossen. 2004. EuroWordNet: A multilingual database with lexical semantic networks. *International Journal of Lexicography*, 17(2):161–173.

M. Yatskar, B. Pang, C. Danescu-Niculescu-Mizil, and L. Lee. 2010. For the sake of simplicity: Unsupervised extraction of lexical simplifications from Wikipedia. In *Proc. ACL'10*, pages 365–368, Uppsala, Sweden.

# Simple task-specific bilingual word embeddings*

**Stephan Gouws**
Stellenbosch University
stephan@ml.sun.ac.za

**Anders Søgaard**
University of Copenhagen
soegaard@hum.ku.dk

## Abstract

We introduce a simple wrapper method that uses off-the-shelf word embedding algorithms to learn task-specific bilingual word embeddings. We use a small dictionary of easily-obtainable task-specific word equivalence classes to produce mixed context-target pairs that we use to train off-the-shelf embedding models. Our model has the advantage that it (a) is independent of the choice of embedding algorithm, (b) does not require parallel data, and (c) can be adapted to specific tasks by re-defining the equivalence classes. We show how our method outperforms off-the-shelf bilingual embeddings on the task of unsupervised cross-language part-of-speech (POS) tagging, as well as on the task of semi-supervised cross-language super sense (SuS) tagging.

## 1 Introduction

Using multi-layered neural networks to learn word embeddings has become standard in NLP (Turian et al., 2010; Guo et al., 2014). While there is still some controversy whether such methods are superior to older methods (Levy and Goldberg, 2014; Baroni et al., 2014), there is little doubt that continuous word representations can potentially solve some of the data sparsity problems inherent in NLP.

Most research on word embeddings has focused on learning representations for the words in a single language, making syntactically or semantically similar words appear close in the embedding space. Embeddings have been applied to many tasks, from named entity recognition (Turian et al., 2010) to dependency parsing (Bansal et al., 2014). It has furthermore been shown that weakly supervised embedding algorithms can also lead to huge improvements for tasks like sentiment analysis (Tang et al., 2014). In this work, we also use weak or distant supervision, relying on small dictionary seeds.

This paper, however, considers the problem of learning *bilingual* word embeddings, i.e., word embeddings such that similar words in two different languages end up close in the embedding space. Such bilingual word embeddings can potentially be used for better cross-language transfer of NLP models, as we show in this paper. Previous work on bilingual word embeddings have defined similar words as translation equivalents and evaluated embeddings in the context of document classification tasks (Klementiev et al., 2012; Kocisky et al., 2014). In this paper, we present a simple wrapper method to existing monolingual word embedding algorithms that can learn task-specific bilingual embeddings, e.g., for POS tagging, named entity recognition, or sentiment analysis. Our algorithm is simpler and performs better on the tasks where we could compare performance to existing algorithms. Also, we note that our approach, unlike existing algorithms (Klementiev et al., 2012), is as fast as learning monolingual embeddings.

**Our contributions** In this paper we introduce a new approach for learning bilingual word embeddings and revisit the task of unsupervised cross-language POS tagging (Das and Petrov, 2011). Our bilingual embedding model, which we call *Bilingual Adaptive Reshuffling with Individual Stochastic Alternatives* (BARISTA), takes two (non-parallel) corpora and a small dictionary as input. The dictio-

*The authors contributed equally to this work. The second author is funded by the ERC Starting Grant LOWLANDS No. 313695.



*Human Language Technologies: The 2015 Annual Conference of the North American Chapter of the ACL*, pages 1386–1390,
Denver, Colorado, May 31 – June 5, 2015. 

nary is essentially a list of words in the two languages that are equivalent with respect to some task, e.g., English *car* and French *maison* ('house') are both nouns, and hence "equivalent" in POS tagging; English *clerk* and *chauffeur* are both persons, and hence "equivalent" in SuS tagging; *house* and *maison* are equivalent in machine translation. BARISTA has the advantage that it (a) is independent of the choice of embedding algorithm, (b) does not require parallel data, and (c) can be adapted to specific tasks by using appropriate dictionaries. We use the bilingual embeddings directly to train a target language POS tagger on source language training data. Instead of lexical features, we use the bilingual embeddings. We show our bilingual embedding method outperforms using off-the-shelf bilingual embeddings on this task, and that our system is competitive to state-of-the-art approaches for cross-language POS tagging. Finally, we show that the same embeddings also lead to significantly better performance in semi-supervised cross-language SuS tagging. The code will be made publicly available at `https://github.com/gouwsmeister/barista`.

## 2 Our approach

Standard monolingual neural language models are unsupervised models that train on raw text, learning word features that enable the model to predict the next word (the target) from a sequence of words (the context). In the process, the model learns to cluster words into soft equivalence classes (words that have similar distributions).

Several authors have proposed bilingual clustering and embedding algorithms based on parallel data (Täckström et al., 2012; Klementiev et al., 2012; Zou et al., 2013; Kocisky et al., 2014; Hermann and Blunsom, 2014b). These authors have all evaluated their embeddings on document classification and machine translation, and not yet structured prediction tasks like POS/SuS tagging or syntactic parsing. A notable exception is Hermann and Blunsom (2014a), who do not rely on parallel data and do not use word alignments, but they still use comparable data and sentence alignments, and they only evaluate their embeddings in document classification.

The assumption that large amounts of parallel data exists for a language pair of interest is sometimes too strong (Hermann and Blunsom, 2014a). On the other hand, we often have access to small samples of near-equivalences from knowledge bases of various forms. For example, for POS tagging, we often have access to small-to-sizeable crowd-sourced tag dictionaries (e.g. Wiktionary). For SuS tagging, which is the other example considered in this paper, we sometimes have access to WordNets or similar resources. If we have such resources for both source and target language, we can extract word-equivalences from them and use these to learn bilingual embeddings using our proposed method.

In this paper, we experiment with using *both* equivalences based on word alignments (e.g., *house* $\sim$ *maison*), and equivalences based on knowledge bases (e.g., *car* $\sim$ *maison*). Crucially, our approach to learning bilingual embeddings only assumes a small seed of equivalences, no parallel data. It then uses these to produce a set of mixed context-target pairs.

Our input is a source corpus $C_s$ and a target corpus $C_t$, as well as a set of bilingual equivalences $R_\sim$. We begin by shuffling the concatenation of $C_s$ and $C_t$. We then pass over this mixed corpus, and for each word $w$, if $\{w' \mid w, w' \in R_\sim\}$ is non-empty and of cardinality $k$, i.e., $w$ is in the seed list of equivalences, we replace $w$ with $w'$ with probability $1/2k$. In other words, we flip a coin whether to replace $w$, and then randomly choose one of its equivalences as our replacement. For example, using translation equivalence classes, one could generate any of the following mixed texts from the English sentence *build the house*: *construire the house*, *build la maison*, *build the maison*, etc., or any other combination of English and French words with the English word order. With POS equivalence classes, any of the words in *build the house* can be replaced with words with overlapping syntactic categories, e.g., *build the voiture*.

## 3 Experiments

In our experiments we balance the source and target corpora, by subsampling from the bigger corpus. The vocabularies for all models are kept unrestricted, and result in around $1M$ words per language pair. We train with a window of 4 words on either side of the target word, using linear discounting of the initial learning rate of $0.1$. These parameters were set on the Spanish POS data (see §3.2). We

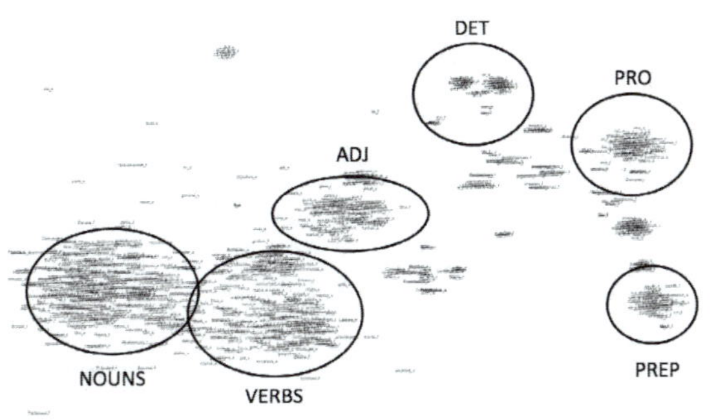


Figure 1: t-SNE visualization of BARISTA embeddings trained with POS classes.

use the CBOW model in `word2vec` for training the word embeddings.[1]

Both our POS tagging evaluation datasets, as well as the Wiktionaries,[2] are mapped to Google's universal tagset (Petrov et al., 2011). We use the derived dictionaries for extracting bilingual POS equivalence classes. For SuS tagging, we only consider English-Danish and extract equivalence classes from Princeton WordNet and DanNet. For translation equivalents, we made use of Google Translate.

### 3.1 Qualitative Evaluation

In our main experiments (§3.2–3.3), we use data from Wikipedia, but we first present a qualitative evaluation of English-German bilingual embeddings learned from the smaller Europarl corpus.[3] Note that while this is parallel data, we do not exploit its parallel nature.

**POS classes** The embeddings learned from English-German Europarl using POS classes from Wiktionary were visualized using the t-SNE technique (Van der Maaten and Hinton, 2008), and are shown in Fig 1. The model learns to cluster words very distinctively by their POS tag. Monolingual word embedding models with short context windows typically cluster by POS, but here we see the same effect for bilingual embeddings, i.e. words from **both** languages with the same POS tag cluster together. Individual words, on the other hand, do not appear to retain the fine-grained relationships we normally observe in word embeddings (where similar words cluster closer together). The question thus is whether such embeddings are more or less useful for cross-language POS tagging than bilingual embeddings based on translation equivalencies.

[1] `https://code.google.com/p/word2vec/`

[2] `https://code.google.com/p/wikily-supervised-pos-tagger/`

[3] http://www.statmt.org/europarl/

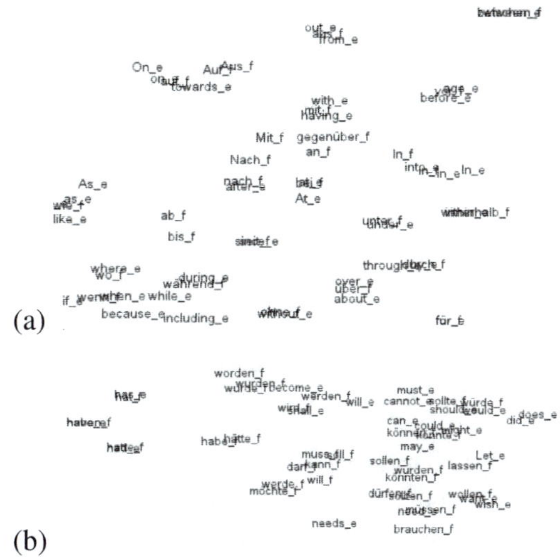


Figure 2: t-SNE visualizations of BARISTA embedding subspaces for (a) prepositions and (b) modals.

**Translation classes** Next, we induced English-German bilingual embeddings on Europarl using translations obtained from Google Translate. We derived a dictionary of the top $20k$ most frequent words in English, translated into German. The embeddings are shown in Fig 2. The visualizations show that the models are able to extract very fine-grained bilingual relationships, and some clusters still correspond to POS.

### 3.2 Cross-language part-of-speech tagging

Next we evaluated the embeddings in the context of unsupervised cross-language POS tagging (Das and Petrov, 2011). The goal is to train a tagger – in our case, we use SEARN (Daume et al., 2009), following (Johannsen et al., 2014)– on labeled English data decorated with bilingual embeddings, and then evaluate the model on another target language. We use data from Danish, German, Spanish, Italian, Dutch, Portuguese, and Swedish. Training and test data, which are the same used in Das and Petrov (2011), were converted to use the same 12 universal parts of speech proposed by Petrov et al. (2011).

All results in this section were obtained by training bilingual embedding models on the publicly-

| Language | TC-Perc | Random | Klmtv | POS-50 | POS-300 | Tr-50 | Tr-300 | DP | B-K |
|---|---|---|---|---|---|---|---|---|---|
| Spanish | 80.6 | 81.8 | 79.8 | 82.4 | 81 | 81.6 | 82.6 | **84.2** | 80.2 |
| German | 80.4 | 82.7 | 82.8 | 81.8 | 84.1 | 82.6 | **84.8** | 82.8 | 81.3 |
| Danish | 63 | 68.9 | - | 68.9 | 72.4 | 71.8 | 78.4 | **83.2** | 69.1 |
| Swedish | 71.6 | 73.7 | - | 75 | 76 | 75.4 | 77.5 | **80.5** | 70.1 |
| Italian | 80.1 | 81.3 | - | 82.1 | 80.9 | 82.1 | 80.7 | **86.8** | 68.1 |
| Dutch | 74.5 | 77.2 | - | 78.3 | 77.4 | 78.7 | **80.3** | 79.5 | 65.1 |
| Portuguese | 76.9 | 78.1 | - | 77.3 | 76.1 | 80.6 | 80.5 | **87.9** | 78.4 |
| Avg | 75.3 | 77.7 | - | 78 | 78.3 | 79 | 80.7 | **83.6** | 73.2 |

Table 1: Cross-language POS tagging. TC-Perc: type-constrained structured perceptron.

available, pre-tokenized versions of Wikipedia,[4] and then using the trained embeddings as features in a publicly available implementation of the structured perceptron.[5] We use ortographic features, as well as the embedding vector of the target word. In addition, we use type constraints from Wiktionary to prune the search lattice during decoding (Täckström et al., 2013). We scaled the embedding features in the same way as Turian et al. (2010) with scaling parameter 0.01 (set on Spanish POS data).

Our baseline method is a type-constrained structured perceptron with only ortographic features, which are expected to transfer across languages. We also experiment with using *random* embeddings, as well as the embeddings provided by Klementiev et al. (2012) (Klmtv).[6] Our results are displayed in Table 1. POS-X refer to $X$-dimensional BARISTA embeddings trained with POS equivalence classes, and Tr-X is $X$-dimensional BARISTA embeddings trained using translation equivalence classes. We note that random embeddings improve over our baseline, suggesting that the random features act as regularizers. The embeddings provided by Klementiev et al. (2012) seem to lead to worse performance than random embeddings, presumably because they capture mostly semantic (topic) similarity. We also compare our results to those reported by Berg-Kirkpatrick et al. (2010) (B-K) and Das and Petrov (2011) (DP), but note that their approaches require in-sample unlabeled data, and in the latter case, also parallel bilingual data.

While training with POS classes improves over the random baseline, training with translation equivalence classes gives even better performance. For both approaches, using more embedding features improves the performance (500 dimensions did not improve significantly over 300). Our model is generally better than Berg-Kirkpatrick et al. (2010) – but worse than Das and Petrov (2011).

### 3.3 Cross-language super sense tagging

Finally, we also tried using the BARISTA-embeddings for English-Danish (with parameters still set on Spanish POS) on *another* task, namely super sense tagging (Ciaramita and Altun, 2006). We train a system on a mixture of 1000 randomly sampled sentences from English SemCor[7]and 320 labeled Danish sentences (see below) and compare using bilingual embeddings trained with equivalence classes from English and Danish wordnets (WN-300), to embeddings trained using translation equivalence classes (Tr-300). We use 300 dimensional embeddings. We use a POS-sensitive most frequent sense baseline (MFS), as well as structured perceptron model trained only with ortographic and POS features, as well as MFS features (Johannsen et al., 2014). Our metric is a weighted average over $F_1$-scores for the (41) semantic classes. Note that using the knowledge base is superior to using translation equivalences, but both embeddings are superior to both our baselines. The Danish training (newswire only) and test data (six different domains) – is made publicly available.[8]

[4] https://sites.google.com/site/rmyeid/projects/polyglot

[5] https://github.com/coastalcph/rungsted

[6] http://people.mmci.uni-saarland.de/~aklement/data/distrib/

[7] http://web.eecs.umich.edu/~mihalcea/downloads.html#semcor

[8] https://github.com/coastalcph/noda2015_sst

| | Baselines | | BARISTA | |
|---|---|---|---|---|
| | MFS | TC-Searn | Tr-300 | WN-300 |
| blogs | 49.1 | 46.7 | 50.5 | **61.9** |
| forum | 44.5 | 41.2 | 45.0 | **53.9** |
| magazine | 46.5 | 45.2 | 50.4 | **51.5** |
| newswire | 48.4 | 45.4 | 52.7 | **60.9** |
| reviews | 48.4 | 44.9 | 50.4 | **55.8** |
| speech | 51.1 | 48.4 | 51.5 | **58.4** |
| Avg | 48.1 | 45.4 | 50.5 | **58.3** |

Table 2: Cross-language SuS tagging.

## 4 Conclusions

We presented a simple approach, BARISTA, to learning bilingual embeddings. BARISTA has the advantages that it (a) is independent of the choice of embedding algorithm, (b) does not require parallel data, and (c) can be adapted to specific tasks by using appropriate dictionaries. Our embeddings proved useful for cross-language POS/SuS tagging.

## References


Mohit Bansal, Kevin Gimpel, and Karen Livescu. 2014. Tailoring continuous word representations for dependency parsing. In *ACL*.

Marco Baroni, Georgiana Dinu, and German Kruszewski. 2014. Don't count, predict! a systematic comparison of context-counting vs. context-predicting semantic vectors. In *ACL*.

Taylor Berg-Kirkpatrick, Alexandre Cote, John DeNero, and Dan Klein. 2010. Painless unsupervised learning with features. In *NAACL*.

Massimiliano Ciaramita and Yasemin Altun. 2006. Broad-coverage sense disambiguation and information extraction with a supersense sequence tagger. In *Proc. of EMNLP*, pages 594–602, Sydney, Australia, July.

Dipanjan Das and Slav Petrov. 2011. Unsupervised part-of-speech tagging with bilingual graph-based projections. In *ACL*.

Hal Daume, John Langford, and Daniel Marcu. 2009. Search-based structured prediction. *Machine Learning*, 75:297–325.

Jiang Guo, Wanxiang Che, Haifeng Wang, and Ting Liu. 2014. Revisiting embedding features for simple semi-supervised learning. In *EMNLP*.

Karl Hermann and Phil Blunsom. 2014a. Multilingual distributed representations without word alignment. In *ICLR*.

Karl Hermann and Phil Blunsom. 2014b. Multilingual models for compositional distributed semantics. In *ACL*.

Anders Johannsen, Dirk Hovy, Hector Martinez Alonso, and Anders Søgaard. 2014. More or less supervised super-sense tagging of twitter. In **SEM*.

Alexandre Klementiev, Ivan Titov, and Binod Bhattarai. 2012. Inducing crosslingual distributed representations of words. In *COLING*.

Tomas Kocisky, Moritz Hermann, and Phil Blunsom. 2014. Learning bilingual word representations by marginalizing alignments. In *ACL*.

Omer Levy and Yoav Goldberg. 2014. Neural word embeddings as implicit matrix factorization. In *NIPS*.

Slav Petrov, Dipanjan Das, and Ryan McDonald. 2011. A universal part-of-speech tagset. CoRR abs/1104.2086.

Oscar Täckström, Ryan McDonald, and Jakob Uszkoreit. 2012. Cross-lingual word clusters for direct transfer of linguistic structure. In *NAACL*.

Oscar Täckström, Dipanjan Das, Slav Petrov, Ryan McDonald, and Joakim Nivre. 2013. Token and type constraints for cross-lingual part-of-speech tagging. *TACL*, 1:1–12.

Duyu Tang, Furu Wei, Nan Yang, Ming Zhou, Ting Liu, and Bing Qin. 2014. Learning sentiment-specific word embedding for Twitter sentiment classification. In *ACL*.

Joseph Turian, Lev Ratinov, and Yoshua Bengio. 2010. Word representations: a simple and general method for semi-supervised learning. In *ACL*.

Laurens Van der Maaten and Geoffrey Hinton. 2008. Visualizing data using t-sne. *Journal of Machine Learning Research*, 9(2579-2605):85.

Will Zou, Richard Socher, Daniel Cer, and Chris Manning. 2013. Bilingual word embeddings for phrase-based machine translation. In *EMNLP*.

# Sampling Techniques for Streaming Cross Document Coreference Resolution

**Luke Shrimpton*** **Victor Lavrenko**[†] **Miles Osborne**[§]
* School of Informatics, University of Edinburgh: luke.shrimpton@ed.ac.uk
[†] School of Informatics, University of Edinburgh: vlavrenk@inf.ed.ac.uk
[§] Bloomberg, London: mosborne29@bloomberg.net

## Abstract

We present the first truly streaming cross document coreference resolution (CDC) system. Processing infinite streams of mentions forces us to use a constant amount of memory and so we maintain a representative, fixed sized sample at all times. For the sample to be representative it should represent a large number of entities whilst taking into account both temporal recency and distant references. We introduce new sampling techniques that take into account a notion of streaming discourse (current mentions depend on previous mentions). Using the proposed sampling techniques we are able to get a CEAFe score within 5% of a non-streaming system while using only 30% of the memory.

## 1 Introduction

Cross document coreference resolution (CDC) - identifying mentions that refer to the same entity across documents - is a prerequisite when combining entity specific information from multiple documents. Typically large scale CDC involves applying a scalable clustering algorithm to all the mentions. We consider *streaming* CDC, hence our system must conform to the streaming computational resource model (Muthukrishnan, 2005). Each mention is processed in bounded time and only a constant amount of memory is used. Honoring these constraints ensures our system can be applied to infinite streams such as newswire or social media.

Storing all the mentions in memory is clearly infeasible, hence we need to either compress mentions or store a *sample*. Compression is more computationally expensive as it involves merging/forgetting mention components (for example: components of a vector) whereas sampling decides to store or forget whole mentions. We investigate sampling techniques due to their computational efficiency. We explore which mentions should be stored while performing streaming CDC. A sample should represent a diverse set of entities while taking into account both temporal recency and distant mentions. We show that using a notion of streaming discourse, where what is currently being mentioned depends on what was previously mentioned significantly improves performance on a new CDC annotated Twitter corpus.

## 2 Related Work

There are many existing approaches to CDC (Bagga and Baldwin, 1998; Lee et al., 2012; Andrews et al., 2014). Few of them scale to large datasets. Singh et al. (2011) proposed a distributed hierarchical factor graph approach. While it can process large datasets, the scalability comes from distributing the problem. Wick et al. (2012) proposed a similar approach based on compressing mentions, while scalable it does not conform to the streaming resource model. The only prior work that addressed online/streaming CDC (Rao et al., 2010) was also not constrained to the streaming model. None of these approaches operate over an unbounded stream processing mentions in constant time/memory.



*Human Language Technologies: The 2015 Annual Conference of the North American Chapter of the ACL*, pages 1391–1396,
Denver, Colorado, May 31 – June 5, 2015. 

## 3 Entities in Streams

Streams like Twitter are well known as being real-time and highly bursty. Some entities are continually mentioned throughout the stream (eg: President Obama) whereas others burst, suddenly peak in popularity then decay (eg: Phillip Hughes, a cricketer who died following a bowling injury).

Capturing the information required to perform streaming CDC in constant space requires us to *sample* from the stream. For example we may consider only the most recent information (eg: the previous 24 hours worth of mentions). This may not be ideal as it would result in a sample biased towards bursting entities, neglecting the continually mentioned entities. We propose three properties that are important when sampling mentions from a stream of tweets:

- **Recency:** There should be some bias towards recent mentions to take into account the real-time nature of the stream. The set of entities mentioned one day is likely to be similar to the set of entities mentioned on the following day.
- **Distant Reference:** The temporal gap between mentions of the same entity can vary drastically, recency captures the small gaps though to capture the larger gaps older mentions should be stored. A mention should be correctly resolved if the last mention of the entity was either a day or a week ago.
- **Entity Diversity:** The sample should contain mentions of many entities instead of storing lots of mentions about a few entities. If the sample only contains mentions of the most tweeted about entity (the one that is bursting) it is impossible to resolve references to other entities.

These properties suggest we should take into account a notion of streaming discourse when sampling: mentions sampled should depend on the previous mentions (informed sampling).

## 4 Approach

We implemented a representative pairwise streaming CDC system using single link clustering. Mention similarity is a linear combination of mention text and contextual similarity (weighted 0.8 and 0.2 respectively) similar to Rao et al. (2010). Mention text similarity is measured using cosine similarity of character skip bigram indicator vectors and contextual similarity is measured using tf-idf weighted cosine similarity of tweet terms. The stream is processed sequentially: we resolve each mention by finding its nearest neighbor in the sample, linking the two mentions if the similarity is above the linking threshold.

## 5 Sampling Techniques

The sampling techniques we investigate are summarized below. Each technique has an insertion and removal policy that are followed each time a mention is processed. New sampling techniques are indicated by a star (*). The new sampling techniques require the nearest neighbor to be identified. As this is already computed during resolution hence the overhead of these new techniques is very low. Parameters particular to each sampling technique are noted in square brackets and are set using a standard grid search on a training dataset.

- **Exact:** To provide an upper bound on performance we forgo the constraints of the streaming resource model and store all previously seen mentions:

  **Insertion:** Add current mention to sample. **Removal:** Do nothing.

- **Window:** We sample a moving window of the most recent mentions (first in, first out). For example this technique assumes that if we are processing mentions on Monday with a window of approximately 24 hours all relevant entities were mentioned since Sunday.

  **Insertion:** Add current mention to sample. **Removal:** Remove oldest mention.

- **Uniform Reservoir Sampling (Uniform-R):** A uniform sample of previously seen mentions will capture a diverse set of entities from the entire stream - taking into account diversity and distant references. This can be achieved using a reservoir sample (Vitter, 1985). We assume each previously seen mention is equally likely to help resolve the current mention.

**Insertion:** Add current mention with probability $p_i$. **Removal:** If a mention was inserted choose a mention uniformly at random to remove.

Setting $p_i = k/N$ where $k$ is the sample size and $N$ is the number of items seen ensures the sample is uniform (Vitter, 1985).

- **Biased Reservoir Sampling (Biased-R):** To resolve both distant and recent references we should store recent mentions and some older mentions. An uninformed approach from randomized algorithms is to use an exponentially biased reservoir sample (Aggarwal, 2006; Osborne et al., 2014). It will store mostly recent mentions but will probabilistically allow older mentions to stay in the sample. For example this technique will sample lots of mentions from yesterday and less from the day before yesterday.

  **Insertion:** Add current mention with probability $p_i$ **Removal:** If a mention was inserted choose a mention uniformly at random to remove.

  Unlike uniform reservoir sampling $p_i$ is constant. A higher value puts more emphasis on the recent past. [$p_i$]

- **Cache*:** We should keep past mentions critical to resolving current references (an informed implementation of recency) and allow mentions to stay in the sample for an arbitrary period of time to help resolve distance references. For example if the same mention is used to resolve a reference on Saturday and Sunday it should be in the sample on Monday.

  **Insertion:** Add current mention to sample. **Removal:** Choose a mention that was not recently used to resolve a reference uniformly at random and remove it.

  When a mention is resolved we find its most similar mention in the sample, recording its use in a first in, first out cache of size $n$. The mention to be removed is chosen from the set of mentions not in the cache. We set $n$ equal to a proportion of the sample size. [Proportion of mentions to keep]

- **Diversity*:** If we store fewer mentions about each distinct entity we can represent more entities in the sample. For example if news breaks that a famous person died yesterday the sample should not be full of mentions about that entity at the expense of other entities mentioned today.

  **Insertion:** Add current mention to sample. **Removal:** If there is a sufficiently similar mention in the sample remove it else choose uniformly at random to be removed.

  We remove the past mention most similar to the current mention, but only if the similarity exceeds a threshold. [Replacement Threshold]

- **Diversity-Cache (D-C)*:** We combine Diversity and Cache sampling.

  **Insertion:** Add current mention to sample. **Removal:** If there is a sufficiently similar mention in the sample remove it else remove a mention that has not recently been used to resolve a reference chosen uniformly at random.

  For this technique we first choose the replacement threshold then the proportion of mentions to keep. [Replacement threshold and proportion of mentions to keep]

## 6 Dataset

We collected 52 million English tweets from the 1% sample of all tweets sent over a 77 day period. We performed named entity recognition using Ritter et al. (2011). It is clearly infeasible for us to annotate all the mentions in the dataset. Hence we annotated a sample of the entities. As with most prior work we focused on person named entity mentions (of which there is approximately 6 million in the dataset).

To select the entities we first sampled two names based on how frequently they occur in the dataset: 'Roger' was chosen randomly from the low frequency names (between 1,000 and 10,000 occurrences) and 'Jessica' was chosen similarly from medium frequency names (10,000 to 100,0000 occurrences). We first annotated all mentions of the names 'Roger' and 'Jessica' discarding entities mentioned once. For the remaining entities we annotated all their mentions (not restricting to mentions that contained the words 'Roger' or 'Jessica').

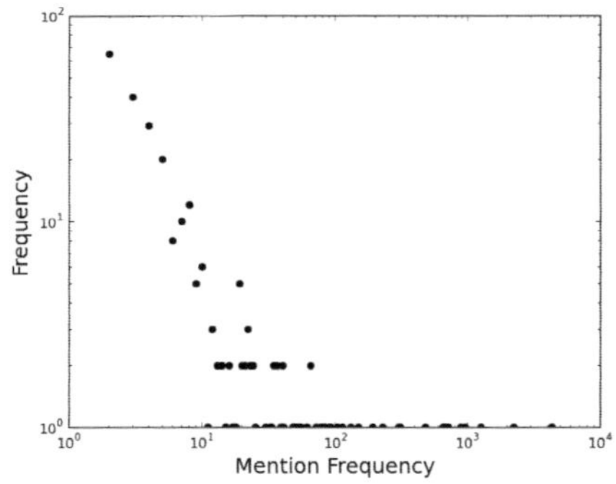


Figure 1: Mention Frequency Distribution.

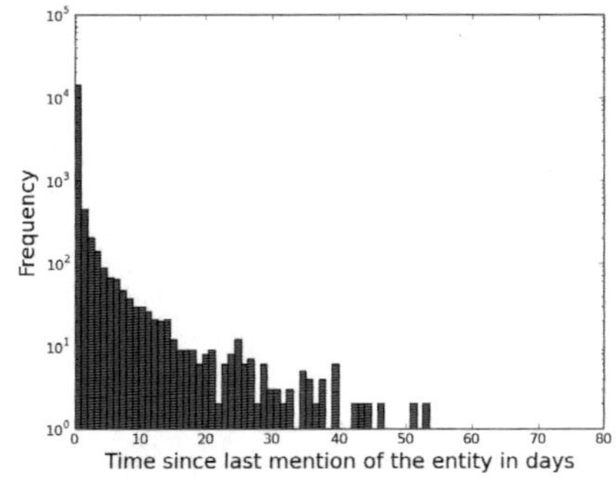


Figure 2: Distribution of time since previous mention of the same entity (gap). Each bar represents 24 hours.

This covers a diverse selection of people including: 'Roger Federer' (tennis player) and 'Jessie J' (the singer whose real name is 'Jessica Cornish') as well as less popular entities such as porn stars and journalists[1].

Some statistics of the dataset are summarized in table 1. We also plot the mention frequency (how often each entity was mentioned) distribution in figure 1 which shows a clear power law distribution similar to what Rao et al. (2010) reported on the New York Times annotated corpus. We show that recency and distant reference are important aspects by plotting the time since previous mention of the same entity (gap) for each mention in figure 2. The gap is often less than 24 hours demonstrating the importance of recency. There are also plenty of mentions with much larger gaps, demonstrating the need to be able to resolve distant references.

| Source | Mentions | Entities | Wiki Page Exists |
|---|---|---|---|
| Roger | 5,794 | 137 | 69% |
| Jessica | 10,543 | 129 | 46% |
| All | 16,337 | 266 | 58% |

Table 1: Mention/entity counts and percentage of entities that have a Wikipedia page.

## 7 Experiments

As we are processing a stream we use a rolling evaluation protocol. Our corpus is split up into 11 constant sized temporally adjacent blocks each lasting approximately one week. Parameters are set using a standard grid search on one block then we progress to the next block to evaluate. The first block is reserved for setting the linking threshold prior to our rolling evaluation. We report the average over the remaining blocks. For all sampling techniques that have a randomized component we report an average over 10 runs.

As the sample size will have a large effect on performance we evaluate using various sample sizes. We base our sample size on the average amount of mentions per day (78,450) and evaluate our system with sample sizes of 0.25,0.5,1,2 times the average amount of mentions per day.

We evaluate using CEAFe (Luo, 2005), it is the only coreference evaluation metric that can be trivially adapted to datasets with a sample of annotated entities. With no adaption it measures how well a small amount of entities align with a system output over a large amount. To make the evaluation more representative we only use response clusters that contain an annotated mention. This scales precision and maintains interpretability. We determine if observed differences are significant by using a Wilcoxon signed-rank test with a p value of 5% over the 9 testing points. Results are shown in table 2.

- **Window:** This shows the performance that can be achieved by only considering recency.
- **Uniform Reservoir Sampling (Uniform-R):** This shows the performance achieved by using an uninformed technique to store a diverse set of older mentions.

[1]The annotations, including links to Wikipedia pages when available, can be downloaded from `https://sites.google.com/site/lukeshr/`.

| Sample Size | Sampling Technique | CEAFe P | CEAFe R | CEAFe F |
|---|---|---|---|---|
| 0.25 Days | Window | 24.2 | 67.2 | 35.6 |
| | Uniform-R | 23.0 | 67.2 | 34.3 |
| | Biased-R | 24.8 | 67.8 | 36.3 |
| 19,613 | Cache ∗ | 25.5 | 67.2 | 37.0 |
| Mentions | Diversity ∗ | 27.6 | 69.2 | 39.4 |
| | D-C ∗ † | **30.1** | **69.7** | **42.0** |
| 0.5 Days | Window | 31.3 | 69.4 | 43.1 |
| | Uniform-R | 29.9 | 69.1 | 41.7 |
| | Biased-R | 31.6 | 69.9 | 43.5 |
| 39,225 | Cache ∗ | 32.9 | 69.7 | 44.7 |
| Mentions | Diversity ∗ | 37.5 | 71.6 | 49.2 |
| | D-C ∗ † | **40.1** | **72.3** | **51.6** |
| 1.0 Days | Window | 40.7 | 72.0 | 52.0 |
| | Uniform-R | 39.3 | 71.4 | 50.6 |
| | Biased-R | 40.9 | 72.3 | 52.3 |
| 78,450 | Cache ∗ | 42.0 | 72.0 | 53.1 |
| Mentions | Diversity ∗ | 48.5 | 74.3 | 58.7 |
| | D-C ∗ † | **49.8** | **74.5** | **59.7** |
| 2.0 Days | Window | 50.2 | 74.1 | 59.8 |
| | Uniform-R | 49.2 | 73.7 | 58.9 |
| | Biased-R | 50.3 | 74.1 | 59.9 |
| 156,900 | Cache ∗ | 50.9 | 74.1 | 60.4 |
| Mentions | Diversity ∗ | 55.2 | 75.2 | 63.7 |
| | D-C ∗ | **55.5** | **75.3** | **63.9** |
| ≈600,000 Mentions | Exact | 59.7 | 75.4 | 66.6 |

Table 2: CEAFe performance for various sample sizes and sampling techniques. ∗ indicates significant improvement over Window sampling. † indicates significant improvement over Diversity sampling

- **Biased Reservoir Sampling (Biased-R):** Uninformed sampling of older mentions is not sufficient to significantly improve performance.

- **Cache:** By using an informed model of recency we keep mentions critical to resolving references currently being tweeted resulting in a significant performance improvement.

- **Diversity:** By using an informed technique to increase the amount of distinct entities represented in the sample we significantly improve performance.

- **Diversity-Cache (D-C):** By combining the new sampling techniques we significantly improve performance. Once we have increased the amount of entities represented in the sample we are still able to benefit from an informed model of recency.

Using uninformed sampling techniques (reservoir sampling) does not result in a significant performance improvement over Window sampling, only informed sampling techniques show a significant improvement. As the sample size increases the performance difference decreases. With larger samples there is space to represent more entities and it is less likely to remove a useful mention at random.

## 8 Conclusion

We presented the first truly streaming CDC system, showing that significantly better performance is achieved by using an informed sampling technique that takes into account a notion of streaming discourse. We are able to get to within 5% of an exact system's performance while using only 30% of the memory required. Instead of improving performance by using an uninformed sampling technique and doubling the memory available, similar performance can be achieved by using the same amount of memory and a informed sampling technique. Further work could look at improving the similarity metric used, applying these sampling techniques to other streaming problems or adding a mention compression component.

## References


Charu C Aggarwal. 2006. On biased reservoir sampling in the presence of stream evolution. In *Proceedings of the 32nd international conference on Very large data bases*, pages 607–618. VLDB Endowment.

Nicholas Andrews, Jason Eisner, and Mark Dredze. 2014. Robust entity clustering via phylogenetic inference. In *Association for Computational Linguistics (ACL)*.

Amit Bagga and Breck Baldwin. 1998. Entity-based cross-document coreferencing using the vector space model. In *Proceedings of the 17th international conference on Computational linguistics-Volume 1*, pages 79–85. Association for Computational Linguistics.

Heeyoung Lee, Marta Recasens, Angel Chang, Mihai Surdeanu, and Dan Jurafsky. 2012. Joint entity and event coreference resolution across documents. In *Proceedings of the 2012 Joint Conference on Empirical Methods in Natural Language Processing and Computational Natural Language Learning*, pages 489–500. Association for Computational Linguistics.

Xiaoqiang Luo. 2005. On coreference resolution performance metrics. In *Proceedings of Human Language Technology Conference and Conference on Empirical Methods in Natural Language Processing*.

S Muthukrishnan. 2005. *Data streams: Algorithms and applications*. Now Publishers Inc.

Miles Osborne, Ashwin Lall, and Benjamin Van Durme. 2014. Exponential reservoir sampling for streaming language models. In *Proceedings of the 52nd Annual Meeting of the Association for Computational Linguistics (Volume 2: Short Papers)*, pages 687–692. Association for Computational Linguistics.

Saša Petrović, Miles Osborne, and Victor Lavrenko. 2010. Streaming first story detection with application to twitter. In *Human Language Technologies: The 2010 Annual Conference of the North American Chapter of the Association for Computational Linguistics*, pages 181–189. Association for Computational Linguistics.

Delip Rao, Paul McNamee, and Mark Dredze. 2010. Streaming cross document entity coreference resolution. In *Coling 2010: Posters*, pages 1050–1058. Coling 2010 Organizing Committee.

Alan Ritter, Sam Clark, Mausam, and Oren Etzioni. 2011. Named entity recognition in tweets: An experimental study. In *EMNLP*.

Sameer Singh, Amarnag Subramanya, Fernando Pereira, and Andrew McCallum. 2011. Large-scale cross-document coreference using distributed inference and hierarchical models. In *Proceedings of the 49th Annual Meeting of the Association for Computational Linguistics: Human Language Technologies*, pages 793–803. Association for Computational Linguistics.

Jeffrey S Vitter. 1985. Random sampling with a reservoir. *ACM Transactions on Mathematical Software (TOMS)*, 11(1):37–57.

Michael Wick, Sameer Singh, and Andrew McCallum. 2012. A discriminative hierarchical model for fast coreference at large scale. In *Proceedings of the 50th Annual Meeting of the Association for Computational Linguistics (Volume 1: Long Papers)*, pages 379–388. Association for Computational Linguistics.

# On the Automatic Learning of Sentiment Lexicons

**Aliaksei Severyn**
DISI, University of Trento
38123 Povo (TN), Italy
severyn@disi.unitn.it

**Alessandro Moschitti**
Qatar Computing Research Institue
5825 Doha, Qatar
amoschitti@qf.org.qa

## Abstract

This paper describes a simple and principled approach to automatically construct sentiment lexicons using distant supervision. We induce the sentiment association scores for the lexicon items from a model trained on a weakly supervised corpora. Our empirical findings show that features extracted from such a machine-learned lexicon outperform models using manual or other automatically constructed sentiment lexicons. Finally, our system achieves the state-of-the-art in Twitter Sentiment Analysis tasks from Semeval-2013 and ranks 2nd best in Semeval-2014 according to the average rank.

## 1 Introduction

One of the early and rather successful models for sentiment analysis (Pang and Lee, 2004; Pang and Lee, 2008) relied on manually constructed lexicons that map words to their sentiment, e.g., *positive*, *negative* or *neutral*. The document-level polarity is then assigned by performing some form of averaging, e.g., majority voting, of individual word polarities found in the document. These systems show an acceptable level of accuracy, they are easy to build and are highly computationally efficient as the only operation required to assign a polarity label are the word lookups and averaging. However, the information about word polarities in a document are best exploited when using machine learning models to train a sentiment classifier.

In fact, most successful sentiment classification systems rely on supervised learning. Interestingly, a simple bag of words model using just unigrams and bigrams with an SVM has shown excellent results (Wang and Manning, 2012) performing on par or beating more complicated models, e.g., using neural networks (Socher et al., 2011).

Regarding Twitter sentiment analysis, the top performing system (Mohammad et al., 2013) from Semeval-2013 Twittter Sentiment Analysis task (Nakov et al., 2013) follows this recipe by training an SVM on various surface form, sentiment and semantic features. Perhaps, the most valuable finding is that sentiment lexicons appear to be the most useful source of features accounting for over 8 point gains in the F-measure on top of the standard feature sets.

Sentiment lexicons are mappings from words to scores capturing the degree of the sentiment expressed by a given word. While several manually constructed lexicons are made available, e.g., the MPQA (Wilson et al., 2005), the Bing and Liu (Hu and Liu, 2004) and NRC Emoticon (Mohammad and Turney, 2013) lexicons, providing high quality word-sentiment associations compiled by humans, still their main drawback is low recall.

For example, the largest NRC Emoticon lexicon contains only 14k items, whereas tweets with extremely sparse surface forms are known to form very large vocabularies. Hence, using larger lexicons with better recall has the potential of learning more accurate models. Extracting such lexicons automatically is a challenging and interesting problem (Lau et al., 2011; Bro and Ehrig, 2013; Liu et al., 2013; Tai and Kao, 2013; Yang et al., 2014; Huang et al., 2014). However, different from previous work our goal is not to extract human-interpretable lexicons but to use them as a source of features to improve the classifier accuracy.



*Human Language Technologies: The 2015 Annual Conference of the North American Chapter of the ACL*, pages 1397–1402,
Denver, Colorado, May 31 – June 5, 2015. 

Following this idea, the authors in (Mohammad et al., 2013) use features derived from the lexicons to build a state-of-the-art sentiment classifier for Twitter. They construct automatic lexicons using noisy labels automatically inferred from emoticons and hashtags present in the tweets. The word-sentiment association scores are estimated using pointwise mutual information (PMI) computed between a word and a tweet label.

While the idea to model statistical correlations between the words and tweet labels using PMI or any other metric is rather intuitive, we believe there is a more effective way to exploit noisy labels for estimating the word-sentiment association scores. Our method relies on the idea of distant supervision (Marchetti-Bowick and Chambers, 2012). We use a large distantly supervised Twitter corpus, which contains noisy opinion labels (positive or negative) to learn a supervised polarity classifier. We encode tweets using words and multi-word expressions as features (which are also entries in our lexicon). The weights from the learned model are then used to define which lexicon items to keep, i.e., items that constitute a good sentiment lexicon. The scores for the lexicon items can be then directly used to encode new tweets or used to derive more advanced features. Using machine learning to induce the scores for the lexicon items has an advantage of learning the scores that are directly optimized for the classification task, where lexicon items with higher discriminative power tend to receive higher weights.

To assess the effectiveness of our approach, we reimplemented the state-of-the-art system ranking 1st in Semeval-2013 Twitter Sentiment Analysis challenge and used it as our baseline. We show that adding features from our machine-learned sentiment lexicon yields better results than any of the automatic PMI lexicons used in the baseline and all of them combined together. Our system obtains new state-of-the-art results on the SemEval-2013 message level task with an F-score of 71.32 – a 2% of absolute improvement over the previous best system in SemEval-2013. We also evaluate the utility of the ML lexicon on the five test sets from a recent Semeval-2014 task showing significant improvement over a strong baseline. Finally, our system shows high accuracy among the 42 systems participating in the Semeval-2014 challenge ranking 2nd best according to the average rank across all test sets.

## 2 Our model

We treat the task of sentiment analysis as a supervised learning problem, where we are given labeled data $\{(\mathbf{x}_i, \mathbf{y}_i)\}_{i=1}^n$ and the goal is to estimate a decision function $f(\mathbf{x}) \to \mathbf{y}$ that maps input examples to labels. In particular, we use a linear SVM model with the prediction function of the following form: $f = sign(\mathbf{w}^T\mathbf{x} + b)$, where the model weights $\mathbf{w}$ are estimated from the training set.

In the following we describe our approach to construct sentiment lexicons by learning an SVM model on the the distant supervised dataset. Finally, we describe our baseline model.

### 2.1 Distant Supervision for Automatic Lexicon Construction

Our sentiment lexicon consists of words and word sequences (we only use word unigrams and bigrams). To select lexicon items from a set of all unigrams and bigrams, we propose the following process:

1. Collect a large unlabelled corpus of tweets $C$.
2. For each tweet $t_i \in C$ use cues (hashtags or emoticons) to automatically infer its label (positive or negative): $y_i \in \{-1, +1\}$. For example, positive or negative emoticons, such as ':-)' or ':(' are good indicators of the general sentiment expressed by a tweet.
3. Extract unigram and bigram features to encode a tweet $t_i$ into a feature vector $\mathbf{x}_i \in \mathbb{R}^{|L|}$, where the lexicon $L$ is a set of unigrams and bigrams.
5. Train an SVM model $\mathbf{w} = \sum_{i=1..N} \alpha_i y_i \mathbf{x}_i$ on the encoded corpus $C = \{(\mathbf{x}_i, y_i)\}_{i=1}^N$. The model $\mathbf{w} \in \mathbb{R}^{|L|}$ is a dense vector whose components are obtained from a weighted combination of training examples $\mathbf{x}_i$ (support vectors) and their labels $y_i$ (only those instances with $\alpha_i > 0$ contribute to the components of $\mathbf{w}$).
6. Given that the each component $w^j$ of the model $\mathbf{w}$ directly corresponds to the lexicon entry $l_j \in L$ its raw score is used as a sentiment association score.

Different from manually constructed lexicons compiled by humans where each item is assigned with an interpretable sentiment score, the scores in the automatic lexicon are learned automatically on a weakly supervised task. We use the weights from an SVM model whose weights are formed by the support vectors, i.e., the most difficult instances close to the decision boundary, hence most useful for the classification task. Additionally, due to its regularisation properties, SVM is known to select only the most robust features, which is important in the case of noisy labeled data. Hence, our method is a more principled way grounded in the statistical learning theory to exploit the noisy labels for estimating the word-sentiment association scores for the lexicon entries. Moreover, feature engineering with our lexicon appears to be more helpful (see Sec. 3) on a supervised task.

### 2.2 Baseline model

We re-implement the state-of-the-art NRC model from (Mohammad et al., 2013), which ranked 1st in the Semeval-2013, and use it as our baseline. This system relies on various n-gram, surface form and lexicon features. Briefly, we engineered the following feature sets:[1]

- **Word and character grams**: we use 1,2,3 n-grams for words and 3,4,5 n-grams for character sequences;
- **Negation**: the number of negated contexts – a span of words between a negation word (*not, never*), and a punctuation mark.
- **Lexicons**: given a word, we lookup its sentiment polarity score in the lexicon: $score(w)$. The following *aggregate* features are produced for the lexicon items found in a tweet: the total count, the total sum, the maximal score and the score of the last token. These features are produced for unigrams, bigrams, each part-of-speech tag, hashtags and all-caps tokens.
- **Other**: number of hashtags, capitalized words, elongated words, positive and negative emoticons, punctuation.

## 3 Experiments

In the following experiments our goal is to assess the value of our distant supervision method to automatically extract sentiment lexicons. We compare its performance with other automatically constructed lexicons extracted from large Twitter corpora, e.g., auto lexicons built using the PMI approach from (Mohammad et al., 2013).

| Negative | Positive |
|---|---|
| (disappointing,) | (no, problem) |
| (depressing,) | (not, bad) |
| (bummer,) | (not, sad) |
| (sadly,) | (cannot, wait) |
| (passed, away) | (no, prob) |

Table 1: Lexicon items learned from Emoticon140 corpus with top negative and positive scores.

### 3.1 Lexicon learning

We extract our lexicon from a freely available Emoticon140 Twitter corpus (Go et al., 2009), where the sentiment labels are automatically inferred from emoticons contained in a tweet[2]. The major advantage of such corpora is that it is easy to build as emoticons serve as fairly good cues for the general sentiment expressed in a tweet, thus they can be used as noisy labels. Hence, large datasets can be collected without incurring any annotation costs.

Tweets with positive emoticons, like ':)', are assumed to be positive, and tweets with negative emoticons, like ':(', are labeled as negative. The corpus contains 1.6 million tweets with equal distribution between positive and negative tweets. We use a tokeniser from the CMU Twitter tagger (Gimpel et al., 2011) extracting only unigrams and bigrams[3] to encode training instances. To make the extraction of word-sentiment association weights from the model straight-forward, we ignore neutral labels thus converting the task to a binary classification task. We use LibLinear (Fan et al., 2008) with L2 regularization and default parameters to learn a model. Preprocessing, feature extraction and learning is very fast taking only a few minutes. As the number of unique unigrams and bigrams can be very large and we would like to keep our sentiment lexicon rea-

[1] our baseline system, lexicon and the code to construct it are freely available at: `https://github.com/yyy`

[2] unfortunately, the corpus to build the NRC Hashtag lexicon (Mohammad et al., 2013) is not freely available due to Twitter data distribution policies.

[3] Adding tri-grams yielded a very minor improvement, yet the size of the dictionary exploded, so to keep the size of the dictionary relatively small we use only uni- and bi-grams.

| Dataset | Size | Pos | Neg. | Neu. |
|---|---|---|---|---|
| Train'13 | 9,728 | 38% | 15% | 47% |
| Dev'13 | 1,654 | 35% | 21% | 45% |
| Twitter'13 | 3,813 | 41% | 16% | 43% |
| SMS'13 | 2093 | 24% | 19% | 58% |
| Twitter'14 | 1,853 | 53% | 11% | 36% |
| Sarcasm'14 | 86 | 38% | 47% | 15% |
| LiveJournal'14 | 1,142 | 37% | 27% | 36% |

Table 2: Datasets.

sonably small, we filter entries with small weights. In particular, we found that selecting items with a weight greater than $1e-6$ did not cause any drop in accuracy, while the resulting lexicon is reasonably compact — it contains about 3 million entries.

Table 1 gives an example of top 10 lexicon entries with highest positive and negative scores. Interestingly, one would expect to find words such as *amazing*, *cool*, etc. as having the highest positive sentiment score. However, an SVM model assigns higher scores to bigrams containing negative words *problem, bad, worries*, to outweigh their negative impact. This helps to handle the inversion of the sentiment due to negations.

It is important to note that our goal is different from constructing sentiment lexicons that are interpretable by humans, e.g., manually built lexicons, but, similar to (Mohammad et al., 2013), we build automatic lexicons to derive highly discriminative features improving the accuracy of our sentiment prediction models.

### 3.2 Setup

**Task.** We focused on the Twitter Sentiment Analysis (Task 2) from Semeval-2013 (Nakov et al., 2013) and its rerun (Task 9) from Semeval-2014 (Rosenthal et al., 2014). Both tasks include two subtasks: an expression-level and a message-level subtasks. Being more general, we focus only on predicting the sentiment of tweets at the message level, where given a tweet, the goal is to classify whether it expresses *positive*, *negative*, or *neutral* sentiment.

**Evaluation.** We used the official scorers from the Semeval 2013 & 2014, which compute the average between F-measures for the positive and negative classes.

**Data.** We evaluated our models on both Semeval-2013 and Semeval-2014 tasks with 44 and 42 participating systems correspondingly. The Semeval-2013 task released the training set containing 9,728 tweets, dev and two test sets: *Twitter'13* and *SMS'13*. We train our model on a combined train and dev sets[4]. The Semeval-2014 re-uses the same training data and systems are evaluated on 5 test sets: two test sets from Semeval-2013 and three new test sets: *LiveJournal'14*, *Twitter'14* and *Sarcasm'14*. The datasets are summarized in Table 3.1.

| n-grams | Manual | | | PMI | | ML | | Twitter'13 |
|---|---|---|---|---|---|---|---|---|
| | M | B | N | hash | s140 | raw | agg | |
| • | | | | | | | | 63.53 |
| • | • | | | | | | | 64.96 (+1.43) |
| • | | • | | | | | | 66.74 (+3.21) |
| • | | | • | | | | | 64.21 (+0.68) |
| • | • | • | • | | | | | 67.44 (+3.91) |
| • | • | • | • | • | | | | 68.47 (+4.94) |
| • | • | • | • | | • | | | 69.08 (+5.55) |
| • | • | • | • | • | • | | | 70.06 (+6.53) |
| • | • | • | • | | | • | | 69.47 (+5.94) |
| • | • | • | • | | | | • | 69.89 (+6.36) |
| • | • | • | • | | | • | • | 70.93 (+7.40) |
| • | • | • | • | • | • | • | • | **71.32** (+7.79) |
| best Semeval'13 system | | | | | | | | 69.06 |

Table 3: Results on Semeval-2013 test set. Used feature sets: n-grams; features from *Manual* lexicons using MPQA (M), BingLiu (B) and NRCEmoticon (N) lexicons; PMI lexicon extracted from NRC-hashtag and Emoticon140 (s140) datasets; our ML lexicon using *raw* and aggregate (*agg*) features. The numbers in parenthesis indicate absolute improvement w.r.t. baseline *n-grams* model.

### 3.3 Results

We report the results on two runs of the Twitter Sentiment Analysis challenge organized by Semeval from 2013 and 2014.

#### 3.3.1 Semeval-2013

The *n-grams* model includes word and character n-grams, negation and various surface form features as described in Section 2. We use this feature set as a yardstick to assess the value of adding features

[4]While in the real setting it is also possible to include additional weakly labeled data, e.g. Emoticon140, for training a model, we stick to the **constrained** setting of the Semeval tasks, where training is allowed only on the train and dev sets.

from various lexicons. Firstly, we note that using three manual lexicons: MPQA (M), BingLiu (B), and NRC (N) results in almost 4 points of absolute improvement. Notably, among all manual lexicons the *BingLiu* lexicon accounts for the largest improvement. Next, we explore the value of automatically generated lexicons using PMI scoring extracted from two large Twitter datasets: Emoticon140 (s140) and hashtag (hash). Both lexicons rely on PMI scoring formula to derive word-sentiment association scores. Adding features from these automatically generated lexicons results in further improvement over the *n-grams* feature set and yields F-score: 70.06.

Next, we explore the value of features derived from our ML based lexicon. We use the lexicon in two modalities: (i) including the raw scores (raw) of each lexicon entry (unigrams and bigrams) found in the given tweet; (ii) deriving aggregate features (*agg*) from the *raw* scores as described in Sec. 2; and (iii) using both. We note that the features from our ML-based lexicon yield superior performance to any of the PMI lexicons providing at least 2% gains and is even better when the two PMI lexicons are combined. Finally, adding the ML-based lexicon on top of the models including manual and auto lexicons provides the new state-of-the-art result on Semeval-2013 with an improvement of almost 8 points w.r.t. to the *basic* model. Our model achieves the score of 71.32 vs. 69.06 for the previous best system.

### 3.3.2 Semeval-2014

Table 4 shows that adding features from our ML-based vocabulary provides a substantial improvement over the previous best NRC system on 4 out of 5 test sets. Interestingly, we observe a strong drop on the Sarcasm'14 test set. One possible reason is that the labels for Emoticon140 corpus are inferred automatically using emoticons, which may strongly bias our model to incorrectly predict sentiment for those tweets containing sarcasm. With more than 40 systems participating in Semeval-2014 challenge, we note that the majority of systems perform well only on few test sets at once while failing on the others[5]. The performance of our system is rather high across all the test sets with an average rank of 3.4, which is the second best result in Semeval-2014 message-level task (the best system is from the NRC team with an ave-rank 2.4, whereas the closest follow up system has an ave-rank 6).

[5] http://alt.qcri.org/semeval2014/task9/

Table 4: Semeval-2014. Numbers in parenthesis is the absolute rank of a system on a given test set. Bold scores compares using our ML lexicon on top of the NRC system. Results marked with † are statistically significant at $p > 0.05$ (via the paired t-test).

| System | NRC | NRC + ML lex. | best score |
|---|---|---|---|
| LJournal'14 | 75.28 (1) | **76.54**† (1) | 74.84 |
| SMS'13 | 66.86 (5) | **67.20** (5) | 70.28 |
| Twitter'13 | 70.06 (5) | **71.32**† (2) | 72.12 |
| Twitter'14 | 68.71 (6) | **70.51**† (2) | 70.96 |
| Sarcasm'14 | **59.20** (1) | 55.08 (7) | 58.16 |
| ave-rank | 3.8 | 3.4 (2) | 2.4 (1) |

## 4 Conclusions

We demonstrated a simple and principled approach grounded in machine learning to construct sentiment lexicons. We show that using off-the-shelf machine learning tools to automatically extract lexicons greatly outperforms other automatically constructed lexicons that use pointwise mutual information to estimate sentiment scores for the lexicon items.

We have shown that combining our machine-learned lexicon with the previous best system yields state-of-the-art results in Semeval-2013 gaining over 2 points in F-score and ranking our system 2nd according to the average rank over the five test sets of Semeval-2014. Finally, our ML-based lexicon shows excellent results when added on top of the current state-of-the-art NRC system. While our experimental study is focused on Twitter, our method is general enough to be applied to sentiment classification tasks on other domains. In the future, we plan to experiment with constructing ML lexicons from larger Twitter corpora also using hashtags.

Recently, deep convolutional neural networks for sentence modelling (Kalchbrenner et al., 2014; Kim, 2014) have shown promising results on several NLP tasks. In particular, (Tang et al., 2014) showed that learning sentiment-specific word embeddings and using them as features can boost the accuracy of existing sentiment classifiers. In the future work we plan to explore such approaches.

## References


Jrgen Bro and Heiko Ehrig. 2013. Automatic construction of domain and aspect specific sentiment lexicons for customer review mining. In *CIKM*.

Rong-En Fan, Kai-Wei Chang, Cho-Jui Hsieh, Xiang-Rui Wang, and Chih-Jen Lin. 2008. LIBLINEAR: A library for large linear classification. *Journal of Machine Learning Research*, 9:1871–1874.

Kevin Gimpel, Nathan Schneider, Brendan O'Connor, Dipanjan Das, Daniel Mills, Jacob Eisenstein, Michael Heilman, Dani Yogatama, Jeffrey Flanigan, and Noah A. Smith. 2011. Part-of-speech tagging for Twitter: annotation, features, and experiments. In *ACL*.

Alex Go, Richa Bhayani, and Lei Huang. 2009. Twitter sentiment classification using distant supervision. In *CS224N Project Report, Stanford*.

Minqing Hu and Bing Liu. 2004. Mining and summarizing customer reviews. In *KDD*.

Sheng Huang, Zhendong Niu, and Chongyang Shi. 2014. Automatic construction of domain-specific sentiment lexicon based on constrained label propagation. *Knowl.-Based Syst.*

Nal Kalchbrenner, Edward Grefenstette, and Phil Blunsom. 2014. A convolutional neural network for modelling sentences. In *ACL*.

Yoon Kim. 2014. Convolutional neural networks for sentence classification. In *EMNLP*.

Raymond Yiu-Keung Lau, Chun Lam Lai, Peter Bruza, and Kam-Fai Wong. 2011. Leveraging web 2.0 data for scalable semi-supervised learning of domain-specific sentiment lexicons. In *CIKM*.

Lizhen Liu, Mengyun Lei, and Hanshi Wang. 2013. Combining domain-specific sentiment lexicon with hownet for chinese sentiment analysis.

Micol Marchetti-Bowick and Nathanael Chambers. 2012. Learning for microblogs with distant supervision: Political forecasting with twitter. In *EACL*.

Saif Mohammad and Peter Turney. 2013. Crowdsourcing a word-emotion association lexicon. *Computational Intelligence*, 39(3):555–590.

Saif M. Mohammad, Svetlana Kiritchenko, and Xiaodan Zhu. 2013. Nrc-canada: Building the state-of-the-art in sentiment analysis of tweets. In *Semeval*.

Preslav Nakov, Zornitsa Kozareva, Alan Ritter, Sara Rosenthal, Veselin Stoyanov, and Theresa Wilson. 2013. In semeval-2013 task 2: Sentiment analysis in twitter. In *Semeval*.

Bo Pang and Lillian Lee. 2004. A sentimental education: Sentiment analysis using subjectivity summarization based on minimum cuts. In *ACL*.

Bo Pang and Lillian Lee. 2008. Opinion mining and sentiment analysis. *Found. Trends Inf. Retr.*, 2(1-2):1–135, January.

Sara Rosenthal, Alan Ritter, Preslav Nakov, and Veselin Stoyanov. 2014. In semeval-2014 task 9: Sentiment analysis in twitter. In *Semeval*.

Richard Socher, Jeffrey Pennington, Eric H Huang, Andrew Y Ng, and Christopher D Manning. 2011. Semi-supervised recursive autoencoders for predicting sentiment distributions. In *EMNLP*.

Yen-Jen Tai and Hung-Yu Kao. 2013. Automatic domain-specific sentiment lexicon generation with label propagation. In *iiWAS*.

Duyu Tang, Furu Wei, Nan Yang, Ming Zhou, Ting Liu, and Bing Qin. 2014. Learning sentiment-specific word embedding for twitter sentiment classification. In *ACL*.

Sida Wang and Christopher Manning. 2012. Baselines and bigrams: Simple, good sentiment and topic classification. In *ACL*.

Theresa Wilson, Janyce Wiebe, and Paul Hoffmann. 2005. Recognizing contextual polarity in phrase-level sentiment analysis. In *EMNLP*.

Min Yang, Dingju Zhu, Rashed Mustafa, and Kam-Pui Chow. 2014. Learning domain-specific sentiment lexicon with supervised sentiment-aware lda. In *ECAI*.

# Large-scale Native Language Identification with Cross-Corpus Evaluation

**Shervin Malmasi**
Centre for Language Technology
Macquarie University
Sydney, NSW, Australia
shervin.malmasi@mq.edu.au

**Mark Dras**
Centre for Language Technology
Macquarie University
Sydney, NSW, Australia
mark.dras@mq.edu.au

## Abstract

We present a large-scale Native Language Identification (NLI) experiment on new data, with a focus on cross-corpus evaluation to identify corpus- and genre-independent language transfer features. We test a new corpus and show it is comparable to other NLI corpora and suitable for this task. Cross-corpus evaluation on two large corpora achieves good accuracy and evidences the existence of reliable language transfer features, but lower performance also suggests that NLI models are not completely portable across corpora. Finally, we present a brief case study of features distinguishing Japanese learners' English writing, demonstrating the presence of cross-corpus and cross-genre language transfer features that are highly applicable to SLA and ESL research.

## 1 Introduction

Native Language Identification, the task of determining the native language (L1) of an author based on a second language (L2) text, has received much attention recently. Much of this is motivated by Second Language Acquisition (SLA) as NLI, often accomplished via machine learning methods, can be used to study language transfer effects.

Most NLI research hitherto has focused on identifying linguistic phenomena that can capture transfer effects, with little effort towards interpreting discriminant features. Some researchers have now shifted their focus to developing data-driven methods for the automatic extraction and ranking of linguistic features that distinguish specific L1s (Swanson and Charniak, 2014).

Such methods could be used not only to confirm existing SLA hypotheses, but also to create new ones. This hypothesis formulation is an inherently difficult problem requiring copious amounts of data. Contrary to this requirement, researchers have long noted the paucity of suitable corpora[1] for this task (Brooke and Hirst, 2011). This is one of the research issues addressed by this work.

Furthermore, deriving SLA hypotheses from a single corpus may not be entirely useful for SLA research. Many variables like genre and topic are constant within a corpus, restricting the validity of such cross-validation studies to those dimensions.

An alternative, potentially more helpful approach, is to identify transfer features that reliably distinguish an L1 across multiple corpora of differing genres and domains. A cross-corpus methodology may be a more promising avenue to finding features that generalize to diverse text sources, but requires additional large corpora. It is also a more realistic approach, and one we pursue in this work.

Accordingly, the aims of the present work are to: (1) test a large new corpus suitable for NLI, (2) perform within-corpus evaluation with a comparative analysis against equivalent corpora, (3) perform cross-corpus evaluation to determine the efficiency of corpus independent features and (4) analyze the features' utility for SLA & ESL research.

## 2 Background and Motivation

NLI work has been growing in recent years, using a wide range of syntactic and more recently, lexical features to distinguish the L1. A detailed review of NLI methods is omitted here for reasons of space, but a thorough exposition is presented in the report from the very first NLI Shared Task that was held in 2013 (Tetreault et al., 2013).

Most English NLI work has been done using two corpora. The *International Corpus of Learner En-*

[1] An ideal NLI corpus should have multiple L1s, be balanced by topic, proficiency, texts per L1 and be large in size.



*Human Language Technologies: The 2015 Annual Conference of the North American Chapter of the ACL*, pages 1403–1409,
Denver, Colorado, May 31 – June 5, 2015. 

*glish* (Granger et al., 2009) was widely used until recently, despite its shortcomings[2] being widely noted (Brooke and Hirst, 2012a). More recently, TOEFL11, the first corpus designed for NLI was released (Blanchard et al., 2013). While it is the largest NLI dataset available, it only contains argumentative essays, limiting analyses to this genre.

Research has also expanded to use non-English learner corpora (Malmasi and Dras, 2014a; Malmasi and Dras, 2014c). Recently, Malmasi and Dras (2014b) introduced the Chinese Learner Corpus for NLI and their results indicate that feature performance may be similar across corpora and even L1-L2 pairs. This is a claim that we will test here.

NLI is now also moving towards using features to generate SLA hypotheses. Swanson and Charniak (2014) approach this by using both L1 and L2 data to identify features exhibiting non-uniform usage in both datasets, creating lists of candidate transfer features. Malmasi and Dras (2014d) propose a different method, using linear SVM weights to extract lists of overused and underused linguistic features for each L1 group.

Cross-corpus studies have been conducted for various data-driven NLP tasks, including parsing (Gildea, 2001), WSD (Escudero et al., 2000) and NER (Nothman et al., 2009). While most such experiments show a drop in performance, the effect varies widely across tasks, making it hard to predict the expected drop for NLI. We aim to address this question using large training and testing data.

## 3 EFCamDat: A new corpus for NLI

The EF Cambridge Open Language Database (EFCAMDAT) is an English L2 corpus that was released recently (Geertzen et al., 2013). It is composed of texts submitted to *Englishtown*, an online school used by thousands of learners daily.

This corpus is notable for its size, containing some 550k texts from numerous nationalities, making it an ideal candidate for NLI research. While the TOEFL11 is made of argumentative essays, EFCAMDAT has a much wider range of genres including writing emails, descriptions, letters, reviews, instructions and more.

In this work we present an application of NLI to this new data. As some of the texts can be short, we use the methodology of Brooke and Hirst (2011) to concatenate and create texts with at least 300 tokens, much like the TOEFL11.

[2]The issues exist as the corpus was not designed for NLI.

| | |
|---|---|
| **Common** | Arabic, Chinese, French, German, Italian, Japanese, Korean, Spanish, Turkish |
| **EFCAMDAT** | Portuguese, Russian |
| **TOEFL11** | Hindi, Telugu |

Table 1: The 11 L1 classes extracted from the EFCAMDAT corpus, compared to the TOEFL11 corpus. The first 9 classes are common between both.

From the data we choose 850 texts from each of the top 11 nationalities. This subset of EFCAMDAT thus consists of 9,350 documents totalling approximately 3.2m tokens. This is an average of 337 tokens per text, close to the 348 tokens per text in TOEFL11.

This also provides us with the same number of classes as the TOEFL11, as shown in Table 1, facilitating direct performance comparisons. The table also indicates the 9 classes common to both corpora. This subset of common classes enables us to perform large-scale cross-corpus validation experiments that have not been possible until now.

## 4 Methodology

We use the standard NLI classification approach. A linear Support Vector Machine is used for classification and feature vectors are created using relative frequency values. We also combine features with a mean probability ensemble classifier (Polikar, 2006, §4.2) using the probabilities assigned to each class. We compare results with a random baseline and the oracle baseline used by Malmasi et al. (2015). The oracle correctly classifies a text if any ensemble member correctly predicts its label and defines an upper-bound for classification accuracy. We avoid using lexical features as EFCAMDAT is not topic balanced. We extract the following topic-independent feature types:

**Function words** are topic-independent grammatical words such as prepositions which indicate the relations between other words. They are known to be useful for NLI. Frequencies of 400 English function words[3] are extracted as features. We also apply function word bigrams as described in Malmasi et al. (2013).

**Context-free Grammar Production Rules** are extracted after parsing each sentence. Each rule is a classification feature (Wong and Dras, 2011) and captures global syntactic patterns.

[3]Like previous work, this also includes stop words, which we sourced from the Onix Text Retrieval Toolkit: http://www.lextek.com/manuals/onix/stopwords1.html

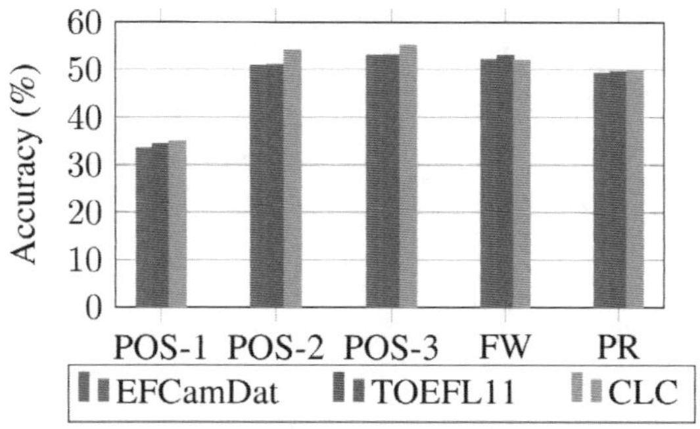


Figure 1: Comparing EFCAMDAT feature performance with the TOEFL11 and Chinese Learner Corpus (CLC). POS-1/2/3: POS uni/bi/trigrams, FW: Function Words, PR: CFG Productions

**Part-of-Speech (POS)** $n$-grams of size 1–3 are extracted as features. They capture preferences for word classes and their localized ordering patterns.

## 5 Within-Corpus Evaluation

Our first experiment applies 10-fold cross-validation within the corpus to assess feature efficacy. The results are shown in the first column of Table 2.

All features perform substantially higher than the 9% baseline. POS trigrams are the best single feature (53%), suggesting there exist significant inter-class syntactic differences. Next, we also combined all features using a classifier ensemble, which has been shown to be helpful for NLI (Tetreault et al., 2012). This yields the best accuracy of 65% against an upper-bound of 87% set by the oracle.

We also compare these results to those from the TOEFL11 and Chinese Learner Corpus (CLC). As shown in Figure 1, we find that feature performance is nearly identical across corpora. Consistent with the results in Malmasi and Dras (2014b), this seems to suggest an invariant degree of transfer across different learners and L1-L2 pairs.

Figure 2 shows the confusion matrix. German is the most correctly classified L1, while the highest confusion is between Japanese–Korean, followed by Spanish–Portuguese and French–Italian. This is not surprising given their syntactic similarity as well as being typologically related in case of the latter two.

## 6 Large-scale Cross-Corpus Evaluation

Our second experiment tests the cross-corpus efficacy of the features by training on EFCAMDAT and testing on TOEFL11,[4] and *vice versa*. As the corpus texts are from different genres, this approach enables

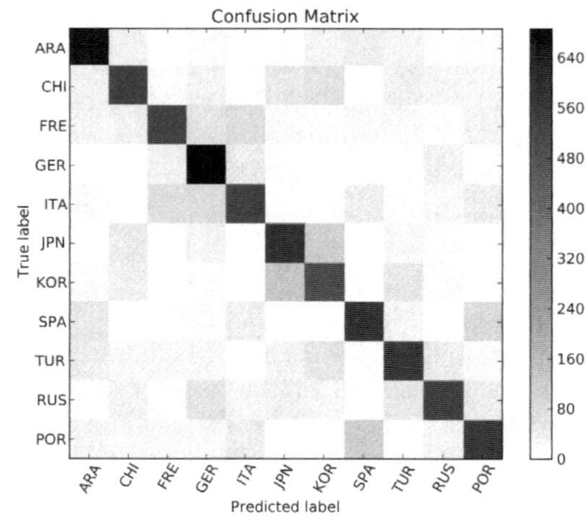


Figure 2: EFCAMDAT 11-class confusion matrix.

| Arabic | German | Japanese |
|---|---|---|
| Saudi | Germany | Japan |
| Arabia | Berlin | Tokyo |
| Arabic | Hamburg | Osaka |
| Mohammed | Frankfurt | Nagoya |
| Ali | Munich | Yen |

Table 3: Selected items from the top 15 most discriminative words for Arabic/German/Japanese.

us to test the cross-corpus and cross-genre generalizability of our features.

Results are shown in the second and third column of Table 2. While lower than the cross-validation results which were on 11 classes *vs* 9 here, the results are far greater than the baseline. The accuracy for training on EFCAMDAT and testing on TOEFL11 is higher (33.45%) than the other way around (28.42%), even though TOEFL11 is the larger corpus. This is possibly because EFCAMDAT has numerous genres while TOEFL11 does not. The cross-corpus oracle is also over 20% lower, despite an increase in the random baseline, showing some features are not portable across corpora. Training on TOEFL11 yields a lower oracle.

Although a performance drop was expected due to the big genre differences, results suggest the presence of some corpus-independent features that capture cross-linguistic influence. However, they also suggest that a large portion of the features helpful for NLI are genre-dependent.

Previously, word $n$-grams have been applied in small-scale cross-corpus studies and found to be the best feature (Brooke and Hirst, 2012b). Word $n$-grams have been previously used in NLI and are believed to capture lexical transfer effects which have been previously noted by researchers and linguists

[4]The 9 common classes discussed in §3 are used.

| Classification Feature | EFCAMDAT 10-fold CV | Train EFCAMDAT Test TOEFL11 | Train TOEFL11 Test EFCAMDAT |
|---|---|---|---|
| Random Baseline | 9.09 | 11.11 | 11.11 |
| Oracle Baseline | 86.84 | 64.92 | 62.43 |
| Function Word unigrams | 52.01 | 27.14 | 21.77 |
| Function Word bigrams | 47.92 | 29.21 | 22.63 |
| Production Rules | 49.12 | 30.73 | 23.91 |
| Part-of-Speech unigrams | 33.21 | 23.42 | 16.71 |
| Part-of-Speech bigrams | 50.43 | 31.02 | 23.09 |
| Part-of-Speech trigrams | 53.05 | 32.38 | 25.55 |
| Ensemble (All features) | **64.95** | **33.45** | **28.42** |
| Word unigrams | – | 41.82 | 42.48 |

Table 2: Classification accuracy (%) for our within- and cross-corpus experiments.

(Odlin, 1989). The effects are mediated not only by cognates and word form similarities, but also semantics and meanings. Other NLI studies have also provided empirical evidence for this hypothesis (Malmasi and Cahill, 2015).

However, issues stemming from topic bias[5] have also limited their use in NLI (Brooke and Hirst, 2012a), although use could be justified in cross-corpus scenarios due to the lower risk of topic-bias across corpora. We applied word unigrams to our cross-corpus experiment, achieving an accuracy of 41.8% for training on the EFCAMDAT and testing on TOEFL11 and 42.5% for the reverse setting. These are the best results in this setup.

To check for any topic-bias effects, we inspected the most discriminative features for each L1 class using the method proposed by Malmasi and Dras (2014d). This analysis revealed that the top features were mostly cultural and geographic references related to the author's country. Table 3 contains words selected from the top 15 most discriminative features found in the cross-corpus experiment for three L1s. We observe that most of these are toponyms or culture-specific terms such as names and currencies. These results reveal another potential issue with using lexical features. Although this isn't topic-bias, the features do not represent genuine linguistic differences or lexical transfer effects between L1 groups. In practical scenarios, this could also make NLI systems vulnerable to content-based manipulation. The exclusion of proper nouns is one way to combat this.

## 7 A Case Study of Japanese Learners

To demonstrate the utility of this cross-corpus approach we present a brief case study of features that characterize English writings of Japanese learners. We extracted the most discriminative cross-corpus features of Japanese learner texts using the method of Malmasi and Dras (2014d).

Table 4 contains the top production rule features. The first rule shows a preference for having a subordinate clause before the main clause. The next two rules show that Japanese learners tend to begin their sentences with adverbs and conjunctions. This preference for placing information at the start of sentences is most likely rooted in the fact that Japanese is an SOV head-final language[6] where dependent clauses generally precede the main clause and relative clauses precede the noun they modify. The influence of this head-direction parameter on English acquisition has been previously investigated (Flynn, 1989).

In contrast, it is quite common for the main clause to precede the subordinate clause in English. Other research has also noted that Japanese speakers have a "long before short" preference[7] (Yamashita and Chang, 2001). This is also evidence by another highly discriminative rule for this L1: `S → S , CC S .`

Japanese writers also seem more likely to split longer arguments into multiple shorter sentences, as suggested by our third production rule. It has also been noted that Japanese and Korean sentences in the TOEFL11 have the shortest mean length (Cimino et al., 2013, p. 211).

Turning to POS trigrams, the POS tag sequence `VBZ JJ NN` is strongly linked to Japanese learn-

[5]Due to correlations between text topics and L1 classes.

[6]Contrasted with English which is SVO.

[7]This refers to how conjuncts are ordered: short-before-long in English, long-before-short in Japanese. Our findings suggest that Japanese writers transfer this internal order-preference into their L2 English writing.

| Production Rule | Example Sentence |
|---|---|
| S → SBAR , NP VP . | If you have spare time, you'll think of shopping. |
| S → ADVP , NP VP . | Therefore, the online studying system is really convenient for me. |
| S → CC NP VP . | But I'm not good at English. / But it wasn't comfortable and cosy. |

Table 4: The top 3 cross-corpus production rule features for Japanese L1 with example lexicalizations.

| Overuse | Underuse |
|---|---|
| however | perhaps |
| though | somebody |
| cannot | everything |
| therefore | behind |
| such | upon |
| into | between |

Table 5: English function words overused and underused by Japanese learners in their writing.

ers. It represents a third person verb, such as *is* or *has* followed by an adjective and a noun. A brief analysis reveals that this is commonly observed in Japanese learner texts because the sequence is missing a determiner before the noun phrase.[8] This likely stems from the fact that Japanese learners have difficulty with English articles, often failing to use them (Butler, 2002; Thomas, 1989). Its prominence in the ranked list shows that it is a common issue across distinct learners and genres.

The top overused and underused function words are listed in Table 5. The words *however* and *therefore* are highly relevant; Japanese writers often use these to start sentences, possibly due to the abovementioned production rules. The word *into* is also predictive and seems to be used in places where *in* is more appropriate. This may be due to the Japanese words for *in*, *to* and *into* being similar.[9] In the underuse list, *perhaps* is never used by Japanese learners. Other words here are low-frequency in Japanese L1 texts in both corpora.

## 8 Discussion

In this work we presented the first application of one of the largest and newest publicly available learner corpora to NLI. Cross-validation experiments mirrored the performance of other corpora and demonstrated its utility for the task. We believe this will motivate future work by equipping researchers with a large-scale corpus that is highly suitable for NLI.

Next, results from the largest cross-corpus NLI evaluation to date were presented, providing strong evidence for the presence of transfer features that generalize across learners, corpora, topics and genres. However, the fact that the cross-corpus accuracy is lower than within-corpus cross-validation highlights that a large portion of the features are highly corpus-specific. This suggests that NLI models are not entirely portable across corpora. Practical applications of NLI to forensic linguistics or SLA must be robust to input from numerous sources and their associated variations, and this finding highlights the need for a cross-corpus approach.

To demonstrate how this methodology could be used for SLA, an examination of the cross-corpus features effective in classifying texts of Japanese learners was conducted. Through feature analysis, we were able to link these patterns of syntactic productions, article use and lexical choices to L1-based SLA hypotheses.

Our output lists hundreds of features, not included or examined here due to space limitations, whose analysis would allow SLA researchers to explore and generate new hypotheses, specially by combining multiple syntactic feature types.

A shortcoming here is that we did not balance texts by proficiency to match the TOEFL11. We expect that a more even sampling of proficiency or using proficiency-segregated models will yield higher accuracy and features more representative of students at each proficiency level.

Directions for future work are manifold. The next phase of this research will focus on developing tools to derive and browse ranked lists of the most discriminative cross-corpus features, which will then be used to formulate SLA hypotheses. Subject to availability of data, this could be expanded to a multiple cross-corpus methodology, using three or more corpora. Its application to other languages besides English is also of interest.

NLI is a young but rapidly growing field of research and this study is but a first step in shifting efforts towards a more interpretive approach to the task. We hope that the new dataset and directions presented here will galvanize future work.

[8] Example lexicalizations from EFCAMDAT include "She *wears black top*" and "This area *is famous park*."

[9] All use the particle *ni*, see Takenobu et al. (2005)

## References


Daniel Blanchard, Joel Tetreault, Derrick Higgins, Aoife Cahill, and Martin Chodorow. 2013. TOEFL11: A Corpus of Non-Native English. Technical report, Educational Testing Service.

Julian Brooke and Graeme Hirst. 2011. Native language detection with 'cheap' learner corpora. Presented at the *Conference of Learner Corpus Research*, University of Louvain, Belgium.

Julian Brooke and Graeme Hirst. 2012a. Measuring interlanguage: Native language identification with L1-influence metrics. In *Proceedings of the Eight International Conference on Language Resources and Evaluation (LREC'12)*, pages 779–784, Istanbul, Turkey, May.

Julian Brooke and Graeme Hirst. 2012b. Robust, Lexicalized Native Language Identification. In *Proc. Internat. Conf. on Computat. Linguistics (COLING)*.

Yuko Goto Butler. 2002. Second language learners' theories on the use of english articles. *Studies in second language acquisition*, 24(03):451–480.

Andrea Cimino, Felice Dell'Orletta, Giulia Venturi, and Simonetta Montemagni. 2013. Linguistic profiling based on general–purpose features and native language identification. In *Proceedings of the Eighth Workshop on Innovative Use of NLP for Building Educational Applications*, pages 207–215, Atlanta, Georgia, June. Association for Computational Linguistics.

Gerard Escudero, Lluís Màrquez, and German Rigau. 2000. An empirical study of the domain dependence of supervised word sense disambiguation systems. In *Proceedings of the 2000 Joint SIGDAT conference on Empirical methods in natural language processing and very large corpora*, pages 172–180. Association for Computational Linguistics.

Suzanne Flynn. 1989. The role of the head-initial/head-final parameter in the acquisition of English relative clauses by adult Spanish and Japanese speakers. *Linguistic perspectives on second language acquisition*, pages 89–108.

Jeroen Geertzen, Theodora Alexopoulou, and Anna Korhonen. 2013. Automatic Linguistic Annotation of Large Scale L2 Databases: The EF-Cambridge Open Language Database (EFCamDat).

Daniel Gildea. 2001. Corpus variation and parser performance. In *Proceedings of the 2001 Conference on Empirical Methods in Natural Language Processing*, pages 167–202.

Sylviane Granger, Estelle Dagneaux, Fanny Meunier, and Magali Paquot. 2009. *International Corpus of Learner English (Version 2)*. Presses Universitaires de Louvain, Louvian-la-Neuve.

Shervin Malmasi and Aoife Cahill. 2015. Measuring Feature Diversity in Native Language Identification. In *Proceedings of the Tenth Workshop on Innovative Use of NLP for Building Educational Applications*, Denver, Colorado, June. Association for Computational Linguistics.

Shervin Malmasi and Mark Dras. 2014a. Arabic Native Language Identification. In *Proceedings of the Arabic Natural Language Processing Workshop (EMNLP 2014)*, pages 180–186, Doha, Qatar, October. Association for Computational Linguistics.

Shervin Malmasi and Mark Dras. 2014b. Chinese Native Language Identification. pages 95–99, Gothenburg, Sweden, April. Association for Computational Linguistics.

Shervin Malmasi and Mark Dras. 2014c. Finnish Native Language Identification. In *Proceedings of the Australasian Language Technology Workshop (ALTA)*, pages 139–144, Melbourne, Australia.

Shervin Malmasi and Mark Dras. 2014d. Language Transfer Hypotheses with Linear SVM Weights. In *Proceedings of the 2014 Conference on Empirical Methods in Natural Language Processing (EMNLP)*, pages 1385–1390, Doha, Qatar, October. Association for Computational Linguistics.

Shervin Malmasi, Sze-Meng Jojo Wong, and Mark Dras. 2013. NLI Shared Task 2013: MQ Submission. In *Proceedings of the Eighth Workshop on Innovative Use of NLP for Building Educational Applications*, pages 124–133, Atlanta, Georgia, June. Association for Computational Linguistics.

Shervin Malmasi, Joel Tetreault, and Mark Dras. 2015. Oracle and Human Baselines for Native Language Identification. In *Proceedings of the Tenth Workshop on Innovative Use of NLP for Building Educational Applications*, Denver, Colorado, June. Association for Computational Linguistics.

Joel Nothman, Tara Murphy, and James R Curran. 2009. Analysing Wikipedia and gold-standard corpora for NER training. In *Proceedings of the 12th Conference of the European Chapter of the Association for Computational Linguistics*, pages 612–620. Association for Computational Linguistics.

Terence Odlin. 1989. *Language Transfer: Cross-linguistic Influence in Language Learning*. Cambridge University Press, Cambridge, UK.

Robi Polikar. 2006. Ensemble based systems in decision making. *Circuits and Systems Magazine, IEEE*, 6(3):21–45.

Ben Swanson and Eugene Charniak. 2014. Data driven language transfer hypotheses. *EACL 2014*, page 169.

Tokunaga Takenobu, Koyama Tomofumi, and Saito Sugguru. 2005. Meaning of japanese spatial nouns. In *Proceedings of the Second ACL-SIGSEM Workshop on the Linguistic Dimensions of Prepositions and their Use in Computational Linguistics Formalisms and Applications*, pages 93–100.

Joel Tetreault, Daniel Blanchard, Aoife Cahill, and Martin Chodorow. 2012. Native Tongues, Lost and Found: Resources and Empirical Evaluations in Native Language Identification. In *Proceedings of COLING 2012*, pages 2585–2602, Mumbai, India, December. The COLING 2012 Organizing Committee.

Joel Tetreault, Daniel Blanchard, and Aoife Cahill. 2013. A Report on the First Native Language Identification Shared Task. In *Proceedings of the Eighth Workshop on Innovative Use of NLP for Building Educational Applications*, pages 48–57, Atlanta, Georgia, June. Association for Computational Linguistics.

Margaret Thomas. 1989. The acquisition of English articles by first-and second-language learners. *Applied Psycholinguistics*, 10(03):335–355.

Sze-Meng Jojo Wong and Mark Dras. 2011. Exploiting Parse Structures for Native Language Identification. In *Proceedings of the 2011 Conference on Empirical Methods in Natural Language Processing*, pages 1600–1610, Edinburgh, Scotland, UK., July. Association for Computational Linguistics.

Hiroko Yamashita and Franklin Chang. 2001. "Long before short" preference in the production of a head-final language. *Cognition*, 81(2):B45–B55.

# Unediting: Detecting Disfluencies Without Careful Transcripts

**Victoria Zayats, Mari Ostendorf and Hannaneh Hajishirzi**
Electrical Engineering Department
University of Washington
Seattle, WA, USA
[vzayats, ostendor, hannaneh]@u.washington.edu

## Abstract

Speech transcripts often only capture semantic content, omitting disfluencies that can be useful for analyzing social dynamics of a discussion. This work describes steps in building a model that can recover a large fraction of locations where disfluencies were present, by transforming carefully annotated text to match the standard transcription style, introducing a two-stage model for handling different types of disfluencies, and applying semi-supervised learning. Experiments show improvement in disfluency detection on Supreme Court oral arguments, nearly 23% improvement in F1.

## 1 Introduction

Many hearings, lectures, news broadcasts and other spoken proceedings are hand-transcribed and made available online for easier searching and increased accessability. For speed and cost reasons, standard transcription services aim at representing semantic content only; thus, filled pauses (uh, um) and many disfluencies (repetitions and self corrections) are omitted, though not all. Careful transcripts represent all the words (and word fragments spoken), as shown below with disfluent regions underlined.

| |
|---|
| ***Careful:*** *<u>It is it is a</u> we submit* |
| *Where there used to be <u>um um um uh</u> the decision* |
| ***Standard:*** *It is, it is, we submit* |
| *Where there used to be the decision* |

These phenomena are quite common in spontaneous speech, even in formal settings such as Supreme Court oral arguments and congressional hearings (Zayats et al., 2014).

While disfluencies may not be important for analyzing the topic of a discussion, the rate and type of disfluencies provide an indication of other factors of interest in spoken language analysis, including cognitive load, emotion, and social cues (Shriberg, 2001). Further, predicting locations of disfluencies in standard transcripts would help to improve time alignments of transcripts to the audio signal, and to provide more useful text data for training language models for speech recognition. Since careful annotation of transcripts with this information is costly, this paper tackles the problem of recovering the disfluencies from clues in the standard orthographic transcripts, or "unediting" the transcripts.[1]

Here, unediting is treated as detection of the reparandum of the disfluencies. Following the structural representation of (Shriberg, 1994), as in:

[ we would + which we would ]
[ would + [ who + who ] wouldn't ]

the task is to detect the words in the brackets preceding the '+' which marks the self-interruption point. Of course, here, some of the words in those regions may not be in the transcript, so location is more important than extent. In addition, some cues used (i.e. filled pauses and word fragments) are not available in standard transcripts.

Three developments are combined to address the problem of unediting with the constraint of limited hand-annotated training data in the target domain: oral arguments from the Supreme Court of the United States (SCOTUS) available from the Oyez Project archive (oyez.org). First, we identify mechanisms for transforming the careful transcripts of the Switchboard corpus (Godfrey et al., 1992) to be

[1]Thanks to Mark Liberman for the term "unediting."



*Human Language Technologies: The 2015 Annual Conference of the North American Chapter of the ACL*, pages 1410–1415,
Denver, Colorado, May 31 – June 5, 2015. 

more similar to the Oyez transcripts. Second, we introduce a multi-stage model that accounts for differences in the rates of repetitions and self-corrections in standard vs. careful transcripts. Lastly, we apply semi-supervised learning to take advantage of the large amount of original Oyez transcripts. The system combining all these techniques, referred to here as UNEDITOR, leads to an improvement in F1 of nearly 23% compared to a baseline of training from the original disfluency-annotated Switchboard corpus.

## 2 Related work

This paper builds on prior work using conditional random field (CRF) models (Liu et al., 2006; Georgila, 2009; Ostendorf and Hahn, 2013; Zayats et al., 2014). More recent work has shown a benefit from Markov networks (Qian and Liu, 2013; Wang et al., 2014). Since our work is on the transcription style mismatch, this work adopts the simpler CRF approach, but can be easily extended to other classification techniques.

In this work, we use only text features. While prosodic features have been shown to be useful (Shriberg, 1999; Kahn et al., 2005; Liu et al., 2006; Wang et al., 2014), the fact that the Oyez transcripts do not capture all the words means that forced time alignments are unreliable and the associated prosodic features are too noisy to be useful. Other studies integrate disfluency detection with parsing, e.g. (Charniak and Johnson, 2001; Johnson and Charniak, 2004; Lease et al., 2006; Hale et al., 2006; Miller, 2009; Miller et al., 2009; Zwarts et al., 2010; Rasooli and Tetreault, 2013; Honnibal and Johnson, 2014), but parsers trained on standard treebank data sets are not effective on the very long and complex sentences in SCOTUS; parser adaptation is left for future work.

There are a few studies that have investigated disfluency detection using cross-domain training data (Georgila et al., 2010; Ostendorf and Hahn, 2013; Zayats et al., 2014), and many more that have used multi-domain data for other language processing tasks. What is different about the task addressed here is that both the domain (topic and speaking style) and the transcription protocol differ between the target and source domain. There have been some attempts to transform written text to a more conversational style for training language models, e.g. Bulyko et al. (2007) inserted pause fillers and word repetitions, which led to reductions in perplexity though not word error rate. The work here differs in that the transformation is in the reverse direction (removing fillers from conversational text) and punctuation cues are emphasized.

## 3 Transforming training data

Here we describe methods for generating training data for use with standard transcripts: i) transferring labels from a small amount of carefully annotated data to corresponding standard transcripts, and ii) transforming the existing Switchboard training set to make it more similar to the target domain.

### 3.1 SCOTUS corpora

The Oyez Project at Chicago-Kent is a multimedia archive containing audio and transcripts of the Supreme Court hearings since 1955. While OYEZ transcripts are consistent with the audio in general, they are not accurate when it comes to disfluencies. We notice that most simple disfluencies such as repetitions have been omitted by OYEZ annotators, while more complex ones are often present and annotators have used the '...' symbol at locations of filled pauses or repetitions. Having those explicit cues indicating interruption points in disfluencies makes it possible to consider recovering the untranscribed disfluencies.

For CAREFUL SCOTUS annotation, we use the data provided by (Zayats et al., 2014), which includes seven cases with carefully transcribed audio and hand-annotated disfluencies, with separately marked repetitions. We develop ANNOTATED OYEZ transcripts, by transferring disfluency labels for those seven cases from CAREFUL SCOTUS to the corresponding files in OYEZ and dropping the deletion markers. As a result, those transcripts are identical to the original OYEZ transcripts, but in addition contain disfluency annotation derived from CAREFUL SCOTUS.

In order to align the CAREFUL SCOTUS and ORIGINAL OYEZ transcripts, we use a dynamic programming algorithm for sequence alignment with matching scores as given in Table 1 and a deletion

| CAREFUL SCOTUS | OYEZ | Score |
|---|---|---|
| exact match | exact match | 4 |
| '+' | '...' | 3 |
| punctuation | punctuation | 2 |
| end of sentence | '...' | 2 |
| word/punct | '...' | 1 |
| word | other word | -1 |
| word | punct | -1 |

Table 1: Matching scores used in dynamic programming transcript alignment.

cost of 1. Some examples of CAREFUL SCOTUS, OYEZ, ALIGNED OYEZ (with deletions marked) and ANNOTATED OYEZ transcripts are shown below. The full corpus is available at `https://ssli.ee.washington.edu/tial/data/oyez`.

CAREFUL SCOTUS: *[ [S It is + it is ] a + ] we submit*
*Where there used to be um um um uh the decision*
OYEZ: *It is, it is, we submit*
*Where there used to be the decision*
ALIGNED OYEZ: *[ [S It is, + it is ], __ + ] we submit*
*Where there used to be __ __ __ __ the decision*
ANNOTATED OYEZ: *[ [S It is, + it is ], + ] we submit*
*Where there used to be the decision*

### 3.2 Switchboard transformation

The ANNOTATED OYEZ training set is a very small dataset, and other work has shown that Switchboard (SWBD) is useful for cross-domain training for SCOTUS (Zayats et al., 2014). However, prior work has been with careful transcripts. SWBD transcripts do not include '...' symbols, and SWBD has many more commas and other punctuation symbols. In order to make best use of the SWBD data, we transform it to be more similar to the OYEZ transcripts in two steps. First, we add '...' after interruption points in SWBD. Second, we remove all punctuations except '...' in the middle of the sentence in both of the corpora.

## 4 Detecting disfluencies

In this section we describe the UNEDITOR system, which is a two-stage CRF model trained on transformed training data and takes advantage of a large pool of unlabeled data with a self-training technique.

**Baseline: CRF** We use a conditional random field (CRF) model that labels each word in a sentence, following a tagging approach with separate repetition and non-repetition reparandum states, as in (Ostendorf and Hahn, 2013). The feature set includes identity and pattern match features widely used in disfluency detection tasks, as well as distance-based and disfluency language model features from (Zayats et al., 2014).

### 4.1 Two-stage model

Using the same features as in the baseline, we introduce a two-stage CRF model motivated by our observation that many repetitions are omitted from the standard transcriptions. Thus, while 62% of disfluencies in CAREFUL SCOTUS are repetitions, only 22% of all disfluencies in ANNOTATED OYEZ are repetitions. We find that training at two separate stages helps to overcome the difference in distributions of two disfluency types between source and target domains, and hence results in a better model for adaptation. In the first stage, we train a model to detect repetitions by only considering repetition states in the training data. In the second stage, we train a model to detect non-repetitions by removing all repetitions from the training data. Similarly at test time, we use the first-stage model to detect repetitions, then remove all the detected repetitions, and apply the second-stage model to detect non-repetitions. In evaluation, we report the disfluencies detected in both stages.

### 4.2 Self-training

A benefit of OYEZ transcripts is that there is a huge amount of unlabeled data available, which makes it natural to use semi-supervised learning. In this work, we use a simple self-training approach. First we apply a CRF model trained on the labeled data to the unlabeled data. Then we augment the training data with automatically labeled sentences that have been detected to contain a disfluency with a confidence score greater than 0.5, and retrain the model with the new augmented training set.

## 5 Experiments and discussion

We evaluate the different sources/transformations of training data, self-training and the two-stage detection model on ANNOTATED OYEZ transcripts from three cases ($\sim$30k words).

| Training set | Prec | Rec | F1 |
|---|---|---|---|
| CAREFUL SCOTUS | 66.1 | 16.7 | 26.7 |
| ANNOT OYEZ | **86.7** | 20.4 | 33.0 |
| ORIG SWBD | 62.2 | 29.1 | 39.7 |
| CAREFUL SCOTUS + ORIG SWBD | 63.7 | 27.8 | 38.7 |
| ANNOT OYEZ + TRANSF SWBD | 70.9 | **49.0** | **57.9** |

Table 2: Disfluency detection of ANNOT OYEZ with different training sets.

| Training set: ANNOT OYEZ+ | Prec | Rec | F1 |
|---|---|---|---|
| ORIGSWBD | 67.8 | 29.3 | 40.9 |
| SWBD WITH ... | 63.1 | 46.8 | 53.7 |
| TRANSF SWBD | **70.9** | **49.0** | **57.9** |

Table 3: The combination of ANNOT OYEZ and SWBD with different SWBD transformation steps.

| Training set | Prec | Rec | F1 |
|---|---|---|---|
| CAREFUL SCOTUS | 57.8 | 21.2 | 31.0 |
| ANNOT OYEZ | **81.7** | 27.3 | 41.0 |
| ORIG SWBD | 59.0 | 31.7 | 41.2 |
| CAREFUL SCOTUS + ORIG SWBD | 64.6 | 33.7 | 44.3 |
| ANNOT OYEZ + TRANSF SWBD | 71.7 | **52.8** | **60.8** |

Table 4: Self-training performance using different initial models.

## 5.1 Transforming training data

First, we assess the utility of different training sources and training data transformation using the baseline model. Note that the two SCOTUS sets are quite small (four cases, ~64k words) compared to Switchboard (1.3M words). Because of the difference in punctuation style between the original Oyez transcripts and the careful transcripts of both corpora, all sentence-internal punctuation is removed in the CAREFUL SCOTUS and ORIG SWBD data.

Table 2 reports results on training the CRF model with the different sources and their combinations. As expected, detection with in-domain training data and transformed SWBD (ANNOT OYEZ+TRANSF SWBD) outperforms training on all other dataset combinations. Training on ANNOT OYEZ alone significantly outperforms detection (especially precision) when only trained on the carefully annotated data because of the matching transcription style. Training with ORIG SWBD outperforms training with ANNOT OYEZ alone mainly due to the availability of more training data in the SWBD dataset, consistent with results in (Ostendorf and Hahn, 2013). Surprisingly, the CAREFUL SCOTUS data did not provide any benefit when added to the ORIG SWBD.

Next, we study the impact of adding '...' symbols and removing punctuation for transforming the SWBD data. Table 3 reports results for training the CRF model with the combination of ANNOT OYEZ and SWBD with different transformation steps. We observe that roughly 30% of the interruption points in CAREFUL SCOTUS are associated with the '...' symbol in the OYEZ transcripts; therefore, we add '...' symbols after $1/3$ of the interruption points in the SWBD. As expected, disfluency detection is improved by transforming SWBD with adding '...'. The largest gain is obtained when we also remove punctuation (the row TRANSF SWBD). All further experiments use this setting for training the models.

## 5.2 Self-training

Here we study the contribution of semi-supervised learning when applied on the baseline model (Table 5). For self-training, we use 1,765 OYEZ transcripts dated 1990 - 2011 as our unlabeled data (~17.5M words), with a confidence threshold of 0.5 for augmenting the training data, as described previously. We use each one of the baseline models in Table 2 as an initial model for the self-training for comparison to the results in Table 4. While adding a lot of in-domain data definitely helps, the quality of the initial model plays a major role in the overall performance.

## 5.3 Two-stage model

Finally, we assess the impact of the two-stage model with and without self-training (Table 5). For the two-stage semi-supervised model, self-training was only used for the second stage (non-repetition detection). As expected, both two-stage and self-training models improve the baseline CRF model, and the combination performs the best. The two-stage model helps to adapt the differences in distribution of repetitions and non-repetitions between the two domains by factoring the different problems to improve the match of the more difficult non-repetition cases. Overall, we obtain nearly 23% im-

| Model | Prec | Rec | F1 |
|---|---|---|---|
| 1-stage | 70.9 | 49.0 | 57.9 |
| 1-stage semi | 71.7 | **52.8** | 60.8 |
| 2-stage | **83.3** | 47.6 | 60.6 |
| UNEDITOR: 2-stage semi | 76.8 | 52.2 | **62.2** |

Table 5: Baseline, two-stages and self-training methods, comparison: baseline self-training method is trained on ...., all the rest methods are trained on ANNOT OYEZ and TRANSF SWBD. Our method, UNEDITOR combines self-training and two-stage models.

provement using the full UNEDITOR system comparing to the model trained on the ORIG SWBD dataset.

## 6 Conclusion

In this paper we present a framework for disfluency detection in non-careful transcripts. Experiments are based on the OYEZ archive of transcriptions of Supreme Court oral arguments. To address the problem of lack of annotated data, we first transfer disfluency annotations from careful transcripts of a few cases to the less precise OYEZ transcripts. Next, we transform Switchboard transcripts to make them more similar to the target domain. In addition, we introduce a two-stage model and self-training to further improve performance.

Experiments show improvement in disfluency detection on Supreme Court oral arguments. Starting from baselines of training from carefully annotated in-domain data (F1=26.1) or Switchboard data (F1=39.7), we achieve a substantial improvement to (F1=62.2) with our best case system UNEDITOR, which corresponds to an improvement of nearly 23% over the stronger baseline.

Possible extensions of this work include exploring graph-based semi-supervised approaches (e.g., (Subramanya et al., 2010)) and combining the text-based approach with flexible ASR forced alignment allowing optional insertion of filled pauses and words that are common as repetitions. In addition, the availability of the automatically annotated disfluencies makes it possible to study the variation in rates for different cases and speakers over an extended time period.


## Acknowledgments

This work was supported in part by DARPA grant FA8750-12-2-0347. The authors thank the anonymous reviewers for their valuable feedback to improve the clarity of paper. The authors also thank Sangyun Hahn for his contribution in the two-stage model. The views and conclusions contained herein are those of the authors and should not be interpreted as necessarily representing the official policies or endorsements, either expressed or implied, of DARPA or the U.S. Government.


## References


[Bulyko et al.2007] I. Bulyko, M. Ostendorf, M. Siu, T. Ng, A. Stolcke, and O. Cetin. 2007. Web resources for language modeling in conversational speech recognition. *IEEE-TSLP*, 5(1).

[Charniak and Johnson2001] E. Charniak and M. Johnson. 2001. Edit detection and parsing for transcribed speech. In *Proc. NAACL*, pages 118–126.

[Georgila et al.2010] K. Georgila, N. Wang, and J. Gratch. 2010. Cross-domain speech disfluency detection. In *Proc. Annual SIGdial Meeting on Discourse and Dialogue*.

[Georgila2009] K. Georgila. 2009. Using integer linear programming for detecting speech disfluencies. In *Proc. NAACL-HLT*.

[Godfrey et al.1992] J. J. Godfrey, E. C. Holliman, and J. McDaniel. 1992. Switchboard: Telephone speech corpus for research and development. In *Proc. ACL*, volume I, pages 517–520.

[Hale et al.2006] John Hale, Izhak Shafran, Lisa Yung, Bonnie Dorr, Mary Harper, Anna Krasnyanskaya, Matthew Lease, Yang Liu, Brian Roark, Matthew Snover, and Robin Stewart. 2006. PCFGs with syntactic and prosodic indicators of speech repairs. In *Proc. COLING-ACL*.

[Honnibal and Johnson2014] Matthew Honnibal and Mark Johnson. 2014. Joint incremental disfluency detection and dependency parsing. *TACL*, 2(1):131–142.

[Johnson and Charniak2004] M. Johnson and E. Charniak. 2004. A tag-based noisy channel model of speech repairs. In *Proc. ACL*.

[Kahn et al.2005] Jeremy G Kahn, Matthew Lease, Eugene Charniak, Mark Johnson, and Mari Ostendorf. 2005. Effective use of prosody in parsing conversational speech. In *Proc. EMNLP-HLT*, pages 233–240.

[Lease et al.2006] Matthew Lease, Mark Johnson, and Eugene Charniak. 2006. Recognizing disfluencies in conversational speech. *IEEE-TASLP*, 14(5):169–177.

[Liu et al.2006] Y. Liu, E. Shriberg, A. Stolcke, D. Hillard, M. Ostendorf, and M. Harper. 2006. Enriching speech recognition with automatic detection of sentence boundaries and disfluencies. *IEEE-TASLP*, 14:1526–1540.

[Miller et al.2009] Tim Miller, Luan Nguyen, and William Schuler. 2009. Parsing speech repair without specialized grammar symbols. In *Proc. ACL-IJCNLP*, pages 277–280.

[Miller2009] Tim Miller. 2009. Improved syntactic models for parsing speech with repairs. In *Proc. NAACL-HLT*.

[Ostendorf and Hahn2013] Mari Ostendorf and Sangyun Hahn. 2013. A sequential repetition model for improved disfluency detection. In *Proc. Interspeech*.

[Qian and Liu2013] Xian Qian and Yang Liu. 2013. Disuency detection using multi-step stacked learning. In *Proc. NAACL-HLT*.

[Rasooli and Tetreault2013] Mohammad Sadegh Rasooli and Joel R Tetreault. 2013. Joint parsing and disfluency detection in linear time. In *Proc. EMNLP*, pages 124–129.

[Shriberg1994] E. Shriberg. 1994. *Preliminaries to a theory of speech disfluencies*. Ph.D. thesis, Department of Psychology, University of California, Berkeley, CA.

[Shriberg1999] E. Shriberg. 1999. Phonetic consequences of speech disfluency. In *Proc. ICPhS*, pages 619–622.

[Shriberg2001] Elizabeth Shriberg. 2001. To errrris human: ecology and acoustics of speech disfluencies. *Journal of the International Phonetic Association*, 31(01):153–169.

[Subramanya et al.2010] Amarnag Subramanya, Slav Petrov, and Fernando Pereira. 2010. Efficient graph-based semi-supervised learning of structured tagging models. In *Proc. EMNLP*, pages 167–176. ACL.

[Wang et al.2014] Xuancong Wang, Hwee Tou Ng, and Khe Chai Sim. 2014. A beam-search decoder for disfluency detection. In *Proc. COLING*.

[Zayats et al.2014] Victoria Zayats, Mari Ostendorf, and Hannaneh Hajishirzi. 2014. Multidomain disfluency and repair detection. In *Proc. Interspeech*.

[Zwarts et al.2010] Simon Zwarts, Mark Johnson, and Robert Dale. 2010. Detecting speech repairs incrementally using a noisy channel approach. In *Proc. COLING*, pages 1371–1378.

# Type-Driven Incremental Semantic Parsing with Polymorphism*

**Kai Zhao**
Graduate Center
City University of New York
kzhao.hf@gmail.com

**Liang Huang**
Queens College and Graduate Center
City University of New York
liang.huang.sh@gmail.com

## Abstract

Semantic parsing has made significant progress, but most current semantic parsers are extremely slow (CKY-based) and rather primitive in representation. We introduce three new techniques to tackle these problems. First, we design the first linear-time incremental shift-reduce-style semantic parsing algorithm which is more efficient than conventional cubic-time bottom-up semantic parsers. Second, our parser, being type-driven instead of syntax-driven, uses type-checking to decide the direction of reduction, which eliminates the need for a syntactic grammar such as CCG. Third, to fully exploit the power of type-driven semantic parsing beyond simple types (such as entities and truth values), we borrow from programming language theory the concepts of subtype polymorphism and parametric polymorphism to enrich the type system in order to better guide the parsing. Our system learns very accurate parses in GEOQUERY, JOBS and ATIS domains.

## 1 Introduction

Most existing semantic parsing efforts employ a CKY-style bottom-up parsing strategy to generate a meaning representation in simply typed lambda calculus (Zettlemoyer and Collins, 2005; Lu and Ng, 2011) or its variants (Wong and Mooney, 2007; Liang et al., 2011). Although these works led to fairly accurate semantic parsers, there are two major drawbacks: efficiency and expressiveness.

First, as many researches in syntactic parsing (Nivre, 2008; Zhang and Clark, 2011) have shown, compared to cubic-time CKY-style parsing, incremental parsing can achieve comparable accuracies while being linear-time, and orders of magnitude faster in practice. We therefore introduce the first incremental parsing algorithm for semantic parsing. More interestingly, unlike syntactic parsing, our incremental semantic parsing algorithm, being strictly **type-driven**, directly employs type checking to automatically determine the direction of function application on-the-fly, thus reducing the search space and eliminating the need for a syntactic grammar such as CCG to explicitly encode the direction of function application.

However, to fully exploit the power of type-driven incremental parsing, we need a more sophisticated type system than simply typed lambda calculus. Compare the following two phrases:

(1) the governor of New York

(2) the mayor of New York

If we know that *governor* is a function from state to person, then the first *New York* can only be of type *state*; similarly knowing *mayor* maps city to person disambiguates the second *New York* to be of type *city*. This can not be done using a simple type system with just entities and booleans.

Now let us consider a more complex question which will be our running example in this paper:

(3) What is the capital of the largest state by area?

Since we know *capital* takes a state as input, we expect *the largest state by area* to return a state. But does *largest* always return a state type? Notice that it is polymorphic, for example, *largest city by population*, or *largest lake by perimeter*. So there is no unique type for *largest*: its return type should depend on the type of its first argument (*city*, *state*, or *lake*). This observation motivates us to introduce the powerful mechanism of parametric polymorphism from programming languages into natural language semantics for the first time.

For example, we can define the type of *largest* to be a template

$$\textbf{largest} : (\texttt{'a}{\rightarrow}\texttt{t}){\rightarrow}(\texttt{'a}{\rightarrow}\texttt{i}){\rightarrow}\texttt{'a}$$

where 'a is a *type variable* that can match any type (for formal details see §3). Just like in functional programming languages such as ML or Haskell, type variables can be bound to a real type (or a range of types) during function application, using the technique of type inference. In the above example, when *largest* is applied to *city*, we know that type variable 'a is bound to type city (or its subtype), so *largest* would eventually return a city.

We make the following contributions:

- We design the first linear-time incremental semantic parsing algorithm (§2), which is much more efficient than the existing semantic parsers that are cubic-time and CKY-based.

*We thank the reviewers for helpful suggestions. We are also grateful to Luke Zettelmoyer, Yoav Artzi, and Tom Kwiatkowski for providing data. This research is supported by DARPA FA8750-13-2-0041 (DEFT), NSF IIS-1449278, and a Google Faculty Research Award.



*Human Language Technologies: The 2015 Annual Conference of the North American Chapter of the ACL*, pages 1416–1421,
Denver, Colorado, May 31 – June 5, 2015. 

- In line with classical Montague theory (Heim and Kratzer, 1998), our parser is type-driven instead of syntax-driven as in CCG-based efforts (Zettlemoyer and Collins, 2005; Kwiatkowski et al., 2011; Krishnamurthy and Mitchell, 2014) (§2.3).

- We introduce parametric polymorphism into natural language semantics (§3), along with proper treatment of subtype polymorphism, and implement Hindley-Milner style type inference (Pierce, 2005, Chap. 10) during parsing (§3.3).[1]

- We adapt the latent-variable max-violation perceptron training from machine translation (Yu et al., 2013), which is a perfect fit for semantic parsing due to its huge search space (§4).

## 2 Type-Driven Incremental Parsing

We start with the simplest meaning representation (MR), *untyped lambda calculus*, and introduce typing and the incremental parsing algorithm for it. Later in §3, we add subtyping and type polymorphism to enrich the system.

### 2.1 Meaning Representation with Types

The untyped MR for the running example is:

Q: What is the capital of the largest state by area?

MR: (**capital** (**argmax** **state** **size**))

Note the binary function **argmax**$(\cdot,\cdot)$ is a higher-order function that takes two other functions as input: the first argument is a "domain" function that defines the set to search for, and second argument is an "evaluation" function that returns a integer for an element in that domain.

The simply typed lambda calculus (Heim and Kratzer, 1998; Lu and Ng, 2011) augments the system with types, including base types (entities e, truth values t, or numbers i), and function types (e.g., e→t). So **capital** is of type e→e, **state** is of type e→t, and **size** is of type e→i. The **argmax** function is of type (e→t)→(e→i)→e.[2] The simply typed MR is now written as

$$(\textbf{capital}:\mathsf{e}\to\mathsf{e}\quad(\textbf{argmax}:(\mathsf{e}\to\mathsf{t})\to(\mathsf{e}\to\mathsf{i})\to\mathsf{e}\quad \textbf{state}:\mathsf{e}\to\mathsf{t}\ \ \textbf{size}:\mathsf{e}\to\mathsf{i}))).$$

### 2.2 Incremental Semantic Parsing: An Example

Similar to a standard shift-reduce parser, we maintain a *stack* and a *queue*. The queue contains words to be parsed, while the stack contains subexpressions of the final MR, each of which is a valid typed lambda expression. At each step, the parser choose to **shift** or **reduce**, but unlike standard shift-reduce parser, there is also a third possible action, **skip**, skipping a semantically vacuous word (e.g., "the", "of", "is", etc.). For example, the first three words of the example question *"What is the ..."* are all skipped (**steps 1–3** in Figure 1 (left)).

The parser then **shifts** the next word, *"capital"*, from the queue to the stack. But unlike incremental syntactic parsing where the word itself is moved onto the stack, here we need to find a **grounded** predicate in the GeoQuery domain for the current word. Triggered by the POS tag NN of word "capital", the template $\lambda P : \mathsf{e}\to\mathsf{e}\ .\ P$ is fetched from a predefined MR templates set like Table 1. In its outermost lambda abstraction, variable $P$ needs to be grounded on-the-fly before we push the expression onto the stack. We find a predicate **capital**: e→e in the GeoQuery domain applicable to the MR template. After the application, we push the result onto the stack (**step 4**).

Next, words *"of the"* are skipped (steps 5–6). For the next word *"largest"*, **argmax** : (e→t)→(e→i)→e is applied to the MR template triggered by its POS tag JJS in Table 1, and the stack becomes (**step 7**)

$$\textbf{capital}:\mathsf{e}\to\mathsf{e}\quad \textbf{argmax}:(\mathsf{e}\to\mathsf{t})\to(\mathsf{e}\to\mathsf{i})\to\mathsf{e}.$$

At this step we have two expressions on the stack and we could attempt to reduce. But type checking fails because for left reduce, **argmax** expects an argument (its "domain" function) of type (e→t) which is different from **capital**'s type (e→e), so is the case for right reduce. So we have to shift again. This time for word *"state"*: **state**: e→t. The stack becomes:

$$\textbf{capital}:\mathsf{e}\to\mathsf{e}\quad \textbf{argmax}:(\mathsf{e}\to\mathsf{t})\to(\mathsf{e}\to\mathsf{i})\to\mathsf{e}\quad \textbf{state}:\mathsf{e}\to\mathsf{t}.$$

### 2.3 Type-Driven Reduce

At this step we can finally perform a **reduce** action, since the top two expressions on the stack pass the type-checking for rightward function application (a partial application): **argmax** expects an (e→t) argument, which is exactly the type of **state**. So we conduct a right-reduce, applying **argmax** on **state**, which results in

$$(\textbf{argmax}\quad \textbf{state}):(\mathsf{e}\to\mathsf{i})\to\mathsf{e}$$

| pattern | λ-expression templates, simple types (§2.2) |
|---|---|
| JJS | $\lambda P:(\mathsf{e}\to\mathsf{t})\to(\mathsf{e}\to\mathsf{i})\to\mathsf{e}\ .\ P$ |
| NN | $\lambda P:\mathsf{e}\to\mathsf{e}\ .\ P;\quad \lambda P:\mathsf{e}\to\mathsf{t}\ .\ P;\quad \lambda P:\mathsf{e}\to\mathsf{i}\ .\ P$ |
| pattern | λ-expression templates, polymorphic types (§3.3) |
| JJS | $\lambda P:(\text{'a}\to\mathsf{t})\to(\text{'a}\to\mathsf{i})\to\text{'a}\ .\ P$ |
| NN | $\lambda P:\text{'b}\to\text{'c}\ .\ P$ |

Table 1: POS-based meaning representation templates used in the running example (see Figure 1). The polymorphic types greatly simplifies the representation for common nouns (NN).

[1] There are three kinds of polymorphisms in programming languages: parametric (e.g., C++ templates), subtyping, and ad-hoc (e.g., operator overloading). See Pierce (2002, Chap. 15) for details.

[2] Note that the type notation is always *curried*, i.e., we represent a binary function as a unary function that returns another unary function. Also the type notation is always *right-associative*, so (e→t)→((e→i)→e) is also written as (e→t)→(e→i)→e.

| step | action | stack after action (simple type) | stack after action (subtyping+polymorphism) |
|---|---|---|---|
| 0 | - | $\phi$ | $\phi$ |
| 1–3 | skip | $\phi$ | $\phi$ |
| 4 | $\mathsf{sh}_{\text{capital}}$ | **capital**:e→e | **capital**:st→ct |
| 7 | $\mathsf{sh}_{\text{largest}}$ | **capital**:e→e **argmax**:(e→t)→(e→i)→e | **capital**:st→ct **argmax**:('a→t)→('a→i)→'a |
| 8 | $\mathsf{sh}_{\text{state}}$ | **capital**:e→e **argmax**:(e→t)→(e→i)→e **state**:e→t | **capital**:st→ct **argmax**:('a→t)→('a→i)→'a **state**:st→t |
| 9 | $\mathsf{re}_{\curvearrowright}$ | **capital**:e→e (**argmax state**):(e→i)→e | **capital**:st→ct (**argmax state**):(st→i)→st † |
| 11 | $\mathsf{sh}_{\text{area}}$ | **capital**:e→e (**argmax state**):(e→i)→e **size**:e→i | **capital**:st→ct (**argmax state**):(st→i)→st **size**:lo→i |
| 12 | $\mathsf{re}_{\curvearrowright}$ | **capital**:e→e (**argmax state size**):e | **capital**:st→ct (**argmax state size**):st ‡ |
| 13 | $\mathsf{re}_{\curvearrowright}$ | (**capital** (**argmax state size**)):e | (**capital** (**argmax state size**)):ct |

Figure 1: Type-driven Incremental Semantic Parsing (TISP) with (a) simple types and (b) subtyping+polymorphism on the example question: "what is the capital of the largest state by area?". Steps 5–6 and 10 are skip actions and thus omitted. The stack and queue in each row are the results *after* each action. †: Type variable 'a is binded to st. ‡: From Eq. 4, st <: lo ⇒ (lo→i) <: (st→i).

while the stack becomes (**step 9**)

**capital**:e→e (**argmax state**):(e→i)→e

Now if we want to continue reduction, it does not type check for either left or right reduction, so we have to shift again. So we move on to shift the final word *"area"* with predicate: **size**:e→i and the stack becomes (**step 11**):

**capital**:e→e (**argmax state**):(e→i)→e **size**:e→i.

Now we can do two consecutive right reduces supported by type checking (**step 12, 13**) and get the final result:

(**capital** (**argmax state size**)):e.

Here we can see the novelty of our shift-reduce parser: its decisions are largely driven by the type system. When we attempt a reduce, **at most** one of the two reduce actions (left, right) is possible thanks to type checking, and when neither is allowed, we have to shift (or skip). This observation suggests that our incremental parser is more deterministic than those syntactic incremental parsers where each step always faces a three-way decision (shift, left-reduce, right-reduce). We also note that this type-checking mechanism, inspired by the classical type-driven theory in linguistics (Heim and Kratzer, 1998), eliminates the need for an *explicit* encoding of direction as in CCG, which makes our formalism much simpler than the synchronous syntactic-semantic ones in most other semantic parsing efforts (Zettlemoyer and Collins, 2005; Zettlemoyer and Collins, 2007; Wong and Mooney, 2007).[3]

## 3 Subtype and Parametric Polymorphisms

Currently in simply typed lambda calculus representation function **capital** can apply to any entity type, for example **capital**(**boston**), which should have been disallowed by the type checker. So we need a more sophisticated system that helps ground with refined types, which will in turn help type-driven parsing.

[3] We need to distinguish between two concepts: a) "direction of reduction": $f(g)$ or $g(f)$. Obviously at any given time, between the top two (unarized) functions $f$ and $g$ on the stack, at most one reduction is possible. b) "order of arguments": $f(x, y)$ or $f(y, x)$. For predicates such as **loc** : lo→lo→t the order does matter. Our parser can not distinguish this purely via types, nor can CCG via its syntactic categories. In practice, it is decided by features such as the voice of the verb.

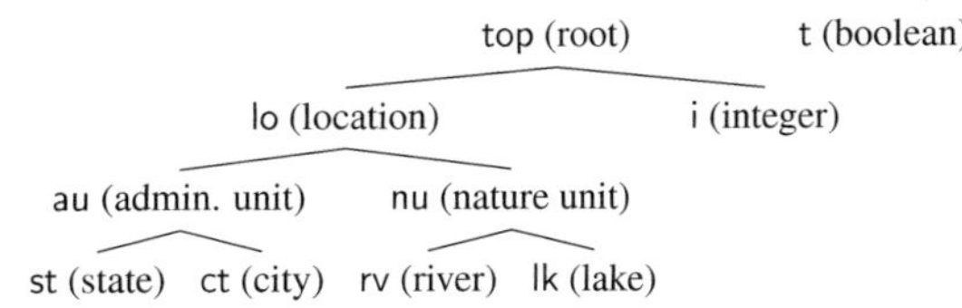


Figure 2: Type hierarchy for GEOQUERY (slightly simplified).

### 3.1 Semantics with Subtype Polymorphism

We first augment the meaning representation with a domain specific type hierarchy. For example Figure 2 shows a (slightly simplified) version of the type hierarchy for GEOQUERY domain. We use <: to denote the (transitive, reflexive, and antisymmetric) **subtyping relation** between types; for example in GEOQUERY, st <: lo.

Each constant in the GEOQUERY domain is well typed. For example, there are states (**michigan**:st), cities (**nyc**:ct), rivers (**mississippi**:rv), and lakes (**tahoe**:lk).

Similarly each predicate is also typed. For example, we can query the length of a river, **len**:rv→i, or the population of some administrative unit, **population**:au→i. Notice that **population**(·) can be applied to both states and cities, since they are subtypes of administrative unit, i.e., st <: au and ct <: au. This is because, as in Java and C++, a function that expects a certain type can always take an argument of a subtype. For example, we can query whether two locations are adjacent, using **next_to**:lo→(lo→t), as the **next_to**(·, ·) function can be applied to two states, or to a river and a city, etc.

Before we move on, there is an important consequence of polymorphism worth mentioning here. For the types of unary predicates such as **city**(·) and **state**(·) that *characterize* its argument, we define theirs argument types to be the required type, i.e., **city** : ct→t, and **state** : st→t. This might look a little weird since everything in the domain of those functions are always mapped to true; i.e., $f(x)$ is either undefined or true, and never false for such $f$'s. This is different from classical simply-typed Montague semantics (Heim and Kratzer, 1998) which defines such predicates as type top→t so that **city**(**mississippi** : st) returns false. The reason for our design is, again, due to subtyping and polymorphism: **capital** takes a state type as input, so **argmax** must returns a state, and therefore its first argument, the **state** function, must have type st→t so that the matched type variable 'a will be bound to st. This more refined design will also help prune unnecessary argument matching using type checking.

### 3.2 Semantics with Parametric Polymorphism

The above type system works smoothly for first-order functions (i.e., predicates taking atomic type arguments), but the situation with higher-order functions (i.e., predicates that take functions as input) is more involved. What is the type of **argmax** in the context "the capital of largest state ..."? One possibility is to define it to be as general as possible, as in the simply typed version (and many conventional semantic parsers):

$$\textbf{argmax}: (\mathsf{top}{\rightarrow}\mathsf{t}){\rightarrow}(\mathsf{top}{\rightarrow}\mathsf{i}){\rightarrow}\mathsf{top}.$$

But this actually no longer works for our sophisticated type system for the following reason.

Intuitively, remember that **capital**:st→ct is a function that takes a state as input, so the return type of **argmax** must be a state or its subtype, rather than top which is a supertype of st. But we can not simply replace top by st, since **argmax** can also be applied in other scenarios such as "the largest city". In other words, **argmax** is a *polymorphic* function, and to assign a correct type for it we have to introduce *type variables*:

$$\textbf{argmax}: (\mathsf{'a}{\rightarrow}\mathsf{t}){\rightarrow}(\mathsf{'a}{\rightarrow}\mathsf{i}){\rightarrow}\mathsf{'a},$$

where type variable 'a is a place-holder for "any type".

### 3.3 Parsing with Subtype Polymorphism and Parametric Polymorphism

We modify the previous parsing algorithm to accommodate subtyping and polymorphic types. Figure 1 (right) shows the derivation of the running example using the new parsing algorithm. Below we focus on the differences brought by the new algorithm.

Note that we also modified the MR templates as in Table 1. The new MR templates are more general due to the polymorphism from type variables. For example, now we use only one MR template $\lambda P$: 'b→'c . $P$ to replace the three NN MR templates for simple types.

In step 4, unlike **capital** : e→e, we shift the predicate **capital** : st→ct; in step 7, we shift the polymorphic expression for *"largest"*: **argmax**: ('a→t)→('a→i)→'a. And after the shift in step 8, the stack becomes

**capital**:st→ct **argmax**:('a→t)→('a→i)→'a **state**:st→t

At **step 9**, in order to apply **argmax** onto **state** : st→t, we simply **bind** type variable 'a to type st, results in (**argmax state**) : (st→i)→st.

After the shift in **step 11**, the stack becomes:

**capital**:st→ct (**argmax state**):(st→i)→st **size**:lo→i.

Can we still apply right reduce here? According to subtyping requirement (§3.1), we want lo→i <: st→i to hold, knowing that st <: lo. Luckily, there is a rule about function types in type theory that exactly fits here:

$$\frac{\mathsf{A} <: \mathsf{B}}{\mathsf{B}{\rightarrow}\mathsf{C} <: \mathsf{A}{\rightarrow}\mathsf{C}} \quad (4)$$

which states the input side is reversed (contravariant). This might look counterintuitive, but the intuition is that, it is safe to allow the function **size**:lo→i to be used in the context where another type st→i is expected, since in that context the argument passed to **size** will be state type (st), which is a subtype of location type (lo) that **size** expects, which in turn will not surprise **size**. See the classical type theory textbook (Pierce, 2002, Chap. 15.2) for details.

Several works in literature (Zettlemoyer and Collins, 2005; Zettlemoyer and Collins, 2007; Wong and Mooney, 2007; Kwiatkowski et al., 2013) employ some primitive type hierarchies and parse with typed lambda calculus. However, simply introducing subtyped predicates without polymorphism will cause type checking failures in handling high-order functions, as we discussed above.

## 4 Training: Latent Variable Perceptron

We follow the latent variable max-violation perceptron algorithm of Yu et al. (2013) for training. This algorithm is based on the "violation-fixing" framework of Huang et al. (2012) which is tailored to structured learning problems with abundant search errors such as parsing or machine translation.

The key challenge in the training is that, for each question, there might be many different unknown derivations that lead to its annotated MR, which is known as the *spurious ambiguity*. In our task, the spurious ambiguity is caused by how the MR templates are chosen and grounded during the shift step, and the different reduce orders that lead to the same result. We treat this unknown information as latent variable.

More formally, we denote $D(x)$ to be the set of *all* partial and full parsing derivations for an input sentence $x$, and $mr(d)$ to be the MR yielded by a full derivation $d$. Then we define the sets of (partial and full) reference derivations as:

$$good_i(x,y) \triangleq \{d \in D(x) \mid |d| = i, \exists \text{full derivation } d' \text{ s.t. } d \text{ is a prefix of } d', mr(d') = y\},$$

Those "bad" partial and full derivations that do not lead to the annotated MR can be defined as:

$$bad_i(x,y) \triangleq \{d \in D(x) \mid d \notin good_i(x,y), |d| = i\}.$$

At step $i$, the best reference partial derivation is

$$d_i^+(x,y) \triangleq \operatorname*{\mathbf{argmax}}_{d \in good_i(x,y)} \mathbf{w} \cdot \mathbf{\Phi}(x,d), \quad (5)$$

| System | GEOQUERY P | R | F1 | JOBS P | R | F1 | ATIS P | R | F1 |
|---|---|---|---|---|---|---|---|---|---|
| Z&C'05 | **96.3** | 79.3 | 87.0 | **97.3** | 79.3 | 87.4 | - | - | - |
| Z&C'07 | 91.6 | 86.1 | 88.8 | - | - | - | **85.8** | **84.6** | **85.2** |
| UBL | 94.1 | 85.0 | 89.3 | - | - | - | 72.1 | 71.4 | 71.7 |
| FUBL | 88.6 | 88.6 | 88.6 | - | - | - | 82.8 | 82.8 | 82.8 |
| TISP (st) | 89.7 | 86.8 | 88.2 | 76.4 | 76.4 | 76.4 | - | - | - |
| TISP | 92.9 | **88.9** | **90.9** | 85.0 | **85.0** | **85.0** | 84.7 | 84.2 | 84.4 |

Table 2: Performances (precision, recall, and F1) of various parsing algorithms on GEOQUERY, JOBS, and ATIS datasets. TISP with simple types are marked "st".

while the Viterbi partial derivation is

$$d_i^-(x,y) \triangleq \underset{d \in bad_i(x,y)}{\mathbf{argmax}} \ \mathbf{w} \cdot \mathbf{\Phi}(x,d), \quad (6)$$

where $\mathbf{\Phi}(x,d)$ is the defined feature set for derivation $d$. In practice, to compute Eq. 6 exactly is intractable, and we resort to beam search. Following Yu et al. (2013), we then find the step $i^*$ with the maximal score difference between the best reference partial derivation and the Viterbi partial derivation:

$$i^* \triangleq \underset{i}{\mathbf{argmax}} \, \mathbf{w} \cdot \Delta\mathbf{\Phi}(x, d_i^+(x,y), d_i^-(x,y)),$$

and do update $\mathbf{w} \leftarrow \mathbf{w} + \Delta\mathbf{\Phi}(x, d_{i^*}^+(x,y), d_{i^*}^-(x,y))$ where $\Delta\mathbf{\Phi}(x,d,d') \triangleq \mathbf{\Phi}(x,d) - \mathbf{\Phi}(x,d')$.

We also use minibatch parallelization of Zhao and Huang (2013); in practice we use 24 cores.

# 5 Experiments

We implement our type-driven incremental semantic parser (TISP) using `Python`, and evaluate its performance on GEOQUERY, JOBS, and ATIS datasets.

Our feature design is inspired by the very effective Word-Edge features in syntactic parsing (Charniak and Johnson, 2005) and MT (He et al., 2008). From each parsing state, we collect atomic features including the types and the leftmost and rightmost words of the span of the top 3 MR expressions on the stack, the top 3 words on the queue, the grounded predicate names and the ID of the MR template used in the shift action. We use budget scheme similar to (Yu et al., 2013) to alleviate the overfitting problem caused by feature sparsity. We get 84 combined feature templates in total. Our final system contains 62 MR expression templates, of which 33 are triggered by POS tags, and 29 are triggered by specific phrases.

In the experiments, we use the same training, development, and testing data splits as Zettlemoyer and Collins (2005) and Zettlemoyer and Collins (2007).

For evaluation, we follow Zettlemoyer and Collins (2005) to use *precision* and *recall*:

$$\text{Precision} = \frac{\#\text{ of correctly parsed questions}}{\#\text{ of successfully parsed questions}},$$

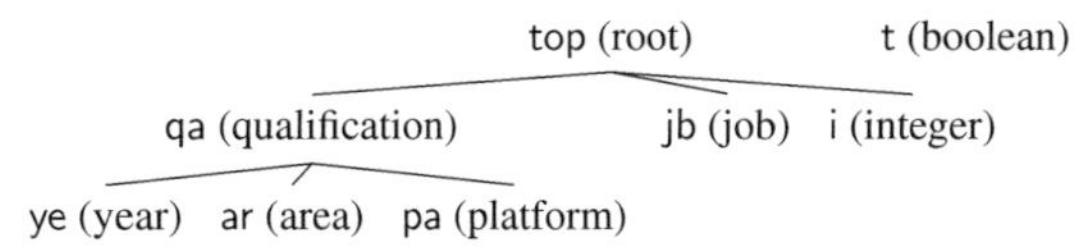

Figure 3: Type hierarchy for JOBS domain (slightly simplified).

$$\text{Recall} = \frac{\#\text{ of correctly parsed questions}}{\#\text{ of questions}}.$$

## 5.1 Evaluation on GEOQUERY Dataset

We first evaluate TISP on GEOQUERY dataset.

In the training and evaluating time, we use a very small beam size of 16, which gives us very fast decoding. In serial mode, our parser takes $\sim$ 83s to decode the 280 sentences (2,147 words) in the testing set, which means $\sim$0.3s per sentence, or $\sim$0.04s per word.

We compare the our accuracy performance with existing methods (Zettlemoyer and Collins, 2005; Zettlemoyer and Collins, 2007; Kwiatkowski et al., 2010; Kwiatkowski et al., 2011) in Table 2. Given that all other methods use CKY-style parsing, our method is well balanced between accuracy and speed.

In addition, to unveil the helpfulness of our type system, we train a parser with only simple types. (Table 2) In this setting, the predicates only have primitive types of location lo, integer i, and boolean t, while the constants still keep their types. It still has the type system, but it is weaker than the polymorphic one. Its accuracy is lower than the standard one, mostly caused by that the type system can not help pruning the wrong applications like (**population**:au→i **mississippi**:rv).

## 5.2 Evaluations on JOBS and ATIS Datasets

We also evaluate the performance of our parser on JOBS and ATIS datasets. Figure 3 shows the type hierarchy for JOBS. We omit the type hierarchy for ATIS due to space constraint. Note that ATIS contains more than 5,000 examples and is a lot larger than GEOQUERY and JOBS.

We show the results in Table 2. In JOBS, we achieves very good recall, but the precision is not as good as Zettlemoyer and Collins (2005), which is actually because we parsed a lot more sentences. Also, TISP with simple types is still weaker than the one with subtyping and parametric polymorphisms. For ATIS, our performance is very close to the state-of-the-art.

# 6 Conclusion

We have presented an incremental semantic parser that is guided by a powerful type system of subtyping and polymorphism. This polymorphism greatly reduced the number of templates and effectively pruned search space during the parsing. Our parser is competitive with state-of-the-art accuracies, but, being linear-time, is faster than CKY-based parsers in theory and in practice.

## References


Eugene Charniak and Mark Johnson. 2005. Coarse-to-fine n-best parsing and maxent discriminative reranking. In *Proceedings of ACL*, pages 173–180, Ann Arbor, Michigan, June.

Zhongjun He, Qun Liu, and Shouxun Lin. 2008. Improving statistical machine translation using lexicalized rule selection. In *Proceedings of COLING*, pages 321–328, Manchester, UK, August.

Irene Heim and Angelika Kratzer. 1998. *Semantics in Generative Grammar*. Blackwell Publishing.

Liang Huang, Suphan Fayong, and Yang Guo. 2012. Structured perceptron with inexact search. In *Proceedings of NAACL*.

Jayant Krishnamurthy and Tom M Mitchell. 2014. Joint syntactic and semantic parsing with combinatory categorial grammar.

Tom Kwiatkowski, Luke Zettlemoyer, Sharon Goldwater, and Mark Steedman. 2010. Inducing probabilistic ccg grammars from logical form with higher-order unification. In *Proceedings of the 2010 conference on empirical methods in natural language processing*, pages 1223–1233. Association for Computational Linguistics.

Tom Kwiatkowski, Luke Zettlemoyer, Sharon Goldwater, and Mark Steedman. 2011. Lexical generalization in ccg grammar induction for semantic parsing. In *Proceedings of EMNLP*, EMNLP '11.

Tom Kwiatkowski, Eunsol Choi, Yoav Artzi, and Luke Zettlemoyer. 2013. Scaling semantic parsers with on-the-fly ontology matching.

Percy Liang, Michael I. Jordan, and Dan Klein. 2011. Learning dependency-based compositional semantics. In *Association for Computational Linguistics (ACL)*, pages 590–599.

Wei Lu and Hwee Tou Ng. 2011. A probabilistic forest-to-string model for language generation from typed lambda calculus expressions. In *Proceedings of EMNLP*.

Joakim Nivre. 2008. Algorithms for deterministic incremental dependency parsing. *Computational Linguistics*, 34(4):513–553.

Benjamin C. Pierce. 2002. *Types and Programming Languages*. MIT Press.

Benjamin Pierce, editor. 2005. *Advanced Topics in Types and Programming Languages*. MIT Press.

Yuk Wah Wong and Raymond J Mooney. 2007. Learning synchronous grammars for semantic parsing with lambda calculus. In *Annual Meeting-Association for computational Linguistics*, volume 45, page 960.

Heng Yu, Liang Huang, Haitao Mi, and Kai Zhao. 2013. Max-violation perceptron and forced decoding for scalable mt training. In *Proceedings of EMNLP 2013*.

Luke Zettlemoyer and Michael Collins. 2005. Learning to map sentences to logical form: Structured classification with probabilistic categorial grammars. In *Proceedings of UAI*.

Luke S Zettlemoyer and Michael Collins. 2007. Online learning of relaxed ccg grammars for parsing to logical form. In *In Proceedings of EMNLP-CoNLL-2007*. Citeseer.

Yue Zhang and Stephen Clark. 2011. Shift-reduce ccg parsing. In *Proceedings of ACL*.

Kai Zhao and Liang Huang. 2013. Minibatch and parallelization for online large margin structured learning. In *Proceedings of NAACL 2013*.

# Template Kernels for Dependency Parsing

**Hillel Taub-Tabib**
Hebrew University
Jerusalem, Israel

**Yoav Goldberg**
Bar-Ilan University
Ramat-Gan, Israel

{hillel.t,yoav.goldberg}@gmail.com

**Amir Globerson**
Hebrew University
Jerusalem, Israel
gamir@cs.huji.ac.il

## Abstract

A common approach to dependency parsing is scoring a parse via a linear function of a set of indicator features. These features are typically manually constructed from templates that are applied to parts of the parse tree. The templates define which properties of a part should combine to create features. Existing approaches consider only a small subset of the possible combinations, due to statistical and computational efficiency considerations. In this work we present a novel kernel which facilitates efficient parsing with feature representations corresponding to a much larger set of combinations. We integrate the kernel into a parse reranking system and demonstrate its effectiveness on four languages from the CoNLL-X shared task.[1]

## 1 Introduction

Dependency parsing is the task of labeling a sentence $x$ with a syntactic dependency tree $y \in \mathcal{Y}(x)$, where $\mathcal{Y}(x)$ denotes the space of valid trees over $x$. Each word in $x$ is represented as a list of linguistic properties (e.g. word form, part of speech, base form, gender, number, etc.). In the graph based approach (McDonald et al., 2005b) parsing is cast as a structured linear prediction problem:

$$h_{\mathbf{v}}(x) = \underset{y \in \mathcal{Y}(x)}{\text{argmax}} \ \mathbf{v}^T \cdot \Phi(x, y) \qquad (1)$$

where $\Phi(x, y) \in \mathbb{R}^d$ is a feature representation defined over a sentence and its parse tree, and $\mathbf{v} \in \mathbb{R}^d$ is a vector of parameters.

To construct an effective representation, $\Phi(x, y)$ is typically decomposed into local representations over parts $p$ of the tree $y$:

$$\Phi(x, y) = \sum_{p \in y} \phi(x, p)$$

Standard decompositions include different types of parts: *arcs*, *sibling arcs*, *grandparent arcs*, etc. Feature templates are then applied to the parts to construct the local representations. The templates determine how the linguistic properties of the words in each part should combine to create features (see Section 2).

Substantial effort has been dedicated to the manual construction of feature templates (McDonald et al., 2005b; Carreras, 2007; Koo and Collins, 2010). Still, for both computational and statistical reasons, existing templates consider only a small subset of the possible combinations of properties. From a computational perspective, solving Eq. 1 involves applying the templates to $y$ and calculating a dot product in the effective dimension of $\Phi$. The use of many templates thus quickly leads to computational infeasibility (the dimensionality of $\mathbf{v}$, as well as the number of non-zero features in $\Phi$, become very large). From a statistical perspective, the use of a large number of feature templates can lead to overfitting.

Several recent works have proposed solutions to the above problem. Lei et al., (2014) represented the space of all possible property combinations in an arc-factored model as a third order tensor and learned the parameter matrix for the tensor under a low rank assumption. In the context of transition parsers, Chen and Manning (2014) have implemented a neural network that uses dense representations of words and parts of speech as its input and implicitly considers combinations in its inner layers. Earlier work on transition-based dependency parsing used SVM classifiers with 2nd order polynomial kernels to achieve similar effects (Hall

[1] See https://bitbucket.org/hillel/templatekernels for implementation.



*Human Language Technologies: The 2015 Annual Conference of the North American Chapter of the ACL*, pages 1422–1427,
Denver, Colorado, May 31 – June 5, 2015. 

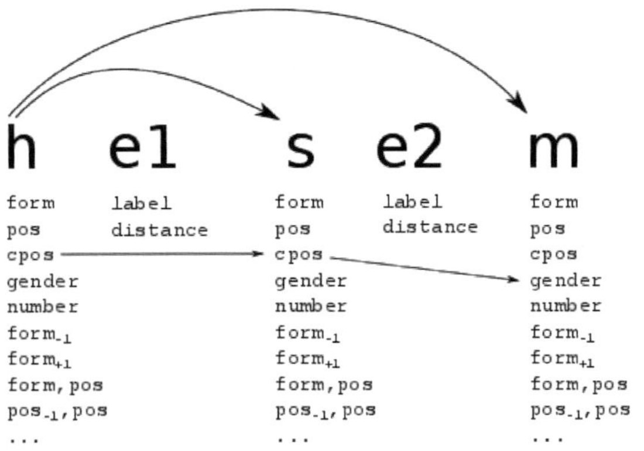


Figure 1: Feature template over the second order consecutive siblings part type. The part type contains slots for the head (h), sibling (s) and modifier (m) words, as well as for the two edges (e1 and e2). Each slot is associated with a set of properties. The directed path skips over the edge properties and defines the partial template <h-cpos=?; s-cpos=?; m-gender=?>.

et al., 2006). While training greedy transition-based parsers such as the ones used in (Chen and Manning, 2014) and (Hall et al., 2006) amounts to training a multiclass classifier, the graph-based parsing framework explored in (Lei et al., 2014) and in the present work is a more involved structured-learning task.

In this paper we present a kernel based approach to automated feature generation in the context of graph-based parsing. Compared to tensors and neural networks, kernel methods have the attractive properties of a convex objective and well understood generalization bounds (Shawe-Taylor and Cristianini, 2004). We introduce a kernel that allows us to learn the parameters for a representation similar to the tensor representation in (Lei et al., 2014) but without the low rank assumption, and without explicitly instantiating the exponentially many possible features.

In contrast to previous works on parsing with kernels (Collins and Duffy, 2002), in which the kernels are defined over trees and count the number of shared subtrees, our focus is on feature combinations. In that sense our work is more closely related to work on tree kernels for relation extraction (Zelenko et al., 2003; Culotta and Sorensen, 2004; Reichartz et al., 2010; Sun and Han, 2014), but the kernel we propose is designed to generate combinations of properties within selected part types and does not involve the all-subtrees representation.

## 2 Template Kernels

For simplicity, we begin with the case where parts $p$ correspond to head modifier pairs $(h, m)$ (i.e. all parts belong to the "arc" part type). The features in $\phi(x, p)$ can then depend on any property of $h, m$ and the sentence $x$. We denote properties related to $h$ using the prefix $h$- (e.g., $h$-pos corresponds to the part-of-speech of the head), and similarly for $m$-. We also use $e$- to denote properties related to the triplets $h, m, x$ (e.g., the surface distance between $h, m$ in $x$ is denoted by $e$-$dist$).

Templates defined over the "arc" part type will then combine different properties of $h, m$ and $e$, to create features. e.g. the template <h-form=?; e-dist=?; m-form=?,m-pos=?>, when applied to a dependency arc, may yield the feature: <h-form=dog;e-dist=1;m-form=black,m-pos=JJ>.

More generally, a parse tree *part* can be seen as ordered lists of slots that contain properties (different part types will contain different lists of slots). The feature templates defined over them select one property from each slot (possibly skipping some slots to produce partial templates). A template can thus be thought of as a directed path between the properties it selects in the different slots. Clearly, the number of possible templates in a given part type is exponential in the number of its slots. Figure 1 depicts the process for sibling parts.

As discussed in Section 1, manually constructed feature templates consider only a small subset of the combinations of properties (i.e. a small number of "good" paths is manually identified and selected). Our goal is to introduce a kernel that allows us to represent all possible paths for a part type in polynomial time.

Formally, let $\Phi(x, y) = \sum_{p \in y} \phi(x, p)$ be a feature representation which associates a feature with any distinct combination of properties in any of the tree parts in the training set. For a given part $p$, the effective dimensionality of $\phi(x, p)$ is thus $O(m^s)$ where $s$ is the number of slots in $p$, and $m$ is the maximal number of properties in a slot.

Explicitly representing $\Phi(x, y)$ is therefore often impractical. However, the well known "kernel trick" (Shawe-Taylor and Cristianini, 2004) implies that linear classifiers depend only on dot products between feature vectors and not on the feature vectors themselves. In the context of reranking (see Section 3), it means we can learn classifiers if we can calculate dot products $K(y_1, y_2) = \Phi^T(x_1, y_1) \cdot \Phi(x_2, y_2)$ for two sentences and candidate parses.[2]

We first note that such dot products can be expressed as sum of dot products over parts:

$$K(y_1, y_2) = \sum_{p \in y_1} \sum_{p' \in y_2} k(p, p')$$

where $k(p, p') = \phi(x_1, p) \cdot \phi(x_2, p)$.

To calculate $k(p, p')$ we'll assume for simplicity that $p$ and $p'$ are of the same type (otherwise $k(p, p') = 0$). Let $p_{ij}$ and $p'_{ij}$ be the values of the $i$'th property in the $j$'th slot in $p, p'$ (e.g., for a second order sibling part as in Figure 1, $p_{1,4}$ will correspond to the label of the edge e2 in $p$) , and let $C_{p \leftrightarrow p'} \in \{0,1\}^{m \times s}$ be a binary matrix comparing $p$ and $p'$ such that $[C_{p \leftrightarrow p'}]_{ij} = 1$ when $p_{ij} = p'_{ij}$ and 0 otherwise. Simple algebra yields that:

$$k(p, p') = \prod_j \vec{1}^T \cdot [C_{p \leftrightarrow p'}]_{:,j}$$

That is, calculating $k(p, p')$ amounts to multiplying the sums of the columns in $C$.[3] The runtime of $k(p, p')$ is then $O(m \times s)$ which means the overall runtime of $K(y_1, y_2)$ is $O(|y_1| \times |y_2| \times |s| \times |m|)$, where $|y_1|, |y_2|$ are the number of parts in $y_1$ and $y_2$.

Finally, note that adding 1 to one of the column counts of $C$ corresponds to a slot that can be skipped to produce a partial template (this simulates a wild card property that is always on).

## 3 Kernel Reranker

We next show how to use the template kernels within a reranker. In the reranking approach (Collins and Koo, 2005; Charniak and Johnson, 2005), a base parser produces a list of k-best candidate parses for an input sentence and a separately trained reranking model is used to select the best one.

[2]For brevity we'll omit x from the kernel parameters and use $K(y_1, y_2)$ instead of $K((x_1, y_1), (x_2, y_2))$.

[3]We omit the proof, but intuitively, the product of column sums is equal to the number of 1 valued paths between elements in the different columns of $C$. Each such path corresponds to a path in $p$ and $p'$ where all the properties have identical values. i.e. it corresponds to a feature that is active in both $\phi(x_1, p)$ and $\phi(x_2, p')$ and thus contributes 1 towards the dot product.

**Features:** Our feature vector will have two parts. One, $\Phi_g(x, y) \in \mathbb{R}^{d_1}$, consists of features obtained from manually constructed templates. The other, $\Phi_k(x, y) \in \mathbb{R}^{d_2}$, corresponds to our kernel features. We will not evaluate or store it, but rather use the kernel trick for implicitly learning with it, as explained below. The score of a candidate parse $y$ for sentence $x$ is calculated via the following linear function:

$$\begin{aligned} \Phi(x, y) &= [\Phi_g(x, y), \Phi_k(x, y)] \\ h_{\mathbf{v}}(x, y) &= \mathbf{v} \cdot \Phi(x, y) \end{aligned} \quad (2)$$

**Learning** For learning we use the passive-aggressive algorithm (Crammer et al., 2006; McDonald et al., 2005a), and adapt it to use with kernels. Formally, let $S = \{(x_i, \mathcal{K}(x_i))\}_{i=1}^n$ be a training set of size $n$ such that $\mathcal{K}(x_i) = \{y_{i1}, \ldots, y_{ik}\}$ is the set of k-best candidate trees produced for the sentence $x_i$. Assume that $y_{i1}$ is the optimal tree in terms of Hamming distance to the gold tree.

A key observation to make is that the $\mathbf{v}$ generated by the PA algorithm will depend on two parameters. One is a weight vector $\mathbf{w} \in \mathbb{R}^{d_1}$, in the manually constructed $\Phi_g$ feature space. The other is a set of weights $\alpha_{ij}$ with $i = 1, \ldots, n$ and $j = 1, \ldots, k$ corresponding to the $j^{th}$ candidate for the $i^{th}$ sample.[4] The score is then given by:

$$f_{\mathbf{w},\alpha}(x, y) = \mathbf{v} \cdot \Phi(x, y) = \mathbf{w} \cdot \Phi_g(x, y) + f_\alpha(x, y)$$

where:

$$f_\alpha(x, y) = \sum_{i,j} \alpha_{ij} \cdot (K(y_{i1}, y) - K(y_{ij}, y))$$

We can now rewrite the updates of the PA algorithm using $\mathbf{w}, \alpha$, as described in Alg 1.[5]

## 4 Implementation

The classifier depends on parameters $\alpha_{ij}$, which are updated using the PA algorithm. In the worst case, all $nk$ of these may be non-zero. For large datasets, this may slow down both learning and prediction.

[4]This follows from tracing the steps of PA and noting their dependence on dot products.

[5]The denominator in line 5 is equal to $\|\Phi_g(x_i, y_{ij}) - \Phi_g(x_i, y_{i1})\|^2 + K(y_{ij}, y_{ij}) - 2K(y_{ij}, y_{i1}) + K(y_{i1}, y_{i1})$ so it can be calculated efficiently using the kernel. $\|y_{i1} - y_{ij}\|_1$ is the hamming distance between $y_{i1}$ and $y_{ij}$. The updates for $\bar{\alpha}$ are equivalent to averaging over all alphas in iterations $1, \ldots, T$. We use this form to save space.

Below we discuss implementation techniques to mitigate this problem. To facilitate the discussion we rewrite the dot-product computation as follows:

$$f_\alpha(x, y) = \sum_{p' \in y} \hat{f}_\alpha(x, p') \tag{3}$$

where:

$$\hat{f}_\alpha(x, p') = \sum_{i,j} \alpha_{ij} \left( \sum_{p \in y_{i1}} k(p, p') - \sum_{p \in y_{ij}} k(p, p') \right)$$

**Reducing Prediction Runtime** From Equation 3 we note several facts. First, prediction involves calculating $k(p, p')$ for every combination of a part $p$ from the support instances (i.e., those for which $\alpha_{ij} > 0$) and part $p'$ from the instances in the k-best list. Our implementation thus maintains its support as a set of parts rather than a set of instances.

Second, parts that appear in both $y_{i1}$ and $y_{ij}$ do not affect the result of $f_\alpha(x, y)$ since they cancel each other out. Our implementation thus only updates the support set with parts that belong exclusively to either $y_{i1}$ or $y_{ij}$. This improves performance significantly since the number of non-overlapping parts in $y_{i1}$ and $y_{ij}$ is typically much smaller than the total number of parts therein.

Another important performance gain is obtained by caching the results of $\hat{f}_\alpha(x, p')$ when calculating $f_\alpha(x, y)$ for the different instances in the k-best list. This avoids recalculating the summation for parts that occur multiple times in the k-best list. Once again, this amounts to a considerable gain, as the number of distinct parts in the k-best list is much smaller than the total number of parts therein.

**Reducing Training Runtime** We greatly improve training speed by caching the results of $f_\alpha(x_i, y_{ij})$ between training iterations so that on each repeating invocation of the function, only the support parts added since the previous iteration need to be considered. Since the predictions of the learning algorithm become increasingly more accurate, the number of added support parts decreases sharply between iterations[6], and so does the runtime. In practice, all iterations from the 3rd onwards have negligible runtime compared to the first and second iterations. This technique allows us to comfortably train the kernel predictor on large datasets.

[6] On correct predictions, $\tau_t$ at line 5 of Alg 1 is 0, so no update is taking place and no support parts are added.

**Algorithm 1** PA Algorithm for Template Kernels

**Input:** $S = \{(x_i, \mathcal{K}(x_i))\}_{i=1}^{n}$, $NumIters$, Aggressiveness parameter $C$

1: $\forall i, j\ \alpha_{ij} \leftarrow 0,\ \bar{\alpha}_{ij} \leftarrow 0; T \leftarrow n \times NumIters$
2: **for** $t = 1$ to $T$ **do**
3: $\quad i \leftarrow t \mod n$
4: $\quad j \leftarrow \underset{j:\, y_{ij} \in \mathcal{K}(x_i)}{\text{argmax}}\ f_{\mathbf{w},\alpha}(x_i, y_{ij})$
5: $\quad \tau_t \leftarrow \min\left\{C, \frac{f_{\mathbf{w},\alpha}(x, y_{ij}) - f_{\mathbf{w},\alpha}(x, y_{i1}) + \|y_{i1} - y_{ij}\|_1}{\|\Phi(x_i, y_{ij}) - \Phi(x_i, y_{i1})\|^2}\right\}$
6: $\quad \alpha_{ij} \leftarrow \alpha_{ij} + \tau_t$
7: $\quad \bar{\alpha}_{ij} \leftarrow \bar{\alpha}_{ij} + \tau_t (T - t + 1)$
8: $\quad \mathbf{w}^{(t+1)} \leftarrow \mathbf{w}^{(t)} + \tau_t (\Phi_g(x_i, y_{i1}) - \Phi_g(x_i, y_{ij}))$
9: **end for**
10: $\forall i, j,\ \bar{\alpha}_{ij} \leftarrow \frac{\bar{\alpha}_{ij}}{T},\ \bar{\mathbf{w}} = \frac{1}{T} \sum_{t=1}^{T} \mathbf{w}^{(t)}$

**Output:** predictor: $\underset{y \in \mathcal{K}(x)}{\text{argmax}} (f_{\bar{\mathbf{w}},\bar{\alpha}}(x, y))$

## 5 Experimental Setup

**Datasets** We test our system on 4 languages from the CoNLL 2006 shared task, all with rich morphological features.[7] The properties provided for each word in these datasets are its *form*, part of speech (*pos*), coarse part of speech (*cpos*), *lemma* and *morph* features (number, gender, person, etc. around 10-20 feats in total). We use 20-fold jackknifing to create the k-best lists for the reranker (Collins and Duffy, 2002).

**Base Parser** The base parser used in experiments was the sampling parser of Lei et al. (2014), augmented to produce the k-best trees encountered during sampling. The parser was set to use feature templates over third order part types, but its tensor component and global templates were deactivated.

**Features** The manual features $\Phi_g$ were based on first to third order templates from Lei et al. (2014). For the kernel features $\Phi_k$ we annotated the nodes and edges in each tree with the properties in Table 1. We used a first order template kernel to train a model using all the the possible combinations of head, edge and modifier properties. Our kernel also produces all the property combinations of the head and modifier words (disregarding the edge properties).

[7] Our property combination approach is less relevant for treebanks that do not specify morphological properties. This is the

| Node Unigram properties: | | |
|---|---|---|
| form | $form_{-1}$ | $form_{+1}$ |
| pos | $pos_{-1}$ | $pos_{+1}$ |
| cpos | $cpos_{-1}$ | $cpos_{+1}$ |
| $\forall i$ $morph_i$ | | |
| **Node Bigram properties:** | | **Edge prop:** |
| $pos_{-1}$, pos | | label |
| pos, $pos_{+1}$ | | len, dist |
| pos, form | | always on |
| $\forall i$ pos, $morph_i$ | | |

Table 1: Linguistic properties for nodes and edges.

**Results** For each language we train a *Kernel Reranker* by running Alg 1 for 10 iterations over the training set, using k-best lists of size 25 and C set to infinity. As baseline, we train a *Base Reranker* in the same setup but with kernel features turned off. Table 2 shows the results for the two systems. Even though they use the same feature set, the base-reranker lags behind the base-parser. We attribute this to the fact that the reranker explores a much smaller fraction of the search space, and that the gold parse tree may not be available to it in either train or test time. However, the kernel-reranker significantly improves over the base-reranker. In Bulgarian and Danish, the kernel-reranker outperforms the base-parser. This is not the case for Slovene and Arabic, which we attribute to the low oracle accuracy of the k-best lists in these languages. As is common in reranking (Jagarlamudi and Daumé III, 2012), our final system incorporates the scores assigned to sentences by the base parser: i.e. $score_{final}(x, y) = \beta score_{base}(x, y) + score_{reranker}(x, y)$. $\beta$ is tuned per language on a development set.[8] Our final system outperforms the base parser, as well as TurboParser (Martins et al., 2013), a parser based on manually constructed feature templates over up to third order parts. The system lags slightly behind the sampling parser of Zhang et al. (2014) which additionally uses global features (not used by our system) and a tensor component for property combinations. Another important difference between the systems is that our search is severely restricted by the use of a reranker. It is likely that using our kernel in a graph-based parser will further improve its accuracy.

| | Arabic | Slovene | Danish | Bulgarian |
|---|---|---|---|---|
| Base Parser | 80.15 | 86.13 | 90.76 | 92.98 |
| Base Reranker | 79.46 | 84.61 | 90.36 | 92.27 |
| Kernel Reranker | 79.48 | 85.25 | 91.04 | 93.28 |
| Final System | 80.19 | 86.44 | 91.56 | 93.4 |
| Turbo Parser | 79.64 | 86.01 | 91.48 | 93.1 |
| Zhang et al. | 80.24 | 86.72 | 91.86 | 93.72 |

Table 2: System Performance (UAS excluding punctuation). TurboParser is (Martins et al., 2013), Zhang et al. is (Zhang et al., 2014)

| | Arabic | Slovene | Danish | Bulgarian |
|---|---|---|---|---|
| Sentences | 1,460 | 1,534 | 5,190 | 12,823 |
| Avg. Sent Len | 37 | 19 | 18 | 15 |
| Support Parts | 15,466 | 10,101 | 31,627 | 58,842 |
| Training Time | 6m | 7m | 31m | 57m |
| tokens/sec | 551 | 432 | 223 | 99 |

Table 3: Runtime statistics, measured on a standard Macbook Pro 2.8 GHz Core i7 using 8 threads.

**Performance** Table 3 lists the performance metrics of our system on the four evaluation treebanks. While training times are reasonable even for large datasets, the increase in support size causes prediction to become slow for medium and large training sets. The number of support instances is a general problem with kernel methods. It has been addressed using techniques like feature maps (Rahimi and Recht, 2007; Lu et al., 2014) and bounded online algorithms (Dekel et al., 2008; Zhao et al., 2012). The application of these techniques to template kernels is a topic for future research.

## 6 Conclusions

We present a kernel approach to graph based dependency parsing. The proposed method facilitates globally optimal parameter estimation in a high dimensional feature space, corresponding to the full set of property combinations. We implemented our solution as part of a parse reranking system, demonstrating state of the art results. Future work will focus on performance improvements, using the kernel on higher order parts, and integrating the kernel directly into a graph based dependency parser.

**Acknowledgments** This work is supported by the US-Israel Binational Science Foundation (BSF, Grant No 2012330) and by the Intel Collaborative Research Institute for Computational Intelligence (ICRI-CI). We thank the NAACL HLT reviewers for their comments.

reason we did not select the English treebank.

[8]To obtain a development set we further split the reranker training sets into tuning training and a development sets (90/10). We then tune $\beta$ per language on the respective development sets by selecting the best value from a list of $\{0, 0.05, \ldots, 3\}$

## References


Xavier Carreras. 2007. Experiments with a higher-order projective dependency parser. In *EMNLP-CoNLL*, pages 957–961.

Eugene Charniak and Mark Johnson. 2005. Coarse-to-fine n-best parsing and maxent discriminative reranking. In *Proceedings of the 43rd Annual Meeting of the Association for Computational Linguistics*, pages 173–180.

Danqi Chen and Christopher D Manning. 2014. A fast and accurate dependency parser using neural networks. In *Proceedings of the 2014 Conference on Empirical Methods in Natural Language Processing (EMNLP)*, volume 1, pages 740–750.

Michael Collins and Nigel Duffy. 2002. New ranking algorithms for parsing and tagging: Kernels over discrete structures, and the voted perceptron. In *Proceedings of the 40th Annual Meeting of the Association for Computational Linguistics*, pages 263–270. Association for Computational Linguistics.

Michael Collins and Terry Koo. 2005. Discriminative reranking for natural language parsing. *Computational Linguistics*, 31(1):25–70.

Koby Crammer, Ofer Dekel, Joseph Keshet, Shai Shalev-Shwartz, and Yoram Singer. 2006. Online passive-aggressive algorithms. *The Journal of Machine Learning Research*, 7:551–585.

Aron Culotta and Jeffrey Sorensen. 2004. Dependency tree kernels for relation extraction. In *Proceedings of the 42nd Annual Meeting on Association for Computational Linguistics*, page 423. Association for Computational Linguistics.

Ofer Dekel, Shai Shalev-Shwartz, and Yoram Singer. 2008. The forgetron: A kernel-based perceptron on a budget. *SIAM Journal on Computing*, 37(5):1342–1372.

Johan Hall, Joakim Nivre, and Jens Nilsson. 2006. Discriminative classifiers for deterministic dependency parsing. In *Proceedings of the COLING/ACL on Main conference poster sessions*, pages 316–323.

Jagadeesh Jagarlamudi and Hal Daumé III. 2012. Low-dimensional discriminative reranking. In *Proceedings of the 2012 Conference of the North American Chapter of the Association for Computational Linguistics: Human Language Technologies*, pages 699–709.

Terry Koo and Michael Collins. 2010. Efficient third-order dependency parsers. In *Proceedings of the 48th Annual Meeting of the Association for Computational Linguistics*, pages 1–11. Association for Computational Linguistics.

Tao Lei, Yu Xin, Yuan Zhang, Regina Barzilay, and Tommi Jaakkola. 2014. Low-rank tensors for scoring dependency structures. In *Proceedings of the 52nd Annual Meeting of the Association for Computational Linguistics*, volume 1, pages 1381–1391.

Zhiyun Lu, Avner May, Kuan Liu, Alireza Bagheri Garakani, Dong Guo, Aurélien Bellet, Linxi Fan, Michael Collins, Brian Kingsbury, Michael Picheny, et al. 2014. How to scale up kernel methods to be as good as deep neural nets. *arXiv preprint arXiv:1411.4000*.

André FT Martins, Miguel Almeida, and Noah A Smith. 2013. Turning on the turbo: Fast third-order non-projective turbo parsers. In *Proceedings of the 51st Annual Meeting of the Association for Computational Linguistics*, pages 617–622.

Ryan McDonald, Koby Crammer, and Fernando Pereira. 2005a. Online large-margin training of dependency parsers. In *Proceedings of the 43rd Annual Meeting of the Association for Computational Linguistics*, pages 91–98.

Ryan McDonald, Fernando Pereira, Kiril Ribarov, and Jan Hajič. 2005b. Non-projective dependency parsing using spanning tree algorithms. In *Proceedings of the conference on Human Language Technology and Empirical Methods in Natural Language Processing*, pages 523–530. Association for Computational Linguistics.

Ali Rahimi and Benjamin Recht. 2007. Random features for large-scale kernel machines. In *Advances in neural information processing systems*, pages 1177–1184.

Frank Reichartz, Hannes Korte, and Gerhard Paass. 2010. Semantic relation extraction with kernels over typed dependency trees. In *Proceedings of the 16th ACM SIGKDD international conference on Knowledge discovery and data mining*, pages 773–782.

John Shawe-Taylor and Nello Cristianini. 2004. *Kernel methods for pattern analysis*. Cambridge university press.

Le Sun and Xianpei Han. 2014. A feature-enriched tree kernel for relation extraction. In *The 52nd Annual Meeting of the Association for Computational Linguistics*, volume 2, pages 61–67.

Dmitry Zelenko, Chinatsu Aone, and Anthony Richardella. 2003. Kernel methods for relation extraction. *The Journal of Machine Learning Research*, 3:1083–1106.

Yuan Zhang, Tao Lei, Regina Barzilay, and Tommi Jaakkola. 2014. Greed is good if randomized: New inference for dependency parsing. In *Proceedings of the 2014 Conference on Empirical Methods in Natural Language Processing (EMNLP)*, pages 1013–1024.

Peilin Zhao, Jialei Wang, Pengcheng Wu, Rong Jin, and Steven CH Hoi. 2012. Fast bounded online gradient descent algorithms for scalable kernel-based online learning. *arXiv preprint arXiv:1206.4633*.

# Embedding a Semantic Network in a Word Space

**Richard Johansson** and **Luis Nieto Piña**
Språkbanken, Department of Swedish, University of Gothenburg
Box 200, SE-40530 Gothenburg, Sweden
{richard.johansson, luis.nieto.pina}@svenska.gu.se

## Abstract

We present a framework for using continuous-space vector representations of word meaning to derive new vectors representing the meaning of *senses* listed in a semantic network. It is a post-processing approach that can be applied to several types of word vector representations. It uses two ideas: first, that vectors for polysemous words can be decomposed into a convex combination of sense vectors; secondly, that the vector for a sense is kept similar to those of its neighbors in the network. This leads to a constrained optimization problem, and we present an approximation for the case when the distance function is the squared Euclidean.

We applied this algorithm on a Swedish semantic network, and we evaluate the quality of the resulting sense representations extrinsically by showing that they give large improvements when used in a classifier that creates lexical units for FrameNet frames.

## 1 Introduction

Representing word meaning computationally is central in natural language processing. Manual, knowledge-based approaches to meaning representation maps word strings to symbolic concepts, which can be described using any knowledge representation framework; using the relations between concepts defined in the knowledge base, we can infer implicit facts from the information stated in a text: a *mouse* is a *rodent*, so it has prominent *teeth*.

Conversely, data-driven meaning representation approaches rely on cooccurrence patterns to derive a vector representation (Turney and Pantel, 2010). There are two classes of methods that compute word vectors: context-counting and context-predicting; while the latter has seen much interest lately, their respective strengths and weaknesses are still being debated (Baroni et al., 2014; Levy and Goldberg, 2014). The most important relation defined in a vector space between the meaning of two words is *similarity*: a *mouse* is something quite similar to a *rat*. Similarity of meaning is operationalized in terms of geometry, by defining a distance metric.

Symbolic representations seem to have an advantage in describing *word sense ambiguity*: when a surface form corresponds to more than one concept. For instance, the word *mouse* can refer to a *rodent* or an *electronic device*. Vector-space representations typically represent surface forms only, which makes it hard to search e.g. for a group of words similar to the rodent sense of *mouse* or to reliably use the vectors in classifiers that rely on the semantics of the word. There have been several attempts to create vectors representing senses, most of them based on some variant of the idea first proposed by Schütze (1998): that senses can be seen as clusters of similar contexts. Recent examples in this tradition include the work by Huang et al. (2012) and Neelakantan et al. (2014). However, because sense distributions are often highly imbalanced, it is not clear that context clusters can be reliably created for senses that occur rarely. These approaches also lack interpretability: if we are interested in the rodent sense of *mouse*, which of the vectors should we use?

In this work, we instead derive sense vectors by embedding the graph structure of a semantic network in the word space. By combining two complementary sources of information – corpus statistics and network structure – we derive useful vectors also for concepts that occur rarely. The method, which can be applied to context-counting as well as context-predicting spaces, works by decompos-



*Human Language Technologies: The 2015 Annual Conference of the North American Chapter of the ACL*, pages 1428–1433,
Denver, Colorado, May 31 – June 5, 2015. 

ing word vectors as linear combinations of sense vectors, and by pushing the sense vectors towards their neighbors in the semantic network. This intuition leads to a constrained optimization problem, for which we present an approximate algorithm.

We applied the algorithm to derive vectors for the senses in a Swedish semantic network, and we evaluated their quality extrinsically by using them as features in a semantic classification task – mapping senses to their corresponding FrameNet frames. When using the sense vectors in this task, we saw a large improvement over using word vectors.

## 2 Embedding a Semantic Network

The goal of the algorithm is to *embed* the semantic network in a geometric space: that is, to associate each sense $s_{ij}$ with a *sense embedding*, a vector $E(s_{ij})$ of real numbers, in a way that reflects the topology of the semantic network but also that the vectors representing the lemmas are related to those corresponding to the senses. We now formalize this intuition, and we start by introducing some notation.

For each lemma $l_i$, there is a set of possible senses $s_{i1}, \ldots, s_{im_i}$ for which $l_i$ is a surface realization. Furthermore, for each sense $s_{ij}$, there is a *neighborhood* consisting of senses semantically related to $s_{ij}$. Each neighbor $n_{ijk}$ of $s_{ij}$ is associated with a weight $w_{ijk}$ representing the degree of semantic relatedness between $s_{ij}$ and $n_{ijk}$. How we define the neighborhood, i.e. our notion of semantical relatedness, will obviously have an impact on the result. In this work, we simply assume that it can be computed from the network, e.g. by picking a number of hypernyms and hyponyms in a lexicon such as WordNet. We then assume that for each lemma $l_i$, we have a $D$-dimensional vector $F(l_i)$ of real numbers; this can be computed using any method described in Section 1. Finally, we assume a *distance function* $\Delta(x, y)$ that returns a non-negative real number for each pair of vectors in $\mathbb{R}^D$.

The algorithm maps each sense $s_{ij}$ to a sense embedding, a real-valued vector $E(s_{ij})$ in the same vector space as the lemma embeddings. The lemma and sense embeddings are related through a *mix constraint*: $F(l_i)$ is decomposed as a convex combination $\sum_j p_{ij} E(s_{ij})$, where the $\{p_{ij}\}$ are picked from the probability simplex. Intuitively, the mix variables correspond to the occurrence probabilities of the senses, but strictly speaking this is only the case when the vectors are built using simple context counting. Since the mix gives an estimate of which sense is the most frequent in the corpus, we get a strong baseline for word sense disambiguation (McCarthy et al., 2007) as a bonus; see our followup paper (Johansson and Nieto Piña, 2015) for a discussion of this.

We can now formalize the intuition above: the weighted sum of distances between each sense and its neighbors is minimized, while satisfying the mix constraint for each lemma. We get the following constrained optimization program:

$$\begin{aligned} \underset{E,p}{\text{minimize}} \quad & \sum_{i,j,k} w_{ijk} \Delta(E(s_{ij}), E(n_{ijk})) \\ \text{subject to} \quad & \sum_j p_{ij} E(s_{ij}) = F(l_i) \qquad \forall i \\ & \sum_j p_{ij} = 1 \qquad \forall i \\ & p_{ij} \geq 0 \qquad \forall i, j \end{aligned} \tag{1}$$

The mix constraints make sure that the solution is nontrivial. In particular, a very large number of words are monosemous, and the procedure will leave the embeddings of these words unchanged.

### 2.1 An Approximate Algorithm

The difficulty of solving the problem stated in Equation (1) obviously depends on the distance function $\Delta$. Henceforth, we focus on the case where $\Delta$ is the squared Euclidean distance. This is an important special case that is related to a number of other distances or similarities, e.g. cosine similarity and Hellinger distance. In this case, (1) is a quadratically constrained quadratic problem, which is NP-hard in general and difficult to handle with off-the-shelf optimization tools. We therefore resort to an approximation; we show empirically in Sections 3 and 4 that it works well in practice.

The approximate algorithm works in an online fashion by considering one lemma at a time. It adjusts the embeddings of the senses as well as their mix in order to minimize the loss function

$$L_i = \sum_{jk} w_{ijk} \|E(s_{ij}) - E(n_{ijk})\|^2. \tag{2}$$

The embeddings of the neighbors $n_{ijk}$ of the sense are kept fixed at each such step. We iterate through the whole set of lemmas for a fixed number of epochs or until the objective is unchanged.

Furthermore, instead of directly optimizing with respect to the sense embeddings (which involves $m_i \cdot D$ scalars), the sense embeddings (and therefore also the loss $L_i$) can be computed analytically if the mix variables $p_{i1}, \ldots, p_{im_i}$ are given, so we have reduced the optimization problem to one involving $m_i - 1$ scalars, i.e. it is univariate in most cases.

Given a sense $s_{ij}$ of a lemma $l_i$, we define the *weighted centroid* of the set of neighbors of $s_{ij}$ as

$$c_{ij} = \frac{\sum_k w_{ijk} E(n_{ijk})}{\sum_k w_{ijk}}. \quad (3)$$

If the mix constraints were removed, $c_{ij}$ would be the solution to the optimization problem: they minimize the weighted sum of squared Euclidean distances to the neighbors. Then, given the mix, the *residual* is defined

$$r_i = \frac{1}{\sum_j \frac{p_{ij}^2}{\sum_k w_{ijk}}} \left( \sum_j p_{ij} c_{ij} - F(l_i) \right). \quad (4)$$

The vector $r_i$ represents the difference between the linear combination of the weighted centroids and the lemma embedding. Finally, we the sense embeddings for the lemma $l_i$ become

$$E(s_{ij}) = c_{ij} - \frac{p_{ij}}{\sum_k w_{ijk}} r_i. \quad (5)$$

Equations (4) and (5) show the role of the mix variables: if $p_{ij} = 0$, then the sense embedding $E(s_{ij})$ is completely determined by the neighbors of the sense (that is, it is equal to the weighted centroid). On the other hand, if $p_{ij} = 1$, then the sense embedding becomes equal to the embedding of the lemma, $F(l_i)$. To optimize the mix variables $p_{i1}, \ldots, p_{im_i}$ with respect to the loss $L_i$, basically any search procedure could be used; we found it easiest to use a variant of a simple randomized gradient-free search method (Matyas, 1965).

## 3 Application to Swedish Data

The algorithm described in Section 2 was applied to Swedish data: we started with lemma embeddings computed from a corpus, and then created sense embeddings by using the SALDO semantic network (Borin et al., 2013). The algorithm was run for a few epochs, which seemed to be enough for reaching a plateau in performance; the total runtime of the algorithm was a few minutes.

### 3.1 Creating Lemma Embeddings

We created a corpus of 1 billion words downloaded from Språkbanken, the Swedish language bank.[1] The corpora are distributed in a format where the text has been tokenized, part-of-speech-tagged and lemmatized. Compounds have been segmented automatically and when a lemma was not listed in SALDO, we used the parts of the compounds instead. The input to the software computing the lemma embedding consisted of lemma forms with concatenated part-of-speech tags, e.g. *dricka..vb* for the verb 'to drink' and *dricka..nn* for the noun 'drink'. We used the `word2vec` tool[2] to build the lemma embeddings. All the default settings were used, except the vector space dimensionality which was set to 512.

### 3.2 SALDO, a Swedish Semantic Network

SALDO (Borin et al., 2013) is the largest freely available lexical resource for Swedish. We used a version from May 2014, which contains 125,781 entries organized into a single semantic network. Compared to WordNet (Fellbaum, 1998), there are similarities but also significant differences. Most significantly, SALDO is organized according to the lexical-semantic relation of *association*, not *is-a* as in WordNet. In SALDO, when we go up in the hierarchy we move from specialized vocabulary to the most central vocabulary of the language (e.g. 'move', 'want', 'who'); in WordNet we move from specific to abstract (e.g. 'entity'). Another difference is that sense distinctions in SALDO tend to be more coarse-grained than in WordNet.

Each entry except a special root is connected to other entries, its *semantic descriptors*. One of the

[1] `http://spraakbanken.gu.se`

[2] `https://code.google.com/p/word2vec`

semantic descriptors is called the *primary* descriptor: this is the semantic neighbor that is conceptually most central. Primary descriptors are most often hypernyms or synonyms, but they can also be e.g. antonyms or meronyms, or be in an argument–predicate relationship with the entry. To exemplify, we consider the word *rock*, which has two senses: a long coat and rock music, respectively. Its first sense has the primary descriptor *kappa* 'coat', while for the second sense it is *musik* 'music'.

When embedding the SALDO network using the algorithm in Section 2, the neighbors $n_{ijk}$ of a SALDO sense $s_{ij}$ are its primary descriptor and inverse primaries (the senses for which $s_{ij}$ is the primary descriptor). We did not use any descriptors beside the primary. The neighborhood weights were set so that the primary descriptor and the set of inverse primaries were balanced, and so that all weights sum to 1. If there were $N$ inverse primaries, we set the weight of the primary descriptor to $\frac{1}{2}$ and of each inverse primary to $\frac{1}{2N}$. We did not see any measurable effect of using a larger set of neighbors (e.g. adding connections to second-order neighbors).

### 3.3 Inspection of Sense Embeddings

Table 1 shows a list of the nearest neighbors of the two senses of *rock*; as we can see, both lists make sense semantically. (A similar query among the lemma embeddings returns a list almost identical to that of the second sense.)

| *rock*-1 'coat' | *rock*-2 'rock music' |
|---|---|
| *syrtut*-1 'overcoat' | *punk*-1 'punk music' |
| *kåpa*-2 'cloak' | *pop*-1 'pop music' |
| *kappa*-1 'coat' | *soul*-1 'soul music' |
| *kavaj*-1 'blazer' | *hårdrock*-1 'hard rock' |
| *jacka*-1 'jacket' | *hot*-2 'hot jazz' |

Table 1: The senses closest to the two senses of *rock*.

A more difficult and interesting use case, where corpus-based methods clearly have an advantage over knowledge-based methods, is to search among the lemmas that have occurred in the corpus but which are not listed in SALDO. Table 2 shows the result of this search, and again the result is very useful. We stress that the list for the first sense would have been hard to derive in a standard word vector space, due to the dominance of the music sense.

| *rock*-1 'coat' | *rock*-2 'rock music' |
|---|---|
| *midjekort* 'doublet' | *indie* 'indie' |
| *trekvartsärm* '3/4 sleeve' | *indierock* 'indie rock' |
| *spetsbh* 'lace bra' | *doo-wop* 'doo-wop' |
| *blåjeans* 'blue jeans' | *psykedelia* 'psychedelia' |
| *treggings* 'treggings' | *R&B* 'R&B' |

Table 2: The unlisted lemmas closest to the two senses of *rock*.

## 4 Evaluation

Evaluating intrinsically using e.g. a correlation between a graph-based similarity measure and geometric similarity would be problematic, since this is in some sense what our algorithm optimizes. We therefore evaluate extrinsically, by using the sense vectors in a classifier that maps senses to semantic classes defined by FrameNet (Fillmore and Baker, 2009). FrameNet is a semantic database consisting of two parts: first, an ontology of *semantic frames* – the classes – and secondly a lexicon that maps word senses to frames. In standard FrameNet terminology, the senses assigned to a frame are called its *lexical units* (LUs). Coverage is often a problem in frame-semantic lexicons, and this has a negative impact on the quality of NLP systems using FrameNet (Palmer and Sporleder, 2010). The task of finding LUs for frames is thus a useful testbed for evaluating lemma and sense vectors.

To evaluate, we used 567 frames from the Swedish FrameNet (Friberg Heppin and Toporowska Gronostaj, 2012); in total we had 28,842 verb, noun, adjective, and adverb LUs, which we split into training (67%) and test sets (33%). For each frame, we trained a SVM with LIBLINEAR (Fan et al., 2008), using the LUs in that frame as positive training instances, and all other LUs as negative instances. Each LU was represented as a vector: its lemma or sense embedding normalized to unit length.

Table 3 shows the precision, recall, and $F$-measure for the classifiers for the five frames with most LUs, and finally the micro-average over all frames. In the overall evaluation as well as in four out of the five largest frames, the classifiers using sense vectors clearly outperform those using lemma vectors. The frame where we do not see any improvement by introducing sense distinctions, PEOPLE_BY_VOCATION, contains terms for professions such as *painter* and *builder*; since SALDO derives such terms from their corresponding verbs rather than from a common hypernym (e.g. *worker*), they do not form a coherent subnetwork in SALDO or subregion in the embedding space.

| Frame | *P* | *R* | *F* |
|---|---|---|---|
| ANIMALS | 0.741 | 0.643 | 0.689 |
| FOOD | 0.684 | 0.679 | 0.682 |
| PEOPLE_BY_VOCATION | 0.595 | 0.651 | 0.622 |
| ORIGIN | 0.789 | 0.691 | 0.737 |
| PEOPLE_BY_ORIGIN | 0.693 | 0.481 | 0.568 |
| Overall | 0.569 | 0.292 | 0.386 |

(a) Using lemma embeddings.

| Frame | *P* | *R* | *F* |
|---|---|---|---|
| ANIMALS | 0.826 | 0.663 | 0.736 |
| FOOD | 0.726 | 0.743 | 0.735 |
| PEOPLE_BY_VOCATION | 0.605 | 0.637 | 0.621 |
| ORIGIN | 0.813 | 0.684 | 0.742 |
| PEOPLE_BY_ORIGIN | 0.756 | 0.508 | 0.608 |
| Overall | 0.667 | 0.332 | 0.443 |

(b) Using sense embeddings.

Table 3: FrameNet lexical unit classification.

## 5 Conclusion

We have presented a new method to embed a semantic network consisting of linked word senses into a continuous-vector word space; the method is agnostic about whether the original word space was produced using a context-counting or context-predicting method. Unlike previous approaches for creating sense vectors, since we rely on the network structure, we can create representations for senses that occur rarely in corpora. While the experiments described in this paper have been carried out using a Swedish corpus and semantic network, the algorithm we have described is generally applicable and the software[3] can be applied to other languages and semantic networks.

The algorithm takes word vectors and uses them and the network structure to induce the sense vectors. It is based on two separate ideas: first, sense embeddings should preserve the structure of the semantic network as much as possible, so two senses should be close if they are neighbors in the graph; secondly, the word vectors are a probablistic mix of sense vectors. These two ideas are stated as an optimization problem where the first becomes the objective and the second a constraint. While this is hard to solve in the general case, we presented an approximation that can be applied when using the squared Euclidean distance.

We implemented the algorithm and used it to embed the senses of a Swedish semantic network into a word space produced using the skip-gram model. While a qualitative inspection of nearest-neighbor lists of a few senses gives very appealing results, our main evaluation was extrinsic: a FrameNet lexical unit classifier saw a large performance boost when using sense vectors instead of word vectors.

In a followup paper (Johansson and Nieto Piña, 2015), we have shown that sense embeddings can be used to build an efficient word sense disambiguation system that is much faster than graph-based systems with a similar accuracy, and that the mix variables can be used to predict the predominant sense of a word. In future work, we plan to investigate whether the sense vectors are useful for retrieving rarely occurring senses in corpora. Furthermore, since we now evaluated extrinsically, it would be useful to devise intrinsic sense-based evaluation schemes, e.g. a sense analogy task similar to the word analogy task used by Mikolov et al. (2013).

## Acknowledgments

This research was funded by the Swedish Research Council under grant 2013–4944, *Distributional methods to represent the meaning of frames and constructions*, and grant 2012–5738, *Towards a knowledge-based culturomics*. The evaluation material used in this work was developed in the project *Swedish FrameNet++*, grant 2010–6013. We also acknowledge the University of Gothenburg for its support of the Centre for Language Technology and Språkbanken.

[3] `http://demo.spraakdata.gu.se/richard/scouse`

## References


Marco Baroni, Georgiana Dinu, and Germán Kruszewski. 2014. Don't count, predict! a systematic comparison of context-counting vs. context-predicting semantic vectors. In *Proceedings of the 52nd Annual Meeting of the Association for Computational Linguistics (Volume 1: Long Papers)*, pages 238–247, Baltimore, United States.

Lars Borin, Markus Forsberg, and Lennart Lönngren. 2013. SALDO: a touch of yin to WordNet's yang. *Language Resources and Evaluation*, 47(4):1191–1211.

Rong-En Fan, Kai-Wei Chang, Cho-Jui Hsieh, Xiang-Rui Wang, and Chih-Jen Lin. 2008. LIBLINEAR: A library for large linear classification. *Journal of Machine Learning Research*, 9:1871–1874.

Christiane Fellbaum, editor. 1998. *WordNet: An electronic lexical database*. MIT Press.

Charles J. Fillmore and Collin Baker. 2009. A frames approach to semantic analysis. In B. Heine and H. Narrog, editors, *The Oxford Handbook of Linguistic Analysis*, pages 313–340. Oxford: OUP.

Karin Friberg Heppin and Maria Toporowska Gronostaj. 2012. The rocky road towards a Swedish FrameNet – creating SweFN. In *Proceedings of the Eighth conference on International Language Resources and Evaluation (LREC-2012)*, pages 256–261, Istanbul, Turkey.

Eric H. Huang, Richard Socher, Christopher D. Manning, and Andrew Y. Ng. 2012. Improving word representations via global context and multiple word prototypes. In *Association for Computational Linguistics 2012 Conference (ACL 2012)*, pages 41–48, Boston, United States.

Richard Johansson and Luis Nieto Piña. 2015. Combining relational and distributional knowledge for word sense disambiguation. In *Proceedings of the 20th Nordic Conference of Computational Linguistics*, Vilnius, Lithuania.

Omer Levy and Yoav Goldberg. 2014. Linguistic regularities in sparse and explicit word representations. In *Proceedings of the Eighteenth Conference on Computational Natural Language Learning*, pages 171–180, Ann Arbor, United States.

J. Matyas. 1965. Random optimization. *Automation and Remote Control*, 26(2):246–253.

Diana McCarthy, Rob Koeling, Julie Weeds, and John Carroll. 2007. Unsupervised acquisition of predominant word senses. *Computational Linguistics*, 33(4):553–590.

Tomáš Mikolov, Wen-tau Yih, and Geoffrey Zweig. 2013. Linguistic regularities in continuous space word representations. In *Proceedings of the 2013 Conference of the North American Chapter of the Association for Computational Linguistics: Human Language Technologies*, pages 746–751, Atlanta, USA.

Arvind Neelakantan, Jeevan Shankar, Alexandre Passos, and Andrew McCallum. 2014. Efficient nonparametric estimation of multiple embeddings per word in vector space. In *Proceedings of the 2014 Conference on Empirical Methods in Natural Language Processing (EMNLP)*, pages 1059–1069, Doha, Qatar, October.

Alexis Palmer and Caroline Sporleder. 2010. Evaluating FrameNet-style semantic parsing: the role of coverage gaps in FrameNet. In *Coling 2010: Posters*, pages 928–936, Beijing, China.

Hinrich Schütze. 1998. Automatic word sense discrimination. *Computational Linguistics*, 24(1):97–123.

Peter D. Turney and Patrick Pantel. 2010. From frequency to meaning: Vector space models of semantics. *Journal of Artificial Intelligence Research*, 37:141–188.

# Random Walks and Neural Network Language Models on Knowledge Bases

**Josu Goikoetxea, Aitor Soroa and Eneko Agirre**
IXA NLP Group
University of the Basque Country
Donostia, Basque Country
{josu.goikoetxea,a.soroa,e.agirre}@ehu.eus

## Abstract

Random walks over large knowledge bases like WordNet have been successfully used in word similarity, relatedness and disambiguation tasks. Unfortunately, those algorithms are relatively slow for large repositories, with significant memory footprints. In this paper we present a novel algorithm which encodes the structure of a knowledge base in a continuous vector space, combining random walks and neural net language models in order to produce novel word representations. Evaluation in word relatedness and similarity datasets yields equal or better results than those of a random walk algorithm, using a dense representation (300 dimensions instead of 117K). Furthermore, the word representations are complementary to those of the random walk algorithm and to corpus-based continuous representations, improving the state-of-the-art in the similarity dataset. Our technique opens up exciting opportunities to combine distributional and knowledge-based word representations.

## 1 Introduction

Graph-based techniques over Knowledge Bases (KB) like WordNet (Fellbaum, 1998) have been widely used in NLP tasks, including word sense disambiguation (Agirre et al., 2014; Moro et al., 2014), semantic similarity and semantic relatedness between terms (Agirre et al., 2009; Agirre et al., 2010; Pilehvar et al., 2013). For instance, Agirre et al. (2009; 2010) apply a random walk algorithm based on Personalized PageRank to WordNet, pre-

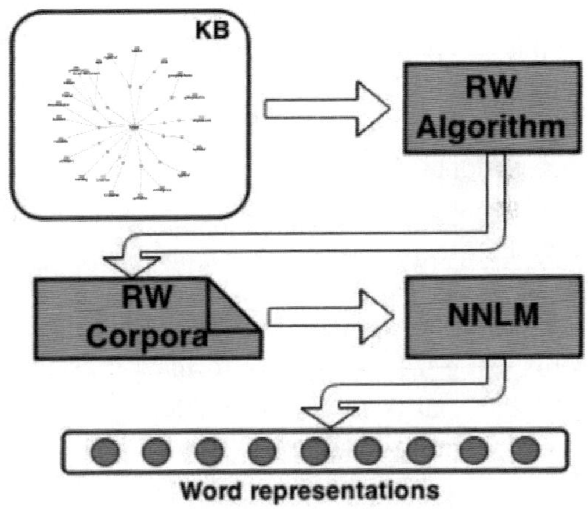


Figure 1: Main architecture for generating KB word embeddings. A random walk algorithm over the KB produces a synthetic corpus, which is fed into a NNLM to produce continuous word representations.

senting the best results to date among WordNet-based methods for the well-known WS353 word-similarity dataset (Finkelstein et al., 2001). For each target word, the method performs a personalized random walk on the WordNet graph. At convergence, the target word is represented as a vector in a multi-dimensional conceptual space, with one dimension for each concept in the KB. The good results of the algorithm contrast with the large dimensionality of the vectors that it needs to produce, 117K dimensions (one per synset) for WordNet.

In recent years a wide variety of Neural Network Language Models (NNLM) have been successfully employed in several tasks, including word similarity (Collobert and Weston, 2008; Socher et al., 2011;



*Human Language Technologies: The 2015 Annual Conference of the North American Chapter of the ACL*, pages 1434–1439,
Denver, Colorado, May 31 – June 5, 2015. 

Turian et al., 2010). NNLM extract meaning from unlabeled corpora following the distributional hypothesis (Harris, 1954), where semantic features of a word are related to its co-occurrence patterns. NNLM learn word representations in the form of dense scalar vectors in n-dimensional spaces (e.g. 300 dimensions), in which each dimension is a latent semantic feature. The representations are obtained by optimizing the likelihood of existing unlabeled text. More recently, Mikolov et al. have developed simpler NNLM architectures (Mikolov et al., 2013a; Mikolov et al., 2013b; Mikolov et al., 2013c), which drastically reduced computational complexity by deleting the hidden layer, enabling to compute accurate word representations from very large corpora. The representations obtained by these methods are compact, taking 1.5G for 3M words on 300-dimensional space, and have been shown to outperform other distributional corpus-based methods on several tasks, including the WS353 word similarity dataset (Baroni et al., 2014).

In this work we propose to encode the meaning of words using the structural information in knowledge bases. That is, instead of modeling the meaning based on the co-occurrences of words in corpora, we model the meaning based on random walks over the knowledge base. Each random walk is seen as a context for words in the vocabulary, and fed into the NNLM architecture, which optimizes the likelihood of those contexts (cf. Fig. 1). The resulting word representations are more compact than those produced by regular random walk algorithms (300 vs. tens of thousands), and produce very good results on two well-known benchmarks on word relatedness and similarity: WS353 (Finkelstein et al., 2001) and SL999 (Hill et al., 2014b), respectively. We also show that the obtained representations are complementary to those of random walks alone and to distributional representations obtained by the same NNLM algorithm, improving the results.

Some recent work has explored embedding KBs in low-dimensional continous vector spaces, representing each entity in a k-dimensional vector and characterizing typed relations between entities in the KB (e.g. born-in-city in Freebase or part-of in WordNet) as operations in the k-dimensional space (Wang et al., 2014). The model estimates the parameters which maximize the likelihood of the triples, which can then be used to infer new typed relations which are missing in the KB. In contrast, we use the relations to explicitly model the context of words, in two complementary approaches to embed information in KBs into continuous spaces.

## 2 NNLM

Neural Network Language Models have become a useful tool in NLP on the last years, specially in semantics. We have used the two models proposed in (Mikolov et al., 2013c) due to their simplicity and effectiveness in word similarity and relatedness tasks (Baroni et al., 2014): Continuous Bag of Words (CBOW) and Skip-gram. The first one is quite similar to the feedforward Neural Network Language Model, but instead of a hidden layer it has a projection layer, and thus all the words are projected in the same position. Word order has thus no influence in the projection. The training criterion is as follows: knowing previous and subsequent words in context, the model maximizes the probability of the predicting the word in the middle. The Skip-gram model uses each current word as an input to a log-linear classifier with a continuous projection layer, and predicts the previous and subsequent words in a context window.

Although the Skip-gram model seems to be more accurate in most of the semantic tasks, we have used both variants in our experiments. We used a publicly available implementation[1].

## 3 Random Walks and NNLM

Our method performs random walks over KB graphs to create synthetic contexts which are fed into the NNLM architecture, creating novel word representations. The algorithm used for creating the contexts is a Monte Carlo method for computing the PageRank algorithm (Avrachenkov et al., 2007).

We consider a KB as undirected graph $G = (V, E)$, where $V$ is the set of concepts and $E$ represents links among concepts. We also need a dictionary, an association from words to KB concepts. We construct an inverse dictionary that maps graph vertices with the words than can be linked to it.

The inputs of the algorithm are: 1) the graph $G = (V, E)$, 2) the inverse dictionary and 3) the damp-

[1] https://code.google.com/p/word2vec/

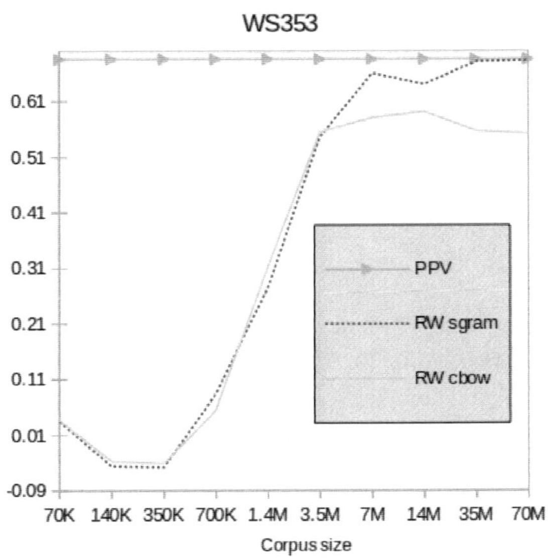


Figure 2: Spearman results on relatedness (WS353) for different corpus sizes (in sentences).

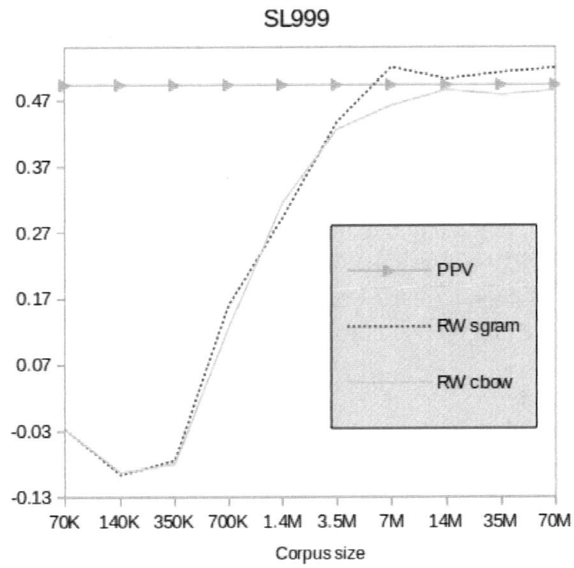


Figure 3: Spearman results on similarity (SL999) for different corpus sizes (in sentences).

ing factor $\alpha^2$. In our experiments we used WordNet 3.0 with gloss relations[3], which has $117.522$ nodes (synsets) and $525.356$ edges (semantic relations). Regarding the dictionary, WordNet already contains links from words to concepts. The dictionary includes the probability of a concept being lexicalized by a specific word, as estimated by the WordNet team from their hand-annotated corpora. Both dictionary and graph are freely available[4].

The method first chooses a vertex at random from the vertex set $V$, and performs a random walk starting from it. At each step, the random walk might terminate with probability $(1-\alpha)$ or choose a neighbor vertex at random with probability $\alpha$. Each time the random walk reaches a vertex, a word is emitted at random using the probabilities in the inverse dictionary. When the random walk terminates, the sequence of emitted words forms the pseudo sentence which is fed to the NNLM architecture, and the process starts again choosing a vertex at random until a maximum number of pseudo sentences have been generated.

Our method creates pseudo sentences like the following:

(1) *amphora wine nebuchadnezzar bear retain long*

(2) *graphology writer write scribble scrawler heedlessly in_haste jot note notebook*

These examples give us clues of the kind of the implicit semantic information that is encoded in the generated pseudo-corpus. Example 1 starts with *amphora* following with *wine* (with which amphoras are usually filled with), *nebuchadnezzar* (a particular bottle size) and finishing with words that are related to wine storage, like *bear,retain* and *long*. Example 2 shows a similar phenomenom; it starts with *graphology*, follows with the closely related *writer*, then *writer*, finishing with names and adjectives of different variants of writing, such as *scribble*, *scrawler*, *heedlessly*, *in_haste* and *jot*; finally, the context ends with *note* and *notebook*. Note that our method also produces multiword terms like *in_haste*.

## 4 Experiments

We have trained two Neural Network models, CBOW and Skip-gram, with several iterations of random walks over WordNet. We trained both models with default parameters (Mikolov et al., 2013a): vector size 300, 3 iterations, 5 negative samples, and

[2] The damping factor is the only parameter of PageRank.
[3] http://wordnet.princeton.edu/glosstag.shtml
[4] `http://ixa2.si.ehu.eus/ukb`

| | SL999 | WS353 |
|---|---|---|
| Skip-gram | 0.442 | **0.686** |
| RWSGRAM | **0.520** | 0.683 |
| RWCBOW | 0.486 | 0.591 |
| PPV | 0.493 | 0.683 |

Table 1: Spearman correlation results for our methods (RWSGRAM, RWCBOW) on WordNet random walks, compared to just random walks (PPV), and Skip-gram on text corpora.

window size 5. In order to check how many iterations of the random walk algorithm are needed to learn good word representations, we produced up to $70 \cdot 10^6$ contexts. The the damping factor ($\alpha$) of the random walk algorithm was set to 0.85, a usual value (Agirre et al., 2010). All parameters were thus set to default, and we only explored different corpus sizes.

The word representations were evaluated on WS353 (Finkelstein et al., 2001) and SL999 (Hill et al., 2014b), two datasets on word relatedness and word similarity, respectively. In order to compute the similarity of two words, it suffices to calculate the cosine between the respective word representations. The evaluation measure computes the rank correlation (Spearman) between the human judgments and the system values.

In order to contrast our results with the two related techniques, we used UKB[5], a publicly available implementation of Personalized PageRank (Agirre et al., 2014), and ran it over the same graph as our proposed methods. We used it out-of-the-box with a damping value of 0.85. We also downloaded the embeddings learnt by (Mikolov et al., 2013a) using Skip-gram over a large text corpus [6]. We used the same cosine algorithm to compute similarity with all word representations. To distinguish one word representation from the other, we will call our models RWCBOW and RWSGRAM respectively (RW for random-walk), in contrast to the original Personalized PageRank algorithm (PPV) and the corpus-based embeddings learned using Skip-grams (Skip-gram).

Figures 2 and 3 show the learning curves on the WS353 and SL999 datasets relative to the number of contexts produced by the random walks on WordNet. The results show that WordNet representations grow quickly (around 7 million contexts), converging around 70M, obtaining practically the same results as PPV for WS353, and better results for SL999[7].

The results at convergence are shown in Table 1, together with those of PPV and Skip-gram. Regarding SL999, we can see that the best results are obtained with RWSGRAM, improving over PPV and Skip-gram. Regarding WS353, all methods except RWSGRAM obtain similar results. The results show that our methods are able to effectively capture the information in WordNet, performing on par to the original PPV algorithm, and better than the corpus-based Skip-gram on the SL999 dataset. Note that the best published results for WS353 using WordNet are those of (Agirre et al., 2010) using PPV, which report 0.685.

In order to see if the word representations that we learn are complementary to those of PPV and Skip-gram, we combined the scores produced by each word representation. Given the potentially different scales of the similarity values, we assigned to each item the average of the ranks of the pair in each output. The top part of Table 2 repeats the three relevant systems. The (a+b) row reports an improvement in both datasets, showing that RWSGRAM on WordNet is complementary to PPV in WordNet, and is thus a different representation, even if both use the same knowledge base. The (a+b) and (a+b+c) show that corpus-based Skip-grams are also complemen-

| | SL999 | WS353 |
|---|---|---|
| (a) RWSGRAM | 0.518 | 0.683 |
| (b) PPV | 0.493 | 0.683 |
| (c) Skip-gram | 0.442 | 0.686 |
| (a+b) | 0.535 | 0.700 |
| (a+c) | 0.533 | 0.748 |
| (a+b+c) | **0.552** | 0.759 |
| Best | 0.520 | **0.800** |

Table 2: Combinations and best published results: SL999 (Hill et al., 2014a), WS353 (Radinsky et al., 2011).

[5] `http://ixa2.si.ehu.eus`

[6] `https://code.google.com/p/word2vec/`

[7] We tried larger context sizes, up to 700M confirming that convergence was around 70M.

tary, yielding incremental improvements. In fact, the combination of all three improves over the best published results on SL999, and approaches the best results for WS353, as shown in the last row of the Table. The state of the art on SL999 corresponds to (Hill et al., 2014a), who training a Recurrent Neural Net model on bilingual text. The best results on WS353 correspond to (Radinsky et al., 2011), who combine a Wikipedia-based algorithm with a corpus-based method which uses date-related information from news to learn word representations.

Note that we have only performed some simple combination to show the complementarity of each information source. More sophisticated combinations (e.g. learning a regression model) could further improve results.

We have performed some qualitative analysis, which indicates that there is a slight tendency for corpus embeddings (with the window size used in the experiments) to group related words (e.g. physics - proton), and not so much similar words (e.g. vodka - gin), while our KB embeddings include both. This analysis agrees with the results in Table 1, where all KB results are better than corpus-based Skip-gram for the semantic similarity dataset (SL999). In passing, note that the best published results to date on similarity (Hill et al., 2014a) use embeddings learnt from bilingual text which suggests that bilingual corpora are better suited to learn embeddings capturing semantic similarity.

## 5 Conclusions

We have presented a novel algorithm which encodes the structure of a knowledge base in a continuous vector space, combining random walks and neural net language models to produce new word representations. Our evaluation in word relatedness and similarity datasets has shown that these new word representations attain similar results to those of the original random walk algorithm, using 300 dimensions instead of tens of thousands. Furthermore, the word representations are complementary to those of the random walk algorithm and to corpus-based continuous representations, producing better results when combined, and improving the state-of-the-art in the similarity dataset. Hand inspection reinforces the observation that WordNet-based

A promising direction of this research is to leverage multilingual Wordnets to produce cross-lingual embeddings.

On another direction, one of the main limitations of KB approaches is that they produce a relatively small number of embeddings, limited by the size of the dictionary. In the future we want to overcome this sparsity problem by combining both textual and KB based embeddings into a unified model. In fact, we think that our technique opens up exciting opportunities to combine distributional and knowledge-based word representations.

It would also be interesting to investigate the influence of the different semantic relations in WordNet, either by removing certain relations or by assigning different weights to them. This investigation could give us deeper insights about the way our knowledge-based approach codes meaning in vector spaces.

## Acknowledgements

This work was partially funded by MINECO (CHIST-ERA READERS project – PCIN-2013-002-C02-01, and SKaTeR project – TIN2012-38584-C06-02), and the European Commission (QTLEAP – FP7-ICT-2013.4.1-610516). The IXA group is funded by the Basque Government (A type Research Group).

## References

Eneko Agirre, Enrique Alfonseca, Keith Hall, Jana Kravalova, Marius Paşca, and Aitor Soroa. 2009. A study on similarity and relatedness using distributional and WordNet-based approaches. In *Proceedings of Human Language Technologies: The 2009 Annual Conference of the North American Chapter of the Association for Computational Linguistics*, pages 19–27. Association for Computational Linguistics.

Eneko Agirre, Montse Cuadros, German Rigau, and Aitor Soroa. 2010. Exploring Knowledge Bases for Similarity. In *LREC*.

Eneko Agirre, Oier Lopez de Lacalle, and Aitor Soroa. 2014. Random walks for knowledge-based word sense disambiguation. *Computational Linguistics*, 40(1):57–84.

K. Avrachenkov, N. Litvak, D. Nemirovsky, and N. Osipova. 2007. Monte carlo methods in pagerank computation: When one iteration is sufficient. *SIAM J. Numer. Anal.*, 45(2):890–904.

Marco Baroni, Georgiana Dinu, and Germán Kruszewski. 2014. Dont count, predict! a systematic comparison of context-counting vs. context-predicting semantic vectors. In *Proceedings of the 52nd Annual Meeting of the Association for Computational Linguistics*, volume 1.

Ronan Collobert and Jason Weston. 2008. A unified architecture for natural language processing: Deep neural networks with multitask learning. In *Proceedings of the 25th international conference on Machine learning*, pages 160–167. ACM.

Christiane Fellbaum. 1998. *WordNet: An Electronic Lexical Database*. Bradford Books.

Lev Finkelstein, Evgeniy Gabrilovich, Yossi Matias, Ehud Rivlin, Zach Solan, Gadi Wolfman, and Eytan Ruppin. 2001. Placing search in context: The concept revisited. In *Proceedings of the 10th international conference on World Wide Web*, pages 406–414. ACM.

Zellig S Harris. 1954. Distributional structure. *Word*.

Felix Hill, KyungHyun Cho, Sébastien Jean, Coline Devin, and Yoshua Bengio. 2014a. Not all neural embeddings are born equal. *CoRR*, abs/1410.0718.

Felix Hill, Roi Reichart, and Anna Korhonen. 2014b. Simlex-999: Evaluating semantic models with (genuine) similarity estimation. *arXiv preprint arXiv:1408.3456*.

Tomas Mikolov, Kai Chen, Greg Corrado, and Jeffrey Dean. 2013a. Efficient estimation of word representations in vector space. *arXiv preprint arXiv:1301.3781*.

Tomas Mikolov, Ilya Sutskever, Kai Chen, Greg S Corrado, and Jeff Dean. 2013b. Distributed representations of words and phrases and their compositionality. In *Advances in Neural Information Processing Systems*, pages 3111–3119.

Tomas Mikolov, Wen-tau Yih, and Geoffrey Zweig. 2013c. Linguistic regularities in continuous space word representations. In *Proceedings of NAACL-HLT*, pages 746–751.

Andrea Moro, Alessandro Raganato, and Roberto Navigli. 2014. Entity linking meets word sense disambiguation: a unied approach. *Transactions of the Association of Computational Linguistics*, 2:231–244, May.

Mohammad Taher Pilehvar, David Jurgens, and Roberto Navigli. 2013. Align, Disambiguate and Walk: a Unified Approach for Measuring Semantic Similarity. In *Proceedings of the 51st Annual Meeting of the Association for Computational Linguistics*, pages 1341–1351, Sofia, Bulgaria.

Kira Radinsky, Eugene Agichtein, Evgeniy Gabrilovich, and Shaul Markovitch. 2011. A word at a time: computing word relatedness using temporal semantic analysis. In *Proceedings of the 20th international conference on World wide web*, WWW '11, pages 337–346, New York, NY, USA. ACM.

Richard Socher, Jeffrey Pennington, Eric H Huang, Andrew Y Ng, and Christopher D Manning. 2011. Semi-supervised recursive autoencoders for predicting sentiment distributions. In *Proceedings of the Conference on Empirical Methods in Natural Language Processing*, pages 151–161. Association for Computational Linguistics.

Joseph Turian, Lev Ratinov, and Yoshua Bengio. 2010. Word representations: a simple and general method for semi-supervised learning. In *Proceedings of the 48th Annual Meeting of the Association for Computational Linguistics*, pages 384–394. Association for Computational Linguistics.

Zhen Wang, Jianwen Zhang, Jianlin Feng, and Zheng Chen. 2014. Knowledge graph and text jointly embedding. In *Proceedings of the 2014 Conference on Empirical Methods in Natural Language Processing (EMNLP)*, pages 1591–1601, Doha, Qatar, October. Association for Computational Linguistics.

# Identification and Characterization of Newsworthy Verbs in World News

**Benjamin Nye**
University of Pennsylvania
bepnye@gmail.com

**Ani Nenkova**
University of Pennsylvania
nenkova@seas.upenn.edu

## Abstract

We present a data-driven technique for acquiring domain-level importance of verbs from the analysis of abstract/article pairs of world news articles. We show that existing lexical resources capture some the semantic characteristics for important words in the domain. We develop a novel characterization of the association between verbs and personal story narratives, which is descriptive of verbs avoided in summaries for this domain.

## 1 Introduction

Summarization, either by people or machine, calls for the ability to identify important content. Computational approaches to identifying important content fall into the two extremes of a possible spectrum. On one end, the types of important information for a given domain and topic are predefined as information extraction templates defined by experts, as in the earliest approaches to multi-document summarization (Radev and McKeown, 1998) and the recently introduced guided summarization (Owczarzak and Dang, 2011). On the other extreme, traditional systems work only with indicators of importance coming solely from the input to be summarized, or possibly also from the context of the input, i.e . analyzing the anchor text of links to a webpage, or comments on a blog post or citations to a scientific article (Nenkova and McKeown, 2012).

Here we explore the feasibility of data-driven identification of important information in the world news domain. We specifically focus on the analysis of verbs, which is the first step of identifying event types of special interest. The goal is to collect evidence of verb importance globally, without regard to a particular input or its context. Such ideas have been explored in the past as subcomponents of extractive summarizers (Schiffman et al., 2002; Hong and Nenkova, 2014) or as features derived from small datasets for sentence compression (Woodsend and Lapata, 2012). In contrast, in our work we rely on large corpora and exclusively focus on the task of acquiring input independent indicators of importance. We also constrain our analysis to a single domain, which allows us to examine the semantic aspects of the verbs that may contribute to their perceived importance.

We leverage a dataset of human-written summaries of news articles to objectively ground the definition of word importance. Summaries are intended to convey important information while omitting the less important pieces, so words that are important in a newsworthy sense will occur more frequently in summaries. The same data and intuition was used recently to develop a large corpus for determining entity salience (Dunietz and Gillick, 2014).

We derive a list of over one thousand verbs that have statistically significant bias to appear in the summaries (important verbs) and verbs with higher rate of occurrence in the original articles (unimportant). This resource of verbs and their domain-level importance may be fruitfully exploited in models of summarization that do not use pre-defined templates but are richer than approaches that rely solely on analysis of the article text.

We furthermore seek to characterize the properties of words that are biased to occur more often



*Human Language Technologies: The 2015 Annual Conference of the North American Chapter of the ACL*, pages 1440–1445,
Denver, Colorado, May 31 – June 5, 2015. 

in either summaries or in articles. We noticed that verbs that tended to be dis-preferred in the summaries related to personal narratives, in which people are described as private entities rather than public personas. We applied the same measures that we used to analyze domain-level importance in world news to a collection of labeled personal and nonpersonal blog entries. Characterizing verbs on the personal vs. nonpersonal dimension indeed turned out to beneficial for explaining domain-level importance of verbs in world news: personal narratives are not considered important in this domain and verbs that tended to get excluded from summaries also tended to appear more frequently in personal blog entries. This characterization offered broad coverage of the article vocabulary and additional explanatory power compared to a characterization derived from General Inquirer categories.[1]

The derived lexical resources may serve as shallow semantics for a range of language processing tasks such as summarization, news filtering and search.[2]

## 2 Determining domain-level importance

To determine domain-level importance, we use summaries and articles from the New York Times Annotated Corpus[3], a collection of NYT articles that includes genre tags and summaries written by library scientists. We use articles published in the world news section between 1996 and 2005 for a total of 36,69 article-summary pairs.

All of the documents were parsed with the Stanford Parser to obtain lemmatized forms of the words and part of speech tags. There are 2,634,850 tokens in the summaries and 32,587,740 tokens in the respective articles.

The overall verb frequency is very similar in the summaries (14.5%) and the articles (14.6%). In our analysis we reduce the corpus of summaries and original articles to only the verbs that occur in them.

[1]The two lists characterizing the domain-level importance and the personal–public dimension are available for download at `http://www.cis.upenn.edu/~nlp/software/importance.html`.

[2]Personal perspective verbs may not be important in reporting world news but may be excellent indicators of celebrity/gossip search for example.

[3]https://catalog.ldc.upenn.edu/LDC2008T19

Then we compare the rate of occurrence of each verb in the two types of writing. Verbs used proportionally more in summaries are likely to correspond to events that are important, while verbs that occur more frequently in the articles are less likely to be related to the key topics of an article. To generate two classes of verbs representing important and non-important verbs, we consider two measurements: the difference of a verb's usage frequency between summaries and articles, and the statistical significance of this bias.

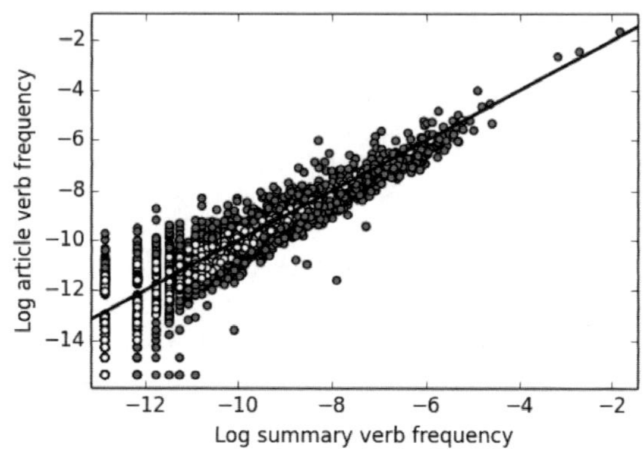


Figure 1: Word frequency in summaries vs. articles. The black line is where the frequencies are equal, and words plotted in grey have statistically significant differences in frequencies for the two classes.

Figure 1 shows the plot of each verb's probability in the summaries, $P_s(w_i)$ vs. in the articles, $P_a(w_i)$. Points above the line are verbs that occur more frequently in articles, while points below the line are more frequent in summaries. Dividing the points along this line produces two classes of verbs. We can further quantify how strongly a word is associated with its class using a variety of metrics (Monroe et al., 2008).

For this application, we chose to use the log odds ratio. To measure how much more likely a word $w$ is to occur in a class $c$, we compute the odds of a word occurring in corpora type $c$, i.e summary ($s$) or original article ($a$):

$$Odds(w, c) = \frac{P(w \mid class = c)}{1 - P(w \mid class = c)}$$

The ratio of the odds with respect to the two different corpora is a measure of how much more frequently a word is used in each case. To make the measure interpretable, we take the log of the odds ratio producing the final weight for a word:

$$\log\left(\frac{Odds(w,s)}{Odds(w,a)}\right) \simeq \log\left(\frac{P(w \mid class = s)}{P(w \mid class = a)}\right)$$

This metric gives an intuitive measure of the usage rate of words. For example, if a word occurs 3 times more often in the summaries it will be given a weight of $\log(3)$, and if it occurs three times more often in the articles it will be given a weight of $-\log(3)$.

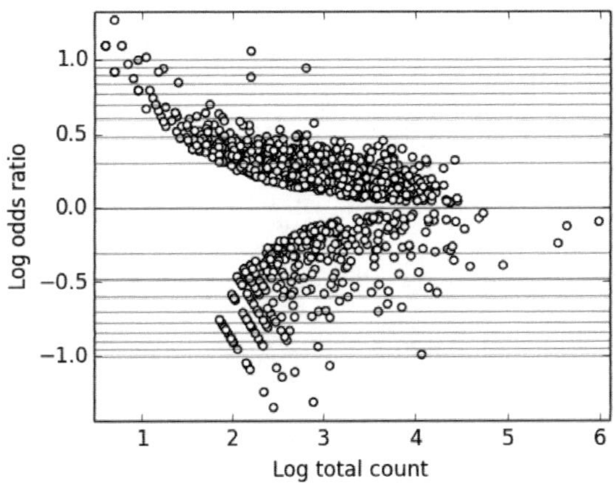


Figure 2: Frequency vs. log odds ratio for each word. Positive odds ratios correspond to summary-biased words and negative correspond to article-biased. The lines indicate integer usage ratios (1:3, 1:2, 1:1, 2:1, 3:1, etc).

However, this metric is unreliable for verbs with low counts in either class of texts. If a verb occurs five times in summaries and only once in articles, it is difficult to say if there is true signal for importance. As the number of counts of a verb in the two classes increases, so does our certainty about the significance of any observed differences in usage rates. To obtain a measure of the statistical significance of the domain-level importance weight of a verb, we treat the set of observed tokens as a Bernoulli trial where each token occurs either in a summary (success) or in an article (failure). We apply a binomial test to compute the probability of the observed distribution of tokens in the two types of text under the null hypothesis that the word has equal frequency in summaries and articles. The $p$-value from the test gives a measure of the certainty that a word is important and not. We can filter out words with $p$-values

| Summary-biased |
|---|
| spur hail allege avert slay exile claim intensify extradite oust overturn underscore cite devastate weigh defuse injure curb defy resign suspect warn quell kidnap stir plot widen charge thwart revive |
| **Article-biased** |
| chant talk sleep hate graduate realize dress understand quote sound add drink sing refer read think imagine remember shout sit happen cry wave like thank love smile accord reply misstate |

Table 1: Words with highest weights, drawn from verbs with frequency greater than the median verb frequency.

above a certain threshold. Moving the threshold closer to 0 enforces more and more certainty about the classification, reducing vocabulary size but also decreasing noise. Discarding verbs with a $p$-value of less than 0.05 reduces the vocabulary size from 3,924 words to 1,210.

In Figure 2, the log odds ratio is plotted against the overall frequency for each verb after discarding unreliable verbs. The most extreme weights occur mostly for the infrequent words, even after filtering out low $p$-value words. Although these words have extremely high bias weights, they tend to be uncommon and not particularly informative. Examples include verbs such as "hostage-take", "muckrake", and "blaspheme." To get a clearer picture of trends in the verbs in each category, we show in Table 1 the verbs with the 30 highest and 30 lowest weights among the verbs in the 50th percentile of total counts across all documents.

In the following two sections, we turn to analyzing *why* certain verbs may be more important in the domain than others. First we examine the relationship between the summary- or article-bias of a word and categories in the General Inquirer lexicon. Then we develop a new characterization of verbs showing their association with person-centered perspective of the narrative.

## 3 General Inquirer

The General Inquirer lexicon provides a list of words manually annotated with a variety of tags (Stone et al., 1966). We considered eight of these tags that were relevant to our task and could explain why

| Tag | Summ. | Article | Examples |
|---|---|---|---|
| none | 0.58 | 0.77 | |
| Negative | 0.21 | 0.05 | counterfeit avert, weep wail |
| Active | 0.26 | 0.15 | intensify overhaul, grasp hop |
| Strong | 0.16 | 0.03 | oust devestate, roar promote |
| Hostile | 0.13 | 0.01 | kidnap ravage, shrug crush |
| Power | 0.08 | 0.01 | curb reclaim, persuade overcome |
| Positive | 0.07 | 0.03 | reinstate mend, reassure hug |
| Passive | 0.05 | 0.05 | deplore mourn, gaze huddle |
| Weak | 0.04 | 0.03 | flounder sag, abandon hesitate |

Table 2: Percentage of words in each class covered by different GI tags. The first two example words come from the summary-biased class and last two come from the article-biased class.

| p-value | 0.01 | 0.001 | 0.0001 | 0.00001 |
|---|---|---|---|---|
| Summary | 0.54 | 0.53 | 0.54 | 0.54 |
| Article | 0.80 | 0.86 | 0.88 | 0.91 |

Table 3: Percentage of words with zero GI tags for increasing p-value cutoff strictness

a verb has domain-level importance: NEGATIVE, POSITIVE, ACTIVE, PASSIVE, STRONG, WEAK, HOSTILE, and POWER.

Table 2 shows some randomly selected words from each of the eight GI tags. The first two words come from the summary-biased class and last two come from the article-biased class. Table 2 also shows the fraction of verbs in each class that occur in the GI with a given tag, as well as the fraction of verbs that do not have any of the eight tags. It becomes immediately clear that the GI categories do have explanatory power but that it has a major problem with coverage, with the majority of verbs in the summary and article corpora not appearing in the GI at all as shown on the first line. Notably, the coverage is considerably better for the summary-biased verbs. Verbs from several GI categories appeared notably more often in summaries than in articles. For example, verbs with the NEGATIVE tag account for 21% of verbs in summaries, but only 5% of verbs in articles. Other such categories include verbs that imply an active physical engagement (ACTIVE), imply that the actor is in a position of power (STRONG), imply that hostility exists between the entities involved (HOSTILE) or that imply that the actor has the influence to affect the policies of others (POWER). POSITIVE, PASSIVE, and WEAK verbs had more similar appearance rates in both classes, but the absolute number of words covered by these tags was low.

Increasing the strictness of the $p$-value cutoff for pruning the vocabulary as described in the previous section reduces the size of the vocabulary but increases the purity of the classes by only including verbs that have sufficiently different usage ratios. As shown in Table 3, as we restrict the vocabulary to increasingly certain verbs, the proportion of verbs in the summary class that are tagged by the GI remains almost constant while the proportion of untagged verbs in the article class steadily increases. This indicates that the summary-biased verbs have a consistent distribution of GI tags across all usage ratios, while verbs tended to be tagged less often as the bias towards the articles increased. Although the GI gives good indicators for which words are likely to be important summary words but no indicators for which words are likely to be of no interest in summarizing world news.

### 3.1 Personal Stories

To get a sense for what aspects of the verb semantics causes a word to be excluded from the summary, we examined the contexts for the verbs with the highest bias weights in each class. To define the context for each verb, we used the dependency relations produced by the Stanford Parser. Any verb, noun, or adverb placed in a dependency relation with a given verb is considered to co-occur with it. For each of the ten most highly weighted verbs in each class, Table 4 shows the lemmas that co-occurred most frequently with it.

The verbs that are biased towards the articles (not important) seem to capture human element of the news reports, corresponding to passages narrating personal stories of ordinary people involved in the larger political situation discussed in the news. The summary-biased verbs are clearly evocative of the NEGATIVE, ACTIVE, STRONG, HOSTILE, and POWER tags given by the GI and the common usages suggested by their contexts tend to be official, non-personal or that of people in public roles.

No existing resources provide descriptions of this personal vs. non-personal dimension of lexical meaning and we decided to derive such a characterization from data unrelated to the NYT.

| Article-biased | |
|---|---|
| add | country,year,get,States,time,people,do,make |
| drink | drink,do,take,glass,much,make,eat |
| sing | song,woman,man,chorus,dance,sing,feel |
| refer | use,official,attack,part,term,program,day,people |
| read | time,report,people,write,statement,book,man |
| think | time,part,get,do,year,take,issue |
| imagine | take,people,get,come,time,make,ask |
| remember | day,year,time,see,decade,many |
| shout | man,people,hear,soldier,get,come,crowd |
| sit | day,man,road,talk,wall,people,watch,table |
| **Summary-biased** | |
| spur | do,action,help,tell,States,effort,concern,man |
| hail | leader,man,call,effort,Clinton,step,election,visit |
| allege | part,case,fraud,arrest,help,people,responsible |
| avert | attack,Iraq,action,month,confrontation,crisis,official |
| slay | week,month,member,attack,many,soldier,day,Americans |
| exile | country,accuse,many,kill,Hussein,family,friend,Arafat |
| claim | member,bombing,describe,part,group,life,leader |
| intensify | country,States,war,week,demand,day,year,effort |
| extradite | Britain,States,try,citizen,Pinochet,trial,member,receive |
| oust | year,Party,Minister,force,coalition,invasion,month,leader |

Table 4: Most frequent co-occurring words for the most extremely weighted verbs.

| Personal-biased |
|---|
| threaten wake rain wander kneel yell grin convulse smile chat hug climb gorge nod crouch laugh sleep perch head park |
| **Nonpersonal-biased** |
| acquit deploy misstate founder besiege decriminalize censure peacekeep headquarter streamline dissociate excommunicate unveil deadlock modify extradite ratify imperil chose |

Table 5: Top weighted words derived from personal and non-personal blog entries

For this purpose, we used a subset of the ICWSM 2009 Spinn3r Blog Dataset that has been annotated with a semi-supervised classifier trained to identify personal stories (Gordon and Swanson, 2009). We took 56,048 blog entries that had been tagged as being a personal story and 2,196,162 blog entries that were not identified as personal.

We then applied the same procedure that we used for the NYT articles to produce two classes of words: those biased towards blogs describing personal stories and those biased towards non-personal blogs. After restricting the vocabulary to only verbs with a binomial test $p$-value of at most 0.05, we obtained log odds ratio weights for 3,143 verbs. Of the 1,210 verbs in the NYT classes, 937 were also present in the restricted blog vocabulary. The 20 most and least personal verbs are shown in Table 5.

| p-value | GI | GI+blog |
|---|---|---|
| 0.05 | 0.134 | 0.098 |
| 0.01 | 0.130 | 0.087 |

Table 6: 10-fold cross-validation mean squared error of a linear regression for increasingly biased vocabularies.

The Pearson correlation between the NYT log odds ratio and the blog log odds ratio is negative and rather high, -0.54, indicating a strong relationship between personal and article-biased words. Restricting the significance to $p$-value cutoff of 0.01 reduces the vocabulary from 937 to 675 verbs, but strengthens the correlation to -0.61. Of the top 100 summary-biased words, only 18 were personal. Of the top 100 article-biased words, 90 were personal.

Not only do the personal/non-personal classes map on to the summary/article classes well, but they supply explanatory information about words that the GI did not cover. In order to measure this effect, we trained a linear regression to predict the NYT log-odds ratio of a word using a binary feature for each GI tag, as well as a binary feature indicating no tags. We were interested in the reduction of error when the personal-biased information was added. Adding the blog log-odds ratio for each word as a feature improved our results in 10-fold cross-validation, reducing the prediction error by almost 30%. The detailed results are shown in Table 6, for experiments performed for two different $p$-value cut-offs.

## 4 Conclusion

We presented a method for data-driven acquisition of domain-level importance of verbs in reports of world news events. Analysis of the acquired verbs reveals that summary-biased words tend to be more negative, active, and hostile, while the article-biased words mostly describe personal actions. This lexicon provides a useful notion of global importance in a domain and can serve as resource for semantic characterization of words in a variety of tasks, including sentence selection in summarization, flagging articles as newsworthy or filtering uninteresting documents. Additionally, we provide a lexicon for personal and non-personal verbs that also captures some of the newsworthiness of the article and summary classes.

## References


Jesse Dunietz and Dan Gillick. A new entity salience task with millions of training examples. *EACL 2014*, page 205, 2014.

Andrew Gordon and Reid Swanson. Identifying personal stories in millions of weblog entries. In *Third International Conference on Weblogs and Social Media, Data Challenge Workshop, San Jose, CA*, 2009.

Kai Hong and Ani Nenkova. Improving the estimation of word importance for news multi-document summarization. *Proceedings of EACL*, 2014.

Burt L Monroe, Michael P Colaresi, and Kevin M Quinn. Fightin'words: Lexical feature selection and evaluation for identifying the content of political conflict. *Political Analysis*, 16(4):372–403, 2008.

Ani Nenkova and Kathleen McKeown. A survey of text summarization techniques. In *Mining Text Data*, pages 43–76. Springer US, 2012.

Karolina Owczarzak and Hoa Trang Dang. Overview of the tac 2011 summarization track: Guided task and aesop task. In *Proceedings of the Text Analysis Conference (TAC 2011), Gaithersburg, Maryland, USA, November*, 2011.

Dragomir R Radev and Kathleen R McKeown. Generating natural language summaries from multiple on-line sources. *Computational Linguistics*, 24 (3):470–500, 1998.

Barry Schiffman, Ani Nenkova, and Kathleen McKeown. Experiments in multidocument summarization. In *Proceedings of the second international conference on Human Language Technology Research*, pages 52–58, 2002.

Philip J Stone, Dexter C Dunphy, and Marshall S Smith. The general inquirer: A computer approach to content analysis. 1966.

Kristian Woodsend and Mirella Lapata. Multiple aspect summarization using integer linear programming. In *Proceedings of the 2012 Joint Conference on Empirical Methods in Natural Language Processing and Computational Natural Language Learning*, pages 233–243, 2012.

# Enhancing Sumerian Lemmatization by Unsupervised Named-Entity Recognition

**Yudong Liu, Clinton Burkhart, James Hearne** and **Liang Luo**
Computer Science Department
Western Washington University
Bellingham, Washington 98226
{yudong.liu@-burkhac@students.-james.hearne@-luol@students.}wwu.edu

## Abstract

Lemmatization for the Sumerian language, compared to the modern languages, is much more challenging due to that it is a long dead language, highly skilled language experts are extremely scarce and more and more Sumerian texts are coming out. This paper describes how our unsupervised Sumerian named-entity recognition (NER) system helps to improve the lemmatization of the Cuneiform Digital Library Initiative (CDLI), a specialist database of cuneiform texts, from the Ur III period. Experiments show that a promising improvement in personal name annotation in such texts and a substantial reduction in expert annotation effort can be achieved by leveraging our system with minimal seed annotation.

## 1 Introduction

Because the Sumerian cuneiform writing system is historically the earliest, Sumerian culture is the earliest recorded civilization. The large number of clay tablets that have been recovered from Mesopotamia reveal "an almost obsessive concern for the preservation of daily events of the time: the digging of ditches, the care of livestock, the storage of grain, and so on. Their survival allows insight into the lives of the city dwellers of remote antiquity" (Garfinkle, 2012). Today, most cuneiform texts are held in public institutions, but the texts are widely separated both from each other and often from scholars by great distances and expensive journeys. Current projects like the Digital Library Initiative (CDLI, 2014) and the Database of Neo-Sumerian Texts (BDTNS, 2014) aim to provide scholars immediate access to virtual collections of tens of thousands of texts.

The Ur III period (2112-2004 BCE) is particularly abundant in surviving texts. Because this era was the specialty of our principle informant, an Assyriologist at our home university, we focus on the tablets that are from this era. The vast majority of these tablets record financial transactions, such as records of cattle deliveries, receipt of metals, repayment of loans, and so forth.

Figure 1 shows a tablet from the CDLI repository. For expository purposes, we arranged the original cuneiform drawings on the left (which are not input to our computations), with its transliteration (a one-to-one transcription of signs in a cuneiform text to computer readable text) in the middle, and the modern English translation on the right. The original CDLI data includes transliterations in ASCII format and inline lemmatization markup. More detail about CDLI data will be introduced in Section 2.

As we can see in Figure 1, in addition to the provider and recipient of transference, tablets consistently enumerate lists of witnesses ("sealed by"). This fact makes the tablet an invaluable resource for the social history of the time since they record, implicitly, on each tablet, lists of persons who knew one another and enjoyed professional relations (Widell, 2008). The recovery of personal names on the tablets suggests the possibility of reconstructing social networks of actors in the mercantile class and also, given the overlap, their social network connections to royalty.

Motivated by this perspective, we built an unsupervised Sumerian named-entity recognition (NER) system, also to accommodate the facts of 1) Sumerian is a dead language; 2) the corpus is of a size too large for even a community of scholars to master; 3) the tablets come in many cases damaged by time and



*Human Language Technologies: The 2015 Annual Conference of the North American Chapter of the ACL*, pages 1446–1451,
Denver, Colorado, May 31 – June 5, 2015. 

the circumstances of their recovery which was, in many cases, looting; 4) new tablets are still being uncovered. More detail on our Decision List Co-Train method (Collins and Singer, 1999) can be found in Section 3. In the process of evaluating our NER system, we noticed that a major inconsistency between our result and the lemmata in CDLI lies in the annotation of personal names with missing signs in damaged tablets. For example, "szu-[x]-lum" is not labeled as a name in the lemmata, but our system does so with a high confidence score. As shown this word contains a damaged sign (indicated by "[x]"). Inconsistencies of this kind account for around 50% of the total false positives in our result. With the help of the Sumerologist at our home university, around 40% of such damaged occurrences have been easily verified as personal names. This suggests that the original lemmatization is performed by a more critical and conservative approach. Our work offers a promising automation tool for the annotation task on this corpus by making good recommendations on name candidates to the annotators.

| Cuneiform Tablet | Transliteration | English Translation |
|---|---|---|
| 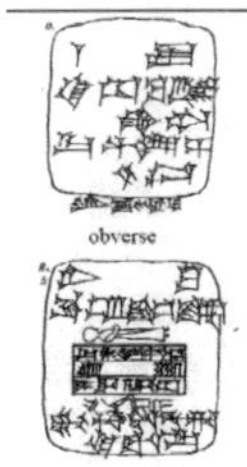 | &P105955 = BIN 03, 149 | *(unique tablet identification)* |
| | @tablet | |
| | @obverse | *(front of tablet)* |
| | 1. 1(disz) sila4 | *1 lamb* |
| | 2. ki ab-ba-sa6-ga-ta | *from Ab-ba-sa-ga (the seller)* |
| | 3. ur-{d}szul-pa-e3 | *Ur-Šul-pa-e (the buyer)* |
| obverse | @reverse | *(back of tablet)* |
| | 1. i3-dab5 | *received* |
| | 2. iti u5-bi2-gu7 | *month: 3* |
| | 3. mu hu-uh2-nu-ri{ki} ba-hul | *year: Ḫuḫnuri was destroyed* |
| | @seal | *(tablet sealed by)* |
| | 1. ur-{d}szul-pa-e3 | *Ur-Šul-pa-e* |
| | 2. dub-sar | *the scribe* |
| reverse | 3. dumu da-a-da kuruszda | *son of Da-a-da the fattener* |

Figure 1: Tablet with ID of P105955 from CDLI.

## 2 CDLI and the Annotations

The CDLI is a collaborative project with cuneiform text capturing and processing efforts underway in North America, Europe and the Middle East. It aims to provide an open access to electronic documentation of ancient cuneiform, consisting of texts, images, transliterations and glossaries of 3500 years of human history. Adhering to the open-source policy, any contribution to the collection by providing electronic catalogues, transliterations, or images of cuneiform artifacts is welcomed (CDLIwiki, 2014).

When represented in Roman script in transliterations, the syllable signs that make up a Sumerian word are written joined together with dashes. As there is no concept of upper- or lowercase in cuneiform writing, signs in transliterations typically occur in lowercase. However, signs rendered in uppercase do occur when the phonetic equivalent of the sign is unclear, tentative or fairly new (Sahala, 2012). One important property of Cuneiform is a high degree of homophony (referred to in the literature on Cuneiform as 'polyvalence'). This phenomenon is conventionally handled by numerical subscripts. For example, "du" means "to go", "$\mathrm{du}_3$" means "to build" (Tablan et al., 2006).

Royal epithets notwithstanding, Sumerian personal names are exclusively comprised of a single word, almost always consisting of at least two signs. In cases where disambiguation is required, a patronymic may added (for example, szu-esz4-tar2 dumu zu-zu, "Su-Estar, son of Zuzu"). This disambiguation is frequent in practice due to the relatively shallow pool of personal names used (Limet, 1960).

In the lemmatization information exposed by CDLI that we make use of in our NER task, when the word is a noun or verbal form, the two types of information included in the lemmata are 1) the *citation form*, rendered as the Sumerian stem; 2) the *guide word*, which functions as a disambiguator and is generally the English translation of the stem; otherwise, the lemma contains only the part of speech, as is the case with proper names and numbers. For example, in the following excerpt (CDLI No: P100032), wherein text is presented with interlinear lemmata (English translation: *Egi-zi-mah received 2 oxen from runner.*), we see both types of lemmatization.

```
1. 2(disz) gu4
#lem: n; gud[ox]
2. ki kas4-ta
#lem: ki[place]; kasz[runner]
3. egi-zi-mah i3-dab5
#lem: PN; dab[seize]
```

On line 3, the verbal form i3-dab5, indicating the receipt of an animate object, is lemmatized with the citation form dab, which is the Sumerian root for this form, and guide word "seize", the best English translation of the citation form. On lines 1 and 3, we have a number lemmatized with the part of speech n and the personal name egi-zi-mah with the part of speech PN, respectively. These annotated

PNs are used as gold standard labels to evaluate our NER system.

In the study of the Ur III corpus, the most exhaustive infrastructure and documentation for lemmatization is that provided for "the Open Richly Annotated Cuneiform Corpus (Oracc)" (ORACC, 2014). The lemmatizer for the Oracc system is accessed via an Emacs interface designed to encourage simultaneous transliteration and lemmatization by a human expert. The process begins with the human expert submitting an unlemmatized transliteration in a format called ATF (ASCII Transliteration Format). This format is the standard interchange format for transliteration across many projects dealing in and exchanging Assyriological textual representations (such as CDLI, BDTNS, the Pennsylvania Sumerian Dictionary (PSD, 2006), and Digital Corpus of Cuneiform Lexical Texts (DCCLT, 2014)). Via the Emacs interface, the transliteration is submitted to the linguistic annotatation system, which identifies an existing project-specific glossary based on directives provided by the human expert in the transliteration, and returns a preliminary lemmatization whose completeness and content depends on the referenced project glossary. The transliterator may then modify any automatically-generated lemmata, or, in the case of new words or new senses in which existing words used, manually lemmatize the word to allow the lemmatizer to "harvest" the new lemma and add it to the glossary. Oracc's lemmatizer also performs normalization and morphological analysis in order to automatically and consistently identify words in the text. The lemmatizer is not designed to "learn" new insights or induce new rules regarding Sumerian morphology on the basis of new lemmata harvested from submissions, but rather serves as a mechanism to consistently apply rules that have been harvested.

Based on our statistics, 53,146 tablets (about 60%) of the CDLI repository are accompanied by the in-line annotations described above. That is the amount of the tablets we used for the NER System.

## 3 Sumerian Personal Name Recognition

### 3.1 Related Work

To our knowledge, no previous empirical research exists directly addressing the question of how to recognize named entities from the Sumerian text. Our very preliminary work on this task (Brewer et al., 2014) uses an existent name list to recognize existing names, and applies simple heuristics and a similarity measure to recognize unseen personal names and dates. And at the time, no comprehensive evaluation and analysis could be done due to the unavailability of the language expert.

The investigation most closely related to ours is found in (Jaworski, 2008), which describes a system for processing Sumerian economic documents. Even though we borrowed 3 rules from their work as our seed rules (more details can be found in Section 3.2), and we are dealing with the same language in the same domain, there are a few important differences between our work and theirs. 1) Their goal is to model the content of the text by using an ontology driven method, whereas our goal is to extract named entities from the text by using some statistical method. 2) Their data set is strictly smaller than ours. The corpus used in their work was restricted to $\sim$12,000 tablets containing transactions involving animals, with the contents of these transactions being extracted via an a priori ontology. Our work is addressed to almost the entire corpus where the lemmatization is available, $\sim$53,000 tablets. 3) Their work involved no learning but rather the application of pre-defined Finite State Methods for entity recognition.

Supervised named entity recognition has achieved excellent performance (Bikel et al., 2002) (Zhou and Su, 2002) (McNamee and Mayfield, 2002) (MaCallum and Li, 2003) (Oliver et al., 2003). Semi-supervised approaches and unsupervised approaches have also achieved notable success on this task. Although our research also has a fairly large amount of data, unlike the previous unsupervised methods (Etzioni et al., 2005) (Nadeau et al., 2006) (Li et al., 2012), we do not have extremely large external corpora such as Wikipedia to retrieve very precise, but sparse features. Our work adopted the DL-Cotrain method proposed in (Collins and Singer, 1999). However, all their features are at the word sequence level, instead of at the token level. As noted in Section 2, there is no concept of upper- or lowercase in cuneiform writing, features on capitalization are not relevant here. Another important observation is that Sumerian personal names are exclusively comprised of a single word, thus our spelling features are on the token level. In addition, unlike their work where POS and parsing information is used for named entity candidate selection, we do not have the candidate selection component given that no Sumerian POS tagger or parser available. In fact, further complicating factors in determining syntactic features include the lack of standardization in spelling and inconsistent scribal quality.

### 3.2 Our System

Our NER system has three components: the preprocessing component, the Decision List Co-Train (DL-CoTrain) (Collins and Singer, 1999) component and the post-processing component.

When the Sumerologists transliterate the tablets, they use metacharacters such as "[...]" and "#" to indicate damage to the text, and "!", "?", "*", and "<...>" to represent correction, querying or collation (Tinney and Robson, 2014). For "[...]" and "<...>" cases, the Sumerologists put their "best guess" within the brackets. For example, in the word "[nu]-su", the first sign was originally damaged but restored by the Sumerologists as the "best guess". Our system removes the metacharacters as noise, and treats the resulting text as if it were otherwise unannotated.

To utilize the pre-knowledge from the language experts and (Weibull, 2004), we apply a tag set of 13 tags to pre-annotate the corpus. The 13 tags in the tag set {"GN", "FN", "TN", "WN", "MN", "n", "TITLE", "UNIT", "GOODS", "OCCUPATION", "YEAR", "MONTH", "DAY"} represent geographical names, field names, temple names, watercourse names, month names, numbers, title names, unit names, trade goods names, occupation names and indicators for year, month and day, respectively.

After the above pre-processing step, we applied the DL-CoTrain method by utilizing contextual and spelling rules to create a decision list.

A contextual rule specifies the context for a named-entity with the window size of 1 or -1 (the right word or the left word). For example, according to the contextual rule "right_context = TITLE $\rightarrow$ Person", "`nam-zi`" is recognized as a personal name in "`nam-zi simug`" given that "`simug`" is pre-tagged as "TITLE" (Smith) in the pre-processing phase.

A spelling rule specifies the spelling of a named-entity. It is a sign sequence that can be either the full string of an entity or is contained as a substring of the entity. For example, "contains(`ab-ba`) $\rightarrow$ Person" is a spelling rule. By applying the rule, the word "`ab-ba-sab-ga-ta`" is recognized as a personal name. With the spelling rule "full-string = `ur-{d}szul-pa-e3` $\rightarrow$ Person", the word "`ur-{d}szul-pa-e3`" is recognized as a personal name.

We use the following three contextual rules (Jaworski, 2008) as the seed rules for the system 1) left_context = `giri3` $\rightarrow$ Person 2) left_context = `kiszib3` $\rightarrow$ Person 3) left_context = `mu-DU` $\rightarrow$ Person.

The first rule indicates that a person is acting as an intermediary in the transaction. The second rule indicates that the tablet was sealed by the named individual, and usually appears in administrative records. The last rule indicates that a delivery was made to the named individual. Since these seed rules have a high specificity to personal names, each of them is given a strength of 0.99999.

The major task of the system is to learn a decision list to classify a word as a personal name. Initialized with the 3 contextual seed rules, the decision list is applied to label the training data to get spelling rules. In the next iteration, the newly obtained spelling rules are applied to label the training data to get new contextual rules. In this alternating process, each iteration produces a new set of rules which are ranked by their strength.

In our NER system, we experimentally settled on a ranking criterion that made use of frequency of some feature x, instead of (smoothed) relative frequency as used in (Collins and Singer, 1999), in order to avoid the problem of some context feature occurs once only as the cue of a personal name, and reverting to the relative frequency formula in the case of ties.

The two post-processing rules are applied to eliminate false positives 1) A word that starts with a number should not be a name; 2) A word following the word "`iti`" (month indicator) should not be a name. The application of these 2 rules improved the performance by 0.5%.

## 4 Experiments and Evaluation

We used a 5-fold cross-validation model to train and test our NER system. In each fold, we randomly picked 85% of the tablets from the corpus for training and the remaining 15% of the tablets for testing. With the top 20 new rules from each iteration being added to the decision list, the system produces a decision list of over 2000 rules and approximately 17,000 personal names in these Sumerian texts, after 150 iterations.

When the lemmata is used as the gold standard data set in this experiment, the system achieved 91.4% recall and 39.6% precision score on average from the 5-fold cross-validation. The low precision motivated us to take a closer look at the cause of the false positives from our system.

Using fold-2 as an example, the system reported 16,657 personal names, and there are 7,406 annotated names in the lemmata. Among all these 7,406 names, 91.4% has been correctly identified by the system. However, 60.6% of the names reported by our system are not labeled as names in the lemmata. Through error analysis, we found that nearly 50% of these false positive names contain"missing" or "damaged" signs in the transliteration (i.e., annotated as [x] or [u] in the lemmata). They were therefore not annotated at all in the lemmata, even though their linguistic context clearly shows that they are personal names. For example, "`szu-x-lum`" in "`giri3 szu-x-lum`" is a word in the testing data labeled as a name by our system after applying one of the seed rules. However, owing to physical damage to the word in the original tablet (flagged by "`x`" in the lemmata), it is unannotated. As a result, it's reported as a false positive in the evaluation.

Based on this observation, we asked the Sumeriologist at our home university to verify the "false positives" that contain "missing" or "damaged" signs (marked in the lemmata as either "unknown" (part of speech `X`) or "unlemmatizable" (part of speech `u`)), restricting our concern to damaged signs to limit the imposition on his time. It turns out that over 40% of such names should have been labeled as a name in the first place. This elevates the precision to 55.8% from 39.4% without sacrificing the recall, for fold-2 testing data. Similar performance gain is obtained for other folds.

Due to the large number of "false positives" and time constraints, we cannot impose on our Assyriologist informant the task of verifying all of the system reported names for us at the moment. However, the current evaluation result reveals that the systematic lemmatization on CDLI, as discussed in Section 2, follows an extremely conservative approach. We suspect that the reason for this is to avoid labeling damaged personal names as such is to prevent partial or potentially incorrect sign information from being reused by the morphological analyzer in future runs of the lemmatizer. Our result suggests that the existing lemmata has its own limitation and should not be fully relied on for evaluation for our NER task. It also suggests that our NER system can be used for automatic annotation task given that it performs well in recovering names based on the context and spelling features, even with the minimal prior knowledge. More details of the algorithms and result can be found in (Liu et al., 2015).

## 5 Conclusions and Future Work

We have shown that a DL-CoTrain based name tagger, with only three initial seed rules and unlabeled data, performs well in recovering personal names from Sumerian texts. This work can potentially make the annotation job much less costly, especially when the expert resource is extremely scarce.

Our results show that the existing lemmatization on CDLI corpus was generated by a, perhaps, excessively conservative policy, especially when one or more signs in the name have sustained damage. As a result, we consider that the existing lemmata cannot be fully relied on, especially for damaged names, for our NER evaluation. Our system is able to make good guesses on such damaged occurrences, based on the context and the spelling features. Confirmed by the language expert, such a high-recall, not-so-high-precision system can be particularly useful for the corpus annotators because they can simply focus on and verify the system's recommended names. Furthermore, we would expect that by applying supervised learning or combining with gazetteer-based method, and by extending the current method to recognizing other types of names in the texts, our system can work even better as an automation tool for such an annotation task.

## References


Steven Garfinkle. 2012. *Entrepreneurs and Enterprise in Early Mesopotamia: A Study of Three Archives from the Third Dynasty of Ur*, 36–136 Cornell University Studies in Assyriology and Sumerology (CUSAS), Ithaca, NY USA.

Michael Collins and Yora Singer. 1999. *Unsupervised Models for Named Entity Classification*, 100–110. In Proceedings of the Joint SIGDAT Conference on Empirical Methods in Natural Language Processing and Very Large Corpora

Wojciech Jaworski. 2008. *Contents Modeling of Neo-Sumerian Ur III Economic Text Corpus*, 369–376. Proceedings of the 22nd International Conference on Computational Linguistics

Aleksi Sahala. 2012. *Notation in Sumerian Transliteration.*

Nikolai Weibull. 2004. *A Historical Survey of Number Systems*, 1–13.

Valentin Tablan, Wim Peters, Diana Maynard, and Hamish Cunningham. 2006. *Creating Tools for Morphological Analysis of Sumerian*, 1762–1765. Proceedings of the Fifth International Conference on Language Resources and Evaluation

Magnus Widell. 2008. *The Ur III Metal Loans from Ur*, 207–223. Consejo Superior de Investigationes Cientficas, Madrid.

Database of Neo-Sumerian Texts. 2014. *http://bdtns.filol.csic.es*

Cuneiform Digital Library Initative. 2014. *http://cdli.ucla.edu*

Cuneiform Digital Library Initative wiki. 2014. *http://cdli.ox.ac.uk/wiki/*

Oracc: The Open Richly Annotated Cuneiform Corpus. 2014. *http://oracc.museum.upenn.edu/*

PSD: The Pennsylvania Sumerian Dictionary. 2006. *http://psd.museum.upenn.edu/*

DCCLT - Digital Corpus of Cuneiform Lexical Texts. 2014. *http://oracc.museum.upenn.edu/dcclt/*

Felicity Brewer, Clinton Burkhart, Joe Houng, Liang Luo, Derek Riley, Brandon Toner, Yudong Liu, and James Hearne. 2014. *A Preliminary Study into Named Entity Recognition in Cuneiform Tablets*, 1–3. The third Pacific Northwest Regional Natural Language Processing Workshop

Daniel Foxvog. 2014. *An Introduction to Sumerian Grammar.*

Henri Limet. 1960. *L'Anthroponymie sumerienne dans les documents de la 3e dynastie d'Ur.* Société d'Édition Les Belles Lettres, Paris.

Manuel Molina. 2008. *The Corpus of Neo-Sumerian Tablets: An Overview*, 19–54. Consejo Superior de Investigationes Cientficas, Madrid.

Steve Tinney and Eleanor Robson. 2014. *Oracc: The Open Richly Annotated Cuneiform Corpus.* http://oracc.museum.upenn.edu/doc/about/aboutoracc/index.html

Roger Woodard. 2008. *The Ancient Languages of Mesopotamia, Egypt and Aksum.* Cambridge University Press, Cambridge, UK.

Steve Tinney and Eleanor Robson. 2014. *Oracc: Linguistic Annotation.* http://build.oracc.org/doc/builder/linganno/

Yudong Liu, Clinton Burkhart, James Hearne, and Liang Luo. 2015. *Unsupervised Sumerian Personal Name Recognition.* Proceedings of the Twenty-eighth International Florida Artificial Intelligence Research Society Conference, May 18-20, 2015, Hollywood, Florida, USA. AAAI Press, 2015.

Andrew McCallum and Wei Li. 2003. *Early results for Named Entity Recognition with Conditional Random Fields, Feature Induction and Web-Enhanced Lexicons.* Proceedings of the Seventh Conference on Natural Language Learning at HLT-NAACL 2003.

Oliver Bender, Franz Josef Och, and Hermann Ney. 2003. *Maximum Entropy Models for Named Entity Recognition.* Proceedings of the Seventh Conference on Natural Language Learning at HLT-NAACL 2003.

Paul McNamee and James Mayfield. 2002. *Entity Extraction Without Language-specific Resources.* Proceedings of the 6th Conference on Natural Language Learning - Volume 20.

Guodong Zhou and Jian Su. 2002. *Named Entity Recognition using an HMM-based Chunk Tagger.* Proceedings of the 40th Annual Meeting on Association for Computational Linguistics.

Daniel M. Bikel and Richard Schwartz and Ralph M. Weischedel. 1999. *An Algorithm That Learns What's in a Name.* Machine Learning.

Etzioni, Oren and Cafarella, Michael and Downey, Doug and Popescu, Ana-Maria and Shaked, Tal and Soderland, Stephen and Weld, Daniel S and Yates, Alexander. 2005. *Unsupervised named-entity extraction from the web: An experimental study.* Artificial intelligence - Volume 165.

Nadeau, David and Turney, Peter and Matwin, Stan. 2006. *Unsupervised named-entity recognition: Generating gazetteers and resolving ambiguity.* Advanced in Artificial Intelligence - Lecture Notes in Computer Science - Volume 14013.

Li, Chenliang, Weng, Jianshu and He, Qi and Yao, Yuxia and Datta, Anwitaman and Sun, Aixin and Lee, Bu-Sun. 2012. *Twiner: named entity recognition in targeted twitter stream.* Proceedings of the 35th international ACM SIGIR conference on Research and development in information retrieva.

# Extracting Information about Medication Use from Veterinary Discussions

**Haibo Ding**
School of Computing
University of Utah
Salt Lake City, UT 84112
hbding@cs.utah.edu

**Ellen Riloff**
School of Computing
University of Utah
Salt Lake City, UT 84112
riloff@cs.utah.edu

## Abstract

Our research aims to extract information about medication use from veterinary discussion forums. We introduce the task of categorizing information about medication use to determine whether a doctor has *prescribed* medication, *changed protocols*, *observed effects*, or *stopped* use of a medication. First, we create a medication detector for informal veterinary texts and show that features derived from the Web can be very powerful. Second, we create classifiers to categorize each medication mention with respect to six categories. We demonstrate that this task benefits from a rich linguistic feature set, domain-specific semantic features produced by a weakly supervised semantic tagger, and balanced self-training.

## 1 Introduction

Natural language processing holds great promise for automatically extracting empirical data about medications, from the perspective of both doctors and patients. A wealth of information about the administration and effectiveness of medications lies within unstructured text, including medical records created by health care professionals (e.g., discharge summaries) as well as informal texts written by medical practitioners and patients (e.g., Web forums).

Previous work has been done on detecting medication terms and recognizing relations between medications and other medical concepts, such as diseases and symptoms. Our research explores a new problem: identifying and categorizing contexts involving the administration of medications, which we call *medication use categorization*. For each mentioned medication, we want to know whether it was used in a patient's care, and if so, what actions or observations are being reported. Our task aims to distinguish between contexts where a doctor *prescribed* a medication, *changed* the protocol of a medication (e.g., dosage or frequency), *stopped* use of a medication, *observed effects* produced by the medication, or *is asking a question* about a medication. Distinguishing these contexts is an important step toward being able to extract empirical data about medication use, such as effectiveness, success under different protocols, and adverse events.

Our research studies veterinary discussion forums, which often contain informal vocabulary such as shortened and abbreviated medication terms (e.g. *"pred"* instead of *"prednisone"*, or *"abx"* for *"antibiotics"*). The first part of our research addresses the problem of medication detection from informal text. We create an effective medication detector using supervised learning with linguistic features as well as contextual features acquired from the Web. We show that the Web context features substantially improve recall, and yield an effective medication detector even with small amounts of training data.

Second, we design supervised classifiers for medication use categorization. We incorporate a rich set of contextual, syntactic, and sentential features as well as a semantic tagger trained for the veterinary domain with bootstrapped learning over a large set of unannotated veterinary texts. We demonstrate additional performance gains by using balanced self-training with the unannotated texts.

## 2 Related Work

Previous work on extracting medication information from text has primarily focused on clinical medical text, such as discharge summaries (e.g., (Doan and Xu, 2010; Halgrim et al., 2010; Doan et al., 2012; Tang et al., 2013; Segura-Bedmar et al.,



*Human Language Technologies: The 2015 Annual Conference of the North American Chapter of the ACL*, pages 1452–1458,
Denver, Colorado, May 31 – June 5, 2015. 

2013)). The Third and Fourth i2b2 Shared Tasks included medication detection from clinical texts (Uzuner et al., 2010; Uzuner et al., 2011), and the Fourth i2b2 Shared Task also included relation classification between treatments (including medications), problems, and tests. Recently, there has been growing interest in extracting medication information from other types of text, such as Twitter, online health forums, and drug review sites (e.g., (Leaman et al., 2010; Bian et al., 2012; Liu et al., 2013; Liu and Chen, 2013; Yates and Goharian, 2013; Segura-Bedmar et al., 2014)). Much of this research is geared toward identifying adverse drug events or drug-drug interactions.

Many methods have been used for medication extraction, including rule based approaches (Levin et al., 2007; Xu et al., 2010), machine learning (Patrick and Li, 2010; Doan and Xu, 2010; Tang et al., 2013), and hybrid methods (Halgrim et al., 2010; Meystre et al., 2010). Rule based and hybrid approaches typically rely on manually created lexicons and rules. RxNorm (Nelson et al., 2011; Liu et al., 2005) is a large knowledge base containing generic and brand names of drugs and it is often used as a component in these systems. We compare our results with the MedEx system (Xu et al., 2010), which uses RxNorm coupled with manually defined rules.

To our knowledge, classifying medication mentions with respect to administration use categories has not yet been studied. A novel aspect of our work is also the use of Web Context features for medication detection. Similar Web features have been exploited for fine-grained person classification (Giuliano, 2009), while we demonstrate that they can be highly beneficial for medical concept extraction.

## 3 Task Description and Data Set

We divide our task into two subproblems: (1) *Medication Detection* aims to identify words corresponding to non-food substances used to treat patients (e.g., drugs, potassium supplements), and (2) *Medication Use Categorization* aims to classify medication mentions based on actions and observations related to their administration and to identify question contexts. We assign each medication mention to one of the six categories below.

**Rx**: The text indicates that a doctor prescribed the medication for a patient, or that a patient is taking (or has previously taken) the medication.
Example: "*I started the dog on abx.*"

**Change**: A change in the administration of the medication was made (e.g., dosage, route, frequency).
Example: "*I increased the pred to 5mg.*"

**Stop**: Use of the medication was discontinued.
Example: "*We took the cat off metacam.*"

**Effect**: The text reports a positive or negative effect from the medication on a patient.
Example: "*The dog responded well to Vetsulin.*"

**Question**: A question is asked about the medication.
Example: "*Do you think we should consider lasix?*"

**Other**: None of the above. This category primarily covers contexts not describing patient use.
Example: "*Aranesp is expensive.*"

Our data consists of discussion forums from the Veterinary Information Network (VIN), which is a web portal (www.vin.com) that hosts message boards for veterinary professionals to discuss cases and issues in their practice. To produce gold standard annotations, we collected the initial post of 500 randomly selected threads from VIN forums about cardiology/pulmonology, endocrinology, and feline internal medicine. We defined annotation guidelines to identify the minimum span of medication mentions.[1] Two people independently annotated 50 texts, and we measured their inter-annotator agreement (IAA) using Cohen's kappa ($\kappa$) statistic. For medication detection, their IAA score was $\kappa = .96$.

For the medication use categories, we measured IAA in two ways. First, we measured agreement on all of the words labeled as a medication by at least one annotator, yielding $\kappa = 0.80$. Second, we measured agreement only on the words labeled as a medication by both annotators (to more directly assess agreement on the six categories), yielding $\kappa = .92$. Finally, the annotators labeled an additional 450 texts, producing a gold standard set of 500 labeled texts. Of the annotated medication mentions, 93% have one word and 6% have two words. The frequency of each category is shown below.

| Rx | Question | Effect | Change | Stop | Other |
|---|---|---|---|---|---|
| 908 | 289 | 181 | 52 | 53 | 470 |

[1]Dosage and duration terms were not included.

## 4 Medication Detection

Detecting medication terms in discussion forums is challenging because of their informal nature. As we will show in Section 4.1, dictionary look-up from lexicons is not sufficient. Therefore the first part of our research aims to create an effective medication detector for these informal veterinary texts. We used the Stanford CoreNLP tools (Manning et al., 2014) for lemmatization, POS tagging and parsing, and created a SVM classifier with a linear kernel using SVMlin (Sindhwani and Keerthi, 2006). The classifier labels each token as a medication term or not a medication term. Adjacent medication tokens are then combined into a single medication mention. We designed three types of features:

**Word Features** include the medication word's string, lemma, and part-of-speech tag. Since drugs often have common affixes (e.g., *"-sone"* is a common suffix for corticosteroids), we also defined features for character sequences of length 2-4 at the beginning and end of a word.

**Local Context Features** represent the word preceding and the word following each medication term. We replace numbers with the symbol "CD". We also defined features to represent the syntactic dependency relations linked to the medication word using the Stanford Parser (De Marneffe et al., 2006).

**Web Context Features** capture information from web sites that mention a term, which provides external context beyond the information available in the training texts. During training, we issued a Google query for each unique word in our training data and collected the title and text snippets of the top 10 retrieved documents. We then defined binary-valued features to represent all of the words in the retrieved texts.[2] We store the results of each query so that additional queries are needed only for previously unseen words.

### 4.1 Medication Detection Results

We conducted 10-fold cross-validation experiments on our data set to evaluate our medication detector.

First, we created three baselines to assess the difficulty of medication detection for this data. The first row of Table 1 shows the performance of a veterinary thesaurus manually created by the VIN.[3] We extracted all of the words in the entries categorized as *Pharmacologic Substance* and label all instances of those words as medication terms. The VIN thesaurus achieved high precision but only 51% recall. Some reasons for the low coverage include abbreviations, misspellings, general terms (e.g., *"drug"*), and pronouns that refer to medications (which are annotated in our data). The second row shows the results of MedEx (Xu et al., 2010), which uses the RxNorm drug lexicon and ranked in second place for the 2009 i2b2 Medication Extraction challenge. MedEx's low precision is primarily due to labeling chemical substances (e.g., *"glucose"*) as medications, but in our data they are often test results (e.g., *"the cat's glucose level..."*). The third row shows the results of creating a Training Lexicon by collecting all nouns annotated as medications in the training data. We labeled all instances of these nouns as medication terms in the test data, which produced slightly higher recall and precision than MedEx.

| Method | Precision | Recall | F |
|---|---|---|---|
| VIN thesaurus | **90.9** | 51.3 | 65.6 |
| MedEX | 52.5 | 73.8 | 61.4 |
| Training Lexicon | 59.4 | 76.9 | 67.0 |
| SVM Classifier | | | |
| Word Features | 88.2 | 79.9 | 83.9 |
| + Local Context | 89.7 | 81.2 | 85.3 |
| + Web Context | 89.2 | **86.1** | **87.6** |

Table 1: Medication Detection Results

The last three rows in Table 1 show the results for our classifier. With only Word Features, the classifier produced an 83.9% F score, outperforming the baselines. Adding the Local Context Features yielded small gains in recall and precision. The Web Context Features further increased recall from 81% to 86%, raising the F score to 87.6%. We tried adding features for the VIN thesaurus and MedEx system, but they did not improve upon the results obtained with the Web Context features.

We observed that the Web Context Features can compensate for small amounts of training data. To demonstrate how powerful they are, we randomly selected 100 gold standard texts to use as a test

[2]We also tried different context windows but found that using the title and entire snippet achieved the best results.

[3]We used a version provided to us in 2013.

set, and trained classifiers using different amounts of training data. Figure 1 shows the results for classifiers using only the Word Features, Word and Local Context Features, and all features. The classifier with Web Context Features achieved an F score > 70% using only 10 training texts, and approached its best performance with just 100 training texts.

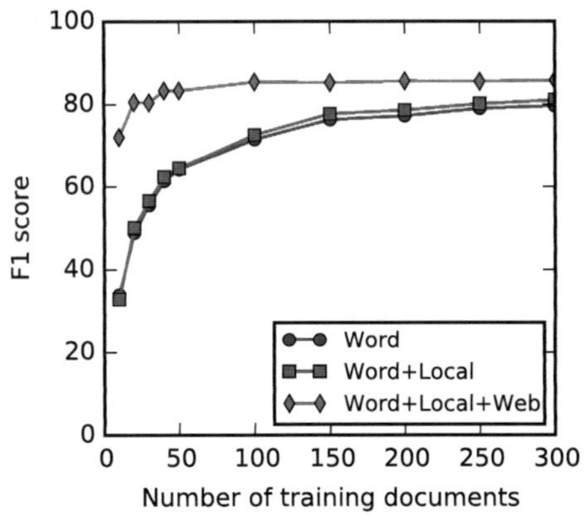


Figure 1: Learning curves with different feature sets

## 5 Medication Use Categorization

We tackled this problem by designing a supervised classifier with linguistic features, and incorporated a semantic tagger trained by bootstrapping on a large collection of veterinary text. We also used a balanced self-training method on unannotated veterinary texts to further improve performance.

First, we created a one-vs-the-rest binary SVM classifier for each category using scikit-learn (Pedregosa et al., 2011).[4] If an instance is labeled with multiple categories, we select the most confident one using the distance from the hyperplane. We designed three sets of features. **N-gram Features** represent a context window of size eight (+/-4) around the medication mention. We define features for lexical unigrams, lexical bigrams, lemma unigrams, and lemma bigrams. **Syntactic Features** capture verb phrases that participate in a dependency relation with the medication, using the Stanford parser. The third set of **Sentential Features** are for the *Question* and *Other* categories to recognize sentences that do not describe use of the medication on a patient, but ask questions, request guidance, describe hypothetical scenarios, etc. The sentential features consist of clause initial part-of-speech (POS) and lemma bigrams; whether the sentence ends with a question mark; whether the word "question" occurs in the same NP as the medication; whether the sentence contains the POS sequence <MD PRP>[5]; and whether the medication is separated by a comma from the ending question mark (for lists).

**Semantic Tagging.** We hypothesized that identifying semantic concepts might be beneficial. For example, the presence of an ANIMAL term suggests a patient, and a SYMPTOM term may indicate the reason for a prescription or an effect of medication use. First, we used WordNet (Miller, 1995) and identified synsets for 4 semantic classes: ANIMAL, DRUG, DISEASE/SYMPTOM, and HUMAN. We assigned any noun phrase with a head in these synsets to the corresponding semantic type. Next, we used a bootstrapping method (Huang and Riloff, 2010) to build domain-specific semantic taggers (**SemTaggers**) for the same four semantic classes as well as TEST, TREATMENT and OTHER. We used 10 seed words[6] for each category and 10,000 unlabeled veterinary forum texts for bootstrapping. Finally, we created **Semantic Features** for our medication use classifier. Each noun phrase tagged with a semantic class was replaced by a semantic type. Then we constructed features from pairs of adjacent terms in a context window of size eight (+/-4) around each medication mention. For example, the word sequence *"for a Boston terrier with diabetes"* would be transformed into *"for* ANIMAL *with* DISSYM*"* and the features for this context would be: <for ANIMAL>, <ANIMAL with>, and <with DISSYM>.

### 5.1 Medication Use Categorization Results

Table 2 shows the results for medication use classification, applied to the mentions identified by our medication detector (from Section 4). The N-gram

[4]Note that for medication detection we used SVMlin, but we switched to scikit-learn for the medication categorization because it supported additional types of classifiers that we wanted to try. Ultimately, however, the SVM performed best. We confirmed that SVM results from both toolkits were very similar.

[5]For question phrases such as "would he".

[6]We used the same seeds as (Huang and Riloff, 2010). However we added one semantic class, TREATMENT, so for this category we manually identified the 10 most frequent words in the unannotated texts that describe treatments.

| Method | Rx<br>P R F | Question<br>P R F | Effect<br>P R F | Change<br>P R F | Stop<br>P R F | Other<br>P R F | Average<br>P R F |
|---|---|---|---|---|---|---|---|
| N-grams | 69 74 71 | 75 65 69 | 69 37 48 | 76 44 56 | 45 23 31 | 50 54 52 | 64.0 49.6 55.9 |
| +Sentential | 68 73 71 | 79 71 **75** | 74 41 53 | 85 45 59 | 49 32 38 | 51 54 53 | 67.8 52.7 59.3 |
| +Syntactic | 69 72 71 | 78 70 74 | 70 40 51 | 77 47 59 | 70 49 58 | 51 56 53 | 69.3 55.7 61.8 |
| All+WordNet | 69 73 71 | 80 70 74 | 73 43 54 | 86 49 63 | 72 39 54 | 50 54 52 | 71.7 54.6 62.0 |
| All+SemTaggers | 69 74 71 | 80 70 **75** | 78 42 55 | 87 51 64 | 73 51 60 | 53 55 54 | **73.2** 57.2 64.2 |
| w/Balanced Self-Training | 71 73 **72** | 81 69 **75** | 69 49 **57** | 76 64 **70** | 67 69 **68** | 55 56 **56** | 70.0 **63.5** **66.6** |

Table 2: Medication Use Categorization Results on detected medications (each cell shows Precision, Recall, F)

| Method | Rx<br>P R F | Question<br>P R F | Effect<br>P R F | Change<br>P R F | Stop<br>P R F | Other<br>P R F | Average<br>P R F |
|---|---|---|---|---|---|---|---|
| N-grams | 75 85 **80** | 84 82 83 | 70 40 51 | 77 44 56 | 46 24 32 | 62 65 63 | 69.1 56.6 62.3 |
| +Sentential | 75 83 79 | 89 88 **89** | 70 45 55 | 86 45 59 | 52 38 44 | 61 64 63 | 72.4 60.4 65.9 |
| +Syntactic | 76 82 79 | 88 87 88 | 70 44 54 | 77 57 59 | 80 55 65 | 61 65 63 | 75.4 63.4 68.9 |
| All+WordNet | 75 83 79 | 89 86 88 | 75 46 57 | 81 54 65 | 82 45 58 | 60 64 62 | 77.2 63.1 69.4 |
| All+SemTaggers | 76 85 **80** | 90 87 88 | 79 47 59 | 89 56 68 | 81 57 67 | 65 65 **65** | **79.8** 65.9 72.2 |
| w/Balanced Self-Training | 78 80 79 | 90 86 88 | 75 54 **63** | 76 71 **74** | 78 80 **79** | 66 65 **65** | 77.2 **73.2** **75.1** |

Table 3: Medication Use Categorization Results on gold medications (each cell shows Precision, Recall, and F)

features alone yield an average F score of 55.9%. Both the Sentential features and Syntactic features (added cumulatively) further improve performance, raising the average F score to 61.8%. The next two rows show the effect of adding the semantic features. WordNet improves performance for **Effect** and **Change** but recall is lower for **Stop** and **Other**. In contrast, the SemTaggers improve performance across all categories, raising the F score to 64.2%. Our ablation studies show the ANIMAL class contributed most to the improvement.

In addition, we explored self-training to exploit unannotated texts. We applied the classifiers to 2,000 unlabeled veterinary texts, and used the newly labeled instances as additional training data. This did not improve performance, presumably because the most common categories dominated the new instances. We then explored a balanced self-training method that enforces an even distribution of the six categories in the new training instances. For this approach, we added exactly $k$ new instances[7] for each class, where $k$ was selected to be the size of the smallest set of newly labeled instances among the six categories. The last row of Table 2 shows that this balanced self-training approach improved the average F score from 64.2% to 66.6%.

[7]The most confident new instances were selected based on the differences between the scores for the winning class and the other classes.

Table 3 shows the results for medication use classification applied to gold standard medication mentions. The same trends hold: the *sentential* and *syntactic* features improve over n-grams, the *SemTagger* semantic features add value and outperform WordNet, and balanced self-training further improves performance. Overall performance increases from 66.6% to 75.1% F score with gold medications.

## 6 Conclusion

This research introduced a new task for classifying medication mentions with respect to their use in patient care. We created an effective medication detector for informal veterinary texts that exploits features derived from Web pages, and we created classifiers to recognize six medication use categories. These classifiers achieved precision $\geq 75\%$ for all categories except Other, with recall ranging from 54% for Effects to 86% for Questions. This research is a first step toward NLP systems that can acquire empirical data about the administration and effectiveness of medications from unstructured text.

## Acknowledgments

This material is based upon work supported by the National Science Foundation under grant IIS-1018314. We are very grateful to the Veterinary Information Network for providing samples of their data, and Ashequl Qadir for help annotating the data.

## References


Jiang Bian, Umit Topaloglu, and Fan Yu. 2012. Towards large-scale twitter mining for drug-related adverse events. In *Proceedings of the 2012 international workshop on Smart health and wellbeing*, pages 25–32. ACM.

Marie-Catherine De Marneffe, Bill MacCartney, Christopher D Manning, et al. 2006. Generating typed dependency parses from phrase structure parses. In *Proceedings of LREC*.

Son Doan and Hua Xu. 2010. Recognizing medication related entities in hospital discharge summaries using support vector machine. In *Proceedings of the 23rd International Conference on Computational Linguistics: Posters*, pages 259–266. Association for Computational Linguistics.

Son Doan, Nigel Collier, Hua Xu, Pham H Duy, and Tu M Phuong. 2012. Recognition of medication information from discharge summaries using ensembles of classifiers. *BMC medical informatics and decision making*, 12(1):36.

Claudio Giuliano. 2009. Fine-grained classification of named entities exploiting latent semantic kernels. In *Proceedings of the Thirteenth Conference on Computational Natural Language Learning*, pages 201–209. Association for Computational Linguistics.

Scott Halgrim, Fei Xia, Imre Solti, Eithon Cadag, and Özlem Uzuner. 2010. Extracting medication information from discharge summaries. In *Proceedings of the NAACL HLT 2010 Second Louhi Workshop on Text and Data Mining of Health Documents*, pages 61–67. Association for Computational Linguistics.

Ruihong Huang and Ellen Riloff. 2010. Inducing domain-specific semantic class taggers from (almost) nothing. In *Proceedings of the 48th Annual Meeting of the Association for Computational Linguistics*, pages 275–285. Association for Computational Linguistics.

Robert Leaman, Laura Wojtulewicz, Ryan Sullivan, Annie Skariah, Jian Yang, and Graciela Gonzalez. 2010. Towards internet-age pharmacovigilance: extracting adverse drug reactions from user posts to health-related social networks. In *Proceedings of the 2010 workshop on biomedical natural language processing*, pages 117–125. Association for Computational Linguistics.

Matthew A Levin, Marina Krol, Ankur M Doshi, and David L Reich. 2007. Extraction and mapping of drug names from free text to a standardized nomenclature. In *AMIA Annual Symposium Proceedings*, volume 2007, page 438. American Medical Informatics Association.

Xiao Liu and Hsinchun Chen. 2013. Azdrugminer: an information extraction system for mining patient-reported adverse drug events in online patient forums. In *Smart Health*, pages 134–150. Springer.

Simon Liu, Wei Ma, Robin Moore, Vikraman Ganesan, and Stuart Nelson. 2005. Rxnorm: prescription for electronic drug information exchange. *IT professional*, 7(5):17–23.

Mei Liu, Ruichu Cai, Yong Hu, Michael E Matheny, Jingchun Sun, Jun Hu, and Hua Xu. 2013. Determining molecular predictors of adverse drug reactions with causality analysis based on structure learning. *Journal of the American Medical Informatics Association*, pages amiajnl–2013.

Christopher D. Manning, Mihai Surdeanu, John Bauer, Jenny Finkel, Steven J. Bethard, and David McClosky. 2014. The Stanford CoreNLP natural language processing toolkit. In *Proceedings of 52nd Annual Meeting of the Association for Computational Linguistics: System Demonstrations*, pages 55–60.

Stéphane M Meystre, Julien Thibault, Shuying Shen, John F Hurdle, and Brett R South. 2010. Textractor: a hybrid system for medications and reason for their prescription extraction from clinical text documents. *Journal of the American Medical Informatics Association*, 17(5):559–562.

George A Miller. 1995. Wordnet: a lexical database for english. *Communications of the ACM*, 38(11):39–41.

Stuart J Nelson, Kelly Zeng, John Kilbourne, Tammy Powell, and Robin Moore. 2011. Normalized names for clinical drugs: Rxnorm at 6 years. *Journal of the American Medical Informatics Association*, 18(4):441–448.

Jon Patrick and Min Li. 2010. High accuracy information extraction of medication information from clinical notes: 2009 i2b2 medication extraction challenge. *Journal of the American Medical Informatics Association*, 17(5):524–527.

F. Pedregosa, G. Varoquaux, A. Gramfort, V. Michel, B. Thirion, O. Grisel, M. Blondel, P. Prettenhofer, R. Weiss, V. Dubourg, J. Vanderplas, A. Passos, D. Cournapeau, M. Brucher, M. Perrot, and E. Duchesnay. 2011. Scikit-learn: Machine learning in Python. *Journal of Machine Learning Research*, 12:2825–2830.

Isabel Segura-Bedmar, Paloma Martınez, and Marıa Herrero-Zazo. 2013. Semeval-2013 task 9: Extraction of drug-drug interactions from biomedical texts (ddiextraction 2013). *Proceedings of Semeval*, pages 341–350.

Isabel Segura-Bedmar, Santiago de la Pena, and Paloma Martınez. 2014. Extracting drug indications and adverse drug reactions from spanish health social media. *ACL 2014*, page 98.

Vikas Sindhwani and S Sathiya Keerthi. 2006. Large scale semi-supervised linear svms. In *Proceedings of the 29th annual international ACM SIGIR conference on Research and development in information retrieval*, pages 477–484. ACM.

Buzhou Tang, Hongxin Cao, Yonghui Wu, Min Jiang, and Hua Xu. 2013. Recognizing clinical entities in hospital discharge summaries using structural support vector machines with word representation features. *BMC medical informatics and decision making*, 13(Suppl 1):S1.

Özlem Uzuner, Imre Solti, and Eithon Cadag. 2010. Extracting medication information from clinical text. *Journal of the American Medical Informatics Association*, 17(5):514–518.

Özlem Uzuner, Brett R South, Shuying Shen, and Scott L DuVall. 2011. 2010 i2b2/va challenge on concepts, assertions, and relations in clinical text. *Journal of the American Medical Informatics Association*.

Hua Xu, Shane P Stenner, Son Doan, Kevin B Johnson, Lemuel R Waitman, and Joshua C Denny. 2010. Medex: a medication information extraction system for clinical narratives. *Journal of the American Medical Informatics Association*, 17(1):19–24.

Andrew Yates and Nazli Goharian. 2013. Adrtrace: detecting expected and unexpected adverse drug reactions from user reviews on social media sites. *Advances in Information Retrieval*, pages 816–819.

# Reserating the awesometastic: An automatic extension of the WordNet taxonomy for novel terms

**David Jurgens**
School of Computer Science
McGill University
jurgens@cs.mcgill.ca

**Mohammad Taher Pilehvar**
Department of Computer Science
Sapienza University of Rome
pilehvar@di.uniroma1.it

## Abstract

This paper presents CROWN, an automatically constructed extension of WordNet that augments its taxonomy with novel lemmas from Wiktionary. CROWN fills the important gap in WordNet's lexicon for slang, technical, and rare lemmas, and more than doubles its current size. In two evaluations, we demonstrate that the construction procedure is accurate and has a significant impact on a WordNet-based algorithm encountering novel lemmas.

## 1 Introduction

Semantic knowledge bases are an essential, enabling component of many NLP applications. A notable example is WordNet (Fellbaum, 1998), which encodes a taxonomy of concepts and semantic relations between them. As a result, WordNet has enabled a wide variety of NLP techniques such as Word Sense Disambiguation (Agirre et al., 2014), information retrieval (Varelas et al., 2005), semantic similarity (Pedersen et al., 2004; Bär et al., 2013), and sentiment analysis (Baccianella et al., 2010). However, semantic knowledge bases such as WordNet are expensive to produce; as a result, their scope and domain are often constrained by the resources available and may omit highly-specific concepts or lemmas, as well as new terminology that emerges after their construction. For example, WordNet does not contain the nouns "stepmom," "broadband," and "prequel."

Because of the coverage limitations of WordNet, several approaches have attempted to enrich WordNet with new relations and concepts. One group of approaches has enriched WordNet by aligning its structure with that of other resources such as Wikipedia or Wiktionary (Ruiz-Casado et al., 2005; Navigli and Ponzetto, 2012; Miller and Gurevych, 2014; Pilehvar and Navigli, 2014). However, because these approaches identify corresponding lemmas with identical lexicalizations, they are often unable to directly add novel lemmas to the existing taxonomic structure. The second group of approaches performs taxonomy induction to learn hypernymy relationships between words (Moro and Navigli, 2012; Meyer and Gurevych, 2012). However, these approaches often produce separate taxonomies from WordNet, which are also generally not readily accessible as resources.

We introduce a new resource CROWN (**C**ommunity-en**R**iched **O**pen **W**ord**N**et) that extends the existing WordNet taxonomy, more than doubling the existing number of synsets, and attaches these novel synsets to their appropriate hypernyms in WordNet. Novel sense data is extracted from Wiktionary, a large-scale collaboratively-constructed dictionary, and attached using multiple heuristics. CROWN fills an important gap in WordNet's limited coverage of both domain-specific lemmas and slang terminology and idioms.[1] In two experiments, we demonstrate that (1) our construction process accurately associates a novel sense with its correct hypernym and (2) the resulting resource has an immediate benefit for existing WordNet-based applications. Importantly, CROWN v1.0 is publicly available and released in WordNet format, making it seamlessly integratable with all existing WordNet libraries and tools.

## 2 Wiktionary

Wiktionary is a multilingual online dictionary that, as of May 2014, contains more than 470K English gloss definitions. Thanks to its collaboratively-constructed nature, Wiktionary provides a high coverage of novel domain-specific, idiomatic and slang terms or meanings, across all parts of speech, while featuring a wide variety of linguistic information such as morphology, etymology, pronunciation and alternative lexicalizations of a lemma. Given these characteristics, Wiktionary is an ideal resource for improving the coverage of hand-crafted lexicons, such as WordNet.

In addition to definitions, Wiktionary contains two sources of semantic relations. First, the Wiktionary entry

[1] For example, "reserate" is correctly included in CROWN as a hypernym of `unlock%2:35:00::` (to open the lock of) and "awesometastic" as a synonym of `fantastic%3:00:00:extraordinary:00` (extraordinarily good or great).



*Human Language Technologies: The 2015 Annual Conference of the North American Chapter of the ACL*, pages 1459–1465,
Denver, Colorado, May 31 – June 5, 2015. ©2015 Association for Computational Linguistics

for a lemma may contain a note stating its relationship with another lemma. Second, Wiktionary includes a separate thesaurus, Wikisaurus, which specifies (1) a lemma and its gloss and (2) all other lemmas sharing a relation with that sense. However, these Wiktionary relations cannot directly be used to enrich WordNet for two reasons. First, Wiktionary entries are defined in terms of lemmas, rather than senses. As a result, directly ontologizing the resource or integrating its semantic relations requires disambiguating each relation's lemmas, which is not always possible due to the limited context. Second, semantic relations in Wiktionary are infrequent, with 19.8% of all words having any specified relation and only 0.3% having a hypernym relation. As a result of this sparsity, structure alignment-based approaches for extending WordNet cannot be directly applied.

# 3 Extending WordNet

CROWN is created by identifying lemmas that are out of vocabulary (OOV) in WordNet but have one or more associated glosses in Wiktionary. A new synset is created for that lemma and a hypernym relation is added to the appropriate WordNet synset. The CROWN attachment process rates hypernym candidates using two methods. First, where possible, we exploit structural or morphological information to identify highly-probable candidates. Second, following previous work on resource alignment showing that lexical overlap accurately measures gloss semantic similarity (Meyer and Gurevych, 2011; Navigli and Ponzetto, 2012), candidates are found by measuring the similarity of the Wiktionary gloss with the glosses of synsets found by a constrained search of the WordNet graph. We note that attaching OOV lemmas by first aligning WordNet and Wiktionary is not possible due to relation sparsity within Wiktionary, where most OOV words would not be connected to the aligned network. Following, we first describe the Wiktionary preprocessing steps and then detail both OOV attachment methods.

## 3.1 Preprocessing

Wiktionary was parsed using JWKTL (Zesch et al., 2008) to extract the text associated with each Wiktionary definition and remove Wiktionary markup. The extracted texts were then partitioned into two sets: (1) those expressing a lexicalization, e.g., "1337" is an alternative spelling of "elite" and (2) those indicating a definition. Novel lexicalizations that are not already handled by the WordNet morphological analyzer (Morphy) were added to the lexicalization exception lists in CROWN.

Definitions are processed using two methods to identify a set of candidate lemmas whose senses might be identical or near to the appropriate hypernym synset. First, candidates are obtained by parsing the gloss with Stanford CoreNLP (Manning et al., 2014) and extracting the head word and all other words joined to it by a conjunction. Second, additional candidates are collected from the first hyperlinked term or phrase in the gloss, which is similar to the approach of Navigli and Velardi (2010) for hypernym extraction in Wikipedia. Candidates are then filtered to ensure that (1) they have the same part of speech as the definition's term and (2) they are defined in WordNet, which is necessary for the attachment.

## 3.2 Structural and Lexical Attachment

Three types of structural or lexical heuristics were used to attach OOV lemmas when the appropriate data was available. First, Wikisaurus or Wiktionary synonym relations create sets of mutually-synonymous lemmas, which may contain OOV lemmas. The common hypernym of these lemmas is estimated by computing the most frequent hypernym synset for all the senses of the set's lemmas that are in WordNet. Any OOV lemma also in the set is then attached to this estimated hypernym.

Second, some Wiktionary glosses follow regular patterns that identify a particular meaning. Two pattern heuristics were used: (1) a group of *Person* patterns and (2) a *Genus* pattern. The *Person* patterns match glosses that start with phrases such as "somebody who." Senses with such glosses have their set of candidate attachments restricted to descendants of the human sense of the noun *person*; the sense is then attached to a descendant using the gloss ranking procedure for lexical attachment (described below). The *Genus* pattern matches glosses that start with "Any member of the" and later contain a proper noun matching a scientific genus in WordNet; in such cases the OOV lemma is attached to the same hypernym as the synsets with a holonymy relation to the genus's synset.

Third, an *Antonymy* heuristic is used to identify OOV lemmas with an antonym relation to lemmas already in WordNet. OOV lemmas are tested for having a prefix indicating it could be an antonym, e.g., "anti." If the lemma formed from the remainder after prefix is in WordNet, then the OOV lemma is treated as its antonym and attached to the antonym's hypernym. Furthermore, the two synsets are marked as antonyms in CROWN.

## 3.3 Gloss-based Attachment

Each OOV lemma is associated with one or more Wiktionary senses, $s_{1...n}$, where each sense $s_i$ is associated with a set of lemmas $l_i$, one of whose senses may be its hypernym. The gloss-based attachment method analyzes each sense separately, first generating a set of candidate hypernym synsets and then ranking each synset according to its gloss similarity, both defined next. Ultimately the OOV lemma is attached to the highest-scoring synset across all of its Wiktionary senses. This procedure is intended to maximize precision by attaching only the

| | |
|---|---|
| **ukWaC** | microsoft, e-learning, helpline, mp3, unsubscribe |
| **Twitter** | selfie, retweet, hella, bday, homie |
| **Wikipedia** | admin, verifiability, bio, sockpuppetry, same-sex |

Table 1: Examples of high-frequency lemmas in CROWN but not in WordNet, from three corpora.

lemma's dominant sense, though we note that most OOV lemmas are monosemous.

The initial set $C$ of candidate hypernym synsets for Wiktionary sense $s_i$ is generated from the union of the synsets of the lemmas in $l_i$. Then, $C$ is expanded by including all WordNet synsets reachable from each synset $c_i \in C$ by a path of hypernym or hyponym edges, where a path (1) has at most three edges and (2) contains at most one hypernym edge. The second constraint is designed to avoid including overly-general concepts.

The glosses of the synsets in $C$ are then compared with the Wiktionary sense's gloss. Directly comparing glosses with string similarity measures omits the important detail that certain lemmas can be highly-specific and most strongly indicate that two glosses refer to the same concept. Therefore, prior to comparison, the lemmas occurring in all glosses are assigned a weight $-\log \frac{1}{f(w)}$, where $f(w)$ denotes the number of glosses in which lemma $w$ appeared. Glosses' similarity is measured by (1) lemmatizing their texts and computing the lemmas in common, and then (2) summing the weights of the in-common lemmas. This similarity function assigns higher scores to glosses sharing more specific concepts.

### 3.4 Resource Creation

The resulting attachments are converted into WordNet lexicography files and then integrated with the existing WordNet taxonomy using the GRIND program. Table 2 shows the resulting statistics for CROWN in comparison to WordNet. The attachment process more than doubles the number of synsets and adds a significant number of new lexicalizations which are essential for capturing common spelling variants that are not reflected in WordNet. Additionally, 4739 new antonym relations were added. Of the OOV lemmas, 87.8% were attached using the lexical attachment procedure. Of the remaining, the *Person* and *Antonymy* heuristics were the most frequently used, accounting for 4.2% and 2.7% of cases respectively. The infrequent use of the structural and lexical heuristics underscores the sparsity of the available data in Wiktionary for straight-forward attachments.

As an initial test of additional content present in CROWN but not in WordNet, all lemmas unique to CROWN were extracted and their occurrences counted in three corpora: (1) all of the English Wikipedia, (2) the web-gathered ukWaC corpus (Ferraresi et al., 2008), and (3) a sample of 50M microtext message from Twitter. Table 1 shows five example high-frequency lemmas from each corpus that are only present in CROWN , highlighting the types of commonly-recognized terms not in WordNet due to their technical, informal, or recently-created nature. Indeed, "selfie" was only recently included in the Merriam Webster dictionary as of 2014,[2] demonstrating the potential for quickly integrating new terminology into CROWN from the frequently-updated entries of Wiktionary.

| PoS | WordNet synsets | new CROWN synsets | new CROWN lex. variants |
|---|---|---|---|
| Noun | 82115 | 124967 | 29563 |
| Verb | 13767 | 16199 | 43318 |
| Adj. | 18156 | 25534 | 6902 |
| Adv. | 3621 | 2031 | 481 |

Table 2: The number of synsets in WordNet and new synsets and lexicalizations added by CROWN.

## 4 Evaluation

Two evaluations were performed. The first estimates attachment accuracy by simulating OOV attachment with lemmas that are already in WordNet. The second calculates the benefit of using CROWN in an example application using a WordNet-based algorithm to measure similarity.

### 4.1 WordNet Replication

No standard dataset exists for where OOV lemmas should be attached to WordNet; therefore in the first evaluation, we assess construction accuracy by simulating the inclusion of OOV lemmas using those already in WordNet, which allows testing on tens of thousands of lemmas. Specifically, the CROWN attachment approach is used to reattach all monosemous lemmas in WordNet. We opted for monosemous terms as they can have only one valid location in the taxonomy.

#### 4.1.1 Methodology

Glosses were extracted for 36,605 of the 101,863 nouns that were monosemous in WordNet and also present in Wiktionary, and for 4668 of the 6277 verbs matching the same condition. These glosses were then provided as input to the CROWN attachment process. We note that these lemmas are not necessarily monosemous in Wiktionary, with nouns and verbs having on average 1.40 and 1.76 senses, respectively; however, the construction process will attach only the highest-scoring of these senses. Once a lemma is attached, accuracy is measured as the number of hyponym or hypernym edges away that CROWN placed the lemma from its original position.

[2] http://www.merriam-webster.com/new-words/2014-update.htm

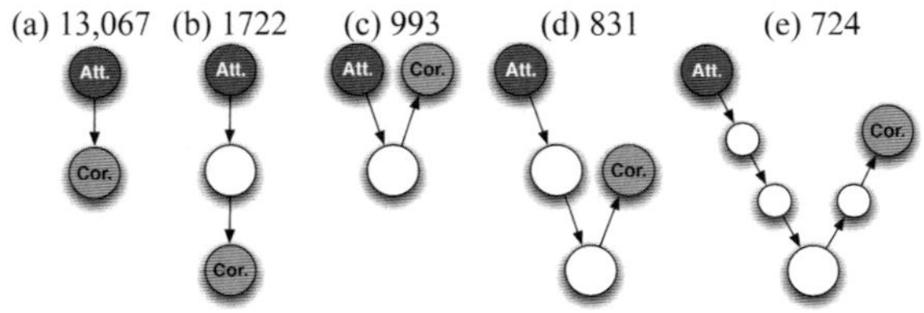


Figure 1: The five most-frequent error patterns and their frequencies seen in the results of monosemous lemma evaluation. Graphs show the attachment point (Att.) and correct hypernym synset (Cor.), with downward edges indicating hypernym relations and upward indicating hyponym. The overall error trend reveals that the vast majority of error was due to attaching a new sense to a more-specific concept than its actual hypernym.

#### 4.1.2 Results

The CROWN construction process was able to attach 34,911 of the 36,605 monosemous noun lemmas (95.4%) and 4209 of the 4668 verb lemmas (90.2%). The median error for attaching monosemous nouns was three edges and for verbs was only one edge, indicating the attachment process is highly accurate for both. The most common form of error was attaching the OOV lemma to a hyponym of the correct hypernym, occurring in 13,067 of the erroneous attachments.

Figure 1 shows the five most common displacement patterns when incorrectly attaching a monosemous noun, revealing that the majority of incorrect placements were to a more-specific concept than what was actually the hypernym. Furthermore, examining the 50 furthest-away noun and verb placements, we find that 28% of nouns and 20% of verbs were attached using a novel sense of the lemma not in WordNet (but in Wiktionary) and the placement is in fact reasonable. As a result, the median error is likely an overestimate of the expected error for the CROWN construction process.

### 4.2 Application-based evaluation

Semantic similarity is one of the core features of many NLP applications. The second evaluation measures the performance improvement of using CROWN instead of WordNet for measuring semantic similarity when faced with slang or OOV lemmas. Notably, prior semantic similarity benchmarks such as SimLex-999 (Hill et al., 2014) and the ESL test questions (Turney, 2001) have largely omitted these types of words. However, the recent dataset of SemEval-2014 Task 3 (Jurgens et al., 2014) includes similarity judgments between a WordNet sense and a word not defined in WordNet's vocabulary or with a slang interpretation not present in WordNet.

| | All | Regular | OOV | Slang |
|---|---|---|---|---|
| WordNet | 0.195 | 0.463 | 0.0 | -0.170 |
| CROWN | 0.248 | 0.452 | 0.448 | 0.138 |
| GST Baseline | 0.148 | 0.283 | 0.148 | 0.018 |
| Best System | 0.389 | 0.529 | 0.501 | 0.146 |

Table 3: The Pearson correlation performance of ADW when using the WordNet and CROWN semantic networks on the word-to-sense test dataset of SemEval-2014 Task 3. We also show results for the string-based baseline system (GST) and for the best participating system in the word-to-sense comparison type of Task 3.

#### 4.2.1 Methodology

Semantic similarity was measured using the similarity algorithm of Pilehvar et al. (2013), ADW,[3] which first represents a given linguistic item (such as a word or a concept) using random walks over the WordNet semantic network, where random walks are initialized from the synsets associated with that item. The similarity between two linguistic items is accordingly computed in terms of the similarity of their corresponding representations. ADW is an ideal candidate for measuring the impact of CROWN for two reasons. First, the algorithm obtains state-of-the-art performance on both word-based and sense-based benchmarks using only WordNet as a knowledge source. Second, the method is both unsupervised and requires no parameter tuning, removing potential performance differences between WordNet and CROWN being due to these factors.

To perform the second experiment, the ADW algorithm was used to generate similarity judgments for the data of Task 3, changing only the underlying semantic network to be either (1) the WordNet 3.0 network, with additional edges from disambiguated glosses,[4] or (2) the same network with novel synsets from CROWN. As the ADW algorithm is unchanged between settings, any performance change is due only to the differences between the two networks. Performance is measured using Pearson correlation with the gold standard judgments.

#### 4.2.2 Results

Of the 60 OOV lemmas and 38 OOV slang terms in the test data, 51 and 26 were contained in CROWN, respectively. Table 3 shows the Pearson correlation performance of ADW in the two settings for all lemmas in the dataset, and for three subsets of the dataset: OOV, slang, and regular lemmas, the latter of which are in WordNet; the bottom rows show the performance of the Task's best participating system for the word-to-sense comparison type (Kashyap et al., 2014) and the most competi-

[3]https://github.com/pilehvar/ADW
[4]http://wordnet.princeton.edu/glosstag.shtml

tive baseline, based on Greedy String Tiling (GST) (Wise, 1996).

ADW sees large performance improvements in the OOV and slang words when using CROWN instead of WordNet, which are both statistically significant at $p<0.01$. The overall improvement of ADW would place it as the fifth best system in this comparison type of Task 3. The performance on regular in-WordNet and OOV lemmas is approximately equal, indicating the high accuracy of OOV hypernym attachment in CROWN. Notably, on OOV and Slang, the unsupervised ADW, when coupled with the additional information in CROWN , produces competitive results with the best performing system, which is a multi-feature supervised system utilizing extensive external dictionaries and distributional methods.

## 5 Related Work

Most related is the work of Poprat et al. (2008), who attempted to automatically build an extension of WordNet with biomedical terminology; however, they were unsuccessful in constructing the resource. Other work has attempted to leverage distributional similarity techniques (Snow et al., 2006) or exploit the structured information in Wikipedia (Ruiz-Casado et al., 2005; Toral et al., 2008; Ponzetto and Navigli, 2009; Yamada et al., 2011) in order to extend WordNet with new synsets. However, structure-based approaches are limited only to the concepts appearing in Wikipedia article titles, which almost always correspond to noun concepts. Distributional and probabilistic approaches are also limited to OOV terms for which it is possible to gather enough statistics. As Wiktionary contains all parts of speech and our method is independent of word frequency, neither limitation applies to this work.

Other related work has attempted to tap resources such as Wikipedia for automatically constructing new ontologies (Suchanek et al., 2007; Dandala et al., 2012; Moro and Navigli, 2012; Meyer and Gurevych, 2012), extending existing ones through either alignment-based methods (Matuschek and Gurevych, 2013; Pilehvar and Navigli, 2014) or inferring the positions of new senses by their shared attributes which are extracted from text (Reisinger and Paşca, 2009). Extension and alignment approaches based on Wikipedia are limited mainly to noun concepts in Wikipedia; furthermore, these techniques cannot be directly applied to Wiktionary because its lack of taxonomic structure would prevent adding most OOV data to the existing WordNet taxonomy.

## 6 Conclusion

This work has introduced CROWN version 1.0, a new extension of WordNet that merges sense definitions from Wiktionary to add new hypernym and antonym relations. The resulting taxonomy has more than doubled the number of synsets in WordNet and includes many technical and slang terms, as well as non-standard lexicalizations. CROWN is released in the same format as WordNet[5] and therefore is fully compatible with all existing WordNet-based tools and libraries. Furthermore, the software for building CROWN has been opened-sourced and will be updated with future versions. In two experiments we demonstrated that the CROWN construction process is accurate and that the resulting resource has a real benefit to WordNet-based applications.

Immediate future work will add support for including new lemmas as synonyms in existing synsets and linking newly-created synsets with all appropriate types of WordNet semantic relationship. Longer-term future work will pursue more sophisticated methods for taxonomy enrichment to improve the quality of integrated content and will aim to integrate additional dictionaries, with a special emphasis on adding domain-specific terminology.

## References


Eneko Agirre, Oier Lopez de Lacalle, and Aitor Soroa. 2014. Random walks for knowledge-based Word Sense Disambiguation. *Computational Linguistics*, 40(1):57–84.

Stefano Baccianella, Andrea Esuli, and Fabrizio Sebastiani. 2010. SentiWordNet 3.0: An enhanced lexical resource for sentiment analysis and opinion mining. In *Proceedings of the Seventh International Conference on Language Resources and Evaluation (LREC)*, volume 10, pages 2200–2204, Valletta, Malta.

Daniel Bär, Torsten Zesch, and Iryna Gurevych. 2013. DKPro Similarity: An open source framework for text similarity. In *Proceedings of the 51st Annual Meeting of the Association for Computational Linguistics (ACL)*, pages 121–126, Sofia, Bulgaria.

Bharath Dandala, Rada Mihalcea, and Razvan Bunescu. 2012. Towards building a multilingual semantic network: Identifying interlingual links in wikipedia. In *Proceedings of the First Joint Conference on Lexical and Computational Semantics (*SEM)*, pages 30–37, Montreal, Canada.

Christiane Fellbaum, editor. 1998. *WordNet: An Electronic Database*. MIT Press, Cambridge, MA.

Adriano Ferraresi, Eros Zanchetta, Marco Baroni, and Silvia Bernardini. 2008. Introducing and evaluating ukWaC, a very large web-derived corpus of English. In *Proceedings of the 4th Web as Corpus Workshop (WAC-4)*, Morocco.

Felix Hill, Roi Reichart, and Anna Korhonen. 2014. Simlex-999: Evaluating semantic models with (genuine) similarity estimation. *arXiv preprint arXiv:1408.3456*.

David Jurgens, Mohammad Taher Pilehvar, and Roberto Navigli. 2014. Semeval-2014 task 3: Cross-level semantic similarity. In *Proceedings of the 8th International Workshop on Semantic Evaluation (SemEval-2014)*, pages 17–26, Dublin, Ireland.


[5] Both the software for creating CROWN and the data itself are available at `https://github.com/davidjurgens/crown`.

Abhay Kashyap, Lushan Han, Roberto Yus, Jennifer Sleeman, Taneeya Satyapanich, Sunil Gandhi, and Tim Finin. 2014. Meerkat mafia: Multilingual and cross-level semantic textual similarity systems. In *Proceedings of the 8th International Workshop on Semantic Evaluation*, pages 416–423, Dublin, Ireland.

Christopher D. Manning, Mihai Surdeanu, John Bauer, Jenny Finkel, Steven J. Bethard, and David McClosky. 2014. The Stanford CoreNLP natural language processing toolkit. In *Proceedings of 52nd Annual Meeting of the Association for Computational Linguistics: System Demonstrations*, pages 55–60, Baltimore, Maryland.

Michael Matuschek and Iryna Gurevych. 2013. Dijkstra-WSA: A graph-based approach to word sense alignment. *Transactions of the Association for Computational Linguistics (TACL)*, 1:151–164.

Christian M. Meyer and Iryna Gurevych. 2011. What psycholinguists know about Chemistry: Aligning Wiktionary and WordNet for increased domain coverage. In *Proceedings of the 5th International Joint Conference on Natural Language Processing*, pages 883–892, Chiang Mai, Thailand.

Christian M. Meyer and Iryna Gurevych. 2012. OntoWiktionary constructing an ontology from the collaborative online dictionary Wiktionary. In *Semi-Automatic Ontology Development: Processes and Resources*, chapter 6, pages 131–161. IGI Global.

Tristan Miller and Iryna Gurevych. 2014. WordNet–Wikipedia–Wiktionary: Construction of a three-way alignment. In *Proceedings of the 9th International Conference on Language Resources and Evaluation (LREC)*, pages 2094–2100, Reykjavik, Iceland.

Andrea Moro and Roberto Navigli. 2012. WiSeNet: Building a Wikipedia-based semantic network with ontologized relations. In *Proceedings of the 21st ACM Conference on Information and Knowledge Management (CIKM)*, pages 1672–1676, Maui, HI, USA.

Roberto Navigli and Simone Paolo Ponzetto. 2012. BabelNet: The automatic construction, evaluation and application of a wide-coverage multilingual semantic network. *Artificial Intelligence*, 193:217–250.

Roberto Navigli and Paola Velardi. 2010. Learning Word-Class Lattices for definition and hypernym extraction. In *Proceedings of the 48th Annual Meeting of the Association for Computational Linguistics (ACL)*, pages 1318–1327.

Ted Pedersen, Siddharth Patwardhan, and Jason Michelizzi. 2004. WordNet:: Similarity: measuring the relatedness of concepts. In *Proceedings of Fifth Annual Meeting of the North American Chapter of the Association for Computational Linguistics (NAACL)*, pages 38–41, Boston, Massachusetts.

Mohammad Taher Pilehvar and Roberto Navigli. 2014. A robust approach to aligning heterogeneous lexical resources. In *Proceedings of the 52nd Annual Meeting of the Association for Computational Linguistics (ACL 2014)*, pages 468–478, Baltimore, Maryland.

Mohammad Taher Pilehvar, David Jurgens, and Roberto Navigli. 2013. Align, Disambiguate and Walk: a Unified Approach for Measuring Semantic Similarity. In *Proceedings of the 51st Annual Meeting of the Association for Computational Linguistics (ACL)*, pages 1341–1351, Sofia, Bulgaria.

Simone Paolo Ponzetto and Roberto Navigli. 2009. Large-scale taxonomy mapping for restructuring and integrating Wikipedia. In *Proceedings of the 21st International Joint Conference on Artificial Intelligence (IJCAI)*, pages 2083–2088, Pasadena, California, USA.

Michael Poprat, Elena Beisswanger, and Udo Hahn. 2008. Building a BioWordNet by using WordNet's data formats and WordNet's software infrastructure: a failure story. In *Proceedings of the Workshop on Software Engineering, Testing, and Quality Assurance for Natural Language Processing*, pages 31–39, Columbus, Ohio.

Joseph Reisinger and Marius Paşca. 2009. Latent variable models of concept-attribute attachment. In *Proceedings of the Joint Conference of the 47th Annual Meeting of the ACL and the 4th International Joint Conference on Natural Language Processing of the AFNLP: Volume 2-Volume 2*, pages 620–628, Suntec, Singapore.

Maria Ruiz-Casado, Enrique Alfonseca, and Pablo Castells. 2005. Automatic assignment of Wikipedia encyclopedic entries to WordNet synsets. In *Proceedings of the Third International Conference on Advances in Web Intelligence*, pages 380–386, Lodz, Poland.

Rion Snow, Daniel Jurafsky, and Andrew Y. Ng. 2006. Semantic Taxonomy Induction from Heterogenous Evidence. In *Proceedings of the 21st International Conference on Computational Linguistics and the 44th Annual Meeting of the Association for Computational Linguistics (COLING-ACL)*, pages 801–808, Sydney, Australia.

Fabian M. Suchanek, Gjergji Kasneci, and Gerhard Weikum. 2007. YAGO: A core of semantic knowledge. unifying WordNet and Wikipedia. In *Proceedings of the 16th World Wide Web Conference (WWW)*, pages 697–706, Banff, Alberta, Canada.

Antonio Toral, Rafael Muoz, and Monica Monachini. 2008. Named Entity WordNet. In *Proceedings of the Sixth International Conference on Language Resources and Evaluation (LREC)*, pages 741–747.

Peter Turney. 2001. Mining the web for synonyms: PMI-IR versus LSA on toefl. In *Proceedings of the Twelfth European Conference on Machine Learning (ECML-2001)*, pages 491–502, London, UK, UK.

Giannis Varelas, Epimenidis Voutsakis, Paraskevi Raftopoulou, Euripides GM Petrakis, and Evangelos E Milios. 2005. Semantic similarity methods in WordNet and their application to information retrieval on the Web. In *Proceedings of the 7th annual ACM international workshop on Web information and data management*, pages 10–16.

Michael J. Wise. 1996. YAP3: improved detection of similarities in computer program and other texts. In *Proceedings of the twenty-seventh SIGCSE technical symposium on Computer science education*, pages 130–134, Philadelphia, Pennsylvania, USA.

Ichiro Yamada, Jong-Hoon Oh, Chikara Hashimoto, Kentaro Torisawa, Jun'ichi Kazama, Stijn De Saeger, and Takuya Kawada. 2011. Extending WordNet with hypernyms and siblings acquired from Wikipedia. In *Proceedings of 5th International Joint Conference on Natural Language Processing*, pages 874–882, Chiang Mai, Thailand.

Torsten Zesch, Christof Müller, and Iryna Gurevych. 2008. Extracting lexical semantic knowledge from Wikipedia and

Wiktionary. In *Proceedings of the 6th International Conference on Language Resources and Evaluation (LREC)*, pages 1646–1652, Morocco.

# Cross-lingual Text Classification Using Topic-Dependent Word Probabilities

**Daniel Andrade** **Akihiro Tamura** **Masaaki Tsuchida** **Kunihiko Sadamasa**
Knowledge Discovery Research Laboratories, NEC Corporation, Japan
{s-andrade@cj, a-tamura@ah,
m-tsuchida@cq, k-sadamasa@az}.jp.nec.com

## Abstract

Cross-lingual text classification is a major challenge in natural language processing, since often training data is available in only one language (target language), but not available for the language of the document we want to classify (source language). Here, we propose a method that only requires a bilingual dictionary to bridge the language gap. Our proposed probabilistic model allows us to estimate translation probabilities that are conditioned on the whole source document. The assumption of our probabilistic model is that each document can be characterized by a distribution over topics that help to solve the translation ambiguity of single words. Using the derived translation probabilities, we then calculate the expected word frequency of each word type in the target language. Finally, these expected word frequencies can be used to classify the source text with any classifier that was trained using only target language documents. Our experiments confirm the usefulness of our proposed method.

## 1 Introduction

Text classification is ubiquitous in natural language processing. It's applications range from simple topic detection, like articles about sport vs articles about computers, to sentimental analysis, and subtle discrimination of Tweets that report the abuse of drugs or the metaphoric use of drugs ("love is like a drug"). Text classification hugely relies on manually annotated training data in one language.

However, creating training data for each language is expensive, and therefore, we are interested in using training data given in only one language (e.g. English, denoted as target language) to classify text written in a different language (e.g. Chinese, or Japanese, denoted as source language).

Our approach addresses this issue by using a simple bilingual dictionary. Bilingual dictionaries have the great advantage that they are available often for free[1], and have good coverage for major languages, like Chinese and Japanese. With the help of the dictionary, we calculate the expected frequency of each word in the target language. Finally, we create a feature vector in the target language that is used as input for the text classifier.

However, due to the translation ambiguity of a word in the source language, it is important to carefully choose the translation probability for calculating the expected frequencies of the target words. For example, consider a Japanese news article that contains the word 拘束 (restrict, restrain, in custody), and we want to find out whether the article is about "foreign policy" or not. The most simple method is to use all its English translations, and assume a uniform distribution over them, i.e. $\{0.33, 0.33$ and $0.33\}$. However, depending on the topic of the news article, the translation "in custody" is more appropriate. For example, if the article reports about a crime/crime suspect, the translation "in custody" is more likely than "restrict" and "restrain". Conversely, if the article is about "military", the translation "in custody" is less likely. Moreover, an article that is about the topic "military" is more likely to belong to the class "foreign policy". This example demonstrates the importance of estimating good translation probabilities in order to improve the clas-

[1]For example from Wikitionay.org under Creative Commons Licence.



*Human Language Technologies: The 2015 Annual Conference of the North American Chapter of the ACL*, pages 1466–1471,
Denver, Colorado, May 31 – June 5, 2015. 

sification of the source text.

Therefore, we propose a probabilistic model that uses latent document topics to help improve the translation probabilities for a source document. Our experiments, on three different pairs of corpora, confirm that our probabilistic model for estimating word translation probabilities is helpful for cross-lingual text classification.

## 2 Related Work

The work in (Wu et al., 2008) and (Shi et al., 2010) uses a bilingual dictionary for cross-lingual text classification. The method described in (Wu et al., 2008) is motivated by transfer learning to adjust the class probability $p(c)$ to account for the differences in distributions between source and target language. Similar to our work, in the first step, they generate a probabilistic bilingual lexicon that contain word translation probabilities $p(e|f)$. However, one main difference to our work is that they translate each source word $f$ in source text $F$ independently, without considering any topic or context information of $F$.

Instead of translating the source text into the target language, the method in (Shi et al., 2010) suggests to translate the target classification model into the source language. They directly estimate the translation probabilities $p(f|e, c)$ using the source and target language data. One limitation of their method is that it assumes that the class of the document, that we want to translate, is given.

Our idea of learning word translation probabilities in context is related to the work in (Koehn and Knight, 2000). They describe an efficient method for learning word translation probabilities $p(f|e)$ using a bilingual dictionary and a pair of comparable corpora[2]. Like our approach, their method has the advantage that no parallel corpora are needed for translation. However, to solve the ambiguity of word-translation they considered only (local) bi-gram context. Moreover, their method assumes that the word order in the languages are the same. This is obviously not the case for language pairs like English and Japanese.

We note that the bilingual paired topic model, suggested in (Jagarlamudi and Gao, 2013), can also be used to disambiguate and select the appropriate word translations by using the topic associated with the given document. However, their model does not consider the use of a document class, and uses fixed word translation probabilities. In Section 3.2, we show that our model can also be used to learn the translation probabilities.

Alternatively, the multi-lingual topic model described in (Ni et al., 2011), and the use of a common low-dimensional projection described in (Platt et al., 2010) have also been applied to the cross-lingual text classification problem. However, both models require for training that cross-lingually aligned documents are available.

## 3 Proposed Method

Our proposed method does not use one translation of $F$, but implicitly generates all translations and weights them by the probability of each translation. More formally, let $E$ be one translation of source text $F$. Moreover, let $count_E(e)$ denote the frequency of word $e$ in E. Instead of using $count_E(e)$, we use the expected number of word occurrences denoted by $\mathbb{E}[count_E(e)|F]$ as features. When we use a simple uni-gram language model in the source language we get:

$$\mathbb{E}[count_E(e)|F] = \sum_{j=1}^{k} p(e_j = e|f_j) \qquad (1)$$

where we might write $F$ as $(f_1, f_2, f_3, ...f_k)$, where $f_j$ is the j-th word in $F$, and $k$ is the number of words in source text $F$.[3] The random variable $e_j$ denotes the translation of the j-th word in $F$. However, such a simple model translates each source word independently and ignores the context of the word.

In the following, we describe a probabilistic model that allows us to consider the whole document context $F$ into account for translating one word $f_j$. The generative story is as follows:

1. For each document, we generate a class label $c$ with probability $v_c$. Here we consider only the binary classification task with class label "positive", or "negative".

[2]Two corpora written in different languages which do not need to be translations of each other

[3]Here "word" refers to a word occurrence (and not unique word). Therefore, $k$ is the length of the source text $F$.

2. For each document, we generate a topic $z$ with probability $\pi_{z|c}$.

3. Given topic $z$, we generate each word $e$ in the target language document independently from a categorical distribution with probability $\vartheta_{e|z}$.

4. For each word $e$ in the target language, we generate a word $f$ in the source language independently from a categorical distribution with probability $\theta_{f|e}$.[4]

Under this model, for one target document $(e_1, ..., e_k)$ and its corresponding source document $(f_1, ..., f_k)$, the joint probability $p(z, c, e_1, ..., e_k, f_1, ..., f_k)$ is

$$
\upsilon_c \pi_{z|c} \prod_{j=1}^{k} \vartheta_{e_j|z} \cdot \theta_{f_j|e_j} \,.
$$

The parameter vector $\boldsymbol{\vartheta}_z$ specifies the target word probabilities $\vartheta_{e|z}$ that can be learned from the target language training data as described in Section 3.1. The parameter vector $\boldsymbol{\theta}_e$ specifies the word translation probability $\theta_{f|e}$ for a target word $e$ into a source language word $f$. These word translation probabilities are determined with the help of the bilingual dictionary as described in Section 3.2.

Our goal is to estimate the translation probability $p(e|f_j, F)$, since this allows us to calculate

$$
\mathbb{E}[count_E(e)|F] = \sum_{j=1}^{k} p(e_j = e|f_j, F) \,. \quad (2)
$$

Note, that under our proposed probabilistic model, it holds that

$$
p(e_j|f_j, F) \;=\; \sum_z p(e_j|f_j, z) \cdot p(z|F) \,.
$$

This can be interpreted as follows. First, the model determines a probability distribution over the latent topics, conditioned on the given input source document, i.e. $p(z|F)$. And then, second, the model uses the conditional probability $p(z|F)$ to determine the translation probability for each word in the source document, i.e. $p(e_j|f_j, z)$.

The actual calculation of $p(e_j = e|f_j, F)$ can be derived as follows.[5]

$$
\begin{aligned}
p(e_j|f_j, F) &= p(e_j|f_1, ..., f_k) \\
&\propto p(e_j, f_1, ..., f_k) \\
&= \sum_c \sum_z p(e_j, f_1, ..., f_k|z) p(z|c) p(c) \,,
\end{aligned}
$$

where the probability $p(e_j, f_1, ..., f_k|z)$ can be efficiently calculated using

$$
\begin{aligned}
& \sum_{e_{l_1} \in V} \cdots \sum_{e_{l_{k-1}} \in V} p(e_1, \ldots, e_k, f_1, \ldots, f_k|z) \\
=\; & \sum_{e_{l_1} \in V} \cdots \sum_{e_{l_{k-1}} \in V} \prod_{j'=1}^{k} \theta_{f_{j'}|e_{j'}} \cdot \vartheta_{e_{j'}|z} \\
=\; & \theta_{f_j|e_j} \cdot \vartheta_{e_j|z} \prod_{j' \in \{l_1 \ldots l_{k-1}\}} \sum_{e_{j'} \in V} \theta_{f_{j'}|e_{j'}} \cdot \vartheta_{e_{j'}|z} \,,
\end{aligned}
$$

where the indexes $l_1 \ldots l_{k-1}$ correspond to $1, \ldots, j-1, j+1, \ldots k$.

### 3.1 Learning $\upsilon_c$, $\pi_{z|c}$, and $\vartheta_{e|z}$

Note that under our model, class $c$ and topic $z$ are independent from $f_1, ..., f_k$ given document $e_1, ..., e_k$ in the target language. Therefore, the parameters $\upsilon_c$, $\pi_{z|c}$, and $\vartheta_{e|z}$ can be learned solely using the training documents in the target language. Given a collection of training documents with known classes $D = \{(E_1, c_1) ..., (E_n, c_n)\}$, we can estimate the parameters as follows.

Parameter $\upsilon_c$ is estimated using the maximum-likelihood (ML), which is

$$
\upsilon_c^* = \frac{\sum_{i=1}^{n} 1_c(c_i)}{n} \,, \quad (3)
$$

where $1_x(y)$ is the indicator function which is 1, if $x = y$, otherwise 0.

The optimal ML-estimate of $\vartheta_{e|z}$ and $\pi_{z|c}$ can be found by maximizing $\log p(D|\vartheta, \pi)$, for which, however, an analytic solution cannot be derived. Therefore, instead, we use the EM-algorithm

[4]It might seem that we need cross-lingually aligned documents, or documents of same length in both languages. However, both is not the case, since in our experiments the translations will always be unobserved, and therefore sum over all possible translations.

[5]When it is clear from the context, we write $p(e_j)$ instead of $p(e_j = e)$.

(Dempster et al., 1977), deriving for the E-step: setting the probability distribution $q$ to

$$p(z_i|D, \vartheta, \pi) \propto \pi_{z_i|c_i} \prod_{j=1}^{k_i} \sum_{e_j} \vartheta_{e_j|z_i}, \quad (4)$$

and in the M-step:

$$\vartheta^*_{e|z} = \frac{\sum_{i=1}^{n} \sum_{j=1}^{k_i} 1_e(e_j) \cdot q(z_i = z)}{\sum_{i=1}^{n} \sum_{j=1}^{k_i} q(z_i = z)} \quad (5)$$

and

$$\pi^*_{z|c} = \frac{\sum_{i=1}^{n} 1_c(c_i) \cdot q(z_i = z)}{\sum_{i=1}^{n} q(z_i = z)}. \quad (6)$$

### 3.2 Learning $\theta_{f|e}$

Here we propose to chose the translation probabilities $\theta_{f|e}$ with highest probability, under our current model, and such that the probability of observing the source documents (without labels) is maximized. Formally, given a collection of source documents $D' := F_1, ..., F_m$, the optimal translation probability $\theta^*_{f|e}$ is

$$\underset{\theta_{f|e}}{\operatorname{argmax}}\, p(D'|\theta_{f|e}, \upsilon^*_c, \pi^*_{z|c}, \vartheta^*_{e|z}),$$

where $\upsilon^*_c, \pi^*_{z|c}, \vartheta^*_{e|z}$ are the parameters learned in the previous section. Unfortunately, the exact optimization is intractable, and therefore, we resort again to an EM-approximation, analogously to before.

The E-step corresponds to setting for each source document $i$, the probability $q(e_{i,1}, ..., e_{i,k_i})$ to

$$p(e_{i,1}, ..., e_{i,k_i}|f_{i,1}, \ldots f_{i,k}, \theta_{f|e})$$
$$\propto \sum_{c_i} \sum_{z_i} p(c_i)p(z_i|c_i) \prod_{j=1}^{k} p(e_{i,j}|z_i)\theta_{f_{i,j}|e_{i,j}}.$$

In the M-step, we update $\theta_{f|e}$ to

$$\theta^*_{f|e} = \frac{\sum_{i=1}^{m} \sum_{j=1}^{k_i} 1_f(f_{j,i}) \cdot q(e_{i,j} = e)}{\sum_{i=1}^{m} \sum_{j=1}^{k_i} q(e_{i,j} = e)}.$$

## 4 Experiments

For our experiments we use three pair of corpora denoted by NEWS, WEB, and TWEETS. The corpora NEWS contains news articles in English and Japanese crawled from Internet news sites during 2012-2013, and were annotated as being related to "foreign policy" or not related. The corpora WEB contains web pages in English and Chinese that are categorized either as "sport" or "computer" in the Open Directory Project (ODP)[6] crawled in 2013. TWEETS contains tweets in English and Chinese gathered during 2013, classified as related to "violence", or not related.[7]

| Method | NEWS | WEB | TWEETS |
|---|---|---|---|
| Co | **0.687** (0.68) | 0.842 (0.84) | **0.430** (0.18) |
| Co (freq) | 0.668 (0.68) | 0.849 (0.83) | 0.424 (0.20) |
| Co (uni) | 0.666 (0.68) | 0.842 (0.83) | 0.426 (0.22) |
| Wu et al. | 0.632 (0.56) | 0.849 (0.74) | 0.391 (0.13) |
| Freq | 0.635 (0.58) | 0.842 (0.76) | 0.376 (0.13) |
| Uniform | 0.628 (0.53) | **0.856** (0.76) | 0.407 (0.13) |
| CN/JA only | 0.816 (0.81) | 0.893 (0.90) | 0.894 (0.89) |
| EN only | 0.718 (0.67) | 0.967 (0.97) | 0.682 (0.67) |

Table 1: Shows the break-even point (f1-score) of the proposed method Co and three baselines for each pair of corpora. Co (freq) and Co (uni) denote the proposed method without estimation of dictionary probabilities, but instead using word frequency and uniform distribution, respectively.

We tokenize and stem the words in the English corpora using Senna (Collobert et al., 2011). For Chinese and Japanese we use the morphological analyzers described in (Qiu et al., 2013), and an in-house analyzer, respectively. The Chinese to English dictionary, and the Japanese to English dictionary contains translations for 94351 and 1483440 words, respectively.

For the classification we use LIBSVM (Chang and Lin, 2011) with linear kernel, and the feature representation as suggested in (Rennie et al., 2003).

For the parameter estimation of our proposed model we use EM, as described in Section 3.1 and 3.2.[8] The number of topics was determined by optimizing the f1-measure using only the English training data when applying the probabilistic model to monolingual text classification. In order to prevent non-zero probabilities, we use a symmetric Dirichlet

[6] www.dmoz.com

[7] The number of documents in the corpora pairs for source/target language are 2472/2289, 1302/6294, and 2005/1499 for NEWS, WEB and TWEETS, respectively.

[8] We observed convergence for less than 50 iterations.

prior.

We compare our proposed method "Co" to four different baselines that also use solely a bilingual dictionary. For all methods (baselines and proposed), we use Equation (2) to estimate the expected word frequencies. The baseline "Wu et al." refers to the method proposed in (Wu et al., 2008). The baseline "Freq" sets the probability $p(e|f)$ to be proportional to the word frequency in the training data. Analogously, the baseline "Uniform" assumes a uniform probability over all translations of $f$.

For measuring the performance of each text classifier we use precision and recall. The break-even point[9] and the f1-measure of our proposed method and all baselines are shown in Table 1. As can be seen, our method performs favorable for the NEWS and TWEETS corpora. For the WEB corpora pair and our proposed method is at par with the baseline "Wu et al.", and looses slightly to the "Uniform" baseline. For reference, we also show the upper bounds "CN/JA only" and "EN only" that train and test in the same source and target language, respectively.[10]

We also analyzed the contribution of using the word translation probabilities learned in Section 3.2. The method "Co (freq)" is the same as our proposed method, except that the translation probabilities $p(f|e)$ are not estimated using the method described in Section 3.2, but instead simply uses the word-frequency distribution. Analogously, the method "Co (uni)" is the same as our proposed method, except that $p(f|e)$ is set to the uniform probability for all translations of $e$. Limiting the discussion to break-even points, we see, in Table 1, an improvement of around 2 percent points for NEWS, but only minor changes in performance for the other two corpora (WEB and TWEETS).

Finally, we give an example which shows the translation probabilities for the word 拘束 (restrict, restrain, custody) for two different source documents in NEWS. The first source document $F_1$ reports a military action, and is labeled as "foreign policy". The second document $F_2$ is a news article about terror, and is labeled as "not foreign policy". The results shown in Table 2, confirm our intuition, that the translation "custody" is more likely in documents related to crime.

| | **e = restrict** | **e = restrain** | **e = custody** |
|---|---|---|---|
| $p(e\|f, F_1)$ | 0.33 | 0.10 | 0.57 |
| $p(e\|f, F_2)$ | 0.02 | 0.00 | 0.98 |

Table 2: Shows the translation probabilities for the source word $f$ = 拘束, within document $F_1$ (military related, class is "foreign policy") and document $F_2$ (terror related, class is not "foreign policy").

## 5 Conclusions

In contrast, to most previous work, we focused on the word translation problem, rather than the domain-adaptation problem for cross-lingual text classification. We have proposed a probabilistic model that allows us to estimate word-translation probabilities that are conditioned on the whole source document. Our experiments on three different pairs of corpora, show that our estimated translation probabilities can improve text classification accuracy, and that our estimated word translation probabilities are able to reflect the topic of a text.

[9]That is the point where precision and recall are equal.

[10]These results were acquired using cross-validation.

## References

Chih-Chung Chang and Chih-Jen Lin. 2011. LIBSVM: A library for support vector machines. *ACM Transactions on Intelligent Systems and Technology*, 2:27:1–27:27. Software available at `http://www.csie.ntu.edu.tw/~cjlin/libsvm`.

Ronan Collobert, Jason Weston, Léon Bottou, Michael Karlen, Koray Kavukcuoglu, and Pavel Kuksa. 2011. Natural language processing (almost) from scratch. *The Journal of Machine Learning Research*, 12:2493–2537.

Arthur P Dempster, Nan M Laird, Donald B Rubin, et al. 1977. Maximum likelihood from incomplete data via the em algorithm. *Journal of the Royal statistical Society*, 39(1):1–38.

Jagadeesh Jagarlamudi and Jianfeng Gao. 2013. Modeling click-through based word-pairs for web search. In *Proceedings of the ACM SIGIR Conference*, pages 483–492. ACM.

P. Koehn and K. Knight. 2000. Estimating word translation probabilities from unrelated monolingual corpora using the em algorithm. In *Proceedings of the National Conference on Artificial Intelligence*, pages 711–715. Association for the Advancement of Artificial Intelligence.

Xiaochuan Ni, Jian-Tao Sun, Jian Hu, and Zheng Chen. 2011. Cross lingual text classification by mining multilingual topics from wikipedia. In *Proceedings of the ACM International Conference on Web Search and Data Mining*, pages 375–384. ACM.

John C Platt, Kristina Toutanova, and Wen-tau Yih. 2010. Translingual document representations from discriminative projections. In *Proceedings of the Conference on Empirical Methods in Natural Language Processing*, pages 251–261. Association for Computational Linguistics.

Xipeng Qiu, Qi Zhang, and Xuanjing Huang. 2013. Fudannlp: A toolkit for chinese natural language processing. In *Proceedings of Annual Meeting of the Association for Computational Linguistics*.

Jason D Rennie, Lawrence Shih, Jaime Teevan, and David R Karger. 2003. Tackling the poor assumptions of naive bayes text classifiers. In *Proceedings of the International Conference on Machine Learning*, volume 3, pages 616–623.

Lei Shi, Rada Mihalcea, and Mingjun Tian. 2010. Cross language text classification by model translation and semi-supervised learning. In *Proceedings of the Conference on Empirical Methods in Natural Language Processing*, pages 1057–1067. Association for Computational Linguistics.

Ke Wu, Xiaolin Wang, and Bao-Liang Lu. 2008. Cross language text categorization using a bilingual lexicon. In *Proceedings of the International Joint Conference on Natural Language Processing*, pages 165–172.

# Testing and Comparing Computational Approaches for Identifying the Language of Framing in Political News

**Eric P. S. Baumer[1,2], Elisha Elovic[2], Ying "Crystal" Qin[2], Francesca Polletta[3], Geri K. Gay[1,2]**
[1]Communication [2]Information Science [3]Sociology
Cornell University University of California, Irvine
Ithaca, NY, USA Irvine, CA, USA
{ericpsb, epe9, yq37, gkg1}@cornell.edu, polletta@uci.edu

## Abstract

The subconscious influence of framing on perceptions of political issues is well-document in political science and communication research. A related line of work suggests that drawing attention to framing may help reduce such framing effects by enabling frame reflection, critical examination of the framing underlying an issue. However, definite guidance on how to identify framing does not exist. This paper presents a technique for identifying frame-invoking language. The paper first describes a human subjects pilot study that explores how individuals identify framing and informs the design of our technique. The paper then describes our data collection and annotation approach. Results show that the best performing classifiers achieve performance comparable to that of human annotators, and they indicate which aspects of language most pertain to framing. Both technical and theoretical implications are discussed.

## 1 Introduction

Contentious political issues are rarely understood *per se* but rather through the lens of framing. Terms such as "tax relief," "death taxes," "racial quotas," "death panels," and others have famously rallied citizens around fairly complex causes. More generally, research has shown that the way an issue is framed (Entman, 1993) – how a problem is defined, to what other problems and people it is linked, etc. – has a significant impact on both perceptions of the issue and prescriptions for action. A variety of work has shown that minor changes in language – "global warming" vs. "climate change" (Schuldt et al., 2011), "gay civil unions" vs. "homosexual marriage" (Price et al., 2005), "not allow" vs. "forbid" (Rugg, 1941) – can significantly impact opinions.

A related but less explored line of research suggests that "frame reflection" (Schön and Rein, 1994), i.e., critical thinking about an issue's framing, can play an important role in understanding issues and reconciling conflicts. Indeed, some recent work suggests that drawing attention to framing may help mitigate framing effects (Baumer et al., 2015). However, such reflection is no mean feat. "Various observers have noted how subtly and unconsciously [framing] operates" (Gamson and Modigliani, 1989, p. 7), making it difficult to acknowledge that an issue is being framed at all, let alone examine that framing critically or consider alternatives. Furthermore, "straightforward guidelines on how to identify [...] a frame in communication do not exist" (Chong and Druckman, 2007, p. 106).

To address this challenge, this paper compares different computational approaches for identifying the language of framing, specifically in political news coverage. The best performing classifiers achieve accuracy around 61% and F1 scores of 0.45 to 0.46, outperforming a dummy baseline and approaching or matching human performance of 73% accuracy and F1 score of 0.46. This work makes two key contributions. First, compares different techniques for identifying language invoking conceptual framing, a novel yet important task. Second, it offers evidence about what language is perceived as related to framing, helping to addressing the gap identified by (Chong and Druckman, 2007).



*Human Language Technologies: The 2015 Annual Conference of the North American Chapter of the ACL*, pages 1472–1482,
Denver, Colorado, May 31 – June 5, 2015. 

## 2 Related Work

### 2.1 Conceptual Framing

Generally speaking, in order to make sense of their interactions, people frame their experiences (Goffman, 1974). Facts "take on their meaning by being embedded in a frame [...] that organizes them and gives them coherence" (Gamson, 1989, p. 157). Frames help people "locate, perceive, identify, and label," i.e., organize and give meaning to, information about experiences in the world. A frame consists of a variety of components, including "keywords, stock phrases, stereotype images, sources of information" (Entman, 1993, p. 52), "metaphors, exemplars, catchphrases, depictions, [...] visual images" (Gamson and Modigliani, 1989, p. 3), and other devices that provide an interpretive lens or "package." Frames define what counts as a problem, diagnose what is causing the problem, make moral judgments about those involved, and suggest remedies for resolving the problem (Entman, 1993). Framing can significantly impact the perception of a variety of political issues. (Schuldt et al., 2011) found that belief in "global warming" was significantly lower than in "climate change," specifically among Republicans. Gamson and Modigliani (1989) show how nuclear power is framed by such phrases as "atoms for peace," "we have created a Frankenstein," and "the war being waged against the environment and our health."

Crucially, framing differs from subjectivity, sentiment, bias, and related constructs. Subjectivity detection may not effectively identify well-established, codified frames (e.g., "tax relief" or "racial quotas"). Sentiment analysis focuses on assessing the valence (e.g., positive, neutral, or negative) of an entity's description. Bias involves a clear, often intentional, preference shown in writing for one position or opinion on an issue. In contrast, there does not exist a one-to-one mapping between framing and opinions (Gamson and Modigliani, 1989). For example, in late 2013, the international community was considering what actions should be taken against Syrian president Bashar al-Assad for using chemical weapons against rebelling citizens. Some viewed the situation as a humanitarian crisis and argued for military intervention. Others argued that al-Assad's actions were a threat to regional security, also arguing for military action. Here, different framings are used to support the same position on an issue.

In contrast, framing involves an ensemble of rhetorical elements to create an "interpretive package" (Gamson and Modigliani, 1989) that functions by altering the relative salience or importance of different aspects of an issue (Chong and Druckman, 2007). In the humanitarian crisis framing vs. regional security framing example above, a regional security framing does not negatively valence human suffering; rather, it shifts the emphasis to make other concerns more apparent. Thus, while we can draw on subjectivity, bias, and sentiment detection, identifying framing requires features and techniques that go beyond any one of these related concepts.

### 2.2 Related Computational Approaches

Some computational work explored concepts related to conceptual framing. For example, Choi et al. (2012) identify hedging in discussion of GMOs using an SVM trained on n-grams from annotated cue phrases. Greene and Resnik (2009) showed how examining grammatical construction (i.e., syntax) can reveal implicit sentiment; for example, passive and active voice imply different degrees of agency and causality. Recasens et al. (2013) used edits from Wikipedia intended to enforce a neutral point of view to identify biased sentences and the terms indicative of that bias.

Relatively little work has been done on identifying frames per se. Lind and Salo (2002) used co-occurrence frequencies to examine the framing of feminism in news media. Matthes and Kohring (2008) take a mixed methods approach, asking human coders to annotate the occurrence of certain features in a text problem definition, attribution of causation, moral evaluation, etc. then cluster the text using that coding to identify high-level frames. Boydstun et al. (2013) suggest that approaches based on hierarchical topic modeling may be an effective means of identifying both issue-specific and generic frames.

Such techniques, while useful from an analytic standpoint, are not as directly relevant here. The work described in this paper does not aim to identify the framing in a text. Rather, it seeks to determine what language is perceived as being most related to framing, especially by lay-persons, as a means of supporting reflection on that framing.

## 3 Exploratory Pilot Study

While the framing literature provides some guidance (Entman, 1993; Chong and Druckman, 2007), little work has explored how exactly non-elites go about identifying framing (Chong and Druckman, 2007). Thus, we conducted a pilot investigating to explore laypersons' understandings and identification of framing.

### 3.1 Methods

We recruited undergraduate students at two major US universities. Participants were asked to read an article that framed the issue of health care in terms of equality (as opposed to cost). Previous work showed that reading this article was associated with stronger support for a national healthcare system (Druckman et al., 2012). Participants were then asked to re-read the article and highlight any words or phrases they believed were related to framing. Specifically, participants were given the following prompt and instructions:

*Political issues can often be complex, contentious, and difficult to understand. One way of making sense of these issues, and the different positions that one can take on an issue, is to think about the frames that structure debate about the issue. Frames help organize facts and information. They help define what counts as a problem, diagnose the problem's causes, and suggest remedies for solving the problem. These ways of thinking have lots of different parts, including stereotypes, metaphors, images, catchphrases, and other elements.*

*These different frames are often associated with a particular way of talking about or communicating about an issue. Certain words or phrases might suggest that one or another frame.*

*Please use the tool at the link below to highlight the words or phrases that help you identify the framings used in the article you just read.*

After a student finished highlighting the article, s/he also participated in a debriefing interview where a researcher asked her or him about what s/he highlighted and why.

We recruited total of 47 students; 20 completed the task in person, who completed the debriefing interview immediately, and 27 used an online annotation tool, who completed the debriefing over the phone within 24 hours.

### 3.2 Results

First, we sought to determine the extent to which study participants' annotations agreed with one another. Do different people see the same words and phrases as being related to framing? An intraclass correlation (ICC) among participants' annotations of 0.757 indicated that the annotators demonstrated a moderately high degree of agreement as to which words and phrases were most related to framing.

As an example, one article about health care contained the sentence: "A good doctor might recognize the regenerative powers of the body politic and come up with a comprehensive treatment plan that also attacks root causesincluding the twin cancers of racism and poverty." Three students highlighted the entire sentence, another three highlighted only the phrase "twin cancers of racism and poverty," and one more highlighted "twinpoverty," "regenerative powers," and "body politic."

Several important insights were also derived from the debriefing interviews. Participants drew a distinction between facts and opinions, the later being more relevant to framing. For example, statistics were rarely seen as related to framing. Also, framing often dealt not only with a word itself but also with aspects of its context and its relationships with other terms in the article. For example, a participant might highlight just the word "but" because it indicates an important rhetorical shift and, implicitly, the article's take on the issue. Similarly, latent relationships between an individual word and the article's main argument also played an important role. For example, the article participants read emphasized "disparities" between healthcare available to the wealthy and to the working class. Many participants indicated that they would highlight any words or phrases that drew attention to such disparities. These insights, in conjunction with the theoretical literature on conceptual framing, were used to guide feature selection.

## 4 Data

We sought to develop a classifier that could automatically identify the language in a text that most related to framing. We chose to focus on news coverage rather than, say, opinion and editorial columns. Framing likely occurs in a more apparent, potentially obvious fashion in opinion articles. In ostensibly "straight" news, though, framing may be harder to identify. Thus, this context would benefit more from a classifier that could automatically draw attention to frame-invoking language.

For training data, we wanted political texts where lay readers had indicated the words and phrases they perceived as most related to framing. Lay annotators were used instead of experts because the classifier's purpose is to support frame reflection among the lay public. Thus, the words and phrases the classifier highlights should align with that population's perception of framing. To our knowledge, no such data set exists. So, we used Mechanical Turk (Snow et al., 2008) and university students to build an annotated dataset that could be used for training and testing.

### 4.1 Collection

We began by collecting political news articles from top 15 online sources of news, as determined by Alexa rankings (http://www.alexa.com/topsites/category/Top/News). We excluded sources outside the US (e.g., BBC), news aggregators (e.g., Yahoo News, Google News), blogs (Huffington Post), and sites without a dedicated politics feed (e.g., USA Today, weather.com). Doing so left eight sources CNN, NYT, Fox, NBC, Washington Post, ABC, LA Times, Reuters.

For each source, we collected all items on their politics-specific RSS feed on two separate days roughly six months apart to provide content about diverse issues and events: Tuesday November 12, 2013, and Thursday May 15, 2014. We manually removed duplicate posts, "round-up" style posts that simply summarized and linked to other stories, video-only posts, and other non-textual content, resulting in a total of 205 documents. Of these, we randomly selected 75 to be annotated.

### 4.2 Annotation

Each article was annotated by five to 13 annotators, who were either Mechanical Turk (MTurk) workers or students at one of two major US universities. The task first asked the annotator to read the article, then gave the same directions from the framing prompt described above.

To encourage MTurk workers to pay attention to the task and complete high-quality work, we provided a scheme for bonus payments. Every word a worker annotated that was also annotated by at least two others (i.e., a majority of the 5 workers annotating each document) would earn the worker a $0.02 bonus (two cents). Each word s/he annotated that was annotated by no other work would reduce the bonus by $0.005 (half a cent). Workers were then linked to our web tool where they could complete and submit their annotations. Student annotators received no agreement-based incentive but were granted extra course credit.

### 4.3 Quality Assurance

Crowd workers do not always provide reliable annotations (Snow et al., 2008). For example, we noted multiple instances where annotators had only annotated about a dozen words in an article of several hundred words. These seemed likely to be cases in which the annotator was completing the task as quickly as possible without paying much attention. By comparing the annotations with those collected during our pilot study, in which participants' justifications during the debriefing ensured higher attention and quality, we developed the following criteria for identifying questionable annotations. Those that did not pass at least three of these five requirements were removed from the analysis.

1. All Annotations Short — While some annotations of short words, such as conjunctions, could be meaningful (see example above), we encountered a number of annotations where every annotated phrase consisted of only one or two words at a time. Thus, we required that the average annotated contiguous segment be at least 3 words long.

2. Few Words Annotated — When very few words in a document are annotated, we suspect the annotator may have been completing the task as quickly as possible and paying little attention. Thus, we required that each annotator's work include enough annotated words to total more than 5% of the document's length.

3. Large Contiguous Passages without Annotation — While pilot study participants pointed out portions of a text that consisted of "facts and figures," these were generally relatively short. Thus, we require the longest block of text without any annotations to be no more than one third the length of

the entire document.

4. Large Contiguous Passages Entirely Annotated — Large, unbroken annotations rarely occurred in our pilot study. Such annotations may also have indicated that the annotator was not attending to the entire content being annotated. Thus, we require that the longest contiguous annotation be no more than 120 words long.

5. Annotating Solely Stop Words — A number of annotations include only very common words, such as articles, prepositions, forms of the verb "to be," etc. Single words such as "but," "all," or "not" could arguably be related to framing. However, accounts from our pilot study participants made us less likely to believe that other single words, such as "an," "of," or "that," instantiated framing. Thus, we require that no more than 3 annotated passages consistent entirely of such stop words1.

We also encountered two situations in which pairs of MTurk workers submitted virtually identical annotations for multiple documents. Following up with the workers, we discovered that in one situation a husband and wife team had actually been working together. Based on our pilot study, we would expect annotators to agree to some degree, but we would not want such agreement to arise because annotators were collaborating. Thus, we also exclude these annotations where we suspect the possibility of collaboration.

We only include in our dataset documents with at least three valid annotations. In total, the resulting data set includes 74 articles containing 53,878 total words (M=728.1 words per particle), each with three to 11 valid annotations (Mdn=6). The data set includes 59,948 annotated words across 507 annotations from 372 annotators (M=122.8 annotated words per article). The full data set is available at http://hdl.handle.net/1813/39216.

## 5 Classifier Design and Implementation

As argued above, drawing attention to framing-related language may both mitigate frame effects (Baumer et al., 2015) and facilitate frame reflection (Schön and Rein, 1994). This section describes the features used to train a classifier to identify framing along with justifications for each, different subsets of features that were tested, our classifier selection, and the training and testing methods.

### 5.1 Features and Subsets

We treat each word as a data point to be classified as framing-related or not. Feature extraction began with splitting each article into sentences with NLTK (Bird et al., 2009) then using Stanford CoreNLP (Klein and Manning, 2003; De Marneffe et al., 2006) to parse each sentence, obtain POSs and lemmatized forms for each word, etc. We then construct a feature vector for each non-stop word. Table 1 lists all features used. The remainder of this subsection describes the justificaton for each feature, as well as several subsets of features.

Framing is often instantiated by specific "keywords, stock phrases," (Entman, 1993, p. 52) or "catchphrases" (Gamson and Modigliani, 1989, p. 3). Therefore, we include lexical features that capture the specific words used. Furthermore, many of our pilot study participants pointed out that a given word might be seen as related to framing because of the other words near which it appears. Therefore, each of these features includes a contextual window of up to two words before and after the word being classified (Recasens et al., 2013).

Participants in our pilot study said physical locations, such as the names of states, were often not related to framing. However, they sometimes saw names of political figures or experts as indicating framing. Thus, we include the named entity type as a feature, both of the word itself and of its context.

Pilot study participants also mentioned that a word's relationship to the remainder of a document and its overall thesis played important roles. A number of similar structural aspects of the document, both explicit and latent, may help draw out these relationships.

Several specific types of terms may be indicative of framing. For example, "depictions," "visual images," and figurative language such as metahpor (Gamson and Modigliani, 1989) often invoke frames. For imagery, we use previously established imagery ratings for 1818 common words (Paivio et al., 1968; van der Veur, 1975). Words that appear in this list are given an imagery rating, either low (first quantile), medium (second and third quantile), or high (fourth quantile) imagery. The context feature represents the average imagery of the

| Feature | Description | Feature Subset(s) |
|---|---|---|
| Token ±1, ±2 | The word token itself and the tokens in its context. | Lexical, Theoretical |
| Lemma ±1, ±2 | The lemmatized word and the lemmas in its context. | Lexical, Theoretical |
| Bigrams and trigrams | All bigrams and trigrams of which the word is a part. | Lexical, Theoretical |
| POS ±1, ±2 | The word's and its context's part(s) of speech. | Grammatical |
| Root | Whether the word is the sentence's parse tree's root. | Grammatical |
| Relation and Role | The grammatical relations in which the word is involved and its role in those relations, e.g., passive subject of a verb. | Grammatical |
| Named Entity ±1, ±2 | Named entity type of the word and its context. | Grammatical |
| In Title | Whether the word appears in the article's title. | Document |
| Sentence Lengeth | The number of words in the sentence. | Document |
| Sentence Position | Whether the word appears in the first third of the sentence, the middle third, or the last third. | Document |
| TFIDF | The word's tf-idf score, grouped into 8 bins of increasing size. | Document |
| Imagery & Context | Imagery rating of the word and average imagery rating of its context (Paivio et al., 1968; van der Veur, 1975). | Theoretical, Dictionaries |
| Figurativeness & Context | Figurativeness rating of the word and average figurativeness rating of its context (Gamson and Modigliani, 1989; Turney et al., 2011). | Theoretical, Dictionaries |
| Abstractness & Context | Abstractness rating of the word and average abstractness rating of its context (Gamson and Modigliani, 1989; Turney et al., 2011). | Theoretical, Dictionaries |
| Dictionaries & Context | One feature each for whether word or context is a subjective word (Riloff and Wiebe, 2003), a report verb (Recasens et al., 2013), a hedge (Hyland, 2005), a factive verb (Hooper, 1975), an entailment (Berant et al., 2012), an assertive word (Hooper, 1975), a bias word (Recasens et al., 2013), a negative word (Liu et al., 2005), or a positive word (Liu et al., 2005). | Theoretical, Dictionaries |

Table 1: Name and description of all features for each word, as well as the set(s) to which each feature belongs.

word's context. For figurative language, we used Turney et al.'s (Turney et al., 2011) approach of measuring figurativeness based on the absolute difference in the concreteness of two terms that are grammatically related. The figurativeness score for a given word is the average absolute difference between its concreteness and the concreteness of every word with which it is in some grammatical relationship. We also used Turney et al.'s (Turney et al., 2011) approach to rate the individual abstractness of each word and its context. Lastly, subjective words, hedges, entailments, and other terms that perform specific psycholinguistic functions (Recasens et al., 2013) may also be useful in identifying framing. For each, we include one feature for the word itself and one feature for the two-word context around the word.

The features used here are informed by a combination of theoretical literature on framing, our own pilot studies, and prior work in computational linguistics. However, we have little means of knowing a priori which of these features will be most important or even necessary. Therefore, in the interest of developing the most perspicacious model, we test several feature subsets, as noted in Table 1. Lexical features involve only words that actually occur in the text. Grammatical features use only aspects of grammatical structure. Document features use various explicit and latent aspects of the document's structure. Theoretical features are those specifically mentioned in the theoretical literature on framing. Finally, the Dictionaries feature set tests whether there might be specific terms that invoke framing.

### 5.2 Training and Testing

We implemented and tested a variety of different classifiers, including Stochastic Gradient Descent (SGD), Multinomial Naïve Bayes, Perceptron, Nearest Neighbor, Logistic Regression, and Passive Aggressive classifiers. In several tests, the Naïve Bayes classifier performed best, so we used a Naïve Bayes classifier throughout.

As described above, our data include three to 11 annotators' annotations for each word in the corpus. To create training data, we aggregated these annotations such that any word highlighted by at least one fourth of the annotators was treated as framing-related (i.e., true positive) for training and testing purposes, and the remaining words were treated as not frame-related (i.e., true negative).

These data, in the combinations of features described above, were used to train our ensemble classifier using scikit-learn (Pedregosa et al., 2011) using ten-fold random shuffle cross-validation, as well as a random dummy classifier based on class distributions in the training set. Performance in terms of f-score, accuracy, precision, and recall was averaged across the ten folds.

## 6 Results

This section summarizes results, highlighting some important aspects thereof, while the subsequent Discussion section considers interpretation and broader implications. Figure 1 presents a summary of results for each feature set, including comparison with the dummy baseline and the aggregate human performance. The Document Structure feature set performed very poorly, identifying 0 true positives, so we exclude it from the detailed results report.

Since overall accuracy does not vary drastically, we focus on other performance metrics. Except for the Dictionaries, all feature sets perform statistically significantly better than the dummy (ANOVA with Tukey's posthoc $p < 0.001$). F1 scores among the top three performers (Lexical, Theoretical, and All

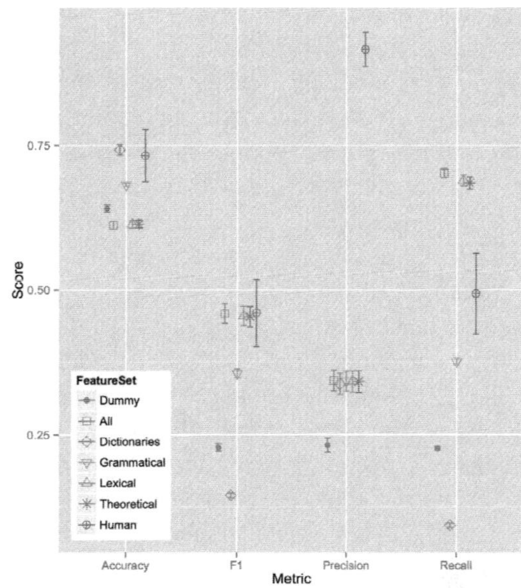


Figure 1: Performance of each feature set, as well as the dummy baseline and human annotators, on accuracy, F1, precision, and recall. Three feature sets (Lexical, Theoretical, and All features) match human annotators on F1 and outperform human recall, but humans demonstrate higher precision.

features) are statistically indistinguishable. Furthermore, each of these three top performers matches aggregate human annotator performance.

Looking at precision and recall, we can see that the classifiers and the human annotators make different trade offs. Precision for all feature sets is around 34% (all statisticially significantly better than the dummy and significantly indistinguishable from one another), while human average precision is 91.5%. On the other hand, the three top performing feature sets (All, Lexical, and Theoretical) all achieve recall around 70%, while average recall for the human annotators is only 49.3%.

It is also important to note that human performance is calculated by comparing each individual annotator to the aggregate of all the annotators. Because each individual is part of that aggregate, precision scores for the humans are fairly high. We consider comparison with human performance further in the discussion below.

We also examine the most influential features for classifiers using each of the three top performing feature sets. For the Lexical feature set, the most informative features for negative cases are bigrams that begin with quotation marks. Since we manually assign all punctuation, including quotation marks, as true negatives, this is perhaps unsurprising. For positive cases, many of the "offset" style features emerge as informative. For example, words that appear one or two words before a comma or period are more likely to involve framing. Similarly, words that occur just before or just after prepositions or conjunctions — to, and, in, of, etc. — are more likely classified as framing (i.e., positive). This result aligns with some of our pilot study findings about the relationships between such function terms the words surrounding them. Interestingly, though, these features do not resemble the catchphrases and keywords described in the framing literature (Entman, 1993; Gamson and Modigliani, 1989).

For the Theoretically Informed feature set, which adds in imagery, figurativeness, and other dictionary-based features, roughly the same kinds of lexical features are most important in identifying negative cases. For positive cases, constructs such as descriptiveness and abstractness play important roles, but mostly when words in the context do *not* appear in these dictionaries, calling into question the importance of imagery, metaphor, and other figurative language (Gamson and Modigliani, 1989). Other dictionary-based features, such as being an entailment word, having an entailment in context, having a bias term in context, or having a subjective term in context, become important in identifying positive cases. Some of the lexical features, such as proximity to a comma or period, also remain informative.

With All features, which adds features for document structure and grammatical structure, two major differences occur. First, some elements of document structure become important features for positive cases, including sentence length and TFIDF. Second, various part of speech tags, mostly NN and NNP, become important to identifying framing. These findings suggest that the choice of terms used to label concepts or entities can indicate framing. Indeed, entity type, both of the word and its context, also emerges as an informative feature.

## 7 Discussion

Chiefly important among the results, three of our feature sets were able to achieve F1 scores on par with those of human annotators. This result provides encouraging evidence that a machine classifier can effectively accomplish the task of identifying the language that invokes framing in political news coverage.

That said, examining the results more closely exposes that, in order to achieve this level of performance, the classifier makes a trade-off. Specifically, the classifier is far more aggressive than humans, resulting in significantly higher recall but lower precision. We did experiment with different post-hoc decision thresholds to make the classifier less aggressive. However, as we the decision threshold rose, recall fell much more quickly than precision increased, resulting in lower overall F1 scores. Moreover, this precision-recall trade off may have different ramifications in different applications. For example, in terms of supporting frame reflection, would it be harmful or distracting for a machine classifier to mark too many words as frame-invoking, thereby potentially overwhelming a potential user? Or would it be worse if the classifier were too sparse, missing certain important key words or phrases? These are questions for later empirical work that incorporates the results of this classifier into interactive systems to support frame reflection.

Also, our results above identifying important features within the classifier contribute to and build on prior computational work. For example, Recasens et al. (Recasens et al., 2013) find entailment (Berant et al., 2012), implicature (Karttunen, 1971), subjectivity (Riloff and Wiebe, 2003), and other related constructs helpful in identifying bias. The results above suggest that, when included, such features also emerge as important for identifying the language of framing. However, the feature sets that include dictionaries of these terms do not perform statistically significantly better than those feature sets without them. This result supports our initial assertion that bias and framing, while conceptually related, are separate constructs that are each perceived and instantiated via different linguistic cues.

These findings also relate to recent efforts at identifying which frame(s) are operating in a text (e.g.,

Boydstun et al., 2013). On the one hand, the performance of the Lexical feature set suggests that topic modeling, especially including certain n-grams, may prove an effective approach. That said, Boydstun et al. are more interested in determining *which* frames are at work in a text as a whole, whereas this paper focuses more on determining *where* within a text frames are invoked. Thus, different computational approaches and features may prove effective for each task.

Interestingly, the grammatical structure feature set is not one of the top performers. Given our expectations, including the importance that pilot study participants placed on structural relationships within the sentence, the role of grammatical construction both in metaphors (Turney et al., 2011) in framing more broadly (Fairclough, 1999), and prior computational work on implicit sentiment (Greene and Resnik, 2009), this result appears fairly surprising. It could be that grammatical structure alone is not sufficient to identify framing, but even combining grammatical structure with other features does not significnatly improve performance. Perhaps, then, grammatical construction matters less than the specific words chosen. On the other hand, lexical features may be topic-specific, such that even obtaining two samples six months apart still resulted in the same buzzwords invoking framing. Future work should examine more closely the role that structural features play, or perhaps do not play, in invoking framing.

This point also draws attention to some practical implications. Performing a full grammatical parse can be computationally intensive. If using other features that do not require a full parse can achieve comparable performance, then perhaps real time applications, such as analyzing live speeches as they happen, could employ only features that are relatively quicker and easier to extract.

Finally, we note that the annotated data analyzed here come from political news stories in US mainstream media. Since these sources ostensibly strive for impartiality, framing in these data may occur implicitly or unconsciously. Future work should compare these results with similar analyses of texts containing more explicit framing, such as opinion columns, campaign speeches, or political advertisements. Differences in how framing is identified may give important clues to how framing operates in different contexts. Similarly informative insights could be gained by comparing lay-persons' annotations with framing experts'.

## 8 Conclusion

"Facts have no intrinsic meaning. They take on their meaning by being embedded in a frame" (Gamson, 1989, p. 157). Given framing's pervasive influence, this paper argues for the importance of computational techniques that can identify and draw attention to the language of framing. Doing so can help support frame reflection (Schön and Rein, 1994) and, thereby, deeper understanding of and engagement with political issues.

This paper both develops a computational approach to identifying framing and tests how well different linguistic features indicate frame-invoking language. Results suggest grammatical structure alone as the most important indicator of framing. However, other data less computationally demanding to extract, such as lexical features (e.g., tokens and n-grams), can prove almost as effective.

In sum, the paper makes two main contributions. First, it provides a technical contribution by identifying a task of importance and demonstrating a technique that performs close to as well as humans. Second, the paper makes a theoretical contribution, helping to provide "guidelines on how to identify [] a frame in communication" (Chong and Druckman, 2007, p. 106). The data set of annotations released with this paper may also prove a valuable resource for future analyses of framing.

## Acknowledgments

This material is based upon work supported by the NSF under Grant No. IIS-1110932. Thanks to the Turker and student annotators, to Andrea Lin for research assistance, and to Cristian Danescu-Niculescu-Mizil and to Peter Turney for sharing technical resources.

## References

Eric P. S. Baumer, Francesca Polletta, Nicole Pierski, and Geri K. Gay. 2015. A Simple Intervention to Reduce Framing Effects in Perceptions of Global Climate Change. *Environmental Communication (to appear)*.

Jonathan Berant, Ido Dagan, Meni Adler, and Jacob Goldberger. 2012. Efficient tree-based approximation for entailment graph learning. In *Proc ACL*, pages 117–125.

Steven Bird, Edward Loper, and Ewan Klein. 2009. *Natural Language Processing with Python*. O'Reilly Media Inc.

Amber E. Boydstun, Justin H. Gross, Philip Resnik, and Noah A. Smith. 2013. Identifying Media Frames and Frame Dynamics Within and Across Policy Issues. In *New Directions in Analyzing Text as Data Workshop*, London.

Eunsol Choi, Chenhao Tan, Lillian Lee, Cristian Danescu-Niculescu-Mizil, and Jennifer Spindel. 2012. Hedge Detection as a Lens on Framing in the GMO Debates: A Position Paper. In *Proc ACL Workshop on Extra-Propositional Aspects of Meaning in Computational Linguistics*, number July, pages 70–79.

Dennis Chong and James N. Druckman. 2007. Framing Theory. *Annual Review of Political Science*, 10(1):103–126, June.

M.C. De Marneffe, Bill MacCartney, and C.D. Manning. 2006. Generating typed dependency parses from phrase structure parses. In *Proc LREC*, Genoa, Italy.

James N. Druckman, Jordan Fein, and Thomas J. Leeper. 2012. A Source of Bias in Public Opinion Stability. *American Political Science Review*, 106(02):430–454, May.

Robert M. Entman. 1993. Framing: Toward Clarification of a Fractured Paradigm. *Journal of Communication*, 43(4):51–58.

Norman Fairclough. 1999. Global Capitalism and Critical Awareness of Language. *Language Awareness*, 8(2):71–83.

William A. Gamson and Andre Modigliani. 1989. Media Discourse and Public Opinion on Nuclear Power: A Constructionist Approach. *The American Journal of Sociology*, 95(1):1–37, July.

William A. Gamson. 1989. News as Framing. *American Behavioral Scientist*, 33(2):157–161, November.

Erving Goffman. 1974. *Frame Analysis*. Harvard University Press, Cambridge, MA.

Stephan Greene and Philip Resnik. 2009. More than Words: Syntactic Packaging and Implicit Sentiment. In *Proc HLT*, number June, pages 503–511, Boulder, CO.

Joan B. Hooper. 1975. On Assertive Predicates. In J. Kimball, editor, *Syntax and Semantics*, pages 91–124. Academic Press, New York, volume 4 edition.

Ken Hyland. 2005. *Metadiscourse: Exploring Interaction in Writing*. Continuum, London and New York.

Lauri Karttunen. 1971. Implicative Verbs. *Language*, 47(2):340–358.

Dan Klein and Christopher D. Manning. 2003. Accurate Unlexicalized Parsing. Sapporo, Japan.

Rebecca Ann Lind and Colleen Salo. 2002. The Framing of Feminists and Feminism in News and Public Affairs Programs in U.S. Electronic Media. *Journal of Communication*, 52(1):211–228.

Bing Liu, Minqing Hu, and Junsheng Cheng. 2005. Opinion Observer: analyzing and comparing opinions on the Web. In *Proc WWW*, pages 342–351.

Jörg Matthes and Matthias Kohring. 2008. The Content Analysis of Media Frames: Toward Improving Reliability and Validity. *Journal of Communication*, 58(2):258–279.

Allan Paivio, John C Yuille, and Stephen A Madigan. 1968. Concreteness, Imagery, and Meaningfulness Values for 925 Nouns. *Journal of Experimental Psychology*, 76(1).

Fabian Pedregosa, Gael Varoquaux, Alexandre Gramfort, Vincent Michel, Bertrand Thirion, Olivier Grisel, Mathieu Blondel, Peter Prettenhofer, Ron Weiss, Vincent Dubourg, Jake Vanderplas, Alexandre Passos, David Cournapeau, Matthieu Brucher, Matthieu Perrot, and Edouard Duchesnay. 2011. Scikit-learn : Machine Learning in Python. *Journal of Machine Learning Research*, 12:2825–2830.

Vincent Price, Lilach Nir, and Joseph N. Cappella. 2005. Framing Public Discussion of Gay Civil Unions. *Public Opinion Quarterly*, 69(2):171–212.

Marta Recasens, Cristian Danescu-Niculescu-Mizil, and Dan Jurafsky. 2013. Linguistic Models for Analyzing and Detecting Biased Language. In *Proc ACL*, pages 1650–1659, Sofia, Bulgaria.

Ellen Riloff and Janyce Wiebe. 2003. Learning extraction patterns for subjective expressions. In *Proc EMNLP*, pages 105–112.

Donald Rugg. 1941. Experiments in Wording Questions: II. *Public Opinion Quarterly*, 5(1):91–92.

Donald A. Schön and Martin Rein. 1994. *Frame Reflection: Toward the Resolution of Intractable Policy Controversies*. Basic Books, New York.

Jonathon P. Schuldt, S. H. Konrath, and N. Schwarz. 2011. "Global warming" or "climate change"?: Whether the planet is warming depends on question wording. *Public Opinion Quarterly*, 75(1):115–124, February.

Rion Snow, Brendan O'Connor, Daniel Jurafsky, Andrew Y Ng, Dolores Labs, and Capp St. 2008. Cheap and Fast But is it Good? Evaluating Non-Expert Annotations for Natural Language Tasks. In *Proc EMNLP*, number October, pages 254–263, Honolulu, HI.

Peter D. Turney, Yair Neuman, Dan Assaf, and Yohai Cohen. 2011. Literal and Metaphorical Sense Identification through Concrete and Abstract Context. In *Proc*

*EMNLP*, volume 2, pages 680–690, Edinburgh, Scotland.

Barbara W. van der Veur. 1975. Imagery Rating of 1,000 Frequently Used Words. *Journal of Educational Psychology*, 67(1):44–56.

# Echoes of Persuasion: The Effect of Euphony in Persuasive Communication


**Marco Guerini**
Trento RISE
Povo, I-38100 Trento
marco.guerini@trentorise.eu

**Gözde Özbal**
FBK-Irst
Povo, I-38100 Trento
gozbalde@gmail.com

**Carlo Strapparava**
FBK-Irst
Povo, I-38100 Trento
strappa@fbk.eu



## Abstract

While the effect of various lexical, syntactic, semantic and stylistic features have been addressed in persuasive language from a computational point of view, the persuasive effect of phonetics has received little attention. By modeling a notion of euphony and analyzing four datasets comprising persuasive and non-persuasive sentences in different domains (political speeches, movie quotes, slogans and tweets), we explore the impact of sounds on different forms of persuasiveness. We conduct a series of analyses and prediction experiments within and across datasets. Our results highlight the positive role of phonetic devices on persuasion.


## 1 Hocus Pocus

Historically, in human sciences, several definitions of persuasion have been proposed – see for example (Toulmin, 1958; Walton, 1996; Chaiken, 1980; Cialdini, 1993; Petty and Cacioppo, 1986). Most of them have a common core addressing: *methodologies aiming to change the mental state of the receiver by means of communication in view of a possible action to be performed by her/him.* (Perelman and Olbrechts-Tyteca, 1969; Moulin et al., 2002).

These methodologies might take into account the overall structure of a text such as the ordering of the arguments or simply single word choices. For a successful text both of them are often required. The focus of persuasion may vary according to the goal of the communication and it can take different forms according to the domain: from memorability (e.g., making people remember a statement or a product) to diffusion (e.g., making people pass on a content in social networks by sharing it), from behavioral change (e.g., political communication) to influencing purchasing decisions (e.g., slogans to convince people to try or buy a product) – see for example (Heath and Heath, 2007). While many techniques such as resorting to expert opinion, utilizing the framing effect, emotive language or exaggeration can be used to obtain such persuasive effects, we devote this study to explore particular techniques pertaining to euphony.

Euphony refers to the inherent pleasantness of the sounds of words, phrases and sentences, and it is utilized to achieve pleasant, rhythmical and harmonious effects. The idea that the pleasantness of the sounds in a sentence can foster its effectiveness is rooted in our culture, and is connected to the concepts of rhythm and music. The fact that language and music interact in our brain has been shown by localizing low-level syntactic processes of music and language in the temporal lobe (Sammler et al., 2013). It has also been shown that changes in the cardiovascular and respiratory systems can be induced by music – specifically tempo, rhythm, melodic structure (Bernardi et al., 2006). The importance of euphony has its roots also in ancient human psychology. As Julian Jaynes suggests (Jaynes, 2000), poetry used to be divine knowledge. It was the sound and tenor of authorization and it commanded where plain prose could only ask. A paradigmatic example of this conception is the act of casting a spell. Spells (incantations) are special linguistic objects that are meant not only to change how




*Human Language Technologies: The 2015 Annual Conference of the North American Chapter of the ACL*, pages 1483–1493,
Denver, Colorado, May 31 – June 5, 2015.

people think or behave but they are also so powerful that they can – allegedly – change reality. Spells are often very euphonic (and meaningless) sentences, e.g. "Hocus Pocus".

Various psycholinguistic studies addressed the effects of phonetics on the audience in different aspects such as memorability (Wales, 2001; Benczes, 2013) or more specifically advertisement (Leech, 1966; Bergh et al., 1984). There are also computational studies that address the problem of recognizing persuasive sentences according to various syntactic, lexical and semantic features (Danescu-Niculescu-Mizil et al., 2012; Tan et al., 2014). However, to the best of our knowledge, the direct impact of phonetic elements on persuasiveness has not been explored in computational settings yet.

In this paper, we fill in this gap by conducting a series of analyses and prediction experiments on four datasets representing different aspects of persuasive language to evaluate the importance of a set of phonetic devices (i.e. rhyme, alliteration, homogeneity and plosives) on various forms of persuasiveness. Our experiments show that phonetic features play an important role in the detection of persuasiveness and encode a notion of "melodious language" that operates both within and across datasets.

## 2 Related Work

In the following, we first revise some NLP studies addressing linguistic features of successful communication. Then, we summarize a selection of studies devoted to the effects of phonetics on persuasion.

### 2.1 NLP studies on persuasion

Berger and Milkman (2009) focus on a particular form of persuasion by using New York Times articles to examine the relationship between virality (i.e., the tendency of a content to be circulated on the Web) and emotions evoked by the content. They conduct semi-automated sentiment analysis to quantify the affectivity and emotionality of each article. Results suggest a strong relationship between affect and virality, in this case measured as the count of how many people emailed each article. As suggested by the authors, this metric represents a form of "narrowcasting", as opposed to other "broadcasting" actions such as sharing on Twitter.

Another line of research investigates the impact of various textual features on audience reactions. The work by Guerini et al. (2011) correlates several viral phenomena with the wording of a post, while Guerini et al. (2012) show that features such as the readability level of an abstract influence the number of downloads, bookmarking and citations.

A particular approach to content virality is presented by Simmons et al. (2011), who explore the impact of different types of modification on memes spreading from one person to another.

Danescu-Niculescu-Mizil et al. (2012) measure a different ingredient of persuasion by analyzing the features of a movie quote that make it "memorable". They compile a corpus consisting of memorable and non-memorable movie quote pairs and conduct a detailed analysis to investigate the lexical and syntactic differences between these pairs.

Louis and Nenkova (2013) focus on influential science articles in newspapers by considering characteristics such as readability, description vividness, use of unusual words and affective content. High quality articles (NYT articles appearing in "The Best American Science Writing" anthology) are compared against typical NYT articles.

Borghol et al. (2012) investigate how differences in textual description affect the spread of content-controlled videos. Lakkaraju et al. (2013) focus on the act of resubmissions (i.e., content that is submitted multiple times with multiple titles to multiple different communities) to understand the extent to which each factor influences the success of a content. Tan et al. (2014) consider how content spreads in an on-line community by pinpointing the effect of wording in terms of content informativeness, generality and affect. Althoff et al. (2014) develop a model that can predict the success of requests for a free pizza gifted from the Reddit community. The authors consider high-level textual features such as politeness, reciprocity, narrative and gratitude.

### 2.2 Studies on the effects of phonetics

Benczes (2013) states that alliteration and rhyme can be considered as attention-seeking devices as they enhance emphasis. The author also suggests that they are useful for acceptability and long-term retention of original expressions, decrypting their meanings, indicating informality, and breaking the ice between an audience and a speaker. Therefore, these devices are commonly used in original metaphorical and metonymical compounds.

According to Leech (1966), phonetic devices such as rhyme and alliteration are systematically exploited by advertisers to achieve memorability. Similarly, Wales (2001) underlines the effectiveness of alliteration and rhyme on emphasis and memorability of an expression.

The relation between the usage of plosives (i.e., consonants in which the vocal tract is blocked so that all airflow ceases, such as "p", "t" or "k") and memorability has also been investigated. According to the study carried out by Bergh et al. (1984) brand names starting with plosive sounds are recalled and recognized more than the ones starting with other sounds. Özbal et al. (2012) carry out an analysis of brand names and discover that plosives are very commonly used.

Danescu-Niculescu-Mizil et al. (2012), whom we previously mentioned, carry out an auxiliary analysis and observe the differences in letter and sound distribution (e.g. usage of labials or front vowels, back sounds, coordinating conjunctions) of memorable and non-memorable quotes.

Özbal et al. (2013) propose a phonetic scorer for creative sentence generation such that generated sentences can contain various phonetic features including alliteration, rhyme and plosive sounds. The authors evaluate the proposed model on automatic slogan generation. In a more recent work (Özbal et al., 2014), they enforce the existence of these features in the sentences that are automatically generated for second language learning to introduce hooks to echoic memory.

## 3 Phonetic Scorer

For the design of the phonetic features, we were mostly inspired by the work of Özbal et al. (2013), who built and used three phonetic scorers for creative sentence generation. Similarly to this work, all the phonetic features that we used are based on the phonetic representation of English words of the Carnegie Mellon University pronouncing dictionary[1]. We selected four classes of phonetic devices, namely plosives, alliteration, rhyme and homogeneity, which can easily be modeled by observing the distribution of specific classes of phonemes within the sentence. The *plosive* score is calculated as the ratio of the number of plosive sounds in a sentence to the overall number of phonemes. For both *alliteration* and *rhyme* scorers, we provide a naïve implementation that does not consider stresses or syllables, but only counts the number of repeated sounds at the beginning or end of words in the sentence. The alliteration score is calculated as the number of repeated phonetic prefixes in a sentence normalized by the total number of phonemes. Similarly, the *rhyme* score is calculated as the ratio of the number of repeated phonetic endings in a sentence to the total number of phonemes. Lastly, the homogeneity scorer simply calculates the degree of homogeneity in terms of phonemes used in a sentence independently from their positions. If we let $d_{\text{ph}}$ be the count of distinct phonemes and $t_{\text{ph}}$ be the total count of phonemes in a sentence, then the homogeneity score is calculated as $1 - (d_{\text{ph}}/t_{\text{ph}})$.

## 4 Dataset

In this section, we describe the four datasets we used to conduct our analyses and experiments. As we mentioned previously, the definition of persuasion is a debated topic and it can comprise distinct strategies or facets. For this reason, we experimented with datasets where at least one ingredient is clearly in the equation. To explore the effects of wording and euphonics on persuasion, the datasets were built in a controlled setting (topic, author, sentence length) to avoid confounding factors such as author or topic popularity, by following the procedure described in (Danescu-Niculescu-Mizil et al., 2012; Tan et al., 2014). In addition, these datasets comprise short texts (mostly single sentences) to focus on surface realization of persuasion, where strategic planning – which might act as a confounding factor – plays a minor role. The idea of using controlled experiments (usually in an A/B test setting) to study persuasive communication can be traced back at least to Hovland et al. (1953). While two of these datasets (Twitter and Movies) were already available, the other two (CORPS and Slogans) were collected by following the methodology proposed in the first two as

[1]The CMU pronunciation dictionary is freely available at `http://www.speech.cs.cmu.edu/cgi-bin/cmudict`. We have used version 0.7a in our implementation.

closely as possible[2].

All datasets are built around the core idea of collecting pairs consisting of a persuasive sentence ($P$) and a non-persuasive counterpart ($\neg P$), where $P$ and $\neg P$ are structurally very similar and controlled for the above mentioned confounding factors.

**Twitter**. A set of 11,404 tweet pairs, where each pair comes from the same user (author control) and contains the same URL (topic control). $P$ and $\neg P$ are determined based on their retweet counts (Tan et al., 2014). It is worth noting that in our experiments we were able to collect only 11,019 of such tweet pairs since some of them were deleted in the meanwhile.

**Movie**. A set of 2,198 single-sentence memorable movie quotes ($P$) paired with non-memorable quotes ($\neg P$). For each $P$, the dataset contains a contrasting quote $\neg P$ from the same movie such that (i) $P$ and $\neg P$ are uttered by the same speaker, (ii) $P$ and $\neg P$ have the same number of words, (iii) $\neg P$ does not occur in the IMDb list of memorable quotes and (iv) $P$ and $\neg P$ are as close as possible to each other in the script (Danescu-Niculescu-Mizil et al., 2012).

**CORPS**. A set of 2,600 sentence pairs uttered by various politicians. We collected these pairs from CORPS, a freely available corpus of political speeches tagged with audience reactions (Guerini et al., 2013). The methodology that we used to build the pairs is very similar to Danescu-Niculescu-Mizil et al. (2012): for each $P$, where $P$ is the sentence preceding an audience reaction (e.g. `APPLAUSE`, `LAUGHTER`), we selected a contrasting single-sentence $\neg P$ from the same speech. We required $\neg P$ to be close to $P$ in the speech transcription, subject to the conditions that (i) $P$ and $\neg P$ are uttered by the same speaker - which is trivial since these are monologues, where a single speaker is addressing the audience - (ii) $P$ and $\neg P$ have the same number of words, and (iii) $\neg P$ is 5 to 15 sentences away from $P$. This last condition had to be imposed since, differently from movie quotes, we do not have the evidence of which fragment of the speech exactly provoked the audience reaction (i.e. it could be the combination of more than one sentence).

**Slogan**. A set of 1,533 slogans taken from online resources paired with non-slogans that are similar in content. We collected the non-slogans from the subset of the New York Times articles in English GigaWord – 5th Edition – released by Linguistic Data Consortium (LDC)[3]. For each slogan, we picked the most similar sentence in the New York Times articles having the same length and the highest LSA similarity (Deerwester et al., 1990) with the slogan. The LSA similarity approach that we used to collect the non-slogans is very similar to the approach used by Louis and Nenkova (2013) to collect the non-persuasive counterparts of successful news articles.

In Table 1, we sum up the criteria used in the construction of each dataset. As can be observed from the table, each dataset satisfies at least two of the three criteria described above. In the last two columns of the table, we also provide the average token length of the persuasive and non-persuasive sentences in each dataset. Finally, in Table 2 we provide examples of euphonic and persuasive sentences for each dataset together with their phonetic scores.

| | Criterion | | | Length | |
|---|---|---|---|---|---|
| DATASET | Author | Length | Topic | $P$ | $\neg P$ |
| CORPS | ✓ | ✓ | ✗ | 14.0 | 14.0 |
| Movie | ✓ | ✓ | ✗ | 9.7 | 9.7 |
| Slogan | ✗ | ✓ | ✓ | 5.0 | 5.0 |
| Twitter | ✓ | ✗ | ✓ | 16.2 | 15.4 |

Table 1: Criteria used in the construction of each dataset and average token length of persuasive and non-persuasive pairs

## 5 Data Analysis

To provide a first insight on the data, in Table 3 we report the average phonetic scores for each data set (Mann-Whitney U Test is used for statistical significance between $P$ and $\neg P$ samples, with Bonferroni correction to ameliorate issues with multiple comparisons). The results are partially in line with our expectations of the euphony phenomena being more relevant in the persuasive sentences across the datasets.

As can be observed from the table, the average rhyme scores are higher in persuasive sentences and

[2]CORPS and Slogans datasets can be downloaded at the following link: `https://github.com/marcoguerini/paired_datasets_for_persuasion/`

[3]`http://www.ldc.upenn.edu/Catalog/catalogEntry.jsp?catalogId=LDC2011T07`

| Dataset | Example | Rhyme | Alliteration | Plosive | Homogeneity |
|---|---|---|---|---|---|
| CORPS | I think we can do better and I think we must do better. | 0.789 | 0.737 | 0.342 | 0.631 |
| | It will be waged with determination and it will be waged until we win. | 0.566 | 0.679 | 0.189 | 0.736 |
| Movie | The night time is the right time. | 0.818 | 0.545 | 0.181 | 0.636 |
| | Beautiful.... beautiful butterfly... | 0.667 | 0.708 | 0.250 | 0.583 |
| | Dog eat dog, brother. | 0.533 | 0.533 | 0.400 | 0.400 |
| Slogan | Different Stores, Different Stories. | 0.621 | 0.896 | 0.207 | 0.690 |
| | Why ask why? Try Bud Dry | 0.625 | 0.625 | 0.312 | 0.437 |
| | Live, Love, Life. | 0.818 | 0.909 | 0.0 | 0.636 |
| Twitter | A Nerd in Need is a Nerd indeed. | 0.636 | 0.727 | 0.227 | 0.681 |
| | Easter cupcake baking!! | 0.0 | 0.0 | 0.412 | 0.470 |

Table 2: Euphonic examples of persuasive sentences from each dataset, along with their phonetic scores.

| | Rhyme | | Alliteration | | Plosive | | Homogeneity | |
|---|---|---|---|---|---|---|---|---|
| Dataset | $\mu$ | $\sigma$ | $\mu$ | $\sigma$ | $\mu$ | $\sigma$ | $\mu$ | $\sigma$ |
| $\text{CORPS}_{\neg P}$ | 0.233 | 0.143 | 0.208 | 0.142 | 0.187 | 0.058 | 0.603 | 0.173 |
| $\text{CORPS}_{P}$ | 0.245† | 0.152 | 0.223** | 0.154 | 0.194*** | 0.060 | 0.588** | 0.179 |
| $\text{Movie}_{\neg P}$ | 0.196 | 0.143 | 0.167 | 0.142 | 0.191 | 0.073 | 0.485 | 0.155 |
| $\text{Movie}_{P}$ | 0.214* | 0.165 | 0.196*** | 0.164 | 0.185† | 0.067 | 0.526*** | 0.164 |
| $\text{Slogan}_{\neg P}$ | 0.071 | 0.111 | 0.047 | 0.092 | 0.204 | 0.098 | 0.343 | 0.163 |
| $\text{Slogan}_{P}$ | 0.140*** | 0.194 | 0.123*** | 0.185 | 0.189*** | 0.098 | 0.366*** | 0.156 |
| $\text{Twitter}_{\neg P}$ | 0.204 | 0.116 | 0.180 | 0.114 | 0.188 | 0.058 | 0.617 | 0.134 |
| $\text{Twitter}_{P}$ | 0.216*** | 0.121 | 0.193*** | 0.120 | 0.185** | 0.055 | 0.636*** | 0.128 |

Table 3: Average phonetic scores for our datasets - ***, $p < .001$; **, $p < .01$; *, $p < .05$; †, not significant

the difference is highly significant for Slogan and Twitter ($p < .001$), slightly significant for Movie quotes ($p < .05$), but not significant for CORPS. The average alliteration scores are again higher in persuasive sentences and all the differences are highly significant in all datasets (apart from CORPS with $p < .01$). Plosives seem not to correlate well with our intuition of persuasiveness and euphony: either there is no significance (movie quotes) or the averages of euphonic scores are higher in the non-persuasive sentences (the difference is highly significant in slogans, and significant in Twitter). The only dataset that meets our expectation is CORPS with a highly significant difference in favor of persuasive sentences. Finally, the average homogeneity scores are significantly ($p < .001$) higher in persuasive sentences in all datasets except CORPS, where the scores of non-persuasive sentences are significantly higher ($p < .01$) than persuasive ones.

Without going into details of cross-dataset comparisons we would like to note that CORPS seems a very peculiar dataset in terms of average scores, as compared to the others. In terms of rhyme and alliteration, the average scores of non-persuasive sentences ($\neg P$) in CORPS are always higher than the persuasive sentences ($P$) in the other datasets ($p < .001$ in all cases), while for homogeneity the same holds apart from Twitter. These results may derive from the fact that a political speech is a carefully crafted text – aimed at influencing the audience – in its entirety, so also "non-persuasive" sentences in CORPS are on average more persuasive than in other datasets.

As a next step, we conducted another analysis on the distribution of "extreme cases", i.e. sentences that have a very high phonetic score at least in one feature. This analysis derives from the intuition that a euphonic sentence might be recognized as such by humans only if its phonetic scores are above a certain threshold. In fact, sound repetition in a sentence may occur by chance, as in "I saw **the** knife in **the** drawer", and the longer the sentence is, the higher the probability that phonetic scores will be non-zero even in absence of a euphonic effect. Therefore, the average scores for each phonetic device, as reported in Table 3, are only partially informative.

Given this premise, to evaluate the "persuasive power" of the phonetic devices taken into account,

| *Dataset* | $\hat{F}_{rh}(t)$ | $\hat{F}_{al}(t)$ | $\hat{F}_{pl}(t)$ | $\hat{F}_{ho}(t)$ |
|---|---|---|---|---|
| $\text{CORPS}_{\neg P}$ | 0.025 | 0.012 | 0.362 | 0.394 |
| $\text{CORPS}_{P}$ | 0.033** | 0.023** | 0.415*** | 0.363† |
| $\text{Movie}_{\neg P}$ | 0.018 | 0.011 | 0.397 | 0.092 |
| $\text{Movie}_{P}$ | 0.041*** | 0.025*** | 0.363† | 0.173*** |
| $\text{Slogan}_{\neg P}$ | 0.005 | 0.003 | 0.460 | 0.011 |
| $\text{Slogan}_{P}$ | 0.055*** | 0.043*** | 0.410*** | 0.018*** |
| $\text{Twitter}_{\neg P}$ | 0.006 | 0.003 | 0.385 | 0.377 |
| $\text{Twitter}_{P}$ | 0.012*** | 0.008*** | 0.364** | 0.449*** |

Table 4: Probability of examples above threshold, - ***, $p < .001$; **, $p < .01$; *, $p < .05$; †, not significant

we compare them in terms of empirical Complementary Cumulative Distribution Functions (CCDFs) of the persuasive/non-persuasive pairs in various datasets. These functions are commonly used to analyze online social networks in terms of growth in size and activity (see for example (Ahn et al., 2007; Jiang et al., 2010; Leskovec, 2008)) and also for measuring content diffusion, e.g. the number of retweets of a given content (Kwak et al., 2010). Here, we use CCDFs to account for the probability $P$ that the score of a phonetic device $d$ will be greater than $n$ indicating it with $\hat{F}_d(n)$. For example, the probability of having a text with more than .75 rhyme score is indicated with $\hat{F}_{rh}(.75) = \text{P}(\#\text{rhyme} > .75)$. To assess whether the CCDFs of the several types of texts we take into account show significant differences, we use the Kolmogorov-Smirnov goodness-of-fit test, which specifically targets cumulative distribution functions. In particular, for each phonetic device and dataset, we use a two-tailed Kolmogorov-Smirnov test (again with Bonferroni correction) to test whether the number of examples above the threshold is higher in the persuasive sentences than in their non-persuasive counterparts for that device.

Since we do not have a theoretical way to define such thresholds, we resort to empirically define them by using a specific dataset of euphonic sentences. Even if it might seem reasonable to consider poems as paradigmatic examples of "euphonic" writing, we discard them as the phonetic devices used in poems may span across sentences. Instead, we resort to tongue twisters as a gold reference of how a euphonic sentence should be. Accordingly, we collected a set of 534 tongue twisters from various online resources. Then, for each phonetic index we defined our thresholds as the average of the phonetic scores in this data, in particular: $t_{rh} = 0.55$ for rhyme, $t_{al} = 0.58$ for alliteration, $t_{pl} = 0.20$ for plosives and $t_{ho} = 0.68$ for homogeneity.

In Table 4, we report the results of our CCDF analysis. After analyzing the "extreme cases", where euphony is granted, we see that the trends found in Table 3 on the correlation between persuasiveness and euphony are confirmed and strengthened. The number of persuasive sentences with a rhyme score above threshold is 30% more than the non-persuasive ones in CORPS, while the difference is 90% in Twitter[4]. The ratio of persuasive sentences above threshold to non-persuasive ones is very high in movies and slogans (more than 2 and 10 respectively). All results are either highly significant or significant. For comparison, in Table 3 these differences are not significant for CORPS and only slightly significant ($p < .05$) for movies. Concerning alliteration, there are 85% more cases above threshold in the persuasive sentences of CORPS than the non-persuasive ones. For movie quotes and Twitter, the persuasive sentences above threshold are more than two times as many as the non-persuasive ones, while the ratio is more than 13 for slogans. All results are either highly significant or significant in line with the results of Table 3. Instead, for plosive scores we observe a negative or no correlation with persuasiveness, the only exception being CORPS. Regarding homogeneity, for CORPS the difference between persuasive and non-persuasive sentences is not significant (in Table 3 it was significantly in favor of non-persuasive sentences), while for the other datasets there is a highly significant difference in favor of persuasive sentences (between 20% and 80%). As a whole, these results confirm our intuition that phonetic features play a significant role with respect to persuasiveness. In the next section we will validate this claim by means of prediction experiments.

## 6 Prediction Experiments

In this section, we describe the prediction tasks (both within and across datasets) that we carried out to in-

[4]In the following the ratios are computed on the real values while Table 4 presents the rounded values.

vestigate the impact of the phonetic features on the detection of various forms of persuasiveness. We compare three different sets of features, namely phonetic, n-grams and their combination to understand whether phonetic information can improve the performance of standard lexical approaches. Similarly to Danescu-Niculescu-Mizil et al. (2012) and Tan et al. (2014), we formulate a pairwise classification problem such that given a pair $(s_1, s_2)$ consisting of sentences $s_1$ and $s_2$, the goal is to determine the more persuasive one (i.e., the one on the *left* or *right*). We can consider this as a binary classification task where for each instance (i.e., pair) the possible labels are *left* or *right*.

### 6.1 Dataset and preprocessing

For the prediction experiments, we used the four datasets described in Section 4 (i.e., CORPS, Twitter, Slogan and Movie), all of which consist of a persuasive sentence $P$ and its non-persuasive counterpart $(\neg P)$ labeled as either *left* or *right*. To make the positions of the sentences in a pair irrelevant (i.e. to provide symmetry), for each instance occurring in the original datasets (e.g., $(s_1, s_2)$ with label *left*), we added another instance including the same sentence pair in reverse order (i.e., $(s_2, s_1)$ with label *right*). As a preprocessing step, all the sentences were tokenized by using Stanford CoreNLP (Manning et al., 2014).

### 6.2 Classifier and features

We performed a 10-fold cross-validation on each dataset and experimented with three feature sets by using a Support Vector Machine (SVM) classifier (Cortes and Vapnik, 1995). We preferred SVM as a classifier due to its characteristic property to especially perform well on high-dimensional data (Weichselbraun et al., 2011).

The first feature set consists of the phonetic features (i.e. plosive, alliteration, rhyme and homogeneity scores as detailed in Section 3). The second feature set is a standard bag of word n-grams including unigrams, bigrams and trigrams. All the non-ascii characters, punctuations and numbers were ignored. The URLs and mentions in Twitter data were replaced with tags (i.e. *_URL_* and *_MENTION_* respectively). In addition, for the unigram features, stop words were filtered out. We did not apply this filtering for bigrams and trigrams to capture longer-range usage patterns such as propositional phrases. The third feature set is simply the union of both phonetic and n-gram features.

To find the best configuration for each dataset and feature set, we conducted a grid search over the degree of the polynomial kernel (1 or 2) and the number of features to be used (in the range between 1,000 and 20,000). Due to the low dimensionality of the phonetic feature set, feature selection was performed only for the feature sets including n-grams. The selection was performed based on the information gain of each feature.

| *Dataset* | *Phonetic* | *N-Gram* | *All* |
|---|---|---|---|
| CORPS | 0.589 (-, 1) | 0.733*** (4k, 1) | 0.736† (2k, 1) |
| Movie | 0.600 (-, 2) | 0.694*** (1k, 1) | 0.722*** (1k, 1) |
| Slogan | 0.700 (-, 2) | 0.826*** (3k, 1) | 0.883*** (5k, 1) |
| Twitter | 0.563 (-, 2) | 0.732*** (5k, 1) | 0.745*** (4k, 1) |

Table 5: Results of the within-dataset experiments.

### 6.3 Within-dataset experiments

For this set of experiments, we conducted a 10-fold cross validation on each dataset separately. In Table 5, for each dataset listed in the first column, in the subsequent columns we report the performance of the best model obtained with 10-fold cross validation using i) only phonetic features (*Phonetic*), ii) only n-grams (*N-Gram*), iii) both phonetic and n-gram features (*All*). As mentioned previously, for each pair $(s_1, s_2)$ consisting of sentences $s_1$ and $s_2$, our dataset contains another pair including the same sentences in reverse order (i.e., $(s_2, s_1)$), resulting in a symmetric and balanced dataset. Therefore, classification performance is measured in terms of accuracy (i.e., the percentage of pairs of which labels were correctly predicted). For each accuracy value, we also report in parenthesis the number of features selected and the kernel degree of the corresponding model. While the kernel degree did not make a big difference in the performance, the number of selected features had an important effect on the accuracy of the models. As can be observed from these values, the best performance on all the datasets is achieved with a relatively small number of features.

Among the values reported in the table, the ones followed by *** are significantly different $(p < .001)$

| *Dataset* | *N-Gram* | *N-Gram+Rhyme* | *N-Gram+Plosive* | *N-Gram+Homogeneity* | *N-Gram+Alliteration* |
|---|---|---|---|---|---|
| CORPS | 0.733 | $0.738^{\dagger}$ (3k, 1) | $0.740^{\dagger}$ (2k, 1) | $0.738^{\dagger}$ (3k, 1) | $0.738^{\dagger}$ (2k, 1) |
| Movie | 0.694 | $0.694^{\dagger}$ (1k, 1) | $0.692^{\dagger}$ (1k, 1) | $0.721^{***}$ (1k, 1) | $0.709^{**}$ (1k, 1) |
| Slogan | 0.826 | $0.864^{***}$ (2k, 1) | $0.824^{\dagger}$ (2k, 1) | $0.867^{***}$ (3k, 1) | $0.859^{***}$ (3k, 1) |
| Twitter | 0.732 | $0.740^{**}$ (4k, 1) | $0.733^{\dagger}$ (4k, 1) | $0.746^{***}$ (4k, 1) | $0.742^{***}$ (4k, 1) |

Table 6: Contribution of the phonetic features.

| | *Test* | | | | | | | | | | | |
|---|---|---|---|---|---|---|---|---|---|---|---|---|
| | CORPS | | | Twitter | | | Slogan | | | Movie | | |
| *Training* | *Phonetic* | *N-Gram* | *All* | *Phonetic* | *N-Gram* | *All* | *Phonetic* | *N-Gram* | *All* | *Phonetic* | *N-Gram* | *All* |
| CORPS | - | - | - | 0.463 | 0.508 | 0.523 | 0.508 | 0.517 | 0.539 | 0.411 | 0.506 | 0.516 |
| Twitter | 0.439 | 0.494 | 0.462 | - | - | - | 0.564 | 0.531 | 0.637 | 0.596 | 0.544 | 0.589 |
| Slogan | 0.535 | 0.512 | 0.514 | 0.535 | 0.510 | 0.539 | - | - | - | 0.532 | 0.545 | 0.588 |
| Movie | 0.431 | 0.513 | 0.498 | 0.562 | 0.533 | 0.560 | 0.581 | 0.537 | 0.589 | - | - | - |

Table 7: Results of the cross-dataset prediction experiments optimized on the training set.

from the ones to their left, while † represents no significance, as calculated according to McNemar's test (McNemar, 1947). For each dataset, the weakest models (i.e. the ones using only the phonetic features in all cases) are still significantly ($p < .001$) more accurate than a random baseline (accuracy = 50%). As can be observed from the table, the models using only n-grams significantly outperform the ones only based on phonetic features in all datasets. However, while the phonetic features are not very strong by themselves, their combination with n-grams results in models outperforming the n-gram based models in all cases. The difference is highly significant for all datasets except CORPS, where n-grams alone are sufficient to achieve a good performance. We speculate that the kind of persuasiveness used in political speeches is more dependent on the lexical choices of the speaker and on the use of a specific set of semantically loaded words such as *bless*, *victory*, *God* and *justice* or *military*. This is in line with the work of Guerini et al. (2008), who built a domain specific lexicon to study the persuasive impact of words in political speeches.

We also conducted an additional set of experiments to investigate if some phonetic features stand out among the others, and to find out the contribution and importance of each phonetic feature in isolation. To achieve that, for each dataset we conducted a 10-fold cross validation to obtain the best four models containing a single phonetic feature on top of n-gram features (i.e. *N-Gram+Rhyme*, *N-Gram+Plosive*, *N-Gram+Homogeneity* and *N-Gram+Alliteration*). In Table 6, we report the accuracy of the n-gram model and these four models for each dataset. Similarly to Table 5, for each accuracy value, we also report in parenthesis the number of features selected and the kernel degree of the corresponding model obtained with grid search. The results demonstrate that homegeneity is the most effective feature when added on top of n-grams, resulting in highly significant improvement against the basic n-gram models in three out of four datasets. Alliteration and rhyme closely follow homogeneity by yielding models that significantly outperform the n-gram models in three and two datasets respectively. Finally, the models containing plosives do not improve over the n-gram models in any of the four datasets. It is worth noting that in CORPS none of the n-gram models enriched with phonetic features improves over the basic n-gram models as in line with the results of the within-dataset experiments reported in Table 5.

### 6.4 Cross-dataset experiments

After observing that the combination of phonetic and n-gram features can be effective in the within-dataset prediction experiments, we took a further step and investigated the interaction of the three feature sets across datasets. More specifically, we classified each dataset with the best models (one for each feature set) trained on the other datasets. With these experiments, we investigated the ability of phonetic features to generalize across the different lexicons of the datasets. As we discussed previously, the four datasets represent different forms of persuasiveness. In this respect, the results of the cross-dataset experiments can also be interpreted as a measure of the degree of compatibility among these kinds of persuasiveness.

In Table 7, we present the results of the cross-dataset prediction experiments. For each training and test set pair, we report the accuracy of the best models, one for each feature set, based on cross-validation on the training set. As can be observed from the table, the figures are generally low and various domain adaptation techniques could be employed to improve the results. However, the objective of this evaluation is not to train an optimized cross-domain classifier, but to assess the potential of the feature sets to model different kinds of persuasiveness.

As expected, n-gram features show poor performance due to the lexical and stylistic differences among the datasets. In many cases, the phonetic models outperform the n-gram models, and in several cases the combination of the two feature sets deteriorates the performance of the phonetic features alone. These findings support our hypothesis that phonetic features, due to their generality, have better correlation with different forms of persuasiveness than lexical features. The experiments involving the CORPS dataset, both for training and testing, do not share this behavior. Indeed, when CORPS is used as a training or test dataset, the performance of the models is quite low (very close to or worse than the baseline in many cases) independently from the feature sets. These results suggest that the notion of persuasiveness encoded in this dataset is remarkably different from the others, as previously discussed in the data analysis in Section 5. As seen in the within dataset experiments (see Table 5), CORPS is the only dataset in which the combination of lexical and phonetic features do not improve the classification accuracy. This explains the inability of the phonetic features to improve the accuracy in cross-dataset experiments when this dataset is employed.

## 7 Conclusion

In this paper, we focused on the impact of a set of phonetic features – namely rhyme, alliteration, homogeneity and plosives – on various forms of persuasiveness including memorability of slogans and movie quotes, re-tweet counts of tweets, and effectiveness of political speeches. We conducted our analysis and experiments on four datasets comprising pairs of a persuasive sentence and a non-persuasive counterpart.

Our data analysis shows that persuasive sentences are generally euphonic. This finding is confirmed by the prediction experiments, in which we observed that phonetic features consistently help in the detection of persuasiveness. When combined with lexical features, they help improving classification performance on three of the four datasets that we considered. The key role played by phonetic features is further underlined by the cross-dataset experiments, in which we observed that phonetic features alone generally outperform the lexical features. To the best of our knowledge, this is the first systematic analysis of the impact of phonetic features on several types of persuasiveness. Our results should encourage researchers dealing with different aspects of persuasiveness to consider the inclusion of phonetic attributes in their models.

As future work, we will investigate the impact of other phonetic devices such as assonance, consonance and rhythm on persuasiveness. It would also be interesting to focus on the connection between sound symbolism and persuasiveness, and investigate how the context or domain of persuasive statements interacts with the sounds in those statements.

We would like to conclude this paper with the most favorite and retweeted tweet of @NAACL2015 (the Twitter account of the conference whose proceedings comprise this paper), which is a good example of the positive effect of euphony in persuasiveness:

*The deadline for @NAACL2015 paper submissions is approaching: Remember, remember, the 4th of December!*

## Acknowledgments

This work has been partially supported by the Trento RISE PerTe project.

## References


Yong-Yeol Ahn, Seungyeop Han, Haewoon Kwak, Sue Moon, and Hawoong Jeong. 2007. Analysis of topological characteristics of huge online social networking services. In *Proceedings of the 16th international conference on World Wide Web*, pages 835–844. ACM.

Tim Althoff, Cristian Danescu-Niculescu-Mizil, and Dan Jurafsky. 2014. How to ask for a favor: A case study on the success of altruistic requests. *Proocedings of ICWSM*.

Rka Benczes. 2013. The role of alliteration and rhyme in novel metaphorical and metonymical compounds. *Metaphor and Symbol*, 28(3):167–184.

Jonah A. Berger and Katherine L. Milkman. 2009. Social Transmission, Emotion, and the Virality of Online Content. *Social Science Research Network Working Paper Series*, December.

Bruce G. Vanden Bergh, Janay Collins, Myrna Schultz, and Keith Adler. 1984. Sound advice on brand names. *Journalism Quarterly*, 61(4):835, dec.

Luciano Bernardi, Cesare Porta, and Peter Sleight. 2006. Cardiovascular, cerebrovascular, and respiratory changes induced by different types of music in musicians and non-musicians: the importance of silence. *Heart*, 92(4):445–452.

Youmna Borghol, Sebastien Ardon, Niklas Carlsson, Derek Eager, and Anirban Mahanti. 2012. The untold story of the clones: Content-agnostic factors that impact youtube video popularity. In *Proceedings of the 18th ACM SIGKDD international conference on Knowledge discovery and data mining*, pages 1186–1194. ACM.

Shelly Chaiken. 1980. Heuristic vs. sistematic information processing and the use of source vs message cues in persuasion. *Journal of Personality and Social Psychology*, 39:752–766.

Robert B. Cialdini. 1993. *Influence. The psychology of persuasion*. William Morrow & Company, Inc., New York.

Corinna Cortes and Vladimir Vapnik. 1995. Support-vector networks. *Mach. Learn.*, 20(3):273–297, September.

Cristian Danescu-Niculescu-Mizil, Justin Cheng, Jon Kleinberg, and Lillian Lee. 2012. You had me at hello: How phrasing affects memorability. In *Proceedings of the ACL*.

Scott Deerwester, Susan T. Dumais, George W. Furnas, Thomas K. Landauer, and Richard Harshman. 1990. Indexing by latent semantic analysis. *Journal of the American Society for Information Science*, 41(6):391–407.

Marco Guerini, Carlo Strapparava, and Oliviero Stock. 2008. Corps: A corpus of tagged political speeches for persuasive communication processing. *Journal of Information Technology & Politics*, 5(1):19–32.

Marco Guerini, Carlo Strapparava, and Gözde Özbal. 2011. Exploring text virality in social networks. In *Proceedings of ICWSM-11*, Barcelona, Spain, July.

Marco Guerini, Alberto Pepe, and Bruno Lepri. 2012. Do linguistic style and readability of scientific abstracts affect their virality. *Proceedings of ICWSM-12*.

Marco Guerini, Danilo Giampiccolo, Giovanni Moretti, Rachele Sprugnoli, and Carlo Strapparava. 2013. The new release of corps: A corpus of political speeches annotated with audience reactions. In *Multimodal Communication in Political Speech. Shaping Minds and Social Action*, pages 86–98. Springer.

Chip Heath and Dan Heath. 2007. *Made to stick: Why some ideas survive and others die*. Random House.

Julian Jaynes. 2000. *The origin of consciousness in the breakdown of the bicameral mind*. Houghton Mifflin Harcourt.

Jing Jiang, Christo Wilson, Xiao Wang, Peng Huang, Wenpeng Sha, Yafei Dai, and Ben Y Zhao. 2010. Understanding latent interactions in online social networks. In *Proceedings of the 10th ACM SIGCOMM conference on Internet measurement*, pages 369–382. ACM.

Haewoon Kwak, Changhyun Lee, Hosung Park, and Sue Moon. 2010. What is twitter, a social network or a news media? In *Proceedings of the 19th international conference on World wide web*, pages 591–600. ACM.

Himabindu Lakkaraju, Julian J McAuley, and Jure Leskovec. 2013. What's in a name? understanding the interplay between titles, content, and communities in social media. In *ICWSM*.

Geoffrey N. Leech. 1966. *English in advertising : a linguistic study of advertising in Great Britain / [by] Geoffrey N. Leech*. Longmans London.

Jurij Leskovec. 2008. *Dynamics of large networks*. ProQuest.

Annie Louis and Ani Nenkova. 2013. What makes writing great? first experiments on article quality prediction in the science journalism domain. *TACL*, 1:341–352.

Christopher D. Manning, Mihai Surdeanu, John Bauer, Jenny Finkel, Steven J. Bethard, and David McClosky. 2014. The Stanford CoreNLP natural language processing toolkit. In *Proceedings of 52nd Annual Meeting of the Association for Computational Linguistics: System Demonstrations*, pages 55–60.

Quinn McNemar. 1947. Note on the sampling error of the difference between correlated proportions or percentages. *Psychometrika*, 12(2):153–157, jun.

Bernard Moulin, Hengameh Irandoust, Micheline Belanger, and Gaëlle Desordes. 2002. Explanation and argumentation capabilities: Towards the creation of more persuasive agents. *Artificial Intelligence Review*, 17:169–222.

Gözde Özbal, Carlo Strapparava, and Marco Guerini. 2012. Brand pitt: A corpus to explore the art of naming. In *Proceedings of the Eighth International Conference on Language Resources and Evaluation (LREC-2012)*. European Language Resources Association (ELRA).

Gözde Özbal, Daniele Pighin, and Carlo Strapparava. 2013. BRAINSUP: Brainstorming Support for Creative Sentence Generation. In *Proceedings of the 51st Annual Meeting of the Association for Computational Linguistics (ACL 2013)*, pages 1446–1455, Sofia, Bulgaria, August. Association for Computational Linguistics.

Gözde Özbal, Daniele Pighin, and Carlo Strapparava. 2014. Automation and evaluation of the keyword method for second language learning. In *Proceedings of the 52nd Annual Meeting of the Association for Computational Linguistics (Volume 2: Short Papers)*, pages 352–357. Association for Computational Linguistics.

Chaim Perelman and Lucie Olbrechts-Tyteca. 1969. *The new Rhetoric: a treatise on Argumentation.* Notre Dame Press.

Richard E. Petty and John T. Cacioppo. 1986. The elaboration likelihood model of persuasion. *Advances in Experimental Social Psychology*, 19:123–205.

Daniela Sammler, Stefan Koelsch, Tonio Ball, Armin Brandt, Maren Grigutsch, Hans-Jürgen Huppertz, Thomas R Knösche, Jörg Wellmer, Guido Widman, Christian E Elger, et al. 2013. Co-localizing linguistic and musical syntax with intracranial eeg. *NeuroImage*, 64:134–146.

Matthew Simmons, Lada A Adamic, and Eytan Adar. 2011. Memes online: Extracted, subtracted, injected, and recollected. *Proceedings of ICWSM-11*.

Chenhao Tan, Lillian Lee, and Bo Pang. 2014. The effect of wording on message propagation: Topic-and author-controlled natural experiments on twitter. *ACL*.

Stephen Toulmin. 1958. *The Use of Arguments*. Cambridge University Press, Cambridge MA.

Katie Wales. 2001. *A dictionary of stylistics*. Harlow, Eng. ; New York : Longman, 2nd ed edition. Includes bibliographical references (p. 413-429).

Douglas N. Walton. 1996. *Argumentation Schemes for Presumptive Reasoning*. Lawrence Erlbaum Associates, Mahwah, New Jersey.

Albert Weichselbraun, Stefan Gindl, and Arno Scharl. 2011. Using games with a purpose and bootstrapping to create domain-specific sentiment lexicons. In *Proceedings of the 20th ACM International Conference on Information and Knowledge Management*, CIKM '11, pages 1053–1060, New York, NY, USA. ACM.

# Translating Videos to Natural Language Using Deep Recurrent Neural Networks


**Subhashini Venugopalan**
UT Austin
Austin, TX
vsub@cs.utexas.edu

**Huijuan Xu**
UMass Lowell
Lowell, MA
hxu1@cs.uml.edu

**Jeff Donahue**
UC Berkeley, ICSI
Berkeley, CA
jdonahue@eecs.berkeley.edu

**Marcus Rohrbach**
UC Berkeley, ICSI
Berkeley, CA
rohrbach@eecs.berkeley.edu

**Raymond Mooney**
UT Austin
Austin, TX
mooney@cs.utexas.edu

**Kate Saenko**
UMass Lowell
Lowell, MA
saenko@cs.uml.edu



## Abstract

Solving the visual symbol grounding problem has long been a goal of artificial intelligence. The field appears to be advancing closer to this goal with recent breakthroughs in deep learning for natural language grounding in static images. In this paper, we propose to translate videos directly to sentences using a unified deep neural network with both convolutional and recurrent structure. Described video datasets are scarce, and most existing methods have been applied to toy domains with a small vocabulary of possible words. By transferring knowledge from 1.2M+ images with category labels and 100,000+ images with captions, our method is able to create sentence descriptions of open-domain videos with large vocabularies. We compare our approach with recent work using language generation metrics, subject, verb, and object prediction accuracy, and a human evaluation.


## 1 Introduction

For most people, watching a brief video and describing what happened (in words) is an easy task. For machines, extracting the meaning from video pixels and generating natural-sounding language is a very complex problem. Solutions have been proposed for narrow domains with a small set of known actions and objects, e.g., (Barbu et al., 2012; Rohrbach et al., 2013), but generating descriptions for "in-the-wild" videos such as the YouTube domain (Figure 1) remains an open challenge.

Progress in open-domain video description has been difficult in part due to large vocabularies and very limited training data consisting of videos with associated descriptive sentences. Another serious obstacle has been the lack of rich models that can capture the joint dependencies of a sequence of frames and a corresponding sequence of words. Previous work has simplified the problem by detecting a fixed set of semantic roles, such as subject, verb, and object (Guadarrama et al., 2013; Thomason et al., 2014), as an intermediate representation. This fixed representation is problematic for large vocabularies and also leads to oversimplified rigid sentence templates which are unable to model the complex structures of natural language.

***Input video:***

***Our output:*** *A cat is playing with a toy.*
***Humans:*** *A Ferret and cat fighting with each other. / A cat and a ferret are playing. / A kitten is playing with a ferret. / A kitten and a ferret are playfully wrestling.*

Figure 1: Our system takes a short video as input and outputs a natural language description of the main activity in the video.

In this paper, we propose to translate from video pixels to natural language with a single deep neural network. Deep NNs can learn powerful features (Donahue et al., 2013; Zeiler and Fergus, 2014), but require a lot of supervised training data. We address the problem by transferring knowledge from auxiliary tasks. Each frame of the video is modeled by a convolutional (spatially-invariant) network pre-trained on 1.2M+ images with category labels (Krizhevsky et al., 2012). The meaning state



*Human Language Technologies: The 2015 Annual Conference of the North American Chapter of the ACL*, pages 1494–1504,
Denver, Colorado, May 31 – June 5, 2015. 

and sequence of words is modeled by a recurrent (temporally invariant) deep network pre-trained on 100K+ Flickr (Hodosh and Hockenmaier, 2014) and COCO (Lin et al., 2014) images with associated sentence captions. We show that such knowledge transfer significantly improves performance on the video task.

Our approach is inspired by recent breakthroughs reported by several research groups in image-to-text generation, in particular, the work by Donahue et al. (2014). They applied a version of their model to video-to-text generation, but stopped short of proposing an end-to-end single network, using an intermediate role representation instead. Also, they showed results only on the narrow domain of cooking videos with a small set of pre-defined objects and actors. Inspired by their approach, we utilize a Long-Short Term Memory (LSTM) recurrent neural network (Hochreiter and Schmidhuber, 1997) to model sequence dynamics, but connect it directly to a deep convolutional neural network to process incoming video frames, avoiding supervised intermediate representations altogether. This model is similar to their image-to-text model, but we adapt it for video sequences.

Our proposed approach has several important advantages over existing video description work. The LSTM model, which has recently achieved state-of-the-art results on machine translation tasks (French and English (Sutskever et al., 2014)), effectively models the sequence generation task without requiring the use of fixed sentence templates as in previous work (Guadarrama et al., 2013). Pre-training on image and text data naturally exploits related data to supplement the limited amount of descriptive video currently available. Finally, the deep convnet, the winner of the ILSVRC2012 (Russakovsky et al., 2014) image classification competition, provides a strong visual representation of objects, actions and scenes depicted in the video.

Our main contributions are as follows:

- We present the first end-to-end deep model for video-to-text generation that simultaneously learns a latent "meaning" state, and a fluent grammatical model of the associated language.

- We leverage still image classification and caption data and transfer deep networks learned on such data to the video domain.

- We provide a detailed evaluation of our model on the popular YouTube corpus (Chen and Dolan, 2011) and demonstrate a significant improvement over the state of the art.

## 2 Related Work

Most of the existing research in video description has focused on narrow domains with limited vocabularies of objects and activities (Kojima et al., 2002; Lee et al., 2008; Khan and Gotoh, 2012; Barbu et al., 2012; Ding et al., 2012; Khan and Gotoh, 2012; Das et al., 2013b; Das et al., 2013a; Rohrbach et al., 2013; Yu and Siskind, 2013). For example, Rohrbach et al. (2013), Rohrbach et al. (2014) produce descriptions for videos of several people cooking in the same kitchen. These approaches generate sentences by first predicting a semantic role representation, e.g., modeled with a CRF, of high-level concepts such as the actor, action and object. Then they use a template or statistical machine translation to translate the semantic representation to a sentence.

Most work on "in-the-wild" online video has focused on retrieval and predicting event tags rather than generating descriptive sentences; examples are tagging YouTube (Aradhye et al., 2009) and retrieving online video in the TRECVID competition (Over et al., 2012). Work on TRECVID has also included clustering both video and text features for video retrieval, e.g., (Wei et al., 2010; Huang et al., 2013).

The previous work on the YouTube corpus we employ (Motwani and Mooney, 2012; Krishnamoorthy et al., 2013; Guadarrama et al., 2013; Thomason et al., 2014) used a two-step approach, first detecting a fixed tuple of role words, such as subject, verb, object, and scene, and then using a template to generate a grammatical sentence. They also utilize language models learned from large text corpora to aid visual interpretation as well as sentence generation. We compare our method to the best-performing method of Thomason et al. (2014). A recent paper by Xu et al. (2015) extracts deep features from video and a continuous vector from language, and projects both to a joint semantic space. They apply their joint embedding to SVO prediction and generation, but do not provide quantitative generation results. Our network learns a joint state vector implicitly, and additionally models sequence dynamics of the language.

Predicting natural language desriptions of still images has received considerable attention, with some of the earliest works by Aker and Gaizauskas (2010), Farhadi et al. (2010), Yao et al. (2010), and Kulkarni et al. (2011) amongst others. Propelled by successes of deep learning, several groups released record breaking results in just the past year (Donahue et al., 2014; Mao et al., 2014; Karpathy et al., 2014; Fang et al., 2014; Kiros et al., 2014; Vinyals et al., 2014; Kuznetsova et al., 2014).

In this work, we use deep recurrent nets (RNNs), which have recently demonstrated strong results for machine translation tasks using Long Short Term Memory (LSTM) RNNs (Sutskever et al., 2014; Cho et al., 2014). In contrast to traditional statistical MT (Koehn, 2010), RNNs naturally combine with vector-based representations, such as those for images and video. Donahue et al. (2014) and Vinyals et al. (2014) simultaneously proposed a multimodal analog of this model, with an architecture which uses a visual convnet to encode a deep state vector, and an LSTM to decode the vector into a sentence.

Our approach to video to text generation is inspired by the work of Donahue et al. (2014), who also applied a variant of their model to video-to-text generation, but stopped short of training an end-to-end model. Instead they converted the video to an intermediate role representation using a CRF, then decoded that representation into a sentence. In contrast, we bypass detection of high-level roles and use the output of a deep convolutional network directly as the state vector that is decoded into a sentence. This avoids the need for labeling semantic roles, which can be difficult to detect in the case of very large vocabularies. It also allows us to first pre-train the model on a large image and caption database, and transfer the knowledge to the video domain where the corpus size is smaller. While Donahue et al. (2014) only showed results on a narrow domain of cooking videos with a small set of pre-defined objects and actors, we generate sentences for open-domain YouTube videos with a vocabulary of thousands of words.

## 3 Approach

Figure 2 depicts our model for sentence generation from videos. Our framework is based on deep image description models in Donahue et al. (2014);Vinyals

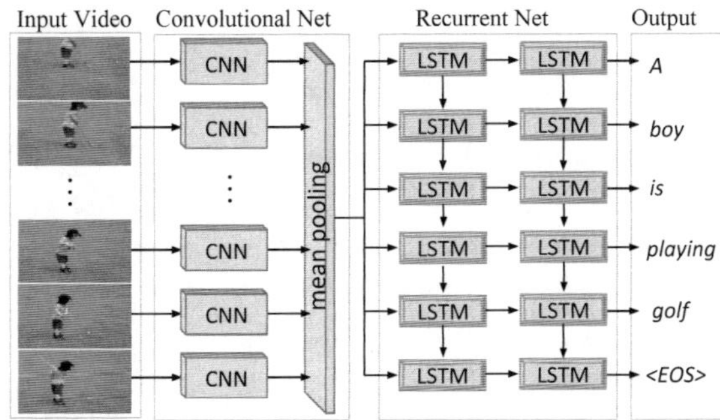

Figure 2: The structure of our video description network. We extract $fc_7$ features for each frame, mean pool the features across the entire video and input this at every time step to the LSTM network. The LSTM outputs one word at each time step, based on the video features (and the previous word) until it picks the end-of-sentence tag.

et al. (2014) and extends them to generate sentences describing events in videos. These models work by first applying a feature transformation on an image to generate a fixed dimensional vector representation. They then use a sequence model, specifically a Recurrent Neural Network (RNN), to "decode" the vector into a sentence (i.e. a sequence of words). In this work, we apply the same principle of "translating" a visual vector into an English sentence and show that it works well for describing dynamic videos as well as static images.

We identify the most likely description for a given video by training a model to maximize the log likelihood of the sentence $S$, given the corresponding video $V$ and the model parameters $\theta$,

$$\theta^* = \underset{\theta}{\operatorname{argmax}} \sum_{(V,S)} \log p(S|V;\theta) \tag{1}$$

Assuming a generative model of $S$ that produces each word in the sequence in order, the log probability of the sentence is given by the sum of the log probabilities over the words and can be expressed as:

$$\log p(S|V) = \sum_{t=0}^{N} \log p(S_{w_t}|V, S_{w_1}, \ldots, S_{w_{t-1}})$$

where $S_{w_i}$ represents the $i^{th}$ word in the sentence and N is the total number of words. Note that we have dropped $\theta$ for convenience.

A sequence model would be apt to model $p(S_{w_t}|V, S_{w_1}, \ldots, S_{w_{t-1}})$, and we choose an RNN. An RNN, parameterized by $\theta$, maps an input $x_t$, and the previously seen words expressed as a hidden state or memory, $h_{t-1}$ to an output $z_t$ and an updated state $h_t$ using a non-linear function $f$:

$$h_t = f_\theta(x_t, h_{t-1}) \quad (2)$$

where ($h_0 = 0$). In our work we use the highly successful Long Short-Term Memory (LSTM) net as the sequence model, since it has shown superior performance on tasks such as speech recognition (Graves and Jaitly, 2014), machine translation (Sutskever et al., 2014; Cho et al., 2014) and the more related task of generating sentence descriptions of images (Donahue et al., 2014; Vinyals et al., 2014). To be specific, we use two layers of LSTMs (one LSTM stacked atop another) as shown in Figure 2. We present details of the network in Section 3.1. To convert videos to a fixed length representation (input $x_t$), we use a Convolutional Neural Network (CNN). We present details of how we apply the CNN model to videos in Section 3.2.

### 3.1 LSTMs for sequence generation

A Recurrent Neural Network (RNN) is a generalization of feed forward neural networks to sequences. Standard RNNs learn to map a sequence of inputs $(x_1, \ldots, x_t)$ to a sequence of hidden states $(h_1, \ldots, h_t)$, and from the hidden states to a sequence of outputs $(z_1, \ldots, z_t)$ based on the following recurrences:

$$h_t = f(W_{xh}x_t + W_{hh}h_{t-1}) \quad (3)$$
$$z_t = g(W_{zh}h_t) \quad (4)$$

where $f$ and $g$ are element-wise non-linear functions such as a sigmoid or hyperbolic tangent, $x_t$ is a fixed length vector representation of the input, $h_t \in \mathbb{R}^N$ is the hidden state with $N$ units, $W_{ij}$ are the weights connecting the layers of neurons, and $z_t$ the output vector.

RNNs can learn to map sequences for which the alignment between the inputs and outputs is known ahead of time (Sutskever et al., 2014) however it's unclear if they can be applied to problems where the inputs ($x_i$) and outputs ($z_i$) are of varying lengths. This problem is solved by learning to map sequences of inputs to a fixed length vector using one RNN, and then map the vector to an output sequence using another RNN. Another known problem with RNNs is that, it can be difficult to train them to learn long-range dependencies (Hochreiter et al., 2001). However, LSTMs (Hochreiter and Schmidhuber, 1997), which incorporate explicitly controllable memory units, are known to be able to learn long-range temporal dependencies. In our work we use the LSTM unit in Figure 3, described in Zaremba and Sutskever (2014), and Donahue et al. (2014).

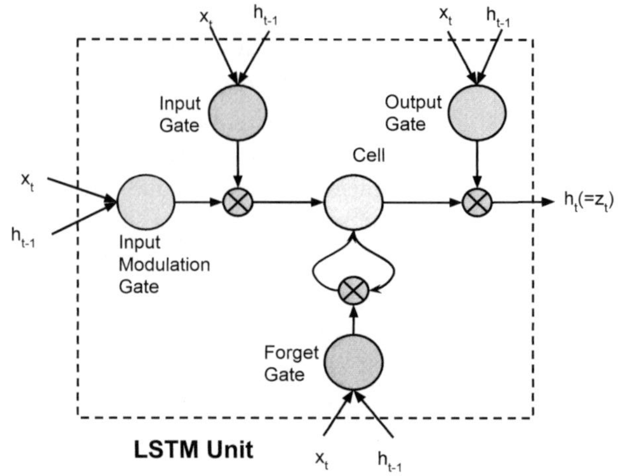


Figure 3: The LSTM unit replicated from (Donahue et al., 2014). The memory cell is at the core of the LSTM unit and it is modulated by the input, output and forget gates controlling how much knowledge is transferred at each time step.

At the core of the LSTM model is a memory cell $c$ which encodes, at every time step, the knowledge of the inputs that have been observed up to that step. The cell is modulated by gates which are all sigmoidal, having range $[0, 1]$, and are applied multiplicatively. The gates determine whether the LSTM keeps the value from the gate (if the layer evaluates to 1) or discards it (if it evaluates to 0). The three gates – input gate ($i$) controlling whether the LSTM considers its current input ($x_t$), the forget gate ($f$) allowing the LSTM to forget its previous memory ($c_{t-1}$), and the output gate ($o$) deciding how much of the memory to transfer to the hidden state ($h_t$), all enable the LSTM to learn complex long-term dependencies. The recurrences for the LSTM are then defined as:

$$i_t = \sigma(W_{xi}x_t + W_{hi}h_{t-1}) \quad (5)$$
$$f_t = \sigma(W_{xf}x_t + W_{hf}h_{t-1}) \quad (6)$$
$$o_t = \sigma(W_{xo}x_t + W_{ho}h_{t-1}) \quad (7)$$
$$c_t = f_t \odot c_{t-1} + i_t \odot \phi(W_{xc}x_t + W_{hc}h_{t-1}) \quad (8)$$
$$h_t = o_t \odot \phi(c_t) \quad (9)$$

where $\sigma$ is the sigmoidal non-linearity, $\phi$ is the hyperbolic tangent non-linearity, $\odot$ represents the product with the gate value, and the weight matrices denoted by $W_{ij}$ are the trained parameters.

### 3.2 CNN-LSTMs for video description

We use a two layer LSTM model for generating descriptions for videos based on experiments by Donahue et al. (2014) which suggest two LSTM layers are better than four and a single layer for image to text tasks. We employ the LSTM to "decode" a visual feature vector representing the video to generate textual output. The first step in this process is to generate a fixed-length visual input that effectively summarizes a short video. For this we use a CNN, specifically the publicly available *Caffe* (Jia et al., 2014) reference model, a minor variant of *AlexNet* (Krizhevsky et al., 2012). The net is pre-trained on the 1.2M image ILSVRC-2012 object classification subset of the ImageNet dataset (Russakovsky et al., 2014) and hence provides a robust initialization for recognizing objects and thereby expedites training. We sample frames in the video (1 in every 10 frames) and extract the output of the $fc_7$ layer and perform a mean pooling over the frames to generate a single 4,096 dimension vector for each video. The resulting visual feature vector forms the input to the first LSTM layer. We stack another LSTM layer on top as in Figure 2, and the hidden state of the LSTM in the first layer is the input to the LSTM unit in the second layer. A word from the sentence forms the target of the output LSTM unit. In this work, we represent words using "one-hot" vectors (i.e 1-of-N coding, where is N is the vocabulary size).

**Training and Inference:** The two-layer LSTM model is trained to predict the next word $S_{w_t}$ in the sentence given the visual features and the previous $t-1$ words, $p(S_{w_t}|V, S_{w_1}, \ldots, S_{w_{t-1}})$. During training the visual feature, sentence pair $(V, S)$ is provided to the model, which then optimizes the log-likelihood (Equation 1) over the entire training dataset using stochastic gradient descent. At each time step, the input $x_t$ is fed to the LSTM along with the previous time step's hidden state $h_{t-1}$ and the LSTM emits the next hidden state vector $h_t$ (and a word). For the first layer of the LSTM $x_t$ is the concatenation of the visual feature vector and the previous encoded word ($S_{w_{t-1}}$, the ground truth word during training and the predicted word during test time). For the second layer of the LSTM $x_t$ is $z_t$ of the first layer. Accordingly, inference must also be performed sequentially in the order $h_1 = f_W(x_1, 0)$, $h_2 = f_W(x_2, h_1)$, until the model emits the end-of-sentence (EOS) token at the final step $T$. In our model the output ($h_t = z_t$) of the second layer LSTM unit is used to obtain the emitted word. We apply the Softmax function, to get a probability distribution over the words $w$ in the vocabulary $D$.

$$p(w|z_t) = \frac{\exp(W_w z_t)}{\sum_{w' \in D} \exp(W_{w'} z_t)} \tag{10}$$

where $W_w$ is a learnt embedding vector for word $w$. At test time, we choose the word $\hat{w}$ with the maximum probability for each time step $t$ until we obtain the EOS token.

### 3.3 Transfer Learning from Captioned Images

Since the training data available for video description is quite limited (described in Section 4.1), we also leverage much larger datasets available for image captioning to train our LSTM model and then fine tune it on the video dataset. Our LSTM model for images is the same as the one described above for single video frames (in Section 3.1, and 3.2). As with videos, we extract $fc_7$ layer features (4096 dimensional vector) from the network (Section 3.2) for the images. This forms the visual feature that is input to the 2-layer LSTM description model. The vocabulary is the combined set of words in the video and image datasets. After the model is trained on the image dataset, we use the weights of the trained model to initialize the LSTM model for the video description task. Additionally, we reduce the learning rate on our LSTM model to allow it to tune to the video dataset. This speeds up training and allows exploiting knowledge previously learned for image description.

## 4 Experiments

### 4.1 Datasets

**Video dataset.** We perform all our experiments on the Microsoft Research Video Description Corpus (Chen and Dolan, 2011). This video corpus is a collection of 1970 YouTube snippets. The duration of each clip is between 10 seconds to 25 seconds, typically depicting a single activity or a short sequence. The dataset comes with several human generated descriptions in a number of languages; we use the roughly 40 available English descriptions per video. This dataset (or portions of it) have been used in several prior works (Motwani and Mooney, 2012; Krishnamoorthy et al., 2013; Guadarrama et al., 2013; Thomason et al., 2014; Xu et al., 2015) on action recognition and video description tasks. For our task we pick 1200 videos to be used as training data, 100 videos for validation and 670 videos for testing, as used by the prior works on video description (Guadarrama et al., 2013; Thomason et al., 2014; Xu et al., 2015).

**Domain adaptation, image description datasets.** Since the number of videos for the description task is quite small when compared to the size of the datasets used by LSTM models in other tasks such as translation (Sutskever et al., 2014) (12M sentences), we use data from the Flickr30k and COCO2014 datasets for training and learn to adapt to the video dataset by fine-tuning the image description models. The Flickr30k (Hodosh and Hockenmaier, 2014) dataset has about 30,000 images, each with 5 or more descriptions. We hold out 1000 images at random for validation and use the remaining for training. In addition to this, we use the recent COCO2014 (Lin et al., 2014) image description dataset consisting of 82,783 training images and 40,504 validation images, each with 5 or more sentence descriptions. We perform ablation experiments by training models on each dataset individually, and on the combination and report results on the YouTube video test dataset.

### 4.2 Models

**HVC** This is the Highest Vision Confidence model described in (Thomason et al., 2014). The model uses strong visual detectors to predict confidence over 45 subjects, 218 verbs and 241 objects.

**FGM** (Thomason et al., 2014) also propose a factor graph model (FGM) that combines knowledge mined from text corpora with visual confidences from the HVC model using a factor graph and performs probabilistic inference to determine the most likely subject, verb, object and scene tuple. They then use a simple template to generate a sentence from the tuple. In this work, we compare the output of our model to the subject, verb, object words predicted by the HVC and FGM models and the sentences generated from the SVO triple.

**Our LSTM models** We present four main models. LSTM-YT is our base two-layer LSTM model trained on the YouTube video dataset. LSTM-YT$_{flickr}$ is the model trained on the Flickr30k (Hodosh and Hockenmaier, 2014) dataset, and fine tuned on the YouTube dataset as descibed in Section 3.3. LSTM-YT$_{coco}$ is first trained on the COCO2014 (Lin et al., 2014) dataset and then fine-tuned on the video dataset. Our final model, LSTM-YT$_{cocoflickr}$ is trained on the combined data of both the Flickr and COCO models and is tuned on YouTube. To compare the overlap in content between the image dataset and YouTube dataset, we use the model trained on just the Flickr images (LSTM$_{flickr}$) and just the COCO images (LSTM$_{coco}$) and evaluate their performance on the test videos.

### 4.3 Evaluation Metrics and Results

**SVO accuracy.** Earlier works (Krishnamoorthy et al., 2013; Guadarrama et al., 2013) that reported results on the YouTube dataset compared their method based on how well their model could predict the subject, verb, and object (SVO) depicted in the video. Since these models first predicted the content (SVO triples) and then generated the sentences, the S,V,O accuracy captured the quality of the content generated by the models. However, in our case the sequential LSTM directly outputs the sentence, so we extract the S,V,O from the dependency parse of the generated sentence. We present, in Table 1 and Table 2, the accuracy of S,V,O words comparing the performance of our model against any valid ground truth triple and the most frequent triple found in human description for each video. The latter evaluation was also reported by (Xu et al., 2015), so we include it here for comparison.

**Sentence Generation.** To evaluate the generated sentences we use the BLEU (Papineni et al., 2002) and METEOR (Banerjee and Lavie, 2005) scores against all ground truth sentences. BLEU is the metric that is seen more commonly in image description literature, but a more recent study (Elliott and Keller, 2014) has shown METEOR to be a better evaluation metric. However, since both metrics have been shown to correlate well with human eval-

| Model | S% | V% | O% |
|---|---|---|---|
| HVC (Thomason et al., 2014) | 86.87 | 38.66 | 22.09 |
| FGM (Thomason et al., 2014) | **88.27** | 37.16 | 24.63 |
| LSTM$_{flickr}$ | 79.95 | 15.47 | 13.94 |
| LSTM$_{coco}$ | 56.30 | 06.90 | 14.86 |
| LSTM-YT | 79.40 | 35.52 | 20.59 |
| LSTM-YT$_{flickr}$ | 84.92 | 38.66 | 21.64 |
| LSTM-YT$_{coco}$ | 86.58 | 42.23 | **26.69** |
| LSTM-YT$_{coco+flickr}$ | 87.27 | **42.79** | 24.23 |

Table 1: SVO accuracy: Binary SVO accuracy compared against any valid S,V,O triples in the ground truth descriptions. We extract S,V,O values from sentences output by our model using a dependency parser. The model is correct if it identifies S,V, or O mentioned in any one of the multiple human descriptions.

| Model | S% | V% | O% |
|---|---|---|---|
| HVC (Thomason et al., 2014) | 76.57 | 22.24 | 11.94 |
| FGM (Thomason et al., 2014) | 76.42 | 21.34 | 12.39 |
| JointEmbed[1] (Xu et al., 2015) | **78.25** | 24.45 | 11.95 |
| LSTM$_{flickr}$ | 70.80 | 10.02 | 07.84 |
| LSTM$_{coco}$ | 47.44 | 02.85 | 07.05 |
| LSTM-YT | 71.19 | 19.40 | 09.70 |
| LSTM-YT$_{flickr}$ | 75.37 | 21.94 | 10.74 |
| LSTM-YT$_{coco}$ | 76.01 | 23.38 | **14.03** |
| LSTM-YT$_{coco+flickr}$ | 75.61 | **25.31** | 12.42 |

Table 2: SVO accuracy: Binary SVO accuracy compared against most frequent S,V,O triple in the ground truth descriptions. We extract S,V,O values from parses of sentences output by our model using a dependency parser. The model is correct only if it outputs the most frequently mentioned S, V, O among the human descriptions.

uations, we compare the generated sentences using both and present our results in Table 3.

**Human Evaluation.** We used Amazon Mechanical Turk to also collect human judgements. We created a task which employed three Turk workers to watch each video, and rank sentences generated by the different models from "Most Relevant" (5) to "Least Relevant" (1). No two sentences could have the same rank unless they were identical. We also evaluate sentences on grammatical correctness. We created a different task which required workers to rate sentences based on grammar. This task

[1]They evaluate against a filtered set of groundtruth SVO words which provides a tiny boost to their scores.

| Model | BLEU | METEOR |
|---|---|---|
| FGM (Thomason et al., 2014) | 13.68 | 23.90 |
| LSTM-YT | 31.19 | 26.87 |
| LSTM-YT$_{flickr}$ | 32.03 | 27.87 |
| LSTM-YT$_{coco}$ | **33.29** | **29.07** |
| LSTM-YT$_{coco+flickr}$ | **33.29** | 28.88 |

Table 3: Scores for BLEU at 4 (combined n-gram 1-4), and METEOR scores from automated evaluation metrics comparing the quality of the generation. All values are reported as percentage (%).

| Model | Relevance | Grammar |
|---|---|---|
| FGM (Thomason et al., 2014) | 2.26 | **3.99** |
| LSTM-YT | 2.74 | 3.84 |
| LSTM-YT$_{coco}$ | **2.93** | 3.46 |
| LSTM-YT$_{coco+flickr}$ | 2.83 | 3.64 |
| GroundTruth | 4.65 | 4.61 |

Table 4: Human evaluation mean scores. Sentences were uniquely ranked between 1 to 5 based on their relevance to a given video. Sentences were rated between 1 to 5 for grammatical correctness. Higher values are better.

displayed only the sentences and did not show any video. Here, workers had to choose a rating between 1-5 for each sentence. Multiple sentences could have the same rating. We discard responses from workers who fail gold-standard items and report the mean ranking/rating for each of the evaluated models in Table 4.

**Individual Frames.** In order to evaluate the effectiveness of mean pooling, we performed experiments to train and test the model on individual frames from the video. Our first set of experiments involved testing how well the image description models performed on a randomly sampled frame in the video. Similar to Tables 1 and 2, the model trained on Flickr30k when tested on random frames from the video scored better on subjects and verbs with any valid accuracy of 75.16% and 11.65% respectively; and 9.01% on objects. The one trained on COCO did better on objects (12.54%, any valid accuracy) but very poorly on subjects and verbs. In our next experiment, we used image description models (trained on Flickr30k, COCO or a combination of both) and fine-tuned them on individual frames in the video by picking a different frame

| Model (individual frames) | BLEU | METEOR |
|---|---|---|
| $\text{LSTM}_{flickr}$ | 08.62 | 18.56 |
| $\text{LSTM}_{coco}$ | 11.39 | 20.03 |
| LSTM-YT-$\text{frame}_{flickr}$ | 26.75 | 26.51 |
| LSTM-YT-$\text{frame}_{coco}$ | **30.77** | **27.66** |
| LSTM-YT-$\text{frame}_{coco+flickr}$ | 29.72 | 27.65 |

Table 5: Scores for BLEU at 4 (combined n-gram 1-4), and METEOR scores comparing the quality of sentence generation by the models trained on Flickr30k and COCO and tested on a random frame from the video. LSTM-YT-frame models were fine tuned on individual frames from the Youtube video dataset. All values are reported as percentage (%).

for each description in the YouTube dataset. These models were tested on a random frame from the test video. The overall trends in the results were similar to those seen in Tables 1 and 2. The model trained on COCO and fine-tuned on individual video frames performed best with any valid S,V,O accuracies $84.8\%, 38.98\%$, and $22.34\%$ respectively. The one trained on both COCO and Flickr30k had any valid S,V,O accuracies of $85.67\%, 38.83\%$, and $19.72\%$. We report the generation results for these models in Table 5.

## 5 Discussion

**Image only models.** The models trained purely on the image description data $\text{LSTM}_{flickr}$ and $\text{LSTM}_{coco}$ achieve lower accuracy on the verbs and objects (Tables 1, 2) since the YouTube videos encompass a wider domain and a variety of actions not detectable from static images.

**Base LSTM model.** We note that in the SVO binary accuracy metrics (Tables 1 and 2), the base LSTM model (LSTM-YT) achieves a slightly lower accuracy compared to prior work. This is likely due to the fact that previous work explicitly optimizes to identify the best subject, verb and object for a video; whereas the LSTM model is trained on objects and actions jointly in a sentence and needs to learn to interpret these in different contexts. However, with regard to the generation metrics BLEU and METEOR, training based on the full sentence helps the LSTM model develop fluency and vocabulary similar to that seen in the training descriptions and allows it to outperform the template based generation.

**Transferring helps.** From our experiments, it is clear that learning from the image description data improves the performance of the model in all criteria of evaluation. We present a few examples demonstrating this in Figure 4. The model that was pre-trained on COCO2014 shows a larger performance improvement, indicating that our model can effectively leverage a large auxiliary source of training data to improve its object and verb predictions. The model pre-trained on the combined data of Flickr30k and COCO2014 shows only a marginal improvement, perhaps due to overfitting. Adding dropout as in (Vinyals et al., 2014) is likely to help prevent overfitting and improve performance.

From the automated evaluation in Table 3 it is clear that the fully deep video-to-text generation models outperform previous work. As mentioned previously, training on the full sentences is probably the main reason for the improvements.

**Testing on individual frames.** The experiments that evaluated models on individual frames (Section 4.3) from the video have trends similar to those seen on mean pooled frame features. Specifically, the model trained on Flickr30k, when directly evaluated on YouTube video frames performs better on subjects and verbs, whereas the one trained on COCO does better on objects. This is explained by the fact that Flickr30k images are more varied but COCO has more examples of a smaller collection of objects, thus increasing object accuracy. Amongst the models trained on images and individual video frames, the ones trained on COCO (and the combination of both) perform well, but are still a bit poorer compared to the models trained on mean-pooled features. One point to note however is that, these models were trained and evaluated on random frames from the video, and not necessarily a key-frame or most-representative frame. It's likely that choosing a representative frame from the video might result in a small improvement. But, on the whole, our experiments show that models trained on images alone do not directly perform well on video frames, and a better representation is required to learn from videos.

**Mean pooling is significant.** Our additional experiments that trained and tested on individual frames in the video, reported in section 4.3, suggest that mean pooling frame features gives significantly better results. This could potentially indicate that mean pooling features across all frames in the video is a reasonable representation for short video clips at least for the task of generating simple sentential descriptions.

**Human evaluation.** We note that the sentences generated by our model have been ranked more relevant (Table 4) to the content in the video than previous models. However, there is still a significant gap between the human ground truth sentence and the ones generated by the LSTM models. Additionally, when we ask Turkers to rate only the sentences (they are not provided the video) on grammatical correctness, the template based FGM (Thomason et al., 2014) achieves the highest ratings. This can be explained by the fact that their work uses a template technique to generate sentences from content, and is hence grammatically well formed. Our model sometimes predicts prepositions and articles more frequently, resulting in duplicates and hence incorrect grammar.

## 6 Conclusion

In this paper we have proposed a model for video description which uses neural networks for the entire pipeline from pixels to sentences and can potentially allow for the training and tuning of the entire network. In an extensive experimental evaluation, we showed that our approach generates better sentences than related approaches. We also showed that exploiting image description data improves performance compared to relying only on video description data. However our approach falls short in better utilizing the temporal information in videos, which is a good direction for future work. We will release our *Caffe*-based implementation, as well as the model and generated sentences.


## Acknowledgments

The authors thank Trevor Darrell for his valuable advice. We would also like to thank reviewers for their comments and suggestions. Marcus Rohrbach was supported by a fellowship within the FITweltweit-Program of the German Academic Exchange Service (DAAD). This research was partially supported by ONR ATL Grant N00014-11-1-010, NSF Awards IIS-1451244 and IIS-1212798.


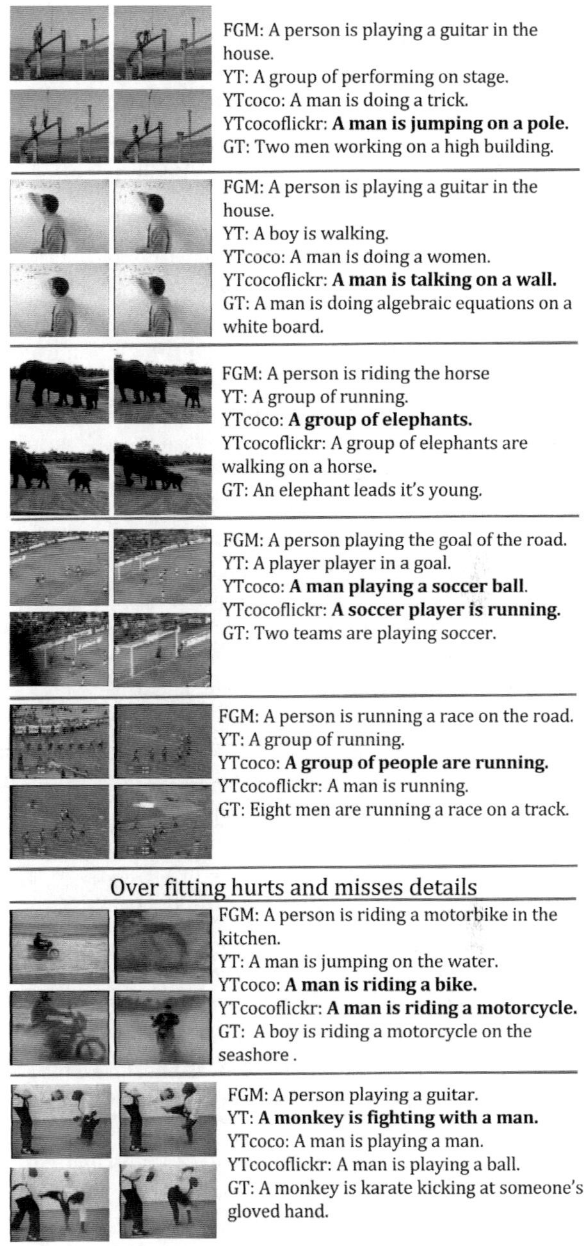


Figure 4: Examples to demonstrate effectiveness of transferring from the image description domain. YT refer to the LSTM-YT, YTcoco to the LSTM-YT$_{coco}$, and YTcocoflickr to the LSTM-YT$_{coco+flickr}$ models. GT is a random human description in the ground truth. Sentences in **bold** highlight the most accurate description for the video amongst the models. Bottom two examples show how transfer can overfit. Thus, while base LSTM-YT model detects water and monkey, the LSTM-YT$_{coco}$ and LSTM-YT$_{cocoflickr}$ models fail to describe the event completely.

## References


Ahmet Aker and Robert Gaizauskas. 2010. Generating image descriptions using dependency relational patterns. In *Association for Computational Linguistics (ACL)*.

H. Aradhye, G. Toderici, and J. Yagnik. 2009. Video2text: Learning to annotate video content. In *IEEE International Conference on Data Mining Workshops (ICDMW)*.

Satanjeev Banerjee and Alon Lavie. 2005. METEOR: An automatic metric for MT evaluation with improved correlation with human judgments. In *Proceedings of the ACL Workshop on Intrinsic and Extrinsic Evaluation Measures for Machine Translation and/or Summarization*.

Andrei Barbu, Alexander Bridge, Zachary Burchill, Dan Coroian, Sven Dickinson, Sanja Fidler, Aaron Michaux, Sam Mussman, Siddharth Narayanaswamy, Dhaval Salvi, Lara Schmidt, Jiangnan Shangguan, Jeffrey Mark Siskind, Jarrell Waggoner, Song Wang, Jinlian Wei, Yifan Yin, and Zhiqi Zhang. 2012. Video in sentences out. In *Association for Uncertainty in Artificial Intelligence (UAI)*.

David L. Chen and William B. Dolan. 2011. Collecting highly parallel data for paraphrase evaluation. In *Association for Computational Linguistics (ACL)*.

Kyunghyun Cho, Bart van Merriënboer, Dzmitry Bahdanau, and Yoshua Bengio. 2014. On the properties of neural machine translation: Encoder-decoder approaches. *arXiv preprint arXiv:1409.1259*.

P. Das, R. K. Srihari, and J. J. Corso. 2013a. Translating related words to videos and back through latent topics. In *Proceedings of Sixth ACM International Conference on Web Search and Data Mining (WSDM)*.

P. Das, C. Xu, R. F. Doell, and J. J. Corso. 2013b. A thousand frames in just a few words: Lingual description of videos through latent topics and sparse object stitching. In *Conference on Computer Vision and Pattern Recognition (CVPR)*.

D. Ding, F. Metze, S. Rawat, P.F. Schulam, S. Burger, E. Younessian, L. Bao, M.G. Christel, and A. Hauptmann. 2012. Beyond audio and video retrieval: towards multimedia summarization. In *Proceedings of the 2nd ACM International Conference on Multimedia Retrieval (ICMR)*. ACM.

Jeff Donahue, Yangqing Jia, Oriol Vinyals, Judy Hoffman, Ning Zhang, Eric Tzeng, and Trevor Darrell. 2013. Decaf: A deep convolutional activation feature for generic visual recognition. *arXiv preprint arXiv:1310.1531*.

Jeff Donahue, Lisa Anne Hendricks, Sergio Guadarrama, Marcus Rohrbach, Subhashini Venugopalan, Kate Saenko, and Trevor Darrell. 2014. Long-term recurrent convolutional networks for visual recognition and description. *CoRR*, abs/1411.4389.

Desmond Elliott and Frank Keller. 2014. Comparing automatic evaluation measures for image description. In *Association for Computational Linguistics (ACL)*.

Hao Fang, Saurabh Gupta, Forrest N. Iandola, Rupesh Srivastava, Li Deng, Piotr Dollár, Jianfeng Gao, Xiaodong He, Margaret Mitchell, John C. Platt, C. Lawrence Zitnick, and Geoffrey Zweig. 2014. From captions to visual concepts and back. *CoRR*, abs/1411.4952.

A. Farhadi, M. Hejrati, M. Sadeghi, P. Young, C. Rashtchian, J. Hockenmaier, and D. Forsyth. 2010. Every picture tells a story: Generating sentences from images. *European Conference on Computer Vision (ECCV)*.

Alex Graves and Navdeep Jaitly. 2014. Towards end-to-end speech recognition with recurrent neural networks. In *Proceedings of the 31st International Conference on Machine Learning (ICML-14)*.

Sergio Guadarrama, Niveda Krishnamoorthy, Girish Malkarnenkar, Subhashini Venugopalan, Raymond Mooney, Trevor Darrell, and Kate Saenko. 2013. Youtube2text: Recognizing and describing arbitrary activities using semantic hierarchies and zero-shot recognition. In *IEEE International Conference on Computer Vision (ICCV)*, December.

Sepp Hochreiter and Jürgen Schmidhuber. 1997. Long short-term memory. *Neural computation*, 9(8).

Sepp Hochreiter, Yoshua Bengio, Paolo Frasconi, and Jürgen Schmidhuber. 2001. Gradient flow in recurrent nets: the difficulty of learning long-term dependencies.

Peter Young Alice Lai Micah Hodosh and Julia Hockenmaier. 2014. From image descriptions to visual denotations: New similarity metrics for semantic inference over event descriptions. *Transactions of the Association for Computational Linguistics (TACL)*.

Haiqi Huang, Yueming Lu, Fangwei Zhang, and Songlin Sun. 2013. A multi-modal clustering method for web videos. In *Trustworthy Computing and Services*. Springer.

Yangqing Jia, Evan Shelhamer, Jeff Donahue, Sergey Karayev, Jonathan Long, Ross Girshick, Sergio Guadarrama, and Trevor Darrell. 2014. Caffe: Convolutional architecture for fast feature embedding. *arXiv preprint arXiv:1408.5093*.

Andrej Karpathy, Armand Joulin, and Li Fei-Fei. 2014. Deep fragment embeddings for bidirectional image sentence mapping. *Advances in Neural Information Processing Systems (NIPS)*.

Muhammad Usman Ghani Khan and Yoshihiko Gotoh. 2012. Describing video contents in natural language.

*Proceedings of the Workshop on Innovative Hybrid Approaches to the Processing of Textual Data.*

Ryan Kiros, Ruslan Salakhuditnov, and Richard. S Zemel. 2014. Unifying visual-semantic embeddings with multimodal neural language models. *arXiv preprint arXiv:1411.2539.*

Philipp Koehn. 2010. *Statistical Machine Translation.* Cambridge University Press.

A. Kojima, T. Tamura, and K. Fukunaga. 2002. Natural language description of human activities from video images based on concept hierarchy of actions. *International Journal of Computer Vision (IJCV)*, 50(2).

Niveda Krishnamoorthy, Girish Malkarnenkar, Raymond J. Mooney, Kate Saenko, and Sergio Guadarrama. 2013. Generating natural-language video descriptions using text-mined knowledge. In *AAAI Conference on Artificial Intelligence (AAAI).*

Alex Krizhevsky, Ilya Sutskever, and Geoffrey E Hinton. 2012. ImageNet classification with deep convolutional neural networks. In *Advances in Neural Information Processing Systems (NIPS).*

Girish Kulkarni, Visruth Premraj, Sagnik Dhar, Siming Li, Yejin Choi, Alexander C Berg, and Tamara L Berg. 2011. Baby talk: Understanding and generating simple image descriptions. In *Conference on Computer Vision and Pattern Recognition (CVPR).*

Polina Kuznetsova, Vicente Ordonez, Tamara L Berg, UNC Chapel Hill, and Yejin Choi. 2014. Treetalk: Composition and compression of trees for image descriptions. *Transactions of the Association for Computational Linguistics*, 2(10).

M.W. Lee, A. Hakeem, N. Haering, and S.C. Zhu. 2008. Save: A framework for semantic annotation of visual events. In *Conference on Computer Vision and Pattern Recognition (CVPR).*

Tsung-Yi Lin, Michael Maire, Serge Belongie, James Hays, Pietro Perona, Deva Ramanan, Piotr Dollár, and C Lawrence Zitnick. 2014. Microsoft COCO: Common objects in context. *arXiv preprint arXiv:1405.0312.*

Junhua Mao, Wei Xu, Yi Yang, Jiang Wang, and Alan L Yuille. 2014. Explain images with multimodal recurrent neural networks. *arXiv preprint arXiv:1410.1090.*

Tanvi S. Motwani and Raymond J. Mooney. 2012. Improving video activity recognition using object recognition and text mining. In *Proceedings of the 20th European Conference on Artificial Intelligence (ECAI).*

Paul Over, George Awad, Martial Michel, Jonathan Fiscus, Greg Sanders, B Shaw, Alan F. Smeaton, and Georges Quéenot. 2012. TRECVID 2012 – an overview of the goals, tasks, data, evaluation mechanisms and metrics. In *Proceedings of TRECVID 2012.*

Kishore Papineni, Salim Roukos, Todd Ward, and Wei-Jing Zhu. 2002. BLEU: a method for automatic evaluation of machine translation. In *Association for Computational Linguistics (ACL).*

Marcus Rohrbach, Wei Qiu, Ivan Titov, Stefan Thater, Manfred Pinkal, and Bernt Schiele. 2013. Translating video content to natural language descriptions. In *IEEE International Conference on Computer Vision (ICCV).*

Anna Rohrbach, Marcus Rohrbach, Wei Qiu, Annemarie Friedrich, Manfred Pinkal, and Bernt Schiele. 2014. Coherent multi-sentence video description with variable level of detail. In *German Conference on Pattern Recognition (GCPR)*, September.

Olga Russakovsky, Jia Deng, Hao Su, Jonathan Krause, Sanjeev Satheesh, Sean Ma, Zhiheng Huang, Andrej Karpathy, Aditya Khosla, Michael Bernstein, Alexander C. Berg, and Li Fei-Fei. 2014. ImageNet Large Scale Visual Recognition Challenge.

Ilya Sutskever, Oriol Vinyals, and Quoc V. Le. 2014. Sequence to sequence learning with neural networks. In *Advances in Neural Information Processing Systems (NIPS).*

J. Thomason, S. Venugopalan, S. Guadarrama, K. Saenko, and R.J. Mooney. 2014. Integrating language and vision to generate natural language descriptions of videos in the wild. In *Proceedings of the 25th International Conference on Computational Linguistics (COLING)*, August.

Oriol Vinyals, Alexander Toshev, Samy Bengio, and Dumitru Erhan. 2014. Show and tell: A neural image caption generator. *CoRR*, abs/1411.4555.

Shikui Wei, Yao Zhao, Zhenfeng Zhu, and Nan Liu. 2010. Multimodal fusion for video search reranking. *IEEE Transactions on Knowledge and Data Engineering,*, 22(8).

R. Xu, C. Xiong, W. Chen, and J. J. Corso. 2015. Jointly modeling deep video and compositional text to bridge vision and language in a unified framework. In *AAAI Conference on Artificial Intelligence (AAAI).*

B.Z. Yao, X. Yang, L. Lin, M.W. Lee, and S.C. Zhu. 2010. I2t: Image parsing to text description. *Proceedings of the IEEE*, 98(8).

Haonan Yu and Jeffrey Mark Siskind. 2013. Grounded language learning from videos described with sentences. In *Association for Computational Linguistics (ACL).*

Wojciech Zaremba and Ilya Sutskever. 2014. Learning to execute. *arXiv preprint arXiv:1410.4615.*

Matthew D Zeiler and Rob Fergus. 2014. Visualizing and understanding convolutional networks. In *European Conference on Computer Vision (ECCV).* Springer.

# Learning to Interpret and Describe Abstract Scenes

**Luis Gilberto Mateos Ortiz, Clemens Wolff** and **Mirella Lapata**
School of Informatics, University of Edinburgh
10 Crichton Street, Edinburgh EH8 9AB
{clemens.wolff,luismattor}@gmail.com, mlap@inf.ed.ac.uk

## Abstract

Given a (static) scene, a human can effortlessly describe what is going on (who is doing what to whom, how, and why). The process requires knowledge about the world, how it is perceived, and described. In this paper we study the problem of interpreting and verbalizing visual information using abstract scenes created from collections of clip art images. We propose a model inspired by machine translation operating over a large parallel corpus of visual relations and linguistic descriptions. We demonstrate that this approach produces human-like scene descriptions which are both fluent and relevant, outperforming a number of competitive alternatives based on templates, sentence-based retrieval, and a multimodal neural language model.

## 1 Introduction

What is going on in the scene in Figure 1? Is the boy trying to feed the dog or play with it? Why is the girl upset? Is it because the dog is wearing her glasses? Or perhaps she is just scared of the dog? Scene interpretation is effortless for humans, almost everyone can summarize Figure 1 in a few words, without probably paying too much attention to the fact the girl is wearing a pink dress, the sun is yellow or that there is a plane in the sky.

Discovering what an image means and relaying it in words is of theoretical importance raising questions about language and its grounding in the perceptual world but also has practical applications. Examples include sentence-based image search and tools that enhance the accessibility of the web for visually impaired (blind and partially sighted) individuals. Indeed, there has been a recent surge of interest in the development of models that automatically describe image content in natural language (see references in Section 2). Due to the complex nature of the problem, existing approaches resort to modeling simplifications, on the generation side (e.g., through the use of templates and sentence-based retrieval methods), or the image processing side (e.g., by avoiding object-detection), or both.

Figure 1: Given an image, humans do not simply see an arrangement of objects, they understand how they relate to each other as well as their attributes and the activities they are involved in.

In this paper we study the problem of interpreting visual scenes and rendering their content using natural language. We approach this problem within the methodology of Zitnick and Parikh (2013), who proposed the use of abstract scenes generated from clip art to model scene understanding (see Figure 1). The use of abstract scenes offers several advantages over real images. Firstly, it allows us to study the scene description problem in isolation, without the noise introduced by automatic object and attribute detectors in real images. Secondly, it is relatively easy to gather large amounts of data, allowing us to compare multiple models on an equal footing, study in more detail the problem of language grounding, and how to identify what is important in an image. Thirdly, information learned from abstract scenes will lead to better understanding of the challenges and data requirements arising when using real images.

We propose a model inspired by machine trans-



*Human Language Technologies: The 2015 Annual Conference of the North American Chapter of the ACL*, pages 1505–1515,
Denver, Colorado, May 31 – June 5, 2015. 

lation, where the task is to transform a source sentence $E$ into its target translation $F$. We argue that generating descriptions for scenes is quite similar, but with a twist: the translation process is very loose and selective; there will always be objects in a scene not worth mentioning, and words in a description that will have no visual counterpart. Our key insight is to represent scenes via visual dependency relations (Elliott and Keller, 2013) corresponding to sentential descriptions. This allows us to create a large parallel corpus for training a statistical machine translation system, which we interface with a content selection component guiding the translation toward interesting or important scene content. Advantageously, our model can be used in the reverse direction, i.e., to generate scenes, without additional engineering effort. Our approach outperforms a number of competitive alternatives, when evaluated both automatically and by humans.

## 2 Related Work

The task of image description generation has recently gained popularity in the natural language processing and computer vision communities. Several methods leverage recent advances in computer vision and generate novel sentences relying on object detectors, attribute predictors, action detectors, and pose estimators. Generation is performed using templates or syntactic rules which piece the description together while leveraging word-co-occurrence statistics (Kulkarni et al., 2011; Yang et al., 2011; Elliott and Keller, 2013; Mitchell et al., 2012). Recent advances in neural language models have led to approaches which generate captions by conditioning on feature vectors from the output of a deep convolutional neural network without the use of templates or syntactic trees (Kiros et al., 2014; Vinyals et al., 2014). Most methods assume no structural information on the image side either (images are represented as unstructured bags of regions or as feature vectors). A notable exception are Elliott and Keller (2013) who introduce visual dependency relations between objects and argue that such structured representations are beneficial for image description.

A large body of work has focused on the complementary problem of matching sentences (Ordonez et al., 2011; Farhadi et al., 2010; Hodosh et al., 2013; Feng and Lapata, 2013; Mason and Charniak, 2014) or phrases (Kuznetsova et al., 2012; Kuznetsova et al., 2014) to an image from existing human authored descriptions. Sentence-based approaches embed images and descriptions into the same multidimensional space, and retrieve descriptions from images most similar to a query image. Phrase-based approaches are more involved in that phrases need to be composed into a description and extraneous information optionally removed. A common modeling choice is the use of Integer Linear Programming (ILP) which naturally allows to encode various well-formedness constraints (e.g., grammaticality).

We are not aware of any previous work generating descriptions for abstract scenes, although the same dataset has been used to model sentence-to-scene generation (Zitnick et al., 2013) and predict object dynamics in scenes (Fouhey and Zitnick, 2014). Using the visual relations put forward in Elliott and Keller (2013), we convert the abstract scenes dataset into a parallel corpus of visual and linguistic descriptions, which allows us to train a statistical machine translation (SMT) model. In contrast to earlier work (Kuznetsova et al., 2014; Kuznetsova et al., 2012), which models the task as an optimization problem end-to-end, we employ ILP for content selection only, deferring the surface realization process entirely to an SMT engine.

## 3 The Abstract Scenes Dataset

The abstract scenes dataset[1] was created with the intent to represent real-world scenes that depict a diverse set of subtle relations. It contains 10,020 images of children playing outside and 60,396 descriptions (on average six per image). The data was collected in three stages. First, Amazon Mechanical Turk (AMT) workers were asked to created scenes for a collection of 80 pieces of clip art depicting a boy and a girl (in different poses and with different facial expressions), and several objects including trees, toys, hats, animals, and so on. Next, a new set of subjects were asked to describe the scenes using a one or two sentence description, finally, semantically similar scenes were generated by asking multiple subjects to create scenes depicting the same writ-

[1] http://research.microsoft.com/en-us/um/people/larryz/clipart/abstract_scenes.html

| | | | | | | |
|---|---|---|---|---|---|---|
| 0 6 | | | | | | |
| s_3s.png | 0 | 3 | 467 | 24 | 2 | 1 |
| hb0_10s.png | 2 | 10 | 145 | 182 | 0 | 1 |
| hb1_19s_png | 3 | 19 | 323 | 188 | 0 | 1 |
| c_9s.png | 5 | 9 | 161 | 116 | 0 | 1 |
| c_5s.png | 7 | 4 | 43 | 172 | 0 | 0 |
| t_4s.png | 7 | 4 | 43 | 173 | 0 | 0 |

"Jenny is upset because Mike isn't sharing the soccer ball.", "Mike is wearing sunglasses.", "Jenny is wearing a silly hat.", "Mike is kicking the soccer ball away from Jenny.", "Jenny is chasing Mike to get the ball.", "Jenny is wearing a silly hat."

Figure 2: Example of a scene, its rendering information (right), and human-written descriptions (bottom).

ten description. By construction, the dataset encodes the objects in each scene, and their position.

An example is shown in Figure 2. The table on the right-hand side specifies how the image was rendered. The top row contains the scene identifier (i.e., 0) and the number of pieces of clip art in the image (i.e., 6). The remaining rows encode rendering information for each individual piece of clipart, i.e., its name (column 1), type (column 2), attribute (column 3), position (columns 4–6), and whether or not it is horizontally flipped (column 7). Six human authored descriptions are shown the bottom. AMT participants were instructed to write simple descriptions using basic words that would appear in a book for young children ages 4–6. Participants who wished to use proper names in their descriptions were provided with names "Mike" and "Jenny" for the boy and girl. The vocabulary consists of 2,705 words, and the average sentence length is 6.3 words. As can be seen in Figure 2, subjects choose to focus on different aspects of the image (e.g., Mike and his sunglasses, the fact that Jenny is chasing Mike). Also notice that even though by design we know which visual objects are present in the image and their spatial relationships (see the right hand-side in Figure 2), the alignment between pieces of clipart and linguistic expressions is hidden. In other words, we do not know which actions the objects depict (e.g., playing, holding) and which words can be used to describe them (e.g., that t_4s.png is called a ball).

## 4 Problem Formulation

We formulate scene description generation as a translation problem from the visual to the linguistic modality. Our approach follows the general paradigm of SMT with two important differences. Firstly, the source side (i.e., scene) is fundamentally different from the target (i.e., linguistic descriptions) both in terms of representation and structure. Secondly, the scene and its corresponding descriptions constitute a very loose parallel corpus: not all visual objects are verbalized (note that no participant chose to mention the sun in Figure 2) and there are multiple valid descriptions for a single scene focusing on different objects and their relations. In the following we first describe how we create a parallel corpus representing the arrangement of objects in a scene and their linguistic realization and then we move on to present our generation model.

### 4.1 Parallel Corpus Creation

As mentioned earlier, each scene in the dataset has six descriptions (on average). For each *linguistic* description we create its corresponding *visual* encoding. We initially ground words and phrases by aligning them to pieces of clipart. We parse the descriptions using a dependency parser, and identify expressions that function as arguments (e.g., subject, object). In our experiments we used the Stanford parser (Klein and Manning, 2003) but any parser with similar output could have been used instead. Next, we compute the mutual information (MI) between arguments and clip-art objects defined as:

$$MI(X,Y) = \sum_{x \in X} \sum_{y \in Y} p(x,y) \log \frac{p(x,y)}{p(x)p(y)} \quad (1)$$

where $X$ is the set of clip-art objects and $Y$ the set of arguments found in the dataset. We assume that the visual rendering of an argument is the clip-art object with which its MI value is highest. Figure 3 shows argument-clipart pairs with high MI values.

Having identified which objects in the scene are talked about, we move on to encode their spatial relations. We adopt the relations outlined in *Visual Dependency Grammar* (VDG; Elliott and Keller (2013)). The latter are defined for pairs of image regions but can also directly apply to clip-art objects. VDR Relations are specified according to

| | |
|---|---|
| *X on Y* | More than 50% of X overlaps with Y |
| *X surrounds Y* | X overlaps entirely with Y |
| *X above Y* | The angle between X and Y is between 225°and 315° |
| *X below Y* | The angle between X and Y is between 45°and 135°. |
| *X opposite Y* | The angle between X and Y is between 315°and 45°or 135°and 225°. The Euclidean distance between X and Y is greater than $w \cdot 0.72$. |
| *X near Y* | Similar to *opposite* but the Euclidean distance between X and Y is greater than $w \cdot 0.36$. |
| *X close Y* | Similar to *opposite* but the Euclidean distance between X and Y is less or equal to $w \cdot 0.36$. |
| *X infront Y* | X is in front Y in the Z-plane |
| *X behind Y* | X is behind Y in the Z-plane |
| *X same Y* | X and Y are at the same depth |

Table 1: VDG relations between pairs of clip art objects. All relations are considered with respect to the centroid of an object and the angle between those centroids. We follow the definition of the unit circle, in which 0°lies to the right and a turn around the circle is counter-clockwise. All regions are mutually exclusive. Parameter $w$ refers to the width of the scene.

three geometric properties: pixel overlap, the angle between regions, and the distance between regions. Table 1 summarizes the relations used in our experiments most of which encode spatial object relations in the $x$-$y$ space; the last three encode relative object position along the $z$ axis. Our relations are broadly similar to those proposed in Elliott and Keller (2013) with the exception of *beside* which we break down into more fine-grained relations (namely *near* and *close*). We also add the *same* relation in the $z$ axis. In cases where object $X$ is facing object $Y$ we subscript relations *opposite*, *near*, and *close* with the letter $\mathcal{F}$.

The procedure described above will generate a visual description for each linguistic description. It also assumes that visual relations hold between pairs of objects. The assumption is not unwarranted, 73.87% of the descriptions in the dataset involve only two arguments. The parallel sentences corresponding to Figure 2 are illustrated in Table 2. In cases where the the original description involves three objects, ternary relations are decomposed into binary ones. We create as many visual representations as there are linguistic descriptions. If two humans generate identical descriptions, we produce identical visual encodings. In total, we were able to create 46,053 parallel descriptions[2] accounting for 79.5% of the sentences in the dataset.

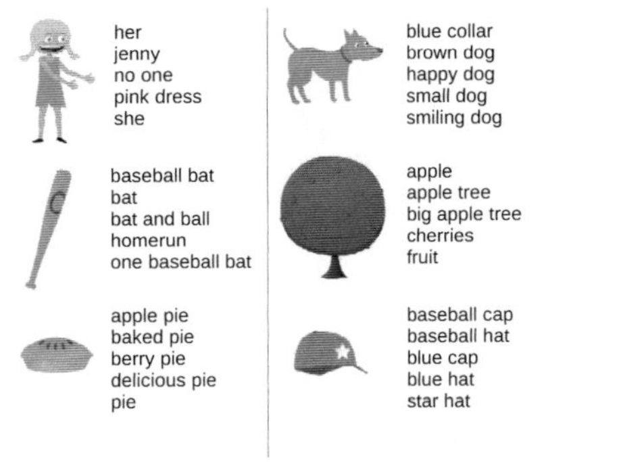


Figure 3: Examples of argument-clipart object pairs with high MI values (shown in descending order).

### 4.2 Generation Model

It is straightforward to train a phrase-based SMT model on the parallel corpus outlined above. The model would learn to translate a visual description (see the source side in Table 2) into natural language. However, when generating linguistic descriptions for a scene at test time, we must first decide "what to say" (content selection) and then "how to say" it (surface realization). What is the most important content in the scene worth describing? Given that visual relations between objects are assumed to be binary (see the VDG grammar in Table 1), there are $n(n-1)$ combinations of pairs of objects in a scene (where $n$ is the number of clipart pieces available) and as many corresponding visual expressions. However, many of these visual expressions will capture unimportant aspects of the scene, or even express atypical relations unattested in the training data. We develop below a content selection component based on the intuition that frequently

[2]Our parallel corpus can be downloaded from http://homepages.inf.ed.ac.uk/mlap/index.php?page=resources.

| | Image | description |
|---|---|---|
| 1. | hb0.10s.png $close_{\mathcal{F}}$ *same* t.4s.png | Mike isn't sharing the soccer ball |
| 2. | hb0.10s.png *surrounds same* c.9s.png | Mike is wearing sunglasses |
| 3. | hb1.19s.png *below same* c.5s.png | Jenny is wearing a silly hat |
| 4. | hb0.10s.png $close_{\mathcal{F}}$ *same* t.4s.png | Mike is kicking the soccer ball |
| 5. | hb1.19s.png $close_{\mathcal{F}}$ *same* hb0.10s.png | Jenny is chasing Mike |
| 6. | hb1.19s.png *below same* c.5s.png | Jenny is wearing a silly hat |

Table 2: Parallel corpus of visual expressions and linguistic descriptions corresponding to Figure 2.

mentioned object pairs probably express important scene content. In addition, it is reasonable to assume that the selected objects will be in close proximity, especially when actions are involved. One would expect the agent of the action to be near the object or person receiving it (e.g., *Mike is kicking the ball, Jenny is holding Mike's hand*). The same is true for instruments, which are typically held by the persons using them (e.g., *Jenny is digging with a shovel*).

**Content Selection** We cast the problem of finding suitable objects to talk about as an integer linear program (ILP). Our model selects clip art object pairs that best describe the content of a scene and ranks them based on their relevance. Indicator variable $y_{stk}$ denotes whether two objects are being selected and how they are ranked (e.g, whether they should be mentioned first or last):

$$y_{stk} = \begin{cases} 1 & \text{if objects } s \text{ and } t \text{ are selected for rank } k \\ & \text{and } s \text{ is before } t \\ 0 & \text{otherwise} \end{cases} \quad (2)$$

where $s$ and $t$ index two clip art objects and $k = 1,..,S$ encodes their rank (based on relevance). Our objective function is given below:

$$Z = \sum_{s \in S, t \in S} F_{st} \cdot D_{st} \cdot \sum_{k \in S} ((card(S)+1)-k) \cdot y_{stk} \quad (3)$$

where $F_{st}$ quantifies the normalized co-occurrence frequency of objects $s$ and $t$ (in the training set) and $D_{st}$ specifies their relative distance. The term $((card(S)+1)-k)$ accounts for the ranking of pairs so that most relevant ones are ranked first. Here, $card(S)$ represents the cardinality of the set $S$ denoting the number of clip art objects in the scene; $k$ ranges over all available ranks (which is limited by the number of clip art objects available). The term

Figure 4: Example of three clip art objects and the most frequent objects they co-occur with.

$((card(S)+1)-k)$ is inversely proportional to $k$, so its highest value is when $k$ is 1. In other words, the value of the term is maximum when the selected objects are ranked first. This way, we ensure that most relevant object pairs are given high ranks.

We compute $F_{st}$ from our parallel corpus (see left-hand side in Table 2), simply by counting the number of times objects $s$ and $t$ co-occur. Figure 4 shows three clip art objects (Mike, a snake, and a bear) and their most frequent co-occurrences. We estimate term $D_{st}$, the distance between objects $s$ and $t$, using function $\sqrt{\Delta x^2 + \Delta y^2 + \Delta z^2}$. Coordinate $z$ has only three possible values (see Table 1). To increase the effect of $\Delta z$, we use a scaling factor. We normalize and invert $D_{st}$ so that it ranges from 0 to 1. In addition, we transform it with a sigmoid function so as to maximize the effect of near and distant objects (distances of relatively close objects are set to 1 and distances of distant objects are set to 0).

The objective function in Equation (3) is too permissive, allowing repetitions of the same object within a pair and of the object pairs themselves. Constraints (4)–(10) avoid repetitions and ensure that the selected objects are varied with the aim of generating logically consistent descriptions. Constraint (4) avoids empty descriptions, by enforcing that at least one clip art object pair is selected. Constraint (5) ensures that an object cannot appear in the same pair twice, whereas constraint (6) requires that at most one pair can be selected for a given rank $k$. We also enforce the selection of different pairs of objects (constraint (7)) at contiguous ranks (constraint (8)).

$$\sum_{s \in S, t \in S} y_{st1} = 1 \tag{4}$$

$$\forall_{stk, s==t}, \; y_{stk} = 0 \tag{5}$$

$$\forall_{k}, \; \sum_{s \in S, t \in S} y_{stk} \leq 1; \tag{6}$$

$$\forall_{st}, \; \sum_{k \in S} (y_{stk} + y_{tsk}) \leq 1 \tag{7}$$

$$\forall_{k=1,..,S-1}, \; \sum_{s \in S, t \in S} y_{stk+1} \leq \sum_{s \in S, t \in S} y_{stk} \tag{8}$$

Finally, to instill some coherence in the descriptions, while avoiding overly repetitive discourse, we disallow objects to be selected more than four times:

$$\forall_{s}, \; sum_s = \sum_{t \in S, k \in S} y_{stk} \tag{9}$$

$$\forall_{t}, \; sum_t = \sum_{s \in S, k \in S} y_{stk} \tag{10}$$

$$\forall_{st, s==t}, \; sum_s + sum_t \leq 4 \tag{11}$$

Auxiliary variables $sum_s$ and $sum_t$ represent the number of times objects $s$ and $t$ are selected to be the first and second object of a pair.

Given a new unseen scene, we obtain the $F_{st}$ values for all pair-wise combinations of the objects in it and compute their distance $D_{st}$. We solve the ILP problem defined above and read the value of the variable $y_{stk}$ which contains the selected clip art object pairs ranked by relevance. So, our model can in principle produce multiple descriptions for a given scene, highlighting potentially different aspects of the visually encoded information. We used GLPK[3] to maximize the objective function subject to the constraints introduced above.

[3] https://www.gnu.org/software/glpk/

**Surface realization** The ILP selects all description-worthy pairs of clip art objects for a scene. Using the rules presented in Table 1 we create visual encodings for them (see Table 2, source side), and finally translate them into natural language using a Phrase-based SMT engine (Koehn et al., 2003). Specifically, given a source visual expression $\mathbf{f}$, our aim is to find an equivalent target natural language description $\hat{\mathbf{e}}$ that maximizes the posterior probability:

$$\hat{\mathbf{e}} = \operatorname*{argmax}_{\mathbf{e}} P(\mathbf{e}|\mathbf{f}) \tag{12}$$

Most recent SMT work models the posterior $P(\mathbf{e}|\mathbf{f})$ directly (Och and Ney, 2002) using a log-linear combination of several models where:

$$P(\mathbf{e}|\mathbf{f}) = \frac{\exp \sum_{k=1}^{K} \lambda_k h_k(\mathbf{f}, \mathbf{e})}{\sum_{e'} \exp \sum_{k=1}^{K} \lambda_k h_k(\mathbf{f}, \mathbf{e}')} \tag{13}$$

and the decision decision rule is given by:

$$\hat{\mathbf{e}} = \operatorname*{argmax}_{\mathbf{e}} \sum_{k=1}^{K} \lambda_k h_k(\mathbf{f}, \mathbf{e}) \tag{14}$$

where $h_k(\mathbf{f}, \mathbf{e})$ is a scoring function representing important features for the translation of $\mathbf{f}$ into $\mathbf{e}$. Examples include the language model of the target language, a reordering model, or several translation models. $K$ is the number of models (or features) and $\lambda_k$ are the weights of the log-linear combination. Typically, the weights $\Lambda = [\lambda_1, \ldots, \lambda_K]^T$ are optimized on a development set, by means of Minimum Error Rate Training (MERT; Och (2003)).

One of the most popular instantiations of loglinear models in SMT are phrase-based (PB) models (Zens et al., 2002; Koehn et al., 2003). PB models allow to learn translations for entire phrases instead of individual words. The basic idea behind PB translation is to segment the source sentence into phrases, then to translate each source phrase into a target phrase, and finally reorder the translated target phrases in order to compose the target sentence. For this purpose, phrase-tables are produced, in which a source phrase is listed together with several target phrases and the probability of translating the former into the latter. Throughout our experiments, we obtained translation models using the PB SMT framework implemented in MOSES (Koehn et al., 2007).

|  |  |
|---|---|
| Mike is kicking the ball | The plane is flying in the sky |
| `nsubj,aux,verb,det,dobj` | `det,nsubj,aux,verb,prep,det,pobj` |

Table 3: Sample scenes with human-written descriptions and corresponding templates.

## 5 Model Comparison

We evaluated the model described above through comparison to four alternatives, representing different modeling paradigms in the literature. Our first comparison model is based on templates, which are commonly used to produce descriptions for images (Elliott and Keller, 2013; Kulkarni et al., 2011). Rather than manually creating template rules we induce them from dependency-parsed scene descriptions. We represent each description in the data as a sequence of typed dependencies. The scene descriptions are relatively simple, and many sentences have similar structure. Overall, 20 templates represent the syntactic structure of more than 44% of all scene descriptions. Examples of scenes, their descriptions, and corresponding templates are shown in Table 3 (template `nsubj,aux,verb,det,dobj` is the most frequent in the data).

We train a logistic regression classifier (Yu et al., 2011) on scene-template pairs, and learn to assign a template for a new unseen scene. The "template-predictor" uses variety of features based on the alignment between clip-art objects and POS-tags as well as objects and dependency roles. The alignments were computed using MI as described in Section 4.1. We also used visual features based on the absolute and relative distance between objects, their co-occurrence, spatial location, depth ordering, facial expression and poses (see Zitnick et al. (2013) for details). In order to transform the templates into natural language sentences we train a "word-predictor" which fills the most likely word for every grammatical function slot in a given template (again using logistic regression and the same feature space as for the template predictor). The word predictor uses a vocabulary of 70 frequently occurring words (attested no less than 150 times in the corpus). For a new scene, candidate templates are predicted and subsequently expanded to descriptions by predicting words for every function slot in the templates. Candidate descriptions are ranked using a trigram language model to ensure grammatical coherence.

We also implemented two sentence-based retrieval approaches. Our first system is conceptually similar to the model proposed by Farhadi et al. (2010). In their work, images and descriptions seen at training time are mapped into a shared meaning space $M$ using a function $f$. Given an unseen image $\lambda$, the description closest to $f(\lambda)$ in $M$ is retrieved and returned by the model. We used the word-predictor described above as a simple way of annotating an unseen scene $\lambda$ with the words that most saliently describe it. These keywords then used as a TFIDF search query against the set $H$ of human scene descriptions seen during training:

$$\begin{aligned} \mathrm{TFIDF}(q,d) &= \sum_{w \in q} \mathrm{TF}(w,d)\mathrm{IDF}(w), \\ \mathrm{TF}(w,q) &= \sqrt{\sum_{w' \in q} \mathbb{1}_{w=w'}}, \\ \mathrm{IDF}(w) &= 1 + \log \frac{\|H\|}{1 + \sum_{d \in H} \sum_{w' \in d} \mathbb{1}_{w=w'}}. \end{aligned} \quad (15)$$

where $H$ is the set of all human descriptions seen at training time, $\|\cdot\|$ is the set-norm, $q$ is a search query, $d$ is any description in $H$ and $\mathbb{1}_{w=w'}$ an indicator variable set to 1 if $w$ and $w'$ are the same word and 0 otherwise. The human description maximizing the TFIDF similarity with the predicted keywords is returned as the description for the new scene.

Our third baseline exploits image similarity (Ordonez et al., 2011). Given an unseen scene $\lambda$, we retrieve from the training set $\lambda'$, the scene most similar to it, and return one of $\lambda'$'s human descriptions selected at random. We used locality sensitivity hashing to find the subset of candidate scenes similar to $\lambda$. Scenes were represented with the same visual features used for the word and template predictors and their similarity was computed with the cosine metric.

Finally, we also trained a multimodal log-bilinear model (Kiros et al., 2014) on the abstract scenes

| System | BLEU | METEOR |
|---|---|---|
| LBL | 7.33 | 17.76 |
| MLBL | 12.30 | 20.40 |
| Image | 12.80 | 21.77 |
| Keyword | 14.70 | 26.60 |
| Template | 40.30 | 30.40 |
| SMT | 43.70 | 35.60 |

Table 4: Model comparison on scene description task using automatic measures.

| System | $1^{st}$ | $2^{nd}$ | $3^{rd}$ | $4^{th}$ | AvgRank |
|---|---|---|---|---|---|
| Keyword | 0.24 | 0.13 | 0.22 | 0.41 | 2.22 |
| Template | 0.25 | 0.16 | 0.13 | 0.46 | 2.21 |
| SMT | 0.53 | 0.24 | 0.12 | 0.11 | 3.19 |
| Human | 0.57 | 0.27 | 0.12 | 0.04 | 3.36 |

Table 5: Rankings (shown as proportions) and mean ratings given to systems by human participants.

dataset. The model essentially implements a feed-forward neural network to predict the next word given the image and previous words.[4] Images were associated with feature representations obtained from the output of a convolutional network, following the feature learning procedure outlined in Kiros et al. (2014).

## 6 Results

We evaluated system output automatically using (smoothed) BLUE and METEOR as calculated by NIST's MultEval software[5] using the human-written descriptions as reference. Elliott and Keller (2014) find that both metrics correlate well with human judgments. For a fair comparison, we force our model to output one description, i.e., the most relevant one.

Our results are summarized in Table 4. As can be seen, our model (SMT) performs best both in terms of BLEU and METEOR. The template-based generator (Template) obtains competitive performance which is not surprising, it incorporates some of the ingredients of the SMT system such as

| Resp | $1^{st}$ | $2^{nd}$ | $3^{rd}$ | $4^{th}$ | $5^{th}$ | $6^{th}$ |
|---|---|---|---|---|---|---|
| YES | 75.5 | 65.8 | 53.0 | 44.7 | 44.0 | 37.5 |
| NO | 18.0 | 24.8 | 31.2 | 31.3 | 37.5 | 58.0 |
| MAYBE | 6.5 | 9.50 | 15.8 | 15.8 | 18.5 | 4.50 |

Table 6: Proportion of SMT descriptions deemed accurate and relevant. System output evaluated for rank placements 1...6.

word-to-clipart alignments, a language model, and is guaranteed to produce grammatical output. The performance of the multimodal log-bilinear model (MLBL) keyword- and image-based retrieval systems is inferior. We conjecture that the image features, and similarity functions used in these models are not fine-grained enough to capture the subtle differences in scenes which humans detect and express in the descriptions. Finally, notice that visual information is critical in doing well on the description generation task. A log-bilinear language model (LBL) trained solely on the descriptions performs poorly (see the top row in Table 4).

We further evaluated system output eliciting human judgments for 100 randomly selected test scenes. Participants were presented with a scene and descriptions generated by our system, the template-based model, the best-performing sentence retrieval model, and a randomly selected human description. Subjects were asked to rank the four descriptions from best to worst (ties are allowed) in order of informativeness (does the description capture what is shown in the scene?) and fluency (is the description written in well-formed English?). We elicited rankings using Amazon's Mechanical Turk crowdsourcing platform. Participants (self-reported native English speakers) saw 10 scenes per session. We collected 5 responses per item.

The results of our human evaluation study are shown in Table 5. Specifically, we show, proportionally, how often our participants ranked each system 1st, 2nd and so on. Perhaps unsurprisingly, the human-written descriptions were considered best (and ranked 1st 57% of the time). Our model is ranked best 0.53% of the time, followed by the template and keyword-based retrieval systems which are only ranked first 25% of the time.[6] We further

[4]We used the implementation at `http://www.cs.toronto.edu/~rkiros/multimodal.html`.

[5]`ftp://jaguar.ncsl.nist.gov/mt/resources/mteval-v13a-20091001.tar.gz`

[6]Percentages do not sum to 100% because ties are allowed.

Jenny is holding a hot dog.
Jenny is wearing a witch hat.
Jenny is scared of the snake.
The snake is under the pine tree.

Jenny is sitting in the sandbox.
Jenny is wearing purple sunglasses.
The cat is sitting in the sandbox.
The cat is watching Jenny.

Figure 5: Examples of descriptions generated by the SMT model for two scenes.

"Mike and Jenny decide to make hot dogs on the grill.", "It's a rainstorm and Jenny runs away to stay dry.", "Mike stays beside the fire.", "Jenny is standing next to the tree.", "Mike is sitting next to the fire.", "The hot dog is on the pit."

Figure 6: Right scene is generated by SMT model (left scene is the original) given descriptions (bottom) as input.

converted the ranks to ratings on a scale of 1 to 4 (assigning ratings 4...1 to rank placements 1...4). This allowed us to perform Analysis of Variance (ANOVA) which revealed a reliable effect of system type. Specifically, post-hoc Tukey tests showed that our SMT model is significantly ($p < 0.01$) better than the other two comparison systems but does not differ significantly from the human goldstandard.

We also evaluated more thoroughly our content selection mechanism. Since our system can in principle generate multiple descriptions for a scene, we were interested to see how many of these are indeed relevant. We let the system generate the six best descriptions per scene and asked AMT participants to assess whether they were accurate (are the people, objects and actions mentioned in the description shown in the scene?) and appropriate (is the description relevant for the scene?). Participants answered with "yes", "no", or "maybe". Again we used 100 items from the test set, and elicited 5 responses per item. Table 6 shows the outcome of this study. The majority of first-best descriptions (75.5%) returned by our system are perceived as relevant and scene appropriate. The same is true for 2nd and 3rd best descriptions, whereas the quality of descriptions deteriorates with lower ranks. This suggests that we could generate short discourses describing different viewpoints in a scene.

Figure 5 illustrates the descriptions produced by our model for two scenes, whereas Figure 6 shows example output when the system is run in reverse, i.e., it takes descriptions as input and generates a scene. This can be done straightforwardly, without any additional effort, however note that the model is unaware of the absolute position of objects, it places the cloud next to Jenny.

## 7 Conclusions

In this paper we presented proof of concept that an SMT-based approach is successful at generating human-like scene descriptions provided that (a) there is a large enough parallel corpus to learn from and (b) a content selection component identifies important scene content. Our results further indicate that instilling some degree of structural information in visual scenes (via the VDG) is beneficial. It allows to describe visual content more accurately and facilitates its rendering in natural language (since the two modalities are structurally similar). The template-based, retrieval, and language modeling systems do not use this structural information, and even though their descriptions are largely grammatical, they are not as felicitous. Our results also point to difficulty of the task. Even when computer vision is taken out of the equation, and the description language is simple, human-written text is still preferable (see Table 5). In the future, we would like to develop better content selection models (e.g., identify surprising aspects in a scene) and more accurate grounding strategies (e.g., via discriminative alignment).

**Acknowledgments** We are grateful to Lukas Dirzys for his help with the LBL and MLBL models. Special thanks to Frank Keller for his comments on an earlier version of this paper and Larry Zitnick whose talk at the UW MSR Summer Institute 2013 insipred this work.

## References


Desmond Elliott and Frank Keller. 2013. Image description using visual dependency representations. In *Proceedings of the 2013 Conference on Empirical Methods in Natural Language Processing*, pages 1292–1302, Seattle, Washington.

Desmond Elliott and Frank Keller. 2014. Comparing automatic evaluation measures for image description. In *Proceedings of the 52nd Annual Meeting of the Association for Computational Linguistics (Volume 2: Short Papers)*, pages 452–457, Baltimore, Maryland.

Ali Farhadi, Mohsen Hejrati, Amin Sadeghi, Peter Yong, Cyrus Rashtchian, Julia Hockenmaier, and David Forsyth. 2010. Every picture tells a story: Generating sentences from images. In *Proceedings of the 11th European Conference on Computer Vision*, pages 25–29, Heraklion, Greece.

Yansong Feng and Mirella Lapata. 2013. Automatic caption generation for news images. *IEEE Transactions on Pattern Analysis and Machine Intelligence*, 35(4):797–812.

David F. Fouhey and C. Lawrence Zitnick. 2014. Predicting object dynamics in scenes. In *Proceedings of the 2014 IEEE Conference on Computer Vision and Pattern Reconition*, pages 2027–2034, Columbus, Ohio.

Micah Hodosh, Peter Young, and Julia Hockenmaier. 2013. Framing image description as a ranking task: Data, models and evaluation metrics. *Journal of Artificial Intelligence Research*, 47:853–899.

Ryan Kiros, Ruslan Slakhutdinov, and Richard Zemel. 2014. Multimodal neural language models. In *Proceedings of the 31st International Conference on Machine Learning*, Beijing, China. volume 32.

Dan Klein and Christopher D. Manning. 2003. Accurate unlexicalized parsing. In *Proceedings of the 41st Annual Meeting of the Association for Computational Linguistics*, pages 423–430, Sapporo, Japan.

Philipp Koehn, Franz Josef Och, and Daniel Marcu. 2003. Statistical phrase-based translation. In *Annual Meeting of the North American Chapter of the Association for Computational Linguistics*, pages 48–54, Edmonton, Canada.

Philipp Koehn, Hieu Hoang, Alexandra Birch, Chris Callison-Burch, Marcello Federico, Nicola Bertoldi, Brooke Cowan, Wade Shen, Christine Moran, Richard Zens, Chris Dyer, Ondrej Bojar, Alexandra Constantin, and Evan Herbst. 2007. Moses: Open source toolkit for statistical machine translation. In *Proceedings of the 45th Annual Meeting of the Association for Computational Linguistics Companion Volume Proceedings of the Demo and Poster Sessions*, pages 177–180, Prague, Czech Republic.

Girish Kulkarni, Visruth Premraj, Sagnik Dhar, Siming Li, Yejin Choi, Alexander C. Berg, and Tamara L. Berg. 2011. Baby talk: Understanding and generating image descriptions. In *Proceedings of the 2011 IEEE Conference on Computer Vision and Pattern Recognition*, pages 1601–1608, Colorado Springs, Colorado.

Polina Kuznetsova, Vicente Ordonez, Alexander Berg, Tamara Berg, and Yejin Choi. 2012. Collective generation of natural image descriptions. In *Proceedings of the 50th Annual Meeting of the Association for Computational Linguistics (Volume 1: Long Papers)*, pages 359–368, Jeju Island, Korea.

Polina Kuznetsova, Vicente Ordonez, Tamara L. Berg, and Yejin Choi. 2014. Treetalk: Composition and compression of trees for image descriptions. *Transactions of the Association for Computational Luingusitics*, 2:351–362.

Rebecca Mason and Eugene Charniak. 2014. Nonparametric method for data-driven image captioning. In *Proceedings of the 52nd Annual Meeting of the Association for Computational Linguistics (Volume 2: Short Papers)*, pages 592–598, Baltimore, Maryland.

Margaret Mitchell, Jesse Dodge, Amit Goyal, Kota Yamaguchi, Karl Stratos, Xufeng Han, Alyssa Mensch, Alex Berg, Tamara Berg, and Hal Daume III. 2012. Midge: Generating image descriptions from computer vision detections. In *Proceedings of the 13th Conference of the European Chapter of the Association for Computational Linguistics*, pages 747–756, Avignon, France.

Franz Josef Och and Hermann Ney. 2002. Discriminative training and maximum entropy models for statistical machine translation. In *Proceedings of 40th Annual Meeting of the Association for Computational Linguistics*, pages 295–302, Philadelphia, Pennsylvania.

Franz Josef Och. 2003. Minimum error rate training in statistical machine translation. In *Proceedings of the 41st Annual Meeting of the Association for Computational Linguistics*, pages 160–167, Sapporo, Japan.

Vicente Ordonez, Girish Kulkarni, and Tamara L. Berg. 2011. Im2text: Describing images using 1 million captioned photographs. In J. Shawe-Taylor, R.S. Zemel, P. Bartlett, F.C.N. Pereira, and K.Q. Weinberger, editors, *Advances in Neural Information Processing Systems 24*, pages 1143–1151. Curran Associates, Inc.

Oriol Vinyals, Alexander Toshev, Samy Bengio, and Dumitru Erhan. 2014. Show and tell: A neural image caption generator. arXiv:1411.4555.

Yezhou Yang, Ching Teo, Hal Daume III, and Yiannis Aloimonos. 2011. Corpus-guided sentence generation of natural images. In *Proceedings of the 2011*

*Conference on Empirical Methods in Natural Language Processing*, pages 444–454, Edinburgh, Scotland.

Hsiang-Fu Yu, Fang-Lan Huang, and Chih-Jen Lin. 2011. Dual coordinate descent methods for logistic regression and maximum entropy models. *Machine Learning*, 85(1-2):41–75.

R. Zens, F. J. Och, and H. Ney. 2002. Phrase-based statistical machine translation. In Springer Verlag, editor, *German Conference on Artificial Intelligence*, pages 18–32.

C. Lawrence Zitnick and Devi Parikh. 2013. Bringing semantics into focus using visual abstraction. In *Proceedings of the 2013 IEEE Conference on Computer Vision and Pattern Recognition*, pages 3009–3016, Portland, Oregon.

C. Lawrewnce Zitnick, Devi Parikh, and Lucy Vanderwende. 2013. Learning the visual interpretation of sentences. In *Proceedings of the 2013 IEEE International Conference on Computer Vision*, pages 1681–1688, Sydney, Australia.

# A Comparison of Update Strategies for Large-Scale Maximum Expected BLEU Training

**Joern Wuebker, Sebastian Muehr, Patrick Lehnen, Stephan Peitz and Hermann Ney**
Human Language Technology and Pattern Recognition Group
RWTH Aachen University
Aachen, Germany
{surname}@cs.rwth-aachen.de

## Abstract

This work presents a flexible and efficient discriminative training approach for statistical machine translation. We propose to use the RPROP algorithm for optimizing a maximum expected BLEU objective and experimentally compare it to several other updating schemes. It proves to be more efficient and effective than the previously proposed growth transformation technique and also yields better results than stochastic gradient descent and AdaGrad. We also report strong empirical results on two large scale tasks, namely BOLT Chinese→English and WMT German→English, where our final systems outperform results reported by Setiawan and Zhou (2013) and on matrix.statmt.org. On the WMT task, discriminative training is performed on the full training data of 4M sentence pairs, which is unsurpassed in the literature.

## 1 Introduction

The main advantage of learning parameters in a discriminative fashion is the possibility to directly optimize towards a quality or error measure on the task that is being performed. This stands in contrast to the generative approach, where parameters are chosen to maximize likelihood under a generative story, which often bears little correspondence with the actual application of the model.

In statistical machine translation (SMT), extending the generative noisy-channel formulation (Brown et al., 1993) as a discriminative, log-linear combination of multiple models (Och, 2003) has become the state of the art. However, most of the component models are still estimated by heuristics or generative training. In this paper, a flexible, efficient and easy to implement discriminative training scheme for SMT is presented. It can be applied to any kind and any number of features. We use the RPROP algorithm to optimize a maximum expected BLEU objective. $n$-best lists approximate the infeasibly large space of translation hypotheses. They are generated with the application of leave-one-out to make them more representative with respect to unseen data.

We make the following main contributions:

1. We propose to apply the RPROP algorithm for maximum expected BLEU training and perform an experimental comparison with growth transformation (GT) (He and Deng, 2012; Setiawan and Zhou, 2013), stochastic gradient descent (Auli et al., 2014) and AdaGrad (Green et al., 2013). RPROP yields superior performance, reaching a total improvement of 1.2 BLEU points over our IWSLT German→English baseline using 5.22M features.

2. In terms of time and memory efficiency, RPROP clearly outperforms GT. The latter needs to update a much larger number of features due to its renormalization component. On the IWSLT data, RPROP is 6.4 times faster than GT and requires a third of the memory.

3. On the WMT German→English task, we perform discriminative training on 4M sentence



*Human Language Technologies: The 2015 Annual Conference of the North American Chapter of the ACL*, pages 1516–1526,
Denver, Colorado, May 31 – June 5, 2015. 

pairs, which, to the best of our knowledge, is 2.4 times the size of the largest training set reported in previous work (1.66M sentences in (Simianer et al., 2012)). This proves the scalability of our approach.

4. On two large scale tasks our experiments show good improvements over strong baselines which include recurrent language modeling components. On the Chinese→English DARPA BOLT task, we achieve nearly twice the improvement reported in (Setiawan and Zhou, 2013) on the same test sets which results in a superior final system. Finally, the best single system reported on matrix.statmt.org is outperformed by 0.8 BLEU points on the WMT German→English *newstest2013* set.

Our experiments also prove that leave-one-out impacts translation quality.

This paper is organized as follows. We review related work in Section 2 and present the translation system in Section 3. In Section 4 we describe the different discriminative update strategies applied in this work and Section 5 derives the complete maximum expected BLEU training algorithm. Finally, experimental results are given in Section 6 and we conclude with Section 7.

## 2 Related Work

Discriminative training is one of the most active research areas in SMT and it can be integrated into the pipeline at various stages.

Och (2003) proposed to apply minimum error rate training (MERT) to optimize the different feature weights in the log-linear model combination on a small development data set. This is still considered to be the state of the art, but is only capable of optimizing a handful of features. More recently, MIRA (Watanabe et al., 2007; Chiang et al., 2008) and PRO (Hopkins and May, 2011) have been presented as optimization procedures that can replace MERT and scale to thousands of parameters.

In a different line of work, Liang et al. (2006) describe a fully discriminative training pipeline, where more than one million features are tuned on the training data using a perceptron-style update algorithm. The Direct Translation Model 2 introduced by Ittycheriah and Roukos (2007) is similar in that it also trains millions of features on the training data. However, the weights are estimated based on a maximum entropy model and the underlying translation paradigm differs from the standard phrase-based model. Gao and He (2013) use gradient ascent to train Markov random field models for phrase translation. These models are interpreted as undirected phrase compatibility scores rather than translation probabilities. Thus, as in our work, they are not subject to a sum-to-one constraint. Simianer et al. (2012) propose a distributed setup for large-scale discriminative training with joint feature selection. The training corpus is divided into several shards, on which features are updated via perceptron-style gradient descent. The authors present results showing that training on large data sets improves results over just using a small development corpus. Another approach based on the AdaGrad method that scales to large numbers of sparse features is proposed in (Green et al., 2013; Green et al., 2014). Different from our work, the authors use either the tuning sets or a small subsample of the training data (15k sentences) for discriminative training.

A notably different idea is pursued by Yu et al. (2013), who present a large-scale training procedure that explicitly minimizes search errors. This is achieved by force-decoding the training data and updating at the point where the correct derivation drops off the beam.

In (Blunsom et al., 2008), conditional random fields (CRFs) are trained within a hierarchical phrase-based translation framework. The hierarchical phrase-based paradigm is used to model the search space in model estimation and search, leaving the hypothesis weighting to CRF features. They constrain search by a beam width for gradient estimation and update the model with the help of L-BFGS. In a similar way Lavergne et al. (2011) use the $n$-gram based approach (Casacuberta and Vidal, 2004; Mariño et al., 2006) to model the reordering, phrase alignment, and the language model. A CRF is applied to estimate the phrase weights. Model updates are carried out by the RPROP algorithm (Riedmiller and Braun, 1993). However, both approaches only improve over constrained baselines.

Our work is inspired by (He and Deng, 2012; Setiawan and Zhou, 2013), where the authors propose to train the standard phrasal and lexical channel models with the growth transformation (GT) algorithm. They use $n$-best lists on the training data and optimize a maximum expected BLEU objective, that provides a clear training criterion, which is missing e.g. in MIRA estimation. Auli et al. (2014) report good results by applying the same objective function to reordering features, which are trained with stochastic gradient descent (SGD).

Our work differs in several key aspects: (i) We propose to apply the RPROP algorithm, which yields superior results to GT, SGD and AdaGrad in our experimental comparison. (ii) For the first time, we apply maximum expected BLEU training on a data set as large as four million sentence pairs. (iii) We apply a leave-one-out heuristic (Wuebker et al., 2010) to make better use of the training data. (iv) We apply phrasal, lexical, reordering and triplet features. (v) Finally, we do not run MERT after each training iteration, which is expensive for large translation systems.

## 3 Statistical Translation System

Our work can be applied to any statistical machine translation paradigm and we will present results on a standard phrase-based translation system (Koehn et al., 2003) and a hierarchical phrase-based translation system (Chiang, 2005). The translation process is implemented as a weighted log-linear combination of several models $h_{m,\Theta}(E, F)$, where $E = e_1, \ldots, e_I$ denotes the translation hypothesis, $F = f_1, \ldots, f_J$ the source sentence, $m$ a model index, and $\Theta$ the model parameters. These models include the phrase translation and lexical smoothing scores in both directions, language model (LM) score, distortion penalty, word penalty and phrase penalty (Och and Ney, 2004). Given a source sentence $F$, the models $h_{m,\Theta}(E, F)$ and the corresponding log-linear feature weights $\lambda_m$, the translation decoder searches for the best scoring translation $\hat{E}$:

$$\hat{E} = \arg\max_{E} \{f_\Theta(E, F)\} \quad (1)$$

$$f_\Theta(E, F) = \sum_{m \in M} \lambda_m h_{m,\Theta}(E, F) \quad (2)$$

where $\ldots, \lambda_m, \ldots$ are the model weighting parameters. In practice, the Viterbi approximation is applied and for simplicity, in the following we will assume the particular derivation for a translation hypothesis to be included in the variable $E$. The log-linear feature weights are optimized with minimum error rate training (MERT) (Och, 2003).

## 4 Update Strategies

### 4.1 Previously Proposed Algorithms

The **Growth Transformation (GT)** or Extended Baum-Welch Algorithm was proposed by He and Deng (2012) for maximum expected BLEU training of the standard phrasal and lexical channel models. It is an algorithm to iteratively optimize polynomials of random variables that are subject to sum-to-one contraints and is therefore suitable for training probability distributions. The disadvantage is that each parameter update requires a renormalization step, which artificially blows up the number of features that need to be changed and has a significant impact on time and memory efficiency. The update formulas are derived in (He and Deng, 2012).

**Stochastic Gradient Descent (SGD)** is a well-known and frequently applied training scheme, which is used for maximum expected BLEU training of reordering models by (Auli et al., 2014). It performs the following update:

$$\vartheta^{(t+1)} = \vartheta^{(t)} + \eta \cdot \nabla_\vartheta^{(t)} \quad (3)$$

Here, the disadvantage is its high sensitivity to the fixed learning rate $\eta$. However, as it does not subject the features to sum-to-one-contraints, it is considerably more time and memory efficient than GT.

As an improvement to SGD, **AdaGrad** (Duchi et al., 2011) is designed for large, sparse feature sets and makes use of an adaptive learning rate. It was proposed for MT training by (Green et al., 2013). Although its main area of application are online algorithms, it is also applicable in our offline setting and is more robust than SGD due to the adaptive learning rate. Following (Green et al., 2013), we apply the approximation with a diagonal outer product matrix, which is computationally cheap. This results in the update equations

$$\vartheta^{(t+1)} = \vartheta^{(t)} + \eta \cdot G_t^{-\frac{1}{2}} \cdot \nabla_\vartheta^{(t)} \quad (4)$$

$$G_t = G_{t-1} + (\nabla_\vartheta^{(t)})^2 \quad (5)$$

### 4.2 RPROP

The resilient backpropagation algorithm (RPROP) proposed by Riedmiller and Braun (1993) is a gradient-based optimization algorithm that emprirically learns the step size without taking the slope into account, making it highly robust and avoiding the need for a learning rate. If the gradient switches algebraic sign compared to the previous iteration, the last step is reverted and the step size reduced. If the sign remains the same, the step size is increased. Formally, given a set of parameters $\Theta$ and an objective function $O(\Theta)$, in iteration $t$ each parameter $\vartheta \in \Theta$ is updated according to

$$\vartheta^{(t+1)} = \begin{cases} \vartheta^{(t-1)} & \text{, if } \nabla_\vartheta^{(t-1)} \cdot \nabla_\vartheta^{(t)} < 0 \\ \vartheta^{(t)} + \Delta\vartheta^{(t)} & \text{, else if } \nabla_\vartheta^{(t)} > 0 \\ \vartheta^{(t)} - \Delta\vartheta^{(t)} & \text{, else if } \nabla_\vartheta^{(t)} < 0 \\ \vartheta^{(t)} & \text{, else} \end{cases}$$

where $\nabla_\vartheta^{(t)} := \frac{\delta O(\Theta^{(t)})}{\delta \vartheta}$ denotes the derivative of the objective function. The step size $\Delta\vartheta^{(t)} > 0$ grows or decreases depending on the sign of the gradient:

$$\Delta\vartheta^{(t)} = \begin{cases} \eta^+ \cdot \Delta\vartheta^{(t-1)} & \text{, if } \nabla_\vartheta^{(t-1)} \cdot \nabla_\vartheta^{(t)} > 0 \\ \eta^- \cdot \Delta\vartheta^{(t-1)} & \text{, if } \nabla_\vartheta^{(t-1)} \cdot \nabla_\vartheta^{(t)} < 0 \\ \Delta\vartheta^{(t-1)} & \text{, else} \end{cases}$$

The strength parameters $0 < \eta^- < 1 \leq \eta^+$ usually have little impact and are fixed to $\eta^- = 0.5$ and $\eta^+ = 1.2$ throughout this work. The RPROP algorithm is simple and easy to implement. It has proven effective for a number of tasks, e.g. in (Wiesler et al., 2013; Heigold et al., 2011; Lavergne et al., 2011; Hahn et al., 2011). Different from growth transformation (cf. Sec. 4.1), it does not assume a probability distribution and performs its updates without a sum-to-one constraint.

Compared to SGD and AdaGrad, RPROP's practical advantage is the absence of a learning rate that needs to be tuned. Further, we see its theoretical advantage in the empirically learned step size. In the first iterations, RPROP's updates are considerably smaller than with the other strategies, resulting in a more careful exploration of the search space. In higher iterations, the update steps for good features keep growing and we observe an exponential increase of the objective function. In contrast, GT, SGD, and AdaGrad determine the size of their update step based on the slope of the gradient, which we believe to be misleading given the complex topology of the feature space in MT.

## 5 Training

### 5.1 Maximum Expected BLEU

Following (He and Deng, 2012), we want to optimize a maximum expected BLEU objective. We denote the universe of possible sentences in the source language as $\mathbb{F}$ and in the target language as $\mathbb{E}$. The expected BLEU score under parameter set $\Theta$ with respect to the joint probability distribution $p_\Theta(\cdot, \cdot)$ is defined as

$$\langle \beta \rangle_\Theta = \sum_{F \in \mathbb{F}} \sum_{E \in \mathbb{E}} p_\Theta(E, F) \beta(E) \quad (6)$$

Here, $\beta(E)$ is the BLEU score for target sentence $E$ (assuming the reference translation to be part of the mapping $\beta$) and we use the notation $\langle \cdot \rangle$ to denote the expectation. Enumerating all possible source and target sentences $F$, $E$ is infeasible. Therefore, we estimate the empirical expectation on a corpus $\mathbb{C} \subset \mathbb{E} \times \mathbb{F}$. We denote the source sentences in $\mathbb{C}$ as $\mathbb{C}_F$ and the size of the corpus as $N = |\mathbb{C}|$. The joint probability $p_\Theta(E, F)$ is decomposed with the help of the Bayes Theorem, resulting in:

$$\langle \beta \rangle_\Theta = \sum_{F \in \mathbb{C}_F} p(F) \sum_{E \in \mathbb{E}_\Theta(F)} p_\Theta(E|F) \beta(E) \quad (7)$$

For $p(F) = \frac{N_F}{N}$ we assume the empirical distribution within the training corpus, where $N_F$ is the count of sentence $F$. The summation over all $E \in \mathbb{E}$ is sampled with a subset $\mathbb{E}_\Theta(F)$ of the most likely hypotheses with respect to the parameterized probability $p_\Theta(E, F)$, which in practice is an $n$-best list generated by the decoder. Iterating over the corpus $\mathbb{C} = \{(E_1, F_1), \ldots, (E_n, F_n), \ldots, (E_N, F_N)\}$ finally results in

$$\langle \beta \rangle_\Theta = \frac{1}{N} \sum_{n=1}^{N} \sum_{E \in \mathbb{E}_\Theta(F_n)} p_\Theta(E|F_n) \beta(E)$$

We use the same unclipped sentence-level BLEU-4 score with smoothed 3-gram and 4-gram precisions as in (He and Deng, 2012), which we denote as $\beta(E) = \text{BLEU}(E, E_n^*)$ with respect to the reference translation $E_n^*$.

The normalized posterior translation probability $p_\Theta(E|F)$ from source sentence $F$ to target sentence $E$ approximates a maximum entropy model normalized on sentence level:

$$p_\Theta(E|F) = \frac{e^{-f_\Theta(E,F)}}{\sum_{E' \in \mathbb{E}_\Theta(F)} e^{-f_\Theta(E',F)}} \quad (8)$$

The denominator of this probability does not depend on the output sentence. Thus, the $\arg\max$ of Equation 8 is equal to the $\arg\max$ of the translation score in Equation 1.

Maximum Entropy models tend to generalize poorly, which can be circumvented by regularization. He and Deng (2012) use Kullback-Leibler regularization, raising the need of having normalized models $h_{m,\Theta}(E,F)$. We employ the more general $L_2$-regularization and the objective function is defined as

$$O(\Theta) = log\langle\beta\rangle_\Theta - \tau \cdot \sum_{\vartheta \in \Theta} \vartheta^2 \quad (9)$$

including the hyper parameter $\tau$ controlling the degree of regularization. The derivative of the objective function, which is needed for the gradient-based training methods, directly follows:

$$\frac{\delta O(\Theta)}{\delta \vartheta} = -\tau \cdot 2\vartheta + \frac{1}{\langle\beta\rangle_\Theta} \cdot \frac{\delta\langle\beta\rangle_\Theta}{\delta\vartheta} \quad (10)$$

With $\frac{\partial h_{m,\Theta}(E,F)}{\partial\vartheta} = \#_\vartheta(E,F)$ the number of times feature $\vartheta$ fires in the derivation for translation hypothesis $E$ given source sentence $F$, the derivative of $p_\Theta(E|F)$ is defined as (for ease of notation $\mathbb{E}_\Theta(F_n)$ is represented by $\mathbb{E}_n$)

$$\frac{\partial p_\Theta(E|F)}{\partial\vartheta} = -p_\Theta(E|F) \cdot \left(\#_\vartheta(E,F) - \sum_{E' \in \mathbb{E}_n} p_\Theta(E'|F)\#_\vartheta(E',F)\right) \quad (11)$$

And the derivative of the expected BLEU is

$$\begin{aligned}\frac{\delta\langle\beta\rangle_\Theta}{\delta\vartheta} &= \frac{1}{N}\sum_{n=1}^{N}\sum_{E\in\mathbb{E}_n}\beta(E)\frac{\partial p_\Theta(E|F_n)}{\partial\vartheta} \\ &= -\frac{1}{N}\sum_{n=1}^{N}\Bigg(\sum_{E\in\mathbb{E}_n}p_\Theta(E|F)\beta(E)\#_\vartheta(E,F) \\ &\quad - \Big(\sum_{E\in\mathbb{E}_n}p_\Theta(E|F)\beta(E)\Big)\cdot \\ &\quad \Big(\sum_{E\in\mathbb{E}_n}p_\Theta(E|F)\#_\vartheta(E,F)\Big)\Bigg)\end{aligned} \quad (12)$$

This can be more compactly expressed by local expectations $\langle\cdot\rangle_n$ of the BLEU score and the feature count $\#_\vartheta$:

$$\frac{\delta\langle\beta\rangle_\Theta}{\delta\vartheta} = -\frac{1}{N}\sum_{n=1}^{N}(\langle\beta\#_\vartheta\rangle_n - \langle\beta\rangle_n\langle\#_\vartheta\rangle_n)$$

In our implementation, $\#_\vartheta$ is moved to the front of the equation to obtain common factors that can be used by all parameter updates:

$$\begin{aligned}\frac{\delta\langle\beta\rangle_\Theta}{\delta\vartheta} &= \frac{1}{N}\sum_{n=1}^{N}\sum_{E\in\mathbb{E}_n}\#_\vartheta(E,F)\cdot \\ &\quad p_\Theta(E|F)(\langle\beta\rangle_n - \beta(E))\end{aligned} \quad (13)$$

### 5.2 Leave-one-out

Although He and Deng (2012) claim that it is not necessary, we apply a leave-one-out heuristic similar to (Wuebker et al., 2010) when generating the $n$-best lists on the training data. The authors have shown this to effectively counteract over-fitting effects and we argue that it helps to bring out the full potential of our discriminative training procedure.

When we decode the training data of our translation model, very long and rare phrases can be used to translate the sentence. The translation probability for these phrases, which are often singletons, are generally over-estimated by the heuristic count model. When they are too dominant in the $n$-best lists they effectively render the training data useless, as they are unlikely to generalize to unseen data. The idea of leave-one-out is that for decoding each sentence, the global counts of the relative frequency estimates are reduced by the local counts extracted from the current sentence pair. This way, the above mentioned rare phrases are penalized and the decoder is encouraged to use more general phrases taken from the remainder of the training data. Singleton phrases are given a fixed penalty. In this work, we apply leave-one-out with all update strategies.

### 5.3 Features

Maximum expected BLEU training facilitates training of arbitrary features. In this work we apply four types of features. (a) A discriminative phrase table, i.e. one feature for each phrase pair. (b) Lexical features, i.e. one feature for each source-target word pair that appear within the same phrase. (c) Source and target triplet features (Hasan et al., 2008), i.e. triples of one source and two target words or one target and two source words appearing within a single phrase pair. (d) The hierarchical lexicalized reordering model (Galley and Manning, 2008), i.e. one feature for each combination of phrase pair, orientation (monotone (M), swap (S) or discontinuous (D)) and orientation direction (forward or backward). GT is only applied with feature set (a), where we reestimate the two phrasal channel models as was done in (He and Deng, 2012). With the other update algorithms we follow the approach taken in (Auli et al., 2014) and condense each feature type into a small number of models for the log-linear combination, which is afterwards tuned with MERT. (a) and (b) result in a single additional model, (c) in two models (source and target triplets) and (d) in six models ($\{$forward,backward$\} \times \{$M,S,D$\}$).

### 5.4 Efficient Implementation

The expected BLEU $\langle\beta\rangle_\Theta$ is efficiently computed in one iteration over the full $n$-best list. As can be seen from Equation 13, the derivative $\frac{\delta\langle\beta\rangle_\Theta}{\delta\vartheta}$ is additive with respect to each firing instance of feature $\vartheta$ in the $n$-best list. The additive factor only depends on the current sentence pair. Therefore, for each sentence of the training data we iterate through its $n$-best list once to compute the expectation of the sentence-level BLEU score $\langle\beta\rangle_n$ and then a second time to update the current derivative for each time the feature fires. The only thing that needs to be kept in memory is a list of the current derivatives for each parameter $\vartheta$.

1. Create the baseline system and run MERT
2. Generate $n$-best list on training corpus
3. Compute sentence-level BLEU $\beta(E_n)$ for each hypothesis $E_n$ in the list
4. Initialize parameters with $\vartheta = 0, \forall\vartheta \in \Theta$
5. Iterate:
   a) Compute the derivatives $\frac{\delta O(\Theta)}{\delta\vartheta}$
   b) Perform update and output $\Theta^{(t)}$
6. Run MERT on `dev` with each table $\Theta^{(t)}$
7. Select best $\Theta^{(t)}$ on `dev`
8. Evaluate on test sets

Figure 1: The complete training algorithm.

### 5.5 Complete Training Algorithm

The complete training and evaluation procedure is shown in Figure 1. We start by building a baseline translation system with MERT-optimized model weights $\lambda$. With the baseline system we generate $n$-best lists on the training data. Now, for each translation hypothesis $E_n$ of the $n$-best list, we compute the sentence-level BLEU score $\beta(E_n)$ and initialize the parameter set for training with the count model. Next, we run the training algorithm for a fixed number of iterations[1] and output the updated feature values $\Theta^{(t)}$ after each iteration $t$. Finally, we run MERT with each $\Theta^{(t)}$, select the best table on `dev` and evaluate on our test sets.

## 6 Experiments

### 6.1 Setup

The experiments are carried out on the IWSLT 2013 German→English shared translation task.[2] For rapid experimentation, the translation model is trained on the in-domain TED portion of the bilingual data, which is also used for maximum expected BLEU training. However, we use a large 4-gram LM with modified Kneser-Ney smoothing (Kneser and Ney, 1995; Chen and Goodman, 1998), trained with the SRILM toolkit (Stolcke, 2002). As additional data sources for the LM we use the complete News Commentary, Europarl v7 and Common Crawl corpora as well as selected parts of the Shuffled News

[1]Note that we keep the $\lambda$ weights fixed throughout all iterations of maximum expected BLEU training.

[2]`http://www.iwslt2013.org`

| | IWSLT | | BOLT | | WMT | |
|---|---|---|---|---|---|---|
| | **German** | **English** | **Chinese** | **English** | **German** | **English** |
| Sentences | 138K | | 4.08M | | 4.09M | |
| Run. Words | 2.63M | 2.70M | 78.3M | 85.9M | 105M | 104M |
| Vocabulary | 75.4K | 50.2K | 384K | 817K | 659K | 649K |

Table 1: Statistics for the bilingual training data of the IWSLT 2013 German→English, the DARPA BOLT Chinese→English and the WMT 2014 German→English tasks.

and LDC English Gigaword corpora. The selection is based on cross-entropy difference (Moore and Lewis, 2010). This makes for a total of 1.7 billion running words for LM training. The baseline further contains a hierarchical reordering model (HRM) (Galley and Manning, 2008) and a 7-gram word class language model (Wuebker et al., 2013). On IWSLT, all results are averages over three independent MERT runs, and we evaluate statistical significance with *MultEval* (Clark et al., 2011).

To confirm our findings, additional experiments are run on two large-scale tasks over strong baselines including recurrent neural language models. On the DARPA BOLT Chinese→English task we use our internal evaluation system as a baseline. It is a powerful hierarchical phrase-based SMT engine with 19 dense features, including an LSTM recurrent neural language model (Sundermeyer et al., 2012) and a hierarchical reordering model (Huck et al., 2013). The 5-gram backoff LM is in total trained on 2.9 billion running words. We use the same data for tuning and testing as Setiawan and Zhou (2013), namely 1275 (tune) and 1239[3] sentences of web data taken from LDC2010E30, the NIST MT06 evaluation set and an additional single-reference test set from the discussion forum (df) domain containing 1124 sentence pairs. Maximum expected BLEU training is performed on the discussion forum portion of the training data, consisting of 67.8K sentence pairs. On the German→English task of the *9th Workshop on Statistical Machine Translation*[4], both translation model and maximum expected BLEU training is performed on all available bilingual data. Our baseline is a phrase-based translation engine with a 4-gram backoff LM trained on 2.5 billion words with `lmplz` (Heafield et al., 2013), a recurrent neural LM, a 7-gram word class LM and the HRM.

[3]named *dev* in (Setiawan and Zhou, 2013)

[4]`http://statmt.org/wmt14/`

| **IWSLT de-en** | **# feat.** | **test** |
|---|---|---|
| baseline | 18 | 30.4 |
| GT (He and Deng, 2012) | 6.08M | 30.9 |
| SGD (Auli et al., 2014) | 921K | 30.8 |
| AdaGrad (Green et al., 2013) | 921K | 31.1 |
| RPROP (this work) | 921K | **31.3** |
| RPROP w/o leave-one-out | 921K | 30.7 |
| RPROP all features | 5.22M | **31.6** |

Table 2: Results for the IWSLT 2013 German→English task in BLEU [%]. The comparison between update strategies is done with feature set (a) and *RPROP all features* uses feature sets (a)-(d). GT, SGD, AdaGrad and RPROP are trained with leave-one-out, unless otherwise specified.

Bilingual data statistics for all tasks are given in Table 1. We use the machine translation toolkit *Jane* (Vilar et al., 2010; Wuebker et al., 2012) and evaluate with case-insensitive BLEU [%] (Papineni et al., 2002) in all experiments.

### 6.2 Experimental Results

Table 2 shows the **IWSLT** results. We first compare the performance of the four update algorithms, for simplicity only on the discriminative phrase table features. Different from previous work the $n$-best lists of the training data were generated with leave-one-out, unless otherwise stated. In all cases we tested different values for the regularization parameter $\tau$ and in the case of SGD and AdaGrad also for the learning rate $\eta$. We selected the best configurations based on a validation set (test2011). For AdaGrad we also experimented with FOBOS regularization and feature selection (Duchi and Singer, 2009), but did not observe improved results. As

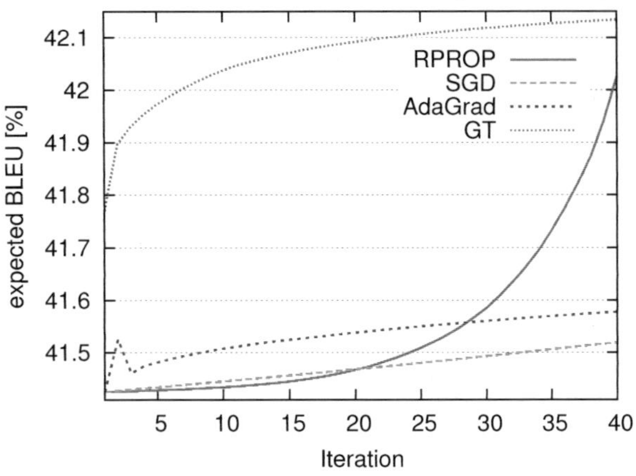


Figure 2: Expected BLEU value on IWSLT German→English for the different update strategies. Note that growth transformation (GT) applies a different regularization term and is therefore not directly comparable with the other techniques.

expected, we found that in all cases regularization is not strictly necessary - results are barely affected as long as $\tau$ is sufficiently small - and that SGD is much more sensitive to $\eta$ than AdaGrad. Further, SGD and RPROP need around 25 iterations to reach good results, where 5-10 iterations are sufficient for GT and AdaGrad. For a fair comparison, however, we run all algorithms for 40 iterations and select the best one on a seletion set, namely iterations 19 (AdaGrad), 23 (GT), 29 (RPROP) and 35 (SGD). Figure 2 shows how the expected BLEU function evolves in training with different update strategies. Although the value for GT is not directly comparable to the others due to a different regularization term, the respective characteristics are clearly visible. SGD exhibits a linear growth pattern, GT resembles a logarithmic and RPROP an exponential function. After initially overshooting and then retracting as the regularization kicks in, AdaGrad also displays logarithmic characteristics.

In terms of BLEU RPROP performs best, followed by AdaGrad, GT and SGD, where the RPROP-AdaGrad and AdaGrad-GT differences are small (0.2% BLEU absolute) but statistically significant on the 95% level. Altogether, RPROP improves over the baseline by 0.9 BLEU points, which is statistically significant at the 99% level. In an additional experiment we verified that leave-one-out has a clear impact on the results. The BLEU difference between RPROP with and without leave-one-out is 0.6% absolute. By adding lexical, triplet and reordering features, we get an additional gain and observe a total improvement of 1.2 BLEU points over the baseline system.

| **BOLT zh-en** | **# feat.** | **df** | **web** | **MT06** |
|---|---|---|---|---|
| baseline | 19 | 18.0 | 34.1 | 39.7 |
| SGD | 12.4M | 18.0 | 34.3 | 39.8 |
| AdaGrad | 12.4M | 18.3 | 34.7 | 40.1 |
| RPROP | 12.4M | **18.7** | **34.8** | **40.5** |
| Setiawan&Zhou (GT) | 150M | - | 32.7 | 40.3 |

Table 3: Results for the BOLT Chinese→English task in BLEU [%] on the discussion forum test set (df), the mixed web test set and NIST MT06. The baseline is our BOLT evaluation system and contains a recurrent neural LM. We compare with (Setiawan and Zhou, 2013) who applied maximum expected BLEU training with growth transformation (GT). Note that the number of features reported by Setiawan and Zhou (2013) is artificially blown up due to renormalization.

**Efficiency comparison.** 921K discriminative phrase table features are active in our training data. Due to the renormalization component, this results in a total of 6.08M features that are updated with GT using the same data. Consequently, it is less time and space efficient than the other algorithms. With our implementation, GT needed around 16 hours and 6.7G memory for 40 iterations, where RPROP, AdaGrad and SGD finished after less than 2.5 hours and required 2.1G memory.

For the **BOLT** task, we directly compare with the GT-trained system in (Setiawan and Zhou, 2013) using the same tune set for MERT and reporting results on the same test sets, see Table 3. With RPROP we achieve nearly twice the improvement reported by Setiawan on both *web* and *MT06* using feature sets (a)-(c)[5]. Our baseline on *web* is already much stronger and RPROP training yields +0.7 BLEU points, as opposed to +0.44 reported by Setiawan. On *MT06* our baseline system is slightly worse, but with the larger gain received by RPROP our final system outperforms the one reported by Se-

[5] Reordering features are not applicable to our hiero system.

| WMT de-en | # feat. | newstest2013 |
|---|---|---|
| baseline | 19 | 28.3 |
| RPROP | 45.0M | **28.9** |
| matrix.statmt.org | 14 | 28.1 |

Table 4: Results for the WMT German→English task in BLEU [%]. The baseline contains a recurrent neural LM. We compare with the best single system that is reported on `matrix.statmt.org`, which was submitted by the Unversity of Edinburgh.

tiawan by 0.2 BLEU points. We would like to stress that this is not a domain adaptation effect, as maximum expected BLEU training was performed on discussion forum (df) data. On the *df* test set, on the other hand, we probably can observe domain adaptation via RPROP training. The improvement here is 0.7% BLEU absolute with a single reference, as opposed to four references on *web* and *MT06*. We also report results training the same feature sets with SGD and AdaGrad, confirming results we observed on IWSLT. Here, SGD yields only minor improvements. AdaGrad performs better, but still 0.1 - 0.4 BLEU points worse than RPROP. Running GT is infeasible in our hierarchical phrase-based setup.

Table 4 shows the results on the **WMT** task. This is our largest setting, where max. exp. BLEU training is performed on the full training data with more than 4M sentence pairs which, to the best of our knowledge, is unsurpassed in the literature. Altogether, training took more than one month, about 3/4 of which were for generating $n$-best lists by decoding the training data. The triplet features did not finish in time, so we applied the feature sets (a), (b) and (d), 45M features in total. With a renormalization step as in GT, this number would grow to 309M. On *newstest2013*, our baseline already outperforms the best single system reported on matrix.statmt.org by 0.2 BLEU points. The discriminatively trained features yield an additional improvement of 0.6% BLEU absolute on this high-end system.

## 7 Conclusion

We have experimentally compared several update strategies for maximum expected BLEU training. The RPROP algorithm proposed in this work shows superior performance compared to AdaGrad, growth transformation (GT) and stochastic gradient descent. In terms of time and memory efficiency, GT is clearly inferior to the other algorithms due to renormalization. Applying phrasal, lexical, triplet and reordering features, the baseline is improved by 1.2% BLEU absolute on the IWSLT German→English task. On two large scale tasks we achieve clearly superior performance compared to results reported in the literature. On BOLT Chinese→English our discriminative training yields nearly twice the improvement reported by Setiawan and Zhou (2013), resulting in a superior final system. On WMT German→English, we outperform the best single system reported on matrix.statmt.org by 0.8% BLEU absolute. Here, we perform maximum expexted BLEU training on more than 4M sentence pairs, which is the largest number reported in the literature to date.

## Acknowledgments

The research leading to these results has received funding from the European Union Seventh Framework Programme (FP7/2007-2013) under grant agreement n° 287658. This material is also partially based upon work supported by the DARPA BOLT project under Contract No. HR0011- 12-C-0015. Any opinions, findings and conclusions or recommendations expressed in this material are those of the authors and do not necessarily reflect the views of DARPA. We further thank the anonymous reviewers for valuable comments.

## References

Michael Auli, Michel Galley, and Jianfeng Gao. 2014. Large-scale Expected BLEU Training of Phrase-based Reordering ModelsI. In *Proceedings of the 2014 Conference on Empirical Methods in Natural Language Processing (EMNLP)*, pages 1250–1260, Doha, Qatar, October.

Phil Blunsom, Trevor Cohn, and Miles Osborne. 2008. A discriminative latent variable model for statistical machine translation. In *Proc. of ACL-HLT*.

Peter F. Brown, Stephan A. Della Pietra, Vincent J. Della Pietra, and Robert L. Mercer. 1993. The Mathematics of Statistical Machine Translation: Parameter Estimation. *Computational Linguistics*, 19(2):263–311, June.

Francisco Casacuberta and Enrique Vidal. 2004. Machine translation with inferred stochastic finite-state transducers. *Computational Linguistics*, 30(2):205–225.

Stanley F. Chen and Joshuo Goodman. 1998. An Empirical Study of Smoothing Techniques for Language Modeling. Technical Report TR-10-98, Computer Science Group, Harvard University, Cambridge, MA, August.

D. Chiang, Y. Marton, and P. Resnik. 2008. Online large-margin training of syntactic and structural translation features. In *Conference on Empirical Methods in Natural Language Processing*, pages 224–233, Honolulu, Hawaii.

David Chiang. 2005. A Hierarchical Phrase-Based Model for Statistical Machine Translation. In *Proceedings of the 43rd Annual Meeting on Association for Computational Linguistics*, pages 263–270, Ann Arbor, Michigan, USA, June.

Jonathan H. Clark, Chris Dyer, Alon Lavie, and Noah A. Smith. 2011. Better hypothesis testing for statistical machine translation: Controlling for optimizer instability. In *49th Annual Meeting of the Association for Computational Linguistics:shortpapers*, pages 176–181, Portland, Oregon, June.

John Duchi and Yoram Singer. 2009. Efficient online and batch learning using forward backward splitting. *Journal of Machine Learning Research*, 10:2899–2934, December.

John Duchi, Elad Hazan, and Yoram Singer. 2011. Adaptive subgradient methods for online learning and stochastic optimization. *Journal of Machine Learning Research*, 12:2121–2159, July.

Michel Galley and Christopher D. Manning. 2008. A simple and effective hierarchical phrase reordering model. In *Proceedings of the Conference on Empirical Methods in Natural Language Processing*, EMNLP '08, pages 848–856, Stroudsburg, PA, USA. Association for Computational Linguistics.

Jianfeng Gao and Xiaodong He. 2013. Training MRF-Based Phrase Translation Models using Gradient Ascent. In *Proceedings of the North American Chapter of the Association for Computational Linguistics - Human Language Technologies conference (NAACL HLT)*, pages 450–459, Atlanta, Georgia, USA, Jun.

Spence Green, Sida Wang, Daniel Cer, and Christopher D. Manning. 2013. Fast and adaptive online training of feature-rich translation models. In *51st Annual Meeting of the Association for Computational Linguistics*, pages 311–321, Sofia, Bulgaria, August.

Spence Green, Daniel Cer, and Christopher D. Manning. 2014. An empirical comparison of features and tunign for phrase-based machine translation. In *Proceedings of the Ninth Workshop on Statistical Machine Translation*, pages 466–476, Baltimore, Maryland, USA, June.

Stefan Hahn, Marco Dinarelli, Christian Raymond, Fabrice Lefevre, Patrick Lehnen, Renato De Mori, Alessandro Moschitti, Hermann Ney, and Giuseppe Riccardi. 2011. Comparing Stochastic Approaches to Spoken Language Understanding in Multiple Languages. *IEEE Transactions on Audio, Speech, and Language Processing*, 19(6):1569–1583, August.

Saša Hasan, Juri Ganitkevitch, Hermann Ney, and Jesús Andrés-Ferrer. 2008. Triplet lexicon models for statistical machine translation. In *Conference on Empirical Methods in Natural Language Processing*, pages 372–381, Honolulu, Hawaii, October. Association for Computational Linguistics.

Xiaodong He and Li Deng. 2012. Maximum Expected BLEU Training of Phrase and Lexicon Translation Models. In *Proceedings of the 50th Annual Meeting of the Association for Computational Linguistics (ACL)*, pages 292–301, Jeju, Republic of Korea, Jul.

Kenneth Heafield, Ivan Pouzyrevsky, Jonathan H. Clark, and Philipp Koehn. 2013. Scalable modified Kneser-Ney language model estimation. In *Proceedings of the 51st Annual Meeting of the Association for Computational Linguistics*, pages 690–696, Sofia, Bulgaria, August.

Georg Heigold, Stefan Hahn, Patrick Lehnen, and Hermann Ney. 2011. EM-Style Optimization of Hidden Conditional Random Fields for Grapheme-to-Phoneme Conversion. In *IEEE International Conference on Acoustics, Speech, and Signal Processing*, pages 4920–4923, Prague, Czech Republic, May.

Mark Hopkins and Jonathan May. 2011. Tuning as ranking. In *In Proceedings of the 2011 Conference on Empirical Methods in Natural Language Processing*, pages 1352–1362, Edinburgh, Scotland, July.

Matthias Huck, Joern Wuebker, Felix Rietig, and Hermann Ney. 2013. A phrase orientation model for hierarchical machine translation. In *Workshop on Statistical Machine Translation*, pages 452–463, Sofia, Bulgaria, August.

Abraham Ittycheriah and Salim Roukos. 2007. Direct Translation Model 2. In *Proceedings of the North American Chapter of the Association for Computational Linguistics - Human Language Technologies conference (NAACL HLT)*, pages 57–64, Rochester, NY, USA, Apr.

Reinerd Kneser and Hermann Ney. 1995. Improved backing-off for M-gram language modeling. In *Proceedings of the International Conference on Acoustics, Speech, and Signal Processingw*, volume 1, pages 181–184, May.

P. Koehn, F. J. Och, and D. Marcu. 2003. Statistical Phrase-Based Translation. In *Proceedings of the 2003 Meeting of the North American chapter of the Association for Computational Linguistics (NAACL-03)*, pages 127–133, Edmonton, Alberta.

Thomas Lavergne, Alexandre Allauzen, Josep Maria Crego, and François Yvon. 2011. From n-gram-based to crf-based translation models. In *Proceedings of the Sixth Workshop on Statistical Machine Translation*, pages 542–553, Edinburgh, Scotland, July. Association for Computational Linguistics.

Percy Liang, Alexandre Buchard-Côté, Dan Klein, and Ben Taskar. 2006. An End-to-End Discriminative Approach to Machine Translation. In *Proceedings of the 21st International Conference on Computational Linguistics and the 44th annual meeting of the Association for Computational Linguistics*, pages 761–768, Sydney, Australia.

José B Mariño, Rafael E Banchs, Josep M Crego, Adrià de Gispert, Patrik Lambert, José A R Fonollosa, and Marta R Costa-jussà. 2006. N-gram-based Machine Translation. *Comput. Linguist.*, 32(4):527–549, December.

R.C. Moore and W. Lewis. 2010. Intelligent Selection of Language Model Training Data. In *ACL (Short Papers)*, pages 220–224, Uppsala, Sweden, July.

Franz Josef Och and Hermann Ney. 2004. The alignment template approach to statistical machine translation. *Computational Linguistics*, 30(4):417–449, December.

Franz Josef Och. 2003. Minimum Error Rate Training in Statistical Machine Translation. In *Proc. of the 41th Annual Meeting of the Association for Computational Linguistics (ACL)*, pages 160–167, Sapporo, Japan, July.

Kishore Papineni, Salim Roukos, Todd Ward, and Wei-Jing Zhu. 2002. Bleu: a Method for Automatic Evaluation of Machine Translation. In *Proceedings of the 41st Annual Meeting of the Association for Computational Linguistics*, pages 311–318, Philadelphia, Pennsylvania, USA, July.

Martin Riedmiller and Heinrich Braun. 1993. A direct adaptive method for faster backpropagation learning: The rprop algorithm. In *IEEE International Conference on Neural Networks*, pages 586–591.

Hendra Setiawan and Bowen Zhou. 2013. Discriminative training of 150 million translation parameters and its application to pruning. In *NAACL-HLT 2013*, pages 335–341, Atlanta, Georgia, June.

Patrick Simianer, Stefan Riezler, and Chris Dyer. 2012. Joint Feature Selection in Distributed Stochastic Learning for Large-Scale Discriminative Training in SMT. In *Proceedings of the 50th Annual Meeting of the Association for Computational Linguistics (Volume 1: Long Papers)*, pages 11–21, Jeju Island, Korea, July. Association for Computational Linguistics.

Andreas Stolcke. 2002. SRILM – An Extensible Language Modeling Toolkit. In *Proc. of the Int. Conf. on Speech and Language Processing (ICSLP)*, volume 2, pages 901–904, Denver, CO, September.

Martin Sundermeyer, Ralf Schlüter, and Hermann Ney. 2012. Lstm neural networks for language modeling. In *Interspeech*, Portland, OR, USA, September.

David Vilar, Daniel Stein, Matthias Huck, and Hermann Ney. 2010. Jane: Open source hierarchical translation, extended with reordering and lexicon models. In *ACL 2010 Joint Fifth Workshop on Statistical Machine Translation and Metrics MATR*, pages 262–270, Uppsala, Sweden, July.

Taro Watanabe, Jun Suzuki, Hajime Tsukada, and Hideki Isozaki. 2007. Online large-margin training for statistical machine translation. In *Proceedings of the 2007 Conference on Empirical Methods in Natural Language Processing*, pages 764–773, Prague, Czech Republic, June.

Simon Wiesler, Alexander Richard, Ralf Schlüter, and Hermann Ney. 2013. A Critical Evaluation of Stochastic Algorithms for Convex Optimization. In *IEEE International Conference on Acoustics, Speech, and Signal Processing*, pages 6955–6959, Vancouver, Canada, May.

Joern Wuebker, Arne Mauser, and Hermann Ney. 2010. Training phrase translation models with leaving-one-out. In *Proceedings of the 48th Annual Meeting of the Assoc. for Computational Linguistics*, pages 475–484, Uppsala, Sweden, July.

Joern Wuebker, Matthias Huck, Stephan Peitz, Malte Nuhn, Markus Freitag, Jan-Thorsten Peter, Saab Mansour, and Hermann Ney. 2012. Jane 2: Open source phrase-based and hierarchical statistical machine translation. In *International Conference on Computational Linguistics*, pages 483–491, Mumbai, India, December.

Joern Wuebker, Stephan Peitz, Felix Rietig, and Hermann Ney. 2013. Improving statistical machine translation with word class models. In *Conference on Empirical Methods in Natural Language Processing*, pages 1377–1381, Seattle, USA, October.

Heng Yu, Liang Huang, Haitao Mi, and Kai Zhao. 2013. Max-violation perceptron and forced decoding for scalable mt training. In *Conference on Empirical Methods in Natural Language Processing*, pages 1112–1123, Seattle, USA, October.

# Learning Translation Models from Monolingual Continuous Representations

**Kai Zhao***
Graduate Center, CUNY
New York, NY 10016, USA
kzhao.hf@gmail.com

**Hany Hassan**
Microsoft Research
Redmond, WA 98502, USA
hanyh@microsoft.com

**Michael Auli***
Facebook AI Research
Menlo Park, CA 94025, USA
michaelauli@fb.com

## Abstract

Translation models often fail to generate good translations for infrequent words or phrases. Previous work attacked this problem by inducing new translation rules from monolingual data with a semi-supervised algorithm. However, this approach does not scale very well since it is very computationally expensive to generate new translation rules for only a few thousand sentences. We propose a much faster and simpler method that directly hallucinates translation rules for infrequent phrases based on phrases with similar continuous representations for which a translation is known. To speed up the retrieval of similar phrases, we investigate approximated nearest neighbor search with redundant bit vectors which we find to be three times faster and significantly more accurate than locality sensitive hashing. Our approach of learning new translation rules improves a phrase-based baseline by up to 1.6 BLEU on Arabic-English translation, it is three-orders of magnitudes faster than existing semi-supervised methods and 0.5 BLEU more accurate.

## 1 Introduction

Statistical translation models (Koehn et al. 2003, Chiang et al. 2005) are trained with bilingual data and a simple solution to improve accuracy is to train on more data. However, for many language pairs we only have a very limited amount of bilingual data and even when dealing with resource-rich languages, we still often perform poorly when dealing with rare words or phrases.

On the other hand, there is plenty of monolingual data and previous work has investigated its use in learning translation models (Rapp, 1995; Callison-Burch et al., 2006; Haghighi et al., 2008; Saluja et al., 2014). However, most methods rely on statistics that are computationally expensive. As a concrete example, the graph propagation algorithm of Saluja et al. (2014) relies on pair-wise mutual information statistics between any pair of phrases in the monolingual corpus that is very expensive to compute, even for moderately sized corpora.

In this paper, we study the use of standard continuous representations for words to generate translation rules for infrequent phrases (§2). We explore linear projections that map continuous representations of rare foreign phrases to English phrases. In particular, we propose to learn many local projections that are specific to a given foreign phrase. We find this to be much more accurate than a single globally learned mapping such as proposed by (Mikolov et al. 2013; §3).

Our method relies on the fast retrieval of similar phrases in continuous space. We explore both Locality Sensitive Hashing (LSH; Indyk and Motwani, 2008) as well as the lesser known Redundant Bit Vector method (RBV; Goldstein et al. 2005) for fast $k$-nearest neighbor ($k$-NN) search. RBV outperforms the popular LSH algorithm by a large margin, both in speed as well as accuracy (§4).

Our results show that the local linear projection method is not only three orders of magnitudes faster than the algorithm of Saluja et al. (2014) but also by 0.5 BLEU more accurate. We achieve a 1.6 BLEU improvement in Arabic-English translation compared to a standard phrase-based baseline (§5).

## 2 Continuous Phrase Representations

Continuous representations of words have been found to capture syntactic and semantic regularities in language (Turian et al., 2014; Collobert et al., 2011; Mikolov et al., 2013c). The induced representations often tend to cluster similar words together as illustrated in Figure 1.

*The entirety of this work was conducted while at Microsoft Research.



*Human Language Technologies: The 2015 Annual Conference of the North American Chapter of the ACL*, pages 1527–1536,
Denver, Colorado, May 31 – June 5, 2015. 

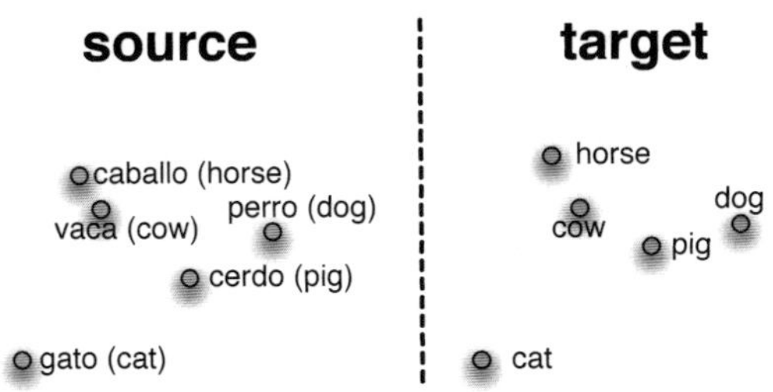


Figure 1: Illustration of word representations in Spanish and English (Figure from Mikolov et al. (2013a)). The plots are based on a two-dimensional projection of the original vectors with principal component analysis.

A logical next step is to learn representations for larger linguistic units, a topic which has received a lot of interest (Mitchell and Lapata, 2010; Socher et al., 2011; Le and Mikolov, 2014). For machine translation there have been efforts to learn representations for entire bilingual phrases (Zou et al., 2013; Zhang et al., 2014; Gao et al., 2014).

In this work, we only require representations for monolingual phrases that are relatively short.[1] We therefore decided to use off-the-shelf word representations to build phrase vectors. In particular, we chose the continuous bag-of-words model (Mikolov et al., 2013b) which is very fast to train and scales very well to large monolingual corpora.

The resulting word vectors are then used to build phrase vectors via simple element-wise addition which has been found to perform very competitively in comparison to alternative approaches (Mitchell and Lapata, 2010). Note that all the algorithms described in this paper are agnostic to the choice of phrase-representation and other schemes may perform better.

We use these monolingual phrase representations to generate translation rules for infrequent, or *unlabeled*, phrases. Unlabeled phrases do not appear in the bilingual data and thus do not have translation rules. The general idea behind the following algorithms is to identify *labeled* phrases for which we know translation rules that are similar to an unlabeled phrase, and to use them to induce translation rules for the unlabeled phrase.

[1]For simplicity, we only consider unigrams and bigrams on the source side, see §5

## 3 Translation Rule Generation

We first describe how we can learn a single mapping between the foreign and English continuous spaces to find translations for an infrequent foreign phrase (§3.1). Next, we make this approach more robust by learning many mappings that are specific to a given foreign phrase (§3.2). Finally, we review the semi-supervised label propagation algorithm of Saluja et al. (2014) which we make much faster using continuous word representations and $k$-NN algorithms (§3.3).

### 3.1 Global Linear Projection

Mikolov et al. (2013a) find that the relative positions between words are preserved between languages (Figure 1), and, thus, it is possible to learn a *linear* projection that maps the continuous representation of source phrases to points on the target side. The hope is to learn a mapping that captures the relationship between the source and target spaces. We call this linear transform *global linear projection*, since we use a single mapping that we apply to every source phrase.

More formally, we denote $f$ and $e$ as source side and target side phrases respectively, and $\mathbf{f} \in \mathbb{R}^{1\times d}$ and $\mathbf{e} \in \mathbb{R}^{1\times d}$ as the corresponding phrasal vectors with dimension $d$. Following Mikolov et al. (2013a), we learn a global linear projection matrix $W \in \mathbb{R}^{d\times d}$ based on the translations of the $n$ most frequent labeled source side phrases: $(\mathbf{f}_1, \mathbf{e}_1), (\mathbf{f}_2, \mathbf{e}_2), \ldots, (\mathbf{f}_n, \mathbf{e}_n), n \geq d$.[2] Let $F = [\mathbf{f}_1^T, \mathbf{f}_2^T, \ldots, \mathbf{f}_n^T]^T$, and $E = [\mathbf{e}_1^T, \mathbf{e}_2^T, \ldots, \mathbf{e}_n^T]^T$. We calculate $W$ by solving the following linear system:

$$FW = E$$

whose solution is:

$$W \approx (F^T F)^{-1} F^T E$$

Using the linear transform $W$, we can compute $\bar{\mathbf{e}} = \mathbf{f}W$ for each unlabeled source phrase $\mathbf{f}$, where $\bar{\mathbf{e}}$ will be close to target phrases that are potential translation candidates for $\mathbf{f}$. We denote the set of all nearby English phrase vectors as $N(\bar{\mathbf{e}})$ and use

[2]We need more than $d$ phrases to be fetched to make the linear system solvable. Similar is for the local linear projection in §3.2.

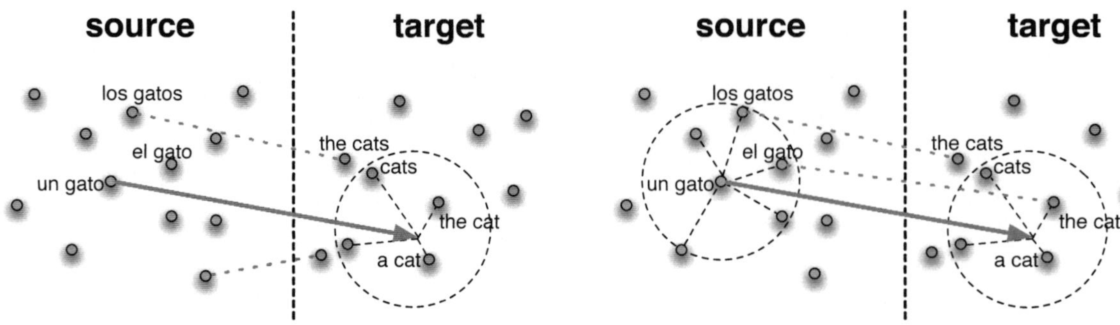


(a) Global Linear Projection (b) Local Linear Projection

Figure 2: (a) Illustration of the global linear projection mapping the unlabeled Spanish phrase "un gato" to the target space. The neighbors of the projected point serve as translation candidates and are fetched via a $k$-NN query. (b) A local linear projection is learned individually for "un gato" based on the translations "the cats", "the cat" of the labeled neighbors "los gatos", "el gato".

fast $k$-NN query algorithms to retrieve this set (§4). Figure 2 (a) illustrates the method.

The translation probability for each translation candidate $\mathbf{e} \in N(\bar{\mathbf{e}})$ is based on the similarity to the projected point $\bar{\mathbf{e}}$:

$$P(e|f) = \frac{\exp\{\text{sim}(\mathbf{e}, \bar{\mathbf{e}})\}}{\sum_{\mathbf{e}' \in N(\bar{\mathbf{e}})} \exp\{\text{sim}(\mathbf{e}', \bar{\mathbf{e}})\}}. \quad (1)$$

Note that we normalize over the neighbor set $N(\bar{\mathbf{e}})$ of the projected point $\bar{\mathbf{e}}$ of foreign phrase $f$. This uses the similarity $\text{sim}(\bar{\mathbf{e}}, \mathbf{e})$ between $\bar{\mathbf{e}}$ and $\mathbf{e}$ which is defined symmetrically as

$$\text{sim}(\bar{\mathbf{e}}, \mathbf{e}) = \frac{1}{1 + \|\bar{\mathbf{e}} - \mathbf{e}\|}, \quad (2)$$

where $\|\bar{\mathbf{e}} - \mathbf{e}\|$ is the Euclidean distance between vectors $\bar{\mathbf{e}}$ and $\mathbf{e}$.

Before adding the generated candidate translations to the MT system, we also calculate the backward maximum likelihood translation probability using Bayes' Theorem:

$$\text{P}(f|e) = \frac{\text{P}(e|f)\text{P}(f)}{\text{P}(e)},$$

where the marginal probabilities are based on the counts of phrases seen in the monolingual corpora.

Similar to Saluja et al. (2014), we use word-based translation probabilities from the baseline system to obtain forward and backward lexicalized translation probabilities.

### 3.2 Local Linear Projection

The global linear projection uses a single projection matrix for all unlabeled source phrases. This is simple and fast but assumes that we can capture all relations between the source and target representation space with a single $\mathbb{R}^{d \times d}$ mapping. We show later that this is clearly not the case (§5.4) and that a single projection struggles particularly with infrequent phrases - the precise situation in which we would like our projection to be robust.

We therefore propose to learn many *local linear projections* which are individually trained for each unlabeled source phrase. Specifically, for each unlabeled source phrase $\mathbf{f}$, we learn a mapping $W_{\mathbf{f}} \in \mathbb{R}^{d \times d}$ based on the translations of $m$ of $\mathbf{f}$'s labeled neighbors: $(\mathbf{f}_1, \mathbf{e}_1), (\mathbf{f}_2, \mathbf{e}_2), \ldots, (\mathbf{f}_m, \mathbf{e}_m)$, $\mathbf{f}_i \in N(\mathbf{f})$, $1 \leq i \leq m$, $m \geq d$ (see Figure 2 (b)).

Compared to the global projection, we require an additional $k$-NN query to find the labeled neighbors for each unlabeled source phrase. However, this extra computation takes only a negligible amount of time, since the number of labeled phrases on the source side is significantly smaller than the number of phrases on the target side.

Our approach of learning many different mappings is similar to the *locality preserving projections* method of He and Niyogi (2004), which also construct a locally precise projection in order to map to another space.

### 3.3 Structured Label Propagation with Continuous Representation

Saluja et al. (2014) use Structured Label Propagation (SLP; Liu et al. 2012) to propagate candidate translations from frequent source phrases that are labeled to unlabeled neighbors that are infrequent.

The algorithm works as follows: for a known translation rule $(f', e')$, SLP propagates the target side phrases $e \in N(e')$, that are similar to $e'$, to the unlabeled source phrases $f \in N(f')$, that are similar to $f'$, as new translation rules. This propagation runs for several iterations. At each iteration, the translation probability between known translations is fixed. More formally, for iteration $t+1$ we have

$$\mathrm{P}^{t+1}(e|f) = \sum_{f' \in N(f)} T(f'|f) \sum_{e' \in H(f')} T(e|e') \mathrm{P}^{t}(e'|f'),$$

where $T(f'|f)$ is the probability that phrase $f$ is propagated through phrase $f'$, similarly for $T(e|e')$; $H(f')$ is the set of translation candidates for source phrase $f'$, which is learned from the bilingual corpus.

In Saluja et al. (2014), both $T(f'|f)$ and $T(e|e')$ are based on the pairwise mutual information (PMI) between two phrases. Computing PMI statistics between any two phrases over a large corpus is infeasible and therefore the authors resort to a simple approximation that only considers co-occurrences with other phrases within a fixed-sized context window. Even after this simplification the running time of the SLP is vastly dominated by gathering similarity statistics and by constructing the resulting graph.

However, once the PMI statistics are collected and the graph is constructed, actual label propagation is very fast. To speed up the algorithm, we replace the costly PMI statistics by continuous phrase representations and adopt the same similarity measure that we used for the global and local projections (see Equation 1). Moreover, we replace the static graph construction with on-demand graph expansion using the fast phrase query mechanisms described in the next section. These modifications allow us to dramatically speed up the original SLP algorithm as demonstrated in our experiments (§5).

## 4 Fast Phrase Query with Continuous Representation

The algorithms presented in the previous section require rapid retrieval of neighboring phrases in continuous space. Linear search over all $n$ candidate phrases is impractical, particularly for the SLP algorithm (§3.3). SLP requires the construction of a graph encoding the nearest neighbors for each target phrase, be it online or offline. To construct this graph naïvely requires $\mathcal{O}(n^2)$ comparisons which is clearly impractical for our setup where we have over one million target phrases (§5). For the linear projections, we still need to run at least one $k$-NN query in the target space for each infrequent foreign phrase.

Various methods, e.g., $k$-d trees, were proposed for fast $k$-NN queries but most of them are not efficient enough in high dimensional space, such as our setting. We therefore investigate *approximated* $k$-NN query methods which sacrifice some accuracy for a large gain in speed. Specifically, we look into locality sensitive hashing (LSH; §4.1), a popular method, as well as redundant bit vectors (RBV; §4.2), which to our knowledge has not been previously used for natural language processing tasks.

### 4.1 Locality Sensitive Hashing

One popular approximated method is Locality Sensitive Hashing (LSH; Indyk and Motwani, 1998), which has been used in many NLP tasks such as noun clustering (Ravichandran et al., 2005), topic detection (Petrović et al., 2010), and fast $k$-NN query for similar words (Goyal et al., 2012).

For our particular task, assume each phrase is represented by a $d$-dimensional vector $\mathbf{p}$ of real values. The core of LSH is a set of hash functions. We choose $p$-stable distribution based functions (Datar et al., 2004) of the following form:

$$h_i(\mathbf{p}) = \lfloor \frac{\mathbf{x}_i \cdot \mathbf{p} + b_i}{w} \rfloor, 1 \le i \le s.$$

This function can be viewed as a quantized random projection, where each element in $\mathbf{x}_i$ is selected randomly from a Gaussian distribution $\mathcal{N}(0,1)$, $w$ is the width of the bin, $b_i$ is a linear bias selected from a uniform distribution $\mathcal{U}(0, w)$ (see Figure 3 (a)).

By concatenating the results from $h_i$, $1 \le i \le s$, phrase $\mathbf{p}$ is projected from $d$-dimensional space to

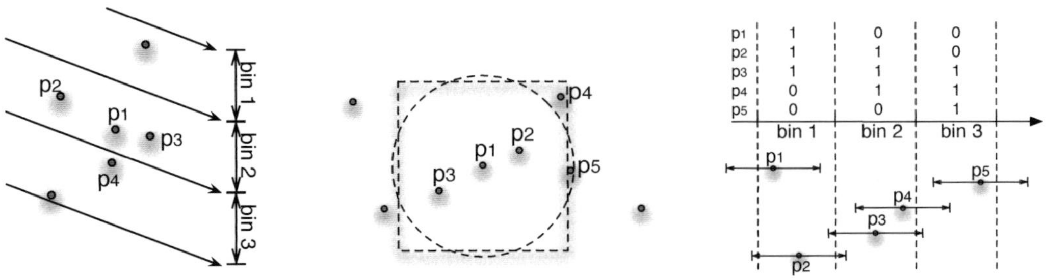


(a) (b) (c)

Figure 3: (a) A quantized random projection in LSH. The arrows show the direction of the projection. Points $p_1$, $p_2$, $p_3$ are correctly projected to the same bin, while $p_4$ falls into another bin, despite being very close to $p_1$. (b) A simplified example illustrating RBV in two dimensions. The circle with radius $r$ is centered at $\mathbf{p}_1$ and contains all neighbors of $\mathbf{p}_1$. RBV approximates the circle by a square of width $d = 2 \times 0.95r$, which contains most of the neighbors of $\mathbf{p}_1$ but also $\mathbf{p}_4$, a false positive, while missing $\mathbf{p}_5$, a closer point. (c) On each dimension, RBV uses bit vectors to maintain the set of points whose hypercubes (represented as the segments on the points in 1-dimensional view) intersect with a bin.

an $s$-dimensional space. Phrases whose projections collide in the $s$-dimensional space are considered candidates to be neighbors. A fast retrieval of those colliding phrases can be done via a hash table. However, since the projection is random, it is very likely that true neighbors in the $d$-dimensional space fall into different bins after projection (false negatives; e.g., $p_1$ and $p_4$ in Figure 3 (a)). To ease this problem, LSH employs a set of such projections and runs a linear search over the *union* of all possible neighbor candidates resulting from these projections to find the approximated $k$-nearest neighbors.

## 4.2 Redundant Bit Vectors

The performance of LSH decreases as the number of dimensions grows. Redundant bit vectors (RBV; Goldstein et al., 2005) address this problem and can quickly search in high dimensional space, which suits our task better.

RBV is a combination of: a) an approximated neighborhood test designed for high dimensional space, and b) an efficient data structure for fast neighborhood query.

First, for a given point $\mathbf{p}$ in high dimensional space, the volume of a hypersphere of radius $r$ centered at $\mathbf{p}$ can be approximately covered by a hypercube of width $d = 2\epsilon r$, $\epsilon \ll 1$.[3] Figure 3 (b) shows an illustration in two dimensional space where a square of width $d = 2 \times 0.95r$ covers most of a circle with radius $r$. In higher dimensional space, e.g., $d = 256$ as in Goldstein et al. (2005), we can cover 99% of the volume of a hypersphere of $r = 1$ with a hypercube whose width is only $\sim 2 \times 0.2r$.[4]

This surprising result allows us to use a very small hypercube to approximate the hypersphere. Furthermore, if two points $\mathbf{q}$ and $\mathbf{p}$ are within a certain radius $r$, i.e., $\|\mathbf{q} - \mathbf{p}\| \leq r$, then frequently $|\mathbf{q}^{(i)} - \mathbf{p}^{(i)}| \leq \epsilon r$, where $\mathbf{x}^{(i)}$ denotes the $i$-th element of vector $\mathbf{x}$. Thus, the neighbor query can be approximated as a check whether the distance between $\mathbf{p}$ and $\mathbf{q}$ on each dimension is less than $\epsilon r$, $\epsilon \ll 1$.

Second, each dimension is quantized into bins. Each bin *redundantly* maintains a set of points whose hypercubes intersect with the bin on that dimension. This set is an approximation of the neighbors of a query point $\mathbf{p}$ that falls into the same bin on this dimension. RBV uses *bit vectors* to store this set of points for each bin. (See Figure 3 (c).)

For a given query vector $\mathbf{p}$, we fetch the bins where $\mathbf{p}$ falls into for each dimension. We then per-

[3]Here we use $\ll$ in an imprecise way. $\epsilon \ll 1$ does not mean $\epsilon$ is smaller than 1 by orders of magnitudes; usually $\epsilon > 0.1$. What we mean is that in high dimensional space, the volume of a hypercube of width $2\epsilon r$ is more than hundreds of magnitudes smaller than a hypercube of width $2r$.

[4]Note that this does not mean the volume of the hypercube is smaller than the hypersphere. It just means that most of the volume of the hypersphere is covered in the hypercube.

| | English | Arabic | Urdu |
|---|---|---|---|
| Token count | 5b | 5b | 75m |
| Word vector count | 2.9m | 2.7m | 0.2m |
| Word vector train time | 100hrs | 100hrs | 3hrs |

Table 1: Monolingual corpora statistics, number of word vectors, and time to learn the word vectors (on single CPU core) for each source language.

| | False Negative (%) | Time (s) |
|---|---|---|
| Linear Search | 0 | 342 |
| LSH | 14.29 | 69 |
| RBV | 9.08 | 19 |

Table 2: Performance of linear search, locality sensitive hashing, and redundant bit vectors, for $k = 200$.

form a bitwise *and* over the corresponding bit vectors to find the set of points that actually fall into $\mathbf{p}$'s hypercube, i.e., the approximated candidate neighbor set of $\mathbf{p}$. Finally, a linear search over this much smaller set finds the approximate $k$-nearest neighbors, similar to LSH.

## 5 Experiments

We first evaluate the speed and accuracy of the presented approximate $k$-NN query algorithms (§5.2). Next we experiment with the translation rule generation approaches (§5.3), and then we analyze the global and local projection methods (§5.4). Following Saluja et al. (2014), we present most results on Arabic-English translation and then validate our findings on Urdu-English (§5.5), a low-resource setting. Lastly, we discuss some qualitative results (§5.6).

### 5.1 Datasets & Preprocessing

We test our approach on both Arabic-English and Urdu-English translation. For Arabic-English our bilingual training data comprises of 685k sentence pairs. The NIST MT08 and MT09 data sets serve as tuning and testing sets, respectively. Both are combinations of newswire and weblog articles, and each Arabic sentence has four reference translations. For Urdu-English our bilingual training corpus contains 165k sentence pairs, and the tuning and testing sets are NIST MT08 and NIST MT09, respectively.

Table 1 shows some statistics for the monolingual data we use. The majority of the data for Arabic and English is drawn from the AFP Gigaword corpus. For Urdu most of the data is mined by a web crawler, mainly because there are not many official resources for this language.

We run standard tokenization and segmentation on the monolingual corpora. After that we use the Word2Vec tool (Mikolov et al., 2013b) to generate word embeddings for each language with the bag-of-words model, where the number of dimensions is set to $d = 300$. See Table 1 for the number of word vectors learned for each language.

To obtain phrases in each language, we use a similar strategy as in Saluja et al. (2014). For Arabic and Urdu, we collect all unigrams and bigrams from the tuning and testing sets. This gives 0.66m phrases for Arabic and 0.2m phrases for Urdu. For English, we collect unigrams and bigrams from the monolingual data instead. However, the English monolingual corpus is much larger than the tuning and testing sets for Arabic and Urdu. We therefore train a language model over the monolingual data, and collect the unigrams and bigrams from the ARPA file, filtering out all candidates that have a probability smaller than $10^{-7}$. Similar to Saluja et al. (2014), we use a baseline MT system to translate the Arabic or Urdu phrases and add their translations to the English phrase set. After this procedure we end up with 1.5m English phrases.

We use simple component-wise addition to generate phrase vectors from word vectors. Some rare words do not receive a vector representation after running Word2Vec, and we simply remove phrases containing those words, resulting in a total of 0.65m phrases for Arabic, 0.18m phrases for Urdu, and 1.2m phrases for English.

### 5.2 Evaluation of Approximated $k$-NN Query

We first evaluate the performances of different $k$-NN query approaches on English word vectors.

There are 2.9m word vectors in $d = 300$ dimensional space. We randomly select 1,000 words, and query for each word the 200 nearest neighbors, $k = 200$, with either linear search, LSH, and RBV. We measure the false negative ratio, i.e., the percentage of true neighbors missed by each query method, as well as time. For LSH and RBV, we tune the parameters for best performance (LSH: number of projected dimensions, number of layers, and width of

| | Tune | Test | Time (hr) |
|---|---|---|---|
| Baseline | 39.33 | 38.09 | - |
| SLP w/ PMI | 40.93 | 39.16 | $\sim$10,000 |
| SLP w/ Cont. Repr. | 41.31 | 39.34 | 120+200 |
| GLP | 40.46 | 38.68 | 20+200 |
| LLP | 41.17 | 39.57 | 30+200 |
| LLP w/ backoff | 41.48 | 39.70 | 30+200 |

Table 3: Arabic-English translation accuracy of structured label propagation with PMI (SLP) and with continuous representations (SLP w/ PMI), the global linear projection (GLP), our local linear projection (LLP) and with an added backoff scheme (LLP w/ backoff). For applicable methods, we list the running time to compute distributional representations as a separate term in the time column. This is usually only required once per language which is why we report it separately.

the bin; RBV: hypercube width and number of bins for each dimension).

Table 2 shows that RBV gives significantly better performance than LSH, both in terms of accuracy and speed. RBV reduces the false negative ratio by $1/3$ compared to LSH and is 3.6 times faster. This is in line with Goldstein et al. (2005) who observed that the performance of LSH degrades in high dimensional space. We therefore use RBV in the following experiments.

### 5.3 Evaluation of Rule Generation

Next, we evaluate the quality of the generated translation rules for Arabic-English translation (Table 3) using either SLP, the global linear projection (GLP), or the local linear projection (LLP).

Our baseline system is an in-house phrase-based system similar to Moses with a 4-gram language model. The underlying log-linear model comprises of 13 features: two maximum likelihood translation probabilities, two lexicalized translation probabilities, five hierarchical reordering model features (Galley and Manning, 2008), one language model, word penalty, phrase length, and distortion penalty), and is tuned with minimum error rate training (MERT; Och 2003). Translation quality is measured with BLEU (Papineni et al., 2002).

For comparison, we reimplemented the graph-based method in Saluja et al. (2014). This method calculates the pairwise mutual information (PMI) between phrases, and employs all the techniques mentioned in Saluja et al. (2014) to speedup the computations. Our reimplementation achieves similar performance to Saluja et al. (2014) (with a negligible $\sim 0.06$ drop in BLEU). We parallelized the algorithm on a cluster since a single core implementation would run for $\sim$10k hours.[5]

Our continuous phrase based version of SLP is orders of magnitudes faster than the SLP variant of Saluja et al. (2014) because it replaces the computationally expensive PMI calculation by an approximated $k$-NN query in distributional space. Moreover, our variant of SLP even improves translation quality by 0.2-0.3 BLEU. Overall, our version of SLP improves the baseline by 2.0 BLEU on the tuning set and by 1.3 BLEU on the test set.

The linear projection based methods, GLP and LLP, are in turn again several times faster than SLP with continuous representations. This is because they require significantly fewer $k$-NN queries. For both GLP and LLP, we retrieve the 200 nearest neighbors of the projected point. For LLP, the local projection is calculated based on the 500 nearest labeled neighbors of the infrequent source phrase. LLP achieves slightly better accuracy on the test set than PMI-based SLP but at four times the speed. GLP is the fastest method but also the least accurate, improving the baseline only by about 0.6 BLEU. We explore this result in more detail in the next section. Overall, our local projection outperforms the global projection by 0.9 BLEU on the test set.

For some infrequent source phrases, approximated $k$-NN query does not retrieve enough ($\geq d$) neighbors to learn a local linear projection. For these phrases, we employ a *backoff* strategy that uses the translations of their neighbors as additional translation candidates. This strategy provides helpful additional rules for LLP (Table 3).[6]

### 5.4 Evaluation of Global Linear Projection

To learn why GLP does not generate high quality translation rules, we run an extra experiment to measure the projection quality of GLP.

We train a global linear projection on an increas-

[5] Confirmed with the authors of Saluja et al. (2014) from personal communication.

[6] The backoff scheme in the Arabic-English setting generates around 15% of the translations rules, which adds 0.13 BLEU on the test set. This is not a big improvement and so we did not employ this scheme for our Urdu-English experiments.

| Training Set | Hit Rate: Freq | Hit Rate: Infreq. |
|---|---|---|
| 500 | 0.87 | 0 |
| 1,000 | 0.6 | 0.01 |
| 5,000 | 0.42 | 0.07 |
| 25,000 | 0.4 | 0.05 |

Table 4: Quality of global linear projection measured by the ratio that GLP can fetch the most possible translation in the 200-nearest neighbors.

| | Tune | Test | Time (hr) |
|---|---|---|---|
| Baseline | 26.32 | 27.41 | - |
| SLP w/ PMI | 27.26 | 27.89 | ~7,000 |
| SLP w/ Cont. Repr. | 27.34 | 27.73 | 100+103 |
| LLP | 27.06 | 27.98 | 30+103 |

Table 5: Urdu-English translation accuracy (cf. Table 3).

ing amount of training data and measure its accuracy on two test sets (Table 4). The first test set contains the 100 most frequent source phrases and their translations. The second test set contains less frequent examples; we choose the 50,000 to 50,100 most frequent source phrases. The training data uses the $l$ most frequent source phrases and their translations which are not already contained in the first test. The projection quality is measured by the ratio of how many times the correct translation is one of the 200-nearest neighbors of the projected point computed by GLP.

The results in Table 4 clearly show that GLP can find the best translation for very frequent source phrases which is in line with previous work Mikolov et al. (2013a). However, the accuracy for infrequent phrases is poor. This explains why GLP helps relatively little in our translation experiments because our setup requires a method that can find good translations for infrequent source phrases.

### 5.5 Evaluation on Urdu-English

Resources for Urdu are limited compared to Arabic (§5.1) which results in fewer word vectors and fewer source phrases. This will also affect the quality of the word vectors in Urdu, since more training data usually results in better representations.

Table 5 shows that the improvements of both SLP and LLP in Urdu-English are not as significant as for Arabic-English. Our reimplementation of SLP is $\sim 1$ BLEU better on the tuning set than the baseline, and $\sim 0.5$ BLEU better on the test set. As expected, the translation quality improvement on small corpora is not as significant as on large corpora like Arabic, since the monolingual data in Urdu is much smaller than for Arabic (75m tokens vs. 5b tokens) which makes it more difficult to learn good representations. In general, with continuous representations, SLP and LLP achieve similar performance to PMI-based SLP but the projection based methods are orders of magnitudes faster.

| Source | Generated target |
|---|---|
| التزاماتها الانسانيه | the humanitarian obligations |
| التزاماتها الانسانيه | humanitarian commitments |
| هاتين المجموعتين | both these two groups |
| هاتين المجموعتين | these two communities |
| بناء مؤسساتهم | building their institutions |
| کوششیں ضرور | certainly efforts |
| کوششیں ضرور | efforts must |
| مند نوجوانوں | healthier youth |
| سپیشل سروسز | services special |
| کمیونٹی ڈیولپمنٹ | community development |

Figure 4: Examples of the generated rules from LLP.

### 5.6 Analysis of Output

Figure 4 shows some examples of the translation rules produced by our system. The first five examples are for the Arabic-English system, while the last five are for the Urdu-English system. All source phrases are unknown to the baseline system which usually results in sub-optimal translations. Our system on the other hand, managed to generate translation rules for them. The Arabic-English examples show mostly morphological variants of phrases which did not appear in the parallel data; this can be helpful for highly inflected languages since most of the inflectional variations are underrepresented in the parallel data. The Urdu-English examples show mostly unknown phrases since there is much less parallel data than for Arabic.

## 6 Conclusion and Future Work

In this work, we showed how simple continuous representations of phrases can be successfully used to induce translation rules for infrequent phrases and demonstrated substantial gains in translation accuracy. Continuous representations not only increase the speed of the semi-supervised approach of Saluja et al. (2014) by two orders of magnitude but also improve its accuracy at the same time. Simpler linear projections are up to three orders of magnitudes faster once phrasal representations have been learned and can be as accurate. Our novel local linear projection is much more accurate than the global projection of Mikolov et al. (2013a) at only a small increase in running time. This brings us closer to generating new translation rules on-the-fly for unseen sentences. Finally, we showed that redundant bit vectors are three times faster but also significantly more accurate than locality sensitive hashing in our setting. To our knowledge this is the first application of redundant bit vectors on a natural language processing task.

In future work, we would like to investigate more elaborate projection schemes that use contextual information from the source side or non-linear projections. Furthermore, we would like to apply redundant bit vectors to other NLP tasks.

## Acknowledgment

We thank the three anonymous reviewers for helpful suggestions. We are also grateful to Chris Quirk, Kristina Toutanova, Jonathan Clark, Qin Gao, Austin Matthews, Liang Huang, Mingbo Ma, and Mo Yu for discussion. Kai Zhao was partially supported by DARPA FA8750-13-2-0041 (DEFT).

## References

Chris Callison-Burch, Philipp Koehn, and Miles Osborne. 2006. Improved statistical machine translation using paraphrases. In *Proceedings of the main conference on Human Language Technology Conference of the North American Chapter of the Association of Computational Linguistics*, pages 17–24. Association for Computational Linguistics.

David Chiang. 2005. A hierarchical phrase-based model for statistical machine translation. In *Proceedings of the 43rd Annual Meeting on Association for Computational Linguistics*, pages 263–270. Association for Computational Linguistics.

Ronan Collobert, Jason Weston, Leon Bottou, Michael Karlen, Koray Kavukcuoglu, and Pavel Kuksa. 2011. Natural language processing (almost) from scratch. *The Journal of Machine Learning Research*, 12:2493–2537.

Mayur Datar, Nicole Immorlica, Piotr Indyk, and Vahab S Mirrokni. 2004. Locality-sensitive hashing scheme based on p-stable distributions. In *Proceedings of the twentieth annual symposium on Computational geometry*, pages 253–262. ACM.

Michel Galley and Christopher D Manning. 2008. A simple and effective hierarchical phrase reordering model. In *Proceedings of the Conference on Empirical Methods in Natural Language Processing*, pages 848–856. Association for Computational Linguistics.

Jianfeng Gao, Xiaodong He, Wen-tau Yih, and Li Deng. 2014. Learning continuous phrase representations for translation modeling. In *Proc. ACL*.

Jonathan Goldstein, John C Plat, and Christopher JC Burges. 2005. Redundant bit vectors for quickly searching high-dimensional regions. In *Deterministic and Statistical Methods in Machine Learning*, pages 137–158. Springer.

Amit Goyal, Hal Daumé III, and Raul Guerra. 2012. Fast large-scale approximate graph construction for nlp. In *Proceedings of the 2012 Joint Conference on Empirical Methods in Natural Language Processing and Computational Natural Language Learning*, pages 1069–1080. Association for Computational Linguistics.

Aria Haghighi, Percy Liang, Taylor Berg-Kirkpatrick, and Dan Klein. 2008. Learning bilingual lexicons from monolingual corpora. In *ACL*, volume 2008, pages 771–779. Citeseer.

Xiaofei He and Partha Niyogi. 2004. Locality preserving projections. In *Neural information processing systems*, volume 16, page 153. MIT.

Piotr Indyk and Rajeev Motwani. 1998. Approximate nearest neighbors: towards removing the curse of dimensionality. In *Proceedings of the thirtieth annual ACM symposium on Theory of computing*, pages 604–613. ACM.

Philipp Koehn, Franz Josef Och, and Daniel Marcu. 2003. Statistical phrase-based translation. In *Proceedings of the 2003 Conference of the North American Chapter of the Association for Computational Linguistics on Human Language Technology-Volume 1*, pages 48–54. Association for Computational Linguistics.

Quoc Le and Tomas Mikolov. 2014. Distributed representations of sentences and documents. In *Proceedings of the 31st International Conference on Machine Learning*.

Shujie Liu, Chi-Ho Li, Mu Li, and Ming Zhou. 2012. Learning translation consensus with structured label propagation. In *Proceedings of the 50th Annual Meeting of the Association for Computational Linguistics: Long Papers-Volume 1*, pages 302–310. Association for Computational Linguistics.

Tomas Mikolov, Quoc V Le, and Ilya Sutskever. 2013a. Exploiting similarities among languages for machine translation. *arXiv preprint arXiv:1309.4168*.

Tomas Mikolov, Ilya Sutskever, Kai Chen, Greg S Corrado, and Jeff Dean. 2013b. Distributed representations of words and phrases and their compositionality. In *Advances in Neural Information Processing Systems*, pages 3111–3119.

Tomas Mikolov, Yih Wen-tau, and Zweig Geoffrey. 2013c. Linguistic regularities in continuous space word representations. In *Proceedings of the 2013 Conference of the North American Chapter of the Association for Computational Linguistics on Human Language Technology*, pages 746–751. Association for Computational Linguistics.

Jeff Mitchell and Mirella Lapata. 2010. Composition in distributional models of semantics. *Cognitive science*, 34(8):1388–1429.

Franz Josef Och. 2003. Minimum error rate training in statistical machine translation. In *Proceedings of the 41st Annual Meeting on Association for Computational Linguistics-Volume 1*, pages 160–167. Association for Computational Linguistics.

Kishore Papineni, Salim Roukos, Todd Ward, and Wei-Jing Zhu. 2002. Bleu: a method for automatic evaluation of machine translation. In *Proceedings of the 40th annual meeting on association for computational linguistics*, pages 311–318. Association for Computational Linguistics.

Saša Petrović, Miles Osborne, and Victor Lavrenko. 2010. Streaming first story detection with application to twitter. In *Human Language Technologies: The 2010 Annual Conference of the North American Chapter of the Association for Computational Linguistics*, pages 181–189. Association for Computational Linguistics.

Reinhard Rapp. 1995. Identifying word translations in non-parallel texts. In *Proceedings of the 33rd annual meeting on Association for Computational Linguistics*, pages 320–322. Association for Computational Linguistics.

Deepak Ravichandran, Patrick Pantel, and Eduard Hovy. 2005. Randomized algorithms and nlp: using locality sensitive hash function for high speed noun clustering. In *Proceedings of the 43rd Annual Meeting on Association for Computational Linguistics*, pages 622–629. Association for Computational Linguistics.

Avneesh Saluja, Hany Hassan, Kristina Toutanova, and Chris Quirk. 2014. Graph-based semi-supervised learning of translation models from monolingual data. In *Proceedings of the 52th Annual Meeting of the Association for Computational Linguistics*. Association for Computational Linguistics.

Richard Socher, Eric Huang, Jeffrey Pennington, Andrew Y Ng, and Christopher D. Manning. 2011. Dynamic pooling and unfolding recursive autoencoders for paraphrase detection. In *Advances in Neural Information Processing Systems 24*.

Joseph Turian, Lev Ratinov, and Yoshua Bengio. 2014. Word representations: a simple and general method for semi-supervised learning. In *Proc. ACL*.

Jiajun Zhang, Shujie Liu, Mu Li, Ming Zhou, and Chengqing Zong. 2014. Bilingually-constrained phrase embeddings for machine translation. In *Proceedings of the 52th Annual Meeting on Association for Computational Linguistics. Association for Computational Linguistics*.

Will Y Zou, Richard Socher, Daniel M Cer, and Christopher D Manning. 2013. Bilingual word embeddings for phrase-based machine translation. In *EMNLP*, pages 1393–1398.

# A Corpus and Model Integrating Multiword Expressions and Supersenses

**Nathan Schneider**
School of Informatics
University of Edinburgh
Edinburgh, Scotland, UK
nschneid@inf.ed.ac.uk

**Noah A. Smith**
School of Computer Science
Carnegie Mellon University
Pittsburgh, Pennsylvania, USA
nasmith@cs.cmu.edu

## Abstract

This paper introduces a task of identifying and semantically classifying lexical expressions in running text. We investigate the online reviews genre, adding semantic supersense annotations to a 55,000 word English corpus that was previously annotated for multiword expressions. The noun and verb supersenses apply to full lexical expressions, whether single- or multiword. We then present a sequence tagging model that jointly infers lexical expressions and their supersenses. Results show that even with our relatively small training corpus in a noisy domain, the joint task can be performed to attain 70% class labeling $F_1$.

## 1 Introduction

The central challenge in computational lexical semantics for text corpora is to develop and apply abstractions that characterize word meanings beyond what can be derived superficially from the orthography. Such abstractions can be found in type-level human-curated lexical resources such as WordNet (Fellbaum, 1998), but such intricate resources are expensive to build and difficult to annotate with at the token level, hindering their applicability beyond a narrow selection of languages and domains. A more portable and scalable—yet still linguistically-grounded—way to represent lexical meanings is with coarse-grained semantic classes. Here we build on prior work with an inventory of semantic classes (for nouns and verbs) known as **supersenses**. The 41 supersenses resemble the types used for named entities (PERSON, LOCATION, etc.), but are more general, with semantic categories relevant to common nouns and verbs as well. As a result, their application to sentences is dense (describing a large proportion of tokens), in contrast to annotations that only describe named entities.

Because most supersense tagging studies have worked with data originally annotated for fine-grained WordNet senses, then automatically mapped to supersenses, the resulting systems have been tied to the lexical coverage of WordNet. Schneider et al. (2012) and Johannsen et al. (2014) overcame this limitation in part by annotating supersenses directly in text; thus, nouns and verbs not in WordNet were not neglected. However, the issue of which *units* ought to receive supersenses has not been addressed satisfactorily. We argue that the semantically holistic nature of **multiword expressions** (MWEs) including idioms, light verb constructions, verb-particle constructions, and many compounds (Baldwin and Kim, 2010) means that they should be considered as units for manual and automatic supersense tagging.

Below, we motivate the need for an integrated representation for broad-coverage lexical semantic analysis that identifies MWEs and labels single- and multiword noun and verb expressions with supersenses (§2). By annotating supersenses directly on sentences with existing comprehensive MWE annotations, we circumvent WordNet's spotty coverage of many kinds of MWEs (§3). Then we demonstrate that the two kinds of information are readily combined in a discriminative sequence tagging model (§4). Notably, our analyzer handles gappy expressions that are ignored by existing supersense taggers, and it marks miscellaneous MWEs even though they do not receive a noun or verb supersense.

Our annotations of the REVIEWS section of the English Web Treebank (Bies et al., 2012), which



*Human Language Technologies: The 2015 Annual Conference of the North American Chapter of the ACL*, pages 1537–1547,
Denver, Colorado, May 31 – June 5, 2015. 

| Noun | | |
|---|---|---|
| GROUP | 1469 | *place* |
| PERSON | 1202 | *people* |
| ARTIFACT | 971 | *car* |
| COGNITION | 771 | *way* |
| FOOD | 766 | *food* |
| ACT | 700 | *service* |
| LOCATION | 638 | *area* |
| TIME | 530 | *day* |
| EVENT | 431 | *experience* |
| COMMUNIC.* | 417 | *review* |
| POSSESSION | 339 | *price* |
| ATTRIBUTE | 205 | *quality* |
| QUANTITY | 102 | *amount* |
| ANIMAL | 88 | *dog* |
| BODY | 87 | *hair* |
| STATE | 56 | *pain* |
| NATURAL OBJ. | 54 | *flower* |
| RELATION | 35 | *portion* |
| SUBSTANCE | 34 | *oil* |
| FEELING | 34 | *discomfort* |
| PROCESS | 28 | *process* |
| MOTIVE | 25 | *reason* |
| PHENOMENON | 23 | *result* |
| SHAPE | 6 | *square* |
| PLANT | 5 | *tree* |
| OTHER | 2 | *stuff* |
| **all 26 NSSTs** | **9018** | |

| Verb | | |
|---|---|---|
| STATIVE | 2922 | *is* |
| COGNITION | 1093 | *know* |
| COMMUNIC.* | 974 | *recommend* |
| SOCIAL | 944 | *use* |
| MOTION | 602 | *go* |
| POSSESSION | 309 | *pay* |
| CHANGE | 274 | *fix* |
| EMOTION | 249 | *love* |
| PERCEPTION | 143 | *see* |
| CONSUMPTION | 93 | *have* |
| BODY | 82 | *get... done* |
| CREATION | 64 | *cook* |
| CONTACT | 46 | *put* |
| COMPETITION | 11 | *win* |
| WEATHER | 0 | — |
| **all 15 VSSTs** | **7806** | |

| **N/A** (see §3.2) | | |
|---|---|---|
| `a | 1191 | *have* |
| ` | 821 | *anyone* |
| `j | 54 | *fried* |

*COMMUNIC. *is short for* COMMUNICATION

**Table 1:** Summary of noun and verb supersense categories. Each entry shows the label along with the count and most frequent lexical item in the STREUSLE corpus.

enrich the MWE annotations of the CMWE corpus[1] (Schneider et al., 2014b), are publicly released under the name STREUSLE.[2] This includes new guidelines for verb supersense annotation. Our open-source tagger, implemented in Python, is available from that page as well.

## 2 Background: Supersense Tags

WordNet's **supersense** categories are the top-level hypernyms in the taxonomy (sometimes known as **semantic fields**) which are designed to be broad enough to encompass all nouns and verbs (Miller, 1990; Fellbaum, 1990).[3]

The 26 noun and 15 verb supersense categories are listed with examples in table 1. Some of the names overlap between the noun and verb inventories, but they are to be considered separate categories; hereafter, we will distinguish the noun and verb categories with prefixes, e.g. N:COGNITION vs. V:COGNITION.

Though WordNet synsets are associated with lexical entries, the supersense categories are unlexicalized. The N:PERSON category, for instance, contains synsets for both *principal* and *student*. A different sense of *principal* falls under N:POSSESSION.

As far as we are aware, the supersenses were originally intended only as a method of organizing the WordNet structure. But Ciaramita and Johnson (2003) pioneered the coarse word sense disambiguation task of **supersense tagging**, noting that the supersense categories provided a natural broadening of the traditional named entity categories to encompass all nouns. Ciaramita and Altun (2006) later expanded the task to include all verbs, and applied a supervised sequence modeling framework adapted from NER. Evaluation was against manually sense-tagged data that had been automatically converted to the coarser supersenses. Similar taggers have since been built for Italian (Picca et al., 2008) and Chinese (Qiu et al., 2011), both of which have their own WordNets mapped to English WordNet.

Although many of the annotated expressions in existing supersense datasets contain multiple words, the relationship between MWEs and supersenses has not received much attention. (Piao et al. (2003, 2005) did investigate MWEs in the context of a lexical tagger with a finer-grained taxonomy of semantic classes.) Consider these examples from online reviews:

(1) IT IS NOT A HIGH END STEAK HOUSE

(2) The white pages allowed me to get in touch with parents of my high school friends so that I could track people down one by one

*HIGH END* functions as a unit to mean 'sophisticated, expensive'. (It is not in WordNet, though

[1] `http://www.ark.cs.cmu.edu/LexSem/`

[2] Supersense-Tagged Repository of English with a Unified Semantics for Lexical Expressions

[3] WordNet synset entries were originally partitioned into **lexicographer files** for these coarse categories, which became known as "supersenses." The `lexname` function in WordNet/NLTK (Bird et al., 2009) returns a synset's lexicographer file. A subtle difference is that a special file called `noun.Tops` contains each noun supersense's root synset (e.g., `group.n.01` for N:GROUP) as well as a few miscellaneous synsets, such as `living_thing.n.01`, that are too abstract to fall under any single supersense. Following Ciaramita and Altun (2006), we treat the latter cases under an N:OTHER supersense category and merge the former under their respective supersense.

it could be added in principle.) Assigning a semantic class such as N:LOCATION to *END* would, in our judgment, be overly literal. To paint a coherent picture of the meaning of this sentence, it is better to treat *HIGH END* as a single unit, and because it serves as an adjective rather than a noun or verb, leave it semantically unclassified.[4]

*STEAK HOUSE* is arguably an entrenched enough compound that it should receive a single supersense—in fact, WordNet spells it without a space. The phrases *white pages*, *high school*, *(get) in touch (with)*, *track... down*, and *one by one* all are listed as MWEs in WordNet. As detailed in §4.1 below, the conventional BIO scheme used in existing supersense taggers is capable of representing most of these. However, it does not allow for gappy (discontinuous) uses of an expression, such as ***track** people **down***.

The corpus and analyzer presented in this work address these shortcomings by integrating a richer, more comprehensive representation of MWEs in the supersense tagging task.

## 3 Supersense Annotation for English

As suggested above, supersense tags offer a practical semantic label space for an integrated analysis of lexical semantics in context. For English, we have created the STREUSLE dataset, which fully annotates the REVIEWS corpus (55k words) for noun and verb supersenses in a manner consistent with Schneider et al.'s (2014b) multiword expression annotations.

Schneider et al. (2012) offered a methodology for noun supersense annotation in Arabic Wikipedia, and predicted that it would port well to other languages and domains. Our experience with English web reviews has borne this out. We generally adhered to the same supersense annotation process (for nouns); the most important difference was that the data had already been annotated for MWEs, and supersense labels apply to any strong[5] MWEs as a whole.

The same annotators had already done the MWE annotation; whenever they encountered an apparent mistake from an earlier stage (usually an oversight), they were encouraged to correct it. Our annotation interface supports modification of MWEs as well as supersense labels in one view.

To lessen the cognitive burden when reasoning about tagsets, supersense annotation was broken into separate phases: first we annotated nearly the entire REVIEWS corpus for noun supersenses; then we made another pass to annotate for verbs. Roughly a tenth of the sentences were saved for a combined noun+verb phase at the end; annotators reported that constantly switching their attention between the two tagsets made this mode of annotation more difficult.

### 3.1 Nouns

**Targets.** Per the annotation standard, all noun singletons and noun-like MWEs should receive a noun supersense label. Annotation targets were determined heuristically from the gold (PTB-style) POS tags in the corpus: all lexical expressions containing a noun[6] were selected. This heuristic overpredicts noun-like MWEs occasionally because it does not check the syntactic status of the MWE as a whole. During this phase, the backtick symbol (`) was therefore reserved for MWEs (such as light verb constructions) that contain a noun but should not receive a noun supersense.[7] The annotation interface prevented submission of blank annotation targets to avoid oversights.

**Tagset conventions.** Several brief annotation rounds were devoted to practice with Schneider et al.'s (2012) noun annotation guidelines,[8] since the annotators were new to the scheme. Metonymy posed the chief difficulty in this domain: institutions with a premises (such as restaurants, hotels, and schools) are frequently ambiguous between N:GROUP (institution as a whole), N:ARTIFACT (the building), and N:LOCATION (site as a whole). Our convention was to use the reading that seemed most salient in context: for example, *restaurant* in a comment about the qual-

[4]Future supersense annotation schemes for additional parts of speech could be assimilated into our framework. Tsvetkov et al. (2014) take a step in this direction for adjectives.

[5]The CMWE corpus distinguishes **strong** and **weak** MWEs—essentially, the former are strongly entrenched and likely noncompositional, whereas weak MWEs are merely statistically collocated. See Schneider et al. (2014b) for details. Because they are deemed semantically compositional, weak MWEs do not receive a supersense as a whole.

[6]Specifically, any POS tag starting with N or ADD (web addresses); pronouns were excluded.

[7]Pronouns like *anything* also fall into this category because they are POS-tagged as nouns.

[8]`http://www.ark.cs.cmu.edu/ArabicSST/corpus/guidelines.html`

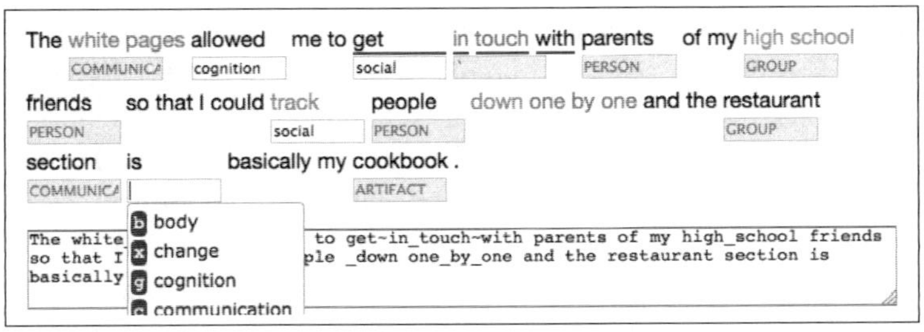


**Figure 1:** Annotation interface, with dropdown menu for verb supersenses. The large text box at the bottom can be used to edit the MWE annotation by typing underscores and tildes to connect tokens.

ity of the service would be labeled N:GROUP.[9] Some subjectivity is involved, suggesting that the scheme is not ideal for such multifaceted concepts.

### 3.2 Verbs

**Targets.** The set of lexical expressions that should receive a verb supersense consists of (a) all verb singletons that are not auxiliaries, and (b) all verb-like MWEs. Again, simple but overly liberal heuristics were used to detect annotation targets, so wherever the heuristics overpredicted, annotators entered:

- `a for auxiliary verbs
- `j for adjectives (some *-ing* and *-ed* adjectives are POS-tagged as VBG and VBD, respectively)
- ` for all other cases

**Tagset conventions.** We wrote new guidelines to characterize the verb supersenses for annotation. They briefly define and exemplify each category, and also relate them via precedence rules: e.g., the rule

$\{$V:PERCEPTION, V:CONSUMPTION$\}$ >
V:BODY > V:CHANGE

stipulates that verbs of perception or consumption (*hear*, *eat*, etc.) be labeled as such rather than the less specific class V:BODY. The precedence rules help to resolve many of the cases of meaning overlap between the categories. The guidelines were developed over several weeks and informed by annotation difficulties and disagreements. We release them along with the STREUSLE corpus.

### 3.3 Interface

We extended the online MWE annotation tool of Schneider et al. (2014b) to also support supersense labeling, as well as grouping tokens into multiword lexical expressions. This is visualized in figure 1. Specifically, singletons and strong MWEs may receive labels (subject to a POS filter). This allows the two types of annotation to be worked on in tandem, especially when a supersense annotator wishes to change a multiword grouping. The tool offers an autocomplete dropdown menu when typing a tag name, and validates that the submitted annotation is complete and internally consistent. Additionally, the tool provides a complete version history of the sentence and a "reconciliation" mode that merges two users' annotations of a sentence, flagging any differences for manual resolution; these features are extremely useful when breaking the annotation down into multiple rounds among several annotators.

### 3.4 Quality Control

There were 2 primary annotators and 3 others who participated in annotation to a lesser degree, including the first author of this paper, whose role was mainly supervisory. All 5 hold bachelor's degrees in linguistics. The annotators were trained in the noun supersense annotation scheme of Schneider et al. (2012) and cooperatively developed and documented interpretations for the verb supersenses. Our main quality control mechanism for the annotation process was to obtain two independent annotations for every sentence—differences between them were reconciled by negotiation (between the two annotators in most cases, and between the two primary annotators in a small number of cases).

To get a sense of the difficulty of the task, we examine the annotation history for a sample of sentences to measure inter-annotator agreement. Estimated between the 2 primary annotators on the batch of sentences annotated last during each phase (350, 302, and 379 sentences, respectively), inter-annotator $F_1$ scores (excluding auxiliaries and other miscellaneous categories) are: 76% for noun expression supersenses after the noun phase, 93% for verb expression supersenses after the verb phase, and 88% for all supersenses after the combined annotation phase.[10] These

[9]This rule is sometimes at odds with WordNet, which only lists N:ARTIFACT for *hotel* and *restaurant*.

[10]Cohen's $\kappa$, limited to tokens for which both annotators

are over different sentences, so they are not directly comparable, but they point to the robustness of the annotation scheme. Thanks to the double annotation plus reconciliation procedure, these numbers should underestimate the reliability of the final annotations.

### 3.5 Corpus Statistics

A total of 9,000 noun mentions (1,300 of them MWEs) and 7,800 verb mentions (1,200 MWEs) incorporating 20,000 word tokens are annotated.[11] Table 1 shows supersense mention counts and the most frequent example of each category in the corpus.

### 3.6 Copenhagen Supersense Data

An independent English noun+verb supersense annotation effort targeting the Twitter domain was undertaken by the COASTAL lab at the University of Copenhagen (Johannsen et al., 2014). The overarching goal of annotating supersenses directly in running text was the same as in the present work, but there are three important differences. First, general-purpose MWE annotations were not considered in that work; second, sentences were pre-annotated by a heuristic system and then manually corrected, whereas here the annotations are supplied from scratch; and third, Johannsen et al. (2014) provided minimal instructions and training to their annotators, whereas here we have worked hard to encourage consistent interpretations of the supersense categories. Johannsen et al. have released their annotations on two samples of tweets (over 18,000 tokens in total).

Johannsen et al.'s dataset illustrates why supersense annotation by itself is not the same as the full scheme for lexical semantic analysis proposed here. Many of the expressions that they have supersense-annotated as single-word nouns/verbs probably would have been part of larger units in MWE annotation: examining Johannsen et al.'s inhouse sample, multiword chunks arguably should have been used for verb phrases like *gain entry*, *make sure*, and *make it* ('succeed'), and for verb-particle constructions like *take over*, *find out*, and *check out* ('ogle'). Moreover, in the traditional supersense annotation scheme, there are no chunks not labeled with a supersense; thus, e.g., PPs such as *on tap*, *of ALL-Time*, and *up to [value limit]* are not chunked.

Many of the nominal expressions in Johannsen et al.'s (2014) data appear to have overly liberal boundaries, grouping perfectly compositional modifiers along with their heads as a multiword chunk: e.g., *Panhandling Ban*, *Panda Cub*, *farm road crash*, and *Tomic's dad*. Presumably, some of these were boundary errors made by the heuristic pre-annotation system that human annotators failed to notice.

## 4 Automatic Tagging

We now turn to automating the combined multiword expression and supersense prediction task in a single statistical model.

### 4.1 Background: Supersense Tagging with a Discriminative Sequence Model

Ciaramita and Altun's (2006) model represents the state of the art for full[12] English supersense tagging on the standard SemCor test set, achieving an $F_1$ score of 77%. It is a feature-based discriminative sequence model learned in a supervised fashion with the structured perceptron (Collins, 2002).

For Ciaramita and Altun (2006) and hereafter, sequences correspond to sentences, with each sentence pre-segmented into words according to some tokenization. Figure 2 shows how token-level tags combine Ramshaw and Marcus (1995)–style BIO flags with supersense class labels to represent the segmentation and supersense labeling of a sentence. These tags are observed during training, predicted at test time, and compared against the gold standard tags.

Ciaramita and Altun's (2006) model uses a simple feature set capturing the lemmas, word shapes, and parts of speech of tokens in a small context window, as well as the supersense category of the first WordNet sense of the current word. (WordNet senses are ordered roughly by frequency.) On SemCor data, the model achieves a 10% absolute improvement in $F_1$ over the first sense baseline.

assigned a supersense, is very similar: .76, .93, and .90, respectively, reflecting strong agreement.

[11] This excludes 1,200 auxiliary verb mentions, 100 of which are MWEs: *have to*, *is going to*, etc.

[12] Paaß and Reichartz (2009) train a similar sequence model for classifying noun and verb supersenses, but treat multiword phrases as single words. Their model is trained as a CRF rather than a structured perceptron, and adds LDA word cluster features, but the effects of these two changes are not separated in the experiments. They also find benefit from constraining the label space according to WordNet for in-vocabulary words (with what they call "lumped labels").

| | | | | | | | | | |
|---|---|---|---|---|---|---|---|---|---|
| United | States | financier | and | philanthropist | ( | 1855 | - | 1937 | ) |
| $_B$N:LOCATION | $_I$N:LOCATION | $_B$N:PERSON | $O$ | $_B$N:PERSON | $O$ | $_B$N:TIME | $O$ | $_B$N:TIME | $O$ |

**Figure 2:** A supersense tagging shown with per-token BIO tags in the style of Ciaramita and Altun (2006).

| | | | | | | | | | | | | | |
|---|---|---|---|---|---|---|---|---|---|---|---|---|---|
| The | white | pages | allowed | me | to | get | in | touch | with | parents | of | my | high | school |
| | $_B$N:COMMUNICATION | Ī | $_O$V:COGNITION | O | O | $_B$V:SOCIAL | Ī | Ī | Ĩ | $_O$N:PERSON | O | O | $_B$N:GROUP | Ī |

| | | | | | | | | | | |
|---|---|---|---|---|---|---|---|---|---|---|
| friends | so | that | I | could | track | people | down | one | by | one |
| $_O$N:PERSON | O | O | O | O | $_B$V:SOCIAL | $_O$N:PERSON | Ī | B | Ī | Ī |

**Figure 3:** Tagging for part of the lexical semantic analysis depicted in figure 1. Note that for nominal and verbal MWEs, the supersense label is only attached to the first tag of the expression.

Though our focus in this paper is on English, automatic supersense tagging has also been explored in Italian (Picca et al., 2008, 2009; Attardi et al., 2010, 2013; Rossi et al., 2013), Chinese (Qiu et al., 2011), and Arabic (Schneider et al., 2013).

### 4.2 Model

Like Ciaramita and Altun (2006) and Schneider et al. (2014a), we train a first-order structured perceptron (Collins, 2002) with averaging. This is a standard discriminative modeling setup, involving: a linear scoring function over features of input–output pairs; a Viterbi search to choose the highest-scoring valid output tag sequence given the input; and an online learning algorithm that makes $M$ passes through the training data, searching for the best tagging given the current model and updating the parameters (linear feature weights) where the best tagging doesn't match the gold tagging. With a first-order Markov assumption and tagset $\mathcal{Y}$, the Viterbi search for a sentence $\mathbf{x}$ requires $O(|\mathcal{Y}|^2 \cdot |\mathbf{x}|)$ runtime. The dataset used to train and evaluate the model, the tagging scheme, and the features are described below.

### 4.3 Data

The STREUSLE dataset, as described in §3, is annotated for multiword expressions as well as noun and verb supersenses and auxiliary verbs. We use this dataset for training and testing an integrated lexical semantic analyzer. Schneider et al. (2014a) used the CMWE dataset—i.e., the same REVIEWS sentences, but annotated only for MWEs. A handful of apparent errors in the MWE analyses were fixed in the course of our supersense annotation.

### 4.4 Tagset

In the STREUSLE dataset, supersense labels apply to *strong* noun and verb expressions—i.e., singleton nouns/verbs as well as strong nominal/verbal MWEs. Weak MWEs are not holistically labeled with a supersense (see fn. 5).

**The 8-way scheme.** To encode the lexical segmentation via token-level tags, we use the 8-way scheme from Schneider et al. (2014a) for positional flags. The 8-way scheme extends Ramshaw and Marcus's (1995) BIO chunking tags to also encode (a) a strong/weak distinction for MWEs, and (b) gappy MWEs (there is no formal limit on the number of gaps per MWE or the number of other lexical expressions occurring within each gap, though there is a limit of one level of nesting). The 4 lowercase positional flags indicate that an expression is within a gap, and otherwise have the same interpretation as their uppercase counterparts, which are:

- O for single-word expressions
- B for the first word of an MWE
- Ī for a word continuing a *strong* MWE
- Ĩ for a word weakly linked to its predecessor, forming a *weak* MWE[13]

As with the original BIO scheme, a globally well-formed sequence of tags in the 8-tag scheme can be constructed by respecting bigram constraints.[14]

**Adding class labels.** The tagset used to annotate the data for our tagger combines 8-way positional flags with supersense class labels. We decorate class labels only on beginners of strong lexical expressions—so this includes O or o on a single-word noun or verb, but always excludes Ī and ī.[15] Figure 3

[13]Weak MWE links may join together strong MWEs.

[14]Among these constraints are: B must always be immediately followed by Ī or Ĩ (because B marks the beginning of an MWE); and within-gap (lowercase-tagged) tokens must immediately follow a tag other than O and precede a tag other than O or B.

[15]Unlike prior work with the plain BIO scheme, we do not include the class in tags continuing a (strong) MWE, though the

gives an example. In this formulation, bigram constraints are sufficient to ensure a globally consistent tagging of the sentence.

There are $|\mathcal{N}| = 26$ noun supersense classes and $|\mathcal{V}| = 16$ verb classes (including the auxiliary verb class, abbreviated `a). In principle, then, there are

$$\underbrace{|\{\mathtt{O\ o\ B\ b\ \tilde{I}\ \tilde{ı}}\}|}_{6} \times \underbrace{(1+|\mathcal{N}|+|\mathcal{V}|)}_{43} + \underbrace{|\{\mathtt{\bar{I}\ \bar{ı}}\}|}_{2} = 260$$

possible tags encoding position and class information, allowing for chunks with no class because they are neither nominal nor verbal expressions. In practice, though, many of these combinations are nonexistent in our data; for experiments we only consider tags occurring in **train**, yielding $|\mathcal{Y}| = 146$.

We also run a condition where the supersense refinements are collapsed, i.e. $\mathcal{Y}$ consists of the 8 MWE tags. This allows us to measure the impact of the supersenses on MWE identification performance.

### 4.5 Features

We constrast three feature sets for full supersense tagging: (a) Schneider et al.'s (2014a) basic MWE features, which include lemmas, POS tags, word shapes, and whether the token potentially matches entries in any of several multiword lexicons; (b) the basic MWE features plus the Brown clusters (Brown et al., 1992) used by Schneider et al. (2014a); and (c) the basic MWE features and Brown clusters, plus several new features shown in figure 4. Chiefly, these new features consult the supersenses of WordNet synsets associated with words in the sentence: the first WordNet supersense feature is inspired by Ciaramita and Altun (2006) and subsequent work on supersense tagging, while the has-supersense feature is novel. There is also a feature aimed at distinguishing auxiliary verbs from main verbs, and new capitalization features take into account the capitalization of the first word in the sentence and the majority of words in the sentence. To keep the system as modular as possible, we refrain from including any features that depend on a syntactic parser.

class label should be interpreted as extending across the entire expression. This is for a technical reason: as our scheme allows for gaps, the classes of the tags flanking a gap in a strong MWE would be required to match for the analysis to be consistent. To enforce this in a bigram tagger, the within-gap tags would have to encode the gappy expression's class as well as their own, leading to an undesirable blowup in the size of the state space.

**New Capitalization Features**

1. capitalized $\wedge$ $[\![i = 0]\!]$ $\wedge$ $[\![$majority of tokens in the sentence are capitalized$]\!]$
2. capitalized $\wedge$ $i > 0 \wedge w_0$ is lowercase

**Auxiliary Verb vs. Main Verb Feature**

3. $pos_i$ is a verb $\wedge$ $[\![pos_{i+1}$ is a verb $\vee$ $(pos_{i+1}$ is an adverb $\wedge\, pos_{i+2}$ is a verb$)]\!]$

**WordNet Supersense Features** (unlexicalized)

*Let $cpos_i$ denote the coarse part-of-speech of token i: common noun, proper noun, pronoun, verb, adjective, adverb, etc. This feature aims primarily to inform the supersense label on the first token of nominal compounds and light verb constructions, where the "semantic head" is usually a common noun subsequent to the beginning of the expression:*

4. subsequent noun's 1st supersense: where $cpos_i$ is a common noun, verb, or adjective, $cpos_i$ $\wedge$ for the smallest $k > i$ such that $pos_k$ is a common noun, the supersense of the first WordNet synset for lemma $\lambda_k$—provided there is no intervening verb ($j$ such that $cpos_j$ is a verb and $i < j < k$)

*The following two feature templates depend on the tag $y_i$. Let $flag(y_i)$ denote the positional flag part of the tag (O, B, etc.) and $sst(y_i)$ denote the supersense class label:*

5. 1st supersense:
   - if $flag(y_i) \in \{\mathtt{O}, \mathtt{o}\}$: the supersense of the first WordNet synset for lemma $\lambda_i$
   - else if $cpos_i$ is a verb and there is a subsequent verb particle at position $k > i$ with no intervening verb: the supersense of the first synset for the compound lemma $\langle \lambda_i, \lambda_k \rangle$ (provided that the particle verb is found in WordNet)
   - otherwise: the supersense of the first WordNet synset for the longest contiguous lemma starting at position $i$ that is present in WordNet: $\langle \lambda_i, \lambda_{i+1}, \ldots, \lambda_j \rangle$ $(j \geq i)$
6. has supersense: same cases as the above, but instead of encoding the highest-ranking synset's supersense, encodes whether $sst(y_i)$ is represented in any of the matched synsets for the given lemma. Note that for a given token, this feature can take on different values for different tags.

**Figure 4:** New features for MWE and supersense tagging. They augment the basic MWE feature set of Schneider et al. (2014a), and are conjoined with the current tag, $y_i$.

The model's percepts (binary or real-valued functions of the input[16]) can be conjoined with any tag $y \in \mathcal{Y}$ to form a feature that receives its own weight

[16]We use the term **percept** rather than "feature" here to emphasize that we are talking about functions of the input only, rather than input–output combinations that each receive a parameter during learning.

(parameter). To avoid having to learn a model with tens of millions of parameters, we impose a percept cutoff during learning: only zero-order percepts that are active at least 5 times in the training data (with any tag) are retained in the model (with features for all tags). There is no minimum threshold for first-order percepts.[17] The resulting models are of a manageable size: about 4 million parameters with the full tagset.

### 4.6 Experimental Setup

Our setup mostly echoes that of Schneider et al. (2014a). We adopt their **train** (3312 sentences/ 48k words) vs. **test** (500 sentences/7k words) split, and tune hyperparameters by 8-fold cross-validation on **train**. By this procedure we chose a percept cutoff of 5 to use throughout, and tuned the number of training iterations for each experimental condition (early stopping within each cross-validation fold so as to greedily maximize tagging accuracy on the held-out portion, and averaging the best number of iterations across folds). For simplicity, we use oracle POS tags in our experiments and do not use Schneider et al.'s (2014a) recall-oriented cost function. Experiments were managed with Jonathan Clark's `ducttape` tool.[18]

### 4.7 Results

Table 2 shows full supersense tagging results, separating the MWE identification performance (measured by link-based precision, recall, and $F_1$; see Schneider et al., 2014a) from the precision, recall, and $F_1$ of class labels on the first token of each expression (segments with no class label are ignored).[19] Exact tagging accuracy (last column) is higher because it rewards true negatives, i.e. single-word segments with no nominal or verbal class label (the `O` and `o` tags).

**Tag space.** The sequence tagging framework makes it simple to model MWE identification jointly with supersense tagging: this is accomplished by packing information about both kinds of output into the tags. But there is always a risk that a larger tag space will impair the model's ability to generalize. By comparing the first two rows of the results, we can see that jointly modeling supersenses along with multiword expressions results in only a minor decrease (<2 $F_1$ points) in MWE identification performance under the most basic feature set. Further, we see that most of that decrease is recovered with richer features. Thus, we conclude that it is empirically reasonable to model these phenomena together.

**Runtime.** Our final system (146 tags; last row of table 2) tags ≈140 words (10 sentences) per second.

**Features.** Comparing the bottom three rows in the table indicates that features that generalize beyond lexical items lead to better supersense labeling. The best model has access to supersense information in the WordNet lexicon; it is 4 $F_1$ points better at choosing the correct class label than its nearest competitor, which relies on word clusters to abstract away from individual lexical items. Nouns, verbs, and auxiliaries all see improvements.

We also inspect the learned parameters. The highest-weighted parameters suggest that the best model relies heavily on the supersense lookup features, whereas the second-best model—lacking those—in large part relies on Brown clusters (cf. Grave et al., 2013). The auxiliary verb vs. main verb feature in the best model is highly weighted as well, helping to distinguish between `` `a`` and V:STATIVE.

**Polysemy.** We have motivated the task of supersense tagging in part as a coarse form of word sense disambiguation. Therefore, it is worth investigating how well the learned model manages to choose the correct supersense for nouns and verbs that are ambiguous in the data. A handful of lemmas in **test** have at least two different supersenses predicted several times; an examination of four such lemmas in table 3 shows that for three of them the tagging accuracy exceeds the majority baseline. In the case of *look*, the model is usually able to distinguish between V:COGNITION (as in *looking for a company with decent rates*) and V:PERCEPTION (as in *sometimes the broccoli looks browned around the edges*).

**Out-of-domain baseline.** To assess the importance of in-domain data for learning, we used a SemCor-trained supersense tagger—a reimplemen-

[17] Zero-order percepts are percepts which are to be conjoined with only the present tag to form zero-order features. First-order percepts are to be conjoined with the present and previous tags.

[18] `https://github.com/jhclark/ducttape/`

[19] We count the class label only once for MWEs—otherwise this measure would be strongly dependent on segmentation performance. However, the MWE predictions do have an effect when the prediction and gold standard disagree on which token begins a strong nominal or verbal expression.

| Feature Set | $\lvert\mathcal{Y}\rvert$ | Model Size | $M$ | MWE ID P | MWE ID R | MWE ID $F_1$ | Class labeling P | Class labeling R | Class labeling $F_1$ | NSST R | VSST R | Aux R | Tag Acc |
|---|---|---|---|---|---|---|---|---|---|---|---|---|---|
| MWE | 8 | 194k | 4 | **72.97** | **55.55** | **63.01** | — | — | — | — | — | — | — |
| MWE | 146 | 3,555k | 5 | 67.77 | 55.76 | 61.14 | 64.68 | 66.78 | 65.71 | 59.14 | 71.64 | 93.71 | 80.73 |
| MWE+clusters | 146 | 4,371k | 5 | 68.55 | **56.73** | 62.04 | 65.69 | 67.76 | 66.71 | 61.49 | 71.34 | 92.45 | 81.20 |
| MWE+clusters+SST | 146 | 4,388k | 4 | **71.05** | 56.24 | **62.74** | **69.47** | **71.90** | **70.67** | **66.95** | **74.17** | **94.97** | **82.49** |

**Table 2:** Results on **test** for lexical semantic analysis of noun and verb supersenses and MWEs with increasingly complex models. Class labeling performance is given in aggregate, and class labeling *recall* is further broken down into noun supersense tagging (NSST), verb supersense tagging (VSST), and auxiliary verb tagging. All of these results use a percept cutoff of 5. The first result row uses a collapsed tagset (just the MWE status) rather than predicting full supersense labels, as described in §4.4. The number of training iterations $M$ was tuned by cross-validation on **train**. The best result in each column and section is bolded.

| lemma | unique SSTs | majority baseline | accuracy |
|---|---|---|---|
| *get* | 7 gold, 8 pred. | **12/28** | 6/28 |
| *look* | 2 gold, 3 pred. | 8/13 | **12/13** |
| *take* | 5 gold, 5 pred. | 8/21 | **11/21** |
| *time(s)* | 3 gold, 2 pred. | 8/14 | **9/14** |

**Table 3:** Four polysemous lemmas and counts of their gold vs. predicted supersenses in **test** (limited to cases where both the gold standard tag and the predicted tag included a supersense). The distribution of gold supersenses for *take*, for example, is V:SOCIAL: 8, V:MOTION: 7, V:POSSESSION: 1, V:STATIVE: 4, V:EMOTION: 1.

tation of Ciaramita and Altun (2006)[20]—to tag our test data in the reviews domain. By our class labeling evaluation, the result is 51.05% precision, 48.93% recall, and 49.97% $F_1$.[21] Even without word clusters or the supersense-tailored features of figure 4, our simplest in-domain model reaches 65.71% $F_1$. Though there are minor differences in features between the two models, both are first-order structured perceptron taggers. We believe that this wide gulf is primarily an artifact of the training data. The annotation methodology was very different (direct MWE and supersense annotation in our case, vs. relying on mappings from WordNet synsets in the case of SemCor), and the vocabulary and style are vastly different between casual online writing and edited prose. Building lexical semantic models that are robust to many domains at once will require further experimentation, and in our estimation, additional annotated resources that cover a fuller spectrum of written language.

## 5 Conclusion

We have integrated the multiword expression identification task formulated in Schneider et al. (2014a) with the supersense tagging task of Ciaramita and Altun (2006). Supersenses offer coarse-grained and broadly applicable semantic labels for lexical expressions and naturally complement multiword expressions in lexical semantic analysis. We have annotated English online reviews for supersenses, including developing detailed annotation criteria for verbs. Experiments with discriminative joint tagging of MWEs and supersenses establish a strong baseline for future work, which may incorporate new features, richer models, and indirect forms of supervision (cf. Grave et al., 2013; Johannsen et al., 2014) for this task. We also expect future investigations will apply our tagger to a downstream task such as semantic parsing or machine translation (for further discussion of potential applications, see Schneider, 2014, pp. 179–189). Our data and open-source software is available at `http://www.ark.cs.cmu.edu/LexSem/`.


## Acknowledgments

We thank our energetic annotators, Nora Kazour, Spencer Onuffer, Emily Danchik, and Michael T. Mordowanec, as well as Chris Dyer, Lori Levin, Ed Hovy, Tim Baldwin, Mark Steedman, and anonymous reviewers for useful feedback on the technical content. This research was supported in part by NSF CAREER grant IIS-1054319 and DARPA grant FA8750-12-2-0342 funded under the DEFT program.


[20] By Michael Heilman (Heilman, 2011, pp. 47–48); downloaded from: `http://www.ark.cs.cmu.edu/mheilman/questions/SupersenseTagger-10-01-12.tar.gz`

[21] Excluding auxiliaries (which are not part of the original supersense representation and thus not predicted by Heilman's tagger) from the evaluation, recall rises to 52.50% and $F_1$ to 51.76%.

## References


Giuseppe Attardi, Luca Baronti, Stefano Dei Rossi, and Maria Simi. 2013. SuperSense Tagging with a Maximum Entropy Markov Model. In Bernardo Magnini, Francesco Cutugno, Mauro Falcone, and Emanuele Pianta, editors, *Evaluation of Natural Language and Speech Tools for Italian*, number 7689 in Lecture Notes in Computer Science, pages 186–194. Springer, Berlin.

Giuseppe Attardi, Stefano Dei Rossi, Giulia Di Pietro, Alessandro Lenci, Simonetta Montemagni, and Maria Simi. 2010. A resource and tool for super-sense tagging of Italian texts. In Nicoletta Calzolari, Khalid Choukri, Bente Maegaard, Joseph Mariani, Jan Odijk, Stelios Piperidis, Mike Rosner, and Daniel Tapias, editors, *Proc. of LREC*, pages 2242–2248. Valletta, Malta.

Timothy Baldwin and Su Nam Kim. 2010. Multiword expressions. In Nitin Indurkhya and Fred J. Damerau, editors, *Handbook of Natural Language Processing, Second Edition*, pages 267–292. CRC Press, Taylor and Francis Group, Boca Raton, FL.

Ann Bies, Justin Mott, Colin Warner, and Seth Kulick. 2012. English Web Treebank. Technical Report LDC2012T13, Linguistic Data Consortium, Philadelphia, PA. URL `http://www.ldc.upenn.edu/Catalog/catalogEntry.jsp?catalogId=LDC2012T13`.

Steven Bird, Ewan Klein, and Edward Loper. 2009. *Natural Language Processing with Python: Analyzing Text with the Natural Language Toolkit.* O'Reilly Media, Inc., Sebastopol, CA.

Peter F. Brown, Peter V. deSouza, Robert L. Mercer, Vincent J. Della Pietra, and Jenifer C. Lai. 1992. Class-based n-gram models of natural language. *Computational Linguistics*, 18(4):467–479.

Massimiliano Ciaramita and Yasemin Altun. 2006. Broad-coverage sense disambiguation and information extraction with a supersense sequence tagger. In *Proc. of EMNLP*, pages 594–602. Sydney, Australia.

Massimiliano Ciaramita and Mark Johnson. 2003. Supersense tagging of unknown nouns in WordNet. In Michael Collins and Mark Steedman, editors, *Proc. of EMNLP*, pages 168–175. Sapporo, Japan.

Michael Collins. 2002. Discriminative training methods for Hidden Markov Models: theory and experiments with perceptron algorithms. In *Proc. of EMNLP*, pages 1–8. Philadelphia, PA, USA.

Christiane Fellbaum. 1990. English verbs as a semantic net. *International Journal of Lexicography*, 3(4):278–301.

Christiane Fellbaum, editor. 1998. *WordNet: an electronic lexical database*. MIT Press, Cambridge, MA.

Edouard Grave, Guillaume Obozinski, and Francis Bach. 2013. Hidden Markov tree models for semantic class induction. In *Proc. of CoNLL*, pages 94–103. Sofia, Bulgaria.

Michael Heilman. 2011. *Automatic factual question generation from text.* Ph.D. dissertation, Carnegie Mellon University, Pittsburgh, Pennsylvania. URL `http://www.ark.cs.cmu.edu/mheilman/questions/papers/heilman-question-generation-dissertation.pdf`.

Anders Johannsen, Dirk Hovy, Héctor Martínez Alonso, Barbara Plank, and Anders Søgaard. 2014. More or less supervised supersense tagging of Twitter. In *Proc. of *SEM*, pages 1–11. Dublin, Ireland.

George A. Miller. 1990. Nouns in WordNet: a lexical inheritance system. *International Journal of Lexicography*, 3(4):245–264.

Gerhard Paaß and Frank Reichartz. 2009. Exploiting semantic constraints for estimating supersenses with CRFs. In *Proc. of the Ninth SIAM International Conference on Data Mining*, pages 485–496. Sparks, Nevada.

Scott S. L. Piao, Paul Rayson, Dawn Archer, Andrew Wilson, and Tony McEnery. 2003. Extracting multiword expressions with a semantic tagger. In *Proc. of the ACL 2003 Workshop on Multiword Expressions: Analysis, Acquisition and Treatment*, pages 49–56. Sapporo, Japan.

Scott Songlin Piao, Paul Rayson, Dawn Archer, and Tony McEnery. 2005. Comparing and combining a semantic tagger and a statistical tool for MWE extraction. *Computer Speech & Language*, 19(4):378–397.

Davide Picca, Alfio Massimiliano Gliozzo, and Simone Campora. 2009. Bridging languages by SuperSense entity tagging. In *Proc. of NEWS*, pages 136–142. Suntec, Singapore.

Davide Picca, Alfio Massimiliano Gliozzo, and Massimiliano Ciaramita. 2008. Supersense Tagger for Italian. In Nicoletta Calzolari, Khalid Choukri, Bente Maegaard, Joseph Mariani, Jan Odjik, Stelios Piperidis, and Daniel Tapias, editors, *Proc. of LREC*, pages 2386–2390. Marrakech, Morocco.

Likun Qiu, Yunfang Wu, Yanqiu Shao, and Alexander Gelbukh. 2011. Combining contextual and structural information for supersense tagging of Chinese unknown words. In *Computational Linguistics and Intelligent Text Processing: Proceedings of the 12th International Conference (CICLing'11)*, volume 6608 of *Lecture Notes in Computer Science*, pages 15–28. Springer, Berlin.

Lance A. Ramshaw and Mitchell P. Marcus. 1995. Text chunking using transformation-based learning. In *Proc. of the Third ACL Workshop on Very Large Corpora*, pages 82–94. Cambridge, MA.

Stefano Dei Rossi, Giulia Di Pietro, and Maria Simi. 2013. Description and results of the SuperSense tagging task. In Bernardo Magnini, Francesco Cutugno, Mauro Falcone, and Emanuele Pianta, editors, *Evaluation of Natural Language and Speech Tools for Italian*, number 7689 in Lecture Notes in Computer Science, pages 166–175. Springer, Berlin.

Nathan Schneider. 2014. *Lexical Semantic Analysis in Natural Language Text*. Ph.D. dissertation, Carnegie Mellon University, Pittsburgh, Pennsylvania, USA. URL `http://www.cs.cmu.edu/~nschneid/thesis/thesis-print.pdf`.

Nathan Schneider, Emily Danchik, Chris Dyer, and Noah A. Smith. 2014a. Discriminative lexical semantic segmentation with gaps: running the MWE gamut. *Transactions of the Association for Computational Linguistics*, 2:193–206.

Nathan Schneider, Behrang Mohit, Chris Dyer, Kemal Oflazer, and Noah A. Smith. 2013. Supersense tagging for Arabic: the MT-in-the-middle attack. In *Proc. of NAACL-HLT*, pages 661–667. Atlanta, Georgia, USA.

Nathan Schneider, Behrang Mohit, Kemal Oflazer, and Noah A. Smith. 2012. Coarse lexical semantic annotation with supersenses: an Arabic case study. In *Proc. of ACL*, pages 253–258. Jeju Island, Korea.

Nathan Schneider, Spencer Onuffer, Nora Kazour, Emily Danchik, Michael T. Mordowanec, Henrietta Conrad, and Noah A. Smith. 2014b. Comprehensive annotation of multiword expressions in a social web corpus. In Nicoletta Calzolari, Khalid Choukri, Thierry Declerck, Hrafn Loftsson, Bente Maegaard, Joseph Mariani, Asuncion Moreno, Jan Odijk, and Stelios Piperidis, editors, *Proc. of LREC*, pages 455–461. Reykjavík, Iceland.

Yulia Tsvetkov, Nathan Schneider, Dirk Hovy, Archna Bhatia, Manaal Faruqui, and Chris Dyer. 2014. Augmenting English adjective senses with supersenses. In Nicoletta Calzolari, Khalid Choukri, Thierry Declerck, Hrafn Loftsson, Bente Maegaard, Joseph Mariani, Asuncion Moreno, Jan Odijk, and Stelios Piperidis, editors, *Proc. of LREC*, pages 4359–4365. Reykjavík, Iceland.

# Good News or Bad News: Using Affect Control Theory to Analyze Readers' Reaction Towards News Articles

**Areej Ahothali**
David R. Cheriton School
of Computer Science
University of Waterloo
Waterloo, Ontario, N2L3G1
aalhotha@cs.uwaterloo.ca

**Jesse Hoey**
David R. Cheriton School
of Computer Science
University of Waterloo
Waterloo, Ontario, N2L3G1
jhoey@cs.uwaterloo.ca

## Abstract

This paper proposes a novel approach to sentiment analysis that leverages work in sociology on symbolic interactionism. The proposed approach uses Affect Control Theory (ACT) to analyze readers' sentiment towards factual (objective) content and towards its entities (subject and object). ACT is a theory of affective reasoning that uses empirically derived equations to predict the sentiments and emotions that arise from events. This theory relies on several large lexicons of words with affective ratings in a three-dimensional space of evaluation, potency, and activity (EPA). The equations and lexicons of ACT were evaluated on a newly collected news-headlines corpus. ACT lexicon was expanded using a label propagation algorithm, resulting in 86,604 new words. The predicted emotions for each news headline was then computed using the augmented lexicon and ACT equations. The results had a precision of 82%, 79%, and 68% towards the event, the subject, and object, respectively. These results are significantly higher than those of standard sentiment analysis techniques.

## 1 Introduction

Natural language texts are often meant to express or impact individuals' emotions. Recognizing the underlying emotions expressed in or triggered by a text is essential to understanding the full meaning that a message conveys. Sentiment analysis (SA) researchers are increasingly interested in investigating natural language processing techniques as well as emotion theories to identify sentiment expressions in natural language texts. They typically focus on analyzing subjective documents from the writer's perspective using frequency-based word representations and mapping them to categorical labels or sentiment polarity, in which text (e.g., sentence or document) is associated, respectively, with either a descriptive label or a point in a continuum.

In this paper, we focus on analyzing objective statements. Unlike subjective statements, that contain an explicit opinion or belief about an object or aspect (e.g., *"Seventh Son is a terrible movie"*), objective statements present only factual information (e.g., *"protestors were arrested in NYC"*). Despite the limited research on fact-based sentiment analysis, many factual statements may carry or evoke sentiments (e.g., news articles, blog comments. etc.). Thus, there is a need for a new approach that attaches sentiment scores to objective (factual) statements as well as to the components that make them up. For example, a sentence like *"x kills y"* will clearly evoke a negative sentiment for the reader, and highly negative (yet different) sentiments towards each *x* and *y* (angry about *x* and sorry about *y*). Further, our affective evaluation of each entity participating in the event might affect our judgement of the situation. For example, if we know that *x* is a victim and *y* is a criminal, then the triggered sentiment will be more positive in general, positive towards *x*, but still negative towards *y*.

The proposed method in this paper builds a contextual model that maps words to a multi-dimensional emotion space by using Affect Control Theory (ACT). ACT is a social psychological



*Human Language Technologies: The 2015 Annual Conference of the North American Chapter of the ACL*, pages 1548–1558,
Denver, Colorado, May 31 – June 5, 2015. 

theory of human social interaction (Heise, 2007). ACT proposes that peoples' social perceptions, actions, and emotional experiences are governed by a psychological need to minimize deflections between culturally shared fundamental sentiments about social situations and transient impressions resulting from the dynamic behaviours of interactants in those situations. Each event in ACT is modeled as a triplet: actor, behavior, and object. Culturally shared "fundamental" sentiments about each of these elements are measured in three-dimensions: Evaluation, Potency, and Activity (EPA). The core idea of ACT is that each of the entities (actor, behaviour and object) participating in an event has a fundamental affective sentiment (EPA value) that is shared among members of a culture, and the combination of entities in the event generates a transient impression or feeling that might be different from the fundamental sentiment. Transient impressions evolve over time according to empirically measured temporal dynamics. Emotions are functions of the difference between fundamental sentiments and transient impressions. EPA profiles of concepts can be measured with the semantic differential (Osgood, 1957), a survey technique whereby respondents rate affective meanings of concepts on numerical scales with opposing adjectives at each end (e.g., {good, nice}$\leftrightarrow${bad, awful} for E; {weak, little}$\leftrightarrow${strong, big} for P; {calm, passive}$\leftrightarrow${exciting, active} for A). Affect control theorists have compiled databases of a few thousand words along with average EPA ratings obtained from survey participants who are knowledgeable about their culture (Heise, 2010). For example, the culturally shared EPA for *"mother"* in Ontario, Canada, is $[2.74, 2.04, 0.67]$, which is quite good, quite powerful, and slightly active. The *"daughter"* EPA is $[2.18, -0.01, 1.92]$, which is quite good, but less powerful and more active than *"mother"*.

ACT is advantageous for sentiment analysis applications, especially those that aim to analyze descriptive events or factual content for the following reasons: (1) EPA space is thought to provide a universal representation of individuals' sentiment; (2) the transient feeling accumulates over the course of several events and, hence, it can model larger structures in text; (3) impression formation can be computed towards different entities in the sentence, giving a more fine-grained description of the sentiments; (4) the EPA values are empirically driven, reflecting a real evaluation of human participants; and (5) the interaction between terms in ACT is compatible with the linguistic principle of a compositional semantic model, which states that the meaning of a sentence is a function of its words (Frege, 1892).

Our method uses the impression and emotion formation equations of ACT to predict human sentiments towards events. We decompose each sentence into subject-verb-object and then associate subject with actor, verb with behaviour, and object with object in ACT. We then compute the predicted emotion towards each of actor, behaviour and object using ACT equations. We use a semi-supervised method based on Wordnet-similarities to assign EPA values to words that are not in ACT lexicons. We evaluated the viability of using ACT in sentiment analysis on a news headlines dataset that we collected and annotated. This approach yielded a precision between 71% and 82% on the news headline dataset. These results are significantly higher than those results from a method that was trained using bag-of-words and Sentiwordnet lexicon.

The rest of the paper is organized as follows: the first section presents the related work in emotions elicitation and sentiment analysis fields; the following two sections describe the proposed method, providing details about affect control theory, impression formation equations, and the lexicon induction method; the last section presents the dataset used in this paper, and discusses the results obtained using our proposed methods.

## 2 Related Work

Emotions have been studied extensively in disciplines like anthropology, psychology, sociology, and more recently in computer science. In recent years, fields like affective computing (AC) (Picard, 2000), human-computer interaction (HCI) (Brave and Nass, 2002), and sentiment analysis (Feldman, 2013) are also contributing to this area of research, by computationally modeling and evaluating existing theories. Most of the proposed methods in SA and AC have used the appraisal theory by representing emotions with discrete labels such as happy, sad, etc. (Ekman, 1992). Only several studies have adopted dimensional theories by representing emotions (core affects) in three- or two-dimensional space: arousal, valence, and sometimes dominance (Russell, 2003). Although psychological evidence show that words or any other events are emotionally perceived in more than one dimension (Barrett, 2006; Russell, 2003), multi-dimensional models have rarely been used in sentiment analysis.

In sentiment analysis research, two main machine learning (ML) methods are used: supervised learning or unsupervised learning methods. Supervised learning methods generally use the occurrence frequencies of words that indicate opinion/sentiment and then classify these occurrences as either positive or negative using one of the common classification methods (e.g., Maximum Entropy, support vector machine (SVM)). Many combinations of features have been tried, such as part-of-speech tagging, n-grams, term weighting, sentiment lexicons, term presence, and syntactic dependencies (Pang et al., 2002; Lin and He, 2009). In contrast, unsupervised learning approaches often determine the semantic orientation (SO) of a sentence or document by calculating the difference between the point-wise mutual information (PMI) (Church and Hanks, 1990) for its phrases or words with sentiment seeds (Turney and Littman, 2002; Turney, 2002).

Other approaches have built more-structured models, augmenting the standard bag-of-words technique with appraisal groups, which are represented as sets of attribute values in a semantic taxonomy (Whitelaw et al., 2005) or considering the interaction between words by using a tree structured CRF based on (Nakagawa et al., 2010). Another study has taken the interaction between words into account by utilizing the compositional formal semantic models based on Frege's principle (Frege, 1892). A framework is proposed in (Coecke et al., 2010) in which a sentence vector is a function of the Kronecker product of its words. This approach was evaluated on several datasets and showed promising results and improvement over non-compositional approaches (Grefenstette et al., 2010; Grefenstette and Sadrzadeh, 2011; Mitchell and Lapata, 2008).

Much sentiment analysis work has focused on extracting emotions from the writer's perspective; only several recent studies have tackled the problem of predicting readers' sentiments. Both (Lin et al., 2008) and (Yang et al., 2009) used bag-of-words and linguistic features to classify Chinese news articles (Yahoo!-Kimo news) into one of the user emotional ratings (happy, sad, surprise, etc.). Another study presents a multi-label classification approach that uses words' polarity, and semantic frame features to classify news article into categorical emotions (Bhowmick, 2009). As a part of the SemEval-2007 task, a number of approaches have been proposed to binary-classify news headlines into positive or negative sentiment (Strapparava and Mihalcea, 2007; Katz et al., 2007; Chaumartin, 2007).

## 3 ACT for Sentiment Analysis

### 3.1 Background

Affect Control theory (ACT) is a new version of symbolic interactionism (Mead, 1938) created by David Heise (Heise, 1987). ACT proposes that individuals process gestures (including words or events) as symbols or concepts shared among groups of people or culture. These fundamental meanings or 'fundamental sentiments' are defined in a three-dimensional space of EPA profile. ACT also proposes that individuals try to maintain the transient impressions, which are generated from the interactions of the events' elements (subject-verb-object), close to the fundamental sentiments in the EPA space. ACT models emotions as arising because of the differences between fundamental sentiments and transient impressions. For example, a person who is powerful but is made to feel powerless will feel "angry". ACT equations (i.e., impression formation equations) are obtained through empirical studies, and they model the process by which the fundamental sentiments of elements in the events are combined to generate a transient impression.

The affective meanings in ACT consist of three components: Evaluation (good versus bad); Potency (powerful versus powerless); and Activity (lively versus inactive). Each affective meaning is measured on a scale from -4.3 (infinitely bad, powerless, or inactive) to +4.3 (infinitely good, powerful, or lively). These meanings are attached to concepts corresponding to identities, behaviors, settings, and modifiers. According to ACT, people from the same cultures and gender share the same fundamental sentiments (EPA) about world concepts (Berger and

Zelditch, 2002; Heise, 2007).

Lexicons of EPA values have been gathered for thousands of words from different languages and cultures including Germany, Japan, Canada and the USA. In general, within-cultural agreement about EPA meanings of social concepts is high even across subgroups of society, and cultural-average EPA ratings from as little as a few dozen survey participants have been shown to be extremely stable over extended periods of time (Heise, 2010). These findings may seem surprising in light of societal conflicts as evidenced, for instance, by competing political ideologies. Research has consistently shown that the number of contested concepts is small relative to the stable and consensual semantic structures that form the basis of our social interactions and shared cultural understanding (Heise, 2010).

### 3.2 Affect Control Theory

In ACT, each event has at least three elements: actor (subject, S), behavior (verb, V), and object (O). Each of these elements is represented by three values (EPA) that capture the fundamental sentiments they evoke in terms of evaluation, potency, and activity. The fundamental sentiment of an event according to ACT grammar is a nine-dimensional vector:

$$f = \{S_e\ S_p\ S_e\ V_e\ V_p\ V_a\ O_e\ O_p\ O_a\}$$

where e.g. $S_e$ represents the fundamental sentiment about the subject (S) on the evaluation (e) dimension. The transient impression evoked by an event is another 9D vector:

$$\tau = \{S'_e\ S'_p\ S'_e\ V'_e\ V'_p\ V'_a\ O'_e\ O'_p\ O'_a\}$$

where fundamental EPA values are denoted by non-primed symbols and post-event EPA values are denoted by primed symbols. The transient impression $\tau$ is computed by multiplying $t$, a vector of features that are combinations of terms from the fundamental sentiment $f$, by a matrix $M$ of prediction coefficients estimated by impression-formation research.

$$\begin{aligned} t = (1\ & S_e\ S_p\ S_a\ V_e\ V_p\ V_a\ O_e\ O_p\ O_a \\ & S_eV_e\ S_eV_p\ S_eV_a\ S_pV_e\ S_pV_p\ S_pO_a\ S_aV_a \\ & V_eO_e\ V_eO_p\ V_pO_e\ V_pO_p\ V_pO_a\ V_aO_e\ V_aO_p \\ & S_eV_eO_e\ S_eV_pO_p\ S_pV_pO_p\ S_pV_pO_a\ S_aV_aO_a) \end{aligned}$$

$$\tau = Mt \tag{1}$$

For example, the transient impression of the subject's valence, $S'_e$, using US male coefficients:

$$\begin{aligned} S'_e = & -.98 + .48\, S_e - .015\, S_p - .015\, S_a \\ & + .425\, V_e - .069\, V_p - .106\, V_a + .055\, O_e ... \end{aligned}$$

This part of the equation shows that our evaluation of the subject/actor is affected mainly by how the valence of this person and action are perceived by others (positive large coefficients .48 and .425 for $S_e$ and $V_e$). It also shows that powerful actors (subject) or behaviours (verb) are seen a bit negatively (negative coefficients -.015, -.069 for $S_p$ and $V_p$).

We also can incorporate the location (settings), which indicates where the event took place such as school, country, and etc., can be achieved by adding the EPA values for the setting and use the coefficient values of the subject-verb-object-location (SVOL) grammar instead of subject-verb-object (SVO).

Modifiers in ACT are adjectives or attributes that modify actor or object (e.g."good friend" or "abusive father"). The impression generated from combinations of identity with modifiers can be calculated as a linear combination of the EPA values of both the identity and modifiers.

$$c = B_1\, p + B_2\, i \tag{2}$$

where $p = \{P_e, P_p, P_a\}, i = \{I_e, I_p, I_a\}$, and $c = \{C_e, C_p, C_a\}$ are the EPA profiles for the modifier, identity, and the combination, respectively, and $B_1$ and $B_2$ are coefficients estimated from survey data. For example, the "father" affective rating is $[1.84, 1.78, 0.02]$, "abusive" is $[-2.23, 0.34, -0.02]$, and "abusive father" is $[-1.51, 1.37, -0.21]$.

The deflection, which is defined as the discrepancy between the fundamental sentiment and the transient impression, is calculated by the squared Euclidean distance between the sentiments and impressions given the following equation.

$$d = \sum_i (f_i - \tau_i)^2 \tag{3}$$

The deflection does not indicate positive or negative emotions, but rather indicates whether or not the event met someone's expectation.

In ACT, the emotion triggered by an event is a function of the fundamental identity for actor or object, $i \equiv \{S_e, S_p, S_a\}$ or $i \equiv \{O_e, O_p, O_a\}$, and the transient identity for actor or object, $i' \equiv \{S'_e, S'_p, S'_a\}$ or $i' \equiv \{O'_e, O'_p, O'_a\}$. ACT uses the following equation to predict emotions, with empirically measured coefficients as follows:

$$\varepsilon \propto E\,(i' - I\,i - \delta) \tag{4}$$

where $E$ is a $3 \times 3$ matrix coefficient of the emotion profile, $I$ is a $3\times3$ matrix coefficient for identity, and $\delta$ is a vector of equation constants.

### 3.3 Emotion Elicitation Using ACT

We implement ACT to predict the triggered sentiment of a single sentence as follows: first we extract the subject, verb, object, setting, and modifiers (adjectives of subject and object) and look them up in the augmented ACT lexicon (see section 3.4) to get EPA values (fundamental sentiments, $f$) for each word (MacKinnon, 2006). We next compute the transient impression $\tau$ using $f$ and Equations 1 and 2. After that, we compute the deflection using Equation 3, and the emotion towards the subject and object using Equation 4. We then map the resulting EPA scores for emotion to the nearest emotions label in ACT. The ACT dataset (MacKinnon, 2006) has 135 emotion labels, each with an EPA score (e.g., delighted= [2.04, 0.96, 1.48]), and we find the closest label using a Euclidean distance measure. We then compare these emotions $\varepsilon$ towards subject and object to corresponding ground truth in the news headline dataset (see Section 4) using root mean squared error (RMSE) and mean absolute error (MAE). We also discretize the predicted $\varepsilon$ and the ground truth into negative or positive EPA values, and compare accuracy of the discretized values.

To extract the sentence's quintet (i.e., subject, verb, object, modifiers, and settings), we implement a search algorithm that takes a treebank parse tree (Socher et al., 2013) and returns a (subject, predicate , and object) triplet (Rusu et al., 2007). As Rusu *et al.*'s algorithm searches a parse tree of grammatically correct English sentences, we make some alterations to consider news headlines' grammar. News headlines are often written to be short and precise (i.e., often not grammatically correct), and usually consist of several noun phrases without articles or the verb "to be". They are written in the present tense for current or past events (e.g, *terror strikes police base*). The past tense verbs are rarely used in news headlines, whereas passive voice sentences are common. The passive voice sentences are often written without an auxiliary verb, which make it hard for standard parsers to distinguish their verbs from past tense verbs and to extract the triplet accurately (e.g, *Six killed in accident*).

Our algorithm takes a parse tree and performs a breadth-first search and identifies the last noun descendent of the first noun phrase (NP) in the sentence as the subject and the previous descendent as the attributes (in Rusu *et al.*'s algorithm the subject is the first noun in (NP)). For example, in the sentence *Super Bowl-winning quarterback Russell Wilson divorces wife*, the actor/subject *"Russell"* is the last noun in the first noun phase and the previous adjectives and nouns are attributes (modifiers) of the subject. To locate the verbs, (similar to Rusu *et al.*'s algorithm) the algorithm searches the deepest verb phrase (VP) and returns the first verb (VB) descendent. If the verb is in the past tense, we transform it to passive voice. The algorithm (similar to Rusu *et al.*'s algorithm) returns the object that is co-located with the verb in the deepest verb phrase (VP). To extract the settings, we look for a noun phrase (NP) sub-tree that has a preposition (at, in, on) and return the last noun. This algorithm yields accuracies of 43%, 53% , and 26% with the ground truth (users' annotations of the subject, verb, and object).

We also consider whether the verb type is transitive, which directly indicates positive or negative sentiment toward something (e.g., $x$ killed $y$), or intransitive, which transfers sentiments into nouns (e.g., $x$ provides help to $y$). For intransitive verbs, we choose the second verb as the behavior (verb) in the sentence (e.g., "$x$ provides help to $y$" will be "$x$ helps $y$"). We also used part-of-speech tagging to determine the elements of an event and to identify the places and names. The gender of the names is considered by training a naïve Bayes classifier on names-gender corpus of 5001 female and 2943 male names[1] which yielded an accuracy of 86% on classifying names according to their gender.

[1] www.nltk.corpus

### 3.4 EPA lexicon Induction

The method described in the last section relies on a lexicon that maps words to EPA values. The ACT lexicon we used originally contains 2,293 words (original-EPA-lexicon) (MacKinnon, 2006). We augmented this lexicon by adding the Affective Norm for English Words (ANEW) (Bradley and Lang, 2010) data-set that contains 2,476 English words, and the Warriner *et al.* data-set (Warriner et al., 2013) that contains 13,915 words. ANEW and Warriner *et al.* data-sets were both scaled from the range of [1,9] to the range of [-4.3,4.3] using max-min scaling formula (Han, 2012). The min-max normalization preforms a linear transformation for a given value $x_i$ of $A$ with a minimum and maximum value of $[min_A,\ max_A]$ to $x'_i$ in range of $[min_B,\ max_B]$ given this formula:

$$x'_i = \frac{x_i - min_A}{max_A - min_A}(max_B - min_B) + min_B$$

Adding ANEW and Warriner lexicons generated lexicon of 17,347 words (extended-EPA-lexicon). We then randomly divided the extended-EPA-lexicon into a training-EPA-lexicon and a testing-EPA-lexicon, with 5,782 and 11,565 words, respectively. We used the training-EPA-lexicon to add more words, using a graph-based semi-supervised learning method called label-propagation, a technique that has been commonly used for NLP (Chen et al., 2006; Niu et al., 2005; Rao and Ravichandran, 2009; Zhu and Ghahramani, 2002; Blair-Goldensohn et al., 2008), and image annotation (Cao et al., 2008; Heckemann et al., 2006). Label-propagation is a transductive algorithm that propagates information from a set of labeled nodes (seed sets) to the rest of the graph through its edges (Zhu and Ghahramani, 2002). The label-propagation algorithm starts by adding all the synonyms and lemmas in WordNet of a specific part-of-speech (verb, noun, adjective, or adverbs) to the training-EPA-lexicon. This generates a set of labeled words $L = (X_l, Y_l)$ (the 5,782 words with EPA labels), and unlabeled words $U = (X_u, Y_u)$, from which we constructed undirected weighted graph $G = \{E, V, W\}$, where $V$ is a set of vertices (all the words in the set), $E$ is the weighted edges, and $W$ is an $n \times n$ weight matrix (affinity matrix) $n$ equal to the size vocabulary $|V|$.

We initialized the labeled nodes/words with the EPA value of the words observed in the training set, and the unlabeled nodes/words with zeroes. We computed the weight matrix using the WordNet similarity (Wu and Palmer, 1994) between the two words $x_i$ and $x_j$. Wu and Palmer's similarity is equal to the depth of the least common subsumer (LCS, the least common ancestor) divided by the summation of the depth of the two words in the WordNet taxonomy.

$$sim_{wup}(w_1, w_2) = \frac{2 * depth(LCS)}{depth(w_1) + depth(w_2)}$$

Each edge $E \in (v_i, v_j)$ has an associated weight $T_{ij}$, which is the row normalized weight $w_{ij}$ of the edge between $v_i$ and $v_j$. The labels are then propagated to adjacent nodes by computing $Y \leftarrow TY$. After each iteration the labeled nodes $Y_l$ are reset to their initial values (see Algorithm 1).

**Algorithm 1** ACT Label Propagation

```
procedure LABEL PROPAGATION(Synests C)
    Construct a Graph G = {V, E, W}
    Initialize T^0 and Y^0 matrices, i ← 0
    repeat
        Y^i ← TY^{i-1}
        Y_l ← L
    until Y converges
end procedure
```

The label propagation algorithm generated 167 adverbs, 3,809 adjectives, 11,531 verbs, and 81,347 nouns, with their EPA ratings in which 10,249 of them are in the testing-EPA-lexicon. To evaluate the validity of this approach, we compare our generated EPA ratings for these 10,249 words with those from the testing-EPA-lexicon (from ACT/ANEW/Warriner datasets). The results are shown in Tables 1 and 2. The resulting EPA are equally distributed between -4.3 and +4.3. We used two metrics to compare the results: root mean squared error (RMSE) and mean absolute error (MAE). These metrics were both close to 1.0 for E, P, and A, suggesting that there is a reasonable degree of agreement between the induced and manually labeled EPA values. It is worth mentioning that due to the limited numbers of adverbs in the ACT lexicon, and because the Wordnet-similarity measure that compares only words of the same part-of-speech, only several adverbs were generated using label-propagation algorithm.

| POS | W | RMSE | | | MSA | | |
|---|---|---|---|---|---|---|---|
| | | E | P | A | E | P | A |
| Adjectives | 378 | 1.2 | 1.2 | 0.9 | 0.9 | 1.0 | 0.8 |
| Adverbs | 5 | 1.0 | 1.1 | 1.3 | 0.7 | 0.8 | 0.9 |
| Verbs | 2,787 | 1.2 | 1.1 | 0.8 | 1.0 | 0.9 | 0.6 |
| Noun | 7,079 | 1.3 | 1.1 | 0.9 | 1.0 | 0.9 | 0.7 |
| Total | 10,249 | 1.3 | 1.1 | 0.9 | 1.0 | 0.9 | 0.7 |

Table 1: The results of comparing the induced lexicon using label propagation and ground truth EPA values (POS= part-of-speech, W= the number of the induced words, MAS=mean absolute error, and RMSE= root mean squared error

## 4 Datasets

We evaluated the proposed method on a newly collected news-headlines dataset. We collected 2080 news-headlines from a group of news websites and archives (BBC, CNN, Reuters, The Telegraph, Times, etc). The news headlines were selected randomly from the period from 1999 to 2014. Through Mechanical Turk, we recruited participants located in North America with more than 500 approved hits and an approved rate above 90%. We asked the participants to locate the subject (actor), behavior (verb), and object of each sentence and to indicate their emotions towards them and towards the event (as a whole) in the EPA format $\in [-4.3, +4.3]$ (where -4.3 indicates strongly negative EPA value and +4.3 indicates strongly positive EPA value). The dataset was annotated by at least three judges per headline. We excluded any ratings that were filled with blanks, zeros, or similar values in all the fields. We also excluded the answers that did not have the appropriate subject, verb, or object form (e.g., behavior=Obama, subject=as). We also excluded all the answers rated by less than three participants. This screening resulted in 1658 headlines that had a mean EPA rating of 0.80, 1.04, and 1.02. Of these, 995 headlines had a positive evaluation score and 663 headlines had a negative evaluation score. Some examples from this dataset can be seen in Table 5.

| Words | Testing-EPA-lexicon | LP-lexicon |
|---|---|---|
| Incapable (adj.) | [-1.83, -1.40, -0.54] | [-1.56, -1.18, -2.59] |
| Wrongly (adv.) | [-1.96, -0.22, 0.17] | [-2.02, -0.23, 0.18] |
| Gauge (v.) | [0.12, -0.55, 0.13] | [0.18, -1.61, 0.25] |
| Loser (n.) | [-1.30, -1.75, 0.30] | [-1.14, -1.52, 0.28] |

Table 2: Words and their EPA ratings from Testing-EPA-lexicon and LP-lexicon=label propagation lexicon

## 5 Results

Our model (the augmented lexicon, and ACT equations) was evaluated in predicting the evoked sentiment towards the headlines as a whole by comparing the discretized evaluation (E) score $\in \{0, 1\}$ (where 0/1 indicates negative/positive emotions, resp.) of the generated EPA to the ground truth. This evaluation was performed using different configurations (Table 3): (1) Using users' annotated triplet (ACT-UA) (i.e., subject, verb and object), the model yielded a precision of 75% compared to the ground truth. (2) Using the parse tree triplet (ACT-PTT) (see Section 3.3 for details), the precision dropped to 71%. (3) Adding the adjectives ( modifiers ) and settings to the subject, verb and object, which we will called parse tree quintet (ACT-PTQ) yielded a higher precision, with 82% precision in comparison with the corresponding ground truth. These results were also compared to the results obtained from a standard sentiment classifier (STD-calssifier) that uses occurrence frequencies of positive vs. negative words using SentiWordNet (Das and Bandyopadhyay, 2010). This classifier yielded a precision of 57% in comparison to the ground truth (Table 3).

The parse tree quintet (ACT-PTQ) were also used to evaluate the ACT predicted emotions towards the actor (subject) and the object in the headline (Table 4). Three metrics were used in this evaluation: precision, MAS, and RMSE. We used precision to compare the disctized EPA scores $\in \{0, 1\}$ and MAS and RMSE to compare the real EPA scores $\in [-4.3, +4.3]$. As shown in Table 4, the RMSE and MAS are almost all less than 1.5, and the precision varies from 67% to 79% across discretized E,P,A for subject and object. To put these results in context, a difference of 1.4 in the EPA space would equate to the difference between "accusing" someone ($\{-1.03, 0.26, 0.29\}$) and "pun-

| Classifier | Precision | Recall | F1-score |
|---|---|---|---|
| **ACT-PTQ** | **82** | **67** | **73** |
| ACT-UA | 75 | 62 | 67 |
| ACT-PTT | 71 | 63 | 66 |
| STD-classifier | 57 | 51 | 53 |

Table 3: Results for sentiment classification of news headlines dataset using ACT and standard sentiment classification method, ACT-PTQ = ACT using the parsing tree quintet, ACT-UA = ACT using users' annotation, ACT-PTT= ACT using the parsing tree triplet, STD-classifier= Standard classifier using SentiWordNet

| Emotions | Precision | | | MAS | | | RMSE | | |
|---|---|---|---|---|---|---|---|---|---|
| | E | P | A | E | P | A | E | P | A |
| ETS | 79 | 74 | 76 | 1.11 | 1.25 | 1.27 | 1.38 | 1.24 | 1.33 |
| ETO | 67 | 68 | 67 | 1.09 | 1.26 | 1.27 | 1.33 | 1.56 | 1.54 |

Table 4: Comparison of predicted emotions towards the subject and object with the ground truth. ETS/ETO = Emotions towards subject/object, MAS=mean absolute error, and RMSE= root mean square error

ishing" someone ($\{0.19, 0.79, 0.76\}$), or between the identity of "mother" ($\{2.48, 1.96, 1.15\}$) and "girl"($\{1.96, 0.67, 0.99\}$), or between the emotion of "joyful" ($\{2.43, 1.97, 1.33\}$) and "euphoric" ($\{1.42, 1.09, 0.99\}$). These words seem quite close in an affective sense, which indicates that our sentiment analysis method is able to uncover sentiments at a level that is reasonable on an intuitive level, and shows the method's power in uncovering sentiments about specific elements of sentences.

## 6 Discussion and Future Work

Human emotions are more complicated than several labels or binary scores. ACT models emotions in a three-dimensional space which is found to be a comprehensive and universal representation of human emotions, and models emotions towards event- or fact-based sentences as a combination of several emotions towards their entities (subject and object). To evaluate the effectiveness of using ACT in sentiment analysis, we chose to analyze news headlines as they represent real-world statements that describe single or multiple events/facts.

Analysing sentiment in news headlines is a challenging task for several reasons: (1) news headlines are ungrammatically structured, which makes it hard for standard parsers to extract their words' part-of-speech and dependency correctly; (2) they are written to be short and precise, providing little information for typical bag-of-word classifiers to work properly; (3) they are objective, containing words that might not exist in the commonly used sentiment lexicon. To overcome the limitation of news headline sentiment analysis, three main contributions that we present in this paper: (1) we extracted the sentences' triplets by considering the headline grammar and structure; (2) we augmented ACT lexicon using label-propagation and word similarity; (3) we model the interaction between the words in the sentence by modelling the transient and fundamental sentiments.

The label propagation algorithm generated 96,853 words in which 10,249 of them are in the testing data set. The EPA values of these words were found to be quite close in the affective space to their corresponding ground truth, Table 1. Table 2 also shows several good examples of the generated EPA and their corresponding ground truth. The label-propagation results could be further improved by adding words antonyms and by employing another similarity measure. The results of predicting the sentiment towards the event and their entities as shown in Tables 4, 3, and 5 are computed using *only* the ACT lexicons and the ACT impression formation equations. With such a simple, parsimonious and theoretically well-grounded approach, we are able to compute fine-grained sentiment analysis in a dimensional space that is known to be a universal representation of human affect. Mapping these three-dimensional EPA scores to a specific emotion provides a detailed label for objects and subjects within a sentence, as shown in Table 5. For example, in a sentence like" *Russia says 4 militants killed in Dagestan siege*", the reader will be feeling negative, yet different emotions towards the subject *"furious"* and the object *"sorry"*.

Table 5 (obtained with ACT-PTQ) shows the deflection ($d$), emotions towards the events ($\varepsilon$), and towards the subject and object ($e_a$) and ($e_o$) of some of the examples in the data set. As shown in Table 5, we can see that the deflection ($d$) is very high when we do not expect an event to occur (e.g.,*"Baby dies after being left in car for over 8 hours"*). The deflection in this sentence is high (17.42) because the EPA value of the object *"Baby"* is equal to

| Headline | $d$ | $ETS$ | $ETO$ | $T_e$ | $\varepsilon$ | $e_s$ | $e_o$ |
|---|---|---|---|---|---|---|---|
| *Press* sees hope in Mecca talks | 2.57 | happy | reverent | 1.33 | 2.50 | 1.53 | 1.59 |
| *Brazil* deploys troops to secure borders for World Cup | 2.32 | proud | apathetic | 1.7 | 1.61 | 0.66 | 1.22 |
| *Gunfire* injures three Napoli fans | 6.80 | furious | melancholy | -1.13 | -0.86 | -1.25 | 0.54 |
| Three political *candidates* slain before Iraqi vote | 11.24 | furious | sorry | -1.33 | -1.46 | -1.80 | 0.05 |
| Lily *Allen* wins web music award | 2.74 | proud | reverent | 1.67 | 2.45 | 1.46 | 1.36 |
| Finland Air *crash* kills skydivers | 12.54 | furious | cheerless | -1.33 | -3.20 | -3.0 | -0.10 |
| *Bomb* kills 18 on military bus in Iran | 3.40 | impatient | overwhelmed | -1.6 | -1.23 | -2.3 | -0.11 |
| *Russia* says 4 militants killed in Dagestan siege | 11.37 | furious | sorry | -0.2 | -1.46 | -2.34 | -0.58 |
| *Baby* dies after being left in car for over 8 hours | 17.42 | furious | overwhelmed | -1.67 | -2.10 | -1.57 | 0.06 |
| Female *astronaut* sets record | 0.79 | contented | reverent | 3.50 | 0.91 | 1.37 | 0.46 |

Table 5: ACT model's results on news headlines, d=deflection, ETS, ETO= emotion towards subject and object, $T_e$ = emotions towards the event (ground truth), $\varepsilon$=emotions towards the event (ACT), and $e_s$, $e_o$ = the evaluation value of the emotion towards subject and object. Parse elements are coded as: *subject*, verb, object, and setting.

$[2.40, -2.28, 2.58]$, which is considered to be quite good, quite weak, and quite active identity and a car is considered to be a quite positive place, with EPA value equal to $[1.62, 1.65, 2.01]$. While if an event took place in a war zone or if the subject has negative evaluation, the deflection will not be very high (e.g., *"Bomb kills 18 on military bus in Iran"*) the deflection is equal to $3.40$ because *"Bomb"* has a negative evaluation. In Table 5, we can see the emotions ($\varepsilon$) and the ground truth evaluation toward the events ($T_e$) are often quite close.

The aforementioned results are obtained by extracting single subject, verb, object, modifier, and setting. These results could further improved by taking adverbs (e.g, *"lived happily"*), phrasal verbs (e.g,*"get along" and "get back"*), numbers (e.g,*"45 killed"*), and negations (e.g.,*"no more funding"*) into consideration. Finally, accumulating the emotions of multiple consequent behaviors could also be very useful. For example, in the sentence *"Man arrested after beating cops in a restaurant"* the behavior will be *"arrested"*, and *"beating"* is not taken into account. We could address this using more complex parse trees and accumulating the emotions of multiple behaviors by considering the previously generated sentiment as the fundamental sentiment. Finally, using ACT predictions to bootstrap supervised learning could also yield improvements.

## 7 Conclusions

We have proposed a new direction for sentiment analysis, employing Affect Control Theory (ACT) to assign different emotions towards events-based/objective statements and their entities (subject, object). Unlike the majority of sentiment analysis models that are trained on highly subjective words to obtain descriptive labels, our model incorporates ACT, that models emotions as points in three-dimensional space, and analyzes how objective texts trigger different emotions. We use a semi-supervised method based on Wordnet similarities to compute emotional ratings for words not in the ACT lexicons. Evaluated on a news headline dataset, our model yielded higher accuracy than a widely used classifier, with a highest precision of 82%. We also analyzed the sentiment evaluation of ACT on (actor/subject and the object) in the news headlines, yielding a precision of 79% and 68% when analyzing the emotions towards the subject and the object, respectively. These results have been obtained without performing any supervised learning and without taking consequent behaviors, phrasal verbs, or sentence negations into account. Thus, they demonstrate the potential of ACT for sentiment analysis. Affect control theory can also handle consequent behaviors and modifiers. In future, we plan to augment our method with more complex levels of detail, gather more extensive datasets, and evaluate ACT for more precise and detailed sentiments.

## Acknowledgments

The authors thank Tobias Schröder and Dan Lizotte for their thoughtful discussion and suggestions. Areej Alhothali acknowledges the sponsorship of King Abdul Aziz University, Jeddah, Saudi Arabia. Jesse Hoey is supported in part by the Natural Sciences and Engineering Council of Canada (NSERC).

## References


Lisa Feldman Barrett. 2006. Are emotions natural kinds? *Perspectives on psychological science*, 1(1):28–58.

Joseph Berger and Morris Zelditch. 2002. *New Directions in Contemporary Sociological Theories*. Rowman & Littlefield.

Plaban Kumar Bhowmick. 2009. Reader perspective emotion analysis in text through ensemble based multi-label classification framework. *Computer and Information Science*, 2(4):P64.

Sasha Blair-Goldensohn, Kerry Hannan, Ryan McDonald, Tyler Neylon, George A Reis, and Jeff Reynar. 2008. Building a sentiment summarizer for local service reviews. In *WWW Workshop on NLP in the Information Explosion Era*, volume 14.

MM Bradley and PJ Lang. 2010. Affective norms for english words (anew): Affective ratings of words and instruction manual (technical report c-2).

Scott Brave and Clifford Nass. 2002. Emotion in human-computer interaction. *The human-computer interaction handbook: fundamentals, evolving technologies and emerging applications*, pages 81–96.

Liangliang Cao, Jiebo Luo, and Thomas S Huang. 2008. Annotating photo collections by label propagation according to multiple similarity cues. In *Proceedings of the 16th ACM international conference on Multimedia*, pages 121–130. ACM.

François-Régis Chaumartin. 2007. Upar7: A knowledge-based system for headline sentiment tagging. In *Proceedings of the 4th International Workshop on Semantic Evaluations*, pages 422–425. Association for Computational Linguistics.

Jinxiu Chen, Donghong Ji, Chew Lim Tan, and Zhengyu Niu. 2006. Relation extraction using label propagation based semi-supervised learning. In *Proceedings of the 21st International Conference on Computational Linguistics and the 44th annual meeting of the Association for Computational Linguistics*, pages 129–136. Association for Computational Linguistics.

Kenneth Ward Church and Patrick Hanks. 1990. Word association norms, mutual information, and lexicography. *Computational linguistics*, 16(1):22–29.

Bob Coecke, Mehrnoosh Sadrzadeh, and Stephen Clark. 2010. Mathematical foundations for a compositional distributional model of meaning. *arXiv preprint arXiv:1003.4394*.

Amitava Das and Sivaji Bandyopadhyay. 2010. Sentiword-net for bangla. *Knowledge Sharing Event-4: Task*, 2.

Paul Ekman. 1992. Are there basic emotions?

Ronen Feldman. 2013. Techniques and applications for sentiment analysis. *Communications of the ACM*, 56(4):82–89.

Gottlob Frege. 1892. On sense and reference. *Ludlow (1997)*, pages 563–584.

Edward Grefenstette and Mehrnoosh Sadrzadeh. 2011. Experimental support for a categorical compositional distributional model of meaning. In *Proceedings of the Conference on Empirical Methods in Natural Language Processing*, pages 1394–1404. Association for Computational Linguistics.

Edward Grefenstette, Mehrnoosh Sadrzadeh, Stephen Clark, Bob Coecke, and Stephen Pulman. 2010. Concrete sentence spaces for compositional distributional models of meaning. *arXiv preprint arXiv:1101.0309*.

Jiawei Han. 2012. *Data mining : concepts and techniques*. Elsevier/Morgan Kaufmann, Amsterdam Boston.

Rolf A Heckemann, Joseph V Hajnal, Paul Aljabar, Daniel Rueckert, and Alexander Hammers. 2006. Automatic anatomical brain mri segmentation combining label propagation and decision fusion. *NeuroImage*, 33(1):115–126.

David R Heise. 1987. Affect control theory: Concepts and model. *Journal of Mathematical Sociology*, 13(1-2):1–33.

David R Heise. 2007. *Expressive order: Confirming sentiments in social actions*. Springer.

David R. Heise. 2010. *Surveying Cultures: Discovering Shared Conceptions and Sentiments*. Wiley.

Phil Katz, Matthew Singleton, and Richard Wicentowski. 2007. Swat-mp: the semeval-2007 systems for task 5 and task 14. In *Proceedings of the 4th International Workshop on Semantic Evaluations*, pages 308–313. Association for Computational Linguistics.

Chenghua Lin and Yulan He. 2009. Joint sentiment/topic model for sentiment analysis. In *Proceedings of the 18th ACM conference on Information and knowledge management*, pages 375–384. ACM.

KH-Y Lin, Changhua Yang, and Hsin-Hsi Chen. 2008. Emotion classification of online news articles from the reader's perspective. In *Web Intelligence and Intelligent Agent Technology, 2008. WI-IAT'08. IEEE/WIC/ACM International Conference on*, volume 1, pages 220–226. IEEE.

Neil J. MacKinnon. 2006. Mean affective ratings of 2, 294 concepts by guelph university undergraduates, ontario, canada. In *2001-3 [Computer file]*.

George Herbert Mead. 1938. *The philosophy of the act*, volume 3. Univ of Chicago Pr.

Jeff Mitchell and Mirella Lapata. 2008. Vector-based models of semantic composition. In *ACL*, pages 236–244.

Tetsuji Nakagawa, Kentaro Inui, and Sadao Kurohashi. 2010. Dependency tree-based sentiment classification using crfs with hidden variables. In *Human Language*

*Technologies: The 2010 Annual Conference of the North American Chapter of the Association for Computational Linguistics*, pages 786–794. Association for Computational Linguistics.

Zheng-Yu Niu, Dong-Hong Ji, and Chew Lim Tan. 2005. Word sense disambiguation using label propagation based semi-supervised learning. In *Proceedings of the 43rd Annual Meeting on Association for Computational Linguistics*, pages 395–402. Association for Computational Linguistics.

Charles Egerton Osgood. 1957. *The measurement of meaning*, volume 47. University of Illinois Press.

Bo Pang, Lillian Lee, and Shivakumar Vaithyanathan. 2002. Thumbs up?: sentiment classification using machine learning techniques. In *Proceedings of the ACL-02 conference on Empirical methods in natural language processing-Volume 10*, pages 79–86. Association for Computational Linguistics.

Rosalind W. Picard. 2000. *Affective computing*. MIT press.

Delip Rao and Deepak Ravichandran. 2009. Semi-supervised polarity lexicon induction. In *Proceedings of the 12th Conference of the European Chapter of the Association for Computational Linguistics*, pages 675–682. Association for Computational Linguistics.

James A Russell. 2003. Core affect and the psychological construction of emotion. *Psychological review*, 110(1):145.

Delia Rusu, Lorand Dali, Blaz Fortuna, Marko Grobelnik, and Dunja Mladenic. 2007. Triplet extraction from sentences. In *Proceedings of the 10th International Multiconference" Information Society-IS*, pages 8–12.

Richard Socher, John Bauer, Christopher D Manning, and Andrew Y Ng. 2013. Parsing with compositional vector grammars. In *In Proceedings of the ACL conference*. Citeseer.

Carlo Strapparava and Rada Mihalcea. 2007. Semeval-2007 task 14: Affective text. In *Proceedings of the 4th International Workshop on Semantic Evaluations*, pages 70–74. Association for Computational Linguistics.

Peter Turney and Michael L Littman. 2002. Unsupervised learning of semantic orientation from a hundred-billion-word corpus.

Peter D Turney. 2002. Thumbs up or thumbs down?: semantic orientation applied to unsupervised classification of reviews. In *Proceedings of the 40th annual meeting on association for computational linguistics*, pages 417–424. Association for Computational Linguistics.

Amy Beth Warriner, Victor Kuperman, and Marc Brysbaert. 2013. Norms of valence, arousal, and dominance for 13,915 english lemmas. *Behavior research methods*, 45(4):1191–1207.

Casey Whitelaw, Navendu Garg, and Shlomo Argamon. 2005. Using appraisal groups for sentiment analysis. In *Proceedings of the 14th ACM international conference on Information and knowledge management*, pages 625–631. ACM.

Zhibiao Wu and Martha Palmer. 1994. Verbs semantics and lexical selection. In *Proceedings of the 32nd annual meeting on Association for Computational Linguistics*, pages 133–138. Association for Computational Linguistics.

Changhua Yang, Kevin Hsin-Yih Lin, and Hsin-Hsi Chen. 2009. Writer meets reader: Emotion analysis of social media from both the writer's and reader's perspectives. In *Proceedings of the 2009 IEEE/WIC/ACM International Joint Conference on Web Intelligence and Intelligent Agent Technology-Volume 01*, pages 287–290. IEEE Computer Society.

Xiaojin Zhu and Zoubin Ghahramani. 2002. Learning from labeled and unlabeled data with label propagation. Technical report, Technical Report CMU-CALD-02-107, Carnegie Mellon University.

# Do We Really Need Lexical Information? Towards a Top-down Approach to Sentiment Analysis of Product Reviews

**Yulia Otmakhova**
Computational Linguistics Lab
Department of Linguistics
Seoul National University
Gwanakro 1, Gwanak-gu
Seoul, 151-742, South Korea
julia.nixie@gmail.com

**Hyopil Shin**
Computational Linguistics Lab
Department of Linguistics
Seoul National University
Gwanakro 1, Gwanak-gu
Seoul, 151-742, South Korea
hpshin@snu.ac.kr

**Abstract**

Most of the current approaches to sentiment analysis of product reviews are dependent on lexical sentiment information and proceed in a bottom-up way, adding new layers of features to lexical data. In this paper, we maintain that a typical product review is not a bag of sentiments, but a narrative with an underlying structure and reoccurring patterns, which allows us to predict its sentiments knowing only its general polarity and discourse cues that occur in it. We hypothesize that knowing only the review's score and its discourse patterns would allow us to accurately predict the sentiments of its individual sentences. The experiments we conducted prove this hypothesis and show a substantial improvement over the lexical baseline.

## 1 Introduction

For years, sentiment analysis has heavily relied on lexical resources, whether compiled by hand (Wilson et al., 2005) or automatically extracted from a large corpus (Hu and Lui, 2004). In addition to an overwhelming task of trying to capture *all* words and expressions that can convey a sentiment there are many other problems to solve: resolving the scope of negation to determine the shift of polarity (Lapponi et al., 2012), determining if an opinion is present in interrogative or conditional sentences (Narayanan et al., 2009), dealing with irony (Tsur, 2010), etc. But even if we manage to solve all aforementioned problems and create an efficient classifier, there will always be cases where reliance on lexical cues for subjectivity will betray us. Consider, for instance, the following examples from reviews of online universities[1]:

(1) The lectures are interactive and recorded. So, if you can't attend you can listen in later.
(2) I assure you, online learning at Capella was the most difficult form of education I have undergone!
(3) UMUC provided really good quality education until about 5 years ago.

In the first example, the author expresses a positive opinion of the university, but it will fail to be detected because it does not include any explicit sentiment cues (such opinions are referred to as "implicit" by Liu (2012) or as "polar facts" by Toprak et al. (2010)). Because the sentiment (and its presence) of such sentences is highly domain-dependent, they cannot be covered by any lexicons or learned in a supervised or a non-supervised way.

The second example does have a sentiment cue *difficult*, and judging by it the sentiment should be

[1] The examples in this section are taken from Darmstadt Service Review Corpus, available from https://www.ukp.tu-darmstadt.de/data/sentiment-analysis/darmstadt-service-review-corpus (Toprak et al., 2010). The corpus was also used as a development set for extracting features for this study.



*Human Language Technologies: The 2015 Annual Conference of the North American Chapter of the ACL*, pages 1559–1568,
Denver, Colorado, May 31 – June 5, 2015. 

negative. However, in this case the author actually expresses a positive view of an online university, defending it from people who claim that online education is "too easy". In the third example, the correct sentiment (negative) would again be impossible to determine because of a complicated structure.

These are just a few examples of what is currently impossible to classify correctly relying on lexical resources. To improve the classification results, there have been attempts to use local discourse information, such as discourse cues and polarity of adjacent sentences, in order to correct some of the misclassified sentences (Somasundaran, 2010). However, though such attempts resulted in some improvements, they also required quite complicated frameworks.

While such bottom-up approach (starting from lexical polarity and adding supplementary information to improve classification on a phrase and text level) is commonly used in sentiment analysis, we are wondering if it is the only valid one. Provided that we have a reliable external measure of a text's general polarity (such as a product rating for a product review) and the narrative has a predictable discourse structure, would not it be possible to classify its sentences in a top-down manner, without using any sentiment lexicons? In this paper, we experiment with this approach and compare its results with those of the traditional bottom-up method.

This paper is organized as follows. Section 2 presents a brief overview of previous studies related to sentiment analysis of product reviews, while section 3 explains the motivation behind taking an alternative approach. In section 4 we give the details of the experiments, and then in section 5 present their results. Lastly, section 6 summarizes our findings.

## 2 Previous Studies

Sentiment analysis so far has largely relied on explicit lexical information, either in the form of sentiment dictionaries and lexicons, such as SentiWordNet[2] or Subjectivity lexicon[3], opinion phrases extracted from a manually-annotated corpus or a dataset compiled in real time using machine learning with such lexical features as bag-of-words features, n-grams, collocations, or more sophisticated lexical patterns (Tang, 2009). As researchers realized the limitations of a purely lexical approach, they tried to augment it by using negation resolution, word meaning disambiguation or hand-crafted rules (Ding, 2008). However, though such efforts improved classification on the sentence level, they were not able to deal with the sentences where an opinion was implicit (i.e. there were no appraisal words or other lexical cues, see example 1 above) or the polarity of the sentiment word was different from the usual one (see example 2 above). To correct such misclassified instances, another level of complexity was added by using discourse features. Somasundaran (2010) defines opinion frames to enforce discourse constraints on the polarity of segments with the same or alternative target relations. Using a similar approach, Zhou et al. (2011) employ simplified Rhetorical Structure Theory (RST) relation cues (contrast, condition, continuation, cause and purpose) to eliminate polarity ambiguities. Yang (2014) concentrates on discovering opinionated sentences which do not have strong sentiment signals (implicit opinions), using discourse knowledge to improve the results of a Conditional Random Fields classifier. While such approaches are a definite improvement over the lexical baseline, they are computationally complex and still overly dependent on the lexical cues.

While machine learning algorithms such as Naïve Bayes or SVM are still the primary tools used for sentiment analysis, lately such texts as product reviews have been recognized as having an internal structure and inter-sentential relations, and thus structural conditional frameworks have been used for their classification. One popular tool is Conditional Random Fields (CRF), which was used, among others, by Zhao (2008) to classify sentiments on a sentence level, by Breck (2007) to identify subjective expressions, and by Li (2010) to summarize product reviews taking their structure into account.

## 3 Motivation behind Top-down Approach

Though most of the previous studies treat product reviews as a bag of sentences or even words, in fact they are narratives that have a specific structure. While their structure is less rigid and

[2] http://sentiwordnet.isti.cnr.it/ (Baccianella et al., 2010)
[3] http://mpqa.cs.pitt.edu/lexicons/subj_lexicon/ (Wilson et al., 2005)

predicable than, say, that of research papers, it nevertheless has some recurring patterns which lend themselves to generalization.

The same principle applies to sentiments appearing in product reviews. The authors of reviews do not simply pile up some random facts about the product or their evaluations of it. To the best of their abilities, they try to convince the reader to buy or not to buy a particular product, and, according to Grice's Maxims (Grice, 1975), they do it in the clearest and most effective way possible. Thus, if an author has in general a positive opinion of a product, the probability of a negative sentence appearing in a review is lower than that of a positive sentence, and even if a negative sentence is introduced, it is likely to appear together with a concession or a contrast marker, such as *although* or *but*, or be modified by a hedging expression, such as *might, only, could* be, which mitigate the negative effect on the reader. Thus the author makes us understand that his primary opinion of the product is still positive, and uses the discourse relation of *contrast* to present an opposite opinion.

Likewise, if an objective sentence appears in a review, it is not a random event, but a tool serving some purpose, such as interacting with a reader by asking questions which do not require an answer (*Where do I start?*) or supporting one's view by showing that you have some expertise necessary to provide a valid opinion. While in this paper we cover only objective sentences that are used to provide background information (the discourse relation of *background*), it is clear that other reasons for usage of objective sentences are present and capable of being formalized.

The facts mentioned above make us consider a product review as a text which has a primary polarity and optionally includes some segments which have an opposite polarity or no polarity at all (objective sentences). Instead of relying on lexical sentiment information, which makes it difficult to distinguish between objective and subjective sentences on one hand (implicit opinions) and between positive and negative opinions on the other (sarcasm, context-dependent polarity), we suggest using a top-down approach: determining the primary polarity of a review based on an external source of information, such as product rating, and then locating segments which do not conform with this polarity (have no polarity or an opposite polarity) by finding cues that mark a change in a discourse flow.

In the next section we describe an experiment which we conducted to confirm that this approach is viable.

## 4 Experiment

### 4.1 Data and Task

For the experiments in this study we use Filatova's Amazon product reviews corpus (so called Sarcasm Corpus[4]), consisting of 817 ironic and regular reviews. We chose to use this corpus because we believed that segments in ironic reviews would be difficult to classify by purely lexical means. Out of these 817 reviews we randomly selected 100 reviews for training and 20 reviews for test data. We did not use the whole dataset because the number of reviews with a particular review score differs greatly (60% of reviews are 5-star, while only 5% are 2-star). To prevent a skew towards positive labels we used equal-size random samples of reviews with all possible scores. Reviews were annotated by one of the authors and an external annotator on a clause level if a sentence contained opinions with opposite polarities, and on a sentence level otherwise. The inter-annotator agreement was measured by using Fleiss' kappa and Krippendorff's alpha, and the results showed that the annotation was highly reliable ($\kappa = 0.912$, $\alpha = 0.913$). Overall the training corpus consisted of 843 segments (438 negative, 268 positive and 137 objective), while the test set contained 145 segments (78 negative, 41 positive and 26 objective).

While the studies in sentiment analysis usually make distinction between subjective and objective sentences on one hand and between negative, positive and neutral sentences on the other, in this paper we make a twofold distinction, first classifying a segment as objective or subjective, and then, in case of subjective (polar) sentences, further subdividing them into positive and negative. To our mind the classification into positive, negative and neutral sentences, commonly adopted for product reviews, is incorrect, as neutral sentiments rarely, if ever, appear in reviews. What is com-

[4] http://storm.cis.fordham.edu/~filatova/SarcasmCorpus.html (Filatova, 2012).

monly referred to as neutral sentences should be classified as objective segments, as they do not carry any sentiment related to the subject matter.

When annotating the corpus we considered the intended semantic orientation of a segment, not its literal meaning and the presence and polarity of lexical cues. Thus, segments without any lexical cues could be annotated both as subjective and objective:

(4) I bought this mobo from Amazon, after buying the same month the DG31PR Classic for my wife. (*objective*)

(5) After I install my new PC, the 2do. day of use, the LAN failed. (*subjective*, *negative*)

Segments with a lexical cue of a certain polarity could be annotated both as positive and negative:

(6) The ring is **nice** and heavy. (*positive*)

(7) It's going to be a **nice** paperweight. (*negative,* from a review of a camera)

Finally, segments where an alternative product was praised or preferred were understood to be a criticism towards the reviewed product:

(8) I will never buy another Panasonic product. There are plenty of other brands that are loyal to their customers. (both segments are *negative)*

We view each of the reviews as a separate discourse with its own sentiment flow, and thus treat the sentiment analysis problem as a sequence classification task. We employ the CRF method, which outperforms other methods of sequence labeling (Lafferty, 2001). In CRFs the probability of a sequence is defined as

$$p_{\lambda}(Y \mid X) = \frac{\exp \lambda \cdot F(Y,X)}{Z_{\lambda}(X)}$$

where

$$Z_{\lambda}(x) = \sum_{y} \exp \lambda \cdot F(y,x)$$

where $X$ is a set of input random variables, $Y$ is a set of labels, and $\lambda$ is a weight for the feature function $F(Y,X)$. (Sha, 2003).

All experiments in this paper were conducted using a C++ implementation of a linear Conditional Random Fields classifier (CRF++)[5]. Though more complex or constrained types of CRF classifiers and models based on them proved to be more suitable for sentiment analysis (Mao, 2006; Yang, 2014), we use the simplest model as a proof of concept in this study.

Each review in the training and test data is converted into a sequence of polarity segments assigned to it. For example, the following short review:

(9) The ring is nice and heavy. Have been wearing if for almost a month and still not a scratch!

is presented as a sequence of tokens POSITIVE POSITIVE, based on the sentiment labels from the annotation. The tokens are assigned features, as defined in the following sections, which are then fed into the classifier.

## 4.2 Features for Experiments

### 4.2.1 Lexical Features

To set a baseline, we use a state-of-art lexical classifier – Stanford Sentiment Analysis Classifier from Stanford CoreNLP toolkit[6] – to determine the lexical polarity of each individual sentence. Thus the *lexical* classifier considers only lexical features available in a particular sentence without looking at neighboring sentences or discourse cues. For the *local context classifier* we also determine the lexical polarity of the previous and next sentences and use the sequence of {prev_polarity, current_polarity, next_polarity} as a feature (a similar approach is taken by Somasundaran (2010)). This is done to disambiguate and, if necessary, to correct the polarity of misclassified instances that are sandwiched between the correctly classified ones. For example, if the lexical classifier fails to detect an implicit opinion

[5] Available from http://taku910.github.io/crfpp/

[6] Available from http://nlp.stanford.edu/sentiment/code.html

in a sentence that appears between two explicit opinions, it might correct it as follows:

POSITIVE OBJECTIVE POSITIVE ->
POSITIVE POSITIVE POSITIVE

#### 4.2.2 Contrast Features

The main drawback of the *local context* classifier is that it can misclassify sentences with the opposite polarity, lumping them together with sentences of the primary polarity. To prevent this, for the *contrast* classifier we add another set of features – discourse cues with a Rhetoric Structure Theory (RST) (Mann and Thompson, 1988) relation of *contrast*. We consider both explicit and implicit discourse markers of contrast for this set of features:

##### 4.2.2.1 Explicit Contrast Markers

Contrast relations are primarily realized by using explicit *discourse markers*, which, depending on their type, mark the sentence they appear in (in case of *although* type) or the previous sentence (in case of *but* type) as contrasting:

(10) The Phillips screwdriver on the end of one of the tines is helpful for things like tightening eyeglasses, POSITIVE CONTR
**but** it is slightly offset from the opposing blade and I've nicked or jabbed myself with it more than once while it's in my pocket. NEGATIVE NCONTR

(11) **Although** it has 10 workable buttons which come in handy for some games, POSITIVE CONTR
it has some major flaws. NEGATIVE NCONTR

The segment with the NCONTR marker usually has the primary polarity of the review, while the segment with a CONTR marker presents a contrasting opinion.

##### 4.2.2.2 Implicit Contrast Relations

Contrast relations can also be manifested implicitly through the use of *hedges*. Hedging is often used when the review's author wants to mention some negative side of a product they like (or a positive aspect of a product they hate), but does not want to put an unnecessary emphasis on it. Such hedging expressions as *the only good/bad point, the only drawback, I would only recommend it…* etc are used for this purpose:

(12) With all the upgrades that Apple has done with their macbooks, I think I finally feel that it's worth the spending to buy my first mac. NHEDGE
My *only complain* is that it's still a lot more expensive than PC laptops with similar specs. HEDGE

#### 4.2.3 Background Classifier

The *background* classifier allows us to capture some of the objective sentences that are related to the polar ones using a *background* RST relation. We identify three types of patterns where background relations are used:

1. *Acquirement patterns*: people often start reviews with an explanation of how they got the product.
2. *Personal background patterns*: people often support their evaluation of a product by stating who there are, what they do for a living, what kind of lifestyle they lead etc.
3. *Personal experience patterns*: again, to support their views the writers prime their readers by describing their experiences or achievements.

Unfortunately, background relations, unlike contrast relations, are almost never explicit. They are paratactic and lack discourse cues, so we need to rely on lexical and grammatical features for classification. However, we believe that because background information is usually presented in easy-to-predict patterns, it is more feasible and computationally inexpensive to use lexical cues to single out objective sentences than to try to capture infinitely large number of ways sentiments can be expressed. In the following subsections, we describe these patterns in more detail and explain which lexical and grammatical cues can be used to detect them.

#### 4.2.3.1 Acquirement Patterns

At the beginning of a review people often explain how they acquired the product:

(13) I bought this camera for my deployment to Iraq. (*objective*)
It was in my cargo pants pocket one day I took it out and the lens was cracked and the silver trim ring had fallen off. (*negative*)

We formalize this feature as follows:

[I | we] [verb synonymous to "acquire"|verb of decision + verb synonymous to "acquire"],

or, more specifically:

[I | we] [ordered | bought | got .* as a gift | purchased | decided to buy…]

All verbs are in past simple tense, as only in this tense they are unlikely to bear any sentiment (compare, for example, sentences with the same verbs in present perfect tense:

(14) However, I am glad that I **have bought** a mac.(*positive*)

(15) This is probably the worst book **I've bought.** (*negative*)

Moreover, this pattern is likely to be used at the beginning of the review, so we add ACQUIRE feature only to those segments which appear in the first 25% of a review.

#### 4.2.3.2 Personal Background Patterns

In these patterns, the authors offer their personal information that is relevant to the subject matter of the review and can support their opinion. For instance, in the following review the author refers to his pets as the major reason for buying a particular vacuum cleaner:

(16) I **have a cat and a dog**, and there is lots of shedding hair, all the time. (*objective, personal background*)
When I saw the DC25 Animal, I **decided to spend the money** hoping that this vacuum would do the job. (*objective, acquirement*)
It has lived up to my wildest dreams, it is wonderfully easy to handle, so easy to maneuver, the 16 lbs make such a difference compared to those very heavy machines I had before, I had no problem carrying it upstairs. (*positive*)

We formalize this feature as follows:

[I|we] [am (a|an)|have (a|an)|'m (a|an)|am not (a|an)]

The indefinite article is used to prevent matching such polar expressions, as *I'm very pleased with the quality of this product.* Again, such patterns are searched for only at the beginning of a review.

#### 4.2.3.3 Personal Experience Patterns

These patterns also serve to provide some background information about user's experiences to back up his opinion on a product:

(17) Usually **I am a huge fan** of hats that look like food. (*objective, personal background*).
My meatloaf hat **has been** a hit for years. (*objective, personal experience*)
When I received my turkey hat I carefully unwrapped the bubble wrap and gazed upon its tan beauty. (*positive*).

To capture this pattern we search for verbs in perfect forms (except for the verbs of possession). We exclude verbs in perfect continuous forms, as they are more often used to describe positive or negative results of using a product. Compare, for example:

(18) I **have been using** it for almost a month and my lashes are so long, they touch my eyebrows... (*positive*)

We also exclude phrases that have "should/could" before "have", as they often express negative sentiments (Liu, 2014):

(19) Would have been nice if the stilts could accommodate multiple/varying heights. (*negative*)

#### 4.2.4 Primary Polarity Features

Lastly, we use reviews' scores to predict their global semantic orientation (primary polarity). The intuition behind this is that the reviews with a higher score will contain more positive sentences than reviews with a lower score, and thus global polarity information might help us to amend incorrect predictions of a lexical classifier (a similar approach was taken, among others, by (Yang, 2014)). This is supported by the statistics of our corpus: the polarity of sentences in a review in general correlates with its score. Highly positive (5-star) and highly negative (1-star) reviews contain few segments of the opposite polarity, and even reviews with a less extreme score demonstrate a clear preference of one of the polarities (see Table 1). Thus it can be predicted that the classifier using this feature will tend to assign the primary polarity (positive for 4- and 5-star reviews, negative for 1-, 2-, and 3-star reviews) unless there is some strong evidence preventing it.

| Review score | Positive | Negative | Objective |
|---|---|---|---|
| 1 | 0.01 | 0.85 | 0.13 |
| 2 | 0.10 | 0.77 | 0.12 |
| 3 | 0.22 | 0.65 | 0.13 |
| 4 | 0.62 | 0.23 | 0.15 |
| 5 | 0.68 | 0.04 | 0.27 |

Table 1. Percentage of positive, negative and objective sentences in reviews with different product ratings

### 4.3 Bottom-up vs Top-down Approach: Experiment Design

#### 4.3.1 Bottom-up Approach

This is a widely-used approach which relies on a lexical polarity classifier to determine the semantic orientation of each segment and then corrects the misclassified segments by employing more general features: discourse features (in our study – *contrast* and *background*) and global semantic orientation features (called *primary polarity* features in this paper).

The bottom-up approach has become a standard in sentiment analysis, so we believe there is no need to explain it in detail. The main focus of this study is on the top-down approach, which we describe below.

#### 4.3.2. Top-down Approach

In this set of experiments, we do not use any lexical information about the presence of sentiments in segments and their types. Instead, we rely on rating scores assigned to the reviews to determine their primary polarity, and then correct the misclassified instances using discourse features. In general, the feature set used for this classifier is the same as for the bottom-up approach. The only important exception is that lexical features are completely omitted.

We adopt the following process for sentiment classification:

1. All sentences in a review are assigned a polarity label determined by the corresponding review rating.
2. We look for discourse patterns that are associated with a change of the primary polarity (POSITIVE -> NEGATIVE, NEGATIVE -> POSITIVE). These are usually manifested through **contrast** relation and enable us to correct some of misclassified polarity labels.
3. We look for discourse patterns where a polar statement is accompanied by an objective statement. A common example of such discourse relations in product reviews is **background**. At this stage, unnecessary POSITIVE and NEGATIVE labels are changed into OBJECTIVE.

Schematically this can be shown as follows using an arbitrary example of a 4-star review, where light-gray blocks stand for positive segments, dark-gray for negative segments and white for objective ones (here we assume that all segments will be initialized as positive, as it is the primary class for 4-star reviews):

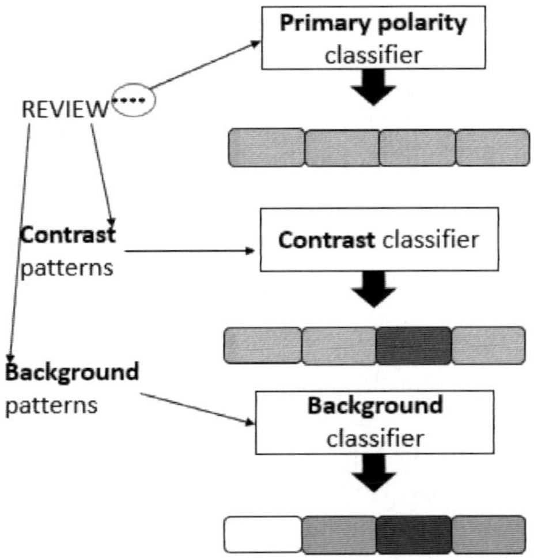


Figure 1. Top-down approach classification flow

In the next section, we discuss the results of experiments conducted to show that such features can improve sentiment classification.

## 5 Experiment Results

In this section, we compare the results achieved by using the top-down approach with those of the traditional bottom-up method.

### 5.1 Bottom-up Approach

The *lexical* classifier results, used as a baseline in this study, are listed in Table 2 below. As can be seen from the results, the recall and precision of positive and especially objective segments is low, which shows that purely lexical classifier cannot reliably distinguish between objective and subjective sentences and between positive and negative ones. The accuracy of the classifier is also low (0.6138).

When we add local discourse context, the recall of positive and negative segments improves, as does the overall accuracy (to 0.6758). However, the *local discourse* classifier completely ignores the objective sentences, assigning polarity to them. The precision of the negative class and overall precision also gets lower, as some positive segments sandwiched between negative ones are assigned a negative label.

Adding *contrast* discourse cues does not help to improve this situation, because it leads to overestimation of positive segments and lower accuracy (0.6620). In fact, the *contrast* classifier performs even worse than the local discourse one. It seems that lexical information introduces too much noise, and building up on such an unreliable basis does not produce expected results.

The *background* classifier improves the performance, especially for objective sentences, classifying them with a high precision and at least some recall. It also improves the overall accuracy (to 0.6896).

However, the most significant improvement is seen after adding the review scores (*primary polarity*) as features. It helps improve almost all scores, including accuracy, which reaches 0.7241.

### 5.2 Top-down Approach

The *primary polarity* classifier, which uses the review's rating to predict its overall polarity, has a high recall and an accuracy of 0.7379 (see Table 3). However, it again ignores the objective class, because it is distributed more or less evenly between reviews with different ratings and thus cannot be correlated with a particular review score.

| | Subjective | | | | Objective | | Total | | | |
|---|---|---|---|---|---|---|---|---|---|---|
| | Negative | | Positive | | | | | | | |
| | Prec | Rec | Prec | Rec | Prec | Rec | Prec | Rec | F1 | Acc |
| Lexical | 0.71 | 0.77 | 0.61 | 0.54 | 0.29 | **0.27** | 0.60 | 0.61 | 0.61 | 0.6138 |
| Local discourse | 0.69 | **0.87** | **0.64** | 0.73 | 0.00 | 0.00 | 0.55 | 0.68 | 0.61 | 0.6758 |
| + Contrast | 0.69 | **0.87** | 0.62 | 0.68 | 0.00 | 0.00 | 0.55 | 0.66 | 0.60 | 0.6620 |
| + Background | 0.73 | 0.85 | 0.60 | 0.75 | **1.00** | 0.12 | 0.74 | 0.69 | 0.65 | 0.6896 |
| + Primary pol. | **0.78** | **0.87** | 0.62 | **0.82** | **1.00** | 0.12 | **0.77** | **0.72** | **0.68** | **0.7241** |

Table 2. Precision, recall, F1 and accuracy scores for the bottom-up approach

| | Subjective | | | | Objective | | Total | | | |
|---|---|---|---|---|---|---|---|---|---|---|
| | Negative | | Positive | | | | | | | |
| | Prec | Rec | Prec | Rec | Prec | Rec | Prec | Rec | F1 | Acc |
| Primary polarity | 0.75 | 0.94 | 0.71 | 0.83 | 0.00 | 0.00 | 0.61 | 0.74 | 0.66 | 0.7379 |
| + Contrast | 0.81 | 0.90 | 0.68 | **0.95** | 0.00 | 0.00 | 0.63 | 0.75 | 0.68 | 0.7517 |
| + Background | **0.82** | **0.91** | **0.73** | **0.95** | **1.00** | **0.19** | **0.83** | **0.79** | **0.76** | **0.7931** |

Table 3. Precision, recall, F1 and accuracy scores for the top-down approach

Also, because 3-star reviews contain more negative sentences than positive ones, all of them are lumped into the negative class. Thus the recall for the positive class is substantially low than for the negative class.

To single out the segments whose polarity is different from the primary one, we add explicit and implicit *contrast* features and train the contrast classifier. *Contrast* features help to raise recall for positive and precision for negative sentences, though, as might be expected, they do not affect the classification of objective segments. However, the overall precision and recall are improved, as well as the overall accuracy (to 0.7517)

The *background* classifier allows us to find some of objective sentences. *Acquirement, personal background* and *personal experience* patterns turn out to be precise features that also guarantee us at least some recall for objective sentences. Overall precision, recall and F1 scores are improved accordingly, as well as accuracy (to 0.7931).

As can be seen from comparing these results, even the most primitive rating-based classifier (*primary polarity*) achieves better recall and accuracy than any of lexical classifiers (even the one with primary polarity features). Moreover, adding discourse features to it consistently improves the results, allowing us to build a high-precision, high-recall sentiment classifier. On the other hand, building up on the lexical classifier does not show such consistent improvements.

## 6 Conclusion

Until now the sentiment analysis has been primarily done in a bottom-up way, starting with the classification of lexical items, then resolving the polarity of the sentence, then using discourse information to improve the lexical classification. However, lexical classifiers so far produce results that are too unreliable to become a basis of a discourse-level classification. We assert that starting from the top by roughly defining a text's polarity and assigning it to all its segments, and then fine-tuning the classification by "chiseling out" incorrect bits based on reliable discourse relations can be a more productive and effective approach. Our experiments show that such approach can lead to a substantial improvement over lexical baseline at least in texts with a predictable structure and recurring patterns, such as product reviews. Because each of the discourse features we tested led to improvement, we believe that the top-down classifier can be made even more accurate by employing other discourse relations in the form of carefully selected linguistic features.

## References

Baccianella, S., Esuli, A., & Sebastiani, F. (2010). SentiWordNet 3.0: An Enhanced Lexical Resource for Sentiment Analysis and Opinion Mining. *LREC, 10*, 2200-2204.

Breck E., Choi Y., & Cardie C. (2007). Identifying Expressions of Opinion in Context. *IJCAI, 7*, 2683-2688.

Ding, X., Liu, B., & Yu, P. S. (2008). A holistic lexicon-based approach to opinion mining. *WSDM*, 231-240.

Filatova, E. (2012). Irony and Sarcasm: Corpus Generation and Analysis Using Crowdsourcing. *LREC*, 392-398.

Grice, P. (1975). Logic and conversation. *Syntax and semantics, 3*, 41-58.

Hu, M., & Liu, B. (2004). Mining opinion features in customer reviews. *AAAI, 4*(4), 755-760.

Lafferty, J., McCallum, A., & Pereira, F. C. (2001). Conditional random fields: Probabilistic models for segmenting and labeling sequence data. *Proceedings of the Eighteenth International Conference on Machine Learning*, 282-289.

Lapponi, E., Read, J., & Ovrelid, L. (2012). Representing and resolving negation for sentiment analysis. *Proceedings of the 2012 ICDM Workshop on Sentiment Elicitation from Natural Text for Information Retrieval and Extraction*, 687-692.

Li F., Han C., Huang M., Zhu X., Xia Y. J., Zhang S., & Yu H. (2010). Structure-aware review mining and summarization. *Proceedings of the 23rd International Conference on Computational Linguistics*, 653-661.

Liu, B. (2012). *Sentiment Analysis and Opinion Mining*. Morgan & Claypool Publishers.

Liu, Y., Yu, X., Liu, B., & Chen, Z. (2014). Sentence-Level Sentiment Analysis in the Presence of Modalities. *Computational Linguistics and Intelligent Text Processing,* 1-16.

Mann, W. & Thompson, S. (1988). Rhetorical structure theory: Towards a functional theory of text organization. *Text*, *8*(3), 243-281.

Mao, Y., & Lebanon, G. (2006). Isotonic conditional random fields and local sentiment flow. *Advances in neural information processing systems*, 961-968.

Narayanan, R., Liu, B., & Choudhary, A. (2009). Sentiment analysis of conditional sentences. *Proceedings of the 2009 Conference on Empirical Methods in Natural Language Processing, 1*, 180-189.

Polanyi, L., & Zaenen, A. (2006). Contextual valence shifters. *Computing attitude and affect in text: Theory and applications,* 1-10.

Sha, F., & Pereira, F. (2003). Shallow parsing with conditional random fields. *Proceedings of the 2003 Conference of the North American Chapter of the Association for Computational Linguistics on Human Language Technology*, *1*, 134-141.

Somasundaran S. (2010). *Discourse-Level Relations for Opinion Analysis* (Doctoral dissertation). University of Pittsburgh.

Tang, H. F., Tan, S. B., & Cheng, X. Q. (2009). A survey on sentiment detection of reviews. *Expert Systems with Applications*, *36*(7), 10760-10773.

Toprak, C., Jakob, N., & Gurevych, I. (2010). Sentence and expression level annotation of opinions in user-generated discourse. *Proceedings of the 48th Annual Meeting of the Association for Computational Linguistics,* 575-584.

Tsur, O., Davidov, D., & Rappoport, A. (2010). Great Catchy Name: Semi-Supervised Recognition of Sarcastic Sentences in Online Product Reviews. *ICWSM,* 162-169.

Wilson, T., Wiebe, J., & Hoffmann, P. (2005). Recognizing contextual polarity in phrase-level sentiment analysis. *Proceedings of the conference on human language technology and empirical methods in natural language processing*, 347-354.

Yang, B., & Cardie, C. (2014). Context-aware learning for sentence-level sentiment analysis with posterior regularization. *Proceedings of ACL.*

Zhao J., Liu K. & Wang G. (2008). Adding Redundant Features for CRFs-based Sentence Sentiment Classification. *Proceedings of the Conference on Empirical Methods in Natural Language Processing,* 117-126.

Zhou L., Li B., Gao W., Wei Z. & Wong K. F. (2011). Unsupervised Discovery of Discourse Relations for Eliminating Intra-sentence Polarity Ambiguities. *Proceedings of the Conference on Empirical Methods in Natural Language Processing*, 162-171.

# How to Memorize a Random 60-Bit String

**Marjan Ghazvininejad**
Information Sciences Institute
Department of Computer Science
University of Southern California
ghazvini@isi.edu

**Kevin Knight**
Information Sciences Institute
Department of Computer Science
University of Southern California
knight@isi.edu

## Abstract

User-generated passwords tend to be memorable, but not secure. A random, computer-generated 60-bit string is much more secure. However, users cannot memorize random 60-bit strings. In this paper, we investigate methods for converting arbitrary bit strings into English word sequences (both prose and poetry), and we study their memorability and other properties.

## 1 Introduction

Passwords chosen by users (e.g., "Scarlet%2") are easy to remember, but not secure (Florencio and Herley, 2007). A more secure method is to use a system-assigned 60-bit random password, such as 0010100010100...00101001. However, this string is hard to memorize. In this paper, we convert such strings into English phrases, in order to improve their memorability, using natural language processing to select fluent passphrases.

Our methods are inspired by an XKCD cartoon[1] that proposes to convert a randomly-chosen 44-bit password into a short, nonsensical sequence of English words. The proposed system divides the 44-bit password into four 11-bit chunks, and each chunk provides an index into a 2048-word English dictionary. XKCD's example passphrase is *correct horse battery staple*:

```
44-bit password    English phrase
---------------    --------------
10101101010     -> correct
10010110101     -> horse
01010101010     -> battery
10110101101     -> staple
```

The four-word sequence is nonsense, but it is easier to memorize than the 44-bit string, and XKCD hypothesizes that users can improve memorability by building an image or story around the four words.

In this paper, we investigate other methods for converting a system-generated bit string into a memorable sequence of English words. Our methods produce whole sentences, e.g.

```
Fox news networks are seeking
views from downtown streets.
```

as well as short poems, e.g.

```
Diversity inside replied,
Soprano finally reside.
```

We also move to 60-bit passwords, for better security. One source claims:

> As of 2011, available commercial products claim the ability to test up to 2,800,000,000 passwords a second on a standard desktop computer using a high-end graphics processor.[2]

If this is correct, a 44-bit password would take one hour to crack, while a 60-bit password would take 11.3 years.

Our concrete task is as follows:

[1] http://xkcd.com/936

[2] http://en.wikipedia.org/wiki/Password_cracking



*Human Language Technologies: The 2015 Annual Conference of the North American Chapter of the ACL*, pages 1569–1575,
Denver, Colorado, May 31 – June 5, 2015. 

| Method Name | Average Number of Words | Average Number of Characters | AVG LM Score | Capacity | Sample Passwords |
|---|---|---|---|---|---|
| XKCD | 4 | 31.2 | -62.42 | 1 | fees wesley inmate decentralization |
| | | | | | photo bros nan plain |
| | | | | | embarrass debating gaskell jennie |
| First Letter Mnemonic | 15 | 87.7 | -61.20 | $2 \cdot 10^{51}$ | It makes me think of union pacific resource said it looks like most commercial networks . |
| | | | | | Some companies keep their windows rolled down so you don't feel connected to any community . |
| | | | | | Contains extreme violence and it was a matter of not only its second straight loss . |
| All Letter Method | 11.8 | 70.8 | -58.83 | $3 \cdot 10^{56}$ | Parking and utilities have been searching for a third straight road win . |
| | | | | | It was the same girl and now a law professor in the former east german town . |
| | | | | | I know a man who said he was chief of staffs in a real and deep conversation . |
| Frequency Method | 9.7 | 55.5 | -52.88 | $6 \cdot 10^{14}$ | Fox news networks are seeking views from downtown streets . |
| | | | | | The review found a silver tree through documents and artifacts . |
| | | | | | These big questions are bothering me a bit stronger . |
| Poetry | 7.2 | 52.7 | -73.15 | $10^{6}$ | Joanna kissing verified<br>soprano finally reside |
| | | | | | Diversity inside replied<br>retreats or colors justified |
| | | | | | Surprise celebrity without<br>the dragging allison throughout |

Table 1: Comparison of methods that convert system-assigned 60-bit strings into English word sequences. Average word lengths range from 4 (XKCD) to 15 (First Letter Mnemonic). Average character lengths include spaces. LM score refers to the log probability assigned by a 5-gram English language model trained on the Gigaword corpus. Capacity tells how many English word sequences are available for an individual 60-bit input string.

- **Input:** A random, system-generated 60-bit password.
- **Output:** An English word sequence with two properties:
  - It is memorable.
  - We can deterministically recover the original input 60-bit string from it.

This implies that we map $2^{60}$ distinct bit strings into $2^{60}$ distinct English sequences. If a user memorizes the English word sequence supplied to them, then they have effectively memorized the 60-bit string.

## 2 Password Generation Methods

We now describe our baseline password generation method, followed by four novel methods. In Section 3 we experimentally test their memorability.

### 2.1 XKCD Baseline

Our baseline is a version of XKCD. Instead of a 2048-word dictionary, we use a 32,7868-word dictionary. We assign each word a distinct 15-bit code.

At runtime, we take a system-assigned 60-bit code and split it into four 15-bit sequences. We then substitute each 15-bit segment with its corresponding word. By doing this, we convert a random 60-bit code into a 4-word password.

The first row of Table 1 shows three sample XKCD passwords, along with other information, such as the average number of characters (including spaces).

### 2.2 First Letter Mnemonic

XKCD passwords are short but nonsensical, so we now look into methods that instead create longer but fluent English sentences. We might think to guarantee fluency by selecting sentences from an already-existing text corpus, but no corpus is large enough to contain $2^{60}$ ($\sim 10^{18}$) distinct sentences. Therefore, we must be able to synthesize new English strings.

In our first sentence generation method (*First Letter Mnemonic*), we store our input 60-bit code in the first letters of each word. We divide the 60-bit code into 4-bit sections, e.g., '0100-1101-1101-...'. Every 4-bit sequence type corresponds to an English letter or two, per Table 2. We build a word-confusion network (or "sausage lattice") by replacing each 4-bit code with all English words that start with a corresponding letter, e.g.:

| Bit Sequence | Mapped Character | Bit Sequence | Mapped Character |
|---|---|---|---|
| 0000 | e | 1000 | r,x |
| 0001 | t | 1001 | d,j |
| 0010 | a | 1010 | l,k |
| 0011 | o | 1011 | c,v |
| 0100 | i | 1100 | u,b |
| 0101 | n | 1101 | m,p |
| 0110 | s,z | 1110 | w,y |
| 0111 | h,q | 1111 | f,g |

Table 2: Mapping function between 4-bit sequences and English letters in the First Letter Mnemonic method.

```
0100     1101     1111           ... 0011
----     ----     ----               ----
income   my       frog           ... octopus
is       miner    feast          ... of
inner    priest   gratuitous     ... oregon
 ...      ...      ...                ...
```

This yields about $10^{74}$ paths, some good (*is my frog...*) and some bad (*income miner feast...*). To select the most fluent path, we train a 5-gram language model with the SRILM toolkit (Stolcke, 2002) on the English Gigaword corpus.[3] SRILM also includes functionality for extracting the best path from a confusion network.

Table 1 shows sample sentences generated by the method. Perhaps surprisingly, even though the sentences are much longer than XKCD (15 words versus 4 words), the n-gram language model (LM) score is a bit better. The sentences are locally fluent, but not perfectly grammatical.

We can easily reconstruct the original 60-bit code by extracting the first letter of each word and applying the Table 2 mapping in reverse.

### 2.3 All Letter Method

Most of the characters in the previous methods seem "wasted", as only the word-initial letters bear information relevant to reconstructing the original 60-

[3]https://catalog.ldc.upenn.edu/LDC2011T07

| Bit Sequence | Mapped Characters |
|---|---|
| 0 | e, o, i, h, r, c, u, f, g, b, v, x ,q |
| 1 | t, a, n, s, d, l, m, w, y, p, k, j, z |

Table 3: Mapping function between bits and English characters in the All Letter Method.

bit string. Our next technique (*All Letter Method*) non-deterministically translates *every* bit into an English letter, per Table 3. Additionally, we non-deterministically introduce a space (or not) between each pair of letters.

This yields $4 \cdot 10^{84}$ possible output strings per input, $3 \cdot 10^{56}$ of which consist of legal English words. From those $3 \cdot 10^{56}$ strings, we choose the one that yields the best word 5-gram score.

It is not immediately clear how to process a letter-based lattice with a word-based language model. We solve this search problem by casting it as one of machine translation from bit-strings to English. We create a phrase translation table by pairing each English word with a corresponding "bit phrase", using Table 3 in reverse. Sample entries include:

```
din ||| 1 0 1
through ||| 1 0 0 0 0 0 0
yields ||| 1 0 0 1 1 1
```

We then use the Moses machine translation toolkit (Koehn et al., 2007) to search for the 1-best translation of our input 60-bit string, using the phrase table and a 5-gram English LM, disallowing re-ordering.

Table 1 shows that these sentences are shorter than the mnemonic method (11.8 words versus 15 words), without losing fluency.

Given a generated English sequence, we can deterministically reconstruct the original 60-bit input string, using the above phrase table in reverse.

### 2.4 Frequency Method

Sentence passwords from the previous method contain 70.8 characters on average (including spaces). Classic studies by Shannon (1951) and others estimate that printed English may ultimately be compressible to about one bit per character. This implies we might be able to produce shorter output (60 characters, including space) while maintaining normal English fluency.

Our next technique (*Frequency Method*) modifies the phrase table by assigning short bit codes to frequent words, and long bit codes to infrequent words. For example:

```
din ||| 0 1 1 0 1 0 1 0 0
through ||| 1 1 1 1
yields ||| 0 1 0 1 1 1 0 1
```

Note that the word *din* is now mapped to a 9-bit sequence rather than a 3-bit sequence. More precisely, we map each word to a random bit sequence of length $\lfloor \max(1, -\alpha \times log\ \mathrm{P}(word) + \beta) \rfloor$. By changing variables $\alpha$ and $\beta$ we can vary between smooth but long sentences ($\alpha = 1$ and $\beta = 0$) to XKCD-style phrases ($\alpha = 0$ and $\beta = 15$).

Table 1 shows example sentences we obtain with $\alpha = 2.5$ and $\beta = -2.5$, yielding sentences of 9.7 words on average.

### 2.5 Poetry

In ancient times, people recorded long, historical epics using poetry, to enhance memorability. We follow this idea by turning each system-assigned 60-bit string into a short, distinct English poem. Our format is the *rhyming iambic tetrameter couplet*:

- The poem contains two lines of eight syllables each.
- Lines are in iambic meter, i.e., their syllables have the stress pattern 01010101, where 0 represents an unstressed syllable, and 1 represents a stressed syllable. We also allow 01010100, to allow a line to end in a word like *Angela*.
- The two lines end in a pair of rhyming words. Words rhyme if their phoneme sequences match from the final stressed vowel onwards. We obtain stress patterns and phoneme sequences from the CMU pronunciation dictionary.[4]

Monosyllabic words cause trouble, because their stress often depends on context (Greene et al., 2010). For example, *eighth* is stressed in *eighth street*, but not in *eighth avenue*. This makes it hard to guarantee that automatically-generated lines will scan as intended. We therefore eject all monosyllabic words

[4]http://www.speech.cs.cmu.edu/cgi-bin/cmudict

from the vocabulary, except for six unstressed ones (*a*, *an*, *and*, *the*, *of*, *or*).

Here is a sample poem password:

```
The le-gen-da-ry Ja-pan-ese
 ↓   ↑  ↓  ↑  ↓  ↑   ↓   ↑
Sub-si-di-ar-ies ov-er-seas
 ↓   ↑  ↓  ↑   ↓  ↑  ↓  ↑
```

Meter and rhyme constraints make it difficult to use the Moses machine translation toolkit to search for fluent output, as we did above; the decoder state must be augmented with additional short- and long-distance information (Genzel et al., 2010).

Instead, we build a large finite-state acceptor (FSA) with a path for each legal poem. In each path, the second line of the poem is reversed, so that we can enforce rhyming locally.

The details of our FSA construction are as follows. First, we create a finite-state transducer (FST) that maps each input English word onto four sequences that capture its essential properties, e.g.:

```
create -> 0 1
create -> 0 1 EY-T
create -> 1r 0r
create -> EY-T 1r 0r
```

Here, `EY-T` represents the rhyme-class of words like *create* and *debate*. The *r* indicates a stress pattern in the right-to-left direction.

We then compose this FST with an FSA that only accepts sequences of the form:

`0 1 0 1 0 1 0 1 X X 1r 0r 1r 0r 1r 0r 1r 0r`

where X and X are identical rhyme classes (e.g., EY-T and EY-T).

It remains to map an arbitrary 60-bit string onto a path in the FSA. Let $k$ be the integer representation of the 60-bit string. If the FSA contains exactly $2^{60}$ paths, we can easily select the $k$th path using the following method. At each node N of the FSA, we store the total number of paths from N to the final state—this takes linear time if we visit states in reverse topological order. We then traverse the FSA deterministically from the start state, using $k$ to guide the path selection.

Our FSA actually contains $2^{79}$ paths, far more than the required $2^{60}$. We can say that the information capacity of the English rhyming iambic tetrameter couplet is 79 bits! Some are very good:

```
Sophisticated potentates
misrepresenting Emirates.

The supervisor notified
the transportation nationwide.

Afghanistan, Afghanistan,
Afghanistan, and Pakistan.
```

while others are very bad:

```
The shirley emmy plebiscite
complete suppressed unlike invite

The shirley emmy plebiscite
complaints suppressed unlike invite

The shirley emmy plebiscite
complaint suppressed unlike invite
```

Fortunately, because our FSA contains over a million times the required $2^{60}$ paths, we can avoid these bad outputs. For any particular 60-bit string, we have a million poems to choose from, and we output only the best one.

More precisely, given a 60-bit input string $k$, we extract not only the $k$th FSA path, but also the $k + i \cdot 2^{60}$ paths, with i ranging from 1 to 999,999. We explicitly list out these paths, reversing the second half of each, and score them with our 5-gram LM. We output the poem with the 1-best LM score. Table 1 shows sample outputs.

To reconstruct the original 60-bit string $k$, we first find the FSA path corresponding to the user-recalled English string (with second half reversed). We use depth-first search to find this path. Once we have the path, it is easy to determine which numbered path it is, lexicographically speaking, using the node-labeling scheme above to recover $k$.

## 3 Experiments

We designed two experiments to compare our methods.

The first experiment tests the memorability of passwords. We asked participants to memorize a password from a randomly selected method[5] and recall it two days later. To give more options to users,

[5]In all experiments, we omit the First Letter Mnemonic, due to its low performance in early tests.

| Method | Participants | Recalls | Correct Recalls |
|---|---|---|---|
| XKCD | 16 | 12 | 58.3% |
| All Letter Method | 15 | 9 | 33.3% |
| Frequency Method | 15 | 10 | 40.0% |
| Poetry | 16 | 13 | 61.5% |

Table 4: Memorability of passwords generated by our methods. "Recalls" indicates how many participants returned to type their memorized English sequences, and "Correct Recalls" tells how many sequences were accurately remembered.

| Method Name | User preference |
|---|---|
| XKCD | 5% |
| All Letter Method | 39% |
| Frequency Method | 37% |
| Poetry | 19% |

Table 5: User preferences among passwords generated by our methods.

we let them select from the 10-best passwords according to the LM score for a given 60-bit code. Note that this flexibility is not available for XKCD, which produces only one password per code.

62 users participated in this experiment, 44 returned to recall the password, and 22 successfully recalled the complete password. Table 4 shows that the Poetry and XKCD methods yield passwords that are easiest to remember.

In the second experiment, we present a separate set of users with passwords from each of the four methods. We ask which they would prefer to use, without requiring any memorization. Table 5 shows that users prefer sentences over poetry, and poetry over XKCD.

## 4 Analysis

Table 4 shows that the Poetry and XKCD methods yield passwords that are easiest to memorize. Complete sentences generated by the All Letter and Frequency Methods are harder to memorize. At the same time Table 5 shows that people like the sentences better than XKCD, so it seems that they overestimate their ability to memorize a sentence of 10-12 words. Here are typical mistakes (S = system-generated, R = as recalled by user):

```
(S) Still looking for ruben sierra could
    be in central michigan
(R) I am still looking for ruben sierra
    in central michigan

(S) That we were required to go to
    college more than action movies
(R) We are required to go to
    college more than action movies

(S) No dressing allowed under canon law
    in the youth group
(R) No dresses allowed under canon law
    for youth groups
```

Users remember the gist of a sentence very well, but have trouble reproducing the exact wording. Post-experiment interview reveal this to be partly an effect of overconfidence. Users put little mental work into memorizing sentences, beyond choosing among the 10-best alternatives presented to them. By contrast, they put much more work into memorizing an XKCD phrase, actively building a mental image or story to connect the four otherwise unrelated words.

## 5 Future Directions

Actually, we can often *automatically* determine that a user-recalled sequence is wrong. For example, when we go to reconstruct the 60-bit input string from a user-recalled sequence, we may find that we get a 62-bit string instead. We can then automatically prod the user into trying again, but we find that this is not effective in practice. An intriguing direction is to do automatic error-correction, i.e., take the user-recalled sequence and find the closest match among the $2^{60}$ English sequences producible by the method. Of course, it is a challenge to do this with 1-best outputs of an MT system that uses heuristic beam search, and we must also ensure that security is maintained.

We may also investigate new ways to re-rank n-best lists. Language model scoring is a good start, but we may prefer vivid, concrete, or other types of words, or we may use text data associated with the user (papers, emails) for secure yet personalized password generation.

## 6 Related Work

Gasser (1975), Crawford and Aycock (2008), and Shay et al. (2012) describe systems that produce meaningless but pronounceable passwords, such as "tufritvi" . However, their systems can only assign $\sim 2^{30}$ distinct passwords.

Jeyaraman and Topkara (2005) suggest generating a random sequence of characters, and finding a mnemonic for it in a text corpus. A limited corpus means they again have a small space of system-assigned passwords. We propose a similar method in Section 2.2, but we automatically synthesize a new mnemonic word sequence.

Kurzban (1985) and Shay et al. (2012) use a method similar to XKCD with small dictionaries. This leads to longer nonsense sequences that can be difficult to remember.

## 7 Conclusion

We introduced several methods for generating secure passwords in the form of English word sequences. We learned that long sentences are seemingly easy to remember, but actually hard to reproduce, and we also learned that our poetry method produced relatively short, memorable passwords that are liked by users.

## Acknowledgments

We would like to thank James Bedell, Aliya Deri, Tomer Levinboim, Jonathan May, Nima Pourdamghani and the anonymous reviewers for their very helpful comments. This work was supported in part by DARPA contract FA-8750-13-2-0045.

## References

Heather Crawford and John Aycock. 2008. Kwyjibo: automatic domain name generation. *Software: Practice and Experience*, 38(14):1561–1567.

Dinei Florencio and Cormac Herley. 2007. A large-scale study of web password habits. In *Proceedings of the 16th international conference on World Wide Web*, pages 657–666. ACM.

Morrie Gasser. 1975. A random word generator for pronounceable passwords. Technical report, Electronic Systems Division, Air Force Systems Command, USAF.

Dmitriy Genzel, Jakob Uszkoreit, and Franz Och. 2010. Poetic statistical machine translation: rhyme and meter. In *Proceedings of the 2010 Conference on Empirical Methods in Natural Language Processing*, pages 158–166. Association for Computational Linguistics.

Erica Greene, Tugba Bodrumlu, and Kevin Knight. 2010. Automatic analysis of rhythmic poetry with applications to generation and translation. In *Proceedings of the Conference on Empirical Methods in Natural Language Processing*, pages 524–533. Association for Computational Linguistics.

Sundararaman Jeyaraman and Umut Topkara. 2005. Have your cake and eat it too–infusing usability into text-password based authentication systems. *In Proceedings of ACSAC.*

Philipp Koehn, Hieu Hoang, Alexandra Birch, Chris Callison-Burch, Marcello Federico, Nicola Bertoldi, Brooke Cowan, Wade Shen, Christine Moran, Richard Zens, et al. 2007. Moses: Open source toolkit for statistical machine translation. In *Proceedings of the 45th Annual Meeting of the ACL, Demo and Poster Sessions*, pages 177–180. Association for Computational Linguistics.

Stanley A Kurzban. 1985. Easily remembered passphrases: a better approach. *ACM SIGSAC Review*, 3(2-4):10–21.

Claude E. Shannon. 1951. Prediction and entropy of printed English. *Bell System Technical Journal*, 30(1):50–64.

Richard Shay, Patrick Gage Kelley, Saranga Komanduri, Michelle L Mazurek, Blase Ur, Timothy Vidas, Lujo Bauer, Nicolas Christin, and Lorrie Faith Cranor. 2012. Correct horse battery staple: Exploring the usability of system-assigned passphrases. In *Proceedings of the Eighth Symposium on Usable Privacy and Security*, page 7. ACM.

Andreas Stolcke. 2002. SRILM-an extensible language modeling toolkit. In *INTERSPEECH*, pages 901–904.

# A Bayesian Model for Joint Learning of Categories and their Features

**Lea Frermann** and **Mirella Lapata**
Institute for Language, Cognition and Computation
School of Informatics, University of Edinburgh
10 Crichton Street, Edinburgh EH8 9AB
`l.frermann@ed.ac.uk`, `mlap@inf.ed.ac.uk`

## Abstract

Categories such as ANIMAL or FURNITURE are acquired at an early age and play an important role in processing, organizing, and conveying world knowledge. Theories of categorization largely agree that categories are characterized by features such as `function` or `appearance` and that feature and category acquisition go hand-in-hand, however previous work has considered these problems in isolation. We present the first model that jointly learns categories and their features. The set of features is shared across categories, and strength of association is inferred in a Bayesian framework. We approximate the learning environment with natural language text which allows us to evaluate performance on a large scale. Compared to highly engineered pattern-based approaches, our model is cognitively motivated, knowledge-lean, and learns categories and features which are perceived by humans as more meaningful.

## 1 Introduction

Categorization is one of the most basic cognitive functions. It allows individuals to organize their subjective experience of their environment by structuring its contents. This ability to group different objects into the same category based on their common characteristics underlies major cognitive activities such as perception, learning, and the use of language. Global categories (such as FURNITURE or ANIMAL) are shared among members of societies, and influence how we perceive, interact with, and argue about the world.

Given its fundamental importance, categorization is one of the most studied problems in cognitive science. The literature is rife with theoretical and experimental accounts, as well as modeling simulations focusing on the emergence, representation, and learning of categories. Most theories assume that basic level concepts such as *dog* or *chair* are characterized by features such as `barks` or `used-for-sitting`, and are grouped into categories based on those features. Although the precise grouping mechanism has been subject to considerable debate (including arguments in favor of *exemplars* (Nosofsky, 1988), *prototypes* (Reed, 1972), and category *utility* (Corter and Gluck, 1992)), it is fairly uncontroversial that categories are associated with featural representations.

Experimental studies show that the development of categories and feature learning mutually influence each other (Goldstone et al., 2001; Schyns and Rodet, 1997): concepts are categorized based on their features, but the perception of features is influenced by already established categories, and, like categories, features evolve over time. There is also evidence that features such as `barks` or `runs` are grouped into types like `behavior` (Ahn, 1998; McRae et al., 2005; Spalding and Ross, 2000), and the distribution of feature types varies across categories. For instance, living-things such as ANIMALS have characteristic `behavior`, whereas artifacts such as TOOLS have characteristic `functions`, and both categories have characteristic `appearance`.

In this paper, we investigate the problem of *jointly* learning categories and their feature types. Previous modeling work has largely considered these problems in isolation, focusing either on category learning with a fixed set of simplistic features (Anderson, 1991; Sanborn et al., 2006) or feature learning (Austerweil and Griffiths, 2013; Baroni et al., 2010;



*Human Language Technologies: The 2015 Annual Conference of the North American Chapter of the ACL*, pages 1576–1586,
Denver, Colorado, May 31 – June 5, 2015. 

Kelly et al., 2014), but not both.

We present a Bayesian model which induces (semantic) categories and feature types from natural language text. Although language is one of many factors influencing category formation (others include the physical world, how we perceive it, and interact with it), large text corpora encode a surprising amount of extralinguistic information (Riordan and Jones, 2011), and can thus be viewed as an approximation of the learning environment. Moreover, focusing on textual data, allows us to build categorization models with theoretically unlimited scope, and evaluate categories and their features on a much larger scale than previous work in the cognitive science literature.

Our model induces categories (e.g., ANIMALS) and their feature types (e.g., `behavior`) from observations of target concepts (e.g., *lion*, *cow*) and their co-occurring contexts (e.g., *eats*, *sleeps*, *large*). While we can directly evaluate learnt categories through comparison against behavioral data, evaluating feature types is less straightforward. Previous work has shown that the kinds of features learnable from text are qualitatively different from those produced by humans, which makes direct comparison difficult (Baroni et al., 2010; Kelly et al., 2014). We circumvent this problem by assessing in a crowd-sourcing experiment whether the induced feature types are *relevant* for a given category and whether they form a *coherent* class. Evaluation results show that our joint model learns accurate categories and feature types achieving results competitive with highly engineered approaches focusing exclusively on feature learning.

## 2 Related Work

The problems of category formation and feature learning have been considered largely independently in the literature. Bayesian categorization models were pioneered by Anderson (1991) and recently reformalized by Sanborn et al. (2006). These models are aimed at replicating human behavior in small scale category acquisition studies, where a fixed set of simple (e.g., binary) features is assumed. Frermann and Lapata (2014) propose a model similar in spirit, which they apply to large scale corpora, while investigating incremental learning in the context of child category acquisition (see also Fountain and Lapata (2011) for a non-Bayesian approach). Their model associates sets of features with categories as a by-product of the learning process, however these feature sets are independent across categories and are not optimized during learning.

Previous approaches on feature learning have primarily focused on emulating or complementing norming studies by automatically extracting norm-like properties from textual corpora (e.g., *elephant* `has-trunk`, *scissors* `used-for-cutting`). A common theme in this line of research is the use of pre-defined syntactic patterns (Baroni et al., 2010), or manually created rules specifying possible connection paths of concepts to features in dependency trees (Devereux et al., 2009; Kelly et al., 2014). Once extracted, the features are typically weighted in order to filter out noisy instances. Features are learnt for individual concepts rather than categories. Austerweil and Griffiths (2013) also focus exclusively on feature learning, however from sensory data. They develop a nonparametric Bayesian model which is able to infer unlimited features, based on distributional patterns as well as category information.

To our knowledge, we propose the first Bayesian model that jointly learns categories and their features, arguing that the two tasks are mutually dependent. Our model is knowledge-lean, it learns from raw text in a single process, without relying on parsing resources, manually crafted rule patterns, or post-processing steps. Our work also differs from approaches which combine topic models with human-produced feature norms (Steyvers, 2010). Our aim is not to boost the generalization performance of a topic model, rather we investigate how both categories and features can be jointly learnt from data.

## 3 The BCF Model

In this section we present our Bayesian model of category and feature induction (henceforth, BCF). BCF jointly learns categories, feature types, and their associations. Specifically, it infers one global set of feature types which is shared across categories (e.g., ANIMALS and VEHICLES can be described in terms of `colors`). However, categories

Generate category distribution, $\theta \sim Dir(\alpha)$
**for** concept type $\ell$ **do**
  Generate category, $k^{\ell} \sim Mult(\theta)$
**for** category $k$ **do**
  Generate feature type distribution, $\mu_k \sim Dir(\beta)$
**for** feature type $g$ **do**
  Generate feature distribution, $\phi_g \sim Dir(\gamma)$
**for** stimulus $d$ **do**
  Observe concept $c^d$ and retrieve category $k^{c^d}$
  Generate a feature type, $g^d \sim Mult(\mu_{k^{c^d}})$
  **for** feature position i **do**
    Generate a feature $f_{d,i} \sim Mult(\phi_{g^d})$

Figure 1: The generative story of the BCF model. Observations $f$ and latent labels $k$ and $g$ are drawn from Multinomial distributions (*Mult*). Parameters for the multinomial distributions are drawn from Dirichlet distributions (*Dir*).

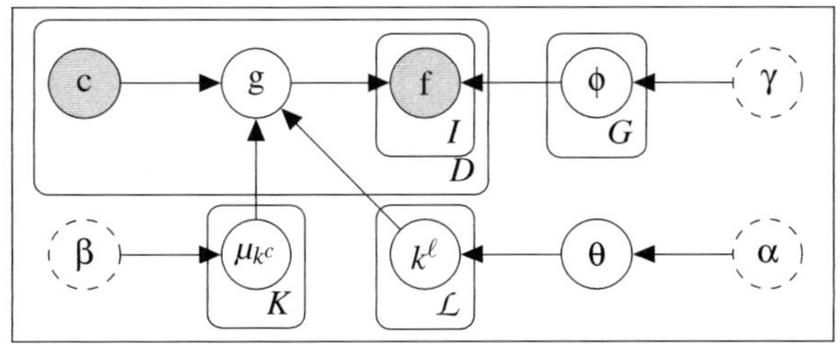


Figure 2: The plate diagram of the BCF model. Shaded nodes indicate observed variables, and dotted nodes indicate hyperparameters.

differ in their strength of association with feature types (e.g., the feature type `function` will be highly associated with TOOLS but less so with ANIMALS). BCF jointly optimizes categories and their featural representation: the learning objective is to obtain a set of meaningful categories, each characterized by relevant and coherent feature types.

The generative story and plate diagram for the BCF model are shown in Figures 1 and 2, respectively. The input to the model is a collection of *stimuli* $d \in \{1..D\}$ extracted from a large text corpus. Each stimulus consists of a target concept $c \in \{1..\mathcal{L}\}$ and its context $\mathbf{f} \in \{1..F\}$. We adopt a simple representation of context as the set of words making up the sentence $c$ occurs in (except $c$). The model assigns concepts to categories $k \in \{1..K\}$ and features to feature types $g \in \{1..G\}$. It learns a set of concept clusters (i.e., categories), as well as a clustering over features (i.e., feature types), and a distribution over those feature clusters for each category (i.e., category-feature type associations). Specifically, the occurrences of a concept will be assigned a category, based on how similar the concept's feature types are compared to the feature types of all other potential categories. Simultaneously, upon observing a stimulus (i.e., a concept in context), the model assigns the context to a particular feature type based on its probability under all potential feature types, and the prior probability of observing that feature type with the concept's assigned category.

More formally, we can describe the model through the generative story given in Figure 1. We assume a global multinomial distribution over categories $Mult(\theta)$, drawn from a symmetric Dirichlet distribution with hyperparameter $\alpha$. For each category $k$, we assume an independent set of multinomial parameters over feature types $\mu_k$, drawn from a symmetric Dirichlet distribution with hyperparameter $\beta$. For each concept type $\ell$, we draw a category $k^{\ell}$ from $Mult(\theta)$. Finally, for each feature type $g$, we draw a multinomial distribution over features $Mult(\phi_g)$ from a symmetric Dirichlet distribution with hyperparameter $\gamma$. With these global assignments in place, we can generate stimuli $d$ as follows: we first retrieve the category $k^{c^d}$ of the observed concept $c^d$; we then generate a feature type $g^d$ from the category's feature type distribution $Mult(\mu_{k^{c^d}})$; and finally, for each feature position $i$ we generate feature $f_{d,i}$ from the feature type's distribution $Mult(\phi_{g^d})$. The joint probability of the model over latent categories, latent feature types, model parameters, and data can be factorized as:

$$P(g,f,\mu,\phi,\theta,k|c,\alpha,\beta,\gamma) = \\ P(\theta|\alpha)\prod_{\ell}P(k^{\ell}|\theta)\prod_{k}P(\mu_k|\beta)\prod_{g}P(\phi_g|\gamma) \\ \prod_{d}P(g^d|\mu_{k^{c^d}})\prod_{i}P(f^{d,i}|\phi_{g^d}). \quad (1)$$

Since we use conjugate priors throughout, we can integrate out the model parameters analytically, and perform inference only over the latent variables, namely the category and feature type labels associ-

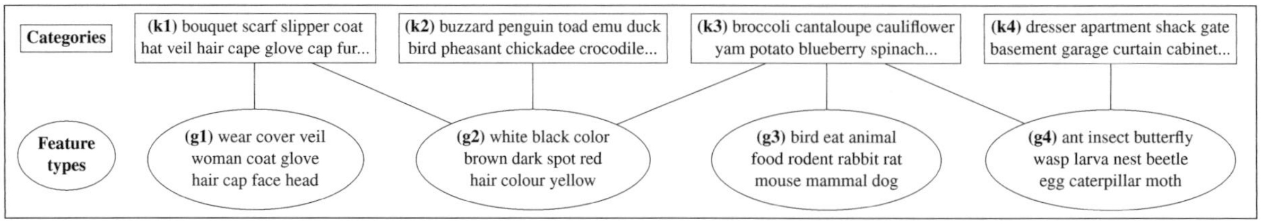


Figure 3: Example of categories (top) and feature types (bottom) inferred by the BCF model. Connecting lines indicate a strong association between the category and the respective feature type.

ated with the stimuli.

Exact inference in the BCF model is intractable, so we turn to approximate posterior inference to discover the assignments of latent variables that best explain our data. We construct a Gibbs sampler (Geman and Geman, 1984) which iteratively re-assigns single variables based on the current assignments of all other variables. One Gibbs iteration for our model consists of one sweep through the input stimuli, resampling feature type assignments from:

$$\begin{aligned} &P(g^d_{k^{c^d}} = i \mid \mathbf{g}^{-d}_{k^{c^d}}, \mathbf{f}^{-}, k^{c^d}, \beta, \gamma) \\ &\quad \propto P(g^d_{k^{c^d}} = i \mid \mathbf{g}^{-d}_{k^{c^d}}, k^{c^d}, \beta) \times P(f^d \mid \mathbf{f}^{-}, g^d_{k^{c^d}} = i, \gamma), \end{aligned} \tag{2}$$

followed by one sweep through the concept types, resampling category assignments from:

$$\begin{aligned} &P(k^\ell = j \mid \mathbf{g}_{k^\ell}, \mathbf{k}^{-}, \alpha, \beta) \\ &\quad \propto P(k^\ell = j \mid \mathbf{k}^{-}, \alpha) \times P(\mathbf{g}_{k^\ell} \mid \mathbf{g}^{-}_{k^\ell}, k^\ell = j, \beta), \end{aligned} \tag{3}$$

where $g^d_{k^{c^d}}$ denotes the feature type assignment to stimulus $d$ given the category $k^{c^d}$ of $d$'s observed target concept $c^d$. $k^\ell$ refers to the category assignment of concept type $\ell$, $\mathbf{g}_{k^\ell}$ refers to the feature type associations of category $k^\ell$, and $f^d$ refers to the observed features in stimulus $d$. The superscript $^{-}$ indicates the absence of the variable assignment(s) which are currently resampled from the current representation of the model state.

Figure 3 illustrates example output produced by our model, in terms of learnt categories, learnt feature types and their associations. Connecting lines indicate category-feature type associations. Feature types are shared across categories, e.g., categories CLOTHING (k1), BIRDS (k2), and FOOD (k3) are all associated with feature type `color` (g2).

## 4 Experimental Design

In this section we outline our experimental set-up for assessing the performance of the BCF model described above. We present our data set, briefly introduce the models used for comparison with our approach, and explain how system output was evaluated. We then report results on a series of experiments which evaluate the quality of the categories and feature types learnt by BCF.

**Data** Our experiments used basic-level target concepts (e.g., *cat* or *chair*) from two norming studies (McRae et al., 2005; Vinson and Vigliocco, 2008). In these studies, humans were presented with concepts and asked for each concept to produce a set of characteristic features. In a subsequent study (Fountain and Lapata, 2010), the concepts were classified into 41 categories (with possible multi-category membership), 34 of which we use as a goldstandard in our categorization experiments (comprising 492 concepts in total). We excluded very general categories such as THING or STRUCTURE, based on the intuition that it is difficult to identify characteristic features for them. As a heuristic concepts were excluded if they were close to the root of WordNet (e.g., with depth 2 or 4).

To obtain the input stimuli for the BCF model, we used a subset of the Wackypedia corpus (Baroni et al., 2009), an automatically extracted and POS tagged dump of the English Wikipedia. For each target concept, we identified one corresponding article in Wackypedia. Next, we extracted a set of stimuli which consists of (a) every sentence from the concept's corresponding article, and (b) any sentence in a different article which mentions the concept. This resulted in a data set of 63,076 stimuli which we split into 60% training, 20% development and 20% test.

We removed stopwords as well as words with a part of speech other than noun, verb, and adjective. Furthermore, we discarded words with an age of acquisition above 10 years (Kuperman et al., 2012) to restrict the vocabulary to frequent and generally familiar words.

**Models and Parameters** We compared the performance of BCF against BayesCat, a Bayesian model of category acquisition (Frermann and Lapata, 2014) and Strudel, a pattern-based model which extracts concept features from text (Baroni et al., 2010).

BayesCat induces categories, which are represented through a distribution over target concepts, and a distribution over features (i.e., individual context words). In contrast to BCF, it does not learn types of features. In addition, while BCF induces a hard assignment of concepts to categories, BayesCat learns soft distributions over target concepts for each category. Soft assignments can be converted into hard assignments by assigning each concept to its most probable category. We ran BayesCat on the same input stimuli as BCF, with the following parameters: the number of categories was set to $K = 40$, and the hyperparameters to $\alpha = 0.7, \beta = 0.1, \gamma = 0.1$. For the BCF model, we used the same number of categories, namely $K = 40$. The number of feature types was set to $G = 75$, and the hyperparameters to $\alpha = 0.5, \beta = 0.5$, and $\gamma = 0.1$. Parameters were tuned on the development set. For both models, we report results averaged over 10 Gibbs runs, each time we ran the sampler for 1,000 iterations. We used annealing during learning which proved effective for avoiding local optima.

Strudel automatically extracts features for concepts from text collections following a pattern-based approach. It takes as input a set of target concepts and a set of patterns, and extracts a list of features for each concept, where each concept-feature pair is weighted with a log-likelihood ratio expressing the pair's strength of association. Baroni et al. (2010) show that the learnt representations can be used as a basis for various tasks such as typicality rating, categorization, or clustering of features into types. In our experiments we obtained Strudel representations from the same Wackypedia corpus used for extracting the input stimuli for BCF (and BayesCat). Note that Strudel, unlike the two Bayesian models, is not a cognitively motivated *acquisition* model, but an optimized system developed with the aim of obtaining the best possible features from data.

### 4.1 Experiment 1: Evaluation of Categories

In our first experiment we evaluate the quality of the categories induced by the three models presented above. The models produce hard categorizations, however, the cognitive gold standard we use for evaluation (Fountain and Lapata, 2010) represents soft categories. We obtained a hard categorization by assigning members of multiple categories to their most typical category (typicality scores are provided with the data).[1]

**Method** BCF and BayesCat learn a set of categories which we can directly compare to the gold standard. For Strudel, we produce a categorization as follows: we represent each concept as a vector over features (obtained from Wackypedia), where each component corresponds to the concept-feature log-likelihood ratios provided by Strudel; following Baroni et al. (2010), we then cluster the vectors using K-means and the Cluto toolkit.[2] As for the other models, we set the number of categories to $K = 40$.

**Metrics** To assess the quality of the clusters produced by the models, we measure purity (*pur*; the extent to which each learnt cluster corresponds to a single gold class) as well as its inverse, collocation (*col*; the extent to which all items of a particular gold class are represented in a single learnt cluster). Both measures are based on set-overlap, and we also report their harmonic mean ($f1$; Lang and Lapata 2011). In addition, we report the V-measure ($v1$; Rosenberg and Hirschberg 2007) and its factors measuring the homogeneity of clusters (*hom*) and their completeness (*com*). The two factors intuitively correspond to purity and collocation, but are based on information-theoretic measures.

**Results** Our results are summarized in Table 1. They show that BCF and Strudel perform almost identically, and both outperform BayesCat. BCF *learns* the categories from data, whereas for Strudel

[1] `http://homepages.inf.ed.ac.uk/s0897549/data/`.

[2] `http://glaros.dtc.umn.edu/gkhome/cluto/cluto/overview`

| | *hom* | *com* | *v*1 | *pur* | *col* | *f*1 |
|---|---|---|---|---|---|---|
| BCF | 0.68 | 0.64 | **0.66** | 0.59 | 0.52 | **0.55** |
| BayesCat | 0.65 | 0.59 | 0.62 | 0.57 | 0.45 | 0.50 |
| Strudel | 0.70 | 0.62 | **0.66** | 0.61 | 0.48 | 0.54 |

Table 1: Model performance on the category induction task.

| | | *pr*@1 | *pr*@10 | *pr*@20 | *avg* |
|---|---|---|---|---|---|
| BCF | full | **0.12** | **0.50** | 0.63 | 56.1 |
| | −tgt | 0.09 | 0.40 | 0.53 | 78.5 |
| BayesCat | full | 0.11 | 0.49 | **0.64** | **37.7** |
| | −tgt | 0.09 | 0.39 | 0.53 | 52.4 |
| Strudel | full | 0.07 | 0.33 | 0.47 | 64.4 |
| | −tgt | 0.07 | 0.35 | 0.49 | 62.2 |

Table 2: Model performance on the concept prediction task. Precision at rank 1, 10, 20, and average rank assigned (*avg*). −tgt refers to the condition where we remove context words which are identical to the target concept as opposed to using the full context.

we construct the categories post-hoc after a highly informed feature extraction process (relying on grammatical patterns). It is therefore not surprising that Strudel performs well, and it is encouraging to see that BCF does too. Also, note that Strudel tends to learn very clean clusters at the cost of recall, whereas the tradeoff is less extreme for BCF. Again, this is expected given Strudel's pattern-based approach. While BCF and Strudel are constrained to assign each concept to only one category, BayesCat induces a soft categorization which is turned into a hard categorization in a post-learning step. While this setting allows for more flexibility, it also induces more uncertainty and results in categorizations which resemble the gold standard less closely compared to the two other models.

### 4.2 Experiment 2: Evaluation of Features

We next investigate the quality of the features our model learns. We do this by letting the model predict the right concept solely from a set of features. If the model has acquired informative features, they will be predictive of the unknown concept. Specifically, the model is presented with a set of previously unseen test stimuli with the target concept removed. For each stimulus, the model ranks all possible target concepts based on the features $\mathbf{f}$ (i.e., context words).

**Method** In our experiments we compared the ranking performance of BCF, BayesCat, and Strudel. For the Bayesian models, we directly exploit the learnt distributions. For BCF, we compute the score of a target concept $c$ given a set of features as:

$$Score(c|\mathbf{f}) = \sum_g P(g|c)P(\mathbf{f}|g). \quad (4)$$

Similarly, for BayesCat we compute the score of a concept $c$ given a set of features as follows:

$$Score(c|\mathbf{f}) = \sum_k P(c|k)P(\mathbf{f}|k). \quad (5)$$

For Strudel, we rank concepts according to the cumulative log-likelihood ratio-based association score over all observed features for a particular concept $c$:

$$Score(c|\mathbf{f}) = \sum_{f \in \mathbf{f}} association(c, f). \quad (6)$$

**Metrics** Since we can directly compare model predictions against the actual target concept of the stimulus, we report precision at rank 1, 10, and 20. We also report the average rank assigned to the correct concept. All results are based on a random test set of 2,000 previously unseen stimuli. To control for the possibility that the models are learning a strong (yet trivial) correlation between target concepts and identical words occurring as features, we also report results on a modification of our test set where we remove any mention of the target concept from the context, if present (the −tgt condition).

**Results** Our results on the concept prediction task are shown in Table 2. The Bayesian models outperform Strudel across all metrics and conditions. Strudel's extraction algorithm, which relies on predefined patterns, might be too restrictive with respect to the set of features it extracts and as a result they are not discriminative. BayesCat and BCF

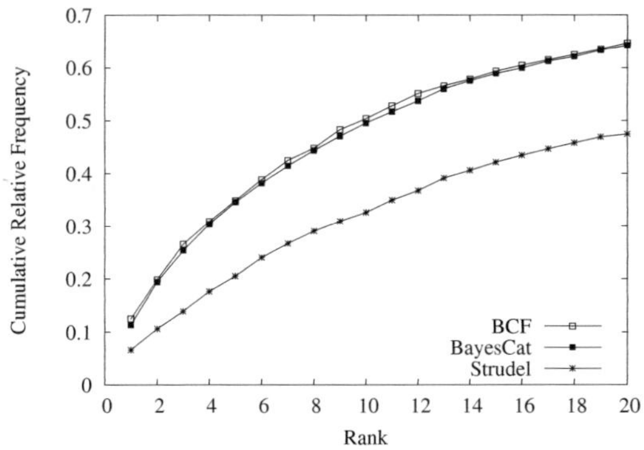


Figure 4: Number of times the correct target concept was placed within the top 20 ranks by BCF, BayesCat, and Strudel.

| ***salmon*** | `journey move hundred mile strong current reproduce` | | | |
|---|---|---|---|---|
| BCF | **salmon** | tuna | goldfish | lobster | fish |
| BayesCat | fish | radio | goldfish | **salmon** | clock |
| Strudel | train | house | apartment | ship | car |

| ***finger*** | `avoid cut quick claw tip painful` | | | | |
|---|---|---|---|---|---|
| BCF | tent | ski | peg | curtain | hut |
| BayesCat | eye | ear | spider | leg | hair |
| Strudel | **finger** | toe | hair | tail | hand |

Table 3: Model output on the concept prediction task for *salmon* (top) and *finger* (bottom): the top part of each table shows the true concept (left) and the context provided to the model as input (right). The bottom part of the table shows the five most highly ranked concepts (left to right) for each model.

perform comparably given that they learn from exactly the same data and exploit local co-occurrence relations in similar ways. BayesCat produces better average rank scores than BCF, while achieving lower precision scores. This can be explained by the fact that BCF assigns low ranks to correct concepts more reliably than BayesCat. Figure 4 shows the relative cumulative frequencies of the ranks assigned by the three models. We display the top ranks 1 through 20 (out of 492). As can be seen, BCF performs slightly better than BayesCat. Pairwise differences between the systems are all statistically significant ($p \ll 0.01$); using a one-way ANOVA with post-hoc Tukey HSD test).

Note that performance decreases for the Bayesian models in the −tgt condition, i.e., when occurrences of the target concept are removed from the context. Strudel is less affected by this given its pattern-based learning mechanism which is not prone to associating target word types with themselves. However, repetitions are a natural phenomenon from a cognitive standpoint and it seems reasonable to consider multiple occurrences of a concept as a canonical feature of the learning environment.

Overall, the precision scores may seem low. However, the models rank a set of 492 target concepts; a random baseline would achieve a *pr*@1 of only 0.002%. In addition, the target concepts we are considering are by design highly confusable: they were selected so that they form categories and are thus bound to share some features which makes the prediction task harder. Example output for all three models is shown in Table 3. The models take context features "*journey move hundred mile strong*" and "*avoid cut quick claw tip*" as input and are expected to predict *salmon* and *finger*, respectively. Unlike Strudel, BCF and BayesCat rank *salmon* almost correctly and the other high ranked concepts are reasonable in the given context as well. For the second example, only Strudel predicts the correct concept correctly, but again the top-ranked concepts of the other two models are reasonable in the given context.

### 4.3 Experiment 3: Evaluation of Feature Types

In this suite of experiments we evaluate two aspects of the feature types induced by our model: (1) Are they *relevant* to their associated category? and (2) Do they form a *coherent* class? Our evaluation followed the intrusion paradigm originally introduced to assess the output of topic models (Chang et al., 2009). We performed two intrusion studies using Amazon's Mechanical Turk crowd-sourcing platform.

In the feature intrusion study, participants were shown examples of categories and their feature types both of which were represented as word clusters (see Figure 6 top). They were asked to detect the feature type which did not belong to the category. If a model creates *relevant* feature types, we would expect participants to be able to identify the intruder relatively easily. We also conducted a word intrusion

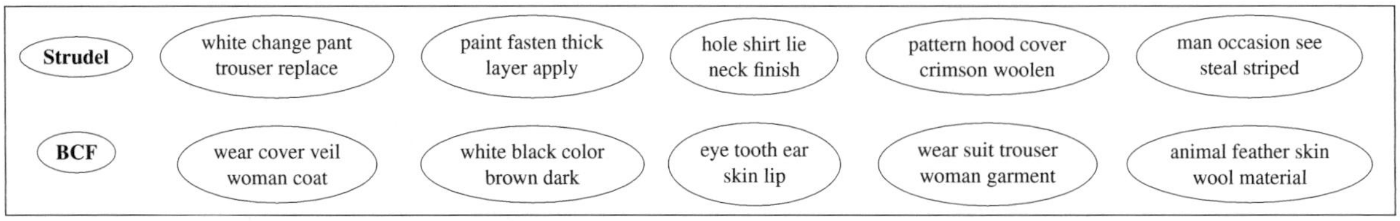


Figure 5: Example feature types learnt for the category CLOTHING by Strudel (top) and BCF (bottom).

| 'Select intruder feature type (right) wrt category (left).' | |
|---|---|
| ***ant hornet*** | ○ `egg female food young bird` |
| ***moth flea*** | ○ `ant insect butterfly wasp larva` |
| ***beetle wasp*** | ● `wear cover veil woman coat` |
| ***cockroach*** | ○ `body air fish blood muscle` |

| 'Select the intruder word.' | | | | |
|---|---|---|---|---|
| ○ | ○ | ● | ○ | ○ |
| `egg` | `female` | `box` | `young` | `bird` |

Figure 6: Illustration of the feature type intrusion task (top); and the word intrusion task (bottom).

study, where participants were shown a single feature type (again represented as a word cluster) and asked to detect the intruder feature/word (see Figure 6 bottom). If the features are overall *coherent* and meaningful, it should be relatively straightforward to identify the intruder.

**Method** We compared the feature types learnt by BCF and Strudel. We omitted BayesCat from this evaluation as it does not naturally produce feature types, rather it associates unstructured lists of features with categories. As mentioned earlier, Strudel does not induce feature types either, however, it associates concepts with features which can be post-processed to obtain feature types as follows. Given a category induced by Strudel (as explained in Experiment 1), we collected the features associated with at least half of the concepts in the category with a log likelihood score no less than 19.51.[3] We then clustered these features with K-means (using the Cluto toolkit) into $K = 5$ feature types.

For BCF, for each category $k$, we select the five feature types $g$ with highest association $P(g|k)$, together with one intruder feature type $g'$ which is highly associated with some other category $k'$ but not with $k$. For Strudel we took the five feature types elicited through the procedure described above, and one random feature type from the global set of feature types. Each feature type was represented by a cluster of five words.

With respect to the word intrusion task, participants were only shown feature types (i.e., word clusters) irrespectively of the associated category. BCF feature types $g$ were represented as the set of the five words $w$ with highest probability $P(f|g)$. In addition, we added one intruder word which had low probability under $g$ but high probability under some other feature type. For Strudel, we represented feature types as a random subset of five words, and added an additional intruder word from the global set of features.

For the feature type intrusion task, We evaluated a total of 40 categories for each model. Each participant assessed 10 categories per session (5 per model). Categories and feature types were presented in random order. For the word intrusion task, we evaluated a total of 66 feature types for each model. Participants saw 11 feature types per session, in randomized order. In both cases, we collected 10 responses per item.

**Metrics** We evaluated feature type relevance and coherence by measuring precision (the proportion of intruders identified correctly). We also use the Kappa coefficient to measure inter-subject agreement (Fleiss, 1981) on our two tasks.

**Results** Our results are presented in Table 4. Participants identify the intruder feature type correctly more than 50% of the time. The performance of Strudel is slightly better compared to BCF, both in terms of accuracy and Kappa (however the dif-

[3]Following Baroni et al. (2010), this number corresponds to a probability of co-occurrence below 0.00001, assuming independence.

| | Feat Type Intrusion | | Word Intrusion | |
|---|---|---|---|---|
| | Prec | Kappa | Prec | Kappa |
| BCF | 0.52 | 0.23 | **0.78** | **0.60** |
| Strudel | **0.56** | **0.26** | 0.36 | 0.21 |

Table 4: Performance of Strudel and BCF on the feature type and word intrusion tasks. We report precision (Prec) and inter-subject agreement (Fleiss' Kappa; all Kappa values are statistically significant at $p \ll 0.05$).

ferences are not statistically significant, using a *t*-test). Again this is not surprising considering that Strudel's feature types were elicited through a highly informed, pipelined process. The results show that the simpler and cognitively plausible BCF model learns feature types of a quality comparable to a highly engineered, competitive system. Examples of feature types discovered by BCF and Strudel are shown in Figure 5, for the category CLOTHING. As can be seen, Strudel obtains a large number of action-related features (e.g., *replace, change, steal*). BCF creates more varied feature types. For example, the second cluster refers to external properties (e.g., color), and the last cluster contains CLOTHING materials.

Concerning the word intrusion task, we observe that participants are able to detect the intruder more accurately when presented with BCF feature types as compared to Strudel feature types (differences between Strudel and BCF are statistically significant at $p \ll 0.05$, again using a *t*-test). The results suggest that the feature types learnt by BCF are more coherent, and indeed express meaningful properties shared by concepts belonging to the same category. While being relevant to the category, Strudel's feature types do not seem to exhibit internal coherence to a similar extent. The mutual dependence of category formation and feature learning allows BCF to learn feature types which are both relevant and individually interpretable.

## 5 Discussion

In this paper we presented a cognitively motivated Bayesian model which jointly learns categories and their features, arguing that the two tasks are codependent. Our model learns from raw text without relying on elaborate post-processing and high-precision patterns. Evaluation of the inferred categories and their features shows that BCF performs competitively compared to a system specifically engineered to extract high quality features, despite the more complex learning objective, and the knowledge-lean approach. We approximate the cognitive learning environment with large text corpora. However, we do not claim to learn features qualitatively similar to features produced in human elicitation studies. Instead, we show, through a crowdsourcing-based human evaluation, that the learnt features are meaningful in that they are relevant to their associated category and form a coherent class.

An interesting direction for future work would be to learn feature types from multiple modalities (not only text) and to investigate how different information sources (e.g., visual or pragmatic input) influence feature learning. The BCF model learns descriptive feature types represented as a collection of feature values. In addition to such descriptive features (e.g., `behavior`) categories also possess *defining* features (e.g., `animate`) which are bound to one particular value. Extending the model in a way that allows to learn qualitatively different types of features is desirable from a cognitive perspective. We will also develop an incremental learning algorithm for joint category and feature learning (e.g., using sequential Monte Carlo methods such as Particle Filtering). In addition, it would be interesting to investigate the emergence of feature types with nonparametric Bayesian methods.

Finally, the BCF model can be applied to tasks beyond those discussed here. For example, one could learn definitions (aka features) of terms (aka concepts) in specialist fields (e.g., finance, law, medicine) or monitor how the meaning of words or concepts as represented by their features changes over time.

**Acknowledgments** We thank Micha Elsner and Charles Sutton for helpful discussions, William Schuler for his comments, and Carina Silberer for providing the Strudel features. We acknowledge the support of EPSRC through project grant EP/I037415/1.

## References


Ahn, Woo-Kyoung. 1998. Why are different features central for natural kinds and artifacts?: the role of causal status in determining feature centrality. *Cognition* 69:135.

Anderson, John R. 1991. The adaptive nature of human categorization. *Psychological Review* 98:409–429.

Austerweil, Joseph L. and Thomas L. Griffiths. 2013. A nonparametric Bayesian framework for constructing flexible feature representations. *Psychological Review* 120(4):817–851.

Baroni, Marco, Silvia Bernardini, Adriano Ferraresi, and Eros Zanchetta. 2009. The WaCky wide web: a collection of very large linguistically processed web-crawled corpora. *Language Resources and Evaluation* 43(3):209–226.

Baroni, Marco, Brian Murphy, Eduard Barbu, and Massimo Poesio. 2010. Strudel: A corpus-based semantic model based on properties and types. *Cognitive Science* 34(2):222–254.

Chang, Jonathan, Jordan Boyd-Graber, Chong Wang, Sean Gerrish, and David M. Blei. 2009. Reading tea leaves: How humans interpret topic models. In *Neural Information Processing Systems*. pages 288–296.

Corter, James E. and Mark A. Gluck. 1992. Explaining basic categories - feature predictability and information. *Psychological Bulletin* 111(2):291–303.

Devereux, Barry, Nicholas Pilkington, Therry Poibeau, and Anna Korhonen. 2009. Towards unrestricted, large-scale acquisition of feature-based conceptual representations from corpus data. *Research on Language & Computation* 7(2-4):137–170.

Fleiss, Joseph L. 1981. *Statistical Methods for Rates and Proportions*. Wiley, New York.

Fountain, Trevor and Mirella Lapata. 2010. Meaning representation in natural language categorization. In *Proceedings of the 32nd Annual Conference of the Cognitive Science Society*. Portland, Oregon, pages 1916–1921.

Fountain, Trevor and Mirella Lapata. 2011. Incremental models of natural language category acquisition. In *Proceedings of the 33nd Annual Conference of the Cognitive Science Society*. Boston, Massachusetts, pages 255–260.

Frermann, Lea and Mirella Lapata. 2014. Incremental Bayesian learning of semantic categories. In *Proceedings of the 14th Conference of the European Chapter of the Association for Computational Linguistics, EACL 2014, April 26-30, 2014, Gothenburg, Sweden*. pages 249–258.

Geman, Stuart and Donald Geman. 1984. Stochastic relaxation, Gibbs distributions and the Bayesian restoration of images. *IEEE Transactions on Pattern Analysis and Machine Intelligence* 6(6):721–741.

Goldstone, Robert L., Yvonne Lippa, and Richard M. Shiffrin. 2001. Altering object representations through category learning. *Cognition* 78:27–43.

Kelly, Colin, Barry Devereux, and Anna Korhonen. 2014. Automatic extraction of property norm-like data from large text corpora. *Cognitive Science* 38(4):638–682.

Kuperman, Victor, Hans Stadthagen-Gonzalez, and Marc Brysbaert. 2012. Age-of-acquisition ratings for 30,000 english words. *Behavior Research Methods* 44(4):978–990.

Lang, Joel and Mirella Lapata. 2011. Unsupervised semantic role induction with graph partitioning. In *Proceedings of the 2011 Conference on Empirical Methods in Natural Language Processing*. Edinburgh, Scotland, UK., pages 1320–1331.

McRae, Ken, George S. Cree, Mark S. Seidenberg, and Chris McNorgan. 2005. Semantic feature production norms for a large set of living and nonliving things. *Behavioral Research Methods* 37(4):547–59.

Nosofsky, Robert M. 1988. Exemplar-based accounts of relations between classification, recognition, and typicality. *Journal of Experimental Psychology: Learning, Memory, and Cognition* 14:700–708.

Reed, Stephen K. 1972. Pattern recognition and categorization. *Cognitive psychology* 3(3):382–407.

Riordan, Brian and Michael N. Jones. 2011. Redundancy in perceptual and linguistic experience:

Comparing feature-based and distributional models of semantic representation. *Topics in Cognitive Science* 3(2):303–345.

Rosenberg, Andrew and Julia Hirschberg. 2007. V-measure: A conditional entropy-based external cluster evaluation measure. In *Proceedings of the 2007 Joint Conference on Empirical Methods in Natural Language Processing and Computational Natural Language Learning*. Prague, Czech Republic, pages 410–420.

Sanborn, Adam N., Thomas L. Griffiths, and Daniel J. Navarro. 2006. A more rational model of categorization. In *Proceedings of the 28th Annual Conference of the Cognitive Science Society*. Vancouver, Canada, pages 726–731.

Schyns, Philippe G and Luc Rodet. 1997. Categorization creates functional features. *Journal of Experimental Psychology: Learning, Memory, and Cognition* 23:681–696.

Spalding, T. L. and B. H. Ross. 2000. Concept learning and feature interpretation. *Memory & Cognition* 28:439–451.

Steyvers, Mark. 2010. Combining feature norms and text data with topic models. *Acta Psychologica* 133(3):234–243.

Vinson, David and Gabriella Vigliocco. 2008. Semantic feature production norms for a large set of objects and events. *Behavior Research Methods* 40(1):183–190.

# Shared common ground influences information density in microblog texts

**Gabriel Doyle**
Dept. of Psychology
Stanford University
Stanford, CA, USA, 94305
gdoyle@stanford.edu

**Michael C. Frank**
Dept. of Psychology
Stanford University
Stanford, CA, USA, 94305
mcfrank@stanford.edu

## Abstract

If speakers use language rationally, they should structure their messages to achieve approximately uniform information density (UID), in order to optimize transmission via a noisy channel. Previous work identified a consistent increase in linguistic information across sentences in text as a signature of the UID hypothesis. This increase was derived from a predicted increase in context, but the context itself was not quantified. We use microblog texts from Twitter, tied to a single shared event (the baseball World Series), to quantify both linguistic and non-linguistic context. By tracking changes in contextual information, we predict and identify gradual and rapid changes in information content in response to in-game events. These findings lend further support to the UID hypothesis and highlights the importance of non-linguistic common ground for language production and processing.

## 1 Introduction

There are many ways express a given message in natural language, so how do speakers decide between potential structures? One prominent hypothesis is that they aim for structures that best convey the intendeed message in the context of the communication. On this view, the use of natural languages is assumed to follow optimal information transmission results from information theory (Shannon, 1948). In particular, speakers should structure their messages to approximate *uniform information density* across symbols (words and phonemes), which is optimal for transmission of information through a noisy channel.

At least three lines of evidence suggest that speakers do make choices to increase the uniformity of information density across their utterances. First, speakers phonologically reduce more predictable material (Aylett and Turk, 2004; Aylett and Turk, 2006; Bell et al., 2003). Second, they omit or reduce optional lexical material in cases where the subsequent syntactic information is relatively more predictable (Levy and Jaeger, 2007; Frank and Jaeger, 2008; Jaeger, 2010). Third, and most relevant to our current hypothesis, speakers appear to increase the complexity of their utterances as a discourse develops (Genzel and Charniak, 2002; Genzel and Charniak, 2003; Qian and Jaeger, 2012). We expand on this finding below.

Following the UID hypothesis, Genzel and Charniak 2002 proposed that $H(Y_i)$, the total entropy of part $i$ of a message (e.g., a word) is constant. They compute this expression by considering $X_i$, the random variable representing the precise word that will appear at position $i$, conditioned on all the previously observed words. They then further factor this expression into two terms:

$$\begin{aligned} H(Y_i) &= H(X_i|C_i, L_i) \\ &= H(X_i|L_i) - I(X_i; C_i|L_i) \quad (1) \end{aligned}$$

where the first term $H(X_i|L_i)$ is the dependence of the current word on only the local linguistic context (e.g. within the rest of the sentence $L_i$) and the second is the mutual information between the current word and the broader linguistic context $C_i$, given the rest of the current sentence. On their logic, with



*Human Language Technologies: The 2015 Annual Conference of the North American Chapter of the ACL*, pages 1587–1596,
Denver, Colorado, May 31 – June 5, 2015. 

greater amounts of contextual information, the predictability of linguistic material based on context, $I(X_i|C_i, L_i)$, must go up. Therefore, they predicted that $H(X_i|L_i)$ should also increase, so as to maintain a constant total amount of information.

Genzel and Charniak then approximated $H(X_i|L_i)$ using a number of methods and showed that it did increase systematically in documents. Later work showed that this increase was strongest within paragraphs and was general across document types (Genzel and Charniak, 2003) and languages (Qian and Jaeger, 2012). This work, however, did not attempt to measure shared context (and its influence on message expectations) directly. This challenge is the focus of our current work.

### 1.1 Contextual effects on complexity

In psycholinguistics, the notion of shared *common ground* is a more precise replacement for the general notion of "context" (Clark, 1996). Common ground is defined as the knowledge that participants in a discourse have and that participants know other participants have, including the current conversational context. A large literature supports the idea that speakers consider referential context and other linguistic common ground in selecting the appropriate expression to refer to a particular physical object (Brennan and Clark, 1996; Metzing and Brennan, 2003; Dale and Reiter, 1995; Sedivy et al., 1999). In principle, Genzel and Charniak's formulation can be considered as capturing the relationship between all of the shared common ground—both linguistic and non-linguistic—and the predictability of language, even though in the previous work only linguistic information was considered.

When there is both linguistic and non-linguistic information passing through the noisy channel, the relevant quantity is not the marginal entropy of only the linguistic stream but the joint entropy of both streams. Let $T_j$ be the linguistic information in part $j$ of the discourse, and $E_j$ be the non-linguistic information in part $j$. If $C_j$ is the built-up context from the preceding parts $\{1, \cdots, j-1\}$ of the discourse, then we can break down the joint entropy as:

$$\begin{aligned} & H(T_j, E_j|C_j) \\ &= H(T_j|E_j, C_j) + H(E_j|C_j) \\ &= H(T_j|C_j) - I(T_j; E_j|C_j) + H(E_j|C_j) \\ &= H(T_j) - I(T_j; C_j) \\ &\quad - I(T_j; E_j|C_j) + H(E_j|C_j) \\ &= H(T_j) - I(T_j; E_j, C_j) + H(E_j|C_j) \qquad (2) \end{aligned}$$

By the UID hypothesis, we expect the left-hand side of this equation, the information content of each part of the discourse, to be constant. The first term of the right-hand side is the out-of-context entropy of the linguistic information. The second term is the mutual information of the linguistic information and the union of the preceding context plus the current non-linguistic information (the events occurring at the time). The third term is the entropy of the non-linguistic information, given the preceding context.

This breakdown suggests that rational participants in a discourse will exhibit both slow and fast adaptation to context in order to maintain overall constant entropy. As context slowly builds, the mutual information term grows (and the non-linguistic entropy likely shrinks), resulting in the time-based increase in $H(T_j)$ that previous work has found. In addition, an individual event can have high or low information content given the context, without having a large effect on the mutual information term. To maintain constant entropy, high-information events should be accompanied by low-information linguistic responses, and vice versa. With an operationalization of shared context, we should be able to observe these two types of adaptation directly, not just via the increasing trend shown in previous work (Genzel and Charniak, 2002; Qian and Jaeger, 2012).

To test this prediction, we leverage Twitter, a popular microblogging service, to operationalize common ground. Because of its structure, Twitter is an ideal platform for this investigation. One common method of using Twitter is to mark messages with hashtags, which serve as ad-hoc categories, allowing anyone interested in a topic to find the messages relevant to that topic. This strategy is especially used when users are commenting on an external event (e.g. a sporting, media, or political event). We focus here on the World Series of baseball, an annual sporting event with large viewership and a single broadcast stream; in this case, the hashtag is `#worldseries`. Hashtagged messages are part of a discourse with extremely limited prior linguistic context, as no two tweeters will have seen the same set of tweets. The total shared context with the audience that can be assumed by the writer of a tweet is the non-linguistic content of the event being hashtagged.

We begin by describing our corpus and our method of calculating linguistic content (by computing entropy within a simple $n$-gram model). We then investigate gradual changes in word-by-word information content as the event goes on (testing adaptation driven by contextual mutual information in Equation 2, replicating Genzel and Charniak 2002) and rapid changes in the total information content of tweets in response to important in-game events (testing adaptation driven by non-linguistic information in Equation 2). We end by considering control analyses that provide evidence against alternative accounts of our results.

## 2 Corpus and Methods

### 2.1 #Worldseries Corpus

Our current analysis looked at tweets during the 2014 World Series, a series of seven baseball games in late October 2014. We obtained these tweets by searching publicly-available tweets through the Twitter API, using an adaptation of SeeTweet (Doyle, 2014) to compile tweets containing the hashtag `#WorldSeries`. To synchronize tweets with game events, we used the Major League Baseball Advance Media XML repository,[1] which contains pitch-by-pitch data including the ongoing state of the game and timestamps at the start of each at-bat. Using this timestamp information, we binned tweets by at-bats so that they could be co-registered with other in-game statistics. These bins extend from the time of the first pitch in an at-bat to the beginning of the next at-bat, and thus provide time for reactions to the events of the at-bat.[2] The mean at-bat length was 2.76 minutes, and there were 512 total at-bats. We limited our analysis to tweets timestamped during one of these at-bats, resulting in a total corpus of 109,207 tweets. Each game had its first pitch at approximately 0008 UTC, and lasted between three and four hours.

Our tweet corpus was compiled from the "gardenhose" Twitter search API, which returns a subset of all relevant tweets. Our searches captured approximately 4% of all relevant tweets; Twitter reported 420,329 relevant tweets during Game 1 of the World Series[3], and our dataset contained 17,538 tweets during the same time period. We address potential confounds from this sampling process in Section 5.2.

### 2.2 Entropy Computation

Estimating the linguistic information content of each tweet is a key task in this work. Social media text has been described as "bad language" (Eisenstein, 2013): It can be difficult to model due to its idiosyncratic abbreviations, typographic errors, and other non-standard forms. Relevant to our goal of assessing information content, it can also be difficult to create an appropriate training corpus for language models, since the vocabulary and composition of tweets of change rapidly (Eisenstein, 2013).

We attempted to minimize these difficulties in two ways. First, we estimated language models with domain-specific corpora. In particular, for tweets from each game we used a training corpus consisting of the tweets from all the other games. This training set provided a vocabulary and structure that was similar in topic and style to the test set. We removed all punctuation and emoji except word-initial @ and #, which refer to users and hashtags, respectively. Usernames were replaced with *[MENTION]* to reduce sparsity; hashtags were not altered, as these often function as words or phrases within the tweet's syntax. Words with fewer than 5 occurrences in the training corpus were marked as out-of-vocabulary items. We estimated trigram models using a modification of NLTK (Bird, 2006)[4] with Witten-Bell smoothing, and estimated per-word and total entropy for each tweet from these models.

Second, we included tweet length (in characters) as an alternative metric of information content (see Section 5.2). Unless information rate varies sys-

[1] `http://gd2.mlb.com/components/game/mlb/`

[2] We tested a series of potential offset times in case Twitter and MLB used different clocks or at-bats were not long enough to capture reactions. We did not adjust the times as there was no significant increase in the correlation between Leverage Index (Sect. 5.1) and tweet rate for these offsets.

[3] `http://Twitter.com/TwitterData/status/524972545930301440`

[4] Smoothing on n-gram models in NLTK can be inaccurate (see `http://github.com/nltk/nltk/issues/367`), so we used a modified version courtesy of B. C. Roy (personal communication).

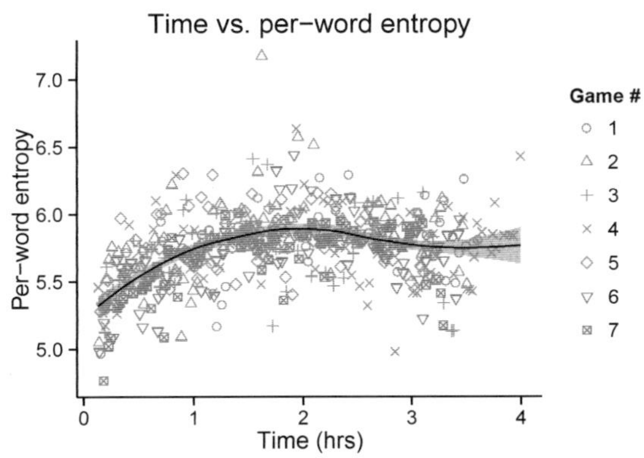


Figure 1: Per-word entropy increases with time for the first two hours of the games, then levels off and slightly declines. Color reflects in-game time; line shows loess fit with 95% confidence intervals.

tematically and substantially across tweets of different lengths—counter to existing results suggesting uniform information density operates at multiple structural levels (e.g., Qian and Jaeger 2009)—longer tweets will generally carry more information.

## 3 Gradual Changes in Information Rate

Our first analytic goal was to examine changes in the information content of tweets due to the long-term build-up of context in a shared event. We predicted that we would see similar developments in information structure as in more traditional conversational settings, even though there was no formal conversation or explicit linguistic history to develop common ground. Specifically, we predicted that the build-up of contextual information would cause the context-independent per-word entropy to rise over time, replicating the effect that has been observed across languages and genres (Genzel and Charniak, 2003; Qian and Jaeger, 2012).

Figure 1 shows evidence for changes in per-word entropy over the course of games. Per-word entropy rises throughout in the first two hours of each game, slowly levels off and finally declines slightly over time. This pattern is consistent with the constant entropy rate proposal of Genzel and Charniak 2002, and more specifically with the context decay model of Qian and Jaeger 2012.[5]

[5]A late decline in per-word entropy also appeared in Qian and Jaeger 2012's analysis of Swedish.

We used mixed-effects linear regression to quantify this relationship, using the time of an at-bat to predict both per-word and per-tweet entropy during the at-bat. Specifically, we used the logarithm of time as our fixed-effect predictor, per the context-decay models of Qian and Jaeger 2012. We added game-specific random intercepts and slopes of log-time to capture cross-game variation. This model showed significant positive effects of time on entropy, using likelihood-ratio tests for both models (per-word entropy: $.348 \pm .045; p < .001, \chi^2(3) = 104.6$, per-tweet entropy: $10.31 \pm 2.08; p = .001, \chi^2(3) = 74.65$).

We hypothesize that this finding—greater linguistic entropy for later tweets—is due to the accrual of common ground across users from shared non-linguistic information. As they watch more of the game, they share more referents and have stronger expectations about what aspects of the game will be discussed. This shared common ground licenses more complex language and more sophisticated linguistic references. Table 1 gives example tweets at different time points; as a game progresses, references can expand from generic references to the teams or series, to specific individuals and events, and eventually to sequences of events.

While this finding is consistent with previous work on the effect of context, it expands the definition of context. In previous work, the context came from explicit linguistic information built up through paragraphs in a formally-structured, written document. In the Twitter dataset, the context comes from real-world events during the games, as there is no canonical shared sequence of tweets that the tweeters can refer back to (indeed, two random users of the #Worldseries hashtag probably have relatively little Twitter context in common). In sum, contextual influences on entropy need not be explicitly linguistic, so long as discourse participants have reason to believe that the other participants share their knowledge.

## 4 Fast Changes In Information Content

Intuitively, after an exciting, game-changing event, tweets will be shorter and make more reference to the shared knowledge that this event has just happened. Such events should also generate more re-

| Minute | Tweet | Per-word entropy |
|---|---|---|
| 0 | It's finally here! #WorldSeries | 4.74 |
| 0 | #WorldSeries Play Ball | 4.96 |
| 0 | IDEA: @mayoredlee, #SanFrancisco can pledge to throw our @SFGiants an #OrangeOctober parade regardless of #WorldSeries outcome! #SFGiants | 8.20 |
| 12 | The guy with the Marlins sweater is behind home plate again. #worldseries | 4.26 |
| 12 | The Giants 3-0! #WorldSeries | 5.43 |
| 12 | Something about Hunter Pence really, really bothers me. Don't ask me what, cause I havent figured it out, but I don't like him. #WorldSeries | 6.64 |
| 73 | Three HORRIBLE at-bats (mixed in with Cain's walk) prevent Royals from breaking through in the third. #WorldSeries | 9.39 |
| 130 | As Hardy Boy #2, Joe Panik just pulled the mask off of Vargas and discovered it's Old Man Withers from down the street. #WorldSeries | 8.12 |
| 178 | #WorldSeries it's funny the non body names have a great hits. Frm now n on consider the Postseson as Cinderla run. No names needed, #MLB | 10.04 |

Table 1: Example tweets, grouped by minutes since the first pitch.

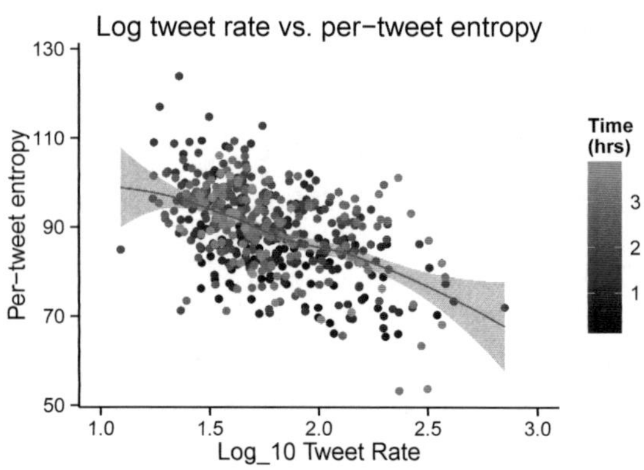


Figure 2: Total tweet entropy plotted against log tweet rate. Color reflects in-game time; line shows loess fit with 95% confidence intervals.

sponses, suggesting that the number of tweets per unit time can serve as a proxy for the information content of an event. This relationship is captured by Equation 2, in which unexpected events have large information content, so linguistic information content should be reduced correspondingly to maintain constant entropy. Our next set of analyses test this relationship.

The examples shown in Table 2 provide anecdotal evidence for the hypothesized relationship between in-game events and linguistic complexity, with examples of consecutive tweets from high-rate and low-rate at-bats, along with their information content. The top triplet comes from one of the highest-rate at-bats, in which Gregor Blanco committed a crucial error in the last inning of the last game. The bottom triplet comes from a low-rate at-bat, mid-game, with one team well ahead of the other; in this case, tweets all refer to different events as there is no single salient shared event.

We quantified the predicted relationship by again fitting a mixed-effect linear regression model, in this case using the logarithm of per-minute tweet rate as a predictor of tweet entropy. Given its significance in the previous model, we included log(time) as a control factor in this analysis, and added by-game random intercepts and slopes for log(rate) and log(time). The log of the tweet rate had a significant negative effect on per-word and per-tweet entropy by likelihood-ratio tests (per-word-entropy: $-.333 \pm .073; p < .001, \chi^2(4) = 59.37$, per-tweet-entropy: $-21.82 \pm 2.43; p < .001, \chi^2(4) = 194.6$).

Log(time) retained significance ($p < .001$) as a predictor for both entropy measures even when rate was accounted for, showing evidence for both

| Log rate | Tweet | Per-word entropy |
|---|---|---|
| 2.49 | Holy shitballs, @Royals! #WorldSeries #Game7 | 3.99 |
| 2.49 | Just when you thought the #WorldSeries was over.... #E8 | 4.76 |
| 2.49 | Fuck you, Blanco. #Giants #WorldSeries | 5.54 |
| 1.66 | Lets Go Giants!!! 5-0 #SFGiants #WorldSeries | 3.26 |
| 1.66 | The guy in Marlins gear behind home plate needs to escorted off property for annoying everybody. #WorldSeries #WhoDoesThat | 4.85 |
| 1.66 | I suppose I appreciate Bochy's "ASG" approach with Bumgarner. Of course, who are any of us to question him in late October? #WorldSeries | 7.42 |

Table 2: Example tweets, grouped by the per-minute tweet rate during each at-bat.

slow and fast adaptation occurring in the discourse. The effects are both in the predicted directions: Entropy increases with time as more informative context builds up, but decreases with tweet rate as more exciting events encourage less information-laden tweets.

## 5 Control Analyses

### 5.1 Non-Rate Metrics of Context

Since tweet rate is an organic reflection of the interest accrued by in-game events, it is an important metric for examining fast adaptation. Nevertheless, it could be confounded with other factors influencing tweet production. For instance, there is evidence that online interactions exhibit rational responses to information overload, the state where the amount of incoming information exceeds a user's ability to process it (Miller, 1956; Schoberth et al., 2003). Previous investigations into forum posting behavior have shown that users adapt to overload by posting shorter messages (Jones et al., 2001b; Jones et al., 2001a; Whittaker et al., 2003; Schoberth et al., 2003), and a similar result was found for the more explicitly conversational setting of IRC chat channels (Jones et al., 2008).

To show that the changes in information content are not merely reactions to increased tweet competition—that they have independent informational motivations—we need metrics of event importance and predictability that are not dependent on social media behavior. Luckily, baseball has a long history of statistical analysis, and as a result, there

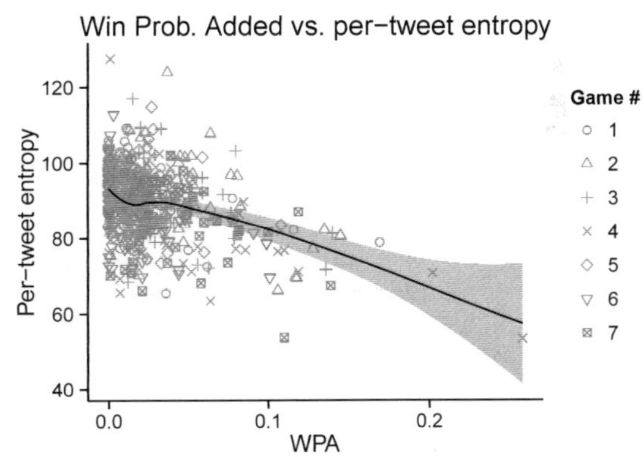


Figure 3: Total entropy decreases for at-bats with greater win probability changes. Loess curve fitting with 95% confidence intervals.

are independently-derived metrics that fit this bill. Two that are appropriate for this purpose are *Leverage Index* (LI)[6] and *Win Probability Added* (WPA) (Tango et al., 2007).

LI is an estimate of how critical an at-bat is to the outcome of the game. It is based on the difference in resultant win probability if the current batter gets a hit or an out, normalized by the mean change in win probability over all at-bats. 1 is the average LI, and greater LI indicates greater importance. LI, as a measure of the expected change in win probability, is similar to non-linguistic entropy term in Equation 2.

WPA depends on the result of an at-bat, and es-

[6]http://www.hardballtimes.com/crucial-situations/

timates how much the win probability changed as a result of what happened during the at-bat. WPA thus provides an estimate of how much information about the game outcome this at-bat has provided, conditioned on the current game context. These measures are well-correlated (Kendall's $\tau = .77$), since a high-LI at-bat's value comes from its ability to affect win probability.

As high LI or WPA values indicate an at-bat whose result has a large effect on the game, these metrics provide an estimate for non-linguistic informativity that is independent of medium-specific influences on tweet production. To assess their effects, we constructed four mixed-effects linear regression models, using LI and WPA to predict per-word and per-tweet entropy in all pairwise combinations (we built separate models for LI and WPA due to their high collinearity). Fixed- and by-game random-effects of log(time) and log(rate) were included as controls in all models; if there is an effect of LI or WPA beyond the effect of rate, this effect can be interpreted as evidence of speaker adaptation to non-linguistic information content.

Both LI and WPA had significant negative effects on per-tweet entropy (LI: $-1.52 \pm .43; p = .001, \chi^2(5) = 20.1$, WPA: $-2.27 \pm .40; p < .001, \chi^2(5) = 44.18$), over and above the effect of tweet rate. Per-word entropy did not show a significant effect of LI or WPA when rate was included as a control factor. Each was a significant factor on per-word entropy ($p = .008, p = .005$) when rate was not included as a control, though, suggesting that the explanatory power of these independent metrics may be subsumed in the more complex factor of tweet rate.

## 5.2 Speaker Normalization

A second alternative hypothesis for the observed behavioral changes with tweet rate is that they arise not from changes in the behavior of individuals but rather from a change in demographics. It is plausible that rising tweet rates come from an influx of new tweeters using the hashtag, and that these new tweeters simply produce shorter, less informative tweets in general. For instance, spambots often include trending hashtags in their spam tweets (Martinez-Romo and Araujo, 2013). To account for this, we treated the users whose tweets are in our corpus as

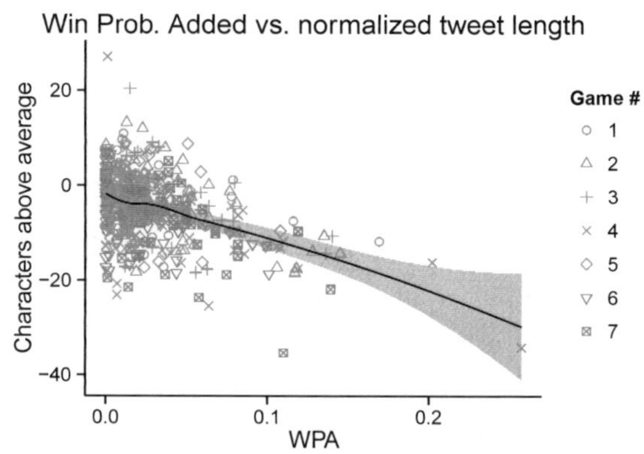


Figure 4: Speaker-normalized tweet length also decreases for at-bats with greater win probability changes. Loess curve fitting with 95% confidence intervals.

a "computational focus group" (Lin et al., 2013; Lin et al., 2014), and used the Twitter API to collected a further 100 tweets from each user outside the time-frame of the games. We used these tweets to estimate an average tweet length for each user, and subtracted this value from the length of their #worldseries tweets during the games.[7] If this baselined metric displays the same effects as shown above, we have reason to believe that users are in fact changing their individual behaviors in response to information factors, rather than that a demographic shift is mimicking a behavioral shift.

For this analysis, we created a mixed-effects model with WPA, log(rate) and log(time) as predictors of tweet length. All three factors were significant (WPA: $-1.64 \pm .36; p < .001, \chi^2(5) = 72.3$; log(rate): $-6.15 \pm .47; p < .001, \chi^2(5) = 303.6$; log(time): $.82 \pm .40; p = .001, \chi^2(5) = 20.6$). We then created a second model using the same factors to predict the mean change in tweet length from the baseline length. Again, all three factors were significant (WPA: $-2.01 \pm .29; p < .001, \chi^2(5) = 70.2$; log(rate): $-5.10 \pm .49; p < .001, \chi^2(5) = 252.6$; log(time): $.61 \pm .35; p = .016, \chi^2(5) = 14.0$). By ruling out demographic shifts (e.g., an influx of terser tweeters), this analysis provides additional support for the idea that tweeters indeed shift their behavior in response to in-game information.

[7] Note that these analyses are conducted over tweet length, rather than total entropy, as there was no obvious way of normalizing entropy by speaker.

## 6 Discussion

We investigated the hypothesis that speakers optimize their language production so as to approximate *uniform information density*, a signature of efficient communication through a noisy channel (Shannon, 1948; Levy and Jaeger, 2007). Previous work had observed indirect evidence for UID via increases in linguistic complexity (which were hypothesized to reflect increasing discourse/contextual knowledge), but this work neither measured contextual information directly nor included non-linguistic measures of context (Genzel and Charniak, 2002; Genzel and Charniak, 2003; Qian and Jaeger, 2012). Our current work takes a first step towards addressing these issues by using microblog texts around shared events (baseball games) as a case study in which a known context can be characterized more precisely. With this approach, we find systematic differences in information rate and total information content as a function of nonlinguistic factors.

We successfully replicated the effect found in previous work: a gradual increase in entropy rate over the course of individual baseball games. But in addition to this effect, we found a striking pattern of short-timescale changes in total message entropy (reflected in the changing lengths of messages). When in-game events were exciting, unpredictable, and outcome-relevant (hence, highly informative), message length and total entropy went down. This regularity suggests that Twitter users were regulating the information content of their messages relative to the total communicative content of the context more broadly, a prediction that can be derived directly from the UID model.

Our work highlights the importance of non-linguistic context for the informational content of language. This relationship is widely acknowledged in theories of pragmatic communication (Grice, 1975; Sperber and Wilson, 1986; Clark, 1996; Frank and Goodman, 2012), but has been largely absent in information-theoretic treatments of linguistic complexity. The omission of this information has largely been for pragmatic, rather than theoretical, reasons: As Genzel and Charniak 2002 note, it is typically very difficult to compute semantic—let alone non-linguistic—information content. Our work suggests that internet communications surrounding shared media events may be a promising source of grounded language use where context can be quantified more effectively due to the existence of substantial metadata.

A growing literature suggests that the information content of language is the critical variable for understanding processing difficulty in language comprehension (Levy, 2008; Demberg and Keller, 2008; Boston et al., 2008; Smith and Levy, 2013). Under surprisal theory (Hale, 2001; Levy, 2008), the overall predictability of individual elements of language is assumed to be due to a predictive model of its likelihood in the current context. Given this model of processing difficulty, our work here makes a strong prediction: that the information processing difficulty of a word or sentence should track with its total information content (including its relationship to the non-linguistic context), rather than its linguistic information content alone. Some preliminary evidence supports this idea. In a study of the processing complexity of negative utterances, Nordmeyer and Frank 2014 found that the processing cost of negation was predicted by the surprisal of encountering the negation in a particular pragmatic context. But future work should test this hypothesis across a wider variety of structures and contexts.

In sum, our work contributes to the growing body of evidence in favor of the UID hypothesis. The mechanisms underlying the tendency to regulate information content are still unknown, however. While UID would follow from a strong form of *audience design*, in which speakers explicitly consider the processing difficulty of different content (Clark, 1996), the UID hypothesis could also emerge from simpler production processes. Untangling these possibilities will not be trivial. Regardless of the resolution of this issue, however, UID appears to be an important descriptive tool in capturing how speakers make production choices.

## Acknowledgments

We gratefully acknowledge the support of ONR Grant N00014-13-1-0287.

## References


Matthew Aylett and Alice Turk. 2004. The smooth signal redundancy hypothesis: A functional explanation for relationships between redundancy, prosodic prominence, and duration in spontaneous speech. *Language and Speech*, 47(1):31–56.

Matthew Aylett and Alice Turk. 2006. Language redundancy predicts syllabic duration and the spectral characteristics of vocalic syllable nuclei. *The Journal of the Acoustical Society of America*, 119(5):3048–3058.

Alan Bell, Daniel Jurafsky, Eric Fosler-Lussier, Cynthia Girand, Michelle Gregory, and Daniel Gildea. 2003. Effects of disfluencies, predictability, and utterance position on word form variation in English conversation. *The Journal of the Acoustical Society of America*, 113(2):1001–1024.

Steven Bird. 2006. NLTK: the natural language toolkit. In *Proceedings of the COLING/ACL on Interactive presentation sessions*, pages 69–72. Association for Computational Linguistics.

Marisa Boston, John Hale, Reinhold Kliegl, Umesh Patil, and Shravan Vasishth. 2008. Parsing costs as predictors of reading difficulty: An evaluation using the potsdam sentence corpus. *Journal of Eye Movement Research*, 2(1):1–12.

Susan E Brennan and Herbert H Clark. 1996. Conceptual pacts and lexical choice in conversation. *Journal of Experimental Psychology: Learning, Memory, and Cognition*, 22(6):1482.

Herbert H Clark. 1996. *Using language*, volume 1996. Cambridge University Press Cambridge.

Robert Dale and Ehud Reiter. 1995. Computational interpretations of the Gricean maxims in the generation of referring expressions. *Cognitive Science*, 19(2):233–263.

Vera Demberg and Frank Keller. 2008. Data from eye-tracking corpora as evidence for theories of syntactic processing complexity. *Cognition*, 109(2):193–210.

Gabriel Doyle. 2014. Mapping dialectal variation by querying social media. In *Proceedings of the European Chapter of the Association for Computational Linguistics*.

Jacob Eisenstein. 2013. What to do about bad language on the internet. In *Proceedings of the 2013 Conference of the North American Chapter of the Association for Computational Linguistics: Human Language Technologies*, pages 359–369.

Michael C Frank and Noah D Goodman. 2012. Predicting pragmatic reasoning in language games. *Science*, 336(6084):998–998.

Austin Frank and T Florian Jaeger. 2008. Speaking rationally: Uniform information density as an optimal strategy for language production. In *Proceedings of the 30th Annual Meeting of the Cognitive Science Society*, pages 933–938. Cognitive Science Society Washington, DC.

Dmitriy Genzel and Eugene Charniak. 2002. Entropy rate constancy in text. In *Proceedings of the 40th Annual Meeting of the Association for Computational Linguistics*, pages 199–206. Association for Computational Linguistics.

Dmitriy Genzel and Eugene Charniak. 2003. Variation of entropy and parse trees of sentences as a function of the sentence number. In *Proceedings of the 2003 Conference on Empirical Methods in Natural Language Processing*, pages 65–72. Association for Computational Linguistics.

H Paul Grice. 1975. Logic and conversation. *Syntax and Semantics*, 3:41–58.

John Hale. 2001. A probabilistic earley parser as a psycholinguistic model. In *Proceedings of the 2nd Meeting of the North American Chapter of the Association for Computational Linguistics on Language Technologies*, pages 1–8. Association for Computational Linguistics.

T Florian Jaeger. 2010. Redundancy and reduction: Speakers manage syntactic information density. *Cognitive Psychology*, 61(1):23–62.

Quentin Jones, Gilad Ravid, and Sheizaf Rafaeli. 2001a. Empirical evidence for information overload in mass interaction. In *CHI'01 Extended Abstracts on Human Factors in Computing Systems*, pages 177–178. ACM.

Quentin Jones, Gilad Ravid, and Sheizaf Rafaeli. 2001b. Information overload and virtual public discourse boundaries. In *INTERACT'01: 13th International Conference on Human-Computer Interaction*, page 43. IOS Press.

Quentin Jones, Mihai Moldovan, Daphne Raban, and Brian Butler. 2008. Empirical evidence of information overload constraining chat channel community interactions. In *Proceedings of the 2008 ACM Conference on Computer Supported Cooperative Work*, pages 323–332. ACM.

Roger Levy and T Florian Jaeger. 2007. Speakers optimize information density through syntactic reduction. In *Advances in Neural Information Processing Systems*, pages 849–856.

Roger Levy. 2008. Expectation-based syntactic comprehension. *Cognition*, 106(3):1126–1177.

Yu-Ru Lin, Drew Margolin, Brian Keegan, and David Lazer. 2013. Voices of victory: A computational focus group framework for tracking opinion shift in real time. In *Proceedings of the 22nd international conference on World Wide Web*, pages 737–748. International World Wide Web Conferences Steering Committee.

Yu-Ru Lin, Brian Keegan, Drew Margolin, and David Lazer. 2014. Rising tides or rising stars?: Dynamics of shared attention on twitter during media events. *PLoS One*, 9(5):e94093.

Juan Martinez-Romo and Lourdes Araujo. 2013. Detecting malicious tweets in trending topics using a statistical analysis of language. *Expert Systems with Applications*, 40(8):2992–3000.

Charles Metzing and Susan E Brennan. 2003. When conceptual pacts are broken: Partner-specific effects on the comprehension of referring expressions. *Journal of Memory and Language*, 49(2):201–213.

George A Miller. 1956. The magical number seven, plus or minus two: some limits on our capacity for processing information. *Psychological Review*, 63(2):81.

Ann E Nordmeyer and Michael C Frank. 2014. A pragmatic account of the processing of negative sentences. In *Proceedings of the 36th Annual Meeting of the Cognitive Science Society*.

Ting Qian and T Florian Jaeger. 2009. Evidence for efficient language production in Chinese. In *Proceedings of the 31st Annual Meeting of the Cognitive Science Society*.

Ting Qian and T Florian Jaeger. 2012. Cue effectiveness in communicatively efficient discourse production. *Cognitive Science*, 36(7):1312–1336.

Thomas Schoberth, Jennifer Preece, and Armin Heinzl. 2003. Online communities: A longitudinal analysis of communication activities. In *Proceedings of the 36th Annual Hawaii International Conference on System Sciences*, pages 10–18. IEEE.

Julie C Sedivy, Michael K Tanenhaus, Craig G Chambers, and Gregory N Carlson. 1999. Achieving incremental semantic interpretation through contextual representation. *Cognition*, 71(2):109–147.

Claude E Shannon. 1948. Bell system tech. j. 27 (1948) 379; ce shannon. *Bell System Tech. J*, 27:623.

Nathaniel J Smith and Roger Levy. 2013. The effect of word predictability on reading time is logarithmic. *Cognition*, 128(3):302–319.

Dan Sperber and Deirdre Wilson. 1986. *Relevance: Communication and Cognition*. Harvard University Press, Cambridge, MA.

Tom M Tango, Mitchel G Lichtman, and Andrew E Dolphin. 2007. *The book: Playing the percentages in baseball*. Potomac Books, Inc.

Steve Whittaker, Loen Terveen, Will Hill, and Lynn Cherny. 2003. The dynamics of mass interaction. In *From Usenet to CoWebs*, pages 79–91. Springer.

# Hierarchic syntax improves reading time prediction

**Marten van Schijndel** **William Schuler**
Department of Linguistics
The Ohio State University
{vanschm,schuler}@ling.osu.edu

## Abstract

Previous work has debated whether humans make use of hierarchic syntax when processing language (Frank and Bod, 2011; Fossum and Levy, 2012). This paper uses an eye-tracking corpus to demonstrate that hierarchic syntax significantly improves reading time prediction over a strong $n$-gram baseline. This study shows that an interpolated 5-gram baseline can be made stronger by combining $n$-gram statistics over entire eye-tracking regions rather than simply using the last $n$-gram in each region, but basic hierarchic syntactic measures are still able to achieve significant improvements over this improved baseline.

## 1 Introduction

In NLP, a concern exists that models of hierarchic syntax may be increasingly used exclusively to compensate for $n$-gram sparsity (Lease et al., 2006). In the context of psycholinguistic modeling, Frank and Bod (2011) find that hierarchic measures of syntactic processing are not as good at predicting reading times as sequential part-of-speech-based models of processing.[1] Fossum and Levy (2012) follow up on this finding and show that, when better $n$-gram information is present in the models, measures of hierarchic syntactic processing cost (PCFG surprisal; Hale, 2001; Levy, 2008) are as good at predicting reading times as the sequential models presented by Frank and Bod.

The present study builds on this finding by showing that cumulative $n$-gram probabilities significantly improve an $n$-gram baseline to better capture sequential frequency statistics. Further, this study shows that measures of hierarchic structural frequencies (as captured by PCFG surprisal) significantly improve reading time predictions over that improved sequential baseline.

First, this work defines a stronger $n$-gram baseline than that used in previous studies by replacing a bigram baseline computed from 101 million words with an interpolated 5-gram baseline computed over 2.96 billion words. Second, while previous work has used $n$-grams from the end of each eye-movement region to model reading times in that region, this paper finds that such models can be significantly improved by combining $n$-gram statistics over the entire region (Section 3). Even when this improved baseline is combined with a standard $n$-gram baseline, this paper demonstrates that PCFG surprisal is a significant predictor of reading times (Section 4). This paper also applies region accumulation to total surprisal and finds that it is not significantly better than non-accumulated total surprisal. In fact, cumulative surprisal is shown not to be a significant predictor of reading times at all when a cumulative $n$-gram factor is included in the baseline. Finally, this paper compares two different models of hierarchic syntax: the Penn Treebank (PTB) representation (Marcus et al., 1993) and the psycholinguistically-motivated Nguyen et al. (2012) Generalized Categorial Grammar (GCG). Each model of syntax is shown to provide orthogonal improvements to reading time predictions (Section 5).

[1] Frank and Bod (2011) find that hierarchic measures significantly improve the descriptive linguistic accuracy of models but that such measures are unable to improve upon a strong linear baseline when predicting reading times.



*Human Language Technologies: The 2015 Annual Conference of the North American Chapter of the ACL*, pages 1597–1605,
Denver, Colorado, May 31 – June 5, 2015. 

| Factors | Durations | |
|---|---|---|
| | $R_{w4}^{w4}$ | $R_{w5}^{w6}$ |
| Bigram | $P(w_4 \mid w_3)$ | $P(w_6 \mid w_5)$ |
| Cumu-Bigram | $P(w_4 \mid w_3)$ | $P(w_6 \mid w_5) \cdot P(w_5 \mid w_4)$ |

Table 1: Bigram factors and their predictions of reading times in example eye-tracking regions. $w_i$ represents word i. $R_{wi}^{wj}$ represents the region from $w_i$ to $w_j$ (inclusive).

Bigram: The red[1] apple that <u>the</u> [girl][2] ate ...

Cumu-Bigram: The <u>red</u>[1] [<u>apple</u>] [<u>that</u>] [<u>the</u>] [girl][2] ate

[X]: bigram targets <u>X</u>: bigram conditions

Table 2: Influences on bigram factor predictions of reading times on *girl* following fixation on *red*.

## 2 Modeling

This study fits models to reading times from the Dundee corpus (Kennedy et al., 2003), which consists of eye-tracking data from 10 subjects who read 2388 sentences of news text from the newspaper, *The Independent*. Prior to using this corpus for evaluations, the first and last fixation of each sentence and of each line are filtered out to avoid potentially confounding wrap-up effects. Additionally, all fixations after saccades (eye movements) over more than 4 words are removed to avoid confounds with eye-tracker track-loss.

All evaluations are done with linear mixed effects models using lme4 (version 1.1-7; Bates et al., 2014).[2] There are two dependent reading time variables of interest in this study: first pass durations and go-past durations. During reading, a person's eye can jump over multiple words each time it moves, this study refers to that span of words as a *region*. First pass durations measure elapsed time until a person's eye leaves a given region. Go-past durations measure elapsed time until a person's eye moves further in the text. For example, in the fixation sequence: word 4, word 6, word 3, word 7, the first region would be from word 4 to word 6 and the second region would be from word 6 to word 7. The first pass duration for the first region would consist of the time fixated on word 6 before leaving the region for word 3, while the go-past duration would consist of the duration from the fixation of word 6 until the fixation of word 7. Separate models are fit to each centered dependent variable.

There are a number of independent variables in all evaluations in this study: sentence position (sentpos), word length (wlen), region length in words (rlen), whether the previous word was fixated (prevfix), and basic 5-gram log probability of the current word given the preceding context (5-gram). All independent predictors are centered and scaled before being added to each model. The 5-gram probabilities are interpolated 5-grams computed over the Gigaword 4.0 corpus (Graff and Cieri, 2003) using KenLM (Heafield et al., 2013). Gigaword 4.0 consists of around 2.96 billion words from around 4 million English newswire documents, which provides appropriate *n*-gram statistics since the Dundee corpus is also English news text.

Each mixed effects model contains random intercepts for subject and word, and random by-subject slopes for all fixed effects. Since the following evaluations use ablative testing to determine whether a fixed effect significantly improves the fit of a model compared to a model without that fixed effect, all models in a given evaluation include random slopes for all fixed effects used in that evaluation, even if the fixed effect is absent from that particular model.

## 3 A Cumulative *N*-gram Predictor

Since *n*-gram frequencies can have such a dramatic impact on the contribution of hierarchic syntax, this study tests whether *n*-gram factors can be improved. Models include a measure of *n*-gram frequencies to capture the rarity of observed sequences. Readers fixate longer on less predictable lexemes than on more predictable lexemes, but the predictability of a lexeme depends on the preceding context. Therefore, it is common for psycholinguistic models to include a measure of *n*-gram predictability for each fixated word conditioned on its context, but unless probabilities for words between fixations are also included, the probabilities used in this calculation are

[2]The models are fit using both the default *bobyqa* and the gradient *nlminb* algorithms to work around convergence issues.

| Model | First Pass | | Go-Past | |
|---|---|---|---|---|
| | Log-Likelihood | AIC | Log-Likelihood | AIC |
| Baseline | $-1212399$ | 2424868 | $-1261582$ | 2523234 |
| Base+$N$-gram | $-1212396^{\dagger}$ | 2424864 | $-1261577^{*}$ | 2523226 |
| Base+Cumu-$N$-gram | $-1212392^{*}$ | 2424856 | $-1261576^{*}$ | 2523224 |
| Base+Both | $-1212387^{*}$ | 2424848 | $-1261570^{*}$ | 2523214 |

Baseline random slopes: sentpos, wlen, rlen, prevfix, 5-gram, cumu-5-gram
Baseline fixed effects: sentpos, wlen, rlen, prevfix

Table 3: Goodness of fit of $N$-gram models to reading times.[3] Significance testing was done between each model and the models in the section above it. Significance for Base+Both applies to improvement over each of the $n$-gram models. $^{\dagger}$ $p < .05$ $^{*}$ $p < .01$

not probabilities of complete word sequences and may miss words that are parafovially previewed or simply inferred.

For example, in Table 1, the standard bigram factor (top line) predicts that the reading time of the region that ends with word 6 depends on word 5, but the probability of word 5 given its context is never included in the model, so an improbable transition between words 4 and 5 would not be caught. This might allow another factor to inappropriately receive credit for an extra long fixation on word 6. Instead, a better model would include the probabilities of every word in the sequence since that is the information that will need to be processed by the reader. Using log-probabilities, a *cumulative* $n$-gram factor can be created simply by summing the log probabilities over each region (comparable to the last line of Table 1). The cumulative $n$-gram predictor is able to account for the frequency of the entire lexical sequence and so should provide a better reading time predictor than the standard fixation-only $n$-gram predictor (see Table 2 for an example).

For this initial evaluation (Table 3), the baseline omits the fixed $n$-gram factor. Instead, a model is constructed without any fixed effects for $n$-gram. Then, the same model is fit to reading times after adding just a fixed effect for $n$-gram and after adding just a fixed effect for cumulative $n$-gram. Finally, a model is fit with both the cumulative and non-cumulative $n$-gram factors as fixed effects.[4] Significance between the models is determined using likelihood ratio testing.[5]

Table 3 shows that both $n$-gram factors significantly improve the fit of the model and the final line shows that each factor provides a significant orthogonal improvement. Both $n$-gram factors will therefore be included as fixed effects and as by-subject random slopes in the baselines of the remaining evaluations in this study.

## 4 Hierarchic Syntax Predictors

This section tests the main hypothesis of this study: that hierarchic syntactic processing is a significant contributor to reading times. For the purposes of this evaluation, total PCFG surprisal (Hale, 2001; Levy, 2008; Roark et al., 2009) will be used as a measure of hierarchic syntactic processing. Specifically, PCFG surprisal will be calculated using the van Schijndel et al. (2013a) incremental parser trained on sections 02-21 of the Wall Street Journal section of the Penn Treebank (Marcus et al., 1993) using 5 iterations of split-merge (Petrov et al., 2006) and a beam width of 5000.

[3]Log-likelihood values are rounded to the nearest whole number, which is why the difference between Base and Base+Both can be larger than the cumulative difference between Base and the other two models.

[4]To ensure effects are not driven by individual subject differences, by-subject random slopes for both predictors of interest are included in the baseline. This practice is repeated throughout this study.

[5]Twice the log-likelihood difference of two nested models can be approximated by a $\chi^2$ distribution with degrees of freedom equal to the difference in degrees of freedom of the models in question. The probability of obtaining a given log-likelihood difference $D$ between the two models is therefore analogous to $P(2 \cdot D)$ under the corresponding $\chi^2$ distribution.

| Factors | Durations | |
|---|---|---|
| | $R_{w4}^{w4}$ | $R_{w5}^{w6}$ |
| surp | $-\log \mathrm{P}(w_4 \mid T_3)$ | $-\log \mathrm{P}(w_6 \mid T_5)$ |
| cumusurp | $-\log \mathrm{P}(w_4 \mid T_3)$ | $\sum_{i=5}^{6} -\log \mathrm{P}(w_i \mid T_{i-1})$ |

Table 4: PCFG surprisal factors and their predictions of reading times in example eye-tracking regions. $w_i$ represents word i. $T_i$ represents the set of trees that can span from $w_1$ to $w_i$. $R_{wi}^{wj}$ represents the region from $w_i$ to $w_j$ (inclusive).

### 4.1 Surprisal

PCFG surprisal (Hale, 2001; Levy, 2008) is a measure of incremental hierarchic syntactic processing. It reflects the information gained by observing a given word in a given context. In PCFG surprisal calculations, *context* is usually taken to refer to the preceding words in the sentence and their underlying syntactic structure. The PCFG surprisal $S(w_i)$ of a word at position $i$ may be calculated as:

$$S(w_i) = \sum_{t \in T_{i-1}} -\log \mathrm{P}(w_i \mid t) \qquad (1)$$

where $T_i$ represents the set of syntactic structures that can span from $w_1$ to $w_i$. PCFG surprisal in psycholinguistic models captures the influence of incremental hierarchic context when processing a given word.

For space considerations, in Table 4, the summation over $T_{i-1}$ is notationally implicit:

$$S(w_i) = -\log \mathrm{P}(w_i \mid T_{i-1}) \qquad (2)$$

### 4.2 Evaluation

As in the previous section, a baseline model is fit to reading times without a fixed effect for surprisal, then surprisal is added as a fixed effect and significance of the fixed effect is determined using a likelihood ratio test with the baseline. The results (Table 5) show that PCFG surprisal is a significant predictor of both first pass and go-past durations even over a strong baseline including both types of $n$-gram factors.

The preceding section showed that applying region accumulation to an $n$-gram factor improves a model's fit to reading times. Previous work suggests region accumulation might improve the fit of syntactic factors to reading times (van Schijndel and Schuler, 2013; van Schijndel et al., 2013b), but the baselines in those studies only included unigram and bigram statistics and did not apply region accumulation to the $n$-gram models. It does make intuitive sense that region accumulation would help improve the fit of total PCFG surprisal for the same reason accumulating $n$-grams helps. For an example, see Table 4. A non-cumulative total PCFG surprisal factor (top line) would predict that duration of region $R_{w5}^{w6}$ depends on $T_5$ (the set of trees that can span from $w_1$ to $w_5$), but the probability of generating the prefix of $T_5$ is never fully calculated by this factor. As with cumulative $n$-grams, cumulative PCFG surprisal of a region can be calculated by simply summing the PCFG surprisal of each word in the region.

When tested, however, the present work does not find any improvement from region accumulation of PCFG surprisal when stronger $n$-gram factors are also included (Table 5, Row 2), suggesting that the improvement in previous studies may have been due to latent $n$-gram information captured by cumulative PCFG surprisal. This finding is interesting because it suggests non-local hierarchic structure does not significantly influence reading times. The next section explores this hypothesis further by testing the fit of a hierarchic syntactic formalism whose strength lies in modeling long-distance dependencies.

## 5 Grammar Formalism Comparison

So far, this study has tried to allay previous concerns that models of hierarchic syntax may just be accounting for the sparsity of $n$-gram statistics (Charniak et al., 2006; Frank and Bod, 2011). This section investigates whether a representation of hierarchic syntax that preserves long-distance dependencies can improve reading time predictions over a hierarchic representation based on the Penn Treebank which discards long-distance dependencies. This evaluation compares total PCFG surprisal as calculated by the original Penn Treebank grammar to total PCFG surprisal calculated by the Nguyen et al. (2012) Generalized Categorial Grammar (GCG).

### 5.1 GCG

A GCG has a category set $C$, which consists of a set of primitive category types $U$, typically labeled

| Model | First Pass | | Go-Past | |
|---|---|---|---|---|
| | Log-Likelihood | AIC | Log-Likelihood | AIC |
| Baseline | −1212260 | 2424627 | −1261488 | 2523084 |
| Base+Surp | −1212253* | 2424617 | −1261481* | 2523072 |
| Base+CumuSurp | −1212259 | 2424627 | −1261487 | 2523085 |
| Base+Both | −1212253* | 2424619 | −1261481* | 2523073 |

Baseline random slopes: sentpos, wlen, rlen, prevfix, 5-gram, cumu-5-gram, surp, cumusurp
Baseline fixed effects: sentpos, wlen, rlen, prevfix, 5-gram, cumu-5-gram

Table 5: Goodness of fit of hierarchic syntax models to reading times. Significance testing was done between each model and the models in the section above it. Significance for Base+Both applies only to improvement over the CumuSurp model. * $p < .01$

with the part of speech of the head of a category (e.g. **V**, **N**, **A**, etc., for phrases or clauses headed by verbs, nouns, adjectives, etc.), followed by one or more unsatisfied dependencies, each consisting of an operator (**-a** and **-b** for adjacent argument dependencies preceding and following a head, **-c** and **-d** for adjacent conjunct dependencies preceding and following a head, **-g** for filler-gap dependencies, **-r** for relative pronoun dependencies, and some others), followed by a dependent category type. For example, the category for a transitive verb would be **V-aN-bN**, since it is headed by a verb and has unsatisfied dependencies to satisfied noun-headed categories preceding and following it (for the subject and direct object noun phrase, respectively).

As in other categorial grammars, inference rules for local argument attachment apply functors of category $c\text{-}\mathbf{a}d$ or $c\text{-}\mathbf{b}d$ to initial or final arguments of category $d$:

$$d \;\; c\text{-}\mathbf{a}d \Rightarrow c \quad \text{(Aa)}$$

$$c\text{-}\mathbf{b}d \;\; d \Rightarrow c \quad \text{(Ab)}$$

However, the Nguyen et al. (2012) GCG uses distinguished inference rules for modifier attachment, which allows modifier categories to be consolidated with categories for modifiers in other contexts (preverbal, post-verbal, etc.), and with certain predicative categories. This allows derivations in the training corpus involving different modifier types to also be consolidated, which increases the power of the extracted statistics. Inference rules for modifier attachment apply initial or final modifiers of category $u\text{-}\mathbf{a}d$ to modificands of category $c$, for $u \in U$ and $c, d \in C$:

$$u\text{-}\mathbf{a}d \;\; c \Rightarrow c \quad \text{(Ma)}$$

$$c \;\; u\text{-}\mathbf{a}d \Rightarrow c \quad \text{(Mb)}$$

The Nguyen et al. (2012) GCG also uses distinguished inference rules to introduce, propagate, and bind missing non-local arguments, similar to the gap or slash rules of Generalized Phrase Structure Grammar (Gazdar et al., 1985) and Head-driven Phrase Structure Grammar (Pollard and Sag, 1994). Inference rules for gap attachment hypothesize gaps as initial arguments, final arguments, or modifiers, for $c, d \in C$:

$$c\text{-}\mathbf{a}d \Rightarrow c\text{-}\mathbf{g}d \quad \text{(Ga)}$$

$$c\text{-}\mathbf{b}d \Rightarrow c\text{-}\mathbf{g}d \quad \text{(Gb)}$$

$$c \Rightarrow c\text{-}\mathbf{g}d \quad \text{(Gc)}$$

Non-local arguments, using non-local operator and argument category $\psi \in \{\text{-}\mathbf{g}, \text{-}\mathbf{h}, \text{-}\mathbf{i}, \text{-}\mathbf{r}\} \times C$, are then propagated to the consequent from all possible combinations of antecedents. For each rule $d \;\; e \Rightarrow c \in \{\text{Aa–b,Ma–b}\}$ :

$$d \;\; e\psi \Rightarrow c\psi \quad \text{(Ac–d,Mc–d)}$$

$$d\psi \;\; e \Rightarrow c\psi \quad \text{(Ae–f,Me–f)}$$

$$d\psi \;\; e\psi \Rightarrow c\psi \quad \text{(Ag–h,Mg–h)}$$

In order to consolidate relative and interrogative pronouns in different pied-piping contexts into just two reusable categories, this grammar uses distinguished inference rules for relative and interrogative pronouns as well as tough constructions (e.g. *this*

| Model | First Pass | | Go-Past | |
|---|---|---|---|---|
| | Log-Likelihood | AIC | Log-Likelihood | AIC |
| Baseline | −1212242 | 2424592 | −1261474 | 2523055 |
| Base+PTB | −1212239* | 2424587 | −1261468* | 2523047 |
| Base+GCG | −1212239† | 2424589 | −1261470* | 2523050 |
| Base+Both | −1212235† | 2424583 | −1261465* | 2523043 |

Baseline random slopes: sentpos, wlen, rlen, prevfix, 5-gram, cumu-5-gram, surp-GCG, surp-PTB
Baseline fixed effects: sentpos, wlen, rlen, prevfix, 5-gram, cumu-5-gram

Table 6: Goodness of fit of models with differing syntactic calculations to reading times. Significance testing was done between each model and the models in the section above it. Base+Both first pass significance applies to improvement over PTB ($p < .05$) and to improvement over GCG ($p < .01$), Base+Both go-past significance applies to improvement over each independent model. † $p < .05$ * $p < .01$

*bread is easy to cut*), which introduce clauses with gap dependencies, for $c, d, e \in C$, $\psi \in \{\textbf{-g}\} \times C$:

$$d\textbf{-i}e \;\; c\textbf{-g}d \Rightarrow c\textbf{-i}e \qquad \text{(Fa)}$$

$$d\textbf{-r}e \;\; c\textbf{-g}d \Rightarrow c\textbf{-r}e \qquad \text{(Fb)}$$

$$c\textbf{-b}(d\psi) \;\; d\psi \Rightarrow c \qquad \text{(Fc)}$$

Also, inference rules for relative pronoun attachment apply pronominal relative clauses of category $c\textbf{-r}d$ to modificands of category $e$:

$$e \;\; c\textbf{-r}d \Rightarrow e \qquad \text{(R)}$$

Because of its richer set of language-specific inference rules, the GCG grammar annotated by Nguyen et al. (2012) does not require different categories for words like *which* in different pied-piping contexts:

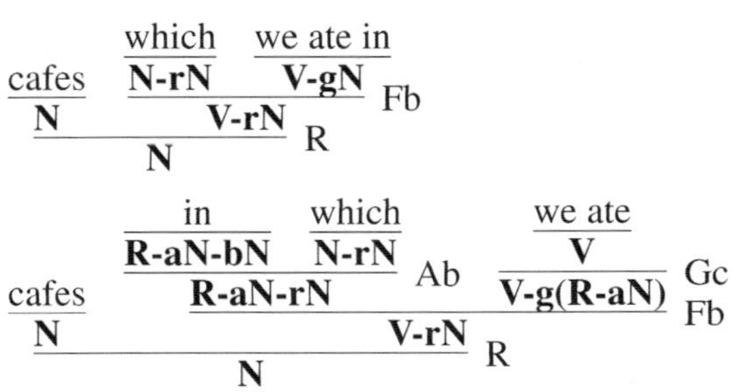


## 5.2 Evaluation

Following van Schijndel et al. (2013b), the GCG calculation of PCFG surprisal comes from a GCG-reannotated version of the Penn Treebank whose grammar rules have undergone 3 iterations of the split-merge algorithm (Petrov et al., 2006). A $k$-best beam with a width of 5000 is used in order to be comparable to the PTB calculation.

Significance testing is done as in the preceding evaluations: a baseline model is fit to reading times, each PCFG surprisal factor is added independently to the baseline, and both PCFG surprisal factors are added concurrently to the baseline. Each model is compared to the next simpler models using likelihood ratio tests.

The results (Table 6) show that GCG PCFG surprisal is a significant predictor of reading times even in the presence of the stronger $n$-gram baseline. Moreover, both PTB and GCG PCFG surprisal significantly improve reading time predictions even when the other PCFG surprisal measure is also included. This suggests that each is contributing something the other is not. Since the GCG grammar is derived from an automatically reannotated version of the Penn Treebank, there may be errors in the GCG annotation which cause errors in the estimates of underlying GCG structure. Since the PTB grammar is manually annotated by experts, the PTB grammar may be receiving credit for correct structural prediction in cases where GCG's estimates are incorrect. However, it seems likely that GCG may be providing a better fit in cases of long-distance dependencies because such relations are omitted from the PTB grammar.

A follow-up evaluation (not shown here) using the experimental design from Section 4 but using GCG PCFG surprisal rather than PTB PCFG surprisal revealed that cumulative PCFG surprisal is still not a significant predictor when calculated using GCG. The failure of cumulative PCFG surprisal to improve over basic GCG PCFG surprisal could be expected

| Predictor | First Pass | | Go-Past | |
|---|---|---|---|---|
| | coef | t value | coef | t value |
| sentpos | −2.47 | −3.59 | −2.82 | −3.38 |
| wlen | 25.90 | 8.67 | 28.98 | 9.97 |
| prevfix | −30.16 | −7.81 | −37.42 | −11.49 |
| $n$-gram | −2.39 | −1.81 | −6.70 | −3.36 |
| cumu-$n$-gram | −14.69 | −7.36 | −11.68 | −5.01 |
| rlen | −5.67 | −1.31 | −12.51 | −2.59 |
| surp-GCG | 4.97 | 2.87 | 5.74 | 2.73 |
| surp-PTB | 4.20 | 3.23 | 4.85 | 3.29 |

Table 7: Fixed effect predictor coefficients for Base+PTB+GCG model.

since a strength of GCG is in enabling non-local decisions on a local basis (by propagating non-local decisions into the category labels), so any non-local advantage cumulative PCFG surprisal might confer is already compressed into the GCG categories.

The results of this evaluation suggest that reading times are mostly affected by local hierarchic structure, but the fact that GCG PCFG surprisal is able to provide a significant fit even in the presence of the PTB PCFG surprisal predictor suggests that some non-local information affects reading times. In particular, while this evaluation showed that accumulated syntactic context is not generally a good predictor of reading times, some or all of the non-local information contained in the GCG categories is used by readers and so influences reading time durations over the local structural information reflected in the PTB PCFG surprisal measure.

## 6 Discussion

The finding that the hierarchic grammars orthogonally improve reading time predictions suggests that hierarchic structural information has a significant influence on reading times. Since both the PTB and GCG calculations of surprisal contain sequential information (e.g., of part-of-speech tags), if the effect in this study was driven by purely sequential information as suggested by Frank and Bod (2011), one might expect either the PTB or the GCG calculations of surprisal (but not both) to be a significant predictor of reading times.

Instead, the present set of results support recent claims made by van Schijndel et al. (2014) that non-local subcategorization decisions are made early during processing and so would have a strong influence on the reading time measures used in the present study. Such decisions would have to be conditioned on hierarchic structural information not present in either PTB PCFG surprisal or the sequential structure models of Frank and Bod (2011).

Further, predictability has been shown to affect word duration during speech production (Jurafsky et al., 2001; Aylett and Turk, 2006), and Demberg et al. (2012) found that hierarchic structure significantly improves over $n$-gram computations of predictability in that domain as well. Together, these findings suggest that hierarchic structure is not only a convenient descriptive tool for linguists, but that such structure is deeply rooted in the human language processor and is used during online language processing.

Previous work has made a distinction between lexical surprisal, syntactic surprisal, and total surprisal (Demberg and Keller, 2008; Roark et al., 2009). Given a prefix derivation of the structure of the context, syntactic surprisal measures the information obtained by generating the structure that will enable the attachment of a newly observed lexical item. Lexical surprisal conveys the amount of information obtained by attaching the particular lexical observation to the new syntactic structure. Total surprisal is the original formulation of surprisal and is the composition of the other two types of surprisal (the information gained by generating a structure for the current lexical observation and attaching the observation to that structure). Fossum and Levy (2012) show that, with a non-cumulative bigram baseline, this distinction is not significant when predicting reading times, so the present study simply uses total surprisal. It may be interesting in future work to see if the distinction between surprisal types becomes more or less useful as the sequential baseline improves.

The finding that cumulative $n$-gram information is useful in predicting reading times bears some resemblance to the finding that the spillover effect of a word is proportional to its logarithmic probability given the context (Smith and Levy, 2013). However, the spillover effect studied by Smith and Levy (2013) is one of a given fixation on the following fixation. The cumulative $n$-grams, in contrast, permit finer predictability of a word given the unfixated intervening context. The two measures are similar in that they both permit better modeling of the predictability of a word given its context, but the spillover measure could also be easily conceived as continued spillover processing from the preceding fixation, while cumulative $n$-grams reflect the predictability of the entire region between one fixation and the next. Further, cumulative $n$-grams could conceivably also capture processing of parafovial preview obtained during the previous fixation. Since the cumulative $n$-gram measure improves the computation of predictability of a word, it could also provide a better measure of the spillover effect a given word will have. Future work could investigate this by using cumulative $n$-grams both to compute the predictability of the current word and to predict the spillover effect from the preceding fixation. The present work suggests that doing so would provide even better reading time predictors.

## 7 Conclusion

First, this work suggests that the standard accounting for $n$-gram frequencies needs to change in psycholinguistic studies. Currently, the standard procedure is to use $n$-gram statistics only from the end of an eye-tracking region. This standard calculates the influence of the final word in each region given the lexical context, but that context is never accounted for in regions greater than one word in length. Instead, psycholinguistic models need to additionally account for the probability of the *context* given its own preceding context to provide a coherent model of the probability of the observed lexical sequence.

This work also shows that, even with good cumulative and non-cumulative estimates of the frequency effects generated by a given lexical sequence, measures of hierarchic structure provide a significant improvement to reading time predictions. Further, even in the presence of both a strong $n$-gram baseline and a linguistically accurate measure of hierarchic structure (PTB with 5 iterations of split-merge), a linguistically-motivated model of hierarchic structure is a significant predictor of reading times. As data coverage grows, some may worry that models of syntax will be superseded by better $n$-gram models. This study suggests that hierarchic syntax retains its value even in a world of big data.

## Acknowledgements

Thanks to Stefan Frank for interesting discussion and helpful feedback on an earlier draft of this paper and to the anonymous reviewers for their comments. This material is based upon work supported by the National Science Foundation Graduate Research Fellowship under Grant No. DGE-1343012. Any opinion, findings, and conclusions or recommendations expressed in this material are those of the authors and do not necessarily reflect the views of the National Science Foundation.

## References

Matthew Aylett and Alice Turk. 2006. Language redundancy predicts syllabic duration and the spectral characteristics of vocalic syllable nuclei. *Journal of the acoustical society of America*, 119(5):3048–3059.

Douglas Bates, Martin Maechler, Ben Bolker, and Steven Walker, 2014. *lme4: Linear mixed-effects models using Eigen and S4*. R package version 1.1-7.

Eugene Charniak, Mark Johnson, Micha Elsner, Joseph Austerweil, David Ellis, Isaac Haxton, Catherine Hill, R. Shrivaths, Jeremy Moore, Michael Pozar, and Theresa Vu. 2006. Multilevel coarse-to-fine pcfg parsing. In *Proceedings of the main conference on Human Language Technology Conference of the North American Chapter of the Association of Computational Linguistics*, pages 168–175.

Vera Demberg and Frank Keller. 2008. Data from eye-tracking corpora as evidence for theories of syntactic processing complexity. *Cognition*, 109(2):193–210.

Vera Demberg, Asad B. Sayeed, Philip J. Gorinski, and Nikolaos Engonopoulos. 2012. Syntactic surprisal affects spoken word duration in conversational contexts. In *Proceedings of the 2012 Joint Conference on Empirical Methods in Natural Language Processing and Computational Natural Language Learning*, pages 356–367.

Victoria Fossum and Roger Levy. 2012. Sequential vs. hierarchical syntactic models of human incremental sentence processing. In *Proceedings of CMCL 2012*. Association for Computational Linguistics.

Stefan Frank and Rens Bod. 2011. Insensitivity of the human sentence-processing system to hierarchical structure. *Psychological Science*.

Gerald Gazdar, Ewan Klein, Geoffrey Pullum, and Ivan Sag. 1985. *Generalized Phrase Structure Grammar*. Harvard University Press, Cambridge, MA.

David Graff and Christopher Cieri, 2003. *English Gigaword LDC2003T05*.

John Hale. 2001. A probabilistic earley parser as a psycholinguistic model. In *Proceedings of the second meeting of the North American chapter of the Association for Computational Linguistics*, pages 159–166, Pittsburgh, PA.

Kenneth Heafield, Ivan Pouzyrevsky, Jonathan H. Clark, and Philipp Koehn. 2013. Scalable modified Kneser-Ney language model estimation. In *Proceedings of the 51st Annual Meeting of the Association for Computational Linguistics*, pages 690–696, Sofia, Bulgaria, August.

Daniel Jurafsky, Alan Bell, Michelle Gregory, and William D. Raymond. 2001. Probabilistic relations between words: Evidence from reduction in lexical production. In Joan Bybee and Paul Hopper, editors, *Frequency and the emergence of linguistic structure*, pages 229–254. John Benjamins, Amsterdam.

Alan Kennedy, James Pynte, and Robin Hill. 2003. The Dundee corpus. In *Proceedings of the 12th European conference on eye movement*.

Matthew Lease, Eugene Charniak, Mark Johnson, and David McClosky. 2006. A look at parsing and its applications. In *Proceedings of AAAI*.

Roger Levy. 2008. Expectation-based syntactic comprehension. *Cognition*, 106(3):1126–1177.

Mitchell P. Marcus, Beatrice Santorini, and Mary Ann Marcinkiewicz. 1993. Building a large annotated corpus of English: the Penn Treebank. *Computational Linguistics*, 19(2):313–330.

Luan Nguyen, Marten van Schijndel, and William Schuler. 2012. Accurate unbounded dependency recovery using generalized categorial grammars. In *Proceedings of the 24th International Conference on Computational Linguistics (COLING '12)*, pages 2125–2140, Mumbai, India.

Slav Petrov, Leon Barrett, Romain Thibaux, and Dan Klein. 2006. Learning accurate, compact, and interpretable tree annotation. In *Proceedings of the 44th Annual Meeting of the Association for Computational Linguistics (COLING/ACL'06)*.

Carl Pollard and Ivan Sag. 1994. *Head-driven Phrase Structure Grammar*. University of Chicago Press, Chicago.

Brian Roark, Asaf Bachrach, Carlos Cardenas, and Christophe Pallier. 2009. Deriving lexical and syntactic expectation-based measures for psycholinguistic modeling via incremental top-down parsing. *Proceedings of the 2009 Conference on Empirical Methods in Natural Langauge Processing*, pages 324–333.

Nathaniel J. Smith and Roger Levy. 2013. The effect of word predictability on reading time is logarithmic. *Cognition*, 128:302–319.

Marten van Schijndel and William Schuler. 2013. An analysis of frequency- and recency-based processing costs. In *Proceedings of NAACL-HLT 2013*. Association for Computational Linguistics.

Marten van Schijndel, Andy Exley, and William Schuler. 2013a. A model of language processing as hierarchic sequential prediction. *Topics in Cognitive Science*, 5(3):522–540.

Marten van Schijndel, Luan Nguyen, and William Schuler. 2013b. An analysis of memory-based processing costs using incremental deep syntactic dependency parsing. In *Proc. of CMCL 2013*. Association for Computational Linguistics.

Marten van Schijndel, William Schuler, and Peter W Culicover. 2014. Frequency effects in the processing of unbounded dependencies. In *Proc. of CogSci 2014*. Cognitive Science Society.

# Retrofitting Word Vectors to Semantic Lexicons

**Manaal Faruqui Jesse Dodge Sujay K. Jauhar**
**Chris Dyer Eduard Hovy Noah A. Smith**
Language Technologies Institute
Carnegie Mellon University
Pittsburgh, PA, 15213, USA
{mfaruqui,jessed,sjauhar,cdyer,ehovy,nasmith}@cs.cmu.edu

## Abstract

Vector space word representations are learned from distributional information of words in large corpora. Although such statistics are semantically informative, they disregard the valuable information that is contained in semantic lexicons such as WordNet, FrameNet, and the Paraphrase Database. This paper proposes a method for refining vector space representations using relational information from semantic lexicons by encouraging linked words to have similar vector representations, and it makes no assumptions about how the input vectors were constructed. Evaluated on a battery of standard lexical semantic evaluation tasks in several languages, we obtain substantial improvements starting with a variety of word vector models. Our refinement method outperforms prior techniques for incorporating semantic lexicons into word vector training algorithms.

## 1 Introduction

Data-driven learning of word vectors that capture lexico-semantic information is a technique of central importance in NLP. These word vectors can in turn be used for identifying semantically related word pairs (Turney, 2006; Agirre et al., 2009) or as features in downstream text processing applications (Turian et al., 2010; Guo et al., 2014). A variety of approaches for constructing vector space embeddings of vocabularies are in use, notably including taking low rank approximations of cooccurrence statistics (Deerwester et al., 1990) and using internal representations from neural network models of word sequences (Collobert and Weston, 2008).

Because of their value as lexical semantic representations, there has been much research on improving the quality of vectors. *Semantic lexicons*, which provide type-level information about the semantics of words, typically by identifying *synonymy*, *hypernymy*, *hyponymy*, and *paraphrase* relations should be a valuable resource for improving the quality of word vectors that are trained solely on unlabeled corpora. Examples of such resources include WordNet (Miller, 1995), FrameNet (Baker et al., 1998) and the Paraphrase Database (Ganitkevitch et al., 2013).

Recent work has shown that by either changing the objective of the word vector training algorithm in neural language models (Yu and Dredze, 2014; Xu et al., 2014; Bian et al., 2014; Fried and Duh, 2014) or by relation-specific augmentation of the cooccurence matrix in spectral word vector models to incorporate semantic knowledge (Yih et al., 2012; Chang et al., 2013), the quality of word vectors can be improved. However, these methods are limited to particular methods for constructing vectors.

The contribution of this paper is a graph-based learning technique for using lexical relational resources to obtain higher quality semantic vectors, which we call "retrofitting." In contrast to previous work, retrofitting is applied as a *post-processing step* by running belief propagation on a graph constructed from lexicon-derived relational information to update word vectors (§2). This allows retrofitting to be used on pre-trained word vectors obtained using *any* vector training model. Intuitively, our method encourages the new vectors to be (i) similar to the vectors of related word types and (ii) similar to their purely distributional representations. The retrofitting process is fast, taking about 5 seconds for a graph of 100,000 words and vector length 300, and its runtime is independent of the original word vector training model.



*Human Language Technologies: The 2015 Annual Conference of the North American Chapter of the ACL*, pages 1606–1615,
Denver, Colorado, May 31 – June 5, 2015. 

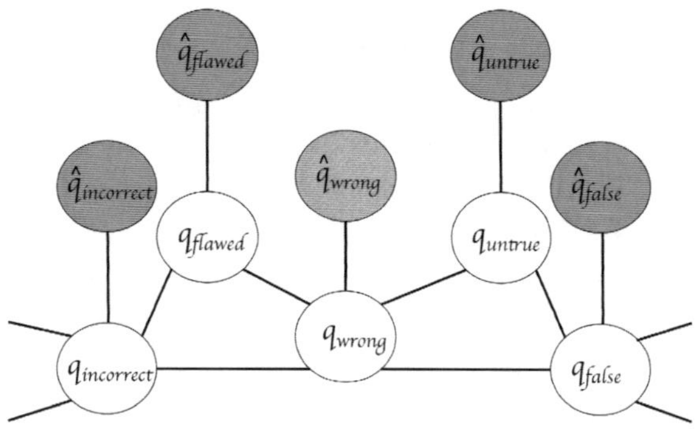


Figure 1: Word graph with edges between related words showing the observed (grey) and the inferred (white) word vector representations.

Experimentally, we show that our method works well with different state-of-the-art word vector models, using different kinds of semantic lexicons and gives substantial improvements on a variety of benchmarks, while beating the current state-of-the-art approaches for incorporating semantic information in vector training and trivially extends to multiple languages. We show that retrofitting gives consistent improvement in performance on evaluation benchmarks with different word vector lengths and show a qualitative visualization of the effect of retrofitting on word vector quality. The retrofitting tool is available at: `https://github.com/mfaruqui/retrofitting`.

## 2 Retrofitting with Semantic Lexicons

Let $V = \{w_1, \ldots, w_n\}$ be a **vocabulary**, i.e, the set of word types, and $\Omega$ be an **ontology** that encodes semantic relations between words in $V$. We represent $\Omega$ as an undirected graph $(V, E)$ with one vertex for each word type and edges $(w_i, w_j) \in E \subseteq V \times V$ indicating a semantic relationship of interest. These relations differ for different semantic lexicons and are described later (§4).

The matrix $\hat{Q}$ will be the collection of vector representations $\hat{q}_i \in \mathbb{R}^d$, for each $w_i \in V$, learned using a standard data-driven technique, where $d$ is the length of the word vectors. Our objective is to learn the matrix $Q = (q_1, \ldots, q_n)$ such that the columns are both close (under a distance metric) to their counterparts in $\hat{Q}$ *and* to adjacent vertices in $\Omega$. Figure 1 shows a small word graph with such edge connections; white nodes are labeled with the $Q$ vectors to be retrofitted (and correspond to $V_\Omega$); shaded nodes are labeled with the corresponding vectors in $\hat{Q}$, which are observed. The graph can be interpreted as a Markov random field (Kindermann and Snell, 1980).

The distance between a pair of vectors is defined to be the Euclidean distance. Since we want the inferred word vector to be close to the observed value $\hat{q}_i$ and close to its neighbors $q_j, \forall j$ such that $(i, j) \in E$, the objective to be minimized becomes:

$$\Psi(Q) = \sum_{i=1}^{n} \left[ \alpha_i \|q_i - \hat{q}_i\|^2 + \sum_{(i,j)\in E} \beta_{ij} \|q_i - q_j\|^2 \right]$$

where $\alpha$ and $\beta$ values control the relative strengths of associations (more details in §6.1).

In this case, we first train the word vectors independent of the information in the semantic lexicons and then retrofit them. $\Psi$ is convex in $Q$ and its solution can be found by solving a system of linear equations. To do so, we use an efficient iterative updating method (Bengio et al., 2006; Subramanya et al., 2010; Das and Petrov, 2011; Das and Smith, 2011). The vectors in $Q$ are initialized to be equal to the vectors in $\hat{Q}$. We take the first derivative of $\Psi$ with respect to one $q_i$ vector, and by equating it to zero arrive at the following online update:

$$q_i = \frac{\sum_{j:(i,j)\in E} \beta_{ij} q_j + \alpha_i \hat{q}_i}{\sum_{j:(i,j)\in E} \beta_{ij} + \alpha_i} \tag{1}$$

In practice, running this procedure for 10 iterations converges to changes in Euclidean distance of adjacent vertices of less than $10^{-2}$. The retrofitting approach described above is modular; it can be applied to word vector representations obtained from any model as the updates in Eq. 1 are agnostic to the original vector training model objective.

**Semantic Lexicons during Learning.** Our proposed approach is reminiscent of recent work on improving word vectors using lexical resources (Yu and Dredze, 2014; Bian et al., 2014; Xu et al., 2014) which alters the learning objective of the original vector training model with a prior (or a regularizer) that encourages semantically related vectors (in $\Omega$) to be close together, except that our technique is applied as a second stage of learning. We describe the prior approach here since it will serve as a baseline. Here semantic lexicons play the role of a prior on $Q$ which we define as follows:

$$p(Q) \propto \exp\left(-\gamma \sum_{i=1}^{n} \sum_{j:(i,j)\in E} \beta_{ij} \|q_i - q_j\|^2\right) \quad (2)$$

Here, $\gamma$ is a hyperparameter that controls the strength of the prior. As in the retrofitting objective, this prior on the word vector parameters forces words connected in the lexicon to have close vector representations as did $\Psi(Q)$ (with the role of $\hat{Q}$ being played by cross entropy of the empirical distribution).

This prior can be incorporated during learning through maximum a posteriori (MAP) estimation. Since there is no closed form solution of the estimate, we consider two iterative procedures. In the first, we use the sum of gradients of the log-likelihood (given by the extant vector learning model) and the log-prior (from Eq. 2), with respect to $Q$ for learning. Since computing the gradient of Eq. 2 has linear runtime in the vocabulary size $n$, we use lazy updates (Carpenter, 2008) for every $k$ words during training. We call this the **lazy** method of MAP. The second technique applies stochastic gradient ascent to the log-likelihood, and after every $k$ words applies the update in Eq. 1. We call this the **periodic** method. We later experimentally compare these methods against retrofitting (§6.2).

## 3 Word Vector Representations

We now describe the various publicly available pre-trained English word vectors on which we will test the applicability of the retrofitting model. These vectors have been chosen to have a balanced mix between large and small amounts of unlabeled text as well as between neural and spectral methods of training word vectors.

**Glove Vectors.** Global vectors for word representations (Pennington et al., 2014) are trained on aggregated global word-word co-occurrence statistics from a corpus, and the resulting representations show interesting linear substructures of the word vector space. These vectors were trained on 6 billion words from Wikipedia and English Gigaword and are of length 300.[1]

| Lexicon | Words | Edges |
|---|---|---|
| PPDB | 102,902 | 374,555 |
| WordNet$_{syn}$ | 148,730 | 304,856 |
| WordNet$_{all}$ | 148,730 | 934,705 |
| FrameNet | 10,822 | 417,456 |

Table 1: Approximate size of the graphs obtained from different lexicons.

**Skip-Gram Vectors (SG).** The `word2vec` tool (Mikolov et al., 2013a) is fast and currently in wide use. In this model, each word's Huffman code is used as an input to a log-linear classifier with a continuous projection layer and words within a given context window are predicted. The available vectors are trained on 100 billion words of Google news dataset and are of length 300.[2]

**Global Context Vectors (GC).** These vectors are learned using a recursive neural network that incorporates both local and global (document-level) context features (Huang et al., 2012). These vectors were trained on the first 1 billion words of English Wikipedia and are of length 50.[3]

**Multilingual Vectors (Multi).** Faruqui and Dyer (2014) learned vectors by first performing SVD on text in different languages, then applying canonical correlation analysis (CCA) on pairs of vectors for words that align in parallel corpora. The monolingual vectors were trained on WMT-2011 news corpus for English, French, German and Spanish. We use the Enligsh word vectors projected in the common English–German space. The monolingual English WMT corpus had 360 million words and the trained vectors are of length 512.[4]

## 4 Semantic Lexicons

We use three different semantic lexicons to evaluate their utility in improving the word vectors. We include both manually and automatically created lexicons. Table 1 shows the size of the graphs obtained

[1] `http://www-nlp.stanford.edu/projects/glove/`

[2] `https://code.google.com/p/word2vec`

[3] `http://nlp.stanford.edu/~socherr/ACL2012_wordVectorsTextFile.zip`

[4] `http://cs.cmu.edu/~mfaruqui/soft.html`

from these lexicons.

**PPDB.** The paraphrase database (Ganitkevitch et al., 2013) is a semantic lexicon containing more than 220 million paraphrase pairs of English.[5] Of these, 8 million are lexical (single word to single word) paraphrases. The key intuition behind the acquisition of its lexical paraphrases is that two words in one language that align, in parallel text, to the same word in a different language, should be synonymous. For example, if the words *jailed* and *imprisoned* are translated as the same word in another language, it may be reasonable to assume they have the same meaning. In our experiments, we instantiate an edge in $E$ for each lexical paraphrase in PPDB. The lexical paraphrase dataset comes in different sizes ranging from S to XXXL, in decreasing order of paraphrasing confidence and increasing order of size. We chose XL for our experiments. We want to give higher edge weights ($\alpha_i$) connecting the retrofitted word vectors ($q$) to the purely distributional word vectors ($\hat{q}$) than to edges connecting the retrofitted vectors to each other ($\beta_{ij}$), so all $\alpha_i$ are set to 1 and $\beta_{ij}$ to be $\mathrm{degree}(i)^{-1}$ (with $i$ being the node the update is being applied to).[6]

**WordNet.** WordNet (Miller, 1995) is a large human-constructed semantic lexicon of English words. It groups English words into sets of synonyms called synsets, provides short, general definitions, and records the various semantic relations between synsets. This database is structured in a graph particularly suitable for our task because it explicitly relates concepts with semantically aligned relations such as hypernyms and hyponyms. For example, the word *dog* is a synonym of *canine*, a hypernym of *puppy* and a hyponym of *animal*. We perform two different experiments with WordNet: (1) connecting a word only to synonyms, and (2) connecting a word to synonyms, hypernyms and hyponyms. We refer to these two graphs as $\mathrm{WN}_{syn}$ and $\mathrm{WN}_{all}$, respectively. In both settings, all $\alpha_i$ are set to 1 and $\beta_{ij}$ to be $\mathrm{degree}(i)^{-1}$.

[5] `http://www.cis.upenn.edu/~ccb/ppdb`

[6] In principle, these hyperparameters can be tuned to optimize performance on a particular task, which we leave for future work.

**FrameNet.** FrameNet (Baker et al., 1998; Fillmore et al., 2003) is a rich linguistic resource containing information about lexical and predicate-argument semantics in English. Frames can be realized on the surface by many different word types, which suggests that the word types evoking the same frame should be semantically related. For example, the frame Cause_change_of_position_on_a_scale is associated with *push*, *raise*, and *growth* (among many others). In our use of FrameNet, two words that group together with any frame are given an edge in $E$. We refer to this graph as FN. All $\alpha_i$ are set to 1 and $\beta_{ij}$ to be $\mathrm{degree}(i)^{-1}$.

## 5 Evaluation Benchmarks

We evaluate the quality of our word vector representations on tasks that test how well they capture both semantic and syntactic aspects of the representations along with an extrinsic sentiment analysis task.

**Word Similarity.** We evaluate our word representations on a variety of different benchmarks that have been widely used to measure word similarity. The first one is the **WS-353** dataset (Finkelstein et al., 2001) containing 353 pairs of English words that have been assigned similarity ratings by humans. The second benchmark is the **RG-65** (Rubenstein and Goodenough, 1965) dataset that contain 65 pairs of nouns. Since the commonly used word similarity datasets contain a small number of word pairs we also use the **MEN** dataset (Bruni et al., 2012) of 3,000 word pairs sampled from words that occur at least 700 times in a large web corpus. We calculate cosine similarity between the vectors of two words forming a test item, and report Spearman's rank correlation coefficient (Myers and Well, 1995) between the rankings produced by our model against the human rankings.

**Syntactic Relations (SYN-REL).** Mikolov et al. (2013b) present a syntactic relation dataset composed of analogous word pairs. It contains pairs of tuples of word relations that follow a common syntactic relation. For example, given *walking* and *walked*, the words are differently inflected forms of the same verb. There are nine different kinds of relations and overall there are 10,675 syntactic pairs of word tuples. The task is to find a word *d* that best fits the following relationship: "*a* is to *b* as *c* is to *d*," given $a$, $b$, and $c$. We use the vector offset method (Mikolov et al., 2013a; Levy and Goldberg, 2014), computing $q = q_a - q_b + q_c$ and returning the vector from $Q$ which has the highest cosine similarity to $q$.

**Synonym Selection (TOEFL).** The TOEFL synonym selection task is to select the semantically closest word to a target from a list of four candidates (Landauer and Dumais, 1997). The dataset contains 80 such questions. An example is "*rug* $\rightarrow$ {*sofa*, *ottoman*, *carpet*, *hallway*}", with *carpet* being the most synonym-like candidate to the target.

**Sentiment Analysis (SA).** Socher et al. (2013) created a treebank containing sentences annotated with fine-grained sentiment labels on phrases and sentences from movie review excerpts. The coarse-grained treebank of positive and negative classes has been split into training, development, and test datasets containing 6,920, 872, and 1,821 sentences, respectively. We train an $\ell_2$-regularized logistic regression classifier on the average of the word vectors of a given sentence to predict the coarse-grained sentiment tag at the sentence level, and report the test-set accuracy of the classifier.

## 6 Experiments

We first show experiments measuring improvements from the retrofitting method (§6.1), followed by comparisons to using lexicons during MAP learning (§6.2) and other published methods (§6.3). We then test how well retrofitting generalizes to other languages (§6.4).

### 6.1 Retrofitting

We use Eq. 1 to retrofit word vectors (§3) using graphs derived from semantic lexicons (§4).

**Results.** Table 2 shows the absolute changes in performance on different tasks (as columns) with different semantic lexicons (as rows). All of the lexicons offer high improvements on the word similarity tasks (the first three columns). On the TOEFL task, we observe large improvements of the order of 10 absolute points in accuracy for all lexicons except for FrameNet. FrameNet's performance is weaker, in some cases leading to worse performance (e.g., with Glove and SG vectors). For the extrinsic sentiment analysis task, we observe improvements using all the lexicons and gain $1.4\%$ (absolute) in accuracy for the Multi vectors over the baseline. This increase is statistically significant ($p < 0.01$, McNemar).

We observe improvements over Glove and SG vectors, which were trained on billions of tokens on all tasks except for SYN-REL. For stronger baselines (Glove and Multi) we observe smaller improvements as compared to lower baseline scores (SG and GC). We believe that FrameNet does not perform as well as the other lexicons because its frames group words based on very abstract concepts; often words with seemingly distantly related meanings (e.g., *push* and *growth*) can evoke the same frame. Interestingly, we almost never improve on the SYN-REL task, especially with higher baselines, this can be attributed to the fact that SYN-REL is inherently a syntactic task and during retrofitting we are incorporating additional semantic information in the vectors. In summary, we find that PPDB gives the best improvement maximum number of times aggreagted over different vetor types, closely followed by $\text{WN}_{all}$, and retrofitting gives gains across tasks and vectors. An ensemble lexicon, in which the graph is the union of the $\text{WN}_{all}$ and PPDB lexicons, on average performed slightly worse than PPDB; we omit those results here for brevity.

### 6.2 Semantic Lexicons during Learning

To incorporate lexicon information during training, and compare its performance against retrofitting, we train log-bilinear (LBL) vectors (Mnih and Teh, 2012). These vectors are trained to optimize the log-likelihood of a language model which predicts a word token $w$'s vector given the set of words in its context ($h$), also represented as vectors:

$$p(w \mid h; Q) \propto \exp\left(\sum_{i \in h} q_i^\top q_j + b_j\right) \qquad (3)$$

We optimize the above likelihood combined with the prior defined in Eq. 2 using the lazy and periodic techniques described in §2. Since it is costly to compute the partition function over the whole vocabulary, we use *noise constrastive estimation* (NCE) to estimate the parameters of the model (Mnih and Teh, 2012) using AdaGrad (Duchi et al., 2010) with a learning rate of $0.05$.

| Lexicon | MEN-3k | RG-65 | WS-353 | TOEFL | SYN-REL | SA |
|---|---|---|---|---|---|---|
| Glove | 73.7 | 76.7 | 60.5 | 89.7 | 67.0 | 79.6 |
| +PPDB | 1.4 | 2.9 | –1.2 | **5.1** | –0.4 | **1.6** |
| +WN$_{syn}$ | 0.0 | 2.7 | 0.5 | **5.1** | –12.4 | 0.7 |
| +WN$_{all}$ | **2.2** | **7.5** | **0.7** | 2.6 | –8.4 | 0.5 |
| +FN | –3.6 | –1.0 | –5.3 | 2.6 | –7.0 | 0.0 |
| SG | 67.8 | 72.8 | 65.6 | 85.3 | 73.9 | 81.2 |
| +PPDB | **5.4** | 3.5 | **4.4** | **10.7** | –2.3 | **0.9** |
| +WN$_{syn}$ | 0.7 | 3.9 | 0.0 | 9.3 | –13.6 | 0.7 |
| +WN$_{all}$ | 2.5 | **5.0** | 1.9 | 9.3 | –10.7 | –0.3 |
| +FN | –3.2 | 2.6 | –4.9 | 1.3 | –7.3 | 0.5 |
| GC | 31.3 | 62.8 | 62.3 | 60.8 | 10.9 | 67.8 |
| +PPDB | **7.0** | 6.1 | 2.0 | **13.1** | **5.3** | **1.1** |
| +WN$_{syn}$ | 3.6 | 6.4 | 0.6 | 7.3 | –1.7 | 0.0 |
| +WN$_{all}$ | 6.7 | **10.2** | **2.3** | 4.4 | –0.6 | 0.2 |
| +FN | 1.8 | 4.0 | 0.0 | 4.4 | –0.6 | 0.2 |
| Multi | 75.8 | 75.5 | 68.1 | 84.0 | 45.5 | 81.0 |
| +PPDB | **3.8** | 4.0 | **6.0** | **12.0** | **4.3** | 0.6 |
| +WN$_{syn}$ | 1.2 | 0.2 | 2.2 | 6.6 | –12.3 | **1.4** |
| +WN$_{all}$ | 2.9 | **8.5** | 4.3 | 6.6 | –10.6 | **1.4** |
| +FN | 1.8 | 4.0 | 0.0 | 4.4 | –0.6 | 0.2 |

Table 2: Absolute performance changes with retrofitting. Spearman's correlation (3 left columns) and accuracy (3 right columns) on different tasks. Higher scores are always better. Bold indicates greatest improvement for a vector type.

| Method | $k, \gamma$ | MEN-3k | RG-65 | WS-353 | TOEFL | SYN-REL | SA |
|---|---|---|---|---|---|---|---|
| LBL (Baseline) | $k = \infty, \gamma = 0$ | 58.0 | 42.7 | 53.6 | 66.7 | 31.5 | 72.5 |
| **LBL + Lazy** | $\gamma = 1$ | –0.4 | 4.2 | 0.6 | –0.1 | 0.6 | 1.2 |
| | $\gamma = 0.1$ | 0.7 | 8.1 | 0.4 | –1.4 | 0.7 | 0.8 |
| | $\gamma = 0.01$ | 0.7 | 9.5 | 1.7 | 2.6 | 1.9 | 0.4 |
| **LBL + Periodic** | $k = 100$M | 3.8 | 18.4 | 3.6 | 12.0 | 4.8 | 1.3 |
| | $k = 50$M | 3.4 | **19.5** | 4.4 | 18.6 | 0.6 | **1.9** |
| | $k = 25$M | 0.5 | 18.1 | 2.7 | **21.3** | –3.7 | 0.8 |
| **LBL + Retrofitting** | – | **5.7** | 15.6 | **5.5** | 18.6 | **14.7** | 0.9 |

Table 3: Absolute performance changes for including PPDB information while training LBL vectors. Spearman's correlation (3 left columns) and accuracy (3 right columns) on different tasks. Bold indicates greatest improvement.

We train vectors of length 100 on the WMT-2011 news corpus, which contains 360 million words, and use PPDB as the semantic lexicon as it performed reasonably well in the retrofitting experiments (§6.1). For the lazy method we update with respect to the prior every $k$ = 100,000 words[7] and test for different values of prior strength $\gamma \in \{1, 0.1, 0.01\}$. For the periodic method, we update the word vectors using Eq. 1 every $k \in \{25, 50, 100\}$ million words.

**Results.** See Table 3. For lazy, $\gamma = 0.01$ performs best, but the method is in most cases not highly sensitive to $\gamma$'s value. For **periodic**, which overall leads to greater improvements over the baseline than **lazy**, $k$ = 50M performs best, although all other values of $k$ also outperform the the baseline. Retrofitting, which can be applied to any word vectors, regardless of how they are trained, is competitive and sometimes better.

[7] $k$ = 10,000 or 50,000 yielded similar results.

| Corpus | Vector Training | MEN-3k | RG-65 | WS-353 | TOEFL | SYN-REL | SA |
|---|---|---|---|---|---|---|---|
| WMT-11 | CBOW | 55.2 | 44.8 | 54.7 | 73.3 | 40.8 | 74.1 |
| | Yu and Dredze (2014) | 50.1 | 47.1 | 53.7 | 61.3 | 29.9 | 71.5 |
| | CBOW + Retrofitting | **60.5** | **57.7** | **58.4** | **81.3** | **52.5** | **75.7** |
| Wikipedia | SG | **76.1** | 66.7 | **68.6** | 72.0 | 40.3 | 73.1 |
| | Xu et al. (2014) | – | – | 68.3 | – | 44.4 | – |
| | SG + Retrofitting | 65.7 | **73.9** | 67.5 | **86.0** | **49.9** | **74.6** |

Table 4: Comparison of retrofitting for semantic enrichment against Yu and Dredze (2014), Xu et al. (2014). Spearman's correlation (3 left columns) and accuracy (3 right columns) on different tasks.

### 6.3 Comparisons to Prior Work

Two previous models (Yu and Dredze, 2014; Xu et al., 2014) have shown that the quality of word vectors obtained using `word2vec` tool can be improved by using semantic knowledge from lexicons. Both these models use constraints among words as a regularization term on the training objective during training, and their methods can only be applied for improving the quality of SG and CBOW vectors produced by the `word2vec` tool. We compared the quality of our vectors against each of these.

**Yu and Dredze (2014).** We train word vectors using their joint model training code[8] while using exactly the same training settings as specified in their best model: CBOW, vector length 100 and PPDB for enrichment. The results are shown in the top half of Table 4 where our model consistently outperforms the baseline and their model.

**Xu et al. (2014).** This model extracts categorical and relational knowledge among words from Freebase[9] and uses it as a constraint while training. Unfortunately, neither their word embeddings nor model training code is publicly available, so we train the SG model by using exactly the same settings as described in their system (vector length 300) and on the same corpus: monolingual English Wikipedia text.[10] We compare the performance of our retrofitting vectors on the SYN-REL and WS-353 task against the best model[11] reported in their paper. As shown in the lower half of Table 4, our model outperforms their model by an absolute 5.5 points absolute on the SYN-REL task, but a slightly inferior score on the WS-353 task.

### 6.4 Multilingual Evaluation

We tested our method on three additional languages: German, French, and Spanish. We used the Universal WordNet (de Melo and Weikum, 2009), an automatically constructed multilingual lexical knowledge base based on WordNet.[12] It contains words connected via different lexical relations to other words both within and across languages. We construct separate graphs for different languages (i.e., only linking words to other words in the same language) and apply retrofitting to each. Since not many word similarity evaluation benchmarks are available for languages other than English, we tested our baseline and improved vectors on one benchmark per language.

We used RG-65 (Gurevych, 2005), RG-65 (Joubarne and Inkpen, 2011) and MC-30 (Hassan and Mihalcea, 2009) for German, French and Spanish, respectively.[13] We trained SG vectors for each language of length 300 on a corpus of 1 billion tokens, each extracted from Wikipedia, and evaluate them on word similarity on the benchmarks before and after retrofitting. Table 5 shows that we obtain high improvements which strongly indicates that our method generalizes across these languages.

## 7 Further Analysis

**Retrofitting vs. vector length.** With more dimensions, word vectors might be able to capture higher orders of semantic information and retrofitting might be less helpful. We train SG vec-

[8]`https://github.com/Gorov/JointRCM`

[9]`https://www.freebase.com`

[10]`http://mattmahoney.net/dc/enwik9.zip`

[11]Their best model is named "RC-NET" in their paper.

[12]`http://www.mpi-inf.mpg.de/yago-naga/uwn`

[13]These benchmarks were created by translating the corresponding English benchmarks word by word manually.

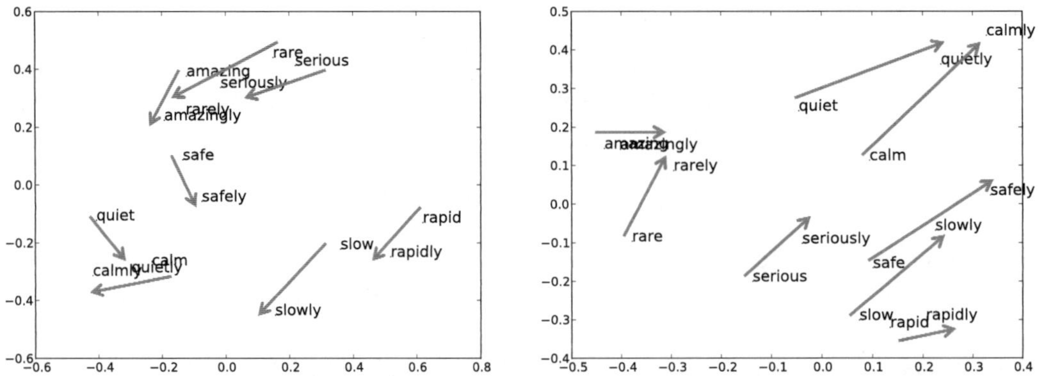


Figure 3: Two-dimensional PCA projections of 100-dimensional SG vector pairs holding the "adjective to adverb" relation, before (left) and after (right) retrofitting.

| Language | Task | SG | Retrofitted SG |
|---|---|---|---|
| German | RG-65 | 53.4 | **60.3** |
| French | RG-65 | 46.7 | **60.6** |
| Spanish | MC-30 | 54.0 | **59.1** |

Table 5: Spearman's correlation for word similarity evaluation using the using original and retrofitted SG vectors.

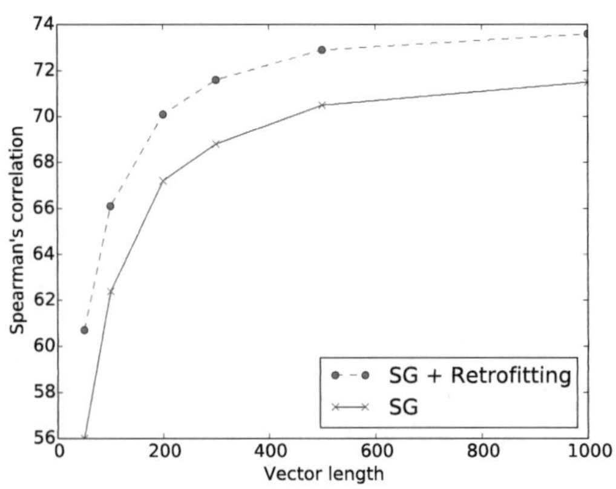


Figure 2: Spearman's correlation on the MEN word similarity task, before and after retrofitting.

tors on 1 billion English tokens for vector lengths ranging from 50 to 1,000 and evaluate on the MEN word similarity task. We retrofit these vectors to PPDB (§4) and evaluate those on the same task. Figure 2 shows consistent improvement in vector quality across different vector lengths.

**Visualization.** We randomly select eight word pairs that have the "adjective to adverb" relation from the SYN-REL task (§5). We then take a two-dimensional PCA projection of the 100-dimensional SG word vectors and plot them in $\mathbb{R}^2$. In Figure 3 we plot these projections before (left) and after (right) retrofitting. It can be seen that in the first case the direction of the analogy vectors is not consistent, but after retrofitting all the analogy vectors are aligned in the same direction.

## 8 Related Work

The use of lexical semantic information in training word vectors has been limited. Recently, word similarity knowledge (Yu and Dredze, 2014; Fried and Duh, 2014) and word relational knowledge (Xu et al., 2014; Bian et al., 2014) have been used to improve the `word2vec` embeddings in a joint training model similar to our regularization approach. In latent semantic analysis, the word cooccurrence matrix can be constructed to incorporate relational information like antonym specific polarity induction (Yih et al., 2012) and multi-relational latent semantic analysis (Chang et al., 2013).

The approach we propose is conceptually similar to previous work that uses graph structures to propagate information among semantic concepts (Zhu, 2005; Culp and Michailidis, 2008). Graph-based belief propagation has also been used to induce POS tags (Subramanya et al., 2010; Das and Petrov, 2011) and semantic frame associations (Das and Smith, 2011). In those efforts, labels for unknown words were inferred using a method similar to ours. Broadly, graph-based semi-supervised learning (Zhu, 2005; Talukdar and Pereira, 2010) has been applied to machine translation (Alexandrescu and Kirchhoff, 2009), unsupervised semantic role induction (Lang and Lapata, 2011), semantic document modeling (Schuhmacher and Ponzetto, 2014), language generation (Krahmer et al., 2003) and sentiment analysis (Goldberg and Zhu, 2006).

## 9 Conclusion

We have proposed a simple and effective method named **retrofitting** to improve word vectors using word relation knowledge found in semantic lexicons. Retrofitting is used as a post-processing step to improve vector quality and is more modular than other approaches that use semantic information while training. It can be applied to vectors obtained from any word vector training method. Our experiments explored the method's performance across tasks, semantic lexicons, and languages and showed that it outperforms existing alternatives. The retrofitting tool is available at: `https://github.com/mfaruqui/retrofitting`.

## Acknowledgements

This research was supported in part by the National Science Foundation under grants IIS-1143703, IIS-1147810, and IIS-1251131; by IARPA via Department of Interior National Business Center (DoI/NBC) contract number D12PC00337; and by DARPA under grant FA87501220342. Part of the computational work was carried out on resources provided by the Pittsburgh Supercomputing Center. The U.S. Government is authorized to reproduce and distribute reprints for Governmental purposes notwithstanding any copyright annotation thereon. Disclaimer: the views and conclusions contained herein are those of the authors and should not be interpreted as necessarily representing the official policies or endorsements, either expressed or implied, of IARPA, DoI/NBC, DARPA, or the U.S. Government.

## References

Eneko Agirre, Enrique Alfonseca, Keith Hall, Jana Kravalova, Marius Paşca, and Aitor Soroa. 2009. A study on similarity and relatedness using distributional and wordnet-based approaches. In *Proceedings of NAACL*.

Andrei Alexandrescu and Katrin Kirchhoff. 2009. Graph-based learning for statistical machine translation. In *Proceedings of NAACL*.

Collin F. Baker, Charles J. Fillmore, and John B. Lowe. 1998. The berkeley framenet project. In *Proceedings of ACL*.

Yoshua Bengio, Olivier Delalleau, and Nicolas Le Roux. 2006. Label propagation and quadratic criterion. In *Semi-Supervised Learning*.

Jiang Bian, Bin Gao, and Tie-Yan Liu. 2014. Knowledge-powered deep learning for word embedding. In *Machine Learning and Knowledge Discovery in Databases*.

Elia Bruni, Gemma Boleda, Marco Baroni, and Nam-Khanh Tran. 2012. Distributional semantics in technicolor. In *Proceedings of ACL*.

Bob Carpenter. 2008. Lazy sparse stochastic gradient descent for regularized multinomial logistic regression. Technical Report Alias-i Inc.

Kai-Wei Chang, Wen-tau Yih, and Christopher Meek. 2013. Multi-relational latent semantic analysis. In *Proceedings of EMNLP*.

Ronan Collobert and Jason Weston. 2008. A unified architecture for natural language processing: deep neural networks with multitask learning. In *Proceedings of ICML*.

Mark Culp and George Michailidis. 2008. Graph-based semisupervised learning. *IEEE Transactions on Pattern Analysis and Machine Intelligence*.

Dipanjan Das and Slav Petrov. 2011. Unsupervised part-of-speech tagging with bilingual graph-based projections. In *Proc. of ACL*.

Dipanjan Das and Noah A. Smith. 2011. Semi-supervised frame-semantic parsing for unknown predicates. In *Proc. of ACL*.

Gerard de Melo and Gerhard Weikum. 2009. Towards a universal wordnet by learning from combined evidence. In *Proceedings of CIKM*.

S. C. Deerwester, S. T. Dumais, T. K. Landauer, G. W. Furnas, and R. A. Harshman. 1990. Indexing by latent semantic analysis. *Journal of the American Society for Information Science*.

John Duchi, Elad Hazan, and Yoram Singer. 2010. Adaptive subgradient methods for online learning and stochastic optimization. Technical Report UCB/EECS 2010 24, Mar.

Manaal Faruqui and Chris Dyer. 2014. Improving vector space word representations using multilingual correlation. In *Proceedings of EACL*.

Charles Fillmore, Christopher Johnson, and Miriam Petruck. 2003. *International Journal of Lexicography*.

Lev Finkelstein, Evgeniy Gabrilovich, Yossi Matias, Ehud Rivlin, Zach Solan, Gadi Wolfman, and Eytan Ruppin. 2001. Placing search in context: the concept revisited. In *Proceedings of WWW*.

Daniel Fried and Kevin Duh. 2014. Incorporating both distributional and relational semantics in word representations. *arXiv preprint arXiv:1412.4369*.

Juri Ganitkevitch, Benjamin Van Durme, and Chris Callison-Burch. 2013. PPDB: The paraphrase database. In *Proceedings of NAACL*.

Andrew B. Goldberg and Xiaojin Zhu. 2006. Seeing stars when there aren't many stars: Graph-based semi-supervised learning for sentiment categorization. TextGraphs-1.

Jiang Guo, Wanxiang Che, Haifeng Wang, and Ting Liu. 2014. Revisiting embedding features for simple semi-supervised learning. In *Proceedings of EMNLP*.

Iryna Gurevych. 2005. Using the structure of a conceptual network in computing semantic relatedness. In *Proceedings of IJCNLP*.

Samer Hassan and Rada Mihalcea. 2009. Cross-lingual semantic relatedness using encyclopedic knowledge. In *Proc. of EMNLP*.

Eric H Huang, Richard Socher, Christopher D Manning, and Andrew Y Ng. 2012. Improving word representations via global context and multiple word prototypes. In *Proceedings of ACL*.

Colette Joubarne and Diana Inkpen. 2011. Comparison of semantic similarity for different languages using the google n-gram corpus and second- order co-occurrence measures. In *Proceedings of CAAI*.

Ross Kindermann and J. L. Snell. 1980. *Markov Random Fields and Their Applications*. AMS.

Emiel Krahmer, Sebastian van Erk, and André Verleg. 2003. Graph-based generation of referring expressions. *Comput. Linguist.*

Thomas K Landauer and Susan T. Dumais. 1997. A solution to plato's problem: The latent semantic analysis theory of acquisition, induction, and representation of knowledge. *Psychological review*.

Joel Lang and Mirella Lapata. 2011. Unsupervised semantic role induction with graph partitioning. In *Proceedings of EMNLP*.

Omer Levy and Yoav Goldberg. 2014. Linguistic regularities in sparse and explicit word representations. In *Proceedings of CoNLL*.

Tomas Mikolov, Kai Chen, Greg Corrado, and Jeffrey Dean. 2013a. Efficient estimation of word representations in vector space. *arXiv preprint arXiv:1301.3781*.

Tomas Mikolov, Wen-tau Yih, and Geoffrey Zweig. 2013b. Linguistic regularities in continuous space word representations. In *Proceedings of NAACL*.

George A Miller. 1995. Wordnet: a lexical database for english. *Communications of the ACM*.

Andriy Mnih and Yee Whye Teh. 2012. A fast and simple algorithm for training neural probabilistic language models. In *Proceedings of ICML*.

Jerome L. Myers and Arnold D. Well. 1995. *Research Design & Statistical Analysis*. Routledge.

Jeffrey Pennington, Richard Socher, and Christopher D. Manning. 2014. Glove: Global vectors for word representation. In *Proceedings of EMNLP*.

Herbert Rubenstein and John B. Goodenough. 1965. Contextual correlates of synonymy. *Commun. ACM*, 8(10):627–633, October.

Michael Schuhmacher and Simone Paolo Ponzetto. 2014. Knowledge-based graph document modeling. In *Proceedings of WSDM*.

Richard Socher, Alex Perelygin, Jean Wu, Jason Chuang, Christopher D. Manning, Andrew Y. Ng, and Christopher Potts. 2013. Recursive deep models for semantic compositionality over a sentiment treebank. In *Proceedings of EMNLP*.

Amarnag Subramanya, Slav Petrov, and Fernando Pereira. 2010. Efficient graph-based semi-supervised learning of structured tagging models. In *Proceedings of EMNLP*.

Partha Pratim Talukdar and Fernando Pereira. 2010. Experiments in graph-based semi-supervised learning methods for class-instance acquisition. In *Proceedings of ACL*.

Joseph Turian, Lev Ratinov, and Yoshua Bengio. 2010. Word representations: a simple and general method for semi-supervised learning. In *Proc. of ACL*.

Peter D. Turney. 2006. Similarity of semantic relations. *Comput. Linguist.*, 32(3):379–416, September.

Chang Xu, Yalong Bai, Jiang Bian, Bin Gao, Gang Wang, Xiaoguang Liu, and Tie-Yan Liu. 2014. Rc-net: A general framework for incorporating knowledge into word representations. In *Proceedings of CIKM*.

Wen-tau Yih, Geoffrey Zweig, and John C. Platt. 2012. Polarity inducing latent semantic analysis. In *Proceedings of EMNLP*.

Mo Yu and Mark Dredze. 2014. Improving lexical embeddings with semantic knowledge. In *ACL*.

Xiaojin Zhu. 2005. *Semi-supervised Learning with Graphs*. Ph.D. thesis, Pittsburgh, PA, USA. AAI3179046.

# “You’re Mr. Lebowski, I’m the Dude”: Inducing Address Term Formality in Signed Social Networks

**Vinodh Krishnan**
College of Computing
Georgia Institute of Technology
Atlanta, GA 30308
krishnan.vinodh@gmail.com

**Jacob Eisenstein**
School of Interactive Computing
Georgia Institute of Technology
Atlanta, GA 30308
jacobe@gatech.edu

## Abstract

We present an unsupervised model for inducing signed social networks from the content exchanged across network edges. Inference in this model solves three problems simultaneously: (1) identifying the sign of each edge; (2) characterizing the distribution over content for each edge type; (3) estimating weights for triadic features that map to theoretical models such as structural balance. We apply this model to the problem of inducing the social function of **address terms**, such as *Madame*, *comrade*, and *dude*. On a dataset of movie scripts, our system obtains a coherent clustering of address terms, while at the same time making intuitively plausible judgments of the formality of social relations in each film. As an additional contribution, we provide a bootstrapping technique for identifying and tagging address terms in dialogue.[1]

## 1 Introduction

One of the core communicative functions of language is to modulate and reproduce **social dynamics**, such as friendship, familiarity, formality, and power (Hymes, 1972). However, large-scale empirical work on understanding this communicative function has been stymied by a lack of labeled data: it is not clear what to annotate, let alone whether and how such annotations can be produced reliably. Computational linguistics has made great progress in modeling language’s informational dimension, but — with a few notable exceptions — computation has had little to contribute to our understanding of language’s social dimension.

Yet there is a rich theoretical literature on social structures and dynamics. In this paper, we focus on one such structure: signed social networks, in which edges between individuals are annotated with information about the nature of the relationship. For example, the individuals in a dyad may be friends or foes; they may be on formal or informal terms; or they may be in an asymmetric power relationship. Several theories characterize signed social networks: in structural balance theory, edge signs indicate friendship and enmity, with some triads of signed edges being stable, and others being unstable (Cartwright and Harary, 1956); conversely, in status theory (Leskovec et al., 2010b), edges indicate status differentials, and triads should obey transitivity. But these theoretical models can only be applied when the sign of each social network connection is known, and they do not answer the sociolinguistic question of how the sign of a social tie relates to the language that is exchanged across it.

We present a unified statistical model that incorporates both network structure and linguistic content. The model connects signed social networks with **address terms** (Brown and Ford, 1961), which include names, titles, and “placeholder names,” such as *dude*. The choice of address terms is an indicator of the level of formality between the two parties: for example, in contemporary North American English, a formal relationship is signaled by the use of titles such as *Ms* and *Mr*, while an informal relationship is signaled by the use of first names and

[1]Code and data for this paper is available at https://github.com/vinodhkris/signed-social.



*Human Language Technologies: The 2015 Annual Conference of the North American Chapter of the ACL*, pages 1616–1626,
Denver, Colorado, May 31 – June 5, 2015. 

placeholder names. These tendencies can be captured with a multinomial distribution over address terms, conditioned on the nature of the relationship. However, the linguistic signal is not the only indicator of formality: network structural properties can also come into play. For example, if two individuals share a mutual friend, with which both are on informal terms, then they too are more likely to have an informal relationship. With a log-linear prior distribution over network structures, it is possible to incorporate such triadic features, which relate to structural balance and status theory.

Given a dataset of unlabeled network structures and linguistic content, inference in this model simultaneously induces three quantities of interest:

- a clustering of network edges into types;
- a probabilistic model of the address terms that are used across each edge type, thus revealing the social meaning of these address terms;
- weights for triadic features of signed networks, which can then be compared with the predictions of existing social theories.

Such inferences can be viewed as a form of **sociolinguistic structure induction**, permitting social meanings to be drawn from linguistic data. In addition to the model and the associated inference procedure, we also present an approach for inducing a lexicon of address terms, and for tagging them in dialogues. We apply this procedure to a dataset of movie scripts (Danescu-Niculescu-Mizil and Lee, 2011). Quantitative evaluation against human ratings shows that the induced clusters of address terms correspond to intuitive perceptions of formality, and that the network structural features improve predictive likelihood over a purely text-based model. Qualitative evaluation shows that the model makes reasonable predictions of the level of formality of social network ties in well-known movies.

We first describe our model for linking network structure and linguistic content in general terms, as it can be used for many types of linguistic content and edge labels. Next we describe a procedure which semi-automatically induces a lexicon of address terms, and then automatically labels them in text. We then describe the application of this procedure to a dataset of movie dialogues, including quantitative and qualitative evaluations.

## 2 Joint model of signed social networks and textual content

We now present a probabilistic model for linking network structure with content exchanged over the network. In this section, the model is presented in general terms, so that it can be applied to any type of event counts, with any form of discrete edge labels. The application of the model to forms of address is described in Sections 4 and 5.

We observe a dataset of undirected graphs $G^{(t)} = \{i, j\}$, with a total ordering on nodes such that $i < j$ in all edges. For each edge $\langle i, j \rangle$, we observe directed content vectors $\boldsymbol{x}_{i \to j}$ and $\boldsymbol{x}_{i \leftarrow j}$, which may represent counts of words or other discrete events, such as up-votes and down-votes for comments in a forum thread. We hypothesize a latent edge label $y_{ij} \in \mathcal{Y}$, so that $\boldsymbol{x}_{i \to j}$ and $\boldsymbol{x}_{i \leftarrow j}$ are conditioned on $y_{ij}$. In this paper we focus on binary labels (e.g., $\mathcal{Y} = \{+, -\}$), but the approach generalizes to larger finite discrete sets, such as directed binary labels (e.g., $\mathcal{Y} = \{++, +-, -+, --\}$) and comparative status labels (e.g., $\mathcal{Y} = \{<, >, \approx\}$).

We model the likelihood of the observations conditioned on the edge labels as multinomial,

$$\boldsymbol{x}_{i \to j} \mid y_{ij} \sim \text{Multinomial}(\boldsymbol{\theta}^{\rightarrow}_{y_{ij}}) \quad (1)$$

$$\boldsymbol{x}_{i \leftarrow j} \mid y_{ij} \sim \text{Multinomial}(\boldsymbol{\theta}^{\leftarrow}_{y_{ij}}). \quad (2)$$

Parameter tying can be employed to handle special cases. For example, if the edge labels are undirected, then we add the constraint $\boldsymbol{\theta}^{\rightarrow}_{y} = \boldsymbol{\theta}^{\leftarrow}_{y}, \forall y$. If the edge labels reflect relative status, then we would instead add the constraints $(\boldsymbol{\theta}^{\rightarrow}_{<} = \boldsymbol{\theta}^{\leftarrow}_{>})$, $(\boldsymbol{\theta}^{\rightarrow}_{>} = \boldsymbol{\theta}^{\leftarrow}_{<})$, and $(\boldsymbol{\theta}^{\rightarrow}_{\approx} = \boldsymbol{\theta}^{\leftarrow}_{\approx})$.

The distribution over edge labelings $P(\boldsymbol{y})$ is modeled in a log-linear framework, with features that can consider network structure and signed triads:

$$P(\boldsymbol{y}; G, \boldsymbol{\eta}, \boldsymbol{\beta}) = \frac{1}{Z(\boldsymbol{\eta}, \boldsymbol{\beta}; G)} \times \exp \sum_{\langle i,j \rangle \in G} \boldsymbol{\eta}^\top \boldsymbol{f}(y_{ij}, i, j, G) \times \exp \sum_{\langle i,j,k \rangle \in \mathcal{T}(G)} \beta_{y_{ij}, y_{jk}, y_{ik}}, \quad (3)$$

where $\mathcal{T}(G)$ is the set of triads in the graph $G$. The first term of Equation 3 represents a normalizing constant. The second term includes weights $\boldsymbol{\eta}$, which apply to network features $\boldsymbol{f}(y_{ij}, i, j, G)$. This can include features like the number of mutual friends between nodes $i$ and $j$, or any number of more elaborate structural features (Liben-Nowell and Kleinberg, 2007). For example, the feature weights $\boldsymbol{\eta}$ could ensure that the edge label $Y_{ij} = +$ is especially likely when nodes $i$ and $j$ have many mutual friends in $G$. However, these features cannot consider any edge labels besides $y_{ij}$.

In the third line of Equation 3, each weight $\beta_{y_{ij}, y_{jk}, y_{ik}}$ corresponds to a signed triad type, invariant to rotation. In a binary signed network, structural balance theory would suggest positive weights for $\beta_{+++}$ (all friends) and $\beta_{+--}$ (two friends and a mutual enemy), and negative weights for $\beta_{++-}$ (two enemies and a mutual friend) and $\beta_{---}$ (all enemies). In contrast, a status-based network theory would penalize non-transitive triads such as $\beta_{>><}$. Thus, in an unsupervised model, we can examine the weights to learn about the semantics of the induced edge types, and to see which theory best describes the signed network configurations that follow from the linguistic signal. This is a natural next step from prior work that computes the frequency of triads in explicitly-labeled signed social networks (Leskovec et al., 2010b).

## 3 Inference and estimation

Our goal is to estimate the parameters $\theta$, $\beta$, and $\boldsymbol{\eta}$, given observations of network structures $G^{(t)}$ and linguistic content $\boldsymbol{x}^{(t)}$, for $t \in \{1, \ldots, T\}$. Eliding the sum over instances $t$, we seek to maximize the variational lower bound on the expected likelihood,

$$\begin{aligned}\mathcal{L}_Q =& E_Q[\log P(\boldsymbol{y}, \boldsymbol{x}; \boldsymbol{\beta}, \boldsymbol{\theta}, G)] - E_Q[\log Q(\boldsymbol{y})] \\ =& E_Q[\log P(\boldsymbol{x} \mid \boldsymbol{y}; \boldsymbol{\theta})] + E_Q[\log P(\boldsymbol{y}; G, \boldsymbol{\beta}, \boldsymbol{\eta})] \\ &- E_Q[\log Q(\boldsymbol{y})]. \end{aligned} \quad (4)$$

The first and third terms factor across edges,

$$\begin{aligned} E_Q[\log P(\boldsymbol{x} \mid \boldsymbol{y}; \boldsymbol{\theta})] =& \sum_{\langle i,j\rangle \in G} \sum_{y' \in \mathcal{Y}} q_{ij}(y') \boldsymbol{x}_{i\rightarrow j}^\top \log \boldsymbol{\theta}_{y'}^{\rightarrow} \\ &+ q_{ij}(y') \boldsymbol{x}_{i\leftarrow j}^\top \log \boldsymbol{\theta}_{y'}^{\leftarrow} \\ E_Q[\log Q(\boldsymbol{y})] =& \sum_{\langle i,j\rangle \in G} \sum_{y' \in \mathcal{Y}} q_{ij}(y') \log q(y'). \end{aligned}$$

The expected log-prior $E_Q[\log P(\boldsymbol{y})]$ is computed from the prior distribution defined in Equation 3, and therefore involves triads of edge labels,

$$\begin{aligned} E_Q[\log P(\boldsymbol{y}; \boldsymbol{\eta}, \boldsymbol{\beta})] =& -\log Z(\boldsymbol{\eta}, \boldsymbol{\beta}; G) \\ &+ \sum_{\langle i,j\rangle \in G} \sum_{y'} q_{ij}(y') \boldsymbol{\eta}^\top \boldsymbol{f}(y', i, j, G) \\ &+ \sum_{\langle i,j,k\rangle \in \mathcal{T}(G)} \sum_{y, y', y''} q_{ij}(y) q_{jk}(y') q_{ik}(y'') \beta_{y, y', y''}. \end{aligned}$$

We can reach a local maximum of the variational bound by applying expectation-maximization (Dempster et al., 1977), iterating between updates to $Q(\boldsymbol{y})$, and updates to the parameters $\boldsymbol{\theta}, \boldsymbol{\beta}, \boldsymbol{\eta}$. This procedure is summarized in Table 1, and described in more detail below.

### 3.1 E-step

In the E-step, we sequentially update each $q_{ij}$, taking the derivative of Equation 4:

$$\begin{aligned} \frac{\partial \mathcal{L}_Q}{\partial q_{ij}(y)} =& \log P(\boldsymbol{x}_{i\rightarrow j} \mid Y_{ij} = y; \boldsymbol{\theta}^{\rightarrow}) \\ &+ \log P(\boldsymbol{x}_{i\leftarrow j} \mid Y_{ij} = y; \boldsymbol{\theta}^{\leftarrow}) \\ &+ E_{Q(\boldsymbol{y}_{-(ij)})}[\log P(\boldsymbol{y} \mid Y_{ij} = y; \boldsymbol{\beta}, \boldsymbol{\eta})] \\ &- \log q_{ij}(y) - 1. \end{aligned} \quad (5)$$

After adding a Lagrange multiplier to ensure that $\sum_y q_{ij}(y) = 1$, we obtain a closed-form solution for each $q_{ij}(y)$. These iterative updates to $q_{ij}$ can be viewed as a form of mean field inference (Wainwright and Jordan, 2008).

### 3.2 M-step

In the general case, the maximum expected likelihood solution for the content parameter $\boldsymbol{\theta}$ is given by the expected counts,

$$\boldsymbol{\theta}_y^{\rightarrow} \propto \sum_{\langle i,j\rangle \in G} q_{ij}(y) \boldsymbol{x}_{i\rightarrow j} \quad (6)$$

$$\boldsymbol{\theta}_y^{\leftarrow} \propto \sum_{\langle i,j\rangle \in G} q_{ij}(y) \boldsymbol{x}_{i\leftarrow j}. \quad (7)$$

As noted above, we are often interested in special cases that require parameter tying, such as $\boldsymbol{\theta}_y^{\rightarrow} = \boldsymbol{\theta}_y^{\leftarrow}, \forall y$. This can be handled by simply computing expected counts across the tied parameters.

1. Initialize $Q(Y^{(t)})$ for each $t \in \{1 \ldots T\}$
2. Iterate until convergence:

   **E-step** update each $q_{ij}$ in closed form, based on Equation 5.

   **M-step: content** Update $\boldsymbol{\theta}$ in closed form from Equations 6 and 7.

   **M-step: structure** Update $\boldsymbol{\beta}, \boldsymbol{\eta}$, and $c$ by applying L-BFGS to the noise-contrastive estimation objective in Equation 8.

Table 1: Expectation-maximization estimation procedure

Obtaining estimates for $\boldsymbol{\beta}$ and $\boldsymbol{\eta}$ is more challenging, as it would seem to involve computing the partition function $Z(\boldsymbol{\eta}, \boldsymbol{\beta}; G)$, which sums over all possible labeling of each network $G^{(t)}$. The number of such labelings is exponential in the number of edges in the network. West et al. (2014) show that for an objective function involving features on triads and dyads, it is NP-hard to find even the single optimal labeling.

We therefore apply noise-contrastive estimation (NCE; Gutmann and Hyvärinen, 2012), which transforms the problem of estimating the density $P(\boldsymbol{y})$ into a classification problem: distinguishing the observed graph labelings $\boldsymbol{y}^{(t)}$ from randomly-generated "noise" labelings $\tilde{\boldsymbol{y}}^{(t)} \sim P_n$, where $P_n$ is a noise distribution. NCE introduces an additional parameter $c$ for the partition function, so that $\log P(\boldsymbol{y}; \boldsymbol{\beta}, \boldsymbol{\eta}, c) = \log P^0(\boldsymbol{y}; \boldsymbol{\beta}, \boldsymbol{\eta}) + c$, with $P^0(\boldsymbol{y})$ representing the unnormalized probability of $\boldsymbol{y}$. We can then obtain the NCE objective by writing $D = 1$ for the case that $\boldsymbol{y}$ is drawn from the data distribution and $D = 0$ for the case that $\boldsymbol{y}$ is drawn from the noise distribution,

$$\begin{aligned} J_{NCE}&(\boldsymbol{\eta}, \boldsymbol{\beta}, c) \\ &= \sum_t \log P(D = 1 \mid \boldsymbol{y}^{(t)}; \boldsymbol{\eta}, \boldsymbol{\beta}, c) \\ &\quad - \log P(D = 0 \mid \tilde{\boldsymbol{y}}^{(t)}; \boldsymbol{\eta}, \boldsymbol{\beta}, c), \end{aligned} \tag{8}$$

where we draw exactly one noise instance $\tilde{\boldsymbol{y}}$ for each true labeling $\boldsymbol{y}^{(t)}$.

Because we are working in an unsupervised setting, we do not observe $\boldsymbol{y}^{(t)}$, so we cannot directly compute the log probability in Equation 8. Instead, we compute the expectations of the relevant log probabilities, under the distribution $Q(\boldsymbol{y})$,

$$\begin{aligned} E_Q[\log P^0(\boldsymbol{y}; \boldsymbol{\beta}, \boldsymbol{\eta})] &= \\ \sum_{\langle i,j \rangle \in G} \sum_{y} & q_{ij}(y) \boldsymbol{\eta}^\top \boldsymbol{f}(y, i, j, G) \\ + \sum_{k : \langle i,j,k \rangle \in \mathcal{T}(G)} \sum_{y, y', y''} & q_{ij}(y) q_{jk}(y') q_{ik}(y'') \beta_{y,y',y''}. \end{aligned} \tag{9}$$

We define the noise distribution $P_n$ by sampling edge labels $y_{ij}$ from their empirical distribution under $Q(\boldsymbol{y})$. The expectation $E_q[\log P_n(\boldsymbol{y})]$ is therefore simply the negative entropy of this empirical distribution, multiplied by the number of edges in $G$. We then plug in these expected log-probabilities to the noise-contrastive estimation objective function, and take derivatives with respect to the parameters $\boldsymbol{\beta}$, $\boldsymbol{\eta}$, and $c$. In each iteration of the M-step, we optimize these parameters using L-BFGS (Liu and Nocedal, 1989).

## 4 Identifying address terms in dialogue

The model described in the previous sections is applied in a study of the social meaning of **address terms** — terms for addressing individual people — which include:

**Names** such as *Barack, Barack Hussein Obama.*

**Titles** such as *Ms., Dr., Private, Reverend.* Titles can be used for address either by preceding a name (e.g., *Colonel Kurtz*), or in isolation (e.g., *Yes, Colonel.*).

**Placeholder names** such as *dude* (Kiesling, 2004), *bro*, *brother*, *sweetie*, *cousin*, and *asshole*. These terms can be used for address only in isolation (for example, in the address *cousin Sue*, the term *cousin* would be considered a title).

Because address terms connote varying levels of formality and familiarity, they play a critical role in establishing and maintaining social relationships. However, we find no prior work on automatically identifying address terms in dialogue transcripts. There are several subtasks: (1) distinguishing addresses from mentions of other individuals, (2) identifying a lexicon of titles, which either precede name addresses or can be used in isolation, (3) identifying

| **Text**: | I | 'm | not | Mr. | Lebowski | ; | you | 're | Mr. | Lebowski | . |
|---|---|---|---|---|---|---|---|---|---|---|---|
| **POS**: | PRP | VBP | RB | NNP | NNP | : | PRP | VBP | NNP | NNP | . |
| **Address**: | O | O | O | B-ADDR | L-ADDR | O | O | O | B-ADDR | L-ADDR | O |

Figure 1: Automatic re-annotation of dialogue data for address term sequences

| Feature | Description |
|---|---|
| **Lexical** | The word to be tagged, and its two predecessors and successors, $w_{i-2:i+2}$. |
| **POS** | The part-of-speech of the token to be tagged, and the POS tags of its two predecessors and successors. |
| **Case** | The case (lower, upper, or title) of the word to be tagged, and its two predessors and successors. |
| **Constituency parse** | First non-NNP ancestor node of the word $w_i$ in the constituent parse tree, and all leaf node siblings in the tree. |
| **Dependency parse** | All dependency relations involving $w_i$. |
| **Location** | Distance of $w_i$ from the start and the end of the sentence or turn. |
| **Punctuation** | All punctuation symbols occurring before and after $w_i$. |
| **Second person pronoun** | All forms of the second person pronoun within the sentence. |

Table 2: Features used to identify address spans

a lexicon of placeholder names, which can only be used in isolation. We now present a tagging-based approach for performing each of these subtasks.

We build an automatically-labeled dataset from the corpus of movie dialogues provided by Danescu-Niculescu-Mizil and Lee (2011); see Section 6 for more details. This dataset gives the identity of the speaker and addressee of each line of dialogue. These identities constitute a minimal form of manual annotation, but in many settings, such as social media dialogues, they could be obtained automatically. We augment this data by obtaining the first (given) and last (family) names of each character, which we mine from the website `rottentomatoes.com`. Next, we apply the CoreNLP part-of-speech tagger (Manning et al., 2014) to identify sequences of the NNP tag, which indicates a proper noun in the Penn Treebank Tagset (Marcus et al., 1993). For each NNP tag sequence that contains the name of the addressee, we label it as an address, using BILOU notation (Ratinov and Roth, 2009): **B**eginning, **I**nside, and **L**ast term of address segments; **O**utside and **U**nit-length sequences. An example of this tagging scheme is shown in Figure 1.

Next, we train a classifier (Support Vector Machine with a linear kernel) on this automatically labeled data, using the features shown in Table 2. For simplicity, we do not perform structured prediction, which might offer further improvements in accuracy. This classifier provides an initial, partial solution to the first problem, distinguishing second-person addresses from references to other individuals (for name references only). On heldout data, the classifier's macro-averaged F-measure is 83%, and its micro-averaged F-measure is 98.7%. Class-by-class breakdowns are shown in Table 3.

### 4.1 Address term lexicons

To our surprise, we were unable to find manually-labeled lexicons for either titles or placeholder names. We therefore employ a semi-automated approach to construct address term lexicons, bootstrapping from the address term tagger to build candidate lists, which we then manually filter.

**Titles** To induce a lexicon of titles, we consider terms that are frequently labeled with the tag B-ADDR across a variety of dialogues, performing a binomial test to obtain a list of terms whose frequency of being labeled as B-ADDR is significantly higher than chance. Of these 34 candidate terms, we manually filter out 17, which are mainly common first names, such as *John*; such names are frequently labeled as B-ADDR across movies. After this manual filtering, we obtain the following titles: *agent, aunt, captain, colonel, commander, cousin, deputy, detective, dr, herr, inspector, judge, lord, master, mayor, miss, mister, miz, monsieur, mr, mrs, ms, professor, queen, reverend, sergeant, uncle.*

**Placeholder names** To induce a lexicon of placeholder names, we remove the CURRENT-WORD feature from the model, and re-run the tagger on all dialogue data. We then focus on terms which are frequently labeled U-ADDR, indicating that they are the sole token in the address (e.g., *I'm*/O *perfectly*/O *calm*/O, *dude*/U-ADDR.) We again perform a binomial test to obtain a list of terms whose frequency of being labeled U-ADDR is significantly higher than chance. We manually filter out 41 terms from a list of 96 possible placeholder terms obtained in the previous step. Most terms eliminated were plural forms of placeholder names, such as *fellas* and *dudes*; these are indeed address terms, but because they are plural, they cannot refer to a single individual, as required by our model. Other false positives were fillers, such as *uh* and *um*, which were ocassionally labeled as I-ADDR by our tagger. After manual filtering, we obtain the following placeholder names: *asshole, babe, baby, boss, boy, bro, bud, buddy, cocksucker, convict, cousin, cowboy, cunt, dad, darling, dear, detective, doll, dude, dummy, father, fella, gal, ho, hon, honey, kid, lad, lady, lover, ma, madam, madame, man, mate, mister, mon, moron, motherfucker, pal, papa, partner, peanut, pet, pilgrim, pop, president, punk, shithead, sir, sire, son, sonny, sport, sucker, sugar, sweetheart, sweetie, tiger.*

### 4.2 Address term tokens

When constructing the content vectors $\boldsymbol{x}_{i \rightarrow j}$ and $\boldsymbol{x}_{i \leftarrow j}$, we run the address span tagger described above, and include counts for the following types of address spans:

- the bare first name, last name, and complete name of individual $j$;
- any element in the title lexicon if labeled as B-ADDR by the tagger;
- any element in the title or placeholder lexicon, if labeled as U-ADDR by the tagger.

## 5 Address terms in a model of formality

Address terms play a key role in setting the formality of a social interaction. However, understanding this role is challenging. While some address terms, like *Ms* and *Sir*, are frequent, there is a long tail of rare terms whose meaning is more difficult to ascertain from data, such as *admiral*, *dude*, and *player*. Moreover, the precise social meaning of address terms can be context-dependent: for example, the term *comrade* may be formal in some contexts, but jokingly informal in others.

| Class | F-measure | Total Instances |
|---|---|---|
| I-ADDR | 0.58 | 53 |
| B-ADDR | 0.800 | 483 |
| U-ADDR | 0.987 | 1864 |
| L-ADDR | 0.813 | 535 |
| O-ADDR | 0.993 | 35975 |

Table 3: Breakdown of f-measure and number of instances by class in the test set.

Both problems can be ameliorated by adding social network structure. We treat $Y = \text{V}$ as indicating formality and $Y = \text{T}$ as indicating informality. (The notation invokes the concept of T/V systems from politeness theory (Brown, 1987), where T refers to the informal Latin second-person pronoun *tu*, and V refers to the formal second-person pronoun *vos*.)

While formality relations are clearly asymmetric in many settings, for simplicity we assume symmetric relations: each pair of individuals is either on formal or informal terms with each other. We therefore add the constraints that $\boldsymbol{\theta}_{\text{V}}^{\leftarrow} = \boldsymbol{\theta}_{\text{V}}^{\rightarrow}$ and $\boldsymbol{\theta}_{\text{T}}^{\leftarrow} = \boldsymbol{\theta}_{\text{T}}^{\rightarrow}$. In this model, we have a soft expectation that triads will obey transitivity: for example, if $i$ and $j$ have an informal relationship, and $j$ and $k$ have an informal relationship, then $i$ and $k$ are more likely to have an informal relationship. After rotation, there are four possible triads, TTT, TTV, TVV, and VVV. The weights estimated for these triads will indicate whether our prior expectations are validated. We also consider a single pairwise feature template, a metric from Adamic and Adar (2003) that sums over the mutual friends of $i$ and $j$, assigning more weight to mutual friends who themselves have a small number of friends:

$$AA(i,j) = \sum_{k \in \Gamma(i) \cap k \in \Gamma(j)} \frac{1}{\log \#|\Gamma(k)|}, \qquad (10)$$

where $\Gamma(i)$ is the set of friends of node $i$. (We also tried simply counting the number of mutual friends, but the Adamic-Adar metric performs slightly better.) This feature appears in the vector $\boldsymbol{f}(y_{ij}, i, j, G)$, as defined in Equation 3.

## 6 Application to movie dialogues

We apply the ideas in this paper to a dataset of movie dialogues (Danescu-Niculescu-Mizil and Lee, 2011), including roughly 300,000 conversational turns between 10,000 pairs of characters in 617 movies. This dataset is chosen because it not only provides the script of each movie, but also indicates which characters are in dialogue in each line. We evaluate on quantitative measures of predictive likelihood (a token-level evaluation) and coherence of the induced address term clusters (a type-level evaluation). In addition, we describe in detail the inferred signed social networks on two films.

We evaluate the effects of three groups of features: address terms, mutual friends (using the Adamic-Adar metric), and triads. We include address terms in all evaluations, and test whether the network features improve performance. Ablating both network features is equivalent to clustering dyads by the counts of address terms, but all evaluations were performed by ablating components of the full model. We also tried ablating the text features, clustering edges using only the mutual friends and triad features, but we found that the resulting clusters were incoherent, with no discernible relationship to the address terms.

### 6.1 Predictive log-likelihood

To compute the predictive log-likelihood of the address terms, we hold out a randomly-selected 10% of films. On these films, we use the first 50% of address terms to estimate the dyad-label beliefs $q_{ij}(y)$. We then evaluate the expected log-likelihood of the second 50% of address terms, computed as $\sum_y q_{ij}(y) \sum_n \log P(x_n \mid \theta_y)$ for each dyad. This is comparable to standard techniques for computing the held-out log-likelihood of topic models (Wallach et al., 2009).

As shown in Table 4, the full model substantially outperforms the ablated alternatives. This indicates that the signed triad features contribute meaningful information towards the understanding of address terms in dialogue.

| Address terms | Mutual friends | Signed triads | Log-likelihood |
|---|---|---|---|
| ✓ | | | -2133.28 |
| ✓ | | ✓ | -2018.21 |
| ✓ | ✓ | | -1884.02 |
| ✓ | ✓ | ✓ | -1582.43 |

Table 4: Predictive log-likelihoods.

| V-cluster | T-cluster |
|---|---|
| *sir* | FIRSTNAME |
| *mr*+LASTNAME | *man* |
| *mr*+FIRSTNAME | *baby* |
| *mr* | *honey* |
| *miss*+LASTNAME | *darling* |
| *son* | *sweetheart* |
| *mister*+FIRSTNAME | *buddy* |
| *mrs* | *sweetie* |
| *mrs*+LASTNAME | *hon* |
| FIRSTNAME+LASTNAME | *dude* |

Table 5: The ten strongest address terms for each cluster, sorted by likelihood ratio.

### 6.2 Cluster coherence

Next, we consider the model inferences that result when applying the EM procedure to the entire dataset. Table 5 presents the top address terms for each cluster, according to likelihood ratio. The cluster shown on the left emphasizes full names, titles, and formal address, while the cluster on the right includes the given name and informal address terms such as *man*, *baby*, and *dude*. We therefore use the labels "V-cluster" and "T-cluster", referring to the formal and informal clusters, respectively.

We perform a quantitative evaluation of this clustering through an intrusion task (Chang et al., 2009). Specifically, we show individual raters three terms, selected so that two terms are from the same cluster, and the third term is from the other cluster; we then ask them to identify which term is least like the other two. Five raters were each given a list of forty triples, with the order randomized. Of the forty triples, twenty were from our full model, and twenty were from a text-only clustering model. The raters agreed with our full model in 73% percent of cases, and agreed with the text-only model in 52% percent

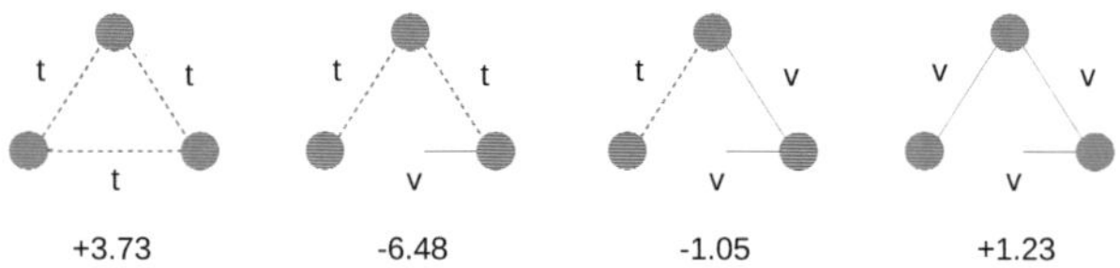


Figure 2: Estimated triad feature weights

of cases. By Fisher's exact test, this difference is statistically significant at $p < 0.01$. Both results are significantly greater than chance agreement (33%) by a binomial test, $p < 0.001$.

### 6.3 Network feature weights

Figure 2 shows the feature weights for each of the four possible triads. Triads with homogeneous signs are preferred, particularly TTT (all informal); heterogeneous triads are dispreferred, particularly TTV, which is when two individuals have a formal relationship despite having a mutual informal tie. Less dispreferred is TVV, when a pair of friends have an informal relationship despite both having a formal relationship with a third person; consider, for example, the situation of two students and their professor. In addition, the informal sign is preferred when the dyad has a high score on the Adamic-Adar metric, and dispreferred otherwise. This coheres with the intuition that highly-embedded edges are likely to be informal, with many shared friends.

### 6.4 Qualitative results

Analysis of individual movies suggests that the induced tie signs are meaningful and coherent. For example, the film "Star Wars" is a space opera, in which the protagonists Luke, Han, and Leia attempt to defeat an evil empire led by Darth Vader. The induced signed social network is shown in Figure 3. The V-edges seem reasonable: C-3PO is a robotic servant, and Blue Leader is Luke's military commander (BLUE LEADER: *Forget it, son.* LUKE: *Yes, sir, but I can get him...*). In contrast, the character pairs with T-edges all have informal relationships: the lesser-known character Biggs is Luke's more experienced friend (BIGGS: *That's no battle, kid*).

The animated film "South Park: Bigger, Longer & Uncut" centers on three children: Stan, Cartman, and Kyle; it also involves their parents, teachers, and friends, as well as a number of political and religious figures. The induced social network is shown in Figure 4. The children and their associates mostly have T-edges, except for the edge to Gregory, a British character with few speaking turns. This part of the network also has a higher clustering coefficient, as the main characters share friends such as Chef and The Mole. The left side of the diagram centers on Kyle's mother, who has more formal relationships with a variety of authority figures.

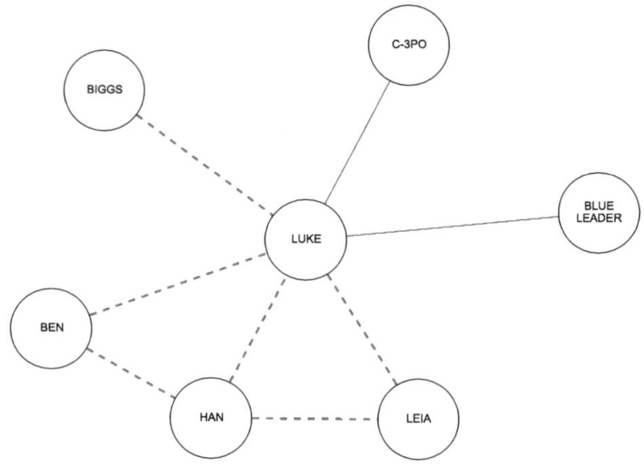


Figure 3: Induced signed social network from the film *Star Wars*. Blue solid edges are in the V-cluster, red dashed edges are in the T-cluster.

## 7 Related work

Recent work has explored the application of signed social network models to social media. Leskovec et al. (2010b) find three social media datasets from which they are able to identify edge polarity; this enables them to compare the frequency of signed triads against baseline expectations, and to build a classifier to predict edge labels (Leskovec et al., 2010a). However, in many of the most popular social media platforms, such as Twitter and Facebook, there is no metadata describing edge labels. We are also interested in new applications of signed social network analysis to datasets outside the realm of social media, such as literary texts (Moretti, 2005; Elson et al., 2010; Agarwal et al., 2013) and movie scripts, but in such corpora, edge labels are not easily available.

In many datasets, it is possible to obtain the textual content exchanged between members of the network, and this content can provide a signal for network structure. For example, Hassan et al. (2012) characterize the sign of each network edge in terms

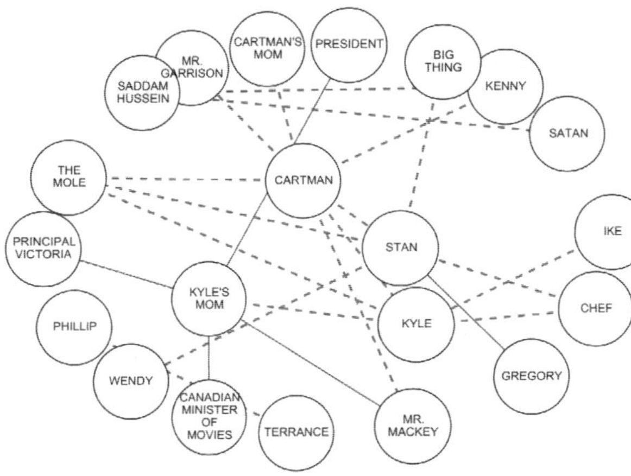


Figure 4: Induced signed social network from the film *South Park: Bigger, Longer & Uncut*. Blue solid edges are in the V-cluster, red dashed edges are in the T-cluster.

of the **sentiment** expressed across it, finding that the resulting networks cohere with the predictions of structural balance theory; similar results are obtained by West et al. (2014), who are thereby able to predict the signs of unlabeled ties. Both papers leverage the relatively mature technology of sentiment analysis, and are restricted to edge labels that reflect sentiment. The unsupervised approach presented here could in principle be applied to lexicons of sentiment terms, rather than address terms, but we leave this for future work.

The issue of address formality in English was considered by Faruqui and Padó (2011), who show that annotators can label the formality of the second person pronoun with agreement of 70%. They use these annotations to train a supervised classifier, obtaining comparable accuracy. If no labeled data is available, annotations can be projected from languages where the T/V distinction is marked in the morphology of the second person pronoun, such as German (Faruqui and Padó, 2012). Our work shows that it is possible to detect formality without labeled data or parallel text, by leveraging regularities across network structures; however, this requires the assumption that the level of formality for a pair of individuals is constant over time. The combination of our unsupervised approach with annotation projection might yield models that attain higher performance while capturing change in formality over time.

More broadly, a number of recent papers have proposed to detect various types of social relationships from linguistic content. Of particular interest are power relationships, which can be induced from n-gram features (Bramsen et al., 2011; Prabhakaran et al., 2012) and from **coordination**, where one participant's linguistic style is asymmetrically affected by the other (Danescu-Niculescu-Mizil et al., 2012). Danescu-Niculescu-Mizil et al. (2013) describe an approach to recognizing politeness in text, lexical and syntactic features motivated by politeness theory. Anand et al. (2011) detect "rebuttals" in argumentative dialogues, and Hasan and Ng (2013) employ extra-linguistic structural features to improve the detection of stances in such debates. In all of these cases, labeled data is used to train supervised model; our work shows that social structural regularities are powerful enough to support accurate induction of social relationships (and their linguistic correlates) without labeled data.

## 8 Conclusion

This paper represents a step towards unifying theoretical models of signed social network structures with linguistic accounts of the expression of social relationships in dialogue. By fusing these two phenomena into a joint probabilistic model, we can induce edge types with robust linguistic signatures and coherent structural properties. We demonstrate the effectiveness of this approach on movie dialogues, where it induces symmetric T/V networks and their linguistic signatures without supervision. Future work should evaluate the capability of this approach to induce asymmetric signed networks, the utility of partial or distant supervision, and applications to non-fictional dialogues.

## Acknowledgments

We thank the reviewers for their detailed feedback. The paper benefitted from conversations with Cristian Danescu-Niculescu-Mizil, Chris Dyer, Johan Ugander, and Bob West. This research was supported by an award from the Air Force Office of Scientific Research, and by Google, through a Focused Research Award for Computational Journalism.

## References


Lada A Adamic and Eytan Adar. 2003. Friends and neighbors on the web. *Social networks*, 25(3):211–230.

Apoorv Agarwal, Anup Kotalwar, and Owen Rambow. 2013. Automatic extraction of social networks from literary text: A case study on alice in wonderland. In *the Proceedings of the 6th International Joint Conference on Natural Language Processing (IJCNLP 2013)*.

Pranav Anand, Marilyn Walker, Rob Abbott, Jean E. Fox Tree, Robeson Bowmani, and Michael Minor. 2011. Cats rule and dogs drool!: Classifying stance in online debate. In *Proceedings of the 2nd Workshop on Computational Approaches to Subjectivity and Sentiment Analysis (WASSA 2.011)*, pages 1–9, Portland, Oregon, June. Association for Computational Linguistics.

Philip Bramsen, Martha Escobar-Molano, Ami Patel, and Rafael Alonso. 2011. Extracting social power relationships from natural language. In *Proceedings of the Association for Computational Linguistics (ACL)*, pages 773–782, Portland, OR.

Roger Brown and Marguerite Ford. 1961. Address in american english. *The Journal of Abnormal and Social Psychology*, 62(2):375.

Penelope Brown. 1987. *Politeness: Some universals in language usage*, volume 4. Cambridge University Press.

Dorwin Cartwright and Frank Harary. 1956. Structural balance: a generalization of heider's theory. *Psychological review*, 63(5):277.

Jonathan Chang, Sean Gerrish, Chong Wang, Jordan L Boyd-graber, and David M Blei. 2009. Reading tea leaves: How humans interpret topic models. In *Neural Information Processing Systems (NIPS)*, pages 288–296.

Cristian Danescu-Niculescu-Mizil and Lillian Lee. 2011. Chameleons in imagined conversations: A new approach to understanding coordination of linguistic style in dialogs. In *Proceedings of the ACL Workshop on Cognitive Modeling and Computational Linguistics*.

Cristian Danescu-Niculescu-Mizil, Lillian Lee, Bo Pang, and Jon Kleinberg. 2012. Echoes of power: Language effects and power differences in social interaction. In *Proceedings of the Conference on World-Wide Web (WWW)*, pages 699–708, Lyon, France.

Cristian Danescu-Niculescu-Mizil, Moritz Sudhof, Dan Jurafsky, Jure Leskovec, and Christopher Potts. 2013. A computational approach to politeness with application to social factors. In *Proceedings of the Association for Computational Linguistics (ACL)*, pages 250–259, Sophia, Bulgaria.

Arthur P Dempster, Nan M Laird, and Donald B Rubin. 1977. Maximum likelihood from incomplete data via the em algorithm. *Journal of the Royal Statistical Society. Series B (Methodological)*, pages 1–38.

David K Elson, Nicholas Dames, and Kathleen R McKeown. 2010. Extracting social networks from literary fiction. In *Proceedings of the Association for Computational Linguistics (ACL)*, pages 138–147, Uppsala, Sweden.

Manaal Faruqui and Sebastian Padó. 2011. "I Thou Thee, Thou Traitor": Predicting Formal vs. Informal Address in English Literature. In *Proceedings of the Association for Computational Linguistics (ACL)*, pages 467–472, Portland, OR.

Manaal Faruqui and Sebastian Padó. 2012. Towards a model of formal and informal address in english. In *Proceedings of the European Chapter of the Association for Computational Linguistics (EACL)*, pages 623–633.

Michael U Gutmann and Aapo Hyvärinen. 2012. Noise-contrastive estimation of unnormalized statistical models, with applications to natural image statistics. *The Journal of Machine Learning Research*, 13(1):307–361.

Kazi Saidul Hasan and Vincent Ng. 2013. Extra-linguistic constraints on stance recognition in ideological debates. In *Proceedings of the Association for Computational Linguistics (ACL)*, pages 816–821, Sophia, Bulgaria.

Ahmed Hassan, Amjad Abu-Jbara, and Dragomir Radev. 2012. Extracting signed social networks from text. In *Workshop Proceedings of TextGraphs-7 on Graph-based Methods for Natural Language Processing*, pages 6–14. Association for Computational Linguistics.

Dell Hymes. 1972. On communicative competence. *Sociolinguistics*, pages 269–293.

Scott F Kiesling. 2004. Dude. *American Speech*, 79(3):281–305.

Jure Leskovec, Daniel Huttenlocher, and Jon Kleinberg. 2010a. Predicting positive and negative links in online social networks. In *Proceedings of the Conference on World-Wide Web (WWW)*, pages 641–650.

Jure Leskovec, Daniel Huttenlocher, and Jon Kleinberg. 2010b. Signed networks in social media. In *Proceedings of Human Factors in Computing Systems (CHI)*, pages 1361–1370.

David Liben-Nowell and Jon Kleinberg. 2007. The link-prediction problem for social networks. *Journal of the American society for information science and technology*, 58(7):1019–1031.

Dong C Liu and Jorge Nocedal. 1989. On the limited memory BFGS method for large scale optimization. *Mathematical programming*, 45(1-3):503–528.

Christopher D. Manning, Mihai Surdeanu, John Bauer, Jenny Finkel, Steven J. Bethard, and David McClosky. 2014. The Stanford CoreNLP natural language processing toolkit. In *Proceedings of 52nd Annual Meeting of the Association for Computational Linguistics: System Demonstrations*, pages 55–60.

Mitchell P Marcus, Mary Ann Marcinkiewicz, and Beatrice Santorini. 1993. Building a large annotated corpus of English: The Penn Treebank. *Computational Linguistics*, 19(2):313–330.

Franco Moretti. 2005. *Graphs, maps, trees: abstract models for a literary history*. Verso.

Vinodkumar Prabhakaran, Owen Rambow, and Mona Diab. 2012. Predicting overt display of power in written dialogs. In *Proceedings of the North American Chapter of the Association for Computational Linguistics (NAACL)*, pages 518–522.

Lev Ratinov and Dan Roth. 2009. Design challenges and misconceptions in named entity recognition. In *Proceedings of the Thirteenth Conference on Computational Natural Language Learning*, pages 147–155. Association for Computational Linguistics.

Martin J Wainwright and Michael I Jordan. 2008. Graphical models, exponential families, and variational inference. *Foundations and Trends® in Machine Learning*, 1(1-2):1–305.

Hanna M Wallach, Iain Murray, Ruslan Salakhutdinov, and David Mimno. 2009. Evaluation methods for topic models. In *Proceedings of the International Conference on Machine Learning (ICML)*, pages 1105–1112.

Robert West, Hristo Paskov, Jure Leskovec, and Christopher Potts. 2014. Exploiting social network structure for person-to-person sentiment analysis. *Transactions of the Association for Computational Linguistics*, 2:297–310.

# Unsupervised Morphology Induction Using Word Embeddings

**Radu Soricut**
Google Inc.
rsoricut@google.com

**Franz Och***
Human Longevity Inc.
och@humanlongevity.com

## Abstract

We present a language agnostic, unsupervised method for inducing morphological transformations between words. The method relies on certain regularities manifest in high-dimensional vector spaces. We show that this method is capable of discovering a wide range of morphological rules, which in turn are used to build morphological analyzers. We evaluate this method across six different languages and nine datasets, and show significant improvements across all languages.

## 1 Introduction

Word representations obtained via neural networks (Bengio et al., 2003; Socher et al., 2011a) or specialized models (Mikolov et al., 2013a) have been used to address various natural language processing tasks (Mnih et al., 2009; Huang et al., 2014; Bansal et al., 2014). These vector representations capture various syntactic and semantic properties of natural language (Mikolov et al., 2013b). In many instances, natural language uses a small set of concepts to render a much larger set of meaning variations via morphology. We show in this paper that morphological transformations can be captured by exploiting regularities present in word-representations as the ones trained using the Skip-Gram model (Mikolov et al., 2013a).

In contrast to previous approaches that combine morphology with vector-based word representations (Luong et al., 2013; Botha and Blunsom, 2014), we do not rely on an external morphological analyzer, such as Morfessor (Creutz and Lagus, 2007). Instead, our method automatically induces morphological rules and transformations, represented as vectors in the same embedding space.

At the heart of our method is the SkipGram model described in (Mikolov et al., 2013a). We further exploit the observations made by Mikolov et al (2013b), and further studied by (Levy and Goldberg, 2014; Pennington et al., 2014), regarding the regularities exhibited by such embedding spaces. These regularities have been shown to allow inferences of certain types (e.g., *king* is to *man* what *queen* is to *woman*). Such regularities also hold for certain morphological relations (e.g., *car* is to *cars* what *dog* is to *dogs*). In this paper, we show that one can exploit these regularities to model, in a principled way, prefix- and suffix-based morphology. The main contributions of this paper are as follows:

1. provides a method by which morphological rules are learned in an unsupervised, language-agnostic fashion;

2. provides a mechanism for applying these rules to known words (e.g., *boldly* is analyzed as *bold+ly*, while *only* is not);

3. provides a mechanism for applying these rules to rare and unseen words;

We show that this method improves state-of-the-art performance on a word-similarity rating task using standard datasets. We also quantify the impact of our morphology treatment when using large amounts of training data (tens/hundreds of billions of words).

The technique we describe is capable of inducing transformations that cover both typical, regular morphological rules, such as adding suffix *ed*

*Work done at Google, now at Human Longevity Inc.



*Human Language Technologies: The 2015 Annual Conference of the North American Chapter of the ACL*, pages 1627–1637,
Denver, Colorado, May 31 – June 5, 2015. 

to verbs in English, as well as exceptions to such rules, such as the fact that pluralization of words that end in *y* require substituting it with *ies*. Because each such transformation is represented in the high-dimensional embedding space, it therefore captures the semantics of the change. Consequently, it allows us to build vector representations for any unseen word for which a morphological analysis is found, therefore covering an unbounded (albeit incomplete) vocabulary.

Our empirical evaluations show that this language-agnostic technique is capable of learning morphological transformations across various language families. We present results for English, German, French, Spanish, Romanian, Arabic, and Uzbek. The results indicate that the induced morphological analysis deals successfully with sophisticated morphological variations.

## 2 Previous Work

Many recent proposals in the literature use word-representations as the basic units for tackling sentence-level tasks such as language modeling (Mnih and Hinton, 2007; Mikolov and Zweig, 2012), paraphrase detection (Socher et al., 2011a), sentiment analysis (Socher et al., 2011b), discriminative parsing (Collobert, 2011), as well as similar tasks involving larger units such as documents (Glorot et al., 2011; Huang et al., 2012; Le and Mikolov, 2014). The main advantage offered by these techniques is that they can be both trained in an unsupervised manner, and also tuned using supervised labels. However, most of these approaches treat words as units, and fail to account for phenomena involving the relationship between various morphological forms that affect word semantics, especially for rare or unseen words.

Previous attempts at dealing with sub-word units and their compositionality have looked at explicitly-engineered features such as stems, cases, POS, etc., and used models such as factored NLMs (Alexandrescu and Kirchhoff, 2006) to obtain representations for unseen words, or compositional distributional semantic models (Lazaridou et al., 2013) to derive representations for morphologically-inflected words, based on the composing morphemes. A more recent trend has seen proposals that deal with morphology using vector-space representations (Luong et al., 2013; Botha and Blunsom, 2014). Given word morphemes (affixes, roots), a neural-network architecture (recursive neural networks in the work of Luong et al (2013), log-bilinear models in the case of Botha and Blunsom (2014)), is used to obtain embedding representations for existing morphemes, and also to combine them into (possibly novel) embedding representations for words that may not have been seen at training time.

Common to these proposals is the fact that the morphological analysis of words is treated as an external, preprocessing-style step. This step is done using off-the-shelf analyzers such as Morfessor (Creutz and Lagus, 2007). As a result, the morphological analysis happens within a different model compared to the model in which the resulting morphemes are consequently used. In contrast, the work presented here uses the same vector-space embedding to achieve both the morphological analysis of words and to compute their representation. As a consequence, the morphological analysis can be justified in terms of the relationship between the resulting representation and other words that exhibit similar morphological properties.

## 3 Morphology Induction using Embedding Spaces

The method we present induces *morphological transformations* supported by evidence in terms of regularities within a word-embedding space. We describe in this section the algorithm used to induce such transformations.

### 3.1 Morphological Transformations

We consider two main transformation types, namely prefix and suffix substitutions. Other transformation types can also be considered, but we restrict the focus of this work to morphological phenomena that can be modeled via prefixes and suffixes.

We provide first a high-level description of our algorithm, followed by details regarding the individual steps. The following steps are applied to monolingual training data over a finite vocabulary $V$:

1. Extract candidate prefix/suffix rules from $V$
2. Train embedding space $E^n \subset \mathbb{R}^n$ for all words in $V$

3. Evaluate quality of candidate rules in $E^n$
4. Generate lexicalized morphological transformations

We provide more detailed descriptions next.

**Extract candidate rules from V**

Starting from $(w_1, w_2) \in V^2$, the algorithm extracts all possible prefix and suffix substitutions from $w_1$ to $w_2$, up to a specified size[1]. We denote such substitutions using triplets of the form `type:from:to`. For instance, triplet `suffix:ed:ing` denotes the substitution of suffix *ed* with suffix *ing*; this substitution is supported by many word pairs in an English vocabulary, e.g. (*bored, boring*), (*stopped, stopping*), etc. We call these triplets candidate rules, because they form the basis of an extended set from which the algorithm extracts morphological rules.

At this stage, the candidate rules set contains both rules that reflect true morphology phenomena, e.g. `suffix:s:`$\epsilon$ (replace suffix *s* with the null suffix, extracted from (*stops, stop*), (*weds, wed*), etc.), or `prefix:un:`$\epsilon$ (replace prefix *un* with the null prefix, from (*undone, done*), etc.), but also rules that simply reflect surface-level coincidences, e.g. `prefix:S:`$\epsilon$ (delete *S* at the beginning of a word, from (*Scream, cream*), (*Scope, cope*), etc.).

**Train embedding space**

Using a large monolingual corpus, we train a word-embedding space $E^n$ of dimensionality $n$ for all words in $V$ using the SkipGram model (Mikolov et al., 2013a). For the experiments reported in this paper, we used our own implementation of this model (which varies only slightly from the publicly-available `word2vec` implementation[2]).

**Evaluate quality of candidate rules**

The extracted candidate rules set is evaluated by using, for each proposed rule $r$, its support set:

$$S_r = \{(w_1, w_2) \in V^2 | w_1 \xrightarrow{r} w_2\}$$

The notation $w_1 \xrightarrow{r} w_2$ means that rule $r$ applies to word $w_1$ (e.g., for rule `suffix:ed:ing`, word $w_1$ ends with suffix *ed*), and the result of applying the rule to word $w_1$ is word $w_2$. To speed up computation, we downsample the sets $S_r$ to a large-enough number of word pairs (1000 has been used in the experiments in this paper).

[1] A maximum size of 6 is used in our experiments.

[2] At `code.google.com/p/word2vec`.

| rule | hit rate | Example $\uparrow d_w$ |
|---|---|---|
| `suffix:er:o` | 0.8 | $\uparrow d_{\text{Vot}\underline{\text{er}}}$ |
| `suffix:ton:`$\epsilon$ | 1.1 | $\uparrow d_{\text{Gale}\underline{\text{ton}}}$ |
| `prefix:S:`$\epsilon$ | 1.6 | $\uparrow d_{\underline{\text{S}}\text{DK}}$ |
| `prefix:`$\epsilon$`:in` | 28.8 | $\uparrow d_{\_\text{competent}}$ |
| `suffix:ly:`$\epsilon$ | 32.1 | $\uparrow d_{\text{official}\underline{\text{ly}}}$ |
| `prefix:`$\epsilon$`:re` | 37.0 | $\uparrow d_{\_\text{sited}}$ |
| `prefix:un:re` | 39.0 | $\uparrow d_{\underline{\text{un}}\text{made}}$ |
| `suffix:st:sm` | 52.5 | $\uparrow d_{\text{egoi}\underline{\text{st}}}$ |
| `suffix:ted:te` | 54.9 | $\uparrow d_{\text{imita}\underline{\text{ted}}}$ |
| `suffix:ed:ing` | 68.1 | $\uparrow d_{\text{procur}\underline{\text{ed}}}$ |
| `suffix:y:ies` | 69.6 | $\uparrow d_{\text{foundr}\underline{\text{y}}}$ |
| `suffix:t:ts` | 73.0 | $\uparrow d_{\text{pugilis}\underline{\text{t}}}$ |
| `suffix:sed:zed` | 80.1 | $\uparrow d_{\text{seriali}\underline{\text{sed}}}$ |

Table 1: Candidate rules evaluated in $E^n$.

We define a generic evaluation function $Ev^F$ over paired couples in $S_r \times S_r$, using a function $F : \mathbb{R}^n \times \mathbb{R}^n \rightarrow \mathbb{R}$, as follows:

$$Ev^F((w_1, w_2), (w, w')) = F_E(w_2, w_1 + \uparrow d_w) \quad (1)$$
$$(w_1, w_2), (w, w') \in S_r, \ \uparrow d_w = w' - w$$

Word-pair combinations in $S_r \times S_r$ are evaluated using Eq. 1 to assess the meaning-preservation property of rule $r$. We use as $F_E$ function $\text{rank}_E$, the cosine-similarity rank function in $E^n$. We can quantitatively measure the assertion "*car* is to *cars* what *dog* is to *dogs*", as $\text{rank}_E(cars, car + \uparrow d_{dog\_})$. We use a single threshold $t^0_{\text{rank}}$ to capture meaning preservation (all the experiments in this paper use $t^0_{\text{rank}} = 100$): for each proposed rule $r$, we compute a hit rate based on the number of times Eq. 1 scores above $t^0_{\text{rank}}$, over the number of times it has been evaluated. In Table 1 we present some of these candidate rules and their hit rate.

We note that rules that are non-meaning–preserving receive low hit rates, while rules that are morphological in nature, such as `suffix:ed:ing` (verb change from past/participle to present-continuous) and `suffix:y:ies` (pluralization of *y*–ending nouns), receive high hit rates.

| $w_1$ | $w_2$ | rank | cosine | transformation |
|---|---|---|---|---|
| create | created | 0 | 0.58 | suffix:$\epsilon$:d:$\uparrow$dethrone |
| create | creates | 0 | 0.65 | suffix:te:tes:$\uparrow$evaluate |
| create | creates | 1 | 0.62 | suffix:$\epsilon$:s:$\uparrow$contradict |
| created | create | 0 | 0.65 | suffix:ed:e$\uparrow$eroded |
| creation | create | 0 | 0.52 | suffix:ion:e:$\uparrow$communication |
| creation | created | 0 | 0.54 | suffix:ion:ed:$\uparrow$disruption |
| recreations | recreate | 2 | 0.59 | suffix:ions:e:$\uparrow$translations |
| recreations | recreating | 1 | 0.53 | suffix:ions:ing:$\uparrow$constructions |
| recreations | Recreations | 81 | 0.64 | prefix:r:R:$\uparrow$remediation |

Table 2: Examples of lexicalized morphological transformations evaluated in $E^n$ using rank and cosine.

**Generate lexicalized morphological transformations**

The results in Table 1 indicate the need for creating *lexicalized* transformations. For instance, rule suffix:ly:$\epsilon$ (drop suffix *ly*, a perfectly reasonable morphological transformation in English) is evaluated to have a hit rate of 32.1%. While such transformations are desirable, we want to avoid applying them when firing without yielding meaning-preserving results (the rest of 67.9%), e.g., for word-pair (*only, on*). We therefore create lexicalized transformations by restricting the rule application to the vocabulary subset of $V$ which passes the meaning-preservation criterion.

The algorithm also computes best direction vectors $\uparrow d_w$ for each rule support set $S_r$. It greedily selects a direction vector $\uparrow d_{w_0}$ that explains (based on Equation 1) the most pairs in $S_r$. After subset $S_r^{w_0}$ is computed for direction vector $\uparrow d_{w_0}$, it applies recursively on set $S_r - S_r^{w_0}$. This yields a new best direction vector $\uparrow d_{w_1}$, and so on. The recursion stops when it finds a direction vector $\uparrow d_{w_k}$ that explains less than a predefined number of words (we used 10 in all the experiments from this paper).

We consider multiple direction vectors $\uparrow d_{w_i}$ because of the possibly-ambiguous nature of a morphological transformation. Consider rule suffix:$\epsilon$:s, which can be applied to the noun *walk* to yield plural-noun *walks*; this case is modeled with a transformation like *walk* + $\uparrow d_{invention\_}$, since $\uparrow d_{invention\_}$=*inventions*$-$*invention* is a direction that our procedure deems to explain well noun pluralization; it can also be applied to the verb *walk* to yield the 3rd-person singular form of the verb, in which case it is modeled as *walk* + $\uparrow d_{enlist\_}$, since $\uparrow d_{enlist\_}$=*enlists*$-$*enlist* is a direction that our procedure deems to explain well 3rd-person singular verb forms. In that sense, our algorithm goes beyond proposing simple surface-level morphemes, with direction vectors encoding well-defined semantics for our morphological analysis.

Lexicalized rules enhanced with direction vectors are called *morphological transformations*. For each morphological transformation, we evaluate again how well it passes a proximity test in $E^n$ for the words it applies to. As evaluation criteria, we use two instances of Eq 1, with $F_E$ instantiated to $\text{rank}_E$ and $\text{cosine}_E$, respectively. We apply more stringent criteria in this second pass, using thresholds on the resulting rank ($t_{\text{rank}}$) and cosine ($t_{\text{cosine}}$) values to indicate meaning preservation (we used $t_{\text{rank}} = 30$ and $t_{\text{cosine}} = 0.5$ in all the experiments in this paper). We present in Table 2 a sample of the results of this procedure. For instance, word *create* can be transformed to *creates* using two different transformations: suffix:te:tes:$\uparrow$evaluate and suffix:$\epsilon$:s:$\uparrow$contradict, passing the meaning-preservation criteria with rank=0, cosine=0.65, and rank=1, cosine=0.62, respectively.

Lexicalized morphological transformations over a vocabulary $V$ have a graph-based interpretation: words represent nodes, transformations represent edges in a labeled, weighted, cyclic, directed multi-graph (weights are $(r, c)$ pairs, rank and cosine values; multiple direction vectors create multiple edges between two nodes; cycles may exist, see

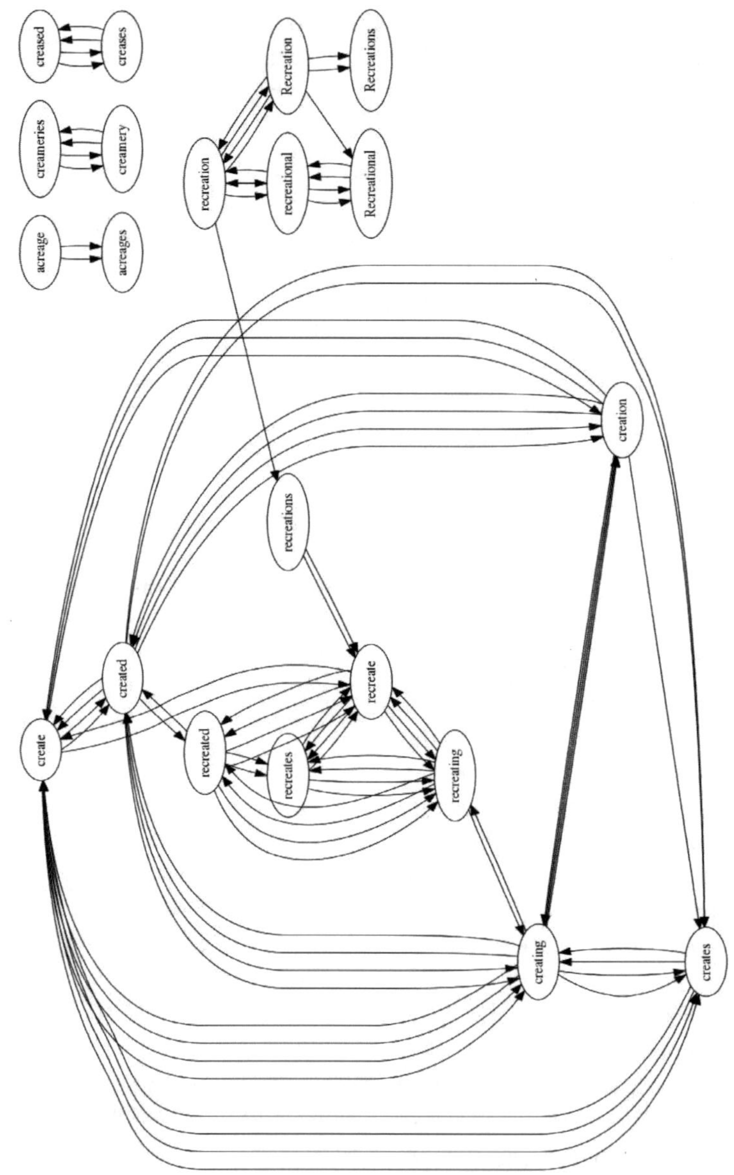


Figure 1: A few strongly connected components of a $G^V_{Morph}$ graph for English.

e.g. *created→create→created* in Table 2). We use the notation $G^V_{Morph}$ to denote such a graph. $G^V_{Morph}$ usually contains many strongly connected components, with components representing families of morphological variations. As an illustration, we present in Figure 1 a few strongly connected components obtained for an English embedding space (for illustration purposes, we show only a maximum of 2 directed edges between any two nodes in this multigraph, even though more may exist).

### 3.2 Inducing 1-to-1 Morphological Mappings

The induced graph $G^V_{Morph}$ encodes a lot of information about words and how they relate to each other. For some applications, however, we want to normalize away morphological diversity by mapping to a canonical surface form. This amounts to selecting, from among all the candidate morphological transformations generated, specific 1-to-1 mappings. In graph terms, this means building a labeled, weighted, acyclic, directed graph $D^V_{Morph}$ starting

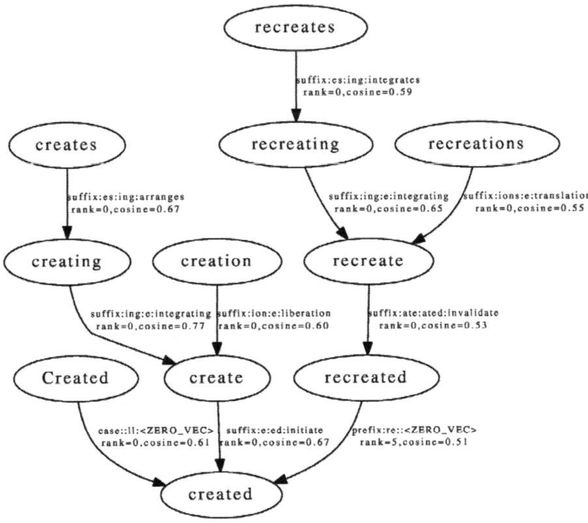


Figure 2: A part of a $D^V_{Morph}$ graph, with the morphological family for the normal-form *created*.

from $G^V_{Morph}$, using the nodes from $G^V_{Morph}$ and retaining only edges that meet certain criteria.

For the experiments presented in Section 4, we build a directed graph $D^V_{Morph}$ as follows:

1. edge $w_1 \overset{(r,c)}{\rightarrow} w_2$ in $G^V_{Morph}$ is considered only if $\text{count}(w_1) \leq \text{count}(w_2)$ in $V$;

2. if multiple such edges exist, chose the one with minimal rank $r$;

3. if multiple such edges still exist, chose the one with the maximal cosine $c$.

The interpretation we give is word-normalization: a normalization of $w$ to $w'$ is guaranteed to be meaning preserving (using the direction-vector semantics), and to a more frequent form. A snippet of the resulting graph $D^V_{Morph}$ is presented in Figure 2.

One notable aspect of this normalization procedure is that these are not "traditional" morphological mappings, with morphology-inflected words mapped to their linguistic roots. Rather, our method produces morphological mappings that favor frequency over linguistic normalization. An example of this can be seen in Figure 2, where the root form *create* is morphologically-explained by mapping it to the form *created*. This choice is purely based on our desire to favor the accuracy of the word-representations for the normal forms; different choices regarding how this pruning procedure is performed lead to different normalization procedures, including some that are more linguistically-motivated (e.g., length-based).

### 3.3 Morphological Transformations for Rare and Unknown Words

For some count threshold $C$, we define $V_C = \{w \in V | C \leq \text{count}(w)\}$. The method we presented up to this point induces a morphology graph $D^{V_C}_{Morph}$ that can be used to perform morphological analysis for any words in $V_C$. We analyze the rest of the words we may encounter (i.e., rare words and OOVs) by mapping them directly to nodes in $D^{V_C}_{Morph}$.

We extract such mappings from $D^{V_C}_{Morph}$ using all the sequences of edges that start at nodes in the graph and end in a normal-form (i.e., nodes that have out-degree 0). The result is a set of rule sequences denoted *RS*. A count cutoff on the rule sequence counts is used, since low-count sequences tend to be less reliable (in the experiments reported in this paper we use a cutoff of 50). We also denote with *R* the set of all edges in $D_{Morph}$. Using sets *RS* and *R*, we map $w \notin V_C$ to a node $w' \in D^{V_C}_{Morph}$, as follows:

1. for rule-sequences $s \in RS$ from highest-to-lowest count, if $w \overset{s}{\rightarrow} w'$ and $w' \in D^{V_C}_{Morph}$, then $s$ is the morphological analysis for $w$;

2. if no $s$ is found, do breadth-first search in $D^{V_C}_{Morph}$ using $r \in R$, up to a predefined[3] depth $d$; for $k \leq d$, word $w'$ with $w \overset{r_1 \ldots r_k}{\longrightarrow} w' \in D^{V_C}_{Morph}$ and the highest count in $V_C$ is the morphological analysis for $w$.

For example, this procedure uses the $RS$ sequence $s$=$\texttt{prefix}:\texttt{un}:\epsilon, \texttt{suffix}:\texttt{ness}:\epsilon$ to perform the OOV morphological analysis *unassertiveness* $\overset{s}{\longrightarrow}$*assertive*. We perform an in-depth analysis of the performance of this procedure in Section 4.2.

## 4 Empirical Results

In this section, we evaluate the performance of the procedure described in Section 3. Our evaluations aim at answering several empirical questions: how

[3]We use $d$=1 in the experiments reported in Section 4.2.

| Lang | \|Tokens\| | $\|V\|$ | $\|G_{Morph}^V\|$ | $\|D_{Morph}^V\|$ |
|---|---|---|---|---|
| EN | 1.1b | 1.2m | 780k | 75,823 |
| DE | 1.2b | 2.9m | 3.7m | 169,017 |
| FR | 1.5b | 1.2m | 1.8m | 92,145 |
| ES | 566m | 941k | 2.2m | 82,379 |
| RO | 1.7b | 963k | 3.8m | 141,642 |
| AR | 453m | 624k | 2.4m | 114,246 |
| UZ | 850m | 2.0m | 5.6m | 194,717 |

Table 3: Statistics regarding the size of the training data and the induced morphology graphs.

well does our method capture morphology, and how does it compare with previous approaches that use word-representations for morphology? How well does this method handle OOVs? How does the impact of morphology analysis change with training data size? We provide both qualitative and quantitative answers for each of these questions next.

### 4.1 Quality of Morphological Analysis

We first evaluate the impact of our morphological analysis on a standard word-similarity rating task. The task measures word-level understanding by comparing the correlation between human-produced similarity ratings for word pairs, e.g. (*intraspecific, interspecies*), with those produced by an algorithm. For the experiments reported here, we train SkipGram models[4] using a dimensionality of $n = 500$. We denote a system using only SkipGram model embeddings as SG. To evaluate the impact of our method, we perform morphological analysis for words below a count threshold $C$. For a word $w \in D_{Morph}^{V_C}$, we simply use the SkipGram vector-representation; for a word $w \notin D_{Morph}^{V_C}$, we use as word-representation its mapping in $D_{Morph}^{V_C}$; we denote such a system SG+Morph. For both SG and SG+Morph systems, we compute the similarity of word-pairs using the cosine distance between the vector-representations.

#### Data

We train both the SG and SG+Morph models from scratch, for all languages considered. For English, we use the Wikipedia data (Shaoul and Westbury, 2010). For German, French, and Spanish, we use the monolingual data released as part of the WMT-2013 shared task (Bojar et al., 2013). For Arabic we use the Arabic GigaWord corpus (Parker et al., 2011). For Romanian and Uzbek, we use collections of News harvested from the web and cleaned (boilerplate removed, formatting removed, encoding made consistent, etc.). All SkipGram models are trained using a count cutoff of 5 (all words with count less than the cutoff are ignored). Table 3 presents statistics on the data and vocabulary size, as well as the size of the induced morphology graphs. These numbers illustrate the richness of the morphological phenomena present in languages such as German, Romanian, Arabic, and Uzbek, compared to English.

As test sets, we use standard, publicly-available word-similarity datasets. Most relevant for our approach is the Stanford English Rare-Word (RW) dataset (Luong et al., 2013), consisting of 2034 word pairs with a higher degree of English morphology compared to other word-similarity datasets. We also use for English the WS353 (Finkelstein et al., 2002) and RG65 datasets (Rubenstein and Goodenough, 1965). For German, we use the Gur350 and ZG222 datasets (Zesch and Gurevych, 2006). For French we use the RG65 French version (Joubarne and Inkpen, 2011); for Spanish, Romanian, and Arabic we use their respective versions of WS353 (Hassan and Mihalcea, 2009).

#### Results

We present in Table 4 the results obtained across 6 language pairs and 9 datasets, using a count threshold for SG+Morph of $C = 100$. We also include the results obtained by two previously-proposed methods, LSM2013 (Luong et al., 2013) and BB2014 (Botha and Blunsom, 2014), which share some of the characteristics of our method.

Even in the absence of any morphological treatment, our word representations are better than previously used ones. For instance, LSM2013 uses exactly the same EN Wikipedia (Shaoul and Westbury, 2010) training data, and achieves 26.8 and 34.4 Spearman $\rho$ correlation on RW, with and without morphological treatment, respectively. The word representations we train yield a $\rho$ of 35.8 for SG, and a $\rho$ of 41.8 for SG+Morph (+7.4 improve-

[4] Additional settings include a window-size of 5 and negative sampling set to 5. Unseen words receive a zero-vector embedding and a cosine score of 0.

| Language / Testset | EN | | | DE | | FR | ES | RO | AR |
|---|---|---|---|---|---|---|---|---|---|
| | Spearman $\rho$ | | | | | | | | |
| System | RW | WS | RG | Gur | ZG | RG | WS | WS | WS |
| LSM2013 w/o morph | 26.8 | 62.6 | 62.8 | - | - | - | - | - | - |
| LSM2013 w/ morph | 34.4 | 64.6 | 65.5 | - | - | - | - | - | - |
| BB2014 w/o morph | 18.0 | 32.0 | 47.0 | 36.0 | 6.0 | 33.0 | 26.0 | - | - |
| BB2014 w/ morph | 30.0 | 40.0 | 41.0 | 56.0 | **25.0** | 45.0 | 28.0 | - | - |
| SG | 35.8 | 71.2 | 75.1 | 62.4 | 16.6 | 63.6 | 36.5 | 51.7 | 37.1 |
| SG+Morph | **41.8** | **71.2** | **75.1** | **64.1** | 21.5 | **67.3** | **47.3** | **53.1** | **43.1** |
| # pairs | 2034 | 353 | 65 | 350 | 222 | 65 | 353 | 353 | 353 |

Table 4: Performance of previously proposed methods, compared to SG and SG+Morph trained on Wiki1b. LSM2013 uses exactly the same training data for EN, whereas BB2014 uses the same training data for DE, FR, ES.

ment under the morphology condition). The morphological treatment used by LSM2013 also has a small effect on the words present in the English WS and RG sets; our method does not propose any separate morphological treatment for the words in these datasets, since all of them have been observed more than our $C = 100$ threshold in the training data (therefore have reliable representations). The SG word-representations for all the other languages (German, French, Spanish, Romanian, and Arabic) also perform well on this task, with much higher Spearman scores obtained by SG compared with the previously-reported scores.

The results in Table 4 also show that our morphology treatment provides consistent gains across all languages considered. For morphologically-rich languages, all datasets reflect the impact of morphology treatment. We observe significant gains between the performance of the SG and SG+Morph systems, on top of the high correlation numbers of the SG system. For German, the relatively small increase we observe is due to the fact the German noun-compounds are not covered by our morphological treatment. For French, Spanish, Romanian, and Arabic, the gains by the SG+Morph support the conclusion that our method, while completely language-agnostic, handles well the variety of morphological phenomena present in these languages.

### 4.2 Quality of Morphological Analysis for Unknown/Rare Words

In this section, we quantify the accuracy of the morphological treatment for OOVs presented in Section 3.3. We assume that the statistics for unseen words (with respect to their morphological make-up) are similar with the statistics for low-frequency words. Therefore, for some relatively-low counts $L$ and $H$, the set $V_{[L,H)} = V_L - V_H$ is a good proxy for the population of OOV words that we see at run-time. We evaluate OOV morphology as follows:

1. Run the procedure for morphology induction on $V_L$, resulting in $D^{V_L}_{Morph}$;
2. Run the procedure for morphology induction on $V_H$, resulting in $D^{V_H}_{Morph}$;
3. Apply OOV morphology using $D^{V_H}_{Morph}$ for each $w \in V_{[L,H]}$; evaluate resulting $w \rightarrow w'$ against reference $w \rightarrow w'_{ref}$ from $D^{V_L}_{Morph}$, as normal-form$(w') \equiv$ normal-form$(w'_{ref})$.

To make the analysis more revealing, we split the entries in $V_{[L,H)}$ in two: type T1 entries are those that have in-degree $> 0$ in $D^{V_L}_{Morph}$ (i.e., words that have a morphological mapping in the reference graph); type T2 entries are those that have 0 in-degree in $D^{V_L}_{Morph}$ (i.e., words with no morphological mapping in the reference, e.g., proper-nouns in English). Note that the T1/T2 distinction reflects a recall/precision trade-off: T1-words should be morphologically analyzed, while T2-words should not; a method that over-analyses has poor performance on T2, while one that under-analyses performs poorly on T1.

We use the same datasets as the ones presented in Section 4.1, see Table 3. The results for all the languages are shown in Table 6, with all rows using

| | EN (RW testset) | | | | DE (RG testset) | | | |
|---|---|---|---|---|---|---|---|---|
| | \|Unmapped\| | | Spearman $\rho$ | | \|Unmapped\| | | Spearman $\rho$ | |
| | Wiki1b | News120b | Wiki1b | News120b | WMT2b | News20b | WMT2b | News20b |
| SG | 80 | 177 | 35.8 | 44.7 | 0 | 20 | 62.4 | 62.1 |
| SG+Morph | 1 | 0 | 41.8 | 52.0 | 0 | 0 | 64.1 | 69.1 |

Table 5: Comparison between models SG and SG+Morph at different training-data sizes.

| | $\|V_{[1000,2000)}\|$ | | Accuracy | |
|---|---|---|---|---|
| Lang | T1 | T2 | T1 | T2 |
| EN | 3421 | 10617 | 89.7% | 89.6% |
| DE | 10778 | 21234 | 90.8% | 93.1% |
| FR | 6435 | 9807 | 90.3% | 90.4% |
| ES | 5724 | 7412 | 91.1% | 90.3% |
| RO | 11905 | 9254 | 86.5% | 85.3% |
| AR | 7913 | 5202 | 92.4% | 69.0% |
| UZ | 11772 | 9027 | 81.3% | 84.1% |

Table 6: Accuracy of Rare&OOV analysis.

| Lang | \|Tokens\| | $\|V\|$ | $\|G^V_{Morph}\|$ | $\|D^V_{Morph}\|$ |
|---|---|---|---|---|
| EN | 120b | 1.0m | 2.9m | 98,268 |
| DE | 20b | 1.8m | 6.7m | 351,980 |

Table 7: Statistics for large training-data sizes.

the same setup. Count $L = 1000$ was chosen such that $D^{V_L}_{Morph}$ is reliable enough to be used as reference. The accuracy results are consistently high (in the 80-90% range) for both T1- and T2-words, even for morphologically-rich languages such as Uzbek. These results indicate that our method does well at both identifying a morphological analysis when appropriate, as well as not proposing one when not justified, and therefore provides accurate morphology analysis for rare and OOV words.

### 4.3 Morphology and Training Data Size

We also evaluate the impact of our morphology analysis under a regime with substantially more training data. To this end, we use large collections of English and German News, harvested from the web and cleaned (boiler-plate removed, formatting removed, encoding made consistent). Statistics regarding the resulting vocabularies and the induced morphology are presented in Table 7 (vocabulary cutoffs of 400 for EN and 50 for DE). We present results using the word-similarity task using the same Stanford Rare-Word (RW) dataset for EN and RG dataset for DE, compared against the setup using only 1-2 billion training tokens. For SG+Morph, we use count thresholds of 3000 for EN and 100 for DE. The results are given in Table 5. For English, a 100x increase in the training data for EN brings a 10-point increase in Spearman $\rho$ (from 35.8 to 44.7, and from 41.8 to 52.0). The morphological analysis provides substantial gains at either level of training-data size: 6 points in $\rho$ for Wiki1b (from 35.8 to 41.8), and 7.3 points for News120b EN (from 44.7 to 52.0). For German, the increase in training-data size does not bring visible improvements (perhaps due the high vocabulary cutoff), but the morphological treatment has a large impact under the large training-data condition (7 points for News20b DE, from 62.1 to 69.1).

## 5 Conclusions and Future Work

We have presented an unsupervised method for morphology induction. The method derives a morphological analyzer from scratch, and only requires a monolingual corpus for training, with no additional knowledge of the language. Our evaluation shows that this method performs well across a large variety of language families, and we present here results that improve on current state-of-the-art for the morphologically-rich Stanford Rare-word dataset.

We acknowledge that certain languages exhibit phenomena (such as word-compounds in German) that require a more focused approach for solving them. But techniques like the ones presented here have the potential to exploit vector-based word representations successfully to address such phenomena as well.

## References


Andrei Alexandrescu and Katrin Kirchhoff. 2006. Factored neural language models. In *Human Language Technology Conference of the North American Chapter of the Association of Computational Linguistics*.

Mohit Bansal, Kevin Gimpel, and Karen Livescu. 2014. Tailoring continuous word representations for dependency parsing. In *Proceedings of the 52nd Annual Meeting of the Association for Computational Linguistics, ACL 2014, June 22-27, Baltimore, MD, USA, Volume 2: Short Papers*, pages 809–815.

Yoshua Bengio, Réjean Ducharme, Pascal Vincent, and Christian Janvin. 2003. A neural probabilistic language model. *Journal of Machine Learning Research*, 3:1137–1155.

Ondřej Bojar, Christian Buck, Chris Callison-Burch, Christian Federmann, Barry Haddow, Philipp Koehn, Christof Monz, Matt Post, Radu Soricut, and Lucia Specia. 2013. Findings of the 2013 Workshop on Statistical Machine Translation. In *Proceedings of the Eighth Workshop on Statistical Machine Translation*, pages 1–44, Sofia, Bulgaria, August. Association for Computational Linguistics.

Jan A. Botha and Phil Blunsom. 2014. Compositional morphology for word representations and language modelling. *CoRR*.

Ronan Collobert. 2011. Deep learning for efficient discriminative parsing. In *Proceedings of the Fourteenth International Conference on Artificial Intelligence and Statistics*, pages 224–232.

Mathias Creutz and Krista Lagus. 2007. Unsupervised models for morpheme segmentation and morphology learning. *TSLP*, 4(1).

Lev Finkelstein, Evgeniy Gabrilovich, Yossi Matias, Ehud Rivlin, Zach Solan, Gadi Wolfman, and Eytan Ruppin. 2002. Placing search in context: the concept revisited. *ACM Trans. Inf. Syst.*, 20(1):116–131.

Xavier Glorot, Antoine Bordes, and Yoshua Bengio. 2011. Domain adaptation for large-scale sentiment classification: A deep learning approach. In *Proceedings of the 28th International Conference on Machine Learning*, pages 513–520.

Samer Hassan and Rada Mihalcea. 2009. Cross-lingual semantic relatedness using encyclopedic knowledge. In *Proceedings of the 2009 Conference on Empirical Methods in Natural Language Processing*, pages 1192–1201.

Eric H. Huang, Richard Socher, Christopher D. Manning, and Andrew Y. Ng. 2012. Improving word representations via global context and multiple word prototypes. In *Proceedings of the 50th Annual Meeting of the Association for Computational Linguistics*, pages 873–882.

Fei Huang, Arun Ahuja, Doug Downey, Yi Yang, Yuhong Guo, and Alexander Yates. 2014. Learning representations for weakly supervised natural language processing tasks. *Computational Linguistics*, 40(1):85–120.

Colette Joubarne and Diana Inkpen. 2011. Comparison of semantic similarity for different languages using the google n-gram corpus and second-order co-occurrence measures. In *Advances in Artificial Intelligence - 24th Canadian Conference on Artificial Intelligence*, pages 216–221.

Angeliki Lazaridou, Marco Marelli, Roberto Zamparelli, and Marco Baroni. 2013. Compositionally derived representations of morphologically complex words in distributional semantics. In *Proceedings of the 51st Annual Meeting of the Association for Computational Linguistics*, pages 1517–1526.

Quoc V. Le and Tomas Mikolov. 2014. Distributed representations of sentences and documents. *CoRR*, abs/1405.4053.

Omer Levy and Yoav Goldberg. 2014. Dependency-based word embeddings. In *Proceedings of the 52nd Annual Meeting of the Association for Computational Linguistics, ACL 2014, June 22-27, 2014, Baltimore, MD, USA, Volume 2: Short Papers*, pages 302–308.

Minh-Thang Luong, Richard Socher, and Christopher D. Manning. 2013. Better word representations with recursive neural networks for morphology. In *CoNLL*, Sofia, Bulgaria.

Tomas Mikolov and Geoffrey Zweig. 2012. Context dependent recurrent neural network language model. In *IEEE Spoken Language Technology Workshop (SLT)*, pages 234–239.

Tomas Mikolov, Kai Chen, Greg Corrado, and Jeff Dean. 2013a. Efficient estimation of word representations in vector space. *CoRR*, abs/1301.3781.

Tomas Mikolov, Wen-tau Yih, and Geoffrey Zweig. 2013b. Linguistic regularities in continuous space word representations. In *Human Language Technologies: Conference of the North American Chapter of the Association of Computational Linguistics*, pages 746–751.

Andriy Mnih and Geoffrey E. Hinton. 2007. Three new graphical models for statistical language modelling. In *Machine Learning, Proceedings of the Twenty-Fourth International Conference*, pages 641–648.

Andriy Mnih, Zhang Yuecheng, and Geoffrey E. Hinton. 2009. Improving a statistical language model through non-linear prediction. *Neurocomputing*, 72(7-9):1414–1418.

Robert Parker, David Graff, Ke Chen, Junbo Kong, and Kazuaki Maedaet. 2011. Arabic gigaword fifth edition ldc2011t11. In *Linguistic Data Consortium*, Philadelphia.

Jeffrey Pennington, Richard Socher, and Christopher D. Manning. 2014. Glove: Global vectors for word representation. In *Proceedings of EMNLP*.

Herbert Rubenstein and John B. Goodenough. 1965. Contextual correlates of synonymy. *Communications of the ACM*, 8(10):627633.

Cyrus Shaoul and Chris Westbury. 2010. The Westbury lab Wikipedia corpus.

Richard Socher, Eric H. Huang, Jeffrey Pennington, Andrew Y. Ng, and Christopher D. Manning. 2011a. Dynamic pooling and unfolding recursive autoencoders for paraphrase detection. In *25th Annual Conference on Neural Information Processing Systems*, pages 801–809.

Richard Socher, Jeffrey Pennington, Eric H. Huang, Andrew Y. Ng, and Christopher D. Manning. 2011b. Semi-supervised recursive autoencoders for predicting sentiment distributions. In *Proceedings of the 2011 Conference on Empirical Methods in Natural Language Processing*, pages 151–161.

Torsten Zesch and Iryna Gurevych. 2006. Automatically creating datasets for measures of semantic relatedness. In *Workshop on Linguistic Distances*, pages 16–24.

# Author Index